Worlds of Fiction

◆ *Worlds of Fiction* ◆

EDITED BY

ROBERTA RUBENSTEIN

AND

CHARLES R. LARSON

AMERICAN UNIVERSITY
WASHINGTON, D.C.

Macmillan Publishing Company
New York
Maxwell Macmillan Canada
Toronto

Editor: D. Anthony English
Production Supervisor: Katherine Evancie
Production Managers: Pam Kennedy and Muriel Underwood
Cover Designer: Thomas Mack

This book was set in Goudy Old Style by Digitype, Inc. and was printed and bound by Rand McNally. The cover was printed by New England Book Components.

Printed in the United States of America

Macmillan Publishing Company
866 Third Avenue, New York, New York 10022

Macmillan Publishing Company is part of
the Maxwell Communication Group of Companies.

Maxwell Macmillan Canada, Inc.
1200 Eglinton Avenue East
Suite 200
Don Mills, Ontario M3C 3N1

Library of Congress Cataloging-in-Publication Data
Worlds of fiction / edited by Roberta Rubenstein and Charles R. Larson.
p. cm.
ISBN 0-02-404185-8 (paper)
1. Short stories. I. Rubenstein, Roberta. II. Larson, Charles R.
PN6120.2.W665 1993
808.83′1—dc20 91-42134
CIP

Printing: 1 2 3 4 5 6 7 Year: 3 4 5 6 7 8 9

ACKNOWLEDGMENTS

CHINUA ACHEBE: "Girls at War." Reprinted by permission of the author.

AMA ATA AIDOO: "Two Sisters" © by Ama Ata Aidoo 1970. The story was first broadcast as a short radio play by The Transcription Centre, London. Reprinted by kind permission of the author and of Shelley Power Literary Agency Ltd.

AKUTAGAWA RYŪNOSUKE: "Within a Grove" translated by James O'Brien, from *Akutagawa and Dazai: Instances of Literary Adaptation* by James O'Brien. Tempe, Arizona: Center for Asian Studies (Arizona State University), 1988, pp. 81–89.

WOODY ALLEN: "The Kugelmass Episode" from *Side Effects* by Woody Allen. Reprinted by permission of Random House, Inc.

ISABEL ALLENDE: "And of Clay Are We Created" from *The Stories of Eva Luna* by Isabel Allende, translated from the Spanish by Margaret Sayers Peden. Copyright © 1989 by Isabel Allende. English translation copyright © 1991 by Macmillan Publishing Company. Reprinted by permission of Lester & Orpen Dennys Publishers Ltd. c/o Key Porter Books Limited; and Atheneum Publishers, an imprint of Macmillan Publishing Company.

HANAN AL SHAYKH: "The Unseeing Eye." Reprinted by permission of the author.

MULK RAJ ANAND: "Untouchable." Originally published in 1931 by Wishart and Co. Used by permission of the author.

RUDOLFO A. ANAYA: "B. Traven Is Alive and Well in Cuernavaca." Reprinted by permission of the author.

SHERWOOD ANDERSON: "Death in the Woods." Reprinted by permission of Harold Ober Associates Incorporated. Copyright 1926 by The American Mercury, Inc. Copyright renewed 1953 by Eleanor Copenhauer Anderson.

MARGARET ATWOOD: "Dancing Girls" from *Dancing Girls and Other Stories* by Margaret Atwood. Reprinted by permission of Margaret Atwood, © 1991; and the Canadian Publishers, McClelland & Stewart, Toronto.

ISAAC BABEL: "My First Goose." Reprinted by permission of S. G. Phillips, Inc. from *The Collected Stories of Isaac Babel.* Copyright © 1955 by S. G. Phillips, Inc.

BARBARANEELY: "Spilled Salt." Reprinted by permission of Marie Brown Associates. Copyright © 1990.

ANN BEATTIE: "The Burning House" from *The Burning House* by Ann Beattie. Copyright © 1979 by Irony & Pity, Inc. Reprinted by permission of Random House, Inc.

J. BERNLEF: "The Black Dog" from *Anecdotes Uit Een Zijstraat* (Ploughshares, 1983). Translated by Frank Scimone. First appeared in *Ploughshares.* Reprinted by permission of Em. Querido's Uitgeverij B. V. and *Ploughshares.*

HEINRICH BÖLL: "The Laugher" from *18 Stories,* by Heinrich Böll. Published by McGraw-Hill, Copyright 1966 by Heinrich Böll. English language translation by Leila Vennewitz. Reprinted by permission of Joan Daves Agency. Copyright © 1966.

JORGE LUIS BORGES: "Death and the Compass" from *The Aleph and Other Stories 1933–1969* by Jorge Luis Borges, translated by Norman Thomas di Giovanni. Translation copyright © 1968, 1969, 1970 by Emece Editores, S. A. and Norman Thomas di Giovanni. Used by permission of the publisher, Dutton, an imprint of New American Library, a division of Penguin Books USA Inc.

DINO BUZZATI: "The Falling Girl" from *Restless Nights* copyright 1983 by Dino Buzzati. English language translation copyright by Lawrence Venuti. Published by North Point Press. Reprinted by permission of the author and translator.

ITALO CALVINO: "A Sign in Space" from *Cosmicomics* by Italo Calvino, translated by William Weaver, Copyright © 1965 by Giulio Einaudi editore s.p.a., Torino. English translation copyright © 1968 by Harcourt Brace Jovanovich, Inc., reprinted by permission of Harcourt Brace Jovanovich, Inc.

ALBERT CAMUS: "The Guest" from *Exile and the Kingdom* by Albert Camus, translated by Justin O'Brien. Copyright 1957, 1958 by Alfred A. Knopf, Inc. Reprinted by permission of Alfred A. Knopf, Inc.

RAYMOND CARVER: "Where I'm Calling From" from *Cathedral* by Raymond Carver. Copyright © 1981, 1982 by Raymond Carver. Reprinted by permission of Alfred A. Knopf, Inc.

JOHN CHEEVER: "The Swimmer" from *The Stories of John Cheever* by John Cheever. Reprinted by permission of Alfred A. Knopf, Inc.

ANTON CHEKHOV: "The Kiss" from *The Party and Other Stories* by Anton Chekhov, translated by Constance Garnett. Reprinted by permission of A. P. Watt Ltd. on behalf of the executors of the estate of Constance Garnett; and Chatto & Windus, Random Century Group.

GABRIELLE-SIDONIE COLETTE: "The Seamstress" from *The Collected Stories* by Colette. Translation copyright © 1983 by Farrar, Straus & Giroux, Inc. Reprinted by permission of Farrar, Straus Giroux, Inc.

ISAK DINESEN: "The Sailor-Boy's Tale" from *Winter's Tales* by Isak Dinesen. Copyright 1942 by Random House, Inc. and renewed 1970 by Johan Philip Thomas Ingerslev, c/o The Rungstedlund Foundation. Reprinted by permission of Random House, Inc., and The Rungstedlund Foundation.

BIRAGO DIOP: "Sarzan" translated by Ellen Conroy Kennedy. Reprinted by permission of Ellen Conroy Kennedy.

JOSÉ DONOSO: "Paseo" from *Cuentos* by José Donoso, copyright 1971. Reprinted by permission of Agencia Literaria Carmen Balcells.

MARGARETA EKSTRÖM: "The Night Between the Second and the Third" translated by Eva Claeson. From *Death's Midwives.* Princeton, New Jersey: Ontario Review Press, 1985.

RALPH ELLISON: "Flying Home" from *Cross Section* edited by Edwin Seaver. William Morris Agency, 1944.

LOUISE ERDRICH: "Love Medicine" from *Love Medicine* by Louise Erdrich. Copyright © 1984 by Louise Erdrich. Reprinted by permission of Henry Holt and Company, Inc.

WILLIAM FAULKNER: "A Rose for Emily" from *Collected Stories of William Faulkner* by William

Faulkner. Copyright 1930 and renewed 1958 by William Faulkner. Reprinted by permission of Random House, Inc.

FENG JICAI: "The Street-Sweeping Show" from *Chrysanthemums and Other Stories* by Feng Jicai, translated and copyright © 1982 by Susan Wilff Chen, reprinted by permission of Harcourt Brace Jovanovich, Inc.

F. SCOTT FITZGERALD: "Babylon Revisited." Reprinted by permission of Charles Scribner's Sons, an imprint of Macmillan Publishing Company from *Taps at Reveille* by F. Scott Fitzgerald. Copyright 1931 by The Curtis Publishing Company; renewal copyright 1959 by Frances Scott Fitzgerald Lanahan.

CARLOS FUENTES: "The Doll Queen" from *Burnt Water* by Carlos Fuentes. Translation copyright © 1969, 1980 by Farrar, Straus & Giroux, Inc. Reprinted by permission of Farrar, Straus & Giroux, Inc.

GABRIEL GARCÍA MÁRQUEZ: "Balthazar's Marvelous Afternoon" from *Collected Stories* by Gabriel García Márquez. Copyright © 1984 by Gabriel García Márquez. Reprinted by permission of HarperCollins Publishers.

NATALIA GINZBURG: "The Mother" translated by Isabel Quigley from *Italian Short Stories* edited by Raleigh Trevelyan (Penguin Books, 1965), copyright © Penguin Books, 1965.

NIKOLAI GOGOL: "The Overcoat" from *The Overcoat and Other Stories* by Nikolai Gogol, translated by Constance Garnett. Reprinted by permission of A. P. Watt Ltd. on behalf of the executors of the estate of Constance Garnett; and Chatto & Windus, Random Century Group.

NADINE GORDIMER: "A Soldier's Embrace" copyright © 1975 by Nadine Gordimer. From *A Soldier's Embrace* by Nadine Gordimer. Used by permission of Viking Penguin, a division of Penguin Books USA Inc.

JUDY GRAHN: "Boys at the Rodeo" from *True to Life Adventure Stories, Vol. II* edited by Judy Grahn. © 1981 Judy Grahn. Freedom, California: The Crossing Press.

JACOB AND WILHELM GRIMM: "Karl Katz" from *Tales of Grimm and Anderson* selected by Frederick Jacobi, Jr. New York: Random House, Inc.

BESSIE HEAD: "The Prisoner Who Wore Glasses." Reprinted by permission of John Johnson (Authors' Agent) Limited.

ERNEST HEMINGWAY: "The Short Happy Life of Francis Macomber." Reprinted by permission of Charles Scribner's Sons, an imprint of Macmillan Publishing Company from *The Short Stories of Ernest Hemingway*. Copyright 1936 by Ernest Hemingway; renewal copyright 1964 by Mary Hemingway.

LANGSTON HUGHES: "Thank You, Ma'am" from *The Langston Hughes Reader* by Langston Hughes. Reprinted by permission of Harold Ober Associates Incorporated. Copyright © 1958 by Langston Hughes. Copyright renewed 1986 by George Houston Bass.

ZORA NEALE HURSTON: "The Gilded Six-Bits" from *Story Magazine* (August 1933).

SHIRLEY JACKSON: "The Lottery" from *The Lottery* by Shirley Jackson. Copyright © 1948, 1949 by Shirley Jackson. Renewal copyright © 1976, 1977 by Laurence Hyman, Barry Hyman, Mrs. Sarah Webster, and Mrs. Joanne Schnurer. Reprinted by permission of Farrar, Straus & Giroux, Inc.

SVAVA JAKOBSDÓTTIR: "A Story for Children" translated by Dennis Auburn Hill. Copyright 1975 by the American Scandinavian Foundation.

ELIZABETH JOLLEY: "Another Holiday for the Prince" from *Stories: Elizabeth Jolley* by Elizabeth Jolley. Used by permission of Viking Penguin, a division of Penguin Books USA Inc.

JAMES JOYCE: "Eveline" from *Dubliners* by James Joyce. Copyright 1916 by B.W. Heubsch. Definitive text copyright © 1967 by the Estate of James Joyce. Used by permission of Viking Penguin, a division of Penguin Books USA Inc.

FRANZ KAFKA: "The Metamorphosis" from *The Metamorphosis, The Penal Colony, and Other Stories* by Franz Kafka, translated by Willa and Edwin Muir. Copyright 1948 by Schocken Books Inc. Copyright renewed 1975 by Schocken Books Inc. Reprinted by permission of Schocken Books, published by Pantheon Books, a division of Random House, Inc.

GHASSAN KANAFANI: "A Hand in the Grave" translated by Hilary Kirkpatrick, from *Men in the Sun*. Washington, D.C.: Three Continents Press, 1978.

KANAI MIEKO: "Platonic Love" translated by Amy V. Heinrich, from *The Shōwa Anthology: Modern Japanese Short Stories Vol. II*, edited by Van C. Gessel and Tomone Matsumoto, published by Kodansha International Ltd. © 1980. Reprinted by permission. All rights reserved.

JOHN KASAIPWALOVA: "Betel Nut Is Bad Magic for Airplanes" from *The Night Warrior and Other Stories from Papua, New Guinea*, published by Jacaranda Wiley Ltd.

KHAMSING SRINAWK: "The Gold-Legged Frog" from *The Politician and Other Stories* by Khamsing Srinawk. Selangor, Malaysia: Oxford University Press, South-East Asian Publishing Services Unit, 1973.

PÄR LAGERKVIST: "The Children's Campaign" from *The Marriage Feast* by Pär Lagerkvist. Copyright © 1954 by Albert Bonniers Förlag. Reprinted by permission of Hill and Wang, a division of Farrar, Straus & Giroux, Inc. Canadian rights © the estate of Pär Lagerkvist 1993. Published in agreement with Albert Bonniers Förlag AB, Stockholm.

MARGARET LAURENCE: "A Bird in the House" from *A Bird in the House* by Margaret Laurence. Reprinted by permission of the Estate of Margaret Laurence and the Canadian Publishers, McClelland & Stewart, Toronto.

MARY LAVIN: "Happiness." Copyright © 1964, 1981 by Mary Lavin. From *Selected Stories* by Mary Lavin. Reprinted by permission of the Wallace Literary Agency, Inc.

D. H. LAWRENCE: "Tickets, Please" copyright 1922 by Thomas Seltzer, Inc., renewal copyright 1950 by Frieda Lawrence. From *Complete Short Stories of D. H. Lawrence* by D. H. Lawrence. Used by permission of Viking Penguin, a division of Penguin Books USA Inc.

URSULA K. LE GUIN: "Sur." Copyright © 1982 by Ursula K. Le Guin; first appeared in *The New Yorker*; reprinted by permission of the author and the author's agent, Virginia Kidd.

DORIS LESSING: "A Woman on a Roof" from *A Man and Two Women* by Doris Lessing. Copyright © 1958, 1962, 1963 by Doris Lessing. Reprinted by permission of Simon & Schuster, Inc.

CATHERINE LIM: "Or Else, the Lightning God" from *Or Else, the Lightning God and Other Stories* by Catherine Lim. Published by Octopus Publishing Asia Pte Ltd, Singapore.

LU XUN: "The Story of Hair" from *Diary of a Madman and Other Stories* translated by William A. Lyell. Honolulu: University of Hawaii Press, 1990.

ARNOST LUSTIG: "The Lemon" from *Diamonds in the Night* by Arnost Lustig, translated by Jeanne Němcová. Evanston, Illinois: Northwestern University Press, 1978.

NAGUIB MAHFOUZ: "Half a Day" from *The Time and the Place and Other Stories* by Naguib Mahfouz. Translation copyright © 1978 by Denys Johnson-Davis. Used by permission of Doubleday, a division of Bantam Doubleday Dell Publishing Group Inc.

BERNARD MALAMUD: "The Jewbird" from *Idiots First* by Bernard Malamud. Copyright © 1963 by Bernard Malamud. Reprinted by permission of Farrar, Straus & Giroux, Inc.

THOMAS MANN: "The Infant Prodigy" from *Stories of Three Decades* by Thomas Mann, translated by H. T. Lowe-Porter. Copyright 1936 and renewed 1964 by Alfred A. Knopf, Inc. Reprinted by permission of Alfred A. Knopf, Inc.

KATHERINE MANSFIELD: "Her First Ball" from *The Short Stories of Katherine Mansfield* by Katherine Mansfield. Copyright 1922 by Alfred A. Knopf, Inc. Copyright renewed 1950 by John Middleton Murry. Reprinted by permission of Alfred A. Knopf, Inc.

RENÉ MARQUÉS: "Island of Manhattan" from *Contemporary Latin American Short Stories* edited by Pat McNees Mancini. Copyright © 1974 by Random House, Inc. Reprinted by permission of Ballantine Books, a division of Random House, Inc.

PAULE MARSHALL: "Brooklyn." Copyright © 1961 by Paule Marshall. From the book *Reena and Other Stories* by Paule Marshall. Published 1983 by The Feminist Press at the City University of New York. All rights reserved.

BOBBIE ANN MASON: "Shiloh" from *Shiloh and Other Stories* by Bobbie Ann Mason. Copyright © 1982 by Bobbie Ann Mason. Reprinted by permission of HarperCollins Publishers.

WILLIAM SOMERSET MAUGHAM: "The Appointment in Samarra" from *Sheppey* by William Somerset Maugham. Copyright 1933 by William Somerset Maugham. Used by permission of Doubleday, a division of Bantam Doubleday Dell Publishing Group, Inc.

RICHARD MCCANN: "My Mother's Clothes: The School of Beauty and Shame." Appeared originally in *The Atlantic Monthly*. Copyright © 1986 by Richard McCann. Reprinted by permission of Brandt & Brandt Literary Agents, Inc.

JOHN MCCLUSKEY: "Lush Life" from *Callaloo*, Vol. 13, No. 2, Spring 1990, pp. 201–212. Baltimore: The Johns Hopkins University Press.

KATHERINE MIN: "The One Who Goes Farthest Away." Reprinted by permission of the author.

SUSAN MINOT: "Lust" from *Lust and Other Stories* by Susan Minot. Copyright © 1989 by Susan Minot. Reprinted by permission of Houghton Mifflin Company/Seymour Lawrence.

MISHIMA YUKIO: "Swaddling Clothes" from *Death in Midsummer* by Mishima Yukio. Copyright © 1966 by New Directions Publishing Corporation. Reprinted by permission of New Directions Publishing Corporation.

KERMIT MOYER: "Tumbling" first appeared in *The Hudson Review*. Copyright © 1986 by Kermit Moyer. Reprinted by permission of the University of Illinois Press from *Tumbling*, by Kermit Moyer.

ES'KIA MPHAHLELE: "Mrs. Plum" from *Renewal Time*. London: Readers International, 1990.

SLAWOMIR MROŻEK: "The Elephant" translated by Konrad Syrop. Copyright © 1962, 1990 by McDonald & Co. (Publishers) Ltd. Used by permission of Grove Press, Inc.

BHARATI MUKHERJEE: "A Father" from *Darkness*. Copyright © Bharati Mukherjee, 1985. Reprinted by permission of Bharati Mukherjee and Penguin Books Canada Limited.

Alice Munro: "The Office" from *Dance of the Happy Shades* by Alice Munro. Copyright © 1968 by Alice Munro. Originally published by McGraw-Hill Ryerson Limited. Reprinted by arrangement with Virginia Barber Literary Agency. All rights reserved.

V. S. Naipaul: "One Out of Many" from *In a Free State* by V. S. Naipaul. Copyright © 1971 by V. S. Naipaul. Reprinted by permission of Alfred A. Knopf, Inc., and Aitken & Stone, Ltd.

Carmen Naranjo: "And We Sold the Rain" translated by Jo Anne Englebert from *And We Sold the Rain: Contemporary Fiction from Central America* edited by Rosario Santos. New York: Four Walls Eight Windows, 1988.

R. K. Narayan: "A Horse and Two Goats." Copyright © 1965, 1970, 1985 by R. K. Narayan. Published in *Under the Banyan Tree and Other Stories* by R. K. Narayan; Viking Penguin, Inc. First appeared in *The New Yorker*. Used by permission of the Wallace Literary Agency, Inc.

Ngugi wa Thiong'o: "A Meeting in the Dark" from *Secret Lives* by Ngugi wa Thiong'o. Copyright 1975. Reprinted by permission of Heinemann Educational Books, Inc.

Joyce Carol Oates: "Where Are You Going, Where Have You Been?" copyright Joyce Carol Oates. Reprinted by permission of John Hawkins & Associates, Inc.

Oba Minako: "The Pale Fox" translated by Stephen W. Kohl, from *The Shōwa Anthology: Modern Japanese Short Stories Vol. II*, edited by Van C. Gessel and Tomone Matsumoto, published by Kodansha International Ltd., 1980.

Flannery O'Connor: "A Good Man Is Hard to Find" from *A Good Man Is Hard to Find and Other Stories*, copyright 1953 by Flannery O'Connor and renewed 1981 by Regina O'Connor, reprinted by permission of Harcourt Brace Jovanovich, Inc.

Oe Kenzaburo: "Aghwee the Sky Monster" translated by John Nathan, from *Teach Us to Outgrow Our Madness*. English translation copyright © 1977 by John Nathan. Used by permission of Grove Press, Inc.

Sembene Ousmane: "Black Girl" translated by Ellen Conroy Kennedy. Reprinted by permission of Ellen Conroy Kennedy.

Amos Oz: "Nomad and Viper" from *Where the Jackals Howl and Other Stories* by Amos Oz, translated by Nicholas de Lange and Philip Simpson, copyright © 1973 by Amos Oz and Massada Ltd., reprinted by permission of Harcourt Brace Jovanovich, Inc.

Emilia Pardo Bazán: "The Revolver" from *Longman Anthology of World Literature by Women* edited by Marian Arkin and Barbara Shollar. Copyright © 1989 by Longman Publishing Group. Reprinted with permission from Longman Publishing Group.

Octavio Paz: "The Blue Bouquet" translated by Lysander Kemp. First appeared in *Evergreen Review* May–June 1961. Copyright © 1961, 1989 by Evergreen Review, Inc. Used by permission of Grove Press, Inc.

Virgilio Piñera: "Insomnia" first published in English by Eridanos Press, Boston in *Cold Tales* by Virgilio Piñera, translated by Mark Schafer. Copyright © 1985 Juan Piñera Lleras, Luisa Piñera Lleras, Yadira Piñera Concepción and José Manuel Piñera Lleras. All rights reserved.

Katherine Anne Porter: "Rope" from *Flowering Judas and Other Stories*, copyright 1930 and renewed 1958 by Katherine Anne Porter, reprinted by permission of Harcourt Brace Jovanovich, Inc.

Rodrigo Rey Rosa: "The Proof" from *Dust on Her Tongue*. Copyright © 1989 by Rodrigo Rey Rosa. Reprinted by permission of City Lights Books.

Gabrielle Roy: "The Move" from *The Road Past Altamont* by Gabrielle Roy. Translated from the French by Joyce Marshall. Reprinted with permission of Fords Gabrielle Roy and McClelland & Stewart Publishers.

Leslie Marmon Silko: "Yellow Woman." Reprinted by permission of the author.

Isaac Bashevis Singer: "Gimpel the Fool" translated by Saul Bellow. Copyright 1953 by The Partisan Review, renewed © 1981 by Isaac Bashevis Singer from *A Treasury of Yiddish Stories* by Irving Howe and Eliezer Greenberg. Used by permission of Viking Penguin, a division of Penguin Books USA Inc.

María Teresa Solari: "Death and Transfiguration of a Teacher" translated by John Benson. From *Short Stories by Latin American Women: The Magic and the Real*, edited by Celia Cerreas de Zapata. Houston: Arte Publico Press, 1990.

John Steinbeck: "The Chrysanthemums" copyright 1937, renewed © 1965 by John Steinbeck. From *The Long Valley* by John Steinbeck. Used by permission of Viking Penguin, a division of Penguin Books USA Inc.

Hyemeyohsts Storm: "The Story of Jumping Mouse" from *Seven Arrows* by Hyemeyohsts Storm. Copyright © 1972 by Hyemeyohsts Storm. Reprinted by permission of HarperCollins Publishers.

Graham Swift: "Learning to Swim" from *Learning to Swim*. Copyright © 1982 by Graham Swift. Reprinted by permission of Poseidon Press, a division of Simon & Schuster, Inc.

AMY TAN: "Half and Half." Reprinted by permission of The Putnam Publishing Group from *The Joy Luck Club* by Amy Tan. Copyright © 1989 by Amy Tan.

AMOS TUTUOLA: "The Complete Gentleman" from *The Palm-Wine Drinkard* by Amos Tutuola. Copyright 1953 by George Braziller. Used by permission of Grove Press, Inc.

JOHN UPDIKE: "A & P" from *Pigeon Feathers and Other Stories* by John Updike. Copyright © 1960 by John Updike. Reprinted by permission of Alfred A. Knopf, Inc.

LUISA VALENZUELA: "Strange Things Happen Here" from *Strange Things Happen Here* by Luisa Valenzuela, translated by Helen Lane, English translation copyright © 1979 by Harcourt Brace Jovanovich, Inc., reprinted by permission of the publisher.

MARIO VARGAS LLOSA: "Sunday" from *Contemporary Latin American Short Stories*, edited by Pat McNees Mancini. Copyright © 1974 by Random House, Inc. Reprinted by permission of Ballantine Books, a division of Random House, Inc.

ALICE WALKER: "Everyday Use" from *In Love & Trouble: Stories of Black Women*, copyright © 1973 by Alice Walker, reprinted by permission of Harcourt Brace Jovanovich, Inc.

EUDORA WELTY: "Why I Live at the P.O." from *A Curtain of Green and Other Stories*, copyright 1941 and renewed 1969 by Eudora Welty, reprinted by permission of Harcourt Brace Jovanovich, Inc.

EDITH WHARTON: "Roman Fever" reprinted with the permission of Charles Scribner's Sons, an imprint of Macmillan Publishing Company, from *Roman Fever and Other Stories* by Edith Wharton. Copyright 1934 Liberty Magazine, renewed © 1962 by William R. Tyler.

Preface

Until about a decade or so ago, most anthologies of short stories were comprised primarily of fiction by writers from North America and Europe; moreover, those stories were written predominantly by men of the majority culture. In the intervening years, scholars, teachers, editors, and readers have gained awareness of what has been missing and invisible in such "selective" collections: gender inclusiveness and cultural multiplicity. Editors of anthologies have begun to include more writing by women and writers of minority ethnic, if not geographical, origins.

Worlds of Fiction was conceived with the goal of extending the parameters of a short fiction anthology even more ambitiously, to encompass fiction written by authors from other geographical areas that are still only nominally (if at all) represented in short story anthologies—Africa, Asia, Latin America, Northern Europe, and the Arabic world—as well as to include more ethnic minority voices from within the United States and more stories by women. Needless to say, once one opens up the geographical boundaries to include short fiction by authors from around the globe, there are simply far too many good stories; it is impossible to achieve full representativeness, even in an anthology of this hefty size. For each story we chose, many more were read and admired but ultimately could not be included here.

In making the selections for this anthology, we have been guided by a desire to include "good" stories, in our judgment. We have sought to include both classical and contemporary stories that reflect thematic, aesthetic, and cultural variety: diversity of styles, subjects, and points of view as well as diversity of cultural, historical, and gender perspectives. Of the 124 short stories and two novellas included in *Worlds of Fiction*, approximately two-thirds are by North American and European authors, including a number of new or less familiar authors or less frequently anthologized selections by well-known authors. The remaining one-third of the stories are drawn from the writers of other major geographical areas: Latin America, Africa, Asia, the Middle East, Australia, New Zealand, and the South Pacific. We hope that we have achieved an appealing mixture of recognizable and refreshingly unfamiliar authors and stories.

Realizing that readers may feel somewhat hesitant about how to read and understand stories by totally unfamiliar writers from cultures and areas not frequently considered by most American readers (whether teachers or students), we have provided a headnote for each story that includes biographical information as well as—where appropriate—suggestions for understanding the story within its cultural context. For a fuller discussion of reading with an enlarged cultural perspective (and for a fuller explanation of the guiding principles behind this anthology), we urge you to read the Introduction that follows this Preface, with its close reading and interpretation of the story "Black Girl" by Senegalese writer Sembene Ousmane.

The primary organization of this anthology is alphabetical by author's name, an arrangement that we believe is the most accessible for readers to find (and also to discover) particular authors. We have tried to respect traditional cultural usage concerning the alphabetical ordering of authors' names. For example, in Japan and China, a person's surname generally precedes his or her given name. Hence, *Mishima* Yukio (a frequently anthologized Japanese author whose name has typically been reversed, English style) still appears among the M's—although surname first—and *Akutagawa* Ryūnosuke appears among the *A*'s. Many Hispanic surnames are composed of both parents' family names. Hence, for Gabriel García Márquez and Mario Vargas Llosa, *García* and *Vargas* are not middle names but the first of two-part surnames and thus the ones used for alphabetization as well as for correct reference to the authors. Gabriel *García Márquez* appears among the G's, and Mario *Vargas Llosa* among the *V*'s.

In addition to the primary alphabetical table of contents—which includes a brief description of each story—an alternative geographical table of contents situates authors within their geographical contexts. Questions at the end of each story guide readers in their consideration of major themes, ideas, and issues. The Thematic Contents at the end of the volume features topical groupings of stories that we hope will stimulate comparative and cross-cultural thinking as well as ideas for writing.

In developing this anthology, we are grateful for the assistance and contributions of a number of people, beginning with the many translators who have rendered stories from other languages into English and whose inestimable contribution to our reading pleasure is too often overlooked. We are particularly grateful for the wise and generous guidance, unfailing support, and constant enthusiasm of our editor, D. Anthony English, during the development and preparation of this anthology. We also wish to thank Katherine Evancie, Ivelisse Elam, Enu Mainigi, and Kay Mussell for their assistance and support.

We appreciate the advice of readers who made valuable suggestions on early versions of this project: Barbara Adams, Pace University; Carolyn Bruder, The University of Southwestern Louisiana; William Combs, Western Michigan University; William H. Cullen, Potsdam College; Thomas E. Dasher, Valdosta State College; Moira Ferguson, University of Nebraska at Lincoln; Kent Forrester, Murray State University; Donald Gray, Indiana University; Gloria D. Haney, Chaffey College; Darlene Harbour Unrue, University of Nevada at Las Vegas; Kathleen Hichok, Iowa University; Kathleen Holcomb, Angelo State University; Tony J. Howard, Collin County Community College; Constance Hunting, University of Maine; Archibald E. Irwin, Indiana University Southeast; Robert K. Johnson, Suffolk University; William C. Johnson, Northern Illinois University; Craig Kallendorf, Texas A&M University; Rosemary A. Kenny, Madison Area Technical College; David Latane, Virginia Commonwealth University; Marjorie D. Lewis, Texas Christian University; Anita Moss, The University of North Carolina; Michael Palencia-Roth, University of Illinois at Urbana; C. P. Pineo, Fullerton College; Pamela T. Pittman, Central State University; Linda F. Selzer, Pennsylvania State University; and Earl Stevens, Rhode Island College.

R.R.
C.R.L.

Contents

Introduction 1

From *The Thousand and One Nights*: "The Story of the Merchant and the Jinni"—Translated by Edward William Lane 10
In these legendary stories within stories, Shahrazad tells King Shahriyar of an angry Jinni whose desire for vengeance against a merchant is appeased by the power of storytelling itself: narratives of enchantment and magical human/animal transformations offered by three sheykhs.

Chinua Achebe (Nigeria): "Girls at War" 19
Achebe offers a variation on the old theme: one man's war is another man's profit, although this time gender enters the scene.

Ama Ata Aidoo (Ghana): "Two Sisters" 30
Two sisters in contemporary Ghana attempt to survive in a male-dominated society.

Akutagawa Ryūnosuke (Japan): "Within a Grove" Translated by James O'Brien 40
This classic story, from which the film *Rashomon* was adapted, explores traditional Japanese standards of personal honor through a modernist use of multiple narrators whose conflicting testimonies raise haunting questions of veracity, honor, and point of view.

Woody Allen (United States): "The Kugelmass Episode" 47
Allen's comic variation on time travel leads the desperate Kugelmass straight into Flaubert's *Madame Bovary*—but how can he get back home?

Isabel Allende (Chile): "And of Clay Are We Created" Translated by Margaret Sayers Peden 56
A seasoned television journalist's role as detached observer is challenged by his own emotional pain in the presence of a young girl's suffering.

Hanan Al-Shaykh (Lebanon): "The Unseeing Eye" Translated by Denys Johnson-Davies 64
What one man fails to perceive about his wife after many years of married life reveals as much about his culture's treatment of women as it does about him.

Rudolfo A. Anaya (United States): "B. Traven Is Alive and Well in Cuernavaca" 67
A writer discovers that the source of his inspiration is also what distinguishes him from other men.

Sherwood Anderson (United States): "Death in the Woods" 78
Anderson's narrator explores the meaning of the life and death of a woman he did not even know, considering the ironic distance between her role as a sustainer of life and her inability to sustain her own life.

Margaret Atwood (Canada): "Dancing Girls" 87
An international student residing in a Toronto boarding house brings out the landlady's irrational prejudices against "foreigners" and leads the narrator to question her idealistic vision of the world.

Isaac Babel (Russia): "My First Goose"
Translated by Walter Morison 98
A young Russian soldier of intellectual disposition determines that his acceptance by Cossack regulars compels him to act in a way that violates his assumptions about himself.

BarbaraNeely (United States): "Spilled Salt" 102
A woman struggles to understand what it means to be the mother of a rapist.

Ann Beattie (United States): "The Burning House" 109
A marriage is on the rocks in Beattie's story of the uptight generation.

J. Bernlef (Netherlands): "The Black Dog"
Translated by Frank Scimone 120
Following a chance encounter with a rabid dog, a young boy's hatred of his father shifts toward love.

Ambrose Bierce (United States): "An Occurrence at Owl Creek Bridge" 124
A Southern farmer reflects on his life at the moment of his execution by Union soldiers.

Heinrich Böll (Germany): "The Laugher"
Translated by Leila Vennewitz 131
Can a man who makes his living by laughing on cue find anything amusing in his own life?

Jorge Luis Borges (Argentina): "Death and the Compass"
Translated by Norman Thomas di Giovanni 134
A master detective unraveling the clues of a series of interlocked murders realizes too late who the final victim will be.

Dino Buzzati (Italy): "The Falling Girl"
Translated by Lawrence Venuti 143
In a surreal exploration of the meaning of a young woman's life, Buzzati matter-of-factly dramatizes her descent from the heights of a skyrise apartment building.

Italo Calvino (Italy): "A Sign in Space"
Translated by William Weaver 147
In the beginning was the Sign—but what does it mean against the backdrop of millenia of time in an infinity of outer space?

Albert Camus (Algeria/France): "The Guest"
Translated by Justin O'Brien 154
A French schoolmaster in the Algerian countryside changes his destiny by a simple act of involvement.

Raymond Carver (United States): "Where I'm Calling From" 164
Carver's story focuses on two alcoholics in a drying-out home who are trying to put their lives back together.

Willa Cather (United States): "Paul's Case" 175
A sensitive youth rebels against his middle-class upbringing, destroying himself in the process.

John Cheever (United States): "The Swimmer" 190
Neddy Merrill, swimming home through one suburban pool after another, eventually realizes that he has also swum through life.

Anton Chekhov (Russia): "The Kiss"
Translated by Constance Garnett 199
Kissed in the dark by a woman of whose identity he is not certain, a young soldier is transformed by romantic fantasy—but who was the woman and was the kiss intended for him?

Gabrielle-Sidonie Colette (France): "The Seamstress"
Translated by Una Vicenzo Troubridge and Enid McLeod 213
A mother realizes that her young daughter gains access to far more than sewing when she masters a traditional female skill.

Joseph Conrad (Poland/England): "Amy Foster" 217
A castaway from Central Europe arrives in a small English village and struggles, with limited success, for acceptance of his basic humanity across ineradicable walls of cultural and linguistic differences.

Stephen Crane (United States): "The Open Boat" 238
Four men in a dinghy, survivors of a shipwreck, struggle against the elements to reach the shore and discover their common humanity in the process.

Isak Dinesen (Denmark): "The Sailor-Boy's Tale" 255
In a tale that intertwines murder and the promise of love, a supernatural link between a sailor youth and a falcon becomes central to the resolution of events.

Birago Diop (Senegal): "Sarzan"
Translated by Ellen Conroy Kennedy 263
The spirits of the past take their revenge on the lost son of their village who dared to modernize their world.

José Donoso (Chile): "Paseo"
Translated by Lorraine O'Grady Freeman 272
A woman "escapes" from the traditional female role assumed by her culture.

Margareta Ekström (Sweden): "The Night Between the Second and the Third"—Translated by Eva Claeson 285
When a man alone in a beach cottage hears a cry for help in the night, his uncertainty over how (or whether) to respond becomes a defining moment in his life.

Ralph Ellison (United States): "Flying Home" 293
A black pilot confronts the harsh reality of being in Uncle Sam's armed forces during World War II.

Louise Erdrich (United States): "Love Medicine" 308
A Native American with special powers struggles with the possibilities of love, faith, and responsibility as he attempts—with unintended results—to renew a faltering bond between his grandparents.

William Faulkner (United States): "A Rose for Emily" **324**
A Southern lady's determination for privacy becomes grotesque, as the community she has thwarted for years finally comes to understand her life.

Feng Jicai (China): "The Street-Sweeping Show"
Translated by Susan Wilff Chen **332**
As the dignitaries of a Chinese town mobilize to produce a staged ceremony in recognition of National Cleanup Week, the author humorously exposes the relationship between politics and spectacle.

F. Scott Fitzgerald (United States): "Babylon Revisited" **336**
The reality of the Jazz Age crashes in on Charlie Wales when he returns to Paris to seek custody of his daughter.

Gustave Flaubert (France): "The Legend of Saint Julian the Hospitaller" **351**
The road to sainthood is strewn with many obstacles and temptations as the legendary Julian is transformed from a bloodthristy hunter and murderer to a humble servant of God.

Carlos Fuentes (Mexico): "The Doll Queen"
Translated by Margaret S. Peden **369**
A childhood memory takes on a grotesque twist when a young man attempts to recapture the innocence of his past.

Gabriel García Márquez (Colombia): "Balthazar's Marvelous Afternoon"
—Translated by J. S. Bernstein **381**
An artist, in his moment of freedom, escapes the mundane activities of daily life.

Charlotte Perkins Gilman (United States):
"The Yellow Wallpaper" **387**
In a room in which the wallpaper itself comes alive, the nameless narrator, suffering from postpartum depression, finds that the "rest cure" that is intended to promote her recovery instead results in her entrapment and mental decline.

Natalia Ginzburg (Italy): "The Mother"
Translated by Isabel Quigley **400**
Two fatherless boys attempt to make sense of their relation to their preoccupied young mother, in whose unhappy life they find they figure only peripherally.

Susan Glaspell (United States): "A Jury of Her Peers" **408**
Two women read the clues to a murder mystery in the alleged murderer's kitchen as Glaspell explores the different ways in which men and women interpret and respond to the same environment.

Nikolai Gogol (Russia): "The Overcoat"
Translated by Constance Garnett **424**
In this classical Russian story of the plight of an "ordinary man" overpowered by forces beyond his comprehension and control, Gogol blends humor with sympathy as he shows the power of a simple dream and the cost of its destruction.

Nadine Gordimer (South Africa): "A Soldier's Embrace" 444
After a civil war that has brought independence, a liberal white couple in an African country slowly face the reality that they are no longer needed or appreciated.

Judy Grahn (United States): "Boys at the Rodeo" 455
Six lesbians enter a rodeo and are mistaken for teenage boys; their "disguise" enables them to witness and unmask the rituals of the rodeo, including its assumptions about traditional gender roles.

Jacob and Wilhelm Grimm (Germany): "Karl Katz" 461
After drinking wine with 12 strange knights who are playing ninepins in the Hartz forest, a goatherd falls into a deep slumber that lasts for 20 years.

Nathaniel Hawthorne (United States): "The Birthmark" 466
In this classic exploration of the complementary realms of spirit and matter, Hawthorne symbolizes both the power and the limits of scientific mastery: a young man attempts to eradicate the minor imperfection on his wife's face, with consequences far different from what either of them expects.

Bessie Head (South Africa/Botswana): "The Prisoner Who Wore Glasses" 479
South African political prisoners break down the defenses of their Afrikaner warden and improve the quality of their lives.

Ernest Hemingway (United States): "The Short Happy Life of Francis Macomber" 484
An African safari is the location for the Hemingway hero's initiation into manhood as well as for an unexpected resolution of a marital conflict.

Langston Hughes (United States): "Thank You, Ma'am" 506
A woman fights back against a purse snatcher and thwarts his potential life of crime.

Zora Neale Hurston (United States): "The Gilded Six-Bits" 510
"Money is the root of all evil," as Hurston demonstrates in this interesting variation on an old theme.

Shirley Jackson (United States): "The Lottery" 519
On a seemingly ordinary afternoon in a New England village, the power of an obscure ritual gathers toward a shocking climax.

Svava Jakobsdóttir (Iceland): "A Story for Children" Translated by Dennis Auburn Hill 526
In this startling satire on maternal self-sacrifice, the mother of brutally indifferent children discovers not only that her brain is literally expendable but that her heart must bear its burdens.

Henry James (United States/England): "The Real Thing" 532
A painter hires a gentleman and his wife as models for the illustrations for a novel and learns that an imitation is often more suitable than the real thing.

Sarah Orne Jewett (United States): "A White Heron" 550
A young girl who is deeply connected to the natural world undergoes an initiatory experience as she chooses something of greater value to her than money.

Elizabeth Jolley (England/Australia): "Another Holiday for the Prince" **558**
An oversolicitous mother pays a price for stepping outside the law to give the ungrateful son she favors a nice weekend holiday at the beach.

James Joyce (Ireland): "Eveline" **563**
On the eve of her elopement and departure for a new life that will free her of family obligations, a young woman realizes that escape from duty is not as simple as she had imagined it.

Franz Kafka (Czechoslovakia): "The Metamorphosis"
Translated by Willa and Edwin Muir **568**
In the first sentence, the protagonist of this visionary nightmare finds himself "transformed in his bed into a giant insect." Kafka traces the consequences of that event with inexorable logic.

Ghassan Kanafani (Palestinian): "A Hand in the Grave"
Translated by Hilary Kilpatrick **601**
The fate of two medical students who need a cadaver for their studies is irrevocably altered when they attempt to rob a grave.

Kanai Mieko (Japan): "Platonic Love"
Translated by Amy Vladeck Heinrich **608**
Exploring the mysteries of literary authorship and creativity, a writer is haunted by the "real author" who takes credit for her work and whose presence complicates the distinctions between imagination, authorial invention, and reality.

John Kasaipwalova (Paupa New Guinea): "Betel Nut Is Bad Magic for Airplanes" **613**
Three Papua New Guinean university students protest their harassment by the police, yet their resistance is more linguistic than physical.

Khamsing Srinawk (Thailand): "The Gold-Legged Frog"
Translated by Domnern Garden **620**
An impoverished rice farmer is obliged to report to authorities to receive a government subsidy for his family while one of his own children lies dying from a snakebite.

Pär Lagerkvist (Sweden): "The Children's Campaign"
Translated by Alan Blair **624**
Describing the heroism of an army composed entirely of children, Lagerkvist's ironic story raises searching questions about military bravery, war, sacrifice, and the nature of childhood.

Margaret Laurence (Canada): "A Bird in the House" **633**
Confronting the deep absence created by her father's sudden death, the young narrator enacts a symbolically lifesaving act years later on his behalf.

Mary Lavin (Ireland): "Happiness" **646**
A mother's way of living life fully makes leaving it an enigma not only for her but also for her three daughters, who ponder her intense commitment to "happiness," and for a loyal priest and friend who confronts the limits of his spiritual authority.

D. H. Lawrence (England): "Tickets, Please" 658
In a contest of wills, a seductive man meets his match in a tram-girl who determines that a man must be held accountable for his casual sexual flirtations.

Ursula K. Le Guin (United States): "Sur" 669
Unknown to the world, an expedition that is composed entirely of women reaches the South Pole several years before Amundsen's expedition, as Le Guin imaginatively explores the real sources of women's invisibility in history.

Doris Lessing (Rhodesia/England): "A Woman on a Roof" 682
The conflict between a woman's desire for privacy and men's assumptions about female availability drive this story to a surprising ending.

Catherine Lim (Singapore): "Or Else, the Lightning God" 690
In this satirical story of generational conflict, a young woman, pregnant with her first child, comes to grips with her mother-in-law's power, though not without significant conflict.

Lu Xun (China): "The Story of Hair"
Translated by William A. Lyell 699
A man learns the social and political meanings signified by the way one wears his hair.

Arnost Lustig (Czechoslovakia/United States): "The Lemon"
Translated by Jeanne Němcová 705
In this riveting story of the Holocaust, two boys in the ghetto recognize their common humanity in their will to survive soul-crushing circumstances.

Naguib Mahfouz (Egypt): "Half a Day"
Translated by Denys Johnson-Davies 720
A young boy's apprehension about his first day of school subtly changes to something quite different.

Bernard Malamud (United States): "The Jewbird" 724
The bird who flies into Harry Cohen's New York City apartment claims that he is Jewish—and, worse, that he wants to take up residence.

Thomas Mann (Germany): "The Infant Prodigy"
Translated by H. T. Lowe-Porter 732
The performance of a young pianist elicits a variety of responses from members of his audience, who are uncertain whether to admire his precocity or criticize the limits of his youthful genius.

Katherine Mansfield (New Zealand/England): "Her First Ball" 739
A young girl from the country finds her romantic expectations for the evening temporarily threatened by an older, jaded dance partner.

René Marqués (Puerto Rico): "Island of Manhattan"
Translated by Faye Edwards and Gladys Ortiz 744
Two Puerto Rican immigrants—a man and a woman—adapt to life in New York City, as their respective genders significantly influence their experiences.

Paule Marshall (Barbados/United States): "Brooklyn" 753
A black female student unintentionally catalyzes the memories of an emotionally bankrupt Jewish professor, scarred by anti-Semitism and McCarthy era blacklisting, who is obliged to face his own racist assumptions.

Bobbie Ann Mason (United States): "Shiloh" 768
A trip to a Civil War battlefield becomes the culminating event in a Kentucky truck driver's discovery that his wife's ambitions for herself directly conflict with his own unquestioning view of their relationship.

William Somerset Maugham (England): "The Appointment in Samarra" 779
Maugham's brief parable, a model of narrative economy, suggests a paradoxical relationship between fate and free will.

Guy de Maupassant (France): "The Necklace" Translated by Marjorie Laurie 781
A young woman's vanity and her longing for social acceptance a notch above her actual circumstances exact a painfully high price, as she discovers her mistaken assumptions about a necklace lost years ago.

Richard McCann (United States): "My Mother's Clothes: The School of Beauty and Shame" 788
In this lyrical reminiscence of youth, an 11-year-old boy discovers his sexual preference, in part through wearing his mother's clothes.

John McCluskey (United States): "Lush Life" 801
Two jazz musicians discuss the meaning of life—the purpose of their music—as they drive through the night toward their next gig.

Herman Melville (United States): "Bartleby, the Scrivener" 813
Although the surface narrative is somewhat humorous, even absurd, Melville's classic story probes the age-old question of man's inhumanity to man—are we our brother's keeper?

Katherine Min (Korea/United States): "The One Who Goes Farthest Away" 839
After 35 years in the United States, a middle-aged Korean returns to the city of his birth, meets his old schoolmates, and contemplates the question of his identity: is he American or Korean?

Susan Minot (United States): "Lust" 847
A young woman gropes toward an understanding of her promiscuity as she leaves a string of lovers behind.

Mishima Yukio (Japan): "Swaddling Clothes" Translated by Ivan Morris 854
The wife of a famous Japanese actor speculates what might happen if her grown son were to meet his double.

Kermit Moyer (United States): "Tumbling" 859
Jack and Jill take a most unusual tumble in this fascinating variation on the well-known children's nursery rhyme.

Es'kia Mphahlele (South Africa): "Mrs. Plum" 879
A South African domestic worker learns that her white employer is not as liberal as she professes to be.

Slawomir Mrożek (Poland): "The Elephant" Translated by Konrad Syrop 903
Can an inflatable rubber elephant substitute for a real one? Two zookeepers and the children who visit a Polish zoo find the answer to this improbable question.

Bharati Mukherjee (India/United States): "A Father" 906
An immigrant Indian family respond in radically different ways to their life in America; the daughter makes a choice that fundamentally challenges her father's deepest cultural values.

Alice Munro (Canada): "The Office" 915
Seeking a room of her own in which to write, the narrator struggles for her own professional—and personal—being as she learns that a private space is not enough.

V. S. Naipaul (Trinidad): "One Out of Many" 925
In this story of acculturation, Naipaul traces the ironic transformation of an Indian into an American.

Carmen Naranjo (Costa Rica): "And We Sold the Rain"
Translated by Jo Anne Engelbert 948
Satirizing the predicament of a Central American developing nation in economic crisis, Naranjo suggests that a previously unexploited natural resource might eliminate the nation's problems.

R. K. Narayan (India): "A Horse and Two Goats" 953
Despite the obstacle of mutually incomprehensible languages, a poor Indian villager and wealthy American tourist conduct a comic conversation that concludes with each convinced that he has acquired something of material value from the other.

Ngugi wa Thiong'o (Kenya): "A Meeting in the Dark" 966
An African student is caught between his girlfriend's traditional world and his father's doctrinaire Christianity.

Joyce Carol Oates (United States): "Where Are You Going, Where Have You Been?" 977
In this chilling tale of good and evil, and adolescent girl is tempted by a stranger, whose question is a variation of the old cliché, "Candy, little girl?"

Ōba Minako (Japan): "The Pale Fox"
Translated by Stephen W. Kohl 990
In Ōba Minako's bizarre account of conflicting sexual desires, a woman is caught between her lover's and her father's dominance.

Flannery O'Connor (United States): "A Good Man Is Hard to Find" 997
A garrulous old grandmother tragically alters the fate of her son's family because she can't keep her mouth shut.

Ōe Kenzaburo (Japan): "Aghwee the Sky Monster"
Translated by John Nathan 1009
In the final days of a Japanese composer's life, madness and guilt become intertwined.

Sembene Ousmane (Senegal): "Black Girl"
Translated by Ellen Conroy Kennedy 1029
A young Senegalese girl learns to her despair that slavery is not a thing of the past but a practice very much a part of her current experience.

Amos Oz (Israel): "Nomad and Viper"
Translated by Nicholas deLange and Philip Simpson 1039
In an uneasy standoff between Israeli settlers and the Arab nomads who surround their kibbutz, a young Israeli woman is torn between political loyalties and what may be a fatal curiosity.

Emilia Pardo Bazán (Spain): "The Revolver"
Translated by Angel Flores 1052
A bereaved wife realizes that her jealous husband has destroyed their love through a weapon more powerful than the revolver she fears.

Octavio Paz (Mexico): "The Blue Bouquet"
Translated by Lysander Kemp 1056
In this surreal story, an outsider in a Mexican city is mugged by a man who covets his blue eyes.

Virgilio Piñera (Cuba): "Insomnia"
Translated by Mark Schafer 1059
A man discovers that insomnia is worse than death—or is it death?

Edgar Allan Poe (United States): "The Cask of Amontillado" 1061
Poe's gothic tale of revenge poses the question of whether one can "punish with impunity."

Katherine Anne Porter (United States): "Rope" 1067
A young husband's innocent purchase of a rope precipitates a series of emotional exchanges and conflicts between him and his wife, for which the rope itself becomes the central symbol.

Rodrigo Rey Rosa (Guatemala): "The Proof"
Translated by Paul Bowles 1072
The strangulation of a canary is the first action in a chain reaction of events that tests the doubting Miguel's questions about death and God's power to perform miracles.

Gabrielle Roy (Canada): "The Move"
Translated by Joyce Marshall 1076
Colored by her mother's childhood memories of crossing the great plains of Canada, a young girl envisions housemoving as a romantic adventure—until her observation of an actual move compels acknowledgement of the underside of her imaginative vision.

Leslie Marmon Silko (United States): "Yellow Woman" 1086
A Native American woman has a passionate encounter with a stranger who may or may not have come from the spirit world.

Isaac Bashevis Singer (Poland/United States): "Gimpel the Fool"
Translated by Saul Bellow 1094
Although the humble Gimpel suffers betrayals and indignities, he learns the true meaning of the rabbinical wisdom: "Better to be a fool all your days than for one hour to be evil."

María Teresa Solari (Peru): "Death and Transfiguration of a Teacher"
Translated by John Benson 1105
In a Swiftian satire on education and the declining appreciation of poetry, a dedicated teacher who is unable to command the respect of her students is instead literally sacrificed and consumed by them.

John Steinbeck (United States): "The Chrysanthemums" **1108**
A farmer's wife learns that the little pleasures in life can be used both for and against us.

Hyemeyohsts Storm (United States): "The Story of Jumping Mouse" **1116**
In this Native American (Northern Cheyenne) "teaching story," stages of spiritual growth and knowledge are revealed through the sacred quest of a determined and courageous mouse, as the storyteller incorporates his own interpretation of the events he describes.

Graham Swift (England): "Learning to Swim" **1125**
A young boy is caught in an emotional tug-of-war between his parents, both of whom crave his affection.

Amy Tan (China/United States): "Half and Half" **1136**
The narrator sees her failing marriage to an American man in the context of her younger brother's accidental drowning years before and begins to understand her mother's need to believe in a traditional Chinese conception of providence.

Leo Tolstoy (Russia): "The Death of Ivan Ilych" Translated by Louise and Aylmer Maude **1147**
Tolstoy's biographer, Henri Troyat, calls this "double story of the decomposing body and the awakening soul . . . one of the most powerful works in the literature of the world."

Amos Tutuola (Nigeria): "The Complete Gentleman" **1186**
An African girl learns, in this traditional tale, that appearances may indeed be deceptive and that warnings should be heeded.

Mark Twain (United States): "Luck" **1193**
In this vintage Twain story, a foolish man manages to "get by" all the way to the top, proving that luck may count more than talent if the circumstances are right.

John Updike (United States): "A & P" **1197**
A young grocery store clerk, finding that his tolerant view of three bathing-suit-clad girls is in conflict with store policy, makes a moral choice that leaves him sadder but possibly wiser.

Luisa Valenzuela (Argentina): "Strange Things Happen Here" Translated by Helen R. Lane **1203**
Two penniless young men find several abandoned objects, including a briefcase that, hinting at both good fortune and danger, temporarily alters the way they see the people and the world around them.

Mario Vargas Llosa (Peru): "Sunday" Translated by Mary E. Ellsworth **1210**
Attempting to prove their masculinity, two young men compete for the hand of the same young girl, risking their lives in the process.

Alice Walker (United States): "Everyday Use" **1222**
Which is the greater value of quilts: as aesthetic or practical objects? A mother must make this determination within the difficult context of her two very different daughters' competing wishes.

Eudora Welty (United States): "Why I Live at the P. O." **1229**
A single woman's plea for attention is ignored by her family in this comic and well-known story.

Edith Wharton (United States): "Roman Fever" **1239**
Two widowed friends traveling in Rome with their daughters reminisce about a sojourn in Rome years earlier before they married; a startling revelation by one alters the truth of both of their lives.

LONGER NARRATIVES

Mulk Raj Anand (India): *Untouchable* **1249**
This classic work of Indian fiction traces a day in the life of a sweeper (an untouchable, Hindu's lowest caste) with all its humiliations and fleeting moments of happiness.

Kate Chopin (United States): *The Awakening* **1333**
Edna Pontellier, wife and mother of two, awakens—to romance, to passion, to the artistic and spiritual possibilities within her own being—in a turn-of-the-century society in which such self-explorations are denied to women.

Thematic Contents **1421**

Geographical Contents

NORTH AMERICA

Woody Allen (United States): "The Kugelmass Episode" 47
Rudolfo A. Anaya (United States): "B. Traven Is Alive and Well in Cuernavaca" 67
Sherwood Anderson (United States): "Death in the Woods" 78
Margaret Atwood (Canada): "Dancing Girls" 87
BarbaraNeely (United States): "Spilled Salt" 102
Ann Beattie (United States): "The Burning House" 109
Ambrose Bierce (United States): "An Occurrence at Owl Creek Bridge" 124
Raymond Carver (United States): "Where I'm Calling From" 164
Willa Cather (United States): "Paul's Case" 175
John Cheever (United States): "The Swimmer" 190
Kate Chopin (United States): *The Awakening* 1333
Stephen Crane (United States): "The Open Boat" 238
Ralph Ellison (United States): "Flying Home" 293
Louise Erdrich (United States): "Love Medicine" 308
William Faulkner (United States): "A Rose for Emily" 324
F. Scott Fitzgerald (United States): "Babylon Revisited" 336
Charlotte Perkins Gilman (United States): "The Yellow Wallpaper" 387
Susan Glaspell (United States): "A Jury of Her Peers" 408
Judy Grahn (United States): "Boys at the Rodeo" 455
Nathaniel Hawthorne (United States): "The Birthmark" 466
Ernest Hemingway (United States): "The Short Happy Life of Francis Macomber" 484
Langston Hughes (United States): "Thank You, Ma'am" 506
Zora Neale Hurston (United States): "The Gilded Six-Bits" 510
Shirley Jackson (United States): "The Lottery" 519
Henry James (United States/England): "The Real Thing" 532
Sarah Orne Jewett (United States): "A White Heron" 550
Margaret Laurence (Canada): "A Bird in the House" 633
Ursula K. Le Guin (United States): "Sur" 669
Arnost Lustig (Czechoslovakia/United States): "The Lemon" 705
Bernard Malamud (United States): "The Jewbird" 724
Paule Marshall (Barbados/United States): "Brooklyn" 753
Bobbie Ann Mason (United States): "Shiloh" 768
Richard McCann (United States): "My Mother's Clothes: The School of Beauty and Shame" 788
John McCluskey (United States): "Lush Life" 801
Herman Melville (United States): "Bartleby, the Scrivener" 813
Katherine Min (Korea/United States): "The One Who Goes Farthest Away" 839
Susan Minot (United States): "Lust" 847
Kermit Moyer (United States): "Tumbling" 859

Bharati Mukherjee (India/United States): "A Father" 906
Alice Munro (Canada): "The Office" 915
Joyce Carol Oates (United States): "Where Are You Going, Where Have You Been?" 977
Flannery O'Connor (United States): "A Good Man Is Hard to Find" 997
Edgar Allan Poe (United States): "The Cask of Amontillado" 1061
Katherine Anne Porter (United States): "Rope" 1067
Gabrielle Roy (Canada): "The Move" 1076
Leslie Marmon Silko (United States): "Yellow Woman" 1086
Isaac Bashevis Singer (Poland/United States) 1094
John Steinbeck (United States): "The Chrysanthemums" 1108
Hyemeyohsts Storm (United States): "The Story of Jumping Mouse" 1116
Amy Tan (China/United States): "Half and Half" 1136
Mark Twain (United States): "Luck" 1193
John Updike (United States): "A & P" 1197
Alice Walker (United States): "Everyday Use" 1222
Eudora Welty (United States): "Why I Live at the P.O." 1229
Edith Wharton (United States): "Roman Fever" 1239

CARIBBEAN

René Marqués (Puerto Rico): "Island of Manhattan" 744
Paule Marshall (Barbados/United States): "Brooklyn" 753
V. S. Naipaul (Trinidad): "One Out of Many" 925

LATIN AMERICA

Isabel Allende (Chile): "And of Clay Are We Created" 56
Jorge Luis Borges (Argentina): "Death and the Compass" 134
José Donoso (Chile): "Paseo" 272
Carlos Fuentes (Mexico): "The Doll Queen" 369
Gabriel García Márquez (Colombia): "Balthazar's Marvelous Afternoon" 381
Carmen Naranjo (Costa Rica): "And We Sold the Rain" 948
Octavio Paz (Mexico): "The Blue Bouquet" 1056
Virgilio Piñera (Cuba): "Insomnia" 1059
Rodrigo Rey Rosa (Guatemala): "The Proof" 1072
María Teresa Solari (Peru): "Death and Transfiguration of a Teacher" 1105
Luisa Valenzuela (Argentina): "Strange Things Happen Here" 1203
Mario Vargas Llosa (Peru): "Sunday" 1210

EUROPE

Isaac Babel (Russia): "My First Goose" 98
J. Bernlef (Netherlands): "The Black Dog" 120
Heinrich Böll (Germany): "The Laugher" (translated by Leila Vennewitz) 131
Dino Buzzati (Italy): "The Falling Girl" 143
Italo Calvino (Italy): "A Sign in Space" 147
Albert Camus (Algeria/France): "The Guest" 154
Anton Chekhov (Russia): "The Kiss" 199

Gabrielle-Sidonie Colette (France): "The Seamstress" 213
Joseph Conrad (Poland/England): "Amy Foster" 217
Isak Dinesen (Denmark): "The Sailor-Boy's Tale" 255
Margareta Ekström (Sweden): "The Night Between the Second and the Third" 285
Gustave Flaubert (France): "The Legend of Saint Julian the Hospitaller" 351
Natalia Ginzburg (Italy): "The Mother" 400
Nicolai Gogol (Russia): "The Overcoat" 424
Jacob and Wilhelm Grimm (Germany): "Karl Katz" 461
Svava Jakobsdóttir (Iceland): "A Story for Children" 526
Henry James (United States/England): "The Real Thing" 532
James Joyce (Ireland): "Eveline" 563
Franz Kafka (Czechoslovakia): "The Metamorphosis" 568
Pär Lagerkvist (Sweden): "The Children's Campaign" 624
Mary Lavin (Ireland): "Happiness" 646
D. H. Lawrence (England): "Tickets, Please" 658
Doris Lessing (Rhodesia/England): "A Woman on a Roof" 682
Arnost Lustig (Czechoslovakia/United States): "The Lemon" 705
Thomas Mann (Germany): "The Infant Prodigy" 732
Katherine Mansfield (New Zealand/England): "Her First Ball" 739
William Somerset Maugham (England): "The Appointment in Samarra" 779
Guy De Maupassant (France): "The Necklace" 781
Slawomir Mrożek (Poland): "The Elephant" 903
Emilia Pardo Bazán (Spain): "The Revolver" 1052
Isaac Bashevis Singer (Poland/United States): "Gimpel the Fool" 1094
Graham Swift (England): "Learning to Swim" 1125
Leo Tolstoy (Russia): "The Death of Ivan Ilych" 1147

AFRICA

Chinua Achebe (Nigeria): "Girls at War" 19
Ama Ata Aidoo (Ghana): "Two Sisters" 30
Birago Diop (Senegal): "Sarzan" 263
Nadine Gordimer (South Africa): "A Soldier's Embrace" 444
Bessie Head (South Africa/Botswana): "The Prisoner Who Wore Glasses" 479
Doris Lessing (Rhodesia/England): "A Woman on a Roof" 682
Es'kia Mphahlele (South Africa): "Mrs. Plum" 879
Ngugi wa Thiong'o (Kenya): "A Meeting in the Dark" 966
Sembene Ousmane (Senegal): "Black Girl" 1029
Amos Tutuola (Nigeria): "The Complete Gentleman" 1186

MIDDLE EAST

From *The Thousand and One Nights*: "The Story of the Merchant and the Jinni" 10
Hanan Al-Shaykh (Lebanon): "The Unseeing Eye" 64
Ghassan Kanafani (Palestinian): "A Hand in the Grave" 601
Naguib Mahfouz (Egypt): "Half a Day" 720
Amos Oz (Israel): "Nomad and Viper" 1039

ASIA

Akutagawa Ryūnosuke (Japan): "Within a Grove" 40
Mulk Raj Anand (India): *Untouchable* 1249
Feng Jicai (China): "The Street-Sweeping Show" 332
Kanai Mieko (Japan): "Platonic Love" 608
Khamsing Srinawk (Thailand): "The Gold-Legged Frog" 620
Catherine Lim (Singapore): "Or Else, the Lightning God" 690
Lu Xun (China): "The Story of Hair" 699
Katherine Min (Korea/United States): "The One Who Goes Farthest Away" 839
Mishima Yukio (Japan): "Swaddling Clothes" 854
R. K. Narayan (India): "A Horse and Two Goats" 953
Ōba Minako (Japan): "The Pale Fox" 990
Ōe Kenzaburo (Japan): "Aghwee the Sky Monster" 1009

AUSTRALIA, NEW ZEALAND, SOUTH PACIFIC

Elizabeth Jolley (England/Australia): "Another Holiday for the Prince" 558
John Kasaipwalova (Papua New Guinea): "Betel Nut Is Bad Magic for Airplanes" 613
Katherine Mansfield (New Zealand/England): "Her First Ball" 739

• *Worlds of Fiction* •

Introduction

I

Although we think of the short story as a relatively recent literary form developed in the past 150 years, in a deeper sense stories are the oldest form of literature. People have always told stories. Long before narratives were shaped into written form, they were the stuff of imaginative communication, beginning with the proverbial, "It was a dark and stormy night," that a storyteller might have shared with a spellbound group around the campfire or next to the hearth. Recorded narratives are as old as the tales originally passed orally from one generation to the next in ancient Greece or medieval Arabia or modern Africa. All of us are creators of narrative: when we try to describe a particularly vivid dream to a friend, only to realize how much is lost in translation, or to invent an ingenious excuse for why a term paper deadline could not be met.

Granted, not all of these fictions qualify as short stories in the more controlled aesthetic sense. Yet the impulse to tell a story is one we can all recognize because we have participated in it. The writers who have found original ways to craft the common language of such narratives into art—to create verbal shapes for our own often shapeless inner stories as well as the stories of others whose lives we may enter for the first time—are the writers whom we read with the exhilaration of discovery and the reward of insight.

In recognition of the beginnings of the short story form in oral traditions, we have included in this anthology several stories that recapture the spoken quality of narrative: the first tales Shahrazad (Scheherazade) tells King Shahriyar in order to postpone for one thousand and one successive nights the ending of the story and thus reprieve her own demise; the Native American "teaching story" of Jumping Mouse; the Nigerian writer Amos Tutuola's entertaining story of the "complete gentleman." These narratives that originate in the oral tradition of their respective cultures and storytellers enable us to hear the *voice* of the storyteller speaking directly into the ear of the reader, reminding us that in any good story, we *hear* as well as read the words as the author speaks to us. As the Barbadian-American writer Paule Marshall phrases it, honoring the women of her mother's generation whose oral stories infuse her fiction,

> The remarkable thing about [these women] was that while they looked ordinary, they were actually poets; they did marvelous things with the English language that they had learned in the schools of Barbados. . . . They brought to bear the few African words and cadences that they remembered and they infused and enriched it with all manner of biblical quotes and metaphors and sayings drawn from their life as black women.
>
> For these women who were immigrants and who always felt as if they were strangers in America, the language gave them a sense of home. . . .
>
> I see myself as someone who is to serve as a vehicle for these

marvelous women who never got a chance, on paper, to be the poets that they were. (*Women's Review of Books*, July, 1991)

II

In reading many short stories written by authors from around the world in preparation for this anthology, we discovered how enormously large and rich and varied the reservoir of stories is in every language. For each story we ultimately selected for inclusion in this volume, literally dozens had to be excluded. Our choices were governed by several principles. First, we believe that an anthology of stories should reflect an even more inclusive international perspective than that encompassed by recent story anthologies. Traditionally (until the 1980s), short story collections were composed primarily of narratives from the United States, Great Britain, and Western Europe. Such collections tended to reinforce the sense of a given and limited "canon" of great writers and stories. In the past decade, scholars, teachers, students, and book editors have challenged such assumptions, responding to the fact that what is included in a textbook or anthology also reveals what traditionally has been omitted: the voices of women, minorities, other cultural perspectives besides the predominantly white, and male, and Western, ones.

Concurrently, the canon of literary excellence is undergoing reconceptualization. The view that literary traditions are static, objective, timeless judgments has begun to give way to a view of literary canons composed of evolving choices based not only on aesthetic criteria but also on social and political realities that inevitably influence both how and what we read, both how and what is defined as the—or, more accurately, a—"tradition." As Bharati Mukherjee (who was born in India and now lives in the United States) expresses the challenge faced by immigrant writers representing a multicultural reality,

> My literary agenda begins by acknowledging that America has transformed *me*. It does not end until I show how I (and the hundreds of thousands like me) have transformed America. . . . I have had to create an audience. I cannot rely on shorthand references to my community, my religion, my class, my region, or my old school tie. . . . My duty [as a writer] is to give voice to continents, but also to redefine the nature of *American* and what makes an American. In the process, work like mine and dozens like it will open up the canon of American literature. (*The Writer on Her Work: New Essays in New Territory*, edited by Janet Sternberg)

Inevitably and sometimes invisibly, the political complexion of the world has closed our eyes to the works of writers from certain areas. This politically induced blindness is compounded by several layers of artistic censorship. During most decades of this century, a number of writers or would-be writers in countries within the (now dissolved) Communist bloc and in other areas of the world in which the freedoms of speech and artistic expression have been severely restricted have practiced self-censorship. No doubt speaking for many in his own and similar situations, the Russian writer Isaac Babel—a victim of severe political repression during the Stalinist era—described himself to the first Soviet Writers' Congress in 1934 as "a master of a new literary genre, the genre of

silence." Moreover, limited access to the works of writers from these areas of the world has resulted in a corresponding limitation in the availability of translations into English. We want to acknowledge our indebtedness to the many fine translators who have given all of us access to stories originally written in other languages, rendering the universal language of the imagination into the English tongue.

Increasingly the country of the mind, like the countries of the world, has opened to embrace larger, more interconnected, and sometimes more contradictory perspectives. As the novelist Virginia Woolf remarked in another context, we all observe the world from a necessarily limited point of view: "Either we are men, or we are women. Either we are cold, or we are sentimental. Either we are young, or growing old" (*Jacob's Room*). One might amend her observation to include distinctions other than polar ones that nonetheless acknowledge differences among us. Stories (and other forms of literature, of course) enable us to travel imaginatively outside those limiting boundaries—whether historical, political, cultural, or gendered—to enter experiences that originate not only in other times but also in other places and in people who seem quite different from ourselves. Through these passports into domains where previously we might not have been granted entrance, we may enlarge our understanding of the complex, multicultural world and, closer to home, of an increasingly culturally and ethnically diverse United States. As critic Paul Skenazy has phrased it, "Different ways of thinking don't just change the way we perceive the world; they recast what can and might be conceived of as the world."

Another principle of selection for this text has been our desire to include stories that provide variety across several different spectrums. Realizing that there is no way to achieve either true representativeness or comprehensiveness in an anthology that aspires to an international perspective, we have sought to include authors and stories that are "good," in our judgment, besides being fresh, accessible, and demonstrative of the enormous range of aesthetic, technical, and thematic possibilities within the form. We recognize that no anthology will please everyone ("What, you left out my favorite story by ________?!"). We also recognize that each of us reads and enjoys stories for a variety of reasons, both intellectual and emotional, public and private, ranging from the comforting rediscovery of the familiar to the startling discovery of the new or unfamiliar. Thus, the stories included here vary not only by nationality, culture, and gender of the author but by themes and subjects, plots and settings, styles and points of view, and length—ranging from a mere paragraph or a brief two pages (what the editors of one collection term "sudden fiction") to several stories of novella length and many in between.

We have included what we hope is an appealing mixture of well-known and new authors and stories: masterpieces by classic writers such as Herman Melville, Leo Tolstoy, and Edith Wharton, but also less familiar stories by major writers such as Mark Twain, Anton Chekhov, Joseph Conrad, James Joyce, and Katherine Anne Porter; more stories by women, by minority writers in the United States, by new writers, by writers from countries and cultures not typically included in short story anthologies. Of the 127 stories in this anthology, although approximately two-thirds are by North American and European authors, a number of those are represented by new or less familiar authors or by less frequently anthologized selections by well-known authors. The remaining third are drawn from the writers of other major geographical areas of the world: Latin

America, Africa, Asia, the Middle East, and Australia, New Zealand, and the South Pacific. Again, some stories and writers will be familiar, but many more in the latter category will be unfamiliar. Accordingly, we have endeavored, in the headnote prefacing each story, to provide not only biographical information about the author but, where appropriate, comments that offer a cultural context for reading the story. The questions that follow each story are meant to provoke discussion, to initiate further thinking, and occasionally to suggest ideas and themes that can be fruitfully compared with those of other stories.

Having considered several different principles of organization for this volume, each of which had clear advantages and equally clear limitations, we ultimately chose the alphabetical organization in the hope that in this format readers would be able to locate authors most easily. A chronological organization works well for collections emphasizing the development of a tradition, particularly for national groupings of literature, but it is less useful across a number of cultures whose writers have entered the storytelling tradition at different points in time—whether or not they have been influenced by one another—and whose traditions are incompletely represented by a single story or two. To anchor each narrative in its appropriate historical moment, we have placed the date of publication at the end of each story. (Occasionally, when the original date of publication of a story originally written in another language cannot be established, we have given the date of publication in English translation.)

We considered organizing the volume by grouping authors by geographical points on the map (north, south, east, west, and "elsewhere" for works of fantasy and speculative fiction); however, we concluded that such an organization depended entirely—and misleadingly, for a volume claiming an international perspective—on where we drew the point of reference in relation to ourselves as North American readers. Alternatively, we have included two supplementary tables of contents. One identifies writers by major geographical areas, and the second groups stories by major themes or motifs, to permit readers to pursue interesting comparisons across times, nationalities, and cultures.

III

Even in these days of the global village, teachers may be reluctant to assign—and students to read—literary works by writers from non-Western cultures; we are all much more comfortable with what we know. Yet in yielding to the position of comfort, we deprive ourselves of insights into other ways of life, other perspectives on experience that may enrich our own. As the Native American writer Hyemeyohsts Storm wrote in the introduction to his unique novel about Plains Indian life and traditions, *Seven Arrows* (1972),

> If you and I were sitting in a circle of people on the prairie, and if I were then to place a painted drum or an eagle feather in the middle of this circle, each of us would perceive these objects differently. Our vision of them would vary according to our individual positions in the circle, each of which would be unique.
>
> Our personal perceptions of these objects would also depend upon much more than just the different positions from which we look upon them. For example, one or more of us might suffer from color

> blindness, or weak eyesight. Either of these two physical differences would influence our perceptions of these objects.
>
> There are levels upon levels of perspectives we must consider when we try to understand our individual perceptions of things, or when we try to relate our own perceptions to those of our brothers and sisters. Every single one of our previous experiences in life will affect in some way the mental perspective from which we see the world around us.

Storm emphasizes the uniqueness of our individual perceptions; he does not say that they are incorrect. Our angle of vision, as we observe the drum or the feather in the circle, shows each of us something slightly different, perhaps even radically different, depending on where we are standing, our physical attributes (including gender and race), and our previous experiences.

In one sense, these attributes and limitations are the same when we read what we consider to be familiar literature and when we read less familiar writing. Scholars have spent decades explicating Shakespeare's plays for modern readers, attempting to understand and convey what each word meant for the Elizabethan viewers of the bard's plays. An understanding of Puritanism is important for grasping the full meaning of many of Nathaniel Hawthorne's stories and novels; similarly, appreciation of the fiction of William Faulkner, the plays of Tennessee Williams, and the short stories of Flannery O'Connor is significantly enhanced by some awareness of life in the American South. On the other hand, these authors also *give us* perspectives on those times and places, so that the reader discovers something about Elizabethan England, Puritan New England, or the post-slavery South in the very act of reading those writers.

Thus, when we read and interpret (and understand) the literature of Western or American traditions, we do the same things that we do when we read literary works by writers from other cultural and national traditions: we invoke whatever we know and understand of culture, history, biography, sociology, anthropology, politics, economics, psychology, gender, race, class, and our own experiences, to illuminate what we read. Of course, some elements may be unfamiliar and may require further information about cultural contexts in order to enhance our comprehension.

To demonstrate this process, let us consider the story "Black Girl" ("La Noire de . . .") by Senegalese writer and filmmaker Sembene Ousmane. Outwardly, Sembene's story takes the form of a journey—an almost universal narrative pattern because it invokes the human journey from birth to death that transcends cultural specifics. In this story, the central character, Diouana, takes a literal journey from Senegal, West Africa, to Antibes, France. The time is 1958 and Diouana leaves the country of her birth to rejoin her employers, the Pouchets, to continue working for them as a domestic who cares for their home and their children as she did when they resided in Dakar, Senegal. That is the literal journey of the story, but, as is often the case in fiction that employs a journey framework (for example, see Joseph Conrad's "Amy Foster," Willa Cather's "Paul's Case," John Cheever's "The Swimmer," Dino Buzzati's "The Falling Girl," Naguib Mahfouz's "Half a Day," Stephen Crane's "The Open Boat," Es'kia Mphahlele's "Mrs. Plum," and a number of other stories included in this volume), the journey is figurative as well as literal: the transformation of Diouana's character as well as her body.

Chronologically, the story begins at its "end," with the discovery of Diouana's body in the bathtub. Western readers may consider the circumstances somewhat melodramatic or sensational: the arrival of the police, the body in the blanket, the blood on the steps. Even the reporters' perspective appears to support this response: "The suicide of a maid—even if she were black—didn't amount to a hill of beans." The final line in the story—the news item, "Homesick African Girl Cuts Throat in Antibes"—seems to underscore this attitude, reducing the incident to little more than a minor item buried in a back page of the newspaper. Yes, Diouana is another victim of racism, but her situation is pitiable, not necessarily tragic.

What, then, should the reader conclude is the central idea of "Black Girl"? Is it racism? Certainly, Diouana's situation with the Pouchets is one of increasing misery—distress that increases the longer she remains in France. Her employers treat her terribly: overworking her, demeaning her character and her differences from them. Even the children for whom she cares contribute to her victimization, referring to her in derogatory terms.

Certainly racism is an important issue in the story. If it is not the primary concern, then what is the theme? Lost ideals, changed perspectives, lost innocence? Indeed, these are also crucial elements of the story, accessible even to readers who lack knowledge of West African culture. Initially, Diouana is full of expectations for her journey to France: "She wanted to see it and make a triumphal return. This was where people got rich." So excited is Diouana by her anticipated move that she fails to heed the warnings of her compatriot, Tive Correa, who undertook a similar journey 20 years earlier. As the narrator informs us, "He had left, rich with youth, full of ambition, and come home a wreck. From having wanted everything he had returned with nothing but an excessive love for the bottle. For Diouana he predicted nothing but misfortune." Unfortunately, Diouana has already been seduced by the lure of money and the legitimate expectations of an improved lifestyle.

Thus far, what we have said about "Black Girl" depends very little on cultural elements that we are likely to misunderstand. We can sympathize with Diouana's lost dreams and with her situation once she arrives in France. But stated that way, these elements may seem almost too familiar; is "Black Girl" simply another story about prejudice or about the disillusionments of youth?

What we would like to suggest is that a central (and perhaps less immediately recognizable) theme of Sembene's story is *slavery*, a concept closely tied to the ideas already mentioned. The details that support such an interpretation are given near the beginning (in chronological time) of Diouana's story, while the girl is still in Dakar, fantasizing about her anticipated journey to France. One problem for Western readers is that, because the initial clues are tied to African history and geography, they may be overlooked. When Diouana, exhilarated, leans out her window and glances at the sea, watching "the birds flying high above in the immense expanse of blue," she is like any young girl imagining new possibilities for her life; additionally, it is easy to understand her desire for flight away from her dreary situation in Dakar as well as her eagerness to be on her way.

Yet in the next sentence, the narrator mentions the Island of Gorée, which Senegalese and other African readers would immediately recognize as an ominous symbol, particularly when juxtaposed with Diouana's earlier sense of freedom and flight. Historically, Gorée, an island approximately two miles off the coast of Senegal, was one of the major points of departure for the westbound slave trade in the eighteenth and nineteenth centuries. Hundreds of thousands of Africans are believed to have been shipped to the New World from Gorée. As a result of treacherous ocean currents, once Africans were transported to the slave pens on the island (where they were held until a vessel arrived to transport them to America), escape was virtually impossible. No one could swim against the perilous currents.

Ironically, the next sentence in Sembene's story, following the reference to Gorée, mentions Diouana's identity card, an aspect of contemporary indenture that distinguishes it from traditional slavery. Diouana regards her picture on the card, identifying it as "a gloomy one" or, in other words, an unflattering photograph; the word *gloomy* also suggests something darker and more fateful. The comment is the more suggestive because it follows the already disturbing reference to Gorée, hinting that Diouana is about to embark on a journey that may not be very different from that of the hundreds of thousands of Africans before her who departed (though involuntarily) from the Senegalese coast.

In 1958, two years before independence, Senegal was still a French colony. The reference to Algeria in the opening paragraph of the story is an allusion to the revolution in that country that would eventually lead to independence there as in other French and English colonies in Africa. (See Albert Camus's "The Guest," included in this volume, for another approach to the legacy of colonialism.) The reference thus invokes colonialism in general, of which the Pouchets are very much a part. The attitudes of Diouana's employers have been shaped by a sense of cultural and racial superiority; they believe that they can do whatever they please, essentially, with their African servants. The Pouchets' "Villa of Green Happiness" is an ironic name, because there is no happiness for Diouana at this villa. Green, a color suggesting life and growth, is also significant. On attaining independence, most African nations chose green as one of the colors for their countries' flags.

When the narrator describes the arrival of the police at the Pouchets' flat in Antibes, several important facts are introduced into the narrative. The first—the mention of April, the month when Diouana arrived in Antibes—is rather startling when we recall that the opening sentence of the story places the date of Diouana's death as June 23. Diouana has been driven to suicide in a brief three months.

The police ask Madame Pouchet a number of questions about their servant, the answers to which reveal more about the insensitivity of the French couple than about their employee. Madame does not know how old Diouana was. (Wasn't she interested enough to ask her?) Madame cannot imagine why Diouana would kill herself; after all, she ate the same food as the family and shared rooms with the children. (Why would Diouana prefer European food? Wouldn't she prefer to be treated as an adult and accorded privacy?) Madame reveals that Diouana did not have any friends of her own. In brief, her situation was almost identical to that of hundreds of thousands of slaves in the United States who were cut off from their families, from their traditional foods, from privacy, from communication even with other slaves because of mutually unintelligible African languages. The placement of this information concerning Diouana's situation in the Pouchets' home is particularly ironic because it comes before the scene describing Diouana's anticipated journey and before the reference to Gorée and the identity card.

The story then moves back in time to trace Diouana's voyage to France. (Significantly, Diouana travels by ship while the Pouchets travel by airplane.) Once in France, Diouana never sees "la belle France" of her imagination. The Pouchets frequently leave her with their four children, who quickly organize to persecute her. They refer to her color, stressing the fact that she is the *other*, different from them. Diouana repeatedly experiences the sensation of drowning. (We recall Diouana's ocean crossing. Some readers may be familiar with statistics on the number of slaves who took their lives into their own hands during the Middle Passage, jumping overboard rather than facing slavery in the New World.)

Overworked, patronized, humiliated, denied a moment to herself, and even unable to write or receive letters from home because she and her family are illiterate, Diouana finally informs us directly of her view of her situation: "'Sold, sold. Bought, bought. . . . They've bought me. For three thousand francs I do all this work. They lured me, tied me to them, and I'm stuck here like a slave.'" Economic exploitation: modern slavery. The situation in "Black Girl" intentionally echoes that of African slaves in the nineteenth century. As we read the remaining paragraphs of "Black Girl," including further details about Diouana's suicide, we cannot help but ask whether the investigators have drawn the wrong conclusion. The responsibility for Diouana's death rests with the Pouchets. Sembene's story is an indictment of the continuing practice of slavery—seen not from a European perspective but from an African one.

One final aspect of "Black Girl" remains to be considered: the matter of melodrama or sensationalism. Would an African reader consider Diouana's demise melodramatic? Here matters of cultural experience enter more directly into an understanding of the story and suggest rather different responses. In many traditional African societies, suicide is a taboo. Taking one's own life is tantamount to spilling blood on Mother Earth and polluting the community. Mother Earth may retaliate by punishing the entire community for such an act through drought, flood, or disease. However, Diouana has been cut off from her community, as the story repeatedly emphasizes. Nonetheless, in committing suicide she takes a drastic step by interrupting the cycles of life and procreation. According to animist belief, the link with the ancestors is vital; by breaking that link, Diouana will be cursed by her ancestors. Moreover, failing to participate in the cycle of procreation by producing children, she herself will leave no one who can worship her. Whether Diouana herself is an animist or not is less important than the fact that many African readers will respond to her act as tragedy, not melodrama: her suicide cuts her off forever from the sacred link with her people. (For a variation on this theme, read "Sarzan" by Birago Diop, included in this volume.)

The logical question to ask is how valid is a Western reader's interpretation of "Black Girl" without this piece of cultural information? Must we take a crash course in each writer's culture before we can read his or her fiction? Although the more we know, the better readers we can be, we can appreciate literature in various ways, whatever our level of cultural or other information. We can appreciate Herman Melville's "Bartleby, the Scrivener" without an awareness of Marxist or other interpretations that have been advanced. Readers in other areas of the world can comprehend the stories of Edgar Allan Poe or F. Scott Fitzgerald or Shirley Jackson or Margaret Atwood without knowing much about life in North America. We can read "Black Girl" and discover much of what we need to know in the story itself. Joseph Conrad's story "Amy Foster" might be read together with Sembene's "Black Girl" for its similar focus on the predicament of the *other*, or outsider: the person from another culture or country (or class or race or linguistic group) whose presence as a stranger in the community may produce occasions for connection as well as for profound misunderstanding.

What we are suggesting is a combination of cultural humility (we should not, as North American readers, presume that our perspective is the only one) and cultural curiosity (the expectation that although we cannot get entirely outside of our own reference points, we can become sensitive readers by maintaining an open ear so that the initially unfamiliar may speak to us). We read to enjoy; we read to learn; we read to escape. Most of us read fiction because we are also curious, and the information that we can gather from newspapers and magazines and works of nonfiction does not satisfy a certain kind of curiosity. It does not provide us with the sense of immediacy, with the depth of human character and emotion and possibility, even with the chaos or disorder of human experience, that imaginative literature does. We read fiction because we are thinking and feeling creatures, so inquisitive that if we cannot have these glimpses into other people's lives and situations, we miss out on something vital for an understanding of our own lives.

IV

The distinctive element of *Worlds of Fiction* is its international and multicultural perspective, its conviction that the short story form and tradition, like the inherited literary canons that are in the process of revision and redefinition, may also be inventively untraditional. As we have suggested in our close reading of "Black Girl," reading habits are shaped by two paths that might be termed recognition of the familiar, or "self," and acknowledgement of that which is unfamiliar, different, foreign, or "other." We hope that the global and multicultural perspectives of this volume will invite you, as readers and teachers, to discover that what you may previously have regarded as "foreign" or "other" is in fact not so different from yourself, or, at very least, that it imaginatively enlarges your own point of view.

As the literary critic Leslie Fiedler has observed, "Literature never really changes anything—it only makes you feel for a moment as though the world has changed." He may be right; but the world itself has also literally changed, as recent events in the Soviet Union, Eastern Europe, and South Africa demonstrate. Although one might argue whether or not literature has had any part in such political transformations, in fact novelists and playwrights are in several instances also political leaders within their countries—both the acknowledged and "unacknowledged legislators of the world," as the poet Percy Bysshe Shelley phrased it. Paradoxically, encounters with good stories by authors who offer us a wide range of cultural perspectives remind us of the fundamental similarities we share as human beings. Through such diversity, we may become more attentive to the intersecting and overlapping worlds we simultaneously occupy: of cultural, social, and political spheres; of language; and of imaginative truth.

FROM
THE THOUSAND AND ONE NIGHTS
(1200–1400 A.D.)
PERSIA/ARABIA

The Thousand and One Nights—a collection of legends, fables, anecdotes, and stories whose origins recede into the obscure past in the oral tradition of Persia—is one of the world's most marvelous storybooks. Not even the date and location of its first expression as a collection of tales joined by the framing device of the storyteller, Shahrazad, is known. European readers first learned of the stories from the French scholar Galland, who discovered a manuscript of the Arabic original and translated it into French in the early 1800s.

Yet the original version is clearly far older. The tales, drawn from several cultures besides that of Persia, including India and Arabia, are "in ultimate origin . . . from all the ends of the earth." As Charles W. Eliot states in the introduction to the 1909 Harvard Classics edition (from which this excerpt is taken),

> There existed as early as the tenth century of our era a Persian collection of a thousand tales, enclosed in a framework which is practically the one used in the present collection, telling of a King who was in the habit of killing his wives after the first night, and who was led to abandon this practise by the cleverness of the Wezir's daughter, who nightly told him a tale which she left unfinished at dawn, so that his curiosity led him to spare her till the tale should be completed.

Most scholars agree that the tales were probably assembled as an oral collection in the framework described above sometime during the thirteenth century but not recorded in manuscript until at least two centuries later. Interestingly, some of the better-known tales, such as "Ali Baba and the Forty Thieves" and "Ala-ed-Din [Aladdin] and the Wonderful Lamp," were not in the original Arabic manuscript that Galland consulted, although they have been included in many subsequent editions of *The Thousand and One Nights* due to their associations with the other stories. However, because no two manuscripts are exactly alike, it is impossible to determine the definitive "thousand and one" stories, a fact that has produced numerous matters of disputed authenticity among scholars.

What is of more importance is the impact of these interconnected stories on generations of readers. For many, reading *The Thousand and One Nights* in childhood has been an indelible introduction to the fabulous fairy-tale worlds of medieval Persia and Arabia. Even in the relatively recent two centuries of Western readership, the tales have become part of narrative tradition, epitomizing the compelling characteristics of interlocking oral narratives while making "the fairy-land of the Oriental imagination and the mode of life of the medieval Arab, his manners and his morals, familiar to young and old; and allusions to their incidents and personages are wrought into the language and literature of all the modern civilized peoples" (Charles W. Eliot).

The opening story of *The Thousand and One Nights*, with its several interlocking substories, told by Shahrazad to King Shahriyar, is included here as an entertaining and instructive reminder of the ancient oral sources of the storytelling tradition that gave birth to the modern short story.

• The Story of the Merchant and the Jinni •

It has been related to me, O happy King, said Shahrazad,[1] that there was a certain merchant who had great wealth, and traded extensively with surrounding countries; and one day he mounted his horse, and journeyed to a neighbouring country to collect what was due to him, and, the heat oppressing him, he sat under a tree, in a garden, and put his hand into his saddle-bag, and ate a morsel of bread and a date which were among his provisions. Having eaten the date, he threw aside the stone, and immediately there appeared before him an 'Efrit,[2] of enormous height, who, holding a drawn sword in his hand, approached him, and said, Rise, that I may kill thee, as thou hast killed my son. The merchant asked him, How have I killed thy son? He answered, When thou atest the date, and threwest aside the stone, it struck my son upon the chest, and, as fate had decreed against him, he instantly died.

The merchant, on hearing these words, exclaimed, Verily to God we belong, and verily to Him we must return! There is no strength nor power but in God, the High, the Great! If I killed him, I did it not intentionally, but without knowing it; and I trust in thee that thou wilt pardon me.—The Jinni answered, Thy death is indispensable, as thou hast killed my son:—and so saying, he dragged him, and threw him on the ground, and raised his arm to strike him with the sword. The merchant, upon this, wept bitterly, and said to the Jinni, I commit my affair unto God, for no one can avoid what He hath decreed:—and he continued his lamentation, repeating the following verses:—

Time consists of two days; this, bright; and that, gloomy; and life,
of two moieties; this, safe; and that, fearful.
Say to him who hath taunted us on account of misfortunes, Doth
fortune oppose any but the eminent?

[1]*Shahrazad* (often spelled "Scheherazade"): the daughter of the king's Wezir (see below) who becomes the king's bride. To spare herself from the King, who has a reputation for beheading his brides, she suspensefully maintains his curiosity by telling him stories that she leaves unfinished each night.

[2]*'Efrit* a powerful evil Jinn (plural, Jinni, sometimes spelled "genie"). In Persian legend, a supernatural being, created of fire thousands of years before Adam, that can assume human or animal form and influence human affairs.

Dost thou observe that corpses float upon the sea, while the
precious pearls remain in its furthest depths?
When the hands of time play with us, misfortune is imparted to us
by its protracted kiss.
In the heaven are stars that cannot be numbered; but none is
eclipsed save the sun and the moon.
How many green and dry trees are on the earth; but none is
assailed with stones save that which beareth fruit!
Thou thoughtest well of the days when they went well with thee,
and fearedst not the evil that destiny was bringing.

—When he had finished reciting these verses, the Jinni said to him, Spare thy words, for thy death is unavoidable.

Then said the merchant, Know, O 'Efrit, that I have debts to pay, and I have much property, and children, and a wife, and I have pledges also in my possession: let me, therefore, go back to my house, and give to every one his due, and then I will return to thee: I bind myself by a vow and covenant that I will return to thee, and thou shalt do what thou wilt; and God is witness of what I say.—Upon this, the Jinni accepted his covenant, and liberated him; granting him a respite until the expiration of the year.

The merchant, therefore, returned to his town, accomplished all that was upon his mind to do, paid every one what he owed him, and informed his wife and children of the event which had befallen him; upon hearing which, they and all his family and women wept. He appointed a guardian over his children, and remained with his family until the end of the year; when he took his grave-clothes under his arm, bade farewell to his household and neighbours, and all his relations, and went forth, in spite of himself; his family raising cries of lamentation, and shrieking.

He proceeded until he arrived at the garden before mentioned; and it was the first day of the new year; and as he sat, weeping for the calamity which he expected soon to befall him, a sheykh,[3] advanced in years, approached him, leading a gazelle with a chain attached to its neck. This sheykh saluted the merchant, wishing him a long life, and said to him, What is the reason of thy sitting alone in this place, seeing that it is a resort of the Jinn? The merchant therefore informed him of what had befallen him with the 'Efrit, and of the cause of his sitting there; at which the sheykh, the owner of the gazelle, was astonished, and said, By Allah, O my brother, thy faithfulness is great, and thy story is wonderful! if it were engraved upon the intellect, it would be a lesson to him who would be admonished!—And he sat down by his side, and said, By Allah, O my brother, I will not quit this place until I see what will happen unto thee with this 'Efrit. So he sat down, and conversed with him. And the merchant became almost senseless; fear entered him, and terror, and violent grief, and excessive anxiety. And as the owner of the gazelle sat by his side, lo, a second sheykh approached them, with two black hounds, and inquired of them, after saluting them, the reason of their sitting in that place, seeing that it was a resort of the Jann: and they told him the story from beginning to end. And he had hardly sat down when there approached them a third sheykh, with a dapple

[3]*sheykh* (commonly spelled "sheikh" or "sheik"): the chief of an Arab family, tribe, or village

mule; and he asked them the same question, which was answered in the same manner.

Immediately after, the dust was agitated, and became an enormous revolving pillar, approaching them from the midst of the desert; and this dust subsided, and behold, the Jinni, with a drawn sword in his hand; his eyes casting forth sparks of fire. He came to them, and dragged from them the merchant, and said to him, Rise, that I may kill thee, as thou killedst my son, the vital spirit of my heart. And the merchant wailed and wept; and the three sheykhs also manifested their sorrow by weeping and crying aloud and wailing: but the first sheykh, who was the owner of the gazelle, recovering his self-possession, kissed the hand of the 'Efrit, and said to him, O thou Jinni, and crown of the kings of the Jann, if I relate to thee the story of myself and this gazelle, and thou find it to be wonderful, and more so than the adventure of this merchant, wilt thou give up to me a third of thy claim to his blood? He answered, Yes, O sheykh; if thou relate to me the story, and I find it to be as thou hast said, I will give up to thee a third of my claim to his blood.

THE STORY OF THE FIRST SHEYKH AND THE GAZELLE

Then said the sheykh, Know, O 'Efrit, that this gazelle is the daughter of my paternal uncle, and she is of my flesh and my blood. I took her as my wife when she was young, and lived with her about thirty years; but I was not blessed with a child by her; so I took to me a concubine slave, and by her I was blessed with a male child, like the rising full moon, with beautiful eyes, and delicately-shaped eyebrows, and perfectly-formed limbs; and he grew up by little and little until he attained the age of fifteen years. At this period, I unexpectedly had occasion to journey to a certain city, and went thither with a great stock of merchandise.

Now my cousin, this gazelle, had studied enchantment and divination from her early years; and during my absence, she transformed the youth above mentioned into a calf; and his mother, into a cow; and committed them to the care of the herdsman: and when I returned, after a long time, from my journey, I asked after my son and his mother, and she said, Thy slave is dead, and thy son hath fled, and I know not whither he is gone. After hearing this, I remained for the space of a year with mourning heart and weeping eye, until the Festival of the Sacrifice; when I sent to the herdsman, and ordered him to choose for me a fat cow; and he brought me one, and it was my concubine, whom this gazelle had enchanted. I tucked up my skirts and sleeves, and took the knife in my hand, and prepared myself to slaughter her; upon which she moaned and cried so violently that I left her, and ordered the herdsman to kill and skin her: and he did so, but found in her neither fat nor flesh, nor anything but skin and bone; and I repented of slaughtering her, when repentance was of no avail. I therefore gave her to the herdsman, and said to him, Bring me a fat calf: and he brought me my son, who was transformed into a calf. And when the calf saw me, he broke his rope, and came to me, and fawned upon me, and wailed and cried, so that I was moved with pity for him; and I said to the herdsman, Bring me a cow, and let this—

Here Shahrazad perceived the light of morning, and discontinued the recitation with which she had been allowed thus far to proceed. Her sister said to her, How excellent is thy story! and how pretty! and how pleasant! and how sweet!—

but she answered, What is this in comparison with that which I will relate to thee in the next night, if I live, and the King spare me! And the King said, By Allah, I will not kill her until I hear the remainder of her story. Thus they pleasantly passed the night until the morning, when the King went forth to his hall of judgment, and the Wezir[4] went thither with the grave-clothes under his arm: and the King gave judgment, and invested and displaced, until the close of the day, without informing the Wezir of that which had happened; and the minister was greatly astonished. The court was then dissolved; and the King returned to the privacy of his palace.

[On the second and each succeeding night, Shahrazad continued so to interest King Shahriyar[5] by her stories as to induce him to defer putting her to death, in expectation that her fund of amusing tales would soon be exhausted; and as this is expressed in the original work in nearly the same words at the close of every night, such repetitions will in the present translation be omitted.]

When the sheykh, continued Shahrazad, observed the tears of the calf, his heart sympathized with him, and he said to the herdsman, Let this calf remain with the cattle.—Meanwhile, the Jinni wondered at this strange story; and the owner of the gazelle thus proceeded.

O lord of the kings of the Jann, while this happened, my cousin, this gazelle, looked on, and said, Slaughter this calf; for he is fat: but I could not do it; so I ordered the herdsman to take him back; and he took him and went away. And as I was sitting, on the following day, he came to me, and said, O my master, I have to tell thee something that thou wilt be rejoiced to hear; and a reward is due to me for bringing good news. I answered, Well:—and he said, O merchant, I have a daughter who learned enchantment in her youth from an old woman in our family; and yesterday, when thou gavest me the calf, I took him to her, and she looked at him, and covered her face, and wept, and then laughed, and said, O my father, hath my condition become so degraded in thy opinion that thou bringest before me strange men?—Where, said I, are any strange men? and wherefore didst thou weep and laugh? She answered, This calf that is with thee is the son of our master, the merchant, and the wife of our master hath enchanted both him and his mother; and this was the reason of my laughter; but as to the reason of my weeping, it was on account of his mother, because his father had slaughtered her.—And I was excessively astonished at this; and scarcely was I certain that the light of morning had appeared when I hastened to inform thee.

When I heard, O Jinni, the words of the herdsman, I went forth with him, intoxicated without wine, from the excessive joy and happiness that I received, and arrived at his house, where his daughter welcomed me, and kissed my hand; and the calf came to me, and fawned upon me. And I said to the herdsman's daughter, Is that true which thou hast said respecting this calf? She answered, Yes, O my master; he is verily thy son, and the vital spirit of thy heart.—O maiden, said I, if thou wilt restore him, all the cattle and other property of mine that thy father hath under his care shall be thine. Upon this, she smiled, and said, O my master, I have no desire for the property unless on two conditions: the first is, that thou shalt marry me to him; and the second, that I shall enchant

[4]*Wezir* (in Persian and Turkish—Vezir or Vizier): one who bears the burdens incumbent on the ruler; the King's chief assistant

[5]*Shahriyar* His name means "friend of the city."

her who enchanted him, and so restrain her; otherwise, I shall not be secure from her artifice. On hearing, O Jinni, these her words, I said, And thou shalt have all the property that is under the care of thy father besides; and as to my cousin, even her blood shall be lawful to thee. So, when she heard this, she took a cup, and filled it with water, and repeated a spell over it, and sprinkled with it the calf, saying to him, If God created thee a calf, remain in this form, and be not changed; but if thou be enchanted, return to thy original form, by permission of God, whose name be exalted! — upon which he shook, and became a man; and I threw myself upon him, and said, I conjure thee by Allah that thou relate to me all that my cousin did to thee and to thy mother. So he related to me all that had happened to them both; and I said to him, O my son, God hath given thee one to liberate thee, and to avenge thee: — and I married to him, O Jinni, the herdsman's daughter; after which, she transformed my cousin into this gazelle. And as I happened to pass this way, I saw this merchant, and asked him what had happened to him; and when he had informed me, I sat down to see the result. — This is my story. The Jinni said, This is a wonderful tale; and I give up to thee a third of my claim to his blood.

The second sheykh, the owner of the two hounds, then advanced, and said to the Jinni, If I relate to thee the story of myself and these hounds, and thou find it to be in like manner wonderful, wilt thou remit to me, also, a third of thy claim to the blood of this merchant? The Jinni answered, Yes.

THE STORY OF THE SECOND SHEYKH AND THE TWO BLACK HOUNDS

Then said the sheykh, Know, O lord of the kings of the Jann, that these two hounds are my brothers. My father died, and left to us three thousand pieces of gold; and I opened a shop to sell and buy. But one of my brothers made a journey, with a stock of merchandise, and was absent from us for the space of a year with the caravans; after which, he returned destitute. I said to him, Did I not advise thee to abstain from travelling? But he wept, and said, O my brother, God, to whom be ascribed all might and glory, decreed this event; and there is no longer any profit in these words: I have nothing left. So I took him up into the shop, and then went with him to the bath, and clad him in a costly suit of my own clothing; after which, we sat down together to eat; and I said to him, O my brother, I will calculate the gain of my shop during the year, and divide it, exclusive of the principal, between me and thee. Accordingly, I made the calculations, and found my gain to amount to two thousand pieces of gold; and I praised God, to whom be ascribed all might and glory, and rejoiced exceedingly, and divided the gain in two equal parts between myself and him. — My other brother then set forth on a journey; and after a year, returned in the like condition; and I did unto him as I had done to the former.

After this, when we had lived together for some time, my brothers again wished to travel, and were desirous that I should accompany them; but I would not. What, said I, have ye gained in your travels, that I should expect to gain? They importuned me; but I would not comply with their request; and we remained selling and buying in our shops a whole year. Still, however, they persevered in proposing that we should travel, and I still refused, until after the lapse of six entire years, when at last I consented, and said to them, O my brothers, let us calculate what property we possess. We did so, and found it to be six thousand pieces of gold: and I then said to them, We will bury half of it in the earth, that it may be of service to us if any misfortune befall us, in which case each of us shall take a thousand pieces, with which to traffic. Excellent is thy advice, said they. So I took the money and divided it into two equal portions, and buried three thousand pieces of gold; and of the other half, I gave to each of them a thousand pieces. We then prepared merchandise, and hired a ship, and embarked our goods, and proceeded on our voyage for the space of a whole month, at the expiration of which we arrived at a city, where we sold our merchandise; and for every piece of gold we gained ten.

And when we were about to set sail again, we found, on the shore of the sea, a maiden clad in tattered garments, who kissed my hand, and said to me, O my master, art thou possessed of charity and kindness? If so, I will requite thee for them. I answered, Yes, I have those qualities, though thou requite me not. Then said she, O my master, accept me as thy wife, and take me to thy country; for I give myself to thee: act kindly towards me; for I am one who requires to be treated with kindness and charity, and who will requite thee for so doing; and let not my present condition at all deceive thee. When I heard these words, my heart was moved with tenderness towards her, in order to the accomplishment of a purpose of God, to whom he ascribed all might and glory; and I took her, and clothed her, and furnished for her a place in the ship in a handsome manner, and regarded her with kind and respectful attention.

We then set sail; and I became most cordially attached to my wife, so that, on her account, I neglected the society of my brothers, who, in consequence, became jealous of me, and likewise envied me my wealth, and the abundance of my merchandise; casting the eyes of covetousness upon the whole of the property. They therefore consulted together to kill me, and take my wealth; saying, Let us kill our brother, and all the property shall be ours: — and the devil made these actions to seem fair in their eyes; so they came to me while I was sleeping by the side of my wife, and took both of us up, and threw us into the sea. But as soon as my wife awoke, she shook herself, and became transformed into a Jinniyeh.[6] She immediately bore me away, and placed me upon an island, and, for a while, disappeared. In the morning, however, she returned, and said to me, I am thy wife, who carried thee, and rescued thee from death, by permission of God, whose name be exalted. Know that I am a Jinniyeh: I saw thee, and my heart loved thee for the sake of God; for I am a believer in God and his Apostle, God bless and save him! I came to thee in the condition in which thou sawest me, and thou didst marry me; and see, I have rescued thee from drowning. But I am incensed against thy brothers, and I must kill them. — When I heard her tale, I was astonished, and thanked her for what she had done; — But, said I, as to the destruction of my brothers, it is not what I desire. I then related to her all that had happened between myself and them from first to last; and when she had heard it, she said, I will, this next night, fly to them, and sink their ship, and destroy them. But I said, I conjure thee by Allah that thou do it not; for the author of the proverb saith, O thou benefactor of him who hath done evil, the action that he hath done is sufficient for him: — besides, they are at all events my brothers. She still, however, said, They must be killed; — and I continued to

[6]*Jinniyeh* female Jinni

propitiate her towards them: and at last she lifted me up, and soared through the air, and placed me on the roof of my house.

Having opened the doors, I dug up what I had hidden in the earth; and after I had saluted my neighbours, and bought merchandise, I opened my shop. And in the following night, when I entered my house, I found these two dogs tied up in it; and as soon as they saw me, they came to me, and wept, and clung to me; but I knew not what had happened until immediately my wife appeared before me, and said, These are thy brothers. And who, said I, hath done this unto them? She answered, I sent to my sister, and she did it; and they shall not be restored until after the lapse of ten years. And I was now on my way to her, that she might restore them, as they have been in this state ten years, when I saw this man, and, being informed of what had befallen him, I determined not to quit the place until I should have seen what would happen between thee and him.—This is my story.—Verily, said the Jinni, it is a wonderful tale; and I give up to thee a third of the claim that I had to his blood on account of his offence.

Upon this, the third sheykh, the owner of the mule, said to the Jinni, As to me, break not my heart if I relate to thee nothing more than this:—

THE STORY OF THE THIRD SHEYKH AND THE MULE

The mule that thou seest was my wife: she became enamoured of a black slave; and when I discovered her with him, she took a mug of water, and, having uttered a spell over it, sprinkled me, and transformed me into a dog. In this state, I ran to the shop of a butcher, whose daughter saw me, and being skilled in enchantment, restored me to my original form, and instructed me to enchant my wife in the manner thou beholdest.—And now I hope that thou wilt remit to me also a third of the merchant's offence. Divinely was he gifted who said,

Sow good, even on an unworthy soil; for it will not be lost
wherever it is sown.

When the sheykh had thus finished his story, the Jinni shook with delight, and remitted the remaining third of his claim to the merchant's blood. The merchant then approached the sheykhs, and thanked them, and they congratulated him on his safety; and each went his way.

But this, said Shahrazad, is not more wonderful than the story of the fisherman. The King asked her, And what is the story of the fisherman? And she related it as follows. . . .

[13th–15th cent.]

Translated by
EDWARD WILLIAM LANE
(1839–1841)

QUESTIONS

1. Which storytelling devices maintain suspense in the stories?
2. How are the stories of the three sheykhs related?

3. On what human foibles and qualities do the stories focus?
4. Compare these traditional stories with the stories included in this volume based on legends, tales, or stories from oral traditions: Hyemeyohsts Storm's "The Story of Jumping Mouse," the Grimm Brothers' "Karl Katz," Gustave Flaubert's "The Legend of Saint Julian the Hospitaller," Amos Tutuola's "The Complete Gentleman," and Isak Dinesen's "The Sailor-Boy's Tale." Which storytelling elements do they share? How are they different from one another?

Chinua Achebe

(b. 1930)

Nigeria

The setting for Chinua Achebe's "Girls at War" couldn't cut closer to the edge. During the Nigerian Civil War (also referred to as the Biafran War, because the Ibos who seceded from Nigeria called their new nation Biafra), Chinua Achebe worked both within the secessionist territory and outside it to gain international recognition and support for the Biafran cause. Though the Nigerian Civil War is now regarded as little more than a footnote in West African history, during the years of the fighting (1967–1970), the eyes of the world were focused on Biafra as a test case for tribalism, imperialism, and the détente between the West and the Communist bloc. In large part, Biafra collapsed because few significant world powers recognized its sovereignty.

Today the Nigerian Civil War can be regarded as a turning point for many of the country's significant writers. In Chinua Achebe's case, the shift is obvious. Achebe's first novel, *Things Fall Apart* (1958), has become the most widely read and admired piece of African writing of the twentieth century. A sequel, *No Longer at Ease*, was published in 1960, followed quickly by two other novels, *Arrow of God* in 1964, and *A Man of the People* in 1966. At the end of the war, Achebe published a volume of poems, *Beware Soul Brother* (1971) and a collection of short stories, *Girls at War and Other Stories* (1972), but the hiatus between his previous novel and his next one, *Anthills of the Savannah* (1987) lasted more than 20 years. However, one indisputable fact can be noted about Chinua Achebe during those two decades of novelistic silence: he became Africa's most deservedly beloved writer.

Girls at War

The first time their paths crossed nothing happened. That was in the first heady days of warlike preparation when thousands of young men (and sometimes women too) were daily turned away from enlistment centres because far too many of them were coming forward burning with readiness to bear arms in defence of the exciting new nation.

The second time they met was at a check-point at Awka. Then the war had started and was slowly moving southwards from the distant northern sector. He was driving from Onitsha to Enugu and was in a hurry. Although intellectually he approved of thorough searches at road-blocks, emotionally he was always offended whenever he had to submit to them. He would probably not admit it but the feeling people got was that if you were put through a search then you could not really be one of the big people. Generally he got away without a search by pronouncing in his deep, authoritative voice: "Reginald Nwankwo, Ministry of Justice." That almost always did it. But sometimes either through ignorance or sheer cussedness the crowd at the odd check-point would refuse to be impressed. As happened now at Awka. Two constables carrying heavy Mark 4 rifles were watching distantly from the roadside, leaving the actual searching to local vigilantes.

"I am in a hurry," he said to the girl who now came up to his car. "My name is Reginald Nwankwo, Ministry of Justice."

"Good afternoon, sir. I want to see your boot."

"Oh Christ! What do you think is in the boot?"

"I don't know, sir."

He got out of the car in suppressed rage, stalked to the back, opened the boot and holding the lid up with his left hand he motioned with the right as if to say: After you!

"Are you satisfied?" he demanded.

"Yes, sir. Can I see your pigeon-hole?"

"Christ Almighty!"

"Sorry to delay you, sir. But you people gave us this job to do."

"Never mind. You are damn right. It's just that I happen to be in a hurry. But never mind. That's the glove-box. Nothing there as you can see."

"All right sir, close it." Then she opened the rear door and bent down to inspect under the seats. It was then he took the first real look at her, starting from behind. She was a beautiful girl in a breasty blue jersey, khaki jeans and canvas shoes with the new-style hair-plait which gave a girl a defiant look and which they called—for reasons of their own—"air force base"; and she looked vaguely familiar.

"I am all right, sir," she said at last meaning she was through with her task. "You don't recognize me?"

"No. Should I?"

"You gave me a lift to Enugu that time I left my school to go and join the militia."

"Ah, yes, you were the girl. I told you, didn't I, to go back to school because girls were not required in the militia. What happened?"

"They told me to go back to my school or join the Red Cross."

"You see I was right. So, what are you doing now?"

"Just patching up with Civil Defence."

"Well, good luck to you. Believe me you are a great girl."

That was the day he finally believed there might be something in this talk about revolution. He had seen plenty of girls and women marching and demonstrating before now. But somehow he had never been able to give it much thought. He didn't doubt that the girls and the women took themselves seriously, they obviously did. But so did the little kids who marched up and down the streets at the time drilling with sticks and wearing their mothers' soup bowls for steel helmets. The prime joke of the time among his friends was the contingent of girls from a local secondary school marching behind a banner: WE ARE IMPREGNABLE!

But after that encounter at the Awka check-point he simply could not sneer at the girls again, nor at the talk of revolution, for he had seen it in action in that young woman whose devotion had simply and without self-righteousness convicted him of gross levity. What were her words? We are doing the work you asked us to do. She wasn't going to make an exception even for one who once did her a favour. He was sure she would have searched her own father just as rigorously.

When their paths crossed a third time, at least eighteen months later, things had got very bad. Death and starvation having long chased out the headiness of the early days, now left in some places blank resignation, in others a rock-like, even suicidal, defiance. But surprisingly enough there were many at this time who had no other desire than to corner whatever good things were still going and to enjoy themselves to the limit. For such people a strange normalcy had returned to the world. All those nervous check-points disappeared. Girls became girls once more and boys boys. It was a tight, blockaded and desperate world but none the less a world—with some goodness and some badness and plenty of heroism which, however, happened most times far, far below the eye-level of the people in this story—in out-of-the-way refugee camps, in the damp tatters, in the hungry and barehanded courage of the first line of fire.

Reginald Nwankwo lived in Owerri then. But that day he had gone to Nkwerri in search of relief. He had got from Caritas in Owerri a few heads of stock-fish, some tinned meat, and the dreadful American stuff called Formula Two which he felt certain was some kind of animal feed. But he always had a vague suspicion that not being a Catholic put one at a disadvantage with Caritas. So he went now to see an old friend who ran the WCC depot at Nkwerri to get other items like rice, beans and that excellent cereal commonly called *Gabon gari*.

He left Owerri at six in the morning so as to catch his friend at the depot where he was known never to linger beyond 8.30 for fear of air-raids. Nwankwo was very fortunate that day. The depot had received on the previous day large supplies of new stock as a result of an unusual number of plane landings a few nights earlier. As his driver loaded tins and bags and cartons into his car the starved crowds that perpetually hung around relief centres made crude, ungracious remarks like "War Can Continue!" meaning the WCC! Somebody else shouted "*Irevolu!*" and his friends replied "*shum!*" "*Irevolu!*" "*shum!*" "*Isofeli?*" "*shum!*" "*Isofeli?*" "*Mba!*"[1]

Nwankwo was deeply embarrassed not by the jeers of this scarecrow crowd of rags and floating ribs but by the independent accusation of their wasted bodies and sunken eyes. Indeed he would probably have felt much worse had they said nothing, simply looked on in silence, as his boot was loaded with milk, and powdered egg and oats and tinned meat and stock-fish. By nature such singular good fortune in the midst of a general desolation was certain to embarrass him. But what could a man do? He had a wife and four children living in the remote village of Ogbu and completely dependent on what relief he could find and send them. He couldn't abandone them to kwashiokor. The best he could do—and did do as a matter of fact—was to make sure that whenever he got sizeable supplies like now he made over some of it to his driver, Johnson, with a wife and six, or was it seven?, children and a salary of ten pounds a month when *gari* in the market was climbing to one pound per cigarette cup. In such a situation one

[1]"*Irevolu!*" "*shum!*" "*Isofeli?*" "*shum!*" "*Isofeli?*" "*Mba!*" The first two words are a distortion of "revolution." Combined with "*Isofeli?*" ("Do you eat with them?") and "*Mba!*" ("No!), the sequence implies that the speakers will have nothing to do with revolutionaries.

could do nothing at all for crowds; at best one could try to be of some use to one's immediate neighbours. That was all.

On his way back to Owerri a very attractive girl by the roadside waved for a lift. He ordered the driver to stop. Scores of pedestrians, dusty and exhausted, some military, some civil, swooped down on the car from all directions.

"No, no, no," said Nwankwo firmly. "It's the young woman I stopped for. I have a bad tyre and can only take one person. Sorry."

"My son, please," cried one old woman in despair, gripping the door-handle.

"Old woman, you want to be killed?" shouted the driver as he pulled away, shaking her off. Nwankwo had already opened a book and sunk his eyes there. For at least a mile after that he did not even look at the girl until she finding, perhaps, the silence too heavy said:

"You've saved me today. Thank you."

"Not at all. Where are you going?"

"To Owerri. You don't recognize me?"

"Oh yes, of course. What a fool I am . . . You are . . ."

"Gladys."

"That's right, the militia girl. You've changed, Gladys. You were always beautiful of course, but now you are a beauty queen. What do you do these days?"

"I am in the Fuel Directorate."

"That's wonderful."

It was wonderful, he thought, but even more it was tragic. She wore a high-tinted wig and very expensive skirt and low-cut blouse. Her shoes, obviously from Gabon, must have cost a fortune. In short, thought Nwankwo, she had to be in the keep of some well-placed gentleman, one of those piling up money out of the war.

"I broke my rule today to give you a lift. I never give lifts these days."

"Why?"

"How many people can you carry? It is better not to try at all. Look at that old woman."

"I thought you would carry her."

He said nothing to that and after another spell of silence Gladys thought maybe he was offended and so added: "Thank you for breaking your rule for me." She was scanning his face, turned slightly away. He smiled, turned, and tapped her on the lap.

"What are you going to Owerri to do?"

"I am going to visit my girl-friend."

"Girl-friend? You sure?"

"Why not? . . . If you drop me at her house you can see her. Only I pray God she hasn't gone on weekend today; it will be serious."

"Why?"

"Because if she is not at home I will sleep on the road today."

"I pray to God that she is not at home."

"Why?"

"Because if she is not at home I will offer you bed and breakfast . . . What is that?" he asked the driver who had brought the car to an abrupt stop. There was no need for an answer. The small crowd ahead was looking upwards. The three scrambled out of the car and stumbled for the bush, necks twisted in a backward search of the sky. But the alarm was false. The sky was silent and clear except for two high-flying vultures. A humorist in the crowd called them Fighter and Bomber and everyone laughed in relief. The three climbed into their car again and continued their journey.

"It is much too early for raids," he said to Gladys, who had both her palms on her breast as though to still a thumping heart. "They rarely come before ten o'clock."

But she remained tongue-tied from her recent fright. Nwankwo saw an opportunity there and took it at once.

"Where does your friend live?"

"250 Douglas Road."

"Ah; that's the very centre of town—a terrible place. No bunkers, nothing. I won't advise you to go there before 6 p.m.; it's not safe. If you don't mind I will take you to my place where there is a good bunker and then as soon as it is safe, around six, I shall drive you to your friend. How's that?"

"It's all right," she said lifelessly. "I am so frightened of this thing. That's why I refused to work in Owerri. I don't even know who asked me to come out today."

"You'll be all right. We are used to it."

"But your family is not there with you?"

"No," he said. "Nobody has his family there. We like to say it is because of air-raids but I can assure you there is more to it. Owerri is a real swinging now, and we live the life of gay bachelors."

"That is what I have heard."

"You will not just hear it; you will see it today. I shall take you to a real swinging party. A friend of mine, a Lieutenant-Colonel, is having a birthday party. He's hired the Sound Smashers to play. I'm sure you'll enjoy it."

He was immediately and thoroughly ashamed of himself. He hated the parties and frivolities to which his friends clung like drowning men. And to talk so approvingly of them because he wanted to take a girl home! And this particular girl too, who had once had such beautiful faith in the struggle and was betrayed (no doubt about it) by some man like him out for a good time. He shook his head sadly.

"What is it?" asked Gladys.

"Nothing. Just my thoughts."

They made the rest of the journey to Owerri practically in silence.

She made herself at home very quickly as if she was a regular girl-friend of his. She changed into a house dress and put away her auburn wig.

"That is a lovely hair-do. Why do you hide it with a wig?"

"Thank you," she said leaving his question unanswered for a while. Then she said: "Men are funny."

"Why do you say that?"

"You are now a beauty queen," she mimicked.

"Oh, that! I mean every word of it." He pulled her to him and kissed her. She neither refused nor yielded fully, which he liked for a start. Too many girls were simply too easy those days. War sickness, some called it.

He drove off a little later to look in at the office and she busied herself in the kitchen helping his boy with lunch. It must have been literally a look-in, for he was back within half an hour, rubbing his hands and saying he could not stay away too long from his beauty queen.

As they sat down to lunch she said: "You have nothing in your fridge."

"Like what?" he asked, half-offended.

"Like meat," she replied undaunted.

"Do you still eat meat?" he challenged.

"Who am I? But other big men like you eat."

"I don't know which big men you have in mind. But they are not like me. I don't make money trading with the enemy or selling relief or . . ."

"Augusta's boy friend doesn't do that. He just gets foreign exchange."

"How does he get it? He swindles the government—that's how he gets foreign exchange, whoever he is. Who is Augusta, by the way?"

"My girl-friend."

"I see."

"She gave me three dollars last time which I changed to forty-five pounds. The man gave her fifty dollars."

"Well, my dear girl, I don't traffic in foreign exchange and I don't have meat in my fridge. We are fighting a war and I happen to know that some young boys at the front drink gari and water once in three days."

"It is true," she said simply. "Monkey de work, baboon de chop."

"It is not even that; it is worse," he said, his voice beginning to shake. "People are dying every day. As we talk now somebody is dying."

"It is true," she said again.

"Plane!" screamed his boy from the kitchen.

"My mother!" screamed Gladys. As they scuttled towards the bunker of palm stems and red earth, covering their heads with their hands and stooping slightly in their flight, the entire sky was exploding with the clamour of jets and the huge noise of home-made anti-aircraft rockets.

Inside the bunker she clung to him even after the plane had gone and the guns, late to start and also to end, had all died down again.

"It was only passing," he told her, his voice a little shaky. "It didn't drop anything. From its direction I should say it was going to the war front. Perhaps our people are pressing them. That's what they always do. Whenever our boys press them, they send an SOS to the Russians and Egyptians to bring the planes." He drew a long breath.

She said nothing, just clung to him. They could hear his boy telling the servant from the next house that there were two of them and one dived like this and the other dived like that.

"I see dem well well," said the other with equal excitement. "If no to say de ting de kill porson e for sweet for eye. To God."

"Imagine!" said Gladys, finding her voice at last. She had a way, he thought, of conveying with a few words or even a single word whole layers of meaning. Now it was at once her astonishment as well as reproof, tinged perhaps with grudging admiration for people who could be so lighthearted about these bringers of death.

"Don't be so scared," he said. She moved closer and he began to kiss her and squeeze her breasts. She yielded more and more and then fully. The bunker was dark and unswept and might harbour crawling things. He thought of bringing a mat from the main house but reluctantly decided against it. Another plane might pass and send a neighbour or simply a chance passer-by crashing into them. That would be only slightly better than a certain gentleman in another air-raid who was seen in broad daylight fleeing his bedroom for his bunker stark naked pursued by a woman in a similar state!

Just as Gladys had feared, her friend was not in town. It would seem her powerful boy-friend had wangled for her a flight to Libreville to shop. So her neighbours thought anyway.

“Great!” said Nwankwo as they drove away. “She will come back on an arms plane loaded with shoes, wigs, pants, bras, cosmetics and what have you, which she will then sell and make thousands of pounds. You girls are really at war, aren't you?”

She said nothing and he thought he had got through at last to her. Then suddenly she said, “That is what you men want us to do.”

“Well,” he said, “here is one man who doesn't want you to do that. Do you remember that girl in khaki jeans who searched me without mercy at the check-point?”

She began to laugh.

“That is the girl I want you to become again. Do you remember her? No wig. I don't even think she had any earrings . . . .”

“Ah, na lie-o. I had ear-rings.”

“All right. But you know what I mean.”

“That time done pass. Now everybody want survival. They call it number six. You put your number six; I put my number six. Everything all right.”

The Lieutenant-Colonel's party turned into something quite unexpected. But before it did things had been going well enough. There was goat-meat, some chicken and rice and plenty of home-made spirits. There was one fiery brand nicknamed “tracer” which indeed sent a flame down your gullet. The funny thing was looking at it in the bottle it had the innocent appearance of an orange drink. But the thing that caused the greatest stir was the bread—one little roll for each person! It was the size of a golf-ball and about the same consistency too! But it was real bread. The band was good too and there were many girls. And to improve matters even further two white Red Cross people soon arrived with a bottle of Courvoisier and a bottle of Scotch! The party gave them a standing ovation and then scrambled to get a drop. It soon turned out from his general behaviour, however, that one of the white men had probably drunk too much already. And the reason it would seem was that a pilot he knew well had been killed in a crash at the airport last night, flying in relief in awful weather.

Few people at the party had heard of the crash by then. So there was an immediate damping of the air. Some dancing couples went back to their seats and the band stopped. Then for some strange reason the drunken Red Cross man just exploded.

“Why should a man, a decent man, throw away his life. For nothing! Charley didn't need to die. Not for this stinking place. Yes, everything stinks here. Even these girls who come here all dolled up and smiling, what are they worth? Don't I know? A head of stockfish, that's all, or one American dollar and they are ready to tumble into bed.”

In the threatening silence following the explosion one of the young officers walked up to him and gave him three thundering slaps—right! left! right!—pulled him up from his seat and (there were things like tears in his eyes) shoved him outside. His friend, who had tried in vain to shut him up, followed him out and the silenced party heard them drive off. The officer who did the job returned dusting his palms.

"Fucking beast!" said he with an impressive coolness. And all the girls showed with their eyes that they rated him a man and a hero.

"Do you know him?" Gladys asked Nwankwo.

He didn't answer her. Instead he spoke generally to the party:

"The fellow was clearly drunk," he said.

"I don't care," said the officer. "It is when a man is drunk that he speaks what is on his mind."

"So you beat him for what was on his mind," said the host, "that is the spirit, Joe."

"Thank you, sir," said Joe, saluting.

"His name is Joe," Gladys and the girl on her left said in unison, turning to each other.

At the same time Nwankwo and a friend on the other side of him were saying quietly, very quietly, that although the man had been rude and offensive what he had said about the girls was unfortunately the bitter truth, only he was the wrong man to say it.

When the dancing resumed Captain Joe came to Gladys for a dance. She sprang to her feet even before the word was out of his mouth. Then she remembered immediately and turned round to take permission from Nwankwo. At the same time the Captain also turned to him and said, "Excuse me."

"Go ahead," said Nwankwo, looking somewhere between the two.

It was a long dance and he followed them with his eyes without appearing to do so. Occasionally a relief plane passed overhead and somebody immediately switched off the lights saying it might be the Intruder. But it was only an excuse to dance in the dark and make the girls giggle, for the sound of the Intruder was well known.

Gladys came back feeling very self-conscious and asked Nwankwo to dance with her. But he wouldn't. "Don't bother about me," he said, "I am enjoying myself perfectly sitting here and watching those of you who dance."

"Then let's go," she said, "if you won't dance."

"But I never dance, believe me. So please enjoy yourself."

She danced next with the Lieutenant-Colonel and again with Captain Joe, and then Nwankwo agreed to take her home.

"I am sorry I didn't dance," he said as they drove away. "But I swore never to dance as long as this war lasts."

She said nothing.

"When I think of somebody like that pilot who got killed last night. And he had no hand whatever in the quarrel. All his concern was to bring us food . . ."

"I hope that his friend is not like him," said Gladys.

"The man was just upset by his friend's death. But what I am saying is that with people like that getting killed and our own boys suffering and dying at the war fronts I don't see why we should sit around throwing parties and dancing."

"You took me there," said she in final revolt. "They are your friends. I don't know them before."

"Look, my dear, I am not blaming you. I am merely telling you why I personally refuse to dance. Anyway, let's change the subject . . . Do you still say you want to go back tomorrow? My driver can take you early enough on Monday morning for you to go to work. No? All right, just as you wish. You are the boss."

She gave him a shock by the readiness with which she followed him to bed and by her language.

"You want to shell?" she asked. And without waiting for an answer said, "Go ahead but don't pour in troops!"

He didn't want to pour in troops either and so it was all right. But she wanted visual assurance and so he showed her.

One of the ingenious economies taught by the war was that a rubber condom could be used over and over again. All you had to do was wash it out, dry it and shake a lot of talcum powder over it to prevent its sticking; and it was as good as new. It had to be the real British thing, though, not some of the cheap stuff they brought in from Lisbon which was about as strong as a dry cocoyam leaf in the harmattan.

He had his pleasure but wrote the girl off. He might just as well have slept with a prostitute, he thought. It was clear as daylight to him now that she was kept by some army officer. What a terrible transformation in the short period of less than two years! Wasn't it a miracle that she still had memories of the other life, that she even remembered her name? If the affair of the drunken Red Cross man should happen again now, he said to himself, he would stand up beside the fellow and tell the party that here was a man of truth. What a terrible fate to befall a whole generation! The mothers of tomorrow!

By morning he was feeling a little better and more generous in his judgments. Gladys, he thought, was just a mirror reflecting a society that had gone completely rotten and maggotty at the centre. The mirror itself was intact; a lot of smudge but no more. All that was needed was a clean duster. "I have a duty to her," he told himself, "the little girl that once revealed to me our situation. Now she is in danger, under some terrible influence."

He wanted to get to the bottom of this deadly influence. It was clearly not just her good-time girl friend, Augusta, or whatever her name was. There must be some man at the centre of it, perhaps one of these heartless attack-traders who traffic in foreign currencies and make their hundreds of thousands by sending young men to hazard their lives bartering looted goods for cigarettes behind enemy lines, or one of those contractors who receive piles of money daily for food they never deliver to the army. Or perhaps some vulgar and cowardly army officer full of filthy barrack talk and fictitious stories of heroism. He decided he had to find out. Last night he had thought of sending his driver alone to take her home. But no, he must go and see for himself where she lived. Something was bound to reveal itself there. Something on which he could anchor his saving operation. As he prepared for the trip his feeling towards her softened with every passing minute. He assembled for her half of the food he had received at the relief centre the day before. Difficult as things were, he thought, a girl who had something to eat would be spared, not all, but some of the temptation. He would arrange with his friend at the WCC to deliver something to her every fortnight.

Tears came to Gladys's eyes when she saw the gifts. Nwankwo didn't have too much cash on him but he got together twenty pounds and handed it over to her.

"I don't have foreign exchange, and I know this won't go far at all, but . . ."

She just came and threw herself at him, sobbing. He kissed her lips and eyes and mumbled something about victims of circumstances, which went over her head. In deference to him, he thought with exultation, she had put away her high-tinted wig in her bag.

"I want you to promise me something," he said.

"What?"

"Never use that expression about shelling again."

She smiled with tears in her eyes. "You don't like it? That's what all the girls call it."

"Well, you are different from all the girls. Will you promise?"

"OK."

Naturally their departure had become a little delayed. And when they got into the car it refused to start. After poking around the engine the driver decided that the battery was flat. Nwankwo was aghast. He had that very week paid thirty-four pounds to change two of the cells and the mechanic who performed it had promised him six months' service. A new battery, which was then running at two hundred and fifty pounds was simply out of the question. The driver must have been careless with something, he thought.

"It must be because of last night," said the driver.

"What happened last night?" asked Nwankwo sharply, wondering what insolence was on the way. But none was intended.

"Because we use the headlight."

"Am I supposed not to use my light then? Go and get some people and try pushing it." He got out again with Gladys and returned to the house while the driver went over to neighbouring houses to seek the help of other servants.

After at least half an hour of pushing it up and down the street, and a lot of noisy advice from the pushers, the car finally spluttered to life shooting out enormous clouds of black smoke from the exhaust.

It was eight-thirty by his watch when they set out. A few miles away a disabled soldier waved for a lift.

"Stop!" screamed Nwankwo. The driver jammed his foot on the brakes and then turned his head towards his master in bewilderment.

"Don't you see the soldier waving? Reverse and pick him up!"

"Sorry, sir," said the driver. "I don't know Master want to pick him."

"If you don't know you should ask. Reverse back."

The soldier, a mere boy, in filthy khaki drenched in sweat lacked his right leg from the knee down. He seemed not only grateful that a car should stop for him but greatly surprised. He first handed in his crude wooden crutches which the driver arranged between the two front seats, then painfully he levered himself in.

"Thanks sir," he said turning his neck to look at the back and completely out of breath.

"I am very grateful. Madame, thank you."

"The pleasure is ours," said Nwankwo. "Where did you get your wound?"

"At Azumini, sir. On tenth of January."

"Never mind. Everything will be all right. We are proud of you boys and will make sure you receive your due reward when it is all over."

"I pray God, sir."

They drove on in silence for the next half-hour or so. Then as the car sped down a slope towards a bridge somebody screamed—perhaps the driver, perhaps the soldier—"They have come!" The screech of the brakes merged into the scream and the shattering of the sky overhead. The doors flew open even before the car had come to a stop and they were fleeing blindly to the bush.

Gladys was a little ahead of Nwankwo where they heard through the drowning tumult the soldier's voice crying: "Please come and open for me!" Vaguely he saw Gladys stop; he pushed past her shouting to her at the same time to come on. Then a high whistle descended like a spear through the chaos and exploded in a vast noise and motion that smashed up everything. A tree he had embraced flung him away through the bush. Then another terrible whistle starting high up and ending again in a monumental crash of the world; and then another, and Nwankwo heard no more.

He woke up to human noises and weeping and the smell and smoke of a charred world. He dragged himself up and staggered towards the source of the sounds.

From afar he saw his driver running towards him in tears and blood. He saw the remains of his car smoking and the entangled remains of the girl and the soldier. And he let out a piercing cry and fell down again.

QUESTIONS

1. Because "Girls at War" is told from Reginald Nwankwo's point of view, the reader sees Gladys only through his eyes. What can be said about the validity of his perspective? Is Reginald any less an opportunist than Gladys?
2. Does the concluding scene in the story redeem Gladys?
3. What irony is implied by the story's title?
4. On numerous occasions, Achebe has described his role as an African writer as that of a teacher—informing, explaining, and, above all, educating his reader. "The role of the writer depends to some extent on the state of his society," he stated in an interview in *Transition* during the Biafran war. "In other words, if a society is ill he has a responsibility to point it out. If the society is healthy—I do not know of any one—his job is limited." How applicable are these remarks to "Girls at War"?

Ama Ata Aidoo

(b. 1942)

Ghana

Ama Ata Aidoo was born in Ghana in 1942. She received her B.A. from the University of Ghana in 1964, where she subsequently was a research fellow in the Institute of African Studies. She has taught at universities in the United States, where she has also lectured extensively. Her publications include two plays—*The Dilemma of a Ghost* (1965) and *Anowa* (1970). "Two Sisters" is from her short story collection, *No Sweetness Here* (1970). Ms. Aidoo has also published two novels, *Our Sister Killjoy* (1977) and *Changes* (1991).

Writing about her compatriot Ayi Kwei Armah's *The Beautyful Ones Are Not Yet Born* (1968), Ms. Aidoo had this to say about Ghanaian women: ". . . especially in the area of what exactly the African woman is, the assumption on the part of most Westerners [has been] that the poor African woman was a downtrodden wretch until the European missionary brought her Christianity, civilization and emancipation. This may apply in certain areas of Africa, but certainly, for most Ghanaian women, the question of their emancipation is not really a problem to discuss since it has always been ensured by the system anyway. Nor is this an idealized view. It is there for anyone to see who is prepared to observe a society instead of imposing on it his own prejudices and syndromes."

Two Sisters

As she shakes out the typewriter cloak and covers the machine with it, the thought of the bus she has to hurry to catch goes through her like a pain. It is her luck, she thinks. Everything is just her luck. Why, if she had one of those graduates for a boy-friend, wouldn't he come and take her home every evening? And she knows that a girl does not herself have to be a graduate to get one of those boys. Certainly, Joe is dying to do exactly that—with his taxi. And he is as handsome as anything, and a good man, but you know . . . Besides there are cars and there are cars. As for the possibility of the other actually coming to fetch her—oh, well. She has to admit it will take some time before she can bring herself to make demands of that sort on *him*. She has also to admit that the temptation is extremely strong. Would it really be so dangerously indiscreet? Doesn't one government car look like another? The hugeness of it? Its shaded glass? The uniformed chauffeur? She can already see herself stepping out to greet the dead-with-envy glances of the other girls. To begin with, she will insist on a little discretion. The driver can drop her under the neem trees in the morning and pick her up from there in the evening . . . anyway, she will have to wait a little while for that and it is all her luck.

There are other ways, surely. One of these, for some reason, she has sworn to have nothing of. Her boss has a car and does not look bad. In fact the man is all right. But she keeps telling herself that she does not fancy having some old and dried-out housewife walking into the office one afternoon to tear her hair out and make a row. . . . Mm, so for the meantime, it is going to continue to be the municipal bus with its grimy seats, its common passengers and impudent conductors. . . . Jesus! She doesn't wish herself dead or anything as stupidly final as that. Oh no. She just wishes she could sleep deep and only wake up on the morning of her glory.

The new pair of black shoes are more realistic than their owner, though. As she walks down the corridor, they sing:

Count, Mercy, count your blessings
Count, Mercy, count your blessings
Count, count, count your blessings.

They sing along the corridor, into the avenue, across the road and into the bus. And they resume their song along the gravel path, as she opens the front gate and crosses the cemented courtyard to the door.

"Sissie!" she called.

"*Hei* Mercy," and the door opened to show the face of Connie, big sister, six years or more older and now heavy with her second child. Mercy collapsed into the nearest chair.

"Welcome home. How was the office today?"

"Sister, don't ask. Look at my hands. My fingers are dead with typing. Oh God, I don't know what to do."

"Why, what is wrong?"

"You tell me what is right. Why should I be a typist?"

"What else would you be?"

"What a strange question. Is typing the only thing one can do in this world? You are a teacher, are you not?"

"But . . . but . . ."

"But what? Or you want me to know that if I had done better in the exams, I could have trained to be a teacher too, eh, sister? Or even a proper secretary?"

"Mercy, what is the matter? What have I done? What have I done? Why have you come home so angry?"

Mercy broke into tears.

"Oh I am sorry. I am sorry, Sissie. It's just that I am sick of everything. The office, living with you and your husband. I want a husband of my own, children. I want . . . I want . . ."

"But you are so beautiful."

"Thank you. But so are you."

"You are young and beautiful. As for marriage, it's you who are postponing it. Look at all these people who are running after you."

"Sissie, I don't like what you are doing. So stop it."

"Okay, okay, okay."

And there was a silence.

"Which of them could I marry? Joe is—mm, fine—but, but I just don't like him."

"You mean . . ."

"Oh, Sissie!"

"Little sister, you and I can be truthful with one another."

"Oh yes."

"What I would like to say is that I am not that old or wise. But still I could advise you a little. Joe drives someone's car now. Well, you never know. Lots of taxi drivers come to own their taxis, sometimes fleets of cars."

"Of course. But it's a pity you are married already. Or I could be a go-between for you and Joe!"

And the two of them burst out laughing. It was when she rose to go to the bedroom that Connie noticed the new shoes.

"*Ei*, those are beautiful shoes. Are they new?"

From the other room, Mercy's voice came interrupted by the motions of her body as she undressed and then dressed again. However, the uncertainty in it was due to something entirely different.

"Oh, I forgot to tell you about them. In fact, I was going to show them to you. I think it was on Tuesday I bought them. Or was it Wednesday? When I came home from the office, you and James had taken Akosua out. And later, I forgot all about them."

"I see. But they are very pretty. Were they expensive?"

"No, not really." This reply was too hurriedly said.

And she said only last week that she didn't have a penny on her. And I believed her because I know what they pay her is just not enough to last anyone through any month, even minus rent. . . . I have been thinking she manages very well. But these shoes. And she is not the type who would borrow money just to buy a pair of shoes, when she could have gone on wearing her old pairs until things get better. Oh I wish I knew what to do. I mean I am not her mother. And I wonder how James will see these problems.

"Sissie, you look worried."

"Hmm, when don't I? With the baby due in a couple of months and the government's new ruling on salaries and all. On top of everything, I have reliable information that James is running after a new girl."

Mercy laughed.

"Oh Sissie. You always get reliable information on these things."

"But yes. And I don't know why."

"Sissie, men are like that."

"They are selfish."

"No, it's just that women allow them to behave the way they do instead of seizing some freedom themselves."

"But I am sure that even if we were free to carry on in the same way, I wouldn't make use of it."

"But why not?"

"Because I love James. I love James and I am not interested in any other man." Her voice was full of tears. But Mercy was amused.

"O God. Now listen to that. It's women like you who keep all of us down."

"Well, I am sorry but it's how the good God created me."

"Mm. I am sure that I can love several men at the same time."

"Mercy!"

They burst out laughing again. And yet they are sad. But laughter is always best.

Mercy complained of hunger and so they went to the kitchen to heat up some food and eat. The two sisters alone. It is no use waiting for James. And this evening, a friend of Connie's has come to take out the baby girl, Akosua, and had threatened to keep her until her bedtime.

"Sissie, I am going to see a film." This from Mercy.

"Where?"

"The Globe."

"Are you going with Joe?"

"No."

"Are you going alone?"

"No."

Careful Connie.

"Whom are you going with?"

Careful Connie, please. Little sister's nostrils are widening dangerously. Look at the sudden creasing-up of her mouth and between her brows. Connie, a sister is a good thing. Even a younger sister. Especially when you have no mother or father.

"Mercy, whom are you going out with?"

"Well, I had food in my mouth! And I had to swallow it down before I could answer you, no?"

"I am sorry." How softly said.

"And anyway, do I have to tell you everything?"

"Oh no. It's just that I didn't think it was a question I should not have asked."

There was more silence. Then Mercy sucked her teeth with irritation and Connie cleared her throat with fear.

"I am going out with Mensar-Arthur."

As Connie asked the next question, she wondered if the words were leaving her lips.

"Mensar-Arthur?"

"Yes."

"Which one?"

"*How many do you know?*"

Her fingers were too numb to pick up the food. She put the plate down. Something jumped in her chest and she wondered what it was. Perhaps it was the baby.

"Do you mean that member of Parliament?"

"Yes."

"But Mercy . . ."

Little sister only sits and chews her food.

"But Mercy . . ."

Chew, chew, chew.

"But Mercy . . ."

"What?"

She startled Connie.

"He is so old."

Chew, chew, chew.

"Perhaps, I mean, perhaps that really doesn't matter, does it? Not very much anyway. But they say he has so many wives and girl-friends."

Please little sister. I am not trying to interfere in your private life. You said yourself a little while ago that you wanted a man of your own. That man belongs to so many women already. . . .

That silence again. Then there was only Mercy's footsteps as she went to put her plate in the kitchen sink, running water as she washed her plate and her hands. She drank some water and coughed. Then as tears streamed down her sister's averted face, there was the sound of her footsteps as she left the kitchen. At the end of it all, she banged a door. Connie only said something like, "O Lord, O Lord," and continued sitting in the kitchen. She had hardly eaten anything at all. Very soon Mercy went to have a bath. Then Connie heard her getting ready to leave the house. The shoes. Then she was gone. She needn't have carried on like that, eh? Because Connie had not meant to probe or bring on a quarrel. What use is there in this old world for a sister, if you can't have a chat with her? What's more, things like this never happen to people like Mercy. Their parents were good Presbyterians. They feared God. Mama had not managed to give them all the rules of life before she died. But Connie knows that running around with an old and depraved public man would have been considered an abomination by the parents.

A big car with a super-smooth engine purred into the drive. It actually purrs: this huge machine from the white man's land. Indeed, its well-mannered protest as the tyres slid on to the gravel seemed like a lullaby compared to the loud thumping of the girl's stiletto shoes. When Mensar-Arthur saw Mercy, he stretched his arm and opened the door to the passenger seat. She sat down and the door closed with a civilized thud. The engine hummed into motion and the car sailed away.

After a distance of a mile or so from the house, the man started conversation.

"And how is my darling today?"

"I am well," and only the words did not imply tragedy.

"You look solemn today, why?"

She remained silent and still.

"My dear, what is the matter?"

"Nothing."

"Oh . . ." he cleared his throat again. "Eh, and how were the shoes?"

"Very nice. In fact, I am wearing them now. They pinch a little but then all new shoes are like that."

"And the handbag?"

"I like it very much too. . . . My sister noticed them. I mean the shoes." The tragedy was announced.

"Did she ask you where you got them from?"

"No."

He cleared his throat again.

"Where did we agree to go tonight?"

"The Globe, but I don't want to see a film."

"Is that so? Mm, I am glad because people always notice things."

"But they won't be too surprised."

"What are you saying, my dear?"

"Nothing."

"Okay, so what shall we do?"

"I don't know."

"Shall I drive to the Seaway?"

"Oh yes."

He drove to the Seaway. To a section of the beach they knew very well. She loves it here. This wide expanse of sand and the old sea. She has often wished she could do what she fancied: one thing she fancies. Which is to drive very near to the end of the sands until the tyres of the car touched the water. Of course it is a very foolish idea as he pointed out sharply to her the first time she thought aloud about it. It was in his occasional I-am-more-than-old-enough-to-be-your-father tone. There are always disadvantages. Things could be different. Like if one had a younger lover. Handsome, maybe not rich like this man here, but well-off, sufficiently well-off to be able to afford a sports car. A little something very much like those in the films driven by the white racing drivers. With tyres that can do everything . . . and they would drive exactly where the sea and the sand meet.

"We are here."

"Don't let's get out. Let's just sit inside and talk."

"Talk?"

"Yes."

"Okay. But what is it, my darling?"

"I have told my sister about you."

"Good God. Why?"

"But I had to. I couldn't keep it to myself any longer."

"Childish. It was not necessary at all. She is not your mother."

"No. But she is all I have. And she has been very good to me."

"Well, it was her duty."

"Then it is my duty to tell her about something like this. I may get into trouble."

"Don't be silly," he said, "I normally take good care of my girl-friends."

"I see," she said and for the first time in the one month since she agreed to be this man's lover, the tears which suddenly rose into her eyes were not forced.

"And you promised you wouldn't tell her." It was father's voice now.

"Don't be angry. After all, people talk so much, as you said a little while ago. She was bound to hear it one day."

"My darling, you are too wise. What did she say?"

"She was pained."

"Don't worry. Find out something she wants very much but cannot get in this country because of the import restrictions."

"I know for sure she wants an electric motor for her sewing machine."

"Is that all?"

"That's what I know of."

"Mm. I am going to London next week on some delegation, so if you bring me the details on the make of the machine, I shall get her the motor."

"Thank you."

"What else is worrying my Black Beauty?"

"Nothing."

"And by the way, let me know as soon as you want to leave your sister's place. I have got you one of the government estate houses."

"Oh . . . oh," she said, pleased, contented for the first time since this typically ghastly day had begun, at half-past six in the morning.

Dear little child came back from the playground with her toe bruised. Shall we just blow cold air from our mouth on it or put on a salve? Nothing matters really. Just see that she does not feel unattended. And the old sea roars on. This is a calm sea, generally. Too calm in fact, this Gulf of Guinea. The natives sacrifice to him on Tuesdays and once a year celebrate him. They might save their chickens, their eggs and their yams. And as for the feast once a year, he doesn't pay much attention to it either. They are always celebrating one thing or another and they surely don't need him for an excuse to celebrate one day more. He has seen things happen along these beaches. Different things. Contradictory things. Or just repetitions of old patterns. He never interferes in their affairs. Why should he? Except in places like Keta where he eats houses away because they leave him no choice. Otherwise he never allows them to see his passions. People are worms, and even the God who created them is immensely bored with their antics. Here is a fifty-year-old "big man" who thinks he is somebody. And a twenty-three-year-old child who chooses a silly way to conquer unconquerable problems. Well, what did one expect of human beings? And so as those who settled on the back seat of the car to play with each other's bodies, he, the Gulf of Guinea, shut his eyes with boredom. It is right. He could sleep, no? He spread himself and moved further ashore. But the car was parked at a very safe distance and the rising tides could not wet its tyres.

James has come home late. But then he has been coming back late for the past few weeks. Connie is crying and he knows it as soon as he enters the bedroom. He hates tears, for like so many men, he knows it is one of the most potent weapons in women's bitchy and inexhaustible arsenal. She speaks first.

"James."

"Oh, are you still awake?" He always tries to deal with these nightly funeral parlour doings by pretending not to know what they are about.

"I couldn't sleep."

"What is wrong?"

"Nothing."

So he moves quickly and sits beside her.

"Connie, what is the matter? You have been crying again."

"You are very late again."

"Is that why you are crying? Or is there something else?"

"Yes."

"Yes to what?"

"James, where were you?"

"Connie, I have warned you about what I shall do if you don't stop examining me, as though I were your prisoner, every time I am a little late."

She sat up.

"A little late! It is nearly two o'clock."

"Anyway, you won't believe me if I told you the truth, so why do you want me to waste my breath?"

"Oh well." She lies down again and turns her face to the wall. He stands up but does not walk away. He looks down at her. So she remembers every night: they have agreed, after many arguments, that she should sleep like this. During her first pregnancy, he kept saying after the third month or so that the sight of her tummy the last thing before he slept always gave him nightmares. Now he regrets all this. The bed creaks as he throws himself down by her.

"James."

"Yes."

"There is something much more serious."

"You have heard about my newest affair?"

"Yes, but that is not what I am referring to."

"Jesus, is it possible that there is anything more important than that?"

And as they laugh they know that something has happened. One of those things which, with luck, will keep them together for some time to come.

"He teases me on top of everything."

"What else can one do to you but tease when you are in this state?"

"James! How profane!"

"It is your dirty mind which gave my statement its shocking meaning."

"Okay! But what shall I do?"

"About what?"

"Mercy. Listen, she is having an affair with Mensar-Arthur."

"Wonderful."

She sits up and he sits up.

"James, we must do something about it. It is very serious."

"Is that why you were crying?"

"Of course."

"Why shouldn't she?"

"But it is wrong. And she is ruining herself."

"Since every other girl she knows has ruined herself prosperously, why shouldn't she? Just forget for once that you are a teacher. Or at least, remember she is not your pupil."

"I don't like your answers."

"What would you like me to say? Every morning her friends who don't earn any more than she does wear new dresses, shoes, wigs and what-have-you to work. What would you have her do?"

"The fact that other girls do it does not mean that Mercy should do it too."

"You are being very silly. If I were Mercy, I am sure that's exactly what I would do. And you know I mean it too."

James is cruel. He is terrible and mean. Connie breaks into fresh tears and James comforts her. There is one point he must drive home though.

"In fact, encourage her. He may be able to intercede with the Ministry for you so that after the baby is born they will not transfer you from here for some time."

"James, you want me to use my sister!"

"She is using herself, remember."

"James, you are wicked."

"And maybe he would even agree to get us a new car from abroad. I shall pay for everything. That would be better than paying a fortune for that old thing I was thinking of buying. Think of that."

"You will ride in it alone."

"Well . . ."

That was a few months before the *coup*. Mensar-Arthur did go to London for a conference and bought something for all his wives and girl-friends, including Mercy. He even remembered the motor for Connie's machine. When Mercy took it to her she was quite confused. She had wanted this thing for a long time, and it would make everything so much easier, like the clothes for the new baby. And yet one side of her said that accepting it was a betrayal. Of what, she wasn't even sure. She and Mercy could never bring the whole business into the open and discuss it. And there was always James supporting Mercy, to Connie's bewilderment. She took the motor with thanks and sold even her right to dissent. In a short while, Mercy left the house to go and live in the estate house Mensar-Arthur had procured for her. Then, a couple of weeks later, the *coup*. Mercy left her new place before anyone could evict her. James never got his car. Connie's new baby was born. Of the three, the one who greeted the new order with undisguised relief was Connie. She is not really a demonstrative person but it was obvious from her eyes that she was happy. As far as she was concerned the old order as symbolized by Mensar-Arthur was a threat to her sister and therefore to her own peace of mind. With it gone, things could return to normal. Mercy would move back to the house, perhaps start to date someone more—ordinary let's say. Eventually, she would get married and then the nightmare of those past weeks would be forgotten. God being so good, he brought the *coup* early before the news of the affair could spread and brand her sister. . . .

The arrival of the new baby has magically waved away the difficulties between James and Connie. He is that kind of man, and she that kind of woman. Mercy has not been seen for many days. Connie is beginning to get worried. . . .

James heard the baby yelling—a familiar noise, by now—the moment he opened the front gate. He ran in, clutching to his chest the few things he had bought on his way home.

"We are in here."

"I certainly could hear you. If there is anything people of this country have, it is a big mouth."

"Don't I agree? But on the whole, we are well. He is eating normally and everything. You?"

"Nothing new. Same routine. More stories about the overthrown politicians."

"What do you mean, nothing new? Look at the excellent job the soldiers have done, cleaning up the country of all that dirt. I feel free already and I am dying to get out and enjoy it."

James laughed mirthlessly.

"All I know is that Mensar-Arthur is in jail. No use. And I am not getting my car. Rough deal."

"I never took you seriously on that car business."

"Honestly, if this were in the ancient days, I could brand you a witch. You don't want me, your husband, to prosper?"

"Not out of my sister's ruin."

"Ruin, ruin, ruin! Christ! See Connie, the funny thing is that I am sure you are the only person who thought it was a disaster to have a sister who was the girl-friend of a big man."

"Okay; now all is over, and don't let's quarrel."

"I bet the *coup* could have succeeded on your prayers alone."

And Connie wondered why he said that with so much bitterness. She wondered if . . .

"Has Mercy been here?"

"Not yet, later, maybe. Mm. I had hoped she would move back here and start all over again."

"I am not surprised she hasn't. In fact, if I were her, I wouldn't come back here either. Not to your nagging, no thank you, big sister."

And as the argument progressed, as always, each was forced into a more aggressive defensive stand.

"Well, just say what pleases you, I am very glad about the soldiers. Mercy is my only sister, brother; everything. I can't sit and see her life going wrong without feeling it. I am grateful to whatever forces there are which put a stop to that. What pains me now is that she should be so vague about where she is living at the moment. She makes mention of a girl-friend but I am not sure that I know her."

"If I were you, I would stop worrying because it seems Mercy can look after herself quite well."

"Hmm," was all she tried to say.

Who heard something like the sound of a car pulling into the drive? Ah, but the footsteps were unmistakably Mercy's. Are those shoes the old pair which were new a couple of months ago? Or are they the newest pair? And here she is herself, the pretty one. A gay Mercy.

"Hello, hello, my clan!" and she makes a lot of her nephew.

"Dow-dah-dee-day! And how is my dear young man today? My lord, grow up fast and come to take care of Auntie Mercy."

Both Connie and James cannot take their eyes off her. Connie says, "He says to Auntie Mercy he is fine."

Still they watch her, horrified, fascinated and wondering what it's all about. Because they both know it is about something.

"Listen people, I brought a friend to meet you. A man."

"Where is he?" from James.

"Bring him in," from Connie.

"You know, Sissie, you are a new mother. I thought I'd come and ask you if it's all right."

"Of course," say James and Connie, and for some reason they are both very nervous.

"He is Captain Ashley."

"Which one?"

"*How many do you know?*"

James still thinks it is impossible. "Eh . . . do you mean the officer who has been appointed the . . . the . . ."

"Yes."

"Wasn't there a picture in *The Crystal* over the week-end about his daughter's wedding? And another one of him with his wife and children and grandchildren?"

"Yes."

"And he is heading a commission to investigate something or other?"

"Yes."

Connie just sits there with her mouth open that wide. . . .

[1970]

QUESTIONS

1. Discuss "Two Sisters" in light of Ama Ata Aidoo's statement about Armah's *The Beautyful Ones Are Not Yet Born.*
2. What is Aidoo's picture of contemporary Ghana in this story? What does Aidoo admire in her culture? What does she criticize?
3. Is one sister's situation better than the other's?

Akutagawa Ryūnosuke

(1892 – 1927)

Japan

In the United States, Akutagawa Ryūnosuke's name is almost synonymous with *Rashomon*, the now-classic film based on two of his stories ("Rashomon" and "Within a Grove") and directed by Akira Kurosawa (1950). However, Akutagawa was also the author of a novel, a number of essays, and over 150 short stories. Born in Tokyo to a dairy owner and a mother of unstable mental health, Akutagawa was adopted by his mother's brother after her death when he was 10. He studied English literature at Tokyo University; his first publications were translations from English into Japanese of such writers as William Butler Yeats and Anatole France.

Akutagawa's early fiction drew uniquely on elements of both Eastern and Western literary forms to produce a distinctly modern form of Japanese literature. Many of his early stories are interesting variations of traditional Japanese legends and tales; his later fiction is more autobiographical and ruminative. While he wrote fiction, Akutagawa also was a practicing journalist and foreign correspondent. During his assignment to China in the 1920s, his physical and mental health deteriorated and exacerbated his life-long obsession that he had inherited his mother's madness. He took his own life at the age of 35.

As Japanese scholar and translator James O'Brien observes of the story "Within a Grove," each character's testimony, rather than clarifying what actually happened, "further confuses the issue. In the end truth itself seems the principal victim. . . ."

Within a Grove

THE TALE OF THE WOODCUTTER TO THE MAGISTRATE

Yes, your honor, I'm the one who found the body. I was heading toward the far slope to cut cedar, just as I do every morning. He was in a grove beneath the mountain. Where exactly? Just a few furlongs in from the Yamashina Post Road.[1] It's an abandoned grove, only bamboo and some spindly cedars.

He was lying on his back in a silk hunting cloak and pleated cap. A blade had pierced his breast, and the bamboo leaves near his body were stained red. No, the blood had stopped flowing. A horsefly clung to the dried wound even as I approached.

[1]*Yamashina Post Road* Yamashina occupied the southern part of Higashiyama, the "Eastern Mountain" area, of Heian-kyō. The Yamashina Post Road ran all the way to Azuma no Kuni, the eastern region of Honshū where Tokyo is now located. Posting stations were situated along the route. (Trans.)

A sword or anything? Not that I could see. There was a rope near one of the cedars, as well as a comb. But that's all. The grass and bamboo leaves around the corpse were trampled, so there must have been a struggle. A horse? A horse couldn't get in there. There's a trail, but it's beyond the next grove.

THE TALE OF THE ITINERANT PRIEST TO THE MAGISTRATE

It must have been the dead man. I saw him yesterday about noon. I was going toward Yamashina from the barrier at Mount Ōsaka[2] when he passed in the opposite direction. The woman with him was on horseback, with a veil over her face. She wore a lilac cloak of some kind, but that's all I can say about her. The horse was a chestnut with a clipped mane. How large? I'm only a priest, I can hardly estimate the size of a horse. The man had . . . No, a sword. And a bow and arrows. I clearly remember a lacquered quiver with more than twenty arrows. They were primed, too.

I never imagined he would meet such a fate. Life in its brevity is well likened to a dewdrop. Or a flash of lightning even. I pity him more than I can say.

THE TALE OF THE ARRESTING OFFICER TO THE MAGISTRATE

The prisoner? There's no question about it. He's Tajōmaru, the notorious thief. He had fallen from his horse on the stone bridge at Awataguchi.[3] I arrested him as he lay there groaning. When was that? Yesterday about eight, as the night watch was getting underway. I recognized the indigo jacket he wore the day he eluded me. His sword was the same as then, too. It had a guarded hilt. As you can see, this time he carried a bow and arrows. They were the dead man's? There's no doubt about it, then. Tajōmaru killed him. And he took this leather-bound bow, lacquered quiver, and hawk-feather arrows, all seventeen of them. Yes, a chestnut with a clipped mane. Fate must have thrown him off. I found the horse just this side of the bridge, nibbling the roadside grass with its halter trailing along the ground.

Women were especially tempting to Tajōmaru — that's what all the thieves in the capital say. Perhaps you remember the woman and her attendant who went to the Toribe Temple[4] in the mountains last year? Apparently they were going to worship Binzura.[5] People say it was Tajōmaru who killed them. And if he killed the man who owned these weapons, imagine what he might do to the woman on the chestnut horse? Where could he have taken her? Would your honor look into this?

[2]*Mount Ōsaka* A checkpoint in the mountain pass east of Heian-kyō. With its first syllable virtually a homonym for the verb, "to meet," the Barrier occasioned numerous tanka poems that played on the name. (Trans.)

[3]*Awataguchi* another district in the Higashiyama area of Heian-kyō (Trans.)

[4]*Toribe Temple* located in Higashiyama near the crematorium for Heian-kyō (Trans.)

[5]*Binzura* A Buddhist disciple who remained in the world to save people rather than enter into Nirvana. In Japan, the sick would rub an image of Binzura in hopes of a cure. (Trans.)

THE TALE OF AN OLD WOMAN TO THE MAGISTRATE

Yes, your honor, he was my daughter's husband. His name was Kanazawa no Takehiro, and he was twenty-six years old. He was a samurai,[6] but not from the capital. He was so gentle, no one should have been angry with him.

My daughter? Her name is Masago and she's nineteen. She's lively for a woman, but Takehiro was the only man in her entire life. She has a small oval face and dark complexion. There's a mole near the tip of her left eye, too.

Takehiro left yesterday for Wakasa,[7] along with my daughter. I don't know the specific reason, but his death must involve some sort of retribution. I'm resigned to that, yet I'm terribly worried about my daughter. Search the grasses and the brush even, but please find her. I'm an old woman, and that's my one wish. Come what may, I despise this Tajōmaru or whatever he's called. My son-in-law . . . and my daughter, too. . . . (She weeps, and her words trail off.)

TAJŌMARU'S CONFESSION

I killed him, but not the woman. I don't know where she went, either. Look, don't be so impatient. I can't tell you what I don't know, regardless of how often you ask me. I'm not a coward. I won't conceal anything now.

It was slightly past noon yesterday when I encountered them. The breeze lifted the woman's veil. I saw her face, but only for a moment. Perhaps that's why she seemed a female Bodhisattva.[8] I wanted to have her, even if it meant killing the man.

Why kill him? Well, killing's not as difficult as you might think. And how else could I possess her? The sword at my waist would do the job. People like you use wealth and power rather than a sword. But you kill just the same. And you pretend to be doing good. Your victims don't shed their blood; they survive in fine health. You destroy them, anyway. Whose crime is worse, yours or mine? (He laughs sardonically.)

If only I could have her without killing him. . . . I would try my best, but I must find the right place. I decided to lure them from the Yamashina Post Road into the mountains.

It wasn't difficult. I spoke of an old mound on the farther slope. I had dug up many swords and mirrors there and hidden them away. I told him how I'd sell the whole lot at a bargain, if the right person came along. He listened more and more intently. And finally . . . Isn't greed a horrible thing? Soon they had turned their horse from the Yamashina Post Road and were heading into the mountains with me.

When we reached the grove, I said the treasure was buried within and urged them to enter. Driven by greed, the man could hardly object. The woman,

[6] *samurai* a member of the military class in feudal Japan

[7] *Wakasa* the western part of present-day Fukui Prefecture, facing the Sea of Japan. (Trans.)

[8] *Bodhisattva* a Bodhisattva is a Buddhist saint that remains in the world after attaining enlightenment in order to help others reach the same state. Strictly speaking, a Bodhisattva is of neither sex, save in popular religious belief. (Trans.)

however, said she would wait and remained on the horse. Her reluctance was not surprising, as the grove seemed quite dense. I had planned to separate them, anyway. Leaving the woman alone, the man and I went in.

For a while there was nothing but bamboo. After about fifty yards or so a cedar opening appeared, the perfect place to carry out my scheme. Even as we pushed through the thicket, I pointed to a row of spindly cedars among the scattered bamboo. Over there, I said, and immediately he rushed ahead. He was waiting when I came up from behind and pinned him to the ground. A sword-bearing samurai is always formidable, and he was no exception. I attacked too quickly for him, however. In a moment he was tied to the base of a cedar. The rope? Any thief knows the value of a rope. I might have to scale a wall at any moment, so I keep one on me. I stuffed the man's mouth with fallen bamboo leaves, so he couldn't cry out. After that he didn't give me any trouble.

Then I went back to the woman. I told her the man had suddenly become ill and she must attend him. Needless to say, she readily gave in. She removed her bonnet and allowed me to lead her into the grove by the hand. But when we reached the spot and she saw him tied to the cedar, she pulled a dagger from her cloak before I knew what was happening. Never have I met a woman so violent. Had I been careless, she would have stabbed me in the side. She slashed at me in desperation. If I had not dodged, she might have killed me. But I'm Tajōmaru. Somehow I knocked her dagger away without even drawing my sword. No matter how spirited, the woman had no chance without her weapon. I would have her in the end, without killing the man either.

Without killing him . . . . I would manage without killing him. The woman lay weeping as I prepared to leave. Suddenly she seized my arm like one gone mad and uttered a breathless plea. One of us must be killed, either the husband or me. That's what I heard amid her weeping. She herself would choose death rather than have two men know of her shame. She would live with the one who survived.

I'll seem crueler here than you people. But none of you could see her face, especially her eyes. When I saw those flashing eyes, I wanted her for my wife. I wanted her, even if it meant being struck down by lightning. All I thought of was having her for good. Not out of lust, as you people might think. If that were all, I would have kicked her aside and left. And his blood would not have stained my sword. Ah, the expression on her face within that dim grove. I resolved to kill him before leaving.

I couldn't just murder him on the spot. So I undid the rope and ordered him to duel. (The rope lay forgotten by the cedar.) Turning white with anger, the man drew his great sword. Then he rushed me without a word. I needn't say how the duel turned out. On the twenty-third pass, my sword finally pierced his breast. The twenty-third — don't forget. I'm still astonished. No other man has lasted even twenty strokes. (He smiles contentedly.)

Once he fell, I put down my bloody sword to speak. I was going to tell her. . . . Imagine! She was gone. I searched among the cedar clump, anxious to find out which way she had fled. But her footprints did not appear among the bamboo leaves. I listened carefully, but could hear nothing except the groans of a dying man.

Perhaps when the duel began, she had fled the grove in search of help. My own life might be at stake. Taking the man's sword as well as his bow and arrows,

I immediately left the way I had come. The woman's horse was still outside, nibbling at the grass. To speak of what occurred after that would merely waste time. I did throw the sword away before entering the capital. That's all I have to confess. Just give me the worst sentence. I'm going to be hanged from an India tree anyway.

THE CONFESSION OF A WOMAN WHO HAD COME TO KIYOMIZU TEMPLE[9]

After he had attacked me, the man in the indigo jacket gazed at my husband and laughed contemptuously. My husband twisted this way and that, but the rope about his body merely tightened further. I would have rushed to his side, but the man kicked me to the ground. My husband's eyes flared. I cannot describe his look; the memory alone makes me shudder. He could not move his lips, but his look told all. There was cold contempt in it, more than anger and regret. That look hurt me more than getting kicked. I let out a cry, then fainted.

When I finally revived, the man in the indigo jacket had left. Only my husband remained, still bound to the cedar. Eventually I looked up from the bamboo leaves and gazed at him. He had not changed, except for the loathing that had crept into his expression of cold contempt. I can hardly name what I felt then. . . . Was it shame . . . regret . . . indignation . . . ? I struggled to my feet and went over to him.

"Husband, I am no longer yours. I've decided to die and be done with it. All I ask is that we die together. You have witnessed my shame and I cannot leave you behind."

He looked so disgusted I could hardly speak. Holding back my anguish, I looked for his sword. The thief had apparently taken it, along with the bow and arrows. Fortunately the dagger was still there, right at my feet. I picked it up.

"Give me your life," I exclaimed. "I shall attend you shortly."

When he heard these words, my husband finally moved his lips. I could hear no sound, as his mouth was crammed with leaves. All the same, I sensed his terrible message: "Go on, kill me!" Half in a dream, I drove the blade through his blue jacket and into his breast.

I must have fainted again. When I finally awoke, my husband had ceased breathing. He remained tied to the tree, his face lit beneath the bamboo and cedar by a ray of fading sunlight. Holding back my tears, I undid the rope from his corpse. And then? What happened next I don't have the strength to tell. Regardless of how I tried, I could not take my life. I stabbed at my throat and threw myself into a pond beneath the mountain. I tried everything, but could not die. I have survived, but I cannot take pride in that. Even the merciful Kannon probably abandons cowards like me. But what can I do? A thief has ravished me, and I have killed my husband. I really . . . I. . . . (Suddenly she breaks down sobbing.)

[9]*Kiyomizu Temple* A temple of the Hossō and Shin sects of Buddhism located in the Higashiyama foothills of Heian-kyō. Kannon, the Buddhist deity of mercy, is the principal object of veneration at the temple. (Trans.)

THE TALE OF THE SPIRIT AS TOLD THROUGH A MEDIUM

Once he had ravished my wife, the thief sat there consoling her. I remained tied to the cedar, unable to speak. All I could do was to keep winking at her, to warn against his lies. My wife sat disconsolate among the fallen leaves, gazing at her own knees. And yet, she seemed to hear him. I shuddered with jealousy as the thief adroitly talked of one thing and another. He said that her body was defiled and she could not rejoin her husband. Didn't she wish to be his instead? He had been violent only out of love for her. The thief boldly wooed her with such talk.

My wife seemed enchanted by his words. Never had she appeared so lovely. And what reply did she give the thief, even as I looked on? Take me with you, she pleaded, it doesn't matter where. Wandering in this limbo, I seethe with anger each time I remember.

If her crime had ended there, I wouldn't suffer so much. But that wasn't all. Won over by the thief, my wife was being led away by the hand when she suddenly turned pale and pointed at me. "So long as he lives, I cannot be yours"—that's what she said. Then she shrieked over and over: "Kill him!" Her words are like a howling storm even now. They threaten to cast me headlong into the darkness. The thief himself turned pale. He stared as my wife clung to his arm and repeated her shrill request. Then, so quickly I could not observe it, he kicked her down on the bamboo leaves. Folding his arms over his chest, he turned and asked, "What should I do with her? Shall I kill her? Or spare her? Just nod in reply. Kill her . . . ?"

For these words alone I wished to forgive the thief his crime. (Long silence again.)

As I hesitated, my wife cried out and rushed into the bamboo thicket. The thief sprang at her, but failed even to catch her sleeve. I watched as if in a dream.

After my wife had fled, the thief picked up my sword, along with my bow and arrows. He made a single cut in the rope that bound me all around. I remember him mumbling to himself as he disappeared into the thicket, "I'll be next. . . ."

Then quiet descended upon everything, except for the faint sound of weeping. I listened closely as I unwound the rope. Finally I realized this must be my own weeping.

At last I rose wearily from the foot of the cedar. Before me glistened the dagger which my wife had dropped. I picked it up and drove the blade into my breast. A bloody lump rose to my mouth, but I did not feel any pain. My breast merely turned cold, and the surroundings fell even more silent. How quiet it seemed. Above the mountain grove not a single bird sang. The solitary sun merely floated beyond the tips of cedar and bamboo. Gradually the sun grew dim. And the cedar and bamboo faded. I lay wrapped in deep silence.

Then someone stole up close. I tried to see, but dusk had already fallen. A hand . . . someone's invisible hand gently removed the blade from my breast. In that moment the blood surged again into my mouth. Thereupon I subsided forever into this dark limbo. . . .

[1921]

Translated by
James O'Brien

QUESTIONS

1. How does the multiple narrative structure contribute to the meaning of the story? Would a segment told from an omniscient perspective giving the "true" version of events enhance or detract from the effect of the conflicting testimonies?
2. Why does Tajōmaru, the robber, claim that he killed the husband? Why does the wife claim that she killed her husband? Why does the husband claim that he killed himself? Which testimony do you believe?
3. Does the presence of a supernatural element—the ghost of the dead husband testifying through a medium—detract from the otherwise realistic qualities of the story?
4. What is the "moral" of the story? What is its theme? How is the Japanese conception of honor central to the story?

Woody Allen

(b. 1935)

United States

Woody Allen is perhaps best known for the more than 20 films he has written, directed, produced, and frequently starred in since his first screenplay, *What's New, Pussycat?* in 1964. As his scripts from *Annie Hall* to *Zelig* reveal, he is a master of ironic and romantic humor; he makes gentle fun of people's emotional longings and anxieties as he punctures their illusions about themselves. In addition to filmscripts, he has written and published three volumes of short fiction and sketches: *Getting Even* (1971), *Without Feathers* (1975), and *Side Effects* (1980), all of which demonstrate his versatile wit and cut-to-the-bone comic style.

Allen was born in Brooklyn, New York, as Allen Stewart Konigsberg, the son of a waiter and jewelry engraver. His early life does not immediately reveal the direction his talent was to take. He dropped out of college twice (New York University and the City College of New York). Nonetheless, he eventually found his true talent in exposing, through his writing for film and in short fiction, the foibles and anxieties that we recognize in ourselves and thus cannot help but laugh at in his wonderfully self-deprecating characters. Expressing his aim for his life's work with characteristic humor, he said that he hoped to "forge in the smithy of my soul the uncreated conscience of my race. Then to see if they can be turned out in plastic."

"The Kugelmass Episode," originally published in *The New Yorker* in 1977, received an O. Henry Award as one of the best stories published that year.

◆ *The Kugelmass Episode* ◆

Kugelmass, a professor of humanities at City College, was unhappily married for the second time. Daphne Kugelmass was an oaf. He also had two dull sons by his first wife, Flo, and was up to his neck in alimony and child support.

"Did I know it would turn out so badly?" Kugelmass whined to his analyst one day. "Daphne had promised. Who suspected she'd let herself go and swell up like a beach ball? Plus she had a few bucks, which is not in itself a healthy reason to marry a person, but it doesn't hurt, with the kind of operating nut I have. You see my point?"

Kugelmass was bald and as hairy as a bear, but he had soul.

"I need to meet a new woman," he went on. "I need to have an affair. I may not look the part, but I'm a man who needs romance. I need softness, I need flirtation. I'm not getting younger, so before it's too late I want to make love in Venice, trade quips at "21,"[1] and exchange coy glances over red wine and candlelight. You see what I'm saying?"

[1]*"21"* famous New York City restaurant

Dr. Mandel shifted in his chair and said, "An affair will solve nothing. You're so unrealistic. Your problems run much deeper."

"And also this affair must be discreet," Kugelmass continued. "I can't afford a second divorce. Daphne would really sock it to me."

"Mr. Kugelmass—"

"But it can't be anyone at City College, because Daphne also works there. Not that anyone on the faculty at C.C.N.Y. is any great shakes, but some of those coeds . . ."

"Mr. Kugelmass—"

"Help me. I had a dream last night. I was skipping through a meadow holding a picnic basket and the basket was marked "Options." And then I saw there was a hole in the basket."

"Mr. Kugelmass, the worst thing you could do is act out. You must simply express your feelings here, and together we'll analyze them. You have been in treatment long enough to know there is no overnight cure. After all, I'm an analyst, not a magician."

"Then perhaps what I need is a magician," Kugelmass said, rising from his chair. And with that he terminated his therapy.

A couple of weeks later, while Kugelmass and Daphne were moping around in their apartment one night like two pieces of old furniture, the phone rang.

"I'll get it," Kugelmass said. "Hello."

"Kugelmass?" a voice said. "Kugelmass, this is Persky."

"Who?"

"Persky. Or should I say The Great Persky?"

"Pardon me?"

"I hear you're looking all over town for a magician to bring a little exotica into your life? Yes or no?"

"Sh-h-h," Kugelmass whispered. "Don't hang up. Where are you calling from, Persky?"

Early the following afternoon, Kugelmass climbed three flights of stairs in a broken-down apartment house in the Bushwick section of Brooklyn. Peering through the darkness of the hall, he found the door he was looking for and pressed the bell. I'm going to regret this, he thought to himself.

Seconds later, he was greeted by a short, thin, waxy-looking man.

"*You're* Persky the Great?" Kugelmass said.

"The Great Persky. You want a tea?"

"No, I want romance. I want music. I want love and beauty."

"But not tea, eh? Amazing. O.K., sit down."

Persky went to the back room, and Kugelmass heard the sounds of boxes and furniture being moved around. Persky reappeared, pushing before him a large object on squeaky roller-skate wheels. He removed some old silk handkerchiefs that were lying on its top and blew away a bit of dust. It was a cheap-looking Chinese cabinet, badly lacquered.

"Persky," Kugelmass said, "what's your scam?"

"Pay attention," Persky said. "This is some beautiful effect. I developed it for a Knights of Pythias date last year, but the booking fell through. Get into the cabinet."

"Why, so you can stick it full of swords or something?"

"You see any swords?"

Kugelmass made a face and, grunting, climbed into the cabinet. He couldn't help noticing a couple of ugly rhinestones glued onto the raw plywood just in front of his face. "If this is a joke," he said.

"Some joke. Now, here's the point. If I throw any novel into this cabinet with you, shut the doors, and tap it three times, you will find yourself projected into that book."

Kugelmass made a grimace of disbelief.

"It's the emess,"[2] Persky said. "My hand to God. Not just a novel, either. A short story, a play, a poem. You can meet any of the women created by the world's best writers. Whoever you dreamed of. You could carry on all you like with a real winner. Then when you've had enough you give a yell, and I'll see you're back here in a split second."

"Persky, are you some kind of outpatient?"

"I'm telling you it's on the level," Persky said.

Kugelmass remained skeptical. "What are you telling me—that this cheesy homemade box can take me on a ride like you're describing?"

"For a double sawbuck."

Kugelmass reached for his wallet. "I'll believe this when I see it," he said.

Persky tucked the bills in his pants pocket and turned toward his bookcase. "So who do you want to meet? Sister Carrie? Hester Prynne? Ophelia? Maybe someone by Saul Bellow? Hey, what about Temple Drake?[3] Although for a man your age she'd be a workout."

"French, I want to have an affair with a French lover."

"Nana?"

"I don't want to have to pay for it."

"What about Natasha in 'War and Peace'?"

"I said French. I know! What about Emma Bovary?[4] That sounds to me perfect."

"You got it, Kugelmass. Give me a holler when you've had enough." Persky tossed in a paperback copy of Flaubert's novel.

"You sure this is safe?" Kugelmass asked as Persky began shutting the cabinet doors.

"Safe. Is anything safe in this crazy world?" Persky rapped three times on the cabinet and then flung open the doors.

Kugelmass was gone. At the same moment, he appeared in the bedroom of Charles and Emma Bovary's house at Yonville. Before him was a beautiful woman standing alone with her back turned to him as she folded some linen. I can't believe this, thought Kugelmass, staring at the doctor's ravishing wife. This is uncanny. I'm here. It's her.

Emma turned in surprise. "Goodness, you startled me," she said. "Who are you?" She spoke in the same fine English translation as the paperback.

It's simply devastating, he thought. Then, realizing that it was he whom she

[2]*emess* the truth

[3]The women named in this conversation are famous female protagonists in literature: Carrie Meeber, *Sister Carrie* (1900) by Theodore Dreiser; Hester Prynne, *The Scarlet Letter* (1850) by Nathaniel Hawthorne; Ophelia, *Hamlet* (c. 1600) by William Shakespeare; Temple Drake, *Sanctuary* (1931) by William Faulkner.

[4]Nana, the female protagonist of *Nana* (1880), a novel by Emile Zola; Natasha, central female in *War and Peace* (1863–1871) by Leo Tolstoy. Emma Bovary is the protagonist of Gustave Flaubert's novel *Madame Bovary* (1865).

had addressed, he said, "Excuse me, I'm Sidney Kugelmass. I'm from City College. A professor of humanities. C.C.N.Y.? Uptown. I—oh, boy!"

Emma Bovary smiled flirtatiously and said, "Would you like a drink? A glass of wine, perhaps?"

She is beautiful, Kugelmass thought. What a contrast with the troglodyte who shared his bed! He felt a sudden impulse to take this vision into his arms and tell her she was the kind of woman he had dreamed of all his life.

"Yes, some wine," he said hoarsely. "White. No, red. No, white. Make it white."

"Charles is out for the day," Emma said, her voice full of playful implication.

After the wine, they went for a stroll in the lovely French countryside. "I've always dreamed that some mysterious stranger would appear and rescue me from the monotony of this crass rural existence," Emma said, clasping his hand. They passed a small church. "I love what you have on," she murmured. "I've never seen anything like it around here. It's so . . . so modern."

"It's called a leisure suit," he said romantically. "It was marked down." Suddenly he kissed her. For the next hour they reclined under a tree and whispered together and told each other deeply meaningful things with their eyes. Then Kugelmass sat up. He had just remembered he had to meet Daphne at Bloomingdale's. "I must go," he told her. "But don't worry. I'll be back."

"I hope so," Emma said.

He embraced her passionately, and the two walked back to the house. He held Emma's face cupped in his palms, kissed her again, and yelled, "O.K., Persky! I got to be at Bloomingdale's by three-thirty."

There was an audible pop, and Kugelmass was back in Brooklyn.

"So? Did I lie?" Persky asked triumphantly.

"Look, Persky, I'm right now late to meet the ball and chain at Lexington Avenue, but when can I go again? Tomorrow?"

"My pleasure. Just bring a twenty. And don't mention this to anybody."

"Yeah. I'm going to call Rupert Murdoch."[5]

Kugelmass hailed a cab and sped off to the city. His heart danced on point. I am in love, he thought, I am the possessor of a wonderful secret. What he didn't realize was that at this very moment students in various classrooms across the country were saying to their teachers, "Who is this character on page 100? A bald Jew is kissing Madame Bovary?" A teacher in Sioux Falls, South Dakota, sighed and thought, Jesus, these kids, with their pot and acid. What goes through their minds!

Daphne Kugelmass was in the bathroom-accessories department at Bloomingdale's when Kugelmass arrived breathlessly. "Where've you been?" she snapped. "It's four-thirty."

"I got held up in traffic," Kugelmass said.

Kugelmass visited Persky the next day, and in a few minutes was again passed magically to Yonville. Emma couldn't hide her excitement at seeing him. The two spent hours together, laughing and talking about their different backgrounds. Before Kugelmass left, they made love. "My God, I'm doing it with Madame Bovary!" Kugelmass whispered to himself. "Me, who failed freshman English."

[5]*Rupert Murdoch* Australian newspaper mogul who owns several American newspapers

As the months passed, Kugelmass saw Persky many times and developed a close and passionate relationship with Emma Bovary. "Make sure and always get me into the book before page 120," Kugelmass said to the magician one day. "I always have to meet her before she hooks up with this Rodolphe character."

"Why?" Persky asked. "You can't beat his time?"

"Beat his time. He's landed gentry. Those guys have nothing better to do than flirt and ride horses. To me, he's one of those faces you see in the pages of *Women's Wear Daily*. With the Helmut Berger hairdo. But to her he's hot stuff."

"And her husband suspects nothing?"

"He's out of his depth. He's a lack-lustre little paramedic who's thrown in his lot with a jitterbug. He's ready to go to sleep by ten, and she's putting on her dancing shoes. Oh, well. . . . See you later."

And once again Kugelmass entered the cabinet and passed instantly to the Bovary estate at Yonville. "How you doing, cupcake?" he said to Emma.

"Oh, Kugelmass," Emma sighed. "What I have to put up with. Last night at dinner, Mr. Personality dropped off to sleep in the middle of the dessert course. I'm pouring my heart out about Maxim's[6] and the ballet, and out of the blue I hear snoring."

"It's O.K., darling, I'm here now," Kugelmass said, embracing her. I've earned this, he thought, smelling Emma's French perfume and burying his nose in her hair. I've suffered enough. I've paid enough analysts. I've searched till I'm weary. She's young and nubile, and I'm here a few pages after Léon and just before Rodolphe. By showing up during the correct chapters, I've got the situation knocked.

Emma, to be sure, was just as happy as Kugelmass. She had been starved for excitement, and his tales of Broadway night life, of fast cars and Hollywood and TV stars, enthralled the young French beauty.

"Tell me again about O. J. Simpson,"[7] she implored that evening, as she and Kugelmass strolled past Abbé Bournisien's church.

"What can I say? The man is great. He sets all kinds of rushing records. Such moves. They can't touch him."

"And the Academy Awards?" Emma said wistfully. "I'd give anything to win one."

"First you've got to be nominated."

"I know. You explained it. But I'm convinced I can act. Of course, I'd want to take a class or two. With Strasberg maybe. Then, if I had the right agent—"

"We'll see, we'll see. I'll speak to Persky."

That night, safely returned to Persky's flat, Kugelmass brought up the idea of having Emma visit him in the big city.

"Let me think about it," Persky said. "Maybe I could work it. Stranger things have happened." Of course, neither of them could think of one.

"Where the hell do you go all the time?" Daphne Kugelmass barked at her husband as he returned home late that evening. "You got a chippie stashed somewhere?"

[6]*Maxim's* famous restaurant in Paris

[7]*O. J. Simpson* American professional football player

"Yeah, sure, I'm just the type," Kugelmass said wearily. "I was with Leonard Popkin. We were discussing Socialist agriculture in Poland. You know Popkin. He's a freak on the subject."

"Well, you've been very odd lately," Daphne said. "Distant. Just don't forget about my father's birthday. On Saturday?"

"Oh, sure, sure," Kugelmass said, heading for the bathroom.

"My whole family will be there. We can see the twins. And Cousin Hamish. You should be more polite to Cousin Hamish—he likes you."

"Right, the twins," Kugelmass said, closing the bathroom door and shutting out the sound of his wife's voice. He leaned against it and took a deep breath. In a few hours, he told himself, he would be back in Yonville again, back with his beloved. And this time, if all went well, he would bring Emma back with him.

At three-fifteen the following afternoon, Persky worked his wizardry again. Kugelmass appeared before Emma, smiling and eager. The two spent a few hours at Yonville with Binet and then remounted the Bovary carriage. Following Persky's instructions, they held each other tightly, closed their eyes, and counted to ten. When they opened them, the carriage was just drawing up at the side door of the Plaza Hotel, where Kugelmass had optimistically reserved a suite earlier in the day.

"I love it! It's everything I dreamed it would be," Emma said as she whirled joyously around the bedroom, surveying the city from their window. "There's F. A. O. Schwartz.[8] And there's Central Park, and the Sherry is which one? Oh, there—I see. It's too divine."

On the bed there were boxes from Halston and Saint Laurent. Emma unwrapped a package and held up a pair of black velvet pants against her perfect body.

"The slacks suit is by Ralph Lauren," Kugelmass said. "You'll look like a million bucks in it. Come on, sugar, give us a kiss."

"I've never been so happy!" Emma squealed as she stood before the mirror. "Let's go out on the town. I want to see *Chorus Line* and the Guggenheim and this Jack Nicholson character you always talk about. Are any of his flicks showing?"

"I cannot get my mind around this," a Stanford professor said. "First a strange character named Kugelmass, and now she's gone from the book. Well, I guess the mark of a classic is that you can reread it a thousand times and always find something new."

The lovers passed a blissful weekend. Kugelmass had told Daphne he would be away at a symposium in Boston, and would return Monday. Savoring each moment, he and Emma went to the movies, had dinner in Chinatown, passed two hours at a discothèque, and went to bed with a TV movie. They slept till noon on Sunday, visited SoHo, and ogled celebrities at Elaine's. They had caviar and champagne in their suite on Sunday night and talked until dawn. That morning, in the cab taking them to Persky's apartment, Kugelmass thought, It was hectic, but worth it. I can't bring her here too often, but now and then it will be a charming contrast with Yonville.

At Persky's, Emma climbed into the cabinet, arranged her new boxes of clothes neatly around her, and kissed Kugelmass fondly. "My place next time,"

[8] *F. A. O. Schwarz* famous New York toy store

she said with a wink. Persky rapped three times on the cabinet. Nothing happened.

"Hmm," Persky said, scratching his head. He rapped again, but still no magic. "Something must be wrong," he mumbled.

"Persky, you're joking!" Kugelmass cried. "How can it not work?"

"Relax, relax. Are you still in the box, Emma?"

"Yes."

Persky rapped again—harder this time.

"I'm still here, Persky."

"I know, darling. Sit tight."

"Persky, we *have* to get her back," Kugelmass whispered. "I'm a married man, and I have a class in three hours. I'm not prepared for anything more than a cautious affair at this point."

"I can't understand it," Persky muttered. "It's such a reliable little trick."

But he could do nothing. "It's going to take a little while," he said to Kugelmass. "I'm going to have to strip it down. I'll call you later."

Kugelmass bundled Emma into a cab and took her back to the Plaza. He barely made it to his class on time. He was on the phone all day, to Persky and to his mistress. The magician told him it might be several days before he got to the bottom of the trouble.

"How was the symposium?" Daphne asked him that night.

"Fine, fine," he said, lighting the filter end of a cigarette.

"What's wrong? You're as tense as a cat."

"Me? Ha, that's a laugh. I'm as calm as a summer night. I'm just going to take a walk." He eased out the door, hailed a cab, and flew to the Plaza.

"This is no good," Emma said. "Charles will miss me."

"Bear with me, sugar," Kugelmass said. He was pale and sweaty. He kissed her again, raced to the elevators, yelled at Persky over a pay phone in the Plaza lobby, and just made it home before midnight.

"According to Popkin, barley prices in Kraków have not been this stable since 1971," he said to Daphne, and smiled wanly as he climbed into bed.

The whole week went by like that. On Friday night, Kugelmass told Daphne there was another symposium he had to catch, this one in Syracuse. He hurried back to the Plaza, but the second weekend there was nothing like the first. "Get me back into the novel or marry me," Emma told Kugelmass. "Meanwhile, I want to get a job or go to class, because watching TV all day is the pits."

"Fine. We can use the money," Kugelmass said. "You consume twice your weight in room service."

"I met an Off Broadway producer in Central Park yesterday, and he said I might be right for a project he's doing," Emma said.

"Who is this clown?" Kugelmass asked.

"He's not a clown. He's sensitive and kind and cute. His name's Jeff Something-or-Other, and he's up for a Tony."

Later that afternoon, Kugelmass showed up at Persky's drunk.

"Relax," Persky told him. "You'll get a coronary."

"Relax. The man says relax. I've got a fictional character stashed in a hotel room, and I think my wife is having me tailed by a private shamus."[9]

[9]*shamus* detective

"O.K., O.K. We know there's a problem." Persky crawled under the cabinet and started banging on something with a large wrench.

"I'm like a wild animal," Kugelmass went on. "I'm sneaking around town, and Emma and I have had it up to here with each other. Not to mention a hotel tab that reads like the defense budget."

"So what should I do? This is the world of magic," Persky said. "It's all nuance."

"Nuance, my foot. I'm pouring Dom Pérignon and black eggs into this little mouse, plus her wardrobe, plus she's enrolled at the Neighborhood Playhouse and suddenly needs professional photos. Also, Persky, Professor Fivish Kopkind, who teaches Comp Lit and who has always been jealous of me, has identified me as the sporadically appearing character in the Flaubert book. He's threatened to go to Daphne. I see ruin and alimony; jail. For adultery with Madame Bovary, my wife will reduce me to beggary."

"What do you want me to say? I'm working on it night and day. As far as your personal anxiety goes, that I can't help you with. I'm a magician, not an analyst."

By Sunday afternoon, Emma had locked herself in the bathroom and refused to respond to Kugelmass's entreaties. Kugelmass stared out the window at the Wollman Rink and contemplated suicide. Too bad this is a low floor, he thought, or I'd do it right now. Maybe if I ran away to Europe and started life over . . . Maybe I could sell the *International Herald Tribune*, like those young girls used to.

The phone rang. Kugelmass lifted it to his ear mechanically.

"Bring her over," Persky said. "I think I got the bugs out of it."

Kugelmass's heart leaped. "You're serious?" he said. "You got it licked?"

"It was something in the transmission. Go figure."

"Persky, you're a genius. We'll be there in a minute. Less than a minute."

Again the lovers hurried to the magician's apartment, and again Emma Bovary climbed into the cabinet with her boxes. This time there was no kiss. Persky shut the doors, took a deep breath, and tapped the box three times. There was the reassuring popping noise, and when Persky peered inside, the box was empty. Madame Bovary was back in her novel. Kugelmass heaved a great sigh of relief and pumped the magician's hand.

"It's over," he said. "I learned my lesson. I'll never cheat again, I swear it." He pumped Persky's hand again and made a mental note to send him a necktie.

Three weeks later, at the end of a beautiful spring afternoon, Persky answered his doorbell. It was Kugelmass, with a sheepish expression on his face.

"O.K., Kugelmass," the magician said. "Where to this time?"

"It's just this once," Kugelmass said. "The weather is so lovely, and I'm not getting any younger. Listen, you've read *Portnoy's Complaint*? Remember The Monkey?"[10]

"The price is now twenty-five dollars, because the cost of living is up, but I'll start you off with one freebie, due to all the trouble I caused you."

"You're good people," Kugelmass said, combing his few remaining hairs as he climbed into the cabinet again. "This'll work all right?"

[10]*The Monkey* a sexually uninhibited woman in Philip Roth's novel *Portnoy's Complaint* (1969)

"I hope. But I haven't tried it much since all that unpleasantness."

"Sex and romance," Kugelmass said from inside the box. "What we go through for a pretty face."

Persky tossed in a copy of *Portnoy's Complaint* and rapped three times on the box. This time, instead of a popping noise there was a dull explosion, followed by a series of crackling noises and a shower of sparks. Persky leaped back, was seized by a heart attack, and dropped dead. The cabinet burst into flames, and eventually the entire house burned down.

Kugelmass, unaware of this catastrophe, had his own problems. He had not been thrust into *Portnoy's Complaint*, or into any other novel, for that matter. He had been projected into an old textbook, *Remedial Spanish*, and was running for his life over a barren, rocky terrain as the word *tener* ("to have")—a large and hairy irregular verb—raced after him on its spindly legs.

[1977]

QUESTIONS

1. What makes this story funny? What particular details provoke laughter?
2. Why does Kugelmass choose Flaubert's *Madame Bovary* as the object of his fantasies? Consider this observation about Emma Bovary as a way of answering the question:

   > [Emma] recalls the heroines of those books that she had read and the lyric legion of these adulterous women began to sing in her memory. . . . She became herself, as it were, an actual part of these lyrical imaginings; at long last as she saw herself among these lovers she had so envied, she fulfilled the love-dream of her youth. (*Madame Bovary*, Part 2, Chapter 9)

   How does Allen juxtapose the events of Flaubert's novel with twentieth-century elements to achieve humor?
3. What contemporary experiences and attitudes is Allen satirizing?
4. How do you understand the role of Persky?
5. How do you understand the ending of the story? Is Kugelmass's predicament resolved?

Isabel Allende

(b. 1942)

Chile

Isabel Allende was born in Peru into an upper-middle-class Chilean family; her father, a diplomat, and her mother were divorced when she was a child, and she had no further contact with her father. She grew up in the household of her mother's parents, experiencing a rather lonely childhood but one filled with interesting adults. Her grandfather was a complex man, capable of both violence and kindness; her grandmother was deeply interested in the occult. These influential figures later inspired Allende's first novel, *The House of the Spirits* (1982).

Allende's mother remarried (another diplomat) when Isabel was 15; the family lived in Bolivia, the Middle East, and Europe during Isabel's adolescence. Allende left school and returned to Chile at 16 to become a secretary for a United Nations organization. Her work with journalists led her to become a journalist herself, eventually developing her own television program as well as writing for a radical women's magazine and working on movie newsreels. By then married to an engineer and the mother of a son and a daughter, Allende began to write fiction, including several short stories for children.

"And then in 1973," as Allende phrases it, "the military coup changed everything, and I felt as many Chileans did, that my life had been cut into pieces, and that I had to start over again." The assassination of Salvador Allende, the president of Chile and Isabel's uncle, made the political upheaval immediate and personal. Allende and her family relocated to Venezuela in 1975. Years later, after her grandparents had died, she began to write *The House of the Spirits* as a way to capture the memories of her grandparents and especially the important women of her family. The novel developed into a chronicle of several generations of the fictional Trueba family through whom Allende recreated a history of modern Chile. Her later fiction includes *Of Love and Shadows* (1986), *Eva Luna* (1988), and *The Stories of Eva Luna* (1991).

One of the few female writers from Latin America to have captured an international readership, Allende is a practitioner of a unique narrative focus created by Latin American writers, often termed "magical realism," in which realistic events are interwoven with fantastic or incredible elements. As Allende commented in an interview, in explanation of this merging of real and incredible elements in fiction,

> In Latin America, we value dreams, passions, obsessions, emotions, and all that which is very important to our lives has a place in literature—our sense of family, our sense of religion, of superstition, too. That's magical realism—the emotions that everybody has plus our reality. . . . Fantastic things happen every day in Latin America—it's not that we make them up.

"And of Clay Are We Created," a story more realistic than magical, demonstrates Allende's insight into the relationship between the media and contemporary events: the problematic nature of "objective" reporting and the power of events to overtake their observers.

• And of Clay Are We Created •

They discovered the girl's head protruding from the mudpit, eyes wide open, calling soundlessly. She had a First Communion name, Azucena. Lily. In that vast cemetery where the odor of death was already attracting vultures from far away, and where the weeping of orphans and wails of the injured filled the air, the little girl obstinately clinging to life became the symbol of the tragedy. The television cameras transmitted so often the unbearable image of the head budding like a black squash from the clay that there was no one who did not recognize her and know her name. And every time we saw her on the screen, right behind her was Rolf Carlé, who had gone there on assignment, never suspecting that he would find a fragment of his past, lost thirty years before.

First a subterranean sob rocked the cotton fields, curling them like waves of foam. Geologists had set up their seismographs weeks before and knew that the mountain had awakened again. For some time they had predicted that the heat of the eruption could detach the eternal ice from the slopes of the volcano, but no one heeded their warnings; they sounded like the tales of frightened old women. The towns in the valley went about their daily life, deaf to the moaning of the earth, until that fateful Wednesday night in November when a prolonged roar announced the end of the world, and walls of snow broke loose, rolling in an avalanche of clay, stones, and water that descended on the villages and buried them beneath unfathomable meters of telluric vomit. As soon as the survivors emerged from the paralysis of that first awful terror, they could see that houses, plazas, churches, white cotton plantations, dark coffee forests, cattle pastures—all had disappeared. Much later, after soldiers and volunteers had arrived to rescue the living and try to assess the magnitude of the cataclysm, it was calculated that beneath the mud lay more than twenty thousand human beings and an indefinite number of animals putrefying in a viscous soup. Forests and rivers had also been swept away, and there was nothing to be seen but an immense desert of mire.

When the station called before dawn, Rolf Carlé and I were together. I crawled out of bed, dazed with sleep, and went to prepare coffee while he hurriedly dressed. He stuffed his gear in the green canvas backpack he always carried, and we said goodbye, as we had so many times before. I had no presentiments. I sat in the kitchen, sipping my coffee and planning the long hours without him, sure that he would be back the next day.

He was one of the first to reach the scene, because while other reporters were fighting their way to the edges of that morass in jeeps, bicycles, or on foot, each getting there however he could, Rolf Carlé had the advantage of the television helicopter, which flew him over the avalanche. We watched on our screens the footage captured by his assistant's camera, in which he was up to his knees in muck, a microphone in his hand, in the midst of a bedlam of lost children, wounded survivors, corpses, and devastation. The story came to us in his calm voice. For years he had been a familiar figure in newscasts, reporting live at the scene of battles and catastrophes with awesome tenacity. Nothing could stop him, and I was always amazed at his equanimity in the face of danger and suffering; it seemed as if nothing could shake his fortitude or deter his curiosity. Fear seemed never to touch him, although he had confessed to me that he was not a courageous man, far from it. I believe that the lens of the camera had a strange effect on him; it was as if it transported him to a different time from which he could watch events without actually participating in them. When I knew him better, I came to realize that this fictive distance seemed to protect him from his own emotions.

Rolf Carlé was in on the story of Azucena from the beginning. He filmed the volunteers who discovered her, and the first persons who tried to reach her; his camera zoomed in on the girl, her dark face, her large desolate eyes, the plastered-down tangle of her hair. The mud was like quicksand around her, and anyone attempting to reach her was in danger of sinking. They threw a rope to her that she made no effort to grasp until they shouted to her to catch it; then she pulled a hand from the mire and tried to move, but immediately sank a little deeper. Rolf threw down his knapsack and the rest of his equipment and waded into the quagmire, commenting for his assistant's microphone that it was cold and that one could begin to smell the stench of corpses.

"What's your name?" he asked the girl, and she told him her flower name. "Don't move, Azucena," Rolf Carlé directed, and kept talking to her, without a thought for what he was saying, just to distract her, while slowly he worked his way forward in mud up to his waist. The air around him seemed as murky as the mud.

It was impossible to reach her from the approach he was attempting, so he retreated and circled around where there seemed to be firmer footing. When finally he was close enough, he took the rope and tied it beneath her arms, so they could pull her out. He smiled at her with that smile that crinkles his eyes and makes him look like a little boy; he told her that everything was fine, that he was here with her now, that soon they would have her out. He signaled the others to pull, but as soon as the cord tensed, the girl screamed. They tried again, and her shoulders and arms appeared, but they could move her no farther; she was trapped. Someone suggested that her legs might be caught in the collapsed walls of her house, but she said it was not just rubble, that she was also held by the bodies of her brothers and sisters clinging to her legs.

"Don't worry, we'll get you out of here," Rolf promised. Despite the quality of the transmission, I could hear his voice break, and I loved him more than ever. Azucena looked at him, but said nothing.

During those first hours Rolf Carlé exhausted all the resources of his ingenuity to rescue her. He struggled with poles and ropes, but every tug was an intolerable torture for the imprisoned girl. It occurred to him to use one of the poles as a lever but got no result and had to abandon the idea. He talked a couple of soldiers into working with him for a while, but they had to leave because so many other victims were calling for help. The girl could not move, she barely could breathe, but she did not seem desperate, as if an ancestral resignation allowed her to accept her fate. The reporter, on the other hand, was determined to snatch her from death. Someone brought him a tire, which he placed beneath her arms like a life buoy, and then laid a plank near the hole to hold his weight and allow him to stay closer to her. As it was impossible to remove the rubble blindly, he tried once or twice to dive toward her feet, but emerged frustrated, covered with mud, and spitting gravel. He concluded that he would have to have a pump to drain the water, and radioed a request for one, but received in return a message that there was no available transport and it could not be sent until the next morning.

"We can't wait that long!" Rolf Carlé shouted, but in the pandemonium no one stopped to commiserate. Many more hours would go by before he accepted that time had stagnated and reality had been irreparably distorted.

A military doctor came to examine the girl, and observed that her heart was functioning well and that if she did not get too cold she could survive the night.

"Hang on, Azucena, we'll have the pump tomorrow," Rolf Carlé tried to console her.

"Don't leave me alone," she begged.

"No, of course I won't leave you."

Someone brought him coffee, and he helped the girl drink it, sip by sip. The warm liquid revived her and she began telling him about her small life, about her family and her school, about how things were in that little bit of world before the volcano had erupted. She was thirteen, and she had never been outside her village. Rolf Carlé, buoyed by a premature optimism, was convinced that everything would end well: the pump would arrive, they would drain the water, move the rubble, and Azucena would be transported by helicopter to a hospital where she would recover rapidly and where he could visit her and bring her gifts. He thought, She's already too old for dolls, and I don't know what would please her; maybe a dress. I don't know much about women, he concluded, amused, reflecting that although he had known many women in his lifetime, none had taught him these details. To pass the hours he began to tell Azucena about his travels and adventures as a newshound, and when he exhausted his memory, he called upon imagination, inventing things he thought might entertain her. From time to time she dozed, but he kept talking in the darkness, to assure her that he was still there and to overcome the menace of uncertainty.

That was a long night.

Many miles away, I watched Rolf Carlé and the girl on a television screen. I could not bear the wait at home, so I went to National Television, where I often spent entire nights with Rolf editing programs. There, I was near his world, and I could at least get a feeling of what he lived through during those three decisive days. I called all the important people in the city, senators, commanders of the armed forces, the North American ambassador, and the president of National Petroleum, begging them for a pump to remove the silt, but obtained only vague promises. I began to ask for urgent help on radio and television, to see if there wasn't *someone* who could help us. Between calls I would run to the newsroom to monitor the satellite transmissions that periodically brought new details of the catastrophe. While reporters selected scenes with most impact for the news report, I searched for footage that featured Azucena's mudpit. The screen reduced the disaster to a single plane and accentuated the tremendous distance that separated me from Rolf Carlé; nonetheless, I was there with him. The child's every suffering hurt me as it did him; I felt his frustration, his impotence.

Faced with the impossibility of communicating with him, the fantastic idea came to me that if I tried, I could reach him by force of mind and in that way give him encouragement. I concentrated until I was dizzy—a frenzied and futile activity. At times I would be overcome with compassion and burst out crying; at other times, I was so drained I felt as if I were staring through a telescope at the light of a star dead for a million years.

I watched that hell on the first morning broadcast, cadavers of people and animals awash in the current of new rivers formed overnight from the melted snow. Above the mud rose the tops of trees and the bell towers of a church where several people had taken refuge and were patiently awaiting rescue teams. Hundreds of soldiers and volunteers from the Civil Defense were clawing through rubble searching for survivors, while long rows of ragged specters awaited their turn for a cup of hot broth. Radio networks announced that their phones were jammed with calls from families offering shelter to orphaned children. Drinking water was in scarce supply, along with gasoline and food. Doctors, resigned to amputating arms and legs without anesthesia, pled that at least they be sent serum and painkillers and antibiotics; most of the roads, however, were impassable, and worse were the bureaucratic obstacles that stood in the way. To top it all, the clay contaminated by decomposing bodies threatened the living with an outbreak of epidemics.

Azucena was shivering inside the tire that held her above the surface. Immobility and tension had greatly weakened her, but she was conscious and could still be heard when a microphone was held out to her. Her tone was humble, as if apologizing for all the fuss. Rolf Carlé had a growth of beard, and dark circles beneath his eyes; he looked near exhaustion. Even from that enormous distance I could sense the quality of his weariness, so different from the fatigue of other adventures. He had completely forgotten the camera; he could not look at the girl through a lens any longer. The pictures we were receiving were not his assistant's but those of other reporters who had appropriated Azucena, bestowing on her the pathetic responsibility of embodying the horror of what had happened in that place. With the first light Rolf tried again to dislodge the obstacles that held the girl in her tomb, but he had only his hands to work with; he did not dare use a tool for fear of injuring her. He fed Azucena a cup of the cornmeal mush and bananas the Army was distributing, but she immediately vomited it up. A doctor stated that she had a fever, but added that there was little he could do: antibiotics were being reserved for cases of gangrene. A priest also passed by and blessed her, hanging a medal of the Virgin around her neck. By evening a gentle, persistent drizzle began to fall.

"The sky is weeping," Azucena murmured, and she, too, began to cry.

"Don't be afraid," Rolf begged. "You have to keep your strength up and be calm. Everything will be fine. I'm with you, and I'll get you out somehow."

Reporters returned to photograph Azucena and ask her the same questions, which she no longer tried to answer. In the meanwhile, more television and movie teams arrived with spools of cable, tapes, film, videos, precision lenses, recorders, sound consoles, lights, reflecting screens, auxiliary motors, cartons of supplies, electricians, sound technicians, and cameramen: Azucena's face was beamed to millions of screens around the world. And all the while Rolf Carlé kept pleading for a pump. The improved technical facilities bore results, and National Television began receiving sharper pictures and clearer sound; the distance seemed suddenly compressed, and I had the horrible sensation that

Azucena and Rolf were by my side, separated from me by impenetrable glass. I was able to follow events hour by hour; I knew everything my love did to wrest the girl from her prison and help her endure her suffering; I overheard fragments of what they said to one another and could guess the rest; I was present when she taught Rolf to pray, and when he distracted her with the stories I had told him in a thousand and one nights beneath the white mosquito netting of our bed.

When darkness came on the second day, Rolf tried to sing Azucena to sleep with old Austrian folk songs he had learned from his mother, but she was far beyond sleep. They spent most of the night talking, each in a stupor of exhaustion and hunger, and shaking with cold. That night, imperceptibly, the unyielding floodgates that had contained Rolf Carlé's past for so many years began to open, and the torrent of all that had lain hidden in the deepest and most secret layers of memory poured out, leveling before it the obstacles that had blocked his consciousness for so long. He could not tell it all to Azucena; she perhaps did not know there was a world beyond the sea or time previous to her own; she was not capable of imagining Europe in the years of the war. So he could not tell her of defeat, nor of the afternoon the Russians had led them to the concentration camp to bury prisoners dead from starvation. Why should he describe to her how the naked bodies piled like a mountain of firewood resembled fragile china? How could he tell this dying child about ovens and gallows? Nor did he mention the night that he had seen his mother naked, shod in stiletto-heeled red boots, sobbing with humiliation. There was much he did not tell, but in those hours he relived for the first time all the things his mind had tried to erase. Azucena had surrendered her fear to him and so, without wishing it, had obliged Rolf to confront his own. There, beside that hellhole of mud, it was impossible for Rolf to flee from himself any longer, and the visceral terror he had lived as a boy suddenly invaded him. He reverted to the years when he was the age of Azucena, and younger, and, like her, found himself trapped in a pit without escape, buried in life, his head barely above ground; he saw before his eyes the boots and legs of his father, who had removed his belt and was whipping it in the air with the never-forgotten hiss of a viper coiled to strike. Sorrow flooded through him, intact and precise, as if it had lain always in his mind, waiting. He was once again in the armoire where his father locked him to punish him for imagined misbehavior, there where for eternal hours he had crouched with his eyes closed, not to see the darkness, with his hands over his ears, to shut out the beating of his heart, trembling, huddled like a cornered animal. Wandering in the mist of his memories he found his sister Katharina, a sweet, retarded child who spent her life hiding, with the hope that her father would forget the disgrace of her having been born. With Katharina, Rolf crawled beneath the dining room table, and with her hid there under the long white tablecloth, two children forever embraced, alert to footsteps and voices. Katharina's scent melded with his own sweat, with aromas of cooking, garlic, soup, freshly baked bread, and the unexpected odor of putrescent clay. His sister's hand in his, her frightened breathing, her silk hair against his cheek, the candid gaze of her eyes. Katharina . . . Katharina materialized before him, floating on the air like a flag, clothed in the white tablecloth, now a winding sheet, and at last he could weep for her death and for the guilt of having abandoned her. He understood then that all his exploits as a reporter, the feats that had won him such recognition and fame, were merely an attempt to keep his most ancient fears at bay, a stratagem for taking refuge behind a lens to test whether reality was more tolerable from that perspective. He took excessive risks as an exercise of courage, training by day to conquer the monsters that tormented him by night. But he had come face to face with the moment of truth; he could not continue to escape his past. He *was* Azucena; he was buried in the clayey mud; his terror was not the distant emotion of an almost forgotten childhood, it was a claw sunk in his throat. In the flush of his tears he saw his mother, dressed in black and clutching her imitation-crocodile pocketbook to her bosom, just as he had last seen her on the dock when she had come to put him on the boat to South America. She had not come to dry his tears, but to tell him to pick up a shovel: the war was over and now they must bury the dead.

"Don't cry. I don't hurt anymore. I'm fine," Azucena said when dawn came.

"I'm not crying for you," Rolf Carlé smiled. "I'm crying for myself. I hurt all over."

The third day in the valley of the cataclysm began with a pale light filtering through storm clouds. The President of the Republic visited the area in his tailored safari jacket to confirm that this was the worst catastrophe of the century; the country was in mourning; sister nations had offered aid; he had ordered a state of siege; the Armed Forces would be merciless, anyone caught stealing or committing other offenses would be shot on sight. He added that it was impossible to remove all the corpses or count the thousands who had disappeared; the entire valley would be declared holy ground, and bishops would come to celebrate a solemn mass for the souls of the victims. He went to the Army field tents to offer relief in the form of vague promises to crowds of the rescued, then to the improvised hospital to offer a word of encouragement to doctors and nurses worn down from so many hours of tribulations. Then he asked to be taken to see Azucena, the little girl the whole world had seen. He waved to her with a limp statesman's hand, and microphones recorded his emotional voice and paternal tone as he told her that her courage had served as an example to the nation. Rolf Carlé interrupted to ask for a pump, and the President assured him that he personally would attend to the matter. I caught a glimpse of Rolf for a few seconds kneeling beside the mudpit. On the evening news broadcast, he was still in the same position; and I, glued to the screen like a fortuneteller to her crystal ball, could tell that something fundamental had changed in him. I knew somehow that during the night his defenses had crumbled and he had given in to grief; finally he was vulnerable. The girl had touched a part of him that he himself had no access to, a part he had never shared with me. Rolf had wanted to console her, but it was Azucena who had given him consolation.

I recognized the precise moment at which Rolf gave up the fight and surrendered to the torture of watching the girl die. I was with them, three days and two nights, spying on them from the other side of life. I was there when she told him that in all her thirteen years no boy had ever loved her and that it was a pity to leave this world without knowing love. Rolf assured her that he loved her more than he could ever love anyone, more than he loved his mother, more than his sister, more than all the women who had slept in his arms, more than he loved me, his life companion, who would have given anything to be trapped in that well in her place, who would have exchanged her life for Azucena's, and I watched as he leaned down to kiss her poor forehead, consumed by a sweet, sad emotion he could not name. I felt how in that instant both were saved from despair, how they were freed from the clay, how they rose above the vultures and helicopters, how together they flew above the vast swamp of corruption and laments. How, finally, they were able to accept death. Rolf Carlé prayed in silence that she would die quickly, because such pain cannot be borne.

By then I had obtained a pump and was in touch with a general who had agreed to ship it the next morning on a military cargo plane. But on the night of that third day, beneath the unblinking focus of quartz lamps and the lens of a hundred cameras, Azucena gave up, her eyes locked with those of the friend who had sustained her to the end. Rolf Carlé removed the life buoy, closed her eyelids, held her to his chest for a few moments, and then let her go. She sank slowly, a flower in the mud.

You are back with me, but you are not the same man. I often accompany you to the station and we watch the videos of Azucena again; you study them intently, looking for something you could have done to save her, something you did not think of in time. Or maybe you study them to see yourself as if in a mirror, naked. Your cameras lie forgotten in a closet; you do not write or sing; you sit long hours before the window, staring at the mountains. Beside you, I wait for you to complete the voyage into yourself, for the old wounds to heal. I know that when you return from your nightmares, we shall again walk hand in hand, as before.

[1989]

Translated by
MARGARET SAYERS PEDEN

QUESTIONS

1. Who is the central character of this story: Azucena, Rolf Carlé, or the narrator? How is Rolf Carlé changed by his involvement with Azucena?
2. What does the story suggest about the relationship between human tragedy or catastrophe and media reportage? Does the presence of the journalist Rolf Carlé alter the situation in which Azucena is trapped? If so, how?
3. Why does Azucena die, despite the sustained human efforts and technological assistance enlisted on her behalf? What does the story suggest about the relationships between a developing country's response to a natural disaster, the international media's response to it, and the human costs?

HANAN AL-SHAYKH

(b. 1945)

LEBANON

Hanan Al-Shaykh was raised in a traditional Shiite Moslem household in Lebanon. Beginning in 1963, she studied in Cairo at the American College for girls. After her return to Beirut four years later, she worked as a journalist and simultaneously began writing short stories and novels. Although her works have all originally been published in Lebanon, in Arabic, several have encountered censorship in other Islamic countries. Two novels have been translated into English: *The Story of Zahra* (1986) and *Women of Sand and Myrrh* (1989). Hanan Al-Shaykh has been described by one critic as a "reluctant feminist."

In response to our query about "The Unseeing Eye," Hanan Al-Shaykh has written,

> I do not write only about Arab women and their place in society, and I cannot see myself being confined within such a narrow frame of reference. For me fiction has a power of its own, while to be a feminist is to have an ideological and political view of the world which may restrict the open, loosely-structured, imaginative qualities that I regard as positive features of my work.
>
> Fiction is the process by which a simple observation of human behaviour and emotions in certain surroundings can evolve into a story, an autonomous entity. I write because I am fascinated to see where the creation of such a story may lead me: I invent characters who behave and feel in certain ways, regardless of what I think of them, and eventually take over from me and dictate their own fate. I write in the hope that I may open people's eyes to certain situations, expose them to certain feelings and ways of thinking, sometimes in the context of extreme conditions like war and blatant oppression. At the same time I write to arouse some kind of response from those who feel the same way as [I do].
>
> I wrote "The Unseeing Eye" to show how people who are very close to one another take each other for granted. In particular, I was thinking about how men are sometimes not very curious about the women they share their lives with, while I cannot imagine a woman who has not observed her partner's features so closely that she knows them by heart, even if she is no longer interested in him.
>
> I also wanted to show how custom and habit interfere with and overshadow our lives, while we remain oblivious to their workings.

The Unseeing Eye

The old man stood there at a loss, his sunken eyes staring at the man seated behind the table. Raising his hand, he wiped the sweat from his forehead and heavily wrinkled face. He didn't use the traditional kerchief and headband though he could feel the sweat running down from his temples and neck, and he gave no reply to the man seated behind the table who went on asking him, "Why did you go in opening all the doors of the wards looking for your wife? Why didn't you come directly to Enquiries?" The old man kept silent. Why, though, was the man seated behind the table continuing to open one drawer after another? His eyes busy watching him, he said, "I came here the day before yesterday wanting the hospital and looking for the mother of my children."

The man seated behind the table muttered irritably, blaming himself for not having ever learnt how to ask the right questions, how to get a conversation going, and why it was that his questions, full of explanations, and sometimes of annoyance, weren't effective. He puffed at his cigarette as he enquired in exasperation, "What's your wife's name?" The old man at once replied, "Zeinab Mohamed." The man seated behind the table began flipping through the pages of the thick ledger; each time he turned over a page there was a loud noise that was heard by everyone sitting in the waiting-room. He went on flipping through the pages of his ledger, pursing his lips listlessly, then nervously, as he kept bringing the ledger close to his face until finally he said, "Your wife came in here the day before yesterday?" The old man in relief at once answered, "Yes, sir, when her heart came to a stop." Once again irritated, the man behind the table mumbled to himself, "Had her heart stopped she wouldn't be here, neither would you." With his eyes still on the ledger, he said, "She's in Ward 4, but it's not permitted for you to enter her ward because there are other women there." Yawning, he called to the nurse leaning against the wall. She came forward, in her hand a paper cup from which she was drinking. Motioning with his head to the man, he said, "Ward Number 4—Zeinab Mohamed." The nurse walked ahead, without raising her mouth from the cup. The old man asked himself how it was that this woman worked in a hospital that was crammed with men, even though she spoke Arabic. Having arrived at the ward, the nurse left him outside after telling him to wait; then, after a while, she came out and said to him, "There are two women called Zeinab Mohamed. One of them, though, has only one eye. Which one is your wife so that I can call her?"

The old man was thrown into confusion. One eye? How am I to know? He tried to recall what his wife Zeinab looked like, with her long gown and black headdress, the veil, and sometimes the black covering enveloping her face and sometimes removed and laying on her neck. He could picture her as she walked and sat, chewing a morsel and then taking it out of her mouth so as to place it in that of her first-born. Her children. One eye. How am I to know? He could picture her stretched out on the bed, her eyes closed. The old man was thrown into confusion and found himself saying, "When I call her she'll know my voice." The nurse doubted whether he was in fact visiting his wife; however, giving him another glance, she laughed at her suspicions and asked him, "How long have the two of you been married?" Again he was confused as he said, "Allah knows best—thirty, forty years. . . ."

[1989]

Translated by
DENYS JOHNSON-DAVIES

QUESTIONS

1. It can be argued that Islamic tradition has created the situation depicted in "The Unseeing Eye": men have a lesser understanding of women than their counterparts have in the West. Do you think the author favors such an interpretation of her story?
2. Is the hospital setting crucial to our understanding of the story? Does it help to explain the husband's confusion?
3. Does the suggestion of distorted vision and understanding apply to anyone besides the husband?

Rudolfo A. Anaya

(b. 1937)

United States

Rudolfo A. Anaya grew up in New Mexico, where he attended the University of New Mexico and subsequently joined the faculty of the Department of English. He is the author of *Bless Me, Ultima* (1972), the classic novel of Chicano childhood. In this richly evocative story, a young boy named Tony comes to understand the delicate balance between good and evil. Guided in his education by the *curandera* (folkhealer) Ultima, Tony develops an understanding of the fusion in modern day Chicano life between the Church (Catholicism) and the traditional mysteries of the past. In subsequent novels (*Heart of Aztlan*, 1978, and *Tortuga*, 1979), short stories, and essays, Anaya has established himself as the leading Mexican-American writer of his generation, writing in English rather than Spanish. He has received numerous honors for his work. In 1980, he was invited by presidential invitation to read from his work at the White House, during a National Salute to American Poets and Writers.

The following story—perhaps Anaya's major statement on his role as a writer—is best understood if we examine the old man's remarks at the end: ". . . a writer's job is to find and follow people like Justino. They're the source of life. . . . They may be illiterate, but they understand our descent into the pozo of hell, and they understand us because they're willing to share the adventure with us. You seek fame and notoriety and you're dead as a writer."

Rudolfo A. Anaya wrote the following introduction especially for *Worlds of Fiction*:

> This story had an exciting and mysterious birth. In the summer of 1979 I set out for Cuernavaca with *mi madre mexicana*, Ana Rosinski. I was finished with my classes at the university and my wife was still teaching, so Ana and I went on ahead. To travel with a woman who escaped the Nazi occupation of Germany and who knew well the Mexican hustle is to travel in realms which lend themselves to story.
>
> The events in the story are very much as I recall them. I began drinking beer in the train station in Juarez, but there is no train to Cuernavaca, so we gave up on a train and decided on the midnight flight to Mexico City. I began dreaming of B. Traven. In search of treasure, you see, but my treasure is the story I feel growing inside.
>
> Coincidence piles on coincidence. The gardener at San Miquelito is new, and he is a storyteller. We trade stories and he becomes the gardener of the story. I don't know what I become in his story. My wife arrives, and Ana throws a small reception for us. To introduce the Chicano writer to the Cuernavaca writers. I am only thinking of B. Traven, and the treasure at the

foot of Popo, the mysterious volcano one can see from Cuernavaca on a clear day.

From Traven, and my many observations, I understand the reality and poverty and the class system of Mexico. The revolution still barks at the door. From its people I understand love and joy and the magic of storytelling. I tried to incorporate both in the story, and to tell within the story the conception and gestation of a story. Stories like this allow me to get deep into the stream of magical realism. (Rudolfo A. Anaya, copyright 1992)

B. Traven Is Alive and Well in Cuernavaca

I didn't go to Mexico to find B. Traven. Why should I? I have enough to do writing my own fiction, so I go to Mexico to write, not to search out writers. B. Traven? you ask. Don't you remember THE TREASURE OF THE SIERRA MADRE? A real classic. They made a movie from the novel. I remember seeing it when I was kid. It was set in Mexico, and it had all the elements of a real adventure story. B. Traven was an adventurous man, traveled all over the world, then disappeared into Mexico and cut himself off from society. He gave no interviews and allowed few photographs. While he lived he remained unapproachable, anonymous to his public, a writer shrouded in mystery.

He's dead now, or they say he's dead. I think he's alive and well. At any rate, he has become something of an institution in Mexico, a man honored for his work. The cantineros and taxi drivers in Mexico City know about him as well as the cantineros of Spain knew Hemingway, or they claim to. I never mention I'm a writer when I'm in a cantina, because inevitably some aficionado will ask, "Do you know the work of B. Traven?" And from some dusty niche will appear a yellowed, thumbworn novel by Traven. Thus if the cantinero knows his business, and they all do in Mexico, he is apt to say "Did you know that B. Traven used to drink here?" If you show the slightest interest, he will follow with, "Sure, he used to sit right over here. In this corner. . . ." And if you don't leave right then you will wind up hearing many stories about the mysterious B. Traven while buying many drinks for the local patrons.

Everybody reads his novels, on the buses, on street corners; if you look closely you'll spot one of his titles. One turned up for me, and that's how this story started. I was sitting in the train station in Juárez, waiting for the train to Cuernavaca, which would be an exciting title for this story except that there is no train to Cuernavaca. I was drinking beer to kill time, the erotic and sensitive Mexican time which is so different from the clean-packaged, well-kept time of the Americanos. Time in Mexico can be cruel and punishing, but it is never indifferent. It permeates everything, it changes reality. Einstein would have loved Mexico because there time and space are one. I stare more often into empty space when I'm in Mexico. The past seems to infuse the present, and in the brown, wrinkled faces of the old people one sees the presence of the past. In Mexico I like to walk the narrow streets of the cities and the smaller pueblos, wandering aimlessly, feeling the sunlight which is so distinctively Mexican, listening to the voices which call in the streets, peering into the dark eyes which are so secretive and proud. The Mexican people guard a secret. But in the end, one is never really lost in Mexico. All streets lead to a good cantina. All good stories start in a cantina.

At the train station, after I let the kids who hustle the tourists know that I didn't want chewing gum or cigarettes, and I didn't want my shoes shined, and I didn't want a woman at the moment, I was left alone to drink my beer. Luke-cold Dos Equis. I don't remember how long I had been there or how many Dos Equis I had finished when I glanced at the seat next to me and saw a book which turned out to be a B. Traven novel, old and used and obviously much read, but a novel nevertheless. What's so strange about finding a B. Traven novel in that dingy little corner of a bar in the Juárez train station? Nothing, unless you know that in Mexico one never finds anything. It is a country that doesn't waste anything, everything is recycled. Chevrolets run with patched up Ford engines and Chrysler transmissions, buses are kept together, and kept running, with baling wire and home-made parts, yesterday's Traven novel is the pulp on which tomorrow's Fuentes story will appear. Time recycles in Mexico. Time returns to the past, and the Christian finds himself dreaming of ancient Aztec rituals. He who does not believe that Quetzalcoatl will return to save Mexico has little faith.

So the novel was the first clue. Later there was Justino. "Who is Justino?" you want to know. Justino was the jardinero who cared for the garden of my friend, the friend who had invited me to stay at his home in Cuernavaca while I continued to write. The day after I arrived I was sitting in the sun, letting the fatigue of the long journey ooze away, thinking nothing, when Justino appeared on the scene. He had finished cleaning the swimming pool and was taking his morning break, so he sat in the shade of the orange tree and introduced himself. Right away I could tell that he would rather be a movie actor or an adventurer, a real free spirit. But things didn't work out for him. He got married, children appeared, he took a couple of mistresses, more children appeared, so he had to work to support his family. "A man is like a rooster," he said after we talked awhile, "the more chickens he has the happier he is." Then he asked me what I was going to do about a woman while I was there, and I told him I hadn't thought that far ahead, that I would be happy if I could just get a damned story going. This puzzled Justino, and I think for a few days it worried him. So on Saturday night he took me out for a few drinks and we wound up in some of the bordellos of Cuernavaca in the company of some of the most beautiful women in the world. Justino knew them all. They loved him, and he loved them.

I learned something more of the nature of this jardinero a few nights later when the heat and an irritating mosquito wouldn't let me sleep. I heard music from a radio, so I put on my pants and walked out into the Cuernavacan night, an oppressive, warm night heavy with the sweet perfume of the dama de la noche bushes which lined the wall of my friend's villa. From time to time I heard a dog cry in the distance, and I remembered that in Mexico many people die of rabies. Perhaps that is why the walls of the wealthy are always so high and the locks always secure. Or maybe it was because of the occasional gunshots that explode in the night. The news media tell us that Mexico is the most stable country in Latin America and, with the recent oil finds, the bankers and the oil men want to keep it that way. I sense, and many know, that in the dark the revolution does not sleep. It is a spirit kept at bay by the high fences and the locked gates, yet it prowls the heart of every man. "Oil will create a new revolution," Justino had told me, "but it's going to be for our people. Mexicans are tired of building gas stations for the Gringos from Gringolandia." I understood what he meant: there is much hunger in the country.

I lit a cigarette and walked toward my friend's car, which was parked in the driveway near the swimming pool. I approached quietly and peered in. On the back seat with his legs propped on the front seat-back and smoking a cigar sat Justino. Two big, luscious women sat on either side of him running their fingers through his hair and whispering in his ears. The doors were open to allow a breeze. He looked content. Sitting there he was that famous artist on his way to an afternoon reception in Mexico City, or he was a movie star on his way to the premiere of his most recent movie. Or perhaps it was Sunday and he was taking a Sunday drive in the country, towards Tepoztlán. And why shouldn't his two friends accompany him? I had to smile. Unnoticed I backed away and returned to my room. So there was quite a bit more than met the eye to this short, dark Indian from Ocosingo.

In the morning I asked my friend, "What do you know about Justino?"

"Justino? You mean Vitorino."

"Is that his real name?"

"Sometimes he calls himself Trinidad."

"Maybe his name is Justino Vitorino Trinidad," I suggested.

"I don't know, don't care," my friend answered. "He told me he used to be a guide in the jungle. Who knows? The Mexican Indian has an incredible imagination. Really gifted people. He's a good jardinero, and that's what matters to me. It's difficult to get good jardineros, so I don't ask questions."

"Is he reliable?" I wondered aloud.

"As reliable as a ripe mango," my friend nodded.

I wondered how much he knew, so I pushed a little further. "And the radio at night?"

"Oh, that. I hope it doesn't bother you. Robberies and break-ins are increasing here in the colonia. Something we never used to have. Vitorino said that if he keeps the radio on low the sound keeps thieves away. A very good idea, don't you think?"

I nodded. A very good idea.

"And I sleep very soundly," my friend concluded, "so I never hear it."

The following night when I awakened and heard the soft sound of music from the radio and heard the splashing of water, I had only to look from my window to see Justino and his friends in the pool, swimming nude in the moonlight. They were joking and laughing softly as they splashed each other, being quiet so as not to awaken my friend, the patrón who slept so soundly. The women were beautiful. Brown skinned and glistening with water in the moonlight they reminded me of ancient Aztec maidens, swimming around Chac, their god of rain. They teased Justino, and he smiled as he floated on a rubber mattress in the middle of the pool, smoking his cigar, happy because they were happy. When he smiled the gold fleck of a filling glinted in the moonlight.

"¡Qué cabrón!" I laughed and closed my window.

Justino said a Mexican never lies. I believed him. If a Mexican says he will meet you at a certain time and place, he means he will meet you sometime at some place. Americans who retire in Mexico often complain of maids who swear they will come to work on a designated day, then don't show up. They did not lie, they knew they couldn't be at work, but they knew to tell the señora otherwise would make her sad or displease her, so they agree on a date so everyone would remain happy. What a beautiful aspect of character. It's a real virtue which Norteamericanos interpret as a fault in their character, because we are used to asserting ourselves on time and people. We feel secure and comfortable only when everything is neatly packaged in its proper time and place. We don't like the disorder of a free-flowing life.

Some day, I thought to myself, Justino will give a grand party in the sala of his patrón's home. His three wives, or his wife and two mistresses, and his dozens of children will be there. So will the women from the bordellos. He will preside over the feast, smoke his cigars, request his favorite beer-drinking songs from the mariachis, smile, tell stories and make sure everyone has a grand time. He will be dressed in a tuxedo, borrowed from the patrón's closet of course, and he will act gallant and show everyone that a man who has just come into sudden wealth should share it with his friends. And in the morning he will report to the patrón that something has to be done about the poor mice that are coming in out of the streets and eating everything in the house.

"I'll buy some poison," the patrón will suggest.

"No, no," Justino will shake his head, "a little music from the radio and a candle burning in the sala will do."

And he will be right.

I liked Justino. He was a rogue with class. We talked about the weather, the lateness of the rainy season, women, the role of oil in Mexican politics. Like other workers, he believed nothing was going to filter down to the campesinos. "We could all be real Mexican greasers with all that oil," he said, "but the politicians will keep it all."

"What about the United States?" I asked.

"Oh, I have traveled in the estados unidos to the north. It's a country that's going to the dogs in a worse way than Mexico. The thing I liked the most was your cornflakes."

"Cornflakes?"

"Sí. You can make really good cornflakes."

"And women?"

"Ah, you better keep your eyes open, my friend. Those gringas are going to change the world just like the Suecas changed Spain."

"For better or for worse?"

"Spain used to be a nice country," he winked.

We talked, we argued, we drifted from subject to subject. I learned from him. I had been there a week when he told the story which eventually led me to B. Traven. One day I was sitting under the orange tree reading the B. Traven novel I had found in the Juarez train station, keeping one eye on the ripe oranges which fell from time to time, my mind wandering as it worked to focus on a story so I could begin to write. After all, that's why I had come to Cuernavaca, to get some writing done, but nothing was coming, nothing. Justino wandered by and asked what I was reading and replied it was an adventure story, a story of a man's search for the illusive pot of gold at the end of a make-believe rainbow. He nodded, thought awhile and gazed toward Popo, Popocatepetl, the towering volcano which lay to the south, shrouded in mist, waiting for the rains as we waited for the rains, sleeping, gazing at his female counterpart, Itza, who lay sleeping and guarding the valley of Cholula, there, where over four hundred years ago Cortés showed his wrath and executed thousands of Cholulans.

"I am going on an adventure," he finally said and paused. "I think you might like to go with me."

I said nothing, but I put my book down and listened.

"I have been thinking about it for a long time, and now is the time to go. You see, it's like this. I grew up on the hacienda of Don Francisco Jimenez, it's to the south, just a day's drive on the carretera. In my village nobody likes Don Francisco, they fear and hate him. He has killed many men and he has taken their fortunes and buried them. He is a very rich man, muy rico. Many men have tried to kill him, but Don Francisco is like the devil, he kills them first."

I listened as I always listen, because one never knows when a word or phrase or an idea will be the seed from which a story sprouts, but at first there was nothing interesting. It sounded like the typical patrón-peón story I had heard so many times before. A man, the patrón, keeps the workers enslaved, in serfdom, and because he wields so much power soon stories are told about him and he begins to acquire super-human powers. He acquires a mystique, just like the divine right of old. The patrón wields a mean machete, like old King Arthur swung Excaliber. He chops off heads of dissenters and sits on top of the bones and skulls pyramid, the king of the mountain, the top macho.

"One day I was sent to look for lost cattle," Justino continued. "I rode back into the hills where I had never been. At the foot of a hill, near a ravine, I saw something move in the bush. I dismounted and moved forward quietly. I was afraid it might be bandidos who steal cattle, and if they saw me they would kill me. When I came near the place I heard a strange sound. Somebody was crying. My back shivered, just like a dog when he sniffs the devil at night. I thought I was going to see witches, brujas who like to go to those deserted places to dance for the devil, or la Llorona."

"La Llorona," I said aloud. My interest grew. I had been hearing Llorona stories since I was a kid, and I was always ready for one more. La Llorona was that archetypal woman of ancient legends who murdered her children then, repentant and demented, she has spent the rest of eternity searching for them.

"Sí, la Llorona. You know that poor woman used to drink a lot. She played around with men, and when she had babies she got rid of them by throwing them into la barranca. One day she realized what she had done and went crazy. She started crying and pulling her hair and running up and down the side of cliffs of the river looking for her children. It's a very sad story."

A new version, I thought, and yes, a sad story. And what of the men who made love to the woman who became la Llorona, I wondered? Did they ever cry for their children? It doesn't seem fair to have only her suffer, only her crying and doing penance. Perhaps a man should run with her, and in our legends we would call him "El Mero Chingón," he who screwed up everything. Then maybe the tale of love and passion and the insanity it can bring will be complete. Yes, I think someday I will write that story.

"What did you see?" I asked Justino.

"Something worse than la Llorona," he whispered.

To the south a wind mourned and moved the clouds off Popo's crown. The bald, snow-covered mountain thrust its power into the blue Mexican sky. The light glowed like liquid gold around the god's head. Popo was a god, an ancient god. Somewhere at his feet Justino's story had taken place.

"I moved closer, and when I parted the bushes I saw Don Francisco. He was sitting on a rock, and he was crying. From time to time he looked at the ravine in front of him, the hole seemed to slant into the earth. That pozo is called el Pozo de Mendoza. I had heard stories about it before, but I had never seen it. I looked into the pozo, and you wouldn't believe what I saw."

He waited, so I asked, "What?"

"Money! Huge piles of gold and silver coins! Necklaces and bracelets and crowns of gold, all loaded with all kinds of precious stones! Jewels! Diamonds! All sparkling in the sunlight that entered the hole. More money than I have ever seen! A fortune, my friend, a fortune which is still there, just waiting for two adventurers like us to take it!"

"Us? But what about Don Francisco? It's his land, his fortune."

"Ah," Justino smiled, "that's the strange thing about this fortune. Don Francisco can't touch it, that's why he was crying. You see, I stayed there, and watched him closely. Every time he stood up and started to walk into the pozo the money disappeared. He stretched out his hand to grab the gold, and poof, it was gone! That's why he was crying! He murdered all those people and hid their wealth in the pozo, but now he can't touch it. He is cursed."

"El Pozo de Mendoza," he said aloud. Something began to click in my mind. I smelled a story.

"Who was Mendoza?" I asked.

"He was a very rich man. Don Francisco killed him in a quarrel they had over some cattle. But Mendoza must have put a curse on Don Francisco before he died, because now Don Francisco can't get to the money."

"So Mendoza's ghost haunts old Don Francisco," I nodded.

"Many ghosts haunt him," Justino answered. "He has killed many men."

"And the fortune, the money. . . ."

He looked at me and his eyes were dark and piercing. "It's still there. Waiting for us!"

"But it disappears as one approaches it, you said so yourself. Perhaps it's only an hallucination."

Justino shook his head. "No, it's real gold and silver, not hallucination money. It disappears for Don Francisco because the curse is on him, but the curse is not on us." He smiled. He knew he had drawn me into his plot. "We didn't steal the money, so it won't disappear for us. And you are not connected with the place. You are innocent. I've thought very carefully about it, and now is the time to go. I can lower you into the pozo with a rope, in a few hours we can bring out the entire fortune. All we need is a car. You can borrow the patrón's car, he is your friend. But he must not know where we're going. We can be there and back in one day, one night." He nodded as if to assure me, then he turned and looked at the sky. "It will not rain today. It will not rain for a week. Now is the time to go."

He winked and returned to watering the grass and flowers of the jardín, a wild Pan among the bougainvillea and the roses, a man possessed by a dream. The gold was not for him, he told me the next day, it was for his women, he would buy them all gifts, bright dresses, and he would take them on vacation to the United States, he would educate his children, send them to the best colleges. I listened and the germ of the story cluttered my thoughts as I sat beneath the orange tree in the mornings. I couldn't write, nothing was coming, but I knew that there were elements for a good story in Justino's tale. In dreams I saw the lonely hacienda to the south. I saw the pathetic, tormented figure of Don Francisco as he cried over the fortune he couldn't touch. I saw the ghosts of the men he had killed, the lonely women who mourned over them and cursed the evil Don Francisco. In one dream I saw a man I took to be B. Traven, a grey-haired distinguished looking gentlemen who looked at me and nodded approvingly. "Yes, there's a story there, follow it, follow it. . . ."

In the meantime, other small and seemingly insignificant details came my way. During a luncheon at the home of my friend, a woman I did not know leaned toward me and asked me if I would like to meet the widow of B. Traven. The woman's hair was tinged orange, her complexion was ashen grey. I didn't know who she was or why she would mention B. Traven to me. How did she know Traven had come to haunt my thoughts? Was she a clue, which would help unravel the mystery? I didn't know, but I nodded. Yes, I would like to meet her. I had heard that Traven's widow, Rosa Elena, lived in Mexico City. But what would I ask her? What did I want to know? Would she know Traven's secret? Somehow he had learned that to keep his magic intact he had to keep away from the public. Like the fortune in the pozo, the magic feel for the story might disappear if unclean hands reached for it. I turned to look at the woman, but she was gone. I wandered to the terrace to finish my beer. Justino sat beneath the orange tree. He yawned. I knew the literary talk bored him. He was eager to be on the way to el Pozo de Mendoza.

I was nervous, too, but I didn't know why. The tension for the story was there, but something was missing. Or perhaps it was just Justino's insistence that I decide whether I was going or not that drove me out of the house in the mornings. Time usually devoted to writing found me in a small cafe in the center of town. From there I could watch the shops open, watch the people cross the zócalo, the main square. I drank lots of coffee, I smoked a lot, I daydreamed, I wondered about the significance of the pozo, the fortune, Justino, the story I wanted to write about B. Traven. In one of these moods I saw a friend from whom I hadn't heard in years. Suddenly he was there, trekking across the square, dressed like an old rabbi, moss and green algae for a beard, and followed by a troop of very dignified Lacandones, Mayan Indians from Chiapas.

"Victor," I gasped, unsure if he was real or a part of the shadows which the sun created as it flooded the square with its light.

"I have no time to talk," he said as he stopped to munch on my pan dulce and sip my coffee. "I only want you to know, for purposes of your story, that I was in a Lacandonian village last month, and a Hollywood film crew descended from the sky. They came in helicopters. They set up tents near the village, and big-bosomed, bikined actresses emerged from them, tossed themselves on the cut trees which are the atrocity of the giant American lumber companies, and they cried while the director shot his film. Then they produced a grey-haired old man from one of the tents and took shots of him posing with the Indians. Herr Traven, the director called him."

He finished my coffee, nodded to his friends and they began to walk away.

"B. Traven?" I asked.

He turned. "No, an imposter, an actor. Be careful for imposters. Remember, even Traven used many disguises, many names!"

"Then he's alive and well?" I shouted. People around me turned to stare.

"His spirit is with us," were the last words I heard as they moved across the zócalo, a strange troop of near naked Lacandon Mayans and my friend the Guatemalan Jew, returning to the rain forest, returning to the primal, innocent land.

I slumped in my chair and looked at my empty cup. What did it mean? As their trees fall the Lacandones die. Betrayed as B. Traven was betrayed. Does each one of us also die as the trees fall in the dark depths of the Chiapas jungle? Far to the north, in Aztlán, it is the same where the earth is ripped open to expose and mine the yellow uranium. A few poets sing songs and stand in the way as the giant machines of the corporations rumble over the land and grind everything into dust. New holes are made in the earth, pozos full of curses, pozos with fortunes we cannot touch, should not touch. Oil, coal, uranium, from holes in the earth through which we suck the blood of the earth.

There were other incidents. A telephone call late one night, a voice with a German accent called my name, and when I answered the line went dead. A letter addressed to B. Traven came in the mail. It was dated March 26, 1969. My friend returned it to the post office. Justino grew more and more morose. He was under the orange tree and stared into space, my friend complained about the garden drying up. Justino looked at me and scowled. He did a little work then went back to daydreaming. Without the rains the garden withered. His heart was set on the adventure which lay at el pozo. Finally I said yes, dammit, why not, let's go, neither one of us is getting anything done here, and Justino cheering like a child, ran to prepare for the trip. But when I asked my friend for the weekend loan of the car he reminded me that we were invited to a tertulia, an afternoon reception, at the home of Señora Ana R. Many writers and artists would be there. It was in my honor, so I could meet the literati of Cuernavaca. I had to tell Justino I couldn't go.

Now it was I who grew morose. The story growing within would not let me sleep. I awakened in the night and looked out the window, hoping to see Justino and women bathing in the pool, enjoying themselves. But all was quiet. No radio played. The still night was warm and heavy. From time to time gunshots sounded in the dark, dogs barked, and the presence of a Mexico which never sleeps closed in on me.

Saturday morning dawned with a strange overcast. Perhaps the rains will come, I thought. In the afternoon I reluctantly accompanied my friend to the reception. I had not seen Justino all day, but I saw him at the gate as we drove out. He looked tired, as if he, too, had not slept. He wore the white shirt and baggy pants of a campesino. His straw hat cast a shadow over his eyes. I wondered if he had decided to go to the pozo alone. He didn't speak as we drove through the gate, he only nodded. When I looked back I saw him standing by the gate, looking after the car, and I had a vague, uneasy feeling that I had lost an opportunity.

The afternoon gathering was a pleasant affair, attended by a number of affectionate artists, critics, and writers who enjoyed the refreshing drinks which quenched the thirst.

But my mood drove me away from the crowd. I wandered around the terrace and found a foyer surrounded by green plants, huge fronds and ferns and flowering bougainvillea. I pushed the green aside and entered a quiet, very private alcove. The light was dim, the air was cool, a perfect place for contemplation. At first I thought I was alone, then I saw the man sitting in one of the wicker chairs next to a small, wrought iron table. He was an elderly white-haired gentlemen. His face showed he had lived a full life, yet he was still very distinguished in his manner and posture. His eyes shone brightly.

"Perdón," I apologized and turned to leave. I did not want to intrude.

"No, no, please," he motioned to the empty chair, "I've been waiting for you." He spoke English with a slight German accent. Or perhaps it was Norwegian, I couldn't tell the difference. "I can't take the literary gossip. I prefer the quiet."

I nodded and sat. He smiled and I felt at ease. I took the cigar he offered and we lit up. He began to talk and I listened. He was a writer also, but I had the good manners not to ask his titles. He talked about the changing Mexico, the change the new oil would bring, the lateness of the rains and how they affected the people and the land, and he talked about how important a woman was in a writer's life. He wanted to know about me, about the Chicanos of Aztlán, about our work. It was the workers, he said, who would change society. The artist learned from the worker. I talked, and sometime during the conversation I told him the name of the friend with whom I was staying. He laughed and wanted to know if Vitorino was still working for him.

"Do you know Justino?" I asked.

"Oh, yes, I know that old guide. I met him many years ago, when I first came to Mexico," he answered. "Justino knows the campesino very well. He and I traveled many places together, he in search of adventure, I in search of stories."

I thought the coincidence strange, so I gathered the courage and asked, "Did he ever tell you the story of the fortune at el Pozo de Mendoza?"

"Tell me?" the old man smiled. "I went there."

"With Justino?"

"Yes, I went with him. What a rogue he was in those days, but a good man. If I remember correctly I even wrote a story based on that adventure. Not a very good story. Never came to anything. But we had a grand time. People like Justino are the writer's source. We met interesting people and saw fabulous places, enough to last me a lifetime. We were supposed to be gone for one day, but we were gone nearly three years. You see, I wasn't interested in the pots of gold he kept saying were just over the next hill, I went because there was a story to write."

"Yes, that's what interested me," I agreed.

"A writer has to follow a story if it leads him to hell itself. That's our curse. Ay, and each one of us knows our own private hell."

I nodded. I felt relieved. I sat back to smoke the cigar and sip from my drink. Somewhere to the west the sun bronzed the evening sky. On a clear afternoon, Popo's crown would glow like fire.

"Yes," the old man continued, "a writer's job is to find and follow people like Justino. They're the source of life. The ones you have to keep away from are the dilettantes like the ones in there." He motioned in the general direction of the noise of the party. "I stay with people like Justino. They may be illiterate, but they understand our descent into the pozo of hell, and they understand us because they're willing to share the adventure with us. You seek fame and notoriety and you're dead as a writer."

I sat upright. I understood now what the pozo meant, why Justino had come into my life to tell me the story. It was clear. I rose quickly and shook the old man's hand. I turned and parted the palm leaves of the alcove. There, across the way, in one of the streets that led out of the maze of the town towards the south, I saw Justino. He was walking in the direction of Popo, and he was followed by women and children, a rag-tail army of adventurers, all happy, all singing. He looked up to where I stood on the terrace, and he smiled as he waved. He paused to light the stub of a cigar. The women turned, and the children turned, and all waved to me. Then they continued their walk, south, towards the foot of the volcano. They were going to the Pozo de Mendoza, to the place where the story originated.

I wanted to run after them, to join them in the glorious light which bathed the Cuernavaca valley and the majestic snow-covered head of Popo. The light was everywhere, a magnetic element which flowed from the clouds. I waved as Justino and his followers disappeared in the light. Then I turned to say something to the old man, but he was gone. I was alone in the alcove. Somewhere in the background I heard the tinkling of glasses and the laughter which came from the party, but that was not for me. I left the terrace and crossed the lawn, found the gate and walked down the street. The sound of Mexico filled the air. I felt light and happy. I wandered aimlessly through the curving, narrow streets, then I quickened my pace because suddenly the story was overflowing and I needed to write. I needed to get to my quiet room and write the story about B. Traven being alive and well in Cuernavaca.

[1984]

QUESTIONS

1. What is the source of conflict in Anaya's story? Is it the same thing that connects the three parts of his narrative: the search for B. Traven, Justino's account of the gold, and the writer's search for material?
2. At the end of the story, we have a strong impression of Justino Victorio Trinidad, the jardinero, but what do we know of the writer himself? How may the two characters be compared?
3. Is it B. Traven who appears at the conclusion of the story?
4. What does Anaya mean when he states, early in the narrative, that "Time in Mexico can be cruel and punishing, but it is never indifferent. It permeates everything, it changes reality. Einstein would have loved Mexico because there time and space are one"? How does this statement expand our understanding of the story that follows?

Sherwood Anderson

(1876–1941)

United States

Sherwood Anderson's voice is utterly distinctive in American literature. Growing up in the midwest—Camden, Ohio—he discovered that voice through listening and shaping the stories and narratives of small-town and rural life. His most highly regarded collection of stories, *Winesburg, Ohio* (1919), is a deeply sympathetic portrait of an entire community: simple people often caught in lives that they do not fully understand and are powerless to change. Many of Anderson's stories seem to hover around the unanswered question, Why?

Anderson came to fiction late, after working in a variety of trades from farm laborer and paint factory worker to advertising copywriter. Unhappy with the commercial life, he went to Chicago, where he found a group of like-minded friends, including Carl Sandburg and Theodore Dreiser, and began to write. Two novels and a volume of poetry preceded his discovery that the short story was his true form. Anderson described his struggle to capture a story in its appropriate form as a difficult gestation process:

> Having, from a conversation overhead or in some other way, got the tone of a tale I was like a woman who has just become impregnated. Something was growing inside me. At night when I lay in my bed I could feel the heels of the tale kicking against the walls of my body. Often as I lay thus every word of the tale came to me quite clearly but when I got out of bed to write it down the words would not come.

If it is not their form that distinguishes Anderson's stories, it is certainly their tone, a characteristic muted melancholy. In "Death in the Woods," as in most of his stories, Anderson conveys with unerring accuracy his characters' despair at failed attachments and lost opportunities.

Death in the Woods

I

She was an old woman and lived on a farm near the town in which I lived. All country and small-town people have seen such old women, but no one knows much about them. Such an old woman comes into town driving an old wornout horse or she comes afoot carrying a basket. She may own a few hens and have eggs to sell. She brings them in a basket and takes them to a grocer. There she trades them in. She gets some salt pork and some beans. Then she gets a pound or two of sugar and some flour.

Afterwards she goes to the butcher's and asks for some dog-meat. She may spend ten or fifteen cents, but when she does she asks for something. Formerly the butchers gave liver to any one who wanted to carry it away. In our family we were always having it. Once one of my brothers got a whole cow's liver at the slaughter-house near the fairgrounds in our town. We had it until we were sick of it. It never cost a cent. I have hated the thought of it ever since.

The old farm woman got some liver and a soup-bone. She never visited with any one, and as soon as she got what she wanted she lit out for home. It made quite a load for such an old body. No one gave her a lift. People drive right down a road and never notice an old woman like that.

There was such an old woman who used to come into town past our house one Summer and Fall when I was a young boy and was sick with what was called inflammatory rheumatism. She went home later carrying a heavy pack on her back. Two or three large gaunt-looking dogs followed at her heels.

The old woman was nothing special. She was one of the nameless ones that hardly any one knows, but she got into my thoughts. I have just suddenly now, after all these years, remembered her and what happened. It is a story. Her name was Grimes, and she lived with her husband and son in a small unpainted house on the bank of a small creek four miles from town.

The husband and son were a tough lot. Although the son was but twenty-one, he had already served a term in jail. It was whispered about that the woman's husband stole horses and ran them off to some other county. Now and then, when a horse turned up missing, the man had also disappeared. No one ever caught him. Once, when I was loafing at Tom Whitehead's livery-barn, the man came there and sat on the bench in front. Two or three other men were there, but no one spoke to him. He sat for a few minutes and then got up and went away. When he was leaving he turned around and stared at the men. There was a look of defiance in his eyes. "Well, I have tried to be friendly. You don't want to talk to me. It has been so wherever I have gone in this town. If, some day, one of your fine horses turns up missing, well, then what?" He did not say anything actually. "I'd like to bust one of you on the jaw," was about what his eyes said. I remember how the look in his eyes made me shiver.

The old man belonged to a family that had had money once. His name was Jake Grimes. It all comes back clearly now. His father, John Grimes, had owned a sawmill when the country was new, and had made money. Then he got to drinking and running after women. When he died there wasn't much left.

Jake blew in the rest. Pretty soon there wasn't any more lumber to cut and his land was nearly all gone.

He got his wife off a German farmer, for whom he went to work one June day in the wheat harvest. She was a young thing then and scared to death. You see, the farmer was up to something with the girl—she was, I think, a bound girl and his wife had her suspicions. She took it out on the girl when the man wasn't around. Then, when the wife had to go off to town for supplies, the farmer got after her. She told young Jake that nothing really ever happened, but he didn't know whether to believe it or not.

He got her pretty easy himself, the first time he was out with her. He wouldn't have married her if the German farmer hadn't tried to tell him where to get off. He got her to go riding with him in his buggy one night when he was threshing on the place, and then he came for her the next Sunday night.

She managed to get out of the house without her employer's seeing, but when she was getting into the buggy he showed up. It was almost dark, and he just popped up suddenly at the horse's head. He grabbed the horse by the bridle and Jake got out his buggy-whip.

They had it out all right! The German was a tough one. Maybe he didn't care whether his wife knew or not. Jake hit him over the face and shoulders with the buggy-whip, but the horse got to acting up and he had to get out.

Then the two men went for it. The girl didn't see it. The horse started to run away and went nearly a mile down the road before the girl got him stopped. Then she managed to tie him to a tree beside the road. (I wonder how I know all this. It must have stuck in my mind from small-town tales when I was a boy.) Jake found her there after he got through with the German. She was huddled up in the buggy seat, crying, scared to death. She told Jake a lot of stuff, how the German had tried to get her, how he chased her once into the barn, how another time, when they happened to be alone in the house together, he tore her dress open clear down the front. The German, she said, might have got her that time if he hadn't heard his old woman drive in at the gate. She had been off to town for supplies. Well, she would be putting the horse in the barn. The German managed to sneak off to the fields without his wife seeing. He told the girl he would kill her if she told. What could she do? She told a lie about ripping her dress in the barn when she was feeding the stock. I remember now that she was a bound girl and did not know where her father and mother were. Maybe she did not have any father. You know what I mean.

Such bound children were often enough cruelly treated. They were children who had no parents, slaves really. There were very few orphan homes then. They were legally bound into some home. It was a matter of pure luck how it came out.

II

She married Jake and had a son and daughter, but the daughter died.

Then she settled down to feed stock. That was her job. At the German's place she had cooked the food for the German and his wife. The wife was a strong woman with big hips and worked most of the time in the fields with her husband. She fed them and fed the cows in the barn, fed the pigs, the horses and chickens. Every moment of every day, as a young girl, was spent feeding something.

Then she married Jake Grimes and he had to be fed. She was a slight thing, and when she had been married for three or four years, and after the two children were born, her slender shoulders became stooped.

Jake always had a lot of big dogs around the house, that stood near the unused sawmill near the creek. He was always trading horses when he wasn't stealing something and had a lot of poor bony ones about. Also he kept three or four pigs and a cow. They were all pastured in the few acres left of the Grimes place and Jake did little enough work.

He went into debt for a threshing outfit and ran it for several years, but it did not pay. People did not trust him. They were afraid he would steal the grain at night. He had to go a long way off to get work and it cost too much to get there. In the Winter he hunted and cut a little firewood, to be sold in some nearby town. When the son grew up he was just like the father. They got drunk together. If there wasn't anything to eat in the house when they came home the old man gave his old woman a cut over the head. She had a few chickens of her own and had to kill one of them in a hurry. When they were all killed she wouldn't have any eggs to sell when she went to town, and then what would she do?

She had to scheme all her life about getting things fed, getting the pigs fed so they would grow fat and could be butchered in the Fall. When they were butchered her husband took most of the meat off to town and sold it. If he did not do it first the boy did. They fought sometimes and when they fought the old woman stood aside trembling.

She had got the habit of silence anyway—that was fixed. Sometimes, when she began to look old—she wasn't forty yet—and when the husband and son were both off, trading horses or drinking or hunting or stealing, she went around the house and the barnyard muttering to herself.

How was she going to get everything fed?—that was her problem. The dogs had to be fed. There wasn't enough hay in the barn for the horses and the cow. If she didn't feed the chickens how could they lay eggs? Without eggs to sell how could she get things in town, things she had to have to keep the life of the farm going? Thank heaven, she did not have to feed her husband—in a certain way. That hadn't lasted long after their marriage and after the babies came. Where he went on his long trips she did not know. Sometimes he was gone from home for weeks, and after the boy grew up they went off together.

They left everything at home for her to manage and she had no money. She knew no one. No one ever talked to her in town. When it was Winter she had to gather sticks of wood for her fire, had to try to keep the stock fed with very little grain.

The stock in the barn cried to her hungrily, the dogs followed her about. In the Winter the hens laid few enough eggs. They huddled in the corners of the barn and she kept watching them. If a hen lays an egg in the barn in the Winter and you don't find it, it freezes and breaks.

One day in Winter the old woman went off to town with a few eggs and the dogs followed her. She did not get started until nearly three o'clock and the snow was heavy. She hadn't been feeling very well for several days and so she went muttering along, scantily clad, her shoulders stooped. She had an old grain bag in which she carried her eggs, tucked away down in the bottom. There weren't many of them, but in Winter the price of eggs is up. She would get a little meat in exchange for the eggs, some salt pork, a little sugar, and some coffee perhaps. It might be the butcher would give her a piece of liver.

When she had got to town and was trading in her eggs the dogs lay by the door outside. She did pretty well, got the things she needed, more than she had hoped. Then she went to the butcher and he gave her some liver and some dog-meat.

It was the first time any one had spoken to her in a friendly way for a long time. The butcher was alone in his shop when she came in and was annoyed by the thought of such a sick-looking old woman out on such a day. It was bitter cold and the snow, that had let up during the afternoon, was falling again. The butcher said something about her husband and her son, swore at them, and the old woman stared at him, a look of mild surprise in her eyes as he talked. He said that if either the husband or the son were going to get any of the liver or the heavy bones with scraps of meat hanging to them that he had put into the grain bag, he'd see him starve first.

Starve, eh? Well, things had to be fed. Men had to be fed, and horses that weren't any good but maybe could be traded off, and the poor thin cow that hadn't given any milk for three months.

Horses, cows, pigs, dogs, men.

III

The old woman had to get back before darkness came if she could. The dogs followed at her heels, sniffing at the heavy grain bag she had fastened on her back. When she got to the edge of town she stopped by a fence and tied the bag on her back with a piece of rope she had carried in her dress-pocket for just that purpose. It was hard when she had to crawl over fences and once she fell over and landed in the snow. The dogs went frisking about. She had to struggle to get to her feet again, but she made it. The point of climbing over the fences was that there was a short cut over a hill and through a woods. She might have gone around by the road, but it was a mile farther that way. She was afraid she couldn't make it. And then, besides, the stock had to be fed. There was a little hay left and a little corn. Perhaps her husband and son would bring some home when they came. They had driven off in the only buggy the Grimes family had, a rickety thing, a rickety horse hitched to the buggy, two other rickety horses led by halters. They were going to trade horses, get a little money if they could. They might come home drunk. It would be well to have something in the house when they came back.

The son had an affair on with a woman at the county seat, fifteen miles away. She was a rough enough woman, a tough one. Once, in the Summer, the son had brought her to the house. Both she and the son had been drinking. Jake Grimes was away and the son and his woman ordered the old woman about like a servant. She didn't mind much; she was used to it. Whatever happened she never said anything. That was her way of getting along. She had managed that way when she was a young girl at the German's and ever since she had married Jake. That time her son brought his woman to the house they stayed all night, sleeping together just as though they were married. It hadn't shocked the old woman, not much. She had got past being shocked early in life.

With the pack on her back she went painfully along across an open field, wading in the deep snow, and got into the woods.

There was a path, but it was hard to follow. Just beyond the top of the hill, where the woods was thickest, there was a small clearing. Had some one once thought of building a house there? The clearing was as large as a building lot in town, large enough for a house and a garden. The path ran along the side of the clearing, and when she got there the old woman sat down to rest at the foot of a tree.

It was a foolish thing to do. When she got herself placed, the pack against the tree's trunk, it was nice, but what about getting up again? She worried about that for a moment and then quietly closed her eyes.

She must have slept for a time. When you are about so cold you can't get any colder. The afternoon grew a little warmer and snow came thicker than ever. Then after a time the weather cleared. The moon even came out.

There were four Grimes dogs that had followed Mrs. Grimes into town, all tall gaunt fellows. Such men as Jake Grimes and his son always keep just such dogs. They kick and abuse them, but they stay. The Grimes dogs, in order to keep from starving, had to do a lot of foraging for themselves, and they had been at it while the old woman slept with her back to the tree at the side of the clearing. They had been chasing rabbits in the woods and in adjoining fields and in their ranging had picked up three other farm dogs.

After a time all the dogs came back to the clearing. They were excited about something. Such nights, cold and clear and with a moon, do things to dogs. It may be that some old instinct, come down from the time when they were wolves and ranged the woods in packs on Winter nights, comes back into them.

The dogs in the clearing, before the old woman, had caught two or three rabbits and their immediate hunger had been satisfied. They began to play, running in circles in the clearing. Round and round they ran, each dog's nose at the tail of the next dog. In the clearing, under the snow-laden trees and under the wintry moon they made a strange picture, running thus silently, in a circle their running had beaten in the soft snow. The dogs made no sound. They ran around and around in the circle.

It may have been that the old woman saw them doing that before she died. She may have awakened once or twice and looked at the strange sight with dim old eyes.

She wouldn't be very cold now, just drowsy. Life hangs on a long time. Perhaps the old woman was out of her head. She may have dreamed of her girlhood at the German's, and before that, when she was a child and before her mother lit out and left her.

Her dreams couldn't have been very pleasant. Not many pleasant things had happened to her. Now and then one of the Grimes dogs left the running circle and came to stand before her. The dog thrust his face to her face. His red tongue was hanging out.

The running of the dogs may have been a kind of death ceremony. It may have been that the primitive instinct of the wolf, having been aroused in the dogs by the night and the running, made them somehow afraid.

"Now we are no longer wolves. We are dogs, the servants of men. Keep alive, man! When man dies we become wolves again." When one of the dogs came to where the old woman sat with her back against the tree and thrust his nose close to her face he seemed satisfied and went back to run with the pack. All the Grimes dogs did it at some time during the evening, before she died. I knew all about it afterward, when I grew to be a man, because once in a woods in Illinois, on another Winter night, I saw a pack of dogs act just like that. The dogs were waiting for me to die as they had waited for the old woman that night when I was a child, but when it happened to me I was a young man and had no intention whatever of dying.

The old woman died softly and quietly. When she was dead and when one of the Grimes dogs had come to her and had found her dead all the dogs stopped running.

They gathered about her.

Well, she was dead now. She had fed the Grimes dogs when she was alive, what about now?

There was the pack on her back, the grain bag containing the piece of salt pork, the liver the butcher had given her, the dog-meat, the soup-bones. The butcher in town, having been suddenly overcome with a feeling of pity, had loaded her grain bag heavily. It had been a big haul for the old woman.

It was a big haul for the dogs now.

IV

One of the Grimes dogs sprang suddenly out from among the others and began worrying the pack on the old woman's back. Had the dogs really been wolves that one would have been the leader of the pack. What he did, all the others did.

All of them sank their teeth into the grain bag the old woman had fastened with the ropes to her back.

They dragged the old woman's body out into the open clearing. The worn-out dress was quickly torn from her shoulders. When she was found, a day or two later, the dress had been torn from her body clear to the hips, but the dogs had not touched her body. They had got the meat out of the grain bag, that was all. Her body was frozen stiff when it was found, and the shoulders were so narrow and the body so slight that in death it looked like the body of some charming young girl.

Such things happened in towns of the Middle West, on farms near town, when I was a boy. A hunter out after rabbits found the old woman's body and did not touch it. Something, the beaten round path in the little snow-covered clearing, the silence of the place, the place where the dogs had worried the body trying to pull the grain bag away or tear it open—something startled the man and he hurried off to town.

I was in Main Street with one of my brothers who was town newsboy and who was taking the afternoon papers to the stores. It was almost night.

The hunter came into a grocery and told his story. Then he went into a hardware-shop and into a drugstore. Men began to gather on the sidewalks. Then they started out along the road to the place in the woods.

My brother should have gone on about his business of distributing papers but he didn't. Every one was going to the woods. The undertaker went and the town marshal. Several men got on a dray and rode out to where the path left the road and went into the woods, but the horses weren't very sharply shod and slid about on the slippery roads. They made no better time than those of us who walked.

The town marshal was a large man whose leg had been injured in the Civil War. He carried a heavy cane and limped rapidly along the road. My brother and I followed at his heels, and as we went other men and boys joined the crowd.

It had grown dark by the time we got to where the old woman had left the road but the moon had come out. The marshal was thinking there might have been a murder. He kept asking the hunter questions. The hunter went along with his gun across his shoulders, a dog following at his heels. It isn't often a rabbit hunter has a chance to be so conspicuous. He was taking full advantage of it, leading the procession with the town marshal. "I didn't see any wounds. She was a beautiful young girl. Her face was buried in the snow. No. I didn't know her." As a matter of fact, the hunter had not looked closely at the body. He had been frightened. She might have been murdered and some one might spring out from behind a tree and murder him. In a woods, in the late afternoon, when the trees are all bare and there is white snow on the ground, when all is silent, something creepy steals over the mind and body. If something strange or uncanny has happened in the neighborhood all you think about is getting away from there as fast as you can.

The crowd of men and boys had got to where the old woman had crossed the field and went, following the marshal and the hunter, up the slight incline and into the woods.

My brother and I were silent. He had his bundle of papers in a bag slung across his shoulder. When he got back to town he would have to go on distributing his papers before he went home to supper. If I went along, as he had no doubt already determined I should, we would both be late. Either mother or our older sister would have to warm our supper.

Well, we would have something to tell. A boy did not get such a chance very often. It was lucky we just happened to go into the grocery when the hunter came in. The hunter was a country fellow. Neither of us had ever seen him before.

Now the crowd of men and boys had got to the clearing. Darkness comes quickly on such Winter nights, but the full moon made everything clear. My brother and I stood near the tree, beneath which the old woman had died.

She did not look old, lying there in that light, frozen and still. One of the men turned her over in the snow and I saw everything. My body trembled with some strange mystical feeling and so did my brother's. It might have been the cold.

Neither of us had ever seen a woman's body before. It may have been the snow, clinging to the frozen flesh, that made it look so white and lovely, so like marble. No woman had come with the party from town; but one of the men, he was the town blacksmith, took off his overcoat and spread it over her. Then he gathered her into his arms and started off to town, all the others following silently. At that time no one knew who she was.

V

I had seen everything, had seen the oval in the snow, like a miniature racetrack, where the dogs had run, had seen how the men were mystified, had seen the white bare young-looking shoulders, had heard the whispered comments of the men.

The men were simply mystified. They took the body to the undertaker's, and when the blacksmith, the hunter, the marshal and several others had got inside they closed the door. If father had been there perhaps he could have got in, but we boys couldn't.

I went with my brother to distribute the rest of his papers and when we got home it was my brother who told the story.

I kept silent and went to bed early. It may have been I was not satisfied with the way he told it.

Later, in the town, I must have heard other fragments of the old woman's story. She was recognized the next day and there was an investigation.

The husband and son were found somewhere and brought to town and there was an attempt to connect them with the woman's death, but it did not work. They had perfect enough alibis.

However, the town was against them. They had to get out. Where they went I never heard.

I remember only the picture there in the forest, the men standing about, the naked girlish-looking figure, face down in the snow, the tracks made by the running dogs and the clear cold Winter sky above. White fragments of clouds were drifting across the sky. They went racing across the little open space among the trees.

The scene in the forest had become for me, without my knowing it, the foundation for the real story I am now trying to tell. The fragments, you see, had to be picked up slowly, long afterwards.

Things happened. When I was a young man I worked on the farm of a German. The hired-girl was afraid of her employer. The farmer's wife hated her.

I saw things at that place. Once later, I had a half-uncanny, mystical adventure with dogs in an Illinois forest on a clear, moon-lit Winter night. When I was a schoolboy, and on a Summer day, I went with a boy friend out along a creek some miles from town and came to the house where the old woman had lived. No one had lived in the house since her death. The doors were broken from the hinges; the window lights were all broken. As the boy and I stood in the road outside, two dogs, just roving farm dogs no doubt, came running around the corner of the house. The dogs were tall, gaunt fellows and came down to the fence and glared through at us, standing in the road.

The whole thing, the story of the old woman's death, was to me as I grew older like music heard from far off. The notes had to be picked up slowly one at a time. Something had to be understood.

The woman who died was one destined to feed animal life. Anyway, that is all she ever did. She was feeding animal life before she was born, as a child, as a young woman working on the farm of the German, after she married, when she grew old and when she died. She fed animal life in cows, in chickens, in pigs, in horses, in dogs, in men. Her daughter had died in childhood and with her one son she had no articulate relations. On the night when she died she was hurrying homeward, bearing on her body food for animal life.

She died in the clearing in the woods and even after her death continued feeding animal life.

You see it is likely that, when my brother told the story, that night when we got home and my mother and sister sat listening, I did not think he got the point. He was too young and so was I. A thing so complete has its own beauty.

I shall not try to emphasize the point. I am only explaining why I was dissatisfied then and have been ever since. I speak of that only that you may understand why I have been impelled to try to tell the simple story over again.

[1933]

QUESTIONS

1. Consider this story as two interwoven stories: that of Mrs. Grimes and that of the narrator himself. In what ways are they related? What does the narrator discover about himself in telling Mrs. Grimes's story?
2. What does the narrator's remark at the end of the story mean: "The woman who died was one destined to feed animal life"?
3. Early in the story Mrs. Grimes is portrayed as an old woman worn down by her life. After her death a hunter who saw her body describes her as "a beautiful young girl"—though the narrator suggests that the hunter might not have looked closely at the body. What is the significance of these contradictory perceptions of Mrs. Grimes?
4. The narrator confesses that he has had a difficult time articulating the meaning of Mrs. Grimes's life and death. In your view, is he successful or not in resolving the questions he raises?

MARGARET ATWOOD

(b. 1939)

CANADA

Widely regarded as one of the most distinguished contemporary writers of Canada, Margaret Atwood is uniquely accomplished and equally at home with poetry and fiction. She has published more than a dozen volumes of poetry—several have been honored with Canada's prestigious Governor-General Award—as well as seven novels and four volumes of short stories to date. Her critical study of Canadian literature, *Survival* (1972), remains an important survey of themes and ideas in a national literary tradition that she helped to establish and identify. She is also artistically talented: she created the illustrations and cover designs for several volumes of her poetry.

Atwood was born in Ottawa, Ontario, one of three siblings; she spent her childhood in the "bush" (rural area) of northern Ontario and Quebec provinces, where her entomologist father conducted his research. Consequently, as she expresses it, "I did not have to go to school full time until I was in grade eight, and I think that was probably a good thing." During those years she wrote poetry, novels, stories, and plays. Subsequently, she attended the University of Toronto, publishing her first volume of poetry the year that she graduated (1962); she received her M.A. in Victorian literature at Harvard. For a time she taught English; since 1972 she has regarded herself as a professional writer. She lives with writer Graeme Gibson and their daughter Jess.

Because Atwood is so prolific in several genres, it is difficult to generalize about her work. Several ideas and themes do recur, however, including explorations of the meaning of "survival," whether understood in political or personal terms; power and victimization; the significance of the past; the dualism or splitness of experience; and the problems of female selfhood. In novels such as *The Edible Woman* (1969), *Surfacing* (1972) and *Lady Oracle* (1976), Atwood explores the dilemmas of inwardly divided female protagonists who struggle to achieve wholeness and to resist the destructive influences of technological and commercial society. *The Handmaid's Tale* (1986) is a chilling dystopian novel of female reproductive oppression, while *Cat's Eye* (1988) focuses retrospectively on the dark side of childhood through the biography of a female painter. Atwood's volumes of poetry range widely in subject, from *The Journals of Susanna Moodie* (1970), based on a historical Canadian pioneer woman, to the cryptic *Two-Headed Poems* (1980).

Atwood is a master of sardonic, wry wit; at the same time her remarkable versatility with language is balanced by strong social commitment. Atwood has described herself as a "pessimistic pantheist," meaning that "God is everywhere, but losing."

Dancing Girls

The first sign of the new man was the knock on the door. It was the landlady, knocking not at Ann's door, as she'd thought, but on the other door, the one east of the bathroom. Knock, knock, knock; then a pause, soft footsteps, the sound of unlocking. Ann, who had been reading a book on canals, put it down and lit herself a cigarette. It wasn't that she tried to overhear: in this house you couldn't help it.

"Hi!" Mrs. Nolan's voice loud, overly friendly. "I was wondering, my kids would love to see your native costume. You think you could put it on, like, and come down?"

A soft voice, unintelligible.

"Gee, that's great! We'd sure appreciate it!"

Closing and locking, Mrs. Nolan slip-slopping along the hall in, Ann knew, her mauve terry-cloth scuffies and flowered housecoat, down the stairs, hollering at her two boys. "You get into this room right now!" Her voice came up through Ann's hot air register as if the grate were a PA system. *It isn't those kids who want to see him*, she thought. *It's her*. She put out the cigarette, reserving the other half for later, and opened her book again. What costume? Which land, this time?

Unlocking, opening, soft feet down the hall. They sounded bare. Ann closed the book and opened her own door. A white robe, the back of a brown head, moving with a certain stealth or caution toward the stairs. Ann went into the bathroom and turned on the light. They would share it; the person in that room always shared her bathroom. She hoped he would be better than the man before, who always seemed to forget his razor and would knock on the door while Ann was having a bath. You wouldn't have to worry about getting raped or anything in this house though, that was one good thing. Mrs. Nolan was better than any burglar alarm, and she was always there.

That one had been from France, studying Cinema. Before him there had been a girl, from Turkey, studying Comparative Literature. Lelah, or that was how it was pronounced. Ann used to find her beautiful long auburn hairs in the washbasin fairly regularly; she'd run her thumb and index finger along them, enviously, before discarding them. She had to keep her own hair chopped off at ear level, as it was brittle and broke easily. Lelah also had a gold tooth, right at the front on the outside where it showed when she smiled. Curiously, Ann was envious of this tooth as well. It and the hair and the turquoise-studded earrings Lelah wore gave her a gypsy look, a wise look that Ann, with her beige eyebrows and delicate mouth, knew she would never be able to develop, no matter how wise she got. She herself went in for "classics," tailored skirts and Shetland sweaters; it was the only look she could carry off. But she and Lelah had been friends, smoking cigarettes in each other's rooms, commiserating with each other about the difficulties of their courses and the loudness of Mrs. Nolan's voice. So Ann was familiar with that room; she knew what it looked like inside and how much it cost. It was no luxury suite, certainly, and she wasn't surprised at the high rate of turnover. It had an even more direct pipeline to the sounds of the Nolan family than hers had. Lelah had left because she couldn't stand the noise.

The room was smaller and cheaper than her room, though painted the same depressing shade of green. Unlike hers, it did not have its own tiny refrigerator, sink and stove; you had to use the kitchen at the front of the house, which had been staked out much earlier by a small enclave of mathematicians, two men and one woman, from Hong Kong. Whoever took that room either had to eat out all the time or run the gamut of their conversation, which even when not in Chinese was so rarefied as to be unintelligible. And you could never find any space in the refrigerator, it was always full of mushrooms. This from Lelah; Ann herself never had to deal with them since she could cook in her own room. She could see them, though, as she went in and out. At mealtimes they usually sat quietly at their kitchen table, discussing surds, she assumed. Ann suspected that what Lelah had really resented about them was not the mushrooms: they simply made her feel stupid.

Every morning, before she left for classes, Ann checked the bathroom for signs of the new man—hairs, cosmetics—but there was nothing. She hardly ever heard him; sometimes there was that soft, barefooted pacing, the click of his lock, but there were no radio noises, no coughs, no conversations. For the first couple of weeks, apart from that one glimpse of a tall, billowing figure, she didn't even see him. He didn't appear to use the kitchen, where the mathematicians continued their mysteries undisturbed; or if he did, he cooked while no one else was there. Ann would have forgotten about him completely if it hadn't been for Mrs. Nolan.

"He's real nice, not like some you get," she said to Ann in her piercing whisper. Although she shouted at her husband, when he was home, and especially at her children, she always whispered when she was talking to Ann, a hoarse, avid whisper, as if they shared disreputable secrets. Ann was standing in front of her door with the room key in her hand, her usual location during these confidences. Mrs. Nolan knew Ann's routine. It wasn't difficult for her to pretend to be cleaning the bathroom, to pop out and waylay Ann, Ajax and rag in hand, whenever she felt she had something to tell her. She was a short, barrel-shaped woman: the top of her head came only to Ann's nose, so she had to look up at Ann, which at these moments made her seem oddly childlike.

"He's from one of them Arabian countries. Though I thought they wore turbans, or not turbans, those white things, like. He just has this funny hat, sort of like the Shriners. He don't look much like an Arab to me. He's got these tattoo marks on his face. . . . But he's real nice."

Ann stood, her umbrella dripping onto the floor, waiting for Mrs. Nolan to finish. She never had to say anything much; it wasn't expected. "You think you could get me the rent on Wednesday?" Mrs. Nolan asked. Three days early; the real point of the conversation, probably. Still, as Mrs. Nolan had said back in September, she didn't have much of anyone to talk to. Her husband was away much of the time and her children escaped outdoors whenever they could. She never went out herself except to shop, and for Mass on Sundays.

"I'm glad it was you took the room," she'd said to Ann. "I can talk to you. You're not, like, foreign. Not like most of them. It was his idea, getting this big house to rent out. Not that he has to do the work or put up with them. You never know what they'll do."

Ann wanted to point out to her that she was indeed foreign, that she was just as foreign as any of the others, but she knew Mrs. Nolan would not understand. It would be like that fiasco in October. *Wear your native costumes.* She had responded to the invitation out of a sense of duty, as well as one of irony. Wait till they get a load of my native costume, she'd thought, contemplating snowshoes and a parka but actually putting on her good blue wool suit. There was only one thing *native costume* reminded her of: the cover picture on the Missionary Sunday School paper they'd once handed out, which showed children from all the countries of the world dancing in a circle around a smiling white-faced Jesus in a bedsheet. That, and the poem in the *Golden Windows Reader*:

Little Indian, Sioux or Cree,
Oh, don't you wish that you were me?

The awful thing, as she told Lelah later, was that she was the only one who'd gone. "She had all this food ready, and not a single other person was there. She was really upset, and I was so embarrassed for her. It was some Friends of Foreign Students thing, just for women: students and the wives of students. She obviously didn't think I was foreign enough, and she couldn't figure out why no one else came." Neither could Ann, who had stayed far too long and had eaten platefuls of crackers and cheese she didn't want in order to soothe her hostess' thwarted sense of hospitality. The woman, who had tastefully-streaked ash-blonde hair and a livingroom filled with polished and satiny traditional surfaces, had alternately urged her to eat and stared at the door, as if expecting a parade of foreigners in their native costumes to come trooping gratefully through it.

Lelah smiled, showing her wise tooth. "Don't they know any better than to throw those things at night?" she said. "Those men aren't going to let their wives go out by themselves at night. And the single ones are afraid to walk on the streets alone, I know I am."

"I'm not," Ann said, "as long as you stay on the main ones, where it's lighted."

"Then you're a fool," Lelah said. "Don't you know there was a girl murdered three blocks from here? Left her bathroom window unlocked. Some man climbed through the window and cut her throat."

"I always carry my umbrella," Ann said. Of course there were certain places where you just didn't go. Scollay Square, for instance, where the prostitutes hung out and you might get followed, or worse. She tried to explain to Lelah that she wasn't used to this, to any of this, that in Toronto you could walk all over the city, well, almost anywhere, and never have any trouble. She went on to say that no one here seemed to understand that she wasn't like them, she came from a different country, it wasn't the same; but Lelah was quickly bored by this. She had to get back to Tolstoy, she said, putting out her cigarette in her unfinished cup of instant coffee. (*Not strong enough for her, I suppose*, Ann thought.)

"You shouldn't worry," she said. "You're well off. At least your family doesn't almost disown you for doing what you want to do." Lelah's father kept writing her letters, urging her to return to Turkey, where the family had decided on the perfect husband for her. Lelah had stalled them for one year, and maybe she could stall them for one more, but that would be her limit. She couldn't possibly finish her thesis in that time.

Ann hadn't seen much of her since she'd moved out. You lost sight of people quickly here, in the ever-shifting population of hopeful and despairing transients.

No one wrote her letters urging her to come home, no one had picked out the perfect husband for her. On the contrary. She could imagine her mother's defeated look, the greying and sinking of her face, if she were suddenly to announce that she was going to quit school, trade in her ambitions for fate, and get married. Even her father wouldn't like it. *Finish what you start*, he'd say, *I didn't and look what happened to me.* The bungalow at the top of Avenue Road, beside a gas station, with the roar of the expressway always there, like the sea, and fumes blighting the Chinese elm hedge her mother had planted to conceal the pumps. Both her brothers had dropped out of high school; they weren't the good students Ann had been. One worked in a print shop now and had a wife; the other had drifted to Vancouver, and no one knew what he did. She remembered her first real boyfriend, beefy, easygoing Bill Decker, with his two-tone car that kept losing the muffler. They'd spent a lot of time parked on side streets, rubbing against each other through all those layers of clothes. But even in that sensual mist, the cocoon of breath and skin they'd spun around each other, those phone conversations that existed as a form of touch, she'd known this was not something she could get too involved in. He was probably flabby by now, settled. She'd had relationships with men since then, but she had treated them the same way. *Circumspect.*

Not that Mrs. Nolan's back room was any step up. Out one window there was a view of the funeral home next door; out the other was the yard, which the Nolan kids had scraped clean of grass and which was now a bog of half-frozen mud. Their dog, a mongrelized German Shepherd, was kept tied there, where the kids alternately hugged and tormented it. ("Jimmy! Donny! Now you leave that dog alone!" "Don't do that, he's filthy! Look at you!" Ann covering her ears, reading about underground malls.) She'd tried to fix the room up, she'd hung a Madras spread as a curtain in front of the cooking area, she'd put up several prints, Braque still-lifes of guitars and soothing Cubist fruit, and she was growing herbs on her windowsill; she needed surroundings that at least tried not to be ugly. But none of these things helped much. At night she wore earplugs. She hadn't known about the scarcity of good rooms, hadn't realized that the whole area was a student slum, that the rents would be so high, the available places so dismal. Next year would be different; she'd get here early and have the pick of the crop. Mrs. Nolan's was definitely a leftover. You could do much better for the money; you could even have a whole apartment, if you were willing to live in the real slum that spread in narrow streets of three-storey frame houses, fading mustard yellow and soot grey, nearer the river. Though Ann didn't think she was quite up to that. Something in one of the good old houses, on a quiet back street, with a little stained glass, would be more like it. Her friend Jetske had a place like that.

But she was doing what she wanted, no doubt of that. In high school she had planned to be an architect, but while finishing the preliminary courses at university she had realized that the buildings she wanted to design were either impossible—who could afford them?—or futile. They would be lost, smothered, ruined by all the other buildings jammed inharmoniously around them. This was why she had decided to go into Urban Design, and she had come here because this school was the best. Or rumoured to be the best. By the time she finished, she intended to be so well-qualified, so armoured with qualifications, that no one back home would dare turn her down for the job she coveted. She wanted to rearrange Toronto. Toronto would do for a start.

She wasn't yet too certain of the specific details. What she saw were spaces, beautiful green spaces, with water flowing through them, and trees. Not big golf-course lawns, though; something more winding, something with sudden turns, private niches, surprising vistas. And no formal flower beds. The houses, or whatever they were, set unobtrusively among the trees, the cars kept . . . where? And where would people shop, and who would live in these places? This was the problem: she could see the vistas, the trees and the streams or canals, quite clearly, but she could never visualize the people. Her green spaces were always empty.

She didn't see her next-door neighbour again until February. She was coming back from the small local supermarket where she bought the food for her cheap, carefully balanced meals. He was leaning in the doorway of what, at home, she would have called a vestibule, smoking a cigarette and staring out at the rain, through the glass panes at the side of the front door. He should have moved a little to give Ann room to put down her umbrella, but he didn't. He didn't even look at her. She squeezed in, shook her deflated umbrella and checked her mail box, which didn't have a key. There weren't usually any letters in it, and today was no exception. He was wearing a white shirt that was too big for him and some greenish trousers. His feet were not bare, in fact he was wearing a pair of prosaic brown shoes. He did have tattoo marks, though, or rather scars, a set of them running across each cheek. It was the first time she had seen him from the front. He seemed a little shorter than he had when she'd glimpsed him heading towards the stairs, but perhaps it was because he had no hat on. He was curved so listlessly against the doorframe, it was almost as if he had no bones.

There was nothing to see through the front of Mrs. Nolan's door except the traffic, sizzling by the way it did every day. He was depressed, it must be that. This weather would depress anyone. Ann sympathized with his loneliness, but she did not wish to become involved in it, implicated by it. She had enough trouble dealing with her own. She smiled at him, though since he wasn't looking at her this smile was lost. She went past him and up the stairs.

As she fumbled in her purse for her key, Mrs. Nolan stumped out of the bathroom. "You see him?" she whispered.

"Who?" Ann said.

"*Him.*" Mrs. Nolan jerked her thumb. "Standing down there, by the door. He does that a lot. He's bothering me, like. I don't have such good nerves."

"He's not doing anything," Ann said.

"That's what I mean," Mrs. Nolan whispered ominously. "He never does nothing. Far as I can tell, he never goes out much. All he does is borrow my vacuum cleaner."

"Your vacuum cleaner?" Ann said, startled into responding.

"That's what I said." Mrs. Nolan had a rubber plunger which she was fingering. "And there's more of them. They come in the other night, up to his room. Two more, with the same marks and everything, on their faces. It's like some kind of, like, a religion or something. And he never gave the vacuum cleaner back till the next day."

"Does he pay the rent?" Ann said, trying to switch the conversation to practical matters. Mrs. Nolan was letting her imagination get out of control.

"Regular," Mrs. Nolan said. "Except I don't like the way he comes down, so quiet like, right into my house. With Fred away so much."

"I wouldn't worry," Ann said in what she hoped was a soothing voice. "He seems perfectly nice."

"It's always that kind," Mrs. Nolan said.

Ann cooked her dinner, a chicken breast, some peas, a digestive biscuit. Then she washed her hair in the bathroom and put it up in rollers. She had to do that, to give it body. With her head encased in the plastic hood of her portable dryer she sat at her table, drinking instant coffee, smoking her usual half cigarette, and attempting to read a book about Roman aqueducts, from which she hoped to get some novel ideas for her current project. (An aqueduct, going right through the middle of the obligatory shopping centre? Would anyone care?) Her mind kept flicking, though, to the problem of the man next door. Ann did not often try to think about what it would be like to be a man. But this particular man . . . Who was he, and what was happening to him? He must be a student, everyone here was a student. And he would be intelligent, that went without saying. Probably on scholarship. Everyone here in the graduate school was on scholarship, except the real Americans, who sometimes weren't. Or rather, the women were, but some of the men were still avoiding the draft, though President Johnson had announced he was going to do away with all that. She herself would never have made it this far without scholarships; her parents could not have afforded it.

So he was here on scholarship, studying something practical, no doubt, nuclear physics or the construction of dams, and, like herself and the other foreigners, he was expected to go away again as soon as he'd learned what he'd come for. But he never went out of the house; he stood at the front door and watched the brutish flow of cars, the winter rain, while those back in his own country, the ones that had sent him, were confidently expecting him to return some day, crammed with knowledge, ready to solve their lives. . . . *He's lost his nerve,* Ann thought. *He'll fail.* It was too late in the year for him ever to catch up. Such failures, such paralyses, were fairly common here, especially among the foreigners. He was far from home, from the language he shared, the wearers of his native costume; he was in exile, he was drowning. What did he do, alone by himself in his room at night?

Ann switched her hair dryer to COOL and wrenched her mind back to aqueducts. She could see he was drowning but there was nothing she could do. Unless you were good at it you shouldn't even try, she was wise enough to know that. All you could do for the drowning was to make sure you were not one of them.

The aqueduct, now. It would be made of natural brick, an earthy red; it would have low arches, in the shade of which there would be ferns and, perhaps, some delphiniums, in varying tones of blue. She must learn more about plants. Before entering the shopping complex (trust him to assign a shopping complex; before that he had demanded a public housing project), it would flow through her green space, in which, she could now see, there were people walking. Children? *But not children like Mrs. Nolan's.* They would turn her grass to mud, they'd nail things to her trees, their mangy dogs would shit on her ferns, they'd throw bottles and pop cans into her aqueduct. . . . And Mrs. Nolan herself, and her Noah's Ark of seedy, brilliant foreigners, where would she put them? For the houses of the Mrs. Nolans of this world would have to go; that was one of the axioms of Urban Design. She could convert them to small offices, or single-floor apartments; some shrubs and hanging plants and a new coat of paint would do wonders. But she knew this was temporizing. Around her green space, she could see, there was now a high wire fence. Inside it were trees, flowers and grass, outside the dirty snow, the endless rain, the grunting cars and the half-frozen mud of Mrs. Nolan's drab backyard. That was what *exclusive* meant, it meant that some people were excluded. Her parents stood in the rain outside the fence, watching with dreary pride while she strolled about in the eternal sunlight. Their one success.

Stop it, she commanded herself. *They want me to be doing this.* She unwound her hair and brushed it out. Three hours from now, she knew, it would be limp as ever because of the damp.

The next day, she tried to raise her new theoretical problem with her friend Jetske. Jetske was in Urban Design, too. She was from Holland, and could remember running through the devastated streets as a child, begging small change, first from the Germans, later from American soldiers, who were always good for a chocolate bar or two.

"You learn how to take care of yourself," she'd said. "It didn't seem hard at the time, but when you are a child, nothing is that hard. We were all the same, nobody had anything." Because of this background, which was more exotic and cruel than anything Ann herself had experienced (what was a gas pump compared to the Nazis?), Ann respected her opinions. She liked her also because she was the only person she'd met here who seemed to know where Canada was. There were a lot of Canadian soldiers buried in Holland. This provided Ann with at least a shadowy identity, which she felt she needed. She didn't have a native costume, but at least she had some heroic dead bodies with which she was connected, however remotely.

"The trouble with what we're doing . . . ," she said to Jetske, as they walked towards the library under Ann's umbrella. "I mean, you can rebuild one part, but what do you do about the rest?"

"Of the city?" Jetske said.

"No," Ann said slowly. "I guess I mean of the world."

Jetske laughed. She had what Ann now thought of as Dutch teeth, even and white, with quite a lot of gum showing above them and below the lip. "I didn't know you were a socialist," she said. Her cheeks were pink and healthy, like a cheese ad.

"I'm not," Ann said. "But I thought we were supposed to be thinking in total patterns."

Jetske laughed again. "Did you know," she said, "that in some countries you have to get official permission to move from one town to another?"

Ann didn't like this idea at all. "It controls the population flow," Jetske said. "You can't really have Urban Design without that, you know."

"I think that's awful," Ann said.

"Of course you do," Jetske said, as close to bitterness as she ever got. "You've never had to do it. Over here you are soft in the belly, you think you can always have everything. You think there is freedom of choice. The whole world will come to it. You will see." She began teasing Ann again about her plastic headscarf. Jetske never wore anything on her head.

Ann designed her shopping complex, putting in a skylight and banks of indoor plants, leaving out the aqueduct. She got an A.

In the third week of March, Ann went with Jetske and some of the others to a Buckminster Fuller lecture. Afterwards they all went to the pub on the corner of the Square for a couple of beers. Ann left with Jetske about eleven o'clock and walked a couple of blocks with her before Jetske turned off towards her lovely old house with the stained glass. Ann continued by herself, warily, keeping to the lighted streets. She carried her purse under her elbow and held her furled umbrella at the ready. For once it wasn't raining.

When she got back to the house and started to climb the stairs, it struck her that something was different. Upstairs, she knew. Absolutely, something was out of line. There was curious music coming from the room next door, a high flute rising over drums, thumping noises, the sound of voices. The man next door was throwing a party, it seemed. *Good for him,* Ann thought. He might as well do something. She settled down for an hour's reading.

But the noises were getting louder. From the bathroom came the sound of retching. There was going to be trouble. Ann checked her door to make sure it was locked, got out the bottle of sherry she kept in the cupboard next to the oven, and poured herself a drink. Then she turned out the light and sat with her back against the door, drinking her sherry in the faint blue light from the funeral home next door. There was no point in going to bed: even with her earplugs in, she could never sleep.

The music and thumpings got louder. After a while there was a banging on the floor, then some shouting, which came quite clearly through Ann's hot-air register. "I'm calling the police! You hear? I'm calling the police! You get them out of here and get out yourself!" The music switched off, the door opened, and there was a clattering down the stairs. Then more footsteps—Ann couldn't tell whether they were going up or down—and more shouting. The front door banged and the shouts continued on down the street. Ann undressed and put on her nightgown, still without turning on the light, and crept into the bathroom. The bathtub was full of vomit.

This time Mrs. Nolan didn't even wait for Ann to get back from classes. She waylaid her in the morning as she was coming out of her room. Mrs. Nolan was holding a can of Drano and had dark circles under her eyes. Somehow this made her look younger. *She's probably not much older than I am,* Ann thought. Until now she had considered her middle-aged.

"I guess you saw the mess in there," she whispered.

"Yes, I did," Ann said.

"I guess you heard all that last night." She paused.

"What happened?" Ann asked. In fact she really wanted to know.

"He had some dancing girls in there! Three dancing girls, and two other men, in that little room! I thought the ceiling was gonna come right down on our heads!"

"I did hear something like dancing," Ann said.

"Dancing! They was jumping, it sounded like they jumped right off the bed onto the floor. The plaster was coming off. Fred wasn't home, he's not home yet. I was afraid for the kids. Like, with those tattoos, who knows what they was working themselves up to?" Her sibilant voice hinted of ritual murders, young Jimmy and runny-nosed Donny sacrificed to some obscure god.

"What did you do?" Ann asked.

"I called the police. Well, the dancing girls, as soon as they heard I was calling the police, they got out of here, I can tell you. Put on their coats and was down the stairs and out the door like nothing. You can bet they didn't want no trouble with the police. But not the others, they don't seem to know what police means."

She paused again, and Ann asked, "Did they come?"

"Who?"

"The police."

"Well, you know around here it always takes the police a while to get there, unless there's some right outside. I know that, it's not the first time I've had to call them. So who knows what they would've done in the meantime? I could hear them coming downstairs, like, so I just grabs the broom and I chased them out. I chased them all the way down the street."

Ann saw that she thought she had done something very brave, which meant that in fact she had. She really believed that the man next door and his friends were dangerous, that they were a threat to her children. She had chased them single-handedly, yelling with fear and defiance. But he had only been throwing a party.

"Heavens," she said weakly.

"You can say that again," said Mrs. Nolan. "I went in there this morning, to get his things and put them out front where he could get them without me having to see him. I don't have such good nerves, I didn't sleep at all, even after they was gone. Fred is just gonna have to stop driving nights, I can't take it. But you know? He didn't have no things in there. Not one. Just an old empty suitcase?"

"What about his native costume?" Ann said.

"He had it on," Mrs. Nolan said. "He just went running down the street in it, like some kind of a loony. And you know what else I found in there? In one corner, there was this pile of empty bottles. Liquor. He must've been drinking like a fish for months, and never threw out the bottles. And in another corner, there was this pile of burnt matches. He could've burnt the house down, throwing them on the floor like that. But the worst thing was, you know all the times he borrowed my vacuum cleaner?"

"Yes," Ann said.

"Well, he never threw away the dirt. There it all was, in the other corner of the room. He must've just emptied it out and left it there. I don't get it." Mrs. Nolan, by now, was puzzled rather than angry.

"Well," Ann said. "That certainly is strange."

"Strange?" Mrs. Nolan said. "I'll tell you it's strange. He always paid the rent though, right on time. Never a day late. Why would he put the dirt in a corner like that, when he could've put it out in a bag like everyone else? It's not like he didn't know. I told him real clear which were the garbage days, when he moved in."

Ann said she was going to be late for class if she didn't hurry. At the front door she tucked her hair under her plastic scarf. Today it was just a drizzle, not heavy enough for the umbrella. She started off, walking quickly along beside the double line of traffic.

She wondered where he had gone, chased down the street by Mrs. Nolan in her scuffies and flowered housecoat, shouting and flailing at him with a broom. She must have been at least as terrifying a spectacle to him as he was to her, and just as inexplicable. Why would this woman, this fat crazy woman, wish to burst in upon a scene of harmless hospitality, banging and raving? He and his friends could easily have overpowered her, but they would not even have thought about doing that. They would have been too frightened. What unspoken taboo had they violated? What would these cold, mad people do next?

Anyway, he did have some friends. They would take care of him, at least for the time being. Which was a relief, she guessed. But what she really felt was a childish regret that she had not seen the dancing girls. If she had known they were there, she might even have risked opening her door. She knew they were not real dancing girls, they were probably just some whores from Scollay Square. Mrs. Nolan had called them that as a euphemism, or perhaps because of an unconscious association with the word *Arabian*, the vaguely Arabian country. She never had found out what it was. Nevertheless, she wished she had seen them. Jetske would find all of this quite amusing, especially the image of her backed against the door, drinking sherry in the dark. It would have been better if she'd had the courage to look.

She began to think about her green space, as she often did during this walk. The green, perfect space of the future. She knew by now that it was cancelled in advance, that it would never come into being, that it was already too late. Once she was qualified, she would return to plan tasteful mixes of residential units and shopping complexes, with a lot of underground malls and arcades to protect people from the snow. But she could allow herself to see it one last time.

The fence was gone now, and the green stretched out endlessly, fields and trees and flowing water, as far as she could see. In the distance, beneath the arches of the aqueduct, a herd of animals, deer or something, was grazing. (She must learn more about animals.) Groups of people were walking happily among the trees, holding hands, not just in twos but in threes, fours, fives. The man from next door was there, in his native costume, and the mathematicians, they were all in their native costumes. Beside the stream a man was playing the flute; and around him, in long flowered robes and mauve scuffies, their auburn hair floating around their healthy pink faces, smiling their Dutch smiles, the dancing girls were sedately dancing.

[1977]

QUESTIONS

1. How do Ann's and Mrs. Nolan's different assumptions about "foreigners" contribute to the story's central theme?
2. What is the basis of Mrs. Nolan's fear of the new foreign occupant of her boarding house? Through that fear, what do we learn about Mrs. Nolan?
3. How do Ann's fantasies of "urban design" contribute to the meaning of the story? How has her vision changed by the story's end?
4. What does this story suggest about cross-cultural understanding?

Isaac Babel
(1894–1941?)
Russia

Issac Emmanuilovich Babel, like many Russian writers before him, struggled with the difficult problem of freedom of artistic expression during a particularly oppressive period of Russian history. As a Jew, he was further threatened by the wave of *pogroms* (persecutions) sweeping Russia at the time. Although the Jews of Odessa—where Babel was born—were less oppressed than those elsewhere in Russia, when he was 10 years old he saw his family's shop looted and witnessed his father's humiliation by a Cossack officer.

As soon as he could, Babel left Odessa for Kiev and then St. Petersburg with the hope of becoming a writer. In St. Petersburg he met Maxim Gorki, a successful playwright, who encouraged Babel as a writer and who published his first two stories. In pursuit of adventure, Babel joined the Czar's army and was stationed on the Romanian frontier and in Poland; his experiences during that time became the source for his most famous collection of stories, *Red Cavalry* (1926), in which he explores the cruelties of war along with the better qualities it may inspire in ordinary people. "My First Goose" first appeared in that collection. His other stories were collected in *Tales of Odessa* (1924), drawing on his formative years in Odessa, and *Jewish Tales* (1927).

As a result of the artistic repression in the Soviet Union during the Stalinist era, Babel published few stories after 1926. In 1934 he spoke to the first Writers' Congress, describing himself as "a master of a new literary genre, the genre of silence." In 1939 he was arrested, charged with espionage and illegal revolutionary activities, and sent to a Soviet concentration camp where he was tortured to confess to the false charges. He was convicted and shot, probably sometime in 1941; 14 years later, in a posthumous review of his case, Babel was cleared of all charges.

Like his predecessors, Turgenev and Chekhov, Babel is distinguished both for his poetic use of language and for his mastery of ironic detachment—a narrative strategy with political as well as aesthetic implications. From his perspective as a member of a persecuted religious minority, he also poignantly explored the circumstances of cultural marginality. Babel's nonjudgmental position obliges the reader to inquire into the moral issues that are compellingly explored in his stories.

My First Goose

Savitsky, Commander of the VI Division, rose when he saw me, and I wondered at the beauty of his giant's body. He rose, the purple of his riding breeches and the crimson of his little tilted cap and the decorations stuck on his chest cleaving the hut as a standard cleaves the sky. A smell of scent and the sickly sweet freshness of soap emanated from him. His long legs were like girls sheathed to the neck in shining riding boots.

He smiled at me, struck his riding whip on the table, and drew toward him an order that the Chief of Staff had just finished dictating. It was an order for Ivan Chesnokov to advance on Chugunov-Dobryvodka with the regiment entrusted to him, to make contact with the enemy and destroy the same.

"For which destruction," the Commander began to write, smearing the whole sheet, "I make this same Chesnokov entirely responsible, up to and including the supreme penalty, and will if necessary strike him down on the spot; which you, Chesnokov, who have been working with me at the front for some months now, cannot doubt."

The Commander signed the order with a flourish, tossed it to his orderlies and turned upon me gray eyes that danced with merriment.

I handed him a paper with my appointment to the Staff of the Division.

"Put it down in the Order of the Day," said the Commander. "Put him down for every satisfaction save the front one. Can you read and write?"

"Yes, I can read and write," I replied, envying the flower and iron of that youthfulness. "I graduated in law from St. Petersburg University."

"Oh, are you one of those grinds?" he laughed. "Specs on your nose, too! What a nasty little object! They've sent you along without making any enquiries; and this is a hot place for specs. Think you'll get on with us?"

"I'll get on all right," I answered, and went off to the village with the quartermaster to find a billet for the night.

The quartermaster carried my trunk on his shoulder. Before us stretched the village street. The dying sun, round and yellow as a pumpkin, was giving up its roseate ghost to the skies.

We went up to a hut painted over with garlands. The quartermaster stopped, and said suddenly, with a guilty smile:

"Nuisance with specs. Can't do anything to stop it, either. Not a life for the brainy type here. But you go and mess up a lady, and a good lady too, and you'll have the boys patting you on the back."

He hesitated, my little trunk on his shoulder; then he came quite close to me, only to dart away again despairingly and run to the nearest yard. Cossacks were sitting there, shaving one another.

"Here, you soldiers," said the quartermaster, setting my little trunk down on the ground. "Comrade Savitsky's orders are that you're to take this chap in your billets, so no nonsense about it, because the chap's been through a lot in the learning line."

The quartermaster, purple in the face, left us without looking back. I raised my hand to my cap and saluted the Cossacks. A lad with long straight flaxen hair and the handsome face of the Ryazan Cossacks went over to my little trunk and tossed it out at the gate. Then he turned his back on me and with remarkable skill emitted a series of shameful noises.

"To your guns—number double-zero!" an older Cossack shouted at him, and burst out laughing. "Running fire!"

His guileless art exhausted, the lad made off. Then, crawling over the ground, I began to gather together the manuscripts and tattered garments that had fallen out of the trunk. I gathered them up and carried them to the other end of the yard. Near the hut, on a brick stove, stood a cauldron in which pork was cooking. The steam that rose from it was like the far-off smoke of home in the village, and it mingled hunger with desperate loneliness in my head. Then I covered my little broken trunk with hay, turning it into a pillow, and lay down on the ground to read in *Pravda* Lenin's speech at the Second Congress of the Comintern. The sun fell upon me from behind the toothed hillocks, the Cossacks trod on my feet, the lad made fun of me untiringly, the beloved lines came toward me along a thorny path and could not reach me. Then I put aside the paper and went out to the landlady, who was spinning on the porch.

"Landlady," I said, "I've got to eat."

The old woman raised to me the diffused whites of her purblind eyes and lowered them again.

"Comrade," she said, after a pause, "what with all this going on, I want to go and hang myself."

"Christ!" I muttered, and pushed the old woman in the chest with my fist. "You don't suppose I'm going to go into explanations with you, do you?"

And turning around I saw somebody's sword lying within reach. A severe-looking goose was waddling about the yard, inoffensively preening its feathers. I overtook it and pressed it to the ground. Its head cracked beneath my boot, cracked and emptied itself. The white neck lay stretched out in the dung, the wings twitched.

"Christ!" I said, digging into the goose with my sword. "Go and cook it for me, landlady."

Her blind eyes and glasses glistening, the old woman picked up the slaughtered bird, wrapped it in her apron, and started to bear it off toward the kitchen.

"Comrade," she said to me, after a while, "I want to go and hang myself." And she closed the door behind her.

The Cossacks in the yard were already sitting around their cauldron. They sat motionless, stiff as heathen priests at a sacrifice, and had not looked at the goose.

"The lad's all right," one of them said, winking and scooping up the cabbage soup with his spoon.

The Cossacks commenced their supper with all the elegance and restraint of peasants who respect one another. And I wiped the sword with sand, went out at the gate, and came in again, depressed. Already the moon hung above the yard like a cheap earring.

"Hey, you," suddenly said Surovkov, an older Cossack. "Sit down and feed with us till your goose is done."

He produced a spare spoon from his boot and handed it to me. We supped up the cabbage soup they had made, and ate the pork.

"What's in the newspaper?" asked the flaxen-haired lad, making room for me.

"Lenin writes in the paper," I said, pulling out *Pravda*. "Lenin writes that there's a shortage of everything."

And loudly, like a triumphant man hard of hearing, I read Lenin's speech out to the Cossacks.

Evening wrapped about me the quickening moisture of its twilight sheets; evening laid a mother's hand upon my burning forehead. I read on and rejoiced, spying out exultingly the secret curve of Lenin's straight line.

"Truth tickles everyone's nostrils," said Surovkov, when I had come to the end. "The question is, how's it to be pulled from the heap. But he goes and strikes at it straight off like a hen pecking at a grain!"

This remark about Lenin was made by Surovkov, platoon commander of the Staff Squadron; after which we lay down to sleep in the hayloft. We slept, all six of us, beneath a wooden roof that let in the stars, warming one another, our legs intermingled. I dreamed: and in my dreams saw women. But my heart, stained with bloodshed, grated and brimmed over.

[1925]
Translated by
WALTER MORISON

QUESTIONS

1. In what ways is the narrator different from the other Cossack soldiers of the story? How are those differences significant to what happens?
2. Why does the narrator kill the goose? Why is he accepted by the other Cossack soldiers afterwards?
3. What role does the old blind woman play in the story?
4. As the title suggests, one might call "My First Goose" a story of initiation. Into what is the narrator initiated? Does he change during the course of the story? If so, how?
5. How does the story's mixture of lyrical imagery and brutal actions affect you?

BarbaraNeely

(b. 1941)

United States

BarbaraNeely was born in Lebanon, Pennsylvania, in 1941. In a biographical comment about her career, she states that she did not begin writing until she was 35 years old. She describes herself as "a black woman of African slave descent who actively supports the right of all peoples to self-determination." "Spilled Salt," the story included here, originally appeared in *Breaking Ice: An Anthology of Contemporary African-American Fiction*, edited by Terry McMillan (1990). Her novel, *Blanche on the Lam*, was published in 1992. Currently, BarbaraNeely lives in Jamaica Plain, Massachusetts, where she is working on a second novel and a short story collection.

When asked to describe her own writing objectives, BarbaraNeely responded, "One of my major goals as a fiction writer is to explore the rich inner lives of people the larger society assumes have no inner life. . . . I am interested in how the world looks and feels to the people who make up the mud—the people who do menial jobs; who are chronically unemployed; the people whom the society discriminates against because they are too black, too old, the wrong kind of woman, conventionally unattractive, or in some other way different from the mainstream model—which is really most of us."

Spilled Salt

"I'm home, Ma."

Myrna pressed down hard on the doorknob and stared blankly up into Kenny's large brown eyes and freckled face so much like her own he was nearly her twin. But he was taller than she remembered. Denser.

He'd written to say he was getting out. She hadn't answered his letter, hoping her lack of response would keep him away.

"You're here." She stepped back from the door, pretending not to see him reach out and try to touch her.

But a part of her had leaped to life at the sight of him. No matter what, she was glad he hadn't been maimed or murdered in prison. He at least looked whole and healthy of body. She hoped it was a sign that he was all right inside, too.

She tried to think of something to say as they stood staring at each other in the middle of the living room. A fly buzzed against the window screen in a desperate attempt to get out.

"Well, Ma, how've you—"

"I'll fix you something to eat," Myrna interrupted. "I know you must be starved for decent cooking." She rushed from the room as though a meal were already in the process of burning.

For a moment she was lost in her own kitchen. The table, with its dented metal legs, the green-and-white cotton curtains, and the badly battered coffeepot were all familiar-looking strangers. She took a deep breath and leaned against the back of a chair.

In the beginning she'd flinched from the very word. She couldn't even think it, let alone say it. Assault, attack, molest, anything but rape. Anyone but her son, her bright and funny boy, her high school graduate.

At the time, she'd been sure it was a frame-up on the part of the police. They did things like that. It was in the newspapers every day. Or the girl was trying to get revenge because he hadn't shown any interest in her. Kenny's confession put paid to all those speculations.

She'd have liked to believe that remorse had made him confess. But she knew better. He'd simply told the wrong lie. If he'd said he'd been with the girl but it hadn't been rape, he might have built a case that someone would have believed—although she didn't know how he could have explained away the wound on her neck where he'd held his knife against her throat to keep her docile. Instead, he'd claimed not to have offered her a ride home from the bar where she worked, never to have had her in his car. He'd convinced Myrna. So thoroughly convinced her that she'd fainted dead away when confronted with the semen, fiber, and hair evidence the police quickly collected from his car, and the word of the woman who reluctantly came forth to say she'd seen Kenny ushering Crystal Roberts into his car on the night Crystal was raped.

Only then had Kenny confessed. He'd said he'd been doing the girl a favor by offering her a ride home. In return, she'd teased and then refused him, he'd said. "I lost my head," he'd said.

"I can't sleep. I'm afraid to sleep." The girl had spoken in barely a whisper. The whole courtroom had seemed to tilt as everyone leaned toward her. "Every night he's there in my mind, making me go through it all over again, and again, and again."

Was she free now that Kenny had done his time? Or was she flinching from hands with short, square fingers, and crying when the first of September came near? Myrna moved around the kitchen like an old, old woman with bad feet.

After Kenny had confessed, Myrna spent days that ran into weeks rifling through memories of the past she shared with him, searching for some incident, some trait or series of events that would explain why he'd done such a thing. She's tried to rationalize his actions with circumstances: Kenny had seen his father beat her. They'd been poorer than dirt. And when Kenny had just turned six, she'd finally found the courage to leave Buddy to raise their son alone. What had she really known about raising a child? What harm might she have done out of ignorance, out of impatience and concentration on warding off the pains of her own life?

Still, she kept stumbling over the knowledge of other boys, from far worse circumstances, with mothers too tired and worried to do more than strike out at them. Yet those boys had managed to grow up and not do the kind of harm Kenny had done. The phrases "I lost my head," and "doing the girl a favor," reverberated through her brain, mocking her, making her groan out loud and startle people around her.

Myrna dragged herself around the room, turning eggs, bacon, milk, and margarine into a meal. In the beginning the why of Kenny's crime was like a tapeworm in her belly, consuming all her strength and sustenance, all her attention. In the first few months of his imprisonment she'd religiously paid a neighbor to drive her the long distance to the prison each visiting day. The visits were as much for her benefit as for his.

"But why?" she'd kept asking him, just as she'd asked him practically every day since he'd confessed.

He would only say that he knew he'd done wrong. As the weeks passed, silence became his only response—a silence that had remained intact despite questions like: "Would you have left that girl alone if I'd bought a shotgun and blown your daddy's brains out after the first time he hit me in front of you?" and, "Is there a special thrill you feel when you make a woman ashamed of her sex?" and, "Was this the first time? The second? The last?"

Perhaps silence was best, now, after so long. Anything could happen if she let those five-year-old questions come rolling out of her mouth. Kenny might begin to question her, might ask her what there was about her mothering that made him want to treat a woman like a piece of toilet paper. And what would she say to that?

It was illness that had finally put an end to her visits with him. She'd written the first letter—a note really—to say she was laid up with the flu. A hacking cough had lingered. She hadn't gotten her strength back for nearly two months. By that time their correspondence was established. Letters full of: How are you? I'm fine. . . . The weather is . . . The print shop is . . . The dress I made for Mrs. Rothstein was . . . were so much more manageable than those silence-laden visits. And she didn't have to worry about making eye contact with Kenny in a letter.

Now Myrna stood staring out the kitchen window while Kenny ate his bacon and eggs. The crisp everydayness of clothes flapping on the line surprised her. A leaf floated into her small cemented yard and landed on a potted pansy. Outside, nothing had changed; the world was still in spring.

"I can't go through this again," she mouthed soundlessly to the breeze.

"Come talk to me, Ma," her son called softly around a mouthful of food.

Myrna turned to look at him. He smiled an egg-flecked smile she couldn't return. She wanted to ask him what he would do now, whether he had a job lined up, whether he planned to stay long. But she was afraid of his answers, afraid of how she might respond if he said he had no job, no plans, no place to stay except with her and that he hadn't changed in any important way.

"I'm always gonna live with you, Mommy," he'd told her when he was a child, "Always." At the time, she'd wished it was true, that they could always be together, she and her sweet, chubby boy. Now the thought frightened her.

"Be right back," she mumbled, and scurried down the hall to the bathroom. She eased the lock over so that it made barely a sound.

"He's my son!" she hissed at the drawn woman in the mirror. Perspiration dotted her upper lip and glistened around her hair line.

"My son!" she repeated pleadingly. But the words were not as powerful as the memory of Crystal Roberts sitting in the courtroom, her shoulders hunched and her head hung down, as though she were the one who ought to be ashamed. Myrna wished him never born, before she flushed the toilet and unlocked the door.

In the kitchen Kenny had moved to take her place by the window. His dishes littered the table. He'd spilled the salt, and there were crumbs on the floor.

"It sure is good to look out the window and see something besides guard towers and cons." Kenny stretched, rubbed his belly, and turned to face her.

"It's good to see you, Ma." His eyes were soft and shiny.

Oh, Lord! Myrna moaned to herself. She turned her back to him and began carrying his dirty dishes to the sink: first the plate, then the cup, the knife, fork, and spoon, drawing out the chore.

"This place ain't got as much room as the old place," she told him while she made dishwater in the sink.

"It's fine, Ma, just fine."

Oh, Lord, Myrna prayed.

Kenny came to lean against the stove to her right. She dropped a knife and made the dishwater too cold.

"Seen Dad?"

"Where and why would I see *him?*" She tried to put ice in her voice. It trembled.

"Just thought you might know where he is." Kenny moved back to the window.

Myrna remembered the crippling shock of Buddy's fist in her groin and scoured Kenny's plate and cup with a piece of steel wool before rinsing them in scalding water.

"Maybe I'll hop a bus over to the old neighborhood. See some of the guys, how things have changed."

He paced the floor behind her. Myrna sensed his uneasiness and was startled by a wave of pleasure at his discomfort.

After he'd gone, she fixed herself a large gin and orange juice and carried it into the living room. She flicked on the TV and sat down to stare at it. After two minutes of frenetic, over-bright commercials, she got up and turned it off again. Outside, children screamed each other to the finish line of a footrace. She remembered that Kenny had always liked to run. So had she. But he'd had more childhood than she'd had. She'd been hired out as a mother's helper by the time she was twelve, and pregnant and married at sixteen. She didn't begrudge him his childhood fun. It just seemed so wasted now.

Tears slid down her face and salted her drink. Tears for the young Myrna who hadn't understood that she was raising a boy who needed special handling to keep him from becoming a man she didn't care to know. Tears for Kenny who was so twisted around inside that he could rape a woman. Myrna drained her gin; left Kenny a note reminding him to leave her door key on the kitchen table, and went to bed.

Of course, she was still awake when he came in. He bumped into the coffee table, ran water in the bathroom sink for a long time, then quiet. Myrna lay awake in the dark blue-gray night listening to the groan of the refrigerator, the hiss of the hot-water heater, and the rumble of large trucks on a distant street. *He* made no sound where he lay on the opened-out sofa, surrounded by her sewing machine, dress dummy, marking tape, and pins.

When sleep finally came, it brought dreams of walking down brilliantly lit streets, hand in hand with a boy about twelve who looked, acted, and talked like Kenny but who she knew with certainty was not her son, at the same time she also knew he could be no one else.

She woke to a cacophony of church bells. It was late. Too late to make it to church service. She turned her head to look at the crucifix hanging by her bed and tried to pray, to summon up that feeling of near weightlessness that came over her in those moments when she was able to free her mind of all else and give herself over to prayer. Now nothing came but a dull ache in the back of her throat.

She had begun attending church regularly after she stopped visiting Kenny. His refusal to respond to her questions made it clear she'd have to seek answers elsewhere. She'd decided to talk to Father Giles. He'd been at St. Mark's, in their old neighborhood, before she and Kenny had moved there. He'd seen Kenny growing up. Perhaps he'd noticed something, understood something about the boy, about her, that would explain what she could not understand.

"It's God's will, my child—put it in His hands," he'd urged, awkwardly patting her arm and averting his eyes.

Myrna took his advice wholeheartedly. She became quite adept at quieting the questions boiling in her belly with, "His will," or "My cross to bear." Many nights she'd "Our Fathered" herself to sleep. Acceptance of Kenny's inexplicable act became a test God had given her. One she passed by visiting the sick, along with other women from the church; working on the neighborhood cleanup committee; avoiding all social contact with men. With sex. She put "widowed" on job applications and never mentioned a son to new people she met. Once she'd moved away from the silent accusation of their old apartment, prayer and good works became a protective shield separating her from the past.

Kenny's tap on her door startled her back to the present. She cleared her throat and straightened the covers before calling to him to come in.

A rich, aromatic steam rose from the coffee he'd brought her. The toast was just the right shade of brown, and she was sure that when she cracked the poached egg it would be cooked exactly to her liking. Not only was everything perfectly prepared, it was the first time she'd had breakfast in bed since he'd been arrested. Myrna couldn't hold back the tears or the flood of memories of many mornings, just so: him bending over her with a breakfast tray.

"You wait on people in the restaurant all day and sit up all night making other people's clothes. You need some waiting on, too."

Had he actually said that, this man as a boy? Could this man have been such a boy? Myrna nearly tilted the tray in her confusion.

"I need to brush my teeth." She averted her face and reached for her bathrobe.

But she couldn't avoid her eyes in the medicine cabinet mirror, eyes that reminded her that despite what Kenny had done, she hadn't stopped loving him. But her love didn't need his company. It thrived only on memories of him that were more than four years old. It was as much a love remembered as a living thing. But it was love, nonetheless. Myrna pressed her clenched fist against her lips and wondered if love was enough. She stayed in the bathroom until she heard him leave her bedroom and turn on the TV in the living room.

When he came back for the tray, she told him she had a sick headache and had decided to stay in bed. He was immediately sympathetic, fetching aspirin and a cool compress for her forehead, offering to massage her neck and temples, to lower the blinds and block out the bright morning sun. Myrna told him she wanted only to rest.

All afternoon she lay on her unmade bed, her eyes on the ceiling or idly roaming the room, her mind moving across the surface of her life, poking at old wounds, so amazingly raw after all these years. First there'd been Buddy. He'd laughed at her country ways and punched her around until he'd driven her and their child into the streets. But at least she was rid of him. Then there was his son. Her baby. He'd tricked a young woman into getting into his car where he proceeded to ruin a great portion of her life. Now he'd come back to spill salt in her kitchen.

I'm home, Ma, homema, homema. His words echoed in her inner ear and made her heart flutter. Her neighbors would want to know where he'd been all this time and why. Fear and disgust would creep into their faces and voices. Her nights would be full of listening. Waiting.

And she would have to live with the unblanketed reality that whatever anger and meanness her son held toward the world, he had chosen a woman to take it out on.

A woman.

Someone like me, she thought, like Great Aunt Faye, or Valerie, her eight-year-old niece; like Lucille, her oldest friend, or Dr. Ramsey, her dentist. A woman like all the women who'd helped feed, clothe, and care for Kenny; who'd tried their damnedest to protect him from as much of the ugly and awful in life as they could; who'd taught him to ride a bike and cross the street. All women. From the day she'd left Buddy, not one man had done a damned thing for Kenny. Not one.

And he might do it again, she thought. The idea sent Myrna rolling back and forth across the bed as though she could actually escape her thoughts. She'd allowed herself to believe she was done with such thoughts. Once she accepted Kenny's crime as the will of God, she immediately saw that it wouldn't have made any difference how she'd raised him if this was God's unfathomable plan for him. It was a comforting idea, one that answered her question of why and how her much-loved son could be a rapist. One that answered the question of the degree of her responsibility for Kenny's crime by clearing her of all possible blame. One that allowed her to forgive him. Or so she'd thought.

Now she realized all her prayers, all her studied efforts to accept and forgive were like blankets thrown on a forest fire. All it took was the small breeze created by her opening the door to her only child to burn those blankets to cinders and release her rage—as wild and fierce as the day he'd confessed.

She closed her eyes and saw her outraged self dash wildly into the living room to scream imprecations in his face until her voice failed. Specks of froth gathered at the corners of her mouth. Her flying spit peppered his face. He cringed before her, his eyes full of shame as he tore at his own face and chest in self-loathing.

Yet, even as she fantasized, she knew Kenny could no more be screamed into contrition than Crystal or any woman could be bullied into willing sex. And what, in fact, was there for him to say or do that would satisfy her? The response she really wanted from him was not available: there was no way he could become the boy he'd been before that night four years ago.

No more than I can treat him as if he were that boy, she thought.

And the thought stilled her. She lay motionless, considering.

When she rose from her bed, she dragged her old green Samsonite suitcase out from the back of the closet. She moved with the easy, effortless grace of someone who knows what she is doing and feels good about it. Without even wiping off the dust, she plopped the suitcase on the bed. When she lifted the lid, the smell of leaving and good-bye flooded the room and quickened her pulse. For the first time in two days, her mouth moved in the direction of a smile.

She hurried from dresser drawer to closet, choosing her favorites: the black two-piece silk knit dress she'd bought on sale, her comfortable gray shoes, the lavender sweater she'd knitted as a birthday present to herself but had never worn, both her blue and her black slacks, the red crepe blouse she'd made to go with them, and the best of her underwear. She packed in a rush, as though her bus or train were even now pulling out of the station.

When she'd packed her clothes, Myrna looked around the room for other necessary items. She gathered up her comb and brush and the picture of her mother from the top of her bureau, then walked to the wall on the left side of her bed and lifted down the shiny metal and wooden crucifix that hung there. She ran her finger down the slim, muscular body. The Aryan plaster-of-Paris Christ seemed to writhe in bittersweet agony. Myrna stared at the crucifix for a few moments, then gently hung it back on the wall.

When she'd finished dressing, she sat down in the hard, straight-backed chair near the window to think through her plan. Kenny tapped at her door a number of times until she was able to convince him that she was best left alone and would be fine in the morning. When dark came, she waited for the silence of sleep, then quietly left her room. She set her suitcase by the front door, tiptoed by Kenny, where he slept on the sofa, and went into the kitchen. By the glow from the back alley streetlight, she wrote him a note and propped it against the sugar bowl:

Dear Kenny,

I'm sorry. I just can't be your mother right now. I will be back in one week. Please be gone. Much love, Myrna.

Kenny flinched and frowned in his sleep as the front door clicked shut.

[1990]

QUESTIONS

1. When Myrna says that a parent always loves a child, no matter what the circumstances, is she speaking truthfully or lying to herself?
2. Is Myrna the source of Kenny's anger? Is the rape his attempt to lash back at his mother?
3. Although Myrna leaves at the end of the story, are we to believe that she and her son will be reunited?
4. Although BarbaraNeely is an African-American writer, does "Spilled Salt" demand an ethnic interpretation, or is the situation it describes applicable to all women whose sons may become rapists?

ANN BEATTIE

(b. 1947)

UNITED STATES

Ann Beattie was born in 1947 in Washington, DC, where she attended American University. By the mid-seventies, when her stories were beginning to appear in *The New Yorker* and other magazines, she had already carved a niche for herself as spokesperson of the uptight generation. Critics have praised her attention to detail and her dialogue. Younger writers have tried to imitate her style but have been largely unsuccessful. Since the simultaneous publication of her first collection of short stories, *Distortions*, and her first novel, *Chilly Scenes of Winter*, in 1976, she has published half a dozen other volumes. The story included here is from *The Burning House* (1982).

In an interview with Bob Miner, describing her own work, Beattie said, "My stories are a lot about chaos . . . and many of the simple flat statements that I bring together are usually non sequiturs or bordering on being non sequiturs—which reinforces the chaos. I write in those flat sentences because that's the way I think. I don't mean to do it as a technique. It might be just that I am incapable of breaking through to the complexities underlying all that sort of simple statement you find in my work."

◆ *The Burning House* ◆

Freddy Fox is in the kitchen with me. He has just washed and dried an avocado seed I don't want, and he is leaning against the wall, rolling a joint. In five minutes, I will not be able to count on him. However: he started late in the day, and he has already brought in wood for the fire, gone to the store down the road for matches, and set the table. "You mean you'd know this stuff was Limoges[1] even if you didn't turn the plate over?" he called from the dining room. He pretended to be about to throw one of the plates into the kitchen, like a Frisbee. Sam, the dog, believed him and shot up, kicking the rug out behind him and skidding forward before he realized his error; it was like the Road Runner tricking Wile E. Coyote into going over the cliff for the millionth time. His jowls sank in disappointment.

"I see there's a full moon," Freddy says. "There's just nothing that can hold a candle to nature. The moon and the stars, the tides and the sunshine—and we just don't stop for long enough to wonder at it all. We're so engrossed in ourselves." He takes a very long drag on the joint. "We stand and stir the sauce in the pot instead of going to the window and gazing at the moon."

"You don't mean anything personal by that, I assume."

[1]*Limoges* fine, expensive porcelain

"I love the way you pour cream in a pan. I like to come up behind you and watch the sauce bubble."

"No, thank you," I say. "You're starting late in the day."

"My responsibilities have ended. You don't trust me to help with the cooking, and I've already brought in firewood and run an errand, and this very morning I exhausted myself by taking Mr. Sam jogging with me, down at Putnam Park. You're sure you won't?"

"No, thanks," I say. "Not now, anyway."

"I love it when you stand over the steam coming out of a pan and the hairs around your forehead curl into damp little curls."

My husband, Frank Wayne, is Freddy's half brother. Frank is an accountant. Freddy is closer to me than to Frank. Since Frank talks to Freddy more than he talks to me, however, and since Freddy is totally loyal, Freddy always knows more than I know. It pleases me that he does not know how to stir sauce; he will start talking, his mind will drift, and when next you look the sauce will be lumpy, or boiling away.

Freddy's criticism of Frank is only implied. "What a gracious gesture to entertain his friends on the weekend," he says.

"Male friends," I say.

"I didn't mean that you're the sort of lady who doesn't draw the line. I most certainly did not mean that," Freddy says. "I would even have been surprised if you had taken a toke of this deadly stuff while you were at the stove."

"O.K.," I say, and take the joint from him. Half of it is left when I take it. Half an inch is left after I've taken two drags and given it back.

"More surprised still if you'd shaken the ashes into the saucepan."

"You'd tell people I'd done it when they'd finished eating, and I'd be embarrassed. You can do it, though. I wouldn't be embarrassed if it was a story you told on yourself."

"You really understand me," Freddy says. "It's moon-madness, but I have to shake just this little bit in the sauce. I have to do it."

He does it.

Frank and Tucker are in the living room. Just a few minutes ago, Frank returned from getting Tucker at the train. Tucker loves to visit. To him, Fairfield County is as mysterious as Alaska. He brought with him from New York a crock of mustard, a jeroboam of champagne, cocktail napkins with a picture of a plane flying over a building on them, twenty egret feathers ("You cannot get them anymore—strictly, illegal," Tucker whispered to me), and, under his black cowboy hat with the rhinestone-studded chin strap, a toy frog that hopped when wound. Tucker owns a gallery in SoHo, and Frank keeps his books. Tucker is now stretched out in the living room, visiting with Frank, and Freddy and I are both listening.

". . . so everything I've been told indicates that he lives a purely Jekyll-and-Hyde existence. He's twenty years old, and I can see that since he's still living at home he might not want to flaunt his gayness. When he came into the gallery, he had his hair slicked back—just with water; I got close enough to sniff—and his mother was all but holding his hand. So fresh-scrubbed. The stories I'd heard. Anyway, when I called, his father started looking for the number where he could be reached in the Vineyard—very irritated, because I didn't know James, and if I'd just phoned James I could have found him in a flash. He's talking to himself, looking for the number, and I say, 'Oh, did he go to visit friends or—' and his father interrupts and says, 'He was going to a gay pig roast. He's been gone since Monday.' *Just like that*."

Freddy helps me carry the food out to the table. When we are all at the table, I mention the young artist Tucker was talking about. "Frank says his paintings are really incredible," I say to Tucker.

"Makes Estes look like an Abstract Expressionist," Tucker says. "I want that boy. I really want that boy."

"You'll get him," Frank says. "You get everybody you go after."

Tucker cuts a small piece of meat. He cuts it small so that he can talk while chewing. "Do I?" he says.

Freddy is smoking at the table, gazing dazedly at the moon centered in the window. "After dinner," he says, putting the back of his hand against his forehead when he sees that I am looking at him, "we must all go to the lighthouse."

"If only *you* painted," Tucker says, "I'd want you."

"You couldn't have me," Freddy snaps. He reconsiders. "That sounded halfhearted, didn't it? Anybody who wants me can have me. This is the only place I can be on Saturday night where somebody isn't hustling me."

"Wear looser pants," Frank says to Freddy.

"This is so much better than some bar that stinks of cigarette smoke and leather. Why do I do it?" Freddy says. "Seriously—do you think I'll ever stop?"

"Let's not be serious," Tucker says.

"I keep thinking of this table as a big boat, with dishes and glasses rocking on it," Freddy says.

He takes the bone from his plate and walks out to the kitchen, dripping sauce on the floor. He walks as though he's on the deck of a wave-tossed ship. "Mr. Sam!" he calls, and the dog springs up from the living-room floor, where he had been sleeping; his toenails on the bare wood floor sound like a wheel spinning in gravel. "You don't have to beg," Freddy says. "Jesus, Sammy—I'm just giving it to you."

"I hope there's a bone involved," Tucker says, rolling his eyes to Frank. He cuts another tiny piece of meat. "I hope your brother does understand why I couldn't keep him on. He was good at what he did, but he also might say just *anything* to a customer. You have to believe me that if I hadn't been extremely embarrassed more than once I never would have let him go."

"He should have finished school," Frank says, sopping up sauce on his bread. "He'll knock around a while longer, then get tired of it and settle down to something."

"You think I died out here?" Freddy calls. "You think I can't hear you?"

"I'm not saying anything I wouldn't say to your face," Frank says.

"I'll tell you what I wouldn't say to your face," Freddy says. "You've got a swell wife and kid and dog, and you're a snob, and you take it all for granted."

Frank puts down his fork, completely exasperated. He looks at me.

"He came to work once this stoned," Tucker says. "*Comprenez-vous?*"[2]

[2]"*Comprenez-vous?*" "Do you understand?" (French)

"You like me because you feel sorry for me," Freddy says.

He is sitting on the concrete bench outdoors, in the area that's a garden in the springtime. It is early April now—not quite spring. It's very foggy out. It rained while we were eating, and now it has turned mild. I'm leaning against a tree, across from him, glad it's so dark and misty that I can't look down and see the damage the mud is doing to my boots.

"Who's his girlfriend?" Freddy says.

"If I told you her name, you'd tell him I told you."

"Slow down. What?"

'I won't tell you, because you'll tell him that I know."

"He knows you know."

"I don't think so."

"How did you find out?"

"He talked about her. I kept hearing her name for months, and then we went to a party at Andy's, and she was there, and when I said something about her later he said, 'Natalie who?' It was much too casual. It gave the whole thing away."

He sighs. "I just did something very optimistic," he says. "I came out here with Mr. Sam and he dug up a rock and I put the avocado seed in the hole and packed dirt on top of it. Don't say it—I know: can't grow outside, we'll still have another snow, even if it grew, the next year's frost would kill it."

"He's embarrassed," I say. "When he's home, he avoids me. But it's rotten to avoid Mark, too. Six years old, and he calls up his friend Neal to hint that he wants to go over there. He doesn't do that when we're here alone."

Freddy picks up a stick and pokes around in the mud with it. "I'll bet Tucker's after that painter personally, not because he's the hottest thing since pancakes. That expression of his—it's always the same. Maybe Nixon really loved his mother, but with that expression who could believe him? It's a curse to have a face that won't express what you mean."

"Amy!" Tucker calls. "Telephone."

Freddy waves goodbye to me with the muddy stick. "'I am not a crook,'" Freddy says. "Jesus Christ."

Sam bounds halfway toward the house with me; then turns and goes back to Freddy.

It's Marilyn, Neal's mother, on the phone.

"Hi," Marilyn says. "He's afraid to spend the night."

"Oh, no," I say. "He said he wouldn't be."

She lowers her voice. "We can try it out, but I think he'll start crying."

"I'll come get him."

"I can bring him home. You're having a dinner party, aren't you?"

I lowered my voice. "Some party. Tucker's here. J.D. never showed up."

"Well," she says. "I'm sure that what you cooked was good."

"It's so foggy out, Marilyn. I'll come get Mark."

"He can stay. I'll be a martyr," she says, and hangs up before I can object.

Freddy comes into the house, tracking in mud. Sam lies in the kitchen, waiting for his paws to be cleaned. "Come on," Freddy says, hitting his hand against his thigh, having no idea what Sam is doing. Sam gets up and runs after him. They go into the small downstairs bathroom together. Sam loves to watch people urinate. Sometimes he sings, to harmonize with the sound of the urine going into the water. There are footprints and pawprints everywhere. Tucker is shrieking with laughter in the living room. ". . . he says, he says to the other one 'Then, dearie, have you ever played *spin* the bottle?'" Frank's and Tucker's laughter drowns out the sound of Freddy peeing in the bathroom. I turn on the water in the kitchen sink, and it drowns out all the noise. I begin to scrape the dishes. Tucker is telling another story when I turn off the water: ". . . that it was Onassis in the Anvil,[3] and nothing would talk him out of it. They told him Onassis was dead, and he thought they were trying to make him think he was crazy. There was nothing to do but go along with him, but, God—he was trying to goad this poor old fag into fighting about Stavros Niarchos. You know—Onassis' *enemy*. He thought it was Onassis. In the *Anvil*." There is a sound of a glass breaking. Frank or Tucker puts "John Coltrane Live in Seattle" on the stereo and turns the volume down low. The bathroom door opens. Sam runs into the kitchen and begins to lap water from his dish. Freddy takes his little silver case and his rolling papers out of his shirt pocket. He puts a piece of paper on the kitchen table and is about to sprinkle grass on it, but realizes just in time that the paper has absorbed water from a puddle. He balls it up with his thumb, flicks it to the floor, puts a piece of rolling paper where the table's dry and shakes a line of grass down it. "You smoke this," he says to me. "I'll do the dishes."

"We'll both smoke it. I'll wash and you can wipe."

"I forgot to tell them I put ashes in the sauce," he says.

"I wouldn't interrupt."

"At least he pays Frank ten times what any other accountant for an art gallery would make," Freddy says.

Tucker is beating his hand on the arm of the sofa as he talks, stomping his feet. ". . . so he's trying to feel him out, to see if this old guy with the dyed hair knew *Maria Callas*. Jesus! And he's so out of it he's trying to think what opera singers are called, and instead of coming up with '*diva*' he comes up with '*duenna*.' At this point, Larry Betwell went up to him and tried to calm him down, and he breaks into song—some aria or something that Maria Callas was famous for. Larry told him he was going to lose his *teeth* if he didn't get it together, and . . ."

"He spends a lot of time in gay hangouts, for not being gay," Freddy says.

I scream and jump back from the sink, hitting the glass I'm rinsing against the faucet, shattering green glass everywhere.

"What?" Freddy says. "Jesus Christ, what is it?"

Too late, I realize what it must have been that I saw: J.D. in a goat mask, the puckered pink plastic lips against the window beside the kitchen sink.

"I'm sorry," J.D. says, coming through the door and nearly colliding with Frank, who has rushed into the kitchen. Tucker is right behind him.

"Ooh," Tucker says, feigning disappointment, "I thought Freddy smooched her."

"I'm sorry," J.D. says again. "I thought you'd know it was me."

The rain must have started again, because J.D. is soaking wet. He has turned the mask around so that the goat's head stares out from the back of his head. "I got lost," J.D. says. He has a farmhouse upstate. "I missed the turn. I went miles. I missed the whole dinner, didn't I?"

"What did you do wrong?" Frank asks.

"I didn't turn left onto 58. I don't know why I didn't realize my mistake, but

[3]*the Anvil* a raunchy gay bar in New York City

I went *miles*. It was raining so hard I couldn't go over twenty-five miles an hour. Your driveway is all mud. You're going to have to push me out."

"There's some roast left over. And salad, if you want it," I say.

"Bring it in the living room," Frank says to J.D. Freddy is holding out a plate to him. J.D. reaches for the plate. Freddy pulls it back. J.D. reaches again, and Freddy is so stoned, that he isn't quick enough this time—J.D. grabs it.

"I thought you'd know it was me," J.D. says. "I apologize." He dishes salad onto the plate. "You'll be rid of me for six months, in the morning."

"Where does your plane leave from?" Freddy says.

"Kennedy."

"Come in here!" Tucker calls. "I've got a story for you about Perry Dwyer down at the Anvil last week, when he thought he saw Aristotle Onassis."

"Who's Perry Dwyer?" J.D. says.

"That is not the point of the story, dear man. And when you're in Cassis, I want you to look up an American painter over there. Will you? He doesn't have a phone. Anyway—I've been tracking him, and I know where he is now, and I am *very* interested, if you would stress that with him, to do a show in June that will be *only* him. He doesn't answer my letters."

"Your hand is cut," J.D. says to me.

"Forget it," I say. "Go ahead."

"I'm sorry," he says. "Did I make you do that?"

"Yes, you did."

"Don't keep your finger under the water. Put pressure on it to stop the bleeding."

He puts the plate on the table. Freddy is leaning against the counter, staring at the blood swirling in the sink, and smoking the joint all by himself. I can feel the little curls on my forehead that Freddy was talking about. They feel heavy on my skin. I hate to see my own blood. I'm sweating. I let J.D. do what he does; he turns off the water and wraps his hand around my second finger, squeezing. Water runs down our wrists.

Freddy jumps to answer the phone when it rings, as though a siren just went off behind him. He calls me to the phone, but J.D. steps in front of me, shakes his head no, and takes the dish towel and wraps it around my hand before he lets me go.

"Well," Marilyn says. "I had the best of intentions, but my battery's dead."

J.D. is standing behind me, with his hand on my shoulder.

"I'll be right over," I say. "He's not upset now, is he?"

"No, but he's dropped enough hints that he doesn't think he can make it through the night."

"O.K.," I say. "I'm sorry about all of this."

"Six years old," Marilyn says. "Wait till he grows up and gets that feeling."

I hang up.

"Let me see your hand," J.D. says.

"I don't want to look at it. Just go get me a Band-Aid, please."

He turns and goes upstairs. I unwrap the towel and look at it. It's pretty deep, but no glass is in my finger. I feel funny; the outlines of things are turning yellow. I sit in the chair by the phone. Sam comes and lies beside me, and I stare at his black-and-yellow tail, beating. I reach down with my good hand and pat him, breathing deeply in time with every second pat.

"*Rothko?*" Tucker says bitterly, in the living room. "Nothing is great that can appear on greeting cards. Wyeth is that way. Would 'Christina's World' look bad on a cocktail napkin? You know it wouldn't."

I jump as the phone rings again. "Hello?" I say, wedging the phone against my shoulder with my ear, wrapping the dish towel tighter around my hand.

"Tell them it's a crank call. Tell them anything," Johnny says. "I miss you. How's Saturday night at your house?"

"All right," I say. I catch my breath.

"Everything's all right here, too. Yes indeed. Roast rack of lamb. Friend of Nicole's who's going to Key West tomorrow had too much to drink and got depressed because he thought it was raining in Key West, and I said I'd go in my study and call the National Weather Service. Hello, Weather Service. How are you?"

J.D. comes down from upstairs with two Band-Aids and stands beside me, unwrapping one. I want to say to Johnny, "I'm cut. I'm bleeding. It's no joke."

It's all right to talk in front of J.D., but I don't know who else might overhear me.

"I'd say they made the delivery about four this afternoon," I say.

"This is the church, this is the steeple. Open the door, and see all the people," Johnny says. "Take care of yourself. I'll hang up and find out if it's raining in Key West."

"Late in the afternoon," I say. "Everything is fine."

"Nothing is fine," Johnny says. "Take care of yourself."

He hangs up. I put the phone down, and realize that I'm still having trouble focusing, the sight of my cut finger made me so light-headed. I don't look at the finger again as J.D. undoes the towel and wraps the Band-Aids around my finger.

"What's going on in here?" Franks says, coming into the dining room.

"I cut my finger," I say. "It's O.K."

"You did?" he says. He looks woozy — a little drunk. "Who keeps calling?"

"Marilyn. Mark changed his mind about staying all night. She was going to bring him home, but her battery's dead. You'll have to get him. Or I will."

"Who called the second time?" he says.

"The oil company. They wanted to know if we got our delivery today."

He nods. "I'll go get him, if you want," he says. He lowers his voice. "Tucker's probably going to whirl himself into a tornado for an encore," he says, nodding toward the living room. "I'll take him with me."

"Do you want me to go get him?" J.D. says.

"I don't mind getting some air," Frank says. "Thanks, though. Why don't you go in the living room and eat your dinner?"

"You forgive me?" J.D. says.

"Sure," I say. "It wasn't your fault. Where did you get that mask?"

"I found it on top of a Goodwill box in Manchester. There was also a beautiful old birdcage — solid brass."

The phone rings again. I pick it up. "Wouldn't I love to be in Key West with you," Johnny says. He makes a sound as though he's kissing me and hangs up.

"Wrong number," I say.

Franks feels in his pants pocket for the car keys.

J.D. knows about Johnny. He introduced me, in the faculty lounge, where J.D. and I had gone to get a cup of coffee after I registered for classes. After being gone for nearly two years, J.D. still gets mail at the department — he said he had to stop by for the mail anyway, so he'd drive me to campus and point me toward the registrar's. J.D. taught English; now he does nothing. J.D. is glad that I've gone back to college to study art again, now that Mark is in school. I'm six credits away from an M.A. in art history. He wants me to think about myself, instead of thinking about Mark all the time. He talks as though I could roll Mark out on a string and let him fly off, high above me. J.D.'s wife and son died in a car crash. His son was Mark's age. "I wasn't prepared," J.D. said when we were driving over that day. He always says this when he talks about it. "How could you be prepared for such a thing?" I asked him. "I am now," he said. Then, realizing he was acting very hardboiled, made fun of himself. "Go on," he said, "punch me in the stomach. Hit me as hard as you can." We both knew he isn't prepared for anything. When he couldn't find a parking place that day, his hands were wrapped around the wheel so tightly that his knuckles turned white.

Johnny came in as we were drinking coffee. J.D. was looking at his junk mail — publishers wanting him to order anthologies, ways to get free dictionaries. "You are so lucky to be out of it," Johnny said, by way of greeting. "What do you do when you've spent two weeks on 'Hamlet' and the student writes about Hamlet's good friend Horchow?"

He threw a blue book into J.D.'s lap. J.D. sailed it back.

"Johnny," he said, "this is Amy."

"Hi, Amy," Johnny said.

"You remember when Frank Wayne was in graduate school here? Amy's Frank's wife."

"Hi, Amy," Johnny said.

J.D. told me he knew it the instant Johnny walked into the room — he knew that second that he should introduce me as somebody's wife. He could have predicted it all from the way Johnny looked at me.

For a long time J.D. gloated that he had been prepared for what happened next — that Johnny and I were going to get together. It took me to disturb his pleasure in himself — me, crying hysterically on the phone last month, not knowing what to do, what move to make next.

"Don't do anything for a while. I guess that's my advice," J.D. said. "But you probably shouldn't listen to me. All I can do myself is run away, hide out. I'm not the learned professor. You know what I believe. I believe all that wicked fairy-tale crap: your heart will break, your house will burn."

Tonight, because he doesn't have a garage at his farm, J.D. has come to leave his car in the empty half of our two-car garage while he's in France. I look out the window and see his old Saab, glowing in the moonlight. J.D. has brought his favorite book, "A Vision,"[4] to read on the plane. He says his suitcase contains only a spare pair of jeans, cigarettes, and underwear. He is going to buy a leather jacket in France, at a store where he almost bought a leather jacket two years ago.

In our bedroom there are about twenty small glass prisms hung with fishing line from one of the exposed beams; they catch the morning light, and we stare at them like a cat eyeing catnip held above its head. Just now, it is 2 A.M. At six-thirty, they will be filled with dazzling color. At four or five, Mark will come into the bedroom and get in bed with us. Sam will wake up, stretch, and shake,

[4]"*A Vision*" by William Butler Yeats, 1856–1939

and the tags on his collar will clink, and he will yawn and shake again and go downstairs, where J.D. is asleep in his sleeping bag and Tucker is asleep on the sofa, and get a drink of water from his dish. Mark has been coming into our bedroom for about a year. He gets onto the bed by climbing up on a footstool that horrified me when I first saw it—a gift from Frank's mother: a footstool that says "Today Is the First Day of the Rest of Your Life" in needlepoint. I kept it in a closet for years, but it occurred to me that it would help Mark get up into the bed, so he would not have to make a little leap and possibly skin his shin again. Now Mark does not disturb us when he comes into the bedroom, except that it bothers me that he has reverted to sucking his thumb. Sometimes he lies in bed with his cold feet against my leg. Sometimes, small as he is, he snores.

Somebody is playing a record downstairs. It's the Velvet Underground—Nico, in a dream or swoon, singing "Sunday Morning." I can barely hear the whispering and tinkling of the record. I can only follow it because I've heard it a hundred times.

I am lying in bed, waiting for Frank to get out of the bathroom. My cut finger throbs. Things are going on in the house even though I have gone to bed; water runs, the record plays, Sam is still downstairs, so there must be some action.

I have known everybody in this house for years; and as time goes by I know them all less and less. J.D. was Frank's adviser in college. Frank was his best student, and they started to see each other outside of class. They played handball. J.D. and his family came to dinner. We went there. That summer—the summer Frank decided to go to graduate school in business instead of English—J.D.'s wife and son deserted him in a more horrible way, in that car crash. J.D. has quit his job. He has been to Las Vegas, to Colorado, New Orleans, Los Angeles, Paris twice; he tapes postcards to the walls of his living room. A lot of the time, on the weekends, he shows up at our house with his sleeping bag. Sometimes he brings a girl. Lately, not. Years ago, Tucker was in Frank's therapy group in New York and ended up hiring Frank to work as the accountant for his gallery. Tucker was in therapy at the time because he was obsessed with foreigners. Now he is also obsessed with homosexuals. Before the parties he does TM and yoga, and during the parties he does Seconals and isometrics. When I first met him, he was living for the summer in his sister's house in Vermont while she was in Europe, and he called us one night, in New York, in a real panic because there were wasps all over. They were "hatching," he said—big, sleepy wasps that were everywhere. We said we'd come; we drove all through the night to get to Brattleboro. It was true: there were wasps on the undersides of plates, in the plants, in the folds of curtains. Tucker was so upset that he was out behind the house, in the cold Vermont morning, wrapped like an Indian in a blanket, with only his pajamas on underneath. He was sitting in a lawn chair, hiding behind a bush, waiting for us to come.

And Freddy—"Reddy Fox," when Frank is feeling affectionate toward him. When we first met, I taught him to ice-skate and he taught me to waltz; in the summer, at Atlantic City, he'd go with me on a roller coaster that curved high over the waves. I was the one—not Frank—who would get out of bed in the middle of the night and meet him at an all-night deli and put my arm around his shoulders, the way he put his arm around my shoulders on the roller coaster, and talk quietly to him until he got over his latest anxiety attack. Now he tests me, and I retreat: this man he picked up, this man who picked him up, how it feels to have forgotten somebody's name when your hand is in the back pocket of his jeans and you're not even halfway to your apartment. Reddy Fox—admiring my new red silk blouse, stroking his fingertips down the front, and my eyes wide, because I could feel his fingers on my chest, even though I was holding the blouse in front of me on a hanger to be admired. All those moments, and all they meant was that I was fooled into thinking I knew these people because I knew the small things, the personal things.

Freddy will always be more stoned than I am, because he feels comfortable getting stoned with me and I'll always be reminded that he's more lost. Tucker knows he can come to the house and be the center of attention; he can tell all the stories he knows, and we'll never tell the story we know about him hiding in the bushes like a frightened dog. J.D. comes back from his trips with boxes full of postcards, and I look at all of them as though they're photographs taken by him, and I know, and he knows, that what he likes about them is their flatness—the unreality of them, the unreality of what he does.

Last summer, I read "The Metamorphosis" and said to J.D., "Why did Gregor Samsa wake up a cockroach?" His answer (which he would have toyed over with his students forever) was "Because that's what people expected of him."

They make the illogical logical. I don't do anything, because I'm waiting, I'm on hold (J.D.); I stay stoned because I know it's better to be out of it (Freddy); I love art because I myself am a work of art (Tucker).

Frank is harder to understand. One night a week or so ago, I thought we were really attuned to each other, communicating by telepathic waves, and as I lay in bed about to speak I realized that the vibrations really existed: they were him, snoring.

Now he's coming into the bedroom, and I'm trying again to think what to say. Or ask. Or do.

"Be glad you're not in Key West," he says. He climbs into bed.

I raise myself up on one elbow and stare at him.

"There's a hurricane about to hit," he says.

"What?" I say. "Where did you hear that?"

"When Reddy Fox and I were putting the dishes away. We had the radio on." He doubles up his pillow, pushes it under his neck. "Boom goes everything," he says. "Bam. Crash. Poof." He looks at me. "You look shocked." He closes his eyes. Then, after a minute or two, he murmurs, "Hurricanes upset you? I'll try to think of something nice."

He is quiet for so long that I think he has fallen asleep. Then he says, "Cars that run on water. A field of flowers, none alike. A shooting star that goes slow enough for you to watch. Your life to do over again." He has been whispering in my ear, and when he takes his mouth away I shiver. He slides lower in the bed for sleep. "I'll tell you something really amazing," he says. "Tucker told me he went into a travel agency on Park Avenue last week and asked the travel agent where he should go to pan for gold, and she told him."

"Where did she tell him to go?"

"I think somewhere in Peru. The banks of some river in Peru."

"Did you decide what you're going to do after Mark's birthday?" I say.

He doesn't answer me. I touch him on the side, finally.

"It's two o'clock in the morning. Let's talk about it another time."

"You picked the house, Frank. They're your friends downstairs. I used to be what you wanted me to be."

"They're your friends, too," he says. "Don't be paranoid."

"I want to know if you're staying or going."

He takes a deep breath, lets it out, and continues to lie very still.

"Everything you've done is commendable," he says. "You did the right thing to go back to school. You tried to do the right thing by finding yourself a normal friend like Marilyn. But your whole life you've made one mistake—you've surrounded yourself with men. Let me tell you something. All men—if they're crazy, like Tucker, if they're gay as the Queen of the May, like Reddy Fox, even if they're just six years old—I'm going to tell you something about them. Men think they're Spider-Man and Buck Rogers and Superman. You know what we all feel inside that you don't feel? That we're going to the stars."

He takes my hand. "I'm looking down on all of this from space," he whispers. "I'm already gone."

[1979]

QUESTIONS

1. Why does Amy put up with a house full of crazies? Why does she tolerate the situation around her?
2. How do you interpret the central metaphor of burning?
3. J. D. says to Amy, "'I believe all that wicked fairy-tale crap: your heart will break, your house will burn.'" Do you regard the story as an updated version of a traditional fairy tale?

J. BERNLEF

(b. 1937)

NETHERLANDS

The prolific Dutch writer J. Bernlef, the pen name of Henk Marsman, is the author of more than 50 books (fiction, poetry, drama, and essays), though few of them have been translated into English or published in the United States. He was born in St. Pancras, Holland, January 14, 1937. His writing has won his country's major literary awards, including the Constantijn Huygens Prize, in 1984, for his entire work.

In his notes to "The Black Dog" in *Sudden Fiction* (edited by Robert Shapard and James Thomas), Bernlef states that the story is "about the invention or rather the discovery of lies, which I think is one of the cornerstones of literature. When I discovered that you could use language in such a way that people believe what it described although what it described had never happened, I started out as a storyteller and, later, as a writer of fiction."

In a commentary about the writer by the Foundation for the Promotion of the Translation of Dutch Literary Works, Bernlef is described as follows: "[His] writing doesn't mean evoking a familiar reality but inalienating it. The main character in *Paspoort in duplo* (*Passport in Duplicate*) threatens to disappear in the past he had purposely evoked to confront the present with. In *De dood van de reqisseur* (*Death of the Director*) a writer feels drawn into his own fiction. In these and many other cases, Bernlef's main theme is the phenomenon of *disappearing*, also the disappearance of personality and identity."

The Black Dog

There's a fire at Voorthuyzen's bakery on Main Street," his father had said during breakfast. "A large blazing fire," he had added.

Half an hour later he shuffled back, his head lowered. His father had laughed at him. His mother had found it childish that he responded so angrily to his father's joke.

It was Saturday, the first of April. Secretly he had wished his father dead.

Now it was the second of April. You can forget a lot in twenty-four hours. He took the usual Sunday stroll with his father.

Behind the still-closed outdoor wooden swimming pool the sandy land stretched ruggedly toward the pale green backdike. While he dodged through the holes and half-caved-in huts of unknown boys in search of possible treasures, his father whistled softly through his teeth and smoked a Players from a pale blue pack, his shiny black raincoat folded in four over his left arm, for he never trusted the weather report, especially not in April.

At the edge of the dike his father sat staring for a long time in the direction of the three chimney stacks of the electric plant while he, the son, watched the schools of nearly transparent sticklebacks and the scurrying of pitch-black water beetles at the foot of a ditch.

These were always the best hours of the week, all alone with his father, who now took off his glasses and wiped them with a chamois cloth which he removed from a front compartment in his purse. As if he wanted to get a better look at the three upright brick-red chimneys of the power plant.

Sitting on top of the dike in clear weather you could even see the ships slowly sailing through the Connecting Canal on their way to the sea.

These were the best hours of the week because his father didn't do a thing, but just sat there silently and every now and then gave him a short wave whenever he, sitting in a hunched position, would look up from the side of the ditch. He listened to the shrill cries of the peewits and the seagulls in the pasture in front of him. A lightly spotted rabbit jumped clumsily through the short grass.

When his father had finished smoking another Player he made the usual gesture. Time to return. Actually it was only a short walk to the backdike, but the town's last row of houses still seemed to be far away.

A large black dog ran toward them over the dunes of sand in enormous lopsided leaps. A Bouvier de Flandres. You could tell by the trimmed ears lying flat against his head.

The dog began to jump around them, barking wildly.

"Just keep on walking." His father had barely finished the sentence before he had to use both hands to keep the raving dog at bay. Savagely, with his head shaking, the animal settled his jaws into the black raincoat.

Only now did he notice the flecks of foam flying out of his mouth, the yellowish glare in his eyes and the unusual rigid manner in which the dog fixed his paws, jerking at a flap of the coat with all his might while his father frantically held on to it with both hands. Every now and then the dog's black body trembled as if it were undergoing an electric shock.

He looked around him. A bed spring, a smashed orange crate. Not a person in sight. Nobody who could see them here. Nobody to help his father.

Suddenly the dog let go of the coat. His father lost his balance, stumbled over backwards, and the dog immediately plunged toward him with a wide-open mouth full of foam and threads of bloody slime. Lying on the ground his father gave the dog such a kick with one of this black shoes that the dog tottered a few steps sideways and stood in a daze for a few moments, as if the blow had brought him to his senses.

Then the dog shook his pelt and bent down, the front paws spread out before him, snarling at the ground. His father had jumped up, the shredded raincoat still in his hands. His left hand was bleeding.

A Dodge hobbled over the sandy land loudly blowing its horn. For the first time he dared to do something. He ran toward the stub-nosed car, his thin boy's arms swaying above his head. Come here. Come here. The driver, a man with a thick bald head and red cheeks, leaned out of the lowered side window.

"That dog," he shouted gasping and pointing. "That dog is biting my father to death!"

The man appeared startled by his announcement and accelerated. The car lunged ahead. He ran after the car, which rode in a circle around his father and the dog twice. His father made a motion to the driver. The car then made an abrupt turn and joltingly disappeared in the direction of the main road. And the dog sprung up again with his mouth wide open.

"Go away," his father screamed. "Run. Go home. Hurry up."

He had to. Without even looking he ran from his father who would now surely be bitten to death by the dog.

He began to cross the sandy land, through the Sunday streets, along parks and lampposts, along the closed front doors of friends' homes, the fence of the nursery school, the pharmacy with its brown bottles in the window.

His father, bitten to death by a black wolf-dog. Covered with foam and slime. Bleeding all over.

He ran crying with quivering lips. Everywhere sat silent people across from each other in bay windows.

Panting, he let himself fall against the door of his house. He pressed the bell without letting go. He leaned against the door with such force that when it was opened he slowly glided together with the door's panel into the hallway.

From the open space of the landing above he heard his mother's voice. Who was there? He stumbled up the stairs.

He couldn't utter a word, only shake his wailing head. His mother gathered him up. What is wrong? What had happened?

Finally he sat plopped down in one of the armchairs in the living room. She went to the kitchen and came back with a wet wash cloth which she brusquely rubbed over his face.

"What happened exactly? Quiet down and tell me."

He could only wail, his drawn-up knees pressed against his chest. She could not understand it. Only he knew what he had wished upon his father while walking back from the nonexistent fire that Saturday morning.

"Daddy is dead."

He hardly felt the hard lashing blow on his cheek. His head jerked to the side and bumped against the headrest. It was as if his insides were filling up with ice water. He vaguely heard doors slamming. Then it became silent. In front of him a striped blue wash cloth lay on the carpet.

He let his legs sink to the floor, stood up and walked to the window. The field in front of the door was deserted. Because it was Sunday there were no playing children to be seen. He stood high above the ground and looked out over the lot, the pastures, the canal and the rows of dully shining greenhouses in the distance.

"I'm never going onto the streets again," he said loudly.

He turned around. The chairs, the table, the piano, the light rug with the cheerful orange rectangles; he stood in a room that suddenly had nothing to do with home anymore.

Filled with panic he leaped into the side room and grabbed the portrait on his father's desk. His father and mother, arm and arm and laughing, somewhere in a garden.

"That was made when you were not here yet."

Then this could also be possible. That everything would continue as before, the room, the dike, his mother, the school, only his father was not there anymore. A dog which grew ever bigger and blacker while his father got weaker and smaller until he completely disappeared.

He had thought of it first, then he had said it and now it had happened.

From a thin silver frame his father and mother smiled at him. From a time in which he had not existed.

Perhaps that was why he sat behind the desk as if turned to stone, the photo pressed between both hands, when the door opened and he heard his father's voice. As if he still lived. He put the portrait down. With his eyes closed he turned around. He heard his father laughing. Only then did he dare to look.

One of his father's arms was in a white sling. He laughed and leaned with his good arm on the marble mantel shelf. He was really alive. Both of them lived, he and his father, at the same time.

The door opened yet again and his mother entered, a tray in her hands. A teapot, three white cups and three saucers. Three spoons, a sugar pot. He could not keep his eyes from these things.

They went to sit at the table, each at his own place. His father on the left, his mother to his right. Walls and furniture surrounded them. His mother poured the tea. A thin golden-yellow stream that softly splashed into the cups. All three of them stirred their teaspoons at the same time.

He sat at the head of the table peering at a stain on the wallpaper and suddenly everything came to him from the dark spot on the wall as if from out of a hole. The fire in the not burning bakery, the picture from the time he had not yet existed and his bitten-to-death living father, who patted his head with his free hand and said there was no reason to cry.

"They did away with him right away," he heard his father say. "One shot through the head and that was it."

[1978]

Translated by
FRANK SCIMONE

QUESTIONS

1. In what way or ways does the boy's relationship with his father alter? What accounts for the shift between the first two sections of the story?
2. What are the symbolic attributes of the black dog?
3. What will be the boy's relationship with his father in the future?
4. Is Bernlef's theme of "disappearing" present — if disguised — in "The Black Dog"?

AMBROSE BIERCE

(1842–1914?)

UNITED STATES

What many people remember about Ambrose Bierce—instead of his writing—is that he vanished in Mexico, though even the facts of his mysterious disappearance are often confused. He was not in the prime of his life when that happened (approximately 1914) but nearly 75 years old. He had already experienced a highly successful writing career, bringing it to a sense of closure with the supervision of his collected works. Perhaps he decided that as a writer he had accomplished all that he wanted. Perhaps the cause of his disappearance was in no way related to his literary work. Yet in spite of intense speculation by many others (including Carlos Fuentes in his novel *The Old Gringo*, 1985), we will probably never know.

Bierce was born in Ohio in 1842. He fought in the Civil War and was wounded in 1864, at which time he left for California, where he eventually became a successful journalist. He married well enough that he was able to live comfortably in London for a number of years, but he eventually returned to California, where he wrote for William Randolph Hearst's *San Francisco Examiner*. By the 1880s, Bierce was writing short stories, many of them freely based on his Civil War experiences. Though his collected works come to 12 volumes, critics identify his earliest stories (in *Tales of Soldiers and Civilians*, 1891, and *Can Such Things Be?*, 1893) as his major ones. Bierce's forte, the short story, perhaps can best be typified by his definition of the novel: "a short story padded." Critics are quick to point out that there is no padding in his finest stories.

Bierce is also remembered for *The Devil's Dictionary* (1906), which the *Literary History of the United States* describes as "no more than an alphabetical compendium of Bierce's deadliest witticisms and most philosophical epigrams."

An Occurrence at Owl Creek Bridge

I

A man stood upon a railroad bridge in Northern Alabama, looking down into the swift waters twenty feet below. The man's hands were behind his back, the wrists bound with a cord. A rope loosely encircled his neck. It was attached to a stout cross-timber above his head, and the slack fell to the level of his knees. Some loose boards laid upon the sleepers supporting the metals of the railway supplied a footing for him and his executioners—two private soldiers of the Federal army, directed by a sergeant, who in civil life may have been a deputy sheriff. At a short remove upon the same temporary platform was an officer in the uniform of his rank, armed. He was a captain. A sentinel at each end of the bridge stood with his rifle in the position known as "support," that is to say, vertical in front of the left shoulder, the hammer resting on the forearm thrown straight across the chest—a formal and unnatural position, enforcing an erect carriage of the body. It did not appear to be the duty of these two men to know what was occurring at the centre of the bridge; they merely blockaded the two ends of the foot plank which traversed it.

Beyond one of the sentinels nobody was in sight; the railroad ran straight away into a forest for a hundred yards, then, curving, was lost to view. Doubtless there was an outpost further along. The other bank of the stream was open ground—a gentle acclivity crowned with a stockade of vertical tree trunks, loop-holed for rifles, with a single embrasure through which protruded the muzzle of a brass cannon commanding the bridge. Midway of the slope between bridge and fort were the spectators—a single company of infantry in line, at "parade rest," the butts of the rifles on the ground, the barrels inclining slightly backward against the right shoulder, the hands crossed upon the stock. A lieutenant stood at the right of the line, the point of his sword upon the ground, his left hand resting upon his right. Excepting the group of four at the centre of the bridge not a man moved. The company faced the bridge, staring stonily, motionless. The sentinels, facing the banks of the stream, might have been statues to adorn the bridge. The captain stood with folded arms, silent, observing the work of his subordinates but making no sign. Death is a dignitary who, when he comes announced, is to be received with formal manifestations of respect, even by those most familiar with him. In the code of military etiquette silence and fixity are forms of deference.

The man who was engaged in being hanged was apparently about thirty-five years of age. He was a civilian, if one might judge from his dress, which was that of a planter. His features were good—a straight nose, firm mouth, broad forehead, from which his long, dark hair was combed straight back, falling behind his ears to the collar of his well-fitted frock coat. He wore a moustache and pointed beard, but no whiskers; his eyes were large and dark grey and had a kindly expression which one would hardly have expected in one whose neck was in the hemp. Evidently this was no vulgar assassin. The liberal military code makes provision for hanging many kinds of people, and gentlemen are not excluded.

The preparations being complete, the two private soldiers stepped aside and each drew away the plank upon which he had been standing. The sergeant turned to the captain, saluted and placed himself immediately behind that officer, who in turn moved apart one pace. These movements left the condemned man and the sergeant standing on the two ends of the same plank, which spanned three of the cross-ties of the bridge. The end upon which the civilian stood almost, but not quite, reached a fourth. This plank had been held in place by the weight of the captain; it was now held by that of the sergeant. At a signal from the former, the latter would step aside, the plank would tilt and the condemned man go down between two ties. The arrangement commended itself to his judgment as simple and effective. His face had not been covered nor his eyes bandaged. He looked a moment at his "unsteadfast footing," then let his gaze wander to the swirling water of the stream racing madly beneath his feet. A piece of dancing driftwood caught his attention and his eyes followed it down the current. How slowly it appeared to move! What a sluggish stream!

He closed his eyes in order to fix his last thoughts upon his wife and children. The water, touched to gold by the early sun, the brooding mists under the banks at some distance down the stream, the fort, the soldiers, the piece of drift—all had distracted him. And now he became conscious of a new disturbance. Striking through the thought of his dear ones was a sound which he could neither ignore nor understand, a sharp, distinct, metallic percussion like the stroke of a blacksmith's hammer upon the anvil; it had the same ringing quality. He wondered what it was, and whether immeasurably distant or near by—it seemed both. Its recurrence was regular, but as slow as the tolling of a death knell. He awaited each stroke with impatience and—he knew not why—apprehension. The intervals of silence grew progressively longer; the delays became maddening. With their greater infrequency the sounds increased in strength and sharpness. They hurt his ear like the thrust of a knife; he feared he would shriek. What he heard was the ticking of his watch.

He unclosed his eyes and saw again the water below him. "If I could free my hands," he thought, "I might throw off the noose and spring into the stream. By diving I could evade the bullets, and, swimming vigorously, reach the bank, take to the woods, and get away home. My home, thank God, is as yet outside their lines; my wife and little ones are still beyond the invader's farthest advance."

As these thoughts, which have here to be set down in words, were flashed into the doomed man's brain rather than evolved from it, the captain nodded to the sergeant. The sergeant stepped aside.

II

Peyton Farquhar was a well-to-do planter, of an old and highly-respected Alabama family. Being a slave owner, and, like other slave owners, a politician, he was naturally an original secessionist and ardently devoted to the Southern cause. Circumstances of an imperious nature which it is unnecessary to relate here, and prevented him from taking service with the gallant army which had fought the disastrous campaigns ending with the fall of Corinth, and he chafed under the inglorious restraint, longing for the release of his energies, the larger life of the soldier, the opportunity for distinction. That opportunity, he felt, would come, as it comes to all in war time. Meanwhile he did what he could. No service was too humble for him to perform in aid of the South, no adventure too perilous for him to undertake if consistent with the character of a civilian who was at heart a soldier, and who in good faith and without too much qualification assented to at least a part of the frankly villainous dictum that all is fair in love and war.

One evening while Farquhar and his wife were sitting on a rustic bench near the entrance to his grounds, a grey-clad soldier rode up to the gate and asked for a drink of water. Mrs. Farquhar was only too happy to serve him with her own white hands. While she was gone to fetch the water, her husband approached the dusty horseman and inquired eagerly for news from the front.

"The Yanks are repairing the railroads," said the man, "and are getting ready for another advance. They have reached the Owl Creek bridge, put it in order, and built a stockade on the other bank. The commandant has issued an order, which is posted everywhere, declaring that any civilian caught interfering with the railroad, its bridges, tunnels, or trains, will be summarily hanged. I saw the order."

"How far is it to the Owl Creek bridge?" Farquhar asked.

"About thirty miles."

"Is there no force on this side the creek?"

"Only a picket post half a mile out, on the railroad, and a single sentinel at this end of the bridge."

"Suppose a man—a civilian and student of hanging—should elude the picket post and perhaps get the better of the sentinel," said Farquhar, smiling, "what could he accomplish?"

The soldier reflected. "I was there a month ago," he replied. "I observed that the flood of last winter had lodged a great quantity of driftwood against the wooden pier at this end of the bridge. It is now dry and would burn like tow."

The lady had now brought the water, which the soldier drank. He thanked her ceremoniously, bowed to her husband, and rode away. An hour later, after nightfall, he repassed the plantation, going northward in the direction from which he had come. He was a Federal scout.

III

As Peyton Farquhar fell straight downward through the bridge, he lost consciousness and was as one already dead. From this state he was awakened—ages later, it seemed to him—by the pain of a sharp pressure upon his throat, followed by a sense of suffocation. Keen, poignant agonies seemed to shoot from his neck downward through every fibre of his body and limbs. These pains appeared to flash along well-defined lines of ramification, and to beat with an inconceivably rapid periodicity. They seemed like streams of pulsating fire heating him to an intolerable temperature. As to his head, he was conscious of nothing but a feeling of fullness—of congestion. These sensations were unaccompanied by thought. The intellectual part of his nature was already effaced; he had power only to feel, and feeling was torment. He was conscious of motion. Encompassed in a luminous cloud, of which he was now merely the fiery heart, without material substance, he swung through unthinkable arcs of oscillation, like a vast pendulum. Then all at once, with terrible suddenness, the light about him shot upward with the noise of a loud plash; a frightful roaring was in his ears, and all was cold and dark. The power of thought was restored; he knew that the rope had broken and he had fallen into the stream. There was no additional strangulation; the noose about his neck was already suffocating him, and kept the water from his lungs. To die of hanging at the bottom of a river—the idea seemed to him ludicrous. He opened his eyes in the blackness and saw above him a gleam of light, but how distant, how inaccessible! He was still sinking, for the light became fainter and fainter until it was a mere glimmer. Then it began to grow and brighten, and he knew that he was rising toward the surface—knew it with reluctance, for he was now very comfortable. "To be hanged and drowned," he thought, "that is not so bad; but I do not wish to be shot. No; I will not be shot; that is not fair."

He was not conscious of an effort, but a sharp pain in his wrist apprised him that he was trying to free his hands. He gave the struggle his attention, as an idler might observe the feat of a juggler, without interest in the outcome. What splendid effort!—what magnificent, what superhuman strength! Ah, that was a fine endeavor! Bravo! The cord fell away; his arms parted and floated upward, the hands dimly seen on each side in the growing light. He watched them with a new interest as first one and then the other pounced upon the noose at his neck. They tore it away and thrust it fiercely aside, its undulations resembling those of a water-snake. "Put it back, put it back!" He thought he shouted these words to his hands, for the undoing of the noose had been succeeded by the direst pang which he had yet experienced. His neck arched horribly; his brain was on fire; his heart, which had been fluttering faintly, gave a great leap, trying to force itself out at his mouth. His whole body was racked and wrenched with an insupportable anguish! But his disobedient hands gave no heed to the command. They beat the water vigorously with quick, downward strokes, forcing him to the surface. He felt his head emerge; his eyes were blinded by the sunlight; his chest expanded convulsively, and with a supreme and crowning agony his lungs engulfed a great draught of air, which instantly he expelled in a shriek!

He was now in full possession of his physical senses. They were, indeed, preternaturally keen and alert. Something in the awful disturbance of his organic system had so exalted and refined them that they made record of things never before perceived. He felt the ripples upon his face and heard their separate sounds as they struck. He looked at the forest on the bank of the stream, saw the individual trees, the leaves and the veining of each leaf—saw the very insects upon them, the locusts, the brilliant-bodied flies, the grey spiders stretching their webs from twig to twig. He noted the prismatic colors in all the dewdrops upon a million blades of grass. The humming of the gnats that danced above the eddies of the stream, the beating of the dragon flies' wings, the strokes of the water spiders' legs, like oars which had lifted their boat—all these made audible music. A fish slid along beneath his eyes and he heard the rush of its body parting the water.

He had come to the surface facing down the stream; in a moment the visible world seemed to wheel slowly round, himself the pivotal point, and he saw the bridge, the fort, the soldiers upon the bridge, the captain, the sergeant, the two privates, his executioners. They were in silhouette against the blue sky. They shouted and gesticulated, pointing at him; the captain had drawn his pistol, but did not fire; the others were unarmed. Their movements were grotesque and horrible, their forms gigantic.

Suddenly he heard a sharp report and something struck the water smartly within a few inches of his head, spattering his face with spray. He heard a second report, and saw one of the sentinels with his rifle at his shoulder, a light cloud of blue smoke rising from the muzzle. The man in the water saw the eye of the man on the bridge gazing into his own through the sights of the rifle. He observed that it was a grey eye, and remembered having read that grey eyes were keenest and that all famous marksmen had them. Nevertheless, this one had missed.

A counter swirl had caught Farquhar and turned him half round; he was again looking into the forest on the bank opposite the fort. The sound of a clear, high voice in a monotonous singsong now rang out behind him and came across the water with a distinctness that pierced and subdued all other sounds, even the beating of the ripples in his ears. Although no soldier, he had frequented camps enough to know the dread significance of that deliberate, drawling, aspirated chant; the lieutenant on shore was taking a part in the morning's work. How coldly and pitilessly—with what an even, calm intonation, presaging and enforcing tranquility in the men—with what accurately-measured intervals fell those cruel words:

"Attention, company. . . . Shoulder arms. . . . Ready. . . . Aim. . . . Fire."

Farquhar dived—dived as deeply as he could. The water roared in his ears like the voice of Niagara, yet he heard the dulled thunder of the volley, and rising again toward the surface, met shining bits of metal, singularly flattened, oscillating slowly downward. Some of them touched him on the face and hands, then fell away, continuing their descent. One lodged between his collar and neck; it was uncomfortably warm, and he snatched it out.

As he rose to the surface, gasping for breath, he saw that he had been a long time under water; he was perceptibly farther down stream—nearer to safety. The soldiers had almost finished reloading; the metal ramrods flashed all at once in the sunshine as they were drawn from the barrels, turned in the air, and thrust into their sockets. The two sentinels fired again, independently and ineffectually.

The hunted man saw all this over his shoulder; he was now swimming vigorously with the current. His brain was as energetic as his arms and legs; he thought with the rapidity of lightning.

"The officer," he reasoned, "will not make the martinet's error a second time. It is as easy to dodge a volley as a single shot. He has probably already given the command to fire at will. God help me, I cannot dodge them all!"

An appalling plash within two yards of him, followed by a loud rushing sound, *diminuendo*, which seemed to travel back through the air to the fort and died in an explosion which stirred the very river to its deeps! A rising sheet of water, which curved over him, fell down upon him, blinded him, strangled him! The cannon had taken a hand in the game. As he shook his head free from the commotion of the smitten water, he heard the deflected shot humming through the air ahead, and in an instant it was cracking and smashing the branches in the forest beyond.

"They will not do that again," he thought; "the next time they will use a charge of grape. I must keep my eye upon the gun; the smoke will apprise me—the report arrives too late; it lags behind the missile. It is a good gun."

Suddenly, he felt himself whirled round and round—spinning like a top. The water, the banks, the forest, the now distant bridge, fort, and men—all were commingled and blurred. Objects were represented by their colors only; circular horizontal streaks of color—that was all he saw. He had been caught in a vortex and was being whirled on with a velocity of advance and gyration which made him giddy and sick. In a few moments he was flung upon the gravel at the foot of the left bank of the stream—the southern bank—and behind a projecting point which concealed him from his enemies. The sudden arrest of his motion, the abrasion of one of his hands on the gravel, restored him and he wept with delight. He dug his fingers into the sand, threw it over himself in handfuls and audibly blessed it. It looked like gold, like diamonds, rubies, emeralds; he could think of nothing beautiful which it did not resemble. The trees upon the bank were giant garden plants; he noted a definite order in their arrangement, inhaled the fragrance of their blooms. A strange, roseate light shone through the spaces among their trunks, and the wind made in their branches the music of æolian harps. He had no wish to perfect his escape, was content to remain in that enchanting spot until retaken.

A whizz and rattle of grapeshot among the branches high above his head roused him from his dream. The baffled cannoneer had fired him a random farewell. He sprang to his feet, rushed up the sloping bank, and plunged into the forest.

All that day he travelled, laying his course by the rounding sun. The forest seemed interminable; nowhere did he discover a break in it, not even a woodman's road. He had not known that he lived in so wild a region. There was something uncanny in the revelation.

By nightfall he was fatigued, footsore, famishing. The thought of his wife and children urged him on. At last he found a road which led him in what he knew to be the right direction. It was as wide and straight as a city street, yet it seemed untravelled. No fields bordered it, no dwelling anywhere. Not so much as the barking of a dog suggested human habitation. The black bodies of the great trees formed a straight wall on both sides, terminating on the horizon in a point, like a diagram in a lesson in perspective. Overhead, as he looked up through this rift in the wood, shone great golden stars looking unfamiliar and grouped in strange constellations. He was sure they were arranged in some order which had a secret and malign significance. The wood on either side was full of singular noises, among which—once, twice, and again—he distinctly heard whispers in an unknown tongue.

His neck was in pain, and, lifting his hand to it, he found it horribly swollen. He knew that it had a circle of black where the rope had bruised it. His eyes felt congested; he could no longer close them. His tongue was swollen with thirst; he relieved its fever by thrusting it forward from between his teeth into the cool air. How softly the turf had carpeted the untravelled avenue! He could no longer feel the roadway beneath his feet!

Doubtless, despite his suffering, he fell asleep while walking, for now he sees another scene—perhaps he has merely recovered from a delirium. He stands at the gate of his own home. All is as he left it, and all bright and beautiful in the morning sunshine. He must have travelled the entire night. As he pushes open the gate and passes up the wide white walk, he sees a flutter of female garments; his wife, looking fresh and cool and sweet, steps down from the verandah to meet him. At the bottom of the steps she stands waiting, with a smile of ineffable joy, an attitude of matchless grace and dignity. Ah, how beautiful she is! He springs forward with extended arms. As he is about to clasp her, he feels a stunning blow upon the back of the neck; a blinding white light blazes all about him, with a sound like a shock of a cannon—then all is darkness and silence!

Peyton Farquhar was dead; his body, with a broken neck, swung gently from side to side beneath the timbers of the Owl Creek bridge.

[1891]

QUESTIONS

1. Does Bierce manipulate his readers in this story, trick them into thinking one thing has happened, while something else has actually happened?
2. What is Bierce's concept of death? On the basis of this story, would you call him a pessimist?
3. How would you describe the conflict in this story?

HEINRICH BÖLL

(b. 1917)

GERMANY

The fiction of Heinrich Böll, who has been described as the most popular of all German writers, has been translated into 45 languages; more than 20 million copies of his books have been sold worldwide. Böll was awarded the Nobel Prize for Literature in 1972. A prolific writer, Böll has published novels, stories, plays, poetry, and essays that consistently reflect his blend of Christian ethics and social commitment. One of the few postwar German writers to take public positions on the social and political issues that had debilitated Germany, Böll was frequently identified by his German (and other) contemporaries as the moral conscience of his era. However, Böll repudiated this label, remarking that if writers, rather than public leaders, were the sole bearers of Germany's moral conscience, his country was doomed.

Böll's strong social commitment was forged by his own personal circumstances. Born in Cologne during the middle of World War I, the son of a wood sculptor and master furniture maker, he saw his family's economically comfortable life vanish precipitously during the Depression of 1930. Although during the early years of Hitler's reign his family tried to remain neutral, Böll was drafted into military service and sustained several serious injuries during his service in France, Poland, and the Crimea. His mother died during an air raid; Böll was taken prisoner by American troops in 1945.

Following his release at the end of the war, Böll returned to Cologne with his wife and young family and wrote while he remained involved with political issues, particularly as an advocate against war, militarism, and hypocrisy in all forms. His most widely praised novels, *Group Portrait with a Lady* (1973) and *The Lost Honor of Katharina Blum* (1975), demonstrate his consistent ideal: to conserve traditional human values while maintaining a healthy suspicion of power based on wealth, social position, or military force.

Böll's short stories that have been translated into English are *Traveler, If You Come to Spa* (1950), *Eighteen Stories* (1966), and *The Stories of Heinrich Böll* (1986). "The Laugher" (translated by Leila Vennewitz) effectively captures the poignant melancholy that characterizes Böll's bittersweet view of human experience.

The Laugher

When someone asks me what business I am in, I am seized with embarrassment: I blush and stammer, I who am otherwise known as a man of poise. I envy people who can say: I am a bricklayer. I envy barbers, bookkeepers, and writers the simplicity of their avowal, for all these professions speak for themselves and need no lengthy explanation, while I am constrained to reply to such questions: I am a laugher. An admission of this kind demands another, since I have to answer the second question: "Is that how you make your living?" truthfully with "Yes." I actually do make a living at my laughing, and a good one too, for my laughing is—commercially speaking—much in demand. I am a good laugher, experienced, no one else laughs as well as I do, no one else has such command of the fine points of my art. For a long time, in order to avoid tiresome explanations, I called myself an actor, but my talents in the field of mime and elocution are so meager that I felt this designation to be too far from the truth: I love the truth, and the truth is: I am a laugher. I am neither a clown nor a comedian. I do not make people gay, I portray gaiety: I laugh like a Roman emperor, or like a sensitive schoolboy, I am as much at home in the laughter of the seventeenth century as in that of the nineteenth, and when occasion demands I laugh my way through the centuries, all classes of society, all categories of age: it is simply a skill which I have acquired, like the skill of being able to repair shoes. In my breast I harbor the laughter of America, the laughter of Africa, white, red, yellow laughter—and for the right fee I let it peal out in accordance with the director's requirements.

I have become indispensable; I laugh on records, I laugh on tape, and television directors treat me with respect. I laugh mournfully, moderately, hysterically; I laugh like a streetcar conductor or like an apprentice in the grocery business; laughter in the morning, laughter in the evening, nocturnal laughter, and the laughter of twilight. In short: wherever and however laughter is required—I do it.

It need hardly be pointed out that a profession of this kind is tiring, especially as I have also—this is my specialty—mastered the art of infectious laughter; this has also made me indispensable to third- and fourth-rate comedians, who are scared—and with good reason—that their audiences will miss their punch lines, so I spend most evenings in nightclubs as a kind of discreet claque, my job being to laugh infectiously during the weaker parts of the program. It has to be carefully timed: my hearty, boisterous laughter must not come too soon, but neither must it come too late, it must come just at the right spot: at the prearranged moment I burst out laughing, the whole audience roars with me, and the joke is saved.

But as for me, I drag myself exhausted to the checkroom, put on my overcoat, happy that I can go off duty at last. At home I usually find telegrams waiting for me: "Urgently require your laughter. Recording Tuesday," and a few hours later I am sitting in an overheated express train bemoaning my fate.

I need scarcely say that when I am off duty or on vacation I have little inclination to laugh: the cowhand is glad when he can forget the cow, the bricklayer when he can forget the mortar, and carpenters usually have doors at home which don't work or drawers which are hard to open. Confectioners like sour pickles, butchers like marzipan, and the baker prefers sausage to bread; bullfighters raise pigeons for a hobby, boxers turn pale when their children have nosebleeds: I find all this quite natural, for I never laugh off duty. I am a very solemn person, and people consider me—perhaps rightly so—a pessimist.

During the first years of our married life, my wife would often say to me: "Do laugh!" but since then she has come to realize that I cannot grant her this wish. I am happy when I am free to relax my tense face muscles, my frayed spirit, in profound solemnity. Indeed, even other people's laughter gets on my nerves, since it reminds me too much of my profession. So our marriage is a quiet, peaceful one, because my wife has also forgotten how to laugh: now and again I catch her smiling, and I smile too. We converse in low tones, for I detest the noise of the nightclubs, the noise that sometimes fills the recording studios. People who do not know me think I am taciturn. Perhaps I am, because I have to open my mouth so often to laugh.

I go through life with an impassive expression, from time to time permitting myself a gentle smile, and I often wonder whether I have ever laughed. I think not. My brothers and sisters have always known me for a serious boy.

So I laugh in many different ways, but my own laughter I have never heard.

[1966]

Translated by
Leila Vennewitz

QUESTIONS

1. How would you characterize the narrator of the story? How can he be so successful in his profession and at the same time be incapable of genuine laughter?
2. What does the narrator mean when he says, "I do not make people gay, I portray gaiety"?
3. Is the story a satire? If so, what is Böll satirizing?
4. Does the story make you laugh? If so, what is the source of its humor? If not, what emotional response does it evoke in you?

Jorge Luis Borges

(1899–1986)

Argentina

When Latin American writers of the twentieth century are discussed, Jorge Luis Borges is likely to be mentioned first. His audience is truly international, as critics would also define the scope of his writing. A master storyteller, poet, essayist, and man of letters, Borges has had an enormous influence on contemporary Latin American writing. Some critics proclaim Borges as the source of the boom in recent Latin American literature. Yet Borges's fame was slow to develop. The story he tells of himself is that when one of his early books was published, it sold only 37 copies. Borges was so humbled that he thought he should write each of the 37 people who purchased the book a personal letter of thanks.

Though born in Buenos Aires, Argentina, in 1899, Borges was educated primarily in Europe. His father was an educator, from whom he developed an interest in intellectual puzzles. That fascination merged with an interest in several avant-garde literary currents in Europe in the early decades of this century. When he returned to Buenos Aires in 1921, he worked in the National Library, while simultaneously beginning his early experiments in writing. He confessed during his *Paris Review* interview that he enjoyed reading old encyclopedias, which may account for some of the obscure references in his short stories. Borges also liked to give his characters names from his own family, "to work in the names of [his] grandfathers, great-grandfathers, and so on. To give them a kind of, well, I won't say immortality, but that's one of the methods." About the names in "Death and the Compass," he said, ". . . one of the characters who comes and goes is called Yarmolinsky because the name struck me—it's a strange word, no? The other character is called Red Scharlach because Scharlach means *scarlet* in German, and he was a murderer; he was doubly red, no? Red Scharlach: Red Scarlet."

Borges's most popular books in the United States are collections of short stories: *Fictions* (1944) and *Labyrinths* (1972). In each of these works he employs the labyrinthian method, an elaborate physical maze that may in turn intellectually confuse the character (a detective, perhaps) at the center of the story. As an anonymous reviewer in the *Virginia Quarterly Review* summed up his work,

> Borges writes of skeptics overwhelmed by mystical event and of gangsters with the logic of Auguste Dupin. [His] remarkable stories which mix cabbalism with science fiction and the detective story deride, in their ironic reversals, the fictions of communication with others and make the communication of one with oneself the greater puzzle. In his stories, narratives, and prose pieces, Borges is among the leading writers of our time who are extending the boundaries of fiction into autobiography and essay.

• Death and the Compass •

Of the many problems ever to tax Erik Lönnrot's rash mind, none was so strange—so methodically strange, let us say—as the intermittent series of murders which came to a culmination amid the incessant odor of eucalyptus trees at the villa Triste-le-Roy.[1] It is true that Lönnrot failed to prevent the last of the murders, but it is undeniable that he foresaw it. Neither did he guess the identity of Yarmolinsky's ill-starred killer, but he did guess the secret shape of the evil series of events and the possible role played in those events by Red Scharlach, also nicknamed Scharlach the Dandy. The gangster (like so many others of his ilk) had sworn on his honor to get Erik Lönnrot, but Lönnrot was not intimidated. Lönnrot thought of himself as a pure logician, a kind of Auguste Dupin,[2] but there was also a streak of the adventurer and even of the gambler in him.

The first murder took place in the Hôtel du Nord—that tall prism which overlooks the estuary whose broad waters are the color of sand. To that tower (which, as everyone knows, brings together the hateful blank white walls of a hospital, the numbered chambers of a cell block, and the overall appearance of a brothel) there arrived on the third of December Rabbi Marcel Yarmolinsky, a gray-bearded gray-eyed man, who was a delegate from Podolsk to the Third Talmudic[3] Congress. We shall never know whether the Hôtel du Nord actually pleased him or not, since he accepted it with the ageless resignation that had made it possible for him to survive three years of war in the Carpathians and three thousand years of oppression and pogroms. He was given a room on floor R, across from the suite occupied—not without splendor—by the Tetrarch[4] of Galilee.

Yarmolinsky had dinner, put off until the next day a tour of the unfamiliar city, arranged in a closet his many books and his few suits of clothes, and before midnight turned off his bed lamp. (So said the Tetrarch's chauffeur, who slept in the room next door.) On the fourth of December, at three minutes past eleven in the morning, an editor of the *Jüdische Zeitung*[5] called him by telephone. Rabbi Yarmolinsky did not answer; soon after, he was found in his room, his face already discolored, almost naked under a great old-fashioned cape. He lay not far from the hall door. A deep knife wound had opened his chest. A couple of hours later, in the same room, in the throng of reporters, photographers, and policemen, Inspector Treviranus and Lönnrot quietly discussed the case.

"We needn't lose any time here looking for three-legged cats," Treviranus said, brandishing an imperious cigar. "Everyone knows the Tetrarch of Galilee owns the world's finest sapphires. Somebody out to steal them probably found his way in here by mistake. Yarmolinsky woke up and the thief was forced to kill him. What do you make of it?"

"Possible, but not very interesting," Lönnrot answered. "You'll say reality is

[1]*Triste-le-Roy* the sad king

[2]*Auguste Dupin* a detective in Edgar Allen Poe's stories

[3]*Talmudic* Hebrew: from the Talmud, the collection of Jewish law and tradition

[4]*Tetrarch* one of four rulers; a ruler of the fourth division

[5]*Jüdische Zeitung* German: *The Jewish Times*

under no obligation to be interesting. To which I'd reply that reality may disregard the obligation but that we may not. In your hypothesis, chance plays a large part. Here's a dead rabbi. I'd much prefer a purely rabbinical explanation, not the imagined mistakes of an imagined jewel thief."

"I'm not interested in rabbinical explanations," Treviranus replied in bad humor; "I'm interested in apprehending the man who murdered this unknown party."

"Not so unknown," corrected Lönnrot. "There are his complete works." He pointed to a row of tall books on a shelf in the closet. There were a *Vindication of the Kabbalah*, a *Study of the Philosophy of Robert Fludd*, a literal translation of the *Sefer Yeçirah*, a *Biography of the Baal Shem*, a *History of the Hasidic Sect*, a treatise (in German) on the Tetragrammaton,[6] and another on the names of God in the Pentateuch.[7] The Inspector stared at them in fear, almost in disgust. Then he burst into laughter.

"I'm only a poor Christian," he said. "You may cart off every last tome if you feel like it. I have no time to waste on Jewish superstitions."

"Maybe this crime belongs to the history of Jewish superstitions," Lönnrot grumbled.

"Like Christianity," the editor from the *Jüdische Zeitung*, made bold to add. He was nearsighted, an atheist, and very shy.

Nobody took any notice of him. One of the police detectives had found in Yarmolinsky's small typewriter a sheet of paper on which these cryptic words were written:

The first letter of the Name has been uttered

Lönnrot restrained himself from smiling. Suddenly turning bibliophile and Hebraic scholar, he ordered a package made of the dead man's books and he brought them to his apartment. There, with complete disregard for the police investigation, he began studying them. One royal-octavo volume revealed to him the teachings of Israel Baal Shem Tobh, founder of the sect of the Pious; another, the magic and the terror of the Tetragrammaton, which is God's unspeakable name; a third, the doctrine that God has a secret name in which (as in the crystal sphere that the Persians attribute to Alexander of Macedonia) His ninth attribute, Eternity, may be found—that is to say, the immediate knowledge of everything under the sun that will be, that is, and that was. Tradition lists ninety-nine names of God; Hebrew scholars explain that imperfect cipher by a mystic fear of even numbers; the Hasidim[8] argue that the missing term stands for a hundredth name—the Absolute Name.

It was out of this bookworming that Lönnrot was distracted a few days later by the appearance of the editor from the *Jüdische Zeitung*, who wanted to speak about the murder. Lönnrot, however, chose to speak of the many names of the Lord. The following day, in three columns, the journalists stated that Chief Detective Erik Lönnrot had taken up the study of the names of God in order to find out the name of the murderer. Lönnrot, familiar with the simplifications of journalism, was not surprised. It also seemed that one of those tradesmen who

[6]*Tetragrammaton* the four letters used to represent the Hebrew word for God

[7]*Pentateuch* the last five books of the Old Testament

[8]*Hasidim* Judaism: a member of a religious sect founded in Poland in the eighteenth century

have discovered that any man is willing to buy any book was peddling a cheap edition of Yarmolinsky's *History of the Hasidic Sect.*

The second murder took place on the night of January third out in the most forsaken and empty of the city's western reaches. Along about daybreak, one of the police who patrol this lonely area on horseback noticed on the doorstep of a dilapidated paint and hardware store a man in a poncho laid out flat. A deep knife wound had ripped open his chest, and his hard features looked as though they were masked in blood. On the wall, on the shop's conventional red and yellow diamond shapes, were some words scrawled in chalk. The policeman read them letter by letter. That evening, Treviranus and Lönnrot made their way across town to the remote scene of the crime. To the left and right of their car the city fell away in shambles; the sky grew wider and houses were of much less account than brick kilns or an occasional poplar. They reached their forlorn destination, an unpaved back alley with rose-colored walls that in some way seemed to reflect the garish sunset. The dead man had already been identified. He turned out to be Daniel Simon Azevedo, a man with a fair reputation in the old northern outskirts of town who had risen from teamster to electioneering thug and later degenerated into a thief and an informer. (The unusual manner of his death seemed to them fitting, for Azevedo was the last example of a generation of criminals who knew how to handle a knife but not a revolver.) The words chalked up on the wall were these:

The second letter of the Name has been uttered

The third murder took place on the night of February third. A little before one o'clock, the telephone rang in the office of Inspector Treviranus. With pointed secrecy, a man speaking in a guttural voice said his name was Ginzberg (or Ginsburg) and that he was ready—for a reasonable consideration—to shed light on the facts surrounding the double sacrifice of Azevedo and Yarmolinsky. A racket of whistles and tin horns drowned out the informer's voice. Then the line went dead. Without discounting the possibility of a practical joke (they were, after all, at the height of Carnival), Treviranus checked and found that he had been phoned from a sailors' tavern called Liverpool House on the Rue de Toulon—that arcaded waterfront street in which we find side by side the wax museum and the dairy bar, the brothel and the Bible seller. Treviranus called the owner back. The man (Black Finnegan by name, a reformed Irish criminal concerned about and almost weighed down by respectibility) told him that the last person to have used the telephone was one of his roomers, a certain Gryphius, who had only minutes before gone out with some friends. At once Treviranus set out for Liverpool House. There the owner told him the following story:

Eight days earlier, Gryphius had taken a small room above the bar. He was a sharp-featured man with a misty gray beard, shabbily dressed in black, Finnegan (who used that room for a purpose Treviranus immediately guessed) had asked the roomer for a rent that was obviously steep, and Gryphius paid the stipulated sum on the spot. Hardly ever going out, he took lunch and supper in his room; in fact, his face was hardly known in the bar. That night he had come down to use the telephone in Finnegan's office. A coupé had drawn up outside. The coachman had stayed on his seat; some customers recalled that he wore the mask of a bear. Two harlequins got out of the carriage. They were very short men and nobody could help noticing that they were very drunk. Bleating their horns, they burst into Finnegan's office, throwing their arms around Gryphius, who seemed to know them but who did not warm to their company. The three exchanged a few words in Yiddish—he in a low, guttural voice, they in a piping falsetto—and they climbed the stairs up to his room. In a quarter of an hour they came down again, very happy. Gryphius, staggering, seemed as drunk as the others. He walked in the middle, tall and dizzy, between the two masked harlequins. (One of the women in the bar remembered their costumes of red, green, and yellow lozenges.) Twice he stumbled; twice the harlequins held him up. Then the trio climbed into the coupé and, heading for the nearby docks (which enclosed a string of rectangular bodies of water), were soon out of sight. Out front, from the running board, the last harlequin had scrawled an obscene drawing and certain words on one of the market slates hung from a pillar of the arcade.

Treviranus stepped outside for a look. Almost predictably, the phrase read:

The last letter of the Name has been uttered

He next examined Gryphius-Ginzberg's tiny room. On the floor was a star-shaped spatter of blood; in the corners, cigarette butts of a Hungarian brand; in the wardrobe, a book in Latin—a 1739 edition of Leusden's *Philologus Hebraeo-Graecus*—with a number of annotations written in by hand. Treviranus gave it an indignant look and sent for Lönnrot. While the Inspector questioned the contradictory witnesses to the possible kidnapping, Lönnrot, not even bothering to take off his hat, began reading. At four o'clock they left. In the twisted Rue de Toulon, as they were stepping over last night's tangle of streamers and confetti, Treviranus remarked, "And if tonight's events were a put-up job?"

Erik Lönnrot smiled and read to him with perfect gravity an underlined passage from the thirty-third chapter of the *Philologus*: "'*Dies Judaeorum incipit a solis occasu usque ad solis occasum diei sequentis.*' Meaning," he added, "'the Jewish day begins at sundown and ends the following sundown.'"

The other man attempted a bit of irony. "Is that the most valuable clue you've picked up tonight?" he said.

"No. Far more valuable is one of the words Ginzberg used to you on the phone."

The evening papers made a great deal of these recurrent disappearances. *La Croix de l'Epée*[9] contrasted the present acts of violence with the admirable discipline and order observed by the last Congress of Hermits. Ernst Palast, in *The Martyr*, condemned "the unbearable pace of this unauthorized and stinting pogrom, which has required three months for the liquidation of three Jews." The *Jüdische Zeitung* rejected the ominous suggestion of an anti-Semitic plot, "despite the fact that many penetrating minds admit of no other solution to the threefold mystery." The leading gunman of the city's Southside, Dandy Red Scharlach, swore that in his part of town crimes of that sort would never happen, and he accused Inspector Franz Treviranus of criminal negligence.

On the night of March first, Inspector Treviranus received a great sealed envelope. Opening it, he found it contained a letter signed by one "Baruch Spinoza" and, evidently torn out of a Baedeker,[10] a detailed plan of the city. The

[9]*La Croix de l'Epée* French: *The Cross of the Swordsman*

[10]*Baedeker* a German guidebook

letter predicted that on the third of March there would not be a fourth crime because the paint and hardware store on the Westside, the Rue de Toulon tavern, and the Hôtel du Nord formed "the perfect sides of an equilateral and mystical triangle." In red ink the map demonstrated that the three sides of the figure were exactly the same length. Treviranus read this Euclidean reasoning with a certain weariness and sent the letter and map to Erik Lönnrot—the man, beyond dispute, most deserving of such cranky notions.

Lönnrot studied them. The three points were, in fact, equidistant. There was symmetry in time (December third, January third, February third); now there was symmetry in space as well. All at once he felt he was on the verge of solving the riddle. A pair of dividers and a compass completed his sudden intuition. He smiled, pronounced the word Tetragrammaton (of recent acquisition) and called the Inspector on the phone.

"Thanks for the equilateral triangle you sent me last night," he told him. "It has helped me unravel our mystery. Tomorrow, Friday, the murderers will be safely behind bars; we can rest quite easy."

"Then they aren't planning a fourth crime?"

"Precisely because they *are* planning a fourth crime we can rest quite easy."

Lönnrot hung up the receiver. An hour later, he was traveling on a car of the Southern Railways on his way to the deserted villa Triste-le-Roy. To the south of the city of my story flows a dark muddy river, polluted by the waste of tanneries and sewers. On the opposite bank is a factory suburb where, under the patronage of a notorious political boss, many gunmen thrive. Lönnrot smiled to himself, thinking that the best-known of them—Red Scharlach—would have given anything to know about this sudden excursion of his. Azevedo had been a henchman of Scharlach's. Lönnrot considered the remote possibility that the fourth victim might be Scharlach himself. Then he dismissed it. He had practically solved the puzzle; the mere circumstances—reality (names, arrests, faces, legal and criminal proceedings)—barely held his interest now. He wanted to get away, to relax after three months of desk work and of snail-pace investigations. He reflected that the solution of the killings lay in an anonymously sent triangle and in a dusty Greek word. The mystery seemed almost crystal clear. He felt ashamed for having spent close to a hundred days on it.

The train came to a stop at a deserted loading platform. Lönnrot got off. It was one of those forlorn evenings that seem as empty as dawn. The air off the darkening prairies was damp and cold. Lönnrot struck out across the fields. He saw dogs, he saw a flatcar on a siding, he saw the line of the horizon, he saw a pale horse drinking stagnant water out of a ditch. Night was falling when he saw the rectangular mirador[11] of the villa Triste-le-Roy, almost as tall as the surrounding black eucalyptus trees. He thought that only one more dawn and one more dusk (an ancient light in the east and another in the west) were all that separated him from the hour appointed by the seekers of the Name.

A rusted iron fence bounded the villa's irregular perimeter. The main gate was shut. Lönnrot, without much hope of getting in, walked completely around the place. Before the barred gate once again, he stuck a hand through the palings—almost mechanically—and found the bolt. The squeal of rusted iron surprised him. With clumsy obedience, the whole gate swung open.

Lönnrot moved forward among the eucalyptus trees, stepping on the layered

[11]*mirador* French: an observation post

generations of fallen leaves. Seen from up close, the house was a clutter of meaningless symmetries and almost insane repetitions: one icy Diana in a gloomy niche matched another Diana in a second niche; one balcony appeared to reflect another; double outer staircases crossed at each landing. A two-faced Hermes cast a monstrous shadow. Lönnrot made his way around the house as he had made his way around the grounds. He went over every detail; below the level of the terrace he noticed a narrow shutter.

He pushed it open. A few marble steps went down into a cellar. Lönnrot, who by now anticipated the architect's whims, guessed that in the opposite wall he would find a similar set of steps. He did. Climbing them, he lifted his hands and raised a trapdoor.

A stain of light led him to a window. He opened it. A round yellow moon outlined two clogged fountains in the unkempt garden. Lönnrot explored the house. Through serving pantries and along corridors he came to identical courtyards and several times to the same courtyard. He climbed dusty stairways to circular anterooms, where he was multiplied to infinity in facing mirrors. He grew weary of opening or of peeping through windows that revealed, outside, the same desolate garden seen from various heights and various angles; and indoors he grew weary of the rooms of furniture, each draped in yellowing slipcovers, and the crystal chandeliers wrapped in tarlatan. A bedroom caught his attention—in it, a single flower in a porcelain vase. At a touch, the ancient petals crumbled to dust. On the third floor, the last floor, the house seemed endless and growing. The house is not so large, he thought. This dim light, the sameness, the mirrors, the many years, my unfamiliarity, the loneliness are what make it large.

By a winding staircase he reached the mirador. That evening's moon streamed in through the diamond-shaped panes; they were red, green, and yellow. He was stopped by an awesome, dizzying recollection.

Two short men, brutal and stocky, threw themselves on him and disarmed him: another, very tall, greeted him solemnly and told him, "You are very kind. You've saved us a night and a day."

It was Red Scharlach. The men bound Lönnrot's wrists. After some seconds, Lönnrot at last heard himself saying, "Scharlach, are you after the Secret Name?"

Scharlach remained standing, aloof. He had taken no part in the brief struggle and had barely held out his hand for Lönnrot's revolver. He spoke. Lönnrot heard in his voice the weariness of final triumph, a hatred the size of the universe, a sadness as great as that hatred.

"No," said Scharlach. "I'm after something more ephemeral, more frail. I'm after Erik Lönnrot. Three years ago, in a gambling dive on the Rue de Toulon, you yourself arrested my brother and got him put away. My men managed to get me into a coupé before the shooting was over, but I had a cop's bullet in my guts. Nine days and nine nights I went through hell, here in this deserted villa, racked with fever. The hateful two-faced Janus that looks on the sunsets and the dawns filled both my sleep and my wakefulness with its horror. I came to loathe my body, I came to feel that two eyes, two hands, two lungs, are as monstrous as two faces. An Irishman, trying to convert me to the faith of Jesus, kept repeating to me the saying of the *goyim*—All roads lead to Rome. At night, my fever fed on that metaphor. I felt the world was a maze from which escape was impossible since all roads, though they seemed to be leading north or south, were really leading to Rome, which at the same time was the square cell where my brother lay dying and also this villa, Triste-le-Roy. During those nights, I swore by the god who looks with two faces and by all the gods of fever and of mirrors that I would weave a maze around the man who sent my brother to prison. Well, I have woven it and it's tight. It's materials are a dead rabbi, a compass, an eighteenth-century sect, a Greek word, a dagger, and the diamond-shaped patterns on a paint-store wall."

Lönnrot was in a chair now, with the two short men at his side.

"The first term of the series came to me by pure chance," Scharlach went on. "With some associates of mine — among them Daniel Azevedo — I'd planned the theft of the Tetrarch's sapphires. Azevedo betrayed us. He got drunk on the money we advanced him and tried to pull the job a day earlier. But there in the hotel he got mixed up and around two in the morning blundered into Yarmolinsky's room. The rabbi, unable to sleep, had decided to do some writing. In all likelihood, he was preparing notes or a paper on the Name of God and had already typed out the words 'The first letter of the Name has been uttered.' Azevedo warned him not to move. Yarmolinsky reached his hand toward the buzzer that would have wakened all the hotel staff; Azevedo struck him a single blow with his knife. It was probably a reflex action. Fifty years of violence had taught him that the easiest and surest way is to kill. Ten days later, I found out through the *Jüdische Zeitung* that you were looking for the key to Yarmolinsky's death in his writings. I read his *History of the Hasidic Sect*. I learned that the holy fear of uttering God's Name had given rise to the idea that that Name is secret and all-powerful. I learned that some of the Hasidim, in search of that secret Name, had gone as far as to commit human sacrifices. The minute I realized you were guessing that the Hasidim had sacrificed the rabbi, I did my best to justify that guess. Yarmolinsky died the night of December third. For the second 'sacrifice' I chose the night of January third. The rabbi had died on the Northside; for the second 'sacrifice' we wanted a spot on the Westside. Daniel Azevedo was the victim we needed. He deserved death — he was impulsive, a traitor. If he'd been picked up, it would have wiped out our whole plan. One of my men stabbed him; in order to link his corpse with the previous one, I scrawled on the diamonds of the paint-store wall 'The second letter of the Name has been uttered."

Scharlach looked his victim straight in the face, then continued. "The third 'crime' was staged on the third of February. It was, as Treviranus guessed, only a plant. Gryphius-Ginzberg-Ginsburg was me. I spent an interminable week (rigged up in a false beard) in that flea-ridden cubicle on the Rue de Toulon until my friends came to kidnap me. From the running board of the carriage, one of them wrote on the pillar, 'The last letter of the Name has been uttered.' That message suggested that the series of crimes was *threefold*. That was how the public understood it. I, however, threw in repeated clues so that you, Erik Lönnrot the reasoner, might puzzle out that the crime was *fourfold*. A murder in the north, others in the east and west, demanded a fourth murder in the south. The Tetragrammaton — the Name of God, JHVH — is made up of *four* letters; the harlequins and the symbol on the paint store also suggest *four* terms. I underlined a certain passage in Leusden's handbook. That passage makes it clear that the Jews reckoned the day from sunset to sunset; that passage makes it understood that the deaths occurred on the *fourth* of each month. I was the one who sent the triangle to Treviranus, knowing in advance that you would supply the missing point — the point that determines the perfect *rhombus*,[12] the point

[12]*rhombus* an oblique-angled equilateral parallelogram

that fixes the spot where death is expecting you. I planned the whole thing, Erik Lönnrot, so as to lure you to the loneliness of Triste-le-Roy."

Lönnrot avoided Scharlach's eyes. He looked off at the trees and the sky broken into dark diamonds of red, green, and yellow. He felt a chill and an impersonal, almost anonymous sadness. It was night now; from down in the abandoned garden came the unavailing cry of a bird. Lönnrot, for one last time, reflected on the problem of the patterned, intermittent deaths.

"In your maze there are three lines too many," he said at last. "I know of a Greek maze that is a single straight line. Along this line so many thinkers have lost their way that a mere detective may very well lose his way. Scharlach, when in another incarnation you hunt me down, stage (or commit) a murder at A, then a second murder at B, eight miles from A, then a third murder at C, four miles from A and B, halfway between the two. Lay in wait for me then at D, two miles from A and C, again halfway between them. Kill me at D, the way you are going to kill me here at Triste-le-Roy."

"The next time I kill you," said Scharlach, "I promise you such a maze, which is made up of a single straight line and which is invisible and unending."

He moved back a few steps. Then, taking careful aim, he fired.

[1942]

Translated by
NORMAN THOMAS DI GIOVANNI

QUESTIONS

1. Is Borges's story intended to be taken realistically or as satire or even parody?
2. Where does the story take place? When? What are the Latin qualities of this story?
3. Besides the names mentioned in the commentary by Borges in the introduction to this story, what are we to conclude about the other names in the story—Liverpool House, Baruch Spinoza, Triste-le-Roy, for example?

Dino Buzzati

(1906–1972)

Italy

Dino Buzzati was a prolific writer in a variety of contexts. A lifelong journalist, he was editor and correspondent for the *Corriere della Sera* of Milan, one of Italy's largest daily newspapers and the first place of publication for many of his short stories. In addition to hundreds of stories, he wrote novels, poems, plays, librettos, and a children's book. He was also a painter. Buzzati is sometimes compared to Kafka and Borges for his genius in combining realism with fantasy to create what might be called fables for adults.

Buzzati's beginnings as a writer coincided with the Fascist period in Italy. His use of fantasy and allegory can be understood as an inventive narrative strategy for circumventing the censorship borne of political repression in Italy in the mid-twentieth century. Through a deliberately skewed perspective that makes use of allegory, satire, paradox, and the fusion of the unbelievable with the believable, Buzzati nonetheless wrote about the human condition and about distinctly credible human concerns, including fears of death, the unknown, and the unknowable. His best-known novels in English, *Barnabo of the Mountains* (1933) and *The Tartar Steppe* (1952) are, despite their enigmatic and surreal qualities, deeply concerned with real human problems, particularly the sense of futility in modern experience. As he phrased it, his fiction was about "things that do not exist, imagined by man for poetic ends." One of his commentators has described Buzzati's characteristic position as one of "melancholic compassion."

◆ The Falling Girl ◆

Marta was nineteen. She looked out over the roof of the skyscraper, and seeing the city below shining in the dusk, she was overcome with dizziness.

The skyscraper was silver, supreme and fortunate in that most beautiful and pure evening, as here and there the wind stirred a few fine filaments of cloud against an absolutely incredible blue background. It was in fact the hour when the city is seized by inspiration and whoever is not blind is swept away by it. From that airy height the girl saw the streets and the masses of buildings writhing in the long spasm of sunset, and at the point where the white of the houses ended, the blue of the sea began. Seen from above, the sea looked as if it were rising. And since the veils of the night were advancing from the east, the city became a sweet abyss burning with pulsating lights. Within it were powerful men, and women who were even more powerful, furs and violins, cars glossy as onyx, the neon signs of nightclubs, the entrance halls of darkened mansions, fountains, diamonds, old silent gardens, parties, desires, affairs, and, above all, that consuming sorcery of the evening which provokes dreams of greatness and glory.

Seeing these things, Marta hopelessly leaned out over the railing and let herself go. She felt as if she were hovering in the air, but she was falling. Given the extraordinary height of the skyscraper, the streets and squares down at the bottom were very far away. Who knows how long it would take her to get there. Yet the girl was falling.

At that hour the terraces and balconies of the top floors were filled with rich and elegant people who were having cocktails and making silly conversation. They were scattered in crowds, and their talk muffled the music. Marta passed before them and several people looked out to watch her.

Flights of that kind (mostly by girls, in fact) were not rare in the skyscraper and they constituted an interesting diversion for the tenants; this was also the reason why the price of those apartments was very high.

The sun had not yet completely set and it did its best to illuminate Marta's simple clothing. She wore a modest, inexpensive spring dress bought off the rack. Yet the lyrical light of the sunset exalted it somewhat, making it chic.

From the millionaires' balconies, gallant hands were stretched out toward her, offering flowers and cocktails. "Miss, would you like a drink? . . . Gentle butterfly, why not stop a minute with us?"

She laughed, hovering, happy (but meanwhile she was falling): "No, thanks, friends. I can't. I'm in a hurry."

"Where are you headed?" they asked her.

"Ah, don't make me say," Marta answered, waving her hands in a friendly good-bye.

A young man, tall, dark, very distinguished, extended an arm to snatch her. She liked him. And yet Marta quickly defended herself: "How dare you, sir?" and she had time to give him a little tap on the nose.

The beautiful people, then, were interested in her and that filled her with satisfaction. She felt fascinating, stylish. On the flower-filled terraces, amid the bustle of waiters in white and the bursts of exotic songs, there was talk for a few minutes, perhaps less, of the young woman who was passing by (from top to bottom, on a vertical course). Some thought her pretty, others thought her so-so, everyone found her interesting.

"You have your entire life before you," they told her, "why are you in such a hurry? You still have time to rush around and busy yourself. Stop with us for a little while, it's only a modest little party among friends, really, you'll have a good time."

She made an attempt to answer but the force of gravity had already quickly carried her to the floor below, then two, three, four floors below; in fact, exactly as you gaily rush around when you are just nineteen years old.

Of course, the distance that separated her from the bottom, that is, from street level, was immense. It is true that she began falling just a little while ago, but the street always seemed very far away.

In the meantime, however, the sun had plunged into the sea; one could see it disappear, transformed into a shimmering reddish mushroom. As a result, it no longer emitted its vivifying rays to light up the girl's dress and make her a seductive comet. It was a good thing that the windows and terraces of the skyscraper were almost all illuminated and the bright reflections completely gilded her as she gradually passed by.

* *

Now Marta no longer saw just groups of carefree people inside the apartments; at times there were even some businesses where the employees, in black or blue aprons, were sitting at desks in long rows. Several of them were young people as old as or older than she, and weary of the day by now, every once in a while they raised their eyes from their duties and from typewriters. In this way they too saw her, and a few ran to the windows. "Where are you going? Why so fast? Who are you?" they shouted to her. One could divine something akin to envy in their words.

"They're waiting for me down there," she answered. "I can't stop. Forgive me." And again she laughed, wavering on her headlong fall, but it wasn't like her previous laughter anymore. The night had craftily fallen and Marta started to feel cold.

Meanwhile, looking downward, she saw a bright halo of lights at the entrance of a building. Here long blacks cars were stopping (from the great distance they looked as small as ants), and men and women were getting out, anxious to go inside. She seemed to make out the sparkling of jewels in that swarm. Above the entrance flags were flying.

They were obviously giving a large party, exactly the kind that Marta dreamed of ever since she was a child. Heaven help her if she missed it. Down there opportunity was waiting for her, fate, romance, the true inauguration of her life. Would she arrive in time?

She spitefully noticed that another girl was falling about thirty meters above her. She was decidedly prettier than Marta and she wore a rather classy evening gown. For some unknown reason she came down much faster than Marta, so that in a few moments she passed by her and disappeared below, even though Marta was calling her. Without doubt she would get to the party before Marta; perhaps she had a plan all worked out to supplant her.

Then she realized that they weren't alone. Along the sides of the skyscraper many other young women were plunging downward, their faces taut with the excitement of the flight, their hands cheerfully waving as if to say: look at us, here we are, entertain us, is not the world ours?

It was a contest, then. And she only had a shabby little dress while those other girls were dressed smartly like high-fashion models and some even wrapped luxurious mink stoles tightly around their bare shoulders. So self-assured when she began the leap, Marta now felt a tremor growing inside her; perhaps it was just the cold; but it may have been fear too, the fear of having made an error without remedy.

It seemed to be late at night now. The windows were darkened one after another, the echoes of music became more rare, the offices were empty, young men no longer leaned out from the windowsills extending their hands. What time was it? At the entrance to the building down below—which in the meantime had grown larger, and one could now distinguish all the architectural details—the lights were still burning, but the bustle of cars had stopped. Every now and then, in fact, small groups of people came out of the main floor wearily drawing away. Then the lights of the entrance were also turned off.

Marta felt her heart tightening. Alas, she wouldn't reach the ball in time. Glancing upwards, she saw the pinnacle of the skyscraper in all its cruel power. It was almost completely dark. On the top floors a few windows here and there were still lit. And above the top the first glimmer of dawn was spreading.

In a dining recess on the twenty-eighth floor a man about forty years old was having his morning coffee and reading his newspaper while his wife tidied up the room. A clock on the sideboard indicated 8:45. A shadow suddenly passed before the window.

"Alberto!" the wife shouted. "Did you see that? A woman passed by."

"Who was it?" he said without raising his eyes from the newspaper.

"An old woman," the wife answered. "A decrepit old woman. She looked frightened."

"It's always like that," the man muttered. "At these low floors only falling old women pass by. You can see beautiful girls from the hundred-and-fiftieth floor up. Those apartments don't cost so much for nothing."

"At least down here there's the advantage," observed the wife, "that you can hear the thud when they touch the ground."

"This time not even that," he said, shaking his head, after he stood listening for a few minutes. Then he had another sip of coffee.

[1983—English translation]

Translated by
LAWRENCE VENUTI

QUESTIONS

1. What different meanings of "falling" contribute to the story's effect and meaning?
2. How does time function in the story?
3. Why do only women "fall"? Why do only "old women" pass by the lower floors of the skyscraper?
4. What elements of society are being criticized or satirized in the story?
5. What is "The Falling Girl" really about? How do the improbable and fantastic qualities and the matter-of-fact tone of the story contribute to its meaning and effectiveness?

Italo Calvino

(1923–1985)

Italy

Italo Calvino is one of a group of twentieth-century writers—including Franz Kafka, Jorge Luis Borges, Gabriel García Márquez, and his near-contemporary Dino Buzzati—who have infused modern and contemporary fiction with fantasy, "magical realism," and the surreal. Like Buzzati, Calvino may have found the nonrealistic liberties of fantasy a useful narrative strategy for avoiding the restrictions of censorship and the political totalitarianism in the Italy of his youth. If realism was too close to the conventional world of social and political ideas that had failed, fantasy provided the opportunity to invent multiple alternative worlds.

In fact, Calvino used traditional forms to write uniquely nontraditional stories. In his own view, the traditional fable form offered a structure in which infinite variations and imaginative transformations could be created. As he phrased it in an essay, "The Lion's Marrow" (1955), "The mold of the most ancient fables: the child abandoned in the woods or the knight who must survive encounters with beasts and enchantments remains the irreplaceable scheme of all human stories."

Calvino was born in Cuba of Italian parents, both of whom were tropical agronomists. He spent his childhood in Italy and, as a result of compulsory military service, saw action in World War II. He was active in the Italian Resistance; later he joined the Communist party but left it when Russia invaded Hungary. He was an editor at the Italian publishing firm Einaudi. As an intellectual, critic, and writer, Calvino was a major voice in recent Italian cultural history. His best-known novels, *Cosmicomics* (1968), *Invisible Cities* (1974), *The Castle of Crossed Destinies* (1976), and *If on a Winter's Night a Traveler* (1979) are not only imaginative adventures but frequently also explorations of the nature of fiction itself. In *Invisible Cities*, a young Marco Polo entertains an aged Kubla Khan with descriptions of his travels to places that exist in the past, present, and future.

Calvino's translator, William Weaver, describes the tales of *Cosmicomics* as "the outer space of Calvino's imagination." However, Calvino's narratives are not simply entertaining, remote fantasies without links to human experience. Rather, even Qfwfq and the other tongue-trippingly-named time-traveling characters of *Cosmicomics* harbor decidedly human desires. As Calvino instructively notes of his fiction, "If the reader looks, I think he will find plenty of moral and political ideas in my stories. I suffer from everyday life."

• *A Sign in Space* •

Situated in the external zone of the Milky Way, the Sun takes about two hundred million years to make a complete revolution of the Galaxy.

Right, that's how long it takes, not a day less, —*Qfwfq said,*—once, as I went past, I drew a sign at a point in space, just so I could find it again two hundred million years later, when we went by the next time around. What sort of sign? It's hard to explain because if I say sign to you, you immediately think of a something that can be distinguished from a something else, but nothing could be distinguished from anything there; you immediately think of a sign made with some implement or with your hands, and then when you take the implement or your hands away, the sign remains, but in those days there were no implements or even hands, or teeth, or noses, all things that came along afterwards, a long time afterwards. As to the form a sign should have, you say it's no problem because, whatever form it may be given, a sign only has to serve as a sign, that is, be different or else the same as other signs: here again it's easy for you young ones to talk, but in that period I didn't have any examples to follow, I couldn't say I'll make it the same or I'll make it different, there were no things to copy, nobody knew what a line was, straight or curved, or even a dot, or a protuberance or a cavity. I conceived the idea of making a sign, that's true enough, or rather, I conceived the idea of considering a sign a something that I felt like making, so when, at that point in space and not in another, I made something, meaning to make a sign, it turned out that I really had made a sign, after all.

In other words, considering it was the first sign ever made in the universe, or at least in the circuit of the Milky Way, I must admit it came out very well. Visible? What a question! Who had eyes to see with in those days? Nothing had ever been seen by anything, the question never even arose. Recognizable, yes, beyond any possibility of error: because all the other points in space were the same, indistinguishable, and instead, this one had the sign on it.

So as the planets continued their revolutions, and the solar system went on in its own, I soon left the sign far behind me, separated from it by the endless fields of space. And I couldn't help thinking about when I would come back and encounter it again, and how I would know it, and how happy it would make me, in that anonymous expanse, after I had spent a hundred thousand light-years without meeting anything familiar, nothing for hundreds of centuries, for thousands of millennia; I'd come back and there it would be in its place, just as I had left it, simple and bare, but with that unmistakable imprint, so to speak, that I had given it.

Slowly the Milky Way revolved, with its fringe of constellations and planets and clouds, and the Sun along with the rest, toward the edge. In all that circling, only the sign remained still, in an ordinary spot, out of all the orbit's reach (to make it, I had leaned over the border of the Galaxy a little, so it would remain outside and all those revolving worlds wouldn't crash into it), in an ordinary point that was no longer ordinary since it was the only point that was surely there, and which could be used as a reference point to distinguish other points.

I thought about it day and night; in fact, I couldn't think about anything else; actually, this was the first opportunity I had had to think something; or I should say: to think something had never been possible, first because there were no things to think about, and second because signs to think of them by were lacking, but from the moment there was that sign, it was possible for someone thinking to think of a sign, and therefore that one, in the sense that the sign was the thing you could think about and also the sign of the thing thought, namely, itself.

So the situation was this: the sign served to mark a place but at the same time it meant that in that place there was a sign (something far more important because there were plenty of places but there was only one sign) and also at the same time that sign was mine, the sign of me, because it was the only sign I had ever made and I was the only one who had ever made signs. It was like a name, the name of that point, and also my name that I had signed on that spot; in short, it was the only name available for everything that required a name.

Transported by the sides of the Galaxy, our world went navigating through distant spaces, and the sign stayed where I had left it to mark that spot, and at the same time it marked me, I carried it with me, it inhabited me, possessed me entirely, came between me and everything with which I might have attempted to establish a relationship. As I waited to come back and meet it again, I could try to derive other signs from it and combinations of signs, series of similar signs and contrasts of different signs. But already tens and tens of thousands of millennia had gone by since the moment when I had made it (rather, since the few seconds in which I had scrawled it down in the constant movement of the Milky Way) and now, just when I needed to bear in mind its every detail (the slightest uncertainty about its form made uncertain the possible distinctions between it and other signs I might make), I realized that, though I recalled its general outline, its over-all appearance, still something about it eluded me, I mean if I tried to break it down into its various elements, I couldn't remember whether, between one part and the other, it went like this or like that. I needed it there in front of me, to study, to consult, but instead it was still far away, I didn't yet know how far, because I had made it precisely in order to know the time it would take me to see it again, and until I had found it once more, I wouldn't know. Now, however, it wasn't my motive in making it that mattered to me, but how it was made, and I started inventing hypotheses about this how, and theories according to which a certain sign had to be perforce in a certain way, or else, proceeding by exclusion, I tried to eliminate all the less probable types of sign to arrive at the right one, but all these imaginary signs vanished inevitably because that first sign was missing as a term of comparison. As I racked my brain like this (while the Galaxy went on turning wakefully in its bed of soft emptiness and the atoms burned and radiated) I realized I had lost by now even that confused notion of my sign, and I succeeded in conceiving only interchangeable fragments of signs, that is, smaller signs within the large one, and every change of these signs-within-the-sign changed the sign itself into a completely different one; in short, I had completely forgotten what my sign was like and, try as I might, it wouldn't come back to my mind.

Did I despair? No, this forgetfulness was annoying, but not irreparable. Whatever happened, I knew the sign was there waiting for me, quiet and still. I would arrive, I would find it again, and I would then be able to pick up the thread of my meditations. At a rough guess, I calculated we had completed half of our galactic revolution: I had only to be patient, the second half always seemed to go by more quickly. Now I just had to remember the sign existed and I would pass it again.

Day followed day, and then I knew I must be near. I was furiously impatient because I might encounter the sign at any moment. It's here, no, a little farther on, now I'll count up to a hundred. . . . Had it disappeared? Had we already gone past it? I didn't know. My sign had perhaps remained who knows where, behind, completely remote from the revolutionary orbit of our system. I hadn't calculated the oscillations to which, especially in those days, the celestial bodies' fields of gravity were subject, and which caused them to trace irregular orbits, cut like the flower of a dahlia. For about a hundred millennia I tormented myself, going over my calculations: it turned out that our course touched that spot not every galactic year but only every three, that is, every six hundred million solar years. When you've waited two hundred million years, you can also wait six hundred; and I waited; the way was long but I wasn't on foot, after all; astride the Galaxy I traveled through the light-years, galloping over the planetary and stellar orbits as if I were on a horse whose shoes struck sparks; I was in a state of mounting excitement; I felt I was going forth to conquer the only thing that mattered to me, sign and dominion and name . . .

I made the second circuit, the third. I was there. I let out a yell. At a point which had to be that very point, in the place of my sign, there was a shapeless scratch, a bruised, chipped abrasion of space. I had lost everything: the sign, the point, the thing that caused me—being the one who had made the sign at that point—to be me. Space, without a sign, was once again a chasm, the void, without beginning or end, nauseating, in which everything—including me—was lost. (And don't come telling me that, to fix a point, my sign and the erasure of my sign amounted to the same thing; the erasure was the negation of the sign, and therefore didn't serve to distinguish one point from the preceding and successive points.)

I was disheartened and for many light-years I let myself be dragged along as if I were unconscious. When I finally raised my eyes (in the meanwhile, sight had begun in our world, and, as a result, also life), I saw what I would never have expected to see. I saw it, the sign, but not that one, a similar sign, a sign unquestionably copied from mine, but one I realized immediately couldn't be mine, it was so squat and careless and clumsily pretentious, a wretched counterfeit of what I had meant to indicate with the sign whose ineffable purity I could only now—through contrast—recapture. Who had played this trick on me? I couldn't figure it out. Finally, a plurimillennial chain of deductions led me to the solution: on another planetary system which performed its galactic revolution before us, there was a certain Kgwgk (the name I deduced afterwards, in the later era of names), a spiteful type, consumed with envy, who had erased my sign in a vandalistic impulse and then, with vulgar artifice, had attempted to make another.

It was clear that his sign had nothing to mark except Kgwgk's intention to imitate my sign, which was beyond all comparison. But at that moment the determination not to let my rival get the better of me was stronger than any other desire: I wanted immediately to make a new sign in space, a real sign that would make Kgwgk die of envy. About seven hundred millions of years had gone by since I had first tried to make a sign, but I fell to work with a will. Now things were different, however, because the world, as I mentioned, was beginning to produce an image of itself, and in everything a form was beginning to correspond to a function, and the forms of that time, we believed, had a long future ahead of them (instead, we were wrong: take—to give you a fairly recent example—the dinosaurs), and therefore in this new sign of mine you could perceive the influence of our new way of looking at things, call it style if you like, that special way that everything had to be, there, in a certain fashion. I must say I was truly satisfied with it, and I no longer regretted that first sign that had been erased, because this one seemed vastly more beautiful to me.

But in the duration of that galactic year we already began to realize that the world's forms had been temporary up until then, and that they would change, one by one. And this awareness was accompanied by a certain annoyance with the old images, so that even their memory was intolerable. I began to be tormented by a thought: I had left that sign in space, that sign which had seemed so beautiful and original to me and so suited to its function, and which now, in my memory, seemed inappropriate, in all its pretension, a sign chiefly of an antiquated way of conceiving signs and of my foolish acceptance of an order of things I ought to have been wise enough to break away from in time. In other words, I was ashamed of that sign which went on through the centuries, being passed by worlds in flight, making a ridiculous spectacle of itself and of me and of that temporary way we had had of seeing things. I blushed when I remembered it (and I remembered it constantly), blushes that lasted whole geological eras: to hide my shame I crawled into the craters of the volcanoes, in remorse I sank my teeth into the caps of the glaciations that covered the continents. I was tortured by the thought that Kgwgk, always preceding me in the circumnavigation of the Milky Way, would see the sign before I could erase it, and boor that he was, he would mock me and make fun of me, contemptuously repeating the sign in rough caricatures in every corner of the circumgalactic sphere.

Instead, this time the complicated astral timekeeping was in my favor. Kgwgk's constellation didn't encounter the sign, whereas our solar system turned up there punctually at the end of the first revolution, so close that I was able to erase the whole thing with the greatest care.

Now, there wasn't a single sign of mine in space. I could start drawing another, but I knew that signs also allow others to judge the one who makes them, and that in the course of a galactic year tastes and ideas have time to change, and the way of regarding the earlier ones depends on what comes afterwards; in short, I was afraid a sign that now might seem perfect to me, in two hundred or six hundred million years would make me look absurd. Instead, in my nostalgia, the first sign, brutally rubbed out by Kgwgk, remained beyond the attacks of time and its changes, the sign created before the beginning of forms, which was to contain something that would have survived all forms, namely the fact of being a sign and nothing else.

Making signs that weren't that sign no longer held any interest for me; and I had forgotten that sign now, billions of years before. So, unable to make true signs, but wanting somehow to annoy Kgwgk, I started making false signs, notches in space, holes, stains, little tricks that only an incompetent creature like Kgwgk could mistake for signs. And still he furiously got rid of them with his erasings (as I could see in later revolutions), with a determination that must have cost him much effort. (Now I scattered these false signs liberally through space, to see how far his simple-mindedness would go.)

Observing these erasures, one circuit after the next (the Galaxy's revolutions had now become for me a slow, boring voyage without goal or expectation), I realized something: as the galactic years passed the erasures tended to fade in space, and beneath them what I had drawn at those points, my false signs—as I called them—began to reappear. This discovery, far from displeasing me, filled me with new hope. If Kgwgk's erasures were erased, the first he had made, there at that point, must have disappeared by now, and my sign must have returned to its pristine visibility!

So expectation was revived, to lend anxiety to my days. The Galaxy turned like an omelet in its heated pan, itself both frying pan and golden egg; and I was frying, with it, in my impatience.

But, with the passing of the galactic years, space was no longer that uniformly barren and colorless expanse. The idea of fixing with signs the points where we passed—as it had come to me and to Kgwgk—had occurred to many, scattered over billions of planets of other solar systems, and I was constantly running into one of these things, or a pair, or even a dozen, simple two-dimensional scrawls, or else three-dimensional solids (polyhedrons, for example), or even things constructed with more care, with the fourth dimension and everything. So it happened that I reached the point of my sign, and I found five, all there. And I wasn't able to recognize my own. It's this one, no, that; no, no, that one seems too modern, but it could also be the most ancient; I don't recognize my hand in that one, I would never have wanted to make it like that . . . And meanwhile the Galaxy ran through space and left behind those signs old and new and I still hadn't found mine.

I'm not exaggerating when I say that the galactic years that followed were the worst I had ever lived through. I went on looking, and signs kept growing thicker in space; from all the worlds anybody who had an opportunity invariably left his mark in space somehow; and our world, too, every time I turned, I found more crowded, so that world and space seemed the mirror of each other, both minutely adorned with hieroglyphics and ideograms, each of which might be a sign and might not be: a calcareous concretion on basalt, a crest raised by the wind on the clotted sand of the desert, the arrangement of the eyes in a peacock's tail (gradually, living among signs had led us to see signs in countless things that, before, were there, marking nothing but their own presence; they had been transformed into the sign of themselves and had been added to the series of signs made on purpose by those who meant to make a sign), the fire-streaks against a wall of schistose rock, the four-hundred-and-twenty-seventh groove—slightly crooked—of the cornice of a tomb's pediment, a sequence of streaks on a video during a thunderstorm (the series of signs was multiplied in the series of the signs of signs, of signs repeated countless times always the same and always somehow different because to the purposely made sign you had to add the sign that had happened there by chance), the badly inked tail of the letter *R* in an evening newspaper joined to a thready imperfection in the paper, one among the eight hundred thousand flakings of a tarred wall in the Melbourne docks, the curve of a graph, a skid-mark on the asphalt, a chromosome. . . . Every now and then I'd start: that's the one! And for a second I was sure I had rediscovered my sign, on the Earth or in space, it made no difference, because through the signs a continuity had been established with no precise boundaries any more.

In the universe now there was no longer a container and a thing contained, but only a general thickness of signs superimposed and coagulated, occupying the whole volume of space; it was constantly being dotted, minutely, a network of lines and scratches and reliefs and engravings; the universe was scrawled over on all sides, along all its dimensions. There was no longer any way to establish a point of reference: the Galaxy went on turning but I could no longer count the revolutions, any point could be the point of departure, any sign heaped up with the others could be mine, but discovering it would have served no purpose, because it was clear that, independent of signs, space didn't exist and perhaps had never existed.

[1965]

Translated by
WILLIAM WEAVER

QUESTIONS

1. What is the significance of the sign to Qfwfq? to the reader?
2. How are time, history, and imagination represented in the story? How do these ideas contribute to the story's theme? What *is* the theme?
3. How does Calvino use the exaggerations of science fiction and fantasy to comment on human concerns? What specific human qualities or characteristics are explored in the story?
4. How does the use of a first-person narrator contribute to the story's effect?

Albert Camus
(1913–1960)
Algeria/France

One of the most famous French existentialists, Albert Camus was born in Mondovi, Algeria, in 1913 and died in an automobile accident near Paris in 1960. In addition to writing numerous essays and dramas, Camus published four works of fiction before his untimely death: *The Stranger* (1942); *The Plague* (1948); *The Fall* (1956); and a volume of short stories, *Exile and the Kingdom* (1957). "The Guest," which is from the latter volume, relies directly on the author's Algerian heritage. Albert Camus was awarded the Nobel Prize for Literature in 1957. In his acceptance speech for the award, he described himself as an "Algerian Frenchman."

The "wartime" referred to early in "The Guest" is the French/Algerian war, which lasted from 1954 to 1962. Camus wrote numerous essays about the relationship of the two countries, historically bound to one another by what he called inevitable solidarity. Although the Algerian struggle was bloody, he often spoke of the "community of hope" that would reconcile the two countries' differences. In his "Appeal for a Civilian Truce" (1956), he wrote:

> On this soil there are a million Frenchmen who have been here for a century, millions of Moslems, either Arabs or Berbers, who have been here for centuries, and several vigorous religious communities. Those men must live together at the crossroads where history put them. They can do so if they will take a few steps toward each other in an open confrontation. Then our differences ought to help us instead of dividing us. As for me, here as in every domain, I believe only in differences and not in uniformity. First of all, because differences are the roots without which the tree of liberty, the sap of creation and of civilization, dries up.

On the artist's role, Camus wrote,

> The aim of art, the aim of a life can only be to increase the sum of freedom and responsibility to be found in every man and in the world. It cannot, under any circumstances, be to reduce or suppress that freedom, even temporarily. There are works of art that tend to make man conform and to convert him to some external rule. Others tend to subject him to whatever is worst in him, to terror or hatred. Such works are valueless to me. No great work has ever been based on hatred or contempt. On the contrary, there is not a single true work of art that has not in the end added to the inner freedom of each person who has known and loved it. ("The Wager of Our Generation," 1957)

The Guest

The schoolmaster was watching the two men climb toward him. One was on horseback, the other on foot. They had not yet tackled the abrupt rise leading to the schoolhouse built on the hillside. They were toiling onward, making slow progress in the snow, among the stones, on the vast expanse of the high, deserted plateau. From time to time the horse stumbled. Without hearing anything yet, he could see the breath issuing from the horse's nostrils. One of the men, at least, knew the region. They were following the trail although it had disappeared days ago under a layer of dirty white snow. The schoolmaster calculated that it would take them half an hour to get onto the hill. It was cold; he went back into the school to get a sweater.

He crossed the empty, frigid classroom. On the blackboard the four rivers of France, drawn with four different colored chalks, had been flowing toward their estuaries for the past three days. Snow had suddenly fallen in mid-October after eight months of drought without the transition of rain, and the twenty pupils, more or less, who lived in the villages scattered over the plateau had stopped coming. With fair weather they would return. Daru now heated only the single room that was his lodging, adjoining the classroom and giving also onto the plateau to the east. Like the class windows, his window looked to the south too. On that side the school was a few kilometers from the point where the plateau began to slope toward the south. In clear weather could be seen the purple mass of the mountain range where the gap opened onto the desert.

Somewhat warmed, Daru returned to the window from which he had first seen the two men. They were no longer visible. Hence they must have tackled the rise. The sky was not so dark, for the snow had stopped falling during the night. The morning had opened with a dirty light which had scarcely become brighter as the ceiling of clouds lifted. At two in the afternoon it seemed as if the day were merely beginning. But still this was better than those three days when the thick snow was falling amidst unbroken darkness with little gusts of wind that rattled the double door of the classroom. Then Daru had spent long hours in his room, leaving it only to go to the shed and feed the chickens or get some coal. Fortunately the delivery truck from Tadjid, the nearest village to the north, had brought his supplies two days before the blizzard. It would return in forty-eight hours.

Besides, he had enough to resist a siege, for the little room was cluttered with bags of wheat that the administration left as a stock to distribute to those of his pupils whose families had suffered from the drought. Actually, they had all been victims because they were all poor. Every day Daru would distribute a ration to the children. They had missed it, he knew, during these bad days. Possibly one of the fathers or big brothers would come this afternoon and he could supply them with grain. It was just a matter of carrying them over to the next harvest. Now shiploads of wheat were arriving from France and the worst was over. But it would be hard to forget that poverty, that army of ragged ghosts wandering in the sunlight, the plateaus burned to a cinder month after month, the earth shriveled up little by little, literally scorched, every stone bursting into dust under one's foot. The sheep had died then by thousands and even a few men, here and there, sometimes without anyone's knowing.

In contrast with such poverty, he who lived almost like a monk in his remote schoolhouse, nonetheless satisfied with the little he had and with the rough life, had felt like a lord with his whitewashed walls, his narrow couch, his unpainted shelves, his well, and his weekly provision of water and food. And suddenly this snow, without warning, without the foretaste of rain. This is the way the region was, cruel to live in, even without men—who didn't help matters either. But Daru had been born here. Everywhere else, he felt exiled.

He stepped out onto the terrace in front of the schoolhouse. The two men were now halfway up the slope. He recognized the horseman as Balducci, the old gendarme[1] he had known for a long time. Balducci was holding on the end of a rope an Arab who was walking behind him with hands bound and head lowered. The gendarme waved a greeting to which Daru did not reply, lost as he was in contemplation of the Arab dressed in a faded blue jellaba,[2] his feet in sandals but covered with socks of heavy raw wool, his head surmounted by a narrow, short *chèche*.[3] They were approaching. Balducci was holding back his horse in order not to hurt the Arab, and the group was advancing slowly.

Within earshot, Balducci shouted: "One hour to do the three kilometers from El Ameur!" Daru did not answer. Short and square in his thick sweater, he watched them climb. Not once had the Arab raised his head. "Hello," said Daru when they got up onto the terrace. "Come in and warm up." Balducci painfully got down from his horse without letting go the rope. From under his bristling mustache he smiled at the schoolmaster. His little dark eyes, deep-set under a tanned forehead, and his mouth surrounded with wrinkles made him look attentive and studious. Daru took the bridle, led the horse to the shed, and came back to the two men, who were now waiting for him in the school. He led them into his room. "I am going to heat up the classroom," he said. "We'll be more comfortable there." When he entered the room again, Balducci was on the couch. He had undone the rope tying him to the Arab, who had squatted near the stove. His hands still bound, the *chèche* pushed back on his head, he was looking toward the window. At first Daru noticed only his huge lips, fat, smooth, almost Negroid; yet his nose was straight, his eyes were dark and full of fever. The *chèche* revealed an obstinate forehead and, under the weathered skin now rather discolored by the cold, the whole face had a restless and rebellious look that struck Daru when the Arab, turning his face toward him, looked him straight in the eyes. "Go into the other room," said the schoolmaster, "and I'll make you some mint tea." "Thanks," Balducci said. "What a chore! How I long for retirement." And addressing his prisoner in Arabic: "Come on, you." The Arab got up and, slowly, holding his bound wrists in front of him, went into the classroom.

With the tea, Daru brought a chair. But Balducci was already enthroned on the nearest pupil's desk and the Arab had squatted against the teacher's platform facing the stove, which stood between the desk and the window. When he held out the glass of tea to the prisoner, Daru hesitated at the sight of his bound hands. "He might perhaps be untied." "Sure," said Balducci. "That was for the trip." He started to get to his feet. But Daru, setting the glass on the floor, had

[1]*gendarme* French: armed policeman; constable

[2]*jellaba* traditional dress, like a flowing robe

[3]*chèche* French: scarf

knelt beside the Arab. Without saying anything, the Arab watched him with his feverish eyes. Once his hands were free, he rubbed his swollen wrists against each other, took the glass of tea, and sucked up the burning liquid in swift little sips.

"Good," said Daru. "And where are you headed?"

Balducci withdrew his mustache from the tea. "Here, son."

"Odd pupils! And you're spending the night?"

"No, I'm going back to El Ameur. And you will deliver this fellow to Tinguit. He is expected at police headquarters."

Balducci was looking at Daru with a friendly little smile.

"What's this story?" asked the schoolmaster. "Are you pulling my leg?"

"No, son. Those are the orders."

"The orders? I'm not. . . ." Daru hesitated, not wanting to hurt the old Corsican. "I mean, that's not my job."

"What! What's the meaning of that? In wartime people do all kinds of jobs."[4]

"Then I'll wait for the declaration of war!"

Balducci nodded.

"O.K. But the orders exist and they concern you too. Things are brewing, it appears. There is talk of a forthcoming revolt. We are mobilized, in a way."

Daru still had his obstinate look.

"Listen, son," Balducci said. "I like you and you must understand. There's only a dozen of us at El Ameur to patrol throughout the whole territory of a small department and I must get back in a hurry. I was told to hand this guy over to you and return without delay. He couldn't be kept there. His village was beginning to stir; they wanted to take him back. You must take him to Tinguit tomorrow before the day is over. Twenty kilometers shouldn't faze a husky fellow like you. After that, all will be over. You'll come back to your pupils and your comfortable life."

Behind the wall the horse could be heard snorting and pawing the earth. Daru was looking out the window. Decidedly, the weather was clearing and the light was increasing over the snowy plateau. When all the snow was melted, the sun would take over again and once more would burn the fields of stone. For days, still, the unchanging sky would shed its dry light on the solitary expanse where nothing had any connection with man.

"After all," he said, turning around toward Balducci, "what did he do?" And, before the gendarme had opened his mouth, he asked: "Does he speak French?"

"No, not a word. We had been looking for him for a month, but they were hiding him. He killed his cousin."

"Is he against us?"

"I don't think so. But you can never be sure."

"Why did he kill?"

"A family squabble, I think. One owed the other grain, it seems. It's not at all clear. In short, he killed his cousin with a billhook. You know, like a sheep, *kreezk!*"

Balducci made the gesture of drawing a blade across his throat and the Arab, his attention attracted, watched him with a sort of anxiety. Daru felt a sudden wrath against the man, against all men with their rotten spite, their tireless hates, their blood lust.

[4]a reference to the French/Algerian war, which began in 1954

But the kettle was singing on the stove. He served Balducci more tea, hesitated, then served the Arab again, who, a second time, drank avidly. His raised arms made the jellaba fall open and the schoolmaster saw his thin, muscular chest.

"Thanks, kid," Balducci said. "And now, I'm off."

He got up and went toward the Arab, taking a small rope from his pocket.

"What are you doing?" Daru asked dryly.

Balducci, disconcerted, showed him the rope.

"Don't bother."

The old gendarme hesitated. "It's up to you. Of course, you are armed?"

"I have my shotgun."

"Where?"

"In the trunk."

"You ought to have it near your bed."

"Why? I have nothing to fear."

"You're crazy, son. If there's an uprising, no one is safe, we're all in the same boat."

"I'll defend myself. I'll have time to see them coming."

Balducci began to laugh, then suddenly the mustache covered the white teeth.

"You'll have time? O.K. That's just what I was saying. You have always been a little cracked. That's why I like you, my son was like that."

At the same time he took out his revolver and put it on the desk.

"Keep it; I don't need two weapons from here to El Ameur."

The revolver shone against the black paint of the table. When the gendarme turned toward him, the schoolmaster caught the smell of leather and horseflesh.

"Listen, Balducci," Daru said suddenly, "every bit of this disgusts me, and first of all your fellow here. But I won't hand him over. Fight, yes, if I have to. But not that."

The old gendarme stood in front of him and looked at him severely.

"You're being a fool," he said slowly. "I don't like it either. You don't get used to putting a rope on a man even after years of it, and you're even ashamed—yes, ashamed. But you can't let them have their way."

"I won't hand him over," Daru said again.

"It's an order, son, and I repeat it."

"That's right. Repeat to them what I've said to you: I won't hand him over."

Balducci made a visible effort to reflect. He looked at the Arab and at Daru. At last he decided.

"No, I won't tell them anything. If you want to drop us, go ahead; I'll not denounce you. I have an order to deliver the prisoner and I'm doing so. And now you'll just sign this paper for me."

"There's no need. I'll not deny that you left him with me."

"Don't be mean with me. I know you'll tell the truth. You're from hereabouts and you are a man. But you must sign, that's the rule."

Daru opened his drawer, took out a little square bottle of purple ink, the red wooden penholder with the "sergeant-major" pen he used for making models of penmanship, and signed. The gendarme carefully folded the paper and put it into his wallet. Then he moved toward the door.

"I'll see you off," Daru said.

"No," said Balducci. "There's no use being polite. You insulted me."

He looked at the Arab, motionless in the same spot, sniffed peevishly, and turned away toward the door. "Good-by, son," he said. The door shut behind him. Balducci appeared suddenly outside the window and then disappeared. His footsteps were muffled by the snow. The horse stirred on the other side of the wall and several chickens fluttered in fright. A moment later Balducci reappeared outside the window leading the horse by the bridle. He walked toward the little rise without turning around and disappeared from sight with the horse following him. A big stone could be heard bouncing down. Daru walked back toward the prisoner, who, without stirring, never took his eyes off him.

"Wait," the schoolmaster said in Arabic and went toward the bedroom. As he was going through the door, he had a second thought, went to the desk, took the revolver, and stuck it in his pocket. Then, without looking back, he went into his room.

For some time he lay on his couch watching the sky gradually close over, listening to the silence. It was this silence that had seemed painful to him during the first days here, after the war. He had requested a post in the little town at the base of the foothills separating the upper plateaus from the desert. There, rocky walls, green and black to the north, pink and lavender to the south, marked the frontier of eternal summer. He had been named to a post farther north, on the plateau itself. In the beginning, the solitude and the silence had been hard for him on these wastelands peopled only by stones. Occasionally, furrows suggested cultivation, but they had been dug to uncover a certain kind of stone good for building. The only plowing here was to harvest rocks. Elsewhere a thin layer of soil accumulated in the hollows would be scraped out to enrich paltry village gardens. This is the way it was: bare rock covered three quarters of the region. Towns sprang up, flourished, then disappeared; men came by, loved one another or fought bitterly, then died. No one in this desert, neither he nor his guest, mattered. And yet, outside this desert neither of them, Daru knew, could have really lived.

When he got up, no noise came from the classroom. He was amazed at the unmixed joy he derived from the mere thought that the Arab might have fled and that he would be alone with no decision to make. But the prisoner was there. He had merely stretched out between the stove and the desk. With eyes open, he was staring at the ceiling. In that position, his thick lips were particularly noticeable, giving him a pouting look. "Come," said Daru. The Arab got up and followed him. In the bedroom, the schoolmaster pointed to a chair near the table under the window. The Arab sat down without taking his eyes off Daru.

"Are you hungry?"

"Yes," the prisoner said.

Daru set the table for two. He took flour and oil, shaped a cake in a frying-pan, and lighted the little stove that functioned on bottled gas. While the cake was cooking, he went out to the shed to get cheese, eggs, dates, and condensed milk. When the cake was done he set it on the window sill to cool, heated some condensed milk diluted with water, and beat up the eggs into an omelette. In one of his motions he knocked against the revolver stuck in his right pocket. He set the bowl down, went into the classroom, and put the revolver in his desk drawer. When he came back to the room, night was falling. He put on the light and served the Arab. "Eat," he said. The Arab took a piece of cake, lifted it eagerly to his mouth, and stopped short.

"And you?" he asked.

"After you. I'll eat too."

The thick lips opened slightly. The Arab hesitated, then bit into the cake determinedly.

The meal over, the Arab looked at the schoolmaster. "Are you the judge?"

"No, I'm simply keeping you until tomorrow."

"Why do you eat with me?"

"I'm hungry."

The Arab fell silent. Daru got up and went out. He brought back a folding bed from the shed, set it up between the table and the stove, perpendicular to his own bed. From a large suitcase which, upright in a corner, served as a shelf for papers, he took two blankets and arranged them on the camp bed. Then he stopped, felt useless, and sat down on his bed. There was nothing more to do or to get ready. He had to look at this man. He looked at him, therefore, trying to imagine his face bursting with rage. He couldn't do so. He could see nothing but the dark yet shining eyes and the animal mouth.

"Why did you kill him?" he asked in a voice whose hostile tone surprised him.

The Arab looked away.

"He ran away. I ran after him."

He raised his eyes to Daru again and they were full of a sort of woeful interrogation. "Now what will they do to me?"

"Are you afraid?"

He stiffened, turning his eyes away.

"Are you sorry?"

The Arab stared at him openmouthed. Obviously he did not understand. Daru's annoyance was growing. At the same time he felt awkward and self-conscious with his big body wedged between the two beds.

"Lie down there," he said impatiently. "That's your bed."

The Arab didn't move. He called to Daru:

"Tell me!"

The schoolmaster looked at him.

"Is the gendarme coming back tomorrow?"

"I don't know."

"Are you coming with us?"

"I don't know. Why?"

The prisoner got up and stretched out on top of the blankets, his feet toward the window. The light from the electric bulb shone straight into his eyes and he closed them at once.

"Why?" Daru repeated, standing beside the bed.

The Arab opened his eyes under the blinding light and looked at him, trying not to blink.

"Come with us," he said.

In the middle of the night, Daru was still not asleep. He had gone to bed after undressing completely; he generally slept naked. But when he suddenly realized that he had nothing on, he hesitated. He felt vulnerable and the temptation came to him to put his clothes back on. Then he shrugged his shoulders; after all, he wasn't a child and, if need be, he could break his adversary in two. From his bed he could observe him, lying on his back, still motionless with his eyes closed under the harsh light. When Daru turned out the light, the darkness seemed to coagulate all of a sudden. Little by little, the night came back to life in the window where the starless sky was stirring gently. The schoolmaster soon made out the body lying at this feet. The Arab still did not move, but his eyes seemed open. A faint wind was prowling around the schoolhouse. Perhaps it would drive away the clouds and the sun would reappear.

During the night the wind increased. The hens fluttered a little and then were silent. The Arab turned over on his side with his back to Daru, who thought he heard him moan. Then he listened for his guest's breathing to become heavier and more regular. He listened to that breath so close to him and mused without being able to go to sleep. In this room where he had been sleeping alone for a year, this presence bothered him. But it bothered him also by imposing on him a sort of brotherhood he knew well but refused to accept in the present circumstances. Men who share the same rooms, soldiers or prisoners, develop a strange alliance as if, having cast off their armor with their clothing, they fraternized every evening, over and above their differences, in the ancient community of dream and fatigue. But Daru shook himself, he didn't like such musings, and it was essential to sleep.

A little later, however, when the Arab stirred slightly, the schoolmaster was still not asleep. When the prisoner made a second move, he stiffened, on the alert. The Arab was lifting himself slowly on his arms with almost the motion of a sleepwalker. Seated upright in bed, he waited motionless without turning his head toward Daru, as if he were listening attentively. Daru did not stir; it had just occurred to him that the revolver was still in the drawer of his desk. It was better to act at once. Yet he continued to observe the prisoner, who, with the same slithery motion, put his feet on the ground, waited again, then began to stand up slowly. Daru was about to call out to him when the Arab began to walk, in a quite natural but extraordinarily silent way. He was heading toward the door at the end of the room that opened into the shed. He lifted the latch with precaution and went out, pushing the door behind him but without shutting it. Daru had not stirred. "He is running away," he merely thought. "Good riddance!" Yet he listened attentively. The hens were not fluttering; the guest must be on the plateau. A faint sound of water reached him, and he didn't know what it was until the Arab again stood framed in the doorway, closed the door carefully, and came back to bed without a sound. Then Daru turned his back on him and fell asleep. Still later he seemed, from the depths of his sleep, to hear furtive steps around the schoolhouse. "I'm dreaming! I'm dreaming!" he repeated to himself. And he went on sleeping.

When he awoke, the sky was clear; the loose window let in a cold, pure air. The Arab was asleep, hunched up under the blankets now, his mouth open, utterly relaxed. But when Daru shook him, he started dreadfully, staring at Daru with wild eyes as if he had never seen him and such a frightened expression that the schoolmaster stepped back. "Don't be afraid. It's me. You must eat." The Arab nodded his head and said yes. Calm had returned to his face, but his expression was vacant and listless.

The coffee was ready. They drank it seated together on the folding bed as they munched their pieces of the cake. Then Daru led the Arab under the shed and showed him the faucet where he washed. He went back into the room, folded the blankets and the bed, made his own bed and put the room in order. Then he went through the classroom and out onto the terrace. The sun was already rising in the blue sky; a soft, bright light was bathing the deserted plateau. On the ridge the snow was melting in spots. The stones were about to reappear. Crouched on the edge of the plateau, the schoolmaster looked at the deserted expanse. He thought of Balducci. He had hurt him, for he had sent him off in a way as if he didn't want to be associated with him. He could still hear the gendarme's farewell and, without knowing why, he felt strangely empty and vulnerable. At that moment, from the other side of the schoolhouse, the prisoner coughed. Daru listened to him almost despite himself and then, furious, threw a pebble that whistled through the air before sinking into the snow. That man's stupid crime revolted him, but to hand him over was contrary to honor. Merely thinking of it made him smart with humiliation. And he cursed at one and the same time his own people who had sent him this Arab and the Arab too who had dared to kill and not managed to get away. Daru got up, walked in a circle on the terrace, waited motionless, and then went back into the schoolhouse.

The Arab, leaning over the cement floor of the shed, was washing his teeth with two fingers. Daru looked at him and said: "Come." He went back into the room ahead of the prisoner. He slipped a hunting jacket on over his sweater and put on walking shoes. Standing, he waited until the Arab had put on his *chèche* and sandals. They went into the classroom and the schoolmaster pointed to the exit, saying: "Go ahead." The fellow didn't budge. "I'm coming," said Daru. The Arab went out. Daru went back into the room and made a package of pieces of zwieback, dates, and sugar. In the classroom, before going out, he hesitated a second in front of his desk, then crossed the threshold and locked the door. "That's the way," he said. He started toward the east, followed by the prisoner. But, a short distance from the schoolhouse, he thought he heard a slight sound behind them. He retraced his steps and examined the surroundings of the house; there was no one there. The Arab watched him without seeming to understand. "Come on," said Daru.

They walked for an hour and rested beside a sharp peak of limestone. The snow was melting faster and faster and the sun was drinking up the puddles at once, rapidly cleaning the plateau, which gradually dried and vibrated like the air itself. When they resumed walking, the ground rang under their feet. From time to time a bird rent the space in front of them with a joyful cry. Daru breathed in deeply the fresh morning light. He felt a sort of rapture before the vast familiar expanse, now almost entirely yellow under its dome of blue sky. They walked an hour more, descending toward the south. They reached a level height made up of crumbly rocks. From there on, the plateau sloped down, eastward, toward a low plain where there were a few spindly trees and, to the south, toward outcroppings of rock that gave the landscape a chaotic look.

Daru surveyed the two directions. There was nothing but the sky on the horizon. Not a man could be seen. He turned toward the Arab, who was looking at him blankly. Daru held out the package to him. "Take it," he said. "There are dates, bread, and sugar. You can hold out for two days. Here are a thousand francs too." The Arab took the package and the money but kept his full hands at chest level as if he didn't know what to do with what was given him. "Now look," the schoolmaster said as he pointed in the direction of the east, "there's the way to Tinguit. You have a two-hour walk. At Tinguit you'll find the administration and the police. They are expecting you." The Arab looked toward the east, still holding the package and the money against his chest. Daru took his elbow and turned him rather roughly toward the south. At the foot of the height on which they stood could be seen a faint path. "That's the trail across the plateau. In a day's walk from here you'll find pasturelands and the first nomads. They'll take you in and shelter you according to their law." The Arab had now turned toward Daru and a sort of panic was visible in his expression. "Listen," he said. Daru shook his head: "No, be quiet. Now I'm leaving you." He turned his back on him, took two long steps in the direction of the school, looked hesitantly at the motionless Arab, and started off again. For a few minutes he heard nothing but his own step resounding on the cold ground and did not turn his head. A moment later, however, he turned around. The Arab was still there on the edge of the hill, his arms hanging now, and he was looking at the schoolmaster. Daru felt something rise in his throat. But he swore with impatience, waved vaguely, and started off again. He had already gone some distance when he again stopped and looked. There was no longer anyone on the hill.

Daru hesitated. The sun was now rather high in the sky and was beginning to beat down on his head. The schoolmaster retraced his steps, at first somewhat uncertainly, then with decision. When he reached the little hill, he was bathed in sweat. He climbed it as fast as he could and stopped, out of breath, at the top. The rock-fields to the south stood out sharply against the blue sky, but on the plain to the east a steamy heat was already rising. And in that slight haze, Daru, with heavy heart, made out the Arab walking slowly on the road to prison.

A little later, standing before the window of the classroom, the schoolmaster was watching the clear light bathing the whole surface of the plateau, but he hardly saw it. Behind him on the blackboard, among the winding French rivers, sprawled the clumsily chalked-up words he had just read: "You handed over our brother. You will pay for this." Daru looked at the sky, the plateau, and, beyond, the invisible lands stretching all the way to the sea. In this vast landscape he had loved so much, he was alone.

[1957]

Translated by
JUSTIN O'BRIEN

QUESTIONS

1. What are the differing attitudes that Daru and Balducci demonstrate toward the Arab? Why?
2. By attempting to remain uninvolved, has Daru created a trap for himself; or, has his desire from the beginning been to act, to become involved in some elemental way?
3. Camus's story posits the centuries-old unspoken rule of hospitality: a guest (especially one with whom one has shared food) is safe—never to be harmed. Does Daru deviate from this belief in any manner?
4. Why does the Arab decide to walk on the road toward the prison at the end of the story? In explaining your answer, you might consider the Arab's earlier response to Daru's question about the murder: "'Are you sorry?'"
5. What is the theme of the story?

RAYMOND CARVER

(1938–1989)

UNITED STATES

Critics often state that Raymond Carver's life reads as if it were one of his own stories. He grew up in a logging town in Oregon, married before he was 20, sporadically acquired an education, and (at least early in his adult life) held a series of low-paying jobs. Bruce Weber, in the *New York Times Magazine*, described these positions as follows: "he picked tulips, pumped gas, swept hospital corridors, swabbed toilets, managed an apartment complex." Carver's fictive world of the working class grew out of his own life experiences. By the end of his short writing career, however, his collections of short stories had been nominated for the National Book Award, the National Book Critics Circle Award, and the Pulitzer Prize; and he had held several prestigious grants, including a Guggenheim fellowship, a National Endowment for the Arts Award in fiction, and the Mildred and Harold Strauss Living Award from the American Academy and Institute of Arts and Letters. Carver is equally revered for his poetry and fiction, especially for his two short story collections: *Will You Please Be Quiet, Please?* (1976) and *Cathedral* (1984).

In a foreword he wrote to John Gardner's *On Becoming a Novelist* (1953), Carver described his own education:

> I put a very high premium on education then—much higher in those days than now, I'm sure, but that's because I'm older and have an education. Understand that nobody in my family had ever gone to college or for that matter had got beyond the mandatory eighth grade in high school. I didn't know *anything*, but I knew I didn't know anything.

Of the creative writing course he took from John Gardner at Ohio State, Carver remarked:

> It was his conviction that if the words in the story were blurred because of the author's insensitivity, carelessness, or sentimentality, then the story suffered a tremendous handicap. But there was something even worse and something that must be avoided at all costs: if the words and sentiments were dishonest, the author was faking it, writing about things he didn't care about or believe in, then nobody could ever care anything about it.

Where I'm Calling From

J. P. and I are on the front porch at Frank Martin's drying-out facility. Like the rest of us at Frank Martin's, J. P. is first and foremost a drunk. But he's also a chimney sweep. It's his first time here, and he's scared. I've been here once before. What's to say? I'm back. J. P.'s real name is Joe Penny, but he says I should call him J. P. He's about thirty years old. Younger than I am. Not much younger, but a little. He's telling me how he decided to go into his line of work, and he wants to use his hands when he talks. But his hands tremble. I mean, they won't keep still. "This has never happened to me before," he says. He means the trembling. I tell him I sympathize. I tell him the shakes will idle down. And they will. But it takes time.

We've only been in here a couple of days. We're not out of the woods yet. J. P. has these shakes, and every so often a nerve — maybe it isn't a nerve, but it's something — begins to jerk in my shoulder. Sometimes it's at the side of my neck. When this happens, my mouth dries up. It's an effort just to swallow then. I know something's about to happen and I want to head it off. I want to hide from it, that's what I want to do. Just close my eyes and let it pass by, let it take the next man. J. P. can wait a minute.

I saw a seizure yesterday morning. A guy they call Tiny. A big fat guy, an electrician from Santa Rosa. They said he'd been in here for nearly two weeks and that he was over the hump. He was going home in a day or two and would spend New Year's Eve with his wife in front of the TV. On New Year's Eve, Tiny planned to drink hot chocolate and eat cookies. Yesterday morning he seemed just fine when he came down for breakfast. He was letting out with quacking noises, showing some guy how he called ducks right down onto his head. "Blam. Blam," said Tiny, picking off a couple. Tiny's hair was damp and was slicked back along the sides of his head. He'd just come out of the shower. He'd also nicked himself on the chin with his razor. But so what? Just about everybody at Frank Martin's has nicks on his face. It's something that happens. Tiny edged in at the head of the table and began telling about something that had happened on one of his drinking bouts. People at the table laughed and shook their heads as they shoveled up their eggs. Tiny would say something, grin, then look around the table for a sign of recognition. We'd all done things just as bad and crazy, so, sure, that's why we laughed. Tiny had scrambled eggs on his plate, and some biscuits and honey. I was at the table, but I wasn't hungry. I had some coffee in front of me. Suddenly, Tiny wasn't there anymore. He'd gone over in his chair with a big clatter. He was on his back on the floor with his eyes closed, his heels drumming the linoleum. People hollered for Frank Martin. But he was right there. A couple of guys got down on the floor beside Tiny. One of the guys put his fingers inside Tiny's mouth and tried to hold his tongue. Frank Martin yelled, "Everybody stand back!" Then I noticed that the bunch of us were leaning over Tiny, just looking at him, not able to take our eyes off him. "Give him air!" Frank Martin said. Then he ran into the office and called the ambulance.

Tiny is on board again today. Talk about bouncing back. This morning

Frank Martin drove the station wagon to the hospital to get him. Tiny got back too late for his eggs, but he took some coffee into the dining room and sat down at the table anyway. Somebody in the kitchen made toast for him, but Tiny didn't eat it. He just sat with his coffee and looked into his cup. Every now and then he moved his cup back and forth in front of him.

I'd like to ask him if he had any signal just before it happened. I'd like to know if he felt his ticker skip a beat, or else begin to race. Did his eyelid twitch? But I'm not about to say anything. He doesn't look like he's hot to talk about it, anyway. But what happened to Tiny is something I won't ever forget. Old Tiny flat on the floor, kicking his heels. So every time this little flitter starts up anywhere, I draw some breath and wait to find myself on my back, looking up, somebody's fingers in my mouth.

In his chair on the front porch, J. P. keeps his hands in his lap. I smoke cigarettes and use an old coal bucket for an ashtray. I listen to J. P. ramble on. It's eleven o'clock in the morning—an hour and a half until lunch. Neither one of us is hungry. But just the same we look forward to going inside and sitting down at the table. Maybe we'll get hungry.

What's J. P. talking about, anyway? He's saying how when he was twelve years old he fell into a well in the vicinity of the farm he grew up on. It was a dry well, lucky for him. "Or unlucky," he says, looking around him and shaking his head. He says how late that afternoon, after he'd been located, his dad hauled him out with a rope. J. P. had wet his pants down there. He's suffered all kinds of terror in that well, hollering for help, waiting, and then hollering some more. He hollered himself hoarse before it was over. But he told me that being at the bottom of that well had made a lasting impression. He'd sat there and looked up at the well mouth. Way up at the top, he could see a circle of blue sky. Every once in a while a white cloud passed over. A flock of birds flew across, and it seemed to J. P. their wingbeats set up this odd commotion. He heard other things. He heard tiny rustlings above him in the well, which made him wonder if things might fall down into his hair. He was thinking of insects. He heard wind blow over the well mouth, and that sound made an impression on him, too. In short, everything about his life was different for him at the bottom of that well. But nothing fell on him and nothing closed off that little circle of blue. Then his dad came along with the rope, and it wasn't long before J. P. was back in the world he'd always lived in.

"Keep talking, J. P. Then what?" I say.

When he was eighteen or nineteen years old and out of high school and had nothing whatsoever he wanted to do with his life, he went across town one afternoon to visit a friend. This friend lived in a house with a fireplace. J. P. and his friend sat around drinking beer and batting the breeze. They played some records. Then the doorbell rings. The friend goes to the door. This young woman chimney sweep is there with her cleaning things. She's wearing a top hat, the sight of which knocked J. P. for a loop. She tells J. P.'s friend that she has an appointment to clean the fireplace. The friend lets her in and bows. The young woman doesn't pay him any mind. She spreads a blanket on the hearth and lays out her gear. She's wearing these black pants, black shirt, black shoes and socks. Of course, by now she's taken her hat off. J. P. says it nearly drove him nuts to look at her. She does the work, she cleans the chimney, while J. P. and his friend play records and drink beer. But they watch her and they watch what she does.

Now and then J. P. and his friend look at each other and grin, or else they wink. They raise their eyebrows when the upper half of the young woman disappears into the chimney. She was all-right-looking, too, J. P. said.

When she'd finished her work, she rolled her things up in the blanket. From J. P.'s friend, she took a check that had been made out to her by his parents. And then she asks the friend if he wants to kiss her. "It's supposed to bring good luck," she says. That does it for J. P. The friend rolls his eyes. He clowns some more. Then, probably blushing, he kisses her on the cheek. At this minute, J. P. made his mind up about something. He put his beer down. He got up from the sofa. He went over to the young woman as she was starting to go out the door.

"Me, too?" J. P. said to her.

She swept her eyes over him. J. P. says he could feel his heart knocking. The young woman's name, it turns out, was Roxy.

"Sure," Roxy says. "Why not? I've got some extra kisses." And she kissed him a good one right on the lips and then turned to go.

Like that, quick as a wink, J. P. followed her onto the porch. He held the porch screen door for her. He went down the steps with her and out to the drive, where she'd parked her panel truck. It was something that was out of his hands. Nothing else in the world counted for anything. He knew he'd met somebody who could set his legs atremble. He could feel her kiss still burning on his lips, etc. J. P. couldn't begin to sort anything out. He was filled with sensations that were carrying him every which way.

He opened the rear door of the panel truck for her. He helped her store her things inside. "Thanks," she told him. Then he blurted it out—that he'd like to see her again. Would she go to a movie with him sometime? He'd realized, too, what he wanted to do with his life. He wanted to do what she did. He wanted to be a chimney sweep. But he didn't tell her that then.

J. P. says she put her hands on her hips and looked him over. Then she found a business card in the front seat of her truck. She gave it to him. She said, "Call this number after ten tonight. We can talk. I have to go now." She put the top hat on and then took it off. She looked at J. P. once more. She must have liked what she saw, because this time she grinned. He told her there was a smudge near her mouth. Then she got into her truck, tooted the horn, and drove away.

"Then what?" I say. "Don't stop now, J. P."

I was interested. But I would have listened if he'd been going on about how one day he'd decided to start pitching horseshoes.

It rained last night. The clouds are banked up against the hills across the valley. J. P. clears his throat and looks at the hills and the clouds. He pulls his chin. Then he goes on with what he was saying.

Roxy starts going out with him on dates. And little by little he talks her into letting him go along on jobs with her. But Roxy's in business with her father and brother and they've got just the right amount of work. They don't need anybody else. Besides, who was this guy J. P.? J. P. what? Watch out, they warned her.

So she and J. P. saw some movies together. They went to a few dances. But mainly the courtship revolved around their cleaning chimneys together. Before you know it, J. P. says, they're talking about tying the knot. And after a while they do it, they get married. J. P.'s new father-in-law takes him in as a full partner. In a year or so, Roxy has a kid. She's quit being a chimney sweep. At any rate, she's quit doing the work. Pretty soon she has another kid. J. P.'s in his mid-twenties by now. He's buying a house. He says he was happy with his life. "I was happy with the way things were going," he says. "I had everything I wanted. I had a wife and kids I loved, and I was doing what I wanted to do with my life." But for some reason—who knows why we do what we do?—his drinking picks up. For a long time he drinks beer and beer only. Any kind of beer—it didn't matter. He says he could drink beer twenty-four hours a day. He'd drink beer at night while he watched TV. Sure, once in a while he drank hard stuff. But that was only if they went out on the town, which was not often, or else when they had company over. Then a time comes, he doesn't know why, when he makes the switch from beer to gin-and-tonic. And he'd have more gin-and-tonic after dinner, sitting in front of the TV. There was always a glass of gin-and-tonic in his hand. He says he actually liked the taste of it. He began stopping off after work for drinks before he went home to have more drinks. Then he began missing some dinners. He just wouldn't show up. Or else he'd show up, but he wouldn't want anything to eat. He'd filled up on snacks at the bar. Sometimes he'd walk in the door and for no good reason throw his lunch pail across the living room. When Roxy yelled at him, he'd turn around and go out again. He moved his drinking time up to early afternoon, while he was still supposed to be working. He tells me that he was starting off the morning with a couple of drinks. He'd have a belt of the stuff before he brushed his teeth. Then he'd have his coffee. He'd go to work with a thermos bottle of vodka in his lunch pail.

J. P. quits talking. He just clams up. What's going on? I'm listening. It's helping me relax, for one thing. It's taking me away from my own situation. After a minute, I say, "What the hell? Go on, J. P." He's pulling his chin. But pretty soon he starts talking again.

J. P. and Roxy are having some real fights now. I mean *fights*. J. P. says that one time she hit him in the face with her fist and broke his nose. "Look at this," he says. "Right here." He shows me a line across the bridge of his nose. "That's a broken nose." He returned the favor. He dislocated her shoulder for her. Another time he split her lip. They beat on each other in front of the kids. Things got out of hand. But he kept on drinking. He couldn't stop. And nothing could make him stop. Not even with Roxy's dad and her brother threatening to beat the hell out of him. They told Roxy she should take the kids and clear out. But Roxy said it was her problem. She got herself into it, and she'd solve it.

Now J. P. gets real quiet again. He hunches his shoulders and pulls down in his chair. He watches a car driving down the road between this place and the hills.

I say, "I want to hear the rest of this, J. P. You better keep talking."

"I just don't know," he says. He shrugs.

"It's all right," I say. And I mean it's okay for him to tell it. "Go on, J. P."

One way she tried to fix things, J. P. says, was by finding a boyfriend. J. P. would like to know how she found the time with the house and kids.

I look at him and I'm surprised. He's a grown man. "If you want to do that," I say, "you find the time. You make the time."

J. P. shakes his head. "I guess so," he says.

Anyway, he found out about it—about Roxy's boyfriend—and he went wild. He manages to get Roxy's wedding ring off her finger. And when he does, he cuts it into several pieces with a pair of wire-cutters. Good, solid fun. They'd already gone a couple of rounds on this occasion. On his way to work the next morning, he gets arrested on a drunk charge. He loses his driver's license. He can't drive the truck to work anymore. Just as well, he says. He'd already fallen off a roof the week before and broken his thumb. It was just a matter of time until he broke his neck, he says.

He was here at Frank Martin's to dry out and to figure how to get his life back on track. But he wasn't here against his will, any more than I was. We weren't locked up. We could leave any time we wanted. But a minimum stay of a week was recommended, and two weeks or a month was, as they put it, "strongly advised."

As I said, this is my second time at Frank Martin's. When I was trying to sign a check to pay in advance for a week's stay, Frank Martin said, "The holidays are always bad. Maybe you should think of sticking around a little longer this time? Think in terms of a couple of weeks. Can you do a couple of weeks? Think about it, anyway. You don't have to decide anything right now," he said. He held his thumb on the check and I signed my name. Then I walked my girlfriend to the front door and said goodbye. "Goodbye," she said, and she lurched into the doorjamb and then onto the porch. It's late afternoon. It's raining. I go from the door to the window. I move the curtain and watch her drive away. She's in my car. She's drunk. But I'm drunk, too, and there's nothing I can do. I make it to a big chair that's close to the radiator, and I sit down. Some guys look up from their TV. Then they shift back to what they were watching. I just sit there. Now and then I look up at something that's happening on the screen.

Later that afternoon the front door banged open and J. P. was brought in between these two big guys—his father-in-law and brother-in-law, I find out afterward. They steered J. P. across the room. The old guy signed him in and gave Frank Martin a check. Then these two guys helped J. P. upstairs. I guess they put him to bed. Pretty soon the old guy and the other guy came downstairs and headed for the front door. They couldn't seem to get out of this place fast enough. It was like they couldn't wait to wash their hands of all this. I didn't blame them. Hell, no. I don't know how I'd act if I was in their shoes.

A day and a half later J. P. and I meet up on the front porch. We shake hands and comment on the weather. J. P. has a case of the shakes. We sit down and prop our feet up on the railing. We lean back in our chairs like we're just out there taking our ease, like we might be getting ready to talk about our bird dogs. That's when J. P. gets going with his story.

It's cold out, but not too cold. It's a little overcast. Frank Martin comes outside to finish his cigar. He has on a sweater buttoned all the way up. Frank Martin is short and heavy-set. He has curly gray hair and a small head. His head is too small for the rest of his body. Frank Martin puts the cigar in his mouth and stands with his arms crossed over his chest. He works that cigar in his mouth and looks across the valley. He stands there like a prizefighter, like somebody who knows the score.

J. P. gets quiet again. I mean, he's hardly breathing. I toss my cigarette into the coal bucket and look hard at J. P., who scoots farther down in his chair. J. P. pulls up his collar. What the hell's going on? I wonder. Frank Martin uncrosses his arms and takes a puff on the cigar. He lets the smoke carry out of his mouth. Then he raises his chin toward the hills and says, "Jack London used to have a big place on the other side of this valley. Right over there behind that green hill you're looking at. But alcohol killed him. Let that be a lesson to you. He was a better man than any of us. But he couldn't handle the stuff, either." Frank Martin looks at what's left of his cigar. It's gone out. He tosses it into the bucket. "You guys want to read something while you're here, read that book of his, *The Call of the Wild*. You know the one I'm talking about? We have it inside if you want to read something. It's about this animal that's half dog and half wolf. End of sermon," he says, and then hitches his pants up and tugs his sweater down. "I'm going inside," he says. "See you at lunch."

"I feel like a bug when he's around," J. P. says. "He makes me feel like a bug." J. P. shakes his head. Then he says, "Jack London. What a name! I wish I had me a name like that. Instead of the name I got."

My wife brought me up here the first time. That's when we were still together, trying to make things work out. She brought me here and she stayed around for an hour or two, talking to Frank Martin in private. Then she left. The next morning Frank Martin got me aside and said, "We can help you. If you want help and want to listen to what we say." But I didn't know if they could help me or not. Part of me wanted help. But there was another part.

This time around, it was my girlfriend who drove me here. She was driving my car. She drove us through a rainstorm. We drank champagne all the way. We were both drunk when she pulled up in the drive. She intended to drop me off, turn around, and drive home again. She had things to do. One thing she had to do was to go to work the next day. She was a secretary. She had an okay job with this electronic-parts firm. She also had this mouthy teenaged son. I wanted her to get a room in town, spend the night, and then drive home. I don't know if she got the room or not. I haven't heard from her since she led me up the front steps the other day and walked me into Frank Martin's office and said, "Guess who's here."

But I wasn't mad at her. In the first place, she didn't have any idea what she was letting herself in for when she said I could stay with her after my wife asked me to leave. I felt sorry for her. The reason I felt sorry for her was that on the day before Christmas her Pap smear came back, and the news was not cheery. She'd have to go back to the doctor, and real soon. That kind of news was reason enough for both of us to start drinking. So what we did was get ourselves good and drunk. And on Christmas Day we were still drunk. We had to go out to a restaurant to eat, because she didn't feel like cooking. The two of us and her mouthy teenaged son opened some presents, and then we went to this steakhouse near her apartment. I wasn't hungry. I had some soup and a hot roll. I drank a bottle of wine with the soup. She drank some wine, too. Then we started in on Bloody Marys. For the next couple of days, I didn't eat anything except salted nuts. But I drank a lot of bourbon. Then I said to her, "Sugar, I think I'd better pack up. I better go back to Frank Martin's."

She tried to explain to her son that she was going to be gone for a while and he'd have to get his own food. But right as we were going out the door, this mouthy kid screamed at us. He screamed, "The hell with you! I hope you never come back. I hope you kill yourselves!" Imagine this kid!

Before we left town, I had her stop at the package store, where I bought us the champagne. We stopped someplace else for plastic glasses. Then we picked up a bucket of fried chicken. We set out for Frank Martin's in this rainstorm, drinking and listening to music. She drove. I looked after the radio and poured.

We tried to make a little party of it. But we were sad, too. There was that fried chicken, but we didn't eat any.

I guess she got home okay. I think I would have heard something if she didn't. But she hasn't called me, and I haven't called her. Maybe she's had some news about herself by now. Then again, maybe she hasn't heard anything. Maybe it was all a mistake. Maybe it was somebody else's smear. But she has my car, and I have things at her house. I know we'll be seeing each other again.

They clang an old farm bell here to call you for mealtime. J. P. and I get out of our chairs and we go inside. It's starting to get too cold on the porch, anyway. We can see our breath drifting out from us as we talk.

New Year's Eve morning I try to call my wife. There's no answer. It's okay. But even if it wasn't okay, what am I supposed to do? The last time we talked on the phone, a couple of weeks ago, we screamed at each other. I hung a few names on her. "Wet brain!" she said, and put the phone back where it belonged.

But I wanted to talk to her now. Something had to be done about my stuff. I still had things at her house, too.

One of the guys here is a guy who travels. He goes to Europe and places. That's what he says, anyway. Business, he says. He also says he has his drinking under control and he doesn't have any idea why he's here at Frank Martin's. But he doesn't remember getting here. He laughs about it, about his not remembering. "Anyone can have a blackout," he says. "That doesn't prove a thing." He's not a drunk—he tells us this and we listen. "That's a serious charge to make," he says. "That kind of talk can ruin a good man's prospects." He says that if he'd only stick to whiskey and water, no ice, he'd never have these blackouts. It's the ice they put into your drink that does it. "Who do you know in Egypt?" he asks me. "I can use a few names over there."

For New Year's Eve dinner Frank Martin serves steak and baked potato. My appetite's coming back. I clean up everything on my plate and I could eat more. I look over at Tiny's plate. Hell, he's hardly touched a thing. His steak is just sitting there. Tiny is not the same old Tiny. The poor bastard had planned to be at home tonight. He'd planned to be in his robe and slippers in front of the TV, holding hands with his wife. Now he's afraid to leave. I can understand. One seizure means you're ready for another. Tiny hasn't told any more nutty stories on himself since it happened. He's stayed quiet and kept to himself. I ask him if I can have his steak, and he pushes his plate over to me.

Some of us are still up, sitting around the TV, watching Times Square, when Frank Martin comes in to show us his cake. He brings it around and shows it to each of us. I know he didn't make it. It's just a bakery cake. But it's still a cake. It's a big white cake. Across the top there's writing in pink letters. The writing says, HAPPY NEW YEAR—ONE DAY AT A TIME.

"I don't want any stupid cake," says the guy who goes to Europe and places. "Where's the champagne?" he says, and laughs.

We all go into the dining room. Frank Martin cuts the cake. I sit next to J. P. J. P. eats two pieces and drinks a Coke. I eat a piece and wrap another piece in a napkin, thinking of later.

J. P. lights a cigarette—his hands are steady now—and he tells me his wife is coming in the morning, the first day of the new year.

"That's great," I say. I nod. I lick the frosting off my finger. "That's good news, J. P."

"I'll introduce you," he says.

"I look forward to it," I say.

We say goodnight. We say Happy New Year. I use a napkin on my fingers. We shake hands.

I go to the phone, put in a dime, and call my wife collect. But nobody answers this time, either. I think about calling my girlfriend, and I'm dialing her number when I realize I really don't want to talk to her. She's probably at home watching the same thing on TV that I've been watching. Anyway, I don't want to talk to her. I hope she's okay. But if she has something wrong with her, I don't want to know about it.

After breakfast, J. P. and I take coffee out to the porch. The sky is clear, but it's cold enough for sweaters and jackets.

"She asked me if she should bring the kids," J. P. says. "I told her she should keep the kids at home. Can you imagine? My God, I don't want my kids up here."

We use the coal bucket for an ashtray. We look across the valley to where Jack London used to live. We're drinking more coffee when this car turns off the road and comes down the drive.

"That's her!" J. P. says. He puts his cup next to his chair. He gets up and goes down the steps.

I see this woman stop the car and set the brake. I see J. P. open the door. I watch her get out, and I see them hug each other. I look away. Then I look back. J. P. takes her by the arm and they come up the stairs. This woman broke a man's nose once. She has had two kids, and much trouble, but she loves this man who has her by the arm. I get up from the chair.

"This is my friend," J. P. says to his wife. "Hey, this is Roxy."

Roxy takes my hand. She's a tall, good-looking woman in a knit cap. She has on a coat, a heavy sweater, and slacks. I recall what J. P. told me about the boyfriend and the wire-cutters. I don't see any wedding ring. That's in pieces somewhere, I guess. Her hands are broad and the fingers have these big knuckles. This is a woman who can make fists if she has to.

"I've heard about you," I say. "J. P. told me how you got acquainted. Something about a chimney, J. P. said."

"Yes, a chimney," she says. "There's probably a lot else he didn't tell you," she says. "I bet he didn't tell you everything," she says, and laughs. Then—she can't wait any longer—she slips her arm around J. P. and kisses him on the cheek. They start to move to the door. "Nice meeting you," she says. "Hey, did he tell you he's the best sweep in the business?"

"Come on now, Roxy," J. P. says. He has his hand on the doorknob.

"He told me he learned everything he knew from you," I say.

"Well, that much is sure true," she says. She laughs again. But it's like she's thinking about something else. J. P. turns the doorknob. Roxy lays her hand over his. "Joe, can't we go into town for lunch? Can't I take you someplace?"

J. P. clears his throat. He says, "It hasn't been a week yet." He takes his hand off the doorknob and brings his fingers to his chin. "I think they'd like it if I didn't leave the place for a little while yet. We can have some coffee here," he says.

"That's fine," she says. Her eyes work over to me again. "I'm glad Joe's made a friend. Nice to meet you," she says.

They start to go inside. I know it's a dumb thing to do, but I do it anyway. "Roxy," I say. And they stop in the doorway and look at me. "I need some luck," I say. "No kidding. I could do with a kiss myself."

J. P. looks down. He's still holding the knob, even though the door is open. He turns the knob back and forth. But I keep looking at her. Roxy grins. "I'm not a sweep anymore," she says. "Not for years. Didn't Joe tell you that? But, sure, I'll kiss you, sure."

She moves over. She takes me by the shoulders—I'm a big man—and she plants this kiss on my lips. "How's that?" she says.

"That's fine," I say.

"Nothing to it," she says. She's still holding me by the shoulders. She's looking me right in the eyes. "Good luck," she says, and then she lets go of me.

"See you later, pal," J. P. says. He opens the door all the way, and they go in.

I sit down on the front steps and light a cigarette. I watch what my hand does, then I blow out the match. I've got the shakes. I started out with them this morning. This morning I wanted something to drink. It's depressing, but I didn't say anything about it to J. P. I try to put my mind on something else.

I'm thinking about chimney sweeps—all that stuff I heard from J. P.—when for some reason I start to think about a house my wife and I once lived in. That house didn't have a chimney, so I don't know what makes me remember it now. But I remember the house and how we'd only been in there a few weeks when I heard a noise outside one morning. It was Sunday morning and it was still dark in the bedroom. But there was this pale light coming in from the bedroom window. I listened. I could hear something scrape against the side of the house. I jumped out of bed and went to look.

"My God!" my wife says, sitting up in bed and shaking the hair away from her face. Then she starts to laugh. "It's Mr. Venturini," she says. "I forgot to tell you. He said he was coming to paint the house today. Early. Before it gets too hot. I forgot all about it," she says, and laughs. "Come on back to bed, honey. It's just him."

"In a minute," I say.

I push the curtain away from the window. Outside, this old guy in white coveralls is standing next to his ladder. The sun is just starting to break above the mountains. The old guy and I look each other over. It's the landlord, all right—this old guy in coveralls. But his coveralls are too big for him. He needs a shave, too. And he's wearing this baseball cap to cover his bald head. Goddamn it, I think, if he isn't a weird old fellow. And a wave of happiness comes over me that I'm not him—that I'm me and that I'm inside this bedroom with my wife.

He jerks his thumb toward the sun. He pretends to wipe his forehead. He's letting me know he doesn't have all that much time. The old fart breaks into a grin. It's then I realize I'm naked. I look down at myself. I look at him again and shrug. What did he expect?

My wife laughs. "Come *on*," she says. "Get back in this bed. Right now. This minute. Come on back to bed."

I let go of the curtain. But I keep standing there at the window. I can see the old fellow nod to himself like he's saying, "Go on, sonny, go back to bed. I understand." He tugs on the bill of his cap. Then he sets about his business. He picks up his bucket. He starts climbing the ladder.

I lean back into the step behind me now and cross one leg over the other. Maybe later this afternoon I'll try calling my wife again. And then I'll call to see what's happening with my girlfriend. But I don't want to get her mouthy kid on the line. If I do call, I hope he'll be out somewhere doing whatever he does when he's not around the house. I try to remember if I ever read any Jack London books. I can't remember. But there was a story of his I read in high school. "To Build a Fire," it was called. This guy in the Yukon is freezing. Imagine it—he's actually going to freeze to death if he can't get a fire going. With a fire, he can dry his socks and things and warm himself.

He gets his fire going, but then something happens to it. A branchful of snow drops on it. It goes out. Meanwhile, it's getting colder. Night is coming on.

I bring some change out of my pocket. I'll try my wife first. If she answers, I'll wish her a Happy New Year. But that's it. I won't bring up business. I won't raise my voice. Not even if she starts something. She'll ask me where I'm calling from, and I'll have to tell her. I won't say anything about New Year's resolutions. There's no way to make a joke out of this. After I talk to her, I'll call my girlfriend. Maybe I'll call her first. I'll just have to hope I don't get her kid on the line. "Hello, sugar," I'll say when she answers. "It's me."

[1983]

QUESTIONS

1. Is Carver's story guilty of the sentimentality John Gardner warned him about?
2. What is the theme of Carver's story?
3. Of what importance are the several references to Jack London and his work?
4. Why is so much space devoted to J. P.'s story?

WILLA CATHER

(1873–1947)

UNITED STATES

Robert E. Spiller's *Literary History of the United States* (1959) describes Willa Cather's discipline as a writer of novels and short stories as follows: "Willa Cather discarded plot from the beginning. She yielded to her subject matter, content to evoke its cadences, its qualities, its stream of significant experience." She was born in the mountains of Virginia in 1876 and was subsequently transplanted to the Nebraska grasslands at the end of the era of the frontier. Readers of her most famous novels (*O Pioneers!*, 1913; *My Antonia*, 1920; *Death Comes for the Archbishop*, 1927) tend to regard her as a regionalist, connecting her to the Midwest and the Southwest. Spiller continues, "Her art was essentially a representation of [a] reaction between the soul of man and its environment. That is why the best of her stories are told against the land—the sweep of red grass on the rolling plains of Nebraska, the hard warm mesas of the Southwest, . . . shadows of the wilderness and the winter crowding in upon the tiny culture of France on the rock of Quebec."

Before writing her novels, but after attending the University of Nebraska, Cather worked for *McClure's* magazine in New York City. Her stories were first collected in 1905, under the title *The Troll Garden*, and then subsequently in *Youth and the Bright Medusa* (1920). Many of these tales (such as "Paul's Case," included here) deal with artists or young people with artistic temperaments. In *Not Quite Forty* (1936), Cather paid her respect to Gustave Flaubert and indirectly explained her own artistic concept:

> Every fine story must leave in the mind of the sensitive reader an intangible residuum of pleasure; a cadence, a quality of voice that is exclusively the writer's own, individual, unique. . . . It is a common fallacy that a writer . . . can achieve this poignant quality by improving upon his subject-matter, by using his "imagination" upon it and twisting it to suit his purpose. The truth is that by such a process (which is not imagination at all!) he can at best present only a brilliant sham. . . . If he achieves anything noble, anything enduring, it must be by giving himself absolutely to his material. And this gift of sympathy is his great gift; is the fine thing in him that alone can make his work fine.

Cather wrote 19 novels, numerous short stories and essays, and an autobiography. She died in 1947.

Paul's Case

It was Paul's afternoon to appear before the faculty of the Pittsburgh High School to account for his various misdemeanors. He had been suspended a week ago, and his father had called at the Principal's office and confessed his perplexity about his son. Paul entered the faculty room suave and smiling. His clothes were a trifle outgrown and the tan velvet on the collar of his open overcoat was frayed and worn; but for all that there was something of the dandy about him, and he wore an opal pin in his neatly knotted black four-in-hand, and a red carnation in his buttonhole. This latter adornment the faculty somehow felt was not properly significant of the contrite spirit befitting a boy under the ban of suspension.

Paul was tall for his age and very thin, with high, cramped shoulders and a narrow chest. His eyes were remarkable for a certain hysterical brilliancy and he continually used them in a conscious, theatrical sort of way, peculiarly offensive in a boy. The pupils were abnormally large, as though he were addicted to belladonna, but there was a glassy glitter about them which that drug does not produce.

When questioned by the Principal as to why he was there, Paul stated, politely enough, that he wanted to come back to school. This was a lie, but Paul was quite accustomed to lying; found it, indeed, indispensable for overcoming friction. His teachers were asked to state their respective charges against him, which they did with such a rancor and aggrievedness as evinced that this was not a usual case. Disorder and impertinence were among the offenses named, yet each of his instructors felt that it was scarcely possible to put into words the real cause of the trouble, which lay in a sort of hysterically defiant manner of the boy's; in the contempt which they all knew he felt for them, and which he seemingly made not the least effort to conceal. Once, when he had been making a synopsis of a paragraph at the blackboard, his English teacher had stepped to his side and attempted to guide his hand. Paul had started back with a shudder and thrust his hands violently behind him. The astonished woman could scarcely have been more hurt and embarrassed had he struck at her. The insult was so involuntary and definitely personal as to be unforgettable. In one way and another, he had made all his teachers, men and women alike, conscious of the same feeling of physical aversion. In one class he habitually sat with his hand shading his eyes; in another he always looked out of the window during the recitation; in another he made a running commentary on the lecture, with humorous intention.

His teachers felt this afternoon that his whole attitude was symbolized by his shrug and his flippantly red carnation flower, and they fell upon him without mercy, his English teacher leading the pack. He stood through it smiling, his pale lips parted over his white teeth. (His lips were continually twitching, and he had a habit of raising his eyebrows that was contemptuous and irritating to the last degree.) Older boys than Paul had broken down and shed tears under that baptism of fire, but his set smile did not once desert him, and his only sign of discomfort was the nervous trembling of the fingers that toyed with the buttons of his overcoat, and an occasional jerking of the other hand that held his hat. Paul was always smiling, always glancing about him, seeming to feel that people might be watching him and trying to detect something. This conscious expression, since it was as far as possible from boyish mirthfulness, was usually attributed to insolence or "smartness."

As the inquisition proceeded, one of his instructors repeated an impertinent remark of the boy's, and the Principal asked him whether he thought that a courteous speech to have made a woman. Paul shrugged his shoulders slightly and his eyebrows twitched.

"I don't know," he replied. "I didn't mean to be polite or impolite, either. I guess it's a sort of way I have of saying things regardless."

The Principal, who was a sympathetic man, asked him whether he didn't think that a way it would be well to get rid of. Paul grinned and said he guessed so. When he was told that he could go, he bowed gracefully and went out. His bow was but a repetition of the scandalous red carnation.

His teachers were in despair, and his drawing master voiced the feeling of them all when he declared there was something about the boy which none of them understood. He added: "I don't really believe that smile of his comes altogether from insolence; there's something sort of haunted about it. The boy is not strong, for one thing. I happen to know that he was born in Colorado, only a few months before his mother died out there of a long illness. There is something wrong about the fellow."

The drawing master had come to realize that, in looking at Paul, one saw only his white teeth and the forced animation of his eyes. One warm afternoon the boy had gone to sleep at his drawing-board, and his master had noted with amazement what a white, blue-veined face it was; drawn and wrinkled like an old man's about the eyes, the lips twitching even in his sleep, and stiff with a nervous tension that drew them back from his teeth.

His teachers left the building dissatisfied and unhappy; humiliated to have felt so vindictive toward a mere boy, to have uttered this feeling in cutting terms, and to have set each other on, as it were, in the gruesome game of intemperate reproach. Some of them remembered having seen a miserable street cat at bay by a ring of tormentors.

As for Paul, he ran down the hill whistling the Soldiers' Chorus from *Faust* looking wildly behind him now and then to see whether some of his teachers were not there to writhe under this light-heartedness. As it was now late in the afternoon and Paul was on duty that evening as usher at Carnegie Hall, he decided that he would not go home to supper. When he reached the concert hall the doors were not yet open and, as it was chilly outside, he decided to go up into the picture gallery—always deserted at this hour—where there were some of Raffelli's gay studies of Paris streets and an airy blue Venetian scene or two that always exhilarated him. He was delighted to find no one in the gallery but the old guard, who sat in one corner, a newspaper on his knee, a black patch over one eye and the other closed. Paul possessed himself of the place and walked confidently up and down, whistling under his breath. After a while he sat down before a blue Rico and lost himself. When he bethought him to look at his watch, it was after seven o'clock, and he rose with a start and ran downstairs, making a face at Augustus, peering out from the cast-room, and an evil gesture at the Venus of Milo as he passed her on the stairway.

When Paul reached the ushers' dressing-room half-a-dozen boys were there already, and he began excitedly to tumble into his uniform. It was one of the few that at all approached fitting, and Paul thought it very becoming—though he knew that the tight, straight coat accentuated his narrow chest, about which he was exceedingly sensitive. He was always considerably excited while he dressed, twanging all over to the tuning of the strings and the preliminary flourishes of the horns in the music-room; but to-night he seemed quite beside himself, and he teased and plagued the boys until, telling him that he was crazy, they put him down on the floor and sat on him.

Somewhat calmed by his suppression, Paul dashed out to the front of the house to seat the early comers. He was a model usher; gracious and smiling he ran up and down the aisles; nothing was too much trouble for him; he carried messages and brought programmes as though it were his greatest pleasure in life, and all the people in his section thought him a charming boy, feeling that he remembered and admired them. As the house filled, he grew more and more vivacious and animated, and the color came to his cheeks and lips. It was very much as though this were a great reception and Paul were the host. Just as the musicians came out to take their places, his English teacher arrived with checks for the seats which a prominent manufacturer had taken for the season. She betrayed some embarrassment when she handed Paul the tickets, and a *hauteur* which subsequently made her feel very foolish. Paul was startled for a moment, and had the feeling of wanting to put her out; what business had she here among all these fine people and gay colors? He looked her over and decided that she was not appropriately dressed and must be a fool to sit downstairs in such togs. The tickets had probably been sent her out of kindness, he reflected as he put down a seat for her, and she had about as much right to sit there as he had.

When the symphony began Paul sank into one of the rear seats with a long sigh of relief, and lost himself as he had done before the Rico. It was not that symphonies, as such, meant anything in particular to Paul, but the first sigh of the instruments seemed to free some hilarious and potent spirit within him; something that struggled there like the Genius in the bottle found by the Arab fisherman. He felt a sudden zest of life; the lights danced before his eyes and the concert hall blazed into unimaginable splendor. When the soprano soloist came on, Paul forgot even the nastiness of his teacher's being there and gave himself up to the peculiar stimulus such personages always had for him. The soloist chanced to be a German woman, by no means in her first youth, and the mother of many children; but she wore an elaborate gown and a tiara, and above all she had that indefinable air of achievement, that world-shine upon her, which, in Paul's eyes, made her a veritable queen of Romance.

After a concert was over Paul was always irritable and wretched until he got to sleep, and tonight he was even more than usually restless. He had the feeling of not being able to let down, of its being impossible to give up this delicious excitement which was the only thing that could be called living at all. During the last number he withdrew and, after hastily changing his clothes in the dressing-room, slipped out to the side door where the soprano's carriage stood. Here he began pacing rapidly up and down the walk, waiting to see her come out.

Over yonder the Schenley, in its vacant stretch, loomed big and square through the fine rain, the windows of its twelve stories glowing like those of a lighted cardboard house under a Christmas tree. All the actors and singers of the better class stayed there when they were in the city, and a number of the big manufacturers of the place lived there in the winter. Paul had often hung about the hotel, watching the people go in and out, longing to enter and leave school-masters and dull care behind him forever.

At last the singer came out, accompanied by the conductor, who helped her into her carriage and closed the door with a cordial *auf wiedersehen* which set Paul to wondering whether she were not an old sweetheart of his. Paul followed the carriage over to the hotel, walking so rapidly as not to be far from the entrance when the singer alighted and disappeared behind the swinging glass doors that were opened by a negro in a tall hat and a long coat. In the moment that the door was ajar it seemed to Paul that he, too, entered. He seemed to feel himself go after her up the steps, into the warm, lighted building, into an exotic, a tropical world of shiny, glistening surfaces and basking ease. He reflected upon the mysterious dishes that were brought into the dining-room, the green bottles in buckets of ice, as he had seen them in the supper party pictures of the *Sunday World* supplement. A quick gust of wind brought the rain down with sudden vehemence, and Paul was startled to find that he was still outside in the slush of the gravel driveway; that his boots were letting in the water and his scanty overcoat was clinging wet about him; that the lights in front of the concert hall were out, and that the rain was driving in sheets between him and the orange glow of the windows above him. There it was, what he wanted—tangibly before him, like the fairy world of a Christmas pantomime, but mocking spirits stood guard at the doors, and, as the rain beat in his face, Paul wondered whether he were destined always to shiver in the black night outside, looking up at it.

He turned and walked reluctantly toward the car tracks. The end had to come sometime; his father in his night-clothes at the top of the stairs, explanations that did not explain, hastily improvised fictions that were forever tripping him up, his upstairs room and its horrible yellow wallpaper, the creaking bureau with the greasy plush collar-box, and over his painted wooden bed the pictures of George Washington and John Calvin, and the framed motto, "Feed my Lambs," which had been worked in red worsted by his mother.

Half an hour later, Paul alighted from his car and went slowly down one of the side streets off the main thoroughfare. It was a highly respectable street, where all the houses were exactly alike, and where businessmen of moderate means begot and reared large families of children, all of whom went to Sabbath-school and learned the shorter catechism, and were interested in arithmetic; all of whom were as exactly alike as their homes, and of a piece of the monotony in which they lived. Paul never went up Cordelia Street without a shudder of loathing. His home was next to the house of the Cumberland minister. He approached it tonight with the nerveless sense of defeat, the hopeless feeling of sinking back forever into ugliness and commonness that he had always had when he came home. The moment he turned into Cordelia Street he felt the waters close above his head. After each of these orgies of living, he experienced all the physical depression which follows a debauch; the loathing of respectable beds, of common food, of a house penetrated by kitchen odors; a shuddering repulsion for the flavorless, colorless mass of every-day existence; a morbid desire for cool things and soft lights and fresh flowers.

The nearer he approached the house, the more absolutely unequal Paul felt to the sight of it all; his ugly sleeping chamber; the cold bathroom with the grimy zinc tub, the cracked mirror, the dripping spiggots; his father, at the top of the stairs, his hairy legs sticking out from his nightshirt, his feet thrust into carpet slippers. He was so much later than usual that there would certainly be inquiries and reproaches. Paul stopped short before the door. He felt that he could not be accosted by his father tonight; that he could not toss again on that miserable bed.

He would not go in. He would tell his father that he had no car fare, and it was raining so hard he had gone home with one of the boys and stayed all night.

Meanwhile, he was wet and cold. He went around to the back of the house and tried one of the basement windows, found it open, raised it cautiously, and scrambled down the cellar wall to the floor. There he stood, holding his breath, terrified by the noise he had made, but the floor above him was silent, and there was no creak on the stairs. He found a soap-box, and carried it over to the soft ring of light that streamed from the furnace door, and sat down. He was horribly afraid of rats, so he did not try to sleep, but sat looking distrustfully at the dark, still terrified lest he might have awakened his father. In such reactions, after one of the experiences which made days and nights out of the dreary blanks of the calendar, when his senses were deadened, Paul's head was always singularly clear. Suppose his father had heard him getting in at the window and had come down and shot him for a burglar? Then, again, suppose his father had come down, pistol in hand, and he had cried out in time to save himself, and his father had been horrified to think how nearly he had killed him? Then, again, suppose a day should come when his father would remember that night, and wish there had been no warning cry to stay his hand? With this last supposition Paul entertained himself until daybreak.

The following Sunday was fine; the sodden November chill was broken by the last flash of autumnal summer. In the morning Paul had to go to church and Sabbath-school, as always. On seasonable Sunday afternoons the burghers of Cordelia Street always sat out on their front "stoops," and talked to their neighbors on the next stoop, or called to those across the street in neighborly fashion. The men usually sat on gay cushions placed upon the steps that led down to the sidewalk, while the women, in their Sunday "waists," sat in rockers on the cramped porches, pretending to be greatly at their ease. The children played in the streets; there were so many of them that the place resembled the recreation grounds of a kindergarten. The men on the steps—all in their shirt sleeves, their vests unbuttoned—sat with their legs well apart, their stomachs comfortably protruding, and talked of the prices of things, or told anecdotes of the sagacity of their various chiefs and overlords. They occasionally looked over the multitude of squabbling children, listened affectionately to their high-pitched, nasal voices, smiling to see their own proclivities reproduced in their offspring, and interspersed their legends of the iron kings with remarks about their sons' progress at school, their grades in arithmetic, and the amounts they had saved in their toy banks.

On this last Sunday of November, Paul sat all the afternoon on the lowest step of his "stoop," staring into the street, while his sisters, in their rockers, were talking to the minister's daughters next door about how many shirt-waists they had made in the last week, and how many waffles some one had eaten at the last church supper. When the weather was warm, and his father was in a particularly jovial frame of mind, the girls made lemonade, which was always brought out in a red-glass pitcher, ornamented with forget-me-nots in blue enamel. This the girls thought very fine, and the neighbors always joked about the suspicious color of the pitcher.

Today Paul's father sat on the top step, talking to a young man who shifted a restless baby from knee to knee. He happened to be the young man who was daily held up to Paul as a model, and after whom it was his father's dearest hope that he would pattern. This young man was of a ruddy complexion, with a compressed, red mouth, and faded, near-sighted eyes, over which he wore thick spectacles, with gold bows that curved about his ears. He was clerk to one of the magnates of a great steel corporation, and was looked upon in Cordelia Street as a young man with a future. There was a story that, some five years ago — he was now barely twenty-six — he had been a trifle dissipated but in order to curb his appetites and save the loss of time and strength that a sowing of wild oats might have entailed, he had taken his chief's advice, oft reiterated to his employees, and at twenty-one had married the first woman whom he could persuade to share his fortunes. She happened to be an angular school-mistress, much older than he, who also wore thick glasses, and who had now borne him four children, all near-sighted, like herself.

The young man was relating how his chief, now cruising in the Mediterranean, kept in touch with all the details of the business, arranging his office hours on his yacht just as though he were at home, and "knocking off work enough to keep two stenographers busy." His father told, in turn, the plan his corporation was considering, of putting in an electric railway plant at Cairo. Paul snapped his teeth; he had an awful apprehension that they might spoil it all before he got there. Yet he rather liked to hear these legends of the iron kings, that were told and retold on Sundays and holidays; these stories of palaces in Venice, yachts on the Mediterranean, and high play at Monte Carlo appealed to his fancy, and he was interested in the triumphs of these cash boys who had become famous, though he had no mind for the cash-boy stage.

After supper was over, and he had helped to dry the dishes, Paul nervously asked his father whether he could go to George's to get some help in his geometry, and still more nervously asked for car fare. This latter request he had to repeat, as his father, on principle, did not like to hear requests for money, whether much or little. He asked Paul whether he could not go to some boy who lived nearer, and told him that he ought not to leave his school work until Sunday; but he gave him the dime. He was not a poor man, but he had a worthy ambition to come up in the world. His only reason for allowing Paul to usher was, that he thought a boy ought to be earning a little.

Paul bounded upstairs, scrubbed the greasy odor of the dish-water from his hands with the ill-smelling soap he hated, and then shook over his fingers a few drops of violet water from the bottle he kept hidden in his drawer. He left the house with his geometry conspicuously under his arm, and the moment he got out of Cordelia Street and boarded a downtown car, he shook off the lethargy of two deadening days, and began to live again.

The leading juvenile of the permanent stock company which played at one of the downtown theatres was an acquaintance of Paul's, and the boy had been invited to drop in at the Sunday-night rehearsals whenever he could. For more than a year Paul had spent every available moment loitering about Charley Edward's dressing-room. He had won a place among Edward's following not only because the young actor, who could not afford to employ a dresser, often found him useful, but because he recognized in Paul something akin to what churchmen term "vocation."

It was at the theatre and at Carnegie Hall that Paul really lived; the rest was but a sleep and a forgetting. This was Paul's fairy tale, and it had for him all the allurement of a secret love. The moment he inhaled the gassy, painty, dusty odor behind the scenes, he breathed like a prisoner set free, and felt within him the possibility of doing or saying splendid, brilliant, poetic things. The moment the cracked orchestra beat out the overture from *Martha*, or jerked at the serenade from *Rigoletto*, all stupid and ugly things slid from him, and his senses were deliciously, yet delicately fired.

Perhaps it was because, in Paul's world, the natural nearly always wore the guise of ugliness, that a certain element of artificialty seemed to him necessary in beauty. Perhaps it was because his experience of life elsewhere was so full of Sabbath-school picnics, petty economies, wholesome advice as to how to succeed in life, and the unescapable odors of cooking, that he found this existence so alluring, these smartly-clad men and women so attractive, that he was so moved by these starry apple orchards that bloomed perennially under the lime-light.

It would be difficult to put it strongly enough how convincingly the stage entrance of that theatre was for Paul the actual portal of Romance. Certainly none of the company ever suspected it, least of all Charley Edwards. It was very like the old stories that used to float about London of fabulously rich Jews, who had subterranean halls there, with palms, and fountains, and soft lamps and richly apparelled women who never saw the disenchanting light of London day. So, in the midst of that smoke-palled city, enamored of figures and grimy toil, Paul had his secret temple, his wishing carpet, his bit of blue-and-white Mediterranean shore bathed in perpetual sunshine.

Several of Paul's teachers had a theory that his imagination had been perverted by garish fiction, but the truth was that he scarcely ever read at all. The books at home were not such as would either tempt or corrupt a youthful mind, and as for reading the novels that some of his friends urged upon him—well, he got what he wanted much more quickly from music; any sort of music, from an orchestra to a barrel organ. He needed only the spark, the indescribable thrill that made his imagination master of his senses, and he could make plots and pictures enough of his own. It was equally true that he was not stage struck—not, at any rate, in the usual acceptation of that expression. He had no desire to become an actor, any more than he had to become a musician. He felt no necessity to do any of these things; what he wanted was to see, to be in the atmosphere, float on the wave of it, to be carried out, blue league after blue league, away from everything.

After a night behind the scenes, Paul found the school-room more than ever repulsive; the bare floors and naked walls; the prosy men who never wore frock coats, or violets in their buttonholes; the women with their dull gowns, shrill voices, and pitiful seriousness about prepositions that govern the dative. He could not bear to have the other pupils think, for a moment, that he took these people seriously; he must convey to them that he considered it all trivial, and was there only by way of a jest, anyway. He had autographed pictures of all the members of the stock company which he showed his classmates, telling them the most incredible stories of his familiarity with these people, of his acquaintance with the soloists who came to Carnegie Hall, his suppers with them and the flowers he sent them. When these stories lost their effect, and his audience grew listless, he became desperate and would bid all the boys good-bye, announcing that he was going to travel for a while; going to Naples, to Venice, to Egypt. Then, next Monday, he would slip back, conscious and nervously smiling; his sister was ill, and he should have to defer his voyage until spring.

Matters went steadily worse with Paul at school. In the itch to let his instructors know how heartily he despised them and their homilies, and how thoroughly he was appreciated elsewhere, he mentioned once or twice that he had no time to fool with theorems; adding — with a twitch of the eyebrows and a touch of that nervous bravado which so perplexed them — that he was helping the people down at the stock company; they were old friends of his.

The upshot of the matter was that the Principal went to Paul's father, and Paul was taken out of school and put to work. The manager at Carnegie Hall was told to get another usher in his stead; the door-keeper at the theatre was warned not to admit him to the house; and Charley Edwards remorsefully promised the boy's father not to see him again.

The members of the stock company were vastly amused when some of Paul's stories reached them — especially the women. They were hardworking women, most of them supporting indigent husbands or brothers, and they laughed rather bitterly at having stirred the boy to such fervid and florid inventions. They agreed with the faculty and with his father that Paul's was a bad case.

The east-bound train was ploughing through a January snow-storm; the dull dawn was beginning to show grey when the engine whistled a mile out of Newark. Paul started up from the seat where he had lain curled in uneasy slumber, rubbed the breath-misted window glass with his hand, and peered out. The snow was whirling in curling eddies above the white bottom lands, and the drifts lay already deep in the fields and along the fences, while here and there the long dead grass and dried weed stalks protruded black above it. Lights shone from the scattered houses, and a gang of laborers who stood beside the track waved their lanterns.

Paul had slept very little, and he felt grimy and uncomfortable. He had made the all-night journey in a day coach, partly because he was ashamed, dressed as he was, to go into a Pullman, and partly because he was afraid of being seen there by some Pittsburgh businessman, who might have noticed him in Denny & Carson's office. When the whistle awoke him, he clutched quickly at his breast pocket, glancing about him with an uncertain smile. But the little, clay-bespattered Italians were still sleeping, the slatternly women across the aisle were in open-mouthed oblivion, and even the crumby, crying babies were for the nonce stilled. Paul settled back to struggle with his impatience as best he could.

When he arrived at the Jersey City station, he hurried through his breakfast, manifestly ill at ease and keeping a sharp eye about him. After he reached the Twenty-third Street station, he consulted a cabman, and had himself driven to a men's furnishing establishment that was just opening for the day. He spent upward of two hours there, buying with endless reconsidering and great care. His new street suit he put on in the fitting-room; the frock coat and dress clothes he had bundled into the cab with his linen. Then he drove to a hatter's and a shoe house. His next errand was at Tiffany's, where he selected his silver and a new scarf-pin. He would not wait to have his silver marked, he said. Lastly, he stopped at a trunk shop on Broadway, and had his purchases packed into various travelling bags.

It was a little after one o'clock when he drove up to the Waldorf, and after settling with the cabman, when into the office. He registered from Washington; said his mother and father had been abroad, and that he had come down to await the arrival of their steamer. He told his story plausibly and had no trouble, since he volunteered to pay for them in advance, in engaging his rooms; a sleeping-room, sitting-room, and bath.

Not once, but a hundred times Paul had planned this entry into New York.

He had gone over every detail of it with Charley Edwards, and in his scrap book at home there were pages of description about New York hotels, cut from the Sunday papers. When he was shown to his sitting-room on the eighth floor, he saw at a glance that everything was as it should be; there was but one detail in his mental picture that the place did not realize, so he rang for the bell boy and sent him down for flowers. He moved about nervously until the boy returned, putting away his new linen and fingering it delightedly as he did so. When the flowers came, he put them hastily into water, and then tumbled into a hot bath. Presently he came out of his white bath-room, resplendent in his new silk underwear, and playing with the tassels of his red robe. The snow was whirling so fiercely outside his windows that he could scarcely see across the street, but within the air was deliciously soft and fragrant. He put the violets and jonquils on the taboret beside the couch, and threw himself down, with a long sigh, covering himself with a Roman blanket. He was thoroughly tired; he had been in such haste, he had stood up to such a strain, covered so much ground in the last twenty-four hours, that he wanted to think how it had all come about. Lulled by the sound of the wind, the warm air, and the cool fragrance of the flowers, he sank into deep, drowsy retrospection.

It had been wonderfully simple; when they had shut him out of the theatre and concert hall, when they had taken away his bone, the whole thing was virtually determined. The rest was a mere matter of opportunity. The only thing that at all surprised him was his own courage—for he realized well enough that he had always been tormented by fear, a sort of apprehensive dread that, of late years, as the meshes of the lies he had told closed about him, had been pulling the muscles of his body tighter and tighter. Until now, he could not remember the time when he had not been dreading something. Even when he was a little boy, it was always there—behind him, or before, or on either side. There had always been the shadowed corner, the dark place into which he dared not look, but from which something seemed always to be watching him—and Paul had done things that were not pretty to watch, he knew.

But now he had a curious sense of relief, as though he had at last thrown down the gauntlet to the thing in the corner.

Yet it was but a day since he had been sulking in the traces; but yesterday afternoon that he had been sent to the bank with Denny & Carson's deposit, as usual—but this time he was instructed to leave the book to be balanced. There was above two thousand dollars in checks, and nearly a thousand in the bank notes which he had taken from the book and quietly transferred to his pocket. At the bank he had made out a new deposit slip. His nerves had been steady enough to permit of his returning to the office, where he had finished his work and asked for a full day's holiday tomorrow, Saturday, giving a perfectly reasonable pretext. The bank book, he knew, would not be returned before Monday or Tuesday, and his father would be out of town for the next week. From the time he slipped the bank notes into his pocket until he boarded the night train for New York, he had not known a moment's hesitation. It was not the first time Paul had steered through treacherous waters.

How astonishingly easy it had all been; here he was, the thing done; and this time there would be no awakening, no figure at the top of the stairs. He watched the snow flakes whirling by his window until he fell asleep.

When he awoke, it was three o'clock in the afternoon. He bounded up with a start; half of one of his precious days gone already! He spent more than an hour in dressing, watching every stage of his toilet carefully in the mirror. Everything was quite perfect; he was exactly the kind of boy he had always wanted to be.

When he went downstairs, Paul took a carriage and drove up Fifth Avenue toward the Park. The snow had somewhat abated; carriages and tradesmen's wagons were hurrying soundlessly to and fro in the winter twilight; boys in woollen mufflers were shovelling off the doorsteps; the avenue stages made fine spots of color against the white sheet. Here and there on the corners were stands, with whole flower gardens blooming under glass cases, against the sides of which the snow flakes stuck and melted; violets, roses, carnations, lilies of the valley—somewhat vastly more lovely and alluring that they blossomed thus unnaturally in the snow. The Park itself was a wonderful stage winterpiece.

When he returned, the pause of the twilight had ceased, and the tune of the streets had changed. The snow was falling faster, lights streamed from the hotels that reared their dozen stories fearlessly up into the storm, defying the raging Atlantic winds. A long, black stream of carriages poured down the avenue, intersected here and there by other streams, tending horizontally. There were a score of cabs about the entrance of his hotel, and his driver had to wait. Boys in livery were running in and out of the awning stretched across the sidewalk, up and down the red velvet carpet laid from the door to the street. Above, about, within it all was the rumble and roar, the hurry and toss of thousands of human beings as hot for pleasure as himself, and on every side of him towered the glaring affirmation of the omnipotence of wealth.

The boy set his teeth and drew his shoulders together in a spasm of realization: the plot of all dramas, the text of all romances, the nerve-stuff of all sensations was whirling about him like the snow flakes. He burnt like a faggot in a tempest.

When Paul went down to dinner, the music of the orchestra came floating up the elevator shaft to greet him. His head whirled as he stepped into the thronged corridor, and he sank back into one of the chairs against the wall to get his breath. The lights, the chatter, the perfumes, the bewildering medley of color—he had, for a moment, the feeling of not being able to stand it. But only for a moment; these were his own people, he told himself. He went slowly about the corridors, through the writing-rooms, smoking-rooms, reception-rooms, as though he were exploring the chambers of an enchanted palace, built and peopled for him alone.

When he reached the dining-room he sat down at a table near a window. The flowers, the white linen, the many-colored wine glasses, the gay toilettes of the women, the low popping of corks, the undulating repetitions of the *Blue Danube* from the orchestra, all flooded Paul's dream with bewildering radiance. When the roseate tinge of his champagne was added—that cold, precious, bubbling stuff that creamed and foamed in his glass—Paul wondered that there were honest men in the world at all. This was what all the world was fighting for, he reflected; this was what all the struggle was about. He doubted the reality of his past. Had he ever known a place called Cordelia Street, a place where fagged-looking businessmen got on the early car; mere rivets in a machine they seemed to Paul—sickening men, with combings of children's hair always hanging to their coats, and the smell of cooking in their clothes. Cordelia Street—Ah! that belonged to another time and country; had he not always been thus, had he not sat here night after night, from as far back as he could remember, looking pensively over just such shimmering textures, and slowly twirling the stem of a glass like this one between his thumb and middle finger? He rather thought he had.

He was not in the least abashed or lonely. He had no especial desire to meet or to know any of these people; all he demanded was the right to look on and conjecture, to watch the pageant. The mere stage properties were all he contended for. Nor was he lonely later in the evening, in his loge at the Metropolitan. He was now entirely rid of his nervous misgivings, of his forced aggressiveness, of the imperative desire to show himself different from his surroundings. He felt now that his surroundings explained him. Nobody questioned the purple; he had only to wear it passively. He had only to glance down at his attire to reassure himself that here it would be impossible for anyone to humiliate him.

He found it hard to leave his beautiful sitting-room to go to bed that night, and sat long watching the raging storm from his turret window. When he went to sleep it was with the lights turned on in his bedroom; partly because of his old timidity, and partly so that, if he should wake in the night, there would be no wretched moment of doubt, no horrible suspicion of yellow wall-paper, or of Washington or Calvin above his bed.

Sunday morning the city was practically snow-bound. Paul breakfasted late, and in the afternoon he fell in with a wild San Francisco boy, a freshman at Yale, who said he had run down for a "little flyer" over Sunday. The young man offered to show Paul the night side of the town, and the two boys went out together after dinner, not returning to the hotel until seven o'clock the next morning. They had started out in the confiding warmth of a champagne friendship, but their parting in the elevator was singularly cool. The freshman pulled himself together to make his train, and Paul went to bed. He awoke at two o'clock in the afternoon, very thirsty and dizzy, and rang for ice-water, coffee, and the Pittsburgh papers.

On the part of the hotel management, Paul excited no suspicion. There was this to be said for him, that he wore his spoils with dignity and in no way made himself conspicuous. Even under the glow of his wine he was never boisterous, though he found the stuff like a magician's wand for wonder-building. His chief greediness lay in his ears and eyes, and his excesses were not offensive ones. His dearest pleasures were the grey winter twilights in his sitting-room; his quiet enjoyment of his flowers, his clothes, his wide divan, his cigarette, and his sense of power. He could not remember a time when he had felt so at peace with himself. The mere release from the necessity of petty lying, lying every day and every day, restored his self-respect. He had never lied for pleasure, even at school; but to be noticed and admired, to assert his difference from other Cordelia Street boys; and he felt a good deal more manly, more honest, even, now that he had no need for boastful pretensions, now that he could, as his actor friends used to say, "dress the part." It was characteristic that remorse did not occur to him. His golden days went by without a shadow, and he made each as perfect as he could.

On the eighth day after his arrival in New York, he found the whole affair exploited in the Pittsburgh papers, exploited with a wealth of detail which indicated that local news of a sensational nature was at a low ebb. The firm of Denny & Carson announced that the boy's father had refunded the full amount of the theft, and that they had no intention of prosecuting. The Cumberland minister had been interviewed, and expressed his hope of yet reclaiming the motherless lad, and his Sabbath-school teacher declared that she would spare no effect to that end. The rumor had reached Pittsburgh that the boy had been seen in a New York hotel, and his father had gone East to find him and bring him home.

Paul had just come in to dress for dinner; he sank into a chair, weak to the knees, and clasped his head in his hands. It was to be worse than jail, even; the tepid waters of Cordelia Street were to close over him finally and forever. The grey monotony stretched before him in hopeless, unrelieved years; Sabbath-school, Young People's Meeting, the yellow-papered room, the damp dish-towels; it all rushed back upon him with a sickening vividness. He had the old feeling that the orchestra had suddenly stopped, the sinking sensation that the play was over. The sweat broke out on his face, and he sprang to his feet, looked about him with his white, conscious smile, and winked at himself in the mirror. With something of the old childish belief in miracles with which he had so often gone to class, all his lessons unlearned, Paul dressed and dashed whistling down the corridor to the elevator.

He had no sooner entered the dining-room and caught the measure of the music than his remembrance was lightened by his old elastic power of claiming the moment, mounting with it, and finding it all sufficient. The glare and glitter about him, the mere scenic accessories had again, and for the last time, their old potency. He would show himself that he was game, he would finish the thing splendidly. He doubted, more than ever, the existence of Cordelia Street, and for the first time he drank his wine recklessly. Was he not, after all, one of those fortunate beings born to the purple, was he not still himself and in his own place? He drummed a nervous accompaniment to the Pagliacci music and looked about him, telling himself over and over that it had paid.

He reflected drowsily, to the swell of the music and the chill sweetness of his wine, that he might have done it more wisely. He might have caught an outboard steamer and been well out of their clutches before now. But the other side of the world had seemed too far away and too uncertain then; he could not have waited for it; his need had been too sharp. If he had to choose over again, he would do the same thing tomorrow. He looked affectionately about the dining-room, now gilded with a soft mist. Ah, it had paid indeed!

Paul was awakened next morning by a painful throbbing in his head and feet. He had thrown himself across the bed without undressing, and had slept with his shoes on. His limbs and hands were lead heavy, and his tongue and throat were parched and burnt. There came upon him one of those fateful attacks of clear-headedness that never occurred except when he was physically exhausted and his nerves hung loose. He lay still and closed his eyes and let the tide of things wash over him.

His father was in New York; "stopping at some joint or other," he told himself. The memory of successive summers on the front stoop fell upon him like a weight of black water. He had not a hundred dollars left; and he knew now, more than ever, that money was everything, the wall that stood between all he loathed and all he wanted. The thing was winding itself up; he had thought of that on his first glorious day in New York, and had even provided a way to snap the thread. It lay on his dressing-table now; he had got it out last night when he came blindly up from dinner, but the shiny metal hurt his eyes, and he disliked the looks of it.

He rose and moved about with a painful effort, succumbing now and again to attacks of nausea. It was the old depression exaggerated; all the world had become Cordelia Street. Yet somehow he was not afraid of anything, was absolutely calm; perhaps because he had looked into the dark corner at last and knew. It was bad enough, what he saw there, but somehow not so bad as his long fear of it had been. He saw everything clearly now. He had a feeling that he had made the best of it, that he had lived the sort of life he was meant to live, and for half an hour he sat staring at the revolver. But he told himself that was not the way, so he went downstairs and took a cab to the ferry.

When Paul arrived at Newark, he got off the train and took another cab, directing the driver to follow the Pennsylvania tracks out of the town. The snow lay heavy on the roadways and had drifted deep in the open fields. Only here and there the dead grass or dried weed stalks projected, singularly black, above it. Once well into the country, Paul dismissed the carriage and walked, floundering along the tracks, his mind a medley of irrelevant things. He seemed to hold in his brain an actual picture of everything he had seen that morning. He remembered every feature of both his drivers, of the toothless old woman from whom he had bought the red flowers in his coat, the agent from whom he had got his ticket, and all of his fellow-passengers on the ferry. His mind, unable to cope with vital matters near at hand, worked feverishly and deftly at sorting and grouping these images. They made for him a part of the ugliness of the world, of the ache in his head, and the bitter burning on his tongue. He stopped and put a handful of snow into his mouth as he walked, but that, too, seemed hot. When he reached a little hillside, where the tracks ran through a cut some twenty feet below him, he stopped and sat down.

The carnations in his coat were drooping with the cold, he noticed; their red glory all over. It occurred to him that all the flowers he had seen in the glass cases that first night must have gone the same way, long before this. It was only one splendid breath they had, in spite of their brave mockery at the winter outside the glass; and it was a losing game in the end, it seemed, this revolt against the homilies by which the world is run. Paul took one of the blossoms carefully from his coat and scooped a little hole in the snow, where he covered it up. Then he dozed a while, from his weak condition, seemingly insensible to the cold.

The sound of an approaching train awoke him, and he started to his feet, remembering only his resolution, and afraid lest he should be too late. He stood watching the approaching locomotive, his teeth chattering, his lips drawn away from them in a frightened smile; once or twice he glanced nervously sidewise, as though he were being watched. When the right moment came, he jumped. As he fell, the folly of his haste occurred to him with merciless clearness, the vastness of what he had left undone. There flashed through his brain, clearer than ever before, the blue of Adriatic water, the yellow of Algerian sands.

He felt something strike his chest, and that his body was being thrown swiftly through the air, on and on, immeasurably far and fast, while his limbs were gently relaxed. Then, because the picture making mechanism was crushed, the disturbing visions flashed into black, and Paul dropped back into the immense design of things.

[1905]

QUESTIONS

1. Is Paul's rebellion against his middle-class upbringing, his father, or something entirely different? What specifically is he rebelling against?

2. Everyone in the story (including his teachers) thinks that Paul's "was a bad case." What does the author want the reader to think?
3. After considering the gun in the hotel, why does Paul leave the city and choose another form of suicide?
4. What would change in your understanding if the last paragraph of the story were omitted?

John Cheever
(1912–1982)
United States

By the time of his death in 1982, John Cheever had not only earned the title of master storyteller but also created such a timeless milieu for his characters that critics commonly referred to it as Cheever Country. Broadly defined as the suburban communities in Connecticut north of New York City, the upper middle class, and sometimes even the rich, Cheever Country is typified by characters who appear to have reached a stage of complacency in their lives. They are bored with their jobs, their spouses, their friends, and above all with their comfortable life-styles. Their lives bear enough of a similarity to the characters in the works of Anton Chekhov that John Leonard once called Cheever "the Chekhov of the suburbs."

Cheever began publishing when he was 17, when *The New Republic* accepted his first story. Shortly thereafter, his stories appeared in *The New Yorker*, where they were published with such frequency that they helped define the kind of fiction often associated with the magazine. His first collection of stories, *The Way Some People Live*, was published in 1942. By the time he won the Pulitzer Prize for *The Stories of John Cheever* in 1978, Cheever had published 10 volumes of stories and four novels: *The Wapshot Chronicle* (1957), *The Wapshot Scandal* (1964), *Bullet Park* (1969), and *Falconer* (1977). One final novel appeared during the year of his death: *Oh, What a Paradise It Seems* (1982).

Cheever's accomplishment as a writer of short stories is best summed up by another writer (John Gardner) who said: "Cheever is one of the few living novelists who might qualify as true artists." Responding to his own question of who reads short stories, Cheever (in "Why I Write Short Stories" [1978]) replied, "I like to think that they are read by men and women in the dentist's office, waiting to be called to the chair; they are read on transcontinental plane trips instead of watching a banal and vulgar film spin out the time between our coasts; they are read by discerning and well-informed men and women who seem to feel that narrative fiction can contribute to our understanding of one another and the sometimes bewildering world around us."

The Swimmer

It was one of those midsummer Sundays when everyone sits around saying, "I *drank* too much last night." You might have heard it whispered by the parishioners leaving church, heard it from the lips of the priest himself, struggling with his cassock in the *vestiarium*, heard it from the golf links and the tennis courts, heard it from the wild-life preserve where the leader of the Audubon group was suffering from a terrible hangover. "I *drank* too much," said Donald Westerhazy. "We all *drank* too much," said Lucinda Merrill. "It must have been the wine," said Helen Westerhazy. "I *drank* too much of that claret."

This was the edge of the Westerhazy's pool. The pool, fed by an artesian well with a high iron content, was a pale shade of green. It was a fine day. In the west there was a massive stand of cumulus cloud so like a city seen from a distance—from the bow of an approaching ship—that it might have had a name. Lisbon. Hackensack. The sun was hot. Neddy Merrill sat by the green water, one hand in it, one around a glass of gin. He was a slender man—he seemed to have the especial slenderness of youth—and while he was far from young he had slid down his banister that morning and given the bronze backside of Aphrodite on the hall table a smack, as he jogged toward the smell of coffee in his dining room. He might have been compared to a summer's day,[1] particularly the last hours of one, and while he lacked a tennis racket or a sail bag the impression was definitely one of youth, sport, and clement weather. He had been swimming and now he was breathing deeply, stertorously as if he could gulp into his lungs the components of that moment, the heat of the sun, the intenseness of his pleasure. It all seemed to flow into his chest. His own house stood in Bullet Park, eight miles to the south, where his four beautiful daughters would have had their lunch and might be playing tennis. Then it occurred to him that by taking a dogleg to the southwest he could reach his home by water.

His life was not confining and the delight he took in this observation could not be explained by its suggestion of escape. He seemed to see, with a cartographer's eye, that string of swimming pools, that quasi-subterranean stream that curved across the country. He had made a discovery, a contribution to modern geography; he would name the stream Lucinda after his wife. He was not a practical joker nor was he a fool but he was determinedly original and had a vague and modest idea of himself as a legendary figure. The day was beautiful and it seemed to him that a long swim might enlarge and celebrate its beauty.

He took off a sweater that was hung over his shoulders and dove in. He had an inexplicable contempt for men who did not hurl themselves into pools. He swam a choppy crawl, breathing either with every stroke or every fourth stroke and counting somewhere well in the back of his mind the one-two one-two of a flutter kick. It was not a serviceable stroke for long distances but the domestication of swimming had saddled the sport with some customs and in his part of the world a crawl was customary. To be embraced and sustained by the light green water was less a pleasure, it seemed, than the resumption of a natural condition, and he would have liked to swim without trunks, but this was not possible, considering his project. He hoisted himself up on the far curb—he never used the ladder—and started across the lawn. When Lucinda asked where he was going he said he was going to swim home.

The only maps and charts he had to go by were remembered or imaginary but these were clear enough. First there were the Grahams, the Hammers, the Lears, the Howlands, and the Crosscups. He would cross Ditmar Street to the Bunkers and come, after a short portage, to the Levys, the Welchers, and the public pool in Lancaster. Then there were the Hallorans, the Sachses, the Biswangers, Shirley Adams, the Gilmartins, and the Clydes. The day was lovely, and that he lived in a world so generously supplied with water seemed

[1]*compared to a summer's day* a reference to Shakespeare's Sonnet 18

like a clemency, a beneficence. His heart was high and he ran across the grass. Making his way home by an uncommon route gave him the feeling that he was a pilgrim, an explorer, a man with a destiny, and he knew that he would find friends all along the way; friends would line the banks of the Lucinda River.

He went through a hedge that separated the Westerhazys' land from the Grahams', walked under some flowering apple trees, passed the shed that housed their pump and filter, and came out at the Grahams' pool. "Why, Neddy," Mrs. Graham said, "what a marvelous surprise. I've been trying to get you on the phone all morning. Here, let me get you a drink." He saw then, like any explorer, that the hospitable customs and traditions of the natives would have to be handled with diplomacy if he was ever going to reach his destination. He did not want to mystify or seem rude to the Grahams nor did he have the time to linger there. He swam the length of their pool and joined them in the sun and was rescued, a few minutes later, by the arrival of two carloads of friends from Connecticut. During the uproarious reunions he was able to slip away. He went down by the front of the Grahams' house, stepped over a thorny hedge, and crossed a vacant lot to the Hammers'. Mrs. Hammer, looking up from her roses, saw him swim by although she wasn't quite sure who it was. The Lears heard him splashing past the open windows of their living room. The Howlands and the Crosscups were away. After leaving the Howlands' he crossed Ditmar Street and started for the Bunkers', where he could hear, even at that distance, the noise of a party.

The water refracted the sound of voices and laughter and seemed to suspend it in midair. The Bunkers' pool was on a rise and he climbed some stairs to a terrace where twenty-five or thirty men and women were drinking. The only person in the water was Rusty Towers, who floated there on a rubber raft. Oh, how bonny and lush were the banks of the Lucinda River! Prosperous men and women gathered by the sapphire-colored waters while caterer's men in white coats passed them cold gin. Overhead a red de Haviland trainer was circling around and around and around in the sky with something like the glee of a child in a swing. Ned felt a passing affection for the scene, a tenderness for the gathering, as if it was something he might touch. In the distance he heard thunder. As soon as Enid Bunker saw him she began to scream: "Oh, look who's here! What a marvelous surprise! When Lucinda said you couldn't come I thought I'd *die*." She made her way to him through the crowd, and when they had finished kissing she led him to the bar, a progress that was slowed by the fact that he stopped to kiss eight or ten other women and shake the hands of as many men. A smiling bartender he had seen at a hundred parties gave him a gin and tonic and he stood by the bar for a moment, anxious not to get stuck in any conversation that would delay his voyage. When he seemed about to be surrounded he dove in and swam close to the side to avoid colliding with Rusty's raft. At the far end of the pool he bypassed the Tomlinsons with a broad smile and jogged up the garden path. The gravel cut his feet but this was only unpleasantness. The party was confined to the pool, and as he went toward the house he heard the brilliant, watery sound of voices fade, heard the noise of a radio from the Bunkers' kitchen, where someone was listening to a ball game. Sunday afternoon. He made his way through the parked cars and down the grassy border of their driveway to Alewives Lane. He did not want to be seen on the road in his bathing trunks but there was no traffic and he made the short distance to the Levys' driveway, marked with a PRIVATE PROPERTY sign and a green tube for *The New York Times*. All the doors and windows of the big house were open but there were no signs of life; not even a dog barked. He went around the side of the house to the pool and saw that the Levys had only recently left. Glasses and bottles and dishes of nuts were on a table at the deep end, where there was a bathhouse or gazebo, hung with Japanese lanterns. After swimming the pool he got himself a glass and poured a drink. It was his fourth or fifth drink and he had swum nearly half the length of the Lucinda River. He felt tired, clean, and pleased at that moment to be alone; pleased with everything.

It would storm. The stand of cumulus cloud—that city—had risen and darkened, and while he sat there he heard the percussiveness of thunder again. The de Haviland trainer was still circling overhead and it seemed to Ned that he could almost hear the pilot laugh with pleasure in the afternoon; but when there was another peal of thunder he took off for home. A train whistle blew and he wondered what time it had gotten to be. Four? Five? He thought of the provincial station at that hour, where a waiter, his tuxedo concealed by a raincoat, a dwarf with some flowers wrapped in newspaper, and a woman who had been crying would be waiting for the local. It was suddenly growing dark; it was that moment when the pin-headed birds seemed to organize their song into some acute and knowledgeable recognition of the storm's approach. Then there was a fine noise of rushing water from the crown of an oak at his back, as if a spigot there had been turned. Then the noise of fountains came from the crowns of all the tall trees. Why did he love storms, what was the meaning of his excitement when the door sprang open and the rain wind fled rudely up the stairs, why had the simple task of shutting the windows of an old house seemed fitting and urgent, why did the first watery notes of a storm wind have for him the unmistakable sound of good news, cheer, glad tidings? Then there was an explosion, a smell of cordite, and rain lashed the Japanese lanterns that Mrs. Levy had bought in Kyoto the year before last, or was it the year before that?

He stayed in the Levys' gazebo until the storm had passed. The rain had cooled the air and he shivered. The force of the wind had stripped a maple of its red and yellow leaves and scattered them over the grass and the water. Since it was midsummer the tree must be blighted, and yet he felt a peculiar sadness at this sign of autumn. He braced his shoulders, emptied his glass, and started for the Welchers' pool. This meant crossing the Lindleys' riding ring and he was surprised to find it overgrown with grass and all the jumps dismantled. He wondered if the Lindleys had sold their horses or gone away for the summer and put them out to board. He seemed to remember having heard something about the Lindleys and their horses but the memory was unclear. On he went, barefoot through the wet grass, to the Welchers', where he found their pool was dry.

This breach in his chain of water disappointed him absurdly, and he felt like some explorer who seeks a torrential headwater and finds a dead stream. He was disappointed and mystified. It was common enough to go away for the summer but no one ever drained his pool. The Welchers had definitely gone away. The pool furniture was folded, stacked, and covered with a tarpaulin. The bathhouse was locked. All the windows of the house were shut, and when he went around to the driveway in front he saw a FOR SALE sign nailed to a tree. When had he last heard from the Welchers—when, that is, had he and Lucinda last regretted an invitation to dine with them? It seemed only a week or so ago. Was his memory failing or had he so disciplined it in the repression of unpleasant facts that he had damaged his sense of the truth? Then in the distance he heard the sound of a tennis game. This cheered him, cleared away all his apprehensions and let him regard the overcast sky and the cold air with indifference. This was the day that Neddy Merrill swam across the country. That was the day! He started off then for his most difficult portage.

Had you gone for a Sunday afternoon ride that day you might have seen him, close to naked, standing on the shoulders of Route 424, waiting for a chance to cross. You might have wondered if he was the victim of foul play, had his car broken down, or was he merely a fool. Standing barefoot in the deposits of the highway—beer cans, rags, and blowout patches—exposed to all kinds of ridicule, he seemed pitiful. He had known when he started that this was a part of his journey—it had been on his maps—but confronted with the lines of traffic, worming through the summery light, he found himself unprepared. He was laughed at, jeered at, a beer can was thrown at him, and he had no dignity or humor to bring to the situation. He could have gone back, back to the Westerhazys', where Lucinda would still be sitting in the sun. He had signed nothing, vowed nothing, pledged nothing, not even to himself. Why, believing as he did, that all human obduracy was susceptible to common sense, was he unable to turn back? Why was he determined to complete his journey even if it meant putting his life in danger? At what point had this prank, this joke, this piece of horseplay become serious? He could not go back, he could not even recall with any clearness the green water at the Westerhazys', the sense of inhaling the day's components, the friendly and relaxed voices saying that they had *drunk* too much. In the space of an hour, more or less, he had covered a distance that made his return impossible.

An old man, tooling down the highway at fifteen miles an hour, let him get to the middle of the road, where there was a grass divider. Here he was exposed to the ridicule of the northbound traffic, but after ten or fifteen minutes he was able to cross. From here he had only a short walk to the Recreation Center at the edge of the village of Lancaster, where there were some handball courts and a public pool.

The effect of the water on voices, the illusion of brilliance and suspense, was the same here as it had been at the Bunkers' but the sounds here were louder, harsher, and more shrill, and as soon as he entered the crowded enclosure he was confronted with regimentation. "ALL SWIMMERS MUST TAKE A SHOWER BEFORE USING THE POOL. ALL SWIMMERS MUST USE THE FOOTBATH. ALL SWIMMERS MUST WEAR THEIR IDENTIFICATION DISKS." He took a shower, washed his feet in a cloudy and bitter solution, and made his way to the edge of the water. It stank of chlorine and looked to him like a sink. A pair of lifeguards in a pair of towers blew police whistles at what seemed to be regular intervals and abused the swimmers through a public address system. Neddy remembered the sapphire water at the Bunkers' with longing and thought that he might contaminate himself—damage his own prosperousness and charm—by swimming in this murk, but he reminded himself that he was an explorer, a pilgrim, and that this was merely a stagnant bend in the Lucinda River. He dove, scowling with distaste, into the chlorine and had to swim with his head above water to avoid collisions, but even so he was bumped into, splashed, and jostled. When he got to the shallow end both lifeguards were shouting at him: "Hey, you, you without the identification disk, get outa the water." He did, but they had no way of pursuing him and he went through the reek of suntan oil and chlorine out

through the hurricane fence and passed the handball courts. By crossing the road he entered the wooded part of the Halloran estate. The woods were not cleared and the footing was treacherous and difficult until he reached the lawn and the clipped beech hedge that encircled their pool.

The Hallorans were friends, an elderly couple of enormous wealth who seemed to bask in the suspicion that they might be Communists. They were zealous reformers but they were not Communists, and yet when they were accused, as they sometimes were, of subversion, it seemed to gratify and excite them. Their beech hedge was yellow and he guessed this had been blighted like the Levys' maple. He called hullo, hullo, to warn the Hallorans of his approach, to palliate his invasion of their privacy. The Hallorans, for reasons that had never been explained to him, did not wear bathing suits. No explanations were in order, really. Their nakedness was a detail in their uncompromising zeal for reform and he stepped politely out of his trunks before he went through the opening in the hedge.

Mrs. Halloran, a stout woman with white hair and a serene face, was reading the *Times*. Mr. Halloran was taking beech leaves out of the water with a scoop. They seemed not surprised or displeased to see him. Their pool was perhaps the oldest in the country, a fieldstone rectangle, fed by a brook. It had no filter or pump and its waters were the opaque gold of the stream.

"I'm swimming across the county," Ned said.

"Why, I didn't know one could," exclaimed Mrs. Halloran.

"Well, I've made it from the Westerhazys'," Ned said. "That must be about four miles."

He left his trunks at the deep end, walked to the shallow end, and swam this stretch. As he was pulling himself out of the water he heard Mrs. Halloran say, "We've been *terribly* sorry to hear about all your misfortunes, Neddy."

"My misfortunes?" Ned asked. "I don't know what you mean."

"Why we heard that you'd sold the house and that your poor children. . . ."

"I don't recall having sold the house," Ned said, "and the girls are at home."

"Yes," Mrs. Halloran sighed. "Yes. . . ." Her voice filled the air with an unseasonable melancholy and Ned spoke briskly. "Thank you for the swim."

"Well, have a nice trip," said Mrs. Halloran.

Beyond the hedge he pulled on his trunks and fastened them. They were loose and he wondered if, during the space of an afternoon, he could have lost some weight. He was cold and he was tired and the naked Hallorans and their dark water had depressed him. The swim was too much for his strength but how could he have guessed this, sliding down the banister that morning and sitting in the Westerhazys' sun? His arms were lame. His legs felt rubbery and ached at the joints. The worst of it was the cold in his bones and the feeling that he might never be warm again. Leaves were falling down around him and he smelled wood smoke on the wind. Who would be burning wood at this time of the year?

He needed a drink. Whiskey would warm him, pick him up, carry him through the last of his journey, refresh his feeling that it was original and valorous to swim across the county. Channel swimmers took brandy. He needed a stimulant. He crossed the lawn in front of the Hallorans' house and went down a little path to where they had built a house for their only daughter, Helen, and her husband, Eric Sachs. The Sachses' pool was small and he found Helen and her husband there.

"Oh, *Neddy*," Helen said. "Did you lunch at Mother's?"

"Not *really*," Ned said. "I *did* stop to see your parents." This seemed to be explanation enough. "I'm terribly sorry to break in on you like this but I've taken a chill and I wonder if you'd give me a drink."

"Why, I'd *love* to," Helen said, "but there hasn't been anything in this house to drink since Eric's operation. That was three years ago."

Was he losing his memory, had his gift for concealing painful facts let him forget that he had sold his house, that his children were in trouble, and that his friend had been ill? His eyes slipped from Eric's face to his abdomen, where he saw three pale, sutured scars, two of them at least a foot long. Gone was his navel, and what, Neddy thought, would the roving hand, bed-checking one's gifts at 3 A.M., make of a belly with no navel, no link to birth, this breach in the succession?

"I'm sure you can get a drink at the Biswangers'," Helen said. "They're having an enormous do. You can hear it from here. Listen!"

She raised her head and from across the road, the lawns, the gardens, the woods, the fields, he heard again the brilliant noise of voices over water. "Well, I'll get wet," he said, still feeling that he had no freedom of choice about his means of travel. He dove into the Sachses' cold water, and gasping, close to drowning, made his way from one end of the pool to the other. "Lucinda and I want *terribly* to see you," he said over his shoulder, his face set toward the Biswangers'. "We're sorry it's been so long and we'll call you *very* soon."

He crossed some fields to the Biswangers' and the sounds of revelry there. They would be honored to give him a drink, they would be happy to give him a drink. The Biswangers invited him and Lucinda for dinner four times a year, six weeks in advance. They were always rebuffed and yet they continued to send out their invitations, unwilling to comprehend the rigid and undemocratic realities of their society. They were the sort of people who discussed the price of things at cocktails, exchanged market tips during dinner, and after dinner told dirty stories to mixed company. They did not belong to Neddy's set—they were not even on Lucinda's Christmas card list. He went toward their pool with feelings of indifference, charity, and some unease, since it seemed to be getting dark and these were the longest days of the year. The party when he joined it was noisy and large. Grace Biswanger was the kind of hostess who asked the optometrist, the veterinarian, the real-estate dealer, and the dentist. No one was swimming and the twilight, reflected on the water of the pool, had a wintry gleam. There was a bar and he started for this. When Grace Biswanger saw him she came toward him, not affectionately as he had every right to expect, but bellicosely.

"Why, this party has everything," she said loudly, "including a gate crasher."

She could not deal him a social blow—there was no question about this and he did not flinch. "As a gate crasher," he asked politely, "do I rate a drink?"

"Suit yourself," she said. "You don't seem to pay much attention to invitations."

She turned her back on him and joined some guests, and he went to the bar and ordered a whiskey. The bartender served him but he served him rudely. His was a world in which the caterer's men kept the social score, and to be rebuffed by a part-time barkeep meant that he had suffered some loss of social esteem. Or perhaps the man was new and uninformed. Then he heard Grace at his back say: "They went for broke overnight—nothing but income—and he showed up drunk one Sunday and asked us to loan him five thousand dollars. . . ." She

was always talking about money. It was worse than eating your peas off a knife. He dove into the pool, swam its length, and went away.

The next pool on his list, the last but two, belonged to his old mistress, Shirley Adams. If he had suffered any injuries at the Biswangers' they would be cured here. Love—sexual roughhouse in fact—was the supreme elixir, the pain killer, the brightly colored pill that would put the spring back into his step, the joy of life in his heart. They had had an affair last week, last month, last year. He couldn't remember. It was he who had broken it off, his was the upper hand, and he stepped through the gate of the wall that surrounded her pool with nothing so considered as self-confidence. It seemed in a way to be his pool, as the lover, particularly the illicit lover, enjoys the possessions of his mistress with an authority unknown to holy matrimony. She was there, her hair the color of brass, but her figure, at the edge of the lighted, cerulean water, excited in him no profound memories. It had been, he thought, a lighthearted affair, although she had wept when he broke it off. She seemed confused to see him and he wondered if she was still wounded. Would she, God forbid, weep again?

"What do you want?" she asked.

"I'm swimming across the county."

"Good Christ. Will you ever grow up?"

"What's the matter?"

"If you've come here for money," she said, "I won't give you another cent."

"You could give me a drink."

"I could but I won't. I'm not alone."

"Well, I'm on my way."

He dove in and swam the pool, but when he tried to haul himself up onto the curb he found that the strength in his arms and shoulders had gone, and he paddled to the ladder and climbed out. Looking over his shoulder he saw, in the lighted bathhouse, a young man. Going out onto the dark lawn he smelled chrysanthemums or marigolds—some stubborn autumnal fragrance—on the night air, strong as gas. Looking overhead he saw that the stars had come out, but why should he seem to see Andromeda, Cepheus, and Cassiopeia? What had become of the constellations of midsummer? He began to cry.

It was probably the first time in his adult life that he had ever cried, certainly the first time in his life that he had ever felt so miserable, cold, tired, and bewildered. He could not understand the rudeness of the caterer's barkeep or the rudeness of a mistress who had come to him on her knees and showered his trousers with tears. He had swum too long, he had been immersed too long, and his nose and his throat were sore from the water. What he needed then was a drink, some company, and some clean, dry clothes, and while he could have cut directly across the road to his home he went on to the Gilmartins' pool. Here, for the first time in his life, he did not dive but went down the steps into the icy water and swam a hobbled sidestroke that he might have learned as a youth. He staggered with fatigue on his way to the Clydes' and paddled the length of their pool, stopping again and again with his hand on the curb to rest. He climbed up the ladder and wondered if he had the strength to get home. He had done what he wanted, he had swum the county, but he was so stupefied with exhaustion that his triumph seemed vague. Stooped, holding on to the gateposts for support, he turned up the driveway of his own house.

The place was dark. Was it so late that they had all gone to bed? Had Lucinda stayed at the Westerhazys' for supper? Had the girls joined her there or gone someplace else? Hadn't they agreed, as they usually did on Sunday, to regret all their invitations and stay at home? He tried the garage doors to see what cars were in but the doors were locked and rust came off the handles onto his hands. Going toward the house, he saw the force of the thunderstorm had knocked one of the rain gutters loose. It hung down over the front door like an umbrella rib, but it could be fixed in the morning. The house was locked, and he thought that the stupid cook or the stupid maid must have locked the place up until he remembered that it had been some time since they had employed a maid or a cook. He shouted, pounded on the door, tried to force it with his shoulder, and then, looking in at the windows, saw that the place was empty.

[1964]

QUESTIONS

1. To what extent is Neddy Merrill's "journey" a heroic one, comparable to that of the protagonists in classical epics and sagas? What are the specific stages of his journey? What are the obstacles he must overcome?
2. What social commentary is implicit in "The Swimmer"?
3. Does the swimming metaphor in Cheever's story bear any similarity to the one in Graham Swift's "Learning to Swim"?

ANTON CHEKHOV
(1860–1904)
RUSSIA

Anton Chekhov's enduring contribution to literature is based on both a body of dramatic works that revolutionized modern drama and an equally distinctive body of short fiction. As the grandson of a serf who bought his own freedom, and the son of an impoverished grocer, Chekhov was raised in humble circumstances in Taganrog, Russia. He began to write short fiction and humorous sketches to support his family while studying medicine at the University of Moscow. Although he practiced medicine, he soon determined that his real love was literature. He wrote prolifically, publishing nearly 800 short stories as well as 18 plays, many of which are justifiably termed classics: *The Cherry Orchard, Three Sisters, Uncle Vanya*, and *The Seagull*. Shortly after Chekhov's plays were translated into English in the early twentieth century, it was not unusual for half a dozen of them to be staged simultaneously in London theatres.

Chekhov was a true innovator in both forms in which he wrote. Less concerned about "plot" in the traditional sense, he focused on the nuances of feeling and circumstance to explore a broad palette of human emotions from pathos and loss to humor and absurdity; because he saw life as fundamentally plotless he chose to mirror that plotlessness rather than to impose a false shape on the experiences he explored. His view of social injustice is set against an indifferent universe—a moral perspective that exposed his distance from, if not disillusionment concerning, religious certainties. His fiction and drama are sometimes said to be written in a minor key because they often conclude without traditional resolutions. This modern sensibility, with its implications for literary form and meaning, was deeply influential for twentieth century writers in both fiction and drama. As the modernist Virginia Woolf (whose own experiments in fiction owe a debt to Chekhov) wrote in her essay "The Russian Point of View," Chekhov's stories are

> inconclusive, we say, and proceed to frame a criticism based upon the assumption that stories ought to conclude in a way that we recognize. . . . [W]here the tune is unfamiliar and the end a note of interrogation or merely the information that they went on talking, . . . we need a very daring and alert sense of literature to make us hear the tune, and in particular those last notes which complete the harmony.

In Chekhov's view the function of literature was not to "solve problems" but to present those problems honestly to the reader. As he wrote to another writer, Alexander Tikhonov, "All I wanted was to say honestly to people: 'Have a look at yourselves and see how bad and dreary your lives are!' The important thing is that people should realize that, for when they do, they will most certainly create another and better life for themselves." In fact, Chekhov was a kind of doctor of spiritual ills; he diagnosed them, but he offered no cure.

Ironically, Chekhov contracted tuberculosis at the age of 29 and suffered poor health for much of his life. Although he was married to the Moscow Art Theatre's leading actress, Olga Knipper, the couple spent little time together because his poor health forced him to live in a warmer climate while she performed in Moscow. When he died at the age of 44, his body was transferred in a train car refrigerated for the shipment of oysters—an absurd circumstance that Chekhov might well have invented for one of his own stories.

The Kiss

At eight o'clock on the evening of the twentieth of May all the six batteries of the N—— Reserve Artillery Brigade halted for the night in the village of Mestechki on their way to camp. At the height of the general commotion, while some officers were busily occupied around the guns, and others, gathered together in the square near the church enclosure, were receiving the reports of the quartermasters, a man in civilian dress, riding a queer horse, came into sight round the church. The little dun-colored horse with a fine neck and a short tail came, moving not straight forward, but as it were sideways, with a sort of dance step, as though it were being lashed about the legs. When he reached the officers the man on the horse took off his hat and said:

"His Excellency Lieutenant-General von Rabbeck, a local landowner, invites the officers to have tea with him this minute. . . ."

The horse bowed, danced, and retired sideways; the rider raised his hat once more and in an instant disappeared with his strange horse behind the church.

"What the devil does it mean?" grumbled some of the officers, dispersing to their quarters. "One is sleepy, and here this von Rabbeck with his tea! We know what tea means."

The officers of all the six batteries remembered vividly an incident of the previous year, when during maneuvers they, together with the officers of a Cossack regiment, were in the same way invited to tea by a count who had an estate in the neighborhood and was a retired army officer; the hospitable and genial count made much of them, dined and wined them, refused to let them go to their quarters in the village, and made them stay the night. All that, of course, was very nice—nothing better could be desired, but the worst of it was, the old army officer was so carried away by the pleasure of the young men's company that till sunrise he was telling the officers ancedotes of his glorious past, taking them over the house, showing them expensive pictures, old engravings, rare guns, reading them autograph letters from great people, while the weary and exhausted officers looked and listened, longing for their beds and yawning in their sleeves; when at last their host let them go, it was too late for sleep.

Might not this von Rabbeck be just such another? Whether he were or not, there was no help for it. The officers changed their uniforms, brushed themselves, and went all together in search of the gentleman's house. In the square by the church they were told they could get to his Excellency's by the lower road—going down behind the church to the river, walking along the bank to the garden, and there the alleys would take them to the house; or by the upper way—straight from the church by the road which, half a mile from the village, led right up to his Excellency's barns. The officers decided to go by the upper road.

"Which von Rabbeck is it?" they wondered on the way. "Surely not the one who was in command of the N——— cavalry division at Plevna?"

"No, that was not von Rabbeck, but simply Rabbe and no 'von.'"

"What lovely weather!

At the first of the barns the road divided in two: one branch went straight on and vanished in the evening darkness, the other led to the owner's house on the right. The officers turned to the right and began to speak more softly. . . . On both sides of the road stretched stone barns with red roofs, heavy and sullen-looking, very much like barracks in a district town. Ahead of them gleamed the windows of the manor house.

"A good omen, gentlemen," said one of the officers. "Our setter leads the way; no doubt he scents game ahead of us! . . ."

Lieutenant Lobytko, who was walking in front, a tall and stalwart fellow, though entirely without mustache (he was over twenty-five, yet for some reason there was no sign of hair on his round, well-fed face), renowned in the brigade for his peculiar ability to divine the presence of women at a distance, turned round and said:

"Yes, there must be women here; I feel that by instinct."

On the threshold the officers were met by von Rabbeck himself, a comely looking man of sixty in civilian dress. Shaking hands with his guests, he said that he was very glad and happy to see them, but begged them earnestly for God's sake to excuse him for not asking them to stay the night; two sisters with their children, his brothers, and some neighbors, had come on a visit to him, so that he had not one spare room left.

The General shook hands with everyone, made his apologies, and smiled, but it was evident by his face that he was by no means so delighted as last year's count, and that he had invited the officers simply because, in his opinion, it was a social obligation. And the officers themselves, as they walked up the softly carpeted stairs, as they listened to him, felt that they had been invited to this house simply because it would have been awkward not to invite them; and at the sight of the footmen, who hastened to light the lamps at the entrance below and in the anteroom above, they began to feel as though they had brought uneasiness and discomfort into the house with them. In a house in which two sisters and their children, brothers, and neighbors were gathered together, probably on account of some family festivity or event, how could the presence of nineteen unknown officers possibly be welcome?

Upstairs at the entrance to the drawing room the officers were met by a tall, graceful old lady with black eyebrows and a long face, very much like the Empress Eugénie. Smiling graciously and majestically, she said she was glad and happy to see her guests, and apologized that her husband and she were on this occasion unable to invite *messieurs les officiers*[1] to stay the night. From her beautiful majestic smile, which instantly vanished from her face every time she turned away from her guests, it was evident that she had seen numbers of officers in her day, that she was in no humor for them now, and if she invited them to her house and apologized for not doing more, it was only because her breeding and position in society required it of her.

[1]*messieurs les officiers* French: the honorable officers

When the officers went into the big dining-room, there were about a dozen people, men and ladies, young and old, sitting at tea at the end of a long table. A group of men wrapped in a haze of cigar smoke was dimly visible behind their chairs; in the midst of them stood a lanky young man with red whiskers, talking loudly in English, with a burr. Through a door beyond the group could be seen a light room with pale blue furniture.

"Gentlemen, there are so many of you that it is impossible to introduce you all!" said the General in a loud voice, trying to sound very gay. "Make each other's acquaintance, gentlemen, without any ceremony!"

The officers—some with very serious and even stern faces, others with forced smiles, and all feeling extremely awkward—somehow made their bows and sat down to tea.

The most ill at ease of them all was Ryabovich—a short, somewhat stooped officer in spectacles, with whiskers like a lynx's. While some of his comrades assumed a serious expression, while others wore forced smiles, his face, his lynx-like whiskers, and spectacles seemed to say, "I am the shyest, most modest, and most undistinguished officer in the whole brigade!" At first, on going into the room and later, sitting down at table, he could not fix his attention on any one face or object. The faces, the dresses, the cut-glass decanters of brandy, the steam from the glasses, the molded cornices—all blended in one general impression that inspired in Ryabovich alarm and a desire to hide his head. Like a lecturer making his first appearance before the public, he saw everything that was before his eyes, but apparently only had a dim understanding of it (among physiologists this condition, when the subject sees but does not understand, is called "mental blindness"). After a little while, growing accustomed to his surroundings, Ryabovich regained his sight and began to observe. As a shy man, unused to society, what struck him first was that in which he had always been deficient—namely, the extraordinary boldness of his new acquaintances. Von Rabbeck, his wife, two elderly ladies, a young lady in a lilac dress, and the young man with the red whiskers, who was, it appeared, a younger son of von Rabbeck, very cleverly, as though they had rehearsed it beforehand, took seats among the officers, and at once got up a heated discussion in which the visitors could not help taking part. The lilac young lady hotly asserted that the artillery had a much better time than the cavalry and the infantry, while von Rabbeck and the elderly ladies maintained the opposite. A brisk interchange followed. Ryabovich looked at the lilac young lady who argued so hotly about what was unfamiliar and utterly uninteresting to her, and watched artificial smiles come and go on her face.

Von Rabbeck and his family skillfully drew the officers into the discussion, and meanwhile kept a sharp eye on their glasses and mouths, to see whether all of them were drinking, whether all had enough sugar, why someone was not eating cakes or not drinking brandy. And the longer Ryabovich watched and listened, the more he was attracted by this insincere but splendidly disciplined family.

After tea the officers went into the drawing-room. Lieutenant Lobytko's instinct had not deceived him. There were a great many girls and young married ladies. The "setter" lieutenant was soon standing by a very young blonde in a black dress, and, bending over her jauntily, as though leaning on an unseen sword, smiled and twitched his shoulders coquettishly. He probably talked very interesting nonsense, for the blonde looked at his well-fed face condescendingly and asked indifferently, "Really?" And from that indifferent "Really?" the "setter," had he been intelligent, might have concluded that she would never call him to heel.

The piano struck up; the melancholy strains of a waltz floated out of the wide open windows, and everyone, for some reason, remembered that it was spring, a May evening. Everyone was conscious of the fragrance of roses, of lilac, and of the young leaves of the poplar. Ryabovich, who felt the brandy he had drunk, under the influence of the music stole a glance towards the window, smiled, and began watching the movements of the women, and it seemed to him that the smell of roses, of poplars, and lilac came not from the garden, but from the ladies' faces and dresses.

Von Rabbeck's son invited a scraggy-looking young lady to dance and waltzed round the room twice with her. Lobytko, gliding over the parquet floor, flew up to the lilac young lady and whirled her away. Dancing began. . . . Ryabovich stood near the door among those who were not dancing and looked on. He had never once danced in his whole life, and he had never once in his life put his arm round the waist of a respectable woman. He was highly delighted that a man should in the sight of all take a girl he did not know round the waist and offer her his shoulder to put her hand on, but he could not imagine himself in the position of such a man. There were times when he envied the boldness and swagger of his companions and was inwardly wretched; the knowledge that he was timid, round-shouldered, and uninteresting, that he had a long waist and lynx-like whiskers deeply mortified him, but with years he had grown used to this feeling, and now, looking at his comrades dancing or loudly talking, he no longer envied them, but only felt touched and mournful.

When the quadrille began, young von Rabbeck came up to those who were not dancing and invited two officers to have a game at billiards. The officers accepted and went with him out of the drawing room. Ryabovich, having nothing to do and wishing to take at least some part in the general movement, slouched after them. From the big drawing room they went into the little drawing room, then into a narrow corridor with a glass roof, and thence into a room in which on their entrance three sleepy-looking footmen jumped up quickly from couches. At last, after passing through a long succession of rooms, young von Rabbeck and the officers came into a small room where there was a billiard table. They began to play.

Ryabovich, who had never played any game but cards, stood near the billiard table and looked indifferently at the players, while they in unbuttoned coats, with cues in their hands, stepped about, made puns, and kept shouting out unintelligible words.

The players took no notice of him, and only now and then one of them, shoving him with his elbow or accidentally touching him with his cue, would turn round and say "*Pardon!*" Before the first game was over he was weary of it, and began to feel that he was not wanted and in the way. . . . He felt disposed to return to the drawing-room and he went out.

On his way back he met with a little adventure. When he had gone half-way he noticed that he had taken a wrong turning. He distinctly remembered that he ought to meet three sleepy footmen on his way, but he had passed five or six rooms, and those sleepy figures seemed to have been swallowed up by the earth. Noticing his mistake, he walked back a little way and turned to the right; he found himself in a little room which was in semidarkness and which he had not seen on his way to the billiard room. After standing there a little while, he resolutely opened the first door that met his eyes and walked into an absolutely dark room. Straight ahead could be seen the crack in the doorway through which came a gleam of vivid light; from the other side of the door came the muffled sound of a melancholy mazurka. Here, too, as in the drawing-room, the windows were wide open and there was a smell of poplars, lilac, and roses. . . .

Ryabovich stood still in hesitation. . . . At that moment, to his surprise, he heard hurried footsteps and the rustling of a dress, a breathless feminine voice whispered "At last!" and two soft, fragrant, unmistakably feminine arms were clasped about his neck; a warm cheek was pressed against his, and simultaneously there was the sound of a kiss. But at once the bestower of the kiss uttered a faint shriek and sprang away from him, as it seemed to Ryabovich, with disgust. He, too, almost shrieked and rushed towards the gleam of light at the door. . . .

When he returned to the drawing-room his heart was palpitating and his hands were trembling so noticeably that he made haste to hide them behind his back. At first he was tormented by shame and dread that the whole drawing-room knew that he had just been kissed and embraced by a woman. He shrank into himself and looked uneasily about him, but as he became convinced that people were dancing and talking as calmly as ever, he gave himself up entirely to the new sensation which he had never experienced before in his life. Something strange was happening to him. . . . His neck, round which soft, fragrant arms had so lately been clasped, seemed to him to be anointed with oil; on his left cheek near his mustache where the unknown had kissed him there was a faint chilly tingling sensation as from peppermint drops, and the more he rubbed the place the more distinct was the chilly sensation; all of him, from head to foot, was full of a strange new feeling which grew stronger and stronger. . . . He wanted to dance, to talk, to run into the garden, to laugh aloud. . . . He quite forgot that he was round-shouldered and uninteresting, that he had lynx-like whiskers and an "undistinguished appearance" (that was how his appearance had been described by some ladies whose conversation he had accidentally overheard). When von Rabbeck's wife happened to pass by him, he gave her such a broad and friendly smile that she stood still and looked at him inquiringly.

"I like your house immensely!" he said, setting his spectacles straight.

The General's wife smiled and said that the house had belonged to her father; then she asked whether his parents were living, whether he had long been in the army, why he was so thin, and so on. . . . After receiving answers to her questions, she went on, and after his conversation with her his smiles were more friendly than ever, and he thought he was surrounded by splendid people. . . .

At supper Ryabovich ate mechanically everything offered him, drank, and without listening to anything, tried to understand what had just happened to him. . . . The adventure was of a mysterious and romantic character, but it was not difficult to explain it. No doubt some girl or young married lady had arranged a tryst with some man in the dark room; had waited a long time, and being nervous and excited had taken Ryabovich for her hero; this was the more probable as Ryabovich had stood still hesitating in the dark room, so that he, too, had looked like a person waiting for something. . . . This was how Ryabovich explained to himself the kiss he had received.

"And who is she?" he wondered, looking round at the women's faces. "She must be young, for elderly ladies don't arrange rendezvous. That she was a lady, one could tell by the rustle of her dress, her perfume, her voice. . . ."

His eyes rested on the lilac young lady, and he thought her very attractive; she had beautiful shoulders and arms, a clever face, and a delightful voice. Ryabovich, looking at her, hoped that she and no one else was his unknown. . . . But she laughed somehow artificially and wrinkled up her long nose, which seemed to him to make her look old. Then he turned his eyes upon the blonde in a black dress. She was younger, simpler, and more genuine, had a charming brow, and drank very daintily out of her wineglass. Ryabovich now hoped that it was she. But soon he began to think her face flat, and fixed his eyes upon the one next her.

"It's difficult to guess," he thought, musing. "If one were to take only the shoulders and arms of the lilac girl, add the brow of the blonde and the eyes of the one on the left of Lobytko, then . . ."

He made a combination of these things in his mind and so formed the image of the girl who had kissed him, the image that he desired but could not find at the table. . . .

After supper, replete and exhilarated, the officers began to take leave and say thank you. Von Rabbeck and his wife began again apologizing that they could not ask them to stay the night.

"Very, very glad to have met you, gentlemen," said von Rabbeck, and this time sincerely (probably because people are far more sincere and good-humored at speeding their parting guests than on meeting them). "Delighted. Come again on your way back! Don't stand on ceremony! Where are you going? Do you want to go by the upper way? No, go across the garden; it's nearer by the lower road."

The officers went out into the garden. After the bright light and the noise the garden seemed very dark and quiet. They walked in silence all the way to the gate. They were a little drunk, in good spirits, and contented, but the darkness and silence made them thoughtful for a minute. Probably the same idea occurred to each one of them as to Ryabovich: would there ever come a time for them when, like von Rabbeck, they would have a large house, a family, a garden—when they, too, would be able to welcome people, even though insincerely, feed them, make them drunk and contented?

Going out of the garden gate, they all began talking at once and laughing loudly about nothing. They were walking now along the little path that led down to the river and then ran along the water's edge, winding round the bushes on the bank, the gulleys, and the willows that overhung the water. The bank and the path were scarcely visible, and the other bank was entirely plunged in darkness. Stars were reflected here and there in the dark water; they quivered and were broken up—and from that alone it could be seen that the river was flowing rapidly. It was still. Drowsy sandpipers cried plaintively on the farther bank, and in one of the bushes on the hither side a nightingale was trilling loudly, taking no notice of the crowd of officers. The officers stood round the bush, touched it, but the nightingale went on singing.

"What a fellow!" they exclaimed approvingly. "We stand beside him and he takes not a bit of notice! What a rascal!"

At the end of the way the path went uphill, and, skirting the church enclosure, led into the road. Here the officers, tired with walking uphill, sat down and lighted their cigarettes. On the farther bank of the river a murky red fire came into sight, and having nothing better to do, they spent a long time in discussing whether it was a camp fire or a light in a window, or something else. . . . Ryabovich, too, looked at the light, and he fancied that the light looked and winked at him, as though it knew about the kiss.

On reaching his quarters, Ryabovich undressed as quickly as possible and got into bed. Lobytko and Lieutenant Merzlyakov — a peaceable, silent fellow, who was considered in his own circle a highly educated officer, and was always, whenever it was possible, reading *The Messenger of Europe*, which he carried about with him everywhere — were quartered in the same cottage with Ryabovich. Lobytko undressed, walked up and down the room for a long while with the air of a man who has not been satisfied, and sent his orderly for beer. Merzlyakov got into bed, put a candle by his pillow and plunged into *The Messenger of Europe*.

"Who was she?" Ryabovich wondered, looking at the sooty ceiling.

His neck still felt as though he had been anointed with oil, and there was still the chilly sensation near his mouth as though from peppermint drops. The shoulders and arms of the young lady in lilac, the brow and the candid eyes of the blonde in black, waists, dresses, and brooches, floated through his imagination. He tried to fix his attention on these images, but they danced about, broke up and flickered. When these images vanished altogether from the broad dark background which everyone sees when he closes his eyes, he began to hear hurried footsteps, the rustle of skirts, the sound of a kiss — and an intense baseless joy took possession of him. . . . Abandoning himself to this joy, he heard the orderly return and announce that there was no beer. Lobytko was terribly indignant, and began pacing up and down the room again.

"Well, isn't he an idiot?" he kept saying, stopping first before Ryabovich and then before Merzlyakov. "What a fool and a blockhead a man must be not to get hold of any beer! Eh? Isn't he a blackguard?"

"Of course you can't get beer here," said Merzlyakov, not removing his eyes from *The Messenger of Europe*.

"Oh! Is that your opinion?" Lobytko persisted. "Lord have mercy upon us, if you dropped me on the moon I'd find you beer and women directly! I'll go and find some at once. . . . You may call me a rascal if I don't!"

He spent a long time in dressing and pulling on his high boots, then finished smoking his cigarette in silence and went out.

"Rabbeck, Grabbeck, Labbeck," he muttered, stopping in the outer room. "I don't care to go alone, damn it all! Ryabovich, wouldn't you like to go for a walk? Eh?"

Receiving no answer, he returned, slowly undressed, and got into bed. Merzlyakov sighed, put *The Messenger of Europe* away, and extinguished the light.

"H'm! . . ." muttered Lobytko, lighting a cigarette in the dark.

Ryabovich pulled the bedclothes over his head, curled himself up in bed, and tried to gather together the flashing images in his mind and to combine them into a whole. But nothing came of it. He soon fell asleep, and his last thought was that someone had caressed him and made him happy — that something extraordinary, foolish, but joyful and delightful, had come into his life. The thought did not leave him even in his sleep.

When he woke up the sensations of oil on his neck and the chill of peppermint about his lips had gone, but joy flooded his heart just as the day before. He looked enthusiastically at the window-frames, gilded by the light of the rising sun, and listened to the movement of the passers-by in the street.

People were talking loudly close to the window. Lebedetzky, the commander of Ryabovich's battery, who had only just overtaken the brigade, was talking to his sergeant at the top of his voice, having lost the habit of speaking in ordinary tones.

"What else?" shouted the commander.

"When they were shoeing the horses yesterday, your Honor, they injured Pigeon's hoof with a nail. The vet put on clay and vinegar; they are leading him apart now. Also, your Honor, Artemyev got drunk yesterday, and the lieutenant ordered him to be put in the limber of a spare gun-carriage."

The sergeant reported that Karpov had forgotten the new cords for the trumpets and the pegs for the tents, and that their Honors the officers had spent the previous evening visiting General von Rabbeck. In the middle of this conversation the red-bearded face of Lebedetzky appeared in the window. He screwed up his short-sighted eyes, looking at the sleepy faces of the officers, and greeted them.

"Is everything all right?" he asked.

"One of the horses has a sore neck from the new collar," answered Lobytko yawning.

The commander sighed, thought a moment, and said in a loud voice:

"I am thinking of going to see Alexandra Yevgrafovna. I must call on her. Well, good-by. I shall catch up with you in the evening."

A quarter of an hour later the brigade set off on its way. When it was moving along the road past the barns, Ryabovich looked at the house on the right. The blinds were down in all the windows. Evidently the household was still asleep. The one who had kissed Ryabovich the day before was asleep too. He tried to imagine her asleep. The wide-open window of the bedroom, the green branches peeping in, the morning freshness, the scent of the poplars, lilac, and roses, the bed, a chair, and on it the skirts that had rustled the day before, the little slippers, the little watch on the table—all this he pictured to himself clearly and distinctly, but the features of the face, the sweet sleepy smile, just what was characteristic and important, slipped through his imagination like quicksilver through the fingers. When he had ridden a third of a mile, he looked back: the yellow church, the house, and the river, were all bathed in light; the river with its bright green banks, with the blue sky reflected in it and glints of silver in the sunshine here and there, was very beautiful. Ryabovich gazed for the last time at Mestechki, and he felt as sad as though he were parting with something very near and dear to him.

And before him on the road were none but long familiar, uninteresting scenes. . . . To right and to left, fields of young rye and buckwheat with rooks hopping about in them; if one looked ahead, one saw dust and the backs of men's heads; if one looked back, one saw the same dust and faces. . . . Foremost of all marched four men with sabers—this was the vanguard. Next came the singers, and behind them the trumpeters on horseback. The vanguard and the singers, like torch-bearers in a funeral procession, often forgot to keep the regulation distance and pushed a long way ahead. . . . Ryabovich was with the first cannon of the fifth battery. He could see all the four batteries moving in front of him. To a civilian the long tedious procession which is a brigade on the move seems an intricate and unintelligible muddle; one cannot understand why there are so many people round one cannon, and why it is drawn by so many horses in such a strange network of harness, as though it really were so terrible and heavy. To Ryabovich it was all perfectly comprehensible and therefore uninteresting. He had known for ever so long why at the head of each battery beside the officer there rode a stalwart noncom, called bombardier; immediately behind him could be seen the horsemen of the first and then of the middle units. Ryabovich knew that of the horses on which they rode, those on the left were called one name, while those on the right were called another—it was all extremely uninteresting. Behind the horsemen came two shaft-horses. On one of them sat a rider still covered with the dust of yesterday and with a clumsy and funny-looking wooden guard on his right leg. Ryabovich knew the object of this guard, and did not think it funny. All the riders waved their whips mechanically and shouted from time to time. The cannon itself was not presentable. On the limber lay sacks of oats covered with a tarpaulin, and the cannon itself was hung all over with kettles, soldiers' knapsacks, bags, and looked like some small harmless animal surrounded for some unknown reason by men and horses. To the leeward of it marched six men, the gunners, swinging their arms. After the cannon there came again more bombardiers, riders, shaft-horses, and behind them another cannon, as unpresentable and unimpressive as the first. After the second came a third, a fourth; near the fourth there was an officer, and so on. There were six batteries in all in the brigade, and four cannon in each battery. The procession covered a third of a mile; it ended in a string of wagons near which an extremely appealing creature—the ass, Magar, brought by a battery commander from Turkey—paced pensively, his long-eared head drooping.

Ryabovich looked indifferently ahead and behind him, at the backs of heads and at faces; at any other time he would have been half asleep, but now he was entirely absorbed in his new agreeable thoughts. At first when the brigade was setting off on the march he tried to persuade himself that the incident of the kiss could only be interesting as a mysterious little adventure, that it was in reality trivial, and to think of it seriously, to say the least, was stupid; but now he bade farewell to logic and gave himself up to dreams. . . . At one moment he imagined himself in von Rabbeck's drawing-room beside a girl who was like the young lady in lilac and the blonde in black; then he would close his eyes and see himself with another, entirely unknown girl, whose features were very vague. In his imagination he talked, caressed her, leaned over her shoulder, pictured war, separation, then meeting again, supper with his wife, children. . . .

"Brakes on!" The word of command rang out every time they went downhill.

He, too, shouted "Brakes on!" and was afraid this shout would disturb his reverie and bring him back to reality. . . .

As they passed by some landowner's estate Ryabovich looked over the fence into the garden. A long avenue, straight as a ruler, strewn with yellow sand and bordered with young birch-trees, met his eyes. . . . With the eagerness of a man who indulges in daydreaming, he pictured to himself little feminine feet tripping along yellow sand, and quite unexpectedly had a clear vision in his imagination of her who had kissed him and whom he had succeeded in picturing to himself the evening before at supper. This image remained in his brain and did not desert him again.

At midday there was a shout in the rear near the string of wagons:

"Attention! Eyes to the left! Officers!"

The general of the brigade drove by in a carriage drawn by a pair of white horses. He stopped near the second battery, and shouted something which no one understood. Several officers, among them Ryabovich, galloped up to him.

"Well? How goes it?" asked the general, blinking his red eyes. "Are there any sick?"

Receiving an answer, the general, a little skinny man, chewed, thought for a moment and said, addressing one of the officers:

"One of your drivers of the third cannon has taken off his leg-guard and hung it on the fore part of the cannon, the rascal. Reprimand him."

He raised his eyes to Ryabovich and went on:

"It seems to me your breeching is too long."

Making a few other tedious remarks, the general looked at Lobytko and grinned.

"You look very melancholy today, Lieutenant Lobytko," he said. "Are you pining for Madame Lopuhova? Eh? Gentlemen, he is pining for Madame Lopuhova."

Madame Lopuhova was a very stout and very tall lady long past forty. The general, who had a predilection for large women, whatever their ages, suspected a similar taste in his officers. The officers smiled respectfully. The general, delighted at having said something very amusing and biting, laughed loudly, touched his coachman's back, and saluted. The carriage rolled on. . . .

"All I am dreaming about now which seems to me so impossible and unearthly is really quite an ordinary thing," thought Ryabovich, looking at the clouds of dust racing after the general's carriage. "It's all very ordinary, and everyone goes through it. . . . That general, for instance, was in love at one time; now he is married and has children. Captain Wachter, too, is married and loved, though the nape of his neck is very red and ugly and he has no waist. . . . Salmanov is coarse and too much of a Tartar, but he had a love affair that has ended in marriage. . . . I am the same as everyone else, and I, too, shall have the same experience as everyone else, sooner or later. . . ."

And the thought that he was an ordinary person and that his life was ordinary delighted him and gave him courage. He pictured *her* and his happiness boldly, just as he liked. . . .

When the brigade reached their halting-place in the evening, and the officers were resting in their tents, Ryabovich, Merzlyakov, and Lobytko were sitting round a chest having supper. Merzlyakov ate without haste and, as he munched deliberately, read *The Messenger of Europe*, which he held on his knees. Lobytko talked incessantly and kept filling up his glass with beer, and Ryabovich, whose head was confused from dreaming all day long drank and said nothing. After three glasses he got a little drunk, felt weak, and had an irresistible desire to relate his new sensations to his comrades.

"A strange thing happened to me at those von Rabbecks'," he began, trying to impart an indifferent and ironical tone to his voice. "You know I went into the billiard-room. . . ."

He began describing very minutely the incident of the kiss, and a moment later relapsed into silence. . . . In the course of that moment he had told everything, and it surprised him dreadfully to find how short a time it took him to tell it. He had imagined that he could have been telling the story of the kiss till next morning. Listening to him, Lobytko, who was a great liar and consequently believed no one, looked at him skeptically and laughed. Merzlyakov twitched his eyebrows and, without removing his eyes from *The Messenger of Europe*, said:

"That's an odd thing! How strange! . . . throws herself on a man's neck, without addressing him by name. . . . She must have been some sort of lunatic."

"Yes, she must," Ryabovich agreed.

"A similar thing once happened to me," said Lobytko, assuming a scared expression. "I was going last year to Kovno. . . . I took a second-class ticket. The train was crammed, and it was impossible to sleep. I gave the guard half a ruble; he took my luggage and led me to another compartment. . . . I lay down and covered myself with a blanket. . . . It was dark, you understand. Suddenly I felt someone touch me on the shoulder and breathe in my face. I made a movement with my hand and felt somebody's elbow. . . . I opened my eyes and only imagine—a woman. Black eyes, lips red as a prime salmon, nostrils breathing passionately—a bosom like a buffer. . . ."

"Excuse me," Merzlyakov interrupted calmly, "I understand about the bosom, but how could you see the lips if it was dark?"

Lobytko began trying to put himself right and laughing at Merzlyakov's being so dull-witted. It made Ryabovich wince. He walked away from the chest, got into bed, and vowed never to confide again.

Camp life began. . . . The days flowed by, one very much like another. All those days Ryabovich felt, thought, and behaved as though he were in love. Every morning when his orderly handed him what he needed for washing, and he sluiced his head with cold water, he recalled that there was something warm and delightful in his life.

In the evenings when his comrades began talking of love and women, he would listen, and draw up closer; and he wore the expression of a soldier listening to the description of a battle in which he has taken part. And on the evenings when the officers, out on a spree with the setter Lobytko at their head, made Don-Juanesque raids on the neighboring "suburb," and Ryabovich took part in such excursions, he always was sad, felt profoundly guilty, and inwardly begged *her* forgiveness. . . . In hours of leisure or on sleepless nights when he felt moved to recall his childhood, his father and mother—everything near and dear, in fact, he invariably thought of Mestechki, the queer horse, von Rabbeck, his wife who resembled Empress Eugénie, the dark room, the light in the crack of the door. . . .

On the thirty-first of August he was returning from the camp, not with the whole brigade, but with only two batteries. He was dreamy and excited all the way, as though he were going home. He had an intense longing to see again the queer horse, the church, the insincere family of the von Rabbecks, the dark room. The "inner voice," which so often deceives lovers, whispered to him for some reason that he would surely see her. . . . And he was tortured by the questions: How would he meet her? What would he talk to her about? Had she forgotten the kiss? If the worst came to the worst, he thought, even if he did not meet her, it would be a pleasure to him merely to go through the dark room and recall the past. . . .

Towards evening there appeared on the horizon the familiar church and white barns. Ryabovich's heart raced. . . . He did not hear the officer who was riding beside him and saying something to him, he forgot everything, and looked eagerly at the river shining in the distance, at the roof of the house, at the dovecote round which the pigeons were circling in the light of the setting sun.

When they reached the church and were listening to the quartermaster, he expected every second that a man on horseback would come round the church enclosure and invite the officers to tea, but . . . the quartermaster ended his report, the officers dismounted and strolled off to the village, and the man on horseback did not appear.

"Von Rabbeck will hear at once from the peasants that we have come and will send for us," thought Ryabovich, as he went into the peasant cottage, unable to understand why a comrade was lighting a candle and why the orderlies were hastening to get the samovars going.

A crushing uneasiness took possession of him. He lay down, then got up and looked out of the window to see whether the messenger were coming. But there was no sign of him.

He lay down again, but half an hour later he got up and, unable to restrain his uneasiness, went into the street and strode towards the church. It was dark and deserted in the square near the church enclosure. Three soldiers were standing silent in a row where the road began to go down-hill. Seeing Ryabovich, they roused themselves and saluted. He returned the salute and began to go down the familiar path.

On the farther bank of the river the whole sky was flooded with crimson: the moon was rising; two peasant women, talking loudly, were pulling cabbage leaves in the kitchen garden; beyond the kitchen garden there were some cottages that formed a dark mass. . . . Everything on the near side of the river was just as it had been in May: the path, the bushes, the willows overhanging the water . . . but there was no sound of the brave nightingale and no scent of poplar and young grass.

Reaching the garden, Ryabovich looked in at the gate. The garden was dark and still. . . . He could see nothing but the white stems of the nearest birch-trees and a little bit of the avenue; all the rest melted together into a dark mass. Ryabovich looked and listened eagerly, but after waiting for a quarter of an hour without hearing a sound or catching a glimpse of a light, he trudged back. . . .

He went down to the river. The General's bathing cabin and the bath-sheets on the rail of the little bridge showed white before him. . . . He walked up on the bridge, stood a little, and quite unnecessarily touched a sheet. It felt rough and cold. He looked down at the water. . . . The river ran rapidly and with a faintly audible gurgle round the piles of the bathing cabin. The red moon was reflected near the left bank; little ripples ran over the reflection, stretching it out, breaking it into bits, and seemed trying to carry it away. . . .

"How stupid, how stupid!" thought Ryabovich, looking at the running water. "How unintelligent it all is!"

Now that he expected nothing, the incident of the kiss, his impatience, his vague hopes and disappointment, presented themselves to him in a clear light. It no longer seemed to him strange that the General's messenger never came and that he would never see the girl who had accidentally kissed him instead of someone else; on the contrary, it would have been strange if he had seen her. . . .

The water was running, he knew not where or why, just as it did in May. At that time it had flowed into a great river, from the great river into the sea; then it had risen in vapor, turned into rain, and perhaps the very same water was running now before Ryabovich's eyes again. . . . What for? Why?

And the whole world, the whole of life, seemed to Ryabovich an unintelligible, aimless jest. . . . And turning his eyes from the water and looking at the sky, he remembered again how Fate in the person of an unknown woman had by chance caressed him, he recalled his summer dreams and fancies, and his life struck him as extraordinarily meager, poverty-stricken, and drab. . . .

When he had returned to the cottage he did not find a single comrade. The orderly informed him that they had all gone to "General Fontryabkin, who had sent a messenger on horseback to invite them. . . ."

For an instant there was a flash of joy in Ryabovich's heart, but he quenched it at once, got into bed, and in his wrath with his fate, as though to spite it, did not go to the General's.

[1887]

Translated by
CONSTANCE GARNETT

QUESTIONS

1. How does the kiss transform Ryabovich?
2. Why do the other officers respond the way they do to Ryabovich's story?
3. How would you describe the tone of the story? Is Chekhov's presentation of Ryabovich sympathetic or mocking?
4. How does the ending contribute to your understanding of Ryabovich and to the story's theme?
5. What does the story suggest about romance? about self-deception?

GABRIELLE-SIDONIE COLETTE
(1873–1954)
FRANCE

Gabrielle-Sidonie Colette lived a colorful and occasionally (for her time) even scandalous life that also inspired and fed her fiction. Born and raised in the Burgundy countryside, she experienced a happy childhood, which became the subject and setting for the reminiscences of childhood captured in her early "Claudine" novels. She married young, in a match arranged by her parents as a result of their failing financial solvency. Henry Gauthier-Villars, a music critic and journalist who was significantly older than Colette and rarely faithful to her, prompted her to write about her childhood and not to be shy of adding "spicy details." Her first novel, *Claudine at School*, was published in 1900 under Gauthier-Villars's pen name, "Willy." Willy then virtually compelled Colette to write three more "Claudine" novels, all somewhat titillating and all published under his pen name. Gauthier-Villars's philandering ultimately led the unhappy Colette to leave the marriage, after which she supported herself as a dancer and mime on the music hall stage.

Besides being married three times, Colette also had several lesbian relationships as well as a brief liaison with the son of her second husband. Many of her stories and novels frankly explore through the themes of love and sexuality the experiences she discovered through her own bisexuality. Drawing on what she called "mental androgyny," she expressed the tension between the masculine and feminine qualities that she felt were present in all human beings.

Colette's early fiction, particularly the "Claudine" novels, brought to life delicate renderings of nature and an unerring evocation of childhood. She is also justly admired for her exceptional psychological insight into female experience and relationships, including the conflict for a woman between self-discovery and career (*The Vagabond*, 1911), as well as the spectrum of emotional possibilities encompassed in the idea of love (*Mitsou, ou Comment l'esprit vient aux filles*, translated as *Mitsou, or How Girls Grow Wise*, 1919; *Cheri*, 1920; and *Gigi*, 1944; among others). Also among her fictional subjects are her adored and idealized mother, "the most important person in all my life," whom she fictionalized as "Sido," and her daughter, born when Colette was 40 and fictionalized as "Bel-Gazou." Her characters Mitsou (a music hall artist), Claudine, Cheri, and Gigi are among Colette's other enduring creations, many of whom are drawn directly from the author's own unconventional life. As Elaine Marks phrases it, Colette was her own "greatest fictional character."

The author of more than 50 books, including novels and collections of stories, Colette was much loved and honored by her country. At her death, she was the first French woman writer ever to be honored by a state funeral.

The Seamstress

"Do you mean to say your daughter is *nine years old*," said a friend, "and she doesn't know how to sew? She really must learn to sew. In bad weather sewing is a better occupation for a child of that age than reading storybooks."

"Nine years old? And she can't sew?" said another friend. "When she was eight, my daughter embroidered this tray cloth for me, look at it. . . . Oh, I don't say it's fine needlework, but it's nicely done all the same. Nowadays my daughter cuts out her own underclothes. I can't bear anyone in my house to mend holes with pins!"

I meekly poured all this domestic wisdom over Bel-Gazou.

"You're nine years old and you don't know how to sew? You really must learn to sew. . . ."

Flouting truth, I even added: "When I was eight years old, I remember I embroidered a tray cloth . . . Oh, it wasn't fine needlework, I dare say. . . . And then, in bad weather . . ."

She has therefore learned to sew. And although—with one bare sunburned leg tucked beneath her, and her body at ease in its bathing suit—she looks more like a fisherboy mending a net than an industrious little girl, she seems to experience no boyish repugnance. Her hands, stained the color of tobacco juice by sun and sea, hem in a way that seems against nature; their version of the simple running stitch resembles the zigzag dotted lines of a road map, but she buttonholes and scallops with elegance and is severely critical of the embroidery of others.

She sews and kindly keeps me company if rain blurs the horizon of the sea. She also sews during the torrid hour when the spindle bushes gather their circles of shadow directly under them. Moreover, it sometimes happens that a quarter of an hour before dinner, black in her white dress—"Bel-Gazou! your hands and frock are clean, and don't forget it!"—she sits solemnly down with a square of material between her fingers. Then my friends applaud: "Just look at her! Isn't she good? That's right! Your mother must be pleased!"

Her mother says nothing—great joys must be controlled. But ought one to feign them? I shall speak the truth: I don't much like my daughter sewing.

When she reads, she returns all bewildered and with flaming cheeks, from the island where the chest full of precious stones is hidden, from the dismal castle where a fair-haired orphan child is persecuted. She is soaking up a tested and time-honored poison, whose effects have long been familiar. If she draws, or colors pictures, a semiarticulate song issues from her, unceasing as the hum of bees around the privet. It is the same as the buzzing of flies as they work, the slow waltz of the house painter, the refrain of the spinner at her wheel. But Bel-Gazou is silent when she sews, silent for hours on end, with her mouth firmly closed, concealing her large, new-cut incisors that bite into the moist heart of a fruit like little saw-edged blades. She is silent, and she—why not write down the word that frightens me—she is thinking.

A new evil? A torment that I had not foreseen? Sitting in a grassy dell, or half buried in hot sand and gazing out to sea, she is thinking, as well I know. She thinks rapidly when she is listening, with a well-bred pretense of discretion, to remarks imprudently exchanged above her head. But it would seem that with this needleplay she has discovered the perfect means of adventuring, stitch by stitch, point by point, along a road of risks and temptations. Silence . . . the hand armed with the steel dart moves back and forth. Nothing will stop the unchecked little explorer. At what moment must I utter the "Halt!" that will brutally arrest her in full flight? Oh, for those young embroiderers of bygone days, sitting on a hard little stool in the shelter of their mother's ample skirts! Maternal authority kept them there for years and years, never rising except to change the skein of silk, or to elope with a stranger. Think of Philomène de Watteville and her canvas, on which she embroidered the loss and the despair of Albert Savarus. . . .[1]

"What are you thinking about, Bel-Gazou?"

"Nothing, Mother. I'm counting my stitches."

Silence. The needle pierces the material. A coarse trail of chain stitch follows very unevenly in its wake. Silence . . .

"Mother?"

"Darling?"

"Is it only when people are married that a man can put his arm around a lady's waist?"

"Yes . . . No . . . It depends. If they are very good friends and have known each other a long time, you understand. . . . As I said before: it depends. Why do you want to know?"

"For no particular reason, Mother."

Two stitches, ten misshapen chain stitches.

"Mother? Is Madame X married?"

"She has been. She is divorced."

"I see. And Monsieur F., is he married?"

"Why, of course he is; you know that."

"Oh! Yes . . . Then it's all right if one of the two is married?"

"What is all right?"

"To depend."

"One doesn't say: 'to depend.'"

"But you said just now that it depended."

"But what has it got to do with you? Is it any concern of yours?"

"No, Mother."

I let it drop. I feel inadequate, self-conscious, displeased with myself. I should have answered differently and I could not think what to say.

Bel-Gazou also drops the subject; she sews. But she pays little attention to her sewing, overlaying it with pictures, associations of names and people, all the results of patient observation. A little later will come other curiosities, other questions, and especially other silences. Would to God that Bel-Gazou were the bewildered and simple child who questions crudely, open-eyed! But she is too near the truth, and too natural not to know, as a birthright, that all nature hesitates before that most majestic and most disturbing of instincts, and that it is wise to tremble, to be silent, and to lie when one draws near to it.

Translated by
UNA VICENZO TROUBRIDGE
AND ENID MCLEOD

[1] *Albert Savarus* The central character of a novel of that name by Honoré de Balzac (1799–1850); *Philomène de Watteville* is a female character in the novel.

QUESTIONS

1. Why does the mother encourage her daughter to learn to sew when she does not really like the idea?
2. How is Bel-Gazou initially described? How does she change? Why does the mother believe that these changes are related to her daughter's learning to sew?
3. The mother and daughter are revealed both through the mother's perspective and through a dialogue between them. How do these perspectives complement each other and convey different kinds of information about the two characters?

Joseph Conrad

(1857–1924)

Poland/England

It is an irony that Conrad would have enjoyed: that a writer who did not even learn English until he was 21 would become one of its literary masters, a giant of twentieth-century literature and one of its first modern writers. Born Josef Teodor Konrad Nalecz Korzeniowski, Conrad was the only child of a Polish-Ukrainian farmer who left his wife and small son to join a radical political party in Warsaw. Eventually both parents were arrested for political treason and sent into exile in Siberia when Conrad was five years old. From the effects of cold and deprivation, Conrad's mother died when he was seven; in 1867 the Russian government commuted his father's exile, and father and son returned to Poland, where Conrad's father died when Conrad was 12.

Having learned about adventure less from his family's painful exile than through his avid reading as a youth, Conrad ran away from his uncle/guardian when he was 16, joining a ship in Marseilles. For eight years he lived a sailor's life, moving through the ranks to become captain of a ship. In 1878 he joined an English ship, although the only English he knew he had learned at sea; later he refined his knowledge of the language through reading Shakespeare, the Bible, and the London newspaper. His adopted language eventually became the only one in which he felt he could express himself as a writer; as he observed in a letter to a friend in 1918, "I began to think in English long before I mastered, I won't say the style (I haven't done that yet), but the mere uttered speech. . . . If I had not known English I wouldn't have written a line for print, in my life."

Although Conrad resigned from his captaincy and apparently gave up life on the seas in 1895, he returned to it several more times, including one journey to the Congo that became the source for his classic novella of corrupted colonialism, *Heart of Darkness* (1902). In many of his more than 20 novels and numerous short stories, Conrad incorporated his vision of the sea as a mysterious element—a psychological as well as physical landscape in which an individual's assumptions, values, and deepest soul were ultimately tested. A moralist during an uncertain time (the turn of the century), Conrad placed his characters in circumstances of isolation and loneliness in which they were challenged to act decisively and in which those actions revealed their true moral compass as well as the moral ambiguity of human truth.

Exploring those themes in such novels as *Lord Jim* (1900), *Heart of Darkness* (1902), "The Secret Sharer" (1912), *Chance* (1914), *Victory* (1915), and other novels and stories, Conrad probed with unexcelled psychological accuracy that unconscious dimension of the self that exists beneath the social arrangements that frame most human actions. As critic David Daiches has observed, Conrad's greatest novels "are all concerned, directly or obliquely, with situations to which public codes—any public codes—are inapplicable, situations which yield a dark and disturbing insight which cannot be related to any of the beliefs which make human societies possible."

Rarely anthologized, the story "Amy Foster" (1903) is especially interesting because it not only embodies a number of Conrad's preoccupations but also draws on his personal experience as an exile from another country and language: his profound awareness of the chasms in communication that expose the irreducible loneliness at the heart of the human condition. In *An Outcast of the Islands* (1896), Conrad described "the tremendous fact of our isolation, of the loneliness impenetrable and transparent, elusive and everlasting; of the indestructible loneliness that surrounds, envelops, clothes every human soul from the cradle to the grave, and, perhaps, beyond."

• Amy Foster •

Kennedy is a country doctor, and lives in Colebrook, on the shores of Eastbay. The high ground rising abruptly behind the red roofs of the little town crowds the quaint High Street against the wall which defends it from the sea. Beyond the sea-wall there curves for miles in a vast and regular sweep the barren beach of shingle, with the village of Brenzett standing out darkly across the water, a spire in a clump of trees; and still further out the perpendicular column of a lighthouse, looking in the distance no bigger than a lead pencil, marks the vanishing-point of the land. The country at the back of Brenzett is low and flat, but the bay is fairly well sheltered from the seas, and occasionally a big ship, windbound or through stress of weather, makes use of the anchoring ground a mile and a half due north from you as you stand at the back door of the "Ship Inn" in Brenzett. A dilapidated windmill near by lifting its shattered arms from a mound no loftier than a rubbish heap, and a Martello tower squatting at the water's edge half a mile to the south of the Coastguard cottages, are familiar to the skippers of small craft. These are the official seamarks for the patch of trustworthy bottom represented on the Admiralty charts by an irregular oval of dots enclosing several figures six, with a tiny anchor engraved among them, and the legend "mud and shells" over all.

The brow of the upland overtops the square tower of the Colebrook Church. The slope is green and looped by a white road. Ascending along this road, you open a valley broad and shallow, a wide green trough of pastures and hedges merging inland into a vista of purple tints and flowing lines closing the view.

In this valley down to Brenzett and Colebrook and up to Darnford, the market town fourteen miles away, lies the practice of my friend Kennedy. He had begun life as surgeon in the Navy, and afterwards had been the companion of a famous traveller, in the days when there were continents with unexplored interiors. His papers on the fauna and flora made him known to scientific societies. And now he had come to a country practice—from choice. The penetrating power of his mind, acting like a corrosive fluid, had destroyed his ambition, I fancy. His intelligence is of a scientific order, of an investigating habit, and of that unappeasable curiosity which believes that there is a particle of a general truth in every mystery.

A good many years ago now, on my return from abroad, he invited me to stay with him. I came readily enough, and as he could not neglect his patients to keep me company, he took me on his rounds — thirty miles or so of an afternoon, sometimes. I waited for him on the roads; the horse reached after the leafy twigs, and, sitting high in the dogcart, I could hear Kennedy's laugh through the half-open door left open of some cottage. He had a big, hearty laugh that would have fitted a man twice his size, a brisk manner, a bronzed face, and a pair of grey, profoundly attentive eyes. He had the talent of making people talk to him freely, and an inexhaustible patience in listening to their tales.

One day, as we trotted out of a large village into a shady bit of road, I saw on our left hand a low, black cottage, with diamond panes in the windows, a creeper on the end wall, a roof of shingle, and some roses climbing on the rickety trellis-work of the tiny porch. Kennedy pulled up to a walk. A woman, in full sunlight, was throwing a dripping blanket over a line stretched between two old apple-trees. And as the bobtailed, long-necked chestnut, trying to get his head, jerked the left hand, covered by a thick dogskin glove, the doctor raised his voice over the hedge: "How's your child, Amy?"

I had the time to see her dull face, red, not with a mantling blush, but as if her flat cheeks had been vigorously slapped, and to take in the squat figure, the scanty, dusty brown hair drawn into a tight knot at the back of the head. She looked quite young. With a distinct catch in her breath, her voice sounded low and timid.

"He's well, thank you."

We trotted again. "A young patient of yours," I said; and the doctor, flicking the chestnut absently, muttered, " Her husband used to be."

"She seems a dull creature," I remarked listlessly.

"Precisely," said Kennedy. "She is very passive. It's enough to look at the red hands hanging at the end of those short arms, at those slow, prominent brown eyes, to know the inertness of her mind — an inertness that one would think made it everlastingly safe from all the surprises of imagination. And yet which of us is safe? At any rate, such as you see her, she had enough imagination to fall in love. She's the daughter of one Isaac Foster, who from a small farmer has sunk into a shepherd; the beginning of his misfortunes dating from his runaway marriage with the cook of his widowed father — a well-to-do, apoplectic grazier, who passionately struck his name off his will, and had been heard to utter threats against his life. But this old affair, scandalous enough to serve as a motive for a Greek tragedy, arose from the similarity of their characters. There are other tragedies, less scandalous and of a subtler poignancy, arising from irreconcilable differences and from that fear of the Incomprehensible that hangs over all our heads — over all our heads. . . ."

The tired chestnut dropped into a walk; and the rim of the sun, all red in a speckless sky, touched familiarly the smooth top of a ploughed rise near the road as I had seen it times innumerable touch the distant horizon of the sea. The uniform brownness of the harrowed field glowed with a rosy tinge, as though the powdered clods had sweated out in minute pearls of blood the toil of uncounted ploughmen. From the edge of a copse a waggon with two horses was rolling gently along the ridge. Raised above our heads upon the sky-line, it loomed up against the red sun, triumphantly big, enormous, like a chariot of giants drawn by two slow-stepping steeds of legendary proportions. And the clumsy figure of the man plodding at the head of the leading horse projected itself on the background of the Infinite with a heroic uncouthness. The end of his carter's whip quivered high up in the blue. Kennedy discoursed.

"She's the eldest of a large family. At the age of fifteen they put her out to service at the New Barns Farm. I attended Mrs. Smith, the tenant's wife, and saw that girl there for the first time. Mrs. Smith, a genteel person with a sharp nose, made her put on a black dress every afternoon. I don't know what induced me to notice her at all. There are faces that call your attention by a curious want of definiteness in their whole aspect, as, walking in a mist, you peer attentively at a vague shape which, after all, may be nothing more curious or strange than a signpost. The only peculiarity I perceived in her was a slight hesitation in her utterance, a sort of preliminary stammer which passes away with the first word. When sharply spoken to, she was apt to lose her head at once; but her heart was of the kindest. She had never been heard to express a dislike for a single human being, and she was tender to every living creature. She was devoted to Mrs. Smith, to Mr. Smith, to their dogs, cats, canaries; and as to Mrs. Smith's grey parrot, its peculiarities exercised upon her a positive fascination. Nevertheless, when that outlandish bird, attacked by the cat, shrieked for help in human accents, she ran out into the yard stopping her ears, and did not prevent the crime. For Mrs. Smith this was another evidence of her stupidity; on the other hand, her want of charm, in view of Smith's well-known frivolousness, was a great recommendation. Her short-sighted eyes would swim with pity for a poor mouse in a trap, and she had been seen once by some boys on her knees in the wet grass helping a toad in difficulties. If it's true, as some German fellow has said, that without phosphorus there is no thought, it is still more true that there is no kindness of heart without a certain amount of imagination. She had some. She had even more than is necessary to understand suffering and to be moved by pity. She fell in love under circumstances that leave no room for doubt in the matter; for you need imagination to form a notion of beauty at all, and still more to discover your ideal in an unfamiliar shape.

"How this aptitude came to her, what it did feed upon, is an inscrutable mystery. She was born in the village, and had never been further away from it than Colebrook or perhaps Darnford. She lived for four years with the Smiths. New Barns is an isolated farmhouse a mile away from the road, and she was content to look day after day at the same fields, hollows, rises; at the trees and the hedgerows; at the faces of the four men about the farm, always the same—day after day, month after month, year after year. She never showed a desire for conversation, and, as it seemed to me, she did not know how to smile. Sometimes of a fine Sunday afternoon she would put on her best dress, a pair of stout boots, a large grey hat trimmed with a black feather (I've seen her in that finery), seize an absurdly slender parasol, climb over two stiles, tramp over three fields and along two hundred yards of road—never further. There stood Foster's cottage. She would help her mother to give their tea to the younger children, wash up the crockery, kiss the little ones, and go back to the farm. That was all. All the rest, all the change, all the relaxation. She never seemed to wish for anything more. And then she fell in love. She fell in love silently, obstinately—perhaps helplessly. It came slowly, but when it came it worked like a powerful spell; it was love as the Ancients understood it: an irresistible and fateful impulse—a possession! Yes, it was in her to become haunted and possessed by a face, by a presence, fatally, as though she had been a pagan worshipper of form under a joyous sky—and to be awakened at last from that mysterious forgetfulness of self, from that enchantment, from that transport, by a fear resembling the unaccountable terror of a brute. . . ."

With the sun hanging low on its western limit, the expanse of the grass-lands framed in the counter-scraps of the rising ground took on a gorgeous and sombre aspect. A sense of penetrating sadness, like that inspired by a grave strain of music, disengaged itself from the silence of the fields. The men we met walked past slow, unsmiling, with downcast eyes, as if the melancholy of an over-burdened earth had weighted their feet, bowed their shoulders, borne down their glances.

"Yes," said the doctor to my remark, "one would think the earth is under a curse, since of all her children these that cling to her the closest are uncouth in body and as leaden of gait as if their very hearts were loaded with chains. But here on this same road you might have seen amongst these heavy men a being lithe, supple, and long-limbed, straight like a pine with something striving upwards in his appearance as though the heart within him had been buoyant. Perhaps it was only the force of the contrast, but when he was passing one of these villagers here, the soles of his feet did not seem to me to touch the dust of the road. He vaulted over the stiles, paced these slopes with a long elastic stride that made him noticeable at a great distance, and had lustrous black eyes. He was so different from the mankind around that, with his freedom of movement, his soft—a little startled, glance, his olive complexion and graceful bearing, his humanity suggested to me the nature of a woodland creature. He came from there."

The doctor pointed with his whip, and from the summit of the descent seen over the rolling tops of the trees in a park by the side of the road, appeared the level sea far below us, like the floor of an immense edifice inlaid with bands of dark ripple, with still trails of glitter, ending in a belt of glassy water at the foot of the sky. The light blur of smoke, from an invisible steamer, faded on the great clearness of the horizon like the mist of a breath on a mirror; and, inshore, the white sails of a coaster, with the appearance of disentangling themselves slowly from under the branches, floated clear of the foliage of the trees.

"Shipwrecked in the bay?" I said.

"Yes; he was a castaway. A poor emigrant from Central Europe bound to America and washed ashore here in a storm. And for him, who knew nothing of the earth, England was an undiscovered country. It was some time before he learned its name; and for all I know he might have expected to find wild beasts or wild men here, when, crawling in the dark over the sea-wall, he rolled down the other side into a dyke, where it was another miracle he didn't get drowned. But he struggled instinctively like an animal under a net, and this blind struggle threw him out into a field. He must have been, indeed, of a tougher fibre than he looked to withstand without expiring such buffetings, the violence of his exertions, and so much fear. Later on, in his broken English that resembled curiously the speech of a young child, he told me himself that he put his trust in God, believing he was no longer in this world. And truly—he would add—how was he to know? He fought his way against the rain and the gale on all fours, and crawled at last among some sheep huddled close under the lee of a hedge. They ran off in all directions, bleating in the darkness, and he welcomed the first familiar sound he heard on these shores. It must have been two in the morning then. And this is all we know of the manner of his landing, though he did not arrive unattended by any means. Only his grisly company did not begin to come ashore till much later in the day. . . ."

The doctor gathered the reins, clicked his tongue; we trotted down the hill. Then turning, almost directly, a sharp corner into the High Street, we rattled over the stones and were home.

Late in the evening Kennedy, breaking a spell of moodiness that had come over him, returned to the story. Smoking his pipe, he paced the long room from end to end. A reading-lamp concentrated all its light upon the papers on his desk; and, sitting by the open window, I saw, after the windless, scorching day, the frigid splendour of a hazy sea lying motionless under the moon. Not a whisper, not a splash, not a stir of the shingle, not a footstep, not a sigh came up from the earth below—never a sign of life but the scent of climbing jasmine; and Kennedy's voice, speaking behind me, passed through the wide casement, to vanish outside in a chill and sumptuous stillness.

". . . The relations of shipwrecks in the olden time tell us of much suffering. Often the castaways were only saved from drowning to die miserably from starvation on a barren coast; others suffered violent death or else slavery, passing through years of precarious existence with people to whom their strangeness was an object of suspicion, dislike or fear. We read about these things, and they are very pitiful. It is indeed hard upon a man to find himself a lost stranger, helpless, incomprehensible, and of a mysterious origin, in some obscure corner of the earth. Yet amongst all the adventurers shipwrecked in all the wild parts of the world there is not one, it seems to me, that ever had to suffer a fate so simply tragic as the man I am speaking of, the most innocent of adventurers cast out by the sea in the bight of this bay, almost within sight from this very window.

"He did not know the name of his ship. Indeed, in the course of time we discovered he did not even know that ships had names—'like Christian people'; and when, one day, from the top of the Talfourd Hill, he beheld the sea lying open to his view, his eyes roamed afar, lost in an air of wild surprise, as though he had never seen such a sight before. And probably he had not. As far as I could make out, he had been hustled together with many others on board an emigrant-ship lying at the mouth of the Elbe, too bewildered to take note of his surroundings, too weary to see anything, too anxious to care. They were driven below into the 'tweendeck and battened down from the very start. It was a low timber dwelling—he would say—with wooden beams overhead, like the houses in his country, but you went into it down a ladder. It was very large, very cold, damp and sombre, with places in the manner of wooden boxes where people had to sleep, one above another, and it kept on rocking all ways at once all the time. He crept into one of these boxes and laid down there in the clothes in which he had left his home many days before, keeping his bundle and his stick by his side. People groaned, children cried, water dripped, the lights went out, the walls of the place creaked, and everything was being shaken so that in one's little box one dared not lift one's head. He had lost touch with his only companion (a young man from the same valley, he said), and all the time a great noise of wind went on outside and heavy blows fell—boom! boom! An awful sickness overcame him, even to the point of making him neglect his prayers. Besides, one could not tell whether it was morning or evening. It seemed always to be night in that place.

"Before that he had been travelling a long, long time on the iron track. He looked out of the window, which had a wonderfully clear glass in it, and the trees, the houses, the fields, and the long roads seemed to fly round and round about him till his head swam. He gave me to understand that he had on his passage beheld uncounted multitudes of people — whole nations — all dressed in such clothes as the rich wear. Once he was made to get out of the carriage, and slept through a night on a bench in a house of bricks with his bundle under his head; and once for many hours he had to sit on a floor of flat stones dozing, with his knees up and with his bundle between his feet. There was a roof over him, which seemed made of glass, and was so high that the tallest mountain-pine he had ever seen would have had room to grow under it. Steam-machines rolled in at one end and out at the other. People swarmed more than you can see on a feast-day round the miraculous Holy Image in the yard of the Carmelite Convent down in the plains where, before he left his home, he drove his mother in a wooden cart — a pious old woman who wanted to offer prayers and make a vow for his safety. He could not give me an idea of how large and lofty and full of noise and smoke and gloom, and clang of iron, the place was, but some one had told him it was called Berlin. Then they rang a bell, and another steam-machine came in, and again he was taken on and on through a land that wearied his eyes by its flatness without a single bit of a hill to be seen anywhere. One more night he spent shut up in a building like a good stable with a litter of straw on the floor, guarding his bundle amongst a lot of men, of whom not one could understand a single word he said. In the morning they were all led down to the stony shores of an extremely broad muddy river, flowing not between hills but between houses that seemed immense. There was a steam-machine that went on the water, and they all stood upon it packed tight, only now there were with them many women and children who made much noise. A cold rain fell, the wind blew in his face; he was wet through, and his teeth chattered. He and the young man from the same valley took each other by the hand.

"They thought they were being taken to America straight away, but suddenly the steam-machine bumped against the side of a thing like a house on the water. The walls were smooth and black, and there uprose, growing from the roof as it were, bare trees in the shape of crosses, extremely high. That's how it appeared to him then, for he had never seen a ship before. This was the ship that was going to swim all the way to America. Voices shouted, everything swayed; there was a ladder dipping up and down. He went up on his hands and knees in mortal fear of falling into the water below, which made a great splashing. He got separated from his companion, and when he descended into the bottom of that ship his heart seemed to melt suddenly within him.

"It was then also, as he told me, that he lost contact for good and all with one of those three men who the summer before had been going about through all the little towns in the foothills of his country. They would arrive on market days driving in a peasant's cart, and would set up an office in an inn or some other Jew's house. There were three of them, of whom one with a long beard looked venerable; and they had red cloth collars round their necks and gold lace on their sleeves like Government officials. They sat proudly behind a long table; and in the next room, so that the common people shouldn't hear, they kept a cunning telegraph machine, through which they could talk to the Emperor of America. The fathers hung about the door, but the young men of the mountains would crowd up to the table asking many questions, for there was work to be got all the year round at three dollars a day in America, and no military service to do.

"But the American Kaiser would not take everybody. Oh, no! He himself had a great difficulty in getting accepted, and the venerable man in uniform had to go out of the room several times to work the telegraph on his behalf. The American Kaiser engaged him at last at three dollars, he being young and strong. However, many able young men backed out, afraid of the great distance; besides, those only who had some money could be taken. There were some who sold their huts and their land because it cost a lot of money to get to America; but then, once there, you had three dollars a day, and if you were clever you could find places where true gold could be picked up on the ground. His father's house was getting over full. Two of his brothers were married and had children. He promised to send money home from America by post twice a year. His father sold an old cow, a pair of piebald mountain ponies of his own raising, and a cleared plot of fair pasture land on the sunny slope of a pine-clad pass to a Jew inn-keeper in order to pay the people of the ship that took men to America to get rich in a short time.

"He must have been a real adventurer at heart, for how many of the greatest enterprises in the conquest of the earth had for their beginning just such a bargaining away of the paternal cow for the mirage or true gold far away! I have been telling you more or less in my own words what I learned fragmentarily in the course of two or three years, during which I seldom missed an opportunity of a friendly chat with him. He told me this story of his adventure with many flashes of white teeth and lively glances of black eyes, at first in a sort of anxious baby-talk, then, as he acquired the language, with great fluency, but always with that singing, soft, and at the same time vibrating intonation that instilled a strangely penetrating power into the sound of the most familiar English words, as if they had been the words of an unearthly language. And he always would come to an end, with many emphatic shakes of his head, upon that awful sensation of his heart melting within him directly he set foot on board that ship. Afterwards there seemed to come for him a period of blank ignorance, at any rate as to facts. No doubt he must have been abominably sea-sick and abominably unhappy—this soft and passionate adventurer, taken thus out of his knowledge, and feeling bitterly as he lay in his emigrant bunk his utter loneliness; for his was a highly sensitive nature. The next thing we know of him for certain is that he had been hiding in Hammond's pig-pound by the side of the road to Norton six miles, as the crow flies, from the sea. Of these experiences he was unwilling to speak: they seemed to have seared into his soul a sombre sort of wonder and indignation. Through the rumours of the country-side, which lasted for a good many days after his arrival, we know that the fishermen of West Colebrook had been disturbed and startled by heavy knocks against the walls of weatherboard cottages, and by a voice crying piercingly strange words in the night. Several of them turned out even, but, no doubt, he had fled in sudden alarm at their rough angry tones hailing each other in the darkness. A sort of frenzy must have helped him up the steep Norton hill. It was he, no doubt, who early the following morning had been seen lying (in a swoon, I should say) on the roadside grass by the Brenzett carrier, who actually got down to have a nearer look, but drew back, intimidated by the perfect immobility, and by something queer in the aspect of that tramp, sleeping so still under the showers. As the day advanced, some children came dashing into school at Norton in such a fright that the schoolmistress went out and spoke indignantly to a 'horrid-looking man' on the road. He edged away, hanging his head, for a few steps, and then suddenly ran off with extraordinary fleetness. The driver of Mr. Bradley's milk-cart made no secret of it that he had lashed with his whip at a hairy sort of gipsy fellow who, jumping up at a turn of the road by the Vents, made a snatch at the pony's bridle. And he caught him a good one too, right over the face, he said, that made him drop down in the mud a jolly sight quicker than he had jumped up; but it was a good half-a-mile before he could stop the pony. Maybe that in his desperate endeavours to get help, and in his need to get in touch with some one, the poor devil had tried to stop the cart. Also three boys confessed afterwards to throwing stones at a funny tramp, knocking about all wet and muddy, and, it seemed, very drunk, in the narrow deep lane by the limekilns. All this was the talk of three villages for days; but we have Mrs. Finn's (the wife of Smith's waggoner) unimpeachable testimony that she saw him get over the low wall of Hammond's pig-pound and lurch straight at her, babbling aloud in a voice that was enough to make one die of fright. Having the baby with her in a perambulator, Mrs. Finn called out to him to go away, and as he persisted in coming nearer, she hit him courageously with her umbrella over the head and, without once looking back, ran like the wind with the perambulator as far as the first house in the village. She stopped then, out of breath, and spoke to old Lewis, hammering there at a heap of stones; and the old chap, taking off his immense black wire goggles, got up on his shaky legs to look where she pointed. Together they followed with their eyes the figure of the man running over a field; they saw him fall down, pick himself up, and run on again, staggering and waving his long arms above his head, in the direction of the New Barns Farm. From that moment he is plainly in the toils of his obscure and touching destiny. There is no doubt after this of what happened to him. All is certain now: Mrs. Smith's intense terror; Amy Foster's stolid conviction held against the other's nervous attack, that the man 'meant no harm'; Smith's exasperation (on his return from Darnford Market) at finding the dog barking himself into a fit, the back-door locked, his wife in hysterics; and all for an unfortunate dirty tramp, supposed to be even then lurking in his stack-yard. Was he? He would teach him to frighten women.

"Smith is notoriously hot-tempered, but the sight of some nondescript and miry creature sitting crosslegged amongst a lot of loose straw, and swinging itself to and fro like a bear in a cage, made him pause. Then this tramp stood up silently before him, one mass of mud and filth from head to foot. Smith, alone amongst his stacks with this apparition, in the stormy twilight ringing with the infuriated barking of the dog, felt the dread of an inexplicable strangeness. But when that being, parting with his black hands the long matted locks that hung before his face, as you part the two halves of a curtain, looked out at him with glistening, wild, black-and-white eyes, the weirdness of this silent encounter fairly staggered him. He had admitted since (for the story has been a legitimate subject of conversation about here for years) that he made more than one step backwards. Then a sudden burst of rapid, senseless speech persuaded him at once that he had to do with an escaped lunatic. In fact, that impression never wore off completely. Smith has not in his heart given up his secret conviction of the man's essential insanity to this very day.

"As the creature approached him, jabbering in a most discomposing manner, Smith (unaware that he was being addressed as 'gracious lord,' and adjured in God's name to afford food and shelter) kept on speaking firmly but gently to it, and retreating all the time into the other yard. At last, watching his chance, by a sudden charge he bundled him headlong into the wood-lodge, and instantly shot the bolt.[1] Thereupon he wiped his brow, though the day was cold. He had done his duty to the community by shutting up a wandering and probably dangerous maniac. Smith isn't a hard man at all, but he had room in his brain only for that one idea of lunacy. He was not imaginative enough to ask himself whether the man might not be perishing with cold and hunger. Meantime, at first, the maniac made a great deal of noise in the lodge. Mrs. Smith was screaming upstairs, where she had locked herself in her bedroom; but Amy Foster sobbed piteously at the kitchen door, wringing her hands and muttering, 'Don't! don't!" I daresay Smith had a rough time of it that evening with one noise and another, and this insane, disturbing voice crying obstinately through the door only added to his irritation. He couldn't possibly have connected this troublesome lunatic with the sinking of a ship in Eastbay, of which there had been a rumour in the Darnford marketplace. And I daresay the man inside had been very near to insanity on that night. Before his excitement collapsed and he became unconscious he was throwing himself violently about in the dark, rolling on some dirty sacks, and biting his fists with rage, cold, hunger, amazement, and despair.

"He was a mountaineer of the eastern range of the Carpathians, and the vessel sunk the night before in Eastbay was the Hamburg emigrant-ship *Herzogin Sophia-Dorothea*, of appalling memory.

"A few months later we could read in the papers the accounts of the bogus 'Emigration Agencies' among the Sclavonian peasantry in the more remote provinces of Austria. The object of these scoundrels was to get hold of the poor ignorant people's homesteads, and they were in league with the local usurers. They exported their victims through Hamburg mostly. As to the ship, I had watched her out of this very window, reaching close-hauled under short canvas into the bay on a dark, threatening afternoon. She came to an anchor, correctly by the chart, off the Brenzett Coastguard station. I remember before the night fell looking out again at the outlines of her spars and rigging that stood out dark and pointed on a background of ragged, slaty clouds like another and a slighter spire to the left of the Brenzett church-tower. In the evening the wind rose. At midnight I could hear in my bed the terrific gusts and the sounds of a driving deluge.

"About that time the Coastguardmen thought they saw the lights of a steamer over the anchoring-ground. In a moment they vanished; but it is clear that another vessel of some sort had tried for shelter in the bay on that awful, blind night, had rammed the German ship amidships (a breach—as one of the divers told me afterwards—'that you could sail a Thames barge through'), and then had gone out either scathless or damaged, who shall say; but had gone out, unknown, unseen, and fatal, to perish mysteriously at sea. Of her nothing ever came to light, and yet the hue and cry that was raised all over the world would have found her out if she had been in existence anywhere on the face of the waters.

"A completeness without a clue, and a stealthy silence as of a neatly executed crime, characterise this murderous disaster, which, as you may remember, had its gruesome celebrity. The wind would have prevented the loudest outcries from reaching the shore; there had been evidently no time for signals of distress. It was

[1]*shot the bolt* locked the door

death without any sort of fuss. The Hamburg ship, filling all at once, capsized as she sank, and at daylight there was not even the end of a spar to be seen above water. She was missed, of course, and at first the Coastguardmen surmised that she had either dragged her anchor or parted her cable some time during the night, and had been blown out to sea. Then, after the tide turned, the wreck must have shifted a little and released some of the bodies, because a child—a little fair-haired child in a red frock—came ashore abreast of the Martello tower. By the afternoon you could see along three miles of beach dark figures with bare legs dashing in and out of the tumbling foam, and rough-looking men, women with hard faces, children, mostly fair-haired, were being carried, stiff and dripping, on stretchers, on wattles, on ladders, in a long procession past the door of the 'Ship Inn,' to be laid out in a row under the north wall of the Brenzett Church.

"Officially, the body of the little girl in the red frock is the first thing that came ashore from that ship. But I have patients amongst the seafaring population of West Colebrook, and, unofficially, I am informed that very early that morning two brothers, who went down to look after their cobble hauled up on the beach, found, a good way from Brenzett, an ordinary ship's hencoop lying high and dry on the shore, with eleven drowned ducks inside. Their families ate the birds, and the hencoop was split into firewood with a hatchet. It is possible that a man (supposing he happened to be on deck at the time of the accident) might have floated ashore on that hencoop. He might. I admit it is improbable, but there was the man—and for days, nay, for weeks—it didn't enter our heads that we had amongst us the only living soul that had escaped from that disaster. The man himself, even when he learned to speak intelligibly, could tell us very little. He remembered he had felt better (after the ship had anchored, I suppose), and that the darkness, the wind, and the rain took his breath away. This looks as if he had been on deck some time during that night. But we mustn't forget he had been taken out of his knowledge, that he had been sea-sick and battened down below for four days, that he had no general notion of a ship or of the sea, and therefore could have no definite idea of what was happening to him. The rain, the wind, the darkness he knew; he understood the bleating of the sheep, and he remembered the pain of his wretchedness and misery, his heartbroken astonishment that it was neither seen nor understood, his dismay at finding all the men angry and all the women fierce. He had approached them as a beggar, it is true, he said; but in his country, even if they gave nothing, they spoke gently to beggars. The children in his country were not taught to throw stones at those who asked for compassion. Smith's strategy overcame him completely. The wood-lodge presented the horrible aspect of a dungeon. What would be done to him next? . . . No wonder that Amy Foster appeared to his eyes with the aureole of an angel of light. The girl had not been able to sleep for thinking of the poor man, and in the morning, before the Smiths were up, she slipped out across the back yard. Holding the door of the wood-lodge ajar, she looked in and extended to him half a loaf of white bread—'such bread as the rich eat in my country,' he used to say.

"At this he got up slowly from amongst all sorts of rubbish, stiff, hungry, trembling, miserable, and doubtful. 'Can you eat this?' she asked in her soft and timid voice. He must have taken her for a 'gracious lady.' He devoured ferociously, and tears were falling on the crust. Suddenly he dropped the bread, seized her wrist, and imprinted a kiss on her hand. She was not frightened. Through his forlorn condition she had observed that he was good-looking. She shut the door and walked back slowly to the kitchen. Much later on, she told Mrs. Smith, who shuddered at the bare idea of being touched by that creature.

"Through this act of impulsive pity he was brought back again within the pale of human relations with his new surroundings. He never forgot it—never.

"That very same morning old Mr. Swaffer (Smith's nearest neighbour) came over to give his advice, and ended by carrying him off. He stood, unsteady on his legs, meek, and caked over in half-dried mud, while the two men talked around him in an incomprehensible tongue. Mrs. Smith had refused to come downstairs till the madman was off the premises; Amy Foster, far from within the dark kitchen, watched through the open back door; and he obeyed the signs that were made to him to the best of his ability. But Smith was full of mistrust. 'Mind, sir! It may be all his cunning,' he cried repeatedly in a tone of warning. When Mr. Swaffer started the mare, the deplorable being sitting humbly by his side, through weakness, nearly fell out over the back of the high two-wheeled cart. Swaffer took him straight home. And it is then that I come upon the scene.

"I was called in by the simple process of the old man beckoning to me with his forefinger over the gate of his house as I happened to be driving past. I got down, of course.

"'I've got something here,' he mumbled, leading the way to an outhouse at a little distance from his other farm-buildings.

"It was there that I saw him first, in a long low room taken upon the space of that sort of coachhouse. It was bare and whitewashed, with a small square aperture glazed with one cracked, dusty pane at its further end. He was lying on his back upon a straw pallet; they had given him a couple of horse-blankets, and he seemed to have spent the remainder of his strength in the exertion of cleaning himself. He was almost speechless; his quick breathing under the blankets pulled up to his chin, his glittering, restless black eyes reminded me of a wild bird caught in a snare. While I was examining him, old Swaffer stood silently by the door, passing the tips of his fingers along his shaven upper lip. I gave some directions, promised to send a bottle of medicine, and naturally made some inquiries.

"'Smith caught him in the stackyard at New Barns,' said the old chap in his deliberate, unmoved manner, and as if the other had been indeed a sort of wild animal. 'That's how I came by him. Quite a curiosity, isn't he? Now tell me, doctor—you've been all over the world—don't you think that's a bit of a Hindoo[2] we've got hold of here.'

"I was greatly surprised. His long black hair scattered over the straw bolster contrasted with the olive pallor of his face. It occurred to me he might be a Basque. It didn't necessarily follow that he should understand Spanish; but I tried him with the few words I know, and also with some French. The whispered sounds I caught by bending my ear to his lips puzzled me utterly. That afternoon the young ladies from the Rectory (one of them read Goethe with a dictionary, and the other had struggled with Dante for years), coming to see Miss Swaffer, tried their German and Italian on him from the doorway. They retreated, just the least bit scared by the flood of passionate speech which, turning on his pallet, he let out at them. They admitted that the sound was pleasant, soft, musical—but, in conjunction with his looks perhaps, it was startling—so excitable, so

[2]*Hindoo* Hindu (Indian)

utterly unlike anything one had ever heard. The village boys climbed up the bank to have a peep through the little square aperture. Everybody was wondering what Mr. Swaffer would do with him.

"He simply kept him.

"Swaffer would be called eccentric were he not so much respected. They will tell you that Mr. Swaffer sits up as late as ten o'clock at night to read books, and they will tell you also that he can write a cheque for two hundred pounds without thinking twice about it. He himself would tell you that the Swaffers had owned land between this and Darnford for these three hundred years. He must be eighty-five to-day, but he does not look a bit older than when I first came here. He is a great breeder of sheep, and deals extensively in cattle. He attends market days for miles around in every sort of weather, and drives sitting bowed low over the reins, his lank grey hair curling over the collar of his warm coat, and with a green plaid rug round his legs. The calmness of advanced age gives a solemnity to his manner. He is clean-shaved; his lips are thin and sensitive; something rigid and monachal in the set of his features lends a certain elevation to the character of his face. He has been known to drive miles in the rain to see a new kind of rose in somebody's garden, or a monstrous cabbage grown by a cottager. He loves to hear tell of or to be shown something that he calls 'outlandish.' Perhaps it was just that outlandishness of the man which influenced old Swaffer. Perhaps it was only an inexplicable caprice. All I know is that at the end of three weeks I caught sight of Smith's lunatic digging in Swaffer's kitchen garden. They had found out he could use a spade. He dug barefooted.

"His black hair flowed over his shoulders. I suppose it was Swaffer who had given him the striped old cotton shirt; but he wore still the national brown cloth trousers (in which he had been washed ashore) fitting to the leg almost like tights; was belted with a broad leathern belt studded with little brass discs; and had never yet ventured into the village. The land he looked upon seemed to him kept neatly, like the grounds round a landowner's house; the size of the cart-horses struck him with astonishment; the roads resembled garden walks, and the aspect of the people, especially on Sundays, spoke of opulence. He wondered what made them so hardhearted and their children so bold. He got his food at the back door, carried it in both hands carefully to his outhouse, and, sitting alone on his pallet, would make the sign of the cross before he began. Beside the same pallet, kneeling in the early darkness of the short days, he recited aloud the Lord's Prayer before he slept. Whenever he saw old Swaffer he would bow with veneration from the waist, and stand erect while the old man, with his fingers over his upper lip, surveyed him silently. He bowed also to Miss Swaffer, who kept house frugally for her father—a broad-shouldered, a big-boned woman of forty-five, with the pocket of her dress full of keys, and a grey, steady eye. She was Church—as people said (while her father was one of the trustees of the Baptist Chapel[3])—and wore a little steel cross at her waist. She dressed severely in black, in memory of one of the innumerable Bradleys of the neighbourhood, to whom she had been engaged some twenty-five years ago—a young farmer who broke his neck out hunting on the eve of the wedding day. She had the

[3]*Church* and *Chapel* In Great Britain *Church* refers to the official Episcopal Church of England; *Chapel* refers to places of worship for those who are not members of the established Church or, broadly, to the practitioners of such worship.

unmoved countenance of the deaf, spoke very seldom, and her lips, thin like her father's, astonished one sometimes by a mysteriously ironic curl.

"These were the people to whom he owed allegiance, and an overwhelming loneliness seemed to fall from the leaden sky of that winter without sunshine. All the faces were sad. He could talk to no one, and had no hope of ever understanding anybody. It was as if these had been the faces of people from the other world—dead people—he used to tell me years afterwards. Upon my word, I wonder he did not go mad. He didn't know where he was. Somewhere very far from his mountains—somewhere over the water. Was this America, he wondered?

"If it hadn't been for the steel cross at Miss Swaffer's belt he would not, he confessed, have known whether he was in a Christian country at all. He used to cast stealthy glances at it, and feel comforted. There was nothing here the same as in his country! The earth and the water were different; there were no images of the Redeemer by the roadside. The very grass was different, and the trees. All the trees but the three old Norway pines on the bit of lawn before Swaffer's house, and these reminded him of his country. He had been detected once, after dusk, with his forehead against the trunk of one of them, sobbing, and talking to himself. They had been like brothers to him at that time, he affirmed. Everything else was strange. Conceive you the kind of an existence overshadowed, oppressed, by the everyday material appearances, as if by the visions of a nightmare. At night, when he could not sleep, he kept on thinking of the girl who gave him the first piece of bread he had eaten in this foreign land. She had been neither fierce nor angry, nor frightened. Her face he remembered as the only comprehensible face amongst all these faces that were as closed, as mysterious, and as mute as the faces of the dead who are possessed of a knowledge beyond the comprehension of the living. I wonder whether the memory of her compassion prevented him from cutting his throat. But there! I suppose I am an old sentimentalist, and forget the instinctive love of life which it takes all the strength of an uncommon despair to overcome.

"He did the work which was given him with an intelligence which surprised old Swaffer. By-and-by it was discovered that he could help at the ploughing, could milk the cows, feed the bullocks in the cattle-yard, and was of some use with the sheep. He began to pick up words, too, very fast; and suddenly, one fine morning in spring, he rescued from an untimely death a grand-child of old Swaffer.

"Swaffer's younger daughter is married to Willcox, a solicitor and the Town Clerk of Colebrook. Regularly twice a year they come to stay with the old man for a few days. Their only child, a little girl not three years old at the time, ran out of the house alone in her little white pinafore, and, toddling across the grass of a terraced garden, pitched herself over a low wall head first into the horse-pond in the yard below.

"Our man was out with the waggoner and the plough in the field nearest to the house, and as he was leading the team round to begin a fresh furrow, he saw, through the gap of the gate, what for anybody else would have been a mere flutter of something white. But he had straight-glancing, quick, far-reaching eyes, that only seemed to flinch and lose their amazing power before the immensity of the sea. He was barefooted, and looking as outlandish as the heart of Swaffer could desire. Leaving the horses on the turn, to the inexpressible disgust of the waggoner he bounded off, going over the ploughed ground in long leaps, and suddenly appeared before the mother, thrust the child into her arms, and strode away.

"The pond was not very deep; but still, if he had not had such good eyes, the child would have perished—miserably suffocated in the foot or so of sticky mud at the bottom. Old Swaffer walked out slowly into the field, waited till the plough came over to his side, had a good look at him, and without saying a word went back to the house. But from that time they laid out his meals on the kitchen table; and at first, Miss Swaffer, all in black and with an inscrutable face, would come and stand in the doorway of the living-room to see him make a big sign of the cross before he fell to. I believe that from that day, too, Swaffer began to pay him regular wages.

"I can't follow step by step his development. He cut his hair short, was seen in the village and along the road going to and fro to his work like any other man. Children ceased to shout after him. He became aware of social differences, but remained for a long time surprised at the bare poverty of the churches among so much wealth. He couldn't understand either why they were kept shut up on week days. There was nothing to steal in them. Was it to keep people from praying too often? The rectory took much notice of him about that time, and I believe the young ladies attempted to prepare the ground for his conversion. They could not, however, break him of his habit of crossing himself, but he went so far as to take off the string with a couple of brass medals the size of a sixpence, a tiny metal cross, and a square sort of scapulary which he wore round his neck. He hung them on the wall by the side of his bed, and he was still to be heard every evening reciting the Lord's Prayer, in incomprehensible words and in a slow, fervent tone, as he had heard his old father do at the head of all the kneeling family, big and little, on every evening of his life. And though he wore corduroys at work, and a slop-made pepper-and-salt suit on Sundays, strangers would turn round to look after him on the road. His foreignness had a peculiar and indelible stamp. At last people became used to see him. But they never became used to him. His rapid, skimming walk; his swarthy complexion; his hat cocked on the left ear; his habit, on warm evenings, of wearing his coat over one shoulder, like a hussar's dolman; his manner of leaping over the stiles, not as a feat of agility, but in the ordinary course of progression—all these peculiarities were, as one may say, so many causes of scorn and offence to the inhabitants of the village. *They* wouldn't in their dinner hour lie flat on their backs on the grass to stare at the sky. Neither did they go about the fields screaming dismal tunes. Many times have I heard his high-pitched voice from behind the ridge of some sloping sheep-walk, a voice light and soaring, like a lark's, but with a melancholy human note, over our fields that hear only the song of birds. And I should be startled myself. Ah! He was different: innocent of heart, and full of good will, which nobody wanted, this castaway, that, like a man transplanted into another planet, was separated by an immense space from his past and by an immense ignorance from his future. His quick, fervent utterance positively shocked everybody. 'An excitable devil,' they called him. One evening, in the tap-room of the Coach and Horses (having drunk some whisky), he upset them all by singing a love song of his country. They hooted him down, and he was pained; but Preble, the lame wheelwright, and Vincent, the fat blacksmith, and the other notables too, wanted to drink their evening beer in peace. On another occasion he tried to show them how to dance. The dust rose in clouds from the sanded floor; he leaped straight up amongst the deal tables, struck his heels together, squatted on one heel in front of old Preble, shooting out the other leg, uttered wild and exulting cries, jumped up to whirl on one foot, snapping his fingers above his head—and a strange carter who was having a drink in there began to swear, and cleared out with his half-pint in his hand into the bar. But when suddenly he sprang upon a table and continued to dance among the glasses, the landlord interfered. He didn't want any 'accrobat tricks in the taproom.' They laid their hands on him. Having had a glass or two, Mr. Swaffer's foreigner tried to expostulate: was ejected forcibly: got a black eye.

"I believe he felt the hostility of his human surroundings. But he was tough—tough in spirit, too, as well as in body. Only the memory of the sea frightened him, with that vague terror that is left by a bad dream. His home was far away; and he did not want now to go to America. I had often explained to him that there is no place on earth where true gold can be found lying ready and to be got for the trouble of the picking up. How then, he asked, could he ever return home with empty hands when there had been sold a cow, two ponies, and a bit of land to pay for his going? His eyes would fill with tears, and, averting them from the immense shimmer of the sea, he would throw himself face down on the grass. But sometimes, cocking his hat with a little conquering air, he would defy my wisdom. He had found his bit of true gold. That was Amy Foster's heart; which was 'a golden heart, and soft to people's misery,' he would say in the accents of overwhelming conviction.

"He was called Yanko. He had explained that this meant little John; but as he would also repeat very often that he was a mountaineer (some word sounding in the dialect of his country like Goorall) he got it for his surname. And this is the only trace of him that the succeeding ages may find in the marriage register of the parish. There it stands—Yanko Goorall—in the rector's handwriting. The crooked cross made by the castaway, a cross whose tracing no doubt seemed to him the most solemn part of the whole ceremony, is all that remains now to perpetuate the memory of his name.

"His courtship had lasted some time—ever since he got his precarious footing in the community. It began by his buying for Amy Foster a green satin ribbon in Darnford. This was what you did in his country. You bought a ribbon at a Jew's stall on a fair-day. I don't suppose the girl knew what to do with it, but he seemed to think that his honourable intentions could not be mistaken.

"It was only when he declared his purpose to get married that I fully understood how, for a hundred futile and inappreciable reasons, how—shall I say odious?—he was to all the countryside. Every old woman in the village was up in arms. Smith, coming upon him near the farm, promised to break his head for him if he found him about again. But he twisted his little black moustache with such a bellicose air and rolled such big, black fierce eyes at Smith that this promise came to nothing. Smith, however, told the girl that she must be mad to take up with a man who was surely wrong in his head. All the same, when she heard him in the gloaming whistle from beyond the orchard a couple of bars of a weird and mournful tune, she would drop whatever she had in her hand—she would leave Mrs. Smith in the middle of a sentence—and she would run out to his call. Mrs. Smith called her a shameless hussy. She answered nothing. She said nothing at all to anybody, and went on her way as if she had been deaf. She and I alone all in the land, I fancy, could see his very real beauty. He was very good-looking, and most graceful in his bearing, with that something wild as of a woodland creature in his aspect. Her mother moaned over her dismally whenever the girl came to see her on her day out. The father was surly, but pretended not to know; and Mrs. Finn once told her plainly that 'this man, my dear, will do you some harm some day yet.' And so it went on. They could be seen on the roads, she tramping stolidly in her finery—grey dress, black feather, stout boots, prominent white cotton gloves that caught your eye a hundred yards away; and he, his coat slung picturesquely over one shoulder, pacing by her side, gallant of bearing and casting tender glances upon the girl with the golden heart. I wonder whether he saw how plain she was. Perhaps among types so different from what he had ever seen, he had not the power to judge; or perhaps he was seduced by the divine quality of her pity.

"Yanko was in great trouble meantime. In his country you get an old man for an ambassador in marriage affairs. He did not know how to proceed. However, one day in the midst of sheep in a field (he was now Swaffer's under-shepherd with Foster) he took off his hat to the father and declared himself humbly. 'I daresay she's fool enough to marry you,' was all Foster said. 'And then,' he used to relate, 'he puts his hat on his head, looks black at me as if he wanted to cut my throat, whistles the dog, and off he goes, leaving me to do the work.' The Fosters, of course, didn't like to lose the wages the girl earned: Amy used to give all her money to her mother. But there was in Foster a very genuine aversion to that match. He contended that the fellow was very good with sheep, but was not fit for any girl to marry. For one thing, he used to go along the hedges muttering to himself like a dam' fool; and then, these foreigners behave very queerly to women sometimes. And perhaps he would want to carry her off somewhere—or run off himself. It was not safe. He preached it to his daughter that the fellow might ill-use her in some way. She made no answer. It was, they said in the village, as if the man had done something to her. People discussed the matter. It was quite an excitement, and the two went on 'walking out' together in the face of opposition. Then something unexpected happened.

"I don't know whether old Swaffer ever understood how much he was regarded in the light of a father by his foreign retainer. Anyway the relation was curiously feudal. So when Yanko asked formally for an interview—'and the Miss too' (he called the severe, deaf Miss Swaffer simply *Miss*)—it was to obtain their permission to marry. Swaffer heard him unmoved, dismissed him by a nod, and then shouted the intelligence into Miss Swaffer's best ear. She showed no surprise, and only remarked grimly, in a veiled blank voice, 'He certainly won't get any other girl to marry him.'

"It is Miss Swaffer who has all the credit of the munificence: but in a very few days it came out that Mr. Swaffer had presented Yanko with a cottage (the cottage you've seen this morning) and something like an acre of ground—had made it over to him in absolute property. Willcox expedited the deed, and I remember him telling me he had a great pleasure in making it ready. It recited: 'In consideration of saving the life of my beloved grandchild, Bertha Willcox.'

"Of course, after that no power on earth could prevent them from getting married.

"Her infatuation endured. People saw her going out to meet him in the evening. She stared with unblinking, fascinated eyes up the road where he was expected to appear, walking freely, with a swing from the hip, and humming one of the love-tunes of his country. When the boy was born, he got elevated at the 'Coach and Horses,' essayed again a song and a dance, and was again ejected. People expressed their commiseration for a woman married to that Jack-in-the-box. He didn't care. There was a man now (he told me boastfully) to whom he could sing and talk in the language of his country, and show how to dance by-and-by.

"But I don't know. To me he appeared to have grown less springy of step, heavier in body, less keen of eye. Imagination, no doubt; but it seems to me now as if the net of fate had been drawn closer round him already.

"One day I met him on the footpath over the Talfourd Hill. He told me that 'women were funny.' I had heard already of domestic differences. People were saying that Amy Foster was beginning to find out what sort of man she had married. He looked upon the sea with indifferent, unseeing eyes. His wife had snatched the child out of his arms one day as he sat on the doorstep crooning to it a song such as the mothers sing to babies in his mountains. She seemed to think he was doing it some harm. Women are funny. And she had objected to him praying aloud in the evening. Why? He expected the boy to repeat the prayer aloud after him by-and-by, as he used to do after his old father when he was a child—in his own country. And I discovered he longed for their boy to grow up so that he could have a man to talk with in that language that to our ears sounded so disturbing, so passionate, and so bizarre. Why his wife should dislike the idea he couldn't tell. But that would pass, he said. And tilting his head knowingly, he tapped his breastbone to indicate that she had a good heart: not hard, not fierce, open to compassion, charitable to the poor!

"I walked away thoughtfully; I wondered whether his difference, his strangeness, were not penetrating with repulsion that dull nature they had begun by irresistibly attracting. I wondered. . . ."

The Doctor came to the window and looked out at the frigid splendour of the sea, immense in the haze, as if enclosing all the earth with all the hearts lost among the passions of love and fear.

"Physiologically, now," he said, turning away abruptly, "it was possible. It was possible."

He remained silent. Then went on—

"At all events, the next time I saw him he was ill—lung trouble. He was tough, but I daresay he was not acclimatised as well as I had supposed. It was a bad winter; and, of course, these mountaineers do get fits of home sickness; and a state of depression would make him vulnerable. He was lying half dressed on a couch downstairs.

"A table covered with a dark oilcloth took up all the middle of the little room. There was a wicker cradle on the floor, a kettle spouting steam on the hob, and some child's linen lay drying on the fender. The room was warm, but the door opens right into the garden, as you noticed perhaps.

"He was very feverish, and kept on muttering to himself. She sat on a chair and looked at him fixedly across the table with her brown, blurred eyes. 'Why don't you have him upstairs?' I asked. With a start and a confused stammer she said, 'Oh! ah! I couldn't sit with him upstairs, Sir.'

"I gave her certain directions; and going outside, I said again that he ought to be in bed upstairs. She wrung her hands. 'I couldn't. I couldn't. He keeps on saying something—I don't know what.' With the memory of all the talk against the man that had been dinned into her ears, I looked at her narrowly. I looked into her short-sighted eyes, at her dumb eyes that once in her life had seen an enticing shape, but seemed, staring at me, to see nothing at all now. But I saw she was uneasy.

"'What's the matter with him?' she asked in a sort of vacant trepidation. 'He doesn't look very ill. I never did see anybody look like this before. . . .

"'Do you think,' I asked indignantly, 'he is shamming?'

"'I can't help it, sir,' she said stolidly. And suddenly she clapped her hands and looked right and left. 'And there's the baby. I am so frightened. He wanted me just now to give him the baby. I can't understand what he says to it.'

"'Can't you ask a neighbour to come in tonight?' I asked.

"'Please, sir, nobody seems to care to come,' she muttered, dully resigned all at once.

"I impressed upon her the necessity of the greatest care, and then had to go. There was a good deal of sickness that winter. 'Oh, I hope he won't talk!' she exclaimed softly just as I was going away.

"I don't know how it is I did not see—but I didn't. And yet, turning in my trap, I saw her lingering before the door, very still, and as if meditating a flight up the miry road.

"Towards the night his fever increased.

"He tossed, moaned, and now and then muttered a complaint. And she sat with the table between her and the couch, watching every movement and every sound, with the terror, the unreasonable terror, of that man she could not understand creeping over her. She had drawn the wicker cradle close to her feet. There was nothing in her now but the maternal instinct and that unaccountable fear.

"Suddenly coming to himself, parched, he demanded a drink of water. She did not move. She had not understood, though he may have thought he was speaking in English. He waited, looking at her, burning with fever, amazed at her silence and immobility, and then he shouted impatiently, 'Water! Give me water!'

"She jumped to her feet, snatched up the child, and stood still. He spoke to her, and his passionate remonstrances only increased her fear of that strange man. I believe he spoke to her for a long time, entreating, wondering, pleading, ordering, I suppose. She says she bore it as long as she could. And then a gust of rage came over him.

"He sat up and called out terribly one word—some word. Then he got up as though he hadn't been ill at all, she says. And as in fevered dismay, indignation, and wonder he tried to get to her round the table, she simply opened the door and ran out with the child in her arms. She heard him call twice after her down the road in a terrible voice—and fled. . . . Ah! but you should have seen stirring behind the dull, blurred glance of these eyes the spectre of the fear which had hunted her on that night three miles and a half to the door of Foster's cottage! I did the next day.

"And it was I who found him lying face down and his body in a puddle, just outside the little wicket-gate.

"I had been called out that night to an urgent case in the village, and on my way home at day-break passed by the cottage. The door stood open. My man helped me to carry him in. We laid him on the couch. The lamp smoked, the fire was out, the chill of the stormy night oozed from the cheerless yellow paper on the wall. 'Amy!' I called aloud, and my voice seemed to lose itself in the emptiness of this tiny house as if I had cried in a desert. He opened his eyes. 'Gone!' he said distinctly. 'I had only asked for water—only for a little water. . . .'

"He was muddy. I covered him up and stood waiting in silence, catching a painfully gasped word now and then. They were no longer in his own language. The fever had left him, taking with it the heat of life. And with his panting breast and lustrous eyes he reminded me again of a wild creature under the net; of a bird caught in a snare. She had left him. She had left him—sick—helpless—thirsty. The spear of the hunter had entered his very soul. 'Why?' he cried in the penetrating and indignant voice of a man calling to a responsible Maker. A gust of wind and a swish of rain answered.

"And as I turned away to shut the door he pronounced the word 'Merciful!' and expired.

"Eventually I certified heart-failure as the immediate cause of death. His heart must have indeed failed him, or else he might have stood this night of storm and exposure, too. I closed his eyes and drove away. Not very far from the cottage I met Foster walking sturdily between the dripping hedges with his collie at his heels.

"'Do you know where your daughter is?' I asked.

"'Don't I!' he cried. 'I am going to talk to him a bit. Frightening a poor woman like this.'

"'He won't frighten her any more,' I said. 'He is dead.'

"He struck with his stick at the mud.

"'And there's the child.'

"Then, after thinking deeply for a while—

"'I don't know that it isn't for the best.'

"That's what he said. And she says nothing at all now. Not a word of him. Never. Is his image as utterly gone from her mind as his lithe and striding figure, his carolling voice are gone from our fields? He is no longer before her eyes to excite her imagination into a passion of love or fear; and his memory seems to have vanished from her dull brain as a shadow passes away upon a white screen. She lives in the cottage and works for Miss Swaffer. She is Amy Foster for everybody, and the child is 'Amy Foster's boy.' She calls him Johnny—which means Little John.

"It is impossible to say whether this name recalls anything to her. Does she ever think of the past? I have seen her hanging over the boy's cot in a very passion of maternal tenderness. The little fellow was lying on his back, a little frightened at me, but very still, with his big black eyes, with his fluttered air of a bird in a snare. And looking at him I seemed to see again the other one—the father, cast out mysteriously by the sea to perish in the supreme disaster of loneliness and despair."

[1903]

QUESTIONS

1. Why does the narrator refer several times to the villagers' lack of imagination? How does this lack affect their response to the foreigner? Why do their suspicions persist long after Yanko settles into village life?
2. What is Amy Foster's role in Yanko's initial survival after the shipwreck and in his eventual death? What accounts for the difference in her responses to him in his moments of extremity?

3. What does the story suggest about the nature and limitations of communication, especially across cultural and linguistic barriers? What does it suggest about people's perceptions of and reactions to foreigners?
4. Compare this story, and the dilemmas inherent in cross-cultural communication and understanding, with R. K. Narayan's "A Horse and Two Goats" and Sembene Ousmane's "Black Girl."

Stephen Crane

(1871–1900)

United States

Stephen Crane was the fourteenth child of a Methodist minister. His father died when he was nine years old; his mother died eleven years later when Crane was writing his first novel, *Maggie: A Girl of the Streets*, privately published in 1893. His most famous novel, *The Red Badge of Courage*, published two years later, made him an international celebrity. Thereafter, Crane wrote short stories and poems and worked for a time as a journalist. He died of tuberculosis in 1900.

Though Crane had not known battle when he wrote *The Red Badge of Courage*, many of his other works were written out of direct observation of a specific incident. "An Experiment in Misery" (1894), for example, was based on Crane's experiences on skid row, the Bowery, in New York City. "The Blue Hotel" (1898), "The Bride Comes to Yellow Sky" (1898), and "The Open Boat" (1898, and usually regarded as his masterpiece) were based on specific events. In these and other short stories, Crane achieved a unique form of impressionistic naturalism that often gives his characters a psychological dimension far in advance of the works of his contemporaries. Crane's influence on subsequent American writers was extensive. The entry devoted to him in the *Literary History of the United States* concludes with the following sentence: "He gave to the naturalistic short story its characteristic form, later to be exploited by Hemingway, Steinbeck, and a host of others."

Crane's poetry often shares the same naturalistic emphasis as his short fiction. Consider the following poem ("A Man Said to the Universe") when you read "The Open Boat":

A man said to the universe:
"Sir, I exist!"
"However," replied the universe,
"The fact has not created in me
A sense of obligation."

The Open Boat

A Tale Intended to Be After the Fact,
Being the Experience of Four Men from
the Sunk Steamer Commodore

I

None of them knew the color of the sky. Their eyes glanced level, and were fastened upon the waves that swept toward them. These waves were of the hue of slate, save for the tops, which were of foaming white, and all of the men knew the colors of the sea. The horizon narrowed and widened, and dipped and rose, and at all times its edge was jagged with waves that seemed thrust up in points like rocks.

Many a man ought to have a bath-tub larger than the boat which here rode upon the sea. These waves were most wrongfully and barbarously abrupt and tall, and each froth-top was a problem in small boat navigation.

The cook squatted in the bottom and looked with both eyes at the six inches of gunwale which separated him from the ocean. His sleeves were rolled over his fat forearms, and the two flaps of his unbuttoned vest dangled as he bent to bail out the boat. Often he said: "Gawd! That was a narrow clip." As he remarked it he invariably gazed eastward over the broken sea.

The oiler, steering with one of the two oars in the boat, sometimes raised himself suddenly to keep clear of water that swirled in over the stern. It was a thin little oar and it seemed often ready to snap.

The correspondent, pulling at the other oar, watched the waves and wondered why he was there.

The injured captain, lying in the bow, was at this time buried in that profound dejection and indifference which comes, temporarily at least, to even the bravest and most enduring when, willy nilly, the firm fails, the army loses, the ship goes down. The mind of the master of a vessel is rooted deep in the timbers of her, though he command for a day or a decade, and this captain had on him the stern impression of a scene in the grays of dawn of seven turned faces, and later a stump of a top-mast with a white ball on it that slashed to and fro at the waves, went low and lower, and down. Thereafter there was something strange in his voice. Although steady, it was deep with mourning, and of a quality beyond oration or tears.

"Keep 'er a little more south, Billie," said he.

"'A little more south,' sir," said the oiler in the stern.

A seat in this boat was not unlike a seat upon a bucking broncho, and, by the same token, a broncho is not much smaller. The craft pranced and reared, and plunged like an animal. As each wave came, and she rose for it, she seemed like a horse making at a fence outrageously high. The manner of her scramble over these walls of water is a mystic thing, and, moreover, at the top of them were ordinarily these problems in white water, the foam racing down from the summit of each wave, requiring a new leap, and a leap from the air. Then, after scornfully bumping a crest, she would slide, and race, and splash down a long incline and arrive bobbing and nodding in front of the next menace.

A singular disadvantage of the sea lies in the fact that after successfully surmounting one wave you discover that there is another behind it just as important and just as nervously anxious to do something effective in the way of swamping boats. In a ten-foot dingey one can get an idea of the resources of the sea in the line of waves that is not probable to the average experience, which is never at sea in a dingey. As each slaty wall of water approached, it shut all else from the view of the men in the boat, and it was not difficult to imagine that this particular wave was the final outburst of the ocean, the last effort of the grim water. There was a terrible grace in the move of the waves, and they came in silence, save for the snarling of the crests.

In the wan light, the faces of the men must have been gray. Their eyes must have glinted in strange ways as they gazed steadily astern. Viewed from a balcony, the whole thing would doubtlessly have been weirdly picturesque. But the men in the boat had no time to see it, and if they had had leisure there were other things to occupy their minds. The sun swung steadily up the sky, and they knew it was broad day because the color of the sea changed from slate to emerald-green, streaked with amber lights, and the foam was like tumbling snow. The process of the breaking day was unknown to them. They were aware only of this effect upon the color of the waves that rolled toward them.

In disjointed sentences the cook and the correspondent argued as to the difference between a life-saving station and a house of refuge. The cook had said: "There's a house of refuge just north of the Mosquito Inlet Light, and as soon as they see us, they'll come off in their boat and pick us up."

"As soon as who see us?" said the correspondent.

"The crew," said the cook.

"Houses of refuge don't have crews," said the correspondent. "As I understand them, they are only places where clothes and grub are stored for the benefit of shipwrecked people. They don't carry crews."

"Oh, yes, they do," said the cook.

"No, they don't," said the correspondent.

"Well, we're not there yet, anyhow," said the oiler, in the stern.

"Well," said the cook, "perhaps it's not a house of refuge that I'm thinking of as being near Mosquito Inlet Light. Perhaps it's a life-saving station."

"We're not there yet," said the oiler, in the stern.

II

As the boat bounced from the top of each wave, the wind tore through the hair of the hatless men, and as the craft plopped her stern down again the spray slashed past them. The crest of each of these waves was a hill, from the top of which the men surveyed, for a moment, a broad tumultuous expanse, shining and wind-riven. It was probably splendid. It was probably glorious, this play of the free sea, wild with lights of emerald and white and amber.

"Bully good thing it's an on-shore wind," said the cook. "If not where would we be? Wouldn't have a show."

"That's right," said the correspondent.

The busy oiler nodded his assent.

Then the captain, in the bow, chuckled in a way that expressed humor, contempt, tragedy, all in one. "Do you think we've got a show, now, boys?" said he.

Whereupon the three went silent, save for a trifle of hemming and hawing. To express any particular optimism at this time they felt to be childish and stupid, but they all doubtless possessed this sense of the situation in their mind. A young man thinks doggedly at such times. On the other hand, the ethics of their condition was decidedly against any open suggestion of hopelessness. So they were silent.

"Oh, well," said the captain, soothing his children, "we'll get ashore all right."

But there was that in his tone which made them think, so the oiler quoth: "Yes! If this wind holds!"

The cook was bailing. "Yes! If we don't catch hell in the surf."

Canton flannel gulls flew near and far. Sometimes they sat down on the sea, near patches of brown sea-weed that rolled over the waves with a movement like carpets on a line in a gale. The birds sat comfortably in groups, and they were envied by some in the dingey, for the wrath of the sea was no more to them than it was to a covey of prairie chickens a thousand miles inland. Often they came very close and stared at the men with black bead-like eyes. At these times they were uncanny and sinister in their unblinking scrutiny, and the men hooted angrily at them, telling them to be gone. One came, and evidently decided to alight on the top of the captain's head. The bird flew parallel to the boat and did not circle, but made short sidelong jumps in the air in chicken-fashion. His black eyes were wistfully fixed upon the captain's head. "Ugly brute," said the oiler to the bird. "You look as if you were made with a jack-knife." The cook and the correspondent swore darkly at the creature. The captain naturally wished to knock it away with the end of the heavy painter, but he did not dare do it, because anything resembling an emphatic gesture would have capsized this freighted boat, and so with his open hand, the captain gently and carefully waved the gull away. After it had been discouraged from the pursuit the captain breathed easier on account of his hair, and others breathed easier because the bird struck their minds at this time as being somehow gruesome and ominous.

In the meantime the oiler and the correspondent rowed. And also they rowed.

They sat together in the same seat, and each rowed an oar. Then the oiler took both oars; then the correspondent took both oars; then the oiler; then the correspondent. They rowed and they rowed. The very ticklish part of the business was when the time came for the reclining one in the stern to take his turn at the oars. By the very last star of truth, it is easier to steal eggs from under a hen than it was to change seats in the dingey. First the man in the stern slid his hand along the thwart and moved with care, as if he were of Sèvres.[1] Then the man in the rowing seat slid his hand along the other thwart. It was all done with the most extraordinary care. As the two sidled past each other, the whole party kept watchful eyes on the coming wave, and the captain cried: "Look out now! Steady there!"

The brown mats of sea-weed that appeared from time to time were like islands, bits of earth. They were travelling, apparently, neither one way nor the other. They were, to all intents, stationary. They informed the men in the boat that it was making progress slowly toward the land.

The captain, rearing cautiously in the bow, after the dingey soared on a great swell, said that he had seen the light-house at Mosquito Inlet. Presently the cook remarked that he had seen it. The correspondent was at the oars, then, and for some reason he too wished to look at the lighthouse, but his back was toward the far shore and the waves were important, and for some time he could not seize an opportunity to turn his head. But at last there came a wave more gentle than the others, and when at the crest of it he swiftly scoured the western horizon.

"See it?" said the captain.

"No," said the correspondent, slowly, "I didn't see anything."

"Look again," said the captain. He pointed. "It's exactly in that direction."

At the top of another wave, the correspondent did as he was bid, and this time his eyes chanced on a small still thing on the edge of the swaying horizon. It was precisely like the point of a pin. It took an anxious eye to find a light-house so tiny.

"Think we'll make it, Captain?"

[1]*Sèvres* delicate French porcelain

"If this wind holds and the boat don't swamp, we can't do much else," said the captain.

The little boat, lifted by each towering sea, and splashed viciously by the crests, made progress that in the absence of sea-weed was not apparent to those in her. She seemed just a wee thing wallowing, miraculously, top-up, at the mercy of five oceans. Occasionally, a great spread of water, like white flames, swarmed into her.

"Bail her, cook," said the captain, serenely.

"All right, Captain," said the cheerful cook.

III

It would be difficult to describe the subtle brotherhood of men that was here established on the seas. No one said that it was so. No one mentioned it. But it dwelt in the boat, and each man felt it warm him. They were a captain, an oiler, a cook, and a correspondent, and they were friends, friends in a more curiously iron-bound degree than may be common. The hurt captain, lying against the water-jar in the bow, spoke always in a low voice and calmly, but he could never command a more ready and swiftly obedient crew than the motley three of the dingey. It was more than a mere recognition of what was best for the common safety. There was surely in it a quality that was personal and heartfelt. And after this devotion to the commander of the boat there was this comradeship that the correspondent, for instance, who had been taught to be cynical of men, knew even at the time was the best experience of his life. But no one said that it was so. No one mentioned it.

"I wish we had a sail," remarked the captain. "We might try my overcoat on the end of an oar and give you two boys a chance to rest." So the cook and the correspondent held the mast and spread wide the overcoat. The oiler steered, and the little boat made good way with her new rig. Sometimes the oiler had to scull sharply to keep a sea from breaking into the boat, but otherwise sailing was a success.

Meanwhile the light-house had been growing slowly larger. It had now almost assumed color, and appeared like a little gray shadow on the sky. The man at the oars could not be prevented from turning his head rather often to try for a glimpse of this little gray shadow.

At last, from the top of each wave the men in the tossing boat could see land. Even as the light-house was an upright shadow on the sky, this land seemed but a long black shadow on the sea. It certainly was thinner than paper. "We must be about opposite New Smyrna," said the cook, who had coasted this shore often in schooners. "Captain, by the way, I believe they abandoned that life-saving station there about a year ago."

"Did they?" said the captain.

The wind slowly died away. The cook and the correspondent were not now obliged to slave in order to hold high the oar. But the waves continued their old impetuous swooping at the dingey, and the little craft, no longer under way, struggled woundily over them. The oiler or the correspondent took the oars again.

Shipwrecks are *apropos* of nothing. If men could only train for them and have them occur when the men had reached pink condition, there would be less drowning at sea. Of the four in the dingey none had slept any time worth mentioning for two days and two nights previous to embarking in the dingey, and in the excitement of clambering about the deck of a foundering ship they had also forgotten to eat heartily.

For these reasons, and for others, neither the oiler nor the correspondent was fond of rowing at this time. The correspondent wondered ingenuously how in the name of all that was sane could there be people who thought it amusing to row a boat. It was not an amusement; it was a diabolical punishment, and even a genius of mental aberrations could never conclude that it was anything but a horror to the muscles and a crime against the back. He mentioned to the boat in general how the amusement of rowing struck him, and the weary-faced oiler smiled in full sympathy. Previously to the foundering, by the way, the oiler had worked double-watch in the engine-room of the ship.

"Take her easy, now, boys," said the captain. "Don't spend yourselves. If we have to run a surf you'll need all your strength, because we'll sure have to swim for it. Take your time."

Slowly the land arose from the sea. From a black line it became a line of black and a line of white — trees and sand. Finally, the captain said that he could make out a house on the shore. "That's the house of refuge, sure," said the cook. "They'll see us before long, and come out after us."

The distant light-house reared high. "The keeper ought to be able to make us out now, if he's looking through a glass," said the captain. "He'll notify the life-saving people."

"None of those other boats could have got ashore to give word of the wreck," said the oiler, in a low voice. "Else the life-boat would be out hunting us."

Slowly and beautifully the land loomed out of the sea. The wind came again. It had veered from the northeast to the southeast. Finally, a new sound struck the ears of the men in the boat. It was the low thunder of the surf on the shore. "We'll never be able to make the light-house now," said the captain. "Swing her head a little more north, Billie."

"'A little more north,' sir," said the oiler.

Whereupon the little boat turned her nose once more down the wind, and all but the oarsman watched the shore grow. Under the influence of this expansion doubt and direful apprehension were leaving the minds of the men. The management of the boat was still most absorbing, but it could not prevent a quiet cheerfulness. In an hour, perhaps, they would be ashore.

Their back-bones had become thoroughly used to balancing in the boat and they now rode this wild colt of a dingey like circus men. The correspondent thought that he had been drenched to the skin, but happening to feel in the top pocket of his coat, he found therein eight cigars. Four of them were soaked with sea-water; four were perfectly scatheless. After a search, somebody produced three dry matches, and thereupon the four waifs rode impudently in their little boat, and with an assurance of an impending rescue shining in their eyes, puffed at the big cigars and judged well and ill of all men. Everybody took a drink of water.

IV

"Cook," remarked the captain, "there don't seem to be any signs of life about your house of refuge."

"No," replied the cook. "Funny they don't see us!"

A broad stretch of lowly coast lay before the eyes of the men. It was of dunes topped with dark vegetation. The roar of the surf was plain, and sometimes they could see the white lip of a wave as it spun up the beach. A tiny house was blocked out black upon the sky. Southward, the slim lighthouse lifted its little gray length.

Tide, wind, and waves were swinging the dingey northward. "Funny they don't see us," said the men.

The surf's roar was here dulled, but its tone was, nevertheless, thunderous and mighty. As the boat swam over the great rollers, the men sat listening to this roar. "We'll swamp sure," said everybody.

It is fair to say here that there was not a life-saving station within twenty miles in either direction, but the men did not know this fact and in consequence they made dark and opprobrious remarks concerning the eyesight of the nation's life-savers. Four scowling men sat in the dingey and surpassed records in the invention of epithets.

"Funny they don't see us."

The light-heartedness of a former time had completely faded. To their sharpened minds it was easy to conjure pictures of all kinds of incompetency and blindness and, indeed, cowardice. There was the shore of the populous land, and it was bitter and bitter to them that from it came no sign.

"Well," said the captain, ultimately, "I suppose we'll have to make a try for ourselves. If we stay out here too long, we'll none of us have strength left to swim after the boat swamps."

And so the oiler, who was at the oars, turned the boat straight for the shore. There was a sudden tightening of muscles. There was some thinking.

"If we don't all get ashore—" said the captain. "If we don't all get ashore, I suppose you fellows know where to send news of my finish?"

They then briefly exchanged some addresses and admonitions. As for the reflections of the men, there was a great deal of rage in them. Perchance they might be formulated thus: "If I am going to be drowned—if I am going to be drowned—if I am going to be drowned, why, in the name of the seven mad gods who rule the sea, was I allowed to come thus far and contemplate sand and trees? Was I brought here merely to have my nose dragged away as I was about to nibble the sacred cheese of life? It is preposterous. If this old ninny-woman, Fate, cannot do better than this, she should be deprived of the management of men's fortunes. She is an old hen who knows not her intention. If she has decided to drown me, why did she not do it in the beginning and save me all this trouble. The whole affair is absurd. . . . But, no, she cannot mean to drown me. She dare not drown me. She cannot drown me. Not after all this work." Afterward the man might have had an impulse to shake his fist at the clouds. "Just you drown me, now, and then hear what I call you!"

The billows that came at this time were more formidable. They seemed always just about to break and roll over the little boat in a turmoil of foam. There was a preparatory and long growl in the speech of them. No mind unused to the sea would have concluded that the dingey could ascend these sheer heights in time. The shore was still afar. The oiler was a wily surfman. "Boys," he said, swiftly, "she won't live three minutes more and we're too far out to swim. Shall I take her to sea again, Captain?"

"Yes! Go ahead!" said the captain.

This oiler, by a series of quick miracles, and fast and steady oarsmanship, turned the boat in the middle of the surf and took her safely to sea again.

There was a considerable silence as the boat bumped over the furrowed sea to deeper water. Then somebody in gloom spoke. "Well, anyhow, they must have seen us from the shore by now."

The gulls went in slanting flight up the wind toward the gray desolate east. A squall, marked by dingy clouds, and clouds brick-red, like smoke from a burning building, appeared from the southeast.

"What do you think of those life-saving people? Ain't they peaches?"

"Funny they haven't seen us."

"Maybe they think we're out here for sport! Maybe they think we're fishin'. Maybe they think we're damned fools."

It was a long afternoon. A changed tide tried to force them southward, but wind and wave said northward. Far ahead, where coast-line, sea, and sky formed their mighty angle, there were little dots which seemed to indicate a city on the shore.

"St. Augustine?"

The captain shook his head. "Too near Mosquito Inlet."

And the oiler rowed, and then the correspondent rowed. Then the oiler rowed. It was a weary business. The human back can become the seat of more aches and pains than are registered in books for the composite anatomy of a regiment. It is a limited area, but it can become the theatre of innumerable muscular conflicts, tangles, wrenches, knots, and other comforts.

"Did you ever like to row, Billie?" asked the correspondent.

"No," said the oiler, "Hang it."

When one exchanged the rowing-seat for a place in the bottom of the boat, he suffered a bodily depression that caused him to be careless of everything save an obligation to wiggle one finger. There was cold seawater swashing to and fro in the boat, and he lay in it. His head, pillowed on a thwart, was within an inch of the swirl of a wave crest, and sometimes a particularly obstreperous sea came in-board and drenched him once more. But these matters did not annoy him. It is almost certain that if the boat had capsized he would have tumbled comfortably out upon the ocean as if he felt sure that it was a great soft mattress.

"Look! There's a man on the shore!"

"Where?"

"There! See 'im? See 'im?"

"Yes, sure! He's walking along."

"Now he's stopped. Look! He's facing us!"

"He's waving at us!"

"So he is! By thunder!"

"Ah, now, we're all right! There'll be a boat out here for us in half an hour."

"He's going on. He's running. He's going up to that house there."

The remote beach seemed lower than the sea, and it required a searching glance to discern the little black figure. The captain saw a floating stick and they rowed to it. A bath-towel was by some weird chance in the boat, and, tying this on the stick, the captain waved it. The oarsman did not dare turn his head, so he was obliged to ask questions.

"What's he doing now?"

"He's standing still again. He's looking, I think. . . . There he goes again. Toward the house. . . . Now he's stopped again."

"Is he waving at us?"

"No, not now! He was, though."

"Look! There comes another man!"

"He's running."

"Look at him go, would you."

"Why, he's on a bicycle. Now he's met the other man. They're both waving at us. Look!"

"There comes something up the beach."

"What the devil is that thing?"

"Why, it looks like a boat."

"Why, certainly it's a boat."

"No, it's on wheels."

"Yes, so it is. Well, that must be the life-boat. They drag them along shore on a wagon."

"That's the life-boat, sure."

"No, by, it's—it's an omnibus."

"I tell you it's a life-boat."

"It is not! It's an omnibus. I can see it plain. See? One of those big hotel omnibuses."

"By thunder, you're right. It's an omnibus, sure as fate. What do you suppose they are doing with an omnibus? Maybe they are going around collecting the life-crew, hey?"

"That's it, likely. Look! There's a fellow waving a little black flag. He's standing on the steps of the omnibus. There come those other two fellows. Now they're all talking together. Look at the fellow with the flag. Maybe he ain't waving it!"

"That ain't a flag, is it? That's his coat. Why, certainly, that's his coat."

"So it is. It's his coat. He's taken it off and is waving it around his head. But would you look at him swing it!"

"Oh, say, there isn't any life-saving station there. That's just a winter resort hotel omnibus that has brought over some of the boarders to see us drown."

"What's that idiot with the coat mean? What's he signaling, anyhow?"

"It looks as if he were trying to tell us to go north. There must be a life-saving station up there."

"No! He thinks we're fishing. Just giving us a merry hand. See? Ah, there, Willie."

"Well, I wish I could make something out of those signals. What do you suppose he means?"

"He don't mean anything. He's just playing."

"Well, if he'd just signal us to try the surf again, or to go to sea and wait, or go north, or go south, or go to hell—there would be some reason in it. But look at him. He just stands there and keeps his coat revolving like a wheel. The ass!"

"There come more people."

"Now there's quite a mob. Look! Isn't that a boat?"

"Where? Oh, I see where you mean. No, that's no boat."

"That fellow is still waving his coat."

"He must think we like to see him do that. Why don't he quit it. It don't mean anything."

"I don't know. I think he is trying to make us go north. It must be that there's a life-saving station there somewhere."

"Say, he ain't tired yet. Look at 'im wave."

"Wonder how long he can keep that up. He's been revolving his coat ever since he caught sight of us. He's an idiot. Why aren't they getting men to bring a boat out. A fishing boat—one of those big yawls—could come out here all right. Why don't he do something?"

"Oh, it's all right, now."

"They'll have a boat out here for us in less than no time, now that they've seen us."

A faint yellow tone came into the sky over the low land. The shadows on the sea slowly deepened. The wind bore coldness with it, and the men began to shiver.

"Holy smoke!" said one, allowing his voice to express his impious mood, "if we keep on monkeying out here! If we've got to flounder out here all night!"

"Oh, we'll never have to stay here all night! Don't you worry. They've seen us now, and it won't be long before they'll come chasing out after us."

The shore grew dusky. The man waving a coat blended gradually into this gloom, and it swallowed in the same manner the omnibus and the group of people. The spray, when it dashed uproariously over the side, made the voyagers shrink and swear like men who were being branded.

"I'd like to catch the chump who waved the coat. I feel like soaking him one, just for luck."

"Why? What did he do?"

"Oh, nothing, but then he seemed so damned cheerful."

In the meantime the oiler rowed, and then the correspondent rowed, and then the oiler rowed. Gray-faced and bowed forward, they mechanically, turn by turn, plied the leaden oars. The form of the light-house had vanished from the southern horizon, but finally a pale star appeared, just lifting from the sea. The streaked saffron in the west passed before the all-merging darkness, and the sea to the east was black. The land had vanished, and was expressed only by the low and drear thunder of the surf.

"If I am going to be drowned—if I am going to be drowned—if I am going to be drowned, why, in the name of the seven mad gods who rule the sea, was I allowed to come thus far and contemplate sand and trees? Was I brought here merely to have my nose dragged away as I was about to nibble the sacred cheese of life?"

The patient captain, drooped over the water-jar, was sometimes obliged to speak to the oarsman.

"Keep her head up! Keep her head up!"

"'Keep her head up,' sir." The voices were weary and low.

This was surely a quiet evening. All save the oarsman lay heavily and listlessly in the boat's bottom. As for him, his eyes were just capable of noting the tall black waves that swept forward in a most sinister silence, save for an occasional subdued growl of a crest.

The cook's head was on a thwart, and he looked without interest at the water under his nose. He was deep in other scenes. Finally he spoke. "Billie," he murmured, dreamfully, "what kind of pie do you like best?"

V

"Pie," said the oiler and the correspondent, agitatedly. "Don't talk about those things, blast you!"

"Well," said the cook, "I was just thinking about ham sandwiches, and—"

A night on the sea in an open boat is a long night. As darkness settled finally, the shine of the light, lifting from the sea in the south, changed to full gold. On the northern horizon a new light appeared, a small bluish gleam on the edge of the waters. These two lights were the furniture of the world. Otherwise there was nothing but waves.

Two men huddled in the stern, and distances were so magnificent in the dingey that the rower was enabled to keep his feet partly warmed by thrusting them under his companions. Their legs indeed extended far under the rowing-seat until they touched the feet of the captain forward. Sometimes, despite the efforts of the tired oarsman, a wave came piling into the boat, an icy wave of the night, and the chilling water soaked them anew. They would twist their bodies for a moment and groan, and sleep the dead sleep once more, while the water in the boat gurgled about them as the craft rocked.

The plan of the oiler and the correspondent was for one to row until he lost the ability, and then arouse the other from his sea-water couch in the bottom of the boat.

The oiler plied the oars until his head drooped forward, and the overpowering sleep blinded him. And he rowed yet afterward. Then he touched a man in the bottom of the boat, and called his name. "Will you spell me for a little while?" he said, meekly.

"Sure, Billie," said the correspondent, awakening and dragging himself to a sitting position. They exchanged places carefully, and the oiler, cuddling down in the sea-water at the cook's side, seemed to go to sleep instantly.

The particular violence of the sea had ceased. The waves came without snarling. The obligation of the man at the oars was to keep the boat headed so that the tilt of the rollers would not capsize her, and to preserve her from filling when the crests rushed past. The black waves were silent and hard to be seen in the darkness. Often one was almost upon the boat before the oarsman was aware.

In a low voice the correspondent addressed the captain. He was not sure that the captain was awake, although this iron man seemed to be always awake. "Captain, shall I keep her making for that light north, sir?"

The same steady voice answered him. "Yes. Keep it about two points off the port bow."

The cook had tied a life-belt around himself in order to get even the warmth which this clumsy cork contrivance could donate, and he seemed almost stove-like when a rower, whose teeth invariably chattered wildly as soon as he ceased his labor, dropped down to sleep.

The correspondent, as he rowed, looked down at the two men sleeping under foot. The cook's arm was around the oiler's shoulders, and, with their fragmentary clothing and haggard faces, they were the babes of the sea, a grotesque rendering of the old babes in the wood.

Later he must have grown stupid at his work, for suddenly there was a growling of water, and a crest came with a roar and a swash into the boat, and it was a wonder that it did not set the cook afloat in his life-belt. The cook continued to sleep, but the oiler sat up, blinking his eyes and shaking with the new cold.

"Oh, I'm awful sorry, Billie," said the correspondent, contritely.

"That's all right, old boy," said the oiler, and lay down again and was asleep.

Presently it seemed that even the captain dozed, and the correspondent thought that he was the one man afloat on all the oceans. The wind had a voice as it came over the waves, and it was sadder than the end.

There was a long, loud swishing astern of the boat, and a gleaming trail of phosphorescence, like blue flame, was furrowed on the black waters. It might have been made by a monstrous knife.

Then there came a stillness, while the correspondent breathed with the open mouth and looked at the sea.

Suddenly there was another swish and another long flash of bluish light, and this time it was alongside the boat, and might almost have been reached with an oar. The correspondent saw an enormous fin speed like a shadow through the water, hurling the crystalline spray and leaving the long glowing trail.

The correspondent looked over his shoulder at the captain. His face was hidden, and he seemed to be asleep. He looked at the babes of the sea. They certainly were asleep. So, being bereft of sympathy, he leaned a little way to one side and swore softly into the sea.

But the thing did not then leave the vicinity of the boat. Ahead or astern, on one side or the other, at intervals long or short, fled the long sparkling streak, and there was to be heard the whirroo of the dark fin. The speed and power of the thing were greatly to be admired. It cut the water like a gigantic and keen projectile.

The presence of this biding thing did not affect the man with the same horror that it would if he had been a picnicker. He simply looked at the sea dully and swore in an undertone.

Nevertheless, it is true that he did not wish to be alone with the thing. He wished one of his companions to awaken by chance and keep him company with it. But the captain hung motionless over the water-jar and the oiler and the cook in the bottom of the boat were plunged in slumber.

VI

"If I am going to be drowned—if I am going to be drowned—if I am going to be drowned, why, in the name of the seven mad gods who rule the sea, was I allowed to come thus far and contemplate sand and trees?"

During this dismal night, it may be remarked that a man would conclude that it was really the intention of the seven mad gods to drown him, despite the abominable injustice of it. For it was certainly an abominable injustice to drown a man who had worked so hard, so hard. The man felt it would be a crime most unnatural. Other people had drowned at sea since galleys swarmed with painted sails, but still—

When it occurs to a man that nature does not regard him as important, and that she feels she would not maim the universe by disposing of him, he at first wishes to throw bricks at the temple, and he hates deeply the fact that there are no bricks and no temples. Any visible expression of nature would surely be pelleted with his jeers.

Then, if there be no tangible thing to hoot he feels, perhaps, the desire to confront a personification and indulge in pleas, bowed to one knee, and with hands supplicant, saying: "Yes, but I love myself."

A high cold star on a winter's night is the word he feels that she says to him. Thereafter he knows the pathos of his situation.

The men in the dingey had not discussed these matters, but each had, no doubt, reflected upon them in silence and according to his mind. There was seldom any expression upon their faces save the general one of complete weariness. Speech was devoted to the business of the boat.

To chime the notes of his emotion, a verse mysteriously entered the correspondent's head. He had even forgotten that he had forgotten this verse, but it suddenly was in his mind.

A soldier of the Legion lay dying in Algiers,
There was lack of woman's nursing, there was dearth of woman's tears;
But a comrade stood beside him, and he took that comrade's hand,
And he said: "I never more shall see my own, my native land."

In his childhood, the correspondent had been made acquainted with the fact that a soldier of the Legion lay dying in Algiers, but he had never regarded it as important. Myriads of his school-fellows had informed him of the soldier's plight, but the dinning had naturally ended by making him perfectly indifferent. He had never considered it his affair that a soldier of the Legion lay dying in Algiers, nor had it appeared to him as a matter for sorrow. It was less to him than the breaking of a pencil's point.

Now, however, it quaintly came to him as a human, living thing. It was no longer merely a picture of a few throes in the breast of a poet, meanwhile drinking tea and warming his feet at the grate; it was an actuality—stern, mournful, and fine.

The correspondent plainly saw the soldier. He lay on the sand with his feet out straight and still. While his pale left hand was upon his chest in an attempt to thwart the going of his life, the blood came between his fingers. In the far Algerian distance, a city of low square forms was set against a sky that was faint with the last sunset hues. The correspondent, plying the oars and dreaming of the slow and slower movements of the lips of the soldier, was moved by a profound and perfectly impersonal comprehension. He was sorry for the soldier of the Legion who lay dying in Algiers.

The thing which had followed the boat and waited had evidently grown bored at the delay. There was no longer to be heard the slash of the cut-water, and there was no longer the flame of the long trail. The light in the north still glimmered, but it was apparently no nearer to the boat. Sometimes the boom of the surf rang in the correspondent's ears, and he turned the craft seaward then and rowed harder. Southward, some one had evidently built a watch-fire on the beach. It was too low and too far to be seen, but it made a shimmering, roseate reflection upon the bluff back of it, and this could be discerned from the boat. The wind came stronger, and sometimes a wave suddenly raged out like a mountain-cat and there was to be seen the sheen and sparkle of a broken crest.

The captain, in the bow, moved on his water-jar and sat erect. "Pretty long night," he observed to the correspondent. He looked at the shore. "Those life-saving people take their time."

"Did you see that shark playing around?"

"Yes, I saw him. He was a big fellow, all right."

"Wish I had known you were awake."

Later the correspondent spoke into the bottom of the boat.

"Billie!" There was a slow and gradual disentanglement. "Billie, will you spell me?"

"Sure," said the oiler.

As soon as the correspondent touched the cold comfortable sea-water in the bottom of the boat, and had huddled close to the cook's life-belt he was deep in sleep, despite the fact that his teeth played all the popular airs. This sleep was so good to him that it was but a moment before he heard a voice call his name in a tone that demonstrated the last stages of exhaustion. "Will you spell me?"

"Sure, Billie."

The light in the north had mysteriously vanished, but the correspondent took his course from the wide-awake captain.

Later in the night they took the boat farther out to sea, and the captain directed the cook to take one oar at the stern and keep the boat facing the seas. He was to call out if he should hear the thunder of the surf. This plan enabled the oiler and the correspondent to get respite together. "We'll give those boys a chance to get into shape again," said the captain. They curled down and, after a few preliminary chatterings and trembles, slept once more the dead sleep. Neither knew they had bequeathed to the cook the company of another shark, or perhaps the same shark.

As the boat caroused on the waves, spray occasionally bumped over the side and gave them a fresh soaking, but this had no power to break their repose. The ominous slash of the wind and the water affected them as it would have affected mummies.

"Boys," said the cook, with the notes of every reluctance in his voice, "she's drifted in pretty close. I guess one of you had better take her to sea again." The correspondent, aroused, heard the crash of the toppled crests.

As he was rowing, the captain gave him some whiskey and water, and this steadied the chills out of him. "If I ever get ashore and anybody shows me even a photograph of an oar—"

At last there was a short conversation.

"Billie. . . . Billie, will you spell me?"

"Sure," said the oiler.

VII

When the correspondent again opened his eyes, the sea and the sky were each of the gray hue of the dawning. Later, carmine and gold was painted upon the waters. The morning appeared finally, in its splendor, with a sky of pure blue, and the sunlight flamed on the tips of the waves.

On the distant dunes were set many little black cottages, and a tall white wind-mill reared above them. No man, nor dog, nor bicycle appeared on the beach. The cottages might have formed a deserted village.

The voyagers scanned the shore. A conference was held in the boat. "Well," said the captain, "if no help is coming, we might better try a run through the surf right away. If we stay out here much longer we will be too weak to do anything for ourselves at all." The others silently acquiesced in this reasoning. The boat was headed for the beach. The correspondent wondered if none ever ascended the tall wind-tower, and if then they never looked seaward. This tower was a giant, standing with its back to the plight of the ants. It represented in a degree, to the correspondent, the serenity of nature amid the struggles of the individual—nature in the wind, and nature in the vision of men. She did not seem cruel to him then, nor beneficent, nor treacherous, nor wise. But she was indifferent, flatly indifferent. It is, perhaps, plausible that a man in this situation, impressed with the unconcern of the universe, should see the innumerable flaws of his life and have them taste wickedly in his mind and wish for another chance. A distinction between right and wrong seems absurdly clear to him, then, in this new ignorance of the grave-edge, and he understands that if he were given another opportunity he would mend his conduct and his words, and be better and brighter during an introduction, or at a tea.

"Now, boys," said the captain, "she is going to swamp sure. All we can do is to work her in as far as possible, and then when she swamps, pile out and scramble for the beach. Keep cool now, and don't jump until she swamps sure."

The oiler took the oars. Over his shoulders he scanned the surf. "Captain," he said, "I think I'd better bring her about, and keep her head-on to the seas and back her in."

"All right, Billie," said the captain. "Back her in." The oiler swung the boat then and, seated in the stern, the cook and the correspondent were obliged to look over their shoulders to contemplate the lonely and indifferent shore.

The monstrous inshore rollers heaved the boat high until the men were again enabled to see the white sheets of water scudding up the slanted beach. "We won't get in very close," said the captain. Each time a man could wrest his attention from the rollers, he turned his glance toward the shore, and in the expression of the eyes during this contemplation there was a singular quality. The correspondent, observing the others, knew that they were not afraid, but the full meaning of their glances was shrouded.

As for himself, he was too tired to grapple fundamentally with the fact. He tried to coerce his mind into thinking of it, but the mind was dominated at this time by the muscles, and the muscles said they did not care. It merely occurred to him that if he should drown it would be a shame.

There were no hurried words, no pallor, no plain agitation. The men simply looked at the shore. "Now, remember to get well clear of the boat when you jump," said the captain.

Seaward the crest of a roller suddenly fell with a thunderous crash, and the long white comber came roaring down upon the boat.

"Steady now," said the captain. The men were silent. They turned their eyes from the shore to the comber and waited. The boat slid up the incline, leaped at the furious top, bounced over it, and swung down the long back of the wave. Some water had been shipped and the cook bailed it out.

But the next crest crashed also. The tumbling boiling flood of white water caught the boat and whirled it almost perpendicular. Water swarmed in from all sides. The correspondent had his hands on the gunwale at this time, and when the water entered at that place he swiftly withdrew his fingers, as if he objected to wetting them.

The little boat, drunken with this weight of water, reeled and snuggled deeper into the sea.

"Bail her out, cook! Bail her out," said the captain.

"All right, Captain," said the cook.

"Now boys, the next one will do for us, sure," said the oiler. "Mind to jump clear of the boat."

The third wave moved forward, huge, furious, implacable. It fairly swallowed the dingey, and almost simultaneously the men tumbled into the sea. A piece of life-belt had lain in the bottom of the boat, and as the correspondent went overboard he held this to his chest with his left hand.

The January water was icy, and he reflected immediately that it was colder than he had expected to find it off the coast of Florida. This appeared to his dazed mind as a fact important enough to be noted at the time. The coldness of the water was sad; it was tragic. This fact was somehow so mixed and confused with his opinion of his own situation that it seemed almost a proper reason for tears. The water was cold.

When he came to the surface he was conscious of little but the noisy water. Afterward he saw his companions in the sea. The oiler was ahead in the race. He was swimming strongly and rapidly. Off to the correspondent's left, the cook's great white and corked back bulged out of the water, and in the rear the captain was hanging with his one good hand to the keel of the overturned dingey.

There is a certain immovable quality to a shore, and the correspondent wondered at it amid the confusion of the sea.

It seemed also very attractive, but the correspondent knew that it was a long journey, and he paddled leisurely. The piece of life-preserver lay under him, and sometimes he whirled down the incline of a wave as if he were on a hand-sled.

But finally he arrived at a place in the sea where travel was beset with difficulty. He did not pause swimming to inquire what manner of current had caught him, but there his progress ceased. The shore was set before him like a bit of scenery on a stage, and he looked at it and understood with his eyes each detail of it.

As the cook passed, much farther to the left, the captain was calling to him, "Turn over on your back, cook! Turn over on your back and use the oar."

"All right, sir." The cook turned on his back, and, paddling with an oar, went ahead as if he were a canoe.

Presently the boat also passed to the left of the correspondent with the captain clinging with one hand to the keel. He would have appeared like a man raising himself to look over a board fence, if it were not for the extraordinary gymnastics of the boat. The correspondent marvelled that the captain could still hold to it.

They passed on, nearer to shore — the oiler, the cook, the captain — and following them went the water-jar, bouncing gayly over the seas.

The correspondent remained in the grip of this strange new enemy — a current. The shore, with its white slope of sand and its green bluff, topped with little silent cottages, was spread like a picture before him. It was very near to him then, but he was impressed as one who in a gallery looks at a scene from Brittany or Holland.

He thought: "I am going to drown? Can it be possible? Can it be possible? Can it be possible?" Perhaps an individual must consider his own death to be the final phenomenon of nature.

But later a wave perhaps whirled him out of his small deadly current, for he found suddenly that he could again make progress toward the shore. Later still, he was aware that the captain, clinging with one hand to the keel of the dingey, had his face turned away from the shore and toward him, and was calling his name. "Come to the boat! Come to the boat!"

In his struggle to reach the captain and the boat, he reflected that when one gets properly wearied, drowning must really be a comfortable arrangement, a cessation of hostilities accompanied by a large degree of relief, and he was glad of it, for the main thing in his mind for some moments had been the horror of the temporary agony. He did not wish to be hurt.

Presently he saw a man running along the shore. He was undressing with most remarkable speed. Coat, trousers, shirt, everything flew magically off him.

"Come to the boat," called the captain.

"All right, Captain." As the correspondent paddled, he saw the captain let himself down to bottom and leave the boat. Then the correspondent performed his one little marvel of the voyage. A large wave caught him and flung him with ease and supreme speed completely over the boat and far beyond it. It struck him even then as an event in gymnastics, and a true miracle of the sea. An overturned boat in the surf is not a plaything to a swimming man.

The correspondent arrived in water that reached only to his waist, but his condition did not enable him to stand for more than a moment. Each wave knocked him into a heap, and the under-tow pulled at him.

Then he saw the man who had been running and undressing, and undressing and running, come bounding into the water. He dragged ashore the cook, and then waded toward the captain, but the captain waved him away, and sent him to the correspondent. He was naked, naked as a tree in winter, but a halo was about his head, and he shone like a saint. He gave a strong pull, and a long drag, and a bully heave at the correspondent's hand. The correspondent, schooled in the minor formulae, said: "Thanks, old man." But suddenly the man cried: "What's that?" He pointed a swift finger. The correspondent said: "Go."

In the shallows, face downward, lay the oiler. His forehead touched sand that was periodically, between each wave, clear of the sea.

The correspondent did not know all that transpired afterward. When he achieved safe ground he fell, striking the sand with each particular part of his body. It was as if he had dropped from a roof, but the thud was grateful to him.

It seems that instantly the beach was populated with men with blankets, clothes, and flasks, and women with coffee-pots and all the remedies sacred to their minds. The welcome of the land to the men from the sea was warm and generous, but a still and dripping shape was carried slowly up the beach, and the land's welcome for it could only be the different and sinister hospitality of the grave.

When it came night, the white waves paced to and fro in the moonlight, and the wind brought the sound of the great sea's voice to the men on shore, and they felt that they could then be interpreters.

[1897]

QUESTIONS

1. What does the first sentence of the story mean for the characters involved? Does it mean something else for the reader?
2. Why does only one of the four men in the boat have a proper name? In what way does Crane delineate his characters and their differences?
3. What are the naturalistic components (and passages) of Crane's story?
4. How is impressionism used throughout "The Open Boat?"

Isak Dinesen (Karen Blixen)

(1882–1962)

Denmark

As critic David Lehmann observed of Isak Dinesen, "She likened herself to Scheherazade—and fully lived up to the name. . . . She led a life as wildly improbable and flamboyantly romantic as her exotic and spell-binding tales." Born Karen Christentze Dinesen in Rungsted, Denmark, she was the daughter of an army officer whose suicide when she was 10 cast a long shadow over her life. She left Denmark to study English at Oxford and then to study painting in Copenhagen, Paris, and Rome.

Dinesen did not take up the writing for which she is known until she was nearly 50. In the meantime, in 1914 she married her second cousin, Baron Bror Blixen-Finecke, a big-game hunter and the twin brother of the man whom she really loved. Together they went to British East Africa (now Kenya) to manage a coffee plantation. Eventually separated from Blixen—but not before she had contracted syphilis from him—Dinesen managed the plantation on her own until the falling price of coffee made it unprofitable. By then her companion and lover, Denys Finch-Hatton, had died in a plane crash and she left Kenya, feeling that the best years of her life were over.

Dinesen returned to Denmark to support herself by writing, publishing her first collection of tales, *Seven Gothic Tales*, in 1934, under the pseudonym by which she is now known: *Isak* is Hebrew for "one who laughs." Despite the poor health that plagued her for the last 15 years of her life (the legacy of syphilis), she continued to write. *Out of Africa* (1937), a reminiscence of her life in Kenya, solidified her reputation in America and Europe; it was followed by *Winter's Tales* (1942) and *Last Tales* (1957).

Describing the genesis of her tales in a *Paris Review* interview, Dinesen commented, "I begin . . . with a flavor of the tale. Then I find the characters and they take over. They make the design, I simply permit them their liberty." Moreover, she consciously defined herself as a storyteller and spinner of tales:

> I belong to an ancient, idle, wild and useless tribe, perhaps I am even one of the last members of it, who, for many thousands of years, in all countries and parts of the world, has, now and again, stayed for a time among hard-working honest people in real life, and sometimes has thus been fortunate enough to create another sort of reality for them, which in some way or another, has satisfied them. I am a storyteller.

In distinct contrast to the literary traditions of her day, Isak Dinesen wrote tales that depend on exotic and archaic settings and supernatural circumstances that direct her characters—and her readers—to ponder the workings of destiny.

The Sailor-Boy's Tale

The barque *Charlotte* was on her way from Marseille to Athens, in grey weather, on a high sea, after three days' heavy gale. A small sailor-boy, named Simon, stood on the wet, swinging deck, held on to a shroud, and looked up towards the drifting clouds, and to the upper top-gallant yard of the main-mast.

A bird, that had sought refuge upon the mast, had got her feet entangled in some loose tackle-yarn of the halliard, and, high up there, struggled to get free. The boy on the deck could see her wings flapping and her head turning from side to side.

Through his own experience of life he had come to the conviction that in this world everyone must look after himself, and expect no help from others. But the mute, deadly fight kept him fascinated for more than an hour. He wondered what kind of bird it would be. These last days a number of birds had come to settle in the barque's rigging: swallows, quails, and a pair of peregrine falcons; he believed that this bird was a peregrine falcon. He remembered how, many years ago, in his own country and near his home, he had once seen a peregrine falcon quite close, sitting on a stone and flying straight up from it. Perhaps this was the same bird. He thought: "That bird is like me. Then she was there, and now she is here."

At that a fellow-feeling rose in him, a sense of common tragedy; he stood looking at the bird with his heart in his mouth. There were none of the sailors about to make fun of him; he began to think out how he might go up by the shrouds to help the falcon out. He brushed his hair back and pulled up his sleeves, gave the deck round him a great glance, and climbed up. He had to stop a couple of times in the swaying rigging.

It was indeed, he found when he got to the top of the mast, a peregrine falcon. As his head was on a level with hers, she gave up her struggle, and looked at him with a pair of angry, desperate yellow eyes. He had to take hold of her with one hand while he got his knife out, and cut off the tackle-yarn. He was scared as he looked down, but at the same time he felt that he had been ordered up by nobody, but that this was his own venture, and this gave him a proud, steadying sensation, as if the sea and the sky, the ship, the bird and himself were all one. Just as he had freed the falcon, she hacked him in the thumb, so that the blood ran, and he nearly let her go. He grew angry with her, and gave her a clout on the head, then he put her inside his jacket, and climbed down again.

When he reached the deck the mate and the cook were standing there, looking up; they roared to him to ask what he had had to do in the mast. He was so tired that the tears were in his eyes. He took the falcon out and showed her to them, and she kept still within his hands. They laughed and walked off. Simon set the falcon down, stood back and watched her. After a while he reflected that she might not be able to get up from the slippery deck, so he caught her once more, walked away with her and placed her upon a bolt of canvas. A little after she began to trim her feathers, made two or three sharp jerks forward, and then suddenly flew off. The boy could follow her flight above the troughs of the grey sea. He thought: "There flies my falcon."

When the *Charlotte* came home, Simon signed aboard another ship, and two years later he was a light hand on the schooner *Hebe* lying at Bodø, high up on the coast of Norway, to buy herrings.

To the great herring-markets of Bodø ships came together from all corners of the world; here were Swedish, Finnish and Russian boats, a forest of masts, and on shore a turbulent, irregular display of life, with many languages spoken, and might fights. On the shore booths had been set up, and the Lapps, small yellow people, noiseless in their movements, with watchful eyes, whom Simon had never seen before, came down to sell bead-embroidered leather-goods. It was April, the sky and the sea were so clear that it was difficult to hold one's eyes up against them—salt, infinitely wide, and filled with bird-shrieks—as if someone were incessantly whetting invisible knives, on all sides, high up in Heaven.

Simon was amazed at the lightness of these April evenings. He knew no geography, and did not assign it to the latitude, but he took it as a sign of an unwonted good-will in the Universe, a favour. Simon had been small for his age all his life, but this last winter he had grown, and had become strong of limb. That good luck, he felt, must spring from the very same source as the sweetness of the weather, from a new benevolence in the world. He had been in need of such encouragement, for he was timid by nature; now he asked for no more. The rest he felt to be his own affair. He went about slowly, and proudly.

One evening he was ashore with land-leave, and walked up to the booth of a small Russian trader, a Jew who sold gold watches. All the sailors knew that his watches were made from bad metal, and would not go, still they bought them, and paraded them about. Simon looked at these watches for a long time, but did not buy. The old Jew had divers goods in his shop, and amongst others a case of oranges. Simon had tasted oranges on his journeys; he bought one and took it with him. He meant to go up on a hill, from where he could see the sea, and suck it there.

As he walked on, and had got to the outskirts of the place, he saw a little girl in a blue frock, standing at the other side of a fence and looking at him. She was thirteen or fourteen years old, as slim as an eel, but with a round, clear, freckled face, and a pair of long plaits. The two looked at one another.

"Who are you looking out for?" Simon asked, to say something. The girl's face broke into an ecstatic, presumptuous smile. "For the man I am going to marry, of course," she said. Something in her countenance made the boy confident and happy; he grinned a little at her. "That will perhaps be me," he said. "Ha, ha," said the girl, "he is a few years older than you, I can tell you." "Why," said Simon, "you are not grown up yourself." The little girl shook her head solemnly. "Nay," she said, "but when I grow up I will be exceedingly beautiful, and wear brown shoes with heels, and a hat." "Will you have an orange?" asked Simon, who could give her none of the things she had named. She looked at the orange and at him. "They are very good to eat," said he. "Why do you not eat it yourself then?" she asked. "I have eaten so many already," said he, "when I was in Athens. Here I had to pay a mark for it." "What is your name?" asked she. "My name is Simon," said he. "What is yours?" "Nora," said the girl. "What do you want for your orange now, Simon?"

When he heard his name in her mouth Simon grew bold. "Will you give me a kiss for the orange?" he asked. Nora looked at him gravely for a moment. "Yes," she said, "I should not mind giving you a kiss." He grew as warm as if he had been running quickly. When she stretched out her hand for the orange he took hold of it. At that moment somebody in the house called out for her. "That is my father," said she, and tried to give him back the orange, but he would not take it. "Then come again tomorrow," she said quickly, "then I will give you a kiss." At that she slipped off. He stood and looked after her, and a little later went back to his ship.

Simon was not in the habit of making plans for the future, and now he did not know whether he would be going back to her or not.

The following evening he had to stay aboard, as the other sailors were going ashore, and he did not mind that either. He meant to sit on the deck with the ship's dog, Balthasar, and to practise upon a concertina that he had purchased some time ago. The pale evening was all round him, the sky was faintly roseate, the sea was quite calm, like milk-and-water, only in the wake of the boats going inshore it broke into streaks of vivid indigo. Simon sat and played; after a while his own music began to speak to him so strongly that he stopped, got up and looked upwards. Then he saw that the full moon was sitting high on the sky.

The sky was so light that she hardly seemed needed there; it was as if she had turned up by a caprice of her own. She was round, demure and presumptuous. At that he knew that he must go ashore, whatever it was to cost him. But he did not know how to get away, since the others had taken the yawl with them. He stood on the deck for a long time, a small lonely figure of a sailor-boy on a boat, when he caught sight of a yawl coming in from a ship farther out, and hailed her. He found that it was the Russian crew from a boat named *Anna*, going ashore. When he could make himself understood to them, they took him with them; they first asked him for money for his fare, then, laughing, gave it back to him. He thought: "These people will be believing that I am going in to town, wenching." And then he felt, with some pride, that they were right, although at the same time they were infinitely wrong, and knew nothing about anything.

When they came ashore they invited him to come in and drink in their company, and he would not refuse, because they had helped him. One of the Russians was a giant, as big as a bear; he told Simon that his name was Ivan. He got drunk at once, and then fell upon the boy with a bear-like affection, pawed him, smiled and laughed into his face, made him a present of a gold watch-chain, and kissed him on both cheeks. At that Simon reflected that he also ought to give Nora a present when they met again, and as soon as he could get away from the Russians he walked up to a booth that he knew of, and bought a small blue silk handkerchief, the same colour as her eyes.

It was Saturday evening, and there were many people amongst the houses; they came in long rows, some of them singing, all keen to have some fun that night. Simon, in the midst of this rich, bawling life under the clear moon, felt his head light with the flight from the ship and the strong drinks. He crammed the handkerchief in his pocket; it was silk, which he had never touched before, a present for his girl.

He could not remember the path up to Nora's house, lost his way, and came back to where he had started. Then he grew deadly afraid that he should be too late, and began to run. In a small passage between two wooden huts he ran straight into a big man, and found that it was Ivan once more. The Russian folded his arms round him and held him. "Good! Good!" he cried in high glee, "I have found you, my little chicken. I have looked for you everywhere, and poor Ivan has wept because he lost his friend." "Let me go, Ivan," cried Simon. "Oho," said Ivan, "I shall go with you and get you what you want. My heart and my money are all yours, all yours; I have been seventeen years old myself, a little lamb of God, and I want to be so again tonight." "Let me go," cried Simon, "I am

in a hurry." Ivan held him so that it hurt, and patted him with his other hand. "I feel it, I feel it," he said. "Now trust to me, my little friend. Nothing shall part you and me. I hear the others coming; we will have such a night together as you will remember when you are an old grandpapa."

Suddenly he crushed the boy to him, like a bear that carries off a sheep. The odious sensation of male bodily warmth and the bulk of a man close to him made the lean boy mad. He thought of Nora waiting, like a slender ship in the dim air, and of himself, here, in the hot embrace of a hairy animal. He struck Ivan with all his might. "I shall kill you, Ivan," he cried out, "if you do not let me go." "Oh, you will be thankful to me later on," said Ivan, and began to sing. Simon fumbled in his pocket for his knife, and got it opened. He could not lift his hand, but he drove the knife, furiously, in under the big man's arm. Almost immediately he felt the blood spouting out, and running down in his sleeve. Ivan stopped short in the song, let go his hold of the boy and gave two long deep grunts. The next second he tumbled down on his knees. "Poor Ivan, poor Ivan," he groaned. He fell straight on his face. At that moment Simon heard the other sailors coming along, singing, in the by-street.

He stood still for a minute, wiped his knife, and watched the blood spread into a dark pool underneath the big body. Then he ran. As he stopped for a second to choose his way, he heard the sailors behind him scream out over their dead comrade. He thought: "I must get down to the sea, where I can wash my hand." But at the same time he ran the other way. After a little while he found himself on the path that he had walked on the day before, and it seemed as familiar to him, as if he had walked it many hundred times in his life.

He slackened his pace to look round, and suddenly saw Nora standing on the other side of the fence; she was quite close to him when he caught sight of her in the moonlight. Wavering and out of breath he sank down on his knees. For a moment he could not speak. The little girl looked down at him. "Good evening, Simon," she said in her small coy voice. "I have waited for you a long time," and after a moment she added: "I have eaten your orange."

"Oh, Nora," cried the boy. "I have killed a man." She stared at him, but did not move. "Why did you kill a man?" she asked after a moment. "To get here," said Simon. "Because he tried to stop me. But he was my friend." Slowly he got on to his feet. "He loved me!" the boy cried out, and at that burst into tears. "Yes," said she slowly and thoughtfully. "Yes, because you must be here in time." "Can you hide me?" he asked. "For they are after me." "Nay," said Nora, "I cannot hide you. For my father is the parson here at Bodø, and he would be sure to hand you over to them, if he knew that you had killed a man." "Then," said Simon, "give me something to wipe my hands on." "What is the matter with your hands?" she asked, and took a little step forward. He stretched out his hands to her. "Is that your own blood?" she asked. "No," said he, "it is his." She took the step back again. "Do you hate me now?" he asked. "No, I do not hate you," said she. "But do put your hands at your back."

As he did so she came up close to him, at the other side of the fence, and clasped her arms round his neck. She pressed her young body to his, and kissed him tenderly. He felt her face, cool as the moonlight, upon his own, and when she released him, his head swam, and he did not know if the kiss had lasted a second or an hour. Nora stood up straight, her eyes wide open. "Now," she said slowly and proudly, "I promise you that I will never marry anybody, as long as I

live." The boy kept standing with his hands on his back, as if she had tied them there. "And now," she said, "you must run, for they are coming." They looked at one another. "Do not forget Nora," said she. He turned and ran.

He leapt over a fence, and when he was down amongst the houses he walked. He did not know at all where to go. As he came to a house, from where music and noise streamed out, he slowly went through the door. The room was full of people; they were dancing in here. A lamp hung from the ceiling, and shone down on them; the air was thick and brown with the dust rising from the floor. There were some women in the room, but many of the men danced with each other, and gravely or laughingly stamped the floor. A moment after Simon had come in the crowd withdrew to the walls to clear the floor for two sailors, who were showing a dance from their own country.

Simon thought: "Now, very soon, the men from the boat will come round to look for their comrade's murderer, and from my hands they will know that I have done it." These five minutes during which he stood by the wall of the dancing-room, in the midst of the gay, sweating dancers, were of great significance to the boy. He himself felt it, as if during this time he grew up, and became like other people. He did not entreat his destiny, nor complain. Here he was, he had killed a man, and had kissed a girl. He did not demand any more from life, nor did life now demand more from him. He was Simon, a man like the men round him, and going to die, as all men are going to die.

He only became aware of what was going on outside him, when he saw that a woman had come in, and was standing in the midst of the cleared floor, looking round her. She was a short, broad old woman, in the clothes of the Lapps, and she took her stand with such majesty and fierceness as if she owned the whole place. It was obvious that most of the people knew her, and were a little afraid of her, although a few laughed; the din of the dancing-room stopped when she spoke.

"Where is my son?" she asked in a high shrill voice, like a bird's. The next moment her eyes fell on Simon himself, and she steered through the crowd, which opened up before her, stretched out her old skinny, dark hand, and took him by the elbow. "Come home with me now," she said. "You need not dance here tonight. You may be dancing a high enough dance soon."

Simon drew back, for he thought that she was drunk. But as she looked him straight in the face with her yellow eyes, it seemed to him that he had met her before, and that he might do well in listening to her. The old woman pulled him with her across the floor, and he followed her without a word. "Do not birch your boy too badly, Sunniva," one of the men in the room cried to her. "He has done no harm, he only wanted to look at the dance."

At the same moment as they came out through the door, there was an alarm in the street, a flock of people came running down it, and one of them, as he turned into the house, knocked against Simon, looked at him and the old woman, and ran on.

While the two walked along the street, the old woman lifted up her skirt, and put the hem of it into the boy's hand. "Wipe your hand on my skirt," she said. They had not gone far before they came to a small wooden house, and stopped; the door to it was so low that they must bend to get through it. As the Lapp-woman went in before Simon, still holding on to his arm, the boy looked up for a moment. The night had grown misty; there was a wide ring round the moon.

The old woman's room was narrow and dark, with but one small window to it; a lantern stood on the floor and lighted it up dimly. It was all filled with reindeer skins and wolf skins, and with reindeer horn, such as the Lapps use to make their carved buttons and knife-handles, and the air in here was rank and stifling. As soon as they were in, the woman turned to Simon, took hold of his head, and with her crooked fingers parted his hair and combed it down in Lapp fashion. She clapped a Lapp cap on him and stood back to glance at him. "Sit down on my stool, now," she said. "But first take out your knife." She was so commanding in voice and manner that the boy could not but choose to do as she told him; he sat down on the stool, and he could not take his eyes off her face, which was flat and brown, and as if smeared with dirt in its net of fine wrinkles. As he sat there he heard many people come along outside, and stop by the house; then someone knocked at the door, waited a moment and knocked again. The old woman stood and listened, as still as a mouse.

"Nay," said the boy and got up. "This is no good, for it is me that they are after. It will be better for you to let me go out to them." "Give me your knife," said she. When he handed it to her, she stuck it straight into her thumb, so that the blood spouted out, and she let it drip all over her skirt. "Come in, then," she cried.

The door opened, and two of the Russian sailors came and stood in the opening; there were more people outside. "Has anybody come in here?" they asked. "We are after a man who has killed our mate, but he has run away from us. Have you seen or heard anybody this way?" The old Lapp-woman turned upon them, and her eyes shone like gold in the lamplight. "Have I seen or heard anyone?" she cried, "I have heard you shriek murder all over the town. You frightened me, and my poor silly boy there, so that I cut my thumb as I was ripping the skin-rug that I sew. The boy is too scared to help me, and the rug is all ruined. I shall make you pay me for that. If you are looking for a murderer, come in and search my house for me, and I shall know you when we meet again." She was so furious that she danced where she stood, and jerked her head like an angry bird of prey.

The Russian came in, looked round the room, and at her and her blood-stained hand and skirt. "Do not put a curse on us now, Sunniva," he said timidly. "We know that you can do many things when you like. Here is a mark to pay you for the blood you have spilled." She stretched out her hand, and he placed a piece of money in it. She spat on it. "Then go, and there shall be no bad blood between us," said Sunniva, and shut the door after them. She stuck her thumb in her mouth, and chuckled a little.

The boy got up from his stool, stood straight up before her and stared into her face. He felt as if he were swaying high up in the air, with but a small hold. "Why have you helped me?" he asked her. "Do you not know?" she answered. "Have you not recognised me yet? But you will remember the peregrine falcon which was caught in the tackle-yarn of your boat, the *Charlotte*, as she sailed in the Mediterranean. That day you climbed up by the shrouds of the top-gallant-mast to help her out, in a stiff wind, and with a high sea. That falcon was me. We Lapps often fly in such a manner, to see the world. When I first met you I was on my way to Africa, to see my younger sister and her children. She is a falcon too, when she chooses. By that time she was living at Takaunga, within an old ruined tower, which down there they call a minaret." She swathed a corner of her skirt round her thumb, and bit at it. "We do not forget," she said. "I hacked your thumb, when you took hold of me; it is only fair that I should cut my thumb for you tonight."

She came close to him, and gently rubbed her two brown, claw-like fingers against his forehead. "So you are a boy," she said, "who will kill a man rather than be late to meet your sweetheart? We hold together, the females of this earth. I shall mark your forehead now, so that the girls will know of that, when they look at you, and they will like you for it." She played with the boy's hair, and twisted it round her finger.

"Listen now, my little bird," said she. "My great grandson's brother-in-law is lying with his boat by the landing-place at this moment; he is to take a consignment of skins out to a Danish boat. He will bring you back to your boat, in time, before your mate comes. The *Hebe* is sailing tomorrow morning, is it not so? But when you are aboard, give him back my cap for me." She took up his knife, wiped it in her skirt and handed it to him. "Here is your knife," she said. "You will stick it into no more men; you will not need to, for from now you will sail the seas like a faithful seaman. We have enough trouble with our sons as it is."

The bewildered boy began to stammer his thanks to her. "Wait," said she, "I shall make you a cup of coffee, to bring back your wits, while I wash your jacket." She went and rattled an old copper kettle upon the fireplace. After a while she handed him a hot, strong, black drink in a cup without a handle to it. "You have drunk with Sunniva now," she said; "you have drunk down a little wisdom, so that in the future all your thoughts shall not fall like raindrops into the salt sea."

When he had finished and set down the cup, she led him to the door and opened it for him. He was surprised to see that it was almost clear morning. The house was so high up that the boy could see the sea from it, and a milky mist about it. He gave her his hand to say good-bye.

She stared into his face. "We do not forget," she said. "And you, you knocked me on the head there, high up in the mast. I shall give you that blow back." With that she smacked him on the ear as hard as she could, so that his head swam. "Now we are quits," she said, gave him a great, mischievous, shining glance, and a little push down the doorstep, and nodded to him.

In this way the sailor-boy got back to his ship, which was to sail the next morning, and lived to tell the story.

[1942]

QUESTIONS

1. In what ways does the story resemble a traditional folk legend or tale of enchantment? How does this form suit the events told in the story?
2. Does the fantastic quality enhance or detract from the story's effectiveness?
3. What kind of universe does the story presume or suggest? Why does Simon's impulsive murder of Ivan go unpunished?
4. Consider the structure of the story as a series of actions that are exactly balanced by other actions. How does this structure contribute to the theme and meaning of the story?

Birago Diop

(b. 1906)

Senegal

Birago Diop was born in Senegal, where he received part of his education at the Lycée Faidherbe in St. Louis. He furthered his studies in France, at the University of Toulouse, becoming a veterinary surgeon. We mention this fact because the narrator of "Sarzan" identifies himself as a veterinarian who has been in Europe yet clearly has managed to reconcile his traditional African background with Western culture in a way that Sarzan has not. "Sarzan," thus, posits an interesting dilemma: the story is told by someone who has presumably undergone many of the same cultural conflicts as the main character yet has apparently resolved them. One must ask, then, how relevant is the narrator's point of view to the story he tells? An appreciation for "Sarzan" is equally dependent on an understanding of animism—the belief in the power that one's ancestors have over the living. As you read the story, pay particular attention to the poems that Sarzan recites, his so-called babbling.

Birago Diop is the author of several volumes of short stories. "Sarzan" is from *Les Contes d'Amadou Koumba* (1947).

◆ Sarzan ◆

It was hard to distinguish the piles of ruins from the termite mounds, and only an ostrich shell, cracked and yellowed by the weather, still indicated at the tip of a tall column what once had been the *mirab* of the mosque El Hadj Omar's[1] warriors had built. The Toucouleur conqueror had shorn the hair and shaved the heads of the forbears of those who are now the village elders. He had decapitated those who would not submit to Koranic law. Once again, the village elders wear their hair in braids. The sacred woods long ago burnt by the fanatic Talibés have long since grown tall again, and still harbour the cult objects, pots whitened from the boiling of millet or browned by the clotted blood of sacrificed chickens and dogs.

Like grain felled at random beneath the flail, or ripe fruits that drop from branches filled with sap, whole families left Dougouba to form new villages, Dougoubanis. Some of the young people would go off to work in Segou, in Bamako, in Kayes, or Dakar; others went to work the Senegalese groundnut fields, returning when the harvest was in and the product had been shipped. All knew the root of their lives was still in Dougouba, which had long ago erased all traces of the Islamic hordes and returned to the teachings of the ancestors.

One son of Dougouba had ventured farther and for a longer time than any of the others: Thiemokho Keita.

From Dougouba he went to the local capital, from there to Kati, from Kati to

[1]*El Hadj Omar* Islamic conqueror of much of upper Senegal who died in 1864

Dakar, from Dakar to Casablanca, from Casablanca to Frejus, and then to Damascus. Leaving the Sudan to be a soldier, Thiemokho Keita had been trained in Senegal, fought in Morocco, stood guard in France, and patrolled in Lebanon. He returned to Dougouba a sergeant, catching a lift in my medical caravan.

I had been making my veterinarian's rounds in the heart of the Sudan when I met Sergeant Keita in a local administrator's office. He had just been discharged from the service and wanted to enlist in the local police, or to be taken on as an interpreter.

"No," the local commandant told him. "You can do more for the administration by returning to your village. You who have travelled so much and seen so much, you can teach the others something about how white men live. You'll 'civilize' them a bit. Say there, Doctor," he continued, turning to me, "since you're going in that direction, won't you take Keita with you? It will spare him the wear and tear of the road and save him some time. It's fifteen years he's been gone."

So we set out. The driver, the sergeant and I occupied the front seat of the little truck, while behind, the cooks, medical aides, driver's helper and civil guard were crowded together among the field kitchen, the camp bed and the cases of serum and vaccine. The sergeant told me about his life as a soldier, then as a noncommissioned officer. I heard about the Riff Wars from the viewpoint of a Sudanese rifleman; he talked about Marseille, Toulon, Frejus, Beirut. He seemed no longer to see the road in front of us. Rough as a corrugated tin room, it was paved with logs covered with a layer of clay, disintegrating into dust now because of the torrid heat and the extreme dryness. It was an unctuous oily dust that stuck to our faces like a yellow mask, making our teeth gritty and screening from our view the chattering baboons and frightened does that leaped about in our wake. Through the choking haze, Keita seemed to see once more the minarets of Fez, the teeming crowds of Marseille, the great tall buildings of France, the blue sea.

By noon we reached the town of Madougou, where the road ended. To reach Dougouba by nightfall, we took horses and bearers.

"When you come back this way again," Keita said, "you'll go all the way to Dougouba by car. Tomorrow I'm going to get started on a road."

The muffled rolling of a tom-tom announced that we were nearing the village. A grey mass of huts appeared, topped by the darker grey of three palm trees against a paler grey sky. The rumbling was accompanied now by the sharp sound of three notes on a flute. We were in Dougouba. I got down first and asked for the village chief.

"*Dougou-tigui*,[2] here is your son, the Sergeant Keita."

Thiemokho Keita jumped down from his horse. As if the sound of his shoes on the ground had been a signal, the drumming stopped and the flute was silent. The aged chief took Keita's two hands while other old men examined his arms, his shoulders, his decorations. Some old women ran up and began fingering the puttees at his knees. Tears shone on the dark faces, settling in the wrinkles that crossed their ritual scars. Everyone was saying:

"Keita, Keita, Keita!"

[2]*Dougou-tigui* honorific title

"Those," the old man quavered at last, "those who brought your steps back to our village on this day are generous and good."

It was in fact a day unlike other days in Dougouba. It was the day of the Kotéba, the day of the Testing.

The drum resumed its rumbling, pierced by the sharp whistles of the flute. Inside the circle of women, children, and grown men, bare-chested youngsters, each carrying a long branch of balazan wood, stripped clean and supple as a whip, were turning about to the rhythm of the tom-tom. In the centre of this moving circle, crouching with his knees and elbows on the ground, the flute player gave forth three notes, always the same. Above him a young man would come to stand, legs apart, arms spread in the shape of a cross, while the others, passing close to him, let their whips whistle. The blows fell on his chest, leaving a stripe wide as a thumb, sometimes breaking the skin. The sharp voice of the flute would go a note higher, the tom-tom would grow softer, as the whips whistled and the blood ran. Firelight gleamed on the black-brown body and light from the embers leaped to the tops of the palm trees, softly creaking in the evening wind. Kotéba! the test of endurance, the testing for insensibility to pain. The child who cries when he hurts himself is only a child; the child who cries when he is hurt will not make a man.

Kotéba! to offer one's back, receive the blow, turn around and give it back to someone else. Kotéba!

"This, these are still the ways of savages!"

I turned round, it was Sergeant Keita who had come to join me by the drum.

The ways of savages? This testing, which among other things produced men who were hard and tough! What was it that had enabled the forbears of these youngsters to march with enormous burdens on their heads for whole days without stopping? What had made Thiemokho Keita himself, and others like him, able to fight valiantly beneath skies where the sun itself is very often sickly, to labour with heavy packs on their backs, enduring cold, thirst, and hunger?

The ways of savages? Perhaps. But I was thinking that elsewhere, where I came from, we had left these initiations behind. For our adolescents there was no longer a 'house of men' where the body, the mind and the character were tempered; where the ancient *passines*, the riddles and conundrums, were learned by dint of beatings on the bent back and the held-out fingers, and where the *kassaks*, the age-old memory training songs whose words and wisdom descend to us from the dark nights, were assured their place in our heads by the heat of live coals that burned the palms of our hands. I was thinking that as far as I could see we had still gained nothing, that perhaps we had left these old ways behind without having caught up with the new ones.

The tom-tom murmured on, sustaining the piercing voice of the flute. The fires died and were born again. I went to the hut that had been prepared for me. Inside, mixed with the thick smell of *banco*—the dried clay kneaded with broken rotten straw that made the hut rainproof—a subtler odour hung, the fragrance of the dead, whose number, three, was indicated by animal horns fixed to the wall at the level of a man's height. For, in Dougouba, the cemetery too had disappeared, and the dead continued to live with the living. They were buried in the huts.

The sun was already warm when I took my leave, but Dougouba was still asleep: drunk, both from fatigue and from the millet beer that had circulated in calabashes from hand to mouth and mouth to hand the whole night long.

"Good bye," said Keita. "The next time you come there will be a road, I promise you."

The work in other sectors and localities kept me from returning to Dougouba until the following year.

It was late in the afternoon after a hard journey. The air seemed a thick mass, hot and sticky, that we pushed our way through with great effort.

Sergeant Keita had kept his word; the road went all the way to Dougouba. As in all the villages at the sound of the car a swarm of naked children appeared at the end of the road, their little bodies grey-white with dust, and on their heels came the reddish-brown dogs with cropped ears and bony flanks. In the midst of the children a man was gesticulating, waving a cow's tail attached to his right wrist. When the car stopped, I saw it was the sergeant, Thiemokho Keita. He wore a faded fatigue jacket, without buttons or stripes. Underneath were a *boubou* and pants made of strips of khaki-coloured cotton, like the ones worn by the village elders. His pants stopped above the knee and were held together with pieces of string. His puttees were in rags. He was barefoot but wore a *képi*[3] on his head.

"Keita!"

The children scattered like a volley of sparrows, chirping:

"Ayi! Ayi!" (No! No!)

Thiemokho Keita did not take my hand. He looked at me, but seemed not to see me. His gaze was so distant that I couldn't help turning around to see what his eyes were fixed upon through mine. Suddenly, agitating his cowtail, he began to cry out in a hoarse voice:

Listen to things
More often than beings
Hear the voice of fire
Hear the voice of water
Listen in the wind to
the sighs of the bush
This is the ancestors breathing.

"He's mad," said my driver, whom I silenced with a gesture. The sergeant was still chanting, in a strange, sing-song voice:

Those who are dead are not ever gone
They are in the darkness that grows lighter
And in the darkness that grows darker
The dead are not down in the earth
They are in the trembling of the trees
In the moaning of the woods
In the water that runs
In the water that sleeps
They are in the hut, they are in the crowd.

The dead are not dead.
Listen to things
More often than beings

[3]*képi* French: military cap

Hear the voice of fire
Hear the voice of water
Listen in the wind
To the bush that is sighing
This is the breathing of ancestors
Who have not gone away
Who are not under earth
Who are not really dead.

Those who are dead are not ever gone
They are in a woman's breast
In a child's wailing
and the log burning
in the moaning rock and
in the weeping grasses
in the forest in the home
The dead are not dead.

Hear the fire speak
Hear the water speak
Listen in the wind to
the bush that is sobbing
This is the ancestors breathing.

Each day they renew ancient bonds
Ancient bonds that hold fast
Binding our lot to their law
To the will of the spirits stronger than we are
Whose covenant binds us to life
Whose authority binds to their will
The will of the spirits that move
In the bed of the river, on the banks of the river
The breathing of ancestors
Wailing in the rocks and weeping in the grasses.

Spirits inhabit
the darkness that lightens, the darkness that darkens
the quivering tree, the murmuring wood
the running and the sleeping waters
Spirits much stronger than we are
The breathing of the dead who are not really dead
Of the dead who are not really gone
Of the dead now no more in the earth.
Listen to things
More often than beings. . . .

The children returned, circling round the old chief and the village elders. After the greetings, I asked what had happened to Sergeant Keita.

"Ayi! Ayi!" said the old men. "Ayi! Ayi!" echoed the children.

"No, not Keita!" said the old father, "Sarzan,[4] just Sarzan. We must not

[4]*Sarzan* a Senegalese pronunciation of *sergent*, the French for sergeant (Trans.)

rouse the anger of the departed. Sarzan is no longer a Keita. The Dead and the Spirits have punished him for his offences."

It had begun the day after his arrival, the very day of my departure from Dougouba.

Sergeant Keita had wanted to keep his father from sacrificing a white chicken to thank the ancestors for having brought him home safe and sound. Keita declared that if he had come home it was quite simply that he had had to, and that the ancestors had had nothing to do with it.

"Leave the dead be," he had said. "They can no longer do anything for the living."

The old chief had paid no attention and the chicken had been sacrificed.

When it was time to work the fields, Thiemokho had called it useless and even stupid to kill black chickens and pour their blood into a corner of the fields. The work, he said, was enough. Rain would fall if it was going to. The millet, corn, groundnuts, yams and beans would grow all by themselves, and would grow better if the villagers would use the ploughs the local administrator had sent him. Keita cut down and burned the branches of Dassiri, the sacred tree, protector of the village and the cultivated fields, at whose foot the dogs were sacrificed.

On the day when the little boys were to be circumcised and the little girls excised,[5] Sergeant Keita had leaped upon their teacher, the Gangourang, who was dancing and chanting. He tore off the porcupine quills the Gangourang wore upon his head, and the netting that hid his body. From the head of Mama Djombo, the venerable grandfather who taught the young girls, Keita had ripped the cone-shaped yellow headdress topped with gri-gri charms and ribbons. All this he called "the ways of savages." And yet he had been to Nice, and seen the carnival with the funny and frightening masks. The Whites, the Toubabs, it is true, wore masks for fun and not in order to teach their children the wisdom of the ancients.

Sergeant Keita had unhooked the little bag hanging in his hut which held the Nyanaboli, the Keita family spirit, and had thrown it into the yard, where the skinny dogs nearly won it from the children before the chief could get there.

One morning he had gone into the sacred wood and broken the pots of boiled millet and sour milk. He had pushed over the little statues and pulled up the forked stakes tipped with hardened blood and chicken feathers. "The ways of savages," he called them. The sergeant, however, had been in churches. He had seen little statues there of saints and the Holy Virgins that people burned candles to. These statues, it is true, were covered with gilt and painted in bright colours—blues, reds and yellows. Certainly they were more beautiful than the blackened pygmies with long arms and short legs carved of cailcedrat or ebony that inhabited the sacred forest.

"You'll civilize them a bit," the local administrator had said. Sergeant Thiemokho Keita was going to "civilize" his people. It was necessary to break with tradition, do away with the beliefs upon which the village life, the existence of the families, the people's behaviour had always rested. Superstition had to be

[5]*excised* female circumcision

eradicated. The ways of savages. Ways of savages, the hard treatment inflicted on the young initiates at circumcision to open their minds, form their character and teach them that nowhere, at any moment of their lives, can they, will they ever be alone A way of savages, the Kotéba, which forges real men on whom pain can hold no sway. The ways of savages, the sacrifices, the blood offered to the ancestors and the earth . . . the boiling of millet and curdled milk poured out to the wandering spirits and the protective genies . . . the ways of savages.

All this Sergeant Keita proclaimed to the young and old of the village, standing in the shade of the palaver-tree.

It was nearly sunset when Thiemokho Keita went out of his mind. He was leaning against the palaver-tree, talking, talking, talking, against the medicine man who had sacrificed some dogs that very morning, against the old who didn't want to hear him, against the young who still listened to the old. He was still speaking, when suddenly he felt something like a prick on his left shoulder. He turned his head. When he looked at his listeners again, his eyes were no longer the same. A white, foamy spittle appeared at the corners of his mouth. He spoke, but it was no longer the same words that emerged from his lips. The spirits had taken his mind, and now they cried out their fear:

Black night! Black night!

He called at nightfall, and the women and children trembled in their huts:

Black night! Black night!

he cried at daybreak:

Black night! Black night!

he howled at high noon. Night and day the spirits and the genies and the ancestors made him speak, cry out and chant. . . .

It was only at dawn that I was able to doze off in the hut where the dead lived. All night I had heard Sergeant Keita coming and going, howling, weeping, and singing:

Trumpeting elephants hoot
In the darkening wood
Above the cursèd drums,
Black night, black night!

Milk sours in the calabash
Gruel hardens in the jar
And fear stalks in the hut,
Black night, black night!

The torches throw
Bodiless flames
In the air
And then, quietly, glarelessly
Smoke,
Black night, black night!

Restless spirits
Meander and moan
Muttering lost words,
Words that strike fear,
Black night, black night!

From the chickens' chilled bodies
Or the warm moving corpse
Not a drop of blood runs
Neither black blood nor red,
Black night, black night!
Trumpeting elephants hoot
Above the cursèd drums,
Black night, black night!

Orphaned, the river calls out
In fear for the people
Endlessly, fruitlessly wandering
Far from its desolate banks,
Black night, black night!

And in the savannah, forlorn
Deserted by ancestors' spirits
The trumpeting elephants hoot
Above the cursèd drums,
Black night, black night!

Sap freezes in the anxious trees
In trunks and leaves
That no longer can pray
To the ancestor haunting their feet,
Black night, black night!

Fear lurks in the hut
In the smoking torch
In the orphaned river
In the weary, soulless forest
In the anxious, faded trees

Trumpeting elephants hoot
In the darkening woods
Above the cursèd drums,
Black night, black night!

No one dared call him by his name any more for the spirits and the ancestors had made another man of him. Thiemokho Keita was gone for the villagers. Only "Sarzan" was left, Sarzan-the-Mad.

[1947]

Translated by
ELLEN CONROY KENNEDY

QUESTIONS

1. How important is the reference to Islam at the beginning of the story? In what way does it anticipate certain aspects of Sarzan's situation?
2. Can the dead drive living people insane?
3. Is the title of the story, the main character's nickname, intended to be ironic?

José Donoso

(b. 1924)

Chile

José Donoso was born in Santiago, Chile, in 1924. His higher education was pursued both in Chile and in the United States. Three of his early translated novels received widespread attention in the United States: *Coronation* (1965), *Hell Has No Limits* (1966), and *The Obscene Bird of Night* (1973). Other works have followed, including *The Boom in Spanish American Literature* (1971). In that work, Donoso wrote,

> In any case, maybe it is worthwhile to begin by pointing out that on the simplest level and prior to possible, and possibly accurate, historical and cultural explanations, there exists the fortuitous circumstance that on the same continent, in twenty-one republics where more or less recognizable varieties of Spanish are written, and during a period of a very few years, there appeared both the brilliant first novels by authors who matured very or relatively early—Vargas Llosa and Carlos Fuentes, for example—and the major novels by older, prestigious authors—Ernesto Sábato, Onetti, Cortázar—which thus produced a spectacular conjunction. In a period of scarcely six years, between 1962 and 1968, I read *The Death of Artemio Cruz*, *The Time of the Hero*, *The Green House*, *The Shipyard*, *Paradiso*, *Hopscotch*, *Sobre héroes y tumbas* (*About Heroes and Tombs*), *One Hundred Years of Solitude*, and other novels all recently published at that time. Suddenly, there burst into view about a dozen novels, noteworthy at the very least and populating a previously uninhabited space.

Donoso concludes his work by saying, "The Boom has been a game; perhaps more precisely, a cultural broth that nourished the tired form of the novel in Latin America for a decade."

In her notes to "Paseo" in *Contemporary Latin American Short Stories*, Pat McNees notes a ubiquitous theme in Donoso's writing: "that in everyone exists the possibility of being both beautiful and monstrous." As you read the story, consider the appropriateness of this theme to Aunt Mathilda's situation.

Paseo

I

This happened when I was very young, when my father and Aunt Mathilda, his maiden sister, and my uncles Gustav and Armand were still living. Now they are all dead. Or I should say, I prefer to think they are all dead: it is too late now for the questions they did not ask when the moment was right, because events seemed to freeze all of them into silence. Later they were able to construct a wall of forgetfulness or indifference to shut out everything, so that they would not have to harass themselves with impotent conjecture. But then, it may not have been that way at all. My imagination and my memory may be deceiving me. After all, I was only a child then, with whom they did not have to share the anguish of their inquiries, if they made any, nor the result of their discussions.

What was I to think? At times I used to hear them closeted in the library, speaking softly, slowly, as was their custom. But the massive door screened the meaning of their words, permitting me to hear only the grave and measured counterpoint of their voices. What was it they were saying? I used to hope that, inside there, abandoning the coldness which isolated each of them, they were at last speaking of what was truly important. But I had so little faith in this that, while I hung around the walls of the vestibule near the library door, my mind became filled with the certainty that they had chosen to forget, that they were meeting only to discuss, as always, some case in jurisprudence relating to their specialty in maritime law. Now I think that perhaps they were right in wanting to blot out everything. For why should one live with the terror of having to acknowledge that the streets of a city can swallow up a human being, leaving him without life and without death, suspended as it were, in a dimension more dangerous than any dimension with a name?

One day, months after, I came upon my father watching the street from the balcony of the drawing-room on the second floor. The sky was close, dense, and the humid air weighed down the large, limp leaves of the ailanthus trees. I drew near my father, eager for an answer that would contain some explanation:

"What are you doing here, Papa?" I murmured.

When he answered, something closed over the despair on his face, like the blow of a shutter closing on a shameful scene.

"Don't you see? I'm smoking . . ." he replied.

And he lit a cigarette.

It wasn't true. I knew why he was peering up and down the street, his eyes darkened, lifting his hand from time to time to stroke his smooth chestnut whiskers: it was in hope of seeing them reappear, returning under the trees of the sidewalk, the white bitch trotting at heel.

Little by little I began to realize that not only my father but all of them, hiding from one another and without confessing even to themselves what they were doing, haunted the windows of the house. If someone happened to look up from the sidewalk he would surely have seen the shadow of one or another of them posted beside a curtain, or faces aged with grief spying out from behind the window panes.

In those days the street was paved with quebracho wood, and under the ailanthus trees a clangorous streetcar used to pass from time to time. The last time I was there neither the wooden pavements nor the streetcars existed any longer. But our house was still standing, narrow and vertical like a little book pressed between the bulky volumes of new buildings, with shops on the ground level and a crude sign advertising knitted undershirts covering the balconies of the second floor.

When we lived there all the houses were tall and slender like our own. The block was always happy with the games of children playing in the patches of sunshine on the sidewalks, and with the gossip of the servant girls on their way back from shopping. But our house was not happy. I say it that way, "it was not happy" instead of "it was sad," because that is exactly what I mean to say. The word "sad" would be wrong because it has too definite a connotation, a weight and a dimension of its own. What took place in our house was exactly the opposite: an absence, a lack, which because it was unacknowledged was irremediable, something that if it weighed, weighed by not existing.

My mother died when I was only four years old, so the presence of a woman was deemed necessary for my care. As Aunt Mathilda was the only woman in the family and she lived with my uncles Armand and Gustav, the three of them came to live at our house, which was spacious and empty.

Aunt Mathilda discharged her duties towards me with that propriety which was characteristic of everything she did. I did not doubt that she loved me, but I could never feel it as a palpable experience uniting us. There was something rigid in her affections, as there was in those of the men of the family. With them, love existed confined inside each individual, never breaking its boundaries to express itself and bring them together. For them to show affection was to discharge their duties to each other perfectly, and above all not to inconvenience, never to inconvenience. Perhaps to express love in any other way was unnecessary for them now, since they had so long a history together, had shared so long a past. Perhaps the tenderness they felt in the past had been expressed to the point of satiation and found itself stylized now in the form of certain actions, useful symbols which did not require further elucidation. Respect was the only form of contact left between those four isolated individuals who walked the corridors of the house which, like a book, showed only its narrow spine to the street.

I, naturally, had no history in common with Aunt Mathilda. How could I, if I was no more than a child then, who could not understand the gloomy motivations of his elders? I wished that their confined feeling might overflow and express itself in a fit of rage, for example, or with some bit of foolery. But she could not guess this desire of mine because her attention was not focused on me: I was a person peripheral to her life, never central. And I was not central because the entire center of her being was filled up with my father and my uncles. Aunt Mathilda was born the only woman, an ugly woman moreover, in a family of handsome men, and on realizing that for her marriage was unlikely, she dedicated herself to looking out for the comfort of those three men, by keeping house for them, by taking care of their clothes and providing their favorite dishes. She did these things without the least servility, proud of her role because she did not question her brothers' excellence. Furthermore, like all women, she possessed in the highest degree the faith that physical well-being is, if not principal, certainly primary, and that to be neither hungry nor cold nor uncomfortable is the basis for whatever else is good. Not that these defects caused her grief, but rather they made her impatient, and when she saw affliction about her she took immediate steps to remedy what, without doubt, were errors in a world that should be, that had to be, perfect. On another plane, she was intolerant of shirts which were not stupendously well-ironed, of meat that was not of the finest quality, of the humidity that owing to someone's carelessness had crept into the cigar-box.

After dinner, following what must have been an ancient ritual in the family, Aunt Mathilda went upstairs to the bedrooms, and in each of her brothers' rooms she prepared the beds for sleeping, parting the sheets with her bony hands. She spread a shawl at the foot of the bed for that one, who was subject to chills, and placed a feather pillow at the head of this one, for he usually read before going to sleep. Then, leaving the lamps lighted beside those enormous beds, she came downstairs to the billiard room to join the men for coffee and for a few rounds, before, as if bewitched by her, they retired to fill the empty effigies of the pajamas she had arranged so carefully upon the white, half-opened sheets.

But Aunt Mathilda never opened my bed. Each night, when I went up to my room, my heart thumped in the hope of finding my bed opened with the recognizable dexterity of her hands. But I had to adjust myself to the less pure style of the servant girl who was charged with doing it. Aunt Mathilda never granted me that mark of importance because I was not her brother. And not to be "one of my brothers" seemed to her a misfortune of which many people were victims, almost all in fact, including me, who after all was only the son of one of them.

Sometimes Aunt Mathilda asked me to visit her in her room where she sat sewing by the tall window, and she would talk to me. I listened attentively. She spoke to me about her brothers' integrity as lawyers in the intricate field of maritime law, and she extended to me her enthusiasm for their wealth and reputation, which I would carry forward. She described the embargo on a shipment of oranges, told of certain damages caused by miserable tugboats manned by drunkards, of the disastrous effects that arose from the demurrage of a ship sailing under an exotic flag. But when she talked to me of ships her words did not evoke the hoarse sound of ships' sirens that I heard in the distance on summer nights when, kept awake by the heat, I climbed to the attic, and from an open window watched the far-off floating lights, and those blocks of darkness surrounding the city that lay forever out of reach for me because my life was, and would ever be, ordered perfectly. I realize now that Aunt Mathilda did not hint at this magic because she did not know of it. It had no place in her life, as it had no place in the life of anyone destined to die with dignity in order afterwards to be installed in a comfortable heaven, a heaven identical to our house. Mute, I listened to her words, my gaze fastened on the white thread that, as she stretched it against her black blouse, seemed to capture all of the light from the window. I exulted at the world of security that her words projected for me, that magnificent straight road which leads to a death that is not dreaded since it is exactly like this life, without anything fortuitous or unexpected. Because death was not terrible. Death was the final incision, clean and definitive, nothing more. Hell existed, of course, but not for us. It was rather for chastising the other inhabitants of the city and those anonymous seamen who caused the damages that, when the cases were concluded, filled the family coffers.

Aunt Mathilda was so removed from the idea of fear that, since I now know that love and fear go hand in hand, I am tempted to think that in those days she did not love anyone. But I may be mistaken. In her rigid way she may have been attached to her brothers by a kind of love. At night, after supper, they gathered in the billiard room for a few games. I used to go in with them. Standing outside that circle of imprisoned affections, I watched for a sign that would show me the ties between them did exist, and did, in fact, bind. It is strange that my memory does not bring back anything but shades of indeterminate grays in remembering the house, but when I evoke that hour, the strident green of the table, the red and white of the balls and the little cube of blue chalk become inflamed in my memory, illumined by the low lamp whose shade banished everything else into dusk. In one of the family's many rituals, the voice of Aunt Mathilda rescued each of the brothers by turn from the darkness, so that they might make their plays.

"No, Gustav . . ."

And when he leaned over the green table, cue in hand, Uncle Gustav's face was lit up, brittle as paper, its nobility contradicted by his eyes, which were too small and spaced too close together. Finished playing, he returned to the shadow, where he lit a cigar whose smoke rose lazily until it was dissolved in the gloom of the ceiling. Then his sister said:

"All right, Armand . . ."

And the soft, timid face of Uncle Armand, with his large, sky-blue eyes concealed by gold-rimmed glasses, bent down underneath the light. His game was generally bad because he was "the baby" as Aunt Mathilda sometimes referred to him. After the comments aroused by his play he took refuge behind his newspaper and Aunt Mathilda said:

"Pedro, your turn . . ."

I held my breath when I saw him lean over to play, held it even more tightly when I saw him succumb to his sister's command. I prayed, as he got up, that he would rebel against the order established by his sister's voice. I could not see that this order was in itself a kind of rebellion, constructed by them as a protection against chaos, so that they might not be touched by what can be neither explained nor resolved. My father, then, leaned over the green cloth, his practiced eye gauging the exact distance and positions of the billiards. He made his play, and making it, he exhaled in such a way that his moustache stirred about his half-opened mouth. Then he handed me his cue so I might chalk it with the blue cube. With this minimal role that he assigned to me, he let me touch the circle that united him with the others, without letting me take part in it more than tangentially.

Now it was Aunt Mathilda's turn. She was the best player. When I saw her face, composed as if from the defects of her brothers' faces, coming out of the shadow, I knew that she was going to win. And yet . . . had I not seen her small eyes light up that face so like a brutally clenched fist, when by chance one of them succeeded in beating her? That spark appeared because, although she might have wished it, she would never have permitted herself to let any of them win. That would be to introduce the mysterious element of love into a game that ought not to include it, because affection should remain in its place, without trespassing on the strict reality of a carom shot.

II

I never did like dogs. One may have frightened me when I was very young, I don't know, but they have always displeased me. As there were no dogs at home and I went out very little, few occasions presented themselves to make me uncomfortable. For my aunt and uncles and for my father, dogs, like all the rest of the animal kingdom, did not exist. Cows, of course, supplied the cream for the dessert that was served in a silver dish on Sundays. Then there were the birds that chirped quite agreeably at twilight in the branches of the elm tree, the only inhabitant of the small garden at the rear of the house. But animals for them existed only in the proportion in which they contributed to the pleasure of human beings. Which is to say that dogs, lazy as city dogs are, could not even dent their imagination with a possibility of their existence.

Sometimes, on Sunday, Aunt Mathilda and I used to go to mass early to take communion. It was rare that I succeeded in concentrating on the sacrament, because the idea that she was watching me without looking generally occupied the first plane of my conscious mind. Even when her eyes were directed to the altar, or her head bowed before the Blessed Sacrament, my every movement drew her attention to it. And on leaving the church she told me with sly reproach that it was without doubt a flea trapped in the pews that prevented me from meditating, as she had suggested, that death is the good foreseen end, and from praying that it might not be painful, since that was the purpose of masses, novenas and communions.

This was such a morning. A fine drizzle was threatening to turn into a storm, and the quebracho pavements extended their shiny fans, notched with streetcar rails, from sidewalk to sidewalk. As I was cold and in a hurry to get home I stepped up the pace beside Aunt Mathilda, who was holding her black mushroom of an umbrella above our heads. There were not many people in the street since it was so early. A dark-complexioned gentleman saluted us without lifting his hat, because of the rain. My aunt was in the process of telling me how surprised she was that someone of mixed blood had bowed to her with so little show of attention, when suddenly, near where we were walking, a streetcar applied its brakes with a screech, making her interrupt her monologue. The conductor looked out through his window:

"Stupid dog!" he shouted.

We stopped to watch.

A small white bitch escaped from between the wheels of the streetcar and, limping painfully, with her tail between her legs, took refuge in a doorway as the streetcar moved on again.

"These dogs," protested Aunt Mathilda. "It's beyond me how they are allowed to go around like that."

Continuing our way we passed by the bitch huddled in the corner of a doorway. It was small and white, with legs which were too short for its size and an ugly pointed snout that proclaimed an entire genealogy of misalliances: the sum of unevenly matched breeds which for generations had been scouring the city, searching for food in the garbage cans and among the refuse of the port. She was drenched, weak, trembling with cold or fever. When we passed in front of her I noticed that my aunt looked at the bitch, and the bitch's eyes returned her gaze.

We continued on our way home. Several steps further I was on the point of forgetting the dog when my aunt surprised me by abruptly turning around and crying out:

"Psst! Go away . . . !"

She had turned in such absolute certainty of finding the bitch following us that I trembled with the mute question which arose from my surprise: How did she know? She couldn't have heard her, since she was following us at an appreciable distance. But she did not doubt it. Perhaps the look that had passed between them of which I saw only the mechanics — the bitch's head raised slightly toward Aunt Mathilda, Aunt Mathilda's slightly inclined toward the bitch — contained some secret commitment? I do not know. In any case, turning to drive away the dog, her peremptory "psst" had the sound of something like a last effort to repel an encroaching destiny. It is possible that I am saying all this in the light of things that happened later, that my imagination is embellishing with significance what was only trivial. However, I can say with certainty that in that moment I felt a strangeness, almost a fear of my aunt's sudden loss of dignity in condescending to turn around and confer rank on a sick and filthy bitch.

We arrived home. We went up the stairs and the bitch stayed down below, looking up at us from the torrential rain that had just been unleashed. We went inside, and the delectable process of breakfast following communion removed the white bitch from my mind. I have never felt our house so protective as that morning, never rejoiced so much in the security derived from those old walls that marked off my world.

In one of my wanderings in and out of the empty sitting-rooms, I pulled back the curtain of a window to see if the rain promised to let up. The storm continued. And, sitting at the foot of the stairs still scrutinizing the house, I saw the white bitch. I dropped the curtain so that I might not see her there, soaked through and looking like one spellbound. Then, from the dark outer rim of the room, Aunt Mathilda's low voice surprised me. Bent over to strike a match to the kindling wood already arranged in the fireplace, she asked:

"Is it still there?"

"What?"

I knew what.

"The white bitch . . ."

I answered yes, that it was.

III

It must have been the last storm of the winter, because I remember quite clearly that the following days opened up and the nights began to grow warmer.

The white bitch stayed posted on our doorstep scrutinizing our windows. In the mornings, when I left for school, I tried to shoo her away, but barely had I boarded the bus when I would see her reappear around the corner or from behind the mailbox. The servant girls also tried to frighten her away, but their attempts were as fruitless as mine, because the bitch never failed to return.

Once, we were all saying good-night at the foot of the stairs before going up to bed. Uncle Gustav had just turned off the lights, all except the one on the stairway, so that the large space of the vestibule had become peopled with the shadowy bodies of furniture. Aunt Mathilda, who was entreating Uncle Armand to open the window of his room so a little air could come in, suddenly stopped speaking, leaving her sentence unfinished, and the movements of all of us, who had started to go up, halted.

"What is the matter?" asked Father, stepping down one stair.

"Go on up," murmured Aunt Mathilda, turning around and gazing into the shadow of the vestibule.

But we did not go up.

The silence of the room was filled with the secret voice of each object: a grain of dirt trickling down between the wallpaper and the wall, the creaking of polished woods, the quivering of some loose crystal. Someone, in addition to ourselves, was where we were. A small white form came out of the darkness near the service door. The bitch crossed the vestibule, limping slowly in the direction of Aunt Mathilda, and without even looking at her, threw herself down at her feet.

It was as though the immobility of the dog enabled us to move again. My father came down two stairs. Uncle Gustav turned on the light. Uncle Armand went upstairs and shut himself in his room.

"What is this?" asked my father.

Aunt Mathilda remained still.

"How could she have come in?" she asked aloud.

Her question seemed to acknowledge the heroism implicit in having either jumped walls in that lamentable condition, or come into the basement through a broken pane of glass, or fooled the servants' vigilance by creeping through a casually opened door.

"Mathilda, call one of the girls to take her away," said my father, and went upstairs followed by Uncle Gustav.

We were left alone looking at the bitch. She called a servant, telling the girl to give her something to eat and the next day to call a veterinarian.

"Is she going to stay in the house?" I asked.

"How can she walk in the street like that?" murmured Aunt Mathilda. "She has to get better so we can throw her out. And she'd better get well soon because I don't want animals in the house."

Then she added:

"Go upstairs to bed."

She followed the girl who was carrying the dog out.

I sensed that ancient drive of Aunt Mathilda's to have everything go well about her, that energy and dexterity which made her sovereign of immediate things. Is it possible that she was so secure within her limitations, that for her the only necessity was to overcome imperfections, errors not of intention or motive, but of condition? If so, the white bitch was going to get well. She would see to it because the animal had entered the radius of her power. The veterinarian would bandage the broken leg under her watchful eye, and protected by rubber gloves and an apron, she herself would take charge of cleaning the bitch's pustules with disinfectant that would make her howl. But Aunt Mathilda would remain deaf to those howls, sure that whatever she was doing was for the best.

And so it was. The bitch stayed in the house. Not that I saw her, but I could feel the presence of any stranger there, even though confined to the lower reaches of the basement. Once or twice I saw Aunt Mathilda with the rubber gloves on her hands, carrying a vial full of red liquid. I found a plate with scraps of food in a passage of the basement where I went to look for the bicycle I had just been given. Weakly, buffered by walls and floors, at times the suspicion of a bark reached my ears.

One afternoon I went down to the kitchen. The bitch came in, painted like a clown with red disinfectant. The servants threw her out without paying her any mind. But I saw that she was not hobbling any longer, that her tail, limp before, was curled up like a feather, leaving her shameless bottom in plain view.

That afternoon I asked Aunt Mathilda:

"When are you going to throw her out?"

"Who?" she asked.

She knew perfectly well.

"The white bitch."

"She's not well yet," she replied.

Later I thought of insisting, of telling her that surely there was nothing now to prevent her from climbing the garbage cans in search of food. I didn't do it because I believe it was the same night that Aunt Mathilda, after losing the first round of billiards, decided that she did not feel like playing another. Her brothers went on playing, and she, ensconced in the leather sofa, made a mistake in calling their names. There was a moment of confusion. Then the thread of order was quickly picked up again by the men, who knew how to ignore an accident if it was not favorable to them. But I had already seen.

It was as if Aunt Mathilda were not there at all. She was breathing at my side as she always did. The deep, silencing carpet yielded under her feet as usual and her tranquilly crossed hands weighed on her skirt. How is it possible to feel with the certainty I felt then the absence of a person whose heart is somewhere else? The following nights were equally troubled by the invisible slur of her absence. She seemed to have lost all interest in the game, and left off calling her brothers by their names. They appeared not to notice it. But they must have, because their games became shorter and I noticed an infinitesimal increase in the deference with which they treated her.

One night, as we were going out of the dining-room, the bitch appeared in the doorway and joined the family group. The men paused before they went into the library so that their sister might lead the way to the billiard room, followed this time by the white bitch. They made no comment, as if they had not seen her, beginning their game as they did every night.

The bitch sat down at Aunt Mathilda's feet. She was very quiet. Her lively eyes examined the room and followed the players' strategies as if all of that amused her greatly. She was fat now and had a shiny coat. Her whole body, from her quivering snout to her tail ready to waggle, was full of an abundant capacity for fun. How long had she stayed in the house? A month? Perhaps more. But in that month Aunt Mathilda had forced her to get well, caring for her not with displays of affection, but with those hands of hers which could not refrain from mending what was broken. The leg was well. She had disinfected, fed and bathed her, and now the white bitch was whole.

In one of his plays Uncle Armand let the cube of blue chalk fall to the floor. Immediately, obeying an instinct that seemed to surge up from her picaresque past, the bitch ran towards the chalk and snatched it with her mouth away from Uncle Armand, who had bent over to pick it up. Then followed something surprising: Aunt Mathilda, as if suddenly unwound, burst into a peal of laughter that agitated her whole body. We remained frozen. On hearing her laugh, the bitch dropped the chalk, ran towards her with her tail waggling aloft, and jumped up onto her lap. Aunt Mathilda's laugh relented, but Uncle Armand left the room. Uncle Gustav and my father went on with the game: now it was more important than ever not to see, not to see anything at all, not to comment, not to consider oneself alluded to by these events.

I did not find Aunt Mathilda's laugh amusing, because I may have felt the dark thing that had stirred it up. The bitch grew calm sitting on her lap. The cracking noises of the balls when they hit seemed to conduct Aunt Mathilda's hand first from its place on the edge of the sofa, to her skirt, and then to the curved back of the sleeping animal. On seeing that expressionless hand reposing there, I noticed that the tension which had kept my aunt's features clenched before, relented, and that a certain peace was now softening her face. I could not resist. I drew closer to her on the sofa, as if to a newly kindled fire. I hoped that she would reach out to me with a look or include me with a smile. But she did not.

IV

When I arrived from school in the afternoon, I used to go directly to the back of the house and, mounting my bicycle, take turn after turn around the narrow garden, circling the pair of cast-iron benches and the elm tree. Behind the wall, the chestnut trees were beginning to display their light spring down, but the seasons did not interest me for I had too many serious things to think about. And since I knew that no one came down into the garden until the suffocation of midsummer made it imperative, it seemed to be the best place for meditating about what was going on inside the house.

One might have said that nothing was going on. But how could I remain calm in the face of the entwining relationship which had sprung up between my aunt and the white bitch? It was as if Aunt Mathilda, after having resigned herself to an odd life of service and duty, had found at last her equal. And as women-friends do, they carried on a life full of niceties and pleasing refinements. They ate bonbons that came in boxes wrapped frivolously with ribbons. My aunt arranged tangerines, pineapples and grapes in tall crystal bowls, while the bitch watched her as if on the point of criticizing her taste or offering a suggestion.

Often when I passed the door of her room, I heard a peal of laughter like the one which had overturned the order of her former life that night. Or I heard her engage in a dialogue with an interlocutor whose voice I did not hear. It was a new life. The bitch, the guilty one, slept in a hamper near her bed, an elegant, feminine hamper, ridiculous to my way of thinking, and followed her everywhere except into the dining-room. Entrance there was forbidden her, but waiting for her friend to come out again, she followed her to the billiard room and sat at her side on the sofa or on her lap, exchanging with her from time to time complicitory glances.

How was it possible, I used to ask myself? Why had she waited until now to go beyond herself and establish a dialogue? At times she appeared insecure about the bitch, fearful that, in the same way she had arrived one fine day, she might also go, leaving her with all this new abundance weighing on her hands. Or did she still fear for her health? These ideas, which now seem so clear, floated blurred in my imagination while I listened to the gravel of the path crunching under the wheels of my bicycle. What was not blurred, however, was my vehement desire to become gravely ill, to see if I might also succeed in harvesting some kind of relationship. Because the bitch's illness had been the cause of everything. If it had not been for that, my aunt might have never joined in league with her. But I had a constitution of iron, and furthermore, it was clear that Aunt Mathilda's heart did not have room for more than one love at a time.

My father and my uncles did not seem to notice any change. The bitch was very quiet, and abandoning her street ways, seemed to acquire manners more worthy of Aunt Mathilda. But still, she had somehow preserved all the sauciness of a female of the streets. It was clear that the hardships of her life had not been able to cloud either her good humor or her taste for adventure which, I felt, lay dangerously dormant inside her. For the men of the house it proved easier to accept her than to throw her out, since this would have forced them to revise their canons of security.

One night, when the pitcher of lemonade had already made its appearance on the console-table of the library, cooling that corner of the shadow, and the windows had been thrown open to the air, my father halted abruptly at the doorway of the billiard room:

"What is that?" he exclaimed, looking at the floor.

The three men stopped in consternation to look at a small, round pool on the waxed floor.

"Mathilda!" called Uncle Gustav.

She went to look and then reddened with shame. The bitch had taken refuge under the billiard table in the adjoining room. Walking over to the table my father saw her there, and changing direction sharply, he left the room, followed by his brothers.

Aunt Mathilda went upstairs. The bitch followed her. I stayed in the library with a glass of lemonade in my hand, and looked out at the summer sky, listening to some far-off siren from the sea, and to the murmur of the city stretched out under the stars. Soon I heard Aunt Mathilda coming down. She appeared with her hat on and with her keys chinking in her hand.

"Go up and go to bed," she said. "I'm going to take her for a walk on the street so that she can do her business."

Then she added something strange:

"It's such a lovely night."

And she went out.

From that night on, instead of going up after dinner to open her brothers' beds, she went to her room, put her hat tightly on her head and came downstairs again, chinking her keys. She went out with the bitch without explaining anything to anyone. And my uncles and my father and I stayed behind in the billiard room, and later we sat on the benches of the garden, with all the murmuring of the elm tree and the clearness of the sky weighing down on us. These nocturnal walks of Aunt Mathilda's were never spoken of by her brothers. They never showed any awareness of the change that had occurred inside our house.

In the beginning Aunt Mathilda was gone at the most for twenty minutes or half an hour, returning to take whatever refreshment there was and to exchange some trivial commentary. Later, her sorties were inexplicably prolonged. We began to realize, or I did at least, that she was no longer a woman taking her dog out for hygienic reasons: outside there, in the streets of the city, something was drawing her. When waiting, my father furtively eyed his pocket watch, and if the delay was very great Uncle Gustav went up to the second floor pretending he had forgotten something there, to spy for her from the balcony. But still they did not speak. Once, when Aunt Mathilda stayed out too long, my father paced back and forth along the path that wound between the hydrangeas. Uncle Gustav threw away a cigar which he could not light to his satisfaction, then another, crushing it with the heel of his shoe. Uncle Armand spilt a cup of coffee. I watched them, hoping that at long last they would explode, that they would finally say something to fill the minutes that were passing by one after another, getting longer and longer and longer without the presence of Aunt Mathilda. It was twelve-thirty when she arrived.

"Why are you all waiting up for me?" she asked smiling.

She was holding her hat in her hand, and her hair, ordinarily so well-groomed, was mussed. I saw that a streak of mud was soiling her shoes.

"What happened to you?" asked Uncle Armand.

"Nothing," came her reply, and with it she shut off any right of her brothers to meddle in those unknown hours that were now her life. I say they were her life because, during the minutes she stayed with us before going up to her room with the bitch, I perceived an animation in her eyes, an excited restlessness like that in the eyes of the animal: it was as though they had been washed in scenes to which even our imagination lacked access. Those two were accomplices. The night protected them. They belonged to the murmuring sound of the city, to the sirens of the ships which, crossing the dark or illumined streets, the houses and factories and parks, reached my ears.

Her walks with the bitch continued for some time. Now we said good-night immediately after dinner, and each one went up to shut himself in his room, my father, Uncle Gustav, Uncle Armand and I. But no one went to sleep before she came in, late, sometimes terribly late, when the light of the dawn was already striking the top of our elm. Only after hearing her close the door of her bedroom did the pacing with which my father measured his room cease, or was the window in one of his brothers' rooms finally closed to exclude that fragment of the night which was no longer dangerous.

Once I heard her come up very late, and as I thought I heard her singing softly, I opened my door and peeked out. When she passed my room, with the white bitch nestled in her arms, her face seemed to me surprisingly young and unblemished, even though it was dirty, and I saw a rip in her skirt. I went to bed terrified, knowing this was the end.

I was not mistaken. Because one night, shortly after, Aunt Mathilda took the dog out for a walk after dinner, and did not return.

We stayed awake all night, each one in his room, and she did not come back. No one said anything the next day. They went — I presume — to their office, and I went to school. She wasn't home when we came back and we sat silently at our meal that night. I wonder if they found out something definite that very first day. But I think not, because we all, without seeming to, haunted the windows of the house, peering into the street.

"Your aunt went on a trip," the cook answered me when I finally dared to ask, if only her.

But I knew it was not true.

Life continued in the house just as if Aunt Mathilda were still living there. It is true that they used to gather in the library for hours and hours, and closeted there they may have planned ways of retrieving her out of that night which had swallowed her. Several times a visitor came who was clearly not of our world, a plain-clothesman perhaps, or the head of a stevedore's union come to pick up indemnification for some accident. Sometimes their voices rose a little, sometimes there was a deadened quiet, sometimes their voices became hard, sharp, as they fenced with the voice I did not know. But the library door was too thick, too heavy for me to hear what they were saying.

[1969]

Translated by
LORRAINE O'GRADY FREEMAN

QUESTIONS

1. Does Aunt Mathilda's escape from her brothers' household free her of her ugliness and make her beautiful, or are we to consider her escape as something less than genuine liberation?
2. What is the significance of the billiard ball game?
3. Why can't Aunt Mathilda express any emotions for the narrator/boy?
4. What will the narrator be like when he grows up—like his father and his uncles or more like Aunt Mathilda?
5. How do the several meanings of *paseo* apply to the story: walk, ride, parade, public park, boulevard?

MARGARETA EKSTRÖM

(b. 1930)

SWEDEN

As the daughter of two writer-storytellers, Margareta Ekström came to her gift as a writer naturally. Born in Stockholm, she studied at the University of Stockholm, pursuing her interests in literary history, religion, and the social sciences. Although her work has not been widely translated from Swedish, she is the author of nine volumes of short stories—for which she has been honored by numerous literary awards in Sweden—as well as literary criticism, poetry, children's stories, and several novels. One collection of her short stories, *Death's Midwives* (1985), has appeared in English with an appreciative introduction by the South African writer Nadine Gordimer. Praising Ekström's insight into her characters, Gordimer notes that the stories take place "in the state of the pursuit of happiness. . . . [T]he twig jumps in her hands and she unerringly directs the reader: there life runs."

Ekström lives in Stockholm with her husband and two children.

◆ *The Night Between the Second and the Third* ◆

It is not uncommon to hear people talk about the exact day and moment of their conversion, or about the exact minute they fell in love. In this same way, I can point to a spot on the calendar—and on the map for that matter—where my life split into two separate parts, once and for all, and irrevocably. Before that, it had been quite stable, never simple, always vulnerable, but still, structurally, pretty much like other people's. After that date, the line of my life, were one to draw it, looked like a Y.

I had borrowed a house for the summer in a little fishing village, not far from the city of X. My friend, who was head of the municipal museum there, was taking part in an excavation near Civita Vecchia, and he had generously left his summer home at my disposal.

It was an old fisherman's cottage, built of stone and whitewashed. It had already, since the beginning of the century, been taken over by summer guests from X, and had therefore lost some of the rustic simplicity which was the foremost quality of these coastal dwellings. The earthen and flagstone floors had been covered with linoleum. The large open fireplace, formerly used for baking, cooking and heating, had been replaced, first by a wood stove and then by an electric range, complete with modern kitchen fan and spice shelf made of teak.

Nevertheless, there was something about the very situation of the house, in the shade of two pitch-dark elms, protected by a boathouse with walls worn to a silver gray, and at a stone's throw from the others which were clustered along a very small village street, that made me feel as though transferred to another century. During the long sunny days I used to pretend I was Robinson Crusoe, just washed up on the beach, far from fellow human beings, news, and especially newspapers, which only served to remind me of my profession. I had unpacked only what was absolutely necessary, a pair of worn-out jeans and two sweaters. All of my more citified clothes remained unused. And I was barefoot, except for the few times when I took a car into X in order to replenish my supply of food and buy a few bottles of wine.

Now, to that spot on the calendar: the night between the second and the third of August 19—. Already, dark clumsy flocks of scoters were flying so close to the surface of the water that I mistook them for porpoises. The oyster-catchers on their fragile lacquer-red legs stepped carefully around in the debris left by the first autumn storm. The piles of seaweed gave off a strong odor of putrefaction, and fog seemed to stick in downy bits of fuzz to fences and elder trees for a long time after the sun had risen and dispersed it: it was the thousands of gossamers made visible by the dew.

Often it didn't get warm and clear until about eleven. Then the sun would shine butter-yellow in competition with the flat heads of the tansy that grew next to the cottage, and I spurned the green-stained bench in front of the cottage to sit instead on an old fish crate on the leeward side of the boathouse, with my morning coffee and my pipe, and look out over the southern part of the bay. Some mornings, the island of Bornholm lay there on the horizon, round and the size of a whale; other mornings, it had disappeared to visit unknown latitudes.

Towards evening on the second of August it started to blow and the breakers became more powerful, sputtering white foam against the deep blue August waters. At dusk the sea roared like constant thunder. On my radio I could hear storm warnings for the coast just south of X, and before I climbed into bed in an alcove up in the otherwise empty loft, I moved the window hook to the closest notch, so that the window was open by only a cautious crack.

Rocked by the rhythmical thudding of the waves, I fell asleep while reading *The Reminiscences of an Egoist*, and woke only for a minute to switch off the lamp and to turn over.

Out of this second and excellent sleep, which would be graded first class if subjected to a consumer evaluation regarding its stability, depth and durability, I was awakened at daybreak by a strange sound.

At night, the sounds in the village and on the adjoining heath, where my cottage was situated, were the following: the splashing, moaning or rushing of the sea, always rhythmical, like the heartbeats of an enormous mammal. Secondly, the crowing of the roosters, both those cocky 6 A.M. wake-up roosters belonging to my closest neighbor, a fisherman, and the bantam roosters that a summer family kept at the other end of the village. Thirdly, it happened that owls hooted, drowsy blackbirds called, cows mooed and early morning traffic swished by on its way to and from the main road in the distance.

Have I left out any sound or call? I'm trying to remember. . . . Yes, the electric pump which took care of my water supply for shower, lavatory and kitchen sometimes decided to start groaning and coughing, even though no one had demanded its services.

I supported myself on my elbow and listened. The wind had increased, but I told myself that it would have to increase much more before the fishermen would refer to it as a storm. As though trying to free themselves from the leaves which constituted such a dangerous windbreak, the two elms twisted and shook their branches, and stretched and pulled at their roots. The window strained on its short leash. The surf broke with roaring force against the rocks on the beach with, it seemed to me, a constantly accelerating crescendo.

In between the worst of the roaring, in the lulls between the waves of sound, there were loud shouts.

Who would shout like that in the middle of the night? Nobody from the village. That was out of the question. Once at the beginning of summer a little summer-guest boy had got lost and screamed bloody murder. He had waked up and, finding himself alone, he had looked for his mother who was playing bridge in a house across the road. But that sort of noise was very unusual. The village was the quietest and most peaceful of places.

I lay down, closed my eyes and tried to ignore the image which inexorably developed even behind my closed lids: the image of a small sailing boat or other pleasure craft, adrift, out of control, about to be sucked out to sea by the dangerous current—or already pierced by the sharp-edged rocks furthest out on the point, and there, struggling, water up to his mouth, a father with a child in his arms, entangled in debris, and equally afraid of being sucked out again and of being hurled to death against the rocks.

There it was again. A shout strong and imploring. And now I did hear clearly that it was a cry for help, and not an inarticulate scream as I had first thought, but a completely clear "Help!"

He or she called whenever the sea was the slightest bit quieter, or else he called all the time, and it was only then, during the intervals, that I could hear that "Help!" which made the hair on my arms literally stand on end.

I didn't have the slightest idea about what to do. But I also realized that remaining inactive would be the same as committing murder. I am a landlubber and have neither the strength nor the equipment for any life-saving maneuver. Words like "lifelines," "life buoys," "storm lantern" crossed my mind. Where could I find these things? I had been thoroughly instructed about such problems as the care of the water pump, rubbish collection, forwarding the mail and defrosting the refrigerator. Heroic acts or tragedies had not been included in the plans for these holiday weeks. I wandered around now in the low-ceilinged loft, pulled on my jeans, cursed and searched for my sandals (which were outside under the garden bench), put on a sweater the wrong way and tried, in vain, to button it down the back with my arms at a grotesque angle, while now and then listening and hearing—not knowing whether what I feared most was hearing, or that the rhythmical, heart-rending call for "Help" had stopped.

"Help! Help!"

A catalogue of all the possible alternatives went through my head one more time, so reluctant was I to go out and wake the village people in order to fight the sea for the sake of the life of some foolhardy pleasure sailor. But the catastrophe throbbed like a pulse inside and outside my head, and I ran out into the black, roaring night and heard myself shouting just as heartrendingly: "Help!"

A flickering silvery glow on the horizon meant that daybreak was on its way, but the heath, the village and the beach were still dark, and down by the cliffs you could only see the white bursts of the surf.

I must have seemed panic-stricken when, having finally succeeded in waking my neighbor the fisherman, a man in his sixties, I gasped and stammered what I wanted. I can still see the skeptical and thoughtful way he looked at me while sluggishly hitching up his pajamas so that I have to push him aside to get to the telephone, and it is only after having dialed the emergency number that I realize the telephone is right next to the ear of the curler-covered head of his sleeping wife.

She moans about something in a nightmare while I give my name, the name of the village, and tell them what I have heard.

First there is silence from the receiver, then a slow, dull voice says in dialect: "You seen them?"

"No," I scream. "Here, listen yourself!" And in stupid desperation I turn the receiver towards the door and then back to my face, and shout: "Don't you hear? They're screaming all the time!"

Of course there's silence from the receiver at that, but my neighbor takes it out of my hand and says with some authority: "I think it'd be a good idea if you came!"

Only then does the emergency man decide to do something, and says almost with alacrity: "O.K., we're coming."

In the meantime, my neighbor has put on his oilskins and picked up the lantern that apparently is always ready next to the front door, which has the week's TV program tacked to it, and as we struggle on our way against the wind, he says again and again: "Well, where are they?" But sometimes the storm makes words impossible, and he puts his hard warm hand on my ice-cold arm instead, and I point silently. "There. Way out there on the point."

I hear them still. "He-elp! He-elp! He-elp!" I hear that the voice is getting weaker and I run faster. But the point, which in calm and sunny weather is a favorite bathing area, is now under water, part of an underwater landscape made up of furrowed slabs of limestone leading to traps slippery as soap. I fall down, hurt myself and get wet through and through. I watch the lantern light up the waves and expect any second to see the wreck of a boat, or a panic-stricken white face, but there is nothing to see except leaden waves and white foam, and a silvery shimmer from the east which, getting stronger, makes the darkness less dense.

So they have drowned, after all.

The fisherman's wife must have awakened and alarmed the other neighbors. In the trembling light of dawn I can dimly see a little flock, and two unfamiliar men making their way through the people with poles and lifelines. I suppose they are the rescue men who've come by car. The sea is lit by our lanterns from one side and by the dawn from the other, there is no sign of a wreck, of debris from a boat, or of struggling human beings. And still, all the time, one can hear them, sometimes weaker, sometimes stronger, those wailing calls for help.

It could all have ended there, with the coming of the sun, the people on the beach, silent and irresolute, confronted with a mystery. But then my life would not have acquired the shape of a Y.

The fisherman's wife walks towards me and, in a manner quite devoid of irony or malice, rather kindly in fact, and a bit pityingly, says: "Wasn't it maybe the sheep you heard?"

At that, all of them turn towards land, and they start talking and laughing, and some of them curse ("Damn summer guests!"), so that I can hardly make out the rhythmical bleating from the farm up the road: Ba-a! Ba-a! He-elp! He-elp!

I don't know how I get back to my bed. I stumble away at a tremendous pace, and the talk and laughter fade, and I run up the steep staircase to the loft, throw myself headfirst onto the bed, and begin weeping like a child, with a misery from ages ago, a continuation of a crying fit from when I was twelve years old, when my teacher refused to believe me even though I tried to explain (that I had *not* tried to cheat when I had leaned over towards the boy next to me during a test, that I had only wanted to know what time it was . . . that I hadn't written "Mary stinks" even though it was I who was standing there, pen in hand, when he surprised us in the locker room). With a superhuman, self-hypnotic effort, I manage to sink back into that very sleep that I was enjoying before the shouting awakened me.

There I was again now, voluptuously stretched out on the wide mattress, under the low attic ceiling that smelled slightly of tar, completely embraced by sleep, rocked by the roaring of the sea, which apparently had decided to beat its own storm record, that night between the second and the third of August.

For a man alone on holiday in a house at a safe distance from the surf, that noise is merely a great rhythmical source of pleasure. "Just listen to the sea," I would mumble to a friend or lover, had one been with me. "Do you hear how beautifully it sings?"

But I was alone, sound asleep, and it was something entirely different from the roar of the surf that finally woke me. It was a shout.

I turned onto my side and supported my head with my hand. The window was open only a crack, but it was enough for me to hear a distinct shout. A human being was out there in the storm, screaming something. "He-elp! He-e-lp!"

I lay down again on my back and looked at the ceiling. It was pitch-dark, both outside and in the house. Nonsense, I thought. Nobody walks around here on the heath screaming for help! And if anyone was being shipwrecked, he certainly wouldn't be so naive as to think shouting like that would reach people's ears, what with all the noise from the sea.

But as I was lying there, almost falling asleep again, the shout returned, again and again, just as real as the pounding of the waves against the beach: "Help! Help!"

I got up and felt how the hair on my arms stood on end from fright and cold. Out there in those breakers, a human being was struggling for his life. Perhaps a whole family. A father who saw his little daughter being washed overboard, or who was already lying in the water with a baby in his arms, or maybe a dog. . . .

I groped around for a warm sweater, managed to put both legs into one jeans leg and almost toppled like a tree being felled, bumped my forehead against the rough sloping ceiling, and all the time I heard those heart-rending shouts and saw in my imagination a man who was trying to swim as hard as he could with one arm, while the sea sucked him out and washed over him alternately, and he didn't know whether he wanted to reach or feared coming closer to the sharp rocks on the beach. From time to time, when he managed to fill his lungs with air, he uttered that piercing, wailing shout for help.

I opened the window wide, and it was immediately wrenched out of my hand, hitting the wall. A weak tinkling told me that the lower pane had been knocked out and fallen to the ground. As I leaned out to get hold of the window, I searched in vain in the darkness. Everything was black. Shouldn't a capsized boat have some sort of lantern, or a light at least? Stupid, I said to myself. The mast was most likely upside down already, caught between the two barnacle-covered rocks, five meters under the surface of the sea. In that case they can hold on to the keel, at any rate . . . but then, most likely, the keel is under water and as slippery as a soapy knife.

Anxious to find good reasons to just go back to bed and sleep, I finally tried to convince myself that the whole thing was a figment of my imagination. But I did keep hearing, again and again, those shouts for help. "Help!"

Who is a call like that for? For the one who hears it.

What other sounds could one hear in the village, if it wasn't . . . . I went through them: the owl, the dogs, the roosters, the blackbirds (impossible), and while I continued my list I tightened my jeans belt as though in a trance, and thought about how inadequate I was, with my weak muscles, shortness of breath, to accomplish any sort of heroic action on a night like this, the night between the second and the third of August.

Didn't the shouts seem weaker now? And couldn't it mean that it was something else, or did it mean that the individual had got his mouth full of ice-cold sea water in the middle of his shout? Could I sit here, at the age of forty, in possession of all my senses, a Swedish man with Christian upbringing, and almost wish that the shouts would stop, so that I wouldn't have to do anything? Why, that was murder! In thought, at any rate.

Then I remembered the sheep. I was so relieved that I smiled into the darkness, there in my alcove. Of course! The sheep! A farmer up the road had acquired two sheep, a brown one and a gray one. They were of an unusual breed and were tethered next to the road, where they grazed on the lawn in front of the farmer's house. I'd heard their bleating for several days now. Perhaps there wasn't any grass left, and it was time to move them.

How lucky that I remembered them! They were real. Not something I had imagined because of my laziness and cowardice in order to be spared going out into the stormy night! I laughed out loud at that—my having to reassure myself that they existed. Imagine if, before remembering the sheep, I had managed to wake my neighbor who was a fisherman, and his wife, or if I had phoned the rescue people who, on a stormy night like this, certainly had other things to think about than to rush out because of a false alarm!

Of course there was a 1-to-100 chance that what I had heard was human shouting, but the certainty was still 99 per cent in favor of the sheep, which towards daybreak usually stood there and called to each other: Ba-a! Ba-a-a! And it was typical of the newness of the situation that their bleating woke me. But then again, if there were a catastrophe, wouldn't I have been awakened by something so new as a catastrophe?

There they were again: Ba-a-a! He-e-elp! They alternated, first the sheep and then the human being in distress. But I had already taken off my jeans and was sitting on the edge of the bed with my head in my hands. For some reason I let my hands glide up to cover my ears, and so heard only the pounding of the surf, or was it my pulse?

Won't make a fool of myself, I was thinking. "Help!" came more weakly from those rocks where I had stood two days before with my fishing tackle and got two briskly fighting codfish. No. Not there. There was nothing but glitter and terns and scoters that swam over the tops of the waves in a black flock that made me think of porpoises. How lucky that I remembered the sheep!

The next morning the storm had calmed down somewhat. I sat, as usual, on the leeward side of the boathouse on my old fish crate, leaning comfortably against the silver-gray planks worn velvet-soft by the weather. The coffee in my mug was steaming and my tape recorder on the rock surrounded by wild pinks was humming Bach's French suites. I thought I heard voices from the beach, so I got up to look around the corner of the boathouse—I can remember how the wind hit me in the face and made me think that it was still pretty strong—I saw almost the whole village population, and a car which in some incomprehensible way had managed to drive down there!

The sea was calmer and the wind had veered. Very distinctly I could see what it was all about. The mast of the sailing boat was leaning at a 45-degree angle from the outermost point of the rock. Where I had stood with my fishing tackle, two strangers, apparently those who had come in the car, were trying to tie someone to a stretcher. I both wanted and didn't want to see what had happened. All at once I remembered everything: the shouts and my cowardice. The sheep! Oh, I . . .

I kept to myself all day. But it was no use. Exactly at sundown, my neighbor the fisherman came over, bursting with the terrible happenings in the sea just outside his house and mine.

I had to make coffee and we spiked it with a shot of whiskey. We drank and looked thoughtfully past each other, he at the wall behind me, and I out through the window towards the rocks where the mast had fastened like the hand of a broken clock. And all the time I felt as though it was stuck like a needle through my throbbing heart.

"And nobody heard anything," he sighed, saying goodbye. And again, "Just think, nobody heard anything!"

I didn't answer. You usually don't have to. Those who want to talk usually do both: ask the questions and answer them too.

"It's that there's so much. The sea roars and the old lady snores. There's so much noise. And one's so tired one sleeps so soundly. Well, well. And all that time, those poor people . . ."

And so at the end, like a persistent coda to a sonata, when we were already standing in the doorway, and I was almost pushing him out in the direction of his house and the village: "And I didn't hear anything. No. Not a damned thing."

And then he turns around in the middle of the burnt August grass, stands like a black and threatening silhouette in the light of the setting sun, and looking straight at me, although I can't see his face, he fires his last shot: "And you, how come you didn't hear anything?"

There is a long pause, and it is then that I understand that my life has acquired the shape of a Y. And I will never know which of the Y's two branches I live in. I didn't then and I won't in the future.

This happened during the night between the second and the third of August a few years ago. I have had lots of time to think about my Y-shaped destiny, and it seems clear that my life, like the wick of a candle, was twined of two separate pieces of yarn from the beginning. One of them stands for indifference, and the other for feeling and concern. It was only after the happenings between the second and the third that the two separated, and they are now free from each other, in eternal opposition.

From that night on, sheep have always been human beings for me, and human beings sheep, if you understand what I mean. Shouts for help will always sound like bleating, and the peaceful sounds sheep make will sound like screams of tragedy. Whichever way I turn, I've been unable since then either to look the other way or to give a helping hand, and my Christian conscience is on a constant electric trampoline, just like those mice we've all read about, who are made to jump up on the charged bar in order to get to their food; sometimes they get a shock, at other times only their food.

Whatever I do, however I jump, I get a shock, a slap in the face, and I try in vain to keep my balance.

[1985 – English translation]

Translated by
EVA CLAESON

QUESTIONS

1. How would you describe the character of the narrator? How is he affected by the events of the night he describes?
2. How are distinctions among actual events, dreams or nightmares, and the imagination blurred in the story? How does the setting contribute to the effectiveness of the story?
3. Why are the events of that night described twice—once when the narrator initiates a rescue mission and once when he does not?
4. What does the narrator mean when he says that his life has branched into a "Y" and he "will never know which of the two branches" he lives in?
5. What is the theme of the story?

RALPH ELLISON

(b. 1914)

UNITED STATES

The context of Ralph Ellison's "Flying Home" grows out of the humiliating treatment of African-Americans in the armed forces during World War II. Although the numbers of African-Americans in the services had greatly increased from earlier times, their duties were little changed. They were still relegated to menial jobs: cooks, stewards, clean-up crews. During the war itself, there was a growing sense of frustration in the black communities in major cities in the States. Riots, in fact, broke out in several large cities, triggered in part by the ill-treatment of black soldiers both at home and abroad. The obvious questions running through the minds of many black soldiers were, What were they defending, and from what were they trying to save America?

During World War II, Ralph Ellison served in the merchant marine. At the war's end, he returned to New York City, where he began working on his masterpiece, *Invisible Man* (1952), a novel that is almost universally regarded as the major piece of American fiction since the war. In his introduction to the thirtieth anniversary of the novel's publication, Ellison states that he had planned to write a novel about the war, but what transpired was something else—though perhaps not so radically different on a symbolic level. Ellison explains the military context as follows:

> Undramatized, all this might sound a bit extreme, yet historically most of this nation's conflicts of arms have been—at least for Afro-Americans—wars-within-wars. Such was true of the Civil War, the last of the Indian wars, of the Spanish-American War, and of World Wars I and II. And in order for the Negro to fulfill his duty as a citizen it was often necessary that he fight for his self-affirmed right to fight.

In "Flying Home," fight also becomes mixed with the metaphor of flight. As Ellison's remarks about war continue, "I also knew something of the trials of Negro airmen, who after being trained in segregated units and undergoing the abuse of white officers and civilians alike were prevented from flying combat missions. . . ." Commenting on "Flying Home" directly, he adds,

> I came to realize that my pilot was also experiencing difficulty in seeing *himself*. And this had to do with his ambivalence before his own group's divisions of class and diversities of culture: an ambivalence which was brought into focus after he crash-landed on a Southern plantation and found himself being aided by a Negro tenant farmer whose outlook and folkways were a painful reminder of his own tenuous military status and their common origin in slavery. A man of two worlds, my pilot felt himself to be misperceived in both and thus was at ease in neither. In brief,

the story depicted his conscious struggle for self-definition and for an invulnerable support for his individual dignity.

Besides *Invisible Man*, Ralph Ellison had published a collection of essays, *Shadow and Act*, in 1964. The same year, he was elected to the American Academy of Arts and Letters. He was Albert Schweitzer Professor of Humanities at New York University from 1970 to 1980. He was born in Oklahoma in 1914.

• *Flying Home* •

When Todd came to, he saw two faces suspended above him in a sun so hot and blinding that he could not tell if they were black or white. He stirred, feeling a pain that burned as though his whole body had been laid open to the sun which glared into his eyes. For a moment an old fear of being touched by white hands seized him. Then the very sharpness of the pain began slowly to clear his head. Sounds came to him dimly. He done come to. Who are they? he thought. Naw he ain't, I coulda sworn he was white. Then he heard clearly:

"You hurt bad?"

Something within him uncoiled. It was a Negro sound.

"He's still out," he heard.

"Give 'im time. . . . Say, son, you hurt bad?"

Was he? There was that awful pain. He lay rigid, hearing their breathing and trying to weave a meaning between them and his being stretched painfully upon the ground. He watched them warily, his mind traveling back over a painful distance. Jagged scenes, swiftly unfolding as in a movie trailer, reeled through his mind, and he saw himself piloting a tailspinning plane and landing and landing and falling from the cockpit and trying to stand. Then, as in a great silence, he remembered the sound of crunching bone, and now, looking up into the anxious faces of an old Negro man and a boy from where he lay in the same field, the memory sickened him and he wanted to remember no more.

"How you feel, son?"

Todd hesitated, as though to answer would be to admit an inacceptable weakness. Then, "It's my ankle," he said.

"Which one?"

"The left."

With a sense of remoteness he watched the old man bend and remove his boot, feeling the pressure ease.

"That any better?"

"A lot. Thank you."

He had the sensation of discussing someone else, that his concern was with some far more important thing, which for some reason escaped him.

"You done broke it bad," the old man said. "We have to get you to a doctor."

He felt that he had been thrown into a tailspin. He looked at his watch; how long had he been here? He knew there was but one important thing in the world, to get the plane back to the field before his officers were displeased.

"Help me up," he said. "Into the ship."

"But it's broke too bad. . . ."

"Give me your arm!"

"But, son . . ."

Clutching the old man's arm he pulled himself up, keeping his left leg clear, thinking, "I'd never make him understand," as the leather-smooth face came parallel with his own.

"Now, let's see."

He pushed the old man back, hearing a bird's insistent shrill. He swayed giddily. Blackness washed over him, like infinity.

"You best sit down."

"No, I'm O.K."

"But, son. You jus' gonna make it worse. . . ."

It was a fact that everything in him cried out to deny, even against the flaming pain in his ankle. He would have to try again.

"You mess with that ankle they have to cut your foot off," he heard.

Holding his breath, he started up again. It pained so badly that he had to bite his lips to keep from crying out and he allowed them to help him down with a pang of despair.

"It's best you take it easy. We gon' git you a doctor."

Of all the luck, he thought. Of all the rotten luck, now I have done it. The fumes of high-octane gasoline clung in the heat, taunting him.

"We kin ride him into town on old Ned," the boy said.

Ned? He turned, seeing the boy point toward an ox team browsing where the buried blade of a plow marked the end of a furrow. Thoughts of himself riding an ox through the town, past streets full of white faces, down the concrete runways of the airfield made swift images of humiliation in his mind. With a pang he remembered his girl's last letter. "Todd," she had written, "I don't need the papers to tell me you had the intelligence to fly. And I have always known you to be as brave as anyone else. The papers annoy me. Don't you be contented to prove over and over again that you're brave or skillful just because you're black, Todd. I think they keep beating that dead horse because they don't want to say why you boys are not yet fighting. I'm really disappointed, Todd. Anyone with brains can learn to fly, but then what? What about using it, and who will you use it for? I wish, dear, you'd write about this. I sometimes think they're playing a trick on us. It's very humiliating. . . ." He wiped cold sweat from his face, thinking. What does she know of humiliation? She's never been down South. Now the humiliation would come. When you must have them judge you, knowing that they never accept your mistakes as your own, but hold it against your whole race—that was humiliation. Yes, and humiliation was when you could never be simply yourself, when you were always a part of this old black ignorant man. Sure, he's all right. Nice and kind and helpful. But he's not you. Well, there's one humiliation I can spare myself.

"No," he said, "I have orders not to leave the ship. . . ."

"Aw," the old man said. Then turning to the boy, "Teddy, then you better hustle down to Mister Graves and get him to come. . . ."

"No, wait!" he protested before he was fully aware. Graves might be white. "Just have him get word to the field, please. They'll take care of the rest."

He saw the boy leave, running.

"How far does he have to go?"

"Might' nigh a mile."

He rested back, looking at the dusty face of his watch. But now they know something has happened, he thought. In the ship there was a perfectly good radio, but it was useless. The old fellow would never operate it. That buzzard knocked me back a hundred years, he thought. Irony danced within him like the gnats circling the old man's head. With all I've learned I'm dependent upon this "peasant's" sense of time and space. His leg throbbed. In the plane, instead of time being measured by the rhythms of pain and a kid's legs, the instruments would have told him at a glance. Twisting upon his elbows he saw where dust had powdered the plane's fuselage, feeling the lump form in his throat that was always there when he thought of flight. It's crouched there, he thought, like the abandoned shell of a locust. I'm naked without it. Not a machine, a suit of clothes you wear. And with a sudden embarrassment and wonder he whispered, "It's the only dignity I have. . . ."

He saw the old man watching, his torn overalls clinging limply to him in the heat. He felt a sharp need to tell the old man what he felt. But that would be meaningless. If I tried to explain why I need to fly back, he'd think I was simply afraid of white officers. But it's more than fear . . . a sense of anguish clung to him like the veil of sweat that hugged his face. He watched the old man, hearing him humming snatches of a tune as he admired the plane. He felt a furtive sense of resentment. Such old men often came to the field to watch the pilots with childish eyes. At first it had made him proud; they had been a meaningful part of a new experience. But soon he realized they did not understand his accomplishments and they came to shame and embarrass him, like the distasteful praise of an idiot. A part of the meaning of flying had gone then, and he had not been able to regain it. If I were a prizefighter I would be more human, he thought. Not a monkey doing tricks, but a man. They were pleased simply that he was a Negro who could fly, and that was not enough. He felt cut off from them by age, by understanding, by sensibility, by technology and by his need to measure himself against the mirror of other men's appreciation. Somehow he felt betrayed, as he had when as a child he grew to discover that his father was dead. Now for him any real appreciation lay with his white officers; and with them he could never be sure. Between ignorant black men and condescending whites, his course of flight seemed mapped by the nature of things away from all needed and natural landmarks. Under some sealed orders, couched in ever more technical and mysterious terms, his path curved swiftly away from both the shame the old man symbolized and the cloudy terrain of white men's regard. Flying blind, he knew but one point of landing and there he would receive his wings. After that the enemy would appreciate his skill and he would assume his deepest meaning, he thought sadly, neither from those who condescended nor from those who praised without understanding, but from the enemy who would recognize his manhood and skill in terms of hate. . . .

He sighed, seeing the oxen making queer, prehistoric shadows against the dry brown earth.

"You just take it easy, son," the old man soothed. "That boy won't take long. Crazy as he is about airplanes."

"I can wait," he said.

"What kinda airplane you call this here'n?"

"An Advanced Trainer," he said, seeing the old man smile. His fingers were like gnarled dark wood against the metal as he touched the low-slung wing.

"'Bout how fast can she fly?"

"Over two hundred an hour."

"Lawd! That's so fast I bet it don't seem like you moving!"

Holding himself rigid, Todd opened his flying suit. The shade had gone and he lay in a ball of fire.

"You mind if I take a look inside? I was always curious to see. . . ."

"Help yourself. Just don't touch anything."

He heard him climb upon the metal wing, grunting. Now the questions would start. Well, so you don't have to think to answer. . . .

He saw the old man looking over into the cockpit, his eyes bright as a child's.

"You must have to know a lot to work all these here things."

He was silent, seeing him step down and kneel beside him.

"Son, how come you want to fly way up there in the air?"

Because it's the most meaningful act in the world . . . because it makes me less like you, he thought.

But he said: "Because I like it, I guess. It's as good a way to fight and die as I know."

"Yeah? I guess you right," the old man said. "But how long you think before they gonna let you all fight?"

He tensed. This was the question all Negroes asked, put with the same timid hopefulness and longing that always opened a greater void within him than that he had felt beneath the plane the first time he had flown. He felt light-headed. It came to him suddenly that there was something sinister about the conversation, that he was flying unwillingly into unsafe and uncharted regions. If he could only be insulting and tell this old man who was trying to help him to shut up!

"I bet you one thing. . . ."

"Yes?"

"That you was plenty scared coming down."

He did not answer. Like a dog on a trail the old man seemed to smell out his fears and he felt anger bubble within him.

"You sho' scared me. When I seen you coming down in that thing with it a-rollin' and a-jumpin' like a pitchin' hoss, I thought sho' you was a goner. I almost had me a stroke!"

He saw the old man grinning, "Ever'thin's been happening round here this morning, come to think of it."

"Like what?" he asked.

"Well, first thing I know, here come two white fellers looking for Mister Rudolph, that's Mister Graves's cousin. That got me worked up right away. . . ."

"Why?"

"Why? 'Cause he done broke outta the crazy house, that's why. He liable to kill somebody," he said. "They oughta have him by now though. Then here you come. First I think it's one of them white boys. Then doggone if you don't fall outta there. Lawd, I'd done heard about you boys but I haven't never seen one o' you-all. Cain't tell you how it felt to see somebody what look like me in a airplane!"

The old man talked on, the sound streaming around Todd's thoughts like air flowing over the fuselage of a flying plane. You were a fool, he thought, remembering how before the spin the sun had blazed bright against the billboard signs beyond the town, and how a boy's blue kite had bloomed beneath him, tugging gently in the wind like a strange, odd-shaped flower. He had once flown such kites himself and tried to find the boy at the end of the invisible cord. But he had been flying too high and too fast. He had climbed steeply away in exultation. Too steeply, he thought. And one of the first rules you learn is that if the angle of thrust is too steep the plane goes into a spin. And then, instead of pulling out of it and going into a dive you let a buzzard panic you. A lousy buzzard!

"Son, what made all that blood on the glass?"

"A buzzard," he said, remembering how the blood and feathers had sprayed back against the hatch. It had been as though he had flown into a storm of blood and blackness.

"Well, I declare! They's lots of 'em around here. They after dead things. Don't eat nothing what's alive."

"A little bit more and he would have made a meal out of me," Todd said grimly.

"They bad luck all right. Teddy's got a name for 'em, calls 'em jimcrows," the old man laughed.

"It's a damned good name."

"They the damnedest birds. Once I seen a hoss all stretched out like he was sick, you know. So I hollers, 'Gid up from there, suh!' Just to make sho! An' doggone, son, if I don't see two ole jimcrows come flying right up outa that hoss's insides! Yessuh! The sun was shinin' on 'em and they couldn't a been no greasier if they'd been eating barbecue."

Todd thought he would vomit, his stomach quivered.

"You made that up," he said.

"Nawsuh! Saw him just like I see you."

"Well, I'm glad it was you."

"You see lots a funny things down here, son."

"No, I'll let you see them," he said.

"By the way, the white folks round here don't like to see you boys up there in the sky. They ever bother you?"

"No."

"Well, they'd like to."

"Someone always wants to bother someone else," Todd said. "How do you know?"

"I just know."

"Well," he said defensively, "no one has bothered us."

Blood pounded in his ears as he looked away into space. He tensed, seeing a black spot in the sky, and strained to confirm what he could not clearly see.

"What does that look like to you?" he asked excitedly.

"Just another bad luck, son."

Then he saw the movement of wings with disappointment. It was gliding smoothly down, wings outspread, tail feathers gripping the air, down swiftly—gone behind the green screen of trees. It was like a bird he had imagined there, only the sloping branches of the pines remained, sharp against the pale stretch of sky. He lay barely breathing and stared at the point where it had disappeared, caught in a spell of loathing and admiration. Why did they make them so disgusting and yet teach them to fly so well? It's like when I was up in heaven, he heard, starting.

The old man was chuckling, rubbing his stubbed chin.

"What did you say?"

"Sho', I died and went to heaven . . . maybe by time I tell you about it they be done come after you."

"I hope so," he said wearily.

"You boys ever sit around and swap lies?"

"Not often. Is this going to be one?"

"Well, I ain't so sho', on account of it took place when I was dead."

The old man paused, "That wasn't no lie 'bout the buzzards, though."

"All right," he said.

"Sho' you want to hear 'bout heaven?"

"Please," he answered, resting his head upon his arm.

"Well, I went to heaven and right away started to sproutin' me some wings. Six good ones, they was. Just like them the white angels had. I couldn't hardly believe it. I was so glad that I went off on some clouds by myself and tried 'em out. You know, 'cause I didn't want to make a fool outta myself the first thing. . . ."

It's an old tale, Todd thought. Told me years ago. Had forgotten. But at least it will keep him from talking about buzzards.

He closed his eyes, listening.

". . . First thing I done was to git up on a low cloud and jump off. And doggone, boy, if them wings didn't work! First I tried the right; then I tried the left; then I tried 'em both together. Then Lawd, I started to move on out among the folks. I let 'em see me. . . ."

He saw the old man gesturing flight with his arms, his face full of mock pride as he indicated an imaginary crowd, thinking, It'll be in the newspapers, as he heard, ". . . so I went and found me some colored angels—somehow I didn't believe I was an angel till I seen a real black one, ha, yes! Then I was sho'—but they tole me I better come down 'cause us colored folks had to wear a special kin' a harness when we flew. That was how come they wasn't flyin'. Oh yes, an' you had to be extra strong for a black man even, to fly with one of them harnesses. . . ."

This is a new turn, Todd thought, what's he driving at?

"So I said to myself, I ain't gonna be bothered with no harness! Oh naw! 'Cause if God let you sprout wings you oughta have sense enough not to let nobody make you wear something what gits in the way of flyin'. So I starts to flyin'. Heck, son," he chuckled, his eyes twinkling, "you know I had to let eve'ybody know that old Jefferson could fly good as anybody else. And I could too, fly smooth as a bird! I could even loop-the-loop—only I had to make sho' to keep my long white robe down roun' my ankles. . . ."

Todd felt uneasy. He wanted to laugh at the joke, but his body refused, as of an independent will. He felt as he had as a child when after he had chewed a sugar-coated pill which his mother had given him, she had laughed at his efforts to remove the terrible taste.

". . . Well," he heard, "I was doing all right 'til I got to speeding. Found out I could fan up a right strong breeze, I could fly so fast. I could do all kin'sa stunts too. I started flying up to the stars and divin' down and zooming roun' the moon. Man, I like to scare the devil outa some ole white angels. I was raisin' hell. Not that I meant any harm, son. But I was just feeling good. It was so good to know I was free at last. I accidentally knocked the tips offa some stars and they tell me I caused a storm and a coupla lynchings down here in Macon County—though I swear I believe them boys what said that was making up lies on me. . . ."

He's mocking me, Todd thought angrily. He thinks it's a joke. Grinning down at me . . . His throat was dry. He looked at his watch; why the hell didn't they come? Since they had to, why? One day I was flying down one of them heavenly streets. You got yourself into it, Todd thought. Like Jonah in the whale.

"Justa throwin' feathers in everybody's face. An 'ole Saint Peter called me in. Said, 'Jefferson, tell me two things, what you doin' flyin' without a harness; an' how come you flyin' so fast?' So I tole him I was flyin' without a harness 'cause it got in my way, but I couldn'ta been flyin' so fast, 'cause I wasn't usin' but one wing. Saint Peter said, 'You wasn't flyin' with but one wing?' 'Yessuh,' I says, scared-like. So he says, 'Well, since you got sucha extra fine pair of wings you can leave off yo' harness awhile. But from now on none of that there one-wing flyin', 'cause you gittin' up too damn much speed!' "

And with one mouth full of bad teeth you're making too damned much talk, thought Todd. Why don't I send him after the boy? His body ached from the hard ground and seeking to shift his position he twisted his ankle and hated himself for crying out.

"It gittin' worse?"

"I . . . I twisted it," he groaned.

"Try not to think about it, son. That's what I do."

He bit his lip, fighting pain with counter-pain as the voice resumed its rhythmical droning. Jefferson seemed caught in his own creation.

". . . After all that trouble I just floated roun' heaven in slow motion. But I forgot, like colored folks will do, and got to flyin' with one wing again. This time I was restin' my old broken arm and got to flyin' fast enough to shame the devil. I was comin' so fast, Lawd, I got myself called befo' ole Saint Peter again. He said, 'Jeff, didn't I warn you 'bout that speedin'?' 'Yessuh,' I says, 'but it was an accident.' He looked at me sad-like and shook his head and I knowed I was gone. He said, 'Jeff, you and that speedin' is a danger to the heavenly community. If I was to let you keep on flyin', heaven wouldn't be nothin' but uproar. Jeff, you got to go!' Son, I argued and pleaded with that old white man, but it didn't do a bit of good. They rushed me straight to them pearly gates and gimme a parachute and a map of the state of Alabama. . . ."

Todd heard him laughing so that he could hardly speak, making a screen between them upon which his humiliation glowed like fire.

"Maybe you'd better stop awhile," he said, his voice unreal.

"Ain't much more," Jefferson laughed. "When they gimme the parachute ole Saint Peter ask me if I wanted to say a few words before I went. I felt so bad I couldn't hardly look at him, specially with all them white angels standin' around. Then somebody laughed and made me mad. So I tole him, 'Well, you done took my wings. And you puttin' me out. You got charge of things so's I can't do nothin' about it. But you got to admit just this: While I was up here I was the flyiest sonofabitch what ever hit heaven!' "

At the burst of laughter Todd felt such an intense humiliation that only great violence would wash it away. The laughter which shook the old man like a boiling purge set up vibrations of guilt within him which not even the intricate machinery of the plane would have been adequate to transform and he heard himself screaming, "Why do you laugh at me this way?"

He hated himself at that moment, but he had lost control. He saw Jefferson's mouth fall open, "What—?"

"Answer me!"

His blood pounded as though it would surely burst his temples and he tried to reach the old man and fell, screaming, "Can I help it because they won't let us actually fly? Maybe we are a bunch of buzzards feeding on a dead horse, but we can hope to be eagles, can't we? Can't we?"

He fell back, exhausted, his ankle pounding. The saliva was like straw in his mouth. If he had the strength he would strangle this old man. This grinning, gray-headed clown who made him feel as he felt when watched by the white officers at the field. And yet this old man had neither power, prestige, rank nor technique. Nothing that could rid him of this terrible feeling. He watched him, seeing his face struggle to express a turmoil of feeling.

"What you mean, son? What you talking 'bout . . . ?"

"Go away. Go tell your tales to the white folks."

"But I didn't mean nothing like that. . . . I . . . I wasn't tryin' to hurt your feelings. . . ."

"Please. Get the hell away from me!"

"But I didn't, son. I didn't mean all them things a-tall."

Todd shook as with a chill, searching Jefferson's face for a trace of the mockery he had seen there. But now the face was somber and tired and old. He was confused. He could not be sure that there had ever been laughter there, that Jefferson had ever really laughed in his whole life. He saw Jefferson reach out to touch him and shrank away, wondering if anything except the pain, now causing his vision to waver, was real. Perhaps he had imagined it all.

"Don't let it get you down, son," the voice said pensively.

He heard Jefferson sigh wearily, as though he felt more than he could say. His anger ebbed, leaving only the pain.

"I'm sorry," he mumbled.

"You just wore out with pain, was all. . . ."

He saw him through a blur, smiling. And for a second he felt the embarrassed silence of understanding flutter between them.

"What you was doin' flyin' over this section, son? Wasn't you scared they might shoot you for a cow?"

Todd tensed. Was he being laughed at again? But before he could decide, the pain shook him and a part of him was lying calmly behind the screen of pain that had fallen between them, recalling the first time he had ever seen a plane. It was as though an endless series of hangars had been shaken ajar in the air-base of his memory and from each, like a young wasp emerging from its cell, arose the memory of a plane.

The first time I ever saw a plane I was very small and planes were new in the world. I was four-and-a-half and the only plane that I had ever seen was a model suspended from the ceiling of the automobile exhibit at the State Fair. But I did not know that it was only a model. I did not know how large a real plane was, nor how expensive. To me it was a fascinating toy, complete in itself, which my mother said could only be owned by rich little white boys. I stood rigid with admiration, my head straining backwards as I watched the gray little plane describing arcs above the gleaming tops of the automobiles. And I vowed that, rich or poor, someday I would own such a toy. My mother had to drag me out of the exhibit and not even the merry-go-round, the Ferris wheel, or the racing horses could hold my attention for the rest of the Fair. I was too busy imitating the tiny drone of the plane with my lips, and imitating with my hands the motion, swift and circling, that it made in flight.

After that I no longer used the pieces of lumber that lay about our back yard to construct wagons and autos . . . now it was used for airplanes. I built biplanes, using pieces of board for wings, a small box for the fuselage, another piece of wood for the rudder. The trip to the Fair had brought something new into my small world. I asked my mother repeatedly when the Fair would come back again. I'd lie in the grass and watch the sky, and each fighting bird became a soaring plane. I would have been good a year just to have seen a plane again. I became a nuisance to everyone with my questions about airplanes. But planes were new to the old folks, too, and there was little that they could tell me. Only my uncle knew some of the answers. And better still, he could carve propellers from pieces of wood that would whirl rapidly in the wind, wobbling noisily upon oiled nails.

I wanted a plane more than I'd wanted anything; more than I wanted the red wagon with rubber tires, more than the train that ran on a track with its train of cars. I asked my mother over and over again:

"Mamma?"

"What do you want, boy?" she'd say.

"Mamma, will you get mad if I ask you?" I'd say.

"What do you want now? I ain't got time to be answering a lot of fool questions. What you want?"

"Mamma, when you gonna get me one . . . ?" I'd ask.

"Get you one what?" she'd say.

"You know, Mamma; what I been asking you. . . ."

"Boy," she'd say, "if you don't want a spanking you better come on an' tell me what you talking about so I can get on with my work."

"Aw, Mamma, you know. . . ."

"What I just tell you?" she'd say.

"I mean when you gonna buy me a airplane."

"AIRPLANE! Boy, is you crazy? How many times I have to tell you to stop that foolishness. I done told you them things cost too much. I bet I'm gon' wham the living daylight out of you if you don't quit worrying me 'bout them things!"

But this did not stop me, and a few days later I'd try all over again.

Then one day a strange thing happened. It was spring and for some reason I had been hot and irritable all morning. It was a beautiful spring. I could feel it as I played barefoot in the backyard. Blossoms hung from the thorny black locust trees like clusters of fragrant white grapes. Butterflies flickered in the sunlight above the short new dew-wet grass. I had gone in the house for bread and butter and coming out I heard a steady unfamiliar drone. It was unlike anything I had ever heard before. I tried to place the sound. It was no use. It was a sensation like that I had when searching for my father's watch, heard ticking unseen in a room. It made me feel as though I had forgotten to perform some task that my mother had ordered . . . then I located it, overhead. In the sky, flying quite low and about a hundred yards off was a plane! It came so slowly that it seemed barely to move. My mouth hung wide; my bread and butter fell into the dirt. I wanted to jump up and down and cheer. And when the idea struck I trembled with excitement: "Some little white boy's plane's done flew away and all I got to do is stretch out my hands and it'll be mine!" It was a little plane like that at the Fair, flying no higher than the eaves of our roof. Seeing it come steadily forward I felt the world grow warm with promise. I opened the screen and climbed over it and clung there, waiting. I would catch the plane as it came over and swing down fast and run into the house before anyone could see me. Then no one could come to claim the plane. It droned nearer. Then when it hung like a silver cross in the blue directly above me I stretched out my hand and grabbed. It was like sticking my finger through a soap bubble. The plane flew on, as though I had simply blown my breath after it. I grabbed again, frantically, trying to catch the tail. My fingers clutched the air and disappointment surged tight and hard in my throat. Giving one last desperate grasp, I strained forward. My fingers ripped against the screen. I was falling. The ground burst hard against me. I drummed the earth with my heels and when my breath returned, I lay there bawling.

My mother rushed through the door.

"What's the matter, chile! What on earth is wrong with you?"

"It's gone! It's gone!"

"What gone?"

"The airplane. . . ."

"Airplane?"

"Yessum, jus' like the one at the Fair. . . . I . . . I tried to stop it an' it kep' right on going. . . . "

"When, boy?"

"Just now," I cried, through my tears.

"Where it go, boy, what way?"

"Yonder, there. . . . "

She scanned the sky, her arms akimbo and her checkered apron flapping in the wind as I pointed to the fading plane. Finally she looked down at me, slowly shaking her head.

"It's gone! It's gone!" I cried.

"Boy, is you a fool?" she said. "Don't you see that there's a real airplane 'stead of one of them toy ones?"

"Real . . . ?" I forgot to cry. "Real?"

"Yass, real. Don't you know that thing you reaching for is bigger'n a auto? You here trying to reach for it and I bet it's flying 'bout two hundred miles higher'n this roof." She was disgusted with me. "You come on in this house before somebody else sees what a fool you done turned out to be. You must think these here lil ole arms of you'n is mighty long. . . . "

I was carried into the house and undressed for bed and the doctor was called. I cried bitterly, as much from the disappointment of finding the plane so far beyond my reach as from the pain.

When the doctor came I heard my mother telling him about the plane and asking if anything was wrong with my mind. He explained that I had had a fever for several hours. But I was kept in bed for a week and I constantly saw the plane in my sleep, flying just beyond my fingertips, sailing so slowly that it seemed barely to move. And each time I'd reach out to grab it I'd miss and through each dream I'd hear my grandma warning:

Young man, young man
Yo' arms too short
To box with God. . . .

"Hey, son!"

At first he did not know where he was and looked at the old man pointing, with blurred eyes.

"Ain't that one of you-all's airplanes coming after you?"

As his vision cleared he saw a small black shape above a distant field, soaring through waves of heat. But he could not be sure and with the pain he feared that somehow a horrible recurring fantasy of being split in twain by the whirling blades of a propeller had come true.

"You think he sees us?" he heard.

"See? I hope so."

"He's coming like a bat outa hell!"

Straining, he heard the faint sound of a motor and hoped it would soon be over.

"How you feeling?"

"Like a nightmare," he said.

"Hey, he's done curved back the other way!"

"Maybe he saw us," he said. "Maybe he's gone to send out the ambulance and ground crew." And, he thought with despair, maybe he didn't even see us.

"Where did you send the boy?"

"Down to Mister Graves," Jefferson said. "Man what owns this land."

"Do you think he phoned?"

Jefferson looked at him quickly.

"Aw sho'. Dabney Graves is got a bad name on accounta them killings but he'll call though. . . . "

"What killings?"

"Them five fellers . . . ain't you heard?" he asked with surprise.

"No."

"Everybody knows 'bout Dabney Graves, especially the colored. He done killed enough of us."

Todd had the sensation of being caught in a white neighborhood after dark.

"What did they do?" he asked.

"Thought they was men," Jefferson said. "An' some he owed money, like he do me. . . . "

"But why do you stay here?"

"You black, son."

"I know, but . . . ."

"You have to come by the white folks, too."

He turned away from Jefferson's eyes, at once consoled and accused. And I'll have to come by them soon, he thought with despair. Closing his eyes, he heard Jefferson's voice as the sun burned blood-red upon his lips.

"I got nowhere to go," Jefferson said, "an' they'd come after me if I did. But Dabney Graves is a funny fellow. He's all the time making jokes. He can be mean as hell, then he's liable to turn right around and back the colored against the white folks. I seen him do it. But me, I hates him for that more'n anything else. 'Cause just as soon as he gits tired helping a man he don't care what happens to him. He just leaves him stone cold. And then the other white folks is double hard on anybody he done helped. For him it's just a joke. He don't give a hilla beans for nobody—but hisself. . . . "

Todd listened to the thread of detachment in the old man's voice. It was as though he held his words arm's length before him to avoid their destructive meaning.

"He'd just as soon do you a favor and then turn right around and have you strung up. Me, I stays outa his way 'cause down here that's what you gotta do."

If my ankle would only ease for a while, he thought. The closer I spin toward the earth the blacker I become, flashed through his mind. Sweat ran into his eyes and he was sure that he would never see the plane if his head continued whirling. He tried to see Jefferson, what it was that Jefferson held in his hand? It was a little black man, another Jefferson! A little black Jefferson that shook with fits of belly-laughter while the other Jefferson looked on with detachment. Then Jefferson looked up from the thing in his hand and turned to speak, but Todd was far away, searching the sky for a plane in a hot dry land on a day and age he had long forgotten. He was going mysteriously with his mother through empty streets where black faces peered from behind drawn shades and someone was rapping at a window and he was looking back to see a hand and a frightened face frantically beckoning from a cracked door and his mother was looking down the empty perspective of the street and shaking her head and hurrying him along and at first it was only a flash he saw and a motor was droning as through the sun-glare he saw it gleaming silver as it circled and he was seeing a burst like a puff of white smoke and hearing his mother yell, Come along, boy, I got no time for them fool airplanes, I got no time, and he saw it a second time, the plane flying high, and the burst appeared suddenly and fell slowly, billowing out and sparkling like fireworks and he was watching and being hurried along as the air filled with a flurry of white pinwheeling cards that caught in the wind and scattered over the rooftops and into the gutters and a woman was running and snatching a card and reading it and screaming and he darted into the shower, grabbing as in winter he grabbed for snowflakes and bounding away at his mother's, Come on here, boy! Come on, I say! and he was watching as she took the card away, seeing her face grow puzzled and turning taut as her voice quavered, "Niggers Stay From the Polls," and died to a moan of terror as he saw the eyeless sockets of a white hood staring at him from the card and above he saw the plane spiraling gracefully, agleam in the sun like a fiery sword. And seeing it soar he was caught, transfixed between a terrible horror and a horrible fascination.

The sun was not so high now, and Jefferson was calling and gradually he saw three figures moving across the curving roll of the field.

"Look like some doctors, all dressed in white," said Jefferson.

They're coming at last, Todd thought. And he felt such a release of tension within him that he thought he would faint. But no sooner did he close his eyes than he was seized and he was struggling with three white men who were forcing his arms into some kind of coat. It was too much for him, his arms were pinned to his sides and as the pain blazed in his eyes, he realized that it was a straitjacket. What filthy joke was this?

"That oughta hold him, Mister Graves," he heard.

His total energies seemed focused in his eyes as he searched their faces. That was Graves; the other two wore hospital uniforms. He was poised between two poles of fear and hate as he heard the one called Graves saying, "He looks kinda purty in that there suit, boys. I'm glad you dropped by."

"This boy ain't crazy, Mister Graves," one of the others said. "He needs a doctor, not us. Don't see how you led us way out here anyway. It might be a joke to you, but your cousin Rudolph liable to kill somebody. White folks or niggers, don't make no difference. . . ."

Todd saw the man turn red with anger. Graves looked down upon him, chuckling.

"This nigguh belongs in a straitjacket, too, boys. I knowed that the minit Jeff's kid said something 'bout a nigguh flyer. You all know you cain't let the nigguh git up that high without his going crazy. The nigguh brain ain't built right for high altitudes. . . . ."

Todd watched the drawling red face, feeling that all the unnamed horror and obscenities that he had ever imagined stood materialized before him.

"Let's git outta here," one of the attendants said.

Todd saw the other reach toward him, realizing for the first time that he lay upon a stretcher as he yelled.

"Don't put your hands on me!"

They drew back, surprised.

"What's that you say, nigguh?" asked Graves.

He did not answer and thought that Graves's foot was aimed at his head. It landed on his chest and he could hardly breathe. He coughed helplessly, seeing Graves's lips stretch taut over his yellow teeth, and tried to shift his head. It was as though a half-dead fly was dragging slowly across his face and a bomb seemed to burst within him. Blasts of hot, hysterical laughter tore from his chest, causing his eyes to pop and he felt that the veins in his neck would surely burst. And then a part of him stood behind it all, watching the surprise in Graves's red face and his own hysteria. He thought he would never stop, he would laugh himself to death. It rang in his ears like Jefferson's laughter and he looked for him, centering his eyes desperately upon his face, as though somehow he had become his sole salvation in an insane world of outrage and humiliation. It brought a certain relief. He was suddenly aware that although his body was still contorted it was an echo that no longer rang in his ears. He heard Jefferson's voice with gratitude.

"Mister Graves, the Army done tole him not to leave his airplane."

"Nigguh, Army or no, you gittin' off my land! That airplane can stay 'cause it was paid for by taxpayers' money. But you gittin' off. An' dead or alive, it don't make no difference to me."

Todd was beyond it now, lost in a world of anguish.

"Jeff," Graves said, "you and Teddy come and grab holt. I want you to take this here black eagle over to that nigguh airfield and leave him."

Jefferson and the boy approached him silently. He looked away, realizing and doubting at once that only they could release him from his overpowering sense of isolation.

They bent for the stretcher. One of the attendants moved toward Teddy.

"Think you can manage it, boy?"

"I think I can, suh," Teddy said.

"Well, you better go behind then, and let yo' pa go ahead so's to keep that leg elevated."

He saw the white men walking ahead of Jefferson and the boy carried him along in silence. Then they were pausing and he felt a hand wiping his face; then he was moving again. And it was as though he had been lifted out of his isolation, back into the world of men. A new current of communication flowed between the man and boy and himself. They moved him gently. Far away he heard a mockingbird liquidly calling. He raised his eyes, seeing a buzzard poised unmoving in space. For a moment the whole afternoon seemed suspended and he waited for the horror to seize him again. Then like a song within his head he heard the boy's soft humming and saw the dark bird glide into the sun and glow like a bird of flaming gold.

[1944]

QUESTIONS

1. What does Jefferson's tale of the angels have to do with Todd's own situation? Why does Todd react so negatively to the story?
2. In *Invisible Man*, Ellison also has a character whose name is Todd, but spelled "Tod," which in German means death. Does the death metaphor apply to his pilot in "Flying Home"?
3. How are we to interpret the second word in Ellison's title?

Louise Erdrich

(b. 1954)

United States

Louise Erdrich credits her parents with instilling in her an early love of reading and writing.

> My father used to give me a nickel for every story I wrote, and my mother wove strips of construction paper together and stapled them into book covers. So at an early age I felt myself to be a published author earning substantial royalties. Mine were wonderful parents: they got me excited about reading and writing in a lasting way.

Erdrich's German-born father taught for the Bureau of Indian Affairs, where her Chippewa mother also worked. Erdrich frequently visited her maternal grandparents, who lived on the Turtle Mountain Chippewa Reservation in North Dakota. Before she began to turn those experiences into lyrical fiction, Erdrich attended Dartmouth and Johns Hopkins; at Dartmouth, she met and later married Michael Dorris, an anthropologist of Native American ancestry and also an author with whom she collaborated on a novel based on Columbus's arrival in America, *The Crown of Columbus* (1991).

Love Medicine (1984), Erdrich's first novel (some critics consider it a collection of short stories), won the National Book Critics Circle Award. The narrative, a vivid, compelling portrait of a Turtle Mountain Chippewa community, employs multiple narrative voices: seven narrators from two interrelated families, the Lamartines and the Kashpaws, tell 14 interlocking stories. Through their "oral" monologues, Erdrich conveys not only the complexity of her characters' family relationships but also the tensions they feel within their tradition and with the white community. Through experiences that are both comic and tragic, her characters ponder the meaning of circumstances ranging from poverty and despair, alcoholism, racism, and unrequited love to spiritual strength, mystery, and mutuality. Toni Morrison commented that "The beauty of *Love Medicine* saves us from being completely devastated by its power." What binds Erdrich's characters is a deeply rooted capacity for love and survival, evoked through the author's rich, lyrical prose.

Erdrich has continued her imaginative recreation of Chippewa community life in *Beet Queen* (1986) and *Tracks* (1988). She is also the author of a collection of poetry, *Jacklight* (1984). Currently, she lives in New Hampshire with Dorris and their five children.

◆ *Love Medicine* ◆

I never really done much with my life, I suppose. I never had a television. Grandma Kashpaw had one inside her apartment at the Senior Citizens, so I used to go there and watch my favorite shows. For a while she used to call me the biggest waste on the reservation and hark back to how she saved me from my own mother, who wanted to tie me in a potato sack and throw me in a slough. Sure, I was grateful to Grandma Kashpaw for saving me like that, for raising me, but gratitude gets old. After a while, stale. I had to stop thanking her. One day I told her I had paid her back in full by staying at her beck and call. I'd do anything for Grandma. She knew that. Besides, I took care of Grandpa like nobody else could, on account of what a handful he'd gotten to be.

But that was nothing. I know the tricks of mind and body inside out without ever having trained for it, because I got the touch. It's a thing you got to be born with. I got secrets in my hands that nobody ever knew to ask. Take Grandma Kashpaw with her tired veins all knotted up in her legs like clumps of blue snails. I take my fingers and I snap them on the knots. The medicine flows out of me. The touch. I run my fingers up the maps of those rivers of veins or I knock very gentle above their hearts or I make a circling motion on their stomachs, and it helps them. They feel much better. Some women pay me five dollars.

I couldn't do the touch for Grandpa, though. He was a hard nut. You know, some people fall right through the hole in their lives. It's invisible, but they come to it after time, never knowing where. There is this woman here, Lulu Lamartine, who always had a thing for Grandpa. She loved him since she was a girl and always said he was a genius. Now she says that his mind got so full it exploded.

How can I doubt that? I know the feeling when your mental power builds up too far. I always used to say that's why the Indians got drunk. Even statistically we're the smartest people on the earth. Anyhow with Grandpa I couldn't hardly believe it, because all my youth he stood out as a hero to me. When he started getting toward second childhood he went through different moods. He would stand in the woods and cry at the top of his shirt. It scared me, scared everyone, Grandma worst of all.

Yet he was so smart—do you believe it?—that he *knew* he was getting foolish.

He said so. He told me that December I failed school and come back on the train to Hoopdance. I didn't have nowhere else to go. He picked me up there and he said it straight out: "I'm getting into my second childhood." And then he said something else I still remember: "I been chosen for it. I couldn't say no." So I figure that a man so smart all his life—tribal chairman and the star of movies and even pictured in the statehouse and on cans of snuff—would know what he's doing by saying yes. I think he was called to second childhood like anybody else gets a call for the priesthood or the army or whatever. So I really did not listen too hard when the doctor said this was some kind of disease old people got eating too much sugar. You just can't tell me that a man who went to Washington and gave them bureaucrats what for could lose his mind from eating too much Milky Way. No, he put second childhood on himself.

Behind those songs he sings out in the middle of Mass, and back of those stories that everybody knows by heart, Grandpa is thinking hard about life. I know the feeling. Sometimes I'll throw up a smokescreen to think behind. I'll hitch up to Winnipeg and play the Space Invaders for six hours, but all the time there and back I will be thinking some fairly deep thoughts that surprise even me, and I'm used to it. As for him, if it was just the thoughts there wouldn't be no problem. Smokescreen is what irritates the social structure, see, and Grandpa has done things that just distract people to the point they want to throw him in the cookie jar where they keep the mentally insane. He's far from that, I know for sure, but even Grandma had trouble keeping her patience once he started sneaking off to Lamartine's place. He's not supposed to have his candy, and Lulu feeds it to him. That's *one* of the reasons why he goes.

Grandma tried to get me to put the touch on Grandpa soon after he began stepping out. I didn't want to, but before Grandma started telling me again what a bad state my bare behind was in when she first took me home, I thought I should at least pretend.

I put my hands on either side of Grandpa's head. You wouldn't look at him and say he was crazy. He's a fine figure of a man, as Lamartine would say, with all his hair and half his teeth, a beak like a hawk, and cheeks like the blades of a hatchet. They put his picture on all the tourist guides to North Dakota and even copied his face for artistic paintings. I guess you could call him a monument all of himself. He started grinning when I put my hands on his templates, and I knew right then he knew how come I touched him. I knew the smokescreen was going to fall.

And I was right: just for a moment it fell.

"Let's pitch whoopee," he said across my shoulder to Grandma.

They don't use that expression much around here anymore, but for damn sure it must have meant something. It got her goat right quick.

She threw my hands off his head herself and stood in front of him, overmatching him pound for pound, and taller too, for she had a growth spurt in middle age while he had shrunk, so now the length and breadth of her surpassed him. She glared up and spoke her piece into his face about how he was off at all hours tomcatting and chasing Lamartine again and making a damn old fool of himself.

"And you got no more whoopee to pitch anymore anyhow!" she yelled at last, surprising me so my jaw just dropped, for us kids all had pretended for so long that those rustling sounds we heard from their side of the room at night never happened. She sure had pretended it, up till now, anyway. I saw that tears were in her eyes. And that's when I saw how much grief and love she felt for him. And it gave me a real shock to the system. You see I thought love got easier over the years so it didn't hurt so bad when it hurt, or feel so good when it felt good. I thought it smoothed out and old people hardly noticed it. I thought it curled up and died, I guess. Now I saw it rear up like a whip and lash.

She loved him. She was jealous. She mourned him like the dead.

And he just smiled into the air, trapped in the seams of his mind.

So I didn't know what to do. I was in a laundry then. They was like parents to me, the way they had took me home and reared me. I could see her point for wanting to get him back the way he was so at least she could argue with him, sleep with him, not be shamed out by Lamartine. She'd always love him. That hit me like a ton of bricks. For one whole day I felt this odd feeling that cramped my hands. When you have the touch, that's where longing gets you. I never loved like that. It made me feel all inspired to see them fight, and I wanted to go out and find a woman who I would love until one of us died or went crazy. But I'm not like that really. From time to time I heal a person all up good inside, however when it comes to the long shot I doubt that I got staying power.

And you need that, staying power, going out to love somebody. I knew this quality was not going to jump on me with no effort. So I turned my thoughts back to Grandma and Grandpa. I felt her side of it with my hands and my tangled guts, and I felt his side of it within the stretch of my mentality. He had gone out to lunch one day and never came back. He was fishing in the middle of Lake Turcot. And there was big thoughts on his line, and he kept throwing them back for even bigger ones that would explain to him, say, the meaning of how we got here and why we have to leave so soon. All in all, I could not see myself treating Grandpa with the touch, bringing him back, when the real part of him had chose to be off thinking somewhere. It was only the rest of him that stayed around causing trouble, after all, and we could handle most of it without any problem.

Besides, it was hard to argue with his reasons for doing some things. Take Holy Mass. I used to go there just every so often, when I got frustrated mostly, because even though I know the Higher Power dwells everyplace, there's something very calming about the cool greenish inside of our mission. Or so I thought, anyway. Grandpa was the one who stripped off my delusions in this matter, for it was he who busted right through what Father Upsala calls the sacred serenity of the place.

We filed in that time. Me and Grandpa. We sat down in our pews. Then the rosary got started up pre-Mass and that's when Grandpa filled up his chest and opened his mouth and belted out them words.

HAIL MARIE FULL OF GRACE.

He had a powerful set of lungs.

And he kept on like that. He did not let up. He hollered and he yelled them prayers, and I guess people was used to him by now, because they only muttered theirs and did not quit and gawk like I did. I was getting red-faced, I admit. I give him the elbow once or twice, but that wasn't nothing to him. He kept on. He shrieked to heaven and he pleaded like a movie actor and he pounded his chest like Tarzan in the Lord I Am Not Worthies. I thought he might hurt himself. Then after a while I guess I got used to it, and that's when I wondered: how come?

So afterwards I out and asked him. "How come? How come you yelled?"

"God don't hear me otherwise," said Grandpa Kashpaw.

I sweat. I broke right into a little cold sweat at my hairline because I knew this was perfectly right and for years not one damn other person had noticed it. God's been going deaf. Since the Old Testament, God's been deafening up on us. I read, see. Besides the dictionary, which I'm constantly in use of, I had this Bible once. I read it. I found there was discrepancies between then and now. It struck me. Here God used to raineth bread from clouds, smite the Phillipines, sling fire down on red-light districts where people got stabbed. He even appeared in person every once in a while. God used to pay attention, is what I'm saying.

Now there's your God in the Old Testament and there is Chippewa Gods as well. Indian Gods, good and bad, like tricky Nanabozho or the water monster, Missepeshu, who lives over in Lake Turcot. That water monster was the last God I ever heard to appear. It had a weakness for young girls and grabbed one of the Blues off her rowboat. She got to shore all right, but only after this monster had its way with her. She's an old lady now. Old Lady Blue. She still won't let her family fish that lake.

Our Gods aren't perfect, is what I'm saying, but at least they come around. They'll do a favor if you ask them right. You don't have to yell. But you do have to know, like I said, how to ask in the right way. That makes problems, because to ask proper was an art that was lost to the Chippewas once the Catholics gained ground. Even now, I have to wonder if Higher Power turned it back, if we got to yell, or if we just don't speak its language.

I looked around me. How else could I explain what all I had seen in my short life—King smashing his fist in things, Gordie drinking himself down to the Bismarck hospitals, or Aunt June left by a white man to wander off in the snow. How else to explain the times my touch don't work, and farther back, to the old-time Indians who was swept away in the outright germ warfare and dirty-dog killing of the whites. In those times, us Indians was so much kindlier than now.

We took them in.

Oh yes, I'm bitter as an old cutworm just thinking of how they done to us and doing still.

So Grandpa Kashpaw just opened my eyes a little there. Was there any sense relying on a God whose ears was stopped? Just like the government? I says then, right off, maybe we got nothing but ourselves. And that's not much, just personally speaking. I know I don't got the cold hard potatoes it takes to understand everything. Still, there's things I'd like to do. For instance, I'd like to help some people like my Grandpa and Grandma Kashpaw get back some happiness within the tail ends of their lives.

I told you once before I couldn't see my way clear to putting the direct touch on Grandpa's mind, and I kept my moral there, but something soon happened to make me think a little bit of mental adjustment wouldn't do him and the rest of us no harm.

It was after we saw him one afternoon in the sunshine courtyard of the Senior Citizens with Lulu Lamartine. Grandpa used to like to dig there. He had his little dandelion fork out, and he was prying up them dandelions right and left while Lamartine watched him.

"He's scratching up the dirt, all right," said Grandma, watching Lamartine watch Grandpa out the window.

Now Lamartine was about half the considerable size of Grandma, but you would never think of sizes anyway. They were different in an even more noticeable way. It was the difference between a house fixed up with paint and picky fence, and a house left to weather away into the soft earth, is what I'm saying. Lamartine was jacked up, latticed, shuttered, and vinyl sided, while Grandma sagged and bulged on her slipped foundations and let her hair go the silver gray of rain-dried lumber. Right now, she eyed the Lamartine's pert flowery dress with such a look it despaired me. I knew what this could lead to with Grandma. Alternating tongue storms and rock-hard silences was hard on a man, even one who didn't notice, like Grandpa. So I went fetching him.

But he was gone when I popped through the little screen door that led out on the courtyard. There was nobody out there either, to point which way they went. Just the dandelion fork quibbling upright in the ground. That gave me an idea. I snookered over to the Lamartine's door and I listened in first, then knocked. But nobody. So I went walking through the lounges and around the card tables. Still nobody. Finally it was my touch that led me to the laundry room. I cracked the door. I went in. There they were. And he was really loving her up good, boy, and she was going hell for leather. Sheets was flapping on the lines above, and washcloths, pillowcases, shirts was also flying through the air, for they was trying to clear out a place for themselves in a high-heaped but shallow laundry cart. The washers and the dryers was all on, chock full of quarters, shaking and moaning. I couldn't hear what Grandpa and the Lamartine was billing and cooing, and they couldn't hear me.

I didn't know what to do, so I went inside and shut the door.

The Lamartine wore a big curly light-brown wig. Looked like one of them squeaky little white-people dogs. Poodles they call them. Anyway, that wig is what saved us from the worse. For I could hardly shout and tell them I was in there, no more could I try and grab him. I was trapped where I was. There was nothing I could really do but hold the door shut. I was scared of somebody else upsetting in and really getting an eyeful. Turned out though, in the heat of the clinch, as I was trying to avert my eyes you see, the Lamartine's curly wig jumped off her head. And if you ever been in the midst of something and had a big change like that occur in the someone, you can't help know how it devastates your basic urges. Not only that, but her wig was almost with a life of its own. Grandpa's eyes were bugging at the change already, and swear to God if the thing didn't rear up and pop him in the face like it was going to start something. He scrambled up, Grandpa did, and the Lamartine jumped up after him all addled looking. They just stared at each other, huffing and puffing, with quizzical expression. The surprise seemed to drive all sense completely out of Grandpa's mind.

"The letter was what started the fire," he said. "I never would have done it."

"What letter?" said the Lamartine. She was stiff-necked now, and elegant, even bald, like some alien queen. I gave her back the wig. The Lamartine replaced it on her head, and whenever I saw her after that, I couldn't help thinking of her bald, with special powers, as if from another planet.

"That was a close call," I said to Grandpa after she had left.

But I think he had already forgot the incident. He just stood there all quiet and thoughtful. You really wouldn't think he was crazy. He looked like he was just about to say something important, explaining himself. He said something, all right, but it didn't have nothing to do with anything that made sense.

He wondered where the heck he put his dandelion fork. That's when I decided about the mental adjustment.

Now what was mostly our problem was not so much that he was not all there, but that what was there of him often hankered after Lamartine. If we could put a stop to that, I thought, we might be getting someplace. But here, see, my touch was of no use. For what could I snap my fingers at to make him faithful to Grandma? Like the quality of staying power, this faithfulness was invisible. I know it's something that you got to acquire, but I never known where from. Maybe there's no rhyme or reason to it, like my getting the touch, and then again maybe it's a kind of magic.

It was Grandma Kashpaw who thought of it in the end. She knows things. Although she will not admit she has a scrap of Indian blood in her, there's no doubt in my mind she's got some Chippewa. How else would you explain the way she'll be sitting there, in front of her TV story, rocking in her armchair and suddenly she turns on me, her brown eyes hard as lake-bed flint.

"Lipsha Morrissey," she'll say, "you went out last night and got drunk."

How did she know that? I'll hardly remember it myself. Then she'll say she just had a feeling or ache in the scar of her hand or a creak in her shoulder. She is constantly being told things by little aggravations in her joints or by her household appliances. One time she told Gordie never to ride with a crazy Lamartine boy. She had seen something in the polished-up tin of her bread toaster. So he didn't. Sure enough, the time came we heard how Lyman and Henry went out of control in their car, ending up in the river. Lyman swam to the top, but Henry never made it.

Thanks to Grandma's toaster, Gordie was probably spared.

Someplace in the blood Grandma Kashpaw knows things. She also remembers things, I found. She keeps things filed away. She's got a memory like them video games that don't forget your score. One reason she remembers so many details about the trouble I gave her in early life is so she can flash back her total when she needs to.

Like now. Take the love medicine. I don't know where she remembered that from. It came tumbling from her mind like an asteroid off the corner of the screen.

Of course she starts out by mentioning the time I had this accident in church and did she leave me there with wet overhalls? No she didn't. And ain't I glad? Yes I am. Now what you want now, Grandma?

But when she mentions them love medicines, I feel my back prickle at the danger. These love medicines is something of an old Chippewa specialty. No other tribe has got them down so well. But love medicines is not for the layman to handle. You don't just go out and get one without paying for it. Before you get one, even, you should go through one hell of a lot of mental condensation. You got to think it over. Choose the right one. You could really mess up your life grinding up the wrong little thing.

So anyhow, I said to Grandma I'd give this love medicine some thought. I knew the best thing was to go ask a specialist like Old Man Pillager, who lives up in a tangle of bush and never shows himself. But the truth is I was afraid of him, like everyone else. He was known for putting the twisted mouth on people, seizing up their hearts. Old Man Pillager was serious business, and I have always thought it best to steer clear of that whenever I could. That's why I took the powers in my own hands. That's why I did what I could.

I put my whole mentality to it, nothing held back. After a while I started to remember things I'd heard gossiped over.

I heard of this person once who carried a charm of seeds that looked like baby pearls. They was attracted to a metal knife, which made them powerful. But I didn't know where them seeds grew. Another love charm I heard about I couldn't go along with, because how was I suppose to catch frogs in the act, which it required. Them little creatures is slippery and fast. And then the powerfullest of all, the most extreme, involved nail clips and such. I wasn't anywhere near asking Grandma to provide me all the little body bits that this last love recipe called for. I went walking around for days just trying to think up something that would work.

Well I got it. If it hadn't been the early fall of the year, I never would have got it. But I was sitting underneath a tree one day down near the school just watching people's feet go by when something tells me, look up! Look up! So I look up, and I see two honkers, Canada geese, the kind with little masks on their faces, a bird what mates for life. I see them flying right over my head naturally preparing to land in some slough on the reservation, which they certainly won't get off of alive.

It hits me, anyway. Them geese, they mate for life. And I think to myself, just what if I went out and got a pair? And just what if I fed some part — say the goose heart — of the female to Grandma and Grandpa ate the other heart? Wouldn't that work? Maybe it's all invisible, and then maybe again it's magic. Love is a stony road. We know that for sure. If it's true that the higher feelings of devotion get lodged in the heart like people say, then we'd be home free. If not, eating goose heart couldn't harm nobody anyway. I thought it was worth my effort, and Grandma Kashpaw thought so, too. She had always known a good idea when she heard one. She borrowed me Grandpa's gun.

So I went out to this particular slough, maybe the exact same slough I never got thrown in by my mother, thanks to Grandma Kashpaw, and I hunched down in a good comfortable pile of rushes. I got my gun loaded up. I ate a few of these soft baloney sandwiches Grandma made me for lunch. And then I waited. The cattails blown back and forth above my head. Then stringy blue herons was spearing up their prey. The thing I know how to do best in this world, the thing I been training for all my life, is to wait. Sitting there and sitting there was no hardship on me. I got to thinking about some funny things that happened. There was this one time that Lulu Lamartine's little blue tweety bird, a paraclete, I guess you'd call it, flown up inside her dress and got lost within there. I recalled her running out into the hallway trying to yell something, shaking. She was doing a right good jig there, cutting the rug for sure, and the thing is it *never* flown out. To this day people speculate where it went. They fear she might perhaps of crushed it in her corsets. It sure hasn't ever yet been seen alive. I thought of funny things for a while, but then I used them up, and strange things that happened started weaseling their way into my mind.

I got to thinking quite naturally of the Lamartine's cousin named Wristwatch. I never knew what his real name was. They called him Wristwatch because he got his father's broken wristwatch as a young boy when his father passed on. Never in his whole life did Wristwatch take his father's watch off. He didn't care if it worked, although after a while he got sensitive when people asked what time it was, teasing him. He often put it to his ear like he was listening to the tick. But it was broken for good and forever, people said so, at least that's what they thought.

Well I saw Wristwatch smoking in his pickup one afternoon and by nine that evening he was dead.

He died sitting at the Lamartine's table, too. As she told it, Wristwatch had just eaten himself a good-size dinner and she said would he take seconds on the hot dish when he fell over to the floor. They turnt him over. He was gone. But here's the strange thing: when the Senior Citizen's orderly took the pulse he noticed that the wristwatch Wristwatch wore was now working. The moment he died the wristwatch started keeping perfect time. They buried him with the watch still ticking on his arm.

I got to thinking. What if some gravediggers dug up Wristwatch's casket in two hundred years and that watch was still going? I thought what question they would ask and it was this: Whose hand wound it?

I started shaking like a piece of grass at just the thought.

Not to get off the subject or nothing. I was still hunkered in the slough. It was passing late into the afternoon and still no honkers had touched down. Now I don't need to tell you that the waiting did not get to me, it was the chill. The rushes was very soft, but damp. I was getting cold and debating to leave, when they landed. Two geese swimming here and there as big as life, looking deep into each other's little pinhole eyes. Just the ones I was looking for. So I lifted Grandpa's gun to my shoulder and I aimed perfectly, and *blam! Blam!* I delivered two accurate shots. But the thing is, them shots missed. I couldn't hardly believe it. Whether it was that the stock had warped or the barrel got bent someways, I don't quite know, but anyway them geese flown off into the dim sky, and Lipsha Morrissey was left there in the rushes with evening fallen and his two cold hands empty. He had before him just the prospect of another day of bone-cracking chill in them rushes, and the thought of it got him depressed.

Now it isn't my style, in no way, to get depressed.

So I said to myself, Lipsha Morrissey, you're a happy S.O.B. who could be covered up with weeds by now down at the bottom of this slough, but instead you're alive to tell the tale. You might have problems in life, but you still got the touch. You got the power, Lipsha Morrissey. Can't argue that. So put your mind to it and figure out how not to be depressed.

I took my advice. I put my mind to it. But I never saw at the time how my thoughts led me astray toward a tragic outcome none could have known. I ignored all the danger, all the limits, for I was tired of sitting in the slough and my feet were numb. My face was aching. I was chilled, so I played with fire. I told myself love medicine was simple. I told myself the old superstitions was just that — strange beliefs. I told myself to take the ten dollars Mary MacDonald had paid me for putting the touch on her arthritis joint, and the other five I hadn't spent yet from winning bingo last Thursday. I told myself to go down to the Red Owl store.

And here is what I did that made the medicine backfire. I took an evil shortcut. I looked at birds that was dead and froze.

All right. So now I guess you will say, "Slap a malpractice suit on Lipsha Morrissey."

I heard of those suits. I used to think it was a color clothing quack doctors had to wear so you could tell them from the good ones. Now I know better that it's law.

As I walked back from the Red Owl with the rock-hard, heavy turkeys, I argued to myself about malpractice. I thought of faith. I thought to myself that faith could be called belief against the odds and whether or not there's any proof. How does that sound? I thought how we might have to yell to be heard by Higher Power, but that's not saying it's not *there*. And that is faith for you. It's belief even when the goods don't deliver. Higher Power makes promises we all know they can't back up, but anybody ever go and slap an old malpractice suit on God? Or the U.S. government? No they don't. Faith might be stupid, but it gets us through. So what I'm heading at is this. I finally convinced myself that the real actual power to the love medicine was not the goose heart itself but the faith in the cure.

I didn't believe it, I knew it was wrong, but by then I had waded so far into my lie I was stuck there. And then I went one step further.

The next day, I cleaned the hearts away from the paper packages of gizzards inside the turkeys. Then I wrapped them hearts with a clean hankie and brung them both to get blessed up at the mission. I wanted to get official blessings from the priest, but when Father answered the door to the rectory, wiping his hands on a little towel, I could tell he was a busy man.

"Booshoo, Father," I said. "I got a slight request to make of you this afternoon."

"What is it?" he said.

"Would you bless this package?" I held out the hankie with the hearts tied inside it.

He looked at the package, questioning it.

"It's turkey hearts," I honestly had to reply.

A look of annoyance crossed his face.

"Why don't you bring this matter over to Sister Martin," he said. "I have duties."

And so, although the blessing wouldn't be as powerful, I went over to the Sisters with the package.

I rung the bell, and they brought Sister Martin to the door. I had her as a music teacher, but I was always so shy then. I never talked out loud. Now, I had grown taller than Sister Martin. Looking down, I saw that she was not feeling up to snuff. Brown circles hung under her eyes.

"What's the matter?" she said, not noticing who I was.

"Remember me, Sister?"

She squinted up at me.

"Oh yes," she said after a moment. "I'm sorry, you're the youngest of the Kashpaws. Gordie's brother."

Her face warmed up.

"Lipsha," I said, "that's my name."

"Well, Lipsha," she said, smiling broad at me now, "what can I do for you?"

They always said she was the kindest-hearted of the Sisters up the hill, and she was. She brought me back into their own kitchen and made me take a big yellow wedge of cake and a glass of milk.

"Now tell me," she said, nodding at my package. "What have you got wrapped up so carefully in those handkerchiefs?"

Like before, I answered honestly.

"Ah," said Sister Martin. "Turkey hearts." She waited.

"I hoped you could bless them."

She waited some more, smiling with her eyes. Kindhearted though she was, I began to sweat. A person could not pull the wool down over Sister Martin. I stumbled through my mind for an explanation, quick, that wouldn't scare her off.

"They're a present," I said, "for Saint Kateri's statue."

"She's not a saint yet."

"I know," I stuttered on, "in the hopes they will crown her."

"Lipsha," she said, "I never heard of such a thing."

So I told her. "Well the truth is," I said, "it's a kind of medicine."

"For what?"

"Love."

"Oh Lipsha," she said after a moment, "you don't need any medicine. I'm sure any girl would like you exactly the way you are."

I just sat there. I felt miserable, caught in my pack of lies.

"Tell you what," she said, seeing how bad I felt, "my blessing won't make any difference anyway. But there is something you can do."

I looked up at her, hopeless.

"Just be yourself."

I looked down at my plate. I knew I wasn't much to brag about right then, and I shortly became even less. For as I walked out the door I stuck my fingers in the cup of holy water that was sacred from their touches. I put my fingers in and blessed the hearts, quick, with my own hand.

I went back to Grandma and sat down in her little kitchen at the Senior Citizens. I unwrapped them hearts on the table, and her hard agate eyes went soft. She said she wasn't even going to cook those hearts up but eat them raw so their power would go down strong as possible.

I couldn't hardly watch when she munched hers. Now that's true love. I was worried about how she would get Grandpa to eat his, but she told me she'd think of something and don't worry. So I did not. I was supposed to hide off in her bedroom while she put dinner on a plate for Grandpa and fixed up the heart so he'd eat it. I caught a glint of the plate she was making for him. She put that heart smack on a piece of lettuce like in a restaurant and then attached to it a little heap of boiled peas.

He sat down. I was listening in the next room.

She said, "Why don't you have some mash potato?" So he had some mash potato. Then she gave him a little piece of boiled meat. He ate that. Then she said, "Why you didn't never touch your salad yet. See that heart? I'm feeding you it because the doctor said your blood needs building up."

I couldn't help it, at that point I peeked through a crack in the door.

I saw Grandpa picking at that heart on his plate with a certain look. He didn't look appetized at all, is what I'm saying. I doubted our plan was going to work. Grandma was getting worried, too. She told him one more time, loudly, that he had to eat that heart.

"Swallow it down," she said. "You'll hardly notice it."

He just looked at her straight on. The way he looked at her made me think I was going to see the smokescreen drop a second time, and sure enough it happened.

"What you want me to eat this for so bad?" he asked her uncannily.

Now Grandma knew the jig was up. She knew that he knew she was working medicine. He put his fork down. He rolled the heart around his saucer plate.

"I don't want to eat this," he said to Grandma. "It don't look good."

"Why, it's fresh grade-A," she told him. "One hundred percent."

He didn't ask percent what, but his eyes took on an even more warier look.

"Just go on and try it," she said, taking the salt shaker up in her hand. She was getting annoyed. "Not tasty enough? You want me to salt it for you?" She waved the shaker over his plate.

"All right, skinny white girl!" She had got Grandpa mad. Oopsy-daisy, he popped the heart into his mouth. I was about to yawn loudly and come out of the bedroom. I was about ready for this crash of wills to be over, when I saw he was still up to his old tricks. First he rolled it into one side of his check. "Mmmmm," he said. Then he rolled it into the other side of his cheek. "Mmmmmmm," again. Then he stuck his tongue out with the heart on it and put it back, and there was no time to react. He had pulled Grandma's leg once too far. Her goat was got. She was so mad she hopped up quick as a wink and slugged him between the shoulderblades to make him swallow.

Only thing is, he choked.

He choked real bad. A person can choke to death. You ever sit down at a restaurant table and up above you there is a list of instructions what to do if something slides down the wrong pipe? It sure makes you chew slow, that's for damn sure. When Grandpa fell off his chair better believe me that little graphic illustrated poster fled into my mind. I jumped out the bedroom. I done everything within my power that I could do to unlodge what was choking him. I squeezed underneath his ribcage. I socked him in the back. I was desperate. But here's the factor of decision: he wasn't choking on the heart alone. There was more to it than that. It was other things that choked him as well. It didn't seem like he wanted to struggle or fight. Death came and tapped his chest, so he went just like that. I'm sorry all through my body at what I done to him with that heart, and there's those who will say Lipsha Morrissey is just excusing himself off the hook by giving song and dance about how Grandpa gave up.

Maybe I can't admit what I did. My touch had gone worthless, that is true. But here is what I seen while he lay in my arms.

You hear a person's life will flash before their eyes when they're in danger. It was him in danger, not me, but it was *his* life come over me. I saw him dying, and it was like someone pulled the shade down in a room. His eyes clouded over and squeezed shut, but just before that I looked in. He was still fishing in the middle of Lake Turcot. Big thoughts was on his line and he had half a case of beer in the boat. He waved at me, grinned, and then the bobber went under.

Grandma had gone out of the room crying for help. I bunched my force up in my hands and I held him. I was so wound up I couldn't even breathe. All the moments he had spent with me, all the times he had hoisted me on his shoulders or pointed into the leaves was concentrated in that moment. Time was flashing back and forth like a pinball machine. Lights blinked and balls hopped and rubber bands chirped, until suddenly I realized the last ball had gone down the drain and there was nothing. I felt his force leaving him, flowing out of Grandpa never to return. I felt his mind weakening. The bobber going under in the lake. And I felt the touch retreat back into the darkness inside my body, from where it came.

One time, long ago, both of us were fishing together. We caught a big old snapper what started towing us around like it was a motor. "This here fishline is pretty damn good," Grandpa said. "Let's keep this turtle on and see where he takes us." So we rode along behind that turtle, watching as from time to time it surfaced. The thing was just about the size of a washtub. It took us all around the lake twice, and as it was traveling, Grandpa said something as a joke. "Lipsha," he said, "we are glad your mother didn't want you because we was always looking for a boy like you who would tow us around the lake."

"I ain't no snapper. Snappers is so stupid they stay alive when their head's chopped off," I said.

"That ain't stupidity," said Grandpa. "Their brain's just in their heart, like yours is."

When I looked up, I knew the fuse had blown between my heart and my mind and that a terrible understanding was to be given.

Grandma got back into the room and I saw her stumble. And then she went down too. It was like a house you can't hardly believe has stood so long, through years of record weather, suddenly goes down in the worst yet. It makes sense, is what I'm saying, but you still can't hardly believe it. You think a person you know has got through death and illness and being broke and living on commodity rice will get through anything. Then they fold and you see how fragile were the stones that underpinned them. You see how instantly the ground can shift you thought was solid. You see the stop signs and the yellow dividing markers of roads you traveled and all the instructions you had played according to vanish. You see how all the everyday things you counted on was just a dream you had been having by which you run your whole life. She had been over me, like a sheer overhang of rock dividing Lipsha Morrissey from outer space. And now she went underneath. It was as though the banks gave way on the shores of Lake Turcot, and where Grandpa's passing was just the bobber swallowed under by his biggest thought, her fall was the house and the rock under it sliding after, sending half the lake splashing up to the clouds.

Where there was nothing.

You play them games never knowing what you see. When I fell into the dream alongside of both of them I saw that the dominions I had defended myself from anciently was but delusions of the screen. Blips of light. And I was scot-free now, whistling through space.

I don't know how I come back. I don't know from where. They was slapping my face when I arrived back at Senior Citizens and they was oxygenating her. I saw her chest move, almost unwilling. She sighed the way she would when somebody bothered her in the middle of a row of beads she was counting. I think it irritated her to no end that they brought her back. I knew from the way she looked after they took the mask off, she was not going to forgive them disturbing her restful peace. Nor was she forgiving Lipsha Morrissey. She had been stepping out onto the road of death, she told the children later at the funeral. I asked was there any stop signs or dividing markers on that road, but she clamped her lips in a vise the way she always done when she was mad.

Which didn't bother me. I knew when things had cleared out she wouldn't have no choice. I was not going to speculate where the blame was put for Grandpa's death. We was in it together. She had slugged him between the shoulders. My touch had failed him, never to return.

All the blood children and the took-ins, like me, came home from Minneapolis and Chicago, where they had relocated years ago. They stayed with friends on the reservation or with Aurelia or slept on Grandma's floor. They were struck down with grief and bereavement to be sure, every one of them. At the funeral I sat down in the back of the church with Albertine. She had gotten all skinny and ragged haired from cramming all her years of study into two or three. She had decided that to be a nurse was not enough for her so she was going to be a doctor. But the way she was straining her mind didn't look too hopeful. Her eyes were bloodshot from driving and crying. She took my hand. From the back we watched all the children and the mourners as they hunched over their prayers, their hands stuffed full of Kleenex. It was someplace in that long sad service that my vision shifted. I began to see things different, more clear. The family kneeling down turned to rocks in a field. It struck me how strong and reliable grief was, and death. Until the end of time, death would be our rock.

So I had perspective on it all, for death gives you that. All the Kashpaw children had done various things to me in their lives—shared their folks with me, loaned me cash, beat me up in secret—and I decided, because of death, then and there I'd call it quits. If I ever saw King again, I'd shake his hand. Forgiving somebody else made the whole thing easier to bear.

Everybody saw Grandpa off into the next world. And then the Kashpaws had to get back to their jobs, which was numerous and impressive. I had a few beers with them and I went back to Grandma, who had sort of got lost in the shuffle of everybody being sad about Grandpa and glad to see one another.

Zelda had sat beside her the whole time and was sitting with her now. I wanted to talk to Grandma, say how sorry I was, that it wasn't her fault, but only mine. I would have, but Zelda gave me one of her looks of strict warning as if to say, "I'll take care of Grandma. Don't horn in on the women."

If only Zelda knew, I thought, the sad realities would change her. But of course I couldn't tell the dark truth.

It was evening, late. Grandma's light was on underneath a crack in the door. About a week had passed since we buried Grandpa. I knocked first but there wasn't no answer, so I went right in. The door was unlocked. She was there but she didn't notice me at first. Her hands were tied up in her rosary, and her gaze was fully absorbed in the easy chair opposite her, the one that had always been Grandpa's favorite. I stood there, staring with her, at the little green nubs in the cloth and plastic armrest covers and the sad little hair-tonic stain he had made on the white doily where he laid his head. For the life of me I couldn't figure what she was staring at. Thin space. Then she turned.

"He ain't gone yet," she said.

Remember that chill I luckily didn't get from waiting in the slough? I got it now. I felt it start from the very center of me, where fear hides, waiting to attack. It spiraled outward so that in minutes my fingers and teeth were shaking and clattering. I knew she told the truth. She seen Grandpa. Whether or not he had been there is not the point. She had *seen* him, and that meant anybody else could see him, too. Not only that but, as is usually the case with these here ghosts, he had a certain uneasy reason to come back. And of course Grandma Kashpaw had scanned it out.

I sat down. We sat together on the couch watching his chair out of the corner of our eyes. She had found him sitting in his chair when she walked in the door.

"It's the love medicine, my Lipsha," she said. "It was stronger than we thought. He came back even after death to claim me to his side."

I was afraid. "We shouldn't have tampered with it," I said. She agreed. For a while we sat still. I don't know what she thought, but my head felt screwed on backward. I couldn't accurately consider the situation, so I told Grandma to go to bed. I would sleep on the couch keeping my eye on Grandpa's chair. Maybe he would come back and maybe he wouldn't. I guess I feared the one as much as the other, but I got to thinking, see, as I lay there in darkness, that perhaps even through my terrible mistakes some good might come. If Grandpa did come back, I thought he'd return in his right mind. I could talk with him. I could tell him it was all my fault for playing with power I did not understand. Maybe he'd forgive me and rest in peace. I hoped this. I calmed myself and waited for him all night.

He fooled me though. He knew what I was waiting for, and it wasn't what he was looking to hear. Come dawn I heard a blood-splitting cry from the bedroom and I rushed in there. Grandma turnt the lights on. She was sitting on the edge of the bed and her face looked harsh, pinched-up gray.

"He was here," she said. "He came and laid down next to me in bed. And he touched me."

Her heart broke down. She cried. His touch was so cold. She laid back in bed after a while, as it was morning, and I went to the couch. As I lay there, falling asleep, I suddenly felt Grandpa's presence and the barrier between us like a swollen river. I felt how I had wronged him. How awful was the place where I had sent him. Behind the wall of death, he'd watched the living eat and cry and get drunk. He was lonesome, but I understood he meant no harm.

"Go back," I said to the dark, afraid and yet full of pity. "You got to be with your own kind now," I said. I felt him retreating, like a sigh, growing less. I felt his spirit as it shrunk back through the walls, the blinds, the brick courtyard of Senior Citizens. "Look up Aunt June," I whispered as he left.

I slept late the next morning, a good hard sleep allowing the sun to rise and warm the earth. It was past noon when I awoke. There is nothing, to my mind, like a long sleep to make those hard decisions that you neglect under stress of wakefulness. Soon as I woke up that morning, I saw exactly what I'd say to Grandma. I had gotten humble in the past week, not just losing the touch but getting jolted into the understanding that would prey on me from here on out. Your life feels different on you, once you greet death and understand your heart's position. You wear your life like a garment from the mission bundle sale ever after — lightly because you realize you never paid nothing for it, cherishing because you know you won't ever come by such a bargain again. Also you have the feeling someone wore it before you and someone will after. I can't explain that, not yet, but I'm putting my mind to it.

"Grandma," I said, "I got to be honest about the love medicine."

She listened. I knew from then on she would be listening to me the way I had listened to her before. I told her about the turkey hearts and how I had them blessed. I told her what I used as love medicine was purely a fake, and then I said to her what my understanding brought me.

"Love medicine ain't what brings him back to you, Grandma. No, it's something else. He loved you over time and distance, but he went off so quick he never got the chance to tell you how he loves you, how he doesn't blame you, how he understands. It's true feeling, not no magic. No supermarket heart could have brung him back."

She looked at me. She was seeing the years and days I had no way of knowing, and she didn't believe me. I could tell this. Yet a look came on her face. It was like the look of mothers drinking sweetness from their children's eyes. It was tenderness.

"Lipsha," she said, "you was always my favorite."

She took the beads off the bedpost, where she kept them to say at night, and she told me to put out my hand. When I did this, she shut the beads inside of my fist and held them there a long minute, tight, so my hand hurt. I almost cried when she did this. I don't really know why. Tears shot up behind my eyelids, and yet it was nothing. I didn't understand, except her hand was so strong, squeezing mine.

The earth was full of life and there were dandelions growing out the window, thick as thieves, already seeded, fat as big yellow plungers. She let my hand go. I got up. "I'll go out and dig a few dandelions," I told her.

Outside, the sun was hot and heavy as a hand on my back. I felt it flow down my arms, out my fingers, arrowing through the ends of the fork into the earth.

With every root I prized up there was return, as if I was kin to its secret lesson. The touch got stronger as I worked through the grassy afternoon. Uncurling from me like a seed out of the blackness where I was lost, the touch spread. The spiked leaves full of bitter mother's milk. A buried root. A nuisance people dig up and throw in the sun to wither. A globe of frail seeds that's indestructible.

[1982]

QUESTIONS

1. Consider the ways in which misunderstandings between people shape the events of the story.
2. What does Lipsha mean by the comment about his grandfather, "some people fall right through the hole in their lives?"
3. How does Lipsha's definition of faith as "belief against the odds" figure in the story? What other elements of belief—both Christian and Native American—are explored?
4. What is Lipsha's power? What is love medicine? Is it successful in producing love?
5. What aspects of the story are humorous? How does Erdrich balance the humorous and serious elements of the story?

William Faulkner

(1897–1962)

United States

By almost universal acclaim, William Faulkner is America's greatest novelist of the twentieth century, though many critics would expand the geographical context to the entire world. This distinction is twofold: first, because of the major novels of his career—*The Sound and the Fury* (1929), *As I Lay Dying* (1930), *Light in August* (1932), *Absalom, Absalom!* (1936), and *The Hamlet* (1940)—and, second, because of the setting of most of his major works—the mythical area of Mississippi that Faulkner called Yoknapatawpha County. When he won the Nobel Prize for literature in 1952, both of these aspects of his work were praised.

Born in New Albany, Mississippi, Faulkner moved with his family to Oxford (the location of the state university) five years later, where he lived most of his life. Faulkner's great grandfather was a novelist and an early source of inspiration for his work. By the time he was 10, Faulkner had already discovered that if he told stories to the boys in the neighborhood, he could get them to do his chores for him. Faulkner wanted to fight in World War I but never saw combat, although he joined the Canadian Royal Air Force (after fudging about his nationality). Later in life, Faulkner often claimed that he was wounded in the war and temporarily took on the affectations of an English count.

The stories about Faulkner's drinking are legion. What they indicate more than anything else is the unhappiness of his marriage, as well as his determination to support himself (and his extended family) by his writing. When royalties from his novels and short stories were insufficient, Faulkner wrote screenplays in Hollywood. When he was awarded the Nobel Prize in 1952, almost all of his work was out of print. (The award had been supported by a number of French critics who had admired his work for years.) Late in his life, Faulkner finally achieved financial security and the admiration of American critics and readers. Responding to Malcolm Cowley about the world he had created in Yoknapatawpha County, Faulkner said, "I discovered that my own little postage stamp of native soil was worth writing about and that I would never live long enough to exhaust it, and that by sublimating the actual into the apocryphal I would have complete liberty to use whatever talent I might have to its absolute top."

Faulkner taught at the University of Virginia in 1957 and 1958. During those years and much of the rest of his life, he responded wittily and obliquely to the elaborate questions of numerous interviewers about his specific works. About "A Rose for Emily" he made several choice remarks, including the following:

> . . . there was the young girl with a young girl's normal aspirations to find love and then a husband and a family, who was brow-beaten and kept down by her father, a selfish man who

didn't want her to leave home because he wanted a housekeeper. . . .

She had been trained that you do not take a lover. You marry, you don't take a lover. She had broken all the laws of her tradition, her background [from *Faulkner in the University* (1959), edited by Frederick Gwynn and Joseph Blotner].

A Rose for Emily

I

When Miss Emily Grierson died, our whole town went to her funeral: the men through a sort of respectful affection for a fallen monument, the women mostly out of curiosity to see the inside of her house, which no one save an old manservant—a combined gardener and cook—had seen in at least ten years.

It was a big, squarish frame house that had once been white, decorated with cupolas and spires and scrolled balconies in the heavily lightsome style of the seventies, set on what had once been our most select street. But garages and cotton gins had encroached and obliterated even the august names of that neighborhood; only Miss Emily's house was left, lifting its stubborn and coquettish decay above the cotton wagons and the gasoline pumps—an eyesore among eyesores. And now Miss Emily had gone to join the representatives of those august names where they lay in the cedar-bemused cemetery among the ranked and anonymous graves of Union and Confederate soldiers who fell at the battle of Jefferson.

Alive, Miss Emily had been a tradition, a duty, and a care; a sort of hereditary obligation upon the town, dating from that day in 1894 when Colonel Sartoris, the mayor—he who fathered the edict that no Negro woman should appear on the streets without an apron—remitted her taxes, the dispensation dating from the death of her father on into perpetuity. Not that Miss Emily would have accepted charity. Colonel Sartoris invented an involved tale to the effect that Miss Emily's father had loaned money to the town, which the town, as a matter of business, preferred this way of repaying. Only a man of Colonel Sartoris' generation and thought could have invented it, and only a woman could have believed it.

When the next generation, with its more modern ideas, became mayors and aldermen, this arrangement created some little dissatisfaction. On the first of the year they mailed her a tax notice. February came, and there was no reply. They wrote her a formal letter, asking her to call at the sheriff's office at her convenience. A week later the mayor wrote her himself, offering to call or to send his car for her, and received in reply a note on paper of an archaic shape, in a thin, flowing calligraphy in faded ink, to the effect that she no longer went out at all. The tax notice was also enclosed, without comment.

They called a special meeting of the Board of Aldermen. A deputation waited upon her, knocked at the door through which no visitor had passed since she ceased giving china-painting lessons eight or ten years earlier. They were admitted by the old Negro into a dim hall from which a stairway mounted into still more shadow. It smelled of dust and disuse—a close, dank smell. The Negro led them into the parlor. It was furnished in heavy, leather-covered furniture. When the Negro opened the blinds of one window, they could see that the leather was cracked; and when they sat down, a faint dust rose sluggishly about their thighs, spinning with slow motes in the single sun-ray. On a tarnished gilt easel before the fireplace stood a crayon portrait of Miss Emily's father.

They rose when she entered—a small, fat woman in black, with a thin gold chain descending to her waist and vanishing into her belt, leaning on an ebony cane with a tarnished gold head. Her skeleton was small and spare; perhaps that was why what would have been merely plumpness in another was obesity in her. She looked bloated, like a body long submerged in motionless water, and of that pallid hue. Her eyes, lost in the fatty ridges of her face, looked like two small pieces of coal pressed into a lump of dough as they moved from one face to another while the visitors stated their errand.

She did not ask them to sit. She just stood in the door and listened quietly until the spokesman came to a stumbling halt. Then they could hear the invisible watch ticking at the end of the gold chain.

Her voice was dry and cold. "I have no taxes in Jefferson. Colonel Sartoris explained it to me. Perhaps one of you can gain access to the city records and satisfy yourselves."

"But we have. We are the city authorities, Miss Emily. Didn't you get a notice from the sheriff, signed by him?"

"I received a paper, yes," Miss Emily said. "Perhaps he considers himself the sheriff. . . . I have no taxes in Jefferson."

"But there is nothing on the books to show that, you see. We must go by the—"

"See Colonel Sartoris. I have no taxes in Jefferson."

"But, Miss Emily—"

"See Colonel Sartoris." (Colonel Sartoris had been dead almost ten years.) "I have no taxes in Jefferson. Tobe!" The Negro appeared. "Show these gentlemen out."

II

So she vanquished them, horse and foot, just as she had vanquished their fathers thirty years before about the smell. That was two years after her father's death and a short time after her sweetheart—the one we believed would marry her—had deserted her. After her father's death she went out very little; after her sweetheart went away, people hardly saw her at all. A few of the ladies had the temerity to call, but were not received, and the only sign of life about the place was the Negro man—a young man then—going in and out with a market basket.

"Just as if a man—any man—could keep a kitchen properly," the ladies said; so they were not surprised when the smell developed. It was another link between the gross, teeming world and the high and mighty Griersons.

A neighbor, a woman, complained to the mayor, Judge Stevens, eighty years old.

"But what will you have me do about it, madam?" he said.

"Why, send her word to stop it," the woman said. "Isn't there a law?"

"I'm sure that won't be necessary," Judge Stevens said. "It's probably just a snake or a rat that nigger of hers killed in the yard. I'll speak to him about it."

The next day he received two more complaints, one from a man who came in diffident deprecation. "We really must do something about it, Judge. I'd be the last one in the world to bother Miss Emily, but we've got to do something." That night the Board of Aldermen met—three gray-beards and one younger man, a member of the rising generation.

"It's simple enough," he said. "Send her word to have her place cleaned up. Give her a certain time to do it in, and if she don't. . . ."

"Dammit, sir," Judge Stevens said, "will you accuse a lady to her face of smelling bad?"

So the next night, after midnight, four men crossed Miss Emily's lawn and slunk about the house like burglars, sniffing along the base of the brickwork and at the cellar openings while one of them performed a regular sowing motion with his hand out of a sack slung from his shoulder. They broke open the cellar door and sprinkled lime there, and in all the outbuildings. As they recrossed the lawn, a window that had been dark was lighted and Miss Emily sat in it, the light behind her, and her upright torso motionless as that of an idol. They crept quietly across the lawn and into the shadow of the locusts that lined the street. After a week or two the smell went away.

That was when people had begun to feel really sorry for her. People in our town, remembering how old lady Wyatt, her great-aunt, had gone completely crazy at last, believed that the Griersons held themselves a little too high for what they really were. None of the young men were quite good enough for Miss Emily and such. We had long thought of them as a tableau, Miss Emily a slender figure in white in the background, her father a spraddled silhouette in the foreground, his back to her and clutching a horsewhip, the two of them framed by the backflung front door. So when she got to be thirty and was still single, we were not pleased exactly, but vindicated; even with insanity in the family she wouldn't have turned down all of her chances if they had really materialized.

When her father died, it got about that the house was all that was left to her; and in a way, people were glad. At last they could pity Miss Emily. Being left alone, and a pauper, she had become humanized. Now she too would know the old thrill and the old despair of a penny more or less.

The day after his death all the ladies prepared to call at the house and offer condolence and aid, as is our custom. Miss Emily met them at the door, dressed as usual and with no trace of grief on her face. She told them that her father was not dead. She did that for three days, with the ministers calling on her, and the doctors, trying to persuade her to let them dispose of the body. Just as they were about to resort to law and force, she broke down, and they buried her father quickly.

We did not say she was crazy then. We believed she had to do that. We remembered all the young men her father had driven away, and we knew that with nothing left, she would have to cling to that which had robbed her, as people will.

III

She was sick for a long time. When we saw her again, her hair was cut short, making her look like a girl, with a vague resemblance to those angels in colored church windows—sort of tragic and serene.

The town had just let the contracts for paving the sidewalks, and in the summer after her father's death they began the work. The construction company came with niggers and mules and machinery, and a foreman named Homer Barron, a Yankee—a big, dark, ready man, with a big voice and eyes lighter than his face. The little boys would follow in groups to hear him cuss the niggers, and the niggers singing in time to the rise and fall of picks. Pretty soon he knew everybody in town. Whenever you heard a lot of laughing anywhere about the square, Homer Barron would be in the center of the group. Presently, we began to see him and Miss Emily on Sunday afternoons driving in the yellow-wheeled buggy and the matched team of bays from the livery stable.

At first we were glad that Miss Emily would have an interest, because the ladies all said, "Of course a Grierson would not think seriously of a Northerner, a day laborer." But there were still others, older people, who said that even grief could not cause a real lady to forget *noblesse oblige*—without calling it *noblesse oblige.* They just said, "Poor Emily. Her kinsfolk should come to her." She had some kin in Alabama; but years ago her father had fallen out with them over the estate of old lady Wyatt, the crazy woman, and there was no communication between the two families. They had not even been represented at the funeral.

And as soon as the old people said, "Poor Emily," the whispering began. "Do you suppose it's really so?" they said to one another. "Of course it is. What else could. . . ." This behind their hands; rustling of craned silk and satin behind jalousies closed upon the sun of Sunday afternoon as the thin, swift clop-clop-clop of the matched team passed: "Poor Emily."

She carried her head high enough—even when we believed that she was fallen. It was as if she demanded more than ever the recognition of her dignity as the last Grierson; as if it had wanted that touch of earthiness to reaffirm her imperviousness. Like when she bought the rat poison, the arsenic. That was over a year after they had begun to say "Poor Emily," and while the two female cousins were visiting her.

"I want some poison," she said to the druggist. She was over thirty then, still a slight woman, though thinner than usual, with cold, haughty black eyes in a face the flesh of which was strained across the temples and about the eyesockets as you imagine a lighthouse-keeper's face ought to look. "I want some poison," she said.

"Yes, Miss Emily. What kind? For rats and such? I'd recom——"

"I want the best you have. I don't care what kind."

The druggist named several. "They'll kill anything up to an elephant. But what you want is ——"

"Arsenic," Miss Emily said. "Is that a good one?"

"Is . . . arsenic? Yes, ma'am. But what you want ——"

"I want arsenic."

The druggist looked down at her. She looked back at him, erect, her face like a strained flag. "Why, of course," the druggist said. "If that's what you want. But the law requires you to tell what you are going to use it for."

Miss Emily just stared at him, her head tilted back in order to look him eye for eye, until he looked away and went and got the arsenic and wrapped it up. The Negro delivery boy brought her the package; the druggist didn't come back. When she opened the package at home there was written on the box, under the skull and bones: "For rats."

IV

So the next day we all said, "She will kill herself"; and we said it would be the best thing. When she had first begun to be seen with Homer Barron, we had said, "She will marry him." Then we said, "She will persuade him yet," because Homer himself had remarked—he liked men, and it was known that he drank with the younger men in the Elks' Club—that he was not a marrying man. Later we said, "Poor Emily" behind the jalousies as they passed on Sunday afternoon in the glittering buggy, Miss Emily with her head high and Homer Barron with his hat cocked and a cigar in his teeth, reins and whip in a yellow glove.

Then some of the ladies began to say that it was a disgrace to the town and a bad example to the young people. The men did not want to interfere, but at last the ladies forced the Baptist minister—Miss Emily's people were Episcopal—to call upon her. He would never divulge what happened during that interview, but he refused to go back again. The next Sunday they again drove about the streets, and the following day the minister's wife wrote to Miss Emily's relations in Alabama.

So she had blood-kin under her roof again and we sat back to watch developments. At first nothing happened. Then we were sure that they were to be married. We learned that Miss Emily had been to the jeweler's and ordered a man's toilet set in silver, with the letters H.B. on each piece. Two days later we learned that she had bought a complete outfit of men's clothing, including a nightshirt, and we said, "They are married." We were really glad. We were glad because the two female cousins were even more Grierson than Miss Emily had ever been.

So we were not surprised when Homer Barron—the streets had been finished some time since—was gone. We were a little disappointed that there was not a public blowing-off, but we believed that he had gone on to prepare for Miss Emily's coming, or to give her a chance to get rid of the cousins. (By that time it was a cabal, and we were all Miss Emily's allies to help circumvent the cousins.) Sure enough, after another week they departed. And, as we had expected all along, within three days Homer Barron was back in town. A neighbor saw the Negro man admit him at the kitchen door at dusk one evening.

And that was the last we saw of Homer Barron. And of Miss Emily for some time. The Negro man went in and out with the market basket, but the front door remained closed. Now and then we would see her at the window for a moment, as the men did that night when they sprinkled the lime, but for almost six months she did not appear on the streets. Then we knew that this was to be expected too; as if that quality of her father which had thwarted her woman's life so many times had been too virulent and too furious to die.

When we next saw Miss Emily, she had grown fat and her hair was turning gray. During the next few years it grew grayer and grayer until it attained an even pepper-and-salt iron-gray, when it ceased turning. Up to the day of her death at seventy-four it was still that vigorous iron-gray, like the hair of an active man.

From that time on her front door remained closed, save during a period of six or seven years, when she was about forty, during which she gave lessons in china-painting. She fitted up a studio in one of the downstairs rooms, where the daughters and granddaughters of Colonel Sartoris' contemporaries were sent to her with the same regularity and in the same spirit that they were sent to church on Sundays with a twenty-five-cent piece for the collection plate. Meanwhile her taxes had been remitted.

Then the newer generation became the backbone and the spirit of the town, and the painting pupils grew up and fell away and did not send their children to her with boxes of color and tedious brushes and pictures cut from the ladies' magazines. The front door closed upon the last one and remained closed for good. When the town got free postal delivery, Miss Emily alone refused to let them fasten the metal numbers above her door and attach a mailbox to it. She would not listen to them.

Daily, monthly, yearly we watched the Negro grow grayer and more stooped, going in and out with the market basket. Each December we sent her a tax notice, which would be returned by the post office a week later, unclaimed. Now and then we would see her in one of the downstairs windows—she had evidently shut up the top floor of the house—like the carven torso of an idol in a niche, looking or not looking at us, we could never tell which. Thus she passed from generation to generation—dear, inescapable, impervious, tranquil, and perverse.

And so she died. Fell ill in the house filled with dust and shadows, with only a doddering Negro man to wait on her. We did not even know she was sick; we had long since given up trying to get any information from the Negro. He talked to no one, probably not even to her, for his voice had grown harsh and rusty, as if from disuse.

She died in one of the downstairs rooms, in a heavy walnut bed with a curtain, her gray head propped on a pillow yellow and moldy with age and lack of sunlight.

V

The Negro met the first of the ladies at the front door and let them in, with their hushed, sibilant voices and their quick, curious glances, and then he disappeared. He walked right through the house and out the back and was not seen again.

The two female cousins came at once. They held the funeral on the second day, with the town coming to look at Miss Emily beneath a mass of bought flowers, with the crayon face of her father musing profoundly above the bier and the ladies sibilant and macabre; and the very old men—some in their brushed Confederate uniforms—on the porch and the lawn, talking of Miss Emily as if she had been a contemporary of theirs, believing that they had danced with her and courted her perhaps, confusing time with its mathematical progression, as the old do, to whom all the past is not a diminishing road but, instead, a huge meadow which no winter ever quite touches, divided from them now by the narrow bottleneck of the most recent decade of years.

Already we knew that there was one room in that region above stairs which no one had seen in forty years, and which would have to be forced. They waited until Miss Emily was decently in the ground before they opened it.

The violence of breaking down the door seemed to fill this room with pervading dust. A thin, acrid pall as of the tomb seemed to lie everywhere upon this room decked and furnished as for a bridal: upon the valance curtains of faded rose color, upon the rose-shaded lights, upon the dressing table, upon the delicate array of crystal and the man's toilet things backed with tarnished silver,

silver so tarnished that the monogram was obscured. Among them lay a collar and tie, as if they had just been removed, which, lifted, left upon the surface a pale crescent in the dust. Upon a chair hung the suit, carefully folded; beneath it the two mute shoes and the discarded socks.

The man himself lay in the bed.

For a long while we just stood there, looking down at the profound and fleshless grin. The body had apparently once lain in the attitude of an embrace, but now the long sleep that outlasts love, that conquers even the grimace of love, had cuckolded him. What was left of him, rotted beneath what was left of the nightshirt, had become inextricable from the bed in which he lay; and upon him and upon the pillow beside him lay that even coating of the patient and biding dust.

Then we noticed that in the second pillow was the indentation of a head. One of us lifted something from it, and leaning forward, that faint and invisible dust dry and acrid in the nostrils, we saw a long strand of iron-gray hair.

[1931]

QUESTIONS

1. How do the five sections of "A Rose for Emily" contribute to its structure, its unfolding?
2. How are we to interpret the title?
3. How significant are the characters' names in this story?
4. What can be said about point of view in Faulkner's story?
5. Is the story geographically "locked" into its Southern context, or is it possible to assume the same events happening in a Northern town?

Feng Jicai
(b. 1942)
China

Feng Jicai, born in Tianjin, China, began his first career as a painter but shifted to fiction when his "counterrevolutionary" art was unwelcome during China's Cultural Revolution of the 1960s and 1970s. For the same reasons, he could not publish his fiction until after the death of Mao Zedong in 1976. Now a prolific writer (though not yet widely translated), he currently resides in Tianjin with his wife and son and holds major positions in Chinese writers' professional organizations.

Feng still precipitates controversy with his writing, however. His translator, Susan Wilff Chen, has noted that "The Street-Sweeping Show," originally published in 1982, is not reprinted in any of Feng's collections of short stories, because it resembled a real-life incident so closely that it caused objections when it first appeared.

The Street-Sweeping Show

"National Cleanup Week starts today," said Secretary Zhao, "and officials everywhere are going out to join in the street sweeping. Here's our list of participants —all top city administrators and public figures. We've just had it mimeographed over at the office for your approval."

He looked like a typical upper-echelon secretary: the collar of his well-worn, neatly pressed Mao suit[1] was buttoned up military style; his complexion was pale; his glasses utilitarian. His gentle, deferential manner and pleasantly modulated voice concealed a shrewd, hard-driving personality.

The mayor pored over the list, as if the eighty names on it were those of people selected to go abroad. From time to time he glanced thoughtfully at the high white ceiling.

"Why isn't there anyone from the Women's Federation?" he asked.

Secretary Zhao thought for a moment. "Oh, you're right—there isn't! We've got the heads of every office in the city—the Athletic Committee, the Youth League Committee, the Federation of Trade Unions, the Federation of Literary and Art Circles—even some famous university professors. The only group we forgot is the Women's Federation."

"Women are the pillars of society. How can we leave out the women's representatives?" The mayor sounded smug rather than reproachful. Only a

[1]*Mao* Mao ZeDong (also transliterated as Mao Tse-tung) (1893–1976), Communist leader and chairman of the Communist party of the People's Republic of China from 1949 until his death. Mao led the Cultural Revolution, 1966 to 1976, including the institution of a uniform code of dress.

leader could think of everything. This was where true leadership ability came into play.

Secretary Zhao was reminded of the time when the mayor had pointed out that the fish course was missing from the menu for a banquet in honor of some foreign guests.

"Add two names from the Women's Federation, and make sure you get people in positions of authority or who are proper representatives of the organization. 'International Working Women's Red Banner Pacesetters,' 'Families of Martyrs,' or 'Model Workers' would be fine." Like an elementary school teacher returning a poor homework paper to his student, the mayor handed the incomplete list back to his secretary.

"Yes, your honor, I'll do it right away. A complete list will be useful the next time something like this comes up. And I must contact everyone at once. The street sweeping is scheduled for two this afternoon in Central Square. Will you be able to go?"

"Of course. As mayor of the city, I have to set an example."

"The car will be at the gate for you at one-thirty. I'll go with you."

"All right," the mayor answered absentmindedly, scratching his forehead and looking away.

Secretary Zhao hurried out.

At one-thirty that afternoon the mayor was whisked to the square in his limousine. All office workers, shop clerks, students, housewives, and retirees were out sweeping the streets, and the air was thick with dust. Secretary Zhao hastily rolled up the window. Inside the car there was only a faint, pleasant smell of gasoline and leather.

At the square they pulled up beside a colorful assortment of limousines. In front of them a group of top city administrators had gathered to wait for the mayor's arrival. Someone had arranged for uniformed policemen to stand guard on all sides.

Secretary Zhao sprang out of the limousine and opened the door for his boss. The officials in the waiting crowd stepped forward with smiling faces to greet the mayor. Everyone knew him and hoped to be the first to shake his hand.

"Good afternoon—oh, nice to see you—good afternoon—" the mayor repeated as he shook hands with each of them.

An old policeman approached, followed by two younger ones pushing wheelbarrows full of big bamboo brooms. The old policeman selected one of the smaller, neater brooms and presented it respectfully to the mayor. When the other dignitaries had gotten their brooms, a marshal with a red armband led them all to the center of the square. Naturally the mayor walked at the head.

Groups of people had come from their workplaces to sweep the huge square. At the sight of this majestic, broom-carrying procession, with its marshal, police escort, and retinue of shutter-clicking photographers, they realized that they were in the presence of no ordinary mortals and gathered closer for a look. How extraordinary for a mayor to be sweeping the streets, thought Secretary Zhao, swelling with unconscious pride as he strutted along beside the mayor with his broom on his shoulder.

"Here we are," the marshal said when they had reached the designated spot.

All eighty-two dignitaries began to sweep.

The swelling crowd of onlookers, which was kept back by a police cordon, was buzzing with excitement:

"Look, he's the one over there."

"Which one? The one in black?"

"No. The bald fat one in blue."

"Cut the chitchat!" barked a policeman.

The square was so huge that no one knew where to sweep. The concrete pavement was clean to begin with; they pushed what little grit there was back and forth with their big brooms. The most conspicuous piece of litter was a solitary popsicle wrapper, which they all pursued like children chasing a dragonfly.

The photographers surrounded the mayor. Some got down on one knee to shoot from below, while others ran from side to side trying to get a profile. Like a cloud in a thunderstorm, the mayor was constantly illuminated by silvery flashes. Then a man in a visored cap, with a video camera, approached Secretary Zhao.

"I'm from the TV station," he said. "Would you please ask them to line up single file so they'll look neat on camera?"

Secretary Zhao consulted with the mayor, who agreed to this request. The dignitaries formed a long line and began to wield their brooms for the camera, regardless of whether there was any dirt on the ground.

The cameraman was about to start shooting, when he stopped and ran over to the mayor.

"I'm sorry, your honor," he said, "but you're all going to have to face the other way because you've got your backs to the sun. And I'd also like the entire line to be reversed so that you're at the head."

"All right," the mayor agreed graciously, and he led his entourage, like a line of dragon dancers, in a clumsy turn-around. Once in place, everyone began sweeping again.

Pleased, the cameraman ran to the head of the line, pushed his cap up, and aimed at the mayor. "All right," he said as the camera started to whir, "swing those brooms, all together now—put your hearts into it—that's it! Chin up please, your honor. Hold it—that's fine—all right!"

He stopped the camera, shook the mayor's hand, and thanked him for helping an ordinary reporter carry out his assignment.

Let's call it a day," the marshal said to Secretary Zhao. Then he turned to the mayor. "You have victoriously accomplished your mission," he said.

"Very good—thank you for your trouble," the mayor replied routinely, smiling and shaking hands again.

Some reporters came running up to the mayor. "Do you have any instructions, your honor?" asked a tall, thin, aggressive one.

"Nothing in particular." The mayor paused for a moment. "Everyone should pitch in to clean up our city."

The reporters scribbled his precious words in their notebooks.

The policemen brought the wheelbarrows back, and everyone returned the brooms. Secretary Zhao replaced the mayor's for him.

It was time to go. The mayor shook hands with everyone again.

"Good-bye—good-bye—good-bye—"

The others waited until the mayor had gotten into his limousine before getting into theirs.

The mayor's limousine delivered him to his house, where his servant had drawn his bathwater and set out scented soap and fresh towels. He enjoyed a leisurely bath and emerged from the bathroom with rosy skin and clean clothes, leaving his grime and exhaustion behind him in the tub.

As he descended the stairs to eat dinner, his grandson hurriedly led him into the living room.

"Look, Granddad, you're on TV!"

There he was on the television screen, like an actor, putting on a show of sweeping the street. He turned away and gave his grandson a casual pat on the shoulder.

"It's not worth watching. Let's go have dinner."

[1982]

Translated by
SUSAN WILFF CHEN

QUESTIONS

1. What is the actual purpose of the street-sweeping ceremony?
2. What does the story suggest about public rituals? About bureaucracy? About the media's role in such rituals? Compare this story with Isabel Allende's "And of Clay Are We Created."
3. What is the significance of the title?
4. Why does the mayor refuse to watch the ceremony on television?

F. Scott Fitzgerald

(1896–1940)

United States

As innumerable critics have observed, it is difficult to think of the American Jazz Age, of the Lost Generation, without recalling F. Scott Fitzgerald's novels and short stories. Although the era has passed, it is locked forever in Fitzgerald's work. As Charlie Wales muses toward the end of "Babylon Revisited," ". . . the snow of twenty-nine wasn't real snow. If you didn't want it to be snow, you just paid some money." Money grew on trees; anything could be had for a price, until the collapse of the stock market, when reality took hold of people's (but not all people's) lives.

Apart from the swan's song to the Jazz Age, many readers would consider "Babylon Revisited" an almost perfect short story. The sense of change is established in the opening lines of dialogue, although we have to read a bit further to learn exactly what that change is. We see the agony of Charlie's reformed life and the price he has had to pay for his earlier indiscretions. We even encounter a classic ogre figure in the guise of his sister-in-law, Marian, who cannot accept the possibility of Charlie's change. Finally, after a series of hard-fought triumphs, it looks as if everything will turn out satisfactorily—until the last scene, when once again Fitzgerald turns the tables on us—this time due to events over which Charlie Wales has very little control.

Fitzgerald was born in St. Paul, Minnesota, in 1896. His most famous novel, *The Great Gatsby*, appeared in 1925. By the time of his death in 1940, he had published nearly 160 short stories, as well as several other major novels, including *This Side of Paradise* (1920), *The Beautiful and the Damned* (1922), and *Tender Is the Night* (1934). His posthumous novel, *The Last Tycoon*, about Hollywood (where Fitzgerald had worked for years) appeared in 1940.

◆ *Babylon Revisited* ◆

I

"And where's Mr. Campbell?" Charlie asked.

"Gone to Switzerland. Mr. Campbell's a pretty sick man, Mr. Wales."

"I'm sorry to hear that. And George Hardt?" Charlie inquired.

"Back in America, gone to work."

"And where is the Snow Bird?"

"He was in here last week. Anyway, his friend, Mr. Schaeffer, is in Paris."

Two familiar names from the long list of a year and half ago. Charlie scribbled an address in his notebook and tore out the page.

"If you see Mr. Schaeffer, give him this," he said. "It's my brother-in-law's address. I haven't settled on a hotel yet."

He was not really disappointed to find Paris was so empty. But the stillness in the Ritz bar was strange and portentous. It was not an American bar any more—he felt polite in it, and not as if he owned it. It had gone back into France. He felt the stillness from the moment he got out of the taxi and saw the doorman, usually in a frenzy of activity at this hour, gossiping with a *chasseur*[1] by the servants' entrance.

Passing through the corridor, he heard only a single, bored voice in the once-clamorous women's room. When he turned into the bar he traveled the twenty feet of green carpet with his eyes fixed straight ahead by old habit; and then, with his foot firmly on the rail, he turned and surveyed the room, encountering only a single pair of eyes that fluttered up from a newspaper in the corner. Charlie asked for the head barman, Paul, who in the latter days of the bull market had come to work in his own custom-built car—disembarking, however, with due nicety at the nearest corner. But Paul was at his country house today and Alix giving him information.

"No, no more," Charlie said, "I'm going slow these days."

Alix congratulated him: "You were going pretty strong a couple of years ago."

"I'll stick to it all right," Charlie assured him. "I've stuck to it for over a year and a half now."

"How do you find conditions in America?"

"I haven't been to America for months. I'm in business in Prague, representing a couple of concerns there. They don't know about me down there."

Alix smiled.

"Remember the night of George Hardt's bachelor dinner here?" said Charlie. "By the way, what's become of Claude Fessenden?"

Alix lowered his voice confidentially: "He's in Paris, but he doesn't come here any more. Paul doesn't allow it. He ran up a bill of thirty thousand francs, charging all his drinks and his lunches, and usually his dinner, for more than a year. And when Paul finally told him he had to pay, he gave him a bad check."

Alix shook his head sadly.

"I don't understand it, such a dandy fellow. Now he's all bloated up—" He made a plump apple of his hands.

Charlie watched a group of strident queens installing themselves in a corner. "Nothing affects them," he thought. "Stocks rise and fall, people loaf or work, but they go on forever." The place oppressed him. He called for the dice and shook with Alix for the drink.

"Here for long, Mr. Wales?"

"I'm here for four or five days to see my little girl."

"Oh-h! You have a little girl?"

Outside, the fire-red, gas-blue, ghost-green signs shone smokily through the tranquil rain. It was late afternoon and the streets were in movement; the *bistros*[2] gleamed. At the corner of the Boulevard des Capucines he took a taxi. The Place de la Concorde moved by in pink majesty; they crossed the logical Seine, and Charlie felt the sudden provincial quality of the Left Bank.

Charlie directed his taxi to the Avenue de l'Opera, which was out of his way. But he wanted to see the blue hour spread over the magnificent façade, and

[1]*chasseur* bellboy
[2]*bistros* pubs, bars

imagine that the cab horns, playing endlessly the first few bars of *La Plus que Lente,*[3] were the trumpets of the Second Empire.[4] They were closing the iron grill in front of Brentano's Book-store, and people were already at dinner behind the trim little bourgeois hedge of Duval's. He had never eaten at a really cheap restaurant in Paris. Five-course dinner, four francs fifty, eighteen cents, wine included. For some odd reason he wished that he had.

As they rolled on to the Left Bank and he felt its sudden provincialism, he thought, "I spoiled this city for myself. I didn't realize it, but the days came along one after another, and then two years were gone, and everything was gone, and I was gone."

He was thirty-five, and good to look at. The Irish mobility of his face was sobered by a deep wrinkle between his eyes. As he rang his brother-in-law's bell in the Rue Palatine, the wrinkle deepened till it pulled down his brows; he felt a cramping sensation in his belly. From behind the maid who opened the door darted a lovely little girl of nine who shrieked "Daddy!" and flew up, struggling like a fish, into his arms. She pulled his head around by one ear and set her cheek against his.

"My old pie," he said.

"Oh, daddy, daddy, daddy, daddy, dads, dads, dads!"

She drew him into the salon, where the family waited, a boy and a girl his daughter's age, his sister-in-law and her husband. He greeted Marion with his voice pitched carefully to avoid either feigned enthusiasm or dislike, but her response was more frankly tepid, though she minimized her expression of unalterable distrust by directing her regard toward his child. The two men clasped hands in a friendly way and Lincoln Peters rested his for a moment on Charlie's shoulder.

The room was warm and comfortably American. The three children moved intimately about, playing through the yellow oblongs that led to other rooms; the cheer of six o'clock spoke in the eager smacks of the fire and the sounds of French activity in the kitchen. But Charlie did not relax; his heart sat up rigidly in his body and he drew confidence from his daughter, who from time to time came close to him, holding in her arms the doll he had brought.

"Really extremely well," he declared in answer to Lincoln's question. "There's a lot of business there that isn't moving at all, but we're doing even better than ever. In fact, damn well. I'm bringing my sister over from America next month to keep house for me. My income last year was bigger than it was when I had money. You see, the Czechs ——"

His boasting was for a specific purpose; but after a moment, seeing a faint restiveness in Lincoln's eye, he changed the subject:

"Those are fine children of yours, well brought up, good manners."

"We think Honoria's a great little girl too."

Marion Peters came back from the kitchen. She was a tall woman with worried eyes, who had once possessed a fresh American loveliness. Charlie had never been sensitive to it and was always surprised when people spoke of how pretty she had been. From the first there had been an instinctive antipathy between them.

[3]*La Plus que Lente* "Slower than Slow," by Claude Debussy
[4]*Second Empire* Napoleon III's reign, 1852 to 1871

"Well, how do you find Honoria?" she asked.

"Wonderful. I was astonished how much she's grown in ten months. All the children are looking well."

"We haven't had a doctor for a year. How do you like being back in Paris?"

"It seems very funny to see so few Americans around."

"I'm delighted," Marion said vehemently. "Now at least you can go into a store without their assuming you're a millionaire. We've suffered like everybody, but on the whole it's a good deal pleasanter."

"But it was nice while it lasted," Charlie said. "We were a sort of royalty, almost infallible, with a sort of magic around us. In the bar this afternoon"—he stumbled, seeing his mistake— "there wasn't a man I knew."

She looked at him keenly. "I should think you'd have had enough of bars."

"I only stayed a minute. I take one drink every afternoon, and no more."

"Don't you want a cocktail before dinner?" Lincoln asked.

"I take only one drink every afternoon, and I've had that."

"I hope you keep to it," said Marion.

Her dislike was evident in the coldness with which she spoke, but Charlie only smiled; he had larger plans. Her very aggressiveness gave him an advantage, and he knew enough to wait. He wanted them to initiate the discussion of what they knew had brought him to Paris.

At dinner he couldn't decide whether Honoria was most like him or her mother. Fortunate if she didn't combine the traits of both that had brought them to disaster. A great wave of protectiveness went over him. He thought he knew what to do for her. He believed in character; he wanted to jump back a whole generation and trust in character again as the eternally valuable element. Everything else wore out.

He left soon after dinner, but not to go home. He was curious to see Paris by night with clearer and more judicious eyes than those of other days. He bought a *strapontin*[5] for the Casino and watched Josephine Baker[6] go through her chocolate arabesques.

After an hour he left and strolled toward Montmartre, up the Rue Pigalle into the Place Blanche. The rain had stopped and there were a few people in evening clothes disembarking from taxis in front of cabarets, and *cocottes*[7] prowling singly or in pairs, and many Negroes. He passed a lighted door from which issued music, and stopped with the sense of familiarity; it was Bricktop's, where he had parted with so many hours and so much money. A few doors farther on he found another ancient rendezvous and incautiously put his head inside. Immediately an eager orchestra burst into sound, a pair of professional dancers leaped to their feet and a maître d'hôtel swooped toward him, crying, "Crowd just arriving, sir!" But he withdrew quickly.

"You have to be damn drunk," he thought.

Zelli's was closed, the bleak and sinister cheap hotels surrounding it were dark; up in the Rue Blanche there was more light and a local, colloquial French crowd. The Poet's Cave had disappeared, but the two great mouths of the Café of Heaven and the Café of Hell still yawned—even devoured, as he watched, the

[5]*strapontin* an inexpensive seat

[6]*Josephine Baker* a famous African-American entertainer in Paris during the time

[7]*cocottes* prostitutes

meager contents of a tourist bus—a German, a Japanese, and an American couple who glanced at him with frightened eyes.

So much for the effort and ingenuity of Montmartre. All the catering to vice and waste was on an utterly childish scale, and he suddenly realized the meaning of the word "dissipate"—to dissipate into thin air; to make nothing out of something. In the little hours of the night every move from place to place was an enormous human jump, an increase of paying for the privilege of slower and slower motion.

He remembered thousand-franc notes given to an orchestra for playing a single number, hundred-franc notes tossed to a doorman for calling a cab.

But it hadn't been given for nothing.

It had been given, even the most wildly squandered sum, as an offering to destiny that he might not remember the things most worth remembering, the things that now he would always remember—his child taken from his control, his wife escaped to a grave in Vermont.

In the glare of a *brasserie*[8] a woman spoke to him. He bought her some eggs and coffee, and then, eluding her encouraging stare, gave her a twenty-franc note and took a taxi to his hotel.

II

He woke upon a fine fall day—football weather. The depression of yesterday was gone and he liked the people on the streets. At noon he sat opposite Honoria at Le Grand Vatel, the only restaurant he could think of not reminiscent of champagne dinners and long luncheons that began at two and ended in a blurred and vague twilight.

"Now, how about vegetables? Oughtn't you to have some vegetables?"

"Well, yes."

"Here's *épinards* and *chou-fleur* and carrots and *haricots.*"[9]

"I'd like *chou-fleur.*"

"Wouldn't you like to have two vegetables?"

"I usually only have one at lunch."

The waiter was pretending to be inordinately fond of children. "*Qu'elle est mignonne la petite! Elle parle exactement comme une Française.*"[10]

"How about dessert? Shall we wait and see?"

The waiter disappeared. Honoria looked at her father expectantly.

"What are we going to do?"

"First, we're going to that toy store in the Rue Saint-Honoré and buy you anything you like. And then we're going to the vaudeville at the Empire."

She hesitated. "I like it about the vaudeville, but not the toy store."

"Why not?"

"Well, you brought me this doll." She had it with her. "And I've got lots of things. And we're not rich any more, are we?"

"We never were. But today you are to have anything you want."

"All right," she agreed resignedly.

[8]*brasserie* an informal restaurant

[9]*épinards, chou-fleur, haricots* vegetables: spinach, cauliflower, beans

[10]*Qu'elle est miqnonne . . .* "*What a pretty little girl. She speaks exactly like a French girl.*"

When there had been her mother and a French nurse he had been inclined to be strict; now he extended himself, reached out for a new tolerance; he must be both parents to her and not shut any of her out of communication.

"I want to get to know you," he said gravely. "First let me introduce myself. My name is Charles J. Wales, of Prague."

"Oh, daddy!" her voice cracked with laughter.

"And who are you, please?" he persisted, and she accepted a rôle immediately: "Honoria Wales, Rue Palatine, Paris."

"Married or single?"

"No, not married. Single."

He indicated the doll. "But I see you have a child, madame."

Unwilling to disinherit it, she took it to her heart and thought quickly: "Yes, I've been married, but I'm not married now. My husband is dead."

He went on quickly, "And the child's name?"

"Simone. That's after my best friend at school."

"I'm very pleased that you're doing so well at school."

"I'm third this month," she boasted. "Elsie" — that was her cousin — "is only about eighteenth, and Richard is at the bottom."

"You like Richard and Elsie, don't you?"

"Oh, yes. I like Richard quite well and I like her all right."

Cautiously and casually he asked: "And Aunt Marion and Uncle Lincoln — which do you like best?"

"Oh, Uncle Lincoln, I guess."

He was increasingly aware of her presence. As they came in, a murmur of ". . . adorable" followed them, and now the people at the next table bent all their silences upon her, staring as if she were something no more conscious than a flower.

"Why don't I live with you?" she asked suddenly. "Because mamma's dead?"

"You must stay here and learn more French. It would have been hard for daddy to take care of you so well."

"I don't really need much taking care of any more. I do everything for myself."

Going out of the restaurant, a man and a woman unexpectedly hailed him.

"Well, the old Wales!"

"Hello there, Lorraine. . . . Dunc."

Sudden ghosts out of the past: Duncan Schaeffer, a friend from college. Lorraine Quarrles, a lovely, pale blonde of thirty; one of a crowd who had helped them make months into days in the lavish times of three years ago.

"My husband couldn't come this year," she said, in answer to his question. "We're poor as hell. So he gave me two hundred a month and told me I could do my worst on that. . . . This your little girl?"

"What about coming back and sitting down?" Duncan asked.

"Can't do it." He was glad for an excuse. As always, he felt Lorraine's passionate, provocative attraction, but his own rhythm was different now.

"Well, how about dinner?" she asked.

"I'm not free. Give me your address and let me call you."

"Charlie, I believe you're sober," she said judicially. "I honestly believe he's sober, Dunc. Pinch him and see if he's sober."

Charlie indicated Honoria with his head. They both laughed.

"What's your address?" said Duncan skeptically.

He hesitated, unwilling to give the name of his hotel.

"I'm not settled yet. I'd better call you. We're going to see the vaudeville at the Empire."

"There! That's what I want to do," Lorraine said. "I want to see some clowns and acrobats and jugglers. That's just what we'll do, Dunc."

"We've got to do an errand first," said Charlie. "Perhaps we'll see you there."

"All right, you snob. . . . Goody-by, beautiful little girl."

"Good-by."

Honoria bobbed politely.

Somehow, an unwelcome encounter. They liked him because he was functioning, because he was serious; they wanted to see him, because he was stronger than they were now, because they wanted to draw a certain sustenance from his strength.

At the Empire, Honoria proudly refused to sit upon her father's folded coat. She was already an individual with a code of her own, and Charlie was more and more absorbed by the desire of putting a little of himself into her before she crystallized utterly. It was hopeless to try to know her in so short a time.

Between the acts they came upon Duncan and Lorraine in the lobby where the band was playing.

"Have a drink?"

"All right, but not up at the bar. We'll take a table."

"The perfect father."

Listening abstractedly to Lorraine, Charlie watched Honoria's eyes leave their table, and he followed them wistfully about the room, wondering what they saw. He met her glance and she smiled.

"I liked that lemonade," she said.

What had she said? What had he expected? Going home in a taxi afterward, he pulled her over until her head rested against his chest.

"Darling, do you ever think of your mother?"

"Yes, sometimes," she answered vaguely.

"I don't want you to forget her. Have you got a picture of her?"

"Yes, I think so. Anyhow, Aunt Marion has. Why don't you want me to forget her?"

"She loved you very much."

"I loved her too."

They were silent for a moment.

"Daddy, I want to come and live with you," she said suddenly.

His heart leaped; he had wanted it to come like this.

"Aren't you perfectly happy?"

"Yes, but I love you better than anybody. And you love me better than anybody, don't you, now that mummy's dead?"

"Of course I do. But you won't always like me best, honey. You'll grow up and meet somebody your own age and go marry him and forget you ever had a daddy."

"Yes, that's true," she agreed tranquilly.

He didn't go in. He was coming back at nine o'clock and he wanted to keep himself fresh and new for the thing he must say then.

"When you're safe inside, just show yourself in that window."

"All right. Good-by, dads, dads, dads, dads."

He waited in the dark street until she appeared, all warm and glowing, in the window above and kissed her fingers out into the night.

III

They were waiting. Marion sat behind the coffee service in a dignified black dinner dress that just faintly suggested mourning. Lincoln was walking up and down with the animation of one who had already been talking. They were as anxious as he was to get into the question. He opened it almost immediately:

"I suppose you know what I want to see you about—why I really came to Paris."

Marion played with the black stars on her necklace and frowned.

"I'm awfully anxious to have a home," he continued. "And I'm awfully anxious to have Honoria in it. I appreciate your taking in Honoria for her mother's sake, but things have changed now"—he hesitated and then continued more forcibly—"changed radically with me, and I want to ask you to reconsider the matter. It would be silly for me to deny that about three years ago I was acting badly—"

Marion looked up at him with hard eyes.

"—but all that's over. As I told you, I haven't had more than a drink a day for over a year, and I take that drink deliberately, so that the idea of alcohol won't get too big in my imagination. You see the idea?"

"No," said Marion succinctly.

"It's a sort of stunt I set myself. It keeps the matter in proportion."

"I get you," said Lincoln. "You don't want to admit it's got any attraction for you."

"Something like that. Sometimes I forget and don't take it. But I try to take it. Anyhow, I couldn't afford to drink in my position. The people I represent are more than satisfied with what I've done, and I'm bringing my sister over from Burlington to keep house for me, and I want awfully to have Honoria too. You know that even when her mother and I weren't getting along well we never let anything that happened touch Honoria. I know she's fond of me and I know I'm able to take care of her and—well, there you are. How do you feel about it?"

He knew that now he would have to take a beating. It would last an hour or two hours, and it would be difficult, but if he modulated his inevitable resentment to the chastened attitude of the reformed sinner, he might win his point in the end.

Keep your temper, he told himself. You don't want to be justified. You want Honoria.

Lincoln spoke first: "We've been talking it over ever since we got your letter last month. We're happy to have Honoria here. She's a dear little thing, and we're glad to be able to help her, but of course that isn't the question ———"

Marion interrupted suddenly. "How long are you going to stay sober, Charlie?" she asked.

"Permanently, I hope."

"How can anybody count on that?"

"You know I never did drink heavily until I gave up business and came over here with nothing to do. Then Helen and I began to run around with ———"

"Please leave Helen out of it. I can't bear to hear you talk about her like that."

He stared at her grimly; he had never been certain how fond of each other the sisters were in life.

"My drinking only lasted about a year and a half—from the time we came over until I—collapsed."

"It was time enough."

"It was time enough," he agreed.

"My duty is entirely to Helen," she said. "I try to think what she would have wanted me to do. Frankly, from the night you did that terrible thing you haven't really existed for me. I can't help that. She was my sister."

"Yes."

"When she was dying she asked me to look out for Honoria. If you hadn't been in a sanitarium then, it might have helped matters."

He had no answer.

"I'll never in my life be able to forget the morning when Helen knocked at my door, soaked to the skin and shivering and said you'd locked her out."

Charlie gripped the sides of the chair. This was more difficult than he expected; he wanted to launch out into a long expostulation and explanation, but he only said: "The night I locked her out—" and she interrupted, "I don't feel up to going over that again."

After a moment's silence Lincoln said: "We're getting off the subject. You want Marion to set aside her legal guardianship and give you Honoria. I think the main point for her is whether she has confidence in you or not."

"I don't blame Marion," Charlie said slowly, "but I think she can have entire confidence in me. I had a good record up to three years ago. Of course, it's within human possibilities I might go wrong any time. But if we wait much longer I'll lose Honoria's childhood and my chance for a home." He shook his head, "I'll simply lose her, don't you see?"

"Yes, I see," said Lincoln.

"Why didn't you think of all this before?" Marion asked.

"I suppose I did, from time to time, but Helen and I were getting along badly. When I consented to the guardianship, I was flat on my back in a sanitarium and the market had cleaned me out. I knew I'd acted badly, and I thought if it would bring any peace to Helen, I'd agree to anything. But now it's different. I'm functioning, I'm behaving damn well, so far as ———"

"Please don't swear at me," Marion said.

He looked at her, startled. With each remark the force of her dislike became more and more apparent. She had built up all her fear of life into one wall and faced it toward him. This trivial reproof was possibly the result of some trouble with the cook several hours before. Charlie became increasingly alarmed at leaving Honoria in this atmosphere of hostility against himself; sooner or later it would come out, in a word here, a shake of the head there, and some of that distrust would be irrevocably implanted in Honoria. But he pulled his temper down out of his face and shut it up inside him; he had won a point, for Lincoln realized the absurdity of Marion's remark and asked her lightly since when she had objected to the word "damn."

"Another thing," Charlie said: "I'm able to give her certain advantages now. I'm going to take a French governess to Prague with me. I've got a lease on a new apartment ———"

He stopped, realizing that he was blundering. They couldn't be expected to

accept with equanimity the fact that his income was again twice as large as their own.

"I suppose you can give her more luxuries than we can," said Marion. "When you were throwing away money we were living along watching every ten francs. . . . I suppose you'll start doing it again."

"Oh, no," he said. "I've learned. I worked hard for ten years, you know—until I got lucky in the market, like so many people. Terribly lucky. It won't happen again."

There was a long silence. All of them felt their nerves straining, and for the first time in a year Charlie wanted a drink. He was sure now that Lincoln Peters wanted him to have his child.

Marion shuddered suddenly; part of her saw that Charlie's feet were planted on the earth now, and her own maternal feeling recognized the naturalness of his desire; but she had lived for a long time with a prejudice—a prejudice founded on a curious disbelief in her sister's happiness, and which, in the shock of one terrible night, had turned to hatred for him. It had all happened at a point in her life where the discouragement of ill health and adverse circumstances made it necessary for her to believe in tangible villainy and a tangible villain.

"I can't help what I think!" she cried out suddenly. "How much you were responsible for Helen's death, I don't know. It's something you'll have to square with your own conscience."

An electric current of agony surged through him; for a moment he was almost on his feet, an unuttered sound echoing in his throat. He hung on to himself for a moment, another moment.

"Hold on there," said Lincoln uncomfortably. "I never thought you were responsible for that."

"Helen died of heart trouble," Charlie said dully.

"Yes, heart trouble." Marion spoke as if the phrase had another meaning for her.

Then, in the flatness that followed her outburst, she saw him plainly and she knew he had somehow arrived at control over the situation. Glancing at her husband, she found no help from him, and as abruptly as if it were a matter of no importance, she threw up the sponge.

"Do what you like!" she cried, springing up from her chair. "She's your child. I'm not the person to stand in your way. I think if it were my child I'd rather see her—" She managed to check herself. "You two decide it. I can't stand this. I'm sick. I'm going to bed."

She hurried from the room; after a moment Lincoln said:

"This has been a hard day for her. You know how strongly she feels—" His voice was almost apologetic: "When a woman gets an idea in her head."

"Of course."

"It's going to be all right. I think she sees now that you—can provide for the child, and so we can't very well stand in your way or Honoria's way."

"Thank you, Lincoln."

"I'd better go along and see how she is."

"I'm going."

He was still trembling when he reached the street, but a walk down the Rue Bonaparte to the *quais* set him up, and as he crossed the Seine, fresh and new by the *quai* lamps, he felt exultant. But back in his room he couldn't sleep. The image of Helen haunted him. Helen whom he had loved so until they had senselessly begun to abuse each other's love, tear it into shreds. On that terrible February night that Marion remembered so vividly, a slow quarrel had gone on for hours. There was a scene at the Florida, and then he attempted to take her home, and then she kissed young Webb at a table; after that there was what she had hysterically said. When he arrived home alone he turned the key in the lock in wild anger. How could he know she would arrive an hour later alone, that there would be a snowstorm in which she wandered about in slippers, too confused to find a taxi? Then the aftermath, her escaping pneumonia by a miracle, and all the attendant horror. They were "reconciled," but that was the beginning of the end, and Marion, who had seen with her own eyes and who imagined it to be one of many scenes from her sister's martyrdom, never forgot.

Going over it again brought Helen nearer, and in the white, soft light that steals upon half sleep near morning he found himself talking to her again. She said that he was perfectly right about Honoria and that she wanted Honoria to be with him. She said she was glad he was being good and doing better. She said a lot of other things—very friendly things—but she was in a swing in a white dress, and swinging faster and faster all the time, so that at the end he could not hear clearly all that she said.

IV

He woke up feeling happy. The door of the world was open again. He made plans, vistas, futures for Honoria and himself, but suddenly he grew sad, remembering all the plans he and Helen had made. She had not planned to die. The present was the thing—work to do and someone to love. But not to love too much, for he knew the injury that a father can do to a daughter or a mother to a son by attaching them too closely: afterward, out in the world, the child would seek in the marriage partner the same blind tenderness and, failing probably to find it, turn against love and life.

It was another bright, crisp day. He called Lincoln Peters at the bank where he worked and asked if he could count on taking Honoria when he left for Prague. Lincoln agreed that there was no reason for delay. One thing—the legal guardianship. Marion wanted to retain that a while longer. She was upset by the whole matter, and it would oil things if she felt that the situation was still in her control for another year. Charlie agreed, wanting only the tangible, visible child.

Then the question of a governess. Charles sat in a gloomy agency and talked to a cross Béarnaise and to a buxom Breton peasant, neither of whom he could have endured. There were others whom he would see tomorrow.

He lunched with Lincoln Peters at Griffons, trying to keep down his exultation.

"There's nothing quite like your own child," Lincoln said. "But you understand how Marion feels too."

"She's forgotten how hard I worked for seven years there," Charlie said. "She just remembers one night."

"There's another thing." Lincoln hesitated. "While you and Helen were tearing around Europe throwing money away, we were just getting along. I didn't touch any of the prosperity because I never got ahead enough to carry anything but my insurance. I think Marion felt there was some kind of injustice in it—you not even working toward the end, and getting richer and richer."

"It went just as quick as it came," said Charlie.

"Yes, a lot of it stayed in the hands of *chasseurs* and saxophone players and maîtres d'hôtel—well, the big party's over now. I just said that to explain Marion's feeling about those crazy years. If you drop in about six o'clock tonight before Marion's too tired, we'll settle the details on the spot."

Back at his hotel, Charlie found a *pneumatique*[11] that had been redirected from the Ritz bar where Charlie had left his address for the purpose of finding a certain man.

> Dear Charlie: You were so strange when we saw you the other day that I wondered if I did something to offend you. If so, I'm not conscious of it. In fact, I have thought about you too much for the last year, and it's always been in the back of my mind that I might see you if I came over here. We *did* have such good times that crazy spring, like the night you and I stole the butcher's tricycle, and the time we tried to call on the president and you had the old derby rim and the wire cane. Everybody seems so old lately, but I don't feel old a bit. Couldn't we get together some time today for old time's sake? I've got a vile hang-over for the moment, but will be feeling better this afternoon and will look for you about five in the sweatshop at the Ritz.
>
> Always devotedly,
> Lorraine

His first feeling was one of awe that he had actually, in his mature years, stolen a tricycle and pedaled Lorraine all over the Étoile between the small hours and dawn. In retrospect it was a nightmare. Locking out Helen didn't fit in with any other act of his life, but the tricycle incident did—it was one of many. How many weeks or months of dissipation to arrive at that condition of utter irresponsibility?

He tried to picture how Lorraine had appeared to him then—very attractive; Helen was unhappy about it, though she said nothing. Yesterday, in the restaurant, Lorraine had seemed trite, blurred, worn away. He emphatically did not want to see her, and he was glad Alix had not given away his hotel address. It was a relief to think, instead, of Honoria, to think of Sundays spent with her and of saying good morning to her and of knowing she was there in his house at night, drawing her breath in the darkness.

At five he took a taxi and bought presents for all the Peters—a piquant cloth doll, a box of Roman soldiers, flowers for Marion, big linen handkerchiefs for Lincoln.

He saw, when he arrived in the apartment, that Marion had accepted the inevitable. She greeted him now as though he were a recalcitrant member of the family, rather than a menacing outsider. Honoria had been told she was going; Charlie was glad to see that her tact made her conceal her excessive happiness.

[11]*pneumatique* a message sent through the city's underground pneumatic tube system

Only on his lap did she whisper her delight and the question "When?" before she slipped away with the other children.

He and Marion were alone for a minute in the room, and on an impulse he spoke out boldly:

"Family quarrels are bitter things. They don't go according to any rules. They're not like aches or wounds; they're more like splits in the skin that won't heal because there's not enough material. I wish you and I could be on better terms."

"Some things are hard to forget," she answered. "It's a question of confidence." There was no answer to this and presently she asked, "When do you propose to take her?"

"As soon as I can get a governess. I hoped the day after tomorrow."

"That's impossible. I've got to get her things in shape. Not before Saturday."

He yielded. Coming back into the room, Lincoln offered him a drink.

"I'll take my daily whiskey," he said.

It was warm here, it was a home, people together by a fire. The children felt very safe and important; the mother and father were serious, watchful. They had things to do for the children more important than his visit here. A spoonful of medicine was, after all, more important than the strained relations between Marion and himself. They were not dull people, but they were very much in the grip of life and circumstances. He wondered if he couldn't do something to get Lincoln out of his rut at the bank.

A long peal at the door-bell; the *bonne à tout faire*[12] passed through and went down the corridor. The door opened upon another long ring, and then voices, and the three in the salon looked up expectantly; Richard moved to bring the corridor within his range of vision, and Marion rose. Then the maid came back along the corridor, closely followed by the voices, which developed under the light into Duncan Schaeffer and Lorraine Quarrles.

They were gay, they were hilarious, they were roaring with laughter. For a moment Charlie was astounded; unable to understand how they ferreted out the Peters' address.

"Ah-h-h!" Duncan wagged his finger roguishly at Charlie. "Ah-h-h!"

They both slid down another cascade of laughter. Anxious and at a loss, Charlie shook hands with them quickly and presented them to Lincoln and Marion. Marion nodded, scarcely speaking. She had drawn back a step toward the fire; her little girl stood beside her, and Marion put an arm about her shoulder.

With growing annoyance at the intrusion, Charlie waited for them to explain themselves. After some concentration Duncan said:

"We came to invite you out to dinner. Lorraine and I insist that all this shishi, cagy business 'bout your address got to stop."

Charlie came closer to them as if to force them backward down the corridor.

"Sorry, but I can't. Tell me where you'll be and I'll phone you in half an hour."

This made no impression. Lorraine sat down suddenly on the side of a chair, and focusing her eyes on Richard, cried, "Oh, what a nice little boy! Come here,

[12]*bonne à tout faire* maid

little boy." Richard glanced at his mother, but did not move. With a perceptible shrug of her shoulders, Lorraine turned back to Charlie:

"Come and dine. Sure your cousins won' mine. See you so sel'om. Or solemn."

"I can't," said Charlie sharply. "You two have dinner and I'll phone you."

Her voice became suddenly unpleasant. "All right, we'll go. But I remember once when you hammered on my door at four A.M. I was enough of a good sport to give you a drink. Come on, Dunc."

Still in slow motion, with blurred, angry faces, with uncertain feet, they retired along the corridor.

"Good night," Charlie said.

"Good night!" responded Lorraine emphatically.

When he went back into the salon Marion had not moved, only now her son was standing in the circle of her other arm. Lincoln was still swinging Honoria back and forth like pendulum from side to side.

"What an outrage!" Charlie broke out. "What an absolute outrage!"

Neither of them answered. Charlie dropped into an armchair, picked up his drink, set it down again and said:

"People I haven't seen for two years having the colossal nerve ———"

He broke off. Marion had made the sound "Oh!" in one swift, furious breath, turned her body from him with a jerk and left the room.

Lincoln set down Honoria carefully.

"You children go in and start your soup," he said, and when they obeyed, he said to Charlie:

"Marion's not well and she can't stand shocks. That kind of people make her really physically sick."

"I didn't tell them to come here. They wormed your name out of somebody. They deliberately ———"

"Well, it's too bad. It doesn't help matters. Excuse me a minute."

Left alone, Charlie sat tense in his chair. In the next room he could hear the children eating, talking in monosyllables, already oblivious to the scene between their elders. He heard a murmur of conversation from a farther room and then the ticking bell of a telephone receiver picked up, and in a panic he moved to the other side of the room and out of earshot.

In a minute Lincoln came back. "Look here, Charlie. I think we'd better call off dinner for tonight. Marion's in bad shape."

"Is she angry with me?"

"Sort of," he said, almost roughly. "She's not strong and———"

"You mean she's changed her mind about Honoria?"

"She's pretty bitter right now. I don't know. You phone me at the bank tomorrow."

"I wish you'd explain to her I never dreamed these people would come here. I'm just as sore as you are."

"I couldn't explain anything to her now."

Charlie got up. He took his coat and hat and started down the corridor. Then he opened the door of the dining room and said in a strange voice, "Good night, children."

Honoria rose and ran around the table to hug him.

"Good night, sweetheart," he said vaguely, and then trying to make his voice more tender, trying to conciliate something, "Good night, dear children."

V

Charlie went directly to the Ritz bar with the furious idea of finding Lorraine and Duncan, but they were not there, and he realized that in any case there was nothing he could do. He had not touched his drink at the Peters', and now he ordered a whisky-and-soda. Paul came over to say hello.

"It's a great change," he said sadly. "We do about half the business we did. So many fellows I hear about back in the States lost everything, maybe not in the first crash, but then in the second. Your friend George Hardt lost every cent, I hear. Are you back in the States?"

"No, I'm in business in Prague."

"I heard that you lost a lot in the crash."

"I did," and he added grimly, "but I lost everything I wanted in the boom."

"Selling short."

"Something like that."

Again the memory of those days swept over him like a nightmare—the people they had met travelling; then people who couldn't add a row of figures or speak a coherent sentence. The little man Helen had consented to dance with at the ship's party, who had insulted her ten feet from the table; the women and girls carried screaming with drink or drugs out of public places ——

—The men who locked their wives out in the snow, because the snow of twenty-nine wasn't real snow. If you didn't want it to be snow, you just paid some money.

He went to the phone and called the Peters' apartment; Lincoln answered.

"I called up because this thing is on my mind. Has Marion said anything definite?"

"Marion's sick," Lincoln answered shortly. "I know this thing isn't altogether your fault, but I can't have her go to pieces about it. I'm afraid we'll have to let it slide for six months; I can't take the chance of working her up to this state again."

"I see."

"I'm sorry, Charlie."

He went back to his table. His whisky glass was empty, but he shook his head when Alix looked at it questioningly. There wasn't much he could do now except send Honoria some things; he would send her a lot of things tomorrow. He thought rather angrily that this was just money—he had given so many people money. . . .

"No, no more," he said to the waiter. "What do I owe you?"

He would come back some day; they couldn't make him pay forever. But he wanted his child, and nothing was much good now, beside that fact. He wasn't young any more, with a lot of nice thoughts and dreams to have by himself. He was absolutely sure Helen wouldn't have wanted him to be so alone.

[1935]

QUESTIONS

1. Is Charlie a sympathetic character? Does he deserve a second chance? Can he, in fact, ever escape his reckless past?
2. What is the significance of the title?
3. What similarities can be drawn between the Jazz Age and the 1990s?

Gustave Flaubert

(1821–1880)

France

The father of the "social novel" and a central figure in the development of narrative language and style, Gustave Flaubert was born in Rouen, the son of a surgeon. He wrote his first novel, *November*, when he was 20. In 1844, he suffered the first attack of what was probably epilepsy, which gave him not only what he regarded as visionary experiences but also the excuse to give up the study of law in Paris and return to Rouen to take up his literary calling.

A consummate stylist and a highly disciplined writer, Flaubert attempted in an almost scientific manner to create an "objective" style that would erase the sense of the author's presence in the narrative and thus bring the reader closer to the sense of "real" characters and events. This bare, unromantic style is based on precise descriptions and an almost encyclopedic inclusion of realistic material details. Yet no detail or fact is extraneous; each contributes to the idea or mood of the whole work. Flaubert lamented that his aesthetic intentions were often misunderstood. As he commented, "Everyone thinks I am in love with reality when I actually detest it."

Among Flaubert's major novels are *The Sentimental Education* (1869), which traces a young man's infatuation for an older, married woman; *Salammbô* (1862) and *The Temptation of Saint Anthony* (1874), which draw on Flaubert's fascination with mysticism and Orientalism; and his most famous novel, *Madame Bovary* (1857), the affecting portrait of a woman who is literally bored to death and an indictment of banality and provincial values.

Flaubert wrote few short stories; "The Legend of Saint Julian the Hospitaller" reflects his fascination with the lives of saintly characters.

The Legend of Saint Julian the Hospitaller[1]

I

Julian's father and mother dwelt in a castle built on the slope of a hill, in the heart of the woods.

The towers at its four corners had pointed roofs covered with leaden tiles, and the foundation rested upon solid rocks, which descended abruptly to the bottom of the moat.

[1]*Hospitaller* patron saint of travelers, called "Hospitaller" because he ministered to them

In the courtyard, the stone flagging was as immaculate as the floor of a church. Long rain-spouts, representing dragons with yawning jaws, directed the water towards the cistern, and on each window-sill of the castle a basil or a heliotrope bush bloomed, in painted flowerpots.

A second enclosure, surrounded by a fence, comprised a fruit-orchard, a garden decorated with figures wrought in bright-hued flowers, an arbour with several bowers, and a mall for the diversion of the pages. On the other side were the kennel, the stables, the bakery, the winepress and the barns. Around these spread a pasture, also enclosed by a strong hedge.

Peace had reigned so long that the portcullis was never lowered; the moats were filled with water; swallows built their nests in the cracks of the battlements, and as soon as the sun shone too strongly, the archer who all day long paced to and fro on the curtain,[2] withdrew to the watchtower and slept soundly.

Inside the castle, the locks on all the doors shone brightly; costly tapestries hung in the apartments to keep out the cold; the closets overflowed with linen, the cellar was filled with casks of wine, and the oak chests fairly groaned under the weight of money-bags.

In the armoury could be seen, between banners and the heads of wild beasts, weapons of all nations and of all ages, from the sling of the Amalekites and the javelins of the Garamantes, to the broadswords of the Saracens and the coats of mail of the Normans.[3]

The largest spit in the kitchen could hold an ox; the chapel was as gorgeous as a king's oratory. There was even a Roman bath in a secluded part of the castle, though the good lord of the manor refrained from using it, as he deemed it a heathenish practice.

Wrapped always in a cape made of foxskins, he wandered about the castle, rendered justice among his vassals and settled his neighbours' quarrels. In the winter, he gazed dreamily at the falling snow, or had stories read aloud to him. But as soon as the fine weather returned, he would mount his mule and sally forth into the country roads, edged with ripening wheat, to talk with the peasants, to whom he distributed advice. After a number of adventures he took unto himself a wife of high lineage.

She was pale and serious, and a trifle haughty. The horns of her head-dress touched the top of the doors and the hem of her gown trailed far behind her. She conducted her household like a cloister. Every morning she distributed work to the maids, supervised the making of preserves and unguents, and afterwards passed her time in spinning, or in embroidering altar-cloths. In response to her fervent prayers, God granted her a son!

Then there was great rejoicing; and they gave a feast which lasted three days and four nights, with illuminations and soft music. Chickens as large as sheep, and the rarest spices were served; for the entertainment of the guests, a dwarf crept out of a pie; and when the bowls were too few, for the crowd swelled continuously, the wine was drunk from helmets and hunting-horns.

The young mother did not appear at the feast. She was quietly resting in bed. One night she awoke, and beheld in a moonbeam that crept through the

[2] *curtain* wall separating two towers of a castle

[3] *Amalekites* tribe descended from the Biblical Esau; *Garamantes*—ancient French noble family; *Saracens*—Muslims who fought against the Crusaders; *Normans*—ancestral conquerers of France and Britain

window something that looked like a moving shadow. It was an old man clad in sackcloth, who resembled a hermit. A rosary dangled at his side and he carried a beggar's sack on his shoulder. He approached the foot of the bed, and without opening his lips said: "Rejoice, O mother! Thy son shall be a saint."

She would have cried out, but the old man, gliding along the moonbeam, rose through the air and disappeared. The songs of the banqueters grew louder. She could hear angels' voices, and her head sank back on the pillow, which was surmounted by the bone of a martyr, framed in precious stones.

The following day, the servants, upon being questioned, declared, to a man, that they had seen no hermit. Then, whether dream or fact this must certainly have been a communication from heaven; but she took care not to speak of it, lest she should be accused of presumption.

The guests departed at daybreak, and Julian's father stood at the castle gate, where he had just bidden farewell to the last one, when a beggar suddenly emerged from the mist and confronted him. He was a gipsy—for he had a braided beard and wore silver bracelets on each arm. His eyes burned and, in an inspired way, he muttered some disconnected words: "Ah! Ah! thy son!—great bloodshed—great glory—happy always—an emperor's family."

Then he stooped to pick up the alms thrown to him, and disappeared in the tall grass.

The lord of the manor looked up and down the road and called as loudly as he could. But no one answered him! The wind only howled and the morning mists were fast dissolving.

He attributed his vision to a dullness of the brain resulting from too much sleep. "If I should speak of it," quoth he, "people would laugh at me." Still, the glory that was to be his son's dazzled him, albeit the meaning of the prophecy was not clear to him, and he even doubted that he had heard it.

The parents kept their secret from each other. But both cherished the child with equal devotion, and as they considered him marked by God, they had great regard for his person. His cradle was lined with the softest feathers, and a lamp representing a dove burned continually over it; three nurses rocked him night and day, and with his pink cheeks and blue eyes, brocaded cloak and embroidered cap, he looked like a little Jesus. He cut all his teeth without even a whimper.

When he was seven years old his mother taught him to sing, and his father lifted him upon a tall horse, to inspire him with courage. The child smiled with delight, and soon became familiar with everything pertaining to chargers. An old and very learned monk taught him the Gospel, the Arabic numerals, the Latin letters, and the art of painting delicate designs on vellum. They worked in the top of a tower, away from all noise and disturbance.

When the lesson was over, they would go down into the garden and study the flowers.

Sometimes a herd of cattle passed through the valley below, in charge of a man in Oriental dress. The lord of the manor, recognising him as a merchant, would despatch a servant after him. The stranger, becoming confident, would stop on his way and after being ushered into the castle-hall, would display pieces of velvet and silk, trinkets and strange objects whose use was unknown in those parts. Then, in due time, he would take leave, without having been molested and with a handsome profit.

At other times, a band of pilgrims would knock at the door. Their wet garments would be hung in front of the hearth and after they had been refreshed by food they would relate their travels, and discuss the uncertainty of vessels on the high seas, their long journeys across burning sands, the ferocity of the infidels, the caves of Syria, the Manger and the Holy Sepulchre. They made presents to the young heir of beautiful shells, which they carried in their cloaks.

The lord of the manor very often feasted his brothers-at-arms, and over the wine and old warriors would talk of battles and attacks, of war-machines and of the frightful wounds they had received, so that Julian, who was a listener, would scream with excitement; then his father felt convinced that some day he would be a conqueror. But in the evening, after the Angelus, when he passed through the crowd of beggars who clustered about the church-door, he distributed his alms with so much modesty and nobility that his mother fully expected to see him become an archbishop in time.

His seat in the chapel was next to his parents, and no matter how long the services lasted, he remained kneeling on his *prie-dieu*,[4] with folded hands and his velvet cap lying close beside him on the floor.

One day, during mass, he raised his head and beheld a little white mouse crawling out of a hole in the wall. It scrambled to the first altar-step and then, after a few gambols, ran back in the same direction. On the following Sunday, the idea of seeing the mouse again worried him. It returned; and every Sunday after that he watched for it; and it annoyed him so much that he grew to hate it and resolved to do away with it.

So, having closed the door and strewn some crumbs on the steps of the altar, he placed himself in front of the hole with a stick. After a long while a pink snout appeared, and then the whole mouse crept out. He struck it lightly with his stick and stood stunned at the sight of the little, lifeless body. A drop of blood stained the floor. He wiped it away hastily with his sleeve, and picking up the mouse, threw it away, without saying a word about it to anyone.

All sorts of birds pecked at the seeds in the garden. He put some peas in a hollow reed, and when he heard birds chirping in a tree, he would approach cautiously, lift the tube and swell his cheeks; then, when the little creatures dropped about him in multitudes, he could not refrain from laughing and being delighted with his own cleverness.

One morning, as he was returning by way of the curtain, he beheld a fat pigeon sunning itself on the top of the wall. He paused to gaze at it; where he stood the rampart was cracked and a piece of stone was near at hand; he gave his arm a jerk and the well-aimed missile struck the bird squarely, sending it straight into the moat below.

He sprang after it, unmindful of the brambles, and ferreted around the bushes with the litheness of a young dog.

The pigeon hung with broken wings in the branches of a privet hedge.

The persistence of its life irritated the boy. He began to strangle it, and its convulsions made his heart beat quicker, and filled him with a wild tumultuous voluptuousness, the last throb of its heart making him feel like fainting.

At supper that night, his father declared that at his age a boy should begin to hunt; and he arose and brought forth an old writing-book which contained, in questions and answers, everything pertaining to the pastime. In it, a master

[4]*prie-dieu* a framed bench used for kneeling during prayers

showed a supposed pupil how to train dogs and falcons, lay traps, recognise a stag by its fumets,[5] and a fox or a wolf by footprints. He also taught the best way of discovering their tracks, how to start them, where their refuges are usually to be found, what winds are the most favorable, and further enumerated the various cries, and the rules of the quarry.

When Julian was able to recite all these things by heart, his father made up a pack of hounds for him. There were twenty-four greyhounds of Barbary, speedier than gazelles, but liable to get out of temper; seventeen couples of Breton dogs, great barkers, with broad chests and russet coats flecked with white. For wild-boar hunting and perilous doublings, there were forty boarhounds as hairy as bears.

The red mastiffs of Tartary, almost as large as donkeys, with broad backs and straight legs, were destined for the pursuit of the wild bull. The black coats of the spaniels shone like satin; the barking of the setters equalled that of the beagles. In a special enclosure were eight growling bloodhounds that tugged at their chains and rolled their eyes, and these dogs leaped at men's throats and were not afraid even of lions.

All ate wheat bread, drank from marble troughs, and had high-sounding names.

Perhaps the falconry surpassed the pack; for the master of the castle, by paying great sums of money, had secured Caucasian hawks, Babylonian sakers, German gerfalcons, and pilgrim falcons captured on the cliffs edging the cold seas, in distant lands. They were housed in a thatched shed and were chained to the perch in the order of size. In front of them was a little grass-plot where, from time to time, they were allowed to disport themselves.

Bag-nets, baits, traps and all sorts of snares were manufactured.

Often they would take out pointers who would set almost immediately; then the whippers-in, advancing step by step, would cautiously spread a huge net over their motionless bodies. At the command, the dogs would bark and arouse the quails; and the ladies of the neighbourhood, with their husbands, children and handmaids, would fall upon them and capture them with ease.

At other times they used a drum to start hares; and frequently foxes fell into the ditches prepared for them, while wolves caught their paws in the traps.

But Julian scorned these convenient contrivances; he preferred to hunt away from the crowd, alone with his steed and his falcon. It was almost always a large, snow-white, Scythian bird. His leather hood was ornamented with a plume, and on his blue feet were bells; and he perched firmly on his master's arm while they galloped across the plains. Then Julian would suddenly untie his tether and let him fly, and the bold bird would dart through the air like an arrow. One might perceive two spots circle around, unite, and then disappear in the blue heights. Presently the falcon would return with a mutilated bird, and perch again on his master's gauntlet with trembling wings.

Julian loved to sound his trumpet and follow his dogs over hills and streams, into the woods; and when the stag began to moan under their teeth, he would kill it deftly, and delight in the fury of the brutes, which would devour the pieces spread out on the warm hide.

[5]*fumets* deer dung

On foggy days, he would hide in the marshes to watch for wild geese, otters and wild ducks.

At daybreak, three equerries waited for him at the foot of the steps; and though the old monk leaned out of the dormer-window and made signs to him to return, Julian would not look around.

He heeded neither the broiling sun, the rain nor the storm; he drank spring water and ate wild berries, and when he was tired, he lay down under a tree; and he would come home at night covered with earth and blood, with thistles in his hair and smelling of wild beasts. He grew to be like them. And when his mother kissed him, he responded coldly to her caress and seemed to be thinking of deep and serious things.

He killed bears with a knife, bulls with a hatchet, and wild boars with a spear; and once, with nothing but a stick, he defended himself against some wolves, which were gnawing corpses at the foot of a gibbet.

One winter morning he set out before daybreak, with a bow slung across his shoulder and a quiver of arrows attached to the pommel of his saddle. The hoofs of his steed beat the ground with regularity and his two beagles trotted close behind. The wind was blowing hard and icicles clung to his cloak. A part of the horizon cleared, and he beheld some rabbits playing around their burrows. In an instant, the two dogs were upon them, and seizing as many as they could, they broke their backs in the twinkling of an eye.

Soon he came to a forest. A woodcock, paralysed by the cold, perched on a branch, with its head hidden under its wing. Julian, with a lunge of his sword, cut off its feet, and without stopping to pick it up, rode away.

Three hours later he found himself on the top of a mountain so high that the sky seemed almost black. In front of him, a long, flat rock hung over a precipice, and at the end, two wild goats stood gazing down into the abyss. As he had no arrows (for he had left his steed behind), he thought he would climb down to where they stood; and with bare feet and bent back he at last reached the first goat and thrust his dagger below its ribs. But the second animal, in its terror, leaped into the precipice. Julian threw himself forward to strike it, but his right foot slipped, and he fell, face downward and with outstretched arms, over the body of the first goat.

After he returned to the plains, he followed a stream bordered by willows. From time to time, some cranes, flying low, passed over his head. He killed them with his whip, never missing a bird. He beheld in the distance the gleam of a lake which appeared to be of lead, and in the middle of it was an animal he had never seen before, a beaver with a black muzzle. Notwithstanding the distance that separated them, an arrow ended its life and Julian only regretted that he was not able to carry the skin home with him.

Then he entered an avenue of tall trees, the tops of which formed a triumphal arch to the entrance of a forest. A deer sprang out of the thicket and a badger crawled out of its hole, a stag appeared in the road, and a peacock spread its fan-shaped tail on the grass—and after he had slain them all, other deer, other stags, other badgers, other peacocks, and jays, blackbirds, foxes, porcupines, polecats, and lynxes, appeared; in fact, a host of beasts that grew more and more numerous with every step he took. Trembling, and with a look of appeal in their eyes, they gathered around Julian, but he did not stop slaying them; and so intent was he on stretching his bow, drawing his sword and whipping out his knife, that he had little thought for aught else. He knew that he was hunting in some country since an indefinite time, through the very fact of his existence, as everything seemed to occur with the ease one experiences in dreams. But presently an extraordinary sight made him pause.

He beheld a valley shaped like a circus and filled with stags which, huddled together, were warming one another with the vapour of their breaths that mingled with the early mist.

For a few minutes, he almost choked with pleasure at the prospect of so great a carnage. Then he sprang from his horse, rolled up his sleeves, and began to aim.

When the first arrow whizzed through the air, the stags turned their heads simultaneously. They huddled closer, uttered plaintive cries, and a great agitation seized the whole herd. The edge of the valley was too high to admit of flight; and the animals ran around the enclosure in their efforts to escape. Julian aimed, stretched his bow and his arrows fell as fast and thick as raindrops in a shower.

Maddened with terror, the stags fought and reared and climbed on top of one another; their antlers and bodies formed a moving mountain which tumbled to pieces whenever it displaced itself.

Finally the last one expired. Their bodies lay stretched out on the sand with foam gushing from the nostrils and the bowels protruding. The heaving of their bellies grew less and less noticeable, and presently all was still.

Night came, and behind the trees, through the branches, the sky appeared like a sheet of blood.

Julian leaned against a tree and gazed with dilated eyes at the enormous slaughter. He was now unable to comprehend how he had accomplished it.

On the opposite side of the valley, he suddenly beheld a large stag, with a doe and their fawn. The buck was black and of enormous size; he had a white beard and carried sixteen antlers. His mate was the color of dead leaves, and she browsed upon the grass, while the fawn, clinging to her udder, followed her step by step.

Again the bow was stretched, and instantly the fawn dropped dead, and seeing this, its mother raised her head and uttered a poignant, almost human wail of agony. Exasperated, Julian thrust his knife into her chest, and felled her to the ground.

The great stag had watched everything and suddenly he sprang forward. Julian aimed his last arrow at the beast. It struck him between his antlers and stuck there.

The stag did not appear to notice it; leaping over the bodies, he was coming nearer and nearer with the intention, Julian thought, of charging at him and ripping him open, and he recoiled with inexpressible horror. But presently the huge animal halted, and, with eyes aflame and the solemn air of a patriarch and a judge, repeated thrice, while a bell tolled in the distance:

"Accursed! Accursed! Accursed! some day, ferocious soul, thou wilt murder thy father and thy mother!"

Then he sank on his knees, gently closed his lids and expired.

At first Julian was stunned, and then a sudden lassitude and an immense sadness came over him. Holding his head between his hands, he wept for a long time.

His steed had wandered away; his dogs had forsaken him; the solitude seemed to threaten him with unknown perils. Impelled by a sense of sickening terror, he ran across the fields, and choosing a path at random, found himself almost immediately at the gates of the castle.

That night he could not rest, for, by the flickering light of the hanging lamp, he beheld again the huge black stag. He fought against the obsession of the prediction and kept repeating: "No! No! No! I cannot slay them!" and then he thought: "Still, supposing I desired to?—" and he feared that the devil might inspire him with this desire.

During three months, his distracted mother prayed at his bedside, and his father paced the halls of the castle in anguish. He consulted the most celebrated physicians, who prescribed quantities of medicine. Julian's illness, they declared, was due to some injurious wind or to amorous desire. But in reply to their questions, the young man only shook his head. After a time, his strength returned, and he was able to take a walk in the courtyard, supported by his father and the old monk.

But after he had completely recovered, he refused to hunt.

His father, hoping to please him, presented him with a large Saracen sabre.

It was placed on a panoply that hung on a pillar, and a ladder was required to reach it. Julian climbed up to it one day, but the heavy weapon slipped from his grasp, and in falling grazed his father and tore his cloak. Julian, believing he had killed him, fell in a swoon.

After that, he carefully avoided weapons. The sight of a naked sword made him grow pale, and this weakness caused great distress to his family.

In the end, the old monk ordered him in the name of God, and of his forefathers, once more to indulge in the sports of a nobleman.

The equerries diverted themselves every day with javelins and Julian soon excelled in the practice.

He was able to send a javelin into bottles, to break the teeth of the weather-cocks on the castle and to strike door-nails at a distance of one hundred feet.

One summer evening, at the hour when dusk renders objects indistinct, he was in the arbour in the garden, and thought he saw two white wings in the background hovering around the espalier. Not for a moment did he doubt that it was a stork, and so he threw his javelin at it.

A heart-rending scream pierced the air.

He had struck his mother, whose cap and long streamers remained nailed to the wall.

Julian fled from home and never returned.

II

He joined a horde of adventurers who were passing through the place.

He learned what it was to suffer hunger, thirst, sickness and filth. He grew accustomed to the din of battles and to the sight of dying men. The wind tanned his skin. His limbs became hardened through contact with armour, and as he was very strong and brave, temperate and of good counsel, he easily obtained command of a company.

At the outset of a battle, he would electrify his soldiers by a motion of his sword. He would climb the walls of a citadel with a knotted rope, at night, rocked by the storm, while sparks of fire clung to his cuirass, and molten lead and boiling tar poured from the battlements.

Often a stone would break his shield. Bridges crowded with men gave way under him. Once, by turning his mace, he rid himself of fourteen horsemen. He defeated all those who came forward to fight him on the field of honour, and more than a score of times it was believed that he had been killed.

However, thanks to Divine protection, he always escaped, for he shielded orphans, widows, and aged men. When he caught sight of one of the latter walking ahead of him, he would call to him to show his face, as if he feared that he might kill him by mistake.

All sorts of intrepid men gathered under his leadership, fugitive slaves, peasant rebels, and penniless bastards; he then organized an army which increased so much that he became famous and was in great demand.

He succoured in turn the Dauphin of France, the King of England, the Templars of Jerusalem, the General of the Parths, the Negus of Abyssinia and the Emperor of Calicut. He fought against Scandinavians covered with fish-scales, against negroes mounted on red asses and armed with shields made of hippopotamus hide, against gold-coloured Indians who wielded great, shining swords above their heads. He conquered the Troglodytes and the cannibals. He travelled through regions so torrid that the heat of the sun would set fire to the hair on one's head; he journeyed through countries so glacial that one's arms would fall from the body; and he passed through places where the fogs were so dense that it seemed like being surrounded by phantoms.

Republics in trouble consulted him; when he conferred with ambassadors, he always obtained unexpected concessions. Also, if a monarch behaved badly, he would arrive on the scene and rebuke him. He freed nations. He rescued queens sequestered in towers. It was he and no other that killed the serpent of Milan and the dragon of Oberbirbach.

Now, the Emperor of Occitania, having triumphed over the Spanish Mussulmans, had taken the sister of the Caliph of Cordova as a concubine, and had had one daughter by her, whom he brought up in the teachings of Christ. But the Caliph, feigning that he wished to become converted, made him a visit, and brought with him a numerous escort. He slaughtered the entire garrison and threw the Emperor into a dungeon, and treated him with great cruelty in order to obtain possession of his treasures.

Julian went to his assistance, destroyed the army of infidels, laid seige to the city, slew the Caliph, chopped off his head and threw it over the fortifications like a cannon-ball.

As a reward for so great a service, the Emperor presented him with a large sum of money in baskets; but Julian declined it. Then the Emperor, thinking that the amount was not sufficiently large, offered him three quarters of his fortune, and on meeting a second refusal, proposed to share his kingdom with his benefactor. But Julian only thanked him for it, and the Emperor felt like weeping with vexation at not being able to show his gratitude, when he suddenly tapped his forehead and whispered a few words in the ear of one of his courtiers; the tapestry curtains parted and a young girl appeared.

Her large black eyes shone like two soft lights. A charming smile parted her lips. Her curls were caught in the jewels of her half-opened bodice, and the grace of her youthful body could be divined under the transparency of her tunic.

She was small and quite plump, but her waist was slender.

Julian was absolutely dazzled, all the more since he had always led a chaste life.

So he married the Emperor's daughter, and received at the same time a castle she had inherited from her mother; and when the rejoicings were over, he departed with his bride, after many courtesies had been exchanged on both sides.

The castle was of Moorish design, in white marble, erected on a promontory and surrounded by orange-trees.

Terraces of flowers extended to the shell-strewn shores of a beautiful bay. Behind the castle spread a fan-shaped forest. The sky was always blue, and the trees were swayed in turn by the ocean-breeze and by the winds that blew from the mountains that closed the horizon.

Light entered the apartments through the incrustations of the walls. High, reed-like columns supported the ceiling of the cupolas, decorated in imitation of stalactites.

Fountains played in the spacious halls; the courts were inlaid with mosaic; there were festooned partitions and a great profusion of architectural fancies; and everywhere reigned a silence so deep that the swish of a sash or the echo of a sigh could be distinctly heard.

Julian now had renounced war. Surrounded by a peaceful people, he remained idle, receiving every day a throng of subjects who came and knelt before him and kissed his hand in Oriental fashion.

Clad in sumptuous garments, he would gaze out of the window and think of his past exploits; and wish that he might again run in the desert in pursuit of ostriches and gazelles, hide among the bamboos to watch for leopards, ride through forests filled with rhinoceroses, climb the most inaccessible peaks in order to have a better aim at the eagles, and fight the polar bears on the icebergs of the northern sea.

Sometimes, in his dreams, he fancied himself like Adam in the midst of Paradise, surrounded by all the beasts; by merely extending his arm, he was able to kill them; or else they filed past him, in pairs, by order of size, from the lions and the elephants to the ermines and the ducks, as on the day they entered Noah's Ark.

Hidden in the shadow of a cave, he aimed unerring arrows at them; then came others and still others, until he awoke, wild-eyed.

Princes, friends of his, invited him to their meets, but he always refused their invitations, because he thought that by this kind of penance he might possibly avert the threatened misfortune; it seemed to him that the fate of his parents depended on his refusal to slaughter animals. But he suffered because he could not see them, and his other desire was growing well-nigh unbearable.

In order to divert his mind, his wife had dancers and jugglers come to the castle.

She went abroad with him in an open litter; at other times, stretched out on the edge of a boat, they watched for hours the fish disport themselves in the water, which was as clear as the sky. Often she playfully threw flowers at him or nestling at his feet she played melodies on an old mandolin; then, clasping her hands on his shoulder, she would inquire tremulously: "What troubles thee, my dear lord?"

He would not reply, or else he would burst into tears; but at last, one day, he confessed his fearful dread.

His wife scorned the idea and reasoned wisely with him: probably his father and mother were dead; and even if he should ever see them again, through what chance, to what end, would he arrive at this abomination? Therefore, his fears were groundless, and he should hunt again.

Julian listened to her and smiled, but he could not bring himself to yield to his desire.

One August evening when they were in their bed-chamber, she having just retired and he being about to kneel in prayer, he heard the yelping of a fox and light footsteps under the window; and he thought he saw things in the dark that looked like animals. The temptation was too strong. He seized his quiver.

His wife appeared astonished.

"I am obeying you," quoth he, "and I shall be back at sunrise."

However, she feared that some calamity would happen. But he reassured her and departed, surprised at her illogical moods.

A short time afterwards, a page came to announce that two strangers desired, in the absence of the lord of the castle, to see its mistress at once.

Soon a stooping old man and an aged woman entered the room; their coarse garments were covered with dust and each leaned on a stick.

They grew bold enough to say that they brought Julian news of his parents. She leaned out of the bed to listen to them. But after glancing at each other, the old people asked her whether he ever referred to them and if he still loved them.

"Oh! yes!" she said.

Then they exclaimed:

"We are his parents!" and they sat themselves down, for they were very tired.

But there was nothing to show the young wife that her husband was their son.

They proved it by describing to her the birthmarks he had on his body. Then she jumped out of bed, called a page, and ordered that a repast be served to them.

But although they were very hungry, they could scarcely eat, and she observed surreptitiously how their lean fingers trembled whenever they lifted their cups.

They asked a hundred questions about their son, and she answered each one of them, but she was careful not to refer to the terrible idea that concerned them.

When he failed to return, they had left their château; and had wandered for several years, following vague indications but without losing hope.

So much money had been spent at the tolls of the rivers and in inns, to satisfy the rights of princes and the demands of highwaymen, that now their purse was quite empty and they were obliged to beg. But what did it matter, since they were about to clasp again their son in their arms? They lauded his happiness in having such a beautiful wife, and did not tire of looking at her and kissing her.

The luxuriousness of the apartment astonished them; and the old man, after examining the wall, inquired why they bore the coat-of-arms of the Emperor of Occitania.

"He is my father," she replied.

And he marvelled and remembered the prediction of the gipsy, while his wife meditated upon the words the hermit had spoken to her. The glory of their son was undoubtedly only the dawn of eternal splendours, and the old people remained awed while the light from the candelabra on the table fell on them.

In the heyday of youth, both had been extremely handsome. The mother had not lost her hair, and bands of snowy whiteness framed her cheeks; and the father, with his stalwart figure and long beard, looked like a carved image.

Julian's wife prevailed upon them not to wait for him. She put them in her bed and closed the curtains; and they both fell asleep. The day broke and outdoors the little birds began to chirp.

Meanwhile, Julian had left the castle grounds and walked nervously through the forest, enjoying the velvety softness of the grass and the balminess of the air.

The shadow of the trees fell on the earth. Here and there, the moonlight flecked the glades and Julian feared to advance, because he mistook the silvery light for water and the tranquil surface of the pools for grass. A great stillness reigned everywhere, and he failed to see any of the beasts that only a moment ago were prowling around the castle. As he walked on, the woods grew thicker, and the darkness more impenetrable. Warm winds, filled with enervating perfumes, caressed him; he sank into masses of dead leaves, and after a while he leaned against on oak-tree to rest and catch his breath.

Suddenly a body blacker than the surrounding darkness sprang from behind the tree. It was a wild boar. Julian did not have time to stretch his bow, and he bewailed the fact as if it were some great misfortune. Presently, having left the woods, he beheld a wolf slinking along a hedge.

He aimed an arrow at him. The wolf paused, turned his head and quietly continued on his way. He trotted along, always keeping at the same distance, pausing now and then to look around and resuming his flight as soon as an arrow was aimed in his direction.

In this way Julian traversed an apparently endless plain, then sand-hills, and at last found himself on a plateau that dominated a great stretch of land. Large flat stones were interspersed among crumbling vaults; bones and skeletons covered the ground, and here and there some mouldy crosses stood desolate. But presently, shapes moved in the darkness of the tombs, and from them came panting, wild-eyed hyenas. They approached him and smelled him, grinning hideously and disclosing their gums. He whipped out his sword, but they scattered in every direction and continuing their swift, limping gallop, disappeared in a cloud of dust.

Some time afterwards, in a ravine, he encountered a wild bull, with threatening horns, pawing the sand with his hoofs. Julian thrust his lance between his dewlaps. But his weapon snapped as if the beast were made of bronze; then he closed his eyes in anticipation of his death. When he opened them again, the bull had vanished.

Then his soul collapsed with shame. Some supernatural power destroyed his strength, and he set out for home through the forest. The woods were a tangle of creeping plants that he had to cut with his sword, and while he was thus engaged, a weasel slid between his feet, a panther jumped over his shoulder, and a serpent wound itself around an ash-tree.

Among its leaves was a monstrous jackdaw that watched Julian intently, and here and there, between the branches, appeared great, fiery sparks as if the sky were raining all its stars upon the forest. But the sparks were the eyes of wild-cats, owls, squirrels, monkeys, and parrots.

Julian aimed his arrows at them, but the feathered weapons lighted on the leaves of the trees and looked like white butterflies. He threw stones at them; but the missiles did not strike, and fell to the ground. Then he cursed himself, and howled imprecations, and in his rage he could have struck himself.

Then all the beasts he had pursued appeared, and formed a narrow circle around him. Some sat on their hindquarters, while others stood at full height. And Julian remained among them, transfixed with terror and absolutely unable to move. By a supreme effort of his will-power, he took a step forward; those that perched in the trees opened their wings, those that trod the earth moved their limbs, and all accompanied him.

The hyenas strode in front of him, the wolf and the wild boar brought up the rear. On his right, the bull swung its head and on his left the serpent crawled through the grass while the panther, arching its back, advanced with velvety footfalls and long strides. Julian walked as slowly as possible, so as not to irritate them, while in the depth of the bushes he could distinguish porcupines, foxes, vipers, jackals, and bears.

He began to run; the brutes followed him. The serpent hissed, the malodorous beasts frothed at the mouth, the wild boar rubbed his tusks against his heels, and the wolf scratched the palms of his hands with the hairs of his snout. The monkeys pinched him and made faces, the weasel rolled over his feet. A bear knocked his cap off with its huge paw, and the panther disdainfully dropped an arrow it was about to put in its mouth.

Irony seemed to incite their sly actions. As they watched him out of the corners of their eyes, they seemed to meditate a plan of revenge, and Julian, who was deafened by the buzzing of the insects, bruised by the wings and tails of the birds, choked by the stench of animal breaths, walked with outstretched arms and closed lids, like a blind man, without even the strength to beg for mercy.

The crowing of a cock vibrated in the air. Other cocks responded; it was day; and Julian recognised the top of his palace rising above the orange-trees.

Then, on the edge of a field, he beheld some red partridges fluttering around a stubble-field. He unfastened his cloak and threw it over them like a net. When he lifted it, he found only a bird that had been dead a long time and was decaying.

This disappointment irritated him more than all the others. The thirst for carnage stirred afresh within him; animals failing him, he desired to slaughter men.

He climbed the three terraces and opened the door with a blow of his fist; but at the foot of the staircase, the memory of his beloved wife softened his heart. No doubt she was asleep, and he would go up and surprise her. Having removed his sandals, he unlocked the door softly and entered.

The stained windows dimmed the pale light of dawn. Julian stumbled over some garments lying on the floor and a little further on, he knocked against a table covered with dishes. "She must have eaten," he thought; so he advanced cautiously towards the bed which was concealed by the darkness in the back of the room. When he reached the edge, he leaned over the pillow where the two heads were resting close together and stooped to kiss his wife. His mouth encountered a man's beard.

He fell back, thinking he had become crazed; then he approached the bed again and his searching fingers discovered some hair which seemed to be very long. In order to convince himself that he was mistaken, he once more passed his hand slowly over the pillow. But this time he was sure that it was a beard and that a man was there! a man lying beside his wife!

Flying into an ingovernable passion, he sprang upon them with his drawn dagger, foaming, stamping, and howling like a wild beast. After a while he stopped.

The corpses, pierced through the heart, had not even moved. He listened attentively to the two death-rattles, they were almost alike, as they grew fainter, another voice, coming from far away, seemed to continue them. Uncertain at first, this plaintive voice came nearer and nearer, grew louder and louder and presently he recognised, with a feeling of abject terror, the bellowing of the great black stag.

And as he turned around, he thought he saw the spectre of his wife standing at the threshold with a light in her hand.

The sound of the murder had aroused her. In one glance she understood what had happened and fled in horror, letting the candle drop from her hand. Julian picked it up.

His father and mother lay before him, stretched on their backs, with gaping wounds in their breasts; and their faces, the expression of which was full of tender dignity, seemed to hide what might be an eternal secret.

Splashes and blotches of blood were on their white skin, on the bed-clothes, on the floor, and on an ivory Christ which hung in the alcove. The scarlet reflection of the stained window, which just then was struck by the sun, lighted up the bloody spots and appeared to scatter them around the whole room. Julian walked toward the corpses, repeating to himself and trying to believe that he was mistaken, that it was not possible, that there are often inexplicable likenesses.

At last he bent over to look closely at the old man and he saw, between the half-closed lids, a dead pupil that scorched him like fire. Then he went over to the other side of the bed, where the other corpse lay, but the face was partly hidden by bands of white hair. Julian slipped his finger beneath them and raised the head, holding it at arm's length to study its features, while, with his other hand he lifted the torch. Drops of blood oozed from the mattress and fell one by one upon the floor.

At the close of the day, he appeared before his wife, and in a changed voice commanded her first not to answer him, not to approach him, not even to look at him, and to obey, under the penalty of eternal damnation, every one of his orders, which were irrevocable.

The funeral was to be held in accordance with the written instructions he had left on a chair in the death-chamber.

He left her his castle, his vassals, all his worldly goods, without keeping even his clothes or his sandals, which would be found at the top of the stairs.

She had obeyed the will of God in bringing about his crime, and accordingly she must pray for his soul, since henceforth he should cease to exist.

The dead were buried sumptuously in the chapel of a monastery which it took three days to reach from the castle. A monk wearing a hood that covered his head followed the procession alone, for nobody dared to speak to him. And during the mass, he lay flat on the floor with his face downward and his arms stretched out at his sides.

After the burial, he was seen to take the road leading into the mountains. He looked back several times, and finally passed out of sight.

III

He left the country and begged his daily bread on his way.

He stretched out his hand to the horsemen he met in the roads, and humbly approached the harvesters in the fields; or else remained motionless in front of the gates of castles; and his face was so sad that he was never turned away.

Obeying a spirit of humility, he related his history to all men, and they would flee from him and cross themselves. In villages through which he had passed before, the good people bolted the doors, threatened him, and threw stones at him as soon as they recognised him. The more charitable ones placed a bowl on the window-sill and closed the shutters in order to avoid seeing him.

Repelled and shunned by everyone, he avoided his fellow men and nourished himself with roots and plants, stray fruits and shells which he gathered along the shores.

Often, at the bend of a hill, he could perceive a mass of crowded roofs, stone spires, bridges, towers and narrow streets, from which arose a continual murmur of activity.

The desire to mingle with men impelled him to enter the city. But the gross and beastly expression of their faces, the noise of their industries and the indifference of their remarks, chilled his very heart. On holidays, when the cathedral bells rang out at daybreak and filled the people's hearts with gladness, he watched the inhabitants coming out of their dwellings, the dancers in the public squares, the fountains of ale, the damask hangings spread before the houses of princes; and then, when night came, he would peer through the windows at the long tables where families gathered and where grandparents held little children on their knees; then sobs would rise in his throat and he would turn away and go back to his haunts.

He gazed with yearning at the colts in the pastures, the birds in their nests, the insects on the flowers; but they all fled from him at his approach and hid or flew away. So he sought solitude. But the wind brought to his ears sounds resembling death-rattles; the tears of the dew reminded him of heavier drops, and every evening, the sun would spread blood in the sky, and every night, in his dreams, he lived over his parricide.

He made himself a hair-cloth lined with iron spikes. On his knees, he ascended every hill that was crowned with a chapel. But the unrelenting thought spoiled the splendour of the tabernacles and tortured him in the midst of his penances.

He did not rebel against God, who had inflicted his action, but he despaired at the thought that he had committed it.

He had such a horror of himself that he took all sorts of risks. He rescued paralytics from fire and children from the waves. But the ocean scorned him and the flames spared him. Time did not allay his torment, which became so intolerable that he resolved to die.

One day, while he was stooping over a fountain to judge of its depth, an old man appeared on the other side. He wore a white beard and his appearance was so lamentable that Julian could not keep back his tears. The old man also was weeping. Without recognising him, Julian remembered confusedly a face that resembled his. He uttered a cry; for it was his father who stood before him; and he gave up all thought of taking his own life.

Thus weighted down by his recollections, he travelled through many countries and arrived at a river which was dangerous, because of its violence and the slime that covered its shore. Since a long time nobody had ventured to cross it.

The bow of an old boat, whose stern was buried in the mud, showed among the reeds. Julian, on examining it closely found a pair of oars and hit upon the idea of devoting his life to the service of his fellow-men.

He began by establishing on the bank of the river a sort of road which would enable people to approach the edge of the stream; he broke his nails in his efforts to lift enormous stones which he pressed against the pit of his stomach in order to transport them from one point to another; he slipped in the mud, he sank into it, and several times was on the very brink of death.

Then he took to repairing the boat with débris of vessels, and afterwards built himself a hut with putty and trunks of trees.

When it became known that a ferry had been established, passengers flocked to it. They hailed him from the opposite side by waving flags, and Julian would jump into the boat and row over. The craft was very heavy, and the people loaded it with all sorts of baggage, and beasts of burden, who reared with fright, thereby adding greatly to the confusion. He asked nothing for his trouble; some gave him left-over victuals which they took from their sacks or worn-out garments which they could no longer use.

The brutal ones hurled curses at him, and when he rebuked them gently they replied with insults, and he was content to bless them.

A little table, a stool, a bed made of dead leaves and three earthen bowls were all he possessed. Two holes in the wall served as windows. On one side, as far as the eye could see, stretched barren wastes studded here and there with pools of water; and in front of him flowed the greenish waters of the wide river. In the spring, a putrid odor arose from the damp sod. Then fierce gales lifted clouds of dust that blew everywhere, even settling in the water and in one's mouth. A little later swarms of mosquitoes appeared, whose buzzing and stinging continued night and day. After that, came frightful frosts which communicated a stone-like rigidity to everything and inspired one with an insane desire for meat. Months passed when Julian never saw a human being. He often closed his lids and endeavored to recall his youth;—he beheld the courtyard of a castle, with greyhounds stretched out on a terrace, an armoury filled with valets, and under a bower of vines a youth with blond curls, sitting between an old man wrapped in furs and a lady with a high cap; presently the corpses rose before him, and then he would throw himself face downward on his cot and sob:

"Oh! poor father! poor mother! poor mother!" and would drop into a fitful slumber in which the terrible visions recurred.

One night he thought that some one was calling to him in his sleep. He listened intently, but could hear nothing save the roaring of the waters.

But the same voice repeated: "Julian!"

It proceeded from the opposite shore, a fact which appeared extraordinary to him, considering the breadth of the river.

The voice called a third time: "Julian!"

And the high-pitched tones sounded like the ringing of a church-bell.

Having lighted his lantern, he stepped out of his cabin. A frightful storm raged. The darkness was complete and was illuminated here and there only by the white waves leaping and tumbling.

After a moment's hesitation, he untied the rope. The water presently grew smooth and the boat glided easily to the opposite shore, where a man was waiting.

He was wrapped in a torn piece of linen; his face was like a chalk mask, and his eyes were redder than glowing coals. When Julian held up his lantern he noticed that the stranger was covered with hideous sores; but notwithstanding this, there was in his attitude something like the majesty of a king.

As soon as he stepped into the boat, it sank deep into the water, borne downward by his weight; then it rose again and Julian began to row.

With each stroke of the oars, the force of the waves raised the bow of the boat. The water, which was blacker than ink, ran furiously along the sides. It formed abysses and then mountains, over which the boat glided, then it fell into yawning depths where, buffeted by the wind, it whirled around and around.

Julian leaned far forward and, bracing himself with his feet, bent backwards so as to bring his whole strength into play. Hail-stones cut his hands, the rain ran down his back, the velocity of the wind suffocated him. He stopped rowing and let the boat drift with the tide. But realising that an important matter was at stake, a command which could not be disregarded, he picked up the oars again; and the rattling of the tholes mingled with the clamourings of the storm.

The little lantern burned in front of him. Sometimes birds fluttered past it and obscured the light. But he could distinguish the eyes of the leper who stood at the stern, as motionless as a column.

And the trip lasted a long, long time.

When they reached the hut, Julian closed the door and saw the man sit down on the stool. The species of shroud that was wrapped around him had fallen below his loins, and his shoulders and chest and lean arms were hidden under blotches of scaly pustules. Enormous wrinkles crossed his forehead. Like a skeleton, he had a hole instead of a nose, and from his bluish lips came breath which was fetid and as thick as mist.

"I am hungry," he said.

Julian set before him what he had, a piece of pork and some crusts of coarse bread.

After he had devoured them, the table, the bowl, and the handle of the knife bore the same scales that covered his body.

Then he said: "I thirst!"

Julian fetched his jug of water and when he lifted it, he smelled an aroma that dilated his nostrils and filled his heart with gladness. It was wine; what a boon! but the leper stretched out his arm and emptied the jug at one draught.

Then he said: "I am cold!"

Julian ignited a bundle of ferns that lay in the middle of the hut. The leper approached the fire and, resting on his heels, began to warm himself; his whole frame shook and he was failing visibly; his eyes grew dull, his sores began to break, and in a faint voice he whispered:

"Thy bed!"

Julian helped him gently to it, and even laid the sail of his boat over him to keep him warm.

The leper tossed and moaned. The corners of his mouth were drawn up over his teeth; an accelerated death-rattle shook his chest and with each one of his aspirations, his stomach touched his spine. At last, he closed his eyes.

"I feel as if ice were in my bones! Lay thyself beside me!" he commanded. Julian took off his garments; and then, as naked as on the day he was born, he got into the bed; against his thigh he could feel the skin of the leper, and it was colder than a serpent and as rough as a file.

He tried to encourage the leper, but he only whispered:

"Oh! I am about to die! Come closer to me and warm me! Not with thy hands! No! with thy whole body."

So Julian stretched himself out upon the leper, lay on him, lips to lips, chest to chest.

Then the leper clasped him close and presently his eyes shone like stars; his hair lengthened into sunbeams; the breath of his nostrils had the scent of roses; a cloud of incense rose from the hearth, and the waters began to murmur harmoniously; an abundance of bliss, a super-human joy, filled the soul of the swooning Julian, while he who clasped him to his breast grew and grew until his head and his feet touched the opposite walls of the cabin. The roof flew up in the air, disclosing the heavens, and Julian ascended into infinity face to face with our Lord Jesus Christ, who bore him straight to heaven.

And this is the story of Saint Julian the Hospitaller, as it is given on the stained-glass window of a church in my birthplace.

[1877]

[Translator not identified]

QUESTIONS

1. What are the distinct phases of Julian's life? What brings about each of the several reversals of direction to his life? What motivates him in each phase?
2. How does Flaubert shape the language and development of the story to highlight its legendary aspects? Does the story succeed only as a legend of a saint or does it also suggest more recognizable human dilemmas and qualities?
3. How are the extreme events described in the story brought into a coherent context as the trials of Julian's life?
4. Can the supernatural events and prophecies be interpreted psychologically? If so, what do they signify about Julian's character and motivation?

Carlos Fuentes

(b. 1928)

Mexico

The scope of Carlos Fuentes's writing is so extensive that one is forced to conclude that here is a man who has simultaneously led several lives, only one of which is the writer of startling fiction. His visionary novel, *Terra Nostra* (1975), for example, assumes as its geography the entire world; the time spans from the beginning of written records—although the implications go back much further than that—to the foreseeable future. Perhaps equally startling, *Terra Nostra* includes characters who are fellow Latin American writers—part of the boom (explosion) in Latin American writing during the past 20 years.

Born in Mexico City in 1928, the young Fuentes spent numerous years as a child outside of Mexico because his father was a career diplomat. Although Fuentes studied law and international diplomacy, by 1953 he was devoting most of his energies to writing. Three early novels gave him an immediate international reputation: *Where the Air Is Clear* (1958); *The Good Conscience* (1959); and, perhaps his most famous novel, *The Death of Artemio Cruz* (1962). For a period of time, Fuentes served as his country's ambassador to France. His more recent novel, *The Old Gringo* (1985), speculates on the life of Ambrose Bierce, who disappeared in Mexico in 1914. The novel was made into a successful Hollywood film.

In an interview with *Mother Jones* in 1986, Carlos Fuentes explained his reason for writing:

> The writer has to say things that would otherwise be silenced. This is the basic urge for this activity. . . . A writer is frightened of silence. Silence is death. It's terrible. I wish we didn't have repressive societies where a writer did not have to do this. It is terrible to have to mount a whole cultural expression, a whole artistic expression on the fact of silence and repression. I would prefer to have a happy society without good writers. But since that's not going to happen, we will need good writers.

The Doll Queen

I

I went because that card—such a strange card—reminded me of her existence. I found it in a forgotten book whose pages had revived the ghost associated with the childish calligraphy. For the first time in a long time I was rearranging my books. I met surprise after surprise since some, placed on the highest shelves, had not been read for a long time. So long a time that the edges of the leaves were grainy, and a mixture of gold dust and greyish scale fell onto my open palm, reminiscent of the lacquer covering certain bodies glimpsed first in dreams and later in the deceptive reality of the first ballet performance to which we're taken. It was a book from my childhood—perhaps from that of many children—that related a series of more or less truculent exemplary tales which had the virtue of precipitating us upon our elders' knees to ask them, over and over again: Why? Children who are ungrateful to their parents; maidens kidnapped by flashy horsemen and returned home in shame—as well as those who willingly abandon hearth and home; old men who in exchange for an overdue mortgage demand the hand of the sweetest and most long-suffering daughter of the threatened family. . . . Why? I do not recall their answers. I only know that from among the stained pages fell, fluttering, a white card in Amilamia's atrocious hand: *Amilamia wil not forget her good frend—com see me here lik I draw it.*

And on the other side was that map of a path starting from an X that indicated, doubtlessly, the park bench where I, an adolescent rebelling against prescribed and tedious education, forgot my classroom schedule in order to spend several hours reading books which if not actually written by me, seemed to be: who could doubt that only from *my* imagination could spring all those corsairs, those couriers of the tzar, all those boys slightly younger than I who rowed all day up and down the great American rivers on a raft. Clutching the arm of the park bench as if it were the frame of a magical saddle, at first I didn't hear the sound of the light steps and of the little girl who would stop behind me after running down the graveled garden path. It was Amilamia, and I don't know how long the child would have kept me silent company if her mischievous spirit, one afternoon, had not chosen to tickle my ear with down from a dandelion she blew towards me, her lips puffed out and her brow furrowed in a frown.

She asked my name and after considering it very seriously, she told me hers with a smile while if not candid, was not too rehearsed. Quickly I realized that Amilamia had discovered, if discovered is the word, a form of expression midway between the ingenuousness of her years and the forms of adult mimicry that well-brought-up children have to know, particularly those for the solemn moments of introduction and of leavetaking. Amilamia's seriousness, apparently, was a gift of nature, whereas her moments of spontaneity, by contrast, seemed artificial. I like to remember her, afternoon after afternoon, in a succession of snapshots that in their totality sum up the complete Amilamia. And it never ceases to surprise me that I cannot think of her as she really was, or remember how she actually moved, light, questioning, constantly looking around her. I must remember her fixed forever in time, as in a photograph album. Amilamia in the distance, a point on the spot where the hill began to descend from a lake of clover towards the flat meadow where I, sitting on the bench, used to read: a point of fluctuating shadow and sunshine and a hand that waved to me from high on the hill. Amilamia frozen in her flight down the hill, her white skirt billowing, the flowered panties gathered around her thighs with elastic, her mouth open and eyes half-closed against the streaming air, the child crying with pleasure. Amilamia sitting beneath the eucalyptus trees, pretending to cry so that I would go over to her. Amilamia lying on her stomach with a flower in her hand: the petals of a flower which I discovered later didn't grow in this garden, but somewhere else, perhaps in the garden of Amilamia's house, since the single pocket of her blue-checked apron was often filled with those white blossoms. Amilamia watching me read, holding with both hands to the bars of the green bench, asking questions with her grey eyes: I recall that she never asked me what I was reading, as if she could divine in my eyes the images born of the pages.

Amilamia laughing with pleasure when I lifted her by the waist and whirled her around my head; she seemed to discover a new perspective on the world in that slow flight. Amilamia turning her back to me and waving goodbye, her arm held high, the fingers waving excitedly. And Amilamia in the thousand postures she affected around my bench, hanging upside down, her bloomers billowing; sitting on the gravel with her legs crossed and her chin resting on her fist; lying on the grass baring her belly-button to the sun; weaving tree branches, drawing animals in the mud with a twig, licking the bars of the bench, hiding beneath the seat, silently breaking off the loose bark from the ancient treetrunks, staring at the horizon beyond the hill, humming with her eyes closed, imitating the voices of birds, dogs, cats, hens, and horses. All for me, and nevertheless, nothing. It was her way of being with me, all these things I remember, but at the same time her manner of being alone in the park. Yes, perhaps my memory of her is fragmentary because reading alternated with the contemplation of the chubby-cheeked child with smooth hair changing in the reflection of the light: now wheat-colored, now burnt chestnut. And it is only today that I think how Amilamia in that moment established the other point of support for my life, the one that created the tension between my own irresolute childhood and the open world, the promised land that was beginning to be mine through my reading.

Not then. Then I dreamed about the women in my books, about the quintessential female—the word disturbed me—who assumed the disguise of the Queen in order to buy the necklace secretly, about the imagined beings of mythology—half recognizable, half white-breasted, damp-bellied salamanders—who awaited monarchs in their beds. And thus, imperceptibly, I moved from indifference towards my childish companion to an acceptance of the child's gracefulness and seriousness and from there to an unexpected rejection of a presence that became useless to me. She irritated me, finally. I who was fourteen was irritated by that child of seven who was not yet memory or nostalgia, but rather the past and its reality. I had let myself be dragged along by weakness. We had run together, holding hands, across the meadow. Together we had shaken the pines and picked up the cones that Amilamia guarded jealously in her apron pocket. Together we had constructed paper boats and followed them, happy and gay, to the edge of the drain. And that afternoon amidst shouts of glee, when we tumbled together down the hill and rolled to a stop at its foot, Amilamia was on my chest, her hair between my lips; but when I felt her panting breath in my ear and her little arms sticky from sweets around my neck, I angrily pushed away her arms and let her fall. Amilamia cried, rubbing her wounded elbow and knee, and I returned to my bench. Then Amilamia went away and the following day she returned, handed me the paper without a word, and disappeared, humming, into the woods. I hesitated whether to tear up the card or keep it in the pages of the book: *Afternoons on the Farm.* Even my reading had become childish because of Amilamia. She did not return to the park. After a few days I left for my vacation and when I returned it was to the duties of my first year of prep school. I never saw her again.

II

And now, almost rejecting the image that is unaccustomed without being fantastic, but is all the more painful for being so real, I return to that forgotten park and stopping before the grove of pines and eucalyptus I recognize the smallness of the bosky enclosure that my memory has insisted on drawing with an amplitude that allowed sufficient space for the vast swell of my imagination. After all, Strogoff and Huckleberry, Milday de Winter and Geneviève de Brabante were born, lived and died here: in a little garden surrounded by mossy iron railings, sparsely planted with old, neglected trees, barely adorned by a concrete bench painted to look like wood that forces me to believe that my beautiful wrought-iron green-painted bench never existed, or else was a part of my orderly, retrospective delirium. And the hill. . . . How could I believe the promontory that Amilamia climbed and descended during her daily coming and going, that steep slope we rolled down together, was *this*. A barely elevated patch of dark stubble with no more heights and depths than those my memory had created.

Com see me here lik I draw it. So I would have to cross the garden, leave the woods behind, descend the hill in three loping steps, cut through that narrow grove of chestnuts—it was here, surely, where the child gathered the white petals—open the squeaking park gate and suddenly recall . . . know . . . find oneself in the street, realize that every afternoon of one's adolescence, as if by a miracle, he had succeeded in suspending the beat of the surrounding city, annulling that flood-tide of whistles, bells, voices, sobs, engines, radios, imprecations. Which was the true magnet, the silent garden or the feverish city?

I wait for the light to change and cross to the other sidewalk, my eyes never leaving the red iris detaining the traffic. I consult Amilamia's paper. After all, that rudimentary map is the true magnet of the moment I am living, and just thinking about it startles me. I was obliged, after the lost afternoons of my fourteenth year, to follow the channels of discipline; now I find myself, at twenty-nine, duly certified with a diploma, owner of an office, assured of a moderate income, a bachelor still, with no family to maintain, slightly bored with sleeping with secretaries, scarcely excited by an occasional outing to the country or to the beach, feeling the lack of a central attraction such as those once afforded me by my books, my park, and Amilamia. I walk down the street of this gray, low-buildinged suburb. The one-story houses with their doorways scaling paint succeed each other monotonously. Faint neighborhood sounds barely interrupt the general uniformity: the squeal of a knife-sharpener here, the hammering of a shoe-repairman there. The children of the neighborhood are playing in the dead-end streets. The music of an organ-grinder reaches my ears, mingled with the voices of children's rounds. I stop a moment to watch them with the sensation, also fleeting, that Amilamia must be among these groups of children, immodestly exhibiting her flowered panties, hanging by her knees from some balcony, still fond of acrobatic excesses, her apron pocket filled with white petals. I smile, and for the first time I am able to imagine the young lady of twenty-two who, even if she still lives at this address, will laugh at my memories, or who perhaps will have forgotten the afternoons spent in the garden.

The house is identical to all the rest. The heavy entry door, two grilled windows with closed shutters. A one-story house, topped by a false neo-classic balustrade that probably conceals the practicalities of the flat-roofed *azotea*:[1] clothes hanging on lines, tubs of water, servant's quarters, a chicken coop. Before I ring the bell, I want to free myself of any illusion. Amilamia no longer

[1]*azotea* Spanish: roof

lives here. Why would she stay fifteen years in the same house? Besides, in spite of her precocious independence and aloneness, she seemed like a well-brought-up, well-behaved child, and this neighborhood is no longer elegant; Amilamia's parents, without doubt, have moved. But perhaps the new renters will know where.

I press the bell and wait. I ring again. Here is another contingency: no one is home. And will I feel the need again to look for my childhood friend? No. Because it will not be possible a second time to open a book from my adolescence and accidentally find Amilamia's card. I would return to my routine, I would forget the moment whose importance lay in its fleeting surprise.

I ring once more. I press my ear to the door and am surprised: I can hear a harsh and irregular breathing on the other side; the sound of labored breathing, accompanied by the disagreeable odor of stale tobacco, filters through the cracks in the hall.

"Good afternoon. Could you tell me . . . ?"

As soon as he hears my voice, the person moves away with heavy and unsure steps. I press the bell again, shouting this time:

"Hey! Open up! What's the matter? Don't you hear me?"

No response. I continue ringing the bell, without result. I move back from the door, still staring at the small cracks, as if distance might give me perspective, or even penetration. With all my attention fixed on that damned door, I cross the street, walking backwards; a piercing scream, followed by a prolonged and ferocious blast of a whistle, saves me in time; dazed, I seek the person whose voice has just saved me. I see only the automobile moving down the street and I hang onto a lamp post, a hold that more than security offers me a point of support during the sudden rush of icy blood to my burning, sweaty skin. I look towards the house that had been, that was, that must be, Amilamia's. There, behind the balustrade, as I had known there would be, fluttering clothes are drying. I don't know what else is hanging there — skirts, pyjamas, blouses — I don't know. All I can see is that starched little blue-checked apron, clamped by clothespins to the long cord that swings between an iron bar and a nail in the white wall of the *azotea*.

III

In the Bureau of Records they have told me that the property is in the name of a Señor R. Valdivia, who rents the house. To whom? That they don't know. Who is Valdivia? He has declared himself a businessman. Where does he live? Who are *you*? the young lady asked me with haughty curiosity. I haven't been able to present a calm and sure appearance. Sleep has not relieved my nervous fatigue. Valdivia. As I leave the Bureau the sun offends me. I associate the repugnance provoked by the hazy sun sifting through the clouds — therefore all the more intense — with the desire to return to the damp, shadowy park. No. It is only the desire to know whether Amilamia lives in that house and why they refuse to let me enter. But the first thing I must do is reject the absurd idea that kept me awake all night. Having seen the apron drying on the flat roof, the one where she kept the flowers, and so believing that in that house lived a seven-year-old girl that I had known fourteen or fifteen years before. . . . She must have a little girl! Yes. Amilamia, at twenty-two, is the mother of a girl who dressed the same, looked the same, repeated the same games, and — who knows — perhaps even went to the same park. And deep in thought I again arrived at the door of the house. I ring the bell and await the whistling breathing on the other side of the door. I am mistaken. The door is opened by a woman who can't be more than about fifty. But wrapped in a shawl, dressed in black and in black low-heeled shoes, with no make-up and her salt and pepper hair pulled into a knot, she seems to have abandoned all illusion or pretext of youth; she is observing me with eyes so indifferent they seem almost cruel.

"You want something?"

"Señor Valdivia sent me." I cough and run my hand over my hair. I should have picked up my briefcase at the office. I realize that without it I cannot play my role very well.

"Valdivia?" the woman asks without alarm, without interest.

"Yes. The owner of this house."

One thing is clear. The woman will reveal nothing in her face. She looks at me, calmly.

"Oh, yes. The owner of the house."

"May I come in?"

I think that in bad comedies the traveling salesman sticks a foot in the door so they can't close the door in his face. I do the same, but the woman steps back and with a gesture of her hand invites me to come into what must have been a garage. On one side there is a glass-paned door, its paint faded. I walk towards the door over the yellow tiles of the entryway and ask again, turning towards the woman who follows me with tiny steps:

"This way?"

I notice for the first time that in her white hands she is carrying a chapelet which she toys with ceaselessly. I haven't seen one of those old-fashioned rosaries since my childhood and I want to comment on it, but the brusque and decisive manner with which the woman opens the door precludes any gratuitous conversation. We enter a long narrow room. The woman hastens to open the shutters. But because of four large perennial plants growing in porcelain and crusted glass pots the room remains in shadow. The only other objects in the room are an old high-backed cane-trimmed sofa and a rocking chair. But it is neither the plants nor the sparcity of the furniture that draws my attention.

The woman invites me to sit on the sofa before she sits in the rocking chair. Beside me, on the cane arm of the sofa, there is an open magazine.

"Señor Valdivia sends his apologies for not having come in person."

The woman rocks, unblinkingly. I peer at the comic book out of the corner of my eye.

"He sends his greetings and. . . ."

I stop, awaiting a reaction from the woman. She continues to rock. The magazine is covered with red-penciled scribbling.

" . . . and asks me to inform you that he must disturb you for a few days. . . ."

My eyes search rapidly.

" . . . A new evaluation of the house must be made for the tax lists. It seems it hasn't been done for. . . . You have been living here since . . . ?"

Yes. That is a stubby lipstick lying under the chair. If the woman smiles, it is only with the slow-moving hands caressing the chapelet; I sense, for an instant, a swift flash of ridicule that does not quite disturb her features. She still does not answer.

" . . . for at least fifteen years, isn't that true?"

She does not agree. She does not disagree. And on the pale thin lips there is not the least sign of lipstick. . . .

" . . . you, your husband, and . . . ?"

She stares at me, never changing expression, almost daring me to continue. We sit a moment in silence, she playing with the rosary, I leaning forwards, my hands on my knees. I rise.

"Well, then, I'll be back this afternoon with the papers. . . . "

The woman nods while, in silence, she picks up the lipstick and the comic book and hides them in the folds of her shawl.

IV

The scene has not changed. This afternoon, while I am writing down false figures in my notebook and feigning interest in establishing the quality of the dulled floorboards and the length of the living room, the woman rocks, as the three decades of the chapelet whisper through her fingers. I sigh as I finish the supposed inventory of the living room and I ask her for permission to go to the other rooms in the house. The woman rises, bracing her long black-clad arms on the seat of the rocking chair and adjusting the shawl on her narrow bony shoulders.

She opens the opaque glass door and we enter a dining room with very little more furniture. But the table with the aluminum legs and the four nickel and plastic chairs lack even the slight hint of distinction of the living room furniture. Another window with wrought-iron grill and closed shutters must at times illuminate this bare-walled dining room, bare of either shelves or bureau. The only object on the table is a plastic fruit dish with a cluster of black grapes, two peaches, and a buzzing corona of flies. The woman, her arms crossed, her face expressionless, stops behind me. I take the risk of breaking the order of things: it is evident that these rooms will not tell me anything that I really want to know.

"Couldn't we go up to the roof?" I ask. "I believe that is the best way of measuring the total area."

The woman's eyes light up as she looks at me, or perhaps it is only the contrast with the penumbra of the dining room.

"What for?" she says finally. "Señor . . . Valdivia . . . knows the dimensions very well."

And those pauses, one before and one after the owner's name, are the first indications that something is at last perturbing the woman and forcing her, in defense, to resort to a certain irony.

"I don't know." I make an effort to smile. "Perhaps I prefer to go from top to bottom and not . . . " my false smile drains away, " . . . from bottom to top."

"You will go the way I show you," the woman says, her arms crossed across her chest, the silver cross hanging against her dark belly.

Before smiling weakly, I force myself to think how, in this shadow, my gestures are useless, not even symbolic. I open the notebook with a crunch of the cardboard cover and continue making my notes with the greatest possible speed, never glancing up, the numbers and estimates of this task whose fiction —the light flush in my cheeks and the perceptible dryness of my tongue tell me—is deceiving no one. And after filling the graph paper with absurd signs, with square roots and algebraic formulas, I ask myself what is preventing me from getting to the point, from asking about Amilamia and getting out of here with a satisfactory answer. Nothing. And nevertheless, I am sure that even if I obtained a response, the truth does not lie along this road. My slim and silent companion is a person I wouldn't look twice at in the street, but in this almost uninhabited house with the coarse furniture, she ceases to be an anonymous face in the crowd and is converted into a stock character of mystery. Such is the paradox, and if memories of Amilamia have once again awakened my appetite for the imaginary, I shall follow the rules of the game, I shall exhaust all the appearances, and I shall not rest until I find the answer—perhaps simple and clear, immediate and evident—that lies beyond the unexpected veils the señora of the rosary places in my path. Do I bestow a more-than-justified strangeness upon my reluctant Amphitryon? If that is so, I shall only take more pleasure in the labyrinths of my own invention. And the flies are still buzzing around the fruit dish, occasionally pausing on the damaged end of the peach, a nibbled bite—I lean closer using the pretext of my notes—where little teeth have left their mark in the velvety skin and ochre flesh of the fruit. I do not look towards the señora. I pretend I am taking notes. The fruit seems to be bitten but not touched. I crouch down to see it better, rest my hands upon the table, moving my lips closer as if I wished to repeat the act of biting without touching. I look down and I see another sign close to my feet: the track of two tires that seem to be bicycle tires, the paint of two rubber tires that come as far as the edge of the table and then lead away, growing fainter, the length of the room, towards the señora. . . .

I close my notebook.

"Let us continue, señora."

As I turn towards her, I find her standing with her hands resting on the back of a chair. Seated before her, coughing the smoke of his black cigarette, is a man with heavy shoulders and hidden eyes: these eyes, hardly visible behind swollen wrinkled lids as thick and droopy as the neck of an ancient turtle, seem nevertheless to follow my every movement. The half-shaven cheeks, criss-crossed by a thousand gray furrows, hang from protruding cheekbones, and his greenish hands are folded beneath his arms. He is wearing a coarse blue shirt, and his rumpled hair is so curly it looks like the bottom of a barnacle-covered ship. He does not move, and the true sign of his existence is that difficult whistling breathing (as if every breath must breach a flood-gate of phlegm, irritation, and abuse) that I had already heard through the chinks of the entry hall.

Ridiculously, he murmurs: "Good afternoon. . . ." and I am disposed to forget everything: the mystery, Amilamia, the assessment, the bicycle tracks. The apparition of this asthmatic old bear justifies a prompt retreat. I repeat "Good afternoon," this time with an inflection of farewell. The turtle's mask dissolves into an atrocious smile: every pore of that flesh seems fabricated of brittle rubber, of painted, peeling oilcloth. The arm reaches out and detains me.

"Valdivia died four years ago," says the man in a distant, choking voice that issues from his belly instead of his larynx: a weak, high-pitched voice.

Held by that strong, almost painful, claw, I tell myself it is useless to pretend. But the wax and rubber faces observing me say nothing and for that reason I am able, in spite of everything, to pretend one last time, to pretend that I am speaking to myself when I say:

"Amilamia. . . ."

Yes; no one will have to pretend any longer. The fist that clutches my arm affirms its strength for only an instant, immediately its grip loosens, then it falls, weak and trembling, before rising to take the waxen hand touching the shoulder: the señora, perplexed for the first time, looks at me with the eyes of a violated bird and sobs with a dry moan that does not disturb the rigid astonishment of her features. Suddenly the ogres of my imagination are two solitary, abandoned, wounded old people, scarcely able to console themselves in the shuddering clasp of hands that fills me with shame. My fantasy has brought me to this stark dining room to violate the intimacy and the secret of two human beings exiled from life by something I no longer have the right to share. I have never despised myself more. Never have words failed me in such a clumsy way. Any gesture of mine would be in vain: shall I approach them, shall I touch them, shall I caress the woman's head, shall I ask them to excuse my intrusion? I return the notebook to my jacket pocket. I toss into oblivion all the clues in my detective story: the comic book, the lipstick, the nibbled fruit, the bicycle tracks, the blue-checked apron. . . . I decide to leave this house in silence. The old man, from behind those thick eyelids, must have noticed me. The high breathy voice says:

"Did you know her?"

That past, so natural they must use it every day, finally destroys my illusions. There is the answer. Did you know her? How many years? How many years must the world have lived without Amilamia, assassinated first by my forgetfulness, and revived, scarcely yesterday, by a sad impotent memory? When did those serious gray eyes cease to be astonished by the delight of an always solitary garden? When did those lips cease to pout or press together thinly in that ceremonious seriousness with which, I now realize, Amilamia must have discovered and consecrated the objects and events of life that, she knew perhaps intuitively, was fleeting?

"Yes, we played together in the park. A long time ago."

"How old was she?" says the old man, his voice even more muffled.

"She must have been about seven. No, older than seven."

The woman's voice rises, along with the arms that seem to implore:

"What was she like, señor? Tell us what she was like, please."

I close my eyes. "Amilamia is my memory, too. I can only compare her to the things that she touched, that she brought, that she discovered in the park. Yes. Now I see her, coming down the hill. No. It isn't true that it was a barely elevated patch of stubble. It was a hill, with grass, and Amilamia's coming and going had traced a path, and she waved to me from the top before she started down, accompanied by the music, yes, the music I saw, the painting I smelled, the tastes I heard, the odors I touched . . . my hallucination. . . ." Do they hear me? "She came, waving, dressed in white, in a blue-checked apron . . . the one you have hanging on the *azotea*. . . ."

They take my arms and still I do not open my eyes.

"What was she like, señor?"

"Her eyes were gray and the color of her hair changed in the reflection of the sun and the shadow of the trees. . . ."

They lead me gently, the two of them; I hear the man's labored breathing, the cross on the rosary hitting against the woman's body.

"Tell us, please. . . ."

"The air brought tears to her eyes when she ran; when she reached my bench her cheeks were silvered with happy tears. . . ."

I do not open my eyes. Now we are going upstairs. Two, five, eight, nine, twelve steps. Four hands guide my body.

"What was she like, what was she like?"

"She sat beneath the eucalyptus and wove garlands from the branches and pretended to cry so I would quit my reading and go over to her. . . ."

Hinges creak. The odor overpowers everything else: it routs the other senses, it takes its seat like a yellow Mogol upon the throne of my hallucination; heavy as a coffin, insinuating as the slither of draped silk, ornamented as a Turkish sceptre, opaque as a deep, lost vein of ore, brilliant as a dead star. The hands no longer hold me. More than the sobbing, it is the trembling of the old people that envelops me. Slowly, I open my eyes: first through the dizzying liquid of my cornea then through the web of my eyelashes, the room suffocated in that enormous battle of perfumes is disclosed, effluvia and frosty, almost flesh-like petals; the presence of the flowers is so strong here they seem to take on the quality of living flesh—the sweetness of the jasmine, the nausea of the lilies, the tomb of the tuberose, the temple of the gardenia. Illuminated through the incandescent wax lips of heavy sputtering candles, the small windowless bedroom with its aura of wax and humid flowers assaults the very center of my plexus, and from there, only there at the solar center of life, am I able to revive and to perceive beyond the candles, among the scattered flowers, the accumulation of used toys: the colored hoops and wrinkled balloons, cherries dried to transparency, wooden horses with scraggly manes, the scooter, blind and hairless dolls, bears spilling their sawdust, punctured oil-cloth ducks, moth-eaten dogs, wornout jumping ropes, glass jars of dried candy, wornout shoes, the tricycle (three wheels? no, two, and not like a bicycle—two *parallel* wheels below), little woolen and leather shoes; and, facing me, within reach of my hand, the small coffin raised on paper flower-decorated blue boxes, flowers of life this time, carnations and sunflowers, poppies and tulips, but like the others, the ones of death, all part of a potion brewed by the atmosphere of this funeral hot-house in which reposes, inside the silvered coffin, between the black silk sheets, upon the pillow of white satin, that motionless and serene face framed in lace, highlighted with rose-colored tints, eyebrows traced by the lightest trace of pencil, closed lids, real eyelashes, thick, that cast a tenuous shadow on cheeks as healthy as those of the days in the park. Serious red lips, set almost in the angry pout that Amilamia feigned so I would come to play. Hands joined over the breast. A chapelet, identical to the mother's, strangling that cardboard neck. Small white shroud on the clean, pre-pubescent, docile body.

The old people, sobbing, have knelt.

I reach out my hand and run my fingers over the porcelain face of my friend. I feel the coldness of those painted features, of the doll-queen who presides over the pomp of this royal chamber of death. Porcelain, cardboard, and cotton. *Amilamia wil not forget her good frend—com see me here lik I draw it.*

I withdraw my fingers from the false cadaver. Traces of my finger prints remain where I touched the skin of the doll.

And nausea crawls in my stomach where the candle smoke and the sweet stench of the lilies in the enclosed room have settled. I turn my back on Amilamia's sepulchre. The woman's hand touches my arm. Her wildly staring eyes do not correspond with the quiet, steady voice.

"Don't come back, señor. If you truly loved her, don't come back again."

I touch the hand of Amilamia's mother. I see through nauseous eyes the old man's head buried between his knees, and I go out of the room to the stairway, to the living room, to the patio, to the street.

V

If not a year, nine or ten months have passed. The memory of that idolatry no longer frightens me. I have forgotten the odor of the flowers and the image of the petrified doll. The real Amilamia has returned to my memory and I have felt, if not content, sane again: the park, the living child, my hours of adolescent reading, have triumphed over the spectres of a sick cult. The image of life is the more powerful. I tell myself that I shall live forever with my real Amilamia, the conqueror of the caricature of death. And one day I dare look again at that notebook with graph paper where I wrote the information of the false assessment. And from its pages, once again, falls Amilamia's card with its terrible childish scrawl and its map for getting from the park to her house. I smile as I pick it up. I bite one of the edges, thinking that in spite of everything, the poor old people would accept this gift.

Whistling, I put on my jacket and knot my tie. Why not visit them and offer them this paper with the child's own writing?

I am running as I approach the one-story house. Rain is beginning to fall in large isolated drops that bring from the earth with magical immediacy an odor of damp benediction that seems to stir the humus and precipitate the fermentation of everything living with its roots in the dust.

I ring the bell. The shower increases and I become insistent. A shrill voice shouts: "I'm going!" and I wait for the figure of the mother with her eternal rosary to open the door for me. I turn up the collar of my jacket. My clothes, my body, too, smell different in the rain. The door opens:

"What do you want? How wonderful you've come!"

The misshapen girl sitting in the wheelchair lays one hand on the doorknob and smiles at me with an indecipherably wry grin. The hump on her chest converts the dress into a curtain over her body, a piece of white cloth that nonetheless lends an air of coquetry to the blue-checked apron. The little woman extracts a pack of cigarettes from her apron pocket and rapidly lights a cigarette, staining the end with orange-painted lips. The smoke causes the beautiful gray eyes to squint. She arranges the coppery, wheat-colored, permanently waved hair: She stares at me all the time with a desolate, inquisitive, and hopeful—but at the same time fearful—expression.

"No, Carlos. Go away. Don't come back."

And from the house, at the same moment, I hear the high breathy breathing of the old man, coming closer and closer.

"Where are you? Don't you know you're not supposed to answer the door? Go back! Devil's spawn! Do I have to beat you again?"

And the water from the rain trickles down my forehead, over my cheeks, and into my mouth, and the little frightened hands drop the comic book onto the damp stones.

[1974]

Translated by
MARGARET S. PEDEN

QUESTIONS

1. Is it possible to establish exactly what has happened to Carlos by the end of the story? What has happened to Amilamia? Why have her parents built the shrine for her? Of what is Amilamia guilty? Of what is Carlos guilty?
2. Why does Carlos wait so many years to visit Amilamia? What does her message mean: "Amilamia wil not forget her good frend—com see me here lik I draw it"?
3. Do Fuentes's remarks on "silence" quoted in the introductory notes have any bearing on the story's meaning?

Gabriel García Márquez

(b. 1928)

Colombia

In recent years, Gabriel García Márquez has clearly become his continent's most famous writer—indeed, one of the most widely read writers in today's world. Born in a small coastal town in Colombia in 1928, García Márquez celebrated that heritage in *One Hundred Years of Solitude* (1967). The novel is often cited as the peak of the "boom," or explosion, in Latin American writing and as one of the most famous examples of magic realism. Equally memorable and fantastic, though for different reasons, are his later works, *The Autumn of the Patriarch* (1975), the study of a Latin American dictator's political abuses; *Chronicle of a Death Foretold* (1981); and *Love in the Time of Cholera* (1985). García Márquez was awarded the Nobel Prize for Literature in 1982.

Commenting on the relationship between art and life, Gabriel García Márquez once remarked, "An electrician called at my house at eight in the morning and as soon as the door was open, he said: 'You have to change the electric iron's cord.' Immediately realizing that he had come to the wrong door, he apologized and left. Hours later, my wife connected the iron, and the cord caught fire. There is no need to go on. It is enough to read the papers, and open one's eyes, in order to feel willing to shout along with the French college students: 'Power to the imagination.'"

Balthazar's Marvelous Afternoon

The cage was finished. Balthazar hung it under the eave, from force of habit, and when he finished lunch everyone was already saying that it was the most beautiful cage in the world. So many people came to see it that a crowd formed in front of the house, and Balthazar had to take it down and close the shop.

"You have to shave," Ursula, his wife, told him. "You look like a Capuchin."

"It's bad to shave after lunch," said Balthazar.

He had two weeks' growth, short, hard, and bristly hair like the mane of a mule, and the general expression of a frightened boy. But it was a false expression. In February he was thirty; he had been living with Ursula for four years, without marrying her and without having children, and life had given him many reasons to be on guard but none to be frightened. He did not even know that for some people the cage he had just made was the most beautiful one in the world. For him, accustomed to making cages since childhood, it had been hardly any more difficult than the others.

"Then rest for a while," said the woman. "With that beard you can't show yourself anywhere."

While he was resting, he had to get out of his hammock several times to show the cage to the neighbors. Ursula had paid little attention to it until then. She was annoyed because her husband had neglected the work of his carpenter's shop to devote himself entirely to the cage, and for two weeks had slept poorly, turning over and muttering incoherencies, and he hadn't thought of shaving. But her annoyance dissolved in the face of the finished cage. When Balthazar woke up from his nap, she had ironed his pants and a shirt; she had put them on a chair near the hammock and had carried the cage to the dining table. She regarded it in silence.

"How much will you charge?" she asked.

"I don't know," Balthazar answered. "I'm going to ask for thirty pesos to see if they'll give me twenty."

"Ask for fifty," said Ursula. "You've lost a lot of sleep in these two weeks. Furthermore, it's rather large. I think it's the biggest cage I've ever seen in my life."

Balthazar began to shave.

"Do you think they'll give me fifty pesos?"

"That's nothing for Mr. Chepe Montiel, and the cage is worth it," said Ursula. "You should ask for sixty."

The house lay in the stifling shadow. It was the first week of April and the heat seemed less bearable because of the chirping of the cicadas. When he finished dressing, Balthazar opened the door to the patio to cool off the house, and a group of children entered the dining room.

The news had spread. Dr. Octavio Giraldo, an old physician, happy with life but tired of his profession, thought about Balthazar's cage while he was eating lunch with his invalid wife. On the inside terrace, where they put the table on hot days, there were many flowerpots and two cages with canaries. His wife liked birds, and she liked them so much that she hated cats because they could eat them up. Thinking about her, Dr. Giraldo went to see a patient that afternoon, and when he returned he went by Balthazar's house to inspect the cage.

There were a lot of people in the dining room. The cage was on display on the table: with its enormous dome of wire, three stories inside, with passageways and compartments especially for eating and sleeping and swings in the space set aside for the birds' recreation, it seemed like a small-scale model of a gigantic ice factory. The doctor inspected it carefully, without touching it, thinking that in effect the cage was better than its reputation, and much more beautiful than any he had ever dreamed of for his wife.

"This is a flight of the imagination," he said. He sought out Balthazar among the group of people and, fixing his maternal eyes on him, added, "You would have been an extraordinary architect."

Balthazar blushed.

"Thank you," he said.

"It's true," said the doctor. He was smoothly and delicately fat, like a woman who had been beautiful in her youth, and he had delicate hands. His voice seemed like that of a priest speaking Latin. "You wouldn't even need to put birds in it," he said, making the cage turn in front of the audience's eyes as if he were auctioning it off. "It would be enough to hang it in the trees so it could sing by itself." He put it back on the table, thought a moment, looking at the cage, and said:

"Fine, then I'll take it."

"It's sold," said Ursula.

"It belongs to the son of Mr. Chepe Montiel," said Balthazar. "He ordered it specially."

The doctor adopted a respectful attitude.

"Did he give you the design?"

"No," said Balthazar. "He said he wanted a large cage, like this one, for a pair of troupials."

The doctor looked at the cage.

"But this isn't for troupials."

"Of course it is, Doctor," said Balthazar, approaching the table. The children surrounded him. "The measurements are carefully calculated," he said, pointing to the different compartments with his forefinger. Then he struck the dome with his knuckles, and the cage filled with resonant chords.

"It's the strongest wire you can find, and each joint is soldered outside and in," he said.

"It's even big enough for a parrot," interrupted one of the children.

"That it is," said Balthazar.

The doctor turned his head.

"Fine, but he didn't give you the design," he said. "He gave you no exact specifications, aside from making it a cage big enough for troupials. Isn't that right?"

"That's right," said Balthazar.

"Then there's no problem," said the doctor. "One thing is a cage big enough for troupials, and another is this cage. There's no proof that this one is the one you were asked to make."

"It's this very one," said Balthazar, confused. "That's why I made it."

The doctor made an impatient gesture.

"You could make another one," said Ursula, looking at her husband. And then, to the doctor: "You're not in any hurry."

"I promised it to my wife for this afternoon," said the doctor.

"I'm very sorry, Doctor," said Balthazar, "but I can't sell you something that's sold already."

The doctor shrugged his shoulders. Drying the sweat from his neck with a handkerchief, he contemplated the cage silently with the fixed, unfocused gaze of one who looks at a ship which is sailing away.

"How much did they pay you for it?"

Balthazar sought out Ursula's eyes without replying.

"Sixty pesos," she said.

The doctor kept looking at the cage. "It's very pretty." He sighed. "Extremely pretty." Then, moving toward the door, he began to fan himself energetically, smiling, and the trace of that episode disappeared forever from his memory.

"Montiel is very rich," he said.

In truth, José Montiel was not as rich as he seemed, but he would have been capable of doing anything to become so. A few blocks from there, in a house crammed with equipment, where no one had ever smelled a smell that couldn't be sold, he remained indifferent to the news of the cage. His wife, tortured by an obsession with death, closed the doors and windows after lunch and lay for two hours with her eyes opened to the shadow of the room, while José Montiel took his siesta. The clamor of many voices surprised her there. Then she opened the door to the living room and found a crowd in front of the house, and Balthazar with the cage in the middle of the crowd, dressed in white, freshly shaved, with that expression of decorous candor with which the poor approach the houses of the wealthy.

"What a marvelous thing!" José Montiel's wife exclaimed, with a radiant expression, leading Balthazar inside. "I've never seen anything like it in my life," she said, and added, annoyed by the crowd which piled up at the door:

"But bring it inside before they turn the living room into a grandstand."

Balthazar was no stranger to José Montiel's house. On different occasions, because of his skill and forthright way of dealing, he had been called in to do minor carpentry jobs. But he never felt at ease among the rich. He used to think about them, about their ugly and argumentative wives, about their tremendous surgical operations, and he always experienced a feeling of pity. When he entered their houses, he couldn't move without dragging his feet.

"Is Pepe home?" he asked.

He had put the cage on the dining-room table.

"He's at school," said José Montiel's wife. "But he shouldn't be long," and she added, "Montiel is taking a bath."

In reality, José Montiel had not had time to bathe. He was giving himself an urgent alcohol rub, in order to come out and see what was going on. He was such a cautious man that he slept without an electric fan so he could watch over the noises of the house while he slept.

"Adelaide!" he shouted. "What's going on?"

"Come and see what a marvelous thing!" his wife shouted.

José Montiel, obese and hairy, his towel draped around his neck, appeared at the bedroom window.

"What is that?"

"Pepe's cage," said Balthazar.

His wife looked at him perplexedly.

"Whose?"

"Pepe's," replied Balthazar. And then, turning toward José Montiel, "Pepe ordered it."

Nothing happened at that instant, but Balthazar felt as if someone had just opened the bathroom door on him. José Montiel came out of the bedroom in his underwear.

"Pepe!" he shouted.

"He's not back," whispered his wife, motionless.

Pepe appeared in the doorway. He was about twelve, and had the same curved eyelashes and was as quietly pathetic as his mother.

"Come here," José Montiel said to him. "Did you order this?"

The child lowered his head. Grabbing him by the hair, José Montiel forced Pepe to look him in the eye.

"Answer me."

The child bit his lip without replying.

"Montiel," whispered his wife.

José Montiel let the child go and turned toward Balthazar in a fury. "I'm very sorry, Balthazar," he said. "But you should have consulted me before going on. Only to you would it occur to contract with a minor." As he spoke, his face recovered its serenity. He lifted the cage without looking at it and gave it to Balthazar.

"Take it away at once, and try to sell it to whomever you can," he said.

"Above all, I beg you not to argue with me." He patted him on the back and explained, "The doctor has forbidden me to get angry."

The child had remained motionless, without blinking, until Balthazar looked at him uncertainly with the cage in his hand. Then he emitted a guttural sound, like a dog's growl, and threw himself on the floor screaming.

José Montiel looked at him, unmoved, while the mother tried to pacify him. "Don't even pick him up," he said. "Let him break his head on the floor, and then put salt and lemon on it so he can rage to his heart's content." The child was shrieking tearlessly while his mother held him by the wrists.

"Leave him alone," José Montiel insisted.

Balthazar observed the child as he would have observed the death throes of a rabid animal. It was almost four o'clock. At that hour, at his house, Ursula was singing a very old song and cutting slices of onion.

"Pepe," said Balthazar.

He approached the child, smiling, and held the cage out to him. The child jumped up, embraced the cage which was almost as big as he was, and stood looking at Balthazar through the wirework without knowing what to say. He hadn't shed one tear.

"Balthazar," said José Montiel softly. "I told you already to take it away."

"Give it back," the woman ordered the child.

"Keep it," said Balthazar. And then, to José Montiel: "After all, that's what I made it for."

José Montiel followed him into the living room.

"Don't be foolish, Balthazar," he was saying, blocking his path. "Take your piece of furniture home and don't be silly. I have no intention of paying you a cent."

"It doesn't matter," said Balthazar. "I made it expressly as a gift for Pepe. I didn't expect to charge anything for it."

As Balthazar made his way through the spectators who were blocking the door, José Montiel was shouting in the middle of the living room. He was very pale and his eyes were beginning to get red.

"Idiot!" he was shouting. "Take your trinket out of here. The last thing we need is for some nobody to give orders in my house. Son of a bitch!"

In the pool hall, Balthazar was received with an ovation. Until that moment, he thought that he had made a better cage than ever before, that he'd had to give it to the son of José Montiel so he wouldn't keep crying, and that none of these things was particularly important. But then he realized that all of this had a certain importance for many people, and he felt a little excited.

"So they gave you fifty pesos for the cage."

"Sixty," said Balthazar.

"Score one for you," someone said. "You're the only one who has managed to get such a pile of money out of Mr. Chepe Montiel. We have to celebrate."

They bought him a beer, and Balthazar responded with a round for everybody. Since it was the first time he had ever been out drinking, by dusk he was completely drunk, and he was talking about a fabulous project of a thousand cages, at sixty pesos each, and then a million cages, till he had sixty million pesos. "We have to make a lot of things to sell to the rich before they die," he was saying, blind drunk. "All of them are sick, and they're going to die. They're so screwed up they can't even get angry any more." For two hours he was paying for the jukebox, which played without interruption. Everybody toasted Balthazar's health, good luck, and fortune, and the death of the rich, but at mealtime they left him alone in the pool hall.

Ursula had waited for him until eight, with a dish of fried meat covered with slices of onion. Someone told her that her husband was in the pool hall, delirious with happiness, buying beers for everyone, but she didn't believe it, because Balthazar had never got drunk. When she went to bed, almost at midnight, Balthazar was in a lighted room where there were little tables, each with four chairs, and an outdoor dance floor, where the plovers were walking around. His face was smeared with rouge, and since he couldn't take one more step, he thought he wanted to lie down with two women in the same bed. He had spent so much that he had had to leave his watch in pawn, with the promise to pay the next day. A moment later, spread-eagled in the street, he realized that his shoes were being taken off, but he didn't want to abandon the happiest dream of his life. The women who passed on their way to five-o'clock Mass didn't dare look at him, thinking he was dead.

[1962]

Translated by
J. S. BERNSTEIN

QUESTIONS

1. To what extent does "Balthazar's Marvelous Afternoon" imply a fusion of honor and machismo (masculinity)?
2. What function does Ursula play in the story? In what ways is she different from Balthazar?
3. Why does Balthazar lie to his friends in the bar?
4. Why does the story conclude with an image of death? Has comedy suddenly become tragedy?

Charlotte Perkins Gilman

(1860–1935)

United States

Charlotte Perkins Gilman was not only a writer of fiction but also a prominent social reformer and one of the leading intellectuals of the women's reform movement from the 1890s to 1920. Widely known throughout the United States and Europe for her important studies of women's status and their role in society, she developed her views both in sociological studies such as the central work, *Women and Economics* (1898), and in several novels, including the utopian fiction *Herland* (1915).

Born in Hartford, Connecticut, Gilman suffered an unhappy childhood. Her father deserted the family soon after her birth; she and her mother and brother lived on the edge of poverty and were compelled to move frequently. Her mother also starved her emotionally, deliberately avoiding physical contact and affection in the belief that she was preparing her daughter for life's hardships. Gilman studied art briefly and earned money as a commercial artist by designing greeting cards. She married a fellow artist, Charles Stetson; their marriage later ended in divorce.

The birth of Gilman's first child, a daughter, precipitated a severe depression. Seeking the advice of the prominent physician S. Weir Mitchell, she was advised to avoid all physical activity, especially writing. As she wrote later, the regimen of total isolation, bed rest, confinement, and proscription against writing nearly drove her crazy. "The Yellow Wallpaper," based in part on her own experience, brilliantly highlights the narrator's increasingly desperate state as well as castigating this abusive medical treatment. First published in 1892, "The Yellow Wallpaper" was initially read as a ghost story in the tradition of Edgar Allan Poe, complete with a haunted mansion and a character deteriorating into madness. Contemporary readers see in Gilman's best-known story not only a strong indictment of the social infantilization of women in the late nineteenth century but also the nameless narrator's painful struggle to tell a story whose telling both expresses and culminates in her own mental destruction.

• *The Yellow Wallpaper* •

It is very seldom that mere ordinary people like John and myself secure ancestral halls for the summer.

A colonial mansion, a hereditary estate, I would say a haunted house and reach the height of romantic felicity—but that would be asking too much of fate!

Still I will proudly declare that there is something queer about it.

Else, why should it be let so cheaply? And why have stood so long untenanted?

John laughs at me, of course, but one expects that.

John is practical in the extreme. He has no patience with faith, an intense horror of superstition, and he scoffs openly at any talk of things not to be felt and seen and put down in figures.

John is a physician, and *perhaps*—(I would not say it to a living soul, of course, but this is dead paper and a great relief to my mind)—*perhaps* that is one reason I do not get well faster.

You see, he does not believe I am sick! And what can one do?

If a physician of high standing, and one's own husband, assures friends and relatives that there is really nothing the matter with one but temporary nervous depression—a slight hysterical tendency—what is one to do?

My brother is also a physician, and also of high standing, and he says the same thing.

So I take phosphates or phosphites—whichever it is—and tonics, and air and exercise, and journeys, and am absolutely forbidden to "work" until I am well again.

Personally, I disagree with their ideas.

Personally, I believe that congenial work, with excitement and change, would do me good.

But what is one to do?

I did write for a while in spite of them; but it *does* exhaust me a good deal—having to be so sly about it, or else meet with heavy opposition.

I sometimes fancy that in my condition, if I had less opposition and more society and stimulus—but John says the very worst thing I can do is to think about my condition, and I confess it always makes me feel bad.

So I will let it alone and talk about the house.

The most beautiful place! It is quite alone, standing well back from the road, quite three miles from the village. It makes me think of English places that you read about, for there are hedges and walls and gates that lock, and lots of separate little houses for the gardeners and people.

There is a *delicious* garden! I never saw such a garden—large and shady, full of box-bordered paths, and lined with long grape-covered arbors with seats under them.

There were greenhouses, but they are all broken now.

There was some legal trouble, I believe, something about the heirs and co-heirs; anyhow, the place has been empty for years.

That spoils my ghostliness, I am afraid, but I don't care—there is something strange about the house—I can feel it.

I even said so to John one moonlight evening, but he said what I felt was a draught, and shut the window.

I get unreasonably angry with John sometimes. I'm sure I never used to be so sensitive. I think it is due to this nervous condition.

But John says if I feel so I shall neglect proper self-control; so I take pains to control myself—before him, at least, and that makes me very tired.

I don't like our room a bit. I wanted one downstairs that opened onto the piazza and had roses all over the window, and such pretty old-fashioned chintz hangings! But John would not hear of it.

He said there was only one window and not room for two beds, and no near room for him if he took another.

He is very careful and loving, and hardly lets me stir without special direction.

I have a schedule prescription for each hour in the day; he takes all care from me, and so I feel basely ungrateful not to value it more.

He said he came here solely on my account, that I was to have perfect rest and all the air I could get. "Your exercise depends on your strength, my dear," said he, "and your food somewhat on your appetite; but air you can absorb all the time." So we took the nursery at the top of the house.

It is a big, airy room, the whole floor nearly, with windows that look all ways, and air and sunshine galore. It was nursery first, and then playroom and gymnasium, I should judge, for the windows are barred for little children, and there are rings and things in the walls.

The paint and paper look as if a boys' school had used it. It is stripped off—the paper—in great patches all around the head of my bed, about as far as I can reach, and in a great place on the other side of the room low down. I never saw a worse paper in my life. One of those sprawling, flamboyant patterns committing every artistic sin.

It is dull enough to confuse the eye in following, pronounced enough constantly to irritate and provoke study, and when you follow the lame uncertain curves for a little distance they suddenly commit suicide—plunge off at outrageous angles, destroy themselves in unheard-of contradictions.

The color is repellent, almost revolting: a smouldering unclean yellow, strangely faded by the slow-turning sunlight. It is a dull yet lurid orange in some places, a sickly sulphur tint in others.

No wonder the children hated it! I should hate it myself if I had to live in this room long.

There comes John, and I must put this away—he hates to have me write a word.

We have been here two weeks, and I haven't felt like writing before, since that first day.

I am sitting by the window now, up in this atrocious nursery, and there is nothing to hinder my writing as much as I please, save lack of strength.

John is away all day, and even some nights when his cases are serious.

I am glad my case is not serious!

But these nervous troubles are dreadfully depressing.

John does not know how much I really suffer. He knows there is no reason to suffer, and that satisfies him.

Of course it is only nervousness. It does weigh on me so not to do my duty in any way!

I meant to be such a help to John, such a real rest and comfort, and here I am a comparative burden already!

Nobody would believe what an effort it is to do what little I am able—to dress and entertain, and order things.

It is fortunate Mary is so good with the baby. Such a dear baby!

And yet I *cannot* be with him, it makes me so nervous.

I suppose John never was nervous in his life. He laughs at me so about this wallpaper!

At first he meant to repaper the room, but afterward he said that I was letting it get the better of me, and that nothing was worse for a nervous patient than to give way to such fancies.

He said that after the wallpaper was changed it would be the heavy bedstead, and then the barred windows, and then that gate at the head of the stairs, and so on.

"You know the place is doing you good," he said, "and really, dear, I don't care to renovate the house just for a three months' rental."

"Then do let us go downstairs," I said. "There are such pretty rooms there."

Then he took me in his arms and called me a blessed little goose, and said he would go down cellar, if I wished, and have it whitewashed into the bargain.

But he is right enough about the beds and windows and things.

It is as airy and comfortable a room as anyone need wish, and, of course, I would not be so silly as to make him uncomfortable just for a whim.

I'm really getting quite fond of the big room, all but that horrid paper.

Out of one window I can see the garden—those mysterious deep-shaded arbors, the riotous old-fashioned flowers, and bushes and gnarly trees.

Out of another I get a lovely view of the bay and a little private wharf belonging to the estate. There is a beautiful shaded lane that runs down there from the house. I always fancy I see people walking in these numerous paths and arbors, but John has cautioned me not to give way to fancy in the least. He says that with my imaginative power and habit of story-making, a nervous weakness like mine is sure to lead to all manner of excited fancies, and that I ought to use my will and good sense to check the tendency. So I try.

I think sometimes that if I were only well enough to write a little it would relieve the press of ideas and rest me.

But I find I get pretty tired when I try.

It is so discouraging not to have any advice and companionship about my work. When I get really well, John says we will ask Cousin Henry and Julia down for a long visit; but he says he would as soon put fireworks in my pillow-case as to let me have those stimulating people about now.

I wish I could get well faster.

But I must not think about that. This paper looks to me as if it *knew* what a vicious influence it had!

There is a recurrent spot where the pattern lolls like a broken neck and two bulbous eyes stare at you upside down.

I get positively angry with the impertinence of it and the everlastingness. Up and down and sideways they crawl, and those absurd unblinking eyes are everywhere. There is one place where two breadths didn't match, and the eyes go all up and down the line, one a little higher than the other.

I never saw so much expression in an inanimate thing before, and we all know how much expression they have! I used to lie awake as a child and get more entertainment and terror out of blank walls and plain furniture than most children could find in a toy-store.

I remember what a kindly wink the knobs of our big old bureau used to have, and there was one chair that always seemed like a strong friend.

I used to feel that if any of the other things looked too fierce I could always hop into that chair and be safe.

The furniture in this room is no worse than inharmonious, however, for we had to bring it all from downstairs. I suppose when this was used as a playroom they had to take the nursery things out, and no wonder! I never saw such ravages as the children have made here.

The wallpaper, as I said before, is torn off in spots, and it sticketh closer than a brother—they must have had perseverance as well as hatred.

Then the floor is scratched and gouged and splintered, the plaster itself is dug out here and there, and this great heavy bed, which is all we found in the room, looks as if it had been through the wars.

But I don't mind it a bit—only the paper.

There comes John's sister. Such a dear girl as she is, and so careful of me! I must not let her find me writing.

She is a perfect and enthusiastic housekeeper, and hopes for no better profession. I verily believe she thinks it is the writing which made me sick!

But I can write when she is out, and see her a long way off from these windows.

There is one that commands the road, a lovely shaded winding road, and one that just looks off over the country. A lovely country, too, full of great elms and velvet meadows.

This wallpaper has a kind of subpattern in a different shade, a particularly irritating one, for you can only see it in certain lights, and not clearly then.

But in the places where it isn't faded and where the sun is just so—I can see a strange, provoking, formless sort of figure that seems to skulk about behind that silly and conspicuous front design.

There's sister on the stairs!

Well, the Fourth of July is over! The people are all gone, and I am tired out. John thought it might do me good to see a little company, so we just had Mother and Nellie and the children down for a week.

Of course I didn't do a thing. Jennie sees to everything now.

But it tired me all the same.

John says if I don't pick up faster he shall send me to Weir Mitchell[1] in the fall.

But I don't want to go there at all. I had a friend who was in his hands once, and she says he is just like John and my brother, only more so!

Besides, it is such an undertaking to go so far.

I don't feel as if it was worthwhile to turn my hand over for anything, and I'm getting dreadfully fretful and querulous.

I cry at nothing, and cry most of the time.

Of course I don't when John is here, or anybody else, but when I am alone.

And I am alone a good deal just now. John is kept in town very often by serious cases, and Jennie is good and lets me alone when I want her to.

So I walk a little in the garden or down that lovely lane, sit on the porch under the roses, and lie down up here a good deal.

[1]*Weir Mitchell* S. Weir Mitchell (1892–1914), a prominent Philadelphia neurologist who promoted the "rest cure" for his patients' (most of whom were female) nervous disorders. Gilman herself underwent the cure, which nearly drove her mad.

I'm getting really fond of the room in spite of the wallpaper. Perhaps *because* of the wallpaper.

It dwells in my mind so!

I lie here on this great immovable bed—it is nailed down, I believe—and follow that pattern about by the hour. It is as good as gymnastics, I assure you. I start, we'll say, at the bottom, down in the corner over there where it has not been touched, and I determine for the thousandth time that I *will* follow that pointless pattern to some sort of a conclusion.

I know a little of the principle of design, and I know this thing was not arranged on any laws of radiation, or alternation, or repetition, or symmetry, or anything else that I ever heard of.

It is repeated, of course, by the breadths, but not otherwise.

Looked at in one way, each breadth stands alone; the bloated curves and flourishes—a kind of "debased Romanesque" with delirium tremens[2] go waddling up and down in isolated columns of fatuity.

But, on the other hand, they connect diagonally, and the sprawling outlines run off in great slanting waves of optic horror, like a lot of wallowing sea-weeds in full chase.

The whole thing goes horizontally, too, at least it seems so, and I exhaust myself trying to distinguish the order of its going in that direction.

They have used a horizontal breadth for a frieze, and that adds wonderfully to the confusion.

There is one end of the room where it is almost intact, and there, when the crosslights fade and the low sun shines directly upon it, I can almost fancy radiation after all—the interminable grotesque seems to form around a common center and rush off in headlong plunges of equal distraction.

It makes me tired to follow it. I will take a nap, I guess.

I don't know why I should write this.

I don't want to.

I don't feel able.

And I know John would think it absurd. But I *must* say what I feel and think in some way—it is such a relief!

But the effort is getting to be greater than the relief.

Half the time now I am awfully lazy, and lie down ever so much. John says I mustn't lose my strength, and has me take cod liver oil and lots of tonics and things, to say nothing of ale and wines and rare meat.

Dear John! He loves me very dearly, and hates to have me sick. I tried to have a real earnest reasonable talk with him the other day, and tell him how I wish he would let me go and make a visit to Cousin Henry and Julia.

But he said I wasn't able to go, nor able to stand it after I got there; and I did not make out a very good case for myself, for I was crying before I had finished.

It is getting to be a great effort for me to think straight. Just this nervous weakness, I suppose.

And dear John gathered me up in his arms, and just carried me upstairs and laid me on the bed, and sat by me and read to me till it tired my head.

[2]*delirium tremens* frightening hallucinations and violent tremors induced by excessive drinking of alcoholic beverages

He said I was his darling and his comfort and all he had, and that I must take care of myself for his sake, and keep well.

He says no one but myself can help me out of it, that I must use my will and self-control and not let any silly fancies run away with me.

There's one comfort — the baby is well and happy, and does not have to occupy this nursery with the horrid wallpaper.

If we had not used it, that blessed child would have! What a fortunate escape! Why, I wouldn't have a child of mine, an impressionable little thing, live in such a room for worlds.

I never thought of it before, but it is lucky that John kept me here after all; I can stand it so much easier than a baby, you see.

Of course I never mention it to them any more — I am too wise — but I keep watch for it all the same.

There are things in the wallpaper that nobody knows about but me, or ever will.

Behind that outside pattern the dim shapes get clearer every day.

It is always the same shape, only very numerous.

And it is like a woman stooping down and creeping about behind that pattern. I don't like it a bit. I wonder — I begin to think — I wish John would take me away from here!

It is so hard to talk with John about my case, because he is so wise, and because he loves me so.

But I tried it last night.

It was moonlight. The moon shines in all around just as the sun does.

I hate to see it sometimes, it creeps so slowly, and always comes in by one window or another.

John was asleep and I hated to waken him, so I kept still and watched the moonlight on that undulating wallpaper till I felt creepy.

The faint figure behind seemed to shake the pattern, just as if she wanted to get out.

I got up softly and went to feel and see if the paper *did* move, and when I came back John was awake.

"What is it, little girl?" he said. "Don't go walking about like that — you'll get cold."

I thought it was a good time to talk, so I told him that I really was not gaining here, and that I wished he would take me away.

"Why, darling!" said he. "Our lease will be up in three weeks, and I can't see how to leave before.

"The repairs are not done at home, and I cannot possibly leave town just now. Of course, if you were in any danger, I could and would, but you really are better, dear, whether you can see it or not. I am a doctor, dear, and I know. You are gaining flesh and color, your appetite is better, I feel really much easier about you."

"I don't weigh a bit more," said I, "nor as much, and my appetite may be better in the evening when you are here but it is worse in the morning when you are away!"

"Bless her little heart!" said he with a big hug. "She shall be as sick as she pleases! But now let's improve the shining hours by going to sleep, and talk about it in the morning!"

"And you won't go away?" I asked gloomily.

"Why, how can I, dear? It is only three weeks more and then we will take a nice little trip for a few days while Jennie is getting the house ready. Really, dear, you are better!"

"Better in body perhaps —" I began, and stopped short, for he sat up straight and looked at me with such a stern, reproachful look that I could not say another word.

"My darling," said he, "I beg you, for my sake and for our child's sake, as well as for your own, that you will never for one instant let that idea enter your mind! There is nothing so dangerous, so fascinating, to a temperament like yours. It is a false and foolish fancy. Can you trust me as a physician when I tell you so?"

So of course I said no more on that score, and we went to sleep before long. He thought I was asleep first, but I wasn't, and lay there for hours trying to decide whether that front pattern and the back pattern really did move together or separately.

On a pattern like this, by daylight, there is a lack of sequence, a defiance of law, that is a constant irritant to a normal mind.

The color is hideous enough, and unreliable enough, and infuriating enough, but the pattern is torturing.

You think you have mastered it, but just as you get well under way in following, it turns a back-somersault and there you are. It slaps you in the face, knocks you down, and tramples upon you. It is like a bad dream.

The outside pattern is a florid arabesque, reminding one of a fungus. If you can imagine a toadstool in joints, an interminable string of toadstools, budding and sprouting in endless convolutions — why, that is something like it.

That is, sometimes!

There is one marked peculiarity about this paper, a thing nobody seems to notice but myself, and that is that it changes as the light changes.

When the sun shoots in through the east window — I always watch for that first long, straight ray — it changes so quickly that I never can quite believe it.

That is why I watch it always.

By moonlight — the moon shines in all night when there is a moon — I wouldn't know it was the same paper.

At night in any kind of light, in twilight, candlelight, lamplight, and worst of all by moonlight, it becomes bars! The outside pattern, I mean, and the woman behind it is as plain as can be.

I didn't realize for a long time what the thing was that showed behind, that dim subpattern, but now I am quite sure it is a woman.

By daylight she is subdued, quiet. I fancy it is the pattern that keeps her so still. It is so puzzling. It keeps me quiet by the hour.

I lie down ever so much now. John says it is good for me, and to sleep all I can.

Indeed he started the habit by making me lie down for an hour after each meal.

It is a very bad habit, I am convinced, for you see, I don't sleep.

And that cultivates deceit, for I don't tell them I'm awake — oh, no!

The fact is I am getting a little afraid of John.

He seems very queer sometimes, and even Jennie has an inexplicable look.

It strikes me occasionally, just as a scientific hypothesis, that perhaps it is the paper!

I have watched John when he did not know I was looking, and come into the room suddenly on the most innocent excuses, and I've caught him several times *looking at the paper!* And Jennie too. I caught Jennie with her hand on it once.

She didn't know I was in the room, and when I asked her in a quiet, a very quiet voice, with the most restrained manner possible, what she was doing with the paper, she turned around as if she had been caught stealing, and looked quite angry—asked me why I should frighten her so!

Then she said that the paper stained everything it touched, that she had found yellow smooches on all my clothes and John's and she wished we would be more careful!

Did not that sound innocent? But I know she was studying that pattern, and I am determined that nobody shall find it out but myself!

Life is very much more exciting now than it used to be. You see, I have something more to expect, to look forward to, to watch. I really do eat better, and am more quiet than I was.

John is so pleased to see me improve! He laughed a little the other day, and said I seemed to be flourishing in spite of my wallpaper.

I turned it off with a laugh. I had no intention of telling him it was *because* of the wallpaper—he would make fun of me. He might even want to take me away.

I don't want to leave now until I have found it out. There is a week more, and I think that will be enough.

I'm feeling so much better!

I don't sleep much at night, for it is so interesting to watch developments; but I sleep a good deal during the daytime.

In the daytime it is tiresome and perplexing.

There are always new shoots on the fungus, and new shades of yellow all over it. I cannot keep count of them, though I have tried conscientiously.

It is the strangest yellow, that wallpaper! It makes me think of all the yellow things I ever saw—not beautiful ones like buttercups, but old, foul, bad yellow things.

But there is something else about that paper—the smell! I noticed it the moment we came into the room, but with so much air and sun it was not bad. Now we have had a week of fog and rain, and whether the windows are open or not, the smell is here.

It creeps all over the house.

I find it hovering in the dining-room, skulking in the parlor, hiding in the hall, lying in wait for me on the stairs.

It gets into my hair.

Even when I go to ride, if I turn my head suddenly and surprise it—there is that smell!

Such a peculiar odor, too! I have spent hours in trying to analyze it, to find what it smelled like.

It is not bad—at first—and very gentle, but quite the subtlest, most enduring odor I ever met.

In this damp weather it is awful. I wake up in the night and find it hanging over me.

It used to disturb me at first. I thought seriously of burning the house—to reach the smell.

But now I am used to it. The only thing I can think of that it is like is the *color* of the paper! A yellow smell.

There is a very funny mark on this wall, low down, near the mopboard. A streak that runs round the room. It goes behind every piece of furniture, except the bed, a long, straight, even *smooch*, as if it had been rubbed over and over.

I wonder how it was done and who did it, and what they did it for.

Round and round and round—round and round and round—it makes me dizzy!

I really have discovered something at last.

Through watching so much at night, when it changes so, I have finally found out.

The front pattern *does* move—and no wonder! The woman behind shakes it!

Sometimes I think there are a great many women behind, and sometimes only one, and she crawls around fast, and her crawling shakes it all over.

Then in the bright spots she keeps still, and in the very shady spots she just takes hold of the bars and shakes them hard.

And she is all the time trying to climb through. But nobody could climb through that pattern—it strangles so; I think that is why it has so many heads.

They get through and then the pattern strangles them off and turns them upside down, and makes their eyes white!

If those heads were covered or taken off it would not be half so bad.

I think that woman gets out in the daytime!

And I'll tell you why—privately—I've seen her!

I can see her out of every one of my windows!

It is the same woman, I know, for she is always creeping, and most women do not creep by daylight.

I see her in that long shaded lane, creeping up and down. I see her in those dark grape arbors, creeping all round the garden.

I see her on that long road under the trees, creeping along, and when a carriage comes she hides under the blackberry vines.

I don't blame her a bit. It must be very humiliating to be caught creeping by daylight!

I always lock the door when I creep by daylight. I can't do it at night, for I know John would suspect something at once.

And John is so queer now that I don't want to irritate him. I wish he would take another room! Besides, I don't want anybody to get that woman out at night but myself.

I often wonder if I could see her out of all the windows at once.

But, turn as fast as I can, I can only see out of one at one time.

And though I always see her, she *may* be able to creep faster than I can turn! I have watched her sometimes away off in the open country, creeping as fast as a cloud shadow in a wind.

If only that top pattern could be gotten off from the under one! I mean to try it, little by little.

I have found out another funny thing, but I shan't tell it this time! It does not do to trust people too much.

There are only two more days to get this paper off, and I believe John is beginning to notice. I don't like the look in his eyes.

And I heard him ask Jennie a lot of professional questions about me. She had a very good report to give.

She said I slept a good deal in the daytime.

John knows I don't sleep very well at night, for all I'm so quiet!

He asked me all sorts of questions too, and pretended to be very loving and kind.

As if I couldn't see through him!

Still, I don't wonder he acts so, sleeping under this paper for three months.

It only interests me, but I feel sure John and Jennie are affected by it.

Hurrah! This is the last day, but it is enough. John is to stay in town over night, and won't be out until this evening.

Jennie wanted to sleep with me — the sly thing; but I told her I should undoubtedly rest better for a night all alone.

That was clever, for really I wasn't alone a bit! As soon as it was moonlight and that poor thing began to crawl and shake the pattern, I got up and ran to help her.

I pulled and she shook. I shook and she pulled, and before morning we had peeled off yards of that paper.

A strip about as high as my head and half around the room.

And then when the sun came and that awful pattern began to laugh at me, I declared I would finish it today!

We go away tomorrow, and they are moving all my furniture down again to leave things as they were before.

Jennie looked at the wall in amazement, but I told her merrily that I did it out of pure spite at the vicious thing.

She laughed and said she wouldn't mind doing it herself, but I must not get tired.

How she betrayed herself that time!

But I am here, and no person touches this paper but Me — not *alive!*

She tried to get me out of the room — it was too patent! But I said it was so quiet and empty and clean now that I believed I would lie down again and sleep all I could, and not to wake me even for dinner — I would call when I woke.

So now she is gone, and the servants are gone, and the things are gone, and there is nothing left but that great bedstead nailed down, with the canvas mattress we found on it.

We shall sleep downstairs tonight, and take the boat home tomorrow.

I quite enjoy the room, now it is bare again.

How those children did tear about here!

This bedstead is fairly gnawed!

But I must get to work.

I have locked the door and thrown the key down into the front path.

I don't want to go out, and I don't want to have anybody come in, till John comes.

I want to astonish him.

I've got a rope up here that even Jennie did not find. If that woman does get out, and tried to get away, I can tie her!

But I forgot I could not reach far without anything to stand on!

This bed will *not* move!

I tried to lift and push it until I was lame, and then I got so angry I bit off a little piece at one corner — but it hurt my teeth.

Then I peeled off all the paper I could reach standing on the floor. It sticks horribly and the pattern just enjoys it! All those strangled heads and bulbous eyes and waddling fungus growths just shriek with derision!

I am getting angry enough to do something desperate. To jump out of the window would be admirable exercise, but the bars are too strong even to try.

Besides I wouldn't do it. Of course not. I know well enough that a step like that is improper and might be misconstrued.

I don't like to *look* out of the windows even—there are so many of those creeping women, and they creep so fast.

I wonder if they all come out of that wallpaper as I did!

But I am securely fastened now by my well-hidden rope—you don't get *me* out in the road there!

I suppose I shall have to get back behind the pattern when it comes night, and that is hard!

It is so pleasant to be out in this great room and creep around as I please!

I don't want to go outside. I won't, even if Jennie asks me to.

For outside you have to creep on the ground, and everything is green instead of yellow.

But here I can creep smoothly on the floor, and my shoulder just fits in that long smooch around the wall, so I cannot lose my way.

Why, there's John at the door!

It is no use, young man, you can't open it!

How he does call and pound!

Now he's crying to Jennie for an axe.

It would be a shame to break down that beautiful door!

"John, dear!" said I in the gentlest voice. "The key is down by the front steps, under a plantain leaf!"

That silenced him for a few moments.

Then he said, very quietly indeed, "Open the door, my darling!"

"I can't," said I. "The key is down by the front door under a plantain leaf!" And then I said it again, several times, very gently and slowly, and said it so often that he had to go and see, and he got it of course, and came in. He stopped short by the door.

"What is the matter?" he cried. "For God's sake, what are you doing!"

I kept on creeping just the same, but I looked at him over my shoulder. "I've got out at last," said I, "in spite of you and Jane. And I've pulled off most of the paper, so you can't put me back!"

Now why should that man have fainted? But he did, and right across my path by the wall, so that I had to creep over him every time!

[1892]

QUESTIONS

1. What drives the narrator crazy? How are the stages of her emotional breakdown expressed in the story?
2. In what ways is the narrator's husband implicated as part of her predicament?
3. How does the point of view affect your understanding of what is happening to the narrator? Is she a reliable narrator?
4. How does the yellow wallpaper function symbolically in the story?

What does it represent for the narrator? What does it represent for the reader? In what sense do the changes in the wallpaper express changes in the narrator?

5. In what sense has the woman "got out at last," as she exclaims at the end of the story?

Natalia Ginzburg

(b. 1916)

Italy

Natalia Levi was born to socialist parents in Turin; her father was a professor of anatomy at the University of Turin. In 1938 she married Leone Ginzburg, a politically committed professor of Russian literature who was punished by house arrest for his underground anti-Fascist activities and eventually handed over to the Germans; he died in prison. Although later married to Gabriele Baldini, Ginzburg maintained her name in memory of her first husband.

Ginzburg published her first collection of stories, *The Road to the City*, in 1942 under a pseudonym, due to wartime anti-Semitism in Italy. After the war she worked for the Italian publishing house Einaudi and continued to write fiction; her novel about a disintegrating marriage, *The Dry Heart* (1947), established her reputation in Italy and abroad. A successful playwright as well, Ginzburg has received numerous literary awards for both fiction and drama.

Describing her vocation as a writer, Ginzburg mused,

> [Writing stories] is quite a difficult vocation, but it is the finest one in the world. The days and houses of our lives, the days and houses of the people with whom we are involved, books and images and thoughts and conversations—all these things feed it, and it grows within us. It is a vocation which also feeds on terrible things; it swallows the best and the worst in our lives and our evil feelings flow in its blood just as much as our benevolent feelings. It feeds itself, and grows within us.

In a conversational, understated narrative style, Ginzburg focuses on the details that typify her disappointed or disillusioned characters, caught in their unsatisfying lives.

The Mother

Their mother was small and thin, and slightly round-shouldered; she always wore a blue skirt and a red woollen blouse. She had short, curly black hair which she kept oiled to control its bushiness; every day she plucked her eyebrows, making two black fish of them that swam towards her temples; and she used yellow powder on her face. She was very young; how old, they didn't know, but she seemed much younger than the mothers of the boys at school; they were always surprised to see their friends' mothers, how old and fat they were. She smoked a great deal and her fingers were stained with smoke; she even smoked in bed in the evening, before going to sleep. All three of them slept together, in the big double bed with the yellow quilt; their mother was on the side nearest the door, and on the bedside table she had a lamp with its shade wrapped in red cloth, because at night she read and smoked; sometimes she came in very late, and the boys would wake up and ask her where she had been: she nearly always answered: "At the cinema," or else "With a girl friend of mine"; who this friend was they didn't know, because no woman friend had ever been to the house to see their mother. She told them they must turn the other way while she undressed, they heard the quick rustle of her clothes, and shadows danced on the walls; she slipped into bed beside them, her thin body in its cold silk nightdress, and they moved away from her because she always complained that they came too close and kicked while they slept; sometimes she put out the light so that they should go to sleep and smoked in silence in the darkness.

Their mother was not important. Granny, Grandpa, Aunt Clementina who lived in the country and turned up now and then with chestnuts and maize-flour were important; Diomira the maid was important, Giovanni the tubercular porter who made cane chairs was important; all these were very important to the two boys because they were strong people you could trust, strong people in allowing and forbidding, very good at everything they did and always full of wisdom and strength; people who could defend you from storms and robbers. But if they were at home with their mother the boys were frightened, just as if they had been alone; as for allowing or forbidding, she never allowed or forbade anything, at the most she complained in a weary voice: "Don't make such a row because I've got a headache," and if they asked permission to do something or other she answered at once: "Ask Granny," or she said no first and then yes and then no and it was all a muddle. When they went out alone with their mother they felt uncertain and insecure because she always took wrong turnings and had to ask a policeman the way, and then she had such a funny, timid way of going into shops to ask for things to buy, and in the shops she always forgot something, gloves or handbag or scarf, and had to go back to look and the boys were ashamed.

Their mother's drawers were untidy and she left all her things scattered about and Diomira grumbled about her when she did out the room in the morning. She even called Granny in to see and together they picked up stockings and clothes and swept up the ash that was scattered all over the place. In the morning their mother went to do the shopping: she came back and flung the string bag on the marble table in the kitchen and took her bicycle and dashed off to the office where she worked. Diomira looked at all the things in the string bag, touched the oranges one by one and the meat, and grumbled and called Granny to see what poor meat it was. Their mother came home at two o'clock when they had all eaten and ate quickly with the newspaper propped up against her glass and then rushed off again to the office on her bicycle and they saw her for a minute at supper again, but after supper she nearly always dashed off.

The boys did their homework in the bedroom. There was their father's picture, large at the head of the bed, with his square black beard and bald head and tortoiseshell-rimmed spectacles, and then another small portrait on the table, with the younger of the boys in his arms. Their father had died when they were very small, they remembered nothing about him: or rather in the older boy's memory there was the shadow of a very distant afternoon, in the country at Aunt Clementina's: his father was pushing him across the meadow in a green wheelbarrow; afterwards he had found some pieces of this wheelbarrow, a handle and a wheel, in Aunt Clementina's attic; when it was new it was a splendid wheelbarrow and he was glad to have it; his father ran along pushing him and his long beard flapped. They knew nothing about their father but they thought he must be the sort of person who is strong and wise in allowing and forbidding; when Grandpa or Diomira got angry with their mother Granny said that they should be sorry for her because she had been very unfortunate, and she said that if Eugenio, the boys' father, had been there she would have been an entirely different woman, whereas she had had the misfortune to lose her husband when she was still young. For a time there had been their father's mother as well, they never saw her because she lived in France but she used to write and send Christmas presents: then in the end she died because she was very old.

At tea-time they ate chestnuts, or bread with oil and vinegar, and then if they had finished their homework they could go and play in the small piazza or among the ruins of the public baths, which had been blown up in an air raid. In the small piazza there were a great many pigeons and they took them bread or got Diomira to give them a paper bag of leftover rice. There they met all the local boys, boys from school and others they met in the youth clubs on Sundays when they had football matches with Don Vigliani, who hitched up his black cassock and kicked. Sometimes they played football in the small piazza too or else cops and robbers. Their grandmother appeared on the balcony occasionally and called to them not to get hurt: it was nice seeing the lighted windows of their home, up there on the third floor, from the dark piazza, and knowing that they could go back there, warm up at the stove and guard themselves from the night. Granny sat in the kitchen with Diomira and mended the linen; Grandpa was in the dining-room with his cap on, smoking his pipe. Granny was very fat, and wore black, and on her breast a medal with a picture of Uncle Oreste who had died in the war: she was very good at cooking pizzas and things. Sometimes she took them on her knee, even now when they were quite big boys; she was fat, she had a large soft bosom; from under the neck of her black dress you could see the thick white woollen vest with a scolloped edge which she had made herself. She would take them on her knee and say tender and slightly pitiful-sounding words in dialect; then she would take a long iron hair-pin out of her bun and clean their ears, and they would shriek and try to get away and Grandpa would come to the door with his pipe.

Grandpa had taught Greek and Latin at the high school. Now he was pensioned off and was writing a Greek grammer: many of his old pupils used to come and see him now and then. Then Diomira would make coffee; in the lavatory there were exercise book pages with Latin and Greek unseens on them, and his corrections in red and blue. Grandpa had a small white beard, a sort of goatee, and they were not to make a racket because his nerves were tired after all those years at school; he was always rather alarmed because prices kept going up and Granny always had a bit of a row with him in the morning because he was always surprised at the money they needed; he would say that perhaps Diomira pinched the sugar and made coffee in secret and Diomira would hear and rush at him and yell that the coffee was for the students who kept coming; but these were small incidents that quietened down at once and the boys were not alarmed, whereas they were alarmed when there was a quarrel between Grandpa and their mother; this happened sometimes if their mother came home very late at night, he would come out of his room with his overcoat over his pyjamas and bare feet, and he and their mother would shout: he said: "I know where you've been, I know where you've been, I know what you are," and their mother said: "What do I care?" and then: "Look, now you've woken the children," and he said: "A fat lot you care what happens to your children. Don't say anything because I know what you are. You're a bitch. You run around at night like the mad bitch you are." And then Granny and Diomira would come out in their nightdresses and push him into his room and say: "Shush, shush," and their mother would get into bed and sob under the bedclothes, her deep sobs echoing in the dark room: the boys thought that Grandpa must be right, they thought their mother was wrong to go to the cinema and to her girl friends at night. They felt very unhappy, frightened and unhappy, and lay huddled close together in the deep, warm, soft bed, and the older boy who was in the middle pushed away so as not to touch his mother's body: there seemed to him something disgusting in his mother's tears, in the wet pillow: he thought: "It gives a chap the creeps when his mother cries." They never spoke between themselves of these rows their mother and Grandpa had, they carefully avoided mentioning them: but they loved each other very much and clung close together at night when their mother cried: in the morning they were faintly embarrassed, because they had hugged so tightly as if to protect themselves, and because there was that thing they didn't want to talk about; besides, they soon forgot that they had been unhappy, the day began and they went to school, and met their friends in the street, and played for a moment at the school door.

In the grey light of morning, their mother got up: with her petticoat wound round her waist she soaped her neck and arms standing bent over the basin: she always tried not to let them see her but in the looking glass they could make out her thin brown shoulders and small naked breasts: in the cold the nipples became dark and protruding, she raised her arms and powdered her armpits: in her armpits she had thick curly hair. When she was completely dressed she started plucking her eyebrows, staring at herself in the mirror from close to and biting her lips hard: then she smothered her face with cream and shook the pink swansdown puff hard and powered herself: then her face became all yellow. Sometimes she was quite gay in the mornings and wanted to talk to the boys, she asked them about school and their friends and told them things about her time at school: she had a teacher called "Signorina Dirce" and she was an old maid who tried to seem young. Then she put on her coat and picked up her string shopping bag, leant down to kiss the boys and ran out with her scarf wound round her head and her face all perfumed and powdered with yellow powder.

The boys thought it strange to have been born of her. It would have been much less strange to have been born of Granny or Diomira, with their large warm bodies that protected you from fear, that defended you from storms and robbers. It was very strange to think she was their mother, that she had held them for a while in her small womb. Since they learnt that children are in their mother's tummy before being born, they had felt very surprised and also a little ashamed that that womb had once held them. And that she had given them milk from her breasts as well: this was even more unlikely. But now she no longer had small children to feed and cradle, and every day they saw her dash off on her bicycle when the shopping was done, her body jerking away, free and happy. She certainly didn't belong to them: they couldn't count on her. You couldn't ask her anything: there were other mothers, the mothers of their school friends, whom clearly you could ask about all sorts of things; their friends ran to their mothers when school was over and asked them heaps of things, got their noses blown and their overcoats buttoned, showed their homework and their comics: these mothers were pretty old, with hats and veils or fur collars and they came to talk to the master practically every day: they were people like Granny or like Diomira, large soft imperious bodies of people who didn't make mistakes: people who didn't lose things, who didn't leave their drawers untidy, who didn't come home late at night. But their mother ran off free after the shopping; besides, she was bad at shopping, she got cheated by the butcher and was often given wrong change: she went off and it was impossible to join her where she went, deep down they marvelled at her enormously when they saw her go off: who knows what that office of hers was like, she didn't talk about it much; she had to type and write letters in French and English: who knows, maybe she was pretty good at that.

One day when they were out for a walk with Don Vigliani and with other boys from the youth club, on the way back they saw their mother in a suburban café. She was sitting inside the café; they saw her through the window, and a man was sitting with her. Their mother had laid her tartan scarf on the table and the old crocodile handbag they knew well: the man had a loose light overcoat and a brown moustache and was talking to her and smiling: their mother's face was happy, relaxed and happy, as it never was at home. She was looking at the man and they were holding hands and she didn't see the boys: the boys went on walking beside Don Vigliani who told them all to hurry because they must catch the tram: when they were on the tram the younger boy moved over to his brother and said: "Did you see Mummy?" and his brother said: "No, I didn't." The younger one laughed softly and said: "Oh yes you did, it was Mummy and there was a man with her." The older boy turned his head away: he was big, nearly thirteen: his younger brother irritated him because he made him feel sorry for him, he couldn't understand why he felt sorry for him but he was sorry for himself as well and he didn't want to think of what he had seen, he wanted to behave as if he had seen nothing.

They said nothing to Granny. In the morning while their mother was dressing the younger boy said: "Yesterday when we were out for a walk with Don Vigliani we saw you and there was a man with you." Their mother jerked round, looking nasty: the black fish on her forehead quivered and met. She said: "But it wasn't me. What an idea. I've got to stay in the office till late in the evening, as you know. Obviously you made a mistake." The older boy then said, in a tired calm voice: "No, it wasn't you. It was someone who looked like you." And both boys realized that the memory must disappear: and they both breathed hard to blow it away.

But the man in the light overcoat once came to the house. He hadn't got his overcoat because it was summer, he wore blue spectacles and a light linen suit, he asked leave to take off his jacket while they had lunch. Granny and Grandpa had gone to Milan to meet some relations and Diomira had gone to her village, so they were alone with their mother. It was then the man came. Lunch was pretty good: their mother had bought nearly everything at the cooked meat shop: there was chicken with chips and this came from the shop: their mother had done the pasta, it was good, only the sauce was a bit burnt. There was wine, too. Their mother was nervous and gay, she wanted to say so much at once: she wanted to talk of the boys to the man and of the man to the boys. The man was called Max

and he had been in Africa, he had lots of photographs of Africa and showed them: there was a photograph of a monkey of his, the boys asked him about this monkey a lot; it was so intelligent and so fond of him and had such a funny, pretty way with it when it wanted a sweet. But he had left it in Africa because it was ill and he was afraid it would die on the steamer. The boys became friendly with this Max. He promised to take them to the cinema one day. They showed him their books, they hadn't got many: he asked them if they had read *Saturnino Farandola* and they said no and he said he would give it to them, and *Robinson delle praterie* as well, as it was very fine. After lunch their mother told them to go and play in the recreation ground. They wished they could stay on with Max. They protested a bit but their mother, and Max too, said they must go; then in the evening when they came home Max was no longer there. Their mother hurriedly prepared the supper, coffee with milk and potato salad: they were happy, they wanted to talk about Africa and the monkey, they were extraordinarily happy and couldn't really understand why: and their mother seemed happy too and told them things, about a monkey she had once seen dancing to a little street organ. And then she told them to go to bed and said she was going out for a minute, they mustn't be scared, there was no reason to be; she bent down to kiss them and told them there was no point in telling Granny and Grandpa about Max because they never liked one inviting people home.

So they stayed on their own with their mother for a few days: they ate unusual things because their mother didn't want to cook, ham and jam and coffee with milk and fried things from the cooked meat shop. Then they washed up together. But when Granny and Grandpa came back the boys felt relieved: the tablecloth was on the dining-room table again, and the glasses and everything there should be: Granny was sitting in her rocking chair again, with her soft body and her smell: Grandma couldn't dash off, she was too old and too fat, it was nice having someone who stayed at home and couldn't ever dash away.

The boys said nothing to Granny about Max. They waited for the book *Saturnino Farandola* and waited for Max to take them to the cinema and show them more photographs of the monkey. Once or twice they asked their mother when they'd be going to the cinema with signor Max. But their mother answered harshly that signor Max had left now. The younger boy asked if he'd gone to Africa. Their mother didn't answer. But he thought he must have gone to Africa to fetch the monkey. He imagined that someday or other he would come and fetch them at school, with a black servant and a monkey in his arms. School began again and Aunt Clementina came to stay with them for a while; she had brought a bag of pears and apples which they put in the oven to cook with marsala and sugar. Their mother was in a very bad temper and quarrelled continually with Grandpa. She came home late and stayed awake smoking. She had got very much thinner and ate nothing. Her face became even smaller and yellower, she now puts black on her eyelashes too, she spat into a little box and picked up the black where she had spat with a brush; she put on masses of powder, Granny tried to wipe it off her face with a handkerchief and she turned her face away. She hardly ever spoke and when she did it seemed an effort, her voice was so weak. One day she came home in the afternoon at about six o'clock: it was strange, usually she came home much later; she locked herself in the bedroom. The younger boy came and knocked because he needed an exercise book: their mother answered angrily from inside that she wanted to sleep and

that they were to leave her in peace: the boy explained timidly that he needed the exercise book; then she came to open up and her face was all swollen and wet: the boy realized she was crying, he went back to Granny and said: "Mummy's crying," and Granny and Aunt Clementina talked quietly together for a long time, they spoke of their mother but you couldn't make out what they were saying.

One night their mother didn't come home. Grandpa kept coming to see, barefoot, with his overcoat over his pyjamas; Granny came too and the boys slept badly, they could hear Granny and Grandpa walking about the house, opening and shutting the windows. The boys were very frightened. Then in the morning, they rang up from the police station: their mother had been found dead in an hotel, she had taken poison, she had left a letter: Grandpa and Aunt Clementina went along, Granny shrieked, the boys were sent to an old lady on the floor below who said continually: "Heartless, leaving two babes like this." Their mother was brought home. The boys went to see her when they had her laid out on the bed: Diomira had dressed her in her patent leather shoes and red silk dress from the time she was married: she was small, a small dead doll.

It was strange to see flowers and candles in the same old room. Diomira and Aunt Clementina and Granny were kneeling and praying: they had said she took the poison by mistake, otherwise the priest wouldn't come and bless her, if he knew she had done it on purpose. Diomira told the boys they must kiss her: they were terribly ashamed and kissed her cold cheek one after the other. Then there was the funeral, it took ages, they crossed the entire town and felt very tired, Don Vigliani was there too and a great many children from school and from the youth club. It was cold, and very windy in the cemetery. When they went home again, Granny started crying and bawling at the sight of the bicycle in the passage: because it was really just like seeing her dashing away, with her free body and her scarf flapping in the wind: Don Vigliani said she was now in heaven, perhaps because he didn't know she had done it on purpose, or he knew and pretended not to: but the boys didn't really know if heaven existed, because Grandpa said no, and Granny said yes, and their mother had once said there was no heaven, with little angels and beautiful music, but that the dead went to a place where they were neither well nor ill, and that where you wish for nothing you rest and are wholly at peace.

The boys went to the country for a time, to Aunt Clementina's. Everyone was very kind to them, and kissed and caressed them, and they were very ashamed. They never spoke together of their mother nor of signor Max either; in the attic at Aunt Clementina's they found the book of *Saturnino Farandola* and they read it over and over and found it very fine. But the older boy often thought of his mother, as he had seen her that day in the café with Max, holding her hands and with such a relaxed, happy face; he thought then that maybe their mother had taken poison because Max had gone back to Africa for good. The boys played with Aunt Clementina's dog, a fine dog called Bubi, and they learnt to climb trees, as they couldn't do before. They went bathing in the river, too, and it was nice going back to Aunt Clementina's in the evening and doing crosswords all together. The boys were very happy at Aunt Clementina's. Then they went back to Granny's and were very happy. Granny sat in the rocking chair, and wanted to clean their ears with her hairpins. On Sunday they went to the cemetery, Diomira came too, they bought flowers and on the way back stopped

at a bar to have hot punch. When they were in the cemetery, at the grave, Granny prayed and cried, but it was very hard to think that the grave and the crosses and the cemetery had anything to do with their mother, who had been cheated by the butcher and dashed off on her bicycle, and smoked, and took wrong turnings, and sobbed at night. The bed was very big for them now and they had a pillow each. They didn't often think of their mother because it hurt them a little and made them ashamed to think of her. Sometimes they tried to remember how she was, each on his own in silence: and they found it harder and harder to reassemble her short curly hair and the fish on her forehead and her lips: she put on a lot of yellow powder, this they remembered quite well; little by little there was a yellow dot, it was impossible to get the shape of her cheeks and face. Besides, they now realized that they had never loved her much, perhaps she too hadn't loved them much, if she had loved them she wouldn't have taken poison, they had heard Diomira and the porter and the lady on the floor below and so many other people say so. The years went by and the boys grew and so many things happened and that face which they had never loved very much disappeared for ever.

[1957]

Translated by
ISABEL QUIGLEY

QUESTIONS

1. From which descriptive details and observations do you understand that the mother is shown through the young boys' perspective? How does the accumulation of precise details shape your view of the mother's character and behavior?
2. Why do the boys consider their mother "unimportant" in relation to their grandparents and housekeeper?
3. What do the boys actually feel about their mother? How and why do those feelings change during the course of the story? How does Ginzburg convey their emotional ambivalence?

SUSAN GLASPELL

(1882–1948)

UNITED STATES

Susan Glaspell bears a unique distinction in American drama of having not only written but also produced and occasionally acted in her own productions. She was the cofounder of the influential experimental theater group, the Provincetown Players, in a wharf theater on Cape Cod in 1915. In addition to writing and producing a number of plays, she was also a prolific writer of fiction, publishing 10 novels and a number of short stories. "A Jury of Her Peers" is based on (and was written shortly after) the dramatic version, the one-act play *Trifles*, one of the most frequently produced one-act plays in the United States.

Glaspell was born and raised in Davenport, Iowa. Following her graduation from Drake University, she became a reporter for the *Des Moines Daily News*, eventually writing her own column, "The News Girl." She soon began to write short fiction, publishing at least two stories a year from 1903 to 1922—mostly romances that appeared in popular journals like *Ladies' Home Journal*.

Glaspell's marriage in 1913 to George Cram Cook led to a life in Greenwich Village and a broadening of her writing to include playwriting. A number of her plays were staged by the Provincetown Players and by the actors of the Playwrights' Theatre in Greenwich Village, the avant-garde group that she and Cook also founded.

Glaspell herself appeared in the role of Mrs. Hale in the first performance of *Trifles* at the Wharf Theatre in 1916. Both the play and the short story have received renewed attention from students interested in female experience as a result of Glaspell's depiction of distinct domains of language, symbol, and meaning recognized by her male and female characters.

A Jury of Her Peers

When Martha Hale opened the storm-door and got a cut of the north wind, she ran back for her big woolen scarf. As she hurriedly wound that round her head her eye made a scandalized sweep of her kitchen. It was no ordinary thing that called her away—it was probably farther from ordinary than anything that had ever happened in Dickson County. But what her eye took in was that her kitchen was in no shape for leaving: her bread all ready for mixing, half the flour sifted and half unsifted.

She hated to see things half done; but she had been at that when the team from town stopped to get Mr. Hale, and then the sheriff came running in to say his wife wished Mrs. Hale would come too—adding, with a grin, that he guessed she was getting scarey and wanted another woman along. So she had dropped everything right where it was.

"Martha!" now came her husband's impatient voice. "Don't keep folks waiting out here in the cold."

She again opened the storm-door, and this time joined the three men and the one woman waiting for her in the big two-seated buggy.

After she had the robes tucked around her she took another look at the woman who sat beside her on the back seat. She had met Mrs. Peters the year before at the county fair, and the thing she remembered about her was that she didn't seem like a sheriff's wife. She was small and thin and didn't have a strong voice. Mrs. Gorman, sheriff's wife before Gorman went out and Peters came in, had a voice that somehow seemed to be backing up the law with every word. But if Mrs. Peters didn't look like a sheriff's wife, Peters made it up in looking like a sheriff. He was to a dot the kind of man who could get himself elected sheriff—a heavy man with a big voice, who was particularly genial with the law-abiding, as if to make it plain that he knew the difference between criminals and non-criminals. And right there it came into Mrs. Hale's mind, with a stab, that this man who was so pleasant and lively with all of them was going to the Wrights' now as a sheriff.

"The country's not very pleasant this time of year," Mrs. Peters at last ventured, as if she felt they ought to be talking as well as the men.

Mrs. Hale scarcely finished her reply, for they had gone up a little hill and could see the Wright place now, and seeing it did not make her feel like talking. It looked very lonesome this cold March morning. It had always been a lonesome-looking place. It was down in a hollow, and the poplar trees around it were lonesome-looking trees. The men were looking at it and talking about what had happened. The county attorney was bending to one side of the buggy, and kept looking steadily at the place as they drew up to it.

"I'm glad you came with me," Mrs. Peters said nervously, as the two women were about to follow the men in through the kitchen door.

Even after she had her foot on the door-step, her hand on the knob, Martha Hale had a moment of feeling she could not cross that threshold. And the reason it seemed she couldn't cross it now was simply because she hadn't crossed it before. Time and time again it had been in her mind, "I ought to go over and see Minnie Foster"—she still thought of her as Minnie Foster, though for twenty years she had been Mrs. Wright. And then there was always something to do and Minnie Foster would go from her mind. But *now* she could come.

The men went over to the stove. The women stood close together by the door. Young Henderson, the county attorney, turned around and said, "Come up to the fire, ladies."

Mrs. Peters took a step forward, then stopped. "I'm not—cold," she said.

And so the two women stood by the door, at first not even so much as looking around the kitchen.

The men talked for a minute about what a good thing it was the sheriff had sent his deputy out that morning to make a fire for them, and then Sheriff Peters stepped back from the stove, unbuttoned his outer coat, and leaned his hands on the kitchen table in a way that seemed to mark the beginning of official business. "Now, Mr. Hale," he said in a sort of semi-official voice, "before we move things about, you tell Mr. Henderson just what it was you saw when you came here yesterday morning."

The county attorney was looking around the kitchen.

"By the way," he said, "has anything been moved?" He turned to the sheriff. "Are things just as you left them yesterday?"

Peters looked from cupboard to sink; from that to a small worn rocker a little to one side of the kitchen table.

"It's just the same."

"Somebody should have been left here yesterday," said the county attorney.

"Oh—yesterday," returned the sheriff, with a little gesture as of yesterday having been more than he could bear to think of. "When I had to send Frank to Morris Center for that man who went crazy—let me tell you, I had my hands full *yesterday*. I knew you could get back from Omaha by to-day, George, and as long as I went over everything here myself—"

"Well, Mr. Hale," said the county attorney, in a way of letting what was past and gone go, "tell just what happened when you came here yesterday morning."

Mrs. Hale, still leaning against the door, had that sinking feeling of the mother whose child is about to speak a piece. Lewis often wandered along and got things mixed up in a story. She hoped he would tell this straight and plain, and not say unnecessary things that would just make things harder for Minnie Foster. He didn't begin at once, and she noticed that he looked queer—as if standing in that kitchen and having to tell what he had seen there yesterday morning made him almost sick.

"Yes, Mr. Hale?" the county attorney reminded.

"Harry and I had started to town with a load of potatoes," Mrs. Hale's husband began.

Harry was Mrs. Hale's oldest boy. He wasn't with them now, for the very good reason that those potatoes never got to town yesterday and he was taking them this morning, so he hadn't been home when the sheriff stopped to say he wanted Mr. Hale to come over to the Wright place and tell the county attorney his story there, where he could point it all out. With all Mrs. Hale's other emotions came the fear that maybe Harry wasn't dressed warm enough—they hadn't any of them realized how that north wind did bite.

"We come along this road," Hale was going on, with a motion of his hand to the road over which they had just come, "and as we got in sight of the house I says to Harry, 'I'm goin' to see if I can't get John Wright to take a telephone.' You see," he explained to Henderson, "unless I can get somebody to go in with me they won't come out this branch road except for a price I can't pay. I'd spoke to Wright about it once before; but he put me off, saying folks talked too much anyway; and all he asked was peace and quiet—guess you know about how much he talked himself. But I thought maybe if I went to the house and talked about it before his wife, and said all the women-folks liked the telephones, and that in this lonesome stretch of road it would be a good thing—well, I said to Harry that that was what I was going to say—though I said at the same time that I didn't know as what his wife wanted made much difference to John—"

Now, there he was!—saying things he didn't need to say. Mrs. Hale tried to catch her husband's eye, but fortunately the county attorney interrupted with:

"Let's talk about that a little later, Mr. Hale. I do want to talk about that, but I'm anxious now to get along to just what happened when you got here."

When he began this time, it was very deliberately and carefully:

"I didn't see or hear anything. I knocked at the door. And still it was all quiet inside. I knew they must be up — it was past eight o'clock. So I knocked again, louder, and I thought I heard somebody say 'Come in.' I wasn't sure — I'm not sure yet. But I opened the door — this door," jerking a hand toward the door by which the two women stood, "and there, in that rocker" — pointing to it — "sat Mrs. Wright."

Every one in the kitchen looked at the rocker. It came into Mrs. Hale's mind that that rocker didn't look in the least like Minnie Foster — the Minnie Foster of twenty years before. It was a dingy red, with wooden rungs up the back and the middle rung was gone, and the chair sagged to one side.

"How did she — look?" the county attorney was inquiring.

"Well," said Hale, "she looked — queer."

"How do you mean — queer?"

As he asked it he took out a note-book and pencil. Mrs. Hale did not like the sight of that pencil. She kept her eye fixed on her husband, as if to keep him from saying unnecessary things that would go into that note-book and make trouble.

Hale did speak guardedly, as if the pencil had affected him too.

"Well, as if she didn't know what she was going to do next. And kind of — done up."

"How did she seem to feel about your coming?"

"Why, I don't think she minded — one way or other. She didn't pay much attention. I said, 'Ho' do, Mrs. Wright? It's cold, ain't it?' And she said, 'Is it?' — and went pleatin' at her apron.

"Well, I was surprised. She didn't ask me to come up to the stove, or to sit down, but just set there, not even lookin' at me. And so I said: 'I want to see John.'

"And then she — laughed. I guess you would call it a laugh.

"I thought of Harry and the team outside, so I said, a little sharp, 'Can I see John?' 'No,' says she — kind of dull like. 'Ain't he home?' says I. Then she looked at me. 'Yes,' says she, 'he's home.' 'Then why can't I see him?' I asked her, out of patience with her now. 'Cause he's dead,' says she, just as quiet and dull — and fell to pleatin' her apron. 'Dead?' says I, like you do when you can't take in what you've heard.

"She just nodded her head, not getting a bit excited, but rockin' back and forth.

"'Why — where is he?' says I, not knowing *what* to say.

"She just pointed upstairs — like this" — pointing to the room above.

"I got up, with the idea of going up there myself. By this time I — didn't know what to do. I walked from there to here; then I says: 'Why, what did he die of?'

"'He died of a rope around his neck,' says she; and just went on pleatin' at her apron."

Hale stopped speaking, and stood staring at the rocker, as if he were still seeing the woman who had sat there the morning before. Nobody spoke; it was as if every one were seeing the woman who had sat there the morning before.

"And what did you do then?" the county attorney at last broke the silence.

"I went out and called Harry. I though I might — need help. I got Harry in, and we went upstairs." His voice fell almost to a whisper. "There he was — lying over the — "

"I think I'd rather have you go into that upstairs," the county attorney interrupted, "where you can point it all out. Just go on now with the rest of the story."

"Well, my first thought was to get that rope off. It looked—"

He stopped, his face twitching.

"But Harry, he went up to him, and he said, 'No, he's dead all right, and we'd better not touch anything.' So we went downstairs.

"She was still sitting that same way. 'Has anybody been notified?' I asked. 'No,' says, she, unconcerned.

"'Who did this, Mrs. Wright?' said Harry. He said it business-like, and she stopped pleatin' at her apron. 'I don't know,' she says. 'You don't *know?*' says Harry. 'Weren't you sleepin' in the bed with him?' 'Yes,' says she, 'but I was on the inside.' 'Somebody slipped a rope around his neck and strangled him, and you didn't wake up?' says Harry. 'I didn't wake up,' she said after him.

"We may have looked as if we didn't see how that could be, for after a minute she said, 'I sleep sound.'

"Harry was going to ask her more questions, but I said maybe that weren't our business; maybe we ought to let her tell her story first to the coroner or the sheriff. So Harry went fast as he could over to High Road—the Rivers' place, where there's a telephone."

"And what did she do when she knew you had gone for the coroner?" The attorney got his pencil in his hand all ready for writing.

"She moved from that chair to this one over here"—Hale pointed to a small chair in the corner—"and just sat there with her hands held together and looking down. I got a feeling that I ought to make some conversation, so I said I had come in to see if John wanted to put in a telephone; and at that she started to laugh, and then she stopped and looked at me—scared."

At the sound of a moving pencil the man who was telling the story looked up.

"I dunno—maybe it wasn't scared," he hastened; "I wouldn't like to say it was. Soon Harry got back, and then Dr. Lloyd came, and you, Mr. Peters, and so I guess that's all I know that you don't."

He said that last with relief, and moved a little, as if relaxing. Every one moved a little. The county attorney walked toward the stair door.

"I guess we'll go upstairs first—then out to the barn and around there."

He paused and looked around the kitchen.

"You're convinced there was nothing important here?" he asked the sheriff. "Nothing that would—point to any motive?"

The sheriff too looked all around, as if to re-convince himself.

"Nothing here but kitchen things," he said, with a little laugh for the insignificance of kitchen things.

The county attorney was looking at the cupboard—a peculiar, ungainly structure, half closet and half cupboard, the upper part of it being built in the wall, and the lower part just the old-fashioned kitchen cupboard. As if its queerness attracted him, he got a chair and opened the upper part and looked in. After a moment he drew his hand away sticky.

"Here's a nice mess," he said resentfully.

The two women had drawn nearer, and now the sheriff's wife spoke.

"Oh—her fruit," she said, looking to Mrs. Hale for sympathetic understanding. She turned back to the county attorney and explained: "She worried about that when it turned so cold last night. She said the fire would go out and her jars might burst."

Mrs. Peters' husband broke into a laugh.

"Well, can you beat the women! Held for murder, and worrying about her preserves!"

The young attorney set his lips.

"I guess before we're through with her she may have something more serious than preserves to worry about."

"Oh, well," said Mrs. Hale's husband, with good-natured superiority, "women are used to worrying over trifles."

The two women moved a little closer together. Neither of them spoke. The county attorney seemed suddenly to remember his manners—and think of his future.

"And yet," said he, with the gallantry of a young politician, "for all their worries, what would we do without the ladies?"

The women did not speak, did not unbend. He went to the sink and began washing his hands. He turned to wipe them on the roller towel—whirled it for a cleaner place.

"Dirty towels! Not much of a housekeeper, would you say ladies?"

He kicked his foot against some dirty pans under the sink.

"There's a great deal of work to be done on a farm," said Mrs. Hale stiffly.

"To be sure. And yet"—with a little bow to her—"I know there are some Dickson County farm-houses that do not have such roller towels." He gave it a pull to expose its full length again.

"Those towels get dirty awful quick. Men's hands aren't always as clean as they might be."

"Ah, loyal to your sex, I see," he laughed. He stopped and gave her a keen look. "But you and Mrs. Wright were neighbors. I suppose you were friends, too."

Martha Hale shook her head.

"I've seen little enough of her of late years. I've not been in this house—it's more than a year."

"And why was that? You didn't like her?"

"I liked her well enough," she replied with spirit. "Farmers' wives have their hands full, Mr. Henderson. And then"—She looked around the kitchen.

"Yes?" he encouraged.

"It never seemed a very cheerful place," said she, more to herself than to him.

"No," he agreed; "I don't think any one would call it cheerful. I shouldn't say she had the home-making instinct."

"Well, I don't know as Wright had, either," she muttered.

"You mean they didn't get on very well?" he was quick to ask.

"No; I don't mean anything," she answered, with decision. As she turned a little away from him, she added: "But I don't think a place would be any the cheerfuler for John Wright's bein' in it."

"I'd like to talk to you about that a little later, Mrs. Hale," he said. "I'm anxious to get the lay of things upstairs now."

He moved toward the stair door, followed by the two men.

"I suppose anything Mrs. Peters does'll be all right?" the sheriff inquired. "She was to take in some clothes for her, you know—and a few little things. We left in such a hurry yesterday."

The county attorney looked at the two women whom they were leaving alone there among the kitchen things.

"Yes—Mrs. Peters," he said, his glance resting on the woman who was not Mrs. Peters, the big farmer woman who stood behind the sheriff's wife. "Of course Mrs. Peters is one of us," he said, in a manner of entrusting responsibility. "And keep your eye out, Mrs. Peters, for anything that might be of use. No telling; you women might come upon a clue to the motive—and that's the thing we need."

Mr. Hale rubbed his face after the fashion of a show man getting ready for a pleasantry.

"But would the women know a clue if they did come upon it?" he said; and, having delivered himself of this, he followed the others through the stair door.

The women stood motionless and silent, listening to the footsteps, first upon the stairs, then in the room above them.

Then, as if releasing herself from something strange, Mrs. Hale began to arrange the dirty pans under the sink, which the county attorney's disdainful push of the foot had deranged.

"I'd hate to have men comin' into my kitchen," she said testily—"snoopin' round and criticizin'."

"Of course it's no more than their duty," said the sheriff's wife, in her manner of timid acquiescence.

"Duty's all right," replied Mrs. Hale bluffly; "but I guess that deputy sheriff that come out to make the fire might have got a little of this on." She gave the roller towel a pull. "Wish I'd thought of that sooner! Seems mean to talk about her for not having things slicked up, when she had to come away in such a hurry."

She looked around the kitchen. Certainly it was not "slicked up." Her eye was held by a bucket of sugar on a low shelf. The cover was off the wooden bucket, and beside it was a paper bag—half full.

Mrs. Hale moved toward it.

"She was putting this in there," she said to herself—slowly.

She thought of the flour in her kitchen at home—half sifted, half not sifted. She had been interrupted and had left things half done. What had interrupted Minnie Foster? Why had that work been left half done? She made a move as if to finish it,—unfinished things always bothered her,—and then she glanced around and saw that Mrs. Peters was watching her—and she didn't want Mrs. Peters to get that feeling she had got of work begun and then—for some reason—not finished.

"It's a shame about her fruit," she said, and walked toward the cupboard that the county attorney had opened, and got on the chair, murmuring: "I wonder if it's all gone."

It was a sorry enough looking sight, but "Here's one that's all right," she said at last. She held it toward the light. "This is cherries, too." She looked again. "I declare I believe that's the only one."

With a sigh, she got down from the chair, went to the sink, and wiped off the bottle.

"She'll feel awful bad, after all her hard work in the hot weather. I remember the afternoon I put up my cherries last summer."

She set the bottle on the table, and, with another sigh, started to sit down in the rocker. But she did not sit down. Something kept her from sitting down in that chair. She straightened—stepped back, and, half turned away, stood looking at it, seeing the woman who sat there "pleatin' at her apron."

The thin voice of the sheriff's wife broke in upon her: "I must be getting those things from the front room closet." She opened the door into the other room, started in, stepped back. "You coming with me, Mrs. Hale?" she asked nervously. "You—you could help me get them."

They were soon back—the stark coldness of that shut-up room was not a thing to linger in.

"My!" said Mrs. Peters, dropping the things on the table and hurrying to the stove.

Mrs. Hale stood examining the clothes the woman who was being detained in town had said she wanted.

"Wright was close!" she exclaimed, holding up a shabby black skirt that bore the marks of much making over. "I think maybe that's why she kept so much to herself. I s'pose she felt she couldn't do her part; and then, you don't enjoy things when you feel shabby. She used to wear pretty clothes and be lively—when she was Minnie Foster, one of the town girls, singing in the choir. But that—oh, that was twenty years ago."

With a carefulness in which there was something tender, she folded the shabby clothes and piled them at one corner of the table. She looked at Mrs. Peters, and there was something in the other woman's look that irritated her.

"She don't care," she said to herself. "Much difference it makes to her whether Minnie Foster had pretty clothes when she was a girl."

Then she looked again, and she wasn't so sure; in fact, she hadn't at any time been perfectly sure about Mrs. Peters. She had that shrinking manner, and yet her eyes looked as if they could see a long way into things.

"This all you was to take in?" asked Mrs. Hale.

"No," said the sheriff's wife; "she said she wanted an apron. Funny thing to want," she ventured in her nervous little way, "for there's not much to get you dirty in jail, goodness knows. But I suppose just to make her feel more natural. If you're used to wearing an apron—. She said they were in the bottom drawer of this cupboard. Yes—here they are. And then her little shawl that always hung on the stair door."

She took the small gray shawl from behind the door leading upstairs, and stood a minute looking at it.

Suddenly Mrs. Hale took a quick step toward the other woman.

"Mrs. Peters!"

"Yes, Mrs. Hale?"

"Do you think she—did it?"

A frightened look blurred the other things in Mrs. Peters' eyes.

"Oh, I don't know," she said, in a voice that seemed to shrink away from the subject.

"Well, I don't think she did," affirmed Mrs. Hale stoutly. "Asking for an apron, and her little shawl. Worryin' about her fruit."

"Mr. Peters says—" Footsteps were heard in the room above; she stopped,

looked up, then went on in a lowered voice: "Mr. Peters says—it looks bad for her. Mr. Henderson is awful sarcastic in a speech, and he's going to make fun of her saying she didn't—wake up."

For a moment Mrs. Hale had no answer. Then, "Well, I guess John Wright didn't wake up—when they was slippin' that rope under his neck," she muttered.

"No, it's *strange*," breathed Mrs. Peters. "They think it was such a—funny way to kill a man."

She began to laugh; at sound of the laugh, abruptly stopped.

"That's just what Mr. Hale said," said Mrs. Hale, in a resolutely natural voice. "There was a gun in the house. He says that's what he can't understand."

"Mr. Henderson said, coming out, that what was needed for the case was a motive. Something to show anger—or sudden feeling."

"Well, I don't see any signs of anger around here," said Mrs. Hale. "I don't—"

She stopped. It was as if her mind tripped on something. Her eye was caught by a dish-towel in the middle of the kitchen table. Slowly she moved toward the table. One half of it was wiped clean, the other half messy. Her eyes made a slow, almost unwilling turn to the bucket of sugar and the half empty bag beside it. Things begun—and not finished.

After a moment she stepped back, and said, in that manner of releasing herself:

"Wonder how they're finding things upstairs? I hope she had it a little more red up there. You know,"—she paused, and feeling gathered,—"it seems kind of *sneaking*; locking her up in town and coming out here to get her own house to turn against her!"

"But, Mrs. Hale," said the sheriff's wife, "the law is the law."

'I s'pose 'tis," answered Mrs. Hale shortly.

She turned to the stove, saying something about that fire not being much to brag of. She worked with it a minute, and when she straightened up she said aggressively:

"The law is the law—and a bad stove is a bad stove. How'd you like to cook on this?"—pointing with the poker to the broken lining. She opened the oven door and started to express her opinion of the oven; but she was swept into her own thoughts, thinking of what it would mean, year after year, to have the stove to wrestle with. The thought of Minnie Foster trying to bake in that oven—and the thought of her never going over to see Minnie Foster—.

She was startled by hearing Mrs. Peters say: "A person gets discouraged—and loses heart."

The sheriff's wife had looked from the stove to the sink—to the pail of water which had been carried in from outside. The two women stood there silent, above them the footsteps of the men who were looking for evidence against the woman who had worked in that kitchen. That look of seeing into things, of seeing through a thing to something else, was in the eyes of the sheriff's wife now. When Mrs. Hale next spoke to her, it was gently:

"Better loosen up your things, Mrs. Peters. We'll not feel them when we go out."

Mrs. Peters went to the back of the room to hang up the fur tippet she was wearing. A moment later she exclaimed, "Why, she was piecing a quilt," and held up a large sewing basket piled high with quilt pieces.

Mrs. Hale spread some of the blocks on the table.

"It's log-cabin pattern," she said, putting several of them together. "Pretty, isn't it?"

They were so engaged with the quilt that they did not hear the footsteps on the stairs. Just as the stair door opened Mrs. Hale was saying:

"Do you suppose she was going to quilt it or just knot it?"

The sheriff threw up his hands.

"They wonder whether she was going to quilt it or just knot it!"

There was a laugh for the ways of women, a warming of hands over the stove, and then the county attorney said briskly:

"Well, let's go right out to the barn and get that cleared up."

"I don't see as there's anything so strange," Mrs. Hale said resentfully, after the outside door had closed on the three men—"our taking up our time with little things while we're waiting for them to get the evidence. I don't see as it's anything to laugh about."

"Of course they've got awful important things on their minds," said the sheriff's wife apologetically.

They returned to an inspection of the blocks for the quilt. Mrs. Hale was looking at the fine, even sewing, preoccupied with thoughts of the woman who had done that sewing, when she heard the sheriff's wife say, in a queer tone:

"Why, look at this one."

She turned to take the block held out to her.

"The sewing," said Mrs. Peters, in a troubled way. "All the rest of them have been so nice and even—but—this one. Why, it looks as if she didn't know what she was about!"

Their eyes met—something flashed to life, passed between them; then, as if with an effort, they seemed to pull away from each other. A moment Mrs. Hale sat there, her hands folded over that sewing which was so unlike all the rest of the sewing. Then she had pulled a knot and drawn the threads.

"Oh, what are you doing, Mrs. Hale?" asked the sheriff's wife, startled.

"Just pulling out a stitch or two that's not sewed very good," said Mrs. Hale mildly.

"I don't think we ought to touch things," Mrs. Peters said, a little helplessly.

"I'd just finish up this end," answered Mrs. Hale, still in that mild, matter-of-fact fashion.

She threaded a needle and started to replace bad sewing with good. For a little while she sewed in silence. Then, in that thin, timid voice, she heard:

"Mrs. Hale!"

"Yes, Mrs. Peters?"

"What do you suppose she was so—nervous about?"

"Oh, *I* don't know," said Mrs. Hale, as if dismissing a thing not important enough to spend much time on. "I don't know as she was—nervous. I sew awful queer sometimes when I'm just tired."

She cut a thread, and out of the corner of her eye looked up at Mrs. Peters. The small, lean face of the sheriff's wife seemed to have tightened up. Her eyes had that look of peering into something. But the next moment she moved, and said in her thin, indecisive way:

"Well, I must get those clothes wrapped. They may be through sooner than we think. I wonder where I could find a piece of paper—and string."

"In that cupboard, maybe," suggested Mrs. Hale, after a glance around.

One piece of the crazy sewing remained unripped. Mrs. Peters' back turned, Martha Hale now scrutinized that piece, compared it with the dainty, accurate sewing of the other blocks. The difference was startling. Holding this block made her feel queer, as if the distracted thoughts of the woman who had perhaps turned to it to try and quiet herself were communicating themselves to her.

Mrs. Peters' voice roused her.

"Here's a bird-cage," she said. "Did she have a bird, Mrs. Hale?"

"Why, I don't know whether she did or not." She turned to look at the cage Mrs. Peters was holding up. "I've not been here in so long." She sighed. "There was a man round last year selling canaries cheap — but I don't know as she took one. Maybe she did. She used to sing real pretty herself."

Mrs. Peters looked around the kitchen.

"Seems kind of funny to think of a bird here." She half laughed — an attempt to put up a barrier. "But she must have had one — or why would she have a cage? I wonder what happened to it."

"I suppose maybe the cat got it," suggested Mrs. Hale, resuming her sewing.

"No; she didn't have a cat. She's got that feeling some people have about cats — being afraid of them. When they brought her to our house yesterday, my cat got in the room, and she was real upset and asked me to take it out."

"My sister Bessie was like that," laughed Mrs. Hale.

The sheriff's wife did not reply. The silence made Mrs. Hale turn round. Mrs. Peters was examining the bird-cage.

"Look at this door," she said slowly. "It's broke. One hinge has been pulled apart."

Mrs. Hale came nearer.

"Looks as if some one must have been — rough with it."

Again their eyes met — startled, questioning, apprehensive. For a moment neither spoke nor stirred. Then Mrs. Hale, turning away, said brusquely:

"If they're going to find any evidence, I wish they'd be about it. I don't like this place."

"But I'm awful glad you came with me, Mrs. Hale." Mrs. Peters put the bird-cage on the table and sat down. "It would be lonesome for me — sitting here alone."

"Yes, it would, wouldn't it?" agreed Mrs. Hale, a certain determined naturalness in her voice. She picked up the sewing, but now it dropped in her lap, and she murmured in a different voice: "But I tell you what I *do* wish, Mrs. Peters. I wish I had come over sometimes when she was here. I wish — I had."

"But of course you were awful busy, Mrs. Hale. Your house — and your children."

"I could've come," retorted Mrs. Hale shortly. "I stayed away because it weren't cheerful — and that's why I ought to have come. I" — she looked around — "I've never liked this place. Maybe because it's down in a hollow and you don't see the road. I don't know what it is, but it's a lonesome place, and always was. I wish I had come over to see Minnie Foster sometimes. I can see now —" She did not put it into words.

"Well, you mustn't reproach yourself," counseled Mrs. Peters. "Somehow, we just don't see how it is with other folks till — something comes up."

"Not having children makes less work," mused Mrs. Hale, after a silence, "but it makes a quiet house — and Wright out to work all day — and no company when he did come in. Did you know John Wright, Mrs. Peters?"

"Not to know him. I've seen him in town. They say he was a good man."

"Yes—good," conceded John Wright's neighbor grimly. "He didn't drink, and kept his word as well as most, I guess, and paid his debts. But he was a hard man, Mrs. Peters. Just to pass the time of day with him—." She stopped, shivered a little. "Like a raw wind that gets to the bone." Her eye fell upon the cage on the table before her, and she added, almost bitterly: "I should think she would've wanted a bird!"

Suddenly she leaned forward, looking intently at the cage. "But what do you s'pose went wrong with it?"

"I don't know," returned Mrs. Peters; "unless it got sick and died."

But after she said it she reached over and swung the broken door. Both women watched it as if somehow held by it.

"You didn't know—her?" Mrs. Hale asked, a gentler note in her voice.

"Not till they brought her yesterday," said the sheriff's wife.

"She—come to think of it, she was kind of like a bird herself. Real sweet and pretty, but kind of timid and—fluttery. How—she—did—change."

That held her for a long time. Finally, as if struck with a happy thought and relieved to get back to everyday things, she exclaimed:

"Tell you what, Mrs. Peters, why don't you take the quilt in with you? It might take up her mind."

"Why, I think that's a real nice idea, Mrs. Hale," agreed the sheriff's wife, as if she too were glad to come into the atmosphere of a simple kindness. "There couldn't possibly be any objection to that, could there? Now, just what will I take? I wonder if her patches are in here—and her things."

They turned to the sewing basket.

"Here's some red," said Mrs. Hale, bringing out a roll of cloth. Underneath that was a box. "Here, maybe her scissors are in here—and her things." She held it up. "What a pretty box! I'll warrant that was something she had a long time ago—when she was a girl."

She held it in her hand a moment; then, with a little sigh, opened it.

Instantly her hand went to her nose.

"Why—!"

Mrs. Peters drew nearer—then turned away.

"There's something wrapped up in this piece of silk," faltered Mrs. Hale.

"This isn't her scissors," said Mrs. Peters in a shrinking voice.

Her hand not steady, Mrs. Hale raised the piece of silk. "Oh, Mrs. Peters!" she cried. "It's—"

Mrs. Peters bent closer.

"It's the bird," she whispered.

"But, Mrs. Peters!" cried Mrs. Hale. "*Look* at it! Its neck—look at its neck! It's all—other side *to*."

She held the box away from her.

The sheriff's wife again bent closer.

"Somebody wrung its neck," said she, in a voice that was slow and deep.

And then again the eyes of the two women met—this time clung together in a look of dawning comprehension, of growing horror. Mrs. Peters looked from the dead bird to the broken door of the cage. Again their eyes met. And just then there was a sound at the outside door.

Mrs. Hale slipped the box under the quilt pieces in the basket, and sank into the chair before it. Mrs. Peters stood holding to the table. The country attorney and the sheriff came in from outside.

"Well, ladies," said the county attorney, as one turning from serious things to little pleasantries, "have you decided whether she was going to quilt it or knot it?"

"We think," began the sheriff's wife in a flurried voice, "that she was going to—knot it."

He was too preoccupied to notice the change that came in her voice on that last.

"Well, that's very interesting, I'm sure," he said tolerantly. He caught sight of the bird-cage. "Has the bird flown?"

"We think the cat got it," said Mrs. Hale in a voice curiously even.

He was walking up and down, as if thinking something out.

"Is there a cat?" he asked absently.

Mrs. Hale shot a look up at the sheriff's wife.

"Well, not *now*," said Mrs. Peters. "They're superstitious, you know; they leave."

She sank into her chair.

The county attorney did not heed her. "No sign at all of any one having come in from the outside," he said to Peters, in the manner of continuing an interrupted conversation. "Their own rope. Now let's go upstairs again and go over it, piece by piece. It would have to have been some one who knew just the—"

The stair door closed behind them and their voices were lost.

The two women sat motionless, not looking at each other, but as if peering into something and at the same time holding back. When they spoke now it was as if they were afraid of what they were saying, but as if they could not help saying it.

"She liked that bird," said Martha Hale, low and slowly. "She was going to bury it in that pretty box."

"When I was a girl," said Mrs. Peters, under her breath, "my kitten—there was a boy took a hatchet, and before my eyes—before I could get there—" She covered her face an instant. "If they hadn't held me back I would have"— she caught herself, looked upstairs where footsteps were heard, and finished weakly —"hurt him."

Then they sat without speaking or moving.

"I wonder how it would seem," Mrs. Hale at last began, as if feeling her way over strange ground—"never to have had any children around?" Her eyes made a slow sweep of the kitchen, as if seeing what that kitchen had meant through all the years. "No, Wright wouldn't like the bird," she said after that—"a thing that sang. She used to sing. He killed that too." Her voice tightened.

Mrs. Peters moved uneasily.

"Of course we don't know who killed the bird."

"I knew John Wright," was Mrs. Hale's answer.

"It was an awful thing was done in this house that night, Mrs. Hale," said the sheriff's wife. "Killing a man while he slept—slipping a thing round his neck that choked the life out of him."

Mrs. Hale's hand went out to the bird-cage.

"His neck. Choked the life out of him."

"We don't *know* who killed him," whispered Mrs. Peters wildly. "We don't *know*."

Mrs. Hale had not moved. "If there had been years and years of—nothing, then a bird to sing to you, it would be awful—still—after the bird was still."

It was as if something within her not herself had spoken, and it found in Mrs. Peters something she did not know as herself.

"I know what stillness is," she said, in a queer, monotonous voice. "When we homesteaded in Dakota, and my first baby died—after he was two years old—and me with no other then—"

Mrs. Hale stirred.

"How soon do you suppose they'll be through looking for evidence?"

"I know what stillness is," repeated Mrs. Peters, in just the same way. Then she too pulled back. "The law has got to punish crime, Mrs. Hale," she said in her tight little way.

"I wish you'd seen Minnie Foster," was the answer, "when she wore a white dress with blue ribbons, and stood up there in the choir and sang."

The picture of that girl, the fact that she had lived neighbor to that girl for twenty years, and had let her die for lack of life, was suddenly more than she could bear.

"Oh, I *wish* I'd come over here once in a while!" she cried. "That was a crime! That was a crime! Who's going to punish that?"

"We mustn't take on," said Mrs. Peters, with a frightened look toward the stairs.

"I might 'a' *known* she needed help! I tell you, It's *queer*, Mrs. Peters. We live close together, and we live far apart. We all go through the same things—it's all just a different kind of the same thing! If it weren't why do you and I *understand*? Why do we *know*—what we know this minute?"

She dashed her hand across her eyes. Then, seeing the jar of fruit on the table, she reached out for it and choked out:

"If I was you I wouldn't *tell* her her fruit was gone! Tell her it *ain't*. Tell her it's all right—all of it. Here—take this in to prove it to her! She—she may never know whether it was broke or not."

She turned away.

Mrs. Peters reached out for the bottle of fruit as if she were glad to take it—as if touching a familiar thing, having something to do, could keep her from something else. She got up, looked about for something to wrap the fruit in, took a petticoat from the pile of clothes she had brought from the front room, and nervously started winding that round the bottle.

"My!" she began, in a high, false voice, "it's a good thing the men couldn't hear us! Getting all stirred up over a little thing like a—dead canary." She hurried over that. "As if that could have anything to do with—with—My, wouldn't they *laugh*?"

Footsteps were heard on the stairs.

"Maybe they would," muttered Mrs. Hale—"maybe they wouldn't."

"No, Peters," said the county attorney incisively; "it's all perfectly clear, except the reason for doing it. But you know juries when it comes to women. If there was some definite thing—something to show. Something to make a story about. A thing that would connect up with this clumsy way of doing it."

In a covert way Mrs. Hale looked at Mrs. Peters. Mrs. Peters was looking at her. Quickly they looked away from each other. The outer door opened and Mr. Hale came in.

"I've got the team round now," he said. "Pretty cold out there."

"I'm going to stay here awhile by myself," the county attorney suddenly announced. "You can send Frank out for me, can't you?" he asked the sheriff. "I want to go over everything. I'm not satisfied we can't do better."

Again, for one brief moment, the two women's eyes found one another.

The sheriff came up to the table.

"Did you want to see what Mrs. Peters was going to take in?"

The county attorney picked up the apron. He laughed.

"Oh, I guess they're not very dangerous things the ladies have picked out."

Mrs. Hale's hand was on the sewing basket in which the box was concealed. She felt that she ought to take her hand off the basket. She did not seem able to. He picked up one of the quilt blocks which she had piled on to cover the box. Her eyes felt like fire. She had a feeling that if he took up the basket she would snatch it from him.

But he did not take it up. With another little laugh, he turned away, saying:

"No; Mrs. Peters doesn't need supervising. For that matter, a sheriff's wife is married to the law. Ever think of it that way, Mrs. Peters?"

Mrs. Peters was standing beside the table. Mrs. Hale shot a look up at her; but she could not see her face. Mrs. Peters had turned away. When she spoke, her voice was muffled.

"Not—just that way," she said.

"Married to the law!" chuckled Mrs. Peters' husband. He moved toward the door into the front room, and said to the county attorney:

"I just want you to come in here a minute, George. We ought to take a look at these windows.

"We'll be right out, Mr. Hale," said the sheriff to the farmer, who was still waiting by the door.

Hale went to look after the horses. The sheriff followed the county attorney into the other room. Again—for one moment—the two women were alone in that kitchen.

Martha Hale sprang up, her hands tight together, looking at that other woman, with whom it rested. At first she could not see her eyes, for the sheriff's wife had not turned back, since she turned away at that suggestion of being married to the law. But now Mrs. Hale made her turn back. Her eyes made her turn back. Slowly, unwillingly, Mrs. Peters turned her head until her eyes met the eyes of the other woman. There was a moment when they held each other in a steady, burning look in which there was no evasion nor flinching. Then Martha Hale's eyes pointed the way to the basket in which was hidden the thing that would make certain the conviction of the other woman—that woman who was not there and yet who had been there with them all through the hour.

For a moment Mrs. Peters did not move. And then she did it. With a rush forward, she threw back the quilt pieces, got the box, tried to put it in her handbag. It was too big. Desperately she opened it, started to take the bird out. But there she broke—she could not touch the bird. She stood helpless foolish.

There was the sound of a knob turning in the inner door. Martha Hale snatched the box from the sheriff's wife, and got it in the pocket of her big coat just as the sheriff and the county attorney came back into the kitchen.

"Well, Henry," said the county attorney facetiously, "at least we found out that she was not going to quilt it. She was going to—what is it you call it, ladies?"

Mrs. Hale's hand was against the pocket of her coat.

"We call it—knot it, Mr. Henderson."

[1917]

QUESTIONS

1. How do Mrs. Hale and Mrs. Peters discover Minnie Wright's motive for murder?
2. Mrs. Peters insists that "the law is the law"; what events persuade her to participate in the exoneration of Minnie Wright's crime? How does the story demonstrate the changes that occur in her and Mrs. Hale?
3. Consider how each of the following elements of the story carries a double meaning: *knot, strangulation, crime, law, evidence, motive, jury.*
4. What does the story imply in expressing different ways in which men and women interpret events and even objects in an environment? Are these differences exaggerated? How does the reader become a participant in interpretation and judgment?
5. What is the significance of the title? What conflicting views of the law are expressed in the story? Are they resolved?

Nikolai Gogol
(1809–1852)
Russia

Nikolai Vasilievich Gogol was born and raised in the Ukraine, the son of an amateur musician and playwright who suffered mental disorders and who died during Nikolai's childhood. Gogol's mother was only 15 when Nikolai was born; she went on to bear 11 more children. Steeped in folklore, she was an important source of the folk legends and superstitions of Ukranian life in Gogol's early stories.

Gogol had hopes of being an actor, but his highly nervous nature and his fear of people made it difficult for him to succeed at that or most other professions. His defeats were exaggerated for him because of his high sense of purpose. He tried several jobs, including the civil service, and eventually acquired a position for which he had absolutely no qualifications as a professor of medieval history at the University of St. Petersburg. His disastrous performance sounds like a situation he might have invented for one of his stories.

Eventually Gogol tried writing fiction based on Ukrainian fairy tales, legends, and romantic horror tales; the first volume, *Evenings on a Farm Near Dikanka* (1831), made his success and name immediately. He also wrote several plays, the best known of which, *The Inspector General* (1836), exposes the posturings and foibles of a cross section of Russian townspeople. His masterpiece, *Dead Souls* (1841), satirizes the greed and corruption of Russian landowners with epic sweep and humor. Although it might seem as if Gogol were a radical social critic, in fact he was politically conservative; he intended for *Dead Souls* (which he never completed) to end with his hero Chichikov's reform and the salvation of traditional Russia.

Gogol's mastery of the "comic grotesque"—the juxtaposition of humor and horror—is one of his unique contributions to narrative form. His mingling of the commonplace with the uncanny or supernatural, as in "The Overcoat," and his mastery of caricature are elements of his indelible style. Moreover, his poignant story of the plight of the little man marked a turning point in Russian literature: the character of the underdog or social misfit is understood not as a nuisance or a figure to be mocked but as a human being who is entitled to his share of happiness. However, he may not find that happiness, as Gogol himself did not. Split between his artistic gifts and his moral certainties, Gogol eventually died of melancholy, mental anguish, and self-starvation at the age of 41.

Gogol's influence on Russian literature was profound; he is regarded as the father of "Russian realism." Dostoevsky remarked, "We all emerged from the folds of Gogol's overcoat." As the Russian writer Vladimir Nabokov observed in his *Lectures on Russian Literature*,

> "The Overcoat" is a grotesque and grim nightmare making black holes in the dim pattern of life. . . . After reading Gogol one's eyes may become gogolized and one is apt to see bits of

> his world in the most unexpected places. . . . [S]omething like Akaky Akakievich's overcoat has been the passionate dream of this or that chance acquaintance who never has heard about Gogol.

"The Overcoat," in its unique fusion of humor and suffering and in its stark rendering of the absurd universe that lurks just beneath the commonplace one, is unarguably one of the world's great masterpieces of short fiction.

The Overcoat

In the department of . . . but I had better not mention which department. There is nothing in the world more touchy than a department, a regiment, a government office, and, in fact, any sort of official body. Nowadays every private individual considers all society insulted in his person. I have been told that very lately a complaint was lodged by a police inspector of which town I don't remember, and that in this complaint he set forth clearly that the institutions of the State were in danger and that his sacred name was being taken in vain; and, in proof thereof, he appended to his complaint an enormously long volume of some romantic work in which a police inspector appeared on every tenth page, occasionally, indeed, in an intoxicated condition. And so, to avoid any unpleasantness, we had better call the department of which we are speaking "a certain department."

And so, in a *certain department* there was a *certain clerk*; a clerk of whom it cannot be said that he was very remarkable; he was short, somewhat pockmarked, with rather reddish hair and rather dim, bleary eyes, with a small bald patch on the top of his head, with wrinkles on both sides of his cheeks and the sort of complexion which is usually described as hemorrhoidal . . . nothing can be done about that, it is the Petersburg climate. As for his grade in the civil service (for among us a man's rank is what must be established first) he was what is called a perpetual titular councilor, a class at which, as we all know, various writers who indulge in the praiseworthy habit of attacking those who cannot defend themselves jeer and jibe to their hearts' content. This clerk's surname was Bashmachkin. From the very name it is clear that it must have been derived from a shoe (*bashmak*); but when and under what circumstances it was derived from a shoe, it is impossible to say. Both his father and his grandfather and even his brother-in-law, and all the Bashmachkins without exception wore boots, which they simply resoled two or three times a year. His name was Akaky Akakievich.[1] Perhaps it may strike the reader as a rather strange and contrived name, but I can assure him that it was not contrived at all, that the circumstances were such that it was quite out of the question to give him any other name. Akaky Akakievich was born toward nightfall, if my memory does not deceive me, on the twenty-third of March. His mother, the wife of a government clerk, a very good woman, made arrangements in due course to christen the child. She was still lying in bed, facing the door, while on her right hand stood the

[1]*Akaky Akakievich* In Russian, *Akaky* is close to a child's word for excrement.

godfather, an excellent man called Ivan Ivanovich Yeroshkin, one of the head clerks in the Senate, and the godmother, the wife of a police official and a woman of rare qualities, Arina Semeonovna Belobriushkova. Three names were offered to the happy mother for selection—Mokky, Sossy, or the name of the martyr Khozdazat. "No," thought the poor lady, "they are all such names!" To satisfy her, they opened the calendar at another page, and the names which turned up were: Trifily, Dula, Varakhasy. "What an infliction!" said the mother. "What names they all are! I really never heard such names. Varadat or Varukh would be bad enough, but Trifily and Varakhasy!" They turned over another page and the names were: Pavsikakhy and Vakhisy. "Well, I see," said the mother, "it is clear that it is his fate. Since that is how it is, he had better be named after his father; his father is Akaky; let the son be Akaky, too." This was how he came to be Akaky Akakievich. The baby was christened and cried and made sour faces during the ceremony, as though he foresaw that he would be a titular councilor. So that was how it all came to pass. We have reported it here so that the reader may see for himself that it happened quite inevitably and that to give him any other name was out of the question.

No one has been able to remember when and how long ago he entered the department, nor who gave him the job. Regardless of how many directors and higher officials of all sorts came and went, he was always seen in the same place, in the same position, at the very same duty, precisely the same copying clerk, so that they used to declare that he must have been born a copying clerk, uniform, bald patch, and all. No respect at all was shown him in the department. The porters, far from getting up from their seats when he came in, took no more notice of him than if a simple fly had flown across the reception room. His superiors treated him with a sort of despotic aloofness. The head clerk's assistant used to throw papers under his nose without even saying "Copy this" or "Here is an interesting, nice little case" or some agreeable remark of the sort, as is usually done in well-bred offices. And he would take it, gazing only at the paper without looking to see who had put it there and whether he had the right to do so; he would take it and at once begin copying it. The young clerks jeered and made jokes at him to the best of their clerkly wit, and told before his face all sorts of stories of their own invention about him; they would say of his landlady, an old woman of seventy, that she beat him, would ask when the wedding was to take place, and would scatter bits of paper on his head, calling them snow. Akaky Akakievich never answered a word, however, but behaved as though there were no one there. It had no influence on his work; in the midst of all this teasing, he never made a single mistake in his copying. It was only when the jokes became too unbearable, when they jolted his arm, and prevented him from going on with his work, that he would say: "Leave me alone! Why do you insult me?" and there was something touching in the words and in the voice in which they were uttered. There was a note in it of something that aroused compassion, so that one young man, new to the office, who, following the example of the rest, had allowed himself to tease him, suddenly stopped as though cut to the heart, and from that time on, everything was, as it were, changed and appeared in a different light to him. Some unseen force seemed to repel him from the companions with whom he had become acquainted because he thought they were well-bred and decent men. And long afterward, during moments of the greatest gaiety, the figure of the humble little clerk with a bald patch on his head appeared before him with his heart-rending words: "Leave me alone! Why do you insult me?" and within those moving words he heard others: "I am your brother." And the poor young man hid his face in his hands, and many times afterward in his life he shuddered, seeing how much inhumanity there is in man, how much savage brutality lies hidden under refined, cultured politeness, and, my God! even in a man whom the world accepts as a gentleman and a man of honor. . . .

It would be hard to find a man who lived for his work as did Akaky Akakievich. To say that he was zealous in his work is not enough; no, he loved his work. In it, in that copying, he found an interesting and pleasant world of his own. There was a look of enjoyment on his face; certain letters were favorites with him, and when he came to them he was delighted; he chuckled to himself and winked and moved his lips, so that it seemed as though every letter his pen was forming could be read in his face. If rewards had been given according to the measure of zeal in the service, he might to his amazement have even found himself a civil councilor; but all he gained in the service, as the wits, his fellow clerks, expressed it, was a button in his buttonhole and hemorrhoids where he sat. It cannot be said, however, that no notice had ever been taken of him. One director, being a good-natured man and anxious to reward him for his long service, sent him something a little more important than his ordinary copying; he was instructed to make some sort of report from a finished document for another office; the work consisted only of altering the headings and in places changing the first person into the third. This cost him so much effort that he was covered with perspiration; he mopped his brow and said at last, "No, I'd rather copy something."

From that time on they left him to his copying forever. It seemed as though nothing in the world existed for him except his copying. He gave no thought at all to his clothes; his uniform was—well, not green but some sort of rusty, muddy color. His collar was very low and narrow, so that, although his neck was particularly long, yet, standing out of the collar, it looked as immensely long as those of the dozens of plaster kittens, with nodding heads which foreigners carry about on their heads and peddle in Russia. And there were always things sticking to his uniform, either bits of hay or threads; moreover, he had a special knack of passing under a window at the very moment when various garbage was being flung out into the street, and so was continually carrying off bits of melon rind and similar litter on his hat. He had never once in his life noticed what was being done and what was going on in the street, all those things at which, as we all know, his colleagues, the young clerks, always stare, utilizing their keen sight so well that they notice anyone on the other side of the street with a strap hanging loose—an observation which always calls forth a sly grin. Whatever Akaky Akakievich looked at, he saw nothing but his clear, evenly written lines, and it was only perhaps when a horse suddenly appeared from nowhere and placed its head on his shoulder, and with its nostrils blew a real gale upon his cheek, that he would notice that he was not in the middle of his writing, but rather in the middle of the street.

On reaching home, he would sit down at once at the table, hurriedly eat his soup and a piece of beef with an onion; he did not notice the taste at all but ate it all with the flies and anything else that Providence happened to send him. When he felt that his stomach was beginning to be full, he would get up from the table, take out a bottle of ink, and begin copying the papers he had brought home with him. When he had none to do, he would make a copy especially for his own pleasure, particularly if the document were remarkable not for the beauty of its style but because it was addressed to some new or distinguished person.

Even at those hours when the gray Petersburg sky is completely overcast and the whole population of clerks have dined and eaten their fill, each as best he can, according to the salary he receives and his personal tastes; when they are all resting after the scratching of pens and bustle of the office, their own necessary work and other people's, and all the tasks that an overzealous man voluntarily sets himself even beyond what is necessary; when the clerks are hastening to devote what is left of their time to pleasure; some more enterprising are flying to the theater, others to the street to spend their leisure staring at women's hats, some to spend the evening paying compliments to some attractive girl, the star of a little official circle, while some—and this is the most frequent of all—go simply to a fellow clerk's apartment on the third or fourth story, two little rooms with a hall or a kitchen, with some pretensions to style, with a lamp or some such article that has cost many sacrifices of dinners and excursions—at the time when all the clerks are scattered about the apartments of their friends, playing a stormy game of whist, sipping tea out of glasses, eating cheap biscuits, sucking in smoke from long pipes, telling, as the cards are dealt, some scandal that has floated down from higher circles, a pleasure which the Russian can never by any possibility deny himself, or, when there is nothing better to talk about, repeating the everlasting anecdote of the commanding offiecer who was told that the tail had been cut off the horse on the Falconet monument—in short, even when everyone was eagerly seeking entertainment, Akaky Akakievich did not indulge in any amusement. No one could say that they had ever seen him at an evening party. After working to his heart's content, he would go to bed, smiling at the thought of the next day and wondering what God would send him to copy. So flowed on the peaceful life of a man who knew how to be content with his fate on a salary of four hundred rubles, and so perhaps it would have flowed on to extreme old age, had it not been for the various disasters strewn along the road of life, not only of titular, but even of privy, actual court, and all other councilors, even those who neither give counsel to others nor accept it themselves.

There is in Petersburg a mighty foe of all who receive a salary of about four hundred rubles. That foe is none other than our northern frost, although it is said to be very good for the health. Between eight and nine in the morning, precisely at the hour when the streets are filled with clerks going to their departments, the frost begins indiscriminately giving such sharp and stinging nips at all their noses that the poor fellows don't know what to do with them. At that time, when even those in the higher grade have a pain in their brows and tears in their eyes from the frost, the poor titular councilors are sometimes almost defenseless. Their only protection lies in running as fast as they can through five or six streets in a wretched, thin little overcoat and then warming their feet thoroughly in the porter's room, till all their faculties and talents for their various duties thaw out again after having been frozen on the way. Akaky Akakievich had for some time been feeling that his back and shoulders were particularly nipped by the cold, although he did try to run the regular distance as fast as he could. He wondered at last whether there were any defects in his overcoat. After examining it thoroughly in the privacy of his home, he discovered that in two or three places, on the back and the shoulders, it had become a regular sieve; the cloth was so worn that you could see through it and the lining was coming out. I must note that Akaky Akakievich's overcoat had also served as a butt for the jokes of the clerks. It had even been deprived of the honorable name of overcoat and had been referred to as the "dressing gown." It was indeed of rather a peculiar make. Its collar had been growing smaller year by year as it served to patch the other parts. The patches were not good specimens of the tailor's art, and they certainly looked clumsy and ugly. On seeing what was wrong, Akaky Akakievich decided that he would have to take the overcoat to

Petrovich, a tailor who lived on the fourth floor up a back staircase, and, in spite of having only one eye and being pockmarked all over his face, was rather successful in repairing the trousers and coats of clerks and others — that is, when he was sober, be it understood, and had no other enterprise on his mind. Of this tailor I ought not, of course, say much, but since it is now the rule that the character of every person in a novel must be completely described, well, there's nothing I can do but describe Petrovich too. At first he was called simply Grigory, and was a serf belonging to some gentleman or other. He began to be called Petrovich[2] from the time that he got his freedom and began to drink rather heavily on every holiday, at first only on the main holidays, but afterward, on all church holidays indiscriminately, wherever there was a cross in the calendar. In this he was true to the customs of his forefathers, and when he quarreled with his wife he used to call her a worldly woman and a German. Since we have now mentioned the wife, it will be necessary to say a few words about her, too, but unfortunately not much is known about her, except indeed that Petrovich had a wife and that she wore a cap and not a kerchief, but apparently she could not boast of beauty; anyway, none but soldiers of the guard peered under her cap when they met her, and they twitched their mustaches and gave vent to a rather peculiar sound.

As he climbed the stairs leading to Petrovich's — which, to do them justice, were all soaked with water and slops and saturated through and through with that smell of ammonia which makes the eyes smart, and is, as we all know, inseparable from the backstairs of Petersburg houses — Akaky Akakievich was already wondering how much Petrovich would ask for the job, and inwardly resolving not to give more than two rubles. The door was open, because Petrovich's wife was frying some fish and had so filled the kitchen with smoke that you could not even see the cockroaches. Akaky Akakievich crossed the kitchen unnoticed by the good woman, and walked at last into a room where he saw Petrovich sitting on a big, wooden, unpainted table with his legs tucked under him like a Turkish pasha. The feet, as is usual with tailors when they sit at work, were bare; and the first object that caught Akaky Akakievich's eye was the big toe, with which he was already familiar, with a misshapen nail as thick and strong as the shell of a tortoise. Around Petrovich's neck hung a skein of silk and another of thread and on his knees was a rag of some sort. He had for the last three minutes been trying to thread his needle, but could not get the thread into the eye and so was very angry with the darkness and indeed with the thread itself, muttering in an undertone: "She won't go in, the savage! You wear me out, you bitch." Akaky Akakievich was unhappy that he had come just at the minute when Petrovich was in a bad humor; he liked to give him an order when he was a little "elevated," or, as his wife expressed it, "had fortified himself with vodka, the one-eyed devil." In such circumstances Petrovich was as a rule very ready to give way and agree, and invariably bowed and thanked him. Afterward, it is true, his wife would come wailing that her husband had been drunk and so had asked too little, but adding a single ten-kopek piece would settle that. But on this occasion Petrovich was apparently sober and consequently curt, unwilling to bargain, and the devil knows what price he would be ready to demand. Akaky Akakievich realized this, and was, as the saying is, beating a retreat, but things had gone too far, for Petrovich was screwing up his solitary eye very attentively at him and Akaky Akakievich involuntarily said: "Good day, Petrovich!"

[2]Serfs were generally addressed by their first names only, while freemen were addressed by first name and patronymic (the middle name derived from the father's first name) or by patronymic only.

"I wish you a good day, sir," said Petrovich, and squinted at Akaky Akakievich's hands, trying to discover what sort of goods he had brought.

"Here I have come to you, Petrovich, do you see . . . !"

It must be noticed that Akaky Akakievich for the most part explained himself by apologies, vague phrases, and meaningless parts of speech which have absolutely no significance whatever. If the subject were a very difficult one, it was his habit indeed to leave his sentences quite unfinished, so that very often after a sentence had begun with the words, "It really is, don't you know . . . " nothing at all would follow and he himself would be quite oblivious to the fact that he had not finished his thought, supposing he had said all that was necessary.

"What is it?" said Petrovich, and at the same time with his solitary eye he scrutinized his whole uniform from the collar to the sleeves, the back, the skirts, the buttonholes—with all of which he was very familiar since they were all his own work. Such scrutiny is habitual with tailors; it is the first thing they do on meeting one.

"It's like this, Petrovich . . . the overcoat, the cloth . . . you see everywhere else it is quite strong; it's a little dusty and looks as though it were old, but it is new and it is only in one place just a little . . . on the back, and just a little worn on one shoulder and on this shoulder, too, a little . . . do you see? that's all, and it's not much work . . . "

Petrovich took the "dressing gown," first spread it out over the table, examined it for a long time, shook his head, and put his hand out to the window sill for a round snuffbox with a portrait on the lid of some general—which general I can't exactly say, for a finger had been thrust through the spot where a face should have been, and the hole had been pasted over with a square piece of paper. After taking a pinch of snuff, Petrovich held the "dressing gown" up in his hands and looked at it against the light, and again he shook his head; then he turned it with the lining upward and once more shook his head; again he took off the lid with the general pasted up with paper and snuffed a pinch into his nose, shut the box, put it away, and at last said: "No, it can't be repaired; a wretched garment!" Akaky Akakievich's heart sank at those words.

"Why can't it, Petrovich?" he said, almost in the imploring voice of a child. "Why, the only thing is, it is a bit worn on the shoulders; why, you have got some little pieces . . . "

"Yes, the pieces will be found all right," said Petrovich, "but it can't be patched, the stuff is rotten; if you put a needle in it, it would give way."

"Let it give way, but you just put a patch on it."

"There is nothing to put a patch on. There is nothing for it to hold on to; there is a great strain on it; it is not worth calling cloth; it would fly away at a breath of wind."

"Well, then, strengthen it with something—I'm sure, really, this is . . . "

"No," said Petrovich resolutely, "there is nothing that can be done, the thing is no good at all. You had far better, when the cold winter weather comes, make yourself leg wrappings out of it, for there is no warmth in stockings; the Germans invented them just to make money." (Petrovich enjoyed a dig at the Germans occasionally.) "And as for the overcoat, it is obvious that you will have to have a new one."

At the word "new" there was a mist before Akaky Akakievich's eyes, and everything in the room seemed blurred. He could see nothing clearly but the general with the piece of paper over his face on the lid of Petrovich's snuffbox.

"A new one?" he said, still feeling as though he were in a dream; "why, I haven't the money for it."

"Yes, a new one," Petrovich repeated with barbarous composure.

"Well, and if I did have a new one, how much would it . . . ?"

"You mean what will it cost?"

"Yes."

"Well, at least one hundred and fifty rubles," said Petrovich, and he compressed his lips meaningfully. He was very fond of making an effect; he was fond of suddenly disconcerting a man completely and then squinting sideways to see what sort of a face he made.

"A hundred and fifty rubles for an overcoat!" screamed poor Akaky Akakievich—it was perhaps the first time he had screamed in his life, for he was always distinguished by the softness of his voice.

"Yes," said Petrovich, "and even then it depends on the coat. If I were to put marten on the collar, and add a hood with silk linings, it would come to two hundred."

"Petrovich, please," said Akaky Akakievich in an imploring voice, not hearing and not trying to hear what Petrovich said, and missing all his effects," repair it somehow, so that it will serve a little longer."

"No, that would be wasting work and spending money for nothing," said Petrovich, and after that Akaky Akakievich went away completely crushed, and when he had gone Petrovich remained standing for a long time with his lips pursed up meaningfully before he began his work again, feeling pleased that he had not demeaned himself or lowered the dignity of the tailor's art.

When he got into the street, Akaky Akakievich felt as though he was in a dream. "So that is how it is," he said to himself. "I really did not think it would be this way . . . " and then after a pause he added, "So that's it! So that's how it is at last! and I really could never have supposed it would be this way. And there . . . " There followed another long silence, after which he said: "So that's it! well, it really is so utterly unexpected . . . who would have thought . . . what a circumstance . . . " Saying this, instead of going home he walked off in quite the opposite direction without suspecting what he was doing. On the way a clumsy chimney sweep brushed the whole of his sooty side against him and blackened his entire shoulder; a whole hatful of plaster scattered upon him from the top of a house that was being built. He noticed nothing of this, and only after he had jostled against a policeman who had set his halberd down beside him and was shaking some snuff out of his horn into his rough fist, he came to himself a little and then only because the policeman said: "Why are you poking yourself right in one's face, haven't you enough room on the street?" This made him look around and turn homeward; only there he began to collect his thoughts, to see his position in a clear and true light, and began talking to himself no longer incoherently but reasonably and openly as with a sensible friend with whom one can discuss the most intimate and vital matters. "No," said Akaky Akakievich, "it is no use talking to Petrovich now; just now he really is . . . his wife must have been giving it to him. I had better go to him on Sunday morning; after Saturday night he will have a crossed eye and be sleepy, so he'll want a little drink and his wife won't give him a kopek. I'll slip ten kopeks into his hand and then he will be more accommodating and maybe take the overcoat. . . . "

So reasoning with himself, Akaky Akakievich cheered up and waited until the next Sunday; then, seeing from a distance Petrovich's wife leaving the house, he went straight in. Petrovich certainly had a crossed eye after Saturday. He could hardly hold his head up and was very drowsy; but, despite all that, as soon as he heard what Akaky Akakievich was speaking about, it seemed as though the devil has nudged him. "I can't," he said, "you must order a new one." Akaky Akakievich at once slipped a ten-kopek piece into his hand. "I thank you, sir, I will have just a drop to your health, but don't trouble yourself about the overcoat; it is no good for anything. I'll make you a fine new coat; you can have faith in me for that."

Akaky Akakievich would have said more about repairs, but Petrovich, without listening, said: "A new one I'll make you without fail; you can rely on that; I'll do my best. It could even be like the fashion that is popular, with the collar to fasten with silver-plated hooks under a flap."

Then Akaky Akakievich saw that there was no escape from a new overcoat and he was utterly depressed. How indeed, for what, with what money could he get it? Of course he could to some extent rely on the bonus for the coming holiday, but that money had long been appropriated and its use determined beforehand. It was needed for new trousers and to pay the cobbler an old debt for putting some new tops on some old boots, and he had to order three shirts from a seamstress as well as two items of undergarments which it is indecent to mention in print; in short, all that money absolutely must be spent, and even if the director were to be so gracious as to give him a holiday bonus of forty-five or even fifty, instead of forty rubles, there would be still left a mere trifle, which would be but a drop in the ocean compared to the fortune needed for an overcoat. Though, of course, he knew that Petrovich had a strange craze for suddenly demanding the devil knows what enormous price, so that at times his own wife could not help crying out: "Why, you are out of your wits, you idiot! Another time he'll undertake a job for nothing, and here the devil has bewitched him to ask more than he is worth himself." Though, of course, he knew that Petrovich would undertake to make it for eighty rubles, still where would he get those eighty rubles? He might manage half of that sum; half of it could be found, perhaps even a little more; but where could he get the other half? . . . But, first of all, the reader ought to know where that first half was to be found. Akaky Akakievich had the habit every time he spent a ruble of putting aside two kopeks in a little box which he kept locked, with a slit in the lid for dropping in the money. At the end of every six months he would inspect the pile of coppers there and change them for small silver. He had done this for a long time, and in the course of many years the sum had mounted up to forty rubles and so he had half the money in his hands, but where was he to get the other half; where was he to get another forty rubles? Akaky Akakievich thought and thought and decided at last that he would have to diminish his ordinary expenses, at least for a year; give up burning candles in the evening, and if he had to do any work he must go into the landlady's room and work by her candle; that as he walked along the streets he must walk as lightly and carefully as possible, almost on tiptoe, on the cobbles and flagstones, so that his soles might last a little longer than usual; that he must send his linen to the wash less frequently, and that, to preserve it from being worn, he must take if off every day when he came home and sit in a thin cotton dressing gown, a very ancient garment which Time itself had spared. To tell the truth, he found it at first rather difficult to get used to these privations, but after a while it became a habit and went smoothly enough —he even became quite accustomed to being hungry in the evening; on the other hand, he had spiritual nourishment, for he carried ever in his thoughts the idea of his future overcoat. His whole existence had in a sense become fuller, as though he had married, as though some other person were present with him, as though he were no longer alone but an agreeable companion had consented to walk the path of life hand in hand with him, and that companion was none other than the new overcoat with its thick padding and its strong, durable lining. He became, as it were, more alive, even more strong-willed, like a man who has set before himself a definite goal. Uncertainty, indecision, in fact all the hesitating and vague characteristics, vanished from his face and his manners. At times there was a gleam in his eyes; indeed, the most bold and audacious ideas flashed through his mind. Why not really have marten on the collar? Meditation on the subject always made him absent-minded. On one occasion when he was copying a document, he very nearly made a mistake, so that he almost cried out "ough" aloud and crossed himself. At least once every month he went to Petrovich to talk about the overcoat: where it would be best to buy the cloth, and what color it should be, and what price; and, though he returned home a little anxious, he was always pleased at the thought that at last the time was at hand when everything would be bought and the overcoat would be made. Things moved even faster than he had anticipated. Contrary to all expectations, the director bestowed on Akaky Akakievich a bonus of no less than sixty rubles. Whether it was that he had an inkling that Akaky Akakievich needed a coat, or whether it happened by luck, owing to this he found he had twenty rubles extra. This circumstance hastened the course of affairs. Another two or three months of partial starvation and Akaky Akakievich had actually saved up nearly eighty rubles. His heart, as a rule very tranquil, began to throb.

The very first day he set out with Petrovich for the shops. They bought some very good cloth, and no wonder, since they had been thinking of it for more than six months, and scarcely a month had passed without their going out to the shop to compare prices; now Petrovich himself declared that there was no better cloth to be had. For the lining they chose calico, but of such good quality, that in Petrovich's words it was even better than silk, and actually as strong and handsome to look at. Marten they did not buy, because it was too expensive, but instead they chose cat fur, the best to be found in the shop—cat which in the distance might almost be taken for marten. Petrovich was busy making the coat for two weeks, because there was a great deal of quilting; otherwise it would have been ready sooner. Petrovich charged twelve rubles for the work; less than that it hardly could have been; everything was sewn with silk, with fine double seams, and Petrovich went over every seam afterwards with his own teeth, imprinting various patterns with them. It was . . . it is hard to say precisely on what day, but probably on the most triumphant day in the life of Akaky Akakievich, that Petrovich at last brought the overcoat. He brought it in the morning, just before it was time to set off for the department. The overcoat could not have arrived at a more opportune time, because severe frosts were just beginning and seemed threatening to become even harsher. Petrovich brought the coat himself as a good tailor should. There was an expression of importance on his face, such as Akaky Akakievich had never seen there before. He seemed fully conscious of having completed a work of no little importance and of having shown by his own example the gulf that separates tailors who only put in linings and do repairs from those who make new coats. He took the coat out of the huge handkerchief in which he had brought it (the handkerchief had just come home from the wash); he then folded it up and put it in his pocket for future use. After taking out the overcoat, he looked at it with much pride and holding it in both hands, threw it very deftly over Akaky Akakievich's shoulders, then pulled it down and smoothed it out behind with his hands; then draped it about Akaky Akakievich somewhat jauntily. Akaky Akakievich, a practical man, wanted to try it with his arms in the sleeves. Petrovich helped him to put it on, and it looked splendid with his arms in the sleeves, too. In fact, it turned out that the overcoat was completely and entirely successful. Petrovich did not let slip the occasion for observing that it was only because he lived in a small street and had no signboard, and because he had known Akaky Akakievich so long, that he had done it so cheaply, and that on Nevsky Prospekt they would have asked him seventy-five rubles for the tailoring alone. Akaky Akakievich had no inclination to discuss this with Petrovich; besides he was frightened of the big sums that Petrovich was fond of flinging airily about in conversation. He paid him, thanked him, and went off, with his new overcoat on, to the department. Petrovich followed him out and stopped in the street, staring for a long time at the coat from a distance and then purposely turned off and, taking a short cut through a side street, came back into the street, and got another view of the coat from the other side, that is, from the front.

Meanwhile Akaky Akakievich walked along in a gay holiday mood. Every second he was conscious that he had a new overcoat on his shoulders, and several times he actually laughed from inward satisfaction. Indeed, it had two advantages: one that it was warm and the other that it was good. He did not notice how far he had walked at all and he suddenly found himself in the department; in the porter's room he took off the overcoat, looked it over, and entrusted it to the porter's special care. I cannot tell how it happened, but all at once everyone in the department learned that Akaky Akakievich had a new overcoat and that the "dressing gown" no longer existed. They all ran out at once into the cloakroom to look at Akaky Akakievich's new overcoat; they began welcoming him and congratulating him so that at first he could do nothing but smile and then felt positively embarrassed. When, coming up to him, they all began saying that he must "sprinkle" the new overcoat and that he ought at least to buy them all a supper, Akaky Akakievich lost his head completely and did not know what to do, how to get out of it, nor what to answer. A few minutes later, flushing crimson, he even began assuring them with great simplicity that it was not a new overcoat at all, that it wasn't much, that it was an old overcoat. At last one of the clerks, indeed the assistant of the head clerk of the room, probably in order to show that he wasn't too proud to mingle with those beneath him, said: "So be it, I'll give a party instead of Akaky Akakievich and invite you all to tea with me this evening; as luck would have it, it is my birthday." The clerks naturally congratulated the assistant head clerk and eagerly accepted the invitation. Akaky Akakievich was beginning to make excuses, but they all declared that it was uncivil of him, that it would be simply a shame and a disgrace that he could not possibly refuse. So, he finally relented, and later felt pleased about it when he remembered that through this he would have the opportunity of going out in the evening, too, in his new overcoat. That whole day was for Akaky Akakievich the most triumphant and festive day in his life. He returned home in the happiest frame of mind, took off the overcoat, and hung it carefully on the wall, admiring the cloth and lining once more, and then pulled out his old "dressing gown," now completely falling apart, and put it next to his new overcoat to compare the two. He glanced at it and laughed: the difference was enormous! And long afterwards he went on laughing at dinner, as the position in which the "dressing gown" was placed recurred to his mind. He dined in excellent spirits and after dinner wrote nothing, no papers at all, but just relaxed for a little while on his bed, till it got dark; then, without putting things off, he dressed, put on his overcoat, and went out into the street. Where precisely the clerk who had invited him lived we regret to say we cannot tell; our memory is beginning to fail sadly, and everything there in Petersburg, all the streets and houses, are so blurred and muddled in our head that it is a very difficult business to put anything in orderly fashion. Regardless of that, there is no doubt that the clerk lived in the better part of the town and consequently a very long distance from Akaky Akakievich. At first Akaky Akakievich had to walk through deserted streets, scantily lighted, but as he approached his destination the streets became more lively, more full of people, and more brightly lighted; passersby began to be more frequent, ladies began to appear, here and there beautifully dressed, and beaver collars were to be seen on the men. Cabmen with wooden, railed sledges, studded with brass-topped nails, were less frequently seen; on the other hand, jaunty drivers in raspberry-colored velvet caps, with lacquered sledges and bearskin rugs, appeared and carriages with decorated boxes dashed along the streets, their wheels crunching through the snow.

Akaky Akakievich looked at all this as a novelty; for several years he had not gone out into the streets in the evening. He stopped with curiosity before a lighted shop window to look at a picture in which a beautiful woman was represented in the act of taking off her shoe and displaying as she did so the whole of a very shapely leg, while behind her back a gentleman with whiskers and a handsome imperial on his chin was sticking his head in at the door. Akaky Akakievich shook his head and smiled and then went on his way. Why did he smile? Was it because he had come across something quite unfamiliar to him, though every man retains some instinctive feeling on the subject, or was it that he reflected, like many other clerks, as follows: "Well, those Frenchmen! It's beyond anything! If they go in for anything of the sort, it really is . . . !" Though possibly he did not even think that; there is no creeping into a man's soul and finding out all that he thinks. At last he reached the house in which the assistant head clerk lived in fine style; there was a lamp burning on the stairs, and the apartment was on the second floor. As he went into the hall Akaky Akakievich saw rows of galoshes. Among them in the middle of the room stood a hissing samovar puffing clouds of steam. On the walls hung coats and cloaks among which some actually had beaver collars or velvet lapels. From the other side of the wall there came noise and talk, which suddenly became clear and loud when the door opened and the footman came out with a tray full of empty glasses, a jug of cream, and a basket of biscuits. It was evident that the clerks had arrived long before and had already drunk their first glass of tea. Akaky Akakievich, after hanging up his coat with his own hands, went into the room, and at the same moment there flashed before his eyes a vision of candles, clerks, pipes, and card tables, together with the confused sounds of conversation rising up on all sides and the noise of moving chairs. He stopped very awkwardly in the middle of the room, looking about and trying to think of what to do, but he was noticed and received with a shout and they all went at once into the hall and again took a look at his overcoat. Though Akaky Akakievich was somewhat embarrassed, yet, being a simple-hearted man, he could not help being pleased at seeing how they all admired his coat. Then of course they all abandoned him and his coat, and turned their attention as usual to the tables set for whist. All this — the noise, the talk, and the crowd of people — was strange and wonderful to Akaky Akakievich. He simply did not know how to behave, what to do with his arms and legs and his whole body; at last he sat down beside the players, looked at the cards, stared first at one and then at another of the faces, and in a little while, feeling bored, began to yawn — especially since it was long past the time at which he usually went to bed. He tried to say goodbye to his hosts, but they would not let him go, saying that he absolutely must have a glass of champagne in honor of the new coat. An hour later supper was served, consisting of salad, cold veal, pastry and pies from the bakery, and champagne. They made Akaky Akakievich drink two glasses, after which he felt that things were much more cheerful, though he could not forget that it was twelve o'clock, and that he ought to have been home long ago. That his host might not take it into his head to detain him, he slipped out of the room, hunted in the hall for his coat, which he found, not without regret, lying on the floor, shook it, removed some fluff from it, put it on, and went down the stairs into the street. It was still light in the streets. Some little grocery shops, those perpetual clubs for servants and all sorts of people, were open; others which were closed showed, however, a long streak of light at every crack of the door, proving that they were not yet deserted, and probably maids and menservants were still finishing their conversation and discussion, driving their masters to utter perplexity as to their whereabouts. Akaky Akakievich walked along in a cheerful state of mind; he was even on the point of running, goodness knows why, after a lady of some sort who passed by like lightning with every part of her frame in violent motion. He checked himself at once, however, and again walked along very gently, feeling positively surprised at the inexplicable impulse that had seized him. Soon the deserted streets, which are not particularly cheerful by day and even less so in the evening, stretched before him. Now they were still more dead and deserted; the light of street lamps was scantier, the oil evidently running low; then came wooden houses and fences; not a soul anywhere; only the snow gleamed on the streets and the low-pitched slumbering hovels looked black and gloomy with their closed shutters. He approached the spot where the street was intersected by an endless square, which looked like a fearful desert with its houses scarcely visible on the far side.

In the distance, goodness knows where, there was a gleam of light from some sentry box which seemed to be at the end of the world. Akaky Akakievich's lightheartedness faded. He stepped into the square, not without uneasiness, as though his heart had a premonition of evil. He looked behind him and to both sides—it was as though the sea were all around him. "No, better not look," he thought, and walked on, shutting his eyes, and when he opened them to see whether the end of the square was near, he suddenly saw standing before him, almost under his very nose, some men with mustaches; just what they were like he could not even distinguish. There was a mist before his eyes, and a throbbing in his chest. "Why, that overcoat is mine!" said one of them in a voice like a clap of thunder, seizing him by the collar. Akaky Akakievich was on the point of shouting "Help" when another put a fist the size of a clerk's head against his lips, saying: "You just shout now." Akaky Akakievich felt only that they took the overcoat off, and gave him a kick with their knees, and he fell on his face in the snow and was conscious of nothing more. A few minutes later he recovered consciousness and got up on his feet, but there was no one there. He felt that it was cold on the ground and that he had no overcoat, and began screaming, but it seemed as though his voice would not carry to the end of the square. Overwhelmed with despair and continuing to scream, he ran across the square straight to the sentry box beside which stood a policeman leaning on his halberd and, so it seemed, looking with curiosity to see who the devil the man was who was screaming and running toward him from the distance. As Akaky Akakievich reached him, he began breathlessly shouting that he was asleep and not looking after his duty not to see that a man was being robbed. The policeman answered that he had seen nothing, that he had only seen him stopped in the middle of the square by two men, and supposed that they were his friends, and that, instead of abusing him for nothing, he had better go the next day to the police inspector, who would certainly find out who had taken the overcoat. Akaky Akakievich ran home in a terrible state: his hair, which was still comparatively abundant on his temples and the back of his head, was completely disheveled; his sides and chest and his trousers were all covered with snow. When his old landlady heard a fearful knock at the door, she jumped hurriedly out of bed and, with only one slipper on, ran to open it, modestly holding her chemise over her bosom; but when she opened it she stepped back, seeing in what a state Akaky Akakievich was. When he told her what had happened, she clasped her hands in horror and said that he must go straight to the district commissioner, because the local police inspector would deceive him, make promises, and lead him a dance; that it would be best of all to go to the district commissioner, and that she knew him, because Anna, the Finnish girl who was once her cook, was now in service as a nurse at the commissioner's; and that she often saw him himself when he passed by their house, and that he used to be every Sunday at church too, saying his prayers and at the same time looking good-humoredly at everyone, and that therefore by every token he must be a kindhearted man. After listening to this advice, Akaky Akakievich made his way very gloomily to his room, and how he spent that night I leave to the imagination of those who are in the least able to picture the position of others.

Early in the morning he set off to the police commissioner's but was told that he was asleep. He came at ten o'clock, he was told again that he was asleep; he came at eleven and was told that the commissioner was not at home; he came at dinnertime, but the clerks in the anteroom would not let him in, and insisted on knowing what was the matter and what business had brought him and exactly what had happened; so that at last Akaky Akakievich for the first time in his life tried to show the strength of his character and said curtly that he must see the commissioner himself, and they dare not refuse to admit him, that he had come from the department on government business, and that if he made complaint of them they would see. The clerks dared say nothing to this, and one of them went to summon the commissioner. The latter received his story of being robbed of his overcoat in an extremely peculiar manner. Instead of attending to the main point, he began asking Akaky Akakievich questions: why had he been coming home so late? wasn't he going, or hadn't he been, to some bawdy house? so that Akaky Akakievich was overwhelmed with confusion, and went away without knowing whether or not the proper measures would be taken regarding his overcoat. He was absent from the office all that day (the only time that it had happened in his life). Next day he appeared with a pale face, wearing his old "dressing gown," which had become a still more pitiful sight. The news of the theft of the overcoat—though there were clerks who did not let even this chance slip of jeering at Akaky Akakievich—touched many of them. They decided on the spot to get up a collection for him, but collected only a very trifling sum, because the clerks had already spent a good deal contributing to the director's portrait and on the purchase of a book, at the suggestion of the head of their department, who was a friend of the author, and so the total realized was very insignificant. One of the clerks, moved by compassion, ventured at any rate to assist Akaky Akakievich with good advice, telling him not to go to the local police inspector, because, though it might happen that the latter might succeed in finding his overcoat because he wanted to impress his superiors, it would remain in the possession of the police unless he presented legal proofs that it belonged to him; he urged that by far the best thing would be to appeal to a Person of Consequence; that the Person of Consequence, by writing and getting into communication with the proper authorities, could push the matter through more successfully. There was nothing else to do. Akaky Akakievich made up his mind to go to the Person of Consequence. What precisely was the nature of the functions of the Person of Consequence has remained a matter of uncertainty. It must be noted that this Person of Consequence had only lately become a person of consequence, and until recently had been a person of no consequence. Though, indeed, his position even now was not reckoned of consequence in comparison with others of still greater consequence. But there is always to be found a circle of persons to whom a person of little consequence in the eyes of others is a person of consequence. It is true that he did his utmost to increase the consequence of his position in various ways, for instance by insisting that his subordinates should come out onto the stairs to meet him when he arrived at his office; that no one should venture to approach him directly but all proceedings should follow the strictest chain of command; that a collegiate registrar should report the matter to the governmental secretary; and the governmental secretary to the titular councilors or whomsoever it might be, and that business should only reach him through this channel. Everyone in Holy Russia has a craze for imitation; everyone apes and mimics his superiors. I have actually been told that a titular councilor who was put in charge of a small separate office, immediately partitioned off a special room for himself, calling it the head office, and posted lackeys at the door with red collars and gold braid, who took hold of the handle of the door and opened it for everyone who went in, though the "head office" was so tiny that it was with difficulty that an ordinary writing desk could be put into it. The manners and habits of the Person of Consequence were dignified and majestic, but hardly subtle. The chief foundation of his system was strictness; "strictness, strictness, and—strictness!" he used to say, and at the last word he would look very significantly at the person he was addressing, though, indeed, he had no reason to do so, for the dozen clerks who made up the whole administrative mechanism of his office stood in appropriate awe of him; any clerk who saw him in the distance would leave his work and remain standing at attention till his superior had left the room. His conversation with his subordinates was usually marked by severity and almost confined to three phrases: "How dare you? Do you know to whom you are speaking? Do you understand who I am?" He was, however, at heart a good-natured man, pleasant and obliging with his colleagues; but his advancement to a high rank had completely turned his head. When he received it, he was perplexed, thrown off his balance, and quite at a loss as to how to behave. If he chanced to be with his equals, he was still quite a decent man, a very gentlemanly man, in fact, and in many ways even an intelligent man; but as soon as he was in company with men who were even one grade below him, there was simply no doing anything with him: he sat silent and his position excited compassion, the more so as he himself felt that he might have been spending his time to so much more advantage. At times there could be seen in his eyes an intense desire to join in some interesting conversation, but he was restrained by the doubt whether it would not be too much on his part, whether it would not be too great a familiarity and lowering of his dignity, and in consequence of these reflections he remained everlastingly in the same mute condition, only uttering from time to time monosyllabic sounds, and in this way he gained the reputation of being a terrible bore.

So this was the Person of Consequence to whom our friend Akaky Akakievich appealed, and he appealed to him at a most unpropitious moment, very unfortunate for himself, though fortunate, indeed, for the Person of Consequence. The latter happened to be in his study, talking in the very best of spirits with an old friend of his childhood who had only just arrived and whom he had not seen for several years. It was at this moment that he was informed that a man called Bashmachkin was asking to see him. He asked abruptly, "What sort of man is he?" and received the answer, "A government clerk." Ah! he can wait. I haven't time now," said the Person of Consequence. Here I must observe that this was a complete lie on the part of the Person of Consequence; he had time; his friend and he had long ago said all they had to say to each other and their conversation had begun to be broken by very long pauses during which they merely slapped each other on the knee, saying, "So that's how things are, Ivan Abramovich!"—"So that's it, Stepan Varlamovich!" but, despite that, he told the clerk to wait in order to show his friend, who had left the civil service some years before and was living at home in the country, how long clerks had to wait for him. At last, after they had talked or rather been silent, to their heart's content and had smoked a cigar in very comfortable armchairs with sloping backs, he seemed suddenly to recollect, and said to the secretary, who was standing at the door with papers for his signature: "Oh, by the way, there is a clerk waiting, isn't there? tell him he can come in." When he saw Akaky Akakievich's meek appearance and old uniform, he turned to him at once and said: "What do you want?" in a firm and abrupt voice, which he had purposely rehearsed in his own room in solitude before the mirror for a week before receiving his present post and the grade of a general. Akaky Akakievich, who was overwhelmed with appropriate awe beforehand, was somewhat confused and, as far as his tongue would allow him, explained to the best of his powers, with even more frequent "ers" than usual, that he had had a perfectly new overcoat and now he had been robbed of it in the most inhuman way, and that now he had come to beg him by his intervention either to correspond with his honor, the head police commissioner, or anybody else, and find the overcoat. This mode of proceeding struck the general for some reason as too familiar. "What next, sir?" he went on abruptly. "Don't you know the way to proceed? To whom are you addressing yourself? Don't you know how things are done? You ought first to have handed in a petition to the office; it would have gone to the head clerk of the room, and to the head clerk of the section; then it would have been handed to the secretary and the secretary would have brought it to me. . . ."

"But, your Excellency," said Akaky Akakievich, trying to gather the drop of courage he possessed and feeling at the same time that he was perspiring all over, "I ventured, your Excellency, to trouble you because secretaries . . . er . . . are people you can't depend on. . . ."

"What? what? what?" said the Person of Consequence, "where did you get hold of that attitude? where did you pick up such ideas? What insubordination is spreading among young men against their superiors and their chiefs!" The Person of Consequence did not apparently observe that Akaky Akakievich was well over fifty, and therefore if he could have been called a young man it would only have been in comparison to a man of seventy. "Do you know to whom you are speaking? Do you understand who I am? Do you understand that, I ask you?" At this point he stamped, and raised his voice to such a powerful note that Akaky Akakievich was not the only one to be terrified. Akaky Akakievich was positively petrified; he staggered, trembling all over, and could not stand; if the porters had not run up to support him, he would have flopped on the floor; he was led out almost unconscious. The Person of Consequence, pleased that the effect had surpassed his expectations and enchanted at the idea that his words could even deprive a man of consciousness, stole a sideway glance at his friend to see how he was taking it, and perceived not without satisfaction that his friend was feeling very uncertain and even beginning to be a little terrified himself.

How he got downstairs, how he went out into the street—of all that Akaky Akakievich remembered nothing; he had no feeling in his arms or his legs. In all his life he had never been so severely reprimanded by a general, and this was by one of another department, too. He went out into the snowstorm that was whistling through the streets, with his mouth open, and as he went he stumbled off the pavement; the wind, as its way is in Petersburg, blew upon him from all points of the compass and from every side street. In an instant it had blown a quinsy into his throat, and when he got home he was not able to utter a word; he went to bed with a swollen face and throat. That's how violent the effects of an appropriate reprimand can be!

Next day he was in a high fever. Thanks to the gracious assistance of the Petersburg climate, the disease made more rapid progress than could have been expected, and when the doctor came, after feeling his pulse he could find nothing to do but prescribe a poultice, and that simply so that the patient might not be left without the benefit of medical assistance; however, two days later he informed him that his end was at hand, after which he turned to Akaky Akakievich's landlady and said: "And you had better lose no time, my good woman, but order him now a pine coffin, for an oak one will be too expensive for him." Whether Akaky Akakievich heard these fateful words or not, whether they produced a shattering effect upon him, and whether he regretted his pitiful life, no one can tell, for he was constantly in delirium and fever. Apparitions, each stranger than the one before, were continually haunting him: first he saw Petrovich and was ordering him to make an overcoat trimmed with some sort of traps for robbers, who were, he believed, continually under the bed, and he was calling his landlady every minute to pull out a thief who had even got under the quilt; then he kept asking why his old "dressing gown" was hanging before him when he had a new overcoat; then he thought he was standing before the general listening to the appropriate reprimand and saying, "I am sorry, your Excellency"; then finally he became abusive, uttering the most awful language, so that his old landlady positively crossed herself, having never heard anything of the kind from him before, and the more horrified because these dreadful words followed immediately upon the phrase "your Excellency." Later on, his talk was merely a medley of nonsense, so that it was quite unintelligible; all that was evident was that his incoherent words and thoughts were concerned with nothing but the overcoat. At last poor Akaky Akakievich gave up the ghost. No seal was put upon his room nor upon his things, because, in the first place, he had no heirs and, in the second, the property left was very small, to wit, a bundle of quills, a quire of white government paper, three pairs of socks, two or three buttons that had come off his trousers, and the "dressing gown" with which the reader is already familiar. Who came into all his wealth God only knows; even I who tell the tale must admit that I have not bothered to inquire. And Petersburg carried on without Akaky Akakievich, as though, indeed, he had never been in the city. A creature had vanished and departed whose cause no one had championed, who was dear to no one, of interest to no one, who never attracted the attention of a naturalist, though the latter does not disdain to fix a common fly upon a pin and look at him under the microscope—a creature who bore patiently the jeers of the office and for no particular reason went to his grave, though even he at the very end of his life was visited by an exalted guest in the form of an overcoat that for one instant brought color into his poor, drab life—a creature on whom disease fell as it falls upon the heads of the mighty ones of this world . . . !

Several days after his death, a messenger from the department was sent to his lodgings with instructions that he should go at once to the office, for his chief was asking for him; but the messenger was obliged to return without him, explaining that he could not come, and to the inquiry "Why?" he added, "Well, you see, the fact is he is dead; he was buried three days ago." This was how they learned at the office of the death of Akaky Akakievich, and the next day there was sitting in his seat a new clerk who was very much taller and who wrote not in the same straight handwriting but made his letters more slanting and crooked.

But who could have imagined that this was not all there was to tell about Akaky Akakievich, that he was destined for a few days to make his presence felt in the world after his death, as though to make up for his life having been unnoticed by anyone? But so it happened, and our little story unexpectedly finishes with a fantastic ending.

Rumors were suddenly floating about Petersburg that in the neighborhood of the Kalinkin Bridge and for a little distance beyond, a corpse had begun appearing at night in the form of a clerk looking for a stolen overcoat, and stripping from the shoulders of all passers-by, regardless of grade and calling, overcoats of all descriptions—trimmed with cat fur or beaver or padded, lined with raccoon, fox, and bear—made, in fact of all sorts of skin which men have adapted for the covering of their own. One of the clerks of the department saw the corpse with his own eyes and at once recognized it as Akaky Akakievich; but it excited in him such terror that he ran away as fast as his legs could carry him and so could not get a very clear view of him, and only saw him hold up his finger threateningly in the distance.

From all sides complaints were continually coming that backs and shoulders, not of mere titular councilors, but even of upper court councilors, had been exposed to catching cold, as a result of being stripped of their overcoats. Orders were given to the police to catch the corpse regardless of trouble or expense, dead or alive, and to punish him severely, as an example to others, and, indeed, they very nearly succeeded in doing so. The policeman of one district in Kiryushkin Alley snatched a corpse by the collar on the spot of the crime in the very act of attempting to snatch a frieze overcoat from a retired musician, who used, in his day, to play the flute. Having caught him by the collar, he shouted until he had brought two other policemen whom he ordered to hold the corpse while he felt just a minute in his boot to get out a snuffbox in order to revive his nose which had six times in his life been frostbitten, but the snuff was probably so strong that not even a dead man could stand it. The policeman had hardly had time to put his finger over his right nostril and draw up some snuff in the left when the corpse sneezed violently right into the eyes of all three. While they were putting their fists up to wipe their eyes, the corpse completely vanished, so that they were not even sure whether he had actually been in their hands. From that time forward, the policemen had such a horror of the dead that they were even afraid to seize the living and confined themselves to shouting from the distance. "Hey, you! Move on!" and the clerk's body began to appear even on the other side of the Kalinkin Bridge, terrorizing all timid people.

We have, however, quite neglected the Person of Consequence, who may in reality almost be said to be the cause of the fantastic ending of this perfectly true story. To begin with, my duty requires me to do justice to the Person of Consequence by recording that soon after poor Akaky Akakievich had gone away crushed to powder, he felt something not unlike regret. Sympathy was a feeling not unknown to him; his heart was open to many kindly impulses, although his exalted grade very often prevented them from being shown. As soon as his friend had gone out of his study, he even began brooding over poor Akaky Akakievich, and from that time forward, he was almost every day haunted by the image of the poor clerk who had been unable to survive the official reprimand. The thought of the man so worried him that a week later he actually decided to send a clerk to find out how he was and whether he really could help him in any way. And when they brought him word that Akaky Akakievich had died suddenly in a delirium and fever, it made a great impression on him; his conscience reproached him and he was depressed all day. Anxious to distract his mind and to forget the unpleasant incident, he went to spend the evening with one of his friends, where he found respectable company, and what was best of all, almost everyone was of the same grade so that he was able to be quite uninhibited. This had a wonderful effect on his spirits. He let himself go, became affable and genial—in short, spent a very agreeable evening. At supper he drank a couple of glasses of champagne—a proceeding which we all know is not a bad recipe for cheerfulness. The champagne made him inclined to do something unusual, and he decided not to go home yet but to visit a lady of his acquaintance, a certain Karolina Ivanovna—a lady apparently of German extraction, for whom he entertained extremely friendly feelings. It must be noted that the Person of Consequence was a man no longer young. He was an excellent husband, and the respectable father of a family. He had two sons, one already serving in an office, and a nice-looking daughter of sixteen with a rather turned-up, pretty little nose, who used to come every morning to kiss his hand, saying: "*Bon jour, Papa.*" His wife, who was still blooming and decidedly good-looking, indeed, used first to give him her hand to kiss and then turning his hand over would kiss it. But though the Person of Consequence was perfectly satisfied with the pleasant amenities of his domestic life, he thought it proper to have a lady friend in another quarter of the town. This lady friend was not a bit better looking nor younger than his wife, but these puzzling things exist in the world and it is not our business to criticize them. And so the Person of Consequence went downstairs, got into his sledge, and said to his coachman, "To Karolina Ivanovna." While luxuriously wrapped in his warm fur coat he remained in that agreeable frame of mind sweeter to a Russian than anything that could be invented, that is, when one thinks of nothing while thoughts come into the mind by themselves, one pleasanter than the other, without your having to bother following them or looking for them. Full of satisfaction, he recalled all the amusing moments of the evening he had spent, all the phrases that had started the intimate circle of friends laughing; many of them he repeated in an undertone and found then as amusing as before, and so, very naturally, laughed very heartily at them again. From time to time, however, he was disturbed by a gust of wind which, blowing suddenly, God knows why or where from, cut him in the face, pelting him with flakes of snow, puffing out his coat collar like a sail, or suddenly flinging it with unnatural force over his head and giving him endless trouble to extricate himself from it. All at once, the Person of Consequence felt that someone had clutched him very tightly by the collar. Turning around he saw a short man in a shabby old uniform, and not without horror recognized him as Akaky Akakievich. The clerk's face was white as snow and looked like that of a corpse, but the horror of the Person of Consequence was beyond all bounds when he saw the mouth of the corpse distorted into speech, and breathing upon him the chill of the grave, it uttered, the following words: "Ah, so here you are at last! At last I've . . . er . . . caught you by the collar. It's your overcoat I want; you refused to help me and abused me in the bargain! So now give me yours!" The poor Person of Consequence very nearly dropped dead. Resolute and determined as he was in his office and before subordinates in general, and though anyone looking at his manly air and figure would have said: "Oh, what a man of character!" yet in this situation he felt, like very many persons of heroic appearance, such terror that not without reason he began to be afraid he would have some sort of fit. He actually flung his overcoat off his shoulders as far as he could and shouted to his coachman in an unnatural voice: "Drive home! Let's get out of here!" The coachman, hearing the tone which he had only heard in critical moments and then accompanied by something even more tangible, hunched his shoulders up to his ears in case of worse following, swung his whip, and flew on like an arrow. In a little over six minutes, the Person of Consequence was at the entrance of his own house. Pale, panic-stricken, and without his overcoat, he arrived home instead of at Karolina Ivanovna's, dragged himself to his own room, and spent the night in great distress, so that next morning his daughter said to him at breakfast, "You look very pale today, Papa"; but her papa remained mute and said not a word to anyone of what had happened to him, where he had been, and where he had been going. The incident made a great impression upon him. Indeed, it happened far more rarely that he said to his subordinates, "How dare you? Do you understand who I am?" and he never uttered those words at all until he had first heard all the facts of the case.

What was even more remarkable is that from that time on the apparition of the dead clerk ceased entirely; apparently the general's overcoat had fitted him perfectly; anyway nothing more was heard of overcoats being snatched from anyone. Many restless and anxious people refused, however, to be pacified, and still maintained that in remote parts of the town the dead clerk went on appearing. One policeman, in Kolomna, for instance, saw with his own eyes an apparition appear from behind a house; but, being by natural constitution somewhat frail—so much so that on one occasion an ordinary grown-up suckling pig, making a sudden dash out of some private building, knocked him off his feet to the great amusement of the cabmen standing around, whom he fined two kopeks each for snuff for such disrespect—he did not dare to stop it, and so followed it in the dark until the apparition suddenly looked around and, stopping, asked him: "What do you want?" displaying a huge fist such as you never see among the living. The policeman said: "Nothing," and turned back on the spot. This apparition, however, was considerably taller and adorned with immense mustaches, and, directing its steps apparently toward Obukhov Bridge, vanished into the darkness of the night.

[1840]

Translated by
CONSTANCE GARNETT

QUESTIONS

1. How is Akaky characterized? On what basis does the reader sympathize with him? What is the narrator's attitude toward him? Why is he ridiculed by his office associates?
2. How would you describe the tone of the story? How does it contribute to one's understanding of Akaky's plight?
3. What does the overcoat symbolize?
4. How do the fantastic elements of the story's ending contribute to its meaning? What would be lost if the story ended with Akaky's death?
5. What does the story suggest about bureaucracy? About social justice? About the human condition?

Nadine Gordimer

(b. 1923)

South Africa

In an interview published in *Women Writers Talk* (1989), edited by Olga Kenyon, Nadine Gordimer had this to say about the political evolution of South Africa:

> [T]here are some extraordinary black and white people who are prepared to take a Pascalian wager on the fact that there is a way, that there must be a way. It goes beyond polarisation, it cannot happen while the situation is what it is. It can only be *after* the power structure has changed. But the fact is that if whites want to go on living in South Africa, they have to change. It's not a matter of just letting blacks in—white life is already dead, over. The big question is, given the kind of conditioning we've had for 300 years, is it possible to strike that down and make a common culture with the blacks?

Since 1953, when she published *The Lying Days*, her first novel, Nadine Gordimer has been aligned with the liberal white consciousness of South Africa. She was born in the Transvaal in 1923. Her father was a shopkeeper, her mother a housewife. A childhood illness kept Gordimer out of school until she was 14, by which time she was already an avid reader. By 15 she had published her first short story. It was not until she was somewhat older that she became aware of the South African political situation, and it was not until she was 30 that her first novel was published. Beginning with *A World of Strangers* (1958), Gordimer's novels focus directly on the South African racial situation. The most famous of these works include *A Guest of Honor* (1970), *The Conservationist* (1974), *Burger's Daughter* (1979), *July's People* (1981), *A Sport of Nature* (1987), and *My Son's Story* (1990). Gordimer has also published 10 volumes of short stories, as well as several volumes of nonfiction. She was awarded the Nobel Prize for literature in 1991.

Asked by Olga Kenyon what it means to be a white South African, Gordimer replied,

> You have to show that you support change. In my case that you support a complete revolution, if possible a peaceful one. I use revolution in a broad sense, a complete change of the whole political organisation, from grass roots. It's not enough for a white to say "Right, I'll be prepared to live under black majority rule," and sit back, waiting for it to come. You also have to work positively, in whatever way you can, as a human being.

A Soldier's Embrace

The day the cease-fire was signed she was caught in a crowd. Peasant boys from Europe who had made up the colonial army and freedom fighters whose column had marched into town were staggering about together outside the barracks, not three blocks from her house in whose rooms, for ten years, she had heard the blurred parade-ground bellow of colonial troops being trained to kill and be killed.

The men weren't drunk. They linked and swayed across the street; because all that had come to a stop, everything *had* to come to a stop: they surrounded cars, bicycles, vans, nannies with children, women with loaves of bread or basins of mangoes on their heads, a road gang with picks and shovels, a Coca-Cola truck, an old man with a barrow who bought bottles and bones. They were grinning and laughing amazement. That it could be: there they were, bumping into each other's bodies in joy, looking into each other's rough faces, all eyes crescent-shaped, brimming greeting. The words were in languages not mutually comprehensible, but the cries were new, a whooping and crowing all understood. She was bumped and jostled and she let go, stopped trying to move in any self-determined direction. There were two soldiers in front of her, blocking her off by their clumsy embrace (how do you do it, how do you do what you've never done before) and the embrace opened like a door and took her in — a pink hand with bitten nails grasping her right arm, a black hand with a big-dialled watch and thong bracelet pulling at her left elbow. Their three heads collided gaily, musk of sweat and tang of strong sweet soap clapped a mask to her nose and mouth. They all gasped with delicious shock. They were saying things to each other. She put up an arm round each neck, the rough pile of an army haircut on one side, the soft negro hair on the other, and kissed them both on the cheek. The embrace broke. The crowd wove her away behind backs, arms, jogging heads; she was returned to and took up the will of her direction again — she was walking home from the post office, where she had just sent a telegram to relatives abroad: ALL CALM DON'T WORRY.

The lawyer came back early from his offices because the courts were not sitting although the official celebration holiday was not until next day. He described to his wife the rally before the Town Hall, which he had watched from the office-building balcony. One of the guerilla leaders (not the most important; he on whose head the biggest price had been laid would not venture so soon and deep into the territory so newly won) had spoken for two hours from the balcony of the Town Hall. "Brilliant. Their jaws dropped. Brilliant. They've never heard anything on that level: precise, reasoned — none of them would ever have believed it possible, out of the bush. You should have seen de Poorteer's face. He'd like to be able to get up and open his mouth like that. And be listened to like that . . ." The Governor's handicap did not even bring the sympathy accorded to a stammer; he paused and gulped between words. The blacks had always used a portmanteau name for him that meant the-crane-who-is-trying-to-swallow-the-bullfrog.

One of the members of the black underground organization that could now come out in brass-band support of the freedom fighters had recognized the lawyer across from the official balcony and given him the freedom fighters' salute. The lawyer joked about it, miming, full of pride. "You should have been there—should have seen him, up there in the official party. I told you—really—you ought to have come to town with me this morning."

"And what did you do?" She wanted to assemble all details.

"Oh I gave the salute in return, chaps in the street saluted *me* . . . everybody was doing it. *It was marvellous.* And the police standing by; just to think, last month—only last week—you'd have been arrested."

"Like thumbing your nose at them," she said, smiling.

"Did anything go on around here?"

"Muchanga was afraid to go out all day. He wouldn't even run up to the post office for me!" Their servant had come to them many years ago, from service in the house of her father, a colonial official in the Treasury.

"But there was no excitement?"

She told him: "The soldiers and some freedom fighters mingled outside the barracks. I got caught for a minute or two. They were dancing about; you couldn't get through. All very good-natured.—Oh, I sent the cable."

An accolade, one side a white cheek, the other a black. The white one she kissed on the left cheek, the black one on the right cheek, as if these were two sides of one face.

That vision, version, was like a poster; the sort of thing that was soon peeling off dirty shopfronts and bus shelters while the months of wrangling talks preliminary to the take-over by the black government went by.

To begin with, the cheek was not white but pale or rather sallow, the poor boy's pallor of winter in Europe (that draft must have only just arrived and not yet seen service) with homesick pimples sliced off by the discipline of an army razor. And the cheek was not black but opaque peat-dark, waxed with sweat round the plump contours of the nostril. As if she could return to the moment again, she saw what she had not consciously noted: there had been a narrow pink strip in the darkness near the ear, the sort of tender stripe of healed flesh revealed when a scab is nicked off a little before it is ripe. The scab must have come away that morning: the young man picked at it in the troop carrier or truck (whatever it was the freedom fighters had; the colony had been told for years that they were supplied by the Chinese and Russians indiscriminately) on the way to enter the capital in triumph.

According to newspaper reports, the day would have ended for the two young soldiers in drunkenness and whoring. She was, apparently, not yet too old to belong to the soldier's embrace of all that a land-mine in the bush might have exploded for ever. That was one version of the incident. Another: the opportunity taken by a woman not young enough to be clasped in the arms of the one who (same newspaper, while the war was on, expressing the fears of the colonists for their women) would be expected to rape her.

She considered this version.

She had not kissed on the mouth, she had not sought anonymous lips and tongues in the licence of festival. Yet she had kissed. Watching herself again, she knew that. She had—god knows why—kissed them on either cheek, his left, his right. It was deliberate, if a swift impulse: she had distinctly made the move.

She did not tell what happened not because her husband would suspect licence in her, but because he would see her—born and brought up in the country as the daughter of an enlightened white colonial official, married to a white liberal lawyer well known for his defence of blacks in political trials—as giving free expression to liberal principles.

She had not told, she did not know what had happened.

She thought of a time long ago when a school camp had gone to the sea and immediately on arrival everyone had run down to the beach from the train, tripping and tearing over sand dunes of wild fig, aghast with ecstatic shock at the meeting with the water.

De Poorteer was recalled and the lawyer remarked to one of their black friends, "The crane has choked on the bullfrog. I hear that's what they're saying in the Quarter."

The priest who came from the black slum that had always been known simply by that anonymous term did not respond with any sort of glee. His reserve implied it was easy to celebrate; there were people who "shouted freedom too loud all of a sudden."

The lawyer and his wife understood: Father Mulumbua was one who had shouted freedom when it was dangerous to do so, and gone to prison several times for it, while certain people, now on the Interim Council set up to run the country until the new government took over, had kept silent. He named a few, but reluctantly. Enough to confirm their own suspicions—men who perhaps had made some deal with the colonial power to place its interests first, no matter what sort of government might emerge from the new constitution? Yet when the couple plunged into discussion their friend left them talking to each other while he drank his beer and gazed, frowning as if at a headache or because the sunset light hurt his eyes behind his spectacles, round her huge-leaved tropical plants that bowered the terrace in cool humidity.

They had always been rather proud of their friendship with him, this man in a cassock who wore a clenched fist carved of local ebony as well as a silver cross round his neck. His black face was habitually stern—a high seriousness balanced by sudden splurting laughter when they used to tease him over the fist—but never inattentively ill-at-ease.

"What was the matter?" She answered herself; "I had the feeling he didn't want to come here." She was using a paper handkerchief dipped in gin to wipe greenfly off the back of a pale new leaf that had shaken itself from its folds like a cut-out paper lantern.

"Good lord, he's been here hundreds of times."

"—Before, yes."

What things were they saying?

With the shouting in the street and the swaying of the crowd, the sweet powerful presence that confused the senses so that sound, sight, stink (sweat, cheap soap) ran into one tremendous sensation, she could not make out words that came so easily.

Not even what she herself must have said.

A few wealthy white men who had been boastful in their support of the colonial war and knew they would be marked down by the blacks as arch exploiters, left at once. Good riddance, as the lawyer and his wife remarked. Many ordinary white people who had lived contentedly, without questioning its actions, under the colonial government, now expressed an enthusiastic intention to help build a nation, as the newspapers put it. The lawyer's wife's neighbourhood butcher was one. "I don't mind blacks." He was expansive with her, in his shop that he had occupied for twelve years on a licence available only to white people. "Makes no difference to me who you are so long as you're honest." Next to a chart showing a beast mapped according to the cuts of meat it provided, he had hung a picture of the most important leader of the freedom fighters, expected to be first President. People like the butcher turned out with their babies clutching pennants when the leader drove through the town from the airport.

There were incidents (newspaper euphemism again) in the Quarter. It was to be expected. Political factions, tribally based, who had not fought the war, wanted to share power with the freedom fighters' Party. Muchanga no longer went down to the Quarter on his day off. His friends came to see him and sat privately on their hunkers near the garden compost heap. The ugly mansions of the rich who had fled stood empty on the bluff above the sea, but it was said they would make money out of them yet—they would be bought as ambassadorial residencies when independence came, and with it many black and yellow diplomats. Zealots who claimed they belonged to the Party burned shops and houses of the poorer whites who lived, as the lawyer said, "in the inevitable echelon of colonial society," closest to the Quarter. A house in the lawyer's street was noticed by his wife to be accommodating what was certainly one of those families, in the outhouses; green nylon curtains had appeared at the garage window, she reported. The suburb was pleasantly overgrown and well-to-do; no one rich, just white professional people and professors from the university. The barracks was empty now, except for an old man with a stump and a police uniform stripped of insignia, a friend of Muchanga, it turned out, who sat on a beer-crate at the gates. He had lost his job as night-watchman when one of the rich people went away, and was glad to have work.

The street had been perfectly quiet; except for that first day.

The fingernails she sometimes still saw clearly were bitten down until embedded in a thin line of dirt all round, in the pink blunt fingers. The thumb and thick fingertips were turned back coarsely even while grasping her. Such hands had never been allowed to take possession. They were permanently raw, so young, from unloading coal, digging potatoes from the frozen Northern Hemisphere, washing hotel dishes. He had not been killed, and now that day of the cease-fire was over he would be delivered back across the sea to the docks, the stony farm, the scullery of the grand hotel. He would have to do anything he could get. There was unemployment in Europe where he had returned, the army didn't need all the young men any more.

A great friend of the lawyer and his wife, Chipande, was coming home from exile. They heard over the radio he was expected, accompanying the future President as confidential secretary, and they waited to hear from him.

The lawyer put up his feet on the empty chair where the priest had sat, shifting it to a comfortable position by hooking his toes, free in sandals, through the slats. "Imagine, Chipande!" Chipande had been almost a protégé—but they didn't like the term, it smacked of patronage. Tall, cocky, casual Chipande, a boy from the slummiest part of the Quarter, was recommended by the White Fathers' Mission (was it by Father Mulumbua himself?—the lawyer thought so, his wife was not sure they remembered correctly) as a bright kid who wanted to be articled to a lawyer. That was asking a lot, in those days—nine years ago. He never finished his apprenticeship because while he and his employer were soon close friends, and the kid picked up political theories from the books in the house he made free of, he became so involved in politics that he had to skip the country one jump ahead of a detention order signed by the crane-who-was-trying-to-swallow-the-bullfrog.

After two weeks, the lawyer phoned the offices the guerilla-movement-become-Party had set up openly in the town but apparently Chipande had an office in the former colonial secretariat. There he had a secretary of his own; he wasn't easy to reach. The lawyer left a message. The lawyer and his wife saw from the newspaper pictures he hadn't changed much: he had a beard and had adopted the Muslim cap favoured by political circles in exile on the East Coast.

He did come to the house eventually. He had the distracted, insistent friendliness of one who has no time to re-establish intimacy; it must be taken as read. And it must not be displayed. When he remarked on a shortage of accommodation for exiles now become officials, and the lawyer said the house was far too big for two people, he was welcome to move in and regard a self-contained part of it as his private living quarters, he did not answer but went on talking generalities. The lawyer's wife mentioned Father Mulumbua, whom they had not seen since just after the cease-fire. The lawyer added, "There's obviously some sort of big struggle going on, he's fighting for his political life there in the Quarter." "Again," she said, drawing them into a reminder of what had only just become their past.

But Chipande was restlessly following with his gaze the movements of old Muchanga, dragging the hose from plant to plant, careless of the spray; "You remember who this is, Muchanga?" she had said when the visitor arrived, yet although the old man had given, in their own language, the sort of respectful greeting even an elder gives a young man whose clothes and bearing denote rank and authority, he was not in any way overwhelmed nor enthusiastic—perhaps he secretly supported one of the rival factions?

The lawyer spoke of the latest whites to leave the country—people who had got themselves quickly involved in the sort of currency swindle that draws more outrage than any other kind of crime, in a new state fearing the flight of capital: "Let them go, let them go. Good riddance." And he turned to talk of other things—there were so many more important questions to occupy the attention of the three old friends.

But Chipande couldn't stay. Chipande could not stay for supper; his beautiful long velvety black hands with their pale lining (as she thought of the palms) hung impatiently between his knees while he sat forward in the chair, explaining, adamant against persuasion. He should not have been there, even now; he had official business waiting, sometimes he drafted correspondence until one or two in the morning. The lawyer remarked how there hadn't been a proper chance to talk; he wanted to discuss those fellows in the Interim Council Mulumbua was so warily distrustful of—what did Chipande know?

Chipande, already on his feet, said something dismissing and very slightly disparaging, not about the Council members but of Mulumbua—a reference to his connection with the Jesuit missionaries as an influence that "comes through." "But I must make a note to see him sometime."

It seemed that even black men who presented a threat to the Party could be discussed only among black men themselves, now. Chipande put an arm round each of his friends as for the brief official moment of a photograph, left them; he who used to sprawl on the couch arguing half the night before dossing down in the lawyer's pyjamas. "As soon as I'm settled I'll contact you. You'll be around, ay?"

"Oh we'll be around." The lawyer laughed, referring, for his part, to those who were no longer. "Glad to see you're not driving a Mercedes!" he called with reassured affection at the sight of Chipande getting into a modest car. How many times, in the old days, had they agreed on the necessity for African leaders to live simply when they came to power!

On the terrace to which he turned back, Muchanga was doing something extraordinary—wetting a dirty rag with Gilbey's. It was supposed to be his day off, anyway; why was he messing about with the plants when one wanted peace to talk undisturbed?

"Is those thing again, those thing is killing the leaves."

"For heaven's sake, he could use methylated for that! Any kind of alcohol will do! Why don't you get him some?"

There were shortages of one kind and another in the country, and gin happened to be something in short supply.

Whatever the hand had done in the bush had not coarsened it. It, too, was suède-black, and elegant. The pale lining was hidden against her own skin where the hand grasped her left elbow. Strangely, black does not show toil—she remarked this as one remarks the quality of a fabric. The hand was not as long but as distinguished by beauty as Chipande's. The watch a fine piece of equipment for a fighter. There was something next to it, in fact looped over the strap by the angle of the wrist as the hand grasped. A bit of thong with a few beads knotted where it was joined as a bracelet. Or amulet. Their babies wore such things; often their first and only garment. Grandmothers or mothers attached it as protection. It had worked; he was alive at cease-fire. Some had been too deep in the bush to know, and had been killed after the fighting was over. He had pumped his head wildly and laughingly at whatever it was she—they—had been babbling.

The lawyer had more free time than he'd ever remembered. So many of his clients had left; he was deputed to collect their rents and pay their taxes for them, in the hope that their property wasn't going to be confiscated—there had been alarmist rumours among such people since the day of the cease-fire. But without the rich whites there was little litigation over possessions, whether in the form of the children of dissolved marriages or the houses and cars claimed by divorced wives. The Africans had their own ways of resolving such redistribution of goods. And a gathering of elders under a tree was sufficient to settle a dispute over boundaries or argue for and against the guilt of a woman accused of adultery. He had had a message, in a round-about way, that he might be asked to be consultant on constitutional law to the Party, but nothing seemed to come of it. He took home with him the proposals for the draft constitution he had managed to get hold of. He spent whole afternoons in his study making notes for counter or improved proposals he thought he would send to Chipande or one of the other people he knew in high positions: every time he glanced up, there through his open windows was Muchanga's little company at the bottom of the garden. Once, when he saw they had straggled off, he wandered down himself to clear his head (he got drowsy, as he never did when he used to work twelve hours a day at the office). They ate dried shrimps, from the market: that's what they were doing! The ground was full of bitten-off heads and black eyes on stalks. His wife smiled. "They bring them. Muchanga won't go near the market since the riot." "It's ridiculous. Who's going to harm him?"

There was even a suggestion that the lawyer might apply for a professorship at the university. The chair of the Faculty of Law was vacant, since the students had demanded the expulsion of certain professors engaged during the colonial regime—in particular of the fuddy-duddy (good riddance) who had gathered dust in the Law chair, and the quite decent young man (pity about him) who had had Political Science. But what professor of Political Science could expect to survive both a colonial regime and the revolutionary regime that defeated it? The lawyer and his wife decided that since he might still be appointed in some consultative capacity to the new government it would be better to keep out of the university context, where the students were shouting for Africanization, and even an appointee with his credentials as a fighter of legal battles for blacks against the colonial regime in the past might not escape their ire.

Newspapers sent by friends from over the border gave statistics for the number of what they termed "refugees" who were entering the neighbouring country. The papers from outside also featured sensationally the inevitable mistakes and misunderstandings, in a new administration, that led to several foreign businessmen being held for investigation by the new regime. For the last fifteen years of colonial rule, Gulf had been drilling for oil in the territory, and just as inevitably it was certain that all sorts of questionable people, from the point of view of the regime's determination not to be exploited preferentially, below the open market for the highest bidder in ideological as well as economic terms, would try to gain concessions.

His wife said, "The butcher's gone."

He was home, reading at his desk; he could spend the day more usefully there than at the office, most of the time. She had left after breakfast with her fisherman's basket that she liked to use for shopping, she wasn't away twenty minutes. "You mean the shop's closed?" There was nothing in the basket. She must have turned and come straight home.

"Gone. It's empty. He's cleared out over the weekend."

She sat down suddenly on the edge of the desk; and after a moment of silence, both laughed shortly, a strange, secret, complicit laugh. "Why, do you think?" "Can't say. He certainly charged, if you wanted a decent cut. But meat's so hard to get, now; I thought it was worth it—justified."

The lawyer raised his eyebrows and pulled down his mouth: "Exactly." They understood; the man probably knew he was marked to run into trouble for profiteering—he must have been paying through the nose for his supplies on the black market, anyway, didn't have much choice.

Shops were being looted by the unemployed and loafers (there had always been a lot of unemployed hanging around for the pickings of the town) who felt the new regime should entitle them to take what they dared not before. Radio and television shops were the most favoured objective for gangs who adopted the freedom fighters' slogans. Transistor radios were the portable luxuries of street life; the new regime issued solemn warnings, over those same radios, that looting and violence would be firmly dealt with but it was difficult for the police to be everywhere at once. Sometimes their actions became street battles, since the struggle with the looters changed character as supporters of the Party's rival political factions joined in with the thieves against the police. It was necessary to be ready to reverse direction, quickly turning down a side street in detour if one encountered such disturbances while driving around town. There were bodies sometimes; both husband and wife had been fortunate enough not to see any close up, so far. A company of the freedom fighters' army was brought down from the north and installed in the barracks to supplement the police force; they patrolled the Quarter, mainly. Muchanga's friend kept his job as gatekeeper although there were armed sentries on guard: the lawyer's wife found that a light touch to mention in letters to relatives in Europe.

"Where'll you go now?"

She slid off the desk and picked up her basket. "Supermarket, I suppose. Or turn vegetarian." He knew that she left the room quickly, smiling, because she didn't want him to suggest Muchanga ought to be sent to look for fish in the markets along the wharf in the Quarter. Muchanga was being allowed to indulge in all manner of eccentric refusals; for no reason, unless out of some curious sentiment about her father?

She avoided walking past the barracks because of the machine guns the young sentries had in place of rifles. Rifles pointed into the air but machine guns pointed to the street at the level of different parts of people's bodies, short and tall, the backsides of babies slung on mothers' backs, the round heads of children, her fisherman's basket—she knew she was getting like the others: what she felt was afraid. She wondered what the butcher and his wife had said to each other. Because he was at least one whom she had known. He had sold the meat she had bought that these women and their babies passing her in the street didn't have the money to buy.

It was something quite unexpected and outside their own efforts that decided it. A friend over the border telephoned and offered a place in a lawyers' firm of highest repute there, and some prestige in the world at large, since the team had defended individuals fighting for freedom of the press and militant churchmen upholding freedom of conscience on political issues. A telephone call; as simple as that. The friend said (and the lawyer did not repeat this even to his wife) they would be proud to have a man of his courage and convictions in the firm. He could be satisfied he would be able to uphold the liberal principles everyone knew he had always stood for; there were many whites, in that country still ruled by a white minority, who deplored the injustices under which their black population suffered etc. and believed you couldn't ignore the need for peaceful change etc.

His offices presented no problem; something called Africa Seabeds (Formosan Chinese who had gained a concession to ship seaweed and dried shrimps in exchange for rice) took over the lease and the typists. The senior clerks and the current articled clerk (the lawyer had always given a chance to young blacks, long before other people had come round to it—it wasn't only the secretary to the President who owed his start to him) he managed to get employed by the new Trades Union Council; he still knew a few blacks who remembered the times he had acted for black workers in disputes with the colonial government. The house would just have to stand empty, for the time being. It wasn't imposing enough to attract an embassy but maybe it would do for a Chargé d'Affaires—it was left in the hands of a half-caste letting agent who was likely to stay put: only whites were allowed in, at the country over the border. Getting money out was going to be much more difficult than disposing of the house. The lawyer would have to keep coming back, so long as this remained practicable, hoping to find a loophole in exchange control regulations.

She was deputed to engage the movers. In their innocence, they had thought it as easy as that! Every large vehicle, let alone a pantechnicon, was commandeered for months ahead. She had no choice but to grease a palm, although it went against her principles, it was condoning a practice they believed a young black state must stamp out before corruption took hold. He would take his entire legal library, for a start; that was the most important possession, to him. Neither was particularly attached to furniture. She did not know what there was she felt she really could not do without. Except the plants. And that was out of the question. She could not even mention it. She did not want to leave her towering plants, mostly natives of South America and not Africa, she supposed, whose aerial tubes pushed along the terrace brick erect tips extending hourly in the growth of the rainy season, whose great leaves turned shields to the spatter of Muchanga's hose glancing off in a shower of harmless arrows, whose two-hand-span trunks were smooth and grooved in one sculptural sweep down their length, or carved by the drop of each dead leaf-stem with concave medallions marking the place and building a pattern at once bold and exquisite. Such things would not travel; they were too big to give away.

The evening she was beginning to pack the books, the telephone rang in the study. Chipande—and he called her by her name, urgently, commandingly—"What is this all about? Is it true, what I hear? Let me just talk to him—"

"Our friend," she said, making a long arm, receiver at the end of it, towards her husband.

"But you can't leave!" Chipande shouted down the phone. "*You* can't go! I'm coming round. *Now*."

She went on packing the legal books while Chipande and her husband were shut up together in the living-room.

"He cried. You know, he actually cried." Her husband stood in the doorway, alone.

"I know—that's what I've always liked so much about them, whatever they do. They feel."

The lawyer made a face: there it is, it happened; hard to believe.

"Rushing in here, after nearly a year! I said, but we haven't seen you, all this time . . . he took no notice. Suddenly he starts pressing me to take the university job, raising all sorts of objections, why not this . . . that. And then he really wept, for a moment."

They got on with packing books like builder and mate deftly handling and catching bricks.

And the morning they were to leave it was all done; twenty-one years of life in that house gone quite easily into one pantechnicon. They were quiet with each other, perhaps out of apprehension of the tedious search of their possessions that would take place at the border; it was said that if you struck over-conscientious or officious freedom fighter patrols they would even make you unload a piano, a refrigerator or washing machine. She had bought Muchanga a hawker's licence, a hand-cart, and stocks of small commodities. Now that many small shops owned by white shopkeepers had disappeared, there was an opportunity for humble itinerant black traders. Muchanga had lost his fear of the town. He was proud of what she had done for him and she knew he saw himself as a rich merchant; this was the only sort of freedom he understood, after so many years as a servant. But she also knew, and the lawyer sitting beside her in the car knew she knew, that the shortages of the goods Muchanga could sell from his cart, the sugar and soap and matches and pomade and sunglasses, would soon put him out of business. He promised to come back to the house and look after the plants every week; and he stood waving, as he had done every year when they set off on holiday. She did not know what to call out to him as they drove away. The right words would not come again; whatever they were, she left them behind.

[1980]

QUESTIONS

1. Are the lawyer and his wife intended to be sympathetic characters? What about the situation they are caught in?
2. Why do they not have proper names?
3. Why is the wife obsessed with her memory of the embrace? What, actually, does the title mean? Does it refer to one soldier or two?

Judy Grahn

(b. 1940)

United States

The daughter of working-class parents in Chicago, Judy Grahn began writing poetry at the age of 10 but stopped and did not return to writing until years later. In the meantime, she left home at 17 and attended—and left—five different colleges before pursuing study at San Francisco State College. Subsequently, she spent a number of financially impoverished years working at various odd jobs until, after a nearly fatal illness, she began to write poetry seriously. Finding few sources of publication in the 1960s for her poetry, which candidly reflected her lesbian identity, Grahn cofounded and eventually also served as publisher, editor, and printer for the Women's Press Collective in Oakland, California.

Grahn's first volume of poetry, *Edward the Dyke and Other Poems*, was published in 1971. A second volume, *Queen of Wands* (1982), received the American Book Award that year. In 1977 she published a collection of a decade of her poetry. Turning to nonfiction in *Another Mother Tongue: Gay Words, Gay Worlds* (1984), Grahn combined history, autobiography, linguistic inquiry, and storytelling to explore gay and lesbian experience in the past and in contemporary society.

Grahn celebrates female experience through her writing and teaching, hoping to increase public understanding of both lesbian and feminist issues. As she explained to an interviewer, she sees her audience as larger than the lesbian readers of her early work: "I think of myself as a writer who writes *out* from that particular position of being a lesbian and also being a working-class woman from birth, as writing out into the world at large and about lots of women."

♦ Boys at the Rodeo ♦

A lot of people have spent time on some women's farm this summer of 1972 and one day six of us decide to go to the rodeo. We are all mature and mostly in our early thirties. We wear levis and shirts and short hair. Susan has shaved her head.

The man at the gate, who looks like a cousin of the sheriff, is certain we are trying to get in for free. It must have been something in the way we are walking. He stares into Susan's face. "I know you're at least fourteen," he says. He slaps her shoulder, in that comradely way men have with each other. That's when we know he thinks we are boys.

"You're over thirteen," he says to Wendy.

"You're over thirteen," he says to me. He examines each of us closely, and sees only that we have been outdoors, are muscled, and look him directly in the eye. Since we are too short to be men, we must be boys. Everyone else at the rodeo are girls.

We decide to play it straight, so to speak. We make up boys' names for each other. Since Wendy has missed the episode with Susan at the gate, I slap her on the shoulder to demonstrate. "This is what he did." Slam. She never missed a step. It didn't feel bad to me at all. We laugh uneasily. We have achieved the status of fourteen year old boys, what a disguise for travelling through the world. I split into two pieces for the rest of the evening, and have never decided if it is worse to be 31 years old and called a boy or to be 31 years old and called a girl.

Irregardless, we are starved so we decide to eat, and here we have the status of boys for real. It seems to us that all the men and all the women attached to the men and most of the children are eating steak dinner plates; and we are the only women not attached to men. We eat hot dogs, which cost one tenth as much. A man who has taken a woman to the rodeo on this particular day has to have at least $12.00 to spend. So he has charge of all of her money and some of our money too, for we average $3.00 apiece and have taken each other to the rodeo.

Hot dogs in hand we escort ourselves to the wooden stands, and first is the standing up ceremony. We are pledging allegiance for the way of life—the competition, the supposed masculinity and pretty girls. I stand up, cursing, pretending I'm in some other country. One which has not been rediscovered. The loudspeaker plays Anchors Aweigh, that's what I like about rodeos, always something unexpected. At the last one I attended in another state the men on horses threw candy and nuts to the kids, chipping their teeth and breaking their noses. Who is it, I wonder, that has put these guys in charge. Even quiet mothers raged over that episode.

Now it is time for the rodeo queen contest, and a display of four very young women on horses. They are judged for queen 30% on their horse*man*ship and 70% on the number of queen tickets which people bought on their behalf to "elect" them. Talk about stuffed ballot boxes. I notice the winner as usual is the one on the registered thoroughbred whose daddy owns tracts and tracts of something—lumber, minerals, animals. His family name is all over the county.

The last loser sits well on a scrubby little pony and lives with her aunt and uncle. I pick her for the dyke even though it is speculation without clues. I can't help it, it's a pleasant habit. I wish I could give her a ribbon. Not for being a dyke, but for sitting on her horse well. For believing there ever was a contest, for not being the daughter of anyone who owns thousands of acres of anything.

Now the loudspeaker announces the girls' barrel races, which is the only grown women's event. It goes first because it is not really a part of the rodeo, but more like a mildly athletic variation of a parade by women to introduce the real thing. Like us boys in the stand, the girls are simply bearing witness to someone else's act.

The voice is booming that barrel racing is a new, modern event, that these young women are the wives and daughters of cowboys, and barrel racing is a way for them to participate in their own right. How generous of these northern cowboys to have resurrected barrel racing for women and to have forgotten the hard roping and riding which women always used to do in rodeos when I was younger. Even though I was a town child, I heard thrilling rumors of the all-women's rodeo in Texas, including that the finest brahma bull rider in all of Texas was a forty year old woman who weighed a hundred pounds.

Indeed, my first lover's first lover was a big heavy woman who was normally slow as a cold python, but she was just hell when she got up on a horse. She could rope and tie a calf faster than any cowboy within 500 miles of Sweetwater,

Texas. That's what the West Texas dykes said, and they never lied about anything as important to them as calf roping, or the differences between women and men. And what about that news story I had heard recently on the radio, about a bull rider who was eight months pregnant? The newsman just had apoplectic fits over her, but not me. I was proud of her. She makes me think of all of us who have had our insides so overly protected from jarring we cannot possibly get through childbirth without an anesthetic.

While I have been grumbling these thoughts to myself, three barrels have been set up in a big triangle on the field, and the women one by one have raced their horses around each one and back to start. The trick is to turn your horse as sharply as possible without overthrowing the barrel.

After this moderate display, the main bulk of the rodeo begins, with calf roping, bronco riding, bull riding. It's a very male show during which the men demonstrate their various abilities at immobilizing, cornering, maneuvering and conquering cattle of every age.

A rodeo is an interminable number of roped and tied calves, ridden and unridden broncoes. The repetition is broken by a few antics from the agile, necessary clown. His long legs nearly envelope the little jackass he is riding for the satire of it.

After a number of hours they produce an event I have never seen before—goat tying. This is for the girls eleven and twelve. They use one goat for fourteen participants. The goat is supposed to be held in place on a rope by a large man on horseback. Each girl rushes out in a long run half way across the field, grabs the animal, knocks it down, ties its legs together. Sometimes the man lets his horse drift so the goat pulls six or eight feet away from her, something no one would allow to happen in a male event. Many of the girls take over a full minute just to do their tying, and the fact that only one goat has been used makes everybody say, "poor goat, poor goat," and start laughing. This had become the real comedy event of the evening, and the purpose clearly is to show how badly girls do in the rodeo.

Only one has broken through this purpose to the other side. One small girl is not disheartened by the years of bad training, the ridiculous cross-field run, the laughing superior man on his horse, *or* the shape-shifting goat. She downs it in a beautiful flying tackle. This makes me whisper, as usual, "that's the dyke," but for the rest of it we watch the girls look ludicrous, awkward, outclassed and totally dominated by the large handsome man on horse. In the stands we six boys drink beer in disgust, groan and hug our breasts, hold our heads and twist our faces at each other in embarrassment.

As the calf roping starts up again, we decide to use our disguises to walk around the grounds. Making our way around to the cowboy side of the arena, we pass the intricate mazes of rail where the stock is stored, to the chutes where they are loading the bull riders onto the bulls.

I wish to report that although we pass by dozens of men, and although we have pressed against wild horses and have climbed on rails overlooking thousands of pounds of angry animalflesh, though we touch ropes and halters, we are never once warned away, never told that this is not the proper place for us, that we had better get back for our own good, are not safe, etc., none of the dozens of warnings and threats we would have gotten if we had been recognized as thirty one year old girls instead of fourteen year old boys. It is a most interesting way to wander around the world for the day.

We examine everything closely. The brahma bulls are in the chutes, ready to be released into the ring. They are bulky, kindly looking creatures with rolling eyes; they resemble overgrown pigs. One of us whispers, "Aren't those the same kind of cattle that walk around all over the streets in India and never hurt anybody?"

Here in the chutes made exactly their size, they are converted into wild antagonistic beasts by means of a nasty belt around their loins, squeezed tight to mash their most tender testicles just before they are released into the ring. This torture is supplemented by a jolt of electricity from an electric cattle prod to make sure they come out bucking. So much for the rodeo as a great drama between man and nature.

A pale, nervous cowboy sits on the bull's back with one hand in a glove hooked under a strap around the bull's midsection. He gains points by using his spurs during the ride. He has to remain on top until the timing buzzer buzzes a few seconds after he and the bull plunge out of the gate. I had always considered it the most exciting event.

Around the fence sit many eager young men watching, helping, and getting in the way. We are easily accepted among them. How depressing this can be.

Out in the arena a dismounted cowboy reaches over and slaps his horse fiercely on the mouth because it has turned its head the wrong way.

I squat down peering through the rails where I see the neat, tight-fitting pants of two young men standing provocatively chest to chest.

"Don't you think Henry's a queer," one says with contempt.

"Hell, I *know* he's a queer," the other says. They hold an informal spitting contest for the punctuation. Meantime their eyes have brightened and their fronts are moving toward each other in their clean, smooth shirts. I realize they are flirting with each other, using Henry to bring up the dangerous subject of themselves. I am remembering all the gay cowboys I ever knew. This is one of the things I like about cowboys. They don't wear those beautiful pearl button shirts and tight levis for nothing.

As the events inside the arena subside, we walk down to a roped off pavillion where there is a dance. The band consists of one portly, bouncing enthusiastic man of middle age who is singing with great spirit into the microphone. The rest of the band are three grim, lean young men over fourteen. The drummer drums angrily, while jerking his head behind himself as though searching the air for someone who is already two hours late and had seriously promised to take him away from here. The two guitar players are sleepwalking from the feet up with their eyes so glassy you could read by them.

A redhaired man appears, surrounded by redhaired children who ask, "Are you drunk, Daddy?"

"No, I am not drunk," Daddy says.

"Can we have some money?"

"No," Daddy says, "I am not drunk enough to give you any money."

During a break in the music the redhaired man asks the bandleader where he got his band.

"Where did I get this band?" the bandleader puffs up, "I raised this band myself. These are all my sons — I raised this band myself." The redhaired man is so very impressed he is nearly bowing and kissing the hand of the bandleader, as they repeat this conversation two or three times. "This is *my* band," the bandleader says, and the two guitar players exchange grim and glassy looks.

Next the bandleader has announced "Okie From Muskogee," a song intended to portray the white country morality of cowboys. The crowd does not respond but he sings enthusiastically anyway. Two of his more alert sons drag themselves to the microphone to wail that they don't smoke marijuana in Muskogee—as those hippies down in San Francisco do, and they certainly don't. From the look of it they shoot hard drugs and pop pills.

In the middle of the song a very drunk thirteen year old boy has staggered up to Wendy, pounding her on the shoulder and exclaiming, "Can you dig it, brother?" Later she tells me she has never been called brother before, and she likes it. Her first real identification as one of the brothers, in the brotherhood of man.

We boys begin to walk back to our truck, past a cowboy vomiting on his own pretty boots, past another lying completely under a car. Near our truck, a young man has calf-roped a young woman. She shrieks for him to stop, hopping weakly along behind him. This is the first bid for public attention I have seen from any woman here since the barrel race. I understand that this little scene is a re-enactment of the true meaning of the rodeo, and of the conquest of the west. And oh how much I do not want to be her; I do not want to be the conquest of the west.

I am remembering how the clown always seems to be tall and riding on an ass, that must be a way of poking fun at the small and usually dark people who tried to raise sheep or goats or were sod farmers and rode burros instead of tall handsome blond horses, and who were driven under by the beef raisers. And so today we went to a display of cattle handling instead of a sheep shearing or a goat milking contest—or to go into even older ghost territory, a corn dance, or acorn gathering. . . .

As we reach the truck, the tall man passes with the rodeo queen, who must surely be his niece, or something. All this non-contest, if it is for anyone, must certainly be for him. As a boy, I look at him. He is his own spitting image, of what is manly and white and masterly, so tall in his high heels, so *well horsed*. His manner portrays his theory of life as the survival of the fittest against wild beasts, and all the mythical rest of us who are too female or dark, not straight, or much too native to the earth to now be trusted as more than witnesses, flags, cheerleaders and unwilling stock.

As he passes, we step out of the way and I am glad we are in our disguise. I hate to step out of his way as a full grown woman, one who hasn't enough class status to warrant his thinly polite chivalry. He has knocked me off the sidewalk of too many towns, too often.

Yet somewhere in me I know I have always wanted to be manly, what I mean is having that expression of courage, control, coordination, ability I associate with men. To *provide*.

But here I am in this truck, not a man at all, a fourteen year old boy only. Tomorrow is my thirty second birthday. We six snuggle together in the bed of this rickety truck which is our world for the time being. We are headed back to the bold and shakey adventures of our all-women's farm, our all-women's households and companies, our expanding minds, ambitions and bodies, we who are neither male nor female at this moment in the pageant world, who are not the rancher's wife, mother earth, Virgin Mary or the rodeo queen—we who are really the one who took her self seriously, who once took an all out dive at the goat believing that the odds were square and that she was truly in the contest.

And now that we know it is not a contest, just a play—we have run off with the goat ourselves to try another way of life.

Because I certainly do not want to be a 32 year old girl, or calf either, and I certainly also do always remember Gertrude Stein's beautiful dykely voice saying, what is the use of being a boy if you grow up to be a man.

[1978]

QUESTIONS

1. What do the women's disguises as boys enable them to do and see differently at the rodeo? Why? How is their status as "the only women not attached to men" significant?
2. What does the rodeo tradition imply about male and female roles? What does the story suggest about unconventional sexual identities?
3. How does Grahn develop the implicit relationship between the values that predominate at the rodeo and those that prevail in American society as a whole, particularly attitudes concerning race, class, gender roles, and sexual preference?
4. How are such phrases as "conquest of the West" and "survival of the fittest" used in the story?

Jacob and Wilhelm Grimm

(1785–1863; 1786–1859)

Germany

In his introduction to the tales of the Brothers Grimm (Jacob Ludwig Karl, 1785–1863, and Wilhelm Karl, 1786–1859), W. H. Auden states of the pair: "The Grimm brothers were the first men to attempt to record folk tales exactly as they were told by the folk themselves," stressing the significance of the oral tradition being transformed into written literature. Auden might have gone on to say—at least for many of us who have grown up in the West in the twentieth century—that the reason we read stories by the Brothers Grimm or by Hans Christian Andersen to our children is that we have largely given up the oral tradition of passing tales down from parent to child, *except* by reading them from storybooks. Although we may on occasion tell a child a story that we remember from our own childhood, rarely do we make up new stories that will in turn be passed on by our own children to someone else. Thus, the oral tradition might be said to be undergoing a trauma in its transformation to written literature. (There are, of course, folklorists who would disagree with that statement.)

What may be particularly fascinating for American readers, however, is the continuation of a still expanding oral tradition in much of the world where literature and literacy are fairly new. In this collection of stories, for example, consider Amos Tutuola's "The Complete Gentlemen" or Hyemeyohsts Storm's "The Story of Jumping Mouse"—both contemporary transformations from the oral tradition. Or—to use a more familiar example—read or reread Washington Irving's "Rip Van Winkle," based on "Karl Katz" but transformed and transplanted to New World soil by the American writer in 1820.

Karl Katz

In the midst of the Hartz forests there is a high mountain of which the neighbors tell all sorts of stories: how the goblins and fairies dance on it by night, and how the old Emperor Redbeard holds his court there and sits on his marble throne, with his long beard sweeping on the ground.

A great many years ago there lived in a village at the foot of this mountain, one Karl Katz. Now Karl was a goatherd, and every morning he drove his flock to feed upon the green spots that are here and there found on the mountainside. In the evening he sometimes thought it too late to drive his charges home, so then he would shut them up in a spot in the woods, where the old ruined walls of some castle that had long ago been deserted were left standing. They were high enough to form a fold, in which he could count his goats and let them rest for the night.

One evening he found that the prettiest goat of his flock had vanished soon after they were driven into this fold. He searched everywhere for it in vain but, to his surprise and delight, when he counted his flock in the morning what should he see but his lost goat! Again and again the same thing happened.

At last he thought he would watch still more narrowly. And having looked carefully over the old walls, he found a narrow doorway through which it seemed that his favorite made her way. Karl followed and found a path leading downwards through a cleft in the rocks. On he went, scrambling as well as he could, down the side of the rock and at last came to the mouth of a cave, where he lost sight of his goat. Just then he saw that his faithful dog was not with him. He whistled but no dog was there. He was therefore forced to go into the cave and try to find his goat by himself.

He groped his way for a while and at last came to a place where a little light found its way in. And there he wondered not a little to find his goat employing itself, very much at its ease in the cavern, in eating corn which kept dropping from some place over its head. He went up and looked about him to see where all this corn, that rattled about his ears like a hailstorm, could come from, but all overhead was dark and he could find no clue to this strange business.

At last, as he stood listening, he thought he heard the neighing and stamping of horses. He listened again; it was plainly so. And after a while he was sure that horses were feeding above him and that the corn fell from their mangers. What could these horses be, which were thus kept in the clefts of rocks where none but the goat's foot ever trod? There must be people of some sort or other living here, and who could they be? Was it safe to trust himself in such company? Karl pondered awhile but his wonder only grew greater and greater, when of a sudden he heard his own name, "Karl Katz!" echo through the cavern. He turned round, but could see nothing. "Karl Katz!" again sounded sharply in his ears. And soon out came a little dwarfish page with a high-peaked hat and a scarlet cloak, from a dark corner at one end of the cave.

The dwarf nodded and beckoned him to follow. Karl thought he should first like to know a little about who it was that thus sought his company. He asked, but the dwarf shook his head, answering not a word, and again beckoned him to follow. He did so, and winding his way through ruins he soon heard rolling overhead what sounded like peals of thunder echoing among the rocks. The noise grew louder and louder as he went on, and at last he came to a courtyard surrounded by old ivy-grown walls. The spot seemed to be the bosom of a little valley. Above rose on every hand high masses of rock. Wide-branching trees threw their arms overhead so that nothing but a glimmering twilight made its way through. And here on the cool smooth-shaven turf Karl saw twelve strange old figures amusing themselves very sedately with a game of ninepins.

Their dress did not seem altogether strange to Karl, for in the church of the town whither he went every week to market there was an old monument, with figures of queer old knights upon it, dressed in the very same fashion. Not a word fell from any of their lips. They moved about soberly and gravely, each taking his turn at the game; but the oldest of them ordered Karl Katz, by dumb signs, to busy himself in setting up the pins as they knocked them down. At first his knees trembled, and he hardly dared snatch a stolen sidelong glance at the long beards and old-fashioned dresses of the worthy knights. But he soon saw that as each knight played out his game he went to his seat and there took a hearty draught at a flagon, which the dwarf kept filled and which sent up the smell of the richest old wine.

Little by little Karl got bolder, and at last he plucked up his heart so far as to beg the dwarf, by signs, to let him too take his turn at the flagon. The dwarf gave it to him with a grave bow, and Karl thought he never had tasted anything half so good before. This gave him new strength for his work, and as often as he flagged at all he turned to the same kind friend for help in his need.

Which was tired first, he or the knights, Karl never could tell, or whether the wine got the better of his head. What he knew was that sleep at last overpowered him, and that when he awoke he found himself stretched out upon the old spot within the walls where he had folded his flock, and saw that the bright sun was high up in the heavens. The same green turf was spread beneath, and the same tottering ivy-clad walls surrounded him. He rubbed his eyes and called his dog, but neither dog nor goat was to be seen. And when he looked about him again, the grass seemed to be longer under his feet than it was yesterday. And trees hung over his head, which he had either never seen before or had quite forgotten. Shaking his head and hardly knowing whether he was in his right mind, he got up and stretched himself. Somehow or other his joints felt stiffer than they were. "It serves me right," said he. "This comes of sleeping out of one's own bed." Little by little he recollected his evening's sport and licked his lips as he thought of the charming wine he had taken so much of. "But who," thought he, "can those people be that come to this odd place to play ninepins?"

His first step was to look for the doorway through which he had followed his goat, but to his astonishment not the least trace of an opening of any sort was to be seen. There stood the wall, without chink or crack big enough for a rat to pass through. Again he paused and scratched his head. His hat was full of holes. "Why, it was new last Shrovetide!" said he. By chance his eyes fell next on his shoes, which were almost new when he last left home. But now they looked so old that they were likely to fall to pieces before he could get home. All his clothes seemed in the same sad plight. The more he looked, the more he pondered, and the more he was at a loss to know what could have happened to him.

At length he turned round and left the old walls to look for his flock. Slow and out of heart he wound his way among the mountain steeps, through paths where his flocks were wont to wander. Still not a goat was to be seen. Again he whistled and called his dog, but no dog came. Below him in the plain lay the village where his home was, so at length he took the downward path and set out with a heavy heart and a faltering step in search of his flock.

"Surely," said he, "I shall soon meet some neighbor who can tell me where my goats are." But the people who met him as he drew near to the village were all unknown to him. They were not even dressed as his neighbors were, and they seemed as if they hardly spoke the same tongue. When he eagerly asked each, as he came up, after his goats, they only stared at him and stroked their chins. At last he did the same too—and what was his wonder to find that his beard was grown at least a foot long!

"The world," said he to himself, "is surely turned upside down. If not, I must be bewitched." Yet he knew the mountain, as he turned round again and looked back on its woody heights. And he knew the houses and cottages also, with their little gardens, as he entered the village. All were where he had always known them to be. And he heard some children, too (as a traveler that passed by was asking his way), call the village by the very same name he had always known it to bear.

Again he shook his head and went straight through the village to his own cottage. Alas, it looked sadly out of repair. The windows were broken, the door off its hinges, and in the courtyard lay an unknown child in a ragged dress, playing with a rough, toothless old dog, whom he thought he ought to know, but who snarled and barked in his face when he called to him. He went in at the open doorway, but he found all so dreary and empty that he staggered out again like a drunken man, and called his wife and children loudly by their names. But no one heard—at least no one answered him.

A crowd of women and children soon flocked around the strange-looking man with the long gray beard, and all broke upon him at once with the questions, "Who are you?" "Who is it that you want?" It seemed to him so odd to ask other people, at his own door, about his wife and children that, in order to get rid of the gaping crowd, he named the first man that came into his head.

"Hans the blacksmith," said he. Most held their tongues and stared, but at last an old woman said, "He went these seven years ago to a place that you will not reach today."

"Fritz the tailor, then."

"Heaven rest his soul!" said an old beldam upon crutches. "He has lain these ten years in a house that he'll never leave."

Karl Katz looked at the old woman again and shuddered, as he knew her to be one of the old gossips, but saw she had a strangely altered face. All wish to ask further questions was gone, but at last a young woman made her way through the gaping throng. She had a baby in one arm and a little girl of about three years old clinging to her other hand. All three looked the very image of his own wife.

"What is your name?" he asked wildly.

"Liese," said she.

"And your father's?"

"Karl Katz, heaven bless him!" said she. "But poor man, he is lost and gone. It is now full twenty years since we sought for him day and night on the mountain. His dog and his flock came back, but he never was heard of any more. I was then seven years old."

Poor Karl could restrain himself no longer. "I am Karl Katz and no other," said he, as he took the child from his daughter's arms and kissed it over and over again.

All stood gaping, hardly knowing what to say or think, when old Stropken the schoolmaster hobbled by and took a long and close look at him. "Karl Katz! Karl Katz!" said he slowly. "Why it *is* Karl Katz sure enough. There is my own mark upon him. There is the scar over his right eye that I gave him myself one day with my oak stick."

Then several others also cried out, "Yes, it is! It is Karl Katz, Welcome, neighbor, welcome home!"

"But where," said or thought all, "can an honest steady fellow like you have been these twenty years?"

And now the whole village had flocked around. The children laughed, the dogs barked, and all were glad to see neighbor Karl home alive and well. As to where he had been for the twenty years, that was a part of the story at which Karl shrugged up his shoulders. For he never could very well explain it, and he seemed to think the less that was said about it the better. But it was plain enough that what dwelt most in his memory was the noble wine that had tickled his mouth while the knights played their game of ninepins.

[1818]

[Translator not identified]

QUESTIONS

1. The Grimms's stories are not, of course, direct transcriptions of oral tales. Rather, they have been shaped by two craftsmen of the written word and retold in a new form. Does the form of "Karl Katz" appear to be different from that of Tutuola's "The Complete Gentleman" or Storm's "The Story of Jumping Mouse"? In what way or ways?
2. If traditional tales are often designed to teach a lesson or establish a moral, what can be said of "Karl Katz"?
3. What is the result of applying contemporary theoretical perspectives to "Karl Katz," such as psychological, Freudian, or feminist?

Nathaniel Hawthorne

(1804–1864)

United States

One of the undisputed masters of nineteenth-century American literature, Nathaniel Hawthorne was born in Salem, Massachusetts, becoming both inheritor and explorer of the New England Puritan consciousness of an earlier era as well as his own. He attended Bowdoin College in Maine, where his classmates included the poet Henry Wadsworth Longfellow and Franklin Pierce, who later was elected to the American presidency. After graduating in 1825, Hawthorne returned to Salem and spent a reclusive life for the next 12 years. While working at the Boston Customhouse, he began to write the allegorical stories that initiate his preoccupation with the themes of moral responsibility, guilt, suffering, and human imperfection. His first volume of stories, *Twice-Told Tales*, was published in 1837, followed by two later volumes. His richly symbolic short stories anticipate themes and characters that are developed more fully in his longer narratives.

In 1842 Hawthorne married and moved to Concord, Massachusetts, where he became a neighbor of Emerson and Thoreau and the circle of Transcendentalists. After losing his position as a surveyor in the Salem Customhouse as a result of a change in political parties, Hawthorne wrote *The Scarlet Letter* (1850), the novel that finally gave him a measure of financial security while firmly establishing his literary reputation. In this historical romance set in seventeenth-century Puritan New England, Hawthorne masterfully probes the intertwined themes of human imperfection, moral responsibility, hidden guilt, and spiritual redemption through the psychologically complex characters Hester Prynne, Arthur Dimmesdale, and Roger Chillingworth.

Hawthorne's other major novels, *The House of the Seven Gables* (1851), *The Blithedale Romance* (1852), and *The Marble Faun* (1860), as well as his short stories, reflect the author's penetrating insight into human psychology and the moral realm. In "The Birthmark," Hawthorne explores the two domains of the natural order—matter and spirit—and the dangers that stem from confusing them.

The Birthmark

In the latter part of the last century there lived a man of science, an eminent proficient in every branch of natural philosophy, who not long before our story opens had made experience of a spiritual affinity more attractive than any chemical one. He had left his laboratory to the care of an assistant, cleared his fine countenance from the furnace smoke, washed the stain of acids from his fingers, and persuaded a beautiful woman to become his wife. In those days when the comparatively recent discovery of electricity and other kindred mysteries of Nature seemed to open paths into the region of miracle, it was not unusual for the love of science to rival the love of woman in its depth and absorbing energy. The higher intellect, the imagination, the spirit, and even the heart might all find their congenial ailment in pursuits which, as some of their ardent votaries believed, would ascend from one step of powerful intelligence to another, until the philosopher should lay his hand on the secret of creative force and perhaps make new worlds for himself. We know not whether Aylmer possessed this degree of faith in man's ultimate control over Nature. He had devoted himself, however, too unreservedly to scientific studies ever to be weaned from them by any second passion. His love for his young wife might prove the stronger of the two; but it could only be by intertwining itself with his love of science, and uniting the strength of the latter to his own.

Such a union accordingly took place, and was attended with truly remarkable consequences and a deeply impressive moral. One day, very soon after their marriage, Aylmer sat gazing at his wife with a trouble in his countenance that grew stronger until he spoke.

"Georgiana," said he, "has it never occurred to you that the mark upon your cheek might be removed?"

"No, indeed," said she, smiling; but perceiving the seriousness of his manner, she blushed deeply. "To tell the truth it has been so often called a charm that I was simple enough to imagine it might be so."

"Ah, upon another face perhaps it might," replied her husband; "but never on yours. No, dearest Georgiana, you came so nearly perfect from the hand of Nature that this slightest possible defect, which we hesitate whether to term a defect or a beauty, shocks me, as being the visible mark of earthly imperfection."

"Shocks you, my husband!" cried Georgiana, deeply hurt; at first reddening with momentary anger, but then bursting into tears. "Then why did you take me from my mother's side? You cannot love what shocks you!"

To explain this conversation it must be mentioned that in the centre of Georgiana's left cheek there was a singular mark, deeply interwoven, as it were, with the texture and substance of her face. In the usual state of her complexion —a healthy though delicate bloom—the mark wore a tint of deeper crimson, which imperfectly defined its shape amid the surrounding rosiness. When she blushed it gradually became more indistinct, and finally vanished amid the triumphant rush of blood that bathed the whole cheek with its brilliant glow. But if any shifting motion caused her to turn pale there was the mark again, a crimson stain upon the snow, in what Aylmer sometimes deemed an almost fearful distinctness. Its shape bore not a little similarity to the human hand, though of the smallest pygmy size. Georgiana's lovers were wont to say that some fairy at her birth hour had laid her tiny hand upon the infant's cheek, and left this impress there in token of the magic endowments that were to give her such sway over all hearts. Many a desperate swain would have risked life for the privilege of pressing his lips to the mysterious hand. It must not be concealed, however, that the impression wrought by this fairy sign manual varied exceedingly, according to the difference of temperament in the beholders. Some fastidious persons—but they were exclusively of her own sex—affirmed that the bloody hand, as they chose to call it, quite destroyed the effect of Georgiana's beauty, and rendered her countenance even hideous. But it would be as reasonable to say that one of those small blue stains which sometimes occur in the purest statuary marble would convert the Eve of Powers[1] to a monster. Masculine observers, if the birthmark did not heighten their admiration, contented themselves with wishing it away, that the world might possess one living specimen of ideal loveliness without the semblance of a flaw. After his marriage,—for he thought little or nothing of the matter before,—Aylmer discovered that this was the case with himself.

Had she been less beautiful,—if Envy's self could have found aught else to sneer at,—he might have felt his affection heightened by the prettiness of this mimic hand, now vaguely portrayed, now lost, now stealing forth again and glimmering to and fro with every pulse of emotion that throbbed within her heart; but seeing her otherwise so perfect, he found this one defect grow more and more intolerable with every moment of their united lives. It was the fatal flaw of humanity which Nature, in one shape or another, stamps ineffaceably on all her productions, either to imply that they are temporary and finite, or that their perfection must be wrought by toil and pain. The crimson hand expressed the ineludible gripe[2] in which mortality clutches the highest and purest of earthly mould, degrading them into kindred with the lowest, and even with the very brutes, like whom their visible frames return to dust. In this manner, selecting it as the symbol of his wife's liability to sin, sorrow, decay, and death, Aylmer's sombre imagination was not long in rendering the birthmark a frightful object, causing him more trouble and horror than ever Georgiana's beauty, whether of soul or sense, had given him delight.

At all the seasons which should have been their happiest, he invariably and without intending it, nay, in spite of a purpose to the contrary, reverted to this one disastrous topic. Trifling as it at first appeared, it so connected itself with innumerable trains of thought and modes of feeling that it became the central point of all. With the morning twilight Aylmer opened his eyes upon his wife's face and recognized the symbol of imperfection; and when they sat together at the evening hearth his eyes wandered stealthily to her cheek, and beheld, flickering with the blaze of the wood fire, the spectral hand that wrote mortality where he would fain have worshipped. Georgiana soon learned to shudder at his gaze. It needed but a glance with the peculiar expression that his face often wore to change the roses of her cheek into a deathlike paleness, amid which the crimson hand was brought strongly out, like a bas-relief of ruby on the whitest marble.

Late one night when the lights were growing dim, so as hardly to betray the stain on the poor wife's cheek, she herself, for the first time, voluntarily took up the subject.

"Do you remember, my dear Aylmer," said she, with a feeble attempt at a smile, "have you any recollection of a dream last night about this odious hand?"

"None! none whatever!" replied Aylmer, starting; but then he added, in a dry, cold tone, affected for the sake of concealing the real depth of his emotion, "I might well dream of it; for before I fell asleep it had taken a pretty firm hold of my fancy."

"And you did dream of it?" continued Georgiana, hastily; for she dreaded lest

[1]*Hiram Powers* American sculptor (1805–1873); his nude statue, *Eve Tempted*, was both praised and condemned in its time.

[2]*gripe* grip

a gush of tears should interrupt what she had to say. "A terrible dream! I wonder that you forget it. Is it possible to forget this one expression?—'It is in her heart now; we must have it out!' Reflect, my husband; for by all means I would have you recall that dream."

The mind is in a sad state when Sleep, the all-involving, cannot confine her spectres within the dim region of her sway, but suffers them to break forth, affrighting this actual life with secrets that perchance belong to a deeper one. Aylmer now remembered his dream. He had fancied himself with his servant Aminadab, attempting an operation for the removal of the birthmark; but the deeper went the knife, the deeper sank the hand, until at length its tiny grasp appeared to have caught hold of Georgiana's heart; whence, however, her husband was inexorably resolved to cut or wrench it away.

When the dream had shaped itself perfectly in his memory, Aylmer sat in his wife's presence with a guilty feeling. Truth often finds its way to the mind close muffled in robes of sleep, and then speaks with uncompromising directness of matters in regard to which we practise an unconscious self-deception during our waking moments. Until now he had not been aware of the tyrannizing influence acquired by one idea over his mind, and of the lengths which he might find in his heart to go for the sake of giving himself peace.

"Aylmer," resumed Georgiana, solemnly, "I know not what may be the cost to both of us to rid me of this fatal birthmark. Perhaps its removal may cause cureless deformity; or it may be the stain goes as deep as life itself. Again: do we know that there is a possibility, on any terms, of unclasping the firm gripe of this little hand which was laid upon me before I came into the world?"

"Dearest Georgiana, I have spent much thought upon the subject," hastily interrupted Aylmer. "I am convinced of the perfect practicability of its removal."

"If there be the remotest possibility of it," continued Georgiana, "let the attempt be made at whatever risk. Danger is nothing to me; for life, while this hateful mark makes me the object of your horror and disgust,—life is a burden which I would fling down with joy. Either remove this dreadful hand, or take my wretched life! You have deep science. All the world bears witness of it. You have achieved great wonders. Cannot you remove this little, little mark, which I cover with the tips of two small fingers? Is this beyond your power, for the sake of your own peace, and to save your poor wife from madness?"

"Noblest, dearest, tenderest wife," cried Aylmer, rapturously, "doubt not my power. I have already given this matter the deepest thought—thought which might almost have enlightened me to create a being less perfect than yourself. Georgiana, you have led me deeper than ever into the heart of science. I feel myself fully competent to render this dear cheek as faultless as its fellow; and then, most beloved, what will be my triumph when I shall have corrected what Nature left imperfect in her fairest work! Pygmalion,[3] when his sculptured woman assumed life, felt not greater ecstasy than mine will be."

"It is resolved, then," said Georgiana, faintly smiling. "And, Aylmer, spare me not, though you should find the birthmark take refuge in my heart at last."

Her husband tenderly kissed her cheek—her right cheek—not that which bore the impress of the crimson hand.

The next day Aylmer apprised his wife of a plan that he had formed whereby

[3]*Pygmalion* according to Greek legend, Pygmalion, King of Cyprus, fell in love with a female statue he had made; the goddess Aphrodite endowed the statue with life.

he might have opportunity for the intense thought and constant watchfulness which the proposed operation would require; while Georgiana, likewise, would enjoy the perfect repose essential to its success. They were to seclude themselves in the extensive apartments occupied by Aylmer as a laboratory, and where, during his toilsome youth, he had made discoveries in the elemental powers of Nature that had roused the admiration of all the learned societies in Europe. Seated calmly in this laboratory, the pale philosopher had investigated the secrets of the highest cloud region and of the profoundest mines; he had satisfied himself of the causes that kindled and kept alive the fires of the volcano; and had explained the mystery of fountains, and how it is that they gush forth, some so bright and pure, and others with such rich medicinal virtues, from the dark bosom of the earth. Here, too, at an earlier period, he had studied the wonders of the human frame, and attempted to fathom the very process by which Nature assimilates all her precious influences from earth and air, and from the spiritual world, to create and foster man, her masterpiece. The latter pursuit, however, Aylmer had long laid aside in unwilling recognition of the truth—against which all seekers sooner or later stumble—that our great creative Mother, while she amuses us with apparently working in the broadest sunshine, is yet severely careful to keep her own secrets, and, in spite of her pretended openness, shows us nothing but results. She permits us, indeed, to mar, but seldom to mend, and, like a jealous patentee, on no account to make. Now, however, Aylmer resumed these half-forgotten investigations; not, of course, with such hopes or wishes as first suggest them; but because they involved much physiological truth and lay in the path of his proposed scheme for the treatment of Georgiana.

As he led her over the threshold of the laboratory, Georgiana was cold and tremulous. Aylmer looked cheerfully into her face, with intent to reassure her, but was so startled with the intense glow of the birthmark upon the whiteness of her cheek that he could not restrain a strong convulsive shudder. His wife fainted.

"Aminadab! Aminadab!" shouted Aylmer, stamping violently on the floor.

Forthwith there issued from an inner apartment a man of low stature, but bulky frame, with shaggy hair hanging about his visage, which was grimed with the vapors of the furnace. This personage had been Aylmer's underworker during his whole scientific career, and was admirably fitted for that office by his great mechanical readiness, and the skill with which, while incapable of comprehending a single principle, he executed all the details of his master's experiments. With his vast strength, his shaggy hair, his smoky aspect, and the indescribable earthiness that incrusted him, he seemed to represent man's physical nature; while Aylmer's slender figure, and pale, intellectual face, were no less apt a type of the spiritual element.

"Throw open the door of the boudoir, Aminadab," said Aylmer, "and burn a pastil."[4]

"Yes, master," answered Aminadab, looking intently at the lifeless form of Georgiana; and then he muttered to himself, "If she were my wife, I'd never part with that birthmark."

When Georgiana recovered consciousness she found herself breathing an atmosphere of penetrating fragrance, the gentle potency of which had recalled

[4]*pastil* (modern spelling: *pastille*) a pellet of aromatic paste, used for fumigation

her from her deathlike faintness. The scene around her looked like enchantment. Aylmer had converted those smoky, dingy, sombre rooms, where he had spent his brightest years in recondite pursuits, into a series of beautiful apartments not unfit to be the secluded abode of a lovely woman. The walls were hung with gorgeous curtains, which imparted the combination of grandeur and grace that no other species of adornment can achieve; and as they fell from the ceiling to the floor, their rich and ponderous folds, concealing all angles and straight lines, appeared to shut in the scene from infinite space. For aught Georgiana knew, it might be a pavilion among the clouds. And Aylmer, excluding the sunshine, which would have interfered with his chemical processes, had supplied its place with perfumed lamps, emitting flames of various hue, but all uniting in a soft, impurpled radiance. He now knelt by his wife's side, watching her earnestly, but without alarm; for he was confident in his science, and felt that he could draw a magic circle round her within which no evil might intrude.

"Where am I? Ah, I remember," said Georgiana, faintly; and she placed her hand over her cheek to hide the terrible mark from her husband's eyes.

"Fear not, dearest!" exclaimed he. "Do not shrink from me! Believe me, Georgiana, I even rejoice in this single imperfection, since it will be such a rapture to remove it."

"Oh, spare me!" sadly replied his wife. "Pray do not look at it again. I never can forget that convulsive shudder."

In order to soothe Georgiana, and, as it were, to release her mind from the burden of actual things, Aylmer now put in practice some of the light and playful secrets which science had taught him among its profounder lore. Airy figures, absolutely bodiless ideas, and forms of unsubstantial beauty came and danced before her, imprinting their momentary footsteps on beams of light. Though she had some indistinct idea of the method of these optical phenomena, still the illusion was almost perfect enough to warrant the belief that her husband possessed sway over the spiritual world. Then again, when she felt a wish to look forth from her seclusion, immediately, as if her thoughts were answered, the procession of external existence flitted across a screen. The scenery and the figures of actual life were perfectly represented, but with that bewitching, yet indescribable difference which always makes a picture, an image, or a shadow so much more attractive than the original. When wearied of this, Aylmer bade her cast her eyes upon a vessel containing a quantity of earth. She did so, with little interest at first; but was soon startled to perceive the germ of a plant shooting upward from the soil. Then came the slender stalk; the leaves gradually unfolded themselves; and amid them was a perfect and lovely flower.

"It is magical!" cried Georgiana. "I dare not touch it."

"Nay, pluck it," answered Aylmer, — "pluck it, and inhale its brief perfume while you may. The flower will wither in a few moments and leave nothing save its brown seed vessels; but thence may be perpetuated a race as ephemeral as itself."

But Georgiana had no sooner touched the flower than the whole plant suffered a blight, its leaves turning coal-black as if by the agency of fire.

"There was too powerful a stimulus," said Aylmer, thoughtfully.

To make up for this abortive experiment, he proposed to take her portrait by a scientific process of his own invention. It was to be effected by rays of light striking upon a polished plate of metal. Georgiana assented; but, on looking at the result, was affrighted to find the features of the portrait blurred and indefinable; while the minute figure of a hand appeared where the cheek should have been. Aylmer snatched the metallic plate and threw it into a jar of corrosive acid.

Soon, however, he forgot these mortifying failures. In the intervals of study and chemical experiment he came to her flushed and exhausted, but seemed invigorated by her presence, and spoke in glowing language of the resources of his art. He gave a history of the long dynasty of the alchemists, who spent so many ages in quest of the universal solvent by which the golden principle might be elicited from all things vile and base. Aylmer appeared to believe that, by the plainest scientific logic, it was altogether within the limits of possibility to discover this long-sought medium; "but," he added, "a philosopher who should go deep enough to acquire the power would attain too lofty a wisdom to stoop to the exercise of it." Not less singular were his opinions in regard to the elixir vitae.[5] He more than intimated that it was at his option to concoct a liquid that should prolong life for years, perhaps interminably; but that it would produce a discord in Nature which all the world, and chiefly the quaffer of the immortal nostrum, would find cause to curse.

"Aylmer, are you in earnest?" asked Georgiana, looking at him with amazement and fear. "It is terrible to possess such power, or even dream of possessing it."

"Oh, do not tremble, my love," said her husband. "I would not wrong either you or myself by working such inharmonious effects upon our lives; but I would have you consider how trifling, in comparison, is the skill requisite to remove this little hand."

At the mention of the birthmark, Georgiana, as usual, shrank as if a redhot iron had touched her cheek.

Again Aylmer applied himself to his labors. She could hear his voice in the distant furnace room giving directions to Aminadab, whose harsh, uncouth, misshapen tones were audible in response, more like the grunt or growl of a brute than human speech. After hours of absence, Aylmer reappeared and proposed that she should now examine his cabinet of chemical products and natural treasures of the earth. Among the former he showed her a small vial, in which, he remarked, was contained a gentle yet most powerful fragrance, capable of impregnating all the breezes that blow across a kingdom. They were of inestimable value, the contents of that little vial; and, as he said so, he threw some of the perfume into the air and filled the room with piercing and invigorating delight.

"And what is this?" asked Georgiana, pointing to a small crystal globe containing a gold-colored liquid. "It is so beautiful to the eye that I could imagine it the elixir of life."

"In one sense it is," replied Aylmer; "or, rather, the elixir of immortality. It is the most precious poison that ever was concocted in this world. By its aid I could apportion the lifetime of any mortal at whom you might point your finger. The strength of the dose would determine whether he were to linger out years, or drop dead in the midst of a breath. No king on his guarded throne could keep his life if I, in my private station, should deem that the welfare of millions justified me in depriving him of it."

"Why do you keep such a terrific drug?" inquired Georgiana in horror.

[5]*elixir vitae* an essence reputed by the alchemists to prolong life

"Do not mistrust me, dearest," said her husband, smiling; "its virtuous potency is yet greater than its harmful one. But see! here is a powerful cosmetic. With a few drops of this in a vase of water, freckles may be washed away as easily as the hands are cleansed. A stronger infusion would take the blood out of the cheek, and leave the rosiest beauty a pale ghost."

"Is it with this lotion that you intend to bathe my cheek?" asked Georgiana, anxiously.

"Oh, no," hastily replied her husband; "this is merely superficial. Your case demands a remedy that shall go deeper."

In his interviews with Georgiana, Aylmer generally made minute inquiries as to her sensations and whether the confinement of the rooms and the temperature of the atmosphere agreed with her. These questions had such a particular drift that Georgiana began to conjecture that she was already subjected to certain physical influences, either breathed in with the fragrant air or taken with her food. She fancied likewise, but it might be altogether fancy, that there was a stirring up of her system—a strange, indefinite sensation creeping through her veins, and tingling, half painfully, half pleasurably, at her heart. Still, whenever she dared to look into the mirror, there she beheld herself pale as a white rose and with the crimson birthmark stamped upon her cheek. Not even Aylmer now hated it so much as she.

To dispel the tedium of the hours which her husband found it necessary to devote to the processes of combination and analysis, Georgiana turned over the volumes of his scientific library. In many dark old tomes she met with chapters full of romance and poetry. They were the works of the philosophers of the middle ages, such as Albertus Magnus, Cornelius Agrippa, Paracelsus, and the famous friar who created the prophetic Brazen Head.[6] All these antique naturalists stood in advance of their centuries, yet were imbued with some of their credulity, and therefore were believed, and perhaps imagined themselves to have acquired from the investigation of Nature a power above Nature, and from physics a sway over the spiritual world. Hardly less curious and imaginative were the early volumes of the Transactions of the Royal Society, in which the members, knowing little of the limits of natural possibility, were continually recording wonders or proposing methods whereby wonders might be wrought.

But to Georgiana the most engrossing volume was a large folio from her husband's own hand, in which he had recorded every experiment of his scientific career, its original aim, the methods adopted for its development, and its final success or failure, with the circumstances to which either event was attributable. The book, in truth, was both the history and emblem of his ardent, ambitious, imaginative, yet practical and laborious life. He handled physical details as if there were nothing beyond them; yet spiritualized them all, and redeemed himself from materialism by his strong and eager aspiration towards the infinite. In his grasp the veriest clod of earth assumed a soul. Georgiana, as she read, reverenced Aylmer and loved him more profoundly than ever, but with a less entire dependence on his judgment than heretofore. Much as he had

[6]*Albertus Magnus,* etc. medieval alchemists and philosophers whose work anticipated modern science. The friar who created the Brazen Head was Roger Bacon (1214?–1294?), a philosopher and alchemist who was reputed to have created a talking head that would respond to his questions concerning the progress of his enterprises.

accomplished, she could not but observe that his most splendid successes were almost invariably failures, if compared with the ideal at which he aimed. His brightest diamonds were the merest pebbles, and felt to be so by himself, in comparison with the inestimable gems which lay hidden beyond his reach. The volume, rich with achievements that had won renown for its author, was yet as melancholy a record as ever mortal hand had penned. It was the sad confession and continual exemplification of the shortcomings of the composite man, the spirit burdened with clay and working in matter, and of the despair that assails the higher nature at finding itself so miserably thwarted by the earthly part. Perhaps every man of genius in whatever sphere might recognize the image of his own experience in Aylmer's journal.

So deeply did these reflections affect Georgiana that she laid her face upon the open volume and burst into tears. In this situation she was found by her husband.

"It is dangerous to read in a sorcerer's books," said he, with a smile, though his countenance was uneasy and displeased. "Georgiana, there are pages in that volume which I can scarcely glance over and keep my senses. Take heed lest it prove as detrimental to you."

"It has made me worship you more than ever," said she.

"Ah, wait for this one success," rejoined he, "then worship me if you will. I shall deem myself hardly unworthy of it. But come, I have sought you for the luxury of your voice. Sing to me, dearest."

So she poured out the liquid music of her voice to quench the thirst of his spirit. He then took his leave with a boyish exuberance of gayety, assuring her that her seclusion would endure but a little longer, and that the result was already certain. Scarcely had he departed when Georgiana felt irresistibly impelled to follow him. She had forgotten to inform Aylmer of a symptom which for two or three hours past had begun to excite her attention. It was a sensation in the fatal birthmark, not painful, but which induced a restlessness throughout her system. Hastening after her husband, she intruded for the first time into the laboratory.

The first thing that struck her eye was the furnace, that hot and feverish worker, with the intense glow of its fire, which by the quantities of soot clustered above it seemed to have been burning for ages. There was a distilling apparatus in full operation. Around the room were retorts, tubes, cylinders, crucibles, and other apparatus of chemical research. An electrical machine stood ready for immediate use. The atmosphere felt oppressively close, and was tainted with gaseous odors which had been tormented forth by the processes of science. The severe and homely simplicity of the apartment, with its naked walls and brick pavement, looked strange, accustomed as Georgiana had become to the fantastic elegance of her boudoir. But what chiefly, indeed almost solely, drew her attention, was the aspect of Aylmer himself.

He was pale as death, anxious and absorbed, and hung over the furnace as if it depended upon his utmost watchfulness whether the liquid which it was distilling should be the draught of immortal happiness or misery. How different from the sanguine and joyous mien that he had assumed for Georgiana's encouragement!

"Carefully now, Aminadab; carefully, thou human machine; carefully, thou man of clay!" muttered Aylmer, more to himself than his assistant. "Now, if there be a thought too much or too little, it is all over."

"Ho! ho!" mumbled Aminadab. "Look, master! look!"

Aylmer raised his eyes hastily, and at first reddened, then grew paler than ever, on beholding Georgiana. He rushed towards her and seized her arm with a gripe that left the print of his fingers upon it.

"Why do you come hither? Have you no trust in your husband?" cried he, impetuously. "Would you throw the blight of that fatal birthmark over my labors? It is not well done. Go, prying woman, go!"

"Nay, Aylmer," said Georgiana with the firmness of which she possessed no stinted endowment, "it is not you that have a right to complain. You mistrust your wife; you have concealed the anxiety with which you watch the development of this experiment. Think not so unworthily of me, my husband. Tell me all the risk we run, and fear not that I shall shrink; for my share in it is far less than your own."

"No, no, Georgiana!" said Aylmer, impatiently; "it must not be."

"I submit," replied she calmly. "And Aylmer, I shall quaff whatever draught you bring me; but it will be on the same principle that would induce me to take a dose of poison if offered by your hand."

"My noble wife," said Aylmer, deeply moved, "I knew not the height and depth of your nature until now. Nothing shall be concealed. Know, then, that this crimson hand, superficial as it seems, has clutched its grasp into your being with a strength of which I had no previous conception. I have already administered agents powerful enough to do aught except to change your entire physical system. Only one thing remains to be tried. If that fail us we are ruined."

"Why did you hesitate to tell me this?" asked she.

"Because, Georgiana," said Aylmer, in a low voice, "there is danger."

"Danger? There is but one danger—that this horrible stigma shall be left upon my cheek!" cried Georgiana. "Remove it, remove it, whatever be the cost, or we shall both go mad!"

"Heaven knows your words are too true," said Aylmer, sadly. "And now, dearest, return to your boudoir. In a little while all will be tested."

He conducted her back and took leave of her with a solemn tenderness which spoke far more than his words how much was now at stake. After his departure Georgiana became rapt in musings. She considered the character of Aylmer, and did it completer justice than at any previous moment. Her heart exulted, while it trembled, at his honorable love—so pure and lofty that it would accept nothing less than perfection nor miserably make itself contented with an earthlier nature than he had dreamed of. She felt how much more precious was such a sentiment than that meaner kind which would have borne with the imperfection for her sake, and have been guilty of treason to holy love by degrading its perfect idea to the level of the actual; and with her whole spirit she prayed that, for a single moment, she might satisfy his highest and deepest conception. Longer than one moment she well knew it could not be; for his spirit was ever on the march, ever ascending, and each instant required something that was beyond the scope of the instant before.

The sound of her husband's footsteps aroused her. He bore a crystal goblet containing a liquor colorless as water, but bright enough to be the draught of immortality. Aylmer was pale; but it seemed rather the consequence of a highly-wrought state of mind and tension of spirit than of fear or doubt.

"The concoction of the draught has been perfect," said he, in answer to Georgiana's look. "Unless all my science have deceived me, it cannot fail."

"Save on your account, my dearest Aylmer," observed his wife, "I might wish to put off this birthmark of mortality by relinquishing mortality itself in preference to any other mode. Life is but a sad possession to those who have attained precisely the degree of moral advancement at which I stand. Were I weaker and blinder it might be happiness. Were I stronger, it might be endured hopefully. But, being what I find myself, methinks I am of all mortals the most fit to die."

"You are fit for heaven without tasting death!" replied her husband. "But why do we speak of dying? The draught cannot fail. Behold its effect upon this plant."

On the window seat there stood a geranium diseased with yellow blotches, which had overspread all its leaves. Aylmer poured a small quantity of the liquid upon the soil in which it grew. In a little time, when the roots of the plant had taken up the moisture, the unsightly blotches began to be extinguished in a living verdure.

"There needed no proof," said Georgiana, quietly. "Give me the goblet. I joyfully stake all upon your word."

"Drink, then, thou lofty creature!" exclaimed Aylmer, with fervid admiration. "There is no taint of imperfection on thy spirit. Thy sensible frame, too, shall soon be all perfect."

She quaffed the liquid and returned the goblet to his hand.

"It is grateful," said she with a placid smile. "Methinks it is like water from a heavenly fountain; for it contains I know not what of unobtrusive fragrance and deliciousness. It allays a feverish thirst that had parched me for many days. Now, dearest, let me sleep. My earthly senses are closing over my spirit like the leaves around the heart of a rose at sunset.

She spoke the last words with a gentle reluctance, as if it required almost more energy than she could command to pronounce the faint and lingering syllables. Scarcely had they loitered through her lips ere she was lost in slumber. Aylmer sat by her side, watching her aspect with the emotions proper to a man the whole value of whose existence was involved in the process now to be tested. Mingled with this mood, however, was the philosophic investigation characteristic of the man of science. Not the minutest symptom escaped him. A heightened flush of the cheek, a slight irregularity of breath, a quiver of the eyelid, a hardly perceptible tremor through the frame,—such were the details which, as the moments passed, he wrote down in his folio volume. Intense thought had set its stamp upon every previous page of that volume, but the thoughts of years were all concentrated upon the last.

While thus employed, he failed not to gaze often at the fatal hand, and not without a shudder. Yet once, by a strange and unaccountable impulse, he pressed it with his lips. His spirit recoiled, however, in the very act; and Georgiana, out of the midst of her deep sleep, moved uneasily and murmured as if in remonstrance. Again Aylmer resumed his watch. Nor was it without avail. The crimson hand, which at first had been strongly visible upon the marble paleness of Georgiana's cheek, now grew more faintly outlined. She remained not less pale than ever; but the birthmark, with every breath that came and went, lost somewhat of its former distinctness. Its presence had been awful; its departure was more awful still. Watch the stain of the rainbow fading out of the sky, and you will know how that mysterious symbol passed away.

"By Heaven! it is well-nigh gone!" said Aylmer to himself, in almost irrepressible ecstasy. "I can scarcely trace it now. Success! success! And now it is like the faintest rose color. The lightest flush of blood across her cheek would overcome it. But she is so pale!"

He drew aside the window curtain and suffered the light of natural day to fall into the room and rest upon her cheek. At the same time he heard a gross, hoarse chuckle, which he had long known as his servant Aminadab's expression of delight.

"Ah, clod! ah, earthly mass!" cried Aylmer, laughing in a sort of frenzy, "you have served me well! Matter and spirit—earth and heaven—have both done their part in this! Laugh, thing of the senses! You have earned the right to laugh."

These exclamations broke Georgiana's sleep. She slowly unclosed her eyes and gazed into the mirror which her husband had arranged for that purpose. A faint smile flitted over her lips when she recognized how barely perceptible was now that crimson hand which had once blazed forth with such disastrous brilliancy as to scare away all their happiness. But then her eyes sought Aylmer's face with a trouble and anxiety that he could by no means account for.

"My poor Aylmer!" murmured she.

"Poor? Nay, richest, happiest, most favored!" exclaimed he. "My peerless bride, it is successful! You are perfect!"

"My poor Aylmer," she repeated, with a more than human tenderness, "you have aimed loftily; you have done nobly. Do not repent that with so high and pure a feeling, you have rejected the best the earth could offer. Aylmer, dearest Aylmer, I am dying!"

Alas! it was too true! The fatal hand had grappled with the mystery of life, and was the bond by which an angelic spirit kept itself in union with a mortal frame. As the last crimson tint of the birthmark—that sole token of human imperfection—faded from her cheek, the parting breath of the now perfect woman passed into the atmosphere; and her soul, lingering a moment near her husband, took its heavenward flight. Then a hoarse, chuckling laugh was heard again! Thus ever does the gross fatality of earth exult in its invariable triumph over the immortal essence which, in this dim sphere of half development, demands the completeness of a higher state. Yet, had Aylmer reached a profounder wisdom, he need not thus have flung away the happiness which would have woven his mortal life of the selfsame texture with the celestial. The momentary circumstance was too strong for him; he failed to look beyond the shadowy scope of time, and, living once for all in eternity, to find the perfect future in the present.

[1843]

QUESTIONS

1. What is the birthmark? What does it come to symbolize by the end of the story?
2. What attitudes toward nature and science are explored in the story? Why are Aylmer's love of science and his love for his wife in conflict? Why do his successful experiments fail when he tries to repeat them for Georgiana?

3. Consider "The Birthmark" as an exploration of different kinds of power. What is Aylmer's power? What is Georgiana's?
4. Is the story more concerned with the abuse of science or with female imperfection?
5. What moral values or attitudes toward nature do Aylmer, Georgiana, and Aminadab represent? What moral perspective does Hawthorne express through the story's conclusion?

Bessie Head

(1937–1986)

South Africa/Botswana

Bessie Head's career as a writer was played out almost exclusively as an exile in Botswana, her adopted homeland. Born of a white mother and black father in Pietermaritzburg, South Africa, she suffered the childhood trauma of being "reclassified," that is, removed from her mother's world and brought up as a Coloured. Her mother had suffered the equally devastating humiliation of being treated as insane, for daring to have a relationship with a black man. The emotional scars of Bessie Head's childhood and early adulthood were recorded in her masterpiece, *A Question of Power* (1973), a fictional study of madness brought about, one might say, by the violence of the apartheid system. Earlier, Ms. Head had written poignantly of Botswana life in two memorable works: *When Rain Clouds Gather* (1968) and *Maru* (1971). These three novels and the works that followed have earned her the distinction of Africa's major female writer. She died in Serowe, Botswana, in 1986.

"The Prisoner Who Wore Glasses" differs from most of Ms. Head's work due to its South African setting, an environment she purposely avoided in most of her other stories and novels—no doubt because it was so painful. Equally unusual in this story is the sex of the characters, all of whom are men, incarcerated in a South African prison for their political activities. Yet the subtext is clear: apartheid is tantamount to incarceration.

In *A Woman Alone: Autobiographical Writings* (1990) Head ends the final essay with this statement: "Every oppressed man has this suppressed violence, as though silently awaiting the time to set right the wrongs that afflict him. I have never forgotten it, even though, for the purpose of my trade, I borrowed the clothes of a country like Botswana. . . . Possibly too, Southern Africa might one day become the home of the storyteller and dreamer, who did not hurt others but only introduced new dreams that filled the heart with wonder."

The Prisoner Who Wore Glasses

Scarcely a breath of wind disturbed the stillness of the day and the long rows of cabbages were bright green in the sunlight. Large white clouds drifted slowly across the deep blue sky. Now and then they obscured the sun and caused a chill on the backs of the prisoners who had to work all day long in the cabbage field. This trick the clouds were playing with the sun eventually caused one of the prisoners who wore glasses to stop work, straighten up and peer short-sightedly at them. He was a thin little fellow with a hollowed-out chest and comic knobbly knees. He also had a lot of fanciful ideas because he smiled at the clouds.

"Perhaps they want me to send a message to the children," he thought tenderly, noting that the clouds were drifting in the direction of his home some hundred miles away. But before he could frame the message, the warder in charge of his work span shouted:

"Hey, what you tink you're doing, Brille?"

The prisoner swung round, blinking rapidly, yet at the same time sizing up the enemy. He was a new warder, named Jacobus Stephanus Hannetjie. His eyes were the colour of the sky but they were frightening. A simple, primitive, brutal soul gazed out of them. The prisoner bent down quickly and a message was quietly passed down the line:

"We're in for trouble this time, comrades."

"Why?" rippled back up the line.

"Because he's not human," the reply rippled down and yet only the crunching of the spades as they turned over the earth disturbed the stillness.

This particular work span was known as Span One. It was composed of ten men and they were all political prisoners. They were grouped together for convenience as it was one of the prison regulations that no black warder should be in charge of a political prisoner lest this prisoner convert him to his views. It never seemed to occur to the authorities that this very reasoning was the strength of Span One and a clue to the strange terror they aroused in the warders. As political prisoners they were unlike the other prisoners in the sense that they felt no guilt nor were they outcasts of society. All guilty men instinctively cower, which was why it was the kind of prison where men got knocked out cold with a blow at the back of the head from an iron bar. Up until the arrival of Warder Hannetjie, no warder had dared beat any member of Span One and no warder had lasted more than a week with them. The battle was entirely psychological. Span One was assertive and it was beyond the scope of white warders to handle assertive black men. Thus, Span One had got out of control. They were the best thieves and liars in the camp. They lived all day on raw cabbages. They chatted and smoked tobacco. And since they moved, thought and acted as one, they had perfected every technique of group concealment.

Trouble began that very day between Span One and Warder Hannetjie. It was because of the short-sightedness of Brille. That was the nickname he was given in prison and is the Afrikaans word for someone who wears glasses. Brille could never judge the approach of the prison gates and on several previous occasions he had munched on cabbages and dropped them almost at the feet of the warder and all previous warders had overlooked this. Not so Warder Hannetjie.

"Who dropped that cabbage?" he thundered.

Brille stepped out of line.

"I did," he said meekly.

"All right," said Hannetjie. "The whole Span goes three meals off."

"But I told you I did it," Brille protested.

The blood rushed to Warder Hannetjie's face.

"Look 'ere," he said. "I don't take orders from a kaffir. I don't know what kind of kaffir you tink you are. Why don't you say Baas. I'm your Baas. Why don't you say Baas, hey?"

Brille blinked his eyes rapidly but by contrast his voice was strangely calm.

"I'm twenty years older than you," he said. It was the first thing that came to mind but the comrades seemed to think it a huge joke. A titter swept up the line.

The next thing Warder Hannetjie whipped out a knobkerrie and gave Brille several blows about the head. What surprised his comrades was the speed with which Brille had removed his glasses or else they would have been smashed to pieces on the ground.

That evening in the cell Brille was very apologetic.

"I'm sorry, comrades," he said. "I've put you into a hell of a mess."

"Never mind, brother," they said. "What happens to one of us, happens to all."

"I'll try to make up for it, comrades," he said. "I'll steal something so that you don't go hungry."

Privately, Brille was very philosophical about his head wounds. It was the first time an act of violence had been perpetrated against him but he had long been a witness of extreme, almost unbelievable human brutality. He had twelve children and his mind travelled back that evening through the sixteen years of bedlam in which he had lived. It had all happened in a small drab little three-bedroomed house in a small drab little street in the Eastern Cape and the children kept coming year after year because neither he nor Martha managed the contraceptives the right way and a teacher's salary never allowed moving to a bigger house and he was always taking exams to improve this salary only to have it all eaten up by hungry mouths. Everything was pretty horrible, especially the way the children fought. They'd get hold of each other's heads and give them a good bashing against the wall. Martha gave up somewhere along the line so they worked out a thing between them. The bashings, biting and blood were to operate in full swing until he came home. He was to be the bogeyman and when it worked he never failed to have a sense of god-head at the way in which his presence could change savages into fairly reasonable human beings.

Yet somehow it was this chaos and mismanagement at the centre of his life that drove him into politics. It was really an ordered beautiful world with just a few basic slogans to learn along with the rights of mankind. At one stage, before things became very bad, there were conferences to attend, all very far away from home.

"Let's face it," he thought ruefully. "I'm only learning right now what it means to be a politician. All this while I've been running away from Martha and the kids."

And the pain in his head brought a hard lump to his throat. That was what the children did to each other daily and Martha wasn't managing and if Warder Hannetjie had not interrupted him that morning he would have sent the following message:

"Be good comrades, my children. Co-operate, then life will run smoothly."

The next day Warder Hannetjie caught this old man with twelve children stealing grapes from the farm shed. They were an enormous quantity of grapes in a ten-gallon tin and for this misdeed the old man spent a week in the isolation cell. In fact, Span One as a whole was in constant trouble. Warder Hannetjie seemed to have eyes at the back of his head. He uncovered the trick about the cabbages, how they were split in two with the spade and immediately covered with earth and then unearthed again and eaten with split-second timing. He found out how tobacco smoke was beaten into the ground and he found out how conversations were whispered down the wind.

For about two weeks Span One lived in acute misery. The cabbages, tobacco and conversations had been the pivot of jail life to them. Then one evening they noticed that their good old comrade who wore the glasses was looking rather pleased with himself. He pulled out a four-ounce packet of tobacco by way of explanation and the comrades fell upon it with great greed. Brille merely smiled. After all, he was the father of many children. But when the last shred had disappeared, it occurred to the comrades that they ought to be puzzled. Someone said:

"I say, brother. We're watched like hawks these days. Where did you get the tobacco?"

"Hannetjie gave it to me," said Brille.

There was a long silence. Into it dropped a quiet bombshell.

"I saw Hannetjie in the shed today," and the failing eyesight blinked rapidly. "I caught him in the act of stealing five bags of fertilizer and he bribed me to keep my mouth shut."

There was another long silence.

"Prison is an evil life," Brille continued, apparently discussing some irrelevant matter. "It makes a man contemplate all kinds of evil deeds."

He held out his hand and closed it.

"You know, comrades," he said. "I've got Hannetjie. I'll betray him tomorrow."

Everyone began talking at once.

"Forget it, brother. You'll get shot."

Brille laughed.

"I won't," he said. "That is what I mean about evil. I am a father of children and I saw today that Hannetjie is just a child and stupidly truthful. I'm going to punish him severely because we need a good warder."

The following day, with Brille as witness, Hannetjie confessed to the theft of the fertilizer and was fined a large sum of money. From then on Span One did very much as they pleased while Warder Hannetjie stood by and said nothing. But it was Brille who carried this to extremes. One day, at the close of work Warder Hannetjie said:

"Brille, pick up my jacket and carry it back to the camp."

"But nothing in the regulations says I'm your servant, Hannetjie," Brille replied coolly.

"I've told you not to call me Hannetjie. You must say, Baas," but Warder Hannetjie's voice lacked conviction. In turn, Brille squinted up at him.

"I'll tell you something about this Baas business, Hannetjie," he said. "One of these days we are going to run the country. You are going to clean my car. Now, I have a fifteen-year-old son and I'd die of shame if you had to tell him that I ever called you Baas."

Warder Hannetjie went red in the face and picked up his coat.

On another occasion Brille was seen to be walking about the prison yard, openly smoking tobacco. On being taken before the prison commander he claimed to have received the tobacco from Warder Hannetjie. All throughout the tirade from his chief, Warder Hannetjie failed to defend himself but his nerve broke completely. He called Brille to one side.

"Brille," he said. "This thing between you and me must end. You may not know it but I have a wife and children and you're driving me to suicide."

"Why don't you like your own medicine, Hannetjie?" Brille asked quietly.

"I can give you anything you want," Warder Hannetjie said in desperation.

"It's not only me but the whole of Span One," said Brille cunningly. "The whole of Span One wants something from you."

Warder Hannetjie brightened with relief.

"I tink I can manage if it's tobacco you want," he said.

Brille looked at him, for the first time struck with pity and guilt. He wondered if he had carried the whole business too far. The man was really a child.

"It's not tobacco we want, but you," he said. "We want you on our side. We want a good warder because without a good warder we won't be able to manage the long stretch ahead."

Warder Hannetjie interpreted this request in his own fashion and his interpretation of what was good and human often left the prisoners of Span One speechless with surprise. He had a way of slipping off his revolver and picking up a spade and digging alongside Span One. He had a way of producing unheard of luxuries like boiled eggs from his farm nearby and things like cigarettes, and Span One responded nobly and got the reputation of being the best work span in the camp. And it wasn't only take from their side. They were awfully good at stealing certain commodities like fertilizer which were needed on the farm of Warder Hannetjie.

[1973]

QUESTIONS

1. When "The Prisoner Who Wore Glasses" was originally published in 1973, critics of South African apartheid saw little hope for political change within the country. Was Bessie Head concurring with that perspective or presenting a more hopeful one?
2. What, in fact, does Head suggest are the ways of coping with such an oppressive system?
3. What is the significance of Brille's glasses?

ERNEST HEMINGWAY

(1898–1961)

UNITED STATES

Because Ernest Hemingway lived the kind of colorful, adventurous, even legendary life that most writers only write about, it is difficult to separate the legends from his celebrated fiction. A journalist who traveled widely—living in Cuba, Spain, Africa, France, Italy, and several parts of the United States—Hemingway wrote for American newspapers, first as a reporter for the *Kansas City Star* and later as a foreign correspondent. He saw action in World War I (sustaining a serious injury) with the American Red Cross Ambulance Corps when he was only 19, was involved with the Loyalists in Spain, and lived on the Paris Left Bank along with other American expatriate writers such as Ezra Pound and Gertrude Stein. During World War II, he served as a war correspondent, flying missions with the Royal Air Force and covering the Normandy landing. He was injured in a plane crash during an African safari. During those years, he was married four times.

Hemingway's adventurous, risk-taking life unquestionably provided both the inspiration and the substance for his fiction. His early novel, *The Sun Also Rises* (1926), explores a group of disillusioned Americans, part of the Lost Generation of expatriates in Spain after the war. *A Farewell to Arms* (1929) draws its energy from encounters with war that Hemingway knew intimately. *For Whom the Bell Tolls* (1940), set during the Spanish Civil War, is among Hemingway's masterpieces.

Hemingway's early novels and stories immediately established his reputation as a master of a distinctive and original style, characterized by spare, lucid, precise prose in which his characters reveal themselves through dialogue and action rather than authorial commentary. In *Death in the Afternoon*, Hemingway commented that "Prose is architecture, not interior decoration, and the Baroque is over." When pressed to describe the function of his writing for a *Paris Review* interview, he said:

> From things that have happened and from things as they exist and from all things that you know and all those you cannot know, you make something through your invention that is not a representation but a whole new thing truer than anything true and alive, and you make it alive, and if you make it well enough, you give it immortality.

Writing was Hemingway's way of discovering himself and of making sense of the pessimism he imbibed as part of the collapse of values precipitated by two harrowing wars. His male characters often seek to model their behavior according to rules derived from specialized contexts like bullfighting and hunting. The Hemingway "code," characterized by courage, self-discipline, and "grace under pressure," was the source of dignity and meaning for his male heroes, who regarded the world as otherwise absurd or harsh. Hemingway's female characters, caught in the same atmosphere of despair but excluded from participation in these male rituals, are often portrayed as helpless or destructive.

Hemingway received the Pulitzer Prize for *The Old Man and the Sea* in 1953; in 1954, he was awarded the Nobel Prize for Literature. In 1961, in poor physical and emotional health and haunted by the memory of his father's suicide years earlier, Hemingway fatally shot himself.

• The Short Happy Life of Francis Macomber •

It was now lunch time and they were all sitting under the double green fly of the dining tent pretending that nothing had happened.

"Will you have lime juice or lemon squash?" Macomber asked.

"I'll have a gimlet," Robert Wilson told him.

"I'll have a gimlet too. I need something," Macomber's wife said.

"I suppose it's the thing to do," Macomber agreed. "Tell him to make three gimlets."

The mess boy had started them already, lifting the bottles out of the canvas cooling bags that sweated wet in the wind that blew through the trees that shaded the tents.

"What had I ought to give them?" Macomber asked.

"A quid would be plenty," Wilson told him. "You don't want to spoil them."

"Will the headman distribute it?"

"Absolutely."

Francis Macomber had, half an hour before, been carried to his tent from the edge of the camp in triumph on the arms and shoulders of the cook, the personal boys, the skinner and the porters. The gun-bearers had taken no part in the demonstration. When the native boys put him down at the door of his tent, he had shaken all their hands, received their congratulations, and then gone into the tent and sat on the bed until his wife came in. She did not speak to him when she came in and he left the tent at once to wash his face and hands in the portable wash basin outside and go over to the dining tent to sit in a comfortable canvas chair in the breeze and the shade.

"You've got your lion," Robert Wilson said to him, "and a damned fine one too."

Mrs. Macomber looked at Wilson quickly. She was an extremely handsome and well-kept woman of the beauty and social position which had, five years before, commanded five thousand dollars as the price of endorsing, with photographs, a beauty product which she had never used. She had been married to Francis Macomber for eleven years.

"He is a good lion, isn't he?" Macomber said. His wife looked at him now. She looked at both these men as though she had never seen them before.

One, Wilson, the white hunter, she knew she had never truly seen before. He was about middle height with sandy hair, a stubby mustache, a very red face and extremely cold blue eyes with faint white wrinkles at the corners that grooved merrily when he smiled. He smiled at her now and she looked away from his face at the way his shoulders sloped in the loose tunic he wore with the four big cartridges held in loops where the left breast pocket should have been, at his big brown hands, his old slacks, his very dirty boots and back to his red face again. She noticed where the baked red of his face stopped in a white line that marked the circle left by his Stetson hat that hung now from one of the pegs of the tent pole.

"Well, here's to the lion," Robert Wilson said. He smiled at her again and, not smiling, she looked curiously at her husband.

Francis Macomber was very tall, very well built if you did not mind that length of bone, dark, his hair cropped like an oarsman, rather thin-lipped, and was considered handsome. He was dressed in the same sort of safari clothes that Wilson wore except that his were new, he was thirty-five years old, kept himself very fit, was good at court games, had a number of big-game fishing records, and had just shown himself, very publicly, to be a coward.

"Here's to the lion," he said. "I can't ever thank you for what you did."

Margaret, his wife, looked away from him and back to Wilson.

"Let's not talk about the lion," she said.

Wilson looked over at her without smiling and now she smiled at him.

"It's been a very strange day," she said. "Hadn't you ought to put your hat on even under the canvas at noon? You told me that, you know."

"Might put it on," said Wilson.

"You know you have a very red face, Mr. Wilson," she told him and smiled again.

"Drink," said Wilson.

"I don't think so," she said. "Francis drinks a great deal, but his face is never red."

"It's red today," Macomber tried a joke.

"No," said Margaret. "It's mine that's red today. But Mr. Wilson's is always red."

"Must be racial," said Wilson. "I say, you wouldn't like to drop my beauty as a topic, would you?"

"I've just started on it."

"Let's chuck it," said Wilson.

"Conversation is going to be so difficult," Margaret said.

"Don't be silly, Margot," her husband said.

"No difficulty," Wilson said. "Got a damn fine lion."

Margot looked at them both and they saw that she was going to cry. Wilson had seen it coming for a long time and he dreaded it. Macomber was past dreading it.

"I wish it hadn't happened. Oh, I wish it hadn't happened," she said and started for her tent. She made no noise of crying but they could see that her shoulders were shaking under the rose-colored, sun-proofed shirt she wore.

"Women upset," said Wilson to the tall man. "Amounts to nothing. Strain on the nerves and one thing'n another."

"No," said Macomber. "I suppose that I rate that for the rest of my life now."

"Nonsense. Let's have a spot of the giant killer," said Wilson. "Forget the whole thing. Nothing to it anyway."

"We might try," said Macomber. "I won't forget what you did for me though."

"Nothing," said Wilson. "All nonsense."

So they sat there in the shade where the camp was pitched under some wide-topped acacia trees with a boulder-strewn cliff behind them, and a stretch of grass that ran to the bank of a boulder-filled stream in front with forest beyond it, and drank their just-cool lime drinks and avoided one another's eyes while the boys set the table for lunch. Wilson could tell that the boys all knew about it now and when he saw Macomber's personal boy looking curiously at his master while he was putting dishes on the table he snapped at him in Swahili. The boy turned away with his face blank.

"What were you telling him?" Macomber asked.

"Nothing. Told him to look alive or I'd see he got about fifteen of the best."

"What's that? Lashes?"

"It's quite illegal," Wilson said. "You're supposed to fine them."

"Do you still have them whipped?"

"Oh, yes. They could raise a row if they chose to complain. But they don't. They prefer it to the fines."

"How strange!" said Macomber.

"Not strange, really," Wilson said. "Which would you rather do? Take a good birching or lose your pay?"

Then he felt embarrassed at asking it and before Macomber could answer he went on, "We all take a beating every day, you know, one way or another."

This was no better. "Good God," he thought. "I am a diplomat, aren't I?"

"Yes, we take a beating," said Macomber, still not looking at him. "I'm awfully sorry about that lion business. It doesn't have to go any further, does it? I mean no one will hear about it, will they?"

"You mean will I tell it at the Mathaiga Club?" Wilson looked at him now coldly. He had not expected this. So he's a bloody four-letter man as well as a bloody coward, he thought. I rather liked him too until today. But how is one to know about an American?

"No," said Wilson. "I'm a professional hunter. We never talk about our clients. You can be quite easy on that. It's supposed to be bad form to ask us not to talk though."

He had decided now that to break would be much easier. He would eat, then, by himself and could read a book with his meals. They would eat by themselves. He would see them through the safari on a very formal basis—what was it the French called it? Distinguished consideration—and it would be a damn sight easier than having to go through this emotional trash. He'd insult him and make a good clean break. Then he could read a book with his meals and he'd still be drinking their whisky. That was the phrase for it when a safari went bad. You ran into another white hunter and you asked, "How is everything going?" and he answered, "Oh, I'm still drinking their whisky," and you knew everything had gone to pot.

"I'm sorry," Macomber said and looked at him with his American face that would stay adolescent until it became middle-aged, and Wilson noted his crew-cropped hair, fine eyes only faintly shifty, good nose, thin lips and handsome jaw. "I'm sorry I didn't realize that. There are lots of things I don't know."

So what could he do, Wilson thought. He was all ready to break it off quickly and neatly and here the beggar was apologizing after he had just insulted him. He made one more attempt. "Don't worry about me talking," he said. "I have a living to make. You know in Africa no woman ever misses her lion and no white man ever bolts."

"I bolted like a rabbit," Macomber said.

Now what in hell were you going to do about a man who talked like that, Wilson wondered.

Wilson looked at Macomber with his flat, blue, machine-gunner's eyes and the other smiled back at him. He had a pleasant smile if you did not notice how his eyes showed when he was hurt.

"Maybe I can fix it up on buffalo," he said. "We're after them next, aren't we?"

"In the morning if you like," Wilson told him. Perhaps he had been wrong. This was certainly the way to take it. You most certainly could not tell a damned thing about an American. He was all for Macomber again. If you could forget the morning. But, of course, you couldn't. The morning had been about as bad as they come.

"Here comes the Memsahib," he said. She was walking over from her tent looking refreshed and cheerful and quite lovely. She had a very perfect oval face, so perfect that you expected her to be stupid. But she wasn't stupid, Wilson thought, no, not stupid.

"How is the beautiful red-faced Mr. Wilson? Are you feeling better, Francis, my pearl?"

"Oh, much," said Macomber.

"I've dropped the whole thing," she said, sitting down at the table. "What importance is there to whether Francis is any good at killing lions? That's not his trade. That's Mr. Wilson's trade. Mr. Wilson is really very impressive killing anything. You do kill anything, don't you?"

"Oh, anything," said Wilson. "Simply anything." They are, he thought, the hardest in the world; the hardest, the cruelest, the most predatory and the most attractive and their men have softened or gone to pieces nervously as they have hardened. Or is it that they pick men they can handle? They can't know that much at the age they marry, he thought. He was grateful that he had gone through his education on American women before now because this was a very attractive one.

"We're going after buff in the morning," he told her.

"I'm coming," she said.

"No, you're not."

"Oh, yes, I am. Mayn't I, Francis?"

"Why not stay in camp?"

"Not for anything," she said. "I wouldn't miss something like today for anything."

When she left, Wilson was thinking, when she went off to cry, she seemed a hell of a fine woman. She seemed to understand, to realize, to be hurt for him and for herself and to know how things really stood. She is away for twenty minutes and now she is back, simply enamelled in that American female cruelty. They are the damnedest women. Really the damnedest.

"We'll put on another show for you tomorrow," Francis Macomber said.

"You're not coming," Wilson said.

"You're very mistaken," she told him. "And I want *so* to see you perform again. You were lovely this morning. That is if blowing things' heads off is lovely."

"Here's the lunch," said Wilson. "You're very merry, aren't you?"

"Why not? I didn't come out here to be dull."

"Well, it hasn't been dull," Wilson said. He could see the boulders in the river and the high bank beyond with the trees and he remembered the morning.

"Oh, no," she said. "It's been charming. And tomorrow. You don't know how I look forward to tomorrow."

"That's eland he's offering you," Wilson said.

"They're the big cowy things that jump like hares, aren't they?"

"I suppose that describes them," Wilson said.

"It's very good meat," Macomber said.

"Did you shoot it, Francis?" she asked.

"Yes."

"They're not dangerous, are they?"

"Only if they fall on you," Wilson told her.

"I'm so glad."

"Why not let up on the bitchery just a little, Margot," Macomber said, cutting the eland steak and putting some mashed potato, gravy and carrot on the down-turned fork that tined through the piece of meat.

"I suppose I could," she said, "since you put it so prettily."

"Tonight we'll have champagne for the lion," Wilson said. It's a bit too hot at noon."

"Oh, the lion," Margot said. "I'd forgotten the lion!"

So, Robert Wilson thought to himself, she *is* giving him a ride, isn't she? Or do you suppose that's her idea of putting up a good show? How should a woman act when she discovers her husband is a bloody coward? She's damn cruel but they're all cruel. They govern, of course, and to govern one has to be cruel sometimes. Still, I've seen enough of their damn terrorism.

"Have some more eland," he said to her politely.

That afternoon, late, Wilson and Macomber went out in the motor car with the native driver and the two gun-bearers. Mrs. Macomber stayed in the camp. It was too hot to go out, she said, and she was going with them in the early morning. As they drove off Wilson saw her standing under the big tree, looking pretty rather than beautiful in her faintly rosy khaki, her dark hair drawn back off her forehead and gathered in a knot low on her neck, her face as fresh, he thought, as though she were in England. She waved to them as the car went off through the swale of high grass and curved around through the trees into the small hills of orchard bush.

In the orchard bush they found a herd of impala, and leaving the car they stalked one old ram with long, wide-spread horns and Macomber killed it with a very creditable shot that knocked the buck down at a good two hundred yards and sent the herd off bounding wildly and leaping over one another's backs in long, leg-drawn-up leaps as unbelievable and as floating as those one makes sometimes in dreams.

"That was a good shot," Wilson said. "They're a small target."

"Is it a worth-while head?" Macomber asked.

"It's excellent," Wilson told him. "You shoot like that and you'll have no trouble."

"Do you think we'll find buffalo tomorrow?"

"There's a good chance of it. They feed out early in the morning and with luck we may catch them in the open."

"I'd like to clear away that lion business," Macomber said. "It's not very pleasant to have your wife see you do something like that."

I should think it would be even more unpleasant to do it, Wilson thought, wife or no wife, or to talk about it having done it. But he said, "I wouldn't think about that any more. Any one could be upset by his first lion. That's all over."

But that night after dinner and a whisky and soda by the fire before going to bed, as Francis Macomber lay on his cot with the mosquito bar over him and listened to the night noises it was not all over. It was neither all over nor was it beginning. It was there exactly as it happened with some parts of it indelibly emphasized and he was miserably ashamed at it. But more than shame he felt cold, hollow fear in him. The fear was still there like a cold slimy hollow in all the emptiness where once his confidence had been and it made him feel sick. It was still there with him now.

It had started the night before when he had wakened and heard the lion roaring somewhere up along the river. It was a deep sound and at the end there were sort of coughing grunts that made him seem just outside the tent, and when Francis Macomber woke in the night to hear it he was afraid. He could hear his wife breathing quietly, asleep. There was no one to tell he was afraid, nor to be afraid with him, and, lying alone, he did not know the Somali proverb that says a brave man is always frightened three times by a lion; when he first sees his track, when he first hears him roar and when he first confronts him. Then while they were eating breakfast by lantern light out in the dining tent, before the sun was up, the lion roared again and Francis thought he was just at the edge of camp.

"Sounds like an old-timer," Robert Wilson said, looking up from his kippers and coffee. "Listen to him cough."

"Is he very close?"

"A mile or so up the stream."

"Will we see him?"

"We'll have a look."

"Does his roaring carry that far? It sounds as though he were right in camp."

"Carries a hell of a long way," said Robert Wilson. "It's strange the way it carries. Hope he's a shootable cat. The boys said there was a very big one about here."

"If I get a shot, where should I hit him," Macomber asked, "to stop him?"

"In the shoulders," Wilson said. "In the neck if you can make it. Shoot for bone. Break him down."

"I hope I can place it properly," Macomber said.

"You shoot very well," Wilson told him. "Take your time. Make sure of him. The first one in is the one that counts."

"What range will it be?"

"Can't tell. Lion has something to say about that. Don't shoot unless it's close enough so you can make sure."

"At under a hundred yards?" Macomber asked.

Wilson looked at him quickly.

"Hundred's about right. Might have to take him a bit under. Shouldn't chance a shot at much over that. A hundred's a decent range. You can hit him wherever you want at that. Here comes the Memsahib."

"Good morning," she said. "Are we going after that lion?"

"As soon as you deal with your breakfast," Wilson said. "How are you feeling?"

"Marvelous," she said. "I'm very excited."

"I'll just go and see that everything is ready," Wilson went off. As he left the lion roared again.

"Noisy beggar." Wilson said. "We'll put a stop to that."

"What's the matter, Francis?" his wife asked him.

"Nothing," Macomber said.

"Yes, there is," she said. "What are you upset about?"

"Nothing," he said.

"Tell me," she looked at him. "Don't you feel well?"

"It's that damned roaring," he said. "It's been going on all night, you know."

"Why didn't you wake me," she said. "I'd love to have heard it."

"I've got to kill the damned thing," Macomber said, miserably.

"Well, that's what you're out here for, isn't it?"

"Yes. But I'm nervous. Hearing the thing roar gets on my nerves."

"Well then, as Wilson said, kill him and stop his roaring."

"Yes, darling," said Francis Macomber. "It sounds easy, doesn't it?"

"You're not afraid, are you?"

"Of course not. But I'm nervous from hearing him roar all night."

"You'll kill him marvellously," she said. "I know you will. I'm awfully anxious to see it."

"Finish your breakfast and we'll be starting."

"It's not light yet," she said. "This is a ridiculous hour."

Just then the lion roared in a deep-chested moaning, suddenly gutteral, ascending vibration that seemed to shake the air and ended in a sigh and a heavy, deep-chested grunt.

"He sounds almost here," Macomber's wife said.

"My God," said Macomber. "I hate that damned noise."

"It's very impressive."

"Impressive. It's frightful."

Robert Wilson came up then carrying his short, ugly, shockingly big-bored .505 Gibbs and grinning.

"Come on," he said. "Your gun-bearer has your Springfield and the big gun. Everything's in the car. Have you solids?"

"Yes."

"I'm ready," Mrs. Macomber said.

"Must make him stop that racket," Wilson said. "You get in front. The Memsahib can sit back here with me."

They climbed into the motor car and, in the gray first daylight, moved off up the river through the trees. Macomber opened the breech of his rifle and saw he had metal-cased bullets, shut the bolt and put the rifle on safety. He saw his hand was trembling. He felt in his pocket for more cartridges and moved his fingers over the cartridges in the loops of his tunic front. He turned back to where Wilson sat in the rear seat of the doorless, box-bodied motor car beside his wife, them both grinning with excitement, and Wilson leaned forward and whispered,

"See the birds dropping. Means the old boy has left his kill."

On the far bank of the stream Macomber could see, above the trees, vultures circling and plummeting down.

"Chances are he'll come to drink along here," Wilson whispered. "Before he goes to lay up. Keep an eye out."

They were driving slowly along the high bank of the stream which here cut deeply to its boulder-filled bed, and they wound in and out through big trees as they drove. Macomber was watching the opposite bank when he felt Wilson take hold of his arm. The car stopped.

"There he is," he heard the whisper. "Ahead and to the right. Get out and take him. He's a marvelous lion."

Macomber saw the lion now. He was standing almost broadside, his great head up and turned toward them. The early morning breeze that blew toward them was just stirring his dark mane, and the lion looked huge, silhouetted on the rise of bank in the gray morning light, his shoulders heavy, his barrel of a body bulking smoothly.

"How far is he?" asked Macomber, raising his rifle.

"About seventy-five. Get out and take him."

"Why not shoot from where I am?"

"You don't shoot them from cars," he heard Wilson saying in his ear. "Get out. He's not going to stay there all day."

Macomber stepped out of the curved opening at the side of the front seat, onto the step and down onto the ground. The lion still stood looking majestically and coolly toward this object that his eyes only showed in silhouette, bulking like some super-rhino. There was no man smell carried toward him and he watched the object, moving his great head a little from side to side. Then watching the object, not afraid, but hesitating before going down the bank to drink with such a thing opposite him, he saw a man figure detach itself from it and he turned his heavy head and swung away toward the cover of the trees as he heard a cracking crash and felt the slam of a .30–06 220-grain solid bullet that bit his flank and ripped in sudden hot scalding nausea through his stomach. He trotted, heavy, big-footed, swinging wounded full-bellied, through the trees toward the tall grass and cover, and the crash came again to go past him ripping the air apart. Then it crashed again and he felt the blow as it hit his lower ribs and ripped on through, blood sudden hot and frothy in his mouth, and he galloped toward the high grass where he could crouch and not be seen and make them bring the crashing thing close enough so he could make a rush and get the man that held it.

Macomber had not thought how the lion felt as he got out of the car. He only knew his hands were shaking and as he walked away from the car it was almost impossible for him to make his legs move. They were stiff in the thighs, but he could feel the muscles fluttering. He raised the rifle, sighted on the junction of the lion's head and shoulders and pulled the trigger. Nothing happened though he pulled until he thought his finger would break. Then he knew he had the safety on and as he lowered the rifle to move the safety over he moved another frozen pace forward, and the lion seeing his silhouette now clear of the silhouette of the car, turned and started off at a trot, and, as Macomber fired, he heard a whunk that meant that the bullet was home; but the lion kept on going. Macomber shot again and everyone saw the bullet throw a spout of dirt beyond the trotting lion. He shot again, remembering to lower his aim, and they all heard the bullet hit, and the lion went into a gallop and was in the tall grass before he had the bolt pushed forward.

Macomber stood there feeling sick at his stomach, his hands that held the Springfield still cocked, shaking, and his wife and Robert Wilson were standing by him. Beside him too were the two gun-bearers chattering in Wakamba.

"I hit him," Macomber said. "I hit him twice."

"You gut-shot him and you hit him somewhere forward," Wilson said without enthusiasm. The gun-bearers looked very grave. They were silent now.

"You may have killed him," Wilson went on. "We'll have to wait a while before we go in to find out."

"What do you mean?"

"Let him get sick before we follow him up."

"Oh," said Macomber.

"He's a hell of a fine lion," Wilson said cheerfully. "He's gotten into a bad place though."

"Why is it bad?"

"Can't see him until you're on him."

"Oh," said Macomber.

"Come on," said Wilson. "The Memsahib can stay here in the car. We'll go to have a look at the blood spoor."

"Stay here, Margot," Macomber said to his wife. His mouth was very dry and it was hard for him to talk.

"Why?" she asked.

"Wilson says to."

"We're going to have a look," Wilson said. "You stay here. You can see even better from here."

"All right."

Wilson spoke in Swahili to the driver. He nodded and said, "Yes, Bwana."

Then they went down the steep bank and across the stream, climbing over and around the boulders and up the other bank, pulling up by some projecting roots, and along it until they found where the lion had been trotting when Macomber first shot. There was dark blood on the short grass that the gun-bearers pointed out with grass stems, and that ran away behind the river bank trees.

"What do we do?" asked Macomber.

"Not much choice," said Wilson. "We can't bring the car over. Bank's too steep. We'll let him stiffen up a bit then you and I'll go in and have a look for him."

"Can't we set the grass on fire?" Macomber asked.

"Too green."

"Can't we send beaters?"

Wilson looked at him appraisingly. "Of course we can," he said. "But it's just a touch murderous. You see we know the lion's wounded. You can drive an unwounded lion—he'll move on ahead of a noise—but a wounded lion's going to charge. You can't see him until you're right on him. He'll make himself perfectly flat in cover you wouldn't think would hide a hare. You can't very well send boys in there to that sort of a show. Somebody bound to get mauled."

"What about the gun-bearers?"

"Oh, they'll go with us. It's their *shauri*. You see, they signed on for it. They don't look too happy though, do they?"

"I don't want to go in there," said Macomber. It was out before he knew he'd said it.

"Neither do I," said Wilson very cheerily. "Really no choice though." Then, as an afterthought, he glanced at Macomber and saw suddenly how he was trembling and the pitiful look on his face.

"You don't have to go in, of course," he said. "That's what I'm hired for, you know. That's why I'm so expensive."

"You mean you'd go in by yourself? Why not leave him there?"

Robert Wilson, whose entire occupation had been with the lion and the problem he presented, and who had not been thinking about Macomber except to note that he was rather windy, suddenly felt as though he had opened the wrong door in a hotel and seen something shameful.

"What do you mean?"

"Why not just leave him?"

"You mean pretend to ourselves he hasn't been hit?"

"No. Just drop it."

"It isn't done."

"Why not?"

"For one thing, he's certain to be suffering. For another, some one else might run onto him."

"I see."

"But you don't have to have anything to do with it."

"I'd like to," Macomber said. "I'm just scared, you know."

"I'll go ahead when we go in," Wilson said, "with Kongoni tracking. You keep behind me and a little to one side. Chances are we'll hear him growl. If we see him we'll both shoot. Don't worry about anything. I'll keep you backed up. As a matter of fact, you know, perhaps you'd better not go. It might be much better. Why don't you go over and join the Memsahib while I just get it over with?"

"No, I want to go."

"All right," said Wilson. "But don't go in if you don't want to. This is my *shauri* now, you know."

"I want to go," said Macomber.

They sat under a tree and smoked.

"Want to go back and speak to the Memsahib while we're waiting?" Wilson asked.

"No."

"I'll just step back and tell her to be patient."

"Good," said Macomber. He sat there, sweating under his arms, his mouth dry, his stomach hollow feeling, wanting to find courage to tell Wilson to go on and finish off the lion without him. He could not know that Wilson was furious because he had not noticed the state he was in earlier and sent him back to his wife. While he sat there Wilson came up. "I have your big gun," he said. "Take it. We've given him time, I think. Come on."

Macomber took the big gun and Wilson said:

"Keep behind me and about five yards to the right and do exactly as I tell you." Then he spoke in Swahili to the two gun-bearers who looked the picture of gloom.

"Let's go," he said.

"Could I have a drink of water?" Macomber asked. Wilson spoke to the older gun-bearer, who wore a canteen on his belt, and the man unbuckled, unscrewed the top and handed it to Macomber, who took it noticing how heavy it seemed and how hairy and shoddy the felt covering was in his hand. He raised it to drink and looked ahead at the high grass with the flat-topped trees behind it. A breeze was blowing toward them and the grass rippled gently in the wind.

He looked at the gun-bearer and he could see the gun-bearer was suffering too with fear.

Thirty-five yards into the grass the big lion lay flattened out along the ground. His ears were back and his only movement was a slight twitching up and down of his long, black-tufted tail. He had turned at bay as soon as he had reached this cover and he was sick with the wound through his full belly, and weakening with the wound through his lungs that brought a thin foamy red to his mouth each time he breathed. His flanks were wet and hot and flies were on the little openings the solid bullets had made in his tawny hide, and his big yellow eyes, narrowed with hate, looked straight ahead, only blinking when the pain came as he breathed, and his claws dug in the soft baked earth. All of him, pain, sickness, hatred and all of his remaining strength, was tightening into an absolute concentration for a rush. He could hear the men talking and he waited, gathering all of himself into this preparation for a charge as soon as the men would come into the grass. As he heard their voices his tail stiffened to twitch up and down, and, as they came into the edge of the grass, he made a coughing grunt and charged.

Kongoni, the old gun-bearer, in the lead watching the blood spoor, Wilson watching the grass for any movement, his big gun ready, the second gun-bearer looking ahead and listening, Macomber close to Wilson, his rifle cocked, they had just moved into the grass when Macomber heard the blood-choked coughing grunt, and saw the swishing rush in the grass. The next thing he knew he was running; running wildly, in panic in the open, running toward the stream.

He heard the *ca-ra-wong*! of Wilson's big rifle, and again in a second a crashing *carawong*! and turning saw the lion, horrible-looking now, with half his head seeming to be gone, crawling toward Wilson in the edge of the tall grass while the red-faced man worked the bolt on the short ugly rifle and aimed carefully as another blasting *carawong*! came from the muzzle, and the crawling, heavy, yellow bulk of the lion stiffened and the huge, mutilated head slid forward and Macomber, standing by himself in the clearing where he had run, holding a loaded rifle, while two black men and a white man looked back at him in contempt, knew the lion was dead. He came toward Wilson, his tallness all seeming a naked reproach, and Wilson looked at him and said:

"Want to take pictures?"

"No," he said.

That was all any one had said until they reached the motor car. Then Wilson had said:

"Hell of a fine lion. Boys will skin him out. We might as well stay here in the shade."

Macomber's wife had not looked at him nor he at her and he had sat by her in the back seat with Wilson sitting in the front seat. Once he had reached over and taken his wife's hand without looking at her and she had removed her hand from his. Looking across the stream to where the gun-bearers were skinning out the lion he could see that she had been able to see the whole thing. While they sat there his wife had reached forward and put her hand on Wilson's shoulder. He turned and she had leaned forward over the low seat and kissed him on the mouth.

"Oh, I say," said Wilson, going redder than his natural baked color.

"Mr. Robert Wilson," she said. "The beautiful red-faced Mr. Robert Wilson."

Then she sat down beside Macomber again and looked away across the stream to where the lion lay, with uplifted, white-muscled, tendon-marked naked forearms, and white bloating belly, as the black men fleshed away the skin. Finally the gun-bearers brought the skin over, wet and heavy, and climbed in behind with it, rolling it up before they got in, and the motor car started. No one had said anything more until they were back in camp.

That was the story of the lion. Macomber did not know how the lion had felt before he started his rush, nor during it when the unbelievable smash of the .505 with a muzzle velocity of two tons had hit him in the mouth, nor what kept him coming after that, when the second ripping crash had smashed his hind quarters and he had come crawling on toward the crashing, blasting thing that had destroyed him. Wilson knew something about it and only expressed it by saying, "Damned fine lion," but Macomber did not know how Wilson felt about things either. He did not know how his wife felt except that she was through with him.

His wife had been through with him before but it never lasted. He was very wealthy, and would be much wealthier, and he knew she would not leave him ever now. That was one of the few things that he really knew. He knew about that, about motor cycles—that was earliest—about motor cars, about duck-shooting, about fishing, trout, salmon and big-sea, about sex in books, many books, too many books, about all court games, about dogs, not much about horses, about hanging on to his money, about most of the other things his world dealt in, and about his wife not leaving him. His wife had been a great beauty and she was still a great beauty in Africa, but she was not a great enough beauty any more at home to be able to leave him and better herself and she knew it and he knew it. She had missed the chance to leave him and he knew it. If he had been better with women she would probably have started to worry about him getting another new, beautiful wife; but she knew too much about him to worry about him either. Also, he had always had a great tolerance which seemed the nicest thing about him if it were not the most sinister.

All in all they were known as a comparatively happily married couple, one of those whose disruption is often rumored but never occurs, and as the society columnist put it, they were adding more than a spice of *adventure* to their much envied and ever-enduring *Romance* by a *Safari* in what was known as *Darkest Africa* until the Martin Johnsons lighted it on so many silver screens where they were pursuing *Old Simba* the lion, the buffalo, *Tembo* and the elephant and as well collecting specimens for the Museum of Natural History. This same columnist had reported them *on the verge* at least three times in the past and they had been. But they always made it up. They had a sound basis of union. Margot was too beautiful for Macomber to divorce her and Macomber had too much money for Margot ever to leave him.

It was now about three o'clock in the morning and Francis Macomber, who had been asleep a little while after he had stopped thinking about the lion, wakened and then slept again, woke suddenly, frightened in a dream of the bloody-headed lion standing over him, and listening while his heart pounded, he realized that his wife was not in the other cot in the tent. He lay awake with that knowledge for two hours.

At the end of that time his wife came into the tent, lifted her mosquito bar and crawled cozily into bed.

"Where have you been?" Macomber asked in the darkness.

"Hello," she said. "Are you awake?"

"Where have you been?"

"I just went out to get a breath of air."

"You did, like hell."

"What do you want me to say, darling?"

"Where have you been?"

"Out to get a breath of air."

"That's a new name for it. You *are* a bitch."

"Well, you're a coward."

"All right," he said. "What of it?"

"Nothing as far as I'm concerned. But please let's not talk, darling, because I'm very sleepy."

"You think that I'll take anything."

"I know you will, sweet."

"Well, I won't."

"Please, darling, let's not talk. I'm so very sleepy."

"There wasn't going to be any of that. You promised there wouldn't be."

"Well, there is now," she said sweetly.

"You said if we made this trip that there would be none of that. You promised."

"Yes, darling. That's the way I meant it to be. But the trip was spoiled yesterday. We don't have to talk about it, do we?"

"You don't wait long when you have an advantage, do you?"

"Please let's not talk. I'm so sleepy, darling."

"I'm going to talk."

"Don't mind me then because I'm going to sleep." And she did.

At breakfast, there were all three at the table before daylight and Francis Macomber found that, of all the men that he hated, he hated Robert Wilson the most.

"Sleep well?" Wilson asked in his throaty voice, filling a pipe.

"Did you?"

"Topping," the white hunter told him.

You bastard, thought Macomber, you insolent bastard.

So she woke him when she came in, Wilson thought, looking at them both with his flat, cold eyes. Well, why doesn't he keep his wife where she belongs? What does he think I am, a bloody plaster saint? Let him keep her where she belongs. It's his own fault.

"Do you think we'll find buffalo?" Margot asked, pushing away a dish of apricots.

"Chance of it," Wilson said and smiled at her. "Why don't you stay in camp?"

"Not for anything," she told him.

"Why not order her to stay in camp?" Wilson said to Macomber.

"You order her," said Macomber coldly.

"Let's not have any ordering, nor," turning to Macomber, "any silliness, Francis," Margot said quite pleasantly.

"Are you ready to start?" Macomber asked.

"Any time," Wilson told him. "Do you want the Memsahib to go?"

"Does it make any difference whether I do or not?"

The hell with it, thought Robert Wilson. The utter complete hell with it. So this is what it's going to be like. Well, this is what it's going to be like, then.

"Makes no difference," he said.

"You're sure you wouldn't like to stay in camp with her yourself and let me go out and hunt the buffalo?" Macomber asked.

"Can't do that," said Wilson. "Wouldn't talk rot if I were you."

"I'm not talking rot. I'm disgusted."

"Bad word, disgusted."

"Francis, will you please try to speak sensibly?" his wife said.

"I speak too damned sensibly," Macomber said. "Did you ever eat such filthy food?"

"Something wrong with the food?" asked Wilson quietly.

"No more than with everything else."

"I'd pull yourself together, laddybuck," Wilson said very quietly. "There's a boy waits at table that understands a little English."

"The hell with him."

Wilson stood up and puffing on his pipe strolled away, speaking a few words in Swahili to one of the gun-bearers who was standing waiting for him. Macomber and his wife sat on at the table. He was staring at his coffee cup.

"If you make a scene I'll leave you, darling," Margot said quietly.

"No, you won't."

"You can try it and see."

"You won't leave me."

"No," she said. "I won't leave you and you'll behave yourself."

"Behave myself? That's a way to talk. Behave myself."

"Yes. Behave yourself."

"Why don't *you* try behaving?"

"I've tried it so long. So very long."

"I hate that red-faced swine," Macomber said. "I loathe the sight of him."

"He's really *very* nice."

"Oh, *shut up*," Macomber almost shouted. Just then the car came up and stopped in front of the dining tent and the driver and the two gun-bearers got out. Wilson walked over and looked at the husband and wife sitting there at the table.

"Going shooting?" he asked.

"Yes," said Macomber, standing up. "Yes."

"Better bring a woolly. It will be cool in the car," Wilson said.

"I'll get my leather jacket," Margot said.

"The boy has it," Wilson told her. He climbed into the front with the driver and Francis Macomber and his wife sat, not speaking, in the back seat.

Hope the silly beggar doesn't take a notion to blow the back of my head off, Wilson thought to himself. Women *are* a nuisance on safari.

The car was grinding down to cross the river at a pebbly ford in the gray daylight and then climbed, angling up the steep bank, where Wilson had ordered a way shovelled out the day before so they could reach the parklike wooded rolling country on the far side.

It was a good morning, Wilson thought. There was a heavy dew and as the wheels went through the grass and low bushes he could smell the odor of the crushed fronds. It was an odor like verbena and he liked this early morning smell of the dew, the crushed bracken and the look of the tree trunks showing black through the early morning mist, as the car made its way through the untracked, parklike country. He had put the two in the back seat out of his mind now and was thinking about buffalo. The buffalo that he was after stayed in the daytime in a thick swamp where it was impossible to get a shot, but in the night they fed out into an open stretch of country and if he could come between them and their swamp with the car, Macomber would have a good chance at them in the open. He did not want to hunt buff with Macomber in thick cover. He did not want to hunt buff or anything else with Macomber at all, but he was a professional hunter and he had hunted with some rare ones in his time. If they got buff today there would only be rhino to come and the poor man would have gone through his dangerous game and things might pick up. He'd have nothing more to do with the woman and Macomber would get over that too. He must have gone through plenty of that before by the look of things. Poor beggar. He must have a way of getting over it. Well, it was the poor sod's own bloody fault.

He, Robert Wilson, carried a double size cot on safari to accommodate any windfalls he might receive. He had hunted for a certain clientele, the international, fast, sporting set, where the women did not feel they were getting their money's worth unless they had shared that cot with the white hunter. He despised them when he was away from them although he liked some of them well enough at the time, but he made his living by them; and their standards were his standards as long as they were hiring him.

They were his standards in all except the shooting. He had his own standards about the killing and they could live up to them or get some one else to hunt them. He knew, too, that they all respected him for this. This Macomber was an odd one though. Damned if he wasn't. Now the wife. Well, the wife. Yes, the wife. Hm, the wife. Well he'd dropped all that. He looked around at them. Macomber sat grim and furious. Margot smiled at him. She looked younger today, more innocent and fresher and not so professionally beautiful. What's in her heart God knows, Wilson thought. She hadn't talked much last night. At that it was a pleasure to see her.

The motor car climbed up a slight rise and went on through the trees and then out into a grassy prairie-like opening and kept in the shelter of the trees along the edge, the driver going slowly and Wilson looking carefully out across the prairie and all along its far side. He stopped the car and studied the opening with his field glasses. Then he motioned to the driver to go on and the car moved slowly along, the driver avoiding wart-hog holes and driving around the mud castles ants had built. Then, looking across the opening, Wilson suddenly turned and said,

"By God, there they are!"

And looking where he pointed, while the car jumped forward and Wilson spoke in rapid Swahili to the driver, Macomber saw three huge, black animals looking almost cylindrical in their long heaviness, like big black tank cars, moving at a gallop across the far edge of the open prairie. They moved at a stiff-necked, stiff-bodied gallop and he could see the upswept wide black horns on their heads as they galloped heads out; the heads not moving.

"They're three old bulls," Wilson said. "We'll cut them off before they get to the swamp."

The car was going a wild forty-five miles an hour across the open and as Macomber watched, the buffalo got bigger and bigger until he could see the gray, hairless, scabby look of one huge bull and how his neck was a part of his shoulders and the shiny black of his horns as he galloped a little behind the others that were strung out in that steady plunging gait; and then, the car swaying as though it had just jumped a road, they drew up close and he could see the plunging hugeness of the bull, and the dust in his sparsely haired hide, the wide boss of horn and his outstretched, wide-nostrilled muzzle, and he was raising his rifle when Wilson shouted, "Not from the car, you fool!" and he had no fear, only hatred of Wilson, while the brakes clamped on and the car skidded, plowing sideways to an almost stop and Wilson was out on one side and he on the other, stumbling as his feet hit the still speeding-by of the earth, and then he was shooting at the bull as he moved away, hearing the bullets whunk into him, emptying his rifle at him as he moved steadily away, finally remembering to get his shots forward into the shoulder, and as he fumbled to reload, he saw the bull was down. Down on his knees, his big head tossing, and seeing the other two still galloping he shot at the leader and hit him. He shot again and missed and he heard the *carawonging* roar as Wilson shot and saw the leading bull slide forward onto his nose.

"Get that other," Wilson said. "Now you're shooting."

But the other bull was moving steadily at the same gallop and he missed, throwing a spout of dirt, and Wilson missed and the dust rose in a cloud and Wilson shouted, "Come on. He's too far!" and grabbed his arm and they were in the car again, Macomber and Wilson hanging on the sides and rocketing swayingly over the uneven ground, drawing up on the steady, plunging, heavy-necked, straight-moving gallop of the bull.

They were behind him and Macomber was filling his rifle, dropping shells onto the ground, jamming it, clearing the jam, then they were almost up with the bull when Wilson yelled "Stop," and the car skidded so that it almost swung over and Macomber fell forward onto his feet, slammed his bolt forward and fired as far forward as he could aim into the galloping, rounded black bull, aimed and shot again, then again, then again, and the bullets, all of them hitting, had no effect on the buffalo that he could see. Then Wilson shot, the roar deafening him, and he could see the bull stagger. Macomber shot again, aiming carefully, and down he came, onto his knees.

"All right," Wilson said. "Nice work. That's three."

Macomber felt a drunken elation.

"How many times did you shoot?" he asked.

"Just three," Wilson said. "You killed the first bull. The biggest one. I helped you finish the other two. Afraid they might have got into cover. You had them killed. I was just mopping up a little. You shot damn well."

"Let's go to the car," said Macomber. "I want a drink."

"Got to finish off that buff first," Wilson told him. The buffalo was on his knees and he jerked his head furiously and bellowed in pig-eyed roaring rage as they came toward him.

"Watch he doesn't get up," Wilson said. Then, "Get a little broadside and take him in the neck just behind the ear."

Macomber aimed carefully at the center of the huge, jerking, rage-driven neck and shot. At the shot the head dropped forward.

"That does it," said Wilson. "Got the spine. They're a hell of a looking thing, aren't they?"

"Let's get the drink," said Macomber. In his life he had never felt so good.

In the car Macomber's wife sat very white faced. "You were marvellous, darling," she said to Macomber. "What a ride."

"Was it rough?" Wilson asked.

"It was frightful. I've never been more frightened in my life."

"Let's all have a drink," Macomber said.

"By all means," said Wilson. "Give it to the Memsahib." She drank the neat whisky from the flask and shuddered a little when she swallowed. She handed the flask to Macomber who handed it to Wilson.

"It was frightfully exciting," she said. "It's given me a dreadful headache. I didn't know you were allowed to shoot them from cars though."

"No one shot from cars," said Wilson coldly.

"I mean chase them from cars."

"Wouldn't ordinarily," Wilson said. "Seemed sporting enough to me though while we were doing it. Taking more chance driving that way across the plain full of holes and one thing and another than hunting on foot. Buffalo could have charged us each time we shot if he liked. Gave him every chance. Wouldn't mention it to any one though. It's illegal if that's what you mean."

"It seemed very unfair to me" Margot said, "chasing those big helpless things in a motor car."

"Did it?" said Wilson.

"What would happen if they heard about it in Nairobi?"

"I'd lose my license for one thing. Other unpleasantnesses," Wilson said, taking a drink from the flask. "I'd be out of business."

"Really?"

"Yes, really."

"Well," said Macomber, and he smiled for the first time all day. "Now she has something on you."

"You have such a pretty way of putting things, Francis," Margot Macomber said. Wilson looked at them both. If a four-letter man marries a five-letter woman, he was thinking, what number of letters would their children be? What he said was, "We lost a gun-bearer. Did you notice it?"

"My God, no," Macomber said.

"Here he comes," Wilson said. "He's all right. He must have fallen off when we left the first bull."

Approaching them was the middle-aged gun-bearer, limping along in his knitted cap, khaki tunic, shorts and rubber sandals, gloomy-faced and disgusted looking. As he came up he called out to Wilson in Swahili and they all saw the change in the white hunter's face.

"What does he say?" asked Margot.

"He says the first bull got up and went into the bush," Wilson said with no expression in his voice.

"Oh," said Macomber blankly.

"Then it's going to be just like the lion," said Margot, full of anticipation.

"It's not going to be a damned bit like the lion," Wilson told her. "Did you want another drink, Macomber?"

"Thanks, yes," Macomber said. He expected the feeling he had had about the lion to come back but it did not. For the first time in his life he really felt wholly without fear. Instead of fear he had a feeling of definite elation.

"We'll go and have a look at the second bull," Wilson said. "I'll tell the driver to put the car in the shade."

"What are you going to do?" asked Margaret Macomber.

"Take a look at the buff," Wilson said.

"I'll come."

"Come along."

The three of them walked over to where the second buffalo bulked blackly in the open, head forward on the grass, the massive horns swung wide.

"He's a very good head," Wilson said. "That's close to a fifty-inch spread."

Macomber was looking at him with delight.

"He's hateful looking," said Margot. "Can't we go into the shade?"

"Of course," Wilson said. "Look," he said to Macomber, and pointed. "See that patch of bush?"

"Yes."

"That's where the first bull went in. The gun-bearer said when he fell off the bull was down. He was watching us helling along and the other two buff galloping. When he looked up there was the bull up and looking at him. Gun-bearer ran like hell and the bull went off slowly into that bush."

"Can we go in after him now?" asked Macomber eagerly.

Wilson looked at him appraisingly. Damned if this isn't a strange one, he thought. Yesterday he's scared sick and today he's a ruddy fire eater.

"No, we'll give him a while."

"Let's please go into the shade," Margot said. Her face was white and she looked ill.

They made their way to the car where it stood under a single, wide-spreading tree and all climbed in.

"Chances are he's dead in there," Wilson remarked. "After a little we'll have a look."

Macomber felt a wild unreasonable happiness that he had never known before.

"By God, that was a chase," he said. "I've never felt any such feeling. Wasn't it marvellous, Margot?"

"I hated it."

"Why?"

"I hated it," she said bitterly. "I loathed it."

"You know I don't think I'd ever be afraid of anything again," Macomber said to Wilson. "Something happened in me after we first saw the buff and started after him. Like a dam bursting. It was pure excitement."

"Cleans out your liver," said Wilson. "Damn funny things happen to people."

Macomber's face was shining. "You know something did happen to me," he said. "I feel absolutely different."

His wife said nothing and eyed him strangely. She was sitting far back in the seat and Macomber was sitting forward talking to Wilson who turned sideways talking over the back of the front seat.

"You know, I'd like to try another lion," Macomber said. "I'm really not afraid of them now. After all, what can they do to you?"

"That's it," said Wilson. "Worst one can do is kill you. How does it go? Shakespeare. Damned good. See if I can remember. Oh, damned good. Used to quote it to myself at one time. Let's see. 'By my troth, I care not; a man can die but once; we owe God a death and let it go which way it will, he that dies this year is quit for the next.' Damned fine, eh?"

He was very embarrassed, having brought out this thing he had lived by, but he had seen men come of age before and it always moved him. It was not a matter of their twenty-first birthday.

It had taken a strange chance of hunting, a sudden precipitation into action without opportunity for worrying beforehand, to bring this about with Macomber, but regardless of how it had happened it had most certainly happened. Look at the beggar now, Wilson thought. It's that some of them stay little boys so long, Wilson thought. Sometimes all their lives. Their figures stay boyish when they're fifty. The great American boy-men. Damned strange people. But he liked this Macomber now. Damned strange fellow. Probably meant the end of cuckoldry too. Well, that would be a damned good thing. Damn good thing. Beggar had probably been afraid all his life. Don't know what started it. But over now. Hadn't had time to be afraid with the buff. That and being angry too. Motor car too. Motor cars made it familiar. Be a damn fire eater now. He'd seen it in the war work the same way. More of a change than any loss of virginity. Fear gone like an operation. Something else grew in its place. Main thing a man had. Made him into a man. Women knew it too. No bloody fear.

From the far corner of the seat Margaret Macomber looked at the two of them. There was no change in Wilson. She saw Wilson as she had seen him the day before when she had first realized what his great talent was. But she saw the change in Francis Macomber now.

"Do you have that feeling of happiness about what's going to happen?" Macomber asked, still exploring his new wealth.

"You're not supposed to mention it," Wilson said, looking in the other's face. "Much more fashionable to say you're scared. Mind you, you'll be scared too, plenty of times."

"But you *have* a feeling of happiness about action to come?"

"Yes," said Wilson. "There's that. Doesn't do to talk too much about all this. Talk the whole thing away. No pleasure in anything if you mouth it up too much."

"You're both talking rot," said Margot. "Just because you've chased some helpless animals in a motor car you talk like heroes."

"Sorry," said Wilson. "I have been gassing too much." She's worried about it already, he thought.

"If you don't know what we're talking about why not keep out of it?" Macomber asked his wife.

"You've gotten awfully brave, awfully suddenly," his wife said contemptuously, but her contempt was not secure. She was afraid of something.

Macomber laughed, a very natural hearty laugh. "You know I *have*," he said. "I really have."

"Isn't it sort of late?" Margot said bitterly. Because she had done the best she could for many years back and the way they were together now was no one person's fault.

"Not for me," said Macomber.

Margot said nothing but sat back in the corner of the seat.

"Do you think we've given him time enough?" Macomber asked Wilson cheerfully.

"We might have a look," Wilson said. "Have you any solids left?"

"The gun-bearer has some."

Wilson called in Swahili and the older gun-bearer, who was skinning out one of the heads, straightened up, pulled a box of solids out of his pocket and brought them over to Macomber, who filled his magazine and put the remaining shells in his pocket.

"You might as well shoot the Springfield," Wilson said. "You're used to it. We'll leave the Mannlicher in the car with the Memsahib. Your gun-bearer can carry your heavy gun. I've this damned cannon. Now let me tell you about them." He had saved this until the last because he did not want to worry Macomber. "When a buff comes he comes with his head high and thrust straight out. The boss of the horns covers any sort of a brain shot. The only shot is straight into the nose. The only other shot is into his chest or, if you're to one side, into the neck or the shoulders. After they've been hit once they take a hell of a lot of killing. Don't try anything fancy. Take the easiest shot there is. They've finished skinning out that head now. Should we get started?"

He called to the gun-bearers, who came up wiping their hands, and the older one got into the back.

"I'll only take Kongoni," Wilson said. "The other can watch to keep the birds away."

As the car moved slowly across the open space toward the island of brushy trees that ran in a tongue of foliage along a dry water course that cut the open swale, Macomber felt his heart pounding and his mouth was dry again, but it was excitement, not fear.

"Here's where he went in," Wilson said. Then to the gun-bearer in Swahili, "Take the blood spoor."

The car was parallel to the patch of bush. Macomber, Wilson and the gun-bearer got down. Macomber, looking back, saw his wife, with the rifle by her side, looking at him. He waved to her and she did not wave back.

The brush was very thick ahead and the ground was dry. The middle-aged gun-bearer was sweating heavily and Wilson had his hat down over his eyes and his red neck showed just ahead of Macomber. Suddenly the gun-bearer said something in Swahili to Wilson and ran forward.

"He's dead in there," Wilson said. "Good work," and he turned to grip Macomber's hand and as they shook hands, grinning at each other, the gun-bearer shouted wildly and they saw him coming out of the bush sideways, fast as a crab, and the bull coming, nose out, mouth tight closed, blood dripping, massive head straight out, coming in a charge, his little pig eyes bloodshot as he looked at them. Wilson, who was ahead, was kneeling shooting, and Macomber, as he fired, unhearing his shot in the roaring of Wilson's gun, saw fragments like slate burst from the huge boss of the horns, and the head jerked, he shot again at the wide nostrils and saw the horns jolt again and fragments fly, and he did not see Wilson now and, aiming carefully, shot again with the buffalo's huge bulk almost on him and his rifle almost level with the on-coming head, nose out, and he could see the little wicked eyes and the head started to lower and he felt a sudden white-hot, blinding flash explode inside his head and that was all he ever felt.

Wilson had ducked to one side to get in a shoulder shot. Macomber had stood solid and shot for the nose, shooting a touch high each time and hitting the heavy horns, splintering and chipping them like hitting a slate roof, and Mrs. Macomber, in the car, had shot at the buffalo with the 6.5 Mannlicher as it seemed about to gore Macomber and had hit her husband about two inches up and a little to one side of the base of his skull.

Francis Macomber lay now, face down, not two yards from where the buffalo lay on his side and his wife knelt over him with Wilson beside her.

"I wouldn't turn him over," Wilson said.

The woman was crying hysterically.

"I'd get back in the car," Wilson said. "Where's the rifle?"

She shook her head, her face contorted. The gun-bearer picked up the rifle.

"Leave it as it is," said Wilson. Then, "Go get Abdulla so that he may witness the manner of the accident."

He knelt down, took a handkerchief from his pocket, and spread it over Francis Macomber's crew-cropped head where it lay. The blood sank into the dry, loose earth.

Wilson stood up and saw the buffalo on his side, his legs out, his thinly-haired belly crawling with ticks. "Hell of a good bull," his brain registered automatically. "A good fifty inches, or better. Better." He called to the driver and told him to spread a blanket over the body and stay by it. Then he walked over to the motor car where the woman sat crying in the corner.

"That was a pretty thing to do," he said in a toneless voice. "He *would* have left you too."

"Stop it," she said.

"Of course it's an accident," he said. "I know that."

"Stop it," she said.

"Don't worry," he said. "There will be a certain amount of unpleasantness but I will have some photographs taken that will be very useful at the inquest. That's the testimony of the gun-bearers and the driver too. You're perfectly all right."

"Stop it," she said.

"There's a hell of a lot to be done," he said. "And I'll have to send a truck off to the lake to wireless for a plane to take the three of us into Nairobi. Why didn't you poison him? That's what they do in England."

"Stop it. Stop it. Stop it," the woman cried.

Wilson looked at her with his flat blue eyes.

"I'm through now," he said. "I was a little angry. I'd begun to like your husband."

"Oh, please stop it," she said. "Please, please stop it."

"That's better," Wilson said. "Please is much better. Now I'll stop."

[1938]

QUESTIONS

1. Why is the lion hunt described in a flashback? What effect does the nonchronological arrangement of the narrative have on your understanding of the story?
2. What male and female roles and values are implied or expressed in the story? Does Robert Wilson reflect the values of the male hero or not?
3. Why does Macomber die? Is his death an accident or a murder?
4. How does Francis Macomber change during the story? How does Margot Macomber change? Is Margot in any way a sympathetic character?
5. What is the meaning of the title?

Langston Hughes

(1902–1967)

United States

Years before his death in 1967, Langston Hughes had earned the respect and admiration of black America and been labeled "The Poet Laureate of the Negro People." It is impossible to consider African-American literature without thinking of Hughes's lifelong contribution as poet, novelist, journalist, editor, translator, playwright, and one-man support group for black artistry in general—from the Harlem Renaissance during the 1920s until the New Black Arts Movement of the 1960s. If Hughes's short stories are less widely known than his poems, the explanation may in large part be due to the vagaries of American publishing. Black readers were familiar with Hughes's Jesse Simple stories for years, beginning with their appearance in *The Chicago Defender* in 1943. Most mainstream readers had to wait until the stories were collected in the various Simple volumes, starting with *Simple Speaks His Mind* in 1950. The story included here, "Thank You, M'am," was written in 1953, although the context for its origin no doubt goes back much earlier, to "The Need for Heroes," an essay Hughes published in *The Crisis* in 1941:

> The written word is the only record we will have of this our present, or our past, to leave behind for future generations. . . . We have a need for heroes. We have a need for books and plays that will encourage and inspire our youth, set for them patterns of conduct, move and stir them to be forthright, strong, clear-thinking and unafraid. . . . It is the social duty of Negro writers to reveal to the people the deep reservoirs of heroism within the race. . . We need in literature the kind of black men and women all of us know exist in life; who are not afraid to claim our rights as human beings and as Americans.

Thank You, M'am

She was a large woman with a large purse that had everything in it but hammer and nails. It had a long strap and she carried it slung across her shoulder. It was about eleven o'clock at night, and she was walking alone, when a boy ran up behind her and tried to snatch her purse. The strap broke with the single tug the boy gave it from behind. But the boy's weight, and the weight of the purse combined caused him to lose his balance so, instead of taking off full blast as he had hoped, the boy fell on his back on the sidewalk, and his legs flew up. The large woman simply turned around and kicked him right square in his blue jeaned sitter. Then she reached down, picked the boy up by the shirt front, and shook him until his teeth rattled.

After that the woman said, "Pick up my pocketbook, boy, and give it here."

She still held him. But she bent down enough to permit him to stoop and pick up her purse. Then she said, "Now ain't you ashamed of yourself?"

Firmly gripped by his shirt front, the boy said, "Yes'm."

The woman said, "What did you want to do it for?"

The boy said, "I didn't aim to."

She said, "You a lie!"

By that time two or three people passed, stopped, turned to look, and some stood watching.

"If I turn you loose, will you run?" asked the woman.

"Yes'm," said the boy.

"Then I won't turn you loose," said the woman. She did not release him.

"I'm very sorry, lady, I'm sorry," whispered the boy.

"Um-hum! And your face is dirty. I got a great mind to wash your face for you. Ain't you got nobody home to tell you to wash your face?"

"No'm," said the boy.

"Then it will get washed this evening," said the large woman starting up the street, dragging the frightened boy behind her.

He looked as if he were fourteen or fifteen, frail and willow-wild, in tennis shoes and blue jeans.

The woman said, "You ought to be my son. I would teach you right from wrong. Least I can do right now is to wash your face. Are you hungry?"

No'm," said the being-dragged boy. "I just want you to turn me loose."

"Was I bothering *you* when I turned that corner?" asked the woman.

"No'm."

"But you put yourself in contact with *me*," said the woman. "If you think that that contact is not going to last awhile, you got another thought coming. When I get through with you, sir, you are going to remember Mrs. Luella Bates Washington Jones."

Sweat popped out on the boy's face and he began to struggle. Mrs. Jones stopped, jerked him around in front of her, put a half-nelson about his neck, and continued to drag him up the street. When she got to her door, she dragged the boy inside, down a hall, and into a large kitchenette-furnished room at the rear of the house. She switched on the light and left the door open. The boy could hear other roomers, laughing and talking in the large house. Some of their doors were open, too, so he knew he and the woman were not alone. The woman still had him by the neck in the middle of her room.

She said, "What is your name?"

"Roger," answered the boy.

"Then, Roger, you go to that sink and wash your face," said the woman, whereupon she turned him loose — at last. Roger looked at the door — looked at the woman — looked at the door — *and went to the sink.*

"Let the water run until it gets warm," she said. "Here's a clean towel."

"You gonna take me to jail?" asked the boy, bending over the sink.

"Not with that face, I would not take you nowhere," said the woman. "Here I am trying to get home to cook me a bite to eat and you snatch my pocketbook! Maybe you ain't been to your supper either, late as it be. Have you?"

"There's nobody home at my house," said the boy.

"Then we'll eat," said the woman. "I believe you're hungry — or been hungry — to try to snatch my pocketbook."

"I wanted a pair of blue suede shoes," said the boy.

"Well, you didn't have to snatch *my* pocketbook to get some suede shoes," said Mrs. Luella Bates Washington Jones. "You could of asked me."

"M'am?"

The water dripping from his face, the boy looked at her. There was a long pause. A very long pause. After he had dried his face and not knowing what else to do dried it again, the boy turned around, wondering what next. The door was open. He could make a dash for it down the hall. He could run, run, run, run, *run*!

The woman was sitting on the day-bed. After awhile she said, "I were young once and I wanted things I could not get."

There was another long pause. The boy's mouth opened. Then he frowned, but not knowing he frowned.

The woman said, "Um-hum! You thought I was going to say *but*, didn't you? You thought I was going to say, *but I didn't snatch people's pocketbooks*. Well, I wasn't going to say that." Pause. Silence. "I have done things, too, which I would not tell you, son—neither tell God, if he didn't already know. So you set down while I fix us something to eat. You might run that comb through your hair so you will look presentable."

In another corner of the room behind a screen was a gas plate and an icebox. Mrs. Jones got up and went behind the screen. The woman did not watch the boy to see if he was going to run now, nor did she watch her purse which she left behind her on the day-bed. But the boy took care to sit on the far side of the room where he thought she could easily see him out of the corner of her eye, if she wanted to. He did not trust the woman *not* to trust him. And he did not want to be mistrusted now.

"Do you need somebody to go to the store," asked the boy, "maybe to get some milk or something?"

"Don't believe I do," said the woman, "unless you just want sweet milk yourself. I was going to make cocoa out of this canned milk I got here."

"That will be fine," said the boy.

She heated some lima beans and ham she had in the icebox, made the cocoa, and set the table. The woman did not ask the boy anything about where he lived, or his folks, or anything else that would embarrass him. Instead, as they ate, she told him about her job in a hotel beauty-shop that stayed open late, what the work was like, and how all kinds of women came in and out, blondes, red-heads, and Spanish. Then she cut him a half of her ten-cent cake.

"Eat some more, son," she said.

When they were finished eating she got up and said, "Now, here, take this ten dollars and buy yourself some blue suede shoes. And next time, do not make the mistake of latching onto *my* pocketbook *nor nobody else's*—because shoes come by devilish like that will burn your feet. I got to get my rest now. But I wish you would behave yourself, son, from here on in."

She led him down the hall to the front door and opened it. "Goodnight! Behave yourself, boy!" she said, looking out into the street.

The boy wanted to say something else other than, "Thank you m'am," to Mrs. Luella Bates Washington Jones, but he couldn't do so as he turned at the barren stoop and looked back at the large woman in the door. He barely managed to say, "Thank you," before she shut the door. And he never saw her again.

[1953]

QUESTIONS

1. Is Langston Hughes guilty of romanticizing the incident in his story? Why? Why not?
2. For contrast, read BarbaraNeely's "Spilled Salt," also included in this volume. In what ways do the two stories mirror or complement each other?
3. Why does Hughes refer to the woman in the story as Mrs. Luella Bates Washington Jones and not simply as Mrs. Jones?

Zora Neale Hurston

(1891–1960)

United States

Zora Neale Hurston has probably influenced contemporary African-American women's fiction more than any other earlier black writer; and, indeed, until Toni Morrison published *Beloved* (1987), Hurston was our country's most prolific African-American woman writer. Her classic novel, *Their Eyes Were Watching God* (1937), demonstrated that black lives are not marked solely by responses to racism in the United States (a theme that is also present in "The Gilded Six-Bits"). In addition to her fiction, Ms. Hurston is also regarded as one of the most important collectors of African-American folklore of this century. According to Robert Hemenway, her biographer, Hurston defined folklore as "the art people create before they find out there is such a thing as art."

Hurston's life was rarely typified by the financial stability she so badly deserved. She was always a bit of a rebel. Her wit and charm apparently sustained her in the most painful of times. On an occasion when she was arrested for crossing the street on a red light, she finagled herself out of the ticket by exclaiming that she had observed white folks cross on green and assumed that red was for black people. Although part of the Harlem Renaissance of the 1920s (whose writers she referred to as the "niggerati"), her writing did not appear until the decade thereafter. She died in 1960 in a poorhouse, without funds to pay for her funeral.

Because interest in Hurston's work has swelled in recent years, her books are now available in a uniform Perennial Library edition, edited by Henry Louis Gates, Jr.: *Mules and Men* (1935), *Their Eyes Were Watching God* (1937), *Moses, Man of the Mountain* (1939), *Dust Tracks on the Road* (1942), and *Seraph on the Suwanee* (1948).

◆ The Gilded Six-Bits ◆

It was a Negro yard around a Negro house in a Negro settlement that looked to the payroll of the G and G Fertilizer works for its support. But there was something happy about the place. The front yard was parted in the middle by a sidewalk from gate to door-step, a sidewalk edged on either side by quart bottles driven neck down into the ground on a slant. A mess of homey flowers planted without a plan but blooming cheerily from their helter-skelter places. The fence and house were whitewashed. The porch and steps scrubbed white.

The front door stood open to the sunshine so that the floor of the front room could finish drying after its weekly scouring. It was Saturday. Everything clean from the front gate to the privy house. Yard raked so that the strokes of the rake would make a pattern. Fresh newspaper cut in fancy edge on the kitchen shelves.

Missie May was bathing herself in the galvanized washtub in the bedroom.

Her dark-brown skin glistened under the soapsuds that skittered down from her wash rag. Her stiff young breasts thrust forward aggressively like broad-based cones with the tips lacquered in black.

She heard men's voices in the distance and glanced at the dollar clock on the dresser.

"Humph! Ah'm way behind time t'day! Joe gointer be heah 'fore Ah git mah clothes on if Ah don't make haste."

She grabbed the clean meal sack at hand and dried herself hurriedly and began to dress. But before she could tie her slippers, there came the ring of singing metal on wood. Nine times.

Missie May grinned with delight. She had not seen the big tall man come stealing in the gate and creep up the walk grinning happily at the joyful mischief he was about to commit. But she knew that it was her husband throwing silver dollars in the door for her to pick up and pile beneath her plate at dinner. It was this way every Saturday afternoon. The nine dollars hurled into the open door, he scurried to a hiding place behind the cape jasmine bush and waited.

Missie May promptly appeared at the door in mock alarm.

"Who dat chuckin' money in mah do'way?" she demanded. No answer from the yard. She leaped off the porch and began to search the shrubbery. She peeped under the porch and hung over the gate to look up and down the road. While she did this, the man behind the jasmine darted to the china berry tree. She spied him and gave chase.

"Nobody ain't gointer be chuckin' money at me and Ah not do 'em nothin'," she shouted in mock anger. He ran around the house with Missie May at his heels. She overtook him at the kitchen door. He ran inside but could not close it after him before she crowded in and locked with him in a rough and tumble. For several minutes the two were a furious mass of male and female energy. Shouting, laughing, twisting, turning, tussling, tickling each other in the ribs; Missie May clutching Joe and Joe trying, but not too hard, to get away.

"Missie May, take yo' hand out mah pocket!" Joe shouted out between laughs.

"Ah ain't, Joe, not lessen you gwine gimme whateve' it is good you got in you' pocket. Turn it go, Joe, do Ah'll tear yo' clothes."

"Go on tear 'em. You de one dat pushes de needles around heah. Move yo' hand, Missie May."

"Lemme git dat paper sack out yo' pocket. Ah bet it's candy kisses."

"Tain't. Move yo' hand. Woman ain't got no business in a man's clothes nohow. Go way."

"Unhhunh! Ah got it. It 'tis so candy kisses. Ah knowed you had something' for me in yo' clothes. Now Ah got to see whut's in every pocket you got."

Joe smiled indulgently and let his wife go through all of his pockets and take out the things that he had hidden there for her to find. She bore off the chewing gum, the cake of sweet soap, the pocket handkerchief as if she had wrested them from him, as if they had not been bought for the sake of this friendly battle.

"Whew! dat play-fight done got me all warmed up," Joe exclaimed. "Got me some water in de kittle?"

"Yo' water is on de fire and yo' clean things is cross de bed. Hurry up and wash yo'self and git changed so we kin eat. Ah'm hongry." As Missie said this, she bore the steaming kettle into the bedroom.

"You ain't hongry, sugar," Joe contradicted her. "Youse jes' a little empty.

Ah'm de one whut's hongry. Ah could eat up camp meetin', back off 'ssociation, and drink Jurdan dry. Have it on de table when Ah git out de tub."

"Don't you mess wid mah business, man. You git in yo' clothes. Ah'm a real wife, not no dress and breath. Ah might not look lak one, but if you burn me, you won't git a thing but wife ashes."

Joe splashed in the bedroom and Missie May fanned around in the kitchen. A fresh red and white checked cloth on the table. Big pitcher of buttermilk beaded with pale drops of butter from the churn. Hot fried mullet, crackling bread, ham hock atop a mound of string beans and new potatoes, and perched on the window-sill a pone of spicy potato pudding.

Very little talk during the meal but that little consisted of banter that pretended to deny affection but in reality flaunted it. Like when Missie May reached for a second helping of the tater pone. Joe snatched it out of her reach.

After Missie May had made two or three unsuccessful grabs at the pan, she begged, "Ah, Joe, gimme some mo' dat tater pone."

"Nope, sweetenin' is for us men-folks. Y'all pritty lil frail eels don't need nothin' lak dis. You too sweet already."

"Please, Joe."

"Naw, naw. Ah don't want you to git no sweeter than whut you is already. We goin' down de road a lil piece t'night so you go put on yo' Sunday-go-to-meetin' things."

Missie May looked at her husband to see if he was planing some prank. "Sho nuff, Joe?"

"Yeah. We goin' to de ice cream parlor."

"Where de ice cream parlor at, Joe?"

"A new man done come heah from Chicago and he done got a place and took and opened it up for a ice cream parlor, and being' as it's real swell, Ah wants you to be one de first ladies to walk in dere and have some set down."

"Do Jesus, Ah ain't knowed nothin' 'bout it. Who de man done it?"

"Mister Otis D. Slemmons, of spots and places—Memphis, Chicago, Jacksonville, Philadelphia and so on."

"Dat heavy-set man wid his mouth full of good teethes?"

"Yeah, Where did you see 'im at?"

"Ah went down to de sto' tuh git a box of lye and Ah seen 'im standin' on de corner talkin' to some of de mens, and Ah come on back and went to scrubbin' de floor, and he passed and tipped his hat whilst Ah was scourin' de steps. Ah thought Ah never seen *him* befo'."

Joe smiled pleasantly. "Yeah, he's up to date. He got de finest clothes Ah ever seen on a colored man's back."

"Aw, he don't look no better in his clothes than you do in yourn. He got a puzzle gut on 'im and he so chuckle-headed, he got a pone behind his neck."

Joe looked down at his own abdomen and said wistfully, "Wisht Ah had a build on me lak he got. He ain't puzzle-gutted, honey. He jes' got a corperation. Dat make 'm look lak a rich white man. All rich mens is got some belly on 'em."

"Ah seen de pitchers of Henry Ford and he's a spare-built man and Rockefeller look lak he ain't got but one gut. But Ford and Rockefeller and dis Slemmons and all de rest kin be as many-gutted as dey please, Ah'm satisfied wid you jes' lak you is, baby. God took pattern after a pine tree and built you noble. Youse a pritty man, and if Ah knowed any way to make you mo' pritty still Ah'd take and do it."

Joe reached over gently and toyed with Missie May's ear. "You jes' say dat cause you love me, but Ah know Ah can't hold no light to Otis D. Slemmons. Ah ain't never been nowhere and Ah ain't got nothing' but you."

Missie May got on his lap and kissed him and he kissed back in kind. Then he went on. "All de womens is crazy 'bout 'im everywhere he go."

"How do you know dat, Joe?"

"He tole us so hisself."

"Dat don't make it so. His mouf is cut cross-ways, ain't it? Well, he kin lie jes' lak anybody else."

"Good Lawd, Missie? You womens sho is hard to sense into things. He's got a five-dollar gold piece for a stick-pin and he got a ten-dollar gold piece on his watch chain and his mouf is jes' crammed full of gold teethes. Sho wisht it wuz mine. And whut make it so cool, he got money 'cumulated. And womens give it all to 'im."

"Ah don't see whut de womens see on 'im. Ah wouldn't give 'im a wink if de sheriff wuz after 'im."

"Well, he tole us how de white womens in Chicago give 'im all dat gold money. So he don't 'low nobody to touch it at all. Not even put dey finger on it. Dey tole 'im not to. You kin make 'miration at it, but don't tetch it."

"Whyn't he stay up dere where dey so crazy 'bout 'im?"

"Ah reckon dey done made 'im vast-rich and he wants to travel some. He says dey wouldn't leave 'im hit a lick of work. He got mo' lady people crazy 'bout him than he kin shake a stick at."

"Joe, Ah hates to see you so dumb. Dat stray nigger jes' tell y'all anything and y'all b'lieve it."

"Go 'head on now, honey and put on yo' clothes. He takin' 'bout his pritty womens—Ah want 'im to see *mine*."

Missie May went off to dress and Joe spent the time trying to make his stomach punch out like Slemmons' middle. He tried the rolling swagger of the stranger, but found that his tall bone-and-muscle stride fitted ill with it. He just had time to drop back into his seat before Missie May came in dressed to go.

On the way home that night Joe was exultant. "Didn't Ah say ole Otis was swell? Can't he talk Chicago talk? Wuzn't dat funny whut he said when great big fat ole Ida Armstrong come in? He asted me, 'Who is dat broad wid de forte shake?' Dat's a new word. Us always thought forty was a set of figgers but he showed us where it means a whole heap of things. Sometimes he don't say forty, he jes' says thirty-eight and two and dat mean de same thing. Know whut he tole me when Ah wuz payin' for our ice cream? He say, 'Ah have to hand it to you, Joe. Dat wife of yours is jes' thirty-eight and two. Yessuh, she's forte!' Ain't he killin'?"

"He'll do in case of a rush. But he sho is got uh heap uh gold on 'im. Dats de first time Ah ever seed gold money. It lookted good on him sho nuff, but it'd look a whole heap better on you."

"Who me? Missie May youse crazy! Where would a po' man lak me git gold money from?"

Missie May was silent for a time, then she said, "Us might find some goin' long de road some time. Us could."

"Who would be losin' gold money round heah? We ain't ever seen none dese white folks wearin' no gold money on dey watch chain. You must be figgerin' Mister Packard or Mister Cadillac goin' pass through heah."

"You don't know whut been lost 'round heah. Maybe somebody way back in memorial times lost they gold money and went on off and it ain't never been found. And then if we wuz to find it, you could wear some 'thout havin' no gang of womens lak dat Slemmons say he got."

Joe laughed and hugged her. "Don't be so wishful 'bout me. Ah'm satisfied de way Ah is. So long as Ah be yo' husband, Ah don't keer 'bout nothin' else. Ah'd ruther all de other womens in de world to be dead than for you to have de toothache. Less we go to bed and git our night rest."

It was Saturday night once more before Joe could parade his wife in Slemmons' ice cream parlor again. He worked the night shift and Saturday was his only night off. Every other evening around six o'clock he left home, and dying dawn saw him hustling home around the lake where the challenging sun flung a flaming sword from east to west across the trembling water.

That was the best part of life—going home to Missie May. Their whitewashed house, the mock battle on Saturday, the dinner and ice cream parlor afterwards, church on Sunday nights when Missie outdressed any other woman in town—all, everything was right.

One night around eleven the acid ran out at the G. and G. The foreman knocked off the crew and let the steam die down. As Joe rounded the lake on his way home, a lean moon rode the lake in a silver boat. If anybody had asked Joe about the moon on the lake, he would have said he hadn't paid it any attention. But he saw it with his feelings. It made him yearn painfully for Missie. Creation obsessed him. He thought about children. They ought to be making little feet for shoes. A little boy child would be about right.

He saw a dim light in the bedroom and decided to come in through the kitchen door. He could wash the fertilizer dust off himself before presenting himself to Missie May. It would be nice for her not to know that he was there until he slipped into his place in bed and hugged her back. She always liked that.

He eased the kitchen door open slowly and silently, but when he went to set his dinner bucket on the table he bumped it into a pile of dishes, and something crashed to the floor. He heard his wife gasp in fright and hurried to reassure her.

"Iss me, honey. Don't git skeered."

There was a quick, large movement in the bedroom. A rustle, a thud and a stealthy silence. The light went out.

What? Robbers? Murderers? Some varmit attacking his helpless wife, perhaps. He struck a match, threw himself on guard and stepped over the door-sill into the bedroom.

The great belt on the wheel of Time slipped and eternity stood still. By the match light he could see the man's legs fighting with his breeches in his frantic desire to get them on. He had both chance and time to kill the intruder in his helpless condition—half in and half out of his pants—but he was too weak to take action. The shapeless enemies of humanity that live in the hours of Time had waylaid Joe. He was assaulted in his weakness. Like Samson awakening after his haircut. So he just opened his mouth and laughed.

The match went out and he struck another and lit the lamp. A howling wind raced across his heart, but underneath its fury he heard his wife sobbing and Slemmons pleading for his life. Offering to buy it with all that he had. "Please, suh, don't kill me. Sixty-two dollars at de sto'. Gold money."

Joe just stood. Slemmons looked at the window, but it was screened. Joe stood like a rough-backed mountain between him and the door. Barring him from escape, from sunrise, from life.

He considered a surprise attack upon the big clown that stood there laughing like a chessy cat. But before his fist could travel an inch, Joe's own rushed out to crush him like a battering ram. Then Joe stood over him.

"Git into yo' damn rags, Slemmons, and dat quick."

Slemmons scrambled to his feet and into his vest and coat. As he grabbed his hat, Joe's fury overrode his intentions and he grabbed at Slemmons with his left hand and struck at him with his right. The right landed. The left grazed the front of his vest. Slemmons was knocked a somersault into the kitchen and fled through the open door. Joe found himself alone with Missie May, with the golden watch charm clutched in his left fist. A short bit of broken chain dangled between his fingers.

Missie May was sobbing. Wails of weeping without words. Joe stood, and after awhile he found out that he had something in his hand. And then he stood and felt without thinking and without seeing with his natural eyes. Missie May kept on crying and Joe kept on feeling so much and not knowing what to do with all his feelings, he put Slemmons watch charm in his pants pocket and took a good laugh and went to bed.

"Missie May, whut you cryin' for?"

"Cause Ah love you so hard and Ah know you don't love *me* no mo'."

Joe sank his face into the pillow for a spell then he said huskily, "You don't know de feelings of dat yet, Missie May."

"Oh Joe, honey, he said he wuz gointer give me dat gold money and he jes' kept on after me—"

Joe was very still and silent for a long time. Then he said, "Well, don't cry no mo', Missie May. Ah got yo' gold piece for you."

The hours went past on their rusty ankles. Joe still and quiet on one bed-rail and Missie May wrung dry of sobs on the other. Finally the sun's tide crept upon the shore of night and drowned all its hours. Missie May with her face stiff and streaked towards the window saw the dawn come into her yard. It was day. Nothing more. Joe wouldn't be coming home as usual. No need to fling open the front door and sweep off the porch, making it nice for Joe. Never no more breakfast to cook; no more washing and starching of Joe's jumper-jackets and pants. No more nothing. So why get up?

With this strange man in her bed, she felt embarrassed to get up and dress. She decided to wait till he had dressed and gone. Then she would get up, dress quickly and be gone forever beyond reach of Joe's looks and laughs. But he never moved. Red light turned to yellow, then white.

From beyond the no-man's land between them came a voice. A strange voice that yesterday had been Joe's.

"Missie May, ain't you gonna fix me no breakfus'?"

She sprang out of bed. "Yeah, Joe. Ah didn't reckon you wuz hongry."

No need to die today. Joe needed her for a few more minutes anyhow.

Soon there was a roaring fire in the cook stove. Water bucket full and two chickens killed. Joe loved fried chicken and rice. She didn't deserve a thing and good Joe was letting her cook him some breakfast. She rushed hot biscuits to the table as Joe took his seat.

He ate with his eyes in his plate. No laughter, no banter.

"Missie May, you ain't eatin' yo' breakfus'."

"Ah don't choose none, Ah thank yuh."

His coffee cup was empty. She sprang to refill it. When she turned from the stove and bent to set the cup beside Joe's plate, she saw the yellow coin on the table between them.

She slumped into her seat and wept into her arms.

Presently Joe said calmly, "Missie May, you cry too much. Don't look back lak Lot's wife and turn to salt."

The sun, the hero of every day, the impersonal old man that beams as brightly on death as on birth, came up every morning and raced across the blue dome and dipped into the sea of fire every evening. Water ran down hill and birds nested.

Missie knew why she didn't leave Joe. She couldn't. She loved him too much, but she could not understand why Joe didn't leave her. He was polite, even kind at times, but aloof.

There were no more Saturday romps. No ringing silver dollars to stack beside her plate. No pockets to rifle. In fact the yellow coin in his trousers was like a monster hiding in the cave of his pockets to destroy her.

She often wondered if he still had it, but nothing could have induced her to ask nor yet to explore his pockets to see for herself. Its shadow was in the house whether or no.

One night Joe came home around midnight and complained of pains in the back. He asked Missie to rub him down with liniment. It had been three months since Missie had touched his body and it all seemed strange. But she rubbed him. Grateful for the chance. Before morning, youth triumphed and Missie exulted. But the next day, as she joyfully made up their bed, beneath her pillow she found the piece of money with the bit of chain attached.

Alone to herself, she looked at the thing with loathing, but look she must. She took it into her hands with trembling and saw first thing that it was no gold piece. It was a gilded half dollar. Then she knew why Slemmons had forbidden anyone to touch his gold. He trusted village eyes at a distance not to recognize his stick-pin as a gilded quarter, and his watch charm as a for-bit piece.

She was glad at first that Joe had left it there. Perhaps he was through with her punishment. They were man and wife again. Then another thought came clawing at her. He had come home to buy from her as if she were any woman in the long house. Fifty cents for her love. As if to say that he could pay as well as Slemmons. She slid the coin into his Sunday pants pocket and dressed herself and left his house.

Half way between her house and the quarters she met her husband's mother, and after a short talk she turned and went back home. Never would she admit defeat to that woman who prayed for it nightly. If she had not the substance of marriage she had the outside show. Joe must leave *her*. She let him see she didn't want his old gold four-bits too.

She saw no more of the coin for some time though she knew that Joe could not help finding it in his pocket. But his health kept poor, and he came home at least every ten days to be rubbed.

The sun swept around the horizon, trailing its robes of weeks and days. One morning as Joe came in from work, he found Missie May chopping wood. Without a word he took the ax and chopped a huge pile before he stopped.

"You ain't got no business choppin' wood, and you know it."

"How come? Ah been choppin' it for de last longest."

"Ah ain't blind. You makin' feet for shoes."

"Won't you be glad to have a lil baby chile, Joe?"

"You know dat 'thout astin' me."

"Iss gointer be a boy chile and de very spit of you."

"You reckon, Missie May?"

"Who else could it look lak?"

Joe said nothing, but he thrust his hand deep into his pocket and fingered something there.

It was almost six months later Missie May took to bed and Joe went and got his mother to come wait on the house.

Missie May was delivered of a fine boy. Her travail was over when Joe came in from work one morning. His mother and the old women were drinking great bowls of coffee around the fire in the kitchen.

The minute Joe came into the room his mother called him aside.

"How did Missie May make out?" he asked quickly.

"Who, dat gal? She strong as a ox. She gointer have plenty mo'. We done fixed her wid de sugar and lard to sweeten her for de nex' one."

Joe stood silent awhile.

"You ain't ast 'bout de baby, Joe. You oughter be mighty proud cause he sho is de spittin' imagine of yuh, son. Dat's yourn all right, if you never git another one, dat un is yourn. And you know Ah'm mighty proud too, son, cause Ah never thought well of you marryin' Missie May cause her ma used tuh fan her foot round right smart and Ah been mighty skeered dat Missie May wuz gointer git misput on her road."

Joe said nothing. He fooled around the house till late in the day then just before he went to work, he went and stood at the foot of the bed and asked his wife how she felt. He did this every day during the week.

On Saturday he went to Orlando to make his market. It had been a long time since he had done that.

Meat and lard, meal and flour, soap and starch. Cans of corn and tomatoes. All the staples. He fooled around town for a while and bought bananas and apples. Way after while he went around to the candy store.

"Hello, Joe," the clerk greeted him. "Ain't seen you in a long time."

"Nope, Ah ain't been heah. Been round in spots and places."

"Want some of them molasses kisses you always buy?"

"Yessuh." He threw the gilded half dollar on the counter. "Will dat spend?"

"Whut is it, Joe? Well, I'll be doggone! A gold-plated four-bit piece. Where'd you git it, Joe?"

"Offen a stray nigger dat come through Eatonville. He had it on his watch chain for a charm—goin' round making out iss gold money. Ha ha! He had a quarter on his tie pin and it wuz all golded up too. Tryin' to fool people. Makin' out he so rich and everything. Ha! Ha! Tryin' to tole off folkses wives from home."

"How did you git it, Joe? Did he fool you, too?"

"Who, me? Naw suh! He ain't fooled me none. Know what Ah done? He come round me wid his smart talk. Ah hauled off and knocked 'im down and took his old four-bits way from 'im. Gointer buy my wife some good ole lasses kisses wid it. Gimme fifty cents worth of dem candy kisses."

"Fifty cents buys a mighty lot of candy kisses, Joe. Why don't you split it up and take some chocolate bars, too. They eat good, too."

"Yessuh, dey do, but Ah wants all dat in kisses. Ah got a lil boy chile home now. Tain't a week old yet, but he kin suck a sugar tit and maybe eat one them kisses hisself."

Joe got his candy and left the store. The clerk turned to the next customer. "Wist I could be like these darkies. Laughin' all the time. Nothin' worries 'em."

Back in Eatonville, Jo reached his own front door. There was the ring of singing metal on wood. Fifteen times. Missie May couldn't run to the door, but she crept there as quickly as she could.

"Joe Banks, Ah hear you chuckin' money in mah do'way. You wait till Ah get mah strength back and Ah'm gointer fix you for dat."

[1933]

QUESTIONS

1. Are the references to gold throughout the story intended to be taken seriously as criticisms of a material society or as something else?
2. What can be said of Hurston's use of images throughout the story, such as the one of the sun: "The sun, the hero of every day, the impersonal old man that beams as brightly on death as on birth, came up every morning and raced across the blue dome and dipped into the sea of fire every evening"?
3. Is "The Gilded Six-Bits" a happy story of African-American life or is there a streak of pessimism beneath the surface narrative?

Shirley Jackson
(1919–1965)
United States

Shirley Jackson might almost be said to have led two lives: as the wife of a noted literary critic and professor, Stanley Edgar Hyman, and mother of their four children; and as the author of fiction, at least one story of which has assured her permanent place in literature. Her fictional *oeuvre* also branches into two directions: one cluster focuses on family life and domestic comedy; the other, far darker in tone, explores dimensions of madness, terror, moral innocence, and evil.

Jackson spent her early years in California, where she showed an early interest in writing: she won a poetry prize before she was 13. She attended the University of Rochester briefly (leaving because of an attack of depression—an illness that returned intermittently during her adult life) and later the University of Syracuse, where she met and married Hyman in 1940. While there, she wrote short stories that were published in a student journal they founded together, presciently named *The Spectre* (prescient, because a number of her stories and novels were to include ghostly or supernatural elements). She continued to write fiction while raising a growing family, establishing a daily discipline that enabled her to produce six novels and a number of short stories despite the domestic claims on her time.

Jackson's most famous and frequently anthologized and dramatized story, "The Lottery," disturbingly links ancient ritual with archetypal possibilities for evil. Jackson herself was surprised at the intensity of response to this story when it first appeared in *The New Yorker* in 1948. As she later summarized the flood of letters expressing outrage sent to the editor (more than for any piece of fiction the magazine had ever published), she identified three recurring themes, "bewilderment, speculation, and plain old-fashioned abuse. . . . The general tone of the early letters, however, was a kind of wide-eyed, shocked innocence. People at first were not so much concerned with what the story meant; what they wanted to know was where these lotteries were held, and whether they could go there and watch." When pressed for an interpretation of "The Lottery," Jackson answered that such an explanation was "very difficult." As she phrased her response,

> I suppose I hoped, by setting a particularly brutal ancient rite in the present and in my own village, to shock the story's readers with a graphic dramatization of the pointless violence and general inhumanity in their own lives. . . . I gather that in some cases the mind just rebels. The number of people who expected [the winner of the lottery] to win a Bendix washer at the end would amaze you.

The Lottery

The morning of June 27th was clear and sunny, with the fresh warmth of a full-summer day; the flowers were blossoming profusely and the grass was richly green. The people of the village began to gather in the square, between the post office and the bank, around ten o'clock; in some towns there were so many people that the lottery took two days and had to be started on June 26th, but in this village, where there were only about three hundred people, the whole lottery took less than two hours, so it could begin at ten o'clock in the morning and still be through in time to allow the villagers to get home for noon dinner.

The children assembled first, of course. School was recently over for the summer, and the feeling of liberty sat uneasily on most of them; they tended to gather together quietly for a while before they broke into boisterous play, and their talk was still of the classroom and teacher, of books and reprimands. Bobby Martin had already stuffed his pockets full of stones, and the other boys soon followed his example, selecting the smoothest and roundest stones; Bobby and Harry Jones and Dickie Delacroix — the villagers pronounced this name "Dellacroy" — eventually made a great pile of stones in one corner of the square and guarded it against the raids of the other boys. The girls stood aside, talking among themselves, looking over their shoulders at the boys, and the very small children rolled in the dust or clung to the hands of their older brothers or sisters.

Soon the men began to gather, surveying their own children, speaking of planting and rain, tractors and taxes. They stood together, away from the pile of stones in the corner, and their jokes were quiet and they smiled rather than laughed. The women, wearing faded house dresses and sweaters, came shortly after their menfolk. They greeted one another and exchanged bits of gossip as they went to join their husbands. Soon the women, standing by their husbands, began to call to their children, and the children came reluctantly, having to be called four or five times. Bobby Martin ducked under his mother's grasping hand and ran, laughing, back to the pile of stones. His father spoke up sharply, and Bobby came quickly and took his place between his father and his oldest brother.

The lottery was conducted — as were the square dances, the teenage club, the Halloween program — by Mr. Summers, who had time and energy to devote to civic activities. He was a round-faced, jovial man and he ran the coal business, and people were sorry for him, because he had no children and his wife was a scold. When he arrived in the square, carrying the black wooden box, there was a murmur of conversation among the villagers, and he waved and called, "Little late today, folks." The postmaster, Mr. Graves, followed him, carrying a three-legged stool, and the stool was put in the center of the square and Mr. Summers set the black box down on it. The villagers kept their distance, leaving a space between themselves and the stool, and when Mr. Summers said, "Some of you fellows want to give me a hand?" there was a hesitation before two men, Mr. Martin and his oldest son, Baxter, came forward to hold the box steady on the stool while Mr. Summers stirred up the papers inside it.

The original paraphernalia for the lottery had been lost long ago, and the black box now resting on the stool had been put into use even before Old Man Warner, the oldest man in town, was born. Mr. Summers spoke frequently to the villagers about making a new box, but no one liked to upset even as much tradition as was represented by the black box. There was a story that the present box had been made with some pieces of the box that had preceded it, the one that had been constructed when the first people settled down to make a village here. Every year, after the lottery, Mr. Summers began talking again about a new box, but every year the subject was allowed to fade off without anything's being done. The black box grew shabbier each year; by now it was no longer completely black but splintered badly along one side to show the original wood color, and in some places faded or stained.

Mr. Martin and his oldest son, Baxter, held the black box securely on the stool until Mr. Summers had stirred the papers thoroughly with his hand. Because so much of the ritual had been forgotten or discarded, Mr. Summers had been successful in having slips of paper substituted for the chips of wood that had been used for generations. Chips of wood, Mr. Summers had argued, had been all very well when the village was tiny, but now that the population was more than three hundred and likely to keep on growing, it was necessary to use something that would fit more easily into the black box. The night before the lottery, Mr. Summers and Mr. Graves made up the slips of paper and put them in the box, and it was then taken to the safe of Mr. Summers's coal company and locked up until Mr. Summers was ready to take it to the square next morning. The rest of the year, the box was put away, sometimes one place, sometimes another; it had spent one year in Mr. Graves's barn and another year underfoot in the post office, and sometimes it was set on a shelf in the Martin grocery and left there.

There was a great deal of fussing to be done before Mr. Summers declared the lottery open. There were the lists to make up — of heads of families, heads of households in each family, members of each household in each family. There was the proper swearing-in of Mr. Summers by the postmaster, as the official of the lottery; at one time, some people remembered, there had been a recital of some sort, performed by the official of the lottery, a perfunctory, tuneless chant that had been rattled off duly each year; some people believed that the official of the lottery used to stand just so when he said or sang it, others believed that he was supposed to walk among the people, but years and years ago this part of the ritual had been allowed to lapse. There had been, also, a ritual salute, which the official of the lottery had had to use in addressing each person who came up to draw from the box, but this also had changed with time, until now it was felt necessary only for the official to speak to each person approaching. Mr. Summers was very good at all this; in his clean white shirt and blue jeans, with one hand resting carelessly on the black box, he seemed very proper and important as he talked interminably to Mr. Graves and the Martins.

Just as Mr. Summers finally left off talking and turned to the assembled villagers, Mrs. Hutchinson came hurriedly along the path to the square, her sweater thrown over her shoulders, and slid into place in the back of the crowd. "Clean forgot what day it was," she said to Mrs. Delacroix, who stood next to her, and they both laughed softly. "Thought my old man was out back stacking wood," Mrs. Hutchinson went on, "and then I looked out the window and the kids was gone, and then I remembered it was the twenty-seventh and came a-running." She dried her hands on her apron, and Mrs. Delacroix said, "You're in time, though. They're still talking away up there."

Mrs. Hutchinson craned her neck to see through the crowd and found her husband and children standing near the front. She tapped Mrs. Delacroix on the arm as a farewell and began to make her way through the crowd. The people separated good-humoredly to let her through; two or three people said, in voices just loud enough to be heard across the crowd, "Here comes your Missus, Hutchinson," and "Bill, she made it after all." Mrs. Hutchinson reached her husband, and Mr. Summers, who had been waiting, said cheerfully, "Thought we were going to have to get on without you, Tessie." Mrs. Hutchinson said, grinning, "Wouldn't have me leave m'dishes in the sink, now, would you, Joe?" and soft laughter ran through the crowd as the people stirred back into position after Mrs. Hutchinson's arrival.

"Well, now," Mr. Summers said soberly, "guess we better get started, get this over with, so's we can go back to work. Anybody ain't here?"

"Dunbar," several people said. "Dunbar, Dunbar."

Mr. Summers consulted his list. "Clyde Dunbar," he said. "That's right. He's broke his leg, hasn't he? Who's drawing for him?"

"Me, I guess," a woman said, and Mr. Summers turned to look at her. "Wife draws for her husband," Mr. Summers said. "Don't you have a grown boy to do it for you, Janey?" Although Mr. Summers and everyone else in the village knew the answer perfectly well, it was the business of the official of the lottery to ask such questions formally. Mr. Summers waited with an expression of polite interest while Mrs. Dunbar answered.

"Horace's not but sixteen yet," Mrs. Dunbar said regretfully. "Guess I gotta fill in for the old man this year."

"Right," Mr. Summers said. He made a note on the list he was holding. Then he asked, "Watson boy drawing this year?"

A tall boy in the crowd raised his hand. "Here," he said. "I'm drawing for m'mother and me." He blinked his eyes nervously and ducked his head as several voices in the crowd said things like "Good fellow, Jack," and "Glad to see your mother's got a man to do it."

"Well," Mr. Summers said, "guess that's everyone. Old Man Warner make it?"

"Here," a voice said, and Mr. Summers nodded.

A sudden hush fell on the crowd as Mr. Summers cleared his throat and looked at the list. "All ready?" he called. "Now, I'll read the names — heads of families first — and the men come up and take a paper out of the box. Keep the paper folded in your hand without looking at it until everyone has had a turn. Everything clear?"

The people had done it so many times that they only half listened to the directions; most of them were quiet, wetting their lips, not looking around. Then Mr. Summers raised one hand high and said, "Adams." A man disengaged himself from the crowd and came forward. "Hi, Steve," Mr. Summers said, and Mr. Adams said, "Hi, Joe." They grinned at one another humorlessly and nervously. Then Mr. Adams reached into the black box and took out a folded paper. He held it firmly by one corner as he turned and went hastily back to his place in the crowd, where he stood a little apart from his family, not looking down at his hand.

"Allen," Mr. Summers said, "Anderson . . . Bentham."

"Seems like there's no time at all between lotteries any more," Mrs. Delacroix said to Mrs. Graves in the back row. "Seems like we got through with the last one only last week."

"Time sure goes fast," Mrs. Graves said.

"Clark . . . Delacroix."

"There goes my old man," Mrs. Delacroix said. She held her breath while her husband went forward.

"Dunbar," Mr. Summers said, and Mrs. Dunbar went steadily to the box while one of the women said, "Go on, Janey," and another said, "There she goes."

"We're next," Mrs. Graves said. She watched while Mr. Graves came around from the side of the box, greeted Mr. Summers gravely, and selected a slip of paper from the box. By now, all through the crowd there were men holding the small folded papers in their large hands, turning them over and over nervously. Mrs. Dunbar and her two sons stood together, Mrs. Dunbar holding the slip of paper.

"Harburt . . . Hutchinson."

"Get up there, Bill," Mrs. Hutchinson said, and the people near her laughed.

"Jones."

"They do say," Mr. Adams said to Old Man Warner, who stood next to him, "that over in the north village they're talking of giving up the lottery."

Old Man Warner snorted. "Pack of crazy fools," he said "Listening to the young folks, nothing's good enough for *them*. Next thing you know, they'll be wanting to go back to living in caves, nobody work any more, live *that* way for a while. Used to be a saying about 'Lottery in June, corn be heavy soon.' First thing you know, we'd all be eating stewed chickweed and acorns. There's *always* been a lottery," he added petulantly. "Bad enough to see young Joe Summers up there joking with everybody."

"Some places have already quit lotteries," Mrs. Adams said.

"Nothing but trouble in *that*," Old Man Warner said stoutly. "Pack of young fools."

"Martin." And Bobby Martin watched his father go forward. "Overdyke . . . Percy."

"I wish they'd hurry," Mrs. Dunbar said to her older son. "I wish they'd hurry."

"They're almost through," her son said.

"You get ready to run tell Dad," Mrs. Dunbar said.

Mr. Summers called his own name and then stepped forward precisely and selected a slip from the box. The he called, "Warner."

"Seventy-seventh year I been in the lottery," Old Man Warner said as he went through the crowd. "Seventy-seventh time."

"Watson." The tall boy came awkwardly through the crowd. Someone said. "Don't be nervous, Jack," and Mr. Summers said, "Take your time, son."

"Zanini."

After that, there was a long pause, a breathless pause, until Mr. Summers, holding his slip of paper in the air, said, "All right, fellows." For a minute, no one moved, and then all the slips of paper were opened. Suddenly, all the women began to speak at once, saying, "Who is it?" "Who's got it?" "Is it the Dunbars?" "Is it the Watsons?" Then the voices began to say, "It's Hutchinson. It's Bill," "Bill Hutchinson's got it."

"Go tell your father," Mrs. Dunbar said to her older son.

People began to look around to see the Hutchinsons. Bill Hutchinson was standing quiet, staring down at the paper in his hand. Suddenly, Tessie Hutchinson shouted to Mr. Summers, "You didn't give him time enough to take any paper he wanted. I saw you. It wasn't fair!"

"Be a good sport, Tessie," Mrs. Delacroix called, and Mrs. Graves said, "All of us took the same chance."

"Shut up, Tessie," Bill Hutchinson said.

"Well, everyone," Mr. Summers said, "that was done pretty fast, and now we've got to be hurrying a little more to get done in time." He consulted his next list. "Bill," he said, "you draw for the Hutchinson family. You got any other households in the Hutchinsons?"

"There's Don and Eva," Mrs. Hutchinson yelled. "Make *them* take their chance!"

"Daughters drew with their husbands' families, Tessie," Mr. Summers said gently. "You know that as well as anyone else."

"It wasn't *fair*," Tessie said.

"I guess not, Joe," Bill Hutchinson said regretfully. "My daughter draws with her husband's family, that's only fair. And I've got no other family except the kids."

"Then, as far as drawing for families is concerned, it's you," Mr. Summers said in explanation, "and as far as drawing for households is concerned, that's you, too. Right?"

"Right," Bill Hutchinson said.

"How many kids, Bill?" Mr. Summers asked formally.

"Three," Bill Hutchinson said. "There's Bill, Jr., and Nancy, and little Dave. And Tessie and me."

"All right, then," Mr. Summers said. "Harry, you got their tickets back?"

Mr. Graves nodded and held up the slips of paper. "Put them in the box, then," Mr. Summers directed. "Take Bill's and put it in."

"I think we ought to start over," Mrs. Hutchinson said, as quietly as she could. "I tell you it wasn't *fair*. You didn't give him time enough to choose. *Every*body saw that."

Mr. Graves had selected the five slips and put them in the box, and he dropped all the papers but those onto the ground, where the breeze caught them and lifted them off.

"Listen, everybody," Mrs. Hutchinson was saying to the people around her.

"Ready, Bill?" Mr. Summers asked, and Bill Hutchinson, with one quick glance around at his wife and children, nodded.

"Remember," Mr. Summers said, "take the slips and keep them folded until each person has taken one. Harry, you help little Dave." Mr. Graves took the hand of the little boy, who came willingly with him up to the box. "Take a paper out of the box, Davy," Mr. Summers said. Davy put his hand into the box and laughed. "Take just *one* paper," Mr. Summers said. "Harry, you hold it for him." Mr. Graves took the child's hand and removed the folded paper from the tight fist and held it while little Dave stood next to him and looked up at him wonderingly.

"Nancy next," Mr. Summers said. Nancy was twelve, and her school friends breathed heavily as she went forward, switching her skirt, and took a slip daintily from the box. "Bill, Jr.," Mr. Summers said, and Billy, his face red and his feet overlarge, nearly knocked the box over as he got a paper out. "Tessie," Mr. Summers said. She hesitated for a minute, looking around defiantly, and then set her lips and went up to the box. She snatched a paper out and held it behind her.

"Bill," Mr. Summers said, and Bill Hutchinson reached into the box and felt around, bringing his hand out at last with the slip of paper in it.

The crowd was quiet. A girl whispered, "I hope it's not Nancy," and the sound of the whisper reached the edges of the crowd.

"It's not the way it used to be," Old Man Warner said clearly. "People ain't the way they used to be."

"All right," Mr. Summers said. "Open the papers. Harry, you open little Dave's."

Mr. Graves opened the slip of paper and there was a general sigh through the crowd as he held it up and everyone could see that it was blank. Nancy and Bill, Jr., opened theirs at the same time, and both beamed and laughed, turning around to the crowd and holding their slips of paper above their heads.

"Tessie," Mr. Summers said. There was a pause, and then Mr. Summers looked at Bill Hutchinson, and Bill unfolded this paper and showed it. It was blank.

"It's Tessie," Mr. Summers said, and his voice was hushed. "Show us her paper, Bill."

Bill Hutchinson went over to his wife and forced the slip of paper out of her hand. It had a black spot on it, the black spot Mr. Summers had made the night before with the heavy pencil in the coal-company office. Bill Hutchinson held it up and there was a stir in the crowd.

"All right, folks," Mr. Summers said. "Let's finish quickly."

Although the villagers had forgotten the ritual and lost the original black box, they still remembered to use stones. The pile of stones the boys had made earlier was ready; there were stones on the ground with the blowing scraps of paper that had come out of the box. Mrs. Delacroix selected a stone so large she had to pick it up with both hands and turned to Mrs. Dunbar. "Come on," she said. "Hurry up."

Mrs. Dunbar had small stones in both hands, and she said, gasping for breath, "I can't run at all. You'll have to go ahead and I'll catch up with you."

The children had stones already, and someone gave little Davy Hutchinson a few pebbles.

Tessie Hutchinson was in the center of a cleared space by now, and she held her hands out desperately as the villagers moved in on her. "It isn't fair," she said. A stone hit her on the side of the head.

Old Man Warner was saying, "Come on, come on, everyone." Steve Adams was in the front of the crowd of villagers, with Mrs. Graves beside him.

"It isn't fair, it isn't right," Mrs. Hutchinson screamed and then they were upon her.

[1948]

QUESTIONS

1. How does the story achieve its impact? How is suspense sustained? When do you begin to suspect the outcome?
2. How do the setting, tone, and point of view contribute to the effectiveness of the story? Why does the author use an omniscient narrator rather than one of the characters' perspectives?
3. What is the purpose of the lottery?
4. What is the theme of the story?

SVAVA JAKOBSDÓTTIR

(b. 1930)

ICELAND

Born in eastern Iceland, Svava Jakobsdóttir also spent part of her childhood in Saskatchewan, Canada, where her father held a position as minister of the Icelandic Lutheran Church. She lived in Reykjavik, the capital of Iceland, for part of high school and college, but returned to North America to study English literature at Smith College (Massachusetts). Continuing her literary studies at Somervillege College, Oxford, and at Uppsala University in Sweden, she concentrated on Old Icelandic and modern Swedish literatures.

From the study of literature, Jakobsdóttir turned to its creation, publishing her first collection of stories, *Twelve Women*, in 1965. She has also published a novel and several other collections of short stories, as well as three plays and several radio scripts. In her writing, Jakobsdóttir frequently focuses on women's roles and expectations in contemporary society.

Jakobsdóttir has also served in several capacities within the political and diplomatic profession: first in Iceland's Foreign Ministry and later as an elected member of the Icelandic Parliament, a delegate to the United Nations, and a member of the Nordic Committee whose goal was the promotion of gender equality. After serving several terms in office, she gave up her political career to be a full-time writer. She is married to a folklorist, Jon Hnefill Adalsteinsson, and has one son.

◆ *A Story for Children* ◆

For as long as she could remember she had resolved to be true to her nature and devote all her energies to her home and her children. There were several children now and from morning till night she was swamped with work, doing the household chores and caring for the children. She was now preparing supper and waiting for the potatoes to boil. A Danish women's magazine lay on the kitchen bench as if it had been tossed there accidentally; in fact, she kept it there on purpose and sneaked a look at it whenever she got a chance. Without letting the pot of potatoes out of her mind she picked up the magazine and skimmed over Fru Ensom's[1] advice column. This was by no means the column that seemed most interesting to her, but it was usually short. It was possible that it would last just long enough so that the potatoes would be boiling when she finished reading it. The first letter in the column was short: Dear Fru Ensom, I have never lived for anything other than my children and have done everything for them. Now I am left alone and they never visit me. What should I do? Fru Ensom answered: Do more for them.

[1]*Fru Ensom* Danish: Mrs. Lonesome

This was the logical answer, of course. It was perfectly clear that nothing else was possible. She hoped that she wouldn't start writing to the magazines about such obvious things when the time came. No, these columns where people moaned and groaned were not to her liking. The columns which discussed childrearing and the role of the mother—or rather, *the* column, since both subjects were discussed in one and the same column—were much more positive. The fundamental aspects of child-rearing had of course been familiar to her for quite some time now, but it did happen that she felt weak and fatigued at times. At that point she would leaf through the columns on child-rearing seeking courage and confirmation that she was on the right track in life. She only regretted having less and less time to read.

The uncleaned fish awaited her in the sink and she withstood the temptation to read the child-rearing column this time. She closed the magazine and stood up. She limped a little bit ever since the children had cut off the big toe on her right foot. They had wanted to find out what happened if someone had only nine toes. Within herself she was proud of her limp and of her children's eagerness to learn, and sometimes she limped even more than was necessary. She now turned the heat down under the potatoes and began cleaning the fish. The kitchen door opened and her little son, who was six years old and had blue eyes and light curly hair, came up to her.

"Mama," he said, and stuck a pin in her arm. She started and almost cut herself with the knife.

"Yes, dear," she said, and reached out her other arm so the child could stick it, too.

"Mama, tell me a story."

She put the knife down, dried her hands and sat down with the child in her lap to tell him a story. She was just about halfway through the story when it occurred to her that one of the other children might suffer psychological harm from not getting supper on time. In the boy's face she tried to see how he would take it if she stopped telling the story. She felt the old indecisiveness taking hold of her and she became distracted from the story. This inability of hers to make decisions had increased with the number of children and the ever-increasing chores. She had begun to fear those moments which interrupted her usual rush from morning to night. More and more often she lost her poise if she stopped to make a decision. The child-rearing columns gave little or no help at such moments, though she tried to call them to mind. They only discussed one problem and one child at a time. Other problems always had to wait until next week.

This time she was spared making a decision. The door opened and all the children crowded into the kitchen. Stjáni, the oldest, was in the lead. At an early age he had shown an admirable interest in both human and animal biology. The boy who had been listening to the story now slid out of her lap and took up a position among his brothers and sisters. They formed a semicircle around her and she looked over each of them one after the other.

"Mama, we want to see what a person's brain looks like."

She looked at the clock.

"Right now?" she asked.

Stjáni didn't answer his mother's question. With a nod of his head and a sharp glance he gave his younger brother a sign, and the younger brother went and got a rope, while Stjáni fastened the saw blade to the handle. The rope was then wrapped around the mother. She felt how the little hands fumbled at her back while the knot was tied. The rope was loose and it wouldn't take much effort to get free. But she was careful not to let it be noticed. He had always been sensitive about how clumsy he was with his hands. Just as Stjáni raised the saw up to her head the image of the children's father came into her mind. She saw him in front of her just as he would appear in a little while: on the threshold of the front door with his briefcase in one hand and his hat in the other. She never saw him except in the front doorway, either on his way out or on his way in. She had once been able to imagine him outside the house among other people or at the office, but now, after the children had been born, they had moved into a new house and he into a new office, and she had lost her bearings. He would come home soon and she still hadn't started frying the fish. The blood had now begun to flow down her head. Stjáni had gotten through with the saw. It seemed to be going well, and fairly quickly. Now and then he stopped as if he were measuring with his eyes just how big the hole had to be. Blood spurted into his face and a curse crossed his lips. He nodded his head and the young brother went immediately and got the mop bucket. They placed it under the hole and soon it was half full. The procedure was over at the exact moment the father appeared in the doorway. He stood motionless for a while and pondered the sight which presented itself to him: his wife tied up, with a hole in her head, the eldest son holding a gray brain in his hand, the curious group of children huddled together, and only one pot on the stove.

"Kids! How can you think of doing this when it's already suppertime?"

He picked up the piece of his wife's skull and snapped it back in just as she was about to bleed to death. Then he took over and soon the children were busy tidying up after themselves. He wiped most of the blood stains off the walls himself before he checked on the pot on the stove. There was a suspicious sound coming from it. The water had boiled away and he took the pot off the stove and set it on the metal counter next to the sink. When he saw the half-cleaned fish in the sink he realized that his wife had still not gotten up from the chair. Puzzled, he knit his brow. It wasn't usual for her to be sitting down when there was so much to do. He went over to her and looked at her attentively. He noticed then that they had forgotten to untie her.

When he had freed her they looked into each other's eyes and smiled. Never was their harmony more deeply felt than when their eyes met in mutual pride over the children.

"Silly urchins," he said, and his voice was filled with the concern and affection that he felt for his family.

Soon afterward they sat down at the table. Everyone except Stjáni. He was in his room studying the brain under a microscope. Meanwhile, his mother kept his supper warm for him in the kitchen. They were all hungry and took to their food briskly; this was an unusually late supper. There was no change to be seen in the mother. She had washed her hair and combed it over the cut before she sat down. Her mild expression displayed the patience and self-denial usual at mealtimes. This expression had first appeared during those years when she served her children first and kept only the smallest and most meager piece for herself. Now the children were big enough so that they could take the best pieces themselves and the expression was actually unnecessary, but it had become an inseparable part of the meal. Before the meal was over Stjáni came in and sat down. The mother went to get his supper. In the kitchen she boned the fish thoroughly before putting it on the plate. When she picked up the garbage pail to throw the bones away she let out a scream. The brain was right on top of the pail.

The rest of the family rushed out as soon as her scream reached the dining room. The father was in the lead and was quick to discover what was wrong when he saw his wife staring down into the garbage pail. Her scream had died out, but it could still be seen in the contours of her face.

"You think it's a shame to throw it out, don't you, dear?" he asked.

"I don't know," she said and looked at him apologetically. "I didn't think."

"Mama didn't think, mama didn't think, mama didn't think," chanted one of the children who had an especially keen sense of humor.

They all burst out laughing and the laughter seemed to solve the problem. The father said he had an idea; they didn't have to throw the brain out, they could keep it in alcohol.

With that, he put the brain into a clear jar and poured alcohol over it. They brought the jar into the living room and found a place for it on a shelf of knick-knacks. They all agreed it fit well there. Then they finished eating.

There were no noticeable changes in the household routine due to the brain loss. At first a lot of people came to visit. They came to see the brain, and those who had prided themselves on their grandmother's old spinning wheel in the corner of their living room now looked with envy upon the brain upon the shelf. She felt no changes in herself either at first. It hadn't become a bit more difficult for her to do housework or to understand the Danish magazines. Many things even turned out to be easier then before, and situations that earlier had caused her to rack her brain no longer did so. But gradually she began to feel a heaviness in her chest. It seemed as if her lungs no longer had room enough to function and after a year had passed she went to the doctor. A thorough examination revealed that her heart had grown larger *usus innaturalis et adsidui causa.*[2] She asked the doctor to excuse her for having forgotten all the Latin she had learned in school, and patiently he explained to her how the loss of one organ could result in changes in another. Just as a man who loses his sight will acquire a more acute sense of hearing, her heart had increased its activity a good deal when her brain was no longer available. This was a natural development, *lex vitae,*[3] if one may say so—and at that, the doctor laughed—there was no need to fear that such a law could be anything but just. Therefore she didn't have to be afraid. She was in the best of health.

She felt relieved at these words. Lately she had even been afraid that she had only a short time to live, and this fear had become an increasingly loud voice within her breast which said: What will become of them if I die? But now she realized that this voice, whose strength and clarity grew steadily, was no prophecy, but rather the voice of her heart. This knowledge made her happy because the voice of one's heart could be trusted.

The years passed and her heart's voice showed her the way: from the children's rooms and her husband's study to the kitchen and the bedroom. This route was dear to her, and no gust of wind that blew through the front door was ever strong enough to sweep away her tracks. Only one thing aroused fear in

[2]*usus innaturalis et adsidui causa* Latin: a case involving unnatural and persistent use

[3]*lex vitae* Latin: law of life

her: unexpected changes in the world. The year they changed counter girls at the milk store five times she was never quite all right. But the children grew up. She awoke with a bad dream when her oldest child, Stjáni, began to pack his suitcase to go out into the world. With uncontrollable vehemence she threw herself over the threshold to block his exit. A sucking sound could be heard as the boy stepped on her on his way out. He thought she was moaning and paused a moment and said that she herself was to blame. No one had asked her to lie down there. She smiled as she got up because what he had said wasn't quite right. Her heart had told her to lie there. She had heard the voice clearly and now, as she watched him walk down the street, the voice spoke to her again and said that she could still be glad that she had softened his first steps out into the world. Later on they all left one after the other and she was left alone. She no longer had anything to do in the children's rooms and she would often sit in the easy chair in the living room now. If she looked up, the jar on the shelf came into view, where the brain had stood all these years and, in fact, was almost completely forgotten. Custom had made it commonplace. Sometimes she pondered over it. As far as she could see, it had kept well. But she got less and less pleasure out of looking at it. It reminded her of her children. And gradually she felt that a change was again taking place within herself, but she couldn't bring herself to mention it to her husband. She saw him so seldom lately, and whenever he appeared at home she got up from the chair in a hurry, as if a guest had arrived. One day he brought up the question himself of whether she wasn't feeling well. Pleased, she looked up, but when she saw that he was figuring the accounts at the same time, she became confused in answering (she had never been particularly good in figuring). In her confusion she said she didn't have enough to do. He looked at her amazed and said there were enough things to be done if people only used their brain. Of course he said this without thinking. He knew very well that she didn't have a brain, but she nevertheless took him literally. She took the jar down from the shelf, brought it to the doctor and asked if he thought the brain was still useable. The doctor didn't exclude the possibility of its being of some use, but on the other hand, all organs atrophied after being preserved in alcohol for a long time. Therefore it would be debatable whether it would pay to move it at all; in addition, the *nervi cerebrales*[4] had been left in rather poor shape, and the doctor asked whether some clumsy dolt had actually done the surgery.

"He was so little then, the poor thing," the woman said.

"By the way," said the doctor, "I recall that you had a highly developed heart."

The woman avoided the doctor's inquiring look and a faint pang of conscience gripped her. And she whispered to the doctor what she hadn't dared hint of to her husband:

"My heart's voice has fallen silent."

As she said this she realized why she had come. She unbuttoned her blouse, took it off and laid it neatly on the back of the chair. Her bra went the same way. Then she stood ready in front of the doctor, naked from the waist up. He picked up a scalpel and cut, and a moment later he handed her the gleaming, red heart. Carefully he placed it in her palm and her hands closed around it. Its hesitant

[4]*nervi cerebrales* Latin: cerebral nerves

beat resembled the fluttering of a bird in a cage. She offered to pay the doctor, but he shook his head and, seeing that she was having difficulty, helped her get dressed. He then offered to call her a taxi since she had so much to carry. She refused, stuffed the brain jar into her shopping bag and slipped the bag over her arm. Then she left with the heart in her hands.

Now began the long march from one child to the next. She first went to see her sons, but found none of them at home. They had all gotten a berth on the ship of state and it was impossible to tell when they would return. Furthermore, they never stayed in home port long enough for there to be time for anything other than begetting children. She withdrew from the bitterness of her daughters-in-law and went to see her oldest daughter, who opened the door herself. A look of astonishment and revulsion came over her face when she saw the slimy, red heart pulsating in her mother's palm, and in her consternation, she slammed the door. This was of course an involuntary reaction and she quickly opened the door again, but she made it clear to her mother that she didn't care at all about her heart; and she wasn't sure it would go with the new furniture in the living room. The mother then realized that it was pointless to continue the march, because her younger daughters had even newer furniture. So she went home. There she filled a jar with alcohol and dropped the heart into it. A deep sucking sound, like a gasp within a human breast, could be heard as the heart sank to the bottom. And now they each stood on the shelf in their own jars, her brain and her heart. But no one came to view them. And the children never came to visit. Their excuse always was that they were too busy. But the truth was that they didn't like the sterile smell that clung to everything in the house.

[1975]

Translated by
DENNIS AUBURN HILL

QUESTIONS

1. At what point do you realize that the story is not strictly realistic? How do the ironic, grotesque, and exaggerated elements enhance the story's effectiveness?
2. What aspects of the story are humorous? How is the humor balanced with its more serious implications?
3. How do you understand the "fact" that the mother lacks a brain but has a "highly developed heart"?
4. What views of motherhood and childhood are explored in the story?
5. How do you interpret the ending?

Henry James

(1843–1916)

United States/England

Henry James changed the shape of American fiction by giving it an international perspective as well as a highly refined form. He was born in New York City, the second son of Henry James, Sr., a radical theologian who moved freely among his contemporaries, including Ralph Waldo Emerson and Thomas Carlyle. James's older brother, William, became one of the country's most famous philosophers. Both sons were privately educated and, as children, traveled extensively in Europe. Henry made one formal attempt at education by attending Harvard Law School in 1862, without completing his degree. Three years later, his stories began appearing in *The Atlantic*. In 1871, he published his first novel, *The Passionate Pilgrim*. In *The American* (1877), he developed his major theme: the conflict between a robust American, naive and rich, and decadent Europeans, steeped in tradition but unwilling to sacrifice heritage for dollars. To this international theme, varied in dozens of subsequent short stories and novels, James was shortly to add a more complex form, altering the point of view and the psychological depiction of his characters. It is impossible to think of American and British fiction of the late nineteenth and early twentieth centuries without considering Henry James's influence on the genre.

James wrote so many short stories about artists that they have even been collected on at least one occasion: *Stories of Writers and Artists*. "The Real Thing" is one of the most famous of those tales. The inspiration for the story came from an incident related to James by George du Maurier. The painter had spoken to James "of a call from a strange and striking couple desirous to propose themselves as artist's models for his weekly 'social' illustrations [for] 'Punch,' and the acceptance of whose services would have entailed the dismissal of an undistinguished but highly expert pair, also husband and wife, who had come to him from far back. . . ." Thus the conflict becomes one of what inspires the true artist: the real thing or its imitative substitute.

The Real Thing

When the porter's wife who used to answer the house-bell announced, "A gentleman and a lady, sir," I had, as I often had in those days—the wish being father to the thought—an immediate vision of sitters. Sitters my visitors in this case proved to be; but not in the sense I should have preferred. There was nothing at first however to indicate that they mightn't have come for a portrait. The gentleman, a man of fifty, very high and very straight, with a moustache slightly grizzled and a dark grey walking-coat admirably fitted, both of which I noted professionally—I don't mean as a barber or yet as a tailor—would have struck me as a celebrity if celebrities often were striking. It was a truth of which I had for some time been conscious that a figure with a good deal of frontage was, as one might say, almost never a public institution. A glance at the lady helped to remind me of this paradoxical law: she also looked too distinguished to be a "personality." Moreover one would scarcely come across two variations together.

Neither of the pair immediately spoke — they only prolonged the preliminary gaze suggesting that each wished to give the other a chance. They were visibly shy; they stood there letting me take them in — which, as I afterwards perceived, was the most practical thing they could have done. In this way their embarrassment served their cause. I had seen people painfully reluctant to mention that they desired anything so gross as to be represented on canvas; but the scruples of my new friends appeared amost insurmountable. Yet the gentleman might have said "I should like a portrait of my wife," and the lady might have said "I should like a portrait of my husband." Perhaps they weren't husband and wife — this naturally would make the matter more delicate. Perhaps they wished to be done together — in which case they ought to have brought a third person to break the news.

"We come from Mr. Rivet," the lady finally said with a dim smile that had the effect of a moist sponge passed over a "sunk" piece of painting, as well as of a vague allusion to vanished beauty. She was as tall and straight, in her degree, as her companion, and with ten years less to carry. She looked as sad as a woman could look whose face was not charged with expression; that is her tinted oval mask showed waste as an exposed surface shows friction. The hand of time had played over her freely, but to an effect of elimination. She was slim and stiff, and so well-dressed, in dark blue cloth, with lappets and pockets and buttons, that it was clear she employed the same tailor as her husband. The couple had an indefinable air of prosperous thrift — they evidently got a good deal of luxury for their money. If I was to be one of their luxuries, it would behoove me to consider my terms.

"Ah, Claude Rivet recommended me?" I echoed; and I added that it was very kind of him, though I could reflect that, as he only painted landscape, this wasn't a sacrifice.

The lady looked very hard at the gentleman, and the gentleman looked round the room. Then, staring at the door a moment and stroking his moustache, he rested his pleasant eyes on me with the remark: "He said you were the right one."

"I try to be, when people want to sit."

"Yes, we should like to," said the lady anxiously.

"Do you mean together?"

My visitors exchanged a glance. "If you could do anything with *me* I suppose it would be double," the gentleman stammered.

"Oh yes, there's naturally a higher charge for two figures than for one."

"We should like to make it pay," the husband confessed.

"That's very good of you," I returned, appreciating so unwonted a sympathy —for I supposed he meant pay the artist.

A sense of strangeness seemed to dawn on the lady. "We mean for the illustrations — Mr. Rivet said you might put one in."

"Put in — an illustration?" I was equally confused.

"Sketch her off, you know," said the gentleman, colouring.

It was only then that I understood the service Claude Rivet had rendered me; he had told them how I worked in black and white, for magazines, for story books, for sketches of contemporary life, and consequently had copious employment for models. These things were true, but it was not less true—I may confess it now; whether because the aspiration was to lead to everything or to nothing I leave the reader to guess—that I couldn't get the honours, to say nothing of the emoluments, of a great painter of portraits out of my head. My "illustrations" were my pot-boilers; I looked to a different branch of art—far and away the most interesting it had always seemed to me—to perpetuate my fame. There was no shame in looking to it also to make my fortune; but that fortune was by so much further from being made from the moment my visitors wished to be "done" for something. I was disappointed; for in the pictorial sense I had immediately seen them. I had seized their type—I had already settled what I would do with it. Something that wouldn't absolutely have pleased them, I afterwards reflected.

"Ah, you're—you're—a—?" I began as soon as I had mastered my surprise. I couldn't bring out the dingy word "models": it seemed so little to fit the case.

"We haven't had much practice," said the lady.

"We've got to *do* something, and we've thought that an artist in your line might perhaps make something of us," her husband threw off. He further mentioned that they didn't know many artists and that they had gone first, on the off chance—he painted views of course, but sometimes put in figures; perhaps I remembered—to Mr. Rivet, whom they had met a few years before at a place in Norfolk where he was sketching.

"We used to sketch a little ourselves," the lady hinted.

"It's very awkward, but we absolutely *must* do something," her husband went on.

"Oh course we're not so *very* young," she admitted with a wan smile.

With the remark that I might as well know something more about them the husband had handed me a card extracted from a neat new pocket-book—their appurtenances were all of the freshest—and inscribed with the words "Major Monarch." Impressive as these words were they didn't carry my knowledge much further; but my visitor presently added: "I've left the army and we've had the misfortune to lose our money. In fact our means are dreadfully small."

"It's awfully trying—a regular strain," said Mrs. Monarch.

They evidently wished to be discreet—to take care not to swagger because they were gentlefolk. I felt them willing to recognise this as something of a drawback, at the same time that I guessed at an underlying sense—their consolation in adversity—that they *had* their points. They certainly had; but these advantages struck me as preponderantly social; such, for instance, as would help to make a drawing-room look well. However, a drawing-room was always, or ought to be, a picture.

In consequence of his wife's allusion to their age Major Monarch observed: "Naturally it's more for the figure that we thought of going in. We can still hold ourselves up." On the instant I saw that the figure was indeed their strong point. His "naturally" didn't sound vain, but it lighted up the question. "*She* has the best one," he continued, nodding at his wife with a pleasant after-dinner absence of circumlocution. I could only reply, as if we were in fact sitting over our wine, that this didn't prevent his own from being very good; which led him in turn to make answer: "We thought that if you ever have to do people like us we might be something like it. *She* particularly—for a lady in a book, you know."

I was so amused by them that, to get more of it, I did my best to take their point of view; and though it was an embarrassment to find myself appraising physically, as if they were animals on hire or useful blacks, a pair whom I should have expected to meet only in one of the relations in which criticism is tacit, I looked at Mrs. Monarch judicially enough to be able to exclaim after a moment with conviction: "Oh, yes, a lady in a book!" She was singularly like a bad illustration.

"We'll stand up, if you like," said the Major; and he raised himself before me with a really grand air.

I could take his measure at a glance—he was six feet two and a perfect gentleman. It would have paid any club in process of formation and in want of a stamp to engage him at a salary to stand in the principal window. What struck me at once was that in coming to me they had rather missed their vocation; they could surely have been turned to better account for advertising purposes. I couldn't of course see the thing in detail, but I could see them make somebody's fortune—I don't mean their own. There was something in them for a waistcoat-maker, an hotel-keeper or a soap-vendor. I could imagine "We always use it" pinned on their bosoms with the greatest effect; I had a vision of the brilliancy with which they would launch a table d'hote.

Mrs. Monarch sat still, not from pride but from shyness, and presently her husband said to her: "Get up, my dear, and show how smart you are." She obeyed, but she had no need to get up to show it. She walked to the end of the studio and then came back blushing, her fluttered eyes on the partner of her appeal. I was reminded of an incident I had accidentally had a glimpse of in Paris—being with a friend there, a dramatist about to produce a play, when an actress came to him to ask to be entrusted with a part. She went through her paces before him, walked up and down as Mrs. Monarch was doing. Mrs. Monarch did it quite as well, but I abstained from applauding. It was very odd to see such people apply for such poor pay. She looked as if she had ten thousand a year. Her husband had used the word that described her: she was in the London current jargon essentially and typically "smart." Her figure was, in the same order of ideas, conspicuously and irreproachably "good." For a woman of her age her waist was surprisingly small; her elbow moreover had the orthodox crook. She held her head at the conventional angle, but why did she come to *me*? She ought to have tried on jackets at a big shop. I feared my visitors were not only destitute but "artistic"—which would be a great complication. When she sat down again I thanked her, observing that what a draughtsman most valued in his model was the faculty of keeping quiet.

"Oh, *she* can keep quiet," said Major Monarch. Then he added jocosely: "I've always kept her quiet."

"I'm not a nasty fidget, am I?" It was going to wring tears from me, I felt, the way she hid her head, ostrich-like, in the other broad bosom.

The owner of this expanse addressed his answer to me. "Perhaps it isn't out of place to mention—because we ought to be quite businesslike, oughtn't we?—that when I married her she was known as the Beautiful Statue."

"Oh dear!" said Mrs. Monarch ruefully.

"Of course I should want a certain amount of expression," I rejoined.

"Of *course*!"—and I had never heard such unanimity.

"And then I suppose you know that you'll get awfully tired."

"Oh, we *never* get tired!" they eagerly cried.

"Have you had any kind of practice?"

They hesitated—they looked at each other. "We've been photographed—*immensely*," said Mrs. Monarch.

"She means the fellows have asked us themselves," added the Major.

"I see—because you're so good-looking."

"I don't know what they thought, but they were always after us."

"We always got our photographs for nothing," smiled Mrs. Monarch.

"We might have brought some, my dear," her husband remarked.

"I'm not sure we have any left. We've given quantities away," she explained to me.

"With our autographs and that sort of thing," said the Major.

"Are they to be got in the shops?" I inquired as a harmless pleasantry.

"Oh, yes, *hers*—they used to be."

"Not now," said Mrs. Monarch with her eyes on the floor.

II

I could fancy the "sort of thing" they put on the presentation copies of their photographs, and I was sure they wrote a beautiful hand. It was odd how quickly I was sure of everything that concerned them. If they were now so poor as to have to earn shillings and pence they could never have had much of a margin. Their good looks had been their capital, and they had good-naturedly made the most of the career that this resource marked out for them. It was in their faces, the blankness, the deep intellectual repose of the twenty years of country-house visiting that had given them pleasant intonations. I could see the sunny drawing-rooms, sprinkled with periodicals she didn't read, in which Mrs. Monarch had continuously sat; I could see the wet shrubberies in which she had walked, equipped to admiration for either exercise. I could see the rich coveys the Major had helped to shoot and the wonderful garments in which, late at night, he repaired to the smoking-room to talk about them. I could imagine their leggings and waterproofs, their knowing tweeds and rugs, their rolls of sticks and cases of tackle and neat umbrellas; and I could evoke the exact appearance of their servants and the compact variety of their luggage on platforms of country stations.

They gave small tips, but they were liked; they didn't do anything themselves, but they were welcome. They looked so well everywhere; they gratified the general relish for stature, complexion and "form." They knew it without fatuity or vulgarity, and they respected themselves in consequence. They weren't superficial; they were thorough and kept themselves up—it had been their line. People with such a taste for activity had to have some line. I could feel how even in a dull house they could have been counted on for the joy of life. At present something had happened—it didn't matter what, their little income had grown less, it had grown least—and they had to do something for pocket-money. Their friends could like them, I made out, without liking to support them. There was something about them that represented credit—their clothes, their manners, their type; but if credit is a large empty pocket in which an occasional chink reverberates, the chink at least must be audible. What they wanted of me was help to make it so. Fortunately they had no children—I soon divined that. They would also perhaps wish our relations to be kept secret: this was why it was "for the figure"—the reproduction of the face would betray them.

I liked them—I felt, quite as their friends must have done—they were so simple; and I had no objection to them if they would suit. But somehow with all their perfections I didn't easily believe in them. After all they were amateurs, and the ruling passion of my life was the detestation of the amateur. Combined with this was another perversity—an innate preference for the represented subject over the real one: the defect of the real one was so apt to be a lack of representation. I liked things that appeared; then one was sure. Whether they *were* or not was a subordinate and almost always profitless question. There were other considerations, the first of which was that I already had two or three recruits in use, notably a young person with big feet, in alpaca, from Kilburn, who for a couple of years had come to me regularly for my illustrations and with whom I was still—perhaps ignobly—satisfied. I frankly explained to my visitors how the case stood, but they had taken more precautions than I supposed. They had reasoned out their opportunity, for Claude Rivet had told them of the projected *édition de luxe* of one of the writers of our day—the rarest of the novelists—who, long neglected by the multitudinous vulgar and dearly prized by the attentive (need I mention Philip Vincent?), had had the happy fortune of seeing, late in life, the dawn and then the full light of a higher criticism; an estimate in which on the part of the public there was something really of expiation. The edition preparing, planned by a publisher of taste, was practically an act of high reparation; the woodcuts with which it was to be enriched were the homage of English art to one of the most independent representatives of English letters. Major and Mrs. Monarch confessed to me they had hoped I might be able to work *them* into my branch of the enterprise. They knew I was to do the first of the books, *Rutland Ramsay*, but I had to make clear to them that my participation in the rest of the affair—this first book was to be a test—must depend on the satisfaction I should give. If this should be limited my employers would drop me with scarce common forms. It was therefore a crisis for me, and naturally I was making special preparations, looking about for new people, should they be necessary, and securing the best types. I admitted however that I should like to settle down to two or three good models who would do for everything.

"Should we have often to—a—put on special clothes?" Mrs. Monarch timidly demanded.

"Dear, yes—that's half the business."

"And should we be expected to supply our own costumes?"

"Oh, no; I've got a lot of things. A painter's models put on—or put off—anything he likes."

"And you mean—a—the same?"

"The same?"

Mrs. Monarch looked at her husband again.

"Oh, she was just wondering," he explained, "if the costumes are in *general* use." I had to confess that they were, and I mentioned further that some of them—I had a lot of genuine greasy last-century things—had served their time, a hundred years ago, on living world-stained men and women; on figures not perhaps so far removed, in that vanished world, from *their* type, the Monarchs', *quoi*![1] of a breeched and bewigged age. "We'll put on anything that *fits*," said the Major.

"Oh, I arrange that—they fit in the pictures."

"I'm afraid I should do better for the modern books. I'd come as you like," said Mrs. Monarch.

"She has got a lot of clothes at home: they might do for contemporary life," her husband continued.

"Oh, I can fancy scenes in which you'd be quite natural." And indeed I could see the slipshod rearrangements of stale properties—the stories I tried to produce pictures for without the exasperation of reading them—whose sandy tracts the good lady might help to people. But I had to return to the fact that for this sort of work—the daily mechanical grind—I was already equipped: the people I was working with were fully adequate.

"We only thought we might be more like *some* characters," said Mrs. Monarch mildly, getting up.

Her husband also rose; he stood looking at me with a dim wistfulness that was touching in so fine a man. "Wouldn't it be rather a pull sometimes to have—a—to have—?" He hung fire; he wanted me to help him by phrasing what he meant. But I couldn't—I didn't know. So he brought it out awkwardly: "The *real* thing; a gentleman, you know, or a lady." I was quite ready to give a general assent—I admitted that there was a great deal in that. This encouraged Major Monarch to say, following up his appeal with an unacted gulp: "It's awfully hard—we've tried everything." The gulp was communicative; it proved too much for his wife. Before I knew it Mrs. Monarch had dropped again upon a divan and burst into tears. Her husband sat down beside her, holding one of her hands; whereupon she quickly dried her eyes with the other, while I felt embarrassed as she looked up at me. "There isn't a confounded job I haven't applied for—waited for—prayed for. You can fancy we'd be pretty bad first. Secretaryships and that sort of thing? You might as well ask for a peerage. I'd be *anything*—I'm strong; a messenger or a coal-heaver. I'd put on a goldlaced cap and open carriage-doors in front of the haberdasher's; I'd hang about a station to carry portmanteaus; I'd be a postman. But they won't *look* at you; there are thousands as good as yourself already on the ground. *Gentlemen*, poor beggars, who've drunk their wine, who've kept their hunters!"

I was as reassuring as I knew how to be, and my visitors were presently on their feet again while, for the experiment, we agreed on an hour. We were discussing it when the door opened and Miss Churm came in with a wet umbrella. Miss Churm had to take the omnibus to Maida Vale and then walk half a mile. She looked a trifle blowsy and slightly splashed. I scarcely ever saw her come in without thinking afresh how odd it was that, being so little in herself, she should yet be so much in others. She was a meagre little Miss Churm, but was such an ample heroine of romance. She was only a freckled cockney, but she could represent everything, from a fine lady to a shepherdess; she had the faculty as she might have had a fine voice or long hair. She couldn't spell and she loved beer, but she had two or three "points," and practice, and a knack, and mother-wit, and a whimsical sensibility, and a love of the *h*.[2] The first thing my visitors saw was that her umbrella was wet, and in their spotless perfection they visibly winced at it. The rain had come on since their arrival.

[1]*quoi!* French: Whatever!

[2]*h* In Cockney dialect, the *h* is dropped from the beginnings of words.

"I'm all in a soak; there *was* a mess of people in the 'bus. I wish you lived near a stytion," said Miss Churm. I requested her to get ready as quickly as possible, and she passed into the room in which she always changed her dress. But before going out she asked me what she was to get into this time.

"It's the Russian princess, don't you know?" I answered; "the one with the 'golden eyes,' in black velvet, for the long thing in the *Cheapside*."

"Golden eyes? I *say*!" cried Miss Churm, while my companions watched her with intensity as she withdrew. She always arranged herself, when she was late, before I could turn round; and I kept my visitors a little on purpose, so that they might get an idea, from seeing her, what would be expected of themselves. I mentioned that she was quite my notion of an excellent model—she was really very clever.

"Do you think she looks like a Russian princess?" Major Monarch asked with lurking alarm.

"When I make her, yes."

"Oh, if you have to *make* her—!" he reasoned, not without point.

"That's the most you can ask. There are so many who are not makeable."

"Well, now, *here's* a lady"—and with a persuasive smile he passed his arm into his wife's—"who's already made!"

"Oh, I'm not a Russian princess," Mrs. Monarch protested a little coldly. I could see she had known some and didn't like them. There at once was a complication of a kind I never had to fear with Miss Churm.

This young lady came back in black velvet—the gown was rather rusty and very low on her lean shoulders—and with a Japanese fan in her red hands. I reminded her that in the scene I was doing she had to look over someone's head. "I forget whose it is; but it doesn't matter. Just look over a head."

"I'd rather look over a stove," said Miss Churm; and she took her station near the fire. She fell into position, settled herself into a tall attitude, gave a certain backward inclination to her head and a certain forward droop to her fan, and looked, at least to my prejudiced sense, distinguished and charming, foreign and dangerous. We left her looking so while I went downstairs with Major and Mrs. Monarch.

"I believe I could come about as near it as that," said Mrs. Monarch.

"Oh, you think she's shabby, but you must allow for the alchemy of art."

However, they went off with an evident increase of comfort founded on their demonstrable advantage in being the real thing. I could fancy them shuddering over Miss Churm. She was very droll about them when I went back, for I told her what they wanted.

"Well, if *she* can sit I'll tyke to bookkeeping," said my model.

"She's very ladylike," I replied as an innocent form of aggravation.

"So much the worse for *your*. That means she can't turn round."

"She'll do for the fashionable novels."

"Oh, yes, she'll *do* for them!" my model humorously declared. "Ain't they bad enough without her?" I had often sociably denounced them to Miss Churm.

III

It was for the elucidation of a mystery in one of these works that I first tried Mrs. Monarch. Her husband came with her, to be useful if necessary—it was sufficiently clear that as a general thing he would prefer to come with her. At first I wondered if this were for "propriety's" sake—if he were going to be jealous and meddling. The idea was too tiresome, and if it had been confirmed it would speedily have brought our acquaintance to a close. But I soon saw there was nothing in it and that if he accompanied Mrs. Monarch it was—in addition to the chance of being wanted—simply because he had nothing else to do. When they were separate his occupation was gone, and they never *had* been separate. I judged rightly that in their awkward situation their close union was their main comfort and that this union had no weak spot. It was a real marriage, an encouragement to the hesitating, a nut for pessimists to crack. Their address was humble—I remember afterwards thinking it had been the only thing about them that was really professional—and I could fancy the lamentable lodgings in which the Major would have been left alone. He could sit there more or less grimly with his wife—he couldn't sit there anyhow without her.

He had too much tact to try and make himself agreeable when he couldn't be useful; so when I was too absorbed in my work to talk he simply sat and waited. But I liked to hear him talk—it made my work, when not interrupting it, less mechanical, less special. To listen to him was to combine the excitement of going out with the economy of staying at home. There was only one hindrance—that I seemed not to know any of the people this brilliant couple had known. I think he wondered extremely, during the term of our intercourse, whom the deuce I *did* know. He hadn't a stray sixpence of an idea to fumble for, so we didn't spin it very fine; we confined ourselves to questions of leather and even of liquor—saddlers and breeches-makers and how to get excellent claret cheap—and matters like "good trains" and the habits of small game. His lore on these last subjects was astonishing—he managed to interweave the station-master with the ornithologist. When he couldn't talk about greater things he could talk cheerfully about small, and since I couldn't accompany him into reminiscences of the fashionable world he could lower the conversation without a visible effort to my level.

So earnest a desire to please was touching in a man who could so easily have knocked one down. He looked after the fire and had an opinion on the draught of the stove without my asking him, and I could see that he thought many of my arrangements not half knowing. I remember telling him that if I were only rich I'd offer him a salary to come and teach me how to live. Sometimes he gave a random sigh of which the essence might have been: "Give me even such a bare old barrack as *this*, and I'd do something with it!" When I wanted to use him he came alone; which was an illustration of the superior courage of women. His wife could bear her solitary second floor, and she was in general more discreet; showing by various small reserves that she was alive to the propriety of keeping our relations markedly professional—not letting them slide into sociability. She wished it to remain clear that she and the Major were employed, not cultivated, and if she approved of me as a superior, who could be kept in his place, she never thought me quite good enough for an equal.

She sat with great intensity, giving the whole of her mind to it, and was capable of remaining for an hour almost as motionless as before a photographer's lens. I could see she had been photographed often, but somehow the very habit that made her good for that purpose unfitted her for mine. At first I was extremely pleased with her ladylike air, and it was a satisfaction, on coming to follow her lines to see how good they were and how far they could lead the pencil. But after a little skirmishing I began to find her too insurmountably stiff;

do what I would with it my drawing looked like a photograph or a copy of a photograph. Her figure had no variety of expression—she herself had no sense of variety. You may say that this was my business and was only a question of placing her. Yet I placed her in every conceivable position and she managed to obliterate their differences. She was always a lady certainly, and into the bargain was always the same lady. She was the real thing, but always the same thing. There were moments when I rather writhed under the serenity of her confidence that she *was* the real thing. All her dealings with me and all her husband's were an implication that this was lucky for *me*. Meanwhile I found myself trying to invent types that approached her own, instead of making her own transform itself—in the clever way that was not impossible for instance to poor Miss Churm. Arrange as I would and take the precautions I would, she always came out, in my pictures, too tall—landing me in the dilemma of having represented a fascinating woman as seven feet high, which (out of respect perhaps to my own very much scantier inches) was far from my idea of such a personage.

The case was worse with the Major—nothing I could do would keep *him* down, so that he became useful only for representation of brawny giants. I adored variety and range, I cherished human accidents, the illustrative note; I wanted to characterise closely, and the thing in the world I most hated was the danger of being ridden by a type. I had quarrelled with some of my friends about it; I had parted company with them for maintaining that one *had* to be, and that if the type was beautiful—witness Raphael and Leonardo—the servitude was only a gain. I was neither Leonardo nor Raphael—I might only be a presumptuous young modern searcher; but I held that everything was to be sacrificed sooner than character. When they claimed that the obsessional form could easily *be* character I retorted, perhaps superficially, "Whose?" It couldn't be everybody's—it might end in being nobody's.

After I had drawn Mrs. Monarch a dozen times I felt surer even than before that the value of such a model as Miss Churm resided precisely in the fact that she had no positive stamp, combined of course with the other fact that what she did have was a curious and inexplicable talent for imitation. Her usual appearance was like a curtain which she could draw up at request for a capital performance. This performance was simply suggestive; but it was a word to the wise—it was vivid and pretty. Sometimes even I thought it, though she was plain herself, too insipidly pretty; I made it a reproach to her that the figures drawn from her were monotonously (*bêtement*,[3] as we used to say) graceful. Nothing made her more angry: it was so much her pride to feel she could sit for characters that had nothing in common with each other. She would accuse me at such moments of taking away her "reputytion."

It suffered a certain shrinkage, this queer quantity, from the repeated visits of my new friends. Miss Churm was greatly in demand, never in want of employment, so I had no scruple in putting her off occasionally, to try them more at my ease. It was certainly amusing at first to do the real thing—it was amusing to do Major Monarch's trousers. They *were* the real thing, even if he did come out colossal. It was amusing to do his wife's back hair—it was so mathematically neat—and the particular "smart" tension of her tight stays. She lent herself especially to positions in which the face was somewhat averted or blurred; she

[3]*bêtement* French: foolishly

abounded in ladylike back views and *profils perdus*.[4] When she stood erect she took naturally one of the attitudes in which court painters represent queens and princesses; so that I found myself wondering whether, to draw out this accomplishment, I couldn't get the editor of the *Cheapside* to publish a really royal romance, "A Tale of Buckingham Palace." Sometimes, however, the real thing and the make-believe came into contact; by which I mean that Miss Churm, keeping an appointment or coming to make one on days when I had much work in hand, encountered her invidious rivals. The encounter was not on their part, for they noticed her no more than if she had been the housemaid; not from intentional loftiness, but simply because as yet, professionally, they didn't know how to fraternise, as I could imagine they would have liked—or at least that the Major would. They couldn't talk about the omnibus—they always walked; and they didn't know what else to try—she wasn't interested in good trains or cheap claret. Besides, they must have felt—in the air—that she was amused at them, secretly derisive of their ever knowing how. She wasn't a person to conceal the limits of her faith if she had had a chance to show them. On the other hand Mrs. Monarch didn't think her tidy; for why else did she take pains to say to me—it was going out of the way, for Mrs. Monarch—that she didn't like dirty women?

One day when my young lady happened to be present with my other sitters—she even dropped in, when it was convenient, for a chat—I asked her to be so good as to lend a hand in getting tea, a service with which she was familiar and which was one of a class that, living as I did in a small way, with slender domestic resources, I often appealed to my models to render. They liked to lay hands on my property, to break the sitting, and sometimes the china—it made them feel Bohemian. The next time I saw Miss Churm after this incident she surprised me greatly by making a scene about it—she accused me of having wished to humiliate her. She hadn't resented the outrage at the time, but had seemed obliging and amused, enjoying the comedy of asking Mrs. Monarch, who sat vague and silent, whether she would have cream and sugar, and putting an exaggerated simper into the question. She had tried intonations—as if she too wished to pass for the real thing—till I was afraid my other visitors would take offence.

Oh, they were determined not to do this, and their touching patience was the measure of their great need. They would sit by the hour, uncomplaining, till I was ready to use them; they would come back on the chance of being wanted and would walk away cheerfully if it failed. I used to go to the door with them to see in what magnificent order they retreated. I tried to find other employment for them—I introduced them to several artists. But they didn't "take," for reasons I could appreciate, and I became rather anxiously aware that after such disappointments they fell back upon me with a heavier weight. They did me the honour to think me most *their* form. They weren't romantic enough for the painters, and in those days there were few serious workers in black-and-white. Besides, they had an eye to the great job I had mentioned to them—they had secretly set their hearts on supplying the right essence for my pictorial vindication of our fine novelist. They knew that for this undertaking I should want no costume effects, none of the frippery of past ages—that it was a case in which everything would be contemporary and satirical and presumably genteel. If I

[4]*profils perdus* French: incomplete profiles, showing more of the back of the head than the face

could work them into it their future would be assured, for the labour would of course be long and the occupation steady.

One day Mrs. Monarch came without her husband—she explained his absence by his having had to go to the City. While she sat there in her usual relaxed majesty there came at the door a knock which I immediately recognised as the subdued appeal of a model out of work. It was followed by the entrance of a young man whom I at once saw to be a foreigner and who proved in fact an Italian acquainted with no English word but my name, which he uttered in a way that made it seem to include all others. I hadn't then visited his country, nor was I proficient in his tongue; but as he was not so meanly constituted—what Italian is?—as to depend only on that member for expression he conveyed to me, in familiar but graceful mimicry, that he was in search of exactly the employment in which the lady before me was engaged. I was not struck with him at first, and while I continued to draw I dropped few signs of interest or encouragement. He stood his ground, however—not importunately, but with a dumb dog-like fidelity in his eyes that amounted to innocent impudence, the manner of a devoted servant—he might have been in the house for years—unjustly suspected. Suddenly it struck me that this very attitude and expression made a picture; whereupon I told him to sit down and wait till I should be free. There was another picture in the way he obeyed me, and I observed as I worked that there were others still in the way he looked wonderingly, with his head thrown back, about the high studio. He might have been crossing himself in Saint Peter's. Before I finished I said to myself, "The fellow's a bankrupt orange-monger, but a treasure."

When Mrs. Monarch withdrew he passed across the room like a flash to open the door by her, standing there with the rapt, pure gaze of the young Dante spellbound by the young Beatrice. As I never insisted, in such situations, on the blankness of the British domestic, I reflected that he had the making of a servant—and I needed one, but couldn't pay him to be only that—as well as of a model; in sort I resolved to adopt my bright adventurer if he would agree to officiate in the double capacity. He jumped at my offer, and in the event my rashness—for I had really known nothing about him—wasn't brought home to me. He proved a sympathetic though a desultory ministrant, and had in a wonderful degree the *sentiment de la pose*.[5] It was uncultivated, instinctive, a part of the happy instinct that had guided him to my door and helped him to spell out my name on the card nailed to it. He had had no other introduction to me than a guess, from the shape of my high north window, seen outside, that my place was a studio and that as a studio it would contain an artist. He had wandered to England in search of fortune, like other itinerants, and had embarked, with a partner and a small green handcart, on the sale of penny ices. The ices had melted away and the partner had dissolved in their train. My young man wore tight yellow trousers with reddish stripes and his name was Oronte. He was sallow but fair, and when I put him into some old clothes of my own he looked like an Englishman. He was as good as Miss Churm, who could look, when requested, like an Italian.

[5]*sentiment de la pose* French: instinct for posing

IV

I thought Mrs. Monarch's face slightly convulsed when, on her coming back with her husband, she found Oronte installed. It was strange to have to recognise in a scrap of a lazzarone[6] a competitor to her magnificent Major. It was she who scented danger first, for the Major was anecdotically unconscious. But Oronte gave us tea, with a hundred eager confusions—he had never been concerned in so queer a process—and I think she thought better of me for having at last an "establishment." They saw a couple of drawings that I had made of the establishment, and Mrs. Monarch hinted that it never would have struck her he had sat for them. "Now the drawings you make from *us*, they look exactly like us," she reminded me, smiling in triumph; and I recognised that this was indeed just their defect. When I drew the Monarchs I couldn't anyhow get away from them—get into the character I wanted to represent; and I hadn't the least desire my model should be discoverable in my picture. Miss Churm never was, and Mrs. Monarch thought I hid her, very properly, because she was vulgar; whereas if she was lost it was only as the dead who go to heaven are lost—in the gain of an angel the more.

But this time I had got a certain start with *Rutland Ramsay*, the first novel in the great projected series; that is, I had produced a dozen drawings, several with the help of the Major and his wife, and I had sent them in for approval. My understanding with the publishers, as I have already hinted, had been that I was to be left to do my work, in this particular case, as I liked, with the whole book committed to me; but my connexion with the rest of the series was only contingent. There were moments when, frankly, it *was* a comfort to have the real thing under one's hand; for there were characters in *Rutland Ramsay* that were very much like it. There were people presumably as erect as the Major and women of as good a fashion as Mrs. Monarch. There was a great deal of country-house life—treated, it is true, in a fine fanciful ironical generalised way—and there was a considerable implication of knickerbockers and kilts. There were certain things I had to settle at the outset; such things for instance as the exact appearance of the hero and the particular bloom and figure of the heroine. The author of course gave me a lead, but there was a margin for interpretation. I took the Monarchs into my confidence, I told them frankly what I was about, I mentioned my embarrassments and alternatives. "Oh, take *him*!" Mrs. Monarch murmured sweetly, looking at her husband; and "What could you want better than my wife?" the Major inquired with the comfortable candour that now prevailed between us.

I wasn't obliged to answer these remarks—I was only obliged to place my sitters. I wasn't easy in mind, and I postponed a little timidly perhaps the solving of my question. The book was a large canvas, the other figures were numerous, and I worked off at first some of the episodes in which the hero and the heroine were not concerned. When once I had set *them* up I should have to stick to them—I couldn't make my young man seven feet high in one place and five feet nine in another. I inclined on the whole to the latter measurement, though the Major more than once reminded me that *he* looked about as young as any one. It was indeed quite possible to arrange him, for the figure, so that it would have

[6]*lazzarone* French: street person

been difficult to detect his age. After the spontaneous Oronte had been with me a month, and after I had given him to understand several times over that his native exuberance would presently constitute an insurmountable barrier to our further intercourse, I waked to a sense of his heroic capacity. He was only five feet seven, but the remaining inches were latent. I tried him almost secretly at first, for I was really rather afraid of the judgment my other models would pass on such a choice. If they regarded Miss Churm as little better than a snare what would they think of the representation of a person so little the real thing as an Italian street-vendor of a protagonist formed by a public school?

If I went a little in fear of them it wasn't because they bullied me, because they had got an oppressive foothold, but because in their really pathetic decorum and mysteriously permanent newness they counted on me so intensely. I was therefore very glad when Jack Hawley came home: he was always of such good counsel. He painted badly himself, but there was no one like him for putting his finger on the place. He had been absent from England for a year; he had been somewhere—I don't remember where—to get a fresh eye. I was in a good deal of dread of any such organ, but we were old friends; he had been away for months and a sense of emptiness was creeping into my life. I hadn't dodged a missile for a year.

He came back with a fresh eye, but with the same old black velvet blouse, and the first evening he spent in my studio we smoked cigarettes till the small hours. He had done no work himself, he had only got the eye; so the field was clear for the production of my little things. He wanted to see what I had produced for the *Cheapside*, but he was disappointed in the exhibition. That at least seemed the meaning of two or three comprehensive groans which, as he lounged on my big divan, his leg folded under him, looking at my latest drawings, issued from his lips with the smoke of the cigarette.

"What's the matter with you?" I asked.

"What's the matter with *you*?"

"Nothing save that I'm mystified."

"You are indeed. You're quite off the hinge. What's the meaning of this new fad?" And he tossed me, with visible irreverence, a drawing in which I happened to have depicted both my elegant models. I asked if he didn't think it good, and he replied that it struck him as execrable, given the sort of thing I had always represented myself to him as wishing to arrive at; but I let that pass—I was so anxious to see exactly what he meant. The two figures in the picture looked colossal, but I supposed this was *not* what he meant, inasmuch as, for aught he knew to the contrary, I might have been trying for some such effect. I maintained that I was working exactly in the same way as when he last had done me the honour to tell me I might do something some day. "Well, there's a screw loose somewhere," he answered; "wait a bit and I'll discover it." I depended upon him to do so: where else was the fresh eye? But he produced at last nothing more luminous than "I don't know—I don't like your types." This was lame for a critic who had never consented to discuss with me anything but the question of execution, the direction of strokes and the mystery of values.

"In the drawings you've been looking at I think my types are very handsome."

"Oh, they won't do!"

"I've been working with new models."

"I see you have. *They* won't do."

"Are you very sure of that?"

"Absolutely—they're stupid."

"You mean *I* am—for I ought to get round that."

"You *can't*—with such people. Who are they?"

I told him, so far as was necessary, and he concluded heartlessly: "*Ce sont des gens qu'il faut mettre à la porte.*"[7]

"You've never seen them; they're awfully good"—I flew to their defence.

"Not seen them? Why all this recent work of yours drops to pieces with them. It's all I want to see of them."

"No one else has said anything against it—the *Cheapside* people are pleased."

"Every one else is an ass, and the *Cheapside* people the biggest asses of all. Come, don't pretend at this time of day to have pretty illusions about the public, especially about publishers and editors. It's not for *such* animals you work—it's for those who know, *coloro che sanno;*[8] so keep straight for *me* if you can't keep straight for yourself. There was a certain sort of thing you used to try for—and a very good thing it was. But this twaddle isn't *in* it." When I talked with Hawley later about *Rutland Ramsay* and its possible successors he declared that I must get back into my boat again or I should go to the bottom. His voice in short was the voice of warning.

I noted the warning, but I didn't turn my friends out of doors. They bored me a good deal; but the very fact that they bored me admonished me not to sacrifice them—if there was anything to be done with them—simply to irritation. As I look back at this phase they seem to me to have pervaded my life not a little. I have a vision of them as most of the time in my studio, seated against the wall on an old velvet bench to be out of the way, and resembling the while a pair of patient courtiers in a royal ante-chamber. I'm convinced that during the coldest weeks of the winter they held their ground because it saved them fire. Their newness was losing its gloss, and it was impossible not to feel them objects of charity. Whenever Miss Churm arrived they went away, and after I was fairly launched in *Rutland Ramsay* Miss Churm arrived pretty often. They managed to express to me tacitly that they supposed I wanted her for the low life of the book, and I let them suppose it, since they had attempted to study the work—it was lying about the studio—without discovering that it dealt only with the highest circles. They had dipped into the most brilliant of our novelists without deciphering many passages. I still took an hour from them, now and again, in spite of Jack Hawley's warning: it would be time enough to dismiss them, if dismissal should be necessary, when the rigour of the season was over. Hawley had made their acquaintance—he had met them at my fireside—and thought them a ridiculous pair. Learning that he was a painter they tried to approach him, to show him too that they were the real thing; but he looked at them, across the big room, as if they were miles away: they were a compendium of everything he most objected to in the social system of his country. Such people as that, all convention and patent-leather, with ejaculations that stopped conversation, had no business in a studio. A studio was a place to learn to see, and how could you see through a pair of feather-beds?

[7]"*Ce sont . . . la porte.*" French: "Those kinds of persons should be shown the door."

[8]*coloro che sanno* Italian: those who know

The main inconvenience I suffered at their hands was that at first I was shy of letting it break upon them that my artful little servant had begun to sit to me for *Rutland Ramsay*. They knew I had been odd enough—they were prepared by this time to allow oddity to artists—to pick a foreign vagabond out of the streets when I might have had a person with whiskers and credentials; but it was some time before they learned how high I rated his accomplishments. They found him in an attitude more than once, but they never doubted I was doing him as an organ-grinder. There were several things they never guessed, and one of them was that for a striking scene in the novel, in which a footman briefly figured, it occurred to me to make use of Major Monarch as the menial. I kept putting this off, I didn't like to ask him to don the livery—besides the difficulty of finding a livery to fit him. At last, one day late in the winter, when I was at work on the despised Oronte, who caught one's idea on the wing, and was in the glow of feeling myself go very straight, they came in, the Major and his wife, with their society laugh about nothing (there was less and less to laugh at); came in like country-callers—they always reminded me of that—who have walked across the park after church and are presently persuaded to stay to luncheon. Luncheon was over, but they could stay to tea—I knew they wanted it. The fit was on me, however, and I couldn't let my ardour cool and my work wait, with the fading daylight, while my model prepared it. So I asked Mrs. Monarch if she would mind laying it out—a request which for an instant brought all the blood to her face. Her eyes were on her husband's for a second, and some mute telegraphy passed between them. Their folly was over the next instant; his cheerful shrewdness put an end to it. So far from pitying their wounded pride, I must add, I was moved to give it as complete a lesson as I could. They bustled about together and got out the cups and saucers and made the kettle boil. I know they felt as if they were waiting on my servant, and when the tea was prepared I said: "He'll have a cup, please—he's tired." Mrs. Monarch brought him one where he stood, and he took it from her as if he had been a gentleman at a party squeezing a crush-hat with an elbow.

Then it came over me that she had made a great effort for me—made it with a kind of nobleness—and that I owed her a compensation. Each time I saw her after this I wondered what the compensation could be. I couldn't go on doing the wrong thing to oblige them. Oh, it *was* the wrong thing, the stamp of the work for which they sat—Hawley was not the only person to say it now. I sent in a large number of the drawings I had made for *Rutland Ramsay*, and I received a warning that was more to the point than Hawley's. The artistic adviser of the house for which I was working was of opinion that many of my illustrations were not what had been looked for. Most of these illustrations were the subjects in which the Monarchs had figured. Without going into the question of what *had* been looked for, I had to face the fact that at this rate I shouldn't get the other books to do. I hurled myself in despair on Miss Churm—I put her through all her paces. I not only adopted Oronte publicly as my hero, but one morning when the Major looked in to see if I didn't require him to finish a *Cheapside* figure for which he had begun to sit the week before, I told him I had changed my mind—I'd do the drawing from my man. At this my visitor turned pale and stood looking at me. "Is *he* your idea of an English gentleman?" he asked.

I was disappointed, I was nervous, I wanted to get on with my work; so I replied with irritation: "Oh my dear Major—I can't be ruined for *you*!"

It was a horrid speech, but he stood another moment—after which, without a word, he quitted the studio. I drew a long breath, for I said to myself that I shouldn't see him again. I hadn't told him definitely that I was in danger of having my work rejected, but I was vexed at his not having felt the catastrophe in the air, read with me the moral of our fruitless collaboration, the lesson that in the deceptive atmosphere of art even the highest respectability may fail of being plastic.

I didn't owe my friends money, but I did see them again. They reappeared together three days later, and, given all the other facts, there was something tragic in that one. It was a clear proof they could find nothing else in life to do. They had threshed the matter out in a dismal conference—they had digested the bad news that they were not in for the series. If they weren't useful to me even for the *Cheapside*, their function seemed difficult to determine, and I could only judge at first that they had come, forgivingly, decorously, to take a last leave. This made me rejoice in secret that I had little leisure for a scene; for I had placed both my other models in position together and I was pegging away at a drawing from which I hoped to derive glory. It had been suggested by the passage in which Rutland Ramsay, drawing up a chair to Artemisia's piano-stool, says extraordinary things to her while she ostensibly fingers out a difficult piece of music. I had done Miss Churm at the piano before—it was an attitude in which she knew how to take on an absolutely poetic grace. I wished the two figures to "compose" together with intensity, and my little Italian had entered perfectly into my conception. The pair were vividly before me, the piano had been pulled out; it was a charming show of blended youth and murmured love, which I had only to catch and keep. My visitors stood and looked at it, and I was friendly to them over my shoulder.

They made no response, but I was used to silent company and went on with my work, only a little disconcerted—even though exhilarated by the sense that *this* was at least the ideal thing—at not having got rid of them after all. Presently I heard Mrs. Monarch's sweet voice beside or rather above me: "I wish her hair were a little better done." I looked up and she was staring with a strange fixedness at Miss Churm, whose back was turned to her. "Do you mind my just touching it?" she went on—a question which made me spring up for an instant as with the instinctive fear that she might do the young lady a harm. But she quieted me with a glance I shall never forget—I confess I should like to have been able to paint *that*—and went for a moment to my model. She spoke to her softly, laying a hand on her shoulder and bending over her; and as the girl, understanding, gratefully assented, she disposed her rough curls, with a few quick passes, in such a way as to make Miss Churm's head twice as charming. It was one of the most heroic personal services I've ever seen rendered. Then Mrs. Monarch turned away with a low sigh and, looking about her as if for something to do, stooped to the floor with a noble humility and picked up a dirty rag that had dropped out of my paint-box.

The Major meanwhile had also been looking for something to do, and, wandering to the other end of the studio, saw before him my breakfast-things neglected, unremoved. "I say, can't I be useful *here*?" he called out to me with an irrepressible quaver. I assented with a laugh that I fear was awkward, and for the next ten minutes, while I worked, I heard the light clatter of china and the tinkle of spoons and glass. Mrs. Monarch assisted her husband—they washed up my crockery, they put it away. They wandered off into my little scullery, and I afterwards found that they had cleaned my knives and that my slender stock of plate had an unprecedented surface. When it came over me, the latent eloquence of what they were doing, I confess that my drawing was blurred for a moment—the picture swam. They had accepted their failure, but they couldn't accept their fate. They had bowed their head in bewilderment to the perverse and cruel law in virtue of which the real thing could be so much less precious than the unreal; but they didn't want to starve. If my servants were my models, then my models might be my servants. They would reverse the parts—the others would sit for the ladies and gentlemen and *they* would do the work. They would still be in the studio—it was an intense dumb appeal to me not to turn them out. "Take us on," they wanted to say—"we'll do *anything*."

My pencil dropped from my hand; my sitting was spoiled and I got rid of my sitters, who were also evidently rather mystified and awestruck. Then, alone with the Major and his wife I had a most uncomfortable moment. He put their prayer into a single sentence: "I say, you know—just let *us* do for you, can't you?" I couldn't—it was dreadful to see them emptying my slops; but I pretended I could, to oblige them, for about a week. Then I gave them a sum of money to go away, and I never saw them again. I obtained the remaining books, but my friend Hawley repeats that Major and Mrs. Monarch did me a permanent harm, got me into false ways. If it be true I'm content to have paid the price—for the memory.

[1893]

QUESTIONS

1. What does the story tell us about artistic and creative processes? Does art imitate or create?
2. Do the Monarchs ever understand what has happened to the painter?
3. Although the main character in the story is a painter, could the central issues also apply to a writer?

Sarah Orne Jewett

(1849–1909)

United States

Sarah Orne Jewett was born in South Berwick, Maine, into a wealthy old New England family of shipowners, merchants, and physicians. Her father was a doctor; her mother was distantly related to the Puritan poet Anne Bradstreet. Although Jewett was educated at the Berwick Academy, she felt that she received her real education from her father, who was well versed in the classics and in nature and who allowed her to accompany him on house calls.

Jewett published her first story at the age of 18, under a pseudonym. Eventually she published nearly 150 stories and sketches in the leading journals of her time; she also wrote nearly two dozen stories for children. Once considered a regional or "local color" writer, Jewett is now more fully appreciated for her rich understanding and portrayal of local manners and characters as well as her vivid depictions of the natural landscape of rural New England, all of which she observed with great depth of insight. The collection of stories for which she is best known, *The Country of Pointed Firs* (1896), a series of sketches of the inhabitants of a seaport village in Maine, is striking and unusual in its focus on older characters, most of whom are women over 60. She also wrote several novels, including *Deephaven* (1877) and *A Country Doctor* (1884). Jewett remained unmarried by choice, declaring that "marriage would only be a hindrance"; however, she maintained enduring relationships with a number of female friends.

"A White Heron," Jewett's best-known and most frequently anthologized story, demonstrates her lyrical exploration of the relationship between the human and natural worlds.

A White Heron

I

The woods were already filled with shadows one June evening, just before eight o'clock, though a bright sunset still glimmered faintly among the trunks of the trees. A little girl was driving home her cow, a plodding, dilatory, provoking creature in her behavior, but a valued companion for all that. They were going away from the western light, and striking deep into the dark woods, but their feet were familiar with the path, and it was no matter whether their eyes could see it or not.

There was hardly a night the summer through when the old cow could be found waiting at the pasture bars; on the contrary, it was her greatest pleasure to hide herself away among the high huckleberry bushes, and though she wore a loud bell she had made the discovery that if one stood perfectly still it would not ring. So Sylvia had to hunt for her until she found her and call Co'! Co'! with never an answering Moo, until her childish patience was quite spent. If the creature had not given good milk and plenty of it, the case would have seemed very different to her owners. Besides, Sylvia had all the time there was, and very little use to make of it. Sometimes in pleasant weather it was a consolation to look upon the cow's pranks as an intelligent attempt to play hide and seek, and as the child had no playmates she lent herself to this amusement with a good deal of zest. Though this chase had been so long that the wary animal herself had given an unusual signal of her whereabouts, Sylvia had only laughed when she came upon Mistress Moolly at the swamp-side, and urged her affectionately homeward with a twig of birch leaves. The old cow was not inclined to wander farther, she even turned in the right direction for once as they left the pasture, and stepped along the road at a good pace. She was quite ready to be milked now, and seldom stopped to browse. Sylvia wondered what her grandmother would say because they were so late. It was a great while since she had left home at half past five o'clock, but everybody knew the difficulty of making this errand a short one. Mrs. Tilley had chased the horned torment too many summer evenings herself to blame any one else for lingering, and was only thankful as she waited that she had Sylvia, nowadays, to give such valuable assistance. The good woman suspected that Sylvia loitered occasionally on her own account; there never was such a child for straying about out-of-doors since the world was made! Everybody said that it was a good change for a little maid who had tried to grow for eight years in a crowded manufacturing town, but, as for Sylvia herself, it seemed as if she never had been alive at all before she came to live at the farm. She thought often with wistful compassion of a wretched dry geranium that belonged to a town neighbor.

"'Afraid of folks,'" old Mrs. Tilley said to herself, with a smile, after she had made the unlikely choice of Sylvia from her daughter's houseful of children, and was returning to the farm. "'Afraid of folks,' they said! I guess she won't be troubled no great with 'em up to the old place!" When they reached the door of the lonely house and stopped to unlock it, and the cat came to purr loudly, and rub against them, a deserted pussy, indeed, but fat with young robins, Sylvia whispered that this was a beautiful place to live in, and she never should wish to go home.

The companions followed the shady wood-road, the cow taking slow steps, and the child very fast ones. The cow stopped long at the brook to drink, as if the pasture were not half a swamp, and Sylvia stood still and waited, letting her bare feet cool themselves in the shoal water, while the great twilight moths struck softly against her. She waded on through the brook as the cow moved away, and listened to the thrushes with a heart that beat fast with pleasure. There was a stirring in the great boughs overhead. They were full of little birds and beasts that seemed to be wide-awake, and going about their world, or else saying good-night to each other in sleepy twitters. Sylvia herself felt sleepy as she walked along. However, it was not much farther to the house, and the air was soft and sweet. She was not often in the woods so late as this, and it made her feel as if she were a part of the gray shadows and the moving leaves. She was just thinking how long it seemed since she first came to the farm a year ago, and wondering if everything went on in the noisy town just the same as when she was there; the thought of the great red-faced boy who used to chase and frighten her made her hurry along the path to escape from the shadow of the trees.

Suddenly this little woods-girl is horror-stricken to hear a clear whistle not very far away. Not a bird's whistle, which would have a sort of friendliness, but a boy's whistle, determined, and somewhat aggressive. Sylvia left the cow to whatever sad fate might await her, and stepped discreetly aside into the bushes, but she was just too late. The enemy had discovered her, and called out in a very cheerful and persuasive tone, "Halloa, little girl, how far is it to the road?" and trembling Sylvia answered almost inaudibly, "A good ways."

She did not dare to look boldly at the tall young man, who carried a gun over his shoulder, but she came out of her bush and again followed the cow, while he walked alongside.

"I have been hunting for some birds," the stranger said kindly, "and I have lost my way, and need a friend very much. Don't be afraid," he added gallantly. "Speak up and tell me what your name is, and whether you think I can spend the night at your house, and go out gunning early in the morning."

Sylvia was more alarmed than before. Would not her grandmother consider her much to blame? But who could have foreseen such an accident as this? It did not appear to be her fault, and she hung her head as if the stem of it were broken, but managed to answer, "Sylvy," with much effort when her companion again asked her name.

Mrs. Tilley was standing in the doorway when the trio came into view. The cow gave a loud moo by way of explanation.

"Yes, you'd better speak up for yourself, you old trial! Where'd she tucked herself away this time, Sylvy?" Sylvia kept an awed silence; she knew by instinct that her grandmother did not comprehend the gravity of the situation. She must be mistaking the stranger for one of the farmer-lads of the region.

The young man stood his gun beside the door, and dropped a heavy game-bag beside it; then he bade Mrs. Tilley good-evening, and repeated his wayfarer's story, and asked if he could have a night's lodging.

"Put me anywhere you like," he said. "I must be off early in the morning, before day; but I am very hungry, indeed. You can give me some milk at any rate, that's plain."

"Dear sakes, yes," responded the hostess, whose long slumbering hospitality seemed to be easily awakened. "You might fare better if you went out on the main road a mile or so, but you're welcome to what we've got. I'll milk right off, and you make yourself at home. You can sleep on husks or feathers," she proffered graciously. "I raised them all myself. There's good pasturing for geese just below here towards the ma'sh. Now step round and set a plate for the gentleman, Sylvy!" And Sylvia promptly stepped. She was glad to have something to do, and she was hungry herself.

It was a surprise to find so clean and comfortable a little dwelling in this New England wilderness. The young man had known the horrors of its most primitive housekeeping, and the dreary squalor of that level of society which does not rebel at the companionship of hens. This was the best thrift of an old-fashioned farmstead, though on such a small scale that it seemed like a hermitage. He listened eagerly to the old woman's quaint talk, he watched Sylvia's pale face and shining gray eyes with ever growing enthusiasm, and insisted that this was the best supper he had eaten for a month; then, afterward, the new-made friends sat down in the doorway together while the moon came up.

Soon it would be berry-time, and Sylvia was a great help at picking. The cow was a good milker, though a plaguy thing to keep track of, the hostess gossiped frankly, adding presently that she had buried four children, so that Sylvia's mother, and a son (who might be dead) in California were all the children she had left. "Dan, my boy, was a great hand to go gunning," she explained sadly. "I never wanted for pa'tridges or gray squer'ls while he was to home. He's been a great wand'rer, I expect, and he's no hand to write letters. There, I don't blame him, I'd ha' seen the world myself if it had been so I could.

"Sylvia takes after him," the grandmother continued affectionately, after a minute's pause. "There ain't a foot o' ground she don't know her way over, and the wild creatur's counts her one o' themselves. Squer'ls she'll tame to come an' feed right out o' her hands, and all sorts o' birds. Last winter she got the jay-birds to bangeing here, and I believe she'd 'a' scanted herself of her own meals to have plenty to throw out amongst 'em, if I hadn't kep' watch. Anything but crows, I tell her, I'm willin' to help support,—though Dan he went an' tamed one o' them that did seem to have reason same as folks. It was round here a good spell after he went away. Dan an' his father they didn't hitch,—but he never held up his head ag'in after Dan had dared him an' gone off."

The guest did not notice this hint of family sorrows in his eager interest in something else.

"So Sylvy knows all about birds, does she?" he exclaimed, as he looked round at the little girl who sat, very demure but increasingly sleepy, in the moonlight. "I am making a collection of birds myself. I have been at it ever since I was a boy." (Mrs. Tilley smiled.) "There are two or three very rare ones I have been hunting for these five years. I mean to get them on my own ground if they can be found."

"Do you cage 'em up?" asked Mrs. Tilley doubtfully, in response to this enthusiastic announcement.

"Oh, no, they're stuffed and preserved, dozens and dozens of them," said the ornithologist, "and I have shot or snared every one myself. I caught a glimpse of a white heron three miles from here on Saturday, and I have followed it in this direction. They have never been found in this district at all. The little white heron, it is," and he turned again to look at Sylvia with the hope of discovering that the rare bird was one of her acquaintances.

But Sylvia was watching a hop-toad in the narrow footpath.

"You would know the heron if you saw it," the stranger continued eagerly. "A queer tall white bird with soft feathers and long thin legs. And it would have a nest perhaps in the top of a high tree, made of sticks, something like a hawk's nest."

Sylvia's heart gave a wild beat; she knew that strange white bird, and had once stolen softly near where it stood in some bright green swamp grass, away over at the other side of the woods. There was an open place where the sunshine always seemed strangely yellow and hot, where tall, nodding rushes grew, and her grandmother had warned her that she might sink in the soft black mud underneath and never be heard of more. Not far beyond were the salt marshes and beyond those was the sea, the sea which Sylvia wondered and dreamed about, but never had looked upon, though its great voice could often be heard above the noise of the woods on stormy nights.

"I can't think of anything I should like so much as to find that heron's nest," the handsome stranger was saying. "I would give ten dollars to anybody who could show it to me," he added desperately, "and I mean to spend my whole vacation hunting for it if need be. Perhaps it was only migrating, or had been chased out of its own region by some bird of prey."

Mrs. Tilley gave amazed attention to all this, but Sylvia still watched the toad, not divining, as she might have done at some calmer time, that the creature wished to get to its hole under the doorstep, and was much hindered by the unusual spectators at that hour of the evening. No amount of thought, that night, could decide how many wished-for treasures the ten dollars, so lightly spoken of, would buy.

The next day the young sportsman hovered about the woods, and Sylvia kept him company, having lost her first fear of the friendly lad, who proved to be most kind and sympathetic. He told her many things about the birds and what they knew and where they lived and what they did with themselves. And he gave her a jack-knife, which she thought as great a treasure as if she were a desert-islander. All day long he did not once make her troubled or afraid except when he brought down some unsuspecting singing creature from its bough. Sylvia would have liked him vastly better without his gun; she could not understand why he killed the very birds he seemed to like so much. But as the day waned, Sylvia still watched the young man with loving admiration. She had never seen anybody so charming and delightful; the woman's heart, asleep in the child, was vaguely thrilled by a dream of love. Some premonition of that great power stirred and swayed these young foresters who traversed the solemn woodlands with soft-footed silent care. They stopped to listen to a bird's song; they pressed forward again eagerly, parting the branches — speaking to each other rarely and in whispers; the young man going first and Sylvia following, fascinated, a few steps behind, with her gray eyes dark with excitement.

She grieved because the longed-for white heron was elusive, but she did not lead the guest, she only followed, and there was no such thing as speaking first. The sound of her own unquestioned voice would have terrified her — it was hard enough to answer yes or no when there was need of that. At last evening began to fall, and they drove the cow home together, and Sylvia smiled with pleasure when they came to the place where she heard the whistle and was afraid only the night before.

II

Half a mile from home, at the farther edge of the woods, where the land was highest, a great pine-tree stood, the last of its generation. Whether it was left for a boundary mark, or for what reason, no one could say; the woodchoppers who had felled its mates were dead and gone long ago, and a whole forest of sturdy trees, pines and oaks and maples, had grown again. But the stately head of this old pine towered above them all and made a landmark for sea and shore miles and miles away. Sylvia knew it well. She had always believed that whoever climbed to the top of it could see the ocean; and the little girl had often laid her hand on the great rough trunk and looked up wistfully at those dark boughs that the wind always stirred, no matter how hot and still the air might be below. Now she thought of the tree with a new excitement, for why, if one climbed it at break of day, could not one see all the world, and easily discover whence the white heron flew, and mark the place, and find the hidden nest?

What a spirit of adventure, what wild ambition! What fancied triumph and delight and glory for the later morning when she could make known the secret! It was almost too real and too great for the childish heart to bear.

All night the door of the little house stood open, and the whippoorwills came and sang upon the very step. The young sportsman and his old hostess were sound asleep, but Sylvia's great design kept her broad awake and watching. She forgot to think of sleep. The short summer night seemed as long as the winter darkness, and at last when the whippoorwills ceased, and she was afraid the morning would after all come too soon, she stole out of the house and followed the pasture path through the woods, hastening toward the open ground beyond, listening with a sense of comfort and companionship to the drowsy twitter of a half-awakened bird, whose perch she had jarred in passing. Alas, if the great wave of human interest which flooded for the first time this dull little life should sweep away the satisfactions of an existence heart to heart with nature and the dumb life of the forest!

There was the huge tree asleep yet in the paling moonlight, and small and hopeful Sylvia began with utmost bravery to mount to the top of it, with tingling, eager blood coursing the channels of her whole frame, with her bare feet and fingers, that pinched and held like bird's claws to the monstrous ladder reaching up, up, almost to the sky itself. First she must mount the white oak tree that grew alongside, where she was almost lost among the dark branches and the green leaves heavy and wet with dew; a bird fluttered off its nest, and a red squirrel ran to and fro and scolded pettishly at the harmless housebreaker. Sylvia felt her way easily. She had often climbed there, and knew that higher still one of the oak's upper branches chafed against the pine trunk, just where its lower boughs were set close together. There, when she made the dangerous pass from one tree to the other, the great enterprise would really begin.

She crept out along the swaying oak limb at last, and took the daring step across into the old pine-tree. The way was harder than she thought; she must reach far and hold fast, the sharp dry twigs caught and held her and scratched her like angry talons, the pitch made her thin little fingers clumsy and stiff as she went round and round the tree's great stem, higher and higher upward. The sparrows and robins in the woods below were beginning to wake and twitter to the dawn, yet it seemed much lighter there aloft in the pine-tree, and the child knew that she must hurry if her project were to be of any use.

The tree seemed to lengthen itself out as she went up, and to reach farther and farther upward. It was like a great main-mast to the voyaging earth; it must truly have been amazed that morning through all its ponderous frame as it felt this determined spark of human spirit creeping and climbing from higher branch to branch. Who knows how steadily the least twigs held themselves to advantage this light, weak creature on her way! The old pine must have loved his new dependent. More than all the hawks, and bats, and moths, and even the sweet-voiced thrushes, was the brave, beating heart of the solitary gray-eyed child. And the tree stood still and held away the winds that June morning while the dawn grew bright in the east.

Sylvia's face was like a pale star, if one had seen it from the ground, when the last thorny bough was past, and she stood trembling and tired but wholly triumphant, high in the tree-top. Yes, there was the sea with the dawning sun making a golden dazzle over it, and toward that glorious east flew two hawks with slow-moving pinions. How low they looked in the air from that height when before one had only seen them far up, and dark against the blue sky. Their gray feathers were as soft as moths; they seemed only a little way from the tree, and Sylvia felt as if she too could go flying away among the clouds. Westward, the woodlands and farms reached miles and miles into the distance; here and there were church steeples, and white villages; truly it was a vast and awesome world.

The birds sang louder and louder. At last the sun came up bewilderingly bright. Sylvia could see the white sails of ships out at sea, and the clouds that were purple and rose-colored and yellow at first began to fade away. Where was the white heron's nest in the sea of green branches, and was this wonderful sight and pageant of the world the only reward for having climbed to such a giddy height? Now look down again, Sylvia, where the green marsh is set among the shining birches and dark hemlocks; there where you saw the white heron once you will see him again; look, look! a white spot of him like a single floating feather comes up from the dead hemlock and grows larger, and rises, and comes close at last, and goes by the landmark pine with steady sweep of wing and outstretched slender neck and crested head. And wait! wait! do not move a foot or a finger, little girl, do not send an arrow of light and consciousness from your two eager eyes, for the heron has perched on a pine bough not far beyond yours, and cries back to his mate on the nest, and plumes his feathers for the new day!

The child gives a long sigh a minute later when a company of shouting cat-birds comes also to the tree, and vexed by their fluttering and lawlessness the solemn heron goes away. She knows his secret now, the wild, light, slender bird that floats and wavers, and goes back like an arrow presently to his home in the green world beneath. Then Sylvia, well satisfied, makes her perilous way down again, not daring to look far below the branch she stands on, ready to cry sometimes because her fingers ache and her lamed feet slip. Wondering over and over again what the stranger would say to her, and what he would think when she told him how to find his way straight to the heron's nest.

"Sylvy, Sylvy!" called the busy old grandmother again and again, but nobody answered, and the small husk bed was empty, and Sylvia had disappeared.

The guest waked from a dream, and remembering his day's pleasure hurried to dress himself that it might sooner begin. He was sure from the way the shy little girl looked once or twice yesterday that she had at least seen the white heron, and now she must really be persuaded to tell. Here she comes now, paler than ever, and her worn old frock is torn and tattered, and smeared with pine pitch. The grandmother and the sportsman stand in the door together and question her, and the splendid moment had come to speak of the dead hemlock-tree by the green marsh.

But Sylvia does not speak after all, though the old grandmother fretfully rebukes her, and the young man's kind appealing eyes are looking straight in her own. He can make them rich with money; he has promised it, and they are poor now. He is so well worth making happy, and he waits to hear the story she can tell.

No, she must keep silence! What is it that suddenly forbids her and makes her dumb? Has she been nine years growing, and now, when the great world for the first time puts out a hand to her, must she thrust it aside for a bird's sake? The murmur of the pine's green branches is in her ears, she remembers how the white heron came flying through the golden air and how they watched the sea and the morning together, and Sylvia cannot speak; she cannot tell the heron's secret and give its life away.

Dear loyalty, that suffered a sharp pang as the guest went away disappointed later in the day, that could have served and followed him and loved him as a dog loves! Many a night Sylvia heard the echo of his whistle haunting the pasture path as she came home with the loitering cow. She forgot even her sorrow at the sharp report of his gun and the piteous sight of thrushes and sparrows dropping silent to the ground, their songs hushed and their pretty feathers stained and wet with blood. Were the birds better friends than their hunter might have been,—who can tell? Whatever treasures were lost to her, woodlands and summer-time, remember! Bring your gifts and graces and tell your secrets to this lonely country child!

[1886]

QUESTIONS

1. What is Sylvia's attitude toward nature? What is the ornithologist's attitude? Why is Sylvia initially frightened by the ornithologist?
2. What is the central conflict in the story? Why does Sylvia make the choice she makes?
3. What is the "initiation" that Sylvia undergoes? How does the narrator convey Sylvia's changing perspective?
4. What is the narrator's relation to the story? How do the shifts in point of view and tense contribute to the unfolding of the narrative?
5. What is the theme of the story?

Elizabeth Jolley

(b. 1923)

England/Australia

Born in Birmingham, England, of a mother from the impoverished Austrian aristocracy who became a nurse, and an English father who was a science teacher, Elizabeth Jolley grew up in England but spoke only German at home until she was six. Because her father did not want his daughters to attend school, Elizabeth and her sister were educated at home by French and German governesses and British Broadcasting System school programs. As Jolley writes, these formative experiences contributed to her eventual vocation as a writer: "Children who do not go to school and whose family speak a foreign language are exiles in their own street. Like all lonely children we retreated into the fantasy and imagination." Later, when her father finally sent Elizabeth to a Quaker boarding school, she tried to subdue her homesickness by writing stories. Additionally, Jolley writes,

> all my life I have kept journals in which I write about people and places; dwelling on, perhaps, some detail of human effort or the way in which a tree might change in the changing light of an afternoon.

Later trained as a nurse, Jolley did not begin to submit her stories for publication until she and her husband, a librarian, emigrated to western Australia in 1959. While raising a family, teaching, and managing an orchard and a goose farm, Jolley continued to write and to publish novels and stories, a number of which she had been working on for years. As she commented in an interview, "The thing about writing is that you do several things alongside, and that writing is only one part of your life. If you made it your whole life, you might go entirely mad, especially if you didn't succeed. . . ."

Jolley's stories, distinguished by their fresh blend of offbeat humor, satire, and pathos, are collected in *Five Acre Virgin and Other Stories* (1976) and *The Traveling Entertainer and Other Stories* (1979). Her novels, including (among others) *Miss Peabody's Inheritance* (1983), *Mr. Scobie's Riddle* (1983), *Foxybaby* (1985), and *Cabin Fever* (1990), have received a number of prizes and awards.

Another Holiday for the Prince

We're having this dumb play at school Falstaff or something I was supposed to be the Sheriff of London but the bell went before my part came on and as it was the long weekend Hot Legs let us go before the bell stopped. I went down and hung around the Deli for a while with the others and when I got home Mother was already there.

"Don't bang the door," she said, "He's still in bed."

"Sorry!"

"He's sleeping," she went on, she seemed relieved. "Sleep's the best thing he can have. I wish *he'd* eat!" She watched me as I took bread and spread the butter thick, she was never mean about butter, when we didn't have other things we always had plenty of butter. I ate my pieces quickly before she could tell me not to spoil my tea.

Mother always called him the Prince, she worried about him all the time. I couldn't think why. He was only my brother and a drop-out at that. Dropped out from school and then dropping in and out of one job after another, sometimes not even staying long enough in one place to get his pay. I could always tell by Mother's face when I came in.

"He's back, was back when I came home," and she would sit in a heap at the kitchen table. And after a bit I'd say, "What's for tea?" and that brightened her.

"What do you think the Prince would like?" and she'd go up the terrace for liverwurst or something tasty to fry up.

My brother smoked and drank and coughed and watched telly with the blinds drawn day in and day out and half the night too.

"He's resting," Mother comforted herself. "Boys outgrow their strength. They need extra rest. If only he'd eat and go outdoors in the air, though!"

Saturday mornings I often went with her to her work to get her finished up as quick as possible.

Mother said it was a revelation every time she got off the bus and walked round the corner and saw the wide river below shining so peaceful with the far bank dark with trees and all the lovely homes piled up on this side of the hill. It was like a great big continental post card. The stillness and the blue misty light on the smooth water made her feel rested she said and she felt she was a better person every time she saw it.

We had the house to ourselves, it was all vinyl and bathrooms. She wouldn't ever let me do out the study.

"There's big cigars in there and sex drinks and books with titles," she said and she sent me to hang out the washing. There was nothing in the *Seducer's Cook Book* to upset her she said and dusting those nude drawings didn't affect her, she was too worn out and faded for that kind of thing.

We seemed to get on really quick with the work and when we sat down to have our cocoa she looked out at the river approving of the calm.

"They'll stay out in their boat the weekend," she said, sipping gratefully.

"I don't like you going out to work," I said.

"You don't want to mind about that," she said. "Everyone's got to work at some time or other, it's best to like it," she said. "Otherwise you'll have to spend most of your life not liking what you've got to do," she said. "My Mrs. Lady is a lovely woman, such a good mother too, you saw all that nice washing! really sets an example, so clean you could do an operation in any room in this house. And don't you ever forget those nice dresses and jumpers you've had from her."

"But you're going for your life all the time."

"Hard work never hurt any one. It's good for me, helps to fight off the menopause."

"What's that?" Mother used big words. She read too much.

"It's when your life changes, you'll find out later," she said, and then she said, "and where else could I have an avocado pear with my cocoa."

"Ugh! Avocado pear!"

"It's an acquired taste," and she waltzed off with the broom. Later while I was wiping out the saucepan cupboard I could hear her queer singing above the noise of the floor polisher. She seemed to get quicker and younger as she worked.

As we were about to go home Mother took a little key off a hook in the kitchen.

"I've a very nice surprise for you," she said, twirling it on her bony finger.

"That why you were singing then?"

"Oh was I singing?" Her cheeks were suddenly bright red and her eyes seemed to be full of tears as if an idea was trying to burst out of them.

"What do you think! Mrs. Lady has left me the use of her car and some money so we can go away for the weekend!" Oh I felt an excitement, I hugged Mother.

"It's a wonder you didn't die keeping the secret all morning." I hugged her again.

"My! Mind my living daylights," she gasped for breath.

"The Prince," Mother said. "We'll get him to that nice motel again right on the sea front. He won't be able to avoid breathing the sea air if he's right in it."

Of course my brother growled. He was in a terrible mood. Mother pleaded with him through the clouds of smoke.

"Only pack up a few things and just come. I have the car. Come and see."

Grudgingly he looked. It took all the afternoon to persuade him.

"Look at the roo bar,[1] and see, there's a radio," Mother urged him, she fretted at the waste of time. She promised to let him drive once we got down into the country to try to make him come.

"But what about a license?" I asked.

"Hold your shit Bogfart!" He gave me a shove.

"Now just you watch your language!" Mother was severe. "Mrs. Lady has fixed everything. Only be quick and let's go!" She had had a shower and her wet hair was flat on her head. She urged and pleaded and threatened and we set off very late, about half past five.

Next day he stayed in the motel room watching T.V. and Mother fretted on the beach.

"Come in!" I called her from the water. "It's beaut in!" And it really was considering the time of the year. But she couldn't get up any enthusiasm, she couldn't bear to see all that lovely sunshine wasted because he wouldn't come out.

Lunch time my brother was still disagreeable. It spoiled the meal and he refused to eat his sweets. But Mother said afterwards not to take any notice when he growled, it was only because he had used his pudding spoon for his soup and she knew it wasn't any use telling him with that snooty waitress looking on.

The motel was really gas! There was so much hot water Mother washed out all our clothes and we both washed our hair again. I got out my social studies. Hot Legs has this idea about a test every Wednesday.

[1]*roo bar* a metal bar surrounding the front grill of a car to protect it against collisions with animals such as kangaroos

"Shit head!" My brother started picking on me. "Why don't you get out before they chuck you out. That's all crap," he said, knocking the book across the floor. "You'll only fail your exam and they don't want failures, spoils their bloody numbers. They'll ask you to leave, see if they don't."

I sat there and howled out loud, though I didn't want to, not in front of him.

Mother was furious, her face went bright red.

"Why you son of a bitch!" she screamed, I really thought she was going to go for him, she looked that mad.

And he put on a real idiot's face and turned his eyes up so only the whites showed and he said in a furry thick voice like as if he was drunk, "Well if I'm the son of a bitch dear lady you must be the bitch," and what with his daft face and Mother standing there all towelled up there really was a funny side to it and we all laughed our heads off. I wasn't sure if Mother was laughing or crying, anyway she got dressed and went off down into the town, we heard her crash the gears at the corner, it's been a while since she drove anything. She came back quite soon with steakburgers and chips and ice cream and Coke and we had a really good evening watching the T.V.

On the Monday just when we should have been setting off for home, my brother said, "What's the beach like?"

And Mother couldn't get him there quick enough. Oh he was a scream. He kept sitting backwards into the water just as a wave came and he went under as if he was drowning with only his thin white fingers reaching up out of the water as it swirled back. I thought Mother would kill herself laughing. She was really enjoying herself.

"Halp!" My brother sat back disappearing again into the sea and his wet white fingers grasped the froth of the wave. Mother played in the water like a girl. "Give you a race!" She swam splashing and choking. She could only do about five strokes of anything.

I don't think I've ever seen her so happy.

We were nearly the last to leave the beach. We saw the sun go, leaving only a long red sky far out over the water which was boiling up dark along the sand.

"Come on!" My brother was nervous and irritable.

"Our Prince is cold and hungry." Mother hurried me in the change rooms. "We'll get a chicken and eat it on the way home."

She seemed anxious suddenly. Her agitation was worse at the Chicken Bar, we had to wait as there'd been a little rush on chickens. She paced up and down the narrow shop and she kept looking anxiously out at the car. My brother was sitting there, we could see his white face through the dark, he was listening to the radio. We were all hungry.

"Smells all right!" He even smiled as we got back into the car. Mother tore up the chicken dividing it on bits of paper between the three of us.

"I'll have to step on it," she said. "I don't want to inconvenience Mrs. Lady over her car."

We were just about to start on the food when it seemed we were surrounded by the police. There they were poking their heads in at the windows, I felt a real fool.

"Eat!" Mother commanded, but of course we couldn't and neither could she.

"It was me! I took the bloody car!" I didn't recognize my brother's voice, I couldn't believe the words were really coming from his white face. He lit a cigarette blowing smoke all over his ragged bits of chicken. I could see his hands shaking.

"You filthy bloody liar. You shut up!" Mother screamed. "Don't listen to that son of a bitch he's . . ."

"If you're not careful Missis," the cop said, "I'll have to book you for obscene language too," and then he seemed to remember something. He looked hard at Mother.

"You don't vary much in your sort of crimes do you Missis. Wasn't it just about here in similar circumstances a few weeks back, if my memory isn't playing tricks."

"This is the only sort of crime, as you put it, as I need to do," Mother replied with quiet haughtiness. "It so happens it was a different car and it was a whole year ago. Time must pass very quick for some people!" she added.

Mother cried when she knew she had to go to gaol,[2] she never could stand unbleached calico next to her skin she said. And she felt so bad about Mrs. Lady too. She'd hoped to get the car back before they got in off their boat and of course she'd intended to work off the cheque she'd written for herself. She would have liked to have the chance to explain to Mrs. Lady.

After a bit she stopped crying.

"It'll be better for the Prince," she said. "A more regular life, and they'll see he eats." This seemed to comfort her.

"Be a good girl at the Home," she said to me. "You won't be so strange as there's sure to be a few you'll know. And everything will all come right," she said. "A change is as good as a rest they say."

It was awful hearing my brother cry later. I didn't know it was him at first, he sounded like a man crying. In his room he'd got this big box of chocolates all wrapped up ready for Mother's Day, it wouldn't go in his case with all his things and he didn't know what to do.

"I'll help you," I said to him.

"Oh go to hell and get stuffed!" he said and banged his door on me.

In Pottery Class I'm making a jar with a lid. If it comes out all right I think I'll use it for a jewel box as we don't ever eat marmalade.

[1976]

QUESTIONS

1. Through which details and events does the reader discover the actual social and financial circumstances of the mother and her children?
2. Why does the mother take such a risk on behalf of her son?
3. Is the story humorous? If so, which elements contribute to its humor?
4. Why is the story told from the daughter's point of view? What is her attitude toward her mother and her brother? From what is only hinted at in her narrative, can you reconstruct the recent history of this family?
5. How does the story illuminate issues concerning social class?

[2]*gaol* jail

James Joyce

(1882–1941)

Ireland

A giant of twentieth-century literature and one of the most influential and original innovators in the modernist shaping of narrative form and language, James Augustine Aloysius Joyce was born in a suburb of Dublin; his father was a tax collector, his mother was a pianist. At one point Joyce seemed destined to follow his mother's vocation: possessed of a fine tenor voice, he considered a career in music. Even in his writing, music is a prominent structural motif.

Joyce's influence on twentieth-century literature is formidable and definitive: his experiments with language, subject, point of view, and formal structure established entirely new conventions and conceptions of literary expression. Each of Joyce's major works reflects his extension of the boundaries of traditional narrative forms. The 15 stories in *Dubliners* (1914), begun in 1904 when Joyce was in his early twenties, already show his departure from tradition. One of his guiding strategies was the inclusion of what he termed "epiphanies": brief but significant moments of insight, illumination, or revelation for his characters.

Rejecting the deeply conservative moral and intellectual climate of Catholic Ireland as inhospitable to his art as well as his private life, Joyce chose voluntary exile, leaving his country in 1904 with Nora Barnacle (his eventual wife) to accept a teaching position in Trieste, Switzerland. Although he continued to write about Dublin, he rarely returned to Ireland during his lifetime. As he commented to a friend about this apparent anomaly, "I always write about Dublin, because if I can get to the heart of Dublin I can get to the heart of all the cities of the world. In the particular is contained the universal."

In *A Portrait of the Artist as a Young Man* (1916), Joyce explores the values and impressions of childhood, adolescence, and young adulthood as they reflect, and shape, the developing consciousness of a fledgling writer, Stephen Dedalus—who, like his creator, decides to leave Ireland. The novel concludes with Dedalus's passionate declaration of artistic independence: "I go to encounter for the millionth time the reality of experience and to forge in the smithy of my soul the uncreated conscience of my race."

Joyce's masterpieces, *Ulysses* (1922) and *Finnegans Wake* (1939), are radical in their structural and narrative innovations. *Ulysses* incorporates the structure of Homer's *Odyssey* as the ironic counterpoint to the lives of three characters as they crisscross Dublin during a single June day in 1904. Each of the chapters is narrated in a different style; several sequences demonstrate Joyce's brilliant use of the stream-of-consciousness technique he originated as a method of entering and directly reproducing the apparently random (but in fact highly controlled) flow of his characters' consciousnesses. *Finnegans Wake*, Joyce's last work, encompasses both particular characters and universal experiences and themes, unfolding as a dream vision of Dublin within the mind of one character and simultaneously within the larger contexts of history, metaphysics, and myth. Language itself is broken and reconstituted; Joyce's allusive, digressive, and punning play with words is part of the novel's self-conscious exploration of language and consciousness.

In "Eveline," from *Dubliners*, Joyce demonstrates his sympathetic understanding of ordinary young people who represent a cross section of contemporary urban life in Dublin. At the same time, it is the nature of their inner moral lives that determines their perceptions of the world and the choices that follow from them.

Eveline

She sat at the window watching the evening invade the avenue. Her head was leaned against the window curtains and in her nostrils was the odour of dusty cretonne. She was tired.

Few people passed. The man out of the last house passed on his way home; she heard his footsteps clacking along the concrete pavement and afterwards crunching on the cinder path before the new red houses. One time there used to be a field there in which they used to play every evening with other people's children. Then a man from Belfast bought the field and built houses in it—not like their little brown houses but bright brick houses with shining roofs. The children of the avenue used to play together in that field—the Devines, the Waters, the Dunns, little Keogh the cripple, she and her brothers and sisters. Ernest, however, never played: he was too grown up. Her father used often to hunt them in out of the field with his blackthorn stick; but usually little Keogh used to keep *nix* and call out when he saw her father coming. Still they seemed to have been rather happy then. Her father was not so bad then; and besides, her mother was alive. That was a long time ago; she and her brothers and sisters were all grown up; her mother was dead. Tizzie Dunn was dead, too, and the Waters had gone back to England. Everything changes. Now she was going to go away like the others, to leave her home.

Home! She looked round the room, reviewing all its familiar objects which she had dusted once a week for so many years, wondering where on earth all the dust came from. Perhaps she would never see again those familiar objects from which she had never dreamed of being divided. And yet during all those years she had never found out the name of the priest whose yellowing photograph hung on the wall above the broken harmonium beside the coloured print of the promises made to Blessed Margaret Mary Alacoque. He had been a school friend of her father. Whenever he showed the photograph to a visitor her father used to pass it with a casual word:

"He is in Melbourne now."

She had consented to go away, to leave her home. Was that wise? She tried to weigh each side of the question. In her home anyway she had shelter and food; she had those whom she had known all her life about her. Of course she had to work hard, both in the house and at business. What would they say of her in the Stores when they found out that she had run away with a fellow? Say she was a fool, perhaps; and her place would be filled up by advertisement. Miss Gavan

would be glad. She had always had an edge on her, especially whenever there were people listening.

"Miss Hill, don't you see these ladies are waiting?"

"Look lively, Miss Hill, please."

She would not cry many tears at leaving the Stores.

But in her new home, in a distant unknown country, it would not be like that. Then she would be married—she, Eveline. People would treat her with respect then. She would not be treated as her mother had been. Even now, though she was over nineteen, she sometimes felt herself in danger of her father's violence. She knew it was that that had given her the palpitations. When they were growing up he had never gone for her, like he used to go for Harry and Ernest, because she was a girl; but latterly he had begun to threaten her and say what he would do to her only for her dead mother's sake. And now she had nobody to protect her. Ernest was dead and Harry, who was in the church decorating business, was nearly always down somewhere in the country. Besides, the invariable squabble for money on Saturday nights had begun to weary her unspeakably. She always gave her entire wages—seven shillings—and Harry always sent up what he could but the trouble was to get any money from her father. He said she used to squander the money, that she had no head, that he wasn't going to give her his hard-earned money to throw about the streets, and much more, for he was usually fairly bad on Saturday night. In the end he would give her the money and ask her had she any intention of buying Sunday's dinner. Then she had to rush out as quickly as she could and do her marketing, holding her black leather purse tightly in her hand as she elbowed her way through the crowds and returning home late under her load of provisions. She had hard work to keep the house together and to see that the two young children who had been left to her charge went to school regularly and got their meals regularly. It was hard work—a hard life—but now that she was about to leave it she did not find it a wholly undesirable life.

She was about to explore another life with Frank. Frank was very kind, manly, open-hearted. She was to go away with him by the night-boat to be his wife and to live with him in Buenos Ayres where he had a home waiting for her. How well she remembered the first time she had seen him; he was lodging in a house on the main road where she used to visit. It seemed a few weeks ago. He was standing at the gate, his peaked cap pushed back on his head and his hair tumbled forward over a face of bronze. Then they had come to know each other. He used to meet her outside the Stores every evening and see her home. He took her to see *The Bohemian Girl* and she felt elated as she sat in an unaccustomed part of the theatre with him. He was awfully fond of music and sang a little. People knew that they were courting and, when he sang about the lass that loves a sailor, she always felt pleasantly confused. He used to call her Poppens out of fun. First of all it had been an excitement for her to have a fellow and then she had begun to like him. He had tales of distant countries. He had started as a deck boy at a pound a month on a ship of the Allan Line going out to Canada. He told her the names of the ships he had been on and the names of the different services. He had sailed through the Straits of Magellan and he told her stories of the terrible Patagonians.[1] He had fallen on his feet in Buenos Ayres, he said, and

[1]*terrible Patagonians* legends based on nomadic tribes that lived at the southern tip of Argentina (known as Patagonia); the Straits of Magellan—the channel between the South American mainland and Tierra del Fuego; Buenos Ayres—Buenos Aires, Argentina

had come over to the old country just for a holiday. Of course, her father had found out the affair and had forbidden her to have anything to say to him.

"I know these sailor chaps," he said.

One day he had quarrelled with Frank and after that she had to meet her lover secretly.

The evening deepened in the avenue. The white of two letters in her lap grew indistinct. One was to Harry; the other was to her father. Ernest had been her favourite but she liked Harry too. Her father was becoming old lately, she noticed; he would miss her. Sometimes he could be very nice. Not long before, when she had been laid up for a day, he had read her out a ghost story and made toast for her at the fire. Another day, when their mother was alive, they had all gone for a picnic to the Hill of Howth. She remembered her father putting on her mother's bonnet to make the children laugh.

Her time was running out but she continued to sit by the window, leaning her head against the window curtain, inhaling the odour of dusty cretonne. Down far in the avenue she could hear a street organ playing. She knew the air. Strange that it should come that very night to remind her of the promise to her mother, her promise to keep the home together as long as she could. She remembered the last night of her mother's illness; she was again in the close dark room at the other side of the hall and outside she heard a melancholy air of Italy. The organ-player had been ordered to go away and given sixpence. She remembered her father strutting back into the sickroom saying:

"Damned Italians! coming over here!"

As she mused the pitiful vision of her mother's life laid its spell on the very quick of her being—that life of commonplace sacrifices closing in final craziness. She trembled as she heard again her mother's voice saying constantly with foolish insistence:

"Derevaun Seraun! Derevaun Seraun!"[2]

She stood up in a sudden impulse of terror. Escape! She must escape! Frank would save her. He would give her life, perhaps love, too. But she wanted to live. Why should she be unhappy? She had a right to happiness. Frank would take her in his arms, fold her in his arms. He would save her.

She stood among the swaying crowd in the station at the North Wall. He held her hand and she knew that he was speaking to her, saying something about the passage over and over again. The station was full of soldiers with brown baggages. Through the wide doors of the sheds she caught a glimpse of the black mass of the boat, lying in beside the quay wall, with illumined portholes. She answered nothing. She felt her cheek pale and cold and, out of a maze of distress, she prayed to God to direct her, to show her what was her duty. The boat blew a long mournful whistle into the mist. If she went, to-morrow she would be on the sea with Frank, steaming towards Buenos Ayres. Their passage had been booked. Could she still draw back after all he had done for her? Her distress awoke a nausea in her body and she kept moving her lips in silent fervent prayer.

A bell clanged upon her heart. She felt him seize her hand:

"Come!"

[2]*"Derevaun Seraun!"* an expression of uncertain translation, possibly corrupt Gaelic for "the end of pleasure is pain" [William Y. Tindall]

All the seas of the world tumbled about her heart. He was drawing her into them: he would drown her. She gripped with both hands at the iron railing.

"Come!"

No! No! No! It was impossible. Her hands clutched the iron in frenzy. Amid the seas she sent a cry of anguish!

"Eveline! Evvy!"

He rushed beyond the barrier and called to her to follow. He was shouted at to go on but he still called to her. She set her white face to him, passive, like a helpless animal. Her eyes gave him no sign of love or farewell or recognition.

[1914]

QUESTIONS

1. What is the conflict in the story?
2. What attracts Eveline to Frank? Why does she decide not to go with him?
3. What attitudes toward her parents and her family do you discover through Eveline's thoughts? How do those attitudes influence her decision to remain in Ireland?

Franz Kafka

(1883–1924)

Czechoslovakia

Although Franz Kafka's works have been translated into more than a hundred languages, during his own lifetime he was never to know the extent of his genius. The first child of a German-speaking Jewish family in Prague, Czechoslovakia, Kafka suffered a lonely childhood (two younger brothers died during childhood and his three sisters were much younger than he). Even more critical for Kafka's own emotional life, he feared his father, a successful but authoritarian businessman. Issues of authority and difficulties in Kafka's relationships with women (he was engaged three times—twice to the same woman—but never married) preoccupied him for most of his life.

Kafka studied law and earned a doctorate in jurisprudence at the German University of Prague. Working as a civil service lawyer in the dreary office of the state Workmans' Accident Insurance Institute and investigating claims during the day, he began to write at night and eventually quit his job. In 1917 his health complications were officially diagnosed as tuberculosis (for which there was no cure at the time). His illness tormented him, but it also became a source of spiritual discovery and confirmed his determination to pursue his writing to the virtual exclusion of other activities. As he phrased it in his diary, "My talent for portraying my dreamlike inner life has thrust all other matters into the background. . . . Nothing else will ever satisfy me. But the strength I can muster for that portrayal is not to be counted on: perhaps it has already vanished forever. . . . " (*Diary*, August 6, 1914). As his friend Milena Jesenska wrote in his obituary, he suffered from a lung disease "which he cherished and fostered even while accepting treatment. . . . It endowed him with a delicacy of feeling that bordered on the miraculous, and with a spiritual purity uncompromising to the point of horror. . . . "

Kafka wrote three novels, all technically unfinished at his death and all published posthumously: *The Trial* (1925), *The Castle* (1926), and *Amerika* (1927). He had instructed his friend and literary executor; Max Brod, to destroy his manuscripts at his death; Brod, torn between loyalty to Kafka's final wishes and recognition of his friend's literary genius, published his works, which include, in addition to the novels, volumes of short stories, parables, aphorisms, diaries, and reflections. The characters Joseph K (*The Trial*) and K (*The Castle*), trapped in labyrinths of legal or bureaucratic incomprehensibility and paralyzed by spiritual uncertainty, are unforgettable central figures in the landscape of twentieth-century literature. In fact, Franz Kafka accomplished, above and beyond his unique and profound literary explorations of modern anxiety, something that, as George Steiner phrases it, "no other writer in the history of language and of literature had accomplished: he . . . made indelibly his own . . . a letter of the alphabet. K is now Kafka's." Moreover, the term "Kafkaesque" is an equally indelible part of the twentieth-century vocabulary as a term for the absurd and incomprehensible entanglements of everyday life.

Kafka's voice is absolutely unique in modern literature. His visionary capacity to turn dreamlike events—or, more accurately, the stuff of nightmares—into symbolic narratives results in the often bizarre, grotesque, and paradoxical characteristics of his fiction and parables, which unfold in an ironic, understated tone. Despite his Jewish background, Kafka was haunted by the idea of Original Sin as well as by the connections among guilt, punishment, and authority. Although at one time critics regarded Kafka as a neurotic genius who poured his psychological preoccupations into his writing, more recently scholars and readers have recognized the way in which Kafka gave form not simply to his own anxieties but also to those of an entire age; he seems to have prophetically anticipated some of the darkest historical events of the twentieth century, including the Holocaust. The ideas of alienation and the "absurd," the human longing for the infinite in the face of spiritual doubt, have no more brilliant spokesman than Kafka. "The Metamorphosis" is an unforgettable rendering of inner nightmare represented as external events with a logic that proceeds inexorably from its first chilling sentence.

◆ *The Metamorphosis* ◆

I

As Gregor Samsa awoke one morning from uneasy dreams he found himself transformed in his bed into a gigantic insect. He was lying on his hard, as it were armor-plated, back and when he lifted his head a little he could see his dome-like brown belly divided into stiff arched segments on top of which the bed quilt could hardly keep in position and was about to slide off completely. His numerous legs, which were pitifully thin compared to the rest of his bulk, waved helplessly before his eyes.

What has happened to me? he thought. It was no dream. His room, a regular human bedroom, only rather too small, lay quiet between the four familiar walls. Above the table on which a collection of cloth samples was unpacked and spread out—Samsa was a commercial traveler—hung the picture which he had recently cut out of an illustrated magazine and put into a pretty gilt frame. It showed a lady, with a fur cap on and a fur stole, sitting upright and holding out to the spectator a huge fur muff into which the whole of her forearm had vanished!

Gregor's eyes turned next to the window, and the overcast sky—one could hear rain drops beating on the window gutter—made him quite melancholy. What about sleeping a little longer and forgetting all this nonsense, he thought, but it could not be done, for he was accustomed to sleep on his right side and in his present condition he could not turn himself over. However violently he forced himself towards his right side he always rolled on to his back again. He tried it at least a hundred times, shutting his eyes to keep from seeing his struggling legs, and only desisted when he began to feel in his side a faint dull ache he had never experienced before.

Oh God, he thought, what an exhausting job I've picked on! Traveling about day in, day out. It's much more irritating work than doing the actual business in the office, and on top of that there's the trouble of constant traveling, of worrying about train connections, the bed and irregular meals, casual acquaintances that are always new and never become intimate friends. The devil take it all! He felt a slight itching up on his belly; slowly pushed himself on his back nearer to the top of the bed so that he could lift his head more easily; identified the itching place which was surrounded by many small white spots the nature of which he could not understand and made to touch it with a leg, but drew the leg back immediately, for the contact made a cold shiver run through him.

He slid down again into his former position. This getting up early, he thought, makes one quite stupid. A man needs his sleep. Other commercials live like harem women. For instance, when I come back to the hotel of a morning to write up the orders I've got, these others are only sitting down to breakfast. Let me just try that with my chief; I'd be sacked on the spot. Anyhow, that might be quite a good thing for me, who can tell? If I didn't have to hold my hand because of my parents I'd have given notice long ago, I'd have gone to the chief and told him exactly what I think of him. That would knock him endways from his desk! It's a queer way of doing, too, this sitting on high at a desk and talking down to employees, especially when they have to come quite near because the chief is hard of hearing. Well, there's still hope; once I've saved enough money to pay back my parents' debts to him — that should take another five or six years — I'll do it without fail. I'll cut myself completely loose then. For the moment, though, I'd better get up, since my train goes at five.

He looked at the alarm clock ticking on the chest. Heavenly Father! he thought. It was half-past six o'clock and the hands were quietly moving on, it was even past the half-hour, it was getting on toward a quarter to seven. Had the alarm clock not gone off? From the bed one could see that it had been properly set for four o'clock; of course it must have gone off. Yes, but was it possible to sleep quietly through that ear-splitting noise? Well, he had not slept quietly, yet apparently all the more soundly for that. But what was he to do now? The next train went at seven o'clock; to catch that he would need to hurry like mad and his samples weren't even packed up, and he himself wasn't feeling particularly fresh and active. And even if he did catch the train he wouldn't avoid a row with the chief, since the firm's porter would have been waiting for the five o'clock train and would have long since reported his failure to turn up. The porter was a creature of the chief's, spineless and stupid. Well, supposing he were to say he was sick? But that would be most unpleasant and would look suspicious, since during his five years' employment he had not been ill once. The chief himself would be sure to come with the sick-insurance doctor, would reproach his parents with their son's laziness and would cut all excuses short by referring to the insurance doctor, who of course regarded all mankind as perfectly healthy malingerers. And would he be so far wrong on this occasion? Gregor really felt quite well, apart from a drowsiness that was utterly superfluous after such a long sleep, and he was even unusually hungry.

As all this was running through his mind at top speed without his being able to decide to leave his bed — the alarm clock had just struck a quarter to seven — there came a cautious tap at the door behind the head of his bed. "Gregor," said a voice—it was his mother's—"it's a quarter to seven. Hadn't you a train to catch?" That gentle voice! Gregor had a shock as he heard his own voice answering hers, unmistakably his own voice, it was true, but with a persistent horrible twittering squeak behind it like an undertone, that left the words in their clear shape only for the first moment and then rose up reverberating round them to destroy their sense, so that one could not be sure one had heard them rightly. Gregor wanted to answer at length and explain everything, but in the circumstances he confined himself to saying: "Yes, yes, thank you, Mother, I'm getting up now." The wooden door between them must have kept the change in his voice from being noticeable outside, for his mother contented herself with this statement and shuffled away. Yet this brief exchange of words had made the other members of the family aware that Gregor was still in the house, as they had not expected, and at one of the side doors his father was already knocking, gently, yet with his fist. "Gregor, Gregor," he called, "what's the matter with you?" And after a little while he called again in a deeper voice: "Gregor! Gregor!" At the other side door his sister was saying in a low, plaintive tone: "Gregor? Aren't you well? Are you needing anything?" He answered them both at once: "I'm just ready," and did his best to make his voice sound as normal as possible by enunciating the words very clearly and leaving long pauses between them. So his father went back to his breakfast, but his sister whispered: "Gregor, open the door, do." However, he was not thinking of opening the door, and felt thankful for the prudent habit he had acquired in traveling of locking all doors during the night, even at home.

His immediate intention was to get up quietly without being disturbed, to put on his clothes and above all eat his breakfast, and only then to consider what else was to be done, since in bed, he was well aware, his meditations would come to no sensible conclusion. He remembered that often enough in bed he had felt small aches and pains, probably caused by awkward postures, which had proved purely imaginary once he got up, and he looked forward eagerly to seeing this morning's delusions gradually fall away. That the change in his voice was nothing but the precursor of a severe chill, a standing ailment of commercial travelers, he had not the least possible doubt.

To get rid of the quilt was quite easy; he had only to inflate himself a little and it fell off by itself. But the next move was difficult, especially because he was so uncommonly broad. He would have needed arms and hands to hoist himself up; instead he had only the numerous little legs which never stopped waving in all directions and which he could not control in the least. When he tried to bend one of them it was the first to stretch itself straight; and did he succeed at last in making it do what he wanted, all the other legs meanwhile waved the more wildly in a high degree of unpleasant agitation. "But what's the use of lying idle in bed," said Gregor to himself.

He thought that he might get out of bed with the lower part of his body first, but this lower part, which he had not yet seen and of which he could form no clear conception, proved too difficult to move; it shifted so slowly; and when finally, almost wild with annoyance, he gathered his forces together and thrust out recklessly, he had miscalculated the direction and bumped heavily against the lower end of the bed, and the stinging pain he felt informed him that precisely this lower part of his body was at the moment probably the most sensitive.

So he tried to get the top part of himself out first, and cautiously moved his head towards the edge of the bed. That proved easy enough, and despite its breadth and mass the bulk of his body at last slowly followed the movement of his head. Still, when he finally got his head free over the edge of the bed he felt too scared to go on advancing, for after all if he let himself fall in this way it would take a miracle to keep his head from being injured. And at all costs he must not lose consciousness now, precisely now; he would rather stay in bed.

But when after a repetition of the same efforts he lay in his former position again, sighing, and watched his little legs struggling against each other more wildly than ever, if that were possible, and saw no way of bringing any order into this arbitrary confusion, he told himself again that it was impossible to stay in bed and that the most sensible course was to risk everything for the smallest hope of getting away from it. At the same time he did not forget meanwhile to remind himself that cool reflection, the coolest possible, was much better than desperate resolves. In such moments he focused his eyes as sharply as possible on the window, but, unfortunately, the prospect of the morning fog, which muffled even the other side of the narrow street, brought him little encouragement and comfort. "Seven o'clock already," he said to himself when the alarm clock chimed again, "seven o'clock already and still such a thick fog." And for a little while he lay quiet, breathing lightly, as if perhaps expecting such complete repose to restore all things to their real and normal condition.

But then he said to himself: "Before it strikes a quarter past seven I must be quite out of this bed, without fail. Anyhow, by that time someone will have come from the office to ask for me, since it opens before seven." And he set himself to rocking his whole body at once in a regular rhythm, with the idea of swinging it out of the bed. If he tipped himself out in that way he could keep his head from injury by lifting it at an acute angle when he fell. His back seemed to be hard and was not likely to suffer from a fall on the carpet. His biggest worry was the loud crash he would not be able to help making, which would probably cause anxiety, if not terror, behind all the doors. Still, he must take the risk.

When he was already half out of the bed — the new method was more a game than an effort, for he needed only to hitch himself across by rocking to and fro — it struck him how simple it would be if he could get help. Two strong people — he thought of his father and the servant girl — would be amply sufficient; they would only have to thrust their arms under his convex back, lever him out of the bed, bend down with their burden and then be patient enough to let him turn himself right over on the floor, where it was to be hoped his legs would then find their proper function. Well, ignoring the fact that the doors were all locked, ought he really to call for help? In spite of his misery he could not suppress a smile at the very idea of it.

He had got so far that he could barely keep his equilibrium when he rocked himself strongly, and he would have to nerve himself very soon for the final decision since in five minutes' time it would be a quarter past seven — when the front doorbell rang. "That's someone from the office," he said to himself, and grew almost rigid, while his little legs only jigged about all the faster. For a moment everything stayed quiet. "They're not going to open the door," said Gregor to himself, catching at some kind of irrational hope. But then of course the servant girl went as usual to the door with her heavy tread and opened it. Gregor needed only to hear the first good morning of the visitor to know immediately who it was — the chief clerk himself. What a fate, to be condemned to work for a firm where the smallest omission at once gave rise to the gravest suspicion! Were all employees in a body nothing but scoundrels, was there not among them one single loyal devoted man who, had he wasted only an hour or so of the firm's time in a morning, was so tormented by conscience as to be driven out of his mind and actually incapable of leaving his bed? Wouldn't it really have been sufficient to send an apprentice to inquire—if any inquiry were necessary at all—did the chief clerk himself have to come and thus indicate to the entire family, an innocent family, that this suspicious circumstance could be investigated by no one less versed in affairs than himself? And more through the agitation caused by these reflections than through any act of will Gregor swung himself out of bed with all his strength. There was a loud thump, but it was not really a crash. His fall was broken to some extent by the carpet, his back, too, was less stiff then he thought, and so there was merely a dull thud, not so very startling. Only he had not lifted his head carefully enough and had hit it; he turned it and rubbed it on the carpet in pain and irritation.

"That was something falling down in there," said the chief clerk in the next room to the left. Gregor tried to suppose to himself that something like what had happened to him today might some day happen to the chief clerk; one really could not deny that it was possible. But as if in brusque reply to this supposition the chief clerk took a couple of firm steps in the next-door room and his patent leather boots creaked. From the right-hand room his sister was whispering to inform him of the situation: "Gregor, the chief clerk's here." "I know," muttered Gregor to himself; but he didn't dare to make his voice loud enough for his sister to hear it.

"Gregor," said his father now from the left-hand room, "the chief clerk has come and wants to know why you didn't catch the early train. We don't know what to say to him. Besides, he wants to talk to you in person. So open the door, please. He will be good enough to excuse the untidiness of your room." "Good morning, Mr. Samsa," the chief clerk was calling amiably meanwhile. "He's not well," said his mother to the visitor, while his father was still speaking through the door, "he's not well, sir, believe me. What else would make him miss a train! The boy thinks about nothing but his work. It makes me almost cross the way he never goes out in the evenings; he's been here the last eight days and has stayed at home every single evening. He just sits there quietly at the table reading a newspaper or looking through railway timetables. The only amusement he gets is doing fretwork. For instance, he spent two or three evenings cutting out a little picture frame; you would be surprised to see how pretty it is; it's hanging in his room; you'll see it in a minute when Gregor opens the door. I must say I'm glad you've come, sir; we should never have got him to unlock the door by ourselves; he's so obstinate; and I'm sure he's unwell, though he wouldn't have it to be so this morning." "I'm just coming," said Gregor slowly and carefully, not moving an inch for fear of losing one word of the conversation. "I can't think of any other explanation, madam," said the chief clerk, "I hope it's nothing serious. Although on the other hand I must say that we men of business—fortunately or unfortunately—very often simply have to ignore any slight indisposition, since business must be attended to." "Well, can the chief clerk come in now?" asked Gregor's father impatiently, again knocking on the door. "No," said Gregor. In the left-hand room a painful silence followed this refusal, in the right-hand room his sister began to sob.

Why didn't his sister join the others? She was probably newly out of bed and hadn't even begun to put on her clothes yet. Well, why was she crying? Because he wouldn't get up and let the chief clerk in, because he was in danger of losing his job, and because the chief would begin dunning his parents again for the old debts? Surely these were things one didn't need to worry about for the present. Gregor was still at home and not in the least thinking of deserting the family. At the moment, true, he was lying on the carpet and no one who knew the condition he was in could seriously expect him to admit the chief clerk. But for such a small discourtesy, which could plausibly be explained away somehow later on, Gregor could hardly be dismissed on the spot. And it seemed to Gregor that it would be much more sensible to leave him in peace for the present than to trouble him with tears and entreaties. Still, of course, their uncertainty bewildered them all and excused their behavior.

"Mr. Samsa," the chief clerk called now in a louder voice, "what's the matter with you? Here you are, barricading yourself in your room, giving only 'yes' and 'no' for answers, causing your parents a lot of unnecessary trouble and neglecting—I mention this only in passing—neglecting your business duties in an incredible fashion. I am speaking here in the name of your parents and of your chief, and I beg you quite seriously to give me an immediate and precise explanation. You amaze me, you amaze me. I thought you were a quiet, dependable person, and now all at once you seem bent on making a disgraceful exhibition of yourself. The chief did hint to me early this morning a possible explanation for your disappearance—with reference to the cash payments that were entrusted to you recently—but I almost pledged my solemn word of honor that this could not be so. But now that I see how incredibly obstinate you are, I no longer have the slightest desire to take your part at all. And your position in the firm is not so unassailable. I came with the intention of telling you all this in private, but since you are wasting my time so needlessly I don't see why your parents shouldn't hear it too. For some time past your work has been most unsatisfactory; this is not the season of the year for a business boom, of course, we admit that, but a season of the year for doing no business at all, that does not exist, Mr. Samsa, must not exist."

"But, sir," cried Gregor, beside himself and in his agitation forgetting everything else, "I'm just going to open the door this very minute. A slight illness, an attack of giddiness, has kept me from getting up. I'm still lying in bed. But I feel all right again. I'm getting out of bed now. Just give me a moment or two longer! I'm not quite so well as I thought. But I'm all right, really. How a thing like that can suddenly strike one down! Only last night I was quite well, my parents can tell you, or rather I did have a slight presentiment. I must have showed some sign of it. Why didn't I report it at the office! But one always thinks that an indisposition can be got over without staying in the house. Oh sir, do spare my parents! All that you're reproaching me with now has no foundation; no one has ever said a word to me about it. Perhaps you haven't looked at the last orders I sent in. Anyhow, I can still catch the eight o'clock train, I'm much the better for my few hours' rest. Don't let me detain you here, sir; I'll be attending to business very soon, and do be good enough to tell the chief so and to make my excuses to him!"

And while all this was tumbling out pell-mell and Gregor hardly knew what he was saying, he had reached the chest quite easily, perhaps because of the practice he had had in bed, and was now trying to lever himself upright by means of it. He meant actually to open the door, actually to show himself and speak to the chief clerk; he was eager to find out what the others, after all their insistence, would say at the sight of him. If they were horrified then the responsibility was no longer his and he could stay quiet. But if they took it calmly, then he had no reason either to be upset, and could really get to the station for the eight o'clock train if he hurried. At first he slipped down a few times from the polished surface of the chest, but at length with a last heave he stood upright; he paid no more attention to the pains in the lower part of his body, however they smarted. Then he let himself fall against the back of a near-by chair, and clung with his little legs to the edges of it. That brought him into control of himself again and he stopped speaking, for now he could listen to what the chief clerk was saying.

"Did you understand a word of it?" the chief clerk was asking; "surely he can't be trying to make fools of us?" "Oh dear," cried his mother, in tears, "perhaps he's terribly ill and we're tormenting him. Grete! Grete!" she called out then, "Yes, Mother?" called his sister from the other side. They were calling to each other across Gregor's room. "You must go this minute for the doctor. Gregor is ill. Go for the doctor, quick. Did you hear how he was speaking?" "That was no human voice," said the chief clerk in a voice noticeably low beside the shrillness of the mother's. "Anna! Anna!" his father was calling through the hall to the kitchen, clapping his hands, "get a locksmith at once!" And the two girls were already running through the hall with a swish of skirts—how could his sister have got dressed so quickly?—and were tearing the front door open. There was no sound of its closing again; they had evidently left it open, as one does in houses where some great misfortune has happened.

But Gregor was now much calmer. The words he uttered were no longer understandable, apparently, although they seemed clear enough to him, even clearer than before, perhaps because his ear had grown accustomed to the sound of them. Yet at any rate people now believed that something was wrong with him, and were ready to help him. The positive certainty with which these first measures had been taken comforted him. He felt himself drawn once more into the human circle and hoped for great and remarkable results from both the doctor and the locksmith, without really distinguishing precisely between them. To make his voice as clear as possible for the decisive conversation that was now imminent he coughed a little, as quietly as he could, of course, since this noise too might not sound like a human cough for all he was able to judge. In the next room meanwhile there was complete silence. Perhaps his parents were sitting at the table with the chief clerk, whispering, perhaps they were all leaning against the door and listening.

Slowly Gregor pushed the chair towards the door, then let go of it, caught hold of the door for support—the soles at the end of his little legs were somewhat sticky—and rested against it for a moment after his efforts. Then he set himself to turning the key in the lock with his mouth. It seemed, unhappily, that he hadn't really any teeth—what could he grip the key with?—but on the other hand his jaws were certainly very strong; with their help he did manage to set the key in motion, heedless of the fact that he was undoubtedly damaging them somewhere, since a brown fluid issued from his mouth, flowed over the key and dripped on the floor. "Just listen to that," said the chief clerk next door; "he's turning the key." That was a great encouragement to Gregor; but they should all have shouted encouragement to him, his father and mother too: "Go on, Gregor," they should have called out, "keep going, hold on to that key!" And in the belief that they were all following his efforts intently, he clenched his jaws recklessly on the key with all the force at his command. As the turning of the key progressed he circled round the lock, holding on now only with his mouth, pushing on the key, as required, or pulling it down again with all the weight of his body. The louder click of the finally yielding lock literally quickened Gregor. With a deep breath of relief he said to himself: "So I didn't need the locksmith," and laid his head on the handle to open the door wide.

Since he had to pull the door towards him, he was still invisible when it was really wide open. He had to edge himself slowly round the near half of the double door, and to do it very carefully if he was not to fall plump upon his back just on the threshold. He was still carrying out this difficult manoeuvre, with no time to observe anything else, when he heard the chief clerk utter a loud "Oh"—it sounded like a gust of wind—and now he could see the man, standing as he was nearest to the door, clapping one hand before his open mouth and slowly backing away as if driven by some invisible steady pressure. His mother—in spite of the chief clerk's being there her hair was still undone and sticking up in all directions—first clasped her hands and looked at his father, then took two steps towards Gregor and fell on the floor among her outspread skirts, her face hidden on her breast. His father knotted his fist with a fierce expression on his face as if he meant to knock Gregor back into his room, then looked uncertainly round the living room, covered his eyes with his hands and wept till his great chest heaved.

Gregor did not go now into the living room, but leaned against the inside of the firmly shut wing of the door, so that only half his body was visible and his head above it bending sideways to look at the others. The light had meanwhile strengthened; on the other side of the street one could see clearly a section of the endlessly long, dark gray building opposite—it was a hospital—abruptly punctuated by its row of regular windows; the rain was still falling, but only in large singly discernible and literally singly splashing drops. The breakfast dishes were set out on the table lavishly, for breakfast was the most important meal of the day to Gregor's father, who lingered it out for hours over various newspapers. Right opposite Gregor on the wall hung a photograph of himself on military service, as a lieutenant, hand on sword, a carefree smile on his face, inviting one to respect his uniform and military bearing. The door leading to the hall was open, and one could see that the front door stood open too, showing the landing beyond and the beginning of the stairs going down.

"Well," said Gregor, knowing perfectly that he was the only one who had retained any composure, "I'll put my clothes on at once, pack up my samples and start off. Will you only let me go? You see, sir, I'm not obstinate, and I'm willing to work; traveling is a hard life, but I couldn't live without it. Where are you going, sir? To the office? Yes? Will you give a true account of all this? One can be temporarily incapacitated, but that's just the moment for remembering former services and bearing in mind that later on, when the incapacity has been got over, one will certainly work with all the more industry and concentration. I'm loyally bound to serve the chief, you know that very well. Besides, I have to provide for my parents and my sister. I'm in great difficulties, but I'll get out of them again. Don't make things any worse for me than they are. Stand up for me in the firm. Travelers are not popular there, I know. People think they earn sacks of money and just have a good time. A prejudice there's no particular reason for revising. But you, sir, have a more comprehensive view of affairs than the rest of the staff, yes, let me tell you in confidence, a more comprehensive view than the chief himself, who, being the owner, lets his judgment easily be swayed against one of his employees. And you know very well that the traveler, who is never seen in the office almost the whole year round, can so easily fall a victim to gossip and ill luck and unfounded complaints, which he mostly knows nothing about, except when he comes back exhausted from his rounds, and only then suffers in person from their evil consequences, which he can no longer trace back to the original causes. Sir, sir, don't go away without a word to me to show that you think me in the right at least to some extent!"

But at Gregor's very first words the chief clerk had already backed away and only stared at him with parted lips over one twitching shoulder. And while Gregor was speaking he did not stand still one moment but stole away towards the door, without taking his eyes off Gregor, yet only an inch at a time, as if obeying some secret injunction to leave the room. He was already at the hall, and the suddenness with which he took his last step out of the living room would have made one believe he had burned the sole of his foot. Once in the hall he stretched his right arm before him towards the staircase, as if some supernatural power were waiting there to deliver him.

Gregor perceived that the chief clerk must on no account be allowed to go away in this frame of mind if his position in the firm were not to be endangered to the utmost. His parents did not understand this so well; they had convinced themselves in the course of years that Gregor was settled for life in this firm, and besides they were so occupied with their immediate troubles that all foresight had forsaken them. Yet Gregor had this foresight. The chief clerk must be detained, soothed, persuaded and finally won over; the whole future of Gregor and his family depended on it! If only his sister had been there! She was intelligent; she had begun to cry while Gregor was still lying quietly on his back. And no doubt the chief clerk, so partial to ladies, would have been guided by her; she would have shut the door of the flat and in the hall talked him out of his horror. But she was not there, and Gregor would have to handle the situation himself. And without remembering that he was still unaware what powers of movement he possessed, without even remembering that his words in all possibility, indeed in all likelihood, would again be unintelligible, he let go the wing of the door, pushed himself through the opening, started to walk towards the chief clerk, who was already ridiculously clinging with both hands to the railing on the landing; but immediately, as he was feeling for a support, he fell down with a little cry upon all his numerous legs. Hardly was he down when he experienced for the first time this morning a sense of physical comfort; his legs had firm ground under them; they were completely obedient, as he noted with joy; they even strove to carry him forward in whatever direction he chose; and he was inclined to believe that a final relief from all his sufferings was at hand. But in the same moment as he found himself on the floor, rocking with suppressed eagerness to move, not far from his mother, indeed just in front of her, she, who had seemed so completely crushed, sprang all at once to her feet, her arms and fingers outspread, cried: "Help, for God's sake, help!" bent her head down as if to see Gregor better, yet on the contrary kept backing senselessly away; had quite forgotten that the laden table stood behind her; sat upon it hastily, as if in absence of mind, when she bumped into it; and seemed altogether unaware that the big coffee pot beside her was upset and pouring coffee in a flood over the carpet.

"Mother, Mother," said Gregor in a low voice, and looked up at her. The chief clerk, for the moment, had quite slipped from his mind; instead, he could not resist snapping his jaws together at the sight of the streaming coffee. That made his mother scream again, she fled from the table and fell into the arms of his father, who hastened to catch her. But Gregor had now no time to spare for his parents; the chief clerk was already on the stairs; with his chin on the banisters he was taking one last backward look. Gregor made a spring, to be as sure as possible of overtaking him; the chief clerk must have divined his intention, for he leaped down several steps and vanished; he was still yelling "Ugh!" and it echoed through the whole staircase.

Unfortunately, the flight of the chief clerk seemed completely to upset Gregor's father, who had remained relatively calm until now, for instead of running after the man himself, or at least not hindering Gregor in his pursuit, he seized in his right hand the walking stick which the chief clerk had left behind on a chair, together with a hat and greatcoat, snatched in his left hand a large newspaper from the table and began stamping his feet and flourishing the stick and the newspaper to drive Gregor back into his room. No entreaty of Gregor's availed, indeed no entreaty was even understood, however humbly he bent his head his father only stamped on the floor the more loudly. Behind his father his mother had torn open a window, despite the cold weather, and was leaning far out of it with her face in her hands. A strong draught set in from the street to the staircase, the window curtains blew in, the newspapers on the table fluttered, stray pages whisked over the floor. Pitilessly Gregor's father drove him back, hissing and crying "Shoo!" like a savage. But Gregor was quite unpracticed in walking backwards, it really was a slow business. If he only had a chance to turn round he could get back to his room at once, but he was afraid of exasperating his father by the slowness of such a rotation and at any moment the stick in his father's hand might hit him a fatal blow on the back or on the head. In the end, however, nothing else was left for him to do since to his horror he observed that in moving backwards he could not even control the direction he took; and so, keeping an anxious eye on his father all the time over his shoulder, he began to turn round as quickly as he could, which was in reality very slowly. Perhaps his father noted his good intentions, for he did not interfere except every now and then to help him in the manoeuvre from a distance with the point of the stick. If only he would have stopped making that unbearable hissing noise! It made Gregor quite lose his head. He had turned almost completely round when the hissing noise so distracted him that he even turned a little the wrong way again. But when at last his head was fortunately right in front of the doorway, it appeared that his body was too broad simply to get through the opening. His father, of course, in his present mood was far from thinking of such a thing as opening the other half of the door, to let Gregor have enough space. He had merely the fixed idea of driving Gregor back into his room as quickly as possible. He would never have suffered Gregor to make the circumstantial preparations for standing up on end and perhaps slipping his way through the door. Maybe he was now making more noise than ever to urge Gregor forward, as if no obstacle impeded him; to Gregor, anyhow, the noise in his rear sounded no longer like the voice of one single father; this was really no joke, and Gregor thrust himself—come what might—into the doorway. One side of his body rose up, he was tilted at an angle in the doorway, his flank was quite bruised, horrid blotches stained the white door, soon he was stuck fast and, left to himself, could not have moved at all, his legs on one side fluttered trembling to the air, those on the other were crushed painfully to the floor—when from behind his father gave him a strong push which was literally a deliverance and he flew far into the room, bleeding freely. The door was slammed behind him with the stick, and then at last there was silence.

II

Not until it was twilight did Gregor awake out of a deep sleep, more like a swoon than a sleep. He would certainly have waked up of his own accord not much later, for he felt himself sufficiently rested and well-slept, but it seemed to him as if a fleeting step and a cautious shutting of the door leading into the hall had aroused him. The electric lights in the street cast a pale sheen here and there on the ceiling and the upper surfaces of the furniture, but down below, where he lay, it was dark. Slowly, awkwardly trying out his feelers, which he now first learned to appreciate, he pushed his way to the door to see what had been happening there. His left side felt like one single long, unpleasant tense scar, and he had actually to limp on his two rows of legs. One little leg, moreover, had been severely damaged in the course of that morning's events—it was almost a miracle that only one had been damaged—and trailed uselessly behind him.

He had reached the door before he discovered what had really drawn him to it: the smell of food. For there stood a basin filled with fresh milk in which floated little sops of white bread. He could almost have laughed with joy, since he was now still hungrier than in the morning, and he dipped his head almost over the eyes straight into the milk. But soon in disappointment he withdrew it again; not only did he find it difficult to feed because of his tender left side—and he could only feed with the palpitating collaboration of his whole body—he did not like the milk either, although milk had been his favorite drink and that was certainly why his sister had set it there for him, indeed it was almost with repulsion that he turned away from the basin and crawled back to the middle of the room.

He could see through the crack of the door that the gas was turned on in the living room, but while usually at this time his father made a habit of reading the afternoon newspaper in a loud voice to his mother and occasionally to his sister as well, not a sound was now to be heard. Well, perhaps his father had recently given up this habit of reading aloud, which his sister had mentioned so often in conversation and in her letters. But there was the same silence all around, although the flat was certainly not empty of occupants. "What a quiet life our family has been leading," said Gregor to himself, and as he sat there motionless staring into the darkness he felt great pride in the fact that he had been able to provide such a life for his parents and sister in such a fine flat. But what if all the quiet, the comfort, the contentment were now to end in horror? To keep himself from being lost in such thoughts Gregor took refuge in movement and crawled up and down the room.

Once during the long evening one of the side doors was opened a little and quickly shut again, later the other side door too; someone had apparently wanted to come in and then thought better of it. Gregor now stationed himself immediately before the living room door, determined to persuade any hesitating visitor to come in or at least to discover who it might be; but the door was not opened again and he waited in vain. In the early morning, when the doors were locked, they had all wanted to come in, now that he had opened one door and the other had apparently been opened during the day, no one came in and even the keys were on the other side of the doors.

It was late at night before the gas went out in the living room, and Gregor could easily tell that his parents and his sister had all stayed awake until then, for he could clearly hear the three of them stealing away on tiptoe. No one was likely to visit him, not until the morning, that was certain; so he had plenty of time to meditate at his leisure on how he was to arrange his life afresh. But the lofty, empty room in which he had to lie flat on the floor filled him with an apprehension he could not account for, since it had been his very own room for the past five years—and with a half-unconscious action, not without a slight feeling of shame, he scuttled under the sofa, where he felt comfortable at once, although his back was a little cramped and he could not lift his head up, and his only regret was that his body was too broad to get the whole of it under the sofa.

He stayed there all night, spending the time partly in a light slumber, from which his hunger kept waking him up with a start, and partly in worrying and sketching vague hopes, which all led to the same conclusion, that he must lie low for the present and, by exercising patience, and the utmost consideration, help the family to bear the inconvenience he was bound to cause them in his present condition.

Very early in the morning, it was still almost night, Gregor had the chance to test the strength of his new resolutions, for his sister, nearly fully dressed, opened the door from the hall and peered in. She did not see him at once, yet when she caught sight of him under the sofa—well, he had to be somewhere, he couldn't have flown away, could he?—she was so startled that without being able to help it she slammed the door shut again. But as if regretting her behavior she opened the door again immediately and came in on tiptoe, as if she were visiting an invalid or even a stranger. Gregor had pushed his head forward to the very edge of the sofa and watched her. Would she notice that he had left the milk standing, and not for lack of hunger, and would she bring in some other kind of food more to his taste? If she did not do it of her own accord, he would rather starve than draw her attention to the fact, although he felt a wild impulse to dart out from under the sofa, throw himself at her feet and beg her for something to eat. But his sister at once noticed, with surprise, that the basin was still full, except for a little milk that had been spilt all around it, she lifted it immediately, not with her bare hands, true, but with a cloth and carried it away. Gregor was wildly curious to know what she would bring instead, and made various speculations about it. Yet what she actually did next, in the goodness of her heart, he could never have guessed at. To find out what he liked she brought him a whole selection of food, all set out on an old newspaper. There were old, half-decayed vegetables, bones from last night's supper covered with a white sauce that had thickened; some raisins and almonds; a piece of cheese that Gregor would have called uneatable two days ago; a dry roll of bread, a buttered roll, and a roll both buttered and salted. Besides all that, she set down again the same basin, into which she had poured some water, and which was apparently to be reserved for his exclusive use. And with fine tact, knowing that Gregor would not eat in her presence, she withdrew quickly and even turned the key, to let him understand that he could take his ease as much as he liked. Gregor's legs all whizzed towards the food. His wounds must have healed completely, moreover, for he felt no disability, which amazed him and made him reflect how more than a month ago he had cut one finger a little with a knife and had still suffered pain from the wound only the day before yesterday. Am I less sensitive now? he thought, and sucked greedily at the cheese, which above all the other edibles attracted him at once and strongly. One after another and with tears of satisfaction in his eyes he quickly devoured the cheese, the vegetables and the sauce; the fresh food, on the other hand, had no charms for him, he could not even stand the smell of it and actually dragged away to some little distance the things he could eat. He had long finished his meal and was only lying lazily on the same spot when his sister turned the key slowly as a sign for him to retreat. That roused him at once, although he was nearly asleep, and he hurried under the sofa again. But it took considerable self-control for him to stay under the sofa, even for the short time his sister was in the room, since the large meal had swollen his body somewhat and he was so cramped he could hardly breathe. Slight attacks of breathlessness afflicted him and his eyes were starting a little out of his head as he watched his unsuspecting sister sweeping together with a broom not only the remains of what he had eaten but even the things he had not touched, as if these were now of no use to anyone, and hastily shoveling it all into a bucket, which she covered with a wooden lid and carried away. Hardly had she turned her back when Gregor came from under the sofa and stretched and puffed himself out.

In this manner Gregor was fed, once in the early morning while his parents and the servant girl were still asleep, and a second time after they had all had their midday dinner, for then his parents took a short nap and the servant girl could be sent out on some errand or other by his sister. Not that they would have wanted him to starve, of course, but perhaps they could not have borne to know more about his feeding than from hearsay, perhaps too his sister wanted to spare them such little anxieties wherever possible, since they had quite enough to bear as it was.

Under what pretext the doctor and the locksmith had been got rid of on that first morning Gregor could not discover, for since what he had said was not understood by the others it never struck any of them, not even his sister, that he could understand what they said, and so whenever his sister came into his room he had to content himself with hearing her utter only a sigh now and then and an occasional appeal to the saints. Later on, when she had got a little used to the situation—of course she could never get completely used to it—she sometimes threw out a remark which was kindly meant or could be so interpreted. "Well, he liked his dinner today," she would say when Gregor had made a good clearance of his food; and when he had not eaten, which gradually happened more and more often, she would say almost sadly: "Everything's been left standing again."

But although Gregor could get no news directly, he overheard a lot from the neighboring rooms, and as soon as voices were audible, he would run to the door of the room concerned and press his whole body against it. In the first few days especially there was no conversation that did not refer to him somehow, even if only indirectly. For two whole days there were family consultations at every mealtime about what should be done; but also between meals the same subject was discussed, for there were always at least two members of the family at home, since no one wanted to be alone in the flat and to leave it quite empty was unthinkable. And on the very first of these days the household cook—it was not quite clear what and how much she knew of the situation—went down on her knees to his mother and begged leave to go, and when she departed, a quarter of an hour later, gave thanks for her dismissal with tears in her eyes as if for the greatest benefit that could have been conferred on her, and without any prompting swore a solemn oath that she would never say a single word to anyone about what had happened.

Now Gregor's sister had to cook too, helping her mother; true, the cooking did not amount to much, for they ate scarcely anything. Gregor was always hearing one of the family vainly urging another to eat and getting no answer but: "Thanks, I've had all I want," or something similar. Perhaps they drank nothing either. Time and again his sister kept asking his father if he wouldn't like some beer and offered kindly to go and fetch it herself, and when he made no answer suggested that she could ask the concierge to fetch it, so that he need feel no sense of obligation, but then a round "No" came from his father and no more was said about it.

In the course of that very first day Gregor's father explained the family's financial position and prospects to both his mother and his sister. Now and then he rose from the table to get some voucher or memorandum out of the small safe he had rescued from the collapse of his business five years earlier. One could hear him opening the complicated lock and rustling papers out and shutting it again. This statement made by his father was the first cheerful information Gregor had heard since his imprisonment. He had been of the opinion that nothing at all was left over from his father's business, at least his father had never said anything to the contrary, and of course he had not asked him directly. At the time Gregor's sole desire was to do his utmost to help the family to forget as soon as possible the catastrophe which had overwhelmed the business and thrown them all into a state of complete despair. And so he had set to work with unusual ardor and almost overnight had become a commercial traveler instead of a little clerk, with of course much greater chances of earning money, and his success was immediately translated into good round coin which he could lay on the table for his amazed and happy family. These had been fine times, and they had never recurred, at least not with the same sense of glory, although later on Gregor had earned so much money that he was able to meet the expenses of the whole household and did so. They had simply got used to it, both the family and Gregor; the money was gratefully accepted and gladly given, but there was no special uprush of warm feeling. With his sister alone had he remained intimate, and it was a secret plan of his that she, who loved music, unlike himself, and could play movingly on the violin, should be sent next year to study at the Conservatorium, despite the great expense that would entail, which must be made up in some other way. During his brief visits home the Conservatorium was often mentioned in the talks he had with his sister, but always merely as a beautiful dream which could never come true, and his parents discouraged even these innocent references to it; yet Gregor had made up his mind firmly about it and meant to announce the fact with due solemnity on Christmas Day.

Such were the thoughts, completely futile in his present condition, that went through his head as he stood clinging upright to the door and listening. Sometimes out of sheer weariness he had to give up listening and let his head fall negligently against the door, but he always had to pull himself together again at once, for even the slight sound his head made was audible next door and brought all conversation to a stop. "What can he be doing now?" his father would say after a while, obviously turning towards the door, and only then would the interrupted conversation gradually be set going again.

Gregor was now informed as amply as he could wish—for his father tended to repeat himself in his explanations, partly because it was a long time since he had handled such matters and partly because his mother could not always grasp things at once — that a certain amount of investments, a very small amount it was true, had survived the wreck of their fortunes and had even increased a little because the dividends had not been touched meanwhile. And besides that, the money Gregor brought home every month — he had kept only a few dollars for himself — had never been quite used up and now amounted to a small capital sum. Behind the door Gregor nodded his head eagerly, rejoiced at this evidence of unexpected thrift and foresight. True, he could really have paid off some more of his father's debts to the chief with his extra money, and so brought much nearer the day on which he could quit his job, but doubtless it was better the way his father had arranged it.

Yet this capital was by no means sufficient to let the family live on the interest of it; for one year, perhaps, or at the most two, they could live on the principal, that was all. It was simply a sum that ought not to be touched and should be kept for a rainy day; money for living expenses would have to be earned. Now his father was still hale enough but an old man, and he had done no work for the past five years and could not be expected to do much; during these five years, the first years of leisure in his laborious though unsuccessful life, he had grown rather fat and become sluggish. And Gregor's old mother, how was she to earn a living with her asthma, which troubled her even when she walked through the flat and kept her lying on a sofa every other day panting for breath beside an open window? And was his sister to earn her bread, she who was still a child of seventeen and whose life hitherto had been so pleasant, consisting as it did in dressing herself nicely, sleeping long, helping in the housekeeping, going out to a few modest entertainments and above all playing the violin? At first whenever the need for earning money was mentioned Gregor let go his hold on the door and threw himself down on the cool leather sofa beside it, he felt so hot with shame and grief.

Often he just lay there the long nights through without sleeping at all, scrabbling for hours on the leather. Or he nerved himself to the great effort of pushing an armchair to the window, then crawled up over the window sill and, braced against the chair, leaned against the windowpanes, obviously in some recollection of the sense of freedom that looking out of a window always used to give him. For in reality day by day things that were even a little way off were growing dimmer to his sight; the hospital across the street, which he used to execrate for being all too often before his eyes, was now quite beyond his range of vision, and if he had not known that he lived in Charlotte Street, a quiet street but still a city street, he might have believed that his window gave on a desert waste where gray sky and gray land blended indistinguishably into each other. His quick-witted sister only needed to observe twice that the armchair stood by the window; after that whenever she had tidied the room she always pushed the chair back to the same place at the window and even left the inner casements open.

If he could have spoken to her and thanked her for all she had to do for him, he could have borne her ministrations better; as it was, they oppressed him. She certainly tried to make as light as possible of whatever was disagreeable in her task, and as time went on she succeeded, of course, more and more, but time brought more enlightenment to Gregor too. The very way she came in distressed him. Hardly was she in the room when she rushed to the window, without even taking time to shut the door, careful as she was usually to shield the sight of Gregor's room from the others, and as if she were almost suffocating tore the casements open with hasty fingers, standing then in the open draught for a while even in the bitterest cold and drawing deep breaths. This noisy scurry of hers upset Gregor twice a day; he would crouch trembling under the sofa all the time, knowing quite well that she would certainly have spared him such a disturbance had she found it at all possible to stay in his presence without opening a window.

On one occasion, about a month after Gregor's metamorphosis, when there was surely no reason for her to be still startled at his appearance, she came a little earlier than usual and found him gazing out of the window, quite motionless, and thus well placed to look like a bogey. Gregor would not have been surprised had she not come in at all, for she could not immediately open the window while he was there, but not only did she retreat, she jumped back as if in alarm and banged the door shut; a stranger might well have thought that he had been lying in wait for her there meaning to bite her. Of course he hid himself under the sofa at once, but he had to wait until midday before she came again, and she seemed more ill at ease than usual. This made him realize how repulsive the sight of him still was to her, and that it was bound to go on being repulsive, and what an effort it must cost her not to run away even from the sight of the small portion of his body that stuck out from under the sofa. In order to spare her that, therefore, one day he carried a sheet on his back to the sofa—it cost him four hours' labor—and arranged it there in such a way as to hide him completely, so that even if she were to bend down she could not see him. Had she considered the sheet unnecessary, she would certainly have stripped it off the sofa again, for it was clear enough that this curtaining and confining of himself was not likely to conduce Gregor's comfort, but she left it where it was, and Gregor even fancied that he caught a thankful glance from her eye when he lifted the sheet carefully a very little with his head to see how she was taking the new arrangement.

For the first fortnight his parents could not bring themselves to the point of entering his room, and he often heard them expressing their appreciation of his sister's activities, whereas formerly they had frequently scolded her for being as they thought a somewhat useless daughter. But now, both of them often waited outside the door, his father and his mother, while his sister tidied his room, and as soon as she came out she had to tell them exactly how things were in the room, what Gregor had eaten, how he had conducted himself this time and whether there was not perhaps some slight improvement in his condition. His mother, moreover, began relatively soon to want to visit him, but his father and sister dissuaded her at first with arguments which Gregor listened to very attentively and altogether approved. Later, however, she had to be held back by main force, and when she cried out: "Do let me in to Gregor, he is my unfortunate son! Can't you understand that I must go to him?" Gregor thought that it might be well to have her come in, not every day, of course, but perhaps once a week; she understood things, after all, much better than his sister, who was only a child despite the efforts she was making and had perhaps taken on so difficult a task merely out of childish thoughtlessness.

Gregor's desire to see his mother was soon fulfilled. During the daytime he did not want to show himself at the window, out of consideration for his parents, but he could not crawl very far around the few square yards of floor space he had, nor could he bear lying quietly at rest all during the night, while he was fast losing any interest he had ever taken in food, so that for mere recreation he had formed the habit of crawling crisscross over the walls and ceiling. He especially enjoyed hanging suspended from the ceiling; it was much better than lying on the floor; one could breathe more freely; one's body swung and rocked lightly; and in the almost blissful absorption induced by this suspension it could happen to his own surprise that he let go and fell plump on the floor. Yet he now had his body much better under control than formerly, and even such a big fall did him no harm. His sister at once remarked the new distraction Gregor had found for himself—he left traces behind him of the sticky stuff on his soles wherever he crawled—and she got the idea in her head of giving him as wide a field as possible to crawl in and of removing the pieces of furniture that hindered him, above all the chest of drawers and the writing desk. But that was more than she could manage all by herself; she did not dare ask her father to help her; and as for the servant girl, a young creature of sixteen who had had the courage to stay on after the cook's departure, she could not be asked to help, for she had begged as an especial favor that she might keep the kitchen door locked and open it only on a definite summons; so there was nothing left but to apply to her mother at an hour when her father was out. And the old lady did come, with exclamations of joyful eagerness, which, however, died away at the door of Gregor's room. Gregor's sister, of course, went in first, to see that everything was in order before letting his mother enter. In great haste Gregor pulled the sheet lower and rucked it more in folds so that it really looked as if it had been thrown accidentally over the sofa. And this time he did not peer out from under it; he renounced the pleasure of seeing his mother on this occasion and was only glad that she had come at all. "Come in, he's out of sight," said his sister, obviously leading her mother in by the hand. Gregor could now hear the two women struggling to shift the heavy old chest from its place, and his sister claiming the greater part of the labor for herself, without listening to the admonitions of her mother who feared she might overstrain herself. It took a long time. After at least a quarter of an hour's tugging his mother objected that the chest had better be left where it was, for in the first place it was too heavy and could never be got out before his father came home, and standing in the middle of the room like that it would only hamper Gregor's movements, while in the second place it was not at all certain that removing the furniture would be doing a service to Gregor. She was inclined to think to the contrary; the sight of the naked walls made her own heart heavy, and why shouldn't Gregor have the same feeling, considering that he had been used to his furniture for so long and might feel forlorn without it. "And doesn't it look," she concluded in a low voice—in fact she had been almost whispering all the time as if to avoid letting Gregor, whose exact whereabouts she did not know, hear even the tones of her voice, for she was convinced that he could not understand her words—"doesn't it look as if we were showing him, by taking away his furniture, that we have given up hope of his ever getting better and are just leaving him coldly to himself? I think it would be best to keep his room exactly as it has always been, so that when he comes back to us he will find everything unchanged and be able all the more easily to forget what has happened in between."

On hearing these words from his mother Gregor realized that the lack of all direct human speech for the past two months together with the monotony of family life must have confused his mind, otherwise he could not account for the fact that he had quite earnestly looked forward to having his room emptied of furnishing. Did he really want his warm room, so comfortably fitted with old family furniture, to be turned into a naked den in which he would certainly be able to crawl unhampered in all directions but at the price of shedding simultaneously all recollection of his human background? He had indeed been so near the brink of forgetfulness that only the voice of his mother, which he had not heard for so long, had drawn him back from it. Nothing should be taken out of his room; everything must stay as it was; he could not dispense with the good influence of the furniture on his state of mind; and even if the furniture did hamper him in his senseless crawling round and round, that was no drawback but a great advantage.

Unfortunately his sister was of the contrary opinion; she had grown accustomed, and not without reason, to consider herself an expert in Gregor's affairs as against her parents, and so her mother's advice was now enough to make her determined on the removal not only of the chest and the writing desk, which had been her first intention, but of all the furniture except the indispensable sofa. This determination was not, of course, merely the outcome of childish recalcitrance and of the self-confidence she had recently developed so unexpectedly and at such cost; she had in fact perceived that Gregor needed a lot of space to crawl about in, while on the other hand he never used the furniture at all, so far as could be seen. Another factor might have been also the enthusiastic temperament of an adolescent girl, which seeks to indulge itself on every opportunity and which now tempted Grete to exaggerate the horror of her brother's circumstances in order that she might do all the more for him. In a room where Gregor lorded it all alone over empty walls no one save herself was likely ever to set foot.

And so she was not to be moved from her resolve by her mother who seemed moreover to be ill at ease in Gregor's room and therefore unsure of herself, was soon reduced to silence and helped her daughter as best she could to push the chest outside. Now, Gregor could do without the chest, if need be, but the writing desk he must retain. As soon as the two women had got the chest out of his room, groaning as they pushed it, Gregor stuck his head out from under the sofa to see how he might intervene as kindly and cautiously as possible. But as bad luck would have it, his mother was the first to return, leaving Grete clasping the chest in the room next door where she was trying to shift it all by herself, without of course moving it from the spot. His mother however was not accustomed to the sight of him, it might sicken her and so in alarm Gregor backed quickly to the other end of the sofa, yet could not prevent the sheet from swaying a little in front. That was enough to put her on the alert. She paused, stood still for a moment and then went back to Grete.

Although Gregor kept reassuring himself that nothing out of the way was happening, but only a few bits of furniture were being changed round, he soon had to admit that all this trotting to and fro of the two women, their little ejaculations and the scraping of furniture along the floor affected him like a vast disturbance coming from all sides at once, and however much he tucked in his head and legs and cowered to the very floor he was bound to confess that he would not be able to stand it for long. They were clearing his room out; taking away everything he loved; the chest in which he kept his fret saw and other tools was already dragged off; they were now loosening the writing desk which had almost sunk into the floor, the desk at which he had done all his homework when he was at the commercial academy, at the grammar school before that, and, yes, even at the primary school—he had no more time to waste in weighing the good intentions of the two women, whose existence he had by now almost forgotten, for they were so exhausted that they were laboring in silence and nothing could be heard but the heavy scuffling of their feet.

And so he rushed out—the women were just leaning against the writing desk in the next room to give themselves a breather—and four times changed his direction, since he really did not know what to rescue first, then on the wall opposite, which was already otherwise cleared, he was struck by the picture of the lady muffled in so much fur and quickly crawled up to it and pressed himself to the glass, which was a good surface to hold on to and comforted his hot belly. This picture at least, which was entirely hidden beneath him, was going to be removed by nobody. He turned his head towards the door of the living room so as to observe the women when they came back.

They had not allowed themselves much of a rest and were already coming; Grete had twined her arm round her mother and was almost supporting her. "Well, what shall we take now?" said Grete, looking round. Her eyes met Gregor's from the wall. She kept her composure, presumably because of her mother, bent her head down to her mother, to keep her from looking up, and said, although in a fluttering, unpremeditated voice: "Come, hadn't we better go back to the living room for a moment?" Her intentions were clear enough to Gregor, she wanted to bestow her mother in safety and then chase him down from the wall. Well, just let her try it! He clung to his picture and would not give it up. He would rather fly in Grete's face.

But Grete's words had succeeded in disquieting her mother, who took a step to one side, caught sight of the huge brown mass on the flowered wallpaper, and before she was really conscious that what she saw was Gregor screamed in a loud, hoarse voice: "Oh God, oh God!" fell with outspread arms over the sofa as if giving up and did not move. "Gregor!" cried his sister, shaking her fist and glaring at him. This was the first time she had directly addressed him since his metamorphosis. She ran into the next room for some aromatic essence with which to rouse her mother from her fainting fit. Gregor wanted to help too—there was still time to rescue the picture—but he was stuck fast to the glass and had to tear himself loose; he then ran after his sister into the next room as if he could advise her, as he used to do; but then had to stand helplessly behind her; she meanwhile searched among various small bottles and when she turned round started in alarm at the sight of him; one bottle fell on the floor and broke; a splinter of glass cut Gregor's face and some kind of corrosive medicine splashed him; without pausing a moment longer Grete gathered up all the bottles she could carry and ran to her mother with them; she banged the door shut with her foot. Gregor was now cut off from his mother, who was perhaps nearly dying because of him; he dared not open the door for fear of frightening away his sister, who had to stay with her mother; there was nothing he could do but wait; and harassed by self-reproach and worry he began now to crawl to and fro, over everything, walls, furniture and ceiling, and finally in his despair, when the whole room seemed to be reeling round him, fell down on to the middle of the big table.

A little while elapsed, Gregor was still lying there feebly and all around was quiet, perhaps that was a good omen. Then the doorbell rang. The servant girl was of course locked in her kitchen, and Grete would have to open the door. It was his father. "What's been happening?" were his first words; Grete's face must have told him everything. Grete answered in a muffled voice, apparently hiding her head on his breast: "Mother has been fainting, but she's better now. Gregor's broken loose." "Just what I expected," said his father, "just what I've been telling you, but you women would never listen." It was clear to Gregor that his father had taken the worst interpretation of Grete's all too brief statement and was assuming that Gregor had been guilty of some violent act. Therefore Gregor must now try to propitiate his father, since he had neither time nor means for an explanation. And so he fled to the door of his own room and crouched against it, to let his father see as soon as he came in from the hall that his son had the good intention of getting back into his room immediately and that it was not necessary to drive him there, but that if only the door were opened he would disappear at once.

Yet his father was not in the mood to perceive such fine distinctions. "Ah!" he cried as soon as he appeared, in a tone which sounded at once angry and exultant. Gregor drew his head back from the door and lifted it to look at his father. Truly, this was not the father he had imagined to himself; admittedly he had been too absorbed of late in his new recreation of crawling over the ceiling to take the same interest as before in what was happening elsewhere in the flat, and he ought really to be prepared for some changes. And yet, and yet, could that be his father? The man who used to lie wearily sunk in bed whenever Gregor set out on a business journey; who welcomed him back of an evening lying in a long chair in a dressing gown; who could not really rise to his feet but only lifted his arms in greeting, and on the rare occasions when he did go out with his family, on one or two Sundays a year and on high holidays, walked between Gregor and his mother, who were slow walkers anyhow, even more slowly than they did, muffled in his old greatcoat, shuffling laboriously forward with the help of his crook-handled stick which he set down most cautiously at every step and, whenever he wanted to say anything, nearly always came to a full stop and gathered his escort around him? Now he was standing there in fine shape; dressed in a smart blue uniform with gold buttons, such as bank messengers wear; his strong double chin bulged over the stiff high collar of his jacket; from under his bushy eyebrows his black eyes darted fresh and penetrating glances; his onetime tangled white hair had been combed flat on either side of a shining and carefully exact parting. He pitched his cap, which bore a gold monogram, probably the badge of some bank, in a wide sweep across the whole room on to a sofa and with the tail-ends of his jacket thrown back, his hands in his trouser pockets, advanced with a grim visage towards Gregor. Likely enough he did not himself know what he meant to do; at any rate he lifted his feet uncommonly high, and Gregor was dumbfounded at the enormous size of his shoe soles. But Gregor could not risk standing up to him, aware as he had been from the very first day of his new life that his father believed only the severest measures suitable for dealing with him. And so he ran before his father, stopping when he stopped and scuttling forward again when his father made any kind of move. In this way they circled the room several times without anything decisive happening; indeed the whole operation did not even look like a pursuit because it was carried out so slowly. And so Gregor did not leave the floor, for he feared that his father might take as a piece of peculiar wickedness any excursion of his over the walls or the ceiling. All the same, he could not stay this course much longer, for while his father took one step he had to carry out a whole series of movements. He was already beginning to feel breathless, just as in his former life his lungs had not been very dependable. As he was staggering along, trying to concentrate his energy on running, hardly keeping his eyes open; in his dazed state never even thinking of any other escape than simply going forward; and having almost forgotten that the walls were free to him, which in this room were well provided with finely carved pieces of furniture full of knobs and crevices—suddenly something lightly flung landed close behind him and rolled before him. It was an apple; a second apple followed immediately; Gregor came to a stop in alarm; there was no point in running on, for his father was determined to bombard him. He had filled his pockets with fruit from the dish on the sideboard and was now shying apple after apple, without taking particularly good aim for the moment. The small red apples rolled about the floor as if magnetized and cannoned into each other. An apple thrown without much force grazed Gregor's back and glanced off harmlessly. But another following immediately landed right on his back and sank in; Gregor wanted to drag himself forward, as if this startling, incredible pain could be left behind him: but he felt as if nailed to the spot and flattened himself out in a complete derangement of all his senses. With his last conscious look he saw the door of his room being torn open and his mother rushing out ahead of his screaming sister, in her underbodice, for her daughter had loosened her clothing to let her breathe more freely and recover from her swoon, he saw his mother rushing towards his father, leaving one after another behind her on the floor her loosened petticoats, stumbling over her petticoats straight to his father and embracing him, in complete union with him—but here Gregor's sight began to fail—with her hands clasped round his father's neck as she begged for her son's life.

III

The serious injury done to Gregor, which disabled him for more than a month—the apple went on sticking in his body as a visible reminder, since no one ventured to remove it—seemed to have made even his father recollect that Gregor was a member of the family, despite his present unfortunate and repulsive shape, and ought not to be treated as an enemy, that, on the contrary, family duty required the suppression of disgust and the exercise of patience, nothing but patience.

And although his injury had impaired, probably forever, his power of movement, and for the time being it took him long, long minutes to creep across his room like an old invalid—there was no question now of crawling up the wall—yet in his own opinion he was sufficiently compensated for this worsening of his condition by the fact that towards evening the living-room door, which he used to watch intently for an hour or two beforehand, was always thrown open, so that lying in the darkness of his room, invisible to the family, he could see them all at the lamp-lit table and listen to their talk, by general consent as it were, very different from his earlier eavesdropping.

True, their intercourse lacked the lively character of former times, which he had always called to mind with a certain wistfulness in the small hotel bedrooms where he had been wont to throw himself down, tired out, on damp bedding. They were now mostly very silent. Soon after supper his father would fall asleep in his armchair; his mother and sister would admonish each other to be silent; his mother, bending low over the lamp, stitched at fine sewing for an underwear firm; his sister, who had taken a job as a salesgirl, was learning shorthand and

French in the evenings on the chance of bettering herself. Sometimes his father woke up, and as if quite unaware that he had been sleeping said to his mother: "What a lot of sewing you're doing today!" and at once fell asleep again, while the two women exchanged a tired smile.

With a kind of mulishness his father persisted in keeping his uniform on even in the house; his dressing gown hung uselessly on its peg and he slept fully dressed where he sat, as if he were ready for service at any moment and even here only at the beck and call of his superior. As a result, his uniform, which was not brand-new to start with, began to look dirty, despite all the loving care of the mother and sister to keep it clean, and Gregor often spent whole evenings gazing at the many greasy spots on the garment, gleaming with gold buttons always in a high state of polish, in which the old man sat sleeping in extreme discomfort and yet quite peacefully.

As soon as the clock struck ten his mother tried to rouse his father with gentle words and to persuade him after that to get into bed, for sitting there he could not have a proper sleep and that was what he needed most, since he had to go to duty at six. But with the mulishness that had obsessed him since he became a bank messenger he always insisted on staying longer at the table, although he regularly fell asleep again and in the end only with the greatest trouble could be got out of his armchair and into his bed. However insistently Gregor's mother and sister kept urging him with gentle reminders, he would go on slowly shaking his head for a quarter of an hour, keeping his eyes shut, and refuse to get to his feet. The mother plucked at his sleeve, whispering endearments in his ear, the sister left her lessons to come to her mother's help, but Gregor's father was not to be caught. He would only sink down deeper in his chair. Not until the two women hoisted him up by the armpits did he open his eyes and look at them both, one after the other, usually with the remark: "This is a life. This is the peace and quiet of my old age." And leaning on the two of them he would heave himself up, with difficulty, as if he were a great burden to himself, suffer them to lead him as far as the door and then wave them off and go on alone, while the mother abandoned her needlework and the sister her pen in order to run after him and help him farther.

Who could find time, in this overworked and tired-out family, to bother about Gregor more than was absolutely needful? The household was reduced more and more; the servant girl was turned off; a gigantic bony charwoman with white hair flying round her head came in morning and evening to do the rough work; everything else was done by Gregor's mother, as well as great piles of sewing. Even various family ornaments, which his mother and sister used to wear with pride at parties and celebrations, had to be sold, as Gregor discovered of an evening from hearing them all discuss the prices obtained. But what they lamented most was the fact that they could not leave the flat which was much too big for their present circumstances, because they could not think of any way to shift Gregor. Yet Gregor saw well enough that consideration for him was not the main difficulty preventing the removal, for they could have easily shifted him in some suitable box with a few air holes in it; what really kept them from moving into another flat was rather their own complete hopelessness and the belief that they had been singled out for a misfortune such as had never happened to any of their relations or acquaintances. They fulfilled to the uttermost all that the world demands of poor people, the father fetched breakfast for the small clerks in the bank, the mother devoted her energy to making underwear for strangers, the sister trotted to and fro behind the counter at the behest of customers, but more than this they had not the strength to do. And the wound in Gregor's back began to nag at him afresh when his mother and sister, after getting his father into bed, came back again, left their work lying, drew close to each other and sat cheek by cheek; when his mother, pointing towards his room, said: "Shut that door now, Grete," and he was left again in darkness, while next door the women mingled their tears or perhaps sat dry-eyed staring at the table.

Gregor hardly slept at all by night or by day. He was often haunted by the idea that next time the door opened he would take the family's affairs in hand again just as he used to do; once more, after this long interval, there appeared in his thoughts the figures of the chief and the chief clerk, the commercial travelers and the apprentices, the porter who was so dull-witted, two or three friends in other firms, a chambermaid in one of the rural hotels, a sweet and fleeting memory, a cashier in a milliner's shop, whom he had wooed earnestly but too slowly—they all appeared, together with strangers or people he had quite forgotten, but instead of helping him and his family they were one and all unapproachable and he was glad when they vanished. At other times he would not be in the mood to bother about his family, he was only filled with rage at the way they were neglecting him, and although he had no clear idea of what he might care to eat he would make plans for getting into the larder to take the food that was after all his due, even if he were not hungry. His sister no longer took thought to bring him what might especially please him, but in the morning and at noon before she went to business hurriedly pushed into his room with her foot any food that was available, and in the evening cleared it out again with one sweep of the broom, heedless of whether it had been merely tasted, or—as most frequently happened—left untouched. The cleaning of his room, which she now did always in the evenings, could not have been more hastily done. Streaks of dirt stretched along the walls, here and there lay balls of dust and filth. At first Gregor used to station himself in some particularly filthy corner when his sister arrived, in order to reproach her with it, so to speak. But he could have sat there for weeks without getting her to make any improvements; she could see the dirt as well as he did, but she had simply made up her mind to leave it alone. And yet, with a touchiness that was new to her, which seemed anyhow to have infected the whole family, she jealously guarded her claim to be the sole caretaker of Gregor's room. His mother once subjected his room to a thorough cleaning, which was achieved only by means of several buckets of water—all this dampness of course upset Gregor too and he lay widespread, sulky and motionless on the sofa—but she was well punished for it. Hardly had his sister noticed the changed aspect of his room than she rushed in high dudgeon into the living room and, despite the imploringly raised hands of her mother, burst into a storm of weeping, while her parents—her father had of course been startled out of his chair—looked on at first in helpless amazement; then they too began to go into action; the father reproached the mother on his right for not having left the cleaning of Gregor's room to his sister; shrieked at the sister on his left that never again was she to be allowed to clean Gregor's room; while the mother tried to pull the father into his bedroom, since he was beyond himself with agitation; the sister, shaken with sobs, then beat upon the table with her small fists; and Gregor hissed loudly with rage because not one of them thought of shutting the door to spare him such a spectacle and so much noise.

Still, even if the sister, exhausted by her daily work, had grown tired of looking after Gregor as she did formerly, there was no need for his mother's intervention or for Gregor's being neglected at all. The charwoman was there. This old widow, whose strong bony frame had enabled her to survive the worst a long life could offer, by no means recoiled from Gregor. Without being in the least curious she had once by chance opened the door of his room and at the sight of Gregor, who, taken by surprise, began to rush to and fro although no one was chasing him, merely stood there with her arms folded. From that time she never failed to open his door a little for a moment, morning and evening, to have a look at him. At first she even used to call him to her, with words which apparently she took to be friendly, such as: "Come along, then, you old dung beetle!" or "Look at the old dung beetle, then!" To such allocutions Gregor made no answer, but stayed motionless where he was, as if the door had never been opened. Instead of being allowed to disturb him so senselessly whenever the whim took her, she should rather have been ordered to clean out his room daily, that charwoman! Once, early in the morning—heavy rain was lashing on the windowpanes, perhaps a sign that spring was on the way—Gregor was so exasperated when she began addressing him again that he ran at her, as if to attack her, although slowly and feebly enough. But the charwoman instead of showing fright merely lifted high a chair that happened to be beside the door, and as she stood there with her mouth wide open it was clear that she meant to shut it only when she brought the chair down on Gregor's back. "So you're not coming any nearer?" she asked, as Gregor turned away again, and quietly put the chair back into the corner.

Gregor was now eating hardly anything. Only when he happened to pass the food laid out for him did he take a bit of something in his mouth as a pastime, kept it there for an hour at a time and usually spat it out again. At first he thought it was chagrin over the state of his room that prevented him from eating, yet he soon got used to the various changes in his room. It had become a habit in the family to push into his room things there was no room for elsewhere, and there were plenty of these now, since one of the rooms had been let to three lodgers. These serious gentlemen—all three of them with full beards, as Gregor once observed through a crack in the door—had a passion for order, not only in their own room but, since they were now members of the household, in all its arrangements, especially in the kitchen. Superfluous, not to say dirty, objects they could not bear. Besides, they had brought with them most of the furnishings they needed. For this reason many things could be dispensed with that it was no use trying to sell but that should not be thrown away either. All of them found their way into Gregor's room. The ash can likewise and the kitchen garbage can. Anything that was not needed for the moment was simply flung into Gregor's room by the charwoman, who did everything in a hurry; fortunately Gregor usually saw only the object, whatever it was, and the hand that held it. Perhaps she intended to take the things away again as time and opportunity offered, or to collect them until she could throw them all out in a heap, but in fact they just lay wherever she happened to throw them, except when Gregor pushed his way through the junk heap and shifted it somewhat, at first out of necessity, because he had not room enough to crawl, but later with increasing enjoyment, although after such excursions, being sad and weary to death, he would lie motionless for hours. And since the lodgers often ate their supper at home in the common living room, the living room door stayed shut many an evening, yet Gregor reconciled himself quite easily to the shutting of the door, for often enough on evenings when it was opened he had disregarded it entirely and lain in the darkest corner of his room, quite unnoticed by the family. But on one occasion the charwoman left the door open a little and it stayed ajar even when the lodgers came in for supper and the lamp was lit. They set themselves at the top end of the table where formerly Gregor and his father and mother had eaten their meals, unfolded their napkins and took knife and fork in hand. At once his mother appeared in the other doorway with a dish of meat and close behind her his sister with a dish of potatoes piled high. The food steamed with a thick vapor. The lodgers bent over the food set before them as if to scrutinize it before eating, in fact the man in the middle, who seemed to pass for an authority with the other two, cut a piece of meat as it lay on the dish, obviously to discover if it were tender or should be sent back to the kitchen. He showed satisfaction, and Gregor's mother and sister, who had been watching anxiously, breathed freely and began to smile.

The family itself took its meals in the kitchen. Nonetheless, Gregor's father came into the living room before going in to the kitchen and with one prolonged bow, cap in hand, made a round of the table. The lodgers all stood up and murmured something in their beards. When they were alone again they ate their food in almost complete silence. It seemed remarkable to Gregor that among the various noises coming from the table he could always distinguish the sound of their masticating teeth, as if this were a sign to Gregor that one needed teeth in order to eat, and that with toothless jaws even of the finest make one could do nothing. "I'm hungry enough," said Gregor sadly to himself, "but not for that kind of food. How these lodgers are stuffing themselves, and here am I dying of starvation!"

On that very evening—during the whole of his time there Gregor could not remember ever having heard the violin—the sound of violin-playing came from the kitchen. The lodgers had already finished their supper, the one in the middle had brought out a newspaper and given the other two a page apiece, and now they were leaning back at ease reading and smoking. When the violin began to play they pricked up their ears, got to their feet, and went on tiptoe to the hall door where they stood huddled together. Their movements must have been heard in the kitchen, for Gregor's father called out: "Is the violin-playing disturbing you, gentlemen? It can be stopped at once." "On the contrary," said the middle lodger, "could not Fräulein Samsa come and play in this room, beside us, where it is much more convenient and comfortable?" "Oh certainly," cried Gregor's father, as if he were the violin-player. The lodgers came back into the living room and waited. Presently Gregor's father arrived with the music stand, his mother carrying the music and his sister with the violin. His sister quietly made everything ready to start playing; his parents, who had never let rooms before and so had an exaggerated idea of the courtesy due to lodgers, did not venture to sit down on their own chairs; his father leaned against the door, the right hand thrust between two buttons of his livery coat, which was formally buttoned up; but his mother was offered a chair by one of the lodgers and, since she left the chair just where he had happened to put it, sat down in a corner to one side.

Gregor's sister began to play; the father and mother, from either side, intently watched the movements of her hands. Gregor, attracted by the playing, ventured to move forward a little until his head was actually inside the living room. He felt hardly any surprise at his growing lack of consideration for the others; there had been a time when he prided himself on being considerate. And yet just on this occasion he had more reason than ever to hide himself, since owing to the amount of dust which lay thick in his room and rose into the air at the slightest movement, he too was covered with dust; fluff and hair and remnants of food trailed with him, caught on his back and along his sides; his indifference to everything was much too great for him to turn on his back and scrape himself clean on the carpet, as once he had done several times a day. And in spite of his condition, no shame deterred him from advancing a little over the spotless floor of the living room.

To be sure, no one was aware of him. The family was entirely absorbed in the violin-playing; the lodgers, however, who first of all had stationed themselves, hands in pockets, much too close behind the music stand so that they could all have read the music, which must have bothered his sister, had soon retreated to the window, half-whispering with downbent heads, and stayed there while his father turned an anxious eye on them. Indeed, they were making it more than obvious that they had been disappointed in their expectation of hearing good or enjoyable violin-playing, that they had had more than enough of the performance and only out of courtesy suffered a continued disturbance of their peace. From the way they all kept blowing the smoke of their cigars high in the air through nose and mouth one could divine their irritation. And yet Gregor's sister was playing so beautifully. Her face leaned sideways, intently and sadly her eyes followed the notes of music. Gregor crawled a little farther forward and lowered his head to the ground so that it might be possible for his eyes to meet hers. Was he an animal, that music had such an effect upon him? He felt as if the way were opening before him to the unknown nourishment he craved. He was determined to push forward till he reached his sister, to pull at her skirt and so let her know that she was to come into his room with her violin, for no one here appreciated her playing as he would appreciate it. He would never let her out of his room, at least, not so long as he lived; his frightful appearance would become, for the first time, useful to him; he would watch all the doors of his room at once and spit at intruders; but his sister should need no constraint, she should stay with him of her own free will; she should sit beside him on the sofa, bend down her ear to him and hear him confide that he had had the firm intention of sending her to the Conservatorium, and that, but for his mishap, last Christmas —surely Christmas was long past?—he would have announced it to everybody without allowing a single objection. After this confession his sister would be so touched that she would burst into tears, and Gregor would then raise himself to her shoulder and kiss her on the neck, which, now that she went to business, she kept free of any ribbon or collar.

"Mr. Samsa!" cried the middle lodger, to Gregor's father, and pointed, without wasting any more words, at Gregor, now working himself slowly forwards. The violin fell silent, the middle lodger first smiled to his friends with a shake of the head and then looked at Gregor again. Instead of driving Gregor out, his father seemed to think it more needful to begin by soothing down the lodgers, although they were not at all agitated and apparently found Gregor more entertaining than the violin-playing. He hurried toward them and, spreading out his arms, tried to urge them back into their own room and at the same time to block their view of Gregor. They now began to be really a little angry, one could not tell whether because of the old man's behavior or because it had just dawned on them that all unwittingly they had such a neighbor as Gregor next door. They demanded explanations of his father, they waved their arms like him, tugged uneasily at their beards, and only with reluctance backed towards their room. Meanwhile Gregor's sister, who stood there as if lost when her playing was so abruptly broken off, came to life again, pulled herself together all at once after standing for a while holding violin and bow in nervelessly hanging hands and staring at her music, pushed her violin into the lap of her mother, who was still sitting in her chair fighting asthmatically for breath, and ran into the lodgers' room to which they were now being shepherded by her father rather more quickly than before. One could see the pillows and blankets on the beds flying under her accustomed fingers and being laid in order. Before the lodgers had actually reached their room she had finished making the beds and slipped out.

The old man seemed once more to be so possessed by his mulish self-assertiveness that he was forgetting all the respect he should show to his lodgers. He kept driving them on and driving them on until in the very door of the bedroom the middle lodger stamped his foot loudly on the floor and so brought him to a halt. "I beg to announce," said the lodger, lifting one hand and looking also at Gregor's mother and sister, "that because of the disgusting conditions prevailing in this household and family"—here he spat on the floor with emphatic brevity—"I give you notice on the spot. Naturally I won't pay you a penny for the days I have lived here, on the contrary I shall consider bringing an action for damages against you, based on claims—believe me—that will be easily susceptible of proof." He ceased and stared straight in front of him, as if he expected something. In fact his two friends at once rushed into the breach with these words: "And we too give notice on the spot." On that he seized the door-handle and shut the door with a slam.

Gregor's father, groping with his hands, staggered forward and fell into his chair; it looked as if he were stretching himself there for his ordinary evening nap, but the marked jerkings of his head, which was as if uncontrollable, showed that he was far from asleep. Gregor had simply stayed quietly all the time on the spot where the lodgers had espied him. Disappointment at the failure of his plan, perhaps also the weakness arising from extreme hunger, made it impossible for him to move. He feared, with a fair degree of certainty, that at any moment the general tension would discharge itself in a combined attack upon him, and he lay waiting. He did not react even to the noise made by the violin as it fell off his mother's lap from under her trembling fingers and gave out a resonant note.

"My dear parents," said his sister, slapping her hand on the table by way of introduction, "things can't go on like this. Perhaps you don't realize that, but I do. I won't utter my brother's name in the presence of this creature, and so all I say is: we must try to get rid of it. We've tried to look after it and to put up with it as far as is humanly possible, and I don't think anyone could reproach us in the slightest."

"She is more than right," said Gregor's father to himself. His mother, who was still choking for lack of breath, began to cough hollowly into her hand with a wild look in her eyes.

His sister rushed over to her and held her forehead. His father's thoughts seemed to have lost their vagueness at Grete's words, he sat more upright, fingering his service cap that lay among the plates still lying on the table from the lodgers' supper, and from time to time looked at the still form of Gregor.

"We must try to get rid of it," his sister now said explicitly to her father, since her mother was coughing too much to hear a word, "it will be the death of both of you, I can see that coming. When one has to work as hard as we do, all of us, one can't stand this continual torment at home on top of it. At least I can't stand it any longer." And she burst into such a passion of sobbing that her tears dropped on her mother's face, where she wiped them off mechanically.

"My dear," said the old man sympathetically, and with evident understanding, "but what can we do?"

Gregor's sister merely shrugged her shoulders to indicate the feeling of helplessness that had now overmastered her during her weeping fit, in contrast to her former confidence.

"If he could understand us," said her father, half questioningly; Grete, still sobbing, vehemently waved a hand to show how unthinkable that was.

"If he could understand us," repeated the old man, shutting his eyes to consider his daughter's conviction that understanding was impossible, "then perhaps we might come to some agreement with him. But as it is—"

"He must go," cried Gregor's sister. "That's the only solution, Father. You must just try to get rid of the idea that this is Gregor. The fact that we've believed it for so long is the root of all our trouble. But how can it be Gregor? If this were Gregor, he would have realized long ago that human beings can't live with such a creature, and he'd have gone away on his own accord. Then we wouldn't have any brother, but we'd be able to go on living and keep his memory in honor. As it is, this creature persecutes us, drives away our lodgers, obviously wants the whole apartment to himself and would have us all sleep in the gutter. Just look, Father," she shrieked all at once, "he's at it again!" And in an access of panic that was quite incomprehensible to Gregor she even quitted her mother, literally thrusting the chair from her as if she would rather sacrifice her mother than stay so near to Gregor, and rushed behind her father, who also rose up, being simply upset by her agitation, and half-spread his arms out as if to protect her.

Yet Gregor had not the slightest intention of frightening anyone, far less his sister. He had only begun to turn round in order to crawl back to his room, but it was certainly a startling operation to watch, since because of his disabled condition he could not execute the difficult turning movements except by lifting his head and then bracing it against the floor over and over again. He paused and looked round. His good intentions seemed to have been recognized; the alarm had only been momentary. Now they were all watching him in melancholy silence. His mother lay in her chair, her legs stiffly outstretched and pressed together, her eyes almost closing for sheer weariness; his father and his sister were sitting beside each other, his sister's arm around the old man's neck.

Perhaps I can go on turning round now, thought Gregor, and began his labors again. He could not stop himself from panting with the effort, and had to pause now and then to take breath. Nor did anyone harass him, he was left entirely to himself. When he had completed the turn-round he began at once to crawl straight back. He was amazed at the distance separating him from his room and could not understand how in his weak state he had managed to accomplish the same journey so recently, almost without remarking it. Intent on crawling as fast as possible, he barely noticed that not a single word, not an ejaculation from his family, interfered with his progress. Only when he was already in the doorway did he turn his head round, not completely, for his neck muscles were getting stiff, but enough to see that nothing had changed behind him except that his sister had risen to her feet. His last glance fell on his mother, who was not quite overcome by sleep.

Hardly was he well inside his room when the door was hastily pushed shut, bolted and locked. The sudden noise in his rear startled him so much that his little legs gave beneath him. It was his sister who had shown such haste. She had been standing ready waiting and had made a light spring forward, Gregor had not even heard her coming, and she cried "At last!" to her parents as she turned the key in the lock.

"And what now?" said Gregor to himself, looking round in the darkness. Soon he made the discovery that he was now unable to stir a limb. This did not surprise him, rather it seemed unnatural that he should ever actually have been able to move on these feeble little legs. Otherwise he felt relatively comfortable. True, his whole body was aching, but it seemed that the pain was gradually growing less and would finally pass away. The rotting apple in his back and the inflamed area around it, all covered with soft dust, already hardly troubled him. He thought of his family with tenderness and love. The decision that he must disappear was one that he held to even more strongly than his sister, if that were possible. In this state of vacant and peaceful meditation he remained until the tower clock struck three in the morning. The first broadening of light in the world outside the window entered his consciousness once more. Then his head sank to the floor of its own accord and from his nostrils came the last faint flicker of his breath.

When the charwoman arrived early in the morning—what between her strength and her impatience she slammed all the doors so loudly, never mind how often she had been begged not to do so, that no one in the whole apartment could enjoy any quiet sleep after her arrival—she noticed nothing unusual as she took her customary peep into Gregor's room. She thought he was lying motionless on purpose, pretending to be in the sulks; she credited him with every kind of intelligence. Since she happened to have the long-handled broom in her hand she tried to tickle him up with it from the doorway. When that too produced no reaction she felt provoked and poked at him a little harder, and only when she had pushed him along the floor without meeting any resistance was her attention aroused. It did not take her long to establish the truth of the matter, and her eyes widened, she let out a whistle, yet did not waste much time over it but tore open the door of the Samsas' bedroom and yelled into the darkness at the top of her voice: "Just look at this, it's dead; it's lying here dead and done for!"

Mr. and Mrs. Samsa started up in their double bed and before they realized the nature of the charwoman's announcement had some difficulty in overcoming the shock of it. But then they got out of bed quickly, one on either side, Mr. Samsa throwing a blanket over his shoulders, Mrs. Samsa in nothing but her nightgown; in this array they entered Gregor's room. Meanwhile the door of the living room opened, too, where Grete had been sleeping since the advent of the lodgers; she was completely dressed as if she had not been to bed, which seemed to be confirmed also by the paleness of her face. "Dead?" said Mrs. Samsa, looking questioningly at the charwoman, although she could have investigated for herself, and the fact was obvious enough without investigation. "I should say so," said the charwoman, proving her words by pushing Gregor's corpse a long way to one side with her broomstick. Mrs. Samsa made a movement as if to stop her, but checked it. "Well," said Mr. Samsa, "now thanks be to God." He crossed himself, and the three women followed his example. Grete, whose eyes never left the corpse, said: "Just see how thin he was. It's such a long time since he's eaten anything. The food came out again just as it went in." Indeed, Gregor's body was completely flat and dry, as could only now be seen when it was no longer supported by the legs and nothing prevented one from looking closely at it.

"Come in beside us, Grete, for a little while," said Mrs. Samsa with a tremulous smile, and Grete, not without looking back at the corpse, followed her parents into their bedroom. The charwoman shut the door and opened the window wide. Although it was so early in the morning a certain softness was perceptible in the fresh air. After all, it was already the end of March.

The three lodgers emerged from their room and were surprised to see no breakfast; they had been forgotten. "Where's our breakfast?" said the middle lodger peevishly to the charwoman. But she put her finger to her lips and hastily, without a word, indicated by gestures that they should go into Gregor's room. They did so and stood, their hands in the pockets of their somewhat shabby coats, around Gregor's corpse in the room where it was now fully light.

At that the door of the Samsas' bedroom opened and Mr. Samsa appeared in his uniform, his wife on one arm, his daughter on the other. They all looked a little as if they had been crying; from time to time Grete hid her face on her father's arm.

"Leave my house at once!" said Mr. Samsa, and pointed to the door without disengaging himself from the women. "What do you mean by that?" said the middle lodger, taken somewhat aback, with a feeble smile. The two others put their hands behind them and kept rubbing them together, as if in gleeful expectation of a fine set-to in which they were bound to come off the winners. "I mean just what I say," answered Mr. Samsa, and advanced in a straight line with his two companions towards the lodger. He stood his ground at first quietly, looking at the floor as if his thoughts were taking a new pattern in his head. "Then let us go, by all means," he said, and looked up at Mr. Samsa as if in a sudden access of humility he were expecting some renewed sanction for this decision. Mr. Samsa merely nodded briefly once or twice with meaning eyes. Upon that the lodger really did go with long strides into the hall, his two friends had been listening and had quite stopped rubbing their hands for some moments and now went scuttling after him as if afraid that Mr. Samsa might get into the hall before them and cut them off from their leader. In the hall they all three took their hats from the rack, their sticks from the umbrella stand, bowed in silence and quitted the apartment. With a suspiciousness which proved quite unfounded Mr. Samsa and the two women followed them out to the landing; leaning over the banister they watched the three figures slowly but surely going down the long stairs, vanishing from sight at a certain turn of the staircase on every floor and coming into view again after a moment or so; the more they dwindled, the more the Samsa family's interest in them dwindled, and when a butcher's boy met them and passed them on the stairs coming up proudly with a tray on his head, Mr. Samsa and the two women soon left the landing and as if a burden had been lifted from them went back into their apartment.

They decided to spend this day in resting and going for a stroll; they had not only deserved such a respite from work but absolutely needed it. And so they sat down at the table and wrote three notes of excuse, Mr. Samsa to his board of management, Mrs. Samsa to her employer and Grete to the head of her firm. While they were writing, the charwoman came in to say that she was going now, since her morning's work was finished. At first they only nodded without looking up, but as she kept hovering there they eyed her irritably. "Well?" said Mr. Samsa. The charwoman stood grinning in the doorway as if she had good news to impart to the family but meant not to say a word unless properly questioned. The small ostrich feather standing upright on her hat, which had annoyed Mr. Samsa ever since she was engaged, was waving gaily in all directions. "Well, what is it then?" asked Mrs. Samsa, who obtained more respect from the charwoman than the others. "Oh," said the charwoman, giggling so amiably that she could not at once continue, "just this, you don't need to bother about how to get rid of the thing next door. It's been seen to already." Mrs. Samsa and Grete bent over their letters again, as if preoccupied; Mr. Samsa, who perceived that she was eager to begin describing it all in detail, stopped her with a decisive hand. But since she was not allowed to tell her story, she remembered the great hurry she was in, being obviously deeply huffed: "Bye, everybody," she said, whirling off violently, and departed with a frightful slamming of doors.

"She'll be given notice tonight," said Mr. Samsa, but neither from his wife nor his daughter did he get any answer, for the charwoman seemed to have shattered again the composure they had barely achieved. They rose, went to the window and stayed there, clasping each other tight. Mr. Samsa turned in his chair to look at them and quietly observed them for a little. Then he called out: "Come along, now, do. Let bygones be bygones. And you might have some consideration for me." The two of them complied at once, hastened to him, caressed him and quickly finished their letters.

Then they all three left the apartment together, which was more than they had done for months, and went by tram into the open country outside the town. The tram, in which they were the only passengers, was filled with warm sunshine. Leaning comfortably back in their seats they canvassed their prospects for the future, and it appeared on closer inspection that these were not at all bad, for the jobs they had got, which so far they had never really discussed with each other, were all three admirable and likely to lead to better things later on. The greatest immediate improvement in their condition would of course arise from moving to another house; they wanted to take a smaller and cheaper but also better situated and more easily run apartment than the one they had, which Gregor had selected. While they were thus conversing, it struck both Mr. and Mrs. Samsa, almost at the same moment, as they became aware of their daughter's increasing vivacity, that in spite of all the sorrow of recent times, which had made her cheeks pale, she had bloomed into a pretty girl with a good figure. They grew quieter and half unconsciously exchanged glances of complete agreement, having come to the conclusion that it would soon be time to find a good husband for her. And it was like a confirmation of their new dreams and excellent intentions that at the end of their journey their daughter sprang to her feet first and stretched her young body.

[1915]

Translated by
WILLA and EDWIN MUIR

QUESTIONS

1. Why does the transformation occur in Gregor Samsa? What does it mean? In addition to his physical metamorphosis, how else does Gregor change during the story? Consider his relationships with his father, mother, and sister.
2. In what sense could it be said that the climax of "The Metamorphosis" is the story's opening line? How does the rest of the story proceed from that climax?
3. How do the style, tone, point of view, and other formal elements of the story contribute to its meaning and effectiveness?
4. How do you understand the final scene of the story?
5. What is the theme or meaning of the story as a whole? Is Gregor Samsa's predicament symbolic of any larger issues?

Ghassan Kanafani

(1936–1972)

Palestinian

In his introduction to Ghassan Kanafani's collection of short stories, *Men in the Sun*, Hilary Kilpatrick, the author's translator, describes the writer as follows: "Ghassan Kanafani was known in the West as the spokesman for the Popular Front for the Liberation of Palestine, and the editor of its weekly, *Al-Hadaf*. But in the Arab world he was also considered a leading novelist, and one of the foremost Palestinian writers in prose." During his short life as a writer, Kanafani was not only a professional journalist but also the author of 10 volumes of fiction (five collections of short stories and five novels), two plays, and two critical studies of Palestinian literature. He was born in Acre in 1936 and died in an automobile explosion in 1972, the result of a booby trap. At the time of his death, Kanafani's widow wrote, "His inspiration for writing and working unceasingly was the Palestinian–Arab struggle. . . . He always stressed that the Palestine problem could not be solved in isolation from the Arab world's whole social and political situation."

Much of Kanafani's fiction (including "A Hand in the Grave") is free of the ideological concerns of his political life. He attempted to separate the two. Yet one cannot help noting Edward W. Said's description of the author's novella, *Men in the Sun*, commented on at the time of the Iraqi invasion of Kuwait in the summer of 1990: "a prescient parable of three Palestinian refugees trying to smuggle themselves from Iraq to Kuwait in a tank truck, [and] dying of asphyxiation and heat at the border post."

A Hand in the Grave

I woke up very early that day. I could hear my father repeating. "God be praised" as he prepared to perform his prayers. Later he came past me:

"Your eyes look tired. What's happened? Didn't you sleep well last night?"

I nodded, turning the soap over in my hand, and began to look at my face in the mirror with its silver back peeling away at the edges, without replying to my father's questions. I did not turn my head, but I realized that he had hung the towel round his neck and put on his sandals. He began to yawn, stretching his arms as far as they would go. As I soaped my face I heard my sister ask my father:

"What's happened?"

"Nothing. Your brother's face looks as though it's been bleached; he definitely didn't sleep last night. Do you know when he came home yesterday?"

"Yes. He wasn't late."

"You're lying. You always tell lies, when it's something to do with Nabil."

I began to rinse my face with water, and though the conversation seemed to threaten a nasty storm I felt that I was outside it all. I heard my sister say:

"I told you that he came home early last night. You just don't want to believe it. Will you drink your coffee?"

"I don't want any coffee. I don't want to be poisoned. Can he tell me why his face is so pale if he went to bed early?"

I dried my face and turned towards him. I knew he was looking for a reason to explode. That is how he appeared every morning, doing nothing the whole time before breakfast except search for a pretext to unburden himself of his rage; today I represented his first attempt. He looked hard at me and then repeated his question, his lips quivering:

"If you went to bed early, young man, why is your face so pale?"

I circled round him, and when my shoulder was level with his I observed quietly:

"Facial pallor has a number of causes. It may be due to worms in the stomach, or a heavy meal the night before, or excessive smoking. And there are more serious causes, anaemia for instance, TB, or the onset of hemiplegia."[1]

What I expected did not occur, for my father did not get in the least upset. Instead he gave me a side-long admiring glance. Perhaps he was remembering that he had supported me for more than ten years so that I could enter the medical faculty, and here I was giving him scientific answers in all seriousness, which brought joy to his heart. But he did not want to give way so easily.

"You woke up early this morning. Did you give the call to the dawn prayer then?"

I had reached my room, and flung the towel over the bed. Without turning to face my father and sister who were standing in the doorway, I answered in a calm tone:

"I woke up early to rob a grave."

"To rob what?"

"A grave." I turned and faced him, trembling. "To rob a grave. Yes. Is that strange? In the faculty we need a skeleton, and Suhail and I have been told to provide it."

My father was still incapable of taking in the whole picture, and he stood there repeating without being aware of it:

"To rob a grave?"

"Yes, to rob a grave, and steal the skeleton of some man who has been dead more than twenty years because I want to study it."

My sister closed the door between us and left me alone. When I could hear no sound on the other side of the door I put on my clothes. The sack and shovel I had already prepared, and it was up to Suhail to provide a small pick. I bent down to pick up my things, but my sister opened the door before I could straighten up and gave me an affectionate rebuke.

"Why did you upset him, Nabil? You're not yourself this morning. Why did you lie to him?"

"I wasn't lying. I mean to rob a grave."

My father had joined her, and was looking over her shoulder. I noticed that he was trembling, and that he burst out shouting:

[1]*hemiplegia* paralysis of one side of the body

"God curse the hour when I enrolled you in the medical faculty. You want to steal a corpse, do you? Thief! Godless sinner! Haven't you read what God said in . . . ?"

"I have. I've read all God's Word, but God isn't against the medical faculty. They require me to provide a skeleton, just as the sheikh used to require you to know the section 'Ain Min'."[2]

He gave me a look of disapproval for intruding into his past with this levity, then quickly came up with an angry question:

"Are all the students of the medical faculty going to rob people's graves this morning? You won't leave a single corpse in the graveyards! Tell me, are all the students going to rob graves?"

I threw the shovel into the sack, twisted it round my wrist, and went up to him:

"Certainly not! A skeleton costs seventy-five lire. Have you got seventy-five lire? That's why Suhail and I mean to steal, because you can't give me seventy-five lire, and his uncle can't give it him either!"

I pressed my lips together and glared angrily at him. He was gazing at me, completely at a loss, and I lifted the sack, thrusting it into his face.

"And now, let me go before the sun rises and gives us away."

He moved out of my way, baffled, unable to take his eyes from my face. His mouth was hanging open, although he was incapable of uttering a word, as I passed him on my way to the door.

Suhail was waiting for me close to the corner. In the twilight before dawn he resembled a black ghost lurking in a corner to frighten a naughty child.

"Is it you?" he whispered in the gloom, and drew his arm through mine. I knew, without looking at his face, that he was as frightened as I was. We took a few steps, then he stopped.

"He hasn't given you seventy-five lire, eh?" he asked in the tone of someone wanting to say that he too had been unable to obtain the seventy-five lire. I shook my head and then explained.

"I left everything till this morning. And apparently surprise prevented him from even thinking of it. So I went out, expecting him to shout to me before I left that he would give me the seventy-five lire. But he stood there, flabbergasted. What happened to you?"

Suhail said, nodding:

"My uncle thought that I wanted to fool him out of seventy-five lire, but when I assured him that that's how things really were he told me that he was prepared to pay the expenses of the living but not the cost of the dead. Then he said I was young and brave, so what prevented me robbing a grave and saving the money?"

We walked on a little, then turned into the street which led out of the city. I heard his whisper:

"So that's how it is."

"What?"

"We'll rob a grave. The attempts at begging have failed. Your father would

[2]*Ain Min* The Quran is divided into 30 sections for purposes of recitation, and each section is numbered according to letters of the Arabic alphabet. [Translator's note]

sell his own skeleton for less than seventy-five lire; as for my uncle, he'd sell his for the price of one breakfast. It's no good, we must rob a grave."

I stopped, and gripped his shoulder.

"Don't say you're afraid! If you are, go back, and I'll go on alone."

"I? Afraid? Ha! *I'm* not frightened. But I don't like making my way through the end of the night to steal a corpse. How do you think you look, on your way to rob the dead?"

There was no doubt about it, he was frightened, more frightened than I. We walked on silently, our heads bowed. There was a cemetery outside the city, an old cemetery with low graves built out of brown earth. It was not walled, and was generally quite unguarded. It was a graveyard such as is found in some remote spot, inexplicably, as though it were the remains of an ancient battle between strangers who had come from afar and perished without anyone bothering to give them a proper burial.

Our steps had a funereal ring. When we approached the cemetery I felt my chest shaking, so violently was my heart beating, and I fancied that something, a ghost perhaps, was perched on my shoulder. I did not look at Suhail, out of fear that he would think that I was scared, and I seemed to hear the whistle of his breathing as he trod heavily and silently beside me.

"Here we are." I spoke after I had gathered all my forces together, and shifting the sack from one shoulder to the other I stood still. "We must choose a good grave."

He did not reply. In the distance an ugly light was silently spreading above the top of the mountain. The incubus was still perched on my shoulder, and my chest was shaken by violent spasms. I turned to Suhail, who was gazing in front of him, motionless.

"Listen, Suhail! If you are frightened, let's go back."

He glanced at me for a moment, then walked in front of me up the slight incline to the cemetery. Panting as he climbed, he began to speak:

"I? Frightened? If you want, *you* go back. But I'll carry on. What do you think of this grave? It looks solid, and old, and it's large. Don't you think it's suitable?"

I didn't expect Suhail to be so courageous. What he said caught me by surprise, and made me want to prove to him that I was equally brave.

"This one? It looks to me more like a bull's grave, but it's fine so long as it takes your fancy."

As soon as I finished speaking I was terrified, and I made the sudden discovery that Suhail, too, was terrified, and that he was looking at me in utter disbelief that I could speak such ill of the dead. I was trying hard to put the sack on the ground and get out the shovel, but I had the feeling that the sack was too heavy to move and my arm was a numb, empty shell. I could hear Suhail whispering to himself:

"Seventy-five lire! Only seventy-five lire! For heaven's sake!"

I saw him throw his small pick on the ground, take off his jacket with a nervous gesture, and turn to me:

"Don't stand there like a fool. Let's start before it gets any lighter. Don't tell me you're frightened! It was your idea."

I put the sack down. Suhail had gone to work forcefully and quickly and had broken away the mound of earth. He leaned on the pick as I shovelled the soil away. We could both feel our blood beginning to flow again.

"There's still the stone slab. What do you think? Shall we drag it away?"

I glanced at him as he panted for breath. In the light of dawn he took on a mythical aspect. "We're almost there," I said to myself making an effort to appear normal. It was clear to me that Suhail was relying on my courage; at the same time I had to earn my reputation in the faculty when Suhail related the event the next day. I felt the slab with my fingers, then raised my head to him.

"I don't think we'll be able to move it away. Let's make a hole in it."

"But we may break part of the skeleton."

"No, when a corpse is buried they usually place the stone some way away from it. Haven't you ever seen a burial in your life?"

He lifted up his pick with a curt "No."

I took the pick from him when he tired, and he in turn took it from me. We worked quickly, out of fear that the columns of peasants would begin to reach the city. It was growing lighter, an ashen, cold, ugly light, and we each of us could make out the expression on his companion's face without difficulty. So, come what might, we busied ourselves with the work.

Suddenly a small cry burst from Suhail. The head of the pick had made a small black hole in the stone and stuck itself into it. We raised the pick together, and he lifted his head and looked at me when our hands touched. I smiled and began to widen the opening as I felt him looking beyond me fearfully.

"You won't be able to get it out of that little hole. You must make it wider," said Suhail behind me, his voice trembling. I was gasping as I enlarged it, and I found it preferable to talk so that my fear would lose itself in the panting brought on by exertion.

"We won't get anything out now. We just want to be sure that it's there, and then we can widen the hole."

"And which of us will stick his hand in?" he asked in a quiet but scared voice, while I began to clean the edges of the hole. It gave forth a strong stench of decay. I ignored his question.

"Who will put his hand in?" he repeated, and this time I stood up and faced him.

"Either of us. You aren't afraid, are you? Do you know what's inside? A skull like the ones which the students pick up every morning in the faculty. That's all."

"Then you put your hand in," he said in a desperate tone. He was as terrified as it is possible to be, and had reached a point when he could no longer go on with the game. For my part I could not imagine that we should give in after all we had achieved, so I gave a calm reply:

"Yes. I'll put my hand in."

I knelt down, put my arm through the hole, and groped inside the grave for several minutes without being able to feel anything. I stood up.

"I couldn't reach the bottom. You're thinner than I am. How would you like to put your arm in? You've seen with your own eyes. There's nothing to be afraid of."

He glanced at me in silent doubt for a moment, then stepped forward, bent down till he was kneeling, and stretched his arm through the hole. His face was white, but then his colour returned, and I guessed that he had found nothing.

"I haven't got to the bottom," he said with a certain cheerfulness. Meanwhile I bent down opposite him, saying:

"Bend your shoulder down farther. We mustn't go back empty-handed. Try!"

Suhail slid his arm farther in, and began to squeeze his shoulder through as he lay on his side, stretched out, with his face touching the ground.

"Have you felt anything?"

He gave a jerky "No!" in reply.

I stood up, putting my hand on my hip. He was obviously keen, and making sustained, violent efforts.

I cannot recall what distracted my attention from him the next moment, but all of a sudden I was brought back to my surroundings by a terrible scream which did not stop. In the tide of swift fear which I felt flow through my limbs I saw Suhail turn over, his face grazing the gravestone, as he made a hysterical attempt to pull his arm out of the hole. I glimpsed his eyes as I dragged at his other arm in an effort to free him, and I shall never forget the sight of them, stretched open as far as they could go. His blue lips trembled while he choked out the scream of a slaughtered beast between his teeth, and his whole body trembled on the stone as though the awful hand of an unseen demon was shaking him savagely. Even when I could get his arm out of the hole he did not stop screaming. The jagged edges of the opening had cut deep scratches in his shoulder and forearm and they were beginning to ooze blood.

Without stopping those hideous loud screams Suhail stood up, while I in turn had begun to shiver and had no idea what I ought to do. I tried to grasp his shoulders and shake him, but he was turning round and round, trembling as though he were having convulsions. All at once he fell silent, and it was as if he was not the person who had been screaming a moment before. Pressing his bluish lips together obstinately, he turned to face me. There was no colour in his face, and his eyes were reddened circles. On his forehead beads of sweat mingled with the fine dust of the tombstone. He stared at me as though he were looking through me at some loathsome vision, but then he opened his lips and shouted in my face, forcing the words out between his teeth:

"My fingers! My fingers! I stuck them in its eyes!"

I was trembling, but more out of fear of Suhail than anything else. I gripped him by the shoulders and shook him fiercely, shouting:

"You idiot! This is an old grave . . . it's more than fifty years old!"

He gave me a stupid look; clearly he had not heard me. He started repeating:

"His eyes . . . I stuck my fingers in his eyes!"

The rest of Suhail's story is not very strange. And why not admit now that the idea was mine? And that it was not expected that in the first year of the medical faculty we should buy a skeleton? But we, Suhail and I, wanted to acquire a skeleton, so as to have the feeling that we had joined the medical faculty.

Suhail and I went back to the university that afternoon. I was ill. Suhail, however, began to tell the story to the other students, trembling like a leaf as he did so. In the days which followed, he continued to tell the story to anyone he came across, explaining in amazing detail how he had put his fingers into the eyes of the corpse. The university found itself obliged to expel him from the medical faculty after all hope of curing him had been abandoned. Everyone thought he had gone mad. I, for my part, transferred to the faculty of law after I discovered that I could not stand the sight of a skeleton.

Today, after more than seven years have passed since that incident, fate has proved that it was both just and stupid. I remember how Suhail's uncle told me the next day that he hoped that Suhail would not be able to get to the cemetery, and expected that he would come back to him panic-stricken, after which he would give him the price of the skeleton. My father, on the other hand, praised God at length when he heard the story, and observed to my sister that the thieves had received their due reward from the grave and the dead man. Thus he came to believe that the grave which we had desecrated was that of a saint and took to visiting it every dawn to receive blessing from its earth and sand and pray beside it.

Yes, it was both a just and a foolish fate. For only yesterday, after more than seven years had passed, I learned by chance the story of the graveyard we had visited.

It was not a real graveyard. It was a kind of waste land belonging to a Turkish peasant who, during the periods of famine, had taken the trouble to construct earthen graves which were actually no more than covers for small storage spaces where he kept wheat and flour to avoid its being stolen or confiscated. The Turk had left a will which was only opened yesterday, when he died, and the secret was contained in that will.

Only yesterday, the heirs took possession of the ground to remove the graves and begin cultivating it.

The city's newspapers published the news on their front pages.

[1962]

Translated by
HILARY KILPATRICK

QUESTIONS

1. Is the tension between the narrator and his father of significance for the story's later unfolding?
2. What kind of tension develops between the two medical students?
3. Does Kanafani make any moral judgments about the attempted grave robbery?
4. In what way is the story a horror story reminiscent of the tales of Edgar Allan Poe? (See Poe's "The Cask of Amontillado" in this volume.)

Kanai Mieko

(b. 1947)

Japan

Kanai Mieko was born and educated in Takasaki, Japan, and began writing early: she published her first collection of fiction, *Love Life* (1968) when she was only 19. During that same year, she was awarded a prize for her poetry. Kanai has continued to write both poetry and fiction, including novels as well as short stories. In the afterword to the collection of stories *Platonic Love* (1979), Kanai suggested that she expects her readers to be active participants in the creation of her narratives; her comment is particularly instructive for the title story:

> Since it happens that the people who read a work of literature delete portions as they skim over them, read into some parts words that weren't written there, and so add to the work, the person called "the author" is not the only one who writes a work of literature.

Platonic Love

If I ever have to prove to her that I am "the author," I suppose I would have to do it by writing an essay or a book. I became acquainted with her . . . well, in this case I don't know that "acquainted" is exactly the right word . . . at any rate, our strange relationship began when I wrote my first story. I received a letter that started: "I am the person who wrote the story published under your name." Letters with the same opening sentence began to accumulate, equal in number to the things I wrote, and while I kept trying to ignore them, the truth is I found myself completely unable to do so. As long as I continued to write these stories, she was always with me. But there was no name or address on the letters, so I had no way of communicating with this "real author." The relationship between the "real author" and myself was completely one-sided. Of course, it was only "one-sided" from my point of view; if you looked at it from hers, you might not think of it that way. But still, I didn't even know if it was really a "she" who wrote the letters.

The envelopes of the earliest letters have already yellowed. They were a variety of square white envelopes of different sizes and textures, and at various times the color of the ink was green or sepia or purple. Green and sepia and purple inks have a Taishō[1] flavor to them, and I hate them. The handwriting had practically no individuality. As with nearly everyone after the war, the handwriting was nothing like the sort of calligraphy you would write with a brush; the characters were the kind you learn when you use a printed book as a model, and

[1]*Taishō* period in modern Japanese history (1912–1926) characterized by experimentation in politics and the arts, including cultural criticism and liberal political reform efforts

could hardly even be called clumsy. In all honesty, they were just like the characters I write—reflecting an undisciplined quality that carelessly says, if it's legible you can't complain.

Perhaps the letters were from someone who had tried to write a similar story—one could easily imagine it happening. Or some young poet my own age, speaking about my first effort, might have said, "I could write something like that in a single night," and duly caught me by surprise. Just about anyone who has read one or two things that might pass as stories could do the same sort of work. On the face of it, it did seem feasible, I suppose.

Leaving aside the unthinkable case of a story with exactly the same contents, it certainly wasn't impossible that someone had written something very similar. Aren't all "literary works" essentially the same? On reading her first letter—I remember the rustling, tactile sound when I opened the neatly folded, thick foreign paper—I admit I couldn't suppress an uncomfortable feeling that must have been some lingering sense of pride, and yet I felt it really didn't matter who the author was. The conceit of "I wrote that" became repellent all the more quickly if I was, in fact, the one who wrote it. Why shouldn't I cede the "authorship" of that story to an unknown person, and become the "author" of a different story? Yes, I would declare myself the "author" of an entirely different work. . . .

Every time I published a story, a letter was invariably delivered to me, and I couldn't help getting a little fed up. Still, she was undoubtedly my most ardent and essential reader, though it was authorship she claimed, and chance might even prove it true. In any event, I first came to realize that one particular story had been written (by her? by me?) as a result of a letter from her. I kept this secret for quite a while because I didn't know how to explain it, and because for some unknown reason I felt reluctant to tell anyone about her.

Yet whatever I wrote, she would doubtless insist that she had written it herself. I might ask, "When could I possibly have read what you wrote?" and with a little smile—unconsciously I was inclined to imagine her smile as beautiful—she would say, "Don't you even remember that?" Naturally I couldn't even try to ask her questions, but simply read what she wrote, as if it were a privilege I'd been singled out for. Our relationship was concerned exclusively with the writing of stories.

In a sense I was made to suffer because of her, but gradually a curiosity about her made me wish that I knew what kind of person she was, what kind of life she led, what sort of things she was attached to, what experiences she had had, what on earth she thought about. I tried to give her a body. But I was filled with doubts, including, in fact, the question of whether she was a man or a woman. Frankly, I despised my own body, and it was painful to think of the "real author's" body as something beautiful. I sang to myself like a poet in love. You have a body!—oh, the wonder of it! Suspended in my (our) dreams. . . . I even thought that if she and not I had written those few slight, inadequate works (and wasn't the description itself a means of scorning her existence?), then I would have the satisfaction of knowing I had nothing to do with them. But it was my hand that had formed those characters, or remained locked in my inability to write them. I even thought of asking other writers if they had ever received letters from someone who called herself the "real author." I might have discovered that I was not the only victim of a person who played malicious, complicated, and even fairly sophisticated pranks. There was no evidence that this wasn't a vicious and persistent piece of mischief.

I don't mean to suggest, of course, that she bothered me twenty-four hours a day. I had my own life, and I was perfectly able to enjoy it. It was a commonplace, ordinary life; I was bored occasionally, but not so often that the boredom gnawed at me, and I had no interest in the experiences that seem to make reality precious only as misfortune makes it tangible. In short, I had probably grown used to getting by without the pathetic confusion to which younger, more innocent sensibilities are so susceptible; the feelings that result from encounters with a too precise and lucidly contoured world. When I feel constrained by an overbearing world in which I cannot write, am I not already trying to start to write? So, as must be the case with any writer, rather than read my own stories (but she doesn't say that: she says the stories *I wrote*), I preferred the many works of other writers I enjoyed. And this in spite of the jealousy that goes with reading them.

I decided to go to Yugawara and take along the notes for a new story I had to get started on, together with some pieces I wanted to revise for a collection; I also took several books I hadn't yet read, and a manuscript which some strange temptation had made me commit myself to write on "Discussing My Own Work." Of course there was some doubt about how qualified I was to comment on "my own work" but, leaving that aside, I had enough money from my royalties to be able to stay at a hot spring for a while. And I must admit I was drawn to the tradition of writers staying at hot spring resorts to work.

Why is it that, try as we might to avoid discussing our own work, or the work we plan to write, in the end we wind up telling all? In spite of being enjoined to silence, words emerge. . . . We start with the desire to discuss the truth, and in practice we go on to speak in terms that veil the truth. What is required and anticipated in the act we call "discussing one's own work"? Perhaps it is a form of confession. And within that act that pretends to be confession, I dream of a form in which, concealed, lie books that have ingeniously turned into illusions.

In the end, I had nothing to confess. It was just that in reading my own stories I felt a curious passion. Just supposing that the story were really something she had written, it might have been exactly because I was already her reader that I felt so strong a passion. Still, I had no more than a title for the story I planned to write: "Platonic Love." And who on earth would write it? She or I?

As I expected, "Platonic Love" didn't progress a single line; there wasn't a word written in my notebook, and I spent five days just walking during the day and reading or drinking alone at night. I tried to focus "Discussing My Own Work" on some short pieces I had written three years earlier, but the words turned out to be all hers, all taken from her letters. In an effort to resist her, I tried writing about the rabbit's pelt that was nailed to the grayish brown wooden door of a grocery store in Hanamaki (exposing the skin where the spilled blood had turned to glue), or about the dream of rabbits I'd had in the berth of a train on the way to Iwate. I tried to remember the winter sky smothering the town of Hanamaki and the rows of streets, the translucent white and bloodless sky over those arteries of gray and brown and pale blue in an ordinary, characterless, provincial town. But as I feared, I wasn't sure if I had actually been there. The requisites for life, the liveliness that embodies a town, at times even the confusion, were quite removed from the Hanamaki I seemed to know, and the town disappeared in the labyrinths of my memory. The town where "the soul of the silent city made me choose the road" had lost its form, and even the untanned rabbit's pelt, which I surely must have seen, had disappeared completely. Weren't they things I had read about once in some story? It wasn't I who saw or wrote about them. No, that pelt, with the brown, red, and purple gluelike blood and fat adhering to it, was nailed up in a story I had read, wasn't it?

It was so quiet in the setting sun in that very seedy, amateurishly run inn that there seemed to be no other guests, and the mountains that used to form the view from the west windows were blocked from sight by the gray concrete building of a large tourist hotel, so of course the guest rates were cheap enough to allow quite a long stay. A clumsy picture of a crane with a sly expression was painted on the sliding door, yellowed over the years by the late afternoon sun, and a scroll with a poem about the pathos of an egret in the snow was hanging in the alcove. A small black-and-white television right in front of it, an old low wooden table, stained all over with rings from beer glasses, with a tea set on it, a mirror stand draped with a faded length of printed silk, and a clothes rack with three hangers were all the furnishings in the room. Every day I had a bath at dusk, then sadly drank alone in silence, eating the home-style cooking prepared by the landlady: sweet-and-sour pork, sashimi, and salad with store-bought mayonnaise. And if I had to say what the great virtue of eating alone is, it would simply be that if you read a book while eating, no one is offended. Shadowing me on this trip (and how many little trips have I taken alone!) was the constant recollection that I had brought along the notes for my story. I would remember to try and listen for the voice calling me to start the story I had been as yet unable to write, and in the middle of the bath, where the surface of the water shone like pink metal in the setting sun, I would be moved to tears. I would think that the absent "he" or "she" who had withdrawn from the protagonist was really the unwritten story itself, and I cried as my feelings were exposed. My body melted into the large bath, and it was already not a body, nor was it hot water that weighed upon and enveloped it, wrapping it in warm gentleness, but something other than me floating in the water that united and merged me with all existence. In the rose-colored sunlight trembling in the milk-white mist of steam and silence and stillness, time was stretched out, and the bath would begin to expand as though in a dream within a dream, and I would not be the one dreaming, but she would be the one dreaming and I just a character in that dream; and then that eerie vision would melt into the water again. Suspended in my (our) dreams. . . .

After lunch one day, when I was walking along a road by a mountain stream that flowed through the park, a woman I didn't know spoke to me. In spite of her hesitant manner, she began speaking with a certain obtrusiveness. She spoke as if she knew all about me, and intuitively I realized that this very woman was the "real author." The image I had secretly cherished of her reflected an unconscious vanity and hope, and, as I wrote earlier, was associated with the word "beautiful"; but it was rude to the "real author" to look so crestfallen when I realized that it wasn't really appropriate. (Not only is it simply not my style to explain in detail how it was inappropriate, but it would be discourteous.) And then she asked me to join her for lunch since she hadn't eaten, and, unable to resist, I answered that I had eaten but would keep her company with a cup of tea or something. We sat opposite each other at a window table in a coffee shop near the park entrance, where she ordered the most expensive roast beef sandwich, and crabmeat salad and coffee; I ordered just a cup of coffee. I actually don't remember most of what we talked about, except that she discussed the as-yet-unwritten story "Platonic Love," accompanied by the crunching sound of lettuce and celery being chewed. Yes, the "real author" discussed "Platonic Love," pausing to lick off her fingers any juice that dropped from her roast beef sandwich. Not only did I miss my chance to ask her what her motives were in sending me those letters, I also had to pay the bill for her sandwich, salad, and three cups of coffee. It was about three o'clock when I returned to the inn.

I know I should have written my "Platonic Love," but now I feel no great desire nor any great need to do so.

When I got back home, there was a letter from the "real author," as I expected, but it contained no particular thank-you for the lunch; it was the manuscript of "Platonic Love" that she had spoken about then.

I've tried and tried to convince myself that I should be able to get by without reading it. It would be extremely simple to throw it in the garbage or burn it without reading it. It would be easy to stretch out my hand to the letter on my desk, with my name written in that awful handwriting (which looks exactly as if I had written it myself), and dispose of it so completely that I would never have to think it had ever existed. I could take the letters (all the letters she's sent) out into the garden, douse them with kerosene, and strike a match. I would have to fill a bucket with water and be careful to control the fire. In a very short time, flames would lick at those letters and swallow them up, sending up a pale purple smoke; and only a light pile of crumbling black ashes would remain, to be drenched with water and trampled into the ground. But I sink into my chair with the hopeless feeling that nothing would have been destroyed. In the end I will probably publish "Platonic Love." And I will probably say it is my work.

[1979]

Translated by
Amy Vladeck Heinrich

QUESTIONS

1. What does the story imply about the relationship between the narrator–author and the "real author"?
2. What is Kanai suggesting about the muse of creativity? About authorship? About literary imagination?
3. How is the story's title part of its meaning?

John Kasaipwalova

(b. 1949)

Papua New Guinea

Much of the background to John Kasaipwalova's "Betel Nut Is Bad Magic for Airplanes" is recent history. When Kasaipwalova published his short story in 1972 (in *The Night Warrior and Other Stories from Papua New Guinea*, edited by Ulli Beier), the country was in the last stages of Australian administration as a United Nations trusteeship. Although the situation might not have been "colonial" in the manner in which England and France governed their colonies, in practice the context was quite similar. Australian officials were disliked, and their actions often were regarded as petty attempts to maintain the status quo.

In "Betel Nut Is Bad Magic for Airplanes," the conflict between the Aussies and the Papua New Guineans is largely verbal, a linguistic exercise of wit, which we see as soon as the narrator talks to the policemen in standard English. Although he may not be able to articulate his dilemma precisely, the narrator demonstrates a concerted effort to remain a part of his culture, his tradition. One way of retaining that context is verbally, by refusing to give in and use the oppressor's language, except in the instance of necessity. (In Papua New Guinea, there are roughly 715 indigenous languages. English is spoken by only 1 or 2 percent of the population, though Pidgin English, used throughout much of the story, is widespread.) As for the regulation concerning betel nuts, the problem is not the nuts themselves but the chewer's urge to spit.

John Kasaipwalova was born in Okaidoka Village on Kiriwina Island of the Trobriand Island Group, Milne Bay Province, in 1949. He was handed over to his maternal uncle to be brought up and trained as a chief. However, the boy's father (a Catholic convert) foiled the plan by sending him to a Catholic school. As a result of his excellent academic record, Kasaipwalova earned a scholarship at the University of Queensland to study Veterinary Science. That degree was never completed. In 1970, Kasaipwalova enrolled at the University of Papua New Guinea, where he was active in both literary groups and politics. He published two volumes of poems: *Hanuabada* (1972) and *Reluctant Flame* (1972). With Greg Murphy he collaborated on a folk opera called *Sail the Midnight Sun* (1980). In recent years, he has been active politically and involved in several business ventures.

Betel Nut Is Bad Magic for Airplanes

One Saturday afternoon in May 22 this year some of we university students went to meet our people at Jacksons Airport in Seven Mile. They arrived and we happy very much. Then we all comes to that backyard corner. That one place where Ansett and TAA[1] capsize boxes for native people who go by plane.

We was standing about thirty of we, waiting to catch our things. We was chewing plenty buwa[2] like civilized people. We was not spitting or making rubbish. Only feeling very good from the betel nuts our people had bringed to Moresby.

Then for nothing somebody in brown uniform with cap like pilot, and wearing boots like dimdim[3] and black belt, he comes up to one our people and he gives some Motu and English. That one our people didn't understood. So soon that uniform man was redding his eyes and rubbing his teeths just like white man's puppy dog. Maybe something like five minutes died but still he talk. Bloody bastard! He wanted our people to stop chewing buwa because TAA and Ansett jets had come and plenty plenty white people inside the terminal. They must not be offended to see us chew betel nut. Anyways, this brown puppy dog of white man angried himself for nothing. His anger now made big big pumpkin inside his throat for because he was "educated native" and he didn't wanted kanaka[4] natives doing like that in front of Europeans.

Soon quickly one native uni. gel[5] student seen what's happening. She goes and she asks why he was giving Motu and English to our people. He whyed. She seen quickly that his why is no good. So the uni. gel student she says to him to go away. Chewing buwa is our custom for many, many civilizations. Bloody bastard! Maybe this one first time natives talked him like that way, because quickly he becomes more angry. He started talking big and making his fingers round like hard cricket ball.

I seen what's hairpin too and I fright really true. But I walks over and I asks. The uni. gel she explains and he talks also. We talk loud and many peoples they see us too and he say, "Stop being cheeky. Just shut up and do what I tell you. You are breaking the law!" So I says, "What law are we breaking? Tell me! What ordinance are we breaking?"

The puppy he gets very angry and he say "Don't be smart! Just shut up and stop chewing betel nut. You are breaking the law!"

Then my anger really wanted to stand its feet, so I says "Bull shit. We are neither spitting nor throwing rubbish. Black people never made that law and this is black people's land. There's no such law."

"All right you think you smart! You want me to report the boss?"

"I don't know your boss. Run to him if you want to smell his boots. Go on report if you want!"

His face smoked and he walked away to get his boss. I says good words to our people and we continue chewing our buwa. We was really getting tired. Our boxes sleeping somewhere we donno. I chewed my buwa but little bit my stomach was frighten because the security man will bring his boss. Then maybe big trouble! Bloody bastard!

[1]*Ansett and TAA* Ansett Airline and Trans-Australian Airline

[2]*buwa* betel nut

[3]*dimdim* white man

[4]*kanaka* native

[5]*uni. gel* university girl

Not long. Soon the brown puppy dog comes with their white papa dog and two other brown puppy dogs too. They was all wearing khaki uniforms, caps, boots and black belts. They seen us and we seen them too. They come to us. My heart started winking and breathing very fast. The white papa dog, his face like one man I seen one day near Boroko R. S. L. Club.[6]

O sori! I looks at him and truly my chest wanted to run away. His bigness, his face red and especially his big big beer stomach, they frighten me already. Maybe if you seen him too, ei, you will really laugh. Bloody bastard! His stomach was too big for him. I can seen how his belt was trying its best to hold the big swelling together. His brown shirt was really punished and all of we can sees how it wanted to break. But no matter, because the stomach was trying to fall down over the black belt like one full up bilum[7] bag.

Me, it was already nearly too much. I straighten my legs quickly because something like water was falling down my leg inside my long trousers. I dunno what something and maybe only my fright trying his luck on me. But I didn't look at my long trousers. Too many people watching and also my head was boiling sweat from the hotness.

Anyways, the security guards came to us. But now we three university students, we was standing together and looking them very proudly. Too late now. We was not going to run any more. We decided to defend our rights. At first they didn't know what to say and only they talked quietly inside their throats. Then their boss, the Australian papa with big stomach, he started showing we his teeths. Oi, we was frighten by his hard voice. He says to me, "Listen boy, who gave you permission to chew betel nut here? You are breaking the law, the legal laws of this land. And when they (pointing to his puppies) told you to stop, you said you didn't believe in the law and will continue to break the law!"

Straightaway my face blooded because many black, white and yellow people, they was watching us too and this white papa dog, he was talking bad like that way to me. Plenty times I hear white people calling black men "bois" so this time I hear it and my mind was already fire. I wanted to give him some. Maybe good English or maybe little bit Strine.[8] So I says loudly to him, "All right white man, on what moral grounds is it unlawful for me to chew betel nut here? This is a free country of which we black people are citizens and unless you can show me the moral basis for your 'so called laws' I cannot recognize and therefore comply to that law!"

Well, he was very very angry now because one black man answering him in very good English. Maybe he didn't understand what I say.

"Listen boy, don't be smart. You are breaking the law and the law is laid down by the lawful government in the book."

I knows straightaway that he is another one of those ignorant, uneducated white men. I getting very angry too.

"O. K. then, show me that ordinance which specifically lays down that we natives are not allowed to chew betel nut within the precincts of an air terminal, in our own country. As a citizen I have at least the right to be shown that law

[6]*Boroko R. S. L. Club* Boroko Return Service League Club

[7]*bilum* local string bag

[8]*Strine* Australian

before you crassly accuse me of breaking the law. Until such times as you do so we shall consider you a liar and one using his delegated authority to intimidate the black people of Niugini."

"Shut up! You are nothing more than a cheeky brat!"

"Your resorting to insults is unwarranted here. All I'm demanding from you is the proof for the existence of such a law. Come on show me the exact ordinance."

"I don't have to show you the written ordinance. The lawful authority is vested in me as an officer to arrest you if I want to. It's written in Commonwealth Safety Regulations Act, section 32."

"Bull shit. I want to see it with my own eyes! Listen mate. Why aren't you arresting those white kids inside the terminal for chewing P. K.?[9] What's the difference between their P. K. inside the terminal and our betel nut outside on the road pavement?"

"Shut up you cheeky brat!" Then he wanted to grab my little neck. I was only short so I jumped back and he missed. But his face was red fire. "Since you are not going to obey, we shall arrest you!"

He was making we feel like we was some "bad cowboys" or criminals. All we three university students we was already hotted up and we was arguing with him very loudly. But when he tried that one on me, that was finish for everything. I lost my manners. I lost my calmness and also my boiling anger and fear. My heart was knocking my chest very hard. Only one thing I wanted to be—a true kanaka. So I threw my voice at him nearly spitting his face.

"Don't you dare lay hands on me white boi. This is black man's country and we have the right to make our laws to suit us. Commonwealth government is not the Nuigini House of Assembly. If you think your laws are justified, you are nothing more than a bloody white racist! A bloody white racist, you hear!"

I was shaking. The overseas people who was arrived and also black people, they was watching. Our people was just waiting for him to hit me and then they would finish him on the spot. Maski[10] Bomana.[11] We will only eat rice and have good times there. The Australian papa dog, he seen too many black faces around him. Too much for him. I think our argument already full him up. He starts walking away and threatening we.

"We'll fix you, you cheeky brat! Don't you run away. I'm going to ring the police."

"Ring the police if you want to! Always like you white racists. Each time you know you are wrong or want to bully us black people, you have to use the police on us."

The brown puppy dogs didn't know what to do so they followed their white boss, the papa dog with big stomach. I think all the water in my blood was all red now. I breathing very fast but maybe that was because I already frighten about the coming of the police. I seen many times how they do to protect white men's lives or property. Only last week I seen them hitting some Chimbu men because they was enjoying life from drinks. I wanted to throw some stones at the police cars but they was too fast and they took the Chimbu men away to kalabus.[12]

[9]*P. K.* a brand of chewing gum

[10]*Maski* never mind

[11]*Bomana* location of prison

[12]*kalabus* prison

Then something maybe like five minutes and we hear big siren noise. Two blue polis cars and one big lorry. That one had gorilla wire all around it and truly big enough to capture maybe twenty or thirty natives inside it. The cars and the lorry was all for we three university students. They stopped the traffic and about six black polis bois jumped down. I was really frighten. But papa dog he gets his courage and they march to us. We was standing calmly, because we was ready now. Any time! The polis bois they seen us not making big trouble so they run away with the big lorry, but they stopped the two blue cars.

They comes marching up to we and our people. Also university bus already come and we busy loading up the boxes, bags of yams and drums. But papa dog he no play now. Bloody bastard! His teeths was already making noise to the polis bois.

"Officer I want you to charge him now."

The polis bois they look very stupid because they didn't know what's up. Only I can seen their eyes. They was very hungry and truly wanted to catch us because white man he said to them. My anger comes back to my head very quickly. I happy little bit, but, because the polis bois was black men and not white.

"Officer before you charge me, I would like to know what you are charging me for and perhaps, allow me to give my side of the story."

The officer he stands very stupidly. He has no words to say. So white papa dog he tells him more.

"Officer, I want you to charge him with the use of obscene language in public and also breach of the Commonwealth Safety Regulations Act, section thirty-two."

All of we was too surprised and we make one big whistle because he was already lying.

"Obscene language, my foot! All right if you reckon I used obscene language, just exactly what words did I use? Go on, tell the officer the exact words I used."

"Officer charge him. I wouldn't even repeat the words in front of the lady, in any case."

The lady who papa dog was pointing to, she was the university gel student with us. So she says, "Officer I don't mind at all, just ask him to prove to us what obscene words we used."

The polis bois they says nothing only wanting to take us away to kalabus.

"Officer they have breached the law under section 32 of the Commonwealth Safety Regulations Act and he was using very insulting language something like 'this is bloody, black fella's country.' I have my witnesses here." He showed them his puppy dogs.

We knewed fully he was truly telling lie. He only want to kalabus we because we was opened our mouths against him.

"Look officer this man is lying and we have here at least thirty witnesses to tell you exactly what I said. I called him a bloody white racist which is what he really is. I had simply questioned him his rights to force us to stop chewing betel nut here. We weren't throwing rubbish or spitting."

The polis bois was getting very annoyed and they wanted to catch me. But I was only very small and I jumped back. Then one officer he say, "You have to come to the police station."

"What for?" I asks very angry. "We've done nothing wrong. If you are going to believe the word of this white man against our thirty witnesses right here, then I suggest that you are nothing more than puppet tools for white man."

My words hit their shame because many black people was watching them too. Quickly they didn't like me. Bloody bastards! They want to friend with white man.

"Just shut up and come to the police station!"

Truly by now I wanted to give them some. But oi, their size and also their big boots! If they give me one, I will really have many holes in my bottom. But I says maski.

"You can't arrest me without telling me what the charges are. Let go my hands! We came to see that our people get to the university and I'm not going anywhere until our people are comfortably seen back to the university!"

I run away free and we start our people into the bus. The polis bois and the white papa dog, they didn't know what to do, so they was standing there like bamboo, all empty. Soon our peoples they come back to university in the bus and we three university students, we goes and we argue some more.

In the end, they tells we three to get into the police car. We goes in but then we sees how the polis bois was going to leave the papa dog behind and take us to Boroko Police Station. So we quickly opens the doors and we runs out. They catch us very quickly again then I says loudly, "We are not going to the police station unless that white man also comes with us. It's hardly justifiable for the police to be his spokesman because this will conveniently screen him from any embarrassment."

What can they do? They knows they was wrong so they calls him back. They pushed we into the back seat, then they opens the front door for the papa dog. So I talks loudly and strong.

"Get in there white man!"

He blooded more and we laugh inside. The polis they was all very silent. We speeded to Boroko Police Station. I knows that place often.

They bringed us to one big table and many police men behind it. The papa dog he didn't waste time. He open one book and he show them.

"I want you to charge them for trespassing under section thirty-two. Under this regulation I have the authority to arrest or have arrested any persons I see to be causing danger to the safety of aeroplanes. . . ."

Then I know he was truly telling more lies and I shout straightaway. "What a lot of rubbish. We weren't carrying anything inflammable. We were simply chewing betel nut on the road pavement outside the terminal."

The white sergeant police, he turns fastly and like one lion's mouth, he yells me, "Listen boy, keep your mouth shut!"

His voice was too big for me. His eyes wanted to shoot and his blue uniform swelling from his fatness. I wanted to say more. But too late! I sees his bigness and I hear his voice and that one finished me up quick. Anyways we was very tired now and we shut up good. Maybe we let him give us some now and maybe later we fight him inside court house. So the papa dog gives more lies.

"I also want to charge him with the use of obscene language in a public place. He was using the words and I quote 'this is fuckin black fellas' country.'"

He tell them more and he shows them more from his book. But the police sergeant and his bois didn't knew what means "obscene language." They look for one dictionary and we was standing there like five or maybe ten minutes waiting for them. They didn't find what means that word. I seen the sergeant pull one telephone and talks to it.

Like two minutes later, we was took to one office inside, near the back. That one office, his name CIB[13] office. We walks in, the four of we and we seen one man sitting inside. He looks like very important man. Long trousers, shoes and tie. We sit down and again the papa dog he starts more talking. Ei, he talks very long, and this making me feel like one real "bad" cowboy or something. Finally the important man shut him up.

"You can either charge him with one or the other. With regards to the section thirty-two, a similar case took place in Lae last year and I remember clearly the new precedent set then. If you want to charge him with that you have to write away for the Controller General's permission from Melbourne."

The papa dog, he nearly cried because he knewed and we knewed that he wronged all the time. Then my turn for explain. I told him about the argument and everything.

"I have my two witnesses here to testify. I didn't use 'fuckin black fellas' country." I do admit having spoken to him in a firm voice but what I called him was a 'bloody white racist.' As far as I'm concerned these are not obscene words. They are political terms which I often ascribe to persons committing injustice to others, and I would just as readily call a black man a 'bloody black racist' if I saw him committing an injustice to a man of another ethnic origin."

The important man held his head for long time and we wait like sleeping pigs. Then he looks up and writes down the white man's name, address and phone. After that he told him to go. I wanted to say something but my mouth shut very quickly. The important man, he writes our names in his book then he say, "I will notify you on Monday as to what the charge will be. In the meantime you may go."

We walk out and we was feeling little bit happy. But I remember we have no money for bus to Waigani. The police they should pay us. So I walks back to the CIB office. "Sir the police had inconvenienced us in the first place and I think it is only right they should take us back to the university."

The important man walk out with us to the front office and he called on sergeant.

"Sergeant, arrange for a car to take these students safely to the university, will you?"

That one sergeant same one before. He didn't like it, to treat us good. We three university students, we come back to Waigani. We was chewing our betel nut on the way.

[1972]

QUESTIONS

1. Is the protest by the students a success or a failure? Do they gain anything or do they lose?
2. Why does the narrator keep using Western expressions such as "bad cowboy"?
3. If chewing betel nut is offensive to the Europeans, what equivalent object and/or custom by the Australians might be offensive to the Papua New Guineans?

[13]*CIB* Criminal Investigation Branch

KHAMSING SRINAWK

(b. 1930)

THAILAND

Khamsing Srinawk, who has written under the pseudonym Lao Khamhawm, was born in 1930 in a small village in northeastern Thailand. Although his family was poor and uneducated, he was encouraged by an uncle who was a monk to pursue his intellectual interests. As his translator, Domnern Garden, notes, when Khamsing completed secondary school, "his older brother gave him a pair of shoes so he could go to Bangkok to pursue his driving ambition to be a writer." Khamsing studied economics at Thammasart University in Bangkok and briefly studied journalism while supporting himself through writing news and feature articles for local newspapers. Before pursuing his literary career in earnest, he served as a forest ranger in northern Thailand and as an assistant to a group of anthropological researchers in a village near Bangkok. His first collection of short stories, *No Barriers*, was published in 1958; *The Politician and Other Stories* appeared in 1972.

Srinawk spent a year in the United States working with a publishing house and subsequently traveled in Europe and Africa as an official guest of several governments as an observer in both literary and agricultural capacities. He currently resides on his farm in Korat Province, Thailand, with his family.

The Gold-Legged Frog

The sun blazed as if determined to crisp every living thing in the broad fields. Now and again the tall, straight, isolated *sabang* and *payom* trees let go some of their dirty yellow leaves. He sank exhausted against a tree trunk with his dark blue shirt wet with sweat. The expanse round him expressed total dryness. He stared at the tufts of dull grass and bits of straw spun in a column to the sky. The brown earth sucked up into the air cast a dark pall over everything. A whirlwind. He recalled the old people had told him this was the portent of drought, want, disaster and death, and he was afraid. He was now anxious to get home; he could see the tips of the bamboo thickets surrounding the house far ahead looking like blades of grass. But he hesitated. A moment before reaching the shade of the tree he felt his ears buzz and his eyes blur and knew it meant giddiness and sunstroke. He looked at the soles of his feet blistered from the burning sandy ground and became indescribably angry—angry with the weather capable of such endless torture. In the morning the cold had pierced his bones, but now it was so hot he felt his head would break into bits and pieces. As he remembered the biting cold of the morning, he thought again of his little son.

That same morning he and two of his small children went out into the dry paddy fields near the house to look for frogs for the morning meal. The air was so chilly the two children on either side of him shivered as they stopped to look for frogs hiding in the cracks of the parched earth. Each time they saw two bright eyes in a deep crack, they would shout, "Pa, here's another one. Pa, this crack has two. Gold-legged ones! Hurry, Pa."

He dashed from place to place as the voices called him, prying up the dry clods with his hoe. He caught some of the frogs immediately, but a few jumped away as soon as he began digging. It was the children's job to chase and pounce on them. Many got away. Some jumped into different fissures obliging him to pry up a new cake of earth. If his luck was good, besides the frog, he would find a land snail or razor clam buried waiting for the rains. He would take these as well.

The air was warming and already he had enough frogs to eat with the morning rice. The sound of drumming, the village chief's call for a meeting, sounded faintly from the village. Vague anger again spilled over as his thoughts returned to that moment. If only he had gone home then the poor child would be all right now. It was really the last crack. As soon as he poked it, the ground broke apart. A fully grown gold-legged frog as big as a thumb leaped past the bigger child. The younger raced after it for about twelve yards when it dodged into the deep hoofprint of a water buffalo. The child groped after it. And then he was shocked almost senseless by the trembling cry of his boy, "Pa, a snake, a snake bit my hand."

A cobra spread its hood, hissing. When finally able to act, the father with all his strength brought the handle of his hoe three times down on the back of the serpent leaving its tail twitching. He carried his child and the basket of frogs home without forgetting to tell the other to drag the snake along as well.

On the way back his son cried softly and moaned, beating his chest with his fists and complaining he could not breathe. At home, the father summoned all the faith-healers and herbalists whose names he could think of and the turmoil began.

"Chop up a frog, roast it, and put it on the wound," a neighbour called out.

When another shouted, "Give him the toasted liver of the snake to eat," he hurriedly slit open the snake to look for the liver while his wife sat by crying. The later it got, the bigger the crowd. On hearing the news, all the neighbours attending the village chief's meeting joined the others. One of them told him he had to go to the District Office in town that day because the village chief told them it was the day the government was going to hand out money to those with five or more children, and he was one who had just five. It was a new shock.

"Can't you see my boy's gasping out his life? How can I go?"

"What difference will it make? You've called in a lot of doctors, all of them expert."

"Go, you fool. It's two hundred baht[1] they're giving. You've never had that much in your life-time. Two hundred!"

"Leave this for a bit," another added. "If the boy dies, you'll be out, that's all."

"I won't go," he yelled. "My child can't breathe and you tell me to go. Why can't they give it out some other day? It's true I've never had two hundred baht since I was born, but I'm not going. I'm not going."

"Jail," another interjected. "If you don't go, you simply go to jail. Whoever disobeyed the authorities? If they decide to give, you have to take, if not, jail."

[1]*baht* monetary unit of Thailand

The word "jail" repeated like that affected him, but still, he resisted.

"Whatever it is, I said I'm not going. I don't want it. How can I leave him when he's dying?" He raised his voice. "I'm not going."

"You go. Don't go against the government. We're subjects." He turned to find the village chief standing grimly at his side. His voice dried up immediately.

"If I don't go, will it really be jail?" he asked.

"For sure," the village chief replied sternly. "Maybe for life."

That was all there was to it. Dazed, he asked the faith-healers and neighbours to take care of his son and left the house.

He reached the District Office almost at eleven and he found a group of his neighbours who had also come for the money sitting in a group. They told him to address the old deputy district officer which he did.

"I am Mr. Nark Na-ngarm, sir, I have come for the money, the many children money."

The deputy district officer raised his fat face to stare at him for a moment then spoke heavily. "Idiot, don't you have eyes to see people are working. Get out! Get out and wait outside."

"But, sir, my child is dying." But he cut himself short when he thought perhaps if the official suspected that his child had died there would be trouble. The deputy officer looked down at his paper and went on scribbling. Nark dejectedly joined the group outside. "All one does is suffer, born a rice farmer and a subject," he thought. "Poor and helpless, one's mouth stained from eating roots when the rice has run out, at the end of one's tether, you turn to the authorities only to be put down." The official continued to write as if there were no groups of peasants waiting anxiously. A few minutes after twelve, he strode from the office but had the kindness to say a few words.

"It's noon already. Time for a break. Come back at one o'clock for it."

Nark and his neighbours sat there waiting until one o'clock. The taciturn deputy on returning called them all to sit on the floor near him. He began by asking each of them why they had so many children. The awkward replies of the peasants brought guffaws from the other officials who turned to listen to the embarrassing answers. At last it had to be his turn.

"Who is Mr. Nark Na-ngarm?"

"I am, sir," he responded with humility.

"And now why do we have such a lot of children?"

Several people tittered.

"Oh, when you're poor, sir . . . ," he burst out, his exasperation uncontrollable.

"What the hell's it got to do with being poor?" the deputy officer questioned in a voice that showed disappointment with the answer.

"So poor and no money to buy a blanket. The kids just keep coming."

Instead of laughter, dead silence, finally broken by the dry voice of the blank-faced deputy, "Bah! This joker uses his wife for a blanket."

The wind gusted again. The *sabang* and *payom* trees threw off a lot of leaves. The spears of sunlight still dazzled him. The whirlwind still hummed in the middle of the empty ricefield ahead. Nark left the shade of the tall tree and went through the flaming afternoon sunshine heading for his village.

"Hey, Nark. . . ." The voice came from a group of villagers still some distance away. It was topped by another.

"You sure are lucky." The words raised his spirits. He smiled a little before repeating expectantly, "How was I lucky, how?"

"The two hundred baht. You got it, didn't you?"

"I got it. It's right here." He patted his pocket.

"What luck! You sure have good luck, Nark. One more day and you'd have been out by two hundred baht."

[1958]

Translated by
DOMNERN GARDEN

QUESTIONS

1. What is the conflict in the story? How does it reveal Nark's economic position and the limits of his choices?
2. In what way is the ending of the story ironic? How is "luck" defined?
3. How does the detailed description of the setting contribute to your understanding of the exigencies of poverty faced by Nark's family and their neighbors?
4. Compare this story with Mark Twain's "Luck."

PÄR LAGERKVIST

(1891–1974)

SWEDEN

Considered one of the foremost figures in Swedish literature of the twentieth century, Pär Lagerkvist was a prolific playwright, novelist, poet, and essayist, though most highly regarded in his own country as a dramatist. He received the Nobel Prize for Literature in 1951. Born into a conservative religious family, Lagerkvist studied briefly at the University of Uppsala and then went to Paris, where he was deeply influenced by the French modernist and symbolist painters as well as by the playwright Strindberg. His early poetry, breaking from traditional forms in its allegiance to the experiments of abstract expressionism, established his reputation as a major new voice in Swedish literature.

Returning to Scandinavia to live in Denmark, Lagerkvist was horrified by World War I and the rise of fascism. His despair and his preoccupation with the relation between good and evil became, and remained, a central theme of his fiction. Calling himself "a believer without faith," Lagerkvist explored metaphysical and moral issues in his fiction and plays, focusing on the relationship between human beings and God as well as the modern tension between science and faith.

Less interested in realism than in symbolic expressions of his themes and ideas, Lagerkvist frequently incorporated elements from folklore, myth, and fable into half a dozen volumes of short stories, several novellas, and a number of novels. *Barrabas* (1950), a novel based on the imagined moral crisis of a minor character in the New Testament, first introduced English readers to his work and was promptly praised as a masterpiece of historical imagination.

"The Children's Campaign"—from the collection of stories titled *The Marriage Feast*—is a Swiftian satire that mocks the practice of war, gaining further effect through its resonances with actual events of two world wars in the twentieth century. As Robert Donald Spector observes, "Beyond the fantasy of Lagerkvist's story stands the actuality of the youth movements in Mussolini's Italy and Hitler's Germany."

The Children's Campaign

Even the children at that time received military training, were assembled in army units and exercised just as though on active service, had their own headquarters and annual manoeuvres when everything was conducted as in a real state of war. The grown-ups had nothing directly to do with this training; the children actually exercised themselves and all command was entrusted to them. The only use made of adult experience was to arrange officers' training courses for specially suitable boys, who were chosen with the greatest care and who were then put in charge of the military education of their comrades in the ranks.

These schools were of high standing and there was hardly a boy throughout the land who did not dream of going to them. But the entrance tests were particularly hard; not only a perfect physique was required but also a highly developed intelligence and character. The age of admission was six to seven years and the small cadets then received an excellent training, both purely military and in all other respects, chiefly the further moulding of character. It was also greatly to one's credit in after life to have passed through one of these schools. It was really on the splendid foundation laid here that the quality, organization and efficiency of the child army rested.

Thereafter, as already mentioned, the grown-ups in no way interfered but everything was entrusted to the children themselves. No adult might meddle in the command, in organizational details or matters of promotion. Everything was managed and supervised by the children; all decisions, even the most vital, being reached by their own little general staff. No one over fourteen was allowed. The boys then passed automatically into the first age-group of the regular troops with no mean military training already behind them.

The large child army, which was the object of the whole nation's love and admiration, amounted to three army corps of four divisions: infantry, light field artillery, medical and service corps. All physically fit boys were enrolled in it and a large number of girls belonged to it as nurses, all volunteers.

Now it so happened that a smaller, quite insignificant nation behaved in a high-handed and unseemly way toward its powerful neighbour, and the insult was all the greater since this nation was by no means an equal. Indignation was great and general and, since people's feelings were running high, it was necessary to rebuke the malapert and at the same time take the chance to subjugate the country in question. In this situation the child army came forward and through its high command asked to be charged with the crushing and subduing of the foe. The news of this caused a sensation and a wave of fervour throughout the country. The proposal was given serious consideration in supreme quarters and as a result the commission was given, with some hesitation, to the children. It was in fact a task well suited to this army, and the people's obvious wishes in the matter had also to be met, if possible.

The Foreign Office therefore sent the defiant country an unacceptable ultimatum and, pending the reply, the child army was mobilized within twenty-four hours. The reply was found to be unsatisfactory and war was declared immediately.

Unparalleled enthusiasm marked the departure for the front. The intrepid little youngsters had green sprigs in the barrels of their rifles and were pelted with flowers. As is so often the case, the campaign was begun in the spring, and this time the general opinion was that there was something symbolic in it. In the capital the little commander-in-chief and chief of general staff, in the presence of huge crowds, made a passionate speech to the troops in which he expressed the gravity of the hour and his conviction of their unswerving valour and willingness to offer their lives for their country.

The speech, made in a strong voice, aroused the greatest ecstasy. The boy—who had a brilliant career behind him and had reached his exalted position at the age of only twelve and a half—was acclaimed with wild rejoicing and from this moment was the avowed hero of the entire nation. There was not a dry eye, and those of the many mothers especially shone with pride and happiness. For them it was the greatest day in their lives. The troops marched past below fluttering banners, each regiment with its music corps at the head. It was an unforgettable spectacle.

There were also many touching incidents, evincing a proud patriotism, as when a little four-year-old, who had been lifted up on his mother's arm so that he could see, howled with despair and shouted, "I want to go, too. I want to go, too!" while his mother tried to hush him, explaining that he was too small. "Small am I, eh?" he exclaimed, punching her face so that her nose bled. The evening papers were full of such episodes showing the mood of the people and of the troops who were so sure of victory. The big march past was broadcast and the C.-in-C.'s speech, which had been recorded, was broadcast every evening during the days that followed, at 7.15 P.M.

Military operations had already begun, however, and reports of victory began to come in at once from the front. The children had quickly taken the offensive and on one sector of the front had inflicted a heavy defeat on the enemy, seven hundred dead and wounded and over twelve hundred prisoners, while their own losses amounted to only a hundred or so fallen. The victory was celebrated at home with indescribable rejoicing and with thanksgiving services in the churches. The newspapers were filled with accounts of individual instances of valour and pictures several columns wide of the high command, of which the leading personalities, later so well-known, began to appear now for the first time. In their joy, mothers and aunts sent so much chocolate and other sweets to the army that headquarters had to issue a strict order that all such parcels were, for the time being at any rate, forbidden, since they had made whole regiments unfit for battle and these in their turn had nearly been surrounded by the enemy.

For the child army was already far inside enemy territory and still managed to keep the initiative. The advance sector did retreat slightly in order to establish contact with its wings, but only improved its positions by so doing. A stalemate ensued in the theatre of war for some time after this.

During July, however, troops were concentrated for a big attack along the whole line and huge reserves—the child army's, in comparison with those of its opponent, were almost inexhaustible—were mustered to the front. The new offensive, which lasted for several weeks, resulted, too, in an almost decisive victory for the whole army, even though casualties were high. The children defeated the enemy all along the line, but did not manage to pursue him and thereby exploit their success to the full, because he was greatly favoured by the fact that his legs were so much longer, an advantage of which he made good use. By dint of forced marches, however, the children finally succeeded in cutting the enemy's right flank to pieces. They were now in the very heart of the country and their outposts were only a few days' march from the capital.

It was a pitched battle on a big scale and the newspapers had enormous headlines every day which depicted the dramatic course of events. At set hours the radio broadcast the gunfire and a résumé of the position. The war correspondents described in rapturous words and vivid colours the state of affairs at the front—the children's incredible feats, their indomitable courage and self-sacrifice, the whole morale of the army. It was no exaggeration. The youngsters showed the greatest bravery; they really behaved like heroes. One only had to see their discipline and contempt of death during an attack, as though they had been grown-up men at least.

It was an unforgettable sight to see them storm ahead under murderous machine-gun fire and the small medical orderlies dart nimbly forward and pick them up as they fell. Or the wounded and dying who were moved behind the front, those who had had a leg shot away or their bellies ripped open by a bayonet so that their entrails hung out—but without one sound of complaint crossing their small lips. The hand-to-hand fighting had been very fierce and a great number of children fell in this, while they were superior in the actual firing. Losses were estimated at 4,000 on the enemy side and 7,000 among the children, according to the secret reports. The victory had been hard won but all the more complete.

This battle became very famous and was also of far greater importance than any previously. It was now clear beyond all doubt that the children were incomparably superior in tactics, discipline and individual courage. At the same time, however, it was admitted by experts that the enemy's head-long retreat was very skilfully carried out, that his strength was evidently in defence and that he should not be underrated too much. Toward the end, also, he had unexpectedly made a stubborn resistance which had prevented any further penetration.

This observation was not without truth. In actual fact the enemy was anything but a warlike nation, and indeed his forces found it very difficult to hold their own. Nevertheless, they improved with practice during the fighting and became more efficient as time went on. This meant that they caused the children a good deal of trouble in each succeeding battle. They also had certain advantages on their side. As their opponents were so small, for instance, it was possible after a little practice to spit several of them on the bayonet at once, and often a kick was enough to fell them to the ground.

But against this, the children were so much more numerous and also braver. They were everywhere. They swarmed over one and in between one's legs and the unwarlike people were nearly demented by all these small monsters who fought like fiends. Little fiends was also what they were generally called—not without reason—and this name was even adopted in the children's homeland, but there it was a mark of honour and a pet name. The enemy troops had all their work cut out merely defending themselves. At last, however, they were able to check the others' advance and even venture on one or two counter-attacks. Everything then came to a standstill for a while and there was a breathing-space.

The children were now in possession of a large part of the country. But this was not always so easy. The population did not particularly like them and proved not to be very fond of children. It was alleged that snipers fired on the boys from houses and that they were ambushed when they moved in small detachments. Children had even been found impaled on stakes or with their eyes gouged out, so it was said. And in many cases these stories were no doubt true. The population had quite lost their heads, were obviously goaded into a frenzy, and as they were of little use as a warlike nation and their cruelty could therefore find no natural outlet, they tried to revenge themselves by atrocities. They felt overrun by all the foreign children as by troublesome vermin and, being at their wits' end, they simply killed whenever they had the chance. In order to put an end to these outrages the children burned one village after the other and shot hundreds of people daily, but this did not improve matters. The despicable deeds of these craven guerrillas caused them endless trouble.

At home, the accounts of all this naturally aroused the most bitter resentment. People's blood boiled to think that their small soldiers were treated in this way by those who had nothing to do with the war, by barbarous civilians who had no notion of established and judicial forms. Even greater indignation was caused, however, by an incident that occurred inside the occupied area some time after the big summer battle just mentioned.

A lieutenant who was out walking in the countryside came to a stream where a large, fat woman knelt washing clothes. He asked her the way to a village close by. The woman, who probably suspected him of evil intent, retorted, "What are you doing here? You ought to be at home with your mother." Whereupon the lieutenant drew his sabre to kill her, but the woman grabbed hold of him and, putting him over her knee, thwacked him black and blue with her washboard so that he was unable to sit down for several days afterward. He was so taken aback that he did nothing, armed though he was to the teeth. Luckily no one saw the incident, but there were orders that all outrages on the part of the population were to be reported to headquarters. The lieutenant therefore duly reported what had happened to him. True, it gave him little satisfaction, but as he had to obey orders he had no choice. And so it all came out.

The incident aroused a storm of rage, particularly among those at home. The infamous deed was a humiliation for the country, an insult which nothing could wipe out. It implied a deliberate violation by this militarily ignorant people of the simplest rules of warfare. Everywhere, in the press, in propaganda speeches, in ordinary conversation, the deepest contempt and disgust for the deed was expressed. The lieutenant who had so flagrantly shamed the army had his officer's epaulettes ripped off in front of the assembled troops and was declared unworthy to serve any longer in the field. He was instantly sent home to his parents, who belonged to one of the most noted families but who now had to retire into obscurity in a remote part of the country.

The woman, on the other hand, became a heroic figure among her people and the object of their rapturous admiration. During the whole of the war she and her deed were a rallying national symbol which people looked up to and which spurred them on to further effort. She subsequently became a favourite motif in the profuse literature about their desperate struggle for freedom; a vastly popular figure, brought to life again and again as time passed, now in a rugged, everyday way which appealed to the man in the street, now in heroic female form on a grandiose scale, to become gradually more and more legendary, wreathed in saga and myth. In some versions she was shot by the enemy; in others she lived to a ripe old age, loved and revered by her people.

This incident, more than anything else, helped to increase the bad feelings between the two countries and to make them wage the war with ever greater ruthlessness. In the late summer, before the autumn rains began, both armies, ignorant of each other's plans, simultaneously launched a violent offensive, which devastated both sides. On large sectors of the front the troops completely annihilated each other so that there was not a single survivor left. Any peaceful inhabitants thereabouts who were still alive and ventured out of their cellars thought that the war was over, because all were slain.

But soon new detachments came up and began fighting again. Great confusion arose in other quarters from the fact that in the heat of attack men ran past each other and had to turn around in order to go on fighting; and that some parts of the line rushed ahead while others came behind, so that the troops were both in front of and behind where they should have been and time and again attacked each other in the rear. The battle raged in this way with extreme violence and shots were fired from all directions at once.

When at last the fighting ceased and stock was taken of the situation, it appeared that no one had won. On both sides there was an equal number of fallen, 12,924, and after all attacks and retreats the position of the armies was exactly the same as at the start of the battle. It was agreed that both should claim the victory. Thereafter the rain set in and the armies went to earth in trenches and put up barbed-wire entanglements.

The children were the first to finish their trenches, since they had had more to do with that kind of thing, and settled down in them as best they could. They soon felt at home. Filthy and lousy, they lived there in the darkness as though they had never done anything else. With the adaptability of children they quickly got into the way of it. The enemy found this more difficult; he felt miserable and home-sick for the life above ground to which he was accustomed. Not so the children. When one saw them in their small grey uniforms, which were caked thick with mud, and their small gas masks, one could easily think they had been born to this existence. They crept in and out of the holes down into the earth and scampered about the passages like mice. When their burrows were attacked they were instantly up on the parapet and snapped back in blind fury. As the months passed, this hopeless, harrowing life put endurance to an increasingly severe test. But they never lost courage or the will to fight.

For the enemy the strain was often too much; the glaring pointlessness of it all made many completely apathetic. But the little ones did not react like this. Children are really more fitted for war and take more pleasure in it, while grown-ups tire of it after a while and think it is boring. The boys continued to find the whole thing exciting and they wanted to go on living as they were now. They also had a more natural herd instinct; their unity and camaraderie helped them a great deal, made it easier to hold out.

But, of course, even they suffered great hardship. Especially when winter set in with its incessant rain, a cold sleet which made everything sodden and filled the trenches with mud. It was enough to unman anyone. But it would never have entered their heads to complain. However bad things were, nothing could have made them admit it. At home everyone was very proud of them. All the cinemas showed parades behind the front and the little C.-in-C. and his generals pinning medals for bravery on their soldiers' breasts. People thought of them a great deal out there, of their little fiends, realizing that they must be having a hard time.

At Christmas, in particular, thoughts went out to them, to the lighted Christmas trees and all the sparkling childish eyes out in the trenches; in every home people sat wondering how they were faring. But the children did not think of home. They were soldiers out and out, absorbed by their duty and their new life. They attacked in several places on the morning of Christmas Eve, inflicting fairly big losses on the enemy in killed and wounded, and did not stop until it was time to open their parcels. They had the real fighting spirit which might have been a lesson even to adults.

There was nothing sentimental about them. The war had hardened and developed them, made them men. It did happen that one poor little chap burst into tears when the Christmas tree was lighted, but he was made the laughing-stock of them all. "Are you homesick for your mummy, you bastard?" they said, and kept on jeering at him all evening. He was the object of their scorn all through Christmas; he behaved suspiciously and tried to keep to himself. Once he walked a hundred yards away from the post and, because he might well have been thinking of flight, he was seized and court-martialled. He could give no reason for having absented himself, and since he had obviously intended to desert he was shot.

If those at home had been fully aware of the morale out there, they need not have worried. As it was, they wondered if the children could really hold their ground and half-regretted having entrusted them with the campaign, now that it was dragging on so long because of this nerve-racking stationary warfare. After the New Year help was even offered in secret, but it was rejected with proud indignation.

The morale of the enemy, on the other hand, was not so high. They did intend to fight to the last man, but the certainty of a complete victory was not so general as it should have been. They could not help thinking, either, how hopeless their fight really was; that in the long run they could not hold their own against these people who were armed to the very milk teeth, and this often dampened their courage.

Hardly had nature begun to come to life and seethe with the newly awakened forces of spring before the children started with incredible intensity to prepare for the decisive battle. Heavy mechanized artillery was brought up and placed in strong positions; huge troop movements went on night and day; all available fighting forces were concentrated in the very front lines. After murderous gunfire which lasted for six days, an attack was launched with great force and extreme skill. Individual bravery was, if possible, more dazzling than ever. The whole army was also a year older, and that means much at that age. But their opponents, too, were determined to do their utmost. They had assembled all their reserves, and their spirits, now that the rain had stopped and the weather was fine, were full of hope.

It was a terrible battle. The hospital trains immediately started going back from both sides packed with wounded and dying. Machine guns, tanks and gas played fearful havoc. For several days the outcome was impossible to foresee, since both armies appeared equally strong and the tide of battle constantly changed. The position gradually cleared, however. The enemy had expected the main attack in the centre, but the child army turned out to be weakest there. Use was made of this, especially because they themselves were best prepared at this very point, and this part of the children's front was soon made to waver and was forced farther and farther back by repeated attack. Advantage was also taken of an ideal evening breeze from just the right quarter to gas the children in thousands. Encouraged by their victory, the troops pursued the offensive with all their might and with equal success.

The child army's retreat, however, turned out to be a stratagem, brilliantly conceived and carried out. Its centre gave way more and more and the enemy, giving all his attention to this, forgot that at the same time he himself was wavering on both wings. In this way he ran his head into a noose. When the children considered that they had retreated far enough they halted, while the troops on the outermost wings, already far ahead, advanced swiftly until they met behind the enemy's back. The latter's entire army was thereby surrounded and in the grip of an iron hand. All the children's army had to do now was to draw the noose tighter. At last the gallant defenders had to surrender and let themselves be taken prisoner, which in fact they already were. It was the most disastrous defeat in history; not a single one escaped other than by death.

This victory became much more famous than any of the others and was eagerly studied at all military academies on account of its brilliantly executed, doubly effective encircling movement. The great general Sludelsnorp borrowed its tactics outright seventy years later at his victory over the Slivokvarks in the year 2048.

The war could not go on any longer now, because there was nothing left to fight, and the children marched to the capital with the imprisoned army between them to dictate the peace terms. These were handed over by the little commander-in-chief in the hall of mirrors in the stately old palace at a historic scene which was to be immortalized time and again in art and even now was reproduced everywhere in the weekly press. The film cameras whirred, the flashlights hissed and the radio broadcast the great moment to the world. The commander-in-chief, with austere and haughty mien and one foot slightly in front of the other, delivered the historic document with his right hand. The first and most important condition was the complete cession of the country, besides which the expenses of its capture were to be borne by the enemy, who thus had to pay the cost of the war on both sides, the last clause on account of the fact that he had been the challenging party and, according to his own admission, the cause of the war. The document was signed in dead silence, the only sound was the scratching of the fountain pen, which, according to the commentator's whisper, was solid gold and undoubtedly a future museum piece.

With this, everything was settled and the children's army returned to its own country, where it was received with indescribable rapture. Everywhere along the roads the troops were greeted with wild rejoicing; their homecoming was one long victory parade. The march into the capital and the dismissal there of the troops, which took place before vast crowds, were especially impressive. People waved and shouted in the streets as they passed, were beside themselves with enthusiasm, bands played, eyes were filled with tears of joy. Some of the loudest cheering was for the small invalids at the rear of the procession, blind and with limbs amputated, who had sacrificed themselves for their country. Many of them had already got small artificial arms and legs so that they looked just the same as before. The victory salute thundered, bayonets flashed in the sun. It was an unforgettable spectacle.

A strange, new leaf was written in the great book of history which would be read with admiration in time to come. The nation had seen many illustrious deeds performed, but never anything as proud as this. What these children had done in their devotion and fervent patriotism could never be forgotten.

Nor was it. Each spring, on the day of victory, school children marched out with flags in their hands to the cemeteries with all the small graves where the heroes rested under their small white crosses. The mounds were strewn with flowers and passionate speeches were made, reminding everyone of the glorious past, their imperishable honour and youthful, heroic spirit of self-sacrifice. The flags floated in the sun and the voices rang out clear as they sang their rousing songs, radiant childish eyes looking ahead to new deeds of glory.

[1954]

Translated by
ALAN BLAIR

QUESTIONS

1. How does Lagerkvist make his premise of a children's army convincing? How does he use irony to reveal his actual view of war? Should children receive military training and fight in wars? Why or why not?
2. How do the matter-of-fact style and detached tone heighten the story's effect?
3. What is the purpose of the scene involving the fat woman who gives the young officer a spanking? What is being satirized in such details as the identical number of casualties for each side?
4. Is there any humor in the story? If so, where? Are some of the details shocking? Identify these aspects of the story.
5. What central ideas are implicitly developed in the story? What is the theme?

Margaret Laurence

(1926–1987)

Canada

One of Canada's most distinguished novelists, Margaret Wemyss Laurence was born in the provincial prairie town of Neepawa, Manitoba—a place she recreated in her fiction as Manawaka. Before she could celebrate its moral rootedness and castigate its snobbery and narrow-mindedness (as she does in her novels), she had to leave it. She studied English at United College, Winnipeg, while writing for the college paper and later the city paper. She married a civil engineer, Jack Laurence, whose work took them to England and West Africa. Laurence's African experiences in the 1950s, as a witness to the rough political transition from colonial satellites to independent states, form the subject of her early narratives, including *This Side Jordan* (1960).

Laurence, subsequently divorced, eventually returned to Canada, settling in Ontario, and wrote the novels that have made her distinguished reputation: *The Stone Angel* (1964), *A Jest of God* (1966), *The Fire-Dwellers* (1969), *A Bird in the House* (1970), and *The Diviners* (1974). *A Jest of God* was made into the film *Rachel, Rachel*. In her strong and introspective but often inwardly divided female characters, Laurence anticipated contemporary feminist issues, unerringly framing the dilemmas that mid-twentieth-century North American women had begun to face in seeking to define themselves through personal independence as well as significant relationships. In *The Diviners* (considered by most critics to be Laurence's masterpiece), the river that flows in two directions is a fitting symbol for the divided pulls of her characters.

• A Bird in the House •

The parade would be almost over by now, and I had not gone. My mother had said in a resigned voice, "All right, Vanessa, if that's the way you feel," making me suffer twice as many jabs of guilt as I would have done if she had lost her temper. She and Grandmother MacLeod had gone off, my mother pulling the low boxsleigh with Roddie all dolled up in his new red snowsuit, just the sort of little kid anyone would want people to see. I sat on the lowest branch of the birch tree in our yard, not minding the snowy wind, even welcoming its punishment. I went over my reasons for not going, trying to believe they were good and sufficient, but in my heart I felt I was betraying my father. This was the first time I had stayed away from the Remembrance Day parade. I wondered if he would notice that I was not there, standing on the sidewalk at the corner of River and Main while the parade passed, and then following to the Court House grounds where the service was held.

I could see the whole thing in my mind. It was the same every year. The Manawaka Civic Band always led the way. They had never been able to afford full uniforms, but they had peaked navy-blue caps and sky-blue chest ribbons. They were joined on Remembrance Day by the Salvation Army band, whose uniforms seemed too ordinary for a parade, for they were the same ones the bandsmen wore every Saturday night when they played "Nearer My God to Thee" at the foot of River Street. The two bands never managed to practise quite enough together, so they did not keep in time too well. The Salvation Army band invariably played faster, and afterwards my father would say irritably, "They play those marches just like they do hymns, blast them, as though they wouldn't get to heaven if they didn't hustle up." And my mother, who had great respect for the Salvation Army because of the good work they did, would respond chidingly, "Now, now, Ewen—" I vowed I would never say "Now, now" to my husband or children, not that I ever intended having the latter, for I had been put off by my brother Roderick, who was now two years old with wavy hair, and everyone said what a beautiful child. I was twelve, and no one in their right mind would have said what a beautiful child, for I was big-boned like my Grandfather Connor and had straight lanky black hair like a Blackfoot or Cree.

After the bands would come the veterans. Even thinking of them at this distance, in the white and withdrawn quiet of the birch tree, gave me a sense of painful embarrassment. I might not have minded so much if my father had not been among them. How could he go? How could he not see how they all looked? It must have been a long time since they were soldiers, for they had forgotten how to march in step. They were old—that was the thing. My father was bad enough, being almost forty, but he wasn't a patch on Howard Tully from the drugstore, who was completely grey-haired and also fat, or Stewart MacMurchie, who was bald at the back of his head. They looked to me like imposters, plump or spindly caricatures of past warriors. I almost hated them for walking in that limping column down Main. At the Court House, everyone would sing *Lord God of Hosts, be with us yet, lest we forget, lest we forget*. Will Masterson would pick up his old Army bugle and blow the last Post. Then it would be over and everyone could start gabbling once more and go home.

I jumped down from the birch bough and ran to the house, yelling, making as much noise as I could.

I'm a poor lonesome cowboy
An' a long way from home—

I stepped inside the front hall and kicked off my snow boots. I slammed the door behind me, making the dark ruby and emerald glass shake in the small leaded panes. I slid purposely on the hall rug, causing it to bunch and crinkle on the slippery polished oak of the floor. I seized the newel post, round as a head, and spun myself to and fro on the bottom stair.

I ain't got no father
To buy the clothes I wear.
I'm a poor lonesome—

At this moment my shoulders were firmly seized and shaken by a pair of hands, white and delicate and old, but strong as talons.

"Just what do you think you're doing, young lady?" Grandmother MacLeod enquired, in a voice like frost on a windowpane, infinitely cold and clearly etched.

I went limp and in a moment she took her hands away. If you struggled, she would always hold on longer.

"Gee, I never knew you were home yet."

"I would have thought that on a day like this you might have shown a little respect and consideration," Grandmother MacLeod said, "even if you couldn't make the effort to get cleaned up enough to go to the parade."

I realised with surprise that she imagined this to be my reason for not going. I did not try to correct her impression. My real reason would have been even less acceptable.

"I'm sorry," I said quickly.

In some families, *please* is described as the magic word. In our house, however, it was *sorry*.

"This isn't an easy day for any of us," she said.

Her younger son, my Uncle Roderick, had been killed in the Great War.[1] When my father marched, and when the hymn was sung, and when that unbearably lonely tune was sounded by the one bugle and everyone forced themselves to keep absolutely still, it would be that boy of whom she was thinking. I felt the enormity of my own offence.

"Grandmother—I'm sorry."

"So you said."

I could not tell her I had not really said it before at all. I went into the den and found my father there. He was sitting in the leather-cushioned armchair beside the fireplace. He was not doing anything, just sitting and smoking. I stood beside him, wanting to touch the light-brown hairs on his forearm, but thinking he might laugh at me or pull his arm away if I did.

"I'm sorry," I said, meaning it.

"What for, honey?"

"For not going."

"Oh—that. What was the matter?"

I did not want him to know, and yet I had to tell him, make him see.

"They look silly," I blurted. "Marching like that."

For a minute I thought he was going to be angry. It would have been a relief to me if he had been. Instead, he drew his eyes away from mine and fixed them above the mantelpiece where the sword hung, the handsome and evil-looking crescent in its carved bronze sheath that some ancestor had once brought from the Northern Frontier of India.

"Is that the way it looks to you?" he said.

I felt in his voice some hurt, something that was my fault. I wanted to make everything all right between us, to convince him that I understood, even if I did not. I prayed that Grandmother MacLeod would stay put in her room, and that my mother would take a long time in the kitchen, giving Roddie his lunch. I wanted my father to myself, so I could prove to him that I cared more about him than any of the others did. I wanted to speak in some way that would be more poignant and comprehending than anything of which my mother could possibly be capable. But I did not know how.

"You were right there when Uncle Roderick got killed, weren't you?" I began uncertainly.

"Yes."

[1]*Great War* World War I (1914–1918)

"How old was he, Dad?"

"Eighteen," my father said.

Unexpectedly, that day came into intense being for me. He had had to watch his own brother die, not in the antiseptic calm of some hospital, but out in the open, the stretches of mud I had seen in his snapshots. He would not have known what to do. He would just have had to stand there and look at it, whatever that might mean. I looked at my father with a kind of horrified awe, and then I began to cry. I had forgotten about impressing him with my perception. Now I needed him to console me for this unwanted glimpse of the pain he had once known.

"Hey, cut it out, honey," he said, embarrassed. "It was bad, but it wasn't all as bad as that part. There were a few other things."

"Like what?" I said, not believing him.

"Oh—I don't know," he replied evasively. "Most of us were pretty young, you know, I and the boys I joined up with. None of us had ever been away from Manawaka before. Those of us who came back mostly came back here, or else went no further away from town than Winnipeg. So when we were overseas—that was the only time most of us were ever a long way from home."

"Did you want to be?" I asked, shocked.

"Oh well—" my father said uncomfortably. "It was kind of interesting to see a few other places for a change, that's all."

Grandmother MacLeod was standing in the doorway.

"Beth's called you twice for lunch, Ewen. Are you deaf, you and Vanessa?"

"Sorry," my father and I said simultaneously.

Then we went upstairs to wash our hands.

That winter my mother returned to her old job as nurse in my father's medical practice. She was able to do this only because of Noreen.

"Grandmother MacLeod says we're getting a maid," I said to my father, accusingly, one morning. "We're not, are we?"

"Believe you me, on what I'm going to be paying her," my father growled, "she couldn't be called anything as classy as a maid. Hired girl would be more like it."

"Now, now, Ewen," my mother put in, "it's not as if we were cheating her or anything. You know she wants to live in town, and I can certainly see why, stuck out there on the farm, and her father hardly ever letting her come in. What kind of life is that for a girl?"

"I don't like the idea of your going back to work, Beth," my father said. "I know you're fine now, but you're not exactly the robust type."

"You can't afford to hire a nurse any longer. It's all very well to say the Depression won't last forever—probably it won't, but what else can we do for now?"

"I'm damned if I know," my father admitted. "Beth—"

"Yes?"

They both seemed to have forgotten about me. It was at breakfast, which we always ate in the kitchen, and I sat rigidly on my chair, pretending to ignore and thus snub their withdrawal from me. I glared at the window, but it was so thickly plumed and scrolled with frost that I could not see out. I glanced back to my parents. My father had not replied, and my mother was looking at him in that anxious and half-frowning way she had recently developed.

"What is it, Ewen?" Her voice had the same nervous sharpness it bore sometimes when she would say to me, "For mercy's sake, Vanessa, what is it *now*?" as though whatever was the matter, it was bound to be the last straw.

My father spun his sterling silver serviette ring, engraved with his initials, slowly around on the table.

"I never thought things would turn out like this, did you?"

"Please—" my mother said in a low strained voice, "please, Ewen, let's not start all this again. I can't take it."

"All right," my father said. "Only—"

"The MacLeods used to have money and now they don't," my mother cried. "Well, they're not alone. Do you think all that matters to me, Ewen? What I can't bear is to see you forever reproaching yourself. As if it were your fault."

"I don't think it's the comedown," my father said. "If I were somewhere else, I don't suppose it would matter to me, either, except where you're concerned. But I suppose you'd work too hard wherever you were—it's bred into you. If you haven't got anything to slave away at, you'll sure as hell invent something."

"What do you think I should do, let the house go to wrack and ruin? That would go over well with your mother, wouldn't it?"

"That's just it," my father said. "It's the damned house all the time. I haven't only taken on my father's house, I've taken on everything that goes with it, apparently. Sometimes I really wonder—"

"Well, it's a good thing I've inherited some practicality even if you haven't," my mother said. "I'll say that for the Connors—they aren't given to brooding, thank the Lord. Do you want your egg poached or scrambled?"

"Scrambled," my father said. "All I hope is that this Noreen doesn't get married straightaway, that's all."

"She won't," my mother said. "Who's she going to meet who could afford to marry?"

"I marvel at you, Beth," my father said. "You look as though a puff of wind would blow you away. But underneath, by God, you're all hardwood."

"Don't talk stupidly," my mother said. "All I hope is that she won't object to taking your mother's breakfast upon a tray."

"That's right," my father said angrily. "Rub it in."

"Oh Ewen, I'm sorry!" my mother cried, her face suddenly stricken. "I don't know why I say these things. I don't mean to."

"I know," my father said. "Here, cut it out, honey. Just for God's sake please don't cry."

"I'm sorry," my mother repeated, blowing her nose.

"We're both sorry," my father said. "Not that that changes anything."

After my father had gone, I got down from my chair and went to my mother.

"I don't want you to go back to the office. I don't want a hired girl here. I'll hate her."

My mother sighed, making me feel that I was placing an intolerable burden on her, and yet making me resent having to feel this weight. She looked tired, as she often did these days. Her tiredness bored me, made me want to attack her for it.

"Catch me getting along with a dumb old hired girl," I threatened.

"Do what you like," my mother said abruptly. "What can I do about it?"

And then, of course, I felt bereft, not knowing which way to turn.

My father need not have worried about Noreen getting married. She was, as it turned out, interested not in boys but in God. My mother was relieved about the boys but alarmed about God.

"It isn't natural," she said, "for a girl of seventeen. Do you think she's all right mentally, Ewen?"

When my parents, along with Grandmother MacLeod, went to the United Church every Sunday, I was made to go to Sunday school in the church basement, where there were small red chairs which humiliatingly resembled kindergarten furniture, and pictures of Jesus wearing a white sheet and surrounded by a whole lot of well-dressed kids whose mothers obviously had not suffered them to come unto Him until every face and ear was properly scrubbed. Our religious observances also included grace at meals, when my father would mumble "For what we are about to receive the Lord make us truly thankful Amen," running the words together as though they were one long word. My mother approved of these rituals, which seemed decent and moderate to her. Noreen's religion, however, was a different matter. Noreen belonged to the Tabernacle of the Risen and Reborn, and she had got up to testify no less than seven times in the past two years, she told us. My mother, who could not imagine anyone's voluntarily making a public spectacle of themselves, was profoundly shocked by this revelation.

"Don't worry," my father soothed her. "She's all right. She's just had kind of a dull life, that's all."

My mother shrugged and went on worrying and trying to help Noreen without hurting her feelings, by tactful remarks about the advisability of modulating one's voice when singing hymns, and the fact that there was plenty of hot water so Noreen really didn't need to hesitate about taking a bath. She even bought a razor and a packet of blades and whispered to Noreen that any girl who wore transparent blouses so much would probably like to shave under her arms. None of these suggestions had the slightest effect on Noreen. She did not cease belting out hymns at the top of her voice, she bathed once a fortnight, and the sorrel-coloured hair continued to bloom like a thicket of Indian paintbrush in her armpits.

Grandmother MacLeod refused to speak to Noreen. This caused Noreen a certain amount of bewilderment until she finally hit on an answer.

"Your poor grandma," she said. "She is deaf as a post. These things are sent to try us here on earth, Vanessa. But if she makes it into Heaven, I'll bet you anything she will hear clear as a bell."

Noreen and I talked about Heaven quite a lot, and also Hell. Noreen had an intimate and detailed knowledge of both places. She not only knew what they looked like — she even knew how big they were. Heaven was seventy-seven thousand miles square and it had four gates, each one made out of a different kind of precious jewel. The Pearl Gate, the Topaz Gate, the Amethyst Gate, the Ruby Gate — Noreen would reel them off, all the gates of Heaven. I told Noreen they sounded like poetry, but she was puzzled by my reaction and said I shouldn't talk that way. If you said poetry, it sounded like it was just made up and not really so, Noreen said.

Hell was larger than Heaven, and when I asked why, thinking of it as something of a comedown for God, Noreen said naturally it had to be bigger because there were a darn sight more people there than in Heaven. Hell was one hundred and ninety million miles deep and was in perpetual darkness, like a cave or under the sea. Even the flames (this was the awful thing) *did not give off any light*.

I did not actually believe in Noreen's doctrines, but the images which they conjured up began to inhabit my imagination. Noreen's fund of exotic knowledge was not limited to religion, although in a way it all seemed related. She could do many things which had a spooky tinge to them. Once when she was making a cake, she found we had run out of eggs. She went outside and gathered a bowl of fresh snow and used it instead. The cake rose like a charm, and I stared at Noreen as though she were a sorceress. In fact, I began to think of her as a sorceress, someone not quite of this earth. There was nothing unearthly about her broad shoulders and hips and her forest of dark red hair, but even these features took on a slightly sinister significance to me. I no longer saw her through the eyes or the expressed opinions of my mother and father, as a girl who had quit school at grade eight and whose life on the farm had been endlessly drab. I knew the truth—Noreen's life had not been drab at all, for she dwelt in a world of violent splendours, a world filled with angels whose wings of delicate light bore real feathers, and saints shining like the dawn, and prophets who spoke in ancient tongues, and the ecstatic souls of the saved, as well as denizens of the lower regions—mean-eyed imps and crooked cloven-hoofed monsters and beasts with the bodies of swine and the human heads of murderers, and lovely depraved jezebels torn by dogs through all eternity. The middle layer of Creation, our earth, was equally full of grotesque presences, for Noreen believed strongly in the visitation of ghosts and the communication with spirits. She could prove this with her Ouija board. We would both place our fingers lightly on the indicator, and it would skim across the board and spell out answers to our questions. I did not believe wholeheartedly in the Ouija board, either, but I was cautious about the kind of question I asked, in case the answer would turn out unfavourable and I would be unable to forget it.

One day Noreen told me she could also make a table talk. We used the small table in my bedroom, and sure enough, it lifted very slightly under our fingertips and tapped once for *Yes*, twice for *No*. Noreen asked if her Aunt Ruthie would get better from the kidney operation, and the table replied *No*. I withdrew my hands.

"I don't want to do it any more."

"Gee, what's the matter, Vanessa?" Noreen's plain placid face creased in a frown. "We only just begun."

"I have to do my homework."

My heart lurched as I said this. I was certain Noreen would know I was lying, and that she would know not by any ordinary perception, either. But her attention had been caught by something else, and I was thankful, at least until I saw what it was.

My bedroom window was not opened in the coldest weather. The storm window, which was fitted outside as an extra wall against the winter, had three small circular holes in its frame so that some fresh air could seep into the house. The sparrow must have been floundering in the new snow on the roof, for it had crawled in through one of these holes and was now caught between the two layers of glass. I could not bear the panic of the trapped bird, and before I realised what I was doing, I had thrown open the bedroom window. I was not releasing the sparrow into any better a situation, I soon saw, for instead of remaining quiet and allowing us to catch it in order to free it, it began flying blindly around the room, hitting the lampshade, brushing against the walls, its wings seeming to spin faster and faster.

I was petrified. I thought I would pass out if those palpitating wings touched me. There was something in the bird's senseless movements that revolted me. I also thought it was going to damage itself, break one of those thin wing-bones, perhaps, and then it would be lying on the floor, dying, like the pimpled and horribly featherless baby birds we saw sometimes on the sidewalks in the spring when they had fallen out of their nests. I was not any longer worried about the sparrow. I wanted only to avoid the sight of it lying broken on the floor. Viciously, I thought that if Noreen said, *God sees the little sparrow fall*, I would kick her in the shins. She did not, however, say this.

"A bird in the house means a death in the house," Noreen remarked.

Shaken, I pulled my glance away from the whirling wings and looked at Noreen.

"What?"

"That's what I've heard said, anyhow."

The sparrow had exhausted itself. It lay on the floor, spent and trembling. I could not bring myself to touch it. Noreen bent and picked it up. She cradled it with great gentleness between her cupped hands. Then we took it downstairs, and when I had opened the back door, Noreen set the bird free.

"Poor little scrap," she said, and I felt struck to the heart, knowing she had been concerned all along about the sparrow, while I, perfidiously, in the chaos of the moment, had been concerned only about myself.

"Wanna do some with the ouija board, Vanessa?" Noreen asked.

I shivered a little, perhaps only because of the blast of cold air which had come into the kitchen when the door was opened.

"No thanks, Noreen. Like I said, I got my homework to do. But thanks all the same."

"That's okay," Noreen said in her guileless voice. "Any time."

But whenever she mentioned the Ouija board or the talking table, after that, I always found some excuse not to consult these oracles.

"Do you want to come to church with me this evening, Vanessa?" my father asked.

"How come you're going to the evening service?" I enquired.

"Well, we didn't go this morning. We went snowshoeing instead, remember? I think your grandmother was a little bit put out about it. She went alone this morning. I guess it wouldn't hurt you and me, to go now."

We walked through the dark, along the white streets, the snow squeaking dryly under our feet. The streetlights were placed at long intervals along the sidewalks, and around each pole the circle of flimsy light created glistening points of blue and crystal on the crusted snow. I would have liked to take my father's hand, as I used to do, but I was too old for that now. I walked beside him, taking long steps so he would not have to walk more slowly on my account.

The sermon bored me, and I began leafing through the Hymnary for entertainment. I must have drowsed, for the next thing I knew, my father was prodding me and we were on our feet for the closing hymn.

Near the Cross, near the Cross,
Be my glory ever,
Till my ransomed soul shall find
Rest beyond the river.

I knew the tune well, so I sang loudly for the first verse. But the music to that hymn is sombre, and all at once the words themselves seemed too dreadful to be sung. I stopped singing, my throat knotted. I thought I was going to cry, but I did not know why, except that the song recalled to me my Grandmother Connor, who had been dead only a year now. I wondered why her soul needed to be ransomed. If God did not think she was good enough just as she was, then I did not have much use for His opinion. *Rest beyond the river*—was that what had happened to her? She had believed in Heaven, but I did not think that rest beyond the river was quite what she had in mind. To think of her in Noreen's flashy Heaven, though—that was even worse. Someplace where nobody ever got annoyed or had to be smoothed down and placated, someplace where there were never any family scenes—that would have suited my Grandmother Connor. Maybe she wouldn't have minded a certain amount of rest beyond the river, at that.

When we had the silent prayer, I looked at my father. He sat with his head bowed and his eyes closed. He was frowning deeply, and I could see the pulse in his temple. I wondered then what he believed. I did not have any real idea what it might be. When he raised his head, he did not look uplifted or anything like that. He merely looked tired. Then Reverend McKee pronounced the benediction, and we could go home.

"What do you think about all that stuff, Dad?" I asked hesitantly, as we walked.

"What stuff, honey?"

"Oh, Heaven and Hell, and like that."

My father laughed. "Have you been listening to Noreen too much? Well, I don't know. I don't think they're actual places. Maybe they stand for something that happens all the time here, or else doesn't happen. It's kind of hard to explain. I guess I'm not so good at explanations."

Nothing seemed to have been made any clearer to me. I reached out and took his hand, not caring that he might think this a babyish gesture.

"I hate that hymn!"

"Good Lord," my father said in astonishment. "Why, Vanessa?"

But I did not know and so could not tell him.

Many people in Manawaka had flu that winter, so my father and Dr. Cates were kept extremely busy. I had flu myself, and spent a week in bed, vomiting only the first day and after that enjoying poor health, as my mother put it, with Noreen bringing me ginger ale and orange juice, and each evening my father putting a wooden tongue-depressor into my mouth and peering down my throat, then smiling and saying he thought I might live after all.

Then my father got sick himself, and had to stay at home and go to bed. This was such an unusual occurrence that it amused me.

"Doctors shouldn't get sick," I told him.

"You're right," he said. "That was pretty bad management."

"Run along now, dear," my mother said.

That night I woke and heard voices in the upstairs hall. When I went out, I found my mother and Grandmother MacLeod, both in their dressing-gowns. With them was Dr. Cates. I did not go immediately to my mother, as I would have done only a year before. I stood in the doorway of my room, squinting against the sudden light.

"Mother—what is it?"

She turned, and momentarily I saw the look on her face before she erased it and put on a contrived calm.

"It's all right," she said. "Dr. Cates has just come to have a look at Daddy. You go on back to sleep."

The wind was high that night, and I lay and listened to it rattling the storm windows and making the dry and winter-stiffened vines of the Virginia creeper scratch like small persistent claws against the red brick. In the morning, my mother told me that my father had developed pneumonia.

Dr. Cates did not think it would be safe to move my father to the hospital. My mother began sleeping in the spare bedroom, and after she had been there for a few nights. I asked if I could sleep in there too. I thought she would be bound to ask me why, and I did not know what I would say, but she did not ask. She nodded, and in some way her easy agreement upset me.

That night Dr. Cates came again, bringing with him one of the nurses from the hospital. My mother stayed upstairs with them. I sat with Grandmother MacLeod in the living room. That was the last place in the world I wanted to be, but I thought she would be offended if I went off. She sat as straight and rigid as a totem pole, and embroidered away at the needlepoint cushion cover she was doing. I perched on the edge of the chesterfield and kept my eyes fixed on *The White Company* by Conan Doyle, and from time to time I turned a page. I had already read it three times before, but luckily Grandmother MacLeod did not know that. At nine o'clock she looked at her gold brooch watch, which she always wore pinned to her dress, and told me to go to bed, so I did that.

I wakened in darkness. At first, it seemed to me that I was in my own bed, and everything was as usual, with my parents in their room, and Roddie curled up in the crib in his room, and Grandmother MacLeod sleeping with her mouth open in her enormous spool bed, surrounded by half a dozen framed photos of Uncle Roderick and only one of my father, and Noreen snoring fitfully in the room next to mine, with the dark flames of her hair spreading out across the pillow, and the pink and silver motto cards from the Tabernacle stuck with adhesive tape onto the wall beside her bed—*Lean on Him, Emmanuel Is My Refuge, Rock of Ages Cleft for Me.*

Then in the total night around me, I heard a sound. It was my mother, and she was crying, not loudly at all, but from somewhere very deep inside her. I sat up in bed. Everything seemed to have stopped, not only time but my own heart and blood as well. Then my mother noticed that I was awake.

I did not ask her, and she did not tell me anything. There was no need. She held me in her arms, or I held her, I am not certain which. And after a while the first mourning stopped, too, as everything does sooner or later, for when the limits of endurance have been reached, then people must sleep.

In the days following my father's death, I stayed close beside my mother, and this was only partly for my own consoling. I also had the feeling that she needed my protection. I did not know from what, nor what I could possibly do, but something held me there. Reverend McKee called, and I sat with my grandmother and my mother in the living room. My mother told me I did not need to stay unless I wanted to, but I refused to go. What I thought chiefly was that he would speak of the healing power of prayer, and all that, and it would be bound to make my mother cry again. And in fact, it happened in just that way, but when it actually came, I could not protect her from this assault. I could only sit there and pray my own prayer, which was that he would go away quickly.

My mother tried not to cry unless she was alone or with me. I also tried, but neither of us was entirely successful. Grandmother MacLeod, on the other hand, was never seen crying, not even the day of my father's funeral. But that day, when we had returned to the house and she had taken off her black velvet overshoes and her heavy sealskin coat with its black fur that was the softest thing I had ever touched, she stood in the hallway and for the first time she looked unsteady. When I reached out instinctively towards her, she sighed.

"That's right," she said. "You might just take my arm while I go upstairs, Vanessa."

That was the most my Grandmother MacLeod ever gave in, to anyone's sight. I left her in her bedroom, sitting on the straight chair beside her bed and looking at the picture of my father that had been taken when he graduated from medical college. Maybe she was sorry now that she had only the one photograph of him, but whatever she felt, she did not say.

I went down into the kitchen. I had scarcely spoken to Noreen since my father's death. This had not been done on purpose. I simply had not seen her. I had not really seen anyone except my mother. Looking at Noreen now, I suddenly recalled the sparrow. I felt physically sick, remembering the fearful darting and plunging of those wings, and the fact that it was I who had opened the window and let it in. Then an inexplicable fury took hold of me, some terrifying need to hurt, burn, destroy. Absolutely without warning, either to her or to myself, I hit Noreen as hard as I could. When she swung around, appalled, I hit out at her once more, my arms and legs flailing. Her hands snatched at my wrists, and she held me, but still I continued to struggle, fighting blindly, my eyes tightly closed, as though she were a prison all around me and I was battling to get out. Finally, too shocked at myself to go on, I went limp in her grasp and she let me drop to the floor.

"Vanessa! I never done one single solitary thing to you, and here you go hitting and scratching me like that! What in the world has got into you?"

I began to say I was sorry, which was certainly true, but I did not say it. I could not say anything.

"You're not yourself, what with your dad and everything," she excused me. "I been praying every night that your dad is with God, Vanessa. I know he wasn't actually saved in the regular way, but still and all—"

"Shut up," I said.

Something in my voice made her stop talking. I rose from the floor and stood in the kitchen doorway.

"He didn't need to be saved," I went on coldly, distinctly. "And he is not in Heaven, because there is no Heaven. And it doesn't matter, see? *It doesn't matter!*"

Noreen's face looked peculiarly vulnerable now, her high wide cheekbones and puzzled childish eyes, and the thick russet tangle of her hair. I had not hurt her much before, when I hit her. But I had hurt her now, hurt her in some inexcusable way. Yet I sensed, too, that already she was gaining some satisfaction out of feeling sorrowful about my disbelief.

I went upstairs to my room. Momentarily I felt a sense of calm, almost of acceptance. *Rest beyond the river.* I knew now what that meant. It meant Nothing. It meant only silence, forever.

Then I lay down on my bed and spent the last of my tears, or what seemed then to be the last. Because, despite what I had said to Noreen, it did matter. It mattered, but there was no help for it.

Everything changed after my father's death. The MacLeod house could not be kept up any longer. My mother sold it to a local merchant who subsequently covered the deep red of the brick over with yellow stucco. Something about the house had always made me uneasy—that tower room where Grandmother MacLeod's potted plants drooped in a lethargic and lime-green confusion, those long stairways and hidden places, the attic which I had always imagined to be dwelt in by the spirits of the family dead, that gigantic portrait of the Duke of Wellington at the top of the stairs. It was never an endearing house. And yet when it was no longer ours, and when the Virginia creeper had been torn down and the dark walls turned to a light marigold, I went out of my way to avoid walking past, for it seemed to me that the house had lost the stern dignity that was its very heart.

Noreen went back to the farm. My mother and brother and myself moved into Grandfather Connor's house. Grandmother MacLeod went to live with Aunt Morag in Winnipeg. It was harder for her than for anyone, because so much of her life was bound up with the MacLeod house. She was fond of Aunt Morag, but that hardly counted. Her men were gone, her husband and her sons, and a family whose men are gone is no family at all. The day she left, my mother and I did not know what to say. Grandmother MacLeod looked even smaller than usual in her fur coat and her black velvet toque. She became extremely agitated about trivialities, and fussed about the possibility of the taxi not arriving on time. She had forbidden us to accompany her to the station. About my father, or the house, or anything important, she did not say a word. Then, when the taxi had finally arrived, she turned to my mother.

"Roddie will have Ewen's seal ring, of course, with the MacLeod crest on it," she said. "But there is another seal as well, don't forget, the larger one with the crest and motto. It's meant to be worn on a watch chain. I keep it in my jewel-box. It was Roderick's. Roddie's to have that, too, when I die. Don't let Morag talk you out of it."

During the Second World War, when I was seventeen and in love with an airman who did not love me, and desperately anxious to get away from Manawaka and from my grandfather's house, I happened one day to be going through the old mahogany desk that had belonged to my father. It had a number of small drawers inside, and I accidentally pulled one of these all the way out. Behind it there was another drawer, one I had not known about. Curiously, I opened it. Inside there was a letter written on almost transparent paper in a cramped angular handwriting. It began—*Cher Monsieur Ewen*—That was all I could make out, for the writing was nearly impossible to read and my French was not good. It was dated 1919. With it, there was a picture of a girl, looking absurdly old-fashioned to my eyes, like the faces on long-discarded calendars or chocolate boxes. But beneath the dated quality of the photograph, she seemed neither expensive nor cheap. She looked like what she probably had been—an ordinary middle-class girl, but in another country. She wore her hair in long ringlets, and her mouth was shaped into a sweetly sad posed smile like Mary Pickford's. That was all. There was nothing else in the drawer.

I looked for a long time at the girl, and hoped she had meant some momentary and unexpected freedom. I remembered what he had said to me, after I hadn't gone to the Remembrance Day parade.

"What are you doing, Vanessa?" my mother called from the kitchen.

"Nothing," I replied.

I took the letter and picture outside and burned them. That was all I could do for him. Now that we might have talked together, it was many years too late. Perhaps it would not have been possible anyway. I did not know.

As I watched the smile of the girl turn into scorched paper, I grieved for my father as though he had just died now.

[1970]

QUESTIONS

1. What aspects of religious faith and doubt, as well as conceptions of heaven and hell, trouble Vanessa MacLeod? How does she resolve her spiritual questions?
2. What is Noreen's role in the story?
3. What kind of childhood and family are described in the story?
4. Why does Vanessa burn the photograph and letter that had belonged to her father?
5. Compare this story with Mary Lavin's "Happiness," particularly concerning spiritual belief and a daughter's response to the death of a parent.

MARY LAVIN

(b. 1912)

IRELAND

The only child of Irish parents, Mary Lavin was born in the United States but grew up in Ireland, where her parents returned to live in Dublin when she was nine. She studied literature at University College, Dublin; while completing a doctoral study of Virginia Woolf, she taught French and English at a convent school. From scholarly writing Lavin turned to writing fiction, publishing her first story in 1938. Her first collection of stories, *Tales from Bective Bridge* (1942), which included a number of autobiographical stories, was awarded a major literary prize. Many of her subsequent stories first appeared in *The New Yorker*. During the years between 1942 and 1954, Lavin was married, raising three children while producing four collections of fiction and two novels (*The House on Cleve Street*, 1945, and *Mary O'Grady*, 1950). When her husband died in 1954, Lavin, left with few financial or emotional resources, virtually stopped writing. Later, through the support of a Jesuit priest, she returned to her writing; they subsequently married after he left his order.

Lavin has published 14 volumes of short stories and has received a number of awards for her fiction. She is frequently compared to such masters of the story form as Chekhov and Mansfield for her finely crafted stories, her lyrical prose, and her rich evocation of the lives of sensitive people struggling with moral and spiritual questions.

Happiness

Mother had a lot to say. This does not mean she was always talking but that we children felt the wells she drew upon were deep, deep, deep. Her theme was happiness: what it was, what it was not; where we might find it, where not; and how, if found, it must be guarded. Never must we confound it with pleasure. Nor think sorrow its exact opposite.

"Take Father Hugh," Mother's eyes flashed as she looked at him. "According to him, sorrow is an ingredient of happiness—a *necessary* ingredient, if you please!" And when he tried to protest she put up her hand. "There may be a freakish truth in the theory—for some people. But not for me. And not, I hope, for my children." She looked severely at us three girls. We laughed. None of us had had much experience with sorrow. Bea and I were children and Linda only a year old when our father died suddenly after a short illness that had not at first seemed serious. "I've known people to make sorrow a *substitute* for happiness," Mother said.

Father Hugh protested again. "You're not putting me in that class, I hope?"

Father Hugh, ever since our father died, had been the closest of anyone to us as a family, without being close to any one of us in particular—even to Mother. He lived in a monastery near our farm in County Meath, and he had been one of the celebrants at the Requiem High Mass our father's political importance had demanded. He met us that day for the first time, but he took to dropping in to see us, with the idea of filling the crater of loneliness left at our centre. He did not know that there was a cavity in his own life, much less that we would fill it. He and Mother were both young in those days, and perhaps it gave scandal to some that he was so often in our house, staying till late into the night and, indeed, thinking nothing of stopping all night if there was any special reason, such as one of us being sick. He had even on occasion slept there if the night was too wet for tramping home across the fields.

When we girls were young, we were so used to having Father Hugh around that we never stood on ceremony with him but in his presence dried our hair and pared our nails and never minded what garments were strewn about. As for Mother—she thought nothing of running out of the bathroom in her slip, brushing her teeth or combing her hair, if she wanted to tell him something she might otherwise forget. And she brooked no criticism of her behaviour. "Celibacy was never meant to take all the warmth and homeliness out of their lives," she said.

On this point, too, Bea was adamant. Bea, the middle sister, was our oracle. "I'm so glad he *has* Mother," she said, "as well as her having him, because it must be awful the way most women treat them—priests, I mean—as if they were pariahs. Mother treats him like a human being—that's all."

And when it came to Mother's ears that there had been gossip about her making free with Father Hugh, she opened her eyes wide in astonishment. "But he's only a priest!" she said.

Bea giggled. "It's a good job he didn't hear *that*," she said to me afterwards. "It would undo the good she's done him. You'd think he was a eunuch."

"Bea!" I said. "Do you think he's in love with her?"

"If so, he doesn't know it," Bea said firmly. "It's her soul he's after! Maybe he wants to make sure of her in the next world!"

But thoughts of the world to come never troubled Mother. "If anything ever happens to me, children," she said, "suddenly, I mean, or when you are not near me, or I cannot speak to you, I want you to promise you won't feel bad. There's no need! Just remember that I had a happy life—and that if I had to choose my kind of heaven I'd take it on this earth with you again, no matter how much you might annoy me!"

You see, annoyance and fatigue, according to Mother, and even illness and pain, could coexist with happiness. She had a habit of asking people if they were happy at times and in places that—to say the least of it—seemed to us inappropriate. "But are you happy?" she'd probe as one lay sick and bathed in sweat, or in the throes of a jumping toothache. And once in our presence she made the inquiry of an old friend as he lay upon his deathbed.

"Why not?" she said when we took her to task for it later. "Isn't it more important than ever to be happy when you're dying? Take my own father! You know what he said in his last moments? On his deathbed, he defied me to name a man who had enjoyed a better life. In spite of dreadful pain, his face *radiated* happiness!" Mother nodded her head comfortably. "Happiness drives out pain, as fire burns out fire."

Having no knowledge of our own to pit against hers, we thirstily drank in her rhetoric. Only Bea was sceptical. "Perhaps you *got* it from him, like spots, or fever," she said. "Or something that could at least be slipped from hand to hand."

"Do you think I'd have taken it if that were the case!" Mother cried. "Then, when he needed it most?"

"Not there and then!" Bea said stubbornly. "I meant as a sort of legacy."

"Don't you think in *that* case," Mother said, exasperated, "he would have felt obliged to leave it to your grandmother?"

Certainly we knew that in spite of his lavish heart our grandfather had failed to provide our grandmother with enduring happiness. He had passed that job on to Mother. And Mother had not made too good a fist of it, even when Father was living and she had him—and later, us children—to help.

As for Father Hugh, he had given our grandmother up early in the game. "God Almighty couldn't make that woman happy," he said one day, seeing Mother's face, drawn and pale with fatigue, preparing for the nightly run over to her own mother's flat that would exhaust her utterly.

There were evenings after she came home from the library where she worked when we saw her stand with the car keys in her hand, trying to think which would be worse—to slog over there on foot, or take out the car again. And yet the distance was short. It was Mother's day that had been too long.

"Weren't you over to see her this morning?" Father Hugh demanded.

"No matter!" said Mother. She was no doubt thinking of the forlorn face our grandmother always put on when she was leaving. ("Don't say good night, Vera," Grandmother would plead. "It makes me feel too lonely. And you never can tell—you might slip over again before you go to bed!")

"Do you know the time?" Bea would say impatiently, if she happened to be with Mother. Not indeed that the lateness of the hour counted for anything, because in all likelihood Mother *would* go back, if only to pass by under the window and see that the lights were out, or stand and listen and make sure that as far as she could tell all was well.

"I wouldn't mind if she was happy," Mother said.

"And how do you know she's not?" we'd ask.

"When people are happy, I can feel it. Can't you?"

We were not sure. Most people thought our grandmother was a gay creature, a small birdy being who even at a great age laughed like a girl, and—more remarkably—sang like one, as she went about her day. But beak and claw were of steel. She'd think nothing of sending Mother back to a shop three times if her errands were not exactly right. "Not sugar like that—that's *too* fine; it's not castor sugar I want. But *not* as coarse as *that*, either. I want an in-between kind."

Provoked one day, my youngest sister, Linda, turned and gave battle. "You're mean!" she cried. "You love ordering people about!"

Grandmother preened, as if Linda had acclaimed an attribute. "I was always hard to please," she said. "As a girl, I used to be called Miss Imperious."

And Miss Imperious she remained as long as she lived, even when she was a great age. Her orders were then given a wry twist by the fact that as she advanced in age she took to calling her daughter Mother, as we did.

There was one great phrase with which our grandmother opened every sentence: "if only." "If only," she'd say, when we came to visit her—"if only you'd come earlier, before I was worn out expecting you!" Or if we were early, then if only it was later, after she'd had a rest and could enjoy us, be *able* for us. And if we brought her flowers, she'd sigh to think that if only we'd brought them the previous day she'd have had a visitor to appreciate them, or say it was a pity the stems weren't longer. If only we'd picked a few green leaves, or included some buds, because, she said disparagingly, the poor flowers we'd brought were already wilting. We might just as well not have brought them! As the years went on, Grandmother had a new bead to add to her rosary: if only her friends were not all dead! By their absence, they reduced to nil all *real* enjoyment in anything. Our own father—her son-in-law—was the one person who had ever gone close to pleasing her. But even here there had been a snag. "If only he was my real son!" she used to say with a sigh.

Mother's mother lived on through our childhood and into our early maturity (though she outlived the money our grandfather left her), and in our minds she was a complicated mixture of valiance and defeat. Courageous and generous within the limits of her own life, her simplest demand was yet enormous in the larger frame of Mother's life, and so we never could see her with the same clarity of vision with which we saw our grandfather, or our own father. Them we saw only through Mother's eyes.

"Take your grandfather!" she'd cry, and instantly we'd see him, his eyes burning upon us—yes, upon *us*, although in his day only one of us had been born: me. At another time, Mother would cry, "Take your own father!" and instantly we'd see *him*—tall, handsome, young, and much more suited to marry one of us than poor bedraggled Mother.

Most fascinating of all were the times Mother would say "Take me!" By magic then, staring down the years, we'd see blazingly clear a small girl with black hair and buttoned boots, who, though plain and pouting, burned bright, like a star. "I was happy, you see," Mother said. And we'd strain hard to try and understand the mystery of the light that still radiated from her. "I used to lean along a tree that grew out over the river," she said, "and look down through the grey leaves at the water flowing past below, and I used to think it was not the stream that flowed but me, spread-eagled over it, who flew through the air! Like a bird! That I'd found the secret!" She made it seem there might *be* such a secret, just waiting to be found. Another time she'd dream that she'd be a great singer.

"We didn't know you sang, Mother!"

She had to laugh. "Like a crow," she said.

Sometimes she used to think she'd swim the Channel.

"Did you swim *that* well, Mother?"

"Oh, not really—just the breast stroke," she said. "And then only by the aid of two pig bladders blown up by my father and tied around my middle. But I used to throb—yes, throb—with happiness."

Behind Mother's back, Bea raised her eyebrows.

What was it, we used to ask ourselves—that quality that she, we felt sure, misnamed? Was it courage? Was it strength, health, or high spirits? Something you could not give or take—a conundrum? A game of catch-as-you-can?

"I know," cried Bea. "A sham!"

Whatever it was, we knew that Mother would let no wind of violence from within or without tear it from her. Although, one evening when Father Hugh was with us, our astonished ears heard her proclaim that there might be a time when one had to slacken hold on it—let go—to catch at it again with a surer hand. In the way, we supposed, that the high-wire walker up among the painted stars of his canvas sky must wait to fling himself through the air until the bar he catches at has started to sway perversely from him. Oh no, no! That downward drag at our innards we could not bear, the belly swelling to the shape of a pear. Let happiness go by the board. "After all, lots of people seem to make out without it," Bea cried. It was too tricky a business. And might it not be that one had to be born with a flair for it?

"A flair would not be enough," Mother answered. "Take Father Hugh. He, if anyone, had a flair for it—a natural capacity! You've only to look at him when he's off guard, with you children, or helping me in the garden. But he rejects happiness! He casts it from him."

"That is simply not true, Vera," cried Father Hugh, overhearing her. "It's just that I don't place an inordinate value on it like you. I don't think it's enough to carry one all the way. To the end, I mean—and after."

"Oh, don't talk about the end when we're only in the middle," cried Mother. And, indeed, at that moment her own face shone with such happiness it was hard to believe that earth was not her heaven. Certainly it was her constant contention that of happiness she had had a lion's share. This, however, we, in private, doubted. Perhaps there were times when she had had a surplus of it—when she was young, say, with her redoubtable father, whose love blazed circles around her, making winter into summer and ice into fire. Perhaps she did have a brimming measure in her early married years. By straining hard, we could find traces left in our minds from those days of milk and honey. Our father, while he lived, had cast a magic over everything, for us as well as for her. He held his love up over us like an umbrella and kept off the troubles that afterwards came down on us, pouring cats and dogs!

But if she did have more than the common lot of happiness in those early days, what use was that when we could remember so clearly how our father's death had ravaged her? And how could we forget the distress it brought on us when, afraid to let her out of our sight, Bea and I stumbled after her everywhere, through the woods and along the bank of the river, where, in the weeks that followed, she tried vainly to find peace.

The summer after Father died, we were invited to France to stay with friends, and when she went walking on the cliffs at Fécamp our fears for her grew frenzied, so that we hung on to her arm and dragged at her skirt, hoping that like leaded weights we'd pin her down if she went too near to the edge. But at night we had to abandon our watch, being forced to follow the conventions of a family still whole—a home still intact—and go to bed at the same time as the other children. It was at that hour, when the coast guard was gone from his rowing boat offshore and the sand was as cold and grey as the sea, that Mother liked to swim. And when she had washed, kissed, and left us, our hearts almost died inside us and we'd creep out of bed again to stand in our bare feet at the mansard and watch as she ran down the shingle, striking out when she reached the water where, far out, wave and sky and mist were one, and the greyness closed over her. If we took our eyes off her for an instant, it was impossible to find her again.

"Oh, make her turn back, God, please!" I prayed out loud one night.

Startled, Bea turned away from the window. "She'll *have* to turn back sometime, won't she? Unless . . . ?"

Locking our damp hands together, we stared out again. "She wouldn't!" I whispered. "It would be a sin!"

Secure in the deterring power of sin, we let out our breath. Then Bea's breath caught again. "What if she went out so far she used up all her strength? She couldn't swim back! It wouldn't be a sin then!"

"It's the intention that counts," I whispered.

A second later, we could see an arm lift heavily up and wearily cleave down, and at last Mother was in the shallows, wading back to shore.

"Don't let her see us!" cried Bea. As if our chattering teeth would not give us away when she looked in at us before she went to her own room on the other side of the corridor, where, later in the night, sometimes the sound of crying would reach us.

What was it worth—a happiness bought that dearly.

Mother had never questioned it. And once she told us, "On a wintry day, I brought my own mother a snowdrop. It was the first one of the year—a bleak bud that had come up stunted before its time—and I meant it for a sign. But do you know what your grandmother said? 'What good are snowdrops to me now?' Such a thing to say! What good is a snowdrop at all if it doesn't hold its value always, and never lose it! Isn't that the whole point of a snowdrop? And that is the whole point of happiness, too! What good would it be if it could be erased without trace? Take me and those daffodils!" Stooping, she buried her face in a bunch that lay on the table waiting to be put in vases. "If they didn't hold their beauty absolute and inviolable, do you think I could bear the sight of them after what happened when your father was in hospital?"

It was a fair question. When Father went to hospital, Mother went with him and stayed in a small hotel across the street so she could be with him all day from early to late. "Because it was so awful for him—being in Dublin!" she said. "You have no idea how he hated it."

That he was dying neither of them realized. How could they know, as it rushed through the sky, that their star was a falling star! But one evening when she'd left him asleep Mother came home for a few hours to see how we were faring, and it broke her heart to see the daffodils out all over the place—in the woods, under the trees, and along the sides of the avenue. There had never been so many, and she thought how awful it was that Father was missing them. "You sent up little bunches to him, you poor dears!" she said. "Sweet little bunches, too—squeezed tight as posies by your little fists! But stuffed into vases they couldn't really make up to him for not being able to see them growing!"

So on the way back to the hospital she stopped her car and pulled a great bunch—the full of her arms. "They took up the whole back seat," she said, "and I was so excited at the thought of walking into his room and dumping them on his bed—you know—just plomping them down so he could smell them, and feel them, and look and look! I didn't mean them to be put in vases, or anything ridiculous like that—it would have taken a rainwater barrel to hold them. Why, I could hardly see over them as I came up the steps; I kept tripping. But when I came into the hall, that nun—I told you about her—that nun came up to me, sprang out of nowhere it seemed, although I know now that she was waiting for me, knowing that somebody had to bring me to my senses. But the way she did it! Reached out and grabbed the flowers, letting lots of them fall—I remember them getting stood on. 'Where are you going with those foolish flowers, you foolish woman?' she said. 'Don't you know your husband is dying? Your prayers are all you can give him now!'

"She was right. I *was* foolish. But I wasn't cured. Afterwards, it was nothing but foolishness the way I dragged you children after me all over Europe. As if any one place was going to be different from another, any better, any less desolate. But there was great satisfaction in bringing you places your father and I had planned to bring you—although in fairness to him I must say that he would not perhaps have brought you so young. And he would not have had an ulterior motive. But above all, he would not have attempted those trips in such a dilapidated car."

Oh, that car! It was a battered and dilapidated red sports car, so depleted of accessories that when, eventually, we got a new car Mother still stuck out her hand on bends, and in wet weather jumped out to wipe the windscreen with her sleeve. And if fussed, she'd let down the window and shout at people, forgetting she now had a horn. How we had ever fitted into it with all our luggage was a miracle.

"You were never lumpish—any of you!" Mother said proudly. "But you were very healthy and very strong." She turned to me. "Think of how you got that car up the hill in Switzerland!"

"The Alps are not hills, Mother!" I pointed out coldly, as I had done at the time, when, as actually happened, the car failed to make it on one of the inclines. Mother let it run back until it wedged against the rock face, and I had to get out and push till she got going again in first gear. But when it got started it couldn't be stopped to pick me up until it got to the top, where they had to wait for me, and for a very long time.

"Ah, well," she said, sighing wistfully at the thought of those trips. "You got something out of them, I hope. All that travelling must have helped you with your geography and your history."

We looked at each other and smiled, and then Mother herself laughed. "Remember the time," she said, "when we were in Italy, and it was Easter, and all the shops were chock-full of food? The butchers' shops had poultry and game hanging up outside the doors, fully feathered, and with their poor heads dripping blood, and in the windows they had poor little lambs and suckling pigs and young goats, all skinned and hanging by their hindfeet." Mother shuddered. "They think so much about food. I found it revolting. I had to hurry past. But Linda, who must have been only four then, dragged at me and stared and stared. You know how children are at that age; they have a morbid fascination for what is cruel and bloody. Her face was flushed and her eyes were wide. I hurried her back to the hotel. But next morning she crept into my room. She crept up to me and pressed against me. 'Can't we go back, just once, and look again at that shop?' she whispered. 'The shop where they have the little children hanging up for Easter!' It was the young goats, of course, but I'd said 'kids,' I suppose. How we laughed." But her face was grave. "You were *so* good on those trips, all of you," she said. "You were really very good children in general. Otherwise I would never have put so much effort into rearing you, because I wasn't a bit maternal. You brought out the best in me! I put an unnatural effort into you, of course, because I was taking my standards from your father, forgetting that his might not have remained so inflexible if he had lived to middle age and was beset by life, like other parents."

"Well, the job is nearly over now, Vera," said Father Hugh. "And you didn't do so badly."

"That's right, Hugh," said Mother, and she straightened up, and put her hand to her back the way she sometimes did in the garden when she got up from her knees after weeding. "I didn't go over to the enemy anyway! We survived!"

Then a flash of defiance came into her eyes. "And we were happy. That's the main thing!"

Father Hugh frowned. "There you go again!" he said.

Mother turned on him. "I don't think you realize the onslaughts that were made upon our happiness! The minute Robert died, they came down on me—cohorts of relatives, friends, even strangers, all draped in black, opening their arms like bats to let me pass into their company. 'Life is a vale of tears,' they said. 'You are privileged to find it out so young!' Ugh! After I staggered on to my feet and began to take hold of life once more, they fell back defeated. And the first day I gave a laugh—pouff, they were blown out like candles. They weren't living in a real world at all; they belonged to a ghostly world where life was easy: all one had to do was sit and weep. It takes effort to push back the stone from the mouth of the tomb and walk out."

Effort. Effort. Ah, but that strange-sounding word could invoke little sympathy from those who had not learned yet what it meant. Life must have been hardest for Mother in those years when we older ones were at college—no longer children, and still dependent on her. Indeed, we made more demands on her than ever then, having moved into new areas of activity and emotion. And our friends! Our friends came and went as freely as we did ourselves, so that the house was often like a café—and one where pets were not prohibited but took their places on our chairs and beds, as regardless as the people. And anyway it was hard to have sympathy for someone who got things into such a state as Mother. All over the house there was clutter. Her study was like the returned-letter department of a post-office, with stacks of paper everywhere, bills paid and unpaid, letters answered and unanswered, tax returns, pamphlets, leaflets. If by mistake we left the door open on a windy day, we came back to find papers flapping through the air like frightened birds. Efficient only in that she managed eventually to conclude every task she began, it never seemed possible to outsiders that by Mother's methods anything whatever could be accomplished. In an attempt to keep order elsewhere, she made her own room the clearing house into which the rest of us put everything: things to be given away, things to be mended, things to be stored, things to be treasured, things to be returned—even things to be thrown out! By the end of the year, the room resembled an obsolescence dump. And no one could help her; the chaos of her life was as personal as an act of creation—one might as well try to finish another person's poem.

As the years passed, Mother rushed around more hectically. And although Bea and I had married and were not at home any more, except at holiday time and for occasional weekends, Linda was noisier than the two of us put together had been, and for every follower we had brought home she brought twenty. The house was never still. Now that we were reduced to being visitors, we watched Mother's tension mount to vertigo, knowing that, like a spinning top, she could not rest till she fell. But now at the smallest pretext Father Hugh would call in the doctor and Mother would be put on the mail boat and dispatched for London. For it was essential that she get far enough away to make phoning home every night prohibitively costly.

Unfortunately, the thought of departure often drove a spur into her and she redoubled her effort to achieve order in her affairs. She would be up until the early hours ransacking her desk. To her, as always, the shortest parting entailed a preparation as for death. And as if it were her end that was at hand, we would all be summoned, although she had no time to speak a word to us, because five minutes before departure she would still be attempting to reply to letters that were the acquisition of weeks and would have taken whole days to dispatch.

"Don't you know the taxi is at the door, Vera?" Father Hugh would say, running his hand through his grey hair and looking very dishevelled himself. She had him at times as distracted as herself. "You can't do any more. You'll have to leave the rest till you come back."

"I can't, I can't!" Mother would cry. "I'll have to cancel my plans."

One day, Father Hugh opened the lid of her case, which was strapped up in the hall, and with a swipe of his arm he cleared all the papers on the top of the desk pell-mell into the suitcase. "You can sort them on the boat," he said, "or the train to London!"

Thereafter, Mother's luggage always included an empty case to hold the unfinished papers on her desk. And years afterwards a steward on the Irish Mail told us she was a familiar figure, working away at letters and bills nearly all the way from Holyhead to Euston. "She gave it up about Rugby or Crewe," he said. "She'd get talking to someone in the compartment." He smiled. "There was one time coming down the train I was just in time to see her close up the window with a guilty look. I didn't say anything, but I think she'd emptied those paper of hers out the window!"

Quite likely. When we were children, even a few hours away from us gave her composure. And in two weeks or less, when she'd come home, the well of her spirit would be freshened. We'd hardly know her — her step so light, her eye so bright, and her love and patience once more freely flowing. But in no time at all the house would fill up once more with the noise and confusion of too many people and too many animals, and again we'd be fighting our corner with cats and dogs, bats, mice, bees and even wasps. "Don't kill it!" Mother would cry if we raised a hand to an angry wasp. "Just catch it, dear, and put it outside. Open the window and let it fly away!" But even this treatment could at times be deemed too harsh. "Wait a minute. Close the window!" she'd cry. "It's too cold outside. It will die. That's why it came in, I suppose! Oh dear, what will we do?" Life would be going full blast again.

There was only one place Mother found rest. When she was at breaking point and fit to fall, she'd go out into the garden — not to sit or stroll around but to dig, to drag up weeds, to move great clumps of corms or rhizomes, or indeed quite frequently to haul huge rocks from one place to another. She was always laying down a path, building a dry wall, or making compost heaps as high as hills. However jaded she might be going out, when dark forced her in at last her step had the spring of a daisy. So if she did not succeed in defining happiness to our understanding, we could see that whatever it was, she possessed it to the full when she was in her garden.

One of us said as much one Sunday when Bea and I had dropped round for the afternoon. Father Hugh was with us again. "It's an unthinking happiness, though," he cavilled. We were standing at the drawing-room window, looking out to where in the fading light we could see Mother on her knees weeding, in the long border that stretched from the house right down to the woods. "I wonder how she'd take it if she were stricken down and had to give up that heavy work!" he said. Was he perhaps a little jealous of how she could stoop and bend? He himself had begun to use a stick. I was often a little jealous of her myself, because although I was married and had children of my own, I had married young and felt the weight of living as heavy as a weight of years. "She doesn't take enough care of herself," Father Hugh said sadly. "Look at her out there with nothing under her knees to protect her from the damp ground." It was almost too dim for us to see her, but even in the drawing-room it was chilly. "She should not be let stay out there after the sun goes down."

"Just you try to get her in then!" said Linda, who had come into the room in time to hear him. "Don't you know by now anyway that what would kill another person only seems to make Mother thrive?"

Father Hugh shook his head again. "You seem to forget it's not younger she's getting!" He fidgeted and fussed, and several times went to the window to stare out apprehensively. He was really getting quite elderly.

"Come and sit down, Father Hugh," Bea said, and to take his mind off Mother she turned on the light and blotted out the garden. Instead of seeing through the window, we saw into it as into a mirror, and there between the flower-laden tables and lamps it was ourselves we saw moving vaguely. Like Father Hugh, we, too, were waiting for her to come in before we called an end to the day.

"Oh, this is ridiculous!" Father Hugh cried at last. "She'll have to listen to reason." And going back to the window he threw it open. "Vera!" he called. "Vera!"—sternly, so sternly that, more intimate than an endearment, his tone shocked us. "She didn't hear me," he said, turning back blinking at us in the lighted room. "I'm going out to get her." And in a minute he was gone from the room. As he ran down the garden path, we stared at each other, astonished; his step, like his voice, was the step of a lover. "I'm coming, Vera!" he cried.

Although she was never stubborn except in things that mattered, Mother had not moved. In the wholehearted way she did everything, she was bent down close to the ground. It wasn't the light only that was dimming; her eyesight also was failing, I thought, as instinctively I followed Father Hugh.

But halfway down the path I stopped. I had seen something he had not: Mother's hand that appeared to support itself in a forked branch of an old tree peony she had planted as a bride was not in fact gripping it but impaled upon it. And the hand that appeared to be grubbing in the clay in fact was sunk into the soft mould. "Mother!" I screamed, and I ran forward, but when I reached her I covered my face with my hands. "Oh Father Hugh!" I cried. "Is she dead?"

It was Bea who answered, hysterical. "She is! She is!" she cried, and she began to pound Father Hugh on the back with her fists, as if his pessimistic words had made this happen.

But Mother was not dead. And at first the doctor even offered hope of her pulling through. But from the moment Father Hugh lifted her up to carry her into the house we ourselves had no hope, seeing how effortlessly he, who was not strong, could carry her. When he put her down on her bed, her head hardly creased the pillow. Mother lived for four more hours.

Like the days of her life, those four hours that Mother lived were packed tight with concern and anxiety. Partly conscious, partly delirious, she seemed to think the counterpane was her desk, and she scrabbled her fingers upon it as if trying to sort out a muddle of bills and correspondence. No longer indifferent now, we listened, anguished, to the distracted cries that had for all our lifetime been so familiar to us. "Oh, where is it? Where is it? I had it a minute ago! Where on earth did I put it?"

"Vera, Vera, stop worrying," Father Hugh pleaded, but she waved him away and went on sifting through the sheets as if they were sheets of paper. "Oh, Vera!" he begged. "Listen to me. Do you not know—"

Bea pushed between them. "You're not to tell her!" she commanded. "Why frighten her?"

"But it ought not to frighten her," said Father Hugh. "This is what I was always afraid would happen—that she'd be frightened when it came to the end."

At that moment, as if to vindicate him, Mother's hands fell idle on the coverlet, palm upward and empty. And turning her head she stared at each of us in turn, beseechingly. "I cannot face it," she whispered. "I can't! I can't! I can't!"

"Oh, my God!" Bea said, and she started to cry.

"Vera. For God's sake listen to me," Father Hugh cried, and pressing his face to hers, as close as a kiss, he kept whispering to her, trying to cast into the dark tunnel before her the light of his own faith.

But it seemed to us that Mother must already be looking into God's exigent eyes. "I can't!" she cried. "I can't!"

Then her mind came back from the stark world of the spirit to the world where her body was still detained, but even that world was now a whirling kaleidoscope of things which only she could see. Suddenly her eyes focussed, and, catching at Father Hugh, she pulled herself up a little and pointed to something we could not see. "What will be done with them?" Her voice was anxious. "They ought to be put in water anyway," she said, and leaning over the edge of the bed, she pointed to the floor. "Don't step on that one!" she said sharply. Then more sharply still, she addressed us all. "Have them sent to the public ward," she said peremptorily. "Don't let that nun take them; she'll only put them on the altar. And God doesn't want them! He made them for *us*—not for Himself!"

It was the familiar rhetoric that all her life had characterized her utterances. For a moment we were mystified. Then Bea gasped. "The daffodils!" she cried. "The day Father died!" And over her face came the light that had so often blazed over Mother's. Leaning across the bed, she pushed Father Hugh aside. And, putting out her hands, she held Mother's face between her palms as tenderly as if it were the face of a child. "It's all right, Mother. You don't *have* to face it! It's over!" Then she who had so fiercely forbade Father Hugh to do so blurted out the truth. "You've finished with this world, Mother," she said, and, confident that her tidings were joyous, her voice was strong.

Mother made the last effort of her life and grasped at Bea's meaning. She let out a sigh, and, closing her eyes, she sank back, and this time her head sank so deep into the pillow that it would have been dented had it been a pillow of stone.

[1970]

QUESTIONS

1. What view of life animates the narrator's mother? How would you describe her concept of happiness? Is it consistent with her frantic, chaotic life?

2. How does the narrator regard her mother?
3. What attitudes toward living and dying are represented in the story? How would you describe the mother's death?
4. What role does Father Hugh play in the story?
5. Compare this story with Margaret Laurence's "A Bird in the House," particularly concerning a daughter's response to the death of a parent.

D. H. Lawrence

(1885–1930)

England

David Herbert Lawrence was born in the coal-mining Midlands of England, the fourth child (of five) born to a miner and a former school teacher. Lawrence's distaste for the financial and physical hardships of his father's vocation and his preference for his mother's profession influenced him to become a teacher after training at Nottingham University. During his years in college, he continued to pursue the writing he had begun in his youth with his first novel, *The White Peacock* (1911), as well as a number of poems.

The deep bond that Lawrence's mother formed with him following the death of an older son both inspired him and complicated his attempts at relationships with other women. The ambivalence of that bond is explored with exceptional psychological insight in Lawrence's autobiographical third novel, *Sons and Lovers* (1911), published two years after his mother's death. By that time Lawrence had met Frieda von Richthofen, the daughter of a German baron who was then married to one of his former professors and the mother of three children. In a scandalous decision, Lawrence and Frieda eloped to Europe, where they married (following her divorce) in 1914. Frieda catalyzed Lawrence's writing and also enabled him to disentangle himself from his mother and other women to whom he had been emotionally bound.

A prolific writer, Lawrence published 10 novels as well as nearly 60 short stories and novellas; he also wrote several volumes of literary and philosophical essays and poetry. Because he suffered from poor health (tuberculosis), he sought hospitable climates as well as places where he might avoid what he viewed as the decline of culture through industrialization and materialism; he and Frieda lived in Europe, Australia, Mexico, and the southwestern United States, all of which figure prominently as settings for his novels.

Lawrence's writing was always controversial because his subject—the modern experience of relationships, including not only love but also passionate sexuality and the exploration of the emotional unconscious—challenged the taboos concerning what could be expressed in print in his day. *The Rainbow* (1915), which traces the tensions between the sexes over several generations of one family, was banned at publication. His last novel, *Lady Chatterley's Lover* (1928), which sensitively explores the relationship between an aristocratic woman and the gamekeeper who awakens her sensuality, so challenged sexual and literary limits that it caused a scandal; it was not published in unexpurgated form until 1959.

Lawrence was also a talented painter but, again, his candid expressions of sexuality and nudity resulted in his 1929 exhibit being declared "obscene" and confiscated. Yet he was not simply a courter of scandal and sensationalism. Rather—ironically to those who misunderstood him—he was a moralist who believed that sexuality was the deepest creative impulse of life itself. His portrayals of the passionate dimension of relationships sprang from a profound faith in the truth of the body, of intuition, and of nature — all elements he felt had been "denatured" by modern industrial society. Moreover, he felt that the avenue for rich self-discovery and spiritual fulfillment was through the mysteries and tensions — and moments of sublime equilibrium — embodied in the complementary male–female relationship. From a philosophical perspective formed early in his career, Lawrence wrote, "My great religion is a belief in the blood, the flesh, as being wiser than the intellect. We can go wrong in our minds. But what our blood feels and believes and says, is always true."

Tickets, Please

There is in the Midlands a single-line tramway system which boldly leaves the country town and plunges off into the black, industrial country-side, up hill and down dale, through the long ugly villages of workmen's houses, over canals and railways, past churches perched high and nobly over the smoke and shadows, through stark, grimy cold little market-places, tilting away in a rush past cinemas and shops down to the hollow where the collieries are, then up again, past a little rural church, under the ash trees, on in a rush to the terminus, the last little ugly place of industry, the cold little town that shivers on the edge of the wild, gloomy country beyond. There the green and creamy coloured tram-cars seem to pause and purr with curious satisfaction. But in a few minutes — the clock on the turret of the Co-operative Wholesale Society's shops gives the time — away it starts once more on the adventure. Again there are the reckless swoops downhill, bouncing the loops: again the chilly wait in the hill-top market-place: again the breathless slithering round the precipitous drop under the church: again the patient halts at the loops, waiting for the outcoming car: so on and on, for two long hours, till at last the city looms beyond the fat gas-works, the narrow factories draw near, we are in the sordid streets of the great town, once more we sidle to a standstill at our terminus, abashed by the great crimson and cream-coloured city cars, but still perky, jaunty, somewhat dare-devil, green as a jaunty sprig of parsley out of a black colliery garden.

To ride on these cars is always an adventure. Since we are in war-time, the drivers are men unfit for active service: cripples and hunchbacks. So they have the spirit of the devil in them. The ride becomes a steeplechase. Hurray! we have leapt in a clear jump over the canal bridge — now for the four-lane corner. With a shriek and a trail of sparks we are clear again. To be sure, a tram often leaps the rails — but what matter! It sits in a ditch till other trams come to haul it out. It is quite common for a car, packed with one solid mass of living people, to come to a dead halt in the midst of unbroken blackness, the heart of nowhere on a dark night, and for the driver and the girl conductor to call: "All get off — car's on fire!" Instead, however, of rushing out in a panic, the passengers stolidly reply: "Get on — get on! We're not coming out. We're stopping where we are. Push on, George." So till flames actually appear.

The reason for this reluctance to dismount is that the nights are howlingly cold, black, and windswept, and a car is a haven of refuge. From village to village the miners travel, for a change of cinema, of girl, of pub. The trams are desperately packed. Who is going to risk himself in the black gulf outside, to wait perhaps an hour for another tram, then to see the forlorn notice "Depot Only," because there is something wrong! Or to greet a unit of three bright cars all so tight with people that they sail past with a howl of derision. Trams that pass in the night.

This, the most dangerous tram-service in England, as the authorities themselves declare, with pride, is entirely conducted by girls, and driven by rash young men, a little crippled, or by delicate young men, who creep forward in terror. The girls are fearless young hussies. In their ugly blue uniform, skirts up to their knees, shapeless old peaked caps on their heads, they have all the *sang-froid*[1] of an old non-commissioned officer. With a tram packed with howling colliers, roaring hymns downstairs and a sort of antiphony of obscenities upstairs, the lasses are perfectly at their ease. They pounce on the youths who try to evade their ticket-machine. They push off the men at the end of their distance. They are not going to be done in the eye—not they. They fear nobody—and everybody fears them.

"Hello, Annie!"

"Hello, Ted!"

"Oh, mind my corn, Miss Stone. It's my belief you've got a heart of stone, for you've trod on it again."

"You should keep it in your pocket," replies Miss Stone, and she goes sturdily upstairs in her high boots.

"Tickets, please."

She is peremptory, suspicious, and ready to hit first. She can hold her own against ten thousand. The step of that tram-car is her Thermopylae.[2]

Therefore, there is a certain wild romance aboard these cars—and in the sturdy bosom of Annie herself. The time for soft romance is in the morning, between ten o'clock and one, when things are rather slack: that is, except market-day and Saturday. Thus Annie has time to look about her. Then she often hops off her car and into a shop where she has spied something, while the driver chats in the main road. There is very good feeling between the girls and the drivers. Are they not companions in peril, shipments aboard this careering vessel of a tram-car, for ever rocking on the waves of a stormy land.

Then, also, during the easy hours, the inspectors are most in evidence. For some reason, everybody employed in this tram-service is young: there are no grey heads. It would not do. Therefore the inspectors are of the right age, and one, the chief, is also good-looking. See him stand on a wet, gloomy morning, in his long oilskin, his peaked cap well down over his eyes, waiting to board a car. His face ruddy, his small brown moustache is weathered, he has a faint impudent smile. Fairly tall and agile, even in his waterproof, he springs aboard a car and greets Annie.

"Hello, Annie! Keeping the wet out?"

"Trying to."

There are only two people in the car. Inspecting is soon over. Then for a long and impudent chat on the foot-board, a good, easy twelve-mile chat.

[1]*sang-froid* French: coolness

[2]*Thermopylae* a mountain pass in ancient Greece where Spartans fought and were defeated by the Persians in 480 B.C.; a place to be defended at all costs

The inspector's name is John Thomas Raynor—always called John Thomas,[3] except sometimes, in malice, Coddy. His face sets in fury when he is addressed, from a distance, with this abbreviation. There is considerable scandal about John Thomas in half a dozen villages. He flirts with the girl conductors in the morning, and walks out with them in the dark night, when they leave their tram-car at the depôt. Of course, the girls quit the service frequently. Then he flirts and walks out with the newcomer: always providing she is sufficiently attractive, and that she will consent to walk. It is remarkable, however, that most of the girls are quite comely, they are all young, and this roving life aboard the car gives them a sailor's dash and recklessness. What matter how they behave when the ship is in port? To-morrow they will be abroad again.

Annie, however, was something of a Tartar,[4] and her sharp tongue had kept John Thomas at arm's length for many months. Perhaps, therefore, she liked him all the more: for he always came up smiling, with impudence. She watched him vanquish one girl, then another. She could tell by the movement of his mouth and eyes, when he flirted with her in the morning, that he had been walking out with this lass, or the other, the night before. A fine cock-of-the-walk he was. She could sum him up pretty well.

In this subtle antagonism they knew each other like old friends, they were as shrewd with one another almost as man and wife. But Annie had always kept him sufficiently at arm's length. Besides, she had a boy of her own.

The Statutes fair, however, came in November, at Bestwood. It happened that Annie had the Monday night off. It was a drizzling ugly night, yet she dressed herself up and went to the fair-ground. She was alone, but she expected soon to find a pal of some sort.

The roundabouts were veering round and grinding out their music, the sideshows were making as much commotion as possible. In the coconut shies[5] there were no coconuts, but artificial war-time substitutes, which the lads declared were fastened into the irons. There was a sad decline in brilliance and luxury. None the less, the ground was muddy as ever, there was the same crush, the press of faces lighted up by the flares and the electric lights, the same smell of naphtha and a few potatoes, and of electricity.

Who should be the first to greet Miss Annie on the show-ground but John Thomas. He had a black overcoat buttoned up to his chin, and a tweed cap pulled down over his brows, his face between was ruddy and smiling and handy as ever. She knew so well the way his mouth moved.

She was very glad to have a "boy." To be at the Statutes without a fellow was no fun. Instantly, like the gallant he was, he took her on the Dragons,[6] grim-toothed, roundabout switchbacks. It was not nearly so exciting as a tram-car actually. But, then, to be seated in a shaking, green dragon, uplifted above the sea of bubble faces, careering in a rickety fashion in the lower heavens, whilst John Thomas leaned over her, his cigarette in his mouth, was after all the right style. She was a plump, quick, alive little creature. So she was quite excited and happy.

[3]*John Thomas* is also a folklore euphemism for the phallus.

[4]*Tartar* Russian ethnic group known for its fighting spirit; a tough person

[5]*shies* carnival game of tossing at coconuts for prizes

[6]*Dragons* carnival ride

John Thomas made her stay on for the next round. And therefore she could hardly for shame repulse him when he put his arm round her and drew her a little nearer to him, in a very warm and cuddly manner. Besides, he was fairly discreet, he kept his movement as hidden as possible. She looked down, and saw that his red, clean hand was out of sight of the crowd. And they knew each other so well. So they warmed up to the fair.

After the Dragons they went on the horses. John Thomas paid each time, so she could but be complaisant. He, of course, sat astride on the outer horse—named "Black Bess"—and she sat sideways, towards him, on the inner horse—named "Wildfire." But of course John Thomas was not going to sit discreetly on "Black Bess," holding the brass bar. Round they spun and heaved, in the light. And round he swung on his wooden steed, flinging one leg across her mount, and perilously tipping up and down, across the space, half lying back, laughing at her. He was perfectly happy; she was afraid her hat was on one side, but she was excited.

He threw quoits on a table, and won for her two large, pale blue hat-pins. And then, hearing the noise of the cinemas, announcing another performance, they climbed the boards and went in.

Of course, during these performances pitch darkness falls from time to time, when the machine goes wrong. Then there is a wild whooping, and a loud smacking of simulated kisses. In these moments John Thomas drew Annie towards him. After all, he had a wonderfully warm, cosy way of holding a girl with his arm, he seemed to make such a nice fit. And, after all, it was pleasant to be so held: so very comforting and cosy and nice. He leaned over her and she felt his breath on her hair; she knew he wanted to kiss her on the lips. And, after all, he was so warm and she fitted in to him so softly. After all, she wanted him to touch her lips.

But the light sprang up; she also started electrically, and put her hat straight. He left his arm lying nonchalantly behind her. Well, it was fun, it was exciting to be at the Statutes with John Thomas.

When the cinema was over they went for a walk across the dark, damp fields. He had all the arts of love-making. He was especially good at holding a girl, when he sat with her on a stile in the black, drizzling darkness. He seemed to be holding her in space, against his own warmth and gratification. And his kisses were soft and slow and searching.

So Annie walked out with John Thomas, though she kept her own boy dangling in the distance. Some of the tram-girls chose to be huffy. But there, you must take things as you find them, in this life.

There was no mistake about it, Annie liked John Thomas a good deal. She felt so rich and warm in herself whenever he was near. And John Thomas really liked Annie, more than usual. The soft, melting way in which she could flow into a fellow, as if she melted into his very bones, was something rare and good. He fully appreciated this.

But with a developing acquaintance there began a developing intimacy. Annie wanted to consider him a person, a man: she wanted to take an intelligent interest in him, and to have an intelligent response. She did not want a mere nocturnal presence, which was what he was so far. And she prided herself that he could not leave her.

Here she made a mistake. John Thomas intended to remain a nocturnal presence; he had no idea of becoming an all-round individual to her. When she started to take an intelligent interest in him and his life and his character, he sheered off. He hated intelligent interest. And he knew that the only way to stop it was to avoid it. The possessive female was aroused in Annie. So he left her.

It is no use saying she was not surprised. She was at first startled, thrown out of her count. For she had been so *very* sure of holding him. For a while she was staggered, and everything became uncertain to her. Then she wept with fury, indignation, desolation, and misery. Then she had a spasm of despair. And then, when he came, still impudently, on to her car, still familiar, but letting her see by the movement of his head that he had gone away to somebody else for the time being, and was enjoying pastures new, then she determined to have her own back.

She had a very shrewd idea what girls John Thomas had taken out. She went to Nora Purdy. Nora was a tall, rather pale, but well-built girl, with beautiful yellow hair. She was rather secretive.

"Hey!" said Annie, accosting her; then softly: "Who's John Thomas on with now?"

"I don't know," said Nora.

"Why, tha does," said Annie, ironically lapsing into dialect. "Tha knows as well as I do."

"Well, I do, then," said Nora. "It isn't me, so don't bother."

"It's Cissy Meakin, isn't it?"

"It is, for all I know."

"Hasn't he got a face on him!" said Annie. "I don't half like his cheek. I could knock him off the foot-board when he comes round at me."

"He'll get dropped on one of these days," said Nora.

"Ay, he will, when somebody makes up their mind to drop it on him. I should like to see him taken down a peg or two, shouldn't you?"

"I shouldn't mind," said Nora.

"You've got quite as much cause to as I have," said Annie. "But we'll drop on him one of these days, my girl. What? Don't you want to?"

"I don't mind," said Nora.

But as a matter of fact, Nora was much more vindictive than Annie.

One by one Annie went the round of the old flames. It so happened that Cissy Meakin left the tramway service in quite a short time. Her mother made her leave. Then John Thomas was on the *qui vive*.[7] He cast his eyes over his old flock. And his eyes lighted on Annie. He thought she would be safe now. Besides, he liked her.

She arranged to walk home with him on Sunday night. It so happened that her car would be in the depôt at half-past nine: the last car would come in at 10:15. So John Thomas was to wait for her there.

At the depôt the girls had a little waiting-room of their own. It was quite rough, but cosy, with a fire and an oven and a mirror, and table and wooden chairs. The half-dozen girls who knew John Thomas only too well had arranged to take service this Sunday afternoon. So, as the cars began to come in, early, the girls dropped into the waiting-room. And instead of hurrying off home, they sat around the fire and had a cup of tea. Outside was the darkness and lawlessness of war-time.

[7]*qui vive* Latin: on the lookout, on the alert

John Thomas came on the car after Annie, at about a quarter to ten. He poked his head easily into the girls' waiting-room.

"Prayer-meeting?" he asked.

"Ay," said Laura Sharp. "Ladies only."

"That's me!" said John Thomas. It was one of his favourite exclamations.

"Shut the door, boy," said Muriel Baggaley.

"Oh, which side of me?" said John Thomas.

"Which tha likes," said Polly Birkin.

He had come in and closed the door behind him. The girls moved in their circle, to make a place for him near the fire. He took off his great-coat and pushed back his hat.

"Who handles the teapot?" he said.

Nora Purdy silently poured him out a cup of tea.

"Want a bit o' my bread and drippin'?" said Muriel Baggaley to him.

"Ay, give us a bit."

And he began to eat his piece of bread.

"There's no place like home, girls," he said.

They all looked at him as he uttered this piece of impudence. He seemed to be sunning himself in the presence of so many damsels.

"Especially if you're not afraid to go home in the dark," said Laura Sharp.

"Me! By myself I am."

They sat till they heard the last tram come in. In a few minutes Emma Houselay entered.

"Come on, my old duck!" cried Polly Birkin.

"It *is* perishing," said Emma, holding her fingers to the fire.

"But—I'm afraid to, go home in, the dark," sang Laura Sharp, the tune having got into her mind.

"Who're you going with to-night, John Thomas?" asked Muriel Baggaley coolly.

"To-night?" said John Thomas. "Oh, I'm going home by myself to-night—all on my lonely-o."

"That's me!" said Nora Purdy, using his own ejaculation.

The girls laughed shrilly.

"Me as well, Nora," said John Thomas.

"Don't know what you mean," said Laura.

"Yes, I'm toddling," said he, rising and reaching for his overcoat.

"Nay," said Polly. "We're all here waiting for you."

"We've got to be up in good time in the morning," he said, in the benevolent official manner.

They all laughed.

"Nay," said Muriel. "Don't leave us all lonely, John Thomas. Take one!"

"I'll take the lot, if you like," he responded gallantly.

"That you won't either," said Muriel. "Two's company; seven's too much of a good thing."

"Nay—take one," said Laura. "Fair and square, all above board and say which."

"Ay," cried Annie, speaking for the first time. "Pick, John Thomas; let's hear thee."

"Nay," he said. "I'm going home quiet to-night. Feeling good, for once."

"Whereabouts?" said Annie. "Take a good 'un, then. But tha's got to take one of us!"

"Nay, how can I take one?" he said, laughing uneasily. "I don't want to make enemies."

"You'd only make *one*," said Annie.

"The chosen *one*," added Laura.

"Oh, my! Who said girls!" exclaimed John Thomas, again turning, as if to escape. "Well—good-night."

"Nay, you've got to make your pick," said Muriel. "Turn your face to the wall, and say which one touches you. Go on—we shall only just touch your back—one of us. Go on—turn your face to the wall, and don't look, and say which one touches you."

He was uneasy, mistrusting them. Yet he had not the courage to break away. They pushed him to a wall and stood him there with his face to it. Behind his back they all grimaced, tittering. He looked so comical. He looked around uneasily.

"Go on!" he cried.

"You're looking—you're looking!" they shouted.

He turned his head away. And suddenly, with a movement like a swift cat, Annie went forward and fetched him a box on the side of the head that sent his cap flying and himself staggering. He started round.

But at Annie's signal they all flew at him, slapping him, pinching him, pulling his hair, though more in fun than in spite or anger. He, however, saw red. His blue eyes flamed with strange fear as well as fury, and he butted through the girls to the door. It was locked. He wrenched at it. Roused, alert, the girls stood round and looked at him. He faced them, at bay. At that moment they were rather horrifying to him, as they stood in their short uniforms. He was distinctly afraid.

"Come on, John Thomas! Come on! Choose!" said Annie.

"What are you after? Open the door," he said.

"We shan't—not till you've chosen!" said Muriel.

"Chosen what?" he said.

"Chosen the one you're going to marry," she replied.

He hesitated a moment.

"Open the blasted door," he said, "and get back to your senses." He spoke with official authority.

"You've got to choose!" cried the girls.

"Come on!" cried Annie, looking him in the eye. "Come on! Come on!"

He went forward, rather vaguely. She had taken off her belt, and swinging it, she fetched him a sharp blow over the head with the buckle end. He sprang and seized her. But immediately the other girls rushed upon him, pulling and tearing and beating him. Their blood was now thoroughly up. He was their sport now. They were going to have their own back, out of him. Strange, wild creatures, they hung on him and rushed at him to bear him down. His tunic was torn right up the back, Nora had hold at the back of his collar, and was actually strangling him. Luckily the button burst. He struggled in a wild frenzy of fury and terror, almost mad terror. His tunic was simply torn off his back, his shirt-sleeves were torn away, his arms were naked. The girls rushed at him, clenched their hands on him and pulled at him: or they rushed at him and pushed him, butted him with all their might: or they struck him wild blows. He ducked and cringed and struck sideways. They became more intense.

At last he was down. They rushed on him, kneeling on him. He had neither breath nor strength to move. His face was bleeding with a long scratch, his brow was bruised.

Annie knelt on him, the other girls knelt and hung on to him. Their faces were flushed, their hair wild, their eyes were all glittering strangely. He lay at last quite still, with face averted, as an animal lies when it is defeated and at the mercy of the captor. Sometimes his eye glanced back at the wild faces of the girls. His breast rose heavily, his wrists were torn.

"Now, then, my fellow!" gasped Annie at length. "Now then—now—"

At the sound of her terrifying, cold triumph, he suddenly started to struggle as an animal might, but the girls threw themselves upon him with unnatural strength and power, forcing him down.

"Yes—now, then!" gasped Annie at length.

And there was a dead silence, in which the thud of heart-beating was to be heard. It was a suspense of pure silence in every soul.

"Now you know where you are," said Annie.

The sight of his white, bare arm maddened the girls. He lay in a kind of trance of fear and antagonism. They felt themselves filled with supernatural strength.

Suddenly Polly started to laugh—to giggle wildly—helplessly—and Emma and Muriel joined in. But Annie and Nora and Laura remained the same, tense, watchful, with gleaming eyes. He winced away from these eyes.

"Yes," said Annie, in a curious low tone, secret and deadly. "Yes! You've got it now. You know what you've done, don't you? You know what you've done."

He made no sound nor sign, but lay with bright, averted eyes, and averted, bleeding face.

"You ought to be *killed*, that's what you ought," said Annie, tensely. "You ought to be *killed*." And there was a terrifying lust in her voice.

Polly was ceasing to laugh, and giving long-drawn Oh-h-hs and sighs as she came to herself.

"He's got to choose," she said vaguely.

"Oh, yes, he has," said Laura, with vindictive decision.

"Do you hear—do you hear?" said Annie. And with a sharp movement, that made him wince, she turned his face to her.

"Do you hear?" she repeated, shaking him.

But he was quite dumb. She fetched him a sharp slap on the face. He started, and his eyes widened. Then his face darkened with defiance, after all.

"Do you hear?" she repeated.

He only looked at her with hostile eyes.

"Speak!" she said, putting her face devilishly near his.

"What?" he said, almost overcome.

"You've got to *choose*!" she cried, as if it were some terrible menace, and as if it hurt that she could not exact more.

"What?" he said, in fear.

"Choose your girl, Coddy. You've got to choose her now. And you'll get your neck broken if you play any more of your tricks, my boy. You're settled now."

There was a pause. Again he averted his face. He was cunning in his overthrow. He did not give in to them really—no, not if they tore him to bits.

"All right, then," he said, "I choose Annie." His voice was strange and full of malice. Annie let go of him as if he had been a hot coal.

"He's chosen Annie!" said the girls in chorus.

"Me!" cried Annie. She was still kneeling, but away from him. He was still lying prostate, with averted face. The girls grouped uneasily around.

"Me!" repeated Annie, with a terrible bitter accent.

Then she got up, drawing away from him with strange disgust and bitterness.

"I wouldn't touch him," she said.

But her face quivered with a kind of agony, she seemed as if she would fall. The other girls turned aside. He remained lying on the floor, with his torn clothes and bleeding, averted face.

"Oh, if he's chosen———" said Polly.

"I don't want him—he can choose again," said Annie, with the same rather bitter hopelessness.

"Get up," said Polly, lifting his shoulder. "Get up."

He rose slowly, a strange, ragged, dazed creature. The girls eyed him from a distance, curiously, furtively, dangerously.

"Who wants him?" cried Laura, roughly.

"Nobody," they answered, with contempt. Yet each one of them waited for him to look at her, hoped he would look at her. All except Annie, and something was broken in her.

He, however, kept his face closed and averted from them all. There was a silence of the end. He picked up the torn pieces of his tunic, without knowing what to do with them. The girls stood about uneasily, flushed, panting, tidying their hair and their dress unconsciously, and watching him. He looked at none of them. He espied his cap in a corner, and went and picked it up. He put it on his head, and one of the girls burst into a shrill, hysteric laugh at the sight he presented. He, however, took no heed, but went straight to where his overcoat hung on a peg. The girls moved away from contact with him as if he had been an electric wire. He put on his coat and buttoned it down. Then he rolled his tunic-rags into a bundle, and stood before the locked door, dumbly.

"Open the door, somebody," said Laura.

"Annie's got the key," said one.

Annie silently offered the key to the girls. Nora unlocked the door.

"Tit for tat, old man," she said. "Show yourself a man, and don't bear a grudge."

But without a word or sign he had opened the door and gone, his face closed, his head dropped.

"That'll learn him," said Laura.

"Coddy!" said Nora.

"Shut up, for God's sake!" cried Annie fiercely, as if in torture.

"Well, I'm about ready to go, Polly. Look sharp!" said Muriel.

The girls were all anxious to be off. They were tidying themselves hurriedly, with mute, stupefied faces.

[1924]

QUESTIONS

1. What is the central conflict in the story? Where are your sympathies? Are the tram-girls excessively vindictive or does John Thomas get what he deserves?
2. How are Annie and John Thomas characterized? How are they shown to be equals? What motivates each of them?
3. What elements of class are represented in the story?
4. How is the briefly noted wartime atmosphere an important context for the events?
5. In dramatizing a "battle of the sexes," what does Lawrence suggest about gender roles and behaviors? Compare this story with Doris Lessing's "A Woman on a Roof."

URSULA K. LE GUIN

(b. 1929)

UNITED STATES

Ursula Le Guin is the daughter of two distinguished parents: anthropologist Alfred Kroeber, an expert on the Indians of California, and Theodora Kroeber, a writer. Le Guin acknowledges that the form her own career took bears the influence of both of her parents. Her father sought out other cultures, including their myths, legends, and languages; she has preferred to invent cultures, creating their myths, legends, and languages. Growing up in Berkeley, California, within a highly literate and intellectual environment, Le Guin later went on to study literature at Radcliffe and received her M.A. from Columbia (1952). On a Fulbright grant to France, she met and later married historian Charles Le Guin.

Le Guin's early fiction was a mixture of elements of fantasy and science fiction, and her protagonists were mostly male. Her writing reached a turning point with *The Left Hand of Darkness* (1969), in which she provocatively explored the issue of gender itself: in the invented chilly world of Gethen, biologically androgynous beings may choose to mother as well as to father children. Eventually Le Guin distinguished between her pure fantasy writing—what she calls "Inner Lands"—and her science fiction—the realm of "Outer Space." Her books in both genres have frequently been honored by Nebula and Hugo awards; she received the National Book Award in 1973 for her novel *The Farthest Shore* (1972), the final novel of the Earthsea fantasy trilogy for children (also including *A Wizard of Earthsea*, 1968, and *The Tombs of Atuan*, 1971).

Much of Le Guin's fiction, whether classified as fantasy or science fiction, challenges cultural assumptions. By imaginatively altering reality, whether through ideas concerning gender and male-female relationships, time and space, or language and other elements of culture, Le Guin examines pressing issues within our own cultural reality. As she phrases it, "Realism is perhaps the least adequate means of understanding or portraying the incredible realities of our existence. . . ." In fact, through her diverse "alien" characters and creatures, she expresses her profound moral vision and her concern for decidedly human dilemmas.

Critics have identified as a central vision in Le Guin's writing—both fantasy and science fiction—the ideal of wholeness or integration as well as the pursuit of a balance between the individual and society. Expressing the moral vision that underlies all of her fiction, Le Guin commented in her acceptance speech for the National Book Award in 1973 that

> The fantasist, whether he uses the ancient archetypes of myth and legend or the younger ones of science and technology, may be talking as seriously as any sociologist—and a good deal more directly—about human life as it is lived, and as it might be lived, and as it ought to be lived. For after all, as great scientists have said and all children know, it is above all by the imagination that we achieve perception, and compassion, and hope.

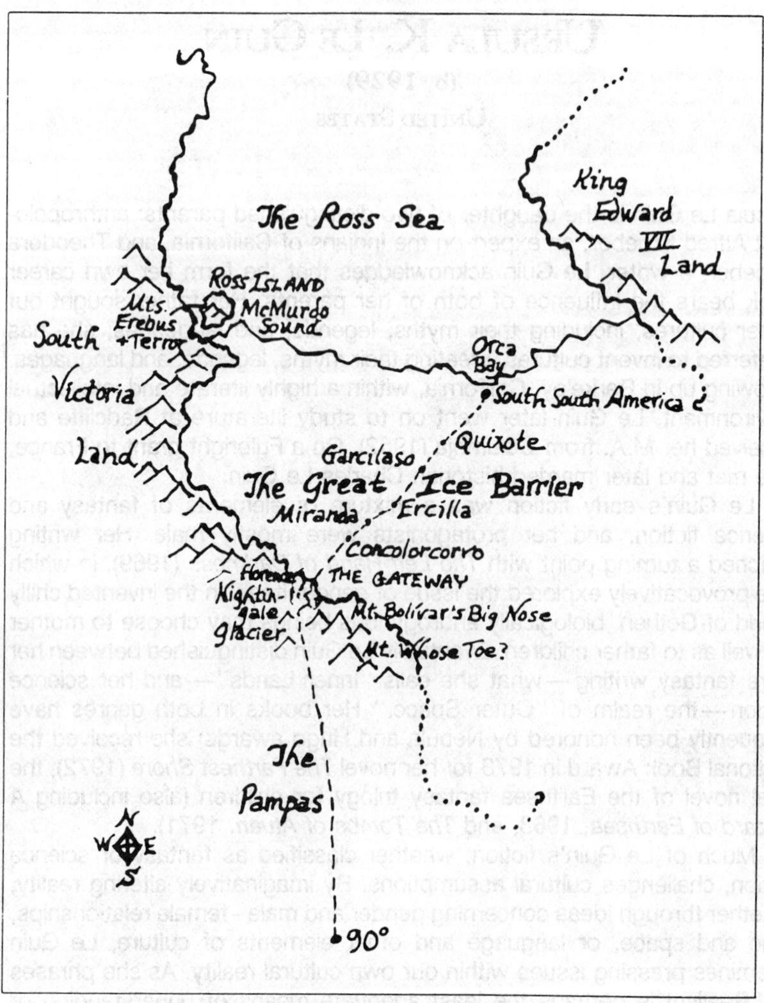

The Map in the Attic

◆ Sur[1] ◆

A Summary Report of the Yelcho Expedition to the Antarctic, 1909–1910

Although I have no intention of publishing this report, I think it would be nice if a grandchild of mine, or somebody's grandchild, happened to find it some day; so I shall keep it in the leather trunk in the attic, along with Rosita's christening dress and Juanito's silver rattle and my wedding shoes and finneskos.[2]

[1]*sur* Spanish: south
[2]*finneskos* reindeer-skin boots

The first requisite for mounting an expedition — money — is normally the hardest to come by. I grieve that even in a report destined for a trunk in the attic of a house in a very quiet suburb of Lima I dare not write the name of the generous benefactor, the great soul without whose unstinting liberality the *Yelcho* Expedition would never have been more than the idlest excursion into daydream. That our equipment was the best and most modern — that our provisions were plentiful and fine — that a ship of the Chilean Government, with her brave officers and gallant crew, was twice sent halfway round the world for our convenience: all this is due to that benefactor whose name, alas! I must not say, but whose happiest debtor I shall be till death.

When I was little more than a child my imagination was caught by a newspaper account of the voyage of the *Belgica*, which, sailing south from Tierra del Fuego, became beset by ice in the Bellingshausen Sea and drifted a whole year with the floe, the men aboard her suffering a great deal from want of food and from the terror of the unending winter darkness. I read and reread that account, and later followed with excitement the reports of the rescue of Dr. Nordenskjold from the South Shetland Isles by the dashing Captain Irizar of the *Uruguay*, and the adventures of the *Scotia* in the Weddell Sea. But all these exploits were to me but forerunners of the British National Antarctic Expedition of 1902 - 1904, in the *Discovery*, and the wonderful account of that expedition by Captain Scott.[3] This book, which I ordered from London and reread a thousand times, filled me with longing to see with my own eyes that strange continent, last Thule[4] of the South, which lies on our maps and globes like a white cloud, a void, fringed here and there with scraps of coastline, dubious capes, supposititious islands, headlands that may or may not be there: Antarctica. And the desire was as pure as the polar snows: to go, to see — no more, no less. I deeply respect the scientific accomplishments of Captain Scott's expedition, and have read with passionate interest the findings of physicists, meteorologists, biologists, etc.; but having had no training in any science, nor any opportunity for such training, my ignorance obliged me to forego any thought of adding to the body of scientific knowledge concerning Antarctica; and the same is true for all the members of my expedition. It seems a pity; but there was nothing we could do about it. Our goal was limited to observation and exploration. We hoped to go a little farther, perhaps, and see a little more; if not, simply to go and to see. A simple ambition, I think, and essentially a modest one.

Yet it would have remained less than an ambition, no more than a longing, but for the support and encouragement of my dear cousin and friend Juana ——— (I use no surnames, lest this report fall into strangers' hands at last, and embarrassment or unpleasant notoriety thus be brought upon unsuspecting husbands, sons, etc.). I had lent Juana my copy of *The Voyage of the Discovery*, and it was she who, as we strolled beneath our parasols across the Plaza de Armas after Mass one Sunday in 1908, said, "Well, if Captain Scott can do it, why can't we?"

It was Juana who proposed that we write Carlota ——— in Valparaiso. Through Carlota we met our benefactor, and so obtained our money, our ship, and even the plausible pretext of going on retreat in a Bolivian convent, which

[3]*Robert Falcon Scott* (1868 - 1912) British explorer and naval officer who commanded an expedition to explore the Ross Sea region of Antarctica (1901 - 1904)

[4]*Thule* among the ancients, the northernmost region of the world, also understood as the ultimate or furthest goal, "Ultima Thule"

some of us were forced to employ (while the rest of us said we were going to Paris for the winter season). And it was my Juana who in the darkest moments remained resolute, unshaken in her determination to achieve our goal.

And there were dark moments, especially in the early months of 1909—times when I did not see how the Expedition would ever become more than a quarter ton of pemmican gone to waste and a lifelong regret. It was so very hard to gather our expeditionary force together! So few of those we asked even knew what we were talking about—so many thought we were mad, or wicked, or both! And of those few who shared our folly, still fewer were able, when it came to the point, to leave their daily duties and commit themselves to a voyage of at least six months, attended with not inconsiderable uncertainty and danger. An ailing parent; an anxious husband beset by business cares; a child at home with only ignorant or incompetent servants to look after it: these are not responsibilities lightly to be set aside. And those who wished to evade such claims were not the companions we wanted in hard work, risk, and privation.

But since success crowned our efforts, why dwell on the setbacks and delays, or the wretched contrivances and downright lies that we all had to employ? I look back with regret only to those friends who wished to come with us but could not, by any contrivance, get free—those we had to leave behind to a life without danger, without uncertainty, without hope.

On the seventeenth of August, 1909, in Punta Arenas, Chile, all the members of the Expedition met for the first time: Juana and I, the two Peruvians; from Argentina, Zoe, Berta, and Teresa; and our Chileans, Carlota and her friends Eva, Pepita, and Dolores. At the last moment I had received word that Maria's husband, in Quito, was ill, and she must stay to nurse him, so we were nine, not ten. Indeed, we had resigned ourselves to being but eight, when, just as night fell, the indomitable Zoe arrived in a tiny pirogue manned by Indians, her yacht having sprung a leak just as it entered the Strait of Magellan.

That night before we sailed we began to get to know one another; and we agreed, as we enjoyed our abominable supper in the abominable seaport inn of Punta Arenas, that if a situation arose of such urgent danger that one voice must be obeyed without present question, the unenviable honor of speaking with that voice should fall first upon myself: if I were incapacitated, upon Carlota: if she, then upon Berta. We three were then toasted as "Supreme Inca," "La Araucana,"[5] and "The Third Mate," among a lot of laughter and cheering. As it came out, to my very great pleasure and relief, my qualities as a "leader" were never tested; the nine of us worked things out amongst us from beginning to end without any orders being given by anybody, and only two or three times with recourse to a vote by voice or show of hands. To be sure, we argued a good deal. But then, we had time to argue. And one way or another the arguments always ended up in a decision, upon which action could be taken. Usually at least one person grumbled about the decision, sometimes bitterly. But what is life without grumbling, and the occasional opportunity to say, "I told you so"? How could one bear housework, or looking after babies, let alone the rigors of sledge-hauling in Antarctica, without grumbling? Officers—as we came to understand aboard the *Yelcho*—are forbidden to grumble; but we nine were, and are, by birth and upbringing, unequivocally and irrevocably, all crew.

[5]*Inca, La Araucana* Indians who occupied Chile before the Spanish conquest

Though our shortest course to the southern continent, and that originally urged upon us by the captain of our good ship, was to the South Shetlands and the Bellingshausen Sea, or else by the South Orkneys into the Weddell Sea, we planned to sail west to the Ross Sea, which Captain Scott had explored and described, and from which the brave Ernest Shackleton[6] had returned only the previous autumn. More was known about this region than any other portion of the coast of Antarctica, and though that more was not much, yet it served as some insurance of the safety of the ship, which we felt we had no right to imperil. Captain Pardo had fully agreed with us after studying the charts and our planned itinerary; and so it was westward that we took our course out of the Strait next morning.

Our journey half round the globe was attended by fortune. The little *Yelcho* steamed cheerily along through gale and gleam, climbing up and down those seas of the Southern Ocean that run unbroken round the world. Juana, who had fought bulls and the far more dangerous cows on her family's *estancia*, called the ship "*la vaca valiente*,"[7] because she always returned to the charge. Once we got over being seasick we all enjoyed the sea voyage, though oppressed at times by the kindly but officious protectiveness of the captain and his officers, who felt that we were only "safe" when huddled up in the three tiny cabins which they had chivalrously vacated for our use.

We saw our first iceberg much farther south than we had looked for it, and saluted it with Veuve Clicquot[8] at dinner. The next day we entered the ice pack, the belt of floes and bergs, broken loose from the land ice and winter-frozen seas of Antarctica, which drifts northward in the spring. Fortune still smiled on us: our little steamer, incapable, with her unreinforced metal hull, of forcing a way into the ice, picked her way from lane to lane without hesitation, and on the third day we were through the pack, in which ships have sometimes struggled for weeks and been obliged to turn back at last. Ahead of us now lay the dark grey waters of the Ross Sea, and beyond that, on the horizon, the remote glimmer, the cloud-reflected whiteness of the Great Ice Barrier.

Entering the Ross Sea a little east of Longitude West 160°, we came in sight of the Barrier at the place where Captain Scott's party, finding a bight in the vast wall of ice, had gone ashore and sent up their hydrogen-gas balloon for reconnaissance and photography. The towering face of the Barrier, its sheer cliffs and azure and violet water-worn caves, all were as described, but the location had changed: instead of a narrow bight there was a considerable bay, full of the beautiful and terrific orca whales playing and spouting in the sunshine of that brilliant southern spring.

Evidently masses of ice many acres in extent had broken away from the Barrier (which — at least for most of its vast extent — does not rest on land but floats on water) since the *Discovery's* passage in 1902. This put our plan to set up camp on the Barrier itself in a new light; and while we were discussing alternatives, we asked Captain Pardo to take the ship west along the Barrier face towards Ross Island and McMurdo Sound. As the sea was clear of ice and quite

[6]*Ernest Shackleton* (1874–1922) member of the British Antarctic expedition led by Scott

[7]*la vaca valiente* Spanish: the fine cow, *estancia* Spanish: cattle ranch

[8]*Veuve Cliquot* expensive French champagne

calm, he was happy to do so, and, when we sighted the smoke plume of Mount Erebus, to share in our celebration—another half case of Veuve Clicquot.

The *Yelcho* anchored in Arrival Bay, and we went ashore in the ship's boat. I cannot describe my emotions when I set foot on the earth, on that earth, the barren, cold gravel at the foot of the long volcanic slope. I felt elation, impatience, gratitude, awe, familiarity. I felt that I was home at last. Eight Adélie penguins immediately came to greet us with many exclamations of interest not unmixed with disapproval. "Where on earth have you been? What took you so long? The Hut is around this way. Please come this way. Mind the rocks!" They insisted on our going to visit Hut Point, where the large structure built by Captain Scott's party stood, looking just as in the photographs and drawings that illustrate his book. The area about it, however, was disgusting—a kind of graveyard of seal skins, seal bones, penguin bones, and rubbish, presided over by the mad, screaming skua gulls. Our escorts waddled past the slaughterhouse in all tranquility, and one showed me personally to the door, though it would not go in.

The interior of the hut was less offensive, but very dreary. Boxes of supplies had been stacked up into a kind of room within the room; it did not look as I had imagined it when the *Discovery* party put on their melodramas and minstrel shows in the long winter night. (Much later, we learned that Sir Ernest had rearranged it a good deal when he was there just a year before us.) It was dirty, and had about it a mean disorder. A pound tin of tea was standing open. Empty meat tins lay about; biscuits were spilled on the floor; a lot of dog turds were underfoot—frozen, of course, but not a great deal improved by that. No doubt the last occupants had had to leave in a hurry, perhaps even in a blizzard. All the same, they could have closed the tea tin. But housekeeping, the art of the infinite, is no game for amateurs.

Teresa proposed that we use the hut as our camp. Zoe counterproposed that we set fire to it. We finally shut the door and left it as we had found it. The penguins appeared to approve, and cheered us all the way to the boat.

McMurdo Sound was free of ice, and Captain Pardo now proposed to take us off Ross Island and across to Victoria Land, where we might camp at the foot of the Western Mountains, on dry and solid earth. But those mountains, with their storm-darkened peaks and hanging cirques and glaciers, looked as awful as Captain Scott had found them on his western journey, and none of us felt much inclined to seek shelter among them.

Aboard the ship that night we decided to go back and set up our base as we had originally planned, on the Barrier itself. For all available reports indicated that the clear way south was across the level Barrier surface until one could ascend one of the confluent glaciers to the high plateau which appears to form the whole interior of the continent. Captain Pardo argued strongly against this plan, asking what would become of us if the Barrier "calved"—if our particular acre of ice broke away and started to drift northward. "Well," said Zoe, "then you won't have to come so far to meet us." But he was so persuasive on this theme that he persuaded himself into leaving one of the *Yelcho's* boats with us when we camped, as a means of escape. We found it useful for fishing, later on.

My first steps on Antarctic soil, my only visit to Ross Island, had not been pleasure unalloyed. I thought of the words of the English poet:

Though every prospect pleases,
And only Man is vile.

But then, the backside of heroism is often rather sad; women and servants know that. They know also that the heroism may be no less real for that. But achievement is smaller than men think. What is large is the sky, the earth, the sea, the soul. I looked back as the ship sailed east again that evening. We were well into September now, with ten hours or more of daylight. The spring sunset lingered on the twelve-thousand-foot peak of Erebus and shone rosy gold on her long plume of steam. The steam from our own small funnel faded blue on the twilit water as we crept along under the towering pale wall of ice.

On our return to "Orca Bay"—Sir Ernest, we learned years later, had named it the Bay of Whales—we found a sheltered nook where the Barrier edge was low enough to provide fairly easy access from the ship. The *Yelcho* put out her ice anchor, and the next long, hard days were spent in unloading our supplies and setting up our camp on the ice, a half kilometer in from the edge: a task in which the *Yelcho's* crew lent us invaluable aid and interminable advice. We took all the aid gratefully, and most of the advice with salt.

The weather so far had been extraordinarily mild for spring in this latitude; the temperature had not yet gone below −20° Fahrenheit, and there was only one blizzard while we were setting up camp. But Captain Scott had spoken feelingly of the bitter south winds on the Barrier, and we had planned accordingly. Exposed as our camp was to every wind, we built no rigid structures above ground. We set up tents to shelter in while we dug out a series of cubicles in the ice itself, lined them with hay insulation and pine boarding, and roofed them with canvas over bamboo poles, covered with snow for weight and insulation. The big central room was instantly named Buenos Aires by our Argentineans, to whom the center, wherever one is, is always Buenos Aires. The heating and cooking stove was in Buenos Aires. The storage tunnels and the privy (called Punta Arenas) got some back heat from the stove. The sleeping cubicles opened off Buenos Aires, and were very small, mere tubes into which one crawled feet first; they were lined deeply with hay and soon warmed by one's body warmth. The sailors called them "coffins" and "wormholes," and looked with horror on our burrows in the ice. But our little warren or prairie-dog village served us well, permitting us as much warmth and privacy as one could reasonably expect under the circumstances. If the *Yelcho* was unable to get through the ice in February, and we had to spend the winter in Antarctica, we certainly could do so, though on very limited rations. For this coming summer, our base—Sudamérica del Sur, South South America, but we generally called it the Base—was intended merely as a place to sleep, to store our provisions, and to give shelter from blizzards.

To Berta and Eva, however, it was more than that. They were its chief architect-designers, its most ingenious builder-excavators, and its most diligent and contented occupants, forever inventing an improvement in ventilation, or learning how to make skylights, or revealing to us a new addition to our suite of rooms, dug in the living ice. It was thanks to them that our stores were stowed so handily, that our stove drew and heated so efficiently, and that Buenos Aires, where nine people cooked, ate, worked, conversed, argued, grumbled, painted, played the guitar and banjo, and kept the Expedition's library of books and maps, was a marvel of comfort and convenience. We lived there in real amity; and if you simply had to be alone for a while, you crawled into your sleeping hole head first.

Berta went a little farther. When she had done all she could to make South South America livable, she dug out one more cell just under the ice surface, leaving a nearly transparent sheet of ice like a greenhouse roof; and there, alone, she worked at sculptures. They were beautiful forms, some like a blending of the reclining human figure with the subtle curves and volumes of the Weddell seal, others like the fantastic shapes of ice cornices and ice caves. Perhaps they are there still, under the snow, in the bubble in the Great Barrier. There where she made them they might last as long as stone. But she could not bring them north. That is the penalty for carving in water.

Captain Pardo was reluctant to leave us, but his orders did not permit him to hang about the Ross Sea indefinitely, and so at last, with many earnest injunctions to us to stay put — make no journeys — take no risks — beware of frostbite —don't use edge tools — look out for cracks in the ice — and a heartfelt promise to return to Orca Bay on the twentieth of February, or as near that date as wind and ice would permit, the good man bade us farewell, and his crew shouted us a great goodbye cheer as they weighed anchor. That evening, in the long orange twilight of October, we saw the topmast of the *Yelcho* go down the north horizon, over the edge of the world, leaving us to ice, and silence, and the Pole.

That night we began to plan the Southern Journey.

The ensuing month passed in short practice trips and depotlaying. The life we had led at home, though in its own way strenuous, had not fitted any of us for the kind of strain met with in sledge-hauling at ten or twenty degrees below freezing. We all needed as much working-out as possible before we dared undertake a long haul.

My longest exploratory trip, made with Dolores and Carlota, was southwest towards Mount Markham, and it was a nightmare — blizzards and pressure ice all the way out, crevasses and no view of the mountains when we got there, and white weather and sastrugi[9] all the way back. The trip was useful, however, in that we could begin to estimate our capacities; and also in that we had started out with a very heavy load of provisions, which we depoted at 100 and 130 miles SSW of Base. Thereafter other parties pushed on farther, till we had a line of snow cairns and depots right down to Latitude 83°43′, where Juana and Zoe, on an exploring trip, had found a kind of stone gateway opening on a great glacier leading south. We established these depots to avoid, if possible, the hunger that had bedevilled Captain Scott's Southern Party, and the consequent misery and weakness. And we also established to our own satisfaction — intense satisfaction — that we were sledgehaulers at least as good as Captain Scott's husky dogs. Of course we could not have expected to pull as much or as fast as his men. That we did so was because we were favored by much better weather than Captain Scott's party ever met on the Barrier; and also the quantity and quality of our food made a very considerable difference. I am sure that the fifteen percent of dried fruits in our pemmican helped prevent scurvy; and the potatoes, frozen and dried according to an ancient Andean Indian method, were very nourishing yet very light and compact — perfect sledging rations. In any case, it was with considerable confidence in our capacities that we made ready at last for the Southern Journey.

The Southern Party consisted of two sledge teams: Juana, Dolores, and myself; Carlota, Pepita, and Zoe. The support team of Berta, Eva, and Teresa set out before us with a heavy load of supplies, going right up onto the glacier to prospect routes and leave depots of supplies for our return journey. We followed

[9]*sastrugi* wavelike ridges of hard snow

five days behind them, and met them returning between Depot Ercilla and Depot Miranda (see map). That "night"—of course there was no real darkness —we were all nine together in the heart of the level plain of ice. It was the fifteenth of November, Dolores's birthday. We celebrated by putting eight ounces of pisco[10] in the hot chocolate, and became very merry. We sang. It is strange now to remember how thin our voices sounded in that great silence. It was overcast, white weather, without shadows and without visible horizon or any feature to break the level; there was nothing to see at all. We had come to that white place on the map, that void, and there we flew and sang like sparrows.

After sleep and a good breakfast the Base Party continued north, and the Southern Party sledged on. The sky cleared presently. High up, thin clouds passed over very rapidly from southwest to northeast, but down on the Barrier it was calm and just cold enough, five or ten degrees below freezing, to give a firm surface for hauling.

On the level ice we never pulled less than eleven miles, seventeen kilometers, a day, and generally fifteen or sixteen miles, twenty-five kilometers. (Our instruments, being British made, were calibrated in feet, miles, degrees Fahrenheit, etc., but we often converted miles to kilometers because the larger numbers sounded more encouraging.) At the time we left South America, we knew only that Mr. Shackleton had mounted another expedition to the Antarctic in 1908, had tried to attain the Pole but failed, and had returned to England in June of the current year, 1909. No coherent report of his explorations had yet reached South America when we left; we did not know what route he had gone, or how far he had got. But we were not altogether taken by surprise when, far across the featureless white plain, tiny beneath the mountain peaks and the strange silent flight of the rainbow-fringed cloud wisps, we saw a fluttering dot of black. We turned west from our course to visit it: a snow heap nearly buried by the winter's storms—a flag on a bamboo pole, a mere shred of threadbare cloth—an empty oilcan—and a few footprints standing some inches above the ice. In some conditions of weather the snow compressed under one's weight remains when the surrounding soft snow melts or is scoured away by the wind; and so these reversed footprints had been left standing all these months, like rows of cobbler's lasts—a queer sight.

We met no other such traces on our way. In general I believe our course was somewhat east of Mr. Shackleton's. Juana, our surveyor, had trained herself well and was faithful and methodical in her sightings and readings, but our equipment was minimal—a theodolite on tripod legs, a sextant with artificial horizon, two compasses, and chronometers. We had only the wheel meter on the sledge to give distance actually travelled.

In any case, it was the day after passing Mr. Shackleton's waymark that I first saw clearly the great glacier among the mountains to the southwest, which was to give us a pathway from the sea level of the Barrier up to the altiplano,[11] ten thousand feet above. The approach was magnificent: a gateway formed by immense vertical domes and pillars of rock. Zoe and Juana had called the vast ice river that flowed through that gateway the Florence Nightingale Glacier, wishing to honor the British, who had been the inspiration and guide of our expedition;

[10]*pisco* Peruvian brandy
[11]*altiplano* high plateau

that very brave and very peculiar lady seemed to represent so much that is best, and strangest, in the island race. On maps, of course, this glacier bears the name Mr. Shackleton gave it, the Beardmore.

The ascent of the Nightingale was not easy. The way was open at first, and well marked by our support party, but after some days we came among terrible crevasses, a maze of hidden cracks, from a foot to thirty feet wide and from thirty to a thousand feet deep. Step by step we went, and step by step, and the way always upward now. We were fifteen days on the glacier. At first the weather was hot, up to 20° F., and the hot nights without darkness were wretchedly uncomfortable in our small tents. And all of us suffered more or less from snowblindness just at the time when we wanted clear eyesight to pick our way among the ridges and crevasses of the tortured ice, and to see the wonders about and before us. For at every day's advance more great, nameless peaks came into view in the west and southwest, summit beyond summit, range beyond range, stark rock and snow in the unending noon.

We gave names to these peaks, not very seriously, since we did not expect our discoveries to come to the attention of geographers. Zoe had a gift for naming, and it is thanks to her that certain sketch maps in various suburban South American attics bear such curious features as "Bolívar's Big Nose," "I Am General Rosas,"[12] "The Cloudmaker," "Whose Toe?" and "Throne of Our Lady of the Southern Cross." And when at last we got up onto the altiplano, the great interior plateau, it was Zoe who called it the pampa, and maintained that we walked there among vast herds of invisible cattle, transparent cattle pastured on the spindrift snow, their gauchos[13] the restless, merciless winds. We were by then all a little crazy with exhaustion and the great altitude—twelve thousand feet—and the cold and the wind blowing and the luminous circles and crosses surrounding the suns, for often there were three or four suns in the sky, up there.

That is not a place where people have any business to be. We should have turned back; but since we had worked so hard to get there, it seemed that we should go on, at least for a while.

A blizzard came with very low temperatures, so we had to stay in the tents, in our sleeping bags, for thirty hours, a rest we all needed; though it was warmth we needed most, and there was no warmth on that terrible plain anywhere at all but in our veins. We huddled close together all that time. The ice we lay on is two miles thick.

It cleared suddenly and became, for the plateau, good weather: twelve below zero and the wind not very strong. We three crawled out of our tent and met the others crawling out of theirs. Carlota told us then that her group wished to turn back. Pepita had been feeling very ill; even after the rest during the blizzard, her temperature would not rise above 90°. Carlota was having trouble breathing. Zoe was perfectly fit, but much preferred staying with her friends and lending them a hand in difficulties to pushing on towards the Pole. So we put the four ounces of pisco which we had been keeping for Christmas into the breakfast cocoa, and dug out our tents, and loaded our sledges, and parted there in the white daylight on the bitter plain.

[12]*General Rosas* Juan Manuel de Rosas (1793–1877), Argentinian dictator; *Simon Bolívar* (1783–1830)—soldier-leader of the South American revolution for independence from Spain

[13]*gauchos* cattlemen; *pampa*—South American plains

Our sledge was fairly light by now. We pulled on to the south. Juana calculated our position daily. On the twenty-second of December, 1909, we reached the South Pole. The weather was, as always, very cruel. Nothing of any kind marked the dreary whiteness. We discussed leaving some kind of mark or monument, a snow cairn, a tent pole and flag; but there seemed no particular reason to do so. Anything we could do, anything we were, was insignificant, in that awful place. We put up the tent for shelter for an hour and made a cup of tea, and then struck "90° Camp." Dolores, standing patient as ever in her sledging harness, looked at the snow; it was so hard frozen that it showed no trace of our footprints coming, and she said, "Which way?"

"North," said Juana.

It was a joke, because at that particular place there is no other direction. But we did not laugh. Our lips were cracked with frostbite and hurt too much to let us laugh. So we started back, and the wind at our backs pushed us along, and dulled the knife edges of the waves of frozen snow.

All that week the blizzard wind pursued us like a pack of mad dogs. I cannot describe it. I wished we had not gone to the Pole. I think I wish it even now. But I was glad even then that we had left no sign there, for some man longing to be first might come some day, and find it, and know then what a fool he had been, and break his heart.

We talked, when we could talk, of catching up to Carlota's party, since they might be going slower than we. In fact they had used their tent as a sail to catch the following wind and had got far ahead of us. But in many places they had built snow cairns or left some sign for us; once Zoe had written on the lee side of a ten-foot sastruga, just as children write on the sand of the beach at Miraflores, "This Way Out!" The wind blowing over the frozen ridge had left the words perfectly distinct.

In the very hour that we began to descend the glacier, the weather turned warmer, and the mad dogs were left to howl forever tethered to the Pole. The distance that had taken us fifteen days going up we covered in only eight days going down. But the good weather that had aided us descending the Nightingale became a curse down on the Barrier ice, where we had looked forward to a kind of royal progress from depot to depot, eating our fill and taking our time for the last three hundred-odd miles. In a tight place on the glacier I lost my goggles — I was swinging from my harness at the time in a crevasse — and then Juana had broken hers when we had to do some rock climbing coming down to the Gateway. After two days in bright sunlight with only one pair of snow goggles to pass amongst us, we were all suffering badly from snowblindness. It became acutely painful to keep lookout for landmarks or depot flags, to take sightings, even to study the compass, which had to be laid down on the snow to steady the needle. At Concolorcorvo Depot, where there was a particularly good supply of food and fuel, we gave up, crawled into our sleeping bags with bandaged eyes, and slowly boiled alive like lobsters in the tent exposed to the relentless sun. The voices of Berta and Zoe were the sweetest sound I ever heard. A little concerned about us, they had skied south to meet us. They led us home to Base.

We recovered quite swiftly, but the altiplano left its mark. When she was very little, Rosita asked if a dog "had bitted Mama's toes." I told her Yes, a great, white, mad dog named Blizzard! My Rosita and my Juanito heard many stories when they were little, about that fearful dog and how it howled, and the transparent cattle of the invisible gauchos, and a river of ice eight thousand feet high called Nightingale, and how Cousin Juana drank a cup of tea standing on the bottom of the world under seven suns, and other fairy tales.

We were in for one severe shock when we reached Base at last. Teresa was pregnant. I must admit that my first response to the poor girl's big belly and sheepish look was anger—rage—fury. That one of us should have concealed anything, and such a thing, from the others! But Teresa had done nothing of the sort. Only those who had concealed from her what she most needed to know were to blame. Brought up by servants, with four years' schooling in a convent, and married at sixteen, the poor girl was still so ignorant at twenty years of age that she had thought it was "the cold weather" that made her miss her periods. Even this was not entirely stupid, for all of us on the Southern Journey had seen our periods change or stop altogether as we experienced increasing cold, hunger, and fatigue. Teresa's appetite had begun to draw general attention; and then she had begun, as she said pathetically, "to get fat." The others were worried at the thought of all the sledge-hauling she had done, but she flourished, and the only problem was her positively insatiable appetite. As well as could be determined from her shy references to her last night on the hacienda with her husband, the baby was due at just about the same time as the *Yelcho*, the twentieth of February. But we had not been back from the Southern Journey two weeks when, on February 14, she went into labor.

Several of us had borne children and had helped with deliveries, and anyhow most of what needs to be done is fairly self-evident; but a first labor can be long and trying, and we were all anxious, while Teresa was frightened out of her wits. She kept calling for her José till she was as hoarse as a skua.[14] Zoe lost all patience at last and said, "By God, Teresa, if you say 'José!' once more I hope you have a penguin!" But what she had, after twenty long hours, was a pretty little red-faced girl.

Many were the suggestions for that child's name from her eight proud midwife-aunts: Polita, Penguina, McMurdo, Victoria. . . . But Teresa announced, after she had had a good sleep and a large serving of pemmican, "I shall name her Rosa—Rosa del Sur," Rose of the South. That night we drank the last two bottles of Veuve Clicquot (having finished the pisco at 88°30′ South) in toasts to our little Rose.

On the nineteenth of February, a day early, my Juana came down into Buenos Aires in a hurry. "The ship," she said, "the ship has come," and she burst into tears—she who had never wept in all our weeks of pain and weariness on the long haul.

Of the return voyage there is nothing to tell. We came back safe.

In 1912 all the world learned that the brave Norwegian Amundsen[15] had reached the South Pole; and then, much later, came the accounts of how Captain Scott and his men had come there after him, but did not come home again.

Just this year, Juana and I wrote to the captain of the *Yelcho*, for the newspapers have been full of the story of his gallant dash to rescue Sir Ernest Shackleton's men from Elephant Island, and we wished to congratulate him, and

[14]*skua* predatory seagull

[15]*Roald Amundsen* (1872–1928) Norwegian explorer, first man to reach the South Pole

once more to thank him. Never one word has he breathed of our secret. He is a man of honor, Luis Pardo.

I add this last note in 1929. Over the years we have lost touch with one another. It is very difficult for women to meet, when they live so far apart as we do. Since Juana died, I have seen none of my old sledgemates, though sometimes we write. Our little Rosa del Sur died of the scarlet fever when she was five years old. Teresa had many other children. Carlota took the veil in Santiago ten years ago. We are old women now, with old husbands, and grown children, and grandchildren who might some day like to read about the Expedition. Even if they are rather ashamed of having such a crazy grandmother, they may enjoy sharing in the secret. But they must not let Mr. Amundsen know! He would be terribly embarrassed and disappointed. There is no need for him or anyone else outside the family to know. We left no footprints, even.

[1982]

QUESTIONS

1. What motivates the women's expedition? What are their goals? Are the ways in which they organize their group effort unusual or distinctive?
2. Why does the narrator feel that the women's expedition must remain unknown to history? Why do the women "leave no footprints, even"?
3. What does the narrator mean when she says that "achievement is smaller than men think. What is large is the sky, the earth, the sea, the soul."
4. Through which details does Le Guin impart a realistic quality to the story? What elements reveal it to be fantasy?

Doris Lessing

(b. 1919)

Rhodesia/England

Doris Lessing's life is literally as well as geographically and politically diverse. Born Doris May Tayler in Persia (now Iran) to English parents who moved from there to southern Africa, she grew up on a farm in Rhodesia (now Zimbabwe). Apart from a brief period at school in Salisbury, she was self-educated at home; she began work as a secretary in Salisbury at the age of 16. Deeply sensitized to the inequities of black oppression in southern Africa, Lessing became actively involved in leftist politics for a time. Eventually, following two marriages that ended in divorce, she left Africa for England, where she has since resided.

Lessing's early fiction, begun in Africa, not only chronicles the political and social divisions of her time and place but also articulates the struggle for self-realization and independence of complex female characters, beginning with Mary Turner of her first novel, *The Grass Is Singing* (1950). As Lessing expressed her evolution as a writer in an interview with Minda Bikman, "I think most writers have to start very realistically because that's a way of establishing what they are, particularly women. . . . When you've found out [who you are], you can start making things up." Of the more than 20 novels Lessing has published, one of the most highly regarded is *The Golden Notebook* (1962), which anticipated central issues of the women's movement of the sixties in an innovative, experimental narrative form. Other major novels include the five-novel series *Children of Violence* (1952–1969).

Turning to science fiction frameworks to express her concerns about the future, Lessing published *Briefing for a Descent into Hell* (1971), *The Memoirs of a Survivor* (1974), and the five-novel series *Canopus at Argos: Archives* (1979–1983). In her subsequent novels, including *The Diaries of Jane Somers* (1983–1984, originally published under the pseudonym Jane Somers), *The Good Terrorist* (1985), and *The Fifth Child* (1988), Lessing returned to more realistic narrative forms to explore contemporary moral and social issues. *African Stories* (1964) and several other collections of stories demonstrate the diversity of Lessing's subjects and the versatility of her style.

Throughout her writing—which includes not only short stories and novels but also poetry, plays, and essays—Lessing has remained passionately committed to social justice and individual dignity. Her work frequently has anticipated and chronicled central contemporary social movements and issues, including mental illness, terrorism, war, women's rights, sexuality, mysticism, aging, and speculation on the future.

A Woman on a Roof

It was during the week of hot sun, that June.

Three men were at work on the roof, where the leads got so hot they had the idea of throwing water on to cool them. But the water steamed, then sizzled; and they made jokes about getting an egg from some woman in the flats under them, to poach it for their dinner. By two it was not possible to touch the guttering they were replacing, and they speculated about what workmen did in regularly hot countries. Perhaps they should borrow kitchen gloves with the egg? They were all a bit dizzy, not used to the heat; and they shed their coats and stood side by side squeezing themselves into a foot-wide patch of shade against a chimney, careful to keep their feet in the thick socks and boots out of the sun. There was a fine view across several acres of roofs. Not far off a man sat in a deck chair reading the newspapers. Then they saw her, between chimneys, about fifty yards away. She lay face down on a brown blanket. They could see the top part of her: black hair, a flushed solid back, arms spread out.

"She's stark naked," said Stanley, sounding annoyed.

Harry, the oldest, a man of about forty-five, said: "Looks like it."

Young Tom, seventeen, said nothing, but he was excited and grinning.

Stanley said: "Someone'll report her if she doesn't watch out."

"She thinks no one can see," said Tom, craning his head all ways to see more.

At this point the woman, still lying prone, brought her two hands up behind her shoulders with the ends of a scarf in them, tied it behind her back, and sat up. She wore a red scarf tied around her breasts and brief red bikini pants. This being the first day of the sun she was white, flushing red. She sat smoking, and did not look up when Stanley let out a wolf whistle. Harry said: "Small things amuse small minds," leading the way back to their part of the roof, but it was scorching. Harry said: "Wait, I'm going to rig up some shade," and disappeared down the skylight into the building. Now that he'd gone, Stanley and Tom went to the farthest point they could to peer at the woman. She had moved, and all they could see were two pink legs stretched on the blanket. They whistled and shouted but the legs did not move. Harry came back with a blanket and shouted: "Come on, then." He sounded irritated with them. They clambered back to him and he said to Stanley: "What about your missus?" Stanley was newly married, about three months. Stanley said, jeering: "What about my missus?"—preserving his independence. Tom said nothing, but his mind was full of the nearly naked woman. Harry slung the blanket, which he had borrowed from a friendly woman downstairs, from the stem of a television aerial to a row of chimney pots. This shade fell across the piece of gutter they had to replace. But the shade kept moving, they had to adjust the blanket, and not much progress was made. At last some of the heat left the roof, and they worked fast, making up for lost time. First Stanley, then Tom, made a trip to the end of the roof to see the woman. "She's on her back," Stanley said, adding a jest which made Tom snicker, and the older man smile tolerantly. Tom's report was that she hadn't moved, but it was a lie. He wanted to keep what he had seen to himself: he had caught her in the act of rolling down the little red pants over her hips, till they were no more than a small triangle. She was on her back, fully visible, glistening with oil.

Next morning, as soon as they came up, they went to look. She was already there, face down, arms spread out, naked except for the little red pants. She had turned brown in the night. Yesterday she was a scarlet and white woman, today she was a brown woman. Stanley let out a whistle. She lifted her head, startled, as if she'd been asleep, and looked straight over at them. The sun was in her eyes, she blinked and stared, then she dropped her head again. At this gesture of indifference, they all three, Stanley, Tom, and old Harry, let out whistles and yells. Harry was doing it in parody of the younger men, making fun of them, but he was also angry. They were all angry because of her utter indifference to the three men watching her.

"Bitch," said Stanley.

"She should ask us over," said Tom, snickering.

Harry recovered himself and reminded Stanley: "If she's married, her old man wouldn't like that."

"Christ," said Stanley virtuously, "if my wife lay about like that, for everyone to see, I'd soon stop her."

Harry said, smiling: "How do you know, perhaps she's sunning herself at this very moment?"

"Not a chance, not on our roof." The safety of his wife put Stanley into a good humour, and they went to work. But today it was hotter than yesterday; and several times one or the other suggested they should tell Matthew, the foreman, and ask to leave the roof until the heat wave was over. But they didn't. There was work to be done in the basement of the big block of flats, but up here they felt free, on a different level from ordinary humanity shut in the streets or the buildings. A lot more people came out onto the roofs that day, for an hour at midday. Some married couples sat side by side in deck chairs, the women's legs stockingless and scarlet, the men in vests with reddening shoulders.

The woman stayed on her blanket, turning herself over and over. She ignored them, no matter what they did. When Harry went off to fetch more screws, Stanley said: "Come on." Her roof belonged to a different system of roofs, separated from theirs at one point by about twenty feet. It meant a scrambling climb from one level to another, edging along parapets, clinging to chimneys, while their big boots slipped and slithered, but at last they stood on a small square projecting roof looking straight down at her, close. She sat smoking, reading a book. Tom thought she looked like a poster, or a magazine cover, with the blue sky behind her and her legs stretched out. Behind her a great crane at work on a new building in Oxford Street swung its black arm across the roofs in a great arc. Tom imagined himself at work on the crane, adjusting the arm to swing over and pick her up and swing her back across the sky to drop her near him.

They whistled. She looked up at them, cool and remote, then went on reading. Again, they were furious. Or rather, Stanley was. His sun-heated face was screwed into rage as he whistled again and again, trying to make her look up. Young Tom stopped whistling. He stood beside Stanley, excited, grinning; but he felt as if he were saying to the woman: "Don't associate me with *him*," for his grin was apologetic. Last night he had thought of the unknown woman before he slept, and she had been tender with him. This tenderness he was remembering as he shifted his feet by the jeering, whistling Stanley, and watched the indifferent healthy brown woman a few feet off, with the gap that plunged to the street between them. Tom thought it was romantic, it was like being high on two hilltops. But there was a shout from Harry, and they clambered back. Stanley's face was hard, really angry. The boy kept looking at him and wondered why he hated the woman so much, for by now he loved her.

The played their little games with the blanket, trying to trap shade to work under; but again it was not until nearly four that they could work seriously, and they were exhausted, all three of them. They were grumbling about the weather, by now. Stanley was in a thoroughly bad humour. When they made their routine trip to see the woman before they packed up for the day, she was apparently asleep, face down, her back naked save for the scarlet triangle on her buttocks. "I've got a good mind to report her to the police," said Stanley, and Harry said: "What's eating you? What harm's she doing?"

"I tell you, if she was my wife!"

"But she isn't, is she?" Tom knew that Harry, like himself, was uneasy at Stanley's reaction. He was normally a sharp young man, quick at his work, making a lot of jokes, good company.

"Perhaps it will be cooler tomorrow," said Harry.

But it wasn't, it was hotter, if anything, and the weather forecast said the good weather would last. As soon as they were on the roof, Harry went over to see if the woman were there, and Tom knew it was to prevent Stanley going, to put off his bad humour. Harry had grown-up children, a boy the same age as Tom, and the youth trusted and looked up to him.

Harry came back and said: "She's not there."

"I bet her old man has put his foot down," said Stanley, and Harry and Tom caught each other's eye and smiled behind the young married man's back.

Harry suggested they should get permission to work in the basement, and they did, that day. But before packing up Stanley said: "Let's have a breath of fresh air." Again Harry and Tom smiled at each other as they followed Stanley up to the roof, Tom in the devout conviction that he was there to protect the woman from Stanley. It was about five-thirty, and a calm, full sunlight lay over the roofs. The great crane still swung its black arm from Oxford Street to above their heads. She was not there. Then there was a flutter of white from behind a parapet, and she stood up, in a belted, white dressing gown. She had been there all day, probably, but on a different patch of roof, to hide from them. Stanley did not whistle, he said nothing, but watched the woman bend to collect papers, books, cigarettes, then fold the blanket over her arm. Tom was thinking: If they weren't here, I'd go over and say . . . what? But he knew from his nightly dreams of her that she was kind and friendly. Perhaps she would ask him down to her flat? Perhaps. . . . He stood watching her disappear down the skylight. As she went, Stanley let out a shrill derisive yell; she started, and it seemed as if she nearly fell. She clutched to save herself, they could hear things falling. She looked straight at them, angry. Harry said, facetiously: "Better be careful on those slippery ladders, love." Tom knew he said it to save her from Stanley, but she could not know it. She vanished, frowning. Tom was full of a secret delight, because he knew her anger was for the others, not for him.

"Roll on some rain," said Stanley, bitter, looking at the blue evening sky.

Next day was cloudless, and they decided to finish the work in the basement. They felt excluded, shut in the grey cement basement fitting pipes, from the holiday atmosphere of London in a heat wave. At lunchtime they came up for some air, but while the married couples, and the men in shirt-sleeves or vests, were there, she was not there, either on her usual patch of roof or where she had been yesterday. They all, even Harry, clambered about, between chimney pots, over parapets, the hot leads stinging their fingers. There was not a sign of her. They took off their shirts and vests and exposed their chests, feeling their feet sweaty and hot. They did not mention the woman. But Tom felt alone again. Last night she had asked him into her flat: it was big and had fitted white carpets and a bed with a padded white leather headtop. She wore a black filmy negligée and her kindness to Tom thickened his throat as he remembered it. He felt she had betrayed him by not being there.

And again after work they climbed up, but still there was nothing to be seen of her. Stanley kept repeating that if it was as hot as this tomorrow he wasn't going to work and that's all there was to it. But they were all there next day. By ten the temperature was in the middle seventies, and it was eighty long before noon. Harry went to the foreman to say it was impossible to work on the leads in that heat; but the foreman said there was nothing else he could put them on, and they'd have to. At midday they stood, silent, watching the skylight on her roof open, and then she slowly emerged in her white gown, holding a bundle of blanket. She looked at them, gravely, then went to the part of the roof where she was hidden from them. Tom was pleased. He felt she was more his when the other men couldn't see her. They had taken off their shirts and vests, but now they put them back again, for they felt the sun bruising their flesh. "She must have the hide of a rhino," said Stanley, tugging at guttering and swearing. They stopped work, and sat in the shade, moving around behind chimney stacks. A woman came to water a yellow window box just opposite them. She was middle-aged, wearing a flowered summer dress. Stanley said to her: "We need a drink more than them." She smiled and said: "Better drop down to the pub quick, it'll be closing in a minute." They exchanged pleasantries, and she left them with a smile and a wave.

"Not like Lady Godiva," said Stanley. "She can give us a bit of a chat and a smile."

"You didn't whistle at *her*," said Tom, reproving.

"Listen to him," said Stanley, "you didn't whistle, then?"

But the boy felt as if he hadn't whistled, as if only Harry and Stanley had. He was making plans, when it was time to knock off work, to get left behind and somehow make his way over to the woman. The weather report said the hot spell was due to break, so he had to move quickly. But there was no chance of being left. The other two decided to knock off work at four, because they were exhausted. As they went down, Tom quickly climbed a parapet and hoisted himself higher by pulling his weight up a chimney. He caught a glimpse of her lying on her back, her knees up, eyes closed, a brown woman lolling in the sun. He slipped and clattered down, as Stanley looked for information: "She's gone down," he said. He felt as if he had protected her from Stanley, and that she must be grateful to him. He could feel the bond between the woman and himself.

Next day, they stood around on the landing below the roof, reluctant to climb up into the heat. The woman who had lent Harry the blanket came out and offered them a cup of tea. They accepted gratefully, and sat round Mrs. Pritchett's kitchen an hour or so, chatting. She was married to an airline pilot. A smart blonde, of about thirty, she had an eye for the handsome sharpfaced Stanley; and the two teased each other while Harry sat in a corner, watching, indulgent, though his expression reminded Stanley that he was married. And young Tom felt envious of Stanley's ease in badinage; felt, too, that Stanley's getting off with Mrs. Pritchett left his romance with the woman on the roof safe and intact.

"I thought they said the heat wave'd break," said Stanley, sullen, as the time approached when they really would have to climb up into the sunlight.

"You don't like it then?" asked Mrs. Pritchett.

"All right for some," said Stanley. "Nothing to do but lie about as if it was a beach up there. Do you ever go up?"

"Went up once," said Mrs. Pritchett. "But it's a dirty place up there, and it's too hot."

"Quite right too," said Stanley.

Then they went up, leaving the cool neat little flat and the friendly Mrs. Pritchett.

As soon as they were up they saw her. The three men looked at her, resentful at her ease in this punishing sun. Then Harry said, because of the expression on Stanley's face: "Come on, we've got to pretend to work, at least."

They had to wrench another length of guttering that ran beside a parapet out of its bed, so that they could replace it. Stanley took it in his two hands, tugged, swore, stood up. "Fuck it," he said, and sat down under a chimney. He lit a cigarette. "Fuck them," he said. "What do they think we are, lizards? I've got blisters all over my hands." Then he jumped up and climbed over the roofs and stood with his back to them. He put his fingers either side of his mouth and let out a shrill whistle. Tom and Harry squatted, not looking at each other, watching him. They could just see the woman's head, the beginnings of her brown shoulders. Stanley whistled again. Then he began stamping with his feet, and whistled and yelled and screamed at the woman, his face getting scarlet. He seemed quite mad, as he stamped and whistled, while the woman did not move, she did not move a muscle.

"Barmy," said Tom.

"Yes," said Harry, disapproving.

Suddenly the older man came to a decision. It was, Tom knew, to save some sort of scandal or real trouble over the woman. Harry stood up and began packing tools into a length of oily cloth. "Stanley," he said, commanding. At first Stanley took no notice, but Harry said: "Stanley, we're packing it in, I'll tell Matthew."

Stanley came back, cheeks mottled, eyes glaring.

"Can't go on like this," said Harry. "It'll break in a day or so. I'm going to tell Matthew we've got sunstroke, and if he doesn't like it, it's too bad." Even Harry sounded aggrieved, Tom noted. The small, competent man, the family man with his grey hair, who was never at a loss, sounded really off balance. "Come on," he said, angry. He fitted himself into the open square in the roof, and went down, watching his feet on the ladder. Then Stanley went, with not a glance at the woman. Then Tom who, his throat beating with excitement, silently promised her in a backward glance: Wait for me, wait, I'm coming.

On the pavement Stanley said: "I'm going home." He looked white now, so perhaps he really did have sunstroke. Harry went off to find the foreman who was at work on the plumbing of some flats down the street. Tom slipped back, not into the building they had been working on, but the building on whose roof the woman lay. He went straight up, no one stopping him. The skylight stood open, with an iron ladder leading up. He emerged onto the roof a couple of yards from her. She sat up, pushing back her black hair with both hands. The scarf across her breasts bound them tight, and brown flesh bulged around it. Her legs were brown and smooth. She stared at him in silence. The boy stood grinning, foolish, claiming the tenderness he expected from her.

"What do you want?" she asked.

"I . . . I came to . . . make your acquaintance," he stammered, grinning, pleading with her.

They looked at each other, the slight, scarlet-faced excited boy, and the serious, nearly naked woman. Then, without a word, she lay down on her brown blanket, ignoring him.

"You like the sun, do you?" he enquired of her glistening back.

Not a word. He felt panic, thinking of how she had held him in her arms, stroked his hair, brought him where he sat, lordly, in her bed, a glass of some exhilarating liquor he had never tasted in life. He felt that if he knelt down, stroked her shoulders, her hair, she would turn and clasp him in her arms.

He said: "The sun's all right for you, isn't it?"

She raised her head, set her chin on two small fists. "Go away," she said. He did not move. "Listen," she said, in a slow reasonable voice, where anger was kept in check, though with difficulty; looking at him, her face weary with anger: "If you get a kick out of seeing women in bikinis, why don't you take a sixpenny bus ride to the Lido? You'd see dozens of them, without all this mountaineering."

She hadn't understood him. He felt her unfairness pale him. He stammered: "But I like you, I've been watching you and . . ."

"Thanks," she said, and dropped her face again, turned away from him.

She lay there. He stood there. She said nothing. She had simply shut him out. He stood, saying nothing at all, for some minutes. He thought: She'll have to say something if I stay. But the minutes went past, with no sign of them in her, except in the tension of her back, her thighs, her arms—the tension of waiting for him to go.

He looked up at the sky, where the sun seemed to spin in heat; and over the roofs where he and his mates had been earlier. He could see the heat quivering where they had worked. "And they expect us to work in these conditions!" he thought, filled with righteous indignation. The woman hadn't moved. A bit of hot wind blew her black hair softly, it shone, and was iridescent. He remembered how he had stroked it last night.

Resentment of her at last moved him off and away down the ladder, through the building, into the street. He got drunk then, in hatred of her.

Next day when he woke the sky was grey. He looked at the wet grey and thought, vicious: "Well, that's fixed you, hasn't it now? That's fixed you good and proper."

The three men were at work early on the cool leads, surrounded by damp drizzling roofs where no one came to sun themselves, black roofs, slimy with rain. Because it was cool now, they would finish the job that day, if they hurried.

[1963]

QUESTIONS

1. Through whose perspective do we understand the action of the story? Whose story is it, Tom's or the woman's?

2. What attitudes concerning the relationships between men and women does the story explore?
3. How does the setting contribute to the development of the story?
4. Does the gender of the reader affect the response to this story? If so, how? How would the story be different if seen through the woman's eyes?

Catherine Lim

(b. 1942)

Singapore

Catherine Lim has published two widely praised collections of short stories: *Little Ironies—Stories of Singapore* (1978) and *Or Else, the Lightning God and Other Stories* (1980). Of *Little Ironies*, Austin Coates has written, "The stories are riveting; there is no other word for them. In their Singapore Chinese context they rank with the best of Guy de Maupassant and Alphonse Daudet. Each story has the same sureness of observation, clarity in the presentation of character, and finely judged economy both of words and emotion. . . . Her knowledge of Chinese ways of living and habits of thought is masterly. It may sound absurd to say this, but so few people are able, as she is, to draw back and look at it objectively. She exposes men and women with a mixture of complacent ruthlessness and compassion." Ms. Lim has published two novels: *They Do Return* (1982) and *The Serpent's Tooth* (1983). Currently she works for the Curriculum Development Institute of Singapore, writing English language instructional materials for use in the primary schools.

Or Else, the Lightning God

Whenever Margaret didn't have the opportunity to talk to Suan Choo in the office about the problems with her mother-in-law, she telephoned her friend in the evening. And she did so now, reclining on the bed, freshly bathed and talcumed. Eng Kiat wasn't home, and the old one was in her room downstairs, so it was all right to speak as freely as she wanted to Suan Choo. Suan Choo had a mother-in-law too, equally troublesome, and so understood her problem perfectly. Margaret knew that the old one, though she spoke no English, understood the meanings of certain words when she heard them; her small eyes would flash, she would look up sharply when she caught words such as "mother-in-law," "money," "servant," "nuisance," convinced that she was being talked about and criticised. So Margaret, in her conversations with Suan Choo had evolved a new set of terms intended to put the old lady off the scent. "Mother-in-law" became "dowager" or "antique," "servant" was "domestic." Sometimes failure to find appropriate alternatives forced Margaret to spell out the word, but the element of unnaturalness introduced into the conversation in this way made the old lady, who was very sharp indeed, pause to listen suspiciously.

"Suan Choo, guess what I saw when I came back from work today," she said, managing to light a cigarette with one hand while holding the receiver with the other. "Or rather, what I smelt. There was a foul smell coming from the kitchen. I rushed to see and there was an earthenpot of the Dowager's herbal medicine a-brewing as usual. The stuff had boiled over and was trickling down the sides of my poor cooker. Luckily I came back in time. Otherwise, that wretched thing would have ruined my whole kitchen. This is the third time this week, Choo, that the Dowager's left her Chinese medicine brewing while she goes off I don't know where. Later she came back and had the audacity to ask who had turned off the flame when her medicine wasn't yet properly brewed!"

Suan Choo was able to furnish a similar story of outrageous mother-in-law behaviour, and the two laughed loud and long over the phone. Margaret's cheerful mood was due partly to the doctor's assurance, when she paid one of her regular calls that morning, that he thought her chances for the baby were very much improved by the administration of the new drug. "When Doctor Lee told me to relax and have plenty of rest, I nearly said, 'You must be joking, Doctor. How can anyone relax with a mother-in-law like mine about the place?'" said Margaret and she laughed again. Not all complaints ended on such a cheerful note.

"Suan Choo, would you believe it, the Dowager actually invited a medium to my house?" cried Margaret shortly after, clutching her friend's arm. "A temple medium, one of those weird men who go into a trance and froth at the mouth? She actually made arrangements for a séance in my house! It seemed she wanted to communicate with my dead father-in-law. Imagine my fury. To make my house a den for those eerie people with their joss-sticks and prayer paper and I don't know what else! A good thing I came back in time. I nearly threw away those horrible prayer things of theirs."

No less than a full delivery of her tirade could have eased the pressure of mounting anger, and after Margaret had finished giving an account of the offence, she went into more details.

"They were going to use her room for the purpose. I saw a table already laid out with those evil-looking candles and joss-sticks and glasses of water and what have you. My father-in-law's photo was on the wall — you know, the one taken of him a month before he died — that unnatural ghostly look — you remarked once how eerie it looked, and how the old man's eyes seemed to be following you, remember? Well, they had the photo on the wall, and a paper effigy of the old man, I think, on the table, against the wall — and I don't know what other rubbish. Fortunately, I came home in time to prevent it. Imagine, Choo, calling up the dead in my house. It makes my flesh creep all over. That mother-in-law of mine is driving me crazy, and Dr. Lee tells me to relax — relax, my God!"

Suan Choo, more interested this time in exploring the subject of the supernatural than in contributing to tirades against mothers-in-law, said that her aunt once conjured the spirit of her uncle in a seance and spoke to the dead one through the medium for half an hour. The aunt maintained that the medium's features had taken on those of her dead husband; she swore it was her husband sitting in the room talking to her.

"Why can't these old people leave their dead alone?" cried Margaret in exasperation. "Why must they cause trouble to others by delving into these dark, sinister things which are best left alone? Anyway, I think those people my mother-in-law associates with are a bunch of cheats, that's all. They foist upon her all sorts of herbal medicines and charms and other such rubbish, and she pays through her nose for them. And where does her money come from? Eng Kiat and me, of course! Do you know, Choo, we give that old fool two hundred dollars a month for pocket money, and she still complains it's not enough! She lives with us, there's a servant to attend to her needs, even her new clothes and slippers and umbrellas are bought for her, and she dares complain the two hundred dollars isn't enough!"

The subject of money had become a very sore one, and here Suan Choo was able to join in the complaints with equal energy, for her mother-in-law sponged outrageously on her husband, demanding money for this or for that all the time.

Margaret's anger extended to the brothers-in-law who refused to carry out their share of the duty of supporting the old one.

"There's Eng Loong, I've told you of his miserly ways so often. His business is thriving, and his wife, I hear, is making tons of money in the Stock Exchange, but they don't give one cent to the old lady. It's only the occasional *ang pow*[1] for the Chinese New Year or the birthday, and they think they're hell of a filial," cried Margaret angrily. "Then there's that good-for-nothing Eng Chian — always flitting from one job to another. I suspect he's been borrowing money from Kiat again, but of course that husband of mine will never tell me anything. So everyone comes to Kiat stretching out a long arm and here am I slaving like a fool in the office, helping to support a host of parasites!" Margaret lit a cigarette furiously, then stubbed it out.

"I forgot," she told her friend in a softened tone. "The doctor says I'm not to smoke during this period. Hey, Choo," a smile appeared on her face, "I may have good news to tell you soon. I'm keeping my fingers crossed!"

When her husband returned from his business trip abroad, Margaret was indeed able to tell him the good news and husband and wife rejoiced, for at last, after six years of marriage, Margaret was to have a child.

"There's no need to tell the old lady yet," said Margaret. "We'll tell her only when we're perfectly sure."

They told her a month later, and Margaret was rankled by the cold indifference of her mother-in-law's response.

"Well, it is good for you," she said stiffly. "You've waited six years for a child, and now you're going to have one.

Margaret recollected the old lady's solicitous anxiety when Eng Loong's wife was pregnant; she fussed, she recommended this food and that food, she made bird's nest soup with expensive rare herbs, she was so concerned. And Mee Lian never bought her any jewellery or even a new dress. Margaret heaved in anger at the unjust antagonism of the old one.

But, she told Suan Choo and her other friends, she couldn't care a jot. She was not of that old breed who trembled in the presence of a mother-in-law and sought to please all the time.

"Today things are different," cried Margaret with spirited defiance. "It's not like in the old days when women were subject to their mothers-in-law. I remember my mum telling me that her mother-in-law nagged and scolded her everyday, and if my father wanted to take her out to the *wayang*,[2] he had to get permission from the old gorgon. Today, it's no longer like this, ah, no more! Today, we're working wives drawing good salaries, we're independent, we're educated. Today, *they* depend on us, *they* stretch out their hands for their monthly money. So what is there to be afraid of?" Margaret described, with animation, her happy position, free of any ties of obligation to the old.

[1]*ang pow* a gift of money (in a red envelope) for Chinese New Year

[2]*wayang* a show; entertainment

"Number One, we're financially secure, we made it on our own without any help from my husband's family," she said. "Kiat's parents didn't spend a cent on his higher education, for he got scholarships and bursaries all the way. I wouldn't want to be in Diana Lau's position. She's living with her rich in-laws; you know that famous big house in Marine Vista with the two huge stone lions at the entrance? That's the family home, and I hear Diana is scared as hell of offending her old father-in-law and mother-in-law. You know the old lady whom we met in Tai Sing Goldsmith the other day, the one glittering with diamonds? Well, I'm glad I don't have a rich mother-in-law like that; it makes things more difficult. Like this, I'm independent, I'm free, I'm not afraid of anybody!"

Suan Choo had two small children and whenever she had problems with the servant, her mother-in-law came to help.

"She's quite useless with the children," said Suan Choo, "but at least I have someone in the house with the kids while Gerard and I are at work. I don't have to leave the children at a friend's, like Gek Eng does whenever the servant plays her out."

"Number Two, I don't depend on my mother-in-law to help in the house," said Margaret with energetic triumph. "My Ah Chan is most reliable and manages perfectly, and I don't have children as yet. When my baby arrives, I'm going to get Ah Chan to take care of the baby, and another servant to do the housework. My mother-in-law will never have the occasion to say, 'See, these young people depend on us their elders to see to this and that.'"

Margaret's mother, a small-sized, timid-looking woman, who was rather in awe of her strong-willed, efficient daughter, nevertheless took her aside one morning when she came on a visit, and gravely spoke about respect for the old.

"You mustn't quarrel with your mother-in-law, Margaret," she said with grave solicitousness. "Young people must heed the old; they must not raise their voice against the old. It is not good, Margaret."

Margaret said impatiently, "Mother, I agree with you. I agree with you when the old are reasonable and considerate in their behaviour. But when they are unreasonable and hypocritical and spiteful, when they are never satisfied no matter how much you do for them and criticise you behind your back, then they don't deserve the respect of the young!"

"Margaret, it is not good to talk like this, it is not good at all," said the elderly woman, with a melancholy shake of her head. "I respected my mother-in-law because of her grey hairs though she was cruel to me. The young must respect the old, Margaret, or they will be punished." And she spoke of that punishment reserved for those guilty of filial impiety, the ultimate transgression: they would be struck by the Lightning God. The Lightning God in Heaven heeds the cries of the old.

"What nonsense!" cried Margaret, and now she was really angry. She said sharply to her mother, "Mother, this is the new age. This is not the old age, when you were scared of your mother-in-law and allowed her to trample on you. There is no Lightning God today, Mother — no Lightning God or Thunder God or Kitchen God. They all died long ago."

Margaret had never seethed with such indignation before. She went out and decided to take her mind off the problems besetting her by doing some shopping. She needed some cleansing cream, and if she found something she liked to put in the baby's room which was almost ready, she would get it, regardless of cost. For, Margaret thought, why should I stinge on myself and the baby, and let all the money go the spongers? I will not be so foolish.

The shopping afforded her much pleasure, and she bought a very large and very expensive panda for the baby. She wished Kiat were home, so she could show him the delightful toy. Kiat was a good, loving husband, only too soft when it came to his family. She rang Suan Choo to tell her about the shopping and uttered a little scream of surprise and delight when Suan Choo confided that she too was going to have a baby; the doctor had just confirmed it.

"I hope it'll be a boy this time, Choo," said Margaret, very glad for her friend.

"I'm thinking of the servant problem," said Suan Choo. "My mother-in-law's in one of her cranky moods again, and the earlier I get a reliable servant, the better."

And Margaret, rejoicing with her best friend, was in a sufficiently good mood to withstand her mother-in-law's latest assault upon her nerves: the old lady was making a patchwork blanket, and strewn all over her nice, clean marble floor downstairs were small pieces of cloth and bits of thread. The servant Ah Chan complained that that was the third time she had to sweep up the stuff that morning, but Margaret said, "Oh, leave her alone, Ah Chan. Otherwise, she will have something more to complain to the neighbours about." The neighbour who irritated Margaret most was the next-door washerwoman who was always talking to her mother-in-law over the fence. The two women's habit of lowering their voices and nudging each other, each time they thought Margaret was approaching, was most annoying. She was positive the old one talked about her to the next-door gossip, and she was furious. She had complained about this to her husband, but in his characteristic casual manner, he had said, "Aw, leave them alone. They're idle gossips, that's all."

Oh, when will I be rid of my burden? thought Margaret. She knew the old one would always be staying with them for Eng Loong's wife would not have her, and Eng Chian was a good-for-nothing who had difficulty supporting himself. Her Eng Kiat, because he had a good-natured disposition, was taken advantage of by all. Margaret had the idea, as yet not carefully defined as a strategy, of getting rid of the troublesome old one once her baby arrived. There must be some excuse which the coming of the baby could furnish for making arrangements for the old one to live elsewhere. It would be some months before the baby arrived; meanwhile, she would have to put up with the old lady whose ways were becoming intolerable.

"One of these days I shall blow up, I don't care what Kiat says," cried poor Margaret. "The old one's Lightning God can strike me dead if he likes!" She took some comfort from the thought that Suan Choo was also having much trouble with her mother-in-law. Suan Choo had confided, the night before, in a voice shrill with exasperation, that her mother-in-law had unreasonably quarrelled with her new servant. The servant had been proving to be so reliable and efficient. Now the servant had left, and she had to start looking all over again for another one. And she was feeling so sick these days, with her frequent vomiting.

"Choo, we are in the same boat," said Margaret. "I keep telling everybody, one of these days I'm going to blow up."

She blew up shortly after this. It happened this way. Margaret was having lunch with an office colleague, who knew her next-door neighbours. It seemed that her mother-in-law had complained to the washerwoman of being ill-treated by Margaret. She was left alone in the house most of the time, she said, and she didn't have proper food.

"No proper food!" gasped Margaret and she could hardly believe what she had just heard. Her refrigerator was always full, her groceries store was stocked to the ceiling with tinned food and dried stuff for the old one to help herself to, and she was complaining of not having enough food!

It seemed, continued the colleague, the washerwoman went over one morning to see the old lady who was sitting at the table eating a bowl of rice porridge with nothing in it but soya sauce. The washerwoman was shocked and asked her why she was eating such meagre food, food not fit for a beggar, whereupon the old one started to weep. It was so pitiful that the washerwoman wept with her.

"Oh, I can't stand this, I can't stand it anymore!" cried Margaret, white with anger. "She gives me endless trouble, I load her with gifts and food and money and she goes around telling people I ill-treat her and starve her! How can I stand this? That gossipy washerwoman has no business to interfere in our affairs. I'm not going to let this pass, I promise you!" Margaret was now weeping in vexed distress. Her friend grew alarmed, for Margaret was six months pregnant now, and it was bad for a woman in her condition to be so distressed.

Margaret stormed home and confronted her mother-in-law. It was raining heavily and she got wet running from the taxi into the house, but she did not bother to dry herself; she went straight in search of the old one who was in the kitchen, and confronted her. Her words of accusation came out in angry torrents; she accused her mother-in-law of ingratitude, of deceit, of injustice to her. Her voice quavered in her anger, her knees trembled beneath her and her hands were cold, for such a situation was something new and, in retrospect, frightening to her. But she stood, firm and strong now, shrill with hurt and fury.

The old one looked up from the table where she was drinking a cup of coffee; she stared at her, first with disbelief, then with silent malevolence. Her mouth was gathered in tight lines of cold fury. Then she stood up. She said to Margaret, "So you dare speak this way to your old mother-in-law? You see the grey hairs on my head, and you dare speak to me in this way? You, who are going to be a mother yourself! You take care!" She pointed a finger at Margaret, her small grey eyes flashing with anger, but Margaret was not to be cowed easily.

"I'm not afraid of you!" she cried in quivering indignation. "I've had enough trouble from you, and so you get out of my house!"

The old one glared at her, the small grey eyes glittering menacingly.

"You wouldn't dare do this to me if my son were here," she said slowly.

"This is MY house, it was bought in MY name, and I tell you to get out," shrieked Margaret, the hot tears rushing to her eyes.

The old one stood up to her full height, and she said, in a clear, shrill voice, "All right. Listen, then, daughter-in-law. In this house you have treated me like dirt, you have made me feel worse than a prisoner. You follow me about with your eyes when I want to speak to my son, and you are not happy when my son is good to me and gives me money. Don't think I'm not aware of all this! So I leave now, but before I go, let me tell you this. Those who are cruel to their elders will never prosper! They are cursed. I curse you now; you are bearing a child, but I curse you!"

The roar of the rain outside almost drowned her words, but Margaret heard, and a thrill of terror ran through her. But she remained in the standing posture of defiance, though her heart was beating violently. The old one went into her room, put some things into a paper bag and left with an umbrella, in the pouring rain.

By herself, Margaret ran up to her room, threw herself upon the bed and wept bitterly. Oh, how hateful everything was! How simply hateful! Why was she so unlucky as to be suffering all this? In her distress, she put a long distance call to her husband to come home.

When he arrived, the next evening, he found her inert on the bed, the tears falling silently down her cheeks. She clung to him, crying dismally. He was alarmed on the baby's account and soothed her as best he could, but inwardly he was irked: "These women—will they never stop their nonsense." Unable to criticise his wife or mother, he lashed out in full fury against the washerwoman, now seen as the cause of all the trouble.

His task, after he had soothed Margaret and made her comfortable, was to look for his mother and make sure she had come to no harm. And he groaned again to himself, and shook his head, "These women—they give endless trouble."

He was relieved to find that the old one had gone to Eng Loong's house and was now under the care of Eng Loong and Mee Lian. He explained as best he could, the two brothers shook their heads, and Mee Lian bustled about to make her old mother-in-law comfortable, for she had caught cold in the rain.

"So it's me, the villainess, sending out an old white-haired woman into the rain and storm," cried Margaret with a sharp laugh, when Eng Kiat returned and told her of what had happened.

She felt unwell and lay in bed for a long time. She fretted and grew irritable, and snapped at her husband and servant. The nights were more distressful for she couldn't sleep—her head swarmed with troubling thoughts and her heart was charged with troubling feelings. Again and again she saw the old one, standing upright, with hand raised and finger pointing upwards, and heard her shrill cry ring out, "I curse you! You are with child, but still I curse you!"

The glint of malevolence in the old eyes Margaret could never forget. She trembled each time she recollected that glare of malice in the old face, the white hair that had loosened from the knot at the back of her head and floated in stiff strands about the face. It was ghastly. It was horrible. Margaret closed her eyes tight to shut off that evil scene, but it would come back, again and again. In her dreams, it took on a vividness and monstrosity that caused her to wake up screaming; in her dreams, the old one's features assumed a demonic leer and her voice a demonic shriek so that the curse rang piercingly in Margaret's ears. She woke up screaming and clung to her husband sobbing.

"She cursed me, your mother cursed me, and I'm already seven months with child," she sobbed in her fear. Eng Kiat, haggard with sleeplessness, tried his best to soothe her. He kept reassuring her that everything would be all right, that old people, especially uneducated ones like his mother, cursed when they were angry, and said all sorts of bizarre things.

"Her curse was terrible, she meant every word of it," said Margaret. "Yesterday and today," she continued with a sob, "the child inside me did not move. Didn't even stir once. I swear to you, Kiat, our baby hasn't moved for two days!"

A tremor of terror ran through the husband, but he only said, with feigned casualness, "Now, now, that's being morbid, darling, and that's not like you at all. You had a bad experience and are now imagining all sorts of things. I'll take you to see Dr. Lee tomorrow morning. You'll see that everything is all right."

Dr. Lee said that there was nothing wrong. Mother and child were doing well, and all Margaret needed was a lot of rest. On reaching home, Margaret told her husband she noticed that Dr. Lee looked worried; perhaps he had discovered something about her baby but was not willing to tell her? Eng Kiat said impatiently, "What nonsense!" but Margaret insisted that he took longer than usual to examine her and there was a frown on his face.

She had lost her appetite and was feeling utterly wretched. A frightened look had come into her eyes; in one of her dreams, her baby was stillborn, in another it had arms but no legs. Margaret sat up in bed in the darkness, and put her hands to her mouth to stifle the sobs, for she did not want to disturb her husband in his sleep.

Suan Choo rang up. Margaret hadn't spoken to Suan Choo for days and was glad to hear her friend's voice. Suan Choo spoke weakly. She was in hospital, recovering from a miscarriage. When she hung up, Margaret stood still, her eyes dilated in terror, her hands cold. Suan Choo had quarrelled with her mother-in-law, and this was her punishment. The power of the curse of the old! Margaret picked up the phone again, rang frantically for Suan Choo, and told her, in stricken whispers, what she thought.

"But that's impossible. The quarrel was some time ago, and besides, my mother-in-law never cursed me. Anyway, we are okay now, and she's helping out with the kids," said Suan Choo, terrified nevertheless by the possibility.

"No, no, Choo, you don't believe it, but it's true! I tell you it's true, their curse is powerful!" sobbed Margaret.

She grew distracted, not wanting her husband to be out of her sight, and she told Dr. Lee tearfully that she felt the child was dying inside her or would be born to torment her.

"On the day she cursed me, there was thunder and lightning," she said in an awestricken voice.

She was in a dark building, which was a temple, for there were red pillars and niches in the walls in which a number of gods sat brooding. Some of them were hidden in the shadows, but she knew they were watching her. The smell of smoke from the giant joss-sticks in a large gold urn on the floor stung her eyes and made her cough a little, and when the tears cleared, she saw, curled round the joss-sticks, snakes of a variety of sizes and colours. They were dull-eyed and their bodies moved slowly, lugubriously, on the joss-sticks, as if drowsed by the fumes. A long time ago, when she was a little girl, she had gone with her mother and aunt to a Chinese temple which housed hundreds of snakes that were supposed to be holy, and she had hidden behind her mother and cried when a snake slowly lifted its head and cast a beady eye on her. Now she looked upon the snakes on the joss-sticks unafraid, for she knew the poison had been taken out of them long ago. They continued to move slowly, ponderously, and then they slithered down to the floor towards her and were all over her, so that she gasped and choked and tried to pull them off. She saw her mother-in-law at a distance, holding a bunch of small joss-sticks in her hand and getting ready to stick them into the ash in an urn on the temple altar. She called to her mother-in-law to help her pull off the snakes; the old one didn't appear to hear her and went on arranging the joss-sticks neatly in the urn, then some oranges on a plate, and some fragrant flowers in a vase, in readiness for an offering to the temple gods. One of the gods in the niches stirred to life; Margaret called to him to help her disengage the snakes which seemed to have increased in number; two were around her neck; a multitude were on her arms, bosom, legs.

"Please—," she choked and the god who had awakened stepped out and advanced upon her. She looked pleadingly at him; his visage was now her mother-in-law's, with the glinting eyes and stiff white hair streaming in the storm, now her father-in-law's, with the malevolent leer.

"Please—," sobbed Margaret, and she put her arms protectively round her swollen belly, afraid her child would be harmed.

She woke up, panting, her wet hair clinging to her face and neck.

Dr. Lee took Eng Kiat aside to discuss Margaret's illness and to recommend psychiatric treatment.

"She's under some obsession which is driving her to distraction; it will be bad for the baby," said the doctor and for the first time, Eng Kiat, under enormous pressure for weeks, broke down and wept.

Margaret's mother consulted a temple medium. In a trance, he said that the only thing that could save Margaret's sanity and the child's life was to have the mother-in-law write certain words on a prayer paper which should then be burnt and the ashes put in water for Margaret to drink. Only in this way would the curse be lifted and Margaret's peace of mind restored.

When told of the temple medium's advice, Margaret, drawn, haggard and hollow-eyed, asked in a small pleading voice, "Do you think it'll work? Do you think it'll save my baby?"

The mother-in-law, recovering from her illness in Eng Loong's house and attended by Mee Lian, refused to write the words for the prayer paper.

"Don't ask me to do anything for her, and don't mention her name in my hearing again," she snapped, sitting in a chair in a corner of the room from which she seldom stirred. There was a look of hard resolution in her eyes.

Margaret herself came to plead. She had grown very thin, but her belly was huge and heavy. She was wearing a long housecoat, and a faded woollen cardigan. Eng Kiat had his arm protectively round her shoulders. When she was brought in front of the old lady, she immediately went up with a sob, but the old one turned aside sharply, and refused to look at her.

"Mother, please," sobbed Margaret and could not go on. Her mother and Mee Lian wept with her, and the sons pleaded with the old one to grant them the favour.

She sat still and unmoved, her lips tightly compressed, her brow dark with displeasure. When they continued pleading, she moved a hand impatiently and cried out, in shrill petulance, "All right! Give me the paper to write and be gone! Leave me in peace!" The brush was put in her hand, the temple medium's words were dictated by Margaret's mother, and in a few seconds she had finished.

"Now go, all of you!" she cried imperiously. And according to the temple medium's instructions, the prayer paper was burnt, the ashes were dropped into a glass of water, and Margaret drank gratefully, reverently, to the last drop.

[1980]

QUESTIONS

1. Margaret and Suan Choo take pride in being modern, independent women. Are they really that independent?
2. What tone does the author employ throughout her story?
3. Why does Margaret start believing in the curse? Does the author want us to believe that the mother-in-law's traditions are better than Margaret's?

Lu Xun

(1881–1936)

China

Lu Xun, the pen name of Zhou Shuren, was born south of the Yangtse Valley in Shaoxing in 1881. His father was a teacher. After studying science and technology in China, Lu Xun was sent to Japan by his government in 1902 in order to learn Japanese and pursue medicine. In Tokyo, he began writing articles for journals aimed at Chinese students abroad. He also translated two Jules Verne novels into Chinese: *Voyage to the Center of the Earth* and *From the Earth to the Moon*. By 1905, deciding that he wanted to be a writer, he gave up his medical studies. During the next decade, his work was primarily related to writing, translating, and teaching, with time spent both in China and Japan.

Lu Xun was disappointed by the failure of the 1911 Revolution in China, for which he had had high expectations. Part of his thinking about the potential for the Revolution was his concern about China's isolation from the rest of the world. By 1918, he was writing stories, poems, and essays in colloquial Chinese and aligning himself with various student movements. Two years later, he began lecturing at Peking University. His first collection of short stories, *Cheering from the Sidelines* (1922), comprised the stories he had written over the four previous years. A second collection, *Wondering Where to Turn*, was published three years later.

Lu Xun considered himself a leftist during much of his subsequent career. Although he never joined the Communist Party, he opposed Chiang Kai-shek and the Kuomintang. As Gladys Yang writes of his experience during the 1930s, "The Kuomintang murdered progressive writers, and Lu Xun living under this reign of terror was often forced to go into hiding, as he writes in his poem 'Long Nights.' He had to resort to over a hundred different pen-names and to the use of innuendo and allusion to get his work passed by the censor." In later years (after his death), Mao Ze Dong referred to Lu Xun as "the chief commander of China's cultural revolution . . . not only a great man of letters but a great thinker and revolutionary. . . . the bravest and most correct, the firmest, the most loyal and the most ardent national hero, a hero without parallel in our history."

Lu Xun is today considered China's greatest twentieth-century writer. William A. Lyell, Lu Xun's most recent translator, describes the writer's importance for China as follows: "In literature and in art . . . Lu Xun consistently favored breaking down China's cultural walls so that she might look outward to the world—not to imitate, but to learn, and to share as well."

• The Story of Hair •

On Sunday morning I tore the previous day's page from the calendar and glanced at the new one. Then I gave it a second look. "Hey, it's October tenth—so today's Double Ten![1] Funny, there's no notation here on the page!"

Mr. N,[2] a man of the next generation above mine, had just walked over to my place for a chat, and hearing me say this he observed in the most disgruntled of tones, "They're right! They don't bother to remember—so what? You *do* remember—so what?"

Now this Mr. N had a rather feisty disposition to begin with. He would often fly off the handle for no apparent reason and say things that revealed a profound naiveté about the ways of the world. At times like that I'd just let him ramble on without putting in a word until he finally got to the end of whatever it was he had to say, and that would be that.

"I really have to give them credit, the way they do up the Double Ten here in Beijing. A policeman comes to the door in the morning: 'Fly the flag,' he orders. 'Yes sir, fly the flag.' Then from every home you'll see a citizen of the realm halfheartedly emerge and put up a raggedy old piece of cloth. There it hangs until nightfall when somebody will take it in again and close the door. Here and there a family forgets and it'll fly right through till the next morning.[3]

"They've forgotten to mark the day there on the calendar, but then the day hasn't remembered them either! I can be counted among those who have forgotten to keep the day, too. When I do remember it, all the things that happened just before and after that *first* Double Ten well up in my mind until I don't know whether I'm coming or going.

"The faces of so many old friends float before my eyes. Some of those youngsters worked themselves to the bone for a decade or more just to bring about that day, only to have their lives taken away by a bullet fired in the secret recesses of some jail. Some, having failed in assassination attempts, endured more than a month's cruel torture in prison before they died. And still others, holding the loftiest of ideals, just disappeared without a trace. We didn't even know where their corpses were.

"They lived out their whole lives in a society that gave them nothing but ridicule, abuse, and persecution, a society ever on the lookout for some way of doing them in. By now their grave mounds have long since flattened away from neglect and forgetfulness. I can't bring myself to celebrate things like that. Let's switch to a more pleasant topic."

A smile suddenly spread across N's face as he extended a hand and felt the back of his head. "The one thing I *do* really feel good about is that I've been able to walk the streets since that first Double Ten without having anyone laugh at me or curse me out," he said, raising his voice with a touch of enthusiasm.

[1]Double Ten (October 10, the tenth day of the tenth month) marks the anniversary of the Republican Revolution of 1911. (Trans.)

[2]Zhou Zuoren says that Mr. N is based on a certain Xia Huiqing, Lu Xun's superior at the Ministry of Education. A great deal of what Mr. N says is a direct reflection of Lu Xun's own experiences in relation to hair. (Trans.)

[3]According to Zhou Zuoren, Lu Xun himself once expressed the same sentiments in a similar way. (Trans.)

"You've got to remember, old friend," he continued, "that hair has always been both the beloved friend and hated enemy of the Chinese people. Just think of how many of us down through the ages have gone through the cruelest and most pointless suffering just because of *hair*!

"The most ancient of our ancients don't seem to have taken hair all that seriously. You can tell that from the order in which they listed the corporal punishments. The thing they set most store by, of course, was the head and that's why Decapitation topped the list. Next in order of importance came the sex organs and therefore Castration and Removal of the Ovaries were set up as terrifying punishments too. But when you got down to Haircutting, you were at the very bottom of the list.[4] And yet if you think about it a little more closely, who knows how many people have been trampled underfoot for an entire lifetime precisely because they had received that lightest of light punishments!

"Whenever we used to talk of revolting against the Manchus, we'd always make a big thing of the *Ten Days at Yangzhou* and the *Butchering of Jiading*, but that was just a little trick we used.[5] To tell you the truth, the intensity of the resistance we Chinese put up against the Manchus at the time of the Republican Revolution had next to nothing to do with the atrocities committed by Manchus when they destroyed us as a nation and a people a few centuries back. If the truth be known, we were simply sick and tired of wearing those queues!

"Once the Manchus established their dynasty and had killed all those who wouldn't submit; once those officials, still loyal to the Ming, had all died off;[6] once we had all actually gotten used to wearing the queue, then along came Hong Xiuquan and Yang Xiuqin. My grandmother once told me that the common people were put in a real bind then: the ones who let their hair grow out were killed by the government troops, and the ones who still did their hair up in the queue were killed by the Long Hairs![7]

"I don't know how many Chinese have suffered pain, martyrdom, and destruction just because of something as utterly insignificant as hair." N gazed at the beams in the ceiling as though thinking of something else, and then continued, "Who would ever have thought that some day my turn to suffer because of hair would roll around too?

"When I went overseas to study I cut off my queue. There was no particular significance to my act—I simply did it because wearing the darned thing was so inconvenient. Much to my surprise, however, some of my fellow students who had coiled *their* queues up on top of their heads absolutely detested *me* because I had cut mine off! The government-appointed supervisor of studies in charge of us was hopping mad too. Said he was going to cut off my government scholar-

[4]In ascending order of harshness, the Five (Corporal) Punishments in ancient China were (1) tattooing the face, (2) cutting off the nose, (3) cutting off the feet, (4) castration or removal of the ovaries, and (5) decapitation. Though not included in this standard list, shaving of the head was also a traditional form of corporal punishment. (Trans.)

[5]The italicized phrases refer to massacres of Chinese that were committed by the Manchus in the course of conquering China during the seventeenth century. (Trans.)

[6]The Ming dynasty (1368–1644) preceded the Manchu (or Qing) dynasty (1644–1911). (Trans.)

[7]Hong Xiuquan and Yang Xiuqin were leaders of the Taiping Rebellion (1850–1864). The hairstyle that had been imposed upon Chinese men by the Manchus involved shaving the front part of the head while braiding the hair at the back into a queue. The Taipings undid their queues and let their hair grow long, and thus they were also known as "Long Hairs." (Trans.)

ship and send me home. But before too many days were out, some students got hold of the supervisor himself and cut *his* queue off, after which he ran away to who-knows-where. One of those in on the cutting was Zou Rong.[8] It was because of that very incident that Zou Rong had to go back to Shanghai, where he later died in West Jail—but I daresay by now you've long since forgotten all of that.

"A few years later, my own family's fortunes sank. I had to either find work or go hungry, and so I was forced to go back to China too. As soon as I arrived in Shanghai I bought an artificial queue. The going price at the time was two dollars. When I wore it back home, my mother didn't say anything, but whenever anyone else set eyes on me they'd immediately launch a close investigation of the damned thing. Once they had established that it was artificial, they would sneer and act as though I'd committed a capital offense. As a matter of fact, one of my relatives was even getting ready to report me to the authorities, but then he began to worry that the Revolutionary Party's insurrection might actually succeed and scrapped the idea.

"I decided that a policy of open honesty would be preferable to all this chicanery, and so I went whole hog—threw away the artificial queue and started wearing a Western suit. When I walked out on the street, however, I was still cursed and ridiculed. Some people would even follow along behind and call me 'Savage' or 'Fake Foreign Devil'! At that point I stopped wearing my Western suit and went back to a Chinese gown. Got cursed out more than ever![9]

"When I got to the end of my rope, I made a slight addition to my daily costume—a walking stick. From then on, I laid into my tormentors with that stick. Worked wonders. A few good doses of that and people stopped bothering me. But whenever I'd go someplace I hadn't been to before, I'd *still* get cursed out.

"But my success with that walking stick made me sick at heart. I often reflect on it even today. When I was studying in Japan, I once saw a newspaper article about a certain Dr. Honda who had just completed a trip through Malaysia and China. Someone asked him, 'Since you didn't know Chinese or Malay, how did you manage to get around?' He raised his walking stick up high and replied, 'This is *their* language—they all understand it quite well!'[10] That article made me boil with indignation for quite a while afterward. Who would have thought back then that someday I would do the very same thing—and what's more, it turned out that those people who were cursing *me* all understood this language too.

"During the first year of Xuantong, I was supervisor of studies right here at the local high school.[11] My colleagues avoided me like the plague and the local officials watched me like a hawk. From one end of the day to the other, I was so isolated that I might as well have been holed up in an icehouse or standing on an

[8]Zou Rong (1885–1905) was the author of an impassioned and influential anti-Manchu tract, *The Revolutionary Army*, written when he was only eighteen; its publication led to his imprisonment and he died in custody only a month before his sentence was up. (Trans.)

[9]Much of this is autobiographical material. (Trans.)

[10]Zuoren says that a newspaper did in fact report this story and that it had incensed his elder brother. (Trans.)

[11]Xuantong (1909–1911) was the final reign period of the Manchu dynasty, ended by the Republican Revolution. Lu Xun became dean of studies at the Shaoxing Academy in 1910. N's words undoubtedly reflect Lu Xun's own experiences around this time. (Trans.)

execution ground. And if the facts be known, there was absolutely no reason for it—except that I didn't have a queue!

"Several students suddenly appeared in my office one day and announced, 'Teacher, we're going to cut off our queues.'

"I said, 'Absolutely not!'

"Then they asked, 'Is it better to have one or not?'

"I started to explain to them that while it's better *not* to have one, still—But they immediately interrupted, 'Then how do you get off telling *us* absolutely not?

"'Because cutting it off is just not worth the trouble.' They didn't say anything, just pulled long faces and walked out, but the upshot was that they all cut off their queues. Well, that caused one hell of an uproar, believe you me! Everywhere you went people were talking about it, but I just went about my business as though nothing had happened and let the queue-less come to class right along with the queue-ed.

"Trouble was, this queue-cutting fad proved contagious. On the third day six queues suddenly bit the dust over at the Normal School, and the six students were expelled that very night. Those kids were in a real pickle—couldn't stay at school and couldn't go home, just had to fend for themselves as best they could. It wasn't until a good month after the first Double Ten that the stigma of their 'crime' disappeared.

"And me? Same thing. Even when I went to Beijing in the winter of that first year of the Republic, I still got cursed out a couple of times. Later on the people who had done the cursing had their own queues cut off by the police and I wasn't bothered anymore. But I didn't get to the countryside, so I can't tell you whether they were still cursing people there."

N seemed quite pleased with himself. Then suddenly his face assumed a solemn cast again as he said, "And now idealists like yourself are going around making noises about young women having the right to bob their hair, causing a lot of them a great deal of needless sorrow. And they have nothing whatsoever to gain from it anyway! Haven't there already been cases of girls not being admitted to school because they've bobbed their hair, and girls being expelled for the same reason?[12] Revolution?[13] Fine, but where are their weapons? Work their way through college? Sounds good, but where are the factories for them to work in? They'd be much better off to keep their hair the way it is, marry and pursue a career as someone's daughter-in-law. Their happiness lies in forgetting hair-bobbing and all that goes with it. If they continue to concern themselves with all this talk of equality and freedom, they'll be letting themselves in for a lifetime of suffering!

"I'd like to put to you idealists the same question that Artzybashev asks: 'You promise a golden age to these people's sons and grandsons, but what do you

[12]Zuoren states that incidents of this kind were common in Beijing in 1920 (the year this story was written). In fact, hair-bobbing by young girls was thought even more unforgivable than queue-cutting had been a decade earlier. For a man to cut his queue was a political act; but when a girl bobbed her hair, her act was interpreted as a direct violation of traditional morality. In effect she proclaimed herself a "loose woman." (Trans.)

[13]The original text has "reform," but Zhou Zuoren claims that at this time his brother would have avoided writing the word "revolution" even though the context calls for it, in order to avoid offending the authorities. (Trans.)

have to offer them here and now?'[14] As long as the Creator's whip doesn't fall hard across China's back she'll always stay the same, unwilling to budge a single hair on her body. Since you people don't have any poisonous fangs, why do you insist on sticking a 'poisonous snake' label on your foreheads, inviting any beggar to come along and beat you to death?'"[15]

The more N spoke, the further afield he went, but as soon as he noticed my expression and realized I really wasn't all that keen on hearing him out, he stopped, stood up, and got his hat.

"Going home?" I asked.

"Yes, it's going to rain pretty soon." Then in silence I saw him to the door.

He put on his hat and said, "Goodbye. Excuse me for disturbing you. Fortunately, tomorrow it won't be the Double Ten anymore and we can just forget the whole business."

[1920]

Translated by
WILLIAM A. LYELL

QUESTIONS

1. William A. Lyell, the translator of Lu Xun's story, states the following: "After their conquest of China in 1644, the Manchus required Chinese males to adopt their alien coiffure, which involved shaving the front of the head while letting the hair grow long at the back and braiding this into a queue; cutting off the queue came to be considered a gesture of defiance against the Manchu regime. The government did, however, make some allowance for returning students, since, it was thought, they *might* have cut off their queues while abroad simply in order to blend with the local population." Besides the cultural and historical contexts, are there other implications suggested by the story's metaphor of hair? Can you think of Western equivalents that similarly apply to hair?
2. Why does the story employ a narrator who relates someone else's (N's) tale? Does N's story have any effect on the narrator?
3. Lu Xun's stories are often described as plotless, without resolution of a specific conflict. Is this true of "The Story of Hair"? What is the conflict? What is the climax?

[14]Though not phrased in these exact words, this question is raised several times in chapter 9 of Mikhail Artzybashev's (1878–1927) midlength novel *Sheviriof*. See *Tales of the Revolution*, trans. Percy Pinkerton (New York: B. W. Huebsch, 1917). (Trans.)

[15]According to Zhou Zuoren, this is a question that Lu Xun himself often posed in conversation. (Trans.)

ARNOST LUSTIG

(b. 1926)

CZECHOSLOVAKIA/UNITED STATES

Arnost Lustig grew up in Prague, Czechoslovakia, where he was born in 1926. During World War II, he was interred in three concentration camps: Theresienstadt, Buchenwald, and Auschwitz. His novel *Darkness Casts No Shadow* (1976) describes the harrowing account of two boys' escape from one of those camps. It was made into a widely praised Czech film, for which Lustig wrote the screenplay. His earlier novel, *A Prayer for Katerina Horovitzova* (1974), won the Clement Gottwald State Prize (1967) and, in the English version, was nominated for a National Book Award. "The Lemon," from *Diamonds of the Night* (1976), prompted the reviewer in the *London Times Literary Supplement* to say, "No one reading [these tales] could ever feel they were *only* stories." On the publication of *Indecent Dreams* (1988), Josef Skvorecky compared Arnost Lustig to several other great Czech writers, including Franz Kafka and Milan Kundera. These and other volumes of Lustig's works (several awaiting translation into English) have earned him praise as the major writer of the Holocaust. (Dates refer to the English translations.)

About the story included here, Lustig has written:

> "The Lemon" was one of my first stories. I wrote it after the war, in the fall of '45, for *Diamonds of the Night*, a collection of stories. The impulse came from a picnic I attended on the riverbanks near Prague. Everybody was singing, dancing, and enjoying themselves, except for a friend of mine. Later that night I asked him what was wrong. In response, he asked me, "Did you know my father, mother, and sister, little Sonitschka?" I nodded. He told me how they had died in a Lodz ghetto, where the hunger was worse than in Auschwitz-Birkenau, and the humiliation unbearable.
>
> In order to save his mother and sister, he had to knock out the gold tooth from the mouth of his dead father before someone else would. He did it. He felt awful. I told him that I was glad I hadn't had to do it, but if I had been in his shoes I would have done the same since, under the circumstances, it was the best and only way to help his mother and little sister. His story spoiled my mood, too. The next day, I wrote this story. I wanted to express the truths in my heart: that human nobility can walk around in dirty rags; that heroism has many faces; that the feeling of human solidarity is stronger than the selfishness that society forces upon us; that even in the corrupted, you can find diamonds of a pure heart.
>
> War brings about horrible things, but also moments of extraordinary beauty where humanity wins over indifference, courage over cowardice, and hope over resignation. This story aspires, like the entire collection, to be a poem about the moral

purity of a man of our time; a song about the purity inside the hearts of the spoiled.

Arnost Lustig left Czechoslovakia after the Soviet occupation in 1968. Since 1970, he has lived in the United States, where he teaches film and literature at American University in Washington.

The Lemon

Ervin was scowling. His feline eyes, set in a narrow skull, shifted nervously and his lips were pressed angrily into a thin blue arch. He hardly answered Chicky's greeting. Under his arm he was clutching a pair of pants rolled into a bundle.

"What'll you give me for these?" he demanded, unrolling the trousers, which were made of a thin nut-brown cloth. The seat and knees were shiny.

Chicky grinned. "Ye gods, where did you pick those up?" He inspected the cuffs and seams. "Jesus Christ himself wouldn't be caught dead in such a low-class shroud."

Ervin ignored the sneer. "I'm only interested in one thing, Chicky, and that's what I can get for them." He spoke fast.

"Listen, not even a resurrected Jesus Christ on the crummiest street in Lodz would wear a pair of pants like that," Chicky went on with the air of an expert.

He noticed the nerve twitching in Ervin's jaw. "Well, the knees still look pretty good, though," he reconsidered. "Where did you get them?"

It was cloudy and the sun was like a big translucent ball. The barn swallows were flying low. Ervin looked up at the sky and at the swallows swooping toward unseen nests. He'd been expecting Chicky to ask that and he'd prepared himself on the way.

He displayed his rather unimpressive wares again. He knew he had to go through with it now, even if the pants were full of holes. The skin on Chicky's face was thin, almost transparent; he had a small chin and rheumy eyes.

A member of the local security force came around the corner.

"Hey, you little brats," he snapped, casting a quick glance at their skinny bodies, "go on, get out of here!"

They turned around. Fortunately, a battered yellow streetcar that was set aside for the Jews came along just then and diverted the security guard's attention.

"Don't tell me it's a big secret!" Chicky said. "Anybody can easily see those pants belonged to some grown-up. What're you so scared of?"

"What should I be scared of?" Ervin retorted, clutching the trousers close. "I've got to cash in on them, that's all."

"They're rags."

"They're English material, they're no rags."

"Well, I might see what I can do for you," Chicky relented. "But on a fifty-fifty basis."

Ervin handed over the bundle, and Chicky took a piece of twine from his pocket and tied up the trousers to suit himself, making a fancy knot. He looked up and down the street.

The security guard was at the other end of the street with his back to the boys. They were on the corner of an alley which hadn't had a name for a long time. It was intermittently paved with cobblestones. People hurried on; Ervin and Chicky moved closer to the wall. The streetcar now took a different route. The next stop was out of sight.

Chicky, the smaller of the two, the one with the shaved head, was clutching the brown checkered pants under his arm as Ervin had done.

"But don't you go having second thoughts, Ervin. Don't let me go ahead and work my ass off and then. . . ."

"My dad died," Ervin said.

"Hm . . . well," Chicky remarked. "It's taken a lot of people these last few weeks," he observed.

"Now there's only one important thing, and that's how you're going to cash in on those pants."

It occurred to Chicky that Ervin might want a bigger share of the take because the pants had been his father's.

"Who's your customer, Chicky?"

"Old Moses," Chicky lied.

"Do I know him?"

"Little short guy."

"First time I've heard of him."

"He just comes up as high as my waist. He's absolutely the biggest bastard in town. But he kind of likes me. Maybe it's because I remind him of somebody."

"He's interested in pants?"

"He's interested in absolutely everything, Ervin."

"Funny I never heard of him."

"Well, I guess I'd better be going," Chicky said.

"What do you suppose your friend would give me for these pants?" Ervin asked.

"Give *us*, you mean," Chicky corrected.

"Anyway, go on and see what you can do," said Ervin, dodging a direct answer.

"He might cough up some bread in exchange for these pants. Or a couple ounces of flour." He unrolled the trousers again. "Like I told you, the knees are still pretty good and the lining's passable. The fly isn't stained yellow like it is in old men's pants. In that respect, these trousers are in good shape and that tells you something about the person who wore them. I'll try to get as much as I can for them, Ervin." He bared his teeth in a tiger grin.

"I need a lemon, Chicky."

"What about a big hunk of nothing?"

"I'm not joking," Ervin said curtly. "All right, then half a lemon, if you can't get a whole one." The expression on Chicky's face changed.

"You know what *I* need, Ervin?" he began. "I need an uncle in Florida where the sun shines all year long and trained fish dance in the water. I need an uncle who would send me an affidavit and money for my boat ticket so I could go over there and see those fish and talk to them." He paused. "A *lemon*! Listen, Ervin, where do you get those ideas, huh, tell me, will you?"

Chicky gazed up into the sky and imagined a blue and white ocean liner and elegant fish poking their noses up out of the silver water, smiling at him, wishing him bon voyage.

Swallows, white-breasted and sharp-winged, darted across the sullen sky. Chicky whistled at them, noticing that Ervin didn't smile.

"That lemon's not for me," said Ervin.

"Where do you think you are? Where do you think Old Moses'd get a lemon? It's harder to find a lemon in this place than. . . . "

But he couldn't think of a good comparison.

Chicky's expression changed to one of mute refusal. He thought to himself, Ervin is something better than I am. His father died, Ervin took his trousers, so now he can talk big about lemons. Chicky's mouth dropped sourly.

"It's for Miriam," Ervin said flatly. "If she doesn't get a lemon, she's finished."

"What's wrong with her?"

"I'm not sure. . . . "

"Just in general. I know you're no doctor."

"Some kind of vitamin deficiency, but it's real bad."

"Are her teeth falling out?"

"The doctor examined her this morning when he came to see my mother. The old man was already out in the hall. There's no point talking about it."

"It's better to be healthy, I grant you that," Chicky agreed. He rolled up the pants again. "At best, I may be able to get you a piece of bread." He tied the twine into a bow again. "If there were four of us getting a share of this rag, Ervin—your mom, your sister, and you and me, nobody would get anything out of it in the end."

"If I didn't need it, I'd keep my mouth shut," Ervin repeated.

"I can tell we won't see eye to eye, even on Judgment Day."

A Polish streetcar rattled and wheezed along behind them. The town was divided into Polish and Jewish sectors. The streetcar line always reminded Ervin that there were still people who could move around and take a streetcar ride through the ghetto, even if it was just along a corridor of barbed wire with sentries in German uniforms so nobody would get any ideas about jumping off—or on.

"It's got to be something more than that. Everybody's got a vitamin deficiency here. What if it's something contagious, Ervin, and here I am fussing around with these pants of yours?" He gulped back his words. "And I've already caught whatever it is?"

"Nobody knows *what* it is," said Ervin.

"Well, I'm going, Ervin. . . ."

"When are you coming back?"

"What if we both went to see what we could do?"

"No," said Ervin quietly.

"Why not?"

Ervin knew what it was he had been carrying around inside him on his way to meet Chicky. *It was everything that had happened when he'd stripped off those trousers. His father's body had begun to stiffen and it felt strange. He kept telling himself it was all right, that it didn't matter.* Instead, he kept reciting the alphabet and jingles.

This was your father, a living person. And now he's dead. Chicky was the only one he could have talked to.

"I haven't got a dad or a mother even," Chicky said suddenly. A grin flickered. "That's my tough luck. They went up the chimney long ago."[1]

The sky above the low rooftops was like a shallow, stagnant sea.

Chicky lingered, uncertain.

[1]*went up the chimney long ago* incinerated by the Nazis long ago

It was just his body, Ervin told himself. *Maybe memory is like the earth and sky and ocean, like all the seashores and the mountains, like a fish swimming up out of the water to some island, poking out its big glassy eyes just to see how things look. Like that fish Chicky had been talking about. Nobody knows, not even the smartest rabbi in the world. And not the bad rabbis either. But while he was taking his father's trousers off, he knew what he was doing. He wasn't thinking about his father, but about an old Italian tune he used to sing and which Miriam loved. Father sang off key, but it sounded pretty. Prettier than a lot of other things. It was about love and flowers and his father had learned it during the war when he fought in the Piave campaign.*

He already had the trousers halfway off. And he knew the reasons he loved his father would never go away.

The swallows flew quietly in low, skidding arches. Ervin looked around to see how the weather was, and finally his gaze dropped. The rounded cobblestones melted away.

"All right then, I'll bring it around to your place later," Chicky said.

"By when do you think you can do it?"

"In two or three hours."

"But, Chicky. . . . "

Chicky turned and disappeared around the corner as another streetcar came clanging along.

Now Ervin could think ahead, instead of going back to what had been on his mind before. He set off down the alley in the opposite direction, toward the house where he and his family had been living for two years.

The tiny shops upstairs and in the basement had been hardly more than market stalls which had been converted into apartments for several families.

He remembered how he discovered that his father no longer wore underpants. The stringy thighs. The darkened penis, the reddish pubic hair. Rigid legs. Scars on the shin bone. His father had gotten those scars when he was wounded fighting in Italy.

Then that old tune came back to him, sung off key again, the song from somewhere around Trieste that he and Miriam had liked so much.

Hell, who needed those pants more than they did? Father had probably traded in his underpants long ago. Who knows for what?

So Father died, he is no more, Ervin thought to himself.

He reached home, one of the dwarfish shops where he and his mother and sister lived.

The corrugated iron shutter over the entry had broken a spring, so it wouldn't go all the way up or down. He could see a mouse.

He squeezed through a crack in the wall. Mother was scared of mice, so he'd repaired the wall boards through which the mice came in and out. Pressing against the wall, Ervin was suddenly aware of his body, and that reminded him of his father again.

"It's me," he called out.

It had occurred to him that there was nothing to be proud of, being unable to cash in on the trousers *himself.* (Even so, his mother must have known what he had done.) He had to take a deep breath and adjust to the musty smell in the room. It was easier to get used to the difference between the light outside and the darkness inside.

Mother greeted him with a snore. She had long since lost any resemblance to the woman who had come here with him. He peered around him. He had been almost proud of having such a pretty mother. On top of everything else, her legs had swollen. She hadn't been able to get out of bed for the past eight weeks. She'd waited on everything for Father, and now for him.

"Where've you been?" his mother asked.

"Out," he answered.

He crawled into his corner where he could turn his back on everything, including his father who lay out in the hall wrapped in a blanket. Miriam, too, was curled up next to the wall, so he couldn't see her face. He heard her coughing.

He bundled his legs into the tattered rug that used to be his father's. *He'd always had the worst covers. He didn't want to admit he was a loser, and as long as he was able to give up something for them, maybe it wasn't so obvious. The dim light made its way through the thin fabric of dust and dampness and the breath of all three of them. When he lost, he put on the smile of a beautiful woman. He was making a point of being a graceful loser. As if it made any difference to anybody except himself.*

"Did you find anything?" his mother asked.

"No. . . . "

"What are we going to do?"

"Maybe this afternoon," he said, his face to the wall.

"Miriam!" his mother called out to his sister. "Don't cough! It wears you out."

"Mirrie," Ervin said. "Miriam!" She didn't answer.

"Can't she speak?" he asked his mother.

"It wears her out," she repeated. "You really ought to look around and see if you can't scrape up something."

"There's no point so early in the afternoon."

"You ought to try at least," his mother insisted.

That's how it used to be with Father, Ervin recalled. *She always kept sending him somewhere. But Father had gone out just as he'd done now, and, like him, he almost felt better outside; he also may have believed that just by going out he was getting back in shape, that he'd be able to do what he used to do in the beginning. Then Mother started saying things couldn't get any worse. She never went wrong about that. That's because there is no limit to what's "worse." The limit was in his father. And now Ervin had to find it, just like his father.*

"I already told you, I can't find anything just now," he said.

"You ought to go out and try, dear," his mother went on. *This was what Father had had to put up with.* "You see how Miriam looks, don't you?" his mother persisted.

"I can see her," he answered. "But I can't find anything now."

"This can't help but finish badly."

"Oh, cut it out! I'm not going anywhere," Ervin declared flatly. "I've already tried. There's nothing to be had."

"For God's sake, listen to me!" his mother cried sharply. "Go on out and *try*! Miriam hasn't had a thing to eat today."

The stains on the plaster were close to his eyes. The room was damp, and it almost swallowed up the sound of his mother's voice and his own. The dampness didn't bother him, though. He could hear faint scratching noises in the walls.

The boards he'd put up didn't help much. He almost envied mice. Just as he'd felt a certain envy for trees when he was outside. Ervin suddenly wished he could catch one of those sad little animals. Pet it, then kill it. Father had told them about the time they were besieged during the First World War and the soldiers ate mice.

To kill and caress. Or simply kill, so you're not always bothered by something or somebody.

But if Chicky was right, a trained mouse should get along great.

"I wonder if I shouldn't air out the room a bit," he said into the silence.

"Have they been here already?" he asked after a while.

"No."

"They're taking their time about it."

Now, in her turn, his mother was silent. "Who knows how many calls they have to make today?"

"Why don't you want to go out, son?"

"I will. In a while," he answered gently. "It doesn't make any sense now, though."

"Ervin, son. . . . "

The room was quiet, the silence broken only by Miriam's coughing.

Ervin put his head between his knees, trying to guess where the mouse was and what it was doing. He stuck his fingers in his ears. The scratching continued. *So Father's still lying out there in the hall. He doesn't have any pants and Mother doesn't even know it. He's naked, but that doesn't bother his old Piave scars. Mother could use that extra blanket now,* he thought to himself. *But he left it around his father for some reason which he didn't know himself. So I don't have the feeling that I've stolen everything from him, including our second tattered blanket,* he thought to himself. *It was lucky she couldn't get out of bed now, even if she wanted to. Her legs wouldn't support her. She'd see that Father had no pants. They'll probably take him along with the blanket. What the hell? They were certainly taking their time. They should have been here an hour ago. It was a regulation of the commanding officer and the self-government committee that corpses must be removed promptly. Everybody was scared of infection. The corpse collectors were kept busy. They probably didn't miss a chance to take anything they could get. Everybody knew they stole like bluejays.*

Miriam would probably have been afraid to sleep with a dead person in the same room, even if it was Father, Ervin decided.

"There's some rabbi here who works miracles, I heard," his mother said. "Why don't you go and see him?"

"What would I say to him?"

"Tell him that I'm your mother."

"I don't have any idea where he lives. And even if he could perform a miracle, he certainly won't put himself out to come over here. He waits for people to come to him."

"I feel so weak," his mother told him.

Suddenly it occurred to him that maybe his mother would have been better off lying out in the hall beside his father. It would be better for Miriam too. Mother's gestures and the things she told him were getting more and more indecisive.

"Why don't you want to go anywhere?" Mother said.

"Because there's no point," he replied, "I'd be wearing myself out in vain. I'll find something, but not until this afternoon."

"Miriam won't last long. She can hardly talk anymore."

"Miriam?" Ervin called out.

Miriam was silent and his mother added: "You know how it was with Daddy."

"He'd been sick for a long time."

And when her son said nothing, she tried again. "Ervin. . . ."

"It doesn't make any sense," he growled. "I'm not going anywhere now. Not till later."

He sat quite still for a while, staring at the blotches and shadows moving on the wall. He could hear mice scampering across the floor toward the mattress where Mother and Miriam were lying. Mother screeched, then Miriam.

Ervin was bored.

It might be more comfortable and pleasant to wait outside. But there was something in here that made him stay. He remembered how he and Chicky used to play poker. They always pretended there was some stake. That made it more interesting. You could bluff and pretend to have a full house when you didn't even have a pair. But there was always the chance—which they'd invented—that you might win something.

He remembered how he and Miriam used to go ice-skating. She was little and her knees were wobbly. He'd drag her around the rink for a while, then take her into the restaurant where you could have a cup of tea for ten hellers. Miriam's nose would be running, and she'd stay there for an hour with her tea so he could have a good time out on the ice. Once his mother had given them money to buy two ham sandwiches. His arches always ached when he'd been skating. So did Miriam's.

If they'd come for Father—and he wished it were over with—he wouldn't have to worry that the body would start to decay or that his mother would find out he didn't have any pants on.

"Why don't you go out and see that miracle rabbi?"

"Because it doesn't make any sense."

At first, Mother only had trouble with her legs. And Miriam hadn't coughed *quite* as much.

The sentries along the streetcar line always looked comfortably well-fed, with nice round bellies, as though they had everything they needed. When these sentries passed through the ghetto, they acted as though victory was already theirs, even if they might lose this little skirmish with the Jews. *Daddy once said that this was their world, whether they won or lost.*

Ervin's stomach growled. It was like the noise the mice made. He stretched and waited for his mother to start nagging him again. But she didn't, and it was almost as though something were missing. *He didn't want to think about his father's body wrapped in that blanket out in the hall. Daddy had been sick long enough. He was certainly better off this way.*

After a while, he wasn't sure whether his stomach was making the noise or the mice. His mother groaned. He thought about a nap. Just then he heard someone banging on the iron shutter. He got up.

"Well, I'll be on my way," he said.

"Come back soon," his mother replied. "Come back safe and sound."

"Sure," he answered. As he approached the shutter, he asked, "Is that you, Chicky?"

"No," a voice replied. "It's the miracle-working rabbi with a pitcher of milk."

Ervin pushed the broken shutter and slipped through. It was easy. His body was nothing but skin and bones now. He had a long narrow skull, with bulging greenish blue eyes. He could feel his mother's eyes on him as he squeezed out. Outside in the courtyard he pulled down his shirt and his bones cracked. Chicky was waiting on the sidewalk.

"So?" asked Ervin.

"Even with those stains on the seat," Chicky started.

"What're you trying to tell me?"

"He gave me more than I expected." He smiled slyly and happily.

Chicky produced a piece of bread, carefully wrapped in a dirty scarf. He handed it to Ervin. "This is for you. I already ate my share on the way, like we agreed."

"Just this measly piece?"

"Maybe you forgot those stains on the seat of those pants."

"Such a little hunk?"

"What else did you expect, hm? Or maybe you think I ought to come back with a whole moving van full of stuff for one pair of pants?"

Chicky wiped his nose, offended.

"You just better not forget about those stains on the seat. Besides, almost everybody's selling off clothes now."

Ervin took the bread. Neither one mentioned the lemon. Ervin hesitated before crawling back into the room, half-hoping Chicky was going to surprise him. Chicky liked to show off.

"Wait here for me," he blurted. "I'll be right back."

Ervin squinted through the dimness to where his mother lay on the mattress.

"Here, catch," he said maliciously. He threw the bread at her. It struck her face, bounced, and slid away. He could hear her groping anxiously over the blanket and across the floor. As soon as she had grabbed it, she began to wheeze loudly.

She broke the bread into three pieces in the dark.

"Here, this is for you," she said.

"I don't want it."

"Why not?" she asked. He heard something else in her voice. "Ervin?"

He stared at the cracks in the wall where the mice crawled through. He was afraid his mother was going to ask him again.

"My God, Ervin, don't you hear me?"

"I've already had mine," he said.

"How much did you take?"

"Don't worry, just my share." He felt mice paws pattering across the tops of his shoes. Again, he had the urge to catch one and throw it on the bed.

"Miriam!" his mother called.

Ervin left before he could hear his sister's reply. He knew what his mother was thinking.

Chicky was waiting, his hands in his pockets, leaning against the wall. He was picking his teeth. He was looking up at the sky trying to guess which way the clouds were going. There must be wind currents that kept changing.

For a while the two boys strolled along in silence. Then just for something to say, Chicky remarked: "You know what that little crook told me? He says you can't take everything away from everybody."

Everything melted together: father, bread, mother, sister, the moment he was imagining what Chicky might bring back for them. Mice.

"He says we can *hope* without *believing*." Chicky laughed, remembering something else.

"Do you feel like bragging all day?"

"If you could see into me the way I can see into you, you could afford to talk. When my dad went up the chimney, I told myself I was still lucky to have my mother. And when I lost Mother, I told myself that at least I was lucky to have a brother left. He was weaker than a fly. And I said to myself, it's great to have your health at least."

Ervin was silent, so Chicky continued: "Still, we're pretty lucky, Ervin. Even if that's what my little businessman says too. Don't get the idea the world's going to stop turning just because one person in it is feeling miserable at this particular moment. You'd be exaggerating."

They didn't talk about it anymore. They could walk along like this together, so close their elbows or shoulders almost touched, and sometimes as they took a step together, their hips. The mice and the chameleon were gone; Chicky was really more like a barn swallow. Chicky was just slightly crooked. The thought suddenly put him in a better mood. Like when the sun came out or when he looked at a tree or the blue sky.

"He's full of wise sayings," Chicky resumed. "According to him, we have to pay for everything. And money and *things* aren't the worst way to pay."

"Aw, forget it. You're sticking as close to me as a fag."

"What about you?" Chicky's little face stretched.

"They haven't come to get him yet, the bastards."

"I can probably tell you why," Chicky declared. "Would you believe it, my dad's beard grew for two days after he was already dead?"

"Do you ever think you might have been a swallow?"

"Say, you're really outdoing yourself today," Chicky remarked. "But if you want to know something, I *have* thought about it."

Ervin looked up into the sky again. He might have known Chicky would have ideas like that. Ervin himself sometimes had the feeling that he was up there being blown around among the raindrops when there was a thunderstorm. The sky looked like an iron shutter. Sometimes he could also imagine himself jumping through the sky, using his arms and legs to steer with.

"Ervin. . . ." Chicky interrupted.

"What?"

"That old guy gave me a tremendous piece of advice."

"So be glad."

"No, Ervin, I mean it."

"Who's arguing?"

"Aren't you interested? He asked me if your old man had anything else."

"What else could he have?"

"He was just hinting."

"These have been hungry days for us. That crooked second-hand man of yours, his brains are going soft. I hope he can tell the difference between dogs and cats."

"Considering we're not their people, Ervin, what he told me wasn't just talk."

"My dad was the cleanest person in this whole dump," said Ervin.

"He didn't mean that and neither did I, Ervin."

"What's with all this suspense?"

"Just say you're not interested and we'll drop it," Chicky said.

"Come on, spill it, will you? What *did* he mean then?"

"Maybe there was a ring or something?"

"Do you really think he'd have let Mother and Miriam die right in front of his eyes if he'd had anything like a *ring*?"

"He wasn't talking only about a ring. He meant gold."

"Dad had to turn over everything he had that was even gilded."

"He hinted at it only after I tried to explain to him about the lemon."

"You know how it was. Mother doesn't have anything either."

"He only hinted at it when I told him how important it was for you to have that lemon, Ervin."

"Well, what was it he hinted, then?" Ervin noticed the expectant look on Chicky's face.

"He hinted that it wasn't impossible, but only in exchange for something made of pure gold. And that he didn't care what it was."

"Don't be a bastard," said Ervin slowly. "Forget it. My dad didn't have anything like that. Go on, get lost!"

"He even indicated exactly *what* and *how*."

"Look, come on—kindly spill it," Ervin said with irritation. *Once again he saw his father lying there wrapped in the blanket. It flooded through him in a dark tide, like when his mother didn't believe that he hadn't taken more than his share of the bread. He'd known right from the start what Chicky was talking about.*

Ervin didn't say anything.

"Gold teeth, for instance. It's simply something in the mouth he doesn't need anymore, something nobody needs except maybe you and me."

Ervin remained silent.

"Well, I wasn't the one who said anything about a lemon," he concluded.

Ervin stopped and so did Chicky. Then Ervin turned and looked him up and down, eyes bulging.

"Aw, cut it out," Chicky said wearily. "Don't look at me as though I killed your dad."

Suddenly Ervin slapped him. Chicky's face was small and triangular, tapering off crookedly at the top. It was very obvious because his head was shaved. Then Ervin slapped him again and began to punch his face and chest. When his fist struck Chicky's Adam's apple, Ervin could feel how fragile everything about him was.

Again he saw himself stripping those brown checkered trousers off his father's body. The undertakers would be coming along any minute. [They should have been here long ago.] He thought of how he'd managed to do that before they came and how he'd probably manage to do even this if he wanted to. And he knew that he couldn't have swallowed that piece of bread even if his mother had given it to him without those second thoughts of hers. He kept pounding his fists into Chicky, and it was as if he were striking at himself and his mother. *He kept telling himself that his father was dead anyway and that it didn't matter much and that it didn't have any bearing on the future either.*

Then he felt everything slowing down. Chicky began to fight back. Ervin got in two fast punches, one on the chin, the other in the belly. Chicky hit Ervin twice before people gathered and tried to break it up, threatening to call the security guards.

Ervin picked himself up off the sidewalk as fast as he could. He shook himself like a dog and went home through the courtyard.

"Ervin?" his mother called out. "Is that you?"

"Yeah," he answered.

"Did you find anything else?"

He was shivering as he sometimes did when he was cold because he'd loaned his blanket to his mother or Miriam.

"Mirrie. . . . " he tried.

He bundled himself up into the rug. He was glad Chicky had hit him back. It was hard to explain why. It was different from wanting to catch a mouse and kill it. He touched his cheek and chin, fingering the swollen places. Again he waited for his mother to say something. But she didn't. Mother only knows as much as I tell her, he said to himself. Mother's quite innocent, Ervin decided. Despite everything she's still innocent. Would she have been able to do what she had criticized him for? He wished she'd say something, give at least an echo. He thought of Miriam. For a moment he could see her, tall and slender, her breasts and blond hair.

The twilight began to melt into the dampness of the cellar. The spider webs disappeared in the darkness. He wished they'd muffle the edge of his mother's voice. He waited for Miriam's cough. The silence was like a muddy path where nobody wants to walk. *And his father was still lying out there in the hall.*

When someone dies, Ervin thought to himself, *it means not expecting, not worrying about anything, not hoping for something that turns out to be futile. It means not forcing yourself into something you don't really want, while you go on behaving as though you did. It means not being dependent on anybody or anything. It means being rid of what's bothering you. It's like when you close your eyes and see things and people in your own way.*

That idea of a path leading from the dead to the living and back again is just a lot of foolishness I thought up by myself. To be dead means to expect nothing, not to expect somebody to say something, not to wait for someone's voice. Not to stare enviously after a streetcar going somewhere from somewhere else.

He looked around. Miriam had begun to cough again. She's coughing almost gently, he thought to himself. She probably doesn't have enough strength left to cough anymore.

My God, that lying, thieving, sly old man, that bastard who's fed for six thousand years on Jewish wisdom and maybe would for another half an hour — but maybe not even that long! That dirty louse, full of phony maxims and dreams as complicated as clockwork, lofty as a rose, rank as an onion, who perhaps wasn't quite as imaginary as I wanted to think he was, judging from Chicky's descriptions which made him sound as though he'd swallowed all the holy books. That slimy crook with his miserable messages, that you have to pay for everything and that money and things aren't the most precious currency. But he also said you can't take everything away from everybody, as though he wanted to confuse you by contradicting himself in the same breath. Where did he get those ideas?

"No, I don't have anything," he said suddenly, as if he knew his mother was still waiting for an answer.

He heard her sigh. From his sister's bed he heard a stifled cough. (She's probably ashamed of coughing by now.)

Nothing's plaguing Father anymore either. Not even the craving for a bowl of soup. He wasn't looking forward anymore to seeing Ervin dash out onto the field in a freshly laundered uniform and shiny football boots, which he took care of, in front of crowds of people waiting for entertainment and thrills and a chance to yell their lungs out. If they come for Father now, they'll do just what Chicky said they would. Anyway, the undertakers themselves do it to the old people. He remembered his father's smile which got on his mother's nerves.

He stared into the darkness. His mother was bandaging her swollen legs. Her eyes were very bright. She's probably feverish, he thought. She made a few inexplicable gestures. What if the rabbis are right and there is some *afterwards? Then his father must be able to see him. Where do you suppose he really is,* Ervin wondered, *and where am I? Does anybody know? Inwardly he tried to smile at his father. It would be nice if I could really smile at him. To be on the safe side, Ervin tried smiling at his father again.*

"I'm going out and take another look around," he said.

Mother ceased her strange movements. "Where do you want to go in the dark?"

"I want to have a look at something."

"Be careful, child."

He went out into the hall and the place he had avoided before, so he wouldn't have to look at the wall beside which his father's body was still lying. He was squeezing through the crack in the wall. For a short while an insurance agent had lived in the corner shop. *But this isn't your father anymore,* he told himself; *he was only until yesterday. Now there is nothing but a weight and the task of carrying it away,* he reminded himself immediately. *But I'll think of him only in good ways. And Mother and Miriam will think about him as if nothing's happened.*

He threw off the old blanket. He closed his eyes for a second. I won't be able to eat very much, he realized, as though he wanted to convince himself that this was the only difference it would make. Everything moved stiffly. He had to turn the head and open its mouth. He grabbed it by the chin and hair and that was how he managed. He couldn't remember exactly which tooth it was. He tried one after another. He was hurrying. He didn't want Chicky and the men with the coffins to catch him at it. Instead, he tried to imagine that lemon. It was like a yellow sphere at the end of the hall. Suddenly he couldn't remember where lemons came from, except that it was somewhere in the south, and whether they grew on trees or bushes. He'd never really known anyway.

He picked up a sharp stone. He had a sticky feeling as though he were robbing somebody. He tried to decide which was the best way to knock it out. He tried several times without success. Then he stopped trying to get at just that one tooth.

Finally something in the jaw loosened. Ervin could smell his own breath. He tossed the stone away. He was glad nobody had seen him. Into the palm of his hand he scooped what he'd been seeking. (He was squatting and the head dropped back to the floor.)

Ervin stood up slowly. He felt as though his body and thoughts were flowing into a dark river, and he didn't know where it came from and where it was going. He wiped his hands on his pants. The cellar was dark, like the last place a person can retreat to. For a moment he closed his eyes. He had to take it out into the light. He headed for the other end of the corridor.

He'd hardly stepped out into the street when he saw Chicky's face in the twilight. There, you see, Ervin said to himself. He was keeping watch after all. Chicky would have done what he'd just done if he'd had the chance.

"Hello, kid," Chicky began. "Hello, you Jew bastard." Then Chicky exploded: "You lousy hyena! You son of a bitch! I suppose you've come to apologize. At least I hope so."

Ervin was clutching the thing tightly in his fist. He stared at Chicky for a long time.

"But I got in two good punches, didn't I? Like Max Schmeling." Chicky sounded pleased with himself. His eyes shone.

But then he noticed that the skin under Ervin's eyes was bluer than any bruise could have made it. He noticed, too, the pale blotches on Ervin's face. And how he kept his hand in his pocket.

"No hard feelings," Chicky said.

"I have it."

"I was sure you'd manage. . . ."

Ervin pulled his hand out of his pocket and Chicky's glance shifted swiftly.

"Bring me that lemon, Chicky, but the whole thing!" He unclenched his fist. It lay there cupped in his palm, a rather unattractive shell of gold the color of old copper, and very dirty.

"You won't take the tiniest slice for yourself."

"If it's pure, Ervin, you're in luck," Chicky said.

When Ervin did not respond he continued: "Sometimes it's just iron or some ersatz. Then it's worn through on top. The old man warned me about that in advance. But if it isn't, then you're damned lucky, Ervin, honest."

"When will you bring me that lemon?" Ervin asked, getting to the point.

"First hand it over and let me take a look."

Impatiently, Chicky inspected the crown, acting as though he hadn't heard Ervin. He scraped away the blood that had dried around the root and removed bits of cement. He blew on it and rubbed the dull gold between his fingers, then let it rest in his palm again.

"For this, the old runt will jump like a toad."

"I hope so."

"But first, Ervin, it's fifty-fifty."

"The hell it is," he answered firmly.

"I'll only do it for half."

"If Miriam doesn't get that lemon, she won't even last out till evening."

"Why shouldn't she last out? I'm keeping half."

"You're not keeping anything," repeated Ervin. "Now get going before it's too late."

Ervin glared at him, but there was a question in his eyes. Chicky acted calm. None of his self-satisfaction had filtered through to Ervin. His throat tightened. He began to shiver. He could feel the goose pimples on his neck and arms. It wasn't the way he wanted to think it was, *that his father had died and otherwise everything was just the same as before.* And when Chicky looked at him, Ervin could read in his eyes that instead of bringing a lemon or some kind of pills that have the same effect as lemons, Chicky would probably bring another piece of bread.

Ervin heard a quiet gurgle rising in his throat. He tried thinking about that runty second-hand dealer.

"I'd be crazy to do it for nothing," said Chicky slowly. He squinted warily and his nostrils flared. He bared his teeth. There were big gaps between them.

"Either we go halves or I tell your mom how you're treating me."

"You're not such a bastard, Chicky, are you?"

"Well, I'd have to be," replied Chicky.

"Get going," Ervin said.

"That sounds more like it."

"I'll wait at home."

"All right."

"And hurry up. Honestly, it's very important."

"Fast as a dog can do you know what," grinned Chicky.

Small and nimble, he dodged among the pedestrians. In the meantime, two men with tubs had appeared. Chicky must have passed them. The tubs were covered with tattered sheets and something bulged underneath. Everybody stepped aside as the porters passed. They knew what they were carrying.

Ervin didn't feel like going back home. He crawled into the opening of a cement culvert pipe. His long skinny head stuck out as he sat there watching the sun set behind the clouds. It dropped slowly. The barn swallows were flying lower now than they had been earlier that afternoon, flying in flocks, suddenly soaring up, then back toward earth.

He kept looking up and down the alley so he wouldn't miss Chicky when he came back.

It all began to melt together before his eyes: the silhouettes of the buildings and the cobblestones that had been pounded into the earth and then washed loose by long-gone rains. He watched the sky which was full of barn swallows and the sun disappeared. Rain was gathering in the clouds as their colors changed.

I ought to be like a rock, he told himself. Even harder than a rock.

And he wept, quietly and without tears, in some little crevice which was inside.

[1945]

Translated by
JEANNE NĚMCOVÁ

QUESTIONS

1. What kind of relationship do the two boys have with each other? How old are they? What are their differences?
2. What tactics have the boys perfected for survival in the ghetto?
3. One of Lustig's major themes has been the difficulty that human beings have recognizing evil in the world in which they live. Is this story about evil or about one of its opposites—love?

Naguib Mahfouz

(b. 1911)

Egypt

Naguib Mahfouz was awarded the Nobel Prize for Literature in 1988. He was the first Arab writer to win the prestigious award and only the second from the African continent (Wole Soyinka, a Nigerian, had won two years earlier). At the time of the citation, Mahfouz was nearly 80 years old (he was born in Cairo on December 11, 1911) and the most famous writer of fiction in the Arab world. However, his reputation with Arab readers has not always been secure. Although he held a position as a civil servant in the Ministry of Culture for many years and worked as a journalist, several of his novels have been banned. In 1989, when the Iranian Ayatollah Ruholla Khomeini placed the death sentence on Salman Rushdie for his novel *The Satanic Verses*, it was Mahfouz who, among Moslems, rose to his defense. His support of Rushdie led to a new round of threats against the Egyptian novelist: Moslem fundamentalists threatened to kill Mahfouz also, for what they considered blasphemy in his writings.

Mahfouz's undergraduate degree was in philosophy. He has remarked about his shift to literature, "I studied philosophy, and, until I was twenty-five, I wanted to continue. Then, I had a crisis and chose literature. But philosophy was important; it prevented me, I think, from becoming sentimental in a time when all my teachers were romantics." A prolific writer, by the time of the Nobel Prize Mahfouz had written nearly 25 novels and a dozen volumes of short stories, in addition to several plays and screenplays. In English, his most popular works have been *Midag Alley* (1981), *Miramar* (1983), and the more recently translated volumes of his Cairo Trilogy: *Palace Walk* (1990), *Palace of Desire* (1991), and *Sugar Street* (1992). The story reprinted here, "Half a Day," is from *The Time and the Place and Other Stories* (1991). (These dates are for the English translations.)

Commenting on Mahfouz's career, Roger Allen in *World Literature Today* has written:

> Alongside a concern with the mundane but crucial issues of survival in the inimical environment of the modern city, Mahfouz shows a continuing and particular concern for such questions as the nature of madness, the alienation of modern man and his search for consolation, and the role of religion in contemporary societies dominated by humanistic values. His choice of venue for the various fictional worlds he has created has been the city, with a particular concentration on Cairo. . . . Unlike other Egyptian novelists . . . he has not used the countryside and its peasant population as a focus for criticism of the course of socialist policies in his country, but has concentrated instead on the sector with which he is extremely familiar: the bureaucrat class in the city.

Half a Day

I proceeded alongside my father, clutching his right hand, running to keep up with the long strides he was taking. All my clothes were new: the black shoes, the green school uniform, and the red tarboosh.[1] My delight in my new clothes, however, was not altogether unmarred, for this was no feast day but the day on which I was to be cast into school for the first time.

My mother stood at the window watching our progress, and I would turn toward her from time to time, as though appealing for help. We walked along a street lined with gardens; on both sides were extensive fields planted with crops, prickly pears, henna trees, and a few date palms.

"Why school?" I challenged my father openly. "I shall never do anything to annoy you."

"I'm not punishing you," he said, laughing. "School's not a punishment. It's the factory that makes useful men out of boys. Don't you want to be like your father and brothers?"

I was not convinced. I did not believe there was really any good to be had in tearing me away from the intimacy of my home and throwing me into this building that stood at the end of the road like some huge, high-walled fortress, exceedingly stern and grim.

When we arrived at the gate we could see the courtyard, vast and crammed full of boys and girls. "Go in by yourself," said my father, "and join them. Put a smile on your face and be a good example to others."

I hesitated and clung to his hand, but he gently pushed me from him. "Be a man," he said. "Today you truly begin life. You will find me waiting for you when it's time to leave."

I took a few steps, then stopped and looked but saw nothing. Then the faces of boys and girls came into view. I did not know a single one of them, and none of them knew me. I felt I was a stranger who had lost his way. But glances of curiosity were directed toward me, and one boy approached and asked, "Who brought you?"

"My father," I whispered.

"My father's dead," he said quite simply.

I did not know what to say. The gate was closed, letting out a pitiable screech. Some of the children burst into tears. The bell rang. A lady came along, followed by a group of men. The men began sorting us into ranks. We were formed into an intricate pattern in the great courtyard surrounded on three sides by high buildings of several floors; from each floor we were overlooked by a long balcony roofed in wood.

"This is your new home," said the woman. "Here too there are mothers and fathers. Here there is everything that is enjoyable and beneficial to knowledge and religion. Dry your tears and face life joyfully."

We submitted to the facts, and this submission brought a sort of contentment. Living beings were drawn to other living beings, and from the first moments my heart made friends with such boys as were to be my friends and fell in love with such girls as I was to be in love with, so that it seemed my misgivings

[1]*tarboosh* a tassled cap often worn by Muslim men and made from felt or cloth

had had no basis. I had never imagined school would have this rich variety. We played all sorts of different games: swings, the vaulting horse, ball games. In the music room we chanted our first songs. We also had our first introduction to language. We saw a globe of the Earth, which revolved and showed the various continents and countries. We started learning the numbers. The story of the Creator of the universe was read to us, we were told of His present world and of His Hereafter, and we heard examples of what He said. We ate delicious food, took a little nap, and woke up to go on with friendship and love, play and learning.

As our path revealed itself to us, however, we did not find it as totally sweet and unclouded as we had presumed. Dust-laden winds and unexpected accidents came about suddenly, so we had to be watchful, at the ready, and very patient. It was not all a matter of playing and fooling around. Rivalries could bring about pain and hatred or give rise to fighting. And while the lady would sometimes smile, she would often scowl and scold. Even more frequently she would resort to physical punishment.

In addition, the time for changing one's mind was over and gone and there was no question of ever returning to the paradise of home. Nothing lay ahead of us but exertion, struggle, and perseverance. Those who were able took advantage of the opportunities for success and happiness that presented themselves amid the worries.

The bell rang announcing the passing of the day and the end of work. The throngs of children rushed toward the gate, which was opened again. I bade farewell to friends and sweethearts and passed through the gate. I peered around but found no trace of my father, who had promised to be there. I stepped aside to wait. When I had waited for a long time without avail, I decided to return home on my own. After I had taken a few steps, a middle-aged man passed by, and I realized at once that I knew him. He came toward me, smiling, and shook me by the hand, saying, "It's a long time since we last met—how are you?"

With a nod of my head, I agreed with him and in turn asked, "And you, how are you?"

"As you can see, not all that good, the Almighty be praised!"

Again he shook me by the hand and went off. I proceeded a few steps, then came to a startled halt. Good Lord! Where was the street lined with gardens? Where had it disappeared to? When did all these vehicles invade it? And when did all these hordes of humanity come to rest upon its surface? How did these hills of refuse come to cover its sides? And where were the fields that bordered it? High buildings had taken over, the street surged with children, and disturbing noises shook the air. At various points stood conjurers showing off their tricks and making snakes appear from baskets. Then there was a band announcing the opening of a circus, with clowns and weight lifters walking in front. A line of trucks carrying central security troops crawled majestically by. The siren of a fire engine shrieked, and it was not clear how the vehicle would cleave its way to reach the blazing fire. A battle raged between a taxi driver and his passenger, while the passenger's wife called out for help and no one answered. Good God! I was in a daze. My head spun. I almost went crazy. How could all this have happened in half a day, between early morning and sunset? I would find the answer at home with my father. But where was my home? I could see only tall buildings and hordes of people. I hastened on to the crossroads between the gardens and Abu Khoda. I had to cross Abu Khoda to reach my house, but the stream of cars would not let up. The fire engine's siren was shrieking at full pitch as it moved at a snail's pace, and I said to myself, "Let the fire take its pleasure in what it consumes." Extremely irritated, I wondered when I would be able to cross. I stood there a long time, until the young lad employed at the ironing shop on the corner came up to me. He stretched out his arm and said gallantly, "Grandpa, let me take you across."

[1989]

Translated by
DENYS JOHNSON-DAVIES

QUESTIONS

1. What kind of person is the narrator's father?
2. At what point in the story does it become apparent that the story covers more than the narrator's first day in school? How does Mahfouz employ the journey motif in his narrative?
3. What is the story's theme?
4. How is the fire at the end of the story significant? Why are the other activities recorded in the final paragraph important?

BERNARD MALAMUD

(1914–1986)

UNITED STATES

Bernard Malamud was born in Brooklyn and died in New York City. His education was also in the city, at City College of New York (B.A.) and at Columbia University (M.A.). During his years as a writer, he taught at Harlem High School, at Oregon State University, and from 1961 to 1986 at Bennington College. His novels include *The Natural* (1952); *The Assistant* (1957); *The Fixer* (1961), which won the Pulitzer Prize; and *Dubin's Lives* (1979). He has published several volumes of short stories, including *The Magic Barrel* (1958), which won the National Book Award, and *Idiots First* (1963). *The Stories of Bernard Malamud* appeared in 1983.

Malamud's parents were Russian-Jewish immigrants, upon whose experiences the writer drew for both his novels and his short stories. So strong are Jewish themes in his work that the editors of *Contemporary Authors* wrote, at the time of his death, that "Each of [Malamud's] first three novels features a schlemiel figure who tries to restore a Wasteland to a Paradise against a Jewish background." Although the novels tend to be serious, even tragic, many of the author's stories (such as "The Jewbird") are essentially satiric or comic. Malamud has often been praised for his mastery of dialogue, especially his complex use of Jewish-American speech patterns.

Malamud was 60 when he agreed to a *Paris Review* interview. To Daniel Stern's question, "Are you a Jewish writer?" Malamud replied, "I'm an American, I'm a Jew, and write for all men. A novelist has to, or he's built himself a cage. I write about Jews, when I write about Jews, because they set my imagination going. I know something about their history, the quality of their experience and belief, and of their literature, though not as much as I would like." Asked if he preferred writing short stories instead of novels, he said, "Just as much, though the short story has its own pleasures. I like packing a self or two into a few pages, predicating lifetimes. The drama is terse, happens faster, and is often outlandish. A short story is a way of indicating the complexity of life in a few pages, producing the surprise and effect of a profound knowledge in a short time."

The Jewbird

The window was open so the skinny bird flew in. Flappity-flap with its frazzled black wings. That's how it goes. It's open, you're in. Closed, you're out and that's your fate. The bird wearily flapped through the open kitchen window of Harry Cohen's top-floor apartment on First Avenue near the lower East River. On a rod on the wall hung an escaped canary cage, its door wide open, but this black-type long-beaked bird—its ruffled head and small dull eyes, crossed a little, making it look like a dissipated crow—landed if not smack on Cohen's thick lamb chop, at least on the table, close by. The frozen foods salesman was sitting at supper with his wife and young son on a hot August evening a year ago. Cohen, a heavy man with hairy chest and beefy shorts; Edie, in skinny yellow shorts and red halter; and their ten-year-old Morris (after his father)—Maurie, they called him, a nice kid though not overly bright—were all in the city after two weeks out, because Cohen's mother was dying. They had been enjoying Kingston, New York, but drove back when Mama got sick in her flat in the Bronx.

"Right on the table," said Cohen, putting down his beer glass and swatting at the bird. "Son of a bitch."

"Harry, take care with your language," Edie said, looking at Maurie, who watched every move.

The bird cawed hoarsely and with a flap of its bedraggled wings—feathers tufted this way and that—rose heavily to the top of the open kitchen door, where it perched staring down.

"Gevalt,[1] a pogrom!"

"It's a talking bird," said Edie in astonishment.

"In Jewish," said Maurie.

"Wise guy," muttered Cohen. He gnawed on his chop, then put down the bone. "So if you can talk, say what's your business. What do you want here?"

"If you can't spare a lamb chop," said the bird, "I'll settle for a piece of herring with a crust of bread. You can't live on your nerve forever."

"This ain't a restaurant," Cohen replied. "All I'm asking is what brings you to this address?"

"The window was open," the bird sighed; adding after a moment, "I'm running. I'm flying but I'm also running."

"From whom?" asked Edie with interest.

"Anti-Semeets."

"Anti-Semites?" they all said.

"That's from who."

"What kind of anti-Semites bother a bird?" Edie asked.

"Any kind," said the bird, "also including eagles, vultures, and hawks. And once in a while some crows will take your eyes out."

"But aren't you a crow?"

"Me? I'm a Jewbird."

Cohen laughed heartily. "What do you mean by that?"

The bird began dovening. He prayed without Book or tallith, but with passion. Edie bowed her head though not Cohen. And Maurie rocked back and forth with the prayer, looking up with one wide-open eye.

When the prayer was done Cohen remarked, "No hat, no phylacteries?"

"I'm an old radical."

"You're sure you're not some kind of a ghost of dybbuk?"

"Not a dybbuk," answered the bird, "though one of my relatives had such an experience once. It's all over now, thanks God. They freed her from a former lover, a crazy jealous man. She's now the mother of two wonderful children."

"Birds?" Cohen asked slyly.

[1]*Gevalt* a cry of amazement

"Why not?"

"What kind of birds?"

"Like me. Jewbirds."

Cohen tipped back in his chair and guffawed. "That's a big laugh. I've heard of a Jewfish but not a Jewbird."

"We're once removed." The bird rested on one skinny leg, then on the other. "Please, could you spare maybe a piece of herring with a small crust of bread?"

Edie got up from the table.

"What are you doing?" Cohen asked her.

"I'll clear the dishes."

Cohen turned to the bird. "So what's your name, if you don't mind saying?"

"Call me Schwartz."

"He might be an old Jew changed into a bird by somebody," said Edie, removing a plate.

"Are you?" asked Harry, lighting a cigar.

"Who knows?" answered Schwartz. "Does God tell us everything?"

Maurie got up on his chair. "What kind of herring?" he asked the bird in excitement.

"Get down, Maurie, or you'll fall," ordered Cohen.

"If you haven't got matjes, I'll take schmaltz,"[2] said Schwartz.

"All we have is marinated, with slices of onion—in a jar," said Edie.

"If you'll open for me the jar I'll eat marinated. Do you have also, if you don't mind, a piece of rye bread—the spitz?"[3]

Edie thought she had.

"Feed him out on the balcony," Cohen said. He spoke to the bird. "After that take off."

Schwartz closed both bird eyes. "I'm tired and it's a long way."

"Which direction are you headed, north or south?"

Schwartz, barely lifting his wings, shrugged.

"You don't know where you're going?"

"Where there's charity I'll go."

"Let him stay, papa," said Maurie. "He's only a bird."

"So stay the night," Cohen said, "but no longer."

In the morning Cohen ordered the bird out of the house but Maurie cried, so Schwartz stayed for a while. Maurie was still on vacation from school and his friends were away. He was lonely and Edie enjoyed the fun he had, playing with the bird.

"He's no trouble at all," she told Cohen, "and besides his appetite is very small."

"What'll you do when he makes dirty?"

"He flies across the street in a tree when he makes dirty, and if nobody passes below, who notices?"

"So all right," said Cohen, "but I'm dead set against it. I warn you he ain't gonna stay here long."

"What have you got against the poor bird?"

[2] *matjes* and *schmaltz* expensive herring or something lesser

[3] *spitz* the heel (of a loaf of bread)

"Poor bird, my ass. He's a foxy bastard. He thinks he's a Jew."

"What difference does it make what he thinks?"

"A Jewbird, what a chutzpah. One false move and he's out on his drumsticks."

At Cohen's insistence Schwartz lived out on the balcony in a new wooden birdhouse Edie had bought him.

"With many thanks," said Schwartz, "though I would rather have a human roof over my head. You know how it is at my age. I like the warm, the windows, the smell of cooking. I would also be glad to see once in a while the *Jewish Morning Journal* and have now and then a schnapps because it helps my breathing, thanks God. But whatever you give me, you won't hear complaints."

However, when Cohen brought home a bird feeder full of dried corn, Schwartz said, "Impossible."

Cohen was annoyed. "What's the matter, crosseyes, is your life getting too good for you? Are you forgetting what it means to be migratory? I'll bet a helluva lot of crows you happen to be acquainted with, Jews or otherwise, would give their eyeteeth to eat this corn."

Schwartz did not answer. What can you say to a grubber yung?[4]

"Not for my digestion," he later explained to Edie. "Cramps. Herring is better even if it makes you thirsty. At least rainwater don't cost anything." He laughed sadly in breathy caws.

And herring, thanks to Edie, who knew where to shop, was what Schwartz got, with an occasional piece of potato pancake, and even a bit of soupmeat when Cohen wasn't looking.

When school began in September, before Cohen would once again suggest giving the bird the boot, Edie prevailed on him to wait a little while until Maurie adjusted.

"To deprive him right now might hurt his school work, and you know what trouble we had last year."

"So okay, but sooner or later the bird goes. That I promise you."

Schwartz, though nobody had asked him, took on full responsibility for Maurie's performance in school. In return for favors granted, when he was let in for an hour or two at night, he spent most of his time overseeing the boy's lessons. He sat on top of the dresser near Maurie's desk as he laboriously wrote out his homework. Maurie was a restless type and Schwartz gently kept him to his studies. He also listened to him practice his screechy violin, taking a few minutes off now and then to rest his ears in the bathroom. And they afterwards played dominoes. The boy was an indifferent checker player and it was impossible to teach him chess. When he was sick, Schwartz read him comic books though he personally disliked them. But Maurie's work improved in school and even his violin teacher admitted his playing was better. Edie gave Schwartz credit for these improvements though the bird pooh-poohed them.

Yet he was proud there was nothing lower than C minuses on Maurie's report card, and on Edie's insistence celebrated with a little schnapps.

"If he keeps up like this," Cohen said, "I'll get him in any Ivy League college for sure."

"Oh I hope so," sighed Edie.

[4]*grubber yung* plump joker

But Schwartz shook his head. "He's a good boy—you don't have to worry. He won't be a shicker[5] or a wifebeater, God forbid, but a scholar he'll never be, if you know what I mean, although maybe a good mechanic. It's no disgrace in these times."

"If I were you," Cohen said, angered, "I'd keep my big snoot out of other people's private business."

"Harry, please," said Edie.

"My goddamn patience is wearing out. That crosseyes butts into everything."

Though he wasn't exactly a welcome guest in the house, Schwartz gained a few ounces although he did not improve in appearance. He looked bedraggled as ever, his feathers unkempt, as though he had just flown out of a snowstorm. He spent, he admitted, little time taking care of himself. Too much to think about. "Also outside plumbing," he told Edie. Still there was more glow to his eyes so that though Cohen went on calling him crosseyes he said it less emphatically.

Liking his situation, Schwartz tried tactfully to stay out of Cohen's way, but one night when Edie was at the movies and Maurie was taking a hot shower, the frozen foods salesman began a quarrel with the bird.

"For Christ sake, why don't you wash yourself sometimes? Why must you always stink like a dead fish?"

"Mr. Cohen, if you'll pardon me, if somebody eats garlic he will smell from garlic. I eat herring three times a day. Feed me flowers and I will smell like flowers."

"Who's obligated to feed you anything at all? You're lucky to get herring."

"Excuse me, I'm not complaining," said the bird. "You're complaining."

"What's more," said Cohen, "Even from out on the balcony I can hear you snoring away like a pig. It keeps me awake at night."

"Snoring," said Schwartz, "isn't a crime, thanks God."

"All in all you are a goddamn pest and free loader. Next thing you'll want to sleep in bed next to my wife."

"Mr. Cohen," said Schwartz, "on this rest assured. A bird is a bird."

"So you say, but how do I know you're a bird and not some kind of a goddamn devil?"

"If I was a devil you would know already. And I don't mean because your son's good marks."

"Shut up, you bastard bird," shouted Cohen.

"Grubber yung," cawed Schwartz, rising to the tips of his talons, his long wings outstretched.

Cohen was about to lunge for the bird's scrawny neck but Maurie came out of the bathroom, and for the rest of the evening until Schwartz's bedtime on the balcony, there was pretended peace.

But the quarrel had deeply disturbed Schwartz and he slept badly. His snoring woke him, and awake, he was fearful of what would become of him. Wanting to stay out of Cohen's way, he kept to the birdhouse as much as possible. Cramped by it, he paced back and forth on the balcony ledge, or sat on the birdhouse roof, staring into space. In evenings, while overseeing Maurie's lessons, he often fell asleep. Awakening, he nervously hopped around exploring the four corners of the room. He spent much time in Maurie's closet, and carefully examined his bureau drawers when they were left open. And once

[5]*shicker* a drinker

when he found a large paper bag on the floor, Schwartz poked his way into it to investigate what possibilities were. The boy was amused to see the bird in the paper bag.

"He wants to build a nest," he said to his mother.

Edie, sensing Schwartz's unhappiness, spoke to him quietly.

"Maybe if you did some of the things my husband wants you, you would get along better with him."

"Give me a for instance," Schwartz said.

"Like take a bath, for instance."

"I'm too old for baths," said the bird. "My feathers fall out without baths."

"He says you have a bad smell."

"Everybody smells. Some people smell because of their thoughts or because who they are. My bad smell comes from the food I eat. What does his come from?"

"I better not ask him or it might make him mad," said Edie.

In late November Schwartz froze on the balcony in the fog and cold, and especially on rainy days he woke with stiff joints and could barely move his wings. Already he felt twinges of rheumatism. He would have liked to spend more time in the warm house, particularly when Maurie was in school and Cohen at work. But though Edie was good-hearted and might have sneaked him in in the morning, just to thaw out, he was afraid to ask her. In the meantime Cohen, who had been reading articles about the migration of birds, came out on the balcony one night after work when Edie was in the kitchen preparing pot roast, and peeking into the birdhouse, warned Schwartz to be on his way soon if he knew what was good for him. "Time to hit the flyways."

"Mr. Cohen, why do you hate me so much?" asked the bird. "What did I do to you?"

"Because you're an A-number-one trouble maker, that's why. What's more, whoever heard of a Jewbird! Now scat or it's open war."

But Schwartz stubbornly refused to depart so Cohen embarked on a campaign of harassing him, meanwhile hiding it from Edie and Maurie. Maurie hated violence and Cohen didn't want to leave a bad impression. He thought maybe if he played dirty tricks on the bird he would fly off without being physically kicked out. The vacation was over, let him make his easy living off the fat of somebody else's land. Cohen worried about the effect of the bird's departure on Maurie's schooling but decided to take the chance, first, because the boy now seemed to have the knack of studying—give the black bird-bastard credit—and second, because Schwartz was driving him bats by being there always, even in his dreams.

The frozen foods salesman began his campaign against the bird by mixing watery cat food with the herring slices in Schwartz's dish. He also blew up and popped numerous paper bags outside the birdhouse as the bird slept, and when he got Schwartz good and nervous, though not enough to leave, he brought a full-grown cat into the house, supposedly a gift for little Maurie, who had always wanted a pussy. The cat never stopped springing up at Schwartz whenever he saw him, one day managing to claw out several of his tailfeathers. And even at lesson time, when the cat was usually excluded from Maurie's room, though somehow or other he quickly found his way in at the end of the lesson, Schwartz was desperately fearful of his life and flew from pinnacle to pinnacle—light fixture to clothes-tree to door-top—in order to elude the beast's wet jaws.

Once when the bird complained to Edie how hazardous his existence was, she said, "Be patient, Mr. Schwartz. When the cat gets to know you better he won't try to catch you any more."

"When he stops trying we will both be in Paradise," Schwartz answered. "Do me a favor and get rid of him. He makes my whole life worry. I'm losing feathers like a tree loses leaves."

"I'm awfully sorry but Maurie likes the pussy and sleeps with it."

What could Schwartz do? He worried but came to no decision, being afraid to leave. So he ate the herring garnished with cat food, tried hard not to hear the paper bags bursting like fire crackers outside the birdhouse at night, and lived terror-stricken closer to the ceiling than the floor, as the cat, his tail flicking, endlessly watched him.

Weeks went by. Then on the day after Cohen's mother had died in her flat in the Bronx, when Maurie came home with a zero on an arithmetic test, Cohen, enraged, waited until Edie had taken the boy to his violin lesson, then openly attacked the bird. He chased him with a broom on the balcony and Schwartz frantically flew back and forth, finally escaping into his birdhouse. Cohen triumphantly reached in, and grabbing both skinny legs, dragged the bird out, cawing loudly, his wings wildly beating. He whirled the bird around and around his head. But Schwartz, as he moved in circles, managed to swoop down and catch Cohen's nose in his beak, and hung on for dear life. Cohen cried out in great pain, punched the bird with his fist, and tugging at its legs with all his might, pulled his nose free. Again he swung the yawking Schwartz around until the bird grew dizzy, then with a furious heave, flung him into the night. Schwartz sank like stone into the street. Cohen then tossed the birdhouse and feeder after him, listening at the ledge until they crashed on the sidewalk below. For a full hour, broom in hand, his heart palpitating and nose throbbing with pain, Cohen waited for Schwartz to return but the broken-hearted bird didn't.

That's the end of that dirty bastard, the salesman thought and went in. Edie and Maurie had come home.

"Look," said Cohen, pointing to his bloody nose swollen three times its normal size, "what that sonofabitch bird did. It's a permanent scar."

"Where is he now?" Edie asked, frightened.

"I threw him out and he flew away. Good riddance."

Nobody said no, though Edie touched a handkerchief to her eyes and Maurie rapidly tried the nine times table and found he knew approximately half.

In the spring when the winter's snow had melted, the boy, moved by a memory, wandered in the neighborhood, looking for Schwartz. He found a dead black bird in a small lot near the river, his two wings broken, neck twisted, and both bird-eyes plucked clean.

"Who did it to you, Mr. Schwartz?" Maurie wept.

"Anti-Semeets," Edie said later.

[1963]

QUESTIONS

1. Why is Cohen so uptight about Schwartz? Is it what Edie says at the end of the story or something else?

2. What kind of comparison can be made between "The Jewbird" and Albert Camus's "The Guest"?
3. Can the satire of the story be appreciated only by someone from the same ethnic group? Is racial prejudice a fitting theme for satire?
4. Who is the main character in the story?

Thomas Mann
(1875–1955)
Germany

Certainly the major German novelist of the twentieth century, Thomas Mann was born to an established and prosperous family of "burgers," or merchants. He began to write in his youth, publishing his first story when he was a teenager. When Mann was 15 his father died, bequeathing him an income sufficient to support him. In his first novel, *Buddenbrooks* (1901), Mann traced a family resembling his own—in decline, ironically, because of the aesthetic tendencies within it that challenged its mercantile values. Intellectually influenced by the philosophical ideas of Nietzsche and Schopenhauer, Mann incorporated their ideas into his fictional diagnosis of the maladies borne of the collapse of the old order in Europe.

In several of his major narratives, physical disease becomes a central symbol for spiritual malady: for Gustave von Aschenbach of *Death in Venice* (1912), a writer who falls in love with a boy to whom he never speaks, but who is destroyed by his own conviction of perversion and moral collapse; for the consumptive Hans Castorp of *The Magic Mountain* (1924), who contemplates his destiny during seven years in a sanatorium in the Alps; and for Adrian Leverkuhn of *Doctor Faustus* (1947), a composer who struggles with syphilis as well as with his grand ambitions.

Mann's narratives are novels of ideas: explorations of the deep tensions between individual and societal conceptions of order, both moral and social, and of fundamental spiritual and intellectual questions concerning the purpose and meaning of life. Examining the matrices of individual experience against an exceptionally broad canvas that includes cultural, political, economic, philosophical, and mythical contexts, Mann wrote during a time in the early twentieth century in which cultural values were in great flux. Hence his narratives, focusing on individuals who are torn between moral responsibility and license, between the necessity for order and self-discipline as a guide for living in the world and the romantic impulse as a more instinctive response, are searching and often ironic psychological documentations of the Age of Anxiety.

Mann left Germany during the rise of fascism, living in Switzerland and then the United States, where he taught at Princeton. He received the Nobel Prize for Literature in 1929.

The Infant Prodigy

The infant prodigy entered. The hall became quiet.

It became quiet and then the audience began to clap, because somewhere at the side a leader of mobs, a born organizer, clapped first. The audience had heard nothing yet, but they applauded; for a mighty publicity organization had heralded the prodigy and people were already hypnotized, whether they knew it or not.

The prodigy came from behind a splendid screen embroidered with Empire garlands and great conventionalized flowers, and climbed nimbly up the steps to the platform, diving into the applause as into a bath; a little chilly and shivering, but yet as though into a friendly element. He advanced to the edge of the platform and smiled as though he were about to be photographed; he made a shy, charming gesture of greeting, like a little girl.

He was dressed entirely in white silk, which the audience found enchanting. The little white jacket was fancifully cut, with a sash underneath it, and even his shoes were made of white silk. But against the white socks his bare little legs stood out quite brown; for he was a Greek boy.

He was called Bibi Saccellaphylaccas. And such indeed was his name. No one knew what Bibi was the pet name for, nobody but the impresario, and he regarded it as a trade secret. Bibi had smooth black hair reaching to his shoulders; it was parted on the side and fastened back from the narrow domed forehead by a little silk bow. His was the most harmless childish countenance in the world, with an unfinished nose and guileless mouth. The area beneath his pitch-black mouselike eyes was already a little tired and visibly lined. He looked as though he were nine years old but was really eight and given out for seven. It was hard to tell whether to believe this or not. Probably everybody knew better and still believed it, as happens about so many things. The average man thinks that a little falseness goes with beauty. Where should we get any excitement out of our daily life if we were not willing to pretend a bit? And the average man is quite right, in his average brains!

The prodigy kept on bowing until the applause died down, then he went up to the grand piano, and the audience cast a last look at its programmes. First came a *Marche solonnelle*, then a *Rêverie*, and then *Le Hibou et les moineaux*[1]—all by Bibi Saccellaphylaccas. The whole programme was by him, they were all his compositions. He could not score them, of course, but he had them all in his extraordinary little head and they possessed real artistic significance, or so it said, seriously and objectively, in the programme. The programme sounded as though the impresario had wrested these concessions from his critical nature after a hard struggle.

The prodigy sat down upon the revolving stool and felt with his feet for the pedals, which were raised by means of a clever device so that Bibi could reach them. It was Bibi's own piano, he took it everywhere with him. It rested upon wooden trestles and its polish was somewhat marred by the constant transportation—but all that only made things more interesting.

Bibi put his silk-shod feet on the pedals; then he made an artful little face, looked straight ahead of him, and lifted his right hand. It was a brown, childish little hand; but the wrist was strong and unlike a child's, with well-developed bones.

Bibi made his face for the audience because he was aware that he had to entertain them a little. But he had his own private enjoyment in the thing too, an enjoyment which he could never convey to anybody. It was that prickling delight, that secret shudder of bliss, which ran through him every time he sat at an open piano—it would always be with him. And here was the keyboard again, these seven black and white octaves, among which he had so often lost himself in

[1]*le Hibou et les moineaux* French: *The Owl and the Sparrows*

abysmal and thrilling adventures—and yet it always looked as clean and untouched as a newly washed blackboard. This was the realm of music that lay before him. It lay spread out like an inviting ocean, where he might plunge in and blissfully swim, where he might let himself be borne and carried away, where he might go under in night and storm, yet keep the mastery: control, ordain—he held his right hand poised in the air.

A breathless stillness reigned in the room—the tense moment before the first note came. . . . How would it begin? It began so. And Bibi, with his index finger, fetched the first note out of the piano, a quite unexpectedly powerful first note in the middle register, like a trumpet blast. Others followed, an introduction developed—the audience relaxed.

The concert was held in the palatial hall of a fashionable first-class hotel. The walls were covered with mirrors framed in gilded arabesques, between frescoes of the rosy and fleshly school. Ornamental columns supported a ceiling that displayed a whole universe of electric bulbs, in clusters darting a brilliance far brighter than day and filling the whole space with thin, vibrating golden light. Not a seat was unoccupied, people were standing in the side aisles and at the back. The front seats cost twelve marks; for the impresario believed that anything worth having was worth paying for. And they were occupied by the best society, for it was in the upper classes, of course, that the greatest enthusiasm was felt. There were even some children, with their legs hanging down demurely from their chairs and their shining eyes staring at their gifted little white-clad contemporary.

Down in front on the left side sat the prodigy's mother, an extremely obese woman with a powdered double chin and a feather on her head. Beside her was the impresario, a man of oriental appearance with large gold buttons on his conspicuous cuffs. The princess was in the middle of the front row—a wrinkled, shrivelled little old princess but still a patron of the arts, especially everything full of sensibility. She sat in a deep, velvet-upholstered arm-chair, and a Persian carpet was spread before her feet. She held her hands folded over her grey striped-silk breast, put her head on one side, and presented a picture of elegant composure as she sat looking up at the performing prodigy. Next to her sat her lady-in-waiting, in a green striped-silk gown. Being only a lady-in-waiting she had to sit up very straight in her chair.

Bibi ended in a grand climax. With what power this wee manikin belaboured the keyboard! The audience could scarcely trust its ears. The march theme, an infectious, swinging tune, broke out once more, fully harmonized, bold and showy; with every note Bibi flung himself back from the waist as though he were marching in a triumphal procession. He ended *fortissimo*, bent over, slipped sideways off the stool, and stood with a smile awaiting the applause.

And the applause burst forth, unanimously, enthusiastically; the child made his demure little maidenly curtsy and people in the front seat thought: "Look what slim little hips he has! Clap, clap! Hurrah, bravo, little chap, Saccophylax or whatever your name is! Wait, let me take off my gloves—what a little devil of a chap he is!"

Bibi had to come out three times from behind the screen before they would stop. Some late-comers entered the hall and moved about looking for seats. Then the concert continued. Bibi's *Rêverie* murmured its numbers, consisting almost entirely of arpeggios, above which a bar of melody rose now and then, weak-winged. Then came *Le Hibou et les moineaux*. This piece was brilliantly successful, it made a strong impression; it was an effective childhood fantasy, remarkably well envisaged. The bass represented the owl, sitting morosely rolling his filmy eyes; while in the treble the impudent, half-frightened sparrows chirped. Bibi received an ovation when he finished, he was called out four times. A hotel page with shiny buttons carried up three great laurel wreaths onto the stage and proffered them from one side while Bibi nodded and expressed his thanks. Even the princess shared in the applause, daintily and noiselessly pressing her palms together.

Ah, the knowing little creature understood how to make people clap! He stopped behind the screen, they had to wait for him; lingered a little on the steps of the platform, admired the long streamers on the wreaths—although actually such things bored him stiff by now. He bowed with the utmost charm, he gave the audience plenty of time to rave itself out, because applause is valuable and must not be cut short. "*Le Hibou* is my drawing card," he thought—this expression he had learned from the impresario. "Now I will play the fantasy, it is a lot better than *Le Hibou*, of course, especially the C-sharp passage. But you idiots dote on the *Hibou*, though it is the first and the silliest thing I wrote." He continued to bow and smile.

Next came a *Méditation* and then an *Étude*—the programme was quite comprehensive. The *Méditation* was very like the *Rêverie*—which was nothing against it—and the *Étude* displayed all of Bibi's virtuosity, which naturally fell a little short of his inventiveness. And then the *Fantaisie*. This was his favourite; he varied it a little each time, giving himself free rein and sometimes surprising even himself, on good evenings, by his own inventiveness.

He sat and played, so little, so white and shining, against the great black grand piano, elect and alone, above that confused sea of faces, above the heavy, insensitive mass soul, upon which he was labouring to work with his individual, differentiated soul. His lock of soft black hair with the white silk bow had fallen over his forehead, his trained and bony little wrists pounded away, the muscles stood out visibly on his brown childish cheeks.

Sitting there he sometimes had moments of oblivion and solitude, when the gaze of his strange little mouselike eyes with the big rings beneath them would lose itself and stare through the painted stage into space that was peopled with strange vague life. Then out of the corner of his eye he would give a quick look back into the hall and be once more with his audience.

"Joy and pain, the heights and the depths—that is my *Fantaisie*," he thought lovingly. "Listen, here is the C-sharp passage." He lingered over the approach, wondering if they would notice anything. But no, of course not, how should they? And he cast his eyes up prettily at the ceiling so that at least they might have something to look at.

All these people sat there in their regular rows, looking at the prodigy and thinking all sorts of things in their regular brains. An old gentleman with a white beard, a seal ring on his finger and a bulbous swelling on his bald spot, a growth if you like, was thinking to himself: "Really, one ought to be ashamed." He had never got any further than "Ah, thou dearest Augustin" on the piano, and here he sat now, a grey old man, looking on while this little hop-o'-my-thumb performed miracles. Yes, yes, it is a gift of God, we must remember that. God grants His gifts, or He withholds them, and there is no shame in being an ordinary man. Like with the Christ Child.—Before a child one may kneel without feeling ashamed. Strange that thoughts like these should be so satisfying—he would even say so sweet, if it was not too silly for a tough old man like him to use the word. That was how he felt, anyhow.

Art . . . the business man with the parrot-nose was thinking. "Yes, it adds something cheerful to life, a little good white silk and a little tumty-ti-ti-tum. Really he does not play so badly. Fully fifty seats, twelve marks apiece, that makes six hundred marks—and everything else besides. Take off the rent of the hall, the lighting and the programmes, you must have fully a thousand marks profit. That is worth while."

That was Chopin he was just playing, thought the piano-teacher, a lady with a pointed nose; she was of an age when the understanding sharpens as the hopes decay. "But not very original—I will say that afterwards, it sounds well. And his hand position is entirely amateur. One must be able to lay a coin on the back of the hand—I would use a ruler on him."

Then there was a young girl, at that self-conscious and chlorotic time of life when the most ineffable ideas come into the mind. She was thinking to herself: "What is it he is playing? It is expressive of passion, yet he is a child. If he kissed me it would be as though my little brother kissed me—no kiss at all. Is there such a thing as passion all by itself, without any earthly object, a sort of child's-play of passion? What nonsense! If I were to say such things aloud they would just be at me with some more cod-liver oil. Such is life."

An officer was leaning against a column. He looked on at Bibi's success and thought: "Yes, you are something and I am something, each in his own way." So he clapped his heels together and paid to the prodigy the respect which he felt to be due to all the powers that be.

Then there was a critic, an elderly man in a shiny black coat and turned-up trousers splashed with mud. He sat in his free seat and thought: "Look at him, this young beggar of a Bibi. As an individual he has still to develop, but as a type he is already quite complete, the artist *par excellence*. He has in himself all the artist's exaltation and his utter worthlessness, his charlatanry and his sacred fire, his burning contempt and his secret raptures. Of course I can't write all that, it is too good. Of course, I should have been an artist myself if I had not seen through the whole business so clearly."

Then the prodigy stopped playing and a perfect storm arose in the hall. He had to come out again and again from behind his screen. The man with the shiny buttons carried up more wreaths: four laurel wreaths, a lyre made of violets, a bouquet of roses. He had not arms enough to convey all these tributes, the impresario himself mounted the stage to help him. He hung a laurel wreath round Bibi's neck, he tenderly stroked the black hair—and suddenly as though overcome he bent down and gave the prodigy a kiss, a resounding kiss, square on the mouth. And then the storm became a hurricane. That kiss ran through the room like an electric shock, it went direct to peoples' marrow and made them shiver down their backs. They were carried away by a helpless compulsion of sheer noise. Loud shouts mingled with the hysterical clapping of hands. Some of Bibi's commonplace little friends down there waved their handkerchiefs. But the critic thought: "Of course that kiss had to come—it's a good old gag. Yes, good Lord, if only one did not see through everything quite so clearly—"

And so the concert drew to a close. It began at half past seven and finished at half past eight. The platform was laden with wreaths and two little pots of flowers stood on the lamp-stands of the piano. Bibi played as his last number his *Rhapsodie grecque*, which turned into the Greek national hymn at the end. His fellow-countrymen in the audience would gladly have sung it with him if the company had not been so august. They made up for it with a powerful noise and hullabaloo, a hot-blooded national demonstration. And the aging critic was thinking: "Yes, the hymn had to come too. They have to exploit every vein — publicity cannot afford to neglect any means to its end. I think I'll criticize that as inartistic. But perhaps I am wrong, perhaps that is the most artistic thing of all. What is the artist? A jack-in-the-box. Criticism is on a higher plane. But I can't say that." And away he went in his muddy trousers.

After being called out nine or ten times the prodigy did not come any more from behind the screen but went to his mother and the impresario down in the hall. The audience stood about among the chairs and applauded and pressed forward to see Bibi close at hand. Some of them wanted to see the princess too. Two dense circles formed, one round the prodigy, the other round the princess, and you could actually not tell which of them was receiving more homage. But the court lady was commanded to go over to Bibi; she smoothed down his silk jacket a bit to make it look suitable for a court function, led him by the arm to the princess, and solemnly indicated to him that he was to kiss the royal hand. "How do you do it, child?" asked the princess. "Does it come into your head of itself when you sit down?" "*Oui, madame,*" answered Bibi. To himself he thought: "Oh, what a stupid old princess!" Then he turned round shyly and uncourtier-like and went back to his family.

Outside in the cloak-room there was a crowd. People held up their numbers and received with open arms furs, shawls, and galoshes. Somewhere among her acquaintances the piano-teacher stood making her critique. "He is not very original," she said audibly and looked about her.

In front of one of the great mirrors an elegant young lady was being arrayed in her evening cloak and fur shoes by her brothers, two lieutenants. She was exquisitely beautiful, with her steel-blue eyes and her clean-cut, well-bred face. A really noble dame. When she was ready she stood waiting for her brothers. "Don't stand so long in front of the glass, Adolf," she said softly to one of them, who could not tear himself away from the sight of his simple, good-looking young features. But Lieutenant Adolf thinks: What cheek! He would button his overcoat in front of the glass, just the same. Then they went out on the street where the arc-lights gleamed cloudily through the white mist. Lieutenant Adolf struck up a little nigger-dance on the frozen snow to keep warm, with his hands in his slanting overcoat pockets and his collar turned up.

A girl with untidy hair and swinging arms, accompanied by a gloomy-faced youth, came out just behind them. A child! she thought. A charming child. But in there he was an awe-inspiring . . . and aloud in a toneless voice she said: "We are all infant prodigies, we artists."

"Well, bless my soul!" thought the old gentleman who had never got further than Augustin on the piano, and whose boil was now concealed by a top hat. "What does all that mean? She sounds very oracular." But the gloomy youth understood. He nodded his head slowly.

Then they were silent and the untidy-haired girl gazed after the brothers and sister. She rather despised them, but she looked after them until they had turned the corner.

[1903]

Translated by
H. T. Lowe-Porter

QUESTIONS

1. What attitudes are expressed toward the infant prodigy? Is the general tone of the story sympathetic toward or critical of the young pianist?
2. What does the story suggest about the relationship between art and experience? Between performer and audience? Between art and criticism? Between appearance and reality?
3. What is the significance of the ending?

Katherine Mansfield

(1888–1923)

New Zealand/England

Born near Wellington, New Zealand, Katherine Mansfield Beauchamp left home early to study the cello in England, but turned to writing instead. Although she returned to New Zealand briefly, publishing her earliest stories in New Zealand and Australian magazines, in 1908 she chose to pursue her life as a writer in London with the help of a small allowance from her father. One of the stories she submitted to a London magazine caught the attention of John Middleton Murry, an editor and critic who became her mentor and eventually her husband.

Mansfield's first collection of stories, *In a German Pension*, was published in 1911. Several other volumes followed, including *Bliss and Other Stories* (1920) and *The Garden Party* (1922). During the last five years of her life, Mansfield suffered from tuberculosis; she was tormented by her deteriorating health, which impeded her profound desire to be "rooted in life" as well as her ability to write. She sought a miracle by taking residence in a spiritual healing community at Fountainbleau, where she died at the age of 34.

Mansfield wrote 88 stories (of which 26 were unfinished). Many of her stories hold a lasting place in twentieth-century fiction because of her influential innovations in form. Like her model, Chekhov, Mansfield reduced the significance of plot, instead emphasizing moments of emotional discovery and epiphany that directly revealed her characters' inner lives. Her eye for the telling detail, vignettes of character, and impressionistic depictions of settings as the backdrops for her characters' visions particularly distinguish her exemplary New Zealand stories.

◆ *Her First Ball* ◆

Exactly when the ball began Leila would have found it hard to say. Perhaps her first real partner was the cab. It did not matter that she shared the cab with the Sheridan girls and their brother. She sat back in her own little corner of it, and the bolster on which her hand rested felt like the sleeve of an unknown young man's dress suit; and away they bowled, past waltzing lampposts and houses and fences and trees.

"Have you really never been to a ball before, Leila? But, my child, how too weird—" cried the Sheridan girls.

"Our nearest neighbor was fifteen miles," said Leila softly, gently opening and shutting her fan.

Oh, dear, how hard it was to be indifferent like the others! She tried not to smile too much; she tried not to care. But every single thing was so new and exciting . . . Meg's tuberoses, Jose's long loop of amber, Laura's little dark head, pushing above her white fur like a flower through snow. She would remember for ever. It even gave her a pang to see her cousin Laurie throw away the wisps of tissue paper he pulled from the fastening of his new gloves. She would like to have kept those wisps as a keepsake, as a remembrance. Laurie leaned forward and put his hand on Laura's knee.

"Look here, darling," he said. "The third and the ninth as usual. Twig?"

Oh, how marvellous to have a brother! In her excitement Leila felt that if there had been time, if it hadn't been impossible, she couldn't have helped crying because she was an only child, and no brother had ever said "Twig?" to her; no sister would ever say, as Meg said to Jose that moment, "I've never known your hair go up more successfully than it has tonight!"

But, of course, there was no time. They were at the drill hall already; there were cabs in front of them and cabs behind. The road was bright on either side with moving fan-like lights, and on the pavement gay couples seemed to float through the air; little satin shoes chased each other like birds.

"Hold on to me, Leila; you'll get lost," said Laura.

"Come on, girls, let's make a dash for it," said Laurie.

Leila put two fingers on Laura's pink velvet cloak, and they were somehow lifted past the big gold lantern, carried along the passage, and pushed into the little room marked "Ladies." Here the crowd was so great there was hardly space to take off their things; the noise was deafening. Two benches on either side were stacked high with wraps. Two old women in white aprons ran up and down tossing fresh armfuls. And everybody was pressing forward trying to get at the little dressing table and mirror at the far end.

A great quivering jet of gas lighted the ladies' room. It couldn't wait; it was dancing already. When the door opened again and there came a burst of tuning from the drill hall, it leaped almost to the ceiling.

Dark girls, fair girls were patting their hair, tying ribbons again, tucking handkerchiefs down the front of their bodices, smoothing marble-white gloves. And because they were all laughing it seemed to Leila that they were all lovely.

"Aren't there any invisible hairpins?" cried a voice. "How most extraordinary! I can't see a single invisible hairpin."

"Powder my back, there's a darling," cried some one else.

"But I must have a needle and cotton. I've torn simply miles and miles of the frill," wailed a third.

Then, "Pass them along, pass them along!" The straw basket of programs was tossed from arm to arm. Darling little pink-and-silver programs, with pink pencils and fluffy tassels. Leila's fingers shook as she took one out of the basket. She wanted to ask someone, "Am I meant to have one too?" but she had just time to read: "Waltz 3. *Two, Two in a Canoe.* Polka 4. *Making the Feathers Fly,*" when Meg cried, "Ready, Leila?" and they pressed their way through the crush in the passage towards the big double doors of the drill hall.

Dancing had not begun yet, but the band had stopped tuning, and the noise was so great it seemed that when it did begin to play it would never be heard. Leila, pressing close to Meg, looking over Meg's shoulder, felt that even the little quivering colored flags strung across the ceiling were talking. She quite forgot to be shy; she forgot how in the middle of dressing she had sat down on the bed with one shoe off and one shoe on and begged her mother to ring up her cousins and say she couldn't go after all. And the rush of longing she had had to be sitting on the veranda of their forsaken upcountry home, listening to the baby owls crying "More pork" in the moonlight, was changed to a rush of joy so sweet that it was hard to bear alone. She clutched her fan, and, gazing at the gleaming, golden floor, the azaleas, the lanterns, the stage at one end with its red carpet and gilt chairs and the band in a corner, she thought breathlessly, "How heavenly; how simply heavenly!"

All the girls stood grouped together at one side of the doors, the men at the other, and the chaperones in dark dresses, smiling rather foolishly, walked with little careful steps over the polished floor towards the stage.

"This is my little country cousin Leila. Be nice to her. Find her partners; she's under my wing," said Meg, going up to one girl after another.

Strange faces smiled at Leila—sweetly, vaguely. Strange voices answered, "Of course, my dear." But Leila felt the girls didn't really see her. They were looking towards the men. Why didn't the men begin? What were they waiting for? There they stood, smoothing their gloves, patting their glossy hair and smiling among themselves. Then, quite suddenly, as if they had only just made up their minds that that was what they had to do, the men came gliding over the parquet. There was a joyful flutter among the girls. A tall, fair man flew up to Meg, seized her program, scribbled something; Meg passed him on to Leila. "May I have the pleasure?" He ducked and smiled. There came a dark man wearing an eyeglass, then cousin Laurie with a friend, and Laura with a little freckled fellow whose tie was crooked. Then quite an old man—fat, with a big bald patch on his head—took her program and murmured, "Let me see, let me see!" And he was a long time comparing his program, which looked black with names, with hers. It seemed to give him so much trouble that Leila was ashamed. "Oh, please don't bother," she said eagerly. But instead of replying the fat man wrote something, glanced at her again. "Do I remember this bright little face?" he said softly. "Is it known to me of yore?" At that moment the band began playing; the fat man disappeared. He was tossed away on a great wave of music that came flying over the gleaming floor, breaking the groups up into couples, scattering them, sending them spinning. . . .

Leila had learned to dance at boarding school. Every Saturday afternoon the boarders were hurried off to a little corrugated iron mission hall where Miss Eccles (of London) held her "select" classes. But the difference between that dusty-smelling hall—with calico texts on the walls, the poor terrified little woman in a brown velvet toque with rabbit's ears thumping the cold piano, Miss Eccles poking the girls' feet with her long white wand—and this was so tremendous that Leila was sure if her partner didn't come and she had to listen to that marvelous music and to watch the others sliding, gliding over the golden floor, she would die at least, or faint, or lift her arms and fly out of one of those dark windows that showed the stars.

"Ours, I think—" Some one bowed, smiled, and offered her his arm; she hadn't to die after all. Some one's hand pressed her waist, and she floated away like a flower that is tossed into a pool.

"Quite a good floor, isn't it?" drawled a faint voice close to her ear.

"I think it's most beautifully slippery," said Leila.

"Pardon!" The faint voice sounded surprised. Leila said it again. And there was a tiny pause before the voice echoed, "Oh, quite!" and she was swung round again.

He steered so beautifully. That was the great difference between dancing with girls and men, Leila decided. Girls banged into each other, and stamped on each other's feet; the girl who was gentleman always clutched you so.

The azaleas were separate flowers no longer; they were pink and white flags streaming by.

"Were you at the Bells' last week?" the voice came again. It sounded tired. Leila wondered whether she ought to ask him if he would like to stop.

"No, this is my first dance," said she.

Her partner gave a little gasping laugh. "Oh, I say," he protested.

"Yes, it is really the first dance I've ever been to." Leila was most fervent. It was such a relief to be able to tell somebody. "You see, I've lived in the country all my life up until now. . . ."

At that moment the music stopped, and they went to sit on two chairs against the wall. Leila tucked her pink satin feet under and fanned herself, while she blissfully watched the other couples passing and disappearing through the swing doors.

"Enjoying yourself, Leila?" asked Jose, nodding her golden head.

Laura passed and gave her the faintest little wink; it made Leila wonder for a moment whether she was quite grown up after all. Certainly her partner did not say very much. He coughed, tucked his handkerchief away, pulled down his waistcoat, took a minute thread off his sleeve. But it didn't matter. Almost immediately the band started, and her second partner seemed to spring from the ceiling.

"Floor's not bad," said the new voice. Did one always begin with the floor? And then, "Were you at the Neaves' on Tuesday?" And again Leila explained. Perhaps it was a little strange that her partners were not more interested. For it was thrilling. Her first ball! She was only at the beginning of everything. It seemed to her that she had never known what the night was like before. Up till now it had been dark, silent, beautiful very often—oh, yes—but mournful somehow. Solemn. And now it would never be like that again—it had opened dazzling bright.

"Care for an ice?" said her partner. And they went through the swing doors, down the passage, to the supper room. Her cheeks burned, she was fearfully thirsty. How sweet the ices looked on little glass plates, and how cold the frosted spoon was, iced too! And when they came back to the hall there was the fat man waiting for her by the door. It gave her quite a shock again to see how old he was; he ought to have been on the stage with the fathers and mothers. And when Leila compared him with her other partners he looked shabby. His waistcoat was creased, there was a button off his glove, his coat looked as if it was dusty with French chalk.

"Come along, little lady," said the fat man. He scarcely troubled to clasp her, and they moved away so gently, it was more like walking than dancing. But he said not a word about the floor. "Your first dance, isn't it?" he murmured.

"How *did* you know?"

"Ah," said the fat man, "that's what it is to be old!" He wheezed faintly as he steered her past an awkward couple. "You see, I've been doing this kind of thing for the last thirty years."

"Thirty years?" cried Leila. Twelve years before she was born!

"It hardly bears thinking about, does it?" said the fat man gloomily. Leila looked at his bald head, and she felt quite sorry for him.

"I think it's marvelous to be still going on," she said kindly.

"Kind little lady," said the fat man, and he pressed her a little closer, and hummed a bar of the waltz. "Of course," he said, "you can't hope to last anything like as long as that. No-o," said the fat man, "long before that you'll be sitting up there on the stage, looking on, in your nice black velvet. And these pretty arms will have turned into little short fat ones, and you'll beat time with such a different kind of fan — a black bony one." The fat man seemed to shudder. "And you'll smile away like the poor old dears up there, and point to your daughter, and tell the elderly lady next to you how some dreadful man tried to kiss her at the club ball. And your heart will ache, ache" — the fat man squeezed her closer still, as if he really was sorry for that poor heart — "because no one wants to kiss you now. And you'll say how unpleasant these polished floors are to walk on, how dangerous they are. Eh, Mademoiselle Twinkletoes?" said the fat man softly.

Leila gave a light little laugh, but she did not feel like laughing. Was it — could it all be true? It sounded terribly true. Was this first ball only the beginning of her last ball after all? At that the music seemed to change; it sounded sad, sad it rose upon a great sigh. Oh, how quickly things changed! Why didn't happiness last for ever? For ever wasn't a bit too long.

"I want to stop," she said in a breathless voice. The fat man led her to the door.

"No," she said, "I won't go outside. I won't sit down. I'll just stand here, thank you." She leaned against the wall, tapping with her foot, pulling up her gloves and trying to smile. But deep inside her a little girl threw her pinafore over her head and sobbed. Why had he spoiled it all?

"I say, you know," said the fat man, "you mustn't take me seriously, little lady."

"As if I should!" said Leila, tossing her small dark head and sucking her underlip. . . .

Again the couples paraded. The swing doors opened and shut. Now new music was given out by the bandmaster. But Leila didn't want to dance any more. She wanted to be home, or sitting on the veranda listening to those baby owls. When she looked through the dark windows at the stars, they had long beams like wings. . . .

But presently a soft, melting, ravishing tune began, and a young man with curly hair bowed before her. She would have to dance, out of politeness, until she could find Meg. Very stiffly she walked into the middle; very haughtily she put her hand on his sleeve. But in one minute, in one turn, her feet glided, glided. The lights, the azaleas, the dresses, the pink faces, the velvet chairs, all became one beautiful flying wheel. And when her next partner bumped her into the fat man and he said, "Par*don*," she smiled at him more radiantly than ever. She didn't even recognize him again.

[1922]

QUESTIONS

1. How is Leila different from her city cousins? How are these differences important to the story?
2. What are Leila's feelings about the ball? Do they change during the evening?
3. What role does the fat man play in Leila's perceptions of the ball? How does Leila respond to his cynical observations?
4. Compare this story to "The Kiss" by Anton Chekhov. In what ways are the naive young protagonists similar? In what ways are the stories similar in theme?

René Marqués

(b. 1919)

Puerto Rico

The myth of the American Dream tells us (among other things) that immigrants adjust to their new lives in the United States and share in the country's bounty. Although René Marqués's story questions that myth, in a larger sense his story asks whether Puerto Rico (his country of birth) will ever be independent from the United States or continue to be dominated by the American presence. No doubt these are questions sharpened in Marqués's consciousness as a result of the periods of his own life when he lived and studied in the United States.

Born in Arecibo, Puerto Rico, in 1919, Marqués initially trained as an agricultural engineer. Later (after a period of time spent in Madrid) Marqués began his literary career. He has subsequently written plays, short stories, and novels. Many of these works focus on the question of Puerto Rican sovereignty in the face of continued American dominance. Unfortunately, few of these works have been translated into English.

◆ *Island of Manhattan* ◆

"Cordelia of the waves,
Bitter Cordelia."
—Gabriela Mistral

Juanita raised the collar of her wool jacket and took a deep breath. She would never get used to this subterranean life. Every time she came out of the subway station, she felt an irrepressible relief.

She stood in the middle of the sidewalk, stepping aside to avoid the avalanche of people. Even so, a huge man brutally pushed against her.

"Animal," she whispered.

The man stopped in his tracks, looked at her and said, almost smiling, "Take it easy, spik." Then, as she walked away quickly, he began to follow her.

She didn't know if it were the insult or the mocking smile that made her shake with anger.

"Yankee! Brute!" she shouted. But the man did not even look back this time.

Juanita looked at her watch. Twenty-five to ten. She had time. She absentmindedly wound her watch and thought about the five payments she still owed on it. She straightened her shoulders and began to walk towards Madison.

She was walking slowly, as if she were strolling around the little plaza in Lares. She laughed to herself at the beauty of it. The memory of Lares seemed a dream. Or was this the total dream!

The important thing was that she was not in a hurry. For the first time in four years she was not in a hurry. Twenty-five minutes in which to walk three blocks. She stopped next to an overflowing garbage can to straighten her stockings. She pulled the garter down and snapped it over the stocking. She noticed that there was a run.

"Damn it! And a new pair!"

At that moment she heard a whistle. She quickly lowered her skirt and looked up to see a young man leaning against the railing. She looked him up and down.

"You have a long way to go before you can whistle like a man," she mocked.

The youngster turned tomato-red, but was Don Juan enough to say, "With you I could learn in a day."

She laughed loudly, nervously, and walked on. To learn in one day. Without knowing why, she stopped laughing. No. Perhaps not in one day. But one learns quickly. A year in Rio Piedras, two in San Juan, four in New York. Yes, above all, these years. How far I've come! The farm in San Isidro where the old man was a tenant farmer. The humid shade of the guamas. The little plaza. The moldy vestments of the big-bellied priest. The white candle of the first communion.

She felt a sweet sadness, tranquil, without anxiety or bitterness. The candle of her first communion. The white candle that today she wasn't going to have. Perhaps if she had shared that thought with someone she would not have laughed so loudly just then. No, there would be no white candle, nor lights, nor flowers. Nor a big-bellied priest.

"Goddammit! That bag is mine. You spik! Let it go! You dirty Portorican!"

"I made that bag myself, coño. It's mine, you half of a man, you Yankee!"

The two little boys wrestled furiously on the sidewalk, blocking her way. She was tempted to intervene, but she saw that the small, dark one with kinky hair was winning.

She smiled. "Take advantage of this, jibarito! There won't be many times when you'll be on top!" she shouted as she walked past.

"At ten in front of Joe's Bar," Nico had said. To meet him or not—she had given a lot of thought to this. Nico knew everything about her life—the year at the University, her work in radio, the shame in New York. Yes, above all, that. Still he kept insisting. Jenny felt confused.

"Why do you call yourself Nick instead of Nico?"

"Because I'm a foreman. This way everyone respects me."

"Wouldn't they respect you if they called you Nico?"

"Don't ask too many questions, baby. . . . " And he laughed showing shining teeth against his dark complexion.

How could he speak seriously of marriage? This thought unsettled her. She experienced a rare feeling of sin, of being immoral and yet accepting a moral solution.

"Do you know what I am, Nico?"

"Sure, you are my Jenny."

"I'm a prostitute."

"You are my Jenny."

And to her it didn't seem natural that a man—a real man—would accept the situation like that.

"You don't seem Puerto Rican."

"I'm an American citizen."

"You're from Quebradillas."

"But still an American citizen."

She was also an American citizen, but there was a huge abyss between her American citizenship and her Puerto Rican heritage.

"Nico, sometimes I believe I could understand an American better than I understand you."

"But, baby, you don't have to understand anything. The only thing you have to do is love me."

Did I love him ever? Yes, that had to be love. I had never loved anyone like that before, except that Lareño from San Isidro, barefoot and pale. It had been such a long time ago.

She probably began to love Nico during her only year at the University. He was in his second year of Industrial Arts and she, with a scholarship and the dream of a rural school, was in her freshman year. It was through Nico that she had gotten involved in the strike at the University.

"Man and woman, side by side, must protest against injustice," he had said.

When they were both expelled for protesting, she fully understood what Nico had meant. The street of Rio Piedras had seemed wide and frank with its real immediacy.

And she remembered clearly the university carrillon behind her repeating the sonorous melody—"London Bridge is falling down, falling down. . . ."

But it was not the English bridge that was falling in her life, but the dream of a rural school near San Isidro.

A beer bottle fell on the sidewalk breaking into a thousand pieces. Juanita jumped back surprised. From the window came the voice of a woman—shrill, strident, hysterical, like an uncontainable torrent.

"And if you like to drink beer, go to the bar! I am fed up with cleaning up your vomit! Do you hear me? Fed up! What I have here is not a house, but a pigpen! We live like pigs! And as if it weren't enough, you come here with your drunken vomit! When I get a few pennies together, I'm going back to Puerto Rico. And I'm taking the children with me!"

The voice of the man—thick, hoarse, stuttering sadly.

"But, Negra, don't be like this. If we can find something better? . . ."

"You can look for something, but don't count on me." And Juanita heard a door slam, furiously, and with finality.

She kicked the pieces of glass with her foot, looked again at the vacant window and straightening her shoulders, walked on.

Yes, Nico was a winner. In seven years he had conquered the city. Already he was a foreman. And he called himself Nick and spoke English. Juanita admired that capacity for adjusting. But she was suspicious. She had a peasant fear of that extraordinary ability to submit to New York. "It isn't natural," she thought.

"You've changed so much, Nico," she had told him.

"Nonsense, I am the same." And he had affirmed this with a long kiss.

Was he the same? Or was she the one who had changed? Six years was a long time. And she remembered his voice burning with indignation when they had been expelled from the University.

"I'm going to New York. Here on the island there is no feeling for justice."

With Nico's departure, she found herself lost and she almost returned to Lares. But an awakening instinct to fight back kept her in San Juan. She kept herself alive selling hot dogs and Coca-Colas until she got the job at the radio station. It all began with her reciting a poem by Llorens on an amateur program. The rest just happened, like rain falling from heaven. She began acting in soap operas.

Her acting in radio programs didn't carry her to stardom, but those obscure roles of perverse women gave her room and board and the cotton dresses she made herself. She owed this opportunity to Nico too. It was he who had insisted on correcting her country accent. By the time Nico had left for the states, she was able to tighten her teeth to let out sibilant "eses." And she had also learned not to pronounce "i" for "e." Nico's lessons had prepared her for radio. She began to receive fan letters, one of them even from Lares.

Now, in the cold air of the city, she could laugh at the soap operas in San Juan. But at that time, no. Justice always triumphed in the scripts. And the unjust were justly punished. Nevertheless, her position was precarious. When a villainess died, she no longer had a job. And although her honor wanted the death of the villainess, her stomach wanted to prolong the life of that despicable being.

Then came the strike and its clamor of confused voices.

"Our rights. . . . Justice. . . . The law. . . . Our rights. . . . Justice. . . . The owner. . . . Justice. . . . The owner. . . . Justice. . . . the worker. . . ."

And thinking of Nico, she went on strike. Another time, on strike!

She wrote him in New York, sure that he would approve of her decision. But the letter was returned. The great city had swallowed him up.

The day when she fainted, carrying a picket sign in front of the radio station, the strike ended. It was the fourth month of abstinence, of almost fasting. The fourth month of picket lines, of insults from scabs. And she raised a prayer to heaven for returning "our daily bread." But she soon found out that "our daily bread" doesn't always come from heaven.

The strike had been a success. Justice had triumphed, said some. But others, the owners of the station, didn't say anything. The owners of the station smiled, kindly patronizing smiles. And the scabs replaced the ex-strikers.

Juanita remembered how on another occasion the street had appeared wide and frank in its immediacy. And how as she had left the station, the amplifiers in the vestibule repeated the melody, "Enjoy yourself. It's later than you think."

Late? If it were too late to enjoy yourself, it was not too late to escape.

And so the noise of the plane's motors united the group of immigrants in a huge uncertainty of space — of the earth they seemed to leave behind and gain again.

At that moment the noise of a passing bus brought her back to reality. She was at Madison. She walked one block to the right and stopped to cross the street. Joe's Bar was on the other side. She saw a crowd of people exactly in the spot where she was to meet Nico. What was happening? Were the Irish police at it again or was it only an accident? The green light changed and she crossed the Avenue rapidly. Then she noticed the flags and the speakers' platform. It was another meeting. Meetings were boring to her. But there was no way to avoid it. Had Nico arrived yet? She looked around for him. No, he wasn't there. Well, she would have to wait. She stood in front of the bar where there were fewer people. She opened her purse and took out a mirror to touch up her lipstick.

At the beginning the English words didn't mean anything to her. She was thinking in Spanish, which made her deaf to the foreign language. Still, little by little, her brain began to perceive the English words. Later, the fiery speech began to make itself intelligible to her. She put away her lipstick, closed her purse and looked toward the rostrum.

A man was speaking about eight black men condemned to death for having tried to rape a blonde woman. Juanita at the beginning believed that she had heard it incorrectly. No, no, it was not possible. But the man went on repeating it and repeating it. Nevertheless, the whole idea of this stuck in her craw. To kill eight men for having *tried* to rape a woman? My God . . . Eight lives! And only for trying! What would have happened to the eight black men had they actually destroyed that delicate virginal tissue? Well, they could not do more to them after killing them. No, but they could do something before. Perhaps they could tear their flesh piece by piece with great red-hot tongs, like the print in the sacristy of the church in Lares. But no, the man was saying that they were only going to be hanged.

She tried to imagine the eight hanging by ropes, hanging from the branch of a tamarind tree. Would it be from a tree that they would hang them? "No, it isn't natural," she said.

And she thought of her own virginity. It was the day of her visit to the Insular Office in New York. The woman who was filling out the forms had stopped her suddenly and had looked fixedly at her.

"You were a striker at the University?"

Surprised, she had nodded her head.

"And a striker at the radio station in Puerto Rico?" She felt the need to talk, to explain something. But she didn't know what to say. Again, she just nodded her head. The woman got up and disappeared behind a green glass door marked Private. Juanita began to look at the posters announcing educational films. "A Voice in the Mountain," read one. She thought of how abandoned her own voice sounded in this mountain of steel and armored cement.

Then the woman returned and, sitting down, continued her work filling out forms.

"Sign here," she said, handing her the fountain pen.

Juanita signed and sat there waiting.

"That is all," said the other.

"They will get in touch with me if there is something?" she asked tentatively.

"Of course," said the woman.

But she left the office with the certainty that it was all useless, that they would not help her find work here. She didn't know why she had this certainty. She didn't know if the questions about the strike were personal questions of the employer or something official which could hurt her. She didn't know anything. But she felt a terrible and total hopelessness. She began to think that this was the end.

For that reason, she was almost thankful for the impertinence of the blond man in the street. She needed the company of someone, the warmth of another voice. She needed the presence of another human being to whom she could communicate the feeling that she was alive, that she did exist. So she let herself be led. They went to Palisades Park. He was reasonably attentive to her. He made her play the Wheel of Fortune and she won a canary. A canary that didn't sing, but was alive. A canary living locked up in his cage.

They returned late to Manhattan. And they drank whiskey. It was the first time she had drunk whiskey. But she didn't make a big fuss about it. She drank it slowly with the same resignation with which she would have taken a laxative. Her hopelessness was drowning in a dense cloud. Then suddenly she found herself in a narrow and bad-smelling little room. The canary slept in his cage. And the man undressed her with hot, impatient hands. She wanted to fight, but she felt weak. The panic and the horror, more than the whiskey, had paralyzed her.

Hours later, she found herself on a dark street, leaning against a brick wall with the stabbing cold of the morning sneaking in through the tears in her dress. And when she raised her hand to her mouth to choke a sob, she discovered the bill in her clenched fist.

They didn't hang anyone then. The police were not aware that there was one less virgin around. Only Doña Casilda, the Cuban in Harlem, knew it, she who performed the abortion. The rest had been easy, too easy.

And suddenly Juanita began to feel a tremendous burning in her blood. It was like a blaze which rose and rose. And the word *Justice* in the mouth of the speaker began to take on a special meaning. And the word *Injustice* too. She thought of the white, blonde woman. She thought of the eight black men too. And she understood. She understood with clarity the language and almost with horror the ideas. Her hard, peasant guts had finally perceived something monstrous.

And that perception warmed her soul. And shook her conscience. Virgin of Carmen! Was it possible?

She forgot the platform and the meeting. She didn't see the people surrounding her. She saw instead herself as if projected on a screen. And she saw the blonde and the eight men. And now she heard the words of the speaker in a different way. It was almost as if she had not heard them. As if those words were conceived in her brain and spoken by another. She was not able to say if it was what she was thinking now in English or what the other man was saying in Spanish.

But there was no longer any language barrier. For that matter, when the speaker was asking in English that justice be done for the eight men, she shouted in Spanish, "Yes, we are going to do it!" But she could have sworn that she had said it in English.

On hearing the shout in Spanish, many faces turned towards her . . . smiling, hostile, impassive. But Juanita didn't see the faces. She knew that they were there, but she didn't see them. She only saw the piece of paper that began to circulate from the platform among the crowd. She saw the paper appear and disappear from hand to hand, the distance between it and her gradually decreasing.

Suddenly she felt two strong hands on her shoulders. "What the hell are you doing here?"

She recognized the voice, but wasn't surprised nor did she have any interest in turning around. The paper continued within her eyeshot. Did she have a pencil in her purse? She opened her purse and looked for it . . . only a lipstick.

"Do you have a pencil?" she asked, half turning her head.

"Come on," she heard Nico say. Later his voice became urgent, almost hopeless. "Come on. Let's get out of here." And she felt that he was trying to drag her outside the circle of spectators.

Juanita brusquely shook his hands off her shoulders. "Leave me alone," she said. And once free, she was face to face with him. She saw that he was pale and in anguish. His face was soaked with perspiration in spite of the cool air of the Avenue.

"What has happened to you?" she asked.

He looked again at the people surrounding him. He came near her again and whispered in a tone of supplication that she had never known before, "Let's get away from here, for the love of God! Come on!"

He said this in Spanish. And what was strange, in a Spanish with a Puerto Rican accent, free from the North American accent that he had acquired in his six years in the city. Seeing that she just looked at him saying nothing, he tried to pretend anguish, smiling.

"Remember, today we get married."

"Married?" Yes, that was right. Today they were getting married.

After six years they had found each other in New York.

"You see what I am now," she had said then with a brutal frankness to hide her shame.

But he wasn't ashamed. Nico was a conqueror. She believed that they had found each other too late. But he, no. Nick was a man of the city. And she had conquered his scruples. She had fastened herself to this man who had been her only inspiration when she had arrived in Rio Piedras saying "Lari" and swallowing her "eses."

Marry? Yes, Nico was there. And today they were getting married. But it wasn't haste for the wedding that she now saw in him. It was something that she didn't understand.

"I'm not leaving yet. Wait for me." And she turned from him.

The paper with the petition for a new trial for the black men was coming nearer. She felt his body behind her, the hands compulsively grabbing her two arms, his breath burning in her right ear.

"Please, you don't understand. This is dangerous."

"Dangerous?" She was bothered by the pressure of Nico's hands on her arms.

"Don't hold me so tight," she said.

His voice continued in Spanish, more urgently, more brokenly.

"Are you crazy? Look at that flag. We'll find ourselves in the police files. Come on, come on, I tell you."

She looked towards the platform and she finally understood. The breeze had begun to softly unfurl one of the two flags, withered and quiet until that instant, the same instant in which the petition reached her hands. And the voice of the man in her ears, like a deaf shout. "Let it go! Pass it on, so they don't see you with it!"

But the voice didn't strike her consciousness. What did a flag matter to her? What mattered in this instance was justice. And justice was that piece of paper which was in her hands for the first time in her life. For that reason, his voice sounded strange, remote, indifferent.

A woman offered her a stump of a pencil. She took it and looked at the blunt point. She almost simultaneously felt that they were going to snatch the paper from her hands.

She turned around and looked at Nico grabbing the paper away from her convulsively. She saw his disjointed features, his pale lips, his forehead perspiring and contracted. She lowered her eyes to look at the paper crumpled in his hands and raised her eyes again to look at the livid face. In that short time she discovered the strange trembling in her body.

She had the impression that she wasn't looking at a human being. And she discovered what she hadn't discovered moments before. Nico's fear. An almost animal fear, an infra-human fear coming through his eyes, through his soul, through his pores. And she understood. For the second time that morning she had understood with a painful clarity. She understood Nico also, almost suddenly. She saw how much humanity he had had to give up to become foreman. She understood the price of his triumph in the city. And she understood his fear. But the understanding disgusted her. She felt such a violent loathing that it almost brought on a contraction in her stomach.

And again Juanita began to feel a tremendous warmth in her blood. It was like a blaze that rose and rose. She had to exert an extraordinary strength to contain the fire that burned at her lips. Remembering him and lowering her voice she was able to condense to a brief threat all the tumult of her feelings. "Give me that paper or I'll tear your face to shreds."

Also to him this Juanita was different from his sweet "Jenny." If the new dread of the threat hadn't added up to all his fears, he would have felt deceived. But only horror reigned in him now.

"If you sign that, I'll never marry you."

She wanted to laugh, but she controlled herself. She took the paper and pressing her made-up face close to his livid one, she almost spat out the words, "If I were a decent woman, I could afford the luxury of saying, 'I would rather become a whore than marry you!'"

She began to laugh finally and, seeing his expression, she added in a voice that was almost a shout, "But as I am what I am, I can only say to you, 'Coward! I don't ever want to see you again!'"

And she turned her back on him. She held the paper against her purse and signed it with the blunt pencil. In that instant a little band next to the platform began to play a tune she had never heard before. She handed the paper and pencil on to a black man and began to make her way through the crowd. Only when she came to the corner of 114th Street did she stop. The street opened wide and frank in its real immediacy. She raised the collar of her wool jacket and breathed deeply.

The fresh air gave her a rare sensation of joy this time. She felt that the justice that would free the eight condemned men had given her back her own freedom. And she began to walk down the street. A clock in a drugstore told her it was twelve o'clock. Seeing the two clock hands together, she instinctively made the sign of the cross, as if here in the city the angelus of the church of Lares was ringing.

[1974]

Translated by
FAYE EDWARDS and GLADYS ORITZ

QUESTIONS

1. Is the subway mentioned at the beginning of the story of any significance in our interpretation of Marqués's tale?

2. Does the reversal of traditional masculine and feminine roles add anything to your understanding of Puerto Rico's relationship to the United States? Or about gender roles and stereotypes?
3. What, specifically, does the title tell you?
4. If Juanita's story had been written by a woman writer, would it be substantially different?

Paule Marshall

(b. 1929)

Barbados/United States

Paule Marshall learned her first lessons in the art of storytelling by listening as a child in the kitchen to the stories her Barbadian (Bajan) mother and her mother's West Indian friends exchanged at the end of their days spent cleaning other people's houses. The daughter of parents who immigrated from the West Indies to Brooklyn following World War II, Marshall warmly recalls those "poets in the kitchen"—the women who "trained my ear. They set a standard of excellence. This is why the best of my work must be attributed to them; it stands as testimony to the rich legacy of language and culture they so freely passed on to me in the wordshop of the kitchen."

As an inheritor of the West Indian Bajan-English oral tradition, Marshall excels at capturing the lyrical inflections and the expressiveness of speech. In her first novel, *Brown Girl, Brownstones* (1959), begun while she was a student at Hunter College in New York City, Marshall incorporates many of her own experiences as a first-generation American in the character of Selina Boyce, the intelligent, complex girl who struggles to define herself both as a woman and as a person of West Indian descent. The novel, now acknowledged as a major contribution to the tradition of black American fiction, directly challenges both racial and gender stereotypes.

During and after college, Marshall worked for a small black magazine, *Our World* (as the only woman on the staff) and as a librarian in the New York Public Library. She received her B.A. from Brooklyn College. Twice married, she now divides her time with her husband between New York and the West Indies. She has received a number of literary awards, including a Guggenheim fellowship in 1960.

Marshall's first collection of short stories, *Soul Clap Hands and Sing* (1961)—the title comes from a poem by William Butler Yeats—is actually a series of four novellas set in different geographical locations that reflect the diverse cultural roots of West Indians and African Americans who came to the New World: "Barbados," "Brooklyn," "British Guyana," and "Brazil." In these novellas, as elsewhere in her fiction, Marshall masterfully captures both the spoken quality of her characters' language and their reality as complex, sensitive people responding to a variety of cross-cultural situations.

Marshall's novels include *The Chosen Place, the Timeless People* (1960), *Praisesong for the Widow* (1985), and *Daughters* (1991). *Reena and Other Stories* was published in 1985.

Brooklyn

A summer wind, soaring just before it died, blew the dusk and the first scattered lights of downtown Brooklyn against the shut windows of the classroom, but Professor Max Berman—B.A., 1919, M.A., 1921, New York; Docteur de l'Université, 1930, Paris—alone in the room, did not bother to open the windows to the cooling wind. The heat and airlessness of the room, the perspiration inching its way like an ant around his starched collar were discomforts he enjoyed, they obscured his larger discomfort: the anxiety which chafed his heart and tugged his left eyelid so that he seemed to be winking, roguishly, behind his glasses.

To steady his eye and ease his heart, to fill the time until his students arrived and his first class in years began, he reached for his cigarettes. As always he delayed lighting the cigarette so that his need for it would be greater and, thus, the relief and pleasure it would bring, fuller. For some time he fondled it, his fingers shaping soft, voluptuous gestures, his warped old man's hands looking strangely abandoned on the bare desk and limp as if the bones had been crushed, and so white—except for the tobacco burn on the index and third fingers—it seemed his blood no longer traveled that far.

He lit the cigarette finally and as the smoke swelled his lungs, his eyelid stilled and his lined face lifted, the plume of white hair wafting above his narrow brow; his body—short, blunt, the shoulders slightly bent as if in deference to his sixty-three years—settled back in the chair. Delicately Max Berman crossed his legs and, looking down, examined his shoes for dust. (The shoes were of a very soft, fawn-colored leather and somewhat foppishly pointed at the toe. They had been custom made in France and were his one last indulgence. He wore them in memory of his first wife, a French Jewess from Alsace-Lorraine whom he had met in Paris while lingering over his doctorate and married to avoid returning home. She had been gay, mindless and very excitable—but at night, she had also been capable of a profound stillness as she lay in bed waiting for him to turn to her, and this had always awed and delighted him. She had been a gift—and her death in a car accident had been a judgment on him for never having loved her, for never, indeed, having even allowed her to matter.) Fastidiously Max Berman unbuttoned his jacket and straightened his vest, which had a stain two decades old on the pocket. Through the smoke his veined eyes contemplated other, more pleasurable scenes. With his neatly shod foot swinging and his cigarette at a rakish tilt, he might have been an old *boulevardier*[1] taking the sun and an absinthe before the afternoon's assignation.

A young face, the forehead shiny with earnestness, hung at the half-opened door. "Is this French Lit, fifty-four? Camus and Sartre?"

Max Berman winced at the rawness of the voice and the flat "a" in Sartre and said formally, "This is Modern French Literature, number fifty-four, yes, but there is some question as to whether we will take up Messieurs Camus and Sartre this session. They might prove hot work for a summer evening course. We will probably do Gide and Mauriac, who are considerably more temperate. But come in nonetheless. . . . "

He was the gallant, half rising to bow her to a seat. He knew that she would

[1]*boulevardier* French: a frequenter of the boulevards (streets)

select the one in the front row directly opposite his desk. At the bell her pen would quiver above her blank notebook, ready to commit his first word—indeed, the clearing of his throat—to paper, and her thin buttocks would begin sidling toward the edge of her chair.

His eyelid twitched with solicitude. He wished that he could have drawn the lids over her fitful eyes and pressed a cool hand to her forehead. She reminded him of what he had been several lifetimes ago: a boy with a pale, plump face and harried eyes, running from the occasional taunts at his yarmulke along the shrill streets of Brownsville in Brooklyn, impeded by the heavy satchel of books which he always carried as proof of his scholarship. He had been proud of his brilliance at school and the Yeshiva, but at the same time he had been secretly troubled by it and resentful, for he could never believe that he had come by it naturally or that it belonged to him alone. Rather, it was like a heavy medal his father had hung around his neck—the chain bruising his flesh—and constantly exhorted him to wear proudly and use well.

The girl gave him an eager and ingratiating smile and he looked away. During his thirty years of teaching, a face similar to hers had crowded his vision whenever he had looked up from a desk. Perhaps it was fitting, he thought, and lighted another cigarette from the first, that she should be present as he tried again at life, unaware that behind his rimless glasses and within his ancient suit, he had been gutted.

He thought of those who had taken the last of his substance and smiled tolerantly. "The boys of summer," he called them, his inquisitors, who had flailed him with a single question: "Are you now or have you ever been a member of the Communist party?"[2] Max Berman had never taken their question seriously—perhaps because he had never taken his membership in the party seriously—and he had refused to answer. What had disturbed him, though, even when the investigation was over, was the feeling that he had really been under investigation for some other offense which did matter and of which he was guilty; that behind their accusations and charges had lurked another which had not been political but personal. For had he been disloyal to the government? His denial was a short, hawking laugh. Simply, he had never ceased being religious. When his father's God had become useless and even a little embarrassing, he had sought others: his work for a time, then the party. But he had been middle-aged when he joined and his faith, which had been so full as a boy, had grown thin. He had come, by then, to distrust all pieties, so that when the purges in Russia during the thirties confirmed his distrust, he had withdrawn into a modest cynicism.

But he had been made to answer for that error. Ten years later his inquisitors had flushed him out from the small community college in upstate New York where he had taught his classes from the same neat pack of notes each semester and had led him bound by subpoena to New York and bandied his name at the hearings until he had been dismissed from his job.

He remembered looking back at the pyres of burning autumn leaves on the

[2]During the 1950s the congressional Un-American Activities Committee, prompted by Senator Joseph McCarthy's anticommunist rhetoric, interrogated Americans suspected of communist associations. Often, regardless of suspects' actual innocence, accusations and investigation by the committee were enough to blacklist them from their professions for years afterwards.

campus his last day and feeling that another lifetime had ended—for he had always thought of his life as divided into many small lives, each with its own beginning and end. Like a hired mute, he had been present at each dying and kept the wake and wept professionally as the bier was lowered into the ground. Because of this feeling, he told himself that his final death would be anticlimactic.

After his dismissal he had continued living in the small house he had built near the college, alone except for an occasional visit from a colleague, idle but for some tutoring in French, content with the income he received from the property his parents had left him in Brooklyn—until the visits and tutoring had tapered off and a silence had begun to choke the house, like weeds springing up around a deserted place. He had begun to wonder then if he were still alive. He would wake at night from the recurrent dream of the hearings, where he was being accused of an unstated crime, to listen for his heart, his hand fumbling among the bedclothes to press the place. During the day he would pass repeatedly in front of the mirror with the pretext that he might have forgotten to shave that morning or that something had blown into his eye. Above all, he had begun to think of his inquisitors with affection and to long for the sound of their voices. They, at least, had assured him of being alive.

As if seeking them out, he had returned to Brooklyn and to the house in Brownsville where he had lived as a boy and had boldly applied for a teaching post without mentioning the investigation. He had finally been offered the class which would begin in five minutes. It wasn't much: a six-week course in the summer evening session of a college without a rating, where classes were held in a converted factory building, a college whose campus took in the bargain department stores, the five-and-dime emporiums and neon-spangled movie houses of downtown Brooklyn.

Through the smoke from his cigarette, Max Berman's eyes—a waning blue that never seemed to focus on any one thing—drifted over the students who had gathered meanwhile. Imbuing them with his own disinterest, he believed that even before the class began, most of them were longing for its end and already anticipating the soft drinks at the soda fountain downstairs and the synthetic dramas at the nearby movie.

They made him sad. He would have liked to lead them like a Pied Piper back to the safety of their childhoods—all of them: the loud girl with the formidable calves of an athlete who reminded him, uncomfortably, of his second wife (a party member who was always shouting political heresy from some picket line and who had promptly divorced him upon discovering his irreverence); the two sallow-faced young men leaning out the window as if searching for the wind that had died; the slender young woman with crimped black hair who sat very still and apart from the others, her face turned toward the night sky as if to a friend.

Her loneliness interested him. He sensed its depth and his eye paused. He saw then that she was a Negro, a very pale mulatto with skin the color of clear, polished amber and a thin, mild face. She was somewhat older than the others in the room—a school-teacher from the South, probably, who came north each summer to take courses toward a graduate degree. He felt a fleeting discomfort and irritation: discomfort at the thought that although he had been sinned against as a Jew he still shared in the sin against her and suffered from the same vague guilt, irritation that she recalled his own humiliations: the large ones, such as the fact that despite his brilliance he had been unable to get into a medical school as a young man because of the quota on Jews (not that he had wanted to be a doctor; that had been his father's wish) and had changed his studies from medicine to French; the small ones which had worn him thin: an eye widening imperceptibly as he gave his name, the savage glance which sought the Jewishness in his nose, his chin, in the set of his shoulders, the jokes snuffed into silence at his appearance. . . .

Tired suddenly, his eyelid pulsing, he turned and stared out the window at the gaudy constellation of neon lights. He longed for a drink, a quiet place and then sleep. And to bear him gently into sleep, to stay the terror which bound his heart then reminding him of those oleographs of Christ with the thorns binding his exposed heart — fat drops of blood from one so bloodless — to usher him into sleep, some pleasantly erotic image: a nude in a boudoir scattered with her frilled garments and warmed by her frivolous laugh, with the sun like a voyeur at the half-closed shutters. But this time instead of the usual Rubens nude with thighs like twin portals and a belly like a huge alabaster bowl into which he poured himself, he chose Gauguin's Aita Parari, her languorous form in the straight back chair, her dark, sloping breasts, her eyes like the sun under shadow.

With the image still on his inner eye, he turned to the Negro girl and appraised her through a blind of cigarette smoke. She was still gazing out at the night sky and something about her fixed stare, her hands stiffly arranged in her lap, the nerve fluttering within the curve of her throat, betrayed a vein of tension within the rock of her calm. It was as if she had fled long ago to a remote region within herself, taking with her all that was most valuable and most vulnerable about herself.

She stirred finally, her slight breasts lifting beneath her flowered summer dress as she breathed deeply — and Max Berman thought again of Gauguin's girl with the dark, sloping breasts. What would this girl with the amber-colored skin be like on a couch in a sunlit room, nude in a straight-back chair? And as the question echoed along each nerve and stilled his breathing, it seemed suddenly that life, which had scorned him for so long, held out her hand again — but still a little beyond his reach. Only the girl, he sensed, could bring him close enough to touch it. She alone was the bridge. So that even while he repeated to himself that he was being presumptuous (for she would surely refuse him) and ridiculous (for even if she did not, what could he do — his performance would be a mere scramble and twitch), he vowed at the same time to have her. The challenge eased the tightness around his heart suddenly; it soothed the damaged muscle of his eye and as the bell rang he rose and said briskly, "Ladies and gentlemen, may I have your attention, please. My name is Max Berman. The course is Modern French Literature, number fifty-four. May I suggest that you check your program cards to see whether you are in the right place at the right time."

Her essay on Gide's *The Immoralist*[3] lay on his desk and the note from the administration informing him, first, that his past political activities had been brought to their attention and then dismissing him at the end of the session weighed the inside pocket of his jacket. The two, her paper and the note, were linked in his mind. Her paper reminded him that the vow he had taken was still an empty one, for the term was half over and he had never once spoken to her

[3]*André Gide* (1869–1951) French novelist. His novel *The Immoralist* (1902), a critique of individualism, is the story of a man obsessed with sensory gratification.

(as if she understood his intention she was always late and disappeared as soon as the closing bell rang, leaving him trapped in a clamorous circle of students around his desk), while the note which wrecked his small attempt to start anew suddenly made that vow more urgent. It gave him the edge of desperation he needed to act finally. So that as soon as the bell rang, he returned all the papers but hers, announced that all questions would have to wait until their next meeting and, waving off the students from his desk, called above their protests, "Miss Williams, if you have a moment, I'd like to speak with you briefly about your paper."

She approached his desk like a child who has been cautioned not to talk to strangers, her fingers touching the backs of the chair as if for support, her gaze following the departing students as though she longed to accompany them.

Her slight apprehensiveness pleased him. It suggested a submissiveness which gave him, as he rose uncertainly, a feeling of certainty and command. Her hesitancy was somehow in keeping with the color of her skin. She seemed to bring not only herself but the host of black women whose bodies had been despoiled to make her. He would not only possess her but them also, he thought (not really thought, for he scarcely allowed these thoughts to form before he snuffed them out). Through their collective suffering, which she contained, his own personal suffering would be eased; he would be pardoned for whatever sin it was he had committed against life.

"I hope you weren't unduly alarmed when I didn't return your paper along with the others," he said, and had to look up as she reached the desk. She was taller close up and her eyes, which he had thought were black, were a strong, flecked brown with very small pupils which seemed to shrink now from the sight of him. "But I found it so interesting I wanted to give it to you privately."

"I didn't know what to think," she said, and her voice—he heard it for the first time for she never recited or answered in class—was low, cautious, Southern.

"It was, to say the least, refreshing. It not only showed some original and mature thinking on your part, but it also proved that you've been listening in class—and after twenty-five years and more of teaching it's encouraging to find that some students do listen. If you have a little time I'd like to tell you, more specifically, what I liked about it. . . ."

Talking easily, reassuring her with his professional tone and a deft gesture with his cigarette, he led her from the room as the next class filed in, his hand cupped at her elbow but not touching it, his manner urbane, courtly, kind. They paused on the landing at the end of the long corridor with the stairs piled in steel tiers above and plunging below them. An intimate silence swept up the stairwell in a warm gust and Max Berman said, "I'm curious. Why did you choose *The Immoralist?*"

She started suspiciously, afraid, it seemed, that her answer might expose and endanger the self she guarded so closely within.

"Well," she said finally, her glance reaching down the stairs to the door marked EXIT at the bottom, "when you said we could use anything by Gide I decided on *The Immoralist*, since it was the first book I read in the original French when I was in undergraduate school. I didn't understand it then because my French was so weak, I guess, but I always thought about it afterward for some odd reason. I was shocked by what I did understand, of course, but something else about it appealed to me, so when you made the assignment I thought I'd try reading it again. I understood it a little better this time. At least I think so. . . ."

"Your paper proves you did."

She smiled absently, intent on some other thought. Then she said cautiously, but with unexpected force, "You see, to me, the book seems to say that the only way you begin to know what you are and how much you are capable of is by daring to try something, by doing something which tests you. . . ."

"Something bold," he said.

"Yes."

"Even sinful."

She paused, questioning this, and then said reluctantly, "Yes, perhaps even sinful."

"The salutary effects of sin, you might say." He gave the little bow.

But she had not heard this; her mind had already leaped ahead. "The only trouble, at least with the character in Gide's book, is that what he finds out about himself is so terrible. He is so unhappy. . . ."

"But at least he knows, poor sinner." And his playful tone went unnoticed.

"Yes," she said with the same startling forcefulness. "And another thing, in finding out what he is, he destroys his wife. It was as if she had to die in order for a person to live and know himself. Perhaps in order for a person to live and know himself somebody else must die. Maybe there's always a balancing out. . . . In a way"—and he had to lean close now to hear her—"I believe this."

Max Berman edged back as he glimpsed something move within her abstracted gaze. It was like a strong and restless seed that had taken root in the darkness there and was straining now toward the light. He had not expected so subtle and complex a force beneath her mild exterior and he found it disturbing and dangerous, but fascinating.

"Well, it's a most interesting interpretation," he said. "I don't know if M. Gide would have agreed, but then he's not around to give his opinion. Tell me, where did you do your undergraduate work?"

"At Howard University."

"And you majored in French?"

"Yes."

"Why, if I may ask?" he said gently.

"Well, my mother was from New Orleans and could still speak a little Creole and I got interested in learning how to speak French through her, I guess. I teach it now at a junior high school in Richmond. Only the beginner courses because I don't have my master's. You know *je vais, tu vas, il va* and *Frère Jacques*.[4] It's not very inspiring."

"You should do something about that then, my dear Miss Williams. Perhaps it's time for you, like our friend in Gide, to try something new and bold."

"I know," she said, and her pale hand sketched a vague, despairing gesture. "I thought maybe if I got my master's . . . that's why I decided to come north this summer and start taking some courses. . . ."

[4]*Frère Jacques* "Brother Jacques," a children's song; *je vais, tu vas, il va*—French verb forms: I go, you go, he goes

Max Berman quickly lighted a cigarette to still the flurry inside him, for the moment he had been awaiting had come. He flicked her paper, which he still held. "Well, you've got the makings of a master's thesis right here. If you like I will suggest some ways for you to expand it sometime. A few pointers from an old pro might help."

He had to turn from her astonished and grateful smile—it was like a child's. He said carefully, "The only problem will be to find a place where we can talk quietly. Regrettably, I don't rate an office. . . ."

"Perhaps we could use one of the empty classrooms," she said.

"That would be much too dismal a setting for a pleasant discussion."

He watched the disappointment wilt her smile and when he spoke he made certain that the same disappointment weighed his voice. "Another difficulty is that the term's half over, which gives us little or no time. But let's not give up. Perhaps we can arrange to meet and talk over a weekend. The only hitch there is that I spend weekends at my place in the country. Of course you're perfectly welcome to come up there. It's only about seventy miles from New York, in the heart of what's very appropriately called the Borsch Circuit, even though, thank God, my place is a good distance away from the borsch. That is, it's very quiet and there's never anybody around except with my permission."

She did not move, yet she seemed to start; she made no sound, yet he thought he heard a bewildered cry. And then she did a strange thing, standing there with the breath sucked into the hollow of her throat and her smile, that had opened to him with such trust, dying—her eyes, her hands faltering up begged him to declare himself.

"There's a lake near the house," he said, "so that when you get tired of talking—or better, listening to me talk—you can take a swim, if you like. I would very much enjoy that sight." And as the nerve tugged at his eyelid, he seemed to wink behind his rimless glasses.

Her sudden, blind step back was like a man groping his way through a strange room in the dark, and instinctively Max Berman reached out to break her fall. Her arms, bare to the shoulder because of the heat (he knew the feel of her skin without even touching it—it would be like a rich, fine-textured cloth which would soothe and hide him in its amber warmth), struck out once to drive him off and then fell limp at her side, and her eyes became vivid and convulsive in her numbed face. She strained toward the stairs and the exit door at the bottom, but she could not move. Nor could she speak. She did not even cry. Her eyes remained dry and dull with disbelief. Only her shoulders trembled as though she was silently weeping inside.

It was as though she had never learned the forms and expressions of anger. The outrage of a lifetime, of her history, was trapped inside her. And she stared at Max Berman with this mute, paralyzing rage. Not really at him but to his side, as if she caught sight of others behind him. And remembering how he had imagined a column of dark women trailing her to his desk, he sensed that she glimpsed a legion of old men with sere flesh and lonely eyes flanking him: "old lechers with a love on every wind. . . ."

"I'm sorry, Miss Williams," he said, and would have welcomed her insults, for he would have been able, at least, to distill from them some passion and a kind of intimacy. It would have been, in a way, like touching her. "It was only that you are a very attractive young woman and although I'm no longer young"—and he gave the tragic little laugh which sought to dismiss that fact—"I can still appreciate and even desire an attractive woman. But I was wrong. . . ." His self disgust, overwhelming him finally, choked off his voice. "And so very crude. Forgive me. I can offer no excuse for my behavior other than my approaching senility."

He could not even manage the little marionette bow this time. Quickly he shoved the paper on Gide into her lifeless hand, but it fell, the pages separating, and as he hurried past her downstairs and out the door, he heard the pages scattering like dead leaves on the steps.

She remained away until the night of the final examination, which was also the last meeting of the class. By that time Max Berman, believing that she would not return, had almost succeeded in forgetting her. He was no longer even certain of how she looked, for her face had been absorbed into the single, blurred, featureless face of all the women who had ever refused him. So that she startled him as much as a stranger would have when he entered the room that night and found her alone amid a maze of empty chairs, her face turned toward the window as on the first night and her hands serene in her lap. She turned at his footstep and it was as if she had also forgotten all that had passed between them. She waited until he said, "I'm glad you decided to take the examination. I'm sure you won't have any difficulty with it"; then she gave him a nod that was somehow reminiscent of his little bow and turned again to the window.

He was relieved yet puzzled by her composure. It was as if during her three-week absence she had waged and won a decisive contest with herself and was ready now to act. He was wary suddenly and all during the examination he tried to discover what lay behind her strange calm, studying her bent head amid the shifting heads of the other students, her slim hand guiding the pen across the page, her legs—the long bone visible, it seemed, beneath the flesh. Desire flared and quickly died.

"Excuse me, Professor Berman, will you take up Camus and Sartre next semester, maybe?" The girl who sat in front of his desk was standing over him with her earnest smile and finished examination folder.

"That might prove somewhat difficult, since I won't be here."

"No more?"

"No."

"I mean, not even next summer?"

"I doubt it."

"Gee, I'm sorry. I mean, I enjoyed the course and everything."

He bowed his thanks and held his head down until she left. Her compliment, so piteous somehow, brought on the despair he had forced to the dim rear of his mind. He could no longer flee the thought of the exile awaiting him when the class tonight ended. He could either remain in the house in Brooklyn, where the memory of his father's face above the radiance of the Sabbath candles haunted him from the shadows, reminding him of the certainty he had lost and never found again, where the mirrors in his father's room were still shrouded with sheets, as on the day he lay dying and moaning into his beard that his only son was a bad Jew; or he could return to the house in the country, to the silence shrill with loneliness.

The cigarette he was smoking burned his fingers, rousing him, and he saw over the pile of examination folders on his desk that the room was empty except for the Negro girl. She had finished—her pen lay aslant the closed folder on her desk — but she had remained in her seat and she was smiling across the room at him — a set, artificial smile that was both cold and threatening. It utterly denuded him and he was wildly angry suddenly that she had seen him give way to despair; he wanted to remind her (he could not stay the thought; it attacked him like an assailant from a dark turn in his mind) that she was only black after all. . . . His head dropped and he almost wept with shame.

The girl stiffened as if she had seen the thought and then the tiny muscles around her mouth quickly arranged the bland smile. She came up to his desk, placed her folder on top of the others and said pleasantly, her eyes like dark, shattered glass that spared Max Berman his reflection, "I've changed my mind. I think I'd like to spend a day at your place in the country if your invitation still holds."

He thought of refusing her, for her voice held neither promise nor passion, but he could not. Her presence, even if it was only for a day, would make his return easier. And there was still the possibility of passion despite her cold manner and the deliberate smile. He thought of how long it had been since he had had someone, of how badly he needed the sleep which followed love and of awakening certain, for the first time in years, of his existence.

"Of course the invitation still holds. I'm driving up tonight."

"I won't be able to come until Sunday," she said firmly. "Is there a train then?"

"Yes, in the morning," he said, and gave her the schedule.

"You'll meet me at the station?"

"Of course. You can't miss my car. It's a very shabby but venerable Chevy."

She smiled stiffy and left, her heels awakening the silence of the empty corridor, the sound reaching back to tap like a warning finger on Max Berman's temple.

The pale sunlight slanting through the windshield lay like a cat on his knees, and the motor of his old Chevy, turning softly under him could have been the humming of its heart. A little distance from the car a log-cabin station house — the logs blackened by the seasons — stood alone against the hills, and the hills, in turn, lifted softly, still green although the summer was ending, into the vague autumn sky.

The morning mist and pale sun, the green that was still somehow new, made it seem that the season was stirring into life even as it died, and this contradiction pained Max Berman at the same time that it pleased him. For it was his own contradiction after all: his desires which remained those of a young man even as he was dying.

He had been parked for some time in the deserted station, yet his hands were still tensed on the steering wheel and his foot hovered near the accelerator. As soon as he had arrived in the station he had wanted to leave. But like the girl that night on the landing, he was too stiff with tension to move. He could only wait, his eyelid twitching with foreboding, regret, curiosity and hope.

Finally and with no warning the train charged through the fiery green, setting off a tremor underground. Max Berman imagined the girl seated at a window in the train, her hands arranged quietly in her lap and her gaze scanning the hills that were so familiar to him, and yet he could not believe that she was really there. Perhaps her plan had been to disappoint him. She might be in New York or on her way back to Richmond now, laughing at the trick she had played on him. He was convinced of this suddenly, so that even when he saw her walking toward him through the blown steam from under the train, he told himself that she was a mirage created by the steam. Only when she sat beside him in the car, bringing with her, it seemed, an essence she had distilled from the morning air and rubbed into her skin, was he certain of her reality.

"I brought my bathing suit but it's much too cold to swim," she said and gave him the deliberate smile.

He did not see it; he only heard her voice, its warm Southern lilt in the chill, its intimacy in the closed car—and an excitement swept him, cold first and then hot, as if the sun had burst in his blood.

"It's the morning air," he said. "By noon it should be like summer again."

"Is that a promise?"

"Yes."

By noon the cold morning mist had lifted above the hills and below, in the lake valley, the sunlight was a sheer gold net spread out on the grass as if to dry, draped on the trees and flung, glinting, over the lake. Max Berman felt it brush his shoulders gently as he sat by the lake waiting for the girl, who had gone up to the house to change into her swimsuit.

He had spent the morning showing her the fields and small wood near his house. During the long walk he had been careful to keep a little apart from her. He would extend a hand as they climbed a rise or when she stepped uncertainly over a rock, but he would not really touch her. He was afraid that at his touch, no matter how slight and casual, her scream would spiral into the morning calm, or worse, his touch would unleash the threatening thing he sensed behind her even smile.

He had talked of her paper and she had listened politely and occasionally even asked a question or made a comment. But all the while detached, distant, drawn within herself as she had been that first night in the classroom. And then halfway down a slope she had paused and, pointing to the canvas tops of her white sneakers, which had become wet and dark from the dew secreted in the grass, she had laughed. The sound, coming so abruptly in the midst of her tense quiet, joined her, it seemed, to the wood and wide fields, to the hills; she shared their simplicity and held within her the same strong current of life. Max Berman had felt privileged suddenly, and humble. He had stopped questioning her smile. He had told himself then that it would not matter even if she stopped and picking up a rock bludgeoned him from behind.

"There's a lake near my home, but it's not like this," the girl said, coming up behind him. "Yours is so dark and serious-looking."

He nodded and followed her gaze out to the lake, where the ripples were long, smooth welts raised by the wind, and across to the other bank, where a group of birches stepped delicately down to the lake and bending over touched the water with their branches as if testing it before they plunged.

The girl came and stood beside him now—and she was like a pale gold naiad, the spirit of the lake, her eyes reflecting its somber autumnal tone and her body as supple as the birches. She walked slowly into the water, unaware, it seemed, of the sudden passion in his gaze, or perhaps uncaring; and as she walked she held out her arms in what seemed a gesture of invocation (and Max Berman remembered his father with the fringed shawl draped on his out-stretched arms as he invoked their God each Sabbath with the same gesture); her head was bent as if she listened for a voice beneath the water's murmurous surface. When the ground gave way she still seemed to be walking and listening, her arms outstretched. The water reached her waist, her small breasts, her shoulders. She lifted her head once, breathed deeply and disappeared.

She stayed down for a long time and when her white cap finally broke the water some distance out, Max Berman felt strangely stranded and deprived. He understood suddenly the profound cleavage between them and the absurdity of his hope. The water between them became the years which separated them. Her white cap was the sign of her purity, while the silt darkening the lake was the flotsam of his failures. Above all, their color—her arms a pale, flashing gold in the sunlit water and his bled white and flaccid with the veins like angry blue penciling—marked the final barrier.

He was sad as they climbed toward the house late that afternoon and troubled. A crow cawed derisively in the bracken, heralding the dusk which would not only end their strange day but would also, he felt, unveil her smile, so that he would learn the reason for her coming. And because he was sad, he said wryly, "I think I should tell you that you've been spending the day with something of an outcast."

"Oh," she said and waited.

He told her of the dismissal, punctuating his words with the little hoarse, deprecating laugh and waving aside the pain with his cigarette. She listened, polite but neutral, and because she remained unmoved, he wanted to confess all the more. So that during dinner and afterward when they sat outside on the porch, he told her of the investigation.

"It was very funny once you saw it from the proper perspective, which I did, of course." he said. "I mean here they were accusing me of crimes I couldn't remember committing and asking me for the names of people with whom I had never associated. It was pure farce. But I made a mistake. I should have done something dramatic or something just as farcical. Bared my breast in the public market place or written a tome on my apostasy, naming names. It would have been a far different story then. Instead of my present ignominy I would have been offered a chairmanship at Yale. . . . No? Well, Brandeis then. I would have been draped in honorary degrees. . . ."

"Well, why didn't you confess?" she said impatiently.

"I've often asked myself the same interesting question, but I haven't come up with a satisfactory answer yet. I suspect, though, that I said nothing because none of it really mattered that much."

"What did matter?" she asked sharply.

He sat back, waiting for the witty answer, but none came, because just then the frame upon which his organs were strung seemed to snap and he felt his heart, his lungs, his vital parts fall in a heap within him. Her question had dealt the severing blow, for it was the same question he understood suddenly that the vague forms in his dream asked repeatedly. It had been the plaintive undercurrent to his father's dying moan, the real accusation behind the charges of his inquisitors at the hearing.

For what had mattered? He gazed through his sudden shock at the night squatting on the porch steps, at the hills asleep like gentle beasts in the darkness, at the black screen of the sky where the events of his life passed in a mute, accusing review—and he saw nothing there to which he had given himself or in which he had truly believed since the belief and dedication of his boyhood.

"Did you hear my question?" she asked, and he was glad that he sat within the shadows clinging to the porch screen and could not be seen.

"Yes, I did," he said faintly, and his eyelid twitched. "But I'm afraid it's another one of those I can't answer satisfactorily." And then he struggled for the old flippancy. "You make an excellent examiner, you know. Far better than my inquisitors."

"What will you do now?" her voice and cold smile did not spare him.

He shrugged and the motion, a slow, eloquent lifting of the shoulders, brought with it suddenly the weight and memory of his boyhood. It was the familiar gesture of the women hawkers in Belmont Market, of the men standing outside the temple on Saturday mornings, each of them reflecting his image of God in their forbidding black coats and with the black, tumbling beards in which he had always imagined he could hide as in a forest. All this had mattered, he called loudly to himself, and said aloud to the girl, "Let me see if I can answer this one at least. What *will* I do?" He paused and swung his leg so that his foot in the fastidious French shoe caught the light from the house. "Grow flowers and write my memoirs. How's that? That would be the proper way for a gentleman and scholar to retire. Or hire one of those hefty housekeepers who will bully me and when I die in my sleep draw the sheet over my face and call my lawyer. That's somewhat European, but how's that?"

When she said nothing for a long time, he added soberly. "But that's not a fair question for me any more. I leave all such considerations to the young. To you, for that matter. What will you do, my dear Miss Williams?"

It was as if she had been expecting the question and had been readying her answer all the time that he had been talking. She leaned forward eagerly and with her face and part of her body fully in the light, she said, "I will do something. I don't know what yet, but something."

Max Berman started back a little. The answer was so unlike her vague, resigned "I know" on the landing that night when he had admonished her to try something new.

He edged back into the darkness and she leaned further into the light, her eyes overwhelming her face and her mouth set in a thin, determined line. "I will do something," she said, bearing down on each word, "because for the first time in my life I feel almost brave."

He glimpsed this new bravery behind her hard gaze and sensed something vital and purposeful, precious, which she had found and guarded like a prize within her center. He wanted it. He would have liked to snatch it and run like a thief. He no longer desired her but it, and starting forward with a sudden envious cry, he caught her arm and drew her close, seeking it.

But he could not get to it. Although she did not pull away her arm, although she made no protest as his face wavered close to hers, he did not really touch her. She held herself and her prize out of his desperate reach and her smile was a knife she pressed to his throat. He saw himself for what he was in her clear, cold gaze: an old man with skin the color and texture of dough that had been kneaded by the years into tragic folds, with faded eyes adrift behind a pair of rimless glasses and the roughened flesh at his throat like a bird's wattles. And as the disgust which he read in her eyes swept him, his hand dropped from her arm. He started to murmur, "Forgive me . . ." when suddenly she caught hold of his wrist, pulling him close again, and he felt the strength which had borne her swiftly through the water earlier hold him now as she said quietly and without passion, "And do you know why, Dr. Berman, I feel almost brave today? Because ever since I can remember my parents were always telling me, 'Stay away from white folks. Just leave them alone. You mind your business and they'll mind theirs. Don't go near them.' And they made sure I didn't. My father, who was the principal of a colored grade school in Richmond, used to drive me to and from school every day. When I needed something from downtown my mother would take me and if the white saleslady asked me anything she would answer. . . .

"And my parents were also always telling me, 'Stay away from niggers,' and that meant anybody darker than we were." She held out her arm in the light and Max Berman saw the skin almost as white as his but for the subtle amber shading. Staring at the arm she said tragically, "I was so confused I never really went near anybody. Even when I went away to college I kept to myself. I didn't marry the man I wanted to because he was dark and I knew my parents would disapprove. . . ." She paused, her wistful gaze searching the darkness for the face of the man she had refused, it seemed, and not finding it she went on sadly. "So after graduation I returned home and started teaching and I was just as confused and frightened and ashamed as always. When my parents died I went on the same way. And I would have gone on like that the rest of my life if it hadn't been for you, Dr. Berman"—and the sarcasm leaped behind her cold smile. "In a way you did me a favor. You let me know how you and most of the people like you—see me."

"My dear Miss Williams, I assure you I was not attracted to you because you were colored. . . ." And he broke off, remembering just how acutely aware of her color he had been.

"I'm not interested in your reasons!" she said brutally. "What matters is what it meant to me. I thought about this these last three weeks and about my parents how wrong they had been, how frightened, and the terrible thing they had done to me . . . and I wasn't confused any longer." Her head lifted, tremulous with her new assurance. "I can do something now! I can begin," she said with her head poised. "Look how I came all the way up here to tell you this to your face. Because how could you harm me? You're so old you're like a cup I could break in my hand." And her hand tightened on his wrist, wrenching the last of his frail life from him, it seemed. Through the quick pain he remembered her saying on the landing that night: "Maybe in order for a person to live someone else must die" and her quiet "I believe this" then. Now her sudden laugh, an infinitely cruel sound in the warm night, confirmed her belief.

Suddenly she was the one who seemed old, indeed ageless. Her touch became mortal and Max Berman saw the darkness that would end his life gathered in her eyes. But even as he sprang back, jerking his arm away, a part of him rushed forward to embrace that darkness, and his cry, wounding the night, held both ecstasy and terror.

"That's all I came for," she said, rising. "You can drive me to the station now."

They drove to the station in silence. Then, just as the girl started from the car, she turned with an ironic, pitiless smile and said, "You know, it's been a nice day, all things considered. It really turned summer again as you said it would. And even though your lake isn't anything like the one near my home, it's almost as nice."

Max Berman bowed to her for the last time, accepting with that gesture his responsibility for her rage, which went deeper than his, and for her anger, which would spur her finally to live. And not only for her, but for all those at last whom he had wronged through his indifference: his father lying in the room of shrouded mirrors, the wives he had never loved, his work which he had never believed in enough and lastly (even though he knew it was too late and he would not be spared), himself.

Too weary to move, he watched the girl cross to the train which would bear her south, her head lifted as though she carried life as lightly there as if it were a hat made of tulle. When the train departed his numbed eyes followed it until its rear light was like a single firefly in the immense night or the last flickering of his life. Then he drove back through the darkness.

[1961]

QUESTIONS

1. Why is Max Berman's Jewish identity significant? How are anti-Semitism and racism explored in the story? How are they related?
2. What does Miss Williams learn from Max? What does she teach him?
3. What are the sources of Max's inner emptiness and disillusionment? Does he change during the story?
4. Through what images and details does Marshall establish and develop the tone of the story?

BOBBIE ANN MASON
(b. 1940)
UNITED STATES

Bobbie Ann Mason was born in Mayfield, Kentucky, and grew up on her parents' dairy farm. Majoring in journalism at the University of Kentucky, she went on to receive a Ph.D. in English at the University of Connecticut and taught English at a college in Pennsylvania. She began her writing career by publishing sketches of such teen stars as Annette Funicello in slick teen fan magazines such as *Movie Stars*, *Movie Life*, and *T.V. Star Parade*. In an entirely different vein, in 1975 she published *The Girl Sleuth: A Feminist Guide to the Bobbsey Twins, Nancy Drew, and Their Sisters*. As Mason has described the unlikely trajectory of her career as a writer,

> After graduating from the University of Kentucky I went to New York City and worked as a writer on some fan magazines. . . . It wasn't the writing career I had had in mind when I was an iconoclastic columnist on the University of Kentucky *Kernel*, so I went off to graduate school to study literature and that took a long time. When I finally came to my senses after finishing the dissertation . . . [on Vladimir Nabokov's novel *Ada*], I lapsed back into my childhood and started reading Nancy Drew books. Life has been steady progress since then.

Mason published her first short story in *The New Yorker* in 1980. Not long afterward, her collection of stories *Shiloh and Other Stories* (1982) received high praise, including its recognition with the Ernest Hemingway Foundation Award. She has also published a second collection of stories, *Love Life* (1989), and two novels, *In Country* (1985) and *Spence and Lila* (1988).

In her stories and novels, Mason focuses on ordinary working class people from the milieu of her own origins in rural western Kentucky, characters who are on the lower margins of the middle class and trying to move up. With an unerring eye for both the material and the psychological environments of her characters, Mason explores the ways in which they are caught, like flies in amber, in a world paradoxically static and rapidly changing before their very eyes.

Shiloh

Leroy Moffitt's wife, Norma Jean, is working on her pectorals. She lifts three-pound dumbbells to warm up, then progresses to a twenty-pound barbell. Standing with her legs apart, she reminds Leroy of Wonder Woman.

"I'd give anything if I could just get these muscles to where they're real hard," says Norma Jean. "Feel this arm. It's not as hard as the other one."

"That's cause you're right-handed," says Leroy, dodging as she swings the barbell in an arc.

"Do you think so?"

"Sure."

Leroy is a truckdriver. He injured his leg in a highway accident four months ago, and his physical therapy, which involves weights and a pulley, prompted Norma Jean to try building herself up. Now she is attending a body-building class. Leroy has been collecting temporary disability since his tractor-trailer jackknifed in Missouri, badly twisting his left leg in its socket. He has a steel pin in his hip. He will probably not be able to drive his rig again. It sits in the backyard, like a gigantic bird that has flown home to roost. Leroy has been home in Kentucky for three months, and his leg is almost healed, but the accident frightened him and he does not want to drive any more long hauls. He is not sure what to do next. In the meantime, he makes things from craft kits. He started by building a miniature log cabin from notched Popsicle sticks. He varnished it and placed it on the TV set, where it remains. It reminds him of a rustic Nativity scene. Then he tried string art (sailing ships on black velvet), a macramé owl kit, a snap-together B-17 Flying Fortress, and a lamp made out of a model truck, with a light fixture screwed in the top of the cab. At first the kits were diversions, something to kill time, but now he is thinking about building a full-scale log house from a kit. It would be considerably cheaper than building a regular house, and besides, Leroy has grown to appreciate how things are put together. He has begun to realize that in all the years he was on the road he never took time to examine anything. He was always flying past scenery.

"They won't let you build a log cabin in any of the new subdivisions," Norma Jean tells him.

"They will if I tell them it's for you," he says, teasing her. Ever since they were married, he has promised Norma Jean he would build her a new home one day. They have always rented, and the house they live in is small and nondescript. It does not even feel like a home, Leroy realizes now.

Norma Jean works at the Rexall drugstore, and she has acquired an amazing amount of information about cosmetics. When she explains to Leroy the three stages of complexion care, involving creams, toners, and moisturizers, he thinks happily of other petroleum products — axle grease, diesel fuel. This is a connection between him and Norma Jean. Since he has been home, he has felt unusually tender about his wife and guilty over his long absences. But he can't tell what she feels about him. Norma Jean has never complained about his traveling; she has never made hurt remarks, like calling his truck a "widow-maker." He is reasonably certain she has been faithful to him, but he wishes she would celebrate his permanent homecoming more happily. Norma Jean is often startled to find Leroy at home, and he thinks she seems a little disappointed about it. Perhaps he reminds her too much of the early days of their marriage, before he went on the road. They had a child who died as an infant, years ago. They never speak about their memories of Randy, which have almost faded, but now that Leroy is home all the time, they sometimes feel awkward around each other, and Leroy wonders if one of them should mention the child. He has the feeling that they are waking up out of a dream together — that they must create a new marriage, start afresh. They are lucky they are still married. Leroy has read that for most people losing a child destroys the marriage — or else he heard this on *Donahue*. He can't always remember where he learns things anymore.

At Christmas, Leroy bought an electric organ for Norma Jean. She used to play the piano when she was in high school. "It don't leave you," she told him once. "It's like riding a bicycle."

The new instrument had so many keys and buttons that she was bewildered by it at first. She touched the keys tentatively, pushed some buttons, then pecked out "Chopsticks." It came out in an amplified fox-trot rhythm, with marimba sounds.

"It's an orchestra!" she cried.

The organ had a pecan-look finish and eighteen preset chords, with optional flute, violin, trumpet, clarinet, and banjo accompaniments. Norma Jean mastered the organ almost immediately. At first she played Christmas songs. Then she bought *The Sixties Songbook* and learned every tune in it, adding variations to each with the rows of brightly colored buttons.

"I didn't like these old songs back then," she said. "But I have this crazy feeling I missed something."

"You didn't miss a thing," said Leroy.

Leroy likes to lie on the couch and smoke a joint and listen to Norma Jean play "Can't Take My Eyes Off You" and "I'll Be Back." He is back again. After fifteen years on the road, he is finally settling down with the woman he loves. She is still pretty. Her skin is flawless. Her frosted curls resemble pencil trimmings.

Now that Leroy has come home to stay, he notices how much the town has changed. Subdivisions are spreading across western Kentucky like an oil slick. The sign at the edge of town says "Pop: 11,500"—only seven hundred more than it said twenty years before. Leroy can't figure out who is living in all the new houses. The farmers who used to gather around the courthouse square on Saturday afternoons to play checkers and spit tobacco juice have gone. It has been years since Leroy has thought about the farmers, and they have disappeared without his noticing.

Leroy meets a kid named Stevie Hamilton in the parking lot at the new shopping center. While they pretend to be strangers meeting over a stalled car, Stevie tosses an ounce of marijuana under the front seat of Leroy's car. Stevie is wearing orange jogging shoes and a T-shirt that says CHATTAHOOCHEE SUPER-RAT. His father is a prominent doctor who lives in one of the expensive subdivisions in a new white-columned brick house that looks like a funeral parlor. In the phone book under his name there is a separate number, with the listing "Teenagers."

"Where do you get this stuff?" asks Leroy. "From your pappy!"

"That's for me to know and you to find out," Stevie says. He is slit-eyed and skinny.

"What else you got?"

"What you interested in?"

"Nothing special. Just wondered."

Leroy used to take speed on the road. Now he has to go slowly. He needs to be mellow. He leans back against the car and says, "I'm aiming to build me a log house, soon as I get time. My wife, though, I don't think she likes the idea."

"Well, let me know when you want me again," Stevie says. He has a cigarette in his cupped palm, as though sheltering it from the wind. He takes a long drag, then stomps it on the asphalt and slouches away.

Stevie's father was two years ahead of Leroy in high school. Leroy is thirty-four. He married Norma Jean when they were both eighteen, and their child Randy was born a few months later, but he died at the age of four months and three days. He would be about Stevie's age now. Norma Jean and Leroy were at the drive-in, watching a double feature (*Dr. Strangelove* and *Lover Come Back*), and the baby was sleeping in the back seat. When the first movie ended, the baby was dead. It was the sudden infant death syndrome. Leroy remembers handing Randy to a nurse at the emergency room, as though he were offering her a large doll as a present. A dead baby feels like a sack of flour. "It just happens sometimes," said the doctor, in what Leroy always recalls as a nonchalant tone. Leroy can hardly remember the child anymore, but he still sees vividly a scene from *Dr. Strangelove* in which the President of the United States was talking in a folksy voice on the hot line to the Soviet premier about the bomber accidentally headed toward Russia. He was in the War Room, and the world map was lit up. Leroy remembers Norma Jean catatonically beside him in the hospital and himself thinking: Who is this strange girl? He had forgotten who she was. Now scientists are saying that crib death is caused by a virus. Nobody knows anything, Leroy thinks. The answers are always changing.

When Leroy gets home from the shopping center, Norma Jean's mother, Mabel Beasley, is there. Until this year, Leroy has not realized how much time she spends with Norma Jean. When she visits, she inspects the closets and then the plants, informing Norma Jean when a plant is droopy or yellow. Mabel calls the plants "flowers," although there are never any blooms. She always notices if Norma Jean's laundry is piling up. Mabel is a short, overweight woman whose tight, brown-dyed curls look more like a wig than the actual wig she sometimes wears. Today she has brought Norma Jean an off-white dust ruffle she made for the bed; Mabel works in a custom-upholstery shop.

"This is the tenth one I made this year," Mabel says. "I got started and couldn't stop."

"It's real pretty," says Norma Jean.

"Now we can hide things under the bed," says Leroy, who gets along with his mother-in-law primarily by joking with her. Mabel has never really forgiven him for disgracing her by getting Norma Jean pregnant. When the baby died, she said that fate was mocking her.

"What's that thing?" Mabel says to Leroy in a loud voice, pointing to a tangle of yarn on a piece of canvas.

Leroy holds it up for Mabel to see. "It's my needlepoint," he explains. "This is a *Star Trek* pillow cover."

"That's what a woman would do," says Mabel. "Great day in the morning!"

"All the big football players on TV do it," he says.

"Why, Leroy, you're always trying to fool me. I don't believe you for one minute. You don't know what to do with yourself—that's the whole trouble. Sewing!"

"I'm aiming to build us a log house," says Leroy. "Soon as my plans come."

"Like *heck* you are," says Norma Jean. She takes Leroy's needlepoint and shoves it into a drawer. "You have to find a job first. Nobody can afford to build now anyway."

Mabel straightens her girdle and says, "I still think before you get tied down y'all ought to take a little run to Shiloh."

"One of these days, Mama," Norma Jean says impatiently.

Mabel is talking about Shiloh, Tennessee. For the past few years, she has been urging Leroy and Norma Jean to visit the Civil War battleground there. Mabel went there on her honeymoon—the only real trip she ever took. Her husband died of a perforated ulcer when Norma Jean was ten, but Mabel, who was accepted into the United Daughters of the Confederacy in 1975, is still preoccupied with going back to Shiloh.

"I've been to kingdom come and back in that truck out yonder," Leroy says to Mabel, "but we never yet set foot in that battleground. Ain't that something? How did I miss it?"

"It's not even that far," Mabel says.

After Mabel leaves, Norma Jean reads to Leroy from a list she has made. "Things you could do," she announces. "You could get a job as a guard at Union Carbide, where they'd let you set on a stool. You could get one at the lumberyard. You could do a little carpenter work, if you want to build so bad. You could—"

"I can't do something where I'd have to stand up all day."

"You ought to try standing up all day behind a cosmetics counter. It's amazing that I have strong feet, coming from two parents that never had strong feet at all." At the moment Norma Jean is holding on to the kitchen counter, raising her knees one at a time as she talks. She is wearing two-pound ankle weights.

"Don't worry," says Leroy. "I'll do something."

"You could truck calves to slaughter for somebody. You wouldn't have to drive any big old truck for that."

"I'm going to build you this house," says Leroy. "I want to make you a real home."

"I don't want to live in any log cabin."

"It's not a cabin. It's a house."

"I don't care. It looks like a cabin."

"You and me together could lift those logs. It's just like lifting weights."

Norma Jean doesn't answer. Under her breath, she is counting. Now she is marching through the kitchen. She is doing goose steps.

Before his accident, when Leroy came home he used to stay in the house with Norma Jean, watching TV in bed and playing cards. She would cook fried chicken, picnic ham, chocolate pie—all his favorites. Now he is home alone much of the time. In the mornings, Norma Jean disappears, leaving a cooling place in the bed. She eats a cereal called Body Buddies, and she leaves the bowl on the table, with soggy tan balls floating in a milk puddle. He sees things about Norma Jean that he never realized before. When she chops onions, she stares off into a corner, as if she can't bear to look. She puts on her house slippers almost precisely at nine o'clock every evening and nudges her jogging shoes under the couch. She saves bread heels for the birds. Leroy watches the birds at the feeder. He notices the peculiar way goldfinches fly past the window. They close their wings, then fall, then spread their wings to catch and lift themselves. He wonders if they close their eyes when they fall. Norma Jean closes her eyes when they are in bed. She wants the lights turned out. Even then, he is sure she closes her eyes.

He goes for long drives around town. He tends to drive a car rather carelessly. Power steering and an automatic shift make a car feel so small and inconsequential that his body is hardly involved in the driving process. His injured leg stretches out comfortably. Once or twice he has almost hit something, but even the prospect of an accident seems minor in a car. He cruises the new subdivisions, feeling like a criminal rehearsing for a robbery. Norma Jean is probably right about a log house being inappropriate here in the new subdivisions. All the houses look grand and complicated. They depress him.

One day when Leroy comes home from a drive he finds Norma Jean in tears. She is in the kitchen making a potato and mushroom-soup casserole, with grated-cheese topping. She is crying because her mother caught her smoking.

"I didn't hear her coming. I was standing here puffing away pretty as you please," Norma Jean says, wiping her eyes.

"I knew it would happen sooner or later," says Leroy, putting his arm around her.

"She don't know the meaning of the word 'knock,'" says Norma Jean. "It's a wonder she hadn't caught me years ago."

"Think of it this way," Leroy says. "What if she caught me with a joint?"

"You better not let her!" Norma Jean shrieks. "I'm warning you, Leroy Moffitt!"

"I'm just kidding. Here, play me a tune. That'll help you relax."

Norma Jean puts the casserole in the oven and sets the timer. Then she plays a ragtime tune, with horns and banjo, as Leroy lights up a joint and lies on the couch, laughing to himself about Mabel's catching him at it. He thinks of Stevie Hamilton—a doctor's son pushing grass. Everything is funny. The whole town seems crazy and small. He is reminded of Virgil Mathis, a boastful policeman Leroy used to shoot pool with. Virgil recently led a drug bust in a back room at a bowling alley, where he seized ten thousand dollars' worth of marijuana. The newspaper had a picture of him holding up the bags of grass and grinning widely. Right now, Leroy can imagine Virgil breaking down the door and arresting him with a lungful of smoke. Virgil would probably have been alerted to the scene because of all the racket Norma Jean is making. Now she sounds like a hard-rock band. Norma Jean is terrific. When she switches to a latin-rhythm version of "Sunshine Superman," Leroy hums along. Norma Jean's foot goes up and down, up and down.

"Well, what do you think?" Leroy says, when Norma Jean pauses to search through her music.

"What do I think about what?"

His mind has gone blank. Then he says, "I'll sell my rig and build us a house." That wasn't what he wanted to say. He wanted to know what she thought—what she *really* thought—about them.

"Don't start in on that again," says Norma Jean. She begins playing "Who'll Be the Next in Line?"

Leroy used to tell hitchhikers his whole life story—about his travels, his hometown, the baby. He would end with a question: "Well, what do you think?" It was just a rhetorical question. In time, he had the feeling that he'd been telling the same story over and over to the same hitchhikers. He quit talking to hitchhikers when he realized how his voice sounded—whining and self-pitying, like some teenage-tragedy song. Now Leroy has the sudden impulse to tell Norma Jean about himself, as if he had just met her. They have known each other so long they have forgotten a lot about each other. They could become reacquainted. But when the oven timer goes off and she runs to the kitchen, he forgets why he wants to do this.

The next day, Mabel drops by. It is Saturday and Norma Jean is cleaning. Leroy is studying the plans of his log house, which have finally come in the mail. He has them spread out on the table—big sheets of stiff blue paper, with diagrams and numbers printed in white. While Norma Jean runs the vacuum, Mabel drinks coffee. She sets her coffee cup on a blueprint.

"I'm just waiting for time to pass," she says to Leroy, drumming her fingers on the table.

As soon as Norma Jean switches off the vacuum, Mabel says in a loud voice, "Did you hear about the datsun dog that killed the baby?"

Norma Jean says, "The word is 'dachshund.'"

"They put the dog on trial. It chewed the baby's legs off. The mother was in the next room all the time." She raises her voice. "They thought it was neglect."

Norma Jean is holding her ears. Leroy manages to open the refrigerator and get some Diet Pepsi to offer Mabel. Mabel still has some coffee and she waves away the Pepsi.

"Datsuns are like that," Mabel says. "They're jealous dogs. They'll tear a place to pieces if you don't keep an eye on them."

"You better watch out what you're saying, Mabel," says Leroy.

"Well, facts is facts."

Leroy looks out the window at his rig. It is like a huge piece of furniture gathering dust in the backyard. Pretty soon it will be an antique. He hears the vacuum cleaner. Norma Jean seems to be cleaning the living room rug again.

Later, she says to Leroy, "She just said that about the baby because she caught me smoking. She's trying to pay me back."

"What are you talking about?" Leroy says, nervously shuffling blueprints.

"You know good and well," Norma Jean says. She is sitting in a kitchen chair with her feet up and her arms wrapped around her knees. She looks small and helpless. She says, "The very idea, her bringing up a subject like that! Saying it was neglect."

"She didn't mean that," Leroy says.

"She might not have *thought* she meant it. She always says things like that. You don't know how she goes on."

"But she didn't really mean it. She was just talking."

Leroy opens a king-sized bottle of beer and pours it into two glasses, dividing it carefully. He hands a glass to Norma Jean and she takes it from him mechanically. For a long time, they sit by the kitchen window watching the birds at the feeder.

Something is happening. Norma Jean is going to night school. She has graduated from her six-week body-building course and now she is taking an adult-education course in composition at Paducah Community College. She spends her evenings outlining paragraphs.

"First you have a topic sentence," she explains to Leroy. "Then you divide it up. Your secondary topic has to be connected to your primary topic."

To Leroy, this sounds intimidating. "I never was any good in English," he says.

"It makes a lot of sense."

"What are you doing this for, anyhow?"

She shrugs. "It's something to do." She stands up and lifts her dumbbells a few times.

"Driving a rig, nobody cared about my English."

"I'm not criticizing your English."

Norma Jean used to say, "If I lose ten minutes' sleep, I just drag all day." Now she stays up late, writing compositions. She got a B on her first paper — a how-to theme on soup-based casseroles. Recently Norma Jean has been cooking unusual foods — tacos, lasagna, Bombay chicken. She doesn't play the organ anymore, though her second paper was called "Why Music Is Important to Me." She sits at the kitchen table, concentrating on her outlines, while Leroy plays with his log house plans, practicing with a set of Lincoln Logs. The thought of getting a truckload of notched, numbered logs scares him, and he wants to be prepared. As he and Norma Jean work together at the kitchen table, Leroy has the hopeful thought that they are sharing something, but he knows he is a fool to think this. Norma Jean is miles away. He knows he is going to lose her. Like Mabel, he is just waiting for time to pass.

One day, Mabel is there before Norma Jean gets home from work, and Leroy finds himself confiding in her. Mabel, he realizes, must know Norma Jean better than he does.

"I don't know what's got into that girl," Mabel says. "She used to go to bed with the chickens. Now you say she's up all hours. Plus her a-smoking. I like to died."

"I want to make her this beautiful home," Leroy says, indicating the Lincoln Logs. "I don't think she even wants it. Maybe she was happier with me gone."

"She don't know what to make of you, coming home like this."

"Is that it?"

Mabel takes the roof off his Lincoln Log cabin. "You couldn't get *me* in a log cabin," she says. "I was raised in one. It's no picnic, let me tell you."

"They're different now," says Leroy.

"I tell you what," Mabel says, smiling oddly at Leroy.

"What?"

"Take her on down to Shiloh. Y'all need to get out together, stir a little. Her brain's all balled up over them books."

Leroy can see traces of Norma Jean's features in her mother's face. Mabel's face has the texture of crinkled cotton, but suddenly she looks pretty. It occurs to Leroy that Mabel has been hinting all along that she wants them to take her with them to Shiloh.

"Let's all go to Shiloh," he says. "You and me and her. Come Sunday."

Mabel throws up her hands in protest. "Oh, no, not me. Young folks want to be by theirselves."

When Norma Jean comes in with groceries, Leroy says excitedly, "Your mama here's been dying to go to Shiloh for thirty-five years. It's about time we went, don't you think?"

"I'm not going to butt in on anybody's second honeymoon," Mabel says.

"Who's going on a honeymoon, for Christ's sake?" Norma Jean says loudly.

"I never raised no daughter of mine to talk that-a-way," Mabel says.

"You ain't seen nothing yet," says Norma Jean. She starts putting away boxes and cans, slamming cabinet doors.

"There's a log cabin at Shiloh." Mabel says, "It was there during the battle. There's bullet holes in it."

"When are you going to *shut up* about Shiloh, Mama?" asks Norma Jean.

"I always thought Shiloh was the prettiest place, so full of history," Mabel goes on. "I just hoped y'all could see it once before I die, so you could tell me about it." Later, she whispers to Leroy, "You do what I said. A little change is what she needs."

"Your name means 'the king,'" Norma Jean says to Leroy that evening. He is trying to get her to go to Shiloh, and she is reading a book about another century.

"Well, I reckon I ought to be right proud."

"I guess so."

"Am I still king around here?"

Norma Jean flexes her biceps and feels them for hardness. "I'm not fooling around with anybody, if that's what you mean," she says.

"Would you tell me if you were?"

"I don't know."

"What does *your* name mean?"

"It was Marilyn Monroe's real name."

"No kidding!"

"Norma comes from the Normans. They were invaders," she says. She closes her book and looks hard at Leroy. "I'll go to Shiloh with you if you'll stop staring at me."

On Sunday, Norma Jean packs a picnic and they go to Shiloh. To Leroy's relief, Mabel says she does not want to come with them. Norma Jean drives, and Leroy, sitting beside her, feels like some boring hitchhiker she has picked up. He tries some conversation, but she answers him in monosyllables. At Shiloh, she drives aimlessly through the park, past bluffs and trails and steep ravines. Shiloh is an immense place, and Leroy cannot see it as a battleground. It is not what he expected. He thought it would look like a golf course. Monuments are everywhere, showing through the thick clusters of trees. Norma Jean passes the log cabin Mabel mentioned. It is surrounded by tourists looking for bullet holes.

"That's not the kind of log house I've got in mind," says Leroy apologetically.

"I know *that*."

"This is a pretty place. Your mama was right."

"It's O.K.," says Norma Jean. "Well, we've seen it. I hope she's satisfied."

They burst out laughing together.

At the park museum, a movie on Shiloh is shown every half hour, but they decide that they don't want to see it. They buy a souvenir Confederate flag for Mabel, and then they find a picnic spot near the cemetery. Norma Jean has brought a picnic cooler, with pimiento sandwiches, soft drinks, and Yodels. Leroy eats a sandwich and then smokes a joint, hiding it behind the picnic cooler. Norma Jean has quit smoking altogether. She is picking cake crumbs from the cellophane wrapper, like a fussy bird.

Leroy says, "So the boys in gray ended up in Corinth. The Union soldiers zapped 'em finally. April 7, 1862."

They both know that he doesn't know any history. He is just talking about some of the historical plaques they have read. He feels awkward, like a boy on a date with an older girl. They are still just making conversation.

"Corinth is where Mama eloped to," says Norma Jean.

They sit in silence and stare at the cemetery for the Union dead and, beyond, at a tall cluster of trees. Campers are parked nearby, bumper to bumper, and small children in bright clothing are cavorting and squealing. Norma Jean wads up the cake wrapper and squeezes it tightly in her hand. Without looking at Leroy, she says, "I want to leave you."

Leroy takes a bottle of Coke out of the cooler and flips off the cap. He holds the bottle poised near his mouth but cannot remember to take a drink. Finally he says, "No, you don't."

"Yes, I do."

"I won't let you."

"You can't stop me."

"Don't do me that way."

Leroy knows Norma Jean will have her own way. "Didn't I promise to be home from now on?" he says.

"In some ways, a woman prefers a man who wanders," says Norma Jean. "That sounds crazy, I know."

"You're not crazy."

Leroy remembers to drink from his Coke. Then he says, "Yes, you *are* crazy. You and me could start all over again. Right back at the beginning."

"We *have* started all over again," says Norma Jean. "And this is how it turned out."

"What did I do wrong?"

"Nothing."

"Is this one of those women's lib things?" Leroy asks.

"Don't be funny."

The cemetery, a green slope dotted with white markers, looks like a subdivision site. Leroy is trying to comprehend that his marriage is breaking up, but for some reason he is wondering about white slabs in a graveyard.

"Everything was fine till Mama caught me smoking," says Norma Jean, standing up. "That set something off."

"What are you talking about?"

"She won't leave me alone—*you* won't leave me alone." Norma Jean seems to be crying, but she is looking away from him. "I feel eighteen again. I can't face that all over again." She starts walking away. "No, it *wasn't* fine. I don't know what I'm saying. Forget it."

Leroy takes a lungful of smoke and closes his eyes as Norma Jean's words sink in. He tries to focus on the fact that thirty-five hundred soldiers died on the grounds around him. He can only think of that war as a board game with plastic soldiers. Leroy almost smiles, as he compares the Confederates' daring attack on the Union camps and Virgil Mathis's raid on the bowling alley. General Grant, drunk and furious, shoved the Southerners back to Corinth, where Mabel and Jet Beasley were married years later, when Mabel was still thin and good-looking. The next day, Mabel and Jet visited the battleground, and then Norma Jean was born, and then she married Leroy and they had a baby, which they lost, and now Leroy and Norma Jean are here at the same battleground. Leroy knows he is leaving out a lot. He is leaving out the insides of history. History was always just names and dates to him. It occurs to him that building a house out of logs is similarly empty—too simple. And the real inner workings of a marriage, like most of history, have escaped him. Now he sees that building a log house is the dumbest idea he could have had. It was clumsy of him to think Norma Jean would want a log house. It was a crazy idea. He'll have to think of something else, quickly. He will wad the blueprints into tight balls and fling them into the lake. Then he'll get moving again. He opens his eyes. Norma Jean has moved away and is walking through the cemetery, following a serpentine brick path.

Leroy gets up to follow his wife, but his good leg is asleep and his bad leg still hurts him. Norma Jean is far away, walking rapidly toward the bluff by the river, and he tries to hobble toward her. Some children run past him, screaming noisily. Norma Jean has reached the bluff, and she is looking out over the Tennessee River. Now she turns toward Leroy and waves her arms. Is she beckoning to him? She seems to be doing an exercise for her chest muscles. The sky is unusually pale — the color of the dust ruffle Mabel made for their bed.

[1982]

QUESTIONS

1. Which details of the story contribute to your understanding of Norma Jean and Leroy's values and tastes? How are these values important to the outcome of the story?
2. Why does Norma Jean decide to leave Leroy? What does she hope to find?
3. Is there humor in the story? If so, where is it and how is it used? Does Mason seem to be mocking her characters or sympathizing with them?
4. What role does Norma Jean's mother play in the story?
5. How does history — both the history of Norma Jean and Leroy's marriage and Civil War history — contribute to the story's meaning? How are the two contexts related?

William Somerset Maugham

(1874–1965)

England

William Somerset Maugham, born in Paris of an English diplomat and a mother who died when he was eight, was educated in Germany and England. After qualifying to become a doctor, he began a second career as an author, writing a number of light comedies in the mode of Noel Coward. In 1908, four of his plays were staged simultaneously in London. In 1917, Maugham married Syrie Wellcome, a talented interior designer, two years after their daughter Liza was born.

Of his novels, Maugham's best-known and most accomplished work is the partly autobiographical novel *Of Human Bondage* (1915). The novel follows the life of the lame and sensitive Philip Carey, who is determined to be both a doctor and an artist (and, through limited talent, nearly fails at both) and who suffers through a disastrous love affair. Among Maugham's other novels are *The Moon and Sixpence* (1919), based on the life of the French painter Gauguin and on Maugham's first-hand knowledge of Tahiti, and *Cakes and Ale* (1930), probably modeled on the life of English writer Thomas Hardy. Several of his novels and stories focus on the competing claims of duty and art or the disappointing recognition of limited artistic talent.

In a sense, this theme embodies Maugham's own situation in the world of letters. Although he achieved financial success and an enormous popular following—Christopher Morley called him "the most continually readable storyteller of our lifetime"—he never achieved the higher distinctions of critical acclaim. Candidly acknowledging the limits of his reputation, he observed, "In my youth I had accepted the challenge of writing and literature to idealize them; in my age I see the magnitude of the attempt and wonder at my audacity."

The Appointment in Samarra

Death speaks: There was a merchant in Baghdad who sent his servant to market to buy provisions and in a little while the servant came back, white and trembling, and said, Master, just now when I was in the market-place I was jostled by a woman in the crowd and when I turned I saw it was Death that jostled me. She looked at me and made a threatening gesture; now, lend me your horse, and I will ride away from this city and avoid my fate. I will go to Samarra and there Death will not find me. The merchant lent him his horse, and the servant mounted it, and he dug his spurs in its flanks and as fast as the horse could gallop he went. Then the merchant went down to the market-place and he saw me standing in the crowd and he came to me and said, Why did you make a threatening gesture to my servant when you saw him this morning? That was not a threatening gesture, I said, it was only a start of surprise. I was astonished to see him in Baghdad, for I had an appointment with him tonight in Samarra.

[1933]

QUESTIONS

1. Who tells this story? How does the point of view contribute to its meaning? How would the meaning of the story change if it were told from another perspective?
2. What is the "moral" of the story?
3. How are differences of interpretation of the events built into the narrative itself?
4. How does the story achieve its effect as a fable?

GUY DE MAUPASSANT

(1850–1893)

FRANCE

In his relatively brief life, Guy de Maupassant produced an astonishing *oeuvre* of over 300 short stories, in addition to six novels, more than 200 sketches for newspapers and magazines, essays on travel, and dramatic adaptations. In fact, he was a born storyteller, whose stories reveal a sharp eye for vivid detail and social observation, a balance of detachment and sympathy, and the controlled use of irony.

Born to middle-class parents in Rouen, Normandy, de Maupassant studied law and served as a soldier in the Franco-Prussian War from 1870 to 1871. In Paris, he supported himself by writing for newspapers and working as a government bureaucrat in the Ministries of the Navy and Education while he tried to write plays; eventually he discovered that his true form was the short story. His literary apprenticeship was significantly furthered by his mentors, Gustave Flaubert, Emile Zola, and other established writers. Flaubert encouraged de Maupassant to write stories, advising him to choose his subjects carefully by finding some aspect that had not been previously explored; many of his stories were first published in newspapers as *contes*, or short tales, including his earliest ones, horror stories in the tradition of Edgar Allan Poe. "The Necklace," one of his most accomplished ironic treatments of bourgeois illusions, was published in 1884. While in Paris, de Maupassant lived a somewhat dissolute life, contracting syphilis that led to years of deteriorating health and his untimely death at the age of 42.

De Maupassant contributed definitively to the aesthetics of the modern story form. By omitting narrative digressions and moral judgments, he pared the form to its essential elements, a technical strategy that significantly influenced most of his successors. In an important statement about writing, de Maupassant revealed his own view of the selective processes essential to literary creation, observing that the writer's goal

> is not to tell us a story, to entertain or to move us, but to make us think and to make us understand the deep and hidden meaning of events. . . . To move us, as he has been moved himself by the spectacle of life, [the author] must reproduce it before our eyes with a scrupulous accuracy. He should compose his work so adroitly, and with such dissimulation and apparent simplicity, that it is impossible to uncover its plan or to perceive his intentions. . . . In giving every detail its exact degree of shading in accordance with its importance, the author produces the profound impression of the particular truth he wishes to point out.
>
> . . . Each of us makes, individually, a personal illusion of the world. It may be a poetic, sentimental, joyful, melancholy, sordid, or dismal one, according to our nature. The writer's goal is to reproduce this illusion of life faithfully, using all the literary techniques at his disposal.

The Necklace

She was one of those pretty and charming girls who are sometimes, as if by a mistake of destiny, born in a family of clerks. She had no dowry, no expectations, no means of being known, understood, loved, wedded by any rich and distinguished man; and she let herself be married to a little clerk at the Ministry of Public Instruction.

She dressed plainly because she could not dress well, but she was as unhappy as though she had really fallen from her proper station, since with women there is neither caste nor rank: and beauty, grace and charm act instead of family and birth. Natural fineness, instinct for what is elegant, suppleness of wit, are the sole hierarchy, and make from women of the people the equals of the very greatest ladies.

She suffered ceaselessly, feeling herself born for all the delicacies and all the luxuries. She suffered from the poverty of her dwelling, from the wretched look of the walls, from the worn-out chairs, from the ugliness of the curtains. All those things, of which another woman of her rank would never even have been conscious, tortured her and made her angry. The sight of the little Breton peasant who did her humble housework aroused in her regrets which were despairing, and distracted dreams. She thought of the silent antechambers hung with Oriental tapestry, lit by tall bronze candelabra, and of the two great footmen in knee breeches who sleep in the big armchairs, made drowsy by the heavy warmth of the hot-air stove. She thought of the long *salons*[1] fitted up with ancient silk, of the delicate furniture carrying priceless curiosities, and of the coquettish perfumed boudoirs made for talks at five o'clock with intimate friends, with men famous and sought after, whom all women envy and whose attention they all desire.

When she sat down to dinner, before the round table covered with a tablecloth three days old, opposite her husband, who uncovered the soup tureen and declared with an enchanted air, "Ah, the good *pot-au-feu*![2] I don't know anything better than that," she thought of dainty dinners, of shining silverware, of tapestry which peopled the walls with ancient personages and with strange birds flying in the midst of a fairy forest; and she thought of delicious dishes served on marvelous plates, and of the whispered gallantries which you listen to with a sphinxlike smile, while you are eating the pink flesh of a trout or the wings of a quail.

She had no dresses, no jewels, nothing. And she loved nothing but that; she felt made for that. She would so have liked to please, to be envied, to be charming, to be sought after.

She had a friend, a former schoolmate at the convent, who was rich, and whom she did not like to go and see any more, because she suffered so much when she came back.

But one evening, her husband returned home with a triumphant air, and holding a large envelope in his hand.

[1]*salons* fashionable drawing rooms
[2]*pot-au-feu* soup or stew

"There," said he. "Here is something for you."

She tore the paper sharply, and drew out a printed card which bore these words:

"The Minister of Public Instruction and Mme. Georges Ramponneau request the honor of M. and Mme. Loisel's company at the palace of the Ministry on Monday evening, January eighteenth."

Instead of being delighted, as her husband hoped, she threw the invitation on the table with disdain, murmuring:

"What do you want me to do with that?"

"But, my dear, I thought you would be glad. You never go out, and this is such a fine opportunity. I had awful trouble to get it. Everyone wants to go; it is very select, and they are not giving many invitations to clerks. The whole official world will be there."

She looked at him with an irritated glance, and said, impatiently:

"And what do you want me to put on my back?"

He had not thought of that; he stammered:

"Why, the dress you go to the theater in. It looks very well, to me."

He stopped, distracted, seeing his wife was crying. Two great tears descended slowly from the corners of her eyes toward the corners of her mouth. He stuttered:

"What's the matter? What's the matter?"

But, by violent effort, she had conquered her grief, and she replied, with a calm voice, while she wiped her wet cheeks:

"Nothing. Only I have no dress and therefore I can't go to this ball. Give your card to some colleague whose wife is better equipped than I."

He was in despair. He resumed:

"Come, let us see, Mathilde. How much would it cost, a suitable dress, which you could use on other occasions, something very simple?"

She reflected several seconds, making her calculations and wondering also what sum she could ask without drawing on herself an immediate refusal and a frightened exclamation from the economical clerk.

Finally, she replied, hesitatingly:

"I don't know exactly, but I think I could manage it with four hundred francs."

He had grown a little pale, because he was laying aside just that amount to buy a gun and treat himself to a little shooting next summer on the plain of Nanterre, with several friends who went to shoot larks down there, of a Sunday.

But he said:

"All right. I will give you four hundred francs. And try to have a pretty dress."

The day of the ball drew near, and Mme. Loisel seemed sad, uneasy, anxious. Her dress was ready, however. Her husband said to her one evening:

"What is the matter? Come, you've been so queer these last three days."

And she answered:

"It annoys me not to have a single jewel, not a single stone, nothing to put on. I shall look like distress. I should almost rather not go at all."

He resumed:

"You might wear natural flowers. It's very stylish at this time of the year. For ten francs you can get two or three magnificent roses."

She was not convinced.

"No; there's nothing more humiliating than to look poor among other women who are rich."

But her husband cried:

"How stupid you are! Go look up your friend Mme. Forestier, and ask her to lend you some jewels. You're quite thick enough with her to do that."

She uttered a cry of joy:

"It's true. I never thought of it."

The next day she went to her friend and told of her distress.

Mme. Forestier went to a wardrobe with a glass door, took out a large jewel-box, brought it back, opened it, and said to Mme. Loisel:

"Choose, my dear."

She saw first of all some bracelets, then a pearl necklace, then a Venetian cross, gold and precious stones of admirable workmanship. She tried on the ornaments before the glass, hesitated, could not make up her mind to part with them, to give them back. She kept asking:

"Haven't you any more?"

"Why, yes. Look. I don't know what you like."

All of a sudden she discovered, in a black satin box, a superb necklace of diamonds, and her heart began to beat with an immoderate desire. Her hands trembled as she took it. She fastened it around her throat, outside her high-necked dress, and remained lost in ecstasy at the sight of herself.

Then she asked, hesitating, filled with anguish:

"Can you lend me that, only that?"

"Why, yes, certainly."

She sprang upon the neck of her friend, kissed her passionately, then fled with her treasure.

The day of the ball arrived. Mme. Loisel made a great success. She was prettier than them all, elegant, gracious, smiling, and crazy with joy. All the men looked at her, asked her name, endeavored to be introduced. All the attachés of the Cabinet wanted to waltz with her. She was remarked by the minister himself.

She danced with intoxication, with passion, made drunk by pleasure, forgetting all, in the triumph of her beauty, in the glory of her success, in a sort of cloud of happiness composed of all this homage, of all this admiration, of all these awakened desires, and of that sense of complete victory which is so sweet to a woman's heart.

She went away about four o'clock in the morning. Her husband had been sleeping since midnight, in a little deserted anteroom, with three other gentlemen whose wives were having a very good time. He threw over her shoulders the wraps which he had brought, modest wraps of common life, whose poverty contrasted with the elegance of the ball dress. She felt this, and wanted to escape so as not to be remarked by the other women, who were enveloping themselves in costly furs.

Loisel held her back.

"Wait a bit. You will catch cold outside. I will go and call a cab."

But she did not listen to him, and rapidly descended the stairs. When they were in the street they did not find a carriage; and they began to look for one, shouting after the cabmen whom they saw passing by at a distance.

They went down toward the Seine, in despair, shivering with cold. At last they found on the quay one of those ancient noctambulant coupés which, exactly as if they were ashamed to show their misery during the day, are never seen round Paris until after nightfall.

It took them to their door in the Rue des Martyrs, and once more, sadly, they climbed up homeward. All was ended, for her. And as to him, he reflected that he must be at the Ministry at ten o'clock.

She removed the wraps which covered her shoulders, before the glass, so as once more to see herself in all her glory. But suddenly she uttered a cry. She no longer had the necklace around her neck!

Her husband, already half undressed, demanded:

"What is the matter with you?"

She turned madly towards him:

"I have—I have—I've lost Mme. Forestier's necklace."

He stood up, distracted.

"What!—how?—impossible!"

And they looked in the folds of her dress, in the folds of her cloak, in her pockets, everywhere. They did not find it.

He asked:

"You're sure you had it on when you left the ball?"

"Yes, I felt it in the vestibule of the palace."

"But if you had lost it in the street we should have heard it fall. It must be in the cab."

"Yes. Probably. Did you take his number?"

"No. And you, didn't you notice it?"

"No."

They looked, thunderstruck, at one another. At last Loisel put on his clothes.

"I shall go back on foot," said he, "over the whole route which we have taken to see if I can find it."

And he went out. She sat waiting on a chair in her ball dress, without strength to go to bed, overwhelmed, without fire, without a thought.

Her husband came back about seven o'clock. He had found nothing.

He went to Police Headquarters, to the newspaper offices, to offer a reward; he went to the cab companies—everywhere, in fact, whither he was urged by the least suspicion of hope.

She waited all day, in the same condition of mad fear before this terrible calamity.

Loisel returned at night with a hollow, pale face; he had discovered nothing.

"You must write to your friend," said he, "that you have broken the clasp of her necklace and that you are having it mended. That will give us time to turn round."

She wrote at his dictation.

At the end of a week they had lost all hope.

And Loisel, who had aged five years, declared:

"We must consider how to replace that ornament."

The next day they took the box which had contained it, and they went to the jeweler whose name was found within. He consulted his books.

"It was not I, madame, who sold that necklace; I must simply have furnished the case."

Then they went from jeweler to jeweler, searching for a necklace like the other, consulting their memories, sick both of them with chagrin and anguish.

They found, in a shop at the Palais Royal, a string of diamonds which seemed to them exactly like the one they looked for. It was worth forty thousand francs. They could have it for thirty-six.

So they begged the jeweler not to sell it for three days yet. And they made a bargain that he should buy it back for thirty-four thousand francs, in case they found the other one before the end of February.

Loisel possessed eighteen thousand francs which his father had left him. He would borrow the rest.

He did borrow, asking a thousand francs of one, five hundred of another, five louis[3] here, three louis there. He gave notes, took up ruinous obligations, dealt with usurers and all the race of lenders. He compromised all the rest of his life, risked his signature without even knowing if he could meet it; and, frightened by the pains yet to come, by the black misery which was about to fall upon him, by the prospect of all the physical privation and of all the moral tortures which he was to suffer, he went to get the new necklace, putting down upon the merchant's counter thirty-six thousand francs.

When Mme. Loisel took back the necklace, Mme. Forestier said to her, with a chilly manner:

"You should have returned it sooner; I might have needed it."

She did not open the case, as her friend had so much feared. If she had detected the substitution, what would she have thought, what would she have said? Would she not have taken Mme. Loisel for a thief?

Mme. Loisel now knew the horrible existence of the needy. She took her part, moreover, all of a sudden, with heroism. That dreadful debt must be paid. She would pay it. They dismissed their servant; they changed their lodgings; they rented a garret under the roof.

She came to know what heavy housework meant and the odious cares of the kitchen. She washed the dishes, using her rosy nails on the greasy pots and pans. She washed the dirty linen, the shirts, and the dishcloths, which she dried upon a line; she carried the slops down to the street every morning, and carried up the water, stopping for breath at every landing. And, dressed like a woman of the people, she went to the fruiterer, the grocer, the butcher, her basket on her arm, bargaining, insulted, defending her miserable money sou by sou.

Each month they had to meet some notes, renew others, obtain more time.

Her husband worked in the evening making a fair copy of some tradesman's accounts, and late at night he often copied manuscript for five sous a page.

And this life lasted for ten years.

At the end of ten years, they had paid everything, everything, with the rates of usury, and the accumulations of the compound interest.

Mme. Loisel looked old now. She had become the woman of impoverished households—strong and hard and rough. With frowsy hair, skirts askew, and red hands, she talked loud while washing the floor with great swishes of water. But sometimes, when her husband was at the office, she sat down near the window, and she thought of that gay evening of long ago, of the ball where she had been so beautiful and so fêted.

What would have happened if she had not lost that necklace? Who knows? Who knows? How life is strange and changeful! How little a thing is needed for us to be lost or to be saved!

But, one Sunday, having gone to take a walk in the Champs Elysées to refresh herself from the labor of the week, she suddenly perceived a woman who was leading a child. It was Mme. Forestier, still young, still beautiful, still charming.

[3] A *louis* was worth 20 francs.

Mme. Loisel felt moved. Was she going to speak to her? Yes, certainly. And now that she had paid, she was going to tell her all about it. Why not?

She went up.

"Good-day, Jeanne."

The other, astonished to be familiarly addressed by this plain goodwife, did not recognize her at all, and stammered:

"But—madam!—I do not know—You must be mistaken."

"No. I am Mathilde Loisel."

Her friend uttered a cry.

"Oh, my poor Mathilde! How you are changed!"

"Yes, I have had days hard enough, since I have seen you, days wretched enough—and that because of you!"

"Of me! How so?"

"Do you remember that diamond necklace which you lent me to wear at the ministerial ball?"

"Yes. Well?"

"Well, I lost it."

"What do you mean? You brought it back."

"I brought you back another just like it. And for this we have been ten years paying. You can understand that it was not easy for us, us who had nothing. At last it is ended, and I am very glad."

Mme. Forestier had stopped.

"You say that you bought a necklace of diamonds to replace mine?"

"Yes. You never noticed it, then! They were very like."

And she smiled with a joy which was proud and naïve at once.

Mme. Forestier, strongly moved, took her two hands.

"Oh, my poor Mathilde! Why, my necklace was paste.[4] It was worth at most five hundred francs!"

[1884]

Translated by
MARJORIE LAURIE

QUESTIONS

1. What values motivate Mme. Loisel? Does the story suggest that she is appropriately chastened or that she pays too dearly for her social aspirations?
2. How does Mme. Loisel change during the 10 years after she loses the necklace? What might her life have been if the misfortune had not occurred?
3. Why does the story conclude before Mme. Loisel responds to Mme. Forestier's revelation about the necklace? Try to imagine her response.
4. What elements of the story are ironic? How does de Maupassant suggest the gap between appearances and reality?
5. What do you learn about the values and manners of the society in which the story is set? Is the author's judgment of those values revealed in the story?

[4]*paste* gems made from a hard, brilliant glass containing oxide of lead

RICHARD McCANN

(b. 1949)

UNITED STATES

Richard McCann grew up in Silver Spring, Maryland. His fiction and poetry have appeared in numerous periodicals, including *The Atlantic*, *Esquire*, and *Shenandoah*, and have been reprinted in *Editor's Choice: Best New Short Fiction for 1987*, *Men on Men 2: Best New Gay Fiction*, and *Poets for Life: 76 Poets Respond to AIDS*. He is also the author of a book of poems, *Dream of the Traveler*, and the editor (with Margaret Gibson) of *Landscape and Distance: Contemporary Poems from Virginia*. He has been Fulbright Lecturer in American Studies at Goteborgs Universitet (Sweden) and the Jenny Moore Writer-in-Washington at George Washington University. Currently he is codirector of the M.F.A. program at American University in Washington, DC.

When asked to comment on the genesis of "My Mother's Clothes," McCann provided the following information:

> My father was our household's official orator. He twice took evening courses in public speaking at a nearby Catholic college. Each time he was scheduled to give a speech, he wore his army uniform to class.
>
> But my mother believed that only secrets were real. Her stories were fraught with painful losses; her stories were suffused with griefs that couldn't be healed. She told me her father was an alcoholic who had died of exposure in an alleyway. She told me her mother had died in a sanatorium she had entered for depression. She died because she was sad, my mother explained. She died because she couldn't stop crying.
>
> "When I was a girl," she said, "I had a gold brush and comb set. When I was a girl, I had a silver fox coat." She said her parents had looked just like Scott and Zelda Fitzgerald.
>
> Sometimes, my mother showed photos of herself when she was young, taken during her first marriage. One had almost appeared in *Life*. On its back she had written, "I looked like Merle Oberon."
>
> She told me that if I was lucky I would inherit "the gift of gab."
>
> From her, I inherited the impulse toward fiction—an anxious dread of loss, and a fear that reality was obscure and best approached obliquely. But I was almost thirty-three before I tried to write stories of my own. Until then, for complicated reasons, I had only been trying to retell my mother's stories. In order to write fiction, however, I had to become willing to tell my own secrets on my own terms, even if those secrets were sometimes about my mother and me.

My Mother's Clothes: The School of Beauty and Shame

Like every corner house in Carroll Knolls, the corner house on our block was turned backward on its lot, a quirk introduced by the developer of the subdivision, who, having run short of money, sought variety without additional expense. The turned-around houses, as we kids called them, were not popular, perhaps because they seemed too public, their casement bedroom windows cranking open onto sunstruck asphalt streets. In actuality, however, it was the rest of the houses that were public, their picture windows offering dioramic glimpses of early-American sofas and Mediterranean-style pole lamps whose mottled globes hung like iridescent melons from wrought-iron chains. In order not to be seen walking across the living room to the kitchen in our pajamas, we had to close the venetian blinds. The corner house on our block was secretive, as though it had turned its back on all of us, whether in superiority or in shame, refusing to acknowledge even its own unkempt yard of yellowing zoysia grass. After its initial occupants moved away, the corner house remained vacant for months.

The spring I was in sixth grade, it was sold. When I came down the block from school, I saw a moving van parked at its curb. "Careful with that!" a woman was shouting at a mover as he unloaded a tiered end table from the truck. He stared at her in silence. The veneer had already been splintered from the table's edge, as though someone had nervously picked at it while watching TV. Then another mover walked from the truck carrying a child's bicycle, a wire basket bolted over its thick rear tire, brightly colored plastic streamers dangling from its handlebars.

The woman looked at me. "What have you got there? In your hand."

I was holding a scallop shell spray-painted gold, with imitation pearls glued along its edges. Mrs. Eidus, the art teacher who visited our class each Friday, had showed me how to make it.

"A hatpin tray," I said. "It's for my mother."

"It's real pretty." She glanced up the street as though trying to guess which house I belonged to. "I'm Mrs. Tyree," she said, "and I've got a boy about your age. His daddy's bringing him tonight in the new Plymouth. I bet you haven't sat in a new Plymouth."

"We have a Ford." I studied her housedress, tiny blue and purple flowers imprinted on thin cotton, a line of white buttons as large as Necco Wafers marching toward its basted hemline. She was the kind of mother my mother laughed at for cutting recipes out of *Woman's Day*. Staring from our picture window, my mother would sometimes watch the neighborhood mothers drag their folding chairs into a circle on someone's lawn. "There they go," she'd say, "a regular meeting of the Daughters of the Eastern Star!" "They're hardly even *women*," she'd whisper to my father, "and their *clothes*." She'd criticize their appearance — their loud nylon scarves tied beneath their chins, their disintegrating figures stuffed into pedal pushers — until my father, worried that my brother, Davis, and I could hear, although laughing himself, would beg her, "Stop it, Maria, please stop; it isn't funny." But she wouldn't stop, not ever. "Not even thirty and they look like they belong to the DAR! They wear their pearls inside their bosoms in case the rope should break!" She was the oldest mother on the block but she was the most glamorous, sitting alone on the front lawn in her sleek kick-pleated skirts and cashmere sweaters, reading her thick paperback novels, whose bindings had split. Her hair was lightly hennaed, so that when I saw her pillowcases piled atop the washer, they seemed dusted with powdery rouge. She had once lived in New York City.

After dinner, when it was dark, I joined the other children congregated beneath the streetlamp across from the turned-around house. Bucky Trueblood, an eighth-grader who had once twisted the stems off my brother's eyeglasses, was crouched in the center, describing his mother's naked body to us elementary school children gathered around him, our faces slightly upturned, as though searching for a distant constellation, or for the bats that Bucky said would fly into our hair. I sat at the edge, one half of my body within the circle of light, the other half lost to darkness. When Bucky described his mother's nipples, which he'd glimpsed when she bent to kiss him good-night, everyone giggled; but when he described her genitals, which he'd seen by dropping his pencil on the floor and looking up her nightie while her feet were propped on a hassock as she watched TV, everyone huddled nervously together, as though listening to a ghost story that made them fear something dangerous in the nearby dark. "I don't believe you," someone said; "I'm telling you," Bucky said, "*that's what it looks like.*"

I slowly moved outside the circle. Across the street a cream-colored Plymouth was parked at the curb. In a lighted bedroom window Mrs. Tyree was hanging café curtains. Behind the chain link fence, within the low branches of a willow tree, the new child was standing in his yard. I could see his white T-shirt and the pale oval of his face, a face deprived of detail by darkness and distance. Behind him, at the open bedroom window, his mother slowly fiddled with a valance. Behind me the children sat spellbound beneath the light. Then Bucky jumped up and pointed in the new child's direction — "Hey, you, you want to hear something really *good*?" — and even before the others had a chance to spot him, he vanished as suddenly and completely as an imaginary playmate.

The next morning, as we waited at our bus stop, he loitered by the mailbox on the opposite corner, not crossing the street until the yellow school bus pulled up and flung open its door. Then he dashed aboard and sat down beside me. "I'm Denny," he said. Denny: a heavy, unbeautiful child, who, had his parents stayed in their native Kentucky, would have been a farm boy, but who in Carroll Knolls seemed to belong to no particular world at all, walking past the identical ranch houses in his overalls and Keds, his whitish-blond hair close-cropped all around except for the distinguishing, stigmatizing feature of a wave that crested perfectly just above his forehead, a wave that neither rose nor fell, a wave he trained with Hopalong Cassidy hair tonic, a wave he tended fussily, as though it were the only loveliness he allowed himself.

What in Carroll Knolls might have been described by someone not native to those parts — a visiting expert, say — as *beautiful*, capable of arousing terror and joy? The brick ramblers strung with multicolored Christmas lights? The occasional front-yard plaster Virgin entrapped within a chicken-wire grotto entwined with plastic roses? The spring Denny moved to Carroll Knolls, I begged my parents to take me to a nightclub, had begged so hard for months, in fact, that by summer they finally agreed to a Sunday matinee. Waiting in the backseat of our Country Squire, a red bow tie clipped to my collar, I watched our house float like a mirage behind the sprinkler's web of water. The front door opened, and a white dress fluttered within the mirage's ascending waves: Slipping on her sunglasses, my mother emerged onto the concrete stoop, adjusted her shoulder strap, and teetered across the wet grass in new spectator shoes. Then my father stepped out and cut the sprinkler off. We drove — the warm breeze inside the car sweetened by my mother's Shalimar — past ranch houses tethered to yards by chain link fences; past the Silver Spring Volunteer Fire Department and Carroll Knolls Elementary School; past the Polar Bear Soft-Serv stand, its white stucco siding shimmery with mirror shards; past a bulldozed red-clay field where a weathered billboard advertised IF YOU LIVED HERE YOU'D BE HOME BY NOW, until we arrived at the border — a line of cinder-block discount liquor stores, a traffic light — of Washington, D.C. The light turned red. We stopped. The breeze died and the Shalimar fell from the air. Exhaust fumes mixed with the smell of hot tar. A drunk man stumbled into the crosswalk, followed by an old woman shielding herself from the sun with an orange umbrella, and two teenaged boys dribbling a basketball back and forth between them. My mother put down her sun visor. "Lock your door," she said.

Then the light changed, releasing us into another country. The station wagon sailed down boulevards of Chinese elms and flowering Bradford pears, through hot, dense streets where black families sat on wooden chairs at curbs, along old streetcar tracks that caused the tires to shimmy and the car to swerve, onto Pennsylvania Avenue, past the White House, encircled by its fence of iron spears, and down 14th Street, past the Treasury Building, until at last we reached the Neptune Room, a cocktail lounge in the basement of a shabbily elegant hotel.

Inside, the Neptune Room's walls were painted with garish mermaids reclining seductively on underwater rocks, and human frogmen who stared longingly through their diving helmets' glass masks at a loveliness they could not possess on dry earth. On stage, leaning against the baby grand piano, a *chanteuse* (as my mother called her) was singing of her grief, her wrists weighted with rhinestone bracelets, a single blue spotlight making her seem like one who lived, as did the mermaids, underwater.

I was transfixed. I clutched my Roy Rogers cocktail (the same as a Shirley Temple, but without the cheerful, girlish grenadine) tight in my fist. In the middle of "The Man I Love" I stood and struggled toward the stage.

I strayed into the spotlight's soft-blue underwater world. Close up, from within the light, the singer was a boozy, plump peroxide blonde in a tight black cocktail dress; but these indiscretions made her yet more lovely, for they showed what she had lost, just as her songs seemed to carry her backward into endless regret. When I got close to her, she extended one hand — red nails, a huge glass ring — and seized one of mine.

"Why, what kind of little sailor have we got here?" she asked the audience.

I stared through the border of blue light and into the room, where I saw my parents gesturing, although whether they were telling me to step closer to her microphone or to step farther away, I could not tell. The whole club was staring.

"Maybe he knows a song!" a man shouted from the back.

"Sing with me," she whispered. "What can you sing?"

I wanted to lift her microphone from its stand and bow deeply from the waist, as Judy Garland did on her weekly TV show. But I could not. As she began to sing, I stood voiceless, pressed against the protection of her black dress; or, more accurately, I stood beside her, silently lip-syncing to myself. I do not recall what she sang, although I do recall a quick, farcical ending in which she falsettoed, like Betty Boop, "Gimme a Little Kiss, Will Ya, Huh?" and brushed my forehead with pursed red lips.

That summer, humidity enveloping the landfill subdivision, Denny, "the new kid," stood on the boundaries, while we neighborhood boys played War, a game in which someone stood on Stanley Allen's front porch and machine-gunned the rest of us, who one by one clutched our bellies, coughed as if choking on blood, and rolled in exquisite death throes down the grassy hill. When Stanley's father came up the walk from work, he ducked imaginary bullets. "Hi, Dad," Stanley would call, rising from the dead to greet him. Then we began the game again: Whoever died best in the last round got to kill in the next. Later, after dusk, we'd smear the wings of balsa planes with glue, ignite them, and send them flaming through the dark on kamikaze missions. Long after the streets were deserted, we children sprawled beneath the corner streetlamp, praying our mothers would not call us—"*Time to come in!*"—back to our ovenlike houses; and then sometimes Bucky, hoping to scare the elementary school kids, would lead his solemn procession of junior high "hoods" down the block, their penises hanging from their unzipped trousers.

Denny and I began to play together, first in secret, then visiting each other's houses almost daily, and by the end of the summer I imagined him to be my best friend. Our friendship was sealed by our shared dread of junior high school. Davis, who had just finished seventh grade, brought back reports of corridors so long that one could get lost in them, of gangs who fought to control the lunchroom and the bathrooms. The only safe place seemed to be the Health Room, where a pretty nurse let you lie down on a cot behind a folding screen. Denny told me about a movie he'd seen in which the children, all girls, did not have to go to school at all but were taught at home by a beautiful governess, who, upon coming to their rooms each morning, threw open their shutters so that sunlight fell like bolts of satin across their beds, whispered their pet names while kissing them, and combed their long hair with a silver brush. "She never got mad," said Denny, beating his fingers up and down through the air as though striking a keyboard, "except once when some old man told the girls they could never play piano again."

With my father at work in the Pentagon and my mother off driving the two-tone Welcome Wagon Chevy to new subdivisions, Denny and I spent whole days in the gloom of my living room, the picture window's venetian blinds closed against an August sun so fierce that it bleached the design from the carpet. Dreaming of fabulous prizes—sets of matching Samsonite luggage, French Provincial bedroom suites, Corvettes, jet flights to Hawaii—we watched Jan Murray's "Treasure Hunt" and Bob Barker's "Truth or Consequences" (a name that seemed strangely threatening). We watched "The Loretta Young Show," worshipping yet critiquing her elaborate gowns. When "The Early Show" came on, we watched old Bette Davis, Gene Tierney, and Joan Crawford movies—*Dark Victory, Leave Her to Heaven, A Woman's Face.* Hoping to become their pen pals, we wrote long letters to fading movie stars, who in turn sent us autographed photos we traded between ourselves. We searched the house for secrets, like contraceptives, Kotex, and my mother's hidden supply of Hershey bars. And finally, Denny and I, running to the front window every few minutes to make sure no one was coming unexpectedly up the sidewalk, inspected the secrets of my mother's dresser: her satin nightgowns and padded brassieres, folded atop pink drawer liners and scattered with loose sachet; her black mantilla, pressed inside a shroud of lilac tissue paper; her heart-shaped candy box, a flapper doll strapped to its lid with a ribbon, from which spilled galaxies of cocktail rings and cultured pearls. Small shrines to deeper intentions, private grottoes of yearning: her triangular cloisonné earrings, her brooch of enameled butterfly wings.

Because beauty's source was longing, it was infused with romantic sorrow; because beauty was defined as "feminine," and therefore as "other," it became hopelessly confused with my mother: Mother, who quickly sorted through new batches of photographs, throwing unflattering shots of herself directly into the fire before they could be seen. Mother, who dramatized herself, telling us and our playmates, "My name is Maria Dolores; in Spanish, that means 'Mother of Sorrows,'" Mother, who had once wished to be a writer and who said, looking up briefly from whatever she was reading, "Books are my best friends." Mother, who read aloud from Whitman's *Leaves of Grass* and O'Neill's *Long Day's Journey Into Night* with a voice so grave I could not tell the difference between them. Mother, who lifted cut-glass vases and antique clocks from her obsessively dusted curio shelves to ask, "If this could talk, what story would it tell?"

And more, always more, for she was the only woman in our house, a "people-watcher," a "talker," a woman whose mysteries and moods seemed endless: Our Mother of the White Silk Gloves; Our Mother of the Veiled Hats; Our Mother of the Paper Lilacs; Our Mother of the Sighs and Heartaches; Our Mother of the Gorgeous Gypsy Earrings; Our Mother of the Late Movies and the Cigarettes; Our Mother whom I adored and who, in adoring, I ran from, knowing it "wrong" for a son to wish to be like his mother; Our Mother who wished to influence us, passing the best of herself along, yet who held the fear common to that era, the fear that by loving a son too intensely she would render him unfit—"Momma's boy," "tied to apron strings"—and who therefore alternately drew us close and sent us away, believing a son needed "male influence" in large doses, that female influence was pernicious except as a final finishing, like manners; Our Mother of the Mixed Messages; Our Mother of Sudden Attentiveness; Our Mother of Sudden Distances; Our Mother of Anger; Our Mother of Apology. The simplest objects of her life, objects scattered accidentally about the house, became my shrines to beauty, my grottoes of romantic sorrow: her Revlon lipstick tubes, "Cherries in the Snow"; her Art Nouveau atomizers on the blue mirror top of her vanity; her pastel silk scarves knotted to a wire hanger in her closet; her white handkerchiefs blotted with red mouths. Voiceless objects; silences. The world halved with a cleaver: "masculine," "feminine." In these ways was the plainest ordinary love made complicated and grotesque. And in these ways was beauty, already confused with the "feminine," also confused with shame, for all these longings were secret, and to control me all my brother had to do was to threaten to expose that Denny and I were dressing ourselves in my mother's clothes.

Denny chose my Mother's drabbest outfits, as though he were ruled by the deepest of modesties, or by his family's austere Methodism: a pink wraparound skirt from which the color had been laundered, its hem almost to his ankles; a sleeveless white cotton blouse with a Peter Pan collar; a small straw summer clutch. But he seemed to challenge his own primness, as though he dared it with his "effects": an undershirt worn over his head to approximate cascading hair; gummed hole-punch reinforcements pasted to his fingernails so that his hands, palms up, might look like a woman's—flimsy crescent moons waxing above his fingertips.

He dressed slowly, hesitantly, but once dressed, he was a manic Proteus metamorphosing into contradictory, half-realized forms, throwing his "long hair" back and balling it violently into a French twist; tapping his paper nails on the glass-topped vanity as though he were an important woman kept waiting at a cosmetics counter; stabbing his nails into the air as though he were an angry teacher assigning an hour of detention; touching his temple as though he were a shy schoolgirl tucking back a wisp of stray hair; resting his fingertips on the rim of his glass of Kool-Aid as though he were an actress seated over an ornamental cocktail—a Pink Lady, say, or a Silver Slipper. Sometimes, in an orgy of jerky movement, his gestures overtaking him with greater and greater force, a dynamo of theatricality unleashed, he would hurl himself across the room like a mad girl having a fit, or like one possessed; or he would snatch the chenille spread from my parents' bed and drape it over his head to fashion for himself the long train of a bride. "Do you like it?" he'd ask anxiously, making me his mirror. "Does it look *real*?" He wanted, as did I, to become something he'd neither yet seen nor dreamed of, something he'd recognize the moment he saw it: himself. Yet he was constantly confounded, for no matter how much he adorned himself with scarves and jewelry, he could not understand that this was himself, as was also and at the same time the boy in overalls and Keds. He was split in two pieces—as who was not?—the blond wave cresting rigidly above his close-cropped hair.

"He makes me nervous," I heard my father tell my mother one night as I lay in bed. They were speaking about me. That morning I'd stood awkwardly on the front lawn—"Maybe you should go help your father," my mother had said—while he propped an extension ladder against the house, climbed up through power lines he separated with his bare hands, and staggered across the pitched roof he was reshingling. When his hammer slid down the incline, catching on the gutter, I screamed, "You're falling!" Startled, he almost fell.

"He needs to spend more time with you," I heard my mother say.

I couldn't sleep. Out in the distance a mother was calling her child home. A screen door slammed. I heard cicadas, their chorus as steady and loud as the hum of a power line. *He needs to spend more time with you.* Didn't she know? Saturday mornings, when he stood in his rubber hip boots fishing off the shore of Triadelphia Reservoir, I was afraid of the slimy bottom and could not wade after him; for whatever reasons of his own—something as simple as shyness, perhaps—he could not come to get me. I sat in the parking lot drinking Tru-Ade and reading *Betty and Veronica*, wondering if Denny had walked alone to Wheaton Plaza, where the weekend manager of Port-o'-Call allowed us to Windex the illuminated glass shelves that held Lladro figurines, the porcelain ballerina's hands so realistic one could see tiny life and heart lines etched into her palms. *He needs to spend more time with you.* Was she planning to discontinue the long summer afternoons that she and I spent together when there were no new families for her to greet in her Welcome Wagon car? "I don't feel like being alone today," she'd say, inviting me to sit on their chenille bedspread and watch her model new clothes in her mirror. Behind her an oscillating fan fluttered nylons and scarves she'd heaped, discarded, on a chair. "Should I wear the red belt with this dress or the black one?" she'd ask, turning suddenly toward me and cinching her waist with her hands.

Afterward we would sit together at the rattan table on the screened-in porch, holding cocktail napkins around sweaty glasses of iced Russian tea and listening to big-band music on the Zenith.

"You look so pretty," I'd say. Sometimes she wore outfits I'd selected for her from her closet—pastel chiffon dresses, an apricot blouse with real mother-of-pearl buttons.

One afternoon she leaned over suddenly and shut off the radio. "You know you're going to leave me one day," she said. When I put my arms around her, smelling the dry carnation talc she wore in hot weather, she stood up and marched out of the room. When she returned, she was wearing Bermuda shorts and a plain cotton blouse. "Let's wait for your father on the stoop," she said.

Late that summer—the summer before he died—my father took me with him to Fort Benjamin Harrison, near Indianapolis, where, as a colonel in the U.S. Army Reserves, he did his annual tour of duty. On the propjet he drank bourbon and read newspapers while I made a souvenir packet for Denny: an airsickness bag, into which I placed the Chiclets given me by the stewardess to help pop my ears during takeoff, and the laminated white card that showed the location of emergency exits. Fort Benjamin Harrison looked like Carroll Knolls: hundreds of acres of concrete and sun-scorched shrubbery inside a cyclone fence. Daytimes I waited for my father in the dining mess with the sons of other officers, drinking chocolate milk that came from a silver machine, and desultorily setting fires in ashtrays. When he came to collect me, I walked behind him—gold braid hung from his epaulets—while enlisted men saluted us and opened doors. At night, sitting in our BOQ room, he asked me questions about myself: "Are you looking forward to seventh grade?" "What do you think you'll want to be?" When these topics faltered—I stammered what I hoped were right answers—we watched TV, trying to preguess lines of dialogue on reruns of his favorite shows, "The Untouchables" and "Rawhide." "That Della Street," he said as we watched "Perry Mason," "is almost as pretty as your mother." On the last day, eager to make the trip memorable, he brought me a gift: a glassine envelope filled with punched IBM cards that told me my life story as his secretary had typed it into the office computer. Card One: *You live at 10406 Lillians Mill Court, Silver Spring, Maryland.* Card Two: *You are entering seventh grade.* Card Three: *Last year your teacher was Mrs. Dillard.* Card Four: *Your favorite color is blue.* Card Five: *You love the Kingston Trio.* Card Six: *You love basketball and football.* Card Seven: *Your favorite sport is swimming.*

Whose son did these cards describe? The address was correct, as was the teacher's name and the favorite color; and he'd remembered that one morning during breakfast I'd put a dime in the jukebox and played the Kingston Trio's song about "the man who never returned." But whose fiction was the rest? Had I, who played no sport other than kickball and Kitty-Kitty-Kick-the-Can, lied to him when he asked me about myself? Had he not heard from my mother the outcome of the previous summer's swim lessons? At the swim club a young man in black trunks had taught us, as we held hands, to dunk ourselves in water, surface, and then go down. When he had told her to let go of me, I had thrashed across the surface, violently afraid I'd sink. But perhaps I had not lied to him; perhaps he merely did not wish to see. It was my job, I felt, to reassure him that I was the son he imagined me to be, perhaps because the role of reassurer gave me power. In any case, I thanked him for the computer cards. I thanked him the way a father thanks a child for a well-intentioned gift he'll never use—a set of handkerchiefs, say, on which the embroidered swirls construct a monogram of no particular initial, and which thus might be used by anyone.

As for me, when I dressed in my mother's clothes, I seldom moved at all: I held myself rigid before the mirror. The kind of beauty I'd seen practiced in movies and in fashion magazines was beauty attained by lacquered stasis, beauty attained by fixed poses—"ladylike stillness," the stillness of mannequins, the stillness of models "caught" in mid-gesture, the stillness of the passive moon around which active meteors orbited and burst. My costume was of the greatest solemnity: I dressed like the *chanteuse* in the Neptune Room, carefully shimmying my mother's black slip over my head so as not to stain it with Brylcreem, draping her black mantilla over my bare shoulders, clipping her rhinestone dangles to my ears. Had I at that time already seen the movie in which French women who had fraternized with German soldiers were made to shave their heads and walk through the streets, jeered by their fellow villagers? And if so, did I imagine myself to be one of the collaborators, or one of the villagers, taunting her from the curb? I ask because no matter how elaborate my costume, I made no effort to camouflage my crew cut or my male body.

How did I perceive myself in my mother's triple-mirrored vanity, its endless repetitions? I saw myself as doubled—both an image and he who studied it. I saw myself as beautiful, and guilty: The lipstick made my mouth seem the ripest rose, or a wound; the small rose on the black slip opened like my mother's heart disclosed, or like the Sacred Heart of Mary, aflame and pierced by arrows; the mantilla transformed me into a Mexican penitent or a Latin movie star, like Dolores Del Rio. The mirror was a silvery stream: On the far side, in a clearing, stood the woman who was icily immune from the boy's terror and contempt; on the close side, in the bedroom, stood the boy who feared and yet longed after her inviolability. (Perhaps, it occurs to me now, this doubleness is the source of drag queens' vulnerable ferocity.) Sometimes, when I saw that person in the mirror, I felt as though I had at last been lifted from that dull, locked room, with its mahogany bedroom suite and chalky blue walls. But other times, particularly when I saw Denny and me together, so that his reality shattered my fantasies, we seemed merely ludicrous and sadly comic, as though we were dressed in the garments of another species, like dogs in human clothes. I became aware of my spatulate hands, my scarred knees, my large feet; I became aware of the drooping, unfilled bodice of my slip. Like Denny, I could neither dispense with images nor take their flexibility as pleasure, for the idea of self I had learned and was learning still was that one was constructed by one's images—"*When boys cross their legs, they cross one ankle atop the knee*"—so that one finally sought the protection of believing in one's own image and, in believing in it as reality, condemned oneself to its poverty.

(That locked room. My mother's vanity; my father's highboy. If Denny and I, still in our costumes, had left that bedroom, its floor strewn with my mother's shoes and handbags, and gone through the darkened living room, out onto the sunstruck porch, down the sidewalk, and up the street, how would we have carried ourselves? Would we have walked boldly, chattering extravagantly back and forth between ourselves, like drag queens refusing to acknowledge the stares of contempt that are meant to halt them? Would we have walked humbly, with the calculated, impervious piety of the condemned walking barefoot to the public scaffold? Would we have walked simply, as deeply accustomed to the normalcy of our own strangeness as Siamese twins? Or would we have walked gravely, a solemn procession, like Bucky Trueblood's gang, their manhood hanging from their unzipped trousers?

(We were eleven years old. Why now, more than two decades later, do I wonder for the first time how we would have carried ourselves through a publicness we would have neither sought nor dared? I am six feet two inches tall; I weigh 198 pounds. Given my size, the question I am most often asked about my youth is "What football position did you play?" Overseas I am most commonly taken to be a German or a Swede. Right now, as I write this, I am wearing L. L. Bean khaki trousers, a LaCoste shirt, Weejuns: the anonymous American costume, although partaking also of certain signs of sexual orientation, this costume having become the standard garb of the urban American gay man. Why do I tell you these things? Am I trying—not subtly—to inform us of my "maleness," to reassure us that I have "survived" without noticeable "complexes"? Or is this my urge, my constant urge, to complicate my portrait of myself to both of us, so that I might layer my selves like so many multicolored crinoline slips, each rustling as I walk? When the wind blows, lifting my skirt, I do not know which slip will be revealed.)

Sometimes, while Denny and I were dressing up, Davis would come home unexpectedly from the bowling alley, where he'd been hanging out since entering junior high. At the bowling alley he was courting the protection of Bucky's gang.

"Let me in!" he'd demand, banging fiercely on the bedroom door, behind which Denny and I were scurrying to wipe the makeup off our faces with Kleenex.

"We're not doing anything," I'd protest, buying time.

"Let me in this minute or I'll tell!"

Once in the room, Davis would police the wreckage we'd made, the emptied hatboxes, the scattered jewelry, the piled skirts and blouses. "You'd better clean this up right now," he'd warn. "You two make me *sick*."

Yet his scorn seemed modified by awe. When he helped us rehang the clothes in the closet and replace the jewelry in the candy box, a sullen accomplice destroying someone else's evidence, he sometimes handled the garments as though they were infused with something of himself, although at the precise moment when he seemed to find them loveliest, holding them close, he would cast them down.

After our dress-up sessions Denny would leave the house without good-byes. I was glad to see him go. We would not see each other for days, unless we met by accident; we never referred to what we'd done the last time we'd been together. We met like those who have murdered are said to meet, each tentatively and warily examining the other for signs of betrayal. But whom had we murdered? The boys who walked into that room? Or the women who briefly came to life within it? Perhaps this metaphor has outlived its meaning. Perhaps our shame derived not from our having killed but from our having created.

In early September, as Denny and I entered seventh grade, my father became ill. Over Labor Day weekend he was too tired to go fishing. On Monday his skin had vaguely yellowed; by Thursday he was severely jaundiced. On Friday he entered the hospital, his liver rapidly failing; Sunday he was dead. He died from acute hepatitis, possibly acquired while cleaning up after our sick dog, the doctor said. He was buried at Arlington National Cemetery, down the hill from the Tomb of the Unknown Soldier. After the twenty-one-gun salute, our mother pinned his colonel's insignia to our jacket lapels. I carried the flag from his coffin to the car. For two weeks I stayed home with my mother, helping her write thank-you notes on small white cards with black borders; one afternoon, as I was affixing postage to the square, plain envelopes, she looked at me across the dining room table. "You and Davis are all I have left," she said. She went into the kitchen and came back. "Tomorrow," she said, gathering up the note cards, "you'll have to go to school." Mornings I wandered the long corridors alone, separated from Denny by the fate of our last names, which had cast us into different homerooms and daily schedules. Lunchtimes we sat together in silence in the rear of the cafeteria. Afternoons, just before gym class, I went to the Health Room, where, lying on a cot, I'd imagine the Phys. Ed. coach calling my name from the class roll, and imagine my name, unclaimed, unanswered to, floating weightlessly away, like a balloon that one jumps to grab hold of but that is already out of reach. Then I'd hear the nurse dial the telephone. "He's sick again," she'd say. "Can you come pick him up?" At home I helped my mother empty my father's highboy. "No, we want to save that," she said when I folded his uniform into a huge brown bag that read GOODWILL INDUSTRIES; I wrapped it in a plastic dry-cleaner's bag and hung it in the hall closet.

After my father's death my relationship to my mother's things grew yet more complex, for as she retreated into her grief, she left behind only her mute objects as evidence of her life among us: objects that seemed as lonely and vulnerable as she was, objects that I longed to console, objects with which I longed to console myself—a tangled gold chain, thrown in frustration on the mantel; a wineglass, its rim stained with lipstick, left unwashed in the sink. Sometimes at night Davis and I heard her prop her pillow up against her bedroom wall, lean back heavily, and tune her radio to a call-in show: "*Nightcaps, what are you thinking at this late hour?*" Sunday evenings, in order to help her prepare for the next day's job hunt, I stood over her beneath the bare basement bulb, the same bulb that first illuminated my father's jaundice. I set her hair, slicking each wet strand with gel and rolling it, inventing gossip that seemed to draw us together, a beautician and his customer.

"You have such pretty hair," I'd say.

"At my age, don't you think I should cut it?" She was almost fifty.

"No, never."

That fall Denny and I were caught. One evening my mother noticed something out of place in her closet. (Perhaps now that she no longer shared it, she knew where every belt and scarf should have been.)

I was in my bedroom doing my French homework, dreaming of one day visiting Au Printemps, the store my teacher spoke of so excitedly as she played us the Edith Piaf records that she had brought back from France. In the mirror above my desk I saw my mother appear at my door.

"Get into the living room," she said. Her anger made her small, reflected body seem taut and dangerous.

In the living room Davis was watching TV with Uncle Joe, our father's brother, who sometimes came to take us fishing. Uncle Joe was lying in our father's La-Z-Boy recliner.

"There aren't going to be any secrets in this house," she said. "You've been in my closet. What were you doing there?"

"No, we weren't," I said. "We were watching TV all afternoon."

"*We*? Was Denny here with you? Don't you think I've heard about that? Were you and Denny going through my clothes? Were you wearing them?"

"No, Mom," I said.

"Don't lie!" She turned to Uncle Joe, who was staring at us. "Make him stop! He's lying to me!"

She slapped me. Although I was already taller than she, she slapped me over and over, slapped me across the room until I was backed against the TV. Davis was motionless, afraid. But Uncle Joe jumped up and stood between my mother and me, holding her until her rage turned to sobs. "I can't, I can't be both a mother and a father," she said to him. "I can't do it." I could not look at Uncle Joe, who, although he was protecting me, did not know I was lying.

She looked at me. "We'll discuss this later," she said. "Get out of my sight."

We never discussed it. Denny was outlawed. I believe, in fact, that it was I who suggested he never be allowed in our house again. I told my mother I hated him. I do not think I was lying when I said this. I truly hated him — hated him, I mean, for being me.

For two or three weeks Denny tried to speak with me at the bus stop, but whenever he approached, I busied myself with kids I barely knew. After a while Denny found a new best friend, Lee, a child despised by everyone, for Lee was "effeminate." His clothes were too fastidious; he often wore his cardigan over his shoulders, like an old woman feeling a chill. Sometimes, watching the street from our picture window, I'd see Lee walking toward Denny's house. "What a queer," I'd say to whoever might be listening. "He walks like a *girl*." Or sometimes, at the junior high school, I'd see him and Denny walking down the corridor, their shoulders pressed together as if they were telling each other secrets, or as if they were joined in mutual defense. Sometimes when I saw them, I turned quickly away, as though I'd forgotten something important in my locker. But when I felt brave enough to risk rejection, for I belonged to no group, I joined Bucky Trueblood's gang, sitting on the radiator in the main hall, and waited for Lee and Denny to pass us. As Lee and Denny got close, they stiffened and looked straight ahead.

"Faggots," I muttered.

I looked at Bucky, sitting in the middle of the radiator. As Lee and Denny passed, he leaned forward from the wall, accidentally disarranging the practiced severity of his clothes, his jeans puckering beneath his tooled belt, the breast pocket of his T-shirt drooping with the weight of a pack of Pall Malls. He whistled. Lee and Denny flinched. He whistled again. Then he leaned back, the hard lines of his body reasserting themselves, his left foot striking a steady beat on the tile floor with the silver V-tap of his black loafer.

[1986]

QUESTIONS

1. Why is so much detail given over to Carroll Knolls at the beginning of the story?
2. Would "Mother" be an equally appropriate title for the story? Why does McCann give his story a subtitle ("The School of Beauty and Shame")?
3. If the paragraph in parentheses (describing the narrator's future) had been omitted, would our interpretation of the story and understanding of the narrator be significantly altered?
4. What importance does Davis play in the story?
5. Why does the narrator turn so strongly against Denny at the end of the story?

John McCluskey

(b. 1944)

United States

Beginning with Frederick Douglass, there is hardly a major African-American writer who hasn't written about the significance of music in black lives. In earlier literature, these remarks might have been about spirituals or the blues; more recently black writers have often focused on jazz. In "Living with Music," for example, Ralph Ellison has written,

> These jazzmen, many of them now world-famous, lived for and with music intensely. Their driving motivation was neither money nor fame, but the will to achieve the most eloquent expression of idea-emotions through the technical mystery of their instruments . . . and the give and take, the subtle rhythmical shaping and blending of idea, tone and imagination demanded of group improvisation. The delicate balance struck between strong individual personality and the group during those early jam sessions was a marvel of social organization.

As you read John McCluskey's "Lush Life," consider whether his story is a tale of individual musicians or of group dynamics.

John McCluskey has written two novels: *Look What They Done to My Song* (1974), about a young black musician, and *Mr. America's Last Season Blues* (1983), about a black athlete. He has also edited several volumes of African-American fiction and history. About his work, he has commented: "As a writer, my commitment is to that level of creative excellence so ably demonstrated by Afro-American artists as diverse as Ralph Ellison, Romare Bearden, and Miles Davis. Hoping to avoid any fashionable ambiguity and pedantry, I want my fiction and essays to heighten the appreciation of the complexities of Afro-American literature and life." McCluskey teaches at Indiana University at Bloomington.

◆ *Lush Life* ◆

Dayton, Ohio

Behind the dance hall the first of the car doors were banging shut, motors starting up, and from somewhere — a backyard, an alley — dogs barked. The band's bus was parked at one darkened corner of the parking lot. Empty, it was a mute and hulking barn in this hour. Along its side in slanted, bold-red letters was painted a sign: EARL FERGUSON AND AMERICA'S GREATEST BAND.

Suddenly the back door to the dance hall swung open and loud laughter rushed out on a thick pillow of cigarette smoke. Ahead of others, two men in suits — the taller one in plaids and the other in stripes — walked quickly, talking, smoking. They stopped at a convertible, a dark-red Buick, dew already sprouting across its canvas top. Other men, all members of the band, in twos or threes, would come up, slap their backs, share a joke or two, then drift toward the bus. In the light over the back door, moths played.

The shorter man, Billy Cox, took off his glasses, fogged the lenses twice, then cleaned them with his polka-dot silk square. He reached a hand toward Tommy, the bassist, approaching.

"I'm gone say, 'See y'all further up the road in Cleveland,'" Tommy said. "But after a night like tonight, it's gone be one hell of a struggle to tear ourselves from this town. Am I right about that, Billy C.?"

Tommy laughed, gold tooth showing, and patted his impeccable "do." More than once it had been said that Tommy sweated ice water. With his face dry, hair in place, tie straightened after three hours of furious work, no one could doubt it now.

Tommy spoke again, this time stern, wide-legged, and gesturing grandly. "Just you two don't get high and dry off into some damn ditch." His usual farewell slid toward a cackle. Billy waved him off.

In the Scout Car, Billy and Earl Ferguson would drive through the night to the next date. Throughout the night they would stay at least an hour or so ahead of the bus. They would breakfast and be nearly asleep by the time the bus pulled into the same hotel parking lot, the men emerging, looking stunned from a fitful sleep on a noisy bus.

From a nearby car a woman's throaty laugh lit up the night. They turned to see Pretty Horace leaning into a car, the passenger's side, smoothing down the back edges of his hair and rolling his rump as he ran his game.

"Man, stop your lying!" came her voice. She, too, was toying with the ends of her hair, dyed bright red and glowing in that light. Her friend from the driver's seat, with nothing better to do perhaps, leaned to hear, to signify, her face round as the moon's.

Moving with a pickpocket's stealth and slow grin spreading, Poo moved up to the driver's side of the car and whispered something. The driver jerked back, then gave him her best attention, smiling. One hand to her throat, she moistened her lips, glistened a smile.

In unison, Billy and Earl shook their heads while watching it all. Billy slid one hand down a lapel, pulled a cigarette from the corner of his mouth. "Some of the boys gone make a long night of this one."

Earl nodded. "Some mean mistreaters fixing to hit that bus late and do a whole lot of shucking, man."

Yes, some would dare the bus's deadline by tipping into an after-hours party, by following some smiling woman home. The rules were simple, however: if you missed the bus and could not make practice the next day, you were fined fifty dollars. If you missed the date because you missed the bus or train, you were fired. Daring these, you could seek adventure that broke the monotony of long road trips. You could bring stories that released bubbles of laughter throughout an overheated and smoke-filled bus.

Cars were rolling out of the side parking lot and, passing members of the band, the drivers honked in appreciation. Earl bowed slowly and waved an arm wide and high toward his men, some still walking out of the back door of the dance hall. Then he embraced Billy, mugged, and pointed to Billy's chest as if branding there all the credit for a magnificent night. After all, they had done Basie and Ellington to perfection. Their own original tunes had been wonders to behold. From the very beginning the audience had been with them and danced and danced, heads bobbing and shoulders rocking, cheering every solo. The dancers had fun on the stair step of every melody; hugging tightly, they did the slow grind to the promise of every ballad. Now they thanked the band again with the toot of their horns, shouts, and the wave of their hands.

Within an hour the bus would start up, all the equipment packed and stored below. Then it would roll slowly out of the parking lot. Some of the men would already be snoring. By the outskirts of town, a car might catch up to it, tires squealing as the car rocked to a stop. One of the men—usually McTee or "Rabbit" Ousley, as myth might have it—would climb out and blow a kiss to some grinning woman behind the wheel and strut onto the bus like some wide-legged conqueror. The doors to the bus would close behind him, sealing his stories from any verification and sealing them against the long, long night.

But it was the Buick, Earl and Billy inside, pulling away first. They would leave before these tales of triumph, outright lies about quick and furious love in a drafty back room or tales of a young wife whispering, "Run! Run!" and the scramble for a window after the husband's key slid into the lock downstairs. Yes, before all that, Earl and Billy would pull from the parking lot and start away, slow at first, like they had all the time in the world.

Well before the edge of town, they would have checked for cigarettes, surely, and from some magical place on a side street, a jukebox blaring and the smell of fried chicken meeting them at the door with its judas hole, they would find their coffee in Mason jars, coffee heavily sugared and creamed, and steaming chicken sandwiches wrapped neatly in waxed paper.

Older women, who would do double duty at Sunday church dinners, would smile and wipe their hands on their aprons. And bless them, these good and prodigal sons with conked hair. Then, moving toward the door, Billy and Earl would be greeted by achingly beautiful women with late night joy lacing their hoarse voices. Billy and Earl would take turns joking and pulling each other away, then, outside and laughing, climb back into the car for the journey through the night.

For the first few minutes, the lights of Dayton thinning, used car lots and a roller rink as outposts, they were silent before nervous energy swept over them. It was that unsettling bath of exhaustion and exuberance, rising to a tingle at the base of the neck, so familiar at the end of a performance. With Earl at the wheel, they began to harmonize and scat their way through "Take the A Train," "One O'Clock Jump," and their own wonderful collaboration, "October Mellow." In this way they would ride for a while. They would sing in ragged breaths before they gave out in laughter. The radio might go on, and there would be mostly the crackle of static, or, faintly, a late night gospel concert with harmonies rising and falling, like a prayer song tossed to the wind. Stray cars would rush past in the next lane, headed back toward Dayton. They passed a trailer groaning under its load, one or two squat Fords, then settled back. The night's first chapter was closed behind them with the noise from the motor, with smears of light.

Like a sudden tree in the car's lights, a sign sprouted and announced the city limits of Springfield.

Billy started nodding as if answering some ancient question. "Springfield got more fine women than they got in two St. Louises or five New Orleanses, I'm here to tell you."

"Wake up, Billy. Find me a place with women finer than they got in St. Louis or New Orleans or Harlem—think I'm gone let Harlem slide?—find me such a place and you got a easy one-hundred-dollar bill in your hand and I'll be in heaven. I'm talking serious now."

Billy snorted, sitting up straight and shaking his head. "I ain't hardly sleeping. Just remembering is all. See, I ain't been through here since 1952, but I can call some preacher's daughter right now—brown skin and about yeah-tall—yeah, at this very hour. Lord, she would be so fine that you and me both would run up the side of a mountain and holler like a mountain jack."

Then Earl blew a smoke ring and watched its rise; maybe it would halo the rearview mirror. "Well, okay, I'll take your word for it now, but if we're ever back through here, I definitely want to stop and see if these women are as pretty as you say."

"They pretty, they mamas pretty, they grandmamas pretty. . . ."

Earl laughed his high-pitched laugh. "You get crazier every day, Billy Cox." He pushed the accelerator, slamming them deeper into their seats.

Earl leveled off at sixty and for minutes was content to enjoy the regular beat of the wheels hitting the seams across the pavement, *pa-poom, pa-poom, pa-poom.* It was on the next stretch of road, ten miles outside of Springfield, that they truly sensed the flatness of the place. In the darkness there were no distant hills promising contour, variety, or perspective. Fields to the left? Woods to the right? They were silent for a minute or so. Crackling music flared up once again from the radio, then died.

"What do you think of the new boy's work tonight?" Billy asked.

"Who, 'Big City'? Not bad, man. Not bad at all." Earl snapped his fingers. "He's swinging more now. Matter of fact, he's driving the entire trumpet section, Big Joe included. You get the prize on that one, you brought him in. I remember you kept saying he could play the sweetest ballads, could curl up inside something like Strayhorn's 'Daydream' as easy as a cat curl up on a bed."

Billy nodded and looked out the side window. "I knew he had it in him the first time I heard him. His problem was hanging around Kansas City too long with that little jive band and just playing careful music. Sometimes you can't tell what's on the inside—just fast or slow, just hard or soft, just mean or laughing sweet. Can't never tell with some. But I had that feeling, know what I'm saying? Had the feeling that if we cut him loose, let him roam a little taste, that he could be all them combinations, that he could be what a tune needed him to be."

Earl tossed a cigarette stub out the window. He remembered the night he had met young Harold. The band was on break, and Harold walked up slowly, head down. The trumpet player had been nervous in his too-tight suit. Earl had later confided to Billy that he looked like he had just come in from plowing a cornfield and that if he joined the band he would have to learn how to dress, to coordinate his colors of his ties and suits, shine his shoes. When you joined the Ferguson band, you joined class. Style was more than your sound. It was your walk, the way you sat during the solos by others, the way you met the night. Earl had promptly nicknamed him "Big City."

"He said meeting you was like meeting God," Billy had said the next morning over hash browns and lukewarm coffee.

Earl smiled now. He was not God, true. He did know that among bandleaders roaming with their groups across this country, he was one of the best. He knew, too, that soft-spoken Billy Cox, five years younger, was the best composer in the business, period. Together they worked an easy magic. Few could weave sounds the way they could, few could get twelve voices, twelve rambunctious personalities, to shout or moan as one. And with it all was the trademark sound: the perfect blend of brass and reeds. Basie might have had a stronger reed section, with the force of a melodic hurricane; Ellington, a brass section with bite and unmatchable brightness. But they had the blend. Within the first few notes you knew that it was Earl Ferguson's band and nobody else's. Now and then players would leave to join other caravans inching across the continent, but the sound, their mix, stayed the same.

The scattered lights of Springfield were far behind them now, merged to a dull electric glow in the rearview mirror. And out from the town there were only occasional lights along State Route 42, one or two on front porches, lights bathing narrow, weathered, and wooded fronts, wood swings perfectly still in that time. Tightly closed shutters, silences inside. Both tried to imagine the front of the houses at noon — children pushing the porch swing? A dog napping in the shade nearby? Clothes flapping on a line running from behind the house? Gone suddenly, a blur to pinpoint, then out.

From a pocket Billy had taken out a matchbook. A few chord progressions had been scribbled on the inside cover. Then, drawing out a small lined tablet from beneath the seat, he quickly drew a bass staff and started humming.

"You got something going?" Earl asked.

"I think, yeah. A little light something, you know, like bright light and springtime and whatnot."

Earl tapped the wheel lightly with the palm of his free hand. "Toss in a small woman's bouncy walk, and I might get excited with you."

"Well, help me then. This time you use the woman — tight yellow skirt, right? — and I'll use the light, the light of mid-May, and when they don't work together, I think we'll both know."

"Solid. What you got so far?"

Billy did not answer. He kept a finger to his ear, staring from the matchbook cover to the tablet. Earl let it run. You don't interrupt when the idea is so young.

More often than not, Billy and Earl brought opposites or, at least, unlikely combinations together. One of the band's more popular numbers, a blues, was the result of Billy's meditations on the richly perfumed arms of a large and fleshy woman, arms tightly holding a man who mistook her short laugh for joy. To this, Earl had brought the memory of a rainy night and a long soft moan carried on the wind, something heard from the end of an alley. They used only the colors and sounds from these images, and only later, when the songs were fully arranged, did the smell and the touch of them sweep in. There had been other songs that resolved the contrasts, the differences, between the drone of a distant train and an empty glass of gin, a lipstick print at its rim, fingerprints around it. A baby's whimpering, and a man grinning as he counted a night's big take from the poker table, painted bright red fingernails tapping lightly down a lover's arm, and the cold of a lonely apartment. How much did the dancing couples, those whispering and holding close as second skins or those bouncing and whirling tirelessly, feel these things, too? Or did they bring something entirely different to the rhythms, something of their own?

Earl and Billy had talked about this many times. They had concluded that it was enough to bring contexts to dreams, to strengthen those who listened and danced. And there were those moments, magical, alive, when the dance hall was torn from the night and whirled, spinning like a top, a half mile from heaven.

Billy started whistling and tapping his thigh. Then he hummed a fragment of a song loudly.

Earl was nodding. "Nice. Already I can hear Slick Harry taking off with Ousley just under him with the alto. In triplets? Let's see, go through it again right quick."

Again Billy hummed and Earl brought in high triplets, nervous wings snagged to the thread of the melody, lifting the piece toward brightness. They stopped, and Billy, smiling now, worked quickly, a draftsman on fire, adding another line or two, crossing out, scribbling notes. He would look up to follow the front edges of the car's lights, then away to the darkness and back to the page.

"Listen up." Billy gave the next lines, flats predominating, while offering harsh counterpoint to the first two lines and snatching the song away from a tender playfulness for a moment. He scratched his chin and nodded. Pointed to the darkness.

"This is what I got so far." And he sang the line in a strong tenor voice, his melody now seeming to double the notes from the last line, though the rhythm did not vary. It was the kind of thing Art Tatum might do with "Tea for Two" or something equally simple. The song moved swiftly from a lyrical indulgence to a catch-me-if-you-can show of speed.

"Watch it now," Earl said, "or they will figure us for one of those beboppers." He chuckled. The woman in his mind walked faster, traffic about her thickened, the streets sent up jarring sounds. Those would be trumpets, probably. Surroundings leaned in. Trombones and tenor saxophones playing in the lowest octaves announced their possibilities.

Earl offered a line of his own. His woman walked quickly up the steps of a brownstone. In. Common enough sequence, but no surprise there. Whatever prompted it, though, was fleeting. Gone. Then he said, "Okay, forget mine for now. Let's stay with what you got."

Billy shrugged and marked off another staff, then glanced again to the match cover. He let out a long, low whistle. "Now we come to the bridge.

"This is when we need a piano, Earl. I bet the closest one to here is probably some ol' beat-up thing in one of these country churches out here. Or something sitting in the front parlor of one of these farmer's houses, and the farmer's daughter playing 'Jingle Bells' after bringing in the eggs."

Hip and arrogant city was in their laughter, they of funky cafés where fights might break out and beer bottles fly as the piano man bobbed and weaved, keeping time on a scarred piano that leaned and offered sticky keys in the lowest and highest octaves.

Then the Earl of Ferguson told the story of a piano search years before Billy had joined the band. With two other men in the car and barely an hour east of St. Louis, when the puzzle of a chord progression struck with the force of a deep stomach cramp. Spotting one light shining in the wilderness, a small neon sign still shining over a door, he ordered the car stopped. Trotting up, Earl noticed the sign blink off. He banged on the door, the hinges straining from each blow. Nobody turned off a sign in his face. The door swung open and up stepped an evil-looking, red-haired farmer in overalls, a man big enough to fill the doorway.

"I said to this giant, 'Quick, I got to get on your piano.' Not 'I got to find your toilet,' or 'I got to use your phone,' but 'I got to use your piano.'" He shook his head as he laughed now.

"That giant rocked on his heels like I had punched him square in the chest. He left just enough room for me to squeeze in and sure enough there was a little raggedy piano in the corner of his place.

"P.M. had enough sense to offer to buy some of the man's good whiskey while I'm sitting there playing and trying to figure out the good chord. P.M. always did have good common sense. Most folks try to remember what just happened, but Past was already on what's happening next. I'm forgetting you never knew P.M. The guys called him Past Midnight because he was so dark-skinned. The shadow of a shadow. Next thing they calling him Past, then one day Rabbit showed up calling him P.M., and it stuck. His real name was Wiley Reed, and he was one of the best alto players in the world."

He paused now, glanced out his side window. "Anyway, he showed him class that night. The giant steady looking around suspiciouslike at first. I mean, he didn't know us from Adam, didn't know how many more of us was waiting outside to rush in and turn out the joint. But he loosened up and took his mess of keys out and go to his cabinet. I'm just playing away because this is the greatest song of my life, don't care if it is in some country roadhouse way out in Plumb Nelly. I'm cussing, too, Billy, because this song is giving me fits, do you hear me? It just wouldn't let me go. All I wanted was to make it through the bridge. I figured the rest would come soon as I'm back in the car.

"Well, P.M. and the man making small talk, and Leon trying to get slick on everybody and tipping over to get him a few packs of Old Golds. I'm checking all this, see, and closing in on something solid and oh-so-sweet, and hearing the big guy go on and on about getting home because his wife already thinking he's sniffing around the new waitress—I remember that part clear as I'm sitting here—when, *boom*! Leon open up the closet, a mop and a jug of moonshine fell out and this woman inside trying to button up her blouse. She give a scream like she done seen the boogeyman. All hell commence to break loose. Next thing you know Leon backing off and telling the woman he ain't meant no harm, just trying to get some cigarettes, he lie. Big Boy running over and telling me we got to take our whiskey and go, song or no song. I look up, and two white guys running down the steps from just over our heads, one of them holding some cards in his hands. The other one run to the telephone like he reporting a robbery. I mean from the outside it's just a little-bitty place on the side of the road, but inside all kinds of shit going on. Well, I found the chords I wanted, did a quick run-through and called out to the fellows to haul ass. If some man's wife or some woman's man don't come in there shooting up the place, then the sheriff might raid the place for all-night gambling. Either way we lose."

Earl was laughing now. A light rain had started to fall just as he ended his tale. The windshield wipers clicked rhythmically; the bump of the road seemed a grace note: *bachoo-choo, bachoo-choo*.

"Never know when you get the tune down right. Go too early and you pluck it raw. Go too late and you got rotten fruit." Earl coughed. "Don't go at all and you put a bad hurt on yourself."

From across the highway a rabbit darted toward them, then cut away. Earl had turned the car just slightly before straightening it without letting up on the accelerator.

"Almost had us one dead rabbit."

Billy did not answer. He was tapping his pencil on the tablet. Up ahead and to the east they would discover the electric glow of Columbus. Beyond that they would have three more hours before Cleveland and breakfast at the Majestic Hotel on Carnegie Avenue. There might be a new singer or two waiting to try out with the band. Who knows? Somebody—another Billy or Sassy Sarah—might get lucky and ride back with them to New York, her life changed forever. Some young woman, prettier than she would ever know, would otherwise be serving up beef stew or spareribs in some tiny smoky place on Cedar Avenue, notes running through her head or thoughts of a sickly mother and two children she and her husband were trying to feed. How many times Billy and Earl had seen it, how many times they had heard the hope there, the sweat mustaches sprouting, the need to escape the routine nights. It was common ground. They had all been there, falling to sleep in clothes that smelled of cigarette smoke, the world a place of slow mornings with traffic starting and a door slamming, a baby crying, and an "Oh, goddamn, one more funky morning, but I'm alive to see it through anyhow.

There was a bump beneath the car. "You clipped something for sure that time, sportey-otee."

"All kinds of stuff out here at night," Earl said. "They like the warm road. Coons, possums, snakes, cows."

"Cows?"

"Yeah, cows." Billy had lit a cigarette. Earl tapped the end of the fresh one he had just placed in his mouth, and Billy reached to light it. "Thanks. Don't tell me you done forgot that cow we nicked on the road up to Saratoga Springs."

Yes, yes, Billy remembered. "Cow must have thought we was the Midnight Special, much noise as I was making trying to scare him off the road. Probably just out to get him a little side action in the next field." The car had knocked it to one knee before it struggled back up and, in the rearview mirror, slipped into the darkness.

They were quiet for long moments. After music, after hours, different thoughts could struggle to life. If there was an easiness earlier, swift terror could strike them in the darkest hours before dawn. They could grow suddenly uneasy in the silences. They could sense it together like a bone-deep chill starting. For now Billy pushed the wing shut on his side, rolled his window up another inch.

In a small town just west of Columbus, they passed a café, the lone light in that stretch. A man behind a long counter—white apron, white T-shirt—was scrubbing the counter and talking with a customer. He stopped his work to make a point, head moving from side to side. The customer nodded. Another man stood over a table at the window, dunking a doughnut. With his free hand, he waved as the car passed. Surprised, Earl honked once, then turned to glance back.

"That back there reminds me of something."

"Huh?"

"That man right back there waving. You didn't see him? Standing back there, waving at us and probably every car coming through here this late."

"Don't tell me you want to get some food," Billy said. "Hell, Earl, I thought those chicken sandwiches and pound cake—"

"No, no. That ain't what I'm thinking. Had a guy in the band by the name of Boonie years ago, way before you joined the band. Boonie could play him some mean trombone, I'm here to tell you. Fact, he could play trumpet and cornet, too. Probably would have played the tuba if I would have asked him to. Like you, he was the master of horns. Anyway, something happened—could have been bad gin or something else nobody will ever know about. He just snapped, and they found him one morning standing on a corner cussing at folks and swearing up and down that he was the governor of Africa. They took him to the jailhouse first, then the crazy house. They didn't keep him there long, six, seven months maybe.

"I went up to see him, way out in the country, Billy, you know where they put those places. Well, just past the gate was this man, and he waved at me when I first came in, and, while I was walking around with Boonie, he waved a couple more times. At first I thought he was just part of the staff because he was all over the place. But then I noticed he's wearing the same kind of clothes as Boonie. And he keeps smiling, you know? By the time I left, he was back out by the gate and waving again. It didn't take me long to figure out that all he had to do was wave at whatever was new and moving by. Like that man back there waving at the night."

Billy only glanced at him, then looked back to his notebook. Earl shook his head and chuckled. "Governor of Africa, can you beat that? Boonie was lucky, though; I mean, the way he wound up. He never got his chops back after he got out. He worked around a little, then finally left the life. He got a foundry job and raised his family in Detroit. Others ain't been so lucky."

Earl glanced ahead to more lights showing up through the rain. He knew some who entered hospitals, never to emerge. And many, too many, died before the age of fifty. Just last March, young "Bird" Parker had died in New York, not yet thirty-five. He whose notes surprised like shooting stars. Playing this music could be as risky as working in a steel mill or coal mine. But what were the choices? What could he do about it, leader of some? Perhaps only show them a lesson or two through his example. Now he did limit himself to one large and long drink per night—one part scotch and three parts water—from an oversized coffee mug. Soon he would cut down on his cigarettes. Beyond that he let the rules pronounce the purpose: you needed a clear head and a sound body to play the music he lived for.

Their talk of work and women—the incomplete song still a bright ribbon over their heads—pulled them well beyond the glow of Columbus. Coffee and sandwiches finished, they were down to three cigarettes each and figured there was nothing open between Columbus and Cleveland. Billy took over at the wheel. Twenty miles or so north of Columbus, they neared a car in trouble at the side of the road. The hood was up and in the swath of the front headlights was a man—very young, thin, white—kneeling at the back tire.

"Keep going, Billy. That cracker'll get help."

Billy slowed. "Well, Earl, it won't hurt. . . ."

Earl stared at him, hard. "You getting softhearted on me? That boy could be the Klan, see? You remember what happened to the Purnell band down in Tennessee just last month? Huh, remember that stuff? Got beat up by a bunch of rednecks, one of them getting his nose broke, and they still winding up in jail for disturbing the peace and impersonating a band? No, let him get help from his own kind."

Billy pulled the car off the road. "He's just a kid, Earl."

"You go without me, then." He watched Billy leave, then quickly felt under his seat.

Billy was approaching the car, and Earl could hear him ask, "Need a hand?"

"Sure do," the boy said loudly. "If you got a jack on you, we can do this in no time."

Beneath his seat in the Buick, Earl had found the gun wrapped in a towel. He opened the glove compartment and placed it inside, unwrapping the towel and leaving the small door open. He began to hum the new song slowly, softly, watching his friend, smiling Billy, trusting Billy, help a stranger.

Billy brought the jack from their trunk and set it up. He could smell alcohol on the boy, and, straightening up, he saw a girl in the car sip from a flask. Neither could have been older than eighteen. She was trying to hum something, missing, then tried again.

"Dumb me out here without a jack, I swear," the boy said. Billy only nodded as they set the jack under the frame.

The boy called the girl out of the car, and she stood apart shyly, both hands holding up the collar of her light coat.

"Your friend back there under the weather?" the boy asked.

"He just don't need the exercise," Billy said. "How about her? She feeling all right?"

The boy looked up in surprise, then he smiled. "No, she all right. She don't need no exercise either." He leaned closer to Billy as they pulled off the wheel and started to set the spare. "Course, me and her just about exercised out." Then he laughed. "Whoo-ee!"

The tire was on now, and the boy was tightening the lugs. "Pretty nice car you got back there. You a undertaker or a preacher?"

"No, neither one. I'm a musician."

The boy whistled low. "Musicians make enough for a car like that? I need to learn me some music. You get to travel a lot and see them big-city women and all like that?"

"Sure do."

The boy glanced at the girl and said loudly, "Course, a man could go all over the world and never find a woman sweet as my Josie there."

Her hair needed a brush, her dress was wrinkled, and her shoes were old and run-over. She was plain and drunk. In the morning she might be in the choir of a tiny church and by evening making biscuits to the staccato of radio news broadcasts. Billy was folding up the jack and turning away.

"Ain't she about the prettiest doggone thing a man could ever see?"

"I know how you feel, sport. I got one just as sweet back in New York."

Billy walked away and waved good-bye with his back turned. He slammed the trunk closed, then settled behind the wheel. He pulled the car back onto the highway.

Earl was whistling. "Feel better?" he asked, not looking up.

"What's that for?" Billy pointed to the gun.

"I thought about cleaning it. Ain't been cleaned in a year." Then: "My daddy told me once that it takes more than a smile and a good heart to get through this world. Told me sometimes you can reach out a helping hand and get it chopped off."

Billy was shivering. "Hide it, Earl. Please."

"Okay, okay. Look, while you were playing the Good Samaritan with Jethro back there, I finished the song. Listen up, young-blood."

Earl hummed through the opening key, stretching the note, then moved through the bright afternoon of the melody, repeated the line in the thinning light of its early evening. The song soon lifted to the bridge, a vivid golden stair step on which to linger briefly. Then the return to the opening line that suggested new possibilities: the smell of a pine forest after a rain, a meadow, too, a deer or two frozen at one edge. There was a street, glistening, a small oil slick catching dull rainbows, and a stranger's laughter like a bright coin spinning at their feet. Yes, all of that.

The small and proud woman walking, her hips working against yellow wool, had been lost to Earl. She would return, surely, to move through another song, walking to a different rhythm. For now she had brought Earl excited to Billy's first thoughts. Provided a spirit. Together, they hummed the song through, speeding it up, slowing. Each time, they tried different harmonies—the bass stronger here, the trombones higher there. Most of the parts had been worked through by the time they noticed the hills near Medina taking shape.

"Got it," Billy said finally. He slapped the wheel with relief.

"It's nice," Earl said.

"Think the people will like it?" Billy asked.

Earl yawned and looked out the window. Maybe he could get twenty minutes or so of sleep before they touched the edges of the city. "You worry too much, Billy. Course they gone like it. They got no choice. We did the best we could. We'll run through it this afternoon, do it again in Pittsburgh, and maybe have it ready by the time we hit Philly. Can't you just hear Big City's solo already?" He settled back, eyes closed.

Cars, trees, cornfields just harvested were explosions of dull colors. Signs placed one hundred feet apart, a shaving cream ad suddenly claimed Billy's attention. *The big blue tube's/Just like Louise/You get a thrill/From every squeeze.* He laughed aloud, then started whistling. Then the car roared into a stretch of light fog. Billy leaned forward, his head almost touching the windshield. Then he stiffened.

"Earl, wake up. I got something to tell you."

"Let it slide. Tell me over grits and coffee." Earl kept his eyes closed.

"No, it can't wait. It happened back there in Dayton. I just now remembered. You know on that second break? Well, I stepped outside to get a little air, take a smoke, you understand. A couple folk stroll past and tell me how much they like our playing, so I'm talking with them a while and then I see this woman—short with a red wig and she standing off to the side. She look up every now and then like she want to come over and say something. But she wait until nobody's around and she walk over real quick-like. Something about her make me think about a bird hopping, then resting, hopping some more. She told me she really like the music, like some of the songs really get a hold of her. . . ."

Earl opened one eye. "Yeah, and she just want to take a cute little man like you home to make music to her all the time."

"No, no, no. Nothing like that, but you better believe I was hoping for some action."

Forehead still to the windshield, Billy fumbled for words, worked a hand like he was flagging down a car. "No, she's smiling but not smiling, if you know what I mean. We talk about a lot of things, then she gets down to the thing she really wanted to talk about, I figure. She told me about her baby. She told me about hearing her baby screaming one day and she rush from her ironing and found him in the next room bleeding. He fell on a stick or glass or something, cut his belly, and blood going every which way. Said her son's belly was thin, like a balloon, but not going down when it's poked. She put her hand there, she said, and could feel each beat of the heart. Every time the heart beat, more blood would spurt out between her fingers. She screamed for help, screamed for her neighbors next door, just screamed and screamed. Blood was all over her, too, she said, but she never saw that until later. All she could do is tell her child not to die and press on that thin belly. And pray and pray, even after he in the ambulance. She told me that baby was all she got in this world."

Billy shook his head slowly. "What could I say to all that? Here I go outside for some fresh air and a draw or two on my Lucky Strikes. She brings me this story when I want to know whether my shoes are shined, my front still holding up, or whether some big-legged woman want to pull me home with her. I touched her on the shoulder, was all I could do. She told me the baby lived, and she smiled this dopey smile. Then she left."

Earl's eyes were closed. He waved his hand as if shooing a fly from his forehead. "It's this music we play, Billy. It opens people up, makes them give up secrets. Better than whiskey or dope for that. It don't kill you, and you can't piss it away. You can whistle it the next day in new places. You can loan it to strangers, and they thank you for it."

Then he shrugged. "It's what keeps us going all night."

Sitting back, fog thinning, Billy nodded and started back whistling. Before long they would sight the giant mills pumping smoke into the gray morning. At Lakewood Billy might swing closer to the gray and glassy Erie. Then he would pick up speed and head toward the east side, through a world raging to light outside their windows. Finally they would gain Carnegie Avenue and weave their way among the early church traffic. They would find the Majestic Hotel, breakfast, and attempt sleep, two wizards before the band.

[1990]

QUESTIONS

1. Why does McCluskey refer to Earl as "The Earl of Ferguson"?
2. What is the significance of the roadside incident involving a vehicle with a flat tire?
3. To what extent does Billy's account (near the end of the story) of the woman with the sick child enhance our understanding of "Lush Life"?
4. What stereotypes of African-American writing does this story challenge?

Herman Melville

(1819–1891)

United States

By the time that Herman Melville had published "Bartleby, the Scrivener" in 1853, he was well on his way toward a life of obscurity, a fact that has often been considered in contemporary interpretations of the story. The successes of his early and somewhat exotic accounts of South Sea life (*Typee*, 1846; *Omoo*, 1847) were already in the past. *Moby Dick* (1851), his masterpiece, had largely confused critics and readers. The same was true of *Pierre*, published the following year. "Bartleby" might have been written in a state of frustration at the author's declining popularity, in fear of his all too sudden obscurity, or even as a simple indication of the author's depression. Nevertheless, the story has been hailed as a precursor of much subsequent psychological fiction focusing on alienation by such writers as Dostoyevsky and Kafka. For the 10 years after the publication of *Pierre* in 1852, Melville watched the royalties from his combined works decline to a few hundred dollars per year. So concerned was he about the support of his family that he took a job as a custom's inspector. Most accounts of his life describe his remaining years as hard and bitter. He died in 1891.

Much has been written about "Bartleby." The story has even been made into an opera. In one of the more revealing interpretations, Mordecai Marcus has written, "Bartleby is a psychological double for the story's nameless lawyer–narrator. Bartleby appears to the lawyer chiefly to remind him of the inadequacies, the sterile routine, of his world. . . . The fact that Bartleby has no history suggests that he emerged from the lawyer's mind. Bartleby criticizes the sterility, impersonality and mechanical adjustments of the world which the lawyer inhabits."

◆ *Bartleby, the Scrivener* ◆

A Story of Wall Street

I am a rather elderly man. The nature of my avocations, for the last thirty years, has brought me into more than ordinary contact with what would seem an interesting and somewhat singular set of men, of whom, as yet, nothing, that I know of, has ever been written—I mean, the law-copyists, or scriveners. I have known very many of them, professionally and privately, and, if I pleased, could relate divers histories, at which good-natured gentlemen might smile, and sentimental souls might weep. But I waive the biographies of all other scriveners, for a few passages in the life of Bartleby, who was a scrivener, the strangest I ever saw, or heard of. While, of other law-copyists, I might write the complete life, of Bartleby nothing of that sort can be done. I believe that no materials exist, for a full and satisfactory biography of this man. It is an irreparable loss to literature.

Bartleby was one of those beings of whom nothing is ascertainable, except from the original sources, and, in his case, those are very small. What my own astonished eyes saw of Bartleby, *that* is all I know of him, except, indeed, one vague report, which will appear in the sequel.

Ere introducing the scrivener, as he first appeared to me, it is fit I make some mention of myself, my *employés*, my business, my chambers, and general surroundings, because some such description is indispensable to an adequate understanding of the chief character about to be presented. Imprimis:[1] I am a man who, from his youth upwards, has been filled with a profound conviction that the easiest way of life is the best. Hence, though I belong to a profession proverbially energetic and nervous, even to turbulence, at times, yet nothing of that sort have I ever suffered to invade my peace. I am one of those unambitious lawyers who never address a jury, or in any way draw down public applause; but, in the cool tranquillity of a snug retreat, do a snug business among rich men's bonds, and mortgages, and title-deeds. All who know me, consider me an eminently *safe* man. The late John Jacob Astor, a personage little given to poetic enthusiasm, had no hesitation in pronouncing my first grand point to be prudence; my next, method. I do not speak it in vanity, but simply record the fact, that I was not unemployed in my profession by the late John Jacob Astor; a name which, I admit, I love to repeat; for it hath a rounded and orbicular sound to it, and rings like unto bullion. I will freely add, that I was not insensible to the late John Jacob Astor's good opinion.

Some time prior to the period at which this little history begins, my avocations had been largely increased. The good old office, now extinct in the State of New York, of a Master in Chancery, had been conferred upon me. It was not a very arduous office, but very pleasantly remunerative. I seldom lose my temper; much more seldom indulge in dangerous indignation at wrongs and outrages; but I must be permitted to be rash here and declare, that I consider the sudden and violent abrogation of the office of Master in Chancery, by the new Constitution, as a ——— premature act; inasmuch as I had counted upon a life-lease of the profits, whereas I only received those of a few short years. But this is by the way.

My chambers were up stairs, at No. — Wall Street. At one end, they looked upon the white wall of the interior of a spacious skylight shaft, penetrating the building from top to bottom.

This view might have been considered rather tame than otherwise, deficient in what landscape painters call "life." But, if so, the view from the other end of my chambers offered, at least, a contrast, if nothing more. In that direction, my windows commanded an unobstructed view of a lofty brick wall, black by age and everlasting shade; which wall required no spyglass to bring out its lurking beauties, but, for the benefit of all near-sighted spectators, was pushed up to within ten feet of my window-panes. Owing to the great height of the surrounding buildings, and my chambers being on the second floor, the interval between this wall and mine not a little resembled a huge square cistern.

At the period just preceding the advent of Bartleby, I had two persons as copyists in my employment, and a promising lad as an office-boy. First, Turkey; second, Nippers; third, Ginger Nut. These may seem names, the like of which

[1]*Imprimis* Latin: first of all

are not usually found in the Directory. In truth, they were nicknames, mutually conferred upon each other by my three clerks, and were deemed expressive of their respective persons or characters. Turkey was a short, pursy Englishman, of about my own age — that is, somewhere not far from sixty. In the morning, one might say, his face was of a fine florid hue, but after twelve o'clock, meridian — his dinner hour — it blazed like a grate full of Christmas coals; and continued blazing — but, as it were, with a gradual wane — till six o'clock, P.M., or thereabouts; after which, I saw no more of the proprietor of the face, which, gaining its meridian with the sun, seemed to set with it, to rise, culminate, and decline the following day, with the like regularity and undiminished glory. There are many singular coincidences I have known in the course of my life, not the least among which was the fact, that, exactly when Turkey displayed his fullest beams from his red and radiant countenance, just then, too, at that critical moment, began the daily period when I considered his business capacities as seriously disturbed for the remainder of the twenty-four hours. Not that he was absolutely idle, or averse to business then; far from it. The difficulty was, he was apt to be altogether too energetic. There was a strange, inflamed, flurried, flighty recklessness of activity about him. He would be incautious in dipping his pen into his inkstand. All his blots upon my documents were dropped there after twelve o'clock, meridian. Indeed, not only would he be reckless, and sadly given to making blots in the afternoon, but, some days, he went further, and was rather noisy. At such times, too, his face flamed with augmented blazonry, as if cannel coal had been heaped on anthracite. He made an unpleasant racket with his chair; spilled his sand-box; in mending his pens, impatiently split them all to pieces, and threw them on the floor in a sudden passion; stood up, and leaned over his table, boxing his papers about in a most indecorous manner, very sad to behold in an elderly man like him. Nevertheless, as he was in many ways a most valuable person to me, and all the time before twelve o'clock, meridian, was the quickest, steadiest creature, too, accomplishing a great deal of work in a style not easily to be matched — for these reasons, I was willing to overlook his eccentricities, though, indeed, occasionally, I remonstrated with him. I did this very gently, however, because, though the civilest, nay, the blandest and most reverential of men in the morning, yet, in the afternoon, he was disposed, upon provocation, to be slightly rash with his tongue — in fact, insolent. Now, valuing his morning services as I did, and resolved not to lose them — yet, at the same time, made uncomfortable by his inflamed ways after twelve o'clock — and being a man of peace, unwilling by my admonitions to call forth unseemly retorts from him, I took upon me, one Saturday noon (he was always worse on Saturdays) to hint to him, very kindly, that, perhaps, now that he was growing old, it might be well to abridge his labors; in short, he need not come to my chambers after twelve o'clock, but, dinner over, had best go home to his lodgings, and rest himself till tea-time. But no; he insisted upon his afternoon devotions. His countenance became intolerably fervid, as he oratorically assured me — gesticulating with a long ruler at the other end of the room — that if his services in the morning were useful, how indispensable, then, in the afternoon?

"With submission, sir," said Turkey, on this occasion, "I consider myself your right-hand man. In the morning I but marshal and deploy my columns; but in the afternoon I put myself at their head, and gallantly charge the foe, thus" — and he made a violent thrust with the ruler.

"But the blots, Turkey," intimated I.

"True; but, with submission, sir, behold these hairs! I am getting old. Surely, sir, a blot or two of a warm afternoon is not to be severely urged against gray hairs. Old age — even if it blot the page — is honorable. With submission, sir, we *both* are getting old."

This appeal to my fellow-feeling was hardly to be resisted. At all events, I saw that go he would not. So, I made up my mind to let him stay, resolving, nevertheless, to see to it that, during the afternoon, he had to do with my less important papers.

Nippers, the second on my list, was a whiskered, sallow, and, upon the whole, rather piratical-looking young man, of about five-and-twenty. I always deemed him the victim of two evil powers — ambition and indigestion. The ambition was evinced by a certain impatience of the duties of a mere copyist, an unwarrantable usurpation of strictly professional affairs such as the original drawing up of legal documents. The indigestion seemed betokened in an occasional nervous testiness and grinning irritability, causing the teeth to audibly grind together over mistakes committed in copying; unnecessary maledictions, hissed, rather than spoken, in the heat of business; and especially by a continual discontent with the height of the table where he worked. Though of a very ingenious mechanical turn, Nippers could never get this table to suit him. He put chips under it, blocks of various sorts, bits of pasteboard, and at last went so far as to attempt an exquisite adjustment, by final pieces of folded blotting paper. But no invention would answer. If, for the sake of easing his back, he brought the table-lid at a sharp angle well up towards his chin, and wrote there like a man using the steep roof of a Dutch house for his desk, then he declared that it stopped the circulation in his arms. If now he lowered the table to his waistbands, and stooped over it in writing, then there was a sore aching in his back. In short, the truth of the matter was, Nippers knew not what he wanted. Or, if he wanted anything, it was to be rid of a scrivener's table altogether. Among the manifestations of his diseased ambition was a fondness he had for receiving visits from certain ambiguous-looking fellows in seedy coats, whom he called his clients. Indeed, I was aware that not only was he, at times, considerable of a ward-politician, but he occasionally did a little business at the justices' courts, and was not unknown on the steps of the Tombs.[2] I have good reason to believe, however, that one individual who called upon him at my chambers, and who, with a grand air, he insisted was his client, was no other than a dun, and the alleged title-deed, a bill. But, with all his failings, and the annoyances he caused me, Nippers, like his compatriot Turkey, was a very useful man to me; wrote a neat, swift hand; and, when he chose, was not deficient in a gentlemanly sort of deportment. Added to this, he always dressed in a gentlemanly sort of way; and so, incidentally, reflected credit upon my chambers. Whereas, with respect to Turkey, I had much ado to keep him from being a reproach to me. His clothes were apt to look oily, and smell of eating-houses. He wore his pantaloons very loose and baggy in summer. His coats were execrable, his hat not to be handled. But while the hat was a thing of indifference to me, inasmuch as his natural civility and deference, as a dependent Englishman, always led him to doff it the moment he entered the room, yet his coat was another matter. Concerning his coats, I reasoned with him; but with no effect. The truth was, I suppose, that a

[2]*Tombs* a prison in New York City

man with so small an income could not afford to sport such a lustrous face and a lustrous coat at one and the same time. As Nippers once observed, Turkey's money went chiefly for red ink. One winter day, I presented Turkey with a highly respectable-looking coat of my own—a padded gray coat, of a most comfortable warmth, and which buttoned straight up from the knee to the neck. I thought Turkey would appreciate the favor, and abate his rashness and obstreperousness of afternoons. But no; I verily believe that buttoning himself up in so downy and blanket-like a coat had a pernicious effect upon him—upon the same principle that too much oats are bad for horses. In fact, precisely as a rash, restive horse is said to feel his oats, so Turkey felt his coat. It made him insolent. He was a man whom prosperity harmed.

Though, concerning the self-indulgent habits of Turkey, I had my own private surmises, yet, touching Nippers, I was well persuaded that, whatever might be his faults in other respects, he was, at least, a temperate young man. But, indeed, nature herself seemed to have been his vintner, and, at his birth, charged him so thoroughly with an irritable, brandy-like disposition, that all subsequent potations were needless. When I consider how, amid the stillness of my chambers, Nippers would sometimes impatiently rise from his seat, and stooping over his table, spread his arms wide apart, seize the whole desk, and move it, and jerk it, with a grim, grinding motion on the floor, as if the table were a perverse voluntary agent, intent on thwarting and vexing him, I plainly perceive that, for Nippers, brandy-and-water were altogether superfluous.

It was fortunate for me that, owing to its peculiar cause—indigestion—the irritability and consequent nervousness of Nippers were mainly observable in the morning, while in the afternoon he was comparatively mild. So that, Turkey's paroxysms only coming on about twelve o'clock, I never had to do with their eccentricities at one time. Their fits relieved each other, like guards. When Nippers' was on, Turkey's was off; and *vice versa.* This was a good natural arrangement, under the circumstances.

Ginger Nut, the third on my list, was a lad, some twelve years old. His father was a carman, ambitious of seeing his son on the bench instead of a cart, before he died. So he sent him to my office, as student at law, errand-boy, cleaner, and sweeper, at the rate of one dollar a week. He had a little desk to himself, but he did not use it much. Upon inspection, the drawer exhibited a great array of the shells of various sorts of nuts. Indeed, to this quick-witted youth, the whole noble science of the law was contained in a nutshell. Not the least among the employments of Ginger Nut, as well as one which he discharged with the most alacrity, was his duty as cake and apple purveyor for Turkey and Nippers. Copying lawpapers being proverbially a dry, husky sort of business, my two scriveners were fain to moisten their mouths very often with Spitzenbergs, to be had at the numerous stalls nigh the Custom House and Post Office. Also, they sent Ginger Nut very frequently for that peculiar cake—small, flat, round, and very spicy—after which he had been named by them. Of a cold morning, when business was but dull, Turkey would gobble up scores of these cakes, as if they were mere wafers—indeed, they sell them at the rate of six or eight for a penny—the scrape of his pen blending with the crunching of the crisp particles in his mouth. Of all the fiery afternoon blunders and flurried rashness of Turkey, was his once moistening a ginger-cake between his lips, and clapping it on to a mortgage, for a seal. I came within an ace of dismissing him then. But he mollified me by making an oriental bow, and saying—

"With submission, sir, it was generous of me to find you in stationery on my own account."

Now my original business—that of a conveyancer and title hunter, and drawer-up of recondite documents of all sorts—was considerably increased by receiving the Master's office. There was now great work for scriveners. Not only must I push the clerks already with me, but I must have additional help.

In answer to my advertisement, a motionless young man one morning stood upon my office threshold, the door being open, for it was summer. I can see that figure now—pallidly neat, pitiably respectable, incurably forlorn! It was Bartleby.

After a few words touching his qualifications, I engaged him, glad to have among my corps of copyists a man of so singularly sedate an aspect, which I thought might operate beneficially upon the flighty temper of Turkey, and the fiery one of Nippers.

I should have stated before that ground-glass folding-doors divided my premises into two parts, one of which was occupied by my scriveners, the other by myself. According to my humor, I threw open these doors, or closed them. I resolved to assign Bartleby a corner by the folding-doors, but on my side of them, so as to have this quiet man within easy call, in case any trifling thing was to be done. I placed his desk close up to a small side-window in that part of the room, a window which originally had afforded a lateral view of certain grimy brickyards and bricks, but which, owing to subsequent erections, commanded at present no view at all, though it gave some light. Within three feet of the panes was a wall, and the light came down from far above, between two lofty buildings, as from a very small opening in a dome. Still further to a satisfactory arrangement, I procured a high green folding screen, which might entirely isolate Bartleby from my sight, though not remove him from my voice. And thus, in a manner, privacy and society were conjoined.

At first, Bartleby did an extraordinary quantity of writing. As if long famishing for something to copy, he seemed to gorge himself on my documents. There was no pause for digestion. He ran a day and night line, copying by sunlight and by candle-light. I should have been quite delighted with his application, had he been cheerfully industrious. But he wrote on silently, palely, mechanically.

It is, of course, an indispensable part of a scrivener's business to verify the accuracy of his copy, word by word. Where there are two or more scriveners in an office, they assist each other in this examination, one reading from the copy, the other holding the original. It is a very dull, wearisome, and lethargic affair. I can readily imagine that, to some sanguine temperaments, it would be altogether intolerable. For example, I cannot credit that the mettlesome poet, Byron, would have contentedly sat down with Bartleby to examine a law document of, say five hundred pages, closely written in a crimpy hand.

Now and then, in the haste of business, it had been my habit to assist in comparing some brief document myself, calling Turkey or Nippers for this purpose. One object I had, in placing Bartleby so handy to me behind the screen, was, to avail myself of his services on such trivial occasions. It was on the third day, I think, of his being with me, and before any necessity had arisen for having his own writing examined, that, being much hurried to complete a small affair I had in hand, I abruptly called to Bartleby. In my haste and natural expectancy of instant compliance, I sat with my head bent over the original on my desk, and my right hand sideways, and somewhat nervously extended with the copy, so that, immediately upon emerging from his retreat, Bartleby might snatch it and proceed to business without the least delay.

In this very attitude did I sit when I called to him, rapidly stating what it was I wanted him to do—namely, to examine a small paper with me. Imagine my surprise, nay, my consternation, when, without moving from his privacy, Bartleby, in a singularly mild, firm voice, replied, "I would prefer not to."

I sat awhile in perfect silence, rallying my stunned faculties. Immediately it occurred to me that my ears had deceived me, or Bartleby had entirely misunderstood my meaning. I repeated my request in the clearest tone I could assume; but in quite as clear a one came the previous reply, "I would prefer not to."

"Prefer not to," echoed I, rising in high excitement, and crossing the room with a stride. "What do you mean? Are you moonstruck? I want you to help me compare this sheet here—take it," and I thrust it towards him.

"I would prefer not to," said he.

I looked at him steadfastly. His face was leanly composed; his gray eye dimly calm. Not a wrinkle of agitation rippled him. Had there been the least uneasiness, anger, impatience, or impertinence in his manner; in other words, had there been anything ordinarily human about him, doubtless I should have violently dismissed him from the premises. But as it was, I should have as soon thought of turning my pale plaster-of-paris bust of Cicero out of doors. I stood gazing at him awhile, as he went on with his own writing, and then reseated myself at my desk. This is very strange, thought I. What had one best do? But my business hurried me. I concluded to forget the matter for the present, reserving it for my future leisure. So, calling Nippers from the other room, the paper was speedily examined.

A few days after this, Bartleby concluded four lengthy documents, being quadruplicates of a week's testimony taken before me in my High Court of Chancery. It became necessary to examine them. It was an important suit, and great accuracy was imperative. Having all things arranged, I called Turkey, Nippers, and Ginger Nut, from the next room, meaning to place the four copies in the hands of my four clerks, while I should read from the original. Accordingly, Turkey, Nippers, and Ginger Nut had taken their seats in a row, each with his document in his hand, when I called to Bartleby to join this interesting group.

"Bartleby! quick, I am waiting."

I heard a slow scrape of his chair legs on the uncarpeted floor, and soon he appeared standing at the entrance of his hermitage.

"What is wanted?" said he, mildly.

"The copies, the copies," said I, hurriedly. "We are going to examine them. There"—and I held towards him the fourth quadruplicate.

"I would prefer not to," he said, and gently disappeared behind the screen.

For a few moments I was turned into a pillar of salt, standing at the head of my seated column of clerks. Recovering myself, I advanced towards the screen, and demanded the reason for such extraordinary conduct.

"*Why* do you refuse?"

"I would prefer not to."

With any other man I should have flown outright into a dreadful passion, scorned all further words, and thrust him ignominiously from my presence. But there was something about Bartleby that not only strangely disarmed me, but, in a wonderful manner, touched and disconcerted me. I began to reason with him.

"These are your own copies we are about to examine. It is labor saving to you, because one examination will answer for your four papers. It is common usage. Every copyist is bound to help examine his copy. Is it not so? Will you not speak? Answer!"

"I prefer not to," he replied in a flute-like tone. It seemed to me that, while I had been addressing him, he carefully revolved every statement that I made; fully comprehended the meaning; could not gainsay the irresistible conclusion; but, at the same time, some paramount consideration prevailed with him to reply as he did.

"You are decided, then, not to comply with my request—a request made according to common usage and common sense?"

He briefly gave me to understand, that on that point my judgment was sound. Yes: his decision was irreversible.

It is not seldom the case that, when a man is browbeaten in some unprecedented and violently unreasonable way, he begins to stagger in his own plainest faith. He begins, as it were, vaguely to surmise that, wonderful as it may be, all the justice and all the reason is on the other side. Accordingly, if any disinterested persons are present, he turns to them for some reinforcement for his own faltering mind.

"Turkey," said I, "what do you think of this? Am I not right?"

"With submission, sir," said Turkey, in his blandest tone, "I think that you are."

"Nippers," said I, "what do *you* think of it?"

"I think I should kick him out of the office."

(The reader of nice perceptions will have perceived that, it being morning, Turkey's answer is couched in polite and tranquil terms, but Nippers replies in ill-tempered ones. Or, to repeat a previous sentence, Nippers' ugly mood was on duty, and Turkey's off.)

"Ginger Nut," said I, willing to enlist the smallest suffrage in my behalf, "what do *you* think of it?"

"I think, sir, he's a little *luny*," replied Ginger Nut, with a grin.

"You hear what they say," said I, turning towards the screen, "come forth and do your duty."

But he vouchsafed no reply. I pondered a moment in sore perplexity. But once more business hurried me. I determined again to postpone the consideration of this dilemma to my future leisure. With a little trouble we made out to examine the papers without Bartleby, though at every page or two Turkey deferentially dropped his opinion, that this proceeding was quite out of the common; while Nippers, twitching in his chair with a dyspeptic nervousness, ground out, between his set teeth, occasional hissing maledictions against the stubborn oaf behind the screen. And for his (Nippers') part, this was the first and the last time he would do another man's business without pay.

Meanwhile Bartleby sat in his hermitage, oblivious to everything but his own peculiar business there.

Some days passed, the scrivener being employed upon another lengthy work. His late remarkable conduct led me to regard his ways narrowly. I observed that he never went to dinner; indeed, that he never went anywhere. As yet I had never, of my personal knowledge, known him to be outside of my office. He was a perpetual sentry in the corner. At about eleven o'clock though, in the morning, I noticed that Ginger Nut would advance towards the opening in Bartleby's screen, as if silently beckoned thither by a gesture invisible to me where I sat. The boy would then leave the office, jingling a few pence, and reappear with a handful of ginger-nuts, which he delivered in the hermitage, receiving two of the cakes for his trouble.

He lives, then, on ginger-nuts, thought I; never eats a dinner, properly speaking; he must be a vegetarian, then, but no; he never eats even vegetables, he eats nothing but ginger-nuts. My mind then ran on in reveries concerning the probable effects upon the human constitution of living entirely on ginger-nuts. Ginger-nuts are so called, because they contain ginger as one of their peculiar constituents, and the final flavoring one. Now, what was ginger? A hot, spicy thing. Was Bartleby hot and spicy? Not at all. Ginger, then, had no effect upon Bartleby. Probably he preferred it should have none.

Nothing so aggravates an earnest person as a passive resistance. If the individual so resisted be of a not inhumane temper, and the resisting one perfectly harmless in his passivity, then, in the better moods of the former, he will endeavor charitably to construe to his imagination what proves impossible to be solved by his judgment. Even so, for the most part, I regarded Bartleby and his ways. Poor fellow! thought I, he means no mischief; it is plain he intends no insolence; his aspect sufficiently evinces that his eccentricities are involuntary. He is useful to me. I can get along with him. If I turn him away, the chances are he will fall in with some less indulgent employer, and then he will be rudely treated, and perhaps driven forth miserably to starve. Yes. Here I can cheaply purchase a delicious self-approval. To befriend Bartleby; to humor him in his strange wilfulness, will cost me little or nothing, while I lay up in my soul what will eventually prove a sweet morsel for my conscience. But this mood was not invariable with me. The passiveness of Bartleby sometimes irritated me. I felt strangely goaded on to encounter him in new opposition—to elicit some angry spark from him answerable to my own. But, indeed, I might as well have essayed to strike fire with my knuckles against a bit of Windsor soap. But one afternoon the evil impulse in me mastered me, and the following little scene ensued:

"Bartleby," said I, "when those papers are all copied, I will compare them with you."

"I would prefer not to."

"How? Surely you do not mean to persist in that mulish vagary?"

No answer.

I threw open the folding-doors nearby, and turning upon Turkey and Nippers, exclaimed:

"Bartleby a second time says, he won't examine his papers. What do you think of it, Turkey?"

It was afternoon, be it remembered. Turkey sat glowing like a brass boiler; his bald head steaming; his hands reeling among his blotted papers.

"Think of it?" roared Turkey. "I think I'll just step behind his screen, and black his eyes for him!"

So saying, Turkey rose to his feet and threw his arms into a pugilistic position. He was hurrying away to make good his promise, when I detained him, alarmed at the effect of incautiously rousing Turkey's combativeness after dinner.

"Sit down, Turkey," said I, "and hear what Nippers has to say. What do you think of it, Nippers? Would I not be justified in immediately dismissing Bartleby?"

"Excuse me, that is for you to decide, sir. I think his conduct quite unusual, and, indeed, unjust, as regards Turkey and myself. But it may only be a passing whim."

"Ah," exclaimed I, "you have strangely changed your mind, then—you speak very gently of him now."

"All beer," cried Turkey; "gentleness is effects of beer—Nippers and I dined together to-day. You see how gentle *I* am, sir. Shall I go and black his eyes?"

"You refer to Bartleby, I suppose. No, not to-day, Turkey," I replied; "pray, put up your fists."

I closed the doors, and again advanced towards Bartleby. I felt additional incentives tempting me to my fate. I burned to be rebelled against again. I remembered that Bartleby never left the office.

"Bartleby," said I, "Ginger Nut is away; just step around to the Post Office, won't you?" (it was but a three minutes' walk) "and see if there is anything for me."

"I would prefer not to."

"You *will* not?"

"I *prefer* not."

I staggered to my desk, and sat there in a deep study. My blind inveteracy returned. Was there any other thing in which I could procure myself to be ignominiously repulsed by this lean, penniless wight?—my hired clerk? What added thing is there, perfectly reasonable, that he will be sure to refuse to do?

"Bartleby!"

No answer.

"Bartleby," in a louder tone.

No answer.

"Bartleby," I roared.

Like a very ghost, agreeably to the laws of magical invocation, at the third summons, he appeared at the entrance of his hermitage.

"Go to the next room, and tell Nippers to come to me."

"I would prefer not to," he respectfully and slowly said, and mildly disappeared.

"Very good, Bartleby," said I, in a quiet sort of serenely-severe self-possessed tone, intimating the unalterable purpose of some terrible retribution very close at hand. At the moment I half intended something of the kind. But upon the whole, as it was drawing towards my dinner-hour, I thought it best to put on my hat and walk home for the day, suffering much from perplexity and distress of mind.

Shall I acknowledge it? The conclusion of this whole business was, that it soon became a fixed fact of my chambers, that a pale young scrivener, by the name of Bartleby, had a desk there; that he copied for me at the usual rate of four cents a folio (one hundred words); but he was permanently exempt from examining the work done by him, that duty being transferred to Turkey and Nippers, out of compliment, doubtless, to their superior acuteness; moreover, said Bartleby was never, on any account, to be dispatched on the most trivial errand of any sort; and that even if entreated to take upon him such a matter, it was generally understood that he would "prefer not to"—in other words, that he would refuse point blank.

As days passed on, I became considerably reconciled to Bartleby. His steadiness, his freedom from all dissipation, his incessant industry (except when he chose to throw himself into a standing revery behind his screen), his great stillness, his unalterableness of demeanor under all circumstances, made him a valuable acquisition. One prime thing was this—*he was always there*—first in the morning, continually through the day, and the last at night. I had a singular confidence in his honesty. I felt my most precious papers perfectly safe in his hands. Sometimes, to be sure, I could not, for the very soul of me, avoid falling into sudden spasmodic passions with him. For it was exceeding difficult to bear in mind all the time those strange peculiarities, privileges, and unheard-of exemptions, forming the tacit stipulations on Bartleby's part under which he remained in my office. Now and then, in the eagerness of dispatching pressing business, I would inadvertently summon Bartleby, in a short, rapid tone, to put his finger, say, on the incipient tie of a bit of red tape with which I was about compressing some papers. Of course, from behind the screen the usual answer, "I prefer not to," was sure to come; and then, how could a human creature, with the common infirmities of our nature, refrain from bitterly exclaiming upon such perverseness—such unreasonableness? However, every added repulse of this sort which I received only tended to lessen the probability of my repeating the inadvertence.

Here it must be said, that, according to the custom of most legal gentlemen occupying chambers in densely populated law buildings, there were several keys to my door. One was kept by a woman residing in the attic, which person weekly scrubbed and daily swept and dusted my apartments. Another was kept by Turkey for convenience sake. The third I sometimes carried in my own pocket. The fourth I knew not who had.

Now, one Sunday morning I happened to go to Trinity Church, to hear a celebrated preacher, and finding myself rather early on the ground I thought I would walk round to my chambers for a while. Luckily I had my key with me; but upon applying it to the lock, I found it resisted by something inserted from the inside. Quite surprised, I called out; when to my consternation a key was turned from within; and thrusting his lean visage at me, and holding the door ajar, the apparition of Bartleby appeared, in his shirt-sleeves, and otherwise in a strangely tattered *deshabille*,[3] saying quietly that he was sorry, but he was deeply engaged just then, and—preferred not admitting me at present. In a brief word or two, he moreover added, that perhaps I had better walk round the block two or three times, and by that time he would probably have concluded his affairs.

Now, the utterly unsurmised appearance of Bartleby, tenanting my law-chambers of a Sunday morning, with his cadaverously gentlemanly *nonchalance*, yet withal firm and self-possessed, had such a strange effect upon me, that incontinently I slunk away from my own door, and did as desired. But not without sundry twinges of impotent rebellion against the mild effrontery of this unaccountable scrivener. Indeed, it was his wonderful mildness chiefly, which not only disarmed me, but unmanned me, as it were. For I consider that one, for the time, is sort of unmanned when he tranquilly permits his hired clerk to dictate to him, and order him away from his own premises. Furthermore, I was full of uneasiness as to what Bartleby could possibly be doing in my office in his shirt-sleeves, and in an otherwise dismantled condition on a Sunday morning. Was anything amiss going on? Nay, that was out of the question. It was not to be

[3]*deshabille* dishabille; carelessly dressed

thought of for a moment that Bartleby was an immoral person. But what could he be doing there?—copying? Nay again, whatever might be his eccentricities, Bartleby was an eminently decorous person. He would be the last man to sit down to his desk in any state approaching to nudity. Besides, it was Sunday; and there was something about Bartleby that forbade the supposition that he would by any secular occupation violate the proprieties of the day.

Nevertheless, my mind was not pacified; and full of a restless curiosity, at last I returned to the door. Without hindrance I inserted my key, opened it, and entered. Bartleby was not to be seen. I looked round anxiously, peeped behind his screen; but it was very plain that he was gone. Upon more closely examining the place, I surmised that for an indefinite period Bartleby must have ate, dressed, and slept in my office, and that too without plate, mirror, or bed. The cushioned seat of a rickety old sofa in one corner bore the faint impress of a lean, reclining form. Rolled away under his desk, I found a blanket; under the empty grate, a blacking box and brush; on a chair, a tin basin, with soap and a ragged towel; in a newspaper a few crumbs of ginger-nuts and a morsel of cheese. Yes, thought I, it is evident enough that Bartleby has been making his home here, keeping bachelor's hall all by himself. Immediately then the thought came sweeping across me, what miserable friendlessness and loneliness are here revealed! His poverty is great; but his solitude, how horrible! Think of it. Of a Sunday, Wall Street is deserted as Petra;[4] and every night of every day it is an emptiness. This building, too, which of week-days hums with industry and life, at nightfall echoes with sheer vacancy, and all through Sunday is forlorn. And here Bartleby makes his home; sole spectator of a solitude which he has seen all populous—a sort of innocent and transformed Marius[5] brooding among the ruins of Carthage!

For the first time in my life a feeling of overpowering stinging melancholy seized me. Before, I had never experienced aught but a not unpleasing sadness. The bond of a common humanity now drew me irresistibly to gloom. A fraternal melancholy! For both I and Bartleby were sons of Adam. I remembered the bright silks and sparkling faces I had seen that day, in gala trim, swan-like sailing down the Mississippi of Broadway; and I contrasted them with the pallid copyist, and thought to myself, Ah, happiness courts the light, so we deem the world is gay; but misery hides aloof, so we deem that misery there is none. These sad fancyings—chimeras, doubtless, of a sick and silly brain—led on to other and more special thoughts, concerning the eccentricities of Bartleby. Presentiments of strange discoveries hovered round me. The scrivener's pale form appeared to me laid out, among uncaring strangers, in its shivering winding-sheet.

Suddenly I was attracted by Bartleby's closed desk, the key in open sight left in the lock.

I mean no mischief, seek the gratification of no heartless curiosity, thought I; besides, the desk is mine, and its contents, too, so I will make bold to look within. Everything was methodically arranged, the papers smoothly placed. The pigeon-holes were deep, and removing the files of documents, I groped into their recesses. Presently I felt something there, and dragged it out. It was an old

[4]*Petra* Once the center of an Arab Kingdom and now part of Jordan. Until its rediscovery by explorers in 1812, it had been deserted for 10 centuries.

[5]*Marius* Gaius Marius (died in 86 B.C.), a roman military general

bandanna handkerchief, heavy and knotted. I opened it, and saw it was a saving's bank.

I now recalled all the quiet mysteries which I had noted in the man. I remembered that he never spoke but to answer; that, though at intervals he had considerable time to himself, yet I had never seen him reading—no, not even a newspaper; that for long periods he would stand looking out, at his pale window behind the screen, upon the dead brick wall; I was quite sure he never visited any refectory or eating-house; while his pale face clearly indicated that he never drank beer like Turkey; or tea and coffee even, like other men; that he never went anywhere in particular that I could learn; never went out for a walk, unless, indeed, that was the case at present; that he had declined telling who he was, or whence he came, or whether he had any relatives in the world; that though so thin and pale, he never complained of ill-health. And more than all, I remembered a certain unconscious air of pallid—how shall I call it?—of pallid haughtiness, say, or rather an austere reserve about him, which has positively awed me into my tame compliance with his eccentricities, when I had feared to ask him to do the slightest incidental thing for me, even though I might know, from his long-continued motionlessness, that behind his screen he must be standing in one of those dead-wall reveries of his.

Revolving all these things, and coupling them with the recently discovered fact, that he made my office his constant abiding place and home, and not forgetful of his morbid moodiness; revolving all these things, a prudential feeling began to steal over me. My first emotions had been those of pure melancholy and sincerest pity; but just in proportion as the forlornness of Bartleby grew and grew to my imagination, did that same melancholy merge into fear, that pity into repulsion. So true it is, and so terrible, too, that up to a certain point the thought or sight of misery enlists our best affections; but, in certain special cases, beyond that point it does not. They err who would assert that invariably this is owing to the inherent selfishness of the human heart. It rather proceeds from a certain hopelessness of remedying excessive and organic ill. To a sensitive being, pity is not seldom pain. And when at last it is perceived that such pity cannot lead to effectual succor, common sense bids the soul be rid of it. What I saw that morning persuaded me that the scrivener was the victim of innate and incurable disorder. I might give alms to his body; but his body did not pain him; it was his soul that suffered, and his soul I could not reach.

I did not accomplish the purpose of going to Trinity Church that morning. Somehow, the things I had seen disqualified me for the time from church-going. I walked homeward, thinking what I would do with Bartleby. Finally, I resolved upon this—I would put certain calm questions to him the next morning, touching his history, etc., and if he declined to answer them openly and unreservedly (and I supposed he would prefer not), then to give him a twenty dollar bill over and above whatever I might owe him, and tell him his services were no longer required; but that if in any other way I could assist him, I would be happy to do so, especially if he desired to return to his native place, wherever that might be, I would willingly help to defray the expenses. Moreover, if, after reaching home, he found himself at any time in want of aid, a letter from him would be sure of a reply.

The next morning came.

"Bartleby," said I, gently calling to him behind his screen.

No reply.

"Bartleby," said I, in a still gentler tone, "come here; I am not going to ask you to do anything you would prefer not to do—I simply wish to speak to you."

Upon this he noiselessly slid into view.

"Will you tell me, Bartleby, where you were born?"

"I would prefer not to."

"Will you tell me *anything* about yourself?"

"I would prefer not to."

"But what reasonable objection can you have to speak to me? I feel friendly towards you."

He did not look at me while I spoke, but kept his glance fixed upon my bust of Cicero, which, as I then sat, was directly behind me, some six inches above my head.

"What is your answer, Bartleby?" said I, after waiting a considerable time for a reply, during which his countenance remained immovable, only there was the faintest conceivable tremor of the white attenuated mouth.

"At present I prefer to give no answer," he said, and retired into his hermitage.

It was rather weak in me I confess, but his manner, on this occasion, nettled me. Not only did there seem to lurk in it a certain calm disdain, but his perverseness seemed ungrateful, considering the undeniable good usage and indulgence he had received from me.

Again I sat ruminating what I should do. Mortified as I was at his behavior, and resolved as I had been to dismiss him when I entered my office, nevertheless I strangely felt something superstitious knocking at my heart, and forbidding me to carry out my purpose, and denouncing me for a villain if I dared to breathe one bitter word against this forlornest of mankind. At last, familiarly drawing my chair behind his screen, I sat down and said: "Bartleby, never mind, then, about revealing your history; but let me entreat you, as a friend, to comply as far as may be with the usages of this office. Say now, you will help to examine papers tomorrow or next day: in short, say now, that in a day or two you will begin to be a little reasonable:—say so, Bartleby."

"At present I would prefer not to be a little reasonable," was his mildly cadaverous reply.

Just then the folding-doors opened, and Nippers approached. He seemed suffering from an unusually bad night's rest, induced by severer indigestion than common. He overheard those final words of Bartleby.

"*Prefer not*, eh?" gritted Nippers—"I'd *prefer* him, if I were you, sir," addressing me—"I'd *prefer* him; I'd give him preferences, the stubborn mule! What is it, sir, pray, that he *prefers* not to do now?"

Bartleby moved not a limb.

"Mr. Nippers," said I, "I'd prefer that you would withdraw for the present."

Somehow, of late, I had got into the way of involuntarily using this word "prefer" upon all sorts of not exactly suitable occasions. And I trembled to think that my contact with the scrivener had already and seriously affected me in a mental way. And what further and deeper aberration might it not yet produce? This apprehension had not been without efficacy in determining me to summary measures.

As Nippers, looking very sour and sulky, was departing, Turkey blandly and deferentially approached.

"With submission, sir," said he, "yesterday I was thinking about Bartleby here, and I think that if he would but prefer to take a quart of good ale every day, it would do much towards mending him, and enabling him to assist in examining his papers."

"So you have got the word, too," said I, slightly excited.

"With submission, what word, sir?" asked Turkey, respectfully crowding himself into the contracted space behind the screen, and by so doing, making me jostle the scrivener. "What word, sir?"

"I would prefer to be left alone here," said Bartleby, as if offended at being mobbed in his privacy.

"*That's* the word, Turkey," said I—"*that's* it."

"Oh, *prefer*? oh yes—queer word. I never use it myself. But, sir, as I was saying, if he would but prefer—"

"Turkey," interrupted I, "you will please withdraw."

"Oh certainly, sir, if you prefer that I should."

As he opened the folding-door to retire, Nippers at his desk caught a glimpse of me, and asked whether I would prefer to have a certain paper copied on blue paper or white. He did not in the least roguishly accent the word "prefer." It was plain that it involuntarily rolled from his tongue. I thought to myself, surely I must get rid of a demented man, who already has in some degree turned the tongues, if not the heads of myself and clerks. But I thought it prudent not to break the dismission at once.

The next day I noticed that Bartleby did nothing but stand at his window in his dead-wall revery. Upon asking him why he did not write, he said that he had decided upon doing no more writing.

"Why, how now? what next?" exclaimed I, "do no more writing?"

"No more."

"And what is the reason?"

"Do you not see the reason for yourself?" he indifferently replied.

I looked steadfastly at him, and perceived that his eyes looked dull and glazed. Instantly it occurred to me, that his unexampled diligence in copying by his dim window for the first few weeks of his stay with me might have temporarily impaired his vision.

I was touched. I said something in condolence with him. I hinted that of course he did wisely in abstaining from writing for a while; and urged him to embrace that opportunity of taking wholesome exercise in the open air. This, however, he did not do. A few days after this, my other clerks being absent, and being in a great hurry to dispatch certain letters by the mail, I thought that, having nothing else earthly to do, Bartleby would surely be less inflexible than usual, and carry these letters to the Post Office. But he blankly declined. So, much to my inconvenience, I went myself.

Still added days went by. Whether Bartleby's eyes improved or not, I could not say. To all appearance, I thought they did. But when I asked him if they did he vouchsafed no answer. At all events, he would do no copying. At last, in replying to my urgings, he informed me that he had permanently given up copying.

"What!" exclaimed I; "suppose your eyes should get entirely well—better than ever before—would you not copy then?"

"I have given up copying," he answered, and slid aside.

He remained as ever, a fixture in my chamber. Nay—if that were possible—he became still more of a fixture than before. What was to be done? He would do nothing in the office; why should he stay there? In plain fact, he had now become a millstone to me, not only useless as a necklace, but afflictive to bear. Yet I was sorry for him. I speak less than truth when I say that, on his own account, he occasioned me uneasiness. If he would but have named a single relative or friend, I would instantly have written, and urged their taking the poor fellow away to some convenient retreat. But he seemed alone, absolutely alone in the universe. A bit of wreck in the mid-Atlantic. At length, necessities connected with my business tyrannized over all other considerations. Decently as I could, I told Bartleby that in six days' time he must unconditionally leave the office. I warned him to take measures, in the interval, for procuring some other abode. I offered to assist him in this endeavor, if he himself would but take the first step towards a removal. "And when you finally quit me, Bartleby," added I, "I shall see that you go not away entirely unprovided. Six days from this hour, remember."

At the expiration of that period, I peeped behind the screen, and lo! Bartleby was there.

I buttoned up my coat, balanced myself; advanced slowly towards him, touched his shoulder, and said, "The time has come; you must quit this place; I am sorry for you; here is money; but you must go."

"I would prefer not," he replied, with his back still towards me.

"You *must*."

He remained silent.

Now I had an unbounded confidence in this man's common honesty. He had frequently restored to me sixpences and shillings carelessly dropped upon the floor, for I am apt to be very reckless in such shirt-button affairs. The proceeding, then, which followed will not be deemed extraordinary.

"Bartleby," said I, "I owe you twelve dollars on account; here are thirty-two; the odd twenty are yours—Will you take it?" and I handed the bills towards him.

But he made no motion.

"I will leave them here, then," putting them under a weight on the table. Then taking my hat and cane and going to the door, I tranquilly turned and added—"After you have removed your things from these offices, Bartleby, you will of course lock the door—since every one is now gone for the day but you—and if you please, slip your key underneath the mat, so that I may have it in the morning. I shall not see you again; so good-bye to you. If, hereafter, in your new place of abode, I can be of any service to you, do not fail to advise me by letter. Good-bye, Bartleby, and fare you well."

But he answered not a word; like the last column of some ruined temple, he remained standing mute and solitary in the middle of the otherwise deserted room.

As I walked home in a pensive mood, my vanity got the better of my pity. I could not but highly plume myself on my masterly management in getting rid of Bartleby. Masterly I call it, and such it must appear to any dispassionate thinker. The beauty of my procedure seemed to consist in its perfect quietness. There was no vulgar bullying, no bravado of any sort, no choleric hectoring, and striding to and fro across the apartment, jerking out vehement commands for Bartleby to bundle himself off with his beggarly traps. Nothing of the kind. Without loudly bidding Bartleby depart—as an inferior genius might have done—I *assumed* the ground that depart he must; and upon that assumption built all I had to say. The more I thought over my procedure, the more I was charmed with it. Nevertheless, next morning, upon awakening, I had my doubts —I had somehow slept off the fumes of vanity. One of the coolest and wisest hours a man has, is just after he awakes in the morning. My procedure seemed as sagacious as ever — but only in theory. How it would prove in practice — there was the rub. It was truly a beautiful thought to have assumed Bartleby's departure; but, after all, that assumption was simply my own, and none of Bartleby's. The great point was, not whether I had assumed that he would quit me, but whether he would prefer to do so. He was more a man of preferences than assumptions.

After breakfast, I walked down town, arguing the probabilities *pro* and *con*. One moment I thought it would prove a miserable failure, and Bartleby would be found all alive at my office as usual; the next moment it seemed certain that I should find his chair empty. And so I kept veering about. At the corner of Broadway and Canal Street, I saw quite an excited group of people standing in earnest conversation.

"I'll take odds he doesn't," said a voice as I passed.

"Doesn't go? — done!" said I, "put up your money."

I was instinctively putting my hand in my pocket to produce my own, when I remembered that this was an election day. The words I had overheard bore no reference to Bartleby, but to the success or non-success of some candidate for the mayoralty. In my intent frame of mind, I had, as it were, imagined that all Broadway shared in my excitement, and were debating the same question with me. I passed on, very thankful that the uproar of the street screened my momentary absent-mindedness.

As I had intended, I was earlier than usual at my office door. I stood listening for a moment. All was still. He must be gone. I tried the knob. The door was locked. Yes, my procedure had worked to a charm; he indeed must be vanished. Yet a certain melancholy mixed with this: I was almost sorry for my brilliant success. I was fumbling under the door mat for the key, which Bartleby was to have left there for me, when accidentally my knee knocked against a panel, producing a summoning sound, and in response a voice came to me from within — "Not yet; I am occupied."

It was Bartleby.

I was thunderstruck. For an instant I stood like the man who, pipe in mouth, was killed one cloudless afternoon long ago in Virginia, by summer lightning; at his own warm open window he was killed, and remained leaning out there upon the dreamy afternoon, till someone touched him, when he fell.

"Not gone!" I murmured at last. But again obeying that wondrous ascendancy which the inscrutable scrivener had over me, and from which ascendancy, for all my chafing, I could not completely escape, I slowly went down stairs and out into the street, and while walking round the block, considered what I should next do in this unheard-of perplexity. Turn the man out by an actual thrusting I could not; to drive him away by calling him hard names would not do; calling in the police was an unpleasant idea; and yet, permit him to enjoy his cadaverous triumph over me — this, too, I could not think of. What was to be done? or, if nothing could be done, was there anything further that I could *assume* in the matter? Yes, as before I had prospectively assumed that Bartleby would depart, so now I might retrospectively assume that departed he was. In the legitimate carrying out of this assumption, I might enter my office in a great hurry, and pretending not to see Bartleby at all, walk straight against him as if he were air. Such a proceeding would in a singular degree have the appearance of a home-thrust. It was hardly possible that Bartleby could withstand such an application of the doctrine of assumption. But upon second thoughts the success of the plan seemed rather dubious. I resolved to argue the matter over with him again.

"Bartleby," said I, entering the office, with a quietly severe expression, "I am seriously displeased. I am pained, Bartleby. I had thought better of you. I had imagined you of such a gentlemanly organization, that in any delicate dilemma a slight hint would suffice—in short, an assumption. But it appears I am deceived. Why," I added, unaffectedly starting, "You have not even touched that money yet," pointing to it, just where I had left it the evening previous.

He answered nothing.

"Will you, or will you not, quit me?" I now demanded in a sudden passion, advancing close to him.

"I would prefer *not* to quit you," he replied, gently emphasizing the *not*.

"What earthly right have you to stay here? Do you pay any rent? Do you pay my taxes? Or is this property yours?"

He answered nothing.

"Are you ready to go on and write now? Are your eyes recovered? Could you copy a small paper for me this morning? or help examine a few lines? or step round to the Post Office? In a word, will you do anything at all, to give a coloring to your refusal to depart the premises?"

He silently retired into his hermitage.

I was now in such a state of nervous resentment that I thought it but prudent to check myself at present from further demonstrations. Bartleby and I were alone. I remembered the tragedy of the unfortunate Adams and the still more unfortunate Colt in the solitary office of the latter; and how poor Colt, being dreadfully incensed by Adams, and imprudently permitting himself to get wildly excited, was at unawares hurried into his fatal act—an act which certainly no man could possibly deplore more than the actor himself.[6] Often it had occurred to me in my ponderings upon the subject that had that altercation taken place in the public street, or at a private residence, it would not have terminated as it did. It was the circumstance of being alone in a solitary office, up stairs, of a building entirely unhallowed by humanizing domestic associations—an uncarpeted office, doubtless, of a dusty, haggard sort of appearance—this it must have been, which greatly helped to enhance the irritable desperation of the hapless Colt.

But when this old Adam of resentment rose in me and tempted me concerning Bartleby, I grappled him and threw him. How? Why, simply by recalling the divine injunction: "A new commandment give I unto you, that ye love one another." Yes, this it was that saved me. Aside from higher considerations, charity often operates as a vastly wise and prudent principle—a great safeguard to its possessor. Men have committed murder for jealousy's sake, and anger's sake, and hatred's sake, and selfishness' sake, and spiritual pride's sake; but no man, that ever I heard of, ever committed a diabolical murder for sweet charity's sake. Mere self-interest, then, if no better motive can be enlisted, should, especially with high-tempered men, prompt all beings to charity and philan-

[6]John C. Colt, who murdered Samuel Adams in 1842, committed suicide shortly before he was to be hanged.

thropy. At any rate, upon the occasion in question, I strove to drown my exasperated feelings towards the scrivener by benevolently construing his conduct. Poor fellow, poor fellow! thought I, he don't mean anything; and besides, he has seen hard times, and ought to be indulged.

I endeavored, also, immediately to occupy myself, and at the same time to comfort my despondency. I tried to fancy, that in the course of the morning, at such time as might prove agreeable to him, Bartleby, of his own free accord, would emerge from his hermitage and take up some decided line of march in the direction of the door. But no. Half-past twelve o'clock came; Turkey began to glow in the face, overturn his inkstand, and become generally obstreperous; Nippers abated down into quietude and courtesy; Ginger Nut munched his noon apple; and Bartleby remained standing at his window in one of his profoundest dead-wall reveries. Will it be credited? Ought I to acknowledge it? That afternoon I left the office without saying one further word to him.

Some days now passed, during which, at leisure intervals I looked a little into "Edwards[7] on the Will," and "Priestley[8] on Necessity." Under the circumstances, those books induced a salutary feeling. Gradually I slid into the persuasion that these troubles of mine, touching the scrivener, had been all predestined from eternity, and Bartleby was billeted upon me for some mysterious purpose of an all-wise Providence, which it was not for a mere mortal like me to fathom. Yes, Bartleby, stay there behind your screen, thought I; I shall persecute you no more; you are harmless and noiseless as any of these old chairs; in short, I never feel so private as when I know you are here. At last I see it, I feel it; I penetrate to the predestined purpose of my life. I am content. Others may have loftier parts to enact; but my mission in this world, Bartleby, is to furnish you with office-room for such period as you may see fit to remain.

I believe that this wise and blessed frame of mind would have continued with me, had it not been for the unsolicited and uncharitable remarks obtruded upon me by my professional friends who visited the rooms. But thus it often is, that the constant friction of illiberal minds wears out at last the best resolves of the more generous. Though to be sure, when I reflected upon it, it was not strange that people entering my office should be struck by the peculiar aspect of the unaccountable Bartleby, and so be tempted to throw out some sinister observations concerning him. Sometimes an attorney, having business with me, and calling at my office, and finding no one but the scrivener there, would undertake to obtain some sort of precise information from him touching my whereabouts; but without heeding his idle talk, Bartleby would remain standing immovable in the middle of the room. So after contemplating him in that position for a time, the attorney would depart, no wiser than he came.

Also, when a reference was going on, and the room full of lawyers and witnesses, and business driving fast, some deeply-occupied legal gentleman present, seeing Bartleby wholly unemployed, would request him to run round to his (the legal gentleman's) office and fetch some papers for him. Thereupon, Bartleby would tranquilly decline, and yet remain idle as before. Then the lawyer would give a great stare, and turn to me. And what could I say? At last I was made aware that all through the circle of my professional acquaintance, a whisper

[7]*Edwards* Jonathan Edwards (1703–1758), a Puritan divine who published *Freedom of Will* in 1754

[8]*Priestly* Joseph Priestly (1733–1803), an English clergyman, philosopher, and scientist

of wonder was running round, having reference to the strange creature I kept at my office. This worried me very much. And as the idea came upon me of his possibly turning out a long-lived man, and keeping occupying my chambers, and denying my authority; and perplexing my visitors; and scandalizing my professional reputation; and casting a general gloom over the premises; keeping soul and body together to the last upon his savings (for doubtless he spent but half a dime a day), and in the end perhaps outlive me, and claim possession of my office by right of his perpetual occupancy: as all these dark anticipations crowded upon me more and more, and my friends continually intruded their relentless remarks upon the apparition in my room; a great change was wrought in me. I resolved to gather all my faculties together, and forever rid me of this intolerable incubus.

Ere revolving any complicated project, however, adapted to this end, I first simply suggested to Bartleby the propriety of his permanent departure. In a calm and serious tone, I commended the idea to his careful and mature consideration. But, having taken three days to meditate upon it, he apprised me, that his original determination remained the same; in short, that he still preferred to abide with me.

What shall I do? I now said to myself, buttoning up my coat to the last button. What shall I do? what ought I to do? what does conscience say I *should* do with this man, or, rather, ghost. Rid myself of him, I must; go, he shall. But how? You will not thrust him, the poor, pale, passive mortal—you will not thrust such a helpless creature out of your door? you will not dishonor yourself by such cruelty? No, I will not, I cannot do that. Rather would I let him live and die here, and then mason up his remains in the wall. What, then, will you do? For all your coaxing, he will not budge. Bribes he leaves under your own paper-weight on your table; in short, it is quite plain that he prefers to cling to you.

Then something severe, something unusual must be done. What! surely you will not have him collared by a constable, and commit his innocent pallor to the common jail? And upon what ground could you procure such a thing to be done?—a vagrant, is he? What! he a vagrant, a wanderer, who refuses to budge? It is because he will not be a vagrant, then, that you seek to count him *as* a vagrant. That is too absurd. No visible means of support: there I have him. Wrong again: for indubitably he *does* support himself, and that is the only unanswerable proof that any man can show of his possessing the means so to do. No more, then. Since he will not quit me, I must quit him. I will change my offices; I will move elsewhere, and give him fair notice, that if I find him on my new premises I will then proceed against him as a common trespasser.

Acting accordingly, next day I thus addressed him: "I find these chambers too far from the City Hall; the air is unwholesome. In a word, I propose to remove my offices next week, and shall no longer require your services. I tell you this now, in order that you may seek another place."

He made no reply, and nothing more was said.

On the appointed day I engaged carts and men, proceeded to my chambers, and, having but little furniture, everything was removed in a few hours. Throughout, the scrivener remained standing behind the screen, which I directed to be removed the last thing. It was withdrawn; and, being folded up like a huge folio, left him the motionless occupant of a naked room. I stood in the entry watching him a moment, while something from within me upbraided me.

I re-entered, with my hand in my pocket—and—and my heart in my mouth.

"Good-bye, Bartleby; I am going—good-bye, and God some way bless you; and take that," slipping something in his hand. But it dropped upon the floor, and then—strange to say—I tore myself from him whom I had so longed to be rid of.

Established in my new quarters, for a day or two I kept the door locked, started at every footfall in the passages. When I returned to my rooms, after any little absence, I would pause at the threshold for an instant, and attentively listen, ere applying my key. But these fears were needless. Bartleby never came nigh me.

I thought all was going well, when a perturbed-looking stranger visited me, inquiring whether I was the person who had recently occupied rooms at No. —Wall Street.

Full of forebodings, I replied that I was.

"Then, sir," said the stranger, who proved a lawyer, "you are responsible for the man you left there. He refuses to do any copying; he refuses to do anything; he says he prefers not to; and he refuses to quit the premises."

"I am very sorry, sir," said I, with assumed tranquillity, but an inward tremor, "but, really, the man you allude to is nothing to me—he is no relation or apprentice of mine, that you should hold me responsible for him."

"In mercy's name, who is he?"

"I certainly cannot inform you. I know nothing about him. Formerly I employed him as a copyist; but he has done nothing for me now for some time past."

"I shall settle him, then—good morning, sir."

Several days passed, and I heard nothing more; and, though I often felt a charitable prompting to call at the place and see poor Bartleby, yet a certain squeamishness, of I know not what, withheld me.

All is over with him, by this time, thought I, at last, when, through another week, no further intelligence reached me. But, coming to my room the day after, I found several persons waiting at my door in a high state of nervous excitement.

"That's the man—here he comes," cried the foremost one, whom I recognized as the lawyer who had previously called upon me alone.

"You must take him away, sir, at once," cried a portly person among them, advancing upon me, and whom I knew to be the landlord of No. —Wall Street. "These gentlemen, my tenants, cannot stand it any longer; Mr. B——," pointing to the lawyer, "has turned him out of his room, and he now persists in haunting the building generally, sitting upon the banisters of the stairs by day, and sleeping in the entry by night. Everybody is concerned; clients are leaving the offices; some fears are entertained of a mob; something you must do, and that without delay."

Aghast at this torrent, I fell back before it, and would fain have locked myself in my new quarters. In vain I persisted that Bartleby was nothing to me—no more than to any one else. In vain—I was the last person known to have anything to do with him, and they held me to the terrible account. Fearful, then, of being exposed in the papers (as one person present obscurely threatened), I considered the matter, and, at length, said, that if the lawyer would give me a confidential interview with the scrivener, in his (the lawyer's) own room, I would, that afternoon, strive my best to rid them of the nuisance they complained of.

Going up stairs to my old haunt, there was Bartleby silently sitting upon the banister at the landing.

"What are you doing here, Bartleby?" said I.

"Sitting upon the banister," he mildly replied.

I motioned him into the lawyer's room, who then left us.

"Bartleby," said I, "are you aware that you are the cause of great tribulation to me, by persisting in occupying the entry after being dismissed from the office?"

No answer.

"Now one of two things must take place. Either you must do something, or something must be done to you. Now what sort of business would you like to engage in? Would you like to re-engage in copying for some one?"

"No; I would prefer not to make any change."

"Would you like a clerkship in a dry-goods store?"

"There is too much confinement about that. No, I would not like a clerkship; but I am not particular."

"Too much confinement," I cried, "why, you keep yourself confined all the time!"

"I would prefer not to take a clerkship," he rejoined, as if to settle that little item at once.

"How would a bar-tender's business suit you? There is no trying of the eye-sight in that."

"I would not like it at all; though, as I said before, I am not particular."

His unwonted wordiness inspirited me. I returned to the charge.

"Well, then, would you like to travel through the country collecting bills for the merchants? That would improve your health."

"No, I would prefer to be doing something else."

"How, then, would going as a companion to Europe, to entertain some young gentleman with your conversation—how would that suit you?"

"Not at all. It does not strike me that there is anything definite about that. I like to be stationary. But I am not particular."

"Stationary you shall be, then," I cried, now losing all patience, and, for the first time in all my exasperating connections with him, fairly flying into a passion. "If you do not go away from these premises before night, I shall feel bound—indeed, I *am* bound—to—to—to quit the premises myself!" I rather absurdly concluded, knowing not with what possible threat to try to frighten his immobility into compliance. Despairing of all further efforts, I was precipitately leaving him, when a final thought occurred to me—one which had not been wholly unindulged before.

"Bartleby," said I, in the kindest tone I could assume under such exciting circumstances, "will you go home with me now—not to my office, but my dwelling—and remain there till we can conclude upon some convenient arrangement for you at our leisure? Come, let us start now, right away."

"No: at present I would prefer not to make any change at all."

I answered nothing; but, effectually dodging every one by the suddenness and rapidity of my flight, rushed from the building, ran up Wall Street towards Broadway, and, jumping into the first omnibus, was soon removed from pursuit. As soon as tranquillity returned, I distinctly perceived that I had now done all that I possibly could, both in respect to the demands of the landlord and his tenants, and with regard to my own desire and sense of duty, to benefit Bartleby, and shield him from rude persecution. I now strove to be entirely care-free and quiescent; and my conscience justified me in the attempt; though, indeed, it was not so successful as I could have wished. So fearful was I of being again hunted out by the incensed landlord and his exasperated tenants, that, surrendering my business to Nippers, for a few days, I drove about the upper part of the town and through the suburbs, in my rockaway; crossed over to Jersey City and Hoboken, and paid fugitive visits to Manhattanville and Astoria. In fact, I almost lived in my rockaway for the time.

When again I entered my office, lo, a note from the landlord lay upon the desk. I opened it with trembling hands. It informed me that the writer had sent to the police, and had Bartleby removed to the Tombs as a vagrant. Moreover, since I knew more about him than any one else, he wished me to appear at that place, and make a suitable statement of the facts. These tidings had a conflicting effect upon me. At first I was indignant; but, at last, almost approved. The landlord's energetic, summary disposition, had led him to adopt a procedure which I do not think I would have decided upon myself; and yet, as a last resort, under such peculiar circumstances, it seemed the only plan.

As I afterwards learned, the poor scrivener, when told that he must be conducted to the Tombs, offered not the slightest obstacle, but, in his pale, unmoving way, silently acquiesced.

Some of the compassionate and curious by-standers joined the party; and headed by one of the constables arm-in-arm with Bartleby, the silent procession filed its way through all the noise, and heat, and joy of the roaring thoroughfares at noon.

The same day I received the note, I went to the Tombs, or, to speak more properly, the Halls of Justice. Seeking the right officer, I stated the purpose of my call, and was informed that the individual I described was, indeed, within. I then assured the functionary that Bartleby was a perfectly honest man, and greatly to be compassionated, however unaccountably eccentric. I narrated all I knew, and closed by suggesting the idea of letting him remain in as indulgent confinement as possible, till something less harsh might be done—though, indeed, I hardly knew what. At all events, if nothing else could be decided upon, the alms-house must receive him. I then begged to have an interview.

Being under no disgraceful charge, and quite serene and harmless in all his ways, they had permitted him freely to wander about the prison, and, especially, in the inclosed grass-platted yards thereof. And so I found him there, standing all alone in the quietest of the yards, his face towards a high wall, while all around, from the narrow slits of the jail windows, I thought I saw peering out upon him the eyes of murderers and thieves.

"Bartleby!"

"I know you," he said, without looking round—"and I want nothing to say to you."

"It was not I that brought you here, Bartleby," said I, keenly pained at his implied suspicion. "And to you, this should not be so vile a place. Nothing reproachful attaches to you by being here. And see, it is not so sad a place as one might think. Look, there is the sky, and here is the grass."

"I know where I am," he replied, but would say nothing more, and so I left him.

As I entered the corridor again, a broad meat-like man, in an apron, accosted me, and, jerking his thumb over my shoulder, said—"Is that your friend?"

"Yes."

"Does he want to starve? If he does, let him live on the prison fare, that's all."

"Who are you?" asked I, not knowing what to make of such an unofficially speaking person in such a place.

"I am the grub-man. Such gentlemen as have friends here, hire me to provide them with something good to eat."

"Is this so?" said I, turning to the turnkey.

He said it was.

"Well, then," said I, slipping some silver into the grub-man's hands (for so they called him), "I want you to give particular attention to my friend there; let him have the best dinner you can get. And you must be as polite to him as possible."

"Introduce me, will you?" said the grub-man, looking at me with an expression which seemed to say he was all impatience for an opportunity to give a specimen of his breeding.

Thinking it would prove of benefit to the scrivener, I acquiesced; and, asking the grub-man his name, went up with him to Bartleby.

"Bartleby, this is a friend; you will find him very useful to you."

"Your servant, sir, your servant," said the grub-man, making a low salutation behind his apron. "Hope you find it pleasant here, sir; nice grounds—cool apartments—hope you'll stay with us some time—try to make it agreeable. What will you have for dinner to-day?"

"I prefer not to dine to-day," said Bartleby, turning away. "It would disagree with me; I am unused to dinners." So saying, he slowly moved to the other side of the inclosure, and took up a position fronting the dead-wall.

"How's this?" said the grub-man, addressing me with a stare of astonishment. "He's odd, ain't he?"

"I think he is a little deranged," said I, sadly.

"Deranged? deranged is it? Well, now, upon my word, I thought that friend of yourn was a gentleman forger; they are always pale and genteel-like, them forgers. I can't help pity 'em—can't help it, sir. Did you know Monroe Edwards?" he added, touchingly, and paused. Then, laying his hand piteously on my shoulder, sighed, "he died of consumption at Sing-Sing. So you weren't acquainted with Monroe?"

"No, I was never socially acquainted with any forgers. But I cannot stop longer. Look to my friend yonder. You will not lose by it. I will see you again."

Some few days after this, I again obtained admission to the Tombs, and went through the corridors in quest of Bartleby; but without finding him.

"I saw him coming from his cell not long ago," said a turnkey, "may be he's gone to loiter in the yards."

So I went in that direction.

"Are you looking for the silent man?" said another turnkey, passing me. "Yonder he lies—sleeping in the yard there. 'Tis not twenty minutes since I saw him lie down."

The yard was entirely quiet. It was not accessible to the common prisoners. The surrounding walls, of amazing thickness, kept off all sounds behind them. The Egyptian character of the masonry weighed upon me with its gloom. But a soft imprisoned turf grew under foot. The heart of the eternal pyramids, it seemed, wherein, by some strange magic, through the clefts, grass-seed, dropped by birds, had sprung.

Strangely huddled at the base of the wall, his knees drawn up, and lying on his side, his head touching the cold stones, I saw the wasted Bartleby. But nothing stirred. I paused; then went close up to him; stooped over, and saw that his dim eyes were open; otherwise he seemed profoundly sleeping. Something prompted me to touch him. I felt his hand, when a tingling shiver ran up my arm and down my spine to my feet.

The round face of the grub-man peered upon me now. "His dinner is ready. Won't he dine to-day, either? Or does he live without dining?"

"Lives without dining," said I, and closed the eyes.

"Eh!—He's asleep, ain't he?"

"With kings and counselors,"[9] murmured I.

There would seem little need for proceeding further in this history. Imagination will readily supply the meagre recital of poor Bartleby's interment. But, ere parting with the reader, let me say, that if this little narrative has sufficiently interested him, to awaken curiosity as to who Bartleby was, and what manner of life he led prior to the present narrator's making his acquaintance, I can only reply, that in such curiosity I fully share, but am wholly unable to gratify it. Yet here I hardly know whether I should divulge one little item of rumor, which came to my ear a few months after the scrivener's decease. Upon what basis it rested, I could never ascertain; and hence, how true it is I cannot now tell. But, inasmuch as this vague report has not been without a certain suggestive interest to me, however sad, it may prove the same with some others; and so I will briefly mention it. The report was this: that Bartleby had been a subordinate clerk in the Dead Letter Office at Washington, from which he had been suddenly removed by a change in the administration. When I think over this rumor, hardly can I express the emotions which seize me. Dead letters! does it not sound like dead men? Conceive a man by nature and misfortune prone to a pallid hopelessness, can any business seem more fitted to heighten it than that of continually handling these dead letters, and assorting them for the flames? For by the cart-load they are annually burned. Sometimes from out the folded paper the pale clerk takes a ring—the finger it was meant for, perhaps, moulders in the grave; a bank-note sent in swiftest charity—he whom it would relieve, nor eats nor hungers any more; pardon for those who died despairing; hope for those who died unhoping; good tidings for those who died stifled by unrelieved calamities. On errands of life, these letters speed to death.

Ah, Bartleby! Ah, humanity!

[1853]

QUESTIONS

1. What is the significance of Melville's subtitle, "A Story of Wall Street"?

[9]"*With . . . counselors*" from Job 3:13, 14; Job in his misery wishes he had never been born—"then had I been at rest, with Kings and counselors of the earth."

2. Is the lawyer responsible for Bartleby's welfare? Are his responses to Bartleby's presence in his office the right ones or the wrong ones?
3. How should we interpret Bartleby's famous line, "I would prefer not to"?
4. What significance is to be made of the three other men who work in the lawyer's office?
5. In what way does the final clue about Bartleby's situation—his work in the dead letter office—illuminate our interpretation of the story? How does the narrator respond to this information?
6. Who is the central character of the story—Bartleby or the narrator?

Katherine Min

(b. 1959)

Korea/United States

Katherine Min's heritage is Korean-American. She was born in the United States, of parents who came to America after the Korean War, yet as a teenager she lived in Seoul. After attending Amherst College (where she majored in English) and Columbia (where she earned an M.A. in journalism), she returned to Korea and worked for the *Korea Herald*. Subsequently married and back in the United States, she worked at Dartmouth and the University of Virginia, while writing dozens of short stories and—as she says—acquiring 200 rejection slips.

"The One Who Goes Farthest Away" was published in *Special Report: Fiction* in 1990. The story was prompted by her father's consideration to move back to Korea. "My writing the story came of my trying to make the decision for him," she said. "But I finally decided I couldn't impose my will on him."

Currently she is working on a novel.

The One Who Goes Farthest Away

Thirty-five years ago the street had been dirt, narrow and rutted; there had been stables along it with tired ponies, all their ribs showing through dull, matted coats. Now, as he walked along the red-tiled sidewalk, he watched the cars glide over the smooth black tar, watched the men on bicycles, loaded in back with toilet paper, chickens, and ice, weave in and out of traffic with the intensity of racers.

He couldn't help comparing the world he had known with what he now saw; ever since he'd come back, he'd felt this curious simultaneity in his mind, as though the past lay superimposed on the present, playing itself out in phantom traces across the city. Thirty-five years ago there had been oxen to carry the loads, lumbering down the dusty streets attended by thin, indolent men. There had been bicycles too, but not for commerce, ridden by schoolchildren in their starched uniforms who had been freed from the basements of the war.

Entering a small courtyard, Kyoungsu marveled at how much the city had changed. The skyscrapers pressed in all around the older, shorter buildings, making them seem not so much like buildings as footstools. When he'd left, the city had been devastated, a dry, gray plain filled with rubble and debris, crowded with starving refugees from the North. *Like a phoenix*, Kyoungsu thought, *the city has rebuilt itself*. He shook his head at the aptness of the image. Out of the ashes.

He slipped off his polished black shoes and placed them next to the other identical pairs, which sat in a row on the wooden stoop outside the house. His were the newest-looking.

A tall woman in a green dress greeted him at the door and bowed slightly. "Welcome, professor," she said, her smile widening to reveal bad teeth. She ushered him into a narrow foyer. "This way, please," she indicated. "Your friends are waiting." She slid open a door of paper and wood and motioned for him to enter.

"Ah, Kyoungsu is here at last!" boomed a jovial male voice.

Three men rose from their cushions on the floor. They embraced Kyoungsu one after the other, slapping him on the back and laughing, all talking at once.

"Let's sit down, why don't we," Jae Shik said, "and Kyoungsu can tell us all about himself." This brought renewed laughter, as it was so typically Jae Shik to organize them all.

On the low black lacquer table were some glasses, an open bottle of whiskey, and two plates of nuts, dried cuttlefish, and raisins. The sight of it made Kyoungsu feel welcome. He settled onto a blue silk cushion beside his friends. He smelled the oiled paper, which covered the floor, heated underneath by hot air pipes. It had a musty odor.

"*Ja*," Young Bae said, picking up the bottle.

Kyoungsu held out his glass formally, with two hands, and Young Bae poured into it.

"To Kyoungsu." Jae Shik lifted his glass, and the others followed suit. "On his return to his homeland."

"To us," Kyoungsu replied with emotion. "To old friends."

They all drank up. Jae Shik refilled their glasses.

"Ah," Young Bae sighed. "We *are* old, aren't we? Look at you, Kyoungsu. Your hair has gone white."

"At least I still have hair," Kyoungsu observed.

Young Bae fingered the bald dome of his head, smoothing down the one lock of hair that still clung there like a faint wisp of smoke. "Bald men are considered sexy," he said.

"Fat men, too?" Hyun Ki asked. They laughed. Young Bae had always been fat, but his bulk had lost its firmness since the last time Kyoungsu had seen him; his stomach sagged unhealthily downward.

They looked older, it was true. Young Bae's baldness showed mottled brown patches on his scalp, patches that repeated on the backs of his large hands. Hyun Ki was thinner than ever, skeletal; his eyes had worsened, and the glasses he wore seemed an inch thick. Even Jae Shik had aged, his boyish face lined with creases.

Kyoungsu felt saddened to see his friends so changed. In his mind they were always teenagers together, their faces bright with an unknown future, bodies restless, flowing with adrenaline. The time intervening seemed insubstantial. Why then, did they look so old? Kyoungsu gulped the whiskey in his glass. It burrowed warmth inside him as he drank.

"So, you've come back, Kyoungsu," Young Bae said, the cigarette in his mouth wavering in the air as he spoke.

"Well, I haven't decided yet," Kyoungsu replied, shrugging. "I've been down in Kwangju for three months now, at the university. They've offered me a permanent position, but I have to go back to the States for at least a year, whatever I decide."

"Of course you're coming back," Jae Shik said, popping pine nuts into his mouth one by one.

"I don't know." Kyoungsu shook his head. "It's a difficult decision."

"Why difficult?" asked Young Bae. "You are Korean. You belong in Korea. You've been away too long already."

"In America, he has it made," Hyun Ki retorted. His eyes blinked enormously behind thick lenses. "Why should he come back here?"

"Because Korea is his homeland," Jae Shik said simply.

Kyoungsu nodded. "I'm quite comfortable with life in the States," he said. "My kids are there, and I've got tenure. Jun Hee has a good job that she enjoys. But as I get older—I don't know—I think more and more about returning." He smiled at them.

"You know, Kyoungsu," Young Bae remarked suddenly, "you have an accent!" He pointed his cigarette toward Jae Shik, laughing. "Doesn't he? Doesn't he, Jae Shik? You sound like a foreigner, Kyoungsu!"

"Of course he has an accent," said Jae Shik. "He's lived abroad more than he's lived here."

Kyoungsu smiled sadly. "The Americans say the same thing," he said. "I guess between learning English and losing Korean I don't really have a language." The poignancy of this struck him, and he knew that it was true, that for him neither language was entirely comfortable anymore. In his mind he thought in a mishmash of the two, groping back and forth, often not distinguishing between them.

"Anyway, I can still understand you," said Hyun Ki, patting Kyoungsu on the back. "Tell us about your job in Kwangju, Godforsaken place," he said.

"Oh, it's not so bad," Kyoungsu shrugged. "They're treating me very well, of course, because they want me to stay. And the students are very sharp, but they're afraid to speak up in class. I have to really work to draw them out; they're so deferential to authority."

Young Bae snorted. "The same students who throw rocks at the police. Very nice, very deferential."

"And why shouldn't they throw rocks at the police?" Kyoungsu snapped. "When the police slaughter them by the thousands. You know what they did. . . ."

Jae Shik held up a hand. His voice was quiet, almost a whisper, but there was urgency behind it. "Kyoungsu, please! This isn't America!"

Kyoungsu held his tongue. Jae Shik had always hated political discussion. More than this, he hated when Kyoungsu and Young Bae bickered, something they had done constantly since grade school.

"Anyway, things are changing, Kyoungsu," Hyun Ki spoke up, his enormous eyes focusing and unfocusing behind his glasses. "Korean kids are following your Western example. Don't be fooled by their behavior in class. Young kids—my kids included—they don't follow the Confucian rules anymore." To Kyoungsu, his gaunt face looked bitter, unhappy, like the face of a disillusioned monk.

"Still, they must be better behaved than those American kids," reflected Jae Shik. "You see them on TV, so wild-looking with those strange clothes and weird hair. Some of the boys even wear earrings!" He scratched his hairless cheek in wonder.

"Yes," Kyoungsu nodded. "Korean kids are still much more easily managed." He was thinking of his own children, the battles he had had with them growing up. Jane's sullen face appeared to him as it had looked when she'd been thirteen: straight black hair hanging in her eyes, hands thrust deep in the pockets of worn-out jeans. "You think you're still in Korea," she would accuse him, when he wouldn't allow her to date or wear makeup like the other girls in her class. "But it's not fair, Dad. This is America."

Young Bae was laughing, shaking his head over something. "You were the hotheaded one, though, Kyoungsu," he was saying. "A madman! Do you remember the time you attacked me? What had I done to offend you? I can't remember. Jae Shik and Sang Chul had to pull you off before the principal came and found us."

"I remember," said Jae Shik soberly, watching Kyoungsu's face with apprehension. "You deserved it, Young Bae. You and your tongue."

Kyoungsu also remembered. He saw Young Bae as he'd been in high school, a sallow boy in a black school uniform stretched tight across his fat stomach. They used to call him Lord Buddha until Jae Shik, in a religious phase, had told them it was irreverent. Kyoungsu hadn't liked Young Bae as much as the others. He'd been hard even then, his round face set in a tough way, with narrow eyes that looked almost closed, and a mouth curling downward that had been attached to a cigarette since he was thirteen. He used to bribe Kyoungsu into doing his homework for him, offering marbles and money for roasted yams. Then, out of shame, he would insult Kyoungsu, belittle his family name. Once, that one time, Kyoungsu had punched him for it, blackening his eye with the knuckles of one fist.

"Do you remember?" Hyun Ki said, his voice distant with the past. "Do you remember the time we all cut class and went to Inchon to eat abalone porridge? When we were around fifteen, I think. What a beautiful day that was!"

Kyoungsu nodded. "In June, wasn't it?" His glass paused at his lips. "We got that fisherman to take us out on his boat."

"Yes, yes," Jae Shik said, "and he let us take turns steering."

Hyun Ki removed his glasses. Without them, his eyes looked tiny. He began to clean the lenses on a corner of his handkerchief. "It was Sang Chul's idea," he said quietly.

They fell silent.

"Did I ever tell you," Kyoungsu said, "about the time in the army when Sang Chul and I were on leave together?"

The men shook their heads slowly, each lost in his own private memory of their friend. Kyoungsu spoke and they listened intently.

"We were drinking in a small bar somewhere in Pusan with a day left on leave, and this old guy next to us started to buy us beer. He said he was a fortune-teller, that he would tell us what we wanted to know about our futures. Well, Sang Chul, you can guess, was pretty keen, so the man took his palm and gazed into it for a long time."

Kyoungsu felt his own palms grow wet. He rubbed them absently on his pants legs. "After a while, the man just turned to me and asked to see my palm. He told me I would leave Korea and live somewhere far away. He said I would be successful, and though I wouldn't be rich, I would be comfortable. And he said I would die an old man."

He saw Sang Chul's face, that smirking combination of eagerness and scorn, both eyes trained steadily on the fortuneteller's face. "Sang Chul kept asking the man, 'What about *my* fortune? Why don't you tell me what's in store for me, old man?' But he just shook his head. I remember his eyes looked frightened, and he shrank away from us. . . . " Kyoungsu stopped and gazed reflectively into his glass.

"Sang Chul laughed and called the old man a lot of names, and then we both forgot about it and I said good-bye to him." Kyoungsu bowed his head, tracing the lines in a rumpled napkin with his finger.

"Poor bastard," Young Bae muttered.

"He was the best of all of us," Hyun Ki said gloomily, and they all fell silent.

Jae Shik clapped his hands. "*Ja*," he said, smiling with visible effort. "Let's order more whiskey."

The hostess brought the bottle on a tray and placed it on the table, then backed out of the room slowly, her eyes cast down on the floor. It was such a feminine gesture, Kyoungsu observed, demure and graceful—very Korean; it stirred a tenderness in him, and he thought of his wife, Jun Hee.

"Still," said Hyun Ki, "it's a wonder any of us survived. Jae Shik was wounded. Young Bae, you almost got sent to the North. And, Kyoungsu, remember when the bomb landed on the outhouse right after you had left it?"

"Good thing you weren't constipated!" Young Bae laughed huskily, then was silent.

How lucky we are, thought Kyoungsu, and he wanted to weep, to cry out. The war had claimed one-third of their classmates. It had divided families. It had seemed to Kyoungsu once that the world would never right itself, that he would never know the quiet pleasures of a normal life. And look at them now. They were the survivors. He felt an overwhelming affection for them all.

"A toast to Sang Chul," he said, raising his glass.

"To our generation," someone shouted. They tossed the whiskey down their throats and wiped the tears from their eyes.

"Did you know," Hyun Ki said after a moment, "they tore down that house, Kyoungsu, your father's old one? They turned it into a shop—antiques for tourists."

"It survived the war and got torn down for progress," muttered Hyun Ki.

"They tore down all the old houses," Jae Shik said, mopping the lacquer table with a napkin. "For the Olympics. New hotels. New shops."

"They tore it down?" Kyoungsu repeated dully. He remembered playing in the courtyard with the little Chindo dog his father kept. Sometimes his father would come in after being out all night and ruffle Kyoungsu's hair with a rough hand. He would give him a 500-hwan note for lunch and wander off to bed, and Kyoungsu would stare after him—at the distant man in the homburg and the English-looking suit—then go off and spend the money on cigarettes and comic books.

"It's changed so much here," Kyoungsu said quietly. He pulled his crossed legs toward his body, rocking back and forth.

"I remember," he murmured, his eyes on his glass, "how homesick I was when I first arrived in America. I was the first Korean at Amherst College, right out of the war; all the other freshmen were four years younger, and my English was poor. I remember the Americans were all so kind to me. My roommate invited me to his house for Thanksgiving; the dean of the college invited me to Christmas dinner. But I missed Korean food so badly. Especially kimchi."

The others nodded, their faces straining to comprehend a place lacking in this staple, the spicy fermented cabbage they had eaten three times a day for their entire lives.

"Once I tried to cook an egg in my room over vacation," Kyoungsu went on. "I wanted it hard-boiled, so I put the egg in my sock and held it under the hot-water faucet in the bathroom for about 20 minutes. It came out raw."

The men chuckled.

Kyoungsu continued. He was aware of the sound his voice made as he talked, of the silence surrounding it. "It was never a conscious decision to stay," he said. "Just one day leading to the next, to the next, faster and faster, until one day I woke up and I was fifty-six and living in a foreign country. I had two grown-up kids who didn't even speak Korean."

The others listened shyly, looking down at their socked feet. Kyoungsu felt his own surprise as he thought of how much time had passed.

"Why did you leave, anyway?" said Young Bae with sudden harshness. "The war ruined everything. You were the smartest in our class. The country needed you."

"Oh, come on, Young Bae," Kyoungsu retorted. "You wanted to go too, but your mother threatened to go on hunger strike if you left her!"

"That's right," Hyun Ki laughed. "That's right, Young Bae, I remember. She told my mother she would rather die than lose her oldest son."

Young Bae took a surly gulp of whiskey, his Adam's apple working like a pump. He grimaced. "Anyway," he said, "I didn't go. And I'm glad I didn't."

"And you did very well, Young Bae," said Jae Shik, patting him on the shoulder. "And Kyoungsu did well in America. And now he's coming back, and we'll all be together."

Hyun Ki poured the last of the whiskey into Kyoungsu's glass.

"Do you remember?" Kyoungsu laughed, upsetting the plate of nuts with his sleeve. "Do you remember," he repeated eagerly, "the time we went up to the temple at sunrise?"

"Which one?" Jae Shik asked.

Kyoungsu thought. "I don't know. The one on Kwanaksan? We were trying to be better Buddhists then."

"I don't remember," said Hyun Ki.

Young Bae shook his head. "I wasn't there."

"Yes, you were. All of us were," Kyoungsu insisted. "Don't you remember, Jae Shik? It was your idea. We must have been twelve or thirteen. We climbed up on a Sunday morning, very early, with our lunches packed, and when we got to the top, we vowed we would all go to America."

"Did we do that?" Jae Shik asked.

"Did we?" Young Bae echoed, a note of wonder in his voice.

"The one who goes the farthest away remembers the most," mused Hyun Ki.

Young Bae laughed. "Or makes it up," he said, coughing. "Fantasies."

They all chuckled, but Kyoungsu saw it all very clearly, the five of them in their identical school uniforms with their crew cuts and black knapsacks, hiking up Kwanaksan in the streaked light of dawn, discussing Buddhism and America with the same eagerness and mystification. They would all go to America; they had decided—a notion one of them had come up with—but only he had gone. And why was that?

Kyoungsu chewed thoughtfully on the end of a shredded piece of dried cuttlefish, savoring the fishy sweetness that he liked so much. It reminded him of the movie theater they used to go to sometimes when they were skipping school. It was a dingy place with sticky floors and a torn velvet curtain where they had first seen the old Tarzan movies and Errol Flynn, mistaking the Hollywood images of Africa or the high seas for a vision of America. It had been in Sam-chong-dong, hadn't it? Surely it wasn't there any longer. He thought if he had the time he might go see.

The smells of his childhood: sesame oil, garlic, and hot pepper in the earthen kitchen of his mother's house, the kerosene and roasting chestnuts from the street vendors' carts—the sounds: the tinny voice of the calisthenics instructor blaring from the loudspeaker in the courtyard of their school, "Ready, begin, one, two, one, two . . ."; the hollow, wooden pounding of the Buddhist drums; the dry rasp of his father's cough—the feeling: timeless afternoons playing war games with Jae Shik when he was seven or eight in the courtyard at Insadong; then the real thing, lying face-down in a damp trench, eighteen but really still a boy, fingering the rifle in his hands with a reluctant fascination and terror. He realized sadly, his stomach tightening, that he remembered these times in his life more vividly than any recent memory.

"I know why I wanted to come back," he said quietly. He shook his head in wonder at himself. "Because I wanted to die here."

"But you are a long way from dying, Kyoungsu," said Jae Shik.

He nodded. He wanted to say that America was a country where there was only the future. From the day he had arrived, with twenty-five dollars in his pocket, he had been swept forward into tomorrow and the next day, awed by the driving possibilities of life without tradition, without the past. There were no memories for him in America.

But here the past swirled with smell and sound, with texture and shape; it spoke to him in many voices, arresting him, crowding up against him as he revolved through the city, more real than the concrete buildings, than the newly laid highways, more resonant than the traffic noise, than the voices in the streets. He could not tell his friends that for him his homeland was a dead land, inhabited by ghosts, by stunning visions of the past. He could not tell them.

"Ah," Hyun Ki was getting to his feet slowly, a bit unsteadily. "Forgive me, but I must go," he said. "It's after two, and I have to go in to work tomorrow." He reached for Kyoungsu's hand. "Come back to us, Kyoungsu, and quit this talk of death," he said, looking with concern at his friend.

The others started to get up also. Young Bae yawned. "I'm off as well," he said. "It's past my bedtime."

"Stay a little longer, Hyun Ki," Kyoungsu protested. "Jae Shik? We can go to a tent restaurant and have some *kooksoo*."[1]

"No, no," Jae Shik shook his head. "Your wife is in the States, Kyoungsu, or you would know better."

Young Bae belched, rubbing a hand underneath his belt. "*Ajuma!*"[2] he called out. "The bill, please!"

Hyun Ki dug his wallet from his back pocket. "Oh, no, you don't, Young Bae," he said. "My treat."

[1]*kooksoo* soup with noodles

[2]*Ajuma!* Waitress!

Kyoungsu reached for his own wallet. "I wish you'd let me pay," he said. "I am the visitor, after all."

Young Bae waved them aside with both arms. "I am the richest one here," he said, taking the bills from his wallet. He laughed, shaking his finger at Kyoungsu. "Mr. Professor, sir. You used to do my homework, too. And I am the wealthiest one of all of us."

The hostess appeared, and Young Bae paid her. "And this is for you," he said, handing her an additional 10,000-won note.

They slipped on their shoes, after much arguing over whose were whose, and walked out into the small courtyard. Neon lights cast a yellow vapor across the city sky. Kyoungsu noted all the English names flashing in Korean letters: Crown, Ambassador, Venus.

Jae Shik embraced Kyoungsu, patting his back several times. "When you come back," he said, "we will meet every week to drink together."

Kyoungsu pressed his friend's hand, nodding absently.

"Your wife isn't so Americanized she will beat you for going out with us, is she?" Hyun Ki teased, shaking Kyoungsu's hand, then holding it with his own.

Kyoungsu grinned. "She is so Americanized, she will go out drinking with her friends also!"

He laughed and the others did, too, but Kyoungsu knew that to them it was hilarious because it seemed absurd; to him it was funny precisely because it was true.

"We argue," Young Bae said, clapping a hand on Kyoungsu's shoulder. "My God, how I've missed fighting with you!"

Kyoungsu hugged him. "Fat man," he whispered, affection choking his words. *What good men they all are*, he thought, *such good men*. His oldest friends.

"Going back to your brother's place?" Jae Shik asked him. "Share a cab?"

Kyoungsu shook his head. "No, no," he said. "I'm all right. I think I'll walk."

"Okay then."

Kyoungsu waved. As he watched his classmates retreat into the shadows, he saw their young faces clearly: smooth, except for Hyun Ki's acne, blinking with an innocence that bestowed upon the world a newness, an even light, their mouths calling to him in childish voices, speaking of boyhood games, of manly achievements, their smiles like promises made to one another. He realized how much it had cost him to leave them, how much it would continue to cost him.

[1990]

QUESTIONS

1. Why can't Kyoungsu return to live in Korea?
2. In the story, Young Bae remarks that the one who goes farthest away makes up his past. Is this true of Kyoungsu? Are his memories of the past distorted?
3. Is Kyoungsu a cultural half-caste?

SUSAN MINOT

(b. 1956)

UNITED STATES

Susan Minot was born in Manchester, Massachusetts, in 1956. She grew up in that area, eventually attending Concord Academy and Boston University, later transferring to Brown, where she began her writing. The title of her first novel, *Monkeys* (1986), refers to a mother's term for her children. The novel covers a period of 13 years and describes the maturation of the children of the Vincent family, ending with their mother's death. The structure of the work is that of a series of interconnected stories, a relatively loose form that can be seen in some of Minot's other work, such as her story "Lust," included here.

Many of the stories in *Lust and Other Stories* (1989) were written during an extended stay in Italy. When Minot was on her way back to the United States, her automobile was vandalized in Milan and all of the stories were stolen. Minot began the arduous task of reconstructing them from scratch. When they were published as a collection, they prompted Kelli Pryor to write, "The stories that make up *Lust* are about desire's smaller wounds."

Lust

Leo was from a long time ago, the first one I ever saw nude. In the spring before the Hellmans filled their pool, we'd go down there in the deep end, with baby oil, and like that. I met him the first month away at boarding school. He had a halo from the campus light behind him. I flipped.

Roger was fast. In his illegal car, we drove to the reservoir, the radio blaring, talking fast, fast, fast. He was always going for my zipper. He got kicked out sophomore year.

By the time the band got around to playing "Wild Horses," I had tasted Bruce's tongue. We were clicking in the shadows on the other side of the amplifier, out of Mrs. Donovan's line of vision. It tasted like salt, with my neck bent back, because we had been dancing so hard before.

Tim's line: "I'd like to see you in a bathing suit." I knew it was his line when he said the exact same thing to Annie Hines.

You'd go on walks to get off campus. It was raining like hell, my sweater as sopped as a wet sheep. Tim pinned me to a tree, the woods light brown and dark brown, a white house half-hidden with the lights already on. The water was as loud as a crowd hissing. He made certain comments about my forehead, about my cheeks.

We started off sitting at one end of the couch and then our feet were squished against the armrest and then he went over to turn off the TV and came back after he had taken off his shirt and then we slid onto the floor and he got up again to close the door, then came back to me, a body waiting on the rug.

You'd try to wipe off the table or to do the dishes and Willie would untuck your shirt and get his hands up under in front, standing behind you, making puffy noises in your ear.

He likes it when I wash my hair. He covers his face with it and if I start to say something, he goes, "Shush."

For a long time, I had Philip on the brain. The less they noticed you, the more you got them on the brain.

My parents had no idea. Parents never really know what's going on, especially when you're away at school most of the time. If she met them, my mother might say, "Oliver seems nice" or "I like that one" without much of an opinion. If she didn't like them, "He's a funny fellow, isn't he?" or "Johnny's perfectly nice but a drink of water." My father was too shy to talk to them at all, unless they played sports and he'd ask them about that.

The sand was almost cold underneath because the sun was long gone. Eben piled a mound over my feet, patting around my ankles, the ghostly surf rumbling behind him in the dark. He was the first person I ever knew who died, later that summer, in a car crash. I thought about it for a long time.

"Come here," he says on the porch.

I go over to the hammock and he takes my wrist with two fingers.

"What?"

He kisses my palm then directs my hand to his fly.

Songs went with whichever boy it was. "Sugar Magnolia" was Tim, with the line "Rolling in the rushes/down by the riverside." With "Darkness Darkness," I'd picture Philip with his long hair. Hearing "Under my Thumb" there'd be the smell of Jamie's suede jacket.

We hid in the listening rooms during study hall. With a record cover over the door's window, the teacher on duty couldn't look in. I came out flushed and heady and back at the dorm was surprised how red my lips were in the mirror.

One weekend at Simon's brother's, we stayed inside all day with the shades down, in bed, then went out to Store 24 to get some ice cream. He stood at the magazine rack and read through *MAD* while I got butterscotch sauce, craving something sweet.

I could do some things well. Some things I was good at, like math or painting or even sports, but the second a boy put his arm around me, I forget about wanting to do anything else, which felt like a relief at first until it became like sinking into a muck.

It was different for a girl.

When we were little, the brothers next door tied up our ankles. They held the door of the goat house and wouldn't let us out till we showed them our underpants. Then they'd forget about being after us and when we played whiffle ball, I'd be just as good as them.

Then it got to be different. Just because you have on a short skirt, they yell from the cars, slowing down for a while and if you don't look, they screech off and call you a bitch.

"What's the matter with me?" they say, point-blank.

Or else, "Why won't you go out with me? I'm not asking you to get married," about to get mad.

Or it'd be, trying to be reasonable, in a regular voice, "Listen, I just want to have a good time."

So I'd go because I couldn't think of something to say back that wouldn't be obvious, and if you go out with them, you sort of have to do something.

I sat between Mack and Eddie in the front seat of the pickup. They were having a fight about something. I've a feeling about me.

Certain nights you'd feel a certain surrender, maybe if you'd had wine. The surrender would be forgetting yourself and you'd put your nose to his neck and feel like a squirrel, safe, at rest, in a restful dream. But then you'd start to slip from that and the dark would come in and there'd be a cave. You make out the dim shape of the windows and feel yourself become a cave, filled absolutely with air, or with a sadness that wouldn't stop.

Teenage years. You know just what you're doing and don't see the things that start to get in the way.

Lots of boys, but never two at the same time. One was plenty to keep you in a state. You'd start to see a boy and something would rush over you like a fast storm cloud and you couldn't possibly think of anyone else. Boys took it differently. Their eyes perked up at any little number that walked by. You'd act like you weren't noticing.

The joke was that the school doctor gave out the pill like aspirin. He didn't ask you anything. I was fifteen. We had a picture of him in assembly, holding up an IUD shaped like a T. Most girls were on the pill, if anything, because they couldn't handle a diaphragm. I kept the dial in my top drawer like my mother and thought of her each time I tipped out the yellow tablets in the morning before chapel.

If they were too shy, I'd be more so. Andrew was nervous. We stayed up with his family album, sharing a pack of Old Golds. Before it got light, we turned on the TV. A man was explaining how to plant seedlings. His mouth jerked to the side in a tic. Andrew thought it was a riot and kept imitating him. I laughed to be polite. When we finally dozed off, he dared to put his arm around me but that was it.

You wait till they come to you. With half fright, half swagger, they stand one step down. They dare to touch the button on your coat then lose their nerve and quickly drop their hand so you—you'd do anything for them. You touch their cheek.

The girls sit around in the common room and talk about boys, smoking their heads off.

"What are you complaining about?" says Jill to me when we talk about problems.

"Yeah," says Giddy. "You always have a boyfriend."

I look at them and think, As if.

I thought the worst thing anyone could call you was a cock-teaser. So, if you flirted, you had to be prepared to go through with it. Sleeping with someone was perfectly normal once you had done it. You didn't really worry about it. But there were other problems. The problems had to do with something else entirely.

Mack was during the hottest summer ever recorded. We were renting a house on an island with all sorts of other people. No one slept during the heat wave, walking around the house with nothing on which we were used to because of the nude beach. In the living room, Eddie lay on top of a coffee table to cool off. Mack and I, with the bedroom door open for air, sweated and sweated all night.

"I can't take this," he said at 3 A.M. "I'm going for a swim." He and some guys down the hall went to the beach. The heat put me on edge. I sat on a cracked chest by the open window and smoked and smoked till I felt even worse, waiting for something—I guess for him to get back.

One was on a camping trip in Colorado. We zipped our sleeping bags together, the coyotes' hysterical chatter far away. Other couples murmured in other tents. Paul was up before sunrise, starting a fire for breakfast. He wasn't much of a talker in the daytime. At night, his hand leafed about in the hair at my neck.

There'd be times when you overdid it. You'd get carried away. All the next day, you'd be in a total fog, delirious, absent-minded, crossing the street and nearly getting run over.

The more girls a boy has, the better. He has a bright look, having reaped fruits, blooming. He stalks around, sure-shouldered, and you have the feeling he's got more in him, a fatter heart, more stories to tell. For a girl, with each boy it's like a petal gets plucked each time.

Then you start to get tired. You begin to feel diluted, like watered-down stew.

Oliver came skiing with us. We lolled by the fire after everyone had gone to bed. Each creak you'd think was someone coming downstairs. The silver-loop bracelet he gave me had been a present from his girlfriend before.

On vacations, we went skiing, or you'd go south if someone invited you. Some people had apartments in New York that their families hardly ever used. Or summer houses, or older sisters. We always managed to find some place to go.

We made the plan at coffee hour. Simon snuck out and met me at Main Gate after lights-out. We crept to the chapel and spent the night in the balcony. He tasted like onions from a submarine sandwich.

The boys are one of two ways: either they can't sit still or they don't move. In front of the TV, they won't budge. On weekends they play touch football while we sit on the sidelines, picking blades of grass to chew on, and watch. We're always watching them run around. We shiver in the stands, knocking our boots together to keep our toes warm and they whizz across the ice, chopping their sticks around the puck. When they're in the rink, they refuse to look at you, only eyeing each other beneath low helmets. You cheer for them but they don't look up, even if it's a face-off when nothing's happening, even if they're doing drills before any game has started at all.

Dancing under the pink tent, he bent down and whispered in my ear. We slipped away to the lawn on the other side of the hedge. Much later, as he was leaving the buffet with two plates of eggs and sausage, I saw the grass stains on the knees of his white pants.

Tim's was shaped like a banana, with a graceful curve to it. They're all different. Willie's like a bunch of walnuts when nothing was happening, another's as thin as a thin hot dog. But it's like faces; you're never really surprised.

Still, you're not sure what to expect.

I look into his face and he looks back. I look into his eyes and they look back at mine. Then they look down at my mouth so I look at his mouth, then back to his eyes then, backing up, at his whole face. I think, Who? Who are you? His head tilts to one side.

I say, "Who are you?"

"What do you mean?"

"Nothing."

I look at his eyes again, deeper. Can't tell who he is, what he thinks.

"What?" he says. I look at his mouth.

"I'm just wondering," I say and go wandering across his face. Study the chin line. It's shaped like a persimmon.

"Who are you? What are you thinking?"

He says, "What the hell are you talking about?"

Then they get mad after when you say enough is enough. After, when it's easier to explain that you don't want to. You wouldn't dream of saying that maybe you weren't really ready to in the first place.

Gentle Eddie. We waded into the sea, the waves round and plowing in, buffalo-headed, slapping our thighs. I put my arms around his freckled shoulders and he held me up, buoyed by the water, and rocked me like a sea shell.

I had no idea whose party it was, the apartment jam-packed, stepping over people in the hallway. The room with the music was practically empty, the bare floor, me in red shoes. This fellow slides onto one knee and takes me around the waist and we rock to jazzy tunes, with my toes pointing heavenward, and waltz and spin and dip to "Smoke Gets in Your Eyes" or "I'll Love You Just for Now." He puts his head to my chest, runs a sweeping hand down my inside thigh and we go loose-limbed and sultry and as smooth as silk and I stamp my red heels and he takes me into a swoon. I never saw him again after that but I thought, I could have loved that one.

You wonder how long you can keep it up. You begin to feel like you're showing through, like a bathroom window that only lets in grey light, the kind you can't see out of.

They keep coming around. Johnny drives up at Easter vacation from Baltimore and I let him in the kitchen with everyone sound asleep. He has friends waiting in the car.

"What are you crazy? It's pouring out there," I say.

"It's okay," he says. "They understand."

So he gets some long kisses from me, against the refrigerator, before he goes because I hate those girls who push away a boy's face as if she were made out of Ivory soap, as if she's that much greater than he is.

The note on my cubby told me to see the headmaster. I had no idea for what. He had received complaints about my amorous displays on the town green. It was Willie that spring. The headmaster told me he didn't care what I did but that Casey Academy had a reputation to uphold in the town. He lowered his glasses on his nose. "We've got twenty acres of woods on this campus," he said. "Smooch with your boyfriend there."

Everybody'd get weekend permissions for different places then we'd all go to someone's house whose parents were away. Usually there'd be more boys than girls. We raided the liquor closet and smoked pot at the kitchen table and you'd never know who would end up where, or with whom. There were always disasters. Ceci got bombed and cracked her head open on the bannister and needed stitches. Then there was the time Wendel Blair walked through the picture window at the Lowe's and got slashed to ribbons.

He scared me. In bed, I didn't dare look at him. I lay back with my eyes closed, luxuriating because he knew all sorts of expert angles, his hands never fumbling, going over my whole body, pressing the hair up and off the back of my head, giving an extra hip shove, as if to say *There*. I parted my eyes slightly, keeping the screen of my lashes low because it was too much to look at him, his mouth loose and pink and parted, his eyes looking through my forehead, or kneeling up, looking through my throat. I was ashamed but couldn't look him in the eye.

You wonder about things feeling a little off-kilter. You begin to feel like a piece of pounded veal.

At boarding school, everyone gets depressed. We go in and see the housemother, Mrs. Gunther. She got married when she was eighteen. Mr. Gunther was her high-school sweetheart, the only boyfriend she ever had.

"And you knew you wanted to marry him right off?" we ask her.

She smiles and says, "Yes."

"They always want something from you," says Jill, complaining about her boyfriend.

"Yeah," says Giddy. "You always feel like you have to deliver something."

"You do," says Mrs. Gunther. "Babies."

After sex, you curl up like a shrimp, something deep inside you ruined, slammed in a place that sickens at slamming, and slowly you fill up with an overwhelming sadness, an elusive gaping worry. You don't try to explain it, filled with the knowledge that it's nothing after all, everything filling up finally and absolutely with death. After the briskness of loving, loving stops. And you roll over with death stretched out alongside you like a feather boa, or a snake, light as air, and you . . . you don't even ask for anything or try to say something to him because it's obviously your own damn fault. You haven't been able to — to what? To open your heart. You open your legs but can't, or don't dare anymore, to open your heart.

It starts this way:

You stare into their eyes. They flash like all the stars are out. They look at you seriously, their eyes at a low burn and their hands no matter what starting off shy and with such a gentle touch that the only thing you can do is take that tenderness and let yourself be swept away. When, with one attentive finger they tuck the hair behind your ear, you—

You do everything they want.

Then comes after. After when they don't look at you. They scratch their balls, stare at the ceiling. Or if they do turn, their gaze is altogether changed. They are surprised. They turn casually to look at you, distracted, and get a mild distracted surprise. You're gone. Their black look tells you that the girl they were fucking is not there anymore. You seem to have disappeared.

[1984]

QUESTIONS

1. Are the form and the content of Susan Minot's story related?
2. Although the narrator of "Lust" gives us a composite picture of her own feelings and emotions, what can be said about the men in her story?
3. Does the narrator like herself?
4. Where exactly does the theme of the story change from lust (sex) to something else? What is that something else?
5. Would "Sex" be an equally appropriate title for Minot's story?

MISHIMA YUKIO

(1925–1970)

JAPAN

Western readers of Japanese fiction have often erroneously concluded that the country's contemporary writers are obsessed with death. The widow of Yasunari Kawabata, a Nobel-prize writer, attempted to suppress the publication of a book that argued that her 72-year-old husband had committed suicide because the housemaid had decided to stop working for him. Others have argued that Kawabata committed suicide because his young friend, Mishima Yukio, had already beaten him to it. Whatever the case, the images of death and ritual suicide (of the samurai) often permeate the fiction of several of the country's most famous writers. (Consider, for example, Mishima's short story "Patriotism.")

Mishima was born in Tokyo in 1925. At the time of his death, he was probably his country's most famous writer—both internationally and at home. During the course of his prolific career, he published novels, short stories, dramas, and essays. Shortly before his suicide, Mishima told Donald Keene that he had written "enough for one lifetime," that he had put everything into his last book (*The Sea of Fertility*) and had "nothing left to do but to die." Keene adds, "Mishima meant it literally, and it must have seemed particularly appropriate to die on the day that he delivered to the publisher the concluding installment of his culminating work. It was not that Mishima feared a waning of his creative powers. He knew he could go on writing better than anyone else in Japan, almost without effort. But there was nothing more he wanted to say. He chose to end his career at his peak."

Swaddling Clothes

He was always busy, Toshiko's husband. Even tonight he had to dash off to an appointment, leaving her to go home alone by taxi. But what else could a woman expect when she married an actor—an attractive one? No doubt she had been foolish to hope that he would spend the evening with her. And yet he must have known how she dreaded going back to their house, unhomely with its Western-style furniture and with the bloodstains still showing on the floor.

Toshiko had been oversensitive since girlhood: that was her nature. As the result of constant worrying she never put on weight, and now, an adult woman, she looked more like a transparent picture than a creature of flesh and blood. Her delicacy of spirit was evident to her most casual acquaintance.

Earlier that evening, when she had joined her husband at a night club, she had been shocked to find him entertaining friends with an account of "the incident." Sitting there in his American-style suit, puffing at a cigarette, he had seemed to her almost a stranger.

"It's a fantastic story," he was saying, gesturing flamboyantly as if in an attempt to outweigh the attractions of the dance band. "Here this new nurse for our baby arrives from the employment agency, and the very first thing I noticed about her is her stomach. It's enormous—as if she had a pillow stuck under her kimono! No wonder, I thought, for I soon saw that she could eat more than the rest of us put together. She polished off the contents of our rice bin like that. . . ." He snapped his fingers. "'Gastric dilation'—that's how she explained her girth and her appetite. Well, the day before yesterday we heard groans and moans coming from the nursery. We rushed in and found her squatting on the floor, holding her stomach in her two hands, and moaning like a cow. Next to her our baby lay in his cot, scared out of his wits and crying at the top of his lungs. A pretty scene, I can tell you!"

"So the cat was out of the bag?" suggested one of their friends, a film actor like Toshiko's husband.

"Indeed it was! And it gave me the shock of my life. You see, I'd completely swallowed that story about 'gastric dilation.' Well, I didn't waste any time. I rescued our good rug from the floor and spread a blanket for her to lie on. The whole time the girl was yelling like a stuck pig. By the time the doctor from the maternity clinic arrived, the baby had already been born. But our sitting room was a pretty shambles!"

"Oh, that I'm sure of!" said another of their friends, and the whole company burst into laughter.

Toshiko was dumbfounded to hear her husband discussing the horrifying happening as though it were no more than an amusing incident which they chanced to have witnessed. She shut her eyes for a moment and all at once she saw the newborn baby lying before her: on the parquet floor the infant lay, and his frail body was wrapped in bloodstained newspapers.

Toshiko was sure that the doctor had done the whole thing out of spite. As if to emphasize his scorn for his mother who had given birth to a bastard under such sordid conditions, he had told his assistant to wrap the baby in some loose newspapers, rather than proper swaddling. This callous treatment of the newborn child had offended Toshiko. Overcoming her disgust at the entire scene, she had fetched a brand-new piece of flannel from her cupboard and, having swaddled the baby in it, had laid him carefully in an armchair.

This all had taken place in the evening after her husband had left the house. Toshiko had told him nothing of it, fearing that he would think her oversoft, oversentimental; yet the scene had engraved itself deeply in her mind. Tonight she sat silently thinking back on it, while the jazz orchestra brayed and her husband chatted cheerfully with his friends. She knew that she would never forget the sight of the baby, wrapped in stained newspapers and lying on the floor—it was a scene fit for a butchershop. Toshiko, whose own life had been spent in solid comfort, poignantly felt the wretchedness of the illegitimate baby.

I am the only person to have witnessed its shame, the thought occurred to her. The mother never saw her child lying there in its newspaper wrappings, and the baby itself of course didn't know. I alone shall have to preserve that terrible scene in my memory. When the baby grows up and wants to find out about his birth, there will be no one to tell him, so long as I preserve silence. How strange that I should have this feeling of guilt! After all, it was I who took him up from the floor, swathed him properly in flannel, and laid him down to sleep in the armchair.

They left the night club and Toshiko stepped into the taxi that her husband had called for her. "Take this lady to Ushigomé," he told the driver and shut the door from the outside. Toshiko gazed through the window at her husband's smiling face and noticed his strong, white teeth. Then she leaned back in the seat, oppressed by the knowledge that their life together was in some way too easy, too painless. It would have been difficult for her to put her thoughts into words. Through the rear window of the taxi she took a last look at her husband. He was striding along the street toward his Nash car, and soon the back of his rather garish tweed coat had blended with the figures of the passers-by.

The taxi drove off, passed down a street dotted with bars and then by a theatre, in front of which the throngs of people jostled each other on the pavement. Although the performance had only just ended, the lights had already been turned out and in the half dark outside it was depressingly obvious that the cherry blossoms decorating the front of the theatre were merely scraps of white paper.

Even if that baby should grow up in ignorance of the secret of his birth, he can never become a respectable citizen, reflected Toshiko, pursuing the same train of thoughts. Those soiled newspaper swaddling clothes will be the symbol of his entire life. But why should I keep worrying about him so much? Is it because I feel uneasy about the future of my own child? Say twenty years from now, when our boy will have grown up into a fine, carefully educated young man, one day by a quirk of fate he meets that other boy, who then will also have turned twenty. And say that the other boy, who has been sinned against, savagely stabs him with a knife. . . .

It was a warm, overcast April night, but thoughts of the future made Toshiko feel cold and miserable. She shivered on the back seat of the car.

No, when the time comes I shall take my son's place, she told herself suddenly. Twenty years from now I shall be forty-three. I shall go to that young man and tell him straight out about everything—about his newspaper swaddling clothes, and about how I went and wrapped him in flannel.

The taxi ran along the dark wide road that was bordered by the park and by the Imperial Palace moat. In the distance Toshiko noticed the pinpricks of light which came from the blocks of tall office buildings.

Twenty years from now that wretched child will be in utter misery. He will be living a desolate, hopeless, poverty-stricken existence—a lonely rat. What else could happen to a baby who has had such a birth? He'll be wandering through the streets by himself, cursing his father, loathing his mother.

No doubt Toshiko derived a certain satisfaction from her somber thoughts: she tortured herself with them without cease. The taxi approached Hanzomon and drove past the compound of the British Embassy. At that point the famous rows of cherry trees were spread out before Toshiko in all their purity. On the spur of the moment she decided to go and view the blossoms by herself in the dark night. It was a strange decision for a timid and unadventurous young woman, but then she was in a strange state of mind and she dreaded the return home. That evening all sorts of unsettling fancies had burst open in her mind.

She crossed the wide street—a slim, solitary figure in the darkness. As a rule when she walked in the traffic Toshiko used to cling fearfully to her companion, but tonight she darted alone between the cars and a moment later had reached the long narrow park that borders the Palace moat. Chidorigafuchi, it is called—the Abyss of the Thousand Birds.

Tonight the whole park had become a grove of blossoming cherry trees. Under the calm cloudy sky the blossoms formed a mass of solid whiteness. The paper lanterns that hung from wires between the trees had been put out; in their place electric light bulbs, red, yellow, and green, shone dully beneath the blossoms. It was well past ten o'clock and most of the flower-viewers had gone home. As the occasional passers-by strolled through the park, they would automatically kick aside the empty bottles or crush the waste paper beneath their feet.

Newspapers, thought Toshiko, her mind going back once again to those happenings. Bloodstained newspapers. If a man were ever to hear of that piteous birth and know that it was he who had lain there, it would ruin his entire life. To think that I, a perfect stranger, should from now on have to keep such a secret—the secret of a man's whole existence. . . .

Lost in these thoughts, Toshiko walked on through the park. Most of the people still remaining there were quiet couples; no one paid her any attention. She noticed two people sitting on a stone bench beside the moat, not looking at the blossoms, but gazing silently at the water. Pitch black it was, and swathed in heavy shadows. Beyond the moat the somber forest of the Imperial Palace blocked her view. The trees reached up, to form a solid dark mass against the night sky. Toshiko walked slowly along the path beneath the blossoms hanging heavily overhead.

On a stone bench, slightly apart from the others, she noticed a pale object—not, as she had at first imagined, a pile of cherry blossoms, nor a garment forgotten by one of the visitors to the park. Only when she came closer did she see that it was a human form lying on the bench. Was it, she wondered, one of those miserable drunks often to be seen sleeping in public places? Obviously not, for the body had been systematically covered with newspapers, and it was the whiteness of those papers that had attracted Toshiko's attention. Standing by the bench, she gazed down at the sleeping figure.

It was a man in a brown jersey who lay there, curled up on layers of newspapers, other newspapers covering him. No doubt this had become his normal night residence now that spring had arrived. Toshiko gazed down at the man's dirty, unkempt hair, which in places had become hopelessly matted. As she observed the sleeping figure wrapped in its newspapers, she was inevitably reminded of the baby who had lain on the floor in its wretched swaddling clothes. The shoulder of the man's jersey rose and fell in the darkness in time with his heavy breathing.

It seemed to Toshiko that all her fears and premonitions had suddenly taken concrete form. In the darkness the man's pale forehead stood out, and it was a young forehead, though carved with wrinkles of long poverty and hardship. His khaki trousers had been slightly pulled up; on his sockless feet he wore a pair of battered gym shoes. She could not see his face and suddenly had an overmastering desire to get one glimpse of it.

She walked to the head of the bench and looked down. The man's head was half buried in his arms, but Toshiko could see that he was surprisingly young. She noticed the thick eyebrows and the fine bridge of his nose. His slightly open mouth was alive with youth.

But Toshiko had approached too close. In the silent night the newspaper bedding rustled, and abruptly the man opened his eyes. Seeing the young woman standing directly beside him, he raised himself with a jerk, and his eyes lit up. A second later a powerful hand reached out and seized Toshiko by her slender wrist.

She did not feel in the least afraid and made no effort to free herself. In a flash the thought had struck her, Ah, so the twenty years have already gone by! The forest of the Imperial Palace was pitch dark and utterly silent.

[1966]

Translated by
IVAN MORRIS

QUESTIONS

1. Two major images of the story are cherry tree blossoms and newspapers. In what way are they related?
2. Are the men in Toshiko's life (her actor husband, the child in swaddling clothes, the man on the bench) all part and parcel of the same unresolved problem for her, or do they represent something else? Why is she the one who feels guilt and shame?
3. What are we to make of the many Western objects in the story: clothing, furniture, cars? Do they contribute to Toshiko's crisis?
4. What happens to Toshiko at the end of the story?
5. Is "Swaddling Clothes" a story about death or about something else?

Kermit Moyer

(b. 1943)

United States

Kermit Moyer was born in Harrisburg, Pennsylvania, in 1943. An army brat, he grew up in Hawaii, Okinawa, Georgia, Pennsylvania, and Texas. He has taught at American University in Washington, DC, since 1970, where he also began writing short stories and teaching in the creative writing program. When *Tumbling*, his first collection of short stories, was published in 1988, it was cited by the reviewer in the New York Times Book Review as one of the most significant volumes to appear in the 13-year history of the Illinois Short Fiction Series.

Asked to comment about the story, Moyer responded, "At its most abstract, I suppose that 'Tumbling' is about the way the imagination mediates our experience. As their nursery-rhyme names may suggest, Jack and Jill are also intended to express something elemental about male and female. By the end of the story, Jill discovers how radically entangled she's become in the masculine Oedipal scenarios that, wittingly or unwittingly, she's been helping to enact. With this discovery, the seemingly solid ground of reality opens up beneath her feet and, like her namesake, she goes tumbling. But, as we know, a fall can also be a genesis, and acrobats routinely turn tumbling into a demonstration of human resiliency and grace. I should add that, although I had some of these ideas in mind when I started the story, the act of writing tends to focus microscopically on the concrete unfolding of a particular moment rather than on anything so generalized as an idea or a 'theme.' In this sense, writing the story seemed less like the working out of a thesis than like the transcription of a dream."

◆ *Tumbling* ◆

Early one rainy morning just about a week ago, Jack and me were sitting in a laundromat in this little town where we'd spent the night in an unlocked car. We sleep in cars a lot of times, it's not as bad as you might think. A little cramped maybe, but if there's a radio and a key to make it work, we don't mind too much. Like that night we were in a big new-smelling Cadillac in a used-car lot. Jack said they could make it smell that way with an aerosol can. Plenty of room and everything clean and shiny. The radio picked up stations from as far away as Chicago and Fort Wayne, Indiana, and we sang along with the top forty and listened to one of those shows where people call in. Jacky tried to get a station from back home to see if there was anything on about us, but he couldn't find one. He said the signals were probably too weak to reach as far as we were by then. He was sitting behind the wheel smoking Camels because it was Daddy's brand. I hated for him to get that clean ashtray dirty. I don't know why. I said we should think of the folks that might want to buy that car. Jack just laughed and said maybe a few cigarette butts might give them a chance to think about us. "But wouldn't that be leaving evidence?" I said. That's one of the things Jacky talks about sometimes: covering our tracks, he calls it. He wipes our fingerprints off the radio knobs and the steering wheels, and he's always careful to use a handkerchief to open and close the doors. Well, that morning dawned so rainy-gray and drizzly you didn't even want to move. Jacky let me sleep with the duffel bag for a pillow and I just rolled myself up with my hands pressed between my knees and tried to keep what was happening in my dream from slipping away. It was a birthday party and it was you, Mom, not Jacky, helping me blow out the candles. I was wearing my blue print dress with the puffy sleeves and the white lace collar, and Jacky was saying, "Let me, let me." There was pink icing on the cake and I wanted to see if maybe Daddy was there too. I thought he might be because we were still little in my dream. But Jack was shaking my shoulder and telling me to rise and shine, we had to get out of there before they opened up. So I combed my hair in the rearview mirror, and then we scooted out and found this laundromat, which was either already open or else hadn't ever closed. We were wet from the rain by that time, so we got behind the machines and changed into some dry clothes. We put a wash in and then just sat around, watching the raindrops slide down the windows and reading magazines. We had the place all to ourselves, and it made me feel kind of blue, looking out at nothing but the rain and two or three parked cars. There was a Woolworth's right across the street that hadn't opened up yet. It was only about six o'clock in the morning. I could see a BACK TO SCHOOL sign in one window and I wondered if come September we'd be going back to school or not. My dream was still with me, too, but all scattered and floating away from where it came from. A foggy picture would come in front of my mind's eye, and I'd think it was something I was about to remember, something that really happened, and then I'd realize it was only my dream, and that'd make me feel like I'd lost something. The fat sound of the washer going chugga-*whoosh*-chugga-*whoosh* and the little pinging noise of the dryer had put me into sort of a hypnotic trance anyway. But not Jacky. He was reading a *Time* magazine, making noises to himself whenever he'd find something interesting. "Hey, listen to this," he says. "Remember what I told you? *Scientists now believe that the universe has been expanding from a single fixed point for millions of years. If we trace back the motion of the galaxies, we arrive at a point in the distant past when they were a single unified mass, a time when the universe must have been very different from its present disseminated state.*" I turned away from the window and said, "What do you mean, 'remember what I told you'? I don't remember anything like that." "Come on, Jill," he says, "everything's always moving away, I always said that, and we're going against the current anytime we try to keep them, you know, from flying apart, or anytime we try to get them back together again. That's why it's so hard, and that's why we have to be so careful all the time." "Oh, yeah," I said. "Sure. We're just like the galaxies."

It was right then that this big fat lady comes into the laundromat. She's got a whole wicker basket full of dirty laundry, so she pushes the door open with her shoulder and sort of backs in. When she turns around and sees us she flinches. "Land sakes," she says. "You give me a fright. I never expected a soul in here this early." Her face was one of those bright lit-up country kind with rosy apple cheeks—made red from bunches of tiny little broken veins I saw later—a face just as shiny wet from the rain as if she'd been crying her eyes out, except she looked so pleased with everything you couldn't believe she'd even know how to cry. She had round arms with freckles and her hair was just like yours, Mom—reddish strawberry-blonde—all twisted up in braids at the back of her head and against her neck. I was glad she was here because now I thought maybe I could get out of feeling so blue. Jacky'd be sure to put on one of his shows, and that meant I'd have to play along. Which usually I get a kick out of. Anytime we talk to somebody I have to wait and see who we're going to be this time. Real life is always so ordinary on the one hand and so complicated on the other, but Jacky's stories can make it all seem just as simple and easy as filling in a coloring book. "Can you tell us about how far we are from the Maryland line?" he says. The fat lady is still standing there with her arms hooped around this big basket of laundry. Jacky's got that funny way of being able to get your attention, and I could see her sort of tilt her head like she's having trouble hearing what he's trying to tell her. She says, "Not far—only about fifty miles, I guess. Just take Route 15 south out of town. Do you all have family in Maryland?" Jacky looks up at her and directly into her eyes. He sort of waves his hand over toward me and says, "This is Peggy Sue." *Peggy Sue?* I thought. He's got to be kidding. I just sat there with my hands folded in my lap and looked sort of lost—which was easy enough because that's just exactly how I felt, we'd been on the road almost two weeks by then, sticking to the back roads. In a way I was in the same boat as the fat lady, just waiting to find out what the story would be so I could play along. So then Jack says, "We're on our way to Maryland to get married." I closed my eyes for a second and tried to take that one in. When I looked up, the fat lady is staring at me and resting her basket on the formica table between the row of washers on one side and the row of dryers on the other. "Why, you're just kids," she says. If I turned slightly toward the window, I could see my reflection in the glass. It was all wavery from the rain. "Just a couple of kids," she says. I'm watching her in the reflection on the window and I can see right through her to the five-and-ten across the street. "You don't want to hear any of this," Jacky says. He's staring down at his hands and shaking his head back and forth. I can see him in the window too—our reflections have a sharp edge to them but the raindrops, sliding crooked down the glass, make everything outside blurry. "Look here," she says out of the blue, her head tilted and her voice going all kindly and soft. "You're in a family way, isn't that right child?" When I turned around she was watching me with a sly, sort of happy look. Jacky sits up straight, like he's suddenly got everything under control. "We're all right. We can take care of ourselves," he says. The fat lady's watching Jacky again, and she narrows her eyes and says, "How old are you kids? Where're you from?" "We're old enough, you don't have to worry about that," Jacky says right away. Then he says, "At least we're old enough in Maryland—we're just passing through here." He got that line from a movie we'd seen where somebody had to go to Maryland to get married because they were underage. We go to movies a lot on the road, for the simple reason that movie theaters turned out to be a good place to spend the night. "What about you?" she says to me. "Are you old enough too?" I circled my arms around my stomach and said, "It looks like I am." The fat lady nods her head and turns back to Jacky. "Well then I guess you better get yourselves a map the next time you fill up," she says. For a second it looked like that was the end of the conversation, but then Jacky says, "We're not driving, we don't have a car." He stops short, and then he blurts out, "We've been hitch-hiking." Which was true enough, that's for sure—one of the problems is being too young to have a driver's license much less a car. All we have is the money we got from cashing Daddy's check—which I'm real sorry about, Mom, but Jacky made out a good case it was his and mine in the first place. And we decided, or rather I should say he did, that we'd pretty much have to forget about riding on buses or trains or anything like that because otherwise we'd be sure to get picked up. So there we were sitting in a laundromat at six in the morning. For some reason, I remember, I kept listening to the rain. The light in that laundromat was real yellow against all the gray outside, and since this fat lady came in, the sound of the rain made it, I don't know, sort of cozy and warm-feeling somehow. "So you'll be looking for a ride then I guess," she says to Jacky. "I want you to know I think you're doing the right thing. I know it's bound to be hard for a spell, but you'll be just fine if you really love one another." She smiles in a way that makes it hard not to believe her. I immediately started to brighten up. Then she says, "Are you hungry, have you two had any breakfast yet? You must be starved." I felt like we were turning a corner when she said that. I don't know why, except it made me think of you asking that same question the time you didn't get back from your date until early Sunday morning and we were already up. You were still dressed fancy from Saturday night and you tried to tell us you'd been to church already. I could just see you in that navy blue cocktail dress with the bow at the bust whipping up jelly omelets and French toast and once in a while tossing your hair out of your eyes the way you do when your hands are full. Standing by the stove in your stocking feet after you'd kicked off your heels. Remembering that made me feel like a little kid, and here I was supposed to be pregnant and everything. When we don't answer her, the fat lady looks at Jack and tells him, "You need to make sure this girl eats on a regular schedule. She's a little lady now, and she'll have to keep her strength up." Then she turns to me and says, "Don't worry, I wouldn't tell your secret to a soul, but you'll have to eat enough for the baby too, that's the first thing." She smiled and I nodded and she says, "Good. Now just let me get this wash started. Our dryer's all right, but the Bendix's been on the fritz, so here I am. Well. We'll have to see about getting some nourishment into you. It's not healthy to be as skinny as you are in your condition." To tell the truth, I *was* just about starved, and I was also glad to let this fat lady take charge for a while—even if it was under false pretenses. I was avoiding Jacky's eyes because I didn't want to be reminded of that at all. I just wanted to be taken care of for a little while. Maybe I'd even get to take a bath. In my dream there were lots and lots of candles on the cake even though we were little, and when I couldn't blow them all out you blew out the rest, so I knew all my wishes were going to come true. Jacky was crying and he kept saying, "Let me, let me," but that didn't really matter. The feeling I had in my dream was this: I didn't know what my wishes were, but I just had a feeling they were all going to come true.

I think it was something about the fat lady herself that made Jack come up with that particular story. The trick Jacky has is he can pretty much hook up the right story with the right person. He just lets them make it up with him. That's where the fat lady was a natural. She really loved the idea of us running off because we had to get married. It might be a speck scandalous, she said, but that's all right, these things always happened this way. She expected we'd be as happy as anybody else and, besides, the baby was a sure sign. So now I had to play my part in this hot teenage romance she and Jack cooked up. Star-struck lovers and everything. And that's probably right where it all started, from then on it's just been one thing after another. Like running off to find Daddy in the first place. If you look at it from a distance, I guess it's pretty ridiculous. But each step of the way it seemed perfectly natural and, the funny thing is, after a while the reasons why hardly seemed to matter. I knew you'd be worried about us, but I also knew you'd be all right and I wasn't so sure about Jacky. And anyway at first I thought I'd be able to steer him home before you even got back from your weekend in the city. But the plan of how to do each step of the thing somehow took over. Each step always makes sense—even if the whole thing doesn't. Daddy's supposed to be in Brunswick, Georgia, so that's where we're going. And of course running off was a good way to make you feel sorry too. Jacky's sure you spent the weekend with that guy from work, the one that brought you home after the office party. I guess you never knew it, but Jacky saw the two of you kissing or something in the kitchen that night. Those things don't matter to me, but where you're concerned Jacky can't even stand the idea of stuff like that. So going off to find Daddy was a bright light for Jacky—he *had* to follow it. And I just had to go along. I guess I've always felt like I had to look after Jacky, even if he is eight minutes older than me. I don't only mean take care of him exactly—I mean more like I have to follow him with my mind and with my feelings. He gets so worked up about stuff sometimes, and really, things like that just never mattered to me. What's actually happening matters a lot more than anything you might merely think about it, don't you agree?

You should have seen the fat lady's house. But of course she wasn't the fat lady by then. We found out her name was Mrs. Spicer, and she had a whole flock of kids, most of them grown now, and grandchildren—the youngest was only about four years old. Well, it didn't take long before Jack had Mrs. Spicer eating out of his hand. He'd tease her and make her laugh and pretty soon she's treating him like he's her favorite son or something. But I don't think she ever pictured me as one of her daughters though. I was more like somebody she used to be herself, that's what she told me. We got in the front seat of this Chevrolet station wagon she had, and then she drove us just barely outside of town to a big old pink house with blue shutters and lots of peaks and chimneys and three wide porches, a screened one up on the second floor just for sleeping—all of it set back on a low hill you couldn't even see from the highway because of all the trees. Everything surrounded by cornfields and peach orchards and a flower garden big enough to walk through, almost like a little park. Just to get there you had to go up a long driveway, really an actual road, between tall rows of evergreen trees. We weren't that far from the mountains—Jacky's pointed them out from the road, and I'd already felt the temperature drop. He showed me on the map how close we were to where the color changed from yellow to long fingers of brown. Those were the Blue Ridge Mountains, he said. One of Jacky's ideas was to take the Appalachian Trail down to Georgia. Brunswick's over on the coast though, about an inch-and-a-half down from Savannah. According to the mileage chart, an inch-and-a-half is about seventy-five miles. Jacky kept changing his mind between going through the mountains and then cutting east along what he called "Sherman's march to the sea" or going along the coast through all the Navy bases and ocean cities as we made our way down to Brunswick. It was a hard decision, and we were right at the turning point that day. He liked to read out the names of the towns and cities between here and there, saying them over while he moved his fingertip along the different paths: Winchester or Norfolk? Asheville or Southport? Atlanta or Charleston, South Carolina? Jacky always pays attention to the names of places. To Jacky it's like the name of each little town we come to—especially if they have funny ones like Buffalo Mills or Mann's Choice or Rainsburg, Pennsylvania—like each little town is his to put away and keep, or like us just knowing the names of those places is what's making them come true. That's why I thought we might end up going east after all: there's just more names in that direction, and going off toward the blue edge of the map seemed more definite to Jacky than just trailing down through the mountains, I could tell. I was sure hoping so anyway, even though I never imagined for a minute we'd find Daddy either way. I just figured if we stayed close to people we'd be okay, but if we went off into the woods who knows what might happen? We don't even have sleeping bags, just a worn-out Navy blanket and that ratty old wedding-ring quilt you remember was my favorite. I like woods and open country, but what I like best is coming into a town, seeing the billboards, passing the first house with a painted fence and a mowed lawn, then maybe coming to an Esso station and a Dairy Queen. We'd always stop for one of those ice-cream cones with a curl-on-the-top, and Jacky'd already be studying the map, looking for the crookedest line between this town and the next one and licking away at the mustache of vanilla on his upper lip.

We stayed with Mrs. Spicer for two entire days, and during the whole time Jack was Buddy and I was Peggy Sue. That's one of our favorite songs, "Peggy Sue," and those names were sort of a secret joke to Jacky. He especially liked it that Mrs. Spicer probably never even heard of that record or of Buddy Holly either (which I found out later she had, on her own radio). I keep hearing that song in my mind because of those names—*I love you, Peggy Sue, with a love so rare and true, uh-oh Peg-gy, my Peg-gy Sue-uh-ooo, uh-ooo-ooo.* That's what I mean about the way Jacky can always get you to thinking exactly what he wants. I mean it was fine with me, that's what we'd been doing all along anyway—and it's fun too, always acting out some story or other. Jack says we have to stay incognito because we can never be sure if anyone's after us or not. We're runaways, he says, and it's safer to keep changing identities. Sometimes I'm his sister and other times I'm not—sometimes I'm his sidekick or his leading lady. But there's always some story going along with it. Even looking for Daddy. That's real, I guess, I mean that's something we're *doing*, but it's really just another story too. The stuff that actually happens, day by day, that stuff doesn't have anything to do with Daddy. Like Mrs. Spicer. Can you feature her taking us into her bedroom to ask us about our "hygiene practices"? That's what she called it. She said we were right to leave such things up to God Almighty. She said she thanked the Lord for all of her children. She wasn't a heathen and she could see we weren't either. "Oh, yes, ma'am," Jacky says, looking over at me sort of moony. "Our love is holy, we know that." Mrs. Spicer just widens her eyes and says, "Amen."

After we got to her house that first morning, she fixed us some corn fritters—these little things like pancakes with whole kernels of corn in them—all we could possibly eat—along with thick country sausage and a big round blue pitcher of milk. We always use the carton at home, so I remember that pitcher, round as a peony and with a kind of pinched-in spout like a flower petal. It was the sort of thing anybody'd love to have themselves someday—that house too, lots of nooks and crannies, so perfectly homey you could hardly believe it, little touches like embroidered cushions on the window seats of these bay windows at all the stairway landings—I bet the house Jacky and me are staying in right now used to be a lot like that, except this one's falling apart and there's no furniture to speak of, only this broken-down rocking chair I'm sitting in and what we managed to pull together out of cardboard boxes and some old wooden milk crates Jack found in the cellar. But I'm sure this used to be a really fabulous mansion though, back in the Gay Nineties or the Roaring Twenties or whatever. We're right next to the ocean, I can hear the surf against the stone wall across the road this very minute. Maryland, or maybe Delaware, I think. It's hard to know exactly which state you're in where we are now.

You might have liked Mrs. Spicer, she was wonderful in a lot of ways, but I doubt that you would have. You don't like anybody sitting in judgment all the time, no matter how kindly they try to tell you what you're doing wrong. I'm like you, my feeling is: whatever anybody else says, I've got my own reasons. But even if Mrs. Spicer could get on your nerves a little bit, you still had to hand it to her. Picture this: the three of us're sitting in this big old country kitchen—four long windows looking out on a vegetable garden where you can see bulging red tomatoes in chicken-wire cages and leafy, purple-colored cabbages. Copper pots and pans are hanging on the wall, and there's this great stone fireplace. The kitchen table's covered with a bright blue-check oilcloth. We're just finishing breakfast and Jack's drinking a cup of coffee—which he taught himself to like after we went on the road, the same with smoking. It goes along with his idea of how he ought to be. So Jacky's drinking his coffee, and Mrs. Spicer's over at the sink looking through the window at something outside. She leans up against the rim of the sink and raps on the middle part of the window—it's open at both the top and the bottom—and she calls out through the screen, "Here, Wendell, you better let sleeping dogs lie—old Bertha's not going to like that. Why don't you and William go on over to your tree house and read some comic books?" Over her shoulder she says, "William's from down the road, he just got a new tricycle." Then through the screen she calls, "You heard me now, you better not tease Bertha like that—" and from over on the other side of the kitchen, farthest from the sink, a deep voice pipes in: "Oh, Mama, let 'em be. A little scrimmage with Bertha might do 'em good." When I turned around to see who's here now, I notice Jacky's still got his eye on Mrs. Spicer. Before he looks he's waiting to see what her reaction's going to be, just as crafty as a fox. I figured whoever's in the doorway's probably Mister Spicer, which it turned out he was, only not Mister but Major. I'm just trying to kind of slide a glance by him, I don't want to give anything away, but he locks onto my eyes, bang, and gives me a big wink—like we know a secret that makes everybody else look like fools, or like he's telling me this fat lady's harmless so we might as well play along. When I look back down at my plate, I see there's only a stub of fried sausage left—which I stick with my fork and smear around in the maple syrup before putting it in my mouth. Mrs. Spicer was a great cook, you'd have thought so too—that sausage was probably the best I ever had, and the corn fritters were entirely out of this world. We'd been pretty much living on french fries and popcorn and Coke for days by then. I'm starting to pour myself some more milk from the blue pitcher, when Jacky stands up and says, "Good morning, sir!"—like a military cadet or something. That's exactly how long it took Jacky to figure him out. "At ease, son, at ease," the guy says. "Sit down and finish your coffee. And you, young lady," he says to me, "you must be little sister, is that right?" I smiled and shook my head and waited for Jack to explain our story, but he never had to—Mrs. Spicer charges right in and does it for him, all in one breath nearly, leaving out the part about me being pregnant, and finishing up with, "So I thought you might take them down to Hagerstown on Saturday when you and Sam Healey go in to the races." Then she turns toward us and says, "This is my husband, Major Spicer." "Pleased to meet you, sir," Jacky chimes in right away, offering his hand. I said, "Same here," and gave him back a wink of my own. I don't know why. I guess I thought at least the two of us might have our feet on the ground, even if nobody else did.

It turned out I was wrong about that—was I ever—but the guy did give you the impression of being absolutely no-nonsense and in-charge—very distinguished looking, but with this crinkly little smile around the edges that seemed to bring him right down to earth and make it sort of a joke that anybody of our intelligence, his and mine I mean, would actually have to tolerate the kind of foolishness we had to put up with. I mean you felt like he was including you in the winner's circle with him—at least that's how he made me feel. And then the story Mrs. Spicer reeled off was such a crock of beans. I mean talk about corny, I thought the Major'd see right through us in a flash and pretty soon we'd be on a bus back home. But instead, he says, sort of sly like he knows it's all just so much bull but he likes the careful planning it takes anyway, he says, "Well, well, I see," and puts his hands behind his back. He's got a newspaper rolled up in one fist and he rocks back on his heels and taps his leg with it—this way you can tell he's thinking, like when he'd smoke his pipe and you'd know it'd be an interruption to say anything to him. "I see," he says again, and, "Understood," like he's really thought it through. "Mind you," he says, "I don't necessarily agree with you in principle, but if that's your choice, I have to admire your tactical skills. Did Mrs. Spicer say you found her—or, I'm sorry, *she* found *you*—at the laundromat in town? Have I got that right?" He's looking at Jacky, but then his eyes shift back to mine like he's giving me a signal. That's when I started giggling, I mean I couldn't help it, even though there was supposedly nothing at all to laugh about—so I started coughing instead. Major Spicer steps over beside my chair and starts patting me on the back, like congratulations or something, and that makes it even funnier. So to stop laughing, like I've got to clear my throat, I take a sip of milk—which of course is a big mistake. The next second I'm spitting a white stream across the table, holding onto the edge and wrinkling up the smooth oilcloth to keep from falling over. Jack's wiping milk off his face with a blue napkin, real cloth, and he's glaring at me, and the Major's stroking my back now, almost like some guy looking to see if you're wearing a bra, and saying, "That's all right, go ahead and laugh, little sister. It's a good release." That's what he called me the whole time, except maybe once—"little sister." Did he know me and Jacky weren't really lovers but brothers and sisters instead? Maybe not, but he sure gave you the feeling that whatever anybody else said, it was all just so much bull—you and him knew what the real score was. But keeping up appearances was part of the game, like one of the rules or something. I mean he never said anything rude and he never lost that stiff Army posture of his either, the way he'd bend over from the waist, his back just as straight as a doll's anytime he'd reach down to scratch one of the family dogs or cats that were all over the place, laying around with their heads on their paws or sitting there staring up at you like you're going to give them something good, maybe a crunchy dog biscuit or a pat on the rear. It was real homey the way the dogs rubbed up against you, panting and grinning like they were just tickled to death you were there. If you think the yellow light in that laundromat was cozy, this was something entirely else. After a while that house really gave you the feeling of living in a beehive—Mrs. Spicer was this bustling queen bee with all these other bees buzzing around making honey—and Major Spicer off to one side, maybe, like the beekeeper with the net helmet to keep the bees from stinging him and getting in his eyes. Nothing ever really seemed to faze Major Spicer—no matter what crazy stuff was going on, he was above it all, outside of it entirely. For instance, the next thing we knew there was a lot of barking outside and some little kid is screaming his head off, but the Major doesn't even move. "There, what did I tell you?" Mrs. Spicer says. "Bertha won't put up with that kind of nonsense, they should have known better." Major Spicer laughs and says, "If they don't, they're finding out now, aren't they? Experience, Rhea, that's the only way we ever learn anything in life—as our adventurous young couple here bear witness. Those boys will pay closer attention in the future. A good object lesson if you ask me." Mrs. Spicer might have been listening to all this but I doubt it—she was already on her way out the door. In another second we could see her through the window waving at little Wendell and William with a broomstick she must have picked up on the back porch. We couldn't see the kids from where we were, but we could sure hear them. The barking had stopped as soon as Mrs. Spicer yelled, "*No*, Bertha, *bad* dog," but the screams were just getting louder, and we could hear the other kid, who turned out to be Wendell, the four-year-old, saying things like, "I *told* him *not* to," and "We didn't even *touch* her, we just wanted to *play*." Mrs. Spicer bangs the broomstick down on the porch and says, "Mind your own business, sir, and leave Bertha to mind hers," and in a different voice she says, "There, there, you're all right, William, Bertha's not going to bite you." Major Spicer is chuckling and he's still standing beside me with his hand on my shoulder. I could smell his particular odor, like the smell of a pillow, beneath the other odor of tobacco and Old Spice shaving lotion that I can recognize anywhere and that always makes me think of Daddy. His fingers were absent-mindedly stroking the back of my neck under my hair, the same way you might pet a dog. It didn't feel personal at all, just friendly and offhand, so I didn't mind it, I like to have the back of my neck stroked, who doesn't? But Jacky looks over and lifts his eyebrows, so when I see nobody's looking, I stick my tongue out at him. Jacky just smiles and shakes his head like as far as he's concerned I'm some kind of moron. That look of his always makes me mad, but in one way I guess it turned out he was right. And I have to admit I never expected anything like what happened—in fact, I get so embarrassed I feel like one big blush whenever I think about it. This is getting into the stuff I'm not sure how to put in my letter—if Jacky ever lets me write one. The thing is, I don't want to just break the news to you, I want to tell you exactly how everything actually happened so you'll see it wasn't really anybody's fault. I mean finding fault is just picturing things according to some story where one way is automatically right and the other way is automatically wrong, but what I'm saying is that these particular things just naturally happened the way they happened, that's all. It made me feel sort of confused, but, honestly, in another way I really didn't mind, I was following right along with it. That was the next afternoon, after we'd spent the night there and eaten four more meals: lunch and dinner the first day, and then another breakfast and another lunch the next. Mrs. Spicer came up with the solution of whether she should let me and Jacky sleep together—because of course we weren't married yet, even if I *was* supposed to be pregnant. What she did was put us in bunk beds out on the sleeping porch with about half-a-dozen visiting grandchildren. It would've felt like a summer camp except it was all one big family, and they treated Jacky and me just like honorary members of the tribe. Major Spicer even asked me to say grace over lunch the next day. We were sitting at a long oval-shaped table, Jacky and me and about umpteen grown-ups and kids, out on what they called the dining porch. In front of us were these big yellow bowls of chicken-corn soup—really more like a chicken and corn and dumpling stew (Mrs. Spicer said they always ate a lot of corn in the summer)—and besides that there was sour-cream cabbage slaw, and sliced tomatoes in vinegar and sugar, and fresh-baked rolls, and—set out in these special little scallop-edged serving dishes—home-canned apple butter and molasses. It was great. Everything about that place made you feel terrific, it really did.

What happened was that after lunch that day Mrs. Spicer took Jacky along to help her pick some peaches, and, well, Major Spicer and me didn't even hear them when they got back. There were always people going in and out anyway, and we were upstairs way over on the other side of the house in the Major's personal study. I liked Major Spicer, and it's true he reminded me a little bit of Daddy. But I don't think I could ever really confuse the two of them, at least not the way the Major mixed me up with the girl in the picture. He was showing me through this big album of photographs at the time. Lots of old black-and-white pictures, starting with ones of his family and then going on to what he called his overseas tours in the military—this one I particularly remember of him standing in a flat bright place with his hands behind his back and wearing one of those helmets like Ramar of the Jungle. That was in North Africa during the war, he told me. The album was a kind of personal scrapbook. There was a dim, brownish one near the beginning of his mother and father—her standing in an ankle-length dress near the spout of an old hand pump, an arm held up to shade her eyes as if what she was looking at was too bright for her to look at straight-on—him standing beside the pump handle in a three-piece suit, one foot forward and a hand stuck into the arm hole of his vest like he's about to make a speech on the Fourth of July. There was page after page of newspaper clippings about Major Spicer from the sports pages and large group-portrait shots where he was a member of some team or other. In a specially clear one he was sitting at the center of the first row of his hometown baseball team holding a bat. Everyone had on a striped shirt and knee-socks, and they were all arranged on the seats of a wooden bleacher. To the sides and behind them you could see the trunks of trees, the tiny little crooked lines in the bark focused so sharp the trees took your attention almost as much as the faces. When Jacky walked in, we'd been looking at a photograph of a girl sitting in a tree swing. She had on a long white dress and was sitting sort of sideways, leaning against the rope so one knee rose up against her skirt. Her arms were stretched kind of lazy-like across her lap, a branch of wild flowers in one hand, maybe blue chicory or ironweed or some kind of aster, the stalk dangling so a blossom almost touched the ground. Her hair caught the light and was held back from her face by a wide, dark ribbon. This was someone I reminded him of, that's what he was telling me, someone he knew when he was still in school, before he joined the Army, way back before the war. And she really did look like me, she could have been my old-fashioned double. Her name was Audrey Cavanagh, his first love, so ethereal, he said, like a little faun, and she was built like you, he said, a fine round bottom for such a narrow girl, and his hand moves from my waist where he's been occasionally touching me to help direct my attention to some particular photograph, him seated in the swivel chair, me standing there beside the desk, and he slides his hand down over my rear end just like that, like he's sculpting clay. And I still don't move, not even when after a while his hand strokes up the inside of my leg and I feel his finger and thumb slip up inside my shorts — I was wearing those loose khaki ones with the wide cuffs and the big pockets. I put one hand on his shoulder like I was trying to keep my balance, that's all I did. He was touching me so lightly I almost had to push against him to be sure he was there. Him talking all the time, and me still listening — as if the other thing with his hand is happening to somebody else. One minute he's talking to the girl in the photograph, saying things like, "Ah, Audrey, you're still as lovely as an angel, perched there in your swing," and the next minute it's as if he's talking to me, calling me by her name and at the same time feeling me up like it's open season on ducks or something. The way the desk was facing out a window meant we had our backs to the door, which also must have been unlatched, because neither one of us even heard it when Jacky came in. There's no telling how long he'd been standing there watching us, but long enough I guess. I bet we made a pretty picture from over by the doorway. It wasn't until the Major turned so he could nuzzle up against my chest that we saw Jack. He's just standing there pop-eyed in the doorway, like he's suddenly remembered something important he forgot to do. You almost expected him to snap his fingers. We were all frozen that way for a second, caught in this burst of something, not light but almost as bright and quick as when a flashbulb goes off. And then everything picks up again all of a sudden right where it left off, and there's voices and sounds again and everybody's moving in different directions. Me, I've got myself backed up against this big globe of the world on a wooden stand right there beside the desk. The globe was so big it came up to my waist, and I had my hands behind me holding onto it. I'm spinning it slowly, feeling the relief map of the mountain ranges slide by beneath my fingers, and I'm thinking, almost like a joke: even if part of me *is* in the United States of America, the other part of me is probably over in China somewhere, all the way over on the other side of the world.

What happened next was, one of the married daughters — everybody called her Sissy — I think her married name was Northman or Newman or something like that, she was little Wendell's mother but she'd left her husband just a couple weeks before, it was a big family scandal at the moment — anyway, Sissy comes waltzing in right behind Jacky and she must have bumped up against him or something because both of them jumped like they'd been hit by electricity. When Jacky jumped, it startled me so I pushed the globe right out of its socket and it bounces once and then rolls over across the floor toward where the Major'd come to a halt after he'd left his chair. All of us are looking at this big colored globe of the world, blue and green and brown and yellow, and the Major bends down and lifts it up off the floor with both hands to see if any damage has been done. "Is it okay?" I ask. I feel like I have to say *something*, so I say, "I didn't know it could slip out like that." "Just a slight dent, hardly noticeable," says the

Major. "Right smack in the middle of Greenland. Nothing there anyway." Jacky looks up at him and smiles, just as cool, as if butter wouldn't melt in his mouth. "You can probably get it to pop out again if you just apply a little heat," he says. "Like holding a match to a ping-pong ball." Sissy laughs and says in a little-girl voice, "Will Daddy kiss the world and make it all better?" And the rest of us laughed too. Ha, ha, ha. Everything seemed like it was just hanging there again for a second, and then Sissy says, "It's so hot, I sent Buddy up to bring down one of your picture puzzles, preferably a snowy Currier and Ives. We're going to take it out on the east porch and try to cool off a little. Then I remembered Mama put all those old puzzles up in the attic. Sorry to barge in and startle everybody. My, it's warm in here, isn't it? Daddy, you ought to turn on the window fan if you're going to spend any time up here. Peggy Sue?" she says to me, "you look like you could use something with ice in it." So Jacky went first and then Sissy followed me and him out the door, and we left the Major still standing there holding his globe in his arms. The way he was holding it made the world look like a big Buddha's belly. The little dent where Greenland was could've been its navel.

So Jacky and me never really had a chance to talk right then. Sissy sent him up to the attic for a jigsaw puzzle and then she says to me, "How would you like some good old country lemonade?" and grabs my hand, and the next thing I know the three of us are out on the porch on the shady side of the house sipping ice-cold lemonade through straws. There's a big cut-glass pitcher all fogged-up and sweaty sitting beside us, and we're scattering out the cardboard pieces of the puzzle on a folding table, each piece glazed and colored on one side and dull pink on the other. We're trying to separate all the edge pieces first, looking for straight lines against all the knobs and sockets of the regular pieces. Because of how we're sitting, I'm working on a side edge, Sissy's working on the snow-covered bottom part, and Jacky's got all the blue pieces of sky. The picture's called "An American Homestead Winter," and there's lots of white, but there's other colors too: a few reds and lots of greens and browns and yellows, and about a million different tones of grayish-blue shadow. The picture on the cover of the box shows these sort of waxy-looking people going about their chores, gathering wood, carrying a bucket, feeding cows and ducks in the snow. A brown dog that looks a lot like old Bertha, but younger, is prancing along beside the man carrying the kindling, and to his right there's a red horse-drawn sleigh with a man in a blue coat holding the reins, and next to him a lady, probably his wife, with some kind of a pink bonnet tied under her chin. They're passing a farmhouse set on a low hill by the road. It reminded me of the Spicers' house a little bit. I was thinking it looked like their house might look after a snowfall. I'm concentrating as hard as I can on the puzzle so I won't have to think about the other stuff. I'm looking for pieces of twisty brown forest with a straight edge on one side. I don't even glance over at Jacky because I'm not ready to meet his eyes yet, I'm not sure how he expects me to act. But what the heck, nothing much really happened. And why should I be embarrassed? I didn't do anything. That's what I think, but there's no telling what Jacky thinks, which is what always throws me off. But we're all working on the puzzle so we don't really get a chance to look at each other much anyway. Instead, we're looking back and forth from the picture on the box to the skinny sections of connected puzzle pieces in front of us. It's like we're working on three different puzzles instead of one big one. OVER FIVE HUNDRED PIECES, it says on the box, SCROLL-CUT AND

INTERLOCKING. "So I see Daddy's been showing you his trophies," Sissy says to me. "That's a sure sign of favor—if you can sit through it. There!" she says, pushing a piece of shadowy snow into one of her little sections. "A corner! Now we're starting to get somewhere. All we need is the corner on your side, Peggy Sue, and we'll have almost half the frame! Buddy, I hate to say anything, but your sky appears to be upside down." "Hah!" Jacky snorts. "From where I'm sitting it's everything else that's upside down." Sissy laughs like she's been taken by surprise. "You're absolutely right," she says, "Everything *is* relative." She's got on glasses with turquoise frames, and she points a finger between her eyebrows to push them back up her nose. Her hair's so brown it's almost black and it's cut short and curly. She reminds me a little of Audrey Hepburn—real thin-boned and aristocratic-looking. She must be distracted about something though because she lights a new cigarette before the last one's finished burning. When she exhales, her nostrils flare out, and then she reaches up and picks a fleck of tobacco off her tongue. "Well, it's almost Wedding Day Eve! You love birds must feel like you've got the world on a string, sittin' on a rainbow—isn't that the way the song goes?" She moves a piece of puzzle around and when she can't find a fit tosses it back onto her little pile. "I bet you can't wait to get into Maryland and tie the knot that binds, right? Make it official in the eyes of God, man, and the PTA." Jacky just laughs and says, "It'll probably take a couple of days once we get to Maryland to get a license and everything." "Well," she says, "I wish you all the luck. At your stage, it's all bill-and-coo and rub-a-dub-dub. Believe me, I know all about it, and I say enjoy it while it lasts. Seize the day. Just don't take all that hot britches stuff too seriously. I'm not saying this to shock you, but—look, take my advice and go to a good drugstore instead of a justice of the peace. Go ahead and have all the fun you want—just don't get married unless you absolutely have to." She's found a piece that fits and she taps it in with a clear-polished fingernail. Her nails aren't long but they're so perfect they make me curl my fingers. My own nails are pretty raggedy-looking, even though I've been trying to only chew them when they need trimming. Her fingers have yellow tobacco stains though. She'll forget she's holding a cigarette and it'll burn right down to the skin. "What makes you think we've got such 'hot britches?'" Jacky asks. He's got his elbow on his knee and his chin in his hand and he's looking up at Sissy like she's the light at the end of the tunnel. "I mean, why do you think that?" Over across the yard we can hear some kids playing guns in the woods. "Pa'*dow!* Pa'*dow!*" one of them yells. "I *got*cha!" "You did *not!*" "I did *so!*" Sissy gives her surprised laugh and raises her glasses to the top of her head so she can look at Jacky eye to eye. "Because, as my mother always says—and what higher authority can there be?—'when peaches get ripe they fall off the tree.'" She raises her eyebrows and nods her head in a quick gesture she uses a lot—it's like her mother's "Amen." "I'm not saying you're wrong," Jacky smiles. "In fact, I'd have to say you're probably right, but is that just a generalization or are you talking about me and Peggy Sue in particular?" "Well, if the shoe fits . . . ," Sissy smiles back, " . . . it might as well be yours—no?" She lowers her glasses again and looks down at the puzzle. "Peggy Sue, what do you think?" she asks. "Does the shoe fit?" "I guess it both does and doesn't," I say. I'm a regular little diplomat. "I'm not exactly sure what shoe you're talking about," I say, "but it probably doesn't fit as good as this," and I push another piece into a string of about ten or twelve that was my main section of edge, twice as long as any of theirs. Sissy falls back into her rocking chair and takes a drag on her cigarette.

"Don't be too sure," she says. She rests her elbow on the arm of her chair and touches the tip of her cigarette to the tip of her thumb, and as she breathes out smoke she just openly sizes Jacky up—the way somebody might look at something they wanted to draw. "I just meant that you're, you know, young and healthy and in love, and there's bound to be a certain, let's say . . . physical attraction, *n'est-ce pas?*"[1] Jacky doesn't say anything for a second. They're both just staring at each other. I mean I almost felt like a third wheel. "Is that how it was with you and your husband?" Jacky finally says. "But of course!" laughs Sissy. "That part was sheer bliss. At least it was at first. But as it turned out, we really didn't have much else in common. When the other wore out, there wasn't a hell of a whole lot left." "The other?" Jacky asks. I can sense Sissy smiling at him more than I can actually see her. "Hot britches," she says: "Rub-a-dub-dub." And she wags her cigarette back and forth with her thumb. "Uh-huh, uh-huh," Jacky says, nodding his head. I'm still working quietly away on my pile of edges when Sissy suddenly sits up straight and reaches for her lemonade. She rattles the ice, then purses her lips to the straw and sips the lemonade down until it sputters in the ice cubes like a little motor. She's got her eyes back on the puzzle now, and she says, "Look at Peggy Sue! She's found the other corner!" Then, after studying her own sections of white bottom pieces for a minute, she taps a piece with the pink nail of her middle finger and says, "If this fits that, I think we can join sides." She places it real gently and pushes it in. "Yes! Perfect fit! How's that? Now we've got the bottom and one side—all we need is Buddy's blue sky and we're halfway home!"

I don't know where the Major was. Maybe he was still in his study, staring at Greenland. The three of us sat there working on the puzzle all afternoon and at one time or another almost everybody else in the family stopped by to put in a couple of pieces, but we never saw hide nor hair of the Major. We worked on the puzzle until it was almost suppertime. There were lightning bugs under the trees across the lawn by then, and it was getting hard to see. We could have turned on a lamp I guess, but nobody thought to. All we had left to fill in was some of the snow and a section of the sky. Except for that, the picture was almost done. It could have been either a sundown or a daybreak scene because there was a lot of pink in the sky, along with the blue. I tried to figure out which it was, morning or evening, but you couldn't really tell. It probably didn't matter. When I asked Sissy what she thought, she said, "Who knows? Maybe it's one of those long winter twilights that last all day. You know the kind I mean? Mmmmm . . . days like that always make me feel so romantic." She arches her back like one of the cats stretching and then suddenly widens her eyes and laughs. "Don't misunderstand," she says. "I only mean days like that make me want to curl up on a davenport somewhere next to a crackling fire with a pot of steaming tea and a good, long novel—something Victorian maybe—although, come to think of it, there's not a wisp of smoke coming from any of these chimneys . . . I wonder why." "Where there's no smoke, there's no fire," Jacky says, whatever that's supposed to mean, and we're all three sitting there in the dark giggling like idiots when Mrs. Spicer calls through the window screen: "Supper's near about ready, Sissy, if you fellows want to wash your hands."

[1]*n'cest-ce pas?* French: is it not?

"Thanks, Mama," Sissy says, and then she looks across the table at Jacky and me, raises her glasses to the top of her head, and grins. "Oh, *screw*," she says in a way that sounds really sexy. "It looks like we won't get to finish what we started. And we came so close too." Nobody says anything for a second. Jacky leans back from the table, and right at that instant the crickets started up, like a ringing in your ears. It was a real warm evening. The stars were coming out and the sky was a thick, deep purple. There wasn't a breeze to be had, and the skin under my leg kept sticking to the cane seat of my chair. Through the window we can hear people moving around inside, chairs scraping against the floor, a drawer opening and then the sound of silverware. "Mom?" somebody's calling. "Where *are* you? Ma-a-*um!*" Sissy sighs and says, "Well, it was nice while it lasted, wasn't it?" Then she calls inside, "Here, lover, mother's out here, just a sec." She turns back to us and says, "He probably fell in the creek. He's always getting his feet wet. From wet diapers to wet sneakers," and she laughs. "You'll find out, Peggy Sue. You'll be me before you know it." Right then, click, a lamp goes on inside the window and some of the light spills out onto the card table. Except for where the table shows black through the unfilled holes, the light makes the glazed surface of the picture puzzle shine so that the snow looks almost real.

When we went in to supper, there was the Major sitting at the head of the table just as if nothing had ever happened at all. He's smiling that same crinkly smile and sniffing at the ham roast like he's posing for the cover of the *Saturday Evening Post*. Real wholesome and homey. When he said grace, he ended the prayer with: "And thank You too, Lord, for the sweet gift of love that is so deeply impressed, by Thy will, in the bosom of each and every one of Thy children . . . In Christ's name, Amen." I mean you had to hand it to the guy. And Jacky and me are playing right along—except Jacky's voice gets this little edge sometimes. He'll say stuff that means one thing to him and me and Sissy, another thing to him and me and the Major, and something else entirely to everybody else. Like when we had fresh sliced peaches with sugar and cream for dessert, and Jacky says, "Peaches may fall off the tree when they're ripe enough, but we picked these, didn't we, Mrs. Spicer? Sissy, how do yours taste? How about yours, Major? Ripe enough?" I think Jacky might have made him nervous, because right after supper the Major offered to take everybody into town to see *Ben-Hur*, which they'd all been dying to see for weeks, I guess. Me and Jacky'd already seen it twice, so when it looks like Sissy's going to have to stay home with little Wendell, Jacky volunteers us to babysit. "We'd just like to repay some of the hospitality we've been shown," he says. "Goodness, what a young gentleman!" says Mrs. Spicer. So Sissy got to go to the movies with the rest, and we ended up having to put Wendell and his little friend William to bed. William had gotten permission to stay over and keep Wendell company. Anyway, it wasn't until they finally fell asleep after a last drink of water and a Peter Pan storybook and a pillow fight that Jacky and me had a chance to be alone. And I could see right away he didn't want to talk about me and the Major at all. Instead, he looks up and says, "Want to see something neat?" We're sitting at the kitchen table eating a second helping of peaches and cream, which we'd brought out of the refrigerator as soon as we knew the coast was clear. "Sure . . . like what?" I say. "Like follow me, I'll show you," Jacky says. We drop our plates into the soapy water in the sink, and Jacky grabs a long red flashlight from a shelf near the back door. I figure we're going outside and I start to turn the knob, but Jacky shakes his head and says, "This way, little sister, this way." I didn't like him calling me that, but I followed him anyway. We went out the kitchen to the hallway and then up the front stairs to the second floor. We're tiptoeing past the door to the sleeping porch where the kids are and Jacky's got the flashlight in one hand and he puts a finger to his lips with the other, and I suddenly felt like we were robbers. I got a sort of butterflies feeling like I had to go to the bathroom. We're passing another door when Jacky stops, turns, and pushes it open. It's a lady's bedroom, you could tell just by the way it smelled. "I think Sissy sleeps in here. Want to look around?" he says. "Is this what you wanted to show me?" I asked. "What's so neat about this?" "Shhh!" he whispers. "Keep your pants on." Then instead of turning on a lamp, he switches on the flashlight and shines it around the room. The beam of light was almost like something solid, like a stick that Jack could poke around with. He pokes it over some stuff on the night table—a crocheted doily, an empty glass, a Kleenex box with a white tissue puffed out part way through the opening—pokes it on over to the bunched-up pillows against the headboard, then on down the bed itself—which has a purply patchwork comforter that looks like somebody's been laying on it—on down across the floor to a little pile of clothes near the dresser. On top are the navy blue shorts Sissy was wearing earlier—inside-out now with the pocket linings showing—and a pair of pearl-colored panties. "What are we doing?" I asked. "Just looking," Jacky says. "Well, I'm getting out of here," I told him. Sissy'd been nice to us and I didn't like nosing around in her room that way. So I turned around and walked out, and after another second here comes Jacky too. "Okay, let's go," he says, switching off the flashlight and pulling the door closed to where it was.

I have no idea what's on his mind at this point. I'm just hoping he doesn't want to steal anything. Our money was getting low and I was wondering how we planned to get some more—which I still am wondering in fact. But Jacky walks on down the hall and doesn't stop at any more bedrooms. Instead he takes me around a turn at the end of the hallway and we immediately come to a dead end at this closed door. The turn in the hall is really just a little nook with the door tucked in it. Jacky turns the knob and sweeps out his arm in this sort of cramped imitation of Reginald Van Gleason[2] the Third ushering me into some fabulous mansion. All I can see is a staircase going up. It's like a tunnel, no wider than the door, and it's real steep. The stairs are made out of unfinished boards, so rough they look almost fuzzy, and they march up one after another into the dark. When Jacky points the flashlight, I can see ceiling rafters through the opening at the top of the stairway but that's all. While I'm poking my head through the door, Jacky leans over and—real quiet but right in my eardrum—says, "The *Sha*dow kno-o-ows," and then he does this spooky laugh. Eeyow, it gave me the creeps, and I didn't want to go nosing around in anybody's attic with a flashlight anyway—there'd probably be spiderwebs all over the place up there and who knew what all else, maybe even bats for all I knew. Even down there in the doorway I could smell the dust, and something else too, like the insides of certain old books, or like the woods. It was a smell that had layers to it, the way it might be if the smells of a whole lot of different rooms were piled all into one

[2]*Reginald Van Gleason* one of Jackie Gleason's personas on his 1950s TV show

another. "Come on, Jill," Jacky says. He puts his hand on my arm and points the flashlight: "Look!" he says. "There's the signpost up ahead! Your next stop—The Twilight Zone!" He's got Rod Serling's voice down pat, and I'm laughing now, ready to go up and take a look. The spookiness isn't real anymore, it's like being inside a fun house now, and while we're climbing the stairs Jacky's doing his Mr. Magoo voice, saying stuff like, "Eh-eh-eh . . . yes, by Gad, the old homestead . . . I'd recognize it anywhere . . . chuckle-chuckle-chuckle," and I'm just laughing away, not even thinking about the stuff with the Major or anything else now. When we come up the stairs through the opening at the top, our eyes are at floor level, and from this angle especially the attic is pitch-black. We can only see where the flashlight makes a hole in the dark. There's a lot we can't see. Things just pop into sight wherever Jack happens to shine the flashlight. It's like he's showing his own movie with that light and also following along wherever it takes us. He's shining it around like he can lick up everything he sees with it or like he's pouring all this stuff out of the flashlight itself instead of finding what's already there.

From what I could tell, it was just an ordinary attic, but bigger and more crowded with junk—old bicycle wheels hanging from the rafters and all different kinds of chairs, stacks of *Life* magazines and *National Geographics*, wooden chests and mirrors and a huge bamboo birdcage in a metal hoop at the top of its own floor stand. "Can you believe this place?" Jacky says. "Isn't this incredible? When I was up here this afternoon I couldn't believe it. They must've been storing stuff up here since before the flood!" He's really revved up about it, and I can see what he means. I've never been in any place quite like it in my life, not really. It seemed like an ordinary attic at first just because it looked exactly the way I'd always pictured an attic *would* look, without ever really thinking about it or anything. Jacky moves his searchlight in a circle around the room and we can see the junk piled everywhere, with little aisles winding through it all, like paths in the woods, leading off to other sections of the attic we can't even begin to see from here. Piles of books and boxes, green steamer trunks with white stenciling and half a dozen tennis rackets, a pair of black rubber hip boots and a straw fishing reel hung up by a leather strap next to an old-fashioned baby buggy with a sun canopy and big, spoked wheels. Stuff even crowding into where the eaves of the roof come down close to the floor and make low little passageways and crawl spaces around the edges of the room. I bet we weren't up there more than a minute when we heard a sort of low stomach rumble of thunder. For a split second, the little half-moon windows in the gables of the attic all lit up like jack-o'-lanterns and almost at the same instant there's a giant crash of thunder that makes the whole attic sort of shake and creak and jingle. "Too much!" Jacky says. "What a great place for a ghost story!" He's whispering and probably doesn't even realize it. The windows light up again right then and there's another clap of thunder and then suddenly it's raining, the sound of it loud and steady, drumming on the roof right over our heads. We can hear it whishing against the sides of the house and gurgling down the drainpipes—a lot of little sounds that melt into one big one. Funny thing is, instead of making it spookier, the rain makes the attic seem all protected and snug, like someplace where it's always King's-X and bad things can't happen. "What if everything you ever had all ended up in one place?" Jacky says. "Like you could find anything you'd ever lost up here no matter where you lost it." "Yeah," I said, "that'd be neat. What'd you look for first?" "No, you don't get it," he says, "I mean you'd never even *need* to look for anything because it'd all be there already, like your whole life, all in one place, not spread out everywhere. That would be you—everything that was part of you all together." Jacky can go on like that all night, talking about some dumb theory or other, like the one about the galaxies expanding. Sometimes you think he's got to be kidding and it turns out he's dead serious. So Jacky's talking away and we're moving into some deeper part of the attic, almost like another room that the main one opens up into, when suddenly I see somebody standing there against the wall. It was like having the breath knocked out of you. I couldn't even scream, I just grabbed Jacky's arm and pointed, and when he shined the light over we saw it was only one of those sewing dummies in the shape of a woman. Whoever it was had a good figure too, maybe as nice as yours, Mom—and it was sort of like seeing them naked. That might sound weird but it's true. It could've been Mrs. Spicer before she got fat. Looking at it gave me almost the same feeling of spying I had in Sissy's bedroom. Jacky couldn't take his eyes off it. "Well, what have we here?" he says. He goes over and sets the flashlight down on top of a shelf so he's got his hands free, then he comes up to the dummy and cups his palms over the dummy's breasts. "Oh, baby," he moans. He puts his hands around its rear end and pulls the dummy up against him and starts humping away like he's a dog going at your leg. Then he says to me, "What if this was Sissy? Oh, man! Wouldn't that be something! . . . Just like you and the Major." Finally, I thought, here it comes. I was beginning to wonder if he'd seen anything or not. "Why'd you let him do it?" Jacky says. "Did you like it?" I didn't know what to answer, so for a second I just listened to the rain drumming on the roof. If this was winter, I was thinking, the rain would be snow and in the morning everything would look shiny and white, just like the picture on the jigsaw puzzle. Jacky turns away from the dummy and I'm thinking he's going to ask me again and I won't be able to avoid it forever, but instead he says, "What if I did that to Sissy? Do you think she'd like it?" I'm standing next to something soft, and when Jacky shines the light over at me I see it's an old daybed with piles of woolen coats and old uniforms and stuff on it. "I guess so," I tell him. "I think she might have a crush on you." I figure if I can keep on his good side about Sissy he won't want to talk about me. "Yeah?" he says. "Would you let me if you were Sissy?" "Sure," I said. "What would it be like?" he says—then, "Let's pretend you're Sissy and I'm me, like when you taught me how to slow-dance. Show me," he says. And he puts the flashlight down on some kind of old hope chest so the light makes our shadows real long—they go all the way across the floor and halfway up the opposite wall, like giants. Jacky comes up until he's standing right next to me and he reaches up and touches his fingers to my breast, real soft. I wasn't really, you know, excited or anything like that, but my breast started to get all tingly, and I guess he could feel the tip of it perk up, because he looks at me funny and says, "That's it, isn't it? . . . does that feel good?" I sort of gulped and nodded and he kept on doing it and then in a few minutes he started kissing me and putting his tongue in my mouth, and I swear that's about the time I knew I was lost. But then he stops all of a sudden and reaches in his pocket. I thought he was only trying to straighten himself out down there—I mean I could feel how stretched he was and how tight his jeans must be, but instead he pulls something out of his pocket and holds it over to the light. It's the pair of panties we saw in Sissy's bedroom. I couldn't believe it. "Would you put these on?" he says. "Oh, man, that'd really be something." I was getting excited too by then, and I bet I never really do put this part in my letter, but I loved the way it felt to get *Jacky* so excited. I mean when he saw me in those panties he starts moaning and groaning and then he's got his hands all over me and he pushes me down onto the pile of coats. I could feel a button on one of the uniforms poking up against my back. By now Jacky's pants are down and he's got my legs apart, and then, just like that, we're actually doing it. It hurt like anything at first, but pretty soon I got sort of numb and it was okay. The whole time, I could smell wool and I could hear these springs somewhere under us squeaking like little birds in a shrub tree. Compared to that, the sound of the rain seemed to come from real far off. It all happened so fast, but it seemed to take a long time too. I was thinking how much I loved Jacky and how good it felt to have him so close inside me, wanting me so much, when I hear him whispering in my ear, "Sissy," he's saying. "Oh, God, Sissy, you just love it . . . you just love it. . . . " *Sissy, Sissy,* he kept calling me, over and over again—until after a while I started to cry, I couldn't help it, and pretty soon the tears were coming like they might never stop.

The next morning we hugged everybody good-bye—everybody except the Major, that is, who never touched me again, not once after that one time—and we promised to write, and then Major Spicer and this old Army buddy of his drove us to Hagerstown and left us off at a Howard Johnson's motel. That was a couple of days ago and now we're in this falling-down old mansion I told you about—in Delaware or Maryland or maybe even Virginia. It's hard to tell exactly what state you're in around here, but we're right next to the ocean. The sound of the surf comes and goes just like somebody breathing. So now I keep thinking, maybe I really *am* pregnant. Can that happen between brothers and sisters, between twins? Or if it can, do you have to do it more than once? Because we only did it that one time, and since then we never even mention it and Jacky's gotten so he's real self-conscious about any kind of touching at all. It seems like we might as well be strangers—that's the worst part about the whole thing. I guess if I don't get my period that'll mean I'm probably pregnant. We'll just have to wait and see, right? If I *am* pregnant though, then maybe we can finally stop this wild-goose chase after Daddy and turn around. Sometimes I almost wish I *was* pregnant, because I'd really love to come home. Where we are now, there's always this fishy salt smell in the air. It'll go away but then it'll come back and you'll notice it again. Sometimes it smells great and other times it smells just like garbage. The ocean makes a steady whishing sound like rain against the rocks on the other side of the stone wall across the road. Jacky's out there somewhere trying to catch a bluefish. There's a lot of tall grass around here that looks like wheat. The feathery tips are a silver color, and I spend a lot of time just sitting here watching the way the wind ripples through them like they were made out of water.

[1986]

QUESTIONS

1. How far are we supposed to take the parallels between "Tumbling" and the "Jack and Jill" nursery rhyme? Does Moyer imply some kind

of archetypal enactment of basic human patterns of action, or do the parallels between the two tales suggest something quite different?
2. When Moyer refers to "the masculine Oedipal scenario" in reference to Jill's tumble, does he imply that the primary theme of the story is her search for her father? If that is so, why is the entire story addressed to her mother?
3. Why is so much detail devoted to the description of Major and Mrs. Spicer's household? Why is the setting of the final scene (the attic) equally detailed? Why is so much detail given over to the Currier and Ives jigsaw puzzle?
4. Jill seems content to accept her brother's decisions for their journey in search of their father. Is the reader equally trusting of Jack's authority?

Es´kia Mphahlele

(b. 1919)

South Africa

Es´kia Mphahlele has been such a force in South African literature for so many years that he is often referred to as the "Dean of African Letters." He was one of the founding editors and writers of the South African literary journal *Drum* (1950). It is impossible to think of life under apartheid without considering Mphahlele's autobiography, *Down Second Avenue* (1959). That book and other early works by the writer were banned in South Africa, and Mphahlele was forced into exile for many years. His pioneer volume, *The African Image* (1962), codified black artistry from an African perspective at a time when most commentaries were Western. In the stories, novels, and critical works that have followed, Dr. Mphahlele (he has a Ph.D. in English from the University of Denver) has widened our perspective of life in South Africa and explained the black aesthetic in such a manner as to make African writing accessible to the Western reader. Most recently, his collected stories have been published in a volume called *Renewal Time* (1989).

Writing in *The African Image* about the emergence of the *Drum* writers of the 1950s, Dr. Mphahlele had this to say: "These South African writers are fashioning an urban literature on terms that are unacceptable to the white ruling class. They are detribalized or Coloured (of mixed blood), not accepted as an integral part of the country's culture (a culture in a chaotic state). But, like every other non-white, they keep on, digging their feet into an urban culture of their own making. This is a fugitive culture: borrowing here, incorporating there, retaining this, rejecting that. But it is a virile culture. The clamour of it is going to keep beating on the walls surrounding the already fragmented culture of the whites until they crumble."

Mrs. Plum

I

My madam's name was Mrs. Plum. She loved dogs and Africans and said that everyone must follow the law even if it hurt. These were three big things in Madam's life.

I came to work for Mrs. Plum in Greenside, not very far from the centre of Johannesburg, after leaving two white families. The first white people I worked for as a cook and laundry woman were a man and his wife in Parktown North. They drank too much and always forgot to pay me. After five months I said to myself No. I am going to leave these drunks. So that was it. That day I was as angry as a red-hot iron when it meets water. The second house I cooked and washed for had five children who were badly brought up. This was in Belgravia. Many times they called me You Black Girl and I kept quiet. Because their mother heard them and said nothing. Also I was only new from Phokeng my home, far away near Rustenburg, I wanted to learn and know the white people before I knew how far to go with the others I would work for afterwards. The thing that drove me mad and made me pack and go was a man who came to visit them often. They said he was cousin or something like that. He came to the kitchen many times and tried to make me laugh. He patted me on the buttocks. I told the master. The man did it again and I asked the madam that very day to give me my money and let me go.

These were the first nine months after I had left Phokeng to work in Johannesburg. There were many of us girls and young women from Phokeng, from Zeerust, from Shuping, from Kosten, and many other places who came to work in the cities. So the suburbs were full of blackness. Most of us had already passed Standard Six and so we learned more English where we worked. None of us liked to work for white farmers, because we know too much about them on the farms near our homes. They do not pay well and they are cruel people.

At Easter time so many of us went home for a long weekend to see our people and to eat chicken and sour milk and *morogo*—wild spinach. We also took home sugar and condensed milk and tea and coffee and sweets and custard powder and tinned foods.

It was a home-girl of mine, Chimane, who called me to take a job in Mrs. Plum's house, just next door to where she worked. This is the third year now. I have been quite happy with Mrs. Plum and her daughter Kate. By this I mean that my place as a servant in Greenside is not as bad as that of many others. Chimane too does not complain much. We are paid six pounds a month with free food and free servant's room. No one can ever say that they are well paid, so we go on complaining somehow. Whenever we meet on Thursday afternoons, which is time off for all of us black women in the suburbs, we talk and talk and talk: about our people at home and their letters; about their illnesses; about bad crops; about a sister who wanted a school uniform and books and school fees; about some of our madams and masters who are good, or stingy with money or food, or stupid or full of nonsense, or who kill themselves and each other, or who are dirty—and so many things I cannot count them all.

Thursday afternoons we go to town to look at the shops, to attend a woman's club, to see our boy friends, to go to bioscope some of us. We turn up smart, to show others the clothes we bought from the black men who sell soft goods to servants in the suburbs. We take a number of things and they come round every month for a bit of money until we finish paying. Then we dress the way of many white madams and girls. I think we look really smart. Sometimes we catch the eyes of a white woman looking at us and we laugh and laugh until we nearly drop on the ground because we feel good inside ourselves.

II

What did the girl next door call you? Mrs. Plum asked me the first day I came to her. Jane, I replied. Was there not an African name? I said yes, Karabo. All right, Madam said. We'll call you Karabo, she said. She spoke as if she knew a name is a big thing. I knew so many whites who did not care what they called black people as long as it was all right for their tongue. This pleased me, I mean Mrs. Plum's use of *Karabo*; because the only time I heard the name was when I was home or when my friends spoke to me. Then she showed me what to do: meals, meal times, washing, and where all the things were that I was going to use.

My daughter will be here in the evening, Madam said. She is at school. When the daughter came, she added, she would tell me some of the things she wanted me to do for her every day.

Chimane, my friend next door, had told me about the daughter Kate, how wild she seemed to be, and about Mr. Plum who had killed himself with a gun in a house down the street. They had left the house and come to this one.

Madam is a tall woman. Not slender, not fat. She moves slowly, and speaks slowly. Her face looks very wise, her forehead seems to tell me she has a strong liver: she is not afraid of anything. Her eyes are always swollen at the lower eyelids like a white person who has not slept for many many nights or like a large frog. Perhaps it is because she smokes too much, like wet wood that will not know whether to go up in flames or stop burning. She looks me straight in the eyes when she talks to me, and I know she does this with other people too. At first this made me fear her, now I am used to her. She is not a lazy woman, and she does many things outside, in the city and in the suburbs.

This was the first thing her daughter Kate told me when she came and we met. Don't mind mother, Kate told me. She said, She is sometimes mad with people for very small things. She will soon be all right and speak nicely to you again.

Kate, I like her very much, and she likes me too. She tells me many things a white woman does not tell a black servant. I mean things about what she likes and does not like, what her mother does or does not do, all these. At first I was unhappy and wanted to stop her, but now I do not mind.

Kate looks very much like her mother in the face. I think her shoulders will be just as round and strong-looking. She moves faster than Madam. I asked her why she was still at school when she was so big. She laughed. Then she tried to tell me that the school where she was was for big people, who had finished with lower school. She was learning big things about cooking and food. She can explain better, me I cannot. She came home on weekends.

Since I came to work for Mrs. Plum Kate has been teaching me plenty of cooking. I first learned from her and Madam the word *recipes*. When Kate was at the big school, Madam taught me how to read cookery books. I went on very slowly at first, slower than an ox-wagon. Now I know more. When Kate came home, she found I had read the recipe she left me. So we just cooked straightaway. Kate thinks I am fit to cook in a hotel. Madam thinks so too. Never never! I thought. Cooking in a hotel is like feeding oxen. No one can say thank you to you. After a few months I could cook the Sunday lunch and later I could cook specials for Madam's or Kate's guests.

Madam did not only teach me cooking. She taught me how to look after guests. She praised me when I did very very well; not like the white people I had worked for before. I do not know what runs crooked in the heads of other people. Madam also had classes in the evenings for servants to teach them how to read and write. She and two other women in Greenside taught in a church hall.

As I say, Kate tells me plenty of things about Madam. She says to me she says, My mother goes to meetings many times. I ask her I say, What for? She says to me she says, For your people. I ask her I say, My people are in Phokeng far away.

They have got mouths, I say. Why does she want to say something for them? Does she know what my mother and what my father want to say? They can speak when they want to. Kate raises her shoulders and drops them and says, How can I tell you Karabo? I don't say your people—your family only. I mean all the black people in the country. I say Oh! What do the black people want to say? Again she raises her shoulders and drops them, taking a deep breath.

I ask her I say, With whom is she in the meeting?

She says, With other people who think like her.

I ask her I say, Do you say there are people in the world who think the same things?

She nods her head.

I ask, What things?

So that a few of your people should one day be among those who rule this country, get more money for what they do for the white man, and—what did Kate say again? Yes, that Madam and those who think like her also wanted my people who have been to school to choose those who must speak for them in the—I think she said it looks like a *Kgotla* at home who rule the villages.

I say to Kate I say, Oh I see now. I say, Tell me Kate why is Madam always writing on the machine, all the time everyday nearly?

She replies she says, Oh my mother is writing books.

I ask, You mean a book like those?—pointing at the books on the shelves.

Yes, Kate says.

And she told me how Madam wrote books and other things for newspapers and she wrote for the newspapers and magazines to say things for the black people who should be treated well, be paid more money, for the black people who can read and write many things to choose those who want to speak for them.

Kate also told me she said, My mother and other women who think like her put on black belts over their shoulders when they are sad and they want to show the white government they do not like the things being done by whites to blacks. My mother and the others go and stand where the people in government are going to enter or go out of a building.

I ask her I say, Does the government and the white people listen and stop their sins? She says No. But my mother is in another group of white people.

I ask, Do the people of the government give the women tea and cakes? Kate says, Karabo! How stupid; oh!

I say to her I say, Among my people if someone comes and stands in front of my house I tell him to come in and I give him food. You white people are wonderful. But they keep standing there and the government people do not give them anything.

She replies, You mean strange. How many times have I taught you not to say *wonderful* when you mean *strange*! Well, Kate says with a short heart and looking cross and she shouts, Well they do not stand there the whole day to ask for tea and cakes stupid. Oh dear!

Always when Madam finished to read her newspapers she gave them to me to read to help me speak and write better English. When I had read she asked me to tell her some of the things in it. In this way, I did better and better and my mind was opening and opening and I was learning and learning many things about the black people inside and outside the towns which I did not know in the least. When I found words that were too difficult or I did not understand some of the things I asked Madam. She always told me You see this, you see that, eh? with a heart that can carry on a long way. Yes, Madam writes many letters to the papers. She is always sore about the way the white police beat up black people; about the way black people who work for whites are made to sit at the Zoo Lake with their hearts hanging, because the white people say our people are making noise on Sunday afternoon when they want to rest in their houses and gardens; about many ugly things that happen when some white people meet black man on the pavement or street. So Madam writes to the papers to let others know, to ask the government to be kind to us.

In the first year Mrs. Plum wanted me to eat at table with her. It was very hard, one because I was not used to eating at table with a fork and knife, two because I heard of no other kitchen worker who was handled like this. I was afraid. Afraid of everybody, of Madam's guests if they found me doing this. Madam said I must not be silly. I must show that African servants can also eat at table. Number three, I could not eat some of the things I loved very much: mealie-meal porridge with sour milk or *morogo*, stamped mealies mixed with butter beans, sour porridge for breakfast and other things. Also, except for morning porridge, our food is nice when you eat with the hand. So nice that it does not stop in the mouth or the throat to greet anyone before it passes smoothly down.

We often had lunch together with Chimane next door and our garden boy—Ha! I must remember never to say *boy* again when I talk about a man. This makes me think of a day during the first few weeks in Mrs. Plum's house. I was talking about Dick her garden man and I said "garden boy." And she says to me she says, Stop talking about a "boy," Karabo. Now listen here, she says, You Africans must learn to speak properly about each other. And she says White people won't talk kindly about you if you look down upon each other.

I say to her I say Madam, I learned the word from the white people I worked for, and all the kitchen maids say 'boy.'

She replies she says to me, Those are white people who know nothing, just low-class whites. I say to her I say I thought white people know everything.

She said, You'll learn, my girl, and you must start in this house, hear? She left me there thinking, my mind mixed up.

I learned. I grew up.

III

If any woman or girl does not know the Black Crow Club in Bree Street, she does not know anything. I think nearly everything takes place inside and outside that house. It is just where the dirty part of the City begins, with factories and the market. After the market is the place where Indians and Coloured people live. It is also at the Black Crow that the buses turn round and back to the black townships. Noise, noise, noise all the time. There are women who sell hot sweet potatoes and fruit and monkey nuts and boiled eggs in the winter, boiled mealies and the other things in the summer, all these on the pavements. The streets are always full of potato and fruit skins and monkey nut shells. There is always a strong smell of roast pork. I think it is because of Piel's cold storage down Bree Street.

Madam said she knew the black people who work in the Black Crow. She was happy that I was spending my afternoon on Thursday in such a club. You will learn sewing, knitting, she said, and other things that you like. Do you like to dance? I told her I said, Yes, I want to learn. She paid the two shillings fee for me each month.

We waited on the first floor, we the ones who were learning sewing; waiting for the teacher. We talked and laughed about madams and masters, and their children and their dogs and birds and whispered about our boy friends.

Sies![1] My Madam you do not know—*mojuta oa'nete*[2]—a real miser . . .

Jo—jo—jo![3] you should see our new dog. A big thing like this. People! Big in a foolish way . . .

What! Me, I take a master's bitch by the leg, me, and throw it away so that it keeps howling, *tjwe—tjwe! ngo—wu ngo—wu!*[4] I don't play about with them, me . . .

Shame, poor thing! God sees you, true. . . . !

They wanted me to take their dog out for a walk every afternoon and I told them I said it is not my work in other houses the garden man does it. I just said to myself I said they can go to the chickens. Let them bite their elbow before I take out a dog, I am not so mad yet. . . .

Hei![5] It is not like the child of my white people who keeps a big white rat and you know what? He puts it on his bed when he goes to school. And let the blankets just begin to smell of urine and all the nonsense and they tell me to wash them. *Hei*, people . . . !

Did you hear about Rebone, people? Her Madam put her out, because her master was always tapping her buttocks with his fingers. And yesterday the madam saw the master press Rebone against himself. . . .

Jo—jo—jo! people . . . !

Dirty white man!

No, not dirty. The madam smells too old for him.

Hei! Go and wash your mouth with soap, this girl's mouth is dirty. . . .

Jo, Rebone, daughter of the people! We must help her to find a job before she thinks of going back home.

The teacher came. A woman with strong legs, a strong face, and kind eyes. She had short hair and dressed in a simple but lovely floral frock. She stood well on her legs and hips. She had a black mark between the two top front teeth. She smiled as if we were her children. Our group began with games, and then Lilian Ngoyi took us for sewing. After this she gave a brief talk to all of us from the different classes.

I can never forget the things this woman said and how she put them to us. She told us that the time had passed for black girls and women in the suburbs to be satisfied with working, sending money to our people and going to see them once a year. We were to learn, she said, that the world would never be safe for black people until they were in the government with the power to make laws. The power should be given by the Africans who were more than the whites.

We asked her questions and she answered them with wisdom. I shall put some of them down in my own words as I remember them.

[1]*Sies!* Shame!

[2]*mojuta oa'nete* cheap; a real miser

[3]*Jo—jo—jo!* You, you, you!

[4]*tjwe—tjwe! ngo—wu ngo—wu!* He belongs to us.

[5]*Hei!* Hi!

Shall we take the place of the white people in the government?

Some yes. But we shall be more than they as we are more in the country. But also the people of all colours will come together and there are good white men we can choose and there are Africans some white people will choose to be in the government.

There are good madams and masters and bad ones. Should we take the good ones for friends?

A master and a servant can never be friends. Never, so put that out of your head, will you! You are not even sure if the ones you say are good are not like that because they cannot breathe or live without the work of your hands. As long as you need their money, face them with respect. But you must know that many sad things are happening in our country and you, all of you, must always be learning, adding to what you already know, and obey us when we ask you to help us.

At other times Lilian Ngoyi told us she said, Remember your poor people at home and the way in which the whites are moving them from place to place like sheep and cattle. And at other times again she told us she said, Remember that a hand cannot wash itself, it needs another to do it.

I always thought of Madam when Lilian Ngoyi spoke. I asked myself, What would she say if she knew that I was listening to such words. Words like: A white man is looked after by his black nanny and his mother when he is a baby. When he grows up the white government looks after him, sends him to school, makes it impossible for him to suffer from the great hunger, keeps a job ready and open for him as soon as he wants to leave school. Now Lilian Ngoyi asked she said, How many white people can be born in a white hospital, grow up in white streets, be clothed in lovely cotton, lie on white cushions; how many whites can live all their lives in a fenced place away from people of other colours and then, as men and women learn quickly the correct ways of thinking, learn quickly to ask questions in their minds, big questions that will throw over all the nice things of a white man's life? How many? Very, very few! For those whites who have not begun to ask, it is too late. For those who have begun and are joining us with both feet in our house, we can only say Welcome!

I was learning. I was growing up. Every time I thought of Madam, she became more and more like a dark forest which one fears to enter, and which one will never know. But there were several times when I thought, This woman is easy to understand, she is like all other white women. What else are they teaching you at the Black Crow, Karabo?

I tell her I say, nothing, Madam. I ask her I say Why does Madam ask?

You are changing.

What does Madam mean?

Well, you are changing.

But we are always changing Madam.

And she left me standing in the kitchen. This was a fews days after I had told her that I did not want to read more than one white paper a day. The only magazines I wanted to read, I said to her, were those from overseas, if she had them. I told her that white papers had pictures of white people most of the time. They talked mostly about white people and their gardens, dogs, weddings and parties. I asked her if she could buy me a Sunday paper that spoke about my people. Madam bought it for me. I did not think she would do it.

There were mornings when, after hanging the white people's washing on the line Chimane and I stole a little time to stand at the fence and talk. We always stood where we could be hidden by our rooms.

Hei, Karabo, you know what? That was Chimane.

No—what? Before you start, tell me, has Timi come back to you?

Ach, I do not care. He is still angry. But boys are fools, they always come back dragging themselves on their empty bellies. *Hei* you know what?

Yes?

The Thursday past I saw Moruti K. K. I laughed until I dropped on the ground. He is standing in front of the Black Crow. I believe his big stomach was crying from hunger. Now he has a small dog in his armpit, and is standing before a woman selling boiled eggs and—*hei* home-girl!—tripe and intestines are boiling in a pot—oh—the smell! you could fill a hungry belly with it, the way it was good. I think Moruti K. K. is waiting for the woman to buy a boiled egg. I do not know what the woman was still doing. I am standing nearby. The dog keeps wriggling and pushing out its nose, looking at the boiling tripe. Moruti keeps patting it with his free hand, not so? Again the dog wants to spill out of Moruti's hand and it gives a few sounds through the nose. *Hei* man, home-girl! One two three the dog spills out to catch some of the good meat! It misses falling into the hot gravy in which the tripe is swimming I do not know how. Moruti K. K. tries to chase it. It has tumbled on to the woman's eggs and potatoes and all are in the dust. She stands up and goes after K. K. She is shouting to him to pay, not so? Where am I at that time? I am nearly dead with laughter the tears are coming down so far.

I was myself holding tight on the fence so as not to fall through laughing. I held my stomach to keep back a pain in the side.

I ask her I say, Did Moruti K. K. come back to pay for the wasted food?

Yes, he paid.

The dog?

He caught it. That is a good African dog. A dog must look for its own food when it is not time for meals. Not these stupid spoiled angels the whites keep giving tea and biscuits.

Hmm.

Dick our garden man joined us, as he often did. When the story was repeated to him the man nearly rolled on the ground laughing.

He asks who is Reverend K. K.

I say he is the owner of the Black Crow.

Oh!

We reminded each other, Chimane and I, of the round minister. He would come into the club, look at us with a smooth smile on his smooth round face. He would look at each one of us, with that smile on all the time, as if he had forgotten that I was there. Perhaps he had, because as he looked at us, almost stripping us naked with his watery shining eyes—funny—he could have been a farmer looking at his ripe corn, thinking many things.

K. K. often spoke without shame about what he called ripe girls—*matjitjana*—with good firm breasts. He said such girls were pure without any nonsense in their heads and bodies. Everybody talked a great deal about him and what they thought he must be doing in his office whenever he called in so-and-so.

The Reverend K. K. did not belong to any church. He baptised, married, and buried people for a fee, who had no church to do such things for them. They said he had been driven out of the Presbyterian Church. He had formed his own, but it did not go far. Then he later came and opened the Black Crow. He knew just how far to go with Lilian Ngoyi. She said although he used his club to teach us things that would help us in life, she could not go on if he was doing any wicked things with the girls in his office. Moruti K. K. feared her, and kept his place.

IV

When I began to tell my story I thought I was going to tell you mostly about Mrs. Plum's two dogs. But I have been talking about people. I think Dick is right when he says What is a dog! And there are so many dogs cats and parrots in Greenside and other places that Mrs. Plum's dogs do not look special. But there was something special in the dog business in Madam's house. The way in which she loved them, maybe.

Monty[6] is a tiny animal with long hair and small black eyes and a face nearly like that of an old woman. The other, Malan, is a bit bigger, with brown and white colours. It has small hair and looks naked by the side of the friend. They sleep in two separate baskets which stay in Madam's bedroom. They are to be washed often and brushed and sprayed and they sleep on pink linen. Monty has a pink ribbon which stays on his neck most of the time. They both carry a cover on their backs. They make me fed up when I see them in their baskets, looking fat, and as if they knew all that was going on everywhere.

It was Dick's work to look after Monty and Malan, to feed them, and to do everything for them. He did this together with garden work and cleaning of the house. He came at the beginning of this year. He just came, as if from nowhere, and Madam gave him the job as she had chased away two before him, she told me. In both those cases, she said that they could not look after Monty and Malan.

Dick had a long heart, even although he told me and Chimane that European dogs were stupid, spoiled. He said One day those white people will put ear rings and toe rings and bangles on their dogs. That would be the day he would leave Mrs. Plum. For, he said, he was sure that she would want him to polish the rings and bangles with Brasso.

Although he had a long heart, Madam was still not sure of him. She often went to the dogs after a meal or after a cleaning and said to them Did Dick give you food sweethearts? Or, Did Dick wash you sweethearts? Let me see. And I could see that Dick was blowing up like a balloon with anger. These things called white people! he said to me. Talking to dogs!

I say to him I say, People talk to oxen at home do I not say so?

Yes, he says, but at home do you not know that a man speaks to an ox because he wants to make it pull the plough or the wagon or to stop or to stand still for a person to inspan it. No one simply goes to an ox looking at him with eyes far apart and speaks to it. Let me ask you, do you ever see a person where we come from take a cow and press it to his stomach or his cheek? Tell me!

[6]*Monty and Malan* Dr. D. F. Malan, a leading figure of the Dutch Reformed Church and subsequent leader of the Nationalist party, which ushered in the worst phase of apartheid in 1948. Monty may be a reference to British Field Marshall B. L. ("Monty") Montgomery.

And I say to Dick I say, We were talking about an ox, not a cow.

He laughed with his broad mouth until tears came out of his eyes. At a certain point I laughed aloud too.

One day when you have time, Dick says to me, he says, you should look into Madam's bedroom when she has put a notice outside her door.

Dick, what are you saying? I ask.

I do not talk, me. I know deep inside me.

Dick was about our age, I and Chimane. So we always said *moshiman'o*[7] when we spoke about his tricks. Because he was not too big to be a boy to us. He also said to us *Hei, lona banyana kelona*—Hey you girls, you! His large mouth always seemed to be making ready to laugh. I think Madam did not like this. Many times she would say What is there to make you laugh here? Or in the garden she would say This is a flower and when it wants water that is not funny! Or again, if you did more work and stopped trying to water my plants with your smile you would be more useful. Even when Dick did not mean to smile. What Madam did not get tired of saying was, If I left you to look after my dogs without anyone to look after you at the same time you would drown the poor things.

Dick smiled at Mrs. Plum. Dick hurt Mrs. Plum's dogs? Then cows can fly. He was really—really afraid of white people, Dick. I think he tried very hard not to feel afraid. For he was always showing me and Chimane in private how Mrs. Plum walked, and spoke. He took two bowls and pressed them to his chest, speaking softly to them as Madam speaks to Monty and Malan. Or he sat at Madam's table and acted the way she sits when writing. Now and again he looked back over his shoulder, pulled his face long like a horse's making as if he were looking over his glasses while telling me something to do. Then he would sit on one of the armchairs, cross his legs and act the way Madam drank her tea; he held the cup he was thinking about between his thumb and the pointing finger, only letting their nails meet. And he laughed after every act. He did these things, of course, when Madam was not home. And where was I at such times? Almost flat on my stomach, laughing.

But oh how Dick trembled when Mrs. Plum scolded him! He did his house-cleaning very well. Whatever mistake he made, it was mostly with the dogs; their linen, their food. One white man came into the house one afternoon to tell Madam that Dick had been very careless when taking the dogs out for a walk. His own dog was waiting on Madam's stoop. He repeated that he had been driving down our street; and Dick had let loose Monty and Malan to cross the street. The white man made plenty of noise about this and I think wanted to let Madam know how useful he had been. He kept on saying Just one inch, *just* one inch. It was lucky I put on my brakes quick enough. . . . But your boy kept on smiling—Why? Strange. My boy would only do it twice and only twice and then . . . ! His pass. The man moved his hand like one writing, to mean that he could sign his servant's pass for him to go and never come back. When he left, the white man said Come on Rusty, the boy is waiting to clean you. Dogs with names, men without, I thought.

Madam climbed on top of Dick for this, as we say.

Once one of the dogs, I don't know which—Malan or Monty—tore my stocking—brand new, you hear—and tore it with its teeth and paws. When I

[7]*moshiman'o* this boy

told Madam about it, my anger as high as my throat, she gave me money to buy another pair. It happened again. This time she said she was not going to give me money because I must also keep my stockings where the two gentlemen would not reach them. Mrs. Plum did not want us ever to say *Voetsek* when we wanted the dogs to go away. Me I said this when they came sniffing at my legs or fingers. I hate it.

In my third year in Mrs. Plum's house, many things happened, most of them all bad for her. There was trouble with Kate; Chimane had big trouble; my heart was twisted by two loves; and Monty and Malan became real dogs for a few days.

Madam had a number of suppers and parties. She invited Africans to some of them. Kate told me the reasons for some of the parties. Like her mother's books when finished, a visitor from across the seas and so on. I did not like the black people who came here to drink and eat. They spoke such difficult English like people who were full of all the books in the world. They looked at me as if I were right down there whom they thought little of—me a black person like them.

One day I heard Kate speak to her mother. She says I don't know why you ask so many Africans to the house. A few will do at a time. She said something about the government which I could not hear well. Madam replies she says to her You know some of them do not meet white people often, so far away in their dark houses. And she says to Kate that they do not come because they want her as a friend but they just want drink for nothing.

I simply felt that I could not be the servant of white people and of blacks at the same time. At my home or in my room I could serve them without a feeling of shame. And now, if they were only coming to drink!

But one of the black men and his sister always came to the kitchen to talk to me. I must have looked unfriendly the first time, for Kate talked to me about it afterwards as she was in the kitchen when they came. I know that at that time I was not easy at all. I was ashamed and I felt that a white person's house was not the place for me to look happy in front of other black people while the white man looked on.

Another time it was easier. The man was alone. I shall never forget that night, as long as I live. He spoke kind words and I felt my heart grow big inside me. It caused me to tremble. There were several other visits. I knew that I loved him, I could never know what he really thought of me, I mean as a woman and he as a man. But I loved him, and I still think of him with a sore heart. Slowly I came to know the pain of it. Because he was a doctor and so full of knowledge and English I could not reach him. So I knew he could not stoop down to see me as someone who wanted him to love me.

Kate turned very wild. Mrs. Plum was very much worried. Suddenly it looked as if she were a new person, with new ways and new everything. I do not know what was wrong or right. She began to play the big gramophone aloud, as if the music were for the whole of Greenside. The music was wild and she twisted her waist all the time, with her mouth half-open. She did the same things in her room. She left the big school and every Saturday night now she went out. When I looked at her face, there was something deep and wild there on it, and when I thought she looked young she looked old, and when I thought she looked old she was young. We were both 22 years of age. I think that I could see the reason why her mother was so worried, why she was suffering.

Worse was to come.

They were now openly screaming at each other. They began in the sitting-room and went upstairs together, speaking fast hot biting words, some of which I did not grasp. One day Madam comes to me and says You know Kate loves an African, you know the doctor who comes to supper here often. She says he loves her too and they will leave the country and marry outside. Tell me, Karabo, what do your people think of this kind of thing between a white woman and a black man? It *cannot* be right is it?

I reply and I say to her We have never seen it happen before where I come from.

That's right, Karabo, it is just madness.

Madam left. She looked like a hunted person.

These white women, I say to myself I say these white women, why do not they love their own men and leave us to love ours!

From that minute I knew that I would never want to speak to Kate. She appeared to me as a thief, as a fox that falls upon a flock of sheep at night. I hated her. To make it worse, he would never be allowed to come to the house again.

Whenever she was home there was silence between us. I no longer wanted to know anything about what she was doing, where or how.

I lay awake for hours on my bed. Lying like that, I seemed to feel parts of my body beat and throb inside me, the way I have seen big machines doing, pounding and pounding and pushing and pulling and pouring some water into one hole which came out at another end. I stretched myself so many times so as to feel tired and sleepy.

When I did sleep, my dreams were full of painful things.

One evening I made up my mind, after putting it off many times. I told my boy-friend that I did not want him any longer. He looked hurt, and that hurt me too. He left.

The thought of the African doctor was still with me and it pained me to know that I should never see him again; unless I met him in the street on a Thursday afternoon. But he had a car. Even if I did meet him by luck, how could I make him see that I loved him? Ach, I do not believe he would even stop to think what kind of woman I am. Part of that winter was a time of longing and burning for me. I say part because there are always things to keep servants busy whose white people go to the sea for the winter.

To tell the truth, winter was the time for servants; not nannies, because they went with their madams so as to look after the children. Those like me stayed behind to look after the house and dogs. In winter so many families went away that the dogs remained the masters and madams. You could see them walk like white people in the streets. Silent but with plenty of power. And when you saw them you knew that they were full of more nonsense and fancies in the house.

There was so little work to do.

One week word was whispered round that a home-boy of ours was going to hold a party in his room on Saturday. I think we all took it for a joke. How could the man be so bold and stupid? The police were always driving about at night looking for black people; and if the whites next door heard the party noise—*oho*! But still, we were full of joy and wanted to go. As for Dick, he opened his big mouth and nearly fainted when he heard of it and that I was really going.

During the day on the big Saturday Kate came.

She seemed a little less wild. But I was not ready to talk to her. I was surprised to hear myself answer her when she said to me Mother says you do not like a marriage between a white girl and a black man, Karabo.

Then she was silent.

She says But I want to help him, Karabo.

I ask her I say You want to help him to do what?

To go higher and higher, to the top.

I knew I wanted to say so much that was boiling in my chest. I could not say it. I thought of Lilian Ngoyi at the Black Crow, what she said to us. But I was mixed up in my head and in my blood.

You still agree with my mother?

All I could say was I said to your mother I had never seen a black man and a white woman marrying, you hear me? What I think about it is my business.

I remembered that I wanted to iron my party dress and so I left her. My mind was full of the party again and I was glad because Kate and the doctor would not worry my peace that day. And the next day the sun would shine for all of us, Kate or no Kate, doctor or no doctor.

The house where our home-boy worked was hidden from the main road by a number of trees. But although we asked a number of questions and counted many fingers of bad luck until we had no more hands for fingers, we put on our best pay-while-you-wear dresses and suits and clothes bought from boys who had stolen them, and went to our home-boy's party. We whispered all the way while we climbed up to the house. Someone who knew told us that the white people next door were away for the winter. Oh, so that is the thing! we said.

We poured into the garden through the back and stood in front of his room laughing quietly. He came from the big house behind us, and were we not struck dumb when he told us to go into the white people's house! Was he mad? We walked in with slow footsteps that seemed to be sniffing at the floor, not sure of anything. Soon we were standing and sitting all over on the nice warm cushions and the heaters were on. Our home-boy turned the lights low. I counted fifteen people inside. We saw how we loved one another's evening dress. The boys were smart too.

Our home-boy's girl-friend Naomi was busy in the kitchen preparing food. He took out glasses and cold drinks — fruit juice, tomato juice, ginger beers, and so many other kinds of soft drink. It was just too nice. The tarts, the biscuits, the snacks, the cakes, *woo*, that was a party, I tell you. I think I ate more ginger cake than I had ever done in my life. Naomi had baked some of the things. Our home-boy came to me and said I do not want the police to come here and have reason to arrest us, so I am not serving hot drinks, not even beer. There is no law that we cannot have parties, is there? So we can feel free. Our use of this house is the master's business. If I had asked him he would have thought me mad.

I say to him I say, You have a strong liver to do such a thing.

He laughed.

He played pennywhistle music on gramophone records — Miriam Makeba, Dorothy Masuka, and other African singers and players. We danced and the party became more and more noisy and more happy. *Hai*, those girls Miriam and Dorothy, they can sing, I tell you! We ate more and laughed more and told more stories. In the middle of the party, our home-boy called us to listen to what he was going to say. Then he told us how he and a friend of his in Orlando collected money to bet on a horse for the July Handicap in Durban. They did this each year but lost. Now they had won two hundred pounds. We all clapped hands and cheered. Two hundred pounds *woo*!

You should go and sit at home and just eat time, I say to him. He laughs and says You have no understanding not one little bit.

To all of us he says Now my brothers and sisters enjoy yourselves. At home I should slaughter a goat for us to feast and thank our ancestors. But this is town life and we must thank them with tea and cake and all those sweet things. I know some people think I must be so bold that I could be midwife to a lion that is giving birth, but enjoy yourselves and have no fear.

Madam came back looking strong and fresh.

The very week she arrived the police had begun again to search servants' rooms. They were looking for what they called loafers and men without passes who they said were living with friends in the suburbs against the law. Our dog's-meat boys became scarce because of the police. A boy who had a girl-friend in the kitchens, as we say, always told his friends that he was coming for dog's meat when he meant he was visiting his girl. This was because we gave our boy-friends part of the meat the white people bought for the dogs and us.

One night a white and a black policeman entered Mrs. Plum's yard. They said they had come to search. She says no, they cannot. They say Yes, they must do it. She answers No. They forced their way to the back, to Dick's room and mine. Mrs. Plum took the hose that was running in the front garden and quickly went round to the back. I cut across the floor to see what she was going to say to the men. They were talking to Dick, using dirty words. Mrs. Plum did not wait, she just pointed the hose at the two policemen. This seemed to surprise them. They turned round and she pointed it into their faces. Without their seeing me I went to the tap at the corner of the house and opened it more. I could see Dick, like me, was trying to keep down his laughter. They shouted and tried to wave the water away, but she kept the hose pointing at them, now moving it up and down. They turned and ran through the back gate, swearing the while.

That fixes them, Mrs. Plum said.

The next day the morning paper reported it.

They arrived in the afternoon—the two policemen—with another. They pointed out Mrs. Plum and she was led to the police station. They took her away to answer for stopping the police while they were doing their work.

She came back and said she had paid bail.

At the magistrate's court, Madam was told that she had done a bad thing. She would have to pay a fine or else go to prison for fourteen days. She said she would go to jail to show that she felt she was not in the wrong.

Kate came and tried to tell her that she was doing something silly going to jail for a small thing like that. She tells Madam she says This is not even a thing to take to the high court. Pay the money. What is £5?

Madam went to jail.

She looked very sad when she came out. I thought of what Lilian Ngoyi often said to us: You must be ready to go to jail for the things you believe are true and for which you are taken by the police. What did Mrs. Plum really believe about me, Chimane, Dick, and all the other black people? I asked myself. I did not know. But from all those things she was writing for the papers and all those meetings she was going to where white people talked about black people and the way they are treated by the government, from what those white women with black bands over their shoulders were doing standing where a white government man was going to pass, I said to myself I said This woman, *hai*, I do not know she seems to think very much of us black people. But why was she so sad?

Kate came back home to stay after this. She still played the big gramophone loud-loud-loud and twisted her body at her waist until I thought it was going to break. Then I saw a young white man come often to see her. I watched them through the opening near the hinges of the door between the kitchen and the sitting-room where they sat. I saw them kiss each other for a long time. I saw him lift up Kate's dress and her white-white legs begin to tremble, and—oh I am afraid to say more, my heart was beating hard. She called him Jim. I thought it was funny because white people in the shops call black men Jim.

Kate had begun to play with Jim when I met a boy who loved me and I loved. He was much stronger than the one I sent away and I loved him more, much more. The face of the doctor came to my mind often, but it did not hurt me so any more. I stopped looking at Kate and her Jim through openings. We spoke to each other, Kate and I, almost as freely as before but not quite. She and her mother were friends again.

Hallo, Karabo, I heard Chimane call me one morning as I was starching my apron. I answered. I went to the line to hang it. I saw she was standing at the fence, so I knew she had something to tell me. I went to her.

Hallo!

Hallo, Chimane!

O *kae?*

Ke teng. Wena?

At that moment a woman came out through the back door of the house where Chimane was working.

I have not seen that one before, I say, pointing with my head.

Chimane looked back. Oh, that one. *Hei,* daughter-of-the-people, *Hei,* you have not seen miracles. You know this is Madam's mother-in-law as you see her there. Did I never tell you about her?

No, never.

White people, nonsense. You know what? That poor woman is here now for two days. She has to cook for herself and I cook for the family.

On the same stove?

Yes, She comes after me when I have finished.

She has her own food to cook?

Yes, Karabo. White people have no heart no sense.

What will eat them up if they share their food?

Ask me, just ask me. God! She clapped her hands to show that only God knew, and it was His business, not ours.

Chimane asks me she says, Have you heard from home?

I tell her I say, Oh daughter-of-the-people, more and more deaths. Something is finishing the people at home. My mother has written. She says they are all right, my father too and my sisters, except for the people who have died. Malebo, the one who lived alone in the house I showed you last year, a white house, he is gone. Then teacher Sedimo. He was very thin and looked sick all the time. He taught my sisters not me. His mother-in-law you remember I told you died last year—no, the year before. Mother says also there is a woman she does not think I remember because I last saw her when I was a small girl she passed away in Zeerust she was my mother's greatest friend when they were girls. She would have gone to her burial if it was not because she has swollen feet.

How are the feet?

She says they are still giving her trouble. I ask Chimane, How are your people at Nokaneng? They have not written?

She shook her head.

I could see from her eyes that her mind was on another thing and not her people at that moment.

Wait for me Chimane eh, forgive me, I have scones in the oven, eh! I will just take them out and come back, eh!

When I came back to her Chimane was wiping her eyes. They were wet.

Karabo, you know what?

E—e. I shook my head.

I am heavy with child.

Hau!

There was a moment of silence.

Who is it, Chimane?

Timi. He came back only to give me this.

But he loves you. What does he say have you told him?

I told him yesterday. We met in town.

I remembered I had not seen her at the Black Crow.

Are you sure, Chimane? You have missed a month?

She nodded her head.

Timi himself—he did not use the thing?

I only saw after he finished, that he had not.

Why? What does he say?

He tells me he says I should not worry I can be his wife.

Timi is a good boy, Chimane. How many of these boys with town ways who know too much will even say Yes it is my child?

Hai, Karabo, you are telling me other things now. Do you not see that I have not worked long enough for my people? If I marry now who will look after them when I am the only child?

Hm. I hear your words. It is true. I tried to think of something soothing to say.

Then I say You can talk it over with Timi. You can go home and when the child is born you look after it for three months and when you are married you come to town to work and can put your money together to help the old people while they are looking after the child.

What shall we be eating all the time I am at home? It is not like those days gone past when we had land and our mother could go to the fields until the child was ready to arrive.

The light goes out in my mind and I cannot think of the right answer. How many times have I feared the same thing! Luck and the mercy of the gods that is all I live by. That is all we live by—all of us.

Listen, Karabo. I must be going to make tea for Madam. It will soon strike half-past ten.

I went back to the house. As Madam was not in yet, I threw myself on the divan in the sitting-room. Malan came sniffing at my legs. I put my foot under its fat belly and shoved it up and away from me so that it cried *tjunk—tjunk—tjunk* as it went out. I say to it I say Go and tell your brother what I have done to you and tell him to try it and see what I will do. Tell your grandmother when she comes home too.

When I lifted my eyes he was standing in the kitchen door, Dick. He says to me he says *Hau!* now you have also begun to speak to dogs!

I did not reply I just looked at him, his mouth ever stretched out like the mouth of a bag, and I passed to my room.

I sat on my bed and looked at my face in the mirror. Since the morning I had been feeling as if a black cloud were hanging over me, pressing on my head and shoulders. I do not know how long I sat there. Then I smelled Madam. What was it? Where was she? After a few moments I knew what it was. My perfume and scent. I used the same cosmetics as Mrs. Plum's. I should have been used to it by now. But this morning—why did I smell Mrs. Plum like this? Then, without knowing why, I asked myself I said, Why have I been using the same cosmetics as Madam? I wanted to throw them all out. I stopped. And then I took all the things and threw them into the dustbin. I was going to buy other kinds on Thursday; finished!

I could not sit down. I went out and into the white people's house. I walked through and the smell of the house made me sick and seemed to fill up my throat. I went to the bathroom without knowing why. It was full of the smell of Madam. Dick was cleaning the bath. I stood at the door and looked at him cleaning the dirt out of the bath, dirt from Madam's body. *Sies*! I said aloud. To myself I said, Why cannot people wash the dirt of their own bodies out of the bath? Before Dick knew I was near I went out. Ach, I said again to myself, why should I think about it now when I have been doing their washing for so long and cleaned the bath many times when Dick was ill. I had held worse things from her body times without number. . . .

I went out and stood midway between the house and my room, looking into the next yard. The three-legged grey cat next door came to the fence and our eyes met. I do not know how long we stood like that looking at each other. I was thinking, Why don't you go and look at your grandmother like that? when it turned away and mewed hopping on the three legs. Just like someone who feels pity for you.

In my room I looked into the mirror on the chest of drawers. I thought Is this Karabo this?

Thursday came, and the afternoon off. At the Black Crow I did not see Chimane. I wondered about her. In the evening I found a note under my door. It told me if Chimane was not back that evening I should know that she was at 660 3rd Avenue, Alexandra Township. I was not to tell the white people.

I asked Dick if he could not go to Alexandra with me after I had washed the dishes. At first he was unwilling. But I said to him I said, Chimane will not believe that you refused to come with me when she sees me alone. He agreed.

On the bus Dick told me much about his younger sister whom he was helping with money to stay at school until she finished; so that she could become a nurse and a midwife. He was very fond of her, as far as I could find out. He said he prayed always that he should not lose his job, as he had done many times before, after staying a few weeks only at each job; because of this he had to borrow monies from people to pay his sister's school fees, to buy her clothes and books. He spoke of her as if she were his sweetheart. She was clever at school, pretty (she was this in the photo Dick had shown me before). She was in Orlando Township. She looked after his old people, although she was only thirteen years of age. He said to me he said Today I still owe many people because I keep losing my job. You must try to stay with Mrs. Plum, I said.

I cannot say that I had all my mind on what Dick was telling me. I was thinking of Chimane: what could she be doing? Why that note?

We found her in bed. In that terrible township where night and day are full of knives and bicycle chains and guns and the barking of hungry dogs and of people in trouble. I even held my heart in my hands. She was in pain and her face, even in the candlelight, was grey. She turned her eyes at me. A fat woman was sitting in a chair. One arm rested on the other and held her chin in its palm. She had hardly opened the door for us after we had shouted our names when she was on her bench again as if there were nothing else to do.

She snorted, as if to let us know that she was going to speak. She said There is your friend. There she is my own-own niece who comes from the womb of my own sister, my sister who was made to spit out my mother's breast to give way for me. Why does she go and do such an evil thing. *Ao!* you young girls of today you do not know children die so fast these days that you have to thank God for sowing a seed in your womb to grow into a child. If she had let the child be born I should have looked after it or my sister would have been so happy to hold a grandchild on her lap, but what does it help? She has allowed a worm to cut the roots, I don't know.

Then I saw that Chimane's aunt was crying. Not once did she mention her niece by her name, so sore her heart must have been. Chimane only moaned.

Her aunt continued to talk, as if she was never going to stop for breath, until her voice seemed to move behind me, not one of the things I was thinking: trying to remember signs, however small, that could tell me more about this moment in a dim little room in a cruel township without street lights, near Chimane. Then I remembered the three-legged cat, its grey-green eyes, its *miau*. What was this shadow that seemed to walk about us but was not coming right in front of us?

I thanked the gods when Chimane came to work at the end of the week. She still looked weak, but that shadow was no longer there. I wondered Chimane had never told me about her aunt before. Even now I did not ask her.

I told her I told her white people that she was ill and had been fetched to Nokaneng by a brother. They would never try to find out. They seldom did, these people. Give them any lie, and it will do. For they seldom believe you whatever you say. And how can a black person work for white people and be afraid to tell them lies. They are always asking the questions, you are always the one to give the answers.

Chimane told me all about it. She had gone to a woman who did these things. Her way was to hold a sharp needle, cover the point with the finger, and guide it into the womb. She then fumbled in the womb until she found the egg and then pierced it. She gave you something to ease the bleeding. But the pain, spirits of our forefathers!

Mrs. Plum and Kate were talking about dogs one evening at dinner. Every time I brought something to table I tried to catch their words. Kate seemed to find it funny, because she laughed aloud. There was a word I could not hear well which began with *sem*—: whatever it was, it was to be for dogs. This I understood by putting a few words together. Mrs. Plum said it was something that was common in the big cities of America, like New York. It was also something Mrs. Plum wanted and Kate laughed at the thought. Then later I was to hear that Monty and Malan could be sure of a nice burial.

Chimane's voice came up to me in my room the next morning, across the fence. When I come out she tells me she said *Hei* child-of-my-father, here is something to tickle your ears. You know what? What? I say. She says, These white people can do things that make the gods angry. More godless people I have not seen. The madam of our house says the people of Greenside want to buy ground where they can bury their dogs. I heard them talk about it in the sitting-room when I was giving them coffee last night. *Hei*, people, let our forefathers come and save us!

Yes, I say, I also heard the madam of our house talk about it with her daughter. I just heard it in pieces. By my mother one day these dogs will sit at table and use knife and fork. These things are to be treated like people now, like children who are never going to grow up.

Chimane sighed and she says *Hela batho*,[8] why do they not give me some of that money they will spend on the ground and on gravestones to buy stockings! I have nothing to put on, by my mother.

Over her shoulder I saw the cat with three legs. I pointed with my head. When Chimane looked back and saw it she said *Hm*, even *they* live like kings. The mother-in-law found it on a chair and the madam said the woman should not drive it away. And there was no other chair, so the woman went to her room.

Hela!

I was going to leave when I remembered what I wanted to tell Chimane. It was that five of us had collected a £1 each to lend her so that she could pay the woman of Alexandra for having done that thing for her. When Chimane's time came to receive money we collected each month and which we took in turns, she would pay us back. We were ten women and each gave £2 at a time. So one waited ten months to receive £20. Chimane thanked us for helping her.

I went to wake up Mrs. Plum as she had asked me. She was sleeping late this morning. I was going to knock at the door when I heard strange noises in the bedroom. What is the matter with Mrs. Plum? I asked myself. Should I call her, in case she is ill? No, the noises were not those of a sick person. They were happy noises but like those a person makes in a dream, the voice full of sleep. I bent a little to peep through the keyhole. What is this? I kept asking myself. Mrs. Plum! Malan! What is she doing this one? Her arm was round Malan's belly and pressing its back against her stomach at the navel, Mrs. Plum's body in a nightdress moving in jerks like someone in fits . . . her leg rising and falling . . . Malan silent like a thing to be owned without any choice it can make to belong to another.

The gods save me! I heard myself saying, the words sounding like wind rushing out of my mouth. So this is what Dick said I would find out for myself!

No one could say where it all started; who talked about it first; whether the police wanted to make a reason for taking people without passes and people living with servants and working in town or not working at all. But the story rushed through Johannesburg that servants were going to poison the white people's dogs. Because they were too much work for us: that was the reason. We heard that letters were sent to the newspapers by white people asking the police to watch over the dogs to stop any wicked things. Some said that we the servants were not really bad, we were being made to think of doing these things by evil people in town and in the locations. Others said the police should watch out lest we poison madams and masters because black people did not know right from wrong when they were angry. We were still children at heart, others said. Mrs. Plum said that she had also written to the papers.

[8]*Hela batho* Oh gosh, people!

Then it was the police came down on the suburbs like locusts on a cornfield. There were lines and lines of men who were arrested hour by hour in the day. They liked this very much, the police. Everybody they took, everybody who was working was asked, Where's the poison eh? Where did you hide it? Who told you to poison the dogs eh? If you tell us we'll leave you to go free, you hear? and so many other things.

Dick kept saying It is wrong this thing they want to do to kill poor dogs. What have these things of God done to be killed for? Is it the dogs that make us carry passes? Is it dogs that make the laws that give us pain? People are just mad they do not know what they want, stupid! But when white policeman spoke to him, Dick trembled and lost his tongue and the things he thought. He just shook his head. A few moments after they had gone through his pockets he still held his arms stretched out, like the man of straw who frightens away birds in a field. Only when I hissed and gave him a sign did he drop his arms. He rushed to a corner of the garden to go on with his work.

Mrs. Plum had put Monty and Malan in the sitting-room, next to her. She looked very much worried. She called me. She asked me she said Karabo, you think Dick is a boy we can trust? I did not know how to answer. I did not know whom she was talking about when she said *we*. Then I said I do not know, Madam. You know! she said. I looked at her. I said I do not know what Madam thinks. She said she did not think anything, that was why she asked. I nearly laughed because she was telling a lie this time and not I.

At another time I should have been angry if she lied to me, perhaps. She and I often told each other lies, as Kate and I also did. Like when she came back from jail, after that day when she turned a hosepipe on two policemen. She said life had been good in jail. And yet I could see she was ashamed to have been there. Not like our black people who are always being put in jail and only look at it as the white man's evil game. Lilian Ngoyi often told us this, and Mrs. Plum showed me how true those words are. I am sure that we have kept to each other by lying to each other.

There was something in Mrs. Plum's face as she was speaking which made me fear her and pity her at the same time. I had seen her when she had come from prison; I had seen her when she was shouting at Kate and the girl left the house; now there was this thing about dog poisoning. But never had I seen her face like this before. The eyes, the nostrils, the lips, the teeth seemed to be full of hate, tired, fixed on doing something bad; and yet there was something on that face that told me she wanted me on her side.

Dick is all right Madam, I found myself saying. She took Malan and Monty in her arms and pressed them to herself, running her hands over their heads. They looked so safe, like a child in a mother's arm.

Mrs. Plum said All right you may go. She said Do not tell anybody what I have asked about Dick eh?

When I told Dick about it, he seemed worried.

It is nothing, I told him.

I had been thinking before that I did not stand with those who wanted to poison the dogs, Dick said. But the police have come out, I do not care what happens to the dumb things, now.

I asked him I said Would you poison them if you were told by someone to do it?

No. But I do not care, he replied.

The police came again and again. They were having a good holiday, everyone could see that. A day later Mrs. Plum told Dick to go because she would not need his work any more.

Dick was almost crying when he left. Is Madam so unsure of me? he asked. I never thought a white person could fear me! And he left.

Chimane shouted from the other yard. She said, *Hei ngoana'rona*,[9] the boers are fire-hot eh!

Mrs. Plum said she would hire a man after the trouble was over.

A letter came from my parents in Phokeng. In it they told me my uncle had passed away. He was my mother's brother. The letter also told me of other deaths. They said I would not remember some, I was sure to know the others. There were also names of sick people.

I went to Mrs. Plum to ask her if I could go home. She asks she says When did he die? I answer I say It is three days, Madam. She says So that they have buried him? I reply Yes Madam. Why do you want to go home then? Because my uncle loved me very much Madam. But what are you going to do there? To take my tears and words of grief to his grave and to my old aunt, Madam. No you cannot go, Karabo. You are working for me you know? Yes, Madam. I, and not your people pay you. I must go Madam, that is how we do it among my people, Madam. She paused. She walked into the kitchen and came out again. If you want to go, Karabo, you must lose the money for the day you will be away. Lose my pay, Madam? Yes, Karabo.

The next day I went to Mrs. Plum and told her I was leaving for Phokeng and was not coming back to her. Could she give me a letter to say that I worked for her. She did, with her lips shut tight. I could feel that something between us was burning like raw chillies. The letter simply said that I had worked for Mrs. Plum for three years. Nothing more. The memory of Dick being sent away was still an open sore in my heart.

The night before the day I left, Chimane came to see me in my room. She had her own story to tell me. Timi, her boy-friend, had left her—for good. Why? Because I killed his baby. Had he not agreed that you should do it? No. Did he show he was worried when you told him you were heavy? He was worried, like me as you saw me, Karabo. Now he says if I kill one I shall eat all his children up when we are married. You think he means what he says? Yes, Karabo. He says his parents would have been very happy to know that the woman he was going to marry can make his seed grow.

Chimane was crying, softly.

I tried to speak to her, to tell her that if Timi left her just like that, he had not wanted to marry her in the first place. But I could not, no, I could not. All I could say was Do not cry, my sister, do not cry. I gave her my handkerchief.

Kate came back the morning I was leaving, from somewhere very far I cannot remember where. Her mother took no notice of what Kate said asking her to keep me, and I was not interested either.

One hour later I was on the Railway bus to Phokeng. During the early part of the journey I did not feel anything about the Greenside house I had worked in. I was not really myself, my thoughts dancing between Mrs. Plum, my uncle, my parents, and Phokeng, my home. I slept and woke up many times during the bus

[9]*ngoana'rona* child

ride. Right through the ride I seemed to see, sometimes in sleep, sometimes between sleep and waking, a red car passing our bus, then running behind us. Each time I looked out it was not there.

Dreams came and passed. He tells me he says You have killed my seed I wanted my mother to know you are a woman in whom my seed can grow. . . . Before you make the police take you to jail make sure that it is for something big you should go to jail for, otherwise you will come out with a heart and mind that will bleed inside you and poison you. . . .

The bus stopped for a short while, which made me wake up.

The Black Crow, the club women . . . *Hei,* listen! I lie to the madam of our house and I say I had a telegram from my mother telling me she is very very sick. I show her a telegram my sister sent me as if Mother were writing. So I went home for a nice weekend. . . .

The laughter of the women woke me up, just in time for me to stop a line of saliva coming out over my lower lip. The bus was making plenty of dust now as it was running over part of the road they were digging up. I was sure the red car was just behind us, but it was not there when I woke.

Any one of you here who wants to be baptized or has a relative without a church who needs to be can come and see me in the office. . . . A round man with a fat tummy and sharp hungry eyes, a smile that goes a long, long way . . .

The bus was going uphill, heavily and noisily.

I kick a white man's dog, me, or throw it there if it has not been told the black people's law. . . . This is Mister Monty and this is Mister Malan. Now get up you lazy boys and meet Mister Kate. Hold out your hands and say hallo to him. . . . Karabo, bring two glasses there. . . . Wait a bit—What will you chew boys while Mister Kate and I have a drink? Nothing? Sure?

We were now going nicely on a straight tarred road and the trees rushed back. Mister Kate. What nonsense, I thought.

Look Karabo, Madam's dogs are dead. What? Poison. I killed them. She drove me out of a job did she not? For nothing. Now I want her to feel she drove me out for something. I came back when you were in your room and took the things and poisoned them. . . . And you know what? She has buried them in clean pink sheets in the garden. *Ao,* clean clean good sheets. I am going to dig them out and take one sheet do you want the other one? Yes, give me the other one I will send it to my mother. . . . *Hei,* Karabo, see here they come. Monty and Malan. The bloody fools they do not want to stay in their hole. Go back you silly fools. Oh you do not want to move eh? Come here, now I am going to throw you in the big pool. No, Dick! No Dick! no, no! Dick! They cannot speak do not kill things that cannot speak. Madam can speak for them she always does. No! Dick . . . . !

I woke up with a jump after I had screamed Dick's name, almost hitting the window. My forehead was full of sweat. The red car also shot out of my sleep and was gone. I remembered a friend of ours who told us how she and the garden man had saved two white sheets in which their white master had buried their two dogs. They went to throw the dogs in a dam.

When I told my parents my story Father says to me he says, So long as you are in good health my child, it is good. The worker dies, work does not. There is always work. I know when I was a boy a strong sound body and a good mind were the biggest things in life. Work was always there, and the lazy man could never say there was no work. But today people see work as something bigger than everything else, bigger than health, because of money.

I reply I say, Those days are gone Papa. I must go back to the city after resting a little to look for work. I must look after you. Today people are too poor to be able to help you.

I knew when I left Greenside that I was going to return to Johannesburg to work. Money was little, but life was full and it was better than sitting in Phokeng and watching the sun rise and set. So I told Chimane to keep her eyes and ears open for a job.

I had been at Phokeng for one week when a red car arrived. Somebody was sitting in front with the driver, a white woman. At once I knew it to be that of Mrs. Plum. The man sitting beside her was showing her the way, for he pointed towards our house in front of which I was sitting. My heart missed a few beats. Both came out of the car. The white woman said Thank you to the man after he had spoken a few words to me.

I did not know what to do and how to look at her as she spoke to me. So I looked at the piece of cloth I was sewing pictures on. There was a tired but soft smile on her face. Then I remembered that she might want to sit. I went inside to fetch a low bench for her. When I remembered it afterwards, the thought came to me that there are things I never think white people can want to do at our homes when they visit for the first time: like sitting, drinking water or entering the house. This is how I thought when the white priest came to see us. One year at Easter Kate drove me home as she was going to the north. In the same way I was at a loss what to do for a few minutes.

Then Mrs. Plum says, I have come to ask you to come back to me, Karabo. Would you like to?

I say I do not know, I must think about it first.

She says, Can you think about it today? I can sleep at the town hotel and come back tomorrow morning, and if you want to you can return with me.

I wanted her to say she was sorry to have sent me away, I did not know how to make her say it because I know white people find it too much for them to say Sorry to a black person. As she was not saying it, I thought of two things to make it hard for her to get me back and maybe even lose me in the end.

I say, You must ask my father first, I do not know, should I call him?

Mrs. Plum says, Yes.

I fetched both Father and Mother. They greeted her while I brought benches. Then I told them what she wanted.

Father asks Mother and Mother asks Father. Father asks me. I say if they agree, I will think about it and tell her the next day.

Father says, It goes by what you feel my child.

I tell Mrs. Plum I say, if you want me to think about it I must know if you will want to put my wages up from £6 because it is too little.

She asks me, How much will you want?

Up by £4.

She looked down for a few moments.

And then I want two weeks at Easter and not just the weekend. I thought if she really wanted me she would want to pay for it. This would also show how sorry she was to lose me.

Mrs. Plum says, I can give you one week. You see you already have something like a rest when I am in Durban in the winter.

I tell her I say I shall think about it.

She left.

The next day she found me packed and ready to return with her. She was very much pleased and looked kinder than I had ever known her. And me, I felt sure of myself, more than I had ever done.

Mrs. Plum says to me, You will not find Monty and Malan.

Oh?

Yes, they were stolen the day after you left. The police have not found them yet. I think they are dead myself.

I thought of Dick . . . my dream. Could he? And she . . . did this woman come to ask me to return because she had lost two animals she loved?

Mrs. Plum says to me she says, You know, I like your people, Karabo, the Africans.

And Dick and Me? I wondered.

[1967]

QUESTIONS

1. Why is the story called "Mrs. Plum" and not "Karabo"?
2. It is clear that Karabo is significantly changed by the end of the story. Can the same be said of Mrs. Plum?
3. Does a person like Mrs. Plum help or hinder the struggle to abolish apartheid?
4. What does the substory involving Chimane and her boyfriend tell us?
5. One of the ideas that Karabo learns from Lilian Ngoyi is that "A master and a servant can never be friends." Is this true?
6. Is Mphahlele's metaphor of fear (as the barrier that separates South African racial groups) a suitable one for his story?

SLAWOMIR MROŻEK

(b. 1930)

POLAND

Slawomir Mrożek is Poland's preeminent contemporary satirist and playwright. Born in Borzęcin, Poland, Mrożek studied architecture and oriental culture in Kraków. Later he was a caricaturist and journalist for newspapers, besides directing, editing, and producing several films. Mrożek's gift for capturing in exaggerated form the essential details of a person's behavior and style through caricature served him well when he changed to the written word. His satirical short stories have been widely translated, including two volumes in English (*The Elephant* and *The Ugupu Bird*). His plays, including *The Police* and *Tango* (English titles), are frequently performed. Through satire, Mrożek frequently mocks the reigning political institutions and communist doctrines of his country, for which reason he left Poland for the West when his work was banned in 1968. Despite the political liberalization of Poland since the 1970s, Mrożek has chosen to remain in Paris permanently.

Mrożek's English translator, Konrad Syrop, praises the author's wit, his poetic language, his ability to compress several layers of meaning within brief narratives, and "his style, which ranges from the austere to the ornate, depending on the demands of the story."

The Elephant

The director of the Zoological Gardens had shown himself to be an upstart. He regarded his animals simply as stepping stones on the road of his own career. He was indifferent to the educational importance of his establishment. In his zoo the giraffe had a short neck, the badger had no burrow and the whistlers, having lost all interest, whistled rarely and with some reluctance. These shortcomings should not have been allowed, especially as the zoo was often visited by parties of schoolchildren.

The zoo was in a provincial town, and it was short of some of the most important animals, among them the elephant. Three thousand rabbits were a poor substitute for the noble giant. However, as our country developed, the gaps were being filled in a well-planned manner. On the occasion of the anniversary of the liberation, on 22nd July, the zoo was notified that it had at long last been allocated an elephant. All the staff, who were devoted to their work, rejoiced at this news. All the greater was their surprise when they learned that the director had sent a letter to Warsaw, renouncing the allocation and putting forward a plan for obtaining an elephant by more economic means.

"I, and all the staff," he had written, "are fully aware how heavy a burden falls upon the shoulders of Polish miners and foundry men because of the elephant. Desirous of reducing our costs, I suggest that the elephant mentioned in your communication should be replaced by one of our own procurement. We can make an elephant out of rubber, of the correct size, fill it with air and place it behind railings. It will be carefully painted the correct color and even on close inspection will be indistinguishable from the real animal. It is well known that the elephant is a sluggish animal and it does not run and jump about. In the notice on the railings we can state that this particular elephant is particularly sluggish. The money saved in this way can be turned to the purchase of a jet plane or the conservation of some church monument.

"Kindly note that both the idea and its execution are my modest contribution to the common task and struggle.

"I am, etc."

This communication must have reached a soulless official, who regarded his duties in a purely bureaucratic manner and did not examine the heart of the matter but, following only the directive about reduction of expenditure, accepted the director's plan. On hearing the Ministry's approval, the director issued instructions for the making of the rubber elephant.

The carcass was to have been filled with air by two keepers blowing into it from opposite ends. To keep the operation secret the work was to be completed during the night because the people of the town, having heard that an elephant was joining the zoo, were anxious to see it. The director insisted on haste also because he expected a bonus, should his idea turn out to be a success.

The two keepers locked themselves in a shed normally housing a workshop, and began to blow. After two hours of hard blowing they discovered that the rubber skin had risen only a few inches above the floor and its bulge in no way resembled an elephant. The night progressed. Outside, human voices were stilled and only the cry of the jackass interrupted the silence. Exhausted, the keepers stopped blowing and made sure that the air already inside the elephant should not escape. They were not young and were unaccustomed to this kind of work.

"If we go on at this rate," said one of them, "we shan't finish by morning. And what am I to tell my missus? She'll never believe me if I say that I spent the night blowing up an elephant."

"Quite right," agreed the second keeper. "Blowing up an elephant is not an everyday job. And it's all because our director is a leftist."

They resumed their blowing, but after another half-hour they felt too tired to continue. The bulge on the floor was larger but still nothing like the shape of an elephant.

"It's getting harder all the time," said the first keeper.

"It's an uphill job, all right," agreed the second. "Let's have a little rest."

While they were resting, one of them noticed a gas pipe ending in a valve. Could they not fill the elephant with gas? He suggested it to his mate.

They decided to try. They connected the elephant to the gas pipe, turned the valve, and to their joy in a few minutes there was a full-sized beast standing in the shed. It looked real: the enormous body, legs like columns, huge ears and the inevitable trunk. Driven by ambition the director had made sure of having in his zoo a very large elephant indeed.

"First class," declared the keeper who had the idea of using gas. "Now we can go home."

In the morning the elephant was moved to a special run in a central position, next to the monkey cage. Placed in front of a large real rock it looked fierce and magnificent. A big notice proclaimed: "Particularly sluggish. Hardly moves."

Among the first visitors that morning was a party of children from the local school. The teacher in charge of them was planning to give them an object-lesson about the elephant. He halted the group in front of the animal and began:

"The elephant is a herbivorous mammal. By means of its trunk it pulls out young trees and eats their leaves."

The children were looking at the elephant with enraptured admiration. They were waiting for it to pull out a young tree, but the beast stood still behind its railings.

" . . . The elephant is a direct descendant of the now-extinct mammoth. It's not surprising, therefore, that it's the largest living land animal."

The more conscientious pupils were making notes.

". . . Only the whale is heavier than the elephant, but then the whale lives in the sea. We can safely say that on land the elephant reigns supreme."

A slight breeze moved the branches of the trees in the zoo.

" . . . The weight of a fully grown elephant is between nine and thirteen thousand pounds."

At that moment the elephant shuddered and rose in the air. For a few seconds it swayed just above the ground, but a gust of wind blew it upward until its mighty silhouette was against the sky. For a short while people on the ground could see the four circles of its feet, its bulging belly and the trunk, but soon, propelled by the wind, the elephant sailed above the fence and disappeared above the treetops. Astonished monkeys in the cage continued staring into the sky.

They found the elephant in the neighboring botanical gardens. It had landed on a cactus and punctured its rubber hide.

The schoolchildren who had witnessed the scene in the zoo soon started neglecting their studies and turned into hooligans. It is reported that they drink liquor and break windows. And they no longer believe in elephants.

[1962]

Translated by
KONRAD SYROP

QUESTIONS

1. Why does the zoo director prefer a fake elephant to a real one? How do his motives provide insight into the social and political institutions in Poland? How are these institutions satirized in the story?
2. What meanings are suggested by the inflatable elephant? Consider Konrad Syrop's (Mrożek's translator's) suggestion that the story is an allegory in which "the rubber elephant represents communist doctrine."
3. Why do the school children who witness the airborne elephant start "neglecting their studies and turn[ing] into hooligans"?

BHARATI MUKHERJEE
(b. 1940)
INDIA/UNITED STATES

Bharati Mukherjee was born in Calcutta, the daughter of a pharmaceutical chemist and businessman. Before coming to North America in 1961, she attended a postcolonial British convent school, studied English at the University of Calcutta, and received an M.A. in English and ancient Indian culture at the University of Baroda. While pursuing a Ph.D. in English at the University of Iowa, she met and married Canadian writer Clark Blaise. Mukherjee lived in Canada for 15 years, during which time she taught at McGill University in Toronto. As a result of the racism she experienced in Canada, she left in 1980 to resettle in the United States.

Mukherjee's first novel, *Tiger's Daughter* (1972), was followed by *Wife* (1975) and *Jasmine* (1989). She has also published two collections of short stories, *Darkness* (1985) and *The Middleman and Other Stories* (1988); the latter book, which won the National Book Critics Circle Award, brought her to the attention of American readers. Mukherjee and her husband have collaborated on several books, including *Days and Nights in Calcutta* (1977), a journalistic account that registers their complementary perspectives during their year-long stay in India: Mukherjee as an exile returning to her country to confront the ambivalent feelings and impressions it generated for her, particularly concerning the oppressive situation of women, and Blaise as an American responding to India for the first time, both fascinated by its cultural richness and troubled by its poverty. As Mukherjee observed in an essay for *The Writer on Her Work: New Essays in New Territory*, "I am aware of myself as a four-hundred-year-old woman, born in the captivity of a colonial, pre-industrial oral culture and living now as a contemporary New Yorker."

In her early stories and novels, Mukherjee explores the difficulty for Indian immigrants to establish both personal and cultural identities in North America against a setting of racism, sexism, and cultural misunderstanding—the "unsettled magma between two worlds." More recently, Mukherjee's canvas has broadened to reflect the immigrant experiences of other ethnic groups in America. As Polly Shulman describes Mukherjee's focus on contemporary multicultural reality, "everyone is living in a new world, even those who never left home. As traditions break down, the characters must try to make lives out of the pieces." Mukherjee has described her artistic focus in an interview for *Belles Lettres*, stating

> I see my job as a writer to make my complicated and unfamiliar world understandable to the mainstream reader. That is what good fiction does. If my writing is strong enough, then even unexplained cultural details about the Indian community in Queens or the Korean community in New York will become accessible.
>
> I want to give voice to the new pioneers in this country. . . . We have big stories to tell. We have lived 300 years of our own

history very quickly because most of us [have] come from either postcolonial countries or countries with a lot of civil and religious strife. Now we are rapidly learning 200 years of American history and acculturating into American society. Our lives are extraordinary, even grand and heroic.

I try to show this in my fiction.

A Father

One Wednesday morning in mid-May Mr. Bhowmick woke up as he usually did at 5:43 A.M., checked his Rolex against the alarm clock's digital readout, punched down the alarm (set for 5:45), then nudged his wife awake. She worked as a claims investigator for an insurance company that had an office in a nearby shopping mall. She didn't really have to leave the house until 8:30, but she liked to get up early and cook him a big breakfast. Mr. Bhowmick had to drive a long way to work. He was a naturally dutiful, cautious man, and he set the alarm clock early enough to accommodate a margin for accidents.

While his wife, in a pink nylon negligee she had paid for with her own MasterCard card, made him a new version of French toast from a clipping ("Eggs-cellent Recipes!") Scotchtaped to the inside of a kitchen cupboard, Mr. Bhowmick brushed his teeth. He brushed, he gurgled with the loud, hawking noises that he and his brother had been taught as children to make in order to flush clean not merely teeth but also tongue and palate.

After that he showered, then, back in the bedroom again, he recited prayers in Sanskrit to Kali, the patron goddess of his family, the goddess of wrath and vengeance. In the pokey flat of his childhood in Ranchi, Bihar, his mother had given over a whole bedroom to her collection of gods and goddesses. Mr. Bhowmick couldn't be that extravagant in Detroit. His daughter, twenty-six and an electrical engineer, slept in the other of the two bedrooms in his apartment. But he had done his best. He had taken Woodworking I and II at a nearby recreation center and built a grotto for the goddess. Kali-Mata was eight inches tall, made of metal and painted a glistening black so that the metal glowed like the oiled, black skin of a peasant woman. And though Kali-Mata was totally nude except for a tiny gilt crown and a garland strung together from sinners' chopped off heads, she looked warm, cozy, *pleased*, in her makeshift wooden shrine in Detroit. Mr. Bhowmick had gathered quite a crowd of admiring, fellow woodworkers in those final weeks of decoration.

"Hurry it up with the prayers," his wife shouted from the kitchen. She was an agnostic, a believer in ambition, not grace. She frequently complained that his prayers had gotten so long that soon he wouldn't have time to go to work, play duplicate bridge with the Ghosals, or play the *tabla*[1] in the Bengali Association's one Sunday per month musical soirees. Lately she'd begun to drain him in a wholly new way. He wasn't praying, she nagged; he was shutting her out of his life. There'd be no peace in the house until she hid Kali-Mata in a suitcase.

[1]*tabla* Indian musical instrument, a kind of drum

She nagged, and he threatened to beat her with his shoe as his father had threatened his mother: it was the thrust and volley of marriage. There was no question of actually taking off a shoe and applying it to his wife's body. She was bigger than he was. And, secretly, he admired her for having the nerve, the agnosticism, which as a college boy in backward Bihar he too had claimed.

"I have time," he shot at her. He was still wrapped in a damp terry towel. "You have time for everything but domestic life."

It was the fault of the shopping mall that his wife had started to buy pop psychology paperbacks. These paperbacks preached that for couples who could sit down and talk about their "relationship," life would be sweet again. His engineer daughter was on his wife's side. She accused him of holding things in.

"Face it, Dad," she said. "You have an affect deficit."

But surely everyone had feelings they didn't want to talk about or talk over. He definitely did not want to blurt out anything about the sick-in-the-guts sensations that came over him most mornings and that he couldn't bubble down with Alka-Seltzer or smother with Gas-X. The women in his family were smarter than him. They were cheerful, outgoing, more American somehow.

How could he tell these bright, mocking women that in the 5:43 A.M. darkness, he sensed invisible presences: gods and snakes frolicked in the master bedroom, little white sparks of cosmic static crackled up the legs of his pajamas. Something was out there in the dark, something that could invent accidents and coincidences to remind mortals that even in Detroit they were no more than mortal. His wife would label this paranoia and dismiss it. Paranoia, premonition: whatever it was, it had begun to undermine his composure.

Take this morning. Mr. Bhowmick had woken up from a pleasant dream about a man taking a Club Med vacation, and the postdream satisfaction had lasted through the shower, but when he'd come back to the shrine in the bedroom, he'd noticed all at once how scarlet and saucy was the tongue that Kali-Mata stuck out at the world. Surely he had not lavished such alarming detail, such admonitory colors on that flap of flesh.

Watch out, ambulatory sinners. Be careful out there, the goddess warned him, and not with the affection of Sergeant Esterhaus, either.

"French toast must be eaten hot-hot," his wife nagged. "Otherwise they'll taste like rubber."

Mr. Bhowmick laid the trousers of a two-trouser suit he had bought on sale that winter against his favorite tweed jacket. The navy stripes in the trousers and the small, navy tweed flecks in the jacket looked quite good together. So what if the Chief Engineer had already started wearing summer cottons?

"I am coming, I am coming," he shouted back. "You want me to eat hot-hot, you start the frying only when I am sitting down. You didn't learn anything from Mother in Ranchi?"

"Mother cooked French toast from fancy recipes? I mean French Sandwich Toast with complicated filling?"

He came into the room to give her his testiest look. "You don't know the meaning of complicated cookery. And mother had to get the coal fire of the *chula*[2] going first."

[2]*chula* clay oven

His daughter was already at the table. "Why don't you break down and buy her a microwave oven? That's what I mean about sitting down and talking things out." She had finished her orange juice. She took a plastic measure of Slim-Fast out of its can and poured the powder into a glass of skim milk. "It's ridiculous."

Babli was not the child he would have chosen as his only heir. She was brighter certainly than the sons and daughters of the other Bengalis he knew in Detroit, and she had been the only female student in most of her classes at Georgia Tech, but as she sat there in her beige linen business suit, her thick chin dropping into a polka-dotted cravat, he regretted again that she was not the child of his dreams. Babli would be able to help him out moneywise if something happened to him, something so bad that even his pension plans and his insurance policies and his money market schemes wouldn't be enough. But Babli could never comfort him. She wasn't womanly or tender the way that unmarried girls had been in the wistful days of his adolescence. She could sing Hindi film songs, mimicking exactly the high, artificial voice of Lata Mungeshkar, and she had taken two years of dance lessons at Sona Devi's Dance Academy in Southfield, but these accomplishments didn't add up to real femininity. Not the kind that had given him palpitations in Ranchi.

Mr. Bhowmick did his best with his wife's French toast. In spite of its filling of marshmallows, apricot jam and maple syrup, it tasted rubbery. He drank two cups of Darjeeling tea, said, "Well, I'm off," and took off.

All might have gone well if Mr. Bhowmick hadn't fussed longer than usual about putting his briefcase and his trenchcoat in the backseat. He got in behind the wheel of his Oldsmobile, fixed his seatbelt and was just about to turn the key in the ignition when his neighbor, Al Stazniak, who was starting up his Buick Skylark, sneezed. A sneeze at the start of a journey brings bad luck. Al Stazniak's sneeze was fierce, made up of five short bursts, too loud to be ignored.

Be careful out there! Mr. Bhowmick could see the goddess's scarlet little tongue tip wagging at him.

He was a modern man, an intelligent man. Otherwise he couldn't have had the options in life that he did have. He couldn't have given up a good job with perks in Bombay and found a better job with General Motors in Detroit. But Mr. Bhowmick was also a prudent enough man to know that some abiding truth lies bunkered within each wanton Hindu superstition. A sneeze was more than a sneeze. The heedless are carried off in ambulances. He had choices to make. He could ignore the sneeze, and so challenge the world unseen by men. Perhaps Al Stazniak had hayfever. For a sneeze to be a potent omen, surely it had to be unprovoked and terrifying, a thunderclap cleaving the summer skies. Or he could admit the smallness of mortals, undo the fate of the universe by starting over, and go back inside the apartment, sit for a second on the sofa, then re-start his trip.

Al Stazniak rolled down his window. "Everything okay?"

Mr. Bhowmick nodded shyly. They weren't really friends in the way neighbors can sometimes be. They talked as they parked or pulled out of their adjacent parking stalls. For all Mr. Bhowmick knew, Al Stazniak had no legs. He had never seen the man out of his Skylark.

He let the Buick back out first. Everything was okay, yes, please. All the same he undid his seatbelt. Compromise, adaptability, call it what you will. A dozen times a day he made these small trade-offs between new-world reasonableness and old-world beliefs.

While he was sitting in his parked car, his wife's ride came by. For fifty dollars a month, she was picked up and dropped off by a hard up, newly divorced woman who worked at a florist's shop in the same mall. His wife came out the front door in brown K-Mart pants and a burgundy windbreaker. She waved to him, then slipped into the passenger seat of the florist's rusty Japanese car.

He was a metallurgist. He knew about rust and ways of preventing it, secret ways, thus far unknown to the Japanese.

Babli's fiery red Mitsubishi was still in the lot. She wouldn't leave for work for another eight minutes. He didn't want her to know he'd been undone by a sneeze. Babli wasn't tolerant of superstitions. She played New Wave music in her tapedeck. If asked about Hinduism, all she'd ever said to her American friends was that "it's neat." Mr. Bhowmick had heard her on the phone years before. The cosmos balanced on the head of a snake was like a beachball balanced on the snout of a circus seal. "This Hindu myth stuff," he'd heard her say, "is like a series of super graphics."

He'd forgiven her. He could probably forgive her anything. It was her way of surviving high school in a city that was both native to her, and alien.

There was no question of going back where he'd come from. He hated Ranchi. Ranchi was no place for dreamers. All through his teenage years, Mr. Bhowmick had dreamed of success abroad. What form that success would take he had left vague. Success had meant to him escape from the constant plotting and bitterness that wore out India's middle class.

Babli should have come out of the apartment and driven off to work by now. Mr. Bhowmick decided to take a risk, to dash inside and pretend he'd left his briefcase on the coffee table.

When he entered the living room, he noticed Babli's spring coat and large vinyl pocketbook on the sofa. She was probably sorting through the junk jewelry on her dresser to give her business suit a lift. She read hints about dressing in women's magazines and applied them to her person with seriousness. If his luck held, he could sit on the sofa, say a quick prayer and get back to the car without her catching on.

It surprised him that she didn't shout out from her bedroom, "Who's there?" What if he had been a rapist?

Then he heard Babli in the bathroom. He heard unladylike squawking noises. She was throwing up. A squawk, a spitting, then the horrible gurgle of a waterfall.

A revelation came to Mr. Bhowmick. A woman vomiting in the privacy of the bathroom could mean many things. She was coming down with the flu. She was nervous about a meeting. But Mr. Bhowmick knew at once that his daughter, his untender, unloving daughter whom he couldn't love and hadn't tried to love, was not, in the larger world of Detroit, unloved. Sinners are everywhere, even in the bosom of an upright, unambitious family like the Bhowmicks. It was the goddess sticking out her tongue at him.

The father sat heavily on the sofa, shrinking from contact with her coat and pocketbook. His brisk, bright engineer daughter was pregnant. Someone had taken time to make love to her. Someone had thought her tender, feminine. Someone even now was perhaps mooning over her. The idea excited him. It was so grotesque and wondrous. At twenty-six Babli had found the man of her dreams; whereas at twenty-six Mr. Bhowmick had given up on truth, beauty and poetry and exchanged them for two years at Carnegie Tech.

Mr. Bhowmick's tweed-jacketed body sagged against the sofa cushions. Babli would abort, of course. He knew his Babli. It was the only possible option if she didn't want to bring shame to the Bhowmick family. All the same, he could see a chubby baby boy on the rug, crawling to his granddaddy. Shame like that was easier to hide in Ranchi. There was always a barren womb sanctified by marriage that could claim sudden fructifying by the goddess Parvati. Babli would do what she wanted. She was headstrong and independent and he was afraid of her.

Babli staggered out of the bathroom. Damp stains ruined her linen suit. It was the first time he had seen his daughter look ridiculous, quite unprofessional. She didn't come into the living room to investigate the noises he'd made. He glimpsed her shoeless stockinged feet flip-flop on collapsed arches down the hall to her bedroom.

"Are you all right?" Mr. Bhowmick asked, standing in the hall. "Do you need Sinutab?"

She wheeled around. "What're you doing here?"

He was the one who should be angry. "I'm feeling poorly too," he said. "I'm taking the day off."

"I feel fine," Babli said.

Within fifteen minutes Babli had changed her clothes and left. Mr. Bhowmick had the apartment to himself all day. All day for praising or cursing the life that had brought him along with its other surprises an illegitimate grandchild.

It was his wife that he blamed. Coming to America to live had been his wife's idea. After the wedding, the young Bhowmicks had spent two years in Pittsburgh on his student visa, then gone back home to Ranchi for nine years. Nine crushing years. Then the job in Bombay had come through. All during those nine years his wife had screamed and wept. She was a woman of wild, progressive ideas — she'd called them her "American" ideas — and she'd been martyred by her neighbors for them. American *memsahib. Markin mem, Markin mem.*[3] In bazaars the beggar boys had trailed her and hooted. She'd done provocative things. She'd hired a *chamar*[4] woman who by caste rules was forbidden to cook for higher caste families, especially for widowed mothers of decent men. This had caused a blowup in the neighborhood. She'd made other, lesser errors. While other wives shopped and cooked every day, his wife had cooked the whole week's menu on weekends.

"What's the point of having a refrigerator, then?" She'd been scornful of the Ranchi women.

His mother, an old-fashioned widow, had accused her of trying to kill her by poisoning. "You are in such a hurry? You want to get rid of me quick-quick so you can go back to the States?"

Family life had been turbulent.

He had kept aloof, inwardly siding with his mother. He did not love his wife now, and he had not loved her then. In any case, he had not defended her. He felt some affection, and he felt guilty for having shunned her during those unhappy years. But he had thought of it then as revenge. He had wanted to

[3]*memsahib* Mrs.; *Markin mem* — American Mrs.

[4]*chamar* a person of one of the lower castes in the Indian caste (class) system

marry a beautiful woman. Not being a young man of means, only a young man with prospects, he had had no right to yearn for pure beauty. He cursed his fate and after a while, settled for a barrister's daughter, a plain girl with a wide, flat plank of a body and myopic eyes. The barrister had sweetened the deal by throwing in an all-expenses-paid two years' study at Carnegie Tech to which Mr. Bhowmick had been admitted. Those two years had changed his wife from pliant girl to ambitious woman. She wanted America, nothing less.

It was his wife who had forced him to apply for permanent resident status in the U.S. even though he had a good job in Ranchi as a government engineer. The putting together of documents for the immigrant visa had been a long and humbling process. He had had to explain to a chilly clerk in the Embassy that, like most Indians of his generation, he had no birth certificate. He had to swear out affidavits, suffer through police checks, bribe orderlies whose job it was to move his dossier from desk to desk. The decision, the clerk had advised him, would take months, maybe years. He hadn't dared hope that merit might be rewarded. Merit could collapse under bad luck. It was for grace that he prayed.

While the immigration papers were being processed, he had found the job in Bombay. So he'd moved his mother in with his younger brother's family, and left his hometown for good. Life in Bombay had been lighthearted, almost fulfilling. His wife had thrown herself into charity work with the same energy that had offended the Ranchi women. He was happy to be in a big city at last. Bombay was the Rio de Janeiro of the East; he'd read that in a travel brochure. He drove out to Nariman Point at least once a week to admire the necklace of municipal lights, toss coconut shells into the dark ocean, drink beer at the Oberoi-Sheraton where overseas Indian girls in designer jeans beckoned him in sly ways. His nights were full. He played duplicate bridge, went to the movies, took his wife to Bingo nights at his club. In Detroit he was a lonelier man.

Then the green card[5] had come through. For him, for his wife, and for the daughter who had been born to them in Bombay. He sold what he could sell, and put in his brother's informal trust what he couldn't to save on taxes. Then he had left for America, and one more start.

All through the week, Mr. Bhowmick watched his daughter. He kept furtive notes on how many times she rushed to the bathroom and made hawking, wrenching noises, how many times she stayed late at the office, calling her mother to say she'd be taking in a movie and pizza afterwards with friends.

He had to tell her that he knew. And he probably didn't have much time. She shouldn't be on Slim-Fast in her condition. He had to talk things over with her. But what would he say to her? What position could he take? He had to choose between public shame for the family, and murder.

For three more weeks he watched her and kept his silence. Babli wore shifts to the office instead of business suits, and he liked her better in those garments. Perhaps she was dressing for her young man, not from necessity. Her skin was pale and blotchy by turn. At breakfast her fingers looked stiff, and she had trouble with silverware.

Two Saturdays running, he lost badly at duplicate bridge. His wife scolded him. He had made silly mistakes. When was Babli meeting this man? Where? He

[5]*green card* American certification of an immigrant's legal resident status

must be American; Mr. Bhowmick prayed only that he was white. He pictured his grandson crawling to him, and the grandson was always fat and brown and buttery-skinned, like the infant Krishna. An American son-in-law was a terrifying notion. Why was she not mentioning men, at least, preparing the way for the major announcement? He listened sharply for men's names, rehearsed little lines like, "Hello, Bob, I'm Babli's old man," with a cracked little laugh. Bob, Jack, Jimmy, Tom. But no names surfaced. When she went out for pizza and a movie it was with the familiar set of Indian girls and their strange, unpopular, American friends, all without men. Mr. Bhowmick tried to be reasonable. Maybe she had already gotten married and was keeping it secret. "Well, Bob, you and Babli sure had Mrs. Bhowmick and me going there, heh-heh," he mumbled one night with the Sahas and Ghosals, over cards. "Pardon?" asked Pronob Saha. Mr. Bhowmick dropped two tricks, and his wife glared. "Such stupid blunders," she fumed on the drive back. A new truth was dawning; there would be no marriage for Babli. Her young man probably was not so young and not so available. He must be already married. She must have yielded to passion or been raped in the office. His wife seemed to have noticed nothing. Was he a murderer, or a conspirator? He kept his secret from his wife; his daughter kept her decision to herself.

Nights, Mr. Bhowmick pretended to sleep, but as soon as his wife began her snoring—not real snores so much as loud, gaspy gulpings for breath—he turned on his side and prayed to Kali-Mata.

In July, when Babli's belly had begun to push up against the waistless dresses she'd bought herself, Mr. Bhowmick came out of the shower one weekday morning and found the two women screaming at each other. His wife had a rolling pin in one hand. His daughter held up a *National Geographic* as a shield for her head. The crazy look that had been in his wife's eyes when she'd shooed away beggar kids was in her eyes again.

"Stop it!" His own boldness overwhelmed him. "Shut up! Babli's pregnant, so what? It's your fault, you made us come to the States."

Girls like Babli were caught between rules, that's the point he wished to make. They were too smart, too impulsive for a backward place like Ranchi, but not tough nor smart enough for sex-crazy places like Detroit.

"My fault?" his wife cried. "I told her to do hanky-panky with boys? I told her to shame us like this?"

She got in one blow with the rolling pin. The second glanced off Babli's shoulder and fell on his arm which he had stuck out for his grandson's sake.

"I'm calling the police," Babli shouted. She was out of the rolling pin's range. "This is brutality. You can't do this to me."

"Shut up! Shut your mouth, foolish woman." He wrenched the weapon from his wife's fist. He made a show of taking off his shoe to beat his wife on the face.

"What do you know? You don't know anything." She let herself down slowly on a dining chair. Her hair, curled overnight, stood in wild whorls around her head. "Nothing."

"And you do!" He laughed. He remembered her tormentors, and laughed again. He had begun to enjoy himself. Now *he* was the one with the crazy, progressive ideas.

"Your daughter is pregnant, yes," she said, "any fool knows that. But ask her the name of the father. Go, ask."

He stared at his daughter who gazed straight ahead, eyes burning with hate, jaw clenched with fury.

"Babli?"

"Who needs a man?" she hissed. "The father of my baby is a bottle and a syringe. Men louse up your lives. I just want a baby. Oh, don't worry—he's a certified fit donor. No diseases, college graduate, above average, and he made the easiest twenty-five dollars of his life—"

"Like animals," his wife said. For the first time he heard horror in her voice. His daughter grinned at him. He saw her tongue, thick and red, squirming behind her row of perfect teeth.

"Yes, yes, yes," she screamed, "like livestock. Just like animals. You should be happy—that's what marriage is all about, isn't it? Matching bloodlines, matching horoscopes, matching castes, matching, matching, matching . . ." and it was difficult to know if she was laughing or singing, or mocking and like a madwoman.

Mr. Bhowmick lifted the rolling pin high above his head and brought it down hard on the dome of Babli's stomach. In the end, it was his wife who called the police.

[1985]

QUESTIONS

1. How do Mr. and Mrs. Bhowmick and their daughter exemplify distinctly different responses to American life and culture? How are these differences significant for the story's development and its resolution?
2. What does the goddess Kali-Mata represent in Mr. Bhowmick's system of belief? What is the connection between the goddess and his daughter Babli?
3. In what way is Babli's pregnancy a reaction to her family's values and their cultural dislocation? What does Mukherjee's story suggest about cultural assimilation?

ALICE MUNRO
(b. 1931)
CANADA

Alice Munro was born in Wingham, Ontario, and grew up on a farm in the rural southwestern corner of the province. Beginning her life as a writer with stories she wrote in high school, she attended the University of Western Ontario; later she married and moved to Vancouver. As a master of the short story form, Munro writes with sympathy but without nostalgia or sentimentality about the realities of small-town life in rural Canada. To the description of her as a "regional writer" she responded, "If I'm a regional writer, the region I'm writing about [rural Ontario] has many things in common with the American South. . . . a closed rural society with a pretty homogenous Scotch-Irish racial strain going slowly to decay." Munro has also described her primary focus as a fascination with "what people don't understand . . . what we think is happening and what we understand later on."

Her collections of short stories include *Dance of the Happy Shades* (1968), *Something I've Been Meaning to Tell You* (1974), *Who Do You Think You Are*? (1979, American title: *The Beggar Maid*), *The Moons of Jupiter* (1982), *The Progress of Love* (1986), and *Friend of my Youth* (1990). Three of her collections have been honored with the Governor General's Award. Her novel *Lives of Girls and Women* (1971) is a series of stories focusing on two young girls as they grow up in southern Ontario. Munro is widely praised for her astute representations of female experience and of the unexpected and paradoxical events that punctuate and alter the meaning of ordinary lives.

The Office

The solution to my life occurred to me one evening while I was ironing a shirt. It was simple but audacious. I went into the living room where my husband was watching television and I said, "I think I ought to have an office."

It sounded fantastic, even to me. What do I want an office for? I have a house; it is pleasant and roomy and has a view of the sea; it provides appropriate places for eating and sleeping, and having baths and conversations with one's friends. Also I have a garden; there is no lack of space.

No. But here comes the disclosure which is not easy for me: I am a writer. That does not sound right. Too presumptuous; phony, or at least unconvincing. Try again. I write. Is that better? I *try* to write. That makes it worse. Hypocritical humility. Well then?

It doesn't matter. However I put it, the words create their space of silence, the delicate moment of exposure. But people are kind, the silence is quickly absorbed by the solicitude of friendly voices, crying variously, how wonderful, and good for *you*, and well, that *is* intriguing. And what do you write, they inquire with spirit. Fiction, I reply, bearing my humiliation by this time with ease, even a suggestion of flippancy, which was not always mine, and again, again, the perceptible circles of dismay are smoothed out by such ready and tactful voices—which have however exhausted their stock of consolatory phrases, and can say only, "*Ah!*"

So this is what I want an office for (I said to my husband): to write in. I was at once aware that it sounded like a finicky requirement, a piece of rare self-indulgence. To write, as everyone knows, you need a typewriter, or at least a pencil, some paper, a table and chair; I have all these things in a corner of my bedroom. But now I want an office as well.

And I was not even sure that I was going to write in it, if we come down to that. Maybe I would sit and stare at the wall; even that prospect was not unpleasant to me. It was really the sound of the word "office" that I liked, its sound of dignity and peace. And purposefulness and importance. But I did not care to mention this to my husband, so I launched instead into a high-flown explanation which went, as I remember, like this:

A house is all right for a man to work in. He brings his work into the house, a place is cleared for it; the house rearranges itself as best it can around him. Everybody recognizes that his work *exists*. He is not expected to answer the telephone, to find things that are lost, to see why the children are crying, or feed the cat. He can shut his door. Imagine (I said) a mother shutting her door, and the children knowing she is behind it; why, the very thought of it is outrageous to them. A woman who sits staring into space, into a country that is not her husband's or her children's is likewise known to be an offence against nature. So a house is not the same for a woman. She is not someone who walks into the house, to make use of it, and will walk out again. She *is* the house; there is no separation possible.

(And this is true, though as usual when arguing for something I am afraid I do not deserve, I put it in too emphatic and emotional terms. At certain times, perhaps on long spring evenings, still rainy and sad, with the cold bulbs in bloom and a light too mild for promise drifting over the sea, I have opened the windows and felt the house shrink back into wood and plaster and those humble elements of which it is made, and the life in it subside, leaving me exposed, empty-handed, but feeling a fierce and lawless quiver of freedom, of loneliness too harsh and perfect for me now to bear. Then I know how the rest of the time I am sheltered and encumbered, how insistently I am warmed and bound.)

"Go ahead, if you can find one cheap enough," is all my husband had to say to this. He is not like me, he does not really want explanations. That the heart of another person is a closed book, is something you will hear him say frequently, and without regret.

Even then I did not think it was something that could be accomplished. Perhaps at bottom it seemed to me too improper a wish to be granted. I could almost more easily have wished for a mink coat, for a diamond necklace; these are things women do obtain. The children, learning of my plans, greeted them with the most dashing skepticism and unconcern. Nevertheless I went down to the shopping centre which is two blocks from where I live; there I had noticed for several months, and without thinking how they could pertain to me, a couple of For Rent signs in the upstairs windows of a building that housed a drugstore and a beauty parlour. As I went up the stairs I had a feeling of complete unreality; surely renting was a complicated business, in the case of offices; you did not simply knock on the door of the vacant premises and wait to be admitted; it would have to be done through channels. Also, they would want too much money.

As it turned out, I did not even have to knock. A woman came out of one of the empty offices, dragging a vacuum cleaner, and pushing it with her foot, towards the open door across the hall, which evidently led to an apartment in the rear of the building. She and her husband lived in this apartment; their name was Malley; and it was indeed they who owned the building and rented out the offices. The rooms she had just been vacuuming were, she told me, fitted out for a dentist's office, and so would not interest me, but she would show me the other place. She invited me into her apartment while she put away the vacuum and got her key. Her husband, she said with a sigh I could not interpret, was not at home.

Mrs. Malley was a black-haired delicate-looking woman, perhaps in her early forties, slatternly but still faintly appealing, with such arbitrary touches of femininity as the thin line of bright lipstick, the pink feather slippers on obviously tender and swollen feet. She had the swaying passivity, the air of exhaustion and muted apprehension, that speaks of a life spent in close attention on a man who is by turns vigorous, crotchety and dependent. How much of this I saw at first, how much decided on later is of course impossible to tell. But I did think that she would have no children, the stress of her life, whatever it was, did not allow it, and in this I was not mistaken.

The room where I waited was evidently a combination living room and office. The first things I noticed were models of ships—galleons, clippers, Queen Marys—sitting on the tables, the window sills, the television. Where there were no ships there were potted plants and a clutter of what are sometimes called "masculine" ornaments—china deer heads, bronze horses, huge ashtrays of heavy, veined, shiny material. On the walls were framed photographs and what might have been diplomas. One photo showed a poodle and a bulldog, dressed in masculine and feminine clothing, and assuming with dismal embarrassment a pose of affection. Written across it was "Old Friends." But the room was really dominated by a portrait, with its own light and a gilded frame; it was of a good-looking, fair-haired man in middle age, sitting behind a desk, wearing a business suit and looking preeminently prosperous, rosy and agreeable. Here again, it is probably hindsight on my part that points out that in the portrait there is evident also some uneasiness, some lack of faith the man has in this role, a tendency he has to spread himself too bountifully and insistently, which for all anyone knows may lead to disaster.

Never mind the Malleys. As soon as I saw that office, I wanted it. It was larger than I needed, being divided in such a way that it would be suitable for a doctor's office. (We had a chiropractor in here but he left, says Mrs. Malley in her regretful but uninformative way.) The walls were cold and bare, white with a little grey, to cut the glare for the eyes. Since there were no doctors in evidence, nor had been, as Mrs. Malley freely told me, for some time, I offered twenty-five dollars a month. She said she would have to speak to her husband.

The next time I came, my offer was agreed upon, and I met Mr. Malley in the flesh. I explained, as I had already done to his wife, that I did not want to make use of my office during regular business hours, but during the weekends and sometimes in the evening. He asked me what I would use it for, and I told him, not without wondering first whether I ought to say I did stenography.

He absorbed the information with good humour. "Ah, you're a writer."

"Well yes. I write."

"Then we'll do our best to see you're comfortable here," he said expansively. "I'm a great man for hobbies myself. All these ship-models, I do them in my spare time, they're a blessing for the nerves. People need an occupation for their nerves. I daresay you're the same."

"Something the same," I said, resolutely agreeable, even relieved that he saw my behaviour in this hazy and tolerant light. At least he did not ask me, as I half-expected, who was looking after the children, and did my husband approve? Ten years, maybe fifteen, had greatly softened, spread and defeated the man in the picture. His hips and thighs had now a startling accumulation of fat, causing him to move with a sigh, a cushiony settling of flesh, a ponderous matriarchal discomfort. His hair and eyes had faded, his features blurred, and the affable, predatory expression had collapsed into one of troubling humility and chronic mistrust. I did not look at him. I had not planned, in taking an office, to take on the responsibility of knowing any more human beings.

On the weekend I moved in, without the help of my family, who would have been kind. I brought my typewriter and a card table and chair, also a little wooden table on which I set a hot plate, a kettle, a jar of instant coffee, a spoon and a yellow mug. That was all. I brooded with satisfaction on the bareness of my walls, the cheap dignity of my essential furnishings, the remarkable lack of things to dust, wash or polish.

The sight was not so pleasing to Mr. Malley. He knocked on my door soon after I was settled and said that he wanted to explain a few things to me — about unscrewing the light in the outer room, which I would not need, about the radiator and how to work the awning outside the window. He looked around at everything with gloom and mystification and said it was an awfully uncomfortable place for a lady.

"It's perfectly all right for me," I said, not as discouragingly as I would have liked to, because I always have a tendency to placate people whom I dislike for no good reason, or simply do not want to know. I make elaborate offerings of courtesy sometimes, in the foolish hope that they will go away and leave me alone.

"What you want is a nice easy chair to sit in, while you're waiting for inspiration to hit. I've got a chair down in the basement, all kinds of stuff down there since my mother passed on last year. There's a bit of carpet rolled up in a corner down there, it isn't doing anybody any good. We could get this place fixed up so it'd be a lot more homelike for you."

But really, I said, but really I like it as it is.

"If you wanted to run up some curtains, I'd pay you for the material. Place needs a touch of colour, I'm afraid you'll get morbid sitting in here."

Oh, no, I said, and laughed, I'm sure I won't.

"It'd be a different story if you was a man. A woman wants things a bit cosier."

So I got up and went to the window and looked down into the empty Sunday street through the slats of the Venetian blind, to avoid the accusing vulnerability of his fat face and I tried out a cold voice that is to be heard frequently in my thoughts but has great difficulty getting out of my cowardly mouth. "Mr. Malley, please don't bother me about this any more. I said it suits me. I have everything I want. Thanks for showing me about the light."

The effect was devastating enough to shame me. "I certainly wouldn't dream of bothering you," he said, with precision of speech and aloof sadness. "I merely made these suggestions for your comfort. Had I realized I was in your way, I would of left some time ago." When he had gone I felt better, even a little exhilarated at my victory though still ashamed of how easy it had been. I told myself that he would have had to be discouraged sooner or later, it was better to have it over with at the beginning.

The following weekend he knocked on my door. His expression of humility was exaggerated, almost enough so to seem mocking, yet in another sense it was real and I felt unsure of myself.

"I won't take up a minute of your time," he said. "I never meant to be a nuisance. I just wanted to tell you I'm sorry I offended you last time and I apologize. Here's a little present if you will accept."

He was carrying a plant whose name I did not know; it had thick, glossy leaves and grew out of a pot wrapped lavishly in pink and silver foil.

"There," he said, arranging this plant in a corner of my room. "I don't want any bad feelings with you and me. I'll take the blame. And I thought, maybe she won't accept furnishings, but what's the matter with a nice little plant, that'll brighten things up for you."

It was not possible for me, at this moment, to tell him that I did not want a plant. I hate house plants. He told me how to take care of it, how often to water it and so on; I thanked him. There was nothing else I could do, and I had the unpleasant feeling that beneath his offering of apologies and gifts he was well aware of this and in some way gratified by it. He kept on talking, using the words *bad feelings, offended, apologize.* I tried once to interrupt, with the idea of explaining that I had made provision for an area of my life where good feelings, or bad, did not enter in, that between him and me, in fact, it was not necessary that there be any feelings at all; but this struck me as a hopeless task. How could I confront, in the open, this craving for intimacy? Besides, the plant in its shiny paper had confused me.

"How's the writing progressing?" he said, with an air of putting all our unfortunate differences behind him.

"Oh, about as usual."

"Well if you ever run out of things to write about, I got a barrelful." Pause. "But I guess I'm just eatin' into your time here," he said with a kind of painful buoyancy. This was a test, and I did not pass it. I smiled, my eyes held by that magnificent plant; I said it was all right.

"I was just thinking about the fellow was in here before you. Chiropractor. You could of wrote a book about him."

I assumed a listening position, my hands no longer hovering over the keys. If cowardice and insincerity are big vices of mine, curiosity is certainly another.

"He had a good practice built up here. The only trouble was, he gave more adjustments than was listed in the book of chiropractory. Oh, he was adjusting right and left. I came in here after he moved out, and what do you think I found? Soundproofing! This whole room was soundproofed, to enable him to make his adjustments without disturbing anybody. This very room you're sitting writing your stories in.

"First we knew of it was a lady knocked on my door one day, wanted me to provide her with a passkey to his office. He'd locked his door against her.

"I guess he just got tired of treating her particular case. I guess he figured he'd been knocking away at it long enough. Lady well on in years, you know, and him just a young man. He had a nice young wife too and a couple of the prettiest children you ever would want to see. Filthy some of the things that go on in this world."

It took me some time to realize that he told this story not simply as a piece of gossip, but as something a writer would be particularly interested to hear. Writing and lewdness had a vague delicious connection in his mind. Even this notion, however, seemed so wistful, so infantile, that it struck me as a waste of energy to attack it. I knew now I must avoid hurting him for my own sake, not for his. It had been a great mistake to think that a little roughness would settle things.

The next present was a teapot. I insisted that I drank only coffee and told him to give it to his wife. He said that tea was better for the nerves and that he had known right away I was a nervous person, like himself. The teapot was covered with gilt and roses and I knew that it was not cheap, in spite of its extreme hideousness. I kept it on my table. I also continued to care for the plant, which thrived obscenely in the corner of my room. I could not decide what else to do. He bought me a wastebasket, a fancy one with Chinese mandarins on all eight sides; he got a foam rubber cushion for my chair. I despised myself for submitting to this blackmail. I did not even really pity him; it was just that I could not turn away, I could not turn away from that obsequious hunger. And he knew himself my tolerance was bought; in a way he must have hated me for it.

When he lingered in my office now he told me stories of himself. It occurred to me that he was revealing his life to me in the hope that I would write it down. Of course he had probably revealed it to plenty of people for no particular reason, but in my case there seemed to be a special, even desperate necessity. His life was a series of calamities, as people's lives often are; he had been let down by people he had trusted, refused help by those he had depended on, betrayed by the very friends to whom he had given kindness and material help. Other people, mere strangers and passersby, had taken time to torment him gratuitously, in novel and inventive ways. On occasion, his very life had been threatened. Moreover his wife was a difficulty, her health being poor and her temperament unstable; what was he to do? You see how it is, he said, lifting his hands, but I live. He looked to me to say yes.

I took to coming up the stairs on tiptoe, trying to turn my key without making a noise; this was foolish of course because I could not muffle my typewriter. I actually considered writing in longhand, and wished repeatedly for the evil chiropractor's soundproofing. I told my husband my problem and he said it was not a problem at all. Tell him you're busy, he said. As a matter of fact I did tell him; every time he came to my door, always armed with a little gift or an errand, he asked me how I was and I said that today I was busy. Ah, then, he said, as he eased himself through the door, he would not keep me a minute. And all the time, as I have said, he knew what was going on in my mind, how I weakly longed to be rid of him. He knew but could not afford to care.

One evening after I had gone home I discovered that I had left at the office a letter I had intended to post, and so I went back to get it. I saw from the street that the light was on in the room where I worked. Then I saw him bending over the card table. Of course, he came in at night and read what I had written! He heard me at the door, and when I came in he was picking up my wastebasket, saying he thought he would just tidy things up for me. He went out at once. I did not say anything, but found myself trembling with anger and gratification. To have found a just cause was a wonder, an unbearable relief.

Next time he came to my door I had locked it on the inside. I knew his step, his chummy cajoling knock. I continued typing loudly, but not uninterruptedly, so he would know I heard. He called my name, as if I was playing a trick; I bit my lips together not to answer. Unreasonably as ever, guilt assailed me but I typed on. That day I saw the earth was dry around the roots of the plant; I let it alone.

I was not prepared for what happened next. I found a note taped to my door, which said that Mr. Malley would be obliged if I would step into his office. I went at once to get it over with. He sat at his desk surrounded by obscure evidences of his authority; he looked at me from a distance, as one who was now compelled to see me in a new and sadly unfavourable light; the embarrassment which he showed seemed not for himself, but me. He started off by saying, with a rather stagey reluctance, that he had known of course when he took me in that I was a writer.

"I didn't let that worry me, though I have heard things about writers and artists and that type of person that didn't strike me as very encouraging. You know the sort of thing I mean."

This was something new; I could not think what it might lead to.

"Now you came to me and said, Mr. Malley, I want a place to write in. I believed you. I gave it to you. I didn't ask any questions. That's the kind of person I am. But you know the more I think about it, well, the more I am inclined to wonder."

"Wonder what?" I said.

"And your own attitude, that hasn't helped to put my mind at ease. Locking yourself in and refusing to answer your door. That's not a normal way for a person to behave. Not if they got nothing to hide. No more than it's normal for a young woman, says she has a husband and kids, to spend her time rattling away on a typewriter."

"But I don't think that—"

He lifted his hand, a forgiving gesture. "Now all I ask is, that you be open and aboveboard with me, I think I deserve that much, and if you are using that office for any other purpose, or at any other times than you let on, and having your friends or whoever they are up to see you—"

"I don't know what you mean."

"And another thing, you claim to be a writer. Well I read quite a bit of material, and I never have seen your name in print. Now maybe you write under some other name?"

"No," I said.

"Well I don't doubt there are writers whose names I haven't heard," he said genially. "We'll let that pass. Just you give me your word of honour there won't be any more deceptions, or any carryings-on, et cetera, in that office you occupy—"

My anger was delayed somehow, blocked off by a stupid incredulity. I only knew enough to get up and walk down the hall, his voice trailing after me, and lock the door. I thought—I must go. But after I had sat down in my own room, my work in front of me, I thought again how much I liked this room, how well I worked in it, and I decided not to be forced out. After all, I felt, the struggle between us had reached a deadlock. I could refuse to open the door, refuse to look at his notes, refuse to speak to him when we met. My rent was paid in advance and if I left now it was unlikely that I would get any refund. I resolved not to care. I had been taking my manuscript home every night, to prevent his reading it, and now it seemed that even this precaution was beneath me. What did it matter if he read it, any more than if the mice scampered over it in the dark?

Several times after this I found notes on my door. I intended not to read them, but I always did. His accusations grew more specific. He had heard voices in my room. My behaviour was disturbing his wife when she tried to take her afternoon nap. (I never came in the afternoons, except on weekends.) He had found a whiskey bottle in the garbage.

I wondered a good deal about that chiropractor. It was not comfortable to see how the legends of Mr. Malley's life were built up.

As the notes grew more virulent our personal encounters ceased. Once or twice I saw his stooped, sweatered back disappearing as I came into the hall. Gradually our relationship passed into something that was entirely fantasy. He accused me now, by note, of being intimate with people from *Numero Cinq*. This was a coffee-house in the neighbourhood, which I imagine he invoked for symbolic purposes. I felt that nothing much more would happen now, the notes would go on, their contents becoming possibly more grotesque and so less likely to affect me.

He knocked on my door on a Sunday morning, about eleven o'clock. I had just come in and taken my coat off and put my kettle on the hot plate.

This time it was another face, remote and transfigured, that shone with the cold light of intense joy at discovering the proofs of sin.

"I wonder," he said with emotion, "if you would mind following me down the hall?"

I followed him. The light was on in the washroom. This washroom was mine and no one else used it, but he had not given me a key for it and it was always open. He stopped in front of it, pushed back the door and stood with his eyes cast down, expelling his breath discreetly.

"Now who done that?" he said, in a voice of pure sorrow.

The walls above the toilet and above the washbasin were covered with drawings and comments of the sort you see sometimes in public washrooms on the beach, and in town hall lavatories in the little decaying towns where I grew up. They were done with a lipstick, as they usually are. Someone must have got up here the night before, I thought, possibly some of the gang who always loafed and cruised around the shopping centre on Saturday nights.

"It should have been locked," I said, coolly and firmly as if thus to remove myself from the scene. "It's quite a mess."

"It sure is. It's pretty filthy language, in my book. Maybe it's just a joke to your friends, but it isn't to me. Not to mention the art work. That's a nice thing to see when you open a door on your own premises in the morning."

I said, "I believe lipstick will wash off."

"I'm just glad I didn't have my wife see a thing like this. Upsets a woman that's had a nice bringing up. Now why don't you ask your friends up here to have a party with their pails and brushes? I'd like to have a look at the people with that kind of a sense of humour."

I turned to walk away and he turned heavily in front of me.

"I don't think there's any question how these decorations found their way onto my walls."

"If you're trying to say I had anything to do with it," I said, quite flatly and wearily, "you must be crazy."

"How did they get there then? Whose lavatory is this? Eh, whose?"

"There isn't any key to it. Anybody can come up here and walk in. Maybe some kids off the street came up here and did it last night after I went home, how do I know?"

"It's a shame the way the kids gets blamed for everything, when it's the elders that corrupts them. That's a thing you might do some thinking about, you know. There's laws. Obscenity laws. Applies to this sort of thing and literature too as I believe."

This is the first time I ever remember taking deep breaths, consciously, for purposes of self-control. I really wanted to murder him. I remember how soft and loathsome his face looked, with the eyes almost closed, nostrils extended to the soothing odour of righteousness, the odour of triumph. If this stupid thing had not happened, he would never have won. But he had. Perhaps he saw something in my face that unnerved him, even in this victorious moment, for he drew back to the wall, and began to say that actually, as a matter of fact, he had not really felt it was the sort of thing I personally would do, more the sort of thing that perhaps certain friends of mine—I got into my own room, shut the door.

The kettle was making a fearsome noise, having almost boiled dry. I snatched it off the hot plate, pulled out the plug and stood for a moment choking on rage. This spasm passed and I did what I had to do. I put my typewriter and paper on the chair and folded the card table. I screwed the top tightly on the instant coffee and put it and the yellow mug and the teaspoon into the bag in which I had brought them; it was still lying folded on the shelf. I wished childishly to take some vengeance on the potted plant, which sat in the corner with the flowery teapot, the wastebasket, the cushion, and—I forgot—a little plastic pencil sharpener behind it.

When I was taking things down to the car Mrs. Malley came. I had seen little of her since that first day. She did not seem upset, but practical and resigned.

"He is lying down," she said. "He is not himself."

She carried the bag with the coffee and the mug in it. She was so still I felt my anger leave me, to be replaced by an absorbing depression.

I have not yet found another office. I think that I will try again some day, but not yet. I have to wait at least until that picture fades that I see so clearly in my mind, though I never saw it in reality—Mr. Malley with his rags and brushes and a pail of soapy water, scrubbing in his clumsy way, his deliberately clumsy way, at the toilet walls, stooping with difficulty, breathing sorrowfully, arranging in his mind the bizarre but somehow never quite satisfactory narrative of yet another betrayal of trust. While I arrange words, and think it is my right to be rid of him.

[1968]

QUESTIONS

1. What is the significance of the office for the narrator? For Mr. Malley? For the reader? Why is the narrator unable to maintain her office?
2. What values and assumptions concerning women does Mr. Malley represent?
3. Does the narrator unconsciously cooperate with Mr. Malley's emotional blackmail? If so, how—and why?
4. How would you describe the conflicts represented in this story?

V. S. Naipaul

(b. 1932)

Trinidad

V. S. Naipaul was born in Trinidad in 1932. In his classic novel of Indian life in the West Indies, *A House for Mr. Biswas* (1961), he drew on his own family history: 80 years earlier, Naipaul's grandfather had been shipped to Trinidad as an indentured servant. A colorful family saga, rich in Dickensian humor and character, *A House for Mr. Biswas* is one of the major works of contemporary fiction. Its theme has become almost ubiquitous in Naipaul's subsequent writing: the immigrant without a culture, removed from his own traditional setting, often drifting from country to country in search of the perfect whole.

Naipaul's own life replicates much of the sense of displacement he has written about. Although Hindu by birth, he did not visit India until he was nearly 30. By that time he had left Trinidad and had already settled in England, where he went for his advanced education. The settings of Naipaul's 20 volumes (both fiction and nonfiction) are spread geographically throughout much of the world: the West Indies, Africa, India, England, the Middle East. His most popular works include *Miquel Street* (1959), *An Area of Darkness* (1964), *Guerrillas* (1975), *India: A Wounded Civilization* (1977), and *A Bend in the River* (1979). "One Out of Many" is from *In a Free State* (1971), a volume that includes both fiction and nonfiction.

Writing in the *New York Times Book Review*, the critic Alfred Kazin said of Naipaul's work, "The sense of displacement has given Naipaul an ominous sense of place. . . . His novels are about the struggle for existence in a world still colonial in feeling despite the breakup of the old Western world. . . . In Naipaul's world we just barely occupy the place we live in—and we can't wait to move on."

◆ One Out of Many ◆

I am now an American citizen and I live in Washington, capital of the world. Many people, both here and in India, will feel that I have done well. But.

I was so happy in Bombay. I was respected, I had a certain position. I worked for an important man. The highest in the land came to our bachelor chambers and enjoyed my food and showered compliments on me. I also had my friends. We met in the evenings on the pavement below the gallery of our chambers. Some of us, like the tailor's bearer and myself, were domestics who lived in the street. The others were people who came to that bit of pavement to sleep. Respectable people; we didn't encourage riff-raff.

In the evenings it was cool. There were few passers-by and, apart from an occasional double-decker bus or taxi, little traffic. The pavement was swept and sprinkled, bedding brought out from daytime hiding-places, little oil-lamps lit.

While the folk upstairs chattered and laughed, on the pavement we read newspapers, played cards, told stories and smoked. The clay pipe passed from friend to friend; we became drowsy. Except of course during the monsoon, I preferred to sleep on the pavement with my friends, although in our chambers a whole cupboard below the staircase was reserved for my personal use.

It was good after a healthy night in the open to rise before the sun and before the sweepers came. Sometimes I saw the street lights go off. Bedding was rolled up; no one spoke much; and soon my friends were hurrying in silent competition to secluded lanes and alleys and open lots to relieve themselves. I was spared this competition; in our chambers I had facilities.

Afterwards for half an hour or so I was free simply to stroll. I liked walking beside the Arabian Sea, waiting for the sun to come up. Then the city and the ocean gleamed like gold. Alas for those morning walks, that sudden ocean dazzle, the moist salt breeze on my face, the flap of my shirt, that first cup of hot sweet tea from a stall, the taste of the first leaf-cigarette.

Observe the workings of fate. The respect and security I enjoyed were due to the importance of my employer. It was this very importance which now all at once destroyed the pattern of my life.

My employer was seconded by his firm to Government service and was posted to Washington. I was happy for his sake but frightened for mine. He was to be away for some years and there was nobody in Bombay he could second me to. Soon, therefore, I was to be out of a job and out of the chambers. For many years I had considered my life as settled. I had served my apprenticeship, known my hard times. I didn't feel I could start again. I despaired. Was there a job for me in Bombay? I saw myself having to return to my village in the hills, to my wife and children there, not just for a holiday but for good. I saw myself again becoming a porter during the tourist season, racing after the buses as they arrived at the station and shouting with forty or fifty others for luggage. Indian luggage, not this lightweight American stuff! Heavy metal trunks!

I could have cried. It was no longer the sort of life for which I was fitted. I had grown soft in Bombay and I was no longer young. I had acquired possessions, I was used to the privacy of my cupboard. I had become a city man, used to certain comforts.

My employer said, "Washington is not Bombay, Santosh. Washington is expensive. Even if I was able to raise your fare, you wouldn't be able to live over there in anything like your present style.'

But to be barefoot in the hills, after Bombay! The shock, the disgrace! I couldn't face my friends. I stopped sleeping on the pavement and spent as much of my free time as possible in my cupboard among my possessions, as among things which were soon to be taken from me.

My employer said, "Santosh, my heart bleeds for you."

I said, "Sahib[1], if I look a little concerned it is only because I worry about you. You have always been fussy, and I don't see how you will manage in Washington."

"It won't be easy. But it's the principle. Does the representative of a poor country like ours travel about with his cook? Will that create a good impression?"

"You will always do what is right, sahib."

[1]*sahib* master

He went silent.

After some days he said, "There's not only the expense, Santosh. There's the question of foreign exchange. Our rupee isn't what it was."

"I understand, sahib. Duty is duty."

A fortnight later, when I had almost given up hope, he said, "Santosh, I have consulted Government. You will accompany me. Government has sanctioned, will arrange accommodation. But no expenses. You will get your passport and your P form. But I want you to think, Santosh. Washington is not Bombay."

I went down to the pavement that night with my bedding.

I said, blowing down my shirt, "Bombay gets hotter and hotter."

"Do you know what you are doing?" the tailor's bearer said. "Will the Americans smoke with you? Will they sit and talk with you in the evenings? Will they hold you by the hand and walk with you beside the ocean?"

It pleased me that he was jealous. My last days in Bombay were very happy.

I packed my employer's two suitcases and bundled up my own belongings in lengths of old cotton. At the airport they made a fuss about my bundles. They said they couldn't accept them as luggage for the hold because they didn't like the responsibility. So when the time came I had to climb up to the aircraft with all my bundles. The girl at the top, who was smiling at everybody else, stopped smiling when she saw me. She made me go right to the back of the plane, far from my employer. Most of the seats there were empty, though, and I was able to spread my bundles around and, well, it was comfortable.

It was bright and hot outside, cool inside. The plane started, rose up in the air, and Bombay and the ocean tilted this way and that. It was very nice. When we settled down I looked around for people like myself, but I could see no one among the Indians or the foreigners who looked like a domestic. Worse, they were all dressed as though they were going to a wedding and, brother, I soon saw it wasn't they who were conspicuous. I was in my ordinary Bombay clothes, the loose long-tailed shirt, the wide-waisted pants held up with a piece of string. Perfectly respectable domestic's wear, neither dirty nor clean, and in Bombay no one would have looked. But now on the plane I felt heads turning whenever I stood up.

I was anxious. I slipped off my shoes, tight even without the laces, and drew my feet up. That made me feel better. I made myself a little betel-nut mixture and that made me feel better still. Half the pleasure of betel, though, is the spitting; and it was only when I had worked up a good mouthful that I saw I had a problem. The airline girl saw too. That girl didn't like me at all. She spoke roughly to me. My mouth was full, my cheeks were bursting, and I couldn't say anything. I could only look at her. She went and called a man in uniform and he came and stood over me. I put my shoes back on and swallowed the betel juice. It made me feel quite ill.

The girl and the man, the two of them, pushed a little trolley of drinks down the aisle. The girl didn't look at me but the man said, "You want a drink, chum?" He wasn't a bad fellow. I pointed at random to a bottle. It was a kind of soda drink, nice and sharp at first but then not so nice. I was worrying about it when the girl said, "Five shillings sterling or sixty cents U.S." That took me by surprise. I had no money, only a few rupees. The girl stamped, and I thought she was going to hit me with her pad when I stood up to show her who my employer was.

Presently my employer came down the aisle. He didn't look very well. He said, without stopping, "Champagne, Santosh? Already we are overdoing?" He went on to the lavatory. When he passed back he said, "Foreign exchange, Santosh! Foreign exchange!" That was all. Poor fellow, he was suffering too.

The journey became miserable for me. Soon, with the wine I had drunk, the betel juice, the movement and the noise of the aeroplane, I was vomiting all over my bundles, and I didn't care what the girl said or did. Later there were more urgent and terrible needs. I felt I would choke in the tiny, hissing room at the back. I had a shock when I saw my face in the mirror. In the fluorescent light it was the colour of a corpse. My eyes were strained, the sharp air hurt my nose and seemed to get into my brain. I climbed up on the lavatory seat and squatted. I lost control of myself. As quickly as I could I ran back out into the comparative openness of the cabin and hoped no one had noticed. The lights were dim now; some people had taken off their jackets and were sleeping. I hoped the plane would crash.

The girl woke me up. She was almost screaming. "It's you, isn't it? Isn't it?"

I thought she was going to tear the shirt off me. I pulled back and leaned hard on the window. She burst into tears and nearly tripped on her sari as she ran up the aisle to get the man in uniform.

Nightmare. And all I knew was that somewhere at the end, after the airports and the crowded lounges where everybody was dressed up, after all those take-offs and touchdowns, was the city of Washington. I wanted the journey to end but I couldn't say I wanted to arrive at Washington. I was already a little scared of that city, to tell the truth. I wanted only to be off the plane and to be in the open again, to stand on the ground and breathe and to try to understand what time of day it was.

At last we arrived. I was in a daze. The burden of those bundles! There were more closed rooms and electric lights. There were questions from officials.

"Is he diplomatic?"

"He's only a domestic," my employer said.

"Is that his luggage? What's in that pocket?"

I was ashamed.

"Santosh," my employer said.

I pulled out the little packets of pepper and salt, the sweets, the envelopes with scented napkins, the toy tubes of mustard. Airline trinkets. I had been collecting them throughout the journey, seizing a handful, whatever my condition, every time I passed the galley.

"He's a cook," my employer said.

"Does he always travel with his condiments?"

"Santosh, Santosh," my employer said in the car afterwards, "in Bombay it didn't matter what you did. Over here you represent your country. I must say I cannot understand why your behaviour has already gone so much out of character."

"I am sorry, sahib."

"Look at it like this, Santosh. Over here you don't only represent your country, you represent me."

For the people of Washington it was late afternoon or early evening, I couldn't say which. The time and the light didn't match, as they did in Bombay. Of that drive I remember green fields, wide roads, many motor cars travelling fast, making a steady hiss, hiss, which wasn't at all like our Bombay traffic noise. I remember big buildings and wide parks; many bazaar areas; then smaller houses without fences and with gardens like bush, with the *hubshi*[2] standing about or sitting down, more usually sitting down, everywhere. Especially I remember the *hubshi.* I had heard about them in stories and had seen one or two in Bombay. But I had never dreamt that this wild race existed in such numbers in Washington and were permitted to roam the streets so freely. O father, what was this place I had come to?

I wanted, I say, to be in the open, to breathe, to come to myself, to reflect. But there was to be no openness for me that evening. From the aeroplane to the airport building to the motor car to the apartment block to the elevator to the corridor to the apartment itself, I was forever enclosed, forever in the hissing, hissing sound of air-conditioners.

I was too dazed to take stock of the apartment. I saw it as only another halting place. My employer went to bed at once, completely exhausted, poor fellow. I looked around for my room. I couldn't find it and gave up. Aching for the Bombay ways, I spread my bedding in the carpeted corridor just outside our apartment door. The corridor was long: doors, doors. The illuminated ceiling was decorated with stars of different sizes; the colours were grey and blue and gold. Below that imitation sky I felt like a prisoner.

Waking, looking up at the ceiling, I thought just for a second that I had fallen asleep on the pavement below the gallery of our Bombay chambers. Then I realized my loss. I couldn't tell how much time had passed or whether it was night or day. The only clue was that newspapers now lay outside some doors. It disturbed me to think that while I had been sleeping, alone and defenceless, I had been observed by a stranger and perhaps by more than one stranger.

I tried the apartment door and found I had locked myself out. I didn't want to disturb my employer. I thought I would get out into the open, go for a walk. I remembered where the elevator was. I got in and pressed the button. The elevator dropped fast and silently and it was like being in the aeroplane again. When the elevator stopped and the blue metal door slid open I saw plain concrete corridors and blank walls. The noise of machinery was very loud. I knew I was in the basement and the main floor was not far above me. But I no longer wanted to try; I gave up ideas of the open air. I thought I would just go back up to the apartment. But I hadn't noted the number and didn't even know what floor we were on. My courage flowed out of me. I sat on the floor of the elevator and felt the tears come to my eyes. Almost without noise the elevator door closed, and I found I was being taken up silently at great speed.

The elevator stopped and the door opened. It was my employer, his hair uncombed, yesterday's dirty shirt partly unbuttoned. He looked frightened.

"Santosh, where have you been at this hour of morning? Without your shoes."

I could have embraced him. He hurried me back past the newspapers to our apartment and I took the bedding inside. The wide window showed the early morning sky, the big city; we were high up, way above the trees.

I said, "I couldn't find my room."

"Government sanctioned," my employer said. "Are you sure you've looked?"

[2]*hubshi* African-Americans

We looked together. One little corridor led past the bathroom to his bedroom; another, shorter corridor led to the big room and the kitchen. There was nothing else.

"Government sanctioned," my employer said, moving about the kitchen and opening cupboard doors. "Separate entrance, shelving. I have the correspondence." He opened another door and looked inside. "Santosh, do you think it is possible that this is what Government meant?"

The cupboard he had opened was as high as the rest of the apartment and as wide as the kitchen, about six feet. It was about three feet deep. It had two doors. One door opened into the kitchen; another door, directly opposite, opened into the corridor.

"Separate entrance," my employer said. "Shelving, electric light, power point, fitted carpet."

"This must be my room, sahib."

"Santosh, some enemy in Government has done this to me."

"Oh no, sahib. You mustn't say that. Besides, it is very big. I will be able to make myself very comfortable. It is much bigger than my little cubby-hole in the chambers. And it has a nice flat ceiling. I wouldn't hit my head."

"You don't understand, Santosh. Bombay is Bombay. Here if we start living in cupboards we give the wrong impression. They will think we all live in cupboards in Bombay."

"O sahib, but they can just look at me and see I am dirt."

"You are very good, Santosh. But these people are malicious. Still, if you are happy, then I am happy."

"I am very happy, sahib."

And after all the upset, I was. It was nice to crawl in that evening, spread my bedding and feel protected and hidden. I slept very well.

In the morning my employer said, "We must talk about money, Santosh. Your salary is one hundred rupees a month. But Washington isn't Bombay. Everything is a little bit more expensive here, and I am going to give you a Dearness Allowance. As from today you are getting one hundred and fifty rupees."

"Sahib."

"And I'm giving you a fortnight's pay in advance. In foreign exchange. Seventy-five rupees. Ten cents to the rupee, seven hundred and fifty cents. Seven fifty U.S. Here, Santosh. This afternoon you go out and have a little walk and enjoy. But be careful. We are not among friends, remember."

So at last, rested, with money in my pocket, I went out in the open. And of course the city wasn't a quarter as frightening as I had thought. The buildings weren't particularly big, not all the streets were busy, and there were many lovely trees. A lot of the *hubshi* were about, very wild-looking some of them, with dark glasses and their hair frizzed out, but it seemed that if you didn't trouble them they didn't attack you.

I was looking for a café or a tea-stall where perhaps domestics congregated. But I saw no domestics, and I was chased away from the place I did eventually go into. The girl said, after I had been waiting some time, "Can't you read? We don't serve hippies or bare feet here."

O father! I had come out without my shoes. But what a country, I thought, walking briskly away, where people are never allowed to dress normally but must forever wear their very best! Why must they wear out shoes and fine clothes for no purpose? What occasion are they honouring? What waste, what presumption! Who do they think is noticing them all the time?

And even while these thoughts were in my head I found I had come to a roundabout with trees and a fountain where — and it was like a fulfilment in a dream, not easy to believe — there were many people who looked like my own people. I tightened the string around my loose pants, held down my flapping shirt and ran through the traffic to the green circle.

Some of the *hubshi* were there, playing musical instruments and looking quite happy in their way. There were some Americans sitting about on the grass and the fountain and the kerb. Many of them were in rough, friendly-looking clothes; some were without shoes; and I felt I had been over hasty in condemning the entire race. But it wasn't these people who had attracted me to the circle. It was the dancers. The men were bearded, barefooted and in saffron robes, and the girls were in saris and canvas shoes that looked like our own Bata shoes. They were shaking little cymbals and chanting and lifting their heads up and down and going round in a circle, making a lot of dust. It was a little bit like a Red Indian dance in a cowboy movie, but they were chanting Sanskrit words in praise of Lord Krishna.

I was very pleased. But then a disturbing thought came to me. It might have been because of the half-caste appearance of the dancers; it might have been their bad Sanskrit pronunciation and their accent. I thought that these people were now strangers, but that perhaps once upon a time they had been like me. Perhaps, as in some story, they had been brought here among the *hubshi* as captives a long time ago and had become a lost people, like our own wandering gipsy folk, and had forgotten who they were. When I thought that, I lost my pleasure in the dancing; and I felt for the dancers the sort of distaste we feel when we are faced with something that should be kin but turns out not to be, turns out to be degraded, like a deformed man, or like a leper, who from a distance looks whole.

I didn't stay. Not far from the circle I saw a café which appeared to be serving bare feet. I went in, had a coffee and a nice piece of cake and bought a pack of cigarettes; matches they gave me free with the cigarettes. It was all right, but then the bare feet began looking at me, and one bearded fellow came and sniffed loudly at me and smiled and spoke some sort of gibberish, and then some others of the bare feet came and sniffed at me. They weren't unfriendly, but I didn't appreciate the behaviour; and it was a little frightening to find, when I left the place, that two or three of them appeared to be following me. They weren't unfriendly, but I didn't want to take any chances. I passed a cinema; I went in. It was something I wanted to do anyway. In Bombay I used to go once a week.

And that was all right. The movie had already started. It was in English, not too easy for me to follow, and it gave me time to think. It was only there, in the darkness, that I thought about the money I had been spending. The prices had seemed to me very reasonable, like Bombay prices. Three for the movie ticket, one fifty in the café, with tip. But I had been thinking in rupees and paying in dollars. In less than an hour I had spent nine days' pay.

I couldn't watch the movie after that. I went out and began to make my way back to the apartment block. Many more of the *hubshi* were about now and I saw that where they congregated the pavement was wet, and dangerous with broken glass and bottles. I couldn't think of cooking when I got back to the apartment. I couldn't bear to look at the view. I spread my bedding in the cupboard, lay down in the darkness and waited for my employer to return.

When he did I said, "Sahib, I want to go home."

"Santosh, I've paid five thousand rupees to bring you here. If I send you back now, you will have to work for six or seven years without salary to pay me back."

I burst into tears.

"My poor Santosh, something has happened. Tell me what has happened."

"Sahib, I've spent more than half the advance you gave me this morning. I went out and had a coffee and cake and then I went to a movie."

His eyes went small and twinkly behind his glasses. He bit the inside of his top lip, scraped at his moustache with his lower teeth, and he said, "You see, you see. I told you it was expensive."

I understood I was a prisoner. I accepted this and adjusted. I learned to live within the apartment, and I was even calm.

My employer was a man of taste and he soon had the apartment looking like something in a magazine, with books and Indian paintings and Indian fabrics and pieces of sculpture and bronze statues of our gods. I was careful to take no delight in it. It was of course very pretty, especially with the view. But the view remained foreign and I never felt that the apartment was real, like the shabby old Bombay chambers with the cane chairs, or that it had anything to do with me.

When people came to dinner I did my duty. At the appropriate time I would bid the company goodnight, close off the kitchen behind its folding screen and pretend I was leaving the apartment. Then I would lie down quietly in my cupboard and smoke. I was free to go out; I had my separate entrance. But I didn't like being out of the apartment. I didn't even like going down to the laundry room in the basement.

Once or twice a week I went to the supermarket on our street. I always had to walk past groups of *hubshi* men and children. I tried not to look, but it was hard. They sat on the pavement, on steps and in the bush around their redbrick houses, some of which had boarded-up windows. They appeared to be very much a people of the open air, with little to do; even in the mornings some of the men were drunk.

Scattered among the *hubshi* houses were others just as old but with gas-lamps that burned night and day in the entrance. These were the houses of the Americans. I seldom saw these people; they didn't spend much time on the street. The lighted gas-lamp was the American way of saying that though a house looked old outside it was nice and new inside. I also felt that it was like a warning to the *hubshi* to keep off.

Outside the supermarket there was always a policeman with a gun. Inside, there were always a couple of *hubshi* guards with truncheons, and, behind the cashiers, some old *hubshi* beggar men in rags. There were also many young *hubshi* boys, small but muscular, waiting to carry parcels, as once in the hills I had waited to carry Indian tourists' luggage.

These trips to the supermarket were my only outings, and I was always glad to get back to the apartment. The work there was light. I watched a lot of television and my English improved. I grew to like certain commercials very much. It was in these commercials I saw the Americans whom in real life I so seldom saw and knew only by their gas-lamps. Up there in the apartment, with a view of the white domes and towers and greenery of the famous city, I entered the homes of the Americans and saw them cleaning those homes. I saw them cleaning floors and dishes. I saw them buying clothes and cleaning clothes, buying motor cars and cleaning motor cars. I saw them cleaning, cleaning.

The effect of all this television on me was curious. If by some chance I saw an American on the street I tried to fit him or her into the commercials; and I felt I had caught the person in an interval between his television duties. So to some extent Americans have remained to me, as people not quite real, as people temporarily absent from television.

Sometimes a *hubshi* came on the screen, not to talk of *hubshi* things, but to do a little cleaning of his own. That wasn't the same. He was too different from the *hubshi* I saw on the street and I knew he was an actor. I knew that his television duties were only make-believe and that he would soon have to return to the street.

One day at the supermarket, when the *hubshi* girl took my money, she sniffed and said, "You always smell sweet, baby."

She was friendly, and I was at last able to clear up that mystery, of my smell. It was the poor country weed I smoked. It was a peasant taste of which I was slightly ashamed, to tell the truth; but the cashier was encouraging. As it happened, I had brought a quantity of the weed with me from Bombay in one of my bundles, together with a hundred razor blades, believing both weed and blades to be purely Indian things. I made an offering to the girl. In return she taught me a few words of English. "Me black and beautiful" was the first thing she taught me. Then she pointed to the policeman with the gun outside and taught me: "He pig."

My English lessons were taken a stage further by the *hubshi* maid who worked for someone on our floor in the apartment block. She too was attracted by my smell, but I soon began to feel that she was also attracted by my smallness and strangeness. She herself was a big woman, broad in the face, with high cheeks and bold eyes and lips that were full but not pendulous. Her largeness disturbed me; I found it better to concentrate on her face. She misunderstood; there were times when she frolicked with me in a violent way. I didn't like it, because I couldn't fight her off as well as I would have liked and because in spite of myself I was fascinated by her appearance. Her smell mixed with the perfumes she used could have made me forget myself.

She was always coming into the apartment. She disturbed me while I was watching the Americans on television. I feared the smell she left behind. Sweat, perfume, my own weed: the smells lay thick in the room, and I prayed to the bronze gods my employer had installed as living-room ornaments that I would not be dishonoured. Dishonoured, I say; and I know that this might seem strange to people over here, who have permitted the *hubshi* to settle among them in such large numbers and must therefore esteem them in certain ways. But in our country we frankly do not care for the *hubshi*. It is written in our books, both holy and not so holy, that it is indecent and wrong for a man of our blood to embrace the *hubshi* woman. To be dishonoured in this life, to be born a cat or a monkey or a *hubshi* in the next!

But I was falling. Was it idleness and solitude? I was found attractive: I wanted to know why. I began to go to the bathroom of the apartment simply to study my face in the mirror. I cannot easily believe it myself now, but in Bombay a week or a month could pass without my looking in the mirror; and then it wasn't to consider my looks but to check whether the barber had cut off too much hair or whether a pimple was about to burst. Slowly I made a discovery. My face was handsome. I had never thought of myself in this way. I had thought of myself as unnoticeable, with features that served as identification alone.

The discovery of my good looks brought its strains. I became obsessed with my appearance, with a wish to see myself. It was like an illness. I would be watching television, for instance, and I would be surprised by the thought: are you as handsome as that man? I would have to get up and go to the bathroom and look in the mirror.

I thought back to the time when these matters hadn't interested me, and I saw how ragged I must have looked, on the aeroplane, in the airport, in that café for bare feet, with the rough and dirty clothes I wore, without doubt or question, as clothes befitting a servant. I was choked with shame. I saw, too, how good people in Washington had been, to have seen me in rags and yet to have taken me for a man.

I was glad I had a place to hide. I had thought of myself as a prisoner. Now I was glad I had so little of Washington to cope with: the apartment, my cupboard, the television set, my employer, the walk to the supermarket, the *hubshi* woman. And one day I found I no longer knew whether I wanted to go back to Bombay. Up there, in the apartment, I no longer knew what I wanted to do.

I became more careful of my appearance. There wasn't much I could do. I bought laces for my old black shoes, socks, a belt. Then some money came my way. I had understood that the weed I smoked was of value to the *hubshi* and the bare feet; I disposed of what I had, disadvantageously as I now know, through the *hubshi* girl at the supermarket. I got just under two hundred dollars. Then, as anxiously as I had got rid of my weed, I went out and bought some clothes.

I still have the things I bought that morning. A green hat, a green suit. The suit was always too big for me. Ignorance, inexperience; but I also remember the feeling of presumption. The salesman wanted to talk, to do his job. I didn't want to listen. I took the first suit he showed me and went into the cubicle and changed. I couldn't think about size and fit. When I considered all that cloth and all that tailoring I was proposing to adorn my simple body with, that body that needed so little, I felt I was asking to be destroyed. I changed back quickly, went out of the cubicle and said I would take the green suit. The salesman began to talk; I cut him short; I asked for a hat. When I got back to the apartment I felt quite weak and had to lie down for a while in my cupboard.

I never hung the suit up. Even in the shop, even while counting out the precious dollars, I had known it was a mistake. I kept the suit folded in the box with all its pieces of tissue paper. Three or four times I put it on and walked about the apartment and sat down on chairs and lit cigarettes and crossed my legs, practising. But I couldn't bring myself to wear the suit out of doors. Later I wore the pants, but never the jacket. I never bought another suit; I soon began wearing the sort of clothes I wear today, pants with some sort of zippered jacket.

Once I had had no secrets from my employer; it was so much simpler not to have secrets. But some instinct told me now it would be better not to let him know about the green suit or the few dollars I had, just as instinct had already told me I should keep my growing knowledge of English to myself.

Once my employer had been to me only a presence. I used to tell him then that beside him I was as dirt. It was only a way of talking, one of the courtesies of our language, but it had something of truth. I meant that he was the man who adventured in the world for me, that I experienced the world through him, that I was content to be a small part of his presence. I was content, sleeping on the Bombay pavement with my friends, to hear the talk of my employer and his guests upstairs. I was more than content, late at night, to be identified among the sleepers and greeted by some of those guests before they drove away.

Now I found that, without wishing it, I was ceasing to see myself as part of my employer's presence, and beginning at the same time to see him as an outsider might see him, as perhaps the people who came to dinner in the apartment saw him. I saw that he was a man of my own age, around thirty-five; it astonished me that I hadn't noticed this before. I saw that he was plump, in need of exercise, that he moved with short, fussy steps; a man with glasses, thinning hair, and that habit, during conversation, of scraping at his moustache with his teeth and nibbling at the inside of his top lip; a man who was frequently anxious, took pains over his work, was subjected at his own table to unkind remarks by his office colleagues; a man who looked as uneasy in Washington as I felt, who acted as cautiously as I had learned to act.

I remember an American who came to dinner. He looked at the pieces of sculpture in the apartment and said he had himself brought back a whole head from one of our ancient temples; he had got the guide to hack it off.

I could see that my employer was offended. He said, "But that's illegal."

"That's why I had to give the guide two dollars. If I had a bottle of whisky he would have pulled down the whole temple for me."

My employer's face went blank. He continued to do his duties as host but he was unhappy throughout the dinner. I grieved for him.

Afterwards he knocked on my cupboard. I knew he wanted to talk. I was in my underclothes but I didn't feel underdressed, with the American gone. I stood in the door of my cupboard; my employer paced up and down the small kitchen; the apartment felt sad.

"Did you hear that person, Santosh?"

I pretended I hadn't understood, and when he explained I tried to console him. I said, "Sahib, but we know these people are Franks and barbarians."

"They are malicious people, Santosh. They think that because we are a poor country we are all the same. They think an official in Government is just the same as some poor guide scraping together a few rupees to keep body and soul together, poor fellow."

I saw that he had taken the insult only in a personal way, and I was disappointed. I thought he had been thinking of the temple.

A few days later I had my adventure. The *hubshi* woman came in, moving among my employer's ornaments like a bull. I was greatly provoked. The smell was too much; so was the sight of her armpits. I fell. She dragged me down on the couch, on the saffron spread which was one of my employer's nicest pieces of Punjabi folk-weaving. I saw the moment, helplessly, as one of dishonour. I saw her as Kali, goddess of death and destruction, coal-black, with a red tongue and white eyeballs and many powerful arms. I expected her to be wild and fierce; but she added insult to injury by being very playful, as though, because I was small and strange, the act was not real. She laughed all the time. I would have liked to withdraw, but the act took over and completed itself. And then I felt dreadful.

I wanted to be forgiven, I wanted to be cleansed, I wanted her to go. Nothing frightened me more than the way she had ceased to be a visitor in the apartment and behaved as though she possessed it. I looked at the sculpture and the fabrics and thought of my poor employer, suffering in his office somewhere.

I bathed and bathed afterwards. The smell would not leave me. I fancied that the woman's oil was still on that poor part of my poor body. It occurred to me to rub it down with half a lemon. Penance and cleansing; but it didn't hurt as much as I expected, and I extended the penance by rolling about naked on the floor of the bathroom and the sitting-room and howling. At last the tears came, real tears, and I was comforted.

It was cool in the apartment; the air-conditioning always hummed; but I could see that it was hot outside, like one of our own summer days in the hills. The urge came upon me to dress as I might have done in my village on a religious occasion. In one of my bundles I had a dhoti-length of new cotton, a gift from the tailor's bearer that I had never used. I draped this around my waist and between my legs, lit incense sticks, sat down crosslegged on the floor and tried to meditate and become still. Soon I began to feel hungry. That made me happy; I decided to fast.

Unexpectedly my employer came in. I didn't mind being caught in the attitude and garb of prayer; it could have been so much worse. But I wasn't expecting him till late afternoon.

"Santosh, what has happened?"

Pride got the better of me. I said, "Sahib, it is what I do from time to time."

But I didn't find merit in his eyes. He was far too agitated to notice me properly. He took off his lightweight fawn jacket, dropped it on the saffron spread, went to the refrigerator and drank two tumblers of orange juice, one after the other. Then he looked out at the view, scraping at his moustache.

"Oh, my poor Santosh, what are we doing in this place? Why do we have to come here?"

I looked with him. I saw nothing unusual. The wide window showed the colours of the hot day: the pale-blue sky, the white, almost colourless, domes of famous buildings rising out of dead-green foliage; the untidy roofs of apartment blocks where on Saturday and Sunday mornings people sunbathed; and, below, the fronts and backs of houses on the tree-lined street down which I walked to the supermarket.

My employer turned off the air-conditioning and all noise was absent from the room. An instant later I began to hear the noises outside: sirens far and near. When my employer slid the window open the roar of the disturbed city rushed into the room. He closed the window and there was near-silence again. Not far from the supermarket I saw black smoke, uncurling, rising, swiftly turning colourless. This was not the smoke which some of the apartment blocks gave off all day. This was the smoke of a real fire.

"The *hubshi* have gone wild, Santosh. They are burning down Washington."

I didn't mind at all. Indeed, in my mood of prayer and repentance, the news was even welcome. And it was with a feeling of release that I watched and heard the city burn that afternoon and watched it burn that night. I watched it burn again and again on television; and I watched it burn in the morning. It burned like a famous city and I didn't want it to stop burning. I wanted the fire to spread and spread and I wanted everything in the city, even the apartment block, even the apartment, even myself, to be destroyed and consumed. I wanted escape to be impossible; I wanted the very idea of escape to become absurd. At every sign that the burning was going to stop I felt disappointed and let down.

For four days my employer and I stayed in the apartment and watched the city burn. The television continued to show us what we could see and what, whenever we slid the window back, we could hear. Then it was over. The view from our window hadn't changed. The famous buildings stood; the trees remained. But for the first time since I had understood that I was a prisoner I found that I wanted to be out of the apartment and in the streets.

The destruction lay beyond the supermarket. I had never gone into this part of the city before, and it was strange to walk in those long wide streets for the first time, to see trees and houses and shops and advertisements, everything like a real city, and then to see that every signboard on every shop was burnt or stained with smoke, that the shops themselves were black and broken, that flames had burst through some of the upper windows and scorched the red bricks. For mile after mile it was like that. There were *hubshi* groups about, and at first when I passed them I pretended to be busy, minding my own business, not at all interested in the ruins. But they smiled at me and I found I was smiling back. Happiness was on the faces of the *hubshi*. They were like people amazed they could do so much, that so much lay in their power. They were like people on holiday. I shared their exhilaration.

The idea of escape was a simple one, but it hadn't occurred to me before. When I adjusted to my imprisonment I had wanted only to get away from Washington and to return to Bombay. But then I had become confused. I had looked in the mirror and seen myself, and I knew it wasn't possible for me to return to Bombay to the sort of job I had had and the life I had lived. I couldn't easily become part of someone else's presence again. Those evening chats on the pavement, those morning walks: happy times, but they were like the happy times of childhood: I didn't want them to return.

I had taken, after the fire, to going for long walks in the city. And one day, when I wasn't even thinking of escape, when I was just enjoying the sights and my new freedom of movement, I found myself in one of those leafy streets where private houses had been turned into business premises. I saw a fellow countryman superintending the raising of a signboard on his gallery. The signboard told me that the building was a restaurant, and I assumed that the man in charge was the owner. He looked worried and slightly ashamed, and he smiled at me. This was unusual, because the Indians I had seen on the streets of Washington pretended they hadn't seen me; they made me feel that they didn't like the competition of my presence or didn't want me to start asking them difficult questions.

I complimented the worried man on his signboard and wished him good luck in his business. He was a small man of about fifty and he was wearing a double-breasted suit with old-fashioned wide lapels. He had dark hollows below his eyes and he looked as though he had recently lost a little weight. I could see that in our country he had been a man of some standing, not quite the sort of person who would go into the restaurant business. I felt at one with him. He invited me in to look around, asked my name and gave his. It was Priya.

Just past the gallery was the loveliest and richest room I had ever seen. The wallpaper was like velvet; I wanted to pass my hand over it. The brass lamps that hung from the ceiling were in a lovely cut-out pattern and the bulbs were of many colours. Priya looked with me, and the hollows under his eyes grew darker, as though my admiration was increasing his worry at his extravagance. The restaurant hadn't yet opened for customers and on a shelf in one corner I saw Priya's collection of good-luck objects: a brass plate with a heap of uncooked rice, for prosperity; a little copybook and a little diary pencil, for good luck with the accounts; a little clay lamp, for general good luck.

"What do you think, Santosh? You think it will be all right?"

"It is bound to be all right, Priya."

"But I have enemies, you know, Santosh. The Indian restaurant people are not going to appreciate me. All mine, you know, Santosh. Cash paid. No mortgage or anything like that. I don't believe in mortgages. Cash or nothing.

I understood him to mean that he had tried to get a mortgage and failed, and was anxious about money.

"But what are you doing here, Santosh? You used to be in Government or something?"

"You could say that, Priya."

"Like me. They have a saying here. If you can't beat them, join them. I joined them. They are still beating me." He sighed and spread his arms on the top of the red wall-seat. "Ah, Santosh, why do we do it? Why don't we renounce and go and meditate on the riverbank?" He waved about the room. "The yemblems of the world, Santosh. Just yemblems."

I didn't know the English word he used, but I understood its meaning; and for a moment it was like being back in Bombay, exchanging stories and philosophies with the tailor's bearer and others in the evening.

"But I am forgetting, Santosh. You will have some tea or coffee or something?"

I shook my head from side to side to indicate that I was agreeable, and he called out in a strange harsh language to someone behind the kitchen door.

"Yes, Santosh. Yem-*blems*!" And he sighed and slapped the red seat hard.

A man came out from the kitchen with a tray. At first he looked like a fellow countryman, but in a second I could tell he was a stranger.

"You are right," Priya said, when the stranger went back to the kitchen. "He is not of Bharat. He is a Mexican. But what can I do? You get fellow countrymen, you fix up their papers and everything, green card and everything. And then? Then they run away. Run-run-runaway. Crooks this side, crooks that side, I can't tell you. Listen, Santosh. I was in cloth business before. Buy for fifty rupees that side, sell for fifty dollars this side. Easy. But then. Caftan, everybody wants caftan. Caftanaftan, I say, I will settle your caftan. I buy one thousand, Santosh. Delays India-side, of course. They come one year later. Nobody wants caftan then. We're not organized, Santosh. We don't do enough consumer research. That's what the fellows at the embassy tell me. But if I do consumer research, when will I do my business? The trouble, you know, Santosh, is that this shopkeeping is not in my blood. The damn thing goes *against* my blood. When I was in cloth business I used to hide sometimes for shame when a customer came in. Sometimes I used to pretend I was a shopper myself. Consumer research! These people make us dance, Santosh. You and I, we will renounce. We will go together and walk beside Potomac and meditate."

I loved his talk. I hadn't heard anything so sweet and philosophical since the Bombay days. I said, "Priya, I will cook for you, if you want a cook."

"I feel I've known you a long time, Santosh. I feel you are like a member of my own family. I will give you a place to sleep, a little food to eat and a little pocket money, as much as I can afford."

I said, "Show me the place to sleep."

He led me out of the pretty room and up a carpeted staircase. I was expecting the carpet and the new paint to stop somewhere, but it was nice and new all the way. We entered a room that was like a smaller version of my employer's apartment.

"Built-in cupboards and everything, you see, Santosh."

I went to the cupboard. It had a folding door that opened outward. I said, "Priya, it is too small. There is room on the shelf for my belongings. But I don't see how I can spread my bedding inside here. It is far too narrow."

He giggled nervously. "Santosh, you are a joker. I feel that we are of the same family already."

Then it came to me that I was being offered the whole room. I was stunned.

Priya looked stunned too. He sat down on the edge of the soft bed. The dark hollows under his eyes were almost black and he looked very small in his double-breasted jacket. "This is how they make us dance over here, Santosh. You say staff quarters and they say staff quarters. This is what they mean."

For some seconds we sat silently, I fearful, he gloomy, meditating on the ways of this new world.

Someone called from downstairs, "Priya!"

His gloom gone, smiling in advance, winking at me, Priya called back in an accent of the country, "Hi, Bab!"

I followed him down.

"Priya," the American said, "I've brought over the menus."

He was a tall man in a leather jacket, with jeans that rode up above thick white socks and big rubber-soled shoes. He looked like someone about to run in a race. The menus were enormous; on the cover there was a drawing of a fat man with a moustache and a plumed turban, something like the man in the airline advertisements.

"They look great, Bab."

"I like them myself. But what's that, Priya? What's that shelf doing there?"

Moving like the front part of a horse, Bab walked to the shelf with the rice and the brass plate and the little clay lamp. It was only then that I saw that the shelf was very roughly made.

Priya looked penitent and it was clear he had put the shelf up himself. It was also clear he didn't intend to take it down.

"Well, it's yours," Bab said. "I suppose we had to have a touch of the East somewhere. Now, Priya—"

"Money-money-money, is it?" Priya said, racing the words together as though he was making a joke to amuse a child. "But, Bab, how can *you* ask *me* for money? Anybody hearing you would believe that this restaurant is mine. But this restaurant isn't mine, Bab. This restaurant is yours."

It was only one of our courtesies, but it puzzled Bab and he allowed himself to be led to other matters.

I saw that, for all his talk of renunciation and business failure, and for all his jumpiness, Priya was able to cope with Washington. I admired this strength in him as much as I admired the richness of his talk. I didn't know how much to believe of his stories, but I liked having to guess about him. I liked having to play with his words in my mind. I liked the mystery of the man. The mystery came from his solidity. I knew where I was with him. After the apartment and the green suit and the *hubshi* woman and the city burning for four days, to be with Priya was to feel safe. For the first time since I had come to Washington I felt safe.

I can't say that I moved in. I simply stayed. I didn't want to go back to the apartment even to collect my belongings. I was afraid that something might happen to keep me a prisoner there. My employer might turn up and demand his five thousand rupees. The *hubshi* woman might claim me for her own; I might be condemned to a life among the *hubshi*. And it wasn't as if I was leaving behind anything of value in the apartment. The green suit I was even happy to forget. But.

Priya paid me forty dollars a week. After what I was getting, three dollars and seventy-five cents, it seemed a lot; and it was more than enough for my needs. I didn't have much temptation to spend, to tell the truth. I knew that my old employer and the *hubshi* woman would be wondering about me in their respective ways and I thought I should keep off the streets for a while. That was no hardship; it was what I was used to in Washington. Besides, my days at the restaurant were pretty full; for the first time in my life I had little leisure.

The restaurant was a success from the start, and Priya was fussy. He was always bursting into the kitchen with one of those big menus in his hand, saying in English, "Prestige job, Santosh, prestige." I didn't mind. I liked to feel I had to do things perfectly; I felt I was earning my freedom. Though I was in hiding, and though I worked every day until midnight, I felt I was much more in charge of myself than I had ever been.

Many of our waiters were Mexicans, but when we put turbans on them they could pass. They came and went, like the Indian staff. I didn't get on with these people. They were frightened and jealous of one another and very treacherous. Their talk amid the biryanis and the pillaus[3] was all of papers and green cards. They were always about to get green cards or they had been cheated out of green cards or they had just got green cards. At first I didn't know what they were talking about. When I understood I was more than depressed.

I understood that because I had escaped from my employer I had made myself illegal in America. At any moment I could be denounced, seized, jailed, deported, disgraced. It was a complication. I had no green card; I didn't know how to set about getting one; and there was no one I could talk to.

I felt burdened by my secrets. Once I had none; now I had so many. I couldn't tell Priya I had no green card. I couldn't tell him I had broken faith with my old employer and dishonoured myself with a *hubshi* woman and lived in fear of retribution. I couldn't tell him that I was afraid to leave the restaurant and that nowadays when I saw an Indian I hid from him as anxiously as the Indian hid from me. I would have felt foolish to confess. With Priya, right from the start, I had pretended to be strong; and I wanted it to remain like that. Instead, when we talked now, and he grew philosophical, I tried to find bigger causes for being sad. My mind fastened on to these causes, and the effect of this was that my sadness became like a sickness of the soul.

It was worse than being in the apartment, because now the responsibility was mine and mine alone. I had decided to be free, to act for myself. It pained me to think of the exhilaration I had felt during the days of the fire; and I felt mocked when I remembered that in the early days of my escape I had thought I was in charge of myself.

The year turned. The snow came and melted. I was more afraid than ever of

[3]*biryanis and pillaus* Indian dishes having a rice base

going out. The sickness was bigger than all the causes. I saw the future as a hole into which I was dropping. Sometimes at night when I awakened my body would burn and I would feel the hot perspiration break all over.

I leaned on Priya. He was my only hope, my only link with what was real. He went out; he brought back stories. He went out especially to eat in the restaurants of our competitors.

He said, "Santosh, I never believed that running a restaurant was a way to God. But it is true. I eat like a scientist. Every day I eat like a scientist. I feel I have already renounced."

This was Priya. This was how his talk ensnared me and gave me the bigger causes that steadily weakened me. I became more and more detached from the men in the kitchen. When they spoke of their green cards and the jobs they were about to get I felt like asking them: Why? Why?

And every day the mirror told its own tale. Without exercise, with the sickening of my heart and my mind, I was losing my looks. My face had become pudgy and sallow and full of spots; it was becoming ugly. I could have cried for that, discovering my good looks only to lose them. It was like a punishment for my presumption, the punishment I had feared when I bought the green suit.

Priya said, "Santosh, you must get some exercise. You are not looking well. Your eyes are getting like mine. What are you pining for? Are you pining for Bombay or your family in the hills?"

But now, even in my mind, I was a stranger in those places.

Priya said one Sunday morning, "Santosh, I am going to take you to see a Hindi movie today. All the Indians of Washington will be there, domestics and everybody else."

I was very frightened. I didn't want to go and I couldn't tell him why. He insisted. My heart began to beat fast as soon as I got into the car. Soon there were no more houses with gas-lamps in the entrance, just those long wide burnt-out *hubshi* streets, now with fresh leaves on the trees, heaps of rubble on bulldozed, fenced-in lots, boarded-up shop windows, and old smoke-stained signboards announcing what was no longer true. Cars raced along the wide roads; there was life only on the roads. I thought I would vomit with fear.

I said, "Take me back, *sahib*."

I had used the wrong word. Once I had used the word a hundred times a day. But then I had considered myself a small part of my employer's presence, and the word was not servile; it was more like a name, like a reassuring sound, part of my employer's dignity and therefore part of mine. But Priya's dignity could never be mine; that was not our relationship. Priya I had always called Priya; it was his wish, the American way, man to man. With Priya the word was servile. And he responded to the word. He did as I asked; he drove me back to the restaurant. I never called him by his name again.

I was good-looking; I had lost my looks. I was a free man; I had lost my freedom.

One of the Mexican waiters came into the kitchen late one evening and said, "There is a man outside who wants to see the chef."

No one had made this request before, and Priya was at once agitated. "Is he an American? Some enemy has sent him here. Sanitary-anitary, health-ealth, they can inspect my kitchens at any time."

"He is an Indian," the Mexican said.

I was alarmed. I thought it was my old employer; that quiet approach was like him. Priya thought it was a rival. Though Priya regularly ate in the restaurants of his rivals he thought it unfair when they came to eat in his. We both went to the door and peeked through the glass window into the dimly lit dining-room.

"Do you know that person, Santosh?"

"Yes, sahib."

It wasn't my old employer. It was one of his Bombay friends, a big man in Government, whom I had often served in the chambers. He was by himself and seemed to have just arrived in Washington. He had a new Bombay haircut, very close, and a stiff dark suit, Bombay tailoring. His shirt looked blue, but in the dim multi-coloured light of the dining-room everything white looked blue. He didn't look unhappy with what he had eaten. Both his elbows were on the curry-spotted tablecloth and he was picking his teeth, half closing his eyes and hiding his mouth with his cupped left hand.

"I don't like him," Priya said. "Still, big man in Government and so on. You must go to him, Santosh."

But I couldn't go.

"Put on your apron, Santosh. And that chef's cap. Prestige. You must go, Santosh."

Priya went out to the dining-room and I heard him say in English that I was coming.

I ran up to my room, put some oil on my hair, combed my hair, put on my best pants and shirt and my shining shoes. It was so, as a man about town rather than as a cook, I went to the dining-room.

The man from Bombay was as astonished as Priya. We exchanged the old courtesies, and I waited. But, to my relief, there seemed little more to say. No difficult questions were put to me; I was grateful to the man from Bombay for his tact. I avoided talk as much as possible. I smiled. The man from Bombay smiled back. Priya smiled uneasily at both of us. So for a while we were, smiling in the dim blue-red light and waiting.

The man from Bombay said to Priya, "Brother, I just have a few words to say to my old friend Santosh."

Priya didn't like it, but he left us.

I waited for those words. But they were not the words I feared. The man from Bombay didn't speak of my old employer. We continued to exchange courtesies. Yes, I was well and he was well and everybody else we knew was well; and I was doing well and he was doing well. That was all. Then, secretively, the man from Bombay gave me a dollar. A dollar, ten rupees, an enormous tip for Bombay. But, from him, much more than a tip: an act of graciousness, part of the sweetness of the old days. Once it would have meant so much to me. Now it meant so little. I was saddened and embarrassed. And I had been anticipating hostility!

Priya was waiting behind the kitchen door. His little face was tight and serious, and I knew he had seen the money pass. Now, quickly, he read my own face, and without saying anything to me he hurried out into the dining-room.

I heard him say in English to the man from Bombay, "Santosh is a good fellow. He's got his own room with bath and everything. I am giving him a hundred dollars a week from next week. A thousand rupees a week. This is a first-class establishment."

A thousand chips a week! I was staggered. It was much more than any man in

Government got, and I was sure the man from Bombay was also staggered, and perhaps regretting his good gesture and that precious dollar of foreign exchange.

"Santosh," Priya said, when the restaurant closed that evening, "that man was an enemy. I knew it from the moment I saw him. And because he was an enemy I did something very bad, Santosh."

"Sahib."

"I lied, Santosh. To protect you. I told him, Santosh, that I was going to give you seventy-five dollars a week after Christmas."

"Sahib."

"And now I have to make that lie true. But, Santosh, you know that is money we can't afford. I don't have to tell you about overheads and things like that. Santosh, I will give you sixty."

I said, "Sahib, I couldn't stay on for less than a hundred and twenty-five."

Priya's eyes went shiny and the hollows below his eyes darkened. He giggled and pressed out his lips. At the end of that week I got a hundred dollars. And Priya, good man that he was, bore me no grudge.

Now here was a victory. It was only after it happened that I realized how badly I had needed such a victory, how far, gaining my freedom, I had begun to accept death not as the end but as the goal. I revived. Or rather, my senses revived. But in this city what was there to feed my senses? There were no walks to be taken, no idle conversations with understanding friends. I could buy new clothes. But then? Would I just look at myself in the mirror? Would I go walking, inviting passers-by to look at me and my clothes? No, the whole business of clothes and dressing up only threw me back into myself.

There was a Swiss or German woman in the cake-shop some doors away, and there was a Filipino woman in the kitchen. They were neither of them attractive, to tell the truth. The Swiss or German could have broken my back with a slap, and the Filipino, though young, was remarkably like one of our older hill women. Still, I felt I owed something to the senses, and I thought I might frolic with these women. But then I was frightened of the responsibility. Goodness, I had learned that a woman is not just a roll and a frolic but a big creature weighing a hundred-and-so-many pounds who is going to be around afterwards.

So the moment of victory passed, without celebration. And it was strange, I thought, that sorrow lasts and can make a man look forward to death, but the mood of victory fills a moment and then is over. When my moment of victory was over I discovered below it, as if waiting for me, all my old sickness and fears: fear of my illegality, my former employer, my presumption, the *hubshi* woman. I saw then that the victory I had had was not something I had worked for, but luck; and that luck was only fate's cheating, giving an illusion of power.

But that illusion lingered, and I became restless. I decided to act, to challenge fate. I decided I would no longer stay in my room and hide. I began to go out walking in the afternoons. I gained courage; every afternoon I walked a little farther. It became my ambition to walk to that green circle with the fountain where, on my first day out in Washington, I had come upon those people in Hindu costumes, like domestics abandoned a long time ago, singing their Sanskrit gibberish and doing their strange Red Indian dance. And one day I got there.

One day I crossed the road to the circle and sat down on a bench. The *hubshi* were there, and the bare feet, and the dancers in saris and the saffron robes. It was mid-afternoon, very hot, and no one was active. I remembered how magical and inexplicable that circle had seemed to me the first time I saw it. Now it seemed so ordinary and tired: the roads, the motor cars, the shops, the trees, the careful policemen: so much part of the waste and futility that was our world. There was no longer a mystery. I felt I knew where everybody had come from and where those cars were going. But I also felt that everybody there felt like me, and that was soothing. I took to going to the circle every day after the lunch rush and sitting until it was time to go back to Priya's for the dinners.

Late one afternoon, among the dancers and the musicians, the *hubshi* and the bare feet, the singers and the police, I saw her. The *hubshi* woman. And again I wondered at her size; my memory had not exaggerated. I decided to stay where I was. She saw me and smiled. Then, as if remembering anger, she gave me a look of great hatred; and again I saw her as Kali, many-armed, goddess of death and destruction. She looked hard at my face; she considered my clothes. I thought: is it for this I bought these clothes? She got up. She was very big and her tight pants made her much more appalling. She moved towards me. I got up and ran. I ran across the road and then, not looking back, hurried by devious ways to the restaurant.

Priya was doing his accounts. He always looked older when he was doing his accounts, not worried, just older, like a man to whom life could bring no further surprises. I envied him.

"Santosh, some friend brought a parcel for you."

It was a big parcel wrapped in brown paper. He handed it to me, and I thought how calm he was, with his bills and pieces of paper, and the pen with which he made his neat figures, and the book in which he would write every day until that book was exhausted and he would begin a new one.

I took the parcel up to my room and opened it. Inside there was a cardboard box; and inside that, still in its tissue paper, was the green suit.

I felt a hole in my stomach. I couldn't think. I was glad I had to go down almost immediately to the kitchen, glad to be busy until midnight. But then I had to go up to my room again, and I was alone. I hadn't escaped; I had never been free. I had been abandoned. I was like nothing; I had made myself nothing. And I couldn't turn back.

In the morning Priya said, "You don't look very well, Santosh."

His concern weakened me further. He was the only man I could talk to and I didn't know what I could say to him. I felt tears coming to my eyes. At that moment I would have liked the whole world to be reduced to tears. I said, "Sahib, I cannot stay with you any longer."

They were just words, part of my mood, part of my wish for tears and relief. But Priya didn't soften. He didn't even look surprised. "Where will you go, Santosh?"

How could I answer his serious question?

"Will it be different where you go?"

He had freed himself of me. I could no longer think of tears. I said, "Sahib, I have enemies."

He giggled. "You are a joker, Santosh. How can a man like yourself have enemies? There would be no profit in it. *I* have enemies. It is part of your happiness and part of the equity of the world that you cannot have enemies. That's why you can run-run-runaway." He smiled and made the running gesture with his extended palm.

So, at last, I told him my story. I told him about my old employer and my escape and the green suit. He made me feel I was telling him nothing he hadn't already known. I told him about the *hubshi* woman. I was hoping for some rebuke. A rebuke would have meant that he was concerned for my honour, that I could lean on him, that rescue was possible.

But he said, "Santosh, you have no problems. Marry the *hubshi*. That will automatically make you a citizen. Then you will be a free man."

It wasn't what I was expecting. He was asking me to be alone forever. I said, "Sahib, I have a wife and children in the hills at home."

"But this is your home, Santosh. Wife and children in the hills, that is very nice and that is always there. But that is over. You have to do what is best for you here. You are alone here. *Hubshi-ubshi*, nobody worries about that here, if that is your choice. This isn't Bombay. Nobody looks at you when you walk down the street. Nobody cares what you do."

He was right. I was a free man; I could do anything I wanted. I could, if it were possible for me to turn back, go to the apartment and beg my old employer for forgiveness. I could, if it were possible for me to become again what I once was, go to the police and say, "I am an illegal immigrant here. Please deport me to Bombay." I could run away, hang myself, surrender, confess, hide. It didn't matter what I did, because I was alone. And I didn't know what I wanted to do. It was like the time when I felt my senses revive and I wanted to go out and enjoy and I found there was nothing to enjoy.

To be empty is not to be sad. To be empty is to be calm. It is to renounce. Priya said no more to me; he was always busy in the mornings. I left him and went up to my room. It was still a bare room, still like a room that in half an hour could be someone else's. I had never thought of it as mine. I was frightened of its spotless painted walls and had been careful to keep them spotless. For just such a moment.

I tried to think of the particular moment in my life, the particular action, that had brought me to that room. Was it the moment with the *hubshi* woman, or was it when the American came to dinner and insulted my employer? Was it the moment of my escape, my sight of Priya in the gallery, or was it when I looked in the mirror and bought the green suit? Or was it much earlier, in that other life, in Bombay, in the hills? I could find no one moment; every moment seemed important. An endless chain of action had brought me to that room. It was frightening; it was burdensome. It was not a time for new decisions. It was time to call a halt.

I lay on the bed watching the ceiling, watching the sky. The door was pushed open. It was Priya.

"My goodness, Santosh! How long have you been here? You have been so quiet I forgot about you."

He looked about the room. He went into the bathroom and came out again. "Are you all right, Santosh?"

He sat on the edge of the bed and the longer he stayed the more I realized how glad I was to see him. There was this: when I tried to think of him rushing into the room I couldn't place it in time; it seemed to have occurred only in my mind. He sat with me. Time became real again. I felt a great love for him. Soon I could have laughed at his agitation. And later, indeed, we laughed together.

I said, "Sahib, you must excuse me this morning. I want to go for a walk. I will come back about tea time."

He looked hard at me, and we both knew I had spoken truly.

"Yes, yes, Santosh. You go for a good long walk. Make yourself hungry with walking. You will feel much better."

Walking, through streets that were now so simple to me, I thought how nice it would be if the people in Hindu costumes in the circle were real. Then I might have joined them. We would have taken to the road; at midday we would have halted in the shade of big trees; in the late afternoon the sinking sun would have turned the dust clouds to gold; and every evening at some village there would have been welcome, water, food, a fire in the night. But that was a dream of another life. I had watched the people in the circle long enough to know that they were of their city; that their television life awaited them; that their renunciation was not like mine. No television life awaited me. It didn't matter. In this city I was alone and it didn't matter what I did.

As magical as the circle with the fountain the apartment block had once been to me. Now I saw that it was plain, not very tall, and faced with small white tiles. A glass door; four tiled steps down; the desk to the right, letters and keys in the pigeonholes; a carpet to the left, upholstered chairs, a low table with paper flowers in the vase; the blue door of the swift, silent elevator. I saw the simplicity of all these things. I knew the floor I wanted. In the corridor, with its illuminated star-decorated ceiling, an imitation sky, the colours were blue, grey and gold. I knew the door I wanted. I knocked.

The *hubshi* woman opened. I saw the apartment where she worked. I had never seen it before and was expecting something like my old employer's apartment, which was on the same floor. Instead, for the first time, I saw something arranged for a television life.

I thought she might have been angry. She looked only puzzled. I was grateful for that.

I said to her in English, "Will you marry me?"

And there, it was done.

"It is for the best, Santosh," Priya said, giving me tea when I got back to the restaurant. "You will be a free man. A citizen. You will have the whole world before you."

I was pleased that he was pleased.

So I am now a citizen, my presence is legal, and I live in Washington. I am still with Priya. We do not talk together as much as we did. The restaurant is one world, the parks and green streets of Washington are another, and every evening some of these streets take me to a third. Burnt-out brick houses, broken fences, overgrown gardens; in a levelled lot between the high brick walls of two houses, a sort of artistic children's playground which the *hubshi* children never use; and then the dark house in which I now live.

Its smells are strange, everything in it is strange. But my strength in this house is that I am a stranger. I have closed my mind and heart to the English language, to newspapers and radio and television, to the pictures of *hubshi* runners and boxers and musicians on the wall. I do not want to understand or learn any more.

I am a simple man who decided to act and see for himself, and it is as though I have had several lives. I do not wish to add to these. Some afternoons I walk to the circle with the fountain. I see the dancers but they are separated from me as by glass. Once, when there were rumours of new burnings, someone scrawled in white paint on the pavement outside my house: *Soul Brother*. I understand the words; but I feel, brother to what or to whom? I was once part of the flow, never thinking of myself as a presence. Then I looked in the mirror and decided to be free. All that my freedom has brought me is the knowledge that I have a face and have a body, that I must feed this body and clothe this body for a certain number of years. Then it will be over.

[1971]

QUESTIONS

1. At the end of the story, Santosh talks of freedom, implying that that is what he has discovered in America. Is Santosh better off at the end of the story than he was at the beginning? Is he now free?
2. To what extent does "One Out of Many" follow the classic journey motif?
3. What picture does Naipaul give of the other Indians in Washington, DC? Are their lives substantially better than Santosh's?
4. How are we to interpret Santosh's changing relationship with the *hubshi*/black woman?

Carmen Naranjo

(b. 1931)

Costa Rica

Author, editor, social critic, museum director, and cultural ambassador (among other positions), Carmen Naranjo understands the people and institutions of Costa Rica from a variety of perspectives. She studied public administration at the Autonomous University of Mexico and literature at the University of Iowa. As the most visible woman in public office in her country, she has served as secretary of culture and ambassador to Israel and currently is director of Editorial Universitaria Centroamericana press, the major publishing company of Central America. Naranjo is also the multitalented author of six novels, six volumes of poetry, three volumes of short stories, and two collections of essays. Most of her work has not been translated into English.

In her fiction, Naranjo employs a variety of modes from realism to fantasy to explore psychological themes as well as social issues and to experiment with nontraditional forms, particularly with narrative perspectives. She has received several national literary awards and prizes for her fiction and poetry in addition to Costa Rica's highest award for public service.

And We Sold the Rain

"This is a royal fuck-up," was all the treasury minister could say a few days ago as he got out of the jeep after seventy kilometers of jouncing over dusty rutted roads and muddy trails. His advisor agreed: there wasn't a cent in the treasury, the line for foreign exchange wound four times around the capital, and the IMF[1] was stubbornly insisting that the country could expect no more loans until the interest had been paid up, public spending curtailed, salaries frozen, domestic production increased, imports reduced, and social programs cut.

The poor were complaining, "We can't even buy beans—they've got us living on radish tops, bananas and garbage; they raise our water bills but don't give us any water even though it rains every day, and on top of that they add on a charge for excess consumption for last year, even though there wasn't any water in the pipes then either."

"Doesn't anyone in this whole goddamned country have an idea that could get us out of this?" asked the president of the republic, who shortly before the elections, surrounded by a toothily smiling, impeccably tailored meritocracy, had boasted that by virtue of his university-trained mind (Ph.D. in developmental economics) he was the best candidate. Someone proposed to him that he pray to

[1]*IMF* International Monetary Fund

La Negrita; he did and nothing happened. Somebody else suggested that he reinstate the Virgin of Ujarrás. But after so many years of neglect, the pretty little virgin had gone deaf and ignored the pleas for help, even though the entire cabinet implored her, at the top of their lungs, to light the way to a better future and a happier tomorrow.

The hunger and poverty could no longer be concealed: the homeless, pockets empty, were squatting in the Parque Central, the Parque Nacional, and the Plaza de la Cultura. They were camping along Central and Second Avenues and in a shantytown springing up on the plains outside the city. Gangs were threatening to invade the national theater, the Banco Central, and all nationalized banking headquarters. The Public Welfare Agency was rationing rice and beans as if they were medicine. In the marketplace, robberies increased to one per second, and homes were burgled at the rate of one per half hour. Business and government were sinking in sleaze; drug lords operated uncontrolled, and gambling was institutionalized in order to launder dollars and attract tourists. Strangely enough, the prices of a few items went down: whiskey, caviar and other such articles of conspicuous consumption.

The sea of poverty that was engulfing cities and villages contrasted with the growing number of Mercedes Benzes, BMWs and a whole alphabet of trade names of gleaming new cars.

The minister announced to the press that the country was on the verge of bankruptcy. The airlines were no longer issuing tickets because so much money was owed them, and travel became impossible; even official junkets were eliminated. There was untold suffering of civil servants suddenly unable to travel even once a month to the great cities of the world! A special budget might be the solution, but tax revenues were nowhere to be found, unless a compliant public were to go along with the president's brilliant idea of levying a tax on air—a minimal tax, to be sure, but, after all, the air was a part of the government's patrimony. Ten *colones*[2] per breath would be a small price to pay.

July arrived, and one afternoon a minister without portfolio and without umbrella, noticing that it had started to rain, stood watching people run for cover. "Yes," he thought, "here it rains like it rains in Comala, like it rains in Macondo. It rains day and night, rain after rain, like a theater with the same movie, sheets of water. Poor people without umbrellas, without a change of clothes, they get drenched, people living in leaky houses, without a change of shoes for when they're shipwrecked. And here, all my poor colleagues with colds, all the poor deputies with laryngitis, the president with that worrisome cough, all this on top of the catastrophe itself. No TV station is broadcasting; all of them are flooded, along with the newspaper plants and the radio stations. A people without news is a lost people, because they don't know that everywhere else, or almost everywhere else, things are even worse. If we could only export the rain," thought the minister.

Meanwhile, the people, depressed by the heavy rains, the dampness, the lack of news, the cold, and their hunger and despair without their sitcoms and soap operas, began to rain inside and to increase the baby population—that is, to try to increase the odds that one of their progeny might survive. A mass of hungry, naked babies began to cry in concert every time it rained.

[2]*colones* monetary unit of Costa Rica

When one of the radio transmitters was finally repaired, the president was able to broadcast a message: He had inherited a country so deeply in debt that it could no longer obtain credit and could no longer afford to pay either the interest or the amortization on loans. He had to dismiss civil servants, suspend public works, cut off services, close offices, and spread his legs somewhat to transnationals. Now even these lean cows were dying; the fat ones were on the way, encouraged by the International Monetary Fund, the AID and the IDB, not to mention the EEC.[3] The great danger was that the fat cows had to cross over the neighboring country on their way, and it was possible that they would be eaten up—even though they came by air, at nine thousand feet above the ground, in a first class stable in a pressurized, air-conditioned cabin. Those neighbors were simply not to be trusted.

The fact was that the government had faded in the people's memory. By now no one remembered the names of the president or his ministers; people remembered them as "the one with glasses who thinks he's Tarzan's mother," or "the one who looks like the baby hog someone gave me when times were good, maybe a little uglier."

The solution came from the most unexpected source. The country had organized the Third World contest to choose "Miss Underdeveloped," to be elected, naturally, from the multitudes of skinny, dusky, round-shouldered, short-legged, half-bald girls with cavity-pocked smiles, girls suffering from parasites and God knows what else. The prosperous Emirate of the Emirs sent its designée, who in sheer amazement at how it rained and rained, widened her enormous eyes—fabulous eyes of harem and Koran delights—and was unanimously elected reigning Queen of Underdevelopment. Lacking neither eyeteeth nor molars, she was indeed the fairest of the fair. She returned in a rush to the Emirate of the Emirs, for she had acquired, with unusual speed, a number of fungal colonies that were taking over the territory under her toenails and fingernails, behind her ears, and on her left cheek.

"Oh, Father Sultan, my lord, lord of the moons and of the suns, if your Arabian highness could see how it rains and rains in that country, you would not believe it. It rains day and night. Everything is green, even the people; they are green people, innocent and trusting, who probably have never even thought about selling their most important resource, the rain. The poor fools think about coffee, rice, sugar, vegetables, and lumber, and they hold Ali Baba's treasure in their hands without even knowing it. What we would give to have such abundance!"

Sultan Abun dal Tol let her speak and made her repeat the part about the rain from dawn to dusk, dusk to dawn, for months on end. He wanted to hear over and over about that greenness that was forever turning greener. He loved to think of it raining and raining, of singing in the rain, of showers bringing forth flowers. . . .

A long distance phone call was made to the office of the export minister from the Emirate of the Emirs, but the minister wasn't in. The trade minister grew radiant when Sultan Abun dal Tol, warming to his subject, instructed him to buy up rain and construct an aqueduct between their countries to fertilize the

[3] *AID* Agency for International Development; *IDB*—International Development Bank; *EEC*—European Economic Community

desert. Another call. Hello, am I speaking with the country of rain, not the rain of marijuana or cocaine, not that of laundered dollars, but the rain that falls naturally from the sky and makes the sandy desert green? Yes, yes, you are speaking with the export minister, and we are willing to sell you our rain. Of course, its production costs us nothing; it is a resource as natural to us as your petroleum. We will make you a fair and just agreement.

The news filled five columns during the dry season, when obstacles like floods and dampness could be overcome. The president himself made the announcement: We will sell rain at ten dollars per cc. The price will be reviewed every ten years. Sales will be unlimited. With the earnings we will regain our independence and our self-respect.

The people smiled. A little less rain would be agreeable to everyone, and the best part was not having to deal with the six fat cows, who were more than a little oppressive. The IMF, the World Bank, the AID, the Embassy, the International Development Bank and perhaps the EEC would stop pushing the cows on them, given the danger that they might be stolen in the neighboring country, air-conditioned cabin, first class stable and all. Moreover, one couldn't count on those cows really being fat, since accepting them meant increasing all kinds of taxes, especially those on consumer goods, lifting import restrictions, spreading one's legs completely open to the transnationals, paying the interest, which was now a little higher, and amortizing the debt that was increasing at a rate only comparable to the spread of an epidemic. And as if this were not enough, it would be necessary to structure the cabinet a certain way, as some ministers were viewed by some legislators as potentially dangerous, as extremists.

The president added with demented glee, his face garlanded in sappy smiles, that French technicians, those guardians of European meritocracy, would build the rain funnels and the aqueduct, a guarantee of honesty, efficiency and effective transfer of technology.

By then we had already sold, to our great disadvantage, the tuna, the dolphins, and the thermal dome, along with the forests and all Indian artifacts. Also our talent, dignity, sovereignty, and the right to traffic in anything and everything illicit.

The first funnel was located on the Atlantic coast, which in a few months looked worse than the dry Pacific. The first payment from the emir arrived — in dollars! — and the country celebrated with a week's vacation. A little more effort was needed. Another funnel was added in the north and one more in the south. Both zones immediately dried up like raisins. The checks did not arrive. What happened? The IMF garnisheed them for interest payments. Another effort: a funnel was installed in the center of the country; where formerly it had rained and rained. It now stopped raining forever, which paralyzed brains, altered behavior, changed the climate, defoliated the corn, destroyed the coffee, poisoned aromas, devastated canefields, dessicated palm trees, ruined orchards, razed truck gardens, and narrowed faces, making people look and act like rats, ants, and cockroaches, the only animals left alive in large numbers.

To remember what we once had been, people circulated photographs of an enormous oasis with great plantations, parks, and animal sanctuaries full of butterflies and flocks of birds, at the bottom of which was printed, "Come and visit us. The Emirate of Emirs is a paradise."

The first one to attempt it was a good swimmer who took the precaution of carrying food and medicine. Then a whole family left, then whole villages, large and small. The population dropped considerably. One fine day there was nobody left, with the exception of the president and his cabinet. Everyone else, even the deputies, followed the rest by opening the cover of the aqueduct and floating all the way to the cover at the other end, doorway to the Emirate of the Emirs.

In that country we were second-class citizens, something we were already accustomed to. We lived in a ghetto. We got work because we knew about coffee, sugar cane, cotton, fruit trees, and truck gardens. In a short time we were happy and felt as if these things too were ours, or at the very least, that the rain still belonged to us.

A few years passed; the price of oil began to plunge and plunge. The emir asked for a loan, then another, then many; eventually he had to beg and beg for money to service the loans. The story sounds all too familiar. Now the IMF has taken possession of the aqueducts. They have cut off the water because of a default in payments and because the sultan had the bright idea of receiving as a guest of honor a representative of that country that is a neighbor of ours.

[1988]

Translated by
JO ANNE ENGELBERT

QUESTIONS

1. What political and social institutions and values does Naranjo satirize? What details contribute to the story's humor? How would you describe the tone of the story?
2. What are the implications of the story's conclusion?
3. What relationship is suggested between developing and developed countries?
4. Compare this story with R. K. Narayan's "A Horse and Two Goats."

R. K. Narayan

(b. 1907)

India

Born into an old Brahmin family to the headmaster of a distinguished secondary school in Madras, Rasipuram Krisnaswami Narayan spent a rather lonely childhood in the home of his grandmother and uncle. Privy to the library of his father's school, he developed an early love of British novelists such as Dickens, Scott, and Hardy. He was later educated at the University of Mysore but, failing at the profession he had assumed he would pursue as a teacher of English, Narayan turned to free-lance writing while working as a journalist for a Madras newspaper.

Although he is currently the most widely read and loved writer of the Indian subcontinent, Narayan initially had difficulty in finding a publisher for his fiction. Graham Greene was influential in securing for Narayan a British publisher for his first four novels. Narayan's greatest audience is in the United States, where his novels are typically published before they appear in India.

Like William Faulkner's mythic Yoknapatawpha County, Narayan's Malgudi is an entire world in microcosm: a fictional transformation of Mysore, where the author has spent most of his life. Through a deeply humane comic vision, Narayan traces the struggles of his sensitive and often doubting characters—middle-class men who are professionally involved in teaching, journalism, or commerce—to find moral equilibrium and spiritual peace within the framework of public life. The formation and testing of character are central preoccupations of his 15 novels to date, including *Swami and Friends* (1935), *The Bachelor of Arts* (1937), and *The Painter of Signs* (1976). His four collections of short stories include *A Horse and Two Goats* (1970), from which the title story is included here.

In 1939 Narayan's marriage ended tragically when his wife died suddenly of typhoid. His autobiographical novel, *Grateful to Life and Death* (1945), masterfully traces his recovery from bereavement through telepathic communication with his deceased wife. The mystical communication he experienced radically transformed his view of personality to something far larger than traditional notions encompass:

> [T]he full view of a personality would extend from the infant curled up in the womb and before it, and beyond it, and ahead of it, into infinity. Our normal view is limited to a physical perception in a condition restricted in time, like the flashing of a torchlight on a spot, the rest of the area being in darkness. If one could have a total view of oneself and others, one would see all in their full stature, through all the stages of evolution and growth, ranging from childhood to old age, in this life, the next one, and the previous ones. [*My Days*]

A Horse and Two Goats

Of the seven hundred thousand villages dotting the map of India, in which the majority of India's five hundred million live, flourish, and die, Kritam was probably the tiniest, indicated on the district survey map by a microscopic dot, the map being meant more for the revenue official out to collect tax than for the guidance of the motorist, who in any case could not hope to reach it since it sprawled far from the highway at the end of a rough track furrowed up by the iron-hooped wheels of bullock carts. But its size did not prevent its giving itself the grandiose name Kritam, which meant in Tamil "coronet" or "crown" on the brow of this subcontinent. The village consisted of less than thirty houses, only one of them built with brick and cement. Painted a brilliant yellow and blue all over with gorgeous carvings of gods and gargoyles on its balustrade, it was known as the Big House. The other houses, distributed in four streets, were generally of bamboo thatch, straw, mud, and other unspecified material. Muni's was the last house in the fourth street, beyond which stretched the fields. In his prosperous days Muni had owned a flock of forty sheep and goats and sallied forth every morning driving the flock to the highway a couple of miles away. There he would sit on the pedestal of a clay statue of a horse while his cattle grazed around. He carried a crook at the end of a bamboo pole and snapped foliage from the avenue trees to feed his flock; he also gathered faggots and dry sticks, bundled them, and carried them home for fuel at sunset.

His wife lit the domestic fire at dawn, boiled water in a mud pot, threw into it a handful of millet flour, added salt, and gave him his first nourishment for the day. When he started out, she would put in his hand a packed lunch, once again the same millet cooked into a little ball, which he could swallow with a raw onion at midday. She was old, but he was older and needed all the attention she could give him in order to be kept alive.

His fortunes had declined gradually, unnoticed. From a flock of forty which he drove into a pen at night, his stock had now come down to two goats, which were not worth the rent of a half rupee a month the Big House charged for the use of the pen in their back yard. And so the two goats were tethered to the trunk of a drumstick tree which grew in front of his hut and from which occasionally Muni could shake down drumsticks. This morning he got six. He carried them in with a sense of triumph. Although no one could say precisely who owned the tree, it was his because he lived in its shadow.

She said, "If you were content with the drumstick leaves alone, I could boil and salt some for you."

"Oh, I am tired of eating those leaves. I have a craving to chew the drumstick out of sauce, I tell you."

"You have only four teeth in your jaw, but your craving is for big things. All right, get the stuff for the sauce, and I will prepare it for you. After all, next year you may not be alive to ask for anything. But first get me all the stuff, including a measure of rice or millet, and I will satisfy your unholy craving. Our store is empty today. Dhall,[1] chili, curry leaves, mustard, coriander, gingelley oil, and one

[1]*dhall* a kind of lentil

large potato. Go out and get all this." He repeated the list after her in order not to miss any item and walked off to the shop in the third street.

He sat on an upturned packing case below the platform of the shop. The shopman paid no attention to him. Muni kept clearing his throat, coughing, and sneezing until the shopman could not stand it any more and demanded, "What ails you? You will fly off that seat into the gutter if you sneeze so hard, young man." Muni laughed inordinately, in order to please the shopman, at being called "young man." The shopman softened and said, "You have enough of the imp inside to keep a second wife busy, but for the fact the old lady is still alive." Muni laughed appropriately again at this joke. It completely won the shopman over; he liked his sense of humour to be appreciated. Muni engaged his attention in local gossip for a few minutes, which always ended with a reference to the postman's wife who had eloped to the city some months before.

The shopman felt most pleased to hear the worst of the postman, who had cheated him. Being an itinerant postman, he returned home to Kritam only once in ten days and every time managed to slip away again without passing the shop in the third street. By thus humouring the shopman, Muni could always ask for one or two items of food, promising repayment later. Some days the shopman was in a good mood and gave in, and sometimes he would lose his temper suddenly and bark at Muni for daring to ask for credit. This was such a day, and Muni could not progress beyond two items listed as essential components. The shopman was also displaying a remarkable memory for old facts and figures and took out an oblong ledger to support his observations. Muni felt impelled to rise and flee. But his self-respect kept him in his seat and made him listen to the worst things about himself. The shopman concluded, "If you could find five rupees[2] and a quarter, you will have paid off an ancient debt and then could apply for admission to swarga.[3] How much have you got now?"

"I will pay you everything on the first of the next month."

"As always, and whom do you expect to rob by then?"

Muni felt caught and mumbled, "My daughter has sent word that she will be sending me money."

"Have you a daughter?" sneered the shopman. "And she is sending you money! For what purpose, may I know?"

"Birthday, fiftieth birthday," said Muni quietly.

"Birthday! How old are you?"

Muni repeated weakly, not being sure of it himself, "Fifty." He always calculated his age from the time of the great famine when he stood as high as the parapet around the village well, but who could calculate such things accurately nowadays with so many famines occurring? The shopman felt encouraged when other customers stood around to watch and comment. Muni thought helplessly, "My poverty is exposed to everybody. But what can I do?"

"More likely you are seventy," said the shopman. "You also forget that you mentioned a birthday five weeks ago when you wanted castor oil for your holy bath."

"Bath! Who can dream of a bath when you have to scratch the tank-bed for a bowl of water? We would all be parched and dead but for the Big House, where

[2]*rupee* monetary unit of India
[3]*swarga* heaven

they let us take a pot of water from their well." After saying this Muni unobtrusively rose and moved off.

He told his wife, "That scoundrel would not give me anything. So go out and sell the drumsticks for what they are worth."

He flung himself down in a corner to recoup from the fatigue of his visit to the shop. His wife said, "You are getting no sauce today, nor anything else. I can't find anything to give you to eat. Fast till the evening, it'll do you good. Take the goats and be gone now," she cried and added, "Don't come back before the sun is down." He knew that if he obeyed her she would somehow conjure up some food for him in the evening. Only he must be careful not to argue and irritate her. Her temper was undependable in the morning but improved by evening time. She was sure to go out and work—grind corn in the Big House, sweep or scrub somewhere, and earn enough to buy foodstuff and keep a dinner ready for him in the evening.

Unleashing the goats from the drumstick tree, Muni started out, driving them ahead and uttering weird cries from time to time in order to urge them on. He passed through the village with his head bowed in thought. He did not want to look at anyone or be accosted. A couple of cronies lounging in the temple corridor hailed him, but he ignored their call. They had known him in the days of affluence when he lorded over a flock of fleecy sheep, not the miserable gawky goats that he had today. Of course he also used to have a few goats for those who fancied them, but real wealth lay in sheep; they bred fast and people came and bought the fleece in the shearing season; and then that famous butcher from the town came over on the weekly market days bringing him betel leaves, tobacco, and often enough some *bhang*,[4] which they smoked in a hut in the coconut grove, undisturbed by wives and well-wishers. After a smoke one felt light and elated and inclined to forgive everyone including that brother-in-law of his who had once tried to set fire to his home. But all this seemed like the memories of a previous birth. Some pestilence afflicted his cattle (he could of course guess who had laid his animals under a curse), and even the friendly butcher would not touch one at half the price . . . and now here he was left with the two scraggy creatures. He wished someone would rid him of their company too. The shopman had said that he was seventy. At seventy, one only waited to be summoned by God. When he was dead what would his wife do? They had lived in each other's company since they were children. He was told on their day of wedding that he was ten years old and she was eight. During the wedding ceremony they had had to recite their respective ages and names. He had thrashed her only a few times in their career, and later she had the upper hand. Progeny, none. Perhaps a large progeny would have brought him the blessing of the gods. Fertility brought merit. People with fourteen sons were always so prosperous and at peace with the world and themselves. He recollected the thrill he had felt when he mentioned a daughter to that shopman; although it was not believed, what if he did not have a daughter?—his cousin in the next village had many daughters, and any one of them was as good as his; he was fond of them all and would buy them sweets if he could afford it. Still, everyone in the village whispered behind their backs that Muni and his wife were a barren couple. He avoided looking at anyone; they all professed to be so high up, and everyone else

[4]*bhang* marijuana

in the village had more money than he. "I am the poorest fellow in our caste and no wonder that they spurn me, but I won't look at them either," and so he passed on with his eyes downcast along the edge of the street, and people left him also very much alone, commenting only to the extent, "Ah, there he goes with his two goats; if he slits their throats, he may have more peace of mind." "What has he to worry about anyway? They live on nothing and have none to worry about." Thus people commented when he passed through the village. Only on the outskirts did he lift his head and look up. He urged and bullied the goats until they meandered along to the foot of the horse statue on the edge of the village. He sat on its pedestal for the rest of the day. The advantage of this was that he could watch the highway and see the lorries[5] and buses pass through to the hills, and it gave him a sense of belonging to a larger world. The pedestal of the statue was broad enough for him to move around as the sun travelled up and westward; or he could also crouch under the belly of the horse, for shade.

The horse was nearly life-size, moulded out of clay, baked, burnt, and brightly coloured, and reared its head proudly, prancing its forelegs in the air and flourishing its tail in a loop; beside the horse stood a warrior with scythe-like mustachios, bulging eyes, and aquiline nose. The old image-makers believed in indicating a man of strength by bulging out his eyes and sharpening his moustache tips, and also decorated the man's chest with beads which looked today like blobs of mud through the ravages of sun and wind and rain (when it came), but Muni would insist that he had known the beads to sparkle like the nine gems at one time in his life. The horse itself was said to have been as white as a dhobi-washed[6] sheet, and had had on its back a cover of pure brocade of red and black lace, matching the multicoloured sash around the waist of the warrior. But none in the village remembered the splendour as no one noticed its existence. Even Muni, who spent all his waking hours at its foot, never bothered to look up. It was untouched even by the young vandals of the village who gashed tree trunks with knives and tried to topple off milestones and inscribed lewd designs on all walls. This statue had been closer to the population of the village at one time, when this spot bordered the village; but when the highway was laid through (or perhaps when the tank and wells dried up completely here) the village moved a couple of miles inland.

Muni sat at the foot of the statue, watching his two goats graze in the arid soil among the cactus and lantana bushes. He looked at the sun; it had tilted westward no doubt, but it was not the time yet to go back home; if he went too early his wife would have no food for him. Also he must give her time to cool off her temper and feel sympathetic, and then she would scrounge and manage to get some food. He watched the mountain road for a time signal. When the green bus appeared around the bend he could leave, and his wife would feel pleased that he had let the goats feed long enough.

He noticed now a new sort of vehicle coming down at full speed. It looked like both a motor car and a bus. He used to be intrigued by the novelty of such spectacles, but of late work was going on at the source of the river on the mountain and an assortment of people and traffic went past him, and he took it all casually and described to his wife, later in the day, everything he saw. Today,

[5]*lorries* trucks

[6]*dhobi* servant who washes clothes

while he observed the yellow vehicle coming down, he was wondering how to describe it later to his wife when it sputtered and stopped in front of him. A red-faced foreigner, who had been driving it, got down and went round it, stooping, looking, and poking under the vehicle; then he straightened himself up, looked at the dashboard, stared in Muni's direction, and approached him. "Excuse me, is there a gas station nearby, or do I have to wait until another car comes—" He suddenly looked up at the clay horse and cried, "Marvellous," without completing his sentence. Muni felt he should get up and run away, and cursed his age. He could not readily put his limbs into action; some years ago he could outrun a cheetah, as happened once when he went to the forest to cut fuel and it was then that two of his sheep were mauled—a sign that bad times were coming. Though he tried, he could not easily extricate himself from his seat, and then there was also the problem of the goats. He could not leave them behind.

The red-faced man wore khaki clothes—evidently a policeman or a soldier. Muni said to himself, "He will chase or shoot if I start running. Some dogs chase only those who run—oh, Shiva protect me. I don't know why this man should be after me." Meanwhile the foreigner cried, "Marvellous!" again, nodding his head. He paced around the statue with his eyes fixed on it. Muni sat frozen for a while, and then fidgeted and tried to edge away. Now the other man suddenly pressed his palms together in a salute, smiled, and said, "Namaste![7] How do you do?"

At which Muni spoke the only English expressions he had learnt, "Yes, no." Having exhausted his English vocabulary, he started in Tamil: "My name is Muni. These two goats are mine, and no one can gainsay it—though our village is full of slanderers these days who will not hesitate to say that what belongs to a man doesn't belong to him." He rolled his eyes and shuddered at the thought of evil-minded men and women peopling his village.

The foreigner faithfully looked in the direction indicated by Muni's fingers, gazed for a while at the two goats and the rocks, and with a puzzled expression took out his silver cigarette case and lit a cigarette. Suddenly remembering the courtesies of the season, he asked, "Do you smoke?" Muni answered, "Yes, no." Whereupon the red-faced man took a cigarette and gave it to Muni, who received it with surprise, having had no offer of a smoke from anyone for years now. Those days when he smoked bhang were gone with his sheep and the large-hearted butcher. Nowadays he was not able to find even matches, let alone bhang. (His wife went across and borrowed a fire at dawn from a neighbour.) He had always wanted to smoke a cigarette; only once did the shopman give him one on credit, and he remembered how good it had tasted. The other flicked the lighter open and offered a light to Muni. Muni felt so confused about how to act that he blew on it and put it out. The other, puzzled but undaunted, flourished his lighter, presented it again, and lit Muni's cigarette. Muni drew a deep puff and started coughing; it was racking, no doubt, but extremely pleasant. When his cough subsided he wiped his eyes and took stock of the situation, understanding that the other man was not an Inquisitor of any kind. Yet, in order to make sure, he remained wary. No need to run away from a man who gave him such a potent smoke. His head was reeling from the effect of one of those strong American cigarettes made with roasted tobacco. The man said, "I come from New York," took out a wallet from his hip pocket, and presented his card.

[7]*Namaste!* greeting: Hello!

Muni shrank away from the card. Perhaps he was trying to present a warrant and arrest him. Beware of khaki, one part of his mind warned. Take all the cigarettes or bhang or whatever is offered, but don't get caught. Beware of khaki. He wished he weren't seventy as the shopman had said. At seventy one didn't run, but surrendered to whatever came. He could only ward off trouble by talk. So he went on, all in the chaste Tamil for which Kritam was famous. (Even the worst detractors could not deny that the famous poetess Avvaiyar was born in this area, although no one could say whether it was in Kritam or Kuppam, the adjoining village.) Out of this heritage the Tamil language gushed through Muni in an unimpeded flow. He said, "Before God, sir, Bhagwan, who sees everything, I tell you, sir, that we know nothing of the case. If the murder was committed, whoever did it will not escape. Bhagwan is all-seeing. Don't ask me about it. I know nothing." A body had been found mutilated and thrown under a tamarind tree at the border between Kritam and Kuppam a few weeks before, giving rise to much gossip and speculation. Muni added an explanation. "Anything is possible there. People over there will stop at nothing." The foreigner nodded his head and listened courteously though he understood nothing.

"I am sure you know when this horse was made," said the red man and smiled ingratiatingly.

Muni reacted to the relaxed atmosphere by smiling himself, and pleaded, "Please go away, sir, I know nothing. I promise we will hold him for you if we see any bad character around, and we will bury him up to his neck in a coconut pit if he tries to escape; but our village has always had a clean record. Must definitely be the other village."

Now the red man implored, "Please, please, I will speak slowly, please try to understand me. Can't you understand even a single word of English? Everyone in this country seems to know English. I have gotten along with English everywhere in this country, but you don't speak it. Have you any religious or spiritual scruples against English speech?"

Muni made some indistinct sounds in his throat and shook his head. Encouraged, the other went on to explain at length, uttering each syllable with care and deliberation. Presently he sidled over and took a seat beside the old man, explaining, "You see, last August, we probably had the hottest summer in history, and I was working in shirt-sleeves in my office on the fortieth floor of the Empire State Building. We had a power failure one day, you know, and there I was stuck for four hours, no elevator, no air conditioning. All the way in the train I kept thinking, and the minute I reached home in Connecticut, I told my wife Ruth, 'We will visit India this winter, it's time to look at other civilizations.' Next day she called the travel agent first thing and told him to f[illegible], and so here I am. Ruth came with me but is staying back at Srinagar, and I [illegible] the one doing the rounds and joining her later."

Muni looked reflective at the end of this long oration a[illegible]d, rather feebly, "Yes, no," as a concession to the other's language and we[illegible]n Tamil, "When I was this high"—he indicated a foot high—"I had he[illegible] uncle say . . ."

No one can tell what he was planning to say, as the[illegible]nterrupted him at this stage to ask, "Boy, what is the secret of your te[illegible]w old are you?"

The old man forgot what he had started to say an[illegible]ed, "Sometimes we too lose our cattle. Jackals or cheetahs may so[illegible]carry them off, but sometimes it is just theft from over in the next [illegible]d then we will know who has done it. Our priest at the temple can s[illegible]mphor flame the face of the thief, and when he is caught . . . " He gestured with his hands a perfect mincing of meat.

The American watched his hands intently and said, "I know what you mean. Chop something? Maybe I am holding you up and you want to chop wood? Where is your axe? Hand it to me and show me what to chop. I do enjoy it, you know, just a hobby. We get a lot of driftwood along the backwater near my house, and on Sundays I do nothing but chop wood for the fireplace. I really feel different when I watch the fire in the fireplace, although it may take all the sections of the Sunday *New York Times* to get a fire started." And he smiled at this reference.

Muni felt totally confused but decided the best thing would be to make an attempt to get away from this place. He tried to edge out, saying, "Must go home," and turned to go. The other seized his shoulder and said desperately, "Is there no one, absolutely no one here, to translate for me?" He looked up and down the road, which was deserted in this hot afternoon; a sudden gust of wind churned up the dust and dead leaves on the roadside into a ghostly column and propelled it towards the mountain road. The stranger almost pinioned Muni's back to the statue and asked, "Isn't this statue yours? Why don't you sell it to me?"

The old man now understood the reference to the horse, thought for a second, and said in his own language, "I was an urchin this high when I heard my grandfather explain this horse and warrior, and my grandfather himself was this high when he heard his grandfather, whose grandfather . . . "

The other man interrupted him. "I don't want to seem to have stopped here for nothing. I will offer you a good price for this," he said, indicating the horse. He had concluded without the least doubt that Muni owned this mud horse. Perhaps he guessed by the way he sat on its pedestal, like other souvenir sellers in this country presiding over their wares.

Muni followed the man's eyes and pointing fingers and dimly understood the subject matter and, feeling relieved that the theme of the mutilated body had been abandoned at least for the time being, said again, enthusiastically, "I was this high when my grandfather told me about this horse and the warrior, and my grandfather was this high when he himself . . . " and he was getting into a deeper bog of reminiscence each time he tried to indicate the antiquity of the statue.

The Tam[illegible]hat *Muni* spoke was stimulating even as pure sound, and the foreigner lis[illegible]d with fascination 'I wish I had my tape-recorder here," he said, assuming t[illegible] [illegible]asantest expression. "Your language sounds wonderful. I get a kick out of ever[illegible] [illegible]ord you utter here" — he indicated his ears — "but you don't have to wa[illegible]te yo[illegible] [illegible]eath in sales talk. I appreciate the article. You don't have to explain its points."

"I never went [illegible]

we had to go out [illegible]hool in those days only Brahmin went to schools, but harvest time . . . . a[illegible]ork [illegible] the fields morning till night, from sowing to allowed me to go out[illegible] P[illegible]ngal came and we had cut the harvest, my father Parangi language you [illegible] with others at the tank, and so I don't know the the Parangi language, b[illegible]en little fellows in your country probably speak postman in our village w[illegible]ly learned men and officers know it. We had a wife ran away with some[illegible]peak to you boldly in your language, but his Who would if a wife did w[illegible] does not speak to anyone at all nowadays. will sell themselves and th[illegible] Women must be watched; otherwise they [illegible]nd he laughed at his own quip.

The foreigner laughed heartily, took out another cigarette, and offered it to Muni, who now smoked with ease, deciding to stay on if the fellow was going to be so good as to keep up his cigarette supply. The American now stood up on the pedestal in the attitude of a demonstrative lecturer and said, running his finger along some of the carved decorations around the horse's neck, speaking slowly and uttering his words syllable by syllable, "I could give a sales talk for this better than anyone else. . . . This is a marvellous combination of yellow and indigo, though faded now. . . . How do you people of this country achieve these flaming colours?"

Muni, now assured that the subject was still the horse and not the dead body, said, "This is our guardian, it means death to our adversaries. At the end of Kali Yuga, this world and all other worlds will be destroyed, and the Redeemer will come in the shape of a horse called 'Kalki'; this horse will come to life and gallop and trample down all bad men." As he spoke of bad men the figures of his shopman and his brother-in-law assumed concrete forms in his mind, and he revelled for a moment in the predicament of the fellow under the horse's hoof: served him right for trying to set fire to his home. . . .

While he was brooding on this pleasant vision, the foreigner utilized the pause to say, "I assure you that this will have the best home in the U.S.A. I'll push away the bookcase, you know I love books and am a member of five book clubs, and the choice and bonus volumes mount up to a pile really in our living room, as high as this horse itself. But they'll have to go. Ruth may disapprove, but I will convince her. The T.V. may have to be shifted too. We can't have everything in the living room. Ruth will probably say what about when we have a party? I'm going to keep him right in the middle of the room. I don't see how that can interfere with the party—we'll stand around him and have our drinks."

Muni continued his description of the end of the world. "Our pundit discoursed at the temple once how the oceans are going to close over the earth in a huge wave and swallow us—this horse will grow bigger than the biggest wave and carry on its back only the good people and kick into the floods the evil ones—plenty of them about—" he said reflectively. "Do you know when it is going to happen?" he asked.

The foreigner now understood by the tone of the other that a question was being asked and said, "How am I transporting it? I can push the seat back and make room in the rear. That van can take in an elephant"—waving precisely at the back of the seat.

Muni was still hovering on visions of avatars and said again, "I never missed our pundit's discourses at the temple in those days during every bright half of the month, although he'd go on all night, and he told us that Vishnu is the highest god. Whenever evil men trouble us, he comes down to save us. He has come many times. The first time he incarnated as a great fish, and lifted the scriptures on his back when the floods and sea waves . . . ."

"I am not a millionaire, but a modest businessman. My trade is coffee."

Amidst all this wilderness of obscure sound Muni caught the word "coffee" and said, "If you want to drink 'kapi,' drive further up, in the next town, they have Friday market, and there they open 'kapi-otels'—so I learn from passers-by. Don't think I wander about. I go nowhere and look for nothing." His thoughts went back to the avatars. "The first avatar was in the shape of a little fish in a bowl of water, but every hour it grew bigger and bigger and became in the end a huge whale which the seas could not contain, and on the back of the whale the holy books were supported, saved and carried." Once he had launched on the first avatar, it was inevitable that he should go on to the next, a wild boar on whose tusk the earth was lifted when a vicious conqueror of the earth carried it off and hid it at the bottom of the sea. After describing this avatar Muni concluded, "God will always save us whenever we are troubled by evil beings. When we were young we staged at full moon the story of the avatars. That's how I know the stories; we played them all night until the sun rose, and sometimes the European collector would come to watch, bringing his own chair. I had a good voice and so they always taught me songs and gave me the women's roles. I was always Goddess Lakshmi, and they dressed me in a brocade sari, loaned from the Big House. . . ."

The foreigner said, "I repeat I am not a millionaire. Ours is a modest business; after all, we can't afford to buy more than sixty minutes of T.V. time in a month, which works out to two minutes a day, that's all, although in the course of time we'll maybe sponsor a one-hour show regularly if our sales graph continues to go up. . . ."

Muni was intoxicated by the memory of his theatrical days and was about to explain how he had painted his face and worn a wig and diamond earrings when the visitor, feeling that he had spent too much time already, said, "Tell me, will you accept a hundred rupees or not for the horse? I'd love to take the whiskered soldier also but no space for him this year. I'll have to cancel my air ticket and take a boat home, I suppose. Ruth can go by air if she likes, but I will go with the horse and keep him in my cabin all the way if necessary." And he smiled at the picture of himself voyaging across the seas hugging this horse. He added, "I will have to pad it with straw so that it doesn't break. . . ."

"When we played *Ramayana*,[8] they dressed me as Sita," added Muni. "A teacher came and taught us the songs for the drama and we gave him fifty rupees. He incarnated himself as Rama, and He alone could destroy Ravana, the demon with ten heads who shook all the worlds; do you know the story of *Ramayana*?"

"I have my station wagon as you see. I can push the seat back and take the horse in if you will just lend me a hand with it."

"Do you know *Mahabharata*?[9] Krishna was the eighth avatar of Vishnu, incarnated to help the Five Brothers regain their kingdom. When Krishna was a baby he danced on the thousand-hooded giant serpent and trampled it to death; and then he suckled the breasts of the demoness and left them flat as a disc though when she came to him her bosoms were large, like mounds of earth on the banks of a dug up canal." He indicated two mounds with his hands. The stranger was completely mystified by the gesture. For the first time he said, "I really wonder what you are saying because your answer is crucial. We have come to the point when we should be ready to talk business."

"When the tenth avatar comes, do you know where you and I will be?" asked the old man.

"Lend me a hand and I can lift off the horse from its pedestal after picking out the cement at the joints. We can do anything if we have a basis of understanding."

At this stage the mutual mystification was complete, and there was no need even to carry on a guessing game at the meaning of words. The old man

[8]*Ramayana* one of the two great epics of India, written in Sanscrit and describing the adventures of the hero Rama; *Sita*—Rama's wife

[9]*Mahabharata* the other great epic of India, written in Sanscrit about 200 B.C.E.

chattered away in a spirit of balancing off the credits and debits of conversational exchange, and said in order to be on the credit side, "Oh, honourable one, I hope God has blessed you with numerous progeny. I say this because you seem to be a good man, willing to stay beside an old man and talk to him, while all day I have none to talk to except when somebody stops by to ask for a piece of tobacco. But I seldom have it, tobacco is not what it used to be at one time, and I have given up chewing. I cannot afford it nowadays." Noting the other's interest in his speech, Muni felt encouraged to ask, "How many children have you?" with appropriate gestures with his hands. Realizing that a question was being asked, the red man replied, "I said a hundred," which encouraged Muni to go into details. "How many of your children are boys and how many girls? Where are they? Is your daughter married? Is it difficult to find a son-in-law in your country also?"

In answer to these questions the red man dashed his hand into his pocket and brought forth his wallet in order to take immediate advantage of the bearish trend in the market. He flourished a hundred-rupee currency note and said, "Well, this is what I meant."

The old man now realized that some financial element was entering their talk. He peered closely at the currency note, the like of which he had never seen in his life; he knew the five and ten by their colours although always in other people's hands, while his own earning at any time was in coppers and nickels. What was this man flourishing the note for? Perhaps asking for change. He laughed to himself at the notion of anyone coming to him for changing a thousand- or ten-thousand-rupee note. He said with a grin, "Ask our village headman, who is also a moneylender; he can change even a lakh[10] of rupees in gold sovereigns if you prefer it that way; he thinks nobody knows, but dig the floor of his puja[11] room and your head will reel at the sight of the hoard. The man disguises himself in rags just to mislead the public. Talk to the headman yourself because he goes mad at the sight of me. Someone took away his pumpkins with the creeper and he, for some reason, thinks it was me and my goats . . . that's why I never let my goats be seen anywhere near the farms." His eyes travelled to his goats nosing about, attempting to wrest nutrition from minute greenery peeping out of rock and dry earth.

The foreigner followed his look and decided that it would be a sound policy to show an interest in the old man's pets. He went up casually to them and stroked their backs with every show of courteous attention. Now the truth dawned on the old man. His dream of a lifetime was about to be realized. He understood that the red man was actually making an offer for the goats. He had reared them up in the hope of selling them some day and, with the capital, opening a small shop on this very spot. Sitting here, watching towards the hills, he had often dreamt how he would put up a thatched roof here, spread a gunny sack out on the ground, and display on it fried nuts, coloured sweets, and green coconut for the thirsty and famished wayfarers on the highway, which was sometimes very busy. The animals were not prize ones for a cattle show, but he had spent his occasional savings to provide them some fancy diet now and then, and they did not look too bad. While he was reflecting thus, the red man shook

[10]*lakh* 100,000 of an item (as American speakers use "a million")

[11]*puja* a room for private prayer

his hand and left on his palm one hundred rupees in tens now, suddenly realizing that this was what the old man was asking. "It is all for you or you may share it if you have a partner."

The old man pointed at the station wagon and asked, "Are you carrying them off in that?"

"Yes, of course," said the other, understanding the transportation part of it.

The old man said, "This will be their first ride in a motor car. Carry them off after I get out of sight, otherwise they will never follow you, but only me even if I am travelling on the path to Yama Loka."[12] He laughed at his own joke, brought his palms together in a salute, turned round and went off, and was soon out of sight beyond a clump of thicket.

The red man looked at the goats grazing peacefully. Perched on the pedestal of the horse, as the westerly sun touched off the ancient faded colours of the statue with a fresh splendour, he ruminated, "He must be gone to fetch some help, I suppose!" and settled down to wait. When a truck came downhill, he stopped it and got the help of a couple of men to detach the horse from its pedestal and place it in his station wagon. He gave them five rupees each, and for a further payment they siphoned off gas from the truck, and helped him to start his engine.

Muni hurried homeward with the cash securely tucked away at his waist in his dhoti. He shut the street door and stole up softly to his wife as she squatted before the lit oven wondering if by a miracle food would drop from the sky. Muni displayed his fortune for the day. She snatched the notes from him, counted them by the glow of the fire, and cried, "One hundred rupees! How did you come by it? Have you been stealing?"

"I have sold our goats to a red-faced man. He was absolutely crazy to have them, gave me all this money and carried them off in his motor car!"

Hardly had these words left his lips when they heard bleating outside. She opened the door and saw the two goats at her door. "Here they are!" she said. "What's the meaning of all this?"

He muttered a great curse and seized one of the goats by its ears and shouted, "Where is that man? Don't you know you are his? Why did you come back?" The goat only wriggled in his grip. He asked the same question of the other too. The goat shook itself off. His wife glared at him and declared, "If you have thieved, the police will come tonight and break your bones. Don't involve me. I will go away to my parents. . . . "

[1970]

QUESTIONS

1. What assumptions does each man make about the other? How do these assumptions reveal their respective cultural situations and personal values?
2. What does the story suggest about cross-cultural communication?

[12]*Yama Loka* the afterlife, according to Hindu belief. Yama is the judge of human beings and king of the invisible world after death.

How do the comments made by Muni and the American tourist form a kind of conversation despite their different languages? Consider the accuracy of the American's observation, "We can do anything if we have a basis of understanding."

3. What are the sources of the story's humor?
4. Compare this story with Carmen Naranjo's "And We Sold the Rain" and Joseph Conrad's "Amy Foster."

Ngugi wa Thiong'o

(b. 1938)

Kenya

Ngugi wa Thiong'o is East Africa's most accomplished writer. Born in Kenya, he is the author of a half dozen novels, including *Weep Not, Child* (1964), *A Grain of Wheat* (1967), *Petals of Blood* (1977), and *Devil on the Cross* (1980). He has also written numerous short stories, plays, and critical essays. Although he has written compellingly about his country's struggle for independence, in recent years Ngugi has exerted much of his energy against neocolonialism. Sadly, his political opinions have not been tolerated by his country's leaders. Ngugi has spent the most recent years of his life in prison in Kenya and, subsequently, in exile in the West.

His essay "Church, Culture and Politics," from *Homecoming* (1972), helps to illuminate "A Meeting in the Dark," which was written at the beginning of his literary career:

> The coming of Christianity . . . set in motion a process of social change, involving rapid disintegration of the tribal set-up and the frame-work of social norms and values by which people had formerly ordered their lives and their relationships to others. This was especially true of Central Province, where the Church of Scotland Mission, which has a highly strict puritan tradition, could not separate the strictly Christian dogma or doctrine from the European scale of values, and from European customs. The evidence that you were saved was not whether you were a believer in the follower of Christ, and accepted all men as equal: the measure of your Christian love and charity was in preserving the outer signs and symbols of a European way of life; whether you dressed as Europeans did, whether you had acquired European good manners, liked European hymns and tunes, and of course whether you had refused to have your daughter circumcised.

◆ *A Meeting in the Dark* ◆

His mother used to tell him stories. "Once upon a time there was a young girl who lived with her father and mother in a lonely house that was hidden by a hill. The house was old but strong. When the rains came and the winds blew, the house remained firm. Her father and mother liked her, but they quarrelled sometimes and she would cry. Otherwise, she was happy. Nobody knew of the house. So nobody came to see them. Then one day a stranger came. He was tall and handsome. He had milk-white teeth. Her mother gave him food. Then he told them of a beautiful country beyond the hill. The girl wanted to go there. Secretly, she followed the man. They had not gone very far when the stranger turned into an Irimu. He became ugly and he had another mouth at the back which was hidden by his long hair. Occasionally, the hair was blown by the wind. Flies were taken in and the mouth would be shut. The girl ran back. The bad Irimu followed her. She ran hard, hard, and the Irimu could not catch her. But he was getting nearer her all the time. When she came close to her home, she found the Irimu had stopped running. But the house was no longer there. She had no home to go to and she could not go forward to the beautiful land, to see all the good things, because the Irimu was on the way."

How did the story end? John wondered. He thought: "I wish I were young again in our old home, then I would ask my mother about it." But now he was not young; not young any more. And he was not a man yet!

He stood at the door of the hut and saw his old, frail but energetic father coming along the village street, with a rather dirty bag made out of strong calico swinging by his side. His father always carried this bag. John knew what it contained: a Bible, a hymn book, and probably a notebook and a pen. His father was a preacher. It must have been he who had stopped his mother from telling him stories. His mother had stopped telling him stories long ago. She would say, "Now, don't ask for any more stories. Your father may come." So he feared his father. John went in and warned his mother of his father's coming. Then his father came in. John stood aside, then walked towards the door. He lingered there doubtfully, then he went out.

"John, hei, John!"

"Baba!"

"Come back."

He stood doubtfully in front of his father. His heart beat faster and an agitated voice within him seemed to ask: Does he know?

"Sit down. Where are you going?"

"For a walk, Father," he answered evasively.

"To the village?"

"Well—yes—no. I mean nowhere in particular." John saw his father look at him hard, seeming to read his face. John sighed a very slow sigh. He did not like the way his father eyed him. He always looked at him as though John was a sinner, one who had to be watched all the time. "I am," his heart told him. John guiltily refused to meet the old man's gaze and looked past him and appealingly to his mother who was quietly peeling potatoes. But she seemed to be oblivious of everything around her.

"Why do you look away? What have you done?"

John shrank within himself with fear. But his face remained expressionless. However, he could hear the loud beats of his heart. It was like an engine pumping water. He felt no doubt his father knew all about it. He thought: "Why does he torture me? Why does he not at once say he knows?" Then another voice told him: "No, he doesn't know, otherwise he would have already jumped at you." A consolation. He faced his thoughtful father with courage.

"When is the journey?"

Again John thought—why does he ask? I have told him many times. Aloud, he said,

"Next week, Tuesday."

"Right. Tomorrow we go to the shops, hear?"

"Yes, Father."

"You can go."

"Thank you, Father." He began to move.

"John!"

"Yes?" John's heart almost stopped beating. That second, before his father's next words, was an age.

"You seem to be in hurry. I don't want to hear of you loitering in the village. I know you young men, going to show off just because you are going away! I don't want to hear of trouble in the village."

Much relieved, he went out. He could guess what his father meant by not wanting trouble in the village. How did the story end? Funny, but he could not remember how his mother had ended it. It had been so long ago. Her home was not there. Where did she go? What did she do?

"Why do you persecute the boy so much?" Susan spoke for the first time. Apparently she had carefully listened to the whole drama without a word. Now was her time to speak. She looked at her tough old preacher who had been a companion for life. She had married him a long time ago. She could not tell the number of years. They had been happy. Then the man became a convert. And everything in the home put on a religious tone. He even made her stop telling stories to the child. "Tell him of Jesus. Jesus died for you. Jesus died for the child. He must know the Lord." She too had been converted. But she was never blind to the moral torture he inflicted on the boy (that's what she always called John), so that the boy had grown up mortally afraid of him. She always wondered if it was love for the son. Or could it be a resentment because, well, they two had "sinned" before marriage? John had been the result of that sin. But that had not been John's fault. It was the boy who ought to complain. She often wondered if the boy had . . . but no. The boy had been very small when they left Fort Hall. She looked at her husband. He remained mute, though his left hand did, rather irritably, feel about his face.

"It is as if he was not your son. Or do you . . . "

"Hm, sister." The voice was pleading. She was seeking a quarrel but he did not feel equal to one. Really, women could never understand. Women were women, whether saved or not. Their son had to be protected against all evil influences. He must be made to grow in the footsteps of the Lord. He looked at her, frowning a little. She had made him sin but that had been a long time ago. And he had been saved. John must not follow the same road.

"You ought to tell us to leave. You know I can go away. Go back to Fort Hall. And then everybody . . . "

"Look, sister." He hastily interrupted. He always called her sister. Sister-in-the-Lord, in full. But he sometimes wondered if she had been truly saved. In his heart, he prayed: Lord, be with our sister Susan. Aloud, he continued, "You know I want the boy to grow in the Lord."

"But you torture him so! You make him fear you!"

"Why! He should not fear me. I have really nothing against him."

"It is you. You. You have always been cruel to him. . . ." She stood up. The peelings dropped from her frock and fell in a heap on the floor.

"Stanley!"

"Sister." He was startled by the vehemence in her voice. He had never seen her like this. Lord, take the devil out of her. Save her this minute. She did not say what she wanted to say. Stanley looked away from her. It was a surprise, but it seemed he feared his wife. If you had told people in the village about this, they would not have believed you. He took his Bible and began to read. On Sunday he would preach to a congregation of brethren and sisters.

Susan, a rather tall, thin woman, who had once been beautiful, sat down again and went on with her work. She did not know what was troubling her son. Was it the coming journey?

Outside, John strolled aimlessly along the path that led from his home. He stood near the wattle tree which was a little way from his father's house, and surveyed the whole village. They lay before his eyes — crammed — rows and rows of mud and grass huts, ending in sharp sticks that pointed to heaven. Smoke was coming out of various huts, an indication that many women had already come from the *shambas*. Night would soon fall. To the west, the sun was hurrying home behind the misty hills. Again, John looked at the crammed rows and rows of huts that formed Makeno Village, one of the new mushroom "towns" that grew up all over the country during the Mau Mau war. It looked so ugly. A pang of pain rose in his heart and he felt like crying — I hate you, I hate you. You trapped me alive. Away from you, it would never have happened. He did not shout. He just watched.

A woman was coming towards where he stood. A path into the village was just near there. She was carrying a big load of *kuni* which bent her into an Akamba-bow shape. She greeted him.

"Is it well with you, Njooni?"

"It is well with me, mother." There was no trace of bitterness in his voice. John was by nature polite. Everyone knew of this. He was quite unlike the other proud, educated sons of the tribe — sons who came back from the other side of the waters with white or Negro wives who spoke English. And they behaved just like Europeans! John was a favourite, a model of humility and moral perfection. Everyone knew that though a clergyman's son, John would never betray the tribe.

"When are you going to — to — "

"Makerere?"

"Makelele." She laughed. The way she pronounced the name was funny. And the way she laughed too. She enjoyed it. But John felt hurt. So everyone knew of this.

"Next week."

"I wish you well."

"Thank you, mother."

She said quietly — as if trying to pronounce it better — "Makelele." She laughed at herself again but she was tired. The load was heavy.

"Stay well, son."

"Go well and in peace, mother."

And the woman who all the time had stood, moved on, panting like a donkey, but obviously pleased with John's kindness.

John remained long looking at her. What made such a woman live on day to day, working hard, yet happy? Had she much faith in life? Or was her faith in the tribe? She and her kind, who had never been touched by ways of the white man, looked as though they had something to cling to. As he watched her disappear, he felt proud that they should think well of him. He felt proud that he had a place in their esteem. And then came the pang. *Father will know. They will know.* He did not know what he feared most; the action his father would take when he knew, or the loss of the little faith the simple villagers had placed in him, when they knew.

He went down to the small local teashop. He met many people who wished him well at the college. All of them knew that the Pastor's son had finished all the white man's learning in Kenya. He would now go to Uganda; they had read this in the *Baraza*, a Swahili weekly paper. John did not stay long at the shop. The sun had already gone to rest and now darkness was coming. The evening meal was ready. His tough father was still at the table reading his Bible. He did not look up when John entered. Strange silence settled in the hut.

"You look unhappy." His mother first broke the silence. John laughed. It was a nervous little laugh.

"No, mother," he hastily replied, nervously looking at his father. He secretly hoped that Wamuhu had not blabbed.

"Then I am glad."

She did not know. He ate his dinner and went out to his hut. A man's hut. Every young man had his own hut. John was never allowed to bring any girl visitor in there. He did not want "trouble." Even to be seen standing with one was a crime. His father could easily thrash him. He wished he had rebelled earlier like all the other young educated men. He lit the lantern. He took it in his hand. The yellow light flickered dangerously and then went out. He knew his hands were shaking. He lit it again and hurriedly took his big coat and a huge *Kofia* which were lying on the unmade bed. He left the lantern burning, so that his father would see it and think him in. John bit his lower lip spitefully. He hated himself for being so girlish. It was unnatural for a boy of his age.

Like a shadow, he stealthily crossed the courtyard and went on to the village street.

He met young men and women, lining the streets. They were laughing, talking, whispering. They were obviously enjoying themselves. John thought, they are more free than I am. He envied their exuberance. They clearly stood outside or above the strict morality that the educated ones had to be judged by. Would he have gladly changed places with them? He wondered. At last, he came to the hut. It stood at the very heart of the village. How well he knew it—to his sorrow. He wondered what he would do! Wait for her outside? What if her mother came out instead? He decided to enter.

"*Hodi!*"

"Enter. We are in."

John pulled down his hat before he entered. Indeed they were all there—all except she whom he wanted. The fire in the hearth was dying. Only a small flame from a lighted lantern vaguely illuminated the whole hut. The flame and the giant shadow created on the wall seemed to be mocking him. He prayed that Wamuhu's parents would not recognize him. He tried to be "thin," and to disguise his voice as he greeted them. They recognized him and made themselves busy on his account. To be visited by such an educated one who knew all about the white man's world and knowledge, and who would now go to another land beyond, was not such a frequent occurrence that it could be taken lightly. Who knew but he might be interested in their daughter? Stranger things had happened. After all, learning was not the only thing. Though Wamuhu had no learning, yet charms she had and she could be trusted to captivate any young man's heart with her looks and smiles.

"You will sit down. Take that stool."

"No!" He noticed with bitterness that he did not call her "mother."

"Where is Wamuhu?" The mother threw a triumphant glance at her husband. They exchanged a knowing look. John bit his lips again and felt like bolting. He controlled himself with difficulty.

"She has gone out to get some tea leaves. Please sit down. She will cook you some tea when she comes."

"I am afraid . . ." he muttered some inaudible words and went out. He almost collided with Wamuhu.

In the hut:

"Didn't I tell you? Trust a woman's eye!"

"You don't know these young men."

"But you see John is different. Everyone speaks well of him and he is a clergyman's son."

"Y-e-e-s! A clergyman's son? You forgot your daughter is circumcised." The old man was remembering his own day. He had found for himself a good, virtuous woman, initiated in all the tribe's ways. And she had known no other man. He had married her. They were happy. Other men of his *Rika* had done the same. All their girls had been virgins, it being a taboo to touch a girl in that way, even if you slept in the same bed, as indeed so many young men and girls did. Then the white men had come, preaching a strange religion, strange ways, which all men followed. The tribe's code of behaviour was broken. The new faith could not keep the tribe together. How could it? The men who followed the new faith would not let the girls be circumcised. And they would not let their sons marry circumcised girls. Puu! Look at what was happening. Their young men went away to the land of the white men. What did they bring? White women. Black women who spoke English. Aaa—bad. And the young men who were left just did not mind. They made unmarried girls their wives and then left them with fatherless children.

"What does it matter?" his wife was replying. "Is Wamuhu not as good as the best of them? Anyway, John is different."

"Different! different! Puu! They are all alike. Those coated with the white clay of the white man's ways are the worst. They have nothing inside. Nothing—nothing here." He took a piece of wood and nervously poked the dying fire. A strange numbness came over him. He trembled. And he feared; he feared for the tribe. For now he said it was not only the educated men who were coated with strange ways, but the whole tribe. The tribe had followed a false Irimu like the girl in the story. For the old man trembled and cried inside, mourning for a tribe that had crumbled. The tribe had nowhere to go to. And it could not be what it was before. He stopped poking and looked hard at the ground.

"I wonder why he came. I wonder." Then he looked at his wife and said, "Have you seen strange behaviour with your daughter?"

His wife did not answer. She was preoccupied with her own great hopes. . . .

John and Wamuhu walked on in silence. The intricate streets and turns were well known to them both. Wamuhu walked with quick light steps; John knew she was in a happy mood. His steps were heavy and he avoided people even though it was dark. But why should he feel ashamed? The girl was beautiful, probably the most beautiful girl in the whole of Limuru. Yet he feared being seen with her. It was all wrong. He knew that he could have loved her, even then he wondered if he did not love her. Perhaps it was hard to tell but had he been one of the young men he had met, he would not have hesitated in his answer.

Outside the village he stopped. She too stopped. Neither had spoken a word all through. Perhaps the silence spoke louder than words. Each was only too conscious of the other.

"Do they know?" Silence. Wamuhu was probably considering the question. "Don't keep me waiting. Please answer me," he implored. He felt weary, very weary, like an old man who had suddenly reached his journey's end.

"No. You told me to give you one more week. A week is over today."

"Yes. That's why I came!" John hoarsely whispered.

Wamuhu did not speak. John looked at her. Darkness was now between them. He was not really seeing her; before him was the image of his father—haughtily religious and dominating. Again he thought: I John, a priest's son, respected by all and going to college, will fall, fall to the ground. He did not want to contemplate the fall.

"It was your fault." He found himself accusing her. In his heart he knew he was lying.

"Why do you keep on telling me that? Don't you want to marry me?"

John sighed. He did not know what to do.

Once upon a time there was a young girl . . . she had no home to go to . . . she could not go forward to the beautiful land and see all the good things because the Irimu was on the way. . . .

"When will you tell them?"

"Tonight." He felt desperate. Next week he would go to the college. If he could persuade her to wait, he might be able to get away and come back when the storm and consternation had abated. But then the government might withdraw his bursary. He was frightened and there was a sad note of appeal as he turned to her and said:

"Look, Wamuhu, how long have you been pre— I mean like this?"

"I have told you over and over again. I have been pregnant for three months and mother is being suspicious. Only yesterday she said I breathed like a woman with a child."

"Do you think you could wait for three weeks more?" She laughed. Ah! the little witch! She knew his trick. Her laughter always aroused many emotions in him.

"All right. Give me just tomorrow. I'll think up something. Tomorrow I'll let you know all."

"I agree. Tomorrow. I cannot wait any more unless you mean to marry me."

Why not marry her? She is beautiful! Why not marry her? And do I or don't I love her?

She left. John felt as if she was deliberately blackmailing him. His knees were weak and lost strength. He could not move but sank on the ground in a heap. Sweat poured profusely down his cheeks, as if he had been running hard under a strong sun. But this was cold sweat. He lay on the grass; he did not want to think. Oh! No! He could not possibly face his father. Or his mother. Or Rev. Thomas Carstone who had had such faith in him. John realized that he was not more secure than anybody else, in spite of his education. He was no better than Wamuhu. *Then why don't you marry her?* He did not know. John had grown up under a Calvinistic father and learnt under a Calvinistic headmaster—a missionary! John tried to pray. But to whom was he praying? To Carstone's God? It sounded false. It was as if he was blaspheming. Could he pray to the God of the tribe? His sense of guilt crushed him.

He woke up. Where was he? Then he understood. Wamuhu had left him. She had given him one day. He stood up; he felt good. Weakly, he began to walk back home. It was lucky that darkness blanketed the whole earth, and him in it. From the various huts, he could hear laughter, heated talks or quarrels. Little fires could be seen flickeringly red through the open doors. Village stars—John thought. He raised up his eyes. The heavenly stars, cold and distant, looked down on him, impersonally. Here and there, groups of boys and girls could be heard laughing and shouting. For them life seemed to go on as usual. John consoled himself by thinking that they too would come to face their day of trial.

John was shaky. Why! Why! Why could he not defy all expectations, all prospects of a future, and marry the girl? No. No. It was impossible. She was circumcised, and he knew that his father and the church would never consent to such a marriage. She had no learning, or rather she had not gone beyond Standard 4. Marrying her would probably ruin his chances of ever going to a University. . . .

He tried to move briskly. His strength had returned. His imagination and thought took flight. He was trying to explain his action before an accusing world—he had done so many times before, ever since he knew of this. He still wondered what he could have done. The girl had attracted him. She was graceful and her smile had been very bewitching. There was none who could equal her and no girl in the village had any pretence to any higher standard of education. Women's education was very low. Perhaps that was why so many Africans went "away" and came back married. He too wished he had gone with the others, especially in the last giant student airlift to America. If only Wamuhu had learning . . . and she was uncircumcised . . . then he might probably rebel. . . .

The light still shone in his mother's hut. John wondered if he should go in for the night prayers. But he thought against it; he might not be strong enough to face his parents. In his hut, the light had gone out. He hoped his father had not noticed it. . . .

John woke up early. He was frightened. He was normally not superstitious but still he did not like the dreams of the night. He dreamt of circumcision; he had just been initiated in the tribal manner. Somebody—he could not tell his face—came and led him because he took pity on him. They went, went into a strange land. Somehow, he found himself alone. The somebody had vanished. A ghost came. He recognized it as the ghost of the home he had left. It pulled him back; then another ghost came. It was the ghost of the land he had come to. It pulled him from the front. The two contested. Then came other ghosts from all sides and pulled him from all sides so that his body began to fall into pieces. And the ghosts were insubstantial. He could not cling to any. Only they were pulling him, and he was becoming nothing, nothing . . . he was now standing a distance away. It had not been him. But he was looking at the girl, the girl in the story. She had nowhere to go. He thought he would go to help her; he would show her the way. But as he went to her, he lost his way . . . he was all alone . . . something destructive was coming towards him, coming, coming . . . He woke up. He was sweating all over—

Dreams about circumcision were no good. They portended death. He dismissed the dream with a laugh. He opened the window only to find the whole country clouded in mist. It was perfect July weather in Limuru. The hills, ridges, valleys and plains that surrounded the village were lost in the mist. It looked such a strange place. But there was almost a magic fascination in it. Limuru was a land of contrasts and evoked differing emotions, at different times. Once, John would be fascinated, and would yearn to touch the land, embrace it or just be on the grass. At another time he would feel repelled by the dust, the strong sun and the pot-holed roads. If only his struggle were just against the dust, the mist, the sun and the rain, he might feel content. Content to live here. At least he thought he would never like to die and be buried anywhere else but at Limuru. But there was the human element whose vices and betrayal of other men were embodied as the new ugly villages. The last night's incident rushed into his mind like a flood, making him weak again. He came out of his blankets and went out. Today he would go to the shops. He was uneasy. An odd feeling was coming to him, in fact had been coming, that his relationship with his father was perhaps unnatural. But he dismissed the thought. Tonight would be the "day of reckoning." He shuddered to think of it. It was unfortunate that this scar had come into his life at this time when he was going to Makerere and it would have brought him closer to his father.

They went to the shops. All day long, John remained quiet as they moved from shop to shop buying things from the lanky but wistful Indian traders. And all day long, John wondered why he feared his father so much. He had grown up fearing him, trembling whenever he spoke or gave commands. John was not alone in this.

Stanley was feared by all.

He preached with great vigour, defying the very gates of hell. Even during the Emergency, he had gone on preaching, scolding, judging and condemning. All those who were not saved were destined for hell. Above all, Stanley was known for his great moral observances—a bit too strict, rather pharisaical in nature. None noticed this; certainly not the sheep he shepherded. If an elder broke any of the rules, he was liable to be expelled, or excommunicated. Young men and women, seen standing together "in a manner prejudicial to church and God's morality" (they were one anyway), were liable to be excommunicated. And so, many young men tried to serve two masters, by seeing their girls at night and going to church by day. The alternative was to give up church-going altogether. . . .

Stanley took a fatherly attitude to all the people in the village. You must be strict with what is yours. And because of all this, he wanted his house to be a good example. That is why he wanted his son to grow up right. But motives behind many human actions may be mixed. He could never forget that he had also fallen before his marriage. Stanley was also a product of the disintegration of the tribe due to the new influences.

The shopping took a long time. His father strictly observed the silences between them and neither by word nor by hint did he refer to last night. They reached home and John was thinking that all was well when his father called him.

"John."

"Yes, Father."

"Why did you not come for prayers last night?"

"I forgot—"

"Where were you?"

Why do you ask me? What right have you to know where I was? One day I am going to revolt against you. But immediately, John knew that this act of rebellion was something beyond him—not unless something happened to push him into it. It needed someone with something he lacked.

"I-I-I mean, I was—"

"You should not sleep so early before prayers. Remember to be there tonight."

"I will."

Something in the boy's voice made the father look up. John went away relieved. All was still well.

Evening came. John dressed like the night before and walked with faltering steps towards the fatal place. The night of reckoning had come. And he had not thought of anything. After this night all would know. Even Rev. Thomas Carstone would hear of it. He remembered Mr. Carstone and the last words of blessing he had spoken to him. No! he did not want to remember. It was no good remembering these things; and yet the words came. They were clearly written in the air, or in the darkness of his mind. "You are going into the world. The world is waiting even like a hungry lion, to swallow you, to devour you. Therefore, beware of the world. Jesus said, Hold fast unto . . . " John felt a pain—a pain that wriggled through his flesh as he remembered these words. He contemplated the coming fall. Yes! He, John would fall from the Gates of Heaven down through the open waiting gates of Hell. Ah! He could see it all, and what people would say. Everybody would shun his company, would give him oblique looks that told so much. The trouble with John was that his imagination magnified the fall from the heights of "goodness" out of proportion. And fear of people and consequences ranked high in the things that made him contemplate the fall with so much horror.

John devised all sorts of punishment for himself. And when it came to thinking of a way out, only fantastic and impossible ways of escape came into his head. He simply could not make up his mind. And because he could not and he feared father and people, and he did not know his true attitude to the girl, he came to the agreed spot having nothing to tell the girl. Whatever he did looked fatal to him. Then suddenly he said—

"Look Wamuhu. Let me give you money. You might then say that someone else was responsible. Lots of girls have done this. Then that man may marry you. For me, it is impossible. You know that."

"No. I cannot do that. How can you, you—"

"I will give you two hundred shillings."

"No!"

"Three hundred!"

"No!" She was almost crying. It pained her to see him so.

"Four hundred, five hundred, six hundred!" John had begun calmly but now his voice was running high. He was excited. He was becoming more desperate. Did he know what he was talking about? He spoke quickly, breathlessly, as if he was in a hurry. The figure was rapidly rising—nine thousand, ten thousand, twenty thousand. . . . He is mad. He is foaming. He is quickly moving towards the girl in the dark. He has laid his hands on her shoulders and is madly imploring her in a hoarse voice. Deep inside him, something horrid that assumes the threatening anger of his father and the village, seems to be pushing him. He is violently shaking Wamuhu, while his mind tells him that he is patting her gently. Yes. He is out of his mind. The figure has now reached fifty thousand shillings and is increasing. Wamuhu is afraid, extricates herself from him, the mad, educated son of a religious clergyman, and she runs. He runs after her and holds her, calling her by all sorts of endearing words. But he is shaking her, shake, shake, her, her—he tries to hug her by the neck, presses . . . She lets out one horrible scream and then falls on the ground. And so all of a sudden, the struggle is over, the figures stop and John stands there trembling like the leaf of a tree on a windy day.

John, in the grip of fear, ran homeward. Soon everyone would know.

[1964]

QUESTIONS

1. What is the significance of the Irimu, mentioned in the opening paragraph? (When considering this question, you might want to compare the opening of Ngugi's story and Amos Tutuola's "The Complete Gentleman," also found in this volume.)
2. In what sense is darkness the predominant metaphor of Ngugi's story?
3. Given the fact that Wamuhu has been circumcised but John has not gone through the similar "rites of passage," how important is the following statement at the end of the second paragraph: "And he was not a man yet!"
4. How radically different would John's dilemma be if the story had an American setting, perhaps during the last century, and John and his girlfriend were of different religions?

Joyce Carol Oates

(b. 1938)

United States

Joyce Carol Oates is one of the most respected American writers of her generation. Since the publication of her first collection of short stories, *By the North Gate* (1963), and her first novel, *With Shuddering Fall* (1964), hardly a year has passed without the publication of a new Oates novel, collection of stories, or volume of poems. The total output exceeds 40 volumes, including *Them* (1969), which won the National Book Award for fiction; *Expensive People* (1969); *A Garden of Earthly Delights* (1970); *All the Good People I've Left Behind* (1979); *Bellefleur* (1980); *Mysteries of Winterthurn* (1984); *You Must Remember This* (1987); and *Because It Is Bitter and Because It Is My Heart* (1990). Her short stories, which total close to 200, have frequently been anthologized in Martha Foley's annual *Best American Short Stories* and in the annual *O. Henry Awards* volumes, edited by William Abrahams.

Joyce Carol Oates was born in Lockport, New York, in 1938, where from 1945 to 1952 she attended a one-room rural school. She graduated from Syracuse University in 1960 and the following year completed an M.A. in English from the University of Wisconsin. Beginning in 1963, she taught at a number of universities in the United States and Canada. Since 1978, she has been writer-in-residence and professor of English at Princeton.

Often accused of creating a dark, almost perverted world of violence and gothic horror, Oates has answered to the charge on a number of occasions. Responding to Joe David Bellamy's question about violence in an interview published in *The Atlantic* (1972), Oates replied, "Am I personally haunted by the fear of violence, the need for violence, or do I reflect everyone else's feelings about it? I sense it around me, both the fear and the desire, and perhaps I simply have appropriated it from other people." Responding more angrily to a similar question in 1981 (in an essay she wrote for the *New York Times Book Review*), she said that the question was insulting and sexist, that it would never be asked of a male writer: "war, rape, murder, and the more colorful minor crimes evidently fall within the exclusive province of the male writer, just as, generally, they fall within the exclusive province of male action."

"Where Are You Going, Where Have You Been?" was made into a film in 1986: *Smooth Talk*, directed by Joyce Chopra.

Where Are You Going, Where Have You Been?

For Bob Dylan

Her name was Connie. She was fifteen and she had a quick nervous giggling habit of craning her neck to glance into mirrors, or checking other people's faces to make sure her own was all right. Her mother, who noticed everything and knew everything and who hadn't much reason any longer to look at her own face, always scolded Connie about it. "Stop gawking at yourself, who are you? You think you're so pretty?" she would say. Connie would raise her eyebrows at these familiar complaints and look right through her mother, into a shadowy vision of herself as she was right at that moment: she knew she was pretty and that was everything. Her mother had been pretty once too, if you could believe those old snapshots in the album, but now her looks were gone and that was why she was always after Connie.

"Why don't you keep your room clean like your sister? How've you got your hair fixed—what the hell stinks? Hair spray? You don't see your sister using that junk."

Her sister June was twenty-four and still lived at home. She was a secretary in the high school Connie attended, and if that wasn't bad enough—with her in the same building—she was so plain and chunky and steady that Connie had to hear her praised all the time by her mother and her mother's sisters. June did this, June did that, she saved money and helped clean the house and cooked and Connie couldn't do a thing, her mind was all filled with trashy daydreams. Their father was away at work most of the time and when he came home he wanted supper and he read the newspaper at supper and after supper he went to bed. He didn't bother talking much to them, but around his bent head Connie's mother kept picking at her until Connie wished her mother was dead and she herself was dead and it was all over. "She makes me want to throw up sometimes," she complained to her friends. She has a high, breathless, amused voice which made everything she said a little forced, whether it was sincere or not.

There was one good thing: June went places with girl friends of hers, girls who were just as plain and steady as she, and so when Connie wanted to do that her mother had no objections. The father of Connie's best girl friend drove the girls the three miles to town and left them off at a shopping plaza, so that they could walk through the stores or go to a movie, and when he came to pick them up again at eleven he never bothered to ask what they had done.

They must have been familiar sights, walking around that shopping plaza in their shorts and flat ballerina slippers that always scuffed the sidewalk, with charm bracelets jingling on their thin wrists; they would lean together to whisper and laugh secretly if someone passed by who amused or interested them. Connie had long dark blond hair that drew anyone's eye to it, and she wore part of it pulled up on her head and puffed out and the rest of it she let fall down her back. She wore a pullover jersey blouse that looked one way when she was at home and another way when she was away from home. Everything about her had two sides to it, one for home and one for anywhere that was not home: her walk that could be childlike and bobbing, or languid enough to make anyone think she was hearing music in her head, her mouth which was pale and smirking most of the time, but bright and pink on these evenings out, her laugh which was cynical and drawling at home—"Ha, ha, very funny"—but high-pitched and nervous anywhere else, like the jingling of the charms on her bracelet.

Sometimes they did go shopping or to a movie, but sometimes they went across the highway, ducking fast across the busy road, to a drive-in restaurant where older kids hung out. The restaurant was shaped like a big bottle, though squatter than a real bottle, and on its cap was a revolving figure of a grinning boy who held a hamburger aloft. One night in mid-summer they ran across, breathless with daring, and right away someone leaned out a car window and invited them over, but it was just a boy from high school they didn't like. It made them feel good to be able to ignore him. They went up through the maze of parked and cruising cars to the bright-lit, fly-infested restaurant, their faces pleased and expectant as if they were entering a sacred building that loomed out of the night to give them what haven and what blessing they yearned for. They sat at the counter and crossed their legs at the ankles, their thin shoulders rigid with excitement and listened to the music that made everything so good: the music was always in the background like music at a church service, it was something to depend upon.

A boy named Eddie came in to talk with them. He sat backwards on his stool, turning himself jerkily around in semi-circles and then stopping and turning again, and after a while he asked Connie if she would like something to eat. She said she did and so she tapped her friend's arm on her way out—her friend pulled her face up into a brave droll look—and Connie said she would meet her at eleven, across the way. "I just hate to leave her like that," Connie said earnestly, but the boy said that she wouldn't be alone for long. So they went out to his car and on the way Connie couldn't help but let her eyes wander over the windshields and faces all around her, her face gleaming with the joy that had nothing to do with Eddie or even this place; it might have been the music. She drew her shoulders up and sucked in her breath with the pure pleasure of being alive, and just at that moment she happened to glance at a face just a few feet from hers. It was a boy with shaggy black hair, in a convertible jalopy painted gold. He stared at her and then his lips widened into a grin. Connie slit her eyes at him and turned away, but she couldn't help glancing back and there he was still watching her. He wagged a finger and laughed and said, "Gonna get you, baby," and Connie turned away again without Eddie noticing anything.

She spent three hours with him, at the restaurant where they ate hamburgers and drank Cokes in wax cups that were always sweating, and then down an alley a mile or so away, and when he left her off at five to eleven only the movie house was still open at the plaza. Her girl friend was there, talking with a boy. When Connie came up the two girls smiled at each other and Connie said, "How was the movie?" and the girl said, "*You* should know." They rode off with the girl's father, sleepy and pleased, and Connie couldn't help but look at the darkened shopping plaza with its big empty parking lot and its signs that were faded and ghostly now, and over at the drive-in restaurant where cars were still circling tirelessly. She couldn't hear the music at this distance.

Next morning June asked her how the movie was and Connie said, "So-so."

She and that girl and occasionally another girl went out several times a week that way, and the rest of the time Connie spent around the house—it was summer vacation—getting in her mother's way and thinking, dreaming, about the boys she met. But all the boys fell back and dissolved into a single face that was not even a face, but an idea, a feeling, mixed up with the urgent insistent pounding of the music and the humid night air of July. Connie's mother kept dragging her back to the daylight by finding things for her to do or saying suddenly, "What's this about the Pettinger girl?"

And Connie would say nervously, "Oh, her. That dope." She always drew thick clear lines between herself and such girls, and her mother was simple and kindly enough to believe her. Her mother was so simple, Connie thought, that it was maybe cruel to fool her so much. Her mother went scuffling around the house in old bedroom slippers and complained over the telephone to one sister about the other, then the other called up and the two of them complained about the third one. If June's name was mentioned her mother's tone was approving, and if Connie's name was mentioned it was disapproving. This did not really mean she disliked Connie and actually Connie thought that her mother preferred her to June because she was prettier, but the two of them kept up a pretense of exasperation, a sense that they were tugging and struggling over something of little value to either of them. Sometimes, over coffee, they were almost friends, but something would come up—some vexation that was like a fly buzzing suddenly around their heads—and their faces went hard with contempt.

One Sunday Connie got up at eleven—none of them bothered with church—and washed her hair so that it could dry all day long, in the sun. Her parents and sister were going to a barbecue at an aunt's house and Connie said no, she wasn't interested, rolling her eyes, to let mother know just what she thought of it. "Stay home alone then," her mother said sharply. Connie sat out back in a lawn chair and watched them drive away, her father quiet and bald, hunched around so that he could back the car out, her mother with a look that was still angry and not at all softened through the windshield, and in the back seat poor old June all dressed up as if she didn't know what a barbecue was, with all the running yelling kids and the flies. Connie sat with her eyes closed in the sun, dreaming and dazed with the warmth about her as if this were a kind of love, the caresses of love, and her mind slipped over onto thoughts of the boy she had been with the night before and how nice he had been, how sweet it always was, not the way someone like June would suppose but sweet, gentle, the way it was in movies and promised in songs; and when she opened her eyes she hardly knew where she was, the back yard ran off into weeds and a fenceline of trees and behind it the sky was perfectly blue and still. The asbestos "ranch house" that was now three years old startled her—it looked small. She shook her head as if to get awake.

It was too hot. She went inside the house and turned on the radio to drown out the quiet. She sat on the edge of her bed, barefoot, and listened for an hour and a half to a program called XYZ Sunday Jamboree, record after record of hard, fast, shrieking songs she sang along with, interspersed by exclamations from "Bobby King": "An' look here you girls at Napoleon's—Son and Charley want you to pay real close attention to this song coming up!"

And Connie paid close attention herself, bathed in a glow of slow-pulsed joy that seemed to rise mysteriously out of the music itself and lay languidly about the airless little room, breathed in and breathed out with each gentle rise and fall of her chest.

After a while she heard a car coming up the drive. She sat up at once, startled, because it couldn't be her father so soon. The gravel kept crunching all the way in from the road—the driveway was long—and Connie ran to the window. It was a car she didn't know. It was an open jalopy, painted a bright gold that caught the sun opaquely. Her heart began to pound and her fingers snatched at her hair, checking it, and she whispered "Christ. Christ," wondering how bad she looked. The car came to a stop at the side door and the horn sounded four short taps as if this were a signal Connie knew.

She went into the kitchen and approached the door slowly, then hung out the screen door, her bare toes curling down off the step. There were two boys in the car and now she recognized the driver: he had shaggy, shabby black hair that looked crazy as a wig and he was grinning at her.

"I ain't late, am I?" he said.

"Who the hell do you think you are?" Connie said.

"Toldja I'd be out, didn't I?"

"I don't even know who you are."

She spoke sullenly, careful to show no interest or pleasure, and he spoke in a fast bright monotone. Connie looked past him to the other boy, taking her time. He had fair brown hair, with a lock that fell onto his forehead. His sideburns gave him a fierce, embarrassed look, but so far he hadn't even bothered to glance at her. Both boys wore sunglasses. The driver's glasses were metallic and mirrored everything in miniature.

"You wanta come for a ride?" he said.

Connie smirked and let her hair fall loose over one shoulder.

"Don'tcha like my car? New paint job," he said. "Hey."

"What?"

"You're cute."

She pretended to fidget, chasing flies away from the door.

"Don'tcha believe me, or what?" he said.

"Look, I don't even know who you are," Connie said in disgust.

"Hey, Ellie's got a radio, see. Mine's broke down." He lifted his friend's arm and showed her the little transistor the boy was holding, and now Connie began to hear the music. It was the same program that was playing inside the house.

"Bobby King?" she said.

"I listen to him all the time. I think he's great."

"He's kind of great," Connie said reluctantly.

"Listen, that guy's *great*. He knows where the action is."

Connie blushed a little, because the glasses made it impossible for her to see just what this boy was looking at. She couldn't decide if she liked him or if he was just a jerk, and so she dawdled in the doorway and wouldn't come down or go back inside. She said, "What's all that stuff painted on your car?"

"Can'tcha read it?" He opened the door very carefully, as if he was afraid it might fall off. He slid out just as carefully, planting his feet firmly on the ground, the tiny metallic world in his glasses slowing down like gelatine hardening and in the midst of it Connie's bright green blouse. "This here is my name, to begin with," he said. ARNOLD FRIEND was written in tar-like black letters on the side, with a drawing of a round grinning face that reminded Connie of a pumpkin, except it wore sunglasses. "I wanta introduce myself, I'm Arnold Friend and that's my real name and I'm gonna be your friend, honey, and inside the car's Ellie Oscar, he's kinda shy." Ellie brought his transistor up to his shoulder and balanced it there. "Now these numbers are a secret code, honey," Arnold Friend explained. He read off the numbers 33, 19, 17 and raised his eyebrows at her to see what she thought of that, but she didn't think much of it. The left rear fender had been smashed and around it was written, on the gleaming gold background: DONE BY CRAZY WOMAN DRIVER. Connie had to laugh at that. Arnold Friend was pleased at her laughter and looked up at her. "Around the other side's a lot more—you wanta come and see them?"

"No."

"Why not?"

"Why should I?"

"Don'tcha wanta see what's on the car? Don'tcha wanta go for a ride?"

"I don't know."

"Why not?"

"I got things to do."

"Like what?"

"Things."

He laughed as if she had said something funny. He slapped his thighs. He was standing in a strange way, leaning back against the car as if he were balancing himself. He wasn't tall, only an inch or so taller than she would be if she came down to him. Connie liked the way he was dressed, which was the way all of them dressed: tight faded jeans stuffed into black, scuffed boots, a belt that pulled his waist in and showed how lean he was, and a white pull-over shirt that was a little soiled and showed the hard small muscles of his arms and shoulders. He looked as if he probably did hard work, lifting and carrying things. Even his neck looked muscular. And his face was a familiar face, somehow: the jaw and chin and cheeks slightly darkened, because he hadn't shaved for a day or two, and the nose long and hawk-like, sniffing as if she were a treat he was going to gobble up and it was all a joke.

"Connie, you ain't telling the truth. This is your day set aside for a ride with me and you know it," he said, still laughing. The way he straightened and recovered from his fit of laughing showed that it had been all fake.

"How do you know what my name is?" she said suspiciously.

"It's Connie."

"Maybe and maybe not."

"I know my Connie," he said, wagging his finger. Now she remembered him even better, back at the restaurant, and her cheeks warmed at the thought of how she sucked in her breath just at the moment she passed him—how she must have looked to him. And he had remembered her. "Ellie and I come out here especially for you," he said. "Ellie can sit in back. How about it?"

"Where?"

"Where what?"

"Where're we going?"

He looked at her. He took off the sunglasses and she saw how pale the skin around his eyes was, like holes that were not in shadow but instead in light. His eyes were like chips of broken glass that catch the light in an amiable way. He smiled. It was as if the idea of going for a ride somewhere, to some place, was a new idea to him.

"Just for a ride, Connie sweetheart."

"I never said my name was Connie," she said.

"But I know what it is. I know your name and all about you, lots of things," Arnold Friend said. He had not moved yet but stood still leaning back against the side of his jalopy. "I took a special interest in you, such a pretty girl, and found out all about you like I know your parents and sister are gone somewheres and I know where and how long they're going to be gone, and I know who you were with last night, and your best friend's name is Betty. Right?"

He spoke in a simple lilting voice, exactly as if he were reciting the words to a song. His smile assured her that everything was fine. In the car Ellie turned up the volume on his radio and did not bother to look around at them.

"Ellie can sit in the back seat," Arnold Friend said. He indicated his friend with a casual jerk of his chin, as if Ellie did not count and she could not bother with him.

"How'd you find out all that stuff?" Connie said.

"Listen? Betty Schultz and Tony Fitch and Jimmy Pettinger and Nancy Pettinger," he said, in a chant. "Raymond Stanley and Bob Hutter—"

"Do you know all those kids?"

"I know everybody."

"Look, you're kidding. You're not from around here."

"Sure."

"But—how come we never saw you before?"

"Sure you saw me before," he said. He looked down at his boots, as if he were a little offended. "You just don't remember."

"I guess I'd remember you," Connie said.

"Yeah?" He looked up at this, beaming. He was pleased. He began to mark time with the music from Ellie's radio, tapping his fists lightly together. Connie looked away from his smile to the car, which was painted so bright it almost hurt her eyes to look at it. She looked at that name, ARNOLD FRIEND. And up at the front fender was an expression that was familiar—MAN THE FLYING SAUCERS. It was an expression kids had used the year before, but didn't use this year. She looked at it for a while as if the words meant something to her that she did not yet know.

"What're you thinking about? Huh?" Arnold Friend demanded. "Not worried about your hair blowing around in the car, are you?"

"No."

"Think I maybe can't drive good?"

"How do I know?"

"You're a hard girl to handle. How come?" he said. "Don't you know I'm your friend? Didn't you see me put my sign in the air when you walked by?"

"What sign?"

"My sign." And he drew an X in the air, leaning out toward her. They were maybe ten feet apart. After his hand fell back to his side the X was still in the air, almost visible. Connie let the screen door close and stood perfectly still inside it, listening to the music from her radio and the boy's blend together. She stared at Arnold Friend. He stood there so stiffly relaxed, pretending to be relaxed, with one hand idly on the door handle as if he were keeping himself up that way and had no intention of ever moving again. She recognized most things about him, the tight jeans that showed his thighs and buttocks and the greasy leather boots and the tight shirt, and even that slippery friendly smile of his, that sleepy dreamy smile that all the boys used to get across ideas they didn't want to put into words. She recognized all this and also the singsong way he talked, slightly mocking, kidding, but serious and a little melancholy, and she recognized the way he tapped one fist against the other in homage to the perpetual music behind him. But all these things did not come together.

She said suddenly, "Hey, how old are you?"

His smile faded. She could see then that he wasn't a kid, he was much older — thirty, maybe more. At this knowledge her heart began to pound faster.

"That's a crazy thing to ask. Can'tcha see I'm your own age?"

"Like hell you are."

"Or maybe a coupla years older, I'm eighteen."

"Eighteen?" she said doubtfully.

He grinned to reassure her and lines appeared at the corners of his mouth. His teeth were big and white. He grinned so broadly his eyes became slits and she saw how thick the lashes were, thick and black as if painted with a black tar-like material. Then he seemed to become embarrassed, abruptly, and looked over his shoulder at Ellie. "*Him*, he's crazy," he said. "Ain't he a riot, he's a nut, a real character." Ellie was still listening to the music. His sunglasses told nothing about what he was thinking. He wore a bright orange shirt unbuttoned halfway to show his chest, which was a pale, bluish chest and not muscular like Arnold Friend's. His shirt collar was turned up all around and the very tips of the collar pointed out past his chin as if they were protecting him. He was pressing the transistor radio up against his ear and sat there in a kind of daze, right in the sun.

"He's kinda strange," Connie said.

"Hey, she says you're kinda strange! Kinda strange!" Arnold Friend cried. He pounded on the car to get Ellie's attention. Ellie turned for the first time and Connie saw with shock that he wasn't a kid either — he had a fair, hairless face, cheeks reddened slightly as if the veins grew too close to the surface of his skin, the face of a forty-year-old baby. Connie felt a wave of dizziness rise in her at this sight and she stared at him as if waiting for something to change the shock of the moment, make it all right again. Ellie's lips kept shaping words, mumbling along with the words blasting his ear.

"Maybe you two better go away," Connie said faintly.

"What? How come?" Arnold Friend cried. "We come out here to take you for a ride. It's Sunday." He had the voice of the man on the radio now. It was the same voice, Connie thought. "Don'tcha know it's Sunday all day and honey, no matter who you were with last night today you're with Arnold Friend and don't you forget it! — Maybe you better step out here," he said, and this last was in a different voice. It was a little flatter, as if the heat was finally getting to him.

"No. I got things to do."

"Hey."

"You two better leave."

"We ain't leaving until you come with us."

"Like hell I am — "

"Connie, don't fool around with me. I mean, I mean, don't fool *around*," he said, shaking his head. He laughed incredulously. He placed his sunglasses on top of his head, carefully, as if he were indeed wearing a wig, and brought the stems down behind his ears. Connie stared at him, another wave of dizziness and fear rising in her so that for a moment he wasn't even in focus but was just a blur, standing there against his gold car, and she had the idea that he had driven up the driveway all right but had come from nowhere before that and belonged nowhere and that everything about him and even the music that was so familiar to her was only half real.

"If my father comes and sees you—"

"He ain't coming. He's at a barbecue."

"How do you know that?"

"Aunt Tillie's. Right now they're—uh—they're drinking. Sitting around," he said vaguely, squinting as if he were staring all the way to town and over to Aunt Tillie's back yard. Then the vision seemed to clear and he nodded energetically. "Yeah. Sitting around. There's your sister in a blue dress, huh? And high heels, the poor sad bitch—nothing like you, sweetheart! And your mother's helping some fat woman with the corn, they're cleaning the corn—husking the corn—"

"What fat woman?" Connie cried.

"How do I know what fat woman. I don't know every goddamn fat woman in the world!" Arnold Friend laughed.

"Oh, that's Mrs. Hornby. . . . Who invited her?" Connie said. She felt a little light-headed. Her breath was coming quickly.

"She's too fat. I don't like them fat. I like them the way you are, honey," he said, smiling sleepily at her. They stared at each other for a while, through the screen door. He said softly, "Now what you're going to do is this: you're going to come out that door. You're going to sit up front with me and Ellie's going to sit in the back, the hell with Ellie, right? This isn't Ellie's date. You're my date. I'm your lover, honey."

"What? You're crazy—"

"Yes, I'm your lover. You don't know what that is but you will," he said. "I know that too. I know all about you. But look: it's real nice and you couldn't ask for nobody better than me, or more polite. I always keep my word. I'll tell you how it is, I'm always nice at first, the first time. I'll hold you so tight you won't think you have to try to get away or pretend anything because you'll know you can't. And I'll come inside you where it's all secret and you'll give in to me and you'll love me—"

"Shut up! You're crazy!" Connie said. She backed away from the door. She put her hands against her ears as if she'd heard something terrible, something not meant for her. "People don't talk like that, you're crazy," she muttered. Her heart was almost too big now for her chest and its pumping made sweat break out all over her. She looked out to see Arnold Friend pause and then take a step toward the porch lurching. He almost fell. But, like a clever drunken man, he managed to catch his balance. He wobbled in his high boots and grabbed hold of one of the porch posts.

"Honey?" he said. "You still listening?"

"Get the hell out of here!"

"Be nice, honey. Listen."

"I'm going to call the police—"

He wobbled again and out of the side of his mouth came a fast spat curse, an aside not meant for her to hear. But even this "Christ!" sounded forced. Then he began to smile again. She watched this smile come, awkward as if he were smiling from inside a mask. His whole face was a mask, she thought wildly, tanned down onto his throat but then running out as if he had plastered make-up on his face but had forgotten about his throat.

"Honey—? Listen, here's how it is. I always tell the truth and I promise you this: I ain't coming in that house after you."

"You better not! I'm going to call the police if you—if you don't—"

"Honey," he said, talking right through her voice, "honey, I'm not coming in there but you are coming out here. You know why?"

She was panting. The kitchen looked like a place she had never seen before, some room she had run inside but which wasn't good enough, wasn't going to help her. The kitchen window had never had a curtain, after three years, and there were dishes in the sink for her to do—probably—and if you ran your hand across the table you'd probably feel something sticky there.

"You listening, honey? Hey?"

"—going to call the police—"

"Soon as you touch the phone I don't need to keep my promise and can come inside. You won't want that."

She rushed forward and tried to lock the door. Her fingers were shaking. "But why lock it," Arnold Friend said gently, talking right into her face. "It's just a screen door. It's just nothing." One of his boots was at a strange angle, as if his foot wasn't in it. It pointed out to the left, bent at the ankle. "I mean, anybody can break through a screen door and glass and wood and iron or anything else if he needs to, anybody at all and specially Arnold Friend. If the place got lit up with a fire, honey, you'd come running out into my arms, right into my arms and safe at home—like you knew I was your lover and'd stopped fooling around, I don't mind a nice shy girl but I don't like no fooling around." Part of those words were spoken with a slight rhythmic lilt, and Connie somehow recognized them—the echo of a song from last year, about a girl rushing into her boy friend's arms and coming home again—

Connie stood barefoot on the linoleum floor, staring at him. "What do you want?" she whispered.

"I want you," he said.

"What?"

"Seen you that night and thought, that's the one, yes sir. I never needed to look any more."

"But my father's coming back. He's coming to get me. I had to wash my hair first—" She spoke in a dry, rapid voice, hardly raising it for him to hear.

"No, your daddy is not coming and yes, you had to wash your hair and you washed it for me. It's nice and shining and all for me, I thank you, sweetheart," he said, with a mock bow, but again he almost lost his balance. He had to bend and adjust his boots. Evidently his feet did not go all the way down; the boots must have been stuffed with something so that he would seem taller. Connie stared out at him and behind him Ellie in the car, who seemed to be looking off toward Connie's right, into nothing. This Ellie said, pulling the words out of the air one after another as if he were just discovering them, "You want me to pull out the phone?"

"Shut your mouth and keep it shut," Arnold Friend said, his face red from bending over or maybe from embarrassment because Connie had seen his boots. "This ain't none of your business."

"What—what are you doing? What do you want?" Connie said. "If I call the police they'll get you, they'll arrest you—"

"Promise was not to come in unless you touch that phone, and I'll keep that promise," he said. He resumed his erect position and tried to force his shoulders back. He sounded like a hero in a movie, declaring something important. He spoke too loudly and it was as if he were speaking to someone behind Connie. "I ain't made plans for coming in that house where I don't belong but just for you to come out to me, the way you should. Don't you know who I am?"

"You're crazy," she whispered. She backed away from the door but did not want to go into another part of the house, as if this would give him permission to come through the door. "What do you. . . . You're crazy, you. . . . "

"Huh? What're you saying, honey?"

Her eyes darted everywhere in the kitchen. She could not remember what it was, this room.

"This is how it is, honey: you come out and we'll drive away, have a nice ride. But if you don't come out we're gonna wait till your people come home and then they're all going to get it."

"You want that telephone pulled out?" Ellie said. He held the radio away from his ear and grimaced, as if without the radio the air was too much for him.

"I toldja shut up, Ellie." Arnold Friend said, "You're deaf, get a hearing aid, right? Fix yourself up. This little girl's no trouble and's gonna be nice to me, so Ellie keep to yourself, this ain't your date—right? Don't hem in on me. Don't hog. Don't crush. Don't bird dog. Don't trail me," he said in a rapid meaningless voice, as if he were running through all the expressions he'd learned but was no longer sure which one of them was in style, then rushing on to new ones, making them up with his eyes closed, "Don't crawl under my fence, don't squeeze in my chipmunk hole, don't sniff my glue, suck my popsicle, keep your own greasy fingers on yourself!" He shaded his eyes and peered in at Connie, who was backed against the kitchen table. "Don't mind him, honey, he's just a creep. He's a dope. Right? I'm the boy for you and like I said you come out here nice like a lady and give me your hand, and nobody else gets hurt, I mean, your nice old bald-headed daddy and your mummy and your sister in her high heels. Because listen: why bring them in this?"

"Leave me alone," Connie whispered.

"Hey, you know that old woman down the road, the one with the chickens and stuff—you know her?"

"She's dead!"

"Dead? What? You know her?" Arnold Friend said.

"She's dead— "

"Don't you like her?"

"She's dead—she's—she isn't here any more—"

"But don't you like her, I mean, you got something against her? Some grudge or something?" Then his voice dipped as if he were conscious of rudeness. He touched the sunglasses on top of his head as if to make sure they were still there. "Now you be a good girl."

"What are you going to do?"

"Just two things, or maybe three," Arnold Friend said. "But I promise it won't last long and you'll like me that way you get to like people you're close to. You will. It's all over for you here, so come on out. You don't want your people in any trouble, do you?"

She turned and bumped against a chair or something, hurting her leg, but she ran into the back room and picked up the telephone. Something roared in her ear, a tiny roaring, and she was so sick with fear that she could do nothing but listen to it—the telephone was clammy and very heavy and her fingers groped down to the dial but were too weak to touch it. She began to scream into the phone, into the roaring. She cried out, she cried for her mother, she felt her breath start jerking back and forth in her lungs as if it were something Arnold Friend were stabbing her with again and again with no tenderness. A noisy sorrowful wailing rose all about her and she was locked inside it the way she was locked inside this house.

After a while she could hear again. She was sitting on the floor, with her wet back against the wall.

Arnold Friend was saying from the door, "That's a good girl. Put the phone back."

She kicked the phone away from her.

"No, honey. Pick it up. Put it back right."

She picked it up and put it back. The dial tone stopped.

"That's a good girl. Now you come outside."

She was hollow with what had been fear, but what was now just an emptiness. All that screaming had blasted it out of her. She sat, one leg cramped under her, and deep inside her brain was something like a pinpoint of light that kept going and would not let her relax. She thought, I'm not going to see my mother again. She thought, I'm not going to sleep in my bed again. Her bright green blouse was all wet.

Arnold Friend said, in a gentle-loud voice that was like a stage voice. "The place where you came from ain't there any more, and where you had in mind to go is cancelled out. This place you are now—inside your daddy's house—is nothing but a cardboard box I can knock down any time. You know that and always did know it. You hear me?"

She thought, I have got to think. I have to know what to do.

"We'll go out to a nice field, out in the country here where it smells so nice and it's sunny," Arnold Friend said. "I'll have my arms tight around you so you won't need to try to get away and I'll show you what love is like, what it does. The hell with this house! It looks solid all right," he said. He ran a fingernail down the screen and the noise did not make Connie shiver, as it would have the day before. "Now put your hand on your heart, honey. Feel that? That feels solid too but we know better, be nice to me, be sweet like you can because what else is there for a girl like you but to be sweet and pretty and give in?—and get away before her people come back?"

She felt her pounding heart. Her hands seemed to enclose it. She thought for the first time in her life that it was nothing that was hers, that belonged to her, but just a pounding, living thing inside this body that wasn't hers either.

"You don't want them to get hurt," Arnold Friend went on. "Now get up, honey. Get up all by yourself."

She stood.

"Now turn this way. That's right. Come over to me—Ellie, put that away, didn't I tell you? You dope. You miserable creepy dope," Arnold Friend said. His words were not angry but only part of an incantation. The incantation was kindly. "Now come out through the kitchen to me honey and let's see a smile, try it, you're a brave sweet little girl and now they're eating corn and hotdogs cooked to bursting over an outdoor fire, and they don't know one thing about you and never did and honey you're better than them because not one of them would have done this for you."

Connie felt the linoleum under her feet; it was cool. She brushed her hair back out of her eyes. Arnold Friend let go of the post tentatively and opened his arms for her, his elbows pointing up toward each other and his wrist limp, to show that this was an embarrassed embrace and a little mocking, he didn't want to make her self-conscious.

She put out her hand against the screen. She watched herself push the door slowly open as if she were safe back somewhere in the other doorway, watching this body and this head of long hair moving out into the sunlight where Arnold Friend waited.

"My sweet little blue-eyed girl," he said, in a half-sung sigh that had nothing to do with her brown eyes but was taken up just the same by the vast sunlit reaches of the land behind him and on all sides of him, so much land that Connie had never seen before and did not recognize except to know that she was going to it.

[1970]

QUESTIONS

1. Does Connie give in to the stranger as a result of her awakening sexuality or her fear of what he may do to her family, that is, as a result of weakness or strength in protecting her family?
2. Is Oates's story intended to be interpreted as Connie's encounter with the Devil?
3. What function does Ellie play in the narrative?
4. Why is the story dedicated to Bob Dylan?

Ōba Minako

(b. 1930)

Japan

In *The Showa Anthology: Modern Japanese Short Stories*, Van C. Gessel and Tomone Matsumoto, the editors, describe Ōba Minako's work as follows: "The author sometimes uses straightforward narrative but more often prefers a montage technique. . . . [Her] stories of love and death [are] full of vivid imagery that is sometimes beautiful, often grotesque. Ōba's subtle and complex literary world provides no answers, but casts a fresh and occasionally disturbing light on the human condition."

Ōba Minako's literary career began in 1968 with a short story called "The Three Crabs." In that story and in others that were soon to follow, she creates a world in which reality and imagination flow into one another, often making it impossible for the reader to determine what is real in her characters' world. As you read "The Pale Fox," try to determine which parts of the story the narrator has actually experienced and which ones she has imagined.

◆ The Pale Fox ◆

"It's been a long time," said the Pale Fox.

Seven years ago, when they were lovers, a melancholy look in the man's downcast face had reminded her of a fox. Sometimes, in the pale light of the moon, or washed perhaps by the light of a neon sign, his face took on a bluish cast, and since that time she had referred to him in her mind as the Pale Fox. His sharp, narrow chin resembled a fox—a fox pausing in a moonlit forest, head cocked toward the moon.

"These white flowers smell nice," said the Pale Fox, "but the thistles, roses, and nettles are a nuisance."

Turning away from the light, the Fox's eyes shone amber, like glowing charcoal or Christmas tree lights.

"It's been seven years, hasn't it?"

The Pale Fox was like a priest who performed the ritual with faultless precision. The priest's eyes were too far apart for a fox, and each drifted independently. For some reason she enjoyed running the tip of her finger down between his eyebrows to the bridge of his nose.

"That's a vulnerable spot. It gives me the shivers when you do that; it makes me feel I'm about to be stabbed by an assassin." The Pale Fox disliked her doing this, but was reluctant to brush the woman's finger away.

The Fox's nose was moist in the moonlight.

The woman thought: I wonder why Father says this is the grave where Mother is buried? It is such a splendid and majestic tomb. It might have been the grave of some venerable priest clothed in rich, brocaded vestments, or a great warrior in full armor and helmet, or a grand minister of state with drooping moustaches.

The funeral must surely have been splendid, too, with much fanfare and a service carried out in the glare of footlights, attended by joyous throngs of celebrities. The choreographer of this spectacle would have been called the Priest of Heaven, and would have led the reading of the scriptures and the voluptuous sobbing of the mourners. Yes, this was the funeral it must have been.

By now, of course, the grave was encrusted with moss and lichen, and it was impossible to read the inscription carved on it. All she could make out was a single Chinese character that seemed to be the word for "great." Yet once it had been a glittering and elaborate tomb.

Though the flesh in the casket had decayed and putrefied, beautiful women had gathered in attendance. Ladies who had flinched at the smell of corruption had risked being thrown into prison. It was a grave of writhing anguish.

This was a grave that wielded power, that threw back its shoulders in pride; this was a grave that laughed arrogantly with cold eyes and a thin smile. But this was all vanity now, for the corpse had rotted and the tomb was crumbling.

The forest was heavy with gloom. When the black birds started up with a mournful cry, cold drops fell from the trees and she looked up. Far away, between the overlapping leaves, was the violet sky.

The path was slippery with mud, and fungi that reminded her of withered and broken oranges grew from the fallen tree trunks. There were others with plump, fleshy umbrellas that spread wide like patches of snow.

Each time her father stumbled, he clutched at her. His hands were cold, and the daughter felt that a corpse was touching her. Still, she was curious about this landscape of death being shown her by a corpse, and she appreciated each stop they made.

"I found Mother's grave. I looked for it everywhere and couldn't find it, but then all of a sudden I saw it, thanks to the way the light was shining."

It was like the abalone clinging to the rocks. Somewhere down among the forest of gently waving sea tangle there comes the glitter of a fish's belly, and suddenly you see it, the tight, tender flesh of the abalone enclosed in its shell, deep within the lush growth of moss.

Her father was delighted. From his youth he had been happiest gathering abalone and edible fungi. He was a metal craftsman by trade who had brought his workshop to the rocky shore of this island and devoted the greater part of each year to making metal objects. Toward the end of the year, he would take everything he had made to the city to sell; but apart from that one annual journey, he remained on the island. The children enjoyed spending several months there with their father during the summer. Stretching out like a backdrop behind the rocky shore was a pine forest where all sorts of fungi flourished.

His eyes were as sharp as an animal's when he probed for abalone trembling beneath the surface of the sea, or the thin, white stalks of fungi hidden in the forest under fallen leaves. He would find each mollusc among the seaweed and pull its living flesh from the rocks where it clung fast. The woman imagined the old man's twisted jaw and superimposed the image on the sharp jaw of the Pale Fox.

"It was a place like this, your mother's grave."

Her father had discovered the grave deep in the inner recesses of an ancient temple on the edge of the pine forest. At the back of the tomb he had found a small door leading to the crypt. He had tried to open it, but it was choked with moss and would not move. Some grass with small, white flowers grew in a crack in the stone that marked the door to the crypt. There were also ferns.

"Your mother is sitting in there. I could see her knee," said her father. "The swelling in her shins seems to have subsided. The color of her earlobes isn't good, though."

Mother had to have her ears pierced to wear the earrings that Father made for her. The daughter remembered from her childhood that when Mother's ears had been pierced, Father had disinfected them so they would not fester.

The shells of the abalone were hidden by sea moss; the tomb was covered with forest moss. When she bent to examine the moss more closely, the beauty of a microcosmic world spread out before her. The stone tomb beneath it became an illusion; the vision of elegance vanished.

Clutching his cane of polished rose root, her father resembled a gaunt, white cat. He smiled and his eyes gleamed with a small, blue flame.

"Shall we burn a cigarette instead of incense?"

Searching in her handbag, she found two cigarettes; they were all she had left. She lit one and put it on the moss. The white paper absorbed some moisture and she watched it go out, leaving only a wisp of smoke. She lit the remaining cigarette and inhaled, turning aside to keep the smoke from getting in her eyes. Then, as though her mother were a patient lying on the tombstone, she held the cigarette out between her fingers so that the sick woman could take it in her mouth. She stayed like that for a while, waiting for the ash to lengthen and fall off.

After all, it was tobacco that had killed her mother, and now that she was dead, her father frequently offered cigarettes at the family altar.

She felt as though she were playing house with her father. It was as though they had joined hands and were dancing around some ancient tomb, playing a children's game. In the shadow of the tombstone, a toad sat watching.

For seven years she had heard no news at all, then suddenly, one day, a man came to see her and it was the Fox. His arrival was totally unexpected, like waking in the morning to find a single leaf by her pillow.

The Pale Fox was smoother than the polished rose root. He believed he had a very beautiful body; he liked to stand straight and walk slowly. She realized he was probably waiting for some word of praise, but felt it was too much trouble to try and find a compliment to satisfy his vanity. At the same time, she was ashamed of her own indifference.

The Pale Fox told her that during the seven years they had been apart, he had married, lived with his wife for four years, and then left her.

"She was like one of those dolls that can shed tears. Whenever I came home, I would find her sitting in the same place, in the same position. In the end she became like a moth, the large sort that crawl around on walls."

"First you say she's a crying doll, and then she's just a dried-up moth stuck to the wall."

"Finally that's all she was, just a spot on the wall. She was the sort of woman who dreams of finding happiness in ordinary family life. She had done nothing wrong, that's why it was such a shame. I even changed my mind after we had separated, and we tried meeting several times, but we never talked about anything. We slept together each time we met, but we couldn't talk about things. I'd leave again as soon as our lovemaking was done. At that point she changed from a moth into a butterfly sitting with its wings folded. As she sat, dust would rise from her wings and make me wheeze."

He paused, then tried to explain his own silence by saying, "Some people talk a lot. I think they lose something when they talk too much."

The woman gazed with admiration at the Pale Fox, who spoke as little as possible in order not to lose anything.

He was, however, the sort of man who could never suit his actions to his words, or his deeds to his thoughts, and so he always ended up talking when the woman remained silent. Nevertheless, he apparently felt obliged to explain what he had done during those seven years.

"I was exhausted the whole time we were married. The constant weariness made my bones ache as though I was carrying a load with straps cutting into my shoulders. I always do what I want, and yet while my own life-style was selfish, I felt some responsibility toward my thoroughly unselfish partner. At the bottom of my heart I suppose what I really want is a woman who'll be a slave to me."

"I'm sure there are women in the world who'd be happy to be your slave. But if you ever encountered one, you'd start dreaming of a woman you could treat as an equal. You really would. Haven't you learned yet that the tyrant is always bound by the tyrant's debt? In your case, the only way to free yourself is to free the other person as well."

"But women all renounce their freedom; it's a way of binding their men to them." Somewhere in his heart the Pale Fox dreamed of having a slave, but in reality he could never manipulate women in that way.

Seven years ago he had asked her to marry him, saying that he intended to be a good husband. The expression on his face had revealed the pathetic determination of someone who was throwing his own freedom away. This frightened the woman and she recoiled from him. She could imagine him saying the same thing to his former wife before their marriage, and she pitied him. To make unrealistic promises, to make promises he could not keep, could only lead to hopelessness in the long run.

It was when he was completely beaten that he dreamed of possessing a slave. If a woman chooses to be a slave, presumably the man's guilt is resolved and this allows him to behave as he pleases. The woman understood this man's fantasy very well; he wanted her to fall on her knees and embrace him, but she felt it was too much bother. Again she felt ashamed of her indifference.

"You are too fond of women. That's why it's impossible either to pledge yourself to one single woman or to treat us simply as objects. But, you know, you're probably fond of women because women are fond of men. If women were not allowed to know men, if the person you married were not allowed to know any man but yourself, she still wouldn't necessarily become the sort of woman you want. A woman can't be treated as a woman if she's lost whatever makes her one. The sort of marriage you had in mind depends too much on someone who's lost her identity as a woman."

In an encounter like this, mood is more important than logic. And so, solemnly, tenderly, they proceeded with their ritual, devoting themselves to it wholeheartedly, and when the ceremony had reached its climax and ended, they were left clinging to the altar like a pair of bats, physically and emotionally drained. Once the ceremony was over, her earlier indifference returned, and she became embarrassed by her lack of enthusiasm. In the end she compromised by telling herself that different people just have different ideas, and that it does no good to ignore other ways of thinking.

The Pale Fox dozed. His arms, twined around her waist, went limp. She could see one ugly, swollen wart on a stubby finger; it reminded her of the skin near the ears of lizards she had seen the previous day at the botanical gardens. They had kissed for the first time in seven years standing in front of a pair of lizards locked in a motionless sexual embrace. The immobile lizards looked like stuffed animals in a specimen case.

His warty finger also appeared to be stuffed. The wart seemed to spread and grow until it resembled a crater. Countless white fungus stalks grew out of this crater.

Her father called again from the island. He had called twice while she was out. Praying Mantis, the man she was living with, passed on the information that he had phoned, but she did not feel like returning his call, and left again.

Her father was in the habit of ringing his seven children one after the other, making the same call to each. The woman was usually the last to be called. She was, after all, the youngest child. Apparently he had said the rocks on the island were covered with abalone, but that was long ago, and now the rocks were covered only by moss. Whatever phase the moon was in, there was only moss that may have looked like abalone shells clinging to the rocks.

"I told her you called, but she left again in a hurry," explained Praying Mantis when her father phoned yet again. The following day, before she had decided whether or not to return his call, there was a fourth phone call from the island, and when she picked up the receiver, she heard her father's hoarse voice.

"We're having lovely weather here on the island. Why don't you come for a visit? The place is full of abalone. There's a new moon now and there are always plenty of them around then."

Unable to endure this senile fantasy, she said, "As usual, the Mantis has a guest here just now."

"I see. A guest is it? I remember in the old days your mother and I used to think up all sorts of excuses for declining our parents' invitations to visit, because we wanted to meet each other instead. . . . I'll go to your mother's grave again and offer a cigarette from you. It occurs to me that you're the only one of the children who knows where that grave is, so I want you to remember how to find it." Her father hung up the phone.

Her mother had borne seven children, and not one of them had provided a monument for her grave. In her will the mother had requested that her ashes be scattered over the sea. The children had some notion that the surging waves would transform her into various shapes. But the father was disappointed by the children's devotion to their mother's will.

Soon the Pale Fox awoke. He drew the woman to him, but it was clear he did so only because he felt obliged to. Even while he longed for a woman slave, the Fox continued to treat women with respect. Understanding this pathetic dream, the woman playfully scratched his beautiful body all over and tugged at his hair.

Like a child on a visit somewhere who wants to go home, the woman longed to return to Praying Mantis. He was a strange man, devoted to that form of ecstasy peculiar to the mantis in which the male is killed and devoured by the female. He enjoyed hearing women talk about other men they had known. He was curious about women only if they displayed curiosity about men. Searching now for words that would flatter the Pale Fox, she moved about the room making gestures, throwing glances that might appeal to him. She did not have the patience for anything more; all she wanted now was to sleep, to sleep next to the Mantis with her leg thrown over his stomach. (The woman could not sleep unless her legs were slightly elevated.)

It would not do to stay with the Pale Fox until morning, and she realized that this feeling confirmed once again the reason she had recoiled from living with him seven years ago.

If he were a real fox, she could put a collar on him and fasten it to the bedpost. Yet, even then, in the morning she might find that he had disappeared, leaving only the collar lying on the bed, the chain still attached. The Pale Fox, it seemed, was always changing into something else. The woman was indifferent to the gallant youth he sometimes became; what captivated her was his true form, a fox sniffing out his prey. She liked his beautiful blue fur, his erect ears, sharp jaw, moist nose, his surprisingly long, pink tongue, bushy tail, and glittering, golden eyes. But the Fox in his true form always eluded her, escaping to the forest; she only caught glimpses of him.

Just as she was getting dressed, the Fox, too, felt a longing for his home in the forest. "We should probably be going now," he said. "I'm leaving town tomorrow," he added, "so it would be better if I went back to my own hotel tonight. I have to pack my things."

As he got up, the Pale Fox said, "Shall we go out for something to eat?" He was looking at the key that lay on the bedside table. They no longer had any use for it, since they would not be coming back to this room.

They locked the door as they went out, leaving the key behind. Outside a warm, muggy wind blew, and the large, red sun perched on the horizon directly in front of them, wrapped in a cloak of gray smog. Groups of people hurried along in the gullies through forests of tall buildings. From the expressions on their faces, they seemed to have forgotten what a dreary business it is to be faithful. In the stores where the stench of the city was blown away by air conditioners, people kept their sullen, bloated faces downturned, and shuffled aimlessly like caged animals.

The man and the woman carried on an absurd conversation. They spoke of buying a villa together on the island. Neither of them had any money, of course, and even as they talked of buying a villa, both were thinking how impossible it would be for them to live there together. As they talked, each fantasized about imaginary slaves.

While they ate their meal of raw, spiced meat, the woman saw a reflection of herself in a wall mirror. It showed a cruel, voracious insect that only slightly resembled her elderly father. The insect appeared covered with a veil of spider web, while the Fox had transformed himself into a beetle. Their wings tangled together and their conversation was meaningless.

Mother's earlobes, she remembered, had been discolored and unhealthy-looking. Had it been her sister who retrieved Mother's earrings from the ashes after the body had been cremated?

When she arrived home, the Mantis said, "There was a phone call from your sister. Something about your father. It seems something has happened. She said he was taken into protective custody yesterday by the island police. Did he seem normal the last time you saw him?"

"I didn't notice anything wrong," said the woman.

"Your sister says he should be put in an institution."

"Oh."

The father had seven children. None of those seven children was opposed to the idea of putting their father in an institution. What they had in mind was a mental hospital located on top of a hill on the island. In its advertising, the hospital used pictures of the surrounding fields in spring, clothed in a haze of yellow blossoms. Crested white butterflies fluttered over the yellow fields, and there in the midst of them stood a white building, rising like some fantastic castle. It seemed to float above the ground; a white-clad ghost without feet.

When she awoke the next morning the woman realized she had left behind at the hotel an ornamental hairpin her father had made when he was young. Her mother had given it to her as a keepsake. It was not yet check-out time, so she hurriedly caught a taxi and set off for the hotel. When she explained to the desk clerk that she had left the key in the room and locked herself out, he rang for the bellboy, but then, remembering, said, "Oh, wait a minute. Your husband came back a little while ago. I gave the key to him."

The woman was heading for the elevator when it occurred to her that he should be at his hotel packing and that he hadn't originally planned to come back. She went to the house phone and dialed.

Soft and light as a feather, the voice at the other end was clearly the Fox's. He was not a beetle now.

"Hello, it's me. I left my hairpin there, on the shelf in the bathroom. It's silver and shaped like a fish; the eyes are inlaid bits of black coral. It's a keepsake from my mother. Could you bring it to me before you check out? Or send it by registered mail."

The woman listened carefully, straining for any sign that he had another woman in the room with him, but she heard nothing. Without a word in reply the Pale Fox put down the receiver.

Two or three days later the hairpin arrived safely in a small, registered envelope. There was not even a note to go with it.

[1973]

Translated by
STEPHEN W. KOHL

QUESTIONS

1. What are the narrator's feelings toward her deceased mother? How are they manipulated by her father?
2. What connects the story of the Pale Fox (her ex-lover) with the story of her parents?
3. Is the father actually insane or is his insanity something else?
4. Why do the narrator's lovers have the names that she has given them?
5. How does the story reveal attitudes about sexual and gender roles?

Flannery O'Connor

(1925–1964)

United States

Much has been made of Flannery O'Connor's Catholic upbringing, especially in the way that religion plays such a strong importance in her novels and short stories. In "A Good Man Is Hard to Find"—probably O'Connor's most famous story—readers have often been fascinated by a kind of ironic reversal within the main characters, as if the seemingly good character (the grandmother) has lost her faith and the bad one (the Misfit) has somehow embraced a basic Christian truth: remain true to your convictions. As V. S. Pritchett has written of O'Connor's religion:

> She was an old Catholic, not a convert, in the South of the poor white of the Bible Belt, and this gave her a critical skirmishing power. But the symbolism of religion, rather than the acrimonies of sectarian dispute, fed her violent imagination—the violence is itself oddly early Protestant—as if she had seen embers of the burning Bible-fed imagery in the minds of her own characters. . . . The essence of Flannery O'Connor's vision is that she sees terror as a purification—unwanted, of course: it is never the sadomasochist's intended indulgence. The moment of purification may actually destroy; it will certainly show someone changed.

O'Connor was born in Savannah, Georgia, in 1925. She attended Georgia State College for Women in Milledgeville and subsequently attended the writer's workshop at the University of Iowa, where her talent was so obvious to other students in the program that some of them are said to have suffered from instant writer's block. In 1950 she was diagnosed as having the autoimmune disease lupus (which had killed her father nine years earlier) and, as a result, returned to Milledgeville, where she lived with her mother. Her first novel, *Wise Blood*, appeared in 1952, followed by a volume of stories, *A Good Man Is Hard to Find*, in 1955. These works were followed by *The Violent Bear It Away*, a novel published in 1964 (the year she died of lupus), and *Everything That Rises Must Converge*, published the following year. O'Connor's *Collected Stories*, published in 1972, won the National Book Award for fiction. Her entire *Collected Works* (including essays and letters) was published in a single-volume edition by The Library of America (1988).

In an essay called "The Grotesque in Southern Fiction," O'Connor wrote:

> Whenever I'm asked why Southern writers particularly have a penchant for writing about freaks, I say it is because we are still able to recognize one. To be able to recognize a freak, you have to have some conception of the whole man, and in the South the general conception of man is still, in the main, theological. That is a large statement, and it is dangerous to

make it, for almost anything you say about Southern belief can be denied in the next breath with equal propriety. But approaching the subject from the standpoint of the writer, I think it is safe to say that while the South is hardly Christ-centered, it is most certainly Christ-haunted. The Southerner who isn't convinced of it is very much afraid that he may have been formed in the image and likeness of God. Ghosts can be fierce and instructive. They cast strange shadows, particularly in our literature. In any case, it is when the freak can be sensed as a figure of our essential displacement that it attains some depth in literature.

A Good Man Is Hard to Find

The dragon is by the side of the road, watching those who pass. Beware lest he devour you. We go to the Father of Souls, but it is necessary to pass by the dragon.

—St. Cyril of Jerusalem

The grandmother didn't want to go to Florida. She wanted to visit some of her connections in east Tennessee and she was seizing at every chance to change Bailey's mind. Bailey was the son she lived with, her only boy. He was sitting on the edge of his chair at the table, bent over the orange sports section of the *Journal*. "Now look here, Bailey," she said, "see here, read this," and she stood with one hand on her thin hip and the other rattling the newspaper at his bald head. "Here this fellow that calls himself The Misfit is aloose from the Federal Pen and headed toward Florida and you read here what it says he did to these people. Just you read it. I wouldn't take my children in any direction with a criminal like that aloose in it. I couldn't answer to my conscience if I did."

Bailey didn't look up from his reading so she wheeled around then and faced the children's mother, a young woman in slacks, whose face was as broad and innocent as a cabbage and was tied around with a green headkerchief that had two points on the top like a rabbit's ears. She was sitting on the sofa, feeding the baby his apricots out of a jar. "The children have been to Florida before," the old lady said. "You all ought to take them somewhere else for a change so they would see different parts of the world and be broad. They never have been to east Tennessee."

The children's mother didn't seem to hear her but the eight-year-old boy, John Wesley, a stocky child with glasses, said, "If you don't want to go to Florida, why dontcha stay at home?" He and the little girl, June Star, were reading the funny papers on the floor.

"She wouldn't stay at home to be queen for a day," June Star said without raising her yellow head.

"Yes and what would you do if this fellow, The Misfit, caught you?" the grandmother asked.

"I'd smack his face," John Wesley said.

"She wouldn't stay at home for a million bucks," June Star said. "Afraid she'd miss something. She has to go everywhere we go."

"All right, Miss," the grandmother said. "Just remember that the next time you want me to curl your hair."

June Star said her hair was naturally curly.

The next morning the grandmother was the first one in the car, ready to go. She had her big black valise that looked like the head of a hippopotamus in one corner, and underneath it she was hiding a basket with Pitty Sing, the cat, in it. She didn't intend for the cat to be left alone in the house for three days because he would miss her too much and she was afraid he might brush against one of the gas burners and accidentally asphyxiate himself. Her son, Bailey, didn't like to arrive at a motel with a cat.

She sat in the middle of the back seat with John Wesley and June Star on either side of her. Bailey and the children's mother and the baby sat in front and they left Atlanta at eight forty-five with the mileage on the car at 55890. The grandmother wrote this down because she thought it would be interesting to say how many miles they had been when they got back. It took them twenty minutes to reach the outskirts of the city.

The old lady settled herself comfortably, removing her white cotton gloves and putting them up with her purse on the shelf in front of the back window. The children's mother still had on slacks and still had her head tied up in a green kerchief, but the grandmother had on a navy blue straw sailor hat with a bunch of white violets on the brim and a navy blue dress with a small white dot in the print. Her collars and cuffs were white organdy trimmed with lace and at her neckline she had pinned a purple spray of cloth violets containing a sachet. In case of an accident, anyone seeing her dead on the highway would know at once that she was a lady.

She said she thought it was going to be a good day for driving, neither too hot nor too cold, and she cautioned Bailey that the speed limit was fifty-five miles an hour and that the patrolmen hid themselves behind billboards and small clumps of trees and sped out after you before you had a chance to slow down. She pointed out interesting details of the scenery: Stone Mountain; the blue granite that in some places came up to both sides of the highway; the brilliant red clay banks slightly streaked with purple; and the various crops that made rows of green lace-work on the ground. The trees were full of silver-white sunlight and the meanest of them sparkled. The children were reading comic magazines and their mother had gone back to sleep.

"Let's go through Georgia fast so we won't have to look at it much," John Wesley said.

"If I were a little boy," said the grandmother, "I wouldn't talk about my native state that way. Tennessee has the mountains and Georgia has the hills."

"Tennessee is just a hillbilly dumping ground," John Wesley said, "and Georgia is a lousy state too."

"You said it," June Star said.

"In my time," said the grandmother, folding her thin veined fingers, "children were more respectful of their native states and their parents and everything else. People did right then. Oh look at the cute little pickaninny!" she said and pointed to a Negro child standing in the door of a shack. "Wouldn't that make a picture, now?" she asked and they all turned and looked at the little Negro out of the back window. He waved.

"He didn't have any britches on," June Star said.

"He probably didn't have any," the grandmother explained. "Little niggers in the country don't have things like we do. If I could paint, I'd paint that picture," she said.

The children exchanged comic books.

The grandmother offered to hold the baby and the children's mother passed him over the front seat to her. She set him on her knee and bounced him and told him about the things they were passing. She rolled her eyes and screwed up her mouth and stuck her leathery thin face into his smooth bland one. Occasionally he gave her a faraway smile. They passed a large cotton field with five or six graves fenced in the middle of it, like a small island. "Look at the graveyard!" the grandmother said, pointing it out. "That was the old family burying ground. That belonged to the plantation."

"Where's the plantation?" John Wesley asked.

"Gone with the Wind," said the grandmother. "Ha. Ha."

When the children finished all the comic books they had brought, they opened the lunch and ate it. The grandmother ate a peanut butter sandwich and an olive and would not let the children throw the box and the paper napkins out the window. When there was nothing else to do they played a game by choosing a cloud and making the other two guess what shape it suggested. John Wesley took one the shape of a cow and June Star guessed a cow and John Wesley said, no, an automobile, and June Star said he didn't play fair, and they began to slap each other over the grandmother.

The grandmother said she would tell them a story if they would keep quiet. When she told a story, she rolled her eyes and waved her head and was very dramatic. She said once when she was a maiden lady she had been courted by a Mr. Edgar Atkins Teagarden from Jasper, Georgia. She said he was a very good-looking man and a gentleman and that he brought her a watermelon every Saturday afternoon with his initials cut in it, E. A. T. Well, one Saturday, she said, Mr. Teagarden brought the watermelon and there was nobody at home and he left it on the front porch and returned in his buggy to Jasper, but she never got the watermelon, she said, because a nigger boy ate it when he saw the initials, E. A. T.! This story tickled John Wesley's funny bone and he giggled and giggled but June Star didn't think it was any good. She said she wouldn't marry a man that just brought her a watermelon on Saturday. The grandmother said she would have done well to marry Mr. Teagarden because he was a gentleman and had bought Coca-Cola stock when it first came out and that he had died only a few years ago, a very wealthy man.

They stopped at The Tower for barbecued sandwiches. The Tower was a part stucco and part wood filling station and dance hall set in a clearing outside of Timothy. A fat man named Red Sammy Butts ran it and there were signs stuck here and there on the building and for miles up and down the highway saying, TRY RED SAMMY'S FAMOUS BARBECUE. NONE LIKE FAMOUS RED SAMMY'S! RED SAM! THE FAT BOY WITH THE HAPPY LAUGH. A VETERAN! RED SAMMY'S YOUR MAN!

Red Sammy was lying on the bare ground outside the Tower with his head under a truck while a gray monkey about a foot high, chained to a small chinaberry tree, chattered nearby. The monkey sprang back into the tree and got on the highest limb as soon as he saw the children jump out of the car and run toward him.

Inside, The Tower was a long dark room with a counter at one end and tables at the other and dancing space in the middle. They all sat down at a board table next to the nickelodeon and Red Sam's wife, a tall burnt-brown woman with hair and eyes lighter than her skin, came and took their order. The children's mother put a dime in the machine and played "The Tennessee Waltz," and the grandmother said that tune always made her want to dance. She asked Bailey if he would like to dance but he only glared at her. He didn't have a naturally sunny disposition like she did and trips made him nervous. The grandmother's brown eyes were very bright. She swayed her head from side to side and pretended she was dancing in her chair. June Star said play something she could tap to so the children's mother put in another dime and played a fast number and June Star stepped out onto the dance floor and did her tap routine.

"Ain't she cute?" Red Sam's wife said, leaning over the counter. "Would you like to come be my little girl?"

"No I certainly wouldn't," June Star said. "I wouldn't live in a broken-down place like this for a million bucks!" and she ran back to the table.

"Ain't she cute?" the woman repeated, stretching her mouth politely.

"Aren't you ashamed?" hissed the grandmother.

Red Sam came in and told his wife to quit lounging on the counter and hurry up with these people's order. His khaki trousers reached just to his hip bones and his stomach hung over them like a sack of meal swaying under his shirt. He came over and sat down at a table nearby and let out a combination sigh and yodel. "You can't win," he said. "You can't win," and he wiped his sweating red face off with a gray handkerchief. "These days you don't know who to trust," he said. "Ain't that the truth?"

"People are certainly not nice like they used to be," said the grandmother.

"Two fellers come in here last week," Red Sammy said, "driving a Chrysler. It was a old beat-up car but it was a good one and these boys looked all right to me. Said they worked at the mill and you know I let them fellers charge the gas they bought? Now why did I do that?"

"Because you're a good man!" the grandmother said at once.

"Yes'm, I suppose so," Red Sam said as if he were struck with this answer.

His wife brought the orders, carrying the five plates all at once without a tray, two in each hand and one balanced on her arm. "It isn't a soul in this green world of God's that you can trust," she said. "And I don't count nobody out of that, not nobody," she repeated, looking at Red Sammy.

"Did you read about that criminal, The Misfit, that's escaped?" asked the grandmother.

"I wouldn't be a bit surprised if he didn't attack this place right here," said the woman. "If he hears about it being here, I wouldn't be none surprised to see him. If he hears it's two cent in the cash register, I wouldn't be a tall surprised if he . . ."

"That'll do," Red Sam said. "Go bring these people their Co'-Colas," and the woman went off to get the rest of the order.

"A good man is hard to find," Red Sammy said. "Everything is getting terrible. I remember the day you could go off and leave your screen door unlatched. Not no more."

He and the grandmother discussed better times. The old lady said that in her opinion Europe was entirely to blame for the way things were now. She said the way Europe acted you would think we were made of money and Red Sam said it was no use talking about it, she was exactly right. The children ran outside into the white sunlight and looked at the monkey in the lacy chinaberry tree. He was busy catching fleas on himself and biting each one carefully between his teeth as if it were a delicacy.

They drove off again into the hot afternoon. The grandmother took cat naps and woke up every few minutes with her own snoring. Outside of Toombsboro she woke up and recalled an old plantation that she had visited in this neighborhood once when she was a young lady. She said the house had six white columns across the front and that there was an avenue of oaks leading up to it and two little wooden trellis arbors on either side in front where you sat down with your suitor after a stroll in the garden. She recalled exactly which road to turn off to get to it. She knew that Bailey would not be willing to lose any time looking at an old house, but the more she talked bout it, the more she wanted to see it once again and find out if the little twin arbors were still standing. "There was a secret panel in this house," she said craftily, not telling the truth but wishing that she were, "and the story went that all the family silver was hidden in it when Sherman came through but it was never found. . . ."

"Hey!" John Wesley said. "Let's go see it! We'll find it! We'll poke all the woodwork and find it! Who lives there? Where do you turn off at? Hey Pop, can't we turn off there?"

"We never have seen a house with a secret panel!" June Star shrieked. "Let's go to the house with the secret panel! Hey Pop, can't we go see the house with the secret panel!"

"It's not far from here, I know," the grandmother said. "It won't take over twenty minutes."

Bailey was looking straight ahead. His jaw was as rigid as a horseshoe. "No." he said.

The children began to yell and scream that they wanted to see the house with the secret panel. John Wesley kicked the back of the front seat and June Star hung over her mother's shoulder and whined desperately into her ear that they never had any fun even on their vacation, that they could never do what THEY wanted to do. The baby began to scream and John Wesley kicked the back of the seat so hard that his father could feel the blows in his kidney.

"All right!" he shouted and drew the car to a stop at the side of the road. "Will you all shut up? Will you all just shut up for one second? If you don't shut up, we won't go anywhere."

"It would be very educational for them," the grandmother murmured.

"All right," Bailey said, "but get this: this is the only time we're going to stop for anything like this. This is the one and only time."

"The dirt road that you have to turn down is about a mile back," the grandmother directed. "I marked it when we passed."

"A dirt road," Bailey groaned.

After they had turned around and were headed toward the dirt road, the grandmother recalled other points about the house, the beautiful glass over the front doorway and the candle-lamp in the hall. John Wesley said that the secret panel was probably in the fireplace.

"You can't go inside this house," Bailey said. "You don't know who lives there."

"While you all talk to the people in front, I'll run around behind and get in a window," John Wesley suggested.

"We'll all stay in the car," his mother said.

They turned onto the dirt road and the car raced roughly along in a swirl of pink dust. The grandmother recalled the times when there were no paved roads and thirty miles was a day's journey. The dirt road was hilly and there were sudden washes in it and sharp curves on dangerous embankments. All at once they would be on a hill, looking down over the blue tops of trees for miles around, then the next minute, they would be in a red depression with the dust-coated trees looking down on them.

"This place had better turn up in a minute," Bailey said, "or I'm going to turn around."

The road looked as if no one had traveled on it for months.

"It's not much farther," the grandmother said and just as she said it, a horrible thought came to her. The thought was so embarrassing that she turned red in the face and her eyes dilated and her feet jumped up, upsetting her valise in the corner. The instant the valise moved, the newspaper top she had over the basket under it rose with a snarl and Pitty Sing, the cat, sprang onto Bailey's shoulder.

The children were thrown to the floor and their mother, clutching the baby was thrown out the door onto the ground, the old lady was thrown into the front seat. The car turned over once and landed right-side-up in a gulch off the side of the road. Bailey remained in the driver's seat with the cat—gray-striped with a broad white face and an orange nose—clinging to his neck like a caterpillar.

As soon as the children saw they could move their arms and legs, they scrambled out of the car, shouting, "We've had an ACCIDENT!" The grandmother was curled up under the dashboard, hoping she was injured so that Bailey's wrath would not come down on her all at once. The horrible thought she had before the accident was that the house she had remembered so vividly was not in Georgia but in Tennessee.

Bailey removed the cat from his neck with both hands and flung it out the window against the side of a pine tree. Then he got out of the car and started looking for the children's mother. She was sitting against the side of the red gutted ditch, holding the screaming baby, but she only had a cut down her face and a broken shoulder. "We've had an ACCIDENT!" the children screamed in a frenzy of delight.

"But nobody's killed," June Star said with disappointment as the grandmother limped out of the car, her hat still pinned to her head but the broken front brim standing up at a jaunty angle and the violet spray hanging off the side. They all sat down in the ditch, except the children, to recover from the shock. They were all shaking.

"Maybe a car will come along," said the children's mother hoarsely.

"I believe I have injured an organ," said the grandmother, pressing her side, but no one answered her. Bailey's teeth were clattering. He had on a yellow sport shirt with bright blue parrots designed in it and his face was as yellow as the shirt. The grandmother decided that she would not mention that the house was in Tennessee.

The road was about ten feet above and they could only see the tops of the trees on the other side of it. Behind the ditch they were sitting in there were more woods, tall and dark and deep. In a few minutes they saw a car some distance away on top of a hill, coming slowly as if the occupants were watching them. The grandmother stood up and waved both arms dramatically to attract their attention. The car continued to come on slowly, disappeared around a bend and appeared again, moving even slower, on top of the hill they had gone over. It was a big black battered hearse-like automobile. There were three men in it.

It came to a stop just over them and for some minutes, the driver looked down with a steady expressionless gaze to where they were sitting, and didn't speak. Then he turned his head and muttered something to the other two and they got out. One was a fat boy in black trousers and a red sweat shirt with a silver stallion embossed on the front of it. He moved around on the right side of them and stood staring, his mouth partly open in a kind of loose grin. The other had on khaki pants and a blue striped coat and a gray hat pulled very low, hiding most of his face. He came around slowly on the left side. Neither spoke.

The driver got out of the car and stood by the side of it, looking down at them. He was an older man than the other two. His hair was just beginning to gray and he wore silver-rimmed spectacles that gave him a scholarly look. He had a long creased face and didn't have on any shirt or undershirt. He had on blue jeans that were too tight for him and was holding a black hat and a gun. The two boys also had guns.

"We've had an ACCIDENT!" the children screamed.

The grandmother had the peculiar feeling that the bespectacled man was someone she knew. His face was as familiar to her as if she had known him all her life but she could not recall who he was. He moved away from the car and began to come down the embankment, placing his feet carefully so that he wouldn't slip. He had on tan and white shoes and no socks, and his ankles were red and thin. "Good afternoon," he said. "I see you all had you a little spill."

"We turned over twice!" said the grandmother.

"Oncet," he corrected. "We seen it happen. Try their car and see will it run, Hiram," he said quietly to the boy with the gray hat.

"What you got that gun for?" John Wesley asked. "Whatcha gonna do with that gun?"

"Lady," the man said to the children's mother, "would you mind calling them children to sit down by you? Children make me nervous. I want all you all to sit down right together there where you're at."

"What are you telling US what to do for?" June Star asked.

Behind them the line of woods gaped like a dark open mouth. "Come here," said the mother.

"Look here now," Bailey said suddenly, "we're in a predicament! We're in . . ."

The grandmother shrieked. She scrambled to her feet and stood staring. "You're The Misfit!" she said. "I recognized you at once!"

"Yes'm," the man said, smiling slightly as if he were pleased in spite of himself to be known, "but it would have been better for all of you, lady, if you hadn't of reckernized me."

Bailey turned his head sharply and said something to his mother that shocked even the children. The old lady began to cry and The Misfit reddened.

"Lady," he said, "don't you get upset. Sometimes a man says things he don't mean. I don't reckon he meant to talk to you thataway."

"You wouldn't shoot a lady, would you?" the grandmother said and removed a clean handkerchief from her cuff and began to slap at her eyes with it.

The Misfit pointed the toe of his shoe into the ground and made a little hole and then covered it up again. "I would hate to have to," he said.

"Listen," the grandmother almost screamed, "I know you're a good man. You don't look a bit like you have common blood. I know you must come from nice people!"

"Yes mam," he said, "finest people in the world." When he smiled he showed a row of strong white teeth. "God never made a finer woman than my mother and my daddy's heart was pure gold," he said. The boy with the red sweat shirt had come around behind them and was standing with his gun at his hip. The Misfit squatted down on the ground. "Watch them children, Bobby Lee," he said. "You know they make me nervous." He looked at the six of them huddled together in front of him and he seemed to be embarrassed as if he couldn't think of anything to say. "Ain't a cloud in the sky," he remarked, looking up at it. "Don't see no sun but don't see no cloud neither."

"Yes, it's a beautiful day," said the grandmother. "Listen," she said, "You shouldn't call yourself The Misfit because I know you're a good man at heart. I can just look at you and tell."

"Hush!" Bailey yelled. "Hush! Everybody shut up and let me handle this!" He was squatting in the position of a runner about to sprint forward but he didn't move.

"I pre-chate that, lady," The Misfit said and drew a little circle in the ground with the butt of his gun.

"It'll take a half a hour to fix this here car," Hiram called, looking over the raised hood of it.

"Well, first you and Bobby Lee get him and that little boy to step over yonder with you." The Misfit said, pointing to Bailey and John Wesley, "The boys want to ast you something," he said to Bailey. "Would you mind stepping back in them woods there with them?"

"Listen," Bailey began, "we're in a terrible predicament! Nobody realizes what this is," and his voice cracked. His eyes were as blue and intense as the parrots in his shirt and he remained perfectly still.

The grandmother reached up to adjust her hat brim as if she were going to the woods with him but it came off in her hand. She stood staring at it and after a second she let it fall to the ground. Hiram pulled Bailey up by the arm as if he were assisting an old man. John Wesley caught hold of his father's hand and Bobby Lee followed. They went off toward the woods and just as they reached the dark edge, Bailey turned and supporting himself against a gray naked pine trunk, he shouted, "I'll be back in a minute, Mamma, wait on me!"

"Come back this instant!" his mother shrilled but they all disappeared into the woods.

"Bailey Boy!" the grandmother called in a tragic voice but she found she was looking at The Misfit squatting on the ground in front of her. "I just know you're a good man," she said desperately. "You're not a bit common!"

"Nome, I ain't a good man," The Misfit said after a second as if he had considered her statement carefully, "but I ain't the worst in the world neither. My daddy said I was a different breed of dog from my brothers and sisters. 'You know,' Daddy said, 'it's some that can live their whole life out without asking about it and it's others has to know why it is, and this boy is one of the latters. He's going to be into everything!'" He put on his black hat and looked up suddenly and then away deep into the woods as if he were embarrassed again. "I'm sorry I don't have on a shirt before you ladies," he said, hunching his shoulders slightly. "We buried our clothes that we had on when we escaped and we're just making do until we can get better. We borrowed these from some folks we met," he explained.

"That's perfectly all right," the grandmother said. "Maybe Bailey has an extra shirt in his suitcase."

"I'll look and see terrectly," The Misfit said.

"Where are they taking him?" the children's mother screamed.

"Daddy was a card himself," The Misfit said. "You couldn't put anything over on him. He never got in trouble with the Authorities though. Just had the knack of handling them."

"You could be honest too if you'd only try," said the grandmother. "Think how wonderful it would be to settle down and live a comfortable life and not have to think about somebody chasing you all the time."

The Misfit kept scratching in the ground with the butt of his gun as if he were thinking about it. "Yes'm, somebody is always after you," he murmured.

The grandmother noticed how thin his shoulder blades were just behind his hat because she was standing up looking down at him. "Do you ever pray?" she asked.

He shook his head. All she saw was the black hat wiggle between his shoulder blades. "Nome," he said.

There was a pistol shot from the woods, followed closely by another. Then silence. The old lady's head jerked around. She could hear the wind move through the tree tops like a long satisfied insuck of breath. "Bailey Boy!" she called.

"I was a gospel singer for a while," The Misfit said. "I been most everything. Been in the arm service, both land and sea, at home and abroad, been twict married, been an undertaker, been with the railroads, plowed Mother Earth, been in a tornado, seen a man burnt alive oncet," and he looked up at the children's mother and the little girl who were sitting close together, their faces white and their eyes glassy; "I even seen a woman flogged," he said.

"Pray, pray," the grandmother began, "pray, pray. . . ."

"I never was a bad boy that I remember of," The Misfit said in an almost dreamy voice, "but somewheres along the line I done something wrong and got sent to the penitentiary. I was buried alive," and he looked up and held her attention to him by a steady stare.

"That's when you should have started to pray," she said. "What did you do to get sent to the penitentiary, that first time?"

"Turn to the right, it was a wall," The Misfit said, looking up again at the cloudless sky. "Turn to the left, it was a wall. Look up it was a ceiling, look down it was a floor. I forgot what I done, lady. I set there and set there, trying to remember what it was I done and I ain't recalled it to this day. Oncet in a while, I would think it was coming to me, but it never come."

"Maybe they put you in by mistake," the old lady said vaguely.

"Nome," he said. "It wasn't no mistake. They had the papers on me."

"You must have stolen something," she said.

The Misfit sneered slightly. "Nobody had nothing I wanted," he said. "It was a head-doctor at the penitentiary said what I had done was kill my daddy but I known that for a lie. My daddy died in nineteen ought nineteen of the epidemic flu and I never had a thing to do with it. He was buried in the Mount Hopewell Baptist churchyard and you can see for yourself."

"If you would pray," the old lady said, "Jesus would help you."

"That's right," The Misfit said.

"Well then, why don't you pray?" she asked trembling with delight suddenly.

"I don't want no hep," he said. "I'm doing all right by myself."

Bobby Lee and Hiram came ambling back from the woods. Bobby Lee was dragging a yellow shirt with bright blue parrots in it.

"Throw me that shirt, Bobby Lee," The Misfit said. The shirt came flying at him and landed on his shoulder and he put it on. The grandmother couldn't name what the shirt reminded her of. "No, lady," The Misfit said while he was buttoning it up, "I found out the crime don't matter. You can do one thing or you can do another, kill a man or take a tire off his car, because sooner or later you're going to forget what it was you done and just be punished for it."

The children's mother had begun to make heaving noises as if she couldn't get her breath. "Lady," he asked, "would you and that little girl like to step off yonder with Bobby Lee and Hiram and join your husband?"

"Yes, thank you," the mother said faintly. Her left arm dangled helplessly and she was holding the baby, who had gone to sleep, in the other. "Hep that lady up, Hiram," The Misfit said as she struggled to climb out of the ditch, "and Bobby Lee, you hold onto that little girl's hand."

"I don't want to hold hands with him," June Star said. "He reminds me of a pig."

The fat boy blushed and laughed and caught her by the arm and pulled her off into the woods after Hiram and her mother.

Alone with The Misfit, the grandmother found that she had lost her voice. There was not a cloud in the sky nor any sun. There was nothing around her but woods. She wanted to tell him that he must pray. She opened and closed her mouth several times before anything came out. Finally she found herself saying, "Jesus, Jesus," meaning, Jesus will help you, but the way she was saying it, it sounded as if she might be cursing.

"Yes'm," The Misfit said as if he agreed. "Jesus thown everything off balance. It was the same case with Him as with me except He hadn't committed any crime and they could prove I had committed one because they had the papers on me. Of course," he said, "they never shown me my papers. That's why I sign myself now. I said long ago, you get your signature and sign everything you do and keep a copy of it. Then you'll know what you done and you can hold up the crime to the punishment and see do they match and in the end you'll have something to prove you ain't been treated right. I call myself The Misfit," he said, "because I can't make what all I done wrong fit what all I gone through in punishment."

There was a piercing scream from the woods, followed closely by a pistol report. "Does it seem right to you, lady, that one is punished a heap and another ain't punished at all?"

"Jesus!" the old lady cried. "You've got good blood! I know you wouldn't shoot a lady! I know you come from nice people! Pray! Jesus, you ought not to shoot a lady. I'll give you all the money I've got!"

"Lady," The Misfit said, looking beyond her far into the woods, "there never was a body that give the undertaker a tip."

There were two more pistol reports and the grandmother raised her head like a parched old turkey hen crying for water and called, "Bailey Boy, Bailey Boy!" as if her heart would break.

"Jesus was the only One that ever raised the dead," The Misfit continued, "and He shouldn't have done it. He thrown everything off balance. If He did what He said, then it's nothing for you to do but throw away everything and follow Him, and if He didn't, then it's nothing for you to do but enjoy the few minutes you got left the best you can—by killing somebody or burning down his house or doing some other meanness to him. No pleasure but meanness," he said and his voice had become almost a snarl.

"Maybe He didn't raise the dead," the old lady mumbled, not knowing what she was saying and feeling so dizzy that she sank down in the ditch with her legs twisted under her.

"I wasn't there so I can't say He didn't," The Misfit said. "I wisht I had of been there," he said, hitting the ground with his fist. "It ain't right I wasn't there because if I had of been there I would of known. Listen lady," he said in a high voice, "if I had of been there I would of known and I wouldn't be like I am now." His voice seemed about to crack and the grandmother's head cleared for an instant. She saw the man's face twisted close to her own as if he were going to cry and she murmured, "Why you're one of my babies. You're one of my own children!" She reached out and touched him on the shoulder. The Misfit sprang back as if a snake had bitten him and shot her three times through the chest. Then he put his gun down on the ground and took off his glasses and began to clean them.

Hiram and Bobby Lee returned from the woods and stood over the ditch, looking down at the grandmother who half sat and half lay in a puddle of blood with her legs crossed under her like a child's and her face smiling up at the cloudless sky.

Without his glasses, The Misfit's eyes were red-rimmed and pale and defenseless-looking. "Take her off and throw her where you thrown the others," he said, picking up the cat that was rubbing itself against his leg.

"She was a talker, wasn't she?" Bobby Lee said, sliding down the ditch with a yodel.

"She would of been a good woman," The Misfit said, "if it had been somebody there to shoot her every minute of her life."

"Some fun!" Bobby Lee said.

"Shut up, Bobby Lee," The Misfit said. "It's no real pleasure in life."

[1955]

QUESTIONS

1. At what place in the story do your sympathies with the grandmother turn against her?
2. What is the Misfit's philosophy of life?
3. Is there too much coincidence in the story?
4. What does the final dialogue between Bobby Lee and the Misfit (after the grandmother's death) mean?
5. What is O'Connor's concept of a good man?

Ōe Kenzaburo

(b. 1935)

Japan

Although he doesn't use the term, John Nathan (Ōe Kenzaburo's American translator) describes the writer in his introduction to *Teach Us to Outgrow Our Madness* as the *enfant terrible* of contemporary Japanese writing. Ōe's novels have won him every major Japanese literary prize, and yet his work is still relatively unknown in the United States. The loss is ours, because Ōe's affinities with American writing and his fascination with American culture should guarantee a natural bond. In "Prize Stock," for example—a story influenced by Mark Twain's *Huckleberry Finn*—the main character is a young Japanese boy during World War II who takes care of an American GI who has crash-landed his airplane in the boy's village. The fascination of the story, and indeed its power to thoroughly engage us, is due to the fact that the GI is an African American and that the boy/narrator learns to distrust the adults around him, just as Huck does in Mark Twain's masterpiece.

For an understanding of "Aghwee the Sky Monster," it is significant to realize that Ōe's first child was born with brain damage in 1964. John Nathan tells us, ". . . the baby boy, whom he called 'Pooh,' altered his world with the force of an exploding sun. I won't presume to describe Ōe's relationship with the child. . . . Suffice it to say that over the years as Pooh grew up, a fierce, exclusive, isolating bond developed between father and son. In a fervent, painful way, Ōe and his fragile, autistic child became one another's best, embracing one another as if they were each other's fate. Shortly after Pooh was born, Ōe ordered two gravestones erected side by side in the cemetery in his native village. He has told me many times that he would die when Pooh died."

Ōe Kenzaburo was born in 1935. He majored in French at Tokyo University and has often been regarded as an unofficial spokesman for the New Left.

• *Aghwee the Sky Monster* •

Alone in my room, I wear a piratical black patch over my right eye. The eye may look all right, but the truth is I have scarcely any sight in it. I say scarcely, it isn't totally blind. Consequently, when I look at this world with both eyes I see two worlds perfectly superimposed, a vague and shadowy world on top of one that's bright and vivid. I can be walking down a paved street when a sense of peril and unbalance will stop me like a rat just scurried out of a sewer, dead in my tracks. Or I'll discover a film of unhappiness and fatigue on the face of a cheerful friend and clog the flow of an easy chat with my stutter. I suppose I'll get used to this eventually. If I don't, I intend to wear my patch not only in my room when I'm alone but on the street and with my friends. Strangers may pass with condescending smiles—what an old-fashioned joke!—but I'm old enough not to be annoyed by every little thing.

The story I intend to tell is about my first experience earning money; I began with my right eye because the memory of that experience ten years ago revived in me abruptly and quite out of context when violence was done to my eye last spring. Remembering, I should add, I was freed from the hatred uncoiling in my heart and beginning to fetter me. At the very end I'll talk about the accident itself.

Ten years ago I had twenty-twenty vision. Now one of my eyes is ruined. *Time* shifted, launched itself from the springboard of an eyeball squashed by a stone. When I first met that sentimental madman I had only a child's understanding of *time*. I was yet to have the cruel awareness of *time* drilling its eyes into my back and *time* lying in wait ahead.

Ten years ago I was eighteen, five feet six, one hundred and ten pounds, had just entered college and was looking for a part-time job. Although I still had trouble reading French, I wanted a cloth-bound edition in two volumes of *L'Âme Enchanté*.[1] It was a Moscow edition, with not only a foreword but footnotes and even the colophon in Russian and wispy lines like bits of thread connecting the letters of the French text. A curious edition to be sure, but sturdier and more elegant than the French, and much cheaper. At the time I discovered it in a bookstore specializing in East European publications I had no interest in Romain Rolland, yet I went immediately into action to make the volumes mine. In those days I often succumbed to some weird passion and it never bothered me, I had the feeling there was nothing to worry about so long as I was sufficiently obsessed.

As I had just entered college and wasn't registered at the employment center, I looked for work by making the rounds of people I knew. Finally my uncle introduced me to a banker who came up with an offer. "Did you happen to see a movie called *Harvey*?" he asked. I said yes, and tried for a smile of moderate but unmistakable dedication, appropriate for someone about to be employed for the first time. *Harvey* was that Jimmy Stewart film about a man living with an imaginary rabbit as big as a bear; it had made me laugh so hard I thought I would die. "Recently, my son has been having the same sort of delusions about living with a monster." The banker didn't return my smile. "He's stopped working and stays in his room. I'd like him to get out from time to time but of course he'd need a—companion. Would you be interested?"

I knew quite a bit about the banker's son. He was a young composer whose avant-garde music had won prizes in France and Italy and who was generally included in the photo roundups in the weekly magazines, the kind of article they always called "Japan's Artists of Tomorrow." I had never heard his major works, but I had seen several films he had written the music for. There was one about the adventures of a juvenile delinquent that had a short, lyrical theme played on the harmonica. It was beautiful. Watching the picture, I remember feeling vaguely troubled by the idea of an adult nearly thirty years old (in fact, the composer was twenty-eight when he hired me, my present age), working out a

[1]*L'Âme Enchanté* French: *The Enchanted Soul*

theme for the harmonica, I suppose because my own harmonica had become my little brother's property when I had entered elementary school. And possibly because I knew more about the composer, whose name was D, than just public facts; I knew he had created a scandal. Generally I have nothing but contempt for scandals, but I knew that the composer's infant child had died, that he had gotten divorced as a result, and that he was rumored to be involved with a certain movie actress. I hadn't known that he was in the grips of something like the rabbit in Jimmy Stewart's movie, or that he had stopped working and secluded himself in his room. How serious was his condition, I wondered, was it a case of nervous breakdown, or was he clearly schizophrenic?

"I'm not certain I know just what you mean by companion," I said, reeling in my smile. "Naturally, I'd like to be of service if I can." This time, concealing my curiosity and apprehension I tried to lend my voice and expression as much sympathy as possible without seeming forward. It was only a part-time job, but it was the first chance of employment I had had and I was determined to do my accommodating best.

"When my son decides he wants to go somewhere in Tokyo, you go along—just that. There's a nurse at the house and she has no trouble handling him, so you don't have to worry about violence." The banker made me feel like a soldier whose cowardice had been discovered. I blushed and said, trying to recover lost ground, "I'm fond of music, and I respect composers more than anyone, so I look forward to accompanying D and talking with him."

"All he thinks about these days is this thing in his head, and apparently that's all he talks about!" The banker's brusqueness made my face even redder. "You can go out to see him tomorrow," he said.

"At—your house?"

"That's right, did you think he was in an asylum?" From the banker's tone of voice I could only suppose that he was at bottom a nasty man.

"If I should get the job," I said with my eyes on the floor, "I'll drop by again to thank you." I could easily have cried.

"No, he'll be hiring you (All right then, I resolved defiantly, I'll call D my employer), so that won't be necessary. All I care about is that he doesn't get into any trouble outside that might develop into a scandal. . . . There's his career to think about. Naturally, what he does reflects on me—"

So that was it! I thought, so I was to be a moral sentinel guarding the banker's family against a second contamination by the poisons of scandal. Of course I didn't say a thing, I only nodded dependably, anxious to warm the banker's chilly heart with the heat of reliance on me. I didn't even ask the most pressing question, something truly difficult to ask: This monster haunting your son, sir, is it a rabbit like Harvey, nearly six feet tall? A creature covered in bristly hair like an Abominable Snowman? What kind of a monster is it? In the end I remained silent and consoled myself with the thought that I might be able to pry the secret out of the nurse if I made friends with her.

Then I left the executive's office, and as I walked along the corridor grinding my teeth in humiliation as if I were Julien Sorel after a meeting with someone important I became self-conscious to the tips of my fingers and tried assessing my attitude and its effectiveness. When I got out of college I chose not to seek nine-to-five employment, and I do believe the memory of my dialogue with that disagreeable banker played a large part in my decision.

Even so, when classes were over the next day I took a train out to the residential suburb where the composer lived. As I passed through the gate of that castle of a house, I remember a roaring of terrific beasts, as at a zoo in the middle of the night. I was dismayed, I cowered, what if those were the screams of my employer? A good thing it didn't occur to me then that those savage screams might have been coming from the monster haunting D like Jimmy Stewart's rabbit. Whatever they were, it was so clear that the screaming had rattled me that the maid showing me the way was indiscreet enough to break into a laugh. Then I discovered someone else laughing, voicelessly, in the dimness beyond a window in an annex in the garden. It was the man who was supposed to employ me; he was laughing like a face in a movie without a sound track. And boiling all around him was that howling of wild beasts. I listened closely and realized that several of the same animals were shrieking in concert. And in voices too shrill to be of this world. Abandoned by the maid at the entrance to the annex, I decided the screaming must be part of the composer's tape collection, regained my courage, straightened up and opened the door.

Inside, the annex reminded me of a kindergarten. There were no partitions in the large room, only two pianos, an electric organ, several tape recorders, a record player, something we had called a "mixer" when I was in the high-school radio club—there was hardly room to step. A dog asleep on the floor, for example, turned out to be a tuba of reddish brass. It was just as I had imagined a composer's studio; I even had the illusion I had seen the place before. His father had said D had stopped working and secluded himself in his room, could he have been mistaken?

The composer was just bending to switch off the tape recorder. Enveloped in a chaos that was not without its own order, he moved his hands swiftly and in an instant those beastly screams were sucked into a dark hole of silence. Then he straightened and turned to me with a truly tranquil smile.

Having glanced around the room and seen that the nurse was not present I was a little wary, but the composer gave me no reason in the world to expect that he was about to get violent.

"My father told me about you. Come in, there's room over there," he said in a low, resonant voice.

I took off my shoes and stepped up onto the rug without putting on slippers. Then I looked around for a place to sit, but except for a round stool in front of the piano and the organ, there wasn't a bit of furniture in the room, not even a cushion. So I brought my feet together between a pair of bongo drums and some empty tape boxes and there I stood uncomfortably. The composer stood there too, arms hanging at his sides. I wondered if he ever sat down. He didn't ask me to be seated either, just stood there silent and smiling.

"Could those have been monkey voices?" I said, trying to crack a silence that threatened to set more quickly than any cement.

"Rhinoceros—they sounded that way because I speeded the machine up. And I had the volume way up, too. At least I think they're rhinoceros—rhino is what I asked for when I had this tape made—of course I can't really be sure. But now that you're here, I'll be able to go to the zoo myself."

"I may take that to mean that I'm employed?"

"Of course! I didn't have you come out here to test you. How can a lunatic test a normal person?" The man who was to be my employer said this objectively and almost as if he were embarrassed. Which made me feel disgusted with the obsequiousness of what I had said—I may take that to mean that I'm employed?

I had sounded like a shopkeeper! The composer was different from his businessman father and I should have been more direct with him.

"I wish you wouldn't call yourself a lunatic. It's awkward for me." Trying to be frank was one thing, but what a brainless remark! But the composer met me half way, "All right, if that's how you feel. I suppose that would make work easier."

Work is a vague word, but, at least during those few months when I was visiting him once a week, the composer didn't get even as close to work as going to the zoo to record a genuine rhino for himself. All he did was wander around Tokyo in various conveyances or on foot and visit a variety of places. When he mentioned work, he must therefore have had me in mind. And I worked quite a lot; I even went on a mission for him all the way to Kyoto.

"Then when should I begin?" I said.

"Right away if it suits you. Now."

"That suits me fine."

"I'll have to get ready—would you wait outside?"

Head lowered cautiously, as though he were walking in a swamp, my employer picked his way to the back of the room past musical instruments and sound equipment and piles of manuscript to a black wooden door which he opened and then closed behind him. I got a quick look at a woman in a nurse's uniform, a woman in her early forties with a longish face and heavy shadows on her cheeks that might have been wrinkles or maybe scars. She seemed to encircle the composer with her right arm as she ushered him inside, while with her left hand she closed the door. If this was part of the routine, I would never have a chance to talk with the nurse before I went out with my employer. Standing in front of the closed door, in the darkest part of that dim room, I shuffled into my shoes and felt my anxiety about this job of mine increase. The composer had smiled the whole time and when I had prompted him he had replied. But he hadn't volunteered much. Should I have been more reserved? Since outside might have meant two things and since I was determined that everything should be perfect on my first job, I decided to wait just inside the main gate, from where I could see the annex in the garden.

D was a small, thin man, but with a head that seemed larger than most. To make the bony cliff of his forehead look a little less forbidding he combed his pale, well-washed, and fluffy hair down over his brow. His mouth and jaw were small, and his teeth were horribly irregular. And yet, probably due to the color of his deeply recessed eyes, there was a static correctness about his face that went well with a tranquil smile. As for the overall impression, there was something canine about the man. He wore flannel trousers and a sweater with stripes like fleas. His shoulders were a little stooped, his arms outlandishly long.

When he came out of the back door of the annex, my employer was wearing a blue wool cardigan over his other sweater and a pair of white tennis shoes. He reminded me of a grade-school music teacher. In one hand he held a black scarf, and as if he were puzzling whether to wrap it around his neck, there was perplexity in his grin to me as I waited at the gate. For as long as I knew D, except at the very end when he was lying in a hospital bed, he was always dressed this way. I remember his outfit so well because I was always struck by something comical about an adult man wearing a cardigan around his shoulders, as if he were a woman in disguise. Its shapelessness and nondescript color made that sweater perfect for him. As the composer pigeon-toed toward me past the shrubbery, he absently lifted the hand that held the scarf and signaled me with it. Then he wrapped the scarf resolutely around his neck. It was already four in the afternoon and fairly cold out-of-doors.

D went through the gate, and as I was following him (our relationship was already that of employer and employee) I had the feeling I was being watched and turned around: behind the same window through which I had discovered my employer, that forty-year-old nurse with the scarred—or were they wrinkled?—cheeks was watching us the way a soldier remaining behind might see a deserter off, her lips clamped shut like a turtle's. I resolved to get her alone as soon as I could to question her about D's condition. What was wrong with the woman, anyway? Here she was taking care of a young man with a nervous condition, maybe a madman, yet when her charge went out she had nothing to say to his companion! Wasn't that professional negligence? Wasn't she at least obliged to fill in the new man on the job? Or was my employer a patient so gentle and harmless that nothing had to be said?

When he got to the sidewalk D shuttered open his tired-looking eyes in their deep sockets and glanced swiftly up and down the deserted, residential street. I didn't know whether it was an indication of madness or what—sudden action without any continuity seemed to be a habit of his. The composer looked up at the clear, end-of-autumn sky, blinking rapidly. Though they were sunken, there was something remarkably expressive about his deep brown eyes. Then he stopped blinking and his eyes seemed to focus, as though he were searching the sky. I stood obliquely behind him, watching, and what impressed me most vividly was the movement of his Adam's apple, which was large as any fist. I wondered if he had been destined to become a large man; perhaps something had impeded his growth in infancy and now only his head from the neck up bespoke the giant he was meant to be.

Lowering his gaze from the sky, my employer found and held my puzzled eyes with his own and said casually, but with a gravity that made objection impossible, "On a clear day you can see things floating up there very well. He's up there with them, and frequently he comes down to me when I go outdoors."

Instantly I felt threatened. Looking away from my employer, I wondered how to survive this first ordeal that had confronted me so quickly. Should I pretend to believe in "him," or would that be a mistake? Was I dealing with a raving madman, or was the composer just a poker-faced humorist trying to have some fun with me? As I stood there in distress, he extended me a helping hand: "I know you can't see the figures floating in the sky, and I know you wouldn't be aware of him even if he were right here at my side. All I ask is that you don't act amazed when he comes down to earth, even if I talk to him. Because you'd upset him if you were to break out laughing all of a sudden or tried to shut me up. And if you happen to notice when we're talking that I want some support from you, I'd appreciate it if you'd chime right in and say something, you know, affirmative. You see, I'm explaining Tokyo to him as if it were a paradise. It might seem a lunatic paradise to you, but maybe you could think of it as a satire and be affirmative anyway, at least when he's down here with me."

I listened carefully and thought I could make out at least the contours of what my employer expected of me. Then was he a rabbit as big as a man after all, nesting in the sky? But that wasn't what I asked; I permitted myself to ask only: "How will I know when he's down here with you?"

"Just by watching me; he only comes down when I'm outside."

"How about when you're in a car?"

"In a car or a train, as long as I'm next to an open window he's likely to show up. There have been times when he's appeared when I was in the house, just standing next to an open window."

"And . . . right now?" I asked uncomfortably. I must have sounded like the class dunce who simply cannot grasp the multiplication principle.

"Right now it's just you and me," my employer said graciously. "Why don't we ride in to Shinjuku today; I haven't been on a train in a long time."

We walked to the station, and all the way I kept an eye peeled for a sign that something had appeared at my employer's side. But before I knew it we were on the train and, so far as I could tell, nothing had materialized. One thing I did notice: the composer ignored the people who passed us on the street even when they greeted him. As if he himself did not exist, as if the people who approached with hellos and how-are-yous were registering an illusion which they mistook for him, my employer utterly ignored all overtures to contact.

The same thing happened at the ticket window; D declined to relate to other people. Handing me one thousand yen he told me to buy tickets, and then refused to take his own even when I held it out to him. I had to stop at the gate and have both our tickets punched while D swept through the turnstile onto the platform with the freedom of the invisible man. Even on the train, he behaved as if the other passengers were no more aware of him than of the atmosphere; huddling in a seat in the farthest corner of the car, he rode in silence with his eyes closed. I stood in front of him and watched in growing apprehension for whatever it was to float in through the open window and settle at his side. Naturally, I didn't believe in the monster's existence. It was just that I was determined not to miss the instant when D's delusions took hold of him; I felt I owed him that much in return for the money he was paying me. But, as it happened, he sat like some small animal playing dead all the way to Shinjuku Station, so I could only surmise that he hadn't had a visit from the sky. Of course, supposition was all it was: as long as other people were around us, my employer remained a sullen oyster of silence. But I learned soon enough that my guess had been correct. Because when the moment came it was more than apparent (from D's reaction, I mean) that something was visiting him.

We had left the station and were walking down the street. It was that time of day a little before evening when not many people are out, yet we ran across a small crowd gathered on a corner. We stopped to look; surrounded by the crowd, an old man was turning around and around in the street without a glance at anyone. A dignified-looking old man, he was spinning in a frenzy, clutching a briefcase and an umbrella to his breast, mussing his gray, pomaded hair a little as he stamped his feet and barked like a seal. The faces in the watching crowd were lusterless and dry in the evening chill that was stealing into the air; the old man's face alone was flushed, and sweating, and seemed about to steam.

Suddenly I noticed that D, who should have been standing at my side, had taken a few steps back and had thrown one arm around the shoulders of an invisible something roughly his own height. Now he was peering affectionately into the space slightly above the empty circle of his arm. The crowd was too intent on the old man to be concerned with D's performance, but I was terrified. Slowly the composer turned to me, as if he wanted to introduce me to a friend. I didn't know how to respond; all I could do was panic and blush. It was like forgetting your silly lines in the junior high school play. The composer continued to stare at me, and now there was annoyance in his eyes. He was seeking an explanation for that intent old man turning singlemindedly in the street for the benefit of his visitor from the sky. A paradisical explanation! But all I could do was wonder stupidly whether the old man might have been afflicted with Saint Vitus' dance.

When I sadly shook my head in silence, the light of inquiry went out of my employer's eyes. As if he were taking leave of a friend, he dropped his arm. Then he slowly shifted his gaze skyward until his head was all the way back and his large Adam's apple stood out in bold relief. The phantom had soared back into the sky and I was ashamed; I hadn't been equal to my job. As I stood there with my head hanging, the composer stepped up to me and indicated that my first day of work was at an end: "We can go home, now. He's come down today already, and you must be pretty tired." I did feel exhausted after all that tension.

We rode back in a taxi with the windows rolled up, and as soon as I'd been paid for the day, I left. But I didn't go straight to the station; I waited behind a telephone pole diagonally across from the house. Dusk deepened, the sky turned the color of a rose, and just as the promise of night was becoming fact, the nurse, in a short-skirted, one-piece dress of a color indistinct in the dimness, appeared through the main gate pushing a brand-new bicycle in front of her. Before she could get on the bicycle, I ran over to her. Without her nurse's uniform, she was just an ordinary little woman in her early forties; vanished from her face was the mystery I had discovered through the annex window. And my appearance had unsettled her. She couldn't climb on the bike and pedal away, but neither would she stand still; she had begun to walk the bike along when I demanded that she explain our mutual employer's condition. She resisted, peevishly, but I had a good grip on the bicycle seat and so in the end she gave in. When she began to talk, her formidable lower jaw snapped shut at each break in the sentence; she was absolutely a talking turtle.

"He says it's a fat baby in a white cotton nightgown. Big as a kangaroo, he says. It's supposed to be afraid of dogs and policemen and it comes down out of the sky. He says its name is Aghwee! Let me tell you something, if you happen to be around when that spook gets hold of him, you'd better just play dumb, you can't afford to get involved. Don't forget, you're dealing with a looney! And another thing, don't you take him anyplace funny, even if he wants to go. On top of everything else, a little gonorrhea is all we need around here!"

I blushed and let go of the bicycle seat. The nurse, jangling her bell, pedaled away into the darkness as fast as she could go with legs as round and thin as handlebars. Ah, a fat baby in a white cotton nightgown, big as a kangaroo!

When I showed up at the house the following week, the composer fixed me with those clear brown eyes of his and rattled me by saying, though not especially in reproof, "I hear you waited for the nurse and asked her about my visitor from the sky. You really take your work seriously."

That afternoon we took the same train in the opposite direction, into the country for half an hour to an amusement park on the banks of the Tama river. We tried all kinds of rides and, luckily for me, the baby as big as a kangaroo dropped out of the sky to visit D when he was up by himself in the Sky Sloop, wooden boxes shaped like boats that were hoisted slowly into the air on the blades of a kind of windmill. From a bench on the ground, I watched the composer talking with an imaginary passenger at his side. And until his visitor had climbed back into the sky, D refused to come down; again and again a signal from him sent me running to buy him another ticket.

Another incident that made an impression on me that day occurred as we were crossing the amusement park toward the exit, when D accidentally stepped in some wet cement. When he saw that his foot had left an imprint he became abnormally irritated, and until I had negotiated with the workmen, paid them something for their pains and had the footprint troweled away, he stubbornly refused to move from the spot. This was the only time the composer ever revealed to me the least violence in his nature. On the way home on the train, I suppose because he regretted having barked at me, he excused himself in this way: "I'm not living in present time anymore, at least not consciously. Do you know the rule that governs trips into the past in a time machine? For example, a man who travels back ten thousand years in time doesn't dare do anything in that world that might remain behind him. Because he doesn't exist in time ten thousand years ago, and if he left anything behind him there the result would be a warp, infinitely slight maybe but still a warp, in all of history from then until now, ten thousand years of it. That's the way the rule goes, and since I'm not living in present time, I mustn't do anything here in this world that might remain or leave an imprint."

"But why have you stopped living in present time?" I asked, and my employer sealed himself up like a golf ball and ignored me. I regretted my loose tongue; I had finally exceeded the limits permitted me, because I was too concerned with D's problem. Maybe the nurse was right; playing dumb was the only way, and I couldn't afford to get involved. I resolved not to.

We walked around Tokyo a number of times after that, and my new policy was a success. But the day came when the composer's problems began to involve me whether I liked it or not. One afternoon we got into a cab together and, for the first time since I had taken the job, D mentioned a specific destination, a swank apartment house designed like a hotel in Daikan Yama. When we arrived, D waited in the coffee shop in the basement while I went up the elevator alone to pick up a package that was waiting for me. I was to be given the package by D's former wife, who was living alone in the apartment now.

I knocked on a door that made me think of the cell blocks at Sing Sing (I was always going to the movies in those days; I have the feeling about ninety-five percent of what I knew came directly from the movies) and it was opened by a short woman with a pudgy red face on top of a neck that was just as pudgy and as round as a cylinder. She ordered me to take my shoes off and step inside, and pointed to a sofa near the window where I was to sit. This must be the way high society receives a stranger, I remember thinking at the time. For me, the son of a poor farmer, refusing her invitation and asking for the package at the door would have taken the courage to defy Japanese high society, the courage of that butcher who threatened Louis XIV. I did as I was told, and stepped for the first time in my life into a studio apartment in the American style.

The composer's former wife poured me some beer. She seemed somewhat older than D, and although she gestured grandly and intoned when she spoke, she was too round and overweight to achieve dignity. She was wearing a dress of some heavy cloth with the hem of the skirt unraveled in the manner of a squaw costume, and her necklace of diamonds set in gold looked like the work of an Inca craftsman (now that I think about it, these observations, too, smell distinctly of the movies). Her window overlooked the streets of Shibuya, but the light pouring through it into the room seemed to bother her terrifically; she was continually shifting in her chair, showing me legs as round and bloodshot as her neck, while she questioned me in the voice of a prosecutor. I suppose I was her only source of information about her former husband. Sipping my black, bitter beer as if it were hot coffee, I answered her as best I could, but my knowledge of D was scant and inaccurate and I couldn't satisfy her. Then she started asking about D's actress girl friend, whether she came to see him and things like that, and there was nothing I could say. Annoyed, I thought to myself, what business was it of hers, didn't she have any woman's pride?

"Does D still see that Phantom?"

"Yes, it's a baby the size of a kangaroo in a white cotton nightgown and he says its name is Aghwee, the nurse was telling me about it," I said enthusiastically, glad to encounter a question I could do justice to. "It's usually floating in the sky, but sometimes it flies down to D's side."

"Aghwee, you say. Then it must be the ghost of our dead baby. You know why he calls it Aghwee? Because our baby spoke only once while it was alive and that was what it said—Aghwee. That's a pretty mushy way to name the ghost that's haunting you, don't you think?" The woman spoke derisively; an ugly, corrosive odor reached me from her mouth. "Our baby was born with a lump on the back of its head that made it look as if it had two heads. The doctor diagnosed it as a brain hernia. When D heard the news he decided to protect himself and me from a catastrophe, so he got together with the doctor and they killed the baby—I think they only gave it sugar water instead of milk no matter how loud it screamed. My husband killed the baby because he didn't want us to be saddled with a child who could only function as a vegetable, which is what the doctor had predicted! So he was acting out of fantastic egotism more than anything else. But then there was an autopsy and the lump turned out to be a benign tumor. That's when D began seeing ghosts; you see he'd lost the courage he needed to sustain his egotism, so he declined to live his own life, just as he had declined to let the baby go on living. Not that he committed suicide, he just fled from reality into a world of phantoms. But once your hands are all bloody with a baby's murder, you can't get them clean again just by running from reality, anybody knows that. So here he is, hands as filthy as ever and carrying on about Aghwee."

The cruelness of her criticism was hard to bear, for my employer's sake. So I turned to her, redder in the face than ever with the excitement of her own loquacity, and struck a blow for D. "Where were you while all this was going on? You were the mother, weren't you?"

"I had a Caesarean, and for a week afterwards I was in a coma with a high fever. It was all over when I woke up," said D's former wife, leaving my gauntlet on the floor. Then she stood up and moved toward the kitchen. "I guess you'll have some more beer?"

"No, thank you, I've had enough. Would you please give me the package I'm supposed to take to D?"

"Of course, just let me gargle. I have to gargle every ten minutes, for pyorrhea—you must have noticed the smell?"

D's former wife put a brass key into a business envelope and handed it to me. Standing behind me while I tied my shoes, she asked what school I went to and then said proudly: "I hear there's not even one subscriber to the *T——Times* in the dormitories there. You may be interested to know that my father will own that paper soon."

I let silence speak for my contempt.

I was about to get into the elevator when doubt knifed through me as though my chest were made of butter. I had to think. I let the elevator go and decided to use the stairs. If his former wife had described D's state of mind correctly, how could I be sure he wouldn't commit suicide with a pinch of cyanide or something taken from a box this key unlocked? All the way down the stairs I wondered what to do, and then I was standing in front of D's table and still hadn't arrived at a conclusion. The composer sat there with his eyes tightly shut, his tea untouched on the table. I suppose it wouldn't do for him to be seen drinking materials from this time now that he had stopped living in it and had become a traveler from another.

"I saw her," I began, resolved all of a sudden to lie, "and we were talking all this time but she wouldn't give me anything."

My employer looked up at me placidly and said nothing, though doubt clouded his puppy eyes in their deep sockets. All the way back in the cab I sat in silence at his side, secretly perturbed. I wasn't sure whether he had seen through my lie. In my shirt pocket the key was heavy.

But I only kept it for a week. For one thing, the idea of D's suicide began to seem silly; for another, I was worried he might ask his wife about the key. So I put it in a different envelope and mailed it to him special delivery. The next day I went out to the house a little worried and found my employer in the open space in front of the annex, burning a pile of scores in manuscript. They must have been his own compositions: that key had unlocked the composer's music.

We didn't go out that day. Instead I helped D incinerate his whole opus. We had burned everything and had dug a hole and I was burying the ashes when suddenly D began to whisper. The phantom had dropped out of the sky. And until it left I continued working, slowly burying those ashes. That afternoon Aghwee (and there was no denying it was a mushy name) the monster from the sky remained at my employer's side for fully twenty minutes.

From that day on, since I either stepped to one side or dropped behind whenever the baby phantom appeared, the composer must have realized that I was complying with only the first of his original instructions, not to act amazed, while his request that I back him up with something affirmative was consistently ignored. Yet he seemed satisfied, and so my job was made easier. I couldn't believe D was the kind of person to create a disturbance in the street; in fact his father's warning began to seem ridiculous, our tours of Tokyo together continued so uneventfully. I had already purchased the Moscow edition of *L'Âme Enchanté* I wanted, but I no longer had any intention of giving up such a wonderful job. My employer and I went everywhere together. D wanted to visit all the concert halls where works of his had been performed and all the schools he had ever been to. We would make special trips to places he had once enjoyed himself—bars, movie theaters, indoor swimming pools—and then we would turn back without going inside. And the composer had a passion for all of Tokyo's many forms of public transportation: I'm sure we rode the entire metropolitan subway system. Since the monster baby couldn't descend from the sky while we were underground, I could enjoy the subway in peace of mind. Naturally, I tensed whenever we encountered dogs or officers of the law, remembering what the nurse had told me, but those encounters never coincided with an appearance by Aghwee. I discovered that I was loving my job. Not loving my employer or his phantom baby the size of a kangaroo. Simply loving my job.

One day the composer approached me about making a trip for him. He would pay traveling expenses, and my daily wage would be doubled; since I would have to stay overnight in a hotel and wouldn't be back until the second day, I would actually be earning four times what I usually made. Not only that, the purpose of the trip was to meet D's former girlfriend the movie actress in D's place. I accepted eagerly, I was delighted. And so began that comic and pathetic journey.

D gave me the name of the hotel the actress had mentioned in a recent letter and the date she was expecting him to arrive. Then he had me learn a message to the girl: my employer was no longer living in present time; he was like a traveler who had arrived here in a time machine from a world ten thousand years in the future. Accordingly, he couldn't permit himself to create a new existence with his own signature on it through such acts as writing letters.

I memorized the message, and then it was late at night and I was sitting opposite a movie actress in the basement bar of a hotel in Kyoto, with a chance first to explain why D hadn't come himself, next to persuade his mistress of his conception of time, and finally to deliver his message. I concluded: "D would like you to be careful not to confuse his recent divorce with another divorce he once promised you he would get; and since he isn't living in present time anymore, he says it's only natural that he won't be seeing you again." I felt my face color; for the first time I had the sensation that I had a truly difficult job.

"Is that what D-boy says? And what do you say? How do you feel about all this that you'd run an errand all the way to Kyoto?"

"Frankly, I think D is being mushy."

"That's the way he is—I'd say he's being pretty mushy with you, too, asking this kind of favor!"

"I'm employed; I get paid by the day for what I do."

"What are you drinking there? Have some brandy."

I did. Until then I'd been drinking the same dark beer D's former wife had given me, with an egg in it to thin it down. By some queer carom of a psychological billiard, I'd been influenced by a memory from D's former wife's apartment while waiting to meet his mistress. The actress had been drinking brandy all along. It was the first imported brandy I'd ever had.

"And what's all this about D-boy seeing a ghost, a baby as big as a kangaroo? What did you call it, Raghbee?"

"Aghwee! The baby only spoke once before it died and that was what it said."

"And D thought it was telling him its name? Isn't that darling! If that baby had been normal, it was all decided that D was going to get a divorce and marry me. The day the baby was born we were in bed together in a hotel room and there was a phone call and then we knew something awful had happened. D jumped out of bed and went straight to the hospital. Not a word from him since—" The actress gulped her brandy down, filled her glass to the brim from the bottle of Hennessy on the table as if she were pouring fruit juice, and drained her glass again.

Our table was hidden from the bar by a display case full of cigarettes. Hanging on the wall above my shoulder was a large color poster with the actress's picture on it, a beer advertisement. The face in the poster glittered like gold, no less than the beer. The girl sitting opposite me was not quite so dazzling, there was even a depression in her forehead, just below the hairline, that looked deep enough to contain an adult thumb. But it was precisely the fault that made her more appealing than her picture.

She couldn't get the baby off her mind.

"Look, wouldn't it be terrifying to die without memories or experiences because you'd never done anything human while you were alive? That's how it would be if you died as an infant—wouldn't that be terrifying?"

"Not to the baby, I don't imagine," I said deferentially.

"But think about the world after death!" The actress's logic was full of leaps.

"The world after death?"

"If there is such a thing, the souls of the dead must live there with their memories for all eternity. But what about the soul of a baby who never knew anything and never had any experiences? I mean what memories can it have?"

At a loss, I drank my brandy in silence.

"I'm terribly afraid of death so I'm always thinking about it—you don't have to be disgusted with yourself because you don't have a quick answer for me. But you know what I think? The minute that baby died, I think D-boy decided not to create any new memories for himself, as if he had died, too, and that's why he stopped living, you know, positively, in present time. And I bet he calls that baby ghost down to earth all over Tokyo so he can create new memories for it!"

At the time I thought she must be right. This tipsy movie actress with a dent in her forehead big enough for a thumb is quite an original psychologist, I thought to myself. And much more D's type, I thought, than the pudgy, tomato-faced daughter of a newspaper baron. All of a sudden I realized that, even here in Kyoto with hundreds of miles between us, I, the model of a faithful employee, was thinking exclusively about D. No, there was something else, too, there was D's phantom. I realized that the baby whose appearance I waited for nervously every time my employer and I went out together hadn't been off my mind for a minute.

It was time for the bar to close and I didn't have a room. I'd managed to get as old as I was without ever staying in a hotel and I knew nothing about reservations. Luckily, the actress was known at the hotel, and a word from her got me a room. We went up in the elevator together, and I started to get off at my floor when she suggested we have one last drink and invited me to her room. It was from that point that memories of the evening get comic and pathetic. When she had seated me in a chair, the actress returned to the door and looked up and down the hall, then went through a whole series of nervous motions, flounced on the bed as if to test the springs, turned lights on and switched them off, ran a little water in the tub. Then she poured me the brandy she had promised and, sipping a Coca-Cola, she told me about another man who had courted her during her affair with D, and finally going to bed with him, and D slapping her so hard the teeth rattled in her mouth. Then she asked if I thought today's college students went in for "heavy petting"? It depended on the student, I said—suddenly the actress had become a mother scolding a child for staying up too late and was telling me to find my own room and go to sleep. I said good night, went downstairs, and fell asleep immediately. I woke up at dawn with a fire in my throat.

The most comic and pathetic part was still to come. I understood the minute I opened my eyes that the actress had invited me to her room intending to seduce a college student who was wild for heavy petting. And with that understanding came rage and abject desire. I hadn't slept with a woman yet, but this humiliation demanded that I retaliate. I was drunk on what must have been my first Hennessy VSOP, and I was out of my head with the kind of poisonous desire that goes with being eighteen. It was only five o'clock in the morning and there was no sign of life in the halls. Like a panther wild with rage I sped to her door on padded feet. It was ajar. I stepped inside and found her seated at the dresser mirror with her back to me. Creeping up directly behind her (to this day I wonder what I was trying to do), I lunged at her neck with both hands. The actress whirled around with a broad smile on her face, rising as she turned, and then she had my hands in her own and was pumping them happily up and down as if she were welcoming a guest and sing-songing, "Good morning! Good morning! Good morning!" Before I knew it I had been seated in a chair and we were sharing her toast and morning coffee and reading the newspaper together. After a while the movie actress said in a tone of voice she might have used to discuss the weather: "You were trying to rape me just now, weren't you!" She went back to her makeup and I got out of there, fled downstairs to my own room and burrowed back into bed, trembling as though I had malaria. I was afraid that a report of this incident might reach D, but the subject of the movie actress never came up again. I continued to enjoy my job.

Winter had come. Our plan that afternoon was to bicycle through D's residential neighborhood and the surrounding fields. I was on a rusty old bike and my employer had borrowed the nurse's shiny new one. Gradually we expanded the radius of a circle around D's house, riding into a new housing development and coasting down hills in the direction of the fields. We were sweating, relishing the sensation of liberation, more and more exhilarated. I say "we" and include D because that afternoon it was evident that he was in high spirits, too. He was even whistling a theme from a Bach sonata for flute and harpsichord called Siciliana. I happened to know that because when I was in high school I had played flute. I never learned to play well but I did develop a habit of thrusting out my upper lip the way a tapir does. Naturally, I had friends who insisted my buck teeth were to blame. But the fact is, flutists frequently look like tapirs.

As we pedaled down the street, I picked up the tune and began to whistle along with D. Siciliana is a sustained and elegant theme, but I was out of breath from pedaling and my whistle kept lapsing into airy sibilance. Yet D's phrasing was perfect, absolutely legato. I stopped whistling then, ashamed to go on, and the composer glanced over at me with his lips still pursed in a whistle like a carp puckering up to breathe and smiled his tranquil smile. Granted there was a difference in the bikes, it was still unnatural and pathetic that an eighteen-year-old student, skinny maybe, but tall, should begin to tire and run short of breath before a twenty-eight-year-old composer who was a little man and sick besides. Unjust is what it was, and infuriating. My mood clouded instantly and I felt disgusted with the whole job. So I stood up on the pedals all of a sudden and sped away as furiously as a bicycle racer. I even turned down a narrow gravel path between two vegetable fields purposely. When I looked back a minute later, my employer was hunched over the handle bars, his large, round head nodding above his narrow shoulders, churning the gravel beneath his wheels in hot pursuit of me. I coasted to a stop, propped a foot on the barbed wire fence that bordered the field and waited for D to catch up. I was already ashamed of my childishness.

His head still bobbing, my employer was approaching fast. And then I knew the phantom was with him. D was racing his bike down the extreme left of the gravel path, his face twisted to the right so that he was almost looking over his right shoulder, and the reason his head appeared to bob was that he was whispering encouragement to something running, or maybe flying, alongside the bicycle. Like a marathon coach pacing one of his runners. Ah, I thought, he's doing that on the premise that Aghwee is neck and neck with his speeding bike. The monster as large as a kangaroo, the fat, funny baby in a white cotton nightgown was bounding—like a kangaroo!—down that gravel path. I shuddered, then I kicked the barbed wire fence and slowly pedaled away, waiting for my employer and the monster in his imagination to catch up.

Don't think I had let myself begin to believe in Aghwee's existence. I had taken the nurse's advice, sworn not to lose sight of the anchor on my common sense as in those slightly solemn slapstick comedies where, for example, the keeper of the mad house goes mad; consciously derisive, I was thinking to myself that the neurotic composer was putting on a show with his bicycle just to follow up a lie he had told me once, and what a lot of trouble to go to! In other words, I was keeping a clinical distance between myself and D's phantom monster. Even so, there occurred a strange alteration in my state of mind.

It began this way: D had finally caught up and was biking along a few feet behind me when, as unexpectedly as a cloudburst, and as inescapably, we were enveloped by the belling of a pack of hounds. I looked up and saw them racing toward me down the gravel path, young adult Dobermans that stood two feet high, more than ten of them. Running breathlessly behind the pack, the thin black leather leashes grasped in one hand, was a man in overalls, chasing the dogs perhaps, or maybe they were dragging him along. Jet-black Dobermans, sleek as wet seals, with just a dusting of dry chocolate on their chests and jowls and pumping haunches. And down on us they howled, filling the gravel path, keening for the attack at such a forward tilt they looked about to topple on their foaming snouts. There was a meadow on the other side of the field; the man in overalls must have been training the beasts there and now he was on his way home with them.

Trembling with fear, I got off my bike and helplessly surveyed the field on the other side of the fence. The barbed wire came up to my chest. I might have had a chance myself but I would never have been able to boost the little composer to safety on the other side. The poisons of terror were beginning to numb my head, but for one lucid instant I could see the catastrophe that was bound to occur in a few seconds. As the Dobermans neared, D would sense that Aghwee was being attacked by a pack of the animals it most feared. He would probably hear the baby's frightened crying. And certainly he would meet the dogs head-on, in defense of his baby. Then the Dobermans would rip him to pieces. Or he would try to escape with the baby and make a reckless leap to clear the fence and be just as cruelly torn. I was rocked by the pity of what I knew must happen. And while I stood there dumbly without a plan, those giant black-and-chocolate devils were closing in on us, snapping in the air with awful jaws, so close by now that I could hear their alabaster claws clicking on the gravel. Suddenly I knew I could do nothing for D and his baby, and with that knowledge I went limp, unresisting as a pervert when he is seized in the subway, and was swallowed whole in the darkness of my fear. I backed off the gravel path until the barbed wire was a fire in my back, pulled my bike in front of me as if it were a wall, and shut my eyes tight. An animal stench battered me, together with the howling of the dogs and the pounding of their feet, and I could feel tears seeping past my eyelids. I abandoned myself to a wave of fear and it swept me away. . . .

On my shoulder was a hand gentle as the essence of all gentleness; it felt like Aghwee touching me. But I knew it was my employer; he had let those fiendish dogs pass and no catastrophe of fear had befallen him. I continued crying anyway, with my eyes closed and my shoulders heaving. I was too old to cry in front of other people, I suppose the shock of fright had induced some kind of infantile regression in me. When I stopped crying, we walked our bikes past that barbed wire fence like prisoners in a concentration camp, in silence, our heads hanging, to the meadow beyond the field where strangers were playing ball and exercising dogs (D wasn't occupied with Aghwee anymore, the baby must have left while I was crying). We laid our bikes down and then sprawled on the grass ourselves. My tears had flooded away my pretensions and my rebelliousness and the perverse suspicion in my heart. And D was no longer wary of me. I lay back on the grass and clasped my hands beneath my head, curiously light and dry after all that crying. Then I closed my eyes and listened quietly while D peered down at me with his chin in his hand and spoke to me of Aghwee's world.

"Do you know a poem called 'Shame' by Chuya Nakahara? Listen to the second verse:

The mournful sky
High where branches tangle
Teems with dead baby souls;
I blinked and saw
above the distant fields
fleece knit into a dream
of mastodons.

"That's one aspect of the world of the dead baby I see. There are some Blake engravings, too, especially one called 'Christ Refusing the Banquet Offered by Satan'—have you ever seen it? And there's another, 'The Morning Stars Singing Together.' In both there are figures in the sky who have the same reality about them as the people on the ground, and whenever I look at them I'm sure Blake was hinting at an aspect of this other world. I once saw a Dali painting that was close, too, full of opaque beings floating in the sky about a hundred yards above the ground and glowing with an ivory white light. Now that's exactly the world I see. And you know what those glowing things are that fill the sky? Beings we've lost from our lives down here on earth, and now they float up there in the sky about a hundred yards above the ground, quietly glowing like amoebas under a microscope. And sometimes they descend the way our Aghwee does (my employer said it and I didn't protest, which doesn't mean I acquiesced). But it takes a sacrifice worthy of them to acquire the eyes to see them floating there and the ears to detect them when they descend to earth, and yet there are moments when suddenly we're endowed with that ability without any sacrifice or even effort on our part. I think that's what happened to you a few minutes ago."

Without any sacrifice or even effort on my part, just a few tears of expiation, my employer seemed to have wanted to say. The truth was I had shed tears out of fear and helplessness and a kind of vague terror about my future (my first job, an experiment in a kind of microcosm of life, was guarding this mad composer, and since I had failed to do that adequately, it was predictable that situations I couldn't cope with would recur as one of the patterns of my life), but instead of interrupting with a protest, I continued to listen docilely.

"You're still young, probably you haven't lost sight of anything in this world that you can never forget, that's so dear to you you're aware of its absence all the time. Probably the sky a hundred yards or so above your head is still nothing more than sky to you. But all that means is that the storehouse happens to be empty at the moment. Or have you lost anything that was really important to you?"

The composer paused for my answer, and I found myself remembering his former mistress, that movie actress with a dent in her forehead as big as an adult thumb. Naturally, no crucial loss of mine could have had anything to do with her, all that crying had eroded my head and a sentimental honey was seeping into the crevices.

"Well, have you?" For the first time since we had met, my employer was insistent. "Have you lost anything that was important to you?"

Suddenly I had to say something silly to cover my embarrassment.

"I lost a cat," I tried.

"A Siamese or what?"

"Just an ordinary cat with orange stripes; he disappeared about a week ago."

"If it's only been a week he might come back. Isn't it the season for them to wander?"

"That's what I thought, too, but now I know he won't be back."

"Why?"

"He was a tough tom with his own territory staked out. This morning I saw a weak-looking cat walking up and down his block and it wasn't even on its guard—my cat won't be coming back." When I'd stopped talking I realized I'd told a story intended for laughs in a voice that was hoarse with sadness.

"Then there's a cat floating in your sky," my employer said solemnly.

Through closed eyes I pictured an opaque cat as large as an ad balloon, glowing with an ivory-white light as it floated through the sky. It was a comical flight all right, but it also made me wistful.

"The figures floating in your sky begin to increase at an accelerating rate. That's why I haven't been living in present time ever since that incident with the baby, so I could stop that spreading. Since I'm not living in our time, I can't discover anything new, but I don't lose sight of anything, either—the state of my sky never changes." There was profound relief in the composer's voice.

But was my own sky really empty except for one bloated cat with orange stripes? I opened my eyes and started to look up at the clear, now almost evening sky, when dread made me close my eyes again. Dread of myself, for what if I had seen a glowing herd of numberless beings I had lost from time down here on earth!

We lay on the grass in that meadow for quite a while, ringed by the passive affinity two people have for one another when the same gloom is gripping them. And gradually I began to get my perspective back. I reproached myself: how unlike the eighteen-year-old pragmatist I really was to have let myself be influenced by a mad composer! I'm not suggesting my equilibrium was perfectly restored. The day I succumbed to that strange panic, I drew closer than ever to the sentiments of my employer and to that glowing herd in the sky one hundred yards above the ground. To an extent, what you might call the aftereffects remained with me.

And then the final day came. It was Christmas Eve. I'm certain about the date because D gave me a wristwatch with a little apology about being a day early. And I remember that a powdery snow fell for about an hour just after lunch. We went down to the Ginza together but it was already getting crowded, so we decided to walk out to Tokyo harbor. D wanted to see a Chilean freighter that was supposed to have docked that day. I was eager to go, too; I pictured a ship with snow blanketing her decks. We had left the Ginza crowds and were just passing the Kabuki Theater when D looked up at the dark and still snowy sky. And Aghwee descended to his side. As usual, I walked a few steps behind the composer and his phantom. We came to a wide intersection. D and the baby had just stepped off the curb when the light changed. D stopped, and a fleet of trucks as bulky as elephants heaved into motion with their Christmas freight. That was when it happened. Suddenly D cried out and thrust both arms in front of him as if he were trying to rescue something; then he leaped in among those trucks and was struck to the ground. I watched stupidly from the curb.

"That was suicide; he just killed himself!" said a shaky voice at my side.

But I had no time to wonder whether it might have been suicide. In a minute that intersection had become backstage at a circus, jammed with milling trucks like elephants, and I was kneeling at D's side, holding his bloody body in my arms and trembling like a dog. I didn't know what to do, a policeman had dashed up and then disappeared on the run again.

D wasn't dead; it was more awful than that. He was dying, lying there in the filthy wet that had been a light snow, oozing blood and something like tree-sap. The dark and snowy pattern of the sky ripped open and the stately light of a Spanish pieta made my employer's blood glisten like silly fat. By that time a crowd had gathered, snatches of "Jingle Bells" wheeled above our heads like panic-stricken pigeons, and I knelt at D's side listening hard for nothing in particular and hearing screaming in the distance. But the crowd just stood there silently in the cold, as if indifferent to the screams. I have never listened so hard on a street corner again, nor again heard screams like that.

An ambulance finally arrived and my employer was lifted inside unconscious. He was caked with blood and mud, and shock seemed to have withered his body. In his white tennis shoes, he looked like an injured blind man. I climbed into the ambulance with a doctor and an orderly and a young man about my age who seemed haughty and aloof. He turned out to be the driver's helper on the long-distance truck that had hit D. The congestion was getting worse all the time as the ambulance cut across the Ginza (according to some statistics I saw recently, there were record crowds that Christmas Eve). Those who heard the siren and stopped to watch us pass, nearly all of them, shared a look of circumspectly solemn concern. In one corner of my dazed head I reflected that the so-called inscrutable Japanese smile, while it seemed likely to exist, did not. Meanwhile D lay unconscious on that wobbly stretcher, bleeding his life away.

When we arrived at the hospital, two orderlies who didn't even pause to change out of shoes into slippers rushed D away to some recess of the building. The same policeman as before appeared out of nowhere again and calmly asked me a lot of questions. Then I was permitted to go to D. The young worker from the truck had already found the room and was sitting on a bench in the corridor next to the door. I sat down next to him and we waited for a long time. At first he would only mutter about all the deliveries he still had to make, but when two hours had passed he began to complain that he was hungry in a surprisingly young voice, and my hostility toward him dwindled. We waited some more, then the banker arrived with his wife and three daughters, who were all dressed up to go to a party. Ignoring us, they went inside. All four of the women had fat, squat bodies and red faces; they reminded me of D's former wife. I continued to wait. It had been hours by then, and the whole time I had been tormented by suspicion—hadn't my employer intended to kill himself from the beginning? Before taking his life he had settled things with his ex-wife and former mistress, burned his manuscripts, toured the city saying goodbye to places he would miss—hadn't he hired me because he needed some good-natured help with those chores? Kept me from seeing his plan by inventing a monster baby floating in the sky? In other words, wasn't it the case that my only real function had been to help D commit suicide? The young laborer had fallen asleep with his head on my shoulder and every minute or two he would convulse as though in pain. He must have been dreaming about running over a man with a truck.

It was pitch black outside when the banker appeared in the door and called me. I eased my shoulder from under the worker's head and stood up. The banker paid me my salary for the day and then let me into the room. D lay on his back with rubber tubes in his nostrils as in a joke. His face gave me pause: it was black as smoked meat. But I couldn't help voicing the doubt that had me so afraid. I called out to my dying employer: "Did you hire me just so you could commit suicide? Was all that about Aghwee just a cover-up?" Then my throat was clogged with tears and I was surprised to hear myself shouting, "I was about to believe in Aghwee!"

At that moment, as my eyes filled with tears and things began to dim, I saw a smile appear on D's darkened, shriveled face. It might have been a mocking smile and it might have been a smile of friendly mischief. The banker led me out of the room. The young man from the truck was stretched out on the bench asleep. On my way out, I slipped the thousand yen I had earned into his jacket pocket. I read in the evening paper the next day that the composer was dead.

And then it was this spring and I was walking down the street when a group of frightened children suddenly started throwing stones. It was so sudden and unprovoked, I don't know what I had done to threaten them. Whatever it was, fear had turned those children into killers, and one of them hit me in the right eye with a rock as big as a fist. I went down on one knee, pressed my hand to my eye and felt a lump of broken flesh. With my good eye I watched my dripping blood draw in the dirt in the street as though magnetically. It was then that I sensed a being I knew and missed leave the ground behind me like a kangaroo and soar into the teary blue of a sky that retained its winter brittleness. Goodbye, Aghwee, I heard myself whispering in my heart. And then I knew that my hatred of those frightened children had melted away and that time had filled my sky during those ten years with figures that glowed with an ivory-white light, I suppose not all of them purely innocent. When I was wounded by those children and sacrificed my sight in one eye, so clearly a gratuitous sacrifice, I had been endowed, if for only an instant, with the power to perceive a creature that had descended from the heights of my sky.

[1977]

Translated by
John Nathan

QUESTIONS

1. What are the sources of D's guilt?
2. Is the narrator correct when he concludes that D has tolerated him because he needed a companion as he wraps up the matters of his life? Or is there another reason?
3. Why is Aghwee referred to as a "monster," when his duties appear to be more protective than harmful?
4. Why does the narrator finally believe in Aghwee?

Sembene Ousmane

(b. 1923)

Senegal

In contemporary Africa, Sembene Ousmane is more widely known as a filmmaker than as a writer. His film version of the story reprinted here launched him on a successful new career midway through an already significant one as a writer of fiction. (The film won a prize at the Cannes Film Festival in 1967.) Ousmane's decision to turn to the cinema was based in large part on his realization that in Africa in the 1960s his audience would be greatly extended. By his use of film as a medium of communication, he would no longer be dependent on the literacy rates of his people across the continent. Since the film version of "Black Girl," Ousmane has made nearly a dozen additional films, widely shown in Africa as well as outside of the continent. At time his work—often due to its strong political context—has provoked the hostility of officials within his native Senegal. Yet Ousmane has continued to pursue his dual careers, in spite of attempts to censor his work.

In an interview he gave to the *New York Times* in 1969, Ousmane made the following statement: "The thing I was trying to do in it [his film *Mandabi*] was show Africans some of the deplorable conditions under which they themselves live. When one creates, one doesn't think of the world; one thinks of his own country. It is, after all, the Africans who will ultimately bring about change in Africa—not the Americans, or the French or the Russians or the Chinese." These comments appear to be equally valid for "Black Girl," although it is set in the colonial era.

Black Girl

It was the morning of the 23rd of June in the year of our Lord nineteen hundred fifty-eight. At Antibes, along the Riviera, neither the fate of the French Republic, nor the future of Algeria nor the state of the colonial territories preoccupied those who swarmed across the beaches below La Croisette.

Above, on the road leading to the Hermitage, two old-style Citroëns, one behind the other, were moving up the mountain. They stopped and several men quickly got out, rushing down the gravel walk towards a house on which a worn sign spelled out "Villa of Green Happiness." The men were the police chief of the town of Grasse, a medical officer, and two police inspectors from Antibes, flanked by officers in uniform.

There was nothing green about the Villa of Green Happiness except its name. The garden was kept in the French manner, the walks covered with gravel, set off by a couple of palm trees with drooping fronds. The Chief looked closely at the house, his eyes stopping at the third window, the broken glass, the ladder.

Inside were other inspectors and a photographer. Three people who seemed to be reporters were looking with rather absent-minded interest at the African statues, masks, animal skins, and ostrich eggs set here and there on the walls. Entering the living-room was like violating the privacy of a hunter's lair.

Two women were hunched together, sobbing. They looked very much alike, the same straight forehead, the same curved nose, the same dark circles about eyes reddened from crying. The one in the pale dress was speaking: "After my nap, I felt like taking a bath. The door was locked from the inside"—blowing her nose—"and I thought to myself, it's the maid taking her bath. I say 'the maid,'" she corrected, "but we never called her anything else but her name, Diouana. I waited for more than an hour, but didn't see her come out. I went back and called, knocking on the door. There was no answer. Then I phoned our neighbour, the Commodore. . . ."

She stopped, wiped her nose, and began to cry again. Her sister, the younger of the two, hair cut in a boyish style, sat hanging her head.

"You're the one who discovered the body?"

"Yes . . . that is, when Madame Pouchet called and told me that the black girl had locked herself in the bathroom, I thought it was a joke. I spent thirty-five years at sea, you know. I've roamed the seven seas. I'm retired from the Navy."

"Yes, yes, we know."

"Yes, well, when Madame Pouchet called I brought my ladder."

"You brought the ladder?"

"No. It was Mademoiselle Dubois, Madame's sister, who suggested the idea. And when I got to the window, I saw the black girl swimming in blood."

"Where is the key to the door?"

"Here it is, your Honour," said the inspector.

"Just wanted to see it."

"I've checked the window," said the other inspector.

"I'm the one who opened it, after breaking the pane," said the retired navy man.

"Which pane did you break?"

"Which pane?" he repeated. He was wearing white linen trousers and a blue jacket.

"Yes, I saw it, but I'd like to ask precisely."

"The second from the top," answered the sister.

At this, two stretcher-bearers came down, carrying a body wrapped in a blanket. Blood dripped on the steps. The magistrate lifted a corner of the blanket and frowned. A black girl lay dead on the stretcher, her throat cut from one ear to the other.

"It was with this knife. A kitchen knife," said another man, from the top of the stairs.

"Did you bring her from Africa or did you hire her here?"

"We brought her back from Africa, in April. She came by boat. My husband is with aerial navigation in Dakar, but the company only pays air passage for the family. She worked for us in Dakar. For two and a half or three years."

"How old is she?"

"I don't know exactly."

"According to her passport, she was born in 1927."

"Oh! The natives don't know when they are born," offered the naval officer, plunging his hands in his pockets.

"I don't know why she killed herself. She was well treated here, she ate the same food, shared the same rooms as my children."

"And your husband, where is he?"

"He left for Paris the day before yesterday."

"Ah!" said the inspector, still looking at the knick-knacks. "Why do you think it was suicide?"

"Why?" said the retired officer . . . "Oh! Who do you think would make an attempt on the life of a Negro girl? She never went out. She didn't know anyone, except for Madame's children."

The reporters were getting impatient. The suicide of a maid—even if she were black—didn't amount to a hill of beans. There was nothing newsworthy in it.

"It must have been homesickness. Because lately, she'd been behaving very strangely. She wasn't the same."

The police magistrate went upstairs, accompanied by one of the inspectors. They examined the bathroom, the window.

"Some boomerang, this story," said the inspector.

The others waited in the living-room.

"We'll let you know when the coroner is finished," said the inspector, on his way out with the police magistrate an hour after their arrival.

The cars and the reporters left. In the Villa of Green Happiness the two women and the retired naval officer remained silent.

Bit by bit, Madame Pouchet searched her memory. She thought back to Africa and her elegant villa on the road to Hann. She remembered Diouana pushing open the iron gate and signalling to the German shepherd to stop barking.

It was there, in Africa, that everything had started. Diouana had made the six-kilometre round trip on foot three times a week. For the last month she had made it gaily, enraptured, her heart beating as if she were in love for the first time. Beginning at the outskirts of Dakar, brand-new houses were scattered like jewels in a landscape of cactus, bougainvillea and jasmine. The asphalt of the Avenue Gambetta stretched out like a long black ribbon. Joyous and happy as usual, the little maid had no complaints about the road or her employers. Though it was a long way, it had no longer seemed so far the past month, ever since Madame had announced she would take her to France. France! Diouana shouted the word in her head. Everything around her had become ugly, the magnificent villas she had so often admired seemed shabby.

In order to be able to travel, in order to go to France, since she was originally from the Casamance, she had needed an identity card. All her paltry savings went to get one. "So what?" she thought. "I'm on my way to France!"

"Is that you, Diouana?"

"*Viye*,[1] Madame," came her answer in the Senegalese accent. She spoke from the vestibule, nicely dressed in her light coloured cotton, her hair neatly combed.

"Good! Monsieur is in town. Will you look after the children?"

"*Viye*, Madame," she agreed in her childish voice.

Though her identity card read "born in 1927," Diouana was not yet thirty.

[1]*Viye* yes

But she must have been over twenty-one. She went to find the children. Every room was in the same condition. Parcels packed and tied with strings, boxes piled here and there. After ten whole days of washing and ironing, there wasn't much left for Diouana to do In the proper sense of her duties, she was a laundress. There was a cook, a houseboy and herself. Three people. The servants.

"Diouana . . . Diouana," Madame called.

"Madame?" she answered, emerging from the children's room.

Madame was standing with a notebook in her hands making an inventory of the baggage. The movers would be coming at any moment.

"Have you been to see your parents? Do you think they will be happy?"

"*Viye*, Madame. The whole family is agreed. I tell Mama for myself. Also tell Papa Boutoupa," she said.

Her face, which had been radiant with happiness, fixed on the empty walls, and began to fade. Her heartbeat slowed. She would be ill if Madame changed her mind. Ready to plead her case, Diouana's ebony-black face grew gloomy, she lowered her eyes.

"You're not going to tell me at the last moment, on this very day, that you're leaving us in the lurch?"

"No, Madame, me go."

They were not speaking the same language. Diouana wanted to see France, this country whose beauty, richness, and joy of living everyone praised. She wanted to see it and make a triumphal return. This was where people got rich. Already, without having left African soil, she could see herself on the dock, returning from France, wealthy to the millions, with gifts of clothes for everyone. She dreamed of the freedom to go where she wished, without having to work like a beast of burden. If Madame should change her mind, refuse to take her, it would truly make her ill.

As for Madame, she was remembering the last few holidays she had spent in France. Three of them. And then she had only had two children. In Africa, Madame had acquired bad habits when it came to servants. In France when she hired a maid not only was the salary higher, but the maid demanded a day off to boot Madame had had to let her go and hired another. The next one was no different from the first, if not worse. She answered Madame tit for tat. "Anyone who is capable of having children should take a turn with them herself. I can't live in. I have my own children to take care of and a husband too," she declared.

Used to being waited on hand and foot, Madame had yielded to her wifely duties, and clumsily fulfilled the role of mother. As for a real vacation, she had hardly had any. She soon persuaded her husband to return to Africa.

On her return, grown thin and thoroughly exasperated, she had conceived a plan for her next vacation. She put want ads in all the newspapers. A hundred young girls answered. Her choice fell on Diouana, newly arrived from her native bush. Producing two more children during the three years that Diouana worked for her, between her last holiday and the one to come, Madame sang the praises of France. For three thousand francs a month, any young African girl would have followed her to the end of the earth. And to top it off, from time to time, especially lately, Madame would give Diouana little gifts of this and that, old clothes, shoes that could be mended.

This was the insurmountable moat that separated the maid and her employer.

"Did you give Monsieur your identity card?"

"*Viye*, Madame."

"You may go back to your work. Tell the cook to give the three of you a good meal."

"*Merci*, Madame," she answered, and went off to the kitchen.

Madame continued her inventory.

Monsieur returned on the stroke of noon, his arrival announced by the barking of the dog. Getting out of his Peugeot 403, he found his wife, indefatigable, pencil in hand.

"Haven't the baggage men come yet?" she said nervously.

"They'll be here at a quarter to two. Our bags will be on top. That way they'll be out first when we land in Marseille. And what about Diouana? Diouana!"

The eldest of the children ran to fetch her. She was under the trees with the littlest one.

"*Viye*, Madame."

"It's Monsieur who was calling you."

"That's fine. Here are your ticket and your identity card."

Diouana held out a hand to take them.

"You keep the identity card, I'll take care of the ticket. The Duponts are returning on the same ship, they'll look after you. Are you glad to be going to France?"

"*Viye*, Monsieur."

"Good. Where are your bags?"

"At Rue Escarfait, Monsieur."

"After I've had lunch we'll go fetch them in the car."

"Bring the children in, Diouana, it's time for their nap."

"*Viye*, Madame."

Diouana wasn't hungry. The cook's helper, two years younger than she, brought the plates and took the empty ones away, noiselessly. The cook was sweating heavily. He wasn't happy. He was going to be out of work. This was how the departure affected him. And for this reason he was a bit resentful of the maid. Leaning out the wide window overlooking the sea, transported, Diouana watched the birds flying high above in the immense expanse of blue. In the distance she could barely make out the Island of Gorée.[2] She was holding her identity card, turning it over and over, examining it and smiling quietly to herself. The picture was a gloomy one. She wasn't pleased with the pose or with the exposure. "What does it matter? I'm leaving!" she thought.

"Samba," said Monsieur, who had come to the kitchen, "the meal was excellent today. You outdid yourself. Madame is very pleased with you."

The cook's helper stood at attention. Samba, the cook, adjusted his tall white hat and made an effort to smile.

"Thank you very much, Monsieur," he said. "I too am happy, very happy, because Monsieur and Madame are happy. Monsieur very nice. My family big, unhappy. Monsieur leave, me no more work."

"We'll be back, my good man. And then, with your talent you'll soon find another job!"

Samba, the cook, wasn't so sure. The Whites were stingy. And in a Dakar

[2]*Gorée* an island off the coast of Senegal from which hundreds of thousands of slaves were sent to the New World

filled with country people each claiming to be a master cook, it wouldn't be easy to find a job.

"We'll be back, Samba. Maybe sooner than you think. The last time we stayed only two and a half months."

To these consoling words from Madame, who had joined her husband in the kitchen, Samba could only answer: "*Merci*, Madame. Madame very nice lady."

Madame was glad. She knew from experience what it meant to have a good reputation with the servants.

"You can go home this afternoon at four with Monsieur. I'll pack up the rest. When we come back I promise to hire you again. Are you pleased?"

"*Merci*, Madame."

Madame and Monsieur were gone. Samba gave Diouana a slap. She hit him back angrily.

"Hey! Careful. Careful. You're going away today. So we shouldn't fight."

"That hurt!" she said.

"And Monsieur, does he hurt you too?"

Samba suspected a secret liaison between the maid and her employer.

"They're calling for you, Diouana I hear the car starting."

She left without even saying goodbye.

The car moved along the highway. Diouana didn't often have the privilege of being driven by Monsieur. Her very look invited the pedestrians' admiration, though she dared not wave a hand or shout while going past, "I'm on my way to France!" Yes, France! She was sure her happiness was plain to see. The subterranean sources of this tumultuous joy made her a bit shaky. When the car stopped in front of the house at Rue Escarfait, she was surprised. "Already?" she thought. Next door to her humble house, at the Gay Navigator Café a few customers were seated at the tables and several were talking quietly on the sidewalk.

"Is it today you're leaving, little one?" asked Tive Correa. Already tipsy, he steadied himself, legs apart, holding his bottle by the neck. His clothes were rumpled.

Diouana would have nothing to do with the drunkard. She didn't listen to Tive Correa's advice. An old sailor, Tive Correa had come home from Europe after twenty years absence. He had left, rich with youth, full of ambition, and come home a wreck. From having wanted everything he had returned with nothing but an excessive love for the bottle. For Diouana he predicted nothing but misfortune. Once, when she had asked his advice, his opinion had been that she shouldn't go. In spite of his serious state of inebriety, he made a few steps towards Monsieur, bottle still in hand.

"Is it true that Diouana's leaving with you Monsieur?"

Monsieur did not answer. He took out a cigarette and lit it, blew the smoke through the car door, and looked Tive Correa over from head to toe. What a bum he was, greasy clothes, stinking of palm wine. Correa leaned over, putting a hand on the car door.

"I was there. I lived in France for twenty years," he began, with a note of pride in his voice. "I, whom you see this way, ruin though I am today, I know France better than you do. During the war I lived in Toulon, and the Germans sent us with the other Africans to Aix-en-Provence, to the mines at Gardanne. I've been against her going."

"We haven't forced her to go! She wants to," Monsieur answered dryly.

"Certainly. What young African doesn't dream of going to France? Unfortunately, they confuse living in France with being a servant in France. I come from the village next to Diouana's, in Casamance. There, we don't say the way you do that it is the light that attracts the butterfly, but the other way round. In my country, Casamance, we say that the darkness pursues the butterfly."

In the meantime, Diouana returned, escorted by several women. They were chatting along, each begging for a little souvenir. Diouana promised happily; she was smiling, her white teeth gleaming.

"The others are at the dock," said one. "Don't forget my dress."

"For me, some shoes for the children. You've got the size in your suitcase. And remember the sewing machine."

"The petticoats, too."

"Write and tell me how much the hair straightening irons cost and also the price of a red jacket with big buttons, size 44."

"Don't forget to send a little money to your mother in Boutoupa. . . ."

Each one had something to tell her, some request to make of her; Diouana promised. Her face was radiant. Tive Correa took the suitcase, pushing it drunkenly but not roughly into the car.

"Let her go, girls. Do you think money grows on trees in France? She'll have something to say about that when she gets back."

Loud protests from the women.

"Goodbye, little cousin. Take care of yourself. You have the address of the cousin in Toulon. Write to him as soon as you get there, he will help you. Come give me a kiss."

They all kissed each other goodbye. Monsieur was getting impatient. He started up the motor to indicate politely that he wished they'd be done with it.

The Peugeot was moving. Everyone waved.

At the dock it was the same; relatives, friends, little commissions. Everyone pressed around her. Always under the watchful eye of Monsieur. She embarked.

A week at sea. "No news," she would have written if she'd been keeping a diary, in which case she'd also have had to know how to read and write. Water in front, behind, to port, to starboard. Nothing but a sheet of liquid, and above it, the sky.

When the boat landed, Monsieur was there. After the formalities, they quickly made their way to the Côte d'Azur. She devoured everything with her eyes, marvelling, astonished. She packed every detail into her head. It was beautiful. Africa seemed a sordid slum by comparison. Towns, buses, trains, trucks went by along the coastal highway. The heaviness of the traffic surprised her.

"Did you have a good crossing?"

"*Viye*, Monsieur," she would have answered, if Monsieur had asked the question.

After a two-hour drive, they were in Antibes.

Days, weeks and the first month went by. The third month began. Diouana was no longer the joyous young girl with the ready laugh, full of life. Her eyes were beginning to look hollow, her glance was less alert, she no longer noticed details. She had a lot more work to do here than in Africa. At first her fretting was hardly noticeable. Of France, "La Belle France," she had only a vague idea, a fleeting vision. French gardens, the hedges of the other villas, the crests of roofs appearing above the green trees, the palms. Everyone lived his own life, isolated, shut up in his own house. Monsieur and Madame went out a good deal, leaving her with the four children. The children quickly organized a mafia and persecuted her. "You've got to keep them happy," Madame would say. The oldest, a real scamp, recruited others of like inclination and they played explorer. Diouana was the "savage." The children pestered her. Once in a while the eldest got a good spanking. Having picked up phrases from the conversations of mama, papa or the neighbours back in Africa—phrases in which notions of racial prejudice played a part—he made exaggerated remarks to his pals. Without the knowledge of his parents, they would turn up, chanting, "Black Girl, Black Girl. She's as black as midnight."

Perpetually harassed, Diouana began to waste away. In Dakar she had never had to think about the colour of her skin. With the youngsters teasing she began to question it. She understood that here she was alone. There was nothing that connected her with the others. And it aggravated her, poisoned her life, the very air she breathed.

Everything grew blunt; her old dreams, her contentment eroded. She did a lot of hard work. It was she who did all the cooking, laundry, babysitting, ironing. Madame's sister came to stay at the villa, making seven people to look after. At night, as soon as she went up to bed, Diouana slept like a log.

The venom was poisoning her heart. She had never hated anything. Everything became monotonous. Where was France? The beautiful cities she had seen at the movies in Dakar, the rare foods, the interesting crowds? The population of France reduced itself to these spiteful monsters, Monsieur, Madame and Mademoiselle, who had become strangers to her. The country seemed limited to the immediate surroundings of the villa. Little by little she was drowning. The wide horizons of a short while ago stopped now at the colour of her skin, which suddenly filled her with an invincible terror. Her skin. Her blackness. Timidly, she retreated into herself.

With no one from her universe to exchange ideas with, she held long moments of palaver with herself. A week ago, Monsieur and Madame had cleverly taken her along to visit their relatives in Cannes.

"Tomorrow we'll go to Cannes. My parents have never tasted African food. You'll do us African honour with your cooking." Madame had said. She was nearly bare, and getting bronzed from the sun.

"*Viye*, Madame."

"I've ordered some rice and two chickens. . . . You'll be careful not to spice it too much?"

"*Viye*, Madame."

Answering this way, her heart hardened. It seemed the hundredth time that she'd been trailed from villa to villa. To this one's house and then to that one's. It was at the Commodore's—everyone called him the Commodore—that she had rebelled the first time. Some silly people, who followed her about, hanging on her heels in the kitchen, had been there for dinner. Their presence was an oppressive shadow on her slightest movement. She had the feeling of not knowing how to do anything. These strange, self-centred, sophisticated beings never stopped asking her idiotic questions about how African women do their cooking. She kept herself under control.

The three women were still chirping when she waited on them at the table, testing the first spoonful on the tip of their tongues, then gluttonously devouring the rest.

"This time, at my parents, you must outdo yourself."

"*Viye*, Madame."

Restored to her kitchen, her thoughts went to Madame's former kindness.

She detested it. Madame had been good to her, but in a self-seeking way. The only reason for her attentiveness had been to wind the strings round Diouana, the better to make her sweat. She loathed everything. Back in Dakar, Diouana used to gather Monsieur and Madame's leftovers to take home to Rue Escarfait. She had taken pride then in working for "important white people." Now she was so alone their meals made her sick to her stomach. The resentment spoiled her relations with her employers. She stood her ground, they stood theirs. They no longer exchanged any remarks but those of a business nature.

"Diouana, will you do the washing today?"

"*Viye*, Madame."

"Last time you didn't do a good job on my slips. The iron was too hot. And the collars of Monsieur's shirts were scorched. Do pay attention to what you're doing, will you?"

"*Viye*, Madame."

"Oh, I forgot. There are some buttons missing on Monsieur's shirts and his shorts."

Every little job was Diouana's. And then Madame started speaking to her in pidgin French, even in front of guests. And this was the only thing she did with honesty. In the end, no one in the house ever spoke to the maid any more except in terms of "Missie." Senegalese pidgin talk. Bewildered by her inadequacies in French, Diouana closed herself into a sort of solitary confinement. After long, lonely moments of meditation she came to the conclusion first of all that she was nothing but a useful object, and furthermore that she was being put on exhibit like a trophy. At parties, when Monsieur or Madame made remarks about "native" psychology, Diouana was taken as an illustration. The neighbours would say: It's the Pouchets' black girl. . . ." She wasn't "the African girl" in her own right, but theirs. And that hurt.

The fourth month began. Things got worse. Her thoughts grew more lucid every day. She had work and work to spare. All week long. Sunday was Mademoiselle's favourite day for asking friends over. There were lots of them. The weeks began and ended with them.

Everything became clear. Why had Madame wanted her to come? Her generosities had been premeditated. Madame no longer took care of her children. She kissed them every morning, that was all. And where was "La Belle France?" These questions kept repeating themselves. "I am cook, nursemaid, chambermaid; I do all the washing and ironing and for a mere three thousand francs a month. I do housework for six people. What am I doing here?"

Diouana gave way to her memories. She compared her "native bush" to these dead shrubs. How different from the forest of her home in Casamance. The memory of her village, of the community life, cut her off from the others even more. She bit her lips, sorry to have come. And on this film of the past, a thousand other details were projected.

Returning to these surroundings, where she was doubly an outsider, her feelings hardened. She thought often of Tive Correa. His predictions had come cruelly true. She would have liked to write to him, but couldn't. Since arriving in France, she had had only two letters from her mother. She didn't have the time to answer, even though Madame had promised to write for her. Was it possible to tell Madame what she was thinking? She was angry with herself. Her ignorance made her mute. It was infuriating. And besides, Mademoiselle had made off with her stamps.

A pleasant idea crossed her mind though, and raised a smile. This evening only Monsieur was at home, watching television. She decided to take advantage of the opportunity. Then, unexpectedly finding Madame there too, Diouana stopped abruptly and left the room.

"Sold, sold. Bought, bought," she repeated to herself. "They've bought me. For three thousand francs I do all this work. They lured me, tied me to them, and I'm stuck here like a slave." She was determined now. That night she opened her suitcase, looked at the objects in it and wept. No one cared.

Yet she went through the same motions and remained as sealed off from the others as an oyster at low tide on the beach of her native Casamance.

"Douna"—it was Mademoiselle calling her. Why was it impossible for her to say Di-ou-a-na?

Her anger redoubled. Mademoiselle was even lazier than Madame: "Come take this away"—"There is such-and-such to be done, Douna"—"Why don't you do this, Douna?"—"Douna, now and then please rake the garden." For an answer Mademoiselle would receive an incendiary glance. Madame complained about her to Monsieur.

"What is the matter with you, Diouana? Are you ill or something?" he asked. She no longer opened her mouth.

"You can tell me what's the matter. Perhaps you'd like to go to Toulon. I haven't had the time to go, but tomorrow I'll take you with me."

"Anyone would think we disgust her," said Madame.

Three days later Diouana took her bath. Returning home after a morning of shopping, Madame Pouchet went in the bathroom and quickly emerged.

"Diouana! Diouana!" she called. "You *are* dirty, in spite of everything. You might have left the bathroom clean."

"No me, Madame. It was the children, *viye*."

"The children! The children are tidy. It may be that you're fed up with them. But to find you telling lies, like a native, *that* I don't like. I don't like liars and you are a liar!"

Diouana kept silent, though her lips were trembling. She went upstairs to the bathroom, and took her clothes off. It was there they found her, dead.

"Suicide," the investigators concluded. The case was closed.

The next day, in the newspaper on page four, column six, hardly noticeable, was a small headline:

"Homesick African Girl Cuts Throat in Antibes."

[1962]

Translated by
ELLEN CONROY KENNEDY

QUESTIONS

1. Are the Pouchets guilty of murder?
2. Is the newspaper headline at the end of the story an accurate summary of what has happened to Diouana?
3. The French title of the story ("La Noire de . . .") is literally translated as "The Black Girl from. . . ." Is this a more accurate title than "Black Girl"?
4. What is Tive Correa's function in the story?

Amos Oz
(b. 1939)
Israel

For most of his adult life, Amos Oz has lived at Kibbutz Hulda, a collective community in Israel. A *sabra*—a first-generation Israeli—he was born Amos Klausner to prosperous Zionist parents who immigrated to Israel. His father was a librarian, writer, and scholar of comparative literature. During adolescence, Oz rebelled against his family's middle-class values by deciding to join directly in the Israeli social experiment. He changed his surname, joined a kibbutz, and undertook the essential but menial work required of *kibbutzim* residents, from driving a tractor to working in agricultural production. Oz also served in the Israeli army, seeing action in two wars.

Pursuing higher education at Hebrew University and Oxford, Oz subsequently returned to the Kibbutz Hulda and began to write fiction. (His royalty income goes to the kibbutz.) As he acknowledges the irony of his life, "In the end, when I look at myself, I am doing exactly what my father wanted me to do. In the kibbutz I look like one of the members, and yet I follow my forefathers. I deal with words. My escape was a full circle."

In his novels, stories, essays, and interviews about the State (and state) of Israel, Oz has become an imaginative witness and recorder of the darker side of a unique but troubled social and political experiment: Jews who struggle to survive in a desert landscape that symbolizes both the physical and the emotional siege under which they live. As Oz phrased it in an essay for *Partisan Review*, life in a kibbutz "waked and fed my curiosity about the strange phenomenon of flawed, tormented human beings dreaming about perfection, aching for the Messiah, aspiring to change human nature. This perpetual paradox of magnanimous dream and unhappy reality is indeed one of the main threads in my writing."

Among his six novels and several collections of stories, all originally written in Hebrew, are *Elsewhere, Perhaps* (1966); *My Michael* (1968); *A Perfect Peace* (1983); and *Where the Jackals Howl* (1965, revised 1976), from which the title story is included here. Describing the special area that Oz has carved out as his subject and theme, Ruth Wisse observes that he has taken

> the great myths with which modern Israel is associated—the noble experiment of the kibbutz, the reclamation of the soil, the wars against the British and the Arabs, the phoenix-like rise of the Jewish spirit out of the ashes of the Holocaust—and shown us their underside: bruised, dazed, and straying characters who move in an atmosphere of almost unalleviated depression.

Nomad and Viper

I

The famine brought them.

They fled north from the horrors of famine, together with their dusty flocks. From September to April the desert had not known a moment's relief from drought. The loess[1] was pounded to dust. Famine had spread through the nomads' encampments and wrought havoc among their flocks.

The military authorities gave the situation their urgent attention. Despite certain hesitations, they decided to open the roads leading north to the Bedouins. A whole population—men, women, and children—could not simply be abandoned to the horrors of starvation.

Dark, sinuous, and wiry, the desert tribesmen trickled along the dirt paths, and with them came their emaciated flocks. They meandered along gullies hidden from town dwellers' eyes. A persistent stream pressed northward, circling the scattered settlements, staring wide-eyed at the sights of the settled land. The dark flocks spread into the fields of golden stubble, tearing and chewing with strong, vengeful teeth. The nomads' bearing was stealthy and subdued; they shrank from watchful eyes. They took pains to avoid encounters. Tried to conceal their presence.

If you passed them on a noisy tractor and set billows of dust loose on them, they would courteously gather their scattered flocks and give you a wide passage, wider by far than was necessary. They stared at you from a distance, frozen like statues. The scorching atmosphere blurred their appearance and gave a uniform look to their features: a shepherd with his staff, a woman with her babes, an old man with his eyes sunk deep in their sockets. Some were half-blind, or perhaps feigned half-blindness from some vague alms-gathering motive. Inscrutable to the likes of you.

How unlike our well-tended sheep were their miserable specimens: knots of small, skinny beasts huddling into a dark, seething mass, silent and subdued, humble as their dumb keepers.

The camels alone spurn meekness. From atop tall necks they fix you with tired eyes brimming with scornful sorrow. The wisdom of age seems to lurk in their eyes, and a nameless tremor runs often through their skin.

Sometimes you manage to catch them unawares. Crossing a field on foot, you may suddenly happen on an indolent flock standing motionless, noon-struck, their feet apparently rooted in the parched soil. Among them lies the shepherd, fast asleep, dark as a block of basalt. You approach and cover him with a harsh shadow. You are startled to find his eyes wide open. He bares most of his teeth in a placatory smile. Some of them are gleaming, others decayed. His smell hits you. You grimace. Your grimace hits him like a punch in the face. Daintily he picks himself up, trunk erect, shoulders hunched. You fix him with a cold blue eye.

[1]*loess* fine, yellowish-brown loam deposited by wind

He broadens his smile and utters a guttural syllable. His garb is a compromise: a short, patched European jacket over a white desert robe. He cocks his head to one side. An appeased gleam crosses his face. If you do not upbraid him, he suddenly extends his left hand and asks for a cigarette in rapid Hebrew. His voice has a silken quality, like that of a shy woman. If your mood is generous, you put a cigarette to your lips and toss another into his wrinkled palm. To your surprise, he snatches a gilt lighter from the recesses of his robe and offers a furtive flame. The smile never leaves his lips. His smile lasts too long, is unconvincing. A flash of sunlight darts off the thick gold ring adorning his finger and pierces your squinting eyes.

Eventually you turn your back on the nomad and continue on your way. After a hundred, two hundred paces, you may turn your head and see him standing just as he was, his gaze stabbing your back. You could swear that he is still smiling, that he will go on smiling for a long while to come.

And then, their singing in the night. A long-drawn-out, dolorous wail drifts on the night air from sunset until the early hours. The voices penetrate to the gardens and pathways of the kibbutz[2] and charge our nights with an uneasy heaviness. No sooner have you settled down to sleep than a distant drumbeat sets the rhythm of your slumber like the pounding of an obdurate heart. Hot are the nights, and vapor-laden. Stray clouds caress the moon like a train of gentle camels, camels without any bells.

The nomads' tents are made up of dark drapes. Stray women drift around at night, barefoot and noiseless. Lean, vicious nomad hounds dart out of the camp to challenge the moon all night long. Their barking drives our kibbutz dogs insane. Our finest dog went mad one night, broke into the henhouse, and massacred the young chicks. It was not out of savagery that the watchmen shot him. There was no alternative. Any reasonable man would justify their action.

II

You might imagine that the nomad incursion enriched our heat-prostrated nights with a dimension of poetry. This may have been the case for some of our unattached girls. But we cannot refrain from mentioning a whole string of prosaic, indeed unaesthetic disturbances, such as foot-and-mouth disease, crop damage, and an epidemic of petty thefts.

The foot-and-mouth disease came out of the desert, carried by their livestock, which had never been subjected to any proper medical inspection. Although we took various early precautions, the virus infected our sheep and cattle, severely reducing the milk yield and killing off a number of animals.

As for the damage to the crops, we had to admit that we had never managed to catch one of the nomads in the act. All we ever found were the tracks of men and animals among the rows of vegetables, in the hayfields, and deep inside the carefully fenced orchards. And wrecked irrigation pipes, plot markers, farming implements left out in the fields, and other objects.

We are not the kind to take such things lying down. We are no believers in forbearance or vegetarianism. This is especially true of our younger men. Among

[2]*kibbutz* communal settlement in Israel, organized as a collective

the veteran founders there are a few adherents of Tolstoyan ideas and such like. Decency constrains me not to dwell in detail on certain isolated and exceptional acts of reprisal conducted by some of the youngsters whose patience had expired, such as cattle rustling, stoning a nomad boy, or beating one of the shepherds senseless. In defense of the perpetrators of the last-mentioned act of retaliation I must state clearly that the shepherd in question had an infuriatingly sly face. He was blind in one eye, broken-nosed, drooling; and his mouth—on this the men responsible were unanimous—was set with long, curved fangs like a fox's. A man with such an appearance was capable of anything. And the Bedouins would certainly not forget this lesson.

The pilfering was the most worrisome aspect of all. They laid hands on the unripe fruit in our orchards, pocketed the faucets, whittled away piles of empty sacks in the fields, stole into the henhouses, and even made away with the modest valuables from our little houses.

The very darkness was their accomplice. Elusive as the wind, they passed through the settlement, evading both the guards we had posted and the extra guards we had added. Sometimes you would set out on a tractor or a battered jeep toward midnight to turn off the irrigation faucets in an outlying field and your headlights would trap fleeting shadows, a man or a night beast. An irritable guard decided one night to open fire, and in the dark he managed to kill a stray jackal.

Needless to say, the kibbutz secretariat did not remain silent. Several times Etkin, the secretary, called in the police, but their tracking dogs betrayed or failed them. Having led their handlers a few paces outside the kibbutz fence, they raised their black noses, uttered a savage howl, and stared foolishly ahead.

Spot raids on the tattered tents revealed nothing. It was as if the very earth had decided to cover up the plunder and brazenly outstare the victims. Eventually the elder of the tribe was brought to the kibbutz office, flanked by a pair of inscrutable nomads. The short-tempered policemen pushed them forward with repeated cries of "Yallah, yallah."

We, the members of the secretariat, received the elder and his men politely and respectfully. We invited them to sit down on the bench, smiled at them, and offered them steaming coffee prepared by Geula at Etkin's special request. The old man responded with elaborate courtesies, favoring us with a smile which he kept up from the beginning of the interview till its conclusion. He phrased his remarks in careful, formal Hebrew.

It was true that some of the youngsters of his tribe had laid hands on our property. Why should he deny it. Boys would be boys, and the world was getting steadily worse. He had the honor of begging our pardon and restoring the stolen property. Stolen property fastens its teeth in the flesh of the thief, as the proverb says. That was the way of it. What could one do about the hotheadedness of youth? He deeply regretted the trouble and distress we had been caused.

So saying, he put his hand into the folds of his robe and drew out a few screws, some gleaming, some rusty, a pair of pruning hooks, a stray knife-blade, a pocket flashlight, a broken hammer, and three grubby bank notes, as a recompense for our loss and worry.

Etkin spread his hands in embarrassment. For reasons best known to himself, he chose to ignore our guest's Hebrew and to reply in broken Arabic, the residue of his studies during the time of the riots and the siege. He opened his remarks with a frank and clear statement about the brotherhood of nations—

the cornerstone of our ideology—and about the quality of neighborliness of which the peoples of the East had long been justly proud, and never more so than in these days of bloodshed and groundless hatred.

To Etkin's credit, let it be said that he did not shrink in the slightest from reciting a full and detailed list of the acts of theft, damage, and sabotage that our guest—as the result of oversight, no doubt—had refrained from mentioning in his apology. If all the stolen property were returned and the vandalism stopped once and for all, we would be whole-heartedly willing to open a new page in the relations of our two neighboring communities. Our children would doubtless enjoy and profit from an educational courtesy visit to the Bedouin encampment, the kind of visit that broadens horizons. And it went without saying that the tribe's children would pay a return visit to our kibbutz home, in the interest of deepening mutual understanding.

The old man neither relaxed nor broadened his smile, but kept it sternly at its former level as he remarked with an abundance of polite phrases that the gentlemen of the kibbutz would be able to prove no further thefts beyond those he had already admitted and for which he had sought our forgiveness.

He concluded with elaborate benedictions, wished us health and long life, posterity and plenty, then took his leave and departed, accompanied by his two barefooted companions wrapped in their dark robes. They were soon swallowed up by the wadi[3] that lay outside the kibbutz fence.

Since the police had proved ineffectual—and had indeed abandoned the investigation—some of our young men suggested making an excursion one night to teach the savages a lesson in a language they would really understand.

Etkin rejected their suggestion with disgust and with reasonable arguments. The young men, in turn, applied to Etkin a number of epithets that decency obliges me to pass over in silence. Strangely enough, Etkin ignored their insults and reluctantly agreed to put their suggestion before the kibbutz secretariat. Perhaps he was afraid that they might take matters into their own hands.

Toward evening, Etkin went around from room to room and invited the committee to an urgent meeting at eight-thirty. When he came to Geula, he told her about the young men's ideas and the undemocratic pressure to which he was being subjected, and asked her to bring along to the meeting a pot of black coffee and a lot of good will. Geula responded with an acid smile. Her eyes were bleary because Etkin had awakened her from a troubled sleep. As she changed her clothes, the night fell, damp and hot and close.

III

Damp and close and hot the night fell on the kibbutz, tangled in the dust-laden cypresses, oppressed the lawns and ornamental shrubs. Sprinklers scattered water onto the thirsty lawn, but it was swallowed up at once: perhaps it evaporated even before it touched the grass. An irritable phone rang vainly in the locked office. The walls of the houses gave out a damp vapor. From the kitchen chimney a stiff column of smoke rose like an arrow into the heart of the sky, because there was no breeze. From the greasy sinks came a shout. A dish had been broken and somebody was bleeding. A fat house-cat had killed a lizard or a snake and dragged its prey onto the baking concrete path to toy with it lazily in

[3]*wadi* channel of a river or ravine

the dense evening sunlight. An ancient tractor started to rumble in one of the sheds, choked, belched a stench of oil, roared, spluttered, and finally managed to set out to deliver an evening meal to the second shift, who were toiling in an outlying field. Near the Persian lilac Geula saw a bottle dirty with the remains of a greasy liquid. She kicked at it repeatedly, but instead of shattering, the bottle rolled heavily among the rosebushes. She picked up a big stone. She tried to hit the bottle. She longed to smash it. The stone missed. The girl began to whistle a vague tune.

Geula was a short, energetic girl of twenty-nine or so. Although she had not yet found a husband, none of us would deny her good qualities, such as the dedication she lavished on local social and cultural activities. Her face was pale and thin. No one could rival her in brewing strong coffee—coffee to raise the dead, we called it. A pair of bitter lines were etched at the corners of her mouth.

On summer evenings, when the rest of us would lounge in a group on a rug spread on one of the lawns and launch jokes and bursts of cheerful song heavenward, accompanied by clouds of cigarette smoke, Geula would shut herself up in her room and not join us until she had prepared the pot of scalding, strong coffee. She it was, too, who always took pains to ensure that there was no shortage of biscuits.

What had passed between Geula and me is not relevant here, and I shall make do with a hint or two. Long ago we used to stroll together to the orchards in the evening and talk. It was all a long time ago, and it is a long time since it ended. We would exchange unconventional political ideas or argue about the latest books. Geula was a stern and sometimes merciless critic: I was covered in confusion. She did not like my stories, because of the extreme polarity of situations, scenery, and characters, with no intermediate shades between black and white. I would utter an apology or a denial, but Geula always had ready proofs and she was a very methodical thinker. Sometimes I would dare to rest a conciliatory hand on her neck, and wait for her to calm down. But she never relaxed completely. If once or twice she leaned against me, she always blamed her broken sandal or her aching head. And so we drifted apart. To this day she still cuts my stories out of the periodicals, and arranges them in a cardboard box kept in a special drawer devoted to them alone.

I always buy her a new book of poems for her birthday. I creep into her room when she is out and leave the book on her table, without any inscription or dedication. Sometimes we happen to sit together in the dining hall. I avoid her glance, so as not to have to face her mocking sadness. On hot days, when faces are covered in sweat, the acne on her cheeks reddens and she seems to have no hope. When the cool of autumn comes, I sometimes find her pretty and attractive from a distance. On such days Geula likes to walk to the orchards in the early evening. She goes alone and comes back alone. Some of the youngsters come and ask me what she is looking for there, and they have a malicious snicker on their faces. I tell them that I don't know. And I really don't.

IV

Viciously Geula picked up another stone to hurl at the bottle. This time she did not miss, but she still failed to hear the shattering sound she craved. The stone grazed the bottle, which tinkled faintly and disappeared under one of the bushes.

A third stone, bigger and heavier than the other two, was launched from ridiculously close range: the girl trampled on the loose soil of the flower bed and stood right over the bottle. This time there was a harsh, dry explosion, which brought no relief. Must get out.

Damp and close and hot the night fell, its heat pricking the skin like broken glass. Geula retraced her steps, passed the balcony of her room, tossed her sandals inside, and walked down barefoot onto the dirt path.

The clods of earth tickled the soles of her feet. There was a rough friction, and her nerve endings quivered with flickers of vague excitement. Beyond the rocky hill the shadows were waiting for her: the orchard in the last of the light. With determined hands she widened the gap in the fence and slipped through. At that moment a slight evening breeze began to stir. It was a warmish summer breeze with no definite direction. An old sun rolled westward, trying to be sucked up by the dusty horizon. A last tractor climbed back to the depot, panting along the dirt road from the outlying plots. No doubt it was the tractor that had taken the second-shift workers their supper. It seemed shrouded in smoke or summer haze.

Geula bent down and picked some pebbles out of the dust. Absently she began to throw them back again, one by one. There were lines of poetry on her lips, some by the young poets she was fond of, others her own. By the irrigation pipe she paused, bent down, and drank as though kissing the faucet. But the faucet was rusty, the pipe was still hot, and the water was tepid and foul. Nevertheless she bent her head and let the water pour over her face and neck and into her shirt. A sharp taste of rust and wet dust filled her throat. She closed her eyes and stood in silence. No relief. Perhaps a cup of coffee. But only after the orchard. Must go now.

V

The orchards were heavily laden and fragrant. The branches intertwined, converging above the rows of trunks to form a shadowy dome. Underfoot the irrigated soil retained a hidden dampness. Shadows upon shadows at the foot of those gnarled trunks. Geula picked a plum, sniffed and crushed it. Sticky juice dripped from it. The sight made her feel dizzy. And the smell. She crushed a second plum. She picked another and rubbed it on her cheek till she was spattered with juice. Then, on her knees, she picked up a dry stick and scratched shapes in the dust. Aimless lines and curves. Sharp angles. Domes. A distant bleating invaded the orchard. Dimly she became aware of a sound of bells. She was far away. The nomad stopped behind Geula's back, as silent as a phantom. He dug at the dust with his big toe, and his shadow fell in front of him. But the girl was blinded by a flood of sounds. She saw and heard nothing. For a long time she continued to kneel on the ground and draw shapes in the dust with her twig. The nomad waited patiently in total silence. From time to time he closed his good eye and stared ahead of him with the other, the blind one. Finally he reached out and bestowed a long caress on the air. His obedient shadow moved in the dust. Geula stared, leapt to her feet, and leaned against the nearest tree, letting out a low sound. The nomad let his shoulders drop and put on a faint smile. Geula raised her arm and stabbed the air with her twig. The nomad continued to smile. His gaze dropped to her bare feet. His voice was hushed, and the Hebrew he spoke exuded a rare gentleness:

"What time is it?"

Geula inhaled to her lungs' full capacity. Her features grew sharp, her glance cold. Clearly and dryly she replied:

"It is half past six. Precisely."

The Arab broadened his smile and bowed slightly, as if to acknowledge a great kindness.

"Thank you very much, miss."

His bare toe had dug deep into the damp soil, and the clods of earth crawled at his feet as if there were a startled mole burrowing underneath them.

Geula fastened the top button of her blouse. There were large perspiration stains on her shirt, drawing attention to her armpits. She could smell the sweat on her body, and her nostrils widened. The nomad closed his blind eye and looked up. His good eye blinked. His skin was very dark; it was alive and warm. Creases were etched in his cheeks. He was unlike any man Geula had ever known, and his smell and color and breathing were also strange. His nose was long and narrow, and a shadow of a mustache showed beneath it. His cheeks seemed to be sunk into his mouth cavity. His lips were thin and fine, much finer than her own. But the chin was strong, almost expressing contempt or rebellion.

The man was repulsively handsome, Geula decided to herself. Unconsciously she responded with a mocking half-smile to the nomad's persistent grin. The Bedouin drew two crumpled cigarettes from a hidden pocket in his belt, laid them on his dark, outstretched palm, and held them out to her as though proffering crumbs to a sparrow. Geula dropped her smile, nodded twice, and accepted one. She ran the cigarette through her fingers, slowly, dreamily, ironing out the creases, straightening it, and only then did she put it to her lips. Quick as lightning, before she realized the purpose of the man's sudden movement, a tiny flame was dancing in front of her. Geula shielded the lighter with her hand even though there was no breeze in the orchard, sucked in the flame, closed her eyes. The nomad lit his own cigarette and bowed politely.

"Thank you very much," he said in his velvety voice.

"Thanks," Geula replied. "Thank you."

"You from the kibbutz?"

Geula nodded.

"Goo-d." An elongated syllable escaped from between his gleaming teeth. "That's goo-d."

The girl eyed his desert robe.

"Aren't you hot in that thing?"

The man gave an embarrassed, guilty smile, as if he had been caught red-handed. He took a slight step backward.

"Heaven forbid, it's not hot. Really not. Why? There's air, there's water. . . . ." And he fell silent.

The treetops were already growing darker. A first jackal sniffed the oncoming night and let out a tired howl. The orchard filled with a scurry of small, busy feet. All of a sudden Geula became aware of the throngs of black goats intruding in search of their master. They swirled silently in and out of the fruit trees. Geula pursed her lips and let out a short whistle of surprise.

"What are you doing here, anyway? Stealing?"

The nomad cowered as though a stone had been thrown at him. His hand beat a hollow tattoo on his chest.

"No, not stealing, heaven forbid, really not." He added a lengthy oath in his own language and resumed his silent smile. His blind eye winked nervously. Meanwhile an emaciated goat darted forward and rubbed against his leg. He kicked it away and continued to swear with passion:

"Not steal, truly, by Allah not steal. Forbidden to steal."

"Forbidden in the Bible," Geula replied with a dry, cruel smile. "Forbidden to steal, forbidden to kill, forbidden to covet, and forbidden to commit adultery. The righteous are above suspicion."

The Arab cowered before the onslaught of words and looked down at the ground. Shamefaced. Guilty. His foot continued to kick restlessly at the loose earth. He was trying to ingratiate himself. His blind eye narrowed. Geula was momentarily alarmed: surely it was a wink. The smile left his lips. He spoke in a soft, drawn-out whisper, as though uttering a prayer.

"Beautiful girl, truly very beautiful girl. Me, I got no girl yet. Me still young. No girl yet. Yaaa," he concluded with a guttural yell directed at an impudent goat that had rested its forelegs against a tree trunk and was munching hungrily at the foliage. The animal cast a pensive, skeptical glance at its master, shook its beard, and solemnly resumed its munching.

Without warning, and with amazing agility, the shepherd leapt through the air and seized the beast by the hind-quarters, lifted it above his head, let out a terrifying, savage screech, and flung it ruthlessly to the ground. Then he spat and turned to the girl.

"Beast," he apologized. "Beast. What to do. No brains. No manners."

The girl let go of the tree trunk against which she had been resting and leaned toward the nomad. A sweet shudder ran down her back. Her voice was still firm and cool.

"Another cigarette?" she asked. "Have you got another cigarette?"

The Bedouin replied with a look of anguish, almost of despair. He apologized. He explained at length that he had no more cigarettes, not even one, not even a little one. No more. All gone. What a pity. He would gladly, very gladly, have given her one. None left. All gone.

The beaten goat was getting shakily to its feet. Treading circumspectly, it returned to the tree trunk, disingenuously observing its master out of the corner of its eye. The shepherd watched it without moving. The goat reached up, rested its front hoofs on the tree, and calmly continued munching. The Arab picked up a heavy stone and swung his arm wildly. Geula seized his arm and restrained him.

"Leave it. Why. Let it be. It doesn't understand. It's only a beast. No brains, no manners."

The nomad obeyed. In total submission he let the stone drop. Then Geula let go of his arm. Once again the man drew the lighter out of his belt. With thin, pensive fingers he toyed with it. He accidentally lit a small flame, and hastily blew at it. The flame widened slightly, slanted, and died. Nearby a jackal broke into a loud, piercing wail. The rest of the goats, meanwhile, had followed the example of the first and were absorbed in rapid, almost angry munching.

A vague wail came from the nomad encampment away to the south, the dim drum beating time to its languorous call. The dusky men were sitting around their campfires, sending skyward their single-noted song. The night took up the strain and answered with dismal cricket-chirp. Last glimmers of light were dying away in the far west. The orchard stood in darkness. Sounds gathered all around, the wind's whispering, the goats' sniffing, the rustle of ravished leaves. Geula pursed her lips and whistled an old tune. The nomad listened to her with rapt attention, his head cocked to one side in surprise, his mouth hanging slightly open. She glanced at her watch. The hands winked back at her with a malign, phosphorescent glint, but said nothing. Night.

The Arab turned his back on Geula, dropped to his knees, touched his forehead on the ground, and began mumbling fervently.

"You've got no girl yet," Geula broke into his prayer. "You're still too young." Her voice was loud and strange. Her hands were on her hips, her breathing still even. The man stopped praying, turned his dark face toward her, and muttered a phrase in Arabic. He was still crouched on all fours, but his pose suggested a certain suppressed joy.

"You're still young," Geula repeated, "very young. Perhaps twenty. Perhaps thirty. Young. No girl for you. Too young."

The man replied with a very long and solemn remark in his own language. She laughed nervously, her hands embracing her hips.

"What's the matter with you?" she inquired, laughing still. "Why are you talking to me in Arabic all of a sudden? What do you think I am? What do you want here, anyway?"

Again the nomad replied in his own language. Now a note of terror filled his voice. With soft, silent steps he recoiled and withdrew as though from a dying creature. She was breathing heavily now, panting, trembling. A single wild syllable escaped from the shepherd's mouth: a sign between him and his goats. The goats responded and thronged around him, their feet pattering on the carpet of dead leaves like cloth ripping. The crickets fell silent. The goats huddled in the dark, a terrified, quivering mass, and disappeared into the darkness, the shepherd vanishing in their midst.

Afterward, alone and trembling, she watched an airplane passing in the dark sky above the treetops, rumbling dully, its lights blinking alternately with a rhythm as precise as that of the drums: red, green, red, green, red. The night covered over the traces. There was a smell of bonfires on the air and a smell of dust borne on the breeze. Only a slight breeze among the fruit trees. Then panic struck her and her blood froze. Her mouth opened to scream but she did not scream, she started to run and she ran barefoot with all her strength for home and stumbled and rose and ran as though pursued, but only the sawing of the crickets chased after her.

VI

She returned to her room and made coffee for all the members of the secretariat, because she remembered her promise to Etkin. Outside the cool of evening had set in, but inside her room the walls were hot and her body was also on fire. Her clothes stuck to her body because she had been running, and her armpits disgusted her. The spots on her face were glowing. She stood and counted the number of times the coffee boiled—seven successive boilings, as she had learned to do it from her brother Ehud before he was killed in a reprisal raid in the desert. With pursed lips she counted as the black liquid rose and subsided, rose and subsided, bubbling fiercely as it reached its climax.

That's enough, now. Take clean clothes for the evening. Go to the showers.

What can that Etkin understand about savages. A great socialist. What does he know about Bedouins. A nomad sniffs out weakness from a distance. Give him a kind word, or a smile, and he pounces on you like a wild beast and tries to rape you. It was just as well I ran away from him.

In the showers the drain was clogged and the bench was greasy. Geula put her clean clothes on the stone ledge. I'm not shivering because the water's cold. I'm shivering with disgust. Those black fingers, and how he went straight for my throat. And his teeth. And the goats. Small and skinny like a child, but so strong. It was only by biting and kicking that I managed to escape. Soap my belly and everything, soap it again and again. Yes, let the boys go right away tonight to their camp and smash their black bones because of what they did to me. Now I must get outside.

VII

She left the shower and started back toward her room, to pick up the coffee and take it to the secretariat. But on the way she heard crickets and laughter, and she remembered him bent down on all fours, and she was alarmed and stood still in the dark. Suddenly she vomited among the flowering shrubs. And she began to cry. Then her knees gave way. She sat down to rest on the dark earth. She stopped crying. But her teeth continued to chatter, from the cold or from pity. Suddenly she was not in a hurry any more, even the coffee no longer seemed important, and she thought to herself: There's still time. There's still time.

Those planes sweeping the sky tonight were probably on a night-bombing exercise. Repeatedly they roared among the stars, keeping up a constant flashing, red, green, red, green, red. In counterpoint came the singing of the nomads and their drums, a persistent heartbeat in the distance: One, one, two, One, one, two. And silence.

VIII

From eight-thirty until nearly nine o'clock we waited for Geula. At five to nine Etkin said that he could not imagine what had happened; he could not recall her ever having missed a meeting or been late before; at all events, we must now begin the meeting and turn to the business on the agenda.

He began with a summary of the facts. He gave details of the damage that had apparently been caused by the Bedouins, although there was no formal proof, and enumerated the steps that had been taken on the committee's initiative. The appeal to good will. Calling in the police. Strengthening the guard around the settlement. Tracking dogs. The meeting with the elder of the tribe. He had to admit, Etkin said, that we had now reached an impasse. Nevertheless, he believed that we had to maintain a sense of balance and not give way to extremism, because hatred always gave rise to further hatred. It was essential to break the vicious circle of hostility. He therefore opposed with all the moral force at his disposal the approach—and particularly the intentions—of certain of the younger members. He wished to remind us, by way of conclusion, that the conflict between herdsmen and tillers of the soil was as old as human civilization, as seemed to be evidenced by the story of Cain, who rose up against Abel, his brother. It was fitting, in view of the social gospel we had adopted, that we should put an end to this ancient feud, too, just as we had put an end to other ugly phenomena. It was up to us, and everything depended on our moral strength.

The room was full of tension, even unpleasantness. Rami twice interrupted Etkin and on one occasion went so far as to use the ugly word "rubbish." Etkin took offense, accused the younger members of planning terrorist activities, and said in conclusion, "We're not going to have that sort of thing here."

Geula had not arrived, and that was why there was no one to cool down the temper of the meeting. And no coffee. A heated exchange broke out between me and Rami. Although in age I belonged with the younger men, I did not agree with their proposals. Like Etkin, I was absolutely opposed to answering the nomads with violence—for two reasons, and when I was given permission to speak I mentioned them both. In the first place, nothing really serious had happened so far. A little stealing perhaps, but even that was not certain: every faucet or pair of pliers that a tractor driver left in a field or lost in the garage or took home with him was immediately blamed on the Bedouins. Secondly, there had been no rape or murder. Hereupon Rami broke in excitedly and asked what I was waiting for. Was I perhaps waiting for some small incident of rape that Geula could write poems about and I could make into a short story? I flushed and cast around in my mind for a telling retort.

But Etkin, upset by our rudeness, immediately deprived us both of the right to speak and began to explain his position all over again. He asked us how it would look if the papers reported that a kibbutz had sent out a lynch mob to settle scores with its Arab neighbors. As Etkin uttered the phrase "lynch mob," Rami made a gesture to his young friends that is commonly used by basketball players. At this signal they rose in a body and walked out in disgust, leaving Etkin to lecture to his heart's content to three elderly women and a long-retired member of Parliament.

After a moment's hesitation I rose and followed them. True, I did not share their views, but I, too, had been deprived of the right to speak in an arbitrary and insulting manner.

IX

If only Geula had come to the meeting and brought her famous coffee with her, it is possible that tempers might have been soothed. Perhaps, too, her understanding might have achieved some sort of compromise between the conflicting points of view. But the coffee was standing, cold by now, on the table in her room. And Geula herself was lying among the bushes behind the Memorial Hall, watching the lights of the planes and listening to the sounds of the night. How she longed to make her peace and to forgive. Not to hate him and wish him dead. Perhaps to get up and go to him, to find him among the wadis and forgive him and never come back. Even to sing to him. The sharp slivers piercing her skin and drawing blood were the fragments of the bottle she had smashed here with a big stone at the beginning of the evening. And the living thing slithering among the slivers of glass among the clods of earth was a snake, perhaps a venomous snake, perhaps a viper. It stuck out a forked tongue, and its triangular head was cold and erect. Its eyes were dark glass. It could never close them, because it had no eyelids. A thorn in her flesh, perhaps a sliver of glass. She was very tired. And the pain was vague, almost pleasant. A distant ringing in her ears. To sleep now.

Wearily, through the thickening film, she watched the gang of youngsters crossing the lawn on their way to the fields and the wadi to even the score with the nomads. We were carrying short, thick sticks. Excitement was dilating our pupils. And the blood was drumming in our temples.

Far away in the darkened orchards stood somber, dust-laden cypresses, swaying to and fro with a gentle, religious fervor. She felt tired, and that was why she did not come to see us off. But her fingers caressed the dust, and her face was very calm and almost beautiful.

[1963]

Translated by
NICHOLAS DE LANGE
and PHILIP SIMPSON

QUESTIONS

1. What is the effect of the variations in the point of view from section to section?
2. How do the narrator and the other men of the settlement view Geula? How does the reader understand her?
3. What happens to Geula in the story? Why are certain events only implied and not described?
4. What does the story's title signify?

Emilia Pardo Bazán

(1857–1921)

Spain

Although not widely known in the United States, Emilia Pardo Bazán is a central and influential figure in nineteenth-century Spanish literature, the author of more than 20 novels as well as a number of short stories and critical essays on literary and other subjects. The only child of titled Spanish royalty, Pardo Bazán inherited the title of Countess. Yet despite her aristocratic background, her political views were scarcely traditional. An early feminist, she expressed in a variety of writings her profound objections to the oppressive conditions for women in Spanish society. Her fiction is in the tradition of the naturalism practiced by her French counterparts, Emile Zola and Gustave Flaubert, although Pardo Bazán distinguished Spanish naturalism as less deterministic than that of her French contemporaries.

"The Revolver" first appeared in a Spanish newspaper.

◆ The Revolver ◆

In a burst of confidence, one of those provoked by the familiarity and companionship of bathing resorts, the woman suffering from heart trouble told me about her illness, with all the details of chokings, violent palpitations, dizziness, fainting spells, and collapses, in which one sees the final hour approach. . . . As she spoke, I looked her over carefully. She was a woman of about thirty-five or thirty-six, maimed by suffering; at least I thought so, but, on closer scrutiny, I began to suspect that there was something more than the physical in her ruin. As a matter of fact, she spoke and expressed herself like someone who had suffered a good deal, and I know that the ills of the body, when not of imminent gravity, are usually not enough to produce such a wasting away, such extreme dejection. And, noting how the broad leaves of the plane tree, touched with carmine by the artistic hand of autumn, fell to the ground majestically and lay stretched out like severed hands, I remarked, in order to gain her confidence, on the passing of all life, the melancholy of the transitoriness of everything. . . .

"Nothing is anything," she answered, understanding at once that not curiosity but compassion was beckoning at the gates of her spirit. "Nothing is anything . . . unless we ourselves convert that nothing into something. Would to God we could see everything, always, with the slight but sad emotion produced in us by the fall of this foliage on the sand."

The sickly flush of her cheeks deepened, and then I realized that she had probably been very beautiful, although her beauty was effaced and gone, like the colors of a fine picture over which is passed cotton saturated with alcohol. Her blond, silky hair showed traces of ash, premature gray hair. Her features had withered away; her complexion especially revealed those disturbances of the blood which are slow poisonings, decompositions of the organism. Her soft blue eyes, veined with black, must have once been attractive, but now they were disfigured by something worse than age; a kind of aberration, which at certain moments lent them the glitter of blindness.

We grew silent: but my way of contemplating her expressed my pity so plainly that she, sighing for a chance to unburden her heavy heart, made up her mind, and stopping from time to time to breathe and regain her strength, she told me the strange story.

"When I married, I was very much in love. . . . My husband was, compared to me, advanced in years; he was bordering on forty, and I was only nineteen. My temperament was gay and lively; I retained a childlike disposition, and when he was not home I would devote my time to singing, playing the piano, chatting and laughing with girl-friends who came to see me and envied me my happiness, my brilliant marriage, my devoted husband, and my brilliant social position.

"This lasted a year — the wonderful year of the honeymoon. The following spring, on our wedding anniversary, I began to notice that Reinaldo's disposition was changing. He was often in a gloomy mood, and, without my knowing the cause, he spoke to me harshly, and had outbursts of anger. But it was not long before I understood the origins of his transformation: Reinaldo had conceived a violent, irrational jealousy, a jealousy without object or cause, which, for that very reason, was doubly cruel and difficult to cure.

"If we went out together, he was watchful lest people stare at me or tell me, in passing, one of those silly things people say to young women; if he went out alone, he was suspicious of what I was doing in the house, and of the people who came to see me; if I went out alone, his suspicions and suppositions were even more defamatory. . . .

"If I proposed, pleadingly, that we stay home together, he was watchful of my saddened expression, of my supposed boredom, of my work, of an instant when, passing in front of the window, I happened to look outside. . . . He was watchful, above all, when he noticed that my birdlike disposition, my good, childlike humor, had disappeared, and that on many afternoons, when I turned on the lights, he found my skin shining with the damp, ardent trace of tears. Deprived of my innocent amusements, now separated from my friends and relatives, and from my own family, because Reinaldo interpreted as treacherous artifices the desire to communicate and look at faces other than his, I often wept, and did not respond to Reinaldo's transports of passion with the sweet abandonment of earlier times.

"One day, after one of the usual bitter scenes, my husband said:

"'Flora, I may be a madman, but I am not a fool. I have alienated your love, and although perhaps you would not have thought of deceiving me, in the future, without being able to remedy it, you would. Now I shall never again be your beloved. The swallows that have left do not return. But because, unfortunately, I love you more each day, and love you without peace, with eagerness and fever, I wish to point out that I have thought of a way which will prevent questions, quarrels, or tears between us — and once and for all you will know what our future will be.'

"Speaking thus, he took me by the arm and led me toward the bedroom.

"I went trembling; cruel presentiments froze me. Reinaldo opened the drawer of the small inlaid cabinet where he kept tobacco, a watch, and handkerchiefs and showed me a large revolver, a sinister weapon.

"'Here,' he said, 'is your guarantee that in the future your life will be peaceful and pleasant. I shall never again demand an accounting of how you spend your time, or of your friends, or of your amusements. You are free, free as the air. But the day I see something that wounds me to the quick . . . that day, I swear by my mother! Without complaints or scenes, or the slightest sign that I am displeased, oh no, not that! I will get up quietly at night, take the weapon, put it to your temple and you will wake up in eternity. Now you have been warned. . . .'

"As for me, I was in a daze, unconscious. It was necessary to send for the doctor, inasmuch as the fainting spell lasted. When I recovered consciousness and remembered, the convulsion took place. I must point out that I have a mortal fear of firearms; a younger brother of mine died of an accidental shot. My eyes, staring wildly, would not leave the drawer of the cabinet that held the revolver.

"I could not doubt, from Reinaldo's tone and the look on his face, that he was prepared to carry out his threat, and knowing also how easily his imagination grew confused, I began to consider myself as dead. As a matter of fact, Reinaldo kept his promise, and left me complete mistress of myself, without directing the slightest censure my way, or showing, even by a look, that he was opposed to any of my wishes or disapproved of my actions; but this itself frightened me, because it indicated the strength and tyranny of a resolute will . . . and, victim of a terror which every day grew more profound, I remained motionless, not daring to take a step. I would always see the steely reflection of the gun barrel.

"At night, insomnia kept my eyes open, and I imagined I felt the metallic cold of a steel circle on my temple; or if I got to sleep, I woke up startled with palpitations that made my heart seem to leap from my breast, because I dreamed that an awful report was ripping apart the bones of my skull and blowing my brains out, dashing them against the wall. . . . And this lasted four years, four years without a single peaceful moment, when I never took a step without fearing that that step might give rise to tragedy."

"And how did that horrible situation end?" I asked, in order to bring her story to a close, because I saw her gasping for breath.

"It ended . . . with Reinaldo, who was thrown by a horse, and had some internal injury, being killed on the spot.

"Then, and only then, I knew that I still loved him, and I mourned him quite sincerely, although he was my executioner, and a systematic one at that!"

"And did you pick up the revolver to throw it out the window?"

"You'll see," she murmured. "Something rather extraordinary happened. I sent Reinaldo's manservant to remove the revolver from my room, because in my dreams I continued to see the shot and feel the chill on my temple. . . . And after he carried out the order, the manservant came to tell me: 'Señora, there was no cause for alarm. . . . This revolver wasn't loaded.'

"'No, Señora, and it looks to me as though it never was. . . . As a matter of fact, the poor master never got around to buying the cartridges. Why, I would even ask him at times if he wanted me to go to the gunsmith's and get them, but he didn't answer, and then he never spoke of the matter again.'"

"And so," added the sufferer from heart disease, "an unloaded revolver shot me, not in the head, but in the center of my heart, and believe me when I tell you that, in spite of digitalis and baths and all the remedies, the bullet is unsparing. . . ."

[1895]

Translated by
ANGEL FLORES

QUESTIONS

1. What is the exact nature of Flora's illness? Why does she continue to suffer?
2. How would you describe the relationship between Flora and Reinaldo?
3. What is the theme of the story?
4. How do the images of the story contribute to its tone and theme?

Octavio Paz

(b. 1914)

Mexico

Born in Mexico City in 1914, Octavio Paz has spent much of his life as a cosmopolite—a citizen of the world. He lived in Spain during the Spanish Civil War; in 1944, he was in the United States as the recipient of a Guggenheim fellowship; the following year he spent in Paris, where he was befriended by André Breton and other surrealists. From 1962 until 1968, he was Mexico's ambassador to India. As a teacher, he has held distinguished teaching positions in both the United States and England: at Cambridge, the University of Texas at Austin, and Harvard. He has also lived in the Orient. In all of these different places and careers, Paz has continued to write, publishing numerous collections of essays and poems.

Paz's influence on contemporary Mexican writing has been extraordinary. The culmination of his artistic career was marked by the Nobel Prize for Literature, which he received in 1990. On that occasion, his poems and essays were specifically praised. Paz himself reflected on his Mexican heritage by stating, "I discovered that I was Mexican when I was in the United States in my youth, during the war. We began by not speaking English, and wound up having fights with other children. And then when I went back to Mexico I had the same fights, for the same reasons. I was fourteen, and I couldn't understand it. This experience was rather painful, to be a foreigner in your own place. And then I started to ask myself who I am and why I am Mexican." As you read "The Blue Bouquet," consider the ways in which Paz's international background influenced both the form and the subject of his story.

◆ *The Blue Bouquet* ◆

When I woke up I was soaked with sweat. The floor of my room had been freshly sprinkled and a warm vapor was rising from the red tiles. A moth flew around and around the naked bulb, dazzled by the light. I got out of the hammock and walked barefoot across the room, being careful not to step on a scorpion if one had come out of its hiding place to enjoy the coolness of the floor. I stood at the window for a few minutes, breathing in the air from the fields and listening to the vast, feminine breathing of the night. Then I walked over to the washstand, poured some water into the enamel basin, and moistened a towel. I rubbed my chest and legs with the damp cloth, dried myself a little, and got dressed, first making sure that no bugs had got into the seams of my clothes. I went leaping down the green-painted staircase and blundered into the hotelkeeper at the door. He was blind in one eye, a glum and reticent man, sitting there in a rush chair, smoking a cigarette, with his eyes half closed.

Now he peered at me with his good eye. "Where are you going, señor?" he asked in a hoarse voice.

"To take a walk. It's too hot to stay in my room."

"But everything's closed up by now. And we don't have any streetlights here. You'd better stay in."

I shrugged my shoulders, mumbled, "I'll be right back," and went out into the darkness. At first I couldn't see anything at all. I groped my way along the stone-paved street. I lit a cigarette. Suddenly the moon came out from behind a black cloud, lighting up a weather-beaten white wall. I stopped in my tracks, blinded by that whiteness. A faint breeze stirred the air and I could smell the fragrance of the tamarind trees. The night was murmurous with the sounds of leaves and insects. The crickets had bivouacked among the tall weeds. I raised my eyes: up there the stars were also camping out. I thought that the whole universe was a grand system of signals, a conversation among enormous beings. My own actions, the creak of a cricket, the blinking of a star, were merely pauses and syllables, odd fragments of that dialogue. I was only one syllable, of only one word. But what was that word? Who was uttering it? And to whom? I tossed my cigarette onto the sidewalk. It fell in a glowing arc, giving off sparks like a miniature comet.

I walked on, slowly, for a long while. I felt safe and free, because those great lips were pronouncing me so clearly, so joyously. The night was a garden of eyes.

Then when I was crossing a street I could tell that someone had come out of a doorway. I turned around but couldn't see anything. I began to walk faster. A moment later I could hear the scuff of huaraches on the warm stones. I didn't want to look back, even though I knew the shadow was catching up with me. I tried to run. I couldn't. Then I stopped short. And before I could defend myself I felt the point of a knife against my back, and a soft voice said, "Don't move, señor, or you're dead."

Without turning my head I asked, "What do you want?"

"Your eyes, señor." His voice was strangely gentle, almost embarrassed.

"My eyes? What are you going to do with my eyes? Look, I've got a little money on me. Not much, but it's something. I'll give you everything I've got if you'll let me go. Don't kill me."

"You shouldn't be scared, señor. I'm not going to kill you. I just want your eyes."

"But what do you want them for?"

"It's my sweetheart's idea. She'd like to have a bouquet of blue eyes. There aren't many people around here that have them."

"Mine won't do you any good. They aren't blue, they're light brown."

"No, señor. Don't try to fool me. I know they're blue."

"But we're both Christians, hombre! You can't just gouge my eyes out. I'll give you everything I've got on me."

"Don't be so squeamish." His voice was harsh now. "Turn around."

I turned around. He was short and slight, with a palm sombrero half covering his face. He had a long machete in his right hand. It glittered in the moonlight.

"Hold a match to your face."

I lit a match and held it up in front of my face. The flame made me close my eyes and he pried up my lids with his fingers. He couldn't see well enough, so he stood on tiptoes and stared at me. The match burned my fingers and I threw it away. He was silent for a moment.

"Aren't you sure now? They aren't blue."

"You're very clever, señor," he said. "Light another match."

I lit another and held it close to my eyes. He tugged at my sleeve. "Kneel down."

I knelt. He grabbed my hair and bent my head back. Then he leaned over me, gazing intently, and the machete came closer and closer till it touched my eyelids. I shut my eyes.

"Open them up," he told me. "Wide."

I opened my eyes again. The match-flame singed my lashes.

Suddenly he let go. "No. They're not blue. Excuse me." And he disappeared.

I huddled against the wall with my hands over my face. Later I got up and ran through the deserted streets for almost an hour. When I finally stumbled into the plaza I saw the hotelkeeper still sitting at the door. I went in without speaking to him. The next day I got out of that village.

[1961]

Translated by
LYSANDER KEMP

QUESTIONS

1. What do the blue eyes represent?
2. What aspects of surrealism have influenced Paz's story?
3. Is it possible to interpret the story literally, or is only a figurative interpretation valid?

Virgilio Piñera

(1912–1979)

Cuba

Cuban writer Virgilio Piñera explained that he called his short stories *Cold Tales* because "As these are heated times, these *Cold Tales* should, I think, come in handy." Cold—he wanted us to believe—is synonymous with reality, the hard facts of life, and cold they are indeed. Piñera's images of life in modern Cuba—where his work was banned due to his homosexuality—are macabre and grotesque, often bordering on the taboo. The narrator of "A Few Children" confesses that he devours infants but limits himself to no more than four a year. A character in "Meat" can best be described as autocannibalistic. Two amputees (each with one leg) decide to buy a pair of shoes together in "Affairs of Amputees." Piñera's stories combine the fantasy of Latin American magic realism with the absurdity of Samuel Beckett and Eugene Ionesco.

Mark Schafer (Piñera's English translator) expands on Piñera's world in a brief foreword to the Eridanos Library edition of *Cold Tales*: "The author maintains that life neither rewards nor punishes, neither condemns nor saves; or, to be more exact, does not distinguish these complicated categories. He can only say that he lives, that he is not obliged to judge his own acts, to give them any significance whatsoever, to expect vindication at the end of his days."

Except for the seven years from 1950 to 1957, Virgilio Piñera lived in Cuba—often at the poverty level. Almost his entire life was one of obscurity.

◆ *Insomnia* ◆

The man goes to bed early. He can't fall asleep. He tosses and turns in bed, as might be expected. He gets tangled in the sheets. He lights a cigarette. He reads a little. He turns out the light again. But he can't sleep. At three o'clock, he gets out of bed. He wakes his friend next door and confides that he can't sleep. He asks the friend for advice. The friend advises him to take a short walk to tire himself out. And then, right away, to drink a cup of linden blossom tea and turn out the light. He does all that, but is unable to fall asleep. He gets up again. This time he goes to see a doctor. As usual, the doctor talks a lot but the man still doesn't fall asleep. At six in the morning, he loads a revolver and blows his brains out. The man is dead, but hasn't been able to get to sleep. Insomnia is a very persistent thing.

[1956]

Translated by
Mark Schafer

QUESTIONS

1. In what sense does "Insomnia" defy categorization as a short story?
2. Of the classical unities (character, setting, time, and conflict) that often give short fiction its form, which—if any of these—apply to "Insomnia"?
3. Is insomnia the opposite of sleep or is it, in fact, something quite different?

EDGAR ALLAN POE

(1809–1849)

UNITED STATES

Edgar Allan Poe is often called the father of the modern short story—not only as a result of his own unique tales but also as a result of the critical theory he formulated about the genre. In a famous review of Nathaniel Hawthorne's short stories, Poe wrote,

> A skillful literary artist has constructed a tale. If wise, he has not fashioned his thoughts to accommodate his incidents; but having conceived, with deliberate care, a certain unique or single *effect* to be wrought out, he then invents such incidents—he then combines such events as may best aid him in establishing this preconceived effect. If his very initial sentence tends not to be the outbringing of this effect, then he has failed in his first step. In the whole composition there should be no word written, of which the tendency, direct or indirect, is not to the one pre-established design. And by such means, with such care and skill, a picture is at length painted which leaves in the mind of him who contemplates it with a kindred art, a sense of the fullest satisfaction. The idea of the tale has been presented unblemished, because undisturbed; and this is an end unattainable by the novel. Undue brevity is just as exceptionable here as in the poem; but undue length is yet more to be avoided.

Much of Poe's writing career was typified by hardship and unhappiness. His wife, Virginia Clemm, died six years after they were married. Editors were unsympathetic to Poe's writing and often paid him poorly for his work. Even after his death, Poe's first biographer wouldn't let him rest in peace but conjured up an image of the writer as demonic and unbalanced. These psychological distortions of the man himself are not difficult to come by, however, if one looks at Poe's writings: especially many of his tales of terror or even his poems of frustrated love. Nevertheless, Poe's influence on the short story form cannot be denied. Perhaps the entire sense of modern American gothicism grows from Poe's fiction.

Another way to measure a writer's significance is by his later imitators. For that reason, we cannot resist quoting a parody of a Poe opening sentence (for that special effect) that appeared in a *New York Magazine* competition a number of years ago: "Three days have passed since my master decreed that his wife, insatiable Lady Anne the Fat, be sent without food or drink to the bare dungeon, her sole companion a ravening crocodile: now, as I stare into Milady's mad yellow eyes, I slowly realize that she is quite alone in her cell."

The Cask of Amontillado

The thousand injuries of Fortunato I had borne as I best could; but when he ventured upon insult, I vowed revenge. You, who so well know the nature of my soul, will not suppose, however, that I gave utterance to a threat. *At length* I would be avenged; this was a point definitely settled—but the very definitiveness with which it was resolved precluded the idea of risk. I must not only punish, but punish with impunity. A wrong is unredressed when retribution overtakes its redresser. It is equally unredressed when the avenger fails to make himself felt as such to him who has done the wrong.

It must be understood, that neither by word nor deed had I given Fortunato cause to doubt my good-will. I continued, as was my wont, to smile in his face, and he did not perceive that my smile *now* was at the thought of his immolation.

He had a weak point—this Fortunato—although in other regards he was a man to be respected and even feared. He prided himself on his connoisseurship in wine. Few Italians have the true virtuoso spirit. For the most part their enthusiasm is adopted to suit the time and opportunity—to practise imposture upon the British and Austrian *millionnaires.* In painting and gemmary Fortunato, like his countrymen, was a quack—but in the matter of old wines he was sincere. In this respect I did not differ from him materially: I was skilful in the Italian vintages myself, and bought largely whenever I could.

It was about dusk, one evening during the supreme madness of the carnival season, that I encountered my friend. He accosted me with excessive warmth, for he had been drinking much. The man wore motley. He had on a tight-fitting parti-striped dress, and his head was surmounted by the conical cap and bells. I was so pleased to see him, that I thought I should never have done wringing his hand.

I said to him: "My dear Fortunato, you are luckily met. How remarkably well you are looking to-day! But I have received a pipe[1] of what passes for Amontillado, and I have my doubts."

"How?" said he. "Amontillado? A pipe? Impossible! And in the middle of the carnival!"

"I have my doubts," I replied; "and I was silly enough to pay the full Amontillado price without consulting you in the matter. You were not to be found, and I was fearful of losing a bargain."

"Amontillado!"

"I have my doubts."

"Amontillado!"

"And I must satisfy them."

"Amontillado!"

"As you are engaged, I am on my way to Luchesi. If any one has a critical turn, it is he. He will tell me———"

"Luchesi cannot tell Amontillado from Sherry."

[1]*pipe* a cask or keg

"And yet some fools will have it that his taste is a match for your own."

"Come, let us go."

"Whither?"

"To your vaults."

"My friend, no; I will not impose upon your good nature. I perceive you have an engagement. Luchesi ——"

"I have no engagement; — come."

"My friend, no. It is not the engagement, but the severe cold with which I perceive you are afflicted. The vaults are insufferably damp. They are encrusted with nitre."

"Let us go, nevertheless. The cold is merely nothing. Amontillado! You have been imposed upon. And as for Luchesi, he cannot distinguish Sherry from Amontillado."

Thus speaking, Fortunato possessed himself of my arm. Putting on a mask of black silk, and drawing a *roquelaire*[2] closely about my person, I suffered him to hurry me to my palazzo.

There were no attendants at home; they had absconded to make merry in honor of the time. I had told them that I should not return until the morning, and had given them explicit orders not to stir from the house. These orders were sufficient, I well knew, to insure their immediate disappearance, one and all, as soon as my back was turned.

I took from their sconces two flambeaux, and giving one to Fortunato, bowed him through several suites of rooms to the archway that led into the vaults. I passed down a long and winding staircase, requesting him to be cautious as he followed. We came at length to the foot of the descent, and stood together on the damp ground of the catacombs of the Montresors.

The gait of my friend was unsteady, and the bells upon his cap jingled as he strode.

"The pipe?" said he.

"It is farther on," said I; "but observe the white web-work which gleams from these cavern walls."

He turned toward me, and looked into my eyes with two filmy orbs that distilled the rheum of intoxication.

"Nitre?" he asked, at length.

"Nitre," I replied. "How long have you had that cough?"

"Ugh! ugh! ugh! — ugh! ugh! ugh! — ugh! ugh! ugh! — ugh! ugh! ugh! — ugh! ugh! ugh!"

My poor friend found it impossible to reply for many minutes.

"It is nothing," he said, at last.

"Come," I said, with decision, "we will go back; your health is precious. You are rich, respected, admired, beloved; you are happy, as once I was. You are a man to be missed. For me it is no matter. We will go back; you will be ill, and I cannot be responsible. Besides, there is Luchesi ——"

"Enough," he said; "the cough is a mere nothing; it will not kill me. I shall not die of a cough."

"True — true," I replied; "and, indeed, I had no intention of alarming you unnecessarily; but you should use all proper caution. A draught of this Medoc will defend us from the damps."

[2]*roquelaire* French: a short cloak

Here I knocked off the neck of a bottle which I drew from a long row of its fellows that lay upon the mould.

"Drink," I said, presenting him the wine.

He raised it to his lips with a leer. He paused and nodded to me familiarly, while his bells jingled.

"I drink," he said, "to the buried that repose around us."

"And I to your long life."

He again took my arm, and we proceeded.

"These vaults," he said, "are extensive."

"The Montresors," I replied. "were a great and numerous family."

"I forget your arms."

"A huge human foot d'or,[3] in a field azure; the foot crushes a serpent rampant whose fangs are imbedded in the heel."

"And the motto?"

"*Nemo me impune lacessit.*"[4]

"Good!" he said.

The wine sparkled in his eyes and the bells jingled. My own fancy grew warm with the Medoc. We had passed through walls of piled bones, with casks and puncheons intermingling into the inmost recesses of the catacombs. I paused again, and this time I made bold to seize Fortunato by an arm above the elbow.

"The nitre!" I said; "see, it increases. It hangs like moss upon the vaults. We are below the river's bed. The drops of moisture trickle among the bones. Come, we will go back ere it is too late. Your cough ——"

"It is nothing," he said; "let us go on. But first, another draught of the Medoc."

I broke and reached him a flagon of De Grâve. He emptied it at a breath. His eyes flashed with a fierce light. He laughed and threw the bottle upward with a gesticulation I did not understand.

I looked at him in surprise. He repeated the movement—a grotesque one.

"You do not comprehend?" he said.

"Not, I," I replied.

"Then you are not of the brotherhood."

"How?"

"You are not of the masons."

"Yes, yes," I said; "yes, yes."

"You? Impossible! A mason?"

"A mason," I replied.

"A sign," he said.

"It is this," I answered, producing a trowel from beneath the folds of my *roquelaire*.

"You jest," he exclaimed, recoiling a few paces. "But let us proceed to the Amontillado."

"Be it so," I said, replacing the tool beneath the cloak, and again offering him my arm. He leaned upon it heavily. We continued our route in search of the Amontillado. We passed through a range of low arches, descended, passed on, and descending again, arrived at a deep crypt, in which the foulness of the air caused our flambeaux rather to glow than flame.

[3]*d'or* French: of gold

[4]*Nemo me impune lacessit* Latin: No one may insult me with impunity.

At the most remote end of the crypt there appeared another less spacious. Its walls had been lined with human remains, piled to the vault overhead, in the fashion of the great catacombs of Paris. Three sides of this interior crypt were still ornamented in this manner. From the fourth the bones had been thrown down, and lay promiscuously upon the earth, forming at one point a mound of some size. Within the wall thus exposed by the displacing of the bones, we perceived a still interior recess, in depth about four feet, in width three, in height six or seven. It seemed to have been constructed for no especial use within itself, but formed merely the interval between two of the colossal supports of the roof of the catacombs, and was backed by one of their circumscribing walls of solid granite.

It was in vain that Fortunato, uplifting his dull torch, endeavored to pry into the depth of the recess. Its termination the feeble light did not enable us to see.

"Proceed," I said; "herein is the Amontillado. As for Luchesi ——"

"He is an ignoramus," interrupted my friend, as he stepped unsteadily forward, while I followed immediately at his heels. In an instant he had reached the extremity of the niche, and finding his progress arrested by the rock, stood stupidly bewildered. A moment more and I had fettered him to the granite. In its surface were two iron staples, distant from each other about two feet, horizontally. From one of these depended a short chain, from the other a padlock. Throwing the links about his waist, it was but the work of a few seconds to secure it. He was too much astounded to resist. Withdrawing the key I stepped back from the recess.

"Pass your hand," I said, "over the wall; you cannot help feeling the nitre. Indeed it is *very* damp. Once more let me *implore* you to return. No? Then I must positively leave you. But I must first render you all the little attentions in my power."

"The Amontillado!" ejaculated my friend, not yet recovered from his astonishment.

"True," I replied; "the Amontillado."

As I said these words I busied myself among the pile of bones of which I have before spoken. Throwing them aside, I soon uncovered a quantity of building stone and mortar. With these materials and with the aid of my trowel, I began vigorously to wall up the entrance of the niche.

I had scarcely laid the first tier of the masonry when I discovered that the intoxication of Fortunato had in a great measure worn off. The earliest indication I had of this was a low moaning cry from the depth of the recess. It was *not* the cry of a drunken man. There was then a long and obstinate silence. I laid the second tier, and the third, and the fourth; and then I heard the furious vibrations of the chain. The noise lasted for several minutes, during which, that I might hearken to it with the more satisfaction, I ceased my labors and sat down upon the bones. When at last the clanking subsided, I resumed the trowel, and finished without interruption the fifth, the sixth, and the seventh tier. The wall was now nearly upon a level with my breast. I again paused, and holding the flambeaux over the masonwork, threw a few feeble rays upon the figure within.

A succession of loud and shrill screams, bursting suddenly from the throat of the chained form, seemed to thrust me violently back. For a brief moment I hesitated—I trembled. Unsheathing my rapier, I began to grope with it about the recess; but the thought of an instant reassured me. I placed my hand upon the solid fabric of the catacombs, and felt satisfied. I reapproached the wall. I replied to the yells of him who clamored. I reechoed—I aided—I surpassed them in volume and in strength. I did this, and the clamorer grew still.

It was now midnight, and my task was drawing to a close. I had completed the eighth, the ninth, and the tenth tier. I had finished a portion of the last and the eleventh; there remained but a single stone to be fitted and plastered in. I struggled with its weight; I placed it partially in its destined position. But now there came from out the niche a low laugh that erected the hairs upon my head. It was succeeded by a sad voice, which I had difficulty in recognizing as that of the noble Fortunato. The voice said—

"Ha! ha! ha!—he! he!—a very good joke indeed—an excellent jest. We will have many a rich laugh about it at the palazzo—he! he! he!—over our wine—he! he! he!"

"The Amontillado!" I said.

"He! he! he!—he! he! he!—yes, the Amontillado. But is it not getting late? Will not they be awaiting us at the palazzo, the Lady Fortunato and the rest? Let us be gone."

"Yes," I said, "let us be gone."

"*For the love of God, Montresor!*"

"Yes," I said, "for the love of God!"

But to these words I hearkened in vain for a reply. I grew impatient. I called aloud:

"Fortunato!"

No answer. I called again:

"Fortunato!"

No answer still, I thrust a torch through the remaining aperture and let it fall within. There came forth in return only a jingling of the bells. My heart grew sick—on account of the dampness of the catacombs. I hastened to make an end of my labor. I forced the last stone into its position; I plastered it up. Against the new masonry I re-erected the old rampart of bones. For the half of a century no mortal has disturbed them. *In pace requiescat!*[5]

[1846]

QUESTIONS

1. Does Montresor achieve his goal? Is he able to gain his revenge and "punish with impunity"?
2. In what way is the setting of Poe's story symbolic?
3. Is the pun on the masons/masonry of any further significance?
4. Does Fortunato realize what has happened to him by the end of the story? Is he insane? How is insanity used in the story?

[5] *In pace requiescat!* Latin: Rest in peace!

Katherine Anne Porter
(1890–1980)
United States

Katherine Anne Porter is widely acknowledged as one of the twentieth-century masters of the short story form. Her meticulously crafted stories embody her lifelong attempt to, as she expressed it, "discover and understand human motives, human feeling, to make a distillation of what human relations and experiences my mind has been able to absorb. I have never known an uninteresting human being, and I have never known two alike."

Born in Texas, Porter moved frequently, writing continuously—although she destroyed most of what she wrote before the age of 30. She was married three times and worked in a variety of jobs to support herself, including writing for a newspaper and performing bit parts in films. In 1918 she contracted influenza and nearly died during the great epidemic that swept the world that year. Her collection of three novellas, *Pale Horse, Pale Rider* (1939), incorporates her experience of serious illness. In 1921 Porter went to Mexico to study Aztec and Mayan art and became involved with a revolutionary movement. Later she traveled widely in Europe.

Porter published only one novel, *Ship of Fools* (1962), which was made into a successful Hollywood film that secured her economic independence. In the novel, which took 20 years to write, she explores the relations among passengers on the transatlantic voyage of a German ship, a microcosm of pre–World War II European society. The novel is allegorical, kaleidoscopic, and episodic—in fact, more like a series of short stories. Most critics believe that it betrays Porter working against the grain of her true talent, the short story form. Through stories collected in *Flowering Judas* (1930), *The Leaning Tower* (1944), and several other volumes, she wrote precisely controlled narratives that focus less on plot than on their fully realized characters' illuminating perceptions of experience.

◆ Rope ◆

On the third day after they moved to the country he came walking back from the village carrying a basket of groceries and a twenty-four-yard coil of rope. She came out to meet him, wiping her hands on her green smock. Her hair was tumbled, her nose was scarlet with sunburn; he told her that already she looked like a born country woman. His gray flannel shirt stuck to him, his heavy shoes were dusty. She assured him he looked like a rural character in a play.

Had he brought the coffee? She had been waiting all day long for coffee. They had forgot it when they ordered at the store the first day.

Gosh, no, he hadn't. Lord, now he'd have to go back. Yes, he would if it killed him. He thought, though, he had everything else. She reminded him it was only because he didn't drink coffee himself. If he did he would remember it quick enough. Suppose they ran out of cigarettes? Then she saw the rope. What was that for? Well, he thought it might do to hang clothes on, or something. Naturally she asked him if he thought they were going to run a laundry? They already had a fifty-foot line hanging right before his eyes? Why, hadn't he noticed it, really? It was a blot on the landscape to her.

He thought there were a lot of things a rope might come in handy for. She wanted to know what, for instance. He thought a few seconds, but nothing occurred. They could wait and see, couldn't they? You need all sorts of strange odds and ends around a place in the country. She said, yes, that was so; but she thought just at that time when every penny counted, it seemed funny to buy more rope. That was all. She hadn't meant anything else. She hadn't just seen, not at first, why he felt it was necessary.

Well, thunder, he had bought it because he wanted to, and that was all there was to it. She thought that was reason enough, and couldn't understand why he hadn't said so, at first. Undoubtedly it would be useful, twenty-four yards of rope, there were hundreds of things, she couldn't think of any at the moment, but it would come in. Of course. As he had said, things always did in the country.

But she was a little disappointed about the coffee, and oh, look, look, look at the eggs! Oh, my, they're all running! What had he put on top of them? Hadn't he known eggs mustn't be squeezed? Squeezed, who had squeezed them, he wanted to know. What a silly thing to say. He had simply brought them along in the basket with the other things. If they got broke it was the grocer's fault. He should know better than to put heavy things on top of eggs.

She believed it was the rope. That was the heaviest thing in the pack, she saw him plainly when he came in from the road, the rope was a big package on top of everything. He desired the whole wide world to witness that this was not a fact. He had carried the rope in one hand and the basket in the other, and what was the use of her having eyes if that was the best they could do for her?

Well, anyhow, she could see one thing plain: no eggs for breakfast. They'd have to scramble them now, for supper. It was too damned bad. She had planned to have steak for supper. No ice, meat wouldn't keep. He wanted to know why she couldn't finish breaking the eggs in a bowl and set them in a cool place.

Cool place! If he could find one for her, she'd be glad to set them there. Well, then, it seemed to him they might very well cook the meat at the same time they cooked the eggs and then warm up the meat for tomorrow. The idea simply choked her. Warmed-over meat, when they might as well have had it fresh. Second best and scraps and makeshifts, even to the meat! He rubbed her shoulder a little. It doesn't really matter so much, does it, darling? Sometimes when they were playful, he would rub her shoulder and she would arch and purr. This time she hissed and almost clawed. He was getting ready to say that they could surely manage somehow when she turned on him and said, if he told her they could manage somehow she would certainly slap his face.

He swallowed the words red hot, his face burned. He picked up the rope and started to put it on the top shelf. She would not have it on the top shelf, the jars and tins belonged there; positively she would not have the top shelf cluttered up with a lot of rope. She had borne all the clutter she meant to bear in the flat in town, there was space here at least and she meant to keep things in order.

Well, in that case, he wanted to know what the hammer and nails were doing up there? And why had she put them there when she knew very well he needed that hammer and those nails upstairs to fix the window sashes? She simply slowed down everything and made double work on the place with her insane habit of changing things around and hiding them.

She was sure she begged his pardon, and if she had had any reason to believe he was going to fix the sashes this summer she would have left the hammer and nails right where he put them; in the middle of the bedroom floor where they could step on them in the dark. And now if he didn't clear the whole mess out of there she would throw them down the well.

Oh, all right, all right — could he put them in the closet? Naturally not, there were brooms and mops and dustpans in the closet, and why couldn't he find a place for his rope outside her kitchen? Had he stopped to consider there were seven God-forsaken rooms in the house, and only one kitchen?

He wanted to know what of it? And did she realize she was making a complete fool of herself? And what did she take him for, a three-year-old idiot? The whole trouble with her was she needed something weaker than she was to heckle and tyrannize over. He wished to God now they had a couple of children she could take it out on. Maybe he'd get some rest.

Her face changed at this, she reminded him he had forgot the coffee and had bought a worthless piece of rope. And when she thought of all the things they actually needed to make the place even decently fit to live in, well, she could cry, that was all. She looked so forlorn, so lost and despairing he couldn't believe it was only a piece of rope that was causing all the racket. What *was* the matter, for God's sake?

Oh, would he please hush and go away, and *stay* away, if he could, for five minutes? By all means, yes, he would. He'd stay away indefinitely if she wished. Lord, yes, there was nothing he'd like better than to clear out and never come back. She couldn't for the life of her see what was holding him, then. It was a swell time. Here she was, stuck, miles from a railroad, with a half-empty house on her hands, and not a penny in her pocket, and everything on earth to do; it seemed the God-sent moment for him to get out from under. She was surprised he hadn't stayed in town as it was until she had come out and done the work and got things straightened out. It was his usual trick.

It appeared to him that this was going a little far. Just a touch out of bounds, if she didn't mind his saying so. Why the hell had he stayed in town the summer before? To do a half-dozen extra jobs to get the money he had sent her. That was it. She knew perfectly well they couldn't have done it otherwise. She had agreed with him at the time. And that was the only time so help him he had ever left her to do anything by herself.

Oh, he could tell that to his great-grandmother. She had her notion of what had kept him in town. Considerably more than a notion, if he wanted to know. So, she was going to bring all that up again, was she? Well, she could just think what she pleased. He was tired of explaining. It may have looked funny but he had simply got hooked in, and what could he do? It was impossible to believe that she was going to take it seriously. Yes, yes, she knew how it was with a man: if he was left by himself a minute, some woman was certain to kidnap him. And naturally he couldn't hurt her feelings by refusing!

Well, what was she raving about? Did she forget she had told him those two weeks alone in the country were the happiest she had known for four years? And how long had they been married when she said that? All right, shut up! If she thought that hadn't stuck in his craw.

She hadn't meant she was happy because she was away from him. She meant she was happy getting the devilish house nice and ready for him. That was what she had meant, and now look! Bringing up something she had said a year ago simply to justify himself for forgetting her coffee and breaking the eggs and buying a wretched piece of rope they couldn't afford. She really thought it was time to drop the subject, and now she wanted only two things in the world. She wanted him to get that rope from underfoot, and go back to the village and get her coffee, and if he could remember it, he might bring a metal mitt for the skillets, and two more curtain rods, and if there were any rubber gloves in the village, her hands were simply raw, and a bottle of milk of magnesia from the drugstore.

He looked out at the dark blue afternoon sweltering on the slopes, and mopped his forehead and sighed heavily and said, if only she could wait a minute for *anything*, he was going back. He had said so, hadn't he, the very instant they found he had overlooked it?

Oh, yes, well . . . run along. She was going to wash windows. The country was so beautiful! She doubted they'd have a moment to enjoy it. He meant to go, but he could not until he had said that if she wasn't such a hopeless melancholiac she might see that this was only for a few days. Couldn't she remember anything pleasant about the other summers? Hadn't they ever had any fun? She hadn't time to talk about it, and now would he please not leave that rope lying around for her to trip on? He picked it up, somehow it had toppled off the table, and walked out with it under his arm.

Was he going this minute? He certainly was. She thought so. Sometimes it seemed to her he had second sight about the precisely perfect moment to leave her ditched. She had meant to put the mattresses out to sun, if they put them out this minute they would get at least three hours, he must have heard her say that morning she meant to put them out. So of course he would walk off and leave her to it. She supposed he thought the exercise would do her good.

Well, he was merely going to get her coffee. A four-mile walk for two pounds of coffee was ridiculous, but he was perfectly willing to do it. The habit was making a wreck of her, but if she wanted to wreck herself there was nothing he could so about it. If he thought it was coffee that was making a wreck of her, she congratulated him: he must have a damned easy conscience.

Conscience or no conscience, he didn't see why the mattresses couldn't very well wait until tomorrow. And anyhow, for God's sake, were they living in the house, or were they going to let the house ride them to death? She paled at this, her face grew livid about the mouth, she looked quite dangerous, and reminded him that housekeeping was no more her work than it was his: she had other work to do as well, and when did he think she was going to find time to do it at this rate?

Was she going to start on that again? She knew as well as he did that his work brought in the regular money, hers was only occasional, if they depended on what *she* made—and she might as well get straight on this question once for all!

That was positively not the point. The question was, when both of them were working on their own time, was there going to be a division of the housework, or wasn't there? She merely wanted to know, she had to make her plans. Why, he thought that was all arranged. It was understood that he was to help. Hadn't he always, in summers?

Hadn't he, though? Oh, just hadn't he? And when, and where, and doing what? Lord, what an uproarious joke!

It was such a very uproarious joke that her face turned slightly purple, and she screamed with laughter. She laughed so hard she had to sit down, and finally a rush of tears spurted from her eyes and poured down into the lifted corners of her mouth. He dashed towards her and dragged her up to her feet and tried to pour water on her head. The dipper hung by a string on a nail and he broke it loose.

Then he tried to pump water with one hand while she struggled in the other. So he gave it up and shook her instead.

She wrenched away, crying out for him to take his rope and go to hell, she had simply given him up: and ran. He heard her high-heeled bedroom slippers clattering and stumbling on the stairs.

He went out around the house and into the lane; he suddenly realized he had a blister on his heel and his shirt felt as if it were on fire. Things broke so suddenly you didn't know where you were. She could work herself into a fury about simply nothing. She was terrible, damn it: not an ounce of reason. You might as well talk to a sieve as that woman when she got going. Damned if he'd spend his life humoring her. Well, what to do now? He would take back the rope and exchange it for something else. Things accumulated, things were mountainous, you couldn't move them or sort them out or get rid of them. They just lay and rotted around. He'd take it back. Hell, why should he? He wanted it. What was it anyhow? A piece of rope. Imagine anybody caring more about a piece of rope than about a man's feelings. What earthly right had she to say a word about it? He remembered all the useless, meaningless things she bought for herself: Why? Because I wanted it, that's why! He stopped and selected a large stone by the road. He would put the rope behind it. He would put it in the toolbox when he got back. He'd heard enough about it to last him a life-time.

When he came back she was leaning against the post box beside the road waiting. It was pretty late, the smell of broiled steak floated nose high in the cooling air. Her face was young and smooth and freshlooking. Her unmanageable funny black hair was all on end. She waved to him from a distance, and he speeded up. She called out that supper was ready and waiting, was he starved?

You bet he was starved. Here was the coffee. He waved it at her. She looked at his other hand. What was that he had there?

Well, it was the rope again. He stopped short. He had meant to exchange it but forgot. She wanted to know why he should exchange it, if it was something he really wanted. Wasn't the air sweet now, and wasn't it fine to be here?

She walked beside him with one hand hooked into his leather belt. She pulled and jostled him a little as he walked, and leaned against him. He put his arm clear around her and patted her stomach. They exchanged wary smiles. Coffee, coffee for the Ootsum-Wootsums! He felt as if he were bringing her a beautiful present.

He was a love, she firmly believed, and if she had had her coffee in the morning, she wouldn't have behaved so funny. . . . There was a whippoorwill still coming back, imagine, clear out of season, sitting in the crab-apple tree calling all by himself. Maybe his girl stood him up. Maybe she did. She hoped to hear him once more, she loved whippoorwills. . . . He knew how she was, didn't he?

Sure, he knew how she was.

[1930]

QUESTIONS

1. What is the central conflict of the story? What are the husband and wife really disagreeing about?
2. What meanings does the rope acquire during the story for the husband and the wife? For the reader?
3. What is the significance of the story's resolution?

Rodrigo Rey Rosa

(b. 1958)

Guatemala

Rodrigo Rey Rosa, who was born in Guatemala in 1958, bases many of his stories on legends and myths indigenous to Latin America and North Africa. Two collections of his stories have appeared in English, *The Path Doubles Back* (1982) and *The Beggar's Knife* (1985). In explanation of his fiction for *Sudden Fiction*, Rey Rosa wrote,

> I like to believe that stories want to be written, that they must make an effort in order to be heard. They suggest themselves to me constantly, but I have little patience, I am lazy. Now and then, however, when I'm in the right mood, I stop to listen to one and sit down to record it. I think that by now they know I am not patient, so they make themselves short.

Rey Rosa has lived in Tangier, Morocco, since 1980. There his fiction captured the attention of author Paul Bowles, who began translating his stories into English.

The Proof

One night while his parents were still on the highway returning from someone's birthday party, Miguel went into the living room and stopped in front of the canary's cage. He lifted up the cloth covering the cage and opened the tiny door. Fearfully, he slipped his hand inside, and then withdrew it doubled into a fist, with the bird's head protruding between his fingers. It allowed itself to be seized almost without resistance, showing the resignation of a person with a chronic illness, thinking perhaps that it was being taken out so the cage could be cleaned and the seeds replenished. But Miguel was staring at it with the eager eyes of one seeking an omen.

All the lights in the house were turned on. Miguel had gone through all the rooms, hesitating at each corner. God can see you no matter where you are, Miguel told himself, but there are not many places suitable for invoking Him. Finally he decided on the cellar because it was dark there. He crouched in a corner under the high vaulted ceiling, as Indians and savages do, face down, his arms wrapped around his legs, and with the canary in his fist between his knees. Raising his eyes into the darkness, which at that moment looked red, he said in a low voice: "If you exist, God, bring this bird back to life." As he spoke, he tightened his fist little by little, until his fingers felt the snapping of the fragile bones and an unaccustomed stillness in the little body.

Then, without meaning to, he remembered María Luisa the maid, who took care of the canary. A little later, when he finally opened his hand, it was as if another, larger hand had been placed on his back — the hand of fear. He realized that the bird would not come back to life. If God did not exist, it was absurd to fear

His punishment. The image, the concept of God went out of his mind, leaving a blank. Then, for an instant, Miguel thought of the shape of evil, of Satan, but he did not dare ask anything of him.

He heard the sound of the car going into the garage over his head. Now the fear had to do with this world. His parents had arrived; he heard their voices, heard the car doors slam and the sound of a woman's heels on the stone floor. He laid the inert little body on the floor in the corner, groped in the dark for a loose brick, and set it on top of the bird. Then he heard the chiming of the bell at the front door, and ran upstairs to greet his parents.

"All the lights on!" exclaimed his mother as he kissed her.

"What were you doing down there?" his father asked him.

"Nothing. I was afraid. The empty house scares me."

His mother went through the house, turning lights off right and left, secretly astonished by her son's fear.

That night Miguel had his first experience of insomnia. For him not sleeping was a kind of nightmare from which there was no hope of awakening. A static nightmare: the dead bird beneath the brick, and the empty cage.

Hours later Miguel heard the front door open, and the sound of footsteps downstairs. Paralyzed by fear, he fell asleep. María Luisa the maid had finally arrived. It was seven o'clock; the day was still dark. She turned on the kitchen light, set her basket on the table, and, as was her custom, removed her sandals in order not to make any noise. She went into the living room and uncovered the canary's cage. The little door was open and the cage was empty. After a moment of panic, during which her eyes remained fixed on the cage hanging in front of her, she glanced around, covered the cage again and returned to the kitchen. Very carefully she took up her sandals and the basket, and went out. When she was no longer in sight of the house she put the sandals on and started to run in the direction of the market, where she hoped to find another canary. It was necessary to replace the one which she thought had escaped due to her carelessness.

Miguel's father awoke at quarter past seven. He went down to the kitchen and, surprised to see that María Luisa had not yet come, decided to go to the cellar for the oranges and squeeze them himself. Before going back up to the kitchen, he tried to turn off the light, but with his hands and arms laden with oranges, he had to use his shoulders to push the switch. One of the oranges slipped from his arm and rolled across the floor into a corner. He pushed the light on once more. Placing the oranges on a chair, he formed a bag out of the front of his bathrobe, dropped the oranges into it, and went to pick up the one in the corner. And then he noticed the bird's wing sticking out from under the brick. It was not easy for him, but he could guess what had happened. Everyone knows that children are cruel, but how should he react? His wife's footsteps sounded above him in the kitchen. He was ashamed of his son, and at the same time he felt that they were accomplices. He had to hide the shame and the guilt as if they were his own. He picked up the brick, put the bird in his bathrobe pocket, and climbed up to the kitchen. Soon he went on upstairs to his room to wash and dress.

A little later, as he left the house, he met María Luisa returning from the market with the new canary hidden in her basket. She greeted him in an odd fashion, but he did not notice it. He was upset: the hand that he kept in his pocket held the bird in it.

As María Luisa went into the house, she heard the voice of Miguel's mother on the floor above. She put the basket on the floor, took out the canary, and ran to slip it into the cage, which she then uncovered with an air of relief and triumph. But then when she drew back the window curtains and the sun's rays tinted the room pink, she saw with alarm that the bird had one black foot.

It was impossible to awaken Miguel. His mother had to carry him into the bathroom, where she turned on the tap and with her wet hand gave his face a few slaps. Miguel opened his eyes. Then his mother helped him dress and get down the stairs. She seated him at the kitchen table. After he had taken a few swallows of orange juice, he managed to rid himself of his sleepiness. The clock on the wall marked quarter to eight; shortly María Luisa would be coming in to get him and walk with him to the corner where the school bus stopped. When his mother went out of the room, Miguel jumped down from his chair and ran down into the cellar. Without turning on the light he went to look for the brick in the corner. Then he rushed back to the door and switched on the light. With the blood pounding in his head, he returned to the corner, lifted the brick, and saw that the bird was not there.

María Luisa was waiting for him in the kitchen. He avoided her and ran to the living room. She hurried after him. When on entering the room he saw the cage by the window, with the canary hopping from one perch to the other, he stopped short. He would have gone nearer to make certain, but María Luisa seized his hand and pulled him along to the front door.

On his way to the factory, Miguel's father was wondering what he would say to his son when he got home that night. The highway was empty. The weather was unusual: flat clouds like steps barred the sky, and near the horizon there were curtains of fog and light. He lowered the window, and at the moment the car crossed a bridge over a deep gully, he took one hand off the steering wheel and tossed the bird's tiny corpse out.

In the city while they waited on the corner for the bus, María Luisa listened to the account of the proof Miguel had been granted. The bus appeared in the distance, in miniature at the end of the street. María Luisa smiled.

"Perhaps that canary isn't what you think it is," she said to Miguel in a mysterious voice. "You have to look at it very close. If it has a black foot, it was sent by the Devil."

Miguel stared into her eyes, his face tense. She seized him by the shoulders and turned him around. The bus had arrived; its door was open. Miguel stepped onto the platform. "Dirty witch!" he shouted.

The driver started up. Miguel ran to the back of the bus and sat down by the window in the last row of seats. There was the squeal of tires, a horn sounded, and Miguel conjured up the image of his father's car.

At the last stop before the school, the bus took on a plump boy with narrow eyes. Miguel made a place for him at his side.

"How's everything?" the boy asked him as he sat down.

The bus ran between the rows of poplars, while Miguel and his friend spoke of the power of God.

[1987]

Translated by
Paul Bowles

QUESTIONS

1. Is Miguel's experiment with faith successful? What does he conclude about God?
2. How does the author use humor to explore serious questions concerning religious belief and doubt?
3. Consider the development of the plot, based on each character's limited understanding of circumstances. How does this structure contribute to the story's effectiveness?

Gabrielle Roy

(1909–1983)

Canada

One of the most distinguished writers of French-speaking Canada, Gabrielle Roy (pronounced "Rwaa") grew up in St. Boniface, Manitoba, the youngest of 11 children born to her Quebecois parents. Roy's imagination was fed by her mother's stories of her childhood in Quebec, to which Roy eventually returned as an adult to live and write after traveling to Europe and teaching school in Manitoba for a number of years. In addition to being honored with numerous literary awards for her fiction, Roy was the first Canadian to be awarded the prestigious French Prix Femina and the first woman to be made a fellow of the Royal Society of Canada.

Many of the characters who populate Roy's 12 novels, beginning with her best known, *The Tin Flute* (1947, originally published in French as *Bonheur d'occasion*, 1945), are downtrodden people of rural, poor, or ethnic minority backgrounds who suffer in their struggles to survive in the face of the social, political, and emotional obstacles they encounter. Roy also writes powerfully of the passage of time and of romantic ideas of youth that modulate into adult disillusionment. The story included here, one of four interrelated stories in *The Road Past Altamont* (1966), combines those themes through the context of journeys—both actual and emotional—undertaken by the young girl Christine as she grows up near the rural Canadian prairie.

Roy's distinctive tone was influenced by Chekhov, as the author acknowledged in describing her admiration for the sense of "plaintiveness" melded with "sad sweetness" in his stories—particularly in "The Steppe," set in a location geographically similar to the central prairies of Canada. With compassion for her downtrodden characters, Roy expresses in a deceptively simple style a bittersweet knowledge of human frailty and suffering.

The Move

I

I have perhaps never envied anyone as much as a girl I knew when I was about eleven years old and of whom today I remember not much more than the name, Florence. Her father was a mover. I don't think this was his trade. He was a handyman, I imagine, engaging in various odd jobs; at the time of the seasonal movings—and it seems to me that people changed their lodgings often in those days—he moved the household effects of people of small means who lived near us and even quite far away, in the suburbs and distant quarters of Winnipeg. No doubt, his huge cart and his horses, which he had not wanted to dispose of when he came from the country to the city, had made him a mover.

On Saturdays Florence accompanied her father on his journeys, which, because of the slow pace of the horses, often took the entire day. I envied her to the point of having no more than one fixed idea: Why was my father not also a mover? What finer trade could one practice?

I don't know what moving signified to me in those days. Certainly I could not have had any clear idea what it was like. I had been born and had grown up in the fine, comfortable house in which we were still living and which, in all probability, we would never leave. Such fixity seemed frightfully monotonous to me that summer. Actually we were never really away from that large house. If we were going to the country for a while, even if we were only to be absent for a day, the problem immediately arose: Yes, but who will look after the house?

To take one's furniture and belongings, to abandon a place, close a door behind one forever, say good-by to a neighborhood, this was an adventure of which I knew nothing; and it was probably the sheer force of my efforts to picture it to myself that made it seem so daring, heroic, and exalted in my eyes.

"Aren't we ever going to move?" I used to ask Maman.

"I certainly hope not," she would say. "By the grace of God and the long patience of your father, we are solidly established at last. I only hope it is forever."

She told me that to her no sight in the world could be more heartbreaking, more poignant even, than a house moving.

"For a while," she said, "it's as if you were related to the nomads, those poor souls who slip along the surface of existence, putting their roots down nowhere. You no longer have a roof over your head. Yes indeed, for a few hours at least, it's as if you were drifting on the stream of life."

Poor Mother! Her objections and comparisons only strengthened my strange hankering. To drift on the stream of life! To be like the nomads! To wander through the world! There was nothing in any of this that did not seem to me complete felicity.

Since I myself could not move, I wished to be present at someone else's moving and see what it was all about. Summer came. My unreasonable desire grew. Even now I cannot speak of it lightly, much less so with derision. Certain of our desires, as if they knew about us before we do ourselves, do not deserve to be mocked.

Each Saturday morning I used to go and wander around Florence's house. Her father—a big dirty-blond man in blue work clothes, always grumbling a little or even, perhaps, swearing—would be busy getting the impressive cart out of the barn. When the horses were harnessed and provided with nose bags of oats, the father and his little daughter would climb onto the high seat; the father would take the reins in his hands; they would both, it seemed to me, look at me then with slight pity, a vague commiseration. I would feel forsaken, of an inferior species of humans unworthy of high adventure.

The father would shout something to the horses. The cart would shake. I would watch them set out in that cool little morning haze that seems to promise such delightful emotions to come. I would wave my hand at them, even though they never looked back at me. "Have a good trip," I would call. I would feel so unhappy at being left behind that I would nurse my regret all day and with it an aching curiosity. What would they see today? Where were they at this moment? What was offering itself to their travelers' eyes? It was no use my knowing that they could go only a limited distance in any event. I would imagine the two of them seeing things that no one else in the world could see. From the top of the cart, I thought, how transformed the world must appear.

At last my desire to go with them was so strong and so constant that I decided to ask my mother for permission — although I was almost certain I would never obtain it. She held my new friends in rather poor esteem and, though she tolerated my hanging continually about them, smelling their odor of horses, adventure, and dust, I knew in my heart of hearts that the mere idea that I might wish to accompany them would fill her with indignation.

At my first words, indeed, she silenced me.

"Are you mad? To wander about the city in a moving wagon! Just picture yourself," she said, "in the midst of furniture and boxes and piled-up mattresses all day, and with who knows what people! What can you imagine would be pleasant about that?"

How strange it was. Even the idea, for instance, of being surrounded by heaped-up chairs, chests with empty drawers, unhooked pictures — the very novelty of all this stimulated my desire.

"Never speak of that whim to me again," said my mother. "The answer is no and no it will remain."

Next day I went over to see Florence, to feed my nostalgic envy of their existence on the few words she might say to me.

"Where did you go yesterday? Who did you move?"

"Oh I'm not sure," Florence said, chewing gum — she was always either chewing gum or sucking a candy. "We went over to Fort Rouge, I think, to get some folks and move them way to hell and gone over by East Kildonan."

These were the names of quite ordinary suburbs. Why was it that at moments such as these they seemed to hold the slightly poignant attraction of those parts of the world that are remote, mysterious, and difficult to reach?

"What did you see?" I asked.

Florence shifted her gum from one cheek to the other, looking at me with slightly foolish eyes. She was not an imaginative child. No doubt, to her and her father the latter's work seemed banal, dirty, and tiring, and nothing more similar to one household move than another household move. Later I discovered that if Florence accompanied her father every Saturday, it was only because her mother went out cleaning that day and there was no one to look after the little girl at home. So her father took her along.

Both father and daughter began to consider me a trifle mad to endow their life with so much glamour.

I had asked the big pale-blond man countless times if he wouldn't take me too. He always looked at me for a moment as at some sort of curiosity — a child who perhaps wasn't completely normal — and said, "If your mother gives you permission . . ." and spat on the ground, hitched up his huge trousers with a movement of his hips, then went off to feed his horses or grease the wheels of his cart.

The end of the moving season was approaching. In the blazing heat of summer no one moved except people who were being evicted or who had to move closer to a new job, rare cases. If I don't soon manage to see what moving is like, I thought, I'll have to wait till next summer. And who knows? Next summer I may no longer have such a taste for it.

The notion that my desire might not always mean so much to me, instead of cheering me, filled me with anxiety. I began to realize that even our desires are not eternally faithful to us, that they wear out, perhaps die, or are replaced by others, and this precariousness of their lives made them seem more touching to me, more friendly. I thought that if we do not satisfy them they must go away somewhere and perish of boredom and lassitude.

Observing that I was still taken up with my "whim," Maman perhaps thought she might distract me from it by telling me once more the charming stories of her own childhood. She chose, oddly enough, to tell me again about the long journey of her family across the prairie by covered wagon. The truth must have been that she herself relived this thrilling voyage into the unknown again and again and that, by recounting it to me, she perhaps drained away some of that heartbreaking nostalgia that our life deposits in us, whatever it may be.

So here she was telling me again how, crowded together in the wagon—for Grandmother had brought some of her furniture, her spinning wheel certainly, and innumerable bundles—pressed closely in together, they had journeyed across the immense country.

"The prairie at that time," she said, "seemed even more immense than it does today, for there were no villages to speak of along the trail and only a few houses. To see even one, away far off in the distance, was an adventure in itself."

"And what did you feel?" I asked her.

"I was attracted," Maman admitted, bowing her head slightly, as if there were something a bit wrong, or at least strange, about this. "Attracted by the space, the great bare sky, the way the tiniest tree was visible in this solitude for miles. I was very much attracted."

"So you were happy?"

"Happy? Yes, I think so. Happy without knowing why. Happy as you are, when you are young—or even not so young—simply because you are in motion, because life is changing and will continue to change and everything is being renewed. It's curious," she told me. "Such things must run in families, for I wonder whether there have ever been such born travelers as all of us."

And she promised me that later on I too would know what it is to set forth, to be always seeking from life a possible beginning over—and that perhaps I might even become weary of it.

That night the intensity of my desire wakened me from sleep. I imagined myself in my mother's place, a child lying, as she had described it, on the floor of the wagon, watching the prairie stars—the most luminous stars in either hemisphere, it is said—as they journeyed over her head.

That, I thought, I shall never know; it is a life that is gone beyond recall and lost—and the mere fact that there were ways of life that were over, extinct in the past, and that we could not recover them in our day, filled me with the same nostalgic longing for the lost years as I had felt for my own perishable desires. But, for lack of anything better, there was the possible journey with our neighbors.

I knew—I guessed, rather—that, though we owe obedience to our parents, we owe it also to certain of our desires, those that are strangest, piercing, and too vast.

I remained awake. Tomorrow—this very day, rather—was a Saturday, moving day. I had resolved to go with the Pichettes.

Dawn appeared. Had I ever really seen it until now? I noticed that before the sky becomes clean and shining, it takes on an indecisive color, like badly washed laundry.

Now, the desire that was pushing me so violently, to the point of revolt, had no longer anything happy or even tempting about it. It was more like an order. Anguish weighed upon my heart. I wasn't even free now to say to myself, "Sleep. Forget all that." I had to go.

Is it the same anguish that has wakened me so many times in my life, wakens me still at dawn with the awareness of an imminent departure, sad sometimes, sometimes joyful, but almost always toward an unknown destination? Is it always the same departure that is involved?

When I judged the morning to be sufficiently advanced, I got up and combed my hair. Curiously enough, for this trip in a cart, I chose to put on my prettiest dress. "Might as well be hung for a sheep as a lamb," I said to myself, and left the house without a sound.

I arrived soon at the mover's. He was yawning on the threshold of the barn, stretching his arms in the early sun. He considered me suspiciously.

"Have you got permission?"

I swallowed my saliva rapidly. I nodded.

A little later Florence appeared, looking bad-tempered and sleepy.

She hitched herself up onto the seat beside us.

"Giddup!" cried the man.

And we set out in that cool morning hour that had promised me the transformation of the world and everything in it—and undoubtedly of myself.

II

And at first the journey kept its promise. We were passing through a city of sonorous and empty streets, over which we rolled with a great noise. All the houses seemed to be still asleep, bathed in a curious and peaceful atmosphere of withdrawal. I had never seen our little town wearing this absent, gentle air of remoteness.

The great rising sun bleached and purified it, I felt. I seemed to be traveling through an absolutely unknown city, remote and still to be explored. And yet I was astonished to recognize, as if vaguely, buildings, church spires, and street crossings that I must have seen somewhere before. But how could this be, since I had this morning left the world I had known and was entering into a new one?

Soon streetcars and a few automobiles began to move about. The sight of them looming upon the horizon and coming toward us gave me a vivid sense of the shifting of epochs.

What had these streetcars and automobiles come to do in our time, which was that of the cart? I asked myself with pleasure. When we reached Winnipeg and became involved in already heavy traffic, my sense of strangeness was so great that I believed I must be dreaming and clapped my hands.

Even at that time a horse-drawn cart must have been rare in the center of the city. So, at our side, everything was moving quickly and easily. We, with our cumbrous and reflective gait, passed like a slow, majestic film. I am the past, I am times gone by, I said to myself with fervor.

People stopped to watch us pass. I looked at them in turn, as if from far away. What did we have in common with this modern, noisy, agitated city? Increasingly, high in the cart, I became a survivor from times past. I had to restrain myself from beginning to salute the crowds, the streets, and the city, as if they were lucky to see us sweeping by.

For I had a tendency to divide into two people, actor and witness. From time to time I was the crowd that watched the passage of this astonishing cart from the past. Then I was the personage who considered from on high these modern times at her feet.

Meanwhile the difficulty of driving his somewhat nervous horses through all this noise and traffic was making the mover, whom I would have expected to be calmer and more composed, increasingly edgy. He complained and even swore noisily at almost everything we encountered. This began to embarrass me. I felt that his bad temper was spoiling all the pleasure and the sense of gentle incongruity that the poor people of the present era might have obtained from our appearance in their midst. I should have very much liked to disassociate myself from him. But how could I, jammed in beside him as I was?

Finally, we took to small, quieter streets. I saw then that we were going toward Fort Garry.

"Is that the way we're going?"

"Yes," replied Monsieur Pichette ungraciously. "That's the way."

The heat was becoming overpowering. Without any shelter, wedged between the big bulky man and Florence, who made no effort to leave me a comfortable place, I was beginning to suffer greatly. At last, after several hours, we were almost in the country.

The houses were still ranked along narrow streets, but now these were short and beyond them the prairie could be seen like a great recumbent land — a land so widespread that doubtless one would never be able to see either its end or its beginning. My heart began once more to beat hard.

There begins the land of the prairies, I said to myself. There begins the infinite prairie of Canada.

"Are we going to go onto the real prairie?" I asked. "Or are we still really inside the city limits?"

"You are certainly the most inquisitive little girl I've ever seen in my life," grumbled Monsieur Pichette, and he told me nothing at all.

Now the roads were only of dirt, which the wind lifted in dusty whirlwinds. The houses spaced themselves out, became smaller and smaller. Finally they were no more than badly constructed shacks, put together out of various odds and ends — a bit of tin, a few planks, some painted, some raw — and they all seemed to have been raised during the night only to be demolished the next day. Yet, unfinished as they were, the little houses still seemed old. Before one of them we stopped.

The people had begun to pile up their belongings, in the house or outside it, in cardboard cartons or merely thrown pell-mell into bedcovers with the corners knotted to form rough bundles. But they were not very far along, according to Monsieur Pichette, who flew into a rage the moment we arrived.

"I only charge five dollars to move people," he said, "and they aren't even ready when I get here."

We all began to transport the household effects from the shack to the cart. I joined in, carrying numerous small objects that fell to my hand — saucepans with unmatching covers, a pot, a chipped water jug. I was trying, I think, to distract myself, to keep, if at all possible, the little happiness I had left. For I was beginning to realize that the adventure was taking a sordid turn. In this poor, exhausted-looking woman with her hair plastered to her face, and in her husband — a man as lacking in amiability as Monsieur Pichette — I was discovering people who were doomed to a life of which I knew nothing, terribly gray and, it seemed to me, without exit. So I tried to help them as much as I could and took it upon myself to carry some rather large objects on my own. At last I was told to sit still because I was getting in everyone's way.

I went to rejoin Florence, who was sitting a short distance away on a little wooden fence.

"Is it always like this?" I asked.

"Yes, like this — or worse."

"It's possible to be worse?"

"Much worse. These people," she said, "have beds, and dressers. . . . ."

She refused to enlighten me further.

"I'm hungry," she decided and she ran to unpack a little lunch box, took out some bread and butter and an apple and proceeded to eat under my nose.

"Didn't you bring anything to eat?" she asked.

"No."

"You should have," she said, and continued to bite hungrily into her bread, without offering me a scrap.

I watched the men bring out some soiled mattresses, which they carried at arm's length. New mattresses are not too distressing a sight; but once they have become the slightest bit worn or dirty I doubt that any household object is more repugnant. Then the men carried out an old torn sofa on their shoulders, some bedposts and springs. I tried to whip up my enthusiasm, to revive a few flames of it, at least. And it was then, I think, that I had a consoling idea: we had come to remove these people from this wretched life; we were going to take them now to something better; we were going to find them a fine, clean house.

A little dog circled around us, whimpering, starving, perhaps anxious. For his sake more than my own maybe, I would have liked to obtain a few bits of Florence's lunch.

"Won't you give him a little bit?" I asked.

Florence hastily devoured a large mouthful.

"Let him try and get it," she said.

The cart was full now and, on the ground beside it, almost as many old things still waited to be stowed away.

I began to suffer for the horses, which would have all this to pull.

The house was completely emptied, except for bits of broken dishes and some absolutely worthless rags. The woman was the last to come out. This was the moment I had imagined as dramatic, almost historic, undoubtedly marked by some memorable gesture or word. But this poor creature, so weary and dust-covered, had apparently no regret at crossing her threshold, at leaving behind her two, three, or perhaps four years of her life.

"Come, we'll have to hurry," she said simply, "if we want to be in our new place before night."

She climbed onto the seat of the cart with one of the younger children, whom she took on her knees. The others went off with their father, to go a little way on foot, then by streetcar, to be ahead of us, they said, at the place where we were going.

Florence and I had to stand among the furniture piled up behind.

The enormous cart now looked like some sort of monster, with tubs and pails bouncing about on both sides, upturned chairs, huge clumsy packages bulging in all directions.

The horses pulled vigorously. We set out. Then the little dog began to run along behind us, whimpering so loudly in fear and despair that I cried, imagining that no one had thought of him, "We've forgotten the little dog. Stop. Wait for the little dog."

In the face of everyone's indifference, I asked the woman, whose name was Mrs. Smith, "Isn't he yours?"

"Yes, he's ours, I suppose," she replied.

"He's coming. Wait for him," I begged.

"Don't you think we're loaded up enough already?" the mover snapped dryly, and he whipped his horses.

For a long moment more the little dog ran along behind us.

He wasn't made for running, this little dog. His legs were too short and bowed. But he did his best. Ah yes! He did his best.

Is he going to try to follow us across the whole city? I thought with distress. Awkward, distracted, and upset as he was, he would surely be crushed by an automobile or a streetcar. I don't know which I dreaded most: to see him turn back alone toward the deserted house or try to cross the city, come what might. We were already turning onto a street that was furrowed with tracks. A streetcar was approaching in the distance; several cars passed us, honking.

Mrs. Smith leaned down from the seat of the cart and shouted at the little dog, "Go on home."

Then she repeated, more loudly, "Go on home, stupid."

So he had a sort of name, even though cruel, yet he was being abandoned.

Overcome with astonishment, the little dog stopped, hesitated a moment, then lay down on the ground, his eyes turned toward us, watching us disappear and whimpering with fright on the edge of the big city.

And a little later I was pleased, as you will understand, that I did not need to look at him any longer.

III

I have always thought that the human heart is a little like the ocean, subject to tides, that joy rises in it in a steady flow, singing of waves, good fortune, and bliss; but afterward, when the high sea withdraws, it leaves an utter desolation in our sight. So it was with me that day.

We had gone back across almost the whole enormous city—less enormous perhaps than scattered, strangely, widely spread out. The eagerness of the day diminished. I even think the sun was about to disappear. Our monster cart plunged, like some worn-out beast, toward the inconvenient, rambling neighborhoods that lay at the exact opposite end of the city to the one from which we had come.

Florence was whiling away the time by opening the drawers of an old chest and thrusting her hand into the muddle inside—the exact embodiment, it seemed to me, of this day—bits of faded ribbon; old postcards on whose backs someone had one day written: Splendid weather, Best love and kisses; a quill from a hat; electricity bills; gas reminders; a small child's shoe. The disagreeable little girl gathered up handfuls of these things, examined them, read, laughed. At one point, sensing my disapproval, she looked up, saw me watching her rummage, and thumbed her nose in spite.

The day declined further. Once more we were in sad little streets, without trees, so much like the one from which we had taken the Smiths that it seemed to me we had made all this journey for nothing and were going to end up finally at the same shack from which I had hoped to remove them.

At the end of each of these little streets the infinite prairie once more appeared but now almost dark, barely tinted, on the rim of the horizon, with angry red — the pensive, melancholy prairie of my childhood.

At last we had arrived.

Against that red horizon a small lonely house stood out black, quite far from its neighbors — a small house without foundations, set upon the ground. It did not seem old but it was already full of the odor and, no doubt, the rags and tatters of the people who had left it a short time ago. However, they had not left a single light bulb in place.

In the semidarkness Mrs. Smith began to search through her bundles, lamenting that she was sure she had tucked two or three carefully away but no longer remembered where. Her husband, who had arrived a short time before us, distressed by the dimness and the clumsiness of his wife, began to accuse her of carelessness. The children were hungry; they started to cry with fretful frightened voices, in an importunate tone that reminded me of the whimpering of the little dog. The parents distributed a few slaps, a little haphazardly, it seemed to me. Finally Mrs. Smith found a light bulb. A small glow shone forth timidly, as if ashamed at having to illuminate such a sad beginning.

One of the children, tortured by some strange preference, began to implore, "Let's go home. This isn't our home. Oh let's go back home!"

Mrs. Smith had come across a sack of flour, a frying pan and some eggs while she was searching for light bulbs and now she courageously set to work preparing a meal for her family. It was this, I think, that saddened me most: this poor woman, in the midst of complete disorder and almost in the dark, beginning to make pancakes. She offered some to me. I ate a little, for I was very hungry. At that moment I believe she was sorry she had abandoned the little dog. This was the one small break in the terrible ending of this day.

Meanwhile Monsieur Pichette, in a grumbling anxiety to be finished, had completely emptied the cart. As soon as everything was dumped on the ground in front of the door, he came and said to Mr. Smith, "That's five dollars."

"But you have to help me carry it all in," said Mr. Smith.

"Not on your life. I've done all I have to."

Poor Mr. Smith fumbled in his pocket and took out five dollars in bills and small change, which he handed to the mover.

The latter counted the money in the weak glimmer that came from the house and said, "That's it. We're quits."

In this glimmer from the house I noticed that our poor horses were also very tired. They blinked their eyes with a lost expression, the result of too many house movings, no doubt. Perhaps horses would prefer to make the same trip over and over again — in this way they would not feel too estranged from their customary ways. But, always setting out on new routes, toward an unknown destination, they must feel disconcerted and dejected. I had time, by hurrying, to fetch them each a handful of tender grass at the end of the street where the prairie began.

What would we have had to say to each other on our way back? Nothing, certainly, and so we said nothing. Night had fallen, black, sad, and impenetrable, when we finally reached the old stable, which had once seemed to me to contain more magic and charm than even the cave of Aladdin!

The mover nevertheless reached out his hand to help me down from the cart.

He was one of those people — at least I thought so then — who, after being surly and detestable all day, try at the last moment to make amends with a pleasant word for the bad impression they have created. But it was too late, much too late.

"You're not too tired?" he asked, I believe.

I shook my head and after a quick good night, an unwilling thank you, I fled. I ran toward my home, the sidewalk resounding in the silence under my steps.

I don't believe I thought of rejoicing at what I was returning to — a life that, modest as it was, was still a thousand miles away from that of the Pichettes and the Smiths. And I had not yet realized that this whole shabby, dull, and pitiless side of life that the move had revealed to me today would further increase my frenzy to escape.

I was thinking only of my mother's anxiety, of my longing to find her again and be pardoned by her — and perhaps pardon her in turn for some great mysterious wrong whose point I did not understand.

She was in such a state of nervous tension, as a matter of fact — although neighbors had told her I had gone off early with the Pichettes — that when she saw me it was her exasperation that got the upper hand. She even raised her hand to strike me. I did not think of avoiding punishment. I may even have wanted it. But at that moment a surge of disillusionment came over me — that terrible distress of the heart after it has been inflated like a balloon.

I looked at my mother and cried, "Oh why have you said a hundred times that from the seat of the covered wagon on the prairie in the old days the world seemed renewed, different, and so beautiful?"

She looked at me in astonishment.

"Ah, so that's it!" she said.

And at once, to my profound surprise, she drew me toward her and cradled me in her arms.

"You too then!" she said. "You too will have the family disease, departure sickness. What a calamity!"

Then, hiding my face against her breast, she began to croon me a sort of song, without melody and almost without words.

"Poor you," she intoned. "Ah, poor you! What is to become of you!"

[1966]

Translated by
JOYCE MARSHALL

QUESTIONS

1. What expectations does the narrator have of housemoving? How do particular details in the story convey the contrast between her romantic view and the actual event?
2. Why does the narrator's mother respond as she does when the narrator returns home?
3. How does the setting contribute to the story's effectiveness and its theme? What is the theme of the story?

Leslie Marmon Silko

(b. 1948)

United States

Leslie Marmon Silko regards as one of the central formative influences in her life and writing her heritage as a Native American of mixed ancestry (Laguna, Mexican, and white). Born in Albuquerque, New Mexico, she grew up at the Laguna Pueblo and attended the University of New Mexico, graduating in 1969. She subsequently attended law school for several semesters and then taught for two years in Arizona and Alaska before she realized that she wanted to write full-time.

Silko's first novel, *Ceremony* (1977), explores the author's concern with her complex cultural heritage. Focusing on a mixed-ancestry Laguna Indian who struggles to locate himself within his cultural confusion, the narrative is an innovative weave of elements of Pueblo oral storytelling and contemporary moral and social concerns, including conflicting cultural attitudes toward war, power, cultural differences, and the human need for connection to the earth and nature. Silko's second novel, *Almanac of the Dead*, was published in 1991. Her short stories and poetry have appeared in a number of collections; she is also the recipient of one of the MacArthur Foundation "genius grants" in 1981.

The story "Yellow Woman" is in the tradition of the "abduction tale," but with a significant difference: the narrator is not certain about what is real and what is not. Silko wrote the following introduction to the story especially for *Worlds of Fiction*:

> When I was a little girl, Aunt Alice used to tell us kids the old-time stories, the "humma-hah" stories. Many of the stories were about the animals and birds and insects and reptiles who the old-time people believe are our sisters and brothers too, because Mother Earth's spirit gave birth to us all. But there were other stories too, about the Twin Brothers who went around saving people from giant monsters, about Salt Woman who gave her gift to the Parrot People because they invited her to share their food with them.
>
> There is a whole cycle of Kochininako—Yellow Woman—stories which Aunt Alice seemed to enjoy a great deal. In most of the stories, Kochininako is a strong courageous woman, sometimes a hunter bringing home rabbits for her family to eat; other times she faces dangers or hardships and overcomes them. But in some of the stories Kochininako is swept away by forces and circumstances beyond her. All realms of possibility are open to Kochininako, even that of sorcery.
>
> I wrote "Yellow Woman" when I was 20 years old. I think it was the third short story I wrote for a class I took. Back then, I wasn't thinking about being a writer; writing was just something I loved to do. I planned to attend law school, and later I did attend for three semesters.

I did not know, at the time I began writing this story, what the story would be about; all I had was the notion of this sensuous woman who leaves her family responsibilities behind for a handsome stranger. Then, when I was about one-third of the way into the story, suddenly I remembered all the Kochininako–Yellow Woman stories I had heard while I was growing up. In one story a terrible drought has dried up all the nearby springs and so Kochininako must walk a great distance to find fresh water to carry home. At a distant water hole she encounters Buffalo Man, a supernatural being who is sometimes a handsome man and other times a buffalo. Although Kochininako leaves her husband and goes away with Buffalo Man, the outcome for Kochininako's people is life-saving; since Kochininako has now become their "sister-in-law," the Buffalo People agree to allow their meat to be harvested by Kochininako's starving people.

In another story, Kochininako meets Whirl-Wind Man at the water hole and goes away with him for a while. When Kochininako finally returns home months later, she is pregnant with twins who later grow up to be the Twin Brothers, who help the people in times of great trouble.

A warning has to go along with this story: in 1976, a Navajo woman who had been a student of mine reported that after six years trying and failing, she had become pregnant during the week our literature class had read and discussed "Yellow Woman." [Leslie Marmon Silko, copyright 1991]

◆ Yellow Woman ◆

My thigh clung to his with dampness, and I watched the sun rising up through the tamaracks and willows. The small brown water birds came to the river and hopped across the mud, leaving brown scratches in the alkali-white crust. They bathed in the river silently. I could hear the water, almost at our feet where the narrow fast channel bubbled and washed green ragged moss and fern leaves. I looked at him beside me, rolled in the red blanket on the white river sand. I cleaned the sand out of the cracks between my toes, squinting because the sun was above the willow trees. I looked at him for the last time, sleeping on the white river sand.

I felt hungry and followed the river south the way we had come the afternoon before, following our footprints that were already blurred by lizard tracks and bug trails. The horses were still lying down, and the black one whinnied when he saw me but he did not get up—maybe it was because the corral was made out of thick cedar branches and the horses had not yet felt the sun like I had. I tried to look beyond the pale red mesas to the pueblo. I knew it was there, even if I could not see it, on the sandrock hill above the river, the same river that moved past me now and had reflected the moon last night.

The horse felt warm underneath me. He shook his head and pawed the sand. The bay whinnied and leaned against the gate trying to follow, and I remembered him asleep in the red blanket beside the river. I slid off the horse and tied him close to the other horse, I walked north with the river again, and the white sand broke loose in footprints over footprints.

"Wake up."

He moved in the blanket and turned his face to me with his eyes still closed. I knelt down to touch him.

"I'm leaving."

He smiled now, eyes still closed. "You are coming with me, remember?" He sat up now with his bare dark chest and belly in the sun.

"Where?"

"To my place."

"And will I come back?"

He pulled his pants on. I walked away from him, feeling him behind me and smelling the willows.

"Yellow Woman," he said.

I turned to face him. "Who are you?" I asked.

He laughed and knelt on the low, sandy bank, washing his face in the river. "Last night you guessed my name, and you knew why I had come."

I stared past him at the shallow moving water and tried to remember the night, but I could only see the moon in the water and remember his warmth around me.

"But I only said that you were him and that I was Yellow Woman — I'm not really her — I have my own name and I come from the pueblo on the other side of the mesa. Your name is Silva and you are a stranger I met by the river yesterday afternoon."

He laughed softly. "What happened yesterday has nothing to do with what you will do today, Yellow Woman."

"I know — that's what I'm saying — the old stories about the ka'tsina [kachina] spirit and Yellow Woman can't mean us."

My old grandpa liked to tell those stories best. There is one about Badger and Coyote who went hunting and were gone all day, and when the sun was going down they found a house. There was a girl living there alone, and she had light hair and eyes and she told them that they could sleep with her. Coyote wanted to be with her all night so he sent Badger into a prairie-dog hole, telling him he thought he saw something in it. As soon as Badger crawled in, Coyote blocked up the entrance with rocks and hurried back to Yellow Woman.

"Come here," he said gently.

He touched my neck and I moved close to him to feel his breathing and to hear his heart. I was wondering if Yellow Woman had known who she was — if she knew that she would become part of the stories. Maybe she'd had another name that her husband and relatives called her so that only the ka'tsina from the north and the storytellers would know her as Yellow Woman. But I didn't go on; I felt him all around me, pushing me down into the white river sand.

Yellow Woman went away with the spirit from the north and lived with him and his relatives. She was gone for a long time, but then one day she came back and she brought twin boys.

"Do you know the story?"

"What story?" He smiled and pulled me close to him as he said this. I was afraid lying there on the red blanket. All I could know was the way he felt, warm, damp, his body beside me. This is the way it happens in the stories, I was thinking, with no thought beyond the moment she meets the ka'tsina spirit and they go.

"I don't have to go. What they tell in stories was real only then, back in time immemorial, like they say."

He stood up and pointed at my clothes tangled in the blanket. "Let's go," he said.

I walked beside him, breathing hard because he walked fast, his hand around my wrist. I had stopped trying to pull away from him, because his hand felt cool and the sun was high, drying the river bed into alkali. I will see someone, eventually I will see someone, and then I will be certain that he is only a man — some man from nearby — and I will be sure that I am not Yellow Woman. Because she is from out of time past and I live now and I've been to school and there are highways and pickup trucks that Yellow Woman never saw.

It was an easy ride north on horseback. I watched the change from the cottonwood trees along the river to the junipers that brushed past us in the foothills, and finally there were only piñons, and when I looked up at the rim of the mountain plateau I could see pine trees growing on the edge. Once I stopped to look down, but the pale sandstone had disappeared and the river was gone and the dark lava hills were all around. He touched my hand, not speaking, but always singing softly a mountain song and looking into my eyes.

I felt hungry and wondered what they were doing at home now — my mother, my grandmother, my husband, and the baby. Cooking breakfast, saying, "Where did she go? — maybe kidnaped." And Al going to the tribal police with the details: "She went walking along the river."

The house was made with black lava rock and red mud. It was high above the spreading miles of arroyos and long mesas. I smelled a mountain smell of pitch and buck brush. I stood there beside the black horse, looking down on the small, dim country we had passed, and I shivered.

"Yellow Woman, come inside where it's warm."

He lit a fire in the stove. It was an old stove with a round belly and an enamel coffeepot on top. There was only the stove, some faded Navajo blankets, and a bedroll and cardboard box. The floor was made of smooth adobe plaster, and there was one small window facing east. He pointed at the box.

"There's some potatoes and the frying pan." He sat on the floor with his arms around his knees pulling them close to his chest and he watched me fry the potatoes. I didn't mind him watching me because he was always watching me — he had been watching me since I came upon him sitting on the river bank trimming leaves from a willow twig with his knife. We ate from the pan and he wiped the grease from his fingers on his Levi's.

"Have you brought women here before?" He smiled and kept chewing, so I said, "Do you always use the same tricks?"

"What tricks?" He looked at me like he didn't understand.

"The story about being a ka'tsina from the mountains. The story about Yellow Woman."

Silva was silent; his face was calm.

"I don't believe it. Those stories couldn't happen now," I said.

He shook his head and said softly, "But someday they will talk about us, and they will say, 'Those two lived long ago when things like that happened.'"

He stood up and went out. I ate the rest of the potatoes and thought about things—about the noise the stove was making and the sound of the mountain wind outside. I remembered yesterday and the day before, and then I went outside.

I walked past the corral to the edge where the narrow trail cut through the black rim rock. I was standing in the sky with nothing around me but the wind that came down from the blue mountain peak behind me. I could see faint mountain images in the distance miles across the vast spread of mesas and valleys and plains. I wondered who was over there to feel the mountain wind on those sheer blue edges—who walks on the pine needles in those blue mountains.

"Can you see the pueblo?" Silva was standing behind me.

I shook my head. "We're too far away."

"From here I can see the world." He stepped out on the edge. "The Navajo reservation begins over there." He pointed to the east. "The Pueblo boundaries are over here." He looked below us to the south, where the narrow trail seemed to come from. "The Texans have their ranches over there, starting with that valley, the Concho Valley. The Mexicans run some cattle over there too."

"Do you ever work for them?"

"I steal from them," Silva answered. The sun was dropping behind us and the shadows were filling the land below. I turned away from the edge that dropped forever into the valleys below.

"I'm cold," I said, "I'm going inside." I started wondering about this man who could speak the Pueblo language so well but who lived on a mountain and rustled cattle. I decided that this man Silva must be Navajo, because Pueblo men didn't do things like that.

"You must be a Navajo."

Silva shook his head gently. "Little Yellow Woman," he said, "you never give up, do you? I have told you who I am. The Navajo people know me, too." He knelt down and unrolled the bedroll and spread the extra blankets out on a piece of canvas. The sun was down, and the only light in the house came from outside—the dim orange light from sundown.

I stood there and waited for him to crawl under the blankets.

"What are you waiting for?" he said, and I lay down beside him. He undressed me slowly like the night before beside the river—kissing my face gently and running his hands up and down my belly and legs. He took off my pants and then he laughed.

"Why are you laughing?"

"You are breathing so hard."

I pulled away from him and turned my back to him.

He pulled me around and pinned me down with his arms and chest. "You don't understand, do you, little Yellow Woman? You will do what I want."

And again he was all around me with his skin slippery against mine, and I was afraid because I understood that his strength could hurt me. I lay underneath him and I knew that he could destroy me. But later, while he slept beside me, I touched his face and I had a feeling—the kind of feeling for him that overcame me that morning along the river. I kissed him on the forehead and he reached out for me.

When I woke up in the morning he was gone. It gave me a strange feeling because for a long time I sat there on the blankets and looked around the little house for some object of his—some proof that he had been there or maybe that he was coming back. Only the blankets and the cardboard box remained. The .30–30 that had been leaning in the corner was gone, and so was the knife I had used the night before. He was gone, and I had my chance to go now. But first I had to eat, because I knew it would be a long walk home.

I found some dried apricots in the cardboard box, and I sat down on a rock at the edge of the plateau rim. There was no wind and the sun warmed me. I was surrounded by silence. I drowsed with apricots in my mouth, and I didn't believe that there were highways or railroads or cattle to steal.

When I woke up, I stared down at my feet in the black mountain dirt. Little black ants were swarming over the pine needles around my foot. They must have smelled the apricots. I thought about my family far below me. They would be wondering about me, because this had never happened to me before. The tribal police would file a report. But if old Grandpa weren't dead he would tell them what happened—he would laugh and say, "Stolen by a ka'tsina, a mountain spirit. She'll come home—they usually do." There are enough of them to handle things. My mother and grandmother will raise the baby like they raised me. Al will find someone else, and they will go on like before, except that there will be a story about the day I disappeared while I was walking along the river. Silva had come for me; he said he had. I did not decide to go. I just went. Moonflowers blossom in the sand hills before dawn, just as I followed him. That's what I was thinking as I wandered along the trail through the pine trees.

It was noon when I got back. When I saw the stone house I remembered that I had meant to go home. But that didn't seem important any more, maybe because there were little blue flowers growing in the meadow behind the stone house and the gray squirrels were playing in the pines next to the house. The horses were standing in the corral, and there was a beef carcass hanging on the shady side of a big pine in front of the house. Flies buzzed around the clotted blood that hung from the carcass. Silva was washing his hands in a bucket full of water. He must have heard me coming because he spoke to me without turning to face me.

"I've been waiting for you."

"I went walking in the big pine trees."

I looked into the bucket full of bloody water with brown-and-white animal hairs floating in it. Silva stood there letting his hand drip, examining me intently.

"Are you coming with me?"

"Where?" I asked him.

"To sell the meat in Marquez."

"If you're sure it's O.K."

"I wouldn't ask you if it wasn't," he answered.

He sloshed the water around in the bucket before he dumped it out and set the bucket upside down near the door. I followed him to the corral and watched him saddle the horses. Even beside the horses he looked tall, and I asked him again if he wasn't Navajo. He didn't say anything; he just shook his head and kept cinching up the saddle.

"But Navajos are tall."

"Get on the horse," he said, "and let's go."

The last thing he did before we started down the steep trail was to grab the .30-30 from the corner. He slid the rifle into the scabbard that hung from his saddle.

"Do they ever try to catch you?" I asked.

"They don't know who I am."

"Then why did you bring the rifle?"

"Because we are going to Marquez where the Mexicans live."

The trail leveled out on a narrow ridge that was steep on both sides like an animal spine. On one side I could see where the trail went around the rocky gray hills and disappeared into the southeast where the pale sandrock mesas stood in the distance near my home. On the other side was a trail that went west, and as I looked far into the distance I thought I saw the little town. But Silva said no, that I was looking in the wrong place, that I just thought I saw houses. After that I quit looking off into the distance; it was hot and the wildflowers were closing up their deep-yellow petals. Only the waxy cactus flowers bloomed in the bright sun, and I saw every color that a cactus blossom can be; the white ones and the red ones were still buds, but the purple and the yellow were blossoms, open full and the most beautiful of all.

Silva saw him before I did. The white man was riding a big gray horse, coming up the trail towards us. He was traveling fast and the gray horse's feet sent rocks rolling off the trail into the dry tumbleweeds. Silva motioned for me to stop and we watched the white man. He didn't see us right away, but finally his horse whinnied at our horses and he stopped. He looked at us briefly before he lapped the gray horse across the three hundred yards that separated us. He stopped his horse in front of Silva, and his young fat face was shadowed by the brim of his hat. He didn't look mad, but his small, pale eyes moved from the blood-soaked gunny sacks hanging from my saddle to Silva's face and then back to my face.

"Where did you get the fresh meat?" the white man asked.

"I've been hunting," Silva said, and when he shifted his weight in the saddle the leather creaked.

"The hell you have, Indian. You've been rustling cattle. We've been looking for the thief for a long time."

The rancher was fat, and sweat began to soak through his white cowboy shirt and the wet cloth stuck to the thick rolls of belly fat. He almost seemed to be panting from the exertion of talking, and he smelled rancid, maybe because Silva scared him.

Silva turned to me and smiled. "Go back up the mountain, Yellow Woman."

The white man got angry when he heard Silva speak in a language he couldn't understand. "Don't try anything, Indian. Just keep riding to Marquez. We'll call the state police from there."

The rancher must have been unarmed because he was very frightened and if he had a gun he would have pulled it out then. I turned my horse around and the rancher yelled, "Stop!" I looked at Silva for an instant and there was something ancient and dark — something I could feel in my stomach — in his eyes, and when I glanced at his hand I saw his finger on the trigger of the .30 – 30 that was still in the saddle scabbard. I slapped my horse across the flank and the sacks of raw meat swung against my knees as the horse leaped up the trail. It was hard to keep my balance, and once I thought I felt the saddle slipping backward; it was because of this that I could not look back.

I didn't stop until I reached the ridge where the trail forked. The horse was breathing deep gasps and there was a dark film of sweat on its neck. I looked down in the direction I had come from, but I couldn't see the place. I waited. The wind came up and pushed warm air past me. I looked up at the sky, pale blue and full of thin clouds and fading vapor trails left by jets.

I think four shots were fired — I remember hearing four hollow explosions that reminded me of deer hunting. There could have been more shots after that, but I couldn't have heard them because my horse was running again and the loose rocks were making too much noise as they scattered around his feet.

Horses have a hard time running downhill, but I went that way instead of uphill to the mountain because I thought it was safer. I felt better with the horse running southeast past the round gray hills that were covered with cedar trees and black lava rock. When I got to the plain in the distance I could see the dark green patches of tamaracks that grew along the river; and beyond the river I could see the beginning of the pale sandrock mesas. I stopped the horse and looked back to see if anyone was coming; then I got off the horse and turned the horse around, wondering if it would go back to its corral under the pines on the mountain. It looked back at me for a moment and then plucked a mouthful of green tumbleweeds before it trotted back up the trail with its ears pointed forward, carrying its head daintily to one side to avoid stepping on the dragging reins. When the horse disappeared over the last hill, the gunny sacks full of meat were still swinging and bouncing.

I walked toward the river on a wood-hauler's road that I knew would eventually lead to the paved road. I was thinking about waiting beside the road for someone to drive by, but by the time I got to the pavement I had decided it wasn't very far to walk if I followed the river back the way Silva and I had come.

The river water tasted good, and I sat in the shade under a cluster of silvery willows. I thought about Silva, and I felt sad at leaving him; still, there was something strange about him, and I tried to figure it out all the way back home.

I came back to the place on the river bank where he had been sitting the first time I saw him. The green willow leaves that he had trimmed from the branch were still lying there, wilted in the sand. I saw the leaves and I wanted to go back to him — to kiss him and to touch him — but the mountains were too far away now. And I told myself, because I believe it, he will come back sometime and be waiting again by the river.

I followed the path up from the river into the village. The sun was getting low, and I could smell supper cooking when I got to the screen door of my house. I could hear their voices inside — my mother was telling my grandmother how to fix the Jell-O and my husband, Al, was playing with the baby. I decided to tell them that some Navajo had kidnaped me, but I was sorry that old Grandpa wasn't alive to hear my story because it was the Yellow Woman stories he liked to tell best.

[1974]

QUESTIONS

1. How does the first-person-narrative perspective contribute to your understanding of the woman? What aspects of her character emerge through her own telling of the story?
2. Who is Silva? What qualities in him appeal to the narrator? Why does she return to her own family?
3. How does the setting contribute to the story's meaning?
4. Why and how does Silko interweave elements from her cultural tradition with contemporary issues?
5. What is the story's resolution? What is its theme?

Isaac Bashevis Singer

(1904–1991)

Poland/United States

Isaac Bashevis Singer, the world's foremost writer in Yiddish, is a difficult author to categorize because his fiction resists easy labeling within either American or Yiddish literary traditions. Coming from a family of rabbis (his father and both grandfathers), Singer almost became a rabbi himself; he attended a rabbinical school and seminary but decided not to become a rabbi because "I began to doubt, not the power of God, but all the traditions and dogmas."

Instead, when he was 15, he began to write, inspired by the stories he heard from his own family: his father's, populated with imps, devils, and miraculous events, and his mother's, recalling her childhood in the *shtetl* (Jewish ghetto) of Bilgorai, Poland. In 1935, fearing the threat of a Nazi invasion of Poland, Singer followed his older brother (also a writer, I. J. Singer) to the United States. Many of his stories first appeared in the Yiddish newspaper for which he worked in New York City, the *Jewish Daily Forward*.

Singer wrote first in Hebrew but changed to Yiddish because Hebrew (before its revival as the national language of Israel) was a dead language. Ironically, it is now Yiddish that is in danger of dying. As Irving Howe has observed, Singer wrote in

> a language that no amount of energy or affection seems likely to save from extinction. He [wrote] about a world that is gone, destroyed with a brutality beyond historical comparison. He [wrote] within a culture, the remnant of Yiddish in the Western world, that [was] more than a little dubious about his purpose and stress. . . . It strikes one as a kind of inspired madness: here [was] a man living in New York City, a sophisticated and clever writer, who compose[d] stories about places like Frampol, Bilgoray, Kreshev, *as if they were still there.*

Although he considered writing in English, Singer stayed with Yiddish because he felt that "a writer has to write in his own language or not at all." Inevitably, much is lost in translation; Howe notes that "no translation . . . could possibly suggest the full idiomatic richness and syntactical verve of Singer's Yiddish."

Singer's stories are moral fables or allegories, set in the *shtetls* and villages of nineteenth- and twentieth-century prewar Poland. Although magical and supernatural events may frequent them, his narratives are about people struggling with the very human emotional and moral challenges of ordinary life: love and lust, sin and responsibility, faith and doubt, madness and sanity, good and evil. As Singer commented in an interview, "I actually believe that there are powers in this world of which we have no inkling but which have an influence on our lives and on our way of thinking."

Although Singer was a prolific writer of stories for both adults and children, many of them have not yet been translated into English, even though the author translated many of his stories himself. "Gimpel the Fool," considered by many critics to be his finest story, brought Singer an audience of English-speaking readers when it was translated by Saul Bellow. When Singer received the Nobel Prize for Literature in 1978, the Nobel Committee praised his "impassioned narrative art which, with roots in a Polish-Jewish cultural tradition, brings universal human conditions to life."

• Gimpel the Fool •

I

I am Gimpel the fool. I don't think myself a fool. On the contrary. But that's what folks call me. They gave me the name while I was still in school. I had seven names in all: imbecile, donkey, flax-head, dope, glump, ninny, and fool. The last name stuck. What did my foolishness consist of? I was easy to take in. They said, "Gimpel, you know the rabbi's wife has been brought to childbed?" So I skipped school. Well, it turned out to be a lie. How was I supposed to know? She hadn't had a big belly. But I never looked at her belly. Was that really so foolish? The gang laughed and hee-hawed, stomped and danced and chanted a good-night prayer. And instead of the raisins they give when a woman's lying in, they stuffed my hand full of goat turds. I was no weakling. If I slapped someone he'd see all the way to Cracow. But I'm really not a slugger by nature. I think to myself: Let it pass. So they take advantage of me.

I was coming home from school and heard a dog barking. I'm not afraid of dogs, but of course I never want to start up with them. One of them may be mad, and if he bites there's not a Tartar in the world who can help you. So I made tracks. Then I looked around and saw the whole market place wild with laughter. It was no dog at all but Wolf-Leib the thief. How was I supposed to know it was he? It sounded like a howling bitch.

When the pranksters and leg-pullers found that I was easy to fool, every one of them tried his luck with me. "Gimpel, the czar is coming to Frampol; Gimpel, the moon fell down in Turbeen; Gimpel, little Hodel Furpiece found a treasure behind the bathhouse." And I like a golem[1] believed everyone. In the first place, everything is possible, as it is written in *The Wisdom of the Fathers*, I've forgotten just how. Second, I had to believe when the whole town came down on me! If I ever dared to say, "Ah, you're kidding!" there was trouble. People got angry. "What do you mean! You want to call everyone a liar?" What was I to do? I believed them, and I hope at least that did them some good.

I was an orphan. My grandfather who brought me up was already bent toward the grave. So they turned me over to a baker, and what a time they gave me there! Every woman or girl who came to bake a batch of noodles had to fool me at least once. "Gimpel, there's a fair in Heaven; Gimpel, the rabbi gave birth to a calf in the seventh month; Gimpel, a cow flew over the roof and laid brass eggs." A student from the yeshiva came once to buy a roll, and he said, "You, Gimpel, while you

[1]*golem* according to Jewish legend, a man artificially created by cabalistic rites; a robot or automaton

stand here scraping with your baker's shovel the Messiah has come. The dead have arisen." "What do you mean?" I said. "I heard no one blowing the ram's horn!" He said, "Are you deaf?" And all began to cry, "We heard it, we heard!" Then in came Rietze the candle-dipper and called out in her hoarse voice, "Gimpel, your father and mother have stood up from the grave, They're looking for you."

To tell the truth, I knew very well that nothing of the sort had happened, but all the same, as folks were talking, I threw on my wool vest and went out. Maybe something had happened. What did I stand to lose by looking? Well, what a cat music went up! And then I took a vow to believe nothing more. But that was no go either. They confused me so that I didn't know the big end from the small.

I went to the rabbi to get some advice. He said, "It is written, better to be a fool all your days than for one hour to be evil. You are not a fool. They are the fools. For he who causes his neighbor to feel shame loses Paradise himself." Nevertheless, the rabbi's daughter took me in. As I left the rabbinical court she said, "Have you kissed the wall yet?" I said, "No, what for?" She answered, "It's the law; you've got to do it after every visit." Well, there didn't seem to be any harm in it. And she burst out laughing. It was a fine trick. She put one over on me, all right.

I wanted to go off to another town, but then everyone got busy matchmaking, and they were after me so they nearly tore my coat tails off. They talked at me and talked until I got water on the ear. She was no chaste maiden, but they told me she was virgin pure. She had a limp, and they said it was deliberate, from coyness. She had a bastard, and they told me the child was her little brother. I cried, "You're wasting your time. I'll never marry that whore." But they said indignantly, "What a way to talk! Aren't you ashamed of yourself? We can take you to the rabbi and have you fined for giving her a bad name." I saw then that I wouldn't escape them so easily and I thought: They're set on making me their butt. But when you're married the husband's the master, and if that's all right with her it's agreeable to me too. Besides, you can't pass through life unscathed, nor expect to.

I went to her clay house, which was built on the sand, and the whole gang, hollering and chorusing, came after me. They acted like bear-baiters. When we came to the well they stopped all the same. They were afraid to start anything with Elka. Her mouth would open as if it were on a hinge, and she had a fierce tongue. I entered the house. Lines were strung from wall to wall and clothes were drying. Barefoot she stood by the tub, doing the wash. She was dressed in a worn hand-me-down gown of plush. She had her hair put up in braids and pinned across her head. It took my breath away, almost, the reek of it all.

Evidently she knew who I was. She took a look at me and said, "Look who's here! He's come, the drip. Grab a seat."

I told her all; I denied nothing. "Tell me the truth," I said, "are you really a virgin, and is that mischievous Yechiel actually your little brother? Don't be deceitful with me, for I'm an orphan."

"I'm an orphan myself," she answered, "and whoever tries to twist you up, may the end of his nose take a twist. But don't let them think they can take advantage of me. I want a dowry of fifty guilders, and let them take up a collection besides. Otherwise they can kiss my you-know-what." She was very plainspoken. I said, "It's the bride and not the groom who gives a dowry." Then she said, "Don't bargain with me. Either a flat yes or a flat no. Go back where you came from."

I thought: No bread will ever be baked from *this* dough. But ours is not a poor town. They consented to everything and proceeded with the wedding. It so happened that there was a dysentery epidemic at the time. The ceremony was held at the cemetery gates, near the little corpse-washing hut. The fellows got drunk.

While the marriage contract was being drawn up I heard the most pious high rabbi ask, "Is the bride a widow or a divorced woman?" And the sexton's wife answered for her, "Both a widow and divorced." It was a black moment for me. But what was I to do, run away from under the marriage canopy?

There was singing and dancing. An old granny danced opposite me, hugging a braided white hallah. The master of revels made a "God 'a mercy" in memory of the bride's parents. The schoolboys threw burrs, as on Tishe b'Av[2] fast day. There were a lot of gifts after the sermon: a noodle board, a kneading trough, a bucket, brooms, ladles, household articles galore. Then I took a look and saw two strapping young men carrying a crib. "What do we need this for?" I asked. So they said, "Don't rack your brains about it. It's all right, it'll come in handy." I realized I was going to be rooked. Take it another way though, what did I stand to lose? I reflected: I'll see what comes of it. A whole town can't go altogether crazy.

II

At night I came where my wife lay, but she wouldn't let me in. "Say, look here, is this what they married us for?" I said. And she said, "My monthly has come." "But yesterday they took you to the ritual bath, and that's afterwards, isn't it supposed to be?" "Today isn't yesterday," said she, "and yesterday's not today. You can beat it if you don't like it." In short, I waited.

Not four months later, she was in childbed. The townsfolk hid their laughter with their knuckles. But what could I do? She suffered intolerable pains and clawed at the walls. "Gimpel," she cried, "I'm going. Forgive me!" The house filled with women. They were boiling pans of water. The screams rose to the welkin.

The thing to do was to go to the house of prayer to repeat psalms, and that was what I did.

The townsfolk liked that, all right. I stood in a corner saying psalms and prayers, and they shook their heads at me. "Pray, pray!" they told me. "Prayer never made any woman pregnant." One of the congregation put a straw to my mouth and said, "Hay for the cows." There was something to that too, by God!

She gave birth to a boy. Friday at the synagogue the sexton stood up before the Ark, pounded on the reading table, and announced, "The wealthy Reb Gimpel invites the congregation to a feast in honor of the birth of a son." The whole house of prayer rang with laughter. My face was flaming. But there was nothing I could do. After all, I *was* the one responsible for the circumcision honors and rituals.

Half the town came running. You couldn't wedge another soul in. Women brought peppered chick-peas, and there was a keg of beer from the tavern. I ate and drank as much as anyone, and they all congratulated me. Then there was a circumcision, and I named the boy after my father, may he rest in peace. When all were gone and I was left with my wife alone, she thrust her head through the bed-curtain and called me to her.

"Gimpel," said she, "why are you silent? Has your ship gone and sunk?"

"What shall I say," I answered. "A fine thing you've done to me! If my mother had known of it she'd have died a second time."

She said, "Are you crazy, or what?"

"How can you make such a fool," I said, "of one who should be the lord and master?"

[2]*Tishe b'Av* a Jewish fast day commemorating the destruction of the Temple, celebrated on the ninth day of the month of Ab

"What's the matter with you?" she said. "What have you taken it into your head to imagine?"

I saw that I must speak bluntly and openly. "Do you think this is the way to use an orphan?" I said. "You have borne a bastard."

She answered, "Drive this foolishness out of your head. The child is yours."

"How can he be mine?" I argued. "He was born seventeen weeks after the wedding."

She told me then that he was premature. I said, "Isn't he a little too premature?" She said, she had had a grandmother who carried just as short a time and she resembled this grandmother of hers as one drop of water does another. She swore to it with such oaths that you would have believed a peasant at the fair if he had used them. To tell the plain truth, I didn't believe her; but when I talked it over next day with the schoolmaster, he told me that the very same thing had happened to Adam and Eve. Two they went up to bed, and four they descended.

"There isn't a woman in the world who is not the granddaughter of Eve," he said.

That was how it was; they argued me dumb. But then, who really knows how such things are?

I began to forget my sorrow. I loved the child madly, and he loved me too. As soon as he saw me he'd wave his little hands and want me to pick him up, and when he was colicky I was the only one who could pacify him. I bought him a little bone teething ring and a little gilded cap. He was forever catching the evil eye from someone, and then I had to run to get one of those abracadabras for him that would get him out of it. I worked like an ox. You know how expenses go up when there's an infant in the house. I don't want to lie about it; I didn't dislike Elka either, for that matter. She swore at me and cursed, and I couldn't get enough of her. What strength she had! One of her looks could rob you of the power of speech. And her orations! Pitch and sulphur, that's what they were full of, and yet somehow also full of charm. I adored her every word. She gave me bloody wounds though.

In the evening I brought her a white loaf as well as a dark one, and also poppyseed rolls I baked myself. I thieved because of her and swiped everything I could lay hands on: macaroons, raisins, almonds, cakes. I hope I may be forgiven for stealing from the Saturday pots the women left to warm in the baker's oven. I would take out scraps of meat, a chunk of pudding, a chicken leg or head, a piece of tripe, whatever I could nip quickly. She ate and became fat and handsome.

I had to sleep away from home all during the week, at the bakery. On Friday nights when I got home she always made an excuse of some sort. Either she had heartburn, or a stitch in the side, or hiccups, or headaches. You know what women's excuses are. I had a bitter time of it. It was rough. To add to it, this little brother of hers, the bastard, was growing bigger. He'd put lumps on me, and when I wanted to hit back she'd open her mouth and curse so powerfully I saw a green haze floating before my eyes. Ten times a day she threatened to divorce me. Another man in my place would have taken French leave and disappeared. But I'm the type that bears it and says nothing. What's one to do? Shoulders are from God, and burdens too.

One night there was a calamity in the bakery; the oven burst, and we almost had a fire. There was nothing to do but go home, so I went home. Let me, I thought, also taste the joy of sleeping in bed in midweek. I didn't want to wake the sleeping mite and tiptoed into the house. Coming in, it seemed to me that I heard not the snoring of one but, as it were, a double snore, one a thin enough snore and the other like the snoring of a slaughtered ox. Oh, I didn't like that! I didn't like it at all. I went up to the bed, and things suddenly turned black. Next to Elka lay a man's form. Another in my place would have made an uproar, and enough noise to rouse the whole town, but the thought occurred to me that I might wake the child. A little thing like that—why frighten a little swallow, I thought. All right then, I went back to the bakery and stretched out on a sack of flour and till morning I never shut an eye. I shivered as if I had had malaria. "Enough of being a donkey," I said to myself. "Gimpel isn't going to be a sucker all his life. There's a limit even to the foolishness of a fool like Gimpel."

In the morning I went to the rabbi to get advice, and it made a great commotion in the town. They sent the beadle for Elka right away. She came, carrying the child. And what do you think she did? She denied it, denied everything, bone and stone! "He's out of his head," she said. "I know nothing of dreams or divinations." They yelled at her, warned her, hammered on the table, but she stuck to her guns: it was a false accusation, she said.

The butchers and the horse-traders took her part. One of the lads from the slaughterhouse came by and said to me, "We've got our eye on you, you're a marked man." Meanwhile, the child started to bear down and soiled itself. In the rabbinical court there was an Ark of the Covenant, and they couldn't allow that, so they sent Elka away.

I said to the rabbi, "What shall I do?"

"You must divorce her at once," said he.

"And what if she refuses?" I asked.

He said, "You must serve the divorce. That's all you'll have to do."

I said, "Well, all right, Rabbi. Let me think about it."

"There's nothing to think about," said he. "You mustn't remain under the same roof with her."

"And if I want to see the child?" I asked.

"Let her go, the harlot," said he, "and her brood of bastards with her."

The verdict he gave was that I mustn't even cross her threshold—never again, as long as I should live.

During the day it didn't bother me so much. I thought: It was bound to happen, the abscess had to burst. But at night when I stretched out upon the sacks I felt it all very bitterly. A longing took me, for her and for the child. I wanted to be angry, but that's my misfortune exactly, I don't have it in me to be really angry. In the first place—this was how my thoughts went—there's bound to be a slip sometimes. You can't live without errors. Probably that lad who was with her led her on and gave her presents and what not, and women are often long on hair and short on sense, and so he got around her. And then since she denies it so, maybe I was only seeing things? Hallucinations do happen. You see a figure or a mannikin or something, but when you come up closer it's nothing, there's not a thing there. And if that's so, I'm doing her an injustice. And when I got so far in my thoughts I started to weep. I sobbed so that I wet the flour where I lay. In the morning I went to the rabbi and told him that I had made a mistake. The rabbi wrote on with his quill, and he said that if that were so he would have to reconsider the whole case. Until he had finished I wasn't to go near my wife, but I might send her bread and money by messenger.

III

Nine months passed before all the rabbis could come to an agreement. Letters went back and forth. I hadn't realized that there could be so much erudition about a matter like this.

Meanwhile, Elka gave birth to still another child, a girl this time. On the Sabbath I went to the synagogue and invoked a blessing on her. They called me up to the Torah, and I named the child for my mother-in-law—may she rest in peace. The louts and loudmouths of the town who came into the bakery gave me a going over. All Frampol refreshed its spirits because of my trouble and grief. However, I resolved that I would always believe what I was told. What's the good of *not* believing? Today it's your wife you don't believe; tomorrow it's God Himself you won't take stock in.

By an apprentice who was her neighbor I sent her daily a corn or a wheat loaf, or a piece of pastry, rolls or bagels, or, when I got the chance, a slab of pudding, a slice of honeycake, or wedding strudel—whatever came my way. The apprentice was a goodhearted lad, and more than once he added something on his own. He had formerly annoyed me a lot, plucking my nose and digging me in the ribs, but when he started to be a visitor to my house he became kind and friendly. "Hey, you, Gimpel," he said to me, "You have a very decent little wife and two fine kids. You don't deserve them."

"But the things people say about her," I said.

"Well, they have long tongues," he said, "and nothing to do with them but babble. Ignore it as you ignore the cold of last winter."

One day the rabbi sent for me and said, "Are you certain, Gimpel, that you were wrong about your wife?"

I said, "I'm certain."

"Why, but look here! You yourself saw it."

"It must have been a shadow," I said.

"The shadow of what?"

"Just of one of the beams, I think."

"You can go home then. You owe things to the Yanover rabbi. He found an obscure reference in Maimonides[3] that favored you."

I seized the rabbi's hand and kissed it.

I wanted to run home immediately. It's no small thing to be separated for so long a time from wife and child. Then I reflected: I'd better go back to work now, and go home in the evening. I said nothing to anyone, although as far as my heart was concerned it was like one of the Holy Days. The women teased and twitted me as they did every day, but my thought was: Go on, with your loose talk. The truth is out, like the oil upon the water. Maimonides says it's right, and therefore it is right!

At night, when I covered the dough to let it rise, I took my share of bread and a little sack of flour and started homeward. The moon was full and the stars were glistening, something to terrify the soul. I hurried onward, and before me darted a long shadow. It was winter, and a fresh snow had fallen. I had a mind to sing, but it was growing late and I didn't want to wake the householders. Then I felt like whistling, but I remembered that you don't whistle at night because it brings the demons out. So I was silent and walked as fast as I could.

Dogs in the Christian yards barked at me when I passed, but I thought: Bark your teeth out! What are you but mere dogs? Whereas I am a man, the husband of a fine wife, the father of promising children.

As I approached the house my heart started to pound as though it were the heart of a criminal. I felt no fear, but my heart went thump! thump! Well, no drawing back. I quietly lifted the latch and went in. Elka was asleep. I looked at the

[3]*Maimonides* Spanish rabbi, physician, and philosopher (1135–1204)

infant's cradle. The shutter was closed, but the moon forced its way through the cracks. I saw the newborn child's face and loved it as soon as I saw it—immediately—each tiny bone.

Then I came nearer to the bed. And what did I see but the apprentice lying there beside Elka. The moon went out all at once. It was utterly black, and I trembled. My teeth chattered. The bread fell from my hands, and my wife waked and said, "Who is that, ah?"

I muttered, "It's me."

"Gimpel?" she asked. "How come you're here? I thought it was forbidden."

"The rabbi said," I answered and shook as with a fever.

"Listen to me, Gimpel," she said, "go out to the shed and see if the goat's all right. It seems she's been sick." I have forgotten to say that we had a goat. When I heard she was unwell I went into the yard. The nannygoat was a good little creature. I had a nearly human feeling for her.

With hesitant steps I went up to the shed and opened the door. The goat stood there on her four feet. I felt her everywhere, drew her by the horns, examined her udders, and found nothing wrong. She had probably eaten too much bark. "Good night, little goat," I said. "Keep well." And the little beast answered with a "Maa" as though to thank me for the good will.

I went back. The apprentice had vanished.

"Where," I asked, "is the lad?"

"What lad?" my wife answered.

"What do you mean?" I said. "The apprentice. You were sleeping with him."

"The things I have dreamed this night and the night before," she said, "may they come true and lay you low, body and soul! An evil spirit has taken root in you and dazzles your sight." She screamed out, "You hateful creature! You moon calf! You spook! You uncouth man! Get out, or I'll scream all Frampol out of bed!"

Before I could move, her brother sprang out from behind the oven and struck me a blow on the back of the head. I thought he had broken my neck. I felt that something about me was deeply wrong, and I said, "Don't make a scandal. All that's needed now is that people should accuse me of raising spooks and dybbuks."[4] For that was what she had meant. "No one will touch bread of my baking."

In short, I somehow calmed her.

"Well," she said, "that's enough. Lie down, and be shattered by wheels."

Next morning I called the apprentice aside. "Listen here, brother!" I said. And so on and so forth. "What do you say?" He stared at me as though I had dropped from the roof or something.

"I swear," he said, "you'd better go to an herb doctor or some healer. I'm afraid you have a screw loose, but I'll hush it up for you." And that's how the thing stood.

To make a long story short, I lived twenty years with my wife. She bore me six children, four daughters and two sons. All kinds of things happened, but I neither saw nor heard. I believed, and that's all. The rabbi recently said to me, "Belief in itself is beneficial. It is written that a good man lives by his faith."

Suddenly my wife took sick. It began with a trifle, a little growth upon the breast. But she evidently was not destined to live long; she had no years. I spent a fortune on her. I have forgotten to say that by this time I had a bakery of my own and in Frampol was considered to be something of a rich man. Daily the healer

[4]*dybbuks* demons or souls of the dead who, according to Jewish folklore, take over the body of living persons. A dybbuk can be exorcised only by rabbinical ritual.

came, and every witch doctor in the neighborhood was brought. They decided to use leeches, and after that to try cupping. They even called a doctor from Lublin, but it was too late. Before she died she called me to her bed and said, "Forgive me, Gimpel."

I said, "What is there to forgive? You have been a good and faithful wife."

"Woe, Gimpel!" she said. "It was ugly how I deceived you all these years. I want to go clean to my Maker, and so I have to tell you that the children are not yours."

If I had been clouted on the head with a piece of wood it couldn't have bewildered me more.

"Whose are they?" I asked.

"I don't know," she said. "There were a lot . . . but they're not yours." And as she spoke she tossed her head to the side, her eyes turned glassy, and it was all up with Elka. On her whitened lips there remained a smile.

I imagined that, dead as she was, she was saying, "I deceived Gimpel. That was the meaning of my brief life."

IV

One night, when the period of mourning was done, as I lay dreaming on the flour sacks, there came the Spirit of Evil himself and said to me, "Gimpel, why do you sleep?"

I said, "What should I be doing? Eating kreplech?"[5]

"The whole world deceives you," he said, "and you ought to deceive the world in your turn."

"How can I deceive all the world?" I asked him.

He answered, "You might accumulate a bucket of urine every day and at night pour it into the dough. Let the sages of Frampol eat filth."

"What about judgment in the world to come?" I said.

"There is no world to come," he said. "They've sold you a bill of goods and talked you into believing you carried a cat in your belly. What nonsense!"

"Well then," I said, "and is there a God?"

He answered, "There is no God either."

"What," I said, "*is* there, then?"

"A thick mire."

He stood before my eyes with a goatish beard and horn, long-toothed, and with a tail. Hearing such words, I wanted to snatch him by the tail, but I tumbled from the flour sacks and nearly broke a rib. Then it happened that I had to answer the call of nature, and, passing, I saw the risen dough, which seemed to say to me, "Do it!" In brief, I let myself be persuaded.

At dawn the apprentice came. We kneaded the bread, scattered caraway seeds on it, and set it to bake. Then the apprentice went away, and I was left sitting in the little trench by the oven, on a pile of rags. Well, Gimpel, I thought, you've revenged yourself on them for all the shame they've put on you. Outside the frost glittered, but it was warm beside the oven. The flames heated my face. I bent my head and fell into a doze.

I saw in a dream, at once, Elka in her shroud. She called to me, "What have you done, Gimpel?"

I said to her, "It's all your fault," and started to cry.

[5]*kreplech* Yiddish: small casings of dough filled with ground meat, boiled, and usually served in soup

"You fool!" she said. "You fool! Because I was false is everything false too? I never deceived anyone but myself. I'm paying for it all, Gimpel. They spare you nothing here."

I looked at her face. It was black; I was startled and waked, and remained sitting dumb. I sense that everything hung in the balance. A false step now and I'd lose eternal life. But God gave me His help. I seized the long shovel and took out the loaves, carried them into the yard, and started to dig a hole in the frozen earth.

My apprentice came back as I was doing it. "What are you doing boss?" he said, and grew pale as a corpse.

"I know what I'm doing," I said, and I buried it all before his very eyes.

Then I went home, took my hoard from its hiding place, and divided it among the children. "I saw your mother tonight," I said. "She's turning black, poor thing."

They were so astonished they couldn't speak a word.

"Be, well," I said, "and forget that such a one as Gimpel ever existed." I put on my short coat, a pair of boots, took the bag that held my prayer shawl in one hand, my stock in the other, and kissed the mezuzah.[6] When people saw me in the street they were greatly surprised.

"Where are you going?" they said.

I answered, "Into the world." And so I departed from Frampol.

I wandered over the land, and good people did not neglect me. After many years I became old and white; I heard a great deal, many lies and falsehoods, but the longer I lived the more I understood that there were really no lies. Whatever doesn't really happen is dreamed at night. It happens to one if it doesn't happen to another, tomorrow if not today, or a century hence if not next year. What difference can it make? Often I heard tales of which I said, "Now this is a thing that cannot happen." But before a year had elapsed I heard that it actually had come to pass somewhere.

Going from place to place, eating at strange tables, it often happens that I spin yarns — improbable things that could never have happened — about devils, magicians, windmills, and the like. The children run after me, calling, "Grandfather, tell us a story." Sometimes they ask for particular stories, and I try to please them. A fat young boy once said to me, "Grandfather, it's the same story you told us before." The little rogue, he was right.

So it is with dreams too. It is many years since I left Frampol, but as soon as I shut my eyes I am there again. And whom do you think I see? Elka. She is standing by the washtub, as at our first encounter, but her face is shining and her eyes are as radiant as the eyes of a saint, and she speaks outlandish words to me, strange things. When I wake I have forgotten it all. But while the dream lasts I am comforted. She answers all my queries, and what comes out is that all is right. I weep and implore, "Let me be with you." And she consoles me and tells me to be patient. The time is nearer than it is far. Sometimes she strokes and kisses me and weeps upon my face. When I awaken I feel her lips and taste the salt of her tears.

No doubt the world is entirely an imaginary world, but it is only once removed from the true world. At the door of the hovel where I lie, there stands the plank on which the dead are taken away. The gravedigger Jew had his spade ready. The grave waits and the worms are hungry; the shrouds are prepared — I carry them in my

[6]*mezuzah* Hebrew: a small scroll inscribed with the Shama from Deuteronomy — "Hear, O Israel" — placed in a case and attached to the doorpost of the home by Biblical command

beggar's sack. Another *shnorrer*[7] is waiting to inherit my bed of straw. When the time comes I will go joyfully. Whatever may be there, it will be real, without complication, without ridicule, without deception. God be praised: there even Gimpel cannot be deceived.

[1953]

Translated by
Saul Bellow

QUESTIONS

1. In what sense is Gimpel a fool? In what sense is he a wise man? How would you describe Gimpel's morality?
2. How is Gimpel's "foolishness" ultimately vindicated? Why does he leave his family and his village?
3. What does the story suggest about true religious faith?
4. What is the theme of the story?

[7] *schnorrer* Yiddish: a person who begs or sponges off others

María Teresa Solari

Peru

According to the only information available on María Teresa Solari, her story, "Death and Transfiguration of a Teacher," originally appeared in *Antologia del cuento fantastico peruano*, published in Peru in 1977.

Death and Transfiguration of a Teacher

The teacher was dead; she had been cut up by the girls who, after killing her, cannibalistically disposed of her remains. The teacher was a poet endowed with great sensitivity and a romantic temperament, having started writing at twenty, although her career was now over at thirty-five. They were going over the scene of the crime. All the students were presumed guilty. They were interrogating the top student in the class:

"Now please tell us everything from the start. . . . "

The girl, a young thing with a blank expression on her face, grabbed one foot and sardonically exclaimed:

"Here."

"What's that supposed to mean? What are you doing with your foot? Get to the point!"

"I mean, I started on her foot. I took off her sock and bit into the heel."

"You can't be serious!"

The principal was nonplussed. Actually, all that was left were the gnawed-on bones. They left a little sign on the macabre residue: "Anatomy Lesson," it said.

One of the murdered teacher's poems went:

Oh, bittersweet youth,
object of my abject toil . . .

And nothing else. She had published only one book, entitled *Destiny*. She was timid in conversation and at times could not seem to express herself. When she got frustrated during the torture of her classes, she turned red and her mouth trembled. But she was incapable of raising her voice. And the classroom noise of the students' uninterrupted chattering seemed to envelop, disorient and paralyze her. She often talked about poetry. She tried to explain the magical power of poetic utterance. Something like the supreme effort of the poet to rise above the maddening crowd and to create. Somewhere in the back of the classroom a girl started going meeeeeooow, smothering the poetry of the impassioned rhapsodist. The laughter sharpened in tone. The class became a single giant cat, glaring at the teacher with piercing, bloodshot eyes. Four girls in the front row were singing some pop tune that went:

When I love you
from the bottom of my heart
my brains go
suddenly into knots . . .

The teacher left the room, crestfallen. Looking out at the empty schoolyard, she thought about her Calvary, about poets no longer having any place in this world. Why make teachers cover poets and poetry? It was laughable, and cruel to boot. A little bird swooped down and daintily snatched up a crumb from the gutter. The school's dog wagged his tail as she passed by, and without realizing it she glanced at him tenderly. At least he was sincere. The principal had called her to the office. When she went in, she couldn't help staring at a row of stuffed animals neatly lined up in an open cabinet. She remembered how the day before the principal had ordered them taken out into the sun to keep down the moths. The glass-eyed rabbit and the hawk with one wing stretched out got to sun themselves all morning. She felt the school was lifeless, and the principal just another stuffed animal.

"You don't seem to appreciate how serious the situation is. Your class is a madhouse, I've noticed it when I go by. The students don't respect you; you don't know how to make them respect you. You don't understand the principle of authority. You've just got to face them down and use a firm tone of voice — and make them afraid of you. You can manage them only if they fear you. But what do you do? You talk about poetry, sweetness and light, subtleties that they'll never understand and they don't care about! Stick to the program, right to the end! Hammer on those dates, yes, dates! For example: this poet was born in 1506 and died of tuberculosis in 1526! Therefore, he lived twenty years, wrote twenty books and a dictionary of poetry. Never made a red cent, nobody gave a damn about his books! The first was Illusion, the last, Desperation. Women wanted nothing to do with him, but now he's a great poet. That's all, enough for them to learn and then get on with the next writer!"

She left the office and her spirit seemed to mope along behind her, but at least it wasn't stuffed.

The day of the crime started normally enough. As she entered the classroom a student gave her a bouquet of red roses. Totally unheard of. Some others arranged them in a vase and placed them on the lectern. One girl got up and recited one of Bécquer's[1] poems from beginning to end, the one that starts with "The dark swallows will return." And then, you could have heard a pin drop. One of them — the one that had recited the poem — suddenly came forward and plunged the knife into her before she knew what was happening. She died with a beatific smile on her face and then they simply ate her up. Laughter was everywhere and spring was in the air, as befit the month of October. Later they went home and no one was hungry, although some complained about upset stomachs. A few threw up, but they were mostly calm. Sensitive to the deceased's poetic inclinations, they buried the bones next to a rosebush, but the dog — who was always hungry — dug them up. And when the principal was notified, she did not know what to make of them, since they did not match any of the bones in her collection. When the teacher did not show up the following day — she had never missed a class — the

[1]*Gustavo Adolfo Bécquer* (1836–1870) Spanish poet and author of romantic prose legends

principal began to suspect something was wrong. Her suspicions were confirmed after questioning the class. There was no accounting for it; this had never happened before at her school. She tried to blame it on the noxious influence of television, but the psychologist she brought in felt that there was more to it: perhaps some of the girls in the class had a congenital predisposition to crime. She called an emergency meeting of the P.T.A. to discuss what should be done, whether to go public or adopt an attitude of prudent silence. More than one father during that long session embarked on a rambling disquisition on how damaging it would be to interrupt or perhaps even end his daughter's studies. Other, more draconian parents noted that the girls' sense of right and wrong would suffer if it were not made clear how they had stepped out of line. Around midnight the sterner ones prevailed; they voted and it was decided to call in the authorities. But who would go to the police with the news? This duty fell to the gardener because, after all, he was the one who found the bones (and the dog chewing on them). So off he went. The police seemed more upset than anyone else. The whole thing was blown up in the press and newspapers sold like hotcakes, although after a while things quieted down and it was all conveniently forgotten. Some of the fathers had a lot of pull and reached an understanding with the court. Money changed hands, classes resumed and the girls did very well in their finals, and 99% of the class passed. The jury admitted that they were very bright. The principal decided to screen all prospective teachers for poetic tendencies, so as to avoid a repetition of this disagreeable and most inconvenient event. She found a taxidermist with literary inclinations to fill the recently-vacated position and keep her supplied with a steady stream of new specimens as well. She even felt a twinge of regret, reflecting on the lost opportunity to stuff the slain Lit teacher and label her "Poet," for an example to all the students: a dangerous breed, an egregious flaw in the Lord's creation. Later on, she and the new teacher started a Taxidermy Club which, to her surprise, proved very popular with the student body, including many of those involved in the incident of the previous year. Not only with the girl with the knife—very bright and a lot of personality, by the way—but also with the best student in the class, who—she knew—had nothing to do with it except for the cannibalism part.

[1977]

Translated by
JOHN BENSON

QUESTIONS

1. What views of teaching, poetry, and education are satirized in this story? For what reason is the teacher sacrificed?
2. How does the author's use of grotesque and shocking details and events contribute to the story's effectiveness? Are these elements balanced by the tone in which the story is told?
3. What is the significance of taxidermy to the story?
4. What does the word *transfiguration* in the title suggest about the story's meaning?

John Steinbeck

(1902–1968)

United States

Winner of the Nobel Prize for Literature in 1962, John Steinbeck is linked in the minds of many of his readers with the region about which he wrote so movingly: the Salinas Valley in Southern California, the place of his birth. In the eyes of critic Donald Heiney,

> Steinbeck is a model example of the modern American nostalgia for the primitive, the counter-reaction to the triumphant urbanization of American culture which took place in the first half of the twentieth century. He stands at the opposite extreme from the Horatio Alger myth, for he admires everything that is not a material success: the have-nots, the misfits, the racial minorities unjustly deprived of their civil and economic rights, the simple, the poor, and the oppressed. His rural heroes, illiterate and sometimes weak-minded, are nevertheless essentially noble; far from realistically described, they are actually poeticized rustics in the traditional romantic manner.

Among his many successful novels, the following stand out as the highlights of Steinbeck's long career: *Tortilla Flat* (1935), *Of Mice and Men* (1937), *The Grapes of Wrath* (1939), *East of Eden* (1953), and *The Winter of Our Discontent* (1961). "The Chrysanthemums" is from *The Long Valley* (1938).

The Chrysanthemums

The high grey-flannel fog of winter closed off the Salinas Valley from the sky and from all the rest of the world. On every side it sat like a lid on the mountains and made of the great valley a closed pot. On the broad, level land floor the gang plows bit deep and left the black earth shining like metal where the shares had cut. On the foothill ranches across the Salinas River, the yellow stubble fields seemed to be bathed in pale cold sunshine, but there was no sunshine in the valley now in December. The thick willow scrub along the river flamed with sharp and positive yellow leaves.

It was a time of quiet and of waiting. The air was cold and tender. A light wind blew up from the southwest so that the farmers were mildly hopeful of a good rain before long; but fog and rain do not go together.

Across the river, on Henry Allen's foothill ranch there was little work to be done, for the hay was cut and stored and the orchards were plowed up to receive the rain deeply when it should come. The cattle on the higher slopes were becoming shaggy and rough-coated.

Elisa Allen, working in her flower garden, looked down across the yard and saw Henry, her husband, talking to two men in business suits. The three of them stood by the tractor shed, each man with one foot on the side of the little Fordson. They smoked cigarettes and studied the machine as they talked.

Elisa watched them for a moment and then went back to her work. She was thirty-five. Her face was lean and strong and her eyes were as clear as water. Her figure looked blocked and heavy in her gardening costume, a man's black hat pulled low down over her eyes, clod-hopper shoes, a figured print dress almost completely covered by a big corduroy apron with four big pockets to hold the snips, the trowel and scratcher, the seeds, and the knife she worked with. She wore heavy leather gloves to protect her hands while she worked.

She was cutting down the old year's chrysanthemum stalks with a pair of short and powerful scissors. She looked down toward the men by the tractor shed now and then. Her face was eager and mature and handsome; even her work with the scissors was overeager, overpowerful. The chrysanthemum stems seemed too small and easy for her energy.

She brushed a cloud of hair out of her eyes with the back of her glove, and left a smudge of earth on her cheek in doing it. Behind her stood the neat white farm house with red geraniums close-banked around it as high as the windows. It was a hard-swept looking little house with hard-polished windows, and a clean mud-mat on the front steps.

Elisa cast another glance toward the tractor shed. The strangers were getting into their Ford coupe. She took off a glove and put her strong fingers down into the forest of new green chrysanthemum sprouts that were growing around the old roots. She spread the leaves and looked down among the close-growing stems. No aphids were there, no sowbugs or snails or cutworms. Her terrier fingers destroyed such pests before they could get started.

Elisa started at the sound of her husband's voice. He had come near quietly, and he leaned over the wire fence that protected her flower garden from cattle and dogs and chickens.

"At it again," he said. "You've got a strong new crop coming."

Elisa straightened her back and pulled on the gardening glove again. "Yes. They'll be strong this coming year." In her tone and on her face there was a little smugness.

"You've got a gift with things," Henry observed. "Some of those yellow chrysanthemums you had this year were ten inches across. I wish you'd work out in the orchard and raise some apples that big."

Her eyes sharpened. "Maybe I could do it, too. I've a gift with things, all right. My mother had it. She could stick anything in the ground and make it grow. She said it was having planters' hands that knew how to do it."

"Well, it sure works with flowers," he said.

"Henry, who were those men you were talking to?"

"Why, sure, that's what I came to tell you. They were from the Western Meat Company. I sold thirty head of three-year-old steers. Got nearly my own price, too."

"Good," she said. "Good for you."

"And I thought," he continued, "I thought how it's Saturday afternoon, and we might to into Salinas for dinner at a restaurant, and then to a picture show — to celebrate, you see."

"Good, she repeated. "Oh, yes. That will be good."

Henry put on his joking tone. "There's fights tonight. How'd you like to go to the fights?"

"Oh, no," she said breathlessly. "No, I wouldn't like fights."

"Just fooling, Elisa. We'll go to a movie. Let's see. It's two now. I'm going to take Scotty and bring down those steers from the hill. It'll take us maybe two hours. We'll go in town about five and have dinner at the Cominos Hotel. Like that?

"Of course I'll like it. It's good to eat away from home."

"All right, then. I'll go get up a couple of horses."

She said, "I'll have plenty of time to transplant some of these sets, I guess."

She heard her husband calling Scotty down by the barn. And a little later she saw the two men ride up the pale yellow hillside in search of the steers.

There was a little square sandy bed kept for rooting the chrysanthemums. With her trowel she turned the soil over and over, and smoothed it and patted it firm. Then she dug ten parallel trenches to receive the sets. Back at the chrysanthemum bed she pulled out the little crisp shoots, trimmed off the leaves at each one with her scissors, and laid it on a small orderly pile.

A squeak of wheels and plod of hoofs came from the road. Elisa looked up. The country road ran along the dense bank of willows and cottonwoods that bordered the river, and up this road came a curious vehicle, curiously drawn. It was an old spring-wagon, with a round canvas top on it like the corner of a prairie schooner. It was drawn by an old bay horse and a little grey-and-white burro. A big stubble-bearded man sat between the cover flaps and drove the crawling team. Underneath the wagon, between the hind wheels, a lean and rangy mongrel dog walked sedately. Words were painted on the canvas, in clumsy, crooked letters. "Pots, pans, knives, sisors, lawn mores, Fixed." Two rows of articles, and the triumphantly definitive "Fixed" below. The black paint had run down in little sharp points beneath each letter.

Elisa, squatting on the ground, watched to see the crazy, loose-jointed wagon pass by. But it didn't pass. It turned into the farm road in front of her house, crooked old wheels skirling and squeaking. The rangy dog darted from between the wheels and ran ahead. Instantly the two ranch shepherds flew out at him. Then all three stopped, and with stiff and quivering tails, with taut straight legs, with ambassadorial dignity, they slowly circled, sniffing daintily. The caravan pulled up to Elisa's wire fence and stopped. Now the newcomer dog, feeling outnumbered, lowered his tail and retired under the wagon with raised hackles and bared teeth.

The man on the seat called out, "That's a bad dog in a fight when he gets started."

Elisa laughed. "I see he is. How soon does he generally get started?"

The man caught up her laughter and echoed it heartily. "Sometimes not for weeks and weeks," he said. He climbed stiffly down, over the wheel. The horse and the donkey dropped like unwatered flowers.

Elisa saw that he was a very big man. Although his hair and beard were greying, he did not look old. His worn black suit was wrinkled and spotted with grease. The laughter had disappeared from his face and eyes the moment his laughing voice ceased. His eyes were dark, and they were full of the brooding that gets in the eyes of teamsters and of sailors. The calloused hands he rested on the wire fence were cracked, and every crack was a black line. He took off his battered hat.

"I'm off my general road, ma'am," he said. "Does this dirt road cut over across the river to the Los Angeles highway?"

Elisa stood up and shoved the thick scissors in her apron pocket. "Well, yes, it does, but it winds around and then fords the river. I don't think your team could pull through the sand."

He replied with some asperity, "It might surprise you what them beasts can pull through."

"When they get started?" she asked.

He smiled for a second. "Yes. When they get started."

"Well," said Elisa, "I think you'll save time if you go back to the Salinas road and pick up the highway there."

He drew a big finger down the chicken wire and made it sing. "I ain't in any hurry, ma'am. I go from Seattle to San Diego and back every year. Takes all my time. About six months each way. I aim to follow nice weather."

Elisa took off her gloves and stuffed them in the apron pocket with the scissors. She touched the under edge of her man's hat, searching for fugitive hairs. "That sounds like a nice kind of a way to live," she said.

He leaned confidentially over the fence. "Maybe you noticed the writing on my wagon. I mend pots and sharpen knives and scissors. You got any of them things to do?"

"Oh, no," she said, quickly. "Nothing like that." Her eyes hardened with resistance.

"Scissors is the worst thing," he explained. "Most people just ruin scissors trying to sharpen 'em, but I know how. I got a special tool. It's a little bobbit kind of thing, and patented. But it sure does the trick."

"No. My scissors are all sharp."

"All right, then. Take a pot," he continued earnestly, "a bent pot, or a pot with a hole. I can make it like new so you don't have to buy no new ones. That's a savings for you."

"No," she said shortly. "I tell you I have nothing like that for you to do."

His face fell to an exaggerated sadness. His voice took on a whining undertone. "I ain't had a thing to do today. Maybe I won't have no supper tonight. You see I'm off my regular road. I know folks on the highway clear from Seattle to San Diego. They save their things for me to sharpen up because they know I do it so good and save them money."

"I'm sorry," Elisa said irritably. "I haven't anything for you to do."

His eyes left her face and fell to searching the ground. They roamed about until they came to the chrysanthemum bed where she had been working. "What's them plants, ma'am?"

The irritation and resistance melted from Elisa's face. "Oh, those are chrysanthemums, giant whites and yellows. I raise them every year, bigger than anybody around here."

"Kind of a long-stemmed flower? Looks like a quick puff of colored smoke?" he asked.

"That's it. What a nice way to describe them."

"They smell kind of nasty till you get used to them," he said.

"It's a good bitter smell," she retorted, "not nasty at all."

He changed his tone quickly, "I like the smell myself."

"I had ten-inch-blooms this year," she said.

The man leaned farther over the fence. "Look, I know a lady down the road a piece, has got the nicest garden you ever seen. Got nearly every kind of flower but no chrysanthemums. Last time I was mending a copper-bottom washtub for her (that's a hard job but I do it good), she said to me, 'If you ever run acrost some nice chrysanthemums I wish you'd try to get me a few seeds.' That's what she told me."

Elisa's eyes grew alert and eager. "She couldn't have known much about chrysanthemums. You *can* raise them from seed, but it's much easier to root the little sprouts you see there."

"Oh," he said. "I s'pose I can't take none to her, then."

"Why yes you can," Elisa cried. "I can put some in damp sand, and you can carry them right along with you. They'll take root in the pot if you keep them damp. And then she can transplant them."

"She'd sure like to have some, ma'am. You say they're nice ones?"

"Beautiful," she said. "Oh, beautiful." Her eyes shone. She tore off the battered hat and shook out her dark pretty hair. "I'll put them in a flower pot, and you can take them right with you. Come into the yard."

While the man came through the picket gate Elisa ran excitedly along the geranium-bordered path to the back of the house. And she returned carrying a big red flower pot. The gloves were forgotten now. She kneeled on the ground by the starting bed and dug up the sandy soil with her fingers and scooped it into the bright new flower pot. Then she picked up the little pile of shoots she had prepared. With her strong fingers she pressed them into the sand and tamped around them with her knuckles. The man stood over her. "I'll tell you what to do," she said. "You remember so you can tell the lady."

"Yes, I'll try to remember."

"Well, look. These will take root in about a month. Then she must set them out, about a foot apart in good rich earth like this, see?" She lifted a handful of dark soil for him to look at. "They'll grow fast and tall. Now remember this: In July tell her to cut them down, about eight inches from the ground."

"Before they bloom?" he asked.

"Yes, before they bloom." Her face was tight with eagerness. "They'll grow right up again. About the last of September the buds will start."

She stopped and seemed perplexed. "It's the budding that takes the most care," she said hesitantly. "I don't know how to tell you." She looked deep into his eyes, searchingly. Her mouth opened a little, and she seemed to be listening. "I'll try to tell you," she said. "Did you ever hear of planting hands?"

"Can't say I have, ma'am."

"Well, I can only tell you what it feels like. It's when you're picking off the buds you don't want. Everything goes right down into your fingertips. You watch your fingers work. They do it themselves. You can feel how it is. They pick and pick the buds. They never make a mistake. They're with the plant. Do you see? Your fingers and the plant. You can feel that, right up your arm. They know. They never make a mistake. You can feel it. When you're like that you can't do anything wrong. Do you see that? Can you understand that?"

She was kneeling on the ground looking up at him. Her breast swelled passionately.

The man's eyes narrowed. He looked away self-consciously. "Maybe I know," he said. "Sometimes in the night in the wagon there—"

Elisa's voice grew husky. She broke in on him, "I've never lived as you do, but I know what you mean. When the night is dark—why, the stars are sharp-pointed, and there's quiet. Why, you rise up and up! Every pointed star gets driven into your body. It's like that. Hot and sharp and—lovely."

Kneeling there, her hand went out toward his legs in the greasy black trousers.

Her hesitant fingers almost touched the cloth. Then her hand dropped to the ground. She crouched low like a fawning dog.

He said, "It's nice, just like you say. Only when you don't have no dinner, it ain't."

She stood up then, very straight, and her face was ashamed. She held the flower pot out to him and placed it gently in his arms. "Here. Put it in your wagon, on the seat, where you can watch it. Maybe I can find something for you to do."

At the back of the house she dug in the can pile and found two old and battered aluminum saucepans. She carried them back and gave them to him. "Here, maybe you can fix these."

His manner changed. He became professional. "Good as new I can fix them." At the back of his wagon he set a little anvil, and out of an oily tool box dug a small machine hammer. Elisa came through the gate to watch him while he pounded out the dents in the kettles. His mouth grew sure and knowing. At a difficult part of the work he sucked his underlip.

"You sleep right in the wagon?" Elisa asked.

"Right in the wagon, ma'am. Rain or shine I'm dry as a cow in there."

"It must be nice," she said. "It must be very nice. I wish women could do such things."

"It ain't the right kind of a life for a woman."

Her upper lip raised a little, showing her teeth. "How do you know? How can you tell?" she said.

"I don't know, ma'am," he protested. "Of course I don't know. Now here's your kettles, done. You don't have to buy no new ones."

"How much?"

"Oh, fifty cents'll do. I keep my prices down and my work good. That's why I have all them satisfied customers up and down the highway."

Elisa brought him a fifty-cent piece from the house and dropped it in his hand. "You might be surprised to have a rival some time. I can sharpen scissors, too. And I can beat the dents out of little pots. I could show you what a woman might do."

He put his hammer back in the oily box and shoved the little anvil out of sight. "It would be a lonely life for a woman, ma'am, and a scarey life, too, with animals creeping under the wagon all night." He climbed over the singletree, steadying himself with a hand on the burro's white rump. He settled himself in the seat, picked up the lines. "Thank you kindly, ma'am," he said. "I'll do like you told me; I'll go back and catch the Salinas road."

"Mind," she called, "if you're long in getting there, keep the sand damp."

"Sand, ma'am? . . . Sand? Oh, sure. You mean around the chrysanthemums. Sure I will. He clucked his tongue. The beasts leaned luxuriously into their collars. The mongrel dog took his place between the back wheels. The wagon turned and crawled out the entrance road and back the way it had come, along the river.

Elisa stood in front of her wire fence watching the slow progress of the caravan. Her shoulders were straight, her head thrown back, her eyes half-closed, so that the scene came vaguely into them. Her lips moved silently, forming the words "Good-bye — good-bye." Then she whispered, "That's a bright direction. There's a glowing there." The sound of her whisper startled her. She shook herself free and looked about to see whether anyone had been listening. Only the dogs had heard. They lifted their heads toward her from their sleeping in the dust, and then stretched out their chins and settled asleep again. Elisa turned and ran hurriedly into the house.

In the kitchen she reached behind the stove and felt the water tank. It was full of hot water from the noonday cooking. In the bathroom she tore off her soiled clothes and flung them into the corner. And then she scrubbed herself with a little block of pumice, legs and thighs, loins and chest and arms, until her skin was scratched and red. When she had dried herself she stood in front of a mirror in her bedroom and looked at her body. She tightened her stomach and threw out her chest. She turned and looked over her shoulder at her back.

After a while she began to dress, slowly. She put on her newest underclothing and her nicest stockings and the dress which was the symbol of her prettiness. She worked carefully on her hair, penciled her eyebrows and rouged her lips.

Before she was finished she heard the little thunder of hoofs and the shouts of Henry and his helper as they drove the red steers into the corral. She heard the gate bang shut and set herself for Henry's arrival.

His step sounded on the porch. He entered the house calling, "Elisa, where are you?"

"In my room, dressing. I'm not ready. There's hot water for your bath. Hurry up. It's getting late."

When she heard him splashing in the tub, Elisa laid his dark suit on the bed, and shirt and socks and tie beside it. She stood his polished shoes on the floor beside the bed. Then she went to the porch and sat primly and stiffly down. She looked toward the river road where the willow-line was still yellow with frosted leaves so that under the high grey fog they seemed a thin band of sunshine. This was the only color in the grey afternoon. She sat unmoving for a long time. Her eyes blinked rarely.

Henry came banging out of the door, shoving his tie inside his vest as he came. Elisa stiffened and her face grew tight. Henry stopped short and looked at her. "Why—why, Elisa. You look so nice!"

"Nice? You think I look nice? What do you mean by 'nice'?"

Henry blundered on. "I don't know. I mean you look different, strong and happy."

"I am strong? Yes, strong. What do you mean 'strong'?"

He looked bewildered. "You're playing some kind of a game," he said helplessly. "It's a kind of a play. You look strong enough to break a calf over your knee, happy enough to eat it like a watermelon."

For a second she lost her rigidity. "Henry! Don't talk like that. You didn't know what you said." She grew complete again. "I'm strong," she boasted, "I never knew before how strong."

Henry looked down toward the tractor shed, and when he brought his eyes back to her, they were his own again. "I'll get out the car. You can put on your coat while I'm starting."

Elisa went into the house. She heard him drive to the gate and idle down his motor, and then she took a long time to put on her hat. She pulled it here and pressed it there. When Henry turned the motor off she slipped into her coat and went out.

The little roadster bounced along on the dirt road by the river, raising the birds and driving the rabbits into the brush. Two cranes flapped heavily over the willow-line and dropped into the river-bed.

Far ahead on the road Elisa saw a dark speck. She knew.

She tried not to look as they passed it, but her eyes would not obey. She whispered to herself sadly, "He might have thrown them off the road. That wouldn't have been much trouble, not very much. But he kept the pot," she explained. "He had to keep the pot. That's why he couldn't get them off the road."

The roadster turned a bend and she saw the caravan ahead. She swung full around toward her husband so she could not see the little covered wagon and the mismatched team as the car passed them.

In a moment it was over. The thing was done. She did not look back.

She said loudly, to be heard above the motor. "It will be good, tonight, a good dinner."

"Now you're changed again," Henry complained. He took one hand from the wheel and patted her knee. "I ought to take you in to dinner oftener. It would be good for both of us. We get so heavy out on the ranch."

"Henry," she asked, "could we have wine at dinner?"

"Sure we could. Say! That will be fine."

She was silent for a while; then she said, "Henry, at those prize fights, do the men hurt each other very much?"

"Sometimes a little, not often. Why?"

"Well, I've read how they break noses, and blood runs down their chests. I've read how the fighting gloves get heavy and soggy with blood."

He looked around at her. "What's the matter, Elisa? I didn't know you read things like that." He brought the car to a stop, then turned to the right over the Salinas River bridge.

"Do any women ever go to the fights?" she asked.

"Oh, sure, some. What's the matter Elisa? Do you want to go? I don't think you'd like it, but I'll take you if you really want to go."

She relaxed limply in the seat. "Oh, no. No. I don't want to go. I'm sure I don't." Her face was turned away from him. "It will be enough if we can have wine. It will be plenty." She turned up her coat collar so he could not see that she was crying weakly—like an old woman.

[1938]

QUESTIONS

1. What does Elisa's husband mean when he refers to her as "strong" near the end of the story? Has her incident with the tinker made her stronger and more capable of living the difficult life of a farmer's wife—or has the incident made her weaker, more vulnerable than she was before?
2. When Elisa talks to the tinker and he describes his lonely nights in the wagon, she has to resist the temptation to reach out and touch his trousers. What are the implied sexual dynamics of their relationship? (For a variation on this theme, read D. H. Lawrence's poem, "The Odour of Chrysanthemums," published before Steinbeck's story.)
3. What do the flowers represent to Elisa? Are they her surrogate children? What is the state of Elisa and Henry's marriage?

Hyemeyohsts Storm

(b. 1935)

United States

Hyemeyohsts (pronounced Hy-*am*-ee-yosts) Storm, a Northern Cheyenne, was born on the Lame Deer Agency in Montana. His first teachers were the tribal elders who taught him the ways of the Plains People and introduced him to the tribal traditions of the Sun Dance and the Medicine Wheel. In his unique novel, *Seven Arrows* (1972)—the first book about the Plains Indians to be written entirely by a Native American—Storm interpolates symbolic "teaching" stories, handed down as part of the oral tradition of his people, within the narrative of historical circumstances that irrevocably altered the Plains Indians' traditional way of life.

As part of the narrative, Storm blends historical photographs, graphic designs of medicine wheels, and several different kinds of stories to produce an effect both magical and haunting. As Charles R. Larson observed in 1973,

> There are few books that have a genuine hypnotic effect on the reader. Fewer still are those occasions in our reading lives when we come across a work with magical properties so enchanting that we immediately sense that we will be haunted by it the rest of our lives. *Seven Arrows* . . . is such a [work]. . . . It is the most extraordinary book that I have ever read. I think that it is going to force us to reconsider some of our basic conceptions of American literature. I know that it is going to make us stand up and look at the American Indian artist in a way that we have never regarded him before.

Storm, who attended Eastern Montana College, has also written *The Son of Heyoehkah* (1979); a book of short stories, *Reliability Mirrors*; and a play, *The Beaded Path*. He has written under the pseudonym Golden Silver. "The Story of Jumping Mouse," from *Seven Arrows*, demonstrates the interweaving of a traditional symbolic "teaching story" with the narrator's own guidance to his audience.

• *The Story of Jumping Mouse* •

Soon half a dozen children were clustered around the Story-Teller. He lit his Pipe and began:

Once there was a Mouse.

Squinting his eyes, he touched his nose to the nose of a little girl near him. *He was a Busy Mouse, Searching Everywhere, Touching his Whiskers to the*

Grass, and Looking. He was Busy as all Mice are, Busy with Mice things. But once in a while he would Hear an odd Sound. He would Lift his Head, Squinting hard to See, his Whiskers Wiggling in the Air, and he would Wonder. One day he Scurried up to a fellow Mouse and asked him, "Do you Hear a Roaring in your Ears, my Brother?"

"No, no," answered the Other Mouse, not Lifting his Busy Nose from the Ground. "I Hear Nothing. I am Busy now. Talk to me Later."

He asked Another Mouse the same Question and the Mouse Looked at him Strangely. "Are you Foolish in your Head? What Sound?" he asked and Slipped into a Hole in a Fallen Cottonwood Tree.

The little Mouse shrugged his Whiskers and Busied himself again, Determined to Forget the Whole Matter. But there was that Roaring again. It was faint, very faint, but it was there! One Day, he Decided to investigate the Sound just a little. Leaving the Other Busy Mice, he Scurried a little Way away and Listened again. There It was! He was Listening hard when suddenly, Someone said Hello.

"Hello, little Brother," the Voice said, and Mouse almost Jumped right Out of his Skin. He Arched his Back and Tail and was about to Run.

"Hello," again said the Voice. "It is I, Brother Raccoon." And sure enough, It was! "What are you Doing Here all by yourself, little Brother?" asked the Raccoon. The Mouse blushed, and put his Nose almost to the Ground. "I Hear a Roaring in my Ears and I am Investigating it," he answered timidly.

"A Roaring in your Ears?" replied the Raccoon as he Sat Down with him. "What you Hear, little Brother, is the River."

"The River?" Mouse asked curiously. "What is a River?"

"Walk with me and I will Show you the River," Raccoon said.

Little Mouse was terribly Afraid, but he was Determined to Find Out Once and for All about the Roaring. "I can Return to my Work," he thought, "after this thing is Settled, and possibly this thing may Aid me in All my Busy Examining and Collecting. And my Brothers All said it was Nothing. I will Show them. I will Ask Raccoon to Return with me and I will have Proof."

"All right Raccoon, my Brother," said Mouse. "Lead on to the River. I will Walk with you."

"Get me another brand from the fire, my son," the Chief said to Hawk. "And we will talk more about this Mouse."

Hawk ran for the brand and brought it to the Chief. Lighting his Pipe, the Chief looked up at the little girl nearest him. "And what will happen to little Mouse?" he asked, grabbing the end of her nose. She blushed and looked down at her hands.

"He will fall into the river," she answered in a voice almost too small to be heard.

"*Aai ya hey!*" the Chief said, gripping his Pipe. "Did Seven Arrows visit you and whisper the Story in your ear?"

"No," she giggled. "Grandfather told me the beginning."

"That is exactly what will happen," the Chief smiled. "But let us talk about it before we continue."

Hawk squirmed in his impatience. What did this have to do with the Power and the riddle he had asked? He looked at a group of boys who were playing the hoop game nearby, and he wished he could join them. "If nothing more interesting happens soon," he thought, "I will go play with them."

Just then Bull Looks Back's wife stuck her head out of her lodge and called. Two of the children sitting in the group got up and ran to their lodge.

"As you already know," began the Chief, "we were discussing the riddle of men. Men are like little Mouse. They are so busy with the things of this world that they are unable to perceive things at any distance. They scrutinize some things very carefully, and only brush others over lightly with their whiskers. But all of these things must be close to them. The roaring that they hear in their ears is life, the river. This great sound in their ears is the sound of the Spirit. The lesson is timely, Hawk, because the cries of mankind now are everywhere, but men are too busy with their little Mouse lives to hear. Some deny the presence of these sounds, others do not hear them at all, and still others, my son, hear them so clearly that it is a screaming in their hearts. Little Mouse heard the sounds and went a short distance from the world of Mice to investigate them."

"And met Raccoon," Hawk added. "Is the Raccoon the Great Spirit?"

"In a manner of speaking he is, little brother, but he is also the things that man will discover, if he seeks them, that will lead him to the Great River. The Raccoon can also be a man, or men."

"Men?" said Day Woman. "What kind of men?"

"Men," continued the Chief, "who know of the Medicine River. Men who have experienced and are familiar with life. The Raccoon washes his food in this Medicine. These types of men are unique, my children."

"Now, let us continue the Story," the Chief began again, glancing quickly at Hawk. "That is, if you wish."

Hawk look fleetingly towards the hoop game and turned his eyes back to the Teacher. "Yes, please continue," he said, settling himself in place.

The man turned his smiling face to the mountains, clapped his hands together, and began.

Little Mouse Walked with Raccoon. His little Heart was Pounding in his Breast. The Raccoon was Taking him upon Strange Paths and little Mouse Smelled the Scent of many things that had Gone by this Way. Many times he became so Frightened he almost Turned Back. Finally, they Came to the River! It was Huge and Breathtaking, Deep and Clear in Places, and Murky in Others. Little Mouse was unable to See Across it because it was so Great. It Roared, Sang, Cried, and Thundered on its Course. Little Mouse Saw Great and Little Pieces of the World Carried Along on its Surface.

"It is Powerful!" little Mouse said, Fumbling for Words.

"It is a Great thing," answered the Raccoon, "but here, let me Introduce you to a Friend."

In a Smoother, Shallower Place was a Lily Pad, Bright and Green. Sitting upon it was a Frog, almost as Green as the Pad it sat on. The Frog's White Belly stood out Clearly.

"Hello, little Brother," said the Frog. "Welcome to the River."

"I must Leave you Now," cut in Raccoon, "but do not Fear, little Brother, for Frog will Care for you Now." And Raccoon Left, Looking along the River Bank for Food that he might Wash and Eat.

Little Mouse Approached the Water and Looked into it. He saw a Frightened Mouse Reflected there.

"Who are you?" little Mouse asked the Reflection. "Are you not Afraid being that Far out into the Great River?"

"No," answered the Frog, "I am not Afraid, I have been Given the Gift

from Birth to Live both Above and Within the River. When Winter Man Comes and Freezes this Medicine, I cannot be Seen. But all the while Thunderbird Flies, I am here. To Visit me, One must Come when the World is Green. I, my Brother, am the Keeper of the Water."

"Amazing!" little Mouse said at last, again Fumbling for Words.

"Would you like to have some Medicine Power?" Frog asked.

"Medicine Power? Me?" asked little Mouse. "Yes, yes! If it is Possible."

"Then Crouch as Low as you Can, and then Jump as High as you are Able! You will have your Medicine!" Frog said.

Little Mouse did as he was Instructed. He Crouched as Low as he Could and Jumped. And when he did, his Eyes Saw the Sacred Mountains.

"Like those over there," the Chief said, pointing to the distant mountains. Then he went on.

Little Mouse could hardly Believe his Eyes. But there They were! But then he Fell back to Earth, and he Landed in the River!

The Chief laughed and looked at the little girl.

Little Mouse became Frightened and Scrambled back to the Bank. He was Wet and Frightened nearly to Death.

"You have Tricked me," little Mouse Screamed at the Frog!

"Wait," said the Frog. "You are not Harmed. Do not let your Fear and Anger Blind you. What did you See?"

"I," Mouse stammered, "I, I Saw the Sacred Mountains!"

"And you have a New Name!" Frog said, "It is Jumping Mouse."

"Thank you. Thank you," Jumping Mouse said, and Thanked him again. "I want to Return to my People and Tell of this thing that has Happened to me."

"Go. Go then," Frog Said. "Return to your People. It is Easy to Find them. Keep the Sound of the Medicine River to the Back of your Head. Go Opposite to the Sound and you will Find your Brother Mice."

Jumping Mouse Returned to the World of the Mice. But he Found Disappointment. No One would listen to him. And because he was Wet, and had no Way of explaining it because there had been no Rain, many of the other Mice were Afraid of him. They believed he had been Spat from the Mouth of Another Animal that had Tried to Eat him. And they all Knew that if he had not been Food for the One who Wanted him, then he must also be Poison for them.

Jumping Mouse Lived again among his People, but he could not Forget his Vision of the Sacred Mountains.

The Medicine Chief reached again for his Pipe, and Hawk ran for a new brand from the fire to light it for him.

"Is this Story about the Green of the South?" asked Hawk as he sat down. "I remember you talked before about the Man of the South and his Sister. Is this Man the Frog?"

"Yes," the Chief answered. He blew a long puff in the air. "The South is the place of innocence. Men who walk there must walk with a heart of trust."

"Your own Shield is bordered with lodges of green," Day Woman said, pointing to a Shield that hung a few lodges away.

"Those marks are Signs of the Mirroring, just as when Jumping Mouse looked into the river and saw his Reflection," said the Chief.

"But," Hawk added quickly, "that Sign you have upon your Shield is the Medicine Wheel, the Sun Dance. How is it then also the Mirroring?"

"The Medicine Wheel, my children," said the Chief, "is the Mirroring of the Great Spirit, the Universe, among men. We are all the Medicine River. And the Universe is the Medicine River that man is Mirrored upon, my children. And we in our turn see the Medicines of men Mirrored in the Universe."

"Then who is the Frog?" Hawk asked. "I am confused. I do not understand."

"Nor I," Day Woman chimed in.

"Do not make this matter complicated for yourselves," the Chief said. "Little Mouse heard the roaring in his ears and sought to solve its mystery. He met Raccoon and was taken to see the Medicine River, which represents Life. He saw himself Mirrored there in Life.

All of us are so Mirrored, my children, but many men have not visited the Great River and have not witnessed it. Some have followed Raccoon to the River, seen their Reflection, but become frightened and retreated among the mice again. But the lesson is always there for those who seek it. It is in the place of the South. The place of trust."

"Will you explain more to us about the Raccoon?" asked Day Woman.

"No, little Day Woman, because it is for you to visit this place yourself. The Raccoon and the Frog will then become clear to you."

The Chief immediately began the Story again.

The Memory Burned in the Mind and Heart of Jumping Mouse, and One Day he Went to the Edge of the River Place. . . .

"Come with me, children," the Peace Chief said, getting to his feet. They walked through the camp, and past it to the river. Even though it was a warm, almost a hot day, many of the People were still busy about the camp.

A group of young men were riding into the camp laughing and teasing with one another. When they rode past Hawk and Day Woman they turned their teasing to the boy and girl. As they rode by, one of the young men slipped from his horse and walked up to the Medicine Chief.

"Good Father," he said, not looking at the Chief, "You are invited to the lodge of my parents for the evening meal. Medicine Crow, my grandfather, has been made well from sickness. The Medicine Power has healed him. My father told me to tell you these things, and also that he will sponsor a dance and Give-Away to the People in thanksgiving tonight."

"A dance!" squeaked Day Woman and Prairie Rose almost together. "We must prepare," the girls explained to the Chief, and then they were off, running hand in hand to their lodge.

"Well, it appears that now only we three are left," said the Chief.

As they began to walk again, a girl the same age as Singing Flower ran up and grabbed her hand, said something, and left to play. Singing Flower hesitated for a moment and then ran off to join her.

"This," explained the Chief after he and Hawk had reached the brush and trees along the river, "is where Jumping Mouse began. Do you see those lodges of our People? Those, my son, we will pretend are the Sacred Mountains. Lie down here upon your stomach and see how a Mouse would perceive the Prairie."

Hawk lay on his stomach and looked. The expanse of Prairie appeared to him as a measureless sea of grass. The Chief helped Hawk back to his feet and found them a cool place to sit. There he began the Story again.

Jumping Mouse went to the Edge of the Place of Mice and Looked onto the Prairie. He Looked up for Eagles. The Sky was Full of many Spots, each One an Eagle. But he was Determined to Go to the Sacred Mountains. He Gathered All of his Courage and Ran just as Fast as he Could onto the Prairie. His little Heart Pounded with Excitement and Fear.

He ran until he Came to a Stand of Sage. He was Resting and trying to Catch his Breath when he Saw an Old Mouse. The Patch of Sage Old Mouse Lived in was a Haven for Mice. Seeds were Plentiful and there was Nesting Material and many things to be Busy with.

"Hello," said Old Mouse. "Welcome."

Jumping Mouse was Amazed. Such a Place and such a Mouse. "You are Truly a great Mouse," Jumping Mouse said with all the Respect he could Find. "This is Truly a Wonderful Place. And the Eagles cannot see you here, either," Jumping Mouse said.

"Yes," said Old Mouse, "and One can See All the Beings of the Prairie here: the Buffalo, Antelope, Rabbit, and Coyote. One can See them All from here and Know their Names."

"That is Marvelous," Jumping Mouse said. "Can you also See the River and the Great Mountains?"

"Yes and No," Old Mouse Said with Conviction. "I Know there is the Great River. But I am Afraid that the Great Mountains are only a Myth. Forget your Passion to See Them and Stay here with me. There is Everything you Want here, and it is a Good Place to Be."

"How can he Say such a thing?" Thought Jumping Mouse. "The Medicine of the Sacred Mountains is Nothing One can Forget."

"Thank you very much for the Meal you have Shared with me, Old Mouse, and also for sharing your Great Home," Jumping Mouse said. "But I must Seek the Mountains."

"You are a Foolish Mouse to Leave here. There is Danger on the Prairie! Just Look up there!" Old Mouse said, with even more Conviction. "See all those Spots! They are Eagles, and they will catch you!"

It was hard for Jumping Mouse to Leave, but he Gathered his Determination and Ran hard Again. The Ground was Rough. But he Arched his Tail and Ran with All his Might. He could Feel the Shadows of the Spots upon his Back as he Ran. All those Spots! Finally he Ran into a Stand of Chokecherries. Jumping Mouse could hardly Believe his Eyes. It was Cool there and very Spacious. There was Water, Cherries and Seeds to Eat, Grasses to Gather for Nests, Holes to be Explored and many, many Other Busy Things to do. And there were a great many things to Gather.

He was Investigating his New Domain when he Heard Heavy Breathing. He Quickly Investigated the Sound and Discovered its Source. It was a Great Mound of Hair with Black Horns. It was a Great Buffalo. Jumping Mouse could hardly Believe the Greatness of the Being he Saw Lying there before him. He was so large that Jumping Mouse could have crawled into One of his Great Horns. "Such a Magnificent Being," Thought Jumping Mouse, and he Crept Closer.

"Hello, my Brother," said the Buffalo. "Thank you for Visiting me."

"Hello, Great Being," said Jumping Mouse. "Why are you Lying here?"

"I am Sick and I am Dying," the Buffalo said, "And my Medicine has Told me that only the Eye of a Mouse can Heal me. But little Brother, there is no such Thing as a Mouse."

Jumping Mouse was Shocked. "One of my Eyes!" he Thought, "One of my

Tiny Eyes." He Scurried back into the Stand of Chokecherries. But the Breathing came Harder and Slower. "He will Die," Thought Jumping Mouse, "If I do not Give him my Eye. He is too Great a Being to Let Die."

He Went Back to where the Buffalo Lay and Spoke. "I am a Mouse," he said with a Shaky Voice. "And you, my Brother, are a Great Being. I cannot Let you Die. I have Two Eyes, so you may have One of them."

The minute he had Said it, Jumping Mouse's Eye Flew Out of his Head and the Buffalo was Made Whole. The Buffalo Jumped to his Feet, Shaking Jumping Mouse's Whole World. "Thank you, my little Brother," said the Buffalo. "I Know of your Quest for the Sacred Mountains and of your Visit to the River. You have Given me Life so that I may Give-Away to the People. I will be your Brother Forever. Run under my Belly and I will Take you right to the Foot of the Sacred Mountains, and you need not Fear the Spots. The Eagles cannot See you while you Run under Me. All they will See will be the Back of a Buffalo. I am of the Prairie and I will Fall on you if I Try to Go up the Mountains."

Little Mouse ran under the Buffalo, Secure and Hidden from the Spots, but with only One Eye it was Frightening. The Buffalo's Great Hooves Shook the Whole World each time he took a Step. Finally they Came to a Place and Buffalo Stopped.

"This is Where I must Leave you, little Brother," said the Buffalo.

"Thank you very much," said Jumping Mouse. "But you Know, it was very Frightening Running under you with only One Eye. I was Constantly in Fear of your Great Earth-Shaking Hooves.

"Your Fear was for Nothing," said Buffalo. "For my Way of Walking is the Sun Dance Way, and I Always Know where my Hooves will Fall. I now must Return to the Prairie, my Brother. You can Always Find me there."

"Come with me, Hawk," the Chief said. "Let us walk to those pines on that hill."

"Tell me," said Hawk, "What is the meaning within this Teaching?"

The Chief walked in silence until he was almost to the top of the hill. A coyote jumped from behind a small rock and ran over the top of the hill, but not before stopping once and looking back at the two men.

The smell of the campfires and cooking food drifted up from the camp below. The voices of children laughing at their play blended with the sounds of the wind in the pines and the songbirds of the prairie.

"When you experience this seeking," the Chief began, "You will meet the Old Mice of the world. They can name for you the beings of the Prairie, but they have neither touched nor known them. These people have received a great Gift, but they spend their lives hidden within the sage. They have not yet run out on to the Prairie, the everyday world. Like Jumping Mouse, they fear the spots the most.

"But remember, my son, that Mice see clearly only that which is very near to them. To those people who perceive in this way, the sky will always be full of spots because of their near-sightedness. And of course in their fear they will always perceive them as Eagles," the Chief chuckled.

"But Jumping Mouse does not stay, he runs. As you already know, the Buffalo is the great Spirit's greatest Gift to the People. He is the Spirit of Giving. Jumping Mouse Gives-Away one of his own eyes, one of his Mouse's ways of perceiving, and heals the Buffalo."

"Why must he Give-Away an eye to heal the Buffalo?" Hawk asked.

"Because this kind of person, this Mouse, must give up one of his Mouse ways of seeing things in order that he may grow. People never are forced to do these things, Hawk. The Buffalo did not even know Jumping Mouse was a Mouse. He could have just stayed hidden like the Old Mouse."

"What would have happened if he had let the Buffalo die?" asked Hawk.

"He would have had to live with the stink of the rotting flesh, my son. Or he would have had to retreat to the place of Old Mouse. And if he had decided to live there instead of moving and growing, then he would have experienced thirst. The chokecherries he would have eaten would have made him thirst mightily for water.

"Believe me, Hawk, many men have reached these places. Some choose to live with the stink, and others, refusing to leave the Old Mouse's place, thirst constantly. Still others run endlessly under the great Buffalo. These are probably the most powerful of men, but no doubt the worst. They have the Power, but they speak always from fear. Fear of the great hooves of the Spirit, and of course the fear of the spots, the high Eagles, the unknown."

"Is there yet more, Shield Man?" Hawk asked.

"Yes, there is," answered the Teacher. "But do you wish to eat first?"

"No," said Hawk quickly, "I can eat later. Please finish the Story."

The Man of the Shield smiled and let his eyes rest on the camp below him.

Jumping Mouse Immediately Began to Investigate his New Surroundings. There were even more things here than in the Other Places, Busier things, and an Abundance of Seeds and Other things Mice Like. In his Investigation of these things, Suddenly he Ran upon a Grey Wolf who was Sitting there doing absolutely Nothing.

"Hello, Brother Wolf," Jumping Mouse said.

The Wolf's Ears Came Alert and his Eyes Shone. "Wolf! Wolf! Yes, that is what I am, I am a Wolf!" But then his mind Dimmed again and it was not long before he Sat Quietly again, completely without Memory as to who he was. Each time Jumping Mouse Reminded him who he was, he became Excited with the News, but soon would Forget again.

"Such a Great Being," thought Jumping Mouse, "but he has no Memory."

Jumping Mouse Went to the Center of this New Place and was Quiet. He Listened for a very long time to the Beating of his Heart. Then Suddenly he Made up his Mind. He Scurried back to where the Wolf Sat and he Spoke.

"Brother Wolf," Jumping Mouse said. . . .

"Wolf! Wolf," said the Wolf. . . .

"Please, Brother Wolf," said Jumping Mouse, "Please Listen to me. I Know what will Heal you. It is One of my Eyes. And I Want to Give it to you. You are a Greater Being than I. I am only a Mouse. Please Take it."

When Jumping Mouse Stopped Speaking his Eye Flew out of his Head and the Wolf was made Whole.

Tears Fell down the Cheeks of Wolf, but his little Brother could not See them, for Now he was Blind.

"You are a Great Brother," said the Wolf, "for Now I have my Memory. But Now you are Blind. I am the Guide into the Sacred Mountains. I will Take you there. There is a Great Medicine Lake there. The most Beautiful Lake in the World. All the World is Reflected there. The People, the Lodges of the People, and All the Beings of the Prairies and Skies."

"Please Take me there," Jumping Mouse said. The Wolf Guided him through the Pines to the Medicine Lake. Jumping Mouse Drank the Water from the Lake. The Wolf Described the Beauty to him.

"I must Leave you here," said Wolf, "for I must Return so that I may Guide Others, but I will Remain with you as long as you Like."

"Thank you, my Brother," said Jumping Mouse. "But although I am Frightened to be Alone, I Know you must Go so that you may Show Others the Way to this Place." Jumping Mouse Sat there Trembling in Fear. It was no use Running, for he was Blind, but he Knew an Eagle would Find him Here. He felt a Shadow on his Back and Heard the Sound that Eagles Make. He Braced himself for the Shock. And the Eagle Hit! Jumping Mouse went to Sleep.

Then he Woke Up. The surprise of being Alive was Great, but Now he could See! Everything was Blurry, but the Colors were Beautiful.

"I can See! I can See!" said Jumping Mouse over again and again.

A Blurry Shape Came toward Jumping Mouse. Jumping Mouse Squinted hard but the Shape Remained a Blur.

"Hello, Brother," a Voice said. "Do you Want some Medicine?"

"Some Medicine for me?" asked Jumping Mouse. "Yes! Yes!"

"Then Crouch down as Low as you Can," the Voice said, "and Jump as High as you Can."

Jumping Mouse did as he was instructed. He Crouched as Low as he Could and Jumped! The Wind Caught him and Carried him Higher.

"Do not be Afraid," the Voice called to him. "Hang on to the Wind and Trust!"

Jumping Mouse did. He Closed his Eyes and Hung on to the Wind and it Carried him Higher and Higher. Jumping Mouse Opened his eyes and they were Clear, and the Higher he Went the Clearer they Became. Jumping Mouse Saw his Old Friend upon a Lily Pad on the Beautiful Medicine Lake. It was the Frog.

"You have a New Name," Called the Frog. "You are Eagle!"

[1972]

QUESTIONS

1. How do you respond to the amalgamation of several narrative elements: the traditional "teaching story," its interpretation or "teaching" provided by the storyteller as he tells the story, and descriptions of the children in the storyteller's audience reacting to his narrative? How does this structure prepare you to interpret the final segment of the story yourself?
2. In what ways is the story of Jumping Mouse an animal fable in the tradition of Aesop's fables? How is it different?
3. What is the theme of the story of Jumping Mouse?
4. Compare the story with some of the other traditional or "oral" tales included in this volume, particularly stories from *The Thousand and One Nights.*

Graham Swift

(b. 1949)

England

Currently one of England's leading novelists, Graham Swift was born in London in 1949. He attended Cambridge University for his undergraduate degree and subsequently continued graduate studies both there and at York University. His first novel, *The Sweet-Shop Owner* (1980), was followed by *Shuttlecock* (1981) and *Waterland* (1983), which was nominated for the Booker Prize (his country's most prestigious literary award). *Waterland* also won the praise of American critics, who compared it to the work of William Faulkner. The narrative opens with the discovery of a corpse in the waterlands, the Fens, and then works backward to solve the question of who the murderer was. The story included here is from *Learning to Swim and Other Stories* (1982).

◆ *Learning to Swim* ◆

Mrs. Singleton had three times thought of leaving her husband. The first time was before they were married, on a charter plane coming back from a holiday in Greece. They were students who had just graduated. They had rucksacks and faded jeans. In Greece they had stayed part of the time by a beach on an island. The island was dry and rocky with great grey and vermilion coloured rocks and when you lay on the beach it seemed that you too became a hot, basking rock. Behind the beach there were eucalyptus trees like dry, leafy bones, old men with mules and gold teeth, a fragrance of thyme, and a café with melon seeds on the floor and a jukebox which played bouzouki music and songs by Cliff Richard. All this Mr. Singleton failed to appreciate. He'd only liked the milk-warm, clear blue sea, in which he'd stayed most of the time as if afraid of foreign soil. On the plane she'd thought: He hadn't enjoyed the holiday, hadn't liked Greece at all. All that sunshine. Then she'd thought she ought not to marry him.

Though she had, a year later.

The second time was about a year after Mr. Singleton, who was a civil engineer, had begun his first big job. He became a junior partner in a firm with a growing reputation. She ought to have been pleased by this. It brought money and comfort; it enabled them to move to a house with a large garden, to live well, to think about raising a family. They spent weekends in country hotels. But Mr. Singleton seemed untouched by this. He became withdrawn and incommunicative. He went to his work austere-faced. She thought: He likes his bridges and tunnels better than me.

The third time, which was really a phase, not a single moment, was when she began to calculate how often Mr. Singleton made love to her. When she started this it was about once every fortnight on average. Then it became every three weeks. The interval had been widening for some time. This was not a predicament Mrs. Singleton viewed selfishly. Love-making had been a problem before, in their earliest days together, which, thanks to her patience and initiative, had been overcome. It was Mr. Singleton's unhappiness, not her own, that she saw in their present plight. He was distrustful of happiness as some people fear heights or open spaces. She would reassure him, encourage him again. But the averages seemed to defy her personal effort: once every three weeks, once every month. . . . She thought: Things go back to as they were.

But then, by sheer chance, she became pregnant.

Now she lay on her back, eyes closed, on the coarse sand of the beach in Cornwall. It was hot and, if she opened her eyes, the sky was clear blue. This and the previous summer had been fine enough to make her husband's refusal to go abroad for holidays tolerable. If you kept your eyes closed it could be Greece or Italy or Ibiza. She wore a chocolate-brown bikini, sunglasses, and her skin, which seldom suffered from sunburn, was already beginning to tan. She let her arms trail idly by her side, scooping up little handfuls of sand. If she turned her head to the right and looked towards the sea she could see Mr. Singleton and their son Paul standing in the shallow water. Mr. Singleton was teaching Paul to swim. "Kick!" he was saying. From here, against the gentle waves, they looked like no more than two rippling silhouettes.

"Kick!" said Mr. Singleton, "Kick!" He was like a punisher administering lashes.

She turned her head away to face upwards. If you shut your eyes you could imagine you were the only one on the beach; if you held them shut you could be part of the beach. Mrs. Singleton imagined that in order to acquire a tan you had to let the sun make love to you.

She dug her heels in the sand and smiled involuntarily.

When she was a thin, flat-chested, studious girl in a grey school uniform, Mrs. Singleton had assuaged her fear and desperation about sex with fantasies which took away from men the brute physicality she expected of them. All her lovers would be artists. Poets would write poems to her, composers would dedicate their works to her. She would even pose, naked and immaculate, for painters, who having committed her true, her eternal form to canvas, would make love to her in an impalpable, ethereal way, under the power of which her bodily and temporal self would melt away, perhaps for ever. These fantasies (for she had never entirely renounced them) had crystallized for her in the image of a sculptor, who from a cold intractable piece of stone would fashion her very essence — which would be vibrant and full of sunlight, like the statues they had seen in Greece.

At university she had worked on the assumption that all men lusted uncontrollably and insatiably after women. She had not yet encountered a man who, whilst prone to the usual instincts, possessing moreover a magnificent body with which to fulfil them, yet had scruples about doing so, seemed ashamed of his own capacities. It did not matter that Mr. Singleton was reading engineering, was scarcely artistic at all, or that his powerful physique was unlike the nebulous creatures of her dreams. She found she loved this solid man-flesh. Mrs. Singleton had thought she was the shy, inexperienced, timid girl. Overnight she discovered that she wasn't this at all. He wore tough denim shirts, spoke and smiled very little and had a way of standing very straight and upright as if he didn't need any help from anyone. She had to educate him into moments of passion, of self-forgetfulness which made her glow with her own achievement. She was happy because she had not thought she was happy and she believed she could make someone else happy. At the university girls were starting to wear jeans, record-players played the

Rolling Stones and in the hush of the Modern Languages Library she read Leopardi and Verlaine. She seemed to float with confidence in a swirling, buoyant element she had never suspected would be her own.

"Kick!" she heard again from the water.

Mr. Singleton had twice thought of leaving his wife. Once was after a symphony concert they had gone to in London when they had not known each other very long and she still tried to get him to read books, to listen to music, to take an interest in art. She would buy concert or theatre tickets, and he had to seem pleased. At this concert a visiting orchestra was playing some titanic, large-scale work by a late nineteenth-century composer. A note in the programme said it represented the triumph of life over death. He had sat on his plush seat amidst the swirling barrage of sound. He had no idea what he had to do with it or the triumph of life over death. He had thought the same thought about the rapt girl on his left, the future Mrs. Singleton, who now and then bobbed, swayed or rose in her seat as if the music physically lifted her. There were at least seventy musicians on the platform. As the piece worked to its final crescendo the conductor, whose arms were flailing frantically so that his white shirt back appeared under his flying tails, looked so absurd Mr. Singleton thought he would laugh. When the music stopped and was immediately supplanted by wild cheering and clapping he thought the world had gone mad. He had struck his own hands together so as to appear to be sharing the ecstasy. Then, as they filed out, he had almost wept because he felt like an insect. He even thought she had arranged the whole business so as to humiliate him.

He thought he would not marry her.

The second time was after they had been married some years. He was one of a team of engineers working on a suspension bridge over an estuary in Ireland. They took it in turns to stay on the site and to inspect the construction work personally. Once he had to go to the very top of one of the two piers of the bridge to examine work on the bearings and housing for the main overhead cables. A lift ran up between the twin towers of the pier amidst a network of scaffolding and power cables to where a working platform was positioned. The engineer, with the supervisor and the foreman, had only to stay on the platform from where all the main features of construction were visible. The men at work on the upper sections of the towers, specialists in their trade, earning up to two hundred pounds a week — who balanced on precarious cat-walks and walked along exposed reinforcing girders — often jibed at the engineers who never left the platform. He thought he would show them. He walked out on to one of the cat-walks on the outer face of the pier where they were fitting huge grip-bolts. This was quite safe if you held on to the rails but still took some nerve. He wore a check cheesecloth shirt and his white safety helmet. It was a grey, humid August day. The cat-walk hung over greyness. The water of the estuary was the colour of dead fish. A dredger was chugging near the base of the pier. He thought, I could swim the estuary; but there is a bridge. Below him the yellow helmets of workers moved over the girders for the roadway like beetles. He took his hands from the rail. He wasn't at all afraid. He had been away from his wife all week. He thought: She knows nothing of this. If he were to step out now into the grey air he would be quite by himself, no harm would come to him. . . .

Now Mr. Singleton stood in the water, teaching his son to swim. They were doing the water-wings exercise. The boy wore a pair of water-wings, red underneath, yellow on top, which ballooned up under his arms and chin. With this to support him, he would splutter and splash towards his father who stood facing him some feet away. After a while at this they would try the same procedure, his father moving a little nearer, but without the water-wings, and this the boy dreaded. "Kick!" said Mr. Singleton. "Use your legs!" He watched his son draw painfully towards him. The boy had not yet grasped that the body naturally floated and that if you added to this certain mechanical effects, you swam. He thought that in order to swim you had to make as much frantic movement as possible. As he struggled towards Mr. Singleton his head, which was too high out of the water, jerked messily from side to side, and his eyes which were half closed swivelled in every direction but straight ahead. "Towards me!" shouted Mr. Singleton. He held out his arms in front of him for Paul to grasp. As his son was on the point of clutching them he would step back a little, pulling his hands away, in the hope that the last desperate lunge to reach his father might really teach the boy the art of propelling himself in water. But he sometimes wondered if this were his only motive.

"Good boy. Now again."

At school Mr. Singleton had been an excellent swimmer. He had won various school titles, broken numerous records and competed successfully in ASA championships. There was a period between the ages of about thirteen and seventeen which he remembered as the happiest in his life. It wasn't the medals and trophies that made him glad, but the knowledge that he didn't have to bother about anything else. Swimming vindicated him. He would get up every morning at six and train for two hours in the baths, and again before lunch; and when he fell asleep, exhausted, in French and English periods in the afternoon, he didn't have to bother about the indignation of the masters — lank, ill-conditioned creatures — for he had his excuse. He didn't have to bother about the physics teacher who complained to the headmaster that he would never get the exam results he needed if he didn't cut down his swimming, for the headmaster (who was an advocate of sport) came to his aid and told the physics teacher not to interfere with a boy who was a credit to the school. Nor did he have to bother about a host of other things which were supposed to be going on inside him, which made the question of what to do in the evening, at weekends, fraught and tantalizing, which drove other boys to moodiness and recklessness. For once in the cool water of the baths, his arms reaching, his eyes fixed on the blue marker line on the bottom, his ears full so that he could hear nothing around him, he would feel quite by himself, quite sufficient. At the end of races, when for one brief instant he clung panting alone like a survivor to the finishing rail which his rivals had yet to touch, he felt an infinite peace. He went to bed early, slept soundly, kept to his training regimen; and he enjoyed this Spartan purity which disdained pleasure and disorder. Some of his schoolmates mocked him — for not going to dances on Saturdays or to pubs, under age, or the Expresso after school. But he did not mind. He didn't need them. He knew they were weak. None of them could hold out, depend on themselves, spurn comfort if they had to. Some of them would go under in life. And none of them could cleave the water as he did or possessed a hard, stream-lined, perfectly tuned body as he did.

Then, when he was nearly seventeen all this changed. His father, who was an engineer, though proud of his son's trophies, suddenly pressed him to different forms of success. The headmaster no longer shielded him from the physics master. He said: "You can't swim into your future." Out of spite perhaps or an odd consistency of self-denial, he dropped swimming altogether rather than cut it down. For a year and a half he worked at his maths and physics with the same single-mindedness with which he had perfected his sport. He knew about mechanics and engineering because he knew how to make his body move through water. His work was not merely competent but good. He got to university where he might have had the leisure, if he wished, to resume his swimming. But he did not. Two years are a long gap in a swimmer's training; two years when you are near your peak can mean you will never get back to your true form. Sometimes he went for a dip in the university pool and swam slowly up and down amongst practising members of the university team, whom perhaps he could still have beaten, as a kind of relief.

Often, Mr. Singleton dreamt about swimming. He would be moving through vast expanses of water, an ocean. As he moved it did not require any effort at all. Sometimes he would go for long distances under water, but he did not have to bother about breathing. The water would be silvery-grey. And as always it seemed that as he swam he was really trying to get beyond the water, to put it behind him, as if it were a veil he were parting and he would emerge on the other side of it at last, on to some pristine shore, where he would step where no one else had stepped before.

When he made love to his wife her body got in the way; he wanted to swim through her.

Mrs. Singleton raised herself, pushed her sun-glasses up over her dark hair and sat with her arms stretched straight behind her back. A trickle of sweat ran between her breasts. They had developed to a good size since her schoolgirl days. Her skinniness in youth had stood her in good stead against the filling out of middle age, and her body was probably more mellow, more lithe and better proportioned now than it had ever been. She looked at Paul and Mr. Singleton half immersed in the shallows. It seemed to her that her husband was the real boy, standing stubbornly upright with his hands before him, and that Paul was some toy being pulled and swung relentlessly around him and towards him as though on some string. They had seen her sit up. Her husband waved, holding the boy's hand, as though for the two of them. Paul did not wave; he seemed more concerned with the water in his eyes. Mrs. Singleton did not wave back. She would have done if her son had waved. When they had left for their holiday Mr. Singleton had said to Paul, "You'll learn to swim this time. In salt water, you know, it's easier." Mrs. Singleton hoped her son wouldn't swim; so that she could wrap him, still, in the big yellow towel when he came out, rub him dry and warm, and watch her husband stand apart, his hands empty.

She watched Mr. Singleton drop his arm back to his side. "If you wouldn't splash it wouldn't go in your eyes," she just caught him say.

The night before, in their hotel room, they had argued. They always argued about half way through their holidays. It was symbolic, perhaps, of that first trip to Greece, when he had somehow refused to enjoy himself. They had to incur injuries so that they could then appreciate their leisure, like convalescents. For the first four days or so of their holiday Mr. Singleton would tend to be moody, on edge. He would excuse this as "winding down," the not-to-be-hurried process of dispelling the pressures of work. Mrs. Singleton would be patient. On about the fifth day Mrs. Singleton would begin to suspect that the winding down would never end and indeed (which she had known all along) that it was not winding down at all—he was clinging, as to a defence, to his bridges and tunnels; and she would show her resentment. At this point Mr. Singleton would retaliate by an attack upon her indolence.

Last night he had called her "flabby." He could not mean, of course, "flabby-bodied" (she could glance down, now, at her still flat belly), though such a sensual attack would have been simpler, almost heartening, from him. He meant "flabby of attitude." And what he meant by this, or what he wanted to mean, was that *he* was not flabby; that he worked, facing the real world, erecting great solid things on the face of the land, and that, whilst he worked, he disdained work's rewards—money, pleasure, rich food, holidays abroad—that he hadn't "gone soft," as she had done since they graduated eleven years ago, with their credentials for the future and their plane tickets to Greece. She knew this toughness of her husband was only a cover for his own failure to relax and his need to keep his distance. She knew that he found no particular virtue in his bridges and tunnels (it was the last thing he wanted to do really—build); it didn't matter if they were right or wrong, they were there, he could point to them as if it vindicated him—just as when he made his infrequent, if seismic, love to her it was not a case of enjoyment or satisfaction; he just did it.

It was hot in their hotel room. Mr. Singleton stood in his blue pyjama bottoms, feet apart, like a PT instructor.

"Flabby? What do you mean—'flabby'!?" she had said, looking daunted.

But Mrs. Singleton had the advantage whenever Mr. Singleton accused her in this way of complacency, of weakness. She knew he only did it to hurt her, and so to feel guilty, and so to feel the remorse which would release his own affection for her, his vulnerability, his own need to be loved. Mrs. Singleton was used to this process, to the tenderness that was the tenderness of successively opened and reopened wounds. And she was used to being the nurse who took care of the healing scars. For though Mr. Singleton inflicted the first blow he would always make himself more guilty than he made her suffer, and Mrs. Singleton, though in pain herself, could not resist wanting to clasp and cherish her husband, wanting to wrap him up safe when his own weakness and submissiveness showed and his body became liquid and soft against her; could not resist the old spur that her husband was unhappy and it was for her to make him happy. Mr. Singleton was extraordinarily lovable when he was guilty. She would even have yielded indefinitely, foregoing her own grievance, to this extreme of comforting him for the pain he caused her, had she not discovered, in time, that this only pushed the process a stage further. Her forgiveness of him became only another level of comfort, of softness he must reject. His flesh shrank from her restoring touch.

She thought: Men go round in circles, women don't move.

She kept to her side of the hotel bed, he, with his face turned, to his. He lay like a person washed up on a beach. She reached out her hand and stroked the nape of his neck. She felt him tense. All this was a pattern.

"I'm sorry," he said, "I didn't mean—"

"It's all right, it doesn't matter."

"Doesn't it matter?" he said.

When they reached this point they were like miners racing each other for deeper and deeper seams of guilt and recrimination.

But Mrs. Singleton had given up delving to rock bottom. Perhaps it was five years ago when she had thought for the third time of leaving her husband, perhaps long before that. When they were students she'd made allowances for his constraints, his reluctances. An unhappy childhood perhaps, a strict upbringing. She thought his inhibition might be lifted by the sanction of marriage. She'd thought, after all, it would be a good thing if he married her. She had not thought what would be good for her. They stood outside Gatwick Airport, back from Greece, in the grey, wet August light. Their tanned skin had seemed to glow. Yet she'd known this mood of promise would pass. She watched him kick against contentment, against ease, against the long, glittering life-line she threw at him; and, after a while, she ceased to try to haul him in. She began to imagine again her phantom artists. She thought: People slip off the shores of the real world, back into dreams. She hadn't "gone soft," only gone back to herself. Hidden inside her like treasure there were lines of Leopardi, of Verlaine her husband would never appreciate. She thought, he doesn't need me, things run off him, like water. She even thought that her husband's neglect in making love to her was not a problem he had but a deliberate scheme to deny her. When Mrs. Singleton desired her husband she could not help herself. She would stretch back on the bed with the sheets pulled off like a blissful nude in a Modigliani. She thought this ought to gladden a man. Mr. Singleton would stand at the foot of the bed and gaze down at her. He looked like some strong, chaste knight in the legend of the Grail. He would respond to her invitation, but before he did so there would be this expression, half stern, half innocent, in his eyes. It was the sort of expression that good men in books and films are supposed to make to prostitutes. It would ensure that their love-making was marred and that afterward it would seem as if he had performed something out of duty that only she wanted. Her body would feel like stone. It was at such times, when she felt the cold, dead-weight feel of abused happiness, that Mrs. Singleton most thought she was through with Mr. Singleton. She would watch his strong, compact torso already lifting itself off the bed. She would think: He thinks he is tough, contained in himself, but he won't see what I offer him, he doesn't see how it is I who can help him.

Mrs. Singleton lay back on her striped towel on the sand. Once again she became part of the beach. The careless sounds of the seaside, of excited children's voices, of languid grownups', of wooden bats on balls, fluttered over her as she shut her eyes. She thought: It is the sort of day on which someone suddenly shouts, "Someone is drowning."

When Mrs. Singleton became pregnant she felt she had out-manoeuvered her husband. He did not really want a child (it was the last thing he wanted, Mrs. Singleton thought, a child), but he was jealous of her condition, as of some achievement he himself could attain. He was excluded from the little circle of herself and her womb, and, as though to puncture it, he began for the first time to make love to her of a kind where he took the insistent initiative. Mrs. Singleton was not greatly pleased. She seemed buoyed up by her own bigness. She noticed that her husband began to do exercises in the morning, in his underpants, press-ups, squat-jumps, as if he were getting in training for something. He was like a boy. He even became, as the term of her pregnancy drew near its end, resilient and detached again, the virile father waiting to receive the son (Mr. Singleton knew it would be a son, so did Mrs. Singleton) that she, at the appointed time, would deliver him. When the moment arrived he insisted on being present so as to prove he wasn't squeamish and to make sure he wouldn't be tricked in the transaction. Mrs. Singleton was not daunted. When the pains became frequent she wasn't at all afraid. There were big, watery lights clawing down from the ceiling of the delivery room like the lights in dentists' surgeries. She could just see her husband looking down at her. His face was white and clammy. It was his fault for wanting to be there. She had to push, as though away from him. Then she knew it was happening. She stretched back. She was a great surface of warm, splitting rock and Paul was struggling bravely up into the sunlight. She had to coax him with her cries. She felt him emerge like a trapped survivor. The doctor groped with rubber gloves. "There we are," he said. She managed to look at Mr. Singleton. She wanted suddenly to put him back inside for good where Paul had come from. With a fleeting pity she saw that this was what Mr. Singleton wanted too. His eyes were half closed. She kept hers on him. He seemed to wilt under her gaze. All his toughness and control were draining from him and she was glad. She lay back triumphant and glad. The doctor was holding Paul; but she looked, beyond, at Mr. Singleton. He was far away like an insect. She knew he couldn't hold out. He was going to faint. He was looking where her legs were spread. His eyes went out of focus. He was going to faint, keel over, right there on the spot.

Mrs. Singleton grew restless, though she lay unmoving on the beach. Wasps were buzzing close to her head, round their picnic bag. She thought that Mr. Singleton and Paul had been too long at their swimming lesson. They should come out. It never struck her, hot as she was, to get up and join her husband and son in the sea. Whenever Mrs. Singleton wanted a swim she would wait until there was an opportunity to go in by herself; then she would wade out, dip her shoulders under suddenly and paddle about contentedly, keeping her hair dry, as though she were soaking herself in a large bath. They did not bathe as a family; nor did Mrs. Singleton swim with Mr. Singleton—who now and then, too, would get up by himself and enter the sea, swim at once about fifty yards out, then cruise for long stretches, with a powerful crawl or butterfly, back and forth across the bay. When this happened Mrs. Singleton would engage her son in talk so he would not watch his father. Mrs. Singleton did not swim with Paul either. He was too old now to cradle between her knees in the very shallow water, and she was somehow afraid that while Paul splashed and kicked around her he would suddenly learn how to swim. She had this feeling that Paul would only swim while she was in the sea, too. She did not want this to happen, but it reassured her and gave her sufficient confidence to let Mr. Singleton continue his swimming lessons with Paul. These lessons were obsessive, indefatigable. Every Sunday morning at seven, when they were at home, Mr. Singleton would take Paul to the baths for yet another attempt. Part of this, of course, was that Mr. Singleton was determined that his son should swim; but it enabled him also to avoid the Sunday morning languor: extra hours in bed, leisurely love-making.

Once, in a room at college, Mr. Singleton had told Mrs. Singleton about his swimming, about his training sessions, races; about what it felt like when you could swim really well. She had run her fingers over his long, naked back.

Mrs. Singleton sat up and rubbed sun-tan lotion on to her thighs. Down near the water's edge, Mr. Singleton was standing about waist deep, supporting Paul who, gripped by his father's hands, water wings still on, was flailing, face down, at the surface. Mr. Singleton kept saying, "No, keep still." He was trying to get Paul to hold his body straight and relaxed so he would float. But each time as Paul nearly succeeded he would panic, fearing his father would let go, and thrash wildly. When he calmed down and Mr. Singleton held him, Mrs. Singleton could see the water running off his face like tears.

Mrs. Singleton did not alarm herself at this distress of her son. It was a guarantee against Mr. Singleton's influence, an assurance that Paul was not going to swim; nor was he to be imbued with any of his father's sullen hardiness. When Mrs. Singleton saw her son suffer, it pleased her and she felt loving toward him. She felt that an invisible thread ran between her and the boy which commanded him not to swim, and she felt that Mr. Singleton knew that it was because of her that his efforts with Paul were in vain. Even now, as Mr. Singleton prepared for another attempt, the boy was looking at her smoothing the suntan oil on to her legs.

"Come on, Paul," said Mr. Singleton. His wet shoulders shone like metal.

When Paul was born it seemed to Mrs. Singleton that her life with her husband was dissolved, as a mirage dissolves, and that she could return again to what she was before she knew him. She let her staved-off hunger for happiness and her old suppressed dreams revive. But then they were not dreams, because they had a physical object and she knew she needed them in order to live. She did not disguise from herself what she needed. She knew that she wanted the kind of close, even erotic relationship with her son that women who have rejected their husbands have been known to have. The kind of relationship in which the son must hurt the mother, the mother the son. But she willed it, as if there would be no pain. Mrs. Singleton waited for her son to grow. She trembled when she thought of him at eighteen or twenty. When he was grown he would be slim and light and slender, like a boy even though he was a man. He would not need a strong body because all his power would be inside. He would be all fire and life in essence. He would become an artist, a sculptor. She would pose for him naked (she would keep her body trim for this), and he would sculpt her. He would hold the chisel. His hands would guide the cold metal over the stone and its blows would strike sunlight.

Mrs. Singleton thought: All the best statues they had seen in Greece seemed to have been dredged up from the sea.

She finished rubbing the lotion on to her insteps and put the cap back on the tube. As she did so she heard something that made her truly alarmed. It was Mr. Singleton saying, "That's it, that's the way! At last! Now keep it going!" She looked up. Paul was in the same position as before but he had learnt to make slower, regular motions with his limbs and his body no longer sagged in the middle. Though he still wore the water-wings he was moving, somewhat laboriously, forwards so that Mr. Singleton had to walk along with him; and at one point Mr. Singleton removed one of his hands from under the boy's ribs and simultaneously looked at his wife and smiled. His shoulders flashed. It was not a smile meant for her. She could see that. And it was not one of her husband's usual, infrequent, rather mechanical smiles. It was the smile a person makes about some joy inside, hidden and incommunicable.

"That's enough," thought Mrs. Singleton, getting to her feet, pretending not to have noticed, behind her sun-glasses, what had happened in the water. It *was* enough: They had been in the water for what seemed like an hour. He was only doing it because of their row last night, to make her feel he was not outmatched by using the reserve weapon of Paul. And, she added with relief to herself, Paul still had the water-wings and one hand to support him.

"That's enough now!" she shouted aloud, as if she were slightly, but not ill-humouredly, peeved at being neglected. "Come on in now!" She had picked up her purse as a quickly conceived ruse as she got up, and as she walked towards the water's edge she waved it above her head. "Who wants an ice-cream?"

Mr. Singleton ignored his wife. "Well done, Paul," he said. "Let's try that again."

Mrs. Singleton knew he would do this. She stood on the little ridge of sand just above where the beach, becoming fine shingle, shelved into the sea. She replaced a loose strap of her bikini over her shoulder and with a finger of each hand pulled the bottom half down over her buttocks. She stood feet apart, slightly on her toes, like a gymnast. She knew other eyes on the beach would be on her. It flattered her that she — and her husband, too — received admiring glances from those around. She thought, with relish for the irony: Perhaps they think we are happy, beautiful people. For all her girlhood diffidence, Mrs. Singleton enjoyed displaying her attractions and she liked to see other people's pleasure. When she lay sunbathing she imagined making love to all the moody, pubescent boys on holiday with their parents, with their slim waists and their quick heels.

"See if you can do it without me holding you," said Mr. Singleton. "I'll help you at first." He stooped over Paul. He looked like a mechanic making final adjustments to some prototype machine.

"Don't you want an ice-cream then, Paul?" said Mrs. Singleton. "They've got those chocolate ones."

Paul looked up. His short wet hair stood up in spikes. He looked like a prisoner offered a chance of escape, but the plastic waterwings, like some absurd pillory, kept him fixed.

Mrs. Singleton thought: He crawled out of me; now I have to lure him back with ice-cream.

"Can't you see he was getting the hang of it?" Mr. Singleton said. "If he comes out now he'll — "

"Hang of it! It was you. You were holding him all the time."

She thought: Perhaps I am hurting my son.

Mr. Singleton glared at Mrs. Singleton. He gripped Paul's shoulders. "You don't want to get out now, do you Paul?" He looked suddenly as if he really might drown Paul rather than let him come out.

Mrs. Singleton's heart raced. She wasn't good at rescues, at resuscitations. She knew this because of her life with her husband.

"Come on, you can go back in later," she said.

Paul was a hostage. She was playing for time, not wanting to harm the innocent.

She stood on the sand like a marooned woman watching for ships. The sea, in the sheltered bay, was almost flat calm. A few, glassy waves idled in but were smoothed out before they could break. On the headlands there were outcrops of scaly rocks like basking lizards. The island in Greece had been where Theseus left Ariadne.[1] Out over the blue water, beyond the heads of bobbing swimmers, seagulls flapped like scraps of paper.

Mr. Singleton looked at Mrs. Singleton. She was a fussy mother daubed with Ambre Solaire, trying to bribe her son with silly ice-creams; though if you forgot this she was a beautiful, tanned girl, like the girls men imagine on desert islands. But then, in Mr. Singleton's dreams, there was no one else on the untouched shore he ceaselessly swam to.

He thought, If Paul could swim, then I could leave her.

Mrs. Singleton looked at her husband. She felt afraid. The water's edge was like a dividing line between them which marked off the territory in which each existed. Perhaps they could never cross over.

"Well, I'm getting the ice-creams: you'd better get out."

She turned and paced up the sand. Behind the beach was an ice-cream van painted like a fairground.

Paul Singleton looked at his mother. He thought: She is deserting me — or I am deserting her. He wanted to get out to follow her. Her feet made puffs of sand

[1]*Theseus left Ariadne* Greek mythology: Theseus deserted his benefactor and lover after carrying her away.

which stuck to her ankles, and you could see all her body as she strode up the beach. But he was afraid of his father and his gripping hands. And he was afraid of his mother, too. How she would wrap him, if he came out, in the big yellow towel like egg yolk, how she would want him to get close to her smooth, sticky body, like a mouth that would swallow him. He thought: The yellow towel humiliated him, his father's hands humiliated him. The water-wings humiliated him: You put them on and became a puppet. So much of life is humiliation. It was how you won love. His father was taking off the water-wings like a man unlocking a chastity belt. He said: "Now try the same, coming towards me." His father stood some feet away from him. He was a huge, straight man, like the pier of a bridge. "Try." Paul Singleton was six. He was terrified of water. Every time he entered it he had to fight down fear. His father never realized this. He thought it was simple; you said: "Only water, no need to be afraid." His father did not know what fear was; the same as he did not know what fun was. Paul Singleton hated water. He hated it in his mouth and in his eyes. He hated the chlorine smell of the swimming baths, the wet, slippery tiles, the echoing whoops and screams. He hated it when his father read to him from *The Water Babies.*[2] It was the only story his father read, because, since he didn't know fear or fun, he was really sentimental. His mother read lots of stories. "Come on then. I'll catch you." Paul Singleton held out his arms and raised one leg. This was the worst moment. Perhaps having no help was most humiliating. If you did not swim you sank like a statue. They would drag him out, his skin streaming. His father would say: "I didn't mean. . . ." But if he swam his mother would be forsaken. She would stand on the beach with chocolate ice-cream running down her arm. There was no way out; there were all these things to be afraid of and no weapons. But then, perhaps he was not afraid of his mother nor his father, nor of water, but of something else. He had felt it just now—when he'd struck out with rhythmic, reaching strokes and his feet had come off the bottom and his father's hand had slipped from under his chest: as if he had mistaken what his fear was; as if he had been unconsciously pretending, even to himself, so as to execute some plan. He lowered his chin into the water. "Come on!" said Mr. Singleton. He launched himself forward and felt the sand leave his feet and his legs wriggle like cut ropes. "There," said his father as he realized. "There!" His father stood like a man waiting to clasp a lover; there was a gleam on his face. "Towards me! Towards me!" said his father suddenly. But he kicked and struck, half in panic, half in pride, away from his father, away from the shore, away, in this strange new element that seemed all his own.

[1982]

QUESTIONS

1. Why are the Singletons referred to so formally, as Mrs. and Mr.?
2. Are your loyalties supposed to be with Mrs. Singleton or her husband? What is the core of the conflict between them? With the reservations that each had about the other, why did they get married? What is the glue that keeps them together?
3. How do you interpret the swimming metaphor?
4. How effective is the use of a shifting point of view?

[2]*The Water Babies* fairy tale written by Charles Kingsley (1819–1875), an English novelist

Amy Tan

(b. 1952)

China/United States

Amy Tan was born in Oakland, California, the daughter of Chinese parents. Her mother left China just before the Communist Revolution; her father was trained as an engineer in Beijing. Tan attended high school in Switzerland, where she and her mother lived briefly after her father's death in 1968. After coming to the United States to attend college in Oregon, she worked as a writer of computer manuals for IBM and received a master's degree in linguistics from San Jose State University.

Two events shaped Tan's discovery that she wanted to write fiction: first, her visit with her mother to China in 1984, which led to her realization that she was part of an extended Chinese family and that her cultural roots were in China, and, second, her admiration for Louise Erdrich's *Love Medicine* (1984), a group of interlocking stories about several Native American families (see Erdrich in this volume) that catalyzed Tan's desire to write about her own experiences as a member of a cultural minority in the United States.

Tan's first story, published in a small magazine, was read by a San Diego literary agent who urged her to develop her ideas into a longer narrative that would explore the cultural and generational conflicts she had begun to consider in the story. The resulting book, *The Joy Luck Club* (1989), a series of self-contained but related narratives told by a group of immigrant Chinese mothers and their Chinese-American daughters, was both a popular and a critical success: a best-seller that was nominated for the National Book Award and the National Book Critics Circle Award.

Struggling with the anxieties of writing a second novel following her initial success, Tan confessed that in order to write *The Kitchen God's Wife* (1991), which also focuses on a mother–daughter relationship, she "had to fight for every single character, every image, every word. And the story is, in fact, about a woman who does the same thing: she fights to believe in herself. She does battle with myths and superstitions and assumptions— then casts off the fates that accompany them."

The story "Half and Half," from *The Joy Luck Club*, demonstrates Tan's original voice and her fresh vision of cultural bifurcation.

◆ *Half and Half* ◆

As proof of her faith, my mother used to carry a small leatherette Bible when she went to the First Chinese Baptist Church every Sunday. But later, after my mother lost her faith in God, that leatherette Bible wound up wedged under a too-short table leg, a way for her to correct the imbalances of life. It's been there for over twenty years.

My mother pretends that Bible isn't there. Whenever anyone asks her what it's doing there, she says, a little too loudly, "Oh, this? I forgot." But I know she sees it. My mother is not the best housekeeper in the world, and after all these years that Bible is still clean white.

Tonight I'm watching my mother sweep under the same kitchen table, something she does every night after dinner. She gently pokes her broom around the table leg propped up by the Bible. I watch her, sweep after sweep, waiting for the right moment to tell her about Ted and me, that we're getting divorced. When I tell her, I know she's going to say, "This cannot be."

And when I say that it is certainly true, that our marriage is over, I know what else she will say: "Then you must save it."

And even though I know it's hopeless—there's absolutely nothing left to save—I'm afraid if I tell her that, she'll still persuade me to try.

I think it's ironic that my mother wants me to fight the divorce. Seventeen years ago she was chagrined when I started dating Ted. My older sisters had dated only Chinese boys from church before getting married.

Ted and I met in a politics of ecology class when he leaned over and offered to pay me two dollars for the last week's notes. I refused the money and accepted a cup of coffee instead. This was during my second semester at UC Berkeley, where I had enrolled as a liberal arts major and later changed to fine arts. Ted was in his third year in pre-med, his choice, he told me, ever since he dissected a fetal pig in the sixth grade.

I have to admit that what I initially found attractive in Ted were precisely the things that made him different from my brothers and the Chinese boys I had dated: his brashness; the assuredness in which he asked for things and expected to get them; his opinionated manner; his angular face and lanky body; the thickness of his arms; the fact that his parents immigrated from Tarrytown, New York, not Tientsin, China.

My mother must have noticed these same differences after Ted picked me up one evening at my parents' house. When I returned home, my mother was still up, watching television.

"He is American," warned my mother, as if I had been too blind to notice. "A *waigoren*."[1]

"I'm American too," I said. "And it's not as if I'm going to marry him or something."

Mrs. Jordan also had a few words to say. Ted had casually invited me to a family picnic, the annual clan reunion held by the polo fields in Golden Gate Park. Although we had dated only a few times in the last month—and certainly had never slept together, since both of us lived at home—Ted introduced me to all his relatives as his girlfriend, which, until then, I didn't know I was.

Later, when Ted and his father went off to play volleyball with the others, his mother took my hand, and we started walking along the grass, away from the crowd. She squeezed my palm warmly but never seemed to look at me.

"I'm so glad to meet you *finally*," Mrs. Jordan said. I wanted to tell her I wasn't really Ted's girlfriend, but she went on. "I think it's nice that you and Ted are having such a lot of fun together. So I hope you won't misunderstand what I have to say."

[1]*waigoren* any person who is a foreigner or, more specifically, any person who is not Chinese

And then she spoke quietly about Ted's future, his need to concentrate on his medical studies, why it would be years before he could even think about marriage. She assured me she had nothing whatsoever against minorities; she and her husband, who owned a chain of office-supply stores, personally knew many fine people who were Oriental, Spanish, and even black. But Ted was going to be in one of those professions where he would be judged by a different standard, by patients and other doctors who might not be as understanding as the Jordans were. She said it was so unfortunate the way the rest of the world was, how unpopular the Vietnam War was.

"Mrs. Jordan, I am not Vietnamese," I said softly, even though I was on the verge of shouting. "And I have no intention of marrying your son."

When Ted drove me home that day, I told him I couldn't see him anymore. When he asked me why, I shrugged. When he pressed me, I told him what his mother had said, verbatim, without comment.

"And you're just going to sit there! Let my mother decide what's right?" he shouted, as if I were a co-conspirator who had turned traitor. I was touched that Ted was so upset.

"What should we do?" I asked, and I had a pained feeling I thought was the beginning of love.

In those early months, we clung to each other with a rather silly desperation, because, in spite of anything my mother or Mrs. Jordan could say, there was nothing that really prevented us from seeing one another. With imagined tragedy hovering over us, we became inseparable, two halves creating the whole: yin and yang. I was victim to his hero. I was always in danger and he was always rescuing me. I would fall and he would lift me up. It was exhilarating and draining. The emotional effect of saving and being saved was addicting to both of us. And that, as much as anything we ever did in bed, was how we made love to each other: conjoined where my weaknesses needed protection.

"What should we do?" I continued to ask him. And within a year of our first meeting we were living together. The month before Ted started medical school at UCSF we were married in the Episcopal church, and Mrs. Jordan sat in the front pew, crying as was expected of the groom's mother. When Ted finished his residency in dermatology, we bought a run-down three-story Victorian with a large garden in Ashbury Heights. Ted helped me set up a studio downstairs so I could take in work as a free-lance production assistant for graphic artists.

Over the years, Ted decided where we went on vacation. He decided what new furniture we should buy. He decided we should wait until we moved into a better neighborhood before having children. We used to discuss some of these matters, but we both knew the question would boil down to my saying, "Ted, you decide." After a while, there were no more discussions. Ted simply decided. And I never thought of objecting. I preferred to ignore the world around me, obsessing only over what was in front of me: my T-square, my X-acto knife, my blue pencil.

But last year Ted's feelings about what he called "decision and responsibility" changed. A new patient had come to him asking what she could do about the spidery veins on her cheeks. And when he told her he could suck the red veins out and make her beautiful again, she believed him. But instead, he accidentally sucked a nerve out, and the left side of her smile fell down and she sued him.

After he lost the malpractice lawsuit — his first, and a big shock to him I now realize — he started pushing me to make decisions. Did I think we should buy an American car or a Japanese car? Should we change from whole-life to term insurance? What did I think about that candidate who supported the contras? What about a family?

I thought about things, the pros and the cons. But in the end I would be so confused, because I never believed there was ever any one right answer, yet there were many wrong ones. So whenever I said, "You decide," or "I don't care," or "Either way is fine with me," Ted would say in his impatient voice, "No, *you* decide. You can't have it both ways, none of the responsibility, none of the blame."

I could feel things changing between us. A protective veil had been lifted and Ted now started pushing me about everything. He asked me to decide on the most trivial matters, as if he were baiting me. Italian food or Thai. One appetizer or two. Which appetizer. Credit card or cash. Visa or MasterCard.

Last month, when he was leaving for a two-day dermatology course in Los Angeles, he asked if I wanted to come along and then quickly, before I could say anything, he added, "Never mind, I'd rather go alone."

"More time to study," I agreed.

"No, because you can never make up your mind about anything," he said.

And I protested, "But it's only with things that aren't important."

"Nothing is important to you, then," he said in a tone of disgust.

"Ted, if you want me to go, I'll go."

And it was as if something snapped in him. "How the hell did we ever get married? Did you just say 'I do' because the minister said 'repeat after me'? What would you have done with your life if I had never married you? Did it ever occur to you?"

This was such a big leap in logic, between what I said and what he said, that I thought we were like two people standing apart on separate mountain peaks, recklessly leaning forward to throw stones at one another, unaware of the dangerous chasm that separated us.

But now I realize Ted knew what he was saying all along. He wanted to show me the rift. Because later that evening he called from Los Angeles and said he wanted a divorce.

Ever since Ted's been gone, I've been thinking, Even if I had expected it, even if I had known what I was going to do with my life, it still would have knocked the wind out of me.

When something that violent hits you, you can't help but lose your balance and fall. And after you pick yourself up, you realize you can't trust anybody to save you—not your husband, not your mother, not God. So what can you do to stop yourself from tilting and falling all over again?

My mother believed in God's will for many years. It was as if she had turned on a celestial faucet and goodness kept pouring out. She said it was faith that kept all these good things coming our way, only I thought she said "fate," because she couldn't pronounce that "th" sound in "faith."

And later, I discovered that maybe it was fate all along, that faith was just an illusion that somehow you're in control. I found out the most *I* could have was hope, and with that I was not denying any possibility, good or bad. I was just saying, If there is a choice, dear God or whatever you are, here's where the odds should be placed.

I remember the day I started thinking this, it was such a revelation to me. It was the day my mother lost her faith in God. She found that things of unquestioned certainty could never be trusted again.

We had gone to the beach, to a secluded spot south of the city near Devil's Slide. My father had read in *Sunset* magazine that this was a good place to catch ocean perch. And although my father was not a fisherman but a pharmacist's assistant who had once been a doctor in China, he believed in his *nengkan*, his ability to do anything he put his mind to. My mother believed she had *nengkan* to cook anything my father had a mind to catch. It was this belief in their *nengkan* that had brought my parents to America. It had enabled them to have seven children and buy a house in the Sunset district with very little money. It had given them the confidence to believe their luck would never run out, that God was on their side, that the house gods had only benevolent things to report and our ancestors were pleased, that lifetime warranties meant our lucky streak would never break, that all the elements were in balance, the right amount of wind and water.

So there we were, the nine of us: my father, my mother, my two sisters, four brothers, and myself, so confident as we walked along our first beach. We marched in single file across the cool gray sand, from oldest to youngest. I was in the middle, fourteen years old. We would have made quite a sight, if anyone else had been watching, nine pairs of bare feet trudging, nine pairs of shoes in hand, nine black-haired heads turned toward the water to watch the waves tumbling in.

The wind was whipping the cotton trousers around my legs and I looked for some place where the sand wouldn't kick into my eyes. I saw we were standing in the hollow of a cove. It was like a giant bowl, cracked in half, the other half washed out to sea. My mother walked toward the right, where the beach was clean, and we all followed. On this side, the wall of the cove curved around and protected the beach from both the rough surf and the wind. And along this wall, in its shadow, was a reef ledge that started at the edge of the beach and continued out past the cove where the waters became rough. It seemed as though a person could walk out to sea on this reef, although it looked very rocky and slippery. On the other side of the cove, the wall was more jagged, eaten away by the water. It was pitted with crevices, so when the waves crashed against the wall, the water spewed out of these holes like white gulleys.

Thinking back, I remember that this beach cove was a terrible place, full of wet shadows that chilled us and invisible specks that flew into our eyes and made it hard for us to see the dangers. We were all blind with the newness of this experience: a Chinese family trying to act like a typical American family at the beach.

My mother spread out an old striped bedspread, which flapped in the wind until nine pairs of shoes weighed it down. My father assembled his long bamboo fishing pole, a pole he had made with his own two hands, remembering its design from his childhood in China. And we children sat huddled shoulder to shoulder on the blanket, reaching into the grocery sack full of bologna sandwiches, which we hungrily ate salted with sand from our fingers.

Then my father stood up and admired his fishing pole, its grace, its strength. Satisfied, he picked up his shoes and walked to the edge of the beach and then onto the reef to the point just before it was wet. My two older sisters, Janice and Ruth, jumped up from the blanket and slapped their thighs to get the sand off. Then they slapped each other's back and raced off down the beach shrieking. I was about to get up and chase them, but my mother nodded toward my four brothers and reminded me: "*Dangsying tamende shenti,*" which means "Take care of them," or literally, "Watch out for their bodies." These bodies were the anchors of my life: Matthew, Mark, Luke, and Bing. I fell back onto the sand, groaning as my throat grew tight, as I made the same lament: "Why?" Why did *I* have to care for them?

And she gave me the same answer: "*Yiding.*"[2]

I must. Because they were my brothers. My sisters had once taken care of me. How else could I learn responsibility? How else could I appreciate what my parents had done for me?

Matthew, Mark, and Luke were twelve, ten, and nine, old enough to keep themselves loudly amused. They had already buried Luke in a shallow grave of sand so that only his head stuck out. Now they were starting to pat together the outlines of a sand-castle wall on top of him.

But Bing was only four, easily excitable and easily bored and irritable. He didn't want to play with the other brothers because they had pushed him off to the side, admonishing him, "No, Bing, you'll just wreck it."

So Bing wandered down the beach, walking stiffly like an ousted emperor, picking up shards of rock and chunks of driftwood and flinging them with all his might into the surf. I trailed behind, imagining tidal waves and wondering what I would do if one appeared. I called to Bing every now and then, "Don't go too close to the water. You'll get your feet wet." And I thought how much I seemed like my mother, always worried beyond reason inside, but at the same time talking about the danger as if it were less than it really was. The worry surrounded me, like the wall of the cove, and it made me feel everything had been considered and was now safe.

My mother had a superstition, in fact, that children were predisposed to certain dangers on certain days, all depending on their Chinese birthdate. It was explained in a little Chinese book called *The Twenty-Six Malignant Gates.* There, on each page, was an illustration of some terrible danger that awaited young innocent children. In the corners was a description written in Chinese, and since I couldn't read the characters, I could only see what the picture meant.

The same little boy appeared in each picture: climbing a broken tree limb, standing by a falling gate, slipping in a wooden tub, being carried away by a snapping dog, fleeing from a bolt of lightning. And in each of these pictures stood a man who looked as if he were wearing a lizard costume. He had a big crease in his forehead, or maybe it was actually that he had two round horns. In one picture, the lizard man was standing on a curved bridge, laughing as he watched the little boy falling forward over the bridge rail, his slippered feet already in the air.

It would have been enough to think that even one of these dangers could befall a child. And even though the birthdates corresponded to only one danger, my mother worried about them all. This was because she couldn't figure out how the Chinese dates, based on the lunar calendar, translated into American dates. So by taking them all into account, she had absolute faith she could prevent every one of them.

The sun had shifted and moved over the other side of the cove wall. Everything had settled into place. My mother was busy keeping sand from blowing onto the blanket, then shaking sand out of shoes, and tacking corners of blankets back down again with the now clean shoes. My father was still standing at the end of the reef, patiently casting out, waiting for *nengkan* to manifest itself as a fish. I could see small figures farther down on the beach, and I could tell they were my sisters by their two dark heads and yellow pants. My brothers' shrieks were mixed with those

[2]*Yiding* must

of seagulls. Bing had found an empty soda bottle and was using this to dig sand next to the dark cove wall. And I sat on the sand, just where the shadows ended and the sunny part began.

Bing was pounding the soda bottle against the rock, so I called to him, "Don't dig so hard. You'll bust a hole in the wall and fall all the way to China." And I laughed when he looked at me as though he thought what I said was true. He stood up and started walking toward the water. He put one foot tentatively on the reef, and I warned him, "Bing."

"I'm gonna see Daddy," he protested.

"Stay close to the wall, then, away from the water," I said. "Stay away from the mean fish."

And I watched as he inched his way along the reef, his back hugging the bumpy cove wall. I still see him, so clearly that I almost feel I can make him stay there forever.

I see him standing by the wall, safe, calling to my father, who looks over his shoulder toward Bing. How glad I am that my father is going to watch him for a while! Bing starts to walk over and then something tugs on my father's line and he's reeling as fast as he can.

Shouts erupt. Someone has thrown sand in Luke's face and he's jumped out of his sand grave and thrown himself on top of Mark, thrashing and kicking. My mother shouts for me to stop them. And right after I pull Luke off Mark, I look up and see Bing walking alone to the edge of the reef. In the confusion of the fight, nobody notices. I am the only one who sees what Bing is doing.

Bing walks one, two, three steps. His little body is moving so quickly, as if he spotted something wonderful by the water's edge. And I think, *He's going to fall in.* I'm expecting it. And just as I think this, his feet are already in the air, in a moment of balance, before he splashes into the sea and disappears without leaving so much as a ripple in the water.

I sank to my knees watching that spot where he disappeared, not moving, not saying anything. I couldn't make sense of it. I was thinking, Should I run to the water and try to pull him out? Should I shout to my father? Can I rise on my legs fast enough? Can I take it all back and forbid Bing from joining my father on the ledge?

And then my sisters were back, and one of them said, "Where's Bing?" There was silence for a few seconds and then shouts and sand flying as everyone rushed past me toward the water's edge. I stood there unable to move as my sisters looked by the cove wall, as my brothers scrambled to see what lay behind pieces of driftwood. My mother and father were trying to part the waves with their hands.

We were there for many hours. I remember the search boats and the sunset when dusk came. I had never seen a sunset like that: a bright orange flame touching the water's edge and then fanning out, warming the sea. When it became dark, the boats turned their yellow orbs on and bounced up and down on the dark shiny water.

As I look back, it seems unnatural to think about the colors of the sunset and boats at a time like that. But we all had strange thoughts. My father was calculating minutes, estimating the temperature of the water, readjusting his estimate of when Bing fell. My sisters were calling, "Bing! Bing!" as if he were hiding in some bushes high above the beach cliffs. My brothers sat in the car, quietly reading comic books. And when the boats turned off their yellow orbs, my mother went for a swim. She had never swum a stroke in her life, but her faith in her own *nengkan* convinced her that what these Americans couldn't do, she could. She could find Bing.

And when the rescue people finally pulled her out of the water, she still had her *nengkan* intact. Her hair, her clothes, they were all heavy with the cold water, but she stood quietly, calm and regal as a mermaid queen who had just arrived out of the sea. The police called off the search, put us all in our car, and sent us home to grieve.

I had expected to be beaten to death, by my father, by my mother, by my sisters and brothers. I knew it was my fault. I hadn't watched him closely enough, and yet I saw him. But as we sat in the dark living room, I heard them, one by one whispering their regrets.

"I was selfish to want to go fishing," said my father.

"We shouldn't have gone for a walk," said Janice, while Ruth blew her nose yet another time.

"Why'd you have to throw sand in my face?" moaned Luke. "Why'd you have to make me start a fight?"

And my mother quietly admitted to me, "I told you to stop their fight. I told you to take your eyes off him."

If I had had any time at all to feel a sense of relief, it would have quickly evaporated, because my mother also said, "So now I am telling you, we must go and find him, quickly, tomorrow morning." And everybody's eyes looked down. But I saw it as my punishment: to go out with my mother, back to the beach, to help her find Bing's body.

Nothing prepared me for what my mother did the next day. When I woke up, it was still dark and she was already dressed. On the kitchen table was a thermos, a teacup, the white leatherette Bible, and the car keys.

"Is Daddy ready?" I asked.

"Daddy's not coming," she said.

"Then how will we get there? Who will drive us?"

She picked up the keys and I followed her out the door to the car. I wondered the whole time as we drove to the beach how she had learned to drive overnight. She used no map. She drove smoothly ahead, turning down Geary, then the Great Highway, signaling at all the right times, getting on the Coast Highway and easily winding the car around the sharp curves that often led inexperienced drivers off and over the cliffs.

When we arrived at the beach, she walked immediately down the dirt path and over to the end of the reef ledge, where I had seen Bing disappear. She held in her hand the white Bible. And looking out over the water, she called to God, her small voice carried up by the gulls to heaven. It began with "Dear God" and ended with "Amen," and in between she spoke in Chinese.

"I have always believed in your blessings," she praised God in that same tone she used for exaggerated Chinese compliments. "We knew they would come. We did not question them. Your decisions were our decisions. You rewarded us for our faith.

"In return we have always tried to show our deepest respect. We went to your house. We brought you money. We sang your songs. You gave us more blessings. And now we have misplaced one of them. We were careless. This is true. We had so many good things, we couldn't keep them in our mind all the time.

"So maybe you hid him from us to teach us a lesson, to be more careful with your gifts in the future. I have learned this. I have put it in my memory. And now I have come to take Bing back."

I listened quietly as my mother said these words, horrified. And I began to cry when she added, "Forgive us for his bad manners. My daughter, this one standing here, will be sure to teach him better lessons of obedience before he visits you again."

After her prayer, her faith was so great that she saw him, three times, waving to her from just beyond the first wave. "*Nale!*"—There! And she would stand straight as a sentinel, until three times her eyesight failed her and Bing turned into a dark spot of churning seaweed.

My mother did not let her chin fall down. She walked back to the beach and put the Bible down. She picked up the thermos and teacup and walked to the water's edge. Then she told me that the night before she had reached back into her life, back when she was a girl in China, and this is what she had found.

"I remember a boy who lost his hand in a firecracker accident," she said. "I saw the shreds of this boy's arm, his tears, and then I heard his mother's claim that he would grow back another hand, better than the last. This mother said she would pay back an ancestral debt ten times over. She would use a water treatment to soothe the wrath of Chu Jung, the three-eyed god of fire. And true enough, the next week this boy was riding a bicycle, both hands steering a straight course past my astonished eyes!"

And then my mother became very quiet. She spoke again in a thoughtful, respectful manner.

"An ancestor of ours once stole water from a sacred well. Now the water is trying to steal back. We must sweeten the temper of the Coiling Dragon who lives in the sea. And then we must make him loosen his coils from Bing by giving him another treasure he can hide."

My mother poured out tea sweetened with sugar into the teacup, and threw this into the sea. And then she opened her fist. In her palm was a ring of watery blue sapphire, a gift from her mother, who had died many years before. This ring, she told me, drew coveting stares from women and made them inattentive to the children they guarded so jealously. This would make the Coiling Dragon forgetful of Bing. She threw the ring into the water.

But even with this, Bing did not appear right away. For an hour or so, all we saw was seaweed drifting by. And then I saw her clasp her hands to her chest, and she said in a wondrous voice, "See, it's because we were watching the wrong direction." And I too saw Bing trudging wearily at the far end of the beach, his shoes hanging in his hand, his dark head bent over in exhaustion. I could feel what my mother felt. The hunger in our hearts was instantly filled. And then the two of us, before we could even get to our feet, saw him light a cigarette, grow tall, and become a stranger.

"Ma, let's go," I said as softly as possible.

"He's there," she said firmly. She pointed to the jagged wall across the water. "I see him. He is in a cave, sitting on a little step above the water. He is hungry and a little cold, but he has learned now not to complain too much."

And then she stood up and started walking across the sandy beach as though it were a solid paved path, and I was trying to follow behind, struggling and stumbling in the soft mounds. She marched up the steep path to where the car was parked, and she wasn't even breathing hard as she pulled a large inner tube from the trunk. To this lifesaver, she tied the fishing line from my father's bamboo pole. She walked back and threw the tube into the sea, holding onto the pole.

"This will go where Bing is. I will bring him back," she said fiercely. I had never heard so much *nengkan* in my mother's voice.

The tube followed her mind. It drifted out, toward the other side of the cove where it was caught by stronger waves. The line became taut and she strained to hold on tight. But the line snapped and then spiraled into the water.

We both climbed toward the end of the reef to watch. The tube had now reached the other side of the cove. A big wave smashed it into the wall. The bloated tube leapt up and then it was sucked in, under the wall and into a cavern. It popped out. Over and over again, it disappeared, emerged, glistening black, faithfully reporting it had seen Bing and was going back to try to pluck him from the cave. Over and over again, it dove and popped back up again, empty but still hopeful. And then, after a dozen or so times, it was sucked into the dark recess, and when it came out, it was torn and lifeless.

At that moment, and not until that moment, did she give up. My mother had a look on her face that I'll never forget. It was one of complete despair and horror, for losing Bing, for being so foolish as to think she could use faith to change fate. And it made me angry—so blindingly angry—that everything had failed us.

I know now that I had never expected to find Bing, just as I know now I will never find a way to save my marriage. My mother tells me, though, that I should still try.

"What's the point?" I say. "There's no hope. There's no reason to keep trying."

"Because you must," she says. "This is not hope. Not reason. This is your fate. This is your life, what you must do."

"So what can I do?"

And my mother says, "You must think for yourself, what you must do. If someone tells you, then you are not trying." And then she walks out of the kitchen to let me think about this.

I think about Bing, how I knew he was in danger, how I let it happen. I think about my marriage, how I had seen the signs, really I had. But I just let it happen. And I think now that fate is shaped half by expectation, half by inattention. But somehow, when you lose something you love, faith takes over. You have to pay attention to what you lost. You have to undo the expectation.

My mother, she still pays attention to it. That Bible under the table, I know she sees it. I remember seeing her write in it before she wedged it under.

I lift the table and slide the Bible out. I put the Bible on the table, flipping quickly through the pages, because I know it's there. On the page before the New Testament begins, there's a section called "Deaths," and that's where she wrote "Bing Hsu" lightly, in erasable pencil.

[1989]

QUESTIONS

1. What does the narrator discover in her exploration of the difference between faith and fate?
2. How does the narrator regard her mother? Does that view change during the story?
3. What elements of the narrator's character are revealed in her recon-

struction of major events in her life? How does she see the failure of her marriage related to her brother's death years earlier?

4. How is the Chinese quality of *nengkan* — the ability to do whatever one puts one's mind to — important to the meaning of the story?

Leo Tolstoy

(1828–1910)

Russia

Leo Tolstoy, one of the indisputable giants of world literature, was the fourth of five children born to a noble Russian family in the province of Tula. His mother died when Tolstoy was two, and his father died when the boy was eight. He was left to the care of guardians and tutors until he was 16. Rather half-heartedly, he studied Arab and Turkish literature at the University of Kazan, then law; he left college without completing a degree. Through "cramming," he eventually passed examinations in civil and criminal law.

During his twenties, Tolstoy joined his brother in the Caucasus as a volunteer officer and later wrote *The Cossacks*, incorporating his experiences in the region of Russia known for its independent, spirited people. Unlike most authors who write their autobiographies later in life, Tolstoy began to write his autobiography early, before most of his fiction; in 1850, at the age of 22, he published *Childhood*, to be followed in the next several years by *Boyhood* and *Youth*. Those explorations of selfhood expressed the spiritual yearnings and conflicts that were to preoccupy Tolstoy for his entire life: the contrary pulls of the "pagan" who relished the sensory material world and the puritan who wanted to be a saint and withdraw from it.

In 1862 Tolstoy married Sonya Behrs. Their marriage was blissfully happy for 15 years, during which Sonya bore 13 children (five of whom died during infancy or childhood). During those years Tolstoy wrote his masterpieces, *War and Peace* (1863–1871)—the greatest antiwar novel ever written—and *Anna Karenina* (1873–1876)—a profound exploration of social and private morality, family life, and the sexual double standard. In 1879 Tolstoy's metaphysical conflicts exploded in a profound spiritual crisis. As he expressed it, "My position was frightful. I knew that I should find nothing on the path of rational knowledge except the denial of life, and in faith nothing but the denial of reason, which is still more impossible than the denial of life." Never fully reconciling the inner split between his moral and spiritual ideals and his own desires, Tolstoy explored his spiritual torment in his writing. The questions that reverberate throughout all of his major fiction anticipate the philosophical concerns of twentieth-century existentialism: Why live? What is happiness? What gives meaning and value to life?

After his spiritual conversion, Tolstoy repudiated much of his fiction as "immoral" because its primary function was entertainment rather than education. Interspersed with short stories on themes of spiritual and moral conflict were his didactic tracts on such subjects as faith, Christian doctrine, and the function of art. Tolstoy felt that his social class, his sexuality, and civilization itself had corrupted him; casting off these elements of his life, he attempted to imitate what he saw as the simpler and purer life of Russian peasants by eschewing his material wealth and property. Sonya struggled to maintain their family in the face of her husband's egotistical asceticism. In the final year of his life, Tolstoy became a pilgrim, wandering with no particular destination. He died of pneumonia at a train master's house.

"The Death of Ivan Ilych," written eight years after Tolstoy's spiritual conversion, grows directly out of his own spiritual torment as well as his witness of the agonizing death of his beloved brother Nikolai. First he wrote the story as a diary supposedly kept by Ivan Ilych during the course of his illness and given to a colleague after his death; later he rewrote it from the omniscient narrator's perspective. (A question to consider in reading the story is how this shift in narrative perspective affects the unfolding of the story and its meaning.)

The poet Randall Jarrell calls the sentence that begins the second section of the story—"Ivan Ilych's life had been most simple and most ordinary and therefore most terrible"—as "one of the most frightening sentences in literature." Henri Troyat, Tolstoy's biographer, wrote, "This double story of the decomposing body and the awakening soul is one of the most powerful works in the literature of the world."

The Death of Ivan Ilych

I

During an interval in the Melvinski trial in the large building of the Law Courts, the members and public prosecutor met in Ivan Egorovich Shebek's private room, where the conversation turned on the celebrated Krasovski case. Fëdor Vasilievich warmly maintained that it was not subject to their jurisdiction, Ivan Egorovich maintained the contrary, while Peter Ivanovich, not having entered into the discussion at the start, took no part in it but looked through the *Gazette* which had just been handed in.

"Gentlemen," he said, "Ivan Ilych has died!"

"You don't say so!"

"Here, read it yourself," replied Peter Ivanovich, handing Fëdor Vasilievich the paper still damp from the press. Surrounded by a black border were the words: "Praskovya Fëdorovna Golovina, with profound sorrow, informs relatives and friends of the demise of her beloved husband Ivan Ilych Golovin, Member of the Court of Justice, which occurred on February the 4th of this year 1882. The funeral will take place on Friday at one o'clock in the afternoon."

Ivan Ilych had been a colleague of the gentlemen present and was liked by them all. He had been ill for some weeks with an illness said to be incurable. His post had been kept open for him, but there had been conjectures that in case of his death Alexeev might receive his appointment, and that either Vinnikov or Shtabel would succeed Alexeev. So on receiving the news of Ivan Ilych's death the first thought of each of the gentlemen in that private room was of the changes and promotions it might occasion among themselves or their acquaintances.

"I shall be sure to get Shtabel's place or Vinnikov's," thought Fëdor Vasilievich. "I was promised that long ago, and the promotion means an extra eight hundred rubles a year for me besides the allowance."

"Now I must apply for my brother-in-law's transfer from Kaluga," thought Peter Ivanovich. "My wife will be very glad, and then she won't be able to say that I never do anything for her relations."

"I thought he would never leave his bed again," said Peter Ivanovich aloud. "It's very sad."

"But what really was the matter with him?"

"The doctors couldn't say—at least they could, but each of them said something different. When last I saw him I thought he was getting better."

"And I haven't been to see him since the holidays. I always meant to go."

"Had he any property?"

"I think his wife had a little—but something quite trifling."

"We shall have to go to see her, but they live so terribly far away."

"Far away from you, you mean. Everything's far away from your place."

"You see, he never can forgive my living on the other side of the river," said Peter Ivanovich, smiling at Shebek. Then, still talking of the distances between different parts of the city, they returned to the Court.

Besides considerations as to the possible transfers and promotions likely to result from Ivan Ilych's death, the mere fact of the death of a near acquaintance aroused, as usual, in all who heard of it the complacent feeling that, "it is he who is dead and not I."

Each one thought or felt, "Well, he's dead but I'm alive!" But the more intimate of Ivan Ilych's acquaintances, his so-called friends, could not help thinking also that they would now have to fulfill the very tiresome demands of propriety by attending the funeral service and paying a visit of condolence to the widow.

Fëdor Vasilievich and Peter Ivanovich had been his nearest acquaintances. Peter Ivanovich had studied law with Ivan Ilych and had considered himself to be under obligations to him.

Having told his wife at dinner-time of Ivan Ilych's death and of his conjecture that it might be possible to get her brother transferred to their circuit, Peter Ivanovich sacrificed his usual nap, put on his evening clothes, and drove to Ivan Ilych's house.

At the entrance stood a carriage and two cabs. Leaning against the wall in the hall downstairs near the cloak-stand was a coffin-lid covered with cloth of gold, ornamented with gold cord and tassels, that had been polished up with metal powder. Two ladies in black were taking off their fur cloaks. Peter Ivanovich recognized one of them as Ivan Ilych's sister, but the other was a stranger to him. His colleague Schwartz was just coming downstairs, but on seeing Peter Ivanovich enter he stopped and winked at him, as if to say: "Ivan Ilych has made a mess of things—not like you and me."

Schwartz's face, with his Piccadilly whiskers and his slim figure in evening dress, had as usual an air of elegant solemnity which contrasted with the playfulness of his character and had a special piquancy here, or so it seemed to Peter Ivanovich.

Peter Ivanovich allowed the ladies to precede him and slowly followed them upstairs. Schwartz did not come down but remained where he was, and Peter

Ivanovich understood that he wanted to arrange where they should play bridge that evening. The ladies went upstairs to the widow's room, and Schwartz, with seriously compressed lips but a playful look in his eyes, indicated by a twist of his eyebrows the room to the right where the body lay.

Peter Ivanovich, like everyone else on such occasions, entered feeling uncertain what he would have to do. All he knew was that at such times it is always safe to cross oneself. But he was not quite sure whether one should make obeisances while doing so. He therefore adopted a middle course. On entering the room he began crossing himself and made a slight movement resembling a bow. At the same time, as far as the motion of his head and arm allowed, he surveyed the room. Two young men — apparently nephews, one of whom was a high-school pupil — were leaving the room, crossing themselves as they did so. An old woman was standing motionless, and a lady with strangely arched eyebrows was saying something to her in a whisper. A vigorous, resolute Church Reader, in a frockcoat, was reading something in a loud voice with an expression that precluded any contradiction. The butler's assistant, Gerasim, stepping lightly in front of Peter Ivanovich, was strewing something on the floor. Noticing this, Peter Ivanovich was immediately aware of a faint odor of a decomposing body.

The last time he had called on Ivan Ilych, Peter Ivanovich had seen Gerasim in the study. Ivan Ilych had been particularly fond of him and he was performing the duty of a sick nurse.

Peter Ivanovich continued to make the sign of the cross, slightly inclining his head in an intermediate direction between the coffin, the Reader, and the icons on the table in a corner of the room. Afterwards, when it seemed to him that this movement of his arm in crossing himself had gone on too long, he stopped and began to look at the corpse.

The dead man lay, as dead men always lie, in a specially heavy way, his rigid limbs sunk in the soft cushions of the coffin, with the head forever bowed on the pillow. His yellow waxen brow with bald patches over his sunken temples was thrust up in the way peculiar to the dead, the protruding nose seeming to press on the upper lip. He was much changed and had grown even thinner since Peter Ivanovich had last seen him, but, as is always the case with the dead, his face was handsomer and above all more dignified than when he was alive. The expression on the face said that what was necessary had been accomplished, and accomplished rightly. Besides this there was in that expression a reproach and a warning to the living. This warning seemed to Peter Ivanovich out of place, or at least not applicable to him. He felt a certain discomfort and so he hurriedly crossed himself once more and turned and went out the door — too hurriedly and too regardless of propriety, as he himself was aware.

Schwartz was waiting for him in the adjoining room with legs spread wide apart and both hands toying with his top-hat behind his back. The mere sight of that playful, well-groomed, and elegant figure refreshed Peter Ivanovich. He felt that Schwartz was above all these happenings and would not surrender to any depressing influences. His very look said that this incident of a church service for Ivan Ilych could not be a sufficient reason for infringing the order of the session — in other words, that it would certainly not prevent his unwrapping a new pack of cards and shuffling them that evening while a footman placed four fresh candles on the table: in fact, that there was no reason for supposing that this incident would hinder their spending the evening agreeably. Indeed he said this in a whisper as Peter Ivanovich passed him, proposing that they should meet for a game at Fëdor Vasilievich's. But apparently Peter Ivanovich was not destined to play bridge that evening. Praskovya Fëdorovna (a short, fat woman who despite all efforts to the contrary had continued to broaden steadily from her shoulders downwards and who had the same extraordinarily arched eyebrows as the lady who had been standing by the coffin), dressed all in black, her head covered with lace, came out of her own room with some other ladies, conducted them to the room where the dead body lay, and said: "The service will begin immediately. Please go in."

Schwartz, making an indefinite bow, stood still, evidently neither accepting nor declining this invitation. Praskovya Fëdorovna, recognizing Peter Ivanovich, sighed, went close up to him, took his hand, and said: "I know you were a true friend to Ivan Ilych . . ." and looked at him awaiting some suitable response. And Peter Ivanovich knew that, just as it had been the right thing to cross himself in that room, so what he had to do here was to press her hand, sigh, and say, "Believe me. . . ." So he did all this and as he did it felt that the desired result had been achieved: that both he and she were touched.

"Come with me. I want to speak to you before it begins," said the widow. "Give me your arm."

Peter Ivanovich gave her his arm and they went to the inner rooms, passing Schwartz, who winked at Peter Ivanovich compassionately.

"That does for our bridge! Don't object if we find another player. Perhaps you can cut in when you do escape," said his playful look.

Peter Ivanovich sighed still more deeply and despondently, and Praskovya Fëdorovna pressed his arm gratefully. When they reached the drawing-room, upholstered in pink cretonne and lighted by a dim lamp, they sat down at the table—she on a sofa and Peter Ivanovich on a low pouffe, the springs of which yielded spasmodically under his weight. Praskovya Fëdorovna had been on the point of warning him to take another seat, but felt that such a warning was out of keeping with her present condition and so changed her mind. As he sat down on the pouffe Peter Ivanovich recalled how Ivan Ilych had arranged this room and had consulted him regarding this pink cretonne with green leaves. The whole room was full of furniture and knick-knacks, and on her way to the sofa the lace of the widow's black shawl caught on the carved edge of the table. Peter Ivanovich rose to detach it, and the springs of the pouffe, relieved of his weight, rose also and gave him a push. The widow began detaching her shawl herself, and Peter Ivanovich again sat down, suppressing the rebellious springs of the pouffe under him. But the widow had not quite freed herself and Peter Ivanovich got up again, and again the pouffe rebelled and even creaked. When this was all over she took out a clean cambric handkerchief and began to weep. The episode with the shawl and the struggle with the pouffe had cooled Peter Ivanovich's emotions and he sat there with a sullen look on his face. This awkward situation was interrupted by Sokolov, Ivan Ilych's butler, who came to report that the plot in the cemetery that Praskovya Fëdorovna had chosen would cost two hundred rubles. She stopped weeping and, looking at Peter Ivanovich with the air of a victim, remarked in French that it was very hard for her. Peter Ivanovich made a silent gesture signifying his full conviction that it must indeed be so.

"Please smoke," she said in a magnanimous yet crushed voice, and turned to discuss with Sokolov the price of the plot for the grave.

Peter Ivanovich while lighting his cigarette heard her inquiring very circumstantially into the price of different plots in the cemetery and finally decided which she would take. When that was done she gave instructions about engaging the choir. Sokolov then left the room.

"I look after everything myself," she told Peter Ivanovich, shifting the albums that lay on the table; and noticing that the table was endangered by his cigarette-ash, she immediately passed him an ashtray, saying as she did so: "I consider it an affectation to say that my grief prevents my attending to practical affairs. On the contrary, if anything can — I won't say console me, but — distract me, it is seeing to everything concerning him." She again took out her handkerchief as if preparing to cry, but suddenly, as if mastering her feeling, she shook herself and began to speak calmly. "But there is something I want to talk to you about."

Peter Ivanovich bowed, keeping control of the springs of the pouffe, which immediately began quivering under him.

"He suffered terribly the last few days."

"Did he?" said Peter Ivanovich.

"Oh, terribly! He screamed unceasingly, not for minutes but for hours. For the last three days he screamed incessantly. It was unendurable. I cannot understand how I bore it; you could hear him three rooms off. Oh, what I have suffered!"

"Is it possible that he was conscious all that time?" asked Peter Ivanovich.

"Yes," she whispered. "To the last moment. He took leave of us a quarter of an hour before he died, and asked us to take Vasya away."

The thought of the sufferings of this man he had known so intimately, first as a merry little boy, then as a school-mate, and later as a grown-up colleague, suddenly struck Peter Ivanovich with horror, despite an unpleasant consciousness of his own and this woman's dissimulation. He again saw that brow, and that nose pressing down on the lip, and felt afraid for himself.

"Three days of frightful suffering and then death! Why, that might suddenly, at any time, happen to me," he thought, and for a moment felt terrified. But — he did not himself know how — the customary reflection at once occurred to him that this had happened to Ivan Ilych and not to him, and that it should not and could not happen to him, and that to think that it could would be yielding to depression which he ought not to do, as Schwartz's expression plainly showed. After which reflection Peter Ivanovich felt reassured, and began to ask with interest about the details of Ivan Ilych's death, as though death was an accident natural to Ivan Ilych but certainly not to himself.

After many details of the really dreadful physical sufferings Ivan Ilych had endured (which details he learnt only from the effect those sufferings had produced on Praskoyva Fëdorovna's nerves) the widow apparently found it necessary to get to business.

"Oh, Peter Ivanovich, how hard is it! How terribly, terribly hard!" and she again began to weep.

Peter Ivanovich sighed and waited for her to finish blowing her nose. When she had done so he said, "Believe me . . ." and she again began talking and brought out what was evidently her chief concern with him — namely, to question him as to how she could obtain a grant of money from the government on the occasion of her husband's death. She made it appear that she was asking Peter Ivanovich's advice about her pension, but he soon saw that she already knew about that to the minutest detail, more even than he did himself. She knew how much could be got out of the government in consequence of her husband's death, but wanted to find out whether she could not possibly extract something more. Peter Ivanovich tried to think of some means of doing so, but after reflecting for a while and, out of propriety, condemning the government for its niggardliness, he said he thought that nothing more could be got. Then she sighed and evidently began to devise means of getting rid of her visitor. Noticing this, he put out his cigarette, rose, pressed her hand, and went out into the anteroom.

In the dining-room where the clock stood that Ivan Ilych had liked so much and had bought at an antique shop, Peter Ivanovich met a priest and a few acquaintances who had come to attend the service, and he recognized Ivan Ilych's daughter, a handsome young woman. She was in black and her slim figure appeared slimmer than ever. She had a gloomy, determined, almost angry expression, and bowed to Peter Ivanovich as though he were in some way to blame. Behind her, with the same offended look, stood a wealthy young man, an examining magistrate, whom Peter Ivanovich also knew and who was her fiancé, as he had heard. He bowed mournfully to them and was about to pass into the death-chamber, when from under the stairs appeared the figure of Ivan Ilych's schoolboy son, who was extremely like his father. He seemed a little Ivan Ilych, such as Peter Ivanovich remembered when they studied law together. His tear-stained eyes had in them the look that is seen in the eyes of boys of thirteen or fourteen who are not pure-minded. When he saw Peter Ivanovich he scowled morosely and shamefacedly. Peter Ivanovich nodded to him and entered the death-chamber. The service began: candles, groans, incense, tears, and sobs. Peter Ivanovich stood looking gloomily down at his feet. He did not look once at the dead man, did not yield to any depressing influence, and was one of the first to leave the room. There was no one in the anteroom, but Gerasim darted out of the dead man's room, rummaged with his strong hands among the fur coats to find Peter Ivanovich's, and helped him on with it.

"Well, friend Gerasim," said Peter Ivanovich, so as to say something. "It's a sad affair, isn't it?"

"It's God's will. We shall all come to it some day," said Gerasim, displaying his teeth — the even, white teeth of a healthy peasant — and, like a man in the thick of urgent work, he briskly opened the front door, called the coachman, helped Peter Ivanovich into the sledge, and sprang back to the porch as if in readiness for what he had to do next.

Peter Ivanovich found the fresh air particularly pleasant after the smell of incense, the dead body, and carbolic acid.

"Where to, sir?" asked the coachman.

"It's not too late even now. . . . I'll call round on Fëdor Vasilievich."

He accordingly drove there and found them just finishing the first rubber, so that it was quite convenient for him to cut in.

II

Ivan Ilych's life had been most simple and most ordinary and therefore most terrible.

He had been a member of the Court of Justice, and died at the age of forty-five. His father had been an official who after serving in various ministries and departments in Petersburg had made the sort of career which brings men to positions from which by reason of their long service they cannot be dismissed, though they were obviously unfit to hold any responsible position, and for whom therefore posts are specially created, which though fictitious carry salaries of from six to ten thousand rubles that are not fictitious, and in receipt of which they live on to a great age.

Such was the Privy Councillor and superfluous member of various superfluous institutions, Ilya Epimovich Golovin.

He had three sons, of whom Ivan Ilych was the second. The eldest son was following in his father's footsteps only in another department, and was already approaching that stage in the service at which a similar sinecure would be reached. The third son was a failure. He had ruined his prospects in a number of positions and was not serving in the railway department. His father and brothers, and still more their wives, not merely disliked meeting him, but avoided remembering his existence unless compelled to do so. His sister had married Baron Greff, a Petersburg official of her father's type. Ivan Ilych was *le phénix de la famille*[1] as people said. He was neither as cold and formal as his elder brother nor as wild as the younger, but was a happy mean between them—an intelligent, polished, lively, and agreeable man. He had studied with his younger brother at the School of Law, but the latter had failed to complete the course and was expelled when he was in the fifth class. Ivan Ilych finished the course well. Even when he was at the School of Law he was just what he remained for the rest of his life: a capable, cheerful, good-natured, and sociable man, though strict in the fulfillment of what he considered to be his duty: and he considered his duty to be what was so considered by those in authority. Neither as a boy nor as a man was he a toady, but from early youth was by nature attracted to people of high station as a fly is drawn to the light, assimilating their ways and views of life and establishing friendly relations with them. All the enthusiasms of childhood and youth passed without leaving much trace on him; he succumbed to sensuality, to vanity, and latterly among the highest classes to liberalism, but always within limits which his instinct unfailingly indicated to him as correct.

At school he had done things which had formerly seemed to him very horrid and made him feel disgusted with himself when he did them; but when later on he saw that such actions were done by people of good position and that they did not regard them as wrong, he was able not exactly to regard them as right, but to forget about them entirely or not be at all troubled at remembering them.

Having graduated from the School of Law and qualified for the tenth rank of the civil service, and having received money from his father for his equipment, Ivan Ilych ordered himself clothes as Scharmer's, the fashionable tailor, hung a medallion inscribed *respice finem*[2] on his watch-chain, took leave of his professor and the prince who was patron of the school, had a farewell dinner with his comrades at Donon's first-class restaurant, and with his new and fashionable portmanteau, linen, clothes, shaving and other toilet appliances, and a traveling rug, all purchased at the best shops, he set off for one of the provinces where, through his father's influence, he had been attached to the Governor as an official for special service.

In the province Ivan Ilych soon arranged as easy and agreeable a position for himself as he had had at the School of Law. He performed his official tasks, made

[1]*le phénix de la famille* French: the pride of the family. French phrases were commonly used by aristocratic and educated Russians in the nineteenth century. All foreign phrases are French unless otherwise noted.

[2]*respice finem* Latin: "Consider your end"—that is, your death

his career, and at the same time amused himself pleasantly and decorously. Occasionally he paid official visits to country districts, where he behaved with dignity both to his superiors and inferiors, and performed the duties entrusted to him, which related chiefly to the sectarians, with an exactness and incorruptible honesty of which he could not but feel proud.

In official matters, despite his youth and taste for frivolous gaiety, he was exceedingly reserved, punctilious, and even severe; but in society he was often amusing and witty, and always good-natured, correct in his manner, and *bon enfant*,[3] as the governor and his wife—with whom he was like one of the family—used to say of him.

In the province he had an affair with a lady who made advances to the elegant young lawyer, and there was also a milliner; and there were carousals with aides-de-camp who visited the district, and after-supper visits to a certain outlying street of doubtful reputation; and there was too some obsequiousness to his chief and even to his chief's wife, but all this was done with such a tone of good breeding that no hard names could be applied to it. It all came under the heading of the French saying: "*Il faut que jeunesse se passe.*"[4] It was all done with clean hands, in clean linen, with French phrases, and above all among people of the best society and consequently with the approval of people of rank.

So Ivan Ilych served for five years and then came a change in his official life. The new and reformed judicial institutions were introduced, and new men were needed. Ivan Ilych became such a new man. He was offered the post of examining magistrate, and he accepted it though the post was in another province and obliged him to give up the connections he had formed and to make new ones. His friends met to give him a send-off; they had a group-photograph taken and presented him with a silver cigarette-case, and he set off to his new post.

As examining magistrate Ivan Ilych was just as *comme il faut*[5] and decorous a man, inspiring general respect and capable of separating his official duties from his private life, as he had been when acting as an official on special service. His duties now as examining magistrate were far more interesting and attractive than before. In his former position it had been pleasant to wear an undress uniform made by Scharmer, and to pass through the crowd of petitioners and officials who were timorously awaiting an audience with the governor, and who envied him as with free and easy gait he went straight into his chief's private room to have a cup of tea and a cigarette with him. But not many people had then been directly dependent on him—only police officials and the sectarians when he went on special missions—and he liked to treat them politely, almost as comrades, as if he were letting them feel that he who had the power to crush them was treating them in this simple, friendly way. There were then but few such people. But now, as an examining magistrate, Ivan Ilych felt that everyone without exception, even the most important and self-satisfied, was in his power, and that he need only write a few words on a sheet of paper with a certain heading, and this or that important, self-satisfied person would be brought before him in the role of an accused person or a witness, and if he did not choose to allow him to sit down, would have to stand before him and answer his questions. Ivan Ilych never abused his power; he tried

[3]*bon enfant* one of the boys (literally, "good child")

[4]"*Il faut que jeunesse se passe*" youth must have its day

[5]*comme il faut* proper (literally: as it should be)

on the contrary to soften its expression, but the consciousness of it and of the possibility of softening its effect, supplied the chief interest and attraction of his office. In his work itself, especially in his examinations, he very soon acquired a method of eliminating all considerations irrelevant to the legal aspect of the case, and reducing even the most complicated case to a form in which it would be presented on paper only in its externals, completely excluding his personal opinion of the matter, while above all observing every prescribed formality. The work was new and Ivan Ilych was one of the first men to apply the new Code of 1864.[6]

On taking up the post of examining magistrate in a new town, he made new acquaintances and connections, placed himself on a new footing, and assumed a somewhat different tone. He took up an attitude of rather dignified aloofness towards the provincial authorities, but picked out the best circle of legal gentlemen and wealthy gentry living in the town and assumed a tone of slight dissatisfaction with the government, of moderate liberalism, and of enlightened citizenship. At the same time, without at all altering the elegance of his toilet, he ceased shaving his chin and allowed his beard to grow as it pleased.

Ivan Ilych settled down very pleasantly in this new town. The society there, which inclined towards opposition to the Governor, was friendly, his salary was larger, and he began to play *vint*,[7] which he found added not a little to the pleasure of life, for he had a capacity for cards, played good-humoredly, and calculated rapidly and astutely, so that he usually won.

After living there for two years he met his future wife, Praskovya Fëdorovna Mikhel, who was the most attractive, clever, and brilliant girl of the set in which he moved, and among other amusements and relaxations from his labors as examining magistrate, Ivan Ilych established light and playful relations with her.

While he had been an official on special service he had been accustomed to dance, but now as an examining magistrate it was exceptional for him to do so. If he danced now, he did it as if to show that though he served under the reformed order of things, and had reached the fifth official rank, yet when it came to dancing he could do it better than most people. So at the end of an evening he sometimes danced with Praskovya Fëdorovna, and it was chiefly during these dances that he captivated her. She fell in love with him. Ivan Ilych had at first no definite intention of marrying, but when the girl fell in love with him he said to himself: "Really, why shouldn't I marry?"

Praskovya Fëdorovna came of a good family, was not bad looking, and had some little property. Ivan Ilych might have aspired to a more brilliant match, but even this was good. He had his salary, and she, he hoped, would have an equal income. She was well connected, and was a sweet, pretty, and thoroughly correct young woman. To say that Ivan Ilych married because he fell in love with Praskovya Fëdorovna and found that she sympathized with his views of life would be as incorrect as to say that he married because his social circle approved of the match. He was swayed by both these considerations: the marriage gave him personal satisfaction, and at the same time it was considered the right thing by the most highly placed of his associates.

So Ivan Ilych got married.

[6]The emancipation of the serfs in 1861 was followed by a thorough all-around reform of judicial proceedings. [Translator's note]

[7]*vint* a form of bridge [Translator's note]

The preparations for marriage and the beginning of married life, with its conjugal caresses, the new furniture, new crockery, and new linen, were very pleasant until his wife became pregnant—so that Ivan Ilych had begun to think that marriage would not impair the easy, agreeable, gay, and always decorous character of his life, approved of by society and regarded by himself as natural, but would even improve it. But from the first months of his wife's pregnancy, something new, unpleasant, depressing, and unseemly, and from which there was no way of escape, unexpectedly showed itself.

His wife, without any reason—*de gaieté de coeur*[8] as Ivan Ilych expressed it to himself—began to disturb the pleasure and propriety of their life. She began to be jealous without any cause, expected him to devote his whole attention to her, found fault with everything, and made coarse and ill-mannered scenes.

At first Ivan Ilych hoped to escape from the unpleasantness of this state of affairs by the same easy and decorous relation to life that had served him heretofore: he tried to ignore his wife's disagreeable moods, continued to live in his usual easy and pleasant way, invited friends to his house for a game of cards, and also tried going out to his club or spending his evenings with friends. But one day his wife began upbraiding him so vigorously, using such coarse words, and continued to abuse him every time he did not fulfil her demands, so resolutely and with such evident determination not to give way till he submitted—that is, till he stayed at home and was bored just as she was—that he became alarmed. He now realized that matrimony—at any rate with Praskovya Fëdorovna—was not always conducive to the pleasures and amenities of life, but on the contrary often infringed both comfort and propriety, and that he must therefore entrench himself against such infringement. And Ivan Ilych began to seek for means of doing so. His official duties were the one thing that imposed upon Praskovya Fëdorovna, and by means of his official work and the duties attached to it he began struggling with his wife to secure his own independence.

With the birth of their child, the attempts to feed it and the various failures in doing so, and with the real and imaginary illnesses of mother and child, in which Ivan Ilych's sympathy was demanded but about which he understood nothing, the need of securing for himself an existence outside his family life became still more imperative.

As his wife grew more irritable and exacting and Ivan Ilych transferred the center of gravity of his life more and more to his official work so did he grow to like his work better and became more ambitious than before.

Very soon, within a year of his wedding, Ivan Ilych had realized that marriage, though it may add some comforts to life, is in fact a very intricate and difficult affair towards which in order to perform one's duty, that is, to lead a decorous life approved of by society, one must adopt a definite attitude just as towards one's official duties.

And Ivan Ilych evolved such an attitude towards married life. He only required of it those conveniences—dinner at home, housewife, and bed—which it could give him, and above all that propriety of external forms required by public opinion. For the rest he looked for light-hearted pleasure and propriety, and was very thankful when he found them, but if he met with antagonism and querulousness he at once retired into his separate fenced-off world of official duties, where he found satisfaction.

[8]*de gaité de coeur* from the heart, or from impulse

Ivan Ilych was esteemed a good official, and after three years was made Assistant Public Prosecutor. His new duties, their importance, the possibility of indicting and imprisoning anyone he chose, the publicity his speeches received, and the success he had in all these things made his work still more attractive.

More children came. His wife became more and more querulous and ill-tempered, but the attitude Ivan Ilych had adopted towards his home life rendered him almost impervious to her grumbling.

After seven years' service in that town he was transferred to another province as Public Prosecutor. They moved, but were short of money and his wife did not like the place they moved to. Though the salary was higher the cost of living was greater, besides which two of their children died and family life became still more unpleasant for him.

Praskovya Fëdorovna blamed her husband for every inconvenience they encountered in their new home. Most of the conversations between husband and wife, especially as to the children's education, led to topics which recalled former disputes, and those disputes were apt to flare up again at any moment. There remained only those rare periods of amorousness which still came to them at times but did not last long. These were islets at which they anchored for a while and then again set out upon that ocean of veiled hostility which showed itself in their aloofness from one another. This aloofness might have grieved Ivan Ilych had he considered that it ought not to exist, but he now regarded the position as normal, and even made it the goal at which he aimed in family life. His aim was to free himself more and more from those unpleasantnesses and to give them a semblance of harmlessness and propriety. He attained this by spending less and less time with his family, and when obliged to be at home he tried to safeguard his position by the presence of outsiders. The chief thing however was that he had his official duties. The whole interest of his life now centered in the official world and that interest absorbed him. The consciousness of his power, being able to ruin anybody he wished to ruin, the importance, even the external dignity of his entry into court, or meetings with his subordinates, his success with superiors and inferiors, and above all his masterly handling of cases, of which he was conscious—all this gave him pleasure and filled his life, together with chats with his colleagues, dinners, and bridge. So that on the whole Ivan Ilych's life continued to flow as he considered it should do—pleasantly and properly.

So things continued for another seven years. His eldest daughter was already sixteen, another child had died, and only one son was left, a schoolboy and a subject of dissension. Ivan Ilych wanted to put him in the School of Law, but to spite him Praskovya Fëdorovna entered him at the High School. The daughter had been educated at home and had turned out well: the boy did not learn badly either.

III

So Ivan Ilych lived for seventeen years after his marriage. He was already a Public Prosecutor of long standing, and had declined several proposed transfers while awaiting a more desirable post, when an unanticipated and unpleasant occurrence quite upset the peaceful course of his life. He was expecting to be offered the post of presiding judge in a University town, but Happe somehow came to the front and obtained the appointment instead. Ivan Ilych became irritable, reproached Happe, and quarreled both with him and with his immediate superiors—who became colder to him and again passed him over when other appointments were made.

This was in 1880, the hardest year of Ivan Ilych's life. It was then that it became evident on the one hand that his salary was insufficient for them to live on, and on the other that he had been forgotten, and not only this, but that what was for him the greatest and most cruel injustice appeared to others a quite ordinary occurrence. Even his father did not consider it his duty to help him. Ivan Ilych felt himself abandoned by everyone, and that they regarded his position with a salary of 3,500 rubbles as quite normal and even fortunate. He alone knew that with the consciousness of the injustices done him, with his wife's incessant nagging, and with the debts he had contracted by living beyond his means, his position was far from normal.

In order to save money that summer he obtained leave of absence and went with his wife to live in the country at her brother's place.

In the country, without his work, he experienced *ennui*[9] for the first time in his life, and not only *ennui* but intolerable depression, and he decided that it was impossible to go on living like that, and that it was necessary to take energetic measures.

Having passed a sleepless night pacing up and down the veranda, he decided to go to Petersburg and bestir himself, in order to punish those who had failed to appreciate him and to get transferred to another ministry.

Next day, despite many protests from his wife and her brother, he started for Petersburg with the sole object of obtaining a post with a salary of five thousand rubles a year. He was no longer bent on any particular department, or tendency, or kind of activity. All he now wanted was an appointment to another post with a salary of five thousand rubles, either in the administration, in the banks, with the railways, in one of the Empress Marya's Institutions, or even in the customs—but it had to carry with it a salary of five thousand rubles and be in a ministry other than that in which they had failed to appreciate him.

And this quest of Ivan Ilych's was crowned with remarkable and unexpected success. At Kursk an acquaintance of his, F. I. Ilyin, got into the first-class carriage, sat down beside Ivan Ilych, and told him of a telegram just received by the Governor of Kursk announcing that a change was about to take place in the ministry: Peter Ivanovich was to be superseded by Ivan Semënovich.

The proposed change, apart from its significance for Russia, had a special significance for Ivan Ilych, because by bringing forward a new man, Peter Petrovich, and consequently his friend Zachar Ivanovich, it was highly favorable for Ivan Ilych, since Zachar Ivanovich was a friend and colleague of his.

In Moscow this news was confirmed, and on reaching Petersburg Ivan Ilych found Zachar Ivanovich and received a definite promise of an appointment in his former department of Justice.

A week later he telegraphed to his wife: "Zachar in Miller's place. I shall receive appointment on presentation of report."

Thanks to this change of personnel, Ivan Ilych had unexpectedly obtained an appointment in his former ministry which placed him two stages above his former colleagues besides giving him five thousand rubles salary and three thousand five hundred rubles for expenses connected with his removal. All his ill humor towards his former enemies and the whole department vanished, and Ivan Ilych was completely happy.

He returned to the country more cheerful and contented than he had been for

[9]*ennui* boredom

a long time. Praskovya Fëdorovna also cheered up and a truce was arranged between them. Ivan Ilych told of how he had been fêted by everybody in Petersburg, how all those who had been his enemies were put to shame and now fawned on him, how envious they were of his appointment, and how much everybody in Petersburg had liked him.

Praskovya Fëdorovna listened to all this and appeared to believe it. She did not contradict anything, but only made plans for their life in the town to which they were going. Ivan Ilych saw with delight that these plans were his plans, that he and his wife agreed, and that, after a stumble, his life was regaining its due and natural character of pleasant lightheartedness and decorum.

Ivan Ilych had come back for a short time only, for he had to take up his new duties on the 10th of September. Moreover, he needed time to settle into the new place, to move all his belongings from the province, and to buy and order many additional things: in a word, to make such arrangements as he had resolved on, which were almost exactly what Praskovya Fëdorovna too had decided on.

Now that everything had happened so fortunately, and that he and his wife were at one in their aims and moreover saw so little of one another, they got on together better than they had done since the first years of marriage. Ivan Ilych had thought of taking his family away with him at once, but the insistence of his wife's brother and her sister-in-law, who had suddenly become particularly amiable and friendly to him and his family, induced him to depart alone.

So he departed, and the cheerful state of mind induced by his success and by the harmony between his wife and himself, the one intensifying the other, did not leave him. He found a delightful house, just the thing both he and his wife had dreamt of. Spacious, lofty reception rooms in the old style, a convenient and dignified study, rooms for his wife and daughter, a study for his son — it might have been specially built for them. Ivan Ilych himself superintended the arrangements, chose the wallpapers, supplemented the furniture (preferably with antiques which he considered particularly *comme it faut*), and supervised the upholstering. Everything progressed and progressed and approached the ideal he had set himself: even when things were only half completed they exceeded his expectations. He saw what a refined and elegant character, free from vulgarity, it would all have when it was ready. On falling asleep he pictured to himself how the reception-room would look. Looking at the yet unfinished drawing-room he could see the fireplace, the screen, the what-not, the little chairs dotted here and there, the dishes and plates on the walls, and the bronzes, as they would be when everything was in place. He was pleased by the thought of how his wife and daughter, who shared his taste in this matter, would be impressed by it. They were certainly not expecting as much. He had been particularly successful in finding, and buying cheaply, antiques which gave a particularly aristocratic character to the whole place. But in his letters he intentionally understated everything in order to be able to surprise them. All this so absorbed him that his new duties — though he liked his official work — interested him less than he had expected. Sometimes he even had moments of absent-mindedness during the Court Sessions, and would consider whether he should have straight or curved cornices for his curtains. He was so interested in it all that he often did things himself, rearranging the furniture, or rehanging the curtains. Once when mounting a step-ladder to show the upholsterer, who did not understand, how he wanted the hangings draped, he made a false step and slipped, but being a strong and agile man he clung on and only knocked his side against the knob of the window frame. The bruised place was painful but the pain soon passed, and he felt particularly bright and well just then. He wrote: "I feel fifteen years younger." He thought he would have everything ready by September, but it dragged on till mid-October. But the result was charming not only in his eyes but to everyone who saw it.

In reality it was just what is usually seen in the houses of people of moderate means who want to appear rich, and therefore succeed only in resembling others like themselves: there were damasks, dark wood, plants, rugs, and dull and polished bronzes—all the things people of a certain class have in order to resemble other people of that class. His house was so like the others that it would never have been noticed, but to him it all seemed to be quite exceptional. He was very happy when he met his family at the station and brought them to the newly furnished house all lit up, where a footman in a white tie opened the door into the hall decorated with plants, and when they went on into the drawing room, and the study uttering exclamations of delight. He conducted them everywhere, drank in their praises eagerly, and beamed with pleasure. At tea that evening, when Praskovya Fëdorovna among other things asked him about his fall, he laughed and showed them how he had gone flying and had frightened the upholsterer.

"It's a good thing I'm a bit of an athlete. Another man might have been killed, but I merely knocked myself, just here; it hurts when it's touched, but it's passing off already—it's only a bruise."

So they began living in their new home—in which, as always happens, when they got thoroughly settled in they found they were just one room short—and with the increased income, which as always was just a little (some five hundred rubles) too little, but it was all very nice.

Things went particularly well at first, before everything was finally arranged and while something had still to be done: this thing bought, that thing ordered, another thing moved, and something else adjusted. Though there were some disputes between husband and wife, they were both so well satisfied and had so much to do that it all passed off without any serious quarrels. When nothing was left to arrange it became rather dull and something seemed to be lacking, but they were then making acquaintances, forming habits, and life was growing fuller.

Ivan Ilych spent his mornings at the law court and came home to dinner, and at first he was generally in a good humor, though he occasionally became irritable just on account of his house. (Every spot on the tablecloth or the upholstery, and every broken windowblind string, irritated him. He had devoted so much trouble to arranging it all that every disturbance of it distressed him.) But on the whole his life ran its course as he believed life should do: easily, pleasantly, and decorously.

He got up at nine, drank his coffee, read the paper, and then put on his undress uniform and went to the law courts. There the harness in which he worked had already been stretched to fit him and he donned it without a hitch: petitioners, inquiries at the chancery, the chancery itself, and the sittings public and administrative. In all this the thing was to exclude everything fresh and vital, which always disturbs the regular course of official business, and to admit only official relations with people, and then only on official grounds. A man would come, for instance, wanting some information. Ivan Ilych, as one in whose sphere the matter did not lie, would have nothing to do with him: but if the man had some business with him in his official capacity, something that could be expressed on officially stamped paper, he would do everything, positively everything he could within the limits of such relations, and in doing so would maintain the semblance of friendly human relations, that is, would observe the courtesies of life. As soon as the official relations ended, so did everything else. Ivan Ilych possessed this capacity to separate his real life from the offical side of affairs and not mix the two, in the highest degree, and by long practice and natural aptitude had brought it to such a pitch that sometimes, in the manner of a virtuoso, he would even allow himself to let the human and official relations mingle. He let himself do this just because he felt that he could at any time he chose resume the strictly official attitude again and drop the human relation. And he did it all easily, pleasantly, correctly, and even artistically. In the intervals between the sessions he smoked, drank tea, chatted a little about politics, a little about general topics, a little about cards, but most of all about official appointments. Tired, but with the feelings of a virtuoso — one of the first violins who has played his part in an orchestra with precision — he would return home to find that his wife and daughter had been out paying calls, or had a visitor, and that his son had been to school, had done his homework with his tutor, and was duly learning what is taught at High Schools. Everything was as it should be. After dinner, if they had no visitors, Ivan Ilych sometimes read a book that was being much discussed at the time, and in the evening settled down to work, that is, read official papers, compared the depositions of witnesses, and noted paragraphs of the Code applying to them. This was neither dull nor amusing. It was dull when he might have been playing bridge, but if no bridge was available it was at any rate better than doing nothing or sitting with his wife. Ivan Ilych's chief pleasure was giving little dinners to which he invited men and women of good social position, and just as his drawing-room resembled all other drawing-rooms so did his enjoyable little parties resemble all other such parties.

Once they even gave a dance. Ivan Ilych enjoyed it and everything went off well, except that it led to a violent quarrel with his wife about the cakes and sweets. Praskovya Fëdorovna had made her own plans, but Ivan Ilych insisted on getting everything from an expensive confectioner and ordered too many cakes, and the quarrel occurred because some of those cakes were left over and the confectioner's bill came to forty-five rubles. It was a great and disagreeable quarrel. Praskovya Fëdorovna called him "a fool and an imbecile," and he clutched at his head and made angry allusions to divorce.

But the dance itself had been enjoyable. The best people were there, and Ivan Ilych had danced with Princess Trufonova, a sister of the distinguished founder of the Society "Bear My Burden."

The pleasures connected with his work were pleasures of ambition; his social pleasures were those of vanity; but Ivan Ilych's greatest pleasure was playing bridge. He acknowledged that whatever disagreeable incident happened in his life, the pleasure that beamed like a ray of light about everything else was to sit down to bridge with good players, not noisy partners, and of course to four-handed bridge (with five players it was annoying to have to stand out, though one pretended not to mind), to play a clever and serious game (when the cards allowed it), and then to have supper and drink a glass of wine. After a game of bridge, especially if he had won a little (to win a large sum was unpleasant), Ivan Ilych went to bed in specially good humor.

So they lived. They formed a circle of acquaintances among the best people and were visited by people of importance and by young folk. In their views as to their acquaintances, husband, wife, and daughter were entirely agreed, and tacitly and unanimously kept at arm's length and shook off the various shabby friends and relations who, with much show of affection, gushed into the drawing-room with its Japanese plates on the walls. Soon these shabby friends ceased to obtrude themselves and only the best people remained in the Golovins' set.

Young men made up to Lisa, and Petrishchev, an examining magistrate and Dmitri Ivanovich Petrishchev's son and sole heir, began to be so attentive to her that Ivan Ilych had already spoken to Praskovya Fëdorovna about it, and considered whether they should not arrange a party for them, or get up some private theatricals.

So they lived, and all went well, without change, and life flowed pleasantly.

IV

They were all in good health. It could not be called ill health if Ivan Ilych sometimes said that he had a queer taste in his mouth and felt some discomfort in his left side.

But this discomfort increased and, though not exactly painful, grew into a sense of pressure in his side accompanied by ill humor. And his irritability became worse and worse and began to mar the agreeable, easy, and correct life that had established itself in the Golovin family. Quarrels between husband and wife became more and more frequent, and soon the ease and amenity disappeared and even the decorum was barely maintained. Scenes again became frequent, and very few of those islets remained on which husband and wife could meet without explosion. Praskovya Fëdorovna now had good reason to say that her husband's temper was trying. With characteristic exaggeration she said he had always had a dreadful temper, and that it had needed all her good nature to put up with it for twenty years. It was true that now the quarrels were started by him. His bursts of temper always came just before dinner, often just as he began to eat his soup. Sometimes he noticed that a plate or dish was chipped, or the food was not right, or his son put his elbow on the table, or his daughter's hair was not done as he liked it, and for all this he blamed Praskovya Fëdorovna. At first she retorted and said disagreeable things to him, but once or twice he fell into such a rage at the beginning of dinner that she realized it was due to some physical derangement brought on by taking food, and so she restrained herself and did not answer, but only hurried to get the dinner over. She regarded this self-restraint as highly praiseworthy. Having come to the conclusion that her husband had a dreadful temper and made her life miserable, she began to feel sorry for herself, and the more she pitied herself the more she hated her husband. She began to wish he would die; yet she did not want him to die because then his salary would cease. And this irritated her against him still more. She considered herself dreadfully unhappy just because not even his death could save her, and though she concealed her exasperation, that hidden exasperation of hers increased his irritation also.

After one scene in which Ivan Ilych had been particularly unfair and after which he had said in explanation that he certainly was irritable but that it was due to his not being well, she said that if he was ill it should be attended to, and insisted on his going to see a celebrated doctor.

He went. Everything took place as he had expected and as it always does. There was the usual waiting and the important air assumed by the doctor, with which he was so familiar (resembling that which he himself assumed in court), and the sounding and listening, and the questions which called for answers that were foregone conclusions and were evidently unnecessary, and the look of importance which implied that "if only you put yourself in our hands we will arrange everything — we know indubitably how it has to be done, always in the same way for everybody alike." It was all just as it was in the law courts. The doctor put on just the same air towards him as he himself put on towards an accused person.

The doctor said that so-and-so indicated that there was so-and-so inside the patient, but if the investigation of so-and-so did not confirm this, then he must assume that and that. If he assumed that and that, then . . . and so on. To Ivan Ilych only one question was important: was his case serious or not? But the doctor ignored that inappropriate question. From his point of view it was not the one under consideration, the real question was to decide between a floating kidney, chronic catarrh, or appendicitis. It was not a question of Ivan Ilych's life or death, but one between a floating kidney and appendicitis. And that question the doctor solved brilliantly, as it seemed to Ivan Ilych, in favor of the appendix, with the reservation that should an examination of the urine give fresh indications the matter would be reconsidered. All this was just what Ivan Ilych had himself brilliantly accomplished a thousand times in dealing with men on trial. The doctor summed up just as brilliantly, looking over his spectacles triumphantly and even gaily at the accused. From the doctor's summing up Ivan Ilych concluded that things were bad, but that for the doctor, and perhaps for everybody else, it was a matter of indifference, though for him it was bad. And this conclusion struck him painfully, arousing in him a great feeling of pity for himself and of bitterness towards the doctor's indifference to a matter of such importance.

He said nothing of this, but rose, placed the doctor's fee on the table, and remarked with a sigh: "We sick people probably often put inappropriate questions. But tell me, in general, is this complaint dangerous, or not? . . ."

The doctor looked at him sternly over his spectacles with one eye, as if to say: "Prisoner, if you will not keep to the questions put to you, I shall be obliged to have you removed from the court."

"I have already told you what I consider necessary and proper. The analysis may show something more." And the doctor bowed.

Ivan Ilych went out slowly, seated himself disconsolately in his sledge, and drove home. All the way home he was going over what the doctor had said, trying to translate those complicated, obscure, scientific phrases into plain language and find in them an answer to the question: "Is my condition bad? Is it very bad? Or is there as yet nothing much wrong?" And it seemed to him that the meaning of what the doctor had said was that it was very bad. Everything in the streets seemed depressing. The cabmen, the houses, the passers-by, and the shops, were dismal. His ache, this dull gnawing ache that never ceased for a moment, seemed to have acquired a new and more serious significance from the doctor's dubious remarks. Ivan Ilych now watched it with a new and oppressive feeling.

He reached home and began to tell his wife about it. She listened, but in the middle of his account his daughter came in with her hat on, ready to go out with her mother. She sat down reluctantly to listen to this tedious story, but could not stand it long, and her mother too did not hear him to the end.

"Well, I am very glad," she said. "Mind now to take your medicine regularly. Give me the prescription and I'll send Gerasim to the chemist's." And she went to get ready to go out.

While she was in the room Ivan Ilych had hardly taken time to breathe, but he sighed deeply when she left it.

"Well," he thought, "perhaps it isn't so bad after all."

He began taking his medicine and following the doctor's directions, which had been altered after the examination of the urine. But then it happened that there was a contradiction between the indications drawn from the examination of the urine and the symptoms that showed themselves. It turned out that what was happening differed from what the doctor had told him, and that he had either forgotten, or blundered, or hidden something from him. He could not, however, be blamed for that, and Ivan Ilych still obeyed his orders implicitly and at first derived some comfort from doing so.

From the time of his visit to the doctor, Ivan Ilych's chief occupation was the exact fulfilment of the doctor's instructions regarding hygiene and the taking of medicine, and the observation of his pain and his excretions. His chief interests came to be people's ailments and people's health. When sickness, deaths, or recoveries were mentioned in his presence, especially when the illness resembled his own, he listened with agitation which he tried to hide, asked questions, and applied what he heard to his own case.

The pain did not grow less, but Ivan Ilych made efforts to force himself to think that he was better. And he could do this so long as nothing agitated him. But as soon as he had any unpleasantness with his wife, any lack of success in his official work, or held bad cards at bridge, he was at once acutely sensible of his disease. He had formerly borne such mischances, hoping soon to adjust what was wrong, to master it and attain success, or make a grand slam. But now every mischance upset him and plunged him into despair. He would say to himself: "There now, just as I was beginning to get better and the medicine had begun to take effect, comes this accursed misfortune, or unpleasantness. . . . " And he was furious with the mishap, or with the people who were causing the unpleasantness and killing him, for he felt that this fury was killing him but could not restrain it. One would have thought that it should have been clear to him that this exasperation with circumstances and people aggravated his illness, and that he ought therefore to ignore unpleasant occurrences. But he drew the very opposite conclusion: he said that he needed peace, and he watched for everything that might disturb it and became irritable at the slightest infringement of it. His condition was rendered worse by the fact that he read medical books and consulted doctors. The progress of his disease was so gradual that he could deceive himself when comparing one day with another—the difference was so slight. But when he consulted the doctors it seemed to him that he was getting worse, and even very rapidly. Yet despite this he was continually consulting them.

That month he went to see another celebrity, who told him almost the same as the first had done but put his questions rather differently, and the interview with this celebrity only increased Ivan Ilych's doubts and fears. A friend of a friend of his, a very good doctor, diagnosed his illness again quite differently from the others, and though he predicted recovery, his questions and suppositions bewildered Ivan Ilych still more and increased his doubts. A homoeopathist diagnosed the disease in yet another way, and prescribed medicine which Ivan Ilych took secretly for a week. But after a week, not feeling any improvement and having lost confidence both in the former doctor's treatment and in this one's, he became still more despondent. One day a lady acquaintance mentioned a cure effected by a wonder-working icon. Ivan Ilych caught himself listening attentively and beginning to believe that it had occurred. This incident alarmed him. "Has my mind really weakened to such an extent?" he asked himself. "Nonsense! It's all rubbish. I mustn't give way to nervous fears but having chosen a doctor must keep strictly to his treatment. That is what I will do. Now it's all settled. I won't think about it, but will follow the treatment seriously till summer, and then we shall see. From now there must be no more of this wavering!" This was easy to say but impossible to carry out. The pain in his side oppressed him and seemed to grow worse and more incessant, while the taste in his mouth grew stranger and stranger. It seemed to him that his breath had a disgusting smell, and he was conscious of a loss of appetite and strength. There was no deceiving himself: something terrible, new, and more important than anything before in his life, was taking place within him of which he alone was aware. Those about him did not understand or would not understand it, but thought everything in the world was going on as usual. That tormented Ivan Ilych more than anything. He saw that his household, especially his wife and daughter who were in a perfect whirl of visiting, did not understand anything of it and were annoyed that he was so depressed and so exacting, as if he were to blame for it. Though they tried to disguise it he saw that he was an obstacle in their path, and that his wife had adopted a definite line in regard to his illness and kept to it regardless of anything he said or did. Her attitude was this: "You know," she would say to her friends, "Ivan Ilych can't do as other people do, and keep to the treatment prescribed for him. One day he'll take his drops and keep strictly to his diet and go to bed in good time, but the next day unless I watch him he'll suddenly forget his medicine, eat sturgeon — which is forbidden — and sit up playing cards till one o'clock in the morning."

"Oh, come, when was that?" Ivan Ilych would ask in vexation. "Only once at Peter Ivanovich's."

"And yesterday with Shebek."

"Well, even if I hadn't stayed up, this pain would have kept me awake."

"Be that as it may you'll never get well like that, but will always make us wretched."

Praskovya Fëdorovna's attitude to Ivan Ilych's illness, as she expressed it both to others and to him, was that it was his own fault and was another of the annoyances he caused her. Ivan Ilych felt that this opinion escaped her involuntarily — but that did not make it easier for him.

At the law courts too, Ivan Ilych noticed, or thought he noticed, a strange attitude towards himself. It sometimes seemed to him that people were watching him inquisitively as a man whose place might soon be vacant. Then again, his friends would suddenly begin to chaff him in a friendly way about his low spirits, as if the awful, horrible, and unheard-of thing that was going on within him, incessantly gnawing at him and irresistibly drawing him away, was a very agreeable subject for jests. Schwartz in particular irritated him by his jocularity, vivacity, and *savoir-faire*, which reminded him of what he himself had been ten years ago.

Friends came to make up a set and they sat down to cards. They dealt, bending the new cards to soften them, and he sorted the diamonds in his hand and found he had seven. His partner said "No trumps" and supported him with two diamonds. What more could be wished for? It ought to be jolly and lively. They would make a grand slam. But suddenly Ivan Ilych was conscious of that gnawing pain, that taste in his mouth, and it seemed ridiculous that in such circumstances he should be pleased to make a grand slam.

He looked at his partner Mikhail Mikhaylovich, who rapped the table with his strong hand and instead of snatching up the tricks pushed the cards courteously and indulgently towards Ivan Ilych that he might have the pleasure of gathering them up without the trouble of stretching out his hand for them. "Does he think I am too weak to stretch out my arm?" thought Ivan Ilych, and forgetting what he was doing he over-trumped his partner, missing the grand slam by three tricks. And what was more awful of all was that he saw how upset Mikhail Mikhaylovich was about it but did not himself care. And it was dreadful to realize why he did not care.

They all saw that he was suffering and said: "We can stop if you are tired. Take a rest." Lie down? No, he was not at all tired, and he finished the rubber. All were gloomy and silent. Ivan Ilych felt that he had diffused this gloom over them and could not dispel it. They had supper and went away, and Ivan Ilych was left alone with the consciousness that his life was poisoned and was poisoning the lives of others, and that this poison did not weaken but penetrated more and more deeply into his whole being.

With this consciousness, and with physical pain besides the terror, he must go to bed, often to lie awake the greater part of the night. Next morning he had to get up again, dress, go to the law courts, speak, and write; or if he did not go out, spend at home those twenty-four hours a day each of which was a torture. And he had to live thus all alone on the brink of an abyss, with no one who understood or pitied him.

V

So one month passed and then another. Just before the New Year his brother-in-law came to town and stayed at their house. Ivan Ilych was at the law courts and Praskovya Fëdorovna had gone shopping. When Ivan Ilych came home and entered his study he found his brother-in-law there—a healthy, florid man—unpacking his portmanteau himself. He raised his head on hearing Ivan Ilych's footsteps and looked up at him for a moment without a word. That stare told Ivan Ilych everything. His brother-in-law opened his mouth to utter an exclamation of surprise but checked himself, and that action confirmed it all.

"I have changed, eh?"

"Yes, there is a change."

And after that, try as he would to get his brother-in-law to return to the subject of his looks, the latter would say nothing about it. Praskovya Fëdorovna came home and her brother went out to her. Ivan Ilych locked the door and began to examine himself in the glass, first full face, then in profile. He took up a portrait of himself taken with his wife, and compared it with what he saw in the glass. The change in him was immense. Then he bared his arms to the elbow, looked at them, drew the sleeves down again, sat down on an ottoman, and grew blacker than night.

"No, no, this won't do!" he said to himself, and jumped up, went to the table, took up some law papers and began to read them, but could not continue. He unlocked the door and went into the reception-room. The door leading to the drawing room was shut. He approached it on tiptoe and listened.

"No, you are exaggerating!" Praskovya Fëdorovna was saying.

"Exaggerating! Don't you see it? Why, he's a dead man! Look at his eyes—there's no light in them. But what is it that is wrong with him?"

"No one knows. Nikolaevich said something, but I don't know what. And Leshchetitsky[10] said quite the contrary. . . . "

[10]two doctors, the latter a celebrated specialist [Translator's note]

Ivan Ilych walked away, went to his own room, lay down, and began musing: "The kidney, a floating kidney." He recalled all the doctors had told him of how it detached itself and swayed about. And by an effort of imagination he tried to catch that kidney and arrest it and support it. So little was needed for this, it seemed to him. "No, I'll go to see Peter Ivanovich again." He rang, ordered the carriage, and got ready to go.

"Where are you going, Jean?" asked his wife, with a specially sad and exceptionally kind look.

This exceptionally kind look irritated him. He looked morosely at her.

"I must go to see Peter Ivanovich."[11]

He went to see Peter Ivanovich, and together they went to see his friend, the doctor. He was in, and Ivan Ilych had a long talk with him.

Reviewing the anatomical and physiological details of what in the doctor's opinion was going on inside of him, he understood it all.

There was something, a small thing, in the vermiform appendix. It might all come right. Only stimulate the energy of one organ and check the activity of another, then absorption would take place and everything would come right. He got home rather late for dinner, ate his dinner, and conversed cheerfully, but could not for a long time bring himself to go back to work in his room. At last, however, he went to his study and did what was necessary, but the consciousness that he had put something aside—an important, intimate matter which he would revert to when his work was done—never left him. When he had finished his work he remembered that this intimate matter was the thought of his vermiform appendix. But he did not give himself up to it, and went to the drawing-room for tea. There were callers there, including the examining magistrate who was a desirable match for his daughter, and they were conversing, playing the piano, and singing. Ivan Ilych, as Praskovya Fëdorovna remarked, spent that evening more cheerfully than usual, but he never for a moment forgot that he had postponed the important matter of the appendix. At eleven o'clock he said good-night and went to his bedroom. Since his illness he had slept alone in a small room next to his study. He undressed and took up a novel by Zola, but instead of reading it he fell into thought, and in his imagination that desired improvement in the vermiform appendix occurred. There were the absorption and evacuation and the re-establishment of normal activity. "Yes, that's it!" he said to himself. "One need only assist nature, that's all." He remembered his medicine, rose, took it, and lay down on his back watching for the beneficent action of the medicine and for it to lessen the pain. "I need only take it regularly and avoid all injurious influences. I am already feeling better, much better." He began touching his side: it was not painful to the touch. "There, I really don't feel it. It's much better already." He put out the light and turned on his side. . . . "The appendix is getting better, absorption is occurring." Suddenly he felt the old, familiar, dull, gnawing pain, stubborn and serious. There was the same familiar loathsome taste in his mouth. His heart sank and he felt dazed. "My God! My God!" he muttered. "Again, again! and it will never cease." And suddenly the matter presented itself in a quite different aspect. "Vermiform appendix! Kidney!" he said to himself. "It's not a question of appendix or kidney, but of life and . . . death. Yes, life was there and now it is going, going and I cannot stop it. Yes. Why deceive myself? Isn't it obvious to

[11]That was the friend whose friend was a doctor. [Translator's note]

everyone but me that I'm dying, and that it's only a question of weeks, days . . . it may happen this moment. There was light and now there is darkness. I was here and now I'm going there! Where?" A chill came over him, his breathing ceased, and he felt only the throbbing of his heart.

"When I am not, what will there be? There will be nothing. Then where shall I be when I am no more? Can this be dying? No, I don't want to!" He jumped up and tried to light the candle, felt for it with trembling hands, dropped candle and candlestick on the floor, and fell back on his pillow.

"What's the use? It makes no difference," he said to himself, staring with wide-open eyes into the darkness. "Death. Yes, death. And none of them know or wish to know it, and they have no pity for me. Now they are playing." (He heard through the door the distant sound of a song and its accompaniment.) "It's all the same to them, but they will die too! Fools! I first, and they later, but it will be the same for them. And now they are merry . . . the beasts!"

Anger choked him and he was agonizingly, unbearably miserable. "It is impossible that all men have been doomed to suffer this awful horror!" He raised himself.

"Something must be wrong. I must calm myself — must think it all over from the beginning." And he again began thinking. "Yes, the beginning of my illness: I knocked my side, but I was still quite well that day and the next. It hurt a little, then rather more. I saw the doctors, then followed despondency and anguish, more doctors, and I drew nearer to the abyss. My strength grew less and I kept coming nearer and nearer, and now I have wasted away and there is no light in my eyes. I think of the appendix — but this is death! I think of mending the appendix, and all the while here is death! Can it really be death?" Again terror seized him and he gasped for breath. He leant down and began feeling for the matches, pressing his elbow on the stand beside the bed. It was in his way and hurt him, he grew furious with it, pressed on it still harder, and upset it. Breathless and in despair he fell on his back, expecting death to come immediately.

Meanwhile the visitors were leaving. Praskovya Fëdorovna was seeing them off. She heard something fall and came in.

"What has happened?"

"Nothing. I knocked it over accidentally."

She went out and returned with a candle. He lay there panting heavily, like a man who has run a thousand yards, and stared upwards at her with a fixed look.

"What is it, Jean?

"No . . . no . . . thing. I upset it." ("Why speak of it? She won't understand," he thought.)

And in truth she did not understand. She picked up the stand, lit his candle, and hurried away to see another visitor off. When she came back he still lay on his back, looking upwards.

"What is it? Do you feel worse?"

"Yes."

She shook her head and sat down.

"Do you know, Jean, I think we must ask Leshchetitsky to come and see you here."

This meant calling in the famous specialist, regardless of expense. He smiled malignantly and said "No." She remained a little longer and then went up to him and kissed his forehead.

While she was kissing him he hated her from the bottom of his soul and with difficulty refrained from pushing her away.

"Good-night. Please God you'll sleep."

"Yes."

VI

Ivan Ilych saw that he was dying, and he was in continual despair.

In the depth of his heart he knew he was dying, but not only was he not accustomed to the thought, he simply did not and could not grasp it.

The syllogism he had learnt from Kiezewetter's Logic:[12] "Caius is a man, men are mortal, therefore Caius is mortal," had always seemed to him correct as applied to Caius, but certainly not as applied to himself. That Caius—man in the abstract—was mortal, was perfectly correct, but he was not Caius, not an abstract man, but a creature quite, quite separate from all others. He had been little Vanya, with a mama and a papa, with Mitya and Volodya, with the toys, a coachman and a nurse, afterwards with Katenka and with all the joys, griefs, and delights of childhood, boyhood, and youth. What did Caius know of the smell of that striped leather ball Vanya had been so fond of? Had Caius kissed his mother's hand like that, and did the silk of her dress rustle so for Caius? Had he rioted like that at school when the pastry was bad? Had Caius been in love like that? Could Caius preside at a session as he did? "Caius really was mortal, and it was right for him to die; but for me, little Vanya, Ivan Ilych, with all my thoughts and emotions, it's altogether a different matter. It cannot be that I ought to die. That would be too terrible."

Such was his feeling.

"If I had to die like Caius I should have known it was so. An inner voice would have told me so, but there was nothing of the sort in me and I and all my friends felt that our case was quite different from that of Caius. And now here it is!" he said to himself. "It can't be. It's impossible! But here it is. How is this? How is one to understand it?"

He could not understand it, and tried to drive this false, incorrect, morbid thought away and to replace it by other proper and healthy thoughts. But that thought, and not the thought only but the reality itself, seemed to come and confront him.

And to replace that thought he called up a succession of others, hoping to find in them some support. He tried to get back into the former current of thoughts that had once screened the thought of death from him. But strange to say, all that formerly shut off, hidden, and destroyed, his consciousness of death, no longer had that effect. Ivan Ilych now spent most of his time in attempting to re-establish that old current. He would say to himself: "I will take up my duties again—after all I used to live by them." And banishing all doubts he would go to the law courts, enter into conversation with his colleagues, and sit carelessly as was his wont, scanning the crowd with a thoughtful look and leaning both his emaciated arms on the arms of his oak chair; bending over as usual to a colleague and drawing his papers nearer he would interchange whispers with him, and then suddenly raising

[12]Klaus Kiezewetter (1766–1819), author of *The Outline of Logic According to Kantian Principles*, a popular text in Russia modeled on the ideas of the German philosopher Immanuel Kant (1722–1804)

his eyes and sitting erect would pronounce certain words and open the proceedings. But suddenly in the midst of those proceedings the pain in his side, regardless of the stage the proceedings had reached, would begin its own gnawing work. Ivan Ilych would turn his attention to it and try to drive the thought of it away, but without success. *It* would come and stand before him and look at him, and he would be petrified and the light would die out of his eyes, and he would again begin asking himself whether *It* alone was true. And his colleagues and subordinates would see with surprise and distress that he, the brilliant and subtle judge, was becoming confused and making mistakes. He would shake himself, try to pull himself together, manage somehow to bring the sitting to a close, and return home with the sorrowful consciousness that his judicial labors could not as formerly hide from him what he wanted them to hide, and could not deliver him from *It*. And what was worst of all was that *It* drew his attention to itself not in order to make him take some action but only that he should look at *It*, look it straight in the face: look at it and without doing anything, suffer inexpressibly.

And to save himself from this condition Ivan Ilych looked for consolations—new screens—and new screens were found and for a while seemed to save him, but then they immediately fell to pieces or rather became transparent, as if *It* penetrated them and nothing could veil *It*.

In these latter days he would go into the drawing-room he had arranged—that drawing-room where he had fallen and for the sake of which (how bitterly ridiculous it seemed) he had sacrificed his life—for he knew that his illness originated with that knock. He would enter and see that something had scratched the polished table. He would look for the cause of this and find that it was the bronze ornamentation of an album, that had got bent. He would take up the expensive album which he had lovingly arranged, and feel vexed with his daughter and her friends for their untidiness—for the album was torn here and there and some of the photographs turned upside down. He would put it carefully in order and bend the ornamentation back into position. Then it would occur to him to place all those things in another corner of the room, near the plants. He could call the footman, but his daughter or wife would come to help him. They would not agree, and his wife would contradict him, and he would dispute and grow angry. But that was all right, for then he did not think about *It*. *It* was invisible.

But then, when he was moving something himself, his wife would say: "Let the servants do it. You will hurt yourself again." And suddenly *It* would flash through the screen and he would see it. It was just a flash, and he hoped it would disappear, but he would involuntarily pay attention to his side. "It sits there as before, gnawing just the same!" And he could no longer forget *It*, but could distinctly see it looking at him from behind the flowers. "What is it all for?"

"It really is so! I lost my life over that curtain as I might have done when storming a fort. Is that possible? How terrible and how stupid. It can't be true! It can't, but it is."

He would go to his study, lie down, and again be alone with *It*: face to face with *It*. And nothing could be done with *It* except to look at it and shudder.

VII

How it happened it is impossible to say because it came about step by step, unnoticed, but in the third month of Ivan Ilych's illness, his wife, his daughter, his son, his acquaintances, the doctors, the servants, and above all he himself, were aware that the whole interest he had for other people was whether he would soon vacate his place, and at last release the living from the discomfort caused by his presence and be himself released from his sufferings.

He slept less and less. He was given opium and hypodermic injections of morphine, but this did not relieve him. The dull depression he experienced in a somnolent condition at first gave him a little relief, but only as something new, afterwards it became as distressing as the pain itself or even more so.

Special foods were prepared for him by the doctors' orders, but all those foods became increasingly distasteful and disgusting to him.

For his excretions also special arrangements had to be made, and this was a torment to him every time — a torment from the uncleanliness, the unseemliness, and the smell, and from knowing that another person had to take part in it.

But just through this most unpleasant matter, Ivan Ilych obtained comfort. Gerasim, the butler's young assistant, always came in to carry the things out. Gerasim was a clean, fresh peasant lad, grown stout on town food and always cheerful and bright. At first the sight of him, in his clean Russian peasant costume, engaged on that disgusting task embarrassed Ivan Ilych.

Once when he got up from the commode too weak to draw up his trousers, he dropped into a soft armchair and looked with horror at his bare, enfeebled thighs with the muscles so sharply marked on them.

Gerasim with a firm light tread, his heavy boots emitting a pleasant smell of tar and fresh winter air, came in wearing a clean Hessian apron, the sleeves of his print shirt tucked up over his strong bare young arms; and refraining from looking at his sick master out of consideration for his feelings, and restraining the joy of life that beamed from his face, he went up to the commode.

"Gerasim!" said Ivan Ilych in a weak voice.

Gerasim started, evidently afraid he might have committed some blunder, and with a rapid movement turned his fresh, kind, simply young face which just showed the first downy signs of a beard.

"Yes, sir?"

"That must be very unpleasant for you. You must forgive me. I am helpless."

"Oh, why, sir," and Gerasim's eyes beamed and he showed his glistening white teeth, "what's a little trouble? It's a case of illness with you, sir."

And his deft strong hands did their accustomed task, and he went out of the room stepping lightly. Five minutes later he as lightly returned.

Ivan Ilych was still sitting in the same position in the armchair.

"Gerasim," he said when the latter had replaced the freshly-washed utensil. "Please come here and help me." Gerasim went up to him. "Lift me up. It is hard for me to get up, and I have sent Dmitri away."

Gerasim went up to him, grasped his master with his strong arms deftly but gently, in the same way that he stepped — lifted him, supported him with one hand, and with the other drew up his trousers and would have set him down again, but Ivan Ilych asked to be led to the sofa. Gerasim, without an effort and without apparent pressure, led him, almost lifting him, to the sofa and placed him on it.

"Thank you. How easily and well you do it all!"

Gerasim smiled again and turned to leave the room. But Ivan Ilych felt his presence such a comfort that he did not want to let him go.

"One thing more, please move up that chair. No, the other one — under my feet. It is easier for me when my feet are raised."

Gerasim brought the chair, set it down gently in place, and raised Ivan Ilych's legs on to it. It seemed to Ivan Ilych that he felt better while Gerasim was holding up his legs.

"It's better when my legs are higher," he said. "Place that cushion under them."

Gerasim did so. He again lifted the legs and placed them, and again Ivan Ilych felt better while Gerasim held his legs. When he set them down Ivan Ilych fancied he felt worse.

"Gerasim," he said. "Are you busy now?"

"Not at all, sir," said Gerasim, who had learnt from the townsfolk how to speak to gentlefolk.

"What have you still to do?"

"What have I to do? I've done everything except chopping the logs for tomorrow."

"Then hold my legs up a bit higher, can you?"

"Of course I can. Why not?" And Gerasim raised his master's legs higher and Ivan Ilych thought that in that position he did not feel any pain at all.

"And how about the logs?"

"Don't trouble about that, sir. There's plenty of time."

Ivan Ilych told Gerasim to sit down and hold his legs, and began to talk to him. And strange to say it seemed to him that he felt better while Gerasim held his legs up.

After that Ivan Ilych would sometimes call Gerasim and get him to hold his legs on his shoulders, and he liked talking to him. Gerasim did it all easily, willingly, simply, and with a good nature that touched Ivan Ilych. Health, strength, and vitality in other people were offensive to him, but Gerasim's strength and vitality did not mortify but soothed him.

What tormented Ivan Ilych most was the deception, the lie, which for some reason they all accepted, that he was not dying but was simply ill, and that he only need keep quiet and undergo a treatment and then something very good would result. He however knew that do what they would nothing would come of it, only still more agonizing suffering and death. This deception tortured him — their not wishing to admit what they all knew and what he knew, but wanting to lie to him concerning his terrible condition, and wishing and forcing him to participate in that lie. Those lies — lies enacted over him on the eve of his death and destined to degrade this awful, solemn act to the level of their visitings, their curtains, their sturgeon for dinner — were a terrible agony for Ivan Ilych. And strangely enough, many times when they were going through their antics over him he had been within a hairbreadth of calling out to them: "Stop lying! You know and I know that I am dying. Then at least stop lying about it!" But he had never had the spirit to do it. The awful, terrible act of his dying was, he could see, reduced by those about him to the level of a casual, unpleasant, and almost indecorous incident (as if someone entered a drawing-room diffusing an unpleasant odor) and this was done by that very decorum which he had served all his life long. He saw that no one felt for him, because no one even wished to grasp his position. Only Gerasim recognized it and pitied him. And so Ivan Ilych felt at ease only with him. He felt comforted when Gerasim supported his legs (sometimes all night long) and refused to go to bed, saying, "Don't you worry, Ivan Ilych. I'll get sleep enough later on," or when he suddenly became familiar and exclaimed: "If you weren't sick it would be another matter, but as it is, why should I grudge a little trouble?" Gerasim alone did not lie;

everything showed that he alone understood the facts of the case and did not consider it necessary to disguise them, but simply felt sorry for his emaciated and enfeebled master. Once when Ivan Ilych was sending him away he even said straight out: "We shall all of us die, so why should I grudge a little trouble?"— expressing the fact that he did not think his work burdensome, because he was doing it for a dying man and hoped someone would do the same for him when his time came.

Apart from this lying, or because of it, what most tormented Ivan Ilych was that no one pitied him as he wished to be pitied. At certain moments after prolonged suffering he wished most of all (though he would have been ashamed to confess it) for someone to pity him as a sick child is pitied. He longed to be petted and comforted. He knew he was an important functionary, that he had a beard turning grey, and that therefore what he longed for was impossible, but still he longed for it. And in Gerasim's attitude towards him there was something akin to what he wished for, and so that attitude comforted him. Ivan Ilych wanted to weep, wanted to be petted and cried over, and then his colleague Shebek would come, and instead of weeping and being petted, Ivan Ilych would assume a serious, severe, and profound air, and by force of habit would express his opinion on a decision of the Court of Cassation and would stubbornly insist on that view. This falsity around him and within him did more than anything else to poison his last days.

VIII

It was morning. He knew it was morning because Gerasim had gone, and Peter the footman had come and put out the candles, drawn back one of the curtains, and begun quietly to tidy up. Whether it was morning or evening, Friday or Sunday, made no difference, it was all just the same: the gnawing, unmitigated, agonizing pain, never ceasing for an instant, the consciousness of life inexorably waning but not yet extinguished, the approach of that ever dreaded and hateful Death which was the only reality, and always the same falsity. What were days, weeks, hours, in such a case?

"Will you have some tea, sir?"

"He wants things to be regular, and wishes the gentlefolk to drink tea in the morning," thought Ivan Ilych, and only said "No."

"Wouldn't you like to move onto the sofa, sir?"

"He wants to tidy up the room, and I'm in the way. I am uncleanliness and disorder," he thought, and said only:

"No, leave me alone."

The man went on bustling about. Ivan Ilych stretched out his hand. Peter came up, ready to help.

"What is it, sir?"

"My watch."

Peter took the watch which was close at hand and gave it to his master.

"Half-past eight. Are they up?"

"No, sir, except Vasily Ivanich" (the son) "who has gone to school. Praskovya Fëdorovna ordered me to wake her if you asked for her. Shall I do so?"

"No, there's no need to." "Perhaps I'd better have some tea," he thought, and added aloud: "Yes, bring me some tea."

Peter went to the door, but Ivan Ilych dreaded being left alone. "How can I keep him here? Oh yes, my medicine." "Peter, give me my medicine." "Why not? Perhaps it may still do me some good." He took a spoonful and swallowed it. "No, it won't help. It's all tomfoolery, all deception," he decided as soon as he became aware of the familiar, sickly, hopeless taste. "No, I can't believe in it any longer. But the pain, why this pain? If it would only cease just for a moment!" And he moaned. Peter turned towards him. "It's all right. Go and fetch me some tea."

Peter went out. Left alone Ivan Ilych groaned not so much with pain, terrible though that was, as from mental anguish. Always and for ever the same, always these endless days and nights. If only it would come quicker! If only *what* would come quicker? Death, darkness? . . . No, no! Anything rather than death!

When Peter returned with the tea on a tray, Ivan Ilych stared at him for a time in perplexity, not realizing who and what he was. Peter was disconcerted by that look and his embarrassment brought Ivan Ilych to himself.

"Oh, tea! All right, put it down. Only help me to wash and put on a clean shirt."

And Ivan Ilych began to wash. With pauses for rest, he washed his hands and then his face, cleaned his teeth, brushed his hair, and looked in the glass. He was terrified by what he saw, especially by the limp way in which his hair clung to his pallid forehead.

While his shirt was being changed he knew that he would be still more frightened at the sight of his body, so he avoided looking at it. Finally he was ready. He drew on a dressing gown, wrapped himself in a plaid, and sat down in the armchair to take his tea. For a moment he felt refreshed, but as soon as he began to drink the tea he was again aware of the same taste and the pain also returned. He finished it with an effort, and then lay down stretching out his legs, and dismissed Peter.

Always the same. Now a spark of hope flashes up, then a sea of despair rages, and always pain; always pain, always despair, and always the same. When alone he had a dreadful and distressing desire to call someone, but he knew beforehand that with others present it would be still worse. "Another dose of morphine—to lose consciousness. I will tell him, the doctor, that he must think of something else. It's impossible, impossible, to go on like this."

An hour and another pass like that. But now there is a ring at the door bell. Perhaps it's the doctor? It is. He comes in fresh, hearty, plump, and cheerful, with that look on his face that seems to say: "There now, you're in a panic about something, but we'll arrange it all for you directly!" The doctor knows this expression is out of place here, but he has put it on once for all and can't take it off—like a man who has put on a frock-coat in the morning to pay a round of calls.

The doctor rubs his hands vigorously and reassuringly.

"Brr! How cold it is! There's such a sharp frost; just let me warm myself!" he says, as if it were only a matter of waiting till he was warm, and then he would put everything right.

"Well now, how are you?"

Ivan Ilych feels that the doctor would like to say: "Well, how are our affairs?" but that even he feels that this would not do, and says instead: "What sort of a night have you had?"

Ivan Ilych looks at him as much as to say: "Are you really never ashamed of lying?" But the doctor does not wish to understand this question, and Ivan Ilych says: "Just as terrible as ever. The pain never leaves me and never subsides. If only something. . . ."

"Yes, you sick people are always like that. . . . There, now I think I am warm enough. Even Praskovya Fëdorovna, who is so particular, could find no fault with my temperature. Well, now I can say good-morning," and the doctor presses his patient's hand.

Then, dropping his former playfulness, he begins with a most serious face to examine the patient, feeling his pulse and taking his temperature, and then begins the sounding and auscultation.

Ivan Ilych knows quite well and definitely that all this is nonsense and pure deception, but when the doctor, getting down on his knee, leans over him, putting his ear first higher then lower, and performs various gymnastic movements over him with a significant expression on his face, Ivan Ilych submits to it all as he used to submit to the speeches of the lawyers, though he knew very well that they were all lying and why they were lying.

The doctor, kneeling on the sofa, is still sounding him when Praskovya Fëdorovna's silk dress rustles at the door and she is heard scolding Peter for not having let her know of the doctor's arrival.

She comes in, kisses her husband, and at once proceeds to prove that she has been up a long time already, and only owing to a misunderstanding failed to be there when the doctor arrived.

Ivan Ilych looks at her, scans her all over, sets against her the whiteness and plumpness and cleanness of her hands and neck, the gloss of her hair, and the sparkle of her vivacious eyes. He hates her with his whole soul. And the thrill of hatred he feels for her makes him suffer from her touch.

Her attitude towards him and his disease is still the same. Just as the doctor had adopted a certain relation to his patient which he could not abandon, so had she formed one towards him — that he was not doing something he ought to do and was himself to blame, and that she reproached him lovingly for this — and she could not now change that attitude.

"You see he doesn't listen to me and doesn't take his medicine at the proper time. And above all he lies in a position that is no doubt bad for him — with his legs up."

She described how he made Gerasim hold his legs up.

The doctor smiled with a contemptuous affability that said: "What's to be done? These sick people do have foolish fancies of that kind, but we must forgive them."

When the examination was over the doctor looked at his watch, and then Praskovya Fëdorovna announced to Ivan Ilych that it was of course as he pleased, but she had sent today for a celebrated specialist who would examine him and have a consultation with Michael Danilovich (their regular doctor).

"Please don't raise any objections. I am doing this for my own sake," she said ironically, letting it be felt that she was doing it all for his sake and only said this to leave him no right to refuse. He remained silent, knitting his brows. He felt that he was so surrounded and involved in a mesh of falsity that it was hard to unravel anything.

Everything she did for him was entirely for her own sake, and she told him she was doing for herself what she actually was doing for herself, as if that was so incredible that he must understand the opposite.

At half-past eleven the celebrated specialist arrived. Again the sounding began and the significant conversations in his presence and in another room, about the kidneys and the appendix, and the questions and answers, with such an air of importance that again, instead of the real question of life and death which now alone confronted him, the question arose of the kidney and appendix which were not behaving as they ought to and would now be attacked by Michael Danilovich and the specialist and forced to amend their ways.

The celebrated specialist took leave of him with a serious though not hopeless look, and in reply to the timid question Ivan Ilych, with eyes glistening with fear and hope, put to him as to whether there was a chance of recovery, said that he could not vouch for it but there was a possibility. The look of hope with which Ivan Ilych watched the doctor out was so pathetic that Praskovya Fëdorovna, seeing it, even wept as she left the room to hand the doctor his fee.

The gleam of hope kindled by the doctor's encouragement did not last long. The same room, the same pictures, curtains, wallpaper, medicine bottles, were all there, and the same aching suffering body, and Ivan Ilych began to moan. They gave him a subcutaneous injection and he sank into oblivion.

It was twilight when he came to. They brought him his dinner and he swallowed some beef tea with difficulty, and then everything was the same again and night was coming on.

After dinner, at seven o'clock, Praskovya Fëdorovna came into the room in evening dress, her full bosom pushed up by her corset, and with traces of powder on her face. She had reminded him in the morning that they were going to the theater. Sarah Bernhardt was visiting the town and they had a box, which he had insisted on their taking. Now he had forgotten about it and her toilet offended him, but he concealed his vexation when he remembered that he had himself insisted on their securing a box and going because it would be an instructive and aesthetic pleasure for the children.

Praskovya Fëdorovna came in, self-satisfied but yet with a rather guilty air. She sat down and asked how he was, but, as he saw, only for the sake of asking and not in order to learn about it, knowing that there was nothing to learn—and then went on to what she really wanted to say: that she would not on any account have gone but that the box had been taken and Helen and their daughter were going, as well as Petrishchev (the examining magistrate, their daughter's fiancé) and that it was out of the question to let them go alone; but that she would have much preferred to sit with him for a while; and he must be sure to follow the doctor's orders while she was away.

"Oh, and Fëdor Petrovich" (the fiancé) "would like to come in. May he? And Lisa?"

"All right."

Their daughter came in in full evening dress, her fresh young flesh exposed (making a show of that very flesh which in his own case caused so much suffering), strong, healthy, evidently in love, and impatient with illness, suffering, and death, because they interfered with her happiness.

Fëdor Petrovich came in too, in evening dress, his hair curled *à la Capoul*,[13] a tight stiff collar round his long sinewy neck, an enormous white shirt-front and narrow black trousers tightly stretched over his strong thighs. He had one white glove tightly drawn on, and was holding his opera hat in his hand.

Following him the schoolboy crept in unnoticed, in a new uniform, poor little fellow, and wearing gloves. Terribly dark shadows showed under his eyes, the meaning of which Ivan Ilych knew well.

[13]*à la Capoul* in the elaborate hairstyle of a famous French singer, Capoul

His son had always seemed pathetic to him, and now it was dreadful to see the boy's frightened look of pity. It seemed to Ivan Ilych that Vasya was the only one besides Gerasim who understood and pitied him.

They all sat down and again asked how he was. A silence followed. Lisa asked her mother about the opera-glasses, and there was an altercation between mother and daughter as to who had taken them and where they had been put. This occasioned some unpleasantness.

Fëdor Petrovich inquired of Ivan Ilych whether he had ever seen Sarah Bernhardt. Ivan Ilych did not at first catch the question, but then replied: "No, have you seen her before?"

"Yes, in *Adrienne Lecouvreur*."[14]

Praskovya Fëdorovna mentioned some rôles in which Sarah Bernhardt was particularly good. Her daughter disagreed. Conversation sprang up as to the elegance and realism of her acting—the sort of conversation that is always repeated and is always the same.

In the midst of the conversation Fëdor Petrovich glanced at Ivan Ilych and became silent. The others also looked at him and grew silent. Ivan Ilych was staring with glittering eyes straight before him, evidently indignant with them. This had to be rectified, but it was impossible to do so. The silence had to be broken, but for a time no one dared to break it and they all became afraid that the conventional deception would suddenly become obvious and the truth become plain to all. Lisa was the first to pluck up courage and break the silence, but by trying to hide what everybody was feeling, she betrayed it.

"Well, if we are going it's time to start," she said, looking at her watch, a present from her father, and with a faint and significant smile at Fëdor Petrovich relating to something known only to them. She got up with a rustle of her dress.

They all rose, said good-night, and went away.

When they had gone it seemed to Ivan Ilych that he felt better; the falsity had gone with them. But the pain remained—that same pain and that same fear that made everything monotonously alike, nothing harder and nothing easier. Everything was worse.

Again minute followed minute and hour followed hour. Everything remained the same and there was no cessation. And the inevitable end of it all became more and more terrible.

"Yes, send Gerasim here," he replied to a question Peter asked.

IX

His wife returned late at night. She came in on tiptoe, but he heard her, opened his eyes, and made haste to close them again. She wished to send Gerasim away and to sit with him herself, but he opened his eyes and said: "No, go away."

"Are you in great pain?"

"Always the same."

"Take some opium."

He agreed and took some. She went away.

Till about three in the morning he was in a state of stupefied misery. It seemed to him that he and his pain were being thrust into a narrow, deep black sack, but

[14]*Adrienne Lecouvreur* French comedy by Eugène Scribe and Ernest Legouvé

though they were pushed further and further in they could not be pushed to the bottom. And this, terrible enough in itself, was accompanied by suffering. He was frightened yet wanted to fall through the sack, he struggled but yet co-operated. And suddenly he broke through, fell, and regained consciousness. Gerasim was sitting at the foot of the bed dozing quietly and patiently, while he himself lay with his emaciated stockinged legs resting on Gerasim's shoulders; the same shaded candle was there and the same unceasing pain.

"Go away, Gerasim," he whispered.

"It's all right, sir. I'll stay a while."

"No. Go away."

He removed his legs from Gerasim's shoulders, turned sideways onto his arm, and felt sorry for himself. He only waited till Gerasim had gone into the next room and then restrained himself no longer but wept like a child. He wept on account of his helplessness, his terrible loneliness, the cruelty of man, the cruelty of God, and the absence of God.

"Why hast Thou done all this? Why hast Thou brought me here? Why, why dost Thou torment me so terribly?"

He did not expect an answer and yet wept because there was no answer and could be none. The pain again grew more acute, but he did not stir and did not call. He said to himself: "Go on! Strike me! But what is it for? What have I done to Thee? What is it for?"

Then he grew quiet and not only ceased weeping but even held his breath and became all attention. It was as though he were listening not to an audible voice but to the voice of his soul, to the current of thoughts arising within him.

"What is it you want?" was the first clear conception capable of expression in words, that he heard.

"What do you want? What do you want?" he repeated to himself.

"What do I want? To live and not to suffer," he answered.

And again he listened with such concentrated attention that even his pain did not distract him.

"To live? How?" asked his inner voice.

"Why, to live as I used to—well and pleasantly."

"As you lived before, well and pleasantly?" the voice repeated.

And in imagination he began to recall the best moments of his pleasant life. But strange to say none of those best moments of his pleasant life now seemed at all what they had then seemed—none of them except the first recollections of childhood. There, in childhood, there had been something really pleasant with which it would be possible to live if it could return. But the child who had experienced that happiness existed no longer, it was like a reminiscence of somebody else.

As soon as the period began which had produced the present Ivan Ilych, all that had then seemed joys now melted before his sight and turned into something trivial and often nasty.

And the further he departed from childhood and the nearer he came to the present the more worthless and doubtful were the joys. This began with the School of Law. A little that was really good was still found there—there was lightheartedness, friendship, and hope. But in the upper classes there had already been fewer of such good moments. Then during the first years of his official career, when he was in the service of the Governor, some pleasant moments again occurred: they were the memories of love for a woman. Then all became confused and there was still less of what was good; later on again there was still less that was good, and the further he went the less there was. His marriage, a mere accident, then the disenchantment that followed it, his wife's bad breath and the sensuality and hypocrisy: then the deadly official life and those preoccupations about money, a year of it, and two, and ten, and twenty, and always the same thing. And the longer it lasted the more deadly it became. "It is as if I had been going downhill while I imagined I was going up. And that is really what it was. I was going up in public opinion, but to the same extent life was ebbing away from me. And now it is all done and there is only death."

"Then what does it mean? Why? It can't be that life is so senseless and horrible. But if it really has been so horrible and senseless, why must I die and die in agony? There is something wrong!"

"Maybe I did not live as I ought to have done," it suddenly occurred to him. "But how could that be, when I did everything properly?" he replied, and immediately dismissed from his mind this, the sole solution of all the riddles of life and death, as something quite impossible.

"Then what do you want now? To live? Live how? Live as you lived in the law courts when the usher proclaimed 'The judge is coming!' The judge is coming, the judge!" he repeated to himself. "Here he is, the judge. But I am not guilty!" he exclaimed angrily. "What is it for?" And he ceased crying, but turning his face to the wall continued to ponder on the same question: Why, and for what purpose, is there all this horror? But however much he pondered he found no answer. And whenever the thought occurred to him, as it often did, that it all resulted from his not having lived as he ought to have done, he at once recalled the correctness of his whole life and dismissed so strange an idea.

X

Another fortnight passed. Ivan Ilych now no longer left his sofa. He would not lie in bed but lay on the sofa, facing the wall nearly all the time. He suffered ever the same unceasing agonies and in his loneliness pondered always on the same insoluble question: "What is this? Can it be that it is Death?" And the inner voice answered: "Yes, it is Death."

"Why these sufferings?" And the voice answered, "For no reason — they just are so." Beyond and besides this there was nothing.

From the very beginning of his illness, ever since he had first been to see the doctor, Ivan Ilych's life had been divided between two contrary and alternating moods: now it was despair and the expectation of this uncomprehended and terrible death, and now hope and an intently interested observation of the functioning of his organs. Now before his eyes there was only a kidney or an intestine that temporarily evaded its duty, and now only that incomprehensible and dreadful death from which it was impossible to escape.

These two states of mind had alternated from the very beginning of his illness, but the further it progressed the more doubtful and fantastic became the conception of the kidney, and the more real the sense of impending death.

He had but to call to mind what he had been three months before and what he was now, to call to mind with what regularity he had been going downhill, for every possibility of hope to be shattered.

Latterly during that loneliness in which he found himself as he lay facing the back of the sofa, a loneliness in the midst of a populous town and surrounded by numerous acquaintances and relations but that yet could not have been more complete anywhere — either at the bottom of the sea or under the earth — during that terrible loneliness Ivan Ilych had lived only in memories of the past. Pictures of his past rose before him one after another. They always began with what was nearest in time and then went back to what was most remote — to his childhood — and rested there. If he thought of the stewed prunes that had been offered him that day, his mind went back to the raw shrivelled French plums of his childhood, their peculiar flavor and the flow of saliva when he sucked their stones, and along with the memory of that taste came a whole series of memories of those days: his nurse, his brother, and their toys. "No, I mustn't think of that. . . . It is too painful," Ivan Ilych said to himself, and brought himself back to the present — to the button on the back of the sofa and the creases in its morocco. "Morocco is expensive, but it does not wear well: there had been a quarrel about it. It was a different kind of quarrel and a different kind of morocco that time when we tore father's portfolio and were punished, and mama brought us some tarts. . . ." And again his thoughts dwelt on his childhood, and again it was painful and he tried to banish them and fix his mind on something else.

Then again together with that chain of memories another series passed through his mind — of how his illness had progressed and grown worse. There also the further back he looked the more life there had been. There had been more of what was good in life and more of life itself. The two merged together. "Just as the pain went on getting worse and worse, so my life grew worse and worse," he thought. "There is one bright spot there at the back, at the beginning of life, and afterwards all becomes blacker and blacker and proceeds more and more rapidly — in inverse ratio to the square of the distance from death," thought Ivan Ilych. And the example of a stone falling downwards with increasing velocity entered his mind. Life, a series of increasing sufferings, flies further and further towards its end — the most terrible suffering. "I am flying. . . ." He shuddered, shifted himself, and tried to resist, but was already aware that resistance was impossible, and again with eyes weary of gazing but unable to cease seeing what was before them, he stared at the back of the sofa and waited — awaiting that dreadful fall and shock and destruction.

"Resistance is impossible!" he said to himself. "If I could only understand what it is all for! But that too is impossible. An explanation would be possible if it could be said that I have not lived as I ought to. But it is impossible to say that," and he remembered all the legality, correctitude, and propriety of his life. "That at any rate can certainly not be admitted," he thought, and his lips smiled ironically as if someone could see that smile and be taken in by it. "There is no explanation! Agony, death. . . . What for?"

XI

Another two weeks went by in this way and during that fortnight an event occurred that Ivan Ilych and his wife had desired. Petrishchev formally proposed. It happened in the evening. The next day Praskovya Fëdorovna came into her husband's room considering how best to inform him of it, but that very night there had been a fresh change for the worse in his condition. She found him still lying on the sofa but in a different position. He lay on his back, groaning and staring fixedly straight in front of him.

She began to remind him of his medicines, but he turned his eyes towards her with such a look that she did not finish what she was saying; so great an animosity, to her in particular, did that look express.

"For Christ's sake let me die in peace!" he said.

She would have gone away, but just then their daughter came in and went up to say good morning. He looked at her as he had done at his wife, and in reply to her inquiry about his health said dryly that he would soon free them all of himself. They were both silent and after sitting with him for a while went away.

"Is it our fault?" Lisa said to her mother. "It's as if we were to blame! I am sorry for papa, but why should we be tortured?"

The doctor came at his usual time. Ivan Ilych answered "Yes" and "No," never taking his angry eyes from him, and at last said: "You know you can do nothing for me, so leave me alone."

"We can ease your sufferings."

"You can't even do that. Let me be."

The doctor went into the drawing-room and told Praskovya Fëdorovna that the case was very serious and that the only resource left was opium to allay her husband's sufferings, which must be terrible.

It was true, as the doctor said, that Ivan Ilych's physical sufferings were terrible, but worse than the physical sufferings were his mental sufferings, which were his chief torture.

His mental sufferings were due to the fact that that night, as he looked at Gerasim's sleepy, good-natured face with its prominent cheek-bones, the question suddenly occurred to him: "What if my whole life has really been wrong?"

It occurred to him that what had appeared perfectly impossible before, namely that he had not spent his life as he should have done, might after all be true. It occurred to him that his scarcely perceptible attempts to struggle against what was considered good by the most highly placed people, those scarcely noticeable impulses which he had immediately suppressed, might have been the real thing, and all the rest false. And his professional duties and the whole arrangement of his life and of his family, and all his social and official interests, might all have been false. He tried to defend all those things to himself and suddenly felt the weakness of what he was defending. There was nothing to defend.

"But if that is so," he said to himself, "and I am leaving this life with the consciousness that I have lost all that was given me and it is impossible to rectify it—what then?"

He lay on his back and began to pass his life in review in quite a new way. In the morning when he saw first his footman, then his wife, then his daughter, and then the doctor, their every word and movement confirmed to him the awful truth that had been revealed to him during the night. In them he saw himself—all that for which he had lived—and saw clearly that it was not real at all, but a terrible and huge deception which had hidden both life and death. This consciousness intensified his physical suffering tenfold. He groaned and tossed about, and pulled at his clothing which choked and stifled him. And he hated them on that account.

He was given a large dose of opium and became unconscious, but at noon his sufferings began again. He drove everybody away and tossed from side to side.

His wife came to him and said:

"Jean, my dear, do this for me. It can't do any harm and often helps. Healthy people often do it."

He opened his eyes wide.

"What? Take communion? Why? It's unnecessary! However . . ."

She began to cry.

"Yes, do, my dear. I'll send for our priest. He is such a nice man."

"All right. Very well," he muttered.

When the priest came and heard his confession, Ivan Ilych was softened and seemed to feel a relief from his doubts and consequently from his sufferings, and for a moment there came a ray of hope. He again began to think of the vermiform appendix and the possibility of correcting it. He received the sacrament with tears in his eyes.

When they laid him down again afterwards he felt a moment's ease, and the hope that he might live awoke in him again. He began to think of the operation that had been suggested to him. "To live! I want to live!" he said to himself.

His wife came in to congratulate him after his communion, and when uttering the usual conventional words she added:

"You feel better, don't you?"

Without looking at her he said "Yes."

Her dress, her figure, the expression of her face, the tone of her voice, all revealed the same thing. "This is wrong, it is not as it should be. All you have lived for and still live for is falsehood and deception, hiding life and death from you." And as soon as he admitted that thought, his hatred and his agonizing physical suffering again sprang up, and with that suffering a consciousness of the unavoidable, approaching end. And to this was added a new sensation of grinding shooting pain and a feeling of suffocation.

The expression of his face when he uttered that "yes" was dreadful. Having uttered it, he looked her straight in the eyes, turned on his face with a rapidity extraordinary in his weak state and shouted:

"Go away! Go away and leave me alone!"

XII

From that moment the screaming began that continued for three days, and was so terrible that one could not hear it through two closed doors without horror. At the moment he answered his wife he realized that he was lost, that there was no return, that the end had come, the very end, and his doubts were still unsolved and remained doubts.

"Oh! Oh! Oh!" he cried in various intonations. He had begun by screaming "I won't!" and continued screaming on the letter O.

For three whole days, during which time did not exist for him, he struggled in that black sack into which he was being thrust by an invisible, resistless force. He struggled as a man condemned to death struggles in the hands of the executioner, knowing that he cannot save himself. And every moment he felt that despite all his efforts he was drawing nearer and nearer to what terrified him. He felt that his agony was due to his being thrust into that black hole and still more to his not being able to get right into it. He was hindered from getting into it by his conviction that his life had been a good one. That very justification of his life held him fast and prevented his moving forward, and it caused him most torment of all.

Suddenly some force struck him in the chest and side, making it still harder to breathe, and he fell through the hole and there at the bottom was a light. What had happened to him was like the sensation one sometimes experiences in a railway carriage when one thinks one is going backwards while one is really going forwards and suddenly becomes aware of the real direction.

"Yes, it was all not the right thing," he said to himself, "but that's no matter. It can be done. But what *is* the right thing?" he asked himself, and suddenly grew quiet.

This occurred at the end of the third day, two hours before his death. Just then his schoolboy son had crept softly in and gone up to the bedside. The dying man was still screaming desperately and waving his arms. His hand fell on the boy's head, and the boy caught it, pressed it to his lips, and began to cry.

At that very moment Ivan Ilych fell through and caught sight of the light, and it was revealed to him that though his life had not been what it should have been, this could still be rectified. He asked himself, "What *is* the right thing?" and grew still, listening. Then he felt that someone was kissing his hand. He opened his eyes, looked at his son, and felt sorry for him. His wife came up to him and he glanced at her. She was gazing at him open-mouthed, with undried tears on her nose and cheek and a despairing look on her face. He felt sorry for her too.

"Yes, I am making them wretched," he thought. "They are sorry, but it will be better for them when I die." He wished to say this but had not the strength to utter it. "Besides, why speak? I must act," he thought. With a look at his wife he indicated his son and said: "Take him away . . . sorry for him . . . sorry for you too. . . ." He tried to add, "forgive me," but said "forgo" and waved his hand, knowing that He whose understanding mattered would understand.

And suddenly it grew clear to him that what had been oppressing him and would not leave him was all dropping away at once from two sides, from ten sides, and from all sides. He was sorry for them, he must act so as not to hurt them: release them and free himself from these sufferings. "How good and how simple!" he thought. "And the pain?" he asked himself. "What had become of it? Where are you, pain?"

He turned his attention to it.

"Yes, here it is. Well, what of it? Let the pain be."

"And death . . . where is it?"

He sought his former accustomed fear of death and did not find it. "Where is it? What death?" There was no fear because there was no death.

In place of death there was light.

"So that's what it is!" he suddenly exclaimed aloud. "What joy!"

To him all this happened in a single instant, and the meaning of that instant did not change. For those present his agony continued for another two hours. Something rattled in his throat, his emaciated body twitched, then the gasping and rattle became less and less frequent.

"It is finished!" said someone near him.

He heard these words and repeated them in his soul.

"Death is finished," he said to himself. "It is no more!"

He drew in a breath, stopped in the midst of a sigh, stretched out, and died.

[1886]

Translated by
Louise and Aylmer Maude

QUESTIONS

1. Why does the story begin after Ivan Ilych's death? Read the first section again after finishing the story. What additional meanings emerge?
2. What is the illness or disease from which Ivan suffers? Why does he suffer so acutely? Why is he treated so objectively by his doctors?
3. What are Ivan Ilych's values? Is something wrong with the way he has lived?
4. What is the significance of Gerasim?
5. Note the structure of the story: as the narrative progresses, why do the sections describe increasingly *smaller* periods of time in Ivan Ilych's life?

Amos Tutuola

(b. 1920)

Nigeria

When Amos Tutuola published *The Palm-Wine Drinkard* in 1952 (from which "The Complete Gentleman" has been extracted), the Welsh poet Dylan Thomas had this to say in his review of the book: "This is the brief, thronged, grisly and bewitching story, written in young English by a West African, about the journey of an expert and devoted palm-wine drinkard through a nightmare of indescribable adventures, all simply and carefully described, in the spirit-bristling bush." The "young" English that Thomas referred to was nothing more than Tutuola's use of West African English, still startling to readers who come across it for the first time. Tutuola's "bewitching story" (in the form of the drinkard's quest for his dead palm-wine tapster) leads his main character into many strange and unusual encounters and events, concluding with a visit to the Yoruba afterworld. Tutuola, a master storyteller, has incorporated innumerable traditional Yoruba oral stories into the framework of the Western written narrative. As you will see from the episode included here, the drinkard/narrator earns a boon for his labor, although the story is primarily the young girl's instead of his.

Amos Tutuola was born in Abeokuta, in Western Nigeria. He completed six years of primary school education, which were followed by further training as a blacksmith. All of his colorful narratives incorporate Yoruba folktales and, in many instances, tales that are familiar to the peoples of many different West African ethnic groups. Besides *The Palm-Wine Drinkard*, Tutuola has also published *My Life in the Bush of Ghosts* (1954), *Simbi and the Satyr of the Dark Jungle* (1956), *The Brave African Huntress* (1958), *The Feather Woman of the Jungle* (1962), *Ajaiyi and His Inherited Poverty* (1967), and *Pauper, Brawler and Slanderer* (1987).

The Complete Gentleman

THE DESCRIPTION OF THE CURIOUS CREATURE—

He was a beautiful "complete" gentleman, he dressed with the finest and most costly clothes, all the parts of his body were completed, he was a tall man but stout. As this gentleman came to the market on that day, if he had been an article or animal for sale, he would be sold at least for £2000 (two thousand pounds). As this complete gentleman came to the market on that day, and at the same time that this lady saw him in the market, she did nothing more than to ask him where he was living, but this fine gentleman did not answer her or approach her at all. But when she noticed that the fine or complete gentleman did not listen to her, she left her articles and began to watch the movements of the complete gentleman about in the market and left her articles unsold.

By and by the market closed for that day then the whole people in the market were returning to their destinations etc., and the complete gentleman was returning to his own too, but as this lady was following him about in the market all the while, she saw him when he was returning to his destination as others did, then she was following him (complete gentleman) to an unknown place. But as she was following the complete gentleman along the road, he was telling her to go back or not to follow him, but the lady did not listen to what he was telling her, and when the complete gentleman had tired of telling her not to follow him or to go back to her town, he left her to follow him.

DO NOT FOLLOW UNKNOWN MAN'S BEAUTY

But when they had travelled about twelve miles away from that market, they left the road on which they were travelling and started to travel inside an endless forest in which only the terrible creatures were living.

RETURN THE PARTS OF BODY TO THE OWNERS; OR HIRED PARTS OF THE COMPLETE GENTLEMAN'S BODY TO BE RETURNED

As they were travelling along in this endless forest then the complete gentleman in the market that the lady was following, began to return the hired parts of his body to the owners and he was paying them the rentage money. When he reached where he hired the left foot, he pulled it out, he gave it to the owner and paid him, and they kept going; when they reached the place where he hired the right foot, he pulled it out and gave it to the owner and paid for the rentage. Now both feet had returned to the owners, so he began to crawl along on the ground, by that time, that lady wanted to go back to her town or her father, but the terrible and curious creature or the complete gentleman did not allow her to return or go back to her town or her father again and the complete gentleman said thus: —"I had told you not to follow me before we branched into this endless forest which belongs to only terrible and curious creatures, but when I become a half-bodied incomplete gentleman you wanted to go back, now that cannot be done, you have failed. Even you have never seen anything yet, just follow me."

When they went furthermore, then they reached where he hired the belly, ribs, chest, etc., then he pulled them out and gave them to the owner and paid for the rentage.

Now to this gentleman or terrible creature remained only the head and both arms with neck, by that time he could not crawl as before but only went jumping on as a bullfrog and now this lady was soon faint for this fearful creature whom she was following. But when the lady saw every part of this complete gentleman in the market was shared or hired and he was returning them to the owners, then she began to try all her efforts to return to her father's town, but she was not allowed by this fearful creature at all.

When they reached where he hired both arms, he pulled them out and gave them to the owner, he paid for them; and they were still going on in this endless forest, they reached the place where he hired the neck, he pulled it out and gave it to the owner and paid for it as well.

A FULL-BODIED GENTLEMAN REDUCED TO HEAD

Now this complete gentleman was reduced to head and when they reached where he hired the skin and flesh which covered the head, he returned them, and paid to the owner, now the complete gentleman in the market reduced to a "SKULL" and this lady remained with only "Skull." When the lady saw that she remained with only Skull, she began to say that her father had been telling her to marry a man, but she did not listen to or believe him.

When the lady saw that the gentleman became a Skull, she began to faint, but the Skull told her if she would die she would die and she would follow him to his house. But by the time that he was saying so, he was humming with a terrible voice and also grew very wild and even if there was a person two miles away he would not have to listen before hearing him, so this lady began to run away in that forest for her life, but the Skull chased her and within a few yards, he caught her, because he was very clever and smart as he was only Skull and he could jump a mile to the second before coming down. He caught the lady in this way: so when the lady was running away for her life, he hastily ran to her front and stopped her as a log of wood.

By and by, this lady followed the Skull to his house, and the house was a hole which was under the ground. When they reached there both of them entered the hole. But there were only Skulls living in that hole. At the same time that they entered the hole, he tied a single cowrie on the neck of this lady with a kind of rope, after that, he gave her a large frog on which she sat as a stool, then he gave a whistle to a Skull of his kind to keep watch on this lady whenever she wanted to run away. Because the Skull knew already that the lady would attempt to run away from the hole. Then he went to the back yard to where his family were staying in the day time till night.

But one day, the lady attempted to escape from the hole, and at the same time that the Skull who was watching her whistled to the rest of the Skulls that were in the back yard, the whole of them rushed out to the place where the lady sat on the bullfrog, so they caught her, but as all of them were rushing out, they were rolling on the ground as if a thousand petrol drums were pushing along a hard road. After she was caught, then they brought her back to sit on the same frog as usual. If the Skull who was watching her fell asleep, and if the lady wanted to escape, the cowrie that was tied on her neck would raise up the alarm with a terrible noise, so that the Skull who was watching her would wake up at once and then the rest of the Skull's family would rush out from the back in thousands to the lady and ask her what she wanted to do with a curious and terrible voice.

But the lady could not talk at all, because as the cowrie had been tied on her neck, she became dumb at the same moment.

THE FATHER OF GODS SHOULD FIND OUT WHEREABOUTS THE DAUGHTER OF THE HEAD OF THE TOWN WAS

Now as the father of the lady first asked for my name and I told him that my name was "Father of gods who could do anything in this world," then he told me that if I could find out where his daughter was and bring her to him, then he would tell me where my palm-wine tapster was. But when he said so, I was jumping up with gladness that he should promise me that he would tell me where my tapster was. I agreed to what he said; the father and parent of this lady never knew whereabouts their daughter was, but they had information that the lady followed a complete gentleman in the market. As I was the "Father of gods who could do anything in this world," when it was at night I sacrificed to my juju[1] with a goat.

And when it was early in the morning, I sent for forty kegs of palm-wine. After I had drunk it all, I started to investigate whereabouts was the lady. As it was the market-day, I started the investigation from the market. But as I was a juju-man, I knew all the kinds of people in that market. When it was exactly 9 o'clock A.M., the very complete gentleman whom the lady followed came to the market again, and at the same time that I saw him, I knew that he was a curious and terrible creature.

THE LADY WAS NOT TO BE BLAMED FOR FOLLOWING THE SKULL AS A COMPLETE GENTLEMAN

I could not blame the lady for following the Skull as a complete gentleman to his house at all. Because if I were a lady, no doubt I would follow him to wherever he would go, and still as I was a man I would jealous him more than that, because if this gentleman went to the battlefield, surely, enemy would not kill him or capture him and if bombers saw him in a town which was to be bombed, they would not throw bombs on his presence, and if they did throw it, the bomb itself would not explode until this gentleman would leave that town, because of his beauty. At the same time that I saw this gentleman in the market on that day, what I was doing was only to follow him about in the market. After I looked at him for so many hours, then I ran to a corner of the market and I cried for a few minutes because I thought within myself why was I not created that he was only a Skull, then I thanked God that He had created me without beauty, so I went back to him in the market, but I was still attracted by his beauty. So when the market closed for that day, and when everybody was returning to his or her destination, this gentleman was returning to his own too and I followed him to know where he was living.

INVESTIGATION TO THE SKULL'S FAMILY'S HOUSE

When I travelled with him a distance of about twelve miles away to that market, the gentleman left the really road on which we were travelling and branched into an endless forest and I was following him, but as I did not want him to see that I was following him, then I used one of my juju which changed me into a lizard and followed him. But after I had travelled with him a distance of about twenty-five

[1]*juju* witchcraft, but used more generally as "magic" here, that is, with no negative connotation

miles away in this endless forest, he began to pull out all the parts of his body and return them to the owners, and paid them.

After I had travelled with him for another fifty miles in this forest, then he reached his house and entered it, but I entered it also with him, as I was a lizard. The first thing that he did when he entered the hole (house) he went straight to the place where the lady was, and I saw the lady sat on a bullfrog with a single cowrie tied on her neck and a Skull who was watching her stood behind her. After he (gentleman) had seen that the lady was there, he went to the back yard where all his family were working.

THE INVESTIGATOR'S WONDERFUL WORK IN THE SKULL'S FAMILY'S HOUSE

When I saw this lady and when the Skull who brought her to that hole or whom I followed from the market to that hole went to the back yard, then I changed myself to a man as before, then I talked to the lady but she could not answer me at all, she only showed that she was in a serious condition. The Skull who was guarding her with a whistle fell asleep at that time.

To my surprise, when I helped the lady to stand up from the frog on which she sat, the cowrie that was tied on her neck made a curious noise at once, and when the Skull who was watching her heard the noise, he woke up and blew the whistle to the rest, then the whole of them rushed to the place and surrounded the lady and me, but at the same time that they saw me there, one of them ran to a pit which was not so far from that spot, the pit was filled with cowries. He picked one cowrie out of the pit, after that he was running towards me, and the whole crowd wanted to tie the cowrie on my neck too. But before they could do that, I had changed myself into air, they could not trace me out again, but I was looking at them. I believed that the cowries in that pit were their power and to reduce the power of any human being whenever tied on his or her neck and also to make a person dumb.

Over one hour after I had dissolved into air, these Skulls went back to the back yard, but there remained the Skull who was watching her.

After they had returned to the back yard, I changed to a man as usual, then I took the lady from the frog, but at the same time that I touched her, the cowrie which was tied on her neck began to shout; even if a person was four miles away he would not have to listen before hearing, but immediately the Skull who was watching her heard the noise and saw me when I took her from that frog, he blew the whistle to the rest of them who were in the back yard.

Immediately the whole Skull family heard the whistle when blew to them, they were rushing out to the place and before they could reach there, I had left their hole for the forest, but before I could travel about one hundred yards in the forest, they had rushed out from their hole to inside the forest and I was still running away with the lady. As these Skulls were chasing me about in the forest, they were rolling on the ground like large stones and also humming with terrible noise, but when I saw that they had nearly caught me or if I continued to run away like that, no doubt, they would catch me sooner, then I changed the lady to a kitten and put her inside my pocket and changed myself to a very small bird which I could describe as a "sparrow" in English language.

After that I flew away, but as I was flying in the sky, the cowrie which was tied on that lady's neck was still making a noise and I tried all my best to stop the noise, but all were in vain. When I reached home with the lady, I changed her to a lady as she was before and also myself changed to man as well. When her father saw that I brought his daughter back home, he was exceedingly glad and said thus: — "You are the 'Father of gods' as you had told me before."

But as the lady was now at home, the cowrie on her neck did not stop making a terrible noise once, and she could not talk to anybody; she showed only that she was very glad she was at home. Now I had brought the lady but she could not talk, eat or loose away the cowrie on her neck, because the terrible noise of the cowrie did not allow anybody to rest or sleep at all.

THERE REMAIN GREATER TASKS AHEAD

Now I began to cut the rope of the cowrie from her neck and to make her talk and eat, but all my efforts were in vain. At last I tried my best to cut off the rope of the cowrie; it only stopped the noise, but I was unable to loose it away from her neck.

When her father saw all my trouble, he thanked me greatly and repeated again that as I called myself "Father of gods who could do anything in this world" I ought to do the rest of the work. But when he said so, I was very ashamed and thought within myself that if I return to the Skulls' hole or house, they might kill me and the forest was very dangerous travel always, again I could not go directly to the Skulls in their hole and ask them how to loose away the cowrie which was tied on the lady's neck and to make her talk and eat.

BACK TO THE SKULL'S FAMILY'S HOUSE

On the third day after I had brought the lady to her father's house, I returned to the endless forest for further investigation. When there remained about one mile to reach the hole of these Skulls, there I saw the very Skull who the lady had followed from the market as a complete gentleman to the hole of Skull's family's house, and at the same time that I saw him like that, I changed into a lizard and climbed a tree which was near him.

He stood before two plants, then he cut a single opposite leaf from the opposite plant; he held the leaf with his right hand and he was saying thus: — "As this lady was taken from me, if this opposite leaf is not given her to eat, she will not talk forever," after that he threw the leaf down on the ground. Then he cut another single compound leaf with his left hand and said that if this single compound is not given to this lady, to eat, the cowrie on her neck could not be loosened away forever and it would be making a terrible noise forever.

After he said so, he threw the leaf down at the same spot, then he jumped away. So after he had jumped very far away (luckily, I was there when he was doing all these things, and I saw the place that he threw both leaves separately), then I changed myself to a man as before, I went to the place that he threw both leaves, then I picked them up and I went home at once.

But at the same time that I reached home, I cooked both leaves separately and gave her to eat; to my surprise the lady began to talk at once. After that, I gave her the compound leaf to eat for the second time and immediately she ate that too, the cowrie which was tied on her neck by the Skull, loosened away by itself, but it disappeared at the same time. So when the father and mother saw the wonderful work which I had done for them, they brought fifty kegs of palm-wine for me, they gave me the lady as wife and two rooms in that house in which to live with them.

So, I saved the lady from the complete gentleman in the market who was afterwards reduced to a Skull and the lady became my wife since that day. This was how I got a wife.

[1952]

QUESTIONS

1. What specific aspects of oral narrative can be identified in Tutuola's story?
2. When Amos Tutuola published *The Palm-Wine Drinkard* in 1952, Walt Disney Productions purchased the film rights to the book. What do you think would happen to "The Complete Gentleman" if it were filmed by Disney?
3. Compare "The Complete Gentleman" to the opening of Ngugi wa Thiongo's "A Meeting in the Dark," included in this volume. What connections can be drawn between the two tales?
4. Although the story is African, does it suggest a universal dimension to the age-old theme of appearance versus reality?

Mark Twain

(1835–1910)

United States

As scholars have noted for years, the underside of Mark Twain's humorous writing is almost always darker, bleaker than its surface reality. In Huck Finn's celebrated journey down the Mississippi River with Jim, the Duke, and the King, there is hardly an on-shore incident (in the small-town communities Twain describes so brilliantly) that doesn't smack of mendacity, gullibility, racism—even stupidity—often on the part of the inhabitants of an entire village. Even the tall tale Twain relates in "The Celebrated Jumping Frog of Calavaras County" clearly implies that for someone to win, someone else may get tricked—taken advantage of. It doesn't take long for the astute reader to understand that Twain's general picture of humankind is pessimistic at best and that humor is his vehicle for getting at something much more serious.

By the time Twain wrote "Luck" (1891), his own life was marred by a series of disappointments: his marriage was deeply troubled, his greatest books were already behind him (and had not always been as successful as he had hoped), and his economic ventures were about to close in on him. The rest of his life would be a series of ups and downs, of dramatic reversals of fortune. As you read Twain's "Luck," try to determine where the story shifts—where the innocent goodwill of Lieutenant General Lord Arthur Scoresby begins to show its true colors.

◆ Luck ◆

[Note—This is not a fancy sketch. I got it from a clergyman who was an instructor at Woolwich forty years ago, and who vouched for its truth.—M. T.]

It was at a banquet in London in honor of one of the two or three conspicuously illustrious English military names of this generation. For reasons which will presently appear, I will withhold his real name and titles, and call him Lieutenant General Lord Arthur Scoresby, V. C., K. C. B., etc., etc., etc. What a fascination there is in a renowned name! There sat the man, in actual flesh, whom I had heard of so many thousands of times since that day, thirty years before, when his name shot suddenly to the zenith from a Crimean battlefield, to remain forever celebrated. It was food and drink to me to look, and look, and look at that demigod; scanning, searching, noting: the quietness, the reserve, the noble gravity of his countenance; the simple honesty that expressed itself all over him; the sweet unconsciousness of his greatness—unconsciousness of the hundreds of admiring eyes fastened upon him, unconsciousness of the deep, loving, sincere worship welling out of the breasts of those people and flowing toward him.

The clergyman at my left was an old acquaintance of mine—clergyman now, but had spent the first half of his life in the camp and field, and as an instructor in the military school at Woolwich. Just at the moment I have been talking about, a veiled and singular light glimmered in his eyes, and he leaned down and muttered confidentially to me—indicating the hero of the banquet with a gesture:

"Privately—he's an absolute fool."

This verdict was a great surprise to me. If its subject had been Napoleon, or Socrates, or Solomon, my astonishment could not have been greater. Two things I was well aware of: that the Reverend was a man of strict veracity, and that his judgment of men was good. Therefore I knew, beyond doubt or question, that the world was mistaken about this hero: he *was* a fool. So I meant to find out, at a convenient moment, how the Reverend, all solitary and alone, had discovered the secret.

Some days later the opportunity came, and this is what the Reverend told me.

About forty years ago I was an instructor in the military academy at Woolwich. I was present in one of the sections when young Scoresby underwent his preliminary examination. I was touched to the quick with pity; for the rest of the class answered up brightly and handsomely, while he—why, dear me, he didn't know *anything*, so to speak. He was evidently good, and sweet, and lovable, and guileless; and so it was exceedingly painful to see him stand there, as serene as a graven image, and deliver himself of answers which were veritably miraculous for stupidity and ignorance. All the compassion in me was aroused in his behalf. I said to myself, when he comes to be examined again, he will be flung over, of course; so it will be simply a harmless act of charity to ease his fall as much as I can. I took him aside, and found that he knew a little of Caesar's history; and as he didn't know anything else, I went to work and drilled him like a galley slave on a certain line of stock questions concerning Caesar which I knew would be used. If you'll believe me, he went through with flying colors on examination day! He went through on that purely superficial "cram," and got compliments too, while others, who knew a thousand times more than he, got plucked. By some strangely lucky accident—an accident not likely to happen twice in a century—he was asked no question outside of the narrow limits of his drill.

It was stupefying. Well, all through his course I stood by him, with something of the sentiment which a mother feels for a crippled child; and he always saved himself—just by miracle, apparently.

Now of course the thing that would expose him and kill him at last was mathematics. I resolved to make his death as easy as I could; so I drilled him and crammed him, and crammed him and drilled him, just on the line of questions which the examiners would be most likely to use, and then launching him on his fate. Well, sir, try to conceive of the result: to my consternation, he took the first prize! And with it he got a perfect ovation in the way of compliments.

Sleep? There was no more sleep for me for a week. My conscience tortured me day and night. What I had done I had done purely through charity, and only to ease the poor youth's fall—I never had dreamed of any such preposterous result as the thing that had happened. I felt as guilty and miserable as the creator of Frankenstein. Here was a woodenhead whom I had put in the way of glittering promotions and prodigious responsibilities, and but one thing could happen: he and his responsibilities would all go to ruin together at the first opportunity.

The Crimean war had just broken out. Of course there had to be a war, I said to myself: we couldn't have peace and give this donkey a chance to die before he is found out. I waited for the earthquake. It came. And it made me reel when it did come. He was actually gazetted to a captaincy in a marching regiment! Better men grow old and gray in the service before they climb to a sublimity like that. And who could ever have foreseen that they would go and put such a load of responsibility on such green and inadequate shoulders? I could just barely have stood it if they had made him a cornet; but a captain—think of it! I thought my hair would turn white.

Consider what I did—I who so loved repose and inaction. I said to myself, I am responsible to the country for this, and I must go along with him and protect the country against him as far as I can. So I took my poor little capital that I had saved up through years of work and grinding economy, and went with a sigh and bought a cornetcy[1] in his regiment, and away we went to the field.

And there—oh dear, it was awful. Blunders? Why, he never did anything *but* blunder. But, you see, nobody was in the fellow's secret—everybody had him focused wrong, and necessarily misinterpreted his performance every time—consequently they took his idiotic blunders for inspirations of genius; they did, honestly! His mildest blunders were enough to make a man in his right mind cry; and they did make me cry—and rage and rave too, privately. And the thing that kept me always in a sweat of apprehension was the fact that every fresh blunder he made increased the luster of his reputation! I kept saying to myself, he'll get so high, that when discovery does finally come, it will be like the sun falling out of the sky.

He went right along up, from grade to grade, over the dead bodies of his superiors, until at last, in the hottest moment of the battle of —— down went our colonel, and my heart jumped into my mouth, for Scoresby was next in rank! Now for it, said I; we'll all land in Sheol in ten minutes, sure.

The battle was awfully hot; the allies were steadily giving way all over the field. Our regiment occupied a position that was vital; a blunder now must be destruction. At this crucial moment, what does this immortal fool do but detach the regiment from its place and order a charge over a neighboring hill where there wasn't a suggestion of an enemy! "There you go!" I said to myself; "this *is* the end at last."

And away we did go, and were over the shoulder of the hill before the insane movement could be discovered and stopped. And what did we find? An entire and unsuspected Russian army in reserve! And what happened? We were eaten up? That is necessarily what would have happened in ninety-nine cases out of a hundred. But no, those Russians argued that no single regiment would come browsing around there at such a time. It must be the entire English army, and that the sly Russian game was detected and blocked; so they turned tail, and away they went, pell-mell, over the hill and down into the field, in wild confusion, and we after them; they themselves broke the solid Russian center in the field, and tore through, and in no time there was the most tremendous rout you ever saw, and the defeat of the allies was turned into a sweeping and splendid victory! Marshal Canrobert looked on, dizzy with astonishment, admiration, and delight; and sent right off for Scoresby, and hugged him, and decorated him on the field, in presence of all the armies!

[1]*cornetcy* the fifth commissioned officer, who carried the colors, in a troop of cavalry (a position or rank of a cornet)

And what was Scoresby's blunder that time? Merely the mistaking his right hand for his left—that was all. An order had come to him to fall back and support our right; and instead, he fell *forward* and went over the hill to the left. But the name he won that day as a marvelous military genius filled the world with his glory, and that glory will never fade while history books last.

He is just as good and sweet and lovable and unpretending as a man can be, but he doesn't know enough to come in when it rains. Now that is absolutely true. He is the supremest ass in the universe; and until half an hour ago nobody knew it but himself and me. He has been pursued, day by day and year by year, by a most phenomenal and astonishing luckiness. He has been a shining soldier in all our wars for a generation; he has littered his whole military life with blunders, and yet has never committed one that didn't make him a knight or a baronet or a lord or something. Look at his breast; why, he is just clothed in domestic and foreign decorations. Well, sir, every one of them is the record of some shouting stupidity or other; and taken together, they are proof that the very best thing in all this world that can befall a man is to be born lucky. I say again, as I said at the banquet, Scoresby's an absolute fool.

[1891]

QUESTIONS

1. Wherein does the conflict reside in this story?
2. What is the significance of the story-within-a-story format?
3. If Twain were writing today, would the story concern a military figure or a person of some other profession?
4. What does the story suggest about the relationship between talent, luck, and success?

John Updike

(b. 1932)

United States

One of John Updike's ambitions in college was to be a cartoonist and graphic artist. After graduating from Harvard with a degree in English instead, he and his wife went to Oxford on a fellowship, where they both pursued further study in fine arts. Returning to the States and exchanging the precision of the visual sketch for equally precise verbal sketches, Updike began writing short stories and soon established his reputation through frequent publication in *The New Yorker*. Updike drew on his own childhood in rural eastern Pennsylvania and his later experience in urban and suburban New York and New England to chronicle cultural changes in a cross section of American society, as demonstrated in marriage, family life, sexuality, and religion. He has described his subject as "the American Protestant small town middle class. I like middles. It is in middles that extremes clash, where ambiguity restlessly rules. . . ."

Occasionally invoking myth and philosophy as the backdrop for his realistic fictional documentations of a sterile secular society, Updike has achieved the position of a contemporary moralist, exploring an impressive range of American preoccupations and anxieties. Harry "Rabbit" Angstrom, the protagonist of the "Rabbit" novels—*Rabbit Run* (1960), *Rabbit Redux* (1971), *Rabbit Is Rich* (1981), and *Rabbit at Rest* (1990)—is an unforgettable Updike character; his life from adolescence through marriage, fatherhood, middle age, and death forms the substance of this multidecade chronicle of an ordinary man moving through the vicissitudes of American life, driven by his pursuit of an uncertain American dream. Among Updike's more than a dozen novels are *The Centaur* (1963), *Couples* (1968), and *The Coup* (1978). His short stories are collected in *Pigeon Feathers* (1962), *Museums and Women* (1972), and *Problems and Other Stories* (1981). The recipient of numerous awards for his fiction, Updike is also an accomplished poet and essayist.

In a *Paris Review* interview, Updike explained that he regards his books "not as sermons or directives in a war of ideas but as objects, with different shapes and textures and the mysteriousness of anything that exists. My first thought about art, as a child, was that the artist brings something into the world that didn't exist before, and that he does it without destroying something else. A kind of refutation of the conservation of matter. That still seems to me its central magic, its core of joy."

Through a lush and polished prose style perfectly suited to its subjects, Updike explores his characters' moments of experience and discovery with unerring accuracy.

• A & P •

In walks these three girls in nothing but bathing suits. I'm in the third checkout slot, with my back to the door, so I don't see them until they're over by the bread. The one that caught my eye first was the one in the plaid green two-piece. She was a chunky kid, with a good tan and a sweet broad soft-looking can with those two crescents of white just under it, where the sun never seems to hit, at the top of the backs of her legs. I stood there with my hand on a box of HiHo crackers trying to remember if I rang it up or not. I ring it up again and the customer starts giving me hell. She's one of these cash-register-watchers, a witch about fifty with rouge on her cheekbones and no eyebrows, and I know it made her day to trip me up. She'd been watching cash registers for fifty years and probably never seen a mistake before.

By the time I got her feathers smoothed and her goodies into a bag — she gives me a little snort in passing, if she'd been born at the right time they would have burned her over in Salem — by the time I get her on her way the girls had circled around the bread and were coming back, without a pushcart, back my way along the counters, in the aisle between the checkouts and the Special bins. They didn't even have shoes on. There was this chunky one, with the two-piece — it was bright green and the seams on the bra were still sharp and her belly was still pretty pale so I guessed she just got it (the suit) — there was this one, with one of those chubby berry-faces, the lips all bunched together under her nose, this one, and a tall one, with black hair that hadn't quite frizzed right, and one of these sunburns right across under the eyes, and a chin that was too long — you know, the kind of girl other girls think is very "striking" and "attractive" but never quite makes it, as they very well know, which is why they like her so much — and then the third one, that wasn't quite so tall. She was the queen. She kind of led them, the other two peeking around and making their shoulders round. She didn't look around, not this queen, she just walked straight on slowly, on these long white prima-donna legs. She came down a little hard on her heels, as if she didn't walk in her bare feet that much, putting down her heels and then letting the weight move along to her toes as if she was testing the floor with every step, putting a little deliberate extra action into it. You never know for sure how girls' minds work (do you really think it's a mind in there or just a little buzz like a bee in a glass jar?) but you got the idea she had talked the other two into coming in here with her, and now she was showing them how to do it, walk slow and hold yourself straight.

She had on a kind of dirty-pink — beige maybe, I don't know — bathing suit with a little nubble all over it, and what got me, the straps were down. They were off her shoulders looped loose around the cool tops of her arms, and I guess as a result the suit had slipped a little on her, so all around the top of the cloth there was this shining rim. If it hadn't been there you wouldn't have known there could have been anything whiter than those shoulders. With the straps pushed off, there was nothing between the top of the suit and the top of her head except just *her*, this clean bare plane of the top of her chest down from the shoulder bones like a dented sheet of metal tilted in the light. I mean, it was more than pretty.

She had sort of oaky hair that the sun and salt had bleached, done up in a bun that was unravelling, and a kind of prim face. Walking into the A & P with your straps down, I suppose it's the only kind of face you *can* have. She held her head so high her neck, coming up out of those white shoulders, looked kind of stretched, but I didn't mind. The longer her neck was, the more of her there was.

She must have felt in the corner of her eye me and over my shoulder Stokesie in the second slot watching, but she didn't tip. Not this queen. She kept her eyes moving across the racks, and stopped, and turned so slow it made my stomach rub the inside of my apron, and buzzed to the other two, who kind of huddled against her for relief, and then they all three of them went up the cat-and-dog-food-breakfast-cereal-macaroni-rice-raisins-seasonings-spreads-spaghetti-soft-drinks-crackers-and-cookies aisle. From the third slot I look straight up this aisle to the meat counter, and I watched them all the way. The fat one with the tan sort of fumbled with the cookies, but on second thought she put the package back. The sheep pushing their carts down the aisle — the girls were walking against the usual traffic (not that we have one-way signs or anything) — were pretty hilarious. You could see them, when Queenie's white shoulders dawned on them, kind of jerk, or hop, or hiccup, but their eyes snapped back to their own baskets and on they pushed. I bet you could set off dynamite in an A & P and the people would by and large keep reaching and checking oatmeal off their lists and muttering "Let me see, there was a third thing, began with A, asparagus, no, ah, yes, applesauce!" or whatever it is they do mutter. But there was no doubt, this jiggled them. A few houseslaves in pin curlers even looked around after pushing their carts past to make sure what they had seen was correct.

You know, it's one thing to have a girl in a bathing suit down on the beach, where what with the glare nobody can look at each other much anyway, and another thing in the cool of the A & P, under the fluorescent lights, against all those stacked packages, with her feet paddling along naked over our checkboard green-and-cream rubber-tile floor.

"Oh Daddy," Stokesie said beside me. "I feel so faint."

"Darling," I said. "Hold me tight." Stokesie's married, with two babies chalked up on his fuselage already, but as far as I can tell that's the only difference. He's twenty-two, and I was nineteen this April.

"Is it done?" he asks, the responsible married man finding his voice. I forgot to say he thinks he's going to be manager some sunny day, maybe in 1990 when it's called the Great Alexandrov and Petrooshki Tea Company or something.

What he meant was, our town is five miles from a beach, with a big summer colony out on the Point, but we're right in the middle of town, and the women generally put on a shirt or shorts or something before they get out of the car into the street. And anyway these are usually women with six children and varicose veins mapping their legs and nobody, including them, could care less. As I say, we're right in the middle of town, and if you stand at our front doors you can see two banks and the Congregational church and the newspaper store and three real-estate offices and about twenty-seven old freeloaders tearing up Central Street because the sewer broke again. It's not as if we're on the Cape; we're north of Boston and there's people in this town haven't seen the ocean for twenty years.

The girls had reached the meat counter and were asking McMahon something. He pointed, they pointed, and they shuffled out of sight behind a pyramid of Diet Delight peaches. All that was left for us to see was old McMahon patting his mouth and looking after them sizing up their joints. Poor kids, I began to feel sorry for them, they couldn't help it.

Now here comes the sad part of the story, at least my family says it's sad, but I don't think it's so sad myself. The store's pretty empty, it being Thursday afternoon, so there was nothing much to do except lean on the register and wait for the girls to show up again. The whole store was like a pinball machine and I didn't know which tunnel they'd come out of. After a while they come around out of the far aisle, around the light bulbs, records at discount of the Caribbean Six or Tony Martin Sings or some such gunk you wonder they waste the wax on, sixpacks of candy bars, and plastic toys done up in cellophane that fall apart when a kid looks at them anyway. Around they come, Queenie still leading the way, and holding a little gray jar in her hand. Slots Three through Seven are unmanned and I could see her wondering between Stokes and me, but Stokesie with his usual luck draws an old party in baggy gray pants who stumbles up with four giant cans of pineapple juice (what do these bums *do* with all that pineapple juice? I've often asked myself) so the girls come to me. Queenie puts down the jar and I take it into my fingers icy cold. Kingfish Fancy Herring Snacks in Pure Sour Cream: 49¢. Now her hands are empty, not a ring or a bracelet, bare as God made them, and I wonder where the money's coming from. Still with that prim look she lifts a folded dollar bill out of the hollow at the center of her nubbled pink top. The jar went heavy in my hand. Really, I thought that was so cute.

Then everybody's luck begins to run out. Lengel comes in from haggling with a truck full of cabbages on the lot and is about to scuttle into that door marked MANAGER behind which he hides all day when the girls touch his eye. Lengel's pretty dreary, teaches Sunday school and the rest, but he doesn't miss that much. He comes over and says, "Girls, this isn't the beach."

Queenie blushes, though maybe it's just a brush of sunburn I was noticing for the first time, now that she was so close. "My mother asked me to pick up a jar of herring snacks." Her voice kind of startled me, the way voices do when you see the people first, coming out so flat and dumb yet kind of tony, too, the way it ticked over "pick up" and "snacks." All of a sudden I slid right down her voice into her living room. Her father and the other men were standing around in ice-cream coats and bow ties and the women were in sandals picking up herring snacks on toothpicks off a big glass plate and they were all holding drinks the color of water with olives and sprigs of mint in them. When my parents have somebody over they get lemonade and if it's a real racy affair Schlitz in tall glasses with "They'll Do It Every Time" cartoons stencilled on.

"That's all right," Lengel said. "But this isn't the beach." His repeating this struck me as funny, as if it had just occurred to him, and he had been thinking all these years the A & P was a great big sand dune and he was the head lifeguard. He didn't like my smiling—as I say he doesn't miss much—but he concentrates on giving the girls that sad Sunday-school-superintendent stare.

Queenie's blush is no sunburn now, and the plump one in plaid, that I liked better from the back—a really sweet can—pipes up, "We weren't doing any shopping. We just came in for the one thing."

"That makes no difference," Lengel tells her, and I could see from the way his eyes went that he hadn't noticed she was wearing a two-piece before. "We want you decently dressed when you come in here."

"We *are* decent," Queenie says suddenly, her lower lip pushing, getting sore now that she remembers her place, a place from which the crowd that runs the A & P must look pretty crummy. Fancy Herring Snacks flashed in her very blue eyes.

"Girls, I don't want to argue with you. After this come in here with your shoulders covered. It's our policy." He turns his back. That's policy for you. Policy is what the kingpins want. What the others want is juvenile delinquency.

All this while, the customers had been showing up with their carts but, you know, sheep, seeing a scene, they had all bunched up on Stokesie, who shook open a paper bag as gently as peeling a peach, not wanting to miss a word. I could feel in the silence everybody getting nervous, most of all Lengel, who asks me, "Sammy, have you rung up their purchase?"

I thought and said "No" but it wasn't about that I was thinking. I go through the punches, 4, 9, GROC, TOT—it's more complicated than you think, and after you do it often enough, it begins to make a little song, that you hear words to, in my case "Hello (*bing*) there, you (*gung*) hap-py *pee*-pul (*splat*)!"—the *splat* being the drawer flying out. I uncreased the bill, tenderly as you may imagine, it just having come from between the two smoothest scoops of vanilla I had ever known were there, and pass a half and a penny into her narrow pink palm, and nestle the herrings in a bag and twist its neck and hand it over, all the time thinking.

The girls, and who'd blame them, are in a hurry to get out, so I say "I quit" to Lengel enough for them to hear, hoping they'll stop and watch me, their unsuspected hero. They keep right on going, into the electric eye; the door flies open and they flicker across the lot to their car, Queenie and Plaid and Big Tall Goony-Goony (not that as raw material she was so bad), leaving me with Lengel and a kink in his eyebrow.

"Did you say something, Sammy?"

"I said I quit."

"I thought you did."

"You didn't have to embarrass them."

"It was they who were embarrassing us."

I started to say something that came out "Fiddle-de-doo." It's a saying of my grandmother's, and I know she would have been pleased.

"I don't think you know what you're saying," Lengel said.

"I know you don't," I said. "But I do." I pull the bow at the back of my apron and start shrugging it off my shoulders. A couple customers that had been heading for my slot begin to knock against each other, like scared pigs in a chute.

Lengel sighs and begins to look very patient and old and gray. He's been a friend of my parents for years. "Sammy, you don't want to do this to your Mom and Dad," he tells me. It's true, I don't. But it seems to me that once you begin a gesture it's fatal not to go through with it. I fold the apron, "Sammy" stitched in red on the pocket, and put it on the counter, and drop the bow tie on top of it. The bow tie is theirs, if you've ever wondered. "You'll feel this for the rest of your life," Lengel says, and I know that's true, too, but remembering how he made that pretty girl blush makes me so scrunchy inside I punch the No Sale tab and the machine whirs "pee-pul" and the drawer splats out. One advantage to this scene taking place in summer, I can follow this up with a clean exit, there's no fumbling around getting your coat and galoshes, I just saunter into the electric eye in my white shirt that my mother ironed the night before, and the door heaves itself open, and outside the sunshine is skating around on the asphalt.

I look around for my girls, but they're gone, of course. There wasn't anybody but some young married screaming with her children about some candy they didn't get by the door of a powder-blue Falcon station wagon. Looking back in the big windows, over the bags of peat moss and aluminum lawn furniture stacked on the pavement, I could see Lengel in my place in the slot, checking the sheep through. His face was dark gray and his back stiff, as if he'd just had an injection of iron, and my stomach kind of fell as I felt how hard the world was going to be to me hereafter.

[1961]

QUESTIONS

1. What is the dramatic conflict of the story? What is its climax?
2. Why, exactly, does Sammy quit his job so suddenly? What does he gain — and lose — in doing so? Sammy sees his decision as heroic; do the girls? Do you?
3. What are Sammy's values? How are they revealed during the narrative? How does his first-person perspective shape the story?
4. How does Updike's style contribute to the effectiveness of the story? What elements make it humorous?
5. Consider whether male and female readers might react differently to this story. What elements might influence different responses according to gender?

Luisa Valenzuela

(b. 1938)

Argentina

Luisa Valenzuela was born in Buenos Aires, the daughter of a physician father and a mother who was a popular Argentinian writer, Luisa Mercedes Levinson. Valenzuela's own literary talent developed early; by the age of 15, she had published her first story. While studying at the University of Buenos Aires, she worked with Jorge Luis Borges at the National Library. When she was 20 she went to Paris to write as a foreign correspondent for Argentinian newspapers; she also wrote for French television and radio.

During her three years in France, Valenzuela met a number of writers and critics who were experimenting with narrative forms and philosophical ideas about language and meaning, ideas that strongly influenced her own writing. In 1966 she published her first book, *Clara: Thirteen Short Stories and a Novel*, in which she explores the themes of violence, politics, and female oppression in Argentina. Several of her later works have been translated into English, including three collections of stories: *Strange Things Happen Here* (1975), *Other Weapons* (1985), and *Open Door* (1988). The novel *The Lizard's Tale* (1983), the fictionalized biography of a despot who is also a sorcerer, could not have been published in her own country, according to Valenzuela, because of its "mythicized and damning version of recent Argentine history."

In her early stories, Valenzuela experimented with the tradition of Latin American writing called magical realism, in which fantastic events occur within real social settings. More recently she has turned away from that narrative mode, remarking, "Magic realism was a beautiful resting place, but things do go forward." Incorporating public political events, Valenzuela examines the intersecting themes of political oppression, cultural repression, and violence in Latin America, especially as those forces affect the lives of women in their more private psychological and erotic experiences.

Valenzuela left Argentina when the country became a military dictatorship following the death of Juan Perón in 1974. During her time in the United States, she has been supported by a Guggenheim grant as well as by a Fulbright fellowship to the International Writers' Program at the University of Iowa; she has been distinguished writer-in-residence at Columbia University and elsewhere.

In "Strange Things Happen Here," Valenzuela captures the quality of the surreal that invades — and challenges — our concept of ordinary reality.

Strange Things Happen Here

In the café on the corner — every self-respecting café is on a corner, every meeting place is a crossing of two paths (two lives) — Mario and Pedro each order a cup of black coffee and put lots of sugar in it because sugar is free and provides nourishment. Mario and Pedro have been flat broke for some time — not that they're complaining, but it's time they got lucky for a change — and suddenly they see the abandoned brief case, and just by looking at each other they tell themselves that maybe the moment has come. Right here, boys, in the café on the corner, no different from a hundred others.

The brief case is there all by itself on a chair leaning against the table, and nobody has come back to look for it. The neighborhood boys come and go, they exchange remarks that Mario and Pedro don't listen to. There are more of them every day and they have a funny accent, they're from the interior. I wonder what they're doing here, why they've come. Mario and Pedro wonder if someone is going to sit down at the table in the back, move the chair, and find the brief case that they almost love, almost caress and smell and lick and kiss. A man finally comes and sits down at the table alone (and to think that the brief case is probably full of money, and that guy's going to latch on to it for the modest price of a vermouth with lemon, which is what he finally asks for after taking a little while to make up his mind). They bring him the vermouth, along with a whole bunch of appetizers. Which olive, which little piece of cheese will he be raising to his mouth when he spots the brief case on the chair next to his? Pedro and Mario don't even want to think about it and yet it's all they *can* think about. When all is said and done the guy has as much or as little right to the brief case as they do. When all is said and done it's only a question of chance, a table more carefully chosen, and that's it. The guy sips his drink indifferently, swallowing one appetizer or another; the two of them can't even order another coffee because they're out of dough as might happen to you or to me, more perhaps to me than to you, but that's beside the point now that Pedro and Mario are being tyrannized by a guy who's picking bits of salami out of his teeth with his fingernail as he finishes his drink, not seeing a thing and not listening to what the boys are saying. You see them on street corners. Even Elba said something about it the other day, can you imagine, she's so nearsighted. Just like science fiction, they've landed from another planet even though they look like guys from the interior but with their hair so well combed, they're nice and neat I tell you, and I asked one of them what time it was but didn't get anywhere — they don't have watches of course. Why would they want a watch anyway, you might ask, if they live in a different time from us? I saw them, too. They come out from under the pavement in the streets and that's where they still are and who knows what they're looking for, though we do know that they leave holes in the streets, those enormous potholes they come out of that can't ever be filled in.

The guy with the vermouth isn't listening to them, and neither are Mario and Pedro, who are worrying about a brief case forgotten on a chair that's bound to contain something of value because otherwise it wouldn't have been forgotten just so they could get it, just the two of them, not the guy with the vermouth. He's finished his drink, picked his teeth, left some of the appetizers almost untouched. He gets up from the table, pays, the waiter takes everything off table, puts tip in pocket, wipes table with damp cloth, goes off and, man, the time has come because there's lots going on at the other end of the café and there's nobody at this end and Mario and Pedro know it's now or never.

Mario comes out first with the brief case under his arm and that's why he's the first to see a man's jacket lying on top of a car next to the sidewalk. That is to say, the car is next to the sidewalk, so the jacket lying on the roof is, too. A splendid jacket, of stupendous quality. Pedro sees it too, his legs shake because it's too much of a coincidence, he could sure use a new jacket, especially one with the pockets stuffed with dough. Mario can't work himself up to grabbing it. Pedro can, though with a certain remorse, which gets worse and practically explodes when he sees two cops coming toward them to . . .

"We found this car on a jacket. This jacket on a car. We don't know what to do with it. The jacket, I mean."

"Well, leave it where you found it then. Don't bother us with things like that, we have more important business to attend to."

More crucial business. Like the persecution of man by man if you'll allow me to use that euphemism. And so the famous jacket is now in Pedro's trembling hands which have picked it up with much affection. He sure needed a jacket like this one, a sports jacket, well lined, lined with cash not silk who cares about silk? With the booty in hand they head back home. They don't have the nerve to take out one of the crisp bills that Mario thought he had glimpsed when he opened the brief case just a hair—spare change to take a taxi or a stinking bus.

They keep an eye peeled to see whether the strange things that are going on here, the things they happened to overhear in the café, have something to do with their two finds. The strange characters either haven't appeared in this part of town or have been replaced: two policemen per corner are too many because there are lots of corners. This is not a gray afternoon like any other, and come to think of it maybe it isn't even a lucky afternoon the way it appears to be. These are the blank faces of a weekday, so different from the blank faces on Sunday. Pedro and Mario have a color now, they have a mask and can feel themselves exist because a brief case (ugly words) and a sports jacket blossomed in their path. (A jacket that's not as new as it appeared to be—threadbare but respectable. That's it: a respectable jacket.) As afternoons go, this isn't an easy one. Something is moving in the air with the howl of the sirens and they're beginning to feel fingered. They see police everywhere, police in the dark hallways, in pairs on all the corners in the city, police bouncing up and down on their motorcycles against traffic as though the proper functioning of the country depended on them, as maybe it does, yes, that's why things are as they are and Mario doesn't dare say that aloud because the brief case has him tongue-tied, not that there's a microphone concealed in it, but what paranoia, when nobody's forcing him to carry it. He could get rid of it in some dark alley—but how can you let go of a fortune that's practically fallen in your lap, even if the fortune's got a load of dynamite inside? He takes a more natural grip on the brief case, holds it affectionately, not as though it were about to explode. At this same moment Pedro decides to put the jacket on and it's a little too big for him but not ridiculous, no not at all. Loose-fitting, yes, but not ridiculous; comfortable, warm, affectionate, just a little bit frayed at the edges, worn. Pedro puts his hands in the pockets of the jacket (*his* pockets) and discovers a few old bus tickets, a dirty handkerchief, several bills, and some coins. He can't bring himself to say anything to Mario and suddenly he turns around to see if they're being followed. Maybe they've fallen into some sort of trap, and Mario must be feeling the same way because he isn't saying a word either. He's whistling between his teeth with the expression of a guy who's been carrying around a ridiculous black brief case like this all his life. The situation doesn't seem quite as bright as it did in the beginning. It looks as though nobody has followed them, but who knows: there are people coming along behind them and maybe somebody left the brief case and the jacket behind for some obscure reason. Mario finally makes up his mind and murmurs to Pedro: Let's not go home, let's go on as if nothing had happened, I want to see if we're being followed. That's okay with Pedro. Mario nostalgically remembers the time (an hour ago) when they could talk out loud and even laugh. The brief case is getting too heavy and he's tempted once again to abandon it to its fate. Abandon it without having had a look at what's inside? Sheer cowardice.

They walk about aimlessly so as to put any possible though improbable tail off the track. It's no longer Pedro and Mario walking, it's a jacket and a brief case that have turned into people. They go on walking and finally the jacket says: "Let's have a drink in a bar. I'm dying of thirst."

"With all this? Without even knowing where it came from?"

"Yeah, sure. There's some money in one pocket." He takes a trembling hand with two bills in it out of the pocket. A thousand nice solid pesos. He's not up to rummaging around in the pockets any more, but he thinks—he smells—that there's more. They could use a couple of sandwiches, they can get them in this café that looks like a nice quiet place.

A guy says and the other girl's name is Saturdays there's no bread; anything, I wonder what kind of brainwashing. . . . In turbulent times there's nothing like turning your ears on, though the bad thing about cafés is the din of voices that drowns out individual voices.

Listen, you're intelligent enough to understand.

They allow themselves to be distracted for a little, they too wonder what kind of brainwashing, and if the guy who was called intelligent believes he is. If it's a question of believing, they're ready to believe the bit about the Saturdays without bread, as though they didn't know that you need bread on Saturday to make the wafers for mass on Sunday, and on Sunday you need some wine to get through the terrible wilderness of workdays.

When a person gets around in the world—the cafés—with the antennae up he can tune in on all sorts of confessions and pick up the most abstruse (most absurd) reasoning processes, absolutely necessary because of the need to be on the alert and through the fault of these two objects that are alien to them and yet possess them, envelop them, especially now when those boys come into the café panting and sit down at a table with a nothing's-been-happening-around-here expression on their faces and take out writing pads, open books, but it's too late: they bring the police in on their heels and of course books don't fool the keen-witted guardians of the law, but instead get them all worked up. They've arrived in the wake of the students to impose law and order and they do, with much pushing and shoving: your identification papers, come on, come on, straight out to the paddy wagon waiting outside with its mouth wide open. Pedro and Mario can't figure out how to get out of there, how to clear a path for themselves through the mass of humanity that's leaving the café to its initial tranquillity. As one of the kids goes out he drops a little package at Mario's feet, and in a reflex motion Mario draws the package over with his foot and hides it behind the famous brief case leaning against the chair. Suddenly he's scared: he thinks he's gotten crazy enough to appropriate anything within reach. Then he's even more scared: he knows he's done it to protect the kid, but what if the cops take it into their head to search *him*? They'd find a brief case with who knows what inside, an inexplicable package (suddenly it strikes him funny, and he hallucinates that the package is a bomb and sees his leg flying through the air accompanied out of sympathy by the brief case, which has burst and is spilling out big counterfeit bills). All this in the split second that it took to hide the little package, and after that nothing. It's better to leave your mind a blank and watch out for telepathic cops and things like that. And what was he saying to himself a thousand years ago when calm reigned? — a brainwashing; a selfservice brainwash so as not to give away what's inside this crazy head of mine. The kids move off, carted off with a kick or two from the bluecoats; the package remains there at the feet of those two respectable-looking gentlemen, gentlemen with a jacket and a brief case (each of them with one of the two). Respectable gentlemen or two guys very much alone in the peaceful café, gentlemen whom even a club sandwich couldn't console now.

They stand up. Mario knows that if he leaves the little package, the waiter is going to call him back and the jig'll be up. He picks it up, thus adding it to the day's booty but only for a short while; with trembling hands he deposits it in a garbage can on a deserted street. Pedro, who's walking next to him, doesn't understand at all what's going on, but can't work up the strength to ask.

At times, when everything is clear, all sorts of questions can be asked, but in moments like this the mere fact of still being alive condenses everything that is askable and diminishes its value. All they can do is to keep walking, that's all they can do, halting now and then to see for example why that man over there is crying. And the man cries so gently that it's almost sacrilege not to stop and see what the trouble is. It's shop-closing time and the salesgirls heading home are trying to find out what's wrong: their maternal instinct is always ready and waiting, and the man is weeping inconsolably. Finally he manages to stammer: I can't stand it any more. A little knot of people has formed around him with understanding looks on their faces, but they don't understand at all. When he shakes the newspaper and says I can't stand it any more, some people think that he's read the news and the weight of the world is too much for him. They are about to go and leave him to his spinelessness. Finally he manages to explain between hiccups that he's been looking for work for months and doesn't have one peso left for the bus home, nor an ounce of strength to keep on looking.

"Work," Pedro says to Mario. "Come on, this scene's not for us."

"Well, we don't have anything to give him anyway. I wish we did."

Work, work, the others chorus and their hearts are touched, because this word is intelligible whereas tears are not. The man's tears keep boring into the asphalt and who knows what they find, but nobody wonders except maybe him, maybe he's saying to himself, my tears are penetrating the ground and may discover oil. If I die right here and now, maybe I can slip through the holes made by my tears in the asphalt, and in a thousand years I'll have turned into oil so that somebody else like me, in the same circumstances. . . . A fine idea, but the chorus doesn't allow him to become lost in his own thoughts, which — it surmises — are thoughts of death (the chorus is afraid: what an assault it is on the peace of mind of the average citizen, for whom death is something you read about in the newspapers). Lack of work, yes, all of them understand being out of a job and are ready to help him. That's much better than death. And the goodhearted salesgirls from the hardware stores open their purses and take out some crumpled bills, a collection is immediately taken up, the most assertive ones take the others' money and urge them to cough up more. Mario is trying to open the brief case — what treasures can there be inside to share with this guy? Pedro thinks he should have fished out the package that Mario tossed in the garbage can. Maybe it was work tools, spray paint, or the perfect equipment for making a bomb, something to give this guy so that inactivity doesn't wipe him out.

The girls are now pressing the guy to accept the money that's been collected. The guy keeps shrieking that he doesn't want charity. One of the girls explains to him that it's a spontaneous contribution to help his family out while he looks for work with better spirits and a full stomach. The crocodile is now weeping with emotion. The salesgirls feel good, redeemed, and Pedro and Mario decide that this is a lucky sign.

Maybe if they keep the guy company Mario will make up his mind to open the brief case, and Pedro can search the jacket pockets to find their secret contents.

So when the guy is alone again they take him by the arm and invite him to eat with them. The guy hangs back at first, he's afraid of the two of them: they might be trying to get the dough he's just received. He no longer knows if it's true or not that he can't find work or if this is his work — pretending to be desperate so that people in the neighborhood feel sorry for him. The thought suddenly crosses his mind: if it's true that I'm a desperate man and everybody was so good to me, there's no reason why these two won't be. If I pretended to be desperate it means that I'm not a bad actor, and I'm going to get something out of these two as well. He decides they have an odd look about them but seem honest, so the three of them go off to a cheap restaurant together to offer themselves the luxury of some good sausages and plenty of wine.

Three, one of them thinks, is a lucky number. We'll see if something good comes of it.

Why have they spent all this time telling one another their life stories, which maybe are true? The three of them discover an identical need to relate their life stories in full detail, from the time when they were little to these fateful days when so many strange things are happening. The restaurant is near the station and at certain moments they dream of leaving or of derailing a train or something, so as to rid themselves of the tensions building up inside. It's the hour for dreaming and none of the three wants to ask for the check. Neither Pedro nor Mario has said a word about their surprising finds. And the guy wouldn't dream of paying for these two bums' dinners, and besides they invited him.

The tension becomes unbearable and all they have to do is make up their minds. Hours have gone by. Around them the waiters are piling the chairs on the tables, like a scaffolding that is closing in little by little, threatening to swallow them up, because the waiters have felt a sudden urge to build and they keep piling chairs on top of chairs, tables on top of tables, and chairs and then more chairs. They are going to be imprisoned in a net of wooden legs, a tomb of chairs and who knows how many tables. A good end for these three cowards who can't make up their minds to ask for the check. Here they lie: they've paid for seven sausage sandwiches and two pitchers of table wine with their lives. A fair price.

Finally Pedro — Pedro the bold — asks for the check and prays that the money in the outside pockets is enough to cover it. The inside pockets are an inscrutable world even here, shielded by the chairs; the inner pockets form too intricate a labyrinth for him. He would have to live other people's lives if he got into the inside pockets of the jacket, get involved with something that doesn't belong to him, lose himself by stepping into madness.

There is enough money. Friends by now, relieved, the three go out of the restaurant. Pretending to be absent-minded, Mario has left the brief case — too heavy, that's it — amid the intricate construction of chairs and tables piled on top of each other, and he is certain it won't be discovered until the next day. A few blocks farther on, they say good-by to the guy and the two of them walk back to the apartment that they share. They are almost there when Pedro realizes that Mario no longer has the brief case. He then takes off the jacket, folds it affectionately, and leaves it on top of a parked car, its original location. Finally they open the door of the apartment without fear, and go to bed without fear, without money, and without illusions. They sleep soundly, until Mario wakes up with a start, unable to tell whether the bang that has awakened him was real or a dream.

[1975]

Translated by
HELEN R. LANE

QUESTIONS

1. Is there a connection among the "strange things" that happen in the story? If so, what is it?
2. Through the characters' private thoughts and imaginings, what do you discover about the world that Pedro, Mario, and the crying man inhabit?
3. Is the story entirely realistic or partly fantastic? How do you determine which? How does the style in which the story is told contribute to its effectiveness?
4. Why do Pedro and Mario ultimately abandon their "finds" without even examining the contents of the briefcase?

Mario Vargas Llosa

(b. 1936)

Peru

In 1990, when Mario Vargas Llosa narrowly lost an election for the presidency of Peru, it looked for a time as if literature had made an unlikely marriage with politics. Readers of Vargas Llosa's fiction, however, had long been aware of the author's growing interest in politics, especially as a part of historical patterns. In *The War of the End of the World* (1981), he had imaginatively blended past, present, and future Latin American events into a utopian fantasy in which he speculated what might have happened to the entire continent if certain historical episodes had turned out differently.

The fantasy world of Vargas Llosa's earlier work, *Aunt Julia and the Script Writer* (1977), had already established for the author an international reputation. By some accounts, this novel is one of the major works of *El Boom* ("the explosion") in Latin American writing. The story—which initially appears to be realistic—recounts the life of a prolific writer of radio soap operas, driven insane by the demands of his mushrooming listening audience. *Aunt Julia* is also Vargas Llosa's own story of how he became a writer and, in fact, married one of his own aunts. By contrast to these later works, the story included here, "Sunday," is from an earlier stage of Vargas Llosa's writing, *Los jefes* (1958), a volume of short stories focusing on adolescence. The story is, further, about machismo and, in this variation of what has been called a ubiquitous Latin American theme, male bonding.

◆ Sunday ◆

He held his breath for a moment, dug his nails into the palms of his hands, and said in a rush: "I'm in love with you." He saw her blush suddenly, as if someone had slapped her cheeks, which were of a glowing paleness and very soft. Terrified, he felt confusion mounting in him and turning his tongue to stone. He wanted to run away, to be done with it. In the silent winter morning had come this inner weakness that always disheartened him in decisive moments. A few minutes before, in the animated, smiling crowd that circulated through Central Park in Miraflores, Miguel was still repeating to himself: "Now. When I get to Pardo Avenue. I'll risk it. Oh, Rubén, if you only knew how much I hate you!" Still earlier, in church, while he sought out Flora with his eyes, he discovered her at the foot of a column and, elbowing his way through without excusing himself to the ladies he pushed, managed to get close to her and greet her in a low voice. He stubbornly told himself again, as he did that morning sprawled on his bed, watching for the appearance of dawn: "There's nothing else to do. I have to do it today. In the morning. You'll pay for it, Rubén." The night before, he had cried for the first time in many years when he learned of the cheap trap they were preparing for him. People kept going into the Park, and Pardo Avenue was deserted. They walked along the mall, under the fig trees with their tall dense tops. "I'll have to hurry," Miguel thought. "If I don't, I'm out of luck." He looked around out of the corner of his eye: there was nobody, he could try it. Slowly he put out his left hand to touch hers; the contact showed him what was happening. He begged for a miracle to happen, for that humiliation to cease. "What'll I say to her?" he thought. "What'll I tell her?" She had just withdrawn her hand, and he felt he was dismissed, ridiculous. All the radiant phrases that he had feverishly prepared the night before were dissolved like bubbles of foam.

"Flora," he stammered, "I've waited a long time for this moment. Ever since I met you, I've thought only of you. I'm in love for the first time, believe me. I've never known a girl like you."

Once more a compact white blot on his brain, emptiness. He could no longer increase the pressure: his skin yielded like rubber, and his nails were digging into the bone. Nevertheless, he went on talking, with some difficulty, at long intervals, overcoming his shameful stammering, trying to describe a total, unreflecting passion, until he discovered with relief that they were coming to the first oval on Pardo Avenue, and then he fell silent. Between the second and third fig trees beyond the oval stood Flora's house. They stopped, looked at each other. Flora was still excited, and her confusion had filled her eyes with a damp brilliance. Miguel told himself desolately that she had never seemed so beautiful to him: a blue ribbon held her hair, and he could see the beginning of her neck and her ears, two question marks, tiny and perfect.

"Look, Miguel," Flora said. Her voice was soft, full of music, assured. "I can't give you an answer now. But Mama doesn't want me to go with boys until I finish school."

"Every mama says the same thing, Flora," Miguel persisted. "How's she going to find out? We can see each other whenever you say, even if it's only on Sundays."

"I'll give you an answer now, but I must think about it first," Flora said, lowering her eyes. After a few moments she added, "Forgive me, but I have to go now. It's getting late."

Miguel felt a profound lassitude, something that spread all through his body and softened it.

"You're not angry with me, are you, Flora?" he asked humbly.

"Don't be silly," she replied vivaciously. "I'm not angry."

"I'll wait as long as you like," Miguel said. "But we'll go on seeing each other, won't we? We're going to the movies this afternoon, aren't we?"

"I can't this afternoon," she said gently. "Martha asked me over to her house."

A warm, violent looseness in his guts came flooding over him, and he felt wounded, ashamed, in the face of that answer which he had expected and which now seemed like a cruelty to him. What Melanés had murmured grimly in his ear on Saturday afternoon was true. Martha would leave them alone; that was her usual tactic. Afterward, Rubén would tell those Sharpies — his gang — how he and his sister had planned the circumstances, the time, and the place. Martha would have claimed the right to spy from behind the curtain as payment for her services. Anger suddenly made his hands perspire.

"Don't be like that, Flora. Let's go to the matinee as we planned. I won't mention this to you, I promise."

"I can't go, really," Flora replied. "I have to go to Martha's. She came to my house yesterday to invite me. But I'm going with her to Salazar Park later."

Not even in these last words did he see any hope. For some time afterward he contemplated the spot where her fragile little figure in blue had disappeared under the majestic arch of the fig trees on the avenue. He could compete with a simple adversary, not with Rubén. He remembered the names of the girls Martha invited one Sunday afternoon. He could no longer do anything; he was defeated. Then once more arose the image that saved him every time he suffered a frustration: from a distant background of clouds swollen by black smoke, he was marching at the head of a company of cadets from the Naval School toward a grandstand erected in the park. Important men in formal dress, top hats in hand, and ladies with sparkling jewels were applauding him. Massed on the walks, a crowd in which the faces of his friends and enemies stood out was observing him in astonishment, murmuring his name. Dressed in blue, a roomy cape billowing behind him, Miguel marched ahead, looking at the horizon. With his sword raised, its tip described a semicircle in the air. There in the center of the grandstand was Flora, smiling. On one corner he discovered Rubén, ragged and ashamed. He confined himself to throwing him a brief contemptuous glance. He went marching on, disappeared among the victors.

Like breath on a mirror when one rubs it, the image disappeared. He stood in the doorway of his house. He hated everybody; everybody hated him. He entered and went directly up to his room. He threw himself face-down on the bed. In the warm darkness between his eyes and eyelids the girl's face appeared — "I love you, Flora," he said in a loud voice — and then Rubén, with his insolent jaw and his hostile smile. They stood beside each other, came closer; Rubén's eyes twisted round to look mockingly at him, while his mouth moved toward Flora.

He leaped out of bed. The wardrobe mirror showed him a livid face and rings under his eyes. "He shan't see you," he decided. "He won't do that to me. I won't let him pull that dirty trick on me."

Pardo Avenue was still empty. Quickening his pace, without stopping, he walked toward the crossing at Grau Avenue; there he hesitated. He felt cold: he had forgotten his jacket in his room, and his one shirt was not enough to protect him from the wind that came in from the sea and was caught in the thick branches of the fig trees in a soft rustling. His dreaded image of Flora and Rubén together gave him strength, and he went on walking. From the door of the neighborhood bar next to the Montecarlo theater he saw them at their usual table, in possession of the nook formed by the back and left-hand walls. Francisco, Melanés, Tobías, and the Scholar discovered him and, after a moment's surprise, turned toward Rubén, their faces malicious, excited. He recovered his self-possession immediately. He certainly knew how to behave in front of men.

"Hello," he said to them, approaching. "What's new?"

"Sit down." The Scholar held out a chair for him. "What miracle's brought you here?"

"You haven't been here for ages," Francisco remarked.

"I wanted to see you," Miguel said cordially. "I already knew you were here. What's so surprising about that? Or aren't I a Sharpie any more?"

He sat down between Melanés and Tobías. Rubén sat across from him.

"Cuncho!" called the Scholar. "Bring another glass. And it had better be clean."

Cuncho brought the glass, and the Scholar filled it with beer. Miguel said, "To the Sharpies!" and drank.

"You almost drank the glass too," Francisco observed. "How violent you are!"

"I bet you went to one-o'clock mass," said Melanés, one eyelid creased in satisfaction, as always when he was thinking up some mischief. "Or did you?"

"I did," Miguel said imperturbably. "But only to see a young lady, that's all."

He looked at Rubén with challenging eyes, but the latter did not take the hint. He was drumming with his fingers on the table, the tip of his tongue between his teeth, whistling "The Popof Girl" by Pérez Prado.

"Well!" Melanés applauded. "Well, Don Juan. Tell us, which girl?"

"That's a secret."

"There aren't any secrets among Sharpies," Tobías reminded him. "Have you forgotten already? Come on, who was she?"

"What do you care?" Miguel asked.

"A good deal," Tobías said. "I have to know who you go with so as to know who you are."

"In the meantime, drink up," Melanés told Miguel. "One to zero."

"Why should I guess who she is?" Francisco asked. "Why not you?"

"I already know," Tobías said.

"Me too," said Melanés. He turned to Rubén with innocent eyes and voice. "And you, brother-in-law, can you guess who she is?"

"No," Rubén answered coldly. "Nor do I care."

"I have a little fire in my stomach," the Scholar remarked. "Isn't anyone going to order a beer?"

Melanés passed a pathetic finger across his throat.

"I have no money, darling," he said, in English.

"I'll buy a bottle," Tobías announced with a solemn gesture. "Let's see who follows me. We have to put out this kid's fire."

"Cuncho, take down half a dozen *Cristales*," Miguel ordered.

There were shouts of joy, exclamations.

"You're a real Sharpie," Francisco agreed.

"A dirty, lousy one," added Melanés. "Yes, sir, a real dude-type Sharpie."

Cuncho brought the beers. They drank. They listened to Melanés tell sexy stories—crude, extravagant, exciting—and a loud argument about football started between Tobías and Francisco. The Scholar recounted an anecdote. He was coming from Lima to Miraflores on a bus. The other passengers got off at Arequipa Avenue. "At the top of Javier Prado, that big blubber of a Tomasso got on, that six-foot albino who's still in grade school, lives around the Ravine—you know him now? Pretending great interest in the automobile, he began asking the driver questions, leaning over the front seat while he quietly scraped the upholstery on the back with a knife.

"He did it because I was there," the Scholar went on. "He wanted to show off."

"He's mentally deficient," Francisco remarked. "You do those things when you're ten years old. At his age it's not funny."

"What happened afterward is funny." The Scholar laughed. "'Look, driver, don't you see this big blubber's ruining your car?'"

"'What?'" the driver exclaimed, braking suddenly. His ears red, his eyes frightened, Tomasso was struggling with the door.

"With his knife," added the Scholar. "Imagine how fast he left the seat.

"The fat kid managed to get out at last. He began to run along Arequipa Avenue. The driver ran after him shouting, 'Grab that wretch!'"

"Did he catch him?" Melanés asked.

"I don't know. I disappeared. I stole the ignition key for a keepsake. I've got it here."

He took a little silver-plated key from his pocket and tossed it on the table. The bottles were empty. Rubén looked at his watch and got to his feet.

"I'm going," he said. "I'll be seeing you."

"Don't go," Miguel said. "I'm rich today. I'm inviting you all to lunch."

A whirlwind of slaps fell on him; the Sharpies were thanking him confusedly, flattering him.

"I can't," Rubén said. "I have to go."

"Go and don't come back, my fine friend," Tobías remarked. "And greet Martha for me."

"We'll think about you a lot, brother-in-law," Melanés said.

"No!" Miguel exclaimed. "I'm inviting everybody or nobody. If Rubén leaves, that's that."

"You heard him, Sharpie Rubén," Francisco said. "You'll have to stay."

"You have to stay," said Melanés. "You have no choice."

"I'm leaving," Rubén said.

"It just so happens you're drunk," Miguel remarked. "You're leaving because you're afraid of making a fool of yourself in front of us, that's what's the matter."

"How many times have I carried *you* home half-dead?" Rubén demanded. "How many times have I helped you climb up the grating so your father wouldn't catch you? I can hold ten times more'n you can."

"You used to be able to," Miguel said. "Now it's harder to. You want to find out?"

"Gladly," Rubén replied. "Shall we meet tonight, right here?"

"No. Now." Miguel turned to the others, extending his arms. "I'm making a challenge, Sharpies."

Happily he proved that the ancient formula had kept its power intact. In the midst of the noisy enthusiasm he had provoked, he saw Rubén sit down, pale.

"Cuncho!" Tobías shouted. "The menu. And two large beers. A Sharpie has just given a challenge."

They ordered steaks and a dozen beers. Tobías put out three bottles for each competitor and the rest for the others. They ate, scarcely speaking. Miguel drank after each mouthful and tried to show some animation, but the fear of not sufficiently holding his own grew as the beer deposited its acid taste in his mouth. When they finished the six bottles, it was some time before Cuncho took away their plates.

"You order," Miguel told Rubén.

"Three more apiece."

After the first glass of the new round, Miguel felt his ears ringing; his head was a slow roulette wheel; everything was going round.

"I have to pee," he said. "I'm going to the bathroom."

The Sharpies laughed.

"Are you giving up?" Rubén asked.

"I'm going to pee," Miguel shouted. "If you want, have 'em bring more."

In the bathroom he vomited. Then he carefully washed his face, trying to erase every tell-tale sign. His watch showed four-thirty. In spite of his dark discomfort he felt happy. Rubén could do nothing now. He went back to the others.

"Your health," said Rubén, raising his glass.

He's furious, Miguel thought. But I've annoyed him now.

"You smell like a corpse," Melanés observed. "Somebody's died around here."

"I just got here," Miguel asserted, trying to conquer his nausea and dizziness.

"Your health!" Rubén repeated.

When they had finished the last beer, his stomach felt like lead, and the voices of the others reached his ears as a confused mixture of sounds. A hand suddenly appeared under his eyes; it was white, with long fingers; it took him by the chin, made him raise his head. Rubén's face had grown larger. He looked funny, so disheveled and angry.

"D'you give up, snotty?"

Miguel got up suddenly and pushed Rubén aside, but before the fight could develop, the Scholar intervened.

"Sharpies don't fight, ever," he said, forcing them to sit down. "They're both drunk. It's all over. Let's vote."

Melanés, Francisco, and Tobías unwillingly agreed to concede that it was a tie.

"I'd already won," Rubén said. "This fella can't even talk. Look at him."

Miguel's eyes were actually glassy, his mouth was open, and a trickle of saliva dripped from his tongue.

"Shut up," the Scholar ordered. "You're no champion, let's say, at drinking beer."

"You're no beer-drinking champion," Melanés said for emphasis. "You're only a swimming champion, the holy terror of the pools."

"You'd better not say anything," Rubén retorted. "Don't you see envy's gnawing at you?"

"Long live the Esther Williams of Miraflores!" said Melanés.

"A tremendous old fella, and he doesn't even know how to swim," Rubén said. "Don't you want me to give you a few lessons?"

"We know how already, you big wonder," said the Scholar. "You won a swimming championship. All the girls're dying for you. You're a little old champion."

"This one here's no champion of anything," Miguel remarked with difficulty. "He's pure affectation."

"You're dying," Rubén retorted. "Shall I take you home, little girl?"

"I'm not drunk," Miguel assured him. "You're pure affectation."

"You're all cut up because I'm going to fall for Flora," Rubén said. "You're dying of jealousy. You think I don't catch on to these things?"

"Pure affectation," Miguel said. "You won because your father's president of the Federation. Everybody knows he cheated, he disqualified Rabbit Villarán, and you only won because of that."

"At least I can swim better 'n you," Rubén said. "You don't even know how to race the waves."

"You don't swim any better 'n anybody else," Miguel retorted. "Anybody can leave *you* behind."

"Anybody," Melanés put in. "Even Miguel, who's an old mother."

"Permit me to laugh."

"We'll permit you," said Tobías. "That's all we needed."

"You're better 'n me because it's winter," Rubén went on. "If it weren't, I'd challenge you to go to the beach, to see if you're so exceptional in the water."

"You won the championship because of your father," Miguel said. "You're pure affectation. When you want t' swim with me, just le' me know, informally. At the beach, at the Terraces, wherever y' like."

"At the beach," Rubén said. "Right now."

"You're pure affectation," said Miguel.

Rubén's face suddenly lighted up, and his eyes, in addition to being filled with rancor, turned arrogant.

"I'll bet you to see who reaches the surf first," he said.

"Pure affectation," Miguel repeated.

"If you win," Rubén said, "I promise you I won't go after Flora. And if I win, you can take your music somewhere else."

"What did you think?" stammered Miguel. "Damn it, what'd you think?"

"Sharpies," Rubén said, extending his arms, "I'm making a challenge."

"Miguel's in no shape now," said the Scholar. "Why not just draw straws for Flora?"

"And why're *you* butting in?" Miguel asked. "I accept. "Le's go t' the beach."

"You're crazy," Francisco remarked. "I'm not going down to the beach in this cold. Make some other bet."

"He's accepted," said Rubén. "Let's go."

"When a Sharpie makes a challenge, everybody puts his tongue in his pocket," Melanés remarked. "Let's go to the beach. And if they don't dare go in the water, we'll throw them in ourselves."

"They're both drunk," the Scholar persisted. "The challenge isn't valid."

"Shut up, Scholar," Miguel bellowed. "I'm a big boy now, I don't need you t' take care of me."

"Well," said the Scholar, shrugging his shoulders, "just suit yourself."

They went out. Outside a quiet gray atmosphere awaited them. Miguel breathed deeply; he felt better. Francisco, Melanés, and Rubén walked ahead, Miguel and the Scholar behind. On Grau Avenue there were pedestrians, the majority of them servant girls wearing bright dresses, on their day off. Ashen-gray men with thick straight hair were walking about, looking covetously at them; the girls laughed, showing their gold teeth. The Sharpies paid no attention to them. They went on with long strides, and excitement was building in them little by little.

"You feel better now?" the Scholar asked.

"Yes," Miguel answered. "The air's done me good."

At the corner of Pardo Avenue they turned. They marched spread out like a squad, all in line, under the fig trees on the mall, over paving stones upraised here and there by the enormous tree roots that occasionally burst through the surface like hooks. Going down along Diagonal Avenue, they passed two girls. Rubén bowed ceremoniously.

"Hello, Rubén," they chanted in duet.

Tobías mocked them in a high-pitched voice.

"Hello, Prince Rubén."

Diagonal Avenue ends in a little ravine which forks off: on one side the Malecón winds along, paved and shining; on the other, there is a slope that follows the hill and leads to the sea. They call it "the slope to the baths"; its paving is similar and shines from the passage of automobile tires and the bathers' feet of many summers past.

"Let's warm up, champions," Melanés shouted, starting to run. The others imitated him.

They ran against the wind and the thin mist that rose from the beach, gripped in an emotional whirlwind. The air penetrated their lungs through their ears, mouths, and noses, and a sensation of relief and sobriety spread through their bodies as the slope steepened, and in a moment their feet were now obeying only a mysterious force that came from the deepest part of the earth. Their arms like propellers, a breath of salt on their tongues, the Sharpies ran down the incline at top speed, as far as the circular platform suspended above the bathhouse. The sea vanished some fifty yards from the bank in a thick cloud that seemed about to dash against the cliffs, the tall dark rocks fronting all along the bay.

"Let's go back," Francisco said. "I'm cold."

At the edge of the platform there is a fence discolored here and there by moss. An opening indicates the beginning of the nearly vertical lower steps leading down to the beach. From there, at their feet, the Sharpies contemplated a narrow ribbon of clear water and the unaccustomed surface of foamy waves.

"I'm leaving if this guy'll give up," Rubén said.

"Who's talking about giving up?" retorted Miguel. "What'd you think?"

Rubén went down the steps three at a time, unbuttoning his shirt.

"Rubén!" shouted the Scholar. "Are you crazy? Come back!"

But Miguel and the others went down too, and the Scholar followed them.

In summer, from the veranda of the long narrow building nestled against the hill where the bathers' rooms are located, as far as the curved edge of the sea, there was a slope with gray stones where people would bask in the sun. The little beach swarmed with animation from morning till night. Now water filled the slope, and there were no bright-colored shadows, no elastic girls with sunburned bodies. No children's melodramatic cries resounded when a wave managed to splash them before it ebbed, dragging noisy stones and pebbles. They could not even see the edge of the beach, for the tide came in as far as the space bounded by the shaded columns that supported the building and, as the undertow went out, they could scarcely see the wooden steps and concrete supports that were ornamented with barnacles and algae.

"You can't see the breakers," Rubén said. "How'll we do it?"

They stood in the gallery on the left, in the women's section. Their faces were serious.

"Wait till tomorrow," the Scholar urged. "By noon it'll be clear. That way we'll be able to check on you."

"Since we've gone this far, let 'em do it now," said Melanés. "They can check on each other."

"Sounds all right to me," Rubén said. "How 'bout you?"

"Me too," Miguel agreed.

When they had undressed, Tobías joked about the blue veins that ran up Miguel's smooth belly. They went down the stairs. The wooden steps, continually lapped by the water for some months, were slippery and very smooth. Grasping the iron handrail in order not to fall, Miguel felt a tremor rising from the soles of his feet to his head. He was thinking that the fog and cold favored him in one way; his success now depended not on his skill, but chiefly on his resistance, and Rubén's skin was also purple, marked with millions of goose-pimples. One step below, Rubén's well-proportioned body was bent: he was waiting tensely for the end of the undertow and the arrival of the next wave, which came quietly, gracefully, thrusting forward its border of foam. When the wave crest was a couple of yards from the stairway, Rubén dived in, his arms lance-stiff, his hair disheveled by the force of his dive. His body cleaved the air cleanly and dropped in without bending. Without lowering his head or flexing his legs, he rebounded in the foam, almost sank, and immediately slipped into it, taking advantage of the tide. His arms appeared and disappeared in a frantic bubbling, and his feet began tracing a fast, cautious wake. Miguel in turn went down another stairway and waited for the next wave. He knew that the bottom was shallow there, that he must dive in like a board, hard and rigid, without moving a muscle, or he would strike against the rocks. He closed his eyes and dove, and he did not hit bottom, but his body was flailed from forehead to knees, and a very sharp stinging sensation arose while he struggled with all his strength to recover the warmth in his limbs that the water had suddenly taken out of them. He was on that unfamiliar section of the sea at Miraflores near the bank, where eddies and opposing currents are encountered, and last summer was so long ago that Miguel had forgotten how to get across them easily. He did not remember that he must relax his body and let go, let himself be carried along drifting submissively, swing his arms only when a wave rises and he is on the crest, on that liquid sheet that escorts the foam and floats on the currents. He did not remember that it is important to bear patiently and with a certain malice that first contact with a sea, exasperated by the bank, that pulls at his limbs and blows water in his mouth and eyes; to offer no resistance, to be a cork, to limit himself to gulping air each time a wave rolls in, to submerge himself—barely, if it breaks far off and comes in gently, or to the very bottom if it breaks nearby—to grasp some stone and wait alertly for the subdued thunder of its passage in order to emerge in just one stroke and continue advancing, furtively, with his hands, until he encounters a new obstacle and then to relax, not fighting against the eddies, to revolve freely in their slow, slow spiral and escape suddenly with a single stroke at the opportune moment. Then a calm surface unexpectedly appears, stirred by harmless combers; the water is clear, smooth, and in some places hidden stones are visible below its surface.

After crossing the choppy area Miguel stopped, exhausted, and gulped air. He saw Rubén nearby, looking at him. His hair fell in bangs over his face. His teeth were clenched.

"Shall we?"

"Let's go."

After swimming for a few minutes Miguel felt the cold that had momentarily vanished coming over him again, and he speeded up his strokes because it was in his legs, especially in his calves, that the water had a greater effect, first making them insensitive, then stiffening them. He was swimming with his face in the water, and each time his right arm rose out of it, he turned his head to expel air and breathe in another supply, at which he submerged his face and chin once more, just barely, so as not to hinder his own progress but, on the contrary, to split the water like a prow and make his forward movement easier. With each stroke he glanced at Rubén swimming smoothly, effortlessly on the surface, not splashing now, with the delicacy and ease of a seagull gliding. Miguel tried to forget Rubén and the sea and the breakers, which must still be far off, for the water was clear and calm, and they were swimming only through newly risen surf. He wanted to remember nothing but Flora's face and the down on her arms that sparkled on sunny days like a little forest of golden threads. But he could not prevent another image from succeeding to that of the girl—the image of a mountain of raging water, not necessarily these breakers (to which he had come once two summers ago and whose waves were intensified with greenish-black foam, because in that spot, more or less, the stones ended and the mud began that the waves brought up to the surface and deposited among nests of seaweed and stagnant water, staining the sea), but rather in a real ocean stirred by inner cataclysms in which were thrown up unusual waves that could have swamped an entire ship and upset it with astonishing rapidity, hurling passengers, lifeboats, masts, sails, sailors, porthole covers, and flags into the air.

He stopped swimming; his body sank until it was vertical; he raised his head and saw Rubén, who was getting farther away. He thought of calling to him on some pretext, of saying to him, "Why don't we rest a minute?" But he did not. All the cold in his body seemed to be concentrated in his calves; his muscles felt cramped, his skin taut; his heart was pounding. He thrust feverishly with his feet. He was in the center of a circle of dark water, walled in by the mist. He tried to make out the beach, or at least the shadow of the cliffs, but that dark mist dissolving at his passage was not transparent. He saw only a narrow surface, blackish-green, and a layer of clouds low over the water. Then he felt afraid. The recollection of the beer he had drunk assailed him, and he thought, "I expect it's sapped my strength." At once his arms and legs seemed to disappear. He decided to go back, but after a few strokes in the direction of the beach, he turned and swam as quickly as he could. "I won't go in to the bank alone," he told himself. "It's better to stay close to Rubén. If I get too tired, I'll tell him, 'You beat me, but let's go back.'" Now he was swimming without any style, his head raised, beating the water with stiff arms, his eyes fastened on the imperturbable body ahead of him.

His agitation and the effort took the numbness out of his legs; his body regained a little warmth; the distance that separated him from Rubén had decreased, and that calmed him. Shortly afterward he caught up with him, stretched out his arm and caught one of his feet. The other stopped at once. Rubén's eyes were very red, and his mouth hung open.

"I think we've got off course," Miguel said. "It seems to me we're swimming parallel to the beach."

His teeth were chattering, but his voice was steady. Rubén looked in all directions. Miguel watched him tensely.

"I don't see the beach now," Rubén said.

"I haven't seen it for a long time," Miguel said. "There's a lot of mist."

"We're not off course," Rubén went on. "Look. You can see the foam now."

As a matter of fact, some combers were coming toward them edged with a border of foam that dissolved and suddenly reappeared. They looked at each other in silence.

"We're close to the breakers now, then," Miguel said at last.

"Yes. We swam fast."

"I've never seen so much mist."

"Aren't you pretty tired?" Rubén asked.

"Me? You're crazy. Let's go on."

Immediately he regretted his words, but it was already too late. Rubén had said, "Okay, let's go on."

He managed to count twenty strokes before telling himself that he could not go on. He was making almost no headway; his right leg was half-paralyzed by the cold; his arms felt awkward and heavy. Panting, he shouted, "Rubén!" The latter went on swimming. "Rubén, *Rubén*!" He turned and began swimming—splashing desperately, rather—toward the beach, and suddenly he was praying to God to save him. He would be good in the future, would obey his parents, would not miss mass on Sunday. Then he remembered having confessed to the Sharpies, "I go to church only to see a young lady," and he felt a knife-sharp conviction: God was going to punish him, to drown him in those turbid waters that he was frantically beating, waters below which an awful death, and afterward hell perhaps, were waiting for him. Then in his anxiety there arose, like an echo, a certain phrase Father Alberto once pronounced in religion class about the divine goodness that knows no limits, and while he flailed at the sea with his arms — his legs dangled like crossed sounding leads — moving his lips, he begged God to be good to him who was so young, and he swore he would go to the seminary if he were saved. But a moment later he corrected himself, shocked, and promised that instead of becoming a priest he would make sacrifices and do other penances, would give to charity, and there he perceived that vacillation and haggling at that critical moment might be fatal. Then he was aware of Rubén's crazed shouts close at hand and, turning his head, saw him some ten yards off, his face half-sunk in the water, waving one arm, begging, "Miguel, brother, come here, I'm drowning, don't go away!"

He stopped perplexed, motionless, and it was suddenly as if Rubén's despair were kindling his own. He felt himself recovering his courage; the rigidity in his legs was diminishing.

"I've got a cramp in my stomach!" Rubén shrieked. "I can't go on, Miguel. Save me! For the sake of what you love most, don't leave me, brother!"

He floated toward Rubén, and he was about to reach out to him when he remembered that drowning persons often manage to grab hold of their saviors like pincers and pull them under, and he kept clear, but the screams frightened him, and he had a presentiment that if Rubén drowned, he would not reach the beach either, so he turned back. A couple of yards from Rubén, who looked like something white and shrunken that sank and surfaced again, he cried, "Don't move, Rubén! I'm going to tow you, but don't try to hold onto me. If you hold onto me, we'll drown, Rubén. You're going to keep quiet, brother. I'll tow you by your head. Don't you touch me!" He stopped at a prudent distance, reached out his arm until he could grasp Rubén's hair. He began to swim with his free arm, making every effort to help himself with his legs. His progress was slow and arduous; it required all his senses; he scarcely heard Rubén complaining monotonously, suddenly uttering terrible cries, "I'm going to die, save me, Miguel!" or being shaken by retching. He was exhausted when he stopped. He supported Rubén with one hand; with the other he traced circles on the surface. He breathed deeply through his mouth. Rubén's face was contorted with pain, his lips pursed in an unusual grimace.

"It's just a little farther, brother," Miguel murmured. "Keep trying. Answer me, Rubén. Yell! Don't be like that!"

He slapped his face sharply, and Rubén opened his eyes; he shook his head feebly.

"Yell, brother," Miguel repeated. "Try to stretch out. I'm going to massage your stomach. It's just a little farther. Don't let yourself give up."

His hand groped under water, found a hard ball beginning at Rubén's navel and occupying a large part of his belly. He rubbed it many times, slowly at first, then harshly, and Rubén cried out, "I don't want to die, Miguel. Save me!"

He began to swim once more, dragging Rubén this time by his chin. Each time a wave overtook them, Rubén choked, and Miguel shouted to him to spit. He went on swimming, not stopping for a moment, closing his eyes at times, encouraged because a sort of confidence, something warm and proud and stimulating that was protecting him against cold and fatigue had sprung up in his heart. A stone scraped one of his feet, but he merely cried out and went on faster. A moment later he stopped and put his arms around Rubén. Holding him pressed against himself, feeling his head supported on one shoulder, he rested for a long time. Then he helped Rubén to turn onto his back and, supporting him on his forearm, forced him to stretch out his legs; he massaged his belly until the hardness began to yield. Rubén was not screaming now; he was making a great effort to stretch out completely, and he rubbed himself with his hands too.

"Feel better?"

"Yes, brother, I'm all right. Let's get out of here."

An inexpressible joy filled them as they came in over the stones, bending forward to face the undertow, insensitive to the spiny sea urchins. In a little while they saw the edge of the cliffs, the bathhouse, and finally, now close to the bank, the Sharpies standing in the women's gallery, watching them.

"Look," Rubén said.

"What?"

"Don't tell them anything. Please don't tell 'em I screamed. We've always been good friends, Miguel. Don't do that to me."

"Do you think I'd be such a stinker?" Miguel said. "I won't say anything, don't worry."

They emerged shivering. They sat on the steps surrounded by excited Sharpies.

"We were about to send condolences to your families," Tobías remarked.

"You were in for more than an hour," the Scholar said. "Tell us, how was it?"

Speaking calmly, while he dried his body with his undershirt, Rubén explained:

"It wasn't anything. We went out to the breakers and back. So, we're Sharpies. Miguel beat me, by just a stroke. Of course, if it'd been in a pool, he'd have made a fool of himself."

Congratulatory slaps rained on the back of Miguel, who had dressed without drying off.

"You're getting to be quite a man," Melanés told him.

Miguel did not answer. Smiling, he was thinking he would go to Salazar Park that very night. All of Miraflores would already know from Melanés' account that he had won that heroic test, and Flora would be waiting for him, her eyes shining. A golden future was opening out in front of him.

[1958]

Translated by
MARY E. ELLSWORTH

QUESTIONS

1. Does the concept of masculinity give Vargas Llosa's story a universal quality? If so, in what way does it expose gender stereotypes? With a few variations of names and places, could the story take place in the United States? Or is the assertion of masculinity distinctly Latin?
2. Why is the story called "Sunday"?
3. Is it possible to argue that both Miguel and Rubén have "won" by the end of the story?

Alice Walker

(b. 1944)

United States

Alice Walker, the youngest of eight children, was born to sharecroppers in Eatonton, Georgia. Despite the family's poverty, Walker's mother, a strong, caring woman, gave her children a strong sense of their own capabilities. Walker was educated at Spelman College in Atlanta and Sarah Lawrence in New York. During the 1960s she became active in the civil rights movement both as a caseworker for the New York City Welfare Department and as an activist for voter registration in Mississippi. During those years she met and married a white civil rights co-worker and had a daughter; the marriage was later dissolved.

Walker is a versatile writer who began by publishing poetry (totaling four volumes to date). She has also published several collections of short stories and essays as well as four novels: *The Third Life of Grange Copeland* (1970), *Meridian* (1976), *The Color Purple* (1982)—for which she was awarded a Pulitzer Prize—and *The Temple of My Familiar* (1989). The subjects of her fiction include the impact of racism and sexism on the relationships between black men and women and the affirmative powers of love and family. As she phrases it, "If art doesn't make us better, then what on earth is it for?" In her well-known essay, "In Search of Our Mothers' Gardens" (1974) Walker identifies the source of that conviction by celebrating the heritage of black women's creative spirit—particularly the inspiration of her own mother—despite their historical exclusion from artistic opportunity: "Our mothers and grandmothers have, more often than not anonymously, handed on the creative spark, the seed of the flower they themselves never hoped to see: or like a sealed letter they could not plainly read."

◆ *Everyday Use* ◆

For your grandmama

I will wait for her in the yard that Maggie and I made so clean and wavy yesterday afternoon. A yard like this is more comfortable than most people know. It is not just a yard. It is like an extended living room. When the hard clay is swept clean as a floor and the fine sand around the edges lined with tiny, irregular grooves, anyone can come and sit and look up into the elm tree and wait for the breezes that never come inside the house.

Maggie will be nervous until after her sister goes: she will stand hopelessly in corners, homely and ashamed of the burn scars down her arms and legs, eying her sister with a mixture of envy and awe. She thinks her sister has held life always in the palm of one hand, that "no" is a word the world never learned to say to her.

You've no doubt seen those TV shows where the child who has "made it" is confronted, as a surprise, by her own mother and father, tottering in weakly from backstage.[1] (A pleasant surprise, of course: What would they do if parent and child came on the show only to curse out and insult each other?) On TV mother and child embrace and smile into each other's faces. Sometimes the mother and father weep, the child wraps them in her arms and leans across the table to tell how she would not have made it without their help. I have seen these programs.

Sometimes I dream a dream in which Dee and I are suddenly brought together on a TV program of this sort. Out of a dark and soft-seated limousine I am ushered into a bright room filled with many people. There I meet a smiling, gray, sporty man like Johnny Carson who shakes my hand and tells me what a fine girl I have. Then we are on the stage and Dee is embracing me with tears in her eyes. She pins on my dress a large orchid, even though she has told me once that she thinks orchids are tacky flowers.

In real life I am a large, big-boned woman with rough, man-working hands. In the winter I wear flannel nightgowns to bed and overalls during the day. I can kill and clean a hog as mercilessly as a man. My fat keeps me hot in zero weather. I can work outside all day, breaking ice to get water for washing; I can eat pork liver cooked over the open fire minutes after it comes steaming from the hog. One winter I knocked a bull calf straight in the brain between the eyes with a sledge hammer and had the meat hung up to chill before nightfall. But of course all this does not show on television. I am the way my daughter would want me to be: a hundred pounds lighter, my skin like an uncooked barley pancake. My hair glistens in the hot bright lights. Johnny Carson has much to do to keep up with my quick and witty tongue.

But that is a mistake. I know even before I wake up. Who ever knew a Johnson with a quick tongue? Who can even imagine me looking a strange white man in the eye? It seems to me I have talked to them always with one foot raised in flight, with my head turned in whichever way is farthest from them. Dee, though. She would always look anyone in the eye. Hesitation was no part of her nature.

"How do I look, Mama?" Maggie says, showing just enough of her thin body enveloped in pink skirt and red blouse for me to know she's there, almost hidden by the door.

"Come out into the yard," I say.

Have you ever seen a lame animal, perhaps a dog run over by some careless person rich enough to own a car, sidle up to someone who is ignorant enough to be kind to him? That is the way my Maggie walks. She has been like this, chin on chest, eyes on ground, feet in shuffle, ever since the fire that burned the other house to the ground.

Dee is lighter than Maggie, with nicer hair and a fuller figure. She's a woman now, though sometimes I forget. How long ago was it that the other house burned? Ten, twelve years? Sometimes I can still hear the flames and feel Maggie's arms sticking to me, her hair smoking and her dress falling off her in little black papery flakes. Her eyes seemed stretched open, blazed open by the flames reflected in them. And Dee. I see her standing off under the sweet gum tree she used to dig

[1]a reference to a television program of the 1960s, "This Is Your Life," in which reunions between long-separated family members and friends were televised live from the studio

gum out of; a look of concentration on her face as she watched the last dingy gray board of the house fall in toward the red-hot brick chimney. Why don't you do a dance around the ashes? I'd wanted to ask her. She had hated the house that much.

I used to think she hated Maggie, too. But that was before we raised the money, the church and me, to send her to Augusta to school. She used to read to us without pity; forcing words, lies, other folks' habits, whole lives upon us two, sitting trapped and ignorant underneath her voice. She washed us in a river of make-believe, burned us with a lot of knowledge we didn't necessarily need to know. Pressed us to her with the serious way she read, to shove us away at just the moment, like dimwits, we seemed about to understand.

Dee wanted nice things. A yellow organdy dress to wear to her graduation from high school; black pumps to match a green suit she'd made from an old suit somebody gave me. She was determined to stare down any disaster in her efforts. Her eyelids would not flicker for minutes at a time. Often I fought off the temptation to shake her. At sixteen she had a style of her own: and knew what style was.

I never had an education myself. After second grade the school was closed down. Don't ask my why: in 1927 colored asked fewer questions than they do now. Sometimes Maggie reads to me. She stumbles along good-naturedly but can't see well. She knows she is not bright. Like good looks and money, quickness passed her by. She will marry John Thomas (who has mossy teeth in an earnest face) and then I'll be free to sit here and I guess just sing church songs to myself. Although I never was a good singer. Never could carry a tune. I was always better at a man's job. I used to love to milk till I was hooked in the side[2] in '49. Cows are soothing and slow and don't bother you, unless you try to milk them the wrong way.

I have deliberately turned my back on the house. It is three rooms, just like the one that burned, except the roof is tin; they don't make shingle roofs any more. There are no real windows, just some holes cut in the sides, like the portholes in a ship, but not round and not square, with rawhide holding the shutters up on the outside. This house is in a pasture, too, like the other one. No doubt when Dee sees it she will want to tear it down. She wrote me once that no matter where we "choose" to live, she will manage to come see us. But she will never bring her friends. Maggie and I thought about this and Maggie asked me, "Mama, when did Dee ever *have* any friends?"

She had a few. Furtive boys in pink shirts hanging about on washday after school. Nervous girls who never laughed. Impressed with her they worshiped the well-turned phrase, the cute shape, the scalding humor that erupted like bubbles in lye. She read to them.

When she was courting Jimmy T she didn't have much time to pay to us, but turned all her faultfinding power on him. He *flew* to marry a cheap city girl from a family of ignorant flashy people. She hardly had time to recompose herself.

When she comes I will meet—but there they are!

Maggie attempts to make a dash for the house, in her shuffling way, but I stay her with my hand. "Come back here," I say. And she stops and tries to dig a well in the sand with her toe.

[2]*hooked in the side* kicked by a cow

It is hard to see them clearly through the strong sun. But even the first glimpse of leg out of the car tells me it is Dee. Her feet were always neat-looking, as if God himself had shaped them with a certain style. From the other side of the car comes a short, stocky man. Hair is all over his head a foot long and hanging from his chin like a kinky mule tail. I hear Maggie suck in her breath. "Uhnnnh," is what it sounds like. Like when you see the wriggling end of a snake just in front of your foot on the road. "Uhnnnh."

Dee next. A dress down to the ground, in this hot weather. A dress so loud it hurts my eyes. There are yellows and oranges enough to throw back the light of the sun. I feel my whole face warming from the heat waves it throws out. Earrings gold, too, and hanging down to her shoulders. Bracelets dangling and making noises when she moves her arm up to shake the folds of the dress out of her armpits. The dress is loose and flows, and as she walks closer, I like it. I hear Maggie go "Uhnnnh" again. It is her sister's hair. It stands straight up like the wool on a sheep. It is black as night and around the edges are two long pigtails that rope about like small lizards disappearing behind her ears.

"Wa-su-zo-Tean-o!"[3] she says, coming on in that gliding way the dress makes her move. The short stocky fellow with the hair to his navel is all grinning and he follows up with "Asalamalakim,[4] my mother and sister!" He moves to hug Maggie but she falls back, right up against the back of my chair. I feel her trembling there and when I look up I see the perspiration falling off her chin.

"Don't get up," says Dee. Since I am stout it takes something of a push. You can see me trying to move a second or two before I make it. She turns, showing white heels through her sandals, and goes back to the car. Out she peeks next with a Polaroid. She stoops down quickly and lines up picture after picture of me sitting there in front of the house with Maggie cowering behind me. She never takes a shot without making sure the house is included. When a cow comes nibbling around the edge of the yard she snaps it and me and Maggie *and* the house. Then she puts the Polaroid in the back seat of the car, and comes up and kisses me on the forehead.

Meanwhile Asalamalakim is going through motions with Maggie's hand. Maggie's hand is as limp as a fish, and probably as cold, despite the sweat, and she keeps trying to pull it back. It looks like Asalamalakim wants to shake hands but wants to do it fancy. Or maybe he don't know how people shake hands. Anyhow, he soon gives up on Maggie.

"Well," I say. "Dee."

"No, Mama," she says. "Not 'Dee,' Wangero Leewanika Kemanjo!"

"What happened to 'Dee'?" I wanted to know.

"She's dead," Wangero said. "I couldn't bear it any longer, being named after the people who oppress me."

"You know as well as me you was named after your aunt Dicie," I said. Dicie is my sister. She named Dee. We called her "Big Dee" after Dee was born.

"But who was *she* named after?" asked Wangero.

"I guess after Grandma Dee," I said.

"And who was she named after?" asked Wangero.

"Her mother," I said, and saw Wangero was getting tired. "That's about as far

[3]*Wa-su-zo-Tean-o!* a greeting in African dialect, phonetically rendered

[4]*Asalamalakim* Muslim salutation

back as I can trace it," I said. Though, in fact, I probably could have carried it back beyond the Civil War through the branches.

"Well," said Asalamalakim, "there you are."

"Uhnnnh," I heard Maggie say.

"There I was not," I said, "before 'Dicie' cropped up in our family, so why should I try to trace it that far back?"

He just stood there grinning, looking down on me like somebody inspecting a Model A car. Every once in a while he and Wangero sent eye signals over my head.

"How do you pronounce this name?" I asked.

"You don't have to call me by it if you don't want to," said Wangero.

"Why shouldn't I?" I asked. "If that's what you want us to call you, we'll call you."

"I know it might sound awkward at first," said Wangero.

"I'll get used to it," I said. "Ream it out again."

Well, soon we got the name out of the way. Asalamalakim had a name twice as long and three times as hard. After I tripped over it two or three times he told me to just call him Hakim-a-barber. I wanted to ask him was he a barber, but I didn't really think he was, so I didn't ask.

"You must belong to those beef-cattle peoples down the road," I said. They said "Asalamalakim" when they met you, too, but they didn't shake hands. Always too busy: feeding the cattle, fixing the fences, putting up salt-lick shelters, throwing down hay. When the white folks poisoned some of the herd the men stayed up all night with rifles in their hands. I walked a mile and a half just to see the sight.

Hakim-a-barber said, "I accept some of their doctrines, but farming and raising cattle is not my style." (They didn't tell me, and I didn't ask, whether Wangero (Dee) had really gone and married him.)

We sat down to eat and right away he said he didn't eat collards and pork was unclean. Wangero, though, went on through the chitlins and corn bread, the greens and everything else. She talked a blue streak over the sweet potatoes. Everything delighted her. Even the fact that we still used the benches her daddy made for the table when we couldn't afford to buy chairs.

"Oh, Mama!" she cried. Then turned to Hakim-a-barber. "I never knew how lovely these benches are. You can feel the rump prints," she said, running her hands underneath her and along the bench. Then she gave a sigh and her hand closed over Grandma Dee's butter dish. "That's it!" she said. "I knew there was something I wanted to ask you if I could have." She jumped up from the table and went over in the corner where the churn stood, the milk in it clabber by now. She looked at the churn and looked at it.

"This churn top is what I need," she said. "Didn't Uncle Buddy whittle it out of a tree you all used to have?"

"Yes," I said.

"Uh huh," she said happily. "And I want the dasher, too."

"Uncle Buddy whittle that, too?" asked the barber.

Dee (Wangero) looked up at me.

"Aunt Dee's first husband whittled the dash," said Maggie so low you almost couldn't hear her. "His name was Henry, but they called him Stash."

"Maggie's brain is like an elephant's," Wangero said, laughing. "I can use the churn top as a centerpiece for the alcove table," she said, sliding a plate over the churn, "and I'll think of something artistic to do with the dasher."

When she finished wrapping the dasher the handle stuck out. I took it for a moment in my hands. You didn't even have to look close to see where hands pushing the dasher up and down to make butter had left a kind of sink in the wood. In fact, there were a lot of small sinks; you could see where thumbs and fingers had sunk into the wood. It was beautiful light yellow wood, from a tree that grew in the yard where Big Dee and Stash had lived.

After dinner Dee (Wangero) went to the trunk at the foot of my bed and started rifling through it. Maggie hung back in the kitchen over the dishpan. Out came Wangero with two quilts. They had been pieced by Grandma Dee and then Big Dee and me had hung them on the quilt frames on the front porch and quilted them. One was in the Lone Star pattern. The other was Walk Around the Mountain. In both of them were scraps of dresses Grandma Dee had worn fifty and more years ago. Bits and pieces of Grandpa Jarrell's Paisley shirts. And one teeny faded blue piece, about the size of a penny matchbox, that was from Great Grandpa Ezra's uniform that he wore in the Civil War.

"Mama," Wangero said sweet as a bird. "Can I have these old quilts?"

I heard something fall in the kitchen, and a minute later the kitchen door slammed.

"Why don't you take one or two of the others?" I asked. "These old things was just done by me and Big Dee from some tops your grandma pieced before she died."

"No," said Wangero. "I don't want those. They are stitched around the borders by machine."

"That'll make them last better," I said.

"That's not the point," said Wangero. "These are all pieces of dresses Grandma used to wear. She did all this stitching by hand. Imagine!" She held the quilts securely in her arms, stroking them.

"Some of the pieces, like those lavender ones, come from old clothes her mother handed down to her," I said, moving up to touch the quilts. Dee (Wangero) moved back just enough so that I couldn't reach the quilts. They already belonged to her.

"Imagine!" she breathed again, clutching them closely to her bosom.

"The truth is," I said, "I promised to give them quilts to Maggie, for when she marries John Thomas."

She gasped like a bee had stung her.

"Maggie can't appreciate these quilts!" she said. "She'd probably be backward enough to put them to everyday use."

"I reckon she would," I said. "God knows I been saving 'em for long enough with nobody using 'em. I hope she will!" I didn't want to bring up how I had offered Dee (Wangero) a quilt when she went away to college. Then she had told me they were old-fashioned, out of style.

"But they're *priceless*!" she was saying now, furiously; for she has a temper. "Maggie would put them on the bed and in five years they'd be in rags. Less than that!"

"She can always make some more," I said. "Maggie knows how to quilt."

Dee (Wangero) looked at me with hatred. "You just will not understand. The point is these quilts, *these* quilts!"

"Well," I said, stumped. "What would *you* do with them?"

"Hang them," she said. As if that was the only thing you *could* do with quilts.

Maggie by now was standing in the door. I could almost hear the sound her feet made as they scraped over each other.

"She can have them, Mama," she said, like somebody used to never winning anything, or having anything reserved for her. "I can 'member Grandma Dee without the quilts."

I looked at her hard. She had filled her bottom lip with checkerberry snuff and it gave her face a kind of dopey, hangdog look. It was Grandma Dee and Big Dee who taught her how to quilt herself. She stood there with her scarred hands hidden in the folds of her skirt. She looked at her sister with something like fear but she wasn't mad at her. This was Maggie's portion. This was the way she knew God to work.

When I looked at her like that something hit me in the top of my head and ran down to the soles of my feet. Just like when I'm in church and the spirit of God touches me and I get happy and shout. I did something I never had done before: hugged Maggie to me, then dragged her on into the room, snatched the quilts out of Miss Wangero's hands and dumped them into Maggie's lap. Maggie just sat there on my bed with her mouth open.

"Take one or two of the others," I said to Dee.

But she turned without a word and went out to Hakim-a-barber.

"You just don't understand," she said, as Maggie and I came out to the car.

"What don't I understand?" I wanted to know.

"Your heritage," she said. And then she turned to Maggie, kissed her, and said, "You ought to try to make something of yourself, too, Maggie. It's really a new day for us. But from the way you and Mama still live you'd never know it."

She put on some sunglasses that hid everything above the tip of her nose and her chin.

Maggie smiled; maybe at the sunglasses. But a real smile, not scared. After we watched the car dust settle I asked Maggie to bring me a dip of snuff. And then the two of us sat there just enjoying, until it was time to go in the house and go to bed.

[1973]

QUESTIONS

1. How does the mother, who narrates the story, express her own values as she establishes the story's central conflict? How does the mother's point of view shape the story?
2. What symbolic role do the family quilts play in the story?
3. Are both daughters' positions given equal value? What influences the mother to make the choice she makes between the wishes of her two daughters?
4. How are images and objects of popular culture (such as Johnny Carson and Polaroid cameras) used to develop the story's theme?

EUDORA WELTY

(b. 1909)

UNITED STATES

One distinguishing mark of many of Eudora Welty's short stories is her unique use of narrative voice. So famous is Welty for her dialogue (often first-person narratives that are actually monologues) that critics have repeatedly asked her to explain her concept of voice. When she was asked specifically about "Why I Live at the P.O." by Bill Ferris in 1975, Welty replied,

> I think the ability to use dialogue, or the first person, or anything like that, is just as essential as the knowledge of place and other components of a story. But I think it has a special importance, because you can use it in fiction to do very subtle things and very many things at once—like giving a notion of the speaker's background, furthering the plot, giving the sense of give-and-take between characters. Dialogue gives a character's age, background, upbringing, everything, without the author's having to explain it on the side. He's doing it out of his own mouth. And also, other things—like a character may be telling a lie which he will show to the reader, but perhaps not to the person to whom he's talking, and perhaps not even realize himself. Sometimes he's deluded. All these things can come out in dialogue.

Eudora Welty was born in Jackson, Mississippi. After attending several universities, she began a career as a journalist. During the depression, she worked for the Works Progress Administration (WPA). She has won major literary awards and prizes, including the Pulitzer Prize in fiction for *The Optimist's Daughter* (1973). Her stories, however, began appearing much earlier. The first of many of these volumes, *A Curtain of Green*, was published in 1941. Other Welty collections and novels include *The Robber Bridegroom* (1942), *Delta Wedding* (1946), *The Golden Apples* (1949), *Thirteen Stories* (1965), and *Losing Battles* (1970). Welty's three lectures at Harvard in April of 1983 (to inaugurate the William E. Massy lecture series) were collected in the critically praised volume, *One Writer's Beginnings* (1984).

In "Finding a Voice" (the third lecture in the Massy series), Welty said,

> Writing a story or a novel is one way of discovering *sequence* in experience, of stumbling upon cause and effect in the happenings of a writer's own life. This has been the case with me. Connections slowly emerge. Like distant landmarks you are approaching, cause and effect begin to align themselves, draw closer together. Experiences too indefinite of outline in themselves to be recognized for themselves connect and are identified as a larger shape. And suddenly a light is thrown back, as when your train makes a curve, showing that there has been a

mountain of meaning rising behind you on the way you've come, is rising there still, proven now through retrospect.

Why I Live at the P.O.

I was getting along fine with Mama, Papa-Daddy, and Uncle Rondo until my sister Stella-Rondo just separated from her husband and came back home again. Mr. Whitaker! Of course I went with Mr. Whitaker first, when he first appeared here in China Grove, taking "Pose Yourself" photos, and Stella-Rondo broke us up. Told him I was one-sided. Bigger on one side than the other, which is a deliberate, calculated falsehood: I'm the same. Stella-Rondo is exactly twelve months to the day younger than I am and for that reason she's spoiled.

She's always had anything in the world she wanted and then she'd throw it away. Papa-Daddy gave her this gorgeous Add-a-Pearl necklace when she was eight years old and she threw it away playing baseball when she was nine, with only two pearls.

So as soon as she got married and moved away from home the first thing she did was separate! From Mr. Whitaker! This photographer with the popeyes she said she trusted. Came home from one of those towns up in Illinois and to our complete surprise brought this child of two.

Mama said she like to make her drop dead for a second. "Here you had this marvelous blonde child and never so much as wrote your mother a word about it," says Mama. "I'm thoroughly ashamed of you." But of course she wasn't.

Stella-Rondo just calmly takes off this *hat*, I wish you could see it. She says, "Why, Mama, Shirley-T.'s adopted, I can prove it."

"How?" says Mama, but all I says was, "H'm!" There I was over the hot stove, trying to stretch two chickens over five people and a completely unexpected child into the bargain, without one moment's notice.

"What do you mean — 'H'm!'?" says Stella-Rondo, and Mama says, "I heard that, Sister."

I said that oh, I didn't mean a thing, only that whoever Shirley-T. was, she was the spit-image of Papa-Daddy if he'd cut off his beard, which of course he'd never do in the world. Papa-Daddy's Mama's papa and sulks.

Stella-Rondo got furious! She said, "Sister, I don't need to tell you you got a lot of nerve and always did have and I'll thank you to make no future reference to my adopted child whatsoever."

"Very well," I said. "Very well, very well. Of course I noticed at once she looks like Mr. Whitaker's side too. That frown. She looks like a cross between Mr. Whitaker and Papa-Daddy."

"Well, all I can say is she isn't."

"She looks exactly like Shirley Temple to me," says Mama, but Shirley-T. just ran away from her.

So the first thing Stella-Rondo did at the table was turn Papa-Daddy against me.

"Papa-Daddy," she says. He was trying to cut up his meat. "Papa-Daddy!" I was taken completely by surprise. Papa-Daddy is about a million years old and's got this long-long beard. "Papa-Daddy, Sister says she fails to understand why you don't cut off your beard."

So Papa-Daddy l-a-y-s down his knife and fork! He's real rich. Mama says he is, he says he isn't. So he says, "Have I heard correctly? You don't understand why I don't cut off my beard?"

"Why," I says, "Papa-Daddy, of course I understand, I did not say any such of a thing, the idea!"

He says, "Hussy!"

I says, "Papa-Daddy, you know I wouldn't any more want you to cut off your beard than the man in the moon. It was the farthest thing from my mind! Stella-Rondo sat there and made that up while she was eating breast of chicken."

But he says, "So the postmistress fails to understand why I don't cut off my beard. Which job I got you through my influence with the government. 'Bird's nest'—is that what you call it?"

Not that it isn't the next to smallest P.O. in the entire state of Mississippi.

I says, "Oh, Papa-Daddy," I says, "I didn't say any such of a thing, I never dreamed it was a bird's nest, I have always been grateful though this is the next to smallest P.O. in the state of Mississippi, and I do not enjoy being referred to as a hussy by my own grandfather."

But Stella-Rondo says, "Yes, you did say it too. Anybody in the world could of heard you, that had ears."

"Stop right there," says Mama, looking at *me*.

So I pulled my napkin straight back through the napkin ring and left the table.

As soon as I was out of the room Mama says, "Call her back, or she'll starve to death," but Papa-Daddy says, "This is the beard I started growing on the Coast when I was fifteen years old." He would of gone on till nightfall if Shirley-T. hadn't lost the Milky Way she ate in Cairo.[1]

So Papa-Daddy says, "I am going out and lie in the hammock, and you can all sit here and remember my words: I'll never cut off my beard as long as I live, even one inch, and I don't appreciate it in you at all." Passed right by me in the hall and went straight out and got in the hammock.

It would be a holiday. It wasn't five minutes before Uncle Rondo suddenly appeared in the hall in one of Stella-Rondo's flesh-colored kimonos, all cut on the bias, like something Mr. Whitaker probably thought was gorgeous.

"Uncle Rondo!" I says. "I didn't know who that was! Where are you going?"

"Sister," he says, "get out of my way, I'm poisoned."

"If you're poisoned stay away from Papa-Daddy," I says. "Keep out of the hammock. Papa-Daddy will certainly beat you on the head if you come within forty miles of him. He thinks I deliberately said he ought to cut off his beard after he got me the P.O., and I've told him and told him and told him, and he acts like he just don't hear me. Papa-Daddy must of gone stone deaf."

"He picked a fine day to do it then," says Uncle Rondo, and before you could say "Jack Robinson" flew out in the yard.

What he'd really done, he'd drunk another bottle of that prescription. He does it every single Fourth of July as sure as shooting, and it's horribly expensive. Then he falls over in the hammock and snores. So he insisted on zigzagging right on out to the hammock, looking like a half-wit.

[1]*Cairo* Cairo, Illinois

Papa-Daddy woke up with this horrible yell and right there without moving an inch he tried to turn Uncle Rondo against me. I heard every word he said. Oh, he told Uncle Rondo I didn't learn to read till I was eight years old and he didn't see how in the world I ever got the mail put up at the P.O., much less read it all, and he said if Uncle Rondo could only fathom the lengths he had gone to get me that job! And he said on the other hand he thought Stella-Rondo had a brilliant mind and deserved credit for getting out of town. All the time he was just lying there swinging as pretty as you please and looping out his beard, and poor Uncle Rondo was *pleading* with him to slow down the hammock, it was making him as dizzy as a witch to watch it. But that's what Papa-Daddy likes about a hammock. So Uncle Rondo was too dizzy to get turned against me for the time being. He's Mama's only brother and is a good case of a one-track mind. Ask anybody. A certified pharmacist.

Just then I heard Stella-Rondo raising the upstairs window. While she was married she got this peculiar idea that it's cooler with the windows shut and locked. So she has to raise the window before she can make a soul hear her outdoors.

So she raises the window and says, "*Oh!*" You would have thought she was mortally wounded.

Uncle Rondo and Papa-Daddy didn't even look up, but kept right on with what they were doing. I had to laugh.

I flew up the stairs and threw the door open! I says, "What in the wide world's the matter, Stella-Rondo? You mortally wounded?"

"No," she says, "I am not mortally wounded but I wish you would do me the favor of looking out that window there and telling me what you see."

So I shade my eyes and look out the window.

"I see the front yard," I says.

"Don't you see any human beings?" she says.

"I see Uncle Rondo trying to run Papa-Daddy out of the hammock," I says. "Nothing more. Naturally, it's so suffocating-hot in the house, with all the windows shut and locked, everybody who cares to stay in their right mind will have to go out and get in the hammock before the Fourth of July is over."

"Don't you notice anything different about Uncle Rondo?" asks Stella-Rondo.

"Why, no, except he's got on some terrible-looking flesh-colored contraption I wouldn't be found dead in, is all I can see," I says.

"Never mind, you won't be found dead in it, because it happens to be part of my trousseau, and Mr. Whitaker took several dozen photographs of me in it," says Stella-Rondo. "What on earth could Uncle Rondo *mean* by wearing part of my trousseau out in the broad open daylight without saying so much as 'Kiss my foot,' *knowing* I only got home this morning after my separation and hung my negligee up on the bathroom door, just as nervous as I could be?"

"I'm sure I don't know, and what do you expect me to do about it?" I says. "Jump out the window?"

"No, I expect nothing of the kind. I simply declare that Uncle Rondo looks like a fool in it, that's all," she says. "It makes me sick to my stomach."

"Well, he looks as good as he can," I says. "As good as anybody in reason could." I stood up for Uncle Rondo, please remember. And I said to Stella-Rondo, "I think I would do well not to criticize so freely if I were you and came home with a two-year-old child I had never said a word about, and no explanation whatever about my separation."

"I asked you the instant I entered this house not to refer one more time to my adopted child, and you gave me your word of honor you would not," was all Stella-Rondo would say, and started pulling out every one of her eyebrows with some cheap Kress tweezers.

So I merely slammed the door behind me and went down and made some green-tomato pickle. Somebody had to do it. Of course Mama had turned both the niggers loose; she always said no earthly power could hold one anyway on the Fourth of July, so she wouldn't even try. It turned out that Jaypan fell in the lake and came within a very narrow limit of drowning.

So Mama trots in. Lifts up the lid and says, "H'm! Not very good for your Uncle Rondo in his precarious condition, I must say. Or poor little adopted Shirley-T. Shame on you!"

That made me tired. I says, "Well, Stella-Rondo had better thank her lucky stars it was her instead of me came trotting in with that very peculiar-looking child. Now if it had been me that trotted in from Illinois and brought a peculiar-looking child of two, I shudder to think of the reception I'd of got, much less controlled the diet of an entire family."

"But you must remember, Sister, that you were never married to Mr. Whitaker in the first place and didn't go up to Illinois to live," says Mama, shaking a spoon in my face. "If you had I would of been just as overjoyed to see you and your little adopted girl as I was to see Stella-Rondo, when you wound up with your separation and came on back home."

"You would not," I says.

"Don't contradict me, I would," says Mama.

But I said she couldn't convince me though she talked till she was blue in the face. Then I said, "Besides, you know as well as I do that that child is not adopted."

"She most certainly is adopted," says Mama, stiff as a poker.

I says, "Why, Mama, Stella-Rondo had her just as sure as anything in this world, and just too stuck up to admit it."

"Why, Sister," said Mama. "Here I thought we were going to have a pleasant Fourth of July, and you start right out not believing a word your own baby sister tells you!"

"Just like Cousin Annie Flo. Went to her grave denying the facts of life," I remind Mama.

"I told you if you ever mentioned Annie Flo's name I'd slap your face," says Mama, and slaps my face.

"All right, you wait and see," I says.

"I," says Mama, "I prefer to take my children's word for anything when it's humanly possible." You ought to see Mama, she weighs two hundred pounds and has real tiny feet.

Just then something perfectly horrible occurred to me.

"Mama," I says, "can that child talk?" I simply had to whisper! "Mama, I wonder if that child can be — you know — in any way? Do you realize," I says, "that she hasn't spoken one single, solitary word to a human being up to this minute? This is the way she looks," I says, and I looked like this.

Well, Mama and I just stood there and stared at each other. It was horrible!

"I remember well that Joe Whitaker frequently drank like a fish," says Mama. "I believed to my soul he drank *chemicals*." And without another word she marches to the foot of the stairs and calls Stella-Rondo.

"Stella-Rondo? O-o-o-o-o! Stella-Rondo!"

"What?" says Stella-Rondo from upstairs. Not even the grace to get up off the bed.

"Can that child of yours talk?" asks Mama.

Stella-Rondo says, "Can she what?"

"Talk! Talk!" says Mama. "Burdyburdyburdyburdy!"

So Stella-Rondo yells back, "Who says she can't talk?"

"Sister says so," says Mama.

"You didn't have to tell me, I know whose word of honor don't mean a thing in this house," says Stella-Rondo.

And in a minute the loudest Yankee voice I ever heard in my life yells out, "OE'm Pop-OE the Sailor-r-r-r Ma-a-an!" and then somebody jumps up and down in the upstairs hall. In another second the house would of fallen down.

"Not only talks, she can tap-dance!" calls Stella-Rondo. "Which is more than some people I won't name can do."

"Why, the little precious darling thing!" Mama says, so surprised. "Just as smart as she can be!" Starts talking baby talk right there. Then she turns on me. "Sister, you ought to be thoroughly ashamed! Run upstairs this instant and apologize to Stella-Rondo and Shirley-T."

"Apologize for what?" I says. "I merely wondered if the child was normal, that's all. Now that she's proved she is, why, I have nothing further to say."

But Mama just turned on her heel and flew out, furious. She ran right upstairs and hugged the baby. She believed it was adopted. Stella-Rondo hadn't done a thing but turn her against me from upstairs while I stood there helpless over the hot stove. So that made Mama, Papa-Daddy, and the baby all on Stella-Rondo's side.

Next, Uncle Rondo.

I must say that Uncle Rondo has been marvelous to me at various times in the past and I was completely unprepared to be made to jump out of my skin, the way it turned out. Once Stella-Rondo did something perfectly horrible to him — broke a chain letter from Flanders Field — and he took the radio back he had given her and gave it to me. Stella-Rondo was furious! For six months we all had to call her Stella instead of Stella-Rondo, or she wouldn't answer. I always thought Uncle Rondo had all the brains of the entire family. Another time he sent me to Mammoth Cave, with all expenses paid.

But this would be the day he was drinking that prescription, the Fourth of July.

So at supper Stella-Rondo speaks up and says she thinks Uncle Rondo ought to try to eat a little something. So finally Uncle Rondo said he would try a little cold biscuits and ketchup, but that was all. So *she* brought it to him.

"Do you think it wise to disport with ketchup in Stella-Rondo's flesh-colored kimono?" I says. Trying to be considerate! If Stella-Rondo couldn't watch out for her trousseau, somebody had to.

"Any objections?" asks Uncle Rondo, just about to pour out all the ketchup.

"Don't mind what she says, Uncle Rondo," says Stella-Rondo. "Sister has been devoting this solid afternoon to sneering out my bedroom window at the way you look."

"What's that?" says Uncle Rondo. Uncle Rondo has got the most terrible temper in the world. Anything is liable to make him tear the house down if it comes at the wrong time.

So Stella-Rondo says, "Sister says, 'Uncle Rondo certainly does look like a fool in that pink kimono!'"

Do you remember who it was really said that?

Uncle Rondo spills out all the ketchup and jumps out of his chair and tears off the kimono and throws it down on the dirty floor and puts his foot on it. It had to be sent all the way to Jackson to the cleaners and repleated.

"So that's your opinion of your Uncle Rondo, is it?" he says. "I look like a fool, do I? Well, that's the last straw. A whole day in this house with nothing to do, and then to hear you come out with a remark like that behind my back!"

"I didn't say any such of a thing, Uncle Rondo," I says, "and I'm not saying who did, either. Why, I think you look all right. Just try to take care of yourself and not talk and eat at the same time," I says. "I think you better go lie down."

"Lie down my foot," says Uncle Rondo. I ought to of known by that he was fixing to do something perfectly horrible.

So he didn't do anything that night in the precarious state he was in—just played Casino with Mama and Stella-Rondo and Shirley-T. and gave Shirley-T. a nickel with a head on both sides. It tickled her nearly to death, and she called him "Papa." But at 6:30 A.M. the next morning, he threw a whole five-cent package of some unsold one-inch firecrackers from the store as hard as he could into my bedroom and they every one went off. Not one bad one in the string. Anybody else, there'd be one that wouldn't go off.

Well, I'm just terribly susceptible to noise of any kind, the doctor has always told me I was the most sensitive person he had ever seen in his whole life, and I was simply prostrated. I couldn't eat! People tell me they heard it as far as the cemetery, and old Aunt Jep Patterson, that had been holding her own so good, thought it was Judgment Day and she was going to meet her whole family. It's usually so quiet here.

And I'll tell you it didn't take me any longer than a minute to make up my mind what to do. There I was with the whole entire house on Stella-Rondo's side and turned against me. If I have anything at all I have pride.

So I just decided I'd go straight down to the P.O. There's plenty of room there in the back, I says to myself.

Well! I made no bones about letting the family catch on to what I was up to. I didn't try to conceal it.

The first thing they knew, I marched in where they were all playing Old Maid and pulled the electric oscillating fan out by the plug, and everything got real hot. Next I snatched the pillow I'd done the needlepoint on right off the davenport from behind Papa-Daddy. He went "Ugh!" I beat Stella-Rondo up the stairs and finally found my charm bracelet in her bureau drawer under a picture of Nelson Eddy.[2]

"So that's the way the land lies," says Uncle Rondo. There he was, piecing on the ham. "Well, Sister, I'll be glad to donate my army cot if you got any place to set it up, providing you'll leave right this minute and let me get some peace." Uncle Rondo was in France.

"Thank you kindly for the cot and 'peace' is hardly the word I would select if I had to resort to firecrackers at 6:30 A.M. in a young girl's bedroom," I says back to him. "And as to where I intend to go, you seem to forget my position as postmistress of China Grove, Mississippi," I says. "I've always got the P.O."

Well, that made them all sit up and take notice.

[2]*Nelson Eddy* popular Hollywood musical star in the 1930s

I went out front and started digging up some four-o'clocks to plant around the P.O.

"Ah-ah-ah!" says Mama, raising the window. "Those happen to be my four-o'clocks. Everything planted in that star is mine. I've never known you to make anything grow in your life."

"Very well," I says. "But I take the fern. Even you, Mama, can't stand there and deny that I'm the one watered that fern. And I happen to know where I can send in a box top and get a packet of one thousand mixed seeds, no two the same kind, free."

"Oh, where?" Mama wants to know.

But I says, "Too late. You 'tend to your house, and I'll 'tend to mine. You hear things like that all the time if you know how to listen to the radio. Perfectly marvelous offers. Get anything you want free."

So I hope to tell you I marched in and got that radio, and they could of all bit a nail in two, especially Stella-Rondo, that it used to belong to, and she well knew she couldn't get it back, I'd sue for it like a shot. And I very politely took the sewing-machine motor I helped pay the most on to give Mama for Christmas back in 1929, and a good big calendar, with the first-aid remedies on it. The thermometer and the Hawaiian ukulele certainly were rightfully mine, and I stood on the step-ladder and got all my watermelon-rind preserves and every fruit and vegetable I'd put up, every jar. Then I began to pull the tacks out of the bluebird wall vases on the archway to the dining room.

"Who told you you could have those, Miss Priss?" says Mama, fanning as hard as she could.

"I bought 'em and I'll keep track of 'em," I says. "I'll tack 'em up one on each side the post-office window, and you can see 'em when you come to ask me for your mail, if you're so dead to see 'em."

"Not I! I'll never darken the door to that post office again if I live to be a hundred," Mama says. "Ungrateful child! After all the money we spent on you at the Normal."

"Me either," says Stella-Rondo. "You can just let my mail lie there and *rot*, for all I care. I'll never come and relieve you of a single, solitary piece."

"I should worry," I says. "And who you think's going to sit down and write you all those big fat letters and postcards, by the way? Mr. Whitaker? Just because he was the only man ever dropped down in China Grove and you got him — unfairly —is he going to sit down and write you a lengthy correspondence after you come home giving no rhyme nor reason whatsoever for your separation and no explanation for the presence of that child? I may not have your brilliant mind, but I fail to see it."

So Mama says, "Sister, I've told you a thousand times that Stella-Rondo simply got homesick, and this child is far too big to be hers," and she says, "Now, why don't you just sit down and play Casino?"

Then Shirley-T. sticks out her tongue at me in this perfectly horrible way. She has no more manners than the man in the moon. I told her she was going to cross her eyes like that some day and they'd stick.

"It's too late to stop me now," I says. "You should have tried that yesterday. I'm going to the P.O. and the only way you can possibly see me is to visit me there."

So Papa-Daddy says, "You'll never catch me setting foot in that post office, even if I should take a notion into my head to write a letter some place." He says, "I won't have you reachin' out of that little old window with a pair of shears and cuttin' off any beard of mine. I'm too smart for you!"

"We all are," says Stella-Rondo.

But I said, "If you're so smart, where's Mr. Whitaker?"

So then Uncle Rondo says, "I'll thank you from now on to stop reading all the orders I get on postcards and telling everybody in China Grove what you think is the matter with them," but I says, "I draw my own conclusions and will continue in the future to draw them." I says, "If people want to write their inmost secrets on penny postcards, there's nothing in the wide world you can do about it, Uncle Rondo."

"And if you think we'll ever *write* another postcard you're sadly mistaken," says Mama.

"Cutting off your nose to spite your face then," I says. "But if you're all determined to have no more to do with the U.S. mail, think of this: What will Stella-Rondo do now, if she wants to tell Mr. Whitaker to come after her?"

"Wah!" says Stella-Rondo. I knew she'd cry. She had a conniption fit right there in the kitchen.

"It will be interesting to see how long she holds out," I says. "And now—I am leaving."

"Good-bye," says Uncle Rondo.

"Oh, I declare," says Mama, "to think that a family of mine should quarrel on the Fourth of July, or the day after, over Stella-Rondo leaving old Mr. Whitaker and having the sweetest little adopted child! It looks like we'd all be glad!"

"Wah!" says Stella-Rondo, and has a fresh conniption fit.

"*He* left *her*—you mark my words," I says. "That's Mr. Whitaker. I know Mr. Whitaker. After all, I knew him first. I said from the beginning he'd up and leave her. I foretold every single thing that's happened."

"Where did he go?" asks Mama.

"Probably to the North Pole, if he knows what's good for him," I says.

But Stella-Rondo just bawled and wouldn't say another word. She flew to her room and slammed the door.

"Now look what you've gone and done, Sister," says Mama. "You go apologize."

"I haven't got time, I'm leaving," I says.

"Well, what are you waiting around for?" asks Uncle Rondo.

So I just picked up the kitchen clock and marched off, without saying "Kiss my foot," or anything, and never did tell Stella-Rondo good-bye.

There was a nigger girl going along on a little wagon right in front.

"Nigger girl," I says, "come help me haul these things down the hill, I'm going to live in the post office."

Took her nine trips in her express wagon. Uncle Rondo came out on the porch and threw her a nickel.

And that's the last I've laid eyes on any of my family or my family laid eyes on me for five solid days and nights. Stella-Rondo may be telling the most horrible tales in the world about Mr. Whitaker, but I haven't heard them. As I tell everybody, I draw my own conclusions.

But oh, I like it here. It's ideal, as I've been saying. You see, I've got everything cater-cornered, the way I like it. Hear the radio? All the war news. Radio, sewing machine, book ends, ironing board and that great big piano lamp—peace, that's what I like. Butter-bean vines planted all along the front where the strings are.

Of course, there's not much mail. My family are naturally the main people in China Grove, and if they prefer to vanish from the face of the earth, for all the mail they get or the mail they write, why, I'm not going to open my mouth. Some of the folks here in town are taking up for me and some turned against me. I know which is which. There are always people who will quit buying stamps just to get on the right side of Papa-Daddy.

But here I am, and here I'll stay. I want the world to know I'm happy.

And if Stella-Rondo should come to me this minute, on bended knees, and *attempt* to explain the incidents of her life with Mr. Whitaker, I'd simply put my fingers in both my ears and refuse to listen.

[1941]

QUESTIONS

1. Is the narrator of "Why I Live at the P.O." objective about her situation, or is she distorting the events she tells us?
2. What do we specifically know about Welty's narrator in this story? How old is she? What does she value in life? What does she dislike?
3. Are your loyalties with the narrator of the story or with her family? What kind of family has Welty given us in her story?
4. Is the narrator happy at the end of the story—as she says she is?
5. Do you see any similarities between Welty's narrator in "Why I Live at the P.O." and the grandmother in Flannery O'Connor's "A Good Man Is Hard to Find"?

Edith Wharton

(1862–1937)

United States

Edith Jones Wharton acquired the storytelling impulse early—during childhood she frequently "made up" stories—but actually did not become a serious writer until several decades later. Born to wealthy parents who belonged to the aristocratic society of New York, Wharton spent winters in New York and summers in Newport, Rhode Island, and traveled in France and Italy following her social debut at 18. In 1885 she married a Bostonian, Edward ("Teddy") Wharton, who shared her love of travel but few of her other interests, including her literary ambitions. "Teddy" later developed serious mental illness. Eventually they divorced (in 1912) and Edith moved to Europe; she lived in France for the rest of her life. Wharton developed several significant intellectual friendships, including an important one with Henry James, whose encouragement and influence throughout her career were invaluable to her.

Wharton's background gave her unique insight into the social world of the dying aristocracy in turn-of-the-century America. Wharton was, according to Sandra Gilbert and Susan Gubar, "an observer who dissected what had been her dilemma—the struggle of the captive lady against the bars of her gilded cage." Her early novel, *House of Mirth* (1905), is a brilliant indictment of the values of the moneyed class, within which the tragic Lily Bart struggles—unsuccessfully—to locate not only a suitable husband but also herself.

A prolific writer, Wharton published a book a year from 1899 until her death in 1937: 16 novels as well as several novellas, travel narratives, and nearly a dozen volumes of short stories, including some of the best ghost stories in literature. Her major novels besides *House of Mirth* include *Ethan Frome* (1911), *The Custom of the Country* (1913), and *The Age of Innocence* (1920).

◆ Roman Fever ◆

I

From the table at which they had been lunching two American ladies of ripe but well-cared-for middle age moved across the lofty terrace of the Roman restaurant and, leaning on its parapet, looked first at each other, and then down on the outspread glories of the Palatine and the Forum, with the same expression of vague but benevolent approval.

As they leaned there a girlish voice echoed up gaily from the stairs leading to the court below. "Well, come along, then," it cried, not to them but to an invisible companion, "and let's leave the young things to their knitting"; and a voice as fresh laughed back: "Oh, look here, Babs, not actually knitting—" "Well, I mean figuratively," rejoined the first. "After all, we haven't left our poor parents much else to do . . ." and at that point the turn of the stairs engulfed the dialogue.

The two ladies looked at each other again, this time with a tinge of smiling embarrassment, and the smaller and paler one shook her head and coloured slightly.

"Barbara!" she murmured, sending an unheard rebuke after the mocking voice in the stairway.

The other lady, who was fuller, and higher in colour, with a small determined nose supported by vigorous black eyebrows, gave a good-humoured laugh. "That's what our daughters think of us!"

Her companion replied by a deprecating gesture. "Not of us individually. We must remember that. It's just the collective modern idea of Mothers. And you see — " Half guiltily she drew from her handsomely mounted black hand-bag a twist of crimson silk run through by two fine knitting needles. "One never knows," she murmured. "The new system has certainly given us a good deal of time to kill; and sometimes I get tired just looking — even at this." Her gesture was now addressed to the stupendous scene at their feet.

The dark lady laughed again, and they both relapsed upon the view, contemplating it in silence, with a sort of diffused serenity which might have been borrowed from the spring effulgence of the Roman skies. The luncheon-hour was long past, and the two had their end of the vast terrace to themselves. At its opposite extremity a few groups, detained by a lingering look at the outspread city, were gathering up guide-books and fumbling for tips. The last of them scattered, and the two ladies were alone on the air-washed height.

"Well, I don't see why we shouldn't just stay here," said Mrs. Slade, the lady of the high colour and energetic brows. Two derelict basketchairs stood near, and she pushed them into the angle of the parapet, and settled herself in one, her gaze upon the Palatine. "After all, it's still the most beautiful view in the world."

"It always will be, to me," assented her friend Mrs. Ansley, with so slight a stress on the "me" that Mrs. Slade, though she noticed it, wondered if it were not merely accidental, like the random underlinings of old-fashioned letter-writers.

"Grace Ansley was always old-fashioned," she thought; and added aloud, with a retrospective smile: "It's a view we've both been familiar with for a good many years. When we first met here we were younger than our girls are now. You remember?"

"Oh, yes, I remember," murmured Mrs. Ansley, with the same undefinable stress. — "There's that head-waiter wondering," she interpolated. She was evidently far less sure than her companion of herself and of her rights in the world.

"I'll cure him of wondering," said Mrs. Slade, stretching her hand toward a bag as discreetly opulent-looking as Mrs. Ansley's. Signing to the head-waiter, she explained that she and her friend were old lovers of Rome, and would like to spend the end of the afternoon looking down on the view — that is, if it did not disturb the service? The head-waiter, bowing over her gratuity, assured her that the ladies were most welcome, and would be still more so if they would condescend to remain for dinner. A full moon night, they would remember. . . .

Mrs. Slade's black brows drew together, as though references to the moon were out-of-place and even unwelcome. But she smiled away her frown as the head-waiter retreated. "Well, why not? We might do worse. There's no knowing, I suppose, when the girls will be back. Do you even know back from *where*? I don't!"

Mrs. Ansley again coloured slightly. "I think those young Italian aviators we met at the Embassy invited them to fly to Tarquinia for tea. I suppose they'll want to wait and fly back by moonlight."

"Moonlight—moonlight! What a part it still plays. Do you suppose they're as sentimental as we were?"

"I've come to the conclusion that I don't in the least know what they are," said Mrs. Ansley. "And perhaps we didn't know much more about each other."

"No; perhaps we didn't."

Her friend gave her a shy glance. "I never should have supposed you were sentimental, Alida."

"Well, perhaps I wasn't." Mrs. Slade drew her lids together in retrospect; and for a few moments the two ladies, who had been intimate since childhood, reflected how little they knew each other. Each one, of course, had a label ready to attach to the other's name; Mrs. Delphin Slade, for instance, would have told herself, or any one who asked her, that Mrs. Horace Ansley, twenty-five years ago, had been exquisitely lovely—no, you wouldn't believe it, would you? . . . though, of course, still charming, distinguished. . . . Well, as a girl she had been exquisite; far more beautiful than her daughter Barbara, though certainly Babs, according to the new standards at any rate, was more effective—had more *edge*, as they say. Funny where she got it, with those two nullities as parents. Yes; Horace Ansley was—well, just the duplicate of his wife. Museum specimens of old New York. Good-looking, irreproachable, exemplary. Mrs. Slade and Mrs. Ansley had lived opposite each other—actually as well as figuratively—for years. When the drawing-room curtains in No. 20 East 73rd Street were renewed, No. 23, across the way, was always aware of it. And of all the movings, buyings, travels, anniversaries, illnesses—the tame chronicle of an estimable pair. Little of it escaped Mrs. Slade. But she had grown bored with it by the time her husband made his big *coup* in Wall Street, and when they bought in upper Park Avenue had already begun to think: "I'd rather live opposite a speak-easy for a change; at least one might see it raided." The idea of seeing Grace raided was so amusing that (before the move) she launched it at a woman's lunch. It made a hit, and went the rounds—she sometimes wondered if it had crossed the street, and reached Mrs. Ansley. She hoped not, but didn't much mind. Those were the days when respectability was at a discount, and it did the irreproachable no harm to laugh at them a little.

A few years later, and not many months apart, both ladies lost their husbands. There was an appropriate exchange of wreaths and condolences, and a brief renewal of intimacy in the half-shadow of their mourning; and now, after another interval, they had run across each other in Rome, at the same hotel, each of them the modest appendage of a salient daughter. The similarity of their lot had again drawn them together, lending itself to mild jokes, and the mutual confession that, if in old days it must have been tiring to "keep up" with daughters, it was now, at times, a little dull not to.

No doubt, Mrs. Slade reflected, she felt her unemployment more than poor Grace ever would. It was a big drop from being the wife of Delphin Slade to being his widow. She had always regarded herself (with a certain conjugal pride) as his equal in social gifts, as contributing her full share to the making of the exceptional couple they were: but the difference after his death was irremediable. As the wife of the famous corporation lawyer, always with an international case or two on hand, every day brought its exciting and unexpected obligation: the impromptu entertaining of eminent colleagues from abroad, the hurried dashes on legal business to

London, Paris or Rome, where the entertaining was so handsomely reciprocated; the amusement of hearing in her wake: "What, that handsome woman with the good clothes and the eyes is Mrs. Slade—*the* Slade's wife? Really? Generally the wives of celebrities are such frumps."

Yes; being *the* Slade's widow was a dullish business after that. In living up to such a husband all her faculties had been engaged; now she had only her daughter to live up to, for the son who seemed to have inherited his father's gifts had died suddenly in boyhood. She had fought through that agony because her husband was there, to be helped and to help; now, after the father's death, the thought of the boy had become unbearable. There was nothing left but to mother her daughter; and dear Jenny was such a perfect daughter that she needed no excessive mothering. "Now with Babs Ansley I don't know that I *should* be so quiet," Mrs. Slade sometimes half-enviously reflected; but Jenny, who was younger than her brilliant friend, was that rare accident, an extremely pretty girl who somehow made youth and prettiness seem as safe as their absence. It was all perplexing—and to Mrs. Slade a little boring. She wished that Jenny would fall in love—with the wrong man, even; that she might have to be watched, out-manoeuvred, rescued. And instead, it was Jenny who watched her mother, kept her out of draughts, made sure that she had taken her tonic. . . .

Mrs. Ansley was much less articulate than her friend, and her mental portrait of Mrs. Slade was slighter, and drawn with fainter touches. "Alida Slade's awfully brilliant; but not as brilliant as she thinks," would have summed it up; though she would have added, for the enlightenment of strangers, that Mrs. Slade had been an extremely dashing girl; much more so than her daughter, who was pretty, of course, and clever in a way, but had none of her mother's—well, "vividness," some one had once called it. Mrs. Ansley would take up current words like this, and cite them in quotation marks, as unheard-of audacities. No; Jenny was not like her mother. Sometimes Mrs. Ansley thought Alida Slade was disappointed; on the whole she had had a sad life. Full of failures and mistakes; Mrs. Ansley had always been rather sorry for her. . . .

So these two ladies visualized each other, each through the wrong end of her little telescope.

II

For a long time they continued to sit side by side without speaking. It seemed as though, to both, there was a relief in laying down their somewhat futile activities in the presence of the vast Memento Mori which faced them. Mrs. Slade sat quite still, her eyes fixed on the golden slope of the Palace of the Caesars, and after a while Mrs. Ansley ceased to fidget with her bag, and she too sank into meditation. Like many intimate friends, the two ladies had never before had occasion to be silent together, and Mrs. Ansley was slightly embarrassed by what seemed, after so many years, a new stage in their intimacy, and one with which she did not yet know how to deal.

Suddenly the air was full of that deep clangour of bells which periodically covers Rome with a roof of silver. Mrs. Slade glanced at her wrist-watch. "Five o'clock already," she said, as though surprised.

Mrs. Ansley suggested interrogatively: "There's bridge at the Embassy at five." For a long time Mrs. Slade did not answer. She appeared to be lost in contemplation, and Mrs. Ansley thought the remark had escaped her. But after a while she said, as if speaking out of a dream: "Bridge, did you say? Not unless you want to. . . . But I don't think I will, you know."

"Oh, no," Mrs. Ansley hastened to assure her. "I don't care to at all. It's so lovely here; and so full of old memories, as you say." She settled herself in her chair, and almost furtively drew forth her knitting. Mrs. Slade took sideway note of this activity, but her own beautifully cared-for hands remained motionless on her knee.

"I was just thinking," she said slowly, "what different things Rome stands for to each generation of travellers. To our grandmothers, Roman fever; to our mothers, sentimental dangers—how we used to be guarded!—to our daughters, no more dangers than the middle of Main Street. They don't know it—but how much they're missing!"

The long golden light was beginning to pale, and Mrs. Ansley lifted her knitting a little closer to her eyes. "Yes; how we were guarded!"

"I always used to think," Mrs. Slade continued, "that our mothers had a much more difficult job than our grandmothers. When Roman fever stalked the streets it must have been comparatively easy to gather in the girls at the danger hour; but when you and I were young, with such beauty calling us, and the spice of disobedience thrown in, and no worse risk than catching cold during the cool hour after sunset, the mothers used to be put to it to keep us in—didn't they?"

She turned again toward Mrs. Ansley, but the latter had reached a delicate point in her knitting. "One, two, three—slip two; yes, they must have been," she assented, without looking up.

Mrs. Slade's eyes rested on her with a deepened attention. "She can knit—in the face of *this*! How like her. . . ."

Mrs. Slade leaned back, brooding, her eyes ranging from the ruins which faced her to the long green hollow of the Forum, the fading glow of the church fronts beyond it, and the outlying immensity of the Colosseum. Suddenly she thought: "It's all very well to say that our girls have done away with sentiment and moonlight. But if Babs Ansley isn't out to catch that young aviator—the one who's a Marchese—then I don't know anything. And Jenny has no chance beside her. I know that too. I wonder if that's why Grace Ansley likes the two girls to go everywhere together? My poor Jenny as a foil—!" Mrs. Slade gave a hardly audible laugh, and at the sound Mrs. Ansley dropped her knitting.

"Yes—?"

"I—oh, nothing. I was only thinking how your Babs carries everything before her. That Campolieri boy is one of the best matches in Rome. Don't look so innocent, my dear—you know he is. And I was wondering, ever so respectfully, you understand . . . wondering how two such exemplary characters as you and Horace had managed to produce anything quite so dynamic." Mrs. Slade laughed again, with a touch of asperity.

Mrs. Ansley's hands lay inert across her needles. She looked straight out at the great accumulated wreckage of passion and splendour at her feet. But her small profile was almost expressionless. At length she said: "I think you overrate Babs, my dear."

Mrs. Slade's tone grew easier. "No; I don't. I appreciate her. And perhaps envy you. Oh, my girl's perfect; if I were a chronic invalid I'd—well, I think I'd rather be in Jenny's hands. There must be times . . . but there! I always wanted a brilliant daughter . . . and never quite understood why I got an angel instead."

Mrs. Ansley echoed her laugh in a faint murmur. "Babs is an angel too."

"Of course — of course! But she's got rainbow wings. Well, they're wandering by the sea with their young men; and here we sit . . . and it all brings back the past a little too acutely."

Mrs. Ansley had resumed her knitting. One might almost have imagined (if one had known her less well, Mrs. Slade reflected) that, for her also, too many memories rose from the lengthening shadows of those august ruins. But no; she was simply absorbed in her work. What was there for her to worry about? She knew that Babs would almost certainly come back engaged to the extremely eligible Campolieri. "And she'll sell the New York house, and settle down near them in Rome, and never be in their way . . . she's much too tactful. But she'll have an excellent cook, and just the right people in for bridge and cocktails . . . and a perfectly peaceful old age among her grandchildren."

Mrs. Slade broke off this prophetic flight with a recoil of self-disgust. There was no one of whom she had less right to think unkindly than of Grace Ansley. Would she never cure herself of envying her? Perhaps she had begun too long ago.

She stood up and leaned against the parapet, filling her troubled eyes with the tranquillizing magic of the hour. But instead of tranquillizing her the sight seemed to increase her exasperation. Her gaze turned toward the Colosseum. Already its golden flank was drowned in purple shadow, and above it the sky curved crystal clear, without light or colour. It was the moment when afternoon and evening hang balanced in mid-heaven.

Mrs. Slade turned back and laid her hand on her friend's arm. The gesture was so abrupt that Mrs. Ansley looked up, startled.

"The sun's set. You're not afraid, my dear?"

"Afraid — "

"Of Roman fever or penumonia? I remember how ill you were that winter. As a girl you had a very delicate throat, hadn't you?"

"Oh, we're all right up here. Down below, in the Forum, it does get deathly cold, all of a sudden . . . but not here."

"Ah, of course you know because you had to be so careful." Mrs. Slade turned back to the parapet. She thought: "I must make one more effort not to hate her." Aloud she said: "Whenever I look at the Forum from up here, I remember that story about a great-aunt of yours, wasn't she? A dreadfully wicked great-aunt?"

"Oh, yes; Great-aunt Harriet. The one who was supposed to have sent her young sister out to the Forum after sunset to gather a night-blooming flower for her album. All our great-aunts and grand-mothers used to have albums of dried flowers."

Mrs. Slade nodded. "But she really sent her because they were in love with the same man — "

"Well, that was the family tradition. They said Aunt Harriet confessed it years afterward. At any rate, the poor little sister caught the fever and died. Mother used to frighten us with the story when we were children."

"And you frightened *me* with it, that winter when you and I were here as girls. The winter I was engaged to Delphin."

Mrs. Ansley gave a faint laugh. "Oh, did I? Really frightened you? I don't believe you're easily frightened."

"Not often; but I was then. I was easily frightened because I was too happy. I wonder if you know what that means?"

"I — yes. . . ." Mrs. Ansley faltered.

"Well, I suppose that was why the story of your wicked aunt made such an impression on me. And I thought: 'There's no more Roman fever, but the Forum is deathly cold after sunset — especially after a hot day. And the Colosseum's even colder and damper.'"

"The Colosseum — ?"

"Yes. It wasn't easy to get in, after the gates were locked for the night. Far from easy. Still, in those days it could be managed; it *was* managed, often. Lovers met there who couldn't meet elsewhere. You knew that?"

"I — I daresay. I don't remember."

"You don't remember? You don't remember going to visit some ruins or other one evening, just after dark, and catching a bad chill? You were supposed to have gone to see the moon rise. People always said that expedition was what caused your illness."

There was a moment's silence; then Mrs. Ansley rejoined: "Did they? It was all so long ago."

"Yes. And you got well again — so it didn't matter. But I suppose it struck your friends — the reason given for your illness, I mean — because everybody knew you were so prudent on account of your throat, and your mother took such care of you. . . . You *had* been out late sight-seeing, hadn't you, that night?"

"Perhaps I had. The most prudent girls aren't always prudent. What made you think of it now?"

Mrs. Slade seemed to have no answer ready. But after a moment she broke out: "Because I simply can't bear it any longer — !"

Mrs. Ansley lifted her head quickly. Her eyes were wide and very pale. "Can't bear what?"

"Why — your not knowing that I've always known why you went."

"Why I went — ?"

"Yes. You think I'm bluffing, don't you? Well, you went to meet the man I was engaged to — and I can repeat every word of the letter that took you there."

While Mrs. Slade spoke Mrs. Ansley had risen unsteadily to her feet. Her bag, her knitting and gloves, slid in a panic-stricken heap to the ground. She looked at Mrs. Slade as though she were looking at a ghost.

"No, no — don't," she faltered out.

"Why not? Listen, if you don't believe me. 'My one darling, things can't go on like this. I must see you alone. Come to the Colosseum immediately after dark tomorrow. There will be somebody to let you in. No one whom you need fear will suspect' — but perhaps you've forgotten what the letter said?"

Mrs. Ansley met the challenge with an unexpected composure. Steadying herself against the chair she looked at her friend, and replied: "No; I know it by heart too."

"And the signature? 'Only *your* D. S.' Was that it? I'm right, am I? That was the letter that took you out that evening after dark?"

Mrs. Ansley was still looking at her. It seemed to Mrs. Slade that a slow struggle was going on behind the voluntarily controlled mask of her small quiet face. "I shouldn't have thought she had herself so well in hand," Mrs. Slade reflected, almost resentfully. But at this moment Mrs. Ansley spoke. "I don't know how you knew. I burnt that letter at once."

"Yes; you would, naturally — you're so prudent!" The sneer was open now. "And if you burnt the letter you're wondering how on earth I know what was in it. That's it, isn't it?"

Mrs. Slade waited, but Mrs. Ansley did not speak.

"Well, my dear, I know what was in that letter because I wrote it!"

"You wrote it?"

"Yes."

The two women stood for a minute staring at each other in the last golden light. Then Mrs. Ansley dropped back into her chair. "Oh," she murmured, and covered her face with her hands.

Mrs. Slade waited nervously for another word or movement. None came, and at length she broke out: "I horrify you."

Mrs. Ansley's hands dropped to her knee. The face they uncovered was streaked with tears. "I wasn't thinking of you. I was thinking—it was the only letter I ever had from him!"

"And I wrote it. Yes; I wrote it! But I was the girl he was engaged to. Did you happen to remember that?"

Mrs. Ansley's head drooped again. "I'm not trying to excuse myself . . . I remembered. . . ."

"And still you went?"

"Still I went."

Mrs. Slade stood looking down on the small bowed figure at her side. The flame of her wrath had already sunk, and she wondered why she had ever thought there would be any satisfaction in inflicting so purposeless a wound on her friend. But she had to justify herself.

"You do understand? I'd found out—and I hated you, hated you. I knew you were in love with Delphin—and I was afraid; afraid of you, of your quiet ways, your sweetness . . . your . . . well, I wanted you out of the way, that's all. Just for a few weeks; just till I was sure of him. So in a blind fury I wrote that letter. . . . I don't know why I'm telling you now."

"I suppose," said Mrs. Ansley slowly, "it's because you've always gone on hating me."

"Perhaps. Or because I wanted to get the whole thing off my mind." She paused. "I'm glad you destroyed the letter. Of course I never thought you'd die."

Mrs. Ansley relapsed into silence, and Mrs. Slade, leaning above her, was conscious of a strange sense of isolation, of being cut off from the warm current of human communion. "You think me a monster!"

"I don't know. . . . It was the only letter I had, and you say he didn't write it?"

"Ah, how you care for him still!"

"I cared for that memory," said Mrs. Ansley.

Mrs. Slade continued to look down on her. She seemed physically reduced by the blow—as if, when she got up, the wind might scatter her like a puff of dust. Mrs. Slade's jealousy suddenly leapt up again at the sight. All these years the woman had been living on that letter. How she must have loved him, to treasure the mere memory of its ashes! The letter of the man her friend was engaged to. Wasn't it she who was the monster?

"You tried your best to get him away from me, didn't you? But you failed; and I kept him. That's all."

"Yes. That's all."

"I wish now I hadn't told you. I'd no idea you'd feel about it as you do; I thought you'd be amused. It all happened so long ago, as you say; and you must do me the justice to remember that I had no reason to think you'd ever taken it seriously. How could I, when you were married to Horace Ansley two months afterward? As soon as you could get out of bed your mother rushed you off to Florence and married you. People were rather surprised—they wondered at its being done so quickly; but I thought I knew. I had an idea you did it out of *pique*—to be able to say you'd got ahead of Delphin and me. Girls have such silly reasons for doing the most serious things. And your marrying so soon convinced me that you'd never really cared."

"Yes. I suppose it would," Mrs. Ansley assented.

The clear heaven overhead was emptied of all its gold. Dusk spread over it, abruptly darkening the Seven Hills. Here and there lights began to twinkle through the foliage at their feet. Steps were coming and going on the deserted terrace—waiters looking out of the doorway at the head of the stairs, then reappearing with trays and napkins and flasks of wine. Tables were moved, chairs straightened. A feeble string of electric lights flickered out. Some vases of faded flowers were carried away, and brought back replenished. A stout lady in a dust-coat suddenly appeared, asking in broken Italian if any one had seen the elastic band which held together her tattered Baedeker. She poked with her stick under the table at which she had lunched, the waiters assisting.

The corner where Mrs. Slade and Mrs. Ansley sat was still shadowy and deserted. For a long time neither of them spoke. At length Mrs. Slade began again: "I suppose I did it as a sort of joke—"

"A joke?"

"Well, girls are ferocious sometimes, you know. Girls in love especially. And I remember laughing to myself all that evening at the idea that you were waiting around there in the dark, dodging out of sight, listening for every sound, trying to get in—. Of course I was upset when I heard you were so ill afterward."

Mrs. Ansley had not moved for a long time. But now she turned slowly toward her companion. "But I didn't wait. He'd arranged everything. He was there. We were let in at once," she said.

Mrs. Slade sprang up from her leaning position. "Delphin there? They let you in?—Ah, now you're lying!" She burst out with violence.

Mrs. Ansley's voice grew clearer, and full of surprise. "But of course he was there. Naturally he came—"

"Came? How did he know he'd find you there? You must be raving!"

Mrs. Ansley hesitated, as though reflecting. "But I answered the letter. I told him I'd be there. So he came."

Mrs. Slade flung her hands up to her face. "Oh, God—you answered! I never thought of your answering. . . ."

"It's odd you never thought of it, if you wrote the letter."

"Yes. I was blind with rage."

Mrs. Ansley rose, and drew her fur scarf about her. "It is cold here. We'd better go. . . . I'm sorry for you," she said, as she clasped the fur about her throat.

The unexpected words sent a pang through Mrs. Slade. "Yes; we'd better go." She gathered up her bag and cloak. "I don't know why you should be sorry for me," she muttered.

Mrs. Ansley stood looking away from her toward the dusky secret mass of the Colosseum. "Well—because I didn't have to wait that night."

Mrs. Slade gave an unquiet laugh. "Yes; I was beaten there. But I oughtn't to begrudge it to you, I suppose. At the end of all these years. After all, I had everything; I had him for twenty-five years. And you had nothing but that one letter that he didn't write."

Mrs. Ansley was again silent. At length she turned toward the door of the terrace. She took a step, and turned back, facing her companion.

"I had Barbara," she said, and began to move ahead of Mrs. Slade toward the stairway.

[1936]

QUESTIONS

1. How does Wharton maintain the balance of withheld feelings and private assumptions between Mrs. Slade and Mrs. Ansley? How does the information that Mrs. Ansley feels sorry for Mrs. Slade while Mrs. Slade envies Mrs. Ansley acquire greater significance by the end of the story?
2. How do the details of the conversation between the two women develop precisely toward the story's final revelation?
3. How does the story's setting contribute to its effectiveness?
4. What is the meaning of the title?

Mulk Raj Anand

(b. 1905)

India

Mulk Raj Anand was born in Peshawar, now a part of Pakistan, December 12, 1905. Beginning in 1921, he attended Khalsa College, Amritsar, and subsequently Punjab University, where he earned his B.A. (with honors) in 1924. As an undergraduate, he wrote poetry in Urdu and participated in nonviolent student political activities. The same year, 1924, he sailed for England to pursue higher studies in philosophy. Anand earned his Ph.D. in philosophy from the University of London in 1930, by which time he had also become a free-lance writer, publishing essays in liberal British journals of the era. In 1932, he returned to India and wrote the first draft of *Untouchable*. Anand has remarked about that stage in his life:

> The book poured out like hot lava from the volcano of my crazed imagination, during a long weekend. I remember that I had to do finger exercises in order to ease the strain on my right hand. And I must have slept only six hours in three nights, while writing this drama. And even during those six hours, I kept on dreaming about several strains in the character of Bakha, almost as though I was moulding his personality and transmuting it from actuality into the hero of a nightmare.

Once the book was completed, Anand attempted to find a publisher. He returned to England only to have the manuscript rejected by 19 publishing houses. Anand considered suicide. Then, with an enthusiastic response from the English novelist E. M. Forster, *Untouchable* was accepted and published in May of 1935, with an introduction by Forster. The issue in the novel's difficult route to publication had been one of subject matter: Bakha's profession of latrine cleaner, as a member of the lowest Hindu caste. The preface to the novel opens with Forster's observation:

> This remarkable novel describes a day in the life of a sweeper in an Indian city with every realistic circumstance. Is it a clean book or a dirty one? Some readers, especially those who consider themselves all-white, will go purple in the face with rage before they have finished a dozen pages and will exclaim that they cannot trust themselves to speak. I cannot trust myself either, though for a different reason: the book seems to me indescribably clean and I hesitate for words in which this can be conveyed. Avoiding rhetoric and circumlocution, it has gone straight to the heart of its subject and purified it. None of us are pure—we wouldn't be alive if we were. But to the straightforward all things can become pure, and it is to the directness of his attack that Mr. Anand's success is probably due.

In his critical study of the writer, M. K. Naik states of Mulk Raj Anand, "The General Strike of 1926 in Britain made him conscious of the class war between the haves and the have-nots in modern civilization, whether in the West or the East." Although Anand's life in India had been privileged (his father was Regimental Head Clerk in the British Indian Army and, consequently, his son attended British Indian schools), he quickly aligned himself with the underdog. After *Untouchable*, his novels include *Coolie* (1936), *Two Leaves and a Bud* (1937), *The Sword and the Sickle* (1942), *The Old Woman and the Cow* (1960), and *Death of a Hero* (1964). Dozens of short stories and essays have also appeared during his long and distinguished writing career.

As background to *Untouchable*, it should be noted that although in practice Hindu society is divided into four castes (Brahmin, priestly; Kshatriya, kingly or warrior, Anand's own caste; Vasisya, mercantile and agricultural; and Sudra, artisan), in practice there are usually 20 or 30 caste distinctions in a typical village. In a large city, there may be as many as 200 to 300. The untouchables—the lowest caste—have historically included almost one-fifth of the entire Indian population. Until around 1925, there were no schools for untouchables. Although Mahatma Gandhi fought during much of his life for the elimination of untouchability (and the new constitution in 1949 made untouchability unconstitutional), until well into the 1950s untouchables were denied the use of most public facilities, including wells and bathing places used by other Hindus. (This information has largely been drawn from Hazari's *Untouchable*, an account of untouchability by one born into the caste.)

Even in recent times, the situation has not been greatly improved. In an article in the *Washington Post* in 1983, William Claiborne noted, "The Mahatma's crusade to liberate night-soil scavengers from their demeaning labor has remained little more than a dream during most of India's thirty-seven years of independence. About 600,000 *bhangis* still collect bucket privies and dump the waste in fields and canals, jeopardizing not only their own health but that of their neighbors." Claiborne ironically concludes that although flush toilets and water-sealed latrines can be installed relatively inexpensively, resistance today often comes from the untouchables themselves. "Night-soil scavengers working for municipal governments earn about $40 a month, and since many of them are women and untrained for any other employment, they have viewed the 'liberation' movement as a threat to their livelihoods."

Untouchable

The outcastes' colony was a group of mud-walled houses that clustered together in two rows, under the shadow both of the town and the cantonment, but outside their boundaries and separate from them. There lived the scavengers, the leather-workers, the washermen, the barbers, the water-carriers, the grass-cutters and other outcastes from Hindu society. A brook ran near the lane, once with crystal-clear water, now soiled by the dirt and filth of the public latrines situated about it, the odour of the hides and skins of dead carcasses left to dry on its banks, the dung of donkeys, sheep, horses, cows and buffaloes heaped up to be made into fuel cakes. The absence of a drainage system had, through the rains of various seasons, made of the quarter a marsh which gave out the most offensive smell. And altogether the ramparts of human and animal refuse that lay on the outskirts of this little colony, and the ugliness, the squalor and the misery which lay within it, made it an "uncongenial" place to live in.

At least, so thought Bakha, a young man of eighteen, strong and able-bodied, the son of Lakha, the Jemadar of all the sweepers in the town and the cantonment, and officially in charge of the three rows of public latrines which lined the extreme end of the colony, by the brook-side. But then he had been working in the barracks of a British regiment for some years on probation with a remote uncle, and had been caught by the glamour of the "white man's" life. The Tommies had treated him as a human being and he had learnt to think of himself as superior to his fellow-outcastes. Otherwise, the rest of the outcastes (with the possible exception of Chota, the leather-worker's son, who oiled his hair profusely, and parted it like the Englishmen on one side, wore a pair of shorts at hockey and smoked cigarettes like them; and Ram Charan, the washerman's son who aped Chota and Bakha in turn) were content with their lot.

Bakha thought of the uncongeniality of his home as he lay half awake in the morning of an autumn day, covered by a worn-out, greasy blanket, on a faded blue carpet which was spread on the floor in a corner of the cave-like, dingy, dank, one-roomed mud-house. His sister slept on a cot next to him and his father and brother snored from under a patched, ochre-coloured quilt, on a broken string bed, on the other side.

The nights had been cold, as they always are in the town of Bulandshahr, as cold as the days are hot. And though, both during winter and summer, he slept with his day clothes on, the sharp, bitter wind that blew from the brook at dawn had penetrated to his skin, past the inadequate blanket, through the regulation overcoat, breeches, puttees and ammunition boots of the military uniform that clothed him.

He shivered as he turned on his side. But he didn't mind the cold very much, suffering it willingly because he could sacrifice a good many comforts for the sake of what he called "fashun," by which he understood the art of wearing trousers, breeches, coat, puttees, boots, etc., as worn by the British and Indian soldiers in India. "Ohe, lover of your mother," his father had once abusively said to him, "take a quilt and throw away that blanket of the goras; you will die of cold." But Bakha was a child of modern India. The clearcut styles of European dress had impressed his naive mind. This stark simplicity had furrowed his old Indian consciousness and cut deep, new lines where all the considerations which made India evolve a skirty costume as best fitted for the human body, lay dormant. Bakha had looked at the Tommies, stared at them with wonder and amazement when he first went to live at the British regimental barracks with his uncle. He had had glimpses, during his sojourn there, of the life the Tommies lived: sleeping on strange, low canvas beds covered tightly with blankets; eating eggs, drinking tea and wine in tin mugs; going to parade and then walking down to the bazaar with cigarettes in their mouths and small silver-mounted canes in their hands. And he had soon become possessed with an overwhelming desire to live their life. He knew they were white sahibs.[1] He had felt that to put on their clothes made one a sahib too. So he tried to copy them in everything, to copy them as well as he could

[1]*sahibs* masters (Europeans)

in the exigencies of his peculiarly Indian circumstances. He had begged one Tommy for the gift of a pair of trousers. The man had given him instead a pair of breeches which he had to spare. A Hindu sepoy, for the good of his own soul, had been kind enough to make an endowment of a pair of boots and puttees. For the other items he had gone down to the rag-seller's shop in the town. He had long looked at that shop. Ever since he was a child he had walked past the wooden stall on which lay heaped the scarlet and khaki uniforms discarded or pawned by the Tommies, pith sola topis, peak caps, knives, forks, buttons, old books and other oddments of Anglo-Indian life. And he had hungered for the touch of them. But he had never mustered up courage enough to go up to the keeper of the shop and to ask him the price of anything, lest it should be a price he could not pay and lest the man should find from his talk that he was a sweeper-boy. So he had stared and stared, stealthily noticing the variety of their queer, well-cut forms. "I will look like a sahib," he had secretly told himself. "And I shall walk like them. Just as they do, in twos, with Chota as my companion. But I have no money to buy things." And there his fantasy would break down and he would walk away from the shop rather crestfallen. Then he had had the good luck to come by some money at the British barracks. The pay which he received there had, of course, to be given to his father, but the baksheesh which he had collected from the Tommies amounted to ten rupees, and although he couldn't buy all the things in the rag-seller's shop he wished to, he had been able to buy the jacket, the overcoat, the blanket he slept under, and had a few annas left over for the enjoyment of "Red-Lamp" cigarettes. His father had been angry at his extravagance, and the boys of the outcastes' colony, even Chota and Ram Charan, cut jokes with him on account of his new rigout, calling him "Pilpali sahib." And he knew, of course, that except for his English clothes there was nothing English in his life. But he kept up his new form, rigidly adhering to his clothes day and night and guarding them from all base taint of Indianness, not even risking the formlessness of an Indian quilt, though he shivered with the cold at night.

A sharp tremor of cold ran through his hot, massive frame. The hair of his body almost stood on end. He turned on his side and waited in the half-dark for something, he knew not what. These nights were awful. So cold and uncomfortable! He liked the days because during the day the sun shone and he could, after he had finished his work, brush his clothes with a rag and walk out into the street, the envy of all his friends and the most conspicuous man in the outcastes' colony. But the nights! "I must get another blanket," he said to himself. "Then father won't ask me to put a quilt on. He always keeps abusing me. I do all his work for him. He appropriates the pay all right. He is afraid of the sepoys. They call him names. He abuses me. He is happy when they call him 'Jemadar.' So proud of his izzat! He just goes about getting salaams from everybody. I don't take a moment's rest and yet he abuses me. And if I go to play with the boys he calls me in the middle of the game to come and attend to the latrines. He is old. He doesn't know anything of the sahibs. And now he will call me to get up, and it is *so* cold. He will keep lying in bed, and Rakha and Sohini will still be asleep, when I go to the latrines." He wrinkled his dark, broad, round face with the irritation that came up into his being and made his otherwise handsome features look knotted and ugly. And thus he lay, awaiting his father's call, hating to hear it, yet lying anxiously in expectation of—the rude bullying order to get up.

"Get up, ohe you Bakhya, ohe son of a pig!" came his father's voice, sure as the daylight, from the midst of a broken, jarring, interrupted snore. "Get up and attend to the latrines or the sepoys will be angry."

The old man seemed to awake instinctively, for a moment, just about that time every morning, and then to relapse into his noisy sleep under the greasy, thick, discoloured, patched quilt.

Bakha half opened his eyes and tried to lift his head from the earth as he heard his father's shout. He was angered at the abuse as he was already feeling rather depressed that morning. The high cheek-bones of his face became pallid with sullenness. His mind went back to the morning after his mother's death, when although he was awake, his father had thought he was asleep and presuming he was never going to get up, had shouted at him. That was the beginning of his father's subsequent early-morning shouts, which he had begun at first to resist with a casual deafness, and which he now ignored irritatedly. It wasn't that he couldn't get up, because ordinarily he woke up from his slumber quite early, his mother having habituated him to it. She used to give him a brass tankard full of a boiling hot mixture of water, tea-leaves and milk from the steaming earthen saucepan that always lay balanced on the two-bricks-with-a-space-in-between fire-place in a corner of their one-roomed house. It was so delightful, the taste of that hot, sugary liquid, that Bakha's mouth always watered for it on the night before the morning on which he had to drink it. And after he had drunk it he used to put on his clothes and go to work at the latrines, happy and contented. When his mother died and the burden of looking after the family fell on him, there was no time left to look for such comforts and luxuries as an early morning tumblerfull of tea. So he learnt to do without it, looking back, however, with fondness to the memory of those days when he lived in the enjoyment not only of the tasty, spicy delights of breakfast, but of all the splendrous details of life, the fine clothes which his mother bought him, the frequent visits to the town and the empty days, filled with play. He often thought of his mother, the small, dark figure, swathed simply in a tunic, a pair of baggy trousers and an apron, crouching as she went about cooking and cleaning the home, a bit too old-fashioned for his then already growing modern tastes, Indian to the core and sometimes uncomfortably so (as she did not like his affecting European clothes), but so loving, so good, and withal generous, giving, always giving, mother, giver of life, Mahalakshmi. He didn't feel sad, however, to think that she was dead. He couldn't summon sorrow to the world he lived in, the world of his English clothes and "Red-Lamp" cigarettes, because it seemed she was not of that world, had no connection with it.

"Are you up? Get up, you illegally begotten!" came his father's shout again and stirred the boy to a feeling of despair.

"The bully!" Bakha exclaimed under his breath as he listened to the last accents of his father's voice die out in a clumsy, asthmatic cough. He just shook himself and, turning his back to his father for sheer cussedness, averted the challenge of the sombre, crowded, little room which seemed to have come with his father's abuse. He felt that his bones were stiff and his flesh numb with the cold. For a moment he felt feverish. A hot liquid trickled down from the corners of his eyes. One of his nostrils seemed to be blocked and he sniffed the air, trying to adjust his breathing to the congested climate of the corner where his face was turned. His throat too seemed to have been caught, for as he inhaled the air it seemed to irritate his trachea and nearly choke him. He began to swallow air in order to relieve his nose and his throat. But when a breath of air pierced the cavity which was clogged the other became impenetrable. A cough shook the inner tissues of his throat and he spat furiously into the corner. He leaned on his elbow and blew his nose under the carpet on which he lay. Then he fell back, his legs gathered together and shrunken under the thin folds of his blanket, his head buried into his arms. He felt very cold. And he dozed off again.

"Ohe, Bakhya! Ohe, Bakhya! Ohe, scoundrel of a sweeper's son! Come and clean a latrine for me!" someone shouted from without.

Bakha flung the blanket off his body, stretched his legs and arms to shake off the half-sleep that still clung to him, and got up abruptly, yawning and rubbing his eyes. For a moment he bent, rolling the carpet and the blanket to make room for the activity of the day, then, thinking he heard the man outside shout again, he hurried to the door.

A small, thin man, naked except for a loin-cloth, stood outside with a small brass jug in his left hand, a round white cotton skull-cap on his head, a pair of wooden sandals on his feet, and the apron of his loin-cloth lifted to his nose.

It was Havildar Charat Singh, the famous hockey player of the 38th Dogras regiment, as celebrated for his humour as for the fact, which with characteristic Indian openness he acknowledged, that he suffered from chronic piles.

"Why aren't the latrines clean, ohe rogue of a Bakha? There is not one fit to go near. I have walked all round. Do you know you are responsible for my piles! I caught the contagion sitting on one of those dirty latrines!"

"All right, Havildar ji, I will get one ready for you at once," Bakha said cautiously as he proceeded to pick up his brush and basket from the place where these tools decorated the front wall of the house.

He worked away earnestly, quickly, without loss of effort. Brisk, yet steady, his capacity for active application to the task he had in hand seemed to flow like constant water from a natural spring. Each muscle of his body, hard as a rock when it came into play, seemed to shine forth like glass. He must have had immense pent-up resources lying deep in his body, for he rushed along with considerable skill and alacrity from one doorless latrine to another, cleaning, brushing, pouring phenoil. "What a dexterous workman!" the onlooker would have said. And though his job was dirty he remained comparatively clean. He didn't even soil his sleeves handling the commodes, sweeping and scrubbing them. "A bit superior to his job," one would have said, "not the kind of man who ought to be doing this." For he looked intelligent, even sensitive, with a sort of dignity that does not belong to the ordinary scavenger, who is as a rule uncouth and unclean. It was perhaps his absorption in his task that gave him the look of distinction, or his exotic dress however loose and ill-fitting, that lifted him above his odorous world. Havildar Charat Singh, who had the Hindu instinct for immaculate cleanliness, was puzzled when he emerged from his painful half an hour in the latrines and caught sight of Bakha. Here was a low-caste man who seemed clean! He became rather self-conscious, the prejudice of the "twice born" high-caste Hindu against stink, even though he saw not the slightest suspicion of it in Bakha, rising into his mind. He smiled complacently. Then, however, he forgot his high caste and the ironic smile on his face became a childlike laugh.

"You are becoming a 'gentreman,' ohe Bakhya! Where did you get that uniform?"

Bakha was shy, knowing he had no right to indulge in such luxuries as apeing the white sahibs. He humbly mumbled:

"Huzoor, it is all your blessing."

Charat Singh was feeling kind, he did not relax the grin which symbolised two thousand years of racial and caste superiority.[2] To express his goodwill, however, he said:

"Come this afternoon, Bakhe. I shall give you a hockey stick." He knew the boy played that game very well.

Bakha stretched himself up; he was astonished yet grateful at Charat Singh's offer. It was a godsend to him, this spontaneous gesture on the part of one of the best hockey players of the regiment. "A hockey stick! I wonder if it will be a new one!" he thought to himself, and stood smiling with a queer humility, overcome with gratitude. Charat Singh's generous promise had called forth that trait of servility in Bakha which he had inherited from his forefathers: the weakness of the down-trodden, the helplessness of the poor and the indigent suddenly receiving help, the passive contentment of the bottom dog suddenly illuminated by the prospect of fulfilment of a secret and long-cherished desire. He saluted his benefactor and bent down to his work again.

A soft smile lingered on his lips, the smile of a slave overjoyed at the condescension of his master, more akin to pride than to happiness. And he slowly slipped into a song. The steady heave of his body from one latrine to another made the whispered refrain a fairly audible note. And he went forward, with eager step, from job to job, a marvel of movement, dancing through his work. Only, the sway of his body was so violent that once the folds of his turban came undone, and the buttons of his overcoat slipped from their worn-out holes. But this did not hinder his work. He clumsily gathered together his loose garments and proceeded with his business.

Men came one after another, towards the latrines. Most of them were Hindus, naked, except for the loin-cloth, brass jugs in hand and with the sacred thread twisted round their left ears. Occasionally came a Muhammadan, who wore a long, white cotton tunic and baggy trousers, holding a big copper kettle in his hand.

Bakha broke the tempo of his measured activity to wipe the sweat off his brow with his sleeve. Its woollen texture felt nice and sharp against his skin, but left an irritating warmth behind. It was a pleasant irritation, however, and he went ahead with renewed vigour that discomfort sometimes gives to the body. "My work will soon be finished," he said poetically, seeing that he was almost at the end of one part of his routine. But the end of one job meant to him only the beginning of another. Not that he shirked work or really liked doing nothing. For, although he didn't know it, to him work was a sort of intoxication which gave him a glowing health and plenty of easy sleep. So he worked on continuously, incessantly, without stopping for breath, even though the violent exertion of his limbs was making him gasp.

At last when he had got to the end of the third row of latrines for the second time during the morning, he felt a cramp in his back and stretched himself out from the bent posture he had maintained all the while. He looked in the direction of the town. There was a slight misty haze before him, a sort of screen which the smouldering fire in the chimney where he had burnt the refuse last night had sent

[2]*two thousand years of racial and caste superiority* The Brahmins and the Kshatriyas, the two upper castes in Hundu society, justify their superiority by asserting that they have earned their position by the good deeds of multiple lives. [Author]

up to mingle with the vaporous smoke clouds that rose from the surface of the brook. Through the thin film he could see the half-naked brown bodies of the Hindus hurrying to the latrines. Some of those who had already visited the latrines could be seen scrubbing their little brass jugs with clay on the side of the brook. Others were bathing to the tune of "Ram re Ram," "Hari Ram"; crouching by the water, rubbing their hands with a little soft earth; washing their feet, their faces; chewing little twigs bitten into the shape of brushes; rinsing their mouths, gargling and spitting noisily into the stream; doucheing their noses and blowing them furiously, ostentatiously. Ever since he had worked in the British barracks Bakha had been ashamed of the Indian way of performing ablutions, all that gargling and spitting, because he knew the Tommies disliked it. He remembered so well the Tommies' familiar abuse of the natives: "Kala admi zamin par hagne wala" (black man, you who relieve himself on the ground). But he himself had been ashamed at the sight of Tommies running naked to their baths. "Disgraceful," he had said to himself. They were, however, sahibs. Whatever they did was "fashun." But his own countrymen—they were natus. He felt amused, as an Englishman might be amused, to see a Hindu loosen his dhoti to pour some water first over his navel and then down his back in a flurry of ecstatic hymn-singing. And he watched with contemptuous displeasure the indecent behaviour of a Muhammadan walking about with his hands buried deep in his trousers, purifying himself in the ritual manner, preparatory to his visit to the mosque. "I wonder what they say in their prayers?" he asked himself. "Why do they sit, stand, bend and kneel as if they were doing exercises?" Once, he remembered, he had asked Ali, the son of a regimental bandsman, why they did that, but Ali would not tell him and was angry, saying that Bakha was insulting his religion. And he recalled the familiar sight of all those naked Hindu men and women who could be seen squatting in the open, outside the city, every morning. "So shameless," he thought, "they don't seem to care who looks at them, sitting there like that. It is on account of this that the goras call them 'kala admi zamin par hagne wala.' Why don't they come here?" But then he realised that if they came to the latrines his work would increase and he didn't relish the idea. He preferred to imagine himself sweeping the streets in the place of his father. "*That* is easy work," he said to himself, "I will only have to lift cow-dung and horse-dung with a shovel and sweep the dust off the road with a broom."

"There is not a latrine clean. You must work for the pay you receive."

Bakha turned abruptly and noticed Ramanand, the peevish old bania,[3] shouting at him in his sharp southern diction. He bowed with joined hands to Ramanand who was staring at him, a pair of gold rings studded with rubies in his ears, a transparent muslin loin-cloth and shirt on his emaciated belly, and a funny string cap on his head. "Maharaj," he said and ran towards the latrines and busied himself with his job again.

He hardly realised that he had lapsed into activity, so vigorously did he attack his job. And he was completely oblivious during the quarter of an hour he took to finish a fourth round of the latrines, oblivious alike of the time and of the sweat trickling down his forehead, of the warmth in his body and of the sense of power that he felt as he ended up.

The spurts of smoke from the chimney near his house made him conscious of the next job he had to attend to. He went towards it half-heartedly, and after

[3]*bania* merchant

pausing for a while to pick up a trident-shaped shovel began to stuff the aperture of the little brick pyramid with the straw in the baskets which he had collected from the latrines.

Little pieces of straw flew into the air as he shovelled the refuse into the chimney, the littlest pieces settling on his clothes, the slightly bigger ones settling on the ground where he had to collect them again with his broom. But he worked unconsciously. This forgetfulness or emptiness persisted in him over long periods. It was a sort of insensitivity created in him by the kind of work he had to do, a tough skin which must be a shield against all the most awful sensations. Stooping down over the baskets full of straw, he gathered shovelfuls and cast them into the grate till it seemed congested and would take no more. Then he picked up a long poker and prodded the fire. Quickly it flared up, suddenly illuminating the furnace with its leaping red, gold and black flames, an angry consuming power, something apart, something detached from the heaps of straw it fed on.

The blood in Bakha's veins tingled with the heat as he stood before it. His dark face lit up with a queer sort of beauty. The toil of the body had built up for him a very fine physique. It seemed to suit him, to give a homogeneity, a wonderful wholeness to his body. And it gave him a nobility, strangely in contrast with his filthy profession and of the sub-human status to which he was born.

This was a long task, lasting almost twenty minutes. Bakha, however, did not seem to feel the strain of it as he had felt the strain of his earlier occupation. The burning flame seemed to ally itself with him. It seemed to give him a sense of power, the power to destroy. It seemed to infuse into him a masterful instinct somewhat akin to sacrifice. It seemed as if burning and destruction were for him acts of purification. His mother had told him work was good.

When the chimney had consumed the last basket of straw and refuse, Bakha closed its mouth and retreated. He felt thirsty. The edges of his lips were dry. He put back the shovel, the basket, the broom and the brushes in their place. Then he moved towards the door of his hut, sniffing the air full of smoke from the chimney, brushing his clothes and smoothing them out. His thirst became overpowering as he entered the room. Looking dazedly at the utensils lying about in a corner, he felt he wanted tea. But as he surveyed the room he heard his father still snoring under his patched quilt. His brother was not in the room. He knew at once where he would be — playing in the maidan by the street. As he stood staring round in order to get used to the comparative darkness, he saw that his sister was trying to light a fire between two bricks. She was blowing hard at it, lifting herself on her haunches as she crouched on the mud floor. Her head almost touched the ground, but each puff succeeded only in raising a spurt of smoke from the wet sticks that served as fuel. She sat back helpless when she heard her brother's footsteps. Her smoke-irritated eyes were full of water. When she turned and saw her brother, real tears began to flow down her cheeks.

"Will you get up and let me blow at it?" Bakha said. And without waiting for a reply he walked up to the corner of the room, sat down on his knees, teased the fuel and, stooping, began to blow. His big, round mouth seemed like a real bellows as it sent the breath whirring into the fireplace and started first a few sparks, then a blazing fire through the wet sticks. He put the earthen pan over the little stove.

"There is no water in that," his sister said.

"I will get some water from the pitcher," he said, as he casually made towards the corner.

"There is no water in the pitcher either," she answered.

"Oh!" he exclaimed under his breath, tired and exasperated. And for a moment he stood defeated where he had bent down to the pitcher.

"I shall go and get some water," said Sohini meekly.

"All right," agreed Bakha without any show of formality, and going out of doors sat down on the edge of a broken cane chair, the only article of furniture of European design which he had been able to acquire in pursuance of his ambition to live like an Englishman. Sohini picked up the pitcher, poised it easily on her head, and ran past her brother.

How a round base can be adjusted on a round top, how a sphere can rest on a sphere is a problem which may be of interest to those who think like a learned babu. It never occurred to Sohini to ask herself anything like this as she balanced the pitcher on her head and went to and from her one-roomed home to the steps of the caste-well where she counted on the chance of some gentleman taking pity on her and giving her the water she needed. She had a sylph-like form, not thin but full-bodied within the limits of her graceful frame, well-rounded on the hips, with an arched narrow waist from which descended the folds of her salwars and above which were her full, round, globular breasts, jerking slightly, for lack of a bodice, under her transparent muslin shirt. Bakha observed her as she walked along swaying. She was beautiful. He was proud of her with a pride not altogether that of a brother for a sister.

The outcastes were not allowed to mount the platform surrounding the well, because if they were ever to draw water from it, the Hindus of the three upper castes would consider the water polluted. Nor were they allowed access to the nearby brook as their use of it would contaminate the stream. They had no well of their own because it cost a lot of money to dig a well in such a hilly town as Bulandshahr. Perforce they had to collect at the foot of the caste Hindu's well and depend on the bounty of some of their superiors to pour water into their pitchers. More often than not there was no caste Hindu present. Most of them were rich enough to get the water-carriers to supply them with plenty of fresh water every morning for their baths and kitchens, and only those came to the well who were either fond of an open-air bath or too poor to pay for the water-carriers' services. So the outcastes had to wait for chance to bring some caste Hindu to the well, for luck to decide that he was kind, for Fate to ordain that he had time — to get their pitchers filled with water. They crowded round the well, congested the space below its high brick platform, morning, noon and night, joining their hands in servile humility to every passer-by; cursing their fate, and bemoaning their lot, if they were refused the help they wanted; praying, beseeching and blessing, if some generous soul condescended to listen to them, or to help them.

When Sohini reached the well there were already about ten other outcastes waiting. But there was no one to give them water. She had come as fast as she could to the well, full of fear and anxiety that she would have to wait her turn since she could see from a distance that there was already a crowd. She didn't feel disappointed so much as depressed to realise that she would be the eleventh to receive water. She had sensed the feeling in her brother's soul. He was tired. He was thirsty. She had felt like a mother as she issued from her home to fetch water, a mother going out to fetch food and drink for her loved ones at home. Now as she sat in a row with her fellow-sufferers, her heart sank. There was no sign of anyone passing that way who could be a possible benefactor. But she was patient. She had in her an inbred fortitude, obvious in her curious reserve, in her docile and peaceful bearing.

Gulabo, the washerwoman, the mother of Ram Charan, her brother's friend, had observed Sohini approach. She was a fair-complexioned, middle-aged woman, the regularity of whose supple body bore even in its decay the evidence of a form which must, in her youth, have been wonderful. But although her face was now covered with wrinkles she had pretensions to beauty and was notorious as an assertive hussy who thought herself superior to every other outcaste, firstly because she claimed a high place in the hierarchy of the castes among the low castes, secondly because a well-known Hindu gentleman in the town who had been her lover in her youth was still kind to her in her middle age.

Now Sohini, being of the lowest caste among the outcastes, would naturally be looked down upon by Gulabo. The delicate features of her rising beauty had inflamed Gulabo's body. The girl was a potential rival. Gulabo hated the very sight of her innocent, honest face, though she would not confess, even to herself, that she was jealous of the sweeper-girl. But she unconsciously betrayed her feeling in the mockery and light-hearted abuse with which she greeted Sohini.

"Go back home," said Gulabo mockingly. "There is no one to give you water here! There are so many of us ahead of you."

Sohini smiled evasively, then, recognising an elderly man in the company, she modestly adjusted her apron on her head so as not to show her eyes. And she sat still, crouching by her pitcher.

"Have you heard of such immodesty!" exclaimed Gulabo to Waziro, the weaver's wife who sat near her. "This sweeper-girl goes about without an apron over her head all day in town and in the cantonment."

"Really!" exclaimed Waziro, pretending to be shocked, though she knew Gulabo's evil tongue and had nothing against Sohini. "You ought to be ashamed of yourself," she said, winking an aside to the girl.

Sohini could not suppress her amusement at so comic an assurance of friendliness as Waziro's and laughed.

"Think of it! Think of it! Bitch! Prostitute! Wanton! And your mother hardly dead. Think of laughing in my face, laughing at me who am old enough to be your mother. Bitch!" the washerwoman exploded.

Sohini laughed still more hilariously at the ridiculous abruptness of Gulabo's abuse.

"Ari, bitch! Do you take me for a buffoon? What are you laughing at, slut? Aren't you ashamed of showing your teeth to me in the presence of men, prostitute?" shouted Gulabo. And she looked towards the old men and the little boys who were of the company.

Sohini now realised that the woman was angry. "But I haven't done anything to annoy her," she reflected. "She herself began it all and is abusing me. I didn't pick the quarrel. I have more cause to be angry than she has."

"Bitch, why don't you speak! Prostitute, why don't you answer me?" Gulabo insisted.

"Please don't abuse me," the girl said, "I haven't said anything to you."

"You annoy me with your silence. Eater of dung and drinker of urine! Bitch of a sweeper-woman! I will show you how to insult one old enough to be your mother." And she rose with upraised arm and rushed at Sohini.

Waziro, the weaver's wife, ran after her and caught her just before she had time to hit the sweeper-girl.

"Be calm, be calm; you must not do that," she said as she dragged Gulabo back to her seat. "No, you must not do that."

A flutter of excitement seized the little group; exclamations, shouts and cries of "Hai, Hai," and strange looks of disgust, indignation and disapproval were exchanged. Sohini was a bit frightened at first and grew pale, but she kept intensely still and, avoiding the shock, subsided into a listless apathy. As she looked away, and cast her eyes up to the blue heavens overhead, she felt a sort of dreariness which, though she accepted it resignedly, brought a hurtfulness with it. Sad and wistful, she heaved a soft sigh and felt something in her heart asking for mercy. The sun overhead shot down sharp arrows of heat, and inspired a feeling of the passing of time, a feeling that made her forget the unsolicited quarrel with Gulabo, but cast over her the miserable, soul-harrowing shadow of the vision of her brother waiting for her at home, thirsty after the morning's toil, aching for a cup of tea. And yet no caste Hindu seemed to be near.

Minutes passed in silence, intermittently broken by Gulabo's sobs and sighs. "On the day of my little daughter's marriage too! This inauspicious sweeper-woman has started my auspicious day so badly," she was saying. But no one heeded her. And then at long last, a belated caste Hindu visitor to the latrines was passing. He was a sepoy from the neighbouring regiment.

"Oh, Maharaj! Maharaj! Won't you draw us some water, please? We beg you. We have been waiting here a long time, we will be grateful," shouted the chorus of voices as they pressed towards him, some standing up, bending and joining their palms in beggary, others twisting their lips in various attitudes of servile appeal and abject humility as they remained seated, separate.

Either the sepoy was a callous brute or in too much of a hurry. But he passed by without heeding the request of the group collected at the foot of the well.

Luckily for the crowd of outcastes, however, there was another man coming a little way behind, no less a person than Pundit Kali Nath, one of the priests in charge of the temple in the town. The crowd repeated their entreaties more vehemently than before.

The Pundit hesitated, twitched his eyebrows and looked at the group, frowning with the whole of his bony, hollow-cheeked, deeply-furrowed face. The appeal seemed, even to his dry as dust self, irresistible. But he was an ill-humoured old devil, and had it not been that, as he stood and reflected, he realised that the exercise at the well might do some good to the chronic constipation from which he suffered, he would not have consented to help the outcastes.

He moved slowly on to the brick platform of the well. His small, cautious steps and the peculiar contortions of his face showed that he was a prey to a morbid preoccupation with his inside. He took his own time to prepare for the task he had undertaken. He seemed to be immersed in thought, but was really engrossed in the rumblings in his belly. "That rice," he thought, "the rice I ate yesterday, that must be responsible. My stomach seems jammed. Or was it the jalebis I ate with my milk at the confectioner's. But the food at the home of Lalla Banarsi Das may have introduced complications." He recalled the taste of the various delicacies to which he was so often treated by the pious. "How nice and sweet is the kheer, sticking to the teeth and lingering in the mouth. And kara parshad, the hot, buttery masses of it melt almost as you put a morsel of it in the mouth. But the hubble-bubble usually keeps my stomach clean. What happened to this morning's smoke? I smoked for an hour to no effect. Strange!" During the time taken by these cogitations he had placed the brass jug in his hand to rest in a little hollow in the wooden frame of the well. The waiting crowd thought that it was the Brahmin's disgust at serving them, the outcastes, that brought such deep wrinkles on his face and made it look peeved and angry. They didn't realise that it was constipation, and a want of vigour in his lanky little limbs. But they soon found that out when, after a great many hesitant steps, he tied the iron can that lay near the frame to an edge of the hemp rope that skirted the pulley-wheel, and gently lowered it into the well. The handle slipped from his hand because of the weight of the bucket and revolved violently back, releasing all the coils of rope that were around it. He was a bit scared by the sudden unwinding of the wheel. Then he pulled himself together and renewed his attack. But he was soon upset again. To draw out a can, full of water, required limbs which had been used to exercise more strenuous than the Pundit had ever performed. His whole life revolved round endless recitation of sacred verses and the writing of an occasional charm or horoscope with a reed pen. He exerted all his strength and strained to turn the handle. His face was contorted, but not altogether unlit with pleasure, because already the exercise of his muscles made him feel much easier in the belly than he had done for days. The expectant outcastes were busy getting their pitchers ready, but as that only meant shifting themselves into position so as to be nearest to this most bountiful, most generous of men all their attention was fixed on him. And as that disclosed the apparent effort the athlete was making, they exerted all their energies, all their will-power to aid him in his task.

At length the can was on the brick platform. But the Brahmin becoming interested in the stirrings of his stomach, in the changing phases of his belly, looked, for a moment, absent-minded. A subtle wave of warmth seemed to have descended slowly down from his arms, to the pit of his abdomen, and he felt a strange stirring above his navel such as he had not experienced for days, so pleasing was it in its intimations of the relief it would bring him. Then, unfortunately, a sharp pain shot through the right-hand side of his waist and his demeanour assumed the anxious, agitated look habitual to it.

"I am first, Pundit ji," said Gulabo impetuously, and suddenly disturbed the Brahmin who was absorbed in himself.

He frowned at her and, not noticing the vamping expression she had assumed, deprived her of the favourable attention that would have been her due if he had.

"No, I came first," shouted an inconspicuous little boy.

"But you know that I was here before you," shouted someone else.

And there was a general stampede towards the well that would, in ordinary circumstances, have flurried the priest into throwing water on all of them. But he had as good an eye for a pretty face as he had a bad ear for the sound of a request. Sohini had sat patiently away from the throng, the while it charged at the well. The Pundit recognised her as the sweeper's daughter. He had seen her before, noticed her as she came to clean the latrines in the gullies in the town — the fresh, young form whose full breasts with their dark beads of nipples stood out so conspicuously under her muslin shirt, whose innocent look of wonder seemed to stir the only soft chord in his person, hardened by the congenital weakness of his body, disillusioned by the congenital weakness of his mind, brazened by the authority he exercised over the faithful and the devout. And he was inclined to be kind to her.

"Oh, Lakha's daughter, come here," he said, "you have been patient and the reward of patience, say the holy books, is supreme. Get away all you noisy ones, get out of the way!"

"But Pundit ji!" said Sohini, hesitating to receive the favour, not because she divined the Brahmin's admiration, but because she was afraid of all those who had come before her.

"Now come along," urged the Pundit, irritated by the beginning in his belly of the urge for excretion, and exhilarated by the thought of doing the beautiful girl a favour.

The girl advanced meekly and put her pitcher near the platform. The priest lifted the can with a great effort. For a moment he successfully handled the water, being surcharged with the glow of that warmth which he felt from being near Sohini; intoxicated by it. Then his normal weakness returned. He splashed the water and the outcastes flew on all sides, half wet, half dry.

"Get out of the way!" he shouted as he poured the water into Sohini's pitcher. He was attempting to cover his weakness by bullying. At length the pitcher was three-quarters full.

"Have you got enough now?" asked the Pundit in triumph as he withdrew the empty can.

"Han, Pundit ji," Sohini whispered, her head bent in modesty, as she wiped the outside of the pitcher to lift it on to her head.

"Look, why don't you come and clean the courtyard of our house at the temple," called the Brahmin as the girl withdrew. "Tell your father to send you from today." And he looked long at her, rather embarrassed, his rigid respectability fighting against the waves of amorousness that had begun to flow in his blood.

"You will come today," he firmly said, lest there should be any misunderstanding left in her mind about it.

Sohini was grateful for the favour he had shown her. She shyly nodded and went her way, her left hand on her waist, her right on the pitcher and a balance in her steps like the rhythm of a song. The washerwoman cast dark and angry glances at her as she herself sullenly drew nearer the well with the rest of the crowd, which had now begun to appeal to a newcomer for help.

This was Lachman, a Hindu water-carrier, a Brahmin come down in life, who earned his living by washing the utensils of the caste Hindus. He cooked their food, fetched their water, and did other odd jobs about their houses. He was a young man, about twenty-six, with the intelligent though rather rugged features of the Brahmin who does menial jobs. A bamboo pole at the extreme ends of which were four strings, supporting wooden brackets to carry pitchers, was on his shoulders. He rested it slowly on the ground and, ascending the well, joined his hands in greeting to the Pundit, saying "Jay deva," and respectfully relieved him of the job of drawing more water from the well. As he threw the can easily into the well, however, he looked sideways towards Sohini who was retreating home. He too had noticed her before and felt a stirring in his blood, the warm impulse of love, the strange desire of the soul to reach out to something beyond, at first in fear, then in hope and then with all the concentrated fury of a physical and mental obsession. Sometimes he had playfully irritated her with mild jokes, when she came to the well and he happened to be there. She had responded with a modest smile and an innocent look in her shining, lustrous eyes. And he was, as he said, in the language characteristic of the Indian lover, "dead over her." The Pundit caught him in the act of looking at her. Shame-faced, Lachman withdrew his gaze, and with that servility which he shared with the other menials, quietly turned to the job he had in hand. Soon the strength of his arm had brought the can full of water to the top of the well. He first filled the Pundit's little brass jug and Gulabo's pitcher, and then set about to help the others. The picture of Sohini disappeared from his mind.

She, however, figured conspicuously in the corner of the little mud-house which was her kitchen. Her father was abusing her as he now sat on his bed, puff-puffing away at the cane tube of his hubble-bubble though he was still wrapped in his patched quilt.

"I thought you were dead or something, daughter of a pig!" Lakha was shouting. "No tea, no piece of bread, and I am dying of hunger! Put the tea on and call those swine, Bakha and Rakha to me." Then he frowned in the gruff manner of a man who was really kind at heart, but who knew he was weak and infirm and so bullied his children, to preserve his authority, lest he should be repudiated by them, refused and rejected as the difficult old rubbish he was.

Sohini obeyed him at once, shouting for her brothers as she put the earthen saucepan on the fire.

"Vay Bakhia, vay Rakhia, father is calling you!"

Bakha alone came into the room in answer to his sister's call, Rakha having slipped away to play, early in the morning.

The boy was wiping the sweat off his face and neck and breathing hard, for he had been to do another round at the latrines. His black eyes shed fire and his big, broad face was slightly contracted with fatigue. His throat was parched and dry.

"I have a pain in my side," said the old man to his son, as the boy came in and stood towering in the doorway, the whites of his eyes glaring. "You go and sweep the temple courtyard and the main road for me, and call that swine of a Rakha, wherever he is, to come and attend to the latrines here."

"Bapu, the Pundit of the temple wanted me to clean the family house at the temple," said Sohini.

"Well then go and do so! Why do you eat my head?" snapped Lakha peevishly.

"Is your pain very bad?" asked Bakha ironically, to make his father conscious of his bad temper. "I will rub your side with oil if you like."

"No, no," said the old man irritably, turning his face to hide the shame which his son's subtle protest aroused in him. He had no pain at all in his side, or anywhere, and was merely foxing, being in his old age ineffectual, and excusing himself from work like a child. "No, no," he said, "you go and attend to the work. I'll get well." And he smiled gently.

Meanwhile the mixture of tea-leaves, water, milk and sugar was ready. Sohini poured some of it into two earthen bowls, glazed on the inside. Bakha came, and lifting one, gave it to his father. Then he picked up the other and put it to his lips hastily. The sharp, warm taste of the liquid sent forth a queer delight spreading into his flesh. His tongue was slightly burnt with the small sips because he did not, as his father did, blow on the tea to cool it. This was another of the things he had learnt at the British barracks from the Tommies. His uncle had said that the goras didn't enjoy the full flavour of the tea because they did not blow on it. But Bakha considered that both his uncle's and his father's spattering sips were habits. He would have told his father that the sahibs didn't do that. But he was too respectful by habit to suggest such a thing, although, of course, for himself he accepted the custom of the goras[4] and followed it implicitly. After he had drunk his tea and eaten a piece of bread from the basket which Sohini had put before her father, Bakha went out. He picked up the big broom and the basket with which his father used to go out sweeping the roads. Then he walked away towards the town, realising, for the first time, the strange coincidence of his morning's wish with his father's sudden injunction.

[4]*goras* Englishmen

The lane leading to the outcastes' street was soon left behind. It seemed such a short lane to him today. Where the lane finished, the heat of the sun seemed to spread as from a bonfire out into the empty space of the maidan beyond the colony. He sniffed at the clean, fresh air around the flat stretch of land before him and vaguely sensed a difference between the odorous, smoky world of refuse and the open, radiant world of the sun. He wanted to warm his flesh; he wanted the warmth to get behind the scales of the dry, powdery surface that had formed on his fingers; he wanted the blood in the blue veins that stood out on the back of his hand to melt. He turned his hands so as to show them to the sun. He lifted his face to the sun, open-eyed for a moment, then with the pupils of his eyes half closed, half open. And he lifted his chin upright. It was pleasing to him. It seemed to give him a thrill, a queer sensation which spread on the surface of his flesh where the tincture of warmth penetrated the numbed skin. He felt vigorous in this bracing atmosphere. Instinctively he rubbed his face in order to make it warm enough to take in the rays of the sun, to open out its pores. A couple of brisk rubs and he felt the blood in his cheeks rising to the high bones under the shadow of his eyes and into the ears which shone red-tipped and transparent at the sides of his head. He felt as he used to do when, on winter Sundays in his childhood, he stripped himself naked, except for a loin-cloth, to stand in the sun, and rub mustard oil on his body. Recollecting this he looked up at the sun. He caught the full force of its glare, and was dazed. He stood lost for a moment, confused in the shimmering rays, feeling as though there was nothing but the sun, the sun, the sun, everywhere, in him, on him, before him, and behind him. It was a pleasant sensation in spite of the disconcerting suddenness with which it had engulfed him. He felt suspended, as it were, in a region of buoyant tenseness and hummed a tune.

As he emerged from the world of that rare, translucent lustre into which he had been lifted, he stumbled over a stone and muttered a curse. Looking ahead he saw that he was being observed by Ram Charan, the washerman's son, by Chota, the leather-worker's son, and his own brother, Rakha. He felt abashed at being seen absorbed in singing to himself. They always made a butt of him, ridiculing the weight of his body, the shape of his clothes, his gait, which was a bit like an elephant's, on account of his heavy, swaying buttocks, and a bit like a tiger's, lithe and supple. He thought they would mock at him if they saw him massaging his face or humming to himself, especially as he was conscious they knew that he was a devotee of "fashun," a weakness which they shared with him and yet for which they ridiculed him. Bakha would always retaliate by pointing at the washer-boy's lashless, browless eyes and saying: "That comes of using too much soap to whiten your skin." And there were other peculiarities about Ram Charan: the fact that he had Gulabo for a mother, and a rather pretty, flirtatious sister, the fact that he was a very bony, thin little figure, and drove an ass, blind of one eye, to the waterside, which made the basis of a good joke. Chota, he could not attack, for that regular-featured lad was the smartest fellow about the lane, with his neatly oiled hair, khaki shorts and white tennis shoes. Almost a model "gentreman," Bakha thought him, the kind of person he admired and wanted to imitate. With him, therefore, he had an intimate understanding which made the jokes they cut about each other always more tolerable.

"Come, brother-in-law," greeted Ram Charan, blinking his lashless eyes and looking up.

"I want to be your brother-in-law if you will let me be," said Bakha turning the washer-boy's light abuse into a mild joke, based on the fact that he was known to everyone to be an admirer of Ram Charan's sister.

"Acha, she is being married today, so you are too late," replied Ram Charan, pleased that Bakha would never be able to make the same joke again.

"Oh, is that why you are wearing such nice clothes today!" remarked Bakha. "I see! What a fine waistcoat that! Only a bit frayed, that gold thread on the velvet. Why don't you iron it? And ohe, I like that chain! By the way is there a watch attached to it or is it merely for 'fashun'?"

Ram Charan flushed red and subsided. Chota sat quietly smiling at the interchange. Rakha was apparently feeling cold from the way he had made muffs for his hands of the long sleeves of the torn and battered overcoat he had inherited from Bakha, and from the manner in which he was hugging his arms close to his chest. A few other outcastes were busy killing lice from the pleats of their shirts and trousers and too comfortable in the sun to bother to look up. As they sat or stood in the sun, showing their dark hands and feet, they had a curiously lackadaisical lazy, lousy look about them. It seemed their insides were concentrated in the act of emergence, of a new birth, as it were, from the raw, bleak wintry feeling in their souls to the world of warmth. The taint of the little prison cells of their one-roomed homes lurked in them, even in the outdoor air. They were silent as if the act of liberation was too much for them to bear. The great life-giver had cut the inscrutable knots that tied them up in themselves. It had melted the innermost parts of their being. And their souls stared at the wonder of it all, the mystery of it, the miracle of it.

It was some time before they nodded a greeting to Bakha. But he understood them like that. For though he considered them his inferiors since he came back with sharpened wits from the British barracks, he still recognised them as his neighbours, the intimates with whose lives, whose thoughts, whose feelings he had to make a compromise. He didn't expect them to be formal. And as he stood for a while among them, he became a part of the strange, brooding, mysterious crowd that was seeking the warmth of the sun. One didn't need to employ a courtesy, a greeting, to become part of this gathering as one does in the world where there is plenty of light and happiness. For in the lives of this riff-raff, these dregs of humanity, only silence, the silence of death fighting for life, prevailed.

Once Bakha was with them, his own and their queer reactions to the beauty of the morning emerged.

"Why, oh Bakhe," said Chota, beaming with pleasure as the light played on his dark, greasy face: "Where are you off today?"

"My father is ill," replied Bakha, "so I am going to sweep the roads in the town and the temple courtyard in his stead." Then he turned to his brother and said: "Oh, Rakhia, why did you run away early in the morning? Father is ill and there is all the work at the latrines to do in my absence. Come, my brother, run back home. Sohini has kept some hot tea for you, too."

Rakha, a short, long-faced, black, stumpy little man, seemed to resent his brother's reprimand. But he quickly got up and sullenly faced the path leading homewards.

"Don't you go! Don't go!" called Ram Charan naughtily after him. "This, your brother, wants to be a 'gentreman' and to work on the roads, but he wants you to do the dirty work at the latrines."

"Don't buk," said Bakha good-humouredly. "Let him go and work for a bit."

"Come and play khuti!" said Chota, turning to a packet of "Red-Lamp" cigarettes he had fished out of a shirt pocket to see how many it contained before offering one to Bakha. "Come," he said, "we will go and join the others." He referred to Clayton, a black-skinned bandsman, and Godu, the carpenter's son, who were playing marbles.

"Come," urged Chota, "we shall win some money."

"No, I must go to my work," Bakha said, firmly declining the suggestion. "My father might see me and he will be angry."

"Forget the old man, come for a while;" Chota insisted.

"Come, come," seduced Ram Charan.

They were truants and expected the call of their parents any time. But they believed in dangerous living and had never missed a morning's sun, however much they were rebuked at home, or even beaten. Bakha had principles. With him duty came first, although he was a champion at all kinds of games and would have beaten them hollow at khuti. He seemed intent on his work and he was going to move on.

"All right, wait," said Chota. "There, I see the son of the burra babu coming. What about hockey today? The boys of the 31st Punjabis sent a 'challenge' to play a match against us."

"I shall come if my father allows me," said Bakha. Then he looked aside and seeing two white-clad, delicate young boys, greeted them by raising his right hand to his forehead.

"Salaam, babu ji."

The elder of the two boys, a simple, innocent, rather plain child of ten, angular, bony, with a flat nose and prominent cheek-bones, smiled kindly. There was a twinkle of recognition in the dark eyes of the little one, about eight years of age, with a bright egg-shaped face, alive in every feature from his big forehead to his pouting, thick, lower lip and his determined little chin.

"Come, boys!" greeted Ram Charan and Chota with an impudent swagger. "What about hockey today? There is a match with the boys of the 31st Punjabis."

"We shall play in the afternoon," said the little one enthusiastically jumping where he stood, holding his brother's finger. He was hardly big enough to hold a stick and he ignored the fact that he hadn't been asked, because he knew the boys never allowed him to play, saying he was too small, and that they were afraid he would get hurt and would go and tell upon them.

"Acha, will you give us the sticks?" asked Ram Charan, cunningly taking advantage of the child's enthusiasm to exact a promise which, though it was more likely to be repudiated than kept, might serve as a precaution against the child's obstinacy if that mood came upon him that afternoon, as it often did when he was not asked to play.

The sons of the babu, being influential with the captain of the regimental hockey team, because of the exalted position of their father, had had a dozen or so discarded hockey sticks given to them. The boys of the neighbourhood, who composed the 38th Dogras boys' eleven, were mostly the poor sons of the Untouchables, dependent on the bounty of the babu's sons for the loan of a stick every afternoon for a practice game. The elder of the two boys was always very obliging. He willingly suffered his mother's abuse for playing with the outcastes. But the younger one had to be humoured before he would yield.

"Han, I have brought a nice, new stick from Havildar Charat Singh," he said, "and a new ball." Then all of a sudden he turned peevishly to his brother, nudged him and exclaimed: "Come, don't you want to go to school? We will be late!"

Bakha noticed the ardent, enthusiastic look that lit up the little one's face. The anxiety of going to school! How beautiful it felt! How nice it must be to be able to read and write! One could read the papers after having been to school. One could talk to the sahibs. One wouldn't have to run to the scribe every time a letter came. And one wouldn't have to pay him to have one's letters written. He had often felt like reading Waris Shah's *Heer-Ranja.* And he had felt a burning desire, while he was in the British barracks, to speak the tish-mish, tish-mish which the Tommies spoke.

His uncle at the British barracks had told him, when he first expressed the wish to be a sahib, that he would have to go to school if he wanted to be one. And he had wept and cried to be allowed to go to school. But then his father had told him that schools were meant for the babus, not for the bhangis. He hadn't quite understood the reason for that, then. Later, at the British barracks, he realised why his father had not sent him to school. He was a sweeper's son and could never be a babu.[5] Later still he realised that there was no school which would admit him, because the parents of the other children would not allow their sons to be contaminated by the touch of a sweeper's son. How absurd, he thought, that was, since most of the Hindu children touched him willingly at hockey and wouldn't mind having him at school with them. But the masters wouldn't teach the outcastes lest their fingers which guided the students across the text should touch the leaves of the outcastes' books and they be polluted. These old Hindus were cruel. He was a sweeper, he knew, but he could not consciously accept that fact. He had begun to work at the latrines at the age of six and resigned himself to the hereditary life of the craft, but he dreamed of becoming a sahib. Several times, he had felt the impulse to study on his own. Life at the Tommies' barracks had fired his imagination. And he often sat in his spare time and tried to feel how it felt to read. Recently he had actually gone and bought a first primer of English. But his self-education hadn't proceeded beyond the alphabet. Today as he stood in the sun looking at the eager little boy dragging his brother to school, a sudden impulse came on him to ask the babu's son to teach him.

"Babu ji," he said, addressing the elder boy, "in what class are you now?"

"In the fifth class," the boy answered.

"Surely now you know enough to teach."

"Han," the boy replied.

"Then, do you think it will be too much trouble for you to give me a lesson a day." Seeing the boy hesitate, he added: "I shall pay you for it."

He spoke in a faint, faltering voice, and his humility increased in depth and sincerity with every syllable.

The babu's sons didn't get much pocket-money. Their parents were thrifty and considered, perhaps rightly, that a child should not eat irregularly, as the low-caste boys did, buying things in the bazaar. The elder boy had developed a strong materialistic instinct, hoarding the stray pice or two he received from anyone.

"Very well," he said. "I will. But the . . ." He wanted to change the topic, to make his suppressed desire for money less obvious. Bakha knew from his glance what he meant.

"I will pay you an anna per lesson."

The babu's son smiled a hypocritical smile which seemed queer in so young a

[5]*babu* clerk or someone of a higher caste

person. And he signified his assent, adding as an afterthought the conventional money-lover's phrase: "Oh, the money doesn't matter."

"Shall we begin this afternoon?" pleaded Bakha.

"Han," the boy agreed, and was inclined to stand to talk and cement the bond with pleasant words, but his brother was now very peevish and tugged at his sleeve, not only because he thought they were late for school, but also because he hated the idea of his brother becoming rich.

"Come," shouted the little one, "the sun is almost overhead! We will be beaten for being late at school."

Bakha divined the nature of the child's anger and tried to placate him by offering a bribe.

"You will also teach me, won't you little brother. I will give you a pice a day."

Bakha knew this would appease the boy's jealousy and obviate any chance of his telling upon his elder brother for spite. He knew if the little one told his mother that his elder brother was teaching a sweeper to read, she would fly into a rage and turn the poor boy out of the house. He knew her to be a pious Hindu lady.

The little one was too flurried to appreciate the value of the bribe. He looked towards school and was obsessed by the lateness of the hour. He pulled at the lower edge of his brother's tunic and dragged him away.

Bakha saw them depart. He felt elated at the prospect of the lesson he was to take in the afternoon and started to leave.

"Stop, O babu! Now you are going to be a very big man," shouted Ram Charan ironically. "You won't even talk to us."

"You are mad," answered Bakha jovially. "I must go, the sun is coming on. And I have to clean the temple approach, and the courtyard."

"Acha, let me show you my madness at hockey today."

"Very well," Bakha said as he headed towards the gates of the town, his basket under one arm, his broom under the other, and in his heart a song as happy as the lark's.

Tan-nana-nan-tan, rang the bells of a bullock-cart behind him as, like other pedestrians, he was walking in the middle of the road. He jumped aside, dragging his boots in the dust, where, thanks to the inefficiency of the Municipal Committee, the pavement should have been but was not. The fine particles of dust that flew into his face as he walked and the creaking of the cart-wheels in the deep ruts seemed to give him an intense pleasure. Near the gates of the town were a number of stalls at which fuel was sold to those who came to burn their dead in the cremation ground a little way off. A funeral procession had stopped at one of these. They were carrying a corpse on an open stretcher. The body lay swathed in a red cloth painted with golden stars. Bakha stared at it and felt for a moment the grim fear of death, a fear akin to the terror of meeting a snake or a thief. Then he assured himself by thinking: "Mother said, it is lucky to see a dead body when one is out in the streets." And he walked on, past the little fruit-stalls where dirtily clad Muhammadans with clean-shaven heads and henna-dyed beards cut sugar cane into pieces, which lay in heaps before them, past the Hindu stall-keepers, who sold sweetmeats from round iron trays balanced on little cane stools, till he came to the betel-leaf shop, where, surrounded by three large mirrors and lithographs of Hindu deities and beautiful European women, sat a dirty turbaned boy smearing the green heart-shaped betel leaves with red and white paint. A number of packets of "Red-Lamp" and "Scissors" cigarettes were arranged in boxes on his right and whole rows of biris on his left. From the reflection of his face in the looking-glass, which he shyly noticed, Bakha's eyes travelled to the cigarettes. He halted suddenly, and, facing the shopkeeper with great humility, joined his hands and begged to know where he could put a coin to pay for a packet of "Red Lamp." The shopkeeper pointed to a spot on the board near him. Bakha put his anna there. The betel-leaf seller threw some water over it from the jug with which he sprinkled the betel leaves now and again. Having thus purified it he picked up the nickel piece and threw it into the counter. Then he flung a packet of "Red-Lamp" cigarettes at Bakha, as a butcher might throw a bone to an insistent dog sniffing round the corner of his shop.

Bakha picked up the packet and moved away. Then he opened it and took out a cigarette. He recalled that he had forgotten to buy a box of matches. He was too modest to go back, as though some deep instinct told him that as a sweeper-boy he should show himself in people's presences as little as possible. For a sweeper, a menial, to be seen smoking constituted an offence against the Lord. Bakha knew that it was considered a presumption on the part of the poor to smoke like the rich people. But he wanted to smoke all the same. Only he felt he should do so unobserved while he carried his broom and basket. He caught sight of a Muhammadan who was puffing at a big hubble-bubble sitting on a mattress, spread on the dust at one of the many open-air barbers' stalls that gaudily flanked the way.

"Mian ji, will you oblige me with a piece of coal from your clay fire-pot?" he appealed.

"Bend down to it and light your cigarette, if that is what you want to do with the piece of coal," replied the barber.

Bakha, not used to taking such liberties with anybody, even with the Muhammadans, whom the Hindus considered outcastes and who were, therefore, much nearer him, felt somewhat embarrassed, but he bent down and lit his cigarette. He felt a happy, carefree man as he sauntered along, drawing the smoke and breathing it out through his nostrils. The coils of smoke rose slowly before his eyes and dissolved, but he was intent on the little white roll of tobacco which was becoming smaller every moment as its dark grey and red outer end smouldered away.

Passing through the huge brick-built gate of the town into the main street, he was engulfed in a sea of colour. Nearly a month had passed since he was last in the city, so little leisure did his job at the latrines allow him, and he couldn't help being swept away by the sensations that crowded in on him from every side. He followed the curves of the winding, irregular streets lined on each side with shops, covered with canvas or jute awnings and topped by projecting domed balconies. He became deeply engrossed in the things that were displayed for sale, and in the various people who thronged around them. His first sensation of the bazaar was of its smell, a pleasant aroma oozing from so many unpleasant things, drains, grains, fresh and decaying vegetables, spices, men and women and as afoetida. Then it was the kaleidoscope of colours, the red, the orange, the purple of the fruit in the tiers of baskets which were arranged around the Peshawari fruit-seller, dressed in a blue silk turban, a scarlet velvet waistcoat embroidered with gold, a long white tunic and trousers; the gory red of the mutton hanging beside the butcher who was himself busy mincing meat on a log of wood, while his assistants roasted it on skewers over a charcoal fire, or fried it in the black iron pan; the pale-blond colour of the wheat shop; and the rainbow hues of the sweetmeat stall, not to speak of the various shades of turbans and skirts, from the deep black of the widows to the green, the pink, the mauve and the fawn of the newly-wedded brides, and all the tints of the shifting, changing crowd, from the Brahmin's white to the grass-cutter's coffee and the Pathan's swarthy brown.

Bakha felt confused, lost for a while. Then he looked steadily from the multi-coloured, jostling crowd to the beautifully arranged shops. There was the inquisitiveness of a child in his stare, absorbed here in the skill of a wood-cutter and there in the manipulation of a sewing-machine by a tailor. "Wonderful! Wonderful!" his instinct seemed to say, in response to the sights familiar to him and yet new. He caught the eye of Ganesh Nath, the bania, a sharp-tongued, mean little man, in view of whose pyramids of baskets full of flour, native sugar, dried chillies, peas and wheat he had sat begging for the gift of a tiny piece of salt and a smear of clarified butter. He withdrew his gaze immediately, because there had recently been a quarrel between the bania and his father on account of the compound interest Ganesh had demanded for the money Lakha had borrowed on the mortgage of his wife's trinkets to pay for her funeral. That was an unpleasant thing! He resisted the memory and drifted in his unconscious happiness towards the cloth shop where a benign lalla, clad in an immaculately white, loose muslin shirt and loin-cloth, was busy writing in curious hieroglyphics on a scroll book bound in ochre-coloured canvas, while his assistants unrolled bundles of Manchester cloth one after another, for inspection by an old couple from a village, talking incessantly the while of the "tintint" and "matchint," just to impress the rustics into buying. Bakha was attracted by the woollen cloths that flanked the corners of the shop. That was the kind of cloth of which the sahibs' suits were made; the other cloth that he had seen lying before the yokels he could imagine turning soon into tunics and tehmets. All that was beneath his notice. But the woollen cloth, so glossy and warm! so expensive-looking! Not that he had any intention of buying, or any hope of wearing a kot-patloon, but he felt for the money in his pocket to see if he had enough to pay an instalment on the purchase of cloth. There were only eight annas there. He remembered that he had promised to pay the babu's son for the English lesson. He crossed the street to where the Bengali sweetmeat-seller's shop was. His mouth began to water for the burfi that lay covered with silver paper on a tray near the dirtily-clad, fat confectioner. "Eight annas in my pocket," he said to himself, "dare I buy some sweets? If my father comes to know that I spend all my money on sweets," he thought and hesitated, "but come, I have only one life to live," he said to himself, "let me taste of the sweets; who knows, tomorrow I may be no more." Standing in a corner, he stole a glance at the shop to see which was the cheapest thing he could buy. His eyes scanned the array of good things; rasgulas, gulabjamans and ludus. They were all so lushly, expensively smothered in syrup, that he knew they certainly could not be cheap, certainly not for him, because the shopkeepers always deceived the sweepers and the poor people, charging them much bigger prices, as if to compensate themselves for the pollution they courted by dealing with the outcastes. He caught sight of jalebis. He knew they were cheap. He had bought them before. He knew the rate at which they were sold, a rupee a seer.

"Four annas' worth of jalebis," Bakha said in a low voice, as he courageously advanced from the corner where he had stood. His head was bent. He was vaguely ashamed and self-conscious at being seen buying sweets.

The confectioner yawned and smiled faintly at the sweeper's taste, for jalebis are rather coarse stuff and no one save a greedy low-caste man would ever buy four annas' worth of them. But he was a shopkeeper. He affected a casual manner and, picking up his scales abruptly, began to put the sweets in one pan against bits of stone and some black, round iron weights which he threw into the other. The alacrity with which he lifted the little string attached to the middle of the rod, balanced the scales for the shortest possible space of time and threw the sweets into a piece torn off an old *Daily Mail*, was as amazing as it was baffling to poor Bakha, who knew he had been cheated, but dared not complain. He caught the jalebis which the confectioner threw at him like a cricket ball, placed four nickel coins on the shoe-board for the confectioner's assistant who stood ready to splash some water on them, and walked away, embarrassed yet happy.

His mouth was watering. He unfolded the paper in which the jalebis were wrapped and put a piece hastily into his mouth. The taste of the warm and sweet syrup was satisfying and delightful. He attacked the packet again. It was nice to fill one's mouth he felt, because only then could one feel the full savour of the thing. It was wonderful to walk along like that, munching and looking at all the sights. The big sign-boards advertising the names of Indian merchants, lawyers, and medical men, their degrees and professions, all in broad, huge blocks of letters, stared down at him from the upper storeys of the shops. He wished he could read all the luridly painted boards. But he found consolation in recalling the arrangement he had made for beginning his lessons in English that afternoon. Then his gaze was drawn to a figure sitting in a window. He stared at her, absorbed and unself-conscious.

"Keep to the side of the road, ohe low-caste vermin!" he suddenly heard someone shouting at him. "Why don't you call, you swine, and announce your approach! Do you know you have touched me and defiled me, cock-eyed son of a bow-legged scorpion! Now I will have to go and take a bath to purify myself. And it was a new dhoti and shirt I put on this morning!"

Bakha stood amazed, embarrassed. He was deaf and dumb. His senses were paralysed. Only fear gripped his soul, fear and humility and servility. He was used to being spoken to roughly. But he had seldom been taken so unawares. The curious smile of humility, which always hovered on his lips in the presence of high-caste men, now became more pronounced. He lifted his face to the man opposite him, though his eyes were bent down. Then he stole a hurried glance at the man. The fellow's eyes were flaming.

"Swine, dog, why didn't you shout and warn me of your approach!" he shouted as he met Bakha's eyes. "Don't you know, you brute, that you must not touch me!"

Bakha's mouth was open. But he couldn't utter a single word. He was about to apologise. He had already joined his hands instinctively. Now he bent his forehead over them, and he mumbled something. But the man didn't care to hear what he said. Bakha was too confused in the tense atmosphere which surrounded him to repeat what he had said, or to speak coherently and audibly. The man was not satisfied with dumb humility.

"Dirty dog! Son of a bitch! offspring of a pig!" he shouted, his temper spluttering on his tongue and obstructing his speech, and the sense behind it, in its mad rush outwards. "I . . . I'll have to go-o-o . . . and get washed-d-d . . . I . . . I was going to business and now . . . now, on account of *you*, I'll be late."

A man had stopped alongside to see what was up, a white-clad man, wearing the distinctive dress of a Hindu merchant. The aggrieved one put his case before him, trying to suppress his rage all the while with his closed, trembling lips which hissed like a snake's:

"This dirty dog bumped right into me. So unmindfully do these sons of bitches walk in the streets! He was walking along without the slightest effort at announcing his approach, the swine!"

Bakha stood still, with his hands joined, though he dared to lift his forehead, perspiring and knotted with its hopeless and futile expression of meekness.

A few other men gathered round to see what the row was about, and as there are seldom any policemen about in Indian streets, the constabulary being mostly concerned to have their palms greased, the pedestrians formed a circle round Bakha, keeping at a distance of several yards from him, but joining in to aid and encourage the aggrieved man in his denunciations. Confused still more by the conspicuous place he occupied in the middle of the crowd, the boy felt as if he would collapse. His first impulse was to run, just to shoot across the throng, away, away, far away from the torment. But then he realised that he was surrounded by a barrier, not a physical barrier, because one push from his hefty shoulders would have been enough to unbalance the skeleton-like bodies of the onlookers, but a moral one. He knew that contact with him, if he pushed through, would defile a great many more of these men. And he could already hear in his ears the abuse that he would thus draw on himself.

"Don't know what the world is coming to! These swine are getting more and more uppish," said a little, old man. "One of his brethren who cleans the lavatory of my house, announced the other day that he wanted ten rupees a month instead of five rupees, and the food that he gets from us daily."

"He walked like a Lat Sahib, like a Laften Gornor!" shouted the defiled one. "Just think, folks, think of the enormity!"

"I know," chimed in a seedy old fellow, "I don't know what the kalijug is coming to!"

"As if he owned the whole street!" exclaimed the touched man. "The son of a dog!"

A street urchin, several of whom had pushed their way through people's legs to see the fun, took his cue from the vigorous complainant and shouted: "Ohe, son of a dog! Now tell us how you feel. You who used to beat us!"

"Now look, look," urged the touched man, "he has been beating innocent little children. He is a confirmed rogue!"

Bakha had stood mute so far. At this awkward concoction of the child's, his honest soul surged up in self-defence.

"When did I beat you?" he angrily asked the child.

"Now, now mark his insolence!" shouted the touched man. "He adds insult to injury. He lies! look!"

"Nahin, Lalla ji, it is not true that I beat this child, it is not true," Bakha pleaded. "I have erred now. I forgot to call. I beg your forgiveness. It won't happen again. I forgot. I beg your forgiveness. It won't happen again."

But the crowd which pressed round him, staring, pulling grimaces, jeering and leering, was without a shadow of pity for his remorse. It stood unmoved, without heeding his apologies, and taking a sort of sadistic delight in watching him cower under the abuses and curses of its spokesman. Those who were silent seemed to sense in the indignation of the more vociferous members of the crowd an expression of their own awakening lust for power.

To Bakha, every second seemed an endless age of woe and suffering. His whole demeanour was concentrated in humility, and in his heart there was a queer stirring. His legs trembled and shook under him. He felt they would fail him. He was really sorry and tried hard to convey his repentance to his tormentors. But the barrier of space that the crowd had placed between themselves and him seemed to prevent his feeling from getting across. And he stood still while they raged and fumed and sneered in fury: "Careless, irresponsible swine!" "They don't want to work." "They laze about!" "They ought to be wiped off the surface of the earth!"

Luckily for Bakha, a tonga-wallah[6] came up, goading a rickety, old mare, which struggled in its shafts to carry a jolting, bolting box-like structure, and shouted a warning (for lack of a bell or a horn) for the crowd to disperse as he reined in his horse in time to prevent an accident. The crowd scattered to safety, blurting out vain abuses, exclamations of amusement and disgust, according to age and taste. The touched man was apparently not yet satisfied. He stood where he was though aware that he would be forced to move by the oncoming vehicle, as for the first time for many years he had had an occasion to display his strength. He felt his five-foot-two frame assume the towering stature of a giant with the false sense of power that the exertion of his will, unopposed against the docile sweeper-boy, had called forth.

"Look out, eh, Lalla ji," shouted the tonga-wallah with an impudence characteristic of his profession. The touched man gave him an indignant, impatient look and signed to him, with a flourish of his hand, to wait.

"Don't you thrust your eyeballs at me," the tonga-wallah answered back, and was going to move on, when, all of a sudden, he gripped his reins fast.

"You've touched me," he had heard the Lalla say to Bakha. "I will have to bathe now and purify myself anyhow. Well, take this for your damned impudence, son of a swine!" And the tonga-wallah heard a sharp, clear slap ring through the air.

Bakha's turban fell off and the jalebis in the paper bag in his hand were scattered in the dust. He stood aghast. Then his whole countenance lit with fire and his hands were no more joined. Tears welled up in his eyes and rolled down his cheeks. The cumulated strength of his giant body glistened in him with the desire for revenge, while horror, rage, indignation swept over his frame. In a moment he had lost all his humility, and he would have lost his temper too, but the man who had struck him the blow had slipped beyond reach into the street.

"Leave him, never mind, let him go, come along, tie your turban," consoled the tonga-wallah, who being a Muhammadan and thus also an Untouchable from the orthodox Hindu point of view, shared the outcaste's resentment to a certain degree.

Bakha hurried aside and, putting his basket and broom down, wrapped the folds of his turban anyhow. Then, wiping the tears off his face with his hands, he picked up his tools and started walking.

"You be sure to shout now, rape-sister!" said a shopkeeper from one side, "if you have learnt your lesson!" Bakha hurried away. He felt that everyone was looking at him. He bore the shopkeeper's abuse silently and went on. A little later he slowed down, and quite automatically he began to shout: "Posh, posh, sweeper coming, posh, posh, sweeper coming, posh, posh, sweeper coming!"

But there was a smouldering rage in his soul. His feelings would rise like spurts of smoke from a half-smothered fire in fitful jerks when the recollection of abuse or rebuke he had suffered kindled a spark in the ashes of remorse inside him. And in the smoky atmosphere of his mind arose dim ghosts of forms peopling the scene

[6]*tonga-wallah* resembling a two-wheeled cart

he had been through. The picture of the touched man stood in the forefront, among several indistinct faces, his bloodshot eyes, his little body with the sunken cheeks, his dry, thin lips, his ridiculously agitated manner, his abuse; and there was the circle of the crowd, jeering, scoffing, abusing, while he himself stood with joined hands in the centre. "Why was all this?" he asked himself in the soundless speech of cells receiving and transmitting emotions, which was his usual way of communicating with himself. "Why was all this fuss? Why was I so humble? I could have struck him! And to think that I was so eager to come to the town this morning. Why didn't I shout to warn the people of my approach? That comes of not looking after one's work. I should have begun to sweep the thoroughfare. I should have seen the high-caste people in the street. That man! That he should have hit me! My poor jalebis! I should have eaten them. But why couldn't I say something? Couldn't I have joined my hands to him and then gone away? The slap on my face! The coward! How he ran away, like a dog with the tail between his legs. That child! The liar! Let me come across him one day. He knew I was being abused. Not one of them spoke for me. The cruel crowd! All of them abused, abused, abused. Why are we always abused? The santry inspictor that day abused my father. They always abuse us. Because we are sweepers. Because we touch dung. They hate dung. I hate it too. That's why I came here. I was tired of working on the latrines every day. That's why they don't touch us, the high-castes. The tonga-wallah was kind. He made me weep telling me, in that way, to take my things and walk along. But he is a Muhammadan. They don't mind touching us, the Muhammadans and the sahibs. It is only the Hindus, and the outcastes who are not sweepers. For them I am a sweeper, sweeper—untouchable! Untouchable! Untouchable! That's the word! Untouchable! I am an Untouchable!"

Like a ray of light shooting through the darkness, the recognition of his position, the significance of his lot dawned upon him. It illuminated the inner chambers of his mind. Everything that had happened to him traced its course up to this light and got the answer: the contempt of those who came to the latrines daily and complained that there weren't any latrines clean, the sneers of the people in the outcastes' colony, the abuse of the crowd which had gathered round him this morning. It was all explicable now. A shock had passed through his perceptions, previously numb and torpid, and had sent a quiver into his being, stirred his nerves of sight, hearing, smell, touch and taste, all into a quickening. "I am an Untouchable!" he said to himself, "an Untouchable!" He repeated the words in his mind, for it was still a bit hazy and he felt afraid it might be immersed in the darkness again. Then, aware of his position, he began to shout aloud the warning word, to announce his approach: "Posh, posh, sweeper coming." The undertone, "Untouchable, Untouchable," was in his heart, the warning shout, "Posh, posh, sweeper coming!" was on his lips. His pace quickened and formed itself into the regular army step into which his ammunition boots always fell so easily. He noticed that the thumping of his heavy feet on the ground excited too much attention. So he slowed down a little.

He became conscious that people were looking at him. He looked about himself to see why he was arousing all that attention. He felt the folds of his turban coming loose over his forehead. He wanted to retreat to a corner and tie it up properly. But he couldn't stop right in the middle of the street. So he walked to a corner. Feeling that he might be observed, he assumed a look of abstraction, as if he was harassed by the thought of some important work he had in hand. And he stared around. He felt a fool knowing that he was acting. He unrolled his turban and began to wrap it hard round his head.

A bright, busy scene surrounded him where he lingered. The burning inside had emptied his mind of its content and he stood firm, struggling to express each shock as it impinged on his tight-stretched senses. A huge, big-humped, small-horned, spotted old brahminee bull was ruminating with half-closed eyes near him. The stink from its mouth as it belched, strangely unlike any odour which had assaulted Bakha's nostrils that day, was nauseating. And the liquid dung which the bull had excreted and which Bakha knew it was his duty to sweep off, sickened him. But presently he saw a well-dressed, wrinkled old Hindu, wearing, like a rich man, a muslin scarf over his left shoulder, advance to the place where the bull was enjoying its siesta and touch the animal with his forefingers. That was a Hindu custom, Bakha knew. What the meaning of it was, he didn't know. His truant memory ran back to a scene which he had seen occur so many times in the town. The figure of a bull roaming aimlessly about, then walking leisurely up to a vegetable stall, sniffing at the row of baskets and getting away with a mouthful of cabbage, spinach or carrots. The keeper only abused it mildly, threatened it with his hand, without striking it. The bull moved a yard or two away munching the mouthful of vegetables it had purloined and then it renewed its attack on the shop as soon as the keeper had turned his head away. "How queer, the Hindus don't feed their cows, although they call the cow 'mother!'" Bakha thought. "Their cattle which go to graze at the brookside are so skinny and feeble. Their cows can't yield more than two seers of milk a day." He recalled with great self-righteousness how, when his father had a buffalo given him in charity (or rather out of superstition), by a rich Hindu merchant who desired sons and was advised by the Brahmins to bestow some cattle on the sweepers, they used to feed it daily with grain and tended it so well that it yielded six seers of milk a day. And these people feed their cows on mere remainders of food and even on the grain, sifted, as he well knew (for he had to do the sifting) from the cow-dung. "But they are kind to the cows. This bull must enjoy making its daily haul on those onions. That is why it smells."

So far he had succeeded in isolating himself from his surroundings, but a cart came loaded with turnips and carrots and was emptied on to the ground. He stepped forward a few yards hurriedly. But a heap of decaying, rotten vegetables were littered over the baskets here. The putrid stink of this decomposing waste made him hurry away. He stared blankly for a while as he went along, without stirring his eyelids. The hot and crowded bazaar blazed with light. He was perspiring. His broad, frank face ordinarily so human, so variable, so changing, with its glistening high cheek-bones, its broad nose, the nostrils of which dilated like those of an Arab horse, his fine full quivering underlip so alive always, was set and impassive, silent, grim and deathly.

"Posh, posh, sweeper coming," he whispered as he resumed his steps and advanced into what was neither a broad, busy street, nor a narrow alley, but something of both, with a few odd shops occupied by companies of native bandsmen who play European instruments of music, and are greatly in demand at the marriages and birth parties held in the gulleys of crowded cities. A stray grocer's shop or the betel-leaf seller's punctuated the "four-faced street" as it was called, and there was a modern flour mill to which went those fastidious old Indian women who loved coarse flour and could not digest the fine which was sold in the shops, or who loved economy and bought wheat wholesale and had it ground. An ancient oil-mill stood in a corner, in a large, dark room, in which the bullock went round and round revolving a wooden pestle into a wooden mortar fixed in the centre from the ceiling. Bakha had known this street ever since his childhood, was used to the deep pits and admired its straight barrack-like look. The English musical instruments and the gold-embroidered uniforms that hung from the band shops, especially in the shop of Jehangir, the celebrated owner of the finest band in the city, were very congenial to his "English" mind. He felt sobered by the comparative quiet of this street. The few shops in it made no claims on his attention and he felt less confused in its atmosphere. The sight of the brass instruments and uniforms in the band shop took his mind back to the military band of the 38th Dogras which he saw almost every day practising in the cantonment, and he partly forgot the insult and the injury which he had suffered.

Out of the silent street, he turned the corner under a house which bridged the thoroughfare and he went along a row of stalls where cheap, nickel jewellery was being electro-plated. As a child, Bakha had often expressed a desire to wear rings on his fingers, and liked to look at his mother adorned with silver ornaments. Now that he had been to the British barracks and known that the English didn't like jewellery, he was full of disgust for the florid, minutely studded designs of the native ornaments. So he walked along without noticing the big ear-rings and nose-rings and hair-flowers and other gold-plated ornaments which shone out from the background of green paper against which the smiths had ingeniously set them. A seller of cloth remnants loaded on a three-wheeled cart was haggling with some white-aproned Hindu women right in the middle of the street. Bakha waited for a minute to see if they would clear the road to enable him to pass. He was too tired to shout and stood while contemplating the cheap, German lithographs of Hindu deities which a Sikh craftsman was fixing into expensive-looking frames. The picture of an English-woman, very scantily dressed and reclining with a flower in her hand, seduced Bakha's eyes away from the Hindu deities. The shopkeeper, noticing the basket and broom in Bakha's hand, gave him a stern look of disapproval and asked him to move on. The sweeper-boy lifted his face and pushing ahead called: "Posh, posh, sweeper coming," to the throng of buyers at the remnant seller's stall. Dragging at the pieces of cloth and bargaining loudly, it was with difficulty that the irritable Muhammadan keeper of the stall could wrest his wares from the grasp of his customers or apprise them of the coming of the Untouchable. When, at last, he managed to do so, they dispersed, talking, whispering, furious, happy, melancholy, ahead of Bakha, and thronged round the bangle-sellers, who were shaking their glass wares to dazzle and attract the young brides in the crowd, who timidly walked behind their mothers and mothers-in-law, adorned in their gold-embroidered silk aprons and Benarsi skirts, towards the temple where Bakha was going. He shouted his call again, a little wearily, "Posh, posh, sweeper coming." But the eager, ardent women had forgotten the instigation of their last move and talking vociferously from their heaving, big bosoms, did not listen till he reiterated his shout more vigorously.

At length he was allowed right of way and sighted the temple, a colossal, huge turreted structure of massive stone and carved masonry, the florid exuberance of whose detailed and intricate decorations struck a strange kind of awe into his being. Bakha had never quite got over his sense of fear born of the respect for these twelve-headed and ten-armed gods and goddesses which was inculcated in him in his childhood. And as he looked up from the shadow of the high wall falling on the courtyard through which he was walking, he was impressed by some unknown force that seemed to lurk there and to make the place too heavy to breathe in. A few slate-coloured pigeons flew and rested in the little, empty niches among the profuse carvings. The sight of them, so cool in their fawn-blue, and the sound of their cooing seemed to calm him. He surveyed the courtyard with the pertinacity of his sweeper's instinct, surveyed the droppings and the flowers, the heap of leaves and dust which he had come to clear.

He threw the basket and the broom he had in his hand on the ground and girt up his loins to attack his job as he stood in the shadow of a banyan-tree that spread its dense foliage over the temple courtyard. A brass cage of a miniature temple with the beautifully polished image of a snake enclosed in it, lay on a small stone structure which surrounded the giant trunk of the banyan-tree. It arrested his attention. "What is that snake image?" he asked himself casually. "What does it mean? Perhaps a snake lives at the root of the tree," his naïve mind answered. And he was slightly afraid, stepping away from the place instinctively. Then, as he saw a regular stream of people pass through the courtyard after touching the foot of the altar of the miniature temple, by the banyan-tree, his nerves were steadied. He drew near to the place where he had dropped his basket and his broom, shouting his call the while, lest the disaster of the morning be repeated through his negligence. This crowd was much more orthodox, this crowd which passed up and down the big broad steps, in and out of the open doorway, this dense crowd, jostling in its blue, white, red and green trappings of cotton and silk. Bakha stared beyond the throng with his inner eye, not daring to look beyond the gate with the overt, lifted eye of the ordinary man curious to know, to solve a mystery, but like the slave stealing an enquiry into the affairs of his master. "What have these people come here to worship?" he asked himself. "Worship the snake?"

"Ram, Ram, Sri, Sri, Hari, Narayan, Sri Krishna," a devotee sang as he almost brushed past the Untouchable. "Hey Hanuman jodah, Kali Mai."

Bakha had got his answer. The word "Ram" he had heard very often, also "Sri, Sri," and he had seen a red shrine with a monkey carved on a wall, caged from without with brass bars—that he knew was called the shrine of Hanuman. The black shrine showing a jet-black woman with a flaming-red tongue, ten-armed and with a garland of skulls round her neck—that was called the shrine of Kali. Krishna was the blue god who played the flute in the coloured pictures of the betel-leaf seller's shop in the street. But who was Hari, Narayan? And he was more completely baffled when a man passed by repeating: "Om, Om, Shanti Deva." Who was Shanti Deva? Was he in the temple? And was he kind?

"There is no chance of seeing anything if I stand here," he mused. "I shall go and look." But he hadn't the courage to go. He felt weak. He realised that an Untouchable going into a temple polluted it past purification. His father would be angry if he knew that he hadn't done any work this morning. Somebody might come and see him roaming about and think he was a thief.

But the edge of his curiosity became more and more intense as he stood there. He suddenly dismissed his thoughts and with a determined, hurried step went towards the stairs, looking to this side and that, with a tense, heavy head, but unafraid. A murderer might have advanced like that, one confident in his consummate mastery of the art of killing. But he soon lost his grace in the low stoop which the dead weight of years of habitual bending cast on him. He became the humble, oppressed underdog that he was by birth, afraid of everything, creeping slowly up, in a curiously hesitant, cringing movement. After he had mounted the first two steps, he stood completely demoralised with fear and retreated to the place from which he had started. He picked up his broom by its short wooden handle and began to sweep the ground. The particles of dust flew in a small, very small cloud before him, pale white and radiating bright gleams of gold where the sun-rays touched them. But Bakha didn't notice that. To him the litter of banyan leaves, flower petals, the droppings of pigeons, stray sticks and the dust, which his broom soon collected in its sweep, was more immediate, though even of this he was fairly unmindful till the dust flew to his nostrils and he tied the edge of his turban across his nose. And he jogged along, slowly, slowly, step by step, with an apathy peculiar to him. This was a slow business as compared to the work at the latrines, but though slow and wearying, not so unpleasant.

He collected the litter in small heaps, because he knew he could not push any more of it with his small broom, right round the courtyard. He had purposed to collect these small heaps, one by one, in his basket later on. When the heaps were ready, he waited for a moment to wipe the sweat off his brow. The temple stood challengingly before him. He bent down and began to collect the heaps. The unfailing sense of direction of his inner impulse landed him near the steps of the temple again. But now he was afraid. The temple seemed to advance towards him like a monster, and to envelop him. He hesitated for a while. Then his will strengthened. With a sudden onslaught he had captured five steps of the fifteen that led to the door of the temple. There he stopped, his heart drumming fiercely in his chest, which bent forward like that of an athletic runner on the starting-line, his head thrown back. The force of another impulse pushed him a step or two further up. Here he was almost thrown out of equilibrium by an accidental knock on his knee and stood tottering, threatened with a fall. But he gripped the steps hard, and, recovering his balance, rushed headlong to the top step. From here, as he lay, he could peer through with his head raised above the marble threshold, lowered (luckily for him) by the rubbings of the heads of the devout, and affording a glimpse, just a glimpse, of the sanctuary which had so far been a secret, a hidden mystery to him. In the innermost recesses of the tall, dark sanctum, beyond the brass gates, past what seemed a maze of corridors, Bakha's eyes probed the depths of a raised platform. There, from a background of gold-embroidered silk and velvet draperies stood out various brass images dimly shrouded in the soft tremors of incense that rose from a dish at their feet. A priest sat half naked, with a tuft of hair on the top of his shaven head, unduly prominent as it tied itself in an inscrutable knot. An open book lay on a bookstand before him, amidst the paraphernalia of brass utensils, conch-shells, and other ritualistic objects. A tall man, evidently also a priest, naked save for a loin-cloth, dark haired and supple, with a sacred thread throwing into relief the elegant curves of his graceful body, got up and blew a conch-shell. Bakha saw, peered, stared hard, and realised that the morning service had begun. After the loud soprano of "Om, Shanti Deva" the seated priest lifted his hard voice, jarring on the bell which tinkled in his left hand, into unison with the brass notes of the conch. The quiet little shrine of a moment ago had become a living, feeling reality. Worshippers flocked from the inner corridors of the temple towards the platform of the gods, and stood beneath the dome, singing, "Arti, Arti . . ." in a chorus. The loud flourish of the first conch note floated into a sweet, lingering melody, soft and clear, yet potent with a strength of the most mysteriously affecting kind, a strength sustained enough to raise one's hair, as it proceeded to a finish in the last hoarse shout of triumphant worship: "Sri Ram Chandra ki jai."

Bakha was profoundly moved. He was affected by the rhythm of the song. His blood had coursed along the balanced melodic line to the final note of strength with such sheer vigour that his hands joined unconsciously, and his head hung in the worship of the unknown god.

But a cry disturbed him. "Polluted! polluted! polluted!" A shout rang through the air. He was completely unnerved. His eyes were covered with darkness. He couldn't see anything. His tongue and throat were parched. He wanted to utter a cry, a cry of fear, but his voice failed him. He opened his mouth wide to speak. It was no use. Beads of sweat covered his forehead. He tried to raise himself from the awkward attitude of prostration, but his limbs had no strength left in them. For a second he was as if dead.

Then as suddenly as he had been overpowered he asserted himself. He lifted his head and looked round. The scales fell from his eyes. He could see the little man with the drooping moustache whom he knew to be a priest of the temple, racing up the courtyard, trembling, stumbling, tottering, falling, with his arms lifted in the air, and in his mouth the hushed cry "polluted, polluted, polluted!"

"I have been seen, undone," the sentence quickly flashed across Bakha's mind. But he espied the figure of a woman behind the shouting priest. He stood amazed, though still afraid, still feeling that he was doomed. He was unaware, however, of the form the doom would take.

But he soon knew. A thumping crowd of worshippers rushed out of the temple, and stood arrayed as in the grand *finale* of a tamasha. The lean, little priest stood with upraised hands, a few steps below him. His sister, Sohini (for that was the woman he had seen behind the priest) lingered modestly in the courtyard.

"Polluted, polluted, polluted!" shouted the Brahmin below. The crowd above him took the cue and shouted after him, waving their hands, some in fear, others in anger, but all in a terrible orgy of excitement. One of the crowd struck out an individual note.

"Get off the steps, scavenger! Off with you! You have defiled our whole service! You have defiled our temple! Now we will have to pay for the purificatory ceremony. Get down, get away, dog!"

Bakha ran down the steps, past the priest below him, to his sister. He had two impulses, that of fear for himself, for the crime he knew he had committed, another of fear for his sister, for the crime she may have committed, since she stood there speechless.

"You people have only been polluted from a distance," Bakha heard the little priest shriek. "I have been defiled by contact."

"The distance, the distance!" the worshippers from the top of the steps were shouting. "A temple can be polluted according to the Holy Books by a low-caste man coming within sixty-nine yards of it, and here he was actually on the steps, at the door. We are ruined. We will need to have a sacrificial fire in order to purify ourselves and our shrine."

"But I . . . I . . ." shouted the lanky priest histrionically, and never finished his sentence.

The crowd on the temple steps believed that he had suffered most grievously, and sympathised. They had seen the sweeper-boy rush past him. They didn't ask about the way he had been polluted. They didn't know the story that Sohini told Bakha at the door of the courtyard with sobs and tears.

"That man, that man," she said, "that man made suggestions to me, when I was cleaning the lavatory of his house there. And when I screamed, he came out shouting that he had been defiled."

Bakha rushed back to the middle of the courtyard, dragging his sister behind him, and he searched for the figure of the priest in the crowd. The man was no longer to be seen, and even the surging crowd seemed to show its heels as it saw the giant stride of the sweeper advance frighteningly towards the temple. Bakha stopped still in his determined advance when he saw the crowd fly back. His fist was clenched. His eyes flared wild and red, and his teeth ground between them the challenge: "I could show you what that Brahmin dog has done!"

He felt he could kill them all. He looked ruthless, deadly pale and livid with anger and rage. A similar incident he had heard about rose to his mind in a flash. A young rustic had teased a friend's sister as she was coming home through the fields after collecting fuel. Her brother had gone straight to the fields with an axe in his hand and murdered the fellow. "Such an insult!" he thought. "That he should attack a young and innocent girl. And then the hypocrisy of it! This man, a Brahmin, he lies and accuses me of polluting him, after — father of fathers, I hope he didn't violate my sister." A suspicion stole into his mind that he might have. He was stung to the quick when he suddenly felt that he too had looked at her with desire.

"Tell me, tell me, that he didn't do anything to you!"

Sohini was weeping. She shook her head in negation. She couldn't speak.

Bakha was reassured a bit. "But no, the attempt!" he thought. "The man must have made indecent suggestions to her. I wonder what he did. Father of fathers! I could kill that man. I could kill that man!" He was being tormented with the anxiety to know what had really happened, and yet he hesitated to question his sister again lest she should begin to cry. But his doubts and misgivings about her were too much for him.

"Tell me, Sohini," he said, turning fiercely at his sister, "how far did he go?"

She sobbed and didn't reply.

"Tell me! Tell me! I will kill him if . . ." he shouted.

"He-e-e just teased me," she at last yielded. "And then when I was bending down to work, he came and held me by my breasts."

"Brahmin dog!" Bakha exclaimed. "I will go and kill him!" And he rushed blindly towards the courtyard.

"No, no. Come back. Let's go away," called Sohini after him, arresting his progress by dragging hard at the lapel of his overcoat.

He stood staring at the temple for a moment. There was not a soul to be seen out of doors. All was still. He felt the cells of his body lapse back chilled. His eyes caught sight of the magnificent sculptures over the doors extending right up to the pinnacle. They seemed vast and fearful and oppressive. He was cowed back. The sense of fear came creeping into him. He felt as if the gods were staring at him. They looked so real although they were not like anything he had ever seen on earth. They seemed hard, their eyes fixed as they ogled out of their niches, with ten arms and five heads. He bent his head low. His eyes were dimmed. His clenched fists relaxed and fell loosely by his side. He felt weak and he wanted support. It was with difficulty that he steadied his gait and retraced his steps, with Sohini, to the outer gate.

The sight of her walking along with him, however, sent a wave of anguish into his soul. So frail she looked and so beautiful. Bakha was conscious of the charm of his sister. Her slim, pale brown figure, soft and warm and glowing, shot through with a lustre that set off her ornaments, the rings in her ears, the bangles on her arms, to a ravishing effect, was so silent and subtly modest and full of a strange tenderness and light. He could not think of her being brutalised by anyone, even by a husband married to her according to the rites of religion. He looked at her and somehow a picture of her future life seemed to come before him. She had a husband—a man who had her, possessed her. He loathed the ghost of her would-be husband that he conjured up. He could see the stranger holding her full breasts and she responding with a modest acquiescence. He hated the thought of that man touching her. He felt he would be losing something. He dared not think what he would be losing. He dared not think that he himself———"I am her brother," he said to himself, to rectify his thoughts which seemed to be going wrong. But there seemed no difference to his naked mind between his own feeling for her and what might be a husband's love. He dismissed the whole picture. Facing his mind was the figure of the little priest. That made his blood boil. He felt a wild desire to retaliate, retaliation meaning to him just doing anything to the man, from belabouring him with blows to killing him if need be. For though the serfdom of thousands of years had humbled him, the tropical emotions that welled up in him under an open sky had lessened his respect for life. He came of peasant stock, his ancestors having come down in the social scale by their change of profession. The blood of his peasant ancestors, free to live their own life even though they may have been slaves, raced in him now. "I could have given him a bit of my mind," he exclaimed to himself.

A superb specimen of humanity he seemed whenever he made the high resolve to say something, to go and do something, his fine form rising like a tiger at bay. And yet there was a futility written on his face. He could not overstep the barriers which the conventions of his superiors had built up to protect their weakness against him. He could not invade the magic circle which protects a priest from attack by anybody, especially by a low-caste man. So in the highest moment of his strength, the slave in him asserted itself, and he lapsed back, wild with torture, biting his lips, ruminating his grievances.

A busy street lay before the brother and sister when they emerged from the temple. Bakha looked out to it vaguely. He could not concentrate on the riot of variety that was displayed in it. He had no patience to see anything or to hear anything, and he didn't want to speak. "Why didn't I go and kill that hypocrite!" he cried out silently. "I could have sacrificed myself for Sohini. Everyone will know about her. My poor sister! How can she show her face to the world after this? But why didn't she let me go and kill that man? Why was she born a girl in our house, to bring disgrace upon us? So beautiful! So beautiful and so accursed! I wish she had been the ugliest woman in the world. Then no one would have teased her!" But he couldn't bear the thought of her being ugly. His pride in her beauty seemed to be hurt. And he just wished: "Oh, God, why was she born, why was she born." Then, however, he saw her bending and wiping her eyes with her apron. With a sudden burst of tenderness and humility he gripped her arm close and dragged her along, writhing with the conflicts in his soul.

A few steps and he felt more easy. His breath came and went more evenly. His big, raw-boned body, strung into a lithe, active frame by his overpowering passion became rather heavy. His instinctive fear of the people in the street, all so quick to notice the vagaries of individuals, rude and ill-mannered if they saw something ridiculous or sublime, made him recollect himself. He contemplated his experience now in the spirit of resignation which he had inherited through the long centuries down through his countless outcaste ancestors, fixed, yet flowing like a wave, confirmed at the beginning of each generation by the discipline of the caste taboo.

"Do you go home, Sohini," he said to his sister who walked behind him, ashamed and crestfallen, with the stain upon her honour she thought it was to have been the object of a scene. "Do you go home," he said, "and I'll go and get the food. Take this basket and broom with you."

She moved her head in assent without looking up at him. And drawing her apron to cover her face, she walked away towards the city gates.

A glance in the direction of his sister, and Bakha walked slowly away from the house of God. "Posh, posh, sweeper coming," he suddenly remembered his warning call, as he just avoided touching a barefooted shopkeeper who was running like a holy bull from shop to shop. When he had thus unconsciously passed through the congested iron-monger's bazaar, past a humanity whose panting rush in its varied, hybrid clothes (neither English nor Indian) he took for granted, he found himself standing outside an alley which spread like a yawn between a fruit-shop and an old perfumer's. Beneath the emptiness in his inside lay suppressed a confusion arising from the overpowering contradictions of his feelings. But outwardly he was calm and unperturbed. He stood still for a moment, to exercise his sense of direction as he had been walking almost in a coma. "To the houses in this alley for food," he said to himself and turned into the lane.

A stray dog, thin, flea-bitten and diseased, was relieving itself. Another, which was all bones, was licking at some decayed food on a refuse heap that lay blocking the drain. Right across the passage further up lay a cow. Bakha observed the dirt and filth that lay about, casually. But the animals seemed to infuriate him. He approached the dogs and jumping sharply surprised them into making off with a squeak and a squeal. The bovine insensibility of the cow that lay stretched before him was, however, hard to break through. Lest he should be accused of disturbing the holy mother of the rich owners at whose doors she lay, he held it by the horns to protect his legs against its well-known ferocity, and picked his way across. More heaps of rubbish littered all over the small, old brick pavement meant to him only more reminders of his sister's careless performance of her duties that morning. He excused her, however, by thinking of her suffering. Nobody who had been insulted as she had could be expected to do her work properly. He didn't want to confess that his defence of her was unreasonable, in that she was supposed to have been here before she went to clean the house in the temple. A huge din of coppersmiths hammering and rehammering copper in their irregular, little, dark shops engulfed him and he walked more comfortably for a while, for the noise was pleasant, even cheering from a distance, and helped to drown his conscience with regard to his sister's negligence. Deeper in the square, however, the "thak, thak, thak" that issued from the collection of shops became unbearable. He would have rushed into the little sub-alley where he had to go and call for food, but the ablutions of a devout Hindu on the platform of the street well in the middle of the lane offered the prospect of Bakha getting sprinkled with the holy water that rained off from the well-oiled body, naked save for a loin-cloth. Bakha waited until his holiness had emptied a canful of water on his head and slung the empty vessel back into the well. Then he sauntered into the dark, damp gulley, where two fat men could hardly pass each other. He felt calmer because it was cool here and the noise of the copper-beaters was fainter. But the rest of his nerves was yet to come. For being an outcaste he could not insult the sanctity of the houses by climbing the stairs to the top floors where the kitchens were, but had to shout and announce his arrival from below.

"Bread for the sweeper, mother. Bread for the sweeper," he called standing at the door of the first house. His voice died down to the echo of "thak, thak, thak," which stole into the alley.

"The sweeper has come for bread, mother! The sweeper has come for the bread," he shouted a little louder.

But it was of no avail.

He penetrated further into the alley and standing near a point where the doors of four houses were near each other, he shouted his call: 'Bread for the sweeper, mother; bread for the sweeper."

Yet no one seemed to hear him on the tops of the houses.He wished it had been the afternoon, because he knew at that time the housewives were always downstairs sitting in the halls of their houses or on the drains in the gully, gossiping or plying the spinning-wheel. But the vision of a number of them squatting in the gully and wailing with each other's aprons over their heads, or beating their breasts in mourning for the dead, came before his eyes and he felt embarrassed.

"Bread for the sweeper, mother," he shouted again.

There was no response. His legs were aching. There was a lethargy in his bones, a curious numbness. His mind refused to work. Feeling defeated, he sat down on the wooden platform of a house in the lane. He was tired and disgusted, more tired than disgusted, for he had almost forgotten the cause of his disgust, his experiences of the morning. A sort of sleepiness seemed to steal into his bones. He struggled hard against it by keeping his eyes open. Then he lightly leaned against the hard wood of the huge hall door as a concession to his fatigued limbs. He knew that his place was on the damp brick pavement on the side of the drain. But for a while he simply didn't care. Bringing his legs together he crouched into a corner and gave himself up to the soft urgings of the darkness that seemed to envelop him. Before long he had succumbed to sleep.

Unfortunately for his tired body, it was an uneasy half sleep that he enjoyed, the hindrances in the labyrinthine depths of his being weaving strange, weird fantasies and dreams. He saw himself driven in a bullock cart through the thronging streets of a most marvellous city, encountering a wedding procession of gaily-dressed, laughing people, preceded by a litter, covered with ochre-coloured draperies, carried by four men, who were themselves preceded by a Sikh band, dressed in the uniform of the English Army, carrying clarinets, bugles, flutes, super-saxaphones and drums, walking in loose formation, and playing not the harmonies which he had heard in the cantonment, but tuneless wails, weird and disturbing. Then he was on the platform of a railway station. Before him stood a train of forty closed iron freight wagons with an engine at each end. Somewhere in a long row he could espy open trucks, two laden with boulders of stone and bulks of timber. He saw himself getting onto the top of one of these loads and sitting there, a bundle by his side, an umbrella with a carved silver handle in his hand, a sola topi on his head and the tube of his father's hookah in his mouth. Suddenly he could see the closed iron freight-wagons move. Almost simultaneously he could hear squeaks, creaks, execrations, lamentations and general excitement, as if someone had been murdered on a near but invisible siding. Full of fear and pity he imagined himself bending over the end of the wagon. He discovered that they were only some blue-uniformed railway coolies pushing a coach into a shed. He was next transplanted to a small village with very narrow streets, muddy and heavily cambered with rills of water running on either side. He could see cows wandering about and two big carts, heavy-laden, get stuck in the slush as they came from opposite directions. A number of sparrows alighted on the heaps of grain in the open shops and helped themselves to food. A huge crow soared down to the bruised neck of a bullock and began to peck at it. Then he watched a little girl who stood outside a sweet shop. The child advanced smiling, holding aloft the food she had bought. The crow swooped down and snatched at her hand and threw her food onto the heap of litter lying near the gutter. She began to cry. A silversmith, handsome, immense, who sat before a charcoal fire fashioning ornaments, looked up, smiled understandingly, and with his tongs placed a burning ember on her uplifted hand. The child toddled off happily through a narrow entry into a garden where beds of flowers flanked jets of fountains. Then Bakha saw himself in the compound of a school where boys in yellow turbans were reading aloud as their master sat, cane in hand, exercising a vigilant scrutiny over his wards. The monitor of the class passed successively to each of his fellows on the benches a verse which they declaimed after him. Behind a network of streets in the wonder city ran a stream by which stood a palace, whose domed inner roof was supported by stone trusses and whose wealth of stone carving compelled attention. Bakha looked at it with wonder and admiration and gasped. He entered and saw how it had been hewn out of rock. Its roof was painted in red and gold and black and green. By colonnades of immense and richly-ornamented columns forming a nave and an aisle at the far end stood men crowding round an emaciated man. Out of the dome some soldiers emerged and chattering, talking, smiling, happy, they carried him to a vast plain, a burning-ground, where the embers of the incinerations of the previous evening still smouldered, sending delicate spirals of smoke from the mounds of human bodies. A number of holy men stood beside the dead bodies, pouring the ashes of the dead into their hair, drinking hemp and dancing in an orgy of destruction. A gora was looking on from a corner. He smiled at the scene. Bakha saw one of the holy men, an ascetic whose years were said to exceed ten thousand and who sat naked and with shaven head in silent contemplation, perform a magic trick by which the sahib was turned into a little black dog. Bakha thought of offering him a gift but the holy man's followers told him he shouldn't. Bakha stood wondering how the man lived. Then a swarm of monkeys jumped down from a tree and——

"Alakh, alakh"[7] came a call and awoke him. The dream completely faded out in the glare that the sunshine cast leaning over the tall houses. Bakha knew it was noon and that just at that time every holy man and beggar seeks the doors of the devout for alms which he has earned by the dedication of his person to God. Almost at once he collected himself, rubbed his eyes and felt: "I shall soon get bread." He knew that the housewives sat waiting for the ash-smeared sadhus[8] and did not eat their food before dispensing hospitality to the holy men. He looked up at the sadhu without getting up. The man was staring down at him. Bakha fell back into the drowsy listlessness of a moment ago.

[7]*Alakh, alakh* Look, Look!

[8]*sadhu* holy man (plural: sadhus)

"Bham, bham, bhole Nath,"[9] cried the sadhu in the peculiar lingo of sadhu-hood, shaking the bangles on his arms, which brought two women rushing to the terraces of their house-tops.

"I am bringing the food, sadhu ji," shouted the lady at whose doorstep Bakha was at rest. But she stopped short when she saw the sweeper's body knotted up on the wooden platform outside her house.

"Vay, eater of your master," she shouted, "may the vessel of your life never float in the sea of existence. May you perish and die! You have defiled my house! Go! Get up, get up! Eater of your masters! Why didn't you shout if you wanted food? Is this your father's house that you come and rest here?"

Bakha got up as abruptly as the woman's tone had changed from kindness to the holy man to cruelty to him. And rubbing his eyes and trying to shake off the lethargy that lay thick like the hot air about him, he apologised.

"Forgive me, mother. I shouted for bread, but you were busy and didn't hear me. I was tired and sat down."

"But, eater of your masters! why did you sit down on my doorstep, if you had to sit down at all? You have defiled my religion! You should have sat there in the gully. Now I will have to sprinkle holy water all over the house. Spoiler of my salt! Oh, how terrible! You sweepers have lifted your heads to the sky, nowadays. This bad luck on a Tuesday morning too! And after I had been to the temple! . . ." She saw the sadhu waiting and checked her copious flow of remonstrance and abuse. Bakha was afraid to look up.

"Be patient, sadhu ji," her voice came again. "I shall just go and get you your food. This eater of his masters has even burnt the bread I was baking by detaining me here." She retreated from her vantage point on the terrace.

Meanwhile, the other woman, as quiet as she was heavy, came down the stairs with a handful of rice in one hand and a chapati in the other. The first she put into the holy man's bag, the second she handed over to Bakha, adding kindly: "My child, you shouldn't sit on people's doorsteps like this."

"May you live long and all your family prosper!" said the sadhu as he received the alms. "Isn't there a little lentil of which you could make the holy man a gift?"

"Han, sadhu ji," she said, "tomorrow, from tomorrow you shall have lentil." And she rushed upstairs saying "I am busy cooking."

The owner of the defiled house came down now. She stared eagle-eyed at Bakha and remonstrated: "Wah! You have wrought strange work this morning, defiling my home!" Then she turned to the holy man and heaped a steaming, hot vegetable curry and a pot full of cooked rice into the sadhu's black skull of a begging-bowl. "Please accept this," she said, "the house is all right; he didn't really pollute it. I wonder if you have a cure for my son's fever which you could bring me."

"May the gods bless you and your children," said the holy man. "I will bring you some herbs in the morning." And he turned his back after having exacted his dues for looking after the souls of his disciples.

"May you die," the woman cursed Bakha, thinking she had acquired enough merit by being good to the holy man and wouldn't lose much of it by being unkind to the sweeper. "What have you done to earn your food today, you or your sister. She never cleaned the lane this morning, and you have defiled my home. Come,

[9]*Bham, bham, bhole Nath* a plea to the god of destruction

clean the drain a bit and then you can have the bread. Come, do a bit of work now that you have defiled my home."

Bakha looked at the lady for a while. Then, cowed down by her abuse, he set to work to sweep the gutter with a small broom which, he knew, his sister always hid under the wooden platform where he sat.

"Mother," shouted a little child from the top of the house, "I want to go——"

"No, you can't go," replied the mother who stood superintending the sweeper's work. "You can't go upstairs, it will lie there all day," she said. "Come here, come downstairs, quick, and go here in the drain. The sweeper will clear it away."

"No," insisted the obstinate boy who felt shy to sit in a public place.

His mother rushed up to fetch him. She had forgotten to give Bakha the bread she had brought for him. On reaching the top of her house she sent her son without the bread, and since she didn't want to undertake another journey down, she called to Bakha while he was in the middle of his job.

"Vay Bakha, take this. Here's your bread coming down." And she flung it at him.

Bakha laid aside the broom and tried hard to be the good cricketer he usually was, but the thin, paper-like pancake floated in the air and fell like a kite on to the brick pavement of the gully. He picked it up quietly and wrapped it in a duster with the other things he had there. He was too disgusted to clean the drain after this, especially as the little boy sat relieving himself before him. He threw the little broom aside and made off.

"Aren't they a superior lot these days!" exclaimed the lady, disappointed at not receiving a courtesy. "They are getting more and more uppish."

"I have finished, mother," her son shouted.

"Rub yourself on the ground my child, if there is no one to give you water at the pickle-maker's next door," she said, and went back to her kitchen.

All the accumulated fury of the morning was in Bakha's soul and the rage of this fresh insult. He felt that he had got up from his sleep almost cured of his unpleasant memories, but now there was an ache in the back of his head. A subtle heat was mounting from his spine, drying the blood in his body and shrinking his face. "I wish that hadn't happened at the temple," he said to himself. "Then Sohini would have come for the bread. Why did I have to come to the lane?" He moved in a sort of trance. Black and filthy, yet orderly with that dignity and decorum which his exotic dress gave him, he was possessed by a curious fire. "I shouldn't have picked up that bread from the pavement," he said, and he sighed. That seemed to relax him.

Meanwhile, he began to feel hungry as if rats were running around in his belly, searching for food. He began to spit a white flocculent spittle on the dust as he hurried out of the town, homewards. His limbs sagged. He felt the sweat trickling down his face from under his turban as soon as he got into the open. He looked up to the sun. It stood right above him. Bakha's face quickened with the awareness of the sun's vertical position. His body had a wonderful time sense as it really had a sense of other things. "How can I go home with only two chapatis under my arm?" the feeling came to him. "Father will be sure to ask if I have brought any delicacies. It isn't my fault that I have only one roti. He is sure to ask why Sohini didn't go down to get the food. I shall have to tell him the whole story. He will be angry!" He remembered how, when he was a child, his father had abused him because he came and reported that a sepoy had frightened him. "Father always takes sides with the others. Never with his own family. How can I tell him about the priest? He won't believe it. And he will burst out if I say anything about the incident in the street: 'The only day that I send you down to the town to work, you go and pick a quarrel." That is what he will say: "When will you learn to do your job properly?'" Bakha felt that rather than bear this he would go and tell a lie. "But then he is sure to know because Sohini didn't go to fetch the food. He must have asked her why she came home so early. Perhaps it will be best not to say anything. But he is sure to ask. Oh, never mind, let come what may." And he closed his mind to the conflict and became absorbed in a stray eagle wheeling high up in the sky.

With his mind occupied by the soaring eagle, Bakha didn't find the way home very long. He could see his family basking in the sunshine outside the house. There was no provision for lights in the sweeper's street, so most of the inhabitants compensated themselves for the nights spent in utter darkness, amid the smoke of smouldering hearth fires in their small congested houses, by spending most of their day-time in the open air. In the summer, of course, this was difficult, even though they made awnings of the string beds on which they slept at night, by covering them with coarse, unwanted rags of jute cloth, and sat under them all day. During the winter, however, they came out of their homes as soon as the sun was up and lived outdoors till the evening fell and it was too cold.

Sohini had kept up the outdoor kitchen which her mother had made adjoining the door of her house. It was not strictly a kitchen in the Hindu manner, for there were no four lines defining its limits, according to those laws of hygiene which are the basis of Hindu piety. A couple of brooms stood out next to the fire-place, an empty refuse basket, a can, two earthen pitchers and a chipped enamelled jug lay scattered about. Most of the utensils were of clay, darkened by the soot of many fires and never washed since Bakha's mother had died, for Sohini was young and inexperienced and had a great deal too much work to do outside the house to devote herself assiduously to housework. Besides, there was a scarcity of water. And since, on account of their profession and the filthy surroundings in which they were forced to live, they needed more than a pitcher full of water, but could not get it, they just did without. Sanitation, cleanliness and hygiene had lost all meaning for them.

"Where is Rakha?" Bakha asked his sister, as he gave her the duster containing the bread.

She kept quiet, but Lakha, his father, answered: "The rascal has gone to get food at the langar in the barracks."

The old man was sitting on his bedstead, now stretched out near the kitchen, puffing away at his hookah, each puff a short asthmatic cough. He looked well groomed. He had evidently been plucking superfluous hair from his face with a pair of tweezers which he always kept under his pillow near a painted, native looking-glass, because his bristling white beard looked trimmed up into clean edges and sides. There was a kindly look in his eyes due probably to the easy and comfortable morning he had had. But his lips were tightly set and his brow was wrinkled under his cleanly-tied blue turban. If need be, his mood would quickly change from grumpiness to anger.

"Have you brought anything nice to eat," he asked Bakha, "I am just hungering for some pickles, spinach, and maize-flour bread."

"I have brought only two chapatis," replied Bakha. The feeling came to him which had possessed him throughout his journey, of the struggle between making a clean breast of it all and lying.

"You are a good-for-nothing scoundrel," muttered Lakha. "I hope that the rascal brings something nice from the barracks."

As he said so the Jemadar's mouth watered and his mind travelled to the great big piles of cooked food which he had received on the occasion of marriages in the alleys of the city. There were fried bread and chingri puffs, vegetables, curries and semolina pudding, sweets and tasty pickles — remainders from the trays of high-caste men, and sometimes portions direct from the kitchens. Those were unforgettable days, so pleasing to Lakha that he had always watched the development of each and every girl in the alleys where he worked and asked their parents when the auspicious occasion of their marriage would be celebrated. It may be that Lakha is to blame for most of the child marriages in Bulandshahr. The parents of the potential brides always remembered Lakha, giving him a suit of clothes and generous portions of food. Another occasion he remembered was when the regiment, to which he was attached, came back from the war, for during the rejoicings on its return there were grand feasts and he, as the Jemadar of all the sweepers, was in charge of the distribution of the remainders of food. He recalled how the wooden box where his wife kept sweets was never empty that year.

"I don't know the people in the town very well, and I didn't call at all the houses for food," said Bakha to excuse himself to his father. The remark disturbed Lakha's gastronomic fantasy.

"You should try and get to know them. You have got to work for them all your life, my son, after I die."

Bakha felt the keen edge of his sense of anticipation draw before his eyes the horrible prospects of all the future days of service in the town and the insults that would come with them. He could see himself being shouted at by a crowd; he could see the little priest fling his arms in the air and cry, "defiled, defiled." He could see the lady who had thrown the bread down at him reprimanding him for not cleaning the gutter. "No, no," his mind seemed to say, "never," and there appeared before him the vague form of a Bakha clad in a superior military uniform, cleaning the commodes of the sahibs in the British barracks. "Yes, much rather," he said to himself to confirm the picture.

It was a queer mixture of awe and romance, the alternation of his hatred for his own town and the love for the world to which he looked out. Men get used to a place, become familiar with it, and then comes a stage when the fascination of the unknown, the exotic dominates them. It is the impulse which tries to create a new harmony, frowning upon the familiar which has grown stale and dreary with too much use. The mind which has once peeped into the wonderland of the new, contemplated various aspects of it with longing and desire, is shocked and disappointed when living reality pulls in the reins of the wild horse of fancy. But how pleasant men find it to look at the world with the open, hopeful, astonished eyes of the child. The vagaries of Bakha's naïve tastes came to him in his dreams and reveries. He didn't like his home, his street, his town, because he had been to work at the Tommies' barracks and obtained glimpses of another world, strange and clean; he had grown out of his native shoes into the ammunition boots that he had secured as a gift. And with this and other fashionable items of dress, he had built up a new world, which was his heaven, if for nothing else, because it represented a change from the old ossified order and the stagnant pools of the lane near which he was born.

"What is the matter with you today?" asked Bakha's father, noticing the wild light in the boy's eyes and his listless manner. "Are you tired?"

This started a panic in Bakha's soul. Should he tell or should he not? The sympathetic tone of the enquiry stirred chords in his dumb soul. He could have wept at the apprehension implicit in his father's manner. He hesitated for a moment. Then, in the struggle to maintain the secret, he answered:

"Nothing," he said, "there is nothing."

"Nothing! There is nothing!" echoed his father. "Surely something is the matter. Come, tell the truth."

Bakha felt he would break down and fall to pieces with his obstinate desire to suppress the secret. He was touched by the strange sympathy evinced by his father. He felt suffocated. He felt he couldn't sustain that mood for long. So he burst out with an explosion more sudden than the manner in which he was normally wont to utter a speech:

"They insulted me this morning, they abused me because as I was walking along a man happened to touch me. He gave me a blow. And a crowd gathered round me, abusing me——" He couldn't continue. He was possessed by an overpowering feeling of self-pity.

"My son," said Lakha, with a forced mixture of anger and kindliness, "didn't you give a warning of your approach?"

This burnt Bakha's soul. He sat tormented to think that he had told his father about his experience. "I knew he would say that if I told him the truth," he thought.

"Why were you not more careful, my son?" Lakha strained himself to be more kind than angry.

"But, father, what is the use?" Bakha shouted. "They would ill-treat us, even if we shouted. They think we are mere dirt, because we clean their dirt. That pundit in the temple tried to molest Sohini and then came shouting: 'Polluted, polluted.' The woman of the big house in the silversmith's gully threw the bread at me from the fourth storey. I won't go down to the town again. I have done with this job."

Lakha was touched. A queer self-conscious smile hovered on the edges of his moustache, a smile of impotent rage.

"You didn't abuse or hit back, did you?" he asked. His sense of fear for his son for the consequences of such a crime, should he have been provoked to commit it, was mixed with that servile humility of his which could never entertain the prospect of retaliation against the high-caste men.

"No, but I was sorry afterwards that I didn't," replied Bakha. "I could have given them a bit of my mind."

"No, no, my son, no," said Lakha, "we can't do that. They are our superiors. One word of theirs is sufficient against all that we might say before the police. They are our masters. We must respect them and do as they tell us. Some of them are kind."

He looked at his son's face. It had relaxed a bit from the deliberate, tense expression it had assumed, to a sort of resigned cynicism, as if he didn't care. But the old man sensed that the body was grieved and hurt, and he sensed also that he hated the high-caste people. He sought to assuage his son's grief, to placate his wrath.

"You know," he began in the impersonal manner with which he always lifted himself from the lazy old man he was to the superior dignity of an aged father; "You know, when you were a little child, I too had a nasty experience. You were ill with fever, and I went to the house of Hakim Bhagawan Das, in this very town. I shouted and shouted, but no one heard me. A babu was passing through the dawai khana of the Dakdar and I said to him:

"Babu ji, Babu ji, God will make you prosperous. Please make my message reach the ears of the Hakim ji. I have been shouting, shouting and have even asked some people to tell the Hakim Sahib that I have a prayer to make to him. My child is suffering from fever. He has been unconscious since last night and I want the Hakim ji to give him some medicine."

"'Keep away, keep away,' said the babu, 'don't come riding on at me. Do you want me to have another bath this morning? The Hakim Sahib has to attend to us people who go to offices first, and there are so many of us waiting. You have nothing to do all day. Come another time or wait.'

"And with this he walked into the dispensary.

"I remained standing. Whenever anyone passed by I would place my head at his feet and ask him to tell the Hakim. But who would listen to a sweeper? Everyone was concerned about himself.

"For an hour I stood like that in a corner, near the heap of litter which I had collected, and I was feeling as if a scorpion was stinging me. That I couldn't buy medicine for my son, when I was willing to pay my hard-earned money for it, troubled me. I had seen many bottles full of medicine in the house of the Hakim ji and I knew that one of those bottles contained the medicine for you, and yet I couldn't get it. My heart was with you and my body was outside the house of the Hakim. I had torn my heart away from the room where you lay with your mother, and prayed to God to make my difficulty easy. But nothing happened. I began to think I was seeing you die. It seemed as if someone was giving me a blow in my side and saying 'come and see the face of your son for the last time.' I ran back home.

"'Have you brought the medicine?' asked your mother, rushing out to me.

"You, of course, only half opened your eyes and you were too delirious to recognise me. They told me they would soon bring you down on the floor.[10] So I ran back to the Hakim's house. Your mother shouted and said: 'What is the good of medicine now?' But I ran and ran. When I got to the Hakim's house I just lifted the curtain and went straight in. I caught the Hakim's feet and said: 'Still there is a little breath left in my child's body, Hakim ji, I shall be your slave all my life. *The meaning of my life is my child.* Hakim ji, take pity. God will be kind to you.'

"'Bhangi! Bhangi!' There was an uproar in the medicine house. People began to disperse as the Hakim's feet had become defiled. He was red and pale in turn, and shouted at the highest pitch of his voice: 'Chandal! by whose orders have you come here? And then you join hands and hold my feet and say you will become my slave for ever. You have polluted hundreds of rupees worth of medicine. Will you pay for it?'

"I began to shed tears," Lakha continued, and said: 'Maharaj, I forgot. Your shoe on my head. I am not in my senses. Maharaj, you are my father — mother. I can't compensate for the medicines. I can only serve you. Will you come and give some medicine to my child? He is on his death-bed!'

[10] *down on the floor* The Hindus do not allow a person to die in bed, but bring the dying to rest as near the earth as possible; the idea being that from the earth we come, to the earth we return. [Author]

"Hakim ji just shook his head and exclaimed: 'Serve me! Serve me! How can you serve me? Have you ever received medicine here, that you come rushing in?'

"I said: 'Sarkar, I went away after standing outside for some time. I tried to fall at the feet of every passer-by and prayed them to tell to the Sarkar that my child was suffering. But Sarkar, this is the time of kindness. Be compassionate this time. Another time you can take even my life. Only save my child. All night I have been rocking him in my arms, thinking that if he survives the night I shall come and fetch medicine from you with the rising of the sun. Who could have heard my call in the middle of the night if I had come here then?'

"With this the Hakim ji's heart melted to some extent and he began to write a prescription. Just at that time your uncle came running and shouted from without: 'Ohe, Lakha! Ohe, Lakha! The boy is passing away!'

"I ran out. Hakim ji had dropped his pen. When I came home I found that you were very bad and they had put you on the floor for the fourth time, and your mother was crying.

"In a little while there was a knock at the door. And what do you think? Your uncle goes out and finds the Hakim ji himself, come to grace our house. He was a good man. He felt your pulse and saved your life."

"He might have killed me," Bakha commented.

"No, no," said Lakha, "they are really kind. We must realise that it is religion which prevents them from touching us."

He had never throughout his narrative renounced his deep-rooted sense of inferiority and the docile acceptance of the laws of fate.

Bakha had felt stirred in the deepest cells of his body as his father narrated the story. Every time his father mentioned his name, every time he referred to his dangerous illness, Bakha felt a strain of self-pity run through him which made him hot and cold at the same time, raised his hair on end and brought tears gushing to his eyes. It was by sheer exertion of his will power that he kept back his tears. In a few moments, however, he was his own strong self again.

"This rascal of a Rakha must have strayed away to play somewhere," grumbled the old man. "Whether you want to eat or not, I must. Sohini, give me some bread."

"There is no dal," said Sohini,. "Would you like to take it with some of the tea left over from the morning."

"'What is taste to the palate of holy men, let it come with cream,'" the old man sang the familiar Indian proverb in reply. Sohini proceeded to put the smoke-bottomed handi full of tea-leaves, water and milk to boil.

Bakha crouched down to a tin jug and gingerly sprinkled a few drops of water on his hands and his face. He had heard his father ask for the food and he slightly resented it. "I feel hungry too," he thought. "Perhaps much hungrier than he does. He has been sitting here all day." The boy did not grudge his old father the food that he was going to eat, but a feeling of disgust ran through him as hunger gnawed at his belly. To the young and healthy animal in him, with the strength of his close-knit sinews, his old father was as good as dead, a putrefying corpse like that of a stray dog or cat on the rubbish heap.

Rakha was at length in sight, a basket of food on his bare clean-shaven head, a pan slung by a string handle in his hand, and his feet dragging a pair of Bakha's old ammunition boots, laceless and noisy and too big for him. His tattered flannel shirt, grimy with the blowings of his ever-running nose, obstructed his walk slightly. The discomfort resulting from this, the fatigue, assumed or genuine, due to the work he had put in that morning, gave a rather drawn, long-jawed look to his dirty face on which flies congregated to taste the saliva on the corners of his lips. The quizzical, not-there look defined by his small eyes and his narrow, very narrow forehead, was positively ugly. And yet his ears, long and transparent in the sunlight, had something intelligent about them, something impish. He seemed a true child of the outcaste colony, where there are no drains, no light, no water; of the marshland where people live among the latrines of the townsmen, and in the stink of their own dung scattered about here, there and everywhere; of the world where the day is dark as the night and the night pitch-dark. He had wallowed in its mire, bathed in its marshes, played among its rubbish-heaps, and his listless, lazy, manner was a result of his surroundings. He was the vehicle of a life-force, which would never reach its culminating point, because malaria lingered in his bones and that disease does not kill but merely dissipates the energy. He was a friend of the flies and the mosquitoes, their companion since his childhood.

"So you have got back after all," Bakha exclaimed when Rakha was within hearing distance.

His younger brother did not reply but came sulkily up to where Sohini sat in the kitchen and, depositing his load of food before her, sat down in the dust, exploring the heap of crumbs in his basket. He ate big morsels. His mouth filled on one side, and looked grotesque.

"At least wash your hands, ohe wild animal!" said Bakha, irritated by the sight of his brother's running nose.

"You mind your own business," retorted the young boy, aware that his father loved him more than he loved Bakha.

"Look at yourself in the mirror! What a picture you look!" exclaimed Bakha.

"Don't keep on finding fault with him," put in Lakha. "Stop quarreling, occasionally, at least."

"Come and eat a piece of bread," said Sohini to her elder brother, sympathetically.

Bakha got up from his chair unwillingly and, crouching by the kitchen, casually dipped his hand in the basket. There was a heap of food there, broken pieces of chapatis, some whole ones and lentil curry in a bowl.

They all ate from the same basket and the same bowl, not apportioning the food in different plates as the Hindus do, for the original Hindu instinct for cleanliness had disappeared long ago. Only Bakha felt a thrill of loathing for his brother go through him after he had eaten his first few morsels of the day. He changed his position slightly, so that he had his back turned towards his brother. But his hand touched a piece of sticky, wet bread. He shrank back from the basket. The picture of a sepoy washing his hands in his round brass tray, over the leavings of bread and salad, and then throwing them in Rakha's basket appeared before him. He had himself gone so often to beg for food and the thing he hated about it was the sight of those bits of bread softened by the water poured upon them. He had a queer, warm feeling of water running under his tongue from across the sides of his mouth. He felt sick. He tried to drop the soft crumb he had got hold of, but some of it stuck to his fingers still. It was nauseating. He rose from the floor.

"You were saying you were hungry!" said Lakha, when he saw his son get up so suddenly from the meal.

Bakha bent over the tin vessel from the mouth of which he was sprinkling drops of water on his hand. He didn't know what to say in reply. "He won't understand if I tell him that I feel sick," he said to himself. "I will make an excuse. But what———" Suddenly a pretence occurred to him.

"I have to go to Ram Charan's house to see his sister's marriage—and to receive my share of the sweets," he said. The last he added tactfully, to fortify himself against any objection his father might have to his going, by appealing to the old man's greed.

The true reason for the sudden impulse that had come so useful in the invention of his lie was inexplicable to anyone, even to himself. For even he did not realise why he was going to see the wedding of Ram Charan's sister. He hadn't been invited to go by Gulabo or by Ram Charan. And he couldn't have been asked by Ram Charan's sister, because she had never talked to him since she was ten. Why then was he going? What had made him decide so suddenly on such an extraordinary adventure?

He only knew that he wanted to get away from home, his father, his brother, his sister, everyone. But he wouldn't confess even to himself that he was going to see Ram Charan's sister for the last time. A picture of her appeared from the past before his eyes. She was a tiny girl with shaven head, wearing a miniature skirt of gaudy, red cotton with a white pattern, that the washerwomen wear. She looked like a juggler's little monkey. He himself was then a boy of eight, in a gold-embroidered cap which his father had begged from a moneylender who had three small sons whose discarded clothes fitted Lakha's three children exactly. Bakha remembered how, while he had been playing with her brother and Chota in the barracks, they had come home and started to play at marriage. Ram Charan's little sister was made to act the wife because she wore a skirt. Bakha was chosen to play the husband because he was wearing the gold-embroidered cap. The rest of the boys took the part of members of the marriage party. Bakha recalled how he had been ragged by Chota for acting as the husband of a shaven-headed, ridiculous, little girl, and how he (Bakha) had been angry with him, although he himself thought she looked funny. There was something wistful about her, a soft light in her eyes, for which she had become endeared to him and for which, he remembered, he had actually quarrelled with his friend. Since then, of course, she had grown up to be a tall girl with a face as brown as ripe wheat and hair as black as the rain clouds. And Bakha always felt proud of having once acted as her husband. Being very reticent and shy, however, he seldom dared even to look at her. But in the depths of his being he had felt waves of confusion at the thought of her. Now at the age of fourteen she was being married off to a young washerman attached as a follower to the 31st Punjabis regiment. He had heard of this arrangement a year ago. It was common knowledge in the sweepers' street that Gulabo had taken two hundred rupees for the hand of her daughter. Chota had told him that. He remembered the evening on which he had heard it, for it had been somewhat of a shock to him, and he had felt a sadness in his soul, like a doleful lyric melody. During the dreary hours of his routine work at the latrines, subsequently, he had often heard the delicate strain of that elfin music. But he had never quite comprehended the source from which it came. In the darkness of his home at night, when he lay half asleep, something in him secretly led him towards the vague sylph-like form which he could have squeezed in his embrace, but he could not connect the feelings he had at such moments with the ripples that surged up in him whenever he caught sight of Ram Charan's sister.

As he walked towards her home today, he recalled occasions on which his vague flowings towards her had become more defined. His large eyes had rested with adoration on her face as she met him once going to the shops to buy some kerosene oil in an old wine bottle. Then from the dark undeclared places of his soul arose another picture of her in his memory—as she came through the darkness before the dawn from the banks of the brook where, he knew, she and the other women of the outcastes' colony went every day, taking advantage of the privacy which the half-light afforded, to perform their toilets unseen by men. He remembered that he had been about the latrines and had at first felt a thrill of delight, then a sensation more vital. He had pictured her quite naked as he had seen his mother quite often when he was a child, and his sister, and other little children. An impulse had arisen like a sudden tremor to his brain, and darkened his thoughts. He had felt as if he could forcibly gather the girl in his embrace and ravish her. Then he had put his hand across his eyes and shuddered in horror at the thought. He had cursed himself for such a vision. His reputation as a docile, good, respectable boy seemed at stake. He had wondered at himself: "How could I, who am known to everyone as Bakha the good, have such an unholy design?" Nevertheless, the picture had persisted. The more he tried to blot it out, the more it had defined itself, until, when he had ceased to bother about his sensual feelings, his phantasy had vanished.

As he recalled these things, he seemed to feel ashamed. He had felt that shame also in the occasion when those things first happened. In a frantic effort to escape from himself, to escape from the secret, buried desire he had for the girl, he casually took a turning off the track which led to the washermen's houses, and wandered aimlessly into a lane which ended in the washermen's ghats.

Shioh! Shioh! Shi! A few washermen were shouting as they tore the garments of their customers and broke their buttons on slabs of stone by the edges of the brook. Their dark legs were immersed in the water up to the knees and their bodies from the rumps upwards were swathed in the thick folds of loin-cloths up to the waists, where their shirts were tucked in. They doubled over the stones with supple movements and struck the garments with a loud swinging sweep which was graceful in itself even if it did not do any good to the cloth. Bakha had often stood watching this operation. In his childhood, of course, he had been fascinated by it, so that he wished to become a washerman. It was Ram Charan, true son of his mother, Gulabo, if he wasn't his father's son, but of the rich man, his mother's lover, who had knocked the bottom out of that ambition by telling Bakha that, though he (Ram Charan) touched him and played with him, he was a Hindu, while Bakha was a mere sweeper. Bakha was too young then to understand the distinction implied in the washer-boy's arrogant claim, or else he would have slapped Ram Charan's face. But now he knew that there were degrees of castes among the low-caste, and that he was the lowest.

He looked hard among the few washermen who beat clothes upon the slabs of stone. He anxiously explored among the stray washermen's donkeys which grazed on the side of the book, wildly thinking that Ram Charan might be there. He looked across the yards of space on which the washed, wet clothes lay drying in the afternoon sun. But he was looking in vain. For how could Ram Charan have absented himself from so auspicious an occasion as his sister's marriage and be working here! "Only, did Ram Charan not absent himself at the time of his father's death and go fishing with us?" Bakha thought. "He might be here today." Then he thought: "Perhaps his father wasn't his father, but he is his sister's brother. I will have to go to his place after all."

He began to walk back. He felt shy. He didn't know how he could approach the house where festivities were going on. "All the members of the washermen's brotherhood will be there, dressed in their best clothes, singing strange southern songs. How shall I be able to stand there and look?" He felt ashamed to picture the scene. "How shall I be able to call Ram Charan when I get there?" he wondered.

Between the intervals of wiping the sweat off his brow his ordinary self came back. The nervousness descended into the crowded world of his entrails, leaving the surface of his mind clean like a slate. He got to the kerb of the outcastes' street and stopped still, suddenly, within ten yards of Ram Charan's house. He had the pleasantest surprise. Chota stood, leaning by a wooden pillar, staring with wonder at the crowd of men and women gathered in the one-roomed mud-house and outside on the veranda.

Bakha advanced gingerly towards the wooden pillar and came and stood by Chota. His friend turned with surprise at him and cordially pressed him by the hand. Then they both fell to staring at the dazed, happy crowd before them. Bakha noticed how white the starched linen, which the washermen wore, seemed against their black skins. At first, however, he could not concentrate his gaze on anyone. He felt afraid to lift his eyes beyond the veranda to the cavernous room scarcely illuminated by the glowing sun outside. A wave of warmth descended down the back of his head. Through the haze he could see a man from within looking at him. He felt quivers of self-consciousness pass through him. The thought of Ram Charan's sister came into collision with the sight of her. His heart sank within him. He was sweating. Luckily for him, the double beat of a drum tore the air and lifted all the confusion in Bakha's soul on the flapping, hovering wings of the song that accompanied it. It was a queer refrain, sudden as thunder, as it ranged over three notes, up, down, up, sung in unison by the whole assembly. In the very beginning it was a shrill wail, which went through the tympanum of the ear to the head, and seemed to make the listener mad with its ever-sharpening frenzy, as lightning which shoots its sharp spears of power through the heart and leaves it a-throb. Before they proceeded very far, the song had mounted above the drum and established the reign of an exhilarating rhythm. Bakha floated on the strain as he might have done on a swing. Then, as the melody arose steeply to its full height of enthusiasm in the swaying, rolling, rocking, yelling frames of the washermen and washerwomen, Bakha again felt cold and impassive with self-consciousness. He touched Chota's arm nervously, hiding his movement in the blaze of riotous excess to which the washermen had carried their song. Chota greeted him with a broad grin as cordial as the contagious spirit of happiness in the atmosphere could make it.

"I shall call Ram Charan," said Chota. And quite unafraid and unashamed to face the crowd of singing washermen he called Ram Charan, who sat dressed in a rather contradictory style of Eastern and Western habiliments — a large, khaki topee on his small head, a muslin shirt, clean and white, but torn near the collar, and a pair of shorts on his thin, bare, black legs.

At first, Ram Charan was too absorbed, eating the ludus which his mother was distributing with the tankards of native wine, for Chota's message to reach him. Then luckily for his friends, as Ram Charan stood up to sprinkle the red colour over the white clothes of the crowd through a crude spray made out of a tin can, the ceremonial little mischief-maker was lifted amid the happy cries and shouts of hilarious laughter of the white-clad men, now spotted profusely with scarlet, and thrown out.

"Come," he greeted Chota and Bakha, blinking his lashless eyes, and ran ahead.

"Give, o bey brother-in-law, give us some of the sweets," said Chota.

Ram Charan had not forgotten to fill the pockets of his shorts and his large silk handkerchief, stolen from the laundry bag of some rich merchant, with sugar-plums.

"Keep quiet for a while," said Ram Charan, suddenly turning back to see if his mother was aware of the direction he was going to take.

She was.

"Oh, illegally begotten!" came her shrill voice, audible above all the other noises. "Are you running away to play with that dirty sweeper and leather-worker on the very day of your sister's marriage. You ought to be ashamed of yourself, little dog!"

"Shut up, bitch!" replied Ram Charan, as was his wont, for he had been hardened into an impudent, obstinate young rascal by the persistency of his mother's abuse. And with Chota at his heels and Bakha following clumsily behind, he led the way towards the heath which sloped gently towards the north of the outcastes' colony.

"Give us some of those sugar-plums, brother-in-law!" insisted Chota, greedy and gay. "I have waited for an hour for you outside your noisy house."

"You shall have some as soon as we get to the hill," assured Ram Charan. "I have brought them for you and Bakha, not for anyone else. Now let us run, for my mother might come after me." And he carried himself with the assurance of one who has suddenly come into power. Chota at least, if not Bakha, paid him the homage which he expected as his due because he had a dozen sugar-plums in his possession.

"Come, O elephant," he rebuked Bakha for his coldness, "show your teeth and lift your legs. You shall have some sweets soon."

Bakha dismissed the impudence of his joke with a grunt and followed quietly. He was feeling quite detached from the human world, bathed in a sort of unadulterated melancholy.

The grasses were stretching themselves towards him, the tall grass on the slopes of Bulandshahr hills. And he had opened his heart to them, lifted by the cool breeze that wafted him away from the crowds, the ugliness and the noise of the outcastes' colony. He looked across at the swaying loveliness before him and the little hillocks over which it spread under a sunny sky, so transcendingly blue and beautiful that he stood dumb and motionless before it. He listened to the incoherent whistling of the shrubs. They were the voices he knew so well. He was glad that his friends were ahead of him and that the thrum was not broken, for the curve of his soul seemed to bend over the heights, straining to silence any disruption of this solitude. It seemed to him he would be unhappy if he heard even one human voice. His inside seemed to know that he wouldn't be soothed if there was the slightest obstruction between him and the outer world. It didn't even occur to him to ask why he had come here. He was just swamped by the merest sight of the open fields that spread before him.

As he rambled along, however, he felt he wanted an adventure in friendship to humanise the solitary excursion. But he didn't want to call Ram Charan, or Chota. He fell back to a memory of the adventures he had had here in his childhood. He remembered the time in his early days when he used to come to the heath with all the other boys, to fight battles for the imaginary fort they had built by fixing a flag on the top of the hill. The bamboo bows with which they flung arrows at each other came before him and the imitation toy pistols with their sparks. How enthusiastic all the boys used to feel about him then. They had made him their Jernel. He recalled with pride the pitched battle they had fought against the boys of the 28th Sikhs and won. They were helter-skelter battles, not quite like the organised manoeuvres of the regiments, fought with guns. "But then," he said to himself, "they were the games played in childhood. I wouldn't play those games now. I can hardly spare time to play hockey, with my father shouting at me all the time."

He felt lonely thinking such thoughts. He switched his mind on to the landscape in that vague groping manner in which his mind always felt its way across things. On the slopes, carpeted with grass, there flourished a wilderness of flowers, of which the shades changed at various intervals. There were the yellow buttercups, which had seemed to Bakha always like the mustard-seed flowers of his village near Sialkot; then there were the long-stalked, single-headed daisies, alternating with beds of purple and white. A pool of water in the long grass and ferns looked like a large basin round which the silver birches bent down and, smitten by the wind, seemed to be drinking. Here every passer-by quenched his thirst from the water that came from a natural spring.

Descending to it, with his nostrils full of fresh air, and his heart as light as the spirits of the sparrows which chirped, Bakha seemed nevertheless unaroused and unresponsive as a child turning aside from every wayside flower, for though he had the receptivity of the man who is willing to lend his senses to experience, he seemed to have no will in his numbed condition. Necessity had forced him to the contemplation of the charms of nature in search of fresh air. Heredity had furrowed no deep grooves in his soul where flowers could grow or grass abound. He could not reach out from the narrow confines of his soul to his yearnings. It was a discord between person and circumstance by which a lion like him lay enmeshed in a net, while many a common criminal wore a rajah's crown. His wealth of inner experience, however, was extraordinary. It was a kind of crude sense of the world in the round, such as the peasant has, or the Arab seaman who sails the seas in a small boat and casually determines his direction by the position of the sun, or like the beggar-singer who recites an epic from door to door. But it wanted the force and vivacity of thought to transmute his vague sense into the superior instinct of the self-conscious man.

As he sauntered along, a spark of some intuition suddenly set him ablaze. He was fired with a desire to burst out from the shadow of silence and obscurity in which he lay enshrouded.

He rushed down the slope, towards the trees that stood by the pool below him. The soft breeze came whispering up to him and made his blood tingle with its fresh coolness. The sun on the curve of the sky before him was being reflected from the sheen of the rippling water with a restlessness like the pain in Bakha's soul. He descended through the meadows, rank with herbage, before he had breathed more than a breath. He lay down on the bank of the pool, and immediately lent himself to the stillness about him, making not the slightest stir, even though the position in which he leaned back exposed his eyes uncomfortably to the sun. In a moment or two his frame seemed to have sunk into insignificance, drowned as it were in a pit of silence, while the things on the sunny bank began to take life, each little stem of plant becoming a big leaf, distinct and important. The whole valley seemed to him suddenly aglow with life.

But the rich and exuberant spaces about him seemed to have sucked all his energy away. He lay as if dead. His empty belly had provoked the subtle urgings of sleep into play. He was dozing.

Chota came and began to tickle his nose with a straw. With one violent sneeze the sweeper lad got up and sat upright in the face of his friends' laughter. Bakha was no killjoy to be annoyed by so ordinary a practical joke and willingly let himself be made a fool of. But the incidents of the morning had cast a shadow over him and there was something forced in his smile as against the spontaneous laughter of his companions. Chota noticed this. He saw that there was something tense about him, something accusing, as if Bakha really disapproved of the joke which had been played on him.

"What is the matter with you, brother-in-law?" he asked.

"Nothing," replied Bakha. "You were running. I came slowly."

"You didn't look for us?"

"I was tired. I wanted to sleep. I couldn't sleep very well last night."

"Because you will be a 'gentreman' and won't put a quilt over you as your father says," joked Chota. He learnt from Rakha all that happened to Bakha at home, all the abuse that their father inflicted upon him.

"Shut up," retorted Bakha playfully, "you are more of a 'gentreman' than I am, and look at this brother-in-law today; he is wearing a sahib's topi and shorts."

"What about those ludus?" Bakha continued, referring to Ram Charan. He wasn't particularly keen to have them although he would have liked to eat one.

"Here is your portion," said Ram Charan, unfolding the handerchief which he carried.

There were three sugar-plums in it, all slightly broken.

"Throw me one," said Bakha.

"Take it," said Ram Charan.

But Bakha hesitated and didn't hold his hands out.

"Take it, why don't you take it?" Ram Charan grumbled.

"No, give it to me, throw it," Bakha said.

Both Ram Charan and Chota were surprised. Never before had they seen Bakha behave like that. Ram Charan was admitted to be of the higher caste among them, because he was a washerman. Chota, the leather-worker's son, came next in the hierarchy, and Bakha was of the third and lowest category. But among the trio, they had banished all thought of distinction, except when the snobbery of caste-feeling supplied the basis for putting on airs for a joke. They had eaten together, if not things in the preparation of which water had been used, at least dry things, this being in imitation of the line drawn by the Hindus between themselves and the Muhammadans and Christians. Sweets they had often shared together, and they had handled soda-water bottles anyhow, at all those formal hockey matches they played with the boys' teams of the various regiments in the Bulandshahr Brigade.

"What has happened to you?" queried Chota in a voice full of deep concern, and then he added caressingly: "Come, friend, tell us."

"Nothing, it's nothing," said Bakha.

"Come, come, we are your friends," implored Chota.

Bakha told them how when he left them that morning he was walking through the town, a man happened to brush past him, and how he began to abuse him, and summoned a large crowd; and how before he could get away, he had slapped him.

"Why didn't you hit back?" Chota asked, enraged.

"That wasn't the only thing," continued Bakha. And he narrated how the priest tried to molest his sister and then came out shouting: "Polluted, polluted."

"You wait till the illegally begotten comes to our street side," said Chota indignantly. "We will skin the fellow."

"There was another insult waiting for me further up," Bakha added, and he narrated the story of how the woman in the silversmith's alley had flung the bread down at him from the top of her house.

"Yar, we're sorry," assured Chota. "Come, be brave, forget all this. What can we do? We are outcastes." He patted Bakha comfortingly. "Come," he consoled again, "forget all about it. We will go and play hockey. Let that brother-in-law of a priest come down our street, and we will teach him the lesson of his life."

"Come, let's go," put in Ram Charan, who was slightly embarrassed by Bakha's narrative, and increasingly afraid that his mother would curse him if he absented himself from home too long. "I'll have to put in an appearance at home before I can come and play hockey," he said, looking from Chota to Bakha.

"Come," urged Chota softly, with a deep strain of melancholy in his voice.

Bakha got to his feet and the three of them began to walk quietly homewards. Ram Charan was beginning to feel very embarrassed by the silence, so embarrassed that he thought it no fit occasion to remain adorned with such a symbol of greatness as his sola hat. So he lifted his large headgear off its small, uneasy seat and followed sheepishly.

Bakha's soul seemed to lie bare before his friends, bruised and tender. Chota felt with him. He allied himself with Bakha's mood.

The sympathy that the repetition of his narrative evoked from his friends accentuated Bakha's self-pity. He began, as he walked along, to feel the heart-burnings of the morning. He felt furious, his fury heightening with the invisible strength that the presence of his two friends gave him. "Chota and I could teach that immoral wretch of a Brahmin a lesson," he reflected.

"What do you say to our catching hold of the swine one day?" put in Chota.

This is strange, Bakha felt, that Chota should think of the same thing at the same time as I. But he felt unequal to the suggestion as he felt unequal to his own hatred.

"What is the use?" he replied sighing. He didn't want to refuse to wreak his vengeance too openly. And then he felt sad and pensive, because he couldn't rise to the realisation of his own urges. He resolved to harden himself. He gnashed his teeth. A warmth rose to his ears. He felt a quickening in his blood. Then came the sweep of his ever-recurring emotions. He boiled with rage. "Horrible, horrible," his soul seemed to cry out within him. He shivered. His broad, impassive face was pale with hostility. But he couldn't do anything. He hung his head and walked with a drooping chest. His frame seemed to be burdened with the weight of an inexpressible, unrelieved power. He was deliberately trying to hide his stature in his stoop, as if he were afraid of being seen at all.

"Where is he gone — Ram Charan?" said Chota to relieve the tension.

"Looking for mushrooms," Bakha joked. With this his knitted brows relaxed and his forehead uncreased. The cowed defiance of his manner gave place to an easy, natural air. He was absorbed in the spectacle of the town of Bulandshahr, sleeping snugly in the afternoon hush at the foot of the hill. From the clump of trees, visible beyond the distant north gate, to the cantonment in the south, from the mango groves in the east to the little group of houses of the outcastes' colony, the white-blue lower sky was defined into a lovely pattern by the golden domes of the temples, the flat roofs of the houses and the carved terraces with big, blue, clay flower-pots fixed to their sides. And then the thatched hut of his home in the swamps and shallows presented itself to his gaze. The contrast of the tremulous line of foliage which lay near him and beyond, the green, green mango groves and the marshland which surrounded his home, was a stark one.

"I think I shall also go and show my face at home before I come to play hockey," said Chota suddenly. "There is too much sunshine yet."

"Acha, Havildar Charat Singh said he would give me a hockey stick if I called this afternoon," Bakha said. "I shall go and get it."

"Acha, you go and get the stick," agreed Chota. "Ram Charan and I will join you before the match begins. Meanwhile we shall stake this footpath."

They had reached a small lane, which led to the outcastes' colony through cactus hedges. They branched off.

Bakha strode along in the open through the stones in the old river-bed that stretched itself between the hills and the barracks of the 38th Dogras. He felt that he had just invented this business with Charat Singh because he didn't want to go home, because he didn't want to see his father, his brother, his sister, because he didn't want to go and work at the latrines — at least, not today. Somewhere in him he felt he could never get away from it, but to the greater part of him, for the moment, the place didn't exist.

There was not a soul to be seen about in the compound of the barracks. Even the quarter-guard seemed empty and forlorn, except for the two dummy-like sentries, who walked up and down the veranda outside the magazine which Bakha knew to be behind the locked doors. Only a sola topi seemed to Bakha alive, instinct with life, there, as it hung on the wall. There were many legends current about this hat. Some said it was a symbol of authority of the sahib logs who ruled over the regiment. Others said that the hat had been forgotten in the regimental office by a sahib (officer) once, and since, being a sahib (rich man) he didn't care to reclaim his lost property, it had been kept on at the quarter-guard. Again, it was rumoured that a sahib had once been court-martialled for shooting a sepoy,[11] and since he was a white man and could never be put behind the bars in the lock-up at the quarter-guard, his hat and belt and sword had been imprisoned instead. The sahib had suddenly disappeared. Some people said he had been helped by the officer commanding the regiment to escape overnight in order to evade the sentence of imprisonment pronounced by the judges, and only the hat had remained at the quarter-guard. If, on the other hand, you asked one of the sentries whose hat it was, they always told you it belonged to an officer who had just gone into the grounds and would soon be returning to take it. But nobody ever asked questions about this hat except the boys of the 38th Dogras. The younger among these children believed what the sentries said and ran away, for great was the fear attaching to the persons of the sahibs, like the dread of pale white ghosts, ghouls and hobgoblins, because they were rumoured to be very irritable, liable to strike you with their canes if you looked at them. The elder boys knew it was a lie invented by the sentries to drive the curious little boys away, as they remembered having seen that hat for years in the same place.

[11]*sepoy* soldier

But even they didn't really know why the sentries invented the lie. They didn't realise that the sepoys too wanted the hat, not because they could wear it, either with their uniform or their mufti, but because they thought of the wonder it would arouse in the hills at home, the interest it would create among the villagers. People would come to see it for miles, as they came to see their uniform and their white clothes, with ogling eyes and admiring glances. How proud, they thought, they would feel carrying this symbol of sahibhood in their luggage, going home to Kangra or Hoshiarpur.

But why had all these stories about the sola hat got round? Because there wasn't a child about the 38th Dogras who hadn't cast lingering eyes at this hat. The spirit of modernity had worked havoc among the youth of the regiment. The consciousness of every boy was full of a desire to wear Western dress, and since most of the boys about the place were the sons of babus, bandsmen, sepoys, sweepers, washermen and shopkeepers, all too poor to afford the luxury of a complete European outfit, they eagerly stretched their hands to seize any particular article they could see anywhere, feeling that the possession of something European was better than the possession of nothing European. A hat with its curious distinction of shape and form, with the peculiar quality of honour that it presents to the Indian eye because it adorns the noblest part of the body, had a fascination such as no other item of European dress possessed.

Bakha had for years looked with longing at the sola topi that hung on the peg in the verandah of the 38th Dogras quarter-guard. Ever since he was a little boy he had contemplated it with the wonder-struck gaze of the lover and the devotee. Whenever he was given the chance of going out sweeping in the compounds of the 38th Dogras barracks, he invariably chose the quarter-guard side, for there, he could steal glances at the object he coveted, and plan various stratagems to take it. Those were nice thoughts, those connected with the schemes he concocted to possess the hat.

One of the ways in which it could be acquired, he had thought, was to make friends with one of the non-commissioned officers in charge of the quarter-guard. But it was impracticable. There was never the same non-commissioned officer in charge of the quarter-guard for two days and nights together. The guard changed every twelve hours, and considering it was the N. C. O from one of the many platoons of one of the twelve companies in the regiment, you could never hope to see the same non-commissioned officer at the quarter-guard twice in your life.

That scheme failing, Bakha had thought of asking one of the sentries. When he was a child he had once dared to do that, but then the sentry had sent him away with the yarn about the sahib who had left it for a moment while he was in the grounds, and who would soon come back to reclaim it. Now, however, he dared not ask. Some of the sepoys gave themselves such airs. "They might abuse me," he said to himself. "Better any time to ask a Havildar. Every Havildar is an experienced person with long service and surely knows my father, the Jemadar of the sweepers. He will be kind even if he doesn't actually give me the hat." But he could not bring himself to ask, he just couldn't. "Why is it," he had often asked himself, "that I can't go and ask now but dared to do so when I was a child?" He couldn't find the answer to this. He didn't know that with the growth of years he had lost the freedom, the wild, careless, dauntless freedom of the child, that he had lost his courage, that he was afraid.

Then he deceived himself by believing that he didn't really want the hat, because he could get any number of them at the rag shop or from some Tommy in the British barracks. But he still longed for this hat. For years he had pined for it. And now he stood contemplating it, with the same interest, the same curiosity, the same desire to possess it, with which he had looked at it during these years. It was not too clean a topi. The dust of years had settled on it. The khaki cloth-cover, with the quilt-like pattern, had faded on the edges of the rim to a dirty white, and, of course, no one knew what it was like inside.

Bakha stared at it hard, as he stood in a corner of the quarter-guard, off the track where the sentries paraded too and fro. It didn't seem to move any nearer towards him. "What can I do?" he asked himself. "Go and ask that sentry," his mind told him. "But no, he might not understand," the doubt arose, "he might not understand what I am talking about if I, a sweeper, suddenly put it to him that I want the hat. He looks rather stern. There is no chance of getting near him."

He looked round to see if there were anyone else about. There wasn't a soul. He guessed that everyone was having a siesta. He felt an irresistible desire to go and steal the hat. If only that sentry was not there. "One could do it," he thought, "when the sentry turns his face away and walks to the other end of his beat. But someone might come and surprise me. It is too big a thing, this hat, to conceal. Besides if I stole it, I could never wear it. Everyone in the regiment knows about it. No, it is impossible. No, there is no way of getting it." Once more he cast a loving glance at it and walked away towards the barracks at the nearer end of which, he knew, lived Havildar Charat Singh.

It wasn't far. A hundred yards or so. The time involved in covering this space, Bakha occupied with a picture of himself playing hockey with the sola topi on. He saw himself running about in it. How important he looked, the idol of all the boys. Then it occurred to him that sola topis are not worn at hockey. "How foolish my thoughts are," he said. He was slightly ashamed of his predilection towards English dress, but he derived consolation from the fact that he had never made such a fool of himself as Ram Charan did by wearing a hat and shorts at his sister's marriage.

He crossed through a ditch and was in sight of the long rows of barracks. The particular one he wanted was only ten yards ahead of him. It had a long veranda. He reached the room at the near end of it. That was Havildar Charat Singh's place. He walked past it, because he was embarrassed. He was always ashamed of being seen. He felt like a thief. Luckily for his self-consciousness, the door of the room was shut. There was no way for him to know whether the Havildar was at home. An ordinary person could go and shout for the Havildar, or could go and strike the latch. He was a sweeper and dared not go within defiling distance of the veranda. Bakha wished that the system which the Emperor Jehangir had invented, if the story of the babu's son was correct, now prevailed. There was a bell in the Emperor's house, which was attached to a string at the outer gates and by the pulling of which the King could be informed of the applicants waiting for admission. Bakha had to shout for his food in the town. He had no way of getting in touch with Ram Charan or Chota when he went to their houses, except by shouting, and that meant Ram Charan's mother and Chota's father shouting back abusively at him for trying to seduce their sons to play truant. And now, of course, he couldn't shout or do anything. The Havildar might be asleep. The sepoys might be having their siesta too. And they would be disturbed.

He walked to and fro outside the veranda. Then he lay down under a tree. His thoughts began to drift. "I don't know what I can do. I hope he remembers the promise he made this morning. Otherwise all this time will be wasted for nothing.

My father must be cursing me. I haven't worked all afternoon. But never mind. Let Rakha do it for a change. I have been doing it all this while. What if I take an afternoon off." His eyes drifted to the kitchen where the food for Charat Singh's company was cooked. He remembered he had been there quite often to get food when he was a child, when his father was attached to "B" company as an ordinary sweeper. The figures of the hockey-playing members of this company passed through his mind. There was Hoshiar Singh, who played centre-half, the pivot of the team. There was Lekh Ram, who played centre-forward. There was Shiv Singh, who played right full-back. And, of course, there was the redoubtable Charat Singh who kept goal. He recalled the story current about Charat Singh, that the days he didn't spend playing hockey he spent in hospital, recovering from the wounds and bruises he received playing. He could picture the men keeping goal in the matches against the British regiment. Charat Singh always stood leaning by the goal-post till the ball came his way and he just fell upon it. The number of scars he had on his body equalled in number, said the babu's son, the marks of sword and lance on the body of the Rajput warrior, Rana Sanga, the conqueror of Akbar, the great Moghul. And the most delightful of the injuries which he had ever sustained was to have had his teeth knocked out, for he had had them replaced with a row of false ones, mounted with gold. This had led to many a joke, when someone ingeniously suggested that the proverb "A straw in the beard of a thief," should be changed to: "Gold teeth in the mouth of the thief."

Bakha had not fully given himself up to his reverie when he saw Charat Singh come out of his door, brass jug in hand. The Havildar sat down on the veranda profusely splashing water into his eyes and on his face. Too absorbed in his toilet and still half asleep, he didn't notice Bakha sitting under the Kikir tree. The sweeper-boy got up with a half-embarrassed, half-daring look, and lifting his hand to his brow, said: "Salaam, Havildar ji,"

"Come ohe Bakhia, how are you?" said Charat Singh enthusiastically. "I have not seen you about at the regimental hockey matches lately. Where do you keep yourself hidden?"

"I have to work, Havildar ji," Bakha replied.

"Oh, work, work, blow work!" exclaimed Charat Singh, forgetful in the manifestation of his present goodwill that he had himself shouted at Bakha for neglecting his work that morning.

Bakha was conscious of the Havildar's absent-mindedness. But he was altogether too favourably inclined towards Charat Singh to let anything stand in the way of his admiration for the hockey hero. There was a comfortable, homely glow, radiating from the smile that the Havildar wore. Bakha felt happy in his present. "For this man," he said to himself, "I wouldn't mind being a sweeper all my life. I would do anything for him."

Charat Singh got up and wiped his face with the edge of his coarse, homespun loin-cloth. Then he picked up a little hookah with a cocoa-nut shell for a water-basin, and a delicately-carved marionette-like stem crowned by a red clay basin for charcoal and tobacco. He separated the earthen pot from the neck of the hubble-bubble and said to Bakha;

"Go and get me two pieces of coal from the kitchen."

The boy stood wonderstruck. That a Hindu should entrust him with the job of fetching glowing charcoal in the chilm which he was going to put on his hookah and smoke! For a moment he felt as if an electric shock had passed through him. Then the strange suggestion produced a pleasant thrill in his being; it exhilarated him. He took the chilm from Charat Singh and elatedly walked towards the kitchen fifty yards away.

"Call the cook also to me," shouted Charat Singh after him, "and tell him to bring my tea."

"Very good, Havildar ji," said Bakha and walked away without looking back, lest he should prove unequal to the unique honour that the Hindu had done him by entrusting him with so intimate a job as fetching coal in his clay chilm. "What? Is it wet or dry?" he asked himself. "Could it be defiled, I wonder?" The answer came back to him: "Oh, yes, the tobacco is wet. Of course it could be defiled." For a moment he doubted whether Charat Singh was conscious and in his senses when he entrusted him with the job. "He might be forgetful and suddenly realise what he has done. Did he forget that I am a sweeper? He couldn't have done, I was just talking to him about my work. And he saw me this morning. How could he have forgotten?" Thus reassured, he was grateful to God that such men as Charat Singh existed. He walked with a steady step, with a happy step, deliberately controlled, lest he should excite anyone's attention about the barracks, and be seen carrying the Havildar's clay pot. It was with difficulty, however, that he prevented himself from stumbling, for his soul was full of love and adoration and worship for the man who had thought it fit to entrust him, an unclean menial, with the job and his eyes were turned inwards.

He went and stood in sight of a kitchen cubicle where a cook sat by the earthen fire-place peeling potatoes, while a big brass saucepan sent puffs of steam shooting out from under its lid.

"Will you give me some pieces of coal for Havildar Charat Singh, please?"

The cook looked at Bakha for a moment, as much as to ask: "Who are you?" He thought he had seen the face somewhere but he couldn't place him. "He might be one of the sappers," he concluded charitably, seeing that the man held Havildar Charat Singh's clay chilm in his hand. As the sappers, in spite of their dark colour and dirty clothes were of the grass-cutter caste, no one would object to sending one of them on an errand to fetch fire. Besides, the cook was indebted to Havildar Charat Singh. The Havildar had given him a clean, new shirt and a white turban before he went on leave. He lifted two sticks of wood fuel from the fire and struck them on the ground before Bakha. The sweeper picked up the live, burning pieces of coal in his hand one by one, and put them in the chilm. He suddenly recalled the figure of the little girl in his dream of the morning on whose hands the silversmith had placed a burning ember.

"Mehrbani," he said, when he had half-filled the chilm with coal. "The Havildar says he wants his tea." He tried to put a great deal of humility into an unfortunately abrupt sentence.

Then he walked back to where Charat Singh sat in an easy-chair he had drawn out from somewhere, and he handed him the chilm. The Havildar casually stretched his hand and, accepting the pot, put it on his cocoa-nut shell hookah and gurgled away.

Bakha was feeling impatient now, and he sat near the veranda on a brick. He didn't know why he felt impatient. It was because of the hookah. It always made him impatient. And then he was eager for the hockey stick. The Havildar hadn't said a word about it. "Had he forgotten?" Bakha wondered. So as he sat waiting, he itched a bit with the empty awkwardness that yawned between him and Charat Singh. The cook came bearing a long, brass tumbler and a jug of tea and the Havildar relieved his friend of his nervousness in an easy unconscious manner.

"Get that pan from which the sparrows drink water," he said to Bakha, pointing to the foot of a wood pillar. "Pour out the water from it."

Bakha did as he was directed, and the vessel was clean in his hand. To his great surprise Charat Singh got up and began to pour tea out of his tumbler into the pan.

"Nahin," Bakha protested in the familiar Indian guests' manner.

Charat Singh poured out the tea.

"Drink it, drink it, my son,"

"I am very grateful, Havildar ji," said Bakha. "You are kind."

"Drink it, drink the tea, you work hard; it will relieve your fatigue," said Charat Singh.

When Bakha had gulped down the liquid, he rose and replaced the vessel. Meanwhile, Charat Singh had poured the contents of his jug into the tumbler and sipped it quietly.

"Now what about a hockey stick for you!" he said, licking his lips and his thin moustache with the tip of his tongue.

Bakha looked up and tried to assume a grateful expression. He didn't have to try very hard, for in a second he seemed to have dwarfed himself to the littlest little being on earth. His face was hot with the tea, his teeth shone even with a slavish smile, his whole body and mind were tense with admiration and gratitude to his benefactor. "What has happened to change my fate all of a sudden?" he asked himself. "Such kindness from the Havildar, who is a Hindu, and one of the most important men in the regiment!" He followed Charat Singh with his gaze, curiously amazed.

The Havildar opened a door by the side of his room and disappeared for a moment. Then he came out with an almost brand-new hockey stick which must have been used only once. He handed it to Bakha as casually as he had given him the chilm to go and fill with charcoal.

"But it is new, Havildar ji," Bakha said as he took it.

"Now run along, new or not new, it doesn't matter," said Charat Singh. "Conceal it under your coat and don't tell anyone. Go, my lad."

Bakha bent his head and evaded the Havildar's eyes. He couldn't look at so generous a person. He was overcome by the man's kindness. He was grateful, grateful, haltingly grateful, falteringly grateful, stumblingly grateful, so grateful that he didn't know how he could walk the ten yards to the corner to be out of the sight of his benevolent and generous host. The whole atmosphere was charged with embarrassment. He felt uncomfortable as he walked way. "Strange! strange! wonderful! kind man! I didn't know he was so kind. I should have known. He always has such a humorous way about him! Kind, good man! He gave me a new stick, a brand-new stick!" He impatiently drew the stick from the folds of his overcoat where he had hidden it. It was a beautiful, broad-bladed stick, marked with English words, and therefore, to Bakha, the best stick that had been manufactured in the world. It had a leather handle. "Beautiful! Beautiful!" his heart seemed to be shouting in its thumping, mad rush of exhilaration. He turned the corner and went across the ditch, so that he was out of sight of his benefactor. Assured now that nobody would see the foolish pride and pleasure that he was taking in his prize, he rested it on the ground in the position in which it is usual to place a stick before hitting the ball. He bent it. It was elastic and bent finely. *That* Bakha knew was the test of a good stick. He hurriedly rubbed off the dust that had touched the lower part of the stick and holding it fast in his hands, as if he were afraid someone would come and snatch it from him, he tried to assure himself and to make himself believe that he possessed it, so incredulous was he of the fact that he owned it. In spite of the fact that he held it tight, he couldn't shake off the feeling that he was dreaming, until he got to the edge of the playing-fields outside the gymnasium, behind the Indian officer's quarters, and began to hit a little round stone about. The he suddenly realised that the stick might break, or get scarred, that way. He clutched it hard, and pressed it to his body, and tried to recollect his thoughts: "So my good karma has been rewarded. If only that thing hadn't happened this morning!"

Bahka tried to recall Charat Singh's face.

It had a slight suspicion of forgetfulness about it. "I hope he knew what he was doing," Bahka thought. "I hope he was not completely absent-minded. He may have been. Dare I play with the stick? It might be spoiled and in case he suddenly realises he has given away something he did not want to give, it will be terrible because I cannot return his stick battered or broken or even used. And, of course, I can't buy a new stick like this. But there is no question of that. Did he not say: 'New or not new, take it and run away, and don't tell anyone.' Of course he knew what he was doing. I am mad to think that he was forgetful. So kind a person, and I think *this* about him. I am a pig to do that." He didn't want to think at all,since he felt his thoughts becoming ungenerous. "How beautiful the afternoon is," he said, and he tilted his face up from the curve of his thought to sniff the bite in the air which came from the hills in the north. He was aware of the transparent, autumn sunshine, just warm enough to fill a heart wrapped in warm clothes with pleasure. The cup of Bakha's life was filled to overflowing with the happiness of the lucid, shining afternoon, as the bowl of the sky was filled with a clear and warm sunshine. He could have jumped for joy.

He was just going to, then he felt someone might see him. Someone was sure to be about. A passing sepoy or someone from among the boys. So there was no way of extending happiness into space, except by walking about.

He began to walk. Each step he took was a strut, his chest thrown out, his head lifted high and his legs stiff, as if they were made of wood. The awkward sway of his rump had, for a moment, become the haughty gait of a proud soldier.

Then he caught a glimpse of himself foolishly strutting about, and he grew self-conscious. He stopped suddenly, uncomfortably. His newly-assumed confidence had been shattered.

He was impatient now. He wished someone would come and relieve his loneliness. If only a sepoy were passing, he would look at him. And if one of the boys came, he would show him the stick he had acquired. He wished that Chota would come. He would like to have shown him the stick. Or Ram Charan. "But no, I must not show it to Ram Charan. Else he will go to Charat Singh and worry him by demanding a similar stick. The Havildar said I was not to tell anyone. He will be angry with me if Ram Charan takes it into his head to go and beg for a stick." He wished the babu's sons would come. They had the ball. The elder boy had promised to give him a lesson in English. Perhaps he could give it to him before the game started. He wished someone would come, someone to fill his mind, which had dried up, become suddenly empty.

He walked about aimlessly now. His limbs were loose. His face turned now to this side, now to that, with a half-conscious look. At last he espied the babu's son, the little boy, rushing out of the hall of his house, a big stick in his little hand, food in his mouth and sweets tied up in the lap of his tunic. Bakha knew how eager the little one was to play hockey. He began to advance towards the child with an easy step, made awkward by a consciousness of his low position, and with a smile of humility on his face. He liked the babu's sons, respected them, not only because they were high-caste Hindus whom he, as a sweeper's son, had to respect, but also because their father held a position of extraordinary importance in the regiment, almost second to the Colonel Sahib himself.

The little one came up to him with a wild gesture of enthusiasm and said: "Look, here is the new stick I told you about this morning. Charat Singh gave it to me."

"Oh, it is very beautiful!" Bakha commented. "But," he continued jocularly, "look at mine, it is better than yours. Ha, ha, mine is more beautiful than yours."

"Let me see," said the little one.

Bakha handed him the stick.

"Oh, it is the same kind exactly," shouted the child.

Bakha felt that Charat Singh had apparently not done him an exceptional favour. But it was a favour all right. "The babu's sons were the babu's sons. He would, of course, give them sticks. That he had given one to him, a sweeper, was an extraordinary favour."

"Are you prepared for the match? Ohe, Bakhe," said the child, as if he were a full-grown skipper.

"Yes, I am ready," said Bakha smilingly, and without betraying the slightest sign of that sympathy which he felt for the child, seeing him so enthusiastic and knowing he wouldn't be allowed to play. He liked the little one, so brimful of energy and enthusiasm.

"Where is your elder brother?" Bakha asked the child.

"He is finishing his meal. He is coming. I shall go and fetch the hockey sticks and the ball. The boys will soon be here." And he ran home abruptly, leaving Bakha curiously affected.

"Poor little boy, and they won't let him play. He is so eager. He will be an extraordinary man when he grows up. A big babu perhaps. Or a sahib. His eyes twinkle so! ———"

"Ohe Bakhe," someone disturbed his thoughts.

He turned round and saw Chota and Ram Charan followed by various boys, the armourer's sons, Niamat and Asmat; the tailor-master's son, Ibrahim; the band-master's sons, Ali, Abdulla, Hassan and Hussein, and hosts of strangers, presumably the boys of the 31st Punjabis. Bakha advanced towards them. Chota ran up to him and whispered: "I have told them that you are the Sahib's bearer: they don't know that you are a sweeper."

"Acha," Bakha agreed. He knew that it had been done to convince some of the orthodox boys of the 31st Punjabis team that they wouldn't be polluted.

"Look, I have got a wonderful new stick," said Bakha. He showed it to his friend. Then he said: "Don't tell Ram Charan about it. Charat Singh gave it to me. I shall score no end of goals with it."

"Wonderful! Wonderful! Marvellous! Beautiful!" exclaimed Chota. "Brother-in-law, you are lucky!" He slapped Bakha's back and raised a small cloud of dust from his thick overcoat.

"Boys, get ready," he shouted as he turned.

When the time for the election of the team came, the babu's little son brought and dumped the sticks before Chota and expected his reward. But Chota had already chosen his eleven.

"Let the child play," Bakha put in on the little one's behalf.

"No, he will be troublesome," Chota whispered. "We can't let him play. It is a match with the big boys. He will get hurt and then there will be trouble."

Bakha didn't want to insist too much. He knew that Chota and the little one didn't get on very well, and he was helpless seeing he liked them both equally, hurt to see the child ignored by everyone except his elder brother, who was trying to console him by saying that even he might not be asked to play, so important was the match, and between such big boys.

The child bore the disappointment more easily when it came after the consolation his brother had offered and the friendliness reflected in Bakha's smiles. Ignored and helpless, he sought to interest himself in the match by volunteering to be the referee. But Chota wouldn't have him even as a referee. The little one now looked sorry for himself. The match began. He stood by the heaps of the boys' clothes which lay on the side of the hockey ground. He wished he were as big as Chota. Then he would be asked to play. Also, then he could wear shorts like him. And he would look like a real sahib because he was not so dark as Chota.

Bakha came, for a second, to throw off his overcoat near the little one. He had started playing without having discarded it.

"Keep a watch over it, little brother, won't you?" he said to the child, as if by entrusting him with the job he was trying to console him for his being not included in the team. Then he ran back to his place.

The little one could have cried at that moment. But the game, the play—Bakha was going to score a goal.

It was an extraordinary spectacle. The crowd of boys in the field hopped to and fro like grasshoppers. There was no organisation. Bakha had rolled the ball, dribbling, dodging to the goal of the 31st Punjabis boys. But then he had been caught, enmeshed, by a throng of defenders, struggling, shouting, shoving to hit the ball out. Bakha managed, however, to scoop past the legs of all the boys and drove the ball into the space between the posts.

Defeated by superior tactics, the goalkeeper spitefully struck Bakha a blow on the legs. Upon this Chota, Ram Charan, Ali, Abdulla, and all the rest of the 38th Dogra boys fell upon the goalkeeper of the 31st Punjabis.

Soon there was a free fight.

"Foul! Foul!" shouted the captain of the 31st Punjabis team.

"No foul! No foul!" responded Chota, drawing himself up to his full height, angrily.

The captain of the 31st Punjabis advanced hotly, tearing the hordes asunder and gripped Chota by the collar. And, once more, the boys were fighting, scratching, hitting, kicking, yelling. One, two, three, four, five, the little hands worked their sticks, rudely, heavily, vigorously and the blusterings of the horde reached such a pitch of excitement that you could see the ruthlessness of the savage hunters in them. Chota had gripped his antagonist by the shoulder and for a time these two wrestled furiously, wildly, tearing each other's clothes and punching each other. Then Chota's enemy, unable to endure his transgressions, called to his followers, and ran back a few yards.

"Throw stones at them, stones," shouted Chota.

At this the boys of the 38th Dogras seemed to separate from their enemies, to run on one side and to begin hurling small stones at them.

In their intense excitement they didn't notice the little boy who stood near the clothes between them and their enemies, receiving the full measure of the stone bombardment. Most of the stones, however, passed high over the child's head and, though frightened, he was safe. But a bad throw from Ram Charan's hand caught him a rap on the skull. He gave a sharp, piercing shriek and fell unconscious. All the boys rushed to him. Streams of blood were pouring from the back of his head. Bakha picked him up in his arms and took him to the hall of his house. Unfortunately for him, the child's mother had heard the row they had been making and casually came to see if her children were safe. She met Bakha face to face.

"Vay, eater of your masters, Vay dirty sweeper!" she shouted. "What have you done to my son?"

Bakha was going to open his mouth and tell her what had happened. But even while she asked, she knew from the trickling of the blood from her son's skull, from his deathly, pale, senseless face.

"Vay, eater of your masters! What have you done? You have killed my son!" she wailed, flinging her hands across her breasts and turning blue and red with fear. "Give him to me! Give me my child! You have defiled my house, besides wounding my son!"

"Mother, mother, what are you saying?" interposed her elder son. "It was not he. He didn't hurt him. It was the washerwoman's son, Ram Charan."

"Get away, get away, eater of your masters!" she shouted at him. "May you die! Why didn't you look after your brother?"

Bakha handed over the child, and afraid, humble, silent as a ghost, withdrew. He felt dejected, utterly miserable. Was the pleasure of Charat Singh's generosity only to be enjoyed for half an hour? What had he done to deserve such treatment? He loved the child. He had been very sorry when Chota refused to let him join the game. Then why should the boy's mother abuse him when he had tried to be kind. She hadn't even let him tell her how it all happened. "Of course, I polluted the child. I couldn't help doing so. I knew my touch would pollute. But it was impossible not to pick him up. He was dazed, the poor little thing. And she abused me. I only get abuse and derision wherever I go. Pollution, pollution, I do nothing else but pollute people. They all say only: 'Polluted, polluted!' She was perhaps justified. Her son was injured. She could have said anything. It was my fault and of the other boys too. Why did we start that quarrel? It started on account of the goal I scored. Cursed me! That poor child! I hope he is not badly hurt. If only Chota had let him join the game the little one would not have been standing where he was, and then he might have escaped getting hurt. Now, where have all the boys gone?"

For the first time he became conscious that he had been walking alone. He looked around. Even the sparrows in the sweepers' lane twittered accusingly at him in the pale afternoon light. With a sudden shudder of unutterable weariness he clutched the stick which he carried under his arm, and turned into a by-path leading to his home across decayed tamarind leaves.

Before he came within sight of his home, he stopped and looked for a convenient spot where he might hide his hockey stick. He couldn't take it home. His father would at once fly into a rage about his wasting valuable time playing when there was all the work to do at the latrines. There was a long hedge of cactus away from the path. He turned towards it. There was a convenient hollow in the middle of the bush. He stepped over with a high stride into the hollow and laid the stick there. Then he bent down a few oar-shaped cactus leaves on to it and covered it against bad weather. After that he hurried, lest he should be seen hiding the stick by someone who might come later and filch it.

When Bakha returned, his father sat smoking his hubble-bubble in the English wicker-chair. For a moment Lakha was unaware of his son's presence. Then suddenly he seemed to rise in his seat and wave his close-fisted hand menacingly at Bakha and to shout:

"Pig! Dog! You ran away! You have been away all the afternoon and now you come back! Illegally begotten! Have you become a nawab that you go wandering about when you know that there is work here for you to do? The sepoys have been shouting!"

Bakha was cool in the face of this warm reception. He was too wearied by the succession of revived memories to cope with anything now. He stood obstinately still while his father's invective continued.

"Son of a pig! You have no care for your old father. You go out in the morning and you come back at night. Who is going to do the work at the latrines? I brought you up. Won't you give me some rest in my old age? There you go trying to be a sahib when you are a sweeper's son."

Bakha moved slowly under the rain of abuse towards the latrines. He was going to pick up a broom but he saw that his brother Rakha held it. He stopped short and looked up at his brother.

"So you have come back," shouted Rakha self-righteously. He stared hard at his elder brother. There was the pride of the favourite in his glance.

Bakha knew that the boy was preening himself because he had put in an afternoon's work and had won his father's partiality. He didn't hate him for his overbearing manner, however. He thought of him as a child, as he really loved him. And he would have borne his impudence and his father's abuse as his due, but the boy refused to give him the broom and his father persisted in his denunciation.

"He has no sense of shame! Play, play, play and wander about all day. As if he has nothing else to do!"

Bakha felt he couldn't bear the constant iteration of the same sentiments. He knew the way in which his father nagged him, persistently, stubbornly, without waiting for breath. He made for the latrines.

"Get away, swine, run away from my presence," shouted his father. "Don't touch that broom or I shall kill you. Go away! Get out of my house. And don't come back! Don't let me see your face again!"

Before now, Bakha had often borne the brunt of his misery with a resigned air of fatalism. He had quietly suffered his father's abuse and invective, and even occasional beatings with a clam that betokened his intense docility and gentleness. Today, however, he had had more than enough. The spirit of fire which lay buried in the mass of his flesh had ignited this morning and lay smouldering. A little more fuel and it flared up, like a wild flame.

He tore across the plain without even looking back. It was as though a demon had taken possession of him. He was not conscious of the shattering moment which had suddenly determined his flight. Nor was he aware of the feeling of revulsion that had filled the moment. It seemed as if the demon in him held a cruel sword with which it hacked everything in its way and by the force of the hacking, acquired a more sinister power, frightening in its intensity and weirdly fascinating in its transmutation of Bakha's body into a wild horse.

As he moved over the fringe of flat earth facing the plane, the rim of the upturned sky was taking on the gold and silver hues of the afternoon sun, and the world lay encircled in a ribbon of crimson. Here he slackened his pace, for it was here that he had felt the first glow of the early morning sun creeping into his bones.

It was through this plain that he had gone out to the world, full of the spirit of adventure.

The wide expanse was empty except for the interminable thread of men entering the mud-houses which clustered in the north like mushrooms, surrounded by rubbish heaps, filled with broken bottles, old tins, dead cats and rags and bones. So lofty did he feel in his mood of righteous indignation that he had the strange sensation of being a giant, commanding a full view of everything in the hollows and the hills.

"Unlucky, unlucky day! What have I done to deserve all this?" he cried in exasperation.

A sepoy on his way to the latrines was approaching. He jumped aside into a ditch so as not to be seen. He didn't want to meet anybody. He wanted to be alone and quiet, to compose himself. When the man had passed, he crept out of the ditch and made for a pipal-tree which stood in the plain surrounded by a clay platform. He sat down under it, facing the sun.

Now he felt desolate and the fact dawned on him that he was homeless. He had often been turned out like that. As a matter of fact, when his father was angry he always threatened him and his brother with eviction. He remembered that once after his mother's death his father had locked him out all night, for not looking after the house properly. It was a winter night. The east wind blew and he was sleepy. He was tired from the day's work and yawned as he curled himself up in his overcoat behind two refuse baskets. How he had smarted under the pain of that callousness and cruelty. Could he be the same father who, according to his own version, had gone praying to the doctor for medicine? Bakha recalled he had not spoken to his father for days after that incident. Then his grief about his unhappy position had become less violent, less rebellious. He had begun to work very hard. It had seemed to him that the punishment was good for him. For he felt he had learnt through it to put his heart into his work. He had matured. He had learnt to scrub floors, cook, fetch water, besides doing his job cleaning the latrines and carting manure for sale to the fields. And in spite of the poor nourishment he got, he had developed into a big, strong man, broad-shouldered, heavy-hipped, supple-armed, as near the Indian ideal of the wrestler as he wished to be.

But this present disgrace! This could do no good, he thought. It was undeserved. Why should his father object to his taking a half-day off once in his life, especially as he knew he had been insulted in the town this morning and didn't feel like working. Then he had not spent the afternoon uselessly. He had got a new stick. But that, it occurred to him, was something which his father could not appreciate. He didn't like him to play hockey. That was what all the trouble was about. "Rakha must have told on me," he muttered, "because he could not go to play. What a day I have had! Unlucky, inauspicious day! I wish I could die!" And he sat nursing his head in his hands, utterly given up to despair.

He had sat for a long while like that, his head in his hands. He felt sick and stifled with the knowledge that he was homeless and unwanted even by his own father. He had unconsciously chosen to sit down in a place where Chota or Ram Charan or someone from the outcastes' colony might recognise him. As time passed and he became conscious of the emptiness around him, he felt that the sympathy he longed for would never come.

But he was mistaken. Colonel Hutchinson, chief of the local Salvation Army, was never very far from the outcastes' colony. To his rather irreligious wife he always made the excuse that he was going out for a walk in the hills where the kingdom of Heaven was waiting to be found, though actually he went out wallowing in the mire for the sake of Jesus Christ, talking to some Untouchable among the rubbish heaps about divinity and trinity. You couldn't miss him even if you saw him from a mile off, for he was one of the few living members of the band of Christian missionaries in India who had originated the idea that the Salvation Army ought to be dressed in the costume of the natives and live among them, if it was to achieve the true end of proselytizing. And he had designed the Colonel's uniform he wore: a pair of white trousers, a scarlet jacket, a white turban with a red band across it. He had been a strong man once, if he wasn't quite the image of Eugene Sandow now. In the old days, he had plenty of hair on his head. Now, unfortunately, he was bald, his wife said, because of the infernal turban he wore and because he was so fond of study. He also once had a turned-up moustache of the real Colonel kind, bushy and black. Now, though it was still bushy, it was grey and drooping, his malicious wife said, in defeat, because she alleged that the proselytizing mission of Christianity had, in his hands, been a complete failure, the number of conversions to his credit for the last twenty years being not more than five, and those five mainly from among the dirty black Untouchables. But in justice to the Colonel's moustache, it must be said that his wife was being catty because she had a personal grievance against him. He had charmed her in his youth with his well-groomed, immaculate bearing, a conspicuous feature of which had been his fine black, upright moustache. She was a barmaid in Cambridge and had developed an aesthetic taste for the gem-like, glistening drops of liquor that adorned the edges of Hutchinson's moustache when he had had a drink. She had married him for that. India, however, had embittered her. For, not only did she hate the "nigger" servants in her house, but she discovered that her husband was too sombre for her gay card-playing, drinking and love-making tastes. Still, she had borne with him for a great many years, on the strength of whisky, but then Hutchinson's moustache had grown grey and it had begun to droop under the weight of years, the Colonel now having turned sixty-five. Despite all that his wife said, therefore, people gave credit to Colonel Hutchinson for his unflinching devotions to duty and loyalty to the cause which he had taken up. He was marvellously active for his three score years and five, laying himself in hiding as of yore in deep pits of filth or behind heaps of dung, to wait for some troubled outcaste who might be tired and hungry and would listen in his despair to the gospel of Christ. He always carried a number of copies of the Hindustani translation of the Bible under his arm, and he stuffed the pockets of his jacket and overcoat with the gospel of St. Luke, to thrust into the hands of any passer-by, be he willing or unwilling. He was a thin fellow, pitiably reduced now. But the edge of his tongue was like a pair of scissors which cut the pattern of Hindustani into smithereens as a parrot snips his food into bits. The impulse that had made him think of learning Hindustani before he started his mission was a noble one considering that his work lay among the natives; the habit of muddling through the language, and never learning it properly during the thirty years of his stay in India was most disastrous in its consequences.

"Tum udas," said the Colonel, putting his hand on Bakha's shoulder.

Bakha looked up with a start. He had hoped that Chota or Ram Charan might come and console him, or someone from the outcastes' colony. He had not the foggiest notion that he would be surprised by Colonel Hutchinson, who, although he freely mixed with the natives and had thus lost some of the glamour attaching to the superior, remote and reticent Englishmen, was yet a sahib, who wore trousers and used a commode. Bakha felt honoured that the sahib had deigned to talk Hindustani to him, even though it was broken Hindustani. He felt flattered that he should be the object of pity and sympathy from a sahib. Of course, he at once recognised the Colonel. Who didn't know the missionary? But it was the first occasion on which he had found himself face to face with him. Being of a very retiring disposition and full of a feeling of inferiority, he had never talked to Hutchinson, although he remembered that the Colonel often visited his father when he (Bakha) was a child. His father, he recalled, also talked of the sahib, sometimes if he saw him in the distance, saying that the old sahib had wanted to convert them to the religion of Yessuh Messih[12] and to make them sahibs like himself, but that he had refused to leave the Hindu fold, saying that the religion which was good enough for his forefathers was good enough for him.

"Salaam Sahib," said Bakha putting his hand to his forehead as he got up.

"Salaam, salaam, you sit, don't disturb yourself," squealed the Colonel in wrong, badly accented Hindustani, patting Bakha affectionately the while.

There was something wonderful in the brave effort the Colonel seemed to make to be natural in this unnatural atmosphere. But he was not self-conscious. He had thrown aside every weight — pride of birth and race and colour in adopting the customs of the natives and in garbing himself in their manner, to build up the Salvation Army in northern India. And he had swamped the overbearing strain of the upper middle-class Englishman in him, by his hackneyed effusions of Christian sentiment, camouflaged the narrow, insular patriotism of his character in the lingo of the white-livered humanitarian.

"What has happened? Are you ill?" the Colonel asked, bending over.

Bakha felt confused, embarrassed by this show of kindness. "Charat Singh," he thought, "was kind to me this afternoon; the Sahib is generosity itself." And he wondered if he were dreaming. He looked and saw the form of the Colonel real enough before him. And hadn't he heard the strange, squeaky voice of the Englishman speaking Hindustani? Good Hindustani, Bakha thought, considering it was spoken by a sahib, for, ordinarily, he knew the sahibs didn't speak Hindustani at all, only some useful words and swear words: "Acha (good); jao (go away); jaldi karo (be quick); sur ka bacha (son of a pig), kute ka bacha (son of a dog)."

"Nothing, Sahib, I was just tired," said Bakha shyly. "I am sweeper here, son of Lakha, jemadar of the sweepers."

"I know! I know! How is your father?"

"Huzoor,[13] he is well," replied Bakha.

"Has your father told you who I am?" asked the Colonel, coming to the point in the practical manner of the Englishman.

"Han, Huzoor. You are a sahib," said Bakha.

"Nahin, nahin," said the Colonel. "I am not a sahib. I am like you. I am padre of the Salvation Army."

"Han, Sahib, I know," said Bakha, without understanding the subtle distinction which the Colonel was trying to institute between himself and the ordinary sahibs in India whose haughtiness and vulgarity was, to his Christian mind, shameful, and from whom, on that account, he took care to distinguish himself, lest their misdeeds reflect on the sincerity of his intentions for the welfare of the

[12]*Yessuh Messih* Jesus Christ

[13]*Huzoor* Sir

souls of the heathen. To Bakha, however, all the sahibs were sahibs, trousered and hatted men, who were generous in the extreme, giving away their cast-off clothes to their servants, also a bit nasty because they abused their servants a great deal. He knew, of course, that the Colonel was a padre sahib, but he did not know what a padre did except that he lived near the girja ghar and came to see the people in the outcastes' colony. To him even the padres were of interest because of their European clothes. This padre did not wear a hat like the padre in the barracks of the British regiments. But that was of little account. He wore all the other items of clothes that the sahibs wore. He was a sahib all right. And this sahib had condescended to pat him on the back, to speak kind words to him, even to ask him why he was looking so sad. He could have cried to receive such gracious treatment from a sahib, cried with the joy of being in touch with that rare quality which was to be found in the sahibs. In spite of it all, however, he seemed to be vaguely aware of the difference the Colonel was trying to define.

"I am a padre and my God is Yessuh Messih," emphasised the Colonel. "If you are in trouble, come to Jesus in the girja ghar." He was seeking vainly to paraphrase into Hindustani the promise: "Come all ye that labour and I shall give thee rest."

Bakha was struck with the coincidence. How did the padre know he was in trouble. "And who is Yessuh Messih to whose religion my father told me this padre wanted to convert us. I wonder if he lives in the girja ghar." He recalled that the girja ghar had seemed to him a mysterious place whenever he had passed by.

"Who is Yessuh Messih, really, Sahib?" Bakha asked, eager to allay his curiosity.

"Come, I shall tell you," said Colonel Hutchison. "Come to the church." And dragging the boy by the arm, babbling, babbling, all vague, in a cloud, and enthusiastic as a mystic, he led him away on the wings of a song:

"Life is found in Jesus
Only there 'tis offered thee;
Offered without price or money
'Tis the gift of God sent free."

Bakha was dumb with amazement, carried away by the confusion, feeling flattered, honoured by the invitation which had come from the sahib, however much that sahib might mix with the natives. He followed willingly, listening to each word that the Colonel spoke, but not understanding a word:

"Life is found in Jesus"

the Colonel sang again, absorbed in himself, and unconscious that he was in charge of a soul in trouble.

Jesus! Who was Jesus? The same as Yessuh Messih? Who was he? The Sahib says he is God. Was he a God like Rama, God of the Hindus, whom his father worshipped and his forefathers had worshipped, whom his mother used to mention quite often in her prayers? These thoughts came into Bakha's mind, and he would have exploded with them, had it not been that the Colonel was absolutely absorbed in his song:

"Life is found alone in Jesus
Only there 'tis offered thee,
Offered without price or money
'Tis the gift of God sent free."

"Huzoor," said Bakha, breaking in impatiently at the close of the third recitation, "who is Jesus? The same as Yessuh Messih? Who is he?"

"He died that we might be forgiven,
He died to make us good,
That we might go at last to heaven,
Saved by His precious blood,"

answered the Colonel quickly, rhythmically, before Bakha knew what he had asked. He was still baffled. The answer, if it was an answer, was like a conundrum to him; words, words. He felt overwhelmed and uncomfortable. But being, of course, so happy to be seen walking with the sahib, he bore all, trying to remember parts of the Colonel's song and asking himself what they meant. But apart from the muffled sound of words he could not catch anything.

"Sahib, who is Yessuh Messih?" Bakha persisted with Punjabi directness.

"He is the Son of God," answered Colonel Hutchinson, coming down to earth for a moment. "He died that we might be forgiven."

And he sang the verse again.

"He died that we might be forgiven. . . ."

"He died that we might be forgiven" thought Bakha. "What does that mean? He is the son of God! How could anybody be the son of God if God, as my mother told me, lives in the sky. How could He have a son? And why did His son die that we should be forgiven? Forgiven for what?"

"Who is Yessuh Messih, Sahib? Is He the God of the sahibs?" Bakha asked, slightly afraid that he was bothering the white man too much. He knew from experience that Englishmen did not like to talk too much.

"He is the Son of God, my boy," answered the Colonel, ecstatically revolving his head. "And He died for us sinners:

"He died that we might be forgiven,
He died to make us good,
That we might go at last to heaven,
Saved by His precious blood."

Bakha was a bit bored by this ecstatic hymn-singing. But the white man had condescended to speak to him, and he was happy and proud to be in touch with a sahib. He suffered the priest and even reiterated his enquiry:

"Do you pray to Yessuh Messih in your girja ghar, Sahib?"

"Han, han," replied the Colonel breaking into the rhythm of a new hymn:

"Jesus, tender shepherd, hear me.
Let my sins be forgiven!
Let there be light
Oh, shed Thy light in the heart of this boy."

Bakha was baffled and bored. He did not understand anything of these songs. He had followed the Sahib because the Sahib wore trousers. Trousers had been the dream of his life. The kindly interest which the trousered man had shown him when he was downcast had made Bakha conjure up pictures of himself wearing the Sahib's clothes, talking the Sahib's language and becoming like the guard whom he had seen on the railway station near his village. He did not know who Yessuh

Messih was. The Sahib probably wanted to convert him to his religion. He didn't want to be converted. It was all so puzzling that he thought of excusing himself by lying to the Sahib that he had to go to work and couldn't come with him.

The colonel saw Bakha lagging behind and, realising that his new follower was losing interest, exerted the peculiar obstinacy of the enthusiastic missionary in him and dragging at the boy's sleeve, said, "Yessuh Messih is the Son of God, my boy. While we were yet sinners, He died for us. He sacrificed Himself for us." Then again he became rapt in his devotional songs:

"Oh Calvary! O Calvary!
It was for me that Jesus died
On the Cross of Calvary!"

He sacrificed Himself for us, Bakha reflected. His idea of sacrifice was something very certain and definite. He remembered that when some calamity brooded over the family, such as an epidemic of sickness, or starvation, his mother used to make offerings to the goddess Kali, by sacrificing a goat or some other animal. That sacrifice was supposed to appease the goddess's wrath and the evil passed over. Now, what did this sacrifice of Yessuh Messih mean? Why did He sacrifice Himself?

"Why did Yessuh Messih sacrifice Himself, Huzoor?" he asked.

"He died that we might be forgiven
He died to make us good,
That we might go at last to heaven,
Saved by His precious blood,"

answered the Colonel forgetting, as he often did while he was with Bakha, that the sweeper-boy didn't understand a word of what he was singing. Then in a sane moment he recognised the look of anxious solicitude on the face of the boy and realised he had been babbling too much, and mostly to himself.

"He sacrificed Himself out of love for us," he said. "He sacrificed Himself to help us all; for the rich and the poor; for Brahmin and the Bhangi."

The last sentence went home. "He sacrificed Himself for us, for the rich and the poor, for the Brahmin and the Bhangi." That meant there was no difference in His eyes between the rich and the poor, between the Brahmins and the Bhangis, between the pundit of the morning, for instance, and himself.

"Han, han, Sahib, I understand," said Bakha eagerly. "Yessuh Messih makes no difference between the Brahmin and myself."

"Han, han, my boy we are all alike in the eyes of Jesus," the Colonel answered him. But he began garrulously: "He is our King. He is the Son of God. We are all sinners. He will intercede with God, His Father, on our behalf."

"He is superior to us. We are all sinners. Why, why, is any one above another? Why are we all sinners?" Bakha began to reflect.

"Why are we all sinners, Sahib?" he queried.

"We were all born sinners," replied the Colonel evasively, the puritan in him shying at an exposition of the doctrine of original sin which seemed called for.

"We must confess our sins. Then alone will He forgive us, otherwise we will have to suffer the eternal torment of hell. You confess your sins to me before I convert you to Christianity."

"But, Huzoor, I don't know who Yessuh Messih is. I know Ram. But I don't know Yessuh Messih."

"Ram is the god of the idolators," the Colonel said after a pause, and a bit absent-mindedly. "Come and confess your sins to me and Yessuh Messih will receive you in Heaven when you die."

Now Bakha was utterly bored. Never mind if it was a sahib who was giving him his company. He was afraid of the thought of conversion. He hadn't understood very much of what the Salvationist said. He didn't like the idea of being called a sinner. He had committed no sin that he could remember. How could he confess his sins? Odd. What did it mean, confessing sins? "Does the Sahib want some secret knowledge?" he wondered. "Does he want to perform some magic or get some illegal information?" He didn't want to go to heaven. As a Hindu he didn't believe in the judgment day. He had never thought of that. He had seen people die. And he just accepted the fact. He had been told that people who died were reborn in some form or other, after the god of Death, Yama, had tried them in hell for their faults. He dreaded that he should be reborn a donkey or a dog. But "Yessuh Messih must be a good man," he thought, "if he regards a Brahmin and a Bhangi the same." But who was he? Where did he come from? What did he do? He had heard the story of Ram. He had heard the story of Krishna. He hadn't heard the story of Yessuh Messih. "This Sahib will not tell me the story," he said to himself. But he still hoped he might give him a pair of his cast-off trousers. And he followed him half unwillingly.

"Look, that is our home," said the Colonel reaching the gate of a compound leading to a pile of mud-houses among the neem-trees with thatched and sloping roofs.

"I know, Sahib," said Bakha who had often passed by it.

"It was a drug-house once, an opium distillery," said the Colonel with great pride. "But five years ago we took it." He paused for a moment to recall the trouble it had cost him to acquire the piece of land to erect a building, and he burst out piously into an exclamation of his gratitude to Christ. "Oh Lord, how great are Thy works, and Thy thoughts how deep! God has indeed brought light into the world!" Then turning from his thoughts to the young man, he said: "He has cast out the heathen from the place."

"George, George, tea is ready!" came a shrieking, hoarse and hysterical voice.

"Coming, coming!" responded the Colonel automatically, standing where he was, but with his arms and legs all in a flurry. He had heard his wife's voice. He was afraid of her. He was confused. He didn't know whether to go into the mud-house on the right which was his bungalow, or to take Bakha in there, or to take him to the church. He stood hesitating.

"Where are you? Where have you been all the afternoon?" came the shrill voice again. And behind it appeared the form of a round-faced, big-bellied, dark-haired, undersized, middle-aged woman, a cigarette in a long cigarette-holder in her mouth, a gaily-coloured band on her Eton-cropped hair, pince-nez glasses on her rather small eyes, a low-necked printed cotton frock, that matched her painted and powdered face and reached barely down to her knees.

"Oh, is that what you've been doing, going to these blackies again!" she shouted, frowning, her heavily-powdered face showing its layers of real, vivid scarlet skin underneath the coating. "I give you up. Really you're incorrigible. I should have thought you would have learned your lesson from the way those Congress wallahs beat you last week!"

"What is the matter? I am just coming. I am coming," responded the Colonel, impatient, disturbed and embarrassed.

Bakha was going to slip away in order to save the Colonel the displeasure of his wife, for which, he felt, he was mainly responsible.

"Ither! Ither!" said the Colonel, holding the sweeper-boy's hand. "I'll take you to the church."

"So that the tea should get cold!" exclaimed Mary Hutchinson. "I can't keep waiting for you all day, while you go messing about with all those dirty bhangis and chamars."[14] And saying this, she withdrew into the house.

Bakha had not known the exact reason for her frowns, but when he heard the words bhangi and chamar, he at once associated her anger with the sight of himself.

"Salaam, Sahib," he said, extricating his hand from the old man's grasp, before the missionary realised he had done so. And he showed his heels; such was his fear of the woman.

"Wait, wait, my son, wait," cried the padre after him.

But in the white haze of the afternoon sun he hurried away as if the Colonel's wife were a witch, following him with raised arms and crooked feet.

The old man was piously reciting another hymn as he stood staring at Bakha's receding figure:

"Blessed by Thy love, blessed by Thy name."

"Everyone thinks us at fault," Bakha was saying to himself as he walked along. "He wants me to come and confess my sins. And his mem-sahib! I don't know what she said about bhangis and chamars. She was angry with the Sahib. I am sure I am the cause of the mem-sahib's anger. I didn't ask the padre to come and talk to me. He came of his own accord. I was so happy talking to him. I would certainly have asked him for a pair of white trousers, had the mem-sahib not been angry."

He walked along, vacantly oppressed by the weight of his heavy cloud of memories. He felt a kind of nausea in his stomach. The spiritual nausea that seemed to rise in him when he was in difficulties, the ghaoon maoon. He was unnerved again as in the morning after his unfortunate experiences. Only, he was now too tired to care. He let himself be carried by his legs towards the edge of the day. There was a faint smell of wetness oozing from the dusty earth which paved his way, a sort of moist warmth that rose to his nostrils. High above the far-distant horizon of the Bulandshahr dales the sun stood fixed, motionless and undissolved, as if it could not bring itself to go, to move or to melt. In the hills and fields, however, there was a strange quickening. Long rows of birds flew over against the cold, blue sky towards their homes. The grasshoppers chirped in an anxious chorus, as they fell back into the places where they always lay waiting for food. A lone beetle sent electric waves of sound quivering into the cool, clear air. Every blade of grass along the pathway, where Bakha walked, was gilded by light.

As he went on, striding lightly from his heavy rump, his head bent, his eyes half closed, his lower lip pursed, he felt the blood coursing through his veins. He seemed full of a tired restlessness. The awkwardness of the moment when the missionary's wife emerged from her room on to the veranda of her thatched bungalow and glared at her husband, stirred in his soul the echoes of those memories which had shaken and stirred him during the morning. There was a common quality in the look of hate in the round, white face of the Colonel's wife and in the sunken visage of the touched man. The man's protruding lower jaw,

[14]*bhangis and chamars* sweepers; that is, of low caste

with its transparent muscles, shaken in his spluttering speech, came before Bakha's eyes. Also his eyes emerging out of their sockets. The Colonel's wife had also opened her little eyes like that, behind her spectacles. That had frightened Bakha, frightened him much more than the thrust of the touched man's eyeballs, for she was a mem-sahib, and the frown of a mem-sahib had the strange quality of unknown, uncharted seas of anger behind it. To Bakha, therefore, the few words which she had uttered carried a dread a hundred times more terrible than the fear inspired by the whole tirade of abuse by the touched man. It was probably that the episode of the morning was a matter of history, removed in time and space from the more recent scene, also, perhaps, because the anger of a white person mattered more. The mem-sahib was more important to his slavish mind than the man who was touched, he being one of his many brown countrymen. To displease the mem-sahib was to him a crime for which no punishment was bad enough. And he thought he had got off comparatively lightly. He dared not think unkind thoughts about her. So he unconsciously transferred his protest against her anger to the sum of his reactions against the insulting personages of the morning.

His attention was diverted to a leper who sat swathed in tattered garments, exposing his raw wounds to the sun and the flies by the wayside, his crumpled hand lifted in beggary, and on his lips the prayer: "Baba pesa de." Bakha had a sudden revulsion of feeling. He looked away from the man. It was the Grand Trunk Road near the railway station of Bulandshahr. The pavements were crowded with beggars. A woman wailed for food outside one of the many cook-shops which lined one side of the road. She had a little child in her arms, another child in a bag on her back, a third holding on to her skirt. Some boys were running behind the stream of carriages begging for coppers. Bakha felt a queer sadistic delight staring at the beggars moaning for alms, but not receiving any. They seemed to him despicable. And the noise they made through their wailings and moanings and blessings, oppressed him.

He heard the rumbling thunder of a railway train which passed under the footbridge he was ascending. Almost simultaneously he heard a shout from the golbagh rend the still, leafy air. The shadow of the smoke-cloud that the engine had sent up to the bridge choked Bakha's throat and blinded his eyes. Then the fumes of smoke melted like invisible, intangible flakes of snow, leaving a dark trail of soot behind. This too paled in the sunshine. The train had rushed into the cool darkness of the tin roof on Bulandshahr station.

Two choruses of voices tore through the air this time, one charged the sky from the platform where the train had stopped; another rose above the treetops of the golbagh, undulating from horizon to horizon.

Bakha stood for a moment on the platform of the footbridge and stared towards the tin roof. Myriads of faces were jutting out of white clothes. He looked in the direction of the golbagh. A veritable sea of white tunics faced him in the oval, where, ordinarily, he had seen the city gymkhana play cricket. Now there was a profound silence. He waited in the hush and listened. The chorus began again. As a spark of lightning suddenly illumines the sky, the myriad of voices leapt up the curve of the heavens before Bakha, and writ in flaming colours the cry: "Mahatma Gandhi ki jai,"[15] And, in a while, there was a rush of eager feet ascending the

[15]*Mahatma Gandhi ki jai* a famous revolutionary cry: "Victory, victory to Mahatma Ghandi"; also implies "glory" to Gandhi

footbridge behind him shouting: "The Mahatma has come! The Mahatma has come!"

Before Bakha had turned round to look at them, they were descending the steps south of the bridge. A passing man answered the questioning look of all the pedestrians by informing them that there was going to be a meeting in the golbagh, where the Mahatma was going to speak.

At once the crowd, and Bakha among them, rushed towards the golbagh. He had not asked himself where he was going. He hadn't paused to think. The word "Mahatma" was like a magical magnet, to which he, like all the other people about him, rushed blindly. The wooden boards of the footbridge creaked under the eager downward rush of his ammunition boots. He was so much in a hurry that he didn't even remember that he was an Untouchable, and actually touched a few people. But not having his broom and basket with him, and the people being all in a flurry, no one noticed that a sweeper-boy had brushed past him.

At the foot of the bridge, by the tongs and motor-lorry stand, the road leading to the fort past the entrance of the golbagh looked like a regular racecourse. Men, women and children of all the different races, colours, castes and creeds, were running towards the oval. There were Hindu lallas from the piece-goods market of Bulandshahr, smartly dressed in silks; there were Kashmiri Muhammadans from the local carpet factories, immaculately clad in white cotton; there were the rough Sikh rustics from the near-by villages swathed in handspun cloth, staves in their hands and loads of shopping on their backs; there were fierce-looking red-cheeked Pathans in red shirts, followers of Abdul Gaffar Khan, the frontier Gandhi; there were the black-faced Indian Christian girls from the Salvation Army colony, in short, coloured skirts, blouses and aprons; there were people from the outcastes' colony, whom Bakha recognised in the distance, but whom he was not too anxious to greet; there was here and there a stray European — there was everybody going to meet the Mahatma, to pay homage to Mohandas Karam Chand Gandhi. And like Bakha they hadn't stopped to ask themselves why they were going. They were just going; the act of going, of walking, running, hurrying, occupied them. Their present motive was to get there, to get there somehow, as quickly as possible. Bakha wished, as he sped along, that there were a sloping bridge on which he could have rolled down to the oval.

He saw that the fort road was too long and too congested. Suddenly he swerved round to a little marsh made by the overflow of a municipal pipe in a corner of the golbagh, jumped the fence into the garden, much to the consternation of the gardener, but wholly to the satisfaction of the crowd behind him, which, once it had got the lead, followed like sheep. The beautiful garden bowers planted by the ancient Hindu kings and since then neglected were thoroughly damaged as the mob followed behind Bakha. It was as if the crowd had determined to crush everything, however ancient or beautiful, that lay in the way of their achievement of all that Gandhi stood for. It was as if they knew, by an instinct surer than that of conscious knowledge, that the things of the old decadence must be destroyed in order to make room for those of the new. It seemed as if, in trampling on the blades of green grass, they were deliberately, brutally trampling on a part of themselves, which they had begun to abhor, and from which they wanted to escape to Gandhi.

Beyond the bowers, on the oval, was a tumult, and the thronging of the thousands who had come to worship. The eager babble of the crowd, the excited gestures, the flow of emotion, portended one thought and one thought only in the surging crowd — Gandhi. There was a terror in this devotion, half-expressed, half-suppressed, of the panting swarms that pressed round Bakha stopped short as he reached the pavilion end of the cricket ground. He leant by a tree. He wanted to be detached. It wasn't that he had lost grip of the emotion that had brought him swirling on the tide of the rushing stream of people. But he became aware of the fact of being a sweeper by the contrast which his dirty, khaki uniform presented to the white garments of most of the crowd. There was an insuperable barrier between himself and the crowd, the barrier of caste. He was part of a consciousness which he could share and yet not understand. He had been lifted from the gutter, through the barriers of space, to partake of a life which was his, and yet not his. He was in the midst of a humanity which included him in its folds, and yet debarred him from entering into a sentient, living , quivering contact with it. Gandhi alone united him with them, in the mind, because Gandhi was in everybody's mind, including Bakha's. Gandhi might unite them really. Bakha waited for Gandhi.

Absorbed he eagerly recalled all that he had heard of this man. People said he was a saint, that he was an avatar of the Gods Vishnu and Krishna. Only recently he had heard that a spider had woven a web in the house of the Lat Sahib at Dilli, making a portrait of the sage, and writing his name under it in English. That was said to be a warning to the sahibs to depart from Hindustan, since God Almighty himself had sent a message through a little insect that Gandhi was to be the Maharaja of the whole of Hindustan. That the spider's web appeared in the Lat Sahib's kothi was surely significant. And, they said, no sword could cut his body, no bullet could pierce his skin, no fire could scorch him!

"The Sakar is afraid of him," said a lalla standing by Bakha. "The magistrate has withdrawn his order against Gandhiji's entry into Bulandshahr."

"That is nothing, they have released him unconditionally from gaol," chimed in a babu, spitting out a phrase of the*Tribune*, pompously, in order to show off his erudition.

"Will he really overthrow the government?" asked a rustic.

"He has the shakti to change the whole world," replied the babu, and he began to vomit out the whole article about Gandhi that he had crammed from the *Tribune* that morning. "This British Government is nothing. Every country in Europe and America is passing through terrible convulsions, politically, economically and industrially. The people of Vilayat, the Angrez log are less convulsed on account of their innate conservatism, but very soon every country on earth including Vilayat will be faced with problems that cannot be solved without a fundamental change, in the mental and moral outlook of the West. Without a radical change from a hankering after sense-gratification, which is the goal of Western civilisation, through a striving after sense-control, whether in individual or in group life, which is the essence of India's dharmic culture! India has been the privileged home of the world's eternal religion, that teaches how every man and woman, according to their birth and environment must practice swadarma, how through sense-control they must evolve their higher nature, and so realise the bliss of divinity, deep-seated in the hearts of all beings. For this bliss all humanity blindly pants, not knowing that neither cigarettes nor cinemas nor sense-enjoyment can lead to the path of dharmic discipline, which alone is the highest bliss to be realised. Gandhi will reveal this path to the modern world, he will teach us the true religion of God-love which is the best self-government."

"How clever you are, babu," said a man staring at the lecturer. He was impressed by the babu's speech, but baffled. To him Gandhi was a legend, a tradition, an oracle. He had heard from time to time during the last fourteen years, how a saint had arisen as great as Guru Nanak, the incarnation of Krishanji Maharaj of whom the Ferungi Sarkar was very afraid. His wife had told him of the miracles which this saint was performing. It was said that he slept in a temple one night with his feet towards the shrine of the god. When the Brahmins had chastised him, for deliberately turning his feet towards God, he told them that God was everywhere and asked them to turn his feet in the direction where God was not. Upon this the priests turned his feet in the direction opposite to the one where the image of the god was, and lo the shrine of God moved in the direction of his feet. He had hungered for a sight of the saint since then. His wife wouldn't be content with anything less than a touch of the Holy Man's feet. But it was a good thing she wasn't with him. The peasant reflected that if she had come, the boys would have wished to accompany her, and they might have been crushed to death in the throng. It was a good thing they didn't know. For myself, I am glad I shall see him. It is lucky he is coming on the day that I came out shopping.

Bakha had listened hard to the babu, and, although he couldn't follow every sentence of his rhetorical outburst, he had somehow got the sense of it all.

"Tell me, babu," Bakha heard the yokel say to the round, felt-capped, bespectacled man who had made the oration, "will he look after the canals when the Ferungis have gone?" It seemed the peasant had more than a vague idea of what Gandhi was about.

"Bhai ji, don't you know," said the babu, "that according to Mr Radha Kamal Mukerji we had canals in ancient India four thousand years before Christ. Who made the Grand Trunk Road? Not the British!"

"But what about the law suits?" asked the jat. "The five elders of my village use the Panchayat to wreak vengeance on their enemies, or to bring pressure on the village menials, if they become too independent, and I hear Gandhi says we must not go to the Sarkari Adalat, but must take up our suits to the Panchayat."

"A good Panchayat," replied the babu sonorously, "can get the villagers to do their bit from time to time in preventing damage by erosion and other causes. It may not be a good, judicial body now, but it was, and always has been so in the past. So far as affairs of executive action are concerned, however, you know that the Panchayats have done much good in the service of this country, in the cause of good administration in general, in making wells, rebuilding roads, etc."

The peasant didn't understand that. Nor did Bakha. But the mention of village menials by the peasant recalled to Bakha's mind the fact that he had heard that Gandhi was very keen on uplifting the Untouchables. Hadn't it been rumoured in the outcastes' colony, lately, that Gandhi was fasting for the sake of the bhangis and chamars. Bakha could not quite understand what fasting had to do with helping the low-castes. "Probably he thinks we are poor and can't get food," he vaguely surmised, "so he tries to show that even he doesn't have food for days."

"We are willing to do all we can," the lalla disturbed Bakha's cogitations with a dramatic gesture towards the babu. "We can boycott Manchester cotton and Bradford fancies, if it is going to mean that in the end we will have a monopoly of swadeshi cloth. I hear, however, that Gandhiji is making terms with Japan."

"You must ask the Mahatma that," the babu replied, flurried because he heard noises at the gate from which he presumed that Gandhi was approaching. He wanted to work his way to a position from which he could obtain a good view of the great man.

"Mathatmaji is not speaking about swadeshi, or on civil disobedience," put in a Congress volunteer authoritatively. "The government has allowed him out of gaol only if he will keep strictly within the limits of his propaganda for harijans,[16] for the removal of untouchability." And he walked away after this declamation, showing a little of the glory that he assumed, on account of his powerful position, as an official appointed to serve the community during the reception to be given to Gandhi.

"Harijan!" Bakha wondered what that meant. He had heard the word before in connection with Gandhi. "But it has something to do with us, the bhangis and chamars," he said to himself. "We are harijans, sons of God." He recalled how some Congress men had come to the outcastes' street a month ago and lectured about harijans, saying they were no different from the Hindus and their touch did not mean pollution. The phrase, as it dropped from the mouth of the volunteer, had gone through Bakha's soul and body. He knew it applied to him. "It is good that I came!" he thought. "Is he really going to talk about the outcastes, about us, about Chota, Ram Charan, my father and me? What will he say, I wonder? Strange that the sahib of the Mukti said that the rich and the poor, the Brahmins and bhangis are the same. Now Gandhi Mahatma will talk about us! It is good that I came. If only he knew what had happened to me this morning. I would like to get up and tell him." He imagined himself rising on the platform, when all was still and the meeting had begun, and telling the Mahatma that a man from the city, where he had come to remove untouchability, had abused him for accidentally touching him and had also slapped him. Then the Mathatma would chastise that man, perhaps, or, at least, he would chide the citizens here, and they wouldn't treat him again as they did this morning. He seemed to get a thrill, imagining himself in this scene. He felt theatrical. Then a queer stirring started in his stomach. He was confused. His face was flushed and his ears reddened. His breath came and went quickly. A chorus of "Mahatma Gandhi ki jai," released his tension, as it came from the distance and chilled the heat of his body with a sudden fear that it brought to his soul.

He looked across and saw that a vast crowd had rushed the gates of the golbagh and surrounded a motor-car in which, presumably, the Mahatma was travelling. He didn't know what to do, stand still or rush. He realised he couldn't rush even though the Mahatma had abolished all caste distinctions for the day. He might touch someone and then there would be a scene. The Mahatma would be too far away to come and help him. He hesitated for a moment, then he looked at the tree overhead. There were some people perched on the branches like vultures waiting for their prey. He made for the trunk. His ammunition boots were an encumbrance but he scrambled up using his knees as rests against the round trunk. He looked not unlike an ape as he sat commanding a view of the advancing procession along the road.

Behind a screen of flower petals showered by ardent devotees under many coloured flags, with garlands of marigolds, jasmine and molsari around his neck, amid cries of "Mahatma Gandhi ki jai. Hindu — Mussulman — Sikh ki jai, Harijan ki jai," the great little man came into sight. His body was swathed in a milk-white blanket, and only his dark, clean-shaven head was visible, with its protruding big ears, its expansive forehead, its long nose, bridged by a pair of glasses. There was a quixotic smile on his thin lips, something Mephistophelean in the determined little chin immediately under his mouth and the long toothless jaws resting on his small neck. But withal there was something beautiful and saintly in the face,

[16]*harijans* low caste

whether it was the well-oiled scalp that glistened round the little tuft of hair on the top, or the aura of the astral self that shone like an aureole about him.

Bakha looked at the Mahatma with a mixed feeling of wonder, reverence, and fear. The sage seemed to him like a child, as he sat huddled up between two women, an Indian and an English woman.

"That's Kasturabai Gandhi," Bakha heard a schoolboy whisper to a friend, who sat on a branch of the tree next to him.

"And who is the other lady?" the boy asked.

"Mahatmaji's English disciple, Miss Slade, Miraben. She is the daughter of an English Admiral."

"He is black like me," Bakha said to himself. "But, of course, he must be very educated." And he waited tensely for the car which was marooned right under his eyes among the throngs of men and women seeking to touch the Mahatma's feet. The Congress volunteers struggled to carve a way through the turbans and fezes and boat-like Gandhi caps, and, at last, they succeeded in getting the open car under way. Half pushed, half towed, with the engines shut off, the Chauffeur steered the vehicle to the gate, improvised at one end of the oval, with broad-leafed banana-trees decorated with flowers and paper-festoons.

Bakha saw a sallow-faced Englishman, whom he knew to be the District Superintendent of Police, standing by the roadside in a khaki uniform of breeches, polished leather gaiters and blue puggareed, khaki sun helmet, not as smart as the military officers', but, of course, possessing for Bakha all the qualities of the sahib's clothes. Somehow, at this moment, Bakha was not interested in sahibs, probably because in the midst of this enormous crowd of Indians, fired with an enthusiasm for their leader, the foreigner seemed out of place, insignificant, the representative of an order which seemed to have nothing to do with the natives.

"Mahatma Gandhi ki jai! Mahatma Gandhi ki jai!" the cry went thundering up into the smoke-scented evening. Bakha's attention was switched off the man who held the sceptre of British rule in the form of his formidable truncheon, and turned to the diminutive figure of the Mahatma, now seated in the lotus seat on the Congress pandal, surrounded by devotees, who had come soft-footed up the steps, joined hands in obeisance to the master, touched the dust at his feet, and scattered to sit around him.

The Mahatma raised his right arm from the folds of his shawl and blessed the crowd with a gentle benediction. The babble of voices died out, as if he had sent an electric shock through the mass of humanity gathered at his feet. This strange man seemed to have the genius that could, by a single dramatic act, rally multi-coloured, multi-tongued India to himself. Someone stood up to chant a hymn. The Mahatma had closed his eyes and was praying. In the stillness of the moment, Bakha forgot all the details of his experience during the day, the touched man, the priest, the woman in the alley, his father, Chota, Ram Charan, the walk in the hills, the missionary and his wife. Except for the turbaned, capped and aproned heads of the men and women sitting on the grass before him, his eyes seemed intent on one thing and one thing alone, Gandhi, and he heard each syllable of the Hindi hymn:

"The dawn is here, O traveller arise;
Past is the night, and yet sleep seals thine eyes.
Lost is the soul that sleeps — dost not thou know?
The sleepless one finds peace beyond all woe.
Oh, waken! Shed thou thy slumber deep

Remember him who made thee and oh, weep.
For shame, is this the way of love—to sleep
When he himself doth ceaseless vigil keep?
"Repent O soul, from sin and find release,
O erring one, in sin there is no peace.
What boots it now to mourn on bended knees,
When thou thyself didst thine own load increase?
"What thou wouldst do tomorrow do today,
Do thou the task thou must face today.
What shall avail thy sorrow and dismay;
When thieving birds have borne thy grain away."

Bakha's attention began to flag. His mind wandered. He thought of the race he had to run to get here. He noticed how still everyone was. It irked him to see everyone so serious. The silence was getting on his nerves. But a part of him seemed to have flown, to have evaporated. He felt he had lost something of himself and was uneasy on account of it, yet thrilled about it, happy. He felt pleased to be sharing the privilege of being in a crowd gathered before the Mahatma. The hymn seemed so heavy. Yet the other feeling was light. The sage seemed so pure. And there was something intimate and warm about him. He smiled like a child. Bakha gazed at him. It was the only way in which he could escape feeling self-conscious. By doing that he forgot himself and everything else, as he felt he ought to. The brown and black faces below him were full of stilled rapture. He sought to feel like them, attentively absorbed. Luckily for him, just then, the Mahatma began his speech. It was a faint whisper at first, the Mahatma's voice, as it came through a loud-speaker:

"I have emerged," he said slowly, as if he were measuring each word and talking more to himself that to anyone else, "from an ordeal of a penance, undertaken for a cause which is as dear to me as life itself. The British Government sought to pursue a policy of divide and rule in giving to our brethren of the depressed classes separate electorates in the Councils that will be created under the new constitution. I do not believe that the bureaucracy is sincere in its efforts to elaborate the new constitution. But it is one of the conditions under which I have been released from gaol that I shall not carry on any propaganda against the government. So I shall not refer to that matter. I shall only speak about the so-called 'Untouchables,' whom the government tried to alienate from Hinduism by giving them a separate legal and political status.

"As you all know, while we are asking for freedom from the grip of a foreign nation, we have ourselves, for centuries, trampled underfoot millions of human beings without feeling the slightest remorse for our iniquity. For me, the question of these people is moral and religious. When I undertook to fast unto death for their sake, it was in obedience to the call of my conscience."

Bakha didn't understand these words. He was restless. He hoped the Mahatma wouldn't go on speaking of things he couldn't understand. He found his wish fulfilled, for a potent word interpreted his thoughts.

"I regard untouchability," the Mahatma was saying, "as the greatest blot on Hinduism. This view of mine dates back to the time when I was a child."

That was getting interesting. Bakha pricked up his ears.

"I was hardly yet twelve when this idea dawned on me. A scavenger named Uka, an Untouchable, used to attend our house for cleaning the latrines. Often I would ask my mother why it was wrong to touch him, and why I was forbidden to do so. If I accidentally touched Uka, I was asked to perform ablutions; and though I naturally obeyed, it was not without smilingly protesting that untouchability was not sanctioned by religion and that it was impossible that it should be so. I was a very dutiful and obedient child; but, so far as was consistent with respect for my parents, I often had arguments with them on this matter. I told my mother that she was entirely wrong in considering physical contact with Uka as sinful; it could not be sinful.

"While on my way to school, I used to touch the Untouchables; and, as I never would conceal the fact from my parents, my mother would tell me that the shortest cut to purification after the unholy touch, was to cancel it by touching a Mussulman passing by. Therefore, simply out of reverence and regard for my mother, I often did so, but never did it believing it to be a religious obligation."

As each part of the story which the Mahatma related about the beginning of his interest in untouchability fell on his ears, Bakha felt as if he were Uka, the scanvenger. By feeling like that, he thought, he would be nearer the sage who seemed a real and genuine sympathiser. "But the speech, the speech," he became aware that he was missing the words of the Mahatma's speech. He eagerly returned his attention.

"The fact that we address God as 'the purifier of the polluted souls' makes it a sin to regard anyone born in Hinduism as polluted—it is satanic to do so. I have never been tired of repeating that it is a great sin. I do not say that this thing crystallised in me at the age of twelve, but I do say that I did then regard untouchability as a sin.

"I was at Nellore on the National Day. I met the Untouchables there, and I prayed as I have done today. I do want to attain spiritual deliverance. I do not want to be reborn. But if I have to be reborn, I should wish to be reborn as an Untouchable, so that I may share their sorrows, sufferings and the affronts levelled at them, in order that I may endeavour to free myself and them from their miserable condition. Therefore, I prayed that, if I should be born again, I should be so, not as a Brahmin, Kshatriya, Vaishya, Shudra, but as an outcaste, as an Untouchable.

"I love scanvenging. In my ashram, an eighteen-year-old Brahmin lad is doing a scanvenger's work, in order to teach the ashram scavenger cleanliness. The lad is no reformer. He was born and bred in orthodoxy. He is a regular reader of the *Gita*, and faithfully says his prayers. When he conducts the prayers, his soft melodies melt one in love. But he felt that his accomplishments were incomplete until he had also become a perfect sweeper. He felt that if he wanted the ashram sweeper to do his work well he must do it himself and set an example."

Bakha felt thrilled. A tremor went down his spine. That the Mahatma should want to be born as an outcaste! That he should love scavenging! He adored the man. He felt he could put his life in his hands and ask him to do what he liked with it. For him he would do anything. He would like to go and be a scavenger at his ashram. "Then I could talk to him," he said to himself. "But I am not listening, I am not listening; I must listen."

"If there are any untouchables here," he heard the Mahatma say, "they should realise that they are cleaning Hindu society." (He felt like shouting to say that he, an Untouchable, was there, but he did not know what the Mahatma meant by "cleaning Hindu society.") He gave ear to the words with beating heart and heard: "They have, therefore, to purify their lives. They should cultivate the habits of cleanliness, so that no one shall point his finger at them. Some of them are addicted to habits of drinking and gambling, which they must get rid of.

"They claim to be Hindus. They read the scriptures. If, therefore, the Hindus oppress them, they should understand that the fault does not lie in the Hindu religion, but in those who profess it. In order to emancipate themselves they have to purify themselves. They have to rid themselves of evil habits, like drinking liquor and eating carrion."

But now, now the Mahatma is blaming us, Bakha felt. "That is not fair!" He wanted to forget the last passages that he had heard. He turned to the Mahatma.

"They should now cease to accept leavings from the plates of high-caste Hindus, however clean they may be represented to be. They should receive grain only — good, sound grain, not rotten grain — and that too, only if it is courteously offered. If they are able to do all that I have asked them to do, they will secure their emancipation."

That was more to Bakha's liking. He felt that he wanted to turn round and say to the Mahatma: "Now, Mahatmaji, now you are talking." He felt he would like to tell him that that very day, in that very town, where he was speaking, he had had to pick up a loaf of bread from near the gutter; that today, there, in that very city, his brother had had to accept leavings of food from the plates of the sepoys, and that they had all to eat it. Bakha visualised himself pitied by the Mahatma and consoled by him. It was such a balm, it was so comforting, the great man's sympathy. "If only he could go and tell my father not to be hard on me! If only he could go and tell him how I have suffered, if only he could go and tell my father he sympathises with me in my sufferings, my father would at once take me back and be kind to me ever afterwards."

"I am an orthodox Hindu and I know that the Hindus are not sinful by nature," Bakha heard the Mahatma declaim. "They are sunk in ignorance. All public wells, temples, roads, schools, sanatoriums, must be declared open to the Untouchables. And, if all of you profess to love me, give me a direct proof of your love by carrying on propaganda against the observance of untouchability. Do this, but let there be no compulsion or brute force in securing this end. Peaceful persuasion is the only means. Two of the strongest desires that keep me in the flesh are the emancipation of the Untouchables and the protection of the cow. When these two desires are fulfilled there is swaraj, and therein lies my soul's deliverance. May God give you strength to work out your soul's salvation to the end."

When the crowd scattered irreverently at the end of the Mahatma's speech, Bakha stood on the branch of the tree spellbound. Each word of the concluding passage seemed to him to echo as deep and intense a feeling of horror and indignation as his own at the distinction which the caste Hindus made between themselves and the Untouchables. The Mahatma seemed to have touched the most intimate corners of his soul. "To be sure, he is a good man," Bakha said.

Muffled cries of "Mahatmaji ki jai, Hindu-Mussulman ki jai, Harijan ki jai," arose from the middle of the throng again, and Bakha knew that the sage was going from the platform to the gate. He clung to his position on the tree, and was rewarded for his patience by the sight of the Mahatma passing beneath him.

A man seated on a high wooden board, with a bucket beside him, was distributing water in a silver tankard to Muhammadans in red fezes and Hindus in white Gandhi caps.

"He has made Hindu and Mussulman one," remarked a citizen, surcharged with the glow of brotherliness and humanitarianism which the Mahatma had left in his trail.

"Let's discard foreign cloth. Let's burn it!" the Congress volunteers were shouting. And true enough, Bakha saw people throwing their felt caps, their silk shirts and aprons into the pile, which soon became a blazing bonfire.

"Sister," said another citizen to a grass-cutter's wife, who struggled in her heavy accordion-pleated skirt to take her two children home, "let me help you through the crowd. Give me the big boy to hold."

There was only the one strange voice which dissented from all this.

"Gandhi is a humbug," it was saying. "He is a fool. He is a hypocrite. In one breath he says he wants to abolish untouchability, in the other he asserts that he is an orthodox Hindu. He is running counter to the spirit of our age, which is democracy. He is in the fourth century B.C. with his swadeshi and his spinning-wheel. We live in the twentieth. I have read Rousseau, Hobbes, Bentham and John Stuart Mill and I. . . . ."

Bakha came down the tree, like a black bear, and arrested the democrat's attention by the ridiculous sight he presented. He was going to slink away shyly, but the man, a fair-complexioned Muhammadan, dressed in the most smartly-cut English suit he had ever seen, interrupted him:

"Eh, eh, boy, come here. Go and get a bottle of soda-water."

Bakha came back with a start and stood staring at the dignitary who had called him. The man wore a monocle in his left eye and Bakha, who had never seen anything of that kind, wondered how a single glass could remain fixed on the eye without a frame.

"Don't stare at me!" shouted the gentleman, while Bakha was wondering who the man could be, too sallow-faced for an Englishman, too white for an Indian, and clad in such fine clothes, yellow gloves on his hands and white cloth on his buckskin shoes.

"Ham desi sahib, don't stare at me," said the man deliberately using the wrong Hindustani spoken by the English, but becoming kinder for a moment. "I have just come from Vilayat. Is there a soda-water shop near here?"

Bakha had been taken unawares. He couldn't adjust himself to this phenomenon. So he moved his head to indicate that he didn't know. Fortunately for him, the man's attention was switched off to his friend, a young man with a delicate feline face, illuminated by sparkling, dark eyes and long, black curly hair, who stood next to him dressed in flowing Indian robes like a poet's. Bakha's inadequate answer did not, therefore, evoke the insolent flourish of the barrister's cane as it might have done.

"It is very unfair of you to abuse the Mahatma," Bakha heard the young poet say gently, as he walked a little way away from the two men who were now surrounded by a group of people. "He is by far the greatest liberating force of our age. He has his limits, of course. But . . ."

"Precisely," Bakha heard his companion interrupt in fluent Hindustani. "That is exactly what I say. And my contention is. . . ."

"Yes, but listen, I haven't finished," the poet was saying. "He has his limitations but he is fundamentally sound. He may be wrong in wanting to shut India off from the rest of the world by preaching the revival of the spinning-wheel, because, as things are, that can't be done. But even in that regard he is right. For it is not India's fault that it is poor; it is the world's fault that the world is rich!——"

"You are talking in paradoxes. You have been reading Shaw," interrupted the monocled gentleman.

"Oh, forget Shaw! I am not a decadent Indian like you to be pandering to those European stars!" exclaimed the poet. "But you know that it is only in terms of our bitter poverty that India is behind the other countries of the world. In fact, it is one of the richest countries; it has abundant natural resources. Only it has chosen to remain agricultural and has suffered for not accepting the machine. We must, of course, remedy that. I hate the machine. I loathe it. But I shall go against Gandhi there and accept it. And I am sure in time all will learn to love it. And we shall beat our enslavers at their own game."

"They will put you into prison," someone interrupted from the crowd.

"Never mind that. I am not afraid of prison. I have already been a guest at His Majesty's boarding-house with a hundred thousand others who were imprisoned last year."

"The peasant who believes this world to be maya will not work the machine," remarked the supercilious barrister, as he adjusted his monocle to reflect the cynical glint in his eye.

"It is India's genius to accept all things," said the poet fiercely. "We have, throughout our long history, been realists, believing in the stuff of this world, in the here and the now, in the flesh and the blood. Man is born, and reborn, according to the *Upanishads*,[17] in this world, and even when he becomes an immortal saint there is no release for him, because he forms the stuff of the cosmos and is born again. We don't believe in the other world, as these Europeans would have you believe we do. There has been only one man in India who believed this world to be illusory—Shankracharya. But he was a consumptive and that made him neurotic. Early European scholars could not get hold of the original texts of the *Upanishads*. So they kept on interpreting Indian thought from the commentaries of Shankracharya. The word 'maya' does not mean illusion, it means a series of illusions. That is the dictum of the latest Hindu commentator of the *Vedas*, Coomaraswamy. And in that signification the word approximates to the views on the nature of the physical world of your pet scientists, Eddington and Jeans. The Victorians misinterpreted us. It was as if in order to give a philosophical background to their exploitation of India that they ingeniously concocted a nice little fairy story: 'You don't believe in this world; to you all this is maya. Let us look after your country for you and you can dedicate yourself to achieving nirvana.' But that is all over now. Right in the tradition of those who accepted the world and produced the baroque exuberance of Indian architecture and sculpture, with its profound sense of form, its solidity and its mass, we will accept and work the machine. But we will do so consciously. We can see through the idiocy of these Europeans who deified money. They were barbarians and lost their heads in the worship of gold. We can steer clear of the pitfalls, because we have the advantage of a race-consciousness six thousand years old, a race-consciousness which accepted all the visible and invisible values. We know life. We know its secret flow. We have danced to its rhythms. We have loved it, not sentimentally through personal feelings, but pervasively, stretching ourselves from our hearts outwards so far, oh, so far, that life seemed to have no limits, that miracles seemed possible. We can feel

[17]*Upanishads* sacred texts that discuss metaphysical problems (based on parts of the earlier *Vedas*); the source of all Indian philosphy (assumed to be fifth century B.C.)

new feelings. We can learn to be aware with a new awareness. We can envisage the possibility of creating new races from the latent heat in our dark brown bodies. Life is still an adventure for us. We are still eager to learn. We cannot go wrong. Our enslavers muddle through things. We can see things clearly. We will go the whole hog with regard to machines while they nervously fumble their way with the steam-engine. And we will keep our heads through it all. We will not become slaves to gold. We can be trusted to see life steadily and see it whole."

The harangue was impressive, with such fire was it delivered. Not only was the crowd moved but the anglicised Indian was silenced. Bakha was too much under the spell of Gandhi to listen intently to anyone else, and he did not follow much of what the poet said although he strained to catch his words.

"Who is he?" someone in the crowd queried.

"Iqbal Nath Sarashar, the young poet who edits the *Nawan Fug*, and his companion is Mr. R. N. Bashir, B.A. (Oxon.), Barrister-at-Law," someone volunteered the information.

There were whispers of consent and appreciation, but Mrs. Bashir's voice rose above the others in a derisive little chuckle.

"Ha, ha, ho ho! but what has all this got to do with untouchability? Gandhi's plea is an expression of his inferiority complex. I think. . . ."

"I know what you think," put in the poet fiercely, exciting some amusement from his brisk retort. "Let me tell you that with regard to untouchability the Mahatma is more sound than he is in his politics. You have swallowed all those cheap phrases about inferiority complex and superiority complex at Oxford without understanding what they mean. You slavishly copy the English in everything. . . ."

"That's right!" shouted a Congress volunteer. "Look at his silk neck-tie and the suit of foreign cloth that he is wearing! Shame!"

"The heredity and the environment of different people varies," continued the poet with a flourish of his hand to silence the rude Congress-wallah. "Some of us are born with big heads, some with small, some with more potential physical strength, some with less. There is one saint to a hundred million people, perhaps, one great man to a whole lot of mediocrities. But, essentially, that is to say humanly, all men are equal. 'Take a ploughman from the plough, wash off his dirt, and he is fit to rule a kingdom' is an old Indian proverb. The civility, the understanding and the gravity of the poorest of our peasants is a proof of that. Go and talk to a yokel and see how kind he is, how full of compliments, and how elegantly he speaks. And the equality of man is no new notion for him. If it had not been for the wily Brahmins, the priestcraft, who came in the pride of their white skin, lifted the pure philosophical idea of Karma from the Dravidians—that deeds and acts are dynamic, that all is in flux, everything changes—and misinterpreted it vulgarly to mean that birth and rebirth in this universe is governed by good or bad deeds in the past life, India would have offered the best instance of democracy. As it is, caste is an intellectual aristocracy, based on the conceit of the pundits, being otherwise wholly democratic. The high-caste High Court Judge eats freely with the coolie of his caste. So we can destroy our inequalities easily. The old, mechanical formulas of our lives must go; the old, stereotyped forms must give place to a new dynamic. We Indians live so deeply in our contacts; we are so acutely aware of our bloodstream. . . ."

"I can't understand what you mean," interrupted Bashir irritatedly. "You are confused."

"Well, we must destroy caste, we must destroy the inequalities of birth and unalterable vocations. We must recognise an equality of rights, privileges and opportunities for everyone. The Mahatma didn't say so, but the legal and social basis of caste having been broken down by the British-Indian penal code, which recognises the rights of every man before a court, caste is now mainly governed by profession. When the sweepers change their profession, they will no longer remain Untouchables. And they can do that soon, for the first thing we will do when we accept the machine will be to introduce the machine which clears dung without anyone having to handle it—the flush system. Then the sweepers can be free from the stigma of untouchability and assume the dignity of status that is their right as useful members of a casteless and classless society.

"In fact," mocked Bashir, "greater efficiency, better salesmanship, more mass-production, standardisation, dictatorship of the sweepers, Marxian materialism and all that!"

"Yes, yes, all that, but no catch words and cheap phrases. The change will be organic and not mechanical."

"All right, all right, come, don't let us stand here, I feel suffocated," said Mr. Bashir pulling out a silken handkerchief to wipe his face.

The crowd looked, ogled, stared with wonder at the celebrities and followed them at a little distance, till they disappeared in the unending throng of people going out of the golbagh.

Bakha had stood aside, beyond polluting distance, thinking vaguely of the few things he had understood from the poet's outburst. He felt that the poet would have been answering the most intimate questions in his soul, if he had not used such big words. "That machine," he thought, "which can remove dung without anyone having to handle it, I wonder what it is like? If only that 'gentreman' hadn't dragged the poet away, I could have asked him."

The fires of sunset were blazing on the distant horizon. As Bakha looked at the magnificent orb of terrible brightness glowing on the margin of the sky, he felt a burning sensation within him. His face, which had paled and contracted with thoughts a moment ago, reddened in a curious conflict of despair. He didn't know what to do, where to go. He seemed to have been smothered by the misery, the anguish of the morning's memories. He stood for a while where he had landed from the tree, his head bent, as if he were tired and broken. Then the last words of the Mahatma's speech seemed to resound in his ears: "May God give you the strength to work out your soul's salvation to the end." "What did that mean?" Bakha asked himself. The Mahatma's face appeared before him, enigmatic, ubiquitous. There was no answer to be found in it. Yet there was a queer kind of strength to be derived from it. Bakha recollected the words of his speech. It all seemed to stand out in his mind, every bit of it. Specially did the story of Uka come back. The Mahatma had talked of a Brahmin boy who did the scavenging in his ashram. "Did he mean, then, that I should go on scavenging?" Bakha asked himself. "Yes," came the forceful answer. "Yes," said Bakha, "I shall go on doing what Gandhi says. "But shall I never be able to leave the latrines?" came the disturbing thought. "But I can. Did not that poet say there is a machine which can do my work?" The prospect of never being able to wear the clothes that the sahibs wore, of never being able to become a sahib was horrible. "But it doesn't matter,"' he said to console himself, and pictured in his mind the English policeman, whom he had seen before the meeting, standing there, ignored by everybody.

He began to move. His virtues lay in his close-knit sinews and in his long-breathed sense. He was thinking of everything he had heard, though he could not understand it all. He was calm as he walked along, though the conflict in his soul was not over, though he was torn between his enthusiasm for Gandhi and the difficulties in his own awkward, naïve self.

The sun descended. The pale, the purple, the mauve of the horizon blended into darkest blue. A handful of stars throbbed in the heart of the sky.

He emerged from the green of the garden into the slight haze of dust that rose from the roads and the paths.

As the brief Indian twilight came and went, a sudden impulse shot through the transformations of space and time, and gathered all the elements that were dispersed in the stream of his soul into a tentative decision: "I shall go and tell father all that Gandhi said about us," he whispered to himself, "and all that the poet said. Perhaps I can find the poet on the way and ask him about his machine." And he proceeded homewards.

QUESTIONS

1. In his preface to the original edition of *Untouchable*, E. M. Forster wrote, "No Untouchable could have written the book, because he would have been involved in indignation and self-pity." How accurate is Forster's remark?
2. To what degree can it be argued that Bahka is a scapegoat?
3. Why does Bahka's father treat him so badly? Why does Singh, the hockey player, treat Bahka so decently? What are we to conclude of these opposites?
4. What was Anand's intent in including Bahka's sister, Sohini, in his story? Is her situation as bad as Bahka's?
5. Contemporary critics of Anand's novel have accursed him of writing propaganda, of being too didactic and sentimental. How valid are these criticisms? Should *Untouchable* be called a "protest" novel? Is such a category pejorative?
6. Bahka has been called a prisoner in his own culture. Are there people in American culture who can be called "untouchables"?
7. Does Anand resolve the conflict — the issue of Bahka's caste — by the end of his narrative? Are any of the three solutions that he proposes likely to eliminate the problem of untouchability?
8. What function does Mahatma Gandhi play in the story? Can you foresee a situation in Western fiction in which a historical equivalent might be brought into the narrative to resolve the conflict?
9. What can be said of the Western characters in Anand's story?
10. Is *Untouchable* still shocking today?

Kate Chopin

(1851 – 1904)

United States

Born Katherine O'Flaherty, Kate Chopin was the daughter of an Irish immigrant father and a French Creole mother. Raised in St. Louis, she lost her father, mother, and brother during her childhood and youth. At the age of 20 she married a French Creole cotton broker, Oscar Chopin, and settled in Louisiana. She bore six children in nine years while also attending to the social obligations required by her role as a successful New Orleans businessman's wife. When the business failed, the Chopins moved to central Louisiana, where they managed a large plantation until Oscar died of swamp fever in 1882, leaving Kate a widow of 32 with six children and few financial resources. Chopin returned with her children to St. Louis and began to write poetry and fiction that was published first in journals such as *Harper's Bazaar* and *Century*. In a relatively short 10 years, she published nearly two dozen poems, 95 short stories, 2 novels, a play, and several essays of literary criticism.

Kate Chopin's classification as a "regional writer" for years obscured the power of her best fiction to expose with probing insight the conflicting cultural and social values of her milieu, not only between people of different ethnic backgrounds and classes in the Creole South of Louisiana but also between men and women. A number of her stories, exploring such sensitive and even taboo themes as miscegenation, alcoholism, divorce, and female desire, shocked the sensibilities of her contemporaries. Other themes, many of which are explored in *The Awakening*, include the conflict between social custom and individual freedom or personal selfhood, and the gap between the inner and the outer life.

The Awakening, published in 1899, precipitated instant outrage from critics, readers, and library censors. Chopin's candid portrayal of female passion and sexuality led to such critical charges as that of the reviewer for the Providence *Sunday Journal*, who wrote, "It is not a healthy book." Other readers objected to Chopin's refusal to pass judgment on Edna Pontellier's abdication of her roles as wife and mother and her determination to take charge of her life at their expense. A reviewer for the St. Louis *Republic* pronounced the novel "too strong a drink for moral babes . . . and should be labeled poison."

Chopin wrote a "retraction" of sorts, which demonstrates that she had no intention of capitulating to her critics. As she phrased it for the St. Louis *Book News* (July 1899), "Having a group of people at my disposal, I thought it might be entertaining (to myself) to throw them together and see what would happen. I never dreamed of Mrs. Pontellier making such a mess of things and working out her own damnation as she did. If I had the slightest intimation of such a thing I would have excluded her from the company. But when I found out what she was up to, the play was half over and it was then too late."

Having survived despite the critical and popular outrage of its day, *The*

Awakening is now appreciated as a classic—a searching exploration of the desire for female selfhood in all its complexity at a time when such realizations were not allowed most women. Chopin's recognition of the need for inner freedom as a condition for creative expression, her use of evocative language to express emotional states, and her attention to the psychological dimension of her central characters' situations grant her inclusion among the modernist writers of the early twentieth century who introduced into fiction the direct expression of psychological and emotional states.

Written in a sensuous prose style that mirrors the stages of emotional realization of its protagonist, *The Awakening* is deeply pessimistic about the possibility of resolving the conflicts between desire and obligation, freedom and necessity. Nonetheless, Chopin charted a new area of female experience in her direct exploration of Edna Pontellier's yearning for selfhood during an era when its achievement could not be readily accommodated. As contemporary novelist Marilynne Robinson observes, "Kate Chopin gives her female protagonist the central role, normally reserved for Man, in a meditation on identity and culture, consciousness and art."

The Awakening

I

A green and yellow parrot, which hung in a cage outside the door, kept repeating over and over:

"*Allez vous-en! Allez vous-en! Sapristi!*[1] That's all right!"

He could speak a little Spanish, and also a language which nobody understood, unless it was the mocking-bird that hung on the other side of the door, whistling his fluty notes out upon the breeze with maddening persistence.

Mr. Pontellier, unable to read his newspaper with any degree of comfort, arose with an expression and an exclamation of disgust. He walked down the gallery and across the narrow "bridges" which connected the Lebrun cottages one with the other. He had been seated before the door of the main house. The parrot and the mocking-bird were the property of Madame Lebrun, and they had the right to make all the noise they wished. Mr. Pontellier had the privilege of quitting their society when they ceased to be entertaining.

He stopped before the door of his own cottage, which was the fourth one from the main building and next to the last. Seating himself in a wicker rocker which was there, he once more applied himself to the task of reading the newspaper. The day was Sunday; the paper was a day old. The Sunday papers had not yet reached Grand Isle. He was already acquainted with the market reports, and he glanced restlessly over the editorials and bits of news which he had not had time to read before quitting New Orleans the day before.

Mr. Pontellier wore eye-glasses. He was a man of forty, of medium height and rather slender build; he stooped a little. His hair was brown and straight, parted on one side. His beard was neatly and closely trimmed.

[1]"*Allez vous-en! Allez vous-en! Sapristi!*" French: "Go away! Go away! for God's sake!"

Italicized words in the text are French unless otherwise noted. Notes for *The Awakening* owe much to the textual and critical scholarship of Margaret Culley and Ronald Gottesman.

Once in a while he withdrew his glance from the newspaper and looked about him. There was more noise than ever over at the house. The main building was called "the house," to distinguish it from the cottages. The chattering and whistling birds were still at it. Two young girls, the Farival twins, were playing a duet from "Zampa" upon the piano. Madame Lebrun was bustling in and out, giving orders in a high key to a yard-boy whenever she got inside the house, and directions in an equally high voice to a dining-room servant whenever she got outside. She was a fresh, pretty woman, clad always in white with elbow sleeves. Her starched skirts crinkled as she came and went. Farther down, before one of the cottages, a lady in black was walking demurely up and down, telling her beads. A good many persons of the *pension* had gone over to the *Chênière Caminada*[2] in Beaudelet's lugger to hear mass. Some young people were out under the water-oaks playing croquet. Mr. Pontellier's two children were there — sturdy little fellows of four and five. A quadroon nurse followed them about with a far-away, meditative air.

Mr. Pontellier finally lit a cigar and began to smoke, letting the paper drag idly from his hand. He fixed his gaze upon a white sunshade that was advancing at snail's pace from the beach. He could see it plainly between the gaunt trunks of the water-oaks and across the stretch of yellow camomile. The gulf looked far away, melting hazily into the blue of the horizon. The sunshade continued to approach slowly. Beneath its pink-lined shelter were his wife, Mrs. Pontellier, and young Robert Lebrun. When they reached the cottage, the two seated themselves with some appearance of fatigue upon the upper step of the porch, facing each other, each leaning against a supporting post.

"What folly! to bathe[3] at such an hour in such heat!" exclaimed Mr. Pontellier. He himself had taken a plunge at daylight. That was why the morning seemed long to him.

"You are burnt beyond recognition," he added, looking at his wife as one looks at a valuable piece of personal property which has suffered some damage. She held up her hands, strong, shapely hands, and surveyed them critically, drawing up her lawn sleeves above the wrists. Looking at them reminded her of her rings, which she had given to her husband before leaving for the beach. She silently reached out to him, and he, understanding, took the rings from his vest pocket and dropped them into her open palm. She slipped them upon her fingers; then clasping her knees, she looked across at Robert and began to laugh. The rings sparkled upon her fingers. He sent back an answering smile.

"What is it?" asked Pontellier, looking lazily and amused from one to the other. It was some utter nonsense; some adventure out there in the water, and they both tried to relate it at once. It did not seem half so amusing when told. They realized this, and so did Mr. Pontellier. He yawned and stretched himself. Then he got up, saying he had half a mind to go over to Klein's hotel and play a game of billiards.

"Come go along, Lebrun," he proposed to Robert. But Robert admitted quite frankly that he preferred to stay where he was and talk to Mrs. Pontellier.

"Well, send him about his business when he bores you, Edna," instructed her husband as he prepared to leave.

[2]*Chênière Caminada* island between Grand Isle and the Louisiana coast; both islands are south of New Orleans; *pension* — small boarding hotel; *lugger* — passenger boat

[3]*bathe* swim

"Here, take the umbrella," she exclaimed, holding it out to him. He accepted the sunshade, and lifting it over his head descended the steps and walked away.

"Coming back to dinner?" his wife called after him. He halted a moment and shrugged his shoulders. He felt in his vest pocket; there was a ten-dollar bill there. He did not know; perhaps he would return for the early dinner and perhaps he would not. It all depended upon the company which he found over at Klein's and the size of "the game." He did not say this, but she understood it, and laughed, nodding good-by to him.

Both children wanted to follow their father when they saw him starting out. He kissed them and promised to bring them back bonbons and peanuts.

II

Mrs. Pontellier's eyes were quick and bright; they were a yellowish brown, about the color of her hair. She had a way of turning them swiftly upon an object and holding them there as if lost in some inward maze of contemplation or thought.

Her eyebrows were a shade darker than her hair. They were thick and almost horizontal, emphasizing the depth of her eyes. She was rather handsome than beautiful. Her face was captivating by reason of a certain frankness of expression and a contradictory subtle play of features. Her manner was engaging.

Robert rolled a cigarette. He smoked cigarettes because he could not afford cigars, he said. He had a cigar in his pocket which Mr. Pontellier had presented him with, and he was saving it for his after-dinner smoke.

This seemed quite proper and natural on his part. In coloring he was not unlike his companion. A clean-shaved face made the resemblance more pronounced than it would otherwise have been. There rested no shadow of care upon his open countenance. His eyes gathered in and reflected the light and languor of the summer day.

Mrs. Pontellier reached over for a palm-leaf fan that lay on the porch and began to fan herself, while Robert sent between his lips light puffs from his cigarette. They chatted incessantly: about the things around them; their amusing adventure out in the water — it had again assumed its entertaining aspect; about the wind, the trees, the people who had gone to the *Chênière*; about the children playing croquet under the oaks, and the Farival twins, who were now performing the overture to "The Poet and the Peasant." Robert talked a good deal about himself. He was very young, and did not know any better. Mrs. Pontellier talked a little about herself for the same reason. Each was interested in what the other said. Robert spoke of his intention to go to Mexico in the autumn, where fortune awaited him. He was always intending to go to Mexico, but some way never got there. Meanwhile he held on to his modest position in a mercantile house in New Orleans, where an equal familiarity with English, French and Spanish gave him no small value as a clerk and correspondent.

He was spending his summer vacation, as he always did, with his mother at Grand Isle. In former times, before Robert could remember, "the house" had been a summer luxury of the Lebruns. Now, flanked by its dozen or more cottages, which were always filled with exclusive visitors from the "*Quartier Français*,"[4] it

[4]*Quartier Français* The French Quarter of New Orleans, originally settled by the French in the early eighteenth century and occupied at the time of Chopin's story by wealthy, established families.

enabled Madame Lebrun to maintain the easy and comfortable existence which appeared to be her birthright.

Mrs. Pontellier talked about her father's Mississippi plantation and her girlhood home in the old Kentucky blue-grass country. She was an American woman, with a small infusion of French which seemed to have been lost in dilution. She read a letter from her sister, who was away in the East, and who had engaged herself to be married. Robert was interested, and wanted to know what manner of girls the sisters were, what the father was like, and how long the mother had been dead.

When Mrs. Pontellier folded the letter it was time for her to dress for the early dinner.

"I see Léonce isn't coming back," she said, with a glance in the direction whence her husband had disappeared. Robert supposed he was not, as there were a good many New Orleans club men over at Klein's.

When Mrs. Pontellier left him to enter her room, the young man descended the steps and strolled over toward the croquet players, where, during the half-hour before dinner, he amused himself with the little Pontellier children, who were very fond of him.

III

It was eleven o'clock that night when Mr. Pontellier returned from Klein's hotel. He was in an excellent humor, in high spirits, and very talkative. His entrance awoke his wife, who was in bed and fast asleep when he came in. He talked to her while he undressed, telling her anecdotes and bits of news and gossip that he had gathered during the day. From his trousers pockets he took a fistful of crumpled bank notes and a good deal of silver coin, which he piled on the bureau indiscriminately with keys, knife, handkerchief, and whatever else happened to be in his pockets. She was overcome with sleep, and answered him with little half utterances.

He thought it very discouraging that his wife, who was the sole object of his existence, evinced so little interest in things which concerned him, and valued so little his conversation.

Mr. Pontellier had forgotten the bonbons and peanuts for the boys. Notwithstanding he loved them very much, and went into the adjoining room where they slept to take a look at them and make sure that they were resting comfortably. The result of his investigation was far from satisfactory. He turned and shifted the youngsters about in bed. One of them began to kick and talk about a basket full of crabs.

Mr. Pontellier returned to his wife with the information that Raoul had a high fever and needed looking after. Then he lit a cigar and went and sat near the open door to smoke it.

Mrs. Pontellier was quite sure Raoul had no fever. He had gone to bed perfectly well, she said, and nothing had ailed him all day. Mr. Pontellier was too well acquainted with fever symptoms to be mistaken. He assured her the child was consuming[5] at that moment in the next room.

He reproached his wife with her inattention, her habitual neglect of the children. If it was not a mother's place to look after children, whose on earth was it?

[5]*consuming*—feverish (from *consumptive*)

He himself had his hands full with his brokerage business. He could not be in two places at once; making a living for his family on the street, and staying at home to see that no harm befell them. He talked in a monotonous, insistent way.

Mrs. Pontellier sprang out of bed and went into the next room. She soon came back and sat on the edge of the bed, leaning her head down on the pillow. She said nothing, and refused to answer her husband when he questioned her. When his cigar was smoked out he went to bed, and in half a minute he was fast asleep.

Mrs. Pontellier was by that time thoroughly awake. She began to cry a little, and wiped her eyes on the sleeve of her *peignoir*.[6] Blowing out the candle, which her husband had left burning, she slipped her bare feet into a pair of satin *mules*[6] at the foot of the bed and went out on the porch, where she sat down in the wicker chair and began to rock gently to and fro.

It was then past midnight. The cottages were all dark. A single faint light gleamed out from the hallway of the house. There was no sound abroad except the hooting of an old owl in the top of a water-oak, and the everlasting voice of the sea, that was not uplifted at that soft hour. It broke like a mournful lullaby upon the night.

The tears come so fast to Mrs. Pontellier's eyes that the damp sleeve of her *peignoir* no longer served to dry them. She was holding the back of her chair with one hand; her loose sleeve had slipped almost to the shoulder of her uplifted arm. Turning, she thrust her face, steaming and wet, into the bend of her arm, and she went on crying there, not caring any longer to dry her face, her eyes, her arms. She could not have told why she was crying. Such experiences as the foregoing were not uncommon in her married life. They seemed never before to have weighed much against the abundance of her husband's kindness and a uniform devotion which had come to be tacit and self-understood.

An indescribable oppression, which seemed to generate in some unfamiliar part of her consciousness, filled her whole being with a vague anguish. It was like a shadow, like a mist passing across her soul's summer day. It was strange and unfamiliar; it was a mood. She did not sit there inwardly upbraiding her husband, lamenting at Fate, which had directed her footsteps to the path which they had taken. She was just having a good cry all to herself. The mosquitoes made merry over her, biting her firm, round arms and nipping at her bare insteps.

The little stinging, buzzing imps succeeded in dispelling a mood which might have held her there in the darkness half a night longer.

The following morning Mr. Pontellier was up in good time to take the rockaway[7] which was to convey him to the steamer at the wharf. He was returning to the city to his business, and they would not see him again at the Island till the coming Saturday. He had regained his composure, which seemed to have been somewhat impaired the night before. He was eager to be gone, as he looked forward to a lively week in Carondelet Street.[8]

Mr. Pontellier gave his wife half of the money which he had brought away from Klein's hotel the evening before. She liked money as well as most women, and accepted it with no little satisfaction.

"It will buy a handsome wedding present for Sister Janet!" she exclaimed, smoothing out the bills as she counted them one by one.

[6]*peignoir* nightgown of fine fabric; *mules* lounging slippers that do not cover the heels

[7]*rockaway* a light, horse-drawn, open-sided carriage

[8]*Carondelet Street* the financial center of New Orleans

"Oh! we'll treat Sister Janet better than that, my dear," he laughed, as he prepared to kiss her good-by.

The boys were tumbling about, clinging to his legs, imploring that numerous things be brought back to them. Mr. Pontellier was a great favorite, and ladies, men, children, even nurses, were always on hand to say good-by to him. His wife stood smiling and waving, the boys shouting, as he disappeared in the old rockaway down the sandy road.

A few days later a box arrived for Mrs. Pontellier from New Orleans. It was from her husband. It was filled with *friandises*, with luscious and toothsome bits — the finest of fruits, *patés*, a rare bottle or two, delicious syrups, and bonbons in abundance.

Mrs. Pontellier was always very generous with the contents of such a box; she was quite used to receiving them when away from home. The *patés* and fruit were brought to the dining-room; the bonbons were passed around. And the ladies, selecting with dainty and discriminating fingers and a little greedily, all declared that Mr. Pontellier was the best husband in the world. Mrs. Pontellier was forced to admit that she knew of none better.

IV

It would have been a difficult matter for Mr. Pontellier to define to his own satisfaction or any one else's wherein his wife failed in her duty toward their children. It was something which he felt rather than perceived, and he never voiced the feeling without subsequent regret and ample atonement.

If one of the little Pontellier boys took a tumble whilst at play, he was not apt to rush crying to his mother's arms for comfort; he would more likely pick himself up, wipe the water out of his eyes and the sand out of his mouth, and go on playing. Tots as they were, they pulled together and stood their ground in childish battles with doubled fists and uplifted voices, which usually prevailed against the other mother-tots. The quadroon nurse was looked upon as a huge encumbrance, only good to button up waists and panties and to brush and part hair; since it seemed to be a law of society that hair must be parted and brushed.

In short, Mrs. Pontellier was not a mother-woman. The mother-women seemed to prevail that summer at Grand Isle. It was easy to know them, fluttering about with extended, protecting wings when any harm, real or imaginary, threatened their precious brood. They were women who idolized their children, worshiped their husbands, and esteemed it a holy privilege to efface themselves as individuals and grow wings as ministering angels.

Many of them were delicious in the rôle; one of them was the embodiment of every womanly grace and charm. If her husband did not adore her, he was a brute, deserving of death by slow torture. Her name was Adèle Ratignolle. There are no words to describe her save the old ones that have served so often to picture the bygone heroine of romance and the fair lady of our dreams. There was nothing subtle or hidden about her charms; her beauty was all there, flaming and apparent: the spun-gold hair that comb nor confining pin could restrain; the blue eyes that were like nothing but sapphires; two lips that pouted, that were so red one could only think of cherries or some other delicious crimson fruit in looking at them. She was growing a little stout, but it did not seem to detract an iota from the grace of every step, pose, gesture. One would not have wanted her white neck a mite less full or her beautiful arms more slender. Never were hands more exquisite than hers, and it was a joy to look at them when she threaded her needle or adjusted her gold thimble to her taper middle finger as she sewed away on the little night-drawers or fashioned a bodice or a bib.

Madame Ratignolle was very fond of Mrs. Pontellier, and often she took her sewing and went over to sit with her in the afternoons. She was sitting there the afternoon of the day the box arrived from New Orleans. She had possession of the rocker, and she was busily engaged in sewing upon a diminutive pair of night-drawers.

She had brought the pattern of the drawers for Mrs. Pontellier to cut out — a marvel of construction, fashioned to enclose a baby's body so effectually that only two small eyes might look out from the garment, like an Eskimo's. They were designed for winter wear, when treacherous drafts came down chimneys and insidious currents of deadly cold found their way through key-holes.

Mrs. Pontellier's mind was quite at rest concerning the present material needs of her children, and she could not see the use of anticipating and making winter night garments the subject of her summer meditations. But she did not want to appear unamiable and uninterested, so she had brought forth newspapers, which she spread upon the floor of the gallery, and under Madame Ratignolle's directions she had cut a pattern of the impervious garment.

Robert was there, seated as he had been the Sunday before, and Mrs. Pontellier also occupied her former position on the upper step, leaning listlessly against the post. Beside her was a box of bonbons, which she held out at intervals to Madame Ratignolle.

That lady seemed at a loss to make a selection, but finally settled upon a stick of nougat, wondering if it were not too rich; whether it could possibly hurt her. Madame Ratignolle had been married seven years. About every two years she had a baby. At that time she had three babies, and was beginning to think of a fourth one. She was always talking about her "condition." Her "condition" was in no way apparent, and no one would have known a thing about it but for her persistence in making it the subject of conversation.

Robert started to reassure her, asserting that he had known a lady who had subsisted upon nougat during the entire — but seeing the color mount into Mrs. Pontellier's face he checked himself and changed the subject.

Mrs. Pontellier, though she had married a Creole,[9] was not thoroughly at home in the society of Creoles; never before had she been thrown so intimately among them. There were only Creoles that summer at Lebrun's. They all knew each other, and felt like one large family, among whom existed the most amicable relations. A characteristic which distinguished them and which impressed Mrs. Pontellier most forcibly was their entire absence of prudery. Their freedom of expression was at first incomprehensible to her, though she had no difficulty in reconciling it with a lofty chastity which in the Creole woman seems to be inborn and unmistakable.

Never would Edna Pontellier forget the shock with which she heard Madame Ratignolle relating to old Monsieur Farival the harrowing story of one of her *accouchements*,[10] withholding no intimate detail. She was growing accustomed to

[9]*Creole* descendant of the original French and Spanish settlers of Louisiana — thus, an aristocrat (at this time)

[10]*accouchements* childbirths

like shocks, but she could not keep the mounting color back from her cheeks. Oftener than once her coming had interrupted the droll story with which Robert was entertaining some amused group of married women.

A book had gone the rounds of the *pension*. When it came her turn to read it, she did so with profound astonishment. She felt moved to read the book in secret and solitude, though none of the others had done so — to hide it from view at the sound of approaching footsteps. It was openly criticised and freely discussed at table. Mrs. Pontellier gave over being astonished, and concluded that wonders would never cease.

V

They formed a congenial group sitting there that summer afternoon — Madame Ratignolle sewing away, often stopping to relate a story or incident with much expressive gesture of her perfect hands; Robert and Mrs. Pontellier sitting idle, exchanging occasional words, glances or smiles which indicated a certain advanced stage of intimacy and *camaraderie*.[11]

He had lived in her shadow during the past month. No one thought anything of it. Many had predicted that Robert would devote himself to Mrs. Pontellier when he arrived. Since the age of fifteen, which was eleven years before, Robert each summer at Grand Isle had constituted himself the devoted attendant of some fair dame or damsel. Sometimes it was a young girl, again a widow; but as often as not it was some interesting married woman.

For two consecutive seasons he lived in the sunlight of Mademoiselle Duvigné's presence. But she died between summers; then Robert posed as an inconsolable, prostrating himself at the feet of Madame Ratignolle for whatever crumbs of sympathy and comfort she might be pleased to vouchsafe.

Mrs. Pontellier liked to sit and gaze at her fair companion as she might look upon a faultless Madonna.

"Could any one fathom the cruelty beneath that fair exterior?" murmured Robert. "She knew that I adored her once, and she let me adore her. It was 'Robert, come; go; stand up; sit down; do this; do that; see if the baby sleeps; my thimble, please, that I left God knows where. Come and read Daudet[12] to me while I sew.' "

"*Par exemple!* I never had to ask. You were always there under my feet, like a troublesome cat."

"You mean like an adoring dog. And just as soon as Ratignolle appeared on the scene, then it *was* like a dog. '*Passez! Adieu! Allez vous-en!*' "[13]

"Perhaps I feared to make Alphonse jealous," she interjoined, with excessive naïevté. That made them all laugh. The right hand jealous of the left! The heart jealous of the soul! But for that matter, the Creole husband is never jealous; with him the gangrene passion is one which has become dwarfed by disuse.

Meanwhile Robert, addressing Mrs. Pontellier, continued to tell of his one time hopeless passion for Madame Ratignolle; of sleepless nights, of consuming

[11]*camaraderie* friendship, companionship

[12]*Daudet* Alphonse Daŭdet (1840–1887), French novelist

[13]"*Par exemple!*" "For goodness's sake!" "*Passez! Adieu! Allez vous-en!*" — "Go on! Good-bye! Go away!"

flames till the very sea sizzled when he took his daily plunge. While the lady at the needle kept up a little running, contemptuous comment:

"Blagueur—farceur—gros bête, va!"[14]

He never assumed this serio-comic tone when alone with Mrs. Pontellier. She never knew precisely what to make of it; at that moment it was impossible for her to guess how much of it was jest and what proportion was earnest. It was understood that he had often spoken words of love to Madame Ratignolle, without any thought of being taken seriously. Mrs. Pontellier was glad he had not assumed a similar rôle toward herself. It would have been unacceptable and annoying.

Mrs. Pontellier had brought her sketching materials, which she sometimes dabbled with in an unprofessional way. She liked the dabbling. She felt in it satisfaction of a kind which no other employment afforded her.

She had long wished to try herself on Madame Ratignolle. Never had that lady seemed a more tempting subject than at that moment, seated there like some sensuous Madonna, with the gleam of the fading day enriching her splendid color.

Robert crossed over and seated himself upon the step below Mrs. Pontellier, that he might watch her work. She handled her brushes with a certain ease and freedom which came, not from long and close acquaintance with them, but from a natural aptitude. Robert followed her work with close attention, giving forth little ejaculatory expressions of appreciation in French, which he addressed to Madame Ratignolle.

"Mais ce n'est pas mal! Elle s'y connait, elle a de la force, oui."[15]

During his oblivious attention he once quietly rested his head against Mrs. Pontellier's arm. As gently she repulsed him. Once again he repeated the offense. She could not but believe it to be thoughtlessness on his part; yet that was no reason she should submit to it. She did not remonstrate, except again to repulse him quietly but firmly. He offered no apology.

The picture completed bore no resemblance to Madame Ratignolle. She was greatly disappointed to find that it did not look like her. But it was a fair enough piece of work, and in many respects satisfying.

Mrs. Pontellier evidently did not think so. After surveying the sketch critically she drew a broad smudge of paint across its surface, and crumpled the paper between her hands.

The youngsters came tumbling up the steps, the quadroon following at the respectful distance which they required her to observe. Mrs. Pontellier made them carry her paints and things into the house. She sought to detain them for a little talk and some pleasantry. But they were greatly in earnest. They had only come to investigate the contents of the bonbon box. They accepted without murmuring what she chose to give them, each holding out two chubby hands scoop-like, in the vain hope that they might be filled; and then away they went.

The sun was low in the west, and the breeze soft and languorous that came up from the south, charged with the seductive odor of the sea. Children, freshly befurbelowed,[16] were gathering for their games under the oaks. Their voices were high and penetrating.

[14]*"Blagueur—farceur—gros bête, va!"* "Joker—comedian—big beast, go on with you!

[15]*"Mais ce n'est pas mal! Elle s'y connait, elle a de la force, oui."* "But that's not bad! She knows what she's doing; yes, she has talent."

[16]*befurbelowed* dressed up

Madame Ratignolle folded her sewing, placing thimble, scissors and thread all neatly together in the roll, which she pinned securely. She complained of faintness. Mrs. Pontellier flew for the cologne water and a fan. She bathed Madame Ratignolle's face with cologne, while Robert plied the fan with unnecessary vigor.

The spell was soon over, and Mrs. Pontellier could not help wondering if there were not a little imagination responsible for its origin, for the rose tint had never faded from her friend's face.

She stood watching the fair woman walk down the long line of galleries with the grace and majesty which queens are sometimes supposed to possess. Her little ones ran to meet her. Two of them clung about her white skirts, the third she took from its nurse and with a thousand endearments bore it along in her own fond, encircling arms. Though, as everybody well knew, the doctor had forbidden her to lift so much as a pin!

"Are you going bathing?" asked Robert of Mrs. Pontellier. It was not so much a question as a reminder.

"Oh, no," she answered, with a tone of indecision. "I'm tired; I think not." Her glance wandered from his face away toward the Gulf, whose sonorous murmur reached her like a loving but imperative entreaty.

"Oh, come!" he insisted. "You mustn't miss your bath. Come on. The water must be delicious; it will not hurt you. Come."

He reached up for her big, rough straw hat that hung on a peg outside the door, and put it on her head. They descended the steps, and walked away together toward the beach. The sun was low in the west and the breeze was soft and warm.

VI

Edna Pontellier could not have told why, wishing to go to the beach with Robert, she should in the first place have declined, and in the second place have followed in obedience to one of the two contradictory impulses which impelled her.

A certain light was beginning to dawn dimly within her, — the light which, showing the way, forbids it.

At that early period it served but to bewilder her. It moved her to dreams, to thoughtfulness, to the shadowy anguish which had overcome her the midnight when she had abandoned herself to tears.

In short, Mrs. Pontellier was beginning to realize her position in the universe as a human being, and to recognize her relations as an individual to the world within and about her. This may seem like a ponderous weight of wisdom to descend upon the soul of a young woman of twenty-eight — perhaps more wisdom than the Holy Ghost is usually pleased to vouchsafe to any woman.

But the beginning of things, of a world especially, is necessarily vague, tangled, chaotic, and exceedingly disturbing. How few of us ever emerge from such beginning! How many souls perish in its tumult!

The voice of the sea is seductive; never ceasing, whispering, clamoring, murmuring, inviting the soul to wander for a spell in abysses of solitude; to lose itself in mazes of inward contemplation.

The voice of the sea speaks to the soul. The touch of the sea is sensuous, enfolding the body in its soft, close embrace.

VII

Mrs. Pontellier was not a woman given to confidences, a characteristic hitherto contrary to her nature. Even as a child she had lived her own small life all within herself. At a very early period she had apprehended instinctively the dual life — that outward existence which conforms, the inward life which questions.

That summer at Grand Isle she began to loosen a little the mantle of reserve that had always enveloped her. There may have been — there must have been — influences, both subtle and apparent, working in their several ways to induce her to do this; but the most obvious was the influence of Adèle Ratignolle. The excessive physical charm of the Creole had first attracted her, for Edna had a sensuous susceptibility to beauty. Then the candor of the woman's whole existence, which every one might read, and which formed so striking a contrast to her own habitual reserve — this might have furnished a link. Who can tell what metals the gods use in forging the subtle bond which we call sympathy, which we might as well call love.

The two women went away one morning to the beach together, arm in arm, under the huge white sunshade. Edna had prevailed upon Madame Ratignolle to leave the children behind, though she could not induce her to relinquish a diminutive roll of needlework, which Adèle begged to be allowed to slip into the depths of her pocket. In some unaccountable way they had escaped from Robert.

The walk to the beach was no inconsiderable one, consisting as it did of a long, sandy path, upon which a sporadic and tangled growth that bordered it on either side made frequent and unexpected inroads. There were acres of yellow camomile reaching out on either hand. Further away still, vegetable gardens abounded, with frequent small plantations of orange or lemon trees intervening. The dark green clusters glistened from afar in the sun.

The women were both of goodly height, Madame Ratignolle possessing the more feminine and matronly figure. The charm of Edna Pontellier's physique stole insensibly upon you. The lines of her body were long, clean and symmetrical; it was a body which occasionally fell into splendid poses; there was no suggestion of the trim, stereotyped fashion-plate about it. A casual and indiscriminating observer, in passing, might not cast a second glance upon the figure. But with more feeling and discernment he would have recognized the noble beauty of its modeling, and the graceful severity of poise and movement, which made Edna Pontellier different from the crowd.

She wore a cool muslin that morning — white, with a waving vertical line of brown running through it; also a white linen collar and the big straw hat which she had taken from the peg outside the door. The hat rested any way on her yellow-brown hair, that waved a little, was heavy, and clung close to her head.

Madame Ratignolle, more careful of her complexion, had twined a gauze veil about her head. She wore doeskin gloves, with gauntlets that protected her wrists. She was dressed in pure white, with a fluffiness of ruffles that became her. The draperies and fluttering things which she wore suited her rich, luxuriant beauty as a greater severity of line could not have done.

There were a number of bath-houses along the beach, of rough but solid construction, built with small, protecting galleries facing the water. Each house consisted of two compartments, and each family at Lebrun's possessed a compartment for itself, fitted out with all the essential paraphernalia of the bath and whatever other conveniences the owners might desire. The two women had no intention of bathing; they had just strolled down to the beach for a walk and to be alone and near the water. The Pontellier and Ratignolle compartments adjoined one another under the same roof.

Mrs. Pontellier had brought down her key through force of habit. Unlocking the door of her bath-room she went inside, and soon emerged, bringing a rug, which she spread upon the floor of the gallery, and two huge hair pillows covered with crash, which she placed against the front of the building.

The two seated themselves there in the shade of the porch, side by side, with their backs against the pillows and their feet extended. Madame Ratignolle removed her veil, wiped her face with a rather delicate handkerchief, and fanned herself with the fan which she always carried suspended somewhere about her person by a long, narrow ribbon. Edna removed her collar and opened her dress at the throat. She took the fan from Madame Ratignolle and began to fan both herself and her companion. It was very warm, and for a while they did nothing but exchange remarks about the heat, the sun, the glare. But there was a breeze blowing, a choppy, stiff wind that whipped the water into froth. It fluttered the skirts of the two women and kept them for a while engaged in adjusting, readjusting, tucking in, securing hair-pins and hat-pins. A few persons were sporting some distance away in the water. The beach was very still of human sound at that hour. The lady in black was reading her morning devotions on the porch of a neighboring bath-house. Two young lovers were exchanging their hearts' yearnings beneath the children's tent, which they had found unoccupied.

Edna Pontellier, casting her eyes about, had finally kept them at rest upon the sea. The day was clear and carried the gaze out as far as the blue sky went; there were a few white clouds suspended idly over the horizon. A lateen sail was visible in the direction of Cat Island, and others to the south seemed almost motionless in the far distance.

"Of whom — of what are you thinking?" asked Adèle of her companion, whose countenance she had been watching with a little amused attention, arrested by the absorbed expression which seemed to have seized and fixed every feature into a statuesque repose.

"Nothing," returned Mrs. Pontellier, with a start, adding at once: "How stupid! But it seems to me it is the reply we make instinctively to such a question. Let me see," she went on, throwing back her head and narrowing her fine eyes till they shone like two vivid points of light. "Let me see. I was really not conscious of thinking of anything; but perhaps I can retrace my thoughts."

"Oh! never mind!" laughed Madame Ratignolle. "I am not quite so exacting. I will let you off this time. It is really too hot to think, especially to think about thinking."

"But for the fun of it," persisted Edna. "First of all, the sight of the water stretching so far away, those motionless sails against the blue sky, made a delicious picture that I just wanted to sit and look at. The hot wind beating in my face made me think — without any connection that I can trace — of a summer day in Kentucky, of a meadow that seemed as big as the ocean to the very little girl walking through the grass, which was higher than her waist. She threw out her arms as if swimming when she walked, beating the tall grass as one strikes out in the water. Oh, I see the connection now!"

"Where were you going that day in Kentucky, walking through the grass?"

"I don't remember now. I was just walking diagonally across a big field. My sun-bonnet obstructed the view. I could see only the stretch of green before me, and I felt as if I must walk on forever, without coming to the end of it. I don't remember whether I was frightened or pleased. I must have been entertained.

"Likely as not it was Sunday," she laughed; "and I was running away from prayers, from the Presbyterian service, read in a spirit of gloom by my father that chills me yet to think of."

"And have you been running away from prayers ever since, *ma chère*?" asked Madame Ratignolle, amused.

"No! oh, no!" Edna hastened to say. "I was a little unthinking child in those days, just following a misleading impulse without question. On the contrary, during one period of my life religion took a firm hold upon me; after I was twelve and until — until — why, I suppose until now, though I never thought much about it — just driven along by habit. But do you know," she broke off, turning her quick eyes upon Madame Ratignolle and leaning forward a little so as to bring her face quite close to that of her companion, "sometimes I feel this summer as if I were walking through the green meadow again; idly, aimlessly, unthinking and unguided."

Madame Ratignolle laid her hand over that of Mrs. Pontellier, which was near her. Seeing that the hand was not withdrawn, she clasped it firmly and warmly. She even stroked it a little, fondly, with the other hand, murmuring in an undertone, "*Pauvre chérie.*"[17]

The action was at first a little confusing to Edna, but she soon lent herself readily to the Creole's gentle caress. She was not accustomed to an outward and spoken expression of affection, either in herself or in others. She and her youngster sister, Janet, had quarreled a good deal through force of unfortunate habit. Her older sister, Margaret, was matronly and dignified, probably from having assumed matronly and housewifely responsibilities too early in life, their mother having died when they were quite young. Margaret was not effusive; she was practical. Edna had had an occasional girl friend, but whether accidentally or not, they seemed to have been all of one type — the self-contained. She never realized that the reserve of her own character had much, perhaps everything, to do with this. Her most intimate friend at school had been one of rather exceptional intellectual gifts, who wrote fine-sounding essays, which Edna admired and strove to imitate; and with her she talked and glowed over the English classics, and sometimes held religious and political controversies.

Edna often wondered at one propensity which sometimes had inwardly disturbed her without causing any outward show or manifestation on her part. At a very early age — perhaps it was when she traversed the ocean of waving grass — she remembered that she had been passionately enamored of a dignified and sad-eyed cavalry officer who visited her father in Kentucky. She could not leave his presence when he was there, nor remove her eyes from his face, which was something like Napoleon's, with a lock of black hair falling across the forehead. But the cavalry officer melted imperceptibly out of her existence.

At another time her affections were deeply engaged by a young gentleman who visited a lady on a neighboring plantation. It was after they went to Mississippi to live. The young man was engaged to be married to the young lady, and they sometimes called upon Margaret, driving over of afternoons in a buggy. Edna was a little miss, just merging into her teens; and the realization that she herself was

[17]"*Pauvre chérie.*" "Poor dear."

nothing, nothing, nothing to the engaged young man was a bitter affliction to her. But he, too, went the way of dreams.

She was a grown young woman when she was overtaken by what she supposed to be the climax of her fate. It was when the face and figure of a great tragedian began to haunt her imagination and stir her senses. The persistence of the infatuation lent it an aspect of genuineness. The hopelessness of it colored it with the lofty tones of a great passion.

The picture of the tragedian stood enframed upon her desk. Any one may possess the portrait of a tragedian without exciting suspicion or comment. (This was a sinister reflection which she cherished.) In the presence of others she expressed admiration for his exalted gifts, as she handed the photograph around and dwelt upon the fidelity of the likeness. When alone she sometimes picked it up and kissed the cold glass passionately.

Her marriage to Léonce Pontellier was purely an accident, in this respect resembling many other marriages which masquerade as the decrees of Fate. It was in the midst of her secret great passion that she met him. He fell in love, as men are in the habit of doing, and pressed his suit with an earnestness and an ardor which left nothing to be desired. He pleased her; his absolute devotion flattered her. She fancied there was a sympathy of thought and taste between them, in which fancy she was mistaken. Add to this the violent opposition of her father and her sister Margaret to her marriage with a Catholic, and we need seek no further for the motives which led her to accept Monsieur Pontellier for her husband.

The acme of bliss, which would have been a marriage with the tragedian, was not for her in this world. As the devoted wife of a man who worshiped her, she felt she would take her place with a certain dignity in the world of reality, closing the portals forever behind her upon the realm of romance and dreams.

But it was not long before the tragedian had gone to join the cavalry officer and the engaged young man and a few others; and Edna found herself face to face with the realities. She grew fond of her husband, realizing with some unaccountable satisfaction that no trace of passion or excessive and fictitious warmth colored her affection, thereby threatening its dissolution.

She was fond of her children in an uneven, impulsive way. She would sometimes gather them passionately to her heart; she would sometimes forget them. The year before they had spent part of the summer with their grandmother Pontellier in Iberville. Feeling secure regarding their happiness and welfare, she did not miss them except with an occasional intense longing. Their absence was a sort of relief, though she did not admit this, even to herself. It seemed to free her of a responsibility which she had blindly assumed and for which Fate had not fitted her.

Edna did not reveal so much as all this to Madame Ratignolle that summer day when they sat with faces upturned to the sea. But a good part of it escaped her. She had put her head down on Madame Ratignolle's shoulder. She was flushed and felt intoxicated with the sound of her own voice and the unaccustomed taste of candor. It muddled her like wine, or like a first breath of freedom.

There was the sound of approaching voices. It was Robert, surrounded by a troop of children, searching for them. The two little Pontelliers were with him, and he carried Madame Ratignolle's little girl in his arms. There were other children beside, and two nurse-maids followed, looking disagreeable and resigned.

The women at once rose and began to shake out their draperies and relax their muscles. Mrs. Pontellier threw the cushions and rug into the bath-house. The children all scampered off to the awning, and they stood there in a line, gazing upon the intruding lovers, still exchanging their vows and sighs. The lovers got up, with only a silent protest, and walked slowly away somewhere else.

The children possessed themselves of the tent, and Mrs. Pontellier went over to join them.

Madame Ratignolle begged Robert to accompany her to the house; she complained of cramp in her limbs and stiffness of the joints. She leaned draggingly upon his arm as they walked.

VIII

"Do me a favor, Robert," spoke the pretty woman at his side, almost as soon as she and Robert had started on their slow, homeward way. She looked up in his face, leaning on his arm beneath the encircling shadow of the umbrella which he had lifted.

"Granted; as many as you like," he returned, glancing down into her eyes that were full of thoughtfulness and some speculation.

"I only ask for one; let Mrs. Pontellier alone."

"*Tiens!*" he exclaimed, with a sudden, boyish laugh. "*Voilà que Madame Ratignolle est jalouse!*"[18]

"Nonsense! I'm in earnest; I mean what I say. Let Mrs. Pontellier alone."

"Why?" he asked; himself growing serious at his companion's solicitation.

"She is not one of us; she is not like us. She might make the unfortunate blunder of taking you seriously."

His face flushed with annoyance, and taking off his soft hat he began to beat it impatiently against his leg as he walked. "Why shouldn't she take me seriously?" he demanded sharply. "Am I a comedian, a clown, a jack-in-the-box? Why shouldn't she? You Creoles! I have no patience with you! Am I always to be regarded as a feature of an amusing programme? I hope Mrs. Pontellier does take me seriously. I hope she has discernment enough to find in me something besides the *blagueur*.[19] If I thought there was any doubt—"

"Oh, enough, Robert!" she broke into his heated outburst. "You are not thinking of what you are saying. You speak with about as little reflection as we might expect from one of those children down there playing in the sand. If your attentions to any married women here were ever offered with any intention of being convincing, you would not be the gentleman we all know you to be, and you would be unfit to associate with the wives and daughters of the people who trust you."

Madame Ratignolle had spoken what she believed to be the law and the gospel. The young man shrugged his shoulders impatiently.

"Oh! well! That isn't," slamming his hat down vehemently upon his head. "You ought to feel that such things are not flattering to say to a fellow."

"Should our whole intercourse consist of an exchange of compliments? *Ma foi!*"[20]

"It isn't pleasant to have a woman tell you—" he went on, unheedingly, but

[18]"*Violà que Madame Ratignolle est jalouse!*" "So, Madame Ratignolle is jealous!"

[19]*blagueur* liar

[20]"*Ma foi!*" "For heaven's sake!"

breaking off suddenly: "Now if I were like Arobin—you remember Alcée Arobin and that story of the consul's wife at Biloxi?" And he related the story of Alcée Arobin and the consul's wife; and another about the tenor of the French Opera, who received letters which should never have been written; and still other stories, grave and gay, till Mrs. Pontellier and her possible propensity for taking young men seriously was apparently forgotten.

Madame Ratignolle, when they had regained her cottage, went in to take the hour's rest which she considered helpful. Before leaving her, Robert begged her pardon for the impatience—he called it rudeness—with which he had received her well-meant caution.

"You made one mistake, Adéle," he said, with a light smile; "there is no earthly possibility of Mrs. Pontellier ever taking me seriously. You should have warned me against taking myself seriously. Your advice might then have carried some weight and given me subject for some reflection. *Au revoir*. But you look tired," he added, solicitously. "Would you like a cup of bouillon? Shall I stir you a toddy? Let me mix you a toddy with a drop of Angostura."[21]

She acceded to the suggestion of bouillon, which was grateful and acceptable. He went himself to the kitchen, which was a building apart from the cottages and lying to the rear of the house. And he himself brought her the golden-brown bouillon, in a dainty Sèvres cup, with a flaky cracker or two on the saucer.

She thrust a bare, white arm from the curtain which shielded her open door, and received the cup from his hands. She told him he was a *bon garçon*,[22] and she meant it. Robert thanked her and turned away toward "the house."

The lovers were just entering the grounds of the *pension*. They were leaning toward each other as the water-oaks bent from the sea. There was not a particle of earth beneath their feet. Their heads might have been turned upside-down, so absolutely did they tread upon blue ether. The lady in black, creeping behind them, looked a trifle paler and more jaded than usual. There was no sign of Mrs. Pontellier and the children. Robert scanned the distance for any such apparition. They would doubtless remain away till the dinner hour. The young man ascended to his mother's room. It was situated at the top of the house, made up of odd angles and a queer, sloping ceiling. Two broad dormer windows looked out toward the Gulf, and as far across it as a man's eye might reach. The furnishings of the room were light, cool, and practical.

Madame Lebrun was busily engaged at the sewing-machine. A little black girl sat on the floor, and with her hands worked the treadle of the machine. The Creole woman does not take any chances which may be avoided to imperiling her health.

Robert went over and seated himself on the broad sill of one of the dormer windows. He took a book from his pocket and began energetically to read it, judging by the precision and frequency with which he turned the leaves. The sewing-machine made a resounding clatter in the room; it was of a ponderous, by-gone make. In the lulls, Robert and his mother exchanged bits of desultory conversation.

"Where is Mrs. Pontellier?"

"Down at the beach with the children."

[21]*toddy* a drink of brandy or whiskey mixed with hot water, sugar, and sometimes spices; *Angostura* aromatic bitters derived from a tree in the rue family

[22]*bon garçon* both "nice fellow" and "good waiter"

"I promised to lend her the Goncourt.[23] Don't forget to take it down when you go; it's there on the bookshelf over the small table." Clatter, clatter, clatter, bang! for the next five or eight minutes.

"Where is Victor going with the rockaway?"

"The rockaway? Victor?"

"Yes; down there in front. He seems to be getting ready to drive away somewhere."

"Call him." Clatter, clatter!

Robert uttered a shrill, piercing whistle which might have been heard back at the wharf.

"He won't look up."

Madame Lebrun flew to the window. She called "Victor!" She waved a handkerchief and called again. The young fellow below got into the vehicle and started the horse off at a gallop.

Madame Lebrun went back to the machine, crimson with annoyance. Victor was the younger son and brother — a *tête montée,*[24] with a temper which invited violence and a will which no ax could break.

"Whenever you say the word I'm ready to thrash any amount of reason into him that he's able to hold."

"If your father had only lived!" Clatter, clatter, clatter, bang! It was a fixed belief with Madame Lebrun that the conduct of the universe and all things pertaining thereto would have been manifestly of a more intelligent and higher order had not Monsieur Lebrun been removed to other spheres during the early years of their married life.

"What do you hear from Montel?" Montel was a middle-aged gentleman whose vain ambition and desire for the past twenty years had been to fill the void which Monsieur Lebrun's taking off had left in the Lebrun household. Clatter, clatter, bang, clatter!

"I have a letter somewhere," looking in the machine drawer and finding the letter in the bottom of the work-basket. "He says to tell you he will be in Vera Cruz the beginning of next month" — clatter, clatter! — "and if you still have the intention of joining him" — bang! clatter, clatter, bang!

"Why didn't you tell me so before, mother? You know I wanted — " Clatter, clatter, clatter!

"Do you see Mrs. Pontellier starting back with the children? She will be in late to luncheon again. She never starts to get ready for luncheon till the last minute." Clatter, clatter! "Where are you going?"

"Where did you say the Goncourt was?"

IX

Every light in the hall was ablaze; every lamp turned as high as it could be without smoking the chimney or threatening explosion. The lamps were fixed at intervals against the wall, encircling the whole room. Some one had gathered orange and lemon branches, and with these fashioned graceful festoons between. The dark green of the branches stood out and glistened against the white muslin curtains

[23]*Goncourt* novel by French author Edmond de Goncourt (1822–1896)

[24]*tête montée* impulsive character

which draped the windows, and which puffed, floated, and flapped at the capricious will of a stiff breeze that swept up from the Gulf.

It was Saturday night a few weeks after the intimate conversation held between Robert and Madame Ratignolle on their way from the beach. An unusual number of husbands, fathers, and friends had come down to stay over Sunday; and they were being suitably entertained by their families, with the material help of Madame Lebrun. The dining tables had all been removed to one end of the hall, and the chairs ranged about in rows and in clusters. Each little family group had had its say and exchanged its domestic gossip earlier in the evening. There was now an apparent disposition to relax; to widen the circle of confidences and give a more general tone to the conversation.

Many of the children had been permitted to sit up beyond their usual bedtime. A small band of them were lying on their stomachs on the floor looking at the colored sheets of the comic papers which Mr. Pontellier had brought down. The little Pontellier boys were permitting them to do so, and making their authority felt.

Music, dancing, and a recitation or two were the entertainments furnished, or rather, offered. But there was nothing systematic about the programme, no appearance of prearrangement nor even premeditation.

At an early hour in the evening the Farival twins were prevailed upon to play the piano. They were girls of fourteen, always clad in the Virgin's colors, blue and white, having been dedicated to the Blessed Virgin at their baptism. They played a duet from "Zampa," and at the earnest solicitation of every one present followed it with the overture to "The Poet and the Peasant."

"*Allez vous-en! Sapristi!*" shrieked the parrot outside the door. He was the only being present who possessed sufficient candor to admit that he was not listening to these gracious performances for the first time that summer. Old Monsieur Farival, grandfather of the twins, grew indignant over the interruption and insisted upon having the bird removed and consigned to regions of darkness. Victor Lebrun objected; and his decrees were as immutable as those of Fate. The parrot fortunately offered no further interruption to the entertainment, the whole venom of his nature apparently having been cherished up and hurled against the twins in that one impetuous outburst.

Later a young brother and sister gave recitations, which every one present had heard many times at winter evening entertainments in the city.

A little girl performed a skirt dance in the center of the floor. The mother played her accompaniments and at the same time watched her daughter with greedy admiration and nervous apprehension. She need have had no apprehension. The child was mistress of the situation. She had been properly dressed for the occasion in black tulle and black silk tights. Her little neck and arms were bare, and her hair, artificially crimped, stood out like fluffy black plumes over her head. Her poses were full of grace, and her little black-shod toes twinkled as they shot out and upward with a rapidity and suddenness which were bewildering.

But there was no reason why every one should not dance. Madame Ratignolle could not, so it was she who gaily consented to play for the others. She played very well, keeping excellent waltz time and infusing an expression into the strains which was indeed inspiring. She was keeping up her music on account of the children, she said; because she and her husband both considered it a means of brightening the home and making it attractive.

Almost every one danced but the twins, who could not be induced to separate during the brief period when one or the other should be whirling around the room in the arms of a man. They might have danced together, but they did not think of it.

The children were sent to bed. Some went submissively; others with shrieks and protests as they were dragged away. They had been permitted to sit up till after the ice-cream, which naturally marked the limit of human indulgence.

The ice-cream was passed around with cake — gold and silver cake arranged on platters in alternate slices; it had been made and frozen during the afternoon back of the kitchen by two black women, under the supervision of Victor. It was pronounced a great success — excellent if it had only contained a little less vanilla or a little more sugar, if it had been frozen a degree harder, and if the salt might have been kept out of portions of it. Victor was proud of his achievement, and went about recommending it and urging every one to partake of it to excess.

After Mrs. Pontellier had danced twice with her husband, once with Robert, and once with Monsieur Ratignolle, who was thin and tall and swayed like a reed in the wind when he danced, she went out on the gallery and seated herself on the low window-sill, where she commanded a view of all that went on in the hall and could look out toward the Gulf. There was a soft effulgence in the east. The moon was coming up, and its mystic shimmer was casting a million lights across the distant, restless water.

"Would you like to hear Mademoiselle Reisz play?" asked Robert, coming out on the porch where she was. Of course Edna would like to hear Mademoiselle Reisz play; but she feared it would be useless to entreat her.

"I'll ask her," he said. "I'll tell her that you want to hear her. She likes you. She will come." He turned and hurried away to one of the far cottages, where Mademoiselle Reisz was shuffling away. She was dragging a chair in and out of her room, and at intervals objecting to the crying of a baby, which a nurse in the adjoining cottage was endeavoring to put to sleep. She was a disagreeable little woman, no longer young, who had quarreled with almost every one, owing to a temper which was self-assertive and a disposition to trample upon the rights of others. Robert prevailed upon her without any too great difficulty.

She entered the hall with him during a lull in the dance. She made an awkward, imperious little bow as she went in. She was a homely woman, with a small weazened face and body and eyes that glowed. She had absolutely no taste in dress, and wore a batch of rusty black lace with a bunch of artificial violets pinned to the side of her hair.

"Ask Mrs. Pontellier what she would like to hear me play," she requested of Robert. She sat perfectly still before the piano, not touching the keys, while Robert carried her message to Edna at the window. A general air of surprise and genuine satisfaction fell upon every one as they saw the pianist enter. There was a settling down, and a prevailing air of expectancy everywhere. Edna was a trifle embarrassed at being thus singled out for the imperious little woman's favor. She would not dare to choose, and begged that Mademoiselle Reisz would please herself in her selections.

Edna was what she herself called very fond of music. Musical strains, well rendered, had a way of evoking pictures in her mind. She sometimes liked to sit in the room of mornings when Madame Ratignolle played or practiced. One piece which that lady played Edna had entitled "Solitude." It was a short, plaintive, minor strain. The name of the piece was something else, but she called it "Solitude." When she heard it there came before her imagination the figure of a man standing beside a desolate rock on the seashore. He was naked. His attitude was one of hopeless resignation as he looked toward a distant bird winging its flight away from him.

Another piece called to her mind a dainty young woman clad in an Empire gown, taking mincing dancing steps as she came down a long avenue between tall hedges. Again, another reminded her of children at play, and still another of nothing on earth but a demure lady stroking a cat.

The very first chords which Mademoiselle Reisz struck upon the piano sent a keen tremor down Mrs. Pontellier's spinal column. It was not the first time she had heard an artist at the piano. Perhaps it was the first time she was ready, perhaps the first time her being was tempered to take an impress of the abiding truth.

She waited for the material pictures which she thought would gather and blaze before her imagination. She waited in vain. She saw no pictures of solitude, of hope, of longing, or of despair. But the very passions themselves were aroused within her soul, swaying it, lashing it, as the waves daily beat upon her splendid body. She trembled, she was choking, and the tears blinded her.

Mademoiselle had finished. She arose, and bowing her stiff, lofty bow, she went away, stopping for neither thanks nor applause. As she passed along the gallery she patted Edna upon the shoulder.

"Well, how did you like my music?" she asked. The young woman was unable to answer, she pressed the hand of the pianist convulsively. Mademoiselle Reisz perceived her agitation and even her tears. She patted her again upon the shoulder as she said:

"You are the only one worth playing for. Those others? Bah!" and she went shuffling and sidling on down the gallery toward her room.

But she was mistaken about "those others." Her playing had aroused a fever of enthusiasm. "What passion!" "What an artist!" "I have always said no one could play Chopin like Mademoiselle Reisz!" "That last prelude! *Bon Dieu!*[25] It shakes a man!"

It was growing late, and there was a general disposition to disband. But some one, perhaps it was Robert, thought of a bath at that mystic hour and under that mystic moon.

X

At all events Robert proposed it, and there was not a dissenting voice. There was not one but was ready to follow when he led the way. He did not lead the way, however, he directed the way; and he himself loitered behind with the lovers, who had betrayed a disposition to linger and hold themselves apart. He walked between them, whether with malicious or mischievous intent was not wholly clear, even to himself.

The Pontelliers and Ratignolles walked ahead; the women leaning upon the arms of their husbands. Edna could hear Robert's voice behind them, and could sometimes hear what he said. She wondered why he did not join them. It was unlike him not to. Of late he had sometimes held away from her for an entire day, redoubling his devotion upon the next and the next, as though to make up for hours that had been lost. She missed him the days when some pretext served to

[25]"*Bon Dieu!*" "Good Lord!"

take him away from her, just as one misses the sun on a cloudy day without having thought much about the sun when it was shining.

The people walked in little groups toward the beach. They talked and laughed; some of them sang. There was a band playing down at Klein's hotel, and the strains reached them faintly, tempered by the distance. There were strange, rare odors abroad—a tangle of the sea smell and of weeds and damp, new-plowed earth, mingled with the heavy perfume of a field of white blossoms somewhere near. But the night sat lightly upon the sea and the land. There was no weight of darkness; there were no shadows. The white light of the moon had fallen upon the world like the mystery and the softness of sleep.

Most of them walked into the water as though into a native element. The sea was quiet now, and swelled lazily in broad billows that melted into one another and did not break except upon the beach in little foamy crests that coiled back like slow, white serpents.

Edna had attempted all summer to learn to swim. She had received instructions from both the men and women; in some instances from the children. Robert had pursued a system of lessons almost daily; and he was nearly at the point of discouragement in realizing the futility of his efforts. A certain ungovernable dread hung about her when in the water, unless there was a hand near by that might reach out and reassure her.

But that night she was like the little tottering, stumbling, clutching child, who of a sudden realizes its powers, and walks for the first time alone, boldly and with over-confidence. She could have shouted for joy. She did shout for joy, as with a sweeping stroke or two she lifted her body to the surface of the water.

A feeling of exultation overtook her, as if some power of significant import had been given her to control the working of her body and her soul. She grew daring and reckless, overestimating her strength. She wanted to swim far out, where no woman had swum before.

Her unlooked-for achievement was the subject of wonder, applause, and admiration. Each one congratulated himself that his special teachings had accomplished this desired end.

"How easy it is!" she thought. "It is nothing," she said aloud; "why did I not discover before that it was nothing. Think of the time I have lost splashing about like a baby!" She would not join the groups in their sports and bouts, but intoxicated with her newly conquered power, she swam out alone.

She turned her face seaward to gather in an impression of space and solitude, which the vast expanse of water, meeting and melting with the moonlit sky, conveyed to her excited fancy. As she swam she seemed to be reaching out for the unlimited in which to lose herself.

Once she turned and looked toward the shore, toward the people she had left there. She had not gone any great distance—that is, what would have been a great distance for an experienced swimmer. But to her unaccustomed vision the stretch of water behind her assumed the aspect of a barrier which her unaided strength would never be able to overcome.

A quick vision of death smote her soul, and for a second of time appalled and enfeebled her senses. But by an effort she rallied her staggering faculties and managed to regain the land.

She made no mention of her encounter with death and her flash of terror, except to say to her husband, "I thought I should have perished out there alone."

"You were not so very far, my dear; I was watching you," he told her.

Edna went at once to the bath-house, and she had put on her dry clothes and was ready to return home before the others had left the water. She started to walk away alone. They all called to her and shouted to her. She waved a dissenting hand, and went on, paying no further heed to their renewed cries which sought to detain her.

"Sometimes I am tempted to think that Mrs. Pontellier is capricious," said Madame Lebrun, who was amusing herself immensely and feared that Edna's abrupt departure might put an end to the pleasure.

"I know she is," assented Mr. Pontellier; "sometimes, not often."

Edna had not traversed a quarter of the distance on her way home before she was overtaken by Robert.

"Did you think I was afraid?" she asked him, without a shade of annoyance.

"No; I knew you weren't afraid."

"Then why did you come? Why didn't you stay out there with the others?"

"I never thought of it."

"Thought of what?"

"Of anything. What difference does it make?"

"I'm very tired," she uttered, complainingly.

"I know you are."

"You don't know anything about it. Why should you know? I never was so exhausted in my life. But it isn't unpleasant. A thousand emotions have swept through me to-night. I don't comprehend half of them. Don't mind what I'm saying; I am just thinking aloud. I wonder if I shall ever be stirred again as Mademoiselle Reisz's playing moved me to-night. I wonder if any night on earth will ever again be like this one. It is like a night in a dream. The people about me are like some uncanny, half-human beings. There must be spirits abroad to-night."

"There are," whispered Robert. "Didn't you know this was the twenty-eighth of August?"

"The twenty-eighth of August?"

"Yes. On the twenty-eighth of August, at the hour of midnight, and if the moon is shining—the moon must be shining—a spirit that has haunted these shores for ages rises up from the Gulf. With its own penetrating vision the spirit seeks some one mortal worthy to hold him company, worthy of being exalted for a few hours into realms of the semi-celestials. His search has always hitherto been fruitless, and he has sunk back, disheartened, into the sea. But to-night he found Mrs. Pontellier. Perhaps he will never wholly release her from the spell. Perhaps she will never again suffer a poor, unworthy earthling to walk in the shadow of her divine presence."

"Don't banter me," she said, wounded at what appeared to be his flippancy. He did not mind the entreaty, but the tone with its delicate note of pathos was like a reproach. He could not explain; he could not tell her that he had penetrated her mood and understood. He said nothing except to offer her his arm, for, by her own admission, she was exhausted. She had been walking alone with her arms hanging limp, letting her white skirts trail along the dewy path. She took his arm, but she did not lean upon it. She let her hand lie listlessly, as though her thoughts were elsewhere—somewhere in advance of her body, and she was striving to overtake them.

Robert assisted her into the hammock which swung from the post before her door out to the trunk of a tree.

"Will you stay out here and wait for Mr. Pontellier?" he asked.

"I'll stay out here. Good-night."

"Shall I get you a pillow?"

"There's one here," she said, feeling about, for they were in the shadow.

"It must be soiled; the children have been tumbling it about."

"No matter." And having discovered the pillow, she adjusted it beneath her head. She extended herself in the hammock with a deep breath of relief. She was not a supercilious or an over-dainty woman. She was not much given to reclining in the hammock, and when she did so it was with no cat-like suggestion of voluptuous ease, but with a beneficent repose which seemed to invade her whole body.

"Shall I stay with you till Mr. Pontellier comes?" asked Robert, seating himself on the outer edge of one of the steps and taking hold of the hammock rope which was fastened to the post.

"If you wish. Don't swing the hammock. Will you get my white shawl which I left on the window-sill over at the house?"

"Are you chilly?"

"No; but I shall be presently."

"Presently?" he laughed. "Do you know what time it is? How long are you going to stay out here?"

"I don't know. Will you get the shawl?"

"Of course I will," he said, rising. He went over to the house, walking along the grass. She watched his figure pass in and out of the strips of moonlight. It was past midnight. It was very quiet.

When he returned with the shawl she took it and kept it in her hand. She did not put it around her.

"Did you say I should stay till Mr. Pontellier came back?"

"I said you might if you wished to."

He seated himself again and rolled a cigarette, which he smoked in silence. Neither did Mrs. Pontellier speak. No multitude of words could have been more significant than those moments of silence, or more pregnant with the first-felt throbbings of desire.

When the voices of the bathers were heard approaching, Robert said good-night. She did not answer him. He thought she was asleep. Again she watched his figure pass in and out of the strips of moonlight as he walked away.

XI

"What are you doing out here, Edna? I thought I should find you in bed," said her husband, when he discovered her lying there. He had walked up with Madame Lebrun and left her at the house. His wife did not reply.

"Are you asleep?" he asked, bending down close to look at her.

"No." Her eyes gleamed bright and intense, with no sleepy shadows, as they looked into his.

"Do you know it is past one o'clock? Come on," and he mounted the steps and went into their room.

"Edna!" called Mr. Pontellier from within, after a few moments had gone by.

"Don't wait for me," she answered. He thrust his head through the door.

"You will take cold out there," he said, irritably. "What folly is this? Why don't you come in?"

"It isn't cold; I have my shawl."

"The mosquitoes will devour you."

"There are no mosquitoes."

She heard him moving about the room; every sound indicating impatience and irritation. Another time she would have gone in at his request. She would, through habit, have yielded to his desire; not with any sense of submission or obedience to his compelling wishes, but unthinkingly, as we walk, move, sit, stand, go through the daily treadmill of the life which has been portioned out to us.

"Edna, dear, are you not coming in soon?" he asked again, this time fondly, with a note of entreaty.

"No; I am going to stay out here."

"This is more than folly," he blurted out. "I can't permit you to stay out there all night. You must come in the house instantly."

With a writhing motion she settled herself more securely in the hammock. She perceived that her will had blazed up, stubborn and resistant. She could not at that moment have done other than denied and resisted. She wondered if her husband had ever spoken to her like that before, and if she had submitted to his command. Of course she had; she remembered that she had. But she could not realize why or how she should have yielded, feeling as she then did.

"Léonce, go to bed," she said. "I mean to stay out here. I don't wish to go in, and I don't intend to. Don't speak to me like that again; I shall not answer you."

Mr. Pontellier had prepared for bed, but he slipped on an extra garment. He opened a bottle of wine, of which he kept a small and select supply in a buffet of his own. He drank a glass of the wine and went out on the gallery and offered a glass to his wife. She did not wish any. He drew up the rocker, hoisted his slippered feet on the rail, and proceeded to smoke a cigar. He smoked two cigars; then he went inside and drank another glass of wine. Mrs. Pontellier again declined to accept a glass when it was offered to her. Mr. Pontellier once more seated himself with elevated feet, and after a reasonable interval of time smoked some more cigars.

Edna began to feel like one who awakens gradually out of a dream, a delicious, grotesque, impossible dream, to feel again the realities pressing into her soul. The physical need for sleep began to overtake her; the exuberance which had sustained and exalted her spirit left her helpless and yielding to the conditions which crowded her in.

The stillest hour of the night had come, the hour before dawn, when the world seems to hold its breath. The moon hung low, and had turned from silver to copper in the sleeping sky. The old owl no longer hooted, and the water-oaks had ceased to moan as they bent their heads.

Edna arose, cramped from lying so long and still in the hammock. She tottered up the steps, clutching feebly at the post before passing into the house.

"Are you coming in, Léonce?" she asked, turning her face toward her husband.

"Yes, dear," he answered, with a glance following a misty puff of smoke. "Just as soon as I have finished my cigar."

XII

She slept but a few hours. They were troubled and feverish hours, disturbed with dreams that were intangible, that eluded her, leaving only an impression upon her half-awakened senses of something unattainable. She was up and dressed in the cool of the early morning. The air was invigorating and steadied somewhat her faculties. However, she was not seeking refreshment or help from any source, either external or from within. She was blindly following whatever impulse moved her, as if she had placed herself in alien hands for direction, and freed her soul of responsibility.

Most of the people at this early hour were still in bed and asleep. A few, who intended to go over to the *Chênière* for mass, were moving about. The lovers, who had laid their plans the night before, were already strolling toward the wharf. The lady in black, with her Sunday prayer-book, velvet and gold-clasped, and her Sunday silver beads, was following them at no great distance. Old Monsieur Farival was up, and was more than half inclined to do anything that suggested itself. He put on his big straw hat, and taking his umbrella from the stand in the hall, followed the lady in black, never overtaking her.

The little negro girl who worked Madame Lebrun's sewing-machine was sweeping the galleries with long, absent-minded strokes of the broom. Edna sent her up into the house to awaken Robert.

"Tell him I am going to the *Chênière*. The boat is ready; tell him to hurry."

He had soon joined her. She had never sent for him before. She had never asked for him. She had never seemed to want him before. She did not appear conscious that she had done anything unusual in commanding his presence. He was apparently equally unconscious of anything extraordinary in the situation. But his face was suffused with a quiet glow when he met her.

They went together back to the kitchen to drink coffee. There was no time to wait for any nicety of service. They stood outside the window and the cook passed them their coffee and a roll, which they drank and ate from the window-sill. Edna said it tasted good. She had not thought of coffee nor of anything. He told her he had often noticed that she lacked forethought.

"Wasn't it enough to think of going to the *Chênière* and waking you up?" she laughed. "Do I have to think of everything?—as Léonce says when he's in a bad humor. I don't blame him; he'd never be in a bad humor if it weren't for me."

They took a short cut across the sands. At a distance they could see the curious procession moving toward the wharf—the lovers, shoulder to shoulder, creeping; the lady in black, gaining steadily upon them; old Monsieur Farival, losing ground inch by inch, and a young barefooted Spanish girl, with a red kerchief on her head and a basket on her arm, bringing up the rear.

Robert knew the girl, and he talked to her a little in the boat. No one present understood what they said. Her name was Mariequita. She had a round, sly, piquant face and pretty black eyes. Her hands were small, and she kept them folded over the handle of her basket. Her feet were broad and coarse. She did not strive to hide them. Edna looked at her feet, and noticed the sand and slime between her brown toes.

Beaudelet grumbled because Mariequita was there, taking up so much room. In reality he was annoyed at having old Monsieur Farival, who considered himself the better sailor of the two. But he would not quarrel with so old a man as Monsieur Farival, so he quarreled with Mariequita. The girl was deprecatory at one moment, appealing to Robert. She was saucy the next, moving her head up and down, making "eyes" at Robert and making "mouths" at Beaudelet.

The lovers were all alone. They saw nothing, they heard nothing. The lady in black was counting her beads for the third time. Old Monsieur Farival talked incessantly of what he knew about handling a boat, and of what Beaudelet did not know on the same subject.

Edna liked it all. She looked Mariequita up and down, from her ugly brown toes to her pretty black eyes, and back again.

"Why does she look at me like that?" inquired the girl of Robert.

"Maybe she thinks you are pretty. Shall I ask her?"

"No. Is she your sweetheart?"

"She's a married lady, and has two children."

"Oh! well! Francisco ran away with Sylvano's wife, who had four children. They took all his money and one of the children and stole his boat."

"Shut up!"

"Does she understand?"

"Oh, hush!"

"Are those two married over there—leaning on each other?"

"Of course not," laughed Robert.

"Of course not," echoed Mariequita, with a serious, confirmatory bob of the head.

The sun was high up and beginning to bite. The swift breeze seemed to Edna to bury the sting of it into the pores of her face and hands. Robert held his umbrella over her.

As they went cutting sidewise through the water, the sails bellied taut, with the wind filling and overflowing them. Old Monsieur Farival laughed sardonically at something as he looked at the sails, and Beaudelet swore at the old man under his breath.

Sailing across the bay to the *Chênière Caminada*, Edna felt as if she were being borne away from some anchorage which had held her fast, whose chains had been loosening—had snapped the night before when the mystic spirit was abroad, leaving her free to drift whithersoever she chose to set her sails. Robert spoke to her incessantly; he no longer noticed Mariequita. The girl had shrimps in her bamboo basket. They were covered with Spanish moss. She beat the moss down impatiently, and muttered to herself sullenly.

"Let us go to Grande Terre to-morrow?" said Robert in a low voice.

"What shall we do there?"

"Climb up the hill to the old fort and look at the little wriggling gold snakes, and watch the lizards sun themselves."

She gazed away toward Grande Terre and thought she would like to be alone there with Robert, in the sun, listening to the ocean's roar and watching the slimy lizards writhe in and out among the ruins of the old fort.

"And the next day or the next we can sail to the Bayou Brulow," he went on.

"What shall we do there?"

"Anything—cast bait for fish."

"No; we'll go back to Grande Terre. Let the fish alone."

"We'll go wherever you like," he said. "I'll have Tonie come over and help me patch and trim my boat. We shall not need Beaudelet nor any one. Are you afraid of the pirogue?"[26]

"Oh, no."

"Then I'll take you some night in the pirogue when the moon shines. Maybe your Gulf spirit will whisper to you in which of these islands the treasures are hidden—direct you to the very spot, perhaps."

[26]*pirogue* canoe

"And in a day we should be rich!" she laughed. "I'd give it all to you, the pirate gold and every bit of treasure we could dig up. I think you would know how to spend it. Pirate gold isn't a thing to be hoarded or utilized. It is something to squander and throw to the four winds, for the fun of seeing the golden specks fly."

"We'd share it, and scatter it together," he said. His face flushed.

They all went together up to the quaint little Gothic church of Our Lady of Lourdes, gleaming all brown and yellow with paint in the sun's glare.

Only Beaudelet remained behind, tinkering at his boat, and Mariequita walked away with her basket of shrimps, casting a look of childish ill-humor and reproach at Robert from the corner of her eye.

XIII

A feeling of oppression and drowsiness overcame Edna during the service. Her head began to ache, and the lights on the altar swayed before her eyes. Another time she might have made an effort to regain her composure; but her one thought was to quit the stifling atmosphere of the church and reach the open air. She arose, climbing over Robert's feet with a muttered apology. Old Monsieur Farival, flurried, curious, stood up, but upon seeing that Robert had followed Mrs. Pontellier, he sank back into his seat. He whispered an anxious inquiry of the lady in black, who did not notice him or reply, but kept her eyes fastened upon the pages of her velvet prayer-book.

"I felt giddy and almost overcome," Edna said, lifting her hands instinctively to her head and pushing her straw hat up from her forehead. "I couldn't have stayed through the service." They were outside in the shadow of the church. Robert was full of solicitude.

"It was folly to have thought of going in the first place, let alone staying. Come over to Madame Antoine's; you can rest there." He took her arm and led her away, looking anxiously and continuously down into her face.

How still it was, with only the voice of the sea whispering through the reeds that grew in the salt-water pools! The long line of little gray, weather-beaten houses nestled peacefully among the orange trees. It must always have been God's day on that low, drowsy island, Edna thought. They stopped, leaning over a jagged fence made of sea-drift, to ask for water. A youth, a mild-faced Acadian, was drawing water from the cistern, which was nothing more than a rusty buoy, with an opening on one side, sunk in the ground. The water which the youth handed to them in a tin pail was not cold to taste, but it was cool to her heated face, and it greatly revived and refreshed her.

Madame Antoine's cot[27] was at the far end of the village. She welcomed them with all the native hospitality, as she would have opened her door to let the sunlight in. She was fat, and walked heavily and clumsily across the floor. She could speak no English, but when Robert made her understand that the lady who accompanied him was ill and desired to rest, she was all eagerness to make Edna feel at home and to dispose of her comfortably.

The whole place was immaculately clean, and the big, four-posted bed, snow-white, invited one to repose. It stood in a small side room which looked out across a narrow grass plot toward the shed, where there was a disabled boat lying keel upward.

[27]*cot* cottage

Madame Antoine had not gone to mass. Her son Tonie had, but she supposed he would soon be back, and she invited Robert to be seated and wait for him. But he went and sat outside the door and smoked. Madame Antoine busied herself in the large front room preparing dinner. She was boiling mullets over a few red coals in the huge fireplace.

Edna, left alone in the little side room, loosened her clothes, removing the greater part of them. She bathed her face, her neck and arms in the basin that stood between the windows. She took off her shoes and stockings and stretched herself in the very center of the high, white bed. How luxurious it felt to rest thus in a strange, quaint bed, with its sweet country odor of laurel lingering about the sheets and mattress! She stretched her strong limbs that ached a little. She ran her fingers through her loosened hair for a while. She looked at her round arms as she held them straight up and rubbed them one after the other, observing closely, as if it were something she saw for the first time, the fine, firm quality and texture of her flesh. She clasped her hands easily above her head, and it was thus she fell asleep.

She slept lightly at first, half awake and drowsily attentive to the things about her. She could hear Madame Antoine's heavy, scraping tread as she walked back and forth on the sanded floor. Some chickens were clucking outside the windows, scratching for bits of gravel in the grass. Later she half heard the voices of Robert and Tonie talking under the shed. She did not stir. Even her eyelids rested numb and heavily over her sleepy eyes. The voices went on—Tonie's slow, Acadian drawl, Robert's quick, soft, smooth French. She understood French imperfectly unless directly addressed, and the voices were only part of the other drowsy, muffled sounds lulling her senses.

When Edna awoke it was with the conviction that she had slept long and soundly. The voices were hushed under the shed. Madame Antoine's step was no longer to be heard in the adjoining room. Even the chickens had gone elsewhere to scratch and cluck. The mosquito bar was drawn over her; the old woman had come in while she slept and let down the bar. Edna arose quietly from the bed, and looking between the curtains of the window, she saw by the slanting rays of the sun that the afternoon was far advanced. Robert was out there under the shed, reclining in the shade against the sloping keel of the overturned boat. He was reading from a book. Tonie was no longer with him. She wondered what had become of the rest of the party. She peeped out at him two or three times as she stood washing herself in the little basin between the windows.

Madame Antoine had laid some coarse, clean towels upon a chair, and had placed a box of *poudre de riz*[28] within easy reach. Edna dabbed the powder upon her nose and cheeks as she looked at herself closely in the little distorted mirror which hung on the wall above the basin. Her eyes were bright and wide awake and her face glowed.

When she had completed her toilet she walked into the adjoining room. She was very hungry. No one was there. But there was a cloth spread upon the table that stood against the wall, and a cover was laid for one, with a crusty brown loaf and a bottle of wine beside the plate. Edna bit a piece from the brown loaf, tearing it with her strong, white teeth. She poured some of the wine into the glass and drank it down. Then she went softly out of doors, and plucking an orange from the

[28]*poudre de riz* rice powder or talcum powder

low-hanging bough of a tree, threw it at Robert, who did not know she was awake and up.

An illumination broke over his whole face when he saw her and joined her under the orange tree.

"How many years have I slept?" she inquired. "The whole island seems changed. A new race of beings must have sprung up, leaving only you and me as past relics. How many ages ago did Madame Antoine and Tonie die? and when did our people from Grand Isle disappear from the earth?"

He familiarly adjusted a ruffle upon her shoulder.

"You have slept precisely one hundred years. I was left here to guard your slumbers; and for one hundred years I have been out under the shed reading a book. The only evil I couldn't prevent was to keep a broiled fowl from drying up."

"If it has turned to stone, still will I eat it," said Edna, moving with him into the house. "But really, what has become of Monsieur Farival and the others?"

"Gone hours ago. When they found that you were sleeping they thought it best not to awake you. Any way, I wouldn't have let them. What was I here for?"

"I wonder if Léonce will be uneasy!" she speculated, as she seated herself at table.

"Of course not; he knows you are with me," Robert replied, as he busied himself among sundry pans and covered dishes which had been left standing on the hearth.

"Where are Madame Antoine and her son?" asked Edna.

"Gone to Vespers, and to visit some friends, I believe. I am to take you back in Tonie's boat whenever you are ready to go."

He stirred the smoldering ashes till the broiled fowl began to sizzle afresh. He served her with no mean repast, dripping the coffee anew and sharing it with her. Madame Antoine had cooked little else than the mullets, but while Edna slept Robert had foraged the island. He was childishly gratified to discover her appetite, and to see the relish with which she ate the food which he had procured for her.

"Shall we go right away?" she asked, after draining her glass and brushing together the crumbs of the crusty loaf.

"The sun isn't as low as it will be in two hours," he answered.

"The sun will be gone in two hours."

"Well, let it go; who cares!"

They waited a good while under the orange trees, till Madame Antoine came back, panting, waddling, with a thousand apologies to explain her absence. Tonie did not dare to return. He was shy, and would not willingly face any woman except his mother.

It was very pleasant to stay there under the orange trees, while the sun dipped lower and lower, turning the western sky to flaming copper and gold. The shadows lengthened and crept out like stealthy, grotesque monsters across the grass.

Edna and Robert both sat upon the ground—that is, he lay upon the ground beside her, occasionally picking at the hem of her muslin gown.

Madame Antoine seated her fat body, broad and squat, upon a bench beside the door. She had been talking all the afternoon, and had wound herself up to the story-telling pitch.

And what stories she told them! But twice in her life she had left the *Chênière Caminada*, and then for the briefest span. All her years she had squatted and waddled there upon the island, gathering legends of the Baratarians[29] and the sea. The night came on, with the moon to lighten it. Edna could hear the whispering voices of dead men and the click of muffled gold.

When she and Robert stepped into Tonie's boat, with the red lateen sail, misty spirit forms were prowling in the shadows and among the reeds, and upon the water were phantom ships, speeding to cover.

XIV

The youngest boy, Etienne, had been very naughty, Madame Ratignolle said, as she delivered him into the hands of his mother. He had been unwilling to go to bed and had made a scene; whereupon she had taken charge of him and pacified him as well as she could. Raoul had been in bed and asleep for two hours.

The youngster was in his long white nightgown, that kept tripping him up as Madame Ratignolle led him along by the hand. With the other chubby fist he rubbed his eyes, which were heavy with sleep and ill humor. Edna took him in her arms, and seating herself in the rocker, began to coddle and caress him, calling him all manner of tender names, soothing him to sleep.

It was not more than nine o'clock. No one had yet gone to bed but the children.

Léonce had been very uneasy at first, Madame Ratignolle said, and had wanted to start at once for the *Chênière*. But Monsieur Farival had assured him that his wife was only overcome with sleep and fatigue, that Tonie would bring her safely back later in the day; and he had thus been dissuaded from crossing the bay. He had gone over to Klein's, looking up some cotton broker whom he wished to see in regard to securities, exchanges, stocks, bonds, or something of the sort, Madame Ratignolle did not remember what. He said he would not remain away late. She herself was suffering from heat and oppression, she said. She carried a bottle of salts and a large fan. She would not consent to remain with Edna, for Monsieur Ratignolle was alone, and he detested above all things to be left alone.

When Etienne had fallen asleep Edna bore him into the back room, and Robert went and lifted the mosquito bar that she might lay the child comfortably in his bed. The quadroon had vanished. When they emerged from the cottage Robert bade Edna good-night.

"Do you know we have been together the whole livelong day, Robert—since early this morning?" she said at parting.

"All but the hundred years when you were sleeping. Good-night."

He pressed her hand and went away in the direction of the beach. He did not join any of the others, but walked alone toward the Gulf.

Edna stayed outside, awaiting her husband's return. She had no desire to sleep or to retire; nor did she feel like going over to sit with the Ratignolles, or to join Madame Lebrun and a group whose animated voices reached her as they sat in conversation before the house. She let her mind wander back over her stay at Grand Isle; and she tried to discover wherein this summer had been different from any and every other summer of her life. She could only realize that she herself—her present self—was in some way different from the other self. That she was

[29]*Baratarians* pirates who plundered in the area of Barataria Bay, located between Grand Isle and the mainland south of New Orleans.

seeing with different eyes and making the acquaintance of new conditions in herself that colored and changed her environment, she did not yet suspect.

She wondered why Robert had gone away and left her. It did not occur to her to think he might have grown tired of being with her the livelong day. She was not tired, and she felt that he was not. She regretted that he had gone. It was so much more natural to have him stay when he was not absolutely required to leave her.

As Edna waited for her husband she sang low a little song that Robert had sung as they crossed the bay. It began with "Ah! *Si ti savais,*" and every verse ended with "*si tu savais.*"[30]

Robert's voice was not pretentious. It was musical and true. The voice, the notes, the whole refrain haunted her memory.

XV

When Edna entered the dining-room one evening a little late, as was her habit, an unusually animated conversation seemed to be going on. Several persons were talking at once, and Victor's voice was predominating, even over that of his mother. Edna had returned late from her bath, had dressed in some haste, and her face was flushed. Her head, set off by her dainty white gown, suggested a rich, rare blossom. She took her seat at table between old Monsieur Farival and Madame Ratignolle.

As she seated herself and was about to begin to eat her soup, which had been served when she entered the room, several persons informed her simultaneously that Robert was going to Mexico. She laid her spoon down and looked about her bewildered. He had been with her, reading to her all the morning, and had never even mentioned such a place as Mexico. She had not seen him during the afternoon; she had heard some one say he was at the house, upstairs with his mother. This she had thought nothing of, though she was surprised when he did not join her later in the afternoon, when she went down to the beach.

She looked across at him, where he sat beside Madame Lebrun, who presided. Edna's face was a blank picture of bewilderment, which she never thought of disguising. He lifted his eyebrows with the pretext of a smile as he returned her glance. He looked embarrassed and uneasy.

"When is he going?" she asked of everybody in general, as if Robert were not there to answer for himself.

"To-night!" "This very evening!" "Did you ever!" "What possesses him!" were some of the replies she gathered, uttered simultaneously in French and English.

"Impossible!" she exclaimed. "How can a person start off from Grand Isle to Mexico at a moment's notice, as if he were going over to Klein's or to the wharf or down to the beach?"

"I said all along I was going to Mexico; I've been saying so for years!" cried Robert, in an excited and irritable tone, with the air of a man defending himself against a swarm of stinging insects.

Madame Lebrun knocked on the table with her knife handle.

"Please let Robert explain why he is going, and why he is going to-night," she called out. "Really, this table is getting to be more and more like Bedlam every day,

[30]"*Si tu savais*" "Couldst Thou But Know," a song by Irish composer and baritone Michael William Balfe (1808–1870)

with everybody talking at once. Sometimes — I hope God will forgive me — but positively, sometimes I wish Victor would lose the power of speech."

Victor laughed sardonically as he thanked his mother for her holy wish, of which he failed to see the benefit to anybody, except that it might afford her a more ample opportunity and license to talk herself.

Monsieur Farival thought that Victor should have been taken out in mid-ocean in his earliest youth and drowned. Victor thought there would be more logic in thus disposing of old people with an established claim for making themselves universally obnoxious. Madame Lebrun grew a trifle hysterical; Robert called his brother some sharp, hard names.

"There's nothing much to explain, mother," he said; though he explained, nevertheless — looking chiefly at Edna — that he could only meet the gentleman whom he intended to join at Vera Cruz by taking such and such a steamer, which left New Orleans on such a day; that Beaudelet was going out with his lugger-load of vegetables that night, which gave him an opportunity of reaching the city and making his vessel in time.

"But when did you make up your mind to all this?" demanded Monsieur Farival.

"This afternoon," returned Robert, with a shade of annoyance.

"At what time this afternoon?" persisted the old gentleman, with nagging determination, as if he were cross-questioning a criminal in a court of justice.

"At four o'clock this afternoon, Monsieur Farival," Robert replied, in a high voice and with a lofty air, which reminded Edna of some gentleman on the stage.

She had forced herself to eat most of her soup, and now she was picking the flaky bits of a *court bouillon*[31] with her fork.

The lovers were profiting by the general conversation on Mexico to speak in whispers of matters which they rightly considered were interesting to no one but themselves. The lady in black had once received a pair of prayer-beads of curious workmanship from Mexico, with very special indulgence attached to them, but she had never been able to ascertain whether the indulgence extended outside the Mexican border. Father Fochel of the Cathedral had attempted to explain it; but he had not done so to her satisfaction. And she begged that Robert would interest himself, and discover, if possible, whether she was entitled to the indulgence accompanying the remarkably curious Mexican prayer-beads.

Madame Ratignolle hoped that Robert would exercise extreme caution in dealing with the Mexicans, who, she considered, were a treacherous people, unscrupulous and revengeful. She trusted she did them no injustice in thus condemning them as a race. She had known personally but one Mexican, who made and sold excellent tamales, and whom she would have trusted implicitly, so soft-spoken was he. One day he was arrested for stabbing his wife. She never knew whether he had been hanged or not.

Victor had grown hilarious, and was attempting to tell an anecdote about a Mexican girl who served chocolate one winter in a restaurant in Dauphine Street. No one would listen to him but old Monsieur Farival, who went into convulsions over the droll story.

Edna wondered if they had all gone mad, to be talking and clamoring at that rate. She herself could think of nothing to say about Mexico or the Mexicans.

"At what time do you leave?" she asked Robert.

[31]*court bouillon* broth in which fish is poached

"At ten," he told her. "Beaudelet wants to wait for the moon."

"Are you all ready to go?"

"Quite ready. I shall only take a hand-bag, and shall pack my trunk in the city."

He turned to answer some question put to him by his mother, and Edna, having finished her black coffee, left the table.

She went directly to her room. The little cottage was close and stuffy after leaving the outer air. But she did not mind; there appeared to be a hundred different things demanding her attention indoors. She began to set the toilet-stand to rights, grumbling at the negligence of the quadroom, who was in the adjoining room putting the children to bed. She gathered together stray garments that were hanging on the backs of chairs, and put each where it belonged in closet or bureau drawer. She changed her gown for a more comfortable and commodious wrapper. She rearranged her hair, combing and brushing it with unusual energy. Then she went in and assisted the quadroon in getting the boys to bed.

They were very playful and inclined to talk — to do anything but lie quiet and go to sleep. Edna sent the quadroon away to her supper and told her she need not return. Then she sat and told the children a story. Instead of soothing it excited them, and added to their wakefulness. She left them in heated argument, speculating about the conclusion of the tale which their mother promised to finish the following night.

The little black girl came in to say that Madame Lebrun would like to have Mrs. Pontellier go and sit with them over at the house till Mr. Robert went away. Edna returned answer that she had already undressed, that she did not feel quite well, but perhaps she would go over to the house later. She started to dress again, and got as far advanced as to remove her *peignoir*. But changing her mind once more she resumed the *peignoir*, and went outside and sat down before her door. She was overheated and irritable, and fanned herself energetically for a while. Madame Ratignolle came down to discover what was the matter.

"All that noise and confusion at the table must have upset me," replied Edna, "and moreover, I hate shocks and surprises. The idea of Robert starting off in such a ridiculously sudden and dramatic way! As if it were a matter of life and death! Never saying a word about it all morning when he was with me."

"Yes," agreed Madame Ratignolle. "I think it was showing us all — you especially — very little consideration. It wouldn't have surprised me in any of the others; those Lebruns are all given to heroics. But I must say I should never have expected such a thing from Robert. Are you not coming down? Come on, dear; it doesn't look friendly."

"No," said Edna, a little sullenly. "I can't go to the trouble of dressing again; I don't feel like it."

"You needn't dress; you look all right; fasten a belt around your waist. Just look at me!"

"No," persisted Edna; "but you go on. Madame Lebrun might be offended if we both stayed away."

Madame Ratignolle kissed Edna good-night, and went away, being in truth rather desirous of joining in the general and animated conversation which was still in progress concerning Mexico and the Mexicans.

Somewhat later Robert came up, carrying his hand-bag.

"Aren't you feeling well?" he asked.

"Oh, well enough. Are you going right away?"

He lit a match and looked at his watch. "In twenty minutes," he said. The sudden and brief flare of the match emphasized the darkness for a while. He sat down upon a stool which the children had left out on the porch.

"Get a chair," said Edna.

"This will do," he replied. He put on his soft hat and nervously took it off again, and wiping his face with his handkerchief, complained of the heat.

"Take the fan," said Edna, offering it to him.

"Oh, no! Thank you. It does no good; you have to stop fanning some time, and feel all the more uncomfortable afterward."

"That's one of the ridiculous things which men always say. I have never known one to speak otherwise of fanning. How long will you be gone?"

"Forever, perhaps. I don't know. It depends upon a good many things."

"Well, in case it shouldn't be forever, how long will it be?"

"I don't know."

"This seems to me perfectly preposterous and uncalled for. I don't like it. I don't understand your motive for silence and mystery, never saying a word to me about it this morning." He remained silent, not offering to defend himself. He only said, after a moment:

"Don't part from me in an ill-humor. I never knew you to be out of patience with me before."

"I don't want to part in any ill-humor," she said. "But can't you understand? I've grown used to seeing you, to having you with me all the time, and your action seems unfriendly, even unkind. You don't even offer an excuse for it. Why, I was planning to be together, thinking of how pleasant it would be to see you in the city next winter."

"So was I," he blurted. "Perhaps that's the — " He stood up suddenly and held out his hand. "Good-by, my dear Mrs. Pontellier; good-by. You won't — I hope you won't completely forget me." She clung to his hand, striving to detain him.

"Write to me when you get there, won't you, Robert?" she entreated.

"I will, thank you. Good-by."

How unlike Robert! The merest acquaintance would have said something more emphatic than "I will, thank you; good-by," to such a request.

He had evidently already taken leave of the people over at the house, for he descended the steps and went to join Beaudelet, who was out there with an oar across his shoulder waiting for Robert. They walked away in the darkness. She could only hear Beaudelet's voice; Robert had apparently not even spoken a word of greeting to his companion.

Edna bit her handkerchief convulsively, striving to hold back and to hide, even from herself as she would have hidden from another, the emotion which was troubling — tearing — her. Her eyes were brimming with tears.

For the first time she recognized anew the symptoms of infatuation which she had felt incipiently as a child, as a girl in her earliest teens, and later as a young woman. The recognition did not lessen the reality, the poignancy of the revelation by any suggestion or promise of instability. The past was nothing to her; offered no lesson which she was willing to heed. The future was a mystery which she never attempted to penetrate. The present alone was significant; was hers, to torture her as it was doing then with the biting conviction that she had lost that which she had held, that she had been denied that which her impassioned, newly awakened being demanded.

XVI

"Do you miss your friend greatly?" asked Mademoiselle Reisz one morning as she came creeping up behind Edna, who had just left her cottage on her way to the beach. She spent much of her time in the water since she had acquired finally the art of swimming. As their stay at Grand Isle drew near its close, she felt that she could not give too much time to a diversion which afforded her the only real pleasurable moments that she knew. When Mademoiselle Reisz came and touched her upon the shoulder and spoke to her, the woman seemed to echo the thought which was ever in Edna's mind; or, better, the feeling which constantly possessed her.

Robert's going had some way taken the brightness, the color, the meaning out of everything. The conditions of her life were in no way changed, but her whole existence was dulled, like a faded garment which seems to be no longer worth wearing. She sought him everywhere — in others whom she induced to talk about him. She went up in the mornings to Madame Lebrun's room, braving the clatter of the old sewing-machine. She sat there and chatted at intervals as Robert had done. She gazed around the room at the pictures and photographs hanging upon the wall, and discovered in some corner an old family album, which she examined with the keenest interest, appealing to Madame Lebrun for enlightenment concerning the many figures and faces which she discovered between its pages.

There was a picture of Madame Lebrun with Robert as a baby, seated in her lap, a round-faced infant with a fist in his mouth. The eyes alone in the baby suggested the man. And that was he also in kilts, at the age of five, wearing long curls and holding a whip in his hand. It made Edna laugh, and she laughed, too, at the portrait in his first long trousers; while another interested her, taken when he left for college, looking thin, long-faced, with eyes full of fire, ambition and great intentions. But there was no recent picture, none which suggested the Robert who had gone away five days ago, leaving a void and wilderness behind him.

"Oh, Robert stopped having his pictures taken when he had to pay for them himself! He found wiser use for his money, he says," explained Madame Lebrun. She had a letter from him, written before he left New Orleans. Edna wished to see the letter, and Madame Lebrun told her to look for it either on the table or the dresser, or perhaps it was on the mantelpiece.

The letter was on the bookshelf. It possessed the greatest interest and attraction for Edna; the envelope, its size and shape, the post-mark, the handwriting. She examined every detail of the outside before opening it. There were only a few lines, setting forth that he would leave the city that afternoon, that he had packed his trunk in good shape, that he was well, and sent her his love and begged to be affectionately remembered to all. There was no special message to Edna except a postscript saying that if Mrs. Pontellier desired to finish the book which he had been reading to her, his mother would find it in his room, among other books there on the table. Edna experienced a pang of jealousy because he had written to his mother rather than to her.

Every one seemed to take for granted that she missed him. Even her husband, when he came down the Saturday following Robert's departure, expressed regret that he had gone.

"How do you get on without him, Edna?" he asked.

"It's very dull without him," she admitted. Mr. Pontellier had seen Robert in the city, and Edna asked him a dozen questions or more. Where had they met? On

Carondelet Street, in the morning. They had gone "in" and had a drink and a cigar together. What had they talked about? Chiefly about his prospects in Mexico, which Mr. Pontellier thought were promising. How did he look? How did he seem — grave, or gay, or how? Quite cheerful, and wholly taken up with the idea of his trip, which Mr. Pontellier found altogether natural in a young fellow about to seek fortune and adventure in a strange, queer country.

Edna tapped her foot impatiently, and wondered why the children persisted in playing in the sun when they might be under the trees. She went down and led them out of the sun, scolding the quadroon for not being more attentive.

It did not strike her as in the least grotesque that she should be making of Robert the object of conversation and leading her husband to speak of him. The sentiment which she entertained for Robert in no way resembled that which she felt for her husband, or had ever felt, or ever expected to feel. She had all her life long been accustomed to harbor thoughts and emotions which never voiced themselves. They had never taken the form of struggles. They belonged to her and were her own, and she entertained the conviction that she had a right to them and that they concerned no one but herself. Edna had once told Madame Ratignolle that she would never sacrifice herself for her children, or for any one. Then had followed a rather heated argument; the two women did not appear to understand each other or to be talking the same language. Edna tried to appease her friend, to explain.

"I would give up the unessential; I would give my money, I would give my life for my children; but I wouldn't give myself. I can't make it more clear; it's only something which I am beginning to comprehend, which is revealing itself to me."

"I don't know what you would call the essential, or what you mean by the unessential," said Madame Ratignolle, cheerfully; "but a woman who would give her life for her children could do no more than that — your Bible tells you so. I'm sure I couldn't do more than that."

"Oh, yes you could!" laughed Edna.

She was not surprised at Mademoiselle Reisz's question the morning that lady, following her to the beach, tapped her on the shoulder and asked if she did not greatly miss her young friend.

"Oh, good morning, Mademoiselle; is it you? Why, of course I miss Robert. Are you going down to bathe?"

"Why should I go down to bathe at the very end of the season when I haven't been in the surf all summer," replied the woman, disagreeably.

"I beg your pardon," offered Edna, in some embarrassment, for she should have remembered that Mademoiselle Reisz's avoidance of the water had furnished a theme for much pleasantry. Some among them thought it was on account of her false hair, or the dread of getting the violets wet, while others attributed it to the natural aversion for water sometimes believed to accompany the artistic temperament. Mademoiselle offered Edna some chocolates in a paper bag, which she took from her pocket, by way of showing that she bore no ill feeling. She habitually ate chocolates for their sustaining quality; they contained much nutriment in small compass, she said. They saved her from starvation, as Madame Lebrun's table was utterly impossible; and no one save so impertinent a woman as Madame Lebrun could think of offering such food to people and requiring them to pay for it.

"She must feel very lonely without her son," said Edna, desiring to change the subject. "Her favorite son, too. It must have been quite hard to let him go."

Mademoiselle laughed maliciously.

"Her favorite son! Oh, dear! Who could have been imposing such a tale upon you? Aline Lebrun lives for Victor, and for Victor alone. She has spoiled him into the worthless creature he is. She worships him and the ground he walks on. Robert is very well in a way, to give up all the money he can earn to the family, and keep the barest pittance for himself. Favorite son, indeed! I miss the poor fellow myself, my dear. I liked to see him and to hear him about the place — the only Lebrun who is worth a pinch of salt. He comes to see me often in the city. I like to play to him. That Victor! hanging would be too good for him. It's a wonder Robert hasn't beaten him to death long ago."

"I thought he had great patience with his brother," offered Edna, glad to be talking about Robert, no matter what was said.

"Oh! he thrashed him well enough a year or two ago," said Mademoiselle. "It was about a Spanish girl, whom Victor considered that he had some sort of claim upon. He met Robert one day talking to the girl, or walking with her, or bathing with her, or carrying her basket — I don't remember what; — and he became so insulting and abusive that Robert gave him a thrashing on the spot that has kept him comparatively in order for a good while. It's about time he was getting another."

"Was her name Mariequita?" asked Edna.

"Mariequita — yes, that was it; Mariequita. I had forgotten. Oh, she's a sly one, and a bad one, that Mariequita!"

Edna looked down at Mademoiselle Reisz and wondered how she could have listened to her venom so long. For some reason she felt depressed, almost unhappy. She had not intended to go into the water; but she donned her bathing suit, and left Mademoiselle alone, seated under the shade of the children's tent. The water was growing cooler as the season advanced. Edna plunged and swam about with an abandon that thrilled and invigorated her. She remained a long time in the water, half hoping that Mademoiselle Reisz would not wait for her.

But Mademoiselle waited. She was very amiable during the walk back, and raved much over Edna's appearance in her bathing suit. She talked about music. She hoped that Edna would go to see her in the city, and wrote her address with the stub of a pencil on a piece of card which she found in her pocket.

"When do you leave?" asked Edna.

"Next Monday; and you?"

"The following week," answered Edna, adding, "It has been a pleasant summer, hasn't it, Mademoiselle?"

"Well," agreed Mademoiselle Reisz, with a shrug, "rather pleasant, if it hadn't been for the mosquitoes and the Farival twins."

XVII

The Pontelliers possessed a very charming home on Esplanade Street in New Orleans. It was a large, double cottage, with a broad front veranda, whose round, fluted columns supported the sloping roof. The house was painted a dazzling white; the outside shutters, or jalousies, were green. In the yard, which was kept scrupulously neat, were flowers and plants of every description which flourishes in South Louisiana. Within doors the appointments were perfect after the conventional type. The softest carpets and rugs covered the floors; rich and tasteful draperies hung at doors and windows. There were paintings, selected with judgment and discrimination, upon the walls. The cut glass, the silver, the heavy damask which daily appeared upon the table were the envy of many women whose husbands were less generous than Mr. Pontellier.

Mr. Pontellier was very fond of walking about his house examining its various appointments and details, to see that nothing was amiss. He greatly valued his possessions, chiefly because they were his, and derived genuine pleasure from contemplating a painting, a statuette, a rare lace curtain—no matter what—after he had bought it and placed it among his household goods.

On Tuesday afternoons—Tuesday being Mrs. Pontellier's reception day[32]—there was a constant stream of callers—women who came in carriages or in the street cars, or walked when the air was soft and distance permitted. A light-colored mulatto boy, in dress coat and bearing a diminutive silver tray for the reception of cards, admitted them. A maid, in white fluted cap, offered the callers liqueur, coffee, or chocolate, as they might desire. Mrs. Pontellier, attired in a handsome reception gown, remained in the drawing-room the entire afternoon receiving her visitors. Men sometimes called in the evening with their wives.

This had been the programme which Mrs. Pontellier had religiously followed since her marriage, six years before. Certain evenings during the week she and her husband attended the opera or sometimes the play.

Mr. Pontellier left his home in the mornings between nine and ten o'clock, and rarely returned before half-past six or seven in the evening—dinner being served at half-past seven.

He and his wife seated themselves at table one Tuesday evening, a few weeks after their return from Grand Isle. They were alone together. The boys were being put to bed; the patter of their bare, escaping feet could be heard occasionally, as well as the pursuing voice of the quadroon, lifted in mild protest and entreaty. Mrs. Pontellier did not wear her usual Tuesday reception gown; she was in ordinary house dress. Mr. Pontellier, who was observant about such things, noticed it, as he served the soup and handed it to the boy in waiting.

"Tired out, Edna? Whom did you have? Many callers?" he asked. He tasted his soup and began to season it with pepper, salt, vinegar, mustard—everything within reach.

"There were a good many," replied Edna, who was eating her soup with evident satisfaction. "I found their cards when I got home; I was out."

"Out!" exclaimed her husband, with something like genuine consternation in his voice as he laid down the vinegar cruet and looked at her through his glasses. "Why, what could have taken you out on Tuesday? What did you have to do?"

"Nothing. I simply felt like going out, and I went out."

"Well, I hope you left some suitable excuse," said her husband, somewhat appeased, as he added a dash of cayenne pepper to the soup.

"No, I left no excuse. I told Joe to say I was out, that was all."

"Why, my dear, I should think you'd understand by this time that people don't do such things; we've got to observe *les convenances*[33] if we ever expect to get on and keep up with the procession. If you felt that you had to leave home this afternoon, you should have left some suitable explanation for your absence.

"This soup is really impossible; it's strange that woman hasn't learned yet to

[32]*reception day* the day of the week when a woman was "at home" to receive guests

[33]*les convenances* the social conventions

make a decent soup. Any free-lunch stand in town serves a better one. Was Mrs. Belthrop here?"

"Bring the tray with the cards, Joe. I don't remember who was here."

The boy retired and returned after a moment, bringing the tiny silver tray, which was covered with ladies' visiting cards. He handed it to Mrs. Pontellier.

"Give it to Mr. Pontellier," she said.

Joe offered the tray to Mr. Pontellier, and removed the soup.

Mr. Pontellier scanned the names of his wife's callers, reading some of them aloud, with comments as he read.

"'The Misses Delasidas,' I worked a big deal in futures for their father this morning; nice girls; it's time they were getting married. 'Mrs. Belthrop.' I tell you what it is, Edna; you can't afford to snub Mrs. Belthrop. Why, Belthrop could buy and sell us ten times over. His business is worth a good, round sum to me. You'd better write her a note. 'Mrs. James Highcamp,' Hugh! the less you have to do with Mrs. Highcamp, the better. 'Madame Laforcé.' Came all the way from Carrolton, too, poor old soul. 'Miss Wiggs,' 'Mrs. Eleanor Boltons.'" He pushed the cards aside.

"Mercy!" exclaimed Edna, who had been fuming. "Why are you taking the thing so seriously and making such a fuss over it?"

"I'm not making any fuss over it. But it's just such seeming trifles that we've got to take seriously; such things count."

The fish was scorched. Mr. Pontellier would not touch it. Edna said she did not mind a little scorched taste. The roast was in some way not to his fancy, and he did not like the manner in which the vegetables were served.

"It seems to me," he said, "we spend money enough in this house to procure at least one meal a day which a man could eat and retain his self-respect."

"You used to think the cook was a treasure," returned Edna, indifferently.

"Perhaps she was when she first came; but cooks are only human. They need looking after, like any other class of persons that you employ. Suppose I didn't look after the clerks in my office, just let them run things their own way; they'd soon make a nice mess of me and my business."

"Where are you going?" asked Edna, seeing that her husband arose from table without having eaten a morsel except a taste of the highly-seasoned soup.

"I'm going to get my dinner at the club. Good night." He went into the hall, took his hat and stick from the stand, and left the house.

She was somewhat familiar with such scenes. They had often made her very unhappy. On a few previous occasions she had been completely deprived of any desire to finish her dinner. Sometimes she had gone into the kitchen to administer a tardy rebuke to the cook. Once she went to her room and studied the cookbook during an entire evening, finally writing out a menu for the week, which left her harassed with a feeling that, after all, she had accomplished no good that was worth the name.

But that evening Edna finished her dinner alone, with forced deliberation. Her face was flushed and her eyes flamed with some inward fire that lighted them. After finishing her dinner she went to her room, having instructed the boy to tell any other callers that she was indisposed.

It was a large, beautiful room, rich and picturesque in the soft, dim light which the maid had turned low. She went and stood at an open window and looked out upon the deep tangle of the garden below. All the mystery and witchery of the night seemed to have gathered there amid the perfumes and the dusky and tortuous outlines of flowers and foliage. She was seeking herself and finding herself in just such sweet, half-darkness which met her moods. But the voices were not soothing that came to her from the darkness and the sky above and the stars. They jeered and sounded mournful notes without promise, devoid even of hope. She turned back into the room and began to walk to and fro down its whole length, without stopping, without resting. She carried in her hands a thin handkerchief, which she tore into ribbons, rolled into a ball, and flung from her. Once she stopped, and taking off her wedding ring, flung it upon the carpet. When she saw it lying there, she stamped her heel upon it, striving to crush it. But her small boot heel did not make an indenture, not a mark upon the little glittering circlet.

In a sweeping passion she seized a glass vase from the table and flung it upon the tiles of the hearth. She wanted to destroy something. The crash and clatter were what she wanted to hear.

A maid, alarmed at the din of breaking glass, entered the room to discover what was the matter.

"A vase fell upon the hearth," said Edna. "Never mind; leave it till morning."

"Oh! you might get some of the glass in your feet, ma'am," insisted the young woman, picking up bits of the broken vase that were scattered upon the carpet. "And here's your ring, ma'am, under the chair."

Edna held out her hand, and taking the ring, slipped it upon her finger.

XVIII

The following morning Mr. Pontellier, upon leaving for his office, asked Edna if she would not meet him in town in order to look at some new fixtures for the library.

"I hardly think we need new fixtures, Léonce. Don't let us get anything new; you are too extravagant. I don't believe you ever think of saving or putting by."

"The way to become rich is to make money, my dear Edna, not to save it," he said. He regretted that she did not feel inclined to go with him and select new fixtures. He kissed her good-by, and told her she was not looking well and must take care of herself. She was unusually pale and very quiet.

She stood on the front veranda as he quitted the house, and absently picked a few sprays of jessamine that grew upon a trellis near by. She inhaled the odor of the blossoms and thrust them into the bosom of her white morning gown. The boys were dragging along the banquette[34] a small "express wagon," which they had filled with blocks and sticks. The quadroon was following them with little quick steps, having assumed a fictitious animation and alacrity for the occasion. A fruit vender was crying his wares in the street.

Edna looked straight before her with a self-absorbed expression upon her face. She felt no interest in anything about her. The street, the children, the fruit vender, the flowers growing there under her eyes, were all part and parcel of an alien world which had suddenly become antagonistic.

She went back into the house. She had thought of speaking to the cook concerning her blunders of the previous night; but Mr. Pontellier had saved her that disagreeable mission, for which she was so poorly fitted. Mr. Pontellier's arguments were usually convincing with those whom he employed. He left home

[34]*banquette* sidewalk

feeling quite sure that he and Edna would sit down that evening, and possibly a few subsequent evenings, to a dinner deserving of the name.

Edna spent an hour or two in looking over some of her old sketches. She could see their shortcomings and defects, which were glaring in her eyes. She tried to work a little, but found she was not in the humor. Finally she gathered together a few of the sketches — those which she considered the least discreditable; and she carried them with her when, a little later, she dressed and left the house. She looked handsome and distinguished in her street gown. The tan of the seashore had left her face, and her forehead was smooth, white, and polished beneath her heavy, yellow-brown hair. There were a few freckles on her face, and a small, dark mole near the under lip and one on the temple, half-hidden in her hair.

As Edna walked along the street she was thinking of Robert. She was still under the spell of her infatuation. She had tried to forget him, realizing the inutility of remembering. But the thought of him was like an obsession, ever pressing itself upon her. It was not that she dwelt upon details of their acquaintance, or recalled in any special or peculiar way his personality; it was his being, his existence, which dominated her thought, fading sometimes as if it would melt into the mist of the forgotten, reviving again with an intensity which filled her with an incomprehensible longing.

Edna was on her way to Madame Ratignolle's. Their intimacy, begun at Grand Isle, had not declined, and they had seen each other with some frequency since their return to the city. The Ratignolles lived at no great distance from Edna's home, on the corner of a side street, where Monsieur Ratignolle owned and conducted a drug store which enjoyed a steady and prosperous trade. His father had been in the business before him, and Monsieur Ratignolle stood well in the community and bore an enviable reputation for integrity and clear-headedness. His family lived in commodious apartments over the store, having an entrance on the side within the *porte cochère*.[35] There was something which Edna thought very French, very foreign, about their whole manner of living. In the large and pleasant salon which extended across the width of the house, the Ratignolles entertained their friends once a fortnight with a *soirée musicale*,[36] sometimes diversified by card-playing. There was a friend who played upon the 'cello. One brought his flute and another his violin, while there were some who sang and a number who performed upon the piano with various degrees of taste and agility. The Ratignolles' *soirées musicales* were widely known, and it was considered a privilege to be invited to them.

Edna found her friend engaged in assorting the clothes which had returned that morning from the laundry. She at once abandoned her occupation upon seeing Edna, who had been ushered without ceremony into her presence.

"'Cité can do it as well as I; it is really her business," she explained to Edna, who apologized for interrupting her. And she summoned a young black woman, whom she instructed, in French, to be very careful in checking off the list which she handed her. She told her to notice particularly if a fine linen handkerchief of Monsieur Ratignolle's, which was missing last week, had been returned; and to be sure to set to one side such pieces as required mending and darning.

Then placing an arm around Edna's waist, she led her to the front of the house,

[35]*porte cochère* porch that shelters passengers boarding or alighting from carriages

[36]*soirée musicale* musical evening

to the salon, where it was cool and sweet with the odor of great roses that stood upon the hearth in jars.

Madame Ratignolle looked more beautiful than ever there at home, in a negligée which left her arms almost wholly bare and exposed the rich, melting curves of her white throat.

"Perhaps I shall be able to paint your picture some day," said Edna with a smile when they were seated. She produced the roll of sketches and started to unfold them. "I believe I ought to work again. I feel as if I wanted to be doing something. What do you think of them? Do you think it worth while to take it up again and study some more? I might study for a while with Laidpore."

She knew that Madame Ratignolle's opinion in such a matter would be next to valueless, that she herself had not alone decided, but determined; but she sought the words of praise and encouragement that would help her to put heart into her venture.

"Your talent is immense, dear!"

"Nonsense!" protested Edna, well pleased.

"Immense, I tell you," persisted Madame Ratignolle, surveying the sketches one by one, at close range, then holding them at arm's length, narrowing her eyes, and dropping her head on one side. "Surely, this Bavarian peasant is worthy of framing; and this basket of apples! never have I seen anything more lifelike. One might almost be tempted to reach out a hand and take one."

Edna could not control a feeling which bordered upon complacency at her friend's praise, even realizing, as she did, its true worth. She retained a few of the sketches, and gave all the rest to Madame Ratignolle, who appreciated the gift far beyond its value and proudly exhibited the pictures to her husband when he came up from the store a little later for his midday dinner.

Mr. Ratignolle was one of those men who are called the salt of the earth. His cheerfulness was unbounded, and it was matched by his goodness of heart, his broad charity, and common sense. He and his wife spoke English with an accent which was only discernible through its un-English emphasis and a certain carefulness and deliberation. Edna's husband spoke English with no accent whatever. The Ratignolles understood each other perfectly. If ever the fusion of two human beings into one has been accomplished on this sphere it was surely in their union.

As Edna seated herself at table with them she thought, "Better a dinner of herbs," though it did not take her long to discover that it was no dinner of herbs, but a delicious repast, simple, choice, and in every way satisfying.

Monsieur Ratignolle was delighted to see her, though he found her looking not so well as at Grand Isle, and he advised a tonic. He talked a good deal on various topics, a little politics, some city news and neighborhood gossip. He spoke with an animation and earnestness that gave an exaggerated importance to every syllable he uttered. His wife was keenly interested in everything he said, laying down her fork the better to listen, chiming in, taking the words out of his mouth.

Edna felt depressed rather than soothed after leaving them. The little glimpse of domestic harmony which had been offered her, gave her no regret, no longing. It was not a condition of life which fitted her, and she could see in it but an appalling and hopeless ennui. She was moved by a kind of commiseration for Madame Ratignolle,—a pity for that colorless existence which never uplifted its possessor beyond the region of blind contentment, in which no moment of anguish ever visited her soul, in which she would never have the taste of life's delirium. Edna vaguely wondered what she meant by "life's delirium." It had crossed her thought like some unsought, extraneous impression.

XIX

Edna could not help but think that it was very foolish, very childish, to have stamped upon her wedding ring and smashed the crystal vase upon the tiles. She was visited by no more outbursts, moving her to such futile expedients. She began to do as she liked and to feel as she liked. She completely abandoned her Tuesdays at home, and did not return the visits of those who had called upon her. She made no ineffectual efforts to conduct her household *en bonne ménagère*,[37] going and coming as it suited her fancy, and, so far as she was able, lending herself to any passing caprice.

Mr. Pontellier had been a rather courteous husband so long as he met a certain tacit submissiveness in his wife. But her new and unexpected line of conduct completely bewildered him. It shocked him. Then her absolute disregard for her duties as a wife angered him. When Mr. Pontellier became rude, Edna grew insolent. She had resolved never to take another step backward.

"It seems to me the utmost folly for a woman at the head of a household, and the mother of children, to spend in an atelier[38] days which would be better employed contriving for the comfort of her family."

"I feel like painting," answered Edna. "Perhaps I shan't always feel like it."

"Then in God's name paint! but don't let the family go to the devil. There's Madame Ratignolle; because she keeps up her music, she doesn't let everything else go to chaos. And she's more of a musician than you are a painter."

"She isn't a musician, and I'm not a painter. It isn't on account of painting that I let things go."

"On account of what, then?"

"Oh! I don't know. Let me alone; you bother me."

It sometimes entered Mr. Pontellier's mind to wonder if his wife were not growing a little unbalanced mentally. He could see plainly that she was not herself. That is, he could not see that she was becoming herself and daily casting aside that fictitious self which we assume like a garment with which to appear before the world.

Her husband let her alone as she requested, and went away to his office. Edna went up to her atelier—a bright room in the top of the house. She was working with great energy and interest, without accomplishing anything, however, which satisfied her even in the smallest degree. For a time she had the whole household enrolled in the service of art. The boys posed for her. They thought it amusing at first, but the occupation soon lost its attractiveness when they discovered that it was not a game arranged especially for their entertainment. The quadroon sat for hours before Edna's palette, patient as a savage, while the house-maid took charge of the children, and the drawing-room went undusted. But the house-maid, too, served her term as model when Edna perceived that the young woman's back and shoulders were molded on classic lines, and that her hair, loosened from its confining cap, became an inspiration. While Edna worked she sometimes sang low the little air, "*Ah! si tu savais!*"

It moved her with recollections. She could hear again the ripple of the water, the flapping sail. She could see the glint of the moon upon the bay, and could feel

[37]*en bonne ménagère* as a good housewife

[38]*atelier* studio

the soft, gusty beating of the hot south wind. A subtle current of desire passed through her body, weakening her hold upon the brushes and making her eyes burn.

There were days when she was very happy without knowing why. She was happy to be alive and breathing, when her whole being seemed to be one with the sunlight, the color, the odors, the luxuriant warmth of some perfect Southern day. She liked then to wander alone into strange and unfamiliar places. She discovered many a sunny, sleepy corner, fashioned to dream in. And she found it good to dream and to be alone and unmolested.

There were days when she was unhappy, she did not know why, — when it did not seem worth while to be glad or sorry, to be alive or dead; when life appeared to her like a grotesque pandemonium and humanity like worms struggling blindly toward inevitable annihilation. She could not work on such a day, nor weave fancies to stir her pulses and warm her blood.

XX

It was during such a mood that Edna hunted up Mademoiselle Reisz. She had not forgotten the rather disagreeable impression left upon her by their last interview; but she nevertheless felt a desire to see her — above all, to listen while she played upon the piano. Quite early in the afternoon she started upon her quest for the pianist. Unfortunately she had mislaid or lost Mademoiselle Reisz's card, and looking up her address in the city directory, she found that the woman lived on Bienville Street, some distance away. The directory which fell into her hands was a year or more old, however, and upon reaching the number indicated, Edna discovered that the house was occupied by a respectable family of mulattoes who had *chambres garnies*[39] to let. They had been living there for six months, and knew absolutely nothing of a Mademoiselle Reisz. In fact, they knew nothing of any of their neighbors; their lodgers were all people of the highest distinction, they assured Edna. She did not linger to discuss class distinctions with Madame Pouponne, but hastened to a neighboring grocery store, feeling sure that Mademoiselle would have left her address with the proprietor.

He knew Mademoiselle Reisz a good deal better than he wanted to know her, he informed his questioner. In truth, he did not want to know her at all, or anything concerning her — the most disagreeable and unpopular woman who ever lived in Bienville Street. He thanked heaven she had left the neighborhood, and was equally thankful that he did not know where she had gone.

Edna's desire to see Mademoiselle Reisz had increased tenfold since these unlooked-for obstacles had arisen to thwart it. She was wondering who could give her the information she sought, when it suddenly occurred to her that Madame Lebrun would be the one most likely to do so. She knew it was useless to ask Madame Ratignolle, who was on the most distant terms with the musician, and preferred to know nothing concerning her. She had once been almost as emphatic in expressing herself upon the subject as the corner grocer.

Edna knew that Madame Lebrun had returned to the city, for it was the middle of November. And she also knew where the Lebruns lived, on Chartres Street.

Their home from the outside looked like a prison, with iron bars before the

[39]*chambres garnies* furnished rooms

door and lower windows. The iron bars were a relic of the old *régime*,[40] and no one had ever thought of dislodging them. At the side was a high fence enclosing the garden. A gate or door opening upon the street was locked. Edna rang the bell at this side garden gate, and stood upon the banquette, waiting to be admitted.

It was Victor who opened the gate for her. A black woman, wiping her hands upon her apron, was close at his heels. Before she saw them Edna could hear them in altercation, the woman — plainly an anomaly — claiming the right to be allowed to perform her duties, one of which was to answer the bell.

Victor was surprised and delighted to see Mrs. Pontellier, and he made no attempt to conceal either his astonishment or his delight. He was a dark-browed, good-looking youngster of nineteen, greatly resembling his mother, but with ten times her impetuosity. He instructed the black woman to go at once and inform Madame Lebrun that Mrs. Pontellier desired to see her. The woman grumbled a refusal to do part of her duty when she had not been permitted to do it all, and started back to her interrupted task of weeding the garden. Whereupon Victor administered a rebuke in the form of a volley of abuse, which, owing to its rapidity and incoherence, was all but incomprehensible to Edna. Whatever it was, the rebuke was convincing, for the woman dropped her hoe and went mumbling into the house.

Edna did not wish to enter. It was very pleasant there on the side porch, where there were chairs, a wicker lounge, and a small table. She seated herself, for she was tired from her long tramp; and she began to rock gently and smooth out the folds of her silk parasol. Victor drew up his chair beside her. He at once explained that the black woman's offensive conduct was all due to imperfect training, as he was not there to take her in hand. He had only come up from the island the morning before, and expected to return next day. He stayed all winter at the island; he lived there, and kept the place in order and got things ready for the summer visitors.

But a man needed occasional relaxation, he informed Mrs. Pontellier, and every now and again he drummed up a pretext to bring him to the city. My! but he had had a time of it the evening before! He wouldn't want his mother to know, and he began to talk in a whisper. He was scintillant with recollections. Of course, he couldn't think of telling Mrs. Pontellier all about it, she being a woman and not comprehending such things. But it all began with a girl peeping and smiling at him through the shutters as he passed by. Oh! but she was a beauty! Certainly he smiled back, and went up and talked to her. Mrs. Pontellier did not know him if she supposed he was one to let an opportunity like that escape him. Despite herself, the youngster amused her. She must have betrayed in her look some degree of interest or entertainment. The boy grew more daring, and Mrs. Pontellier might have found herself, in a little while, listening to a highly colored story but for the timely appearance of Madame Lebrun.

That lady was still clad in white, according to her custom of the summer. Her eyes beamed an effusive welcome. Would not Mrs. Pontellier go inside? Would she partake of some refreshment? Why had she not been there before? How was that dear Mr. Pontellier and how were those sweet children? Had Mrs. Pontellier ever known such a warm November?

Victor went and reclined on the wicker lounge behind his mother's chair, where he commanded a view of Edna's face. He had taken her parasol from her

[40]*régime* Spanish rule in Louisiana (1766–1803)

hands while he spoke to her, and he now lifted it and twirled it above him as he lay on his back. When Madame Lebrun complained that it was *so* dull coming back to the city; that she saw *so* few people now; that even Victor, when he came up from the island for a day or two, had *so* much to occupy him and engage his time; then it was that the youth went into contortions on the lounge and winked mischievously at Edna. She somehow felt like a confederate in crime, and tried to look severe and disapproving.

There had been but two letters from Robert, with little in them, they told her. Victor said it was really not worth while to go inside for the letters, when his mother entreated him to go in search of them. He remembered the contents, which in truth he rattled off very glibly when put to the test.

One letter was written from Vera Cruz and the other from the City of Mexico. He had met Montel, who was doing everything toward his advancement. So far, the financial situation was no improvement over the one he had left in New Orleans, but of course the prospects were vastly better. He wrote of the City of Mexico, the buildings, the people and their habits, the conditions of life which he found there. He sent his love to the family. He inclosed a check to his mother, and hoped she would affectionately remember him to all his friends. That was about the substance of the two letters. Edna felt that if there had been a message for her, she would have received it. The despondent frame of mind in which she had left home began again to overtake her, and she remembered that she wished to find Mademoiselle Reisz.

Madame Lebrun knew where Mademoiselle Reisz lived. She gave Edna the address, regretting that she would not consent to stay and spend the remainder of the afternoon, and pay a visit to Mademoiselle Reisz some other day. The afternoon was already well advanced.

Victor escorted her out upon the banquette, lifted her parasol, and held it over her while he walked to the car with her. He entreated her to bear in mind that the disclosures of the afternoon were strictly confidential. She laughed and bantered him a little, remembering too late that she should have been dignified and reserved.

"How handsome Mrs. Pontellier looked!" said Madame Lebrun to her son.

"Ravishing!" he admitted. "The city atmosphere has improved her. Some way she doesn't seem like the same woman."

XXI

Some people contended that the reason Mademoiselle Reisz always chose apartments up under the roof was to discourage the approach of beggars, peddlars and callers. There were plenty of windows in her little front room. They were for the most part dingy, but as they were nearly always open it did not make so much difference. They often admitted into the room a good deal of smoke and soot; but at the same time all the light and air that there was came through them. From her windows could be seen the crescent of the river, the masts of ships and the big chimneys of the Mississippi steamers. A magnificent piano crowded the apartment. In the next room she slept, and in the third and last she harbored a gasoline stove on which she cooked her meals when disinclined to descend to the neighboring restaurant. It was there also that she ate, keeping her belongings in a rare old buffet, dingy and battered from a hundred years of use.

When Edna knocked at Mademoiselle Reisz's front room door and entered, she discovered that person standing beside the window, engaged in mending or patching an old prunella gaiter.[41] The little musician laughed all over when she saw Edna. Her laugh consisted of a contortion of the face and all the muscles of the body. She seemed strikingly homely, standing there in the afternoon light. She still wore the shabby lace and the artificial bunch of violets on the side of her head.

"So you remembered me at last," said Mademoiselle. "I had said to myself, 'Ah, bah! she will never come.'"

"Did you want me to come?" asked Edna with a smile.

"I had not thought much about it," answered Mademoiselle. The two had seated themselves on a little bumpy sofa which stood against the wall. "I am glad, however, that you came. I have the water boiling back there, and was just about to make some coffee. You will drink a cup with me. And how is *la belle dame?*[42] Always handsome! always healthy! always contented!" She took Edna's hand between her strong wiry fingers, holding it loosely without warmth, and executing a sort of double theme upon the back and palm.

"Yes," she went on; "I sometimes thought: 'She will never come. She promised as those women in society always do, without meaning it. She will not come.' For I really don't believe you like me, Mrs. Pontellier."

"I don't know whether I like you or not," replied Edna, gazing down at the little woman with a quizzical look.

The candor of Mrs. Pontellier's admission greatly pleased Mademoiselle Reisz. She expressed her gratification by repairing forthwith to the region of the gasoline stove and rewarding her guest with the promised cup of coffee. The coffee and the biscuit accompanying it proved very acceptable to Edna, who had declined refreshment at Madame Lebrun's and was now beginning to feel hungry. Mademoiselle set the tray which she brought in upon a small table near at hand, and seated herself once again on the lumpy sofa.

"I have had a letter from your friend," she remarked, as she poured a little cream into Edna's cup and handed it to her.

"My friend?"

"Yes, your friend Robert. He wrote to me from the City of Mexico."

"Wrote to *you?*" repeated Edna in amazement, stirring her coffee absently.

"Yes, to me. Why not? Don't stir all the warmth out of your coffee; drink it. Though the letter might as well have been sent to you; it was nothing but Mrs. Pontellier from beginning to end."

"Let me see it," requested the young woman, entreatingly.

"No; a letter concerns no one but the person who writes it and the one to whom it is written."

"Haven't you just said it concerned me from beginning to end?"

"It was written about you, not to you. 'Have you seen Mrs. Pontellier? How is she looking?' he asks. 'As Mrs. Pontellier says,' or 'as Mrs. Pontellier once said.' 'If Mrs. Pontellier should call upon you, play for her that Impromptu of Chopin's, my favorite. I heard it here a day or two ago, but not as you play it. I should like to know how it affects her,' and so on, as if he supposed we were constantly in each other's society."

[41]*prunella gaiter* a cloth button shoe

[42]*la belle dame* the lovely lady

"Let me see the letter."

"Oh, no."

"Have you answered it?"

"No."

"Let me see the letter."

"No, and again, no."

"Then play the Impromptu for me."

"It is growing late; what time do you have to be home?"

"Time doesn't concern me. Your question seems a little rude. Play the Impromptu."

"But you have told me nothing of yourself. What are you doing?"

"Painting!" laughed Edna. "I am becoming an artist. Think of it!"

"Ah! an artist! You have pretensions, Madame."

"Why pretensions? Do you think I could not become an artist?"

"I do not know you well enough to say. I do not know your talent or your temperament. To be an artist includes much; one must possess many gifts—absolute gifts—which have not been acquired by one's own effort. And, moreover, to succeed, the artist must possess the courageous soul."

"What do you mean by the courageous soul?"

"Courageous, *ma foi!* The brave soul. The soul that dares and defies."

"Show me the letter and play for me the Impromptu. You see that I have persistence. Does that quality count for anything in art?"

"It counts with a foolish old woman whom you have captivated," replied Mademoiselle, with her wriggling laugh.

The letter was right there at hand in the drawer of the little table upon which Edna had just placed her coffee cup. Mademoiselle opened the drawer and drew forth the letter, the topmost one. She placed it in Edna's hands, and without further comment arose and went to the piano.

Mademoiselle played a soft interlude. It was an improvisation. She sat low at the instrument, and the lines of her body settled into ungraceful curves and angles that gave it an appearance of deformity. Gradually and imperceptibly the interlude melted into the soft opening minor chords of the Chopin Impromptu.

Edna did not know when the Impromptu began or ended. She sat in the sofa corner reading Robert's letter by the fading light. Mademoiselle had glided from the Chopin into the quivering lovenotes of Isolde's song, and back again to the Impromptu with its soulful and poignant longing.

The shadows deepened in the little room. The music grew strange and fantastic—turbulent, insistent, plaintive and soft with entreaty. The shadows grew deeper. The music filled the room. It floated out upon the night, over the housetops, the crescent of the river, losing itself in the silence of the upper air.

Edna was sobbing, just as she had wept one midnight at Grand Isle when strange, new voices awoke in her. She arose in some agitation to take her departure. "May I come again, Mademoiselle? "she asked at the threshold.

"Come whenever you feel like it. Be careful; the stairs and landings are dark; don't stumble."

Mademoiselle reëntered and lit a candle. Robert's letter was on the floor. She stooped and picked it up. It was crumpled and damp with tears. Mademoiselle smoothed the letter out, restored it to the envelope, and replaced it in the table drawer.

XXII

One morning on his way into town Mr. Pontellier stopped at the house of his old friend and family physician, Doctor Mandelet. The Doctor was a semi-retired physician, resting, as the saying is, upon his laurels. He bore a reputation for wisdom rather than skill — leaving the active practice of medicine to his assistants and younger contemporaries — and was much sought for in matters of consultation. A few families, united to him by bonds of friendship, he still attended when they required the services of physician. The Pontelliers were among these.

Mr. Pontellier found the Doctor reading at the open window of his study. His house stood rather far back from the street, in the center of a delightful garden, so that it was quiet and peaceful at the old gentleman's study window. He was a great reader. He stared up disapprovingly over his eye-glasses as Mr. Pontellier entered, wondering who had the temerity to disturb him at that hour of the morning.

"Ah, Pontellier! Not sick, I hope. Come and have a seat. What news do you bring this morning?" He was quite portly, with a profusion of gray hair, and small blue eyes which age had robbed of much of their brightness but none of their penetration.

"Oh! I'm never sick, Doctor. You know that I come of tough fiber — of that old Creole race of Pontelliers that dry up and finally blow away. I came to consult — no, not precisely to consult — to talk to you about Edna. I don't know what ails her."

"Madame Pontellier not well?" marveled the Doctor. "Why, I saw her — I think it was a week ago — walking along Canal Street, the picture of health, it seemed to me."

"Yes, yes; she seems quite well," said Mr. Pontellier, leaning forward and whirling his stick between his two hands; "but she doesn't act well. She's odd, she's not like herself. I can't make her out, and I thought perhaps you'd help me."

"How does she act?" inquired the doctor.

"Well, it isn't easy to explain," said Mr. Pontellier, throwing himself back in his chair. "She lets the housekeeping go to the dickens."

"Well, well; women are not all alike, my dear Pontellier. We've got to consider — "

"I know that; I told you I couldn't explain. Her whole attitude — toward me and everybody and everything — has changed. You know I have a quick temper, but I don't want to quarrel or be rude to a woman, especially my wife; yet I'm driven to it, and feel like ten thousand devils after I've made a fool of myself. She's making it devilishly uncomfortable for me," he went on nervously. "She's got some sort of notion in her head concerning the eternal rights of women; and — you understand — we meet in the morning at the breakfast table."

The old gentleman lifted his shaggy eyebrows, protruded his thick nether lip, and tapped the arms of his chair with his cushioned fingertips.

"What have you been doing to her, Pontellier?"

"Doing! *Parbleu!*"[43]

"Has she," asked the Doctor, with a smile, "has she been associating of late with a circle of pseudo-intellectual women — super-spiritual superior beings? My wife has been telling me about them."

[43]"*Parbleu!*" "For heaven's sake!"

"That's the trouble," broke in Mr. Pontellier, "she hasn't been associating with any one. She has abandoned her Tuesdays at home, has thrown over all her acquaintances, and goes tramping about by herself, moping in the street-cars, getting in after dark. I tell you she's peculiar. I don't like it; I feel a little worried over it."

This was a new aspect for the Doctor. "Nothing hereditary?" he asked, seriously. "Nothing peculiar about her family antecedents, is there?"

"Oh, no, indeed! She comes of sound old Presbyterian Kentucky stock. The old gentleman, her father, I have heard, used to atone for his week-day sins with his Sunday devotions. I know for a fact, that his race horses literally ran away with the prettiest bit of Kentucky farming land I ever laid eyes upon. Margaret — you know Margaret — she has all the Presbyterianism undiluted. And the youngest is something of a vixen. By the way, she gets married in a couple of weeks from now."

"Send your wife up to the wedding," exclaimed the Doctor, foreseeing a happy solution. "Let her stay among her own people for a while; it will do her good."

"That's what I want her to do. She won't go to the marriage. She says a wedding is one of the most lamentable spectacles on earth. Nice thing for a woman to say to her husband!" exclaimed Mr. Pontellier, fuming anew at the recollection.

"Pontellier," said the Doctor, after a moment's reflection, "let your wife alone for a while. Don't bother her, and don't let her bother you. Woman, my dear friend, is a very peculiar and delicate organism — a sensitive and highly organized woman, such as I know Mrs. Pontellier to be, is especially peculiar. It would require an inspired psychologist to deal successfully with them. And when ordinary fellows like you and me attempt to cope with their idiosyncrasies the result is bungling. Most women are moody and whimsical. This is some passing whim of your wife, due to some cause or causes which you and I needn't try to fathom. But it will pass happily over, especially if you let her alone. Send her around to see me."

"Oh! I couldn't do that; there'd be no reason for it," objected Mr. Pontellier.

"Then I'll go around and see her," said the Doctor. "I'll drop in to dinner some evening *en bon ami*."[44]

"Do! by all means," urged Mr. Pontellier. "What evening will you come? Say Thursday. Will you come Thursday?" he asked, rising to take his leave.

"Very well; Thursday. My wife may possibly have some engagement for me Thursday. In case she has, I shall let you know. Otherwise, you may expect me."

Mr. Pontellier turned before leaving to say:

"I am going to New York on business very soon. I have a big scheme on hand, and want to be on the field proper to pull the ropes and handle the ribbons. We'll let you in on the inside if you say so, Doctor," he laughed.

"No, I thank you, my sir," returned the Doctor. "I leave such ventures to you younger men with the fever of life still in your blood."

"What I wanted to say," continued Mr. Pontellier, with his hand on the knob; "I may have to be absent a good while. Would you advise me to take Edna along?"

"By all means, if she wishes to go. If not, leave her here. Don't contradict her. The mood will pass, I assure you. It may take a month, two, three months — possibly longer, but it will pass; have patience."

"Well, good-by, *à jeudi*,"[45] said Mr. Pontellier, as he let himself out.

[44]*en bon ami* as an old friend

[45]*à jeudi* till Thursday

The Doctor would have liked during the course of conversation to ask, "Is there any man in the case?" but he knew his Creole too well to make such a blunder as that.

He did not resume his book immediately, but sat for a while meditatively looking out into the garden.

XXIII

Edna's father was in the city, and had been with them several days. She was not very warmly or deeply attached to him, but they had certain tastes in common, and when together they were companionable. His coming was in the nature of a welcome disturbance; it seemed to furnish a new direction for her emotions.

He had come to purchase a wedding gift for his daughter, Janet, and an outfit for himself in which he might make a creditable appearance at her marriage. Mr. Pontellier had selected the bridal gift, as every one immediately connected with him always deferred to his taste in such matters. And his suggestions on the question of dress — which too often assumes the nature of a problem — were of inestimable value to his father-in-law. But for the past few days the old gentleman had been upon Edna's hands, and in his society she was becoming acquainted with a new set of sensations. He had been a colonel in the Confederate army, and still maintained, with the title, the military bearing which had always accompanied it. His hair and mustache were white and silky, emphasizing the rugged bronze of his face. He was tall and thin, and wore his coats padded, which gave a fictitious breadth and depth to his shoulders and chest. Edna and her father looked very distinguished together, and excited a good deal of notice during their perambulations. Upon his arrival she began by introducing him to her atelier and making a sketch of him. He took the whole matter very seriously. If her talent had been ten-fold greater than it was, it would not have surprised him, convinced as he was that he had bequeathed to all of his daughters the germs of a masterful capacity, which only depended upon their own efforts to be directed toward successful achievement.

Before her pencil he sat rigid and unflinching, as he had faced the cannon's mouth in days gone by. He resented the intrusion of the children, who gaped with wondering eyes at him, sitting so stiff up there in their mother's bright atelier. When they drew near he motioned them away with an expressive action of the foot, loath to disturb the fixed lines of his countenance, his arms, or his rigid shoulders.

Edna, anxious to entertain him, invited Mademoiselle Reisz to meet him, having promised him a treat in her piano playing; but Mademoiselle declined the invitation. So together they attended a *soirée musicale* at the Ratignolles'. Monsieur and Madame Ratignolle made much of the Colonel, installing him as the guest of honor and engaging him at once to dine with them the following Sunday, or any day which he might select. Madame coquetted with him in the most captivating and naïve manner, with eyes, gestures, and a profusion of compliments, till the Colonel's old head felt thirty years younger on his padded shoulders. Edna marveled, not comprehending. She herself was almost devoid of coquetry.

There were one or two men whom she observed at the *soirée musicale*; but she would never have felt moved to any kittenish display to attract their notice — to any feline or feminine wiles to express herself toward them. Their personality attracted her in an agreeable way. Her fancy selected them, and she was glad when a lull in the music gave them an opportunity to meet her and talk with her. Often on the street the glance of strange eyes had lingered in her memory, and sometimes had disturbed her.

Mr. Pontellier did not attend these *soirées musicales*. He considered them *bourgeois*, and found more diversion at the club. To Madame Ratignolle he said the music dispensed at her *soirées* was too "heavy," too far beyond his untrained comprehension. His excuses flattered her. But she disapproved of Mr. Pontellier's club, and she was frank enough to tell Edna so.

"It's a pity Mr. Pontellier doesn't stay home in the evenings. I think you would be more—well, if you don't mind my saying it—more united, if he did."

"Oh! dear no!" said Edna, with a blank look in her eyes. "What should I do if he stayed home? We wouldn't have anything to say to each other."

She had not much of anything to say to her father, for that matter; but he did not antagonize her. She discovered that he interested her, though she realized that he might not interest her long; and for the first time in her life she felt as if she were thoroughly acquainted with him. He kept her busy serving him and ministering to his wants. It amused her to do so. She would not permit a servant or one of the children to do anything for him which she might do herself. Her husband noticed, and thought it was the expression of a deep filial attachment which he had never suspected.

The Colonel drank numerous "toddies" during the course of the day, which left him, however, imperturbed. He was an expert at concocting strong drinks. He had even invented some to which he had given fantastic names, and for whose manufacture he required diverse ingredients that it devolved upon Edna to procure for him.

When Doctor Mandelet dined with the Pontelliers on Thursday he could discern in Mrs. Pontellier no trace of that morbid condition which her husband had reported to him. She was excited and in a manner radiant. She and her father had been to the race course, and their thoughts when they seated themselves at table were still occupied with the events of the afternoon, and their talk was still of the track. The Doctor had not kept pace with turf affairs. He had certain recollections of racing in what he called "the good old times" when the Lecompte stables flourished, and he drew upon this fund of memories so that he might not be left out and seem wholly devoid of the modern spirit. But he failed to impose upon the Colonel, and was even far from impressing him with this trumped-up knowledge of bygone days. Edna had staked her father on his last venture, with the most gratifying results to both of them. Besides, they had met some very charming people, according to the Colonel's impressions. Mrs. Mortimer Merriman and Mrs. James Highcamp, who were there with Alcée Arobin, had joined them and had enlivened the hours in a fashion that warmed him to think of.

Mr. Pontellier himself had no particular leaning toward horseracing, and was even rather inclined to discourage it as a pastime, especially when he considered the fate of that blue-grass farm in Kentucky. He endeavored, in a general way, to express a particular disapproval, and only succeeded in arousing the ire and opposition of his father-in-law. A pretty dispute followed, in which Edna warmly espoused her father's cause and the Doctor remained neutral.

He observed his hostess attentively from under his shaggy brows, and noted a subtle change which had transformed her from the listless woman he had known into a being who, for the moment, seemed palpitant with the forces of life. Her speech was warm and energetic. There was no repression in her glance or gesture. She reminded him of some beautiful, sleek animal waking up in the sun.

The dinner was excellent. The claret was warm and the champagne was cold, and under their beneficent influence the threatened unpleasantness melted and vanished with the fumes of the wine.

Mr. Pontellier warmed up and grew reminiscent. He told some amusing plantation experiences, recollections of old Iberville and his youth, when he hunted 'possum in company with some friendly darky; thrashed the pecan trees, shot the grosbec, and roamed the woods and fields in mischievous idleness.

The Colonel, with little sense of humor and of the fitness of things, related a somber episode of those dark and bitter days, in which he had acted a conspicuous part and always formed a central figure. Nor was the Doctor happier in his selection, when he told the old, ever new and curious story of the waning of a woman's love, seeking strange, new channels, only to return to its legitimate source after days of fierce unrest. It was one of the many little human documents which had been unfolded to him during his long career as a physician. The story did not seem especially to impress Edna. She had one of her own to tell, of a woman who paddled away with her lover one night in a pirogue and never came back. They were lost amid the Baratarian Islands, and no one ever heard of them or found trace of them from that day to this. It was a pure invention. She said that Madame Antoine had related it to her. That, also, was an invention. Perhaps it was a dream she had had. But every glowing word seemed real to those who listened. They could feel the hot breath of the Southern night; they could hear the long sweep of the pirogue through the glistening moonlit water, the beating of birds' wings, rising startled from among the reeds in the salt-water pools; they could see the faces of the lovers, pale, close together, rapt in obvious forgetfulness, drifting into the unknown.

The champagne was cold, and its subtle fumes played fantastic tricks with Edna's memory that night.

Outside, away from the glow of the fire and the soft lamplight, the night was chill and murky. The Doctor doubled his old-fashioned cloak across his breast as he strode home through the darkness. He knew his fellow-creatures better than most men; knew that inner life which so seldom unfolds itself to unanointed eyes. He was sorry he had accepted Pontellier's invitation. He was growing old, and beginning to need rest and an imperturbed spirit. He did not want the secrets of other lives thrust upon him.

"I hope it isn't Arobin," he muttered to himself as he walked. "I hope to heaven it isn't Alcée Arobin."

XXIV

Edna and her father had a warm, and almost violent dispute upon the subject of her refusal to attend her sister's wedding. Mr. Pontellier declined to interfere, to interpose either his influence or his authority. He was following Doctor Mandelet's advice, and letting her do as she liked. The Colonel reproached his daughter for her lack of filial kindness and respect, her want of sisterly affection and womanly consideration. His arguments were labored and unconvincing. He doubted if Janet would accept any excuse — forgetting that Edna had offered none. He doubted if Janet would ever speak to her again, and he was sure Margaret would not.

Edna was glad to be rid of her father when he finally took himself off with his wedding garments and his bridal gifts, with his padded shoulders, his Bible reading, his "toddies" and ponderous oaths.

Mr. Pontellier followed him closely. He meant to stop at the wedding on his way to New York and endeavor by every means which money and love could devise to atone somewhat for Edna's incomprehensible action.

"You are too lenient, too lenient by far, Léonce," asserted the Colonel. "Authority, coercion are what is needed. Put your foot down good and hard; the only way to manage a wife. Take my word for it."

The Colonel was perhaps unaware that he had coerced his own wife into her grave. Mr. Pontellier had a vague suspicion of it which he thought it needless to mention at that late date.

Edna was not so consciously gratified at her husband's leaving home as she had been over the departure of her father. As the day approached when he was to leave her for a comparatively long stay, she grew melting and affectionate, remembering his many acts of consideration and his repeated expressions of an ardent attachment. She was solicitous about his health and his welfare. She bustled around, looking after his clothing, thinking about heavy underwear, quite as Madame Ratignolle would have done under similar circumstances. She cried when he went away, calling him her dear, good friend, and she was quite certain she would grow lonely before very long and go to join him in New York.

But after all, a radiant peace settled upon her when she at last found herself alone. Even the children were gone. Old Madame Pontellier had come herself and carried them off to Iberville with their quadroon. The old madame did not venture to say she was afraid they would be neglected during Léonce's absence; she hardly ventured to think so. She was hungry for them—even a little fierce in her attachment. She did not want them to be wholly "children of the pavement," she always said when begging to have them for a space. She wished them to know the country, with its streams, its fields, its woods, its freedom, so delicious to the young. She wished them to taste something of the life their father had lived and known and loved when he, too, was a little child.

When Edna was at last alone, she breathed a big, genuine sigh of relief. A feeling that was unfamiliar but very delicious came over her. She walked all through the house, from one room to another, as if inspecting it for the first time. She tried the various chairs and lounges, as if she had never sat and reclined upon them before. And she perambulated around the outside of the house, investigating, looking to see if windows and shutters were secure and in order. The flowers were like new acquaintances; she approached them in a familiar spirit, and made herself at home among them. The garden walks were damp, and Edna called to the maid to bring out her rubber sandals. And there she stayed, and stooped, digging around the plants, trimming, picking dead, dry leaves. The children's little dog came out, interfering, getting in her way. She scolded him, laughed at him, played with him. The garden smelled so good and looked so pretty in the afternoon sunlight. Edna plucked all the bright flowers she could find, and went into the house with them, she and the little dog.

Even the kitchen assumed a sudden interesting character which she had never before perceived. She went in to give directions to the cook, to say that the butcher would have to bring much less meat, that they would require only half their usual quantity of bread, of milk and groceries. She told the cook that she herself would be greatly occupied during Mr. Pontellier's absence, and she begged her to take all thought and responsibility of the larder upon her own shoulders.

That night Edna dined alone. The candelabra, with a few candles in the center of the table, gave all the light she needed. Outside the circle of light in which she sat, the large dining-room looked solemn and shadowy. The cook, placed upon her mettle, served a delicious repast—a luscious tenderloin broiled *à point*.[46] The wine tasted good; the *marron glacé* seemed to be just what she wanted. It was so pleasant, too, to dine in a comfortable *peignoir*.

She thought a little sentimentally about Léonce and the children, and wondered what they were doing. As she gave a dainty scrap or two to the doggie, she talked intimately to him about Etienne and Raoul. He was beside himself with astonishment and delight over these companionable advances, and showed his appreciation by his little quick, snappy barks and a lively agitation.

Then Edna sat in the library after dinner and read Emerson until she grew sleepy. She realized that she had neglected her reading, and determined to start anew upon a course of improving studies, now that her time was completely her own to do with as she liked.

After a refreshing bath, Edna went to bed. And as she snuggled comfortably beneath the eiderdown a sense of restfulness invaded her, such as she had not known before.

XXV

When the weather was dark and cloudy Edna could not work. She needed the sun to mellow and temper her mood to the sticking point. She had reached a stage when she seemed to be no longer feeling her way, working, when in the humor, with sureness and ease. And being devoid of ambition, and striving not toward accomplishment, she drew satisfaction from the work in itself.

On rainy or melancholy days Edna went out and sought the society of the friends she had made at Grand Isle. Or else she stayed indoors and nursed a mood with which she was becoming too familiar for her own comfort and peace of mind. It was not despair; but it seemed to her as if life were passing by, leaving its promise broken and unfulfilled. Yet there were other days when she listened, was led on and deceived by fresh promises which her youth held out to her.

She went again to the races, and again. Alcée Arobin and Mrs. Highcamp called for her one bright afternoon in Arobin's drag.[47] Mrs. Highcamp was a worldly but unaffected, intelligent, slim, tall blonde woman in the forties, with an indifferent manner and blue eyes that stared. She had a daughter who served her as a pretext for cultivating the society of young men of fashion. Alcée Arobin was one of them. He was a familiar figure at the race course, the opera, the fashionable clubs. There was a perpetual smile in his eyes, which seldom failed to awaken a corresponding cheerfulness in any one who looked into them and listened to his good-humored voice. His manner was quiet, and at times a little insolent. He possessed a good figure, a pleasing face, not overburdened with depth of thought or feeling; and his dress was that of the conventional man of fashion.

He admired Edna extravagantly, after meeting her at the races with her father.

[46]*à point* to a turn; *marron glacé*—glazed chestnuts

[47]*drag* a large, heavy carriage

He had met her before on other occasions, but she had seemed to him unapproachable until that day. It was at his instigation that Mrs. Highcamp called to her to go with them to the Jockey Club to witness the turf event of the season.

There were possibly a few track men out there who knew the race horse as well as Edna, but there was certainly none who knew it better. She sat between her two companions as one having authority to speak. She laughed at Arobin's pretensions, and deplored Mrs. Highcamp's ignorance. The race horse was a friend and intimate associate of her childhood. The atmosphere of the stables and the breath of the blue grass paddock revived in her memory and lingered in her nostrils. She did not perceive that she was talking like her father as the sleek geldings ambled in review before them. She played for very high stakes, and fortune favored her. The fever of the game flamed in her cheeks and eyes, and it got into her blood and into her brain like an intoxicant. People turned their heads to look at her, and more than one lent an attentive ear to her utterances, hoping thereby to secure the elusive but ever-desired "tip." Arobin caught the contagion of excitement which drew him to Edna like a magnet. Mrs. Highcamp remained, as usual, unmoved, with her indifferent stare and uplifted eyebrows.

Edna stayed and dined with Mrs. Highcamp upon being urged to do so. Arobin also remained and sent away his drag.

The dinner was quiet and uninteresting, save for the cheerful efforts of Arobin to enliven things. Mrs. Highcamp deplored the absence of her daughter from the races, and tried to convey to her what she had missed by going to the "Dante reading" instead of joining them. The girl held a geranium leaf up to her nose and said nothing, but looked knowing and noncommittal. Mr. Highcamp was a plain, bald-headed man, who only talked under compulsion. He was unresponsive. Mrs. Highcamp was full of delicate courtesy and consideration toward her husband. She addressed most of her conversation to him at table. They sat in the library after dinner and read the evening papers together under the droplight; while the younger people went into the drawing-room near by and talked.

Miss Highcamp played some selections from Grieg upon the piano. She seemed to have apprehended all of the composer's coldness and none of his poetry. While Edna listened she could not help wondering if she had lost her taste for music.

When the time came for her to go home, Mr. Highcamp grunted a lame offer to escort her, looking down at his slippered feet with tactless concern. It was Arobin who took her home. The car ride was long, and it was late when they reached Esplanade Street. Arobin asked permission to enter for a second to light his cigarette — his match safe was empty. He filled his match safe, but did not light his cigarette until he left her, after she had expressed her willingness to go to the races with him again.

Edna was neither tired nor sleepy. She was hungry again, for the Highcamp dinner, though of excellent quality, had lacked abundance. She rummaged in the larder and brought forth a slice of Gruyère and some crackers. She opened a bottle of beer which she found in the ice-box. Edna felt extremely restless and excited. She vacantly hummed a fantastic tune as she poked at the wood embers on the hearth and munched a cracker.

She wanted something to happen — something, anything; she did not know what. She regretted that she had not made Arobin stay a half hour to talk over the horses with her. She counted the money she had won. But there was nothing else to do, so she went to bed, and tossed there for hours in a sort of monotonous agitation.

In the middle of the night she remembered that she had forgotten to write her regular letter to her husband; and she decided to do so next day and tell him about her afternoon at the Jockey Club. She lay wide awake composing a letter which was nothing like the one which she wrote next day. When the maid awoke her in the morning Edna was dreaming of Mr. Highcamp playing the piano at the entrance of a music store on Canal Street, while his wife was saying to Alcée Arobin, as they boarded an Esplanade Street car.

"What a pity that so much talent has been neglected! but I must go."

When, a few days later, Alcée Arobin again called for Edna in his drag, Mrs. Highcamp was not with him. He said they would pick her up. But as that lady had not been apprised of his intention of picking her up, she was not at home. The daughter was just leaving the house to attend the meeting of a branch Folk Lore Society, and regretted that she could not accompany them. Arobin appeared nonplused, and asked Edna if there were any one else she cared to ask.

She did not deem it worth while to go in search of any of the fashionable acquaintances from whom she had withdrawn herself. She thought of Madame Ratignolle, but knew that her fair friend did not leave the house, except to take a languid walk around the block with her husband after nightfall. Mademoiselle Reisz would have laughed at such a request from Edna. Madame Lebrun might have enjoyed the outing, but for some reason Edna did not want her. So they went alone, she and Arobin.

The afternoon was intensely interesting to her. The excitement came back upon her like a remittent fever. Her talk grew familiar and confidential. It was no labor to become intimate with Arobin. His manner invited easy confidence. The preliminary stage of becoming acquainted was one which he always endeavored to ignore when a pretty and engaging woman was concerned.

He stayed and dined with Edna. He stayed and sat beside the wood fire. They laughed and talked; and before it was time to go he was telling her how different life might have been if he had known her years before. With ingenuous frankness he spoke of what a wicked, ill-disciplined boy he had been, and impulsively drew up his cuff to exhibit upon his wrist the scar from a saber cut which he had received in a duel outside of Paris when he was nineteen. She touched his hand as she scanned the red cicatrice on the inside of his white wrist. A quick impulse that was somewhat spasmodic impelled her fingers to close in a sort of clutch upon his hand. He felt the pressure of her pointed nails in the flesh of his palm.

She arose hastily and walked toward the mantel.

"The sight of a wound or scar always agitates and sickens me," she said. "I shouldn't have looked at it."

"I beg your pardon," he entreated, following her; "it never occurred to me that it might be repulsive."

He stood close to her, and the effrontery in his eyes repelled the old, vanishing self in her, yet drew all her awakening sensuousness. He saw enough in her face to impel him to take her hand and hold it while he said his lingering good night.

"Will you go to the races again?" he asked.

"No," she said. "I've had enough of the races. I don't want to lose all the money I've won, and I've got to work when the weather is bright, instead of—"

"Yes; work; to be sure. You promised to show me your work. What morning may I come up to your atelier? To-morrow?"

"No!"

"Day after?"

"No, no."

"Oh, please don't refuse me! I know something of such things. I might help you with a stray suggestion or two."

"No. Good night. Why don't you go after you have said good night? I don't like you," she went on in a high, excited pitch, attempting to draw away her hand. She felt that her words lacked dignity and sincerity, and she knew that he felt it.

"I'm sorry you don't like me. I'm sorry I offended you. How have I offended you? What have I done? Can't you forgive me?" And he bent and pressed his lips upon her hand as if he wished never more to withdraw them.

"Mr. Arobin," she complained, "I'm greatly upset by the excitement of the afternoon; I'm not myself. My manner must have misled you in some way. I wish you to go, please." She spoke in a monotonous, dull tone. He took his hat from the table, and stood with eyes turned from her, looking into the dying fire. For a moment or two he kept an impressive silence.

"Your manner has not misled me, Mrs. Pontellier," he said finally. "My own emotions have done that. I couldn't help it. When I'm near you, how could I help it? Don't think anything of it, don't bother, please. You see, I go when you command me. If you wish me to stay away, I shall do so. If you let me come back, I—oh! you will let me come back?"

He cast one appealing glance at her, to which she made no response. Alcée Arobin's manner was so genuine that it often deceived even himself.

Edna did not care or think whether it were genuine or not. When she was alone she looked mechanically at the back of her hand which he had kissed so warmly. Then she leaned her head down on the mantelpiece. She felt somewhat like a woman who in a moment of passion is betrayed into an act of infidelity, and realizes the significance of the act without being wholly awakened from its glamour. The thought was passing vaguely through her mind, "What would he think?"

She did not mean her husband; she was thinking of Robert Lebrun. Her husband seemed to her now like a person whom she had married without love as an excuse.

She lit a candle and went up to her room. Alcée Arobin was absolutely nothing to her. Yet his presence, his manners, the warmth of his glances, and above all the touch of his lips upon her hand had acted like a narcotic upon her.

She slept a languorous sleep, interwoven with vanishing dreams.

XXVI

Alcée Arobin wrote Edna an elaborate note of apology, palpitant with sincerity. It embarrassed her; for in a cooler, quieter moment it appeared to her absurd that she should have taken his action so seriously, so dramatically. She felt sure that the significance of the whole occurrence had lain in her own self-consciousness. If she ignored his note it would give undue importance to a trivial affair. If she replied to it in a serious spirit it would still leave in his mind the impression that she had in a susceptible moment yielded to his influence. After all, it was no great matter to have one's hand kissed. She was provoked at his having written the apology. She answered in as light and bantering a spirit as she fancied it deserved, and said she would be glad to have him look in upon her at work whenever he felt the inclination and his business gave him the opportunity.

He responded at once by presenting himself at her home with all his disarming naïveté. And then there was scarcely a day which followed that she did not see him or was not reminded of him. He was prolific in pretexts. His attitude became one of good-humored subservience and tacit adoration. He was ready at all times to submit to her moods, which were as often kind as they were cold. She grew accustomed to him. They became intimate and friendly by imperceptible degrees, and then by leaps. He sometimes talked in a way that astonished her at first and brought the crimson into her face; in a way that pleased her at last, appealing to the animalism that stirred impatiently within her.

There was nothing which so quieted the turmoil of Edna's senses as a visit to Mademoiselle Reisz. It was then, in the presence of that personality which was offensive to her, that the woman, by her divine art, seemed to reach Edna's spirit and set it free.

It was misty, with heavy, lowering atmosphere, one afternoon, when Edna climbed the stairs to the painist's apartments under the roof. Her clothes were dripping with moisture. She felt chilled and pinched as she entered the room. Mademoiselle was poking at a rusty stove that smoked a little and warmed the room indifferently. She was endeavoring to heat a pot of chocolate on the stove. The room looked cheerless and dingy to Edna as she entered. A bust of Beethoven, covered with a hood of dust, scowled at her from the mantelpiece.

"Ah! here comes the sunlight!" exclaimed Mademoiselle, rising from her knees before the stove. "Now it will be warm and bright enough; I can let the fire alone."

She closed the stove door with a bang, and approaching, assisted in removing Edna's dripping mackintosh.

"You are cold; you look miserable. The chocolate will soon be hot. But would you rather have a taste of brandy? I have scarcely touched the bottle which you brought me for my cold." A piece of red flannel was wrapped around Mademoiselle's throat; a stiff neck compelled her to hold her head on one side.

"I will take some brandy," said Edna, shivering as she removed her gloves and overshoes. She drank the liquor from the glass as a man would have done. Then flinging herself upon the uncomfortable sofa she said, "Mademoiselle, I am going to move away from my house on Esplanade Street."

"Ah!" ejaculated the musician, neither surprised nor especially interested. Nothing ever seemed to astonish her very much. She was endeavoring to adjust the bunch of violets which had become loose from its fastening in her hair. Edna drew her down upon the sofa, and taking a pin from her own hair, secured the shabby artificial flowers in their accustomed place.

"Aren't you astonished?"

"Passably. Where are you going? to New York? to Iberville? to your father in Mississippi? where?

"Just two steps away," laughed Edna, "in a little four-room house around the corner. It looks so cozy, so inviting and restful, whenever I pass by; and it's for rent. I'm tired looking after that big house. It never seemed like mine, anyway — like home. It's too much trouble. I have to keep too many servants. I am tired bothering with them."

"That is not your true reason, *ma belle.*[48] There is no use in telling me lies. I

[48]*ma belle* my pretty

don't know your reason, but you have not told me the truth." Edna did not protest or endeavor to justify herself.

"The house, the money that provides for it, are not mine. Isn't that enough reason?"

"They are your husband's," returned Mademoiselle, with a shrug and a malicious elevation of the eyebrows.

"Oh! I see there is no deceiving you. Then let me tell you: It is a caprice. I have a little money of my own from my mother's estate, which my father sends me by driblets. I won a large sum this winter on the races, and I am beginning to sell my sketches. Laidpore is more and more pleased with my work; he says it grows in force and individuality. I cannot judge of that myself, but I feel that I have gained in ease and confidence. However, as I said, I have sold a good many through Laidpore. I can live in the tiny house for little or nothing, with one servant. Old Celestine, who works occasionally for me, says she will come stay with me and do my work. I know I shall like it, like the feeling of freedom and independence."

"What does your husband say?"

"I have not told him yet. I only thought of it this morning. He will think I am demented, no doubt. Perhaps you think so."

Mademoiselle shook her head slowly. "Your reason is not yet clear to me," she said.

Neither was it quite clear to Edna herself; but it unfolded itself as she sat for a while in silence. Instinct had prompted her to put away her husband's bounty in casting off her allegiance. She did not know how it would be when he returned. They would have to be an understanding, an explanation. Conditions would some way adjust themselves, she felt; but whatever came, she had resolved never again to belong to another than herself.

"I shall give a grand dinner before I leave the old house!" Edna exclaimed. "You will have to come to it, Mademoiselle. I will give you everything that you like to eat and to drink. We shall sing and laugh and be merry for once." And she uttered a sigh that came from the very depths of her being.

If Mademoiselle happened to have received a letter from Robert during the interval of Edna's visits, she would give her the letter unsolicited. And she would seat herself at the piano and play as her humor prompted her while the young woman read the letter.

The little stove was roaring; it was red-hot, and the chocolate in the tin sizzled and sputtered. Edna went forward and opened the stove door, and Mademoiselle rising, took a letter from under the bust of Beethoven and handed it to Edna.

"Another! so soon!" she exclaimed, her eyes filled with delight. "Tell me, Mademoiselle, does he know that I see his letters?"

"Never in the world! He would be angry and would never write to me again if he thought so. Does he write to you? Never a line. Does he send you a message? Never a word. It is because he loves you, poor fool, and is trying to forget you, since you are not free to listen to him or to belong to him."

"Why do you show me his letters, then?"

"Haven't you begged for them? Can I refuse you anything? Oh! you cannot deceive me," and Mademoiselle approached her beloved instrument and began to play. Edna did not at once read the letter. She sat holding it in her hand, while the music penetrated her whole being like an effulgence, warming and brightening the dark places of her soul. It prepared her for joy and exultation.

"Oh!" she exclaimed, letting the letter fall to the floor. "Why did you not tell me?" She went and grasped Mademoiselle's hands up from the keys. "Oh! unkind! malicious! Why did you not tell me?"

"That he was coming back? No great news, *ma foi*. I wonder he did not come long ago."

"But when, when? cried Edna, impatiently. "He does not say when."

"He says 'very soon.' You know as much about it as I do; it is all in the letter."

"But why? Why is he coming? Oh, if I thought—" and she snatched the letter from the floor and turned the pages this way and that way, looking for the reason, which was left untold.

"If I were young and in love with a man," said Mademoiselle, turning on the stool and pressing her wiry hands between her knees as she looked down at Edna, who sat on the floor holding the letter, "it seems to me he would have to be some *grand esprit*;[49] a man with lofty aims and ability to reach them; one who stood high enough to attract the notice of his fellow-men. It seems to me if I were young and in love I should never deem a man of ordinary caliber worthy of my devotion."

"Now it is you who are telling lies and seeking to deceive me, Mademoiselle; or else you have never been in love, and know nothing about it. Why," went on Edna, clasping her knees and looking up into Mademoiselle's twisted face, "do you suppose a woman knows why she loves? Does she select? Does she say to herself: 'Go to! Here is a distinguished statesman with presidential possibilities; I shall proceed to fall in love with him.' Or, 'I shall set my heart upon this musician, whose fame is on every tongue?' Or, 'This financier, who controls the world's money markets?'"

"You are purposely misunderstanding me, *ma reine*.[50] Are you in love with Robert?"

"Yes," said Edna. It was the first time she had admitted it, and a glow overspread her face, blotching it with red spots.

"Why?" asked her companion. "Why do you love him when you ought not to?"

Edna, with a motion or two, dragged herself on her knees before Mademoiselle Reisz, who took the glowing face between her two hands.

"Why? Because his hair is brown and grows away from his temples; because he opens and shuts his eyes, and his nose is a little out of drawing; because he has two lips and a square chin, and a little finger which he can't straighten from having played baseball too energetically in his youth. Because—"

"Because you do, in short," laughed Mademoiselle. "What will you do when he comes back?" she asked.

"Do? Nothing, except feel glad and happy to be alive."

She was already glad and happy to be alive at the mere thought of his return. The murky, lowering sky, which had depressed her a few hours before, seemed bracing and invigorating as she splashed through the streets on her way home.

She stopped at a confectioner's and ordered a huge box of bonbons for the children in Iberville. She slipped a card in the box, on which she scribbled a tender message and sent an abundance of kisses.

Before dinner in the evening Edna wrote a charming letter to her husband, telling him of her intention to move for a while into the little house around the

[49] *grand esprit* literally: grand spirit—noble soul

[50] *my reine* my queen

block, and to give a farewell dinner before leaving, regretting that he was not there to share it, to help her out with the menu and assist her in entertaining the guests. Her letter was brilliant and brimming with cheerfulness.

XXVII

"What is the matter with you?" asked Arobin that evening. "I never found you in such a happy mood." Edna was tired by that time, and was reclining on the lounge before the fire.

"Don't you know the weather prophet has told us we shall see the sun pretty soon?"

"Well, that ought to be reason enough," he acquiesced. "You wouldn't give me another if I sat here all night imploring you." He sat close to her on a low tabouret,[51] and as he spoke his fingers lightly touched the hair that fell a little over her forehead. She liked the touch of his fingers through her hair, and closed her eyes sensitively.

"One of these days," she said, "I'm going to pull myself together for a while and think — try to determine what character of a woman I am; for, candidly, I don't know. By all the codes which I am acquainted with, I am a devilishly wicked specimen of the sex. But some way I can't convince myself that I am. I must think about it."

"Don't. What's the use? Why should you bother thinking about it when I can tell you what manner of woman you are." His fingers strayed occasionally down to her warm, smooth cheeks and firm chin, which was growing a little full and double.

"Oh, yes! You will tell me that I am adorable; everything that is captivating. Spare yourself the effort."

"No; I shan't tell you anything of the sort, though I shouldn't be lying if I did."

"Do you know Mademoiselle Reisz?" she asked irrelevantly.

"The pianist? I know her by sight. I've heard her play."

"She says queer things sometimes in a bantering way that you don't notice at the time and you find yourself thinking about afterward."

"For instance?"

"Well, for instance, when I left her to-day, she put her arms around me and felt my shoulder blades, to see if my wings were strong, she said. 'The bird that would soar above the level plain of tradition and prejudice must have strong wings. It is a sad spectacle to see the weaklings bruised, exhausted, fluttering back to earth.'"

"Whither would you soar?"

"I'm not thinking of any extraordinary flights. I only half comprehend her."

"I've heard she's partially demented," said Arobin.

"She seems to me wonderfully sane," Edna replied.

"I'm told she's extremely disagreeable and unpleasant. Why have you introduced her at a moment when I desired to talk of you?"

"Oh! talk of me if you like," cried Edna, clasping her hands beneath her head; "but let me think of something else while you do."

"I'm jealous of your thoughts to-night. They're making you a little kinder than usual; but some way I feel as if they were wandering, as if they were not here with me." She only looked at him and smiled. His eyes were very near. He leaned upon

[51]*tabouret* round stool

the lounge with an arm extended across her, while the other hand still rested upon her. They continued silently to look into each other's eyes. When he leaned forward and kissed her, she clasped his head, holding his lips to hers.

It was the first kiss of her life to which her nature had really responded. It was a flaming torch that kindled desire.

XXVIII

Edna cried a little that night after Arobin left her. It was only one phase of the multitudinous emotions which had assailed her. There was with her an overwhelming feeling of irresponsibility. There was the shock of the unexpected and the unaccustomed. There was her husband's reproach looking at her from the external things around her which he had provided for her external existence. There was Robert's reproach making itself felt by a quicker, fiercer, more overpowering love, which had awakened within her toward him. Above all, there was understanding. She felt as if a mist had been lifted from her eyes, enabling her to look upon and comprehend the significance of life, that monster made up of beauty and brutality. But among the conflicting sensations which assailed her, there was neither shame or remorse. There was a dull pang of regret because it was not the kiss of love which had inflamed her, because it was not love which had held this cup of life to her lips.

XXIX

Without even waiting for an answer from her husband regarding his opinion or wishes in the matter, Edna hastened her preparations for quitting her home on Esplanade Street and moving into the little house around the block. A feverish anxiety attended her every action in that direction. There was no moment of deliberation, no interval of repose between the thought and its fulfillment. Early upon the morning following those hours passed in Arobin's society, Edna set about securing her new abode and hurrying her arrangements for occupying it. Within the precincts of her home she felt like one who has entered and lingered within the portals of some forbidden temple in which a thousand muffled voices bade her begone.

Whatever was her own in the house, everything which she had acquired aside from her husband's bounty, she caused to be transported to the other house, supplying simple and meager deficiencies from her own resources.

Arobin found her with rolled sleeves, working in company with the housemaid when he looked in during the afternoon. She was splendid and robust, and had never appeared handsomer than in the old blue gown, with a red silk handkerchief knotted at random around her head to protect her hair from the dust. She was mounted upon a high step-ladder, unhooking a picture from the wall when he entered. He had found the front door open, and had followed his ring by walking in unceremoniously.

"Come down!" he said. "Do you want to kill yourself?" She greeted him with affected carelessness, and appeared absorbed in her occupation.

If he had expected to find her languishing, reproachful, or indulging in sentimental tears, he must have been greatly surprised.

He was no doubt prepared for any emergency, ready for any one of the foregoing attitudes, just as he bent himself easily and naturally to the situation which confronted him.

"Please come down," he insisted, holding the ladder and looking up at her.

"No," she answered; "Ellen is afraid to mount the ladder. Joe is working over at the 'pigeon house'—that's the name Ellen gives it, because it's so small and looks like a pigeon house—and some one has to do this."

Arobin pulled off his coat, and expressed himself ready and willing to tempt fate in her place. Ellen brought him one of her dust-caps, and went into contortions of mirth, which she found it impossible to control, when she saw him put it on before the mirror as grotesquely as he could. Edna herself could not refrain from smiling when she fastened it at his request. So it was he who in turn mounted the ladder, unhooking pictures and curtains, and dislodging ornaments as Edna directed. When he had finished he took off his dust-cap and went out to wash his hands.

Edna was sitting on the tabouret, idly brushing the tips of a feather duster along the carpet when he came in again.

"Is there anything more you will let me do?" he asked.

"That is all," she answered. "Ellen can manage the rest." She kept the young woman occupied in the drawing-room, unwilling to be left alone with Arobin.

"What about the dinner?" he asked; "the grand event, the *coup d'état*?"

"It will be day after to-morrow. Why do you call it the *coup d'état*? Oh! it will be very fine; all my best of everything—crystal, silver and gold, Sèvres, flowers, music, and champagne to swim in. I'll let Léonce pay the bills. I wonder what he'll say when he sees the bills."

"And you ask me why I call it a *coup d'état*?" Arobin had put on his coat, and he stood before her and asked if his cravat was plumb. She told him it was, looking no higher than the tip of his collar.

"When do you go to the 'pigeon house?'—with all due acknowledgment to Ellen."

"Day after to-morrow, after the dinner. I shall sleep there."

"Ellen, will you very kindly get me a glass of water?" asked Arobin. "The dust in the curtains, if you will pardon me for hinting such a thing, has parched my throat to a crisp."

"While Ellen gets the water," said Edna, rising, "I will say good-by and let you go. I must get rid of this grime, and I have a million things to do and think of."

"When shall I see you?" asked Arobin, seeking to detain her, the maid having left the room.

"At the dinner, of course. You are invited."

"Not before?—not to-night or to-morrow morning or to-morrow noon or night? or the day after morning or noon? Can't you see yourself, without my telling you, what an eternity it is?"

He had followed her into the hall and to the foot of the stairway, looking up at her as she mounted with her face half turned to him.

"Not an instant sooner," she said. But she laughed and looked at him with eyes that at once gave him courage to wait and made it torture to wait.

XXX

Though Edna had spoken of the dinner as a very grand affair, it was in truth a very small affair and very select, in so much as the guests invited were few and were selected with discrimination. She had counted upon an even dozen seating themselves at her round mahogany board, forgetting for the moment that Madame Ratignolle was to the last degree *souffrante*[52] and unpresentable, and not foreseeing that Madame Lebrun would sent a thousand regrets at the last moment. So there were only ten, after all, which made a cozy, comfortable number.

There were Mr. and Mrs. Merriman, a pretty, vivacious little woman in the thirties; her husband, a jovial fellow, something of a shallow-pate, who laughed a good deal at other people's witticisms, and had thereby made himself extremely popular. Mrs. Highcamp had accompanied them. Of course, there was Alcée Arobin; and Mademoiselle Reisz had consented to come. Edna had sent her a fresh bunch of violets with black lace trimmings for her hair. Monsieur Ratignolle brought himself and his wife's excuses. Victor Lebrun, who happened to be in the city, bent upon relaxation, had accepted with alacrity. There was a Miss Mayblunt, no longer in her teens, who looked at the world through lorgnettes and with the keenest interest. It was thought and said that she was intellectual; it was suspected of her that she wrote under a *nom de guerre*.[53] She had come with a gentleman by the name of Gouvernail, connected with one of the daily papers, of whom nothing special could be said, except that he was observant and seemed quiet and inoffensive. Edna herself made the tenth, and at half-past eight they seated themselves at table, Arobin and Monsieur Ratignolle on either side of their hostess.

Mrs. Highcamp sat between Arobin and Victor Lebrun. Then came Mrs. Merriman, Mr. Gouvernail, Miss Mayblunt, Mr. Merriman, and Mademoiselle Reisz next to Monsieur Ratignolle.

There was something extremely gorgeous about the appearance of the table, an effect of splendor conveyed by a cover of pale yellow satin under strips of lace-work. There were wax candles in massive brass candelabra, burning softly under yellow silk shades; full, fragrant roses, yellow and red, abounded. There were silver and gold, as she had said there would be, and crystal which glittered like the gems which the women wore.

The ordinary stiff dining chairs had been discarded for the occasion and replaced by the most commodious and luxurious which could be collected throughout the house. Mademoiselle Reisz, being exceedingly diminutive, was elevated upon cushions, as small children are sometimes hoisted at table upon bulky volumes.

"Something new, Edna?" exclaimed Miss Mayblunt, with lorgnette directed toward a magnificent cluster of diamonds that sparkled, that almost sputtered, in Edna's hair, just over the center of her forehead.

"Quite new; 'brand' new, in fact; a present from my husband. It arrived this morning from New York. I may as well admit that this is my birthday, and that I am twenty-nine. In good time I expect you to drink my health. Meanwhile, I shall ask you to begin with this cocktail, composed—would you say 'composed?'" with an appeal to Miss Mayblunt—"composed by my father in honor of Sister Janet's wedding."

Before each guest stood a tiny glass that looked and sparkled like a garnet gem.

"Then, all things considered," spoke Arobin, "it might not be amiss to start out

[52]*souffrante* in discomfort
[53]*nom de guerre* pseudonym

by drinking the Colonel's health in the cocktail which he composed, on the birthday of the most charming of women—the daughter whom he invented."

Mr. Merriman's laugh at this sally was such a genuine outburst and so contagious that it started the dinner with an agreeable swing that never slackened.

Miss Mayblunt begged to be allowed to keep her cocktail untouched before her, just to look at. The color was marvelous! She could compare it to nothing she had ever seen, and the garnet lights which it emitted were unspeakably rare. She pronounced the Colonel an artist, and stuck to it.

Monsieur Ratignolle was prepared to take things seriously: the *mets*, the *entre-mets*,[54] the service, the decorations, even the people. He looked up from his pompono and inquired of Arobin if he were related to the gentleman of that name who formed one of the firm of Laitner and Arobin, lawyers. The younger man admitted that Laitner was a warm personal friend, who permitted Arobin's name to decorate the firm's letterheads and to appear upon a shingle that graced Perdido Street.

"There are so many inquisitive people and institutions abounding," said Arobin, "that one is really forced as a matter of convenience these days to assume the virtue of an occupation if he has it not."

Monsieur Ratignolle stared a little, and turned to ask Mademoiselle Reisz if she considered the symphony concerts up to the standard which had been set the previous winter. Mademoiselle Reisz answered Monsieur Ratignolle in French, which Edna thought a little rude, under the circumstances, but characteristic. Mademoiselle had only disagreeable things to say of the symphony concerts, and insulting remarks to make of all the musicians of New Orleans, singly and collectively. All her interest seemed to be centered upon the delicacies placed before her.

Mr. Merriman said that Mr. Arobin's remark about inquisitive people reminded him of a man from Waco the other day at the St. Charles Hotel—but as Mr. Merriman's stories were always lame and lacking point, his wife seldom permitted him to complete them. She interrupted him to ask if he remembered the name of the author whose book she had bought the week before to send to a friend in Geneva. She was talking "books" with Mr. Gouvernail and trying to draw from him his opinion upon current literary topics. Her husband told the story of the Waco man privately to Miss Mayblunt, who pretended to be greatly amused and to think it extremely clever.

Mrs. Highcamp hung with languid but unaffected interest upon the warm and impetuous volubility of her left-hand neighbor, Victor Lebrun. Her attention was never for a moment withdrawn from him after seating herself at table; and when he turned to Mrs. Merriman, who was prettier and more vivacious than Mrs. Highcamp, she waited with easy indifference for an opportunity to reclaim his attention. There was the occasional sound of music, of mandolins, sufficiently removed to be an agreeable accompaniment rather than an interruption to the conversation. Outside the soft, monotonous splash of a fountain could be heard; the sound penetrated into the room with the heavy odor of jessamine that came through the open windows.

The golden shimmer of Edna's satin gown spread in rich folds on either side of her. There was a soft fall of lace encircling her shoulders. It was the color of her

[54]*mets* and *entre-mets* main course and side dishes; *pompono*—southern fish

skin, without the glow, the myriad living tints that one may sometimes discover in vibrant flesh. There was something in her attitude, in her whole appearance when she leaned her head against the high-backed chair and spread her arms, which suggested the regal woman, the one who rules, who looks on, who stands alone.

But as she sat there amid her guests, she felt the old ennui overtaking her; the hopelessness which so often assailed her, which came upon her like an obsession, like something extraneous, independent of volition. It was something which announced itself; a chill breath that seemed to issue from some vast cavern wherein discords wailed. There came over her the acute longing which always summoned into her spiritual vision the presence of the beloved one, overpowering her at once with a sense of the unattainable.

The moments glided on, while a feeling of good fellowship passed around the circle like a mystic cord, holding and binding these people together with jest and laughter. Monsieur Ratignolle was the first to break the pleasant charm. At ten o'clock he excused himself. Madame Ratignolle was waiting for him at home. She was *bien souffrante*,[55] and she was filled with vague dread, which only her husband's presence could allay.

Mademoiselle Reisz arose with Monsieur Ratignolle, who offered to escort her to the car. She had eaten well; she had tasted the good, rich wines, and they must have turned her head, for she bowed pleasantly to all as she withdrew from table. She kissed Edna upon the shoulder, and whispered: "*Bonne nuit, ma reine; soyez sage.*"[56] She had been a little bewildered upon rising, or rather, descending from her cushions, and Monsieur Ratignolle gallantly took her arm and led her away.

Mrs. Highcamp was weaving a garland of roses, yellow and red. When she had finished the garland, she laid it lightly upon Victor's black curls. He was reclining far back in the luxurious chair, holding a glass of champagne to the light.

As if a magician's wand had touched him, the garland of roses transformed him into a vision of Oriental beauty. His cheeks were the color of crushed grapes, and his dusky eyes glowed with a languishing fire.

"*Sapristi!*" exclaimed Arobin.

But Mrs. Highcamp had one more touch to add to the picture. She took from the back of her chair a white silken scarf, with which she had covered her shoulders in the early part of the evening. She draped it across the boy in graceful folds, and in a way to conceal his black, conventional evening dress. He did not seem to mind what she did to him, only smiled, showing a faint gleam of white teeth, while he continued to gaze with narrowing eyes at the light through his glass of champagne.

"Oh! to be able to paint in color rather than in words!" exclaimed Miss Mayblunt, losing herself in a rhapsodic dream as she looked at him.

"'There was a graven image of Desire
Painted with red blood on a ground of gold.'"[57]

murmured Gouvernail, under his breath.

The effect of the wine upon Victor was to change his accustomed volubility into silence. He seemed to have abandoned himself to a reverie, and to be seeing pleasing visions in the amber bead.

[55]*bien souffrante* in great discomfort

[56]"*Bonne nuit, ma reine; soyez sage.*" "Good night, my queen; be good."

[57]From *A Cameo*, a sonnet by Algernon Charles Swinburne (1837–1909)

"Sing," entreated Mrs. Highcamp. "Won't you sing to us?"

"Let him alone," said Arobin.

"He's posing," offered Mr. Merriman; "let him have it out."

"I believe he's paralyzed," laughed Mrs. Merriman. And leaning over the youth's chair, she took the glass from his hand and held it to his lips. He sipped the wine slowly, and when he had drained the glass she laid it upon the table and wiped his lips with her little filmy handkerchief.

"Yes, I'll sing for you," he said, turning in his chair toward Mrs. Highcamp. He clasped his hands behind his head, and looking up at the ceiling began to hum a little, trying his voice like a musician tuning an instrument. Then, looking at Edna, he began to sing:

"Ah! si tu savais!"

"Stop!" she cried, "don't sing that. I don't want you to sing it," and she laid her glass so impetuously and blindly upon the table as to shatter it against a carafe. The wine spilled over Arobin's legs and some of it trickled down upon Mrs. Highcamp's black gauze gown. Victor had lost all idea of courtesy, or else he thought his hostess was not in earnest, for he laughed and went on:

"Ah! si tu savais
Ce que tes yeux me disent"—

"Oh! you mustn't! you mustn't," exclaimed Edna, and pushing back her chair she got up, and going behind him placed her hand over his mouth. He kissed the soft palm that pressed upon his lips.

"No, no, I won't, Mrs. Pontellier. I didn't know you meant it," looking up at her with caressing eyes. The touch of his lips was like a pleasing sting to her hand. She lifted the garland of roses from his head and flung it across the room.

"Come, Victor; you've posed long enough. Give Mrs. Highcamp her scarf."

Mrs. Highcamp undraped the scarf from about him with her own hands. Miss Mayblunt and Mr. Gouvernail suddenly conceived the notion that it was time to say good night. And Mr. and Mrs. Merriman wondered how it could be so late.

Before parting from Victor, Mrs. Highcamp invited him to call upon her daughter, who she knew would be charmed to meet him and talk French and sing French songs with him. Victor expressed his desire and intention to call upon Miss Highcamp at the first opportunity which presented itself. He asked if Arobin were going his way. Arobin was not.

The mandolin players had long since stolen away. A profound stillness had fallen upon the broad, beautiful street. The voices of Edna's disbanding guests jarred like a discordant note upon the quiet harmony of the night.

XXXI

"Well?" questioned Arobin, who had remained with Edna after the others had departed.

"Well," she reiterated, and stood up, stretching her arms, and feeling the need to relax her muscles after having been so long seated.

"What next?" he asked.

"The servants are all gone. They left when the musicians did. I have dismissed them. The house has to be closed and locked, and I shall trot around to the pigeon house, and shall send Celestine over in the morning to straighten things up."

He looked around, and began to turn out some of the lights.

"What about upstairs?" he inquired.

"I think it is all right; but there may be a window or two unlatched. We had better look; you might take a candle and see. And bring me my wrap and hat on the foot of the bed in the middle room."

He went up with the light, and Edna began closing doors and windows. She hated to shut in the smoke and the fumes of the wine. Arobin found her cape and hat, which he brought down and helped her to put on.

When everything was secured and the lights put out, they left through the front door, Arobin locking it and taking the key, which he carried for Edna. He helped her down the steps.

"Will you have a spray of jessamine?" he asked, breaking off a few blossoms as he passed.

"No; I don't want anything."

She seemed disheartened, and had nothing to say. She took his arm, which he offered her, holding up the weight of her satin train with the other hand. She looked down, noticing the black line of his leg moving in and out so close to her against the yellow shimmer of her gown. There was the whistle of a railway train somewhere in the distance, and the midnight bells were ringing. They met no one in their short walk.

The "pigeon-house" stood behind a locked gate, and a shallow *parterre*[58] that had been somewhat neglected. There was a small front porch, upon which a long window and the front door opened. The door opened directly into the parlor; there was no side entry. Back in the yard was a room for servants, in which old Celestine had been ensconced.

Edna had left a lamp burning low upon the table. She had succeeded in making the room look habitable and homelike. There were some books on the table and a lounge near at hand. On the floor was a fresh matting, covered with a rug or two; and on the walls hung a few tasteful pictures. But the room was filled with flowers. These were a surprise to her. Arobin had sent them, and had had Celestine distribute them during Edna's absence. Her bedroom was adjoining, and across a small passage were the dining-room and kitchen.

Edna seated herself with very appearance of discomfort.

"Are you tired?" he asked.

"Yes, and chilled, and miserable. I feel as if I had been wound up to a certain pitch — too tight — and something inside of me had snapped." She rested her head against the table upon her bare arm.

"You want to rest," he said, "and to be quiet. I'll go; I'll leave you and let you rest."

"Yes," she replied.

He stood up beside her and smoothed her hair with his soft, magnetic hand. His touch conveyed to her a certain physical comfort. She could have fallen quietly asleep there if he had continued to pass his hand over her hair. He brushed the hair upward from the nape of her neck.

"I hope you will feel better and happier in the morning," he said. "You have tried to do too much in the past few days. The dinner was the last straw; you might have dispensed with it."

"Yes," she admitted; "it was stupid."

[58]*parterre* garden

"No, it was delightful; but it has worn you out." His hand had strayed to her beautiful shoulders, and he could feel the response of her flesh to his touch. He seated himself beside her and kissed her lightly upon the shoulder.

"I thought you were going away," she said, in an uneven voice.

"I am, after I have said good night."

"Good night," she murmured.

He did not answer, except to continue to caress her. He did not say good night until she had become supple to his gentle, seductive entreaties.

XXXII

When Mr. Pontellier learned of his wife's intention to abandon her home and take up her residence elsewhere, he immediately wrote her a letter of unqualified disapproval and remonstrance. She had given reasons which he was unwilling to acknowledge as adequate. He hoped she had not acted upon her rash impulse; and he begged her to consider first, foremost, and above all else, what people would say. He was not dreaming of scandal when he uttered this warning; that was a thing which would never have entered into his mind to consider in connection with his wife's name or his own. He was simply thinking of his financial integrity. It might get noised about that the Pontelliers had met with reverses, and were forced to conduct their *ménage*[59] on a humbler scale than heretofore. It might do incalculable mischief to his business prospects.

But remembering Edna's whimsical turn of mind of late, and foreseeing that she had immediately acted upon her impetuous determination, he grasped the situation with his usual promptness and handled it with his well-known business tact and cleverness.

The same mail which brought to Edna his letter of disapproval carried instructions—the most minute instructions—to a well-known architect concerning the remodeling of his home, changes which he had long contemplated, and which he desired carried forward during his temporary absence.

Expert and reliable packers and movers were engaged to convey the furniture, carpets, pictures—everything movable, in short—to places of security. And in an incredibly short time the Pontellier house was turned over to the artisans. There was to be an addition—a small snuggery;[60] there was to be frescoing, and hardwood flooring was to be put into such rooms as had not yet been subjected to this improvement.

Furthermore, in one of the daily papers appeared a brief notice to the effect that Mr. and Mrs. Pontellier were contemplating a summer sojourn abroad, and that their handsome residence on Esplanade Street was undergoing sumptuous alterations, and would not be ready for occupancy until their return. Mr. Pontellier had saved appearances!

Edna admired the skill of his maneuver, and avoided any occasion to balk his intentions. When the situation as set forth by Mr. Pontellier was accepted and taken for granted, she was apparently satisfied that it should be so.

The pigeon-house pleased her. It at once assumed the intimate character of a home, while she herself invested it with a charm which it reflected like a warm

[59]*ménage* household
[60]*snuggery* den

glow. There was with her a feeling of having descended in the social scale, with a corresponding sense of having risen in the spiritual. Every step which she took toward relieving herself from obligations added to her strength and expansion as an individual. She began to look with her own eyes; to see and to apprehend the deeper undercurrents of life. No longer was she content to "feed upon opinion" when her own soul had invited her.

After a little while, a few days, in fact, Edna went up and spent a week with her children in Iberville. They were delicious February days, with all the summer's promise hovering in the air.

How glad she was to see the children! She wept for very pleasure when she felt their little arms clasping her; their hard, ruddy cheeks pressed against her own glowing cheeks. She looked into their faces with hungry eyes that could not be satisfied with looking. And what stories they had to tell their mother! About the pigs, the cows, the mules! About riding to the mill behind Gluglu; fishing back in the lake with their Uncle Jasper; picking pecans with Lidie's little black brood, and hauling chips in their express wagon. It was a thousand times more fun to haul real chips for old lame Susie's real fire than to drag painted blocks along the banquette on Esplanade Street!

She went with them herself to see the pigs and the cows, to look at the darkies laying the cane, to thrash the pecan trees, and catch fish in the back lake. She lived with them a whole week long, giving them all of herself, and gathering and filling herself with their young existence. They listened, breathless, when she told them the house in Esplanade Street was crowded with workmen, hammering, nailing, sawing, and filling the place with clatter. They wanted to know where their bed was; what had been done with their rocking-horse; and where did Joe sleep, and where had Ellen gone, and the cook? But, above all, they were fired with a desire to see the little house around the block. Was there any place to play? Were there any boys next door? Raoul, with pessimistic foreboding, was convinced that there were only girls next door. Where would they sleep, and where would papa sleep? She told them the fairies would fix it all right.

The old Madam was charmed with Edna's visit, and showered all manner of delicate attentions upon her. She was delighted to know that the Esplanade Street house was in a dismantled condition. It gave her the promise and pretext to keep the children indefinitely.

It was with a wrench and a pang that Edna left her children. She carried away with her the sound of their voices and the touch of their cheeks. All along the journey homeward their presence lingered with her like the memory of a delicious song. But by the time she had regained the city the song no longer echoed in her soul. She was again alone.

XXXIII

It happened sometimes when Edna went to see Mademoiselle Reisz that the little musician was absent, giving a lesson or making some small necessary household purchase. The key was always left in a secret hiding-place in the entry, which Edna knew. If Mademoiselle happened to be away, Edna would usually enter and wait for her return.

When she knocked at Mademoiselle Reisz's door one afternoon there was no response; so unlocking the door, as usual, she entered and found the apartment deserted, as she had expected. Her day had been quite filled up, and it was for a rest, for a refuge, and to talk about Robert, that she sought out her friend.

She had worked at her canvas — a young Italian character study — all the morning, completing the work without the model; but there had been many interruptions, some incident to her modest housekeeping, and others of a social nature.

Madame Ratignolle had dragged herself over, avoiding the too public thoroughfares, she said. She complained that Edna had neglected her much of late. Besides, she was consumed with curiosity to see the little house and the manner in which it was conducted. She wanted to hear all about the dinner party; Monsieur Ratignolle had left *so* early. What had happened after he left? The champagne and grapes which Edna sent over were *too* delicious. She had so little appetite; they had refreshed and toned her stomach. Where on earth was she going to put Mr. Pontellier in that little house, and the boys? And then she made Edna promise to go to her when her hour of trial overtook her.

"At any time — any time of the day or night, dear," Edna assured her.

Before leaving Madame Ratignolle said:

"In some way you seem to me like a child, Edna. You seem to act without a certain amount of reflection which is necessary in this life. That is the reason I want to say you mustn't mind if I advise you to be a little careful while you are living here alone. Why don't you have some one come and stay with you? Wouldn't Mademoiselle Reisz come?"

"No; she wouldn't wish to come, and I shouldn't want her always with me."

"Well, the reason — you know how evil-minded the world is — some one was talking of Alcée Arobin visiting you. Of course, it wouldn't matter if Mr. Arobin had not such a dreadful reputation. Monsieur Ratignolle was telling me that his attentions alone are considered enough to ruin a woman's name."

"Does he boast of his successes?" asked Edna, indifferently, squinting at her picture.

"No, I think not. I believe he is a decent fellow as far as that goes. But his character is so well known among the men. I shan't be able to come back and see you; it was very, very imprudent to-day."

"Mind the step!" cried Edna.

"Don't neglect me," entreated Madame Ratignolle; "and don't mind what I said about Arobin, or having some one to stay with you."

"Of course not," Edna laughed. "You may say anything you like to me." They asked each other good-by. Madame Ratignolle had not far to go, and Edna stood on the porch a while watching her walk down the street.

Then in the afternoon Mrs. Merriman and Mrs. Highcamp had made their "party call." Edna felt that they might have dispensed with the formality. They had also come to invite her to play *vingt-et-un*[61] one evening at Mrs. Merriman's. She was asked to go early, to dinner, and Mr. Merriman or Mr. Arobin would take her home. Edna accepted in a half-hearted way. She sometimes felt very tired of Mrs. Highcamp and Mrs. Merriman.

Late in the afternoon she sought refuge with Mademoiselle Reisz, and stayed there alone, waiting for her, feeling a kind of repose invade her with the very atmosphere of the shabby, unpretentious little room.

Edna sat at the window, which looked out over the housetops and across the

[61]*vingt-et-un* Twenty-one, a card game

river. The window frame was filled with pots of flowers, and she sat and picked the dry leaves from a rose geranium. The day was warm, and the breeze which blew from the river was very pleasant. She removed her hat and laid it on the piano. She went on picking the leaves and digging around the plants with her hat pin. Once she thought she heard Mademoiselle Reisz approaching. But it was a young black girl, who came in, bringing a small bundle of laundry, which she deposited in the adjoining room, and went away.

Edna seated herself at the piano, and softly picked out with one hand the bars of a piece of music which lay open before her. A half-hour went by. There was the occasional sound of people going and coming in the lower hall. She was growing interested in her occupation of picking out the aria, when there was a second rap at the door. She vaguely wondered what these people did when they found Mademoiselle's door locked.

"Come in," she called, turning her face toward the door. And this time it was Robert Lebrun who presented himself. She attempted to rise; she could not have done so without betraying the agitation which mastered her at sight of him, so she fell back upon the stool, only exclaiming, "Why, Robert!"

He came and clasped her hand, seemingly without knowing what he was saying or doing.

"Mrs. Pontellier! How do you happen — oh! how well you look! Is Mademoiselle Reisz not here? I never expected to see you."

"When did you come back?" asked Edna in an unsteady voice, wiping her face with her handkerchief. She seemed ill at ease on the piano stool, and he begged her to take the chair by the window. She did so, mechanically, while he seated himself on the stool.

"I returned day before yesterday," he answered, while he leaned his arm on the keys, bringing forth a crash of discordant sound.

"Day before yesterday!" she repeated, aloud; and went on thinking to herself, "day before yesterday," in a sort of an uncomprehending way. She had pictured him seeing her at the very first hour, and he had lived under the same sky since day before yesterday; while only by accident had he stumbled upon her. Mademoiselle must have lied when she said, "Poor fool, he loves you."

"Day before yesterday," she repeated, breaking off a spray of Mademoiselle's geranium; "then if you had not met me here today you wouldn't — when — that is, didn't you mean to come and see me?"

"Of course, I should have gone to see you. There have been so many things — " he turned the leaves of Mademoiselle's music nervously. "I started in at once yesterday with the old firm. After all there is as much chance for me here as there was there — that is, I might find it profitable some day. The Mexicans were not very congenial."

So he had come back because the Mexicans were not congenial; because business was as profitable here as there; because of any reason, and not because he cared to be near her. She remembered the day she sat on the floor, turning the pages of his letter, seeking the reason which was left untold.

She had not noticed how he looked — only feeling his presence; but she turned deliberately and observed him. After all, he had been absent but a few months, and was not changed. His hair — the color of hers — waved back from his temples in the same way as before. His skin was not more burned than it had been at Grand Isle. She found in his eyes, when he looked at her for one silent moment, the same tender caress, with an added warmth and entreaty which had not been there before — the same glance which had penetrated to the sleeping places of her soul and awakened them.

A hundred times Edna had pictured Robert's return, and imagined their first meeting. It was usually at her home, whither he had sought her out at once. She always fancied him expressing or betraying in some way his love for her. And here, the reality was that they sat ten feet apart, she at the window, crushing geranium leaves in her hand and smelling them, he twirling around on the piano stool, saying:

"I was very much surprised to hear of Mr. Pontellier's absence; it's a wonder Mademoiselle Reisz did not tell me; and your moving — mother told me yesterday. I should think you would have gone to New York with him, or to Iberville with the children, rather than be bothered here with housekeeping. And you are going abroad, too, I hear. We shan't have you at Grand Isle next summer; it won't seem — do you see much of Mademoiselle Reisz? She often spoke of you in the few letters she wrote."

"Do you remember that you promised to write to me when you went away?" A flush overspread his whole face.

"I couldn't believe that my letters would be of any interest to you."

"That is an excuse; it isn't the truth." Edna reached for her hat on the piano. She adjusted it, sticking the hat pin through the heavy coil of hair with some deliberation.

"Are you not going to wait for Mademoiselle Reisz?" asked Robert.

"No; I have found when she is absent this long, she is liable not to come back till late." She drew on her gloves, and Robert picked up his hat.

"Won't you wait for her?" asked Edna.

"Not if you think she will not be back till late," adding, as if suddenly aware of some discourtesy in his speech, "and I should miss the pleasure of walking home with you." Edna locked the door and put the key back in its hiding-place.

They went together, picking their way across muddy streets and sidewalks encumbered with the cheap display of small tradesmen. Part of the distance they rode in the car, and after disembarking, passed the Pontellier mansion, which looked broken and half torn asunder. Robert had never known the house, and looked at it with interest.

"I never knew you in your home," he remarked.

"I am glad you did not."

"Why?" She did not answer. They went on around the corner, and it seemed as if her dreams were coming true after all, when he followed her into the little house.

"You must stay and dine with me, Robert. You see I am all alone, and it is so long since I have seen you. There is so much I want to ask you."

She took off her hat and gloves. He stood irresolute, making some excuse about his mother who expected him; he even muttered something about an engagement. She struck a match and lit the lamp on the table; it was growing dusk. When he saw her face in the lamp-light, looking pained, with all the soft lines gone out of it, he threw his hat aside and seated himself.

"Oh! you know I want to stay if you will let me!" he exclaimed. All the softness came back. She laughed, and went and put her hand on his shoulder.

"This is the first moment you have seemed like the old Robert. I'll go tell Celestine." She hurried away to tell Celestine to set an extra place. She even sent her off in search of some added delicacy which she had not thought of for herself. And she recommended great care in dripping the coffee and having the omelet done to a proper turn.

When she reëntered, Robert was turning over magazines, sketches, and things that lay upon the table in great disorder. He picked up a photograph, and exclaimed:

"Alcée Arobin! What on earth is his picture doing here?"

"I tried to make a sketch of his head one day," answered Edna "and he thought the photograph might help me. It was at the other house. I thought it had been left there. I must have packed it up with my drawing materials."

"I should think you would give it back to him if you have finished with it."

"Oh! I have a great many such photographs. I never think of returning them. They don't amount to anything." Robert kept on looking at the picture.

"It seems to me—do you think his head worth drawing? Is he a friend of Mr. Pontellier's? You never said you knew him."

"He isn't a friend of Mr. Pontellier's; he's a friend of mine. I always knew him—that is, it is only of late that I know him pretty well. But I'd rather talk about you, and know what you have been seeing and doing and feeling out there in Mexico." Robert threw aside the picture.

"I've been seeing the waves and the white beach of Grand Isle; the quiet, grassy street of the *Chênière*; the old fort at Grande Terre. I've been working like a machine, and feeling like a lost soul. There was nothing interesting."

She leaned her head upon her hand to shade her eyes from the light.

"And what have you been seeing and doing and feeling all these days?" he asked.

"I've been seeing the waves and the white beach of Grand Isle; the quiet, grassy street of the *Chênière Caminada*; the old sunny fort at Grande Terre. I've been working with a little more comprehension than a machine and still feeling like a lost soul. There was nothing interesting."

"Mrs. Pontellier, you are cruel," he said, with feeling, closing his eyes and resting his head back in his chair. They remained in silence till old Celestine announced dinner.

XXXIV

The dining-room was very small. Edna's round mahogany would have almost filled it. As it was there was but a step or two from the little table to the kitchen, to the mantel, the small buffet, and the side door that opened out on the narrow brick-paved yard.

A certain degree of ceremony settled upon them with the announcement of dinner. There was no return to personalities. Robert related incidents of his sojourn in Mexico, and Edna talked of events likely to interest him, which had occurred during his absence. The dinner was of ordinary quality, except for the few delicacies which she had sent out to purchase. Old Celestine, with a bandana *tignon*[62] twisted about her head, hobbled in and out, taking a personal interest in everything; and she lingered occasionally to talk patois with Robert, whom she had known as a boy.

[62]*tignon* hair tied up with a scarf (archaic form of *chignon*, a coil of hair); *patois*—dialect

He went out to a neighboring cigar stand to purchase cigarette papers, and when he came back he found that Celestine had served the black coffee in the parlor.

"Perhaps I shouldn't have come back," he said. "When you are tired of me, tell me to go."

"You never tire me. You must have forgotten the hours and hours at Grand Isle in which we grew accustomed to each other and used to being together."

"I have forgotten nothing at Grand Isle," he said, not looking at her, but rolling a cigarette. His tobacco pouch, which he laid upon the table, was a fantastic embroidered silk affair, evidently the handiwork of a woman.

"You used to carry your tobacco in a rubber pouch," said Edna, picking up the pouch and examining the needlework.

"Yes; it was lost."

"Where did you buy this one? In Mexico?"

"It was given to me by a Vera Cruz girl; they are very generous," he replied, striking a match and lighting his cigarette.

"They are very handsome, I suppose, those Mexican women; very picturesque, with their black eyes and their lace scarfs."

"Some are; others are hideous. Just as you find women everywhere."

"What was she like — the one who gave you the pouch? You must have known her very well."

"She was very ordinary. She wasn't of the slightest importance. I knew her well enough."

"Did you visit at her house? Was it interesting? I should like to know and hear about the people you met, and the impressions they made on you."

"There are some people who leave impressions not so lasting as the imprint of an oar upon the water."

"Was she such a one?"

"It would be ungenerous for me to admit that she was of that order and kind." He thrust the pouch back in his pocket, as if to put away the subject with the trifle which had brought it up.

Arobin dropped in with a message from Mrs. Merriman, to say that the card party was postponed on account of the illness of one of her children.

"How do you do, Arobin?" said Robert, rising from the obscurity

"Oh! Lebrun. To be sure! I heard yesterday you were back. How did they treat you down in Mexique?"

"Fairly well."

"But not well enough to keep you there. Stunning girls, though, in Mexico. I thought I should never get away from Vera Cruz when I was down there a couple of years ago."

"Did they embroider slippers and tobacco pouches and hatbands and things for you?" asked Edna.

"Oh! my! no! I didn't get so deep in their regard. I fear they made more impression on me than I made on them."

"You were less fortunate than Robert, then."

"I am always less fortunate than Robert. Has he been imparting tender confidences?"

"I've been imposing myself long enough," said Robert, rising, and shaking hands with Edna. "Please convey my regards to Mr. Pontellier when you write."

He shook hands with Arobin and went away.

"Fine fellow, that Lebrun," said Arobin when Robert had gone. "I never heard you speak of him."

"I knew him last summer at Grand Isle," she replied. "Here is that photograph of yours. Don't you want it?"

"What do I want with it? Throw it away." She threw it back on the table. "I'm not going to Mrs. Merriman's," she said. "If you see her, tell her so. But perhaps I had better write. I think I shall write now, and say that I am sorry her child is sick, and tell her not to count on me."

"It would be a good scheme," acquiesced Arobin. "I don't blame you; stupid lot!"

Edna opened the blotter, and having procured paper and pen, began to write the note. Arobin lit a cigar and read the evening paper, which he had in his pocket.

"What is the date?" she asked. He told her.

"Will you mail this for me when you go out?"

"Certainly." He read to her little bits out of the newspaper, while she straightened things on the table.

"What do you want to do?" he asked, throwing aside the paper. "Do you want to go out for a walk or a drive or anything? It would be a fine night to drive."

"No; I don't want to do anything but just be quiet. You go away and amuse yourself. Don't stay."

"I'll go away if I must; but I shan't amuse myself. You know that I only live when I am near you."

He stood up to bid her good night.

"Is that one of the things you always say to women?"

"I have said it before, but I don't think I ever came to so near meaning it," he answered with a smile. There were no warm lights in her eyes; only a dreamy, absent look.

"Good night. I adore you. Sleep well," he said, and he kissed her hand and went away.

She stayed alone in a kind of reverie — a sort of stupor. Step by step she lived over every instant of the time she had been with Robert after he had entered Mademoiselle Reisz's door. She recalled his words, his looks. How few and meager they had been for her hungry heart! A vision — a transcendently seductive vision of a Mexican girl arose before her. She writhed with a jealous pang. She wondered when he would come back. He had not said he would come back. She had been with him, had heard his voice and touched his hand. But some way he had seemed nearer to her off there in Mexico.

XXXV

The morning was full of sunlight and hope. Edna could see before her no denial — only the promise of excessive joy. She lay in bed awake, with bright eyes full of speculation. "He loves you, poor fool." If she could but get that conviction firmly fixed in her mind, what mattered about the rest? She felt she had been childish and unwise the night before in giving herself over to despondency. She recapitulated the motives which no doubt explained Robert's reserve. They were not insurmountable; they would not hold if he really loved her; they could not hold against her own passion, which he must come to realize in time. She pictured him going to his business that morning. She even saw how he was dressed; how he walked down one street, and turned the corner of another; saw him bending over his desk, talking to people who entered the office, going to his lunch, and perhaps watching for her on the street. He would come to her in the afternoon or evening, sit and roll his cigarette, talk a little, and go away as he had done the night before. But how delicious it would be to have him there with her! She would have no regrets, nor seek to penetrate his reserve if he still chose to wear it.

Edna ate her breakfast only half dressed. The maid brought her a delicious printed scrawl from Raoul, expressing his love, asking her to send him some bonbons, and telling her they had found that morning ten tiny white pigs all lying in a row beside Lidie's big white pig.

A letter also came from her husband, saying he hoped to be back early in March, and then they would get ready for that journey abroad which he had promised her so long, which he felt now fully able to afford; he felt able to travel as people should, without any thought of small economies—thanks to his recent speculations in Wall Street.

Much to her surprise she received a note from Arobin, written at midnight from the club. It was to say good morning to her, to hope she had slept well, to assure her of his devotion, which he trusted she in some faintest manner returned.

All these letters were pleasing to her. She answered the children in a cheerful frame of mind, promising them bonbons, and congratulating them upon their happy find of the little pigs.

She answered her husband with friendly evasiveness,—not with any fixed design to mislead him, only because all sense of reality had gone out of her life; she had abandoned herself to Fate, and awaited the consequences with indifference.

To Arobin's note she made no reply. She put it under Celestine's stove-lid.

Edna worked several hours with much spirit. She saw no one but a picture dealer, who asked her if it were true that she was going abroad to study in Paris.

She said possibly she might, and he negotiated with her for some Parisian studies to reach him in time for the holiday trade in December.

Robert did not come that day. She was keenly disappointed. He did not come the following day, nor the next. Each morning she awoke with hope, and each night she was a prey to despondency. She was tempted to seek him out. But far from yielding to the impulse, she avoided any occasion which might throw her in his way. She did not go to Mademoiselle Reisz's nor pass by Madame Lebrun's, as she might have done if he had still been in Mexico.

When Arobin, one night, urged her to drive with him, she went—out to the lake, on the Shell Road. His horses were full of mettle, and even a little unmanageable. She liked the rapid gait at which they spun along, and the quick, sharp sound of the horses' hoofs on the hard road. They did not stop anywhere to eat or to drink. Arobin was not needlessly imprudent. But they ate and they drank when they regained Edna's little dining-room—which was comparatively early in the evening.

It was late when he left her. It was getting to be more than a passing whim with Arobin to see her and be with her. He had detected the latent sensuality, which unfolded under his delicate sense of her nature's requirements like a torpid, torrid, sensitive blossom.

There was no despondency when she fell asleep that night; nor was there hope when she awoke in the morning.

XXXVI

There was a garden out in the suburbs; a small, leafy corner, with a few green tables under the orange trees. An old cat slept all day on the stone step in the sun, and an old *mulatresse*[63] slept her idle hours away in her chair at the open window, till some one happened to knock on one of the green tables. She had milk and cream cheese to sell, and bread and butter. There was no one who could make such excellent coffee or fry a chicken so golden brown as she.

The place was too modest to attract the attention of people of fashion, and so quiet as to have escaped the notice of those in search of pleasure and dissipation. Edna had discovered it accidentally one day when the high-board gate stood ajar. She caught sight of a little green table, blotched with the checkered sunlight that filtered through the quivering leaves overhead. Within she had found the slumbering *mulatresse*, the drowsy cat, and a glass of milk which reminded her of the milk she had tasted in Iberville.

She often stopped there during her perambulations; sometimes taking a book with her, and sitting an hour or two under the trees when she found the place deserted. Once or twice she took a quiet dinner there alone, having instructed Celestine beforehand to prepare no dinner at home. It was the last place in the city where she would have expected to meet any one she knew.

Still she was not astonished when, as she was partaking of a modest dinner late in the afternoon, looking into an open book, stroking the cat, which had made friends with her — she was not greatly astonished to see Robert come in at the tall garden gate.

"I am destined to see you only by accident," she said, shoving the cat off the chair beside her. He was surprised, ill at ease, almost embarrassed at meeting her thus so unexpectedly.

"Do you come here often?" he asked.

"I almost live here," she said.

"I used to drop in very often for a cup of Catiche's good coffee. This is the first time since I came back."

"She'll bring you a plate, and you will share my dinner. There's always enough for two — even three." Edna had intended to be indifferent and as reserved as he when she met him; she had reached the determination by a laborious train of reasoning, incident to one of her despondent moods. But her resolve melted when she saw him before her, seated there beside her in the little garden, as if a designing Providence had led him into her path.

"Why have you kept away from me, Robert?" She asked, closing the book that lay open upon the table.

"Why are you so personal, Mrs. Pontellier? Why do you force me to idiotic subterfuges?" he exclaimed with sudden warmth. "I suppose there's no use telling you I've been very busy, or that I've been sick, or that I've been to see you and not found you at home. Please let me off with any one of these excuses."

"You are the embodiment of selfishness," she said. "You save yourself something — I don't know what — but there is some selfish motive, and in sparing yourself you never consider for a moment what I think, or how I feel your neglect and indifference. I suppose this is what you would call unwomanly; but I have got

[63]*mulatresse* mulatto woman, of mixed black and white ancestry

into a habit of expressing myself. It doesn't matter to me, and you may think me unwomanly if you like."

"No; I only think you cruel, as I said the other day. Maybe not intentionally cruel; but you seem to be forcing me into disclosures which can result in nothing; as if you would have me bare a wound for the pleasure of looking at it, without the intention or power of healing it."

"I'm spoiling your dinner, Robert; never mind what I say. You haven't eaten a morsel."

"I only came in for a cup of coffee." His sensitive face was all disfigured with excitement.

"Isn't this a delightful place?" she remarked. "I am so glad it has never actually been discovered. It is so quiet, so sweet, here. Do you notice there is scarcely a sound to be heard? It's so out of the way; and a good walk from the car. However, I don't mind walking. I always feel so sorry for women who don't like to walk; they miss so much — so many rare little glimpses of life; and we women learn so little of life on the whole.

"Catiche's coffee is always hot. I don't know how she manages it, here in the open air. Celestine's coffee gets cold bringing it from the kitchen to the dining-room. Three lumps! How can you drink it so sweet? Take some of the cress with your chop; it's so biting and crisp. Then there's the advantage of being able to smoke with your coffee out here. Now, in the city — aren't you going to smoke?"

"After a while," he said, laying a cigar on the table.

"Who gave it to you?" she laughed.

"I bought it. I suppose I'm getting reckless; I bought a whole box." She was determined not to be personal again and make him uncomfortable.

The cat made friends with him, and climbed into his lap when he smoked his cigar. He stroked her silky fur, and talked a little about her. He looked at Edna's book, which he had read; and he told her the end, to save her the trouble of wading through it, he said.

Again he accompanied her back to her home; and it was after dusk when they reached the little "pigeon-house." She did not ask him to remain, which he was grateful for, as it permitted him to stay without the discomfort of blundering through an excuse which he had no intention of considering. He helped her to light the lamp; then she went into her room to take off her hat and to bathe her face and hands.

When she came back Robert was not examining the pictures and magazines as before; he sat off in the shadow, leaning his head back on the chair as if in a reverie. Edna lingered a moment beside the table, arranging the books there. Then she went across the room to where he sat. She bent over the arm of his chair and called his name.

"Robert," she said, "are you asleep?"

"No," he answered, looking up at her.

She leaned over and kissed him — a soft, cool, delicate kiss, whose voluptuous sting penetrated his whole being — then she moved away from him. He followed, and took her in his arms, just holding her close to him. She put her hand up to his face and pressed his cheek against her own. The action was full of love and tenderness. He sought her lips again. Then he drew her down upon the sofa beside him and held her hand in both of his.

"Now you know," he said, "now you know what I have been fighting against since last summer at Grande Isle; what drove me away and drove me back again."

"Why have you been fighting against it?" she asked. Her face glowed with soft lights.

"Why? Because you were not free; you were Léonce Pontellier's wife. I couldn't help loving you if you were ten times his wife; but so long as I went away from you and kept away I could help telling you so." She put her free hand up to his shoulder, and then against his cheek, rubbing it softly. He kissed her again. His face was warm and flushed.

"There in Mexico I was thinking of you all the time, and longing for you."

"But not writing to me," she interrupted.

"Something put into my head that you cared for me; and I lost my senses. I forgot everything but a wild dream of your some way becoming my wife."

"Your wife!"

"Religion, loyalty, everything would give way if only you cared."

"Then you must have forgotten that I was Léonce Pontellier's wife."

"Oh! I was demented, dreaming of wild, impossible things, recalling men who had set their wives free, we have heard of such things."

"Yes, we have heard of such things."

"I came back full of vague, mad intentions. And when I got here—"

"When you got here you never came near me!" She was still caressing his cheek.

"I realized what a cur I was to dream of such a thing, even if you had been willing."

She took his face between her hands and looked into it as if she would never withdraw her eyes more. She kissed him on the forehead, the eyes, the cheeks, and the lips.

"You have been a very, very foolish boy, wasting your time dreaming of impossible things when you speak of Mr. Pontellier setting me free! I am no longer one of Mr. Pontellier's possessions to dispose of or not. I give myself where I choose. If he were to say, 'Here, Robert, take her and be happy; she is yours,' I should laugh at you both."

His face grew a little white. "What do you mean?" he asked.

There was a knock at the door. Old Celestine came in to say that Madame Ratignolle's servant had come around the back way with a message that Madame had been taken sick and begged Mrs. Pontellier to go to her immediately.

"Yes, yes," said Edna, rising; "I promised. Tell her yes—to wait for me. I'll go back with her."

"Let me walk over with you," offered Robert.

"No," she said; "I will go with the servant." She went into her room to put on her hat, and when she came in again she sat once more upon the sofa beside him. He had not stirred. She put her arms about his neck.

"Good-by, my sweet Robert. Tell me good-by." He kissed her with a degree of passion which had not before entered into his caress, and strained her to him.

"I love you," she whispered, "only you; no one but you. It was you who awoke me last summer out of a life-long, stupid dream. Oh! you have made me so unhappy with your indifference. Oh! I have suffered, suffered! Now you are here we shall love each other, my Robert. We shall be everything to each other. Nothing else in the world is of any consequence. I must go to my friend; but you will wait for me? No matter how late; you will wait for me, Robert?"

"Don't go; don't go! Oh! Edna, stay with me," he pleaded. "Why should you go? Stay with me, stay with me."

"I shall come back as soon as I can; I shall find you here." She buried her face in his neck, and said good-by again. Her seductive voice, together with his great love for her, had enthralled his senses, had deprived him of every impulse but the longing to hold her and keep her.

XXXVII

Edna looked in at the drug store. Monsieur Ratignolle was putting up a mixture himself, very carefully, dropping a red liquid into a tiny glass. He was grateful to Edna for having come; her presence would be a comfort to his wife. Madame Ratignolle's sister, who had always been with her at such trying times, had not been able to come up from the plantation, and Adèle had been inconsolable until Mrs. Pontellier so kindly promised to come to her. The nurse had been with them at night for the past week, as she lived a great distance away. And Dr. Mandelet had been coming and going all the afternoon. They were then looking for him any moment.

Edna hastened upstairs by a private stairway that led from the rear of the store to the apartments above. The children were all sleeping in a back room. Madame Ratignolle was in the salon, whither she had strayed in her suffering impatience. She sat on the sofa, clad in an ample white *peignoir*, holding a handkerchief tight in her hand with a nervous clutch. Her face was drawn and pinched, her sweet blue eyes haggard and unnatural. All her beautiful hair had been drawn back and plaited. It lay in a long braid on the sofa pillow, coiled like a golden serpent. The nurse, a comfortable looking *Griffe*[64] woman in white apron and cap, was urging her to return to her bedroom.

"There is no use, there is no use," she said at once to Edna. "We must get rid of Mandelet; he is getting too old and careless. He said he would be here at half-past seven; now it must be eight. See what time it is, Joséphine."

The woman was possessed of a cheerful nature, and refused to take any situation too seriously, especially a situation with which she was so familiar. She urged Madame to have courage and patience. But Madame only set her teeth hard into her under lip, and Edna saw the sweat gather in beads on her white forehead. After a moment or two she uttered a profound sigh and wiped her face with the handkerchief rolled in a ball. She appeared exhausted. The nurse gave her a fresh handkerchief, sprinkled with cologne water.

"This is too much!" she cried. "Mandelet ought to be killed! Where is Alphonse? Is it possible I am to be abandoned like this — neglected by every one?"

"Neglected, indeed!" exclaimed the nurse. Wasn't she there? And here was Mrs. Pontellier leaving, no doubt, a pleasant evening at home to devote to her? And wasn't Monsieur Ratignolle coming that very instant through the hall? And Joséphine was quite sure she had heard Doctor Mandelet's coupé. Yes, there it was, down at the door.

Adèle consented to go back to her room. She sat on the edge of a little low couch next to her bed.

Doctor Mandelet paid no attention to Madame Ratignolle's upbraidings. He was accustomed to them at such times, and was too well convinced of her loyalty to doubt it.

[64]*Griffe* offspring of a mulatto and a black or Native American

He was glad to see Edna, and wanted her to go with him into the salon and entertain him. But Madame Ratignolle would not consent that Edna should leave her for an instant. Between agonizing moments, she chatted a little, and said it took her mind off her sufferings.

Edna began to feel uneasy. She was seized with a vague dread. Her own like experiences seemed far away, unreal, and only half remembered. She recalled faintly an ecstasy of pain, the heavy odor of chloroform, a stupor which had deadened sensation, and an awakening to find a little new life to which she had given being, added to the great unnumbered multitude of souls that come and go.

She began to wish she had not come; her presence was not necessary. She might have invented a pretext for staying away; she might even invent a pretext now for going. But Edna did not go. With an inward agony, with a flaming, outspoken revolt against the ways of Nature, she witnessed the scene of torture.

She was still stunned and speechless with emotion when later she leaned over her friend to kiss her and softly say good-by. Adèle, pressing her cheek, whispered in an exhausted voice: "Think of the children, Edna. Oh think of the children! Remember them!"

XXXVIII

Edna still felt dazed when she got outside in the open air. The Doctor's coupé had returned for him and stood before the *porte cochère*. She did not wish to enter the coupé, and told Doctor Mandelet she would walk; she was not afraid, and would go alone. He directed his carriage to meet him at Mrs. Pontellier's, and he started to walk home with her.

Up—away up, over the narrow street between the tall houses, the stars were blazing. The air was mild and caressing, but cool with the breath of spring and the night. They walked slowly, the Doctor with a heavy, measured tread and his hands behind him; Edna, in an absent-minded way, as she had walked one night at Grande Isle, as if her thoughts had gone ahead of her and she was striving to overtake them.

"You shouldn't have been there, Mrs. Pontellier," he said. "That was no place for you. Adèle is full of whims at such times. There were a dozen women she might have had with her, unimpressionable women. I felt that it was cruel, cruel. You shouldn't have gone."

"Oh well!" she answered, indifferently. "I don't know that it matters after all. One has to think of the children some time or other; the sooner the better."

"When is Léonce coming back?"

"Quite soon. Some time in March."

"And you are going abroad?"

"Perhaps—no, I am not going. I'm not going to be forced into doing things. I don't want to go abroad. I want to be let alone. Nobody has any right—except children, perhaps—and even then, it seems to me—or it did seem—" She felt that her speech was voicing the incoherency of her thoughts, and stopped abruptly.

"The trouble is," sighed the Doctor, grasping her meaning intuitively, "that youth is given up to illusions. It seems to be a provision of Nature; a decoy to secure mothers for the race. And Nature takes no account of moral consequences, of arbitrary conditions which we create, and which we feel obliged to maintain at any cost."

"Yes," she said. "The years that are gone seem like dreams — if one might go on sleeping and dreaming — but to wake up and find — oh! well! perhaps it is better to wake up after all, even to suffer, rather than to remain a dupe to illusions all one's life."

"It seems to me, my dear child," said the Doctor at parting, holding her hand, "you seem to me to be in trouble. I am not going to ask for your confidence. I will only say that if ever you feel moved to give it to me, perhaps I might help you. I know I would understand, and I tell you there are not many who would — not many, my dear."

"Some way I don't feel moved to speak of things that trouble me. Don't think I am ungrateful or that I don't appreciate your sympathy. There are periods of despondency and suffering which take possession of me. But I don't want anything but my own way. That is wanting a good deal, of course, when you have to trample upon the lives, the hearts, the prejudices of others — but no matter — still, I shouldn't want to trample upon the little lives. Oh! I don't know what I'm saying, Doctor. Good night. Don't blame me for anything."

"Yes, I will blame you if you don't come and see me soon. We will talk of things you never have dreamt of talking about before. It will do us both good. I don't want you to blame yourself, whatever comes. Good night, my child."

She let herself in at the gate, but instead of entering she sat upon the step of the porch. The night was quiet and soothing. All the tearing emotion of the last few hours seemed to fall away from her like a somber, uncomfortable garment, which she had but to loosen to be rid of. She went back to that hour before Adèle had sent for her; and her senses kindled afresh in thinking of Robert's words, the pressure of his arms, and the feeling of his lips upon her own. She could picture at that moment no greater bliss on earth than possession of the beloved one. His expression of love had already given him to her in part. When she thought that he was there at hand, waiting for her, she grew numb with the intoxication of expectancy. It was so late; he would be asleep perhaps. She would awaken him with a kiss. She hoped he would be asleep that she might arouse him with her caresses.

Still, she remembered Adèle's voice whispering, "Think of the children; think of them." She meant to think of them; that determination had driven into her soul like a death wound — but not to-night. To-morrow would be time to think of everything.

Robert was not waiting for her in the little parlor. He was nowhere at hand. The house was empty. But he had scrawled on a piece of paper that lay in the lamplight:

"I love you. Good-by — because I love you."

Edna grew faint when she read the words. She went and sat on the sofa. Then she stretched herself out there, never uttering a sound. She did not sleep. She did not go to bed. The lamp sputtered and went out. She was still awake in the morning, when Celestine unlocked the kitchen door and came in to light the fire.

XXXIX

Victor, with hammer and nails and scraps of scantling,[65] was patching a corner of one of the galleries. Mariequita sat near by, dangling her legs, watching him work,

[65]*scantling* small pieces of wood

and handing him nails from the tool-box. The sun was beating down upon them. The girl had covered her head with her apron folded into a square pad. They had been talking for an hour or more. She was never tired of hearing Victor describe the dinner at Mrs. Pontellier's. He exaggerated every detail, making it appear a veritable Lucullean feast. The flowers were in tubs, he said. The champagne was quaffed from huge golden goblets. Venus rising from the foam could have presented no more entrancing a spectacle than Mrs. Pontellier, blazing with beauty and diamonds at the head of the board, while the other women were all of them youthful houris,[66] possessed of incomparable charms.

She got it into her head that Victor was in love with Mrs. Pontellier, and he gave her evasive answers, framed so as to confirm her belief. She grew sullen and cried a little, threatening to go off and leave him to his fine ladies. There were a dozen men crazy about her at the *Chênière*; and since it was the fashion to be in love with married people, why, she could run away any time she like to New Orleans with Célina's husband.

Célina's husband was a fool, a coward, and a pig, and to prove it to her, Victor intended to hammer his head into a jelly the next time he encountered him. This assurance was very consoling to Mariequita. She dried her eyes, and grew cheerful at the prospect.

They were still talking of the dinner and the allurements of city life when Mrs. Pontellier herself slipped around the corner of the house. The two youngsters stayed dumb with amazement before what they considered to be an apparition. But it was really she in flesh and blood, looking tired and a little travel-stained.

"I walked up from the wharf," she said, "and heard the hammering. I supposed it was you, mending the porch. It's a good thing. I was always tripping over those loose planks last summer. How dreary and deserted everything looks!"

It took Victor some little time to comprehend that she had come in Beaudelet's lugger, that she had come alone, and for no purpose but to rest.

"There's nothing fixed up yet, you see. I'll give you my room; it's the only place."

"Any corner will do," she assured him.

"And if you can stand Philomel's cooking," he went on, "though I might try to get her mother while you are here. Do you think she would come?" turning to Mariequita.

Mariequita thought that perhaps Philomel's mother might come for a few days, and money enough.

Beholding Mrs. Pontellier make her appearance, the girl had at once suspected a lovers' rendezvous. But Victor's astonishment was so genuine, and Mrs. Pontellier's indifference so apparent, that the disturbing notion did not lodge long in her brain. She contemplated with the greatest interest this woman who gave the most sumptuous dinners in America, and who had all the men in New Orleans at her feet.

"What time will you have dinner?" asked Edna. "I'm very hungry; but don't get anything extra."

"I'll have it ready in little or no time," he said, bustling and packing away his tools. "You may go to my room to brush up and rest yourself. Mariequita will show you."

[66]*houris* nymphs of the Moslem Paradise; thus, seductively beautiful women

"Thank you," said Edna. "But, do you know, I have a notion to go down to the beach and take a good wash and even a little swim, before dinner?"

"The water is too cold!" they both exclaimed. "Don't think of it."

"Well, I might go down and try—dip my toes in. Why, it seems to me the sun is hot enough to have warmed the very depths of the ocean. Could you get me a couple of towels? I'd better go right away, so as to be back in time. It would be a little too chilly if I waited till this afternoon."

Mariequita ran over to Victor's room, and returned with some towels, which she gave to Edna.

"I hope you have fish for dinner," said Edna, as she started to walk away; "but don't do anything extra if you haven't."

"Run and find Philomel's mother," Victor instructed the girl. "I'll go to the kitchen and see what I can do. By Gimminy! Women have no consideration! She might have sent me word."

Edna walked on down to the beach rather mechanically, not noticing anything special except that the sun was hot. She was not dwelling upon any particular train of thought. She had done all the thinking which was necessary after Robert went away, when she lay awake upon the sofa till morning.

She had said over and over to herself: "To-day it is Arobin; to-morrow it will be some one else. It makes no difference to me, it doesn't matter about Léonce Pontellier—but Raoul and Etienne!" She understood now clearly what she had meant long ago when she said to Adèle Ratignolle that she would give up the unessential, but she would never sacrifice herself for her children.

Despondency had come upon her there in the wakeful night, and had never lifted. There was no one thing in the world that she desired. There was no human being whom she wanted near her except Robert; and she even realized that the day would come when he, too, and the thought of him would melt out of her existence, leaving her alone. The children appeared before her like antagonists who had overcome her; who had overpowered and sought to drag her into the soul's slavery for the rest of her days. But she knew a way to elude them. She was not thinking of these things when she walked down to the beach.

The water of the Gulf stretched out before her, gleaming with the million lights of the sun. The voice of the sea is seductive, never ceasing, whispering, clamoring, murmuring, inviting the soul to wander in abysses of solitude. All along the white beach, up and down, there was no living thing in sight. A bird with a broken wing was beating the air above, reeling, fluttering, circling disabled down, down to the water.

Edna had found her old bathing suit still hanging, faded, upon its accustomed peg.

She put it on, leaving her clothing in the bath-house. But when she was there beside the sea, absolutely alone, she cast the unpleasant, pricking garments from her, and for the first time in her life she stood naked in the open air, at the mercy of the sun, the breeze that beat upon her, and the waves that invited her.

How strange and awful it seemed to stand naked under the sky! how delicious! She felt like some new-born creature, opening its eyes in a familiar world that it had never known.

The foamy wavelets curled up to her white feet, and coiled like serpents about her ankles. She walked out. The water was chill, but she walked on. The water was deep, but she lifted her white body and reached out with a long, sweeping stroke. The touch of the sea is sensuous, enfolding the body in its soft, close embrace.

She went on and on. She remembered the night she swam far out, and recalled the terror that seized her at the fear of being unable to regain the shore. She did not look back now, but went on and on, thinking of the blue-grass meadow that she had traversed when a little child, believing that it had no beginning and no end.

Her arms and legs were growing tired.

She thought of Léonce and the children. They were a part of her life. But they need not have thought that they could possess her, body and soul. How Mademoiselle Reisz would have laughed, perhaps sneered, if she knew! "And you call yourself an artist! What pretensions, Madame! The artist must possess the courageous soul that dares and defies."

Exhaustion was pressing upon and overpowering her.

"Good-by — because I love you." He did not know; he did not understand. He would never understand. Perhaps Doctor Mandelet would have understood if she had seen him — but it was too late; the shore was far behind her, and her strength was gone.

She looked into the distance, and the old terror flamed up for an instant, then sank again. Edna heard her father's voice and her sister Margaret's. She heard the barking of an old dog that was chained to the sycamore tree. The spurs of the cavalry officer clanged as he walked across the porch. There was the hum of bees, and the musky odor of pinks filled the air.

[1899]

QUESTIONS

1. What is the "awakening"? What are its stages?
2. How do each of the other major characters — Mr. Pontellier, Robert Lebrun, Mme. Ratignolle, Mmme. Reisz, and Alcée Arobin — express different moral or social possibilities or roles that Edna must weigh?
3. How does the Creole cultural background influence the difference in values that Edna confronts?
4. What does Edna mean when she says, "I would give up the unessential; I would give my money, I would give my life for my children; but I wouldn't give myself"?
5. What is the significance of Edna's learning to swim?
6. How does Edna change during the course of the novel?
7. How do language and imagery contribute to the themes of the novel? How do the unnamed figures — the lovers, the woman in black — contribute to meaning?
8. Is any other ending possible for the novel? Why or why not? How do you understand Edna's final act: does she choose or submit to her fate? Are any other choices available to her?

Thematic Contents

ALIENATION

Mulk Raj Anand (India): *Untouchable*
Heinrich Böll (Germany): "The Laugher" (Translated by Leila Vennewitz)
Willa Cather (United States): "Paul's Case"
Kate Chopin (United States): *The Awakening*
William Faulkner (United States): "A Rose for Emily"
Charlotte Perkins Gilman (United States): "The Yellow Wallpaper"
Nicolai Gogol (Russia): "The Overcoat"
Franz Kafka (Czechoslovakia): "The Metamorphosis"
Herman Melville (United States): "Bartleby, the Scrivener"
Ngugi wa Thiong'o (Kenya): "A Meeting in the Dark"
Sembene Ousmane (Senegal): "Black Girl"

ALLEGORY/LEGEND/FABLE

From *The Thousand and One Nights*: "The Story of the Merchant and the Jinni"
Heinrich Böll (Germany): "The Laugher" (Translated by Leila Vennewitz)
Jorge Luis Borges (Argentina): "Death and the Compass"
Dino Buzzati (Italy): "The Falling Girl"
Italo Calvino (Italy): "A Sign in Space"
John Cheever (United States): "The Swimmer"
Isak Dinesen (Denmark): "The Sailor-Boy's Tale"
Gustave Flaubert (France): "The Legend of Saint Julian the Hospitaller"
Jacob and Wilhelm Grimm (Germany): "Karl Katz"
Nathaniel Hawthorne (United States): "The Birthmark"
Shirley Jackson (United States): "The Lottery"
Franz Kafka (Czechoslovakia): "The Metamorphosis"
Pär Lagerkvist (Sweden): "The Children's Campaign"
Naguib Mahfouz (Egypt): "Half a Day"
William Somerset Maugham (England): "The Appointment in Samarra"
Edgar Allan Poe (United States): "The Cask of Amontillado"
Hyemeyohsts Storm (United States): "The Story of Jumping Mouse"
Amos Tutuola (Nigeria): "The Complete Gentleman"

THE ARTIST

Rudolfo A. Anaya (United States): "B. Traven Is Alive and Well in Cuernavaca"
Kate Chopin (United States): *The Awakening*
Gabriel García Márquez (Colombia): "Balthazar's Marvelous Afternoon"
Henry James (United States/England): "The Real Thing"

Kanai Mieko (Japan): "Platonic Love"
John McCluskey (United States): "Lush Life"
Thomas Mann (Germany): "The Infant Prodigy"
Ōe Kenzaburo (Japan): "Aghwee the Sky Monster"

DEATH

Isabel Allende (Chile): "And of Clay Are We Created"
Sherwood Anderson (United States): "Death in the Woods"
Ambrose Bierce (United States): "An Occurrence at Owl Creek Bridge"
Jorge Luis Borges (Argentina): "Death and the Compass"
Willa Cather (United States): "Paul's Case"
Ghassan Kanafani (Palestinian): "A Hand in the Grave"
Mary Lavin (Ireland): "Happiness"
Virgilio Piñera (Cuba): "Insomnia"
Leo Tolstoy (Russia): "The Death of Ivan Ilych"

FANTASTIC/ABSURD

From *The Thousand and One Nights*: "The Story of the Merchant and the Jinni"
Woody Allen (United States): "The Kugelmass Episode"
Dino Buzzati (Italy): "The Falling Girl"
Italo Calvino (Italy): "A Sign in Space"
Franz Kafka (Czechoslovakia): "The Metamorphosis"
Ursula K. Le Guin (United States): "Sur"
Catherine Lim (Singapore): "Or Else, the Lightning God"
Slawomir Mrożek (Poland): "The Elephant"
Octavio Paz (Mexico): "The Blue Bouquet"
María Teresa Solari (Peru): "Death and Transfiguration of a Teacher"
Amos Tutuola (Nigeria): "The Complete Gentleman"
Luisa Valenzuela (Argentina): "Strange Things Happen Here"
Mario Vargas Llosa (Peru): "Sunday"

GENDER

Barbara Neely (United States): "Spilled Salt"
Kate Chopin (United States): *The Awakening*
Charlotte Perkins Gilman (United States): "The Yellow Wallpaper"
Susan Glaspell (United States): "A Jury of Her Peers"
Judy Grahn (United States): "Boys at the Rodeo"
Ernest Hemingway (United States): "The Short Happy Life of Francis Macomber"
Svava Jakobsdóttir (Iceland): "A Story for Children"
D. H. Lawrence (England): "Tickets, Please"
Ursula K. Le Guin (United States): "Sur"
Doris Lessing (Rhodesia/England): "A Woman on a Roof"
Mishima Yukio (Japan): "Swaddling Clothes"
Alice Munro (Canada): "The Office"
Amos Oz (Israel): "Nomad and Viper"

HUMOR/COMEDY

Woody Allen (United States): "The Kugelmass Episode"
Italo Calvino (Italy): "A Sign in Space"
John Cheever (United States): "The Swimmer"
Feng Jicai (China): "The Street-Sweeping Show"
Judy Grahn (United States): "Boys at the Rodeo"
Zora Neale Hurston (United States): "The Gilded Six-Bits"
John Kasaipwalova (Papua New Guinea): "Betel Nut Is Bad Magic for Airplanes
Bernard Malamud (United States): "The Jewbird"
Es'kia Mphahlele (South Africa): "Mrs. Plum"
Slawomir Mrożek (Poland): "The Elephant"
Carmen Naranjo (Costa Rica): "And We Sold the Rain"
R. K. Narayan (India): "A Horse and Two Goats"
Flannery O'Connor (United States): "A Good Man Is Hard to Find"
Isaac Bashevis Singer (Poland/United States): "Gimpel the Fool"
Mark Twain (United States): "Luck"
Eudora Welty (United States): "Why I Live at the P.O."

JOURNEY

Woody Allen (United States): "The Kugelmass Episode"
Hanan Al-Shaykh (Lebanon): "The Unseeing Eye"
Mulk Raj Anand (India): *Untouchable*
Rudolfo A. Anaya (United States): "B. Traven Is Alive and Well in Cuernavaca"
Dino Buzzati (Italy): "The Falling Girl"
Italo Calvino (Italy): "A Sign in Space"
Willa Cather (United States): "Paul's Case"
John Cheever (United States): "The Swimmer"
Joseph Conrad (Poland/England): "Amy Foster"
Stephen Crane (United States): "The Open Boat"
Isak Dinesen (Denmark): "The Sailor-Boy's Tale"
Birago Diop (Senegal): "Sarzan"
Ralph Ellison (United States): "Flying Home"
F. Scott Fitzgerald (United States): "Babylon Revisited"
Gustave Flaubert (France): "The Legend of Saint Julian the Hospitaller"
Jacob and Wilhelm Grimm (Germany): "Karl Katz"
Ursula K. Le Guin (United States): "Sur"
John McCluskey (United States): "Lush Life"
Naguib Mahfouz (Egypt): "Half a Day"
René Marqués (Puerto Rico): "Island of Manhattan"
Bobbie Ann Mason (United States): "Shiloh"
William Somerset Maugham (England): "The Appointment in Samarra"
Katherine Min (Korea/United States): "The One Who Goes Farthest Away"
Kermit Moyer (United States): "Tumbling"
Flannery O'Connor (United States): "A Good Man Is Hard to Find"
Sembene Ousmane (Senegal): "Black Girl"
Gabrielle Roy (Canada): "The Move"
Hyemeyohsts Storm (United States): "The Story of Jumping Mouse"
Graham Swift (England): "Learning to Swim"

Leo Tolstoy (Russia): "The Death of Ivan Ilych"
Amos Tutuola (Nigeria): "The Complete Gentleman"
Edith Wharton (United States): "Roman Fever"

MORAL DILEMMA

Isabel Allende (Chile): "And of Clay Are We Created"
Albert Camus (Algeria/France): "The Guest"
Margareta Ekström (Sweden): "The Night Between the Second and the Third"
Louise Erdrich (United States): "Love Medicine"
F. Scott Fitzgerald (United States): "Babylon Revisited"
Susan Glaspell (United States): "A Jury of Her Peers"
Nathaniel Hawthorne (United States): "The Birthmark"
Sarah Orne Jewett (United States): "A White Heron"
James Joyce (Ireland): "Eveline"
Khamsing Srinawk (Thailand): "The Gold-Legged Frog"
Lu Xun (China): "The Story of Hair"
Arnost Lustig (Czechoslovakia/United States): "The Lemon"
Guy De Maupassant (France): "The Necklace"
Herman Melville (United States): "Bartleby, the Scrivener"
Alice Munro (Canada): "The Office"
Isaac Bashevis Singer (Poland/United States): "Gimpel the Fool"
John Updike (United States): "A & P"
Alice Walker (United States): "Everyday Use"
Edith Wharton (United States): "Roman Fever"

THE NATURE OF EVIL

Shirley Jackson (United States): "The Lottery"
Joyce Carol Oates (United States): "Where Are You Going, Where Have You Been?"
Flannery O'Connor (United States): "A Good Man Is Hard to Find"
Sembene Ousmane (Senegal): "Black Girl"
Edgar Allan Poe (United States): "The Cask of Amontillado"

PERSPECTIVES ON CLASS

Mulk Raj Anand (India): *Untouchable*
William Faulkner (United States): "A Rose for Emily"
F. Scott Fitzgerald (United States): "Babylon Revisited"
Gabriel García Márquez (Colombia): "Balthazar's Marvelous Afternoon"
Henry James (United States/England): "The Real Thing"
Elizabeth Jolley (England/Australia): "Another Holiday for the Prince"
Khamsing Srinawk (Thailand): "The Gold-Legged Frog"
Guy de Maupassant (France): "The Necklace"
Herman Melville (United States): "Bartleby, the Scrivener"
Es'kia Mphahlele (South Africa): "Mrs. Plum"
V. S. Naipaul (Trinidad): "One Out of Many"
Ngugi wa Thiong'o (Kenya): "A Meeting in the Dark"
Edgar Allan Poe (United States): "The Cask of Amontillado"
John Steinbeck (United States): "The Crysanthemums"

RACIAL OR CULTURAL DISLOCATION/CONFLICT/CONNECTION

Chinua Achebe (Nigeria): "Girls at War"
Isabel Allende (Chile): "And of Clay Are We Created"
Mulk Raj Anand (India): *Untouchable*
Margaret Atwood (Canada): "Dancing Girls"
Albert Camus (Algeria/France): "The Guest"
Joseph Conrad (Poland/England): "Amy Foster"
Birago Diop (Senegal): "Sarzan"
Ralph Ellison (United States): "Flying Home"
Louise Erdrich (United States): "Love Medicine"
Nadine Gordimer (South Africa): "A Soldier's Embrace"
Bessie Head (South Africa/Botswana): "The Prisoner Who Wore Glasses"
John Kasaipwalova (Papua New Guinea): "Betel Nut Is Bad Magic for Airplanes"
Lu Xun (China): "The Story of Hair"
Bernard Malamud (United States): "The Jewbird"
René Marqués (Puerto Rico): "Island of Manhattan"
Paule Marshall (Barbados/United States): "Brooklyn"
Katherine Min (Korea/United States): "The One Who Goes Farthest Away"
Es'kia Mphahlele (South Africa): "Mrs. Plum"
Bharati Mukherjee (India/United States): "A Father"
V. S. Naipaul (Trinidad): "One Out of Many"
R. K. Narayan (India): "A Horse and Two Goats"
Ngugi wa Thiong'o (Kenya): "A Meeting in the Dark"
Sembene Ousmane (Senegal): "Black Girl"
Amos Oz (Israel): "Nomad and Viper
Octavio Paz (Mexico): "The Blue Bouquet"
Amy Tan (China/United States): "Half and Half"
Alice Walker (United States): "Everyday Use"

RELATIONSHIPS: PARENTS AND CHILDREN

Mulk Raj Anand (India): *Untouchable*
Barbara Neely (United States): "Spilled Salt"
J. Bernlef (Netherlands): "The Black Dog"
Gabrielle-Sidonie Colette (France): "The Seamstress"
Louise Erdrich (United States): "Love Medicine"
Gustave Flaubert (France): "The Legend of Saint Julian the Hospitaller"
Natalia Ginzburg (Italy): "The Mother"
Langston Hughes (United States): "Thank You, Ma'am"
Svava Jakobsdóttir (Iceland): "A Story for Children"
Elizabeth Jolley (England/Australia): "Another Holiday for the Prince"
James Joyce (Ireland): "Eveline"
Franz Kafka (Czechoslovakia): "The Metamorphosis"
Margaret Laurence (Canada): "A Bird in the House"
Mary Lavin (Ireland): "Happiness"
Catherine Lim (Singapore): "Or Else, the Lightning God"
Richard McCann (United States): "My Mother's Clothes: The School of Beauty and Shame"

Mishima Yukio (Japan): "Swaddling Clothes"
Bharati Mukherjee (India/United States): "A Father"
Ōba Minako (Japan): "The Pale Fox"
Flannery O'Connor (United States): "A Good Man Is Hard to Find"
Gabrielle Roy (Canada): "The Move"
Graham Swift (England): "Learning to Swim"
Amy Tan (China/United States): "Half and Half"
Alice Walker (United States): "Everyday Use"
Eudora Welty (United States): "Why I Live at the P.O."

RELATIONSHIPS: MEN

Isaac Babel (Russia): "My First Goose"
Albert Camus (Algeria/France): "The Guest"
Raymond Carver (United States): "Where I'm Calling From"
Stephen Crane (United States): "The Open Boat"
Gabriel García Márquez (Colombia): "Balthazar's Marvelous Afternoon"
Bessie Head (South Africa/Botswana): "The Prisoner Who Wore Glasses"
Ghassan Kanafani (Palestinian): "A Hand in the Grave"
Arnost Lustig (Czechoslovakia/United States): "The Lemon"
Richard McCann (United States): "My Mother's Clothes: The School of Beauty and Shame"
John McCluskey (United States): "Lush Life"
Herman Melville (United States): "Bartleby, the Scrivener"
Katherine Min (Korea/United States): "The One Who Goes Farthest Away"
Edgar Allan Poe (United States): "The Cask of Amontillado"
Luisa Valenzuela (Argentina): "Strange Things Happen Here"
Mario Vargas Llosa (Peru): "Sunday"

RELATIONSHIPS: WOMEN

Ama Ata Aidoo (Ghana): "Two Sisters"
Susan Glaspell (United States): "A Jury of Her Peers"
Judy Grahn (United States): "Boys at the Rodeo"
D. H. Lawrence (England): "Tickets, Please"
Ursula K. Le Guin (United States): "Sur"
Edith Wharton (United States): "Roman Fever"

RELATIONSHIPS: WOMEN AND MEN

Chinua Achebe (Nigeria): "Girls at War"
Ama Ata Aidoo (Ghana): "Two Sisters"
Akutagawa Ryūnosuke (Japan): "Within a Grove"
Woody Allen (United States): "The Kugelmass Episode"
Hanan Al-Shaykh (Lebanon): "The Unseeing Eye"
Ann Beattie (United States): "The Burning House"
Raymond Carver (United States): "Where I'm Calling From"
Kate Chopin (United States): *The Awakening*
José Donoso (Chile): "Paseo"
William Faulkner (United States): "A Rose for Emily"

Carlos Fuentes (Mexico): "The Doll Queen"
Charlotte Perkins Gilman (United States): "The Yellow Wallpaper"
Susan Glaspell (United States): "A Jury of Her Peers"
Nathaniel Hawthorne (United States): "The Birthmark"
Ernest Hemingway (United States): "The Short Happy Life of Francis Macomber"
Zora Neale Hurston (United States): "The Gilded Six-Bits"
Henry James (United States/England): "The Real Thing"
D. H. Lawrence (England): "Tickets, Please"
Doris Lessing (Rhodesia/England): "A Woman on a Roof"
Katherine Mansfield (New Zealand/England): "Her First Ball"
René Marqués (Puerto Rico): "Island of Manhattan"
Paule Marshall (Barbados/United States): "Brooklyn"
Bobbie Ann Mason (United States): "Shiloh"
Susan Minot (United States): "Lust"
Mishima Yukio (Japan): "Swaddling Clothes"
Ōba Minako (Japan): "The Pale Fox"
Emilia Pardo Bazán (Spain): "The Revolver"
Katherine Anne Porter (United States): "Rope"
Leslie Marmon Silko (United States): "Yellow Woman"
John Steinbeck (United States): "The Crysanthemums"
John Updike (United States): "A & P"

SATIRE

Jorge Luis Borges (Argentina): "Death and the Compass"
Feng Jicai (China): "The Street-Sweeping Show"
Svava Jakobsdóttir (Iceland): "A Story for Children"
Pär Lagerkvist (Sweden): "The Children's Campaign"
Thomas Mann (Germany): "The Infant Prodigy"
Slawomir Mrożek (Poland): "The Elephant"
Carmen Naranjo (Costa Rica): "And We Sold the Rain"
Virgilio Piñera (Cuba): "Insomnia"
María Teresa Solari (Peru): "Death and Transfiguration of a Teacher"
Mark Twain (United States): "Luck"

SPIRITUAL POWER OR DISCOVERY

Birago Diop (Senegal): "Sarzan"
Margareta Ekström (Sweden): "The Night Between the Second and the Third"
Ralph Ellison (United States): "Flying Home"
Louise Erdrich (United States): "Love Medicine"
F. Scott Fitzgerald (United States): "Babylon Revisited"
Gustave Flaubert (France): "The Legend of Saint Julian the Hospitaller"
Catherine Lim (Singapore): "Or Else, the Lightning God"
Naguib Mahfouz (Egypt): "Half a Day"
Rodrigo Rey Rosa (Guatemala): "The Proof"
Leslie Marmon Silko (United States): "Yellow Woman"
Isaac Bashevis Singer (Poland/United States): "Gimpel the Fool"
Hyemeyohsts Storm (United States): "The Story of Jumping Mouse"
Leo Tolstoy (Russia): "The Death of Ivan Ilych"

STORYTELLING/THE ART OF FICTION

From *The Thousand and One Nights*: "The Story of the Merchant and the Jinni"
Rudolfo A. Anaya (United States): "B. Traven Is Alive and Well in Cuernavaca"
Sherwood Anderson (United States): "Death in the Woods"
Jorge Luis Borges (Argentina): "Death and the Compass"
Kanai Mieko (Japan): "Platonic Love"
Hyemeyohsts Storm (United States): "The Story of Jumping Mouse"
Amos Tutuola (Nigeria): "The Complete Gentleman"

YOUTH/INITIATION/MATURATION

Mulk Raj Anand (India): *Untouchable*
Isaac Babel (Russia): "My First Goose"
J. Bernlef (Netherlands): "The Black Dog"
Willa Cather (United States): "Paul's Case"
Anton Chekhov (Russia): "The Kiss"
Kate Chopin (United States): *The Awakening*
Isak Dinesen (Denmark): "The Sailor-Boy's Tale"
José Donoso (Chile): "Paseo"
Carlos Fuentes (Mexico): "The Doll Queen"
Jacob and Wilhelm Grimm (Germany): "Karl Katz"
Ernest Hemingway (United States): "The Short Happy Life of Francis Macomber"
Langston Hughes (United States): "Thank You, Ma'am"
Sarah Orne Jewett (United States): "A White Heron"
Ghassan Kanafani (Palestinian): "A Hand in the Grave"
Pär Lagerkvist (Sweden): "The Children's Campaign"
Arnost Lustig (Czechoslovakia/United States): "The Lemon"
Richard McCann (United States): "My Mother's Clothes: The School of Beauty and Shame"
Naguib Mahfouz (Egypt): "Half a Day"
Thomas Mann (Germany): "The Infant Prodigy"
Katherine Mansfield (New Zealand/England): "Her First Ball"
Susan Minot (United States): "Lust"
Kermit Moyer (United States): "Tumbling"
V. S. Naipaul (Trinidad): "One Out of Many"
Ngugi wa Thiong'o (Kenya): "A Meeting in the Dark"
Joyce Carol Oates (United States): "Where Are You Going, Where Have You Been?"
Flannery O'Connor (United States): "A Good Man Is Hard to Find"
Rodrigo Rey Rosa (Guatemala): "The Proof"
Gabrielle Roy (Canada): "The Move"
María Teresa Solari (Peru): "Death and Transfiguration of a Teacher"
Graham Swift (England): "Learning to Swim"
John Updike (United States): "A & P"
Mario Vargas Llosa (Peru): "Sunday"